Florentine Gothic Painters

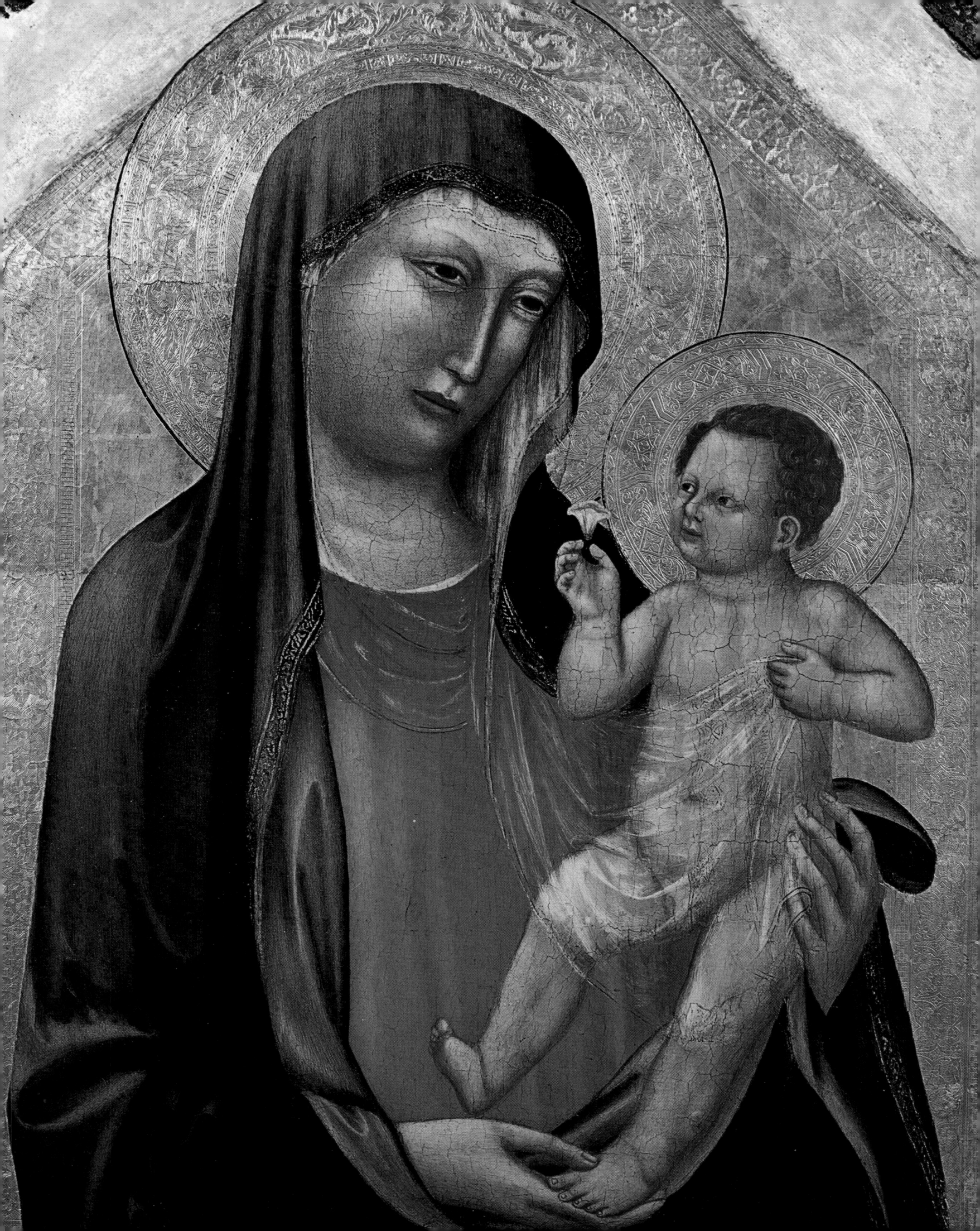

FLORENTINE GOTHIC PAINTERS

From Giotto to Masaccio

A Guide to Painting in and near Florence
1300 to 1450

by

RICHARD FREMANTLE

with 1335 illustrations
and 13 pages of maps

Martin Secker and Warburg
London

First published in England 1975 by
Martin Secker & Warburg Limited
14 Carlisle Street, London W1V 6NN.

Copyright © 1975 Richard Fremantle.
SBN: 436 16468 X.

Printed in Italy.

This work is dedicated with gratitude to

THOMAS HUGHES JACKSON

and to

RICCARDO POSANI

The quotations on pages XII and 2 of this book are:

From Cennini: D. V. Thompson, Jr., *Il Libro dell' Arte*, New Haven, 1933, and New York, 1954.

From Vasari: G. B. Brown, *Vasari on Technique*, London, 1907, and New York, 1960; as well as from the Dent-Everyman edition of the *Lives*, London, 1927.

Reprinted with gratitude.

Maps are reprinted with the kind permission of the Istituto Geografico Militare, autorizzazione n. 754, dated 19.6.74, and of the Touring Club Italiano, from the Road Map of Italy 1:200.000, authorized reproduction. Volume designed by Massimo Barca and Fabrizio Biffoli.

ALSO BY RICHARD FREMANTLE

FLORENTINE PAINTING IN THE UFFIZI
AN INTRODUCTION TO THE HISTORICAL BACKGROUND

..... *And so Adam, recognizing the error which he had committed, after being so royally endowed by God as the source, beginning, and father of us all, realized theoretically that some means of living by labour had to be found. And so he started with the spade, and Eve, with spinning. Man afterward pursued many useful occupations, differing from each other; and some were, and are, more theoretical than others; they could not all be alike, since theory is the most worthy. Close to that man pursued some related to the one which calls for a basis of theory coupled with skill of hand and this is an occupation known as painting, which calls for imagination, and skill of hand, in order to discover things not seen, hiding themselves under the shadow of natural objects, and to give them shape with the hand, presenting to plain sight what does not actually exist. And it justly deserves to be enthroned next to theory, and to be crowned with poetry.*

..... *The basis of the profession, the very beginning of all these manual operations, is drawing and painting. These two sections call for a knowledge of the following: how to work up or grind, how to apply size, to put on cloth, to gesso, to scrape the gessos and smooth them down, to model with gesso, to lay bole, to gild, to burnish; to temper, to lay in; to pounce, to scrape through, to stamp or punch; to mark out, to paint, to embellish, and to varnish, on panel or ancona. To work on a wall you have to wet down, to plaster, to true up, to smooth off, to draw, to paint in fresco. To carry to completion in secco: to temper, to embellish, to finish on the wall.*

Cennino d'Andrea Cennini,
Il Libro dell' Arte, ca. 1395.

Contents

PREFACE pg. XVII
PHOTOGRAPH SOURCES XIX
ACKNOWLEDGEMENTS XIX

Painters *(listed chronologically)*

Giotto *(1266/7-1337)* pg. 3
Pacino di Bonaguida *(active 1310-1330 ?)* 17
Lippo di Benivieni *(mentioned 1296- ?)* 27
Master of Santa Cecilia *(active ca. 1300-1320)* 35
Bernardo Daddi *(active ca. 1312-1348)* 45
Master of San Martino alla Palma *(active ca. 1330-1350)* 61
Taddeo Gaddi *(active 1332-1363)* 71
Puccio di Simone (Master of the Fabriano Altarpiece) *(Active ca. 1335-ca. 1365)* 85
Master of Terenzano (Master of the Dominican Effigies and of the Capella Medici) *(active ca. 1330-1350)* 95
Master of Figline (Master of the Fogg Pietà) *(active 1320-1360 ?)* 105
Jacopo del Casentino *(ca. 1300-1349 ?)* 115
Maso di Banco *(mentioned 1341-1346)* 125
Orcagna *(mentioned 1344-1368)* 135
Nardo di Cione *(active ca. 1343-1365)* 147
Jacopo di Cione *(active ca. 1360-1398)* 161
Niccolò di Tommaso *(active ca. 1350-1380)* 173
Giovanni da Milano *(mentioned 1350-1369)* 181
Master of Rinuccini Chapel *(active 1365-1370 ?)* 193
Andrea da Firenze *(mentioned 1343-1377)* 203
Giovanni Bonsi *(mentioned 1351-1371)* 213
Master of the Giraldi Tabernacle *(active 1370)* 221
Antonio Veneziano *(mentioned 1369-1388)* 229
Giovanni del Biondo *(mentioned 1356-1392)* 239
Cristiani *(mentioned 1366-1398)* 255
Agnolo Gaddi *(ca. 1333 ?-1396)* 265
Master of San Martino a Mensola *(active ca. 1380-1400)* 275
Starnina *(active 1390-1410 ?)* 285
Master of Santa Verdiana Panel *(active ca. 1385-1415)* 293
Master of the Straus Madonna *(active 1390-1420)* 303
Niccolò di Pietro Gerini *(mentioned 1368-1415)* 313
Master of the Arte della Lana *(active 1375 ?)* 323
Pietro Nelli (& Tommaso del Mazza) *(mentioned 1375-1419)* 331
Spinello Aretino *(active 1373-1410)* 343
Giovanni dal Ponte *(ca. 1385-1437)* 355
Lorenzo Monaco *(ca. 1370-ca. 1425)* 367
Cenno di Francesco di Ser Cenni *(mentioned 1400-1415)* 381
Lorenzo di Niccolò *(mentioned 1392-1411)* 391
Pietro di Miniato *(1366-ca. 1430)* 401
Lorenzo di Bicci *(ca. 1350-1427)* 409
Pseudo Ambrogio di Baldese *(active 1410-1420 ?)* 417
Francesco di Antonio *(1393-1433 ?)* 425
Alvaro Portoghese *(mentioned 1411-1434)* 433
Master of the Bambino Vispo *(active ca. 1410-1425)* 441
Mariotto di Nardo *(ca. 1373-1424)* 451
Rossello di Jacopo Franchi *(1376 ?-1457 ?)* 461
Bicci di Lorenzo *(1373-1452)* 471
Masolino *(1383-ca. 1440)* 483
Giovanni Toscani (Master of the Griggs Crucifixion) *(1372-1430)* 493
Masaccio *(1401-ca. 1428)* 503
Andrea di Giusto *(?-1455)* 513
Paolo Schiavo *(1397-1478)* 523
Parri Spinelli *(1387-1453)* 533
Master of Fucecchio (Master of the Adimari Cassone) *(active 1435-1460 ?)* 543
Mariotto di Cristofano *(1393-1457)* 553

Painters *(listed alphabetically)*

Agnolo Gaddi *(ca. 1333 ?-1396)* pg. 265
Alvaro Portoghese *(mentioned 1411-1434)* 433
Andrea da Firenze *(mentioned 1343-1377)* 203
Andrea di Giusto *(?-1455)* 513
Antonio Veneziano *(mentioned 1369-1388)* 229
Bernardo Daddi *(active ca. 1312-1348)* 45
Bicci di Lorenzo *(1373-1452)* 471
Cenno di Francesco di Ser Cenni *(mentioned 1400-1415)* 381
Cristiani *(mentioned 1366-1398)* 255
Francesco di Antonio *(1393-1433 ?)* 425
Giotto *(1266/7-1337)* 3
Giovanni del Biondo *(mentioned 1356-1392)* 239
Giovanni Bonsi *(mentioned 1351-1371)* 213
Giovanni da Milano *(mentioned 1350-1369)* 181
Giovanni dal Ponte *(ca. 1385-1437)* 355
Giovanni Toscani (Master of the Griggs Crucifixion) *(1372-1430)* 493
Jacopo del Casentino *(ca. 1300-1349)* 115
Jacopo di Cione *(active ca. 1360-1398)* 161
Lippo di Benivieni *(mentioned 1296- ?)* 27
Lorenzo di Bicci *(ca. 1350-1427)* 409
Lorenzo Monaco *(ca. 1370-ca. 1425)* 367
Lorenzo di Niccolò *(mentioned 1392-1411)* 391
Mariotto di Cristofano *(1393-1457)* 553
Mariotto di Nardo *(ca. 1373-1424)* 451
Masaccio *(1401-ca. 1428)* 503
Maso di Banco *(mentioned 1341-1346)* 125
Masolino *(1383-ca. 1440)* 483
Master of the Arte della Lana *(active 1375 ?)* 323
Master of Bambino Vispo *(active ca. 1410-1425)* 441
Master of Figline (Master of the Fogg Pietà) *(active ca. 1320-1360 ?)* 105
Master of Fucecchio (Master of the Adimari Cassone) *(active 1435-1460 ?)* 543
Master of the Giraldi Tabernacle *(active 1370)* 221
Master of the Rinuccini Chapel *(active ca. 1365-1370 ?)* 193
Master of Santa Cecilia *(active ca. 1300-1320)* 35
Master of San Martino alla Palma *(active ca. 1330-1350)* 61
Master of San Martino a Mensola *(active ca. 1380-1400)* 275
Master of Santa Verdiana Panel *(active ca. 1385-1415)* 293
Master of the Straus Madonna *(active ca. 1390-1420)* 303
Master of Terenzano (Master of Dominican Effigies, and of the Cappella Medici) *(active ca. 1330-1350)* 95
Nardo di Cione *(active ca. 1343-1365)* 147
Niccolò di Pietro Gerini *(mentioned 1368-1415)* 313
Niccolò di Tommaso *(active ca. 1350-1380 ?)* 173
Orcagna *(mentioned 1344-1368)* 135
Pacino di Bonaguida *(active 1310-1330 ?)* 17
Paolo Schiavo *(1397-1478)* 523
Parri Spinelli *(1387-1453)* 533
Pietro di Miniato *(1366-ca. 1430)* 401
Pietro Nelli (Tommaso del Mazza) *(mentioned 1375-1419)* 331
Pseudo Ambrogio di Baldese *(active 1410-1420)* 417
Puccio di Simone (Master of the Fabriano Altarpiece) *(active ca. 1335-ca. 1365)* 85
Rossello di Jacopo Franchi *(1376 ?-1457 ?)* 461
Spinello Aretino *(active 1373-1410)* 343
Starnina *(active 1390-1410 ?)* 285
Taddeo Gaddi *(active 1332-1363)* 71

Appendices

Appendix A pg. 567

A visual reference list of painters:
  1) who worked in or near Florence just *before* and just *after* the period covered in this compilation;
  2) who worked *during* the period covered, in or near Florence, but either about whom almost nothing is known, or for whom reproductions are easily available.

At the end of this *Appendix A*, is a list of extant dated paintings, arranged chronologically, by unknown hands.
For most of these painters a single work or part of a work is reproduced.

This list as far as possible, has been arranged chronologically, and includes:

Alesso d'Andrea	pg. 581
Allegretto Nuzi	585
Ambrogio di Baldese	593
Amico di Daddi	580
Andrea del Castagno	604
Andrea di Nerio	606
Andrea Tafi	571
Angelico	601
Angelo Puccinelli	585
Antonio da Firenze	603
Antonio di Vita Ricci (Antonio Vite)	591
Apollonio di Giovanni	603
Arcangelo di Cola da Camerino	596
Arrigo di Niccolò	593
Bartolomeo Bertozzo	589
Bartolomeo da Frosino	592
Bartolomeo di Andrea Bocchi	600
Battista da Pisa	593
Battista di Biagio Sanguigni	601
Benozzo Gozzoli	606
Berlinghiero	567
Biadiaolo Illuminator	580
Bonaccorso di Cino	581
Bonaiuto di Corsino	592
Bonaventura Berlinghieri	569
Brunelleschi Master	588
Buffalmacco	574
Buonamico	575
Calvano di Cristofano	595
Cavallini	572
Cennino Cennini	587
Cimabue	571
Cipriani di Simone	600
Compagno d'Agnolo	589
Coppo di Marcovaldo	568
Corsino di Bonaiuto	585
Corso di Buono	572
Crawford-Thebaid Master	594
Dalmasio	582
Dello Delli	596
Dello Samsone	596
Deodato Orlandi	572
Dido Master	604
Dino di Puccio	589
Domenico di Michelino	602
Domenico Veneziano	598
Don Silvestro dei Gherarducci	583
Don Simone	583
Filippo Lippi	605
Fra Diamante	605
Francesco di Andrea Anguilla	591
Francesco Ghissi	584
Francesco di Michele Colonnato	587
Gaddo Gaddi	573
Gentile da Fabriano	596
Giottino	576
Giovanni d'Agnolo di Balduccio	599
Giovanni di Bonino	579
Giovanni di Consalvo	599
Giovanni di Francesco	600
Giovanni di Ser Giovanni	599
Giuliano Amadei	602
Giuliano d'Arrigo	600
Giuliano di Jacopo	597
Giuliano di Simone	588
Giunta di Jacopo Franchi	595
Giusto di Menabuoi	584
Isaac Master	573
Jacopo del Corso	600
Jacopo di Agnolo	589
Jacopo di Antonio	600
Jacopo di Cristofano	597
Jacopo da Firenze	593
Jacopo Torriti	571
Lapo di Firenze	568
Lippo Fiorentino	pg. 590
Lo Scheggia	599
Manfredino da Pistoia	571
Marco del Buono	604
Marco di Filippo	597
Margarito d'Arezzo	568
Master of 1310	574
Master of 1416	594
Master of 1419	595
Master of the Accademia Annunciation	591
Master of the Accademia Humility	583
Master of the Accademia Misericordia	592
Master of the Adimari Cassone	599
Maestro dell'Altare di S. Spirito	576
Maestro degli Arcangeli	598
Master of the Ashmolean Predella	583
Master of Bagnano	571
Master of the Barberino Madonna	590
Master of the Bargello Tondo	597
Master of the Bigallo	567
Master of Borgo alla Collina	596
Master of the Buckingham Palace Madonna	602
Master of Campodonico	583
Maestro delle Canzoni	593
Master of the Cappella Medici Polyptych	580
Maestro della Cappella dei Velluti	572
Master of the Carrand Triptych	601
Master of the Cassoni	604
Master of Castelfiorentino	572
Master of the Castello Nativity	605
Master of Cesi	574
Master of Chantilly	576
Master of the Chiostro degli Aranci	598
Master of the Christ Church Coronation	604
Master of the Cini S. Paolo	582
Master of the Cionesque (Orcagnesque) Humility	583
Maestro Colorista d'Assisi	576
Master of the Contini Madonna	601
Maestro del Convento del T	581
Master of the Corsi Crucifix	574
Master of the Corsini Triptych	580
Master Crawford-Thebaid	594
Maestro del Cristo Docente	588
Master of the Da Filicaia Cross	578
Master of the Dominican Effigies	580
Master of the Fabriano Altarpiece	583
Master of Figline di Prato	591
Master of the Figline di Prato Madonna	591
Maestro Francesco	588
Maestro del Giudizio dell'Ospedale	581
Maestro del Giudizio di Paride	597
Master of the Horne Triptych	575
Master of the Infancy of Christ	584
Master of the Innocenti Madonna	591
Master of the Jarves Cassone	604
Master of the Kahn St Catherine	586
Master of Karlsruhe	599
Master of the Life of the Virgin	597
Master of the Lord Lee Polyptych	580
Master of the Louvre Nativity (active third quarter, fourteenth century)	585
Master of the Louvre Nativity (active second half, fifteenth century)	605
Master of the Maddalena	570
Master of the Madonnas	589
Maestro di Marradi	597
Master of Mezzana	579
Master of Montefalco	577
Master of Montefloscoli	586
Master of Mosciano	570
Master of the Oberlin Cross	578
Master of the Orcagnasque (Cionesque) Humility	583
Master of the Orcagnasque Misericordia	592
Master of Panzano	569
Master of the Pentecost	582
Master of Popiglio	583
Master Prato	597
Master of Pratovecchio	598

Master of the Quarata Predella pg. 599
Master of the Rovezzano Tabernacle 590
Master of Ruballa 579
Master of S. Biagio in Caprile 583
Master of S. Chiara 572
Master of S. Eligio 592
Master of S. Gaggio 580
Master of S. Giacomo 587
Master of S. Giorgio alla Costa 575
Maestro di S. Girolamo 590
Master of S. Jacopo a Mucciana 590
Master of the S. Lorenzo Madonna 577
Master of S. Lucchese 586
Master of the S. Maria Novella Cross 578
Master of S. Martino 567
Master of S. Miniato 603
Master of the St Nicholas Altarpiece 587
Master of S. Pietro in Monticelli 578
Master of S. Remigio (active second half, thirteenth century) 570
Master of S. Remigio (active second quarter, fourteenth century) 580
Master of the S. Reparata Polyptych 579
Master of S. Quirico 579
Master of the S. Spirito Refectory 582
Master of the Sherman Predella 595
Master of Signa 603
Master of the Stefaneschi Altarpiece 576
Maestro delle Storie di S. Niccolò 589
Maestro del Tau 581
Maestro del Trionfo della Morte 575
Maestro Universitas Aurificum 583
Master of Varlungo 573
Maestro Vaticano 590
Maestro delle Vele 573
Maestro del Vescovado 585
Master of Vico l'Abate 568
Master Vicchio-Paris 577
Master of Vicchio a Rimaggio 578
Master of the Vincigliata Madonna 586
Master of the Virgin of Mercy 583
Matteo Pacini 584
Meliore Toscano 570
Meo di Frusino 589
Nanni di Jacopo 594
Neri di Bicci 606
Paolo Uccello 598
Pesellino 604
Pesello 595
Pietro Chellini 595
Prato Master 597
Pseudo Domenico di Michelino 602
Puccio Capanna 577
Salerno di Coppo 569
Ser Monte 585
Stefano di Antonio di Vanni 601
Stefano di Lorenzo 595
Stefano Fiorentino 576
Tommaso del Mazza 585
Torelli 592
Ventura di Moro 597
Vicchio-Paris Master 577
Virgil Master 604
Zanobi Machiavelli 603
Zanobi Strozzi 602

Some dated paintings by unknown hands, listed chronologically pg. 607

Appendix B

Glossary pg. 617
List of saints appearing in this work and their usual symbols. 619

Appendix C

Page references to Offner's Corpus, and Berenson's Florentine Lists. pg. 625

Appendix D

I. A chronological list of known dated works, 1300-1450. pg. 629

II. Three lists, by artist, of:
1) signed works; 631
2) dated works; 633
3) signed and dated works. 635

III. A list, by year, 1300-1450, including:
1) dated works; signed and dated works;
2) documented works;
3) some works dated by Berenson, Marcucci and Offner. 636

Appendix E

Maps of the area around Florence, in the provinces of Florence, Pistoia, Arezzo, Siena and Pisa. pg. 645

List of photographers. 661

Topographical list of locations of paintings reproduced. 663

XV

Preface

The purpose of this work is to provide a handbook of the painters active in Florence during the fourteenth and first half of the fifteenth centuries.

Whereas reproductions of works by Giotto and Masaccio are often published, photographs of paintings by such neglected artists as the Gaddi or the Cioni are difficult to find outside of the various photograph libraries — the Witt in London, the Villa I Tatti, and Kunsthistorisches Institut, in Florence, and a few others. In these *fototeche*, attributions which are correct will be found next to many, frequently scores, which are tentative or even incorrect. The confusion for both the novice and the more experienced frustrates understanding of the individual painters and of the period as a whole. Even when some of the work of an artist has been published, it is often represented by a few paintings badly reproduced in specialized journals. Bibliography for the painters of the period is usually similarily scattered among various journals and exhibition catalogues.

The present compilation makes conveniently available good reproductions of works by almost all the principal, known painters working in Florence from just after the beginning of the fourteenth century until the end of the fifth decade of the fifteenth. Omitted, however, are those painters of the 1430's and 1440's for whom reproductions are easily available. Except in a few cases, there are between twenty and twenty-five illustrations of each painter's work. Examples of the work of Giotto and Masaccio have been included to give two poles of reference within the book itself. A few of the fifteenth century painters included worked after the early death of Masaccio. They were, however, his contemporaries. Although he predeceased them, in a certain sense his painting surpassed theirs.

Together with the illustrations of each painter's work are biographical notes, bibliography, and an indication of his signed or dated paintings.

The paintings illustrated are, first of all, the known *signed and dated*, and known *signed* works of the period. Almost all of these are reproduced. Almost all known *dated* paintings are also illustrated. Many documented pictures are included as well, as are numerous other works representative of the manner of each painter. Further, in *Appendix A* there are reproductions of other dated paintings of less sure attribution. This first appendix contains the names of many painters, mostly Florentines, who worked before or after the period in question. For each of these a biographical note and bibliographical reference is given, while for most an important work is reproduced. This section also contains some Florentines of the period 1300-1450 who were either too minor or too well-known to merit inclusion in the main body of the book.

This catalogue is meant to be representative. There has been no attempt to include reproductions of all the work of an artist: rather it has been the aim to provide enough good illustrations to outline each painter's manner. In any case, problems of attribution are not always resolved by a simple abundance of black and white photographs: colour, brushwork, cracking of the gold-leaf, preservation in general, size, punch-hole and tooling, secret inscriptions, as well as other factors, can often only be known from the paintings themselves.

Obviously, in a period as distant from us in time, as extraordinarily prolific in painting, and as long, the question of attribution sometimes arises. However, the selection of works other than those signed, has been carefully based upon the opinions of the various critics. Those opinions are sometimes, of course, at variance one with another. I have in such cases had to decide which works to illustrate, avoiding controversy as much as possible. I have also in a number of cases attributed new works to a painter where such attribution seems clearly correct. Questions of attribution or of artistic personality are not, however, the primary scope of this handbook: the object is to stimulate study of the period, not to resolve its problems.

Arrangement

The painters are listed chronologically, and each painter's section is arranged in the following way:

— *biographical quotations* about the artist
— *a bibliography* divided into two parts: citings in books; citings in journals. This is done to facilitate research in libraries, where books and journals are usually in separate sections.
— *a list of signed and dated, dated, and signed works by the artist*
— *reproductions of each artist's work.*

Following the last of the painters arranged in this way — Mariotto di Cristofano — are five *Appendices* designed to facilitate further the study of the period.

Biographical quotations. I have tried to provide an indication of opinions of each painter's dates, work and personality by quoting chronologically from the various critics. For clarity I have omitted pages or footnote references, when these occurred in the passage; they can be obtained by returning to the original. The citations reflect the disagreement or progress of criticism. Translations are my own.

Bibliography. Any bibliography for such an important body of work is bound to include almost anything ever written on the period or its painters. Therefore, in order to restrict the bibliography to a fairly workable size, I have included for each painter a limited number of the more recent references, paying particular attention to the various journals. If further references are required, they can easily be obtained in the articles and books cited. For the bibliography before 1917, Lothrop's *Bibliographical Guide....* (etc.) is useful; for that before 1950, see, *Enciclopedia della Pittura Italiana*, Galetti, U., and Camesasca, E., under the individual entries. Extremely useful sources are: the *Index* for the *Rivista d'Arte*, 1903-1942; the *Zeitschrift für Kunstgeschichte*, which publishes art-historical bibliographies regularly; and the *Art Index*. For reference, the Camerani bibliography to the Florentine archives (1956) is included, as are the lists of Tuscan archives of 1956 and 1960. Abbreviations have been adopted, both for the journals and for citings in more general works. Citations in these last are indicated by an asterix, and are listed in the *General Bibliography*, at the end of this *Preface*. The use of *Edit.* merely indicates an un-named author or authors.

Signed and Dated Lists. These are lists of all the works known to me which are either dated, or signed, or both. Sometimes, when it is well known that a panel once formed part of a dated painting, the panel is also considered dated.

Sometimes a date is given, without the letters *d.* for a date, or *s & d.* for a *signed and dated* painting, preceding it: in this case, the painting was probably painted in that year, and there is documentary or other evidence to support the date.

Photographs of paintings. Photographs have been chosen with care to present a valid impression of the painter's style. In some cases, such as those of Bernardo Daddi, Giovanni del Biondo and Lorenzo Monaco, it has been difficult, among all the many attributed paintings, to choose only a limited number to be representative. In other cases, the number of identified extant paintings is limited, so that more details of whole paintings are included. Rather than attempting to arrange the illustrations of the paintings in some real or hypothetical chronological order, I have tried to present them so that they best clarify each painter's style.

Appendix A. This is a list of painters who worked in or near Florence immediately before and after the period of this compendium; with these artists are also listed the names of many others, who worked in or near Florence *during* the period covered, but who are not included in the main body of this work, being either almost entirely unknown, or too well-known to have been included. Further, a few painters from other towns in or near the Arno valley are included, artists who may also have worked in Florence. A biographical note is given for each painter, as well as a bibliographical reference, and, for most, an illustration of an important painting. This list, including but part of the large number of painters actually involved, is obviously inadequate, so certainly are the minimal bibliographical and biographical references. None the less, it is hoped that it will prove useful.

Included also is a short list of extant dated Florentine paintings, by artists whose names are at the moment not known to us, as well as an illustration of each of the pictures in question.

Appendix B is in two parts: the first contains a glossary of some of the more common terms used when studying Florentine painters and paintings of the period; the second lists the saints who appear in the catalogue, and their usual symbols.

Appendix C. The two most useful modern works for the study of painters of the period are Offner's *Corpus* and Berenson's *Florentine* lists. Unfortunately, of the former, only fourteen volumes of the thirty projected in 1930, have so far appeared. Unfortunately, also, neither has a proper index. This is a fairly small matter in the 1963 edition of Berenson's lists; it makes Offner's work very difficult to use. For convenience, I have therefore included in *Appendix C* an alphabetical list of all the relevant painters contained in both works, and page numbers for them. A list of the fourteen Offner volumes which have so far been published, and their general contents, is also included.

Appendix D contains lists of all the *dated, signed,* and *signed and dated* paintings in the main section of this compendium, as well as of the dated Florentine paintings listed in *Appendix A.* These lists should contain almost all of the signed and dated Florentine paintings of the period. Listed also are some documented works, and some of the works to which Berenson, Offner and Marcucci have assigned tentative dates.

Appendix E consists of maps of the Arno valley with adjacent areas, showing the location of the smallest villages, castles and churches.

Some other comments

Dimensions. The correct dimensions of pictures of this period is a complicated question. For frescoes they are rarely cited, or even taken. Until recently these wall-paintings remained where they were painted, but more and more frequently they are being detached, restored and remounted on movable surfaces. After restoration, the paint-

ings are usually returned to their original locations and hung as though part of the wall. Sometimes, however, they are placed in museums or in storage. For purposes of future identification, frescoes should be carefully measured.

Conversely, dimensions for panel paintings are usually available. These, however, are undependable, for it is not always clear *which* dimensions are given. Sometimes the measurement is taken of the picture surface inside the frame; sometimes a slightly different result will be given by taking the measurement without the frame. On other occasions a measurement includes the frame of the picture: *ancone* are a good example of this. On still others, the frame is not included: for example, when the frame is a restoration or an addition. If the picture is a large polyptych, still intact, accompanied by the original predella, would it be correct to measure it with the predella or without? And how does one measure accurately such a picture — which is really a whole group of pictures — giving all the gothic appendages their just due? There are also occasions when the measurements have simply been taken incorrectly. There are others, when the dimensions have changed since the picture was measured, through some alteration, such as the deterioration of the wood backing, or cutting-up for commercial reasons. In any case, I have given no dimensions for frescoes, whether detached or not, as practically speaking few are available anyway. For panel paintings, I have given dimensions whenever they have been available, height before width, as they have been communicated to me: I have however, for consistency, quoted them all in centimetres: *cp* and *sps* refer to the dimensions of *central panel* and *side panels*, as does *lp, left panel,* and *rp, right panel; wf* and *wof* refer to measurements, *with frame* and *without frame.*

Technique. We do not know a great deal about the various techniques of painting in the fourteenth and fifteenth centuries. No doubt these varied considerably from painter to painter. Besides, those techniques must have changed over the years — certainly much more than is generally known or recognized. The *Bibliography* includes the names of a few works on painting methods. The best of these is Cennino Cennini's *Libro dell' Arte,* translated and published by D. V. Thompson, Jr., in 1933. Vasari's comments in the *Preface* to his *Lives* are also excellent. These were published in English in 1907, edited by G. B. Brown, as *Vasari on Technique.* This book has recently been reprinted by Dover Books, of New York (1960). Another good work, also recently re-published, is Merrifield, Mrs., *The Art of Fresco Painting,* London, 1896, 1952. To be recommended also is the work of both Prof. Mojmir Frinta, and of E. Skaug, particularly the former's introductory note on the tooling of gold in mediaeval panel painting, cited among the general articles. Their work gives a good indication of how study of technique can be helpful in the understanding of painting of the period; two similar approaches are B. Klesse's book on patterns in cloth (1967), and M. Cämmerer-George's work on frames (1966). I have, when referring to the two most common categories of pictures made during the fourteenth and fifteenth centuries — pictures on wooden panels and pictures on walls, simply used the terms " panel " and " fresco "; there is a note on these terms in the glossary.

Restoration. Pictures known to be by the same master will sometimes show significant differences. These are due in the first instance to the painter's own development, but often changes are due either to treatment over the last five to six hundred years, or to modern restoration. This last development has been known to leave pictures looking scrubbed, without original shading, outlines or colour. It can also replace not just glazes and varnish, half a millenium old, with new substitutes, but can repaint whole sections of pictures. In fact, two similar pictures by the same painter can not only *seem* to be by different hands, but actually be so altered during restoration as to *be* by differents hands.

Particular Problems of Attribution. Three paintings not usually considered to be by Giotto's hand have been illustrated among his works, as they are all signed.

There are a few places where the styles of painters are particularly similar. Among these is the distinction between *Nardo di Cione* and his brother *Jacopo.* The relationship is not always very clear; it is complicated by the fact that they must have worked a great deal together until the former's death. The paintings of *Niccolò di Tommaso* are also sometimes difficult to distinghish from some of those of the Cioni. Niccolò knew the Cioni and may have worked with them; it is even suggested that he was a pupil of Nardo.

Another problem is that of the differences in style between *Niccolò di Pietro Gerini, Pietro Nelli* and the *Master of the Arte della Lana*. This problem is all the more difficult because of the documented presence of *Tommaso del Mazza* in the large Impruneta polyptych. That altarpiece would seem to be by two distinct painters: one who painted the Madonna and Child (fig. 685); another who painted the twelve saints flanking the central panel (figs. 687 & 691). The hand which painted the central panel — be it that of Pietro Nelli, Tommaso del Mazza or someone else — is similar to that of the painter named by Berenson, the Master of the Arte della Lana (fig. 665). Further, the Master of the Arte della Lana is difficult to distinguish from Niccolò di Pietro Gerini. Instead of abandoning the Master of the Arte della Lana, and grouping those which would seem to be his pictures with the work of Niccolò di Pietro Gerini, or with that of Pietro Nelli, I have retained the usual groupings. All the reproductions of the various panels of the Impruneta altarpiece are to be found under the name of Pietro Nelli. This whole problem has recently been somewhat clarified by Luciano Bellosi.

Both the *Giraldi Master* and the Master of the Arte della Lana seem, too, to be close sometimes to the work — as little as we know of it — of *Giovanni Bonsi*; this is also true of some of the work of the *Master of the Rinuccini Chapel*. This last painter has recently been identified as Matteo Pacini, again by Luciano Bellosi.

There may also be confusion among the works attributed to the *Master of the Straus Madonna*. The panel for which the painter is named, in Houston, seems so much more volumetric, bold and well-painted than many of the paintings attributed to this hand, that we may be dealing with a case of master and imitator: I have however retained the grouping, preferring, as noted above, to point out an apparent problem, open to study.

Another problematic relationship is that of Alvaro Portoghese to the so-called Master of the Bambino Vispo: their forms are often alike. The Master of the Bambino Vispo has now been tentatively identified with Starnina.

PHOTOGRAPH SOURCES

Paintings are reproduced not only with the kind permission of the various collections but also because of assistance proffered. I must thank especially the Staff of the *Gabinetto Fotografico* of the Soprintendenza alle Gallerie in Florence who aided me in all my searches for photographs. For the same reason I would like to make note of the assistance of Signorina Guidotti and Signora Corti, at the firm of Alinari and thank them. I also owe thanks to two photographers: Signor Rodolfo Reali, who sadly died during the compilation of this book. He was among the very finest photographers of works of art, ever. In particular manner, too, I owe much to Marcello Bertoni and to his family, and thank them for all their kindnesses over the last years. I have besides, a very special feeling of gratitude towards Fiorella Superbi, the keeper of photographs at the Villa *I Tatti*, the Villa Berenson. Her kindness and help on literally scores of occasions confirm that marvellous reputation for generosity and efficiency which she enjoys. I thank her warmly.

The source of each photograph is noted in its caption; abbreviations are used for convenience. The abbreviation is given with the photographer's address, at the back of the book. *Museum Photo* means simply that the photograph came from the museum where the work is now located. *Bertoni-Berenson* or *Fototeca Berenson* signifies that the photograph is a copy of a photo in Villa *I Tatti*; *Bertoni-Offner* indicates a copy by Bertoni of a photograph in Offner's *Corpus*. Photographs of pictures in museums and private collections can usually be ordered through the Secretary of the collection in question, whether the negative belongs to the collection or to a professional photographer.

The Courtauld and Berenson Libraries will usually copy photographs in their keeping. Sotheby's take their own photographs; photographs from Christie's can be ordered directly or through A. C. Cooper, the firm which acts for them. Photographs of all pictures from the Kress Collection, except of those pictures now in the National Gallery in

Washington, should be obtained from the Samuel H. Kress Foundation in New York. I thank this Foundation warmly for all the photographs which they offered me free of charge, together with permission to publish them. For reproductions of pictures in or near Florence, either the commercial firm of Alinari (which includes the Anderson and Brogi collections) or the Gabinetto Fotografico attached to the Uffizi, can usually provide photographs, although many of the Alinari negatives are old, and many of the negatives of the Uffizi Gabinetto Fotografico were destroyed in the flood of 1966. Reali, in Florence, is slowly going out of business and their negatives sold. Many of their earlier negatives, particularly those ordered by Offner, are now in the Frick Reference Library, in New York. The Gabinetto Fotografico Nazionale in Rome can also often provide photographs for the whole of Italy, as can that in Pisa for the surrounding area.

I would like to thank those responsible for the care of the public and private collections noted in the captions, and in the topographical list at the end of the book (p. 663), who have given permission to reproduce pictures in their keeping. In particular I want to thank the keepers of collections who generously waived photograph reproduction fees, in the interest of study.

ACKNOWLEDGEMENTS

I am grateful to Mary Davis, Executive Vice-President of the Kress Foundation who was kind and helpful on many occasions.
I should also like to thank the following people, all of whom have aided me, in one way or another:
The late Nicky Mariano, and her sister Baronessa Alda Anrep, who has also recently died. Professor Myron and Mrs Gilmore, Nelda Cantarella Ferace and all the staff of the Villa Berenson; the staff of the Kunsthistorisches Institut ; Michel Laclotte who helped me with many things to do with pictures in French collections; Sir Harold Acton, who allowed me to study his father's collection and aided me with problems of attribution and dimension; Sidney and Frances Alexander; Hanna Kiel; Henry and Esther Clifford, as well as Henry and Byba Coster for hospitality and advice on many occasions; Luisa Vertova for a myriad of things but especially for abundant good advice and friendship; David Friedman; David Kolch; Marcia Early Brocklebank ; Renzo Chiarelli; Cesare Bucci; Penelope Eley; Andrea Rothe; Anna Maria Maetzke, Helen Stephenson, Nancy Isenberg, Margaret Haines, Elizabeth Locke, Kip Baker, and Gino Corti for their generous and various assistance. Anna Barsanti aided me in many ways over a period of almost four years. I thank her warmly. But I owe most, an absurdly enormous debt of gratitude, to Susan Haskins who originally agreed to assist me for six weeks; she, in fact, helped for three and a half years. Always in good humour, she never once, to my knowledge, made any significant error of either advice or fact. Many, many thanks: the book would never have been finished without her patience, hard work, and again, good humor. I should also like to thank all the admirable critics, living and dead, from whom I have not only learned so much, but from whom I have quoted liberally to provide outlines of the lives and work of the painters. For any misinterpretation or misrepresentation that may occur due to translation or cutting, I apologise. I should like to thank: U. Baldini, J. Beck, L. Bellosi, B. Berenson, L. Berti, K. Birkmeyer, M. Boskovits, M. Bucci, E. Camesasca, L. Castelfranchi-Vegas, G. B. Cavalcaselle, B. Cole, L. Coletti, D. E. Colnaghi, W. Cohn, J. A. Crowe, P. Dal Poggetto, C. de Azevedo, U. Galetti, St.-J. Gore, A. Graziani, M. Gregori, H. Gronau, J. S. Held, B. Khvoshinsky, B. Klesse, M. Laclotte, M. Levi D'Ancona, R. Longhi, A. Marabottini, G. Marchini, L. Marcucci, M. Meiss, J. Mesnil, M. L. Moriondo, R. Oertel, R. Offner, A. Parronchi, U. Pasqui, U. Procacci, G. Rossi, A. J. Rusconi, M. Salmi, R. Salvini, F. R. Shapley, C. Shell, O. Sirèn, K. Steinweg, W. Suida, P. Toesca, R. van Marle, J. van Waadenoijen, A. Venturi, F. Zeri. I should also like to express my gratitude to their various publishers for permission to quote.
Finally I would like to express my gratitude to Eugenio Cassin, Ljubivoje and Aleksander Stefanovic, to Massimo Barca, and Fabrizio Biffoli, to Ascanio Lepri, to Peter Murray and to Tom Rosenthal.

General bibliography

Journals and Books with their abbreviations

Abbreviations for Journals

A	L'Arte
AA	Art in America
AAM	Arte Antica e Moderna
AB	The Art Bulletin
ABI	Accademie e Biblioteche d'Italia
AC	Acropoli
ACOL	Atti e Memorie dell'Accademia Fiorentina di Scienze Morale, *La Colombaria*
AE	Archivo Español de Arte y Archeologia
AF	Arti Figurative
AHA	Acta Historiae Artium
AI	Arte Illustrata
AJ	Art Journal
AL	Arte Lombarda
AN	Art News
AP	Apollo
AQ	The Art Quarterly
AS	Arte e Storia
ASNP	Annali della Scuola Normale Superiore di Pisa
ASI	Archivio Storico Italiano
ASP	Archivio Storico Pratese
AST	Art Studies
AV	Antichità Viva
AVN	Arte Veneta
B	Belvedere
BA	Bollettino d'Arte
BAE	Bollettino dell'Accademia degli Euteleti
BCMA	Bulletin of the Cleveland Museum of Art
BDIA	Bulletin of the Detroit Institute of Arts
BFM	Bulletin of the Fogg Museum of Art
BHA	Bulletin du Musée Hongrois des Beaux-Arts
BIB	La Bibliofilia
BIR	Bollettino dell'Istituto Centrale del Restauro
BM	The Burlington Magazine
BMB	Bulletin of the Museum of Fine Arts, Boston
BMNV	Bulletin du Musée National de Varsovie
BSAO	Bollettino dell'Istituto Storico-Artistico Orvietano
BSP	Bullettino Storico Pistoiese
BWAG	Bulletin of the Walters Art Gallery
BWAM	Bulletin of the Worcester Art Museum
C	Commentari
CA	Critica d'Arte
CAJ	College Art Journal
CS	Connoisseur
DD	Dedalo
E	Emporium
GBA	Gazette des Beaux-Arts
GSAT	Giornale Storico degli Archivi Toscani

IS	International Studio
IV	Il Vasari
JA	Journal of Aesthetics and Art Criticism
JBK	Jahrbuch des Museums der Bildenden Kunst
JBM	Jahrbuch der Berliner Museen
JPK	Jahrbuch der Königlich Preussischen Kunstsammlungen
JW	Journal of the Walters Art Gallery
K	Kunstchronik
KGA	Kunstgeschichtliche Anzeigen
LA	Le Arti
LC	Liburni Civitas
M	Marsyas
MA	Magazine of Art
MIAB	Minneapolis Institute of Arts Bulletin
MKIF	Mitteilungen des Kunsthistorischen Instituts in Florenz
MKW	Monatshefte für Kunstwissenschaft
MM	Bulletin of the Metropolitan Museum of Art
MSV	Miscellanea Storica della Valdelsa
NCA	Nuova Critica d'Arte
NN	Napoli Nobilissima
O	L'Oeil
P	Pantheon
PA	Paragone
Pin	Pinacoteca
PMB	Bulletin of the Pennsylvania Museum
Prop	Proporzioni
PR	Princeton Record (Record of the Museum of Historical Art)
R	Rendiconti (Atti della Pontificia Accademia Romana di Archeologia)
RA	Rivista d'Arte
RADA	Rassegna d'Arte
RAI	Reale Accademia d'Italia
RAAM	Revue de l'art ancien et moderne
RAAN	Rassegna d'Arte Antica
RDA	La Revue des Arts
RDL	Revue du Louvre
RIA	Rassegna dell'Istruzione Artistica
RIAS	Rivista del Reale Istituto d'Archeologia e Storia dell'Arte
RJB	Bulletin van het Rijksmuseum
RKW	Repertorium für Kunstwissenschaft
RM	Rassegna Marchigiana
RN	Renaissance

S	Speculum
SAR	Scottish Art Review
SDA	Storia dell'Arte
SLB	Bulletin of the St. Louis City Art Museum
SIM	Simiolus
VA	Vita d'Arte
W	Weltkunst
WAMA	Worcester Art Museum Annual
WCJ	Journal of the Warburg and Courtauld Institutes
WRJ	Wallraf-Richartz-Jahrbuch

ZBK	Zeitschrift für Bildende Kunst
ZBKKK	Zeitschrift für Bildende Kunst, Kunstchronik und Kunst-litteratur
ZK	Zeitschrift für Kunst
ZKG	Zeitschrift für Kunstgeschichte
ZKW	Zeitschrift für Kunstwissenschaft

General Articles

1904   Suida, W., *RKW*, XXVII, 6, pp. 483-90
1905   Suida, W., *JPK*, XXVI, 1, pp. 28-39
1906   Sirèn, O., *JPK*, XXVII, 1, pp. 208-23
1906   Suida, W., *RKW*, XXIX, 1, pp. 108-17
1908   Suida, W., *RKW*, XXXI, 3, pp. 199-214
1920   Fiorilli, C., *ASI*, LXXVIII, 2, pp. 5-74.
1921   Sirèn, O., *A*, XXIV, pp. 97-102
1929   Piattoli, R., *RA*, XI, pp. 221-53, 396-437, 537-79
1930   Piattoli, R., *RA*, XII, pp. 97-150
1929-30 Various Authors, *RA*, XI-XII, 1-2.
1931   Richter, G. M., *BM*, LIX, pp. 250-1
1931   Berenson, B., *DD*, XI, 14, pp. 579-88; XI, 15, pp. 1039-73; XI, 16, pp. 1286-1318
1932   Berenson, B., *DD*, XII, 1, pp. 5-34; XII, 3, pp. 173-93; XII, 7, pp. 512-41; XII, 9, pp. 665-702
1933   Gamba, C., *BA*, XXVII, pp. 145-63
1933   Offner, R., *BM*, LXIII, pp. 72-84, 166-78
1933   Venturi, L., *A*, pp. 141-3
1935   Salmi, M., *RA*, XVII, pp. 411-21
1937   Coletti, L., *BA*, XXXI, III, pp. 49-72
1937   Salmi, M., *E*, XLIII, 7, pp. 349-64
1937   Sandberg-Vavalà, E., *WAMA*, III, pp. 23-44
1946   Meiss, M., *AB*, XXVIII, pp. 1-16
1947   Salmi, M., *ACOL*, XII, pp. 415-32
1954   Coletti, L., *ASNP*, XXII, 1-2, pp. 33-46
1956   Various Authors, *ASI*, CXIV, pp. 410-11 ; II-III, pp. 304-692
1956   Meiss, M., *RDA*, VI, pp. 139-48
1959   Previtali, G., *PA*, IX, 113, pp. 3-32
1959   Previtali, G., *PA*, IX, 115, pp. 3-18
1960   Various Authors, *ASI*, CXVIII, 427-28; III-IV, pp. 313-525
1962   Klesse, B., *ZKG*, XXV, 3-4, pp. 251-77
1963   Longhi, R., *PA*, XIV, 1967, pp. 3-16
1963   Zeri, F., *BA*, XLVIII, 4, pp. 245-58
1964   Tintori, L., and Meiss, M., *AB*, XLVI, 3, pp. 377-80
1965   Bellosi, L., *PA*, XVI, 187/7, pp. 18-43
1965   Frinta, M., *AB*, XLVII, pp. 261-65
1965   Longhi, R., *PA*, XVI, 183, pp. 8-16
1965   Zeri, F., *BM*, CVII, pp. 252-6
1967   Fahy, E., *BM*, CIX, pp. 128-39
1968   Boskovits, M., *AHA*, XIV, pp. 106-9
1968   Zeri, F., *GBA*, LXXI, 110, Feb., 1968, pp. 65-78
1969   Smart, A., *AP*, LXXXIX, pp. 256-63
1970   Cole, B., *AQ*, XXXIII, pp. 306-7
1970   Fremantle, R., *AJ*, XXX/1, pp. 41-44
1971   Meiss, M., *BM*, CXIII, 817, pp. 178-86
1971   Skaug, E., *MKIF*, XV, 2, pp. 141-60
1972   Boskovits, A., *PA*, XXIII, 265, pp. 35-61

General Books

Earlier References

For a list of these, see: Murray, P., *An Index of Attributions made in Tuscan Sources before Vasari*, Florence, 1959, and especially:

Albertini, F.,   *Memoriale di molte statue e pitture della città di Firenze* (1510), ed. by Nozzi, L. A. and Piaggio, L., Florence, 1863.

Anonymous   *Il Codice Magliabechiano* (Anonimo Gaddiano), Frey, C., Berlin, 1832; also see Fabriczy, C. van, in *ASI*, V, XII, 1893, pp. 15-94; as well as, more recently: Ficarra, A., *L'Anonimo Magliabechiano*, Naples, 1968.

Baldinucci, F.,   *Notizie de' professori del disegno da Cimabue in qua*, Florence, 1681-1728.

Billi, A.,   *Il libro di Antonio Billi esistente in due copie nella Biblioteca Nazionale di Firenze*, Frey, C., Florence, 1891, and *ASI*, V, VII, 1891, pp. 299-368.

Repetti, E.   *Dizionario geografico fisico storico della Toscana*, Florence, 1833-46.

Repetti, E.,   *Compendio storico della città di Firenze*, Florence, 1849.

Richa, G.,   *Notizie istoriche delle chiese fiorentine*, Florence, 1754-62.

Vasari, G.,   *Le vite de' più ecc. architetti, pittori ed scultori italiani*, Firenze, 1550, and the 2nd ed., of 1568.

Abbreviations for Books

Date	Title	Abbreviation
1859	Cennini, C., *Il Libro dell' Arte o Trattato della Pittura*, Ed. by G. and C. Milanesi, Florence.	Cennini 1
1893-1901	Milanesi, G., *Sulla Storia dell' Arte Toscana, Scritti Vari*, Siena. *Nuovi documenti per la storia dell' arte Toscana*, Rome, 1893, Florence, 1901.	Milanesi
1876	Pini, C. and Milanesi, G., *La Scrittura di Artisti Italiani*, Vol. I, Florence.	Pini, Milanesi
1878-85	Vasari, G., *Le vite de più eccellenti pittori, scultori, ed architetti*, Ed. Milanesi, Florence.	Vasari
1896	Schlosser, J. von, *Quellenbuch zur Kunstgeschichte des abendländischen Mittelalters*, Vienna.	Schlosser
1902	Brown, J. W., *The Dominican Church of Santa Maria Novella*, Edinburgh.	Brown
1902	Conway, (Sir) W. M., *Early Tuscan Art*, London.	Conway
1903	Crowe, J. A., and Cavalcaselle, G. B., *A History of Painting in Italy*, Vol. II, New York.	C-Cavalcaselle II
1905	Chiapelli, A., *Pagine d' Antica Arte Fiorentina*, Florence.	Chiapelli I
1905	Suida, W., *Florentinische Maler um die Mitte des XIV. Jahrhunderts*, Strassburg.	Suida, 1905
1906	Staley, E., *The Guilds of Florence*, London.	Staley
1907	Brown, G. B., *Vasari on Technique*, London (Reprint N. Y. [Dover], 1960).	Brown Vasari
1907	Cruttwell, M., *A Guide to the Paintings in the Florentine Galleries*, London, New York.	Cruttwell, 1907
1907-50	Thieme, U., and Becker, F., *Allgemeines Lexikon der Bildenden Künstler von der Antike bis zur Gegenwart*, Vols. I-XXXVII, Leipzig.	T-Becker
1907	Venturi, A., *Storia dell' Arte Italiana*, Vol. V, Milan (Vol. VII, 1911).	Venturi, A.
1908	Cruttwell, M., *A Guide to the Paintings in the Churches and Minor Museums of Florence*, London, New York.	Cruttwell, 1908
1911	Crowe, J. A., and Cavalcaselle, G. B., *A History of Painting in Italy*, Vol. IV, London.	C-Cavalcaselle IV
1914	D'Ancona, P., *La Miniatura Fiorentina*, Florence.	D'Ancona, 1914
1914	Khvoshinsky, B., and Salmi, M., *I Pittori Toscani del XIII al XIV Secolo*, Vol. II, Rome.	Khv & Salmi
1914	Laurie, A. P., *The Pigments and Mediums of the Old Masters*, London.	Laurie, 1914
1915	Schubring, P., *Cassoni: Truhen und Truhenbilder der Italienischen Frührenassance*, 2 vols, Leipzig.	Schubring
1916	Drake, M. W., *Saints and their Emblems*, London.	Drake
1917	Lothrop, S., *A Bibliographical Guide to Cavallini and the Florentine Painters before 1450*, Rome (American Academy).	Lothrop
1920	Errera, I., *Répertoire des peintures datées*, Vol. I, Brussels.	Errera
1924-25	van Marle, R., *The Development of the Italian Schools of Painting*, Vols. III, V, The Hague.	v. Marle, 1924, 1925
1924	Vitzhum, G., and Volbach, W. F., *Die Malerei und Plastik des Mittelalters in Italien*, Potsdam.	Vitzhum
1925	de Bles, A., *How to Distinguish the Saints in Art*, New York.	de Bles, 1925
1925	Chiapelli, A., *Arte del Rinascimento*, Rome.	Chiapelli, 1925
1925	D'Ancona, P., *La Miniature Italienne*, Paris.	D'Ancona, 1925
1926	Künstle, K., *Ikonographie der Heiligen*, Freiburg.	Künstle, 1926
1926	Laurie, A. P., *The Painters' Methods and Materials*, London.	Laurie, 1926
1927	Offner, R., *Italian Primitives at Yale University*, New Haven.	Offner, 1927
1927	Offner, R., *Studies in Florentine Painting. The Fourteenth Century*, New York.	Offner, Studies
1927	van Marle, R., *The Development of the Italian Schools of Painting*, The Hague, Vol. IX.	v. Marle, 1927
1928	Colnaghi, D. E., *A Dictionary of Florentine Painters*, London.	Colnaghi
1928	Künstle, K., *Ikonographie der Christlichen Kunst*, Freiburg.	Künstle, 1928
1928	van Marle, R., *The Development of the Italian Schools of Painting*, The Hague, Vol. X.	v. Marle, 1928
1929	*Reale Gallerie degli Uffizi, Firenze. Catalogo Topografico Illustrato*, Sala I., Florence.	Uffizi Cat. 1929
1929	Sandberg-Vavalà, E., *La Croce Dipinta Italiana*, Verona.	Vavalà, 1929
1929	Toesca, P., *Florentine Painting of the Trecento*, Florence.	Toesca, 1929
1930	Berenson, B., *Studies in Medieval Paintings*, New Haven.	Berenson, 1930
1930	Borenius, T., *Florentine Frescoes*, London.	Borenius
1930	Offner, R., *A Critical and Historical Corpus of Florentine Painting*, Sec. III, Vol. I-Sec. IV, Vol. 5 (14 vols., see Appendix A), New York.	Corpus, 1930-1969
1930	Weigelt, C. H., *Die Sienesische Malerei des Vierzehnten Jahrhunderts*, Florence, Munich.	Weigelt
1931	Hautecoeur, L., *Les Primitifs Italiens*, Paris.	Hautecoeur
1932	Berenson, B., *The Italian Painters of the Renaissance*, Oxford.	Berenson, 1932
1933	*Mostra del Tesoro di Firenze Sacra* (Catalogue: S. Marco), Florence.	Firenze, 1933
1933	Thompson, D. V., Jr., *The Craftsman's Handbook* (Cennino Cennini, *Il Libro dell' Arte*), New Haven.	Cennini 2
1933	Venturi, L., *Italian Paintings in America*, Vols. I and II, New York, Milan.	Venturi, L.
1934	Doerner, M., *The Materials of the Artist and their Use in Painting*, New York.	Doerner
1934	van Marle, R., *Le Scuole della Pittura Italiana*, Vol. II, The Hague.	v. Marle, 1934
1935	D'Ancona, P., *Les Primitifs Italiens du XI au XIII Siècles*, Paris.	D'Ancona, 1935
1935	Giglioli, O. H., *Le Scuole Pittoriche della Toscana*, Bergamo.	Giglioli
1936	Lavagnino, E., *Storia dell' Arte Medioevale Italiana*, Turin.	Lavagnino
1936	Procacci, U., *La Reale Galleria dell' Accademia di Firenze*, Rome.	Procacci, 1936
1936	Thompson, D. V., *The Materials of Medieval Paintings*, London.	Thompson
1939 (?)	Bazin, G., *La Peinture Italienne aux XIV et XV Siècles*, Paris.	Bazin
1940-54	Paatz, W., and E., *Die Kirchen von Florenz. Ein Kunstgeschichtliches Handbuch*, Vols. 1-6, Frankfurt.	Paatz
1942	Rivista d'Arte: *Index*, 1903-1942.	RA Index
1943	*Mostra Giottesca*, 1937, Catalogue, 2nd Edition, Bergamo.	M. Giottesca
1945	H. M. Stationery Office, *Works of Art in Italy, Losses and Survivals in the War*, London.	HMSO
1946	Coletti, L., *I Primitivi*, Vol. II (Vol. I, 1942), (Vol. III, 1947), Novara.	Coletti, Vol. I, II, III
1946-47	Procacci, U., *Mostra di Opere d' Arte Restaurate*, I, II, Florence.	Procacci, 1946-1947
1947	Morisani, O., *Ghiberti: I Commentari*, Naples.	Morisani
1948	Antal, F., *Florentine Painting and its Social Background*, London.	Antal
1948	Sandberg-Vavalà, E., *Uffizi Studies, The Development of the Florentine School of Painting*, Florence.	Vavalà, 1948
1949	Garrison, E. B., *Italian Romanesque Paintings*, Florence.	Garrison
s. d.	Pittaluga, M., *L' Arte Italiana*, Vol. II, Florence.	Pittaluga

1950	Galetti, U., and Camesasca, E., *Enciclopedia della Pittura Italiana*, Vols. 1-3, Cernusco sul Naviglio.	*Galetti*
1950	Oertel, R., Catalogue: *Frühe Italienische Tafelmalerei*, Stuttgart.	*Oertel, 1950*
1951	Englebert, O., *The Lives of the Saints*, London.	*Englebert*
1951	Hauser, A., *The Social History of Art*, Vol. I, London.	*Hauser*
1951	Meiss, M., *Painting in Florence and Siena After the Black Death*, Princeton.	*Meiss, 1951*
1951	Procacci, U., *La Galleria dell' Accademia di Firenze*, 2nd Edition, Rome.	*Procacci, 1951*
1951	Toesca, P., *Storia dell' Arte Italiana*, Vol. II, *Il Trecento*, Turin.	*Toesca, 1951*
1952	Kaftal, G., *Iconography of the Saints in Tuscan Painting*, Florence.	*Kaftal, 1952*
1952	Salvini, R., *Catalogo della Galleria degli Uffizi*, Florence.	*Salvini*
1950	Sewter, A. C., *Merrifield's The Art of Fresco Painting*, London.	*Merrifield*
1953	Baldini, U., *Mostra di Opere d' Arte Restaurate VII*, 1953.	*Baldini, 1953*
1953	Salmi, M., *L' Arte Italiana*, Florence.	*Salmi, 1953*
1954	Dupont, J., and Gnudi, C., *Gothic Painting*, Geneva.	*D-Gnudi*
1954	Ferguson, G., *Signs and Symbols in Christian Art*, New York.	*Ferguson*
1954	Muzzioli, G., *Mostra Storica Nazionale della Miniatura*, Rome; Florentine ed. 1953.	*Muzzioli*
1954	Salmi, M., *La Miniatura Fiorentina Gotica*, Rome.	*Salmi, 1954*
1954	Shorr, D. C., *The Christ Child in Devotional Images in Italy during the XIV Century*, New York.	*Shorr*
1956	Chastel, A., *L' Art Italien*, Vol. I, Paris.	*Chastel*
1956	Godfrey, F. M., *Early Italian Paintings*, London.	*Godfrey*
1956	Laclotte, M., *De Giotto à Bellini: Les primitifs Italiens dans les musées de France*, Paris.	*Laclotte*
1956	Lazaref, V. N., *The Origin of the Italian Renaissance*, Moscow.	*Lazaref*
1957	Brandi, C., *Studi in onore di Matteo Marangoni*, Pisa-Florence.	*Marangoni*
1957	Procacci, U., Pamphlet: *Del Distacco degli Affreschi e della loro Conservazione*, Florence.	*Procacci, 1957*
1957	Baldini, U., Berti, L., and Procacci, U., *Mostra di Affreschi Staccati I*, Florence.	*MAS I*
1958	Baldini, U., Berti L., and Procacci, U., *Mostra di Affreschi Staccati II*, Florence.	*MAS II*
1958-61	Carli, E., *Pittura Pisana del Trecento*, Vols. I-II, Milan.	*Carli*
1958	Herberts, K., *The Complete Book of Artists' Techniques*, London.	*Herberts*
1958-60	Procacci, U., *La Tecnica degli Antichi Affreschi e il Loro Distacco e Restauro*, Florence.	*Procacci, 1958, 60*
1958-67	*Enciclopedia Universale dell' Arte*, Venice-Rome, Vigni, G., *EUA, VIII*, pp. 279-83.	*EUA*
1959	*Mostre di Opere d' Arte Restaurate*, VIII, IX, X: 1955, 1958, 1959, Florence.	*MOA, VIII, IX, X*
1959	Carli, E., Gnudi, C., and Salvini, R., *Pittura Italiana*, Vol. I, Milano.	*Carli, 1959*
1959	Sandberg-Vavalà, E., *Studies in Florentine Churches*, Vol. I: *Pre-Renaissance Period*, Florence.	*Vavalà, 1959*
1959	Touring Club Italiano, *Toscana*, Milan.	*TCI, 1959*
1960	Borsook, E., *The Mural Painters of Tuscany, from Cimabue to Andrea del Sarto*, London.	*Borsook, 1960*
1960	Brown, G. B. *Vasari on Technique*, New York (see 1907).	
1960	Bucci, M., and Bertolini, L., *Il Camposanto Monumentale di Pisa*, Pisa-Milan.	*Camposanto*
1960	Gregori, M. (Croce Rossa di Firenze), *Mostra dei tesori segreti delle case fiorentine*, Florence.	*Gregori*
1960	Procacci, U., *Sinopie e Affreschi*, Florence.	*Procacci, 1960*
1961	Catalogue: *La Peinture Italienne des XIV et XV Siècles*, Cracow.	*Cracow*
1961	Davies, M., *National Gallery Catalogue: The Earlier Italian Schools*, 2nd Edition, London.	*Davies*
1961-62	Dewald, E. T., *Italian Painting 1200-1600*, New York.	*Dewald*
1961	Gúkovskii, M. A., *Italiia 1380-1450*, Leningrad.	*Gúkovskii*
1961	Catalogue: *Mostra di Arte Sacra Antica*, Florence.	*MASA*
1961	Oertel, R., *Frühe Italienische Malerei in Altenburg*, Berlin.	*Oertel, 1961*
1929-61	Treccani, Istituto Giovanni, *Enciclopedia Italia*, Vols. I-XXXVI; Appendices Vols. I-III, Milan-Rome.	*Treccani, Vol. I-XXXVI*
1962	Berenson, B., *The Study & Criticism of Italian Art*, New York.	*Berenson, 1962*
1962	Bologna, F., *La Pittura Italiana dalle Origini*, Rome-Dresden.	*Bologna*
1962	Hager, H., *Die Anfänge des Italienischen Altarbildes*, Munich.	*Hager*
1962	Levi D'Ancona, M., *Miniatura e Miniatori a Firenze dal XIV al XVI Secolo*, Florence.	*Levi D'Ancona*
1962	Mariano, N., and Russoli, F., *La Raccolta Berenson*, Milan.	*Mariano*
1962	Melis, F., *Aspetti della Vita Economica Medievale*, Siena.	*Melis*
1962	Tintori, L., and Meiss, M., *The Painting of the Life of St. Francis of Assisi with Notes on the Arena Chapel*, New York (2nd Edition, 1967).	*Tintori, Meiss*
1962	Touring Club Italiano, *Le Marche*, Milan.	*TCI, 1962*
1963	Berenson, B., *Italian Pictures of the Renaissance. Florentine School*, 2 vols., London.	*Berenson, 1963*
1963	Dal Poggetto, P., Catalogue: *Arte in Valdelsa*, Certaldo.	*AIV*
1963	Prunai, G., *Gli archivi storici dei Comuni della Toscana*, Rome.	*Prunai*
1964	Touring Club Italiano, *Firenze e Dintorni*, Milan.	*TCI, 1964*
1965	Boskovits, M., *L' Art du Gothique et de la Renaissance (1300-1500)*, Bibliography, 2 vols., Budapest.	*Boskovits, 1965*
1965	Marcucci, L., *I Dipinti Toscani del Secolo XIV*, Rome.	*Marcucci*
1965	Tintori, L., and Borsook, E., *Giotto, The Peruzzi Chapel*, New York.	*Tintori, Borsook*
1965	Gore, St. J., Wildenstein Catalogue: *The Art of Painting in Florence and Siena from 1250-1500*, London.	*Wildenstein*
1966	Boskovits, M., *Early Italian Panel Paintings*, Budapest.	*Boskovits, 1966*
1966	Castelfranchi-Vegas, L., *Il Gotico Internazionale in Italia*, Rome-Dresden (Eng. ed. Edition Leipzig, 1966)	*Castelfranchi-Vegas*
1966	Cämmerer-George, M., *Die Rahmung der Toskanischen Altarbilder im Trecento*, Strasbourg.	*Cämmerer-George*
1966	Città di Vita (Ed.), *Giotto e Giotteschi in Santa Croce*, Firenze.	*Città di vita*
1966	Gilbert, C., " Florentine Painters & the Origins of Modern Science ", in *Arte in Europa*, Vol. I: *Scritti di Storia dell' Arte in Onore di Edoardo Arslan*, Milan, pp. 333-40.	*AIE, 1966*
1966	Shapley, F. R., *Paintings from the Samuel H. Kress Collection, Italian Schools XIII-XV Century*, London.	*Shapley*
1966	Touring Club Italiano, *Umbria*, Milan.	*TCI, 1966*
1966	White, J., *Art and Architecture in Italy, 1250-1400*, Harmondsworth.	*White*
1967	Byam Shaw, J., *Paintings by Old Masters at Christ Church Oxford*, Oxford.	*Byam Shaw*
1967	Dal Poggetto, P., *Omaggio a Giotto*, Florence.	*Dal Poggetto*
1967	Klesse, B., *Seidenstoffe in der Italienischen Malerei des 14. Jahrhunderts*, Bern.	*Klesse*
1968	Arnoldi, F. N., *Storia dell' Arte*, Vol. II, Milan.	*SDA II*
1968-69	Boskovits, M., *Tuscan Paintings of the Early Renaissance*, Budapest.	*Boskovits, 1968*
1968	de Bosque, A., *Artisti Italiani in Spagna*, Milan.	*Bosque*
1968	Metropolitan Museum of Art, Catalogue: *The Great Age of Fresco*, New York (English edition: Arts	*Fresco Show*

Council of Great Britain: *Frescoes from Florence*, London, 1969).

1968   Oertel, R., *Early Italian Paintings to 1400*, London.   *Oertel, 1968*

1968   Winfield, D. C., *Middle and Later Byzantine Wall Painting Methods*, Dumbarton Oaks Papers XXII,   *Winfield*
pp. 63-139.

1969   Hartt, F., *History of Italian Renaissance Art*, New York.   *Hartt*

1969   Kiel, H., *Bernard Berenson, Homeless Paintings*, London.   *Kiel*

1969   Marchini, G., (Catalogue): *Due Secoli di Pittura Murale a Prato*, Prato.   *Prato, 1969*

1970   Meiss, M., *The Great Age of Fresco*, New York.   *Meiss, 1970*

1970   Seymour, C., Jr., *Early Italian Paintings in the Yale University Art Gallery*, New Haven and London.   *Seymour, 1970*

1970   Wundram, M., *Frührenaissance*, Baden-Baden.   *Wundram*

1971   Edit., *Giotto e il suo tempo: Atti del Congresso Internazionale per la celebrazione del VII centenario della nascita*   *Congresso VII*
di Giotto, Rome.

1971   Fremantle, R., *Florentine Painting in the Uffizi*, Florence.   *Fremantle*

1971   Zeri, F., and Gardner, E. E., *Italian Paintings, Florentine School*. Catalogue: Metropolitan Museum of   *MMOA*
Art, New York.

1972   Fredericksen, B. B., Zeri, F., *Census of Pre-Nineteenth-Century Italian Paintings in North American Public*   *Census*
Collections, Cambridge (Mass.).

1972   Seymour, C. Jr., *Italian Primitives: The Case History of a Collection and its Conservation*, New Haven.   *Seymour, 1972*

1974   Van Os, H. W., and Prakken, M., *The Florentine Paintings in Holland 1300-1500*, Amsterdam-Maarssen.   *Dutch Shon*

1974   Boccia, L. G., Corsi, C., Maetzke, A. M., Secchi, A., *Arte nell'Aretino*, Catalogue.   *Maetzke*

Florentine Gothic Painters

.....Of all the methods that painters employ, painting on the wall is the most masterly and beautiful, because it consists in doing in a single day that which, in the other methods, may be retouched day after day over the work already done..... It is worked on the plaster while it is fresh and must not be left till the day's portion is finished..... There is needed also a hand that is dexterous, resolute and rapid, but most of all a sound and perfect judgment; because while the wall is wet the colours show up in one fashion, and afterwards when dry they are no longer the same.....

..... And these old masters when they laid the gesso ground on their panels, fearing lest they should open at the joints, were accustomed to cover them all over with linen cloth attached with glue of parchment shreds, and then above that they put on the gesso to make their working ground. They then mixed the colours they were going to use with the yolk of an egg or tempera, of the following kind. They whisked up an egg and shredded into it a tender branch of a fig tree, in order that the milk of this with the egg should make the tempera of the colours, which after being mixed with this medium were ready for use. They chose for their panels mineral colours of which some are made by the chemist and some found in the mines.....

..... Nor was it in any way less ingenious to discover the method of spreading the gold over the gesso in such a manner that the wood and other material hidden beneath it should appear a mass of gold. This is how it is done. The wood is covered with the thinnest gesso kneaded with size weak rather than strong, and coarser gesso is laid on in several coats..... When the gesso is scraped and smoothed, white of egg beaten carefully in water is mixed with Armenian bole, which has been reduced with water to the finest paste. The first coat of this is made watery, I mean to say liquid and clear and the next thicker. This is laid on the panel at least three times, until it takes it well all over, then with a brush the worker gradually wets with pure water the parts where the Armenian bole has been applied and there he puts on the gold leaf, which quickly sticks to that soft substance; and when partially but not entirely dry he burnishes it with a dogs tooth or the tooth of a wolf in order to make it become lustrous and beautiful.....

..... The debt owed by many painters to Nature, which serves them continually as an example, that from her they may select the best and finest parts for reproduction and imitation, is due also, in my opinion, to the Florentine painter Giotto; because, when the methods and outlines of good painting had been buried for so many years under the ruins caused by war, he alone, although born in the midst of unskilful artists, through God's gift in him, revived what had fallen into such an evil plight and raised it to a condition which one might call good.....

Giorgio Vasari
Le Vite de più eccellenti architetti, pittori, e scultori italiani, Firenze, 1550

2

GIOTTO

In all probability Giotto was born in 1266; Vasari's statement that it was ten years later is hardly compatible with the facts that towards 1300 we find him already undertaking important works; besides this, Antonio Pucci says in his Centiloquio that Giotto died in 1336 at the age of seventy and Pucci being a contemporary of the artist we have no reason to doubt his word. His birthplace is Colle in the commune of Vespignano to the North of Florence.....

from R. van Marle, p. 3, *The Development of the Italian Schools of Painting*, Vol. III, The Hague, 1924.

Giotto di Bondone, Florentine, born 1266?, died Jan. 8, 1336/7. Painter, Sculptor, Architect, Mosaicist. Member of the Physicians and Apothecaries Guild between 1312-20. Pupil of Cimabue, influenced by Pietro Cavallini, master of Taddeo Gaddi, Bernardo Daddi, Maso di Banco, Stefano Fiorentino, Pucci Capanna, Francesco di Maestro Giotto (?), Guglielmo da Forli, Ottaviano da Faenza, Pace da Faenza, Pietro da Rimini, Giorgio da Firenze (?). Among his Neapolitan followers may be mentioned Maestro Simone Napoletano (?) and Roberto di Oderisio; the friend of Dante and, according to Vasari, of Oderigo da Gubbio. Known to and greatly esteemed by Petrarch; his praises sung by Boccaccio. According to the tradition of early commentators and Vasari, Giotto was the pupil of Cimabue, and, of course, he may have begun under that Master; but apparently the Master from whom he benefited most was the Roman Pietro Cavallini, the author of the frescoes in St. Cecilia and the mosaics in Sta. Maria in Trastevere. In a sense Giotto was the master of the whole school of painting in Italy. His influence was such that he not only changed the character of the Florentine school of painting and determined its direction during the fourteenth century, but also left his mark on the art of many cities throughout Italy, in which he worked.

from D. E. Colnaghi, pp. 125-126, *A Dictionary of Florentine Painters*, London, 1928.

There was a theory at the end of the 19th century, apparently supported by very old documents, that the father of Giotto, Bondone, exercised the trade of smith in Florence until 1260: he appeared to have moved there from Vespignano (Mugello) about 1230: his children, among whom Giotto, or Ambrogiotto, would have thus been born citizens; the dispute which began then still lasts, weakened but not dead; neither have the supporters of Giotto *mugellano*, nor the supporters of Giotto *fiorentino* been able to produce the decisive document. Nonetheless, one is inclined to consider probable his birth at Colle, where a number of entries in the records would seem to mention the artist and his family.....

from U. Galetti & E. Camesasca, p. 1124, *Enciclopedia della Pittura Italiana*," F-O ", Cernusco sul Naviglio, 1950.

Finally, his frescoes having made him famous throughout Italy, Giotto returned lastly to work in his own city. He was commissioned to decorate two chapels in the second greatest Franciscan church after that of Assisi, S. Croce in Florence. Arnolfo's stupendous architectural creation had been born practically under Giotto's own eyes and so recently that the plaster was almost still wet. It was the richest of the Florentine banking families who commissioned him, two who were most representative of the mercantile society of the time: the Bardi and the Peruzzi. The stories from the lives of Sts John the Baptist and John the Evangelist which Giotto frescoed onto the walls of the Peruzzi Chapel to the right of the main chapel in the apse, were painted sometime about the end of the second decade of the Trecento and the beginning of the third. The composition, which is more expansive than that used by the painter in Padua, is more spacious and contains more complex architectural arrangements; the stories have a more melodious and solemn tone which echoes along the whole length of the chapel wall and is not broken into separate scenes. This expansive atmosphere gives the figures' gestures tranquillity and grandeur; they appear less aggressive and sharp, less stony than in Padua.....

from M. Bucci, p. 27, *Giotto*, Florence, 1966.

When Vasari wrote of Giotto as ' the true restorer of the art of painting ' who ' put an end to the crude Greek (Byzantine) manner ', he was echoing a tradition which goes back to the lifetime of Giotto himself. His reputation as the leading Florentine artist of the day was clearly established; Dante (died 1321) refers to it in the " Purgatorio " (Canto XI, line 95), and his responsibility for ' the rise of the art of painting ' was unequivocally affirmed by Ghiberti in the fifteenth century.

Controversy surrounds the activity of Giotto at Assisi during the first decade of the Trecento, when the frescoes in the upper church of San Francesco were probably painted. His first certain works are the frescoes in the Arena Chapel in Padua. This was built by Enrico Scrovegni, consecrated in 1305, and therefore probably decorated between 1304 and 1312-3. Of his work for the church of Santa Croce in Florence, the Bardi (? 1312-20) and Peruzzi (? 1320-26) chapels survive, clearly demonstrating the existence of a large and competent workshop. Between 1329 and 1333 Giotto is known to have worked in Naples under royal patronage, but returned to Florence in 1334 as ' Capomaestro ' or Supervisor of Works for the Duomo in Florence.

from U. Procacci, p. 56, *Frescoes from Florence*, London, 1969.

The foundation and development of Florentine painting reflects a desire to construct and investigate an ideal world. This hoped-for world is placed on a miniature stage within a closed box. The box is open on one side, through which we observe this dream world, the stage being oriented, more or less, towards us, with a background behind. Giotto first uses this box, in the fourteenth century. Masaccio, in the fifteenth, puts air and light into it. And Michelangelo, in the sixteenth, begins to bring an oversized man to the front of the stage, and to destroy the background, thus destroying the spatial box.....

from R. Fremantle, p. 1, *Florentine Painting in the Uffizi*, Florence, 1971.

BIBLIOGRAPHY
BOOKS

An asterisk indicates a work listed in the General Bibliography

Cecchi, E., *Giotto*, Milan, 1937; Salvini, R., *Giotto, Bibliografia*, Rome, 1938; Brunetti, G., and Sinibaldi, G., *M. Giottesca**, 1943, pp. 301-33; *Vavalà, 1948**, pp. 29-39; Coletti, L., *Gli affreschi della basilica di Assisi*, Bergamo, 1949; Brandi, C., pp. 55-85 in *Scritti di Storia dell'Arte in Onore di Lionello Venturi*, Vol. I, Rome, 1950; *Galetti** " F-O ", 1950, pp. 1124-44; Paatz, W., pp. 85-102 in *Eine Gabe der Freunde für Carl Georg Heise zum 28.vi.1950*, Berlin, 1950; Seewald, R., *Giotto. Eine Apologie der Klassiken*, Olten, 1950; Carli, E., *Giotto*, Milan, 1951; Suida, W., *Paintings and Sculpture from the Kress Collection*, Washington, 1951, p. 26; *Toesca, 1951**, pp. 441-99; Salvini, R., *Giotto*, Milan, 1952; Arcangeli, F., *Le storie di Giotto: Gli affreschi della Cappella degli Scrovegni in Padova*, Milan, 1952-3; Bouzet, J., *Giotto: Gli affreschi della Chiesa Superiore di Assisi*, Milan, 1953; Oertel, R., *Die Frühzeit der Italienischen Malerei*, Stuttgart, 1953, pp. 62-76; Brandi, C., in *Scritti di Storia dell'Arte in Onore di Lionello Venturi*, Vol. II, Rome, 1956, pp. 55-85; *Laclotte**, 1956, pp. 7-8; *Offner, 1956**, Sec. III, Vol. VI, p. 6; Schöne, W., pp. 50-116, in *Festschrift Kurt Bauch, Kunstgeschichtliche Beiträge zum 25 November 1957* (n.d.); Gnudi, C., *Giotto*, Milan, 1958; Gnudi, C., *EUA**, Vol. VI, Venice-Rome, 1958, pp. 219-39; *Giotto, Cappella Bardi in Santa Croce* (Coll. " La Minima "), Milan, 1959; Bauch, K., *Giotto*, Berlin, 1959; Cecchi, E., *Giotto*, Milan, 1959; Gnudi, C., *Giotto*, Milan, 1959; Guglielmi, C., *Giotto, Simone Martini, Pietro Lorenzetti ad Assisi*, Rome, 1959; Hetzer, T., *Giotto di Bondone*, Stuttgart, 1959; Schöne, W., pp. 49-63, in *Festschrift Friedrich Winkler*, Berlin, 1959; *Vavalà, 1959**, pp. 26-67; Battisti, E., *Giotto. Etude biographique et critique*, Geneva, 1960; *Borsook, 1960**, pp. 128-31; Gabrielli, M., *Giotto e l'origine del realismo*, Rome, 1960; Meiss, M., *Giotto and Assisi*, New York, 1960; Shapley, F. R., *Catalogue of the North Carolina Museum of Art*, Raleigh, 1960, p. 30; Valsecchi, M., *Giotto*, Milan, 1960; *Cracow**, 1961, pp. 44-45; Gosebruch, M., in *Festschrift Kurt Badt*, Berlin, 1961, pp. 32-65; Gosebruch, M., in *Miscellanea Bibliothecae Hertzianae*, Munich, 1961, pp. 104-130; Gosebruch, M., *Giotto und die Entwicklung des neuzeitlichen Kunstbewusstseins*, Cologne, 1962; Procacci, U., pp. 9-45, in *Scritti di Storia dell'Arte in Onore di Mario Salmi*, Vol. II, Rome, 1962; Rosenthal, E., *The Changing Concept of Reality in Art*, New York, 1962, pp. 15-29, 49-56; Salvini, R., *Tutta la pittura di Giotto*, Milan, 1962 (2nd ed.); Tea, E., *Giotto*, Brescia, 1962; Tintori, L., and Meiss, M., *The Painting of the Life of St Francis in Assisi*, New York, 1962; von Nagy, M., *Die Wandbilder der Scrovegni-Kapelle zu Padua Giottoverhältnis zu seinen Quellen*, Berne and Munich, 1962; *Berenson, 1963**, Vol. I, pp. 79-81, 144; Gioseffi, D., *Giotto architetto*, Milan, 1963; Chastel, A., pp. 37-44, in *Studien zur Toskanischen Kunst. Festschrift für L. H. Heydenreich*, Munich, 1964; Previtali, G., *Giotto* (I Maestri del Colore, nos. 26, 27), Milan, 1964; Schrade, H., *Franz von Assisi und Giotto*, Cologne, 1964; Gilbert, C., pp. 80-6, 114-131, in *Essays in Honor of Walter Friedländer*, (*Marsyas* Supplement No II), New York, 1965; *Marcucci**, 1965, pp. 11-14; Previtali, G., *Gli affreschi di Giotto a Padova*, Milan, 1965; Salvini, R., *Giotto: gli affreschi di Assisi*, Florence, 1965; Salvini, R., *Giotto* (Forma e Colore, 4), Florence, 1965; Semenzato, C., *Giotto* (Forma e Colore, 33), Florence, 1965; Tintori, L., and Borsook, E., *Giotto: la Cappella Peruzzi*, Turin, 1965; Baccheschi, E., *The Complete Paintings of Giotto*, London, 1966; Battista, E., *Giotto*, Cleveland, (Ohio), 1966; Boskovits, M., *La Scuola di Giotto* (I Maestri del Colore, 248), Milan, 1966; Bucci, M., *Giotto* (I Diamanti dell'Arte), Florence, 1966; Chiarelli, R., *Giotto*, Bergamo, 1966; Gilbert, C., *AIE**, 1966, Milan, pp. 334-40; *Shapley**, 1966, pp. 20-22; Various authors, *Giotto e il Mugello, 1967*, Florence, 1967; Dal Poggetto, P., and Procacci, U., *Dal Poggetto**, 1967, pp. 7-14; Hirschfeld, P., pp. 88-90, in *Stil und Überlieferung in der Kunst des Abendlandes: Akten des 21 internationalen Kongresses für Kunstgeschichte in Bonn 1964*, Berlin, 1967; Palumbo, G., *Giotto e i giotteschi in Assisi*, Rome, 1970; Previtali, G., *Giotto e la sua bottega*, Milan, 1967; Procacci, U., *Fresco Show**, 1968, pp. 60-2 (56-8); Bologna, F., *Novità su Giotto: Giotto al tempo della Cappella Peruzzi*, Turin, 1969; Stubblebine, J. H., *Giotto: The Arena Chapel Frescoes*, New York, 1969; Gosebruch, M., and others, *Giotto di Bondone*, Würtzburg, 1970; Edit., *Giotto e il suo tempo: Atti del Congresso Internazionale per la celebrazione del VII° centenario della nascita di Giotto*, Rome, 1971; Fremantle, R., *Florentine Painting in the Uffizi*, Florence, 1971, p. 1; *MMOA**, 1971, pp. 13-16; Smart, A., *The Assisi Problem and the Art of Giotto*, Oxford, 1971; Martindale, A., *Rise of the Artist in the Middle Ages & Early Renaissance*, London, 1972, pp. 22, 37, 38, 40, 41, 100-101, 122; Ragghianti, C. L., *Stefano da Ferrara*, Florence, 1972, pp. 11-27; Gilbert, C., *History of Renaissance Art throughout Europe*, New York, 1973, pp. 29-31.

JOURNALS

Mather, F. S., Jr., *ASI*, 1925, pp. 25-32; Rambaldi, P. L., *RA*, XIX, 1937, pp. 286-348; Procacci, U., *RA*, XIX, 1937, pp. 377-89; Rambaldi, P. L., *RA*, XIX, 1937, pp. 349-56; Suida, W., *P*, XX, 1937, pp. 347-52; Rambaldi, P. L., *RA*, XIX, 1937, pp. 357-69; Oertel, R., *ZKG*, VI, 1937, pp. 218-38; Zanocco, R., *RA*, XIX, 1937, pp. 370-3; Zanocco, R., *RA*, XIX, 1937, pp. 374-6; Sandberg-Vavalà, E., *BM*, LXXXIII, 1946, pp. 102-103; Alpatoff, M., *AB*, XXIX, 1947, pp. 149-54; FF, *AVN*, I, 1947, p. 303; Cellini, P., *Prop*, II, 1948, pp. 55-61; Freyham, R., *WCJ*, XI, 1948, pp. 79-82; Longhi, R., *Prop*, II, 1948, pp. 49-52; Oertel, R., *ZKG*, XII, 1949, pp. 125-130; Hartlaub, GF, *ZKW*, IV, 1950, pp. 19-34; Carrà, C., *MA*, 44, 1951, pp. 261-7; MS., *AN*, 1951, p. 12; Mâle, E., *RDA*, I, 1951, pp. 46-7; Mitchell, C., *WCJ*, XIV, 1951, pp. 1-6; Longhi, R., *PA*, II, 13, 1951, pp. 19-40; Longhi, R., *PA*, III, 31, 1952, pp. 18-24; Brandi, C., *BM*, XCIV, 1952, p. 218; Baldini, U., *BA*, XXXVII, 4, 1952, pp. 254-5; Bush-Brown, A., *AB*, XXXIV, 1952, pp. 42-6; Valentiner, W. R., *AQ*, XV, 2, 1952, pp. 157-158; Frey, D., *WRJ*, XIV, 1952, pp. 73-98; Morisani, O., *BM*, XCV, 1953, pp. 267-70; Murray, P., *WCJ*, XVI, 1953, pp. 58-80; Bauch, K., *MKIF*, VII, 1, 1953, pp. 43-64; Ragghianti, C. L., *NCA*, I, 1954, pp. 1-18; Fisher, M. R., *AB*, XXXVIII, 1956, pp. 47-52; Shorr, D. C., *AB*, XXXVIII, 1956, pp. 207-14; White, J., *BM*, XCVIII, 1956, 344-51; Laclotte, M., *RDA*, VI, 1956, pp. 75-6; Gandolfo, G., *NCA*, III, 1956, pp. 32-55; Marcucci, L., *MKIF*, IX, 3-4, pp. 141-158; Schlegel, U., *ZKG*, XX, 1957, pp. 125-146; Zeri, F., *PA*, VIII, 85, 1957, pp. 79-87; Zeri, F., *PA*, VIII, 85, 1957, pp. 75-9; Chastel, A., *RDA*, VIII, 1958, p. 100; Gilbert, C. E., *BA*, LIII, 4, 1958, pp. 192-7; Gosebruch, M., *K*, XI, 1958, pp. 288-91; Procacci, U., *RA*, XXXIII, 1958, pp. 121-39; Brown, H., *Studies in the Renaissance*, VII, 1960, pp. 27-42; Smart, A., *BM*, CII, 1960, pp. 540-41; Smart, A., *BM*, CII, 1960, pp. 405-13, 431-7; Stöckelová, G., *A*, LIX, 25/4, 1960, pp. 277-88; Kiel, H., *P*, XVIII, 1960, pp. 309-11; Pini, U., *AC*, 1, 1960-1, pp. 7-37; Gioseffi, D., *AVN*, XV, 1961, pp. 11-24; Gosebruch, M., *Miscellanea Bibliothecae Hertziana*, 1961, pp. 104-30; Gilbert, C., *JA*, XX, 1, 1961, pp. 111-12; Virch, C., *MM*, 19, 1961, pp. 185-93; Fisher, M. R., *RN*, XIV, 1961, pp. 252-4; Previtali, G., *PA*, XII, 139, 1961, pp. 69-74; Mellini, G. L., *NCA*, VIII, 1961, pp. 17-26; Borsook, E., *RA*, XXXVI, 1961-2, pp. 89-107; de Tolnay, C., *RA*, XXXVI, 1961-2, pp. 3-10; Klesse, B., *ZKG*, XXV, 1962, pp. 254-264; Smith, M. Q., *BM*, CIV, 1962, p. 110; Previtali, G., *PA*, XIII, 1962, pp. 63-5; Paccagnini, G., *AVN*, XVII, 1963, pp. 224-228; Tintori, L., *Studies in Conservation*, VIII, 2, 1963, pp. 37-41; Volpe, C., *PA*, XIV, 1963, 157, pp. 3-14; Arslan, E., *BA*, XLVIII, 1963, pp. 221-38; Longhi, R., *PA*, XIV, 167, 1963, pp. 3-6; Previtali, G., *PA*, XIV, 165, 1963, pp. 71-80; Becker, M. B., *AB*, XLVI, 1964, pp. 376-77; Tintori, L., and Meiss, M., *AB*, XLVI, 1964, pp. 377-80; Stubblebine, J. H., *AB*, XLVII, 1965, p. 302; Smart, A., *AP*, 81, 1965, pp. 257-263; Romanini, A. M., *BA*, 5, 1, 1965, pp. 160-180; Baro, G., *AA*, LIV, 1966, pp. 100-1; Boskovits, M., *ZKG*, XXIX, 1, 1966, pp. 51-66; Smart, A., *AP*, 83, 1966, p. 268; Bellosi, L., *PA*, XVII, 201/21, 1966, pp. 76-7; Rosenbaum, A., *M*, XIII, 1966-7, pp. 1-7; Toesca, P., *PA*, XVIII, 209/229, 1967, pp. 33-40; Shearman, J., *PA*, XVIII, 203/23, 1967, p. 26; Previtali, G., *PA*, XVIII, 213/33, 1967, pp. 64-65; Herrmann, F., *CS*, 165, 1967, pp. 153-4; Kempt, W., *ZKG*, XXX, 1967, pp. 309-20; Kardos, T., *AHA*, XIII, 1967, pp. 137-48; De Benedictis, C., *AV*, VI, 4, 1967, pp. 33-50; Kruft, H. W., *K*, XX, 1967, pp. 342-46; Hueck, I., *MKIF*, XIII, 1-4, 1967-1968, pp. 1-30; Conti, A., *PA*, XIX, 225, 1968, pp. 10-20; Smart, A., *BM*, CX, 1968, pp. 100-2; Rotondi, P., *A*, I, 1, 1968, pp. 74-97; Weiss, G., *A*, II, 1968, pp. 5-25; d'Arcais, F., *CA*, XV, 97, 1968, pp. 23-34; Bongiorno, L. M., *AB*, L, 1968, pp. 11-20; Mellini, G. L., *CA*, XV, 98, 1968, pp. 49-64; Conti, A., *PA*, XX, 231, 1969, pp. 61-63; Gruenwoldt, R., *AP*, LXXXIX, 1969, pp. 350-355; Kruft, H. W., *ZKG*, XXXII, 1, 1969, pp. 47-51; Ragghianti, C. L., *CA*, XVI, 101-102, 1969, pp. 3-80; Serra, J. R., *C*, XX, 1-2, 1969, pp. 20-36; Nessi, S., *C*, XX, 3, 1969, pp. 157-61; Venturoli, P., *SDA*, 1-2, 1969, pp. 142-158; Calvesi, M., *SDA*, 1-2, 1969, pp. 158-161; White, J., *BM*, CXII, 1970, pp. 114-115; Smart, A., *AP*, XCI, 96, 1970; pp. 163-5; Wilkins, D., *AQ*, XXXIII, 1, 1970, pp. 1-15; Conti, A. and Wilkins, D., *AQ*, XXXIII, 4, 1970, pp. 450-453; Pieper, P., *ZKG*, XXXIII, 1, 1970, pp. 78-85; Wilkins, D., *AQ*, XXXIII, 1, 1970, pp. 1-15; Skaug, E., *MKIF*, XV, 2, 1971, pp. 141-60; Cole, B., *MKIF*, XV, 3, 1971, pp. 259-264; Fahy, E., *MM*, XXIX, 10, 1971, p. 430; Gardner, J., *ZKG*, XXXIV, 2, 1971; pp. 89-114; Gardner, J., *BM*, CXIII, 820, 1971, pp. 391-2; Cole, B., *GBA*, LXXX, 114, 1972, pp. 91-96; Cole, B., *CS*, 181, 727, 1972, pp. 48-53; Falaschi, E., *IS*, XXVII, 1972, pp. 1-27; Schneider, L., *A*, 18/19-20, 1972, pp. 91-104; Volpe, C., *PA*, XXIII, 267, 1972, pp. 6, 9, 11, 12; Boskovits, M., *MKIF*, XVII, 2-3, 1973, pp. 205, note 16, 206, 22; Cole, B., *MKIF*, XVII, 2-3, 1973, pp. 229, 30, 36, 38, 44, and note 11; Hueck, I, *MKIF*, XVII, 2-3, 1973, pp. 277-294; Redig de Campos, D., *MKIF*, XVII, 2-3, 1973, pp. 325-346; Scarpellini, P., *PA*, XXIV, 279, 1973, pp. 7-14; Denny, D., *AB*, LV, 2, 1973, pp. 205-212; White, J., *BM*, CXV, 844, 1973, pp. 439-47; Cole, B., *BM*, CXV, 844, 1973, p. 453; Bucher, F., *AB*, LV, 2, 1973, pp. 290-92; Gilmore, M. P., *AB*, LV, 1, 1973, p. 148; Gregori, M., & Longhi, R., *PA*, XXIV, 281/3, 1973, pp. 16-17; Verga, C., *CA*, XXXIX, 134, 1974, pp. 35-52; Smart, A., *AP*, XCIX, 146, Apr. 1974, pp. 228-231.

SIGNED WORKS

There are no signed works universally accepted as entirely by Giotto's hand; there are however the three signed works illustrated in figs. 23-25, usually attributed to his shop.

Bologna, Pinacoteca Nazionale 102. Polyptych: Madonna and Child with Sts Peter, Gabriel, Michael and Paul (fig. 25).

Florence, S. Croce, Baroncelli Chapel. Polyptych: Coronation of the Virgin with Saints and Angels (central panel, fig. 24).

Paris, Louvre 1312. Panel: Stigmatization of St Francis (fig. 23).

There are no known dated works by Giotto.

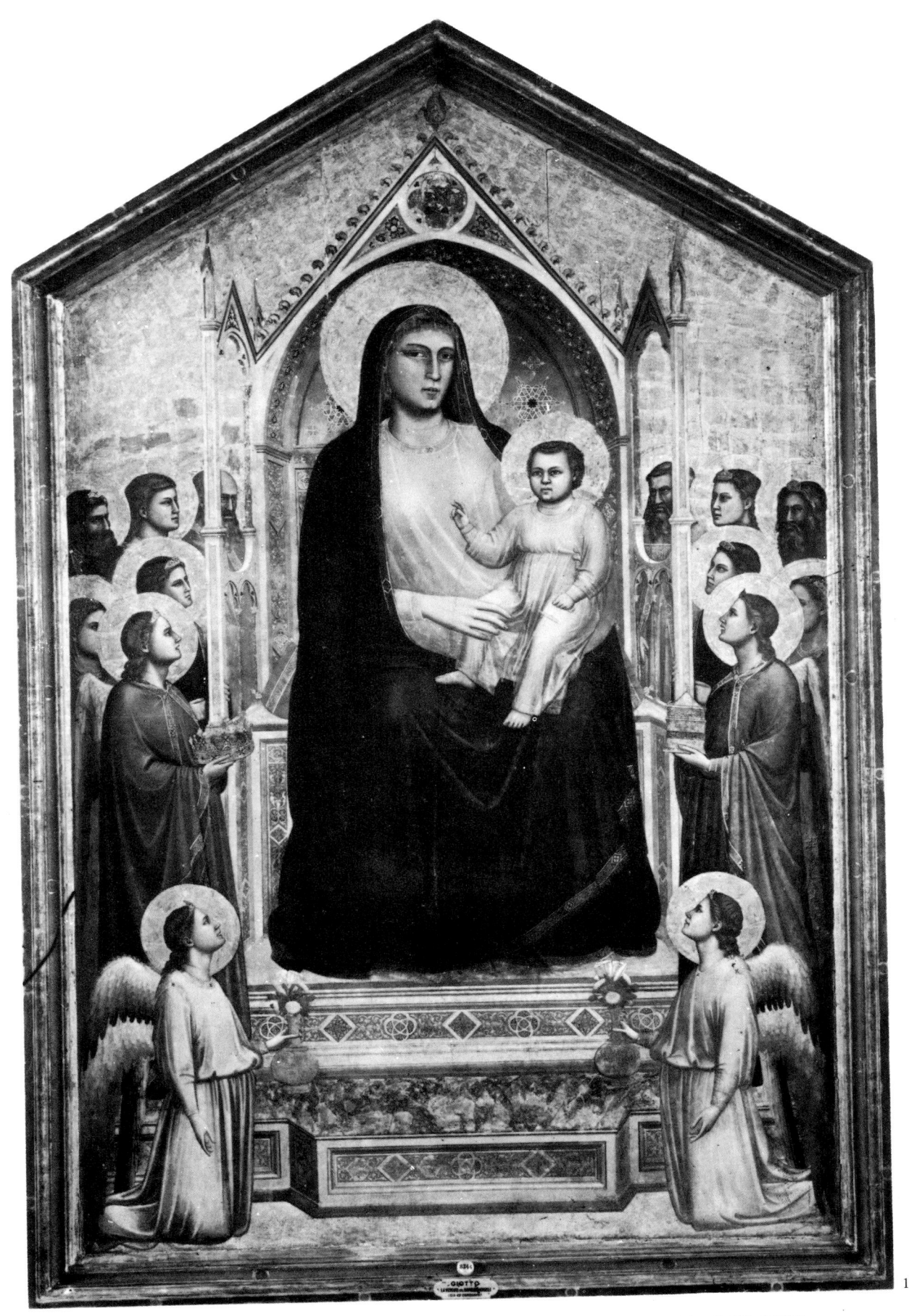

1. *Madonna and Child Enthroned with Saints and Angels. Panel. Florence, Uffizi no. 8344. 325 × 204. SGF 25409.*

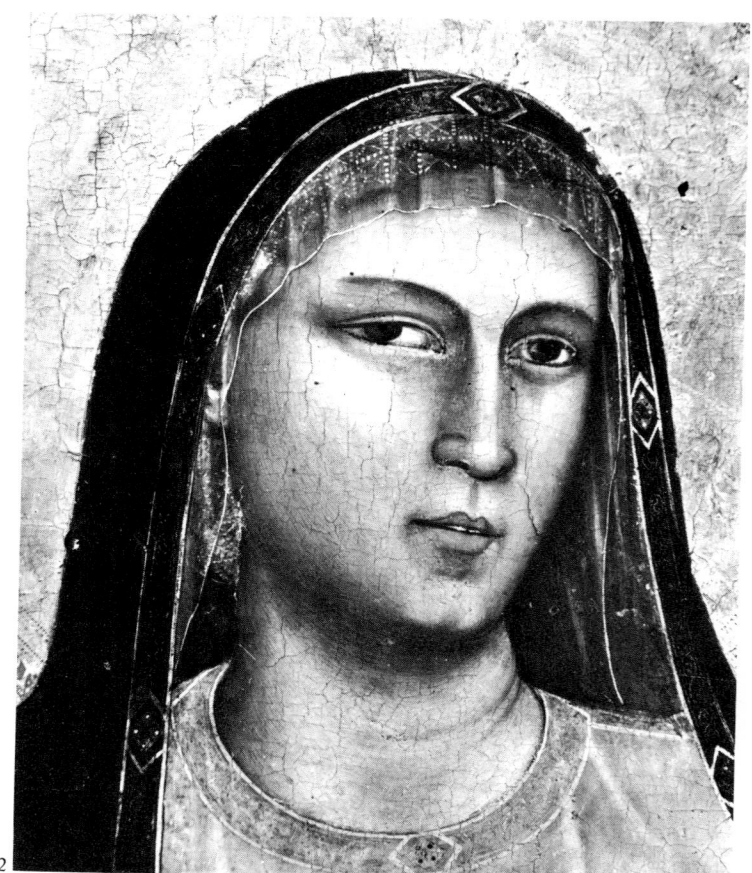

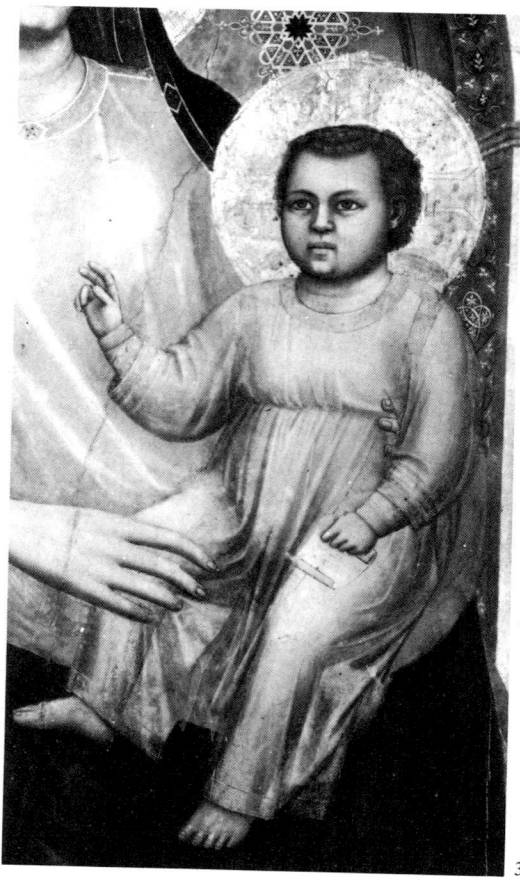

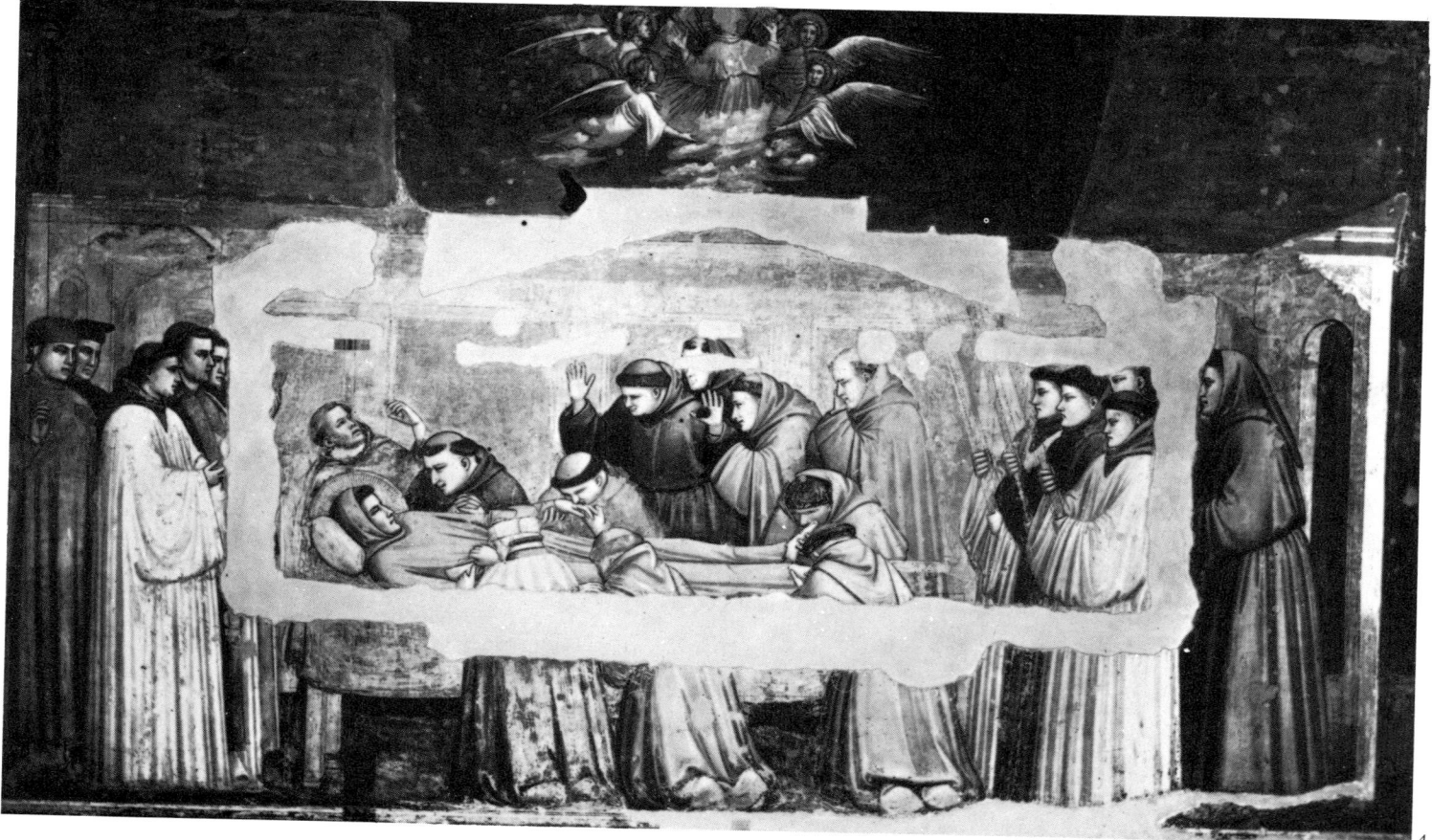

2. *Head of Madonna, detail of fig. 1. Panel. Florence, Uffizi. no. 8344. SGF 26887.*
3. *Infant Christ, detail of fig. 1. Panel. Florence, Uffizi. no. 8344. SGF 26888.*
4. *Death of St. Francis. Fresco. Florence, S. Croce, Bardi Chapel. SGF 105240.*

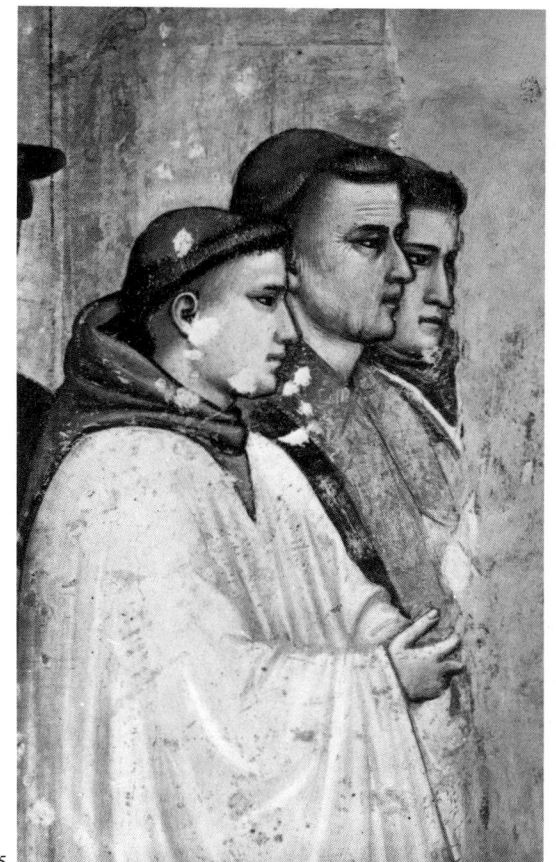

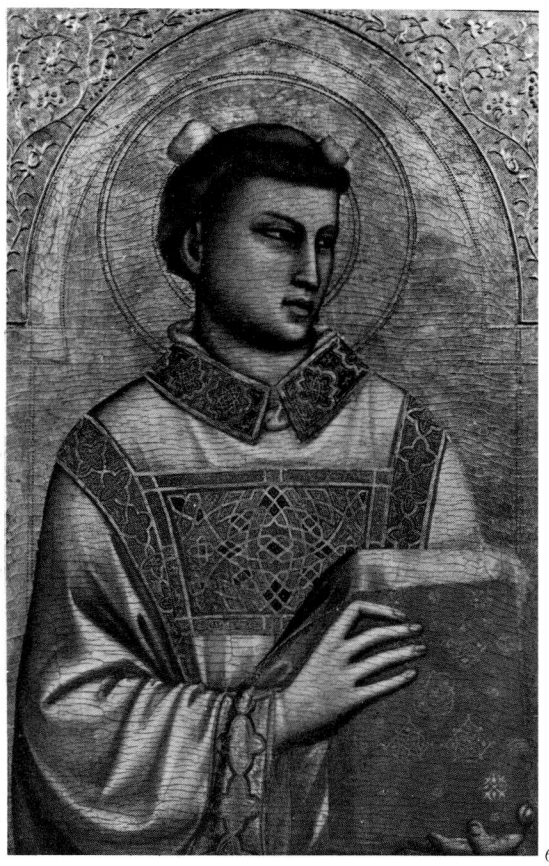

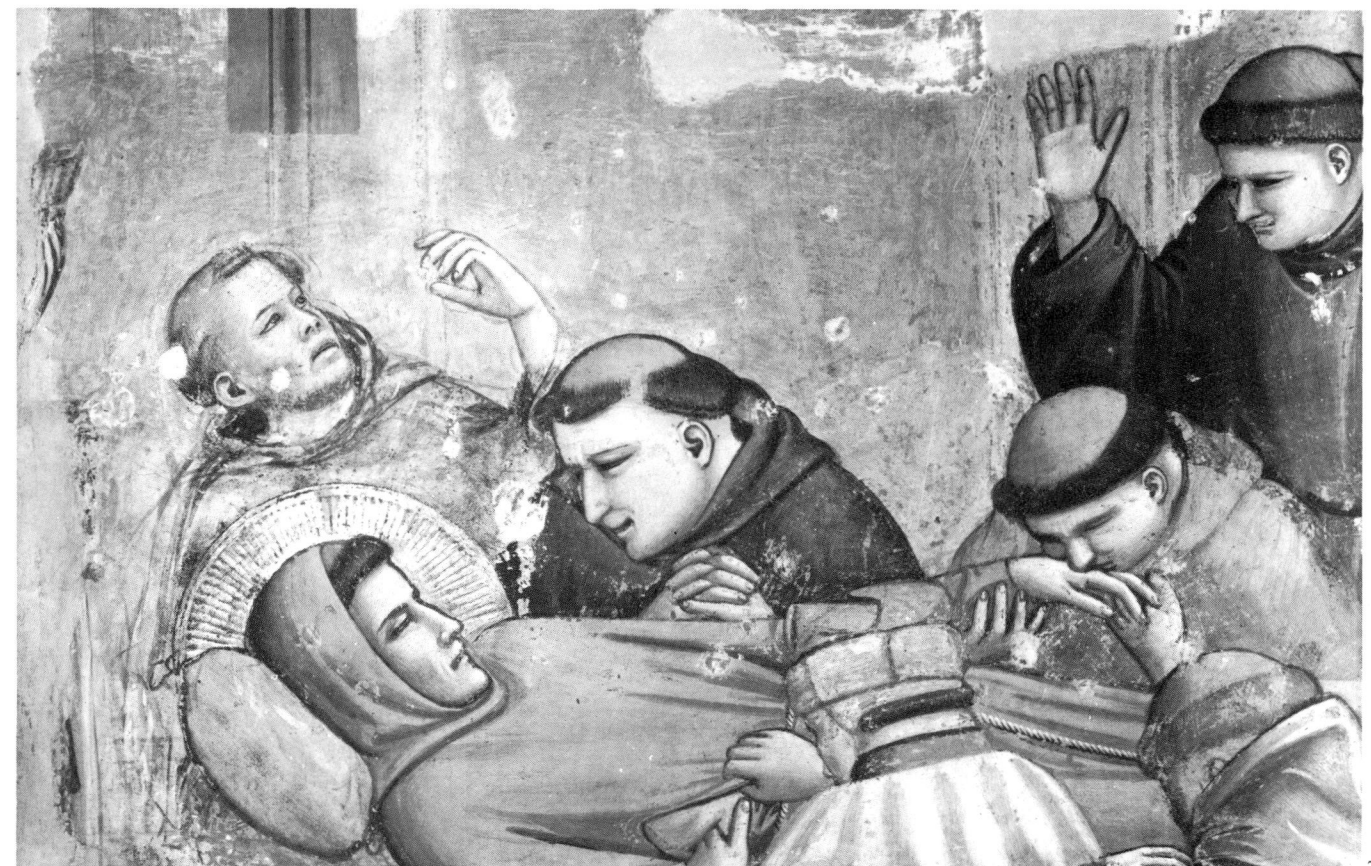

5. *Three Monks, detail of fig. 4. Fresco. Florence, S. Croce, Bardi Chapel. SGF 107814.*
6. *St Stephen. Panel. Florence, Horne Museum. no. 52. 84 × 54. SGF 147783.*
7. *The Death of St Francis, detail of fig. 4. Fresco. Florence, S. Croce, Bardi Chapel. SGF 107815.*

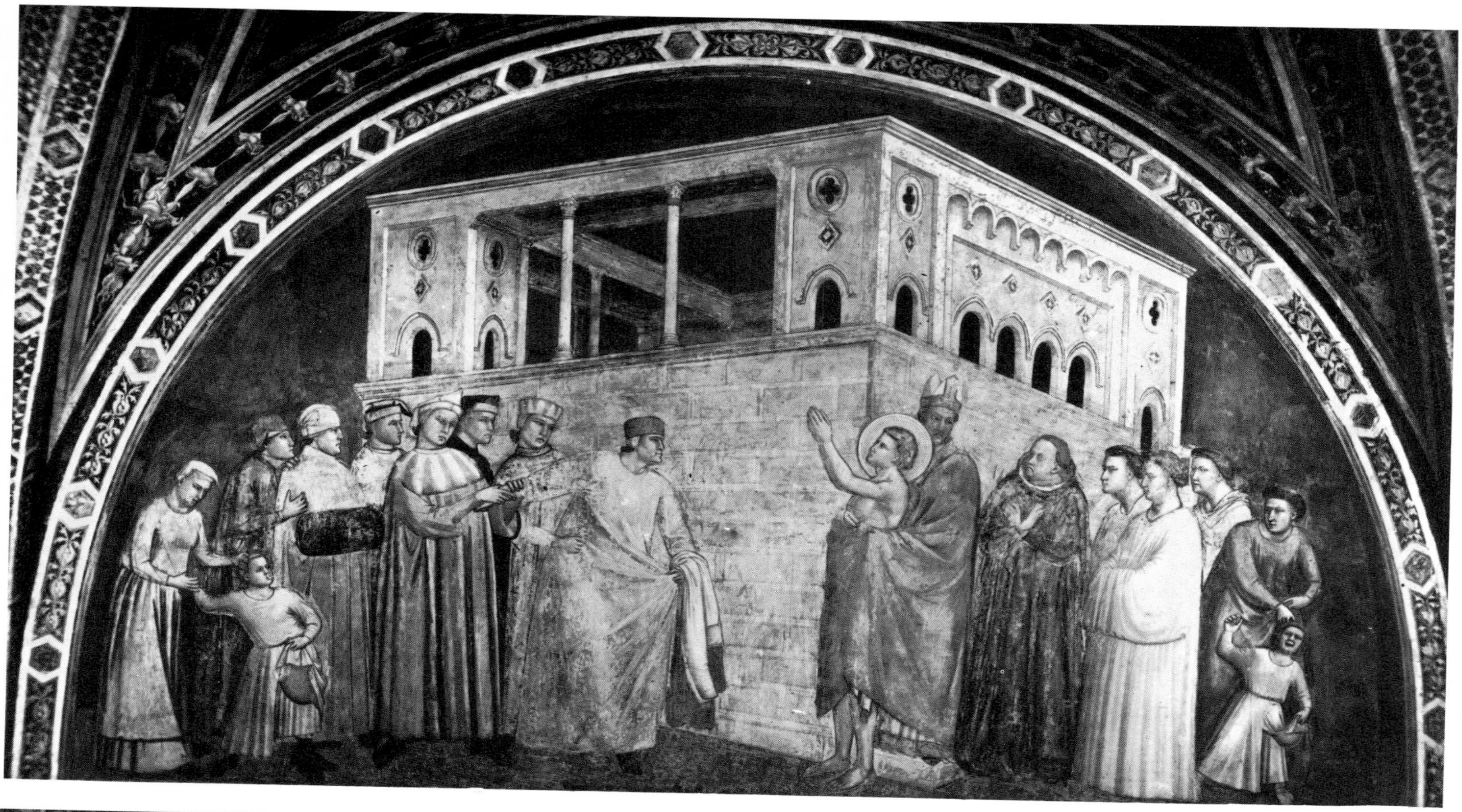

8. *St Francis renouncing his Inheritance. Fresco. Florence, S. Croce, Bardi Chapel. SGF 111564.*
9. *Annunciation to Zaccharias. Fresco. Florence, S. Croce, Peruzzi Chapel. SGF 128982.*

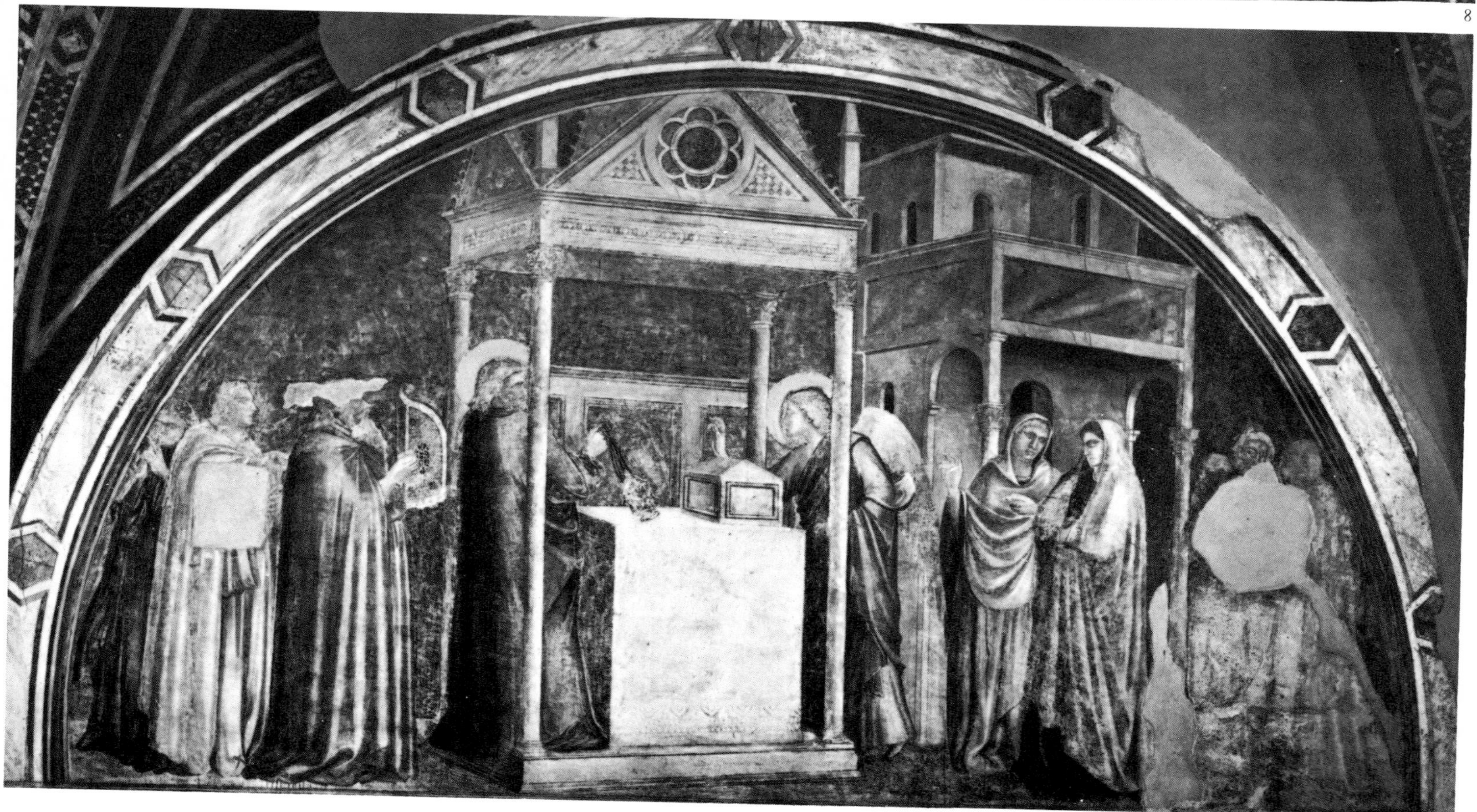

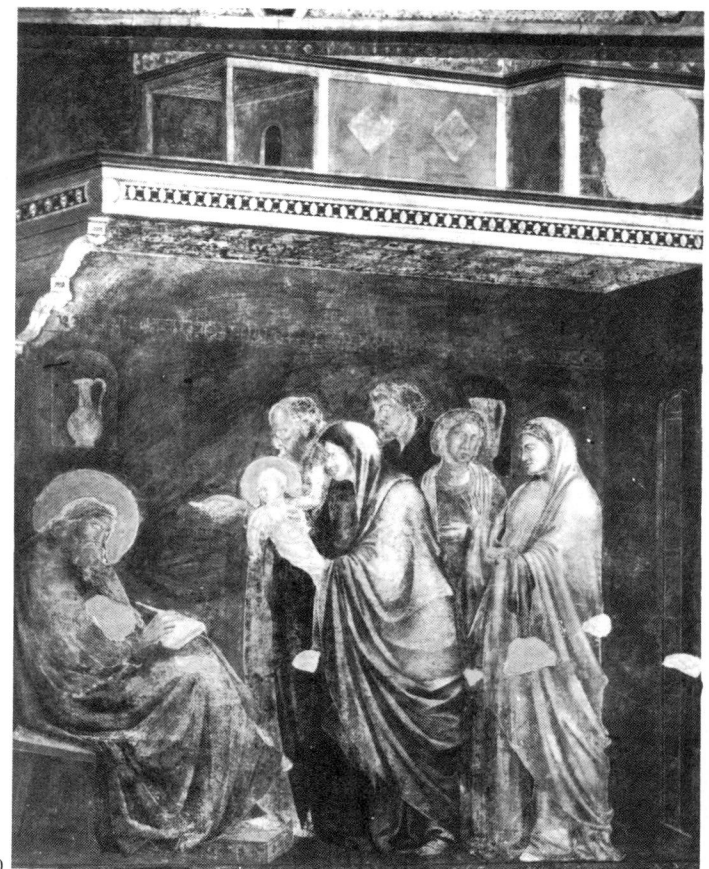

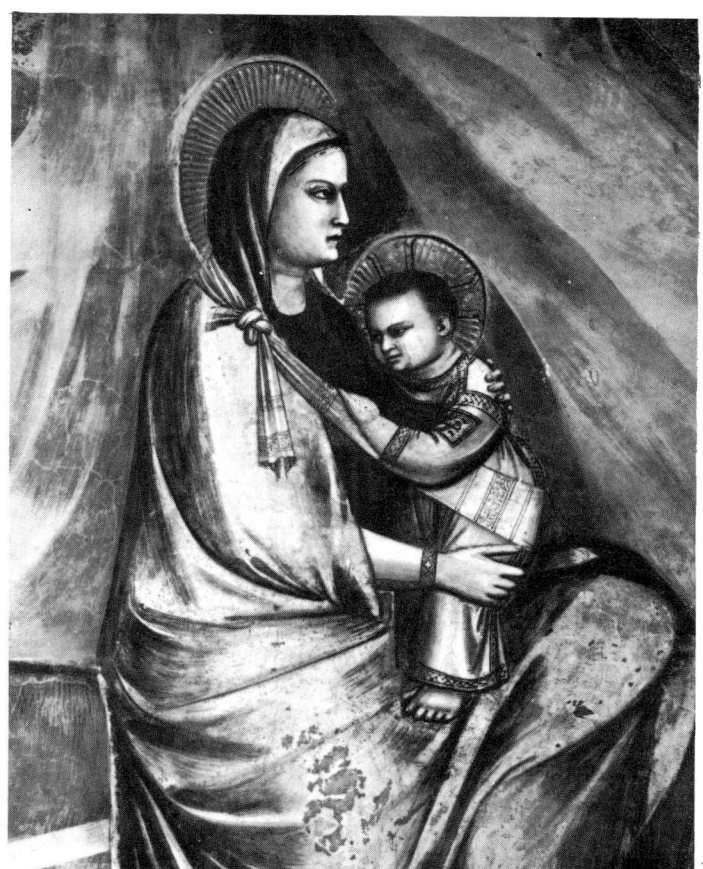

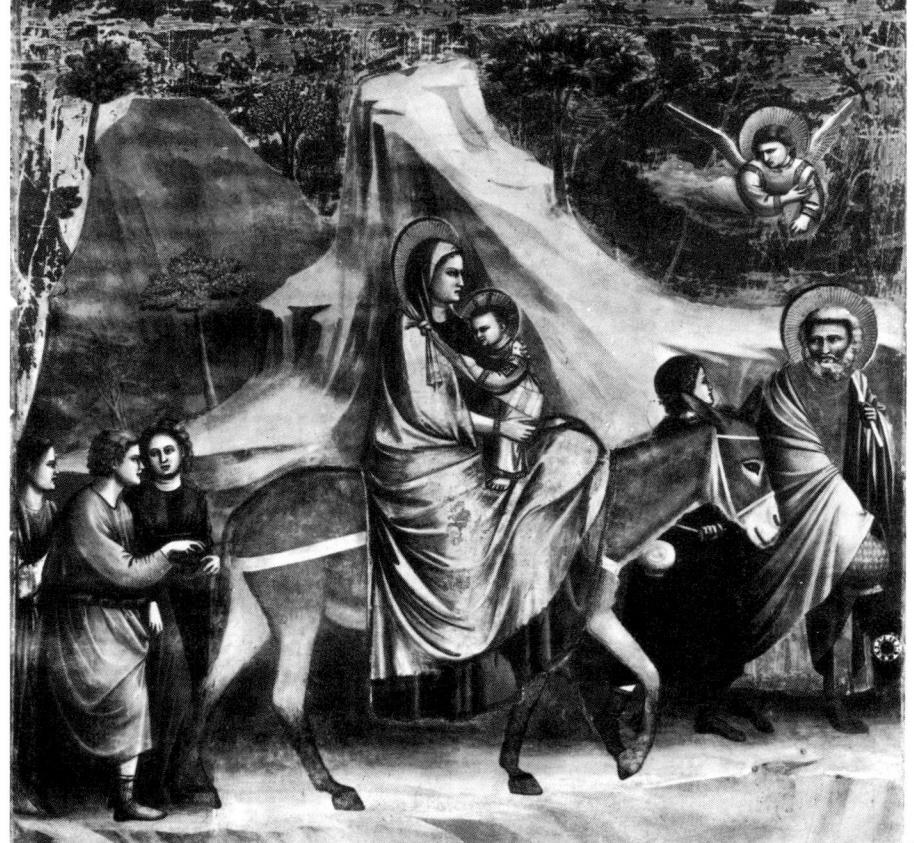

10. *Birth and name-giving of St John the Baptist. Fresco. Florence, S. Croce, Peruzzi Chapel. SGF 129042.*
11. *Madonna and Child, detail of fig. 12. Fresco. Padua, Arena Chapel. Alinari 19332. 1305-06.*
12. *Flight into Egypt. Fresco. Padua, Arena Chapel. Anderson 27030. 1305-06.*

11

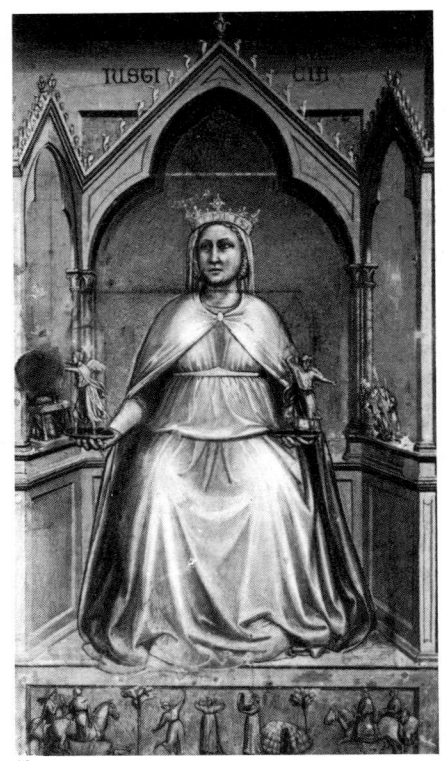

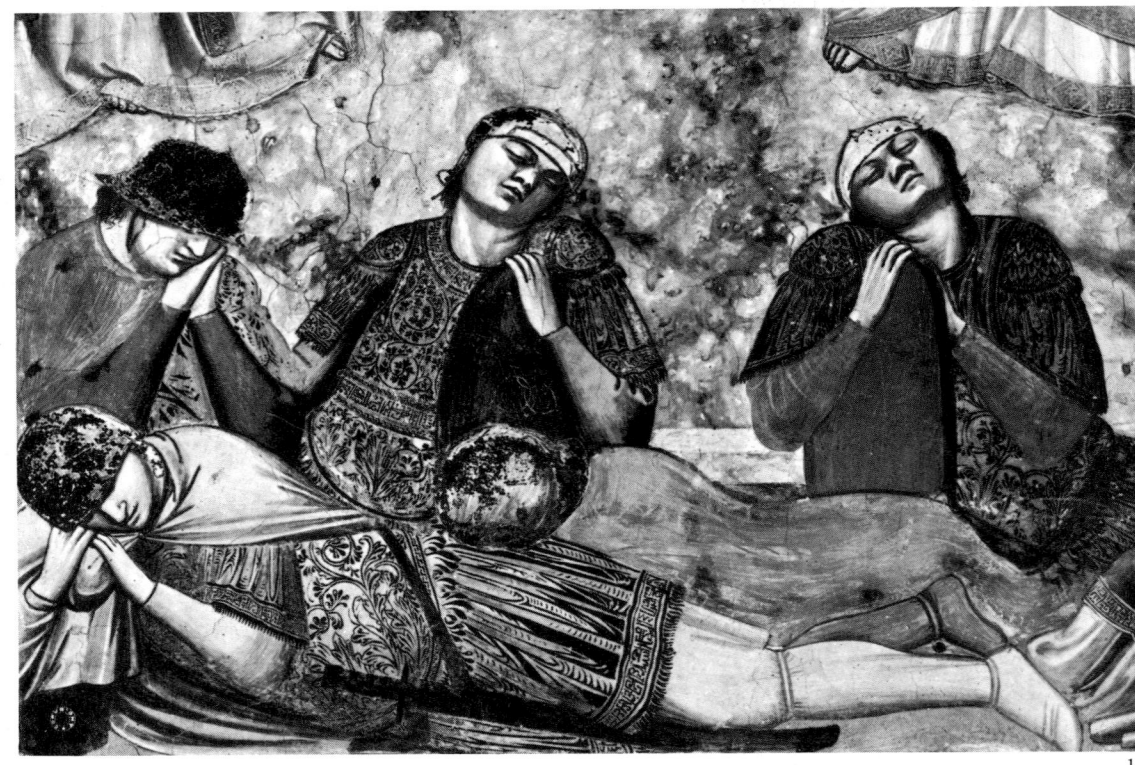

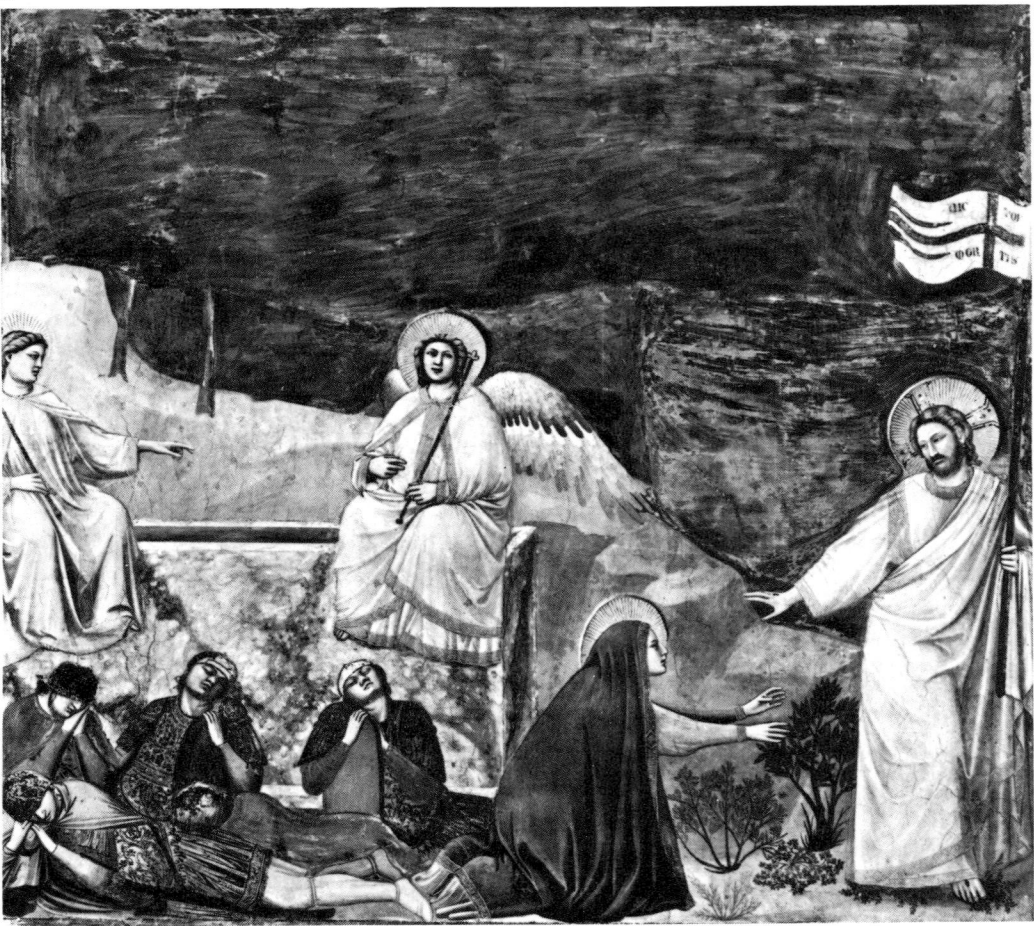

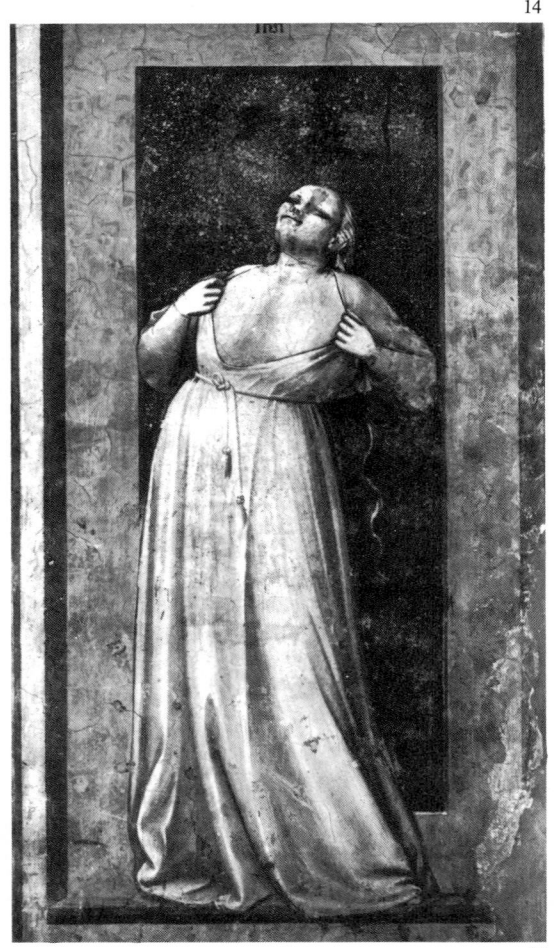

13. *Justice. Fresco. Padua, Arena Chapel. Alinari 19430. 1305-06.*
14. *Sleeping figures, detail of fig. 15. Fresco, Padua, Arena Chapel. Anderson 27074. 1305-06.*
15. *Noli me tangere. Fresco. Padua, Arena Chapel. Anderson 27070. 1305-06.*
16. *Wrath. Fresco. Padua, Arena Chapel. Alinari 19422. 1305-06.*

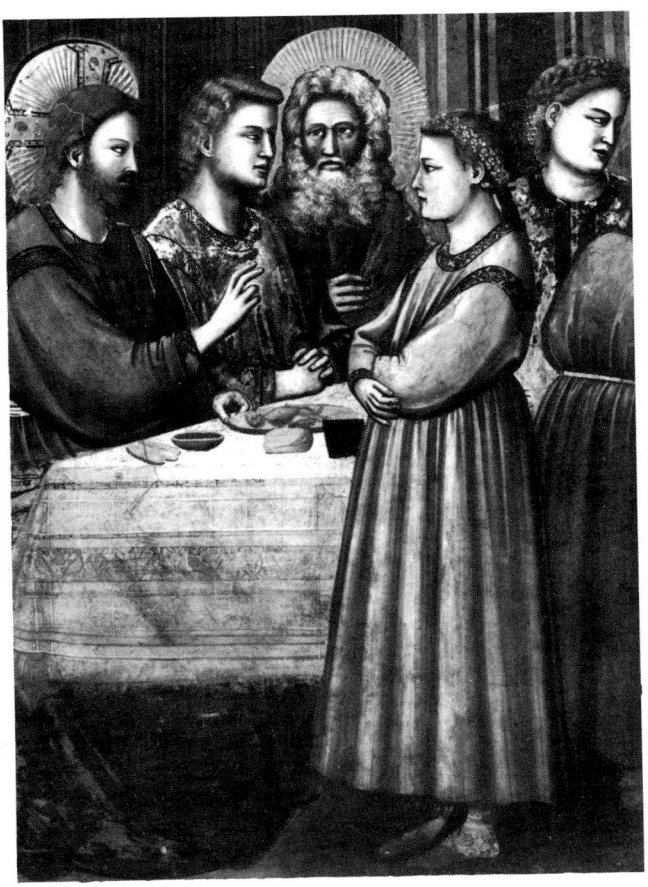

17

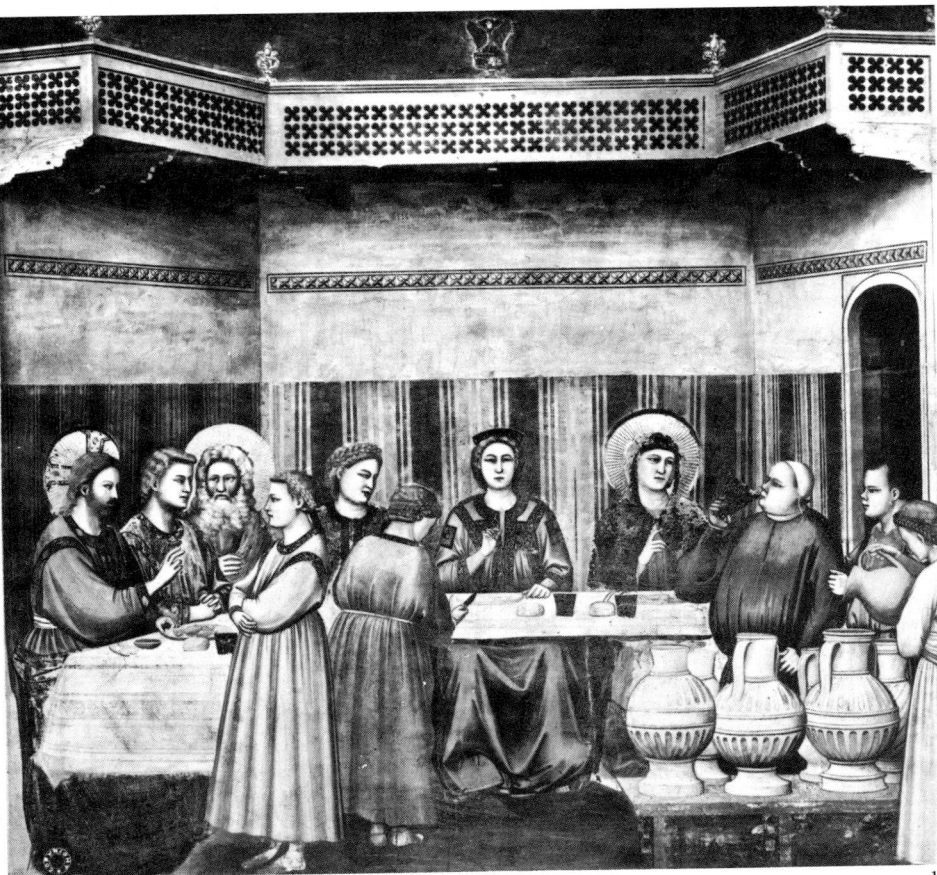

18

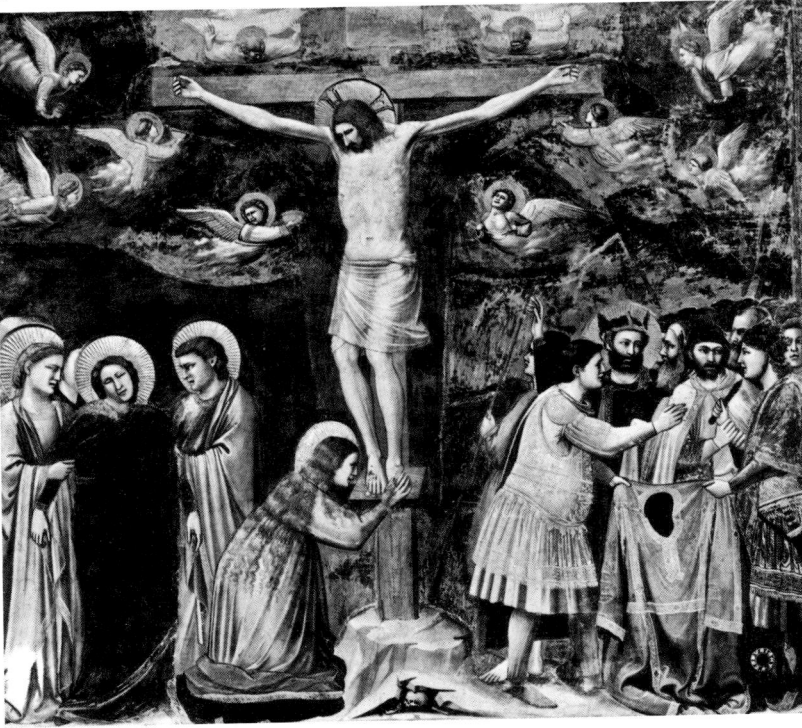

19

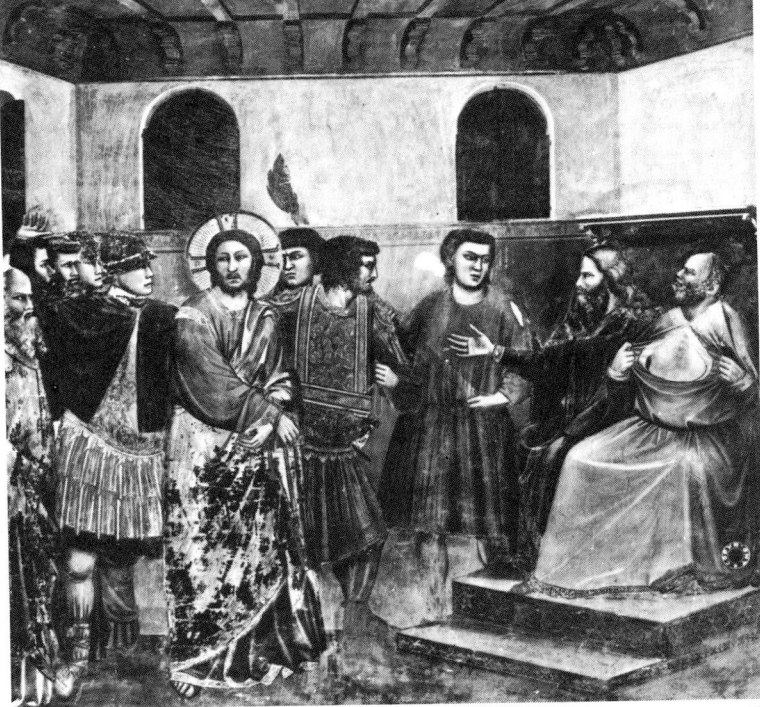

20

17. *Marriage at Cana, detail of fig. 18. Fresco. Padua, Arena Chapel. Alinari 19339. 1305-06.*
18. *Marriage at Cana. Fresco. Padua, Arena Chapel. Alinari 27037. 1305-06.*
19. *Crucifixion. Fresco. Padua, Arena Chapel. Alinari 27061. 1305-06.*
20. *Christ before Caiaphas. Fresco. Padua, Arena Chapel. Anderson 27054. 1305-06.*

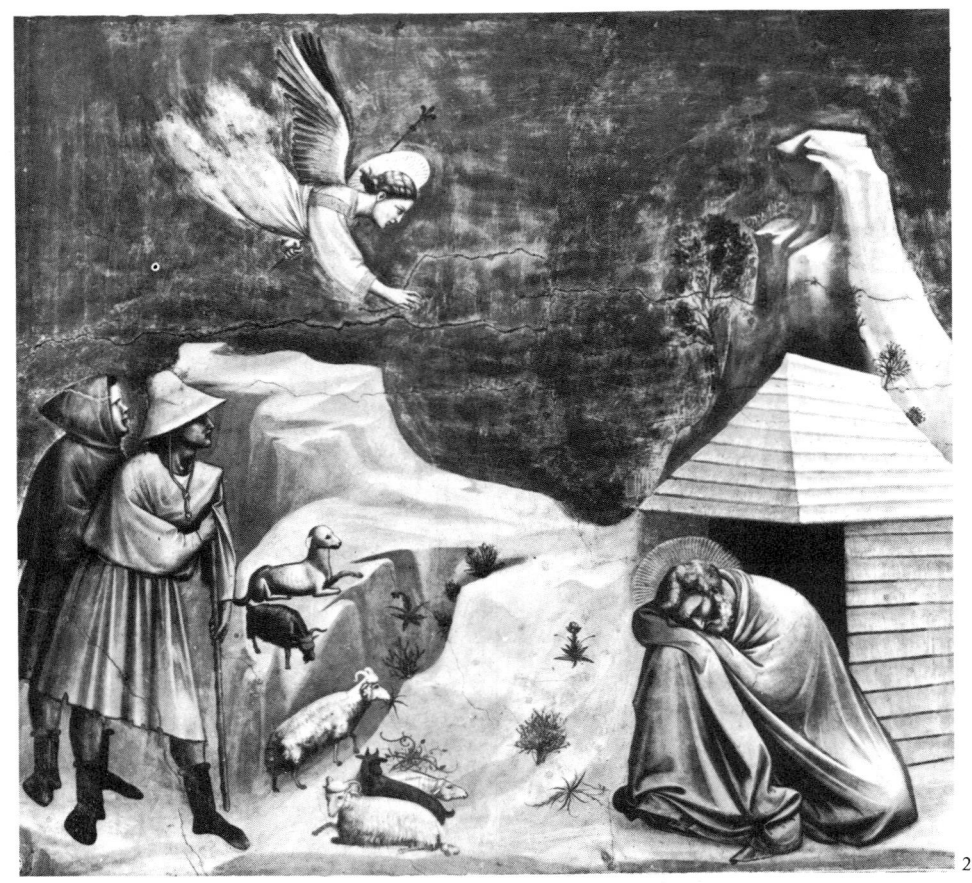

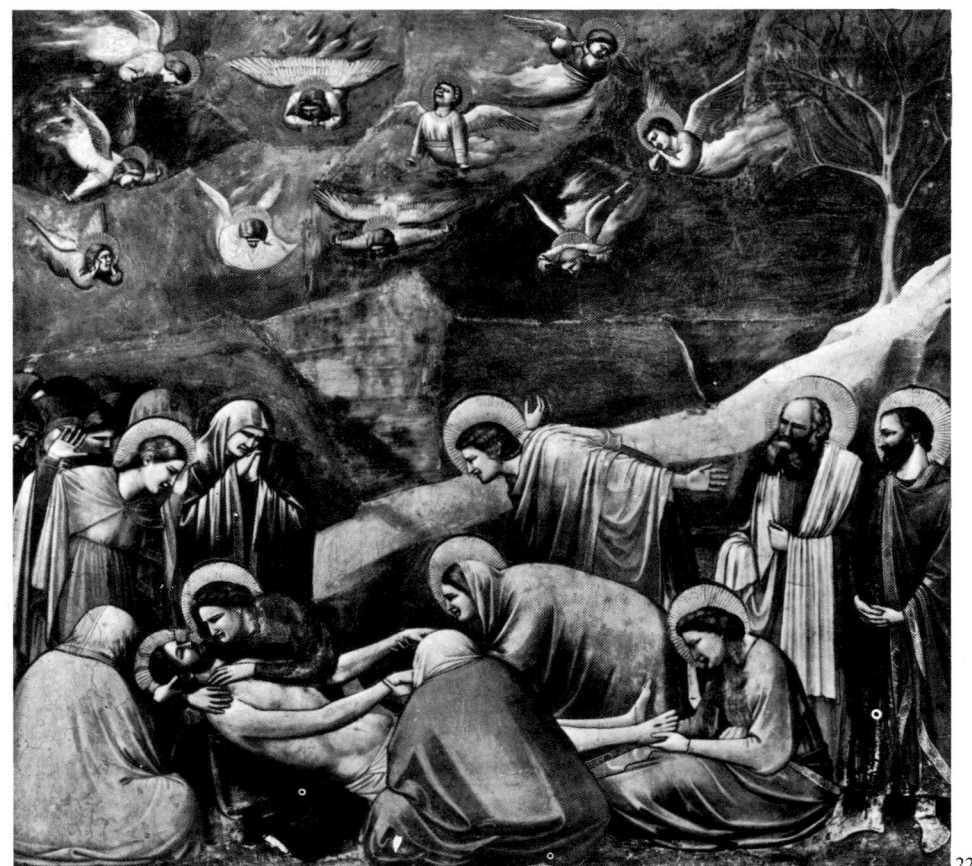

21. *Joachim among the Shepherds. Fresco. Padua, Arena Chapel. Anderson 27007. 1305-06.*
22. *Lamentation. Fresco. Padua, Arena Chapel. Anderson 27066. 1305-06.*

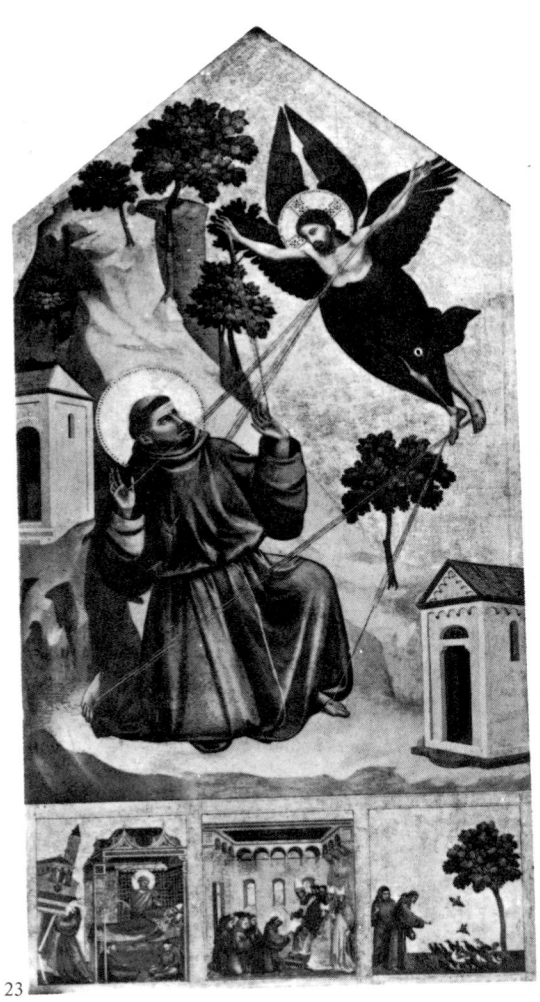

23

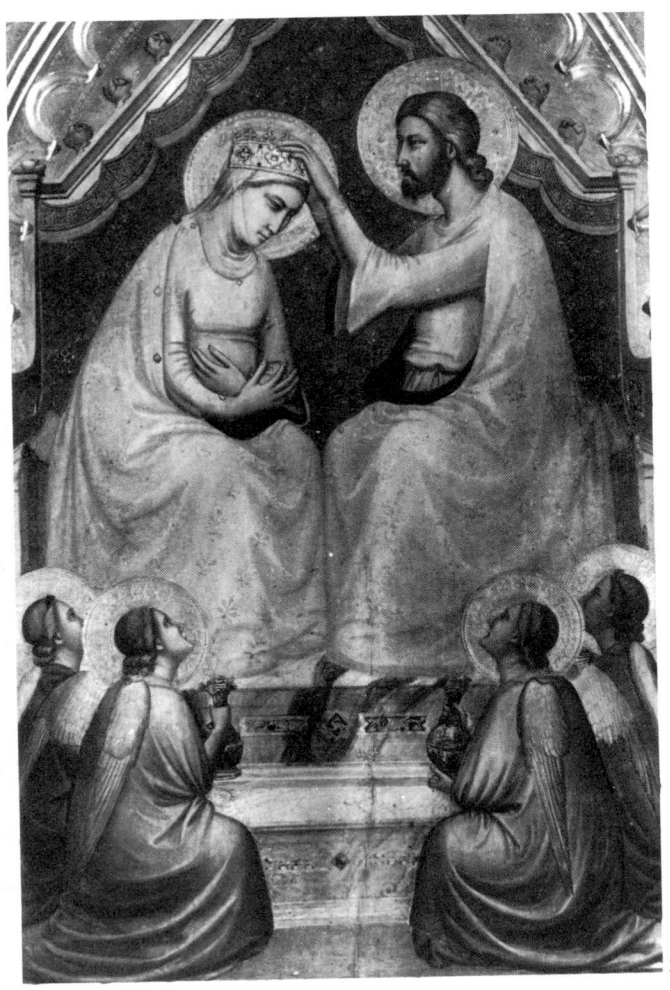

24

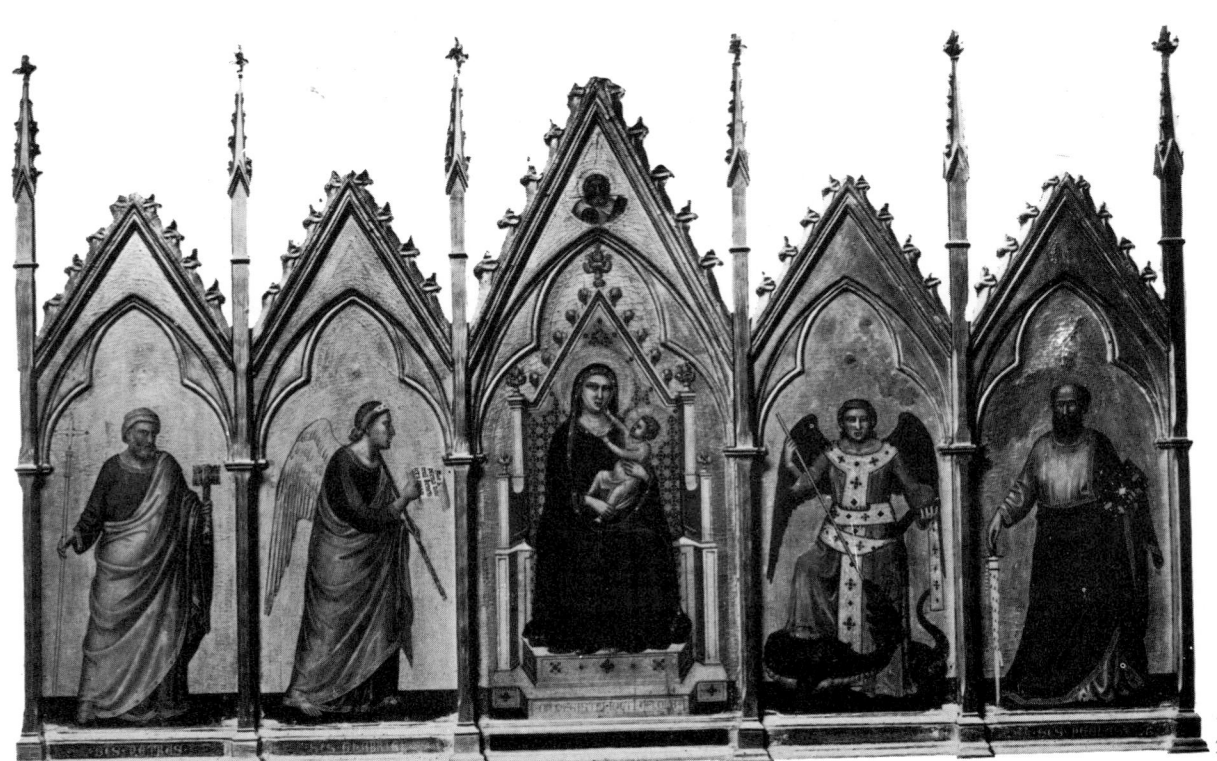

25

23. *Stigmatization of St Francis, and three scenes from his Life. Panel. Paris, Musée du Louvre. no. 1312. Whole panel: 314 × 162. Alinari 23123. s.*
(*In fact, by Giotto's shop*).

24. *Central panel of a polyptych: Coronation of the Virgin, with four Angels. Panel. Florence, S. Croce, Baroncelli Chapel. Whole panel: 185 × 323. SGF 26897. s. (In fact, by Giotto's shop*).

25. *Polyptych: Madonna and Child, with Sts Peter and Paul and the Archangels Gabriel and Michael. Panel. Bologna, Pinacoteca Nazionale. no. 102. 91 × 340. Anderson 6060. s. (In fact, by Giotto's shop*).

PACINO di BONAGUIDA

Amongst the adherents of Giotto there are several artists who, on account of certain particularities of style, may be grouped together. The only one of these whose name has come to us, is Pacino di Bonaguida, who is found mentioned for the first time in 1303 and who matriculated in the corporation of painters in 1320; while the Accademia of Florence possess the only signed work which we have of his and which bears the date MCCCX...., and what I believe to be the beginning of another X.....
From the appearance of the figures, the types and the relief, we may conclude at once that Pacino was a follower of Giotto, but one whose style shows a good deal of variation to the master's. The somewhat curved figures, large and richly draped, remind us more of statuary than do Giotto's.....

from R. van Marle, p. 240, *The Development the Italian Schools of Painting*, Vol. III, The Hague, 1924.

Pacino di Buonaguida, Florentine, born 12- -, died 13- -. Painter. Member of the Physicians and Apothecaries Guild between 1320-28 (probably c. 1320). On Feb. 20, 1302/3, Pacino dissolved partnership with Tambo di Serraglio. The association had lasted for one year. In the deed Pacino, of the popolo di S. Lorenzo, describes himself as " publicus artifex in arte pictorum ", showing that he must have been inscribed in the old Guild of Painters, which probably existed as an independent corporation until after the year 1316.....

from D. E. Colnaghi, pp. 196-197, *A Dictionary of Florentine Painters*, London, 1928.

The facts recorded under Pacino's name prolong the period of his active maturity conjecturally before his earliest known date, 1303, and beyond 1320. He is with Giotto and the St. Cecilia Master the third well-determined figure of a period that art-historically belongs to them. Naturally disposed to book, and panel, miniature, his present conspicuity perhaps exceeds his gifts, which were small, but whimsical and graceful. It is by his wide productivity, in which he was abundantly helped by assistants, that he wins a certain significance in the history of early Trecento painting. His mode of expression emerges out of the blind gap between the Dugento and the Trecento, and suggests he may have formed under the older tradition, to be initiated into the urbanities of Florentine style by the St. Cecilia Master. This style he schematized to a briskly pictographic manner, which was to find a considerable following among his younger contemporaries.....

from R. Offner, p. 1, *A Critical & Historical Corpus of Florentine Painting*, Sec. III, Vol. II, Part I, New York, 1930.

Mentioned from 1303 to 1339. Possibly a pupil of the Master of S. Cecilia.

from B. Berenson, p. 164, *Italian Pictures of the Renaissance, Florentine School*, Vol. I, London, 1963.

Florentine School. Active 1310-30. A contemporary of Giotto, Pacino seems to have been more influenced by the St. Cecilia Master. He was an illuminator, a painter of lively, if somewhat superficial, narrative, developing however in his later work a more monumental style.

from F. R. Shapley, p. 23, *Paintings from the Samuel H. Kress Collection*, London, 1966.

BIBLIOGRAPHY

BOOKS

An asterisk indicates a work listed in the General Bibliography

Cruttwell*, 1907, pp. 278-9; *Venturi, A.**, 1907, pp. 502, 506-8; *Khv & Salmi**, 1914, p. 13; Lafenestre, G., and Richtenberger, E., *La Peinture en Europe*, Florence, 1920, p. 176; *Vitzhum**, 1924, p. 291; *v. Marle, 1924**, pp. 240-250; *v. Marle, 1925**, p. 469; *Chiappelli**, 1925, pp. 283; *Offner, Studies**, 1927, pp. 3-21; *Offner, 1927**, pp. 4, 13; *Colnaghi**, 1928, pp. 196-7; *Vavalà, 1929**, pp. 20-1; *Toesca, 1929**, p. 63, 76, note 19; *Offner, 1930**, Sec. III, Vol. II, Part I, pp. 1-40, and Sec. III, Vol. II, Part II, pp. 215-238; *Hautecoeur**, 1931, p. 111; Gronau, H. D., in *T.-Becker**, 1932, XXVI, p. 126; *Lavagnino**, 1936, pp. 637-8; *Procacci, 1936**, pp. 25-6;; *Paatz**, 1940, Vol. I, pp. 111, 293; *M. Giottesca**, 1943, pp. 400-15; *Coletti, Vol. II**, 1946, pp. 34-5; *Antal**, 1948, pp. 167-9, 184, 217, 225, 252; *Offner, 1947**, Sec. III, Vol. V, pp. 252-3, 255, 258; Collobi-Ragghianti, L., *La casa italiana nei secoli: Mostra delle arti decorative in Italia dal Trecento all'Ottocento*, Florence, 1948, p. 33; *Galetti**, " P-Z ", pp. 1803-4; *Toesca, 1951**, pp. 499, 604-5, 805-9; *Paatz**, 1952, pp. 329, 338; Oertel, R., *Die Frühzeit der Italienischen Malerei*, Stuttgart, 1953, p. 181; Catalogue: *Mostra Storica Nazionale della Miniatura, Roma*, Florence, 1953, p. 214; *Salmi, 1954**, pp. 6-11, 13, 15, 25, 35-7, 39, 41; *Offner, 1956**, Sec. III, Vol. VI, pp. 121-74; Suida, W. E., *Catalogue of the University of Arizona Collection*, Tucson (Arizona), 1957, n. 3; *Berenson, 1963**, Vol. I, p. 164; *Marcucci**, 1965, pp. 18-25; *Shapley** 1966, pp. 22-3; Boskovits, M., *La Scuola di Giotto* (I Maestri del Colore, 248), Milan, 1966; *Dal Poggetto**, 1967, pp. 20-22; *MMOA**, 1971, pp. 17-20; *Dutch Show**, 1974, p. 86.

JOURNALS

Bertaux, E., *NN*, XV, 1906, p. 131; Rintelen, F., *KGA*, 2, 1906, pp. 33-45; Suida, W., *RKW*, XXXI, 1908, p. 206; Bertaux, E., *GBA*, II, 1909, pp. 149, 154; Suida, W., *MKW*, VII, 1914, pp. 1-2; Offner, R., *AA*, XI, 1923, pp. 3-27; Mather, F. J., Jr., *AS*, 1925, p. 29; Hendy, P., *BM*, LII, 1928, p. 290; Hendy, P., *BM*, LIII, 1928, p. 23; Berenson, B., *DD*, 1930-1, p. 980; Salmi, M., *Bib*, XXXIII, 1931, pp. 274-8; Salmi, M., *RIAS*, III, 1931-32, pp. 226-9; Salmi M., *ACOL*, 1931-2, p. 259; Salmi, M., *RIAS*, IV, 1932-33, pp. 145-201; Gamba, C., *BA*, XXVII, 1933, pp. 145-63; Castelfranco, G., *BA*, XXVIII, 1935, pp. 462-5; Rabb, D. M., *AB*, 1936, p. 524; Garrison, E. B., *GBA*, XXIX, 1946, pp. 321-46; Longhi, R., *Prop*, II, 1948, p. 52; Salmi, M., *ABI*, XX, 1952, 13, pp. 16-17; Boskovits, M., *AHA*, XI, 1965, pp. 70-94; Boskovits, M., *ZKG*, XXIX, I, 1966, pp. 51-66; De Benedictis, C., *AV*, 3, 1967, p. 42; Conti, A., *PA*, XIX, 223/43, 1968, p. 4; Fahy, E., *MM*, XXIX, 10, 1971, p. 432; Pieper, P. *ZKG*, XXXIII, I, 1970, p. 81; Volpe, C., *PA*, XXIII, 267, 1972, pp. 7, 11.

SIGNED AND DATED WORK

13?? Florence, Accademia, 8568. Polyptych: Christ on the Cross with the Virgin, St John and Saints. s. & d. (fig. 26).

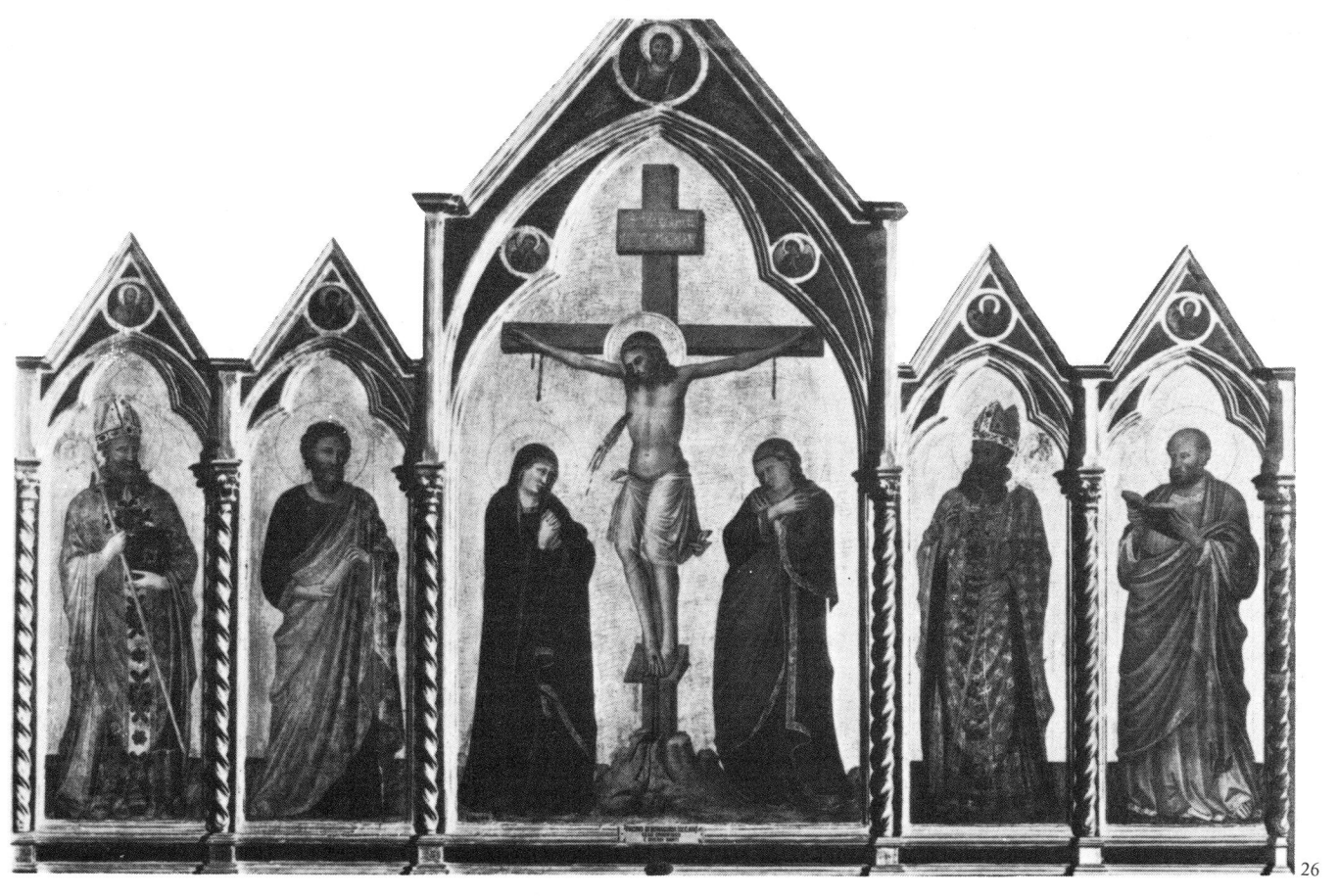

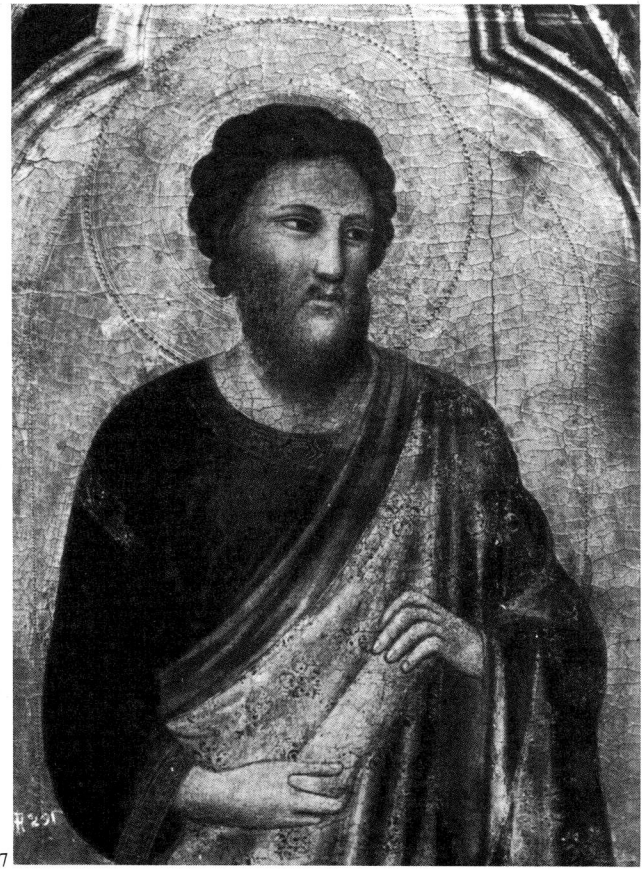

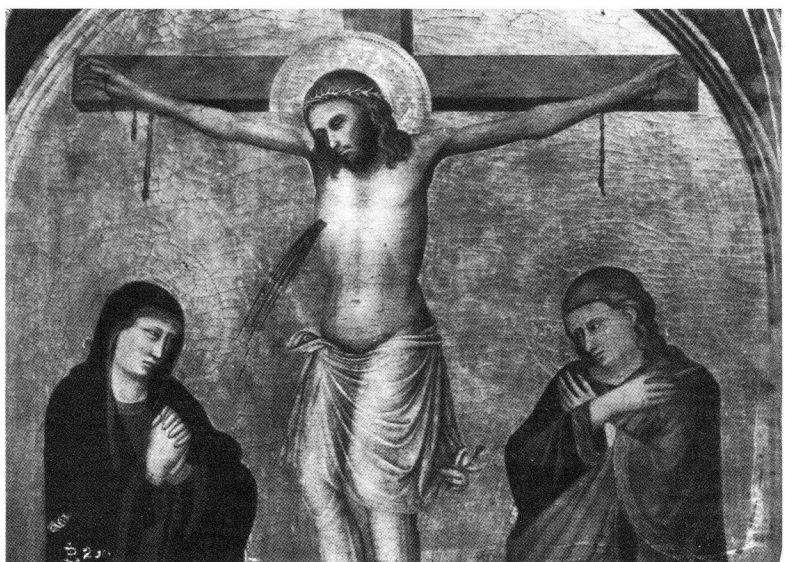

26. *Polyptych: Christ on the Cross with the Virgin and St John, and Sts Nicholas, Bartholomew, Florentius and Luke. Above: Christ blessing, four Prophets, two Angels. Panel. Florence, Accademia. no. 8568. cp: 136 × 78; sps: 136 × 31. Alinari 1598. s & d. 13??*
27. *St Bartholomew, detail of fig. 26. Panel. Florence, Accademia. no. 8568. SGF 20936. s & d. 13??*
28. *Christ on the Cross with the Virgin and St John, detail of fig. 26. Panel. Florence, Accademia. no. 8568. SGF 20935. s & d. 13??*

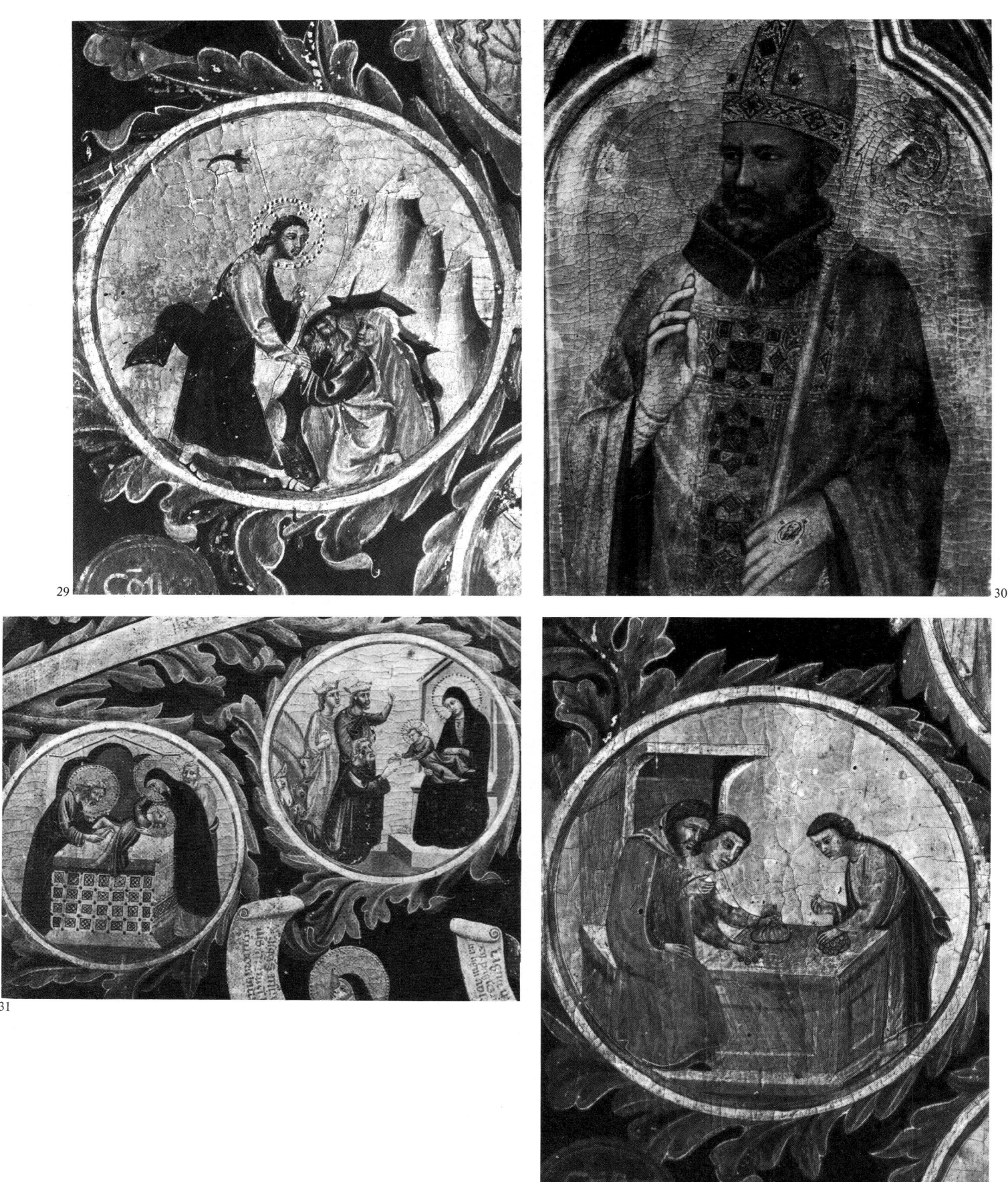

29. *Branches of the True Cross, detail of fig. 33. Panel. Florence, Accademia. no. 8459. SGF 26936.*
30. *St Florentius, detail of fig. 26. Panel. Florence, Accademia. no. 8568. SGF 20939. s & d. 13??*
31. *Branches of the True Cross: Circumcision, and Adoration of the Magi, detail of fig. 33. Panel. Florence, Accademia. no. 8549. Brogi 19996.*
32. *Branches of the True Cross, detail of fig. 33. Panel. Florence, Accademia. no. 8459. SGF 26937.*

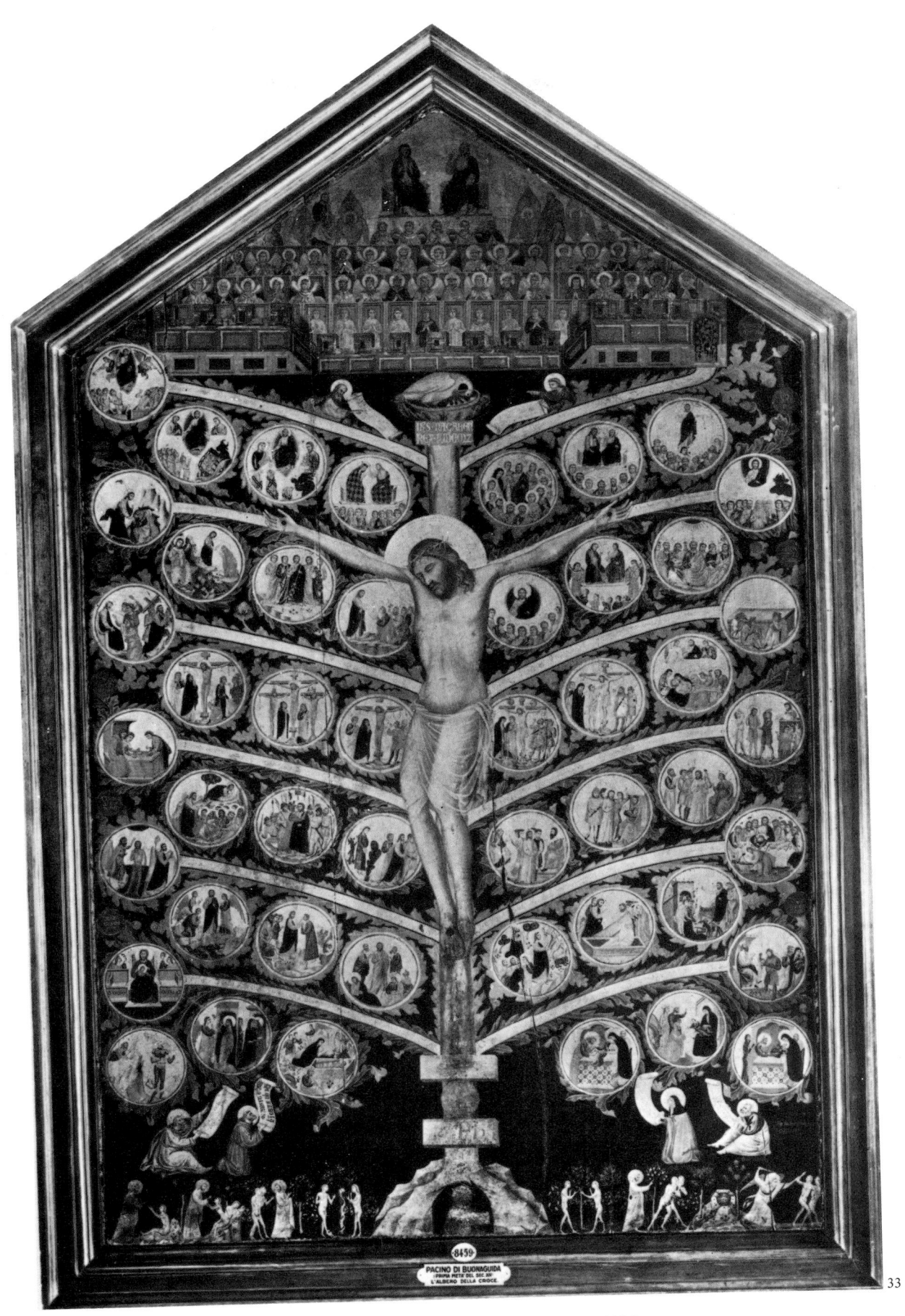

33. *Branches of the True Cross. Panel. Florence, Accademia. no. 8459. 248 × 151. SGF 28936.*

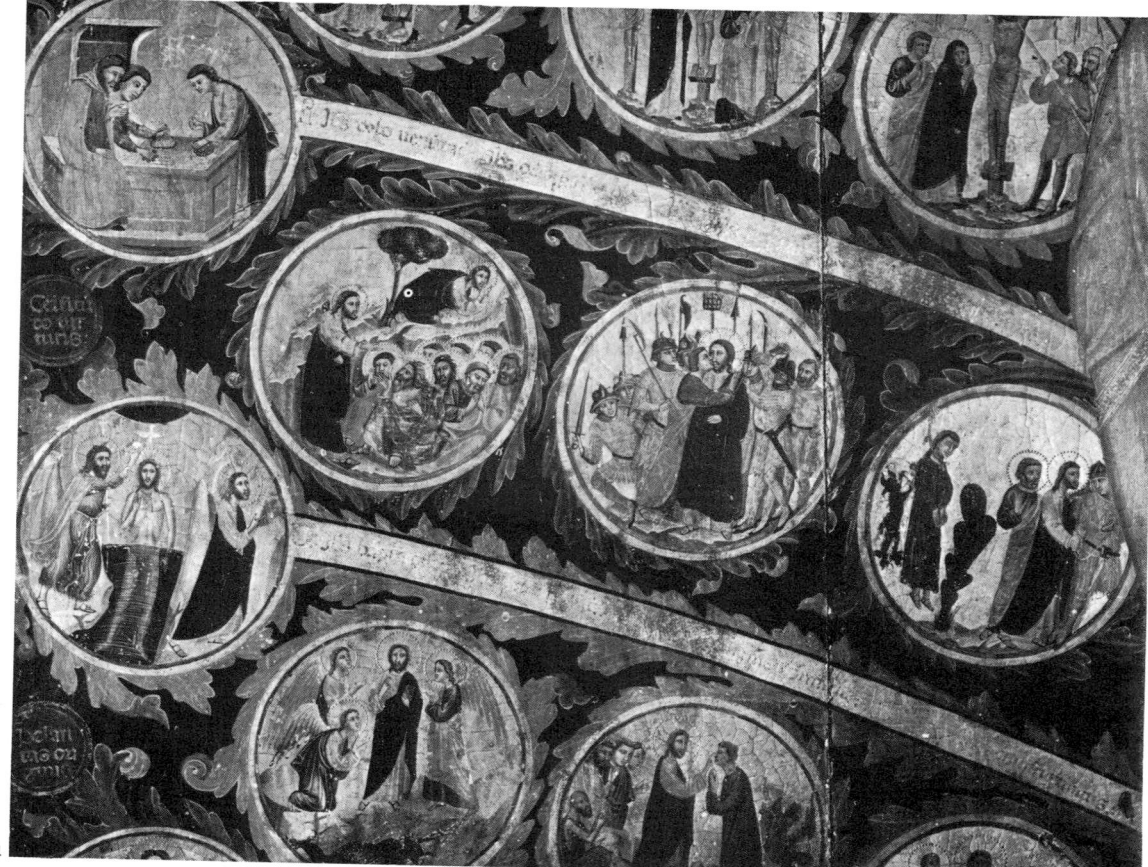

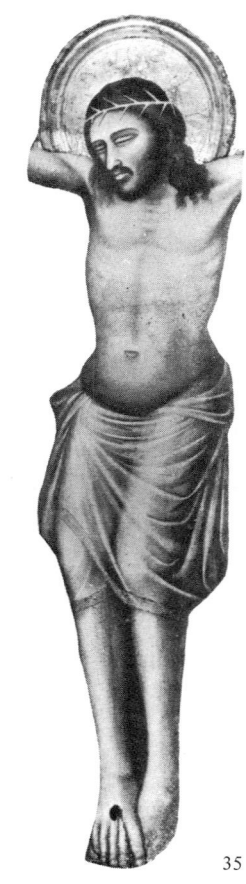

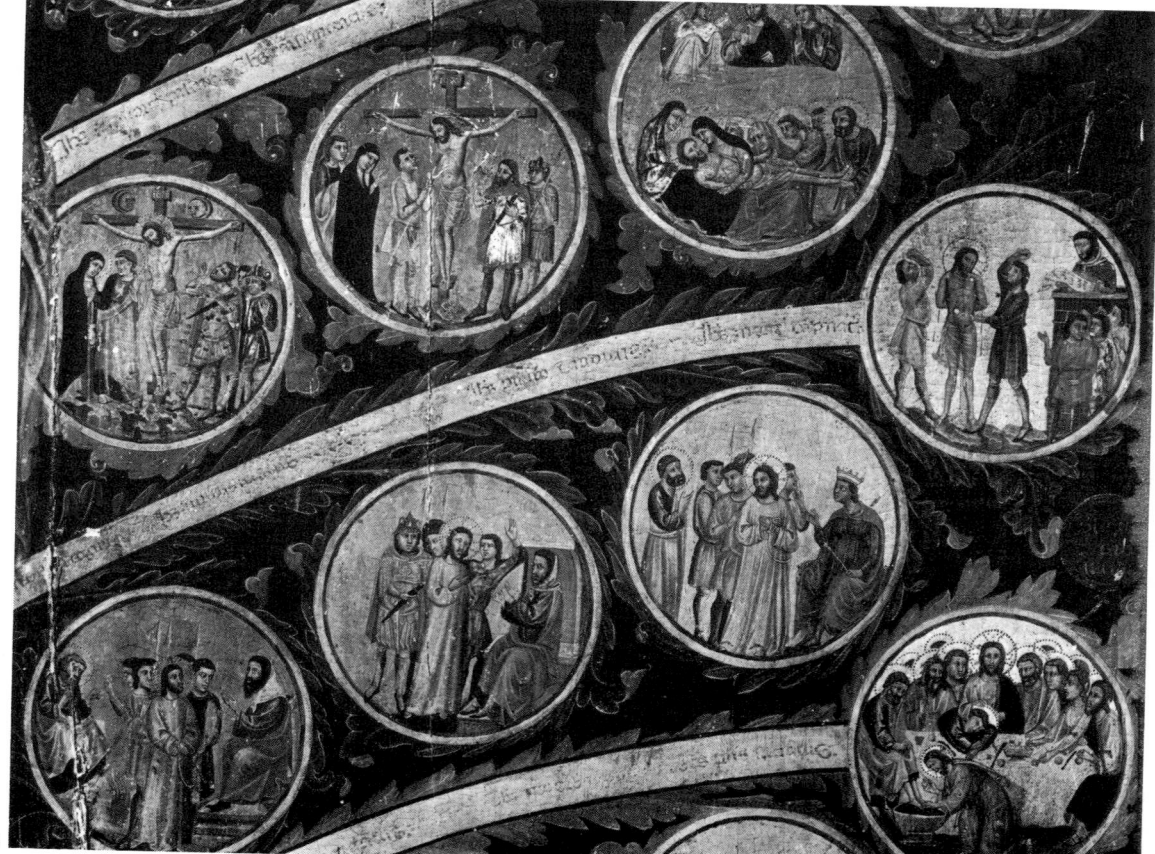

34. *Branches of the True Cross, detail of fig. 33. Panel. Florence, Accademia. no. 8459. SGF 10009.*
35. *Painted Crucifix (damaged). Panel. Ponce (Puerto Rico), Museo de Arte, Kress Study Collection. no. K1262. 139 × 35.5. Kress Foundation photo.*
36. *Branches of the True Cross, detail of fig. 33. Panel. Florence, Accademia no. 8459. SGF 10013.*

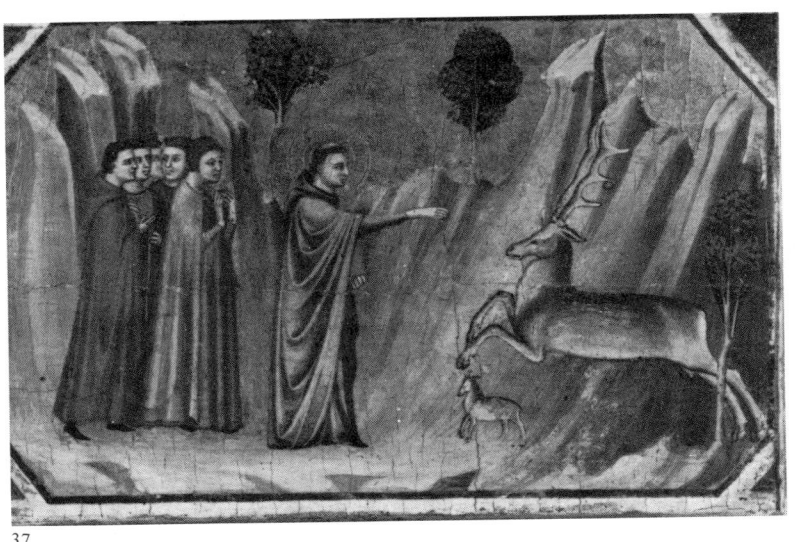

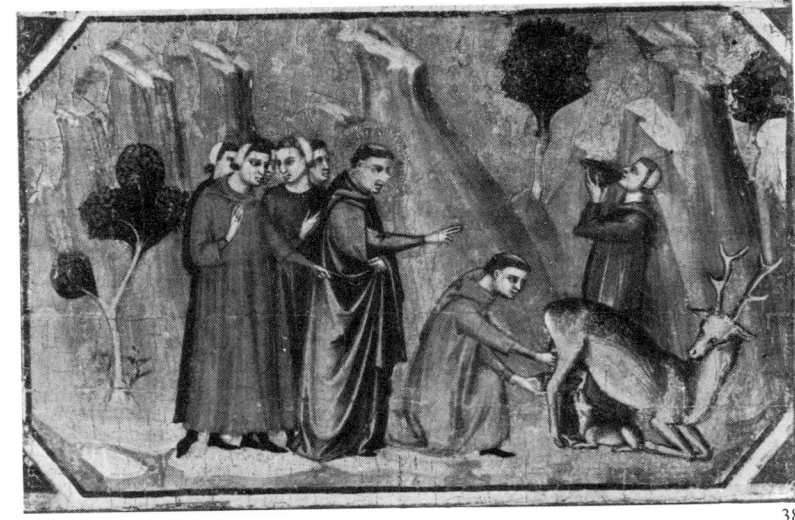

37

38

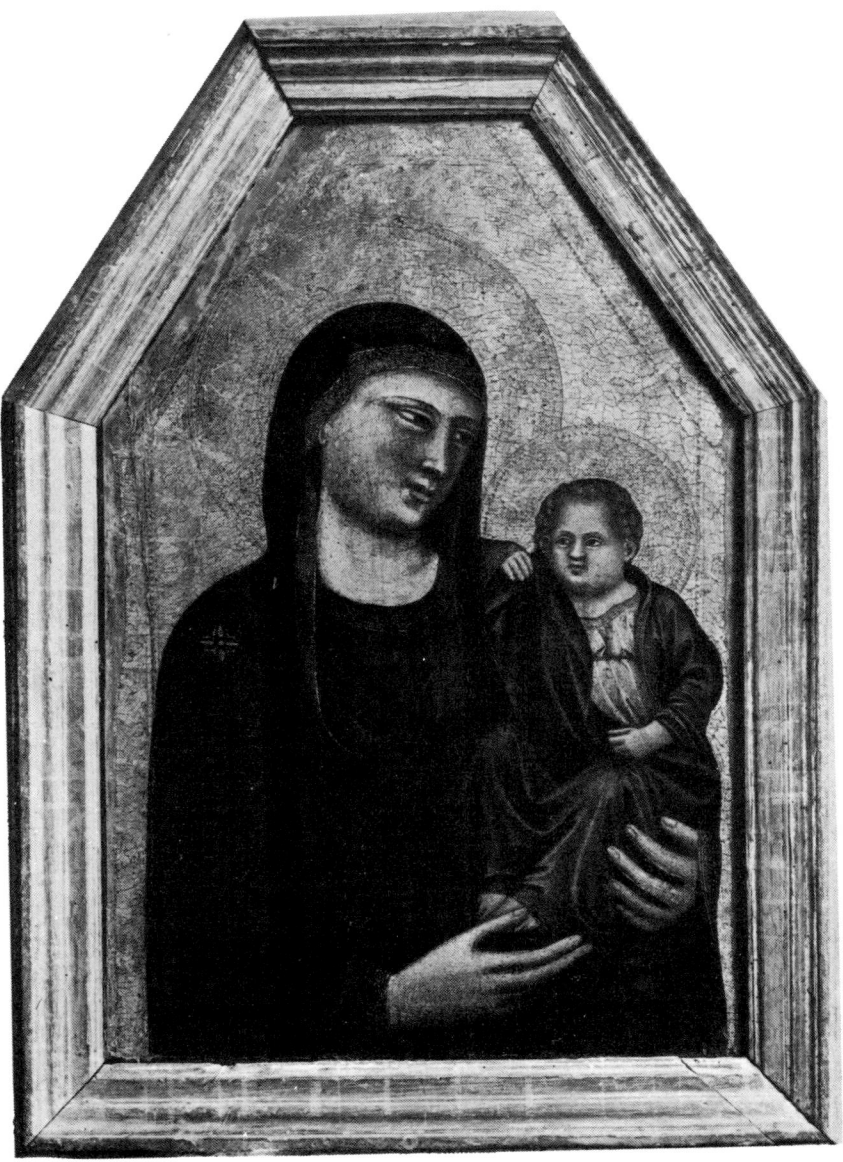

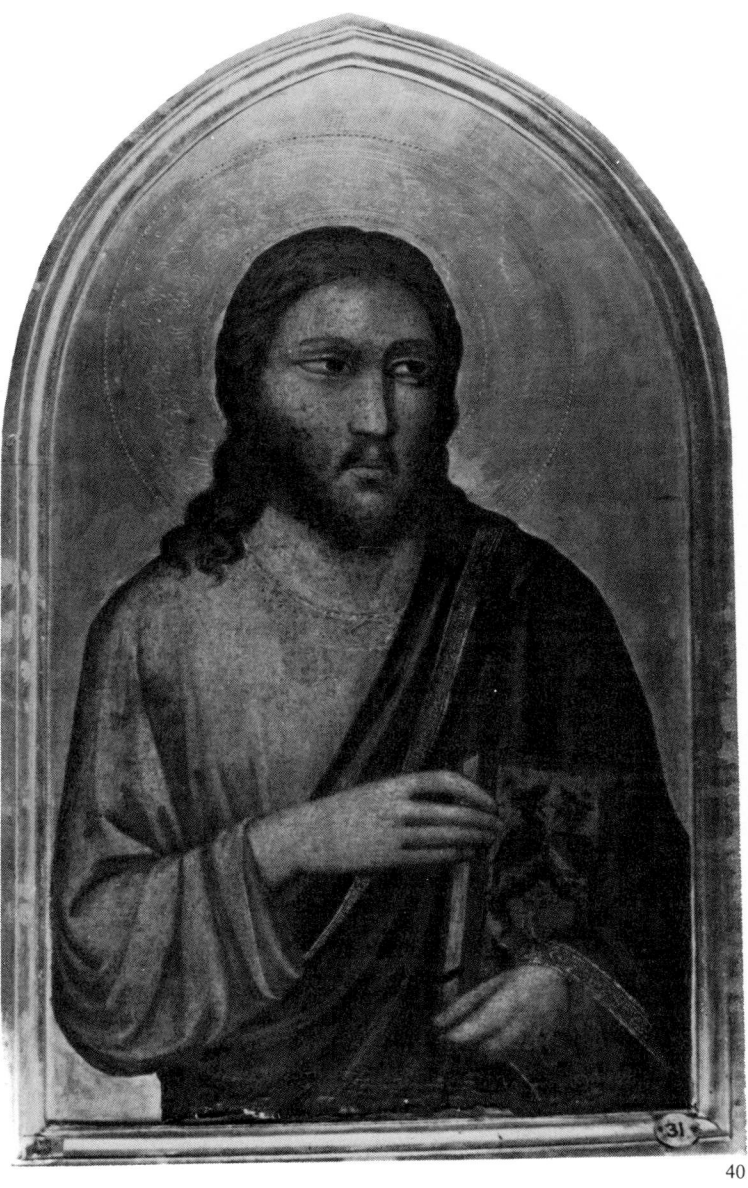

39

40

37. *St Proculus, on a journey, stops a Doe in the Wilderness. Panel. Cambridge (Mass.), Fogg Art Museum, G. L. Winthrop Bequest. no. 1943.110.*
    20.3 × 30.5. Museum photo.
38. *Doe gives milk to St Proculus and his thirsty Companions on the way to Rome. Panel. Cambridge (Mass.), Fogg Art Museum, G. L. Winthrop Bequest.*
    no. 1943.111. 20.3 × 30.5. Museum photo.
39. *Madonna and Child. Panel. Whereabouts unknown. Alinari 43512.*
40. *St John the Evangelist. Panel. Whereabouts unknown. 61 × 35.5. Sotheby A7195.*

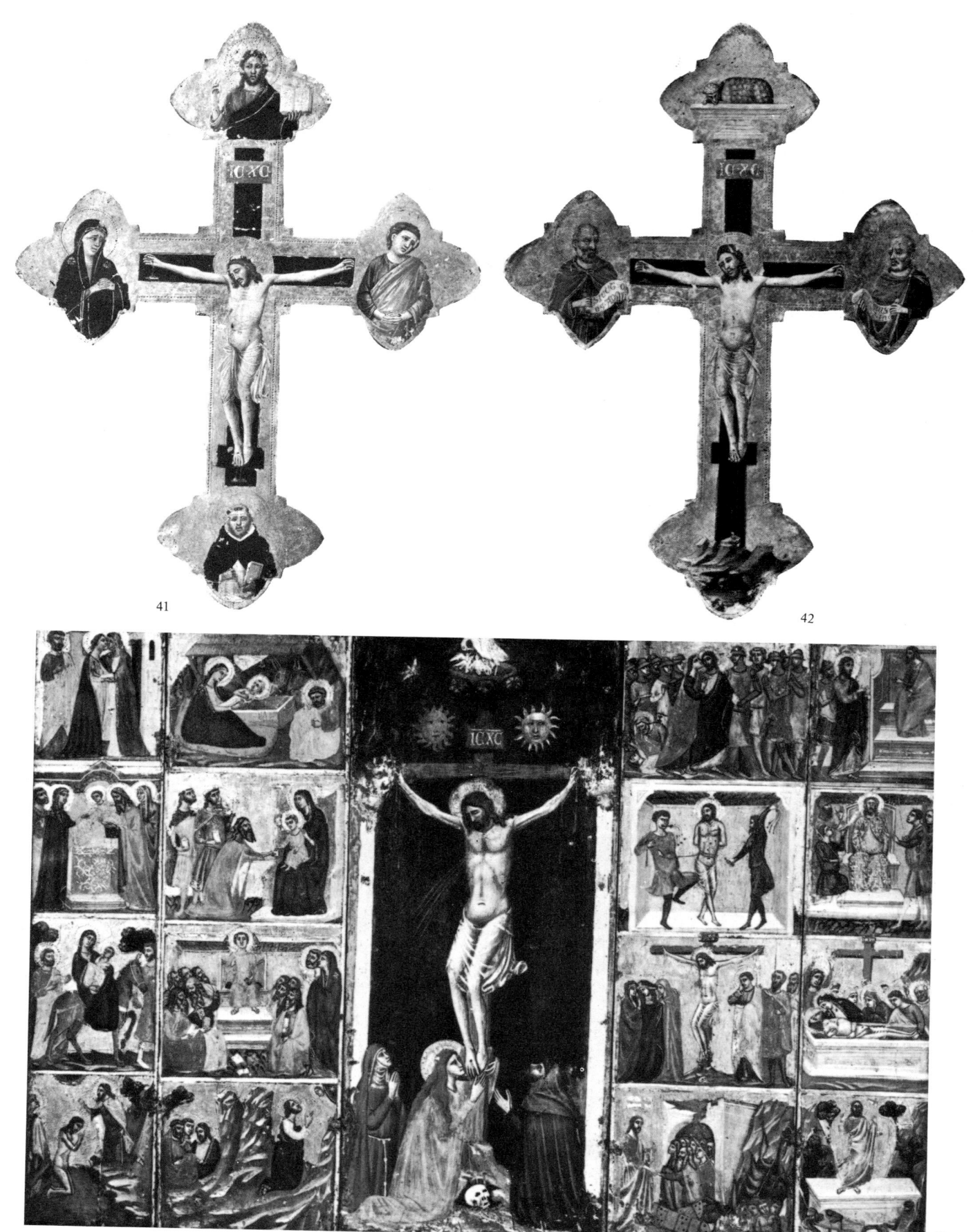

41. *Painted Crucifix, recto of fig. 42. Panel. Florence, Società della Colombaria. 40 × 29.5. SGF 20751.*
42. *Painted Crucifix, verso of fig. 41. Panel. Florence, Società della Colombaria. 40 × 29.5. SGF 20752.*
43. *Scenes from the Life of Christ. Panel. Tucson (Ariz.), University of Arizona, Museum of Art, Kress Gift. no. K. 1717. 44.4 × 63.5. Kress Foundation photo.*

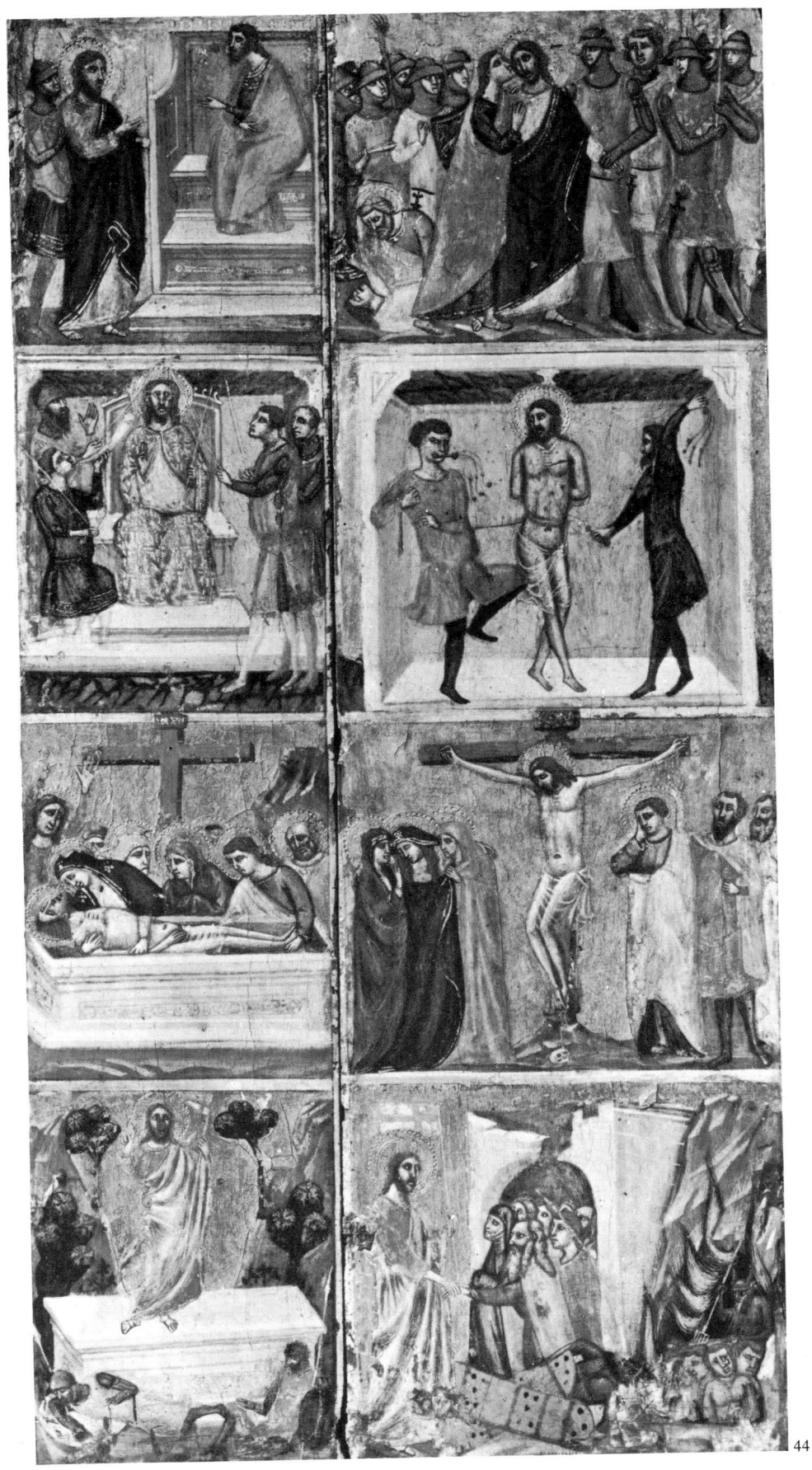

44

44. *Scenes from the Life of Christ, detail of fig. 43. Panel. Tucson (Ariz.), University of Arizona, Museum of Art. no. K. 1717. Reali.*

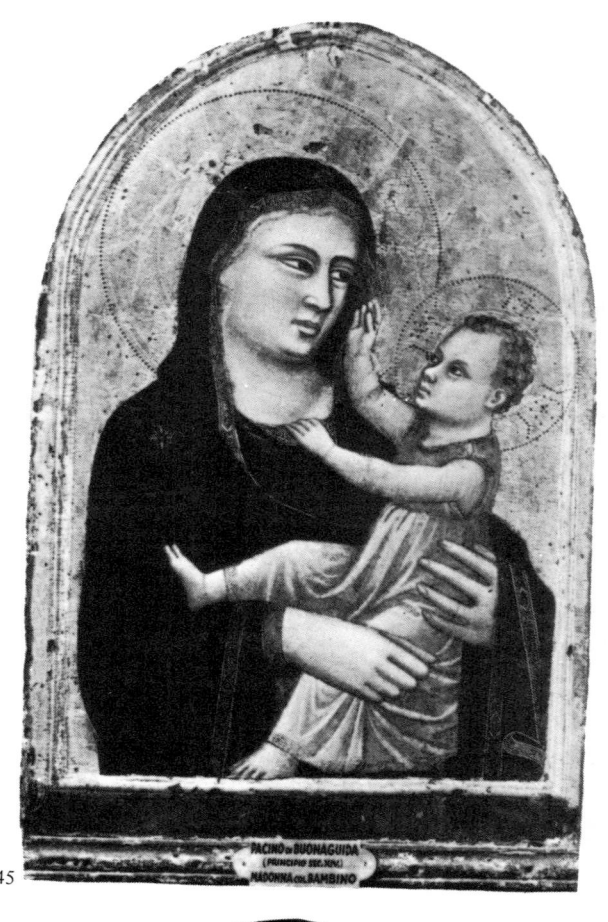

45

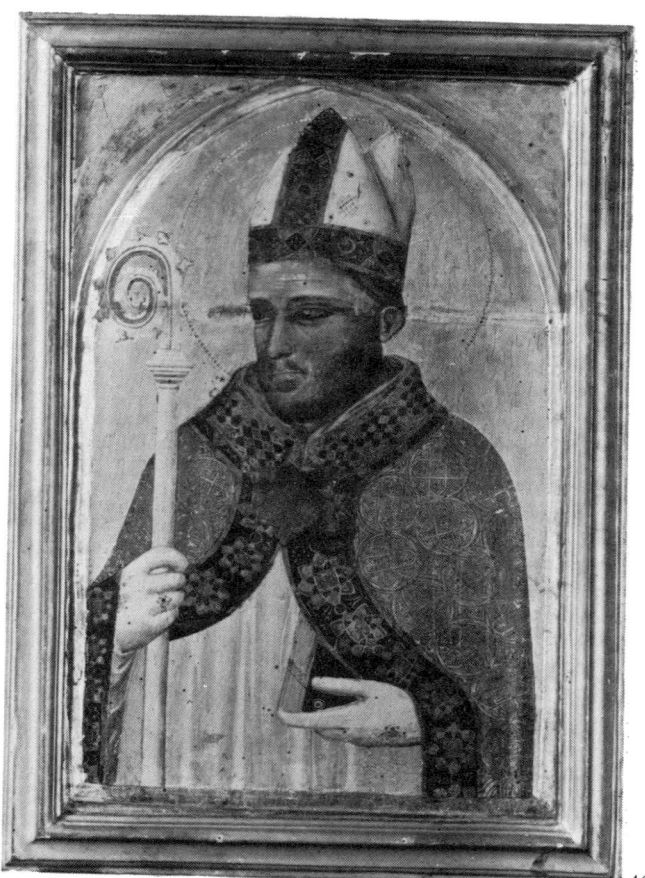

46

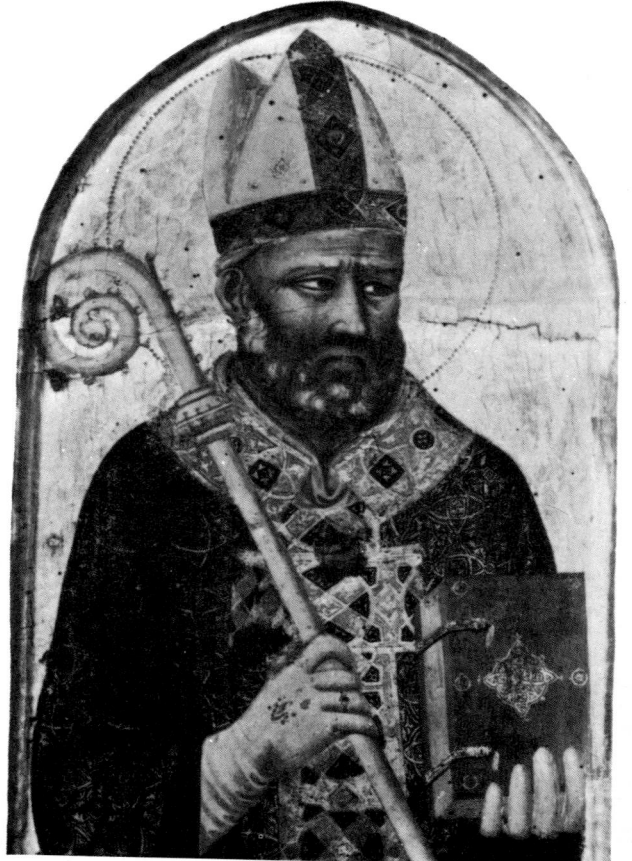

47

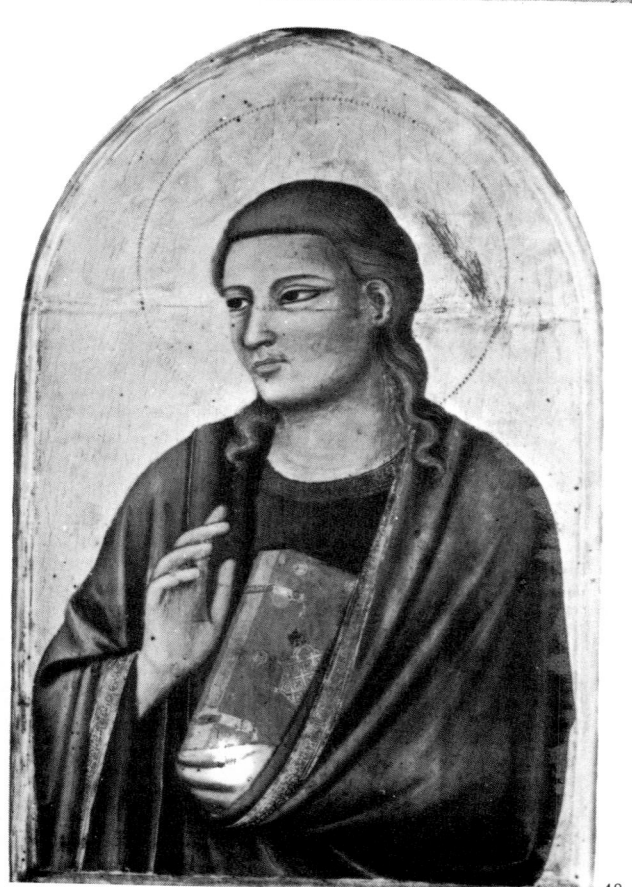

48

45. *Madonna and Child. Panel. Florence, Accademia. no. 6146. 75 × 46. SGF 03760.*
46. *Bishop Saint (St Nicholas?). Panel. Florence, Accademia. no. 8698. 75 × 51. SGF 03760.*
47. *Bishop Saint (St Procolus?). Panel. Florence, Accademia. no. 8700. 75 × 51. SGF 03760.*
48. *St John the Evangelist. Panel. Florence, Accademia. no. 8699. 75 × 51. SGF 03760.*

LIPPO di BENIVIENI

Florentine, born 12- -, died 13- -. Member of the Physicians and Apothecaries Guild between 1312-20..... Master of Neri di Binduccio, who was apprenticed to Lippo for three years on February 20, 1295-6. In 1313 Lippo painted the doors of the tabernacle of S. Giovanni in the baptistery for the Consuls of the Guild of "Calimala". He was elected Superintendent (*Capo Maestro*) of these paintings, which he was then executing and which "enlightened and charmed the heart and eyes of the citizens and of all those who looked at them". They have long ceased to exist.....

> from D. E. Colnaghi, p. 156, *A Dictionary of Florentine Painters*, London, 1928.

If our master owed the direction of his endowments and his chief inspiration initially to the authoritative tradition of Cimabue, that tradition mingled early with a jargon and visual vocabulary taken in with the Florentine air he breathed. What he learned from these two sources passed through the refining process of the Sienese influence: the works of Duccio and of his circle principally. He was uncommonly susceptible to Sienese enchantments and he is the only Florentine of his age whose Sienese borrowings appear at times virtually unaltered in the transcription.....

> from R. Offner, p. VI, *A Critical and Historical Corpus of Florentine Painting*, Sec III, Vol. VI, 1956.

No one, however, has thought to examine the signatures more closely. Both contain the same words and are set down in the same clumsy and unskilled writing. Both are incised in single-line letters without thickness or terminal Gothic flourishes, in summary modern characters, with archaizing intention in the E and the V only. Both deviate from the form of current early Trecento script, and notably from signatures of the period..... If one compares the Acton signature with the two non-Florentine instances one is forced to conclude that it was conceived independently of the painting. The letters are superimposed upon the longitudinal grooves of the sword in a way that leaves no doubt but that the artist himself had not intended an inscription whether written or engraved; if he had, he certainly would have provided a bare interval. Besides, the cutting of these grooves is sharper and of a precision the writer of the signature did not command. The Alessandri signature, in which Milanesi sees the name of the author, would seem a copy of the Acton unless both repeat a common source. It is freer but also looser in the writing, the strokes slenderer, while the letters of Lippus have not been properly aligned. A comparison of the two signatures with the writing upon the Evangelist's open book at Rennes and with the saints' names in the Alessandri dossal discredits the signatures conclusively.....

> from R. Offner, p. VIII, *A Historical and Critical Corpus of Florentine Painting*, Sec. III, Vol. VI, 1956.

This is the centre panel of a polyptych which also includes a panel of St. Paul, with a sword inscribed " Lippus me fecit " as well as other panels of Saints Zenobius, Peter, Paul and Benedict. Once considered a work of the Sienese painter Lippo Memmi, it was attributed by Milanesi, 1878, to the hand of the Florentine Lippo di Benivieni who is recorded by Vasari. The similarity with the Acton polyptych and the coincidence there of another signature on a similar sword confirm that both panels are by this little known Florentine painter, whose stylistic ties with Sienese painting at the beginning of the Trecento can be seen in the usual attribution to Lippo Memmi of these works.....

> from M. Gregori, p. 3, *Mostra dei Tesori Segreti delle Case Fiorentine*, Florence, 1960.

Florentine open to Sienese influence, mentioned from 1296 to 1353.

> from B. Berenson, p. 114, *Italian Pictures of the Renaissance, Florentine School*, Vol. I, London, 1963.

BIBLIOGRAPHY
BOOKS

An asterisk indicates a work listed in the General Bibliography

C-Cavalcaselle II*, 1864, p. 106; *Vasari*, II, 1878, p. 13; *Colnaghi*, 1928, p. 156; *T.-Becker*, Vol. XXIII, 1929, p. 275; *Toesca*, 1951*, p. 517; *Offner, 1956*, Sec. III, Vol. VI, pp. iii-ix, 29-45; *Gregori*, 1960, p. 3; *Cracow*, 1961, pp. 39-40; *Marcucci*, 1965, p. 126; *Berenson, 1963*, Vol. I, p. 114; Boskovits, M., *Giotto* (I Maestri del Colore, 248), Milan, 1966.

JOURNALS

Procacci, U., *RA*, XXXIII, 1958, pp. 129-31; Rozycka-Bryzek, A., *A*, LXI, 27/3-4, 1962, pp. 115-24; Boskovits, M., *ZKG*, XXIX, 1, 1966, pp. 51-66; Salmi, M., *BA*, LII, 1967, p. 223; Volpe, C., *PA*, XXIII, 267, 1972, pp. 3-12.

SIGNED WORKS

Florence, Acton Collection. Panels: Madonna & Child with Sts. Peter and Paul. s. (fig. 59).
Florence, Count Carlo degli Alessandri Collection. Panel: Madonna & Child. s. (fig. 49).
Florence, Count Cosimo degli Alessandri Collection. Two panels: Sts Peter and Paul. s. (figs. 57-58).

There are no known dated works by Lippo di Benivieni.

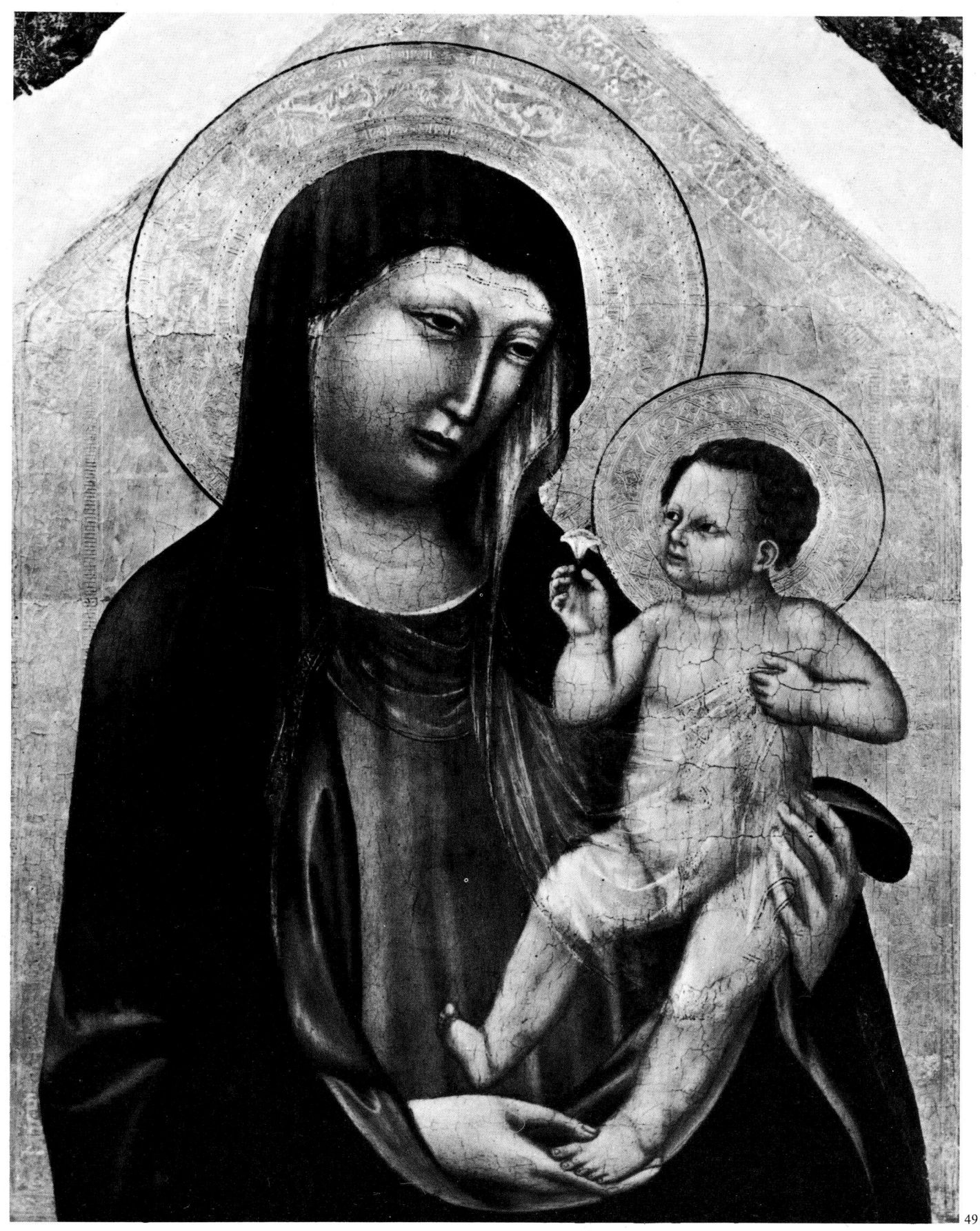

49. *Madonna and Child. Panel. Florence, Conte Carlo degli Alessandri Collection. 75.3 × 56.2. Bertoni-Offner. s.*

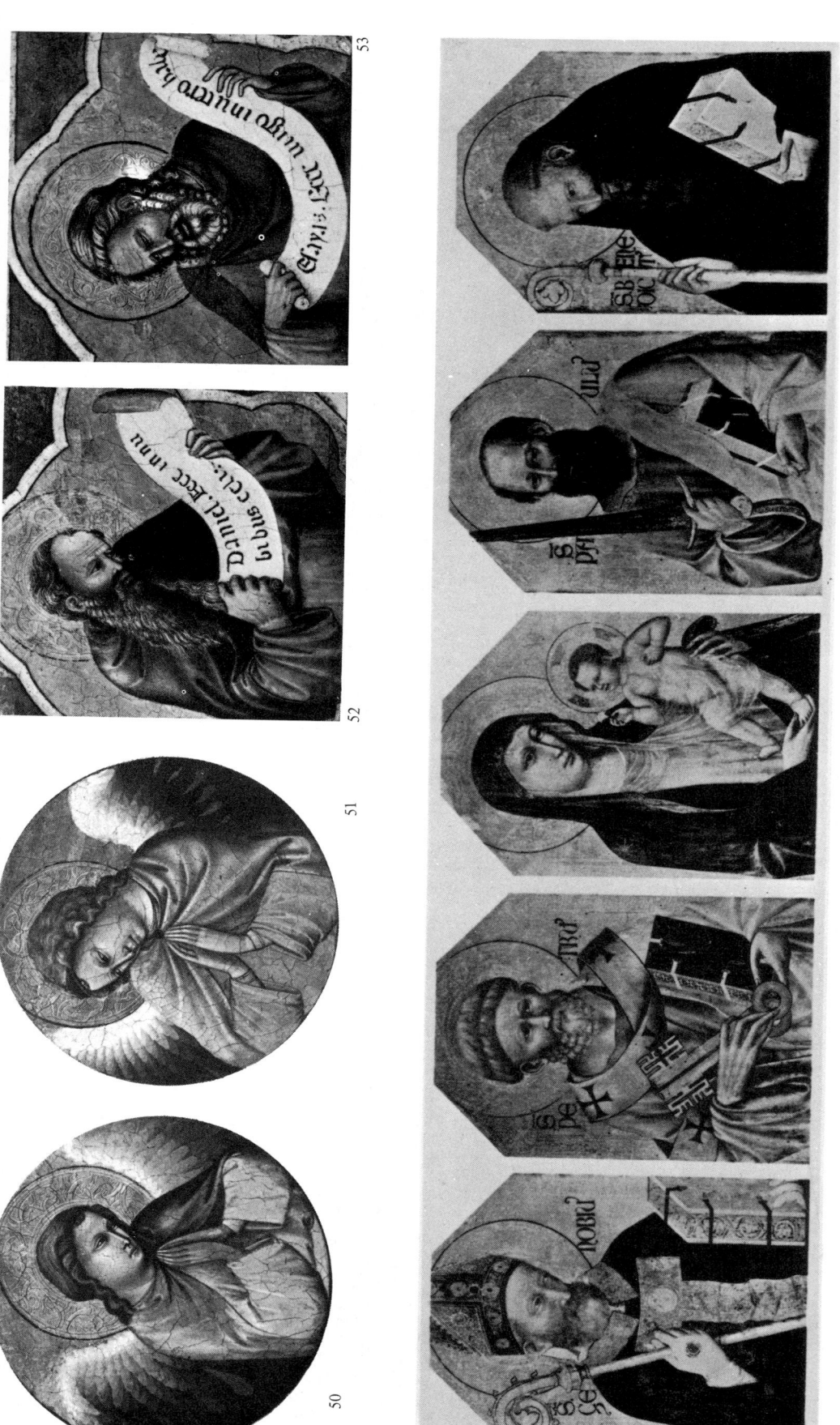

50. *An Angel. Panel. Whereabouts unknown. 16.5 × 15. Perotti 19417.*
51. *An Angel. Panel. Whereabouts unknown. 16 × 19. Perotti 19418.*
52. *Daniel. Panel. Whereabouts unknown. 17.2 × 22. Perotti 19416.*
53. *Elijah. Panel. Whereabouts unknown. 16 × 22. Perotti 19415.*
54. *Reconstruction of Alessandri polyptych. Madonna and Child with four Saints. Panel. SGF 173057.*

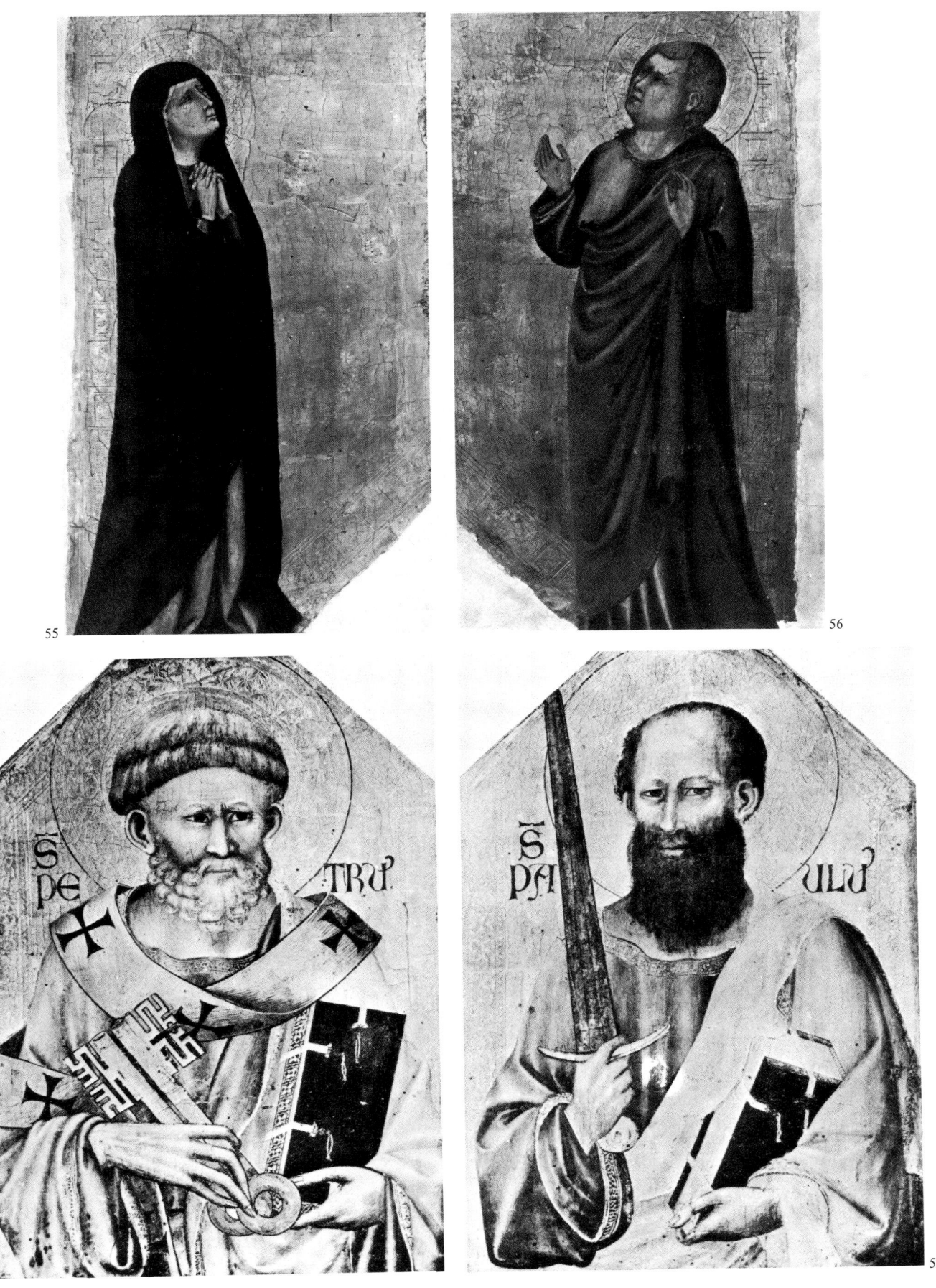

55. *The Virgin. Panel. Whereabouts unknown. 40 × 21. Perotti 19411.*
56. *St John. Panel. Whereabouts unknown. 39.5 × 21. Perotti 19412.*
57. *St Peter. Panel. Florence, Conte Cosimo degli Alessandri Collection. 40 × 21. Bertoni-Offner. s.*
58. *St Paul. Panel. Florence, Conte Cosimo degli Alessandri Collection. 40 × 21. Bertoni-Offner. s.*

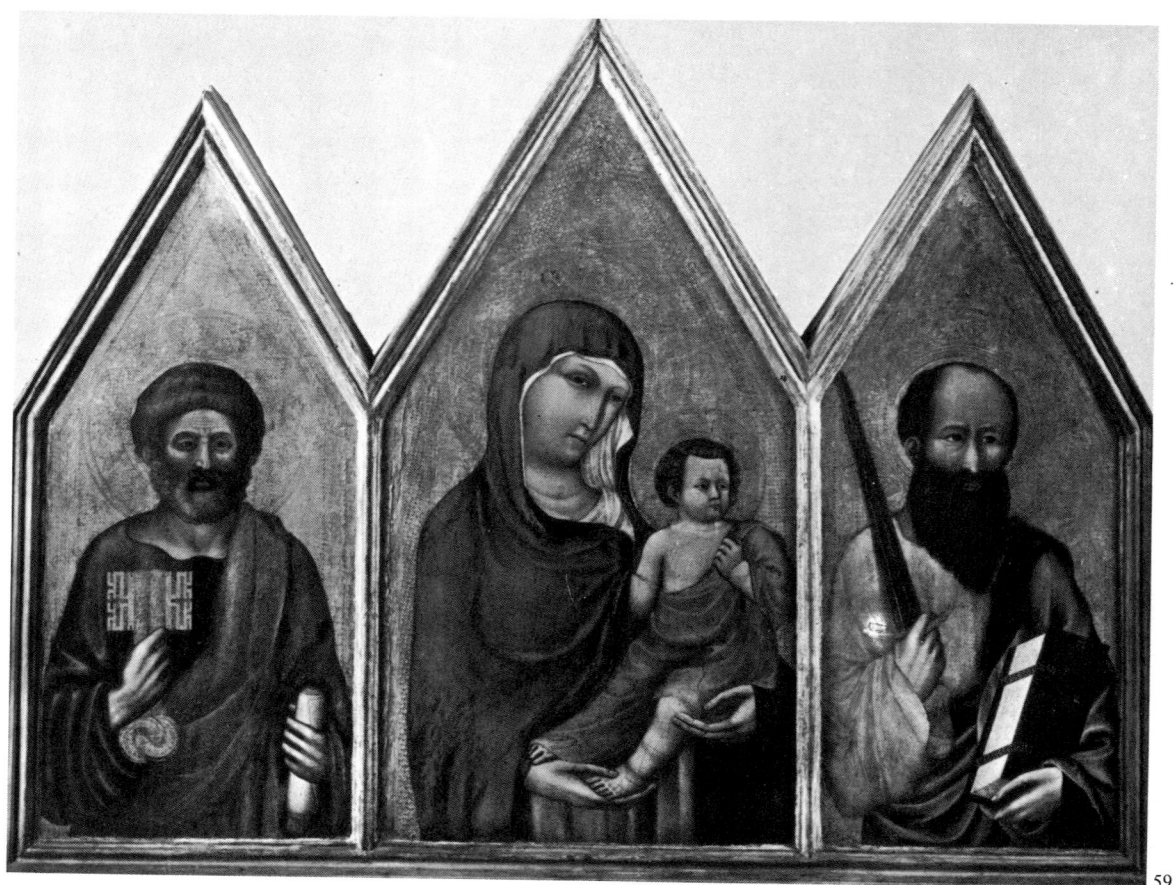

59

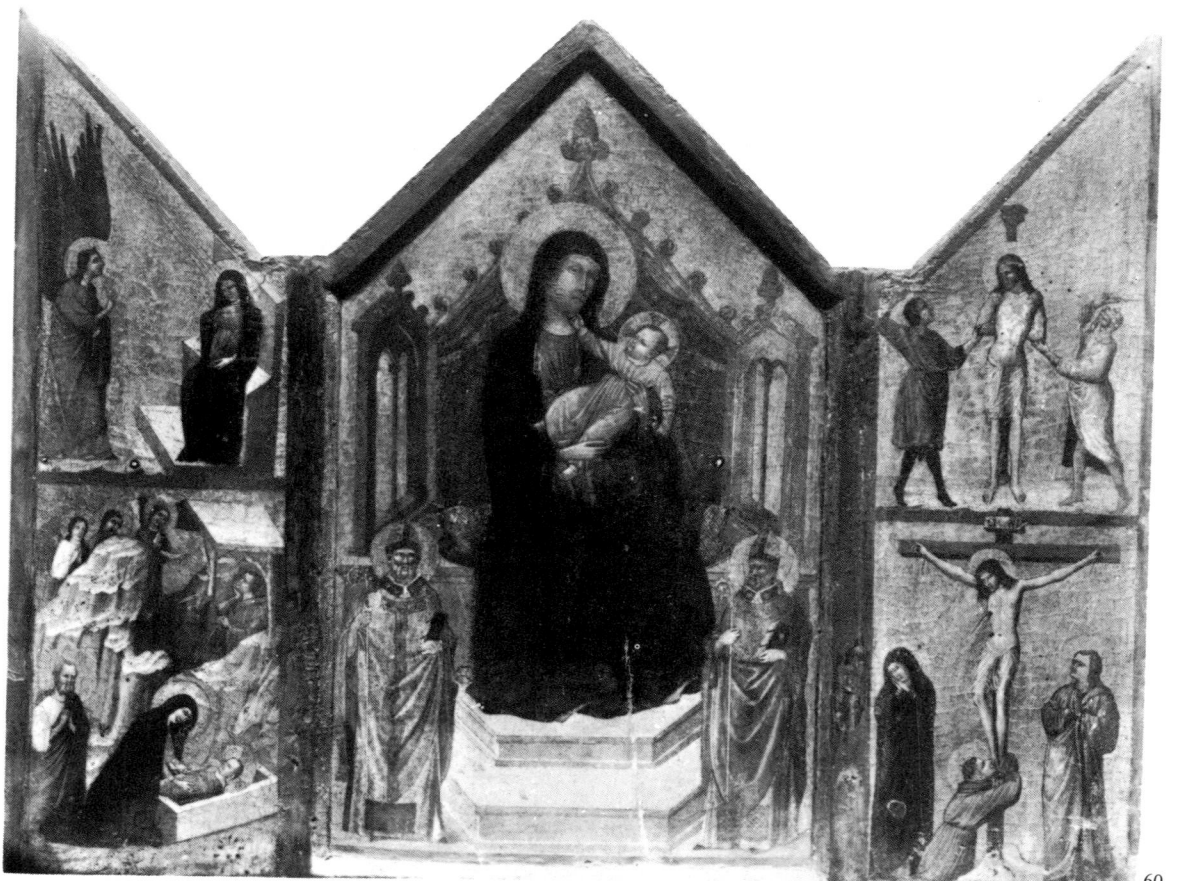

60

59. *Madonna and Child with Sts Peter and Paul.   Panel.   Florence, Acton Collection.   Madonna: 88.7 × 47; Peter: 87.5 × 36.5; Paul: 79 × 33.5. Reali. s.*
60. *Portable triptych: Madonna and Child with two Bishop Saints. Wings: Annunciation; Nativity; Flagellation; Crucifixion. Panel. Cracow, Muzeum Narodowe. XII.188. 47.2 × 60. Museum photo.*

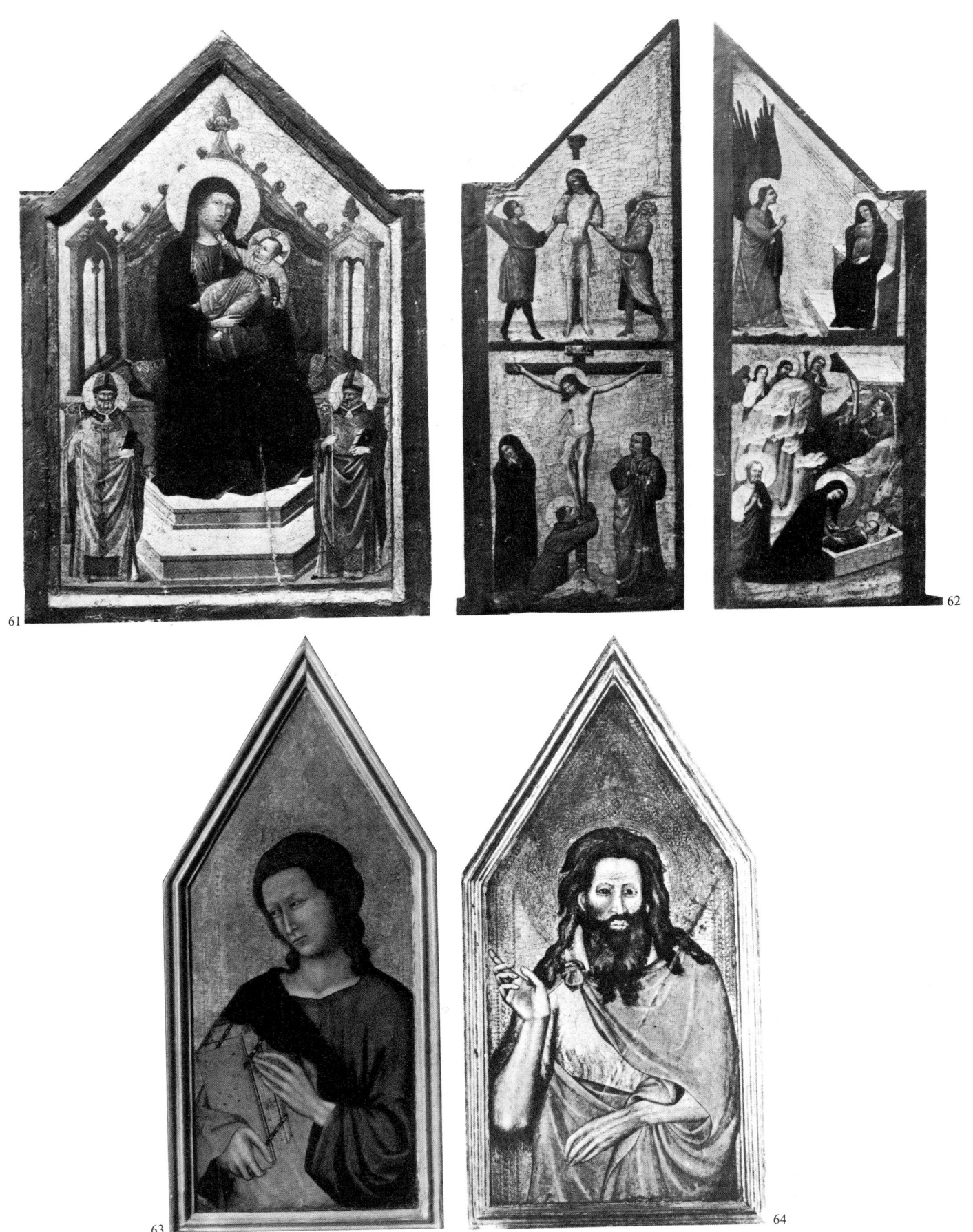

61. *Madonna and Child with two Bishop Saints, detail of fig. 60. Panel. Cracow, Muzeum Narodowe. XII.188. Museum photo.*
62. *Wings: Flagellation, Crucifixion, Annunciation and Nativity, detail of fig. 60. Panel. Cracow, Muzeum Narodowe. XII.188. Museum photo.*
63. *St John the Evangelist. Panel. Ottawa, National Gallery of Canada. 2995. 77.5 × 31.7. Museum photo.*
64. *St John the Baptist. Panel. New York (N.Y.), Maurice Salomon Collection. 77.5 × 31.8. Bertoni-Offner.*

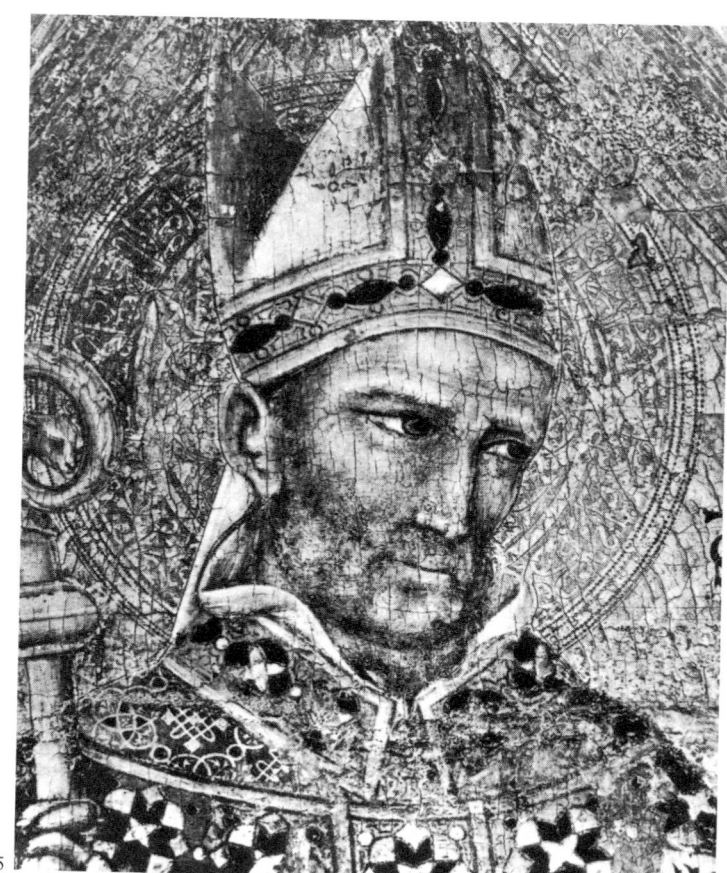

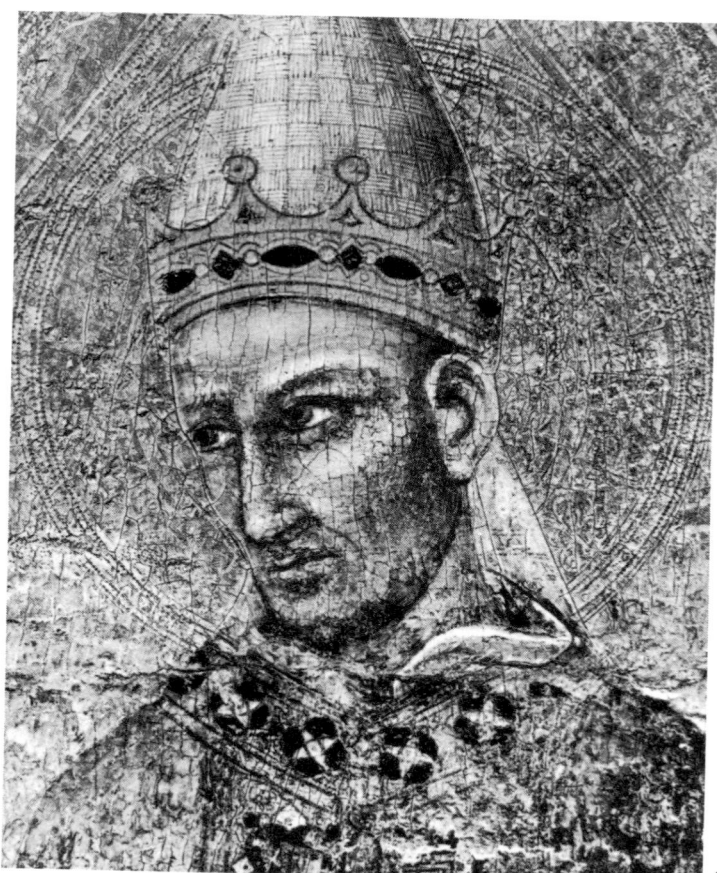

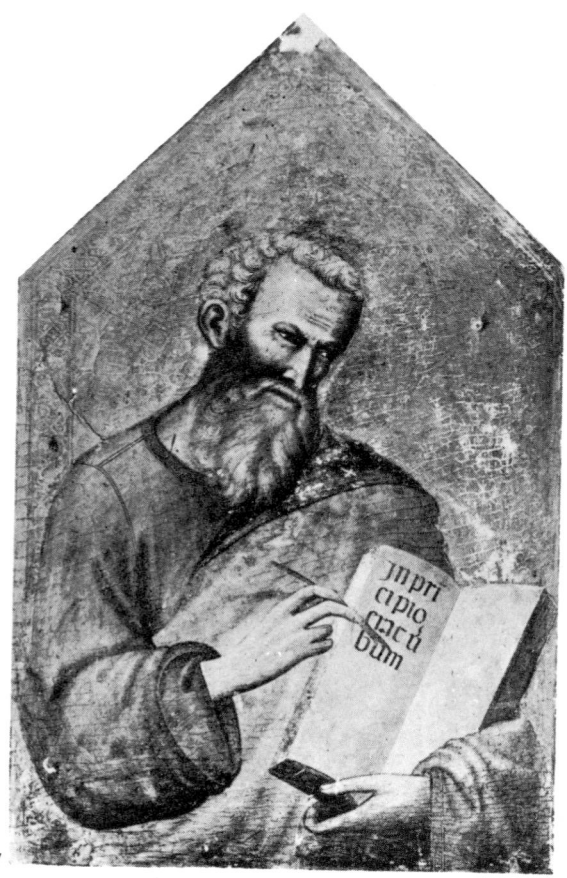

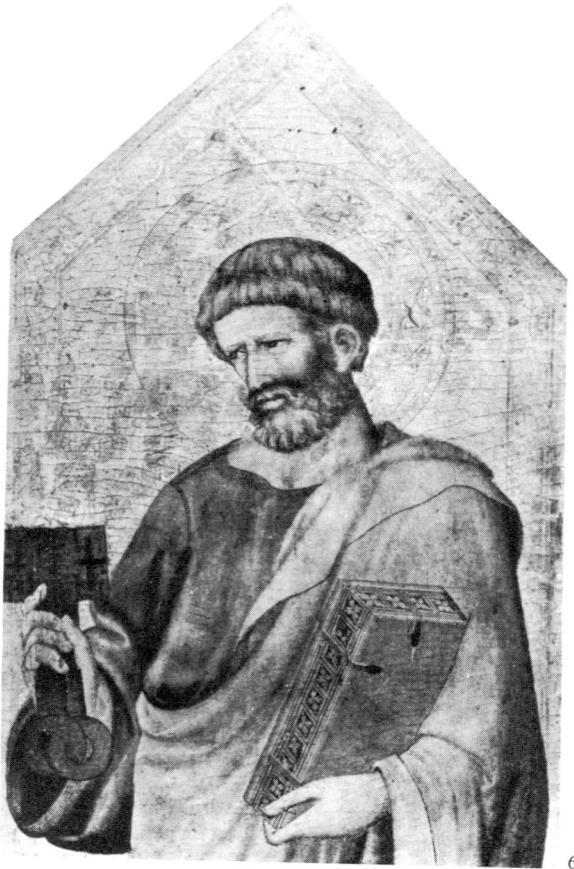

65. *St Nicholas. Panel. Florence, Conte Alessandro Contini-Bonacossi Collection. 97 × 55. Bertoni-Offner.*
66. *A Pope Saint. Panel. Florence, Conte Alessandro Contini-Bonacossi Collection. 97 × 55. Bertoni-Offner.*
67. *St John the Evangelist. Panel. Rennes, Musée des Beaux-Arts. no. 6178. 78 × 48. Bertoni-Offner.*
68. *St Peter. Panel. Rennes, Musée des Beaux-Arts. no. 6177. 78 × 48. Bertoni-Offner.*

MASTER OF SAINT CECILIA

Other than the paintings in the chapel of San Niccolò, and those in the right arm of the transept at Assisi, there are also paintings that are related to the early manner of Giotto by another master, the author of the altar frontal representing Saint Cecilia, which is now in the Uffizi Gallery. The saint is enthroned in the centre, her life story is represented on the sides: at the left is Cecilia at table with Valerian, and the story of the conversion of these, and of her brother Tiburtius; at the right, Cecilia publicly confesses her faith, is betrayed before the prefect and at the end martyred.

For the vivacity of the representations and in the portrayal of particular characters, the panel reminds one of the last scenes of the frescoes of the life of St. Francis in the upper Basilica at Assisi. There one sees the same exaggerated figures, the little heads against a background of very tall buildings. With this picture there is surely a relationship to the *St. Peter Enthroned between Two Angels* formerly on the altar of the destroyed church of San Pier Maggiore and now on the first altar at the right in San Simone in Florence; a *Madonna* and a *Santa Margherita* in the church named for this last saint in Montici; finally a *San Miniato* in the Basilica of the same name near Florence. The first of these paintings, noted by Suida, carries the date of 1307. One is dealing with a Tuscan painter who was younger than Giotto and who was a follower of the old style, painting at the same moment as Giotto was revealing his powerful individuality at Padua.....

from A. Venturi, p. 488, *La Pittura del Trecento*, Vol. V, Milan, 1907.

We recognise by this name a personality who was a contemporary of Giotto, who Suida wishes to identify with Stefano, and Venturi with Buffalmacco.

His characteristics are to make his figures tall, with small heads, and to put his architecture into perspective, with minute decoration on it. He retains, in his vivacity, something of the Byzantine to such an extent that Vasari attributed to Cimabue the altarpiece now in the Uffizi, which is the best example of his style.....

from B. Khvoshinsky and M. Salmi, p. 9, *I Pittori Toscani*, Rome, 1912.

The painter, to whom the name of Master of the St. Cecily altar-piece, has been given, has only been evolved within the last few years and his art gradually established since. Mr. Berenson, I believe, was the first to attribute to the same hand the St. Cecily altar-piece in the Uffizi, the Madonna and St. Margaret panels in the church of Sta. Margarita a Motici, the painting of St. Miniatus in his church near Florence and the continuation of the St. Francis cycle at Assisi. Herr Suida, who has dedicated a long study to this artist, unjustly refused to include in the list of his works any of the last mentioned scenes but rightly added the altar-piece, dated 1307, of St. Peter in the church of S. Simone, Florence, and another originally in Sta. Maria degli Angeli, but now in the collection of Christ Church College, Oxford.....

from R. van Marle, pp. 274-276, *The Development of the Italian Schools of Painting*, Vol. III, The Hague, 1924.

The name is a practical designation for a group of paintings, which among them yield a single unequivocal date: that of 1307 inscribed under the St. Peter in S. Simone. It is the only considerable Florentine group in the XIV century the identity of whose painter still remains problematic. The hypothesis that he is the historical Buffalmacco is rendered difficult chiefly by the irreconcilability of his art with that of the frescoes at Settimo. The St. Cecilia Master inclined with all the delicacy of his genius to miniature painting, in which he was (Daddi excepted) the most exquisite Florentine master before Uccello. But extant examples of such painting withhold any clue to his immediate artistic forebears. The style of his full-sized works, however, issues out of that dark interval between Cimabue and the fully-formed Giotto, in which Rome exerted such profound influence on Florence. This was accessible to our master in Assisi, where he himself painted. He constitutes in Giotto's time the one other great source of formative influence in Florence, and should be regarded the founder of a style. He is responsible for a definite and persistent tendency, narrative in kind, mystical and lyrical in essence; and independent of the monumentalism of Giotto.....

from R. Offner, p. 15, *A Critical & Historical Corpus of Florentine Painting*, Sec. III, Vol. I, New York, 1931.

According to the most recent conclusions of the critics, the " Master of Santa Cecilia" was the painter who continued Giotto's work in the upper church at Assisi, where he would have been the author of the last three scenes from the " Stories from the Life of St Francis ".....

from U. Galetti and E. Camesasca, p. 1480, *Enciclopedia della Pittura Italiana*, " F-O ", Cernusco sul Naviglio, 1950.

BIBLIOGRAPHY
BOOKS

An asterisk indicates a work listed in the General Bibliography

Venturi, A.*, 1907, pp. 488-9; *Cruttwell, 1907**, 1907, p. 8; *Khv & Salmi**, 1912, pp. 9-10; Schmarsow, A., *Kompositionsgesetze der Franzlegende in der Oberkirche zu Assisi*, Leipzig, 1918; *Vitzhum**, 1924, pp. 265-7; *Offner, 1927**, pp. 4-5, 13, 15-16; *v. Marle*, 1924*, pp. 274-94; *Hautecoeur**, 1931, p. 107; *Offner, 1931**, Sec. III, Vol. I; *Berenson, 1932**, pp. 343-4; Catalogue: *Exposition de l'art italien de Cimabue à Tiepolo*, Paris, 1935, p. 127; Cecchi, E., *Giotto*, Milan, 1937, pp. 118-20; *Paatz**, 1940, pp. 444-5; *M. Giottesca**, 1943, pp. 381-93; *Coletti, Vol. II**, 1946, pp. 33-4; *Antal**, 1948, pp. 166-7; *Vavalà, 1948**, pp. 40-8; *Galetti**, " F-O ", 1950, pp. 1480-4; Vollmer, H., *T-Becker**, 1950, XXXVII, pp. 62-3; *Toesca, 1951**, p. 607; Oertel, R., *Die Frühzeit der Italienischen Malerei*, Stuttgart, 1953, p. 220; *Offner, 1956**, Sec. III, Vol. VI, pp. vi-vii, 3 ff.; *Berenson, 1963**, Vol. I, p. 144; *Marcucci**, 1965, pp. 14-17; Boskovits, M., *La Scuola di Giotto* (I Maestri del Colore, 248), Milan, 1966; *Dal Poggetto**, 1967, pp. 15-18; *Edit., Congresso VII**, 1971; Gilbert, C., *History of Renaissance Art throughout Europe*, New York, 1973, p. 27.

JOURNALS

Fry, R., *BM*, II, 1903, p. 118; Suida, W., *RKW*, XXVII, 1904, p. 387; Wulff, O., *RKW*, XXVII, 1904, pp. 221-250; Rintelen, F., *KGA*, 2, 1906, pp. 33-45; Wulff, O., *RKW*, XXIX, 1906, pp. 47-54; Berenson, B., *RADA*, VIII, 3, 1908, p. 45; Salmi, M., *A*, XVI, 1913, pp. 208-27; Offner, R., *MKIF*, III, 1919-32, p. 136; Sirèn, O., *BM*, XXXV, 1919, pp. 229-36; Sirèn, O., *BM*, XXXVI, 1919, pp. 4-11; Sirèn, O., *BM*, XXXVII, 1920, pp. 176-84; Offner, R., *AA*, XI, 1922, p. 22; Sirèn, O., *BM*, XLIV, 1924, pp. 271-8; Offner, R., *BM*, L, 1927, pp. 91-104; Parronchi, A., *RA*, XXI, 1939, pp. 193-228; Tatlock, R., *BM*, LVI, 1930, p. 225; Offner, R., *BM*, LXIII, 1933, p. 80; Oertel, R., *ZKG*, VI, 1937, pp. 218-38; Oertel, R., *MKIF*, V, 6, 1940, pp. 436-7; Oertel, R., *ZKG*, XI, 1943-4, pp. 1-27; Richardson, E. P., *BDIA*, 33, 1953-4, pp. 66-7; *AQ*, XVIII, 1, 1955, pp. 97-9; Meiss, M., *RDA*, VI, 2, 1956, pp. 139-48; Cohn, W., *BA*, LXII, 4, 1957, pp. 335-8; Procacci, U., *RA*, XXXIII, 1958, pp. 121-39; Smart, A., *BM*, CII, 1960, pp. 405-13, 430-7; Longhi, R., *PA*, XIV, 164, 1963, pp. 3-16; Previtali, G., *PA*, XIV, 165, 1963, pp. 71-80; Smart, A., *AP*, LXXXI, 1965, pp. 262-3; Boskovits, M., *ZKG*, XXIX, 1, 1966, pp. 51-66; De Benedictis, C., *AV*, VI, 4, 1967, p. 41; Donati, P. P., *C*, XVIII, 4, 1967, pp. 290-6; Donati, P. P., *PA*, XIX, 215/235, 1968, pp. 36-7; Ragghianti, C. L., *CA*, XVI, 101-102, 1969, pp. 3-80; De Benedictis, C., *AV*, XI, 4, 1972, pp. 3-9; Cole, B., *GBA*, LXXX, 1972, pp. 91-96; Volpe, C., *PA*, XXIII, 267, 1972, pp. 7, 11; Cole, B., *MKIF*, XVII, 2-3, 1973, p. 236, note 35.

DATED WORK

1307 Florence, S. Simone. Panel: St. Peter Enthroned with two Angels. d. (fig. 83).

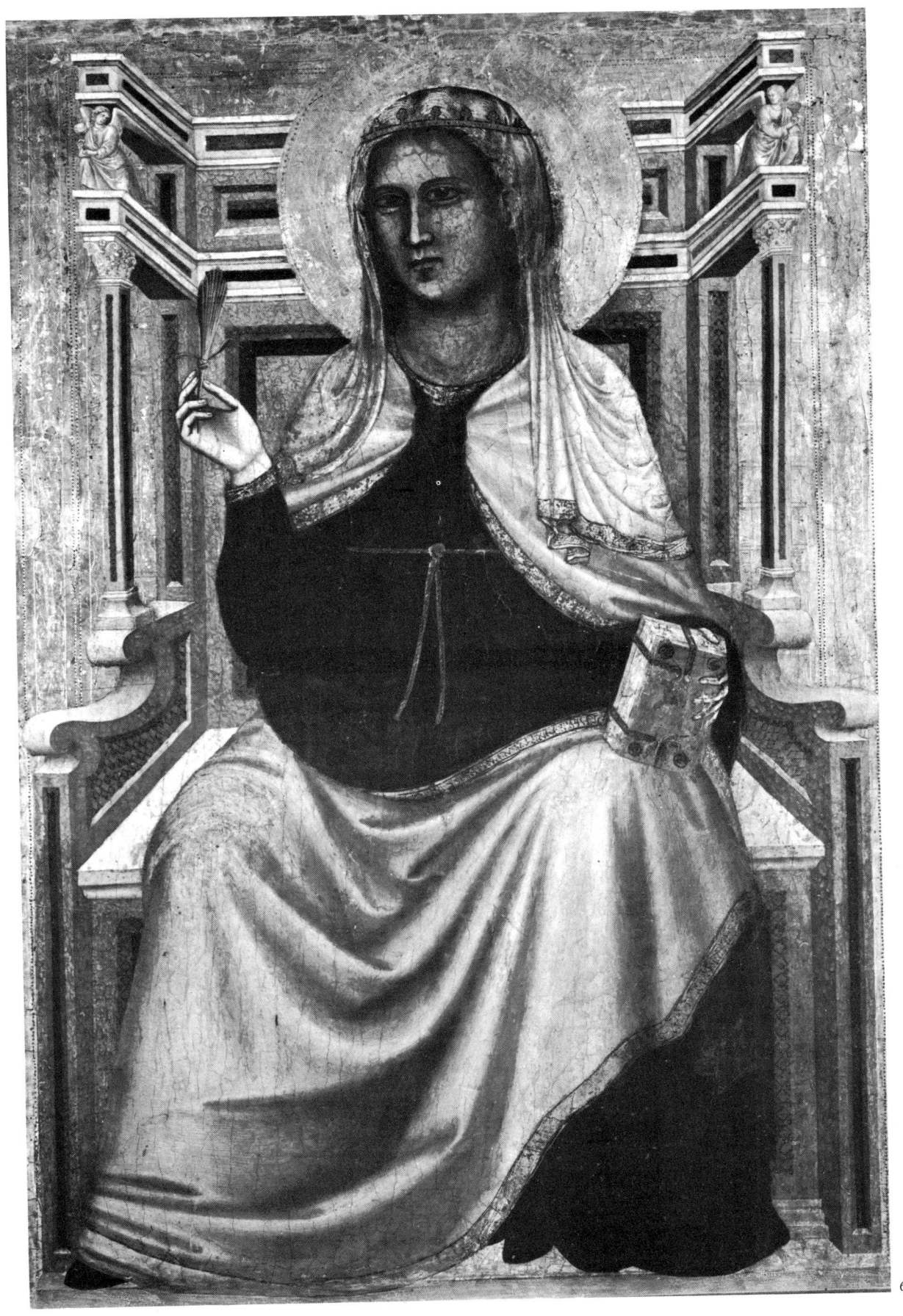

69. *St Cecilia, detail of fig. 70. Panel. Florence, Uffizi. no. 449. SGF 144303.*

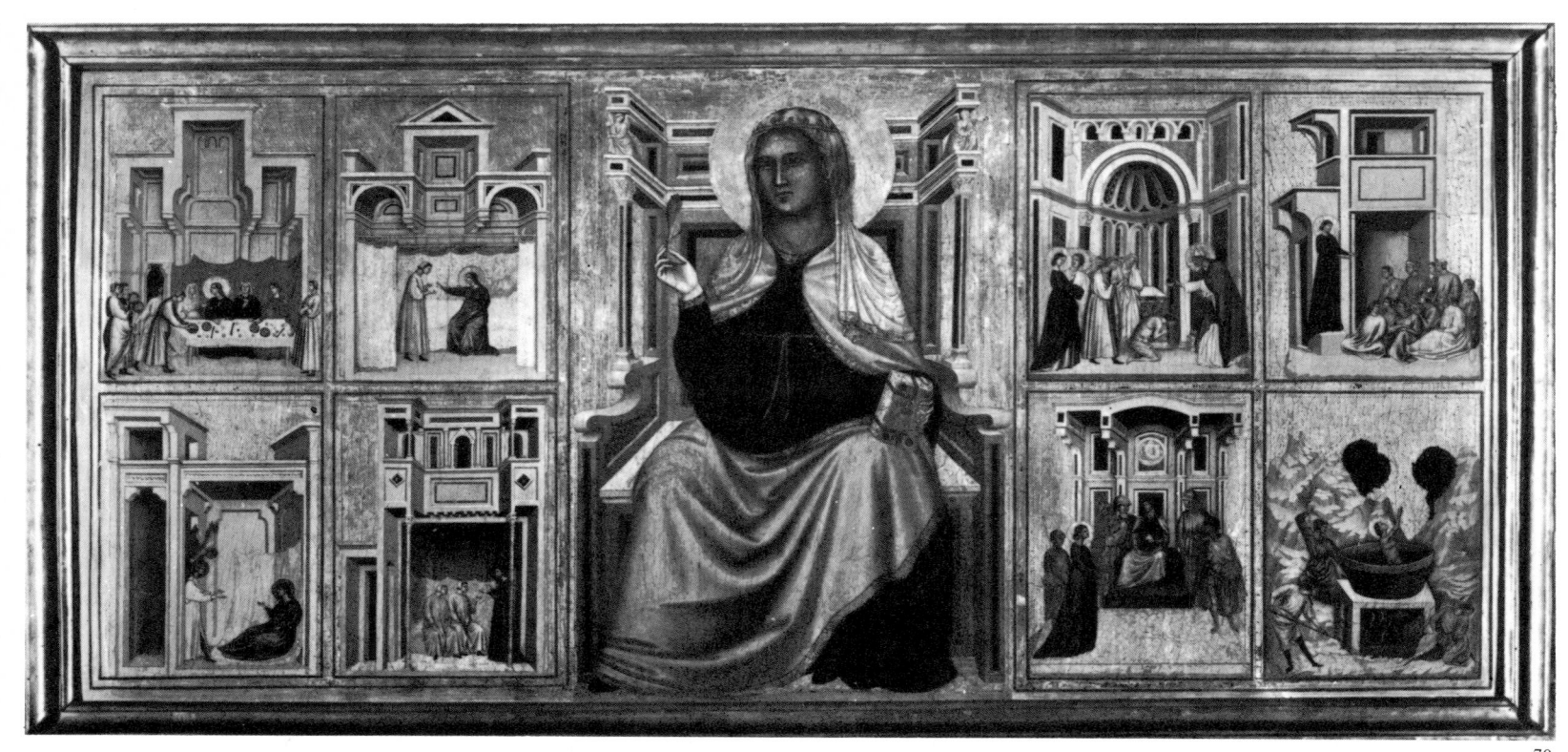

70

70. *St Cecilia and scenes from her Life: Wedding feast of Cecilia and Valerian; being the Bride of Christ, she begs her Husband to live in continence; Valerian crowned with flowers by an Angel; Cecilia preaches to Valerian and Tiburtius; Baptism of Tiburtius; Cecilia preaches; refusing to worship idols, she is sentenced by Almachius; she is put into the cauldron of boiling oil. Panel. Florence, Uffizi. no. 449. 181 × 85. SGF 144302.*

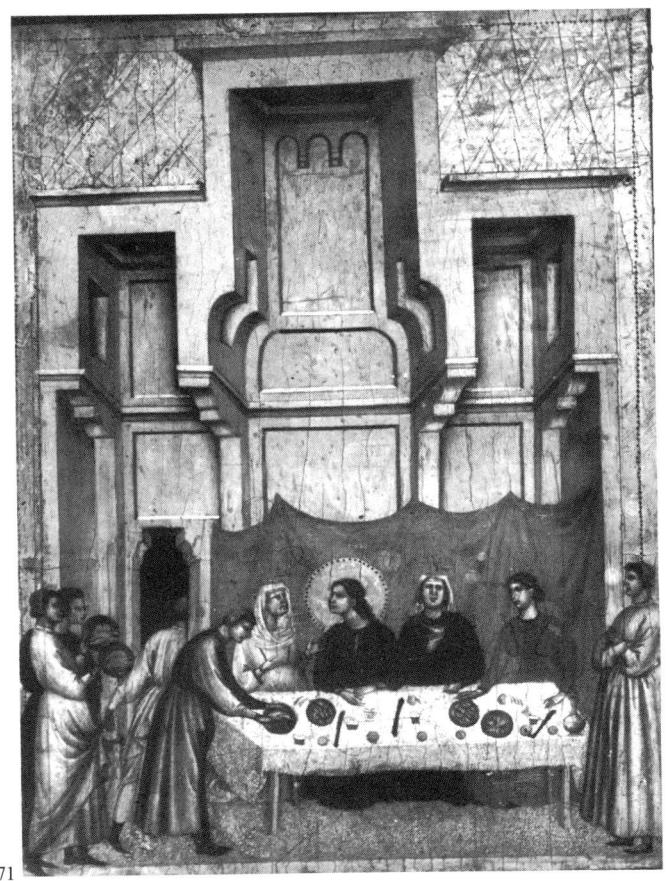

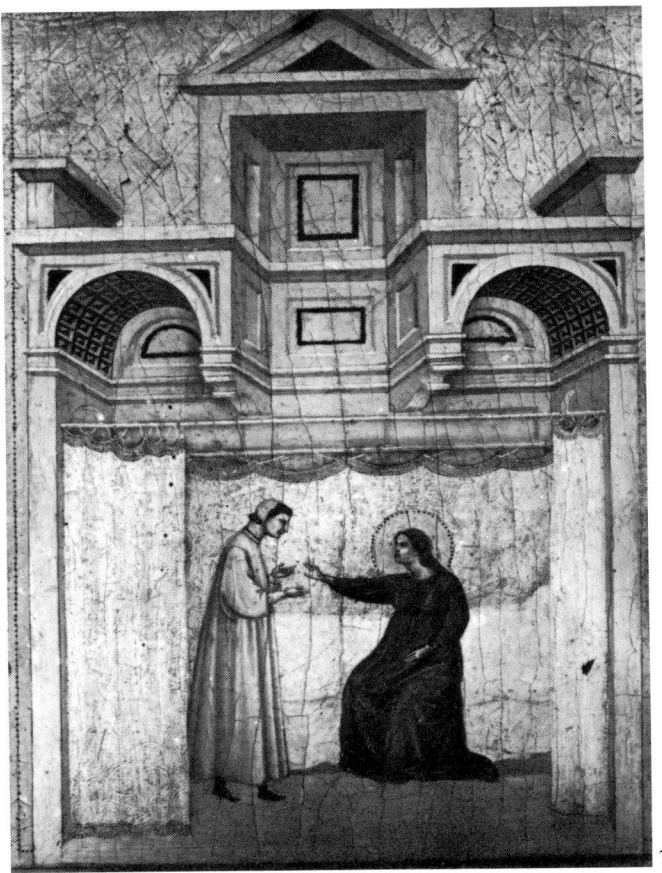

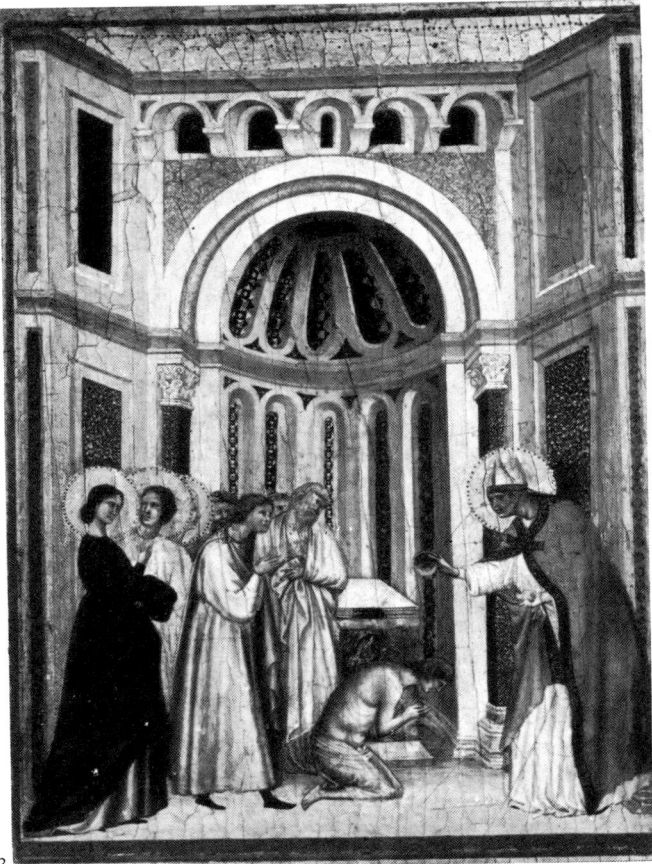

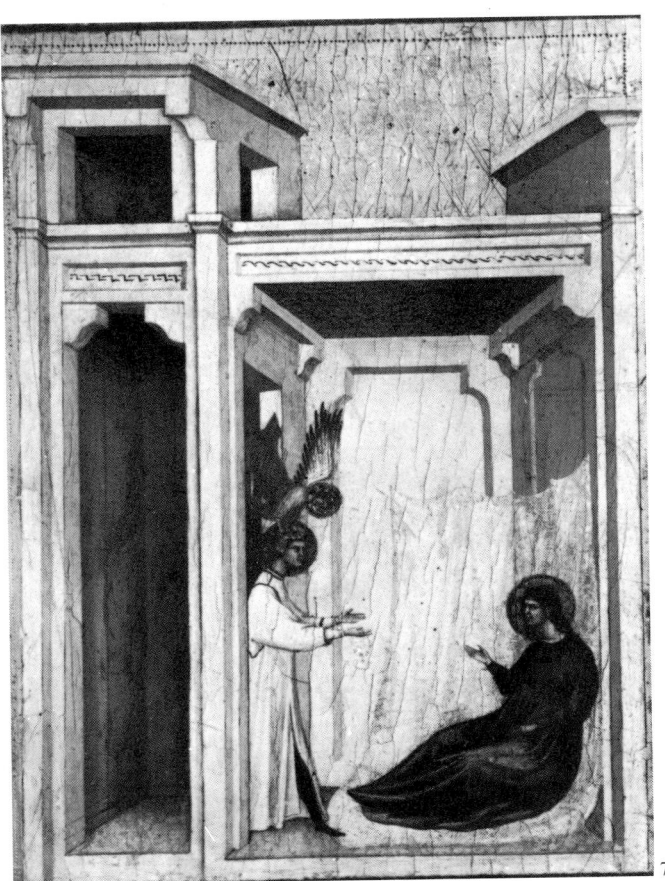

71. *Wedding feast of St Cecilia and Valerian, detail of fig. 70. Panel. Florence. Uffizi. no. 449. SGF 10629.*
72. *Being the Bride of Christ, St Cecilia begs her Husband to live in continence, detail of fig. 70. Panel. Florence, Uffizi. no. 449. SGF 10630.*
73. *Baptism of Tibertius, detail of fig. 70. Panel. Florence, Uffizi. no. 449. SGF 10631.*
74. *Valerian crowned with flowers by an Angel, detail of fig. 70. Panel. Florence, Uffizi. no. 449. SGF 10633.*

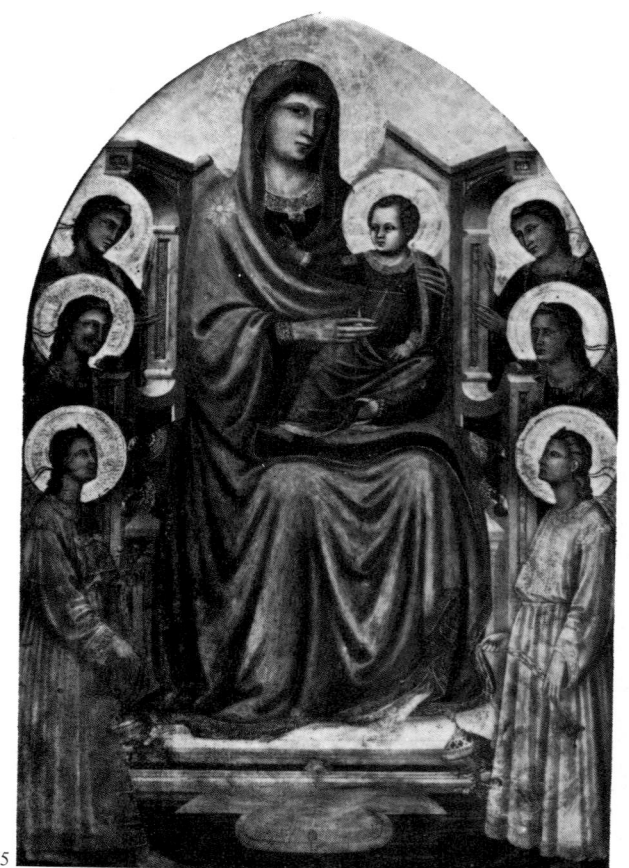

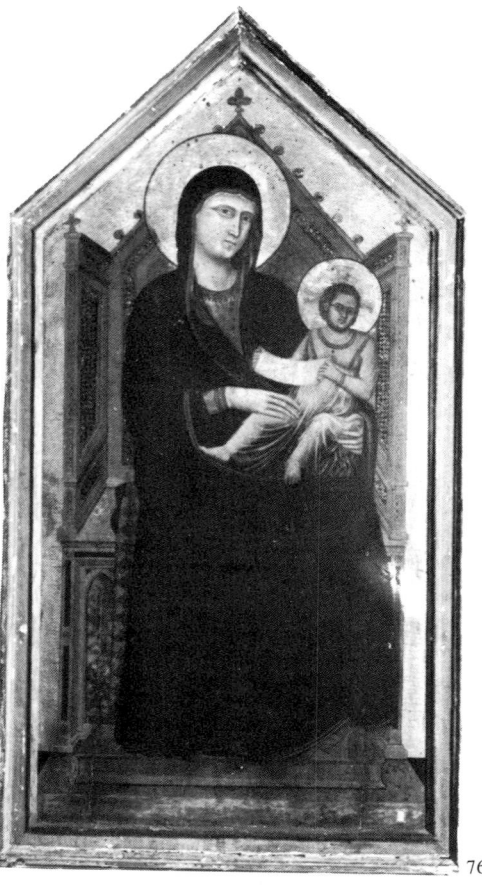

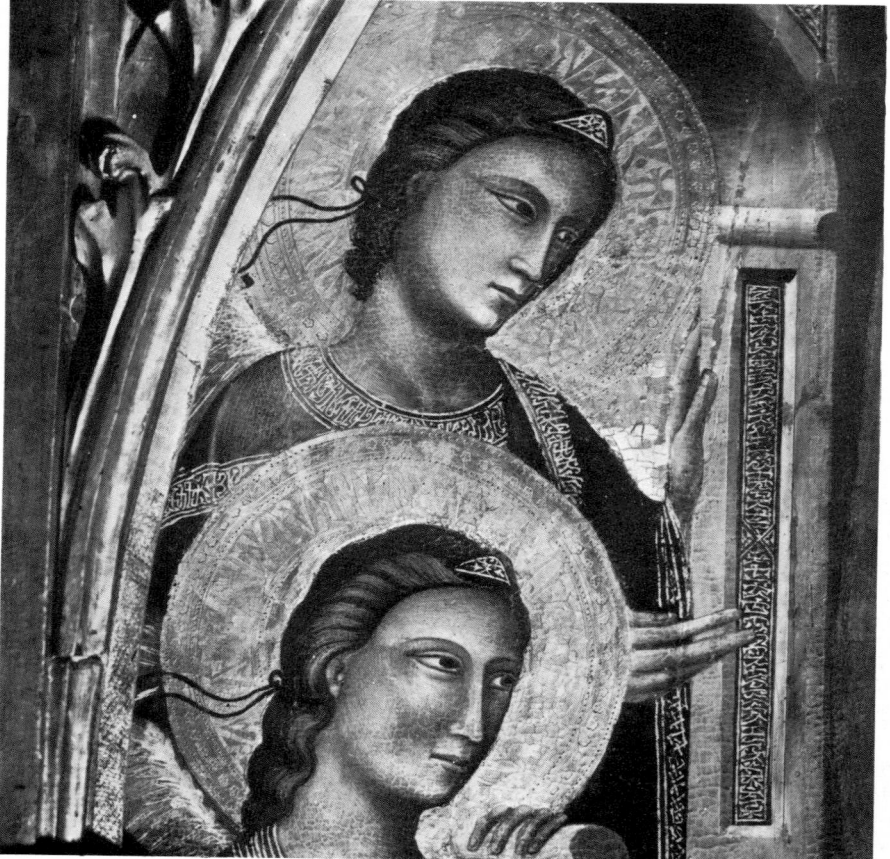

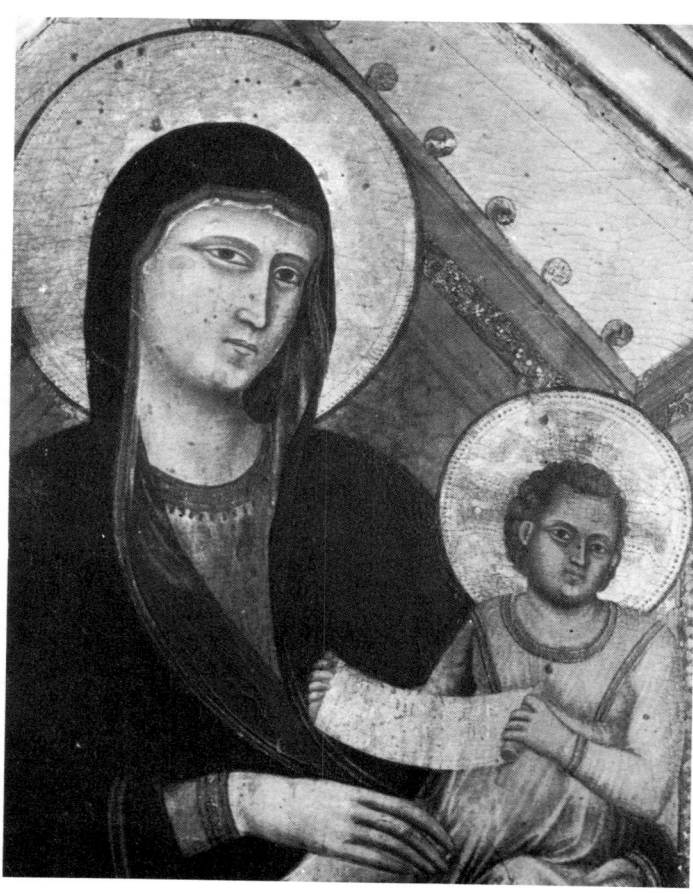

75. *Madonna and Child Enthroned with six Angels. Panel. Caldine (8 km. north of Florence), S. Maria Maddalena. 235 × 155. Brogi 22141.*
76. *Madonna and Child Enthroned. Panel. Pescia (lower Valdarno), Museo della Biblioteca Comunale. no. 10. 185 × 95. Foto Tredici, Pescia.*
77. *Heads of two Angels, detail of fig. 75. Caldine, S. Maria Maddalena. Brogi 22149.*
78. *Heads of Madonna and Child, detail of fig. 76. Panel. Pescia, Museo della Biblioteca Comunale. no. 10. Foto Tredici, Pescia.*

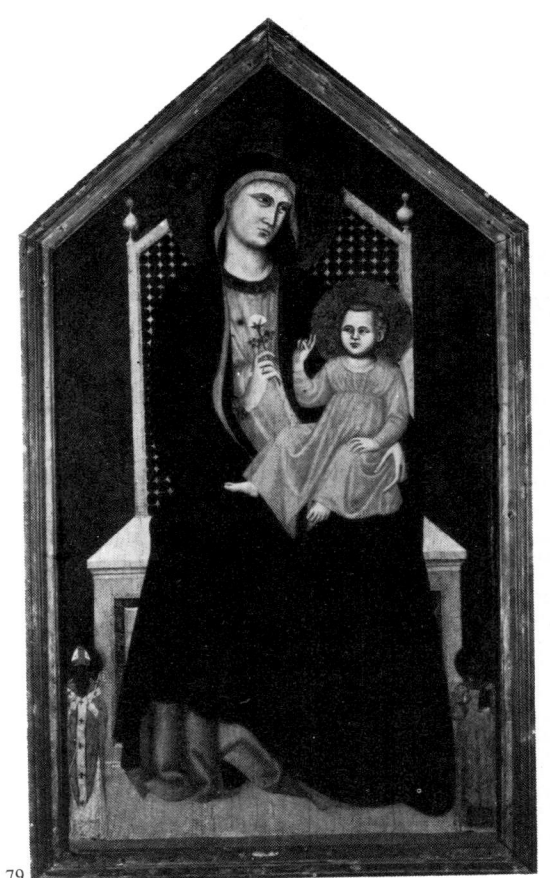

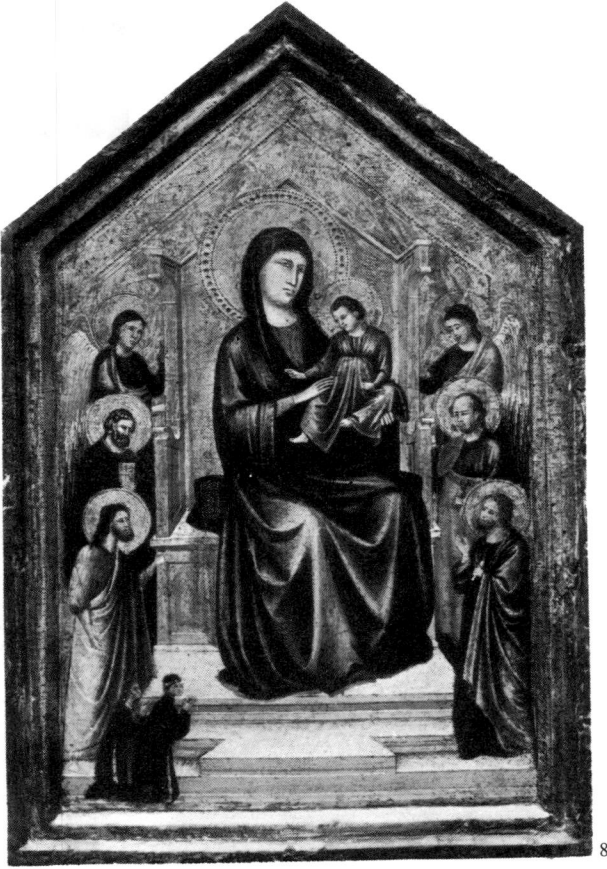

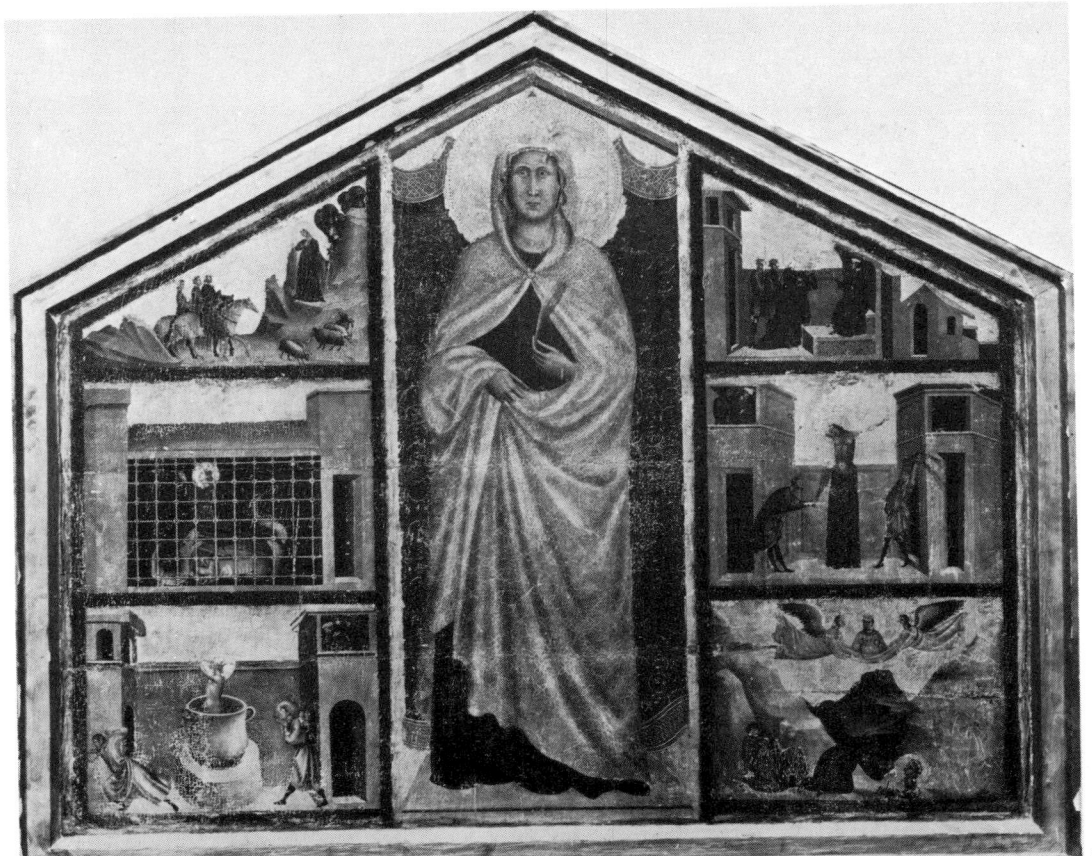

79. *Madonna and Child Enthroned with two Saints. Panel. Venice, Cini Collection. no. 2065. 185 × 102. Collection photo AFI.*

80. *Madonna and Child Enthroned with four Saints, two Angels and two Donors. Panel. Budapest, Musée des Beaux-Arts. no. 10. 39.6 × 25.6 (w.f). Museum photo.*

81. *St Margaret and scenes from her Life: She seduces Olibrius by her beauty; she is arrested and brought before him; she is imprisoned; she is tortured by whipping; she is put in boiling oil; she is beheaded and her Soul is carried to heaven by Angels. Panel. Florence, Arcetri, S. Margherita a Montici. 130 × 163. Alinari 3344.*

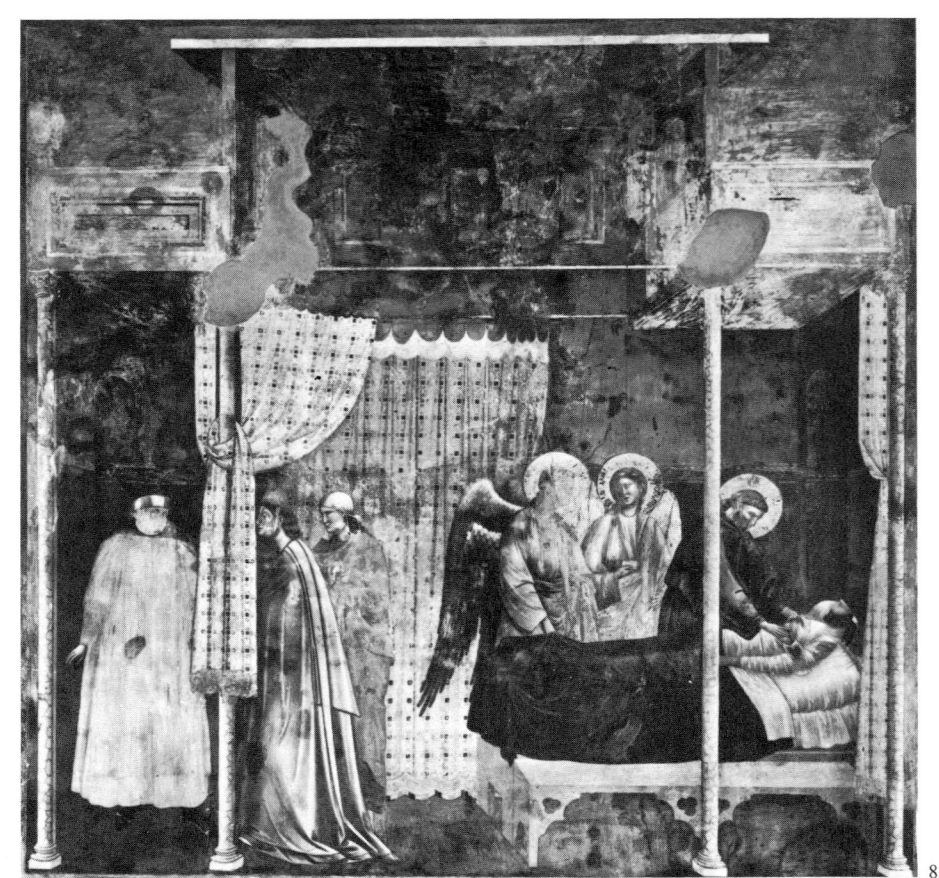

82

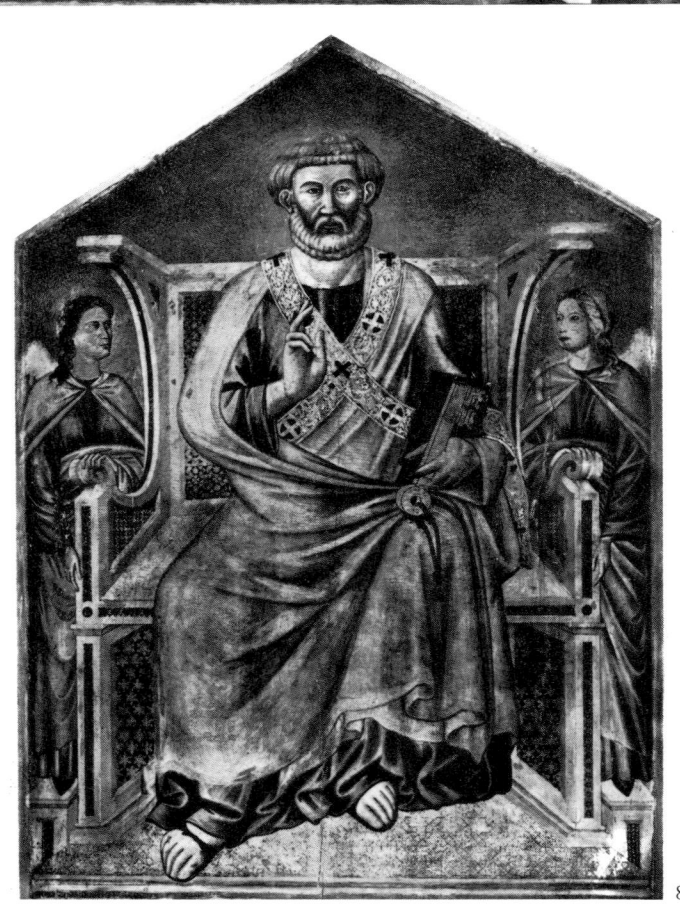

83

82. *St Francis healing. Fresco. Assisi, S. Francesco, Upper Church. Alinari 5275.*
83. *St Peter Enthroned with two Angels. Panel. Florence, S. Simone. 245 × 180. Alinari 30903. d. 1307.*

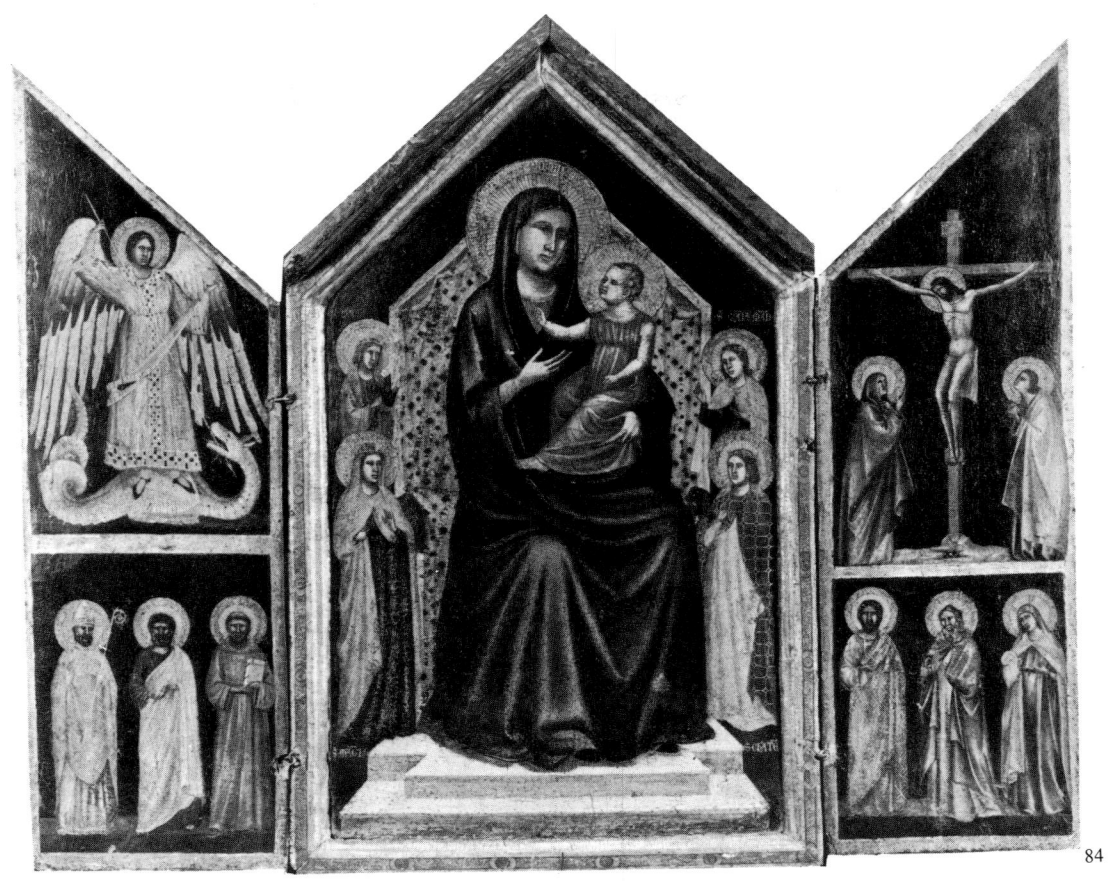

84

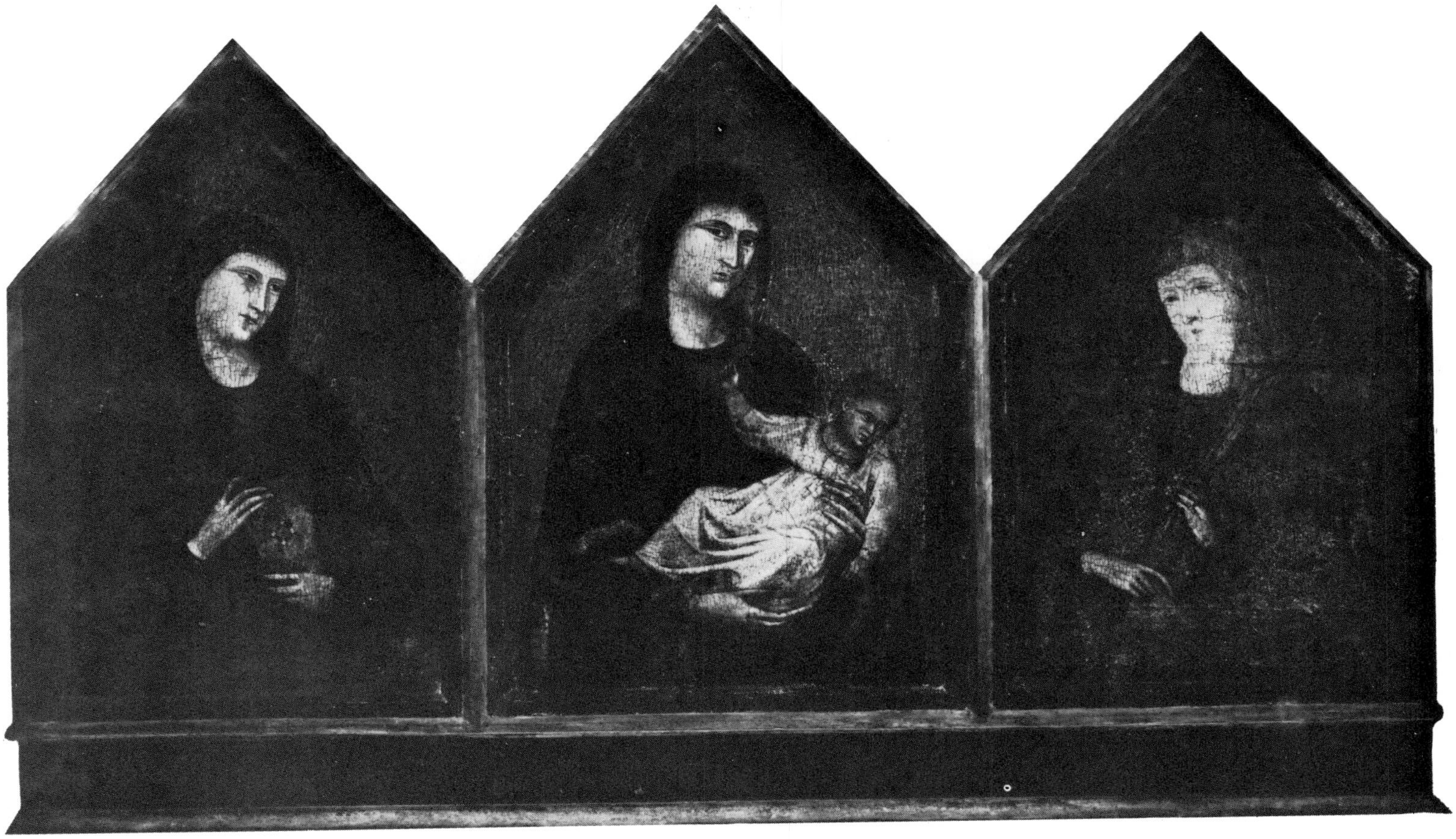

85

84. *Portable triptych: Madonna and Child Enthroned with Sts Lucy, Margaret, Mary Magdalene, Catherine and Archangel Michael; Christ on the Cross with the Virgin and St John the Evangelist; six Saints. Panel. Detroit (Mich.), Detroit Institute of Arts. no. 53.386. cp: 75 × 43.2; lp: 71.7 × 22.9; rp: 71.5 × 21.9. Museum photo 9596.*
85. *Triptych: Madonna and Child and two female Saints. Panel. Florence, Horne Museum. no. 19. 97 × 170. SGF 10868.*

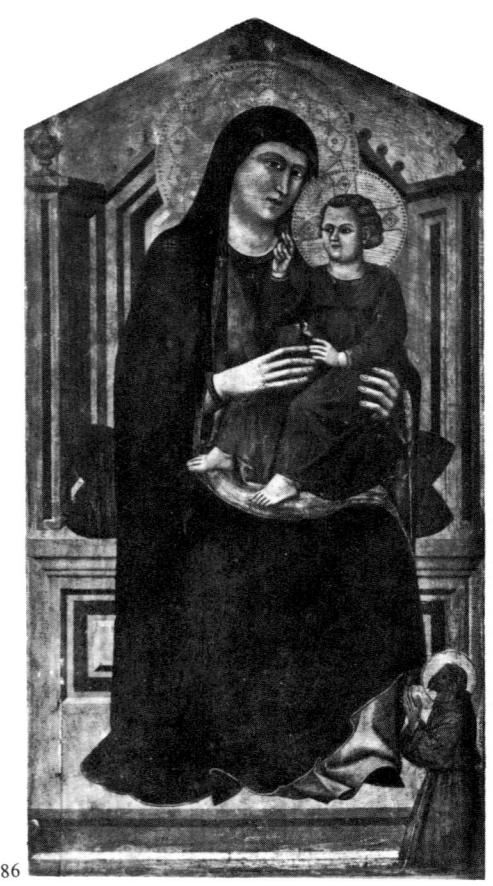

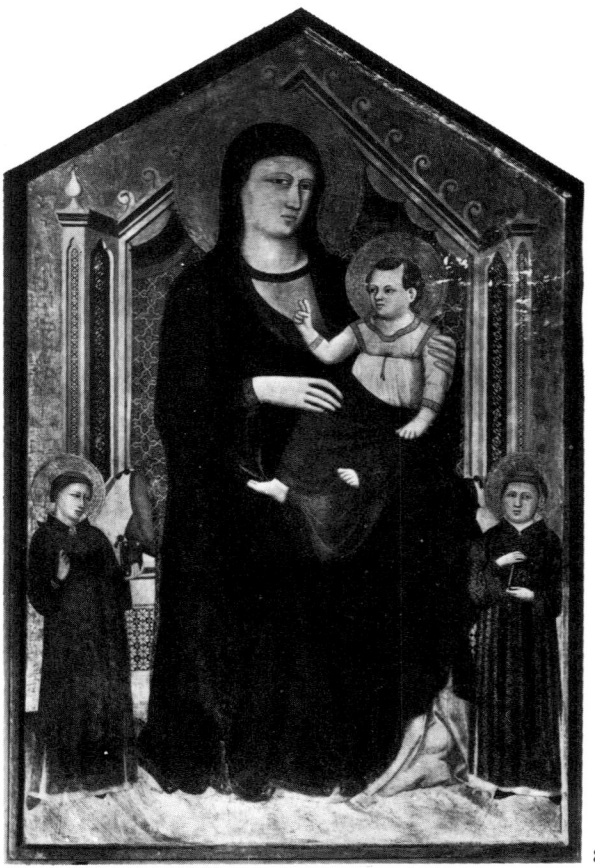

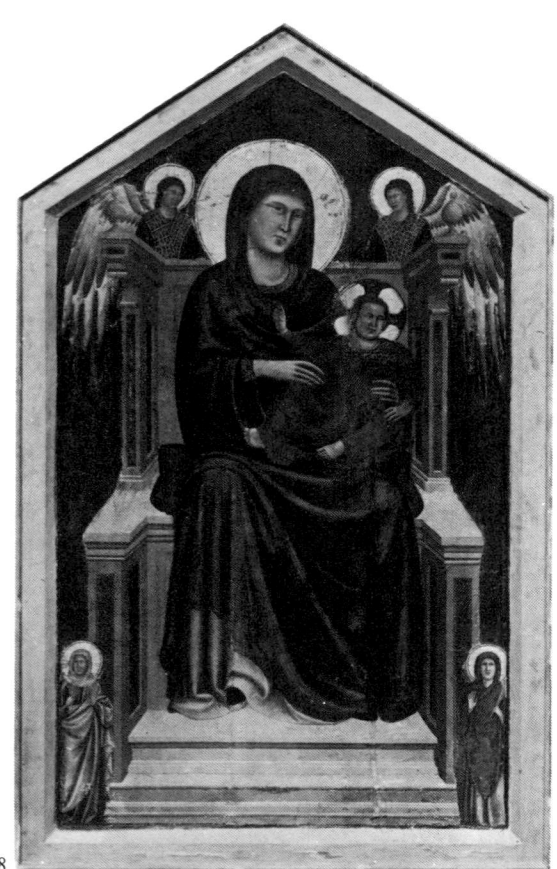

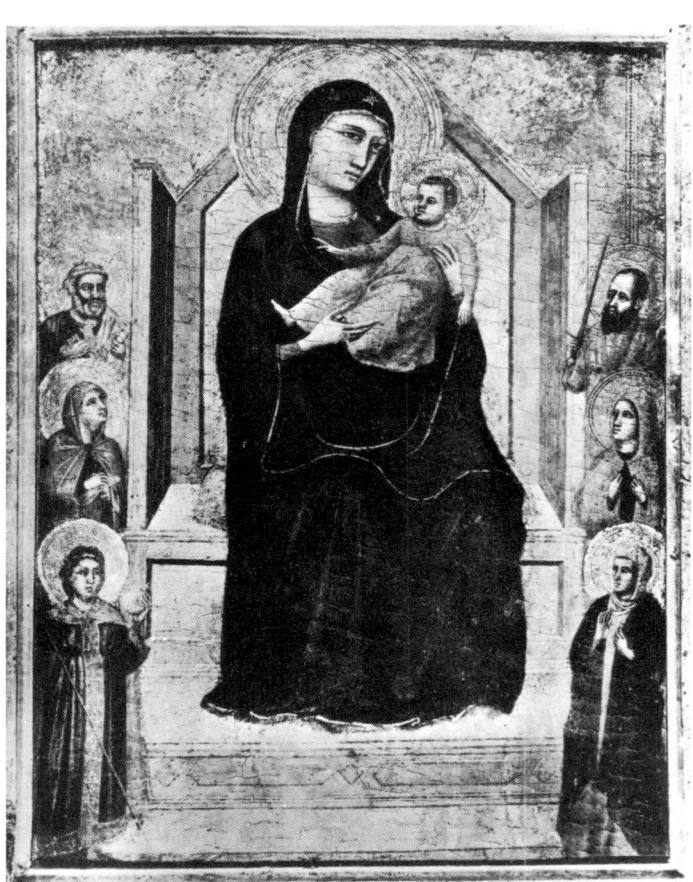

86. *Madonna and blessing Child Enthroned with St Francis. Panel. Florence, Finaly Collection. 124 × 67. Brogi 24857.*
87. *Madonna and Child Enthroned with two Deacon Saints. Panel. Castello (near Sesto), S. Michele a Castello. 183 × 120. Brogi 24684.*
88. *Madonna and Child Enthroned with two female Saints and two Angels. Panel. Florence, Arcetri, S. Margherita a Montici. 200 × 115. Alinari 3344 a.*
89. *Madonna and Child Enthroned with Sts Peter, Lucy, Michael, Paul, Margaret and female Saint. Panel. Private Collection. 35 × 25.5. Bertoni-Offner.*

BERNARDO DADDI

Bernardo di Daddo di Simone has been wrongly understood, firstly by Vasari who calls him a follower of Spinello and who gives the date of his death as 1380, and secondly — which is much rarer — by Crowe and Cavalcaselle who treat him as a negligible figure to whom only a few lines have been devoted.

The truth of the matter is, however, that Bernardo Daddi is one of the most refined painters who may be found in Florence in the early 14th century, a true artist, full of sentiment and possessing a keen sense of beauty.

Daddi was almost a contemporary of Giotto's, only outliving him eleven years although his artistic career must have begun about twenty years after the great Florentine's; Daddi, consequently, belongs to a generation preceding but little that of Taddeo Gaddi.

The first mention we find of Daddi is his matriculation in the corporation of physicians and " speciali " which took place between 1312 and 1320, and as his name is inscribed just after the half of the ledger which covers this period we may take it to have been about 1317.....

As his name in the ledger of the guild is accompanied by the date 1355, it has been assumed that this was the year of his death; it is however certain that Bernardo died in 1348, as in August of that year trustees were chosen for two of his three sons, which would lead us to suppose that their father was not old at the moment of his decease.....

from R. van Marle, pp. 348-349, *The Development of the Italian Schools of Painting*, Vol. III, The Hague, 1924.

An artist of rare and exquisite gifts, Bernardo Daddi is first mentioned in a series of guild-registrations running from 1312 to 1320, and as late as August 18, 1348, the probable day of his death. The earliest of his dated works, the Uffizi Triptych, painted in 1328 — at least eight years after the first occurrence of his name — and his last, the Parry [Courtauld] Polyptych of 1348, can therefore hardly be said to measure the whole span of his independent artistic activity; which, judging from the stylistic maturity of the Uffizi Triptych, might easily have begun at least five years before. The written sources speak of him as Bernardo Daddi, or di Dado whereas he endorses his paintings without a patronymic as Bernardus or Bernardus de Florentia. It is generally agreed that these two classes of designation refer to a single flesh-and-blood individual. And if a ghost of the old doubt — which for a time timidly persisted in separating them — is still abroad, it should have been laid conclusively by the fact that the Or San Michele Altarpiece (authenticated by records of payments to Bernardo Daddi) and the Pulci-Berardi frescoes (attributed by Vasari to Bernardo Daddi) correspond in style with the body of panels signed Bernardus.....

Daddi's paintings show him a master of supreme lyrical inspiration. His expression is like an irradiation of inner light, and his personages are forbearing and detached. His compositions evolve in an exquisite adjustment between flat space and figure, in which the empty intervals expand and determine the meaning of the action, and breathe out a sense of space and silence. This awareness of spatial values, already articulated by the St. Cecilia Master, continues in Orcagna and his brothers.

In the light of the collective development, Daddi's works manifest a share in the revolution of form that swept Italy in the early Trecento. If this revolution had been brought about by Giotto alone, Daddi's share in it might be regarded as due to Giotto's influence, and Daddi possibly as his pupil. The works themselves, however, and particularly Daddi's early works, affirm a closer correspondence in the shapes, in the types, in the proportions and patterning to the Master of the St. Cecilia Altarpiece.....

His lyricism suited a miniature rather than the monumental Giottesque mode of presentation, and his small paintings, which out-number his larger ones, contain the principles that were to survive him in a lasting influence. Whereas his contemporaries within the non-Giottesque group (Pacino di Bonaguida, the Biadaiolo Illuminator, Jacopo del Casentino, the Masters of the Dominican Effigies and of the Cappella Medici Polyptych) die practically without artistic issue, Daddi may be said to be the founder of a style. After Giotto's death it was Daddi's aesthetics that directed the taste and fashion of the second half of the Trecento when Giotto was for the time being eclipsed or forgotten. The essence of Daddi's genius persists in the most popular school in Florence before Fra Angelico, which centred in the shop of the Cioni, and the memory of him lingers on to the end of the century.....

from R. Offner, pp. III, IV, V, *The Works of Bernardo Daddi*, New York, 1930.

Active ca 1312-1348. Pupil of Giotto, influenced by the S. Cecilia Master, Ambrogio Lorenzetti and thirteenth-century French sculpture.....

> from B. Berenson, p. 51, *Italian Pictures of the Renaissance, Florentine School*, Vol. I, London, 1963.

A leading Florentine artist, perhaps a pupil of the St. Cecilia Master, an assistant of Giotto who worked at Assisi. To his early training Daddi united motifs from Florentine painting and sculpture and from Sienese and Gothic art, and his work was thus composed of two strains: the monumental and sculptural qualities of Giovanni Pisano and Giotto and — to some extent — the Lorenzetti on one hand, and on the other the decorative sense and elegance derived from contemporary Sienese painting and French sculpture and ivories. His influence throughout the second half of the century was far-reaching.....

> from St. J. Gore, p. 4, *The Art of Painting in Florence and Siena from 1250-1500*, London, 1965.

Florentine School. Active from 1312; died probably 1348. Although often said to have been a pupil of Giotto, Daddi seems to have been strongly influenced by the Sienese, whose lyricism and sweetness of mood were most congenial to him. He painted a number of monumental altarpieces but scenes on a small scale seem especially well adapted to his style. It is this small scale work that was most frequently emulated by his many followers in the second half of the fourteenth century.....

> from F. R. Shapley, p. 26, *Paintings from the Samuel H. Kress Collection*, London, 1966.

BIBLIOGRAPHY
BOOKS

An asterisk indicates a work listed in the General Bibliography

Vitzhum, G., *Bernardo Daddi*, Leipzig, 1903; *Venturi A.**, 1907, pp. 508-23; Vitzhum, G., *T-Becker**, VIII, 1913, pp. 253-4; *v. Marle 1924**, pp. 348-9; *Uffizi Cat. 1929**, no 3073; *Toesca, 1929**, pp. 54-77; *Offner, 1930**, Sec. III, Vol. III; Catalogue: *Royal Academy* Exhibition, 1930, pp. 39, 54; *Berenson, 1930**, pp. 64-5; Chiti, A., *Pistoia*, Pistoia, 1931, p. 46; *Venturi, L.**, *Pitture Italiane in America*, Milan, 1931, pls. 37-39; *Hautecoeur**, Paris, 1931, pp. 155-9; Golzio, V., *Lorenzo Monaco*, Rome, 1931, pp. 6, 14; Hendy, P., Catalogue: *The Isabella Stewart Gardner Museum*, Boston, 1931, pp. 118-20; Ciaranfi, A. M., *Treccani XII**, Milan, 1931, p. 217; Pacchioni, G., *La Regia Pinacoteca di Torino*, Rome, 1932, p. 27; Quintavalle, A. O., *La Pinacoteca del Museo Nazionale di Napoli*, Rome, 1932, p. 5; *Berenson, 1932**, pp. 164-8; Brandi, C., *La Regia Pinacoteca di Siena*, Rome, 1933, p. 325; *Catalogo della Mostra del Tesoro di Firenze Sacra*, Florence, 1933, p. 141; *Guida della Pinacoteca Vaticana*, Città del Vaticano, 1933, pp. 50-1, 153; Offner, R., *The Works of Bernardo Daddi*, New York, 1933; *Venturi, L.**, 1933, nos 37, 44, 48; Longstreet, G. W., *General Catalogue: Isabella Stewart Gardner Museum: Fenway Court*, Boston, 1935, pp. 98-99; Cecchi, E., *Giotto*, Milan, 1937, pp. 117-21; Quintavalle, A. O., *La Regia Galleria di Parma*, Rome, 1939, p. 158; Bacci, P., *Dipinti inediti e sconosciuti di Pietro Lorenzetti, Bernardo Daddi, etc.*, Siena, 1939; *M. Giottesca**, 1943, pp. 491-535 (with preceding bibliography); Sinibaldi, G., and Brunetti, G., *Pittura Italiana del duecento e trecento*, Florence, 1943; *Coletti, Vol. II**, 1946, pp. 47-9; *Offner, 1947**, Sec. III, Vol. V, p. 145; *Antal**, 1948, pp. 180-4; *Vavalà, 1948**, pp. 49-58; *Galetti**, " A-E", 1950, pp. 771-4; *Oertel, 1950**, pp. 32-4; *Toesca, 1951**, pp. 622-4; Suida, W. E., *Paintings and Sculpture from the Samuel H. Kress Collection*, Washington, 1951, pp. 32-3; *Paatz**, 1954, Vol. VI, p. 56; Suida, W. E., *Catalogue of the William Rockhill Nelson Gallery of Art*, Kansas, 1952, p. 22; Suida, W. E., *Catalogue of the Seattle Art Museum*, Seattle, 1954, pp. 11, 18; *Laclotte**, 1956, p. 4; Longhi, R., *Laclotte**, 1956, pp. 4-5; *Offner, 1958**, Sec. III, Vol. VIII, pp. iii-xx, 1-34; Paccagnini, G., *EUA, IV**, 1960, pp. 182-183; *Cracow**, 1961, pp. 41-42; Contini-Bonacossi, A., *Catalogue of the Columbia Museum of Art*, Columbia, S. Carolina, 1962, pp. 9-10; Santi, F., pp. 59-60 in *Scritti di Storia dell'Arte in Onore di Mario Salmi*, Vol. II, Rome, 1962; *Berenson, 1963**, Vol. I, pp. 51-8; *Marcucci**, 1965, pp. 27-50; *Shapley, 1966**, pp. 25-29; Rossi, F., *Il Museo Horne a Firenze*, Milan, 1966, p. 135; Gore, St. J., *Wildenstein**, 1965, pp. 4-5; *Dal Poggetto**, 1967, pp. 32-5; *MMOA**, 1971, pp. 25-31; Fredericksen, B. B., *Catalogue of the Paintings in the J. Paul Getty Museum*, Malibu (Calif.), 1972, p. 3; Gilbert, C., *History of Renaissance Art throughout Europe*, New York, 1973, p. 30; Klesse, B., *Katalog der Italienischen, Französischen und Spanischen Gemälde bis 1800 im Wallraf-Richartz Museum*, Cologne, 1973, p. 43; *Dutch Show**, 1974, pp. 17, 18, 19, 37-39.

JOURNALS

Suida, W., *RKW*, XXVII, 1904, pp. 385-9; Sirèn, O., *BM*, XIV, 1908, p. 193; Sandberg-Vavalà, E., *Cronache d'Arte*, 1927; Comstock, H., *IS*, LXXXIX, 1928, Feb., pp. 21-6, Mar., pp. 71-6, 90; Constable, W. G., *DD*, X, 1929-30, pp. 723-31; Offner, R., *BM*, LIV, 1929, p. 230; Offner, R., *IS*, XCIII, 1929, pp. 23-26; Piattoli, R., *RA*, XI, 1929, pp. 221-253, 396-437, 537-579; Borenius, T., *AP*, XI, 1930, pp. 92-4, 153-4; Piattoli, R., *RA*, XII, 1930, pp. 97-150; Toesca, P., *A*, XXXIII, 1930, 1, pp. 5-15; Salmi, M., *BA*, X, 1931, pp. 385-406; Berenson, B., *DD*, XI, 4, 1930-1, pp. 957-88; Burroughs, B., *MM*, XXVII, II, 1932, p. 31; Procacci, U., *RA*, XIV, 1932, pp. 341-53, 463-75; van Marle, R., *DD*, XIII, 1, 1933, pp. 237-57; Salmi, M., *DD*, XIII, 1, 1933, pp. 3-17; Offner, R., *BM*, LXIII, 1933, p. 83; Gamba, C., *BA*, XXVII, 1933, pp. 145-63; Colasanti, A., *BA*, XXVII, 1934; pp. 337-50;

Procacci, U., *RA*, XV, 1933, pp. 224-244; Beenken, H., *BM*, LXV, 1934, p. 104; de Vries, A. B., *P*, XIV, 1934, pp. 311-12; Mather, R. G., *A*, XXXIX, 1936, pp. 50-64; Meiss, M., *AB*, XVIII, 1936, p. 442; Procacci, U., *BA*, XXIX, 1936, pp. 371-77; Procacci, U., *RA*, XVIII, 1936, pp. 213-15; Coletti, L., *BA*, XXXI, 1937, pp. 49-72; Marchini, G., *RA*, XX, 1938, pp. 215-41; Oertel, R., *MKIF*, V, 4-5, 1940, pp. 217-314; Oertel, R., *ZKG*, X, 1941-2, pp. 222-23; Gronau, H. D., *BM*, LXXXVI, 1945, p. 143; *AN*, XLIV, 1946, p. 37; Quintavalle, A. O., *BA*, XXXIII, 1948, p. 272; Longhi, R., *PA*, III, 1950, pp. 16-19; Coletti, L., *CA*, VIII, 6, 1950, pp. 443-54; Cohn, W., *RA*, XXXI, 6, 1951, p. 71; Steinweg, K., *RA*, XXXI, 6, 1951, pp. 25-40; Baldini, U., *BA*, XXXVII, 1952, pp. 53-55; Quintavalle, A. O., *A*, LII, Jul., 1951-Jun., 1952, p. 6; Levi d'Ancona, M., *GBA*, VI, 42, 1953, pp. 281-90 (trs: pp. 331-4); Marabottini, A., *RA*, XXVII, 1951-2, pp. 23-55; Pope-Hennessy, J., *BM*, XCV, 1953, p. 346; Steinweg, K., *K*, VI, 1953, p. 326; Steinweg, K., *MKIF*, VII, 1, 1953, pp. 65-70; Coor, G., *WRJ*, XVIII, 1956, pp. 111-131; Steinweg, K., *RA*, XXXI, 1956, pp. 25-40; Eisenberg, M. J., *BA*, XLI, 4, 1956, p. 334; Cohn, W., *BA*, XLII, 4, 1957, pp. 175-6; Procacci, U., *RA*, XXXII, 1958, pp. 121-39; Longhi, R., *PA*, 109, 1959, pp. 31-40; Longhi, R., *PA*, 111, 1959, pp. 3-12; Stöckelovà, G., *A*, LIX, 1960, pp. 277-88; Beccherucci, L., *BA*, XLVI, 1961, 4, pp. 33-40; Birkmeyer, K., *GBA*, LX, VI, 1962, pp. 473-80; Coor, G., *AB*, 44, 1962, pp. 343-4; Rozycka-Bryzek, A., *A*, LXI, 1962, pp. 115-24; Blunt, A., *AP*, 81, 1965, p. 290; Edit., *BM*, 107, 1965, pp. 109-10; Baldini, U., *AV*, V, 6, 1966, pp. 25-32; Gregori, M., *AV*, V, 6, 1966, pp. 40-9; De Benedictis, C., *AV*, 3, 1967, p. 40; Herrmann, F., *CS*, CLXV, 665, 1967, p. 154; Bellosi, L., *PA*, XVIII, 203/23, 1967, p. 85; Conti, A., *PA*, XIX, 1968, p. 17; Friedmann, H., *Sim*, 3, 1968-69, 1, p. 13; Vertova, L., *AV*, VII, 3, 1968, pp. 23-30; Zeri, F., *GBA*, LXXI, 110, 1968, p. 69; Pieper, P., *ZKG*, XXXIII, 1, 1970, p. 82; Gardner, J., *ZKG*, XXXIV, 2, 1971, p. 105; Meiss, M., *BM*, CXIII, 817, 1971, p. 181; Skaug, E., *MKIF*, XV, 2, 1971, pp. 141-60; Bellosi, L., *MKIF*, XVII, 2-3, 1973, pp. 183, 6, 8, 92; Cole, B., *MKIF*, XVII, 2-3, 1973, p. 72, note 53.

SIGNED AND DATED WORKS

1328 Florence, Uffizi 3073. Triptych: Madonna & Child with Sts. Matthew & Nicholas. s & d. (fig. 90).

1333 Florence, Bigallo. Portable triptych: Madonna & Child Enthroned with Donors and 14 Saints, Nativity and Christ on the Cross. d. (fig. 94).

1333 Florence, Depositi 6170. Triptych: Madonna & Child with 2 Angels & Sts. John the Baptist and John the Evangelist. d. (fig. 93).

133(3)? Washington D.C., National Gallery, Mellon Collection 3. Panel: St Paul & Donors. d. (fig. 92).

1334 Philadelphia, John G. Johnson Collection 344. Triptych: Madonna & Child, St John the Baptist and a Bishop Saint. d. (figs. 96a, b, c).

1334 Florence, Museo dell'Opera del Duomo. Panel: Madonna of the Magnificat. d. (fig. 98).

1334 Cambridge (Mass.), Fogg Art Museum 1918.3. Portable triptych: Christ on the Cross, Agony in the Garden & Saints. d. (fig. 97).

1334 Florence, Uffizi 8564. Panel: Madonna & Child Enthroned with Sts. Peter and Paul and eight Angels. s & d. (fig. 99).

1336 Osteria Nuova (Bagno a Ripoli), S. Giorgio a Ruballa. Panel: Madonna & Child Enthroned with Sts. Matthias and George, a Donor and four Angels. d. (fig. 100).

1336 Siena, Pinacoteca 60. Portable triptych: Madonna & Child with 16 Angels and four Saints. d. (fig. 106).

1337 Washington, Dumbarton Oaks Collection. Panel: Madonna & Child Enthroned with Saints and Angels. d. (fig. 105).

1338 Minneapolis (Minn.), Institute of Art. Portable triptych: Madonna & Child Enthroned with Saints. d. (fig. 117).

1338 London, Count Seilern Collection. Portable triptych: Madonna & Child Enthroned with Saints and Angels, Nativity and Annunciation to the Shepherds. d. (fig. 114).

1338 Edinburgh, National Gallery of Scotland 1904. Portable triptych: Crucifixion, Nativity, Madonna & Child Enthroned. d. (fig. 113).

1343 Florence, Accademia 8570. Panel: Christ on the Cross with the Virgin and Saints. d. (fig. 111).

1344 Florence, S. Maria Novella, Cloister of Spanish Chapel. Polyptych: Madonna & Child Enthroned with Saints. s & d. (fig. 119).

1348 London, Courtauld Institute of Art. Polyptych: Crucifixion and Sts. Lawrence, Andrew, Bartholomew, George, Paul, Peter, James and four Evangelists. s & d. (fig. 120).

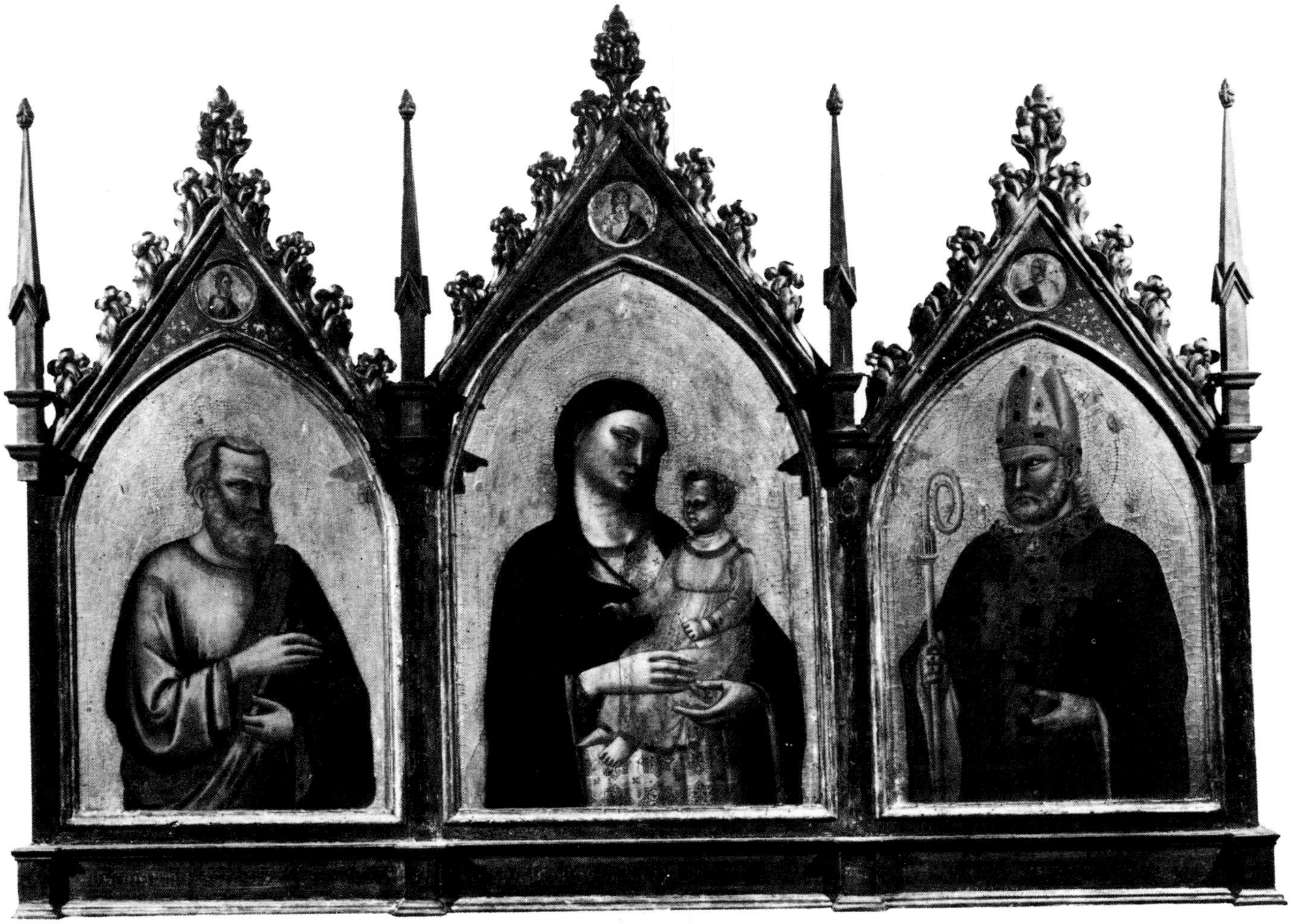

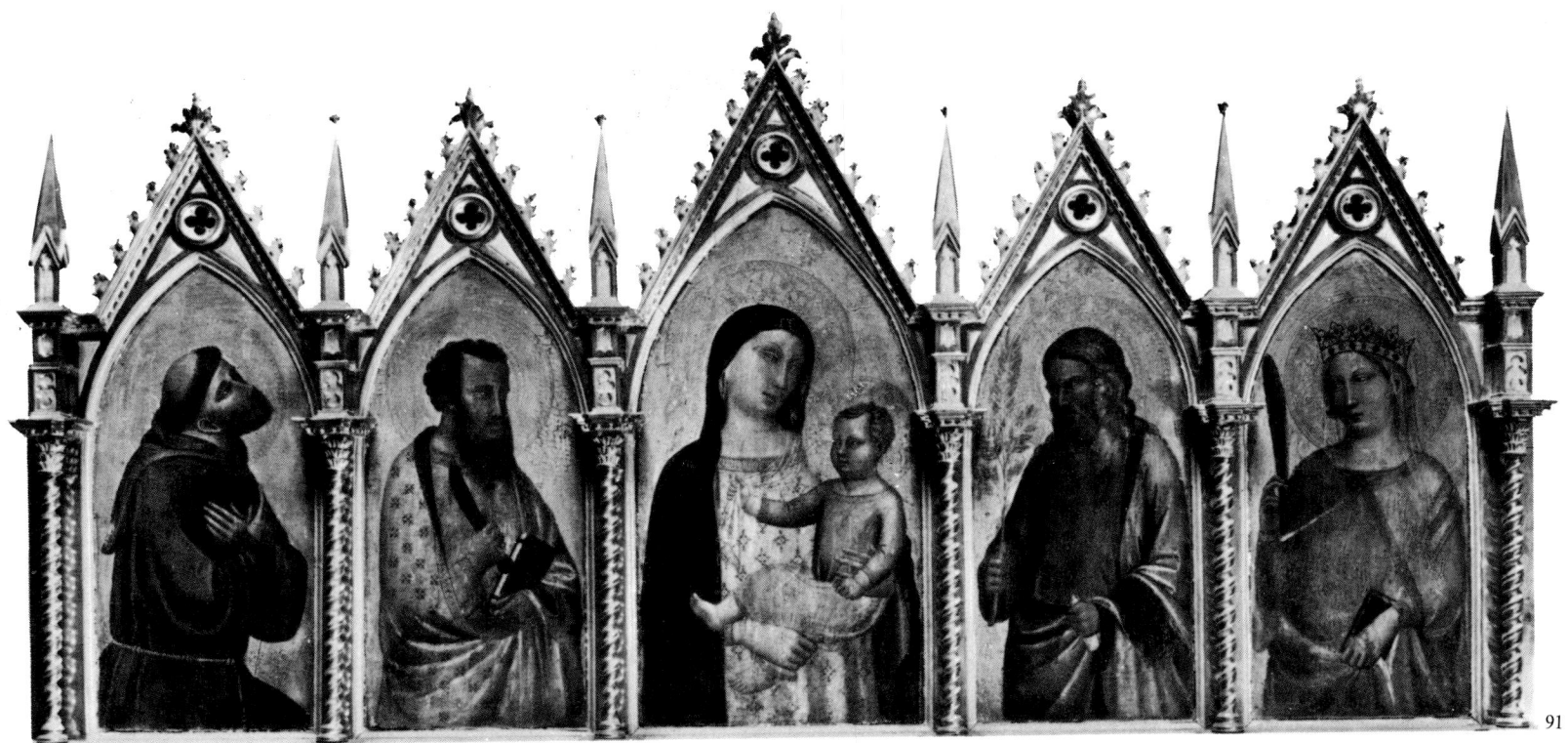

90. *Triptych: Madonna and Child with Sts Matthew and Nicholas.* *Above: Christ blessing and two Angels. Panel. Florence, Uffizi. no. 3073. 144 × 194.*
SGF 144157. s & d. 1328.
91. *Polyptych: Madonna and Child with Sts Francis, Bartholomew, Barnabas and Catherine. Panel. Prato, Galleria Comunale. no. 4. cp: 85 × 45.5;*
sps: 76.5 × 35. Alinari 30780.

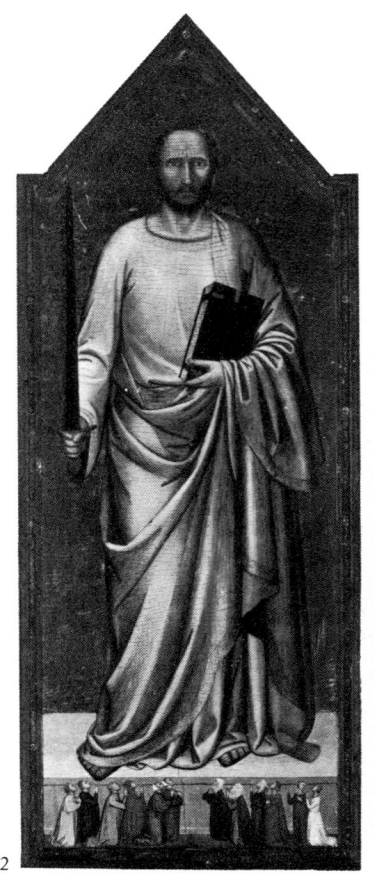

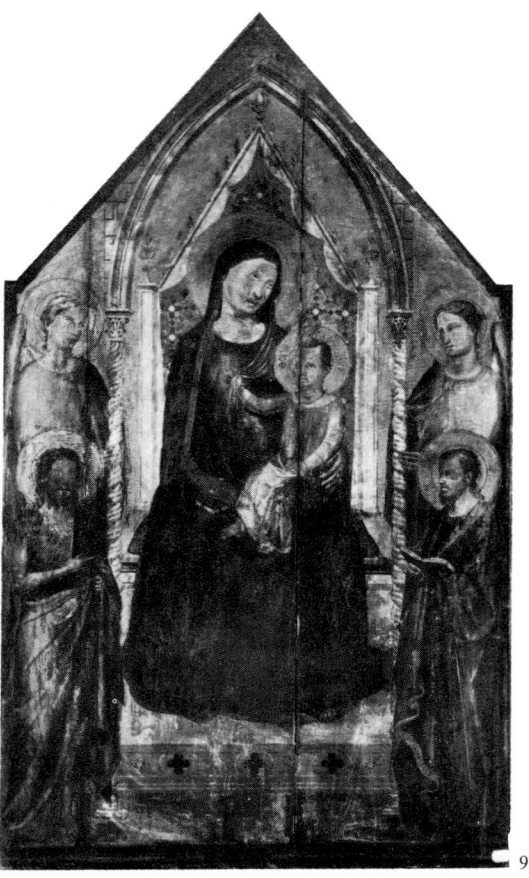

92

93

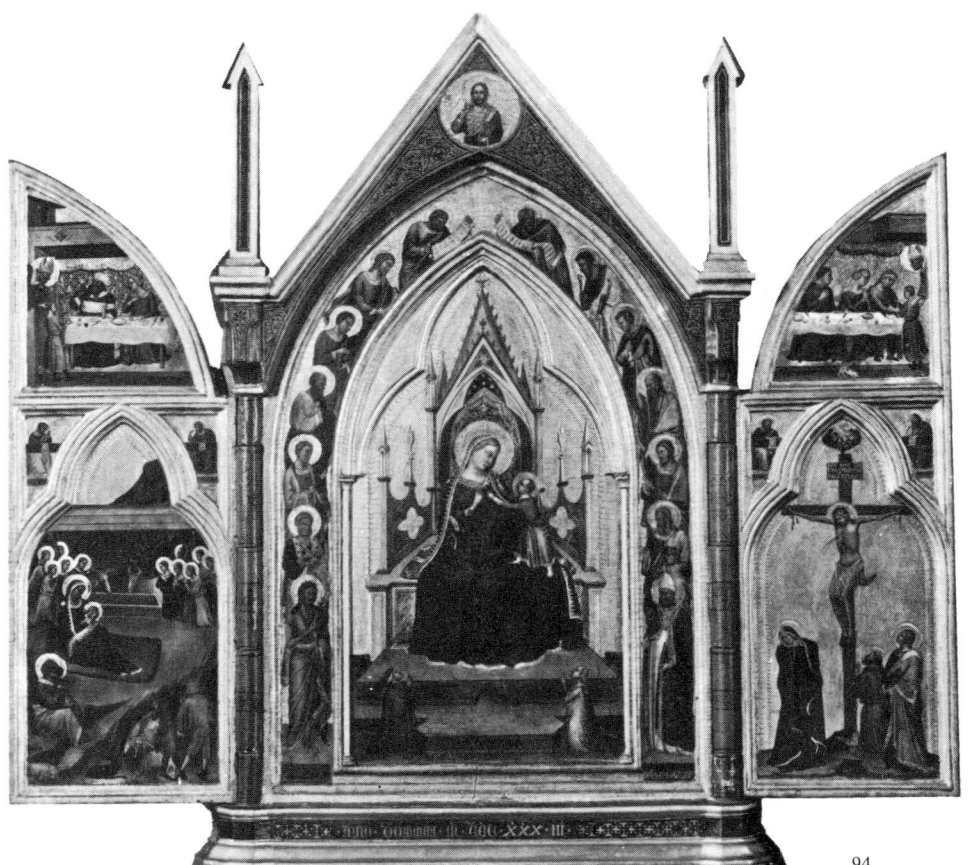

94

92. *St Paul and Donors. Panel. Washington (D.C.), National Gallery, Mellon Collection. no. 3. 234 × 89. Museum photo. d. 133(3)?*
93. *Madonna and Child with Sts John the Baptist, Luke and two Angels. Panel. Florence, Uffizi, Depositi. no. Depositi 6170. 219 × 132. SGF 5432. d. 1333.*
94. *Portable triptych: Madonna and Child Enthroned with Donors and fourteen Saints, Nativity and Christ on the Cross. Above: Christ blessing; St Nicholas rescuing Adeodatus: from the service of the Pagan King; St Nicholas restoring Adeodatus to his Parents. Outside (not shown): Sts Margaret, Martin, Catherine and Christopher. Panel. Florence, Museo del Bigallo. 90 × 82. Alinari 4779. d. 1333.*

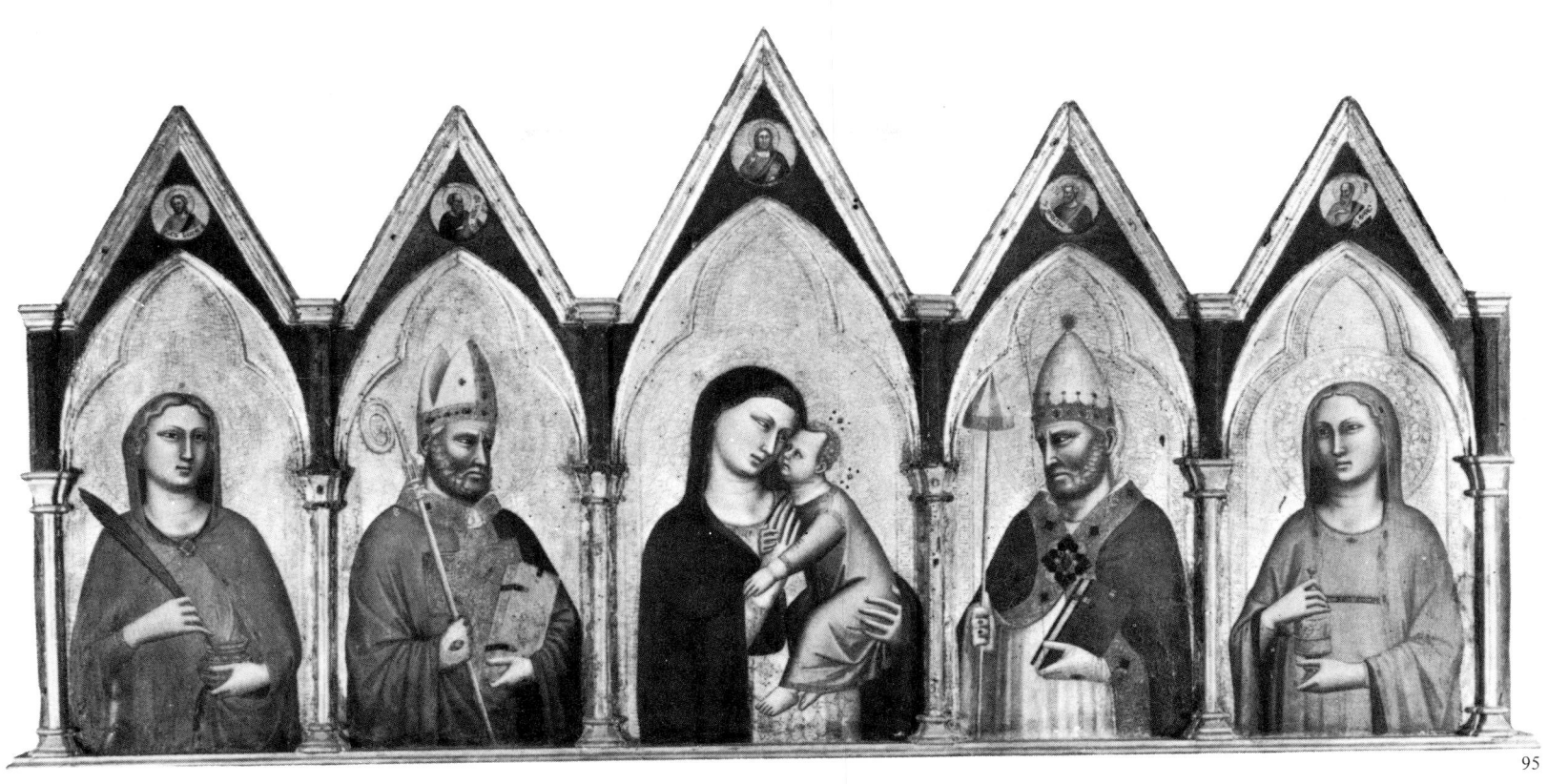

95

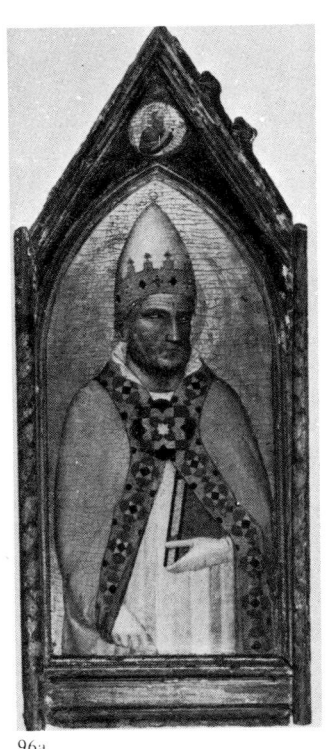

96a

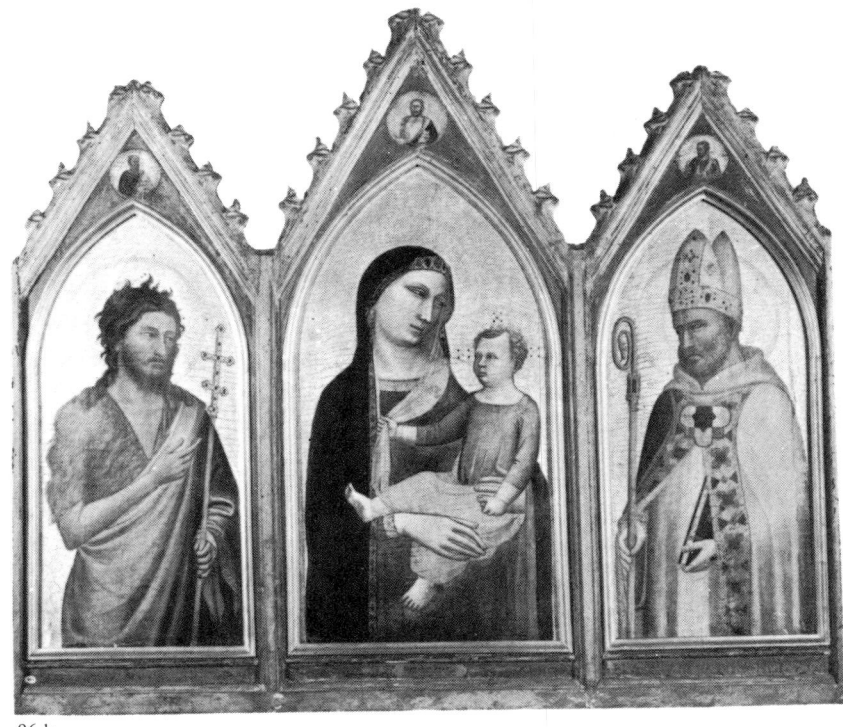

96 b

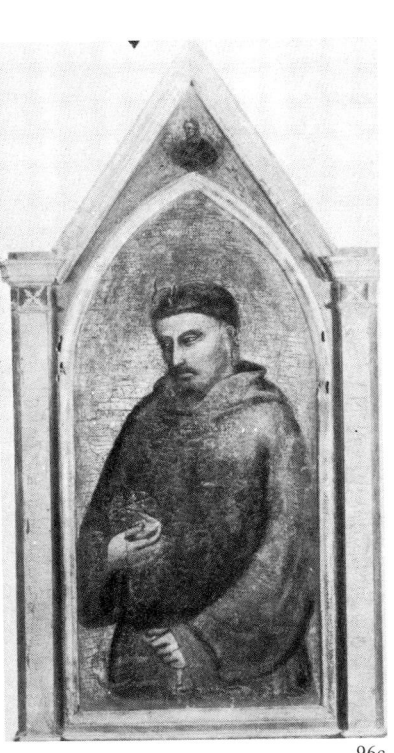

96c

95. *Polyptych: Madonna and Child with Sts Lucy, Nicholas, Gregory and Mary Magdalene. Above: Christ blessing and four Evangelists. Panel. Lucarelli (near Radda in Chianti), S. Martino. cp: 97 × 41; sps: 87 × 34. SGF 94381.*
96a. *St Gregory. Above: a Prophet. Panel. Cambridge (Mass.), Fogg Art Museum. no. 1936.56. 108.9 × 43. Museum photo 1334. (Panel from Daddi's d. 1334 altarpiece).*
96b. *Triptych: Madonna and Child, St John the Baptist, and a Bishop Saint. Panel. Philadelphia (Pa.), Museum of Art, John G. Johnson Collection. no. 344. 123.8 × 140.3. Collection photo. d. 1334.*
96c. *St Francis. Panel. Sherborn (Mass.), Mrs R. F. Pickhardt Collection. 90.8 × 34.3. Collection photo. 1334. (Panel from Daddi's d.1334 altarpiece).*

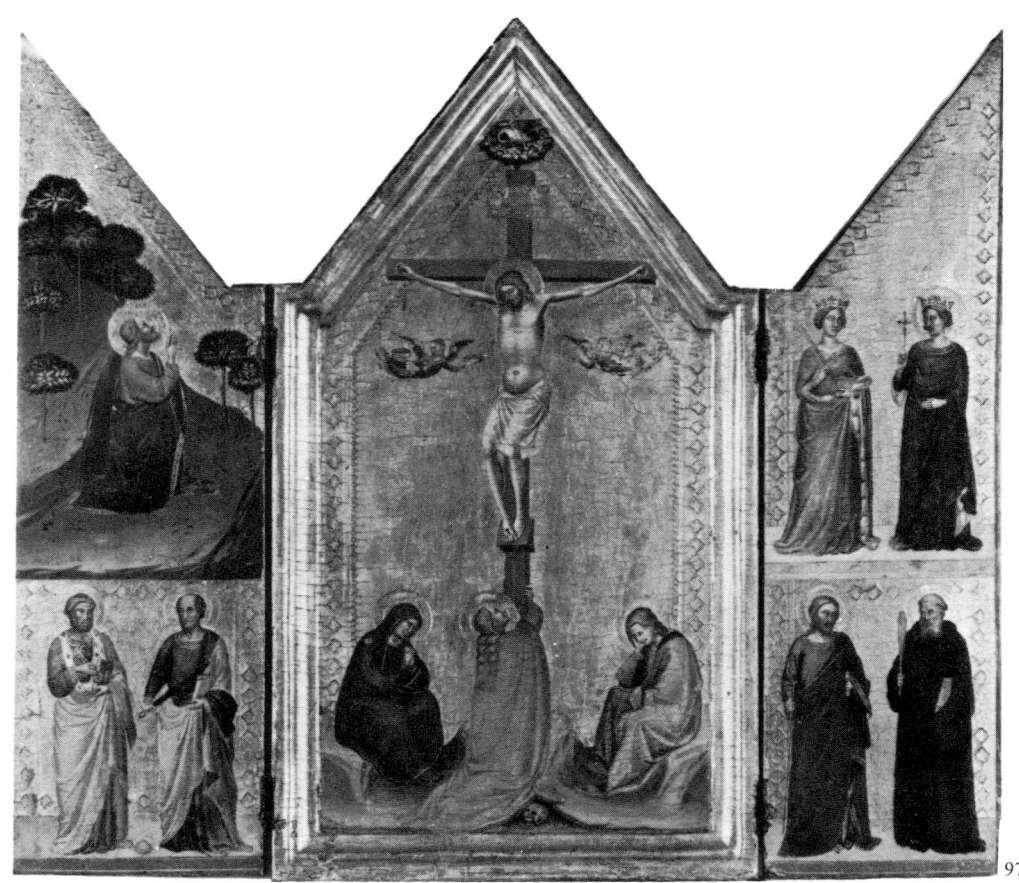

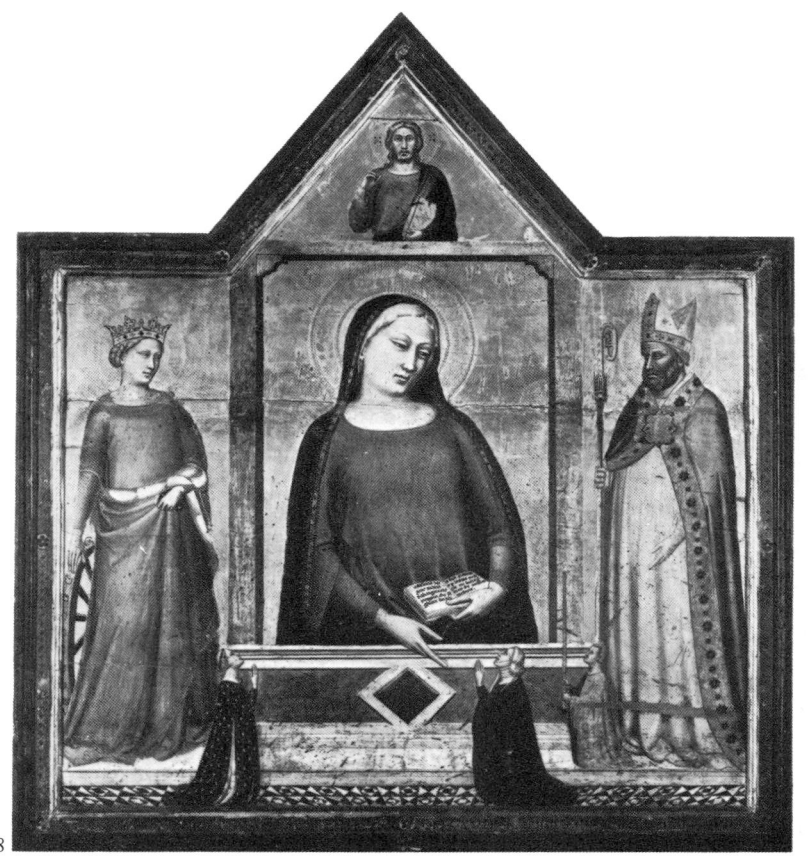

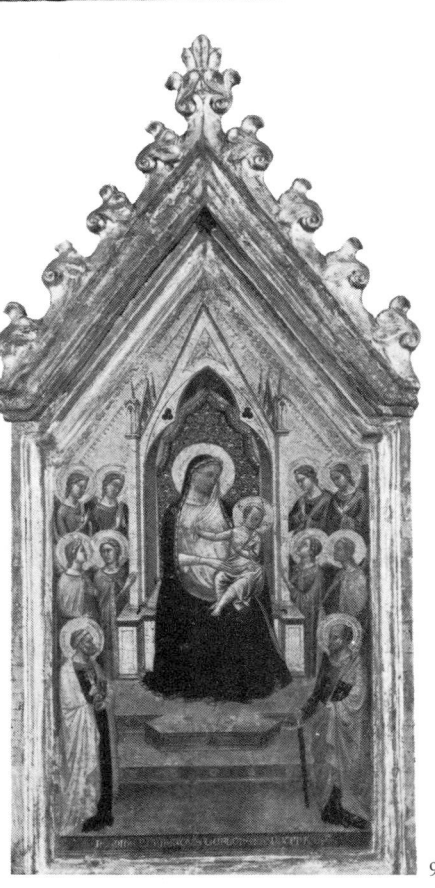

97. *Portable triptych: Christ on the Cross, Agony in the Garden and Sts Peter and Paul, Catherine, Margaret, James and Benedict. Panel. Cambridge (Mass.), Fogg Art Museum. no. 1918.33. cp: 45.4 × 25.4. Museum photo. d. 1334.*
98. *Madonna of the Magnificat. Panel. Florence, Museo dell'Opera del Duomo. no. 89. 131 × 116. SGF 27006. d. 1334.*
99. *Madonna and Child Enthroned with Sts Peter and Paul and eight Angels. Panel. Florence, Uffizi. no. 8564. 56 × 26. SGF 98368. s & d. 1334.*

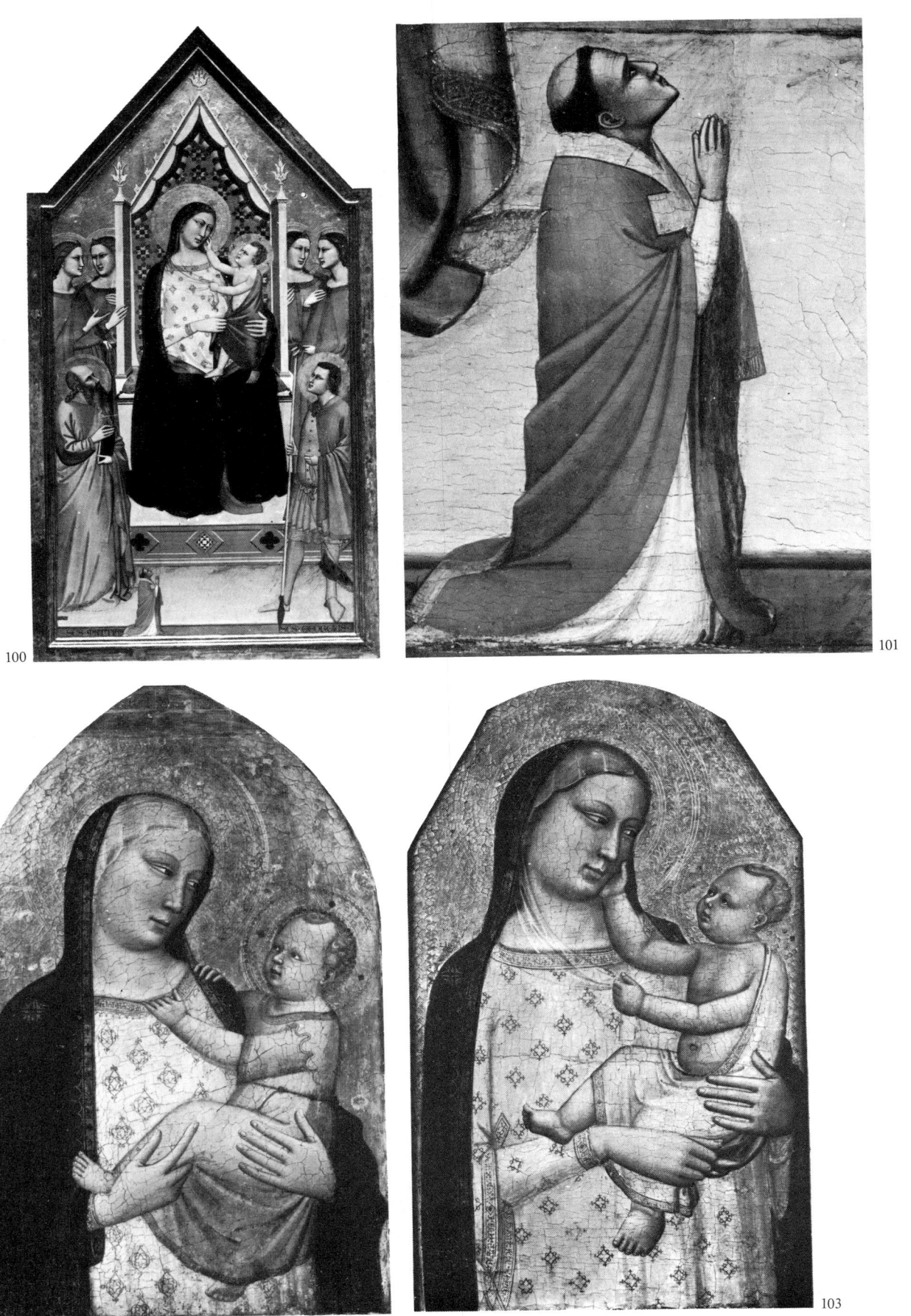

100. *Madonna and Child Enthroned with Sts Matthias and George, a Donor and four Angels. Panel. Osteria Nuova (Bagno a Ripoli, 8 kms east of Florence), S. Giorgio a Ruballa. 208 × 117. SGF 24884. d. 1336.*
101. *Monastic Donor, detail of fig. 100. Panel. Osteria Nuova, S. Giorgio a Ruballa. SGF 24891. d. 1336.*
102. *Madonna and Child. Panel. Baltimore (Md.), Walters Art Gallery. no. 37.553. 76.2 × 55.8. Museum photo.*
103. *Madonna and Child. Panel. Florence, Acton Collection. 37 × 76. Reali.*

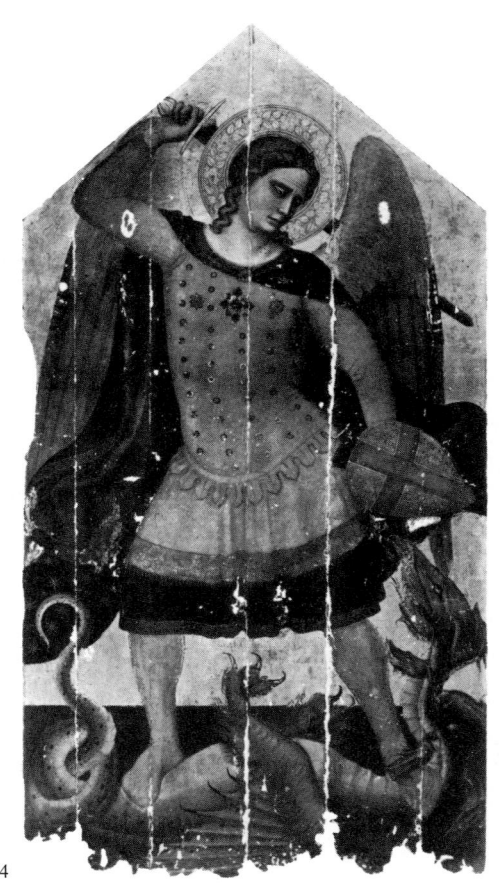

104

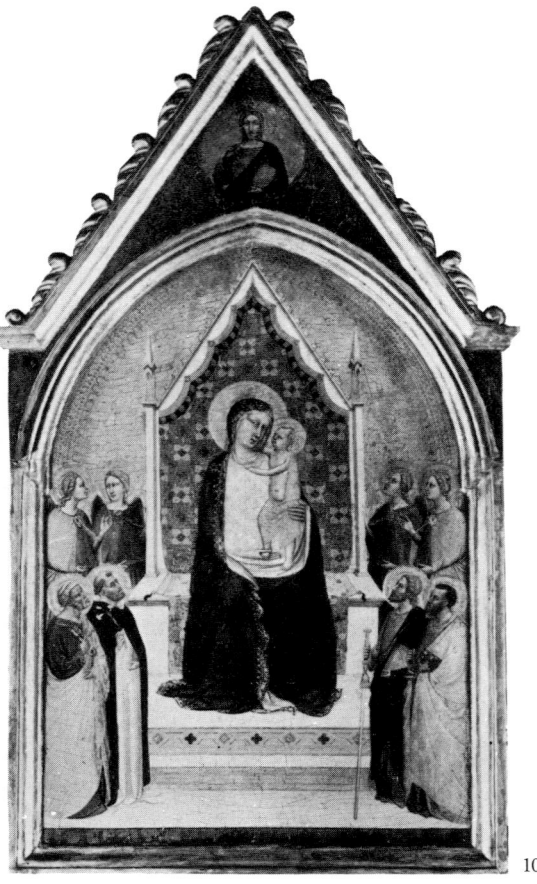

105

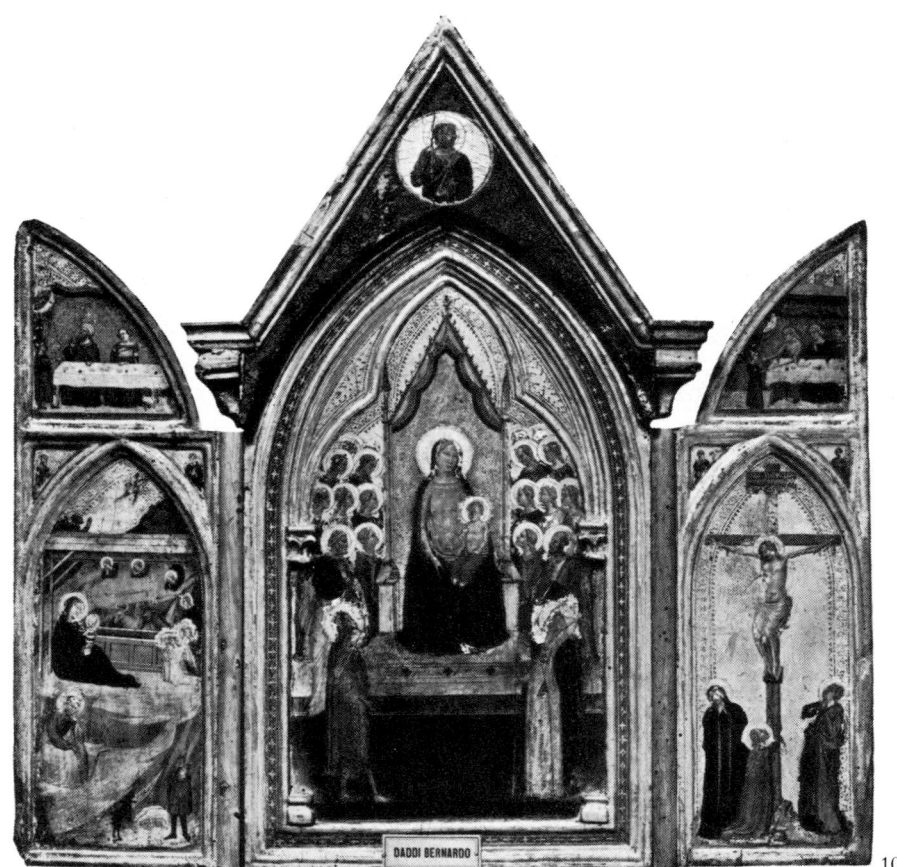

106

104. *St. Michael the Archangel. Panel. Crespina (20 kms south-east of Pisa), S. Michele Arcangelo. SGF 49583.*
105. *Madonna and Child Enthroned with Sts Peter, Dominic, Bartholomew, James and four Angels. Panel. Washington, Dumbarton Oaks Collection. no. 36.57. 90 × 43. Collection photo. d. 1337.*
106. *Portable triptych: Madonna and Child with sixteen Angels and four Saints. Pinnacle: Christ blessing. Wings: St Nicholas rescuing Adeodatus from the service of the Pagan King; Nativity; St Nicholas restoring Adeodatus to his Parents; Crucifixion. Panel. Siena, Pinacoteca Nazionale. no. 60. 80 × 72. Anderson 21075. d. 1336.*

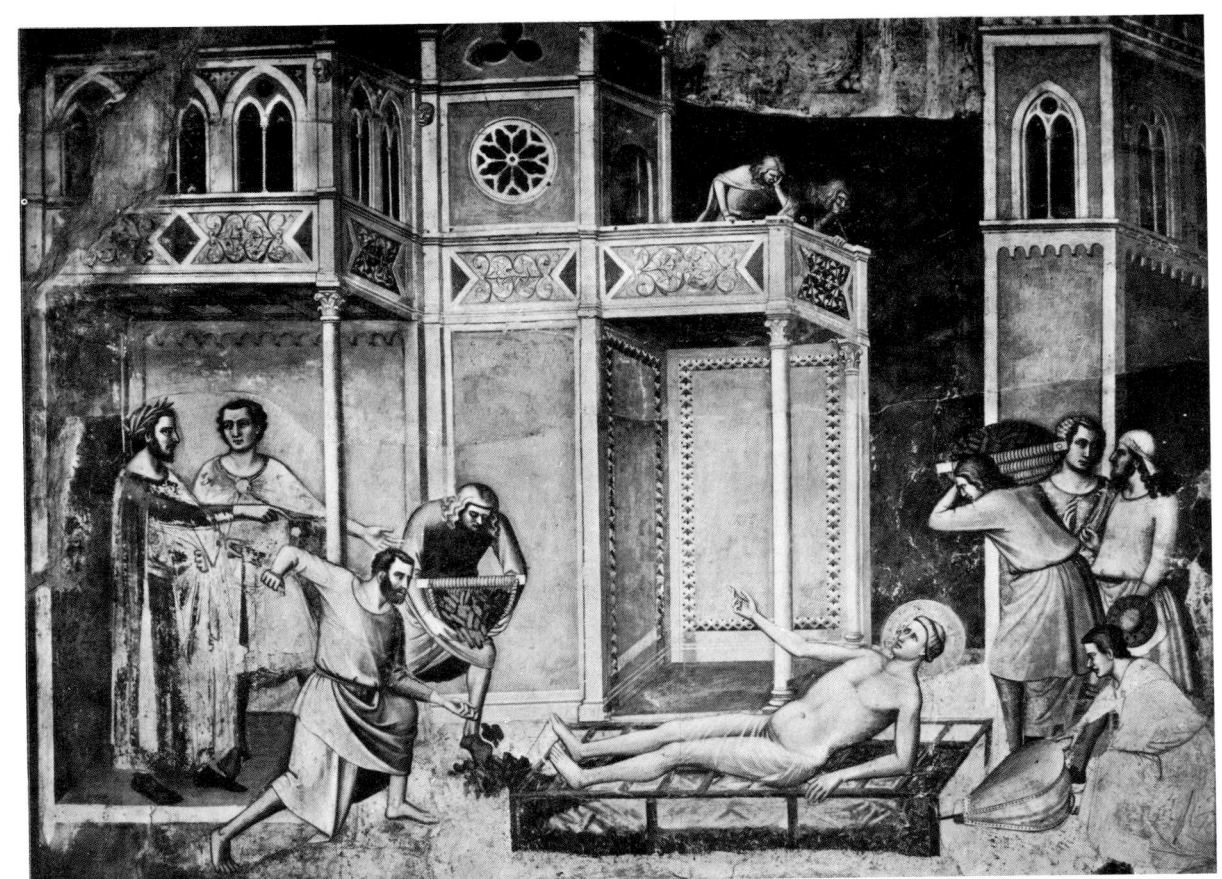

107

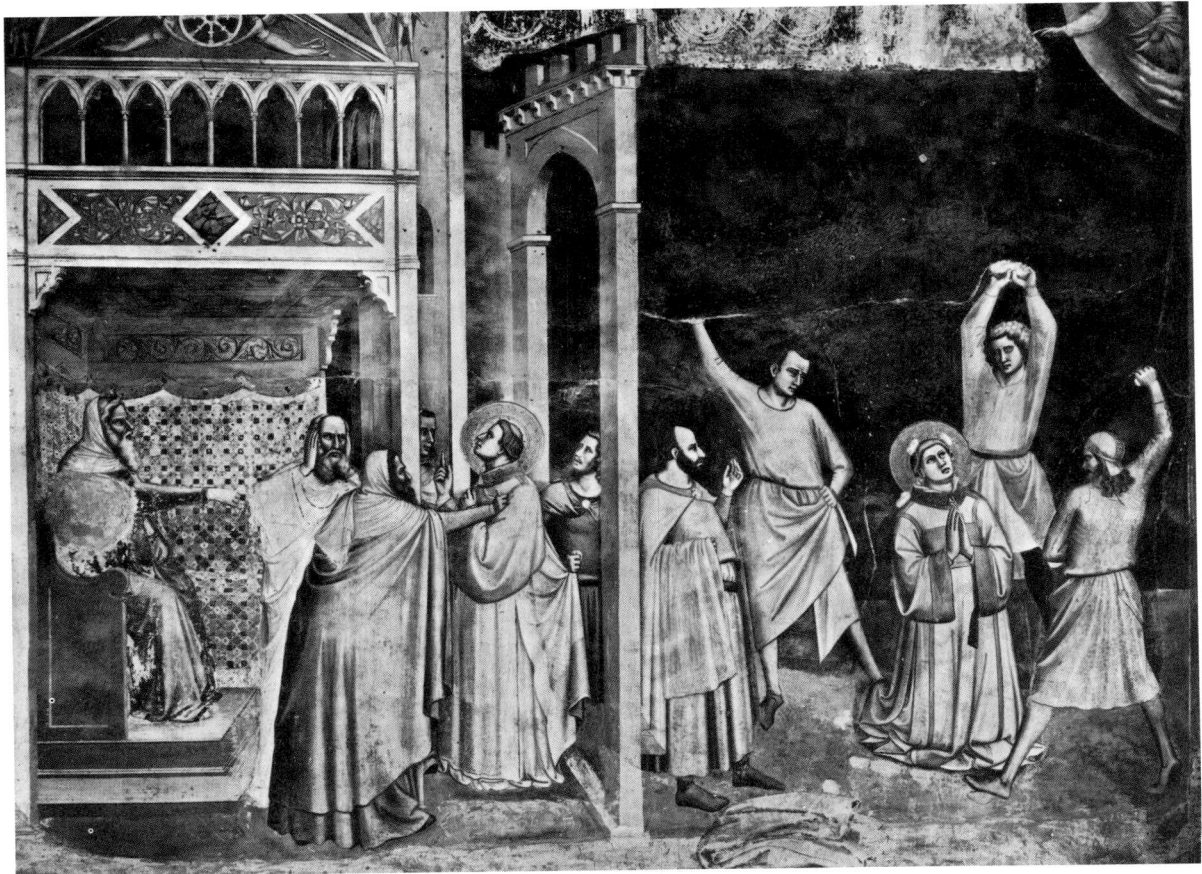

108

107. *Martyrdom of St Lawrence. Fresco. Florence, S. Croce, Pulci and Beraldi Chapel. Alinari 3883.*
108. *Martyrdom of St Stephen. Fresco. Florence, S. Croce, Pulci and Beraldi Chapel. Alinari 3884.*

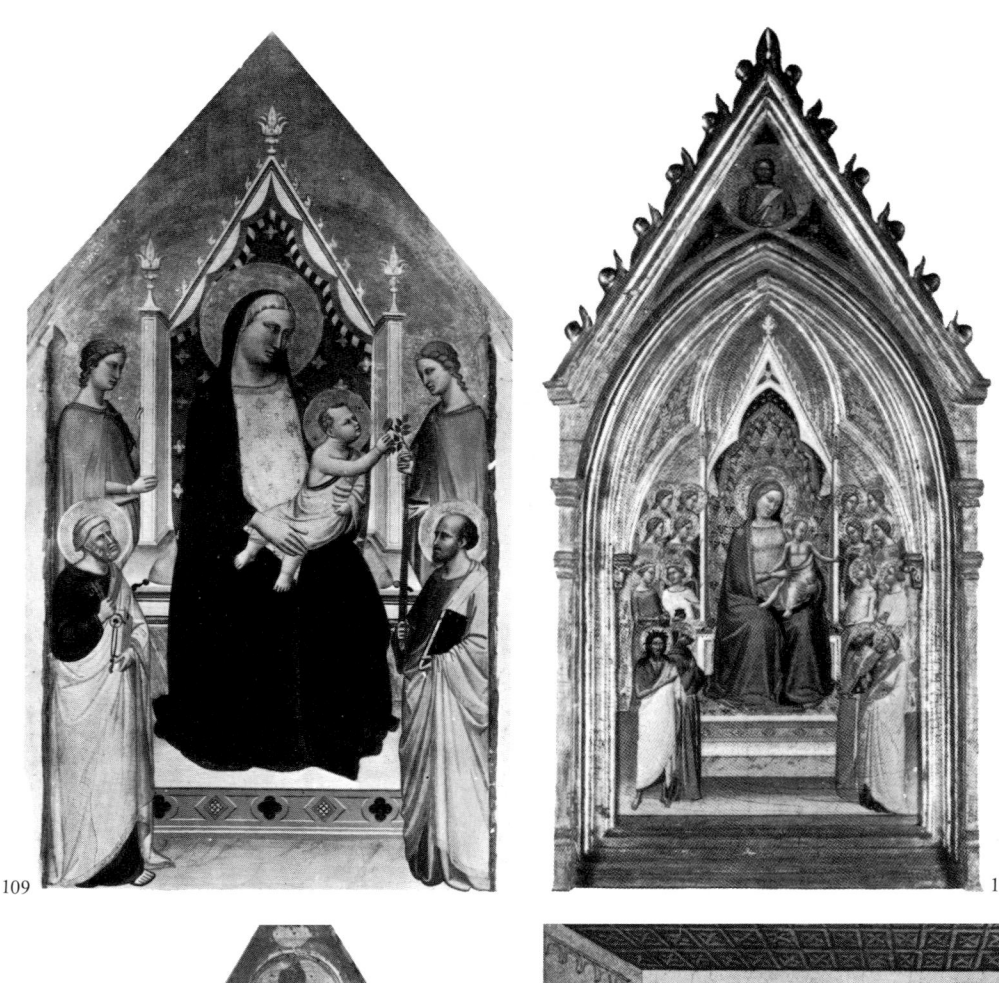

109

110

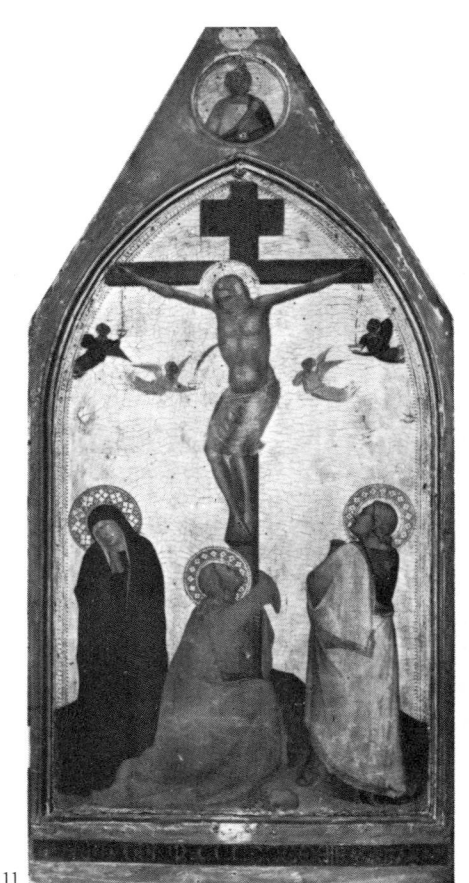

111

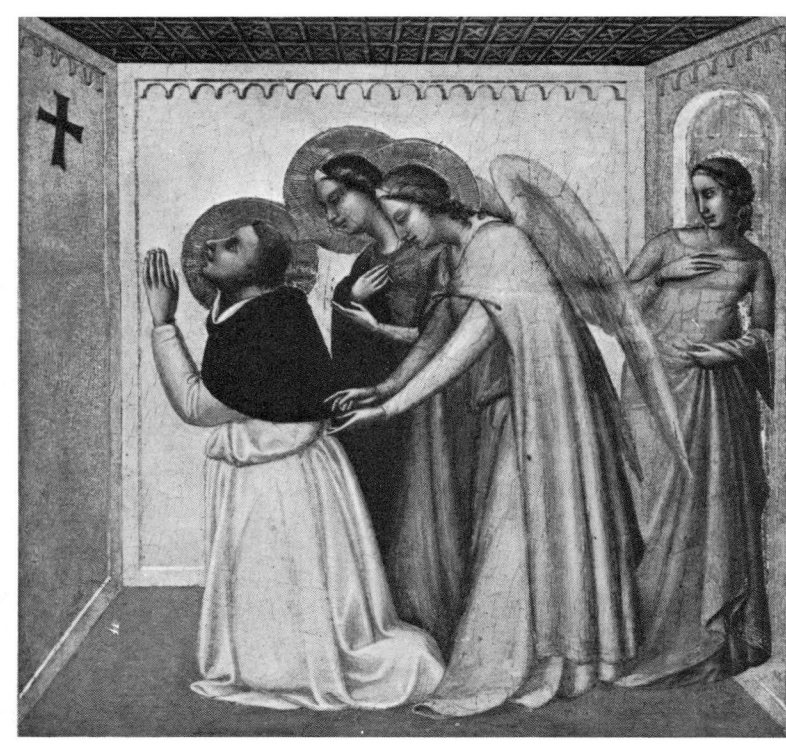

112

109. *Madonna and Child Enthroned with Sts Peter and Paul and two Angels. Panel. Signano (near Scandicci), S. Giusto. 180 × 110. SGF 24358.*

110. *Madonna and Child Enthroned with Sts Dorothy, Lucy, Catherine, Margaret, John the Baptist, Francis, Paul, Peter and eight Angels. Above: Christ blessing. Panel. Kansas City (Mo.), Wm. Rockhill Nelson Gallery of Art, Samuel H. Kress Collection. no. 46.1952. (K1300). 54.6 × 30.5. Kress Foundation photo.*

111. *Christ on the Cross with the Virgin, Sts John the Baptist, Mary Magdalene. Above: Christ blessing. Panel. Florence, Accademia. no. 8570. 125 × 59.5. SGF 92912. d. 1343.*

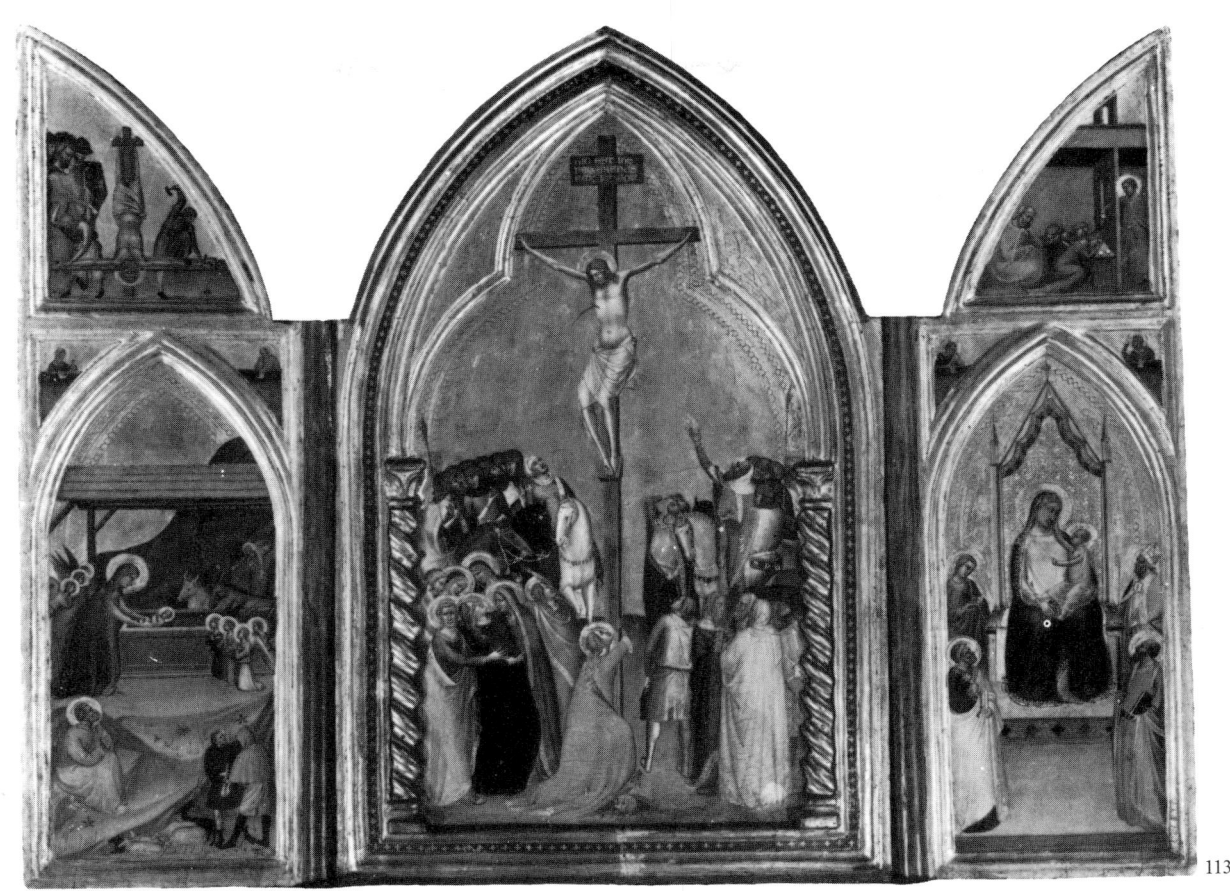

113

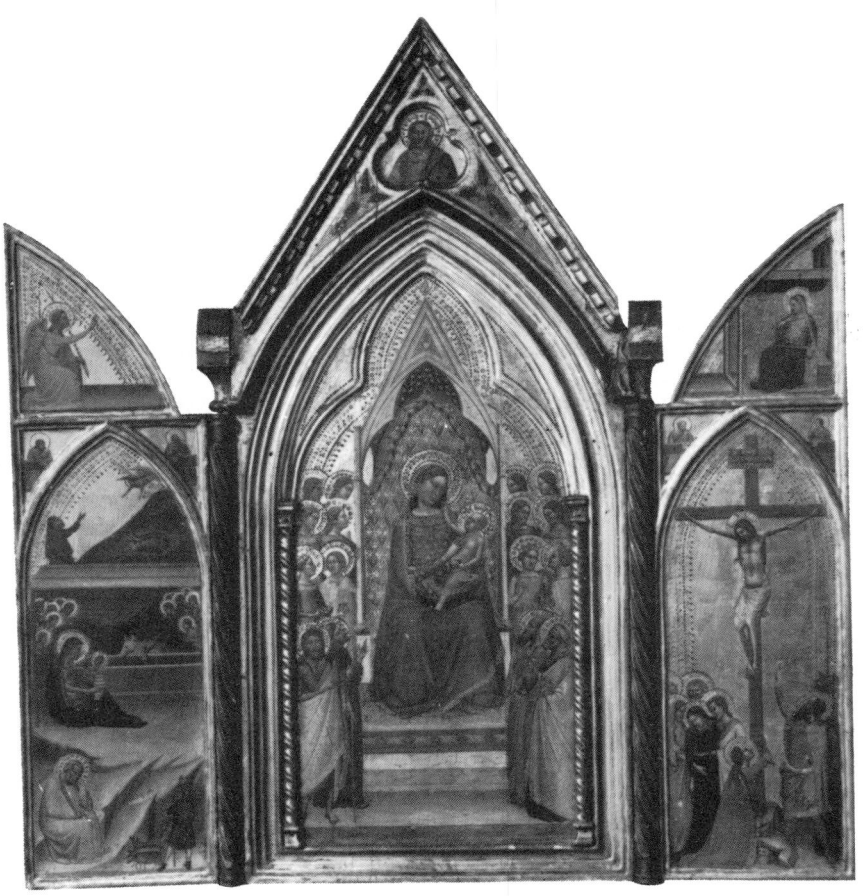

114

112. *Predella scene: St Thomas Aquinas resisting seduction with the aid of Angels. Panel. Berlin, Bodestrasse, Staatliche Museen. no. 1094. 37 × 30. Museum photo. 1338.*

113. *Portable triptych: Crucifixion, Nativity, Madonna and Child Enthroned. Above: Martyrdom of St Peter, St Nicholas and the three Maidens. Panel. Edinburgh, National Gallery of Scotland. no. 1904. cp: 53.3 × 28; sps: 55.8 × 15.2. Museum photo. d. 1338.*

114. *Portable triptych: Madonna and Child Enthroned with Sts Dorothy, Lucy, Margaret, Catherine, John the Baptist, Francis, Paul and Peter and eight Angels, Nativity, Annunciation to the Shepherds, and Christ on the Cross. Above: Annunciation. Panel. London, Count Seilern Collection. cp: 87.5 × 34; sps: 62 × 17. Collection photo. d. 1338.*

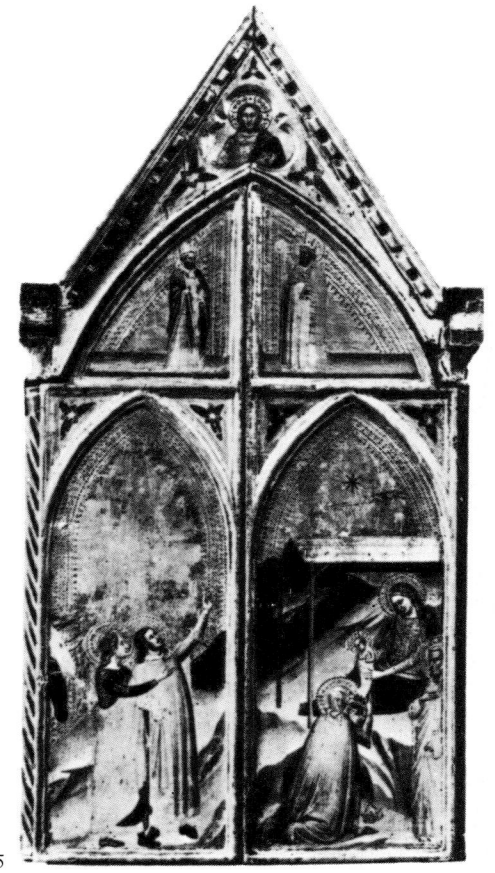

115

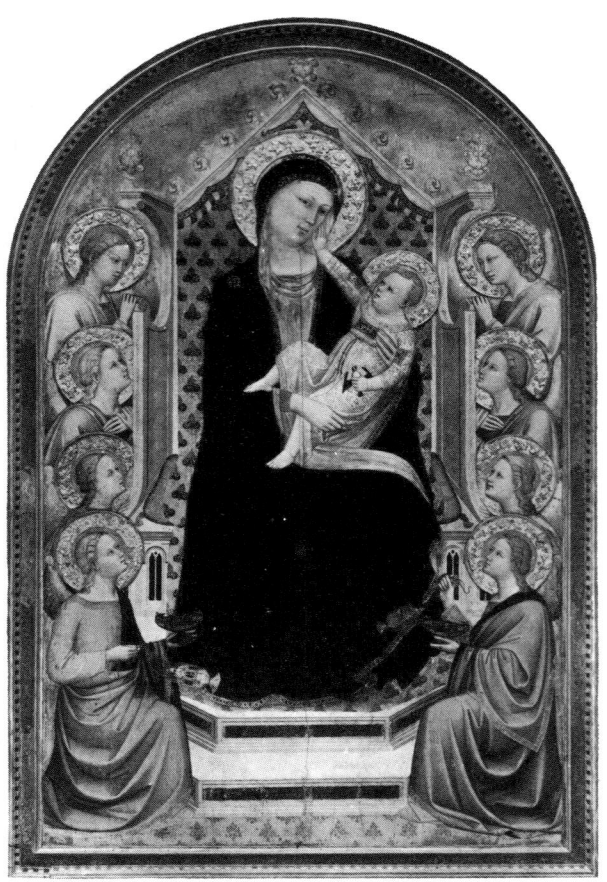

116

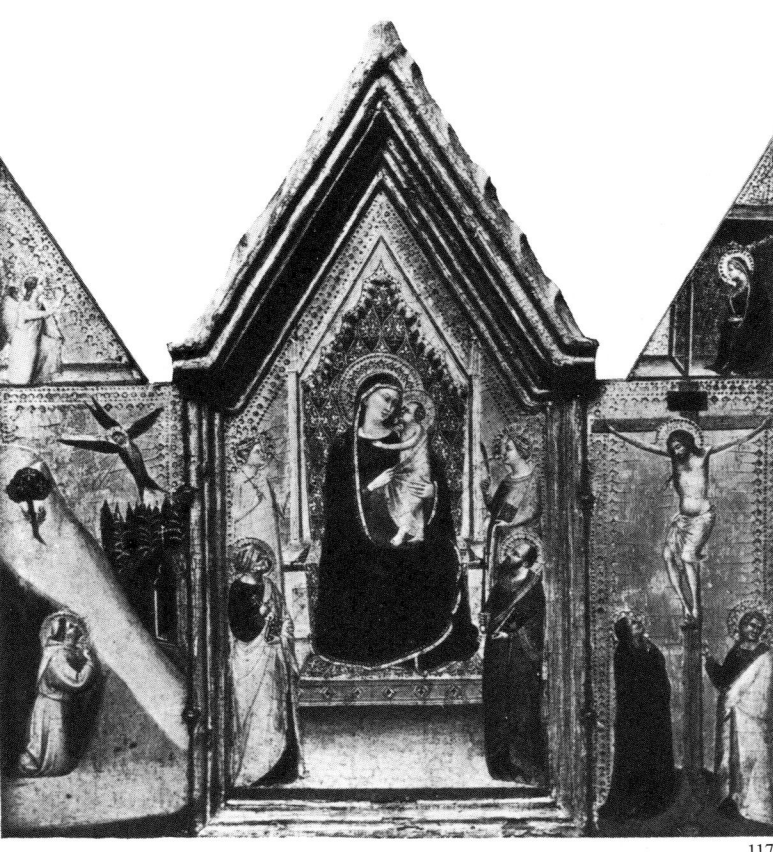

117

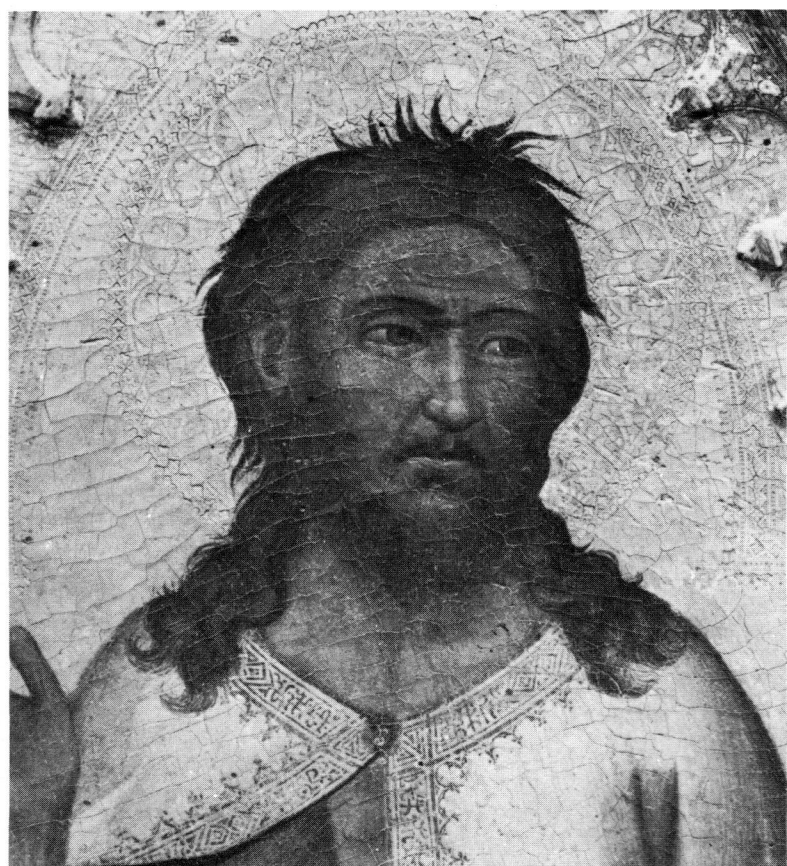

118

115.　*Closed triptych: Adoration of the Magi. Panel. London, Count Seilern Collection. sps: 62 × 17. SGF 94639. d. 1338.*
116.　*Madonna and Child Enthroned with eight Angels. Panel. Florence, Orsanmichele, Tabernacle. 250 × 180. SGF 26997. 1347.*
117.　*Portable triptych: Madonna and Child Enthroned with two female Saints, Sts Peter and Paul, Stigmatization of St Francis and Christ on the Cross.*
　　　Above: Annunciation. Panel. Minneapolis (Minn.), Institute of Art. no. 3420. 59.7 × 50.8. Museum photo. d. 1338.
118.　*Head of St John the Baptist, detail of fig. 119. Panel. Florence, S. Maria Novella, Cloister, Spanish Chapel. SGF 26136. s & d. 1344.*

MASTER OF
S. MARTINO ALLA PALMA

The four paintings which I reproduce form a group that is unknown, or at least little noticed, which I have seen on my trips through the Tuscan countryside, and which are sure to be of some use to historians of art.

At Santa Brigida all'Opaco, within the township of Pontassieve, and about halfway between this latter place and Fiesole, on the lefthand altar as one enters the parish church, there is a panel of the Virgin enthroned holding the Child Jesus upright on her knee; at the sides, standing, two angels — one leaning against the throne, the other in the act of offering a little bird to the Divine Redeemer..... The picture, the unusual beauty of which is evident even in the reproduction, brings immediately to mind another work, known for some time: the large Madonna and Child enthroned with six angels, in the church of San Martino alla Palma near Scandicci.....

The picture in San Martino alla Palma was first published by Perkins in the *Rassegna d'Arte* in 1913, as a work of Bernardo Daddi; this opinion was corroborated by van Marle, Toesca and Berenson.....

Unfortunately for the time being the identity of the painter is unknown: perhaps in the future we will find out that he is one of the finest of Giotto's followers, of whom history has left us only the names; I suggest that for now he should be named the Master of San Martino alla Palma, after the location of his finest work.....

> from U. Procacci, pp. 341-342, 344, *Rivista d'Arte*, XIV, 1932.

The hand of a fully formed master of the same circle appears in the two panels from S. Martino alla Palma and S. Brigida all'Opaco. He is distinguishable by his soft-lipped fragile types, his caressing gentleness, his delicately tinted flesh, and his rich wine-coloured reds and purples. But in these works, as in those of all the non-Giottesque painters, the large figures seem blown-up and oversized, whereas the small worshippers in the lower part of the S. Martino panel are more compact and vivid. It is this pupil of Daddi we discover in the exquisite little diptych of the New York Historical Society (variously attributed to Simone and to Daddi himself) and in a series of other panels.....

> from R. Offner, p. 83, *Burlington Magazine*, LXIII, 1933.

Among the followers of Bernardo Daddi stands out the Master of S. Martino alla Palma. A reconstruction of Procacci, to the work of whom Offner has added two precious panels, *Christ Mocked* and the *Flagellation*; the latter of these two pictures is of an amber colour of great fineness which reminds one of the Rothermere Coronation; but these two pictures are less heavy and ingenuous, less puerile in their bright colour and plain forms; the fundamental works of the Master of S. Martino alla Palma suggest to us a marvellous fourteenth century Lenci.....

> from L. Coletti, p. 70, *Bollettino d'Arte*, XXXI, 1937.

A Florentine painter closely linked with the young manner of Bernardo Daddi, but with a tendency to more grandeur, with louder colours. He was named by Procacci, who first distinguished his personality using as the basis of his reconstruction the painting (a Madonna and Child, with six angels) in the Church of S. Martino alla Palma, near Florence.....

> from U. Baldini, *VIIª Mostra di Opere d'arte Restaurate*, Florence, 1953.

There are a number of new attributions to the Master of S. Martino alla Palma and to his immediate following. To the Master himself, Offner has now attributed the lovely panel of the *Madonna* which is called " La Ninna " and which I assigned to this painter many years ago, even before the restoration which removed from the surface the heavy overpaint and which made even more possible the present attribution.....

from U. Procacci, p. 138, *Rivista d' Arte*, XXXII, 1957.

BIBLIOGRAPHY
BOOKS

An asterisk indicates a work listed in the General Bibliography

Sirèn, O., *Giotto and some of his Followers*, I, London, 1917, p. 122; *van Marle**, III, 1924, p. 352; *Offner, 1934**, Sec. III, Vol. IV, p. 214; *National Gallery of Art, Preliminary Catalogue of Paintings and Sculpture*, Washington, D.C., 1941, p. 51; *M. Giottesca**, 1943, pp. 536-45; *Offner, 1947**, Sec. III, Vol. V, pp. 1-53; *Galetti**, 1950, " F-O ", pp. 1488-9; *Baldini, 1953**, pp. 17-19; Shorr, D. C., *The Christ Child in Devotional Images*, New York, 1954, pp. 162, 166; *Offner 1958**, Sec. III, Vol. VII, pp. 123-33; *Marcucci**, 1965, pp. 67-8; Boskovits, M., *Giotto* (I Maestri del Colore, 248), Milan, 1966; *Shapley**, 1966, p. 30; *Klesse**, 1967, pp. 223, 314; Palumbo, G., *Collezione Federico Mason Perkins*, Rome, 1973, p. 39.

JOURNALS

Procacci, U., *RA*, XIV, 1932, pp. 341-44; Offner, R., *BM*, LXIII, 1933, p. 83; Sanpaolesi, P. ,*BA*, XXVII, III, 1933, pp. 145-63; Gamba, C., *BA*, XXVII, 1933, pp. 145-63; Coletti, L., *BA*, XXXI, III, 1937, pp. 49-72; Goldkuhle, F., *K*, VI, 1953, p. 178; Feudale, C., *M*, VII, 1954-7, pp. 8-24; Procacci, U., *RA*, XXXII, 1957, p. 138; Procacci, U., *RA*, XXXIII, 1958, pp. 121-39; Bellosi, L., *PA*, XVI, 187/7, 1965, p. 19; De Benedictis, C., *AV*, 3, 1967, p. 44.

There are no known dated works by the Master of S. Martino alla Palma.

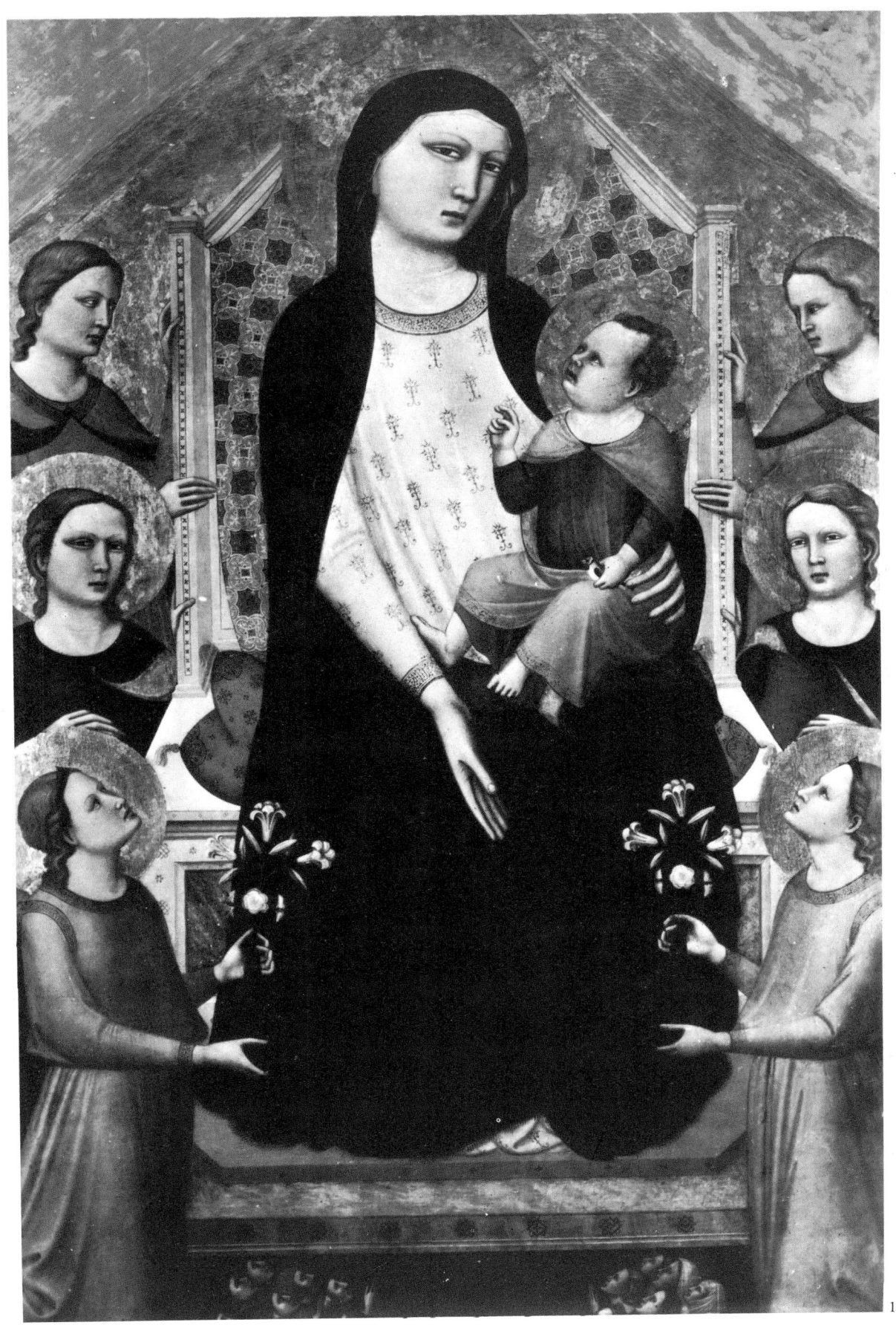

121

121. *Madonna and Child Enthroned with six Angels. Panel. San Martino alla Palma (8 kms south-west of Florence), Pieve.* 190 × 118. *SGF 22607.*

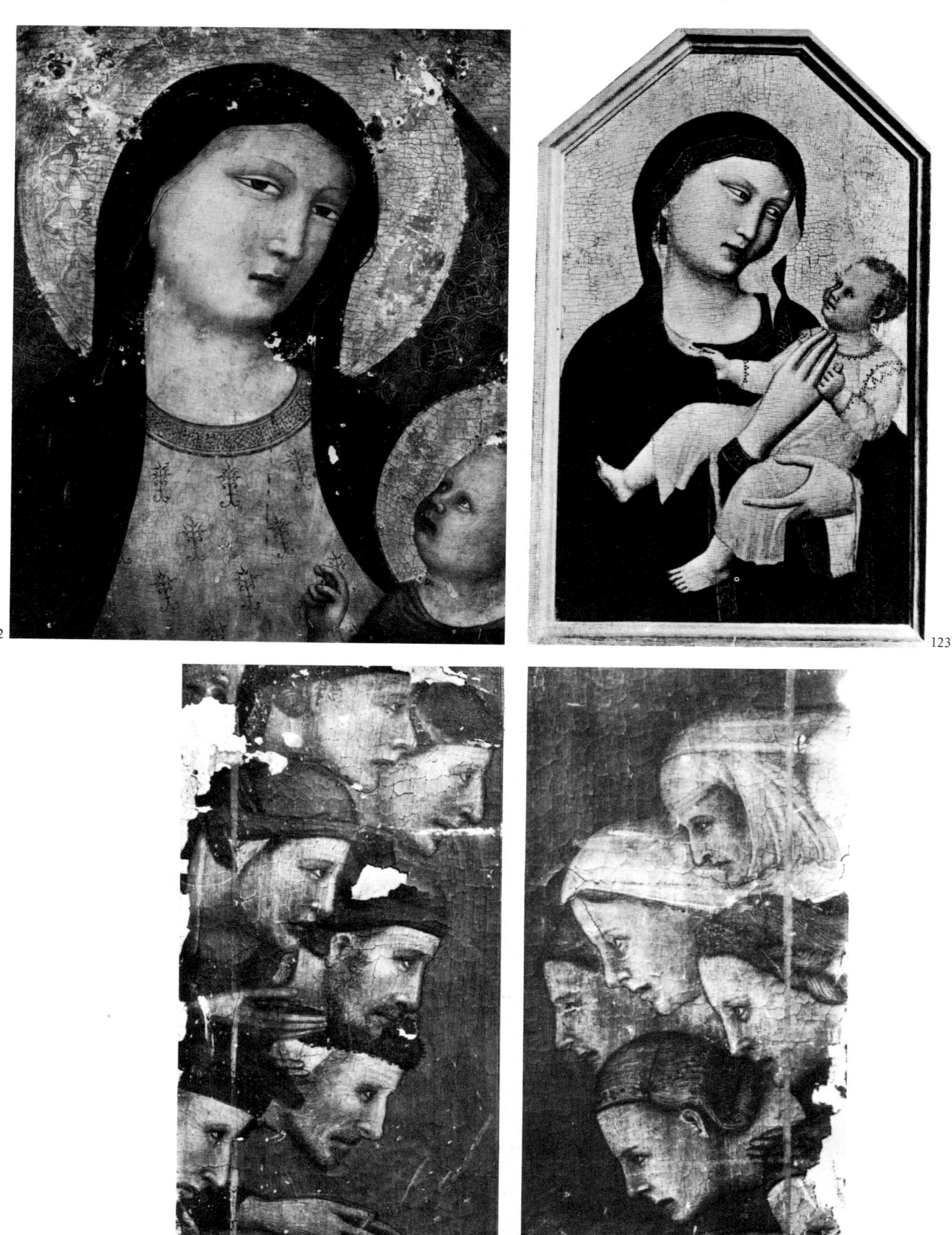

122. Madonna, detail of fig. 121. Panel. San Martino alla Palma, Pieve. Brogi 24732
123. Madonna and Child. Panel. São Paolo, Museu. 65 × 37. Bertoni-Offner.
124. Heads of Worshippers, detail of fig. 121. Panel. San Martino alla Palma, Pieve. Brogi 24740.
125. Heads of Worshippers, detail of fig. 121. Panel. San Martino alla Palma, Pieve. Brogi 24741.

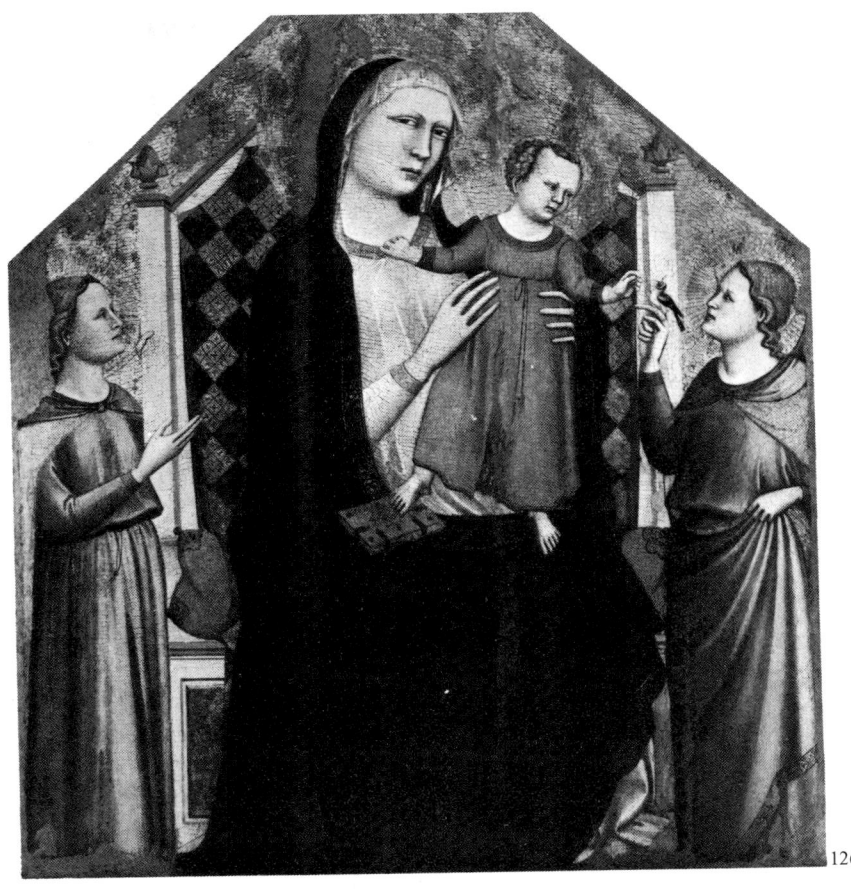

126

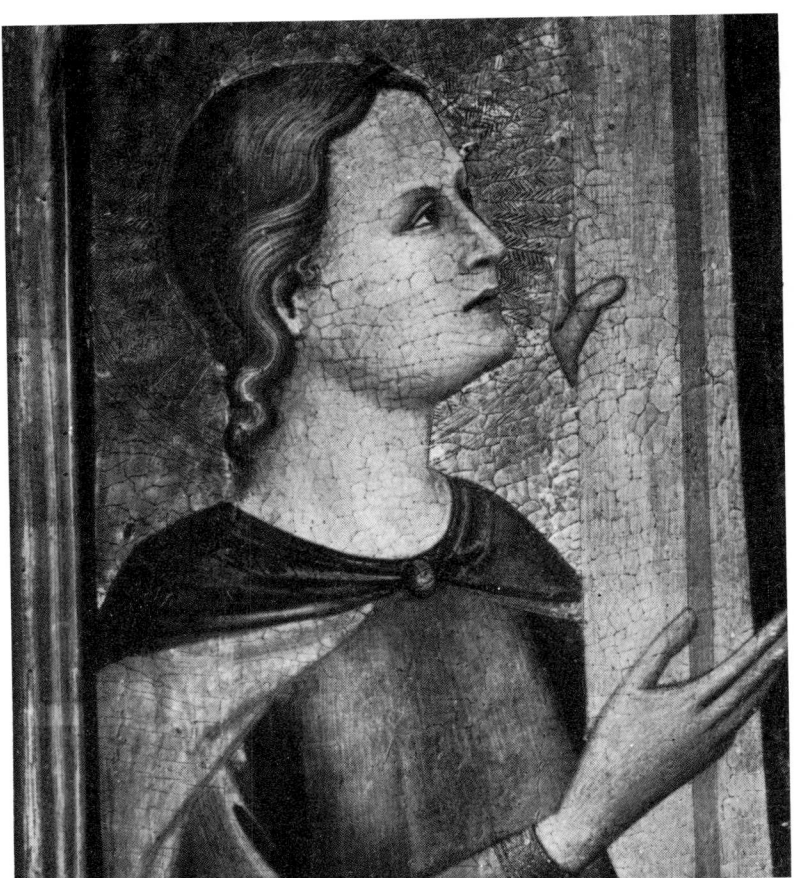

127

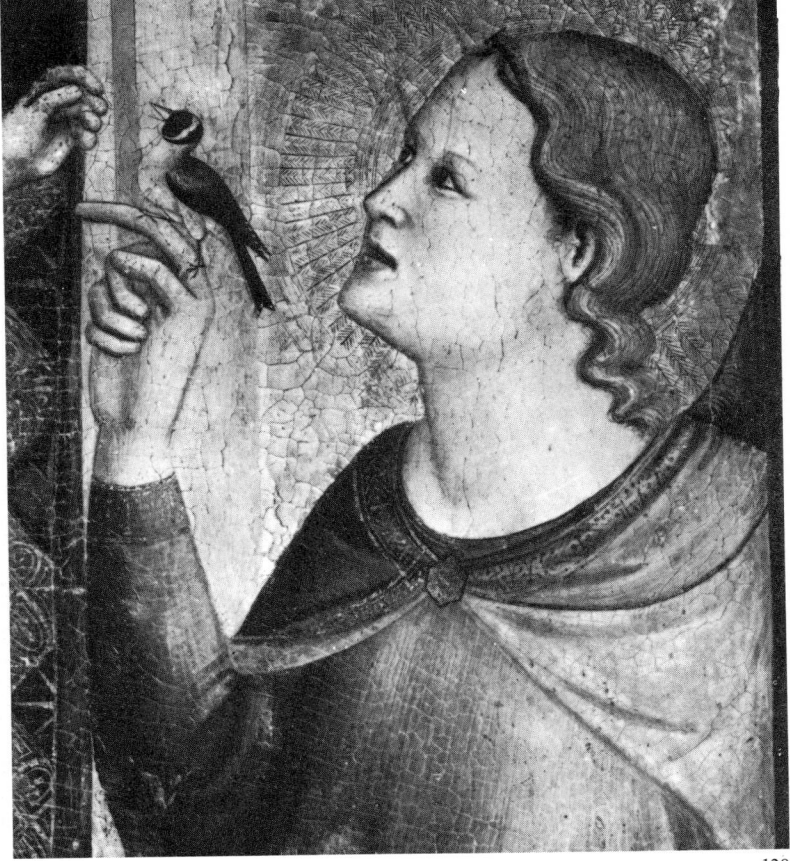

128

126. *Madonna and Child Enthroned with two Angels. Panel. Santa Brigida all'Opaco (near Pontassieve), Pieve. 135 × 120. SGF 03983.*
127. *Angel, detail of fig. 126. Panel. Santa Brigida all'Opaco, Pieve. Brogi 24752.*
128. *Angel, detail of fig. 126. Panel. Santa Brigida all'Opaco, Pieve. Brogi 24751.*

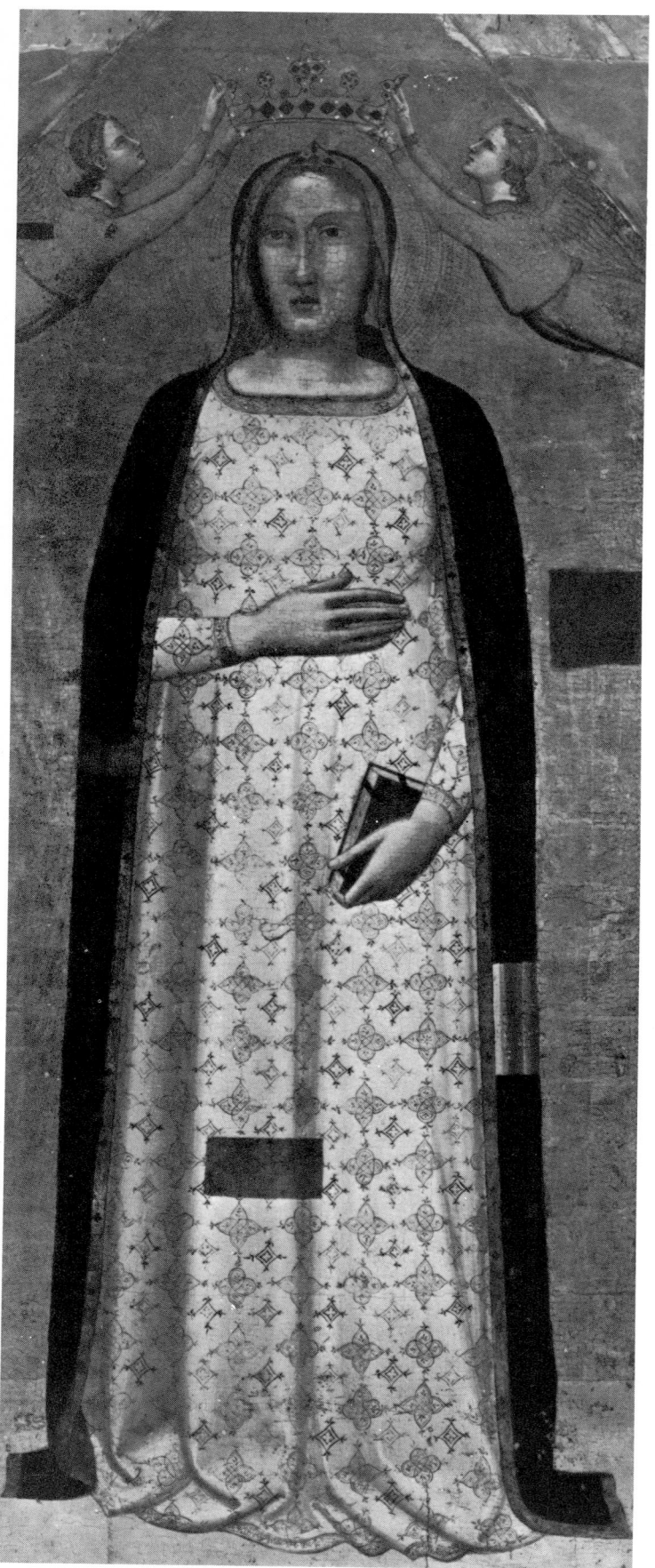

129

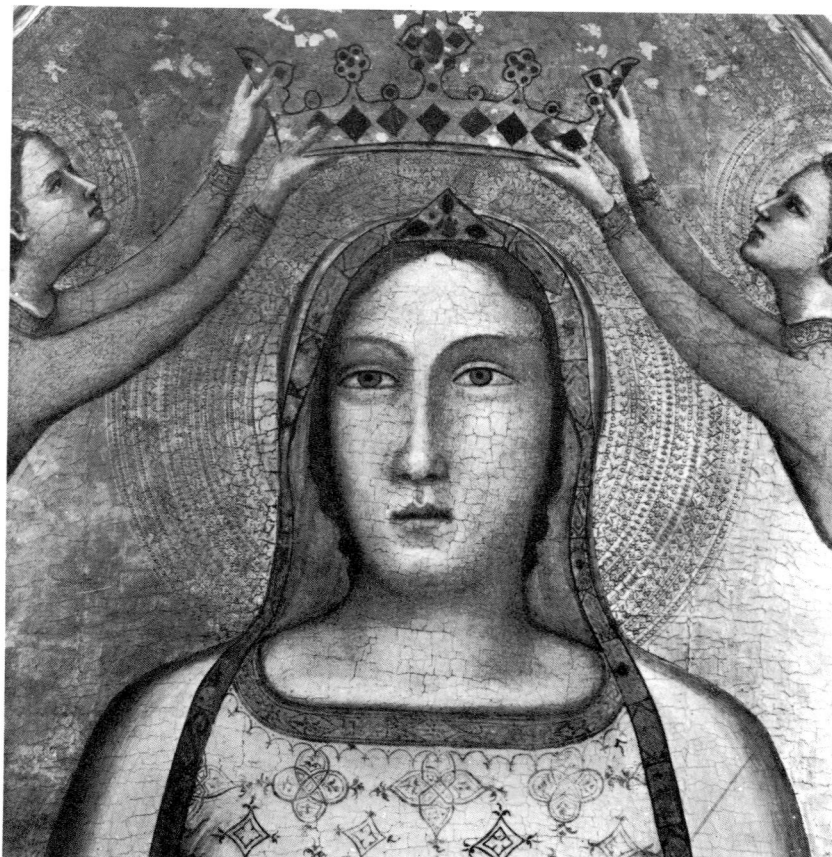

130

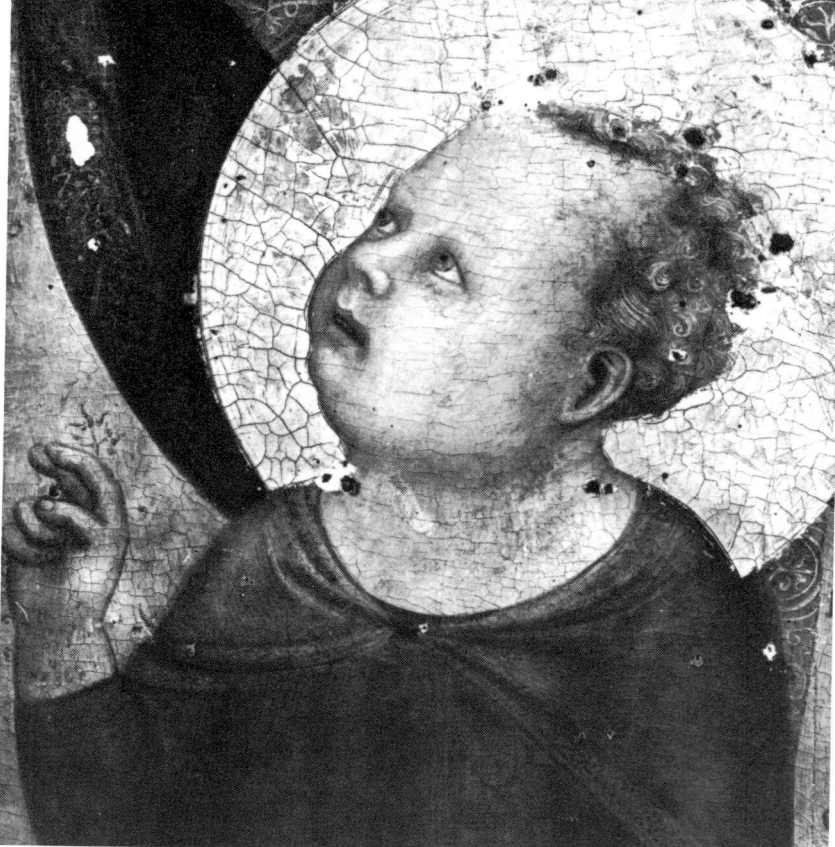

131

129. *Madonna del Parto, " La Ninna ". Panel. Florence, Uffizi, Depositi. no. 1890 :6165. 185 × 93. SGF 94474.*
130. *Head of Madonna, detail of fig. 129. Panel. Florence, Uffizi, Depositi. no. 1890 :6165. SGF 94687.*
131. *Infant Christ, detail of fig. 121. Panel. San Martino alla Palma, Pieve. Brogi 24733.*

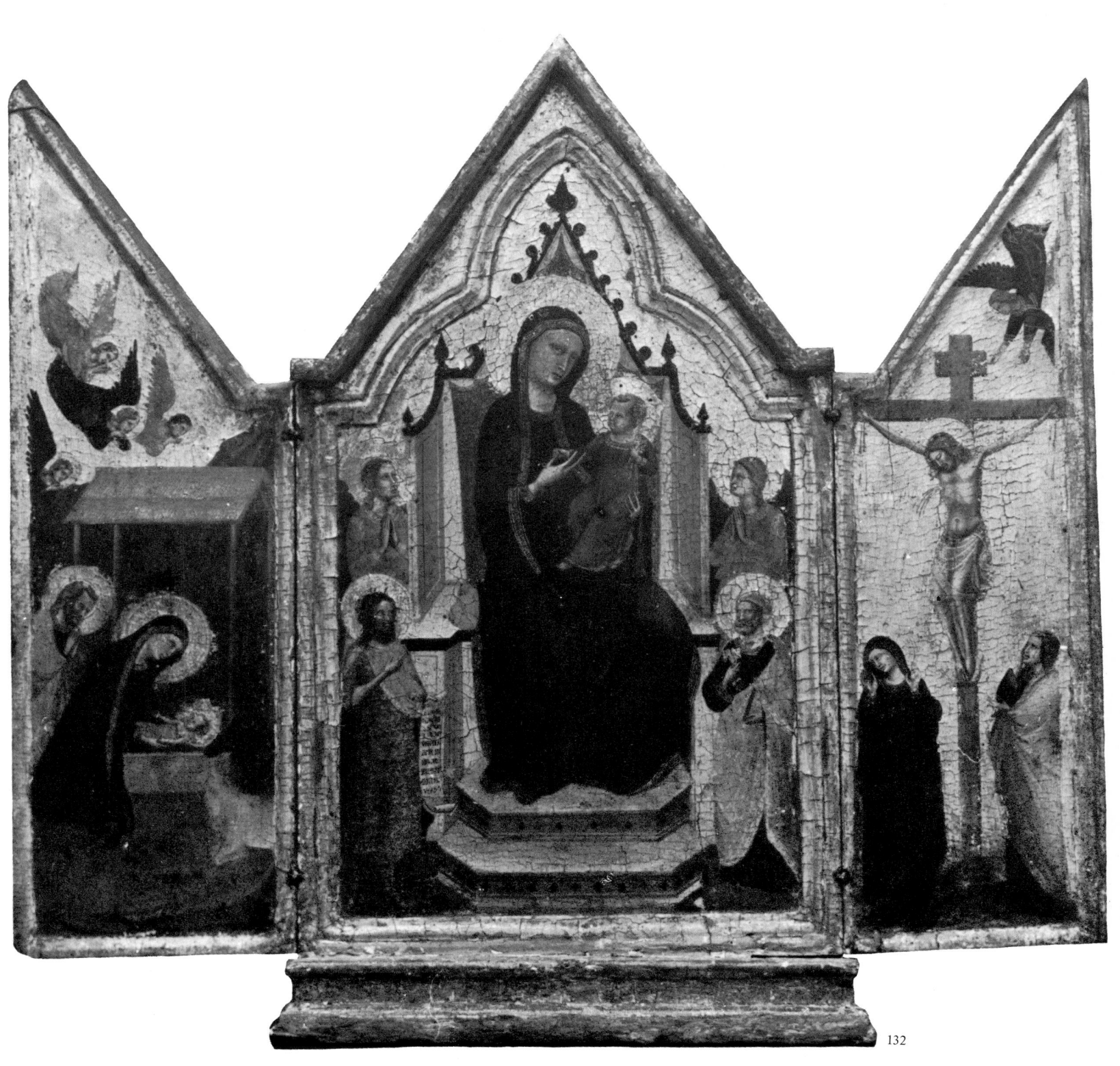

132. *Triptych: Madonna and Child Enthroned with Angels and Saints; Nativity and Crucifixion. Panel. Assisi, F.M. Perkins Collection.* 60 × 57.
Foto de Giovanni.

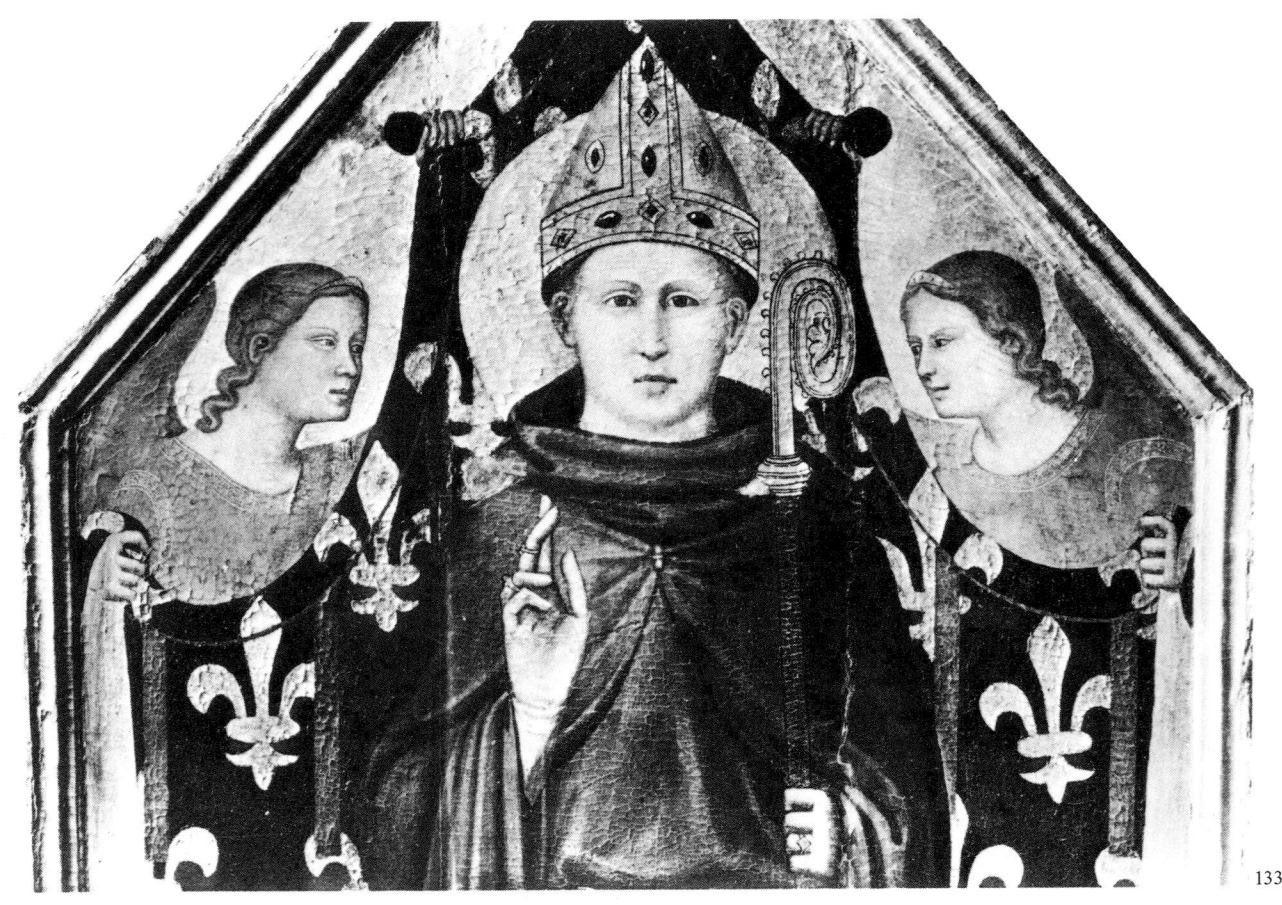

133

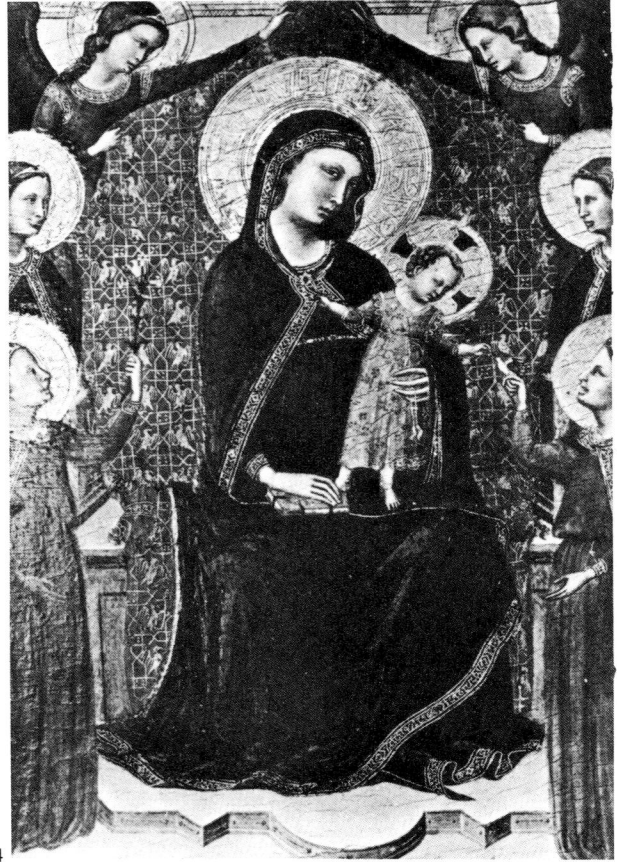

134

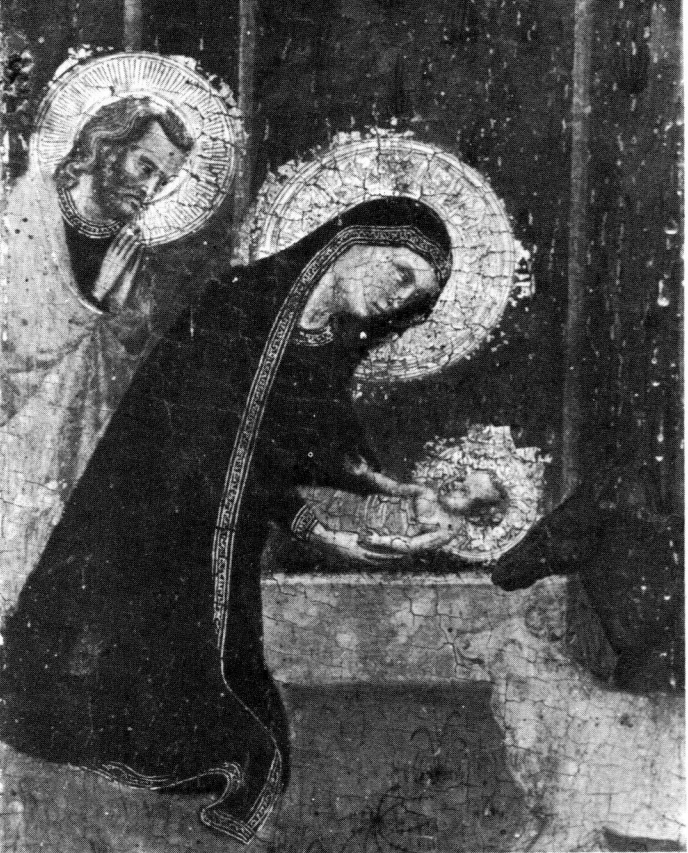

135

133. *Heads of St Louis of Toulouse and two Angels, detail of fig. 138. Panel. Hatfield (Herts.), Walter Burns Collection. Bertoni-Offner.*
134. *Madonna and Child Enthroned with six Angels. Panel. New York (N.Y.), New York Historical Society. 31.7 × 21.6. Bertoni-Offner.*
135. *Nativity, detail of fig. 132. Panel. Assisi, F.M. Perkins Collection. Foto de Giovanni.*

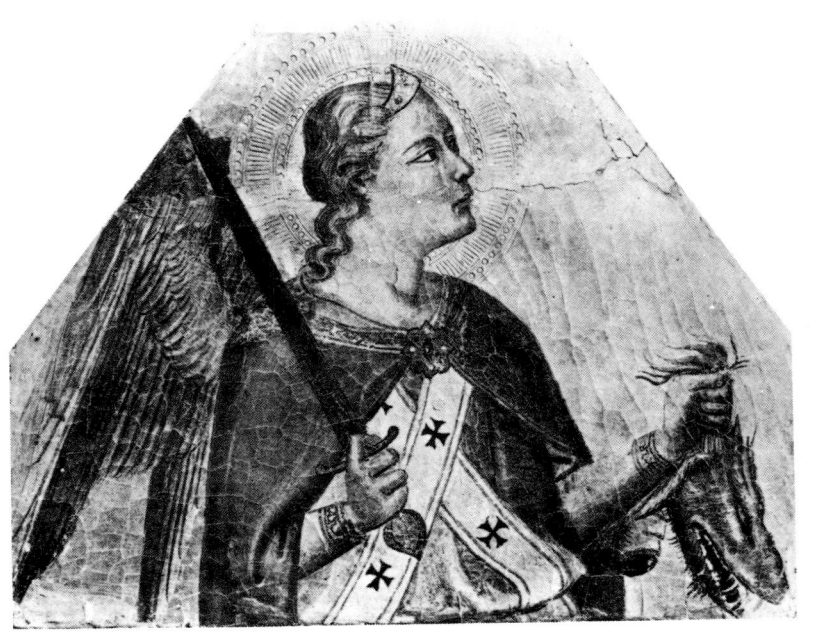

136

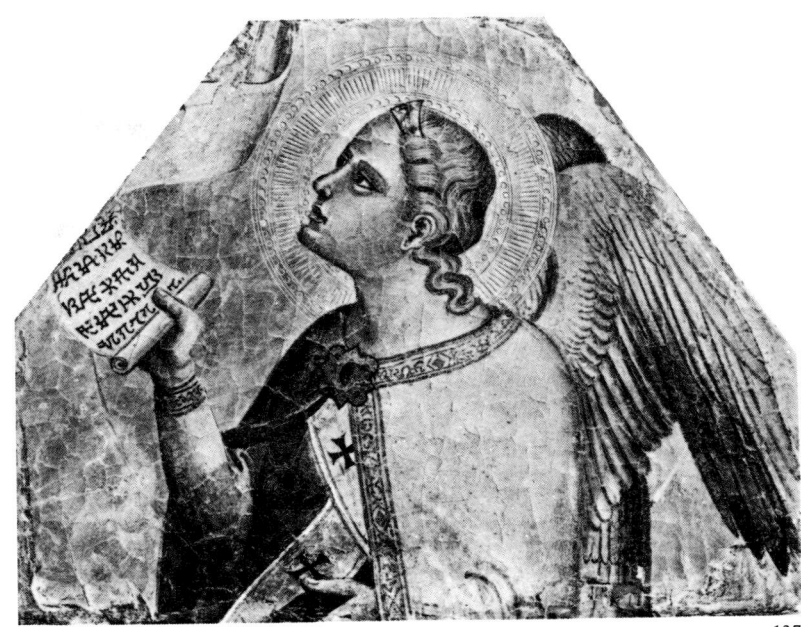

137

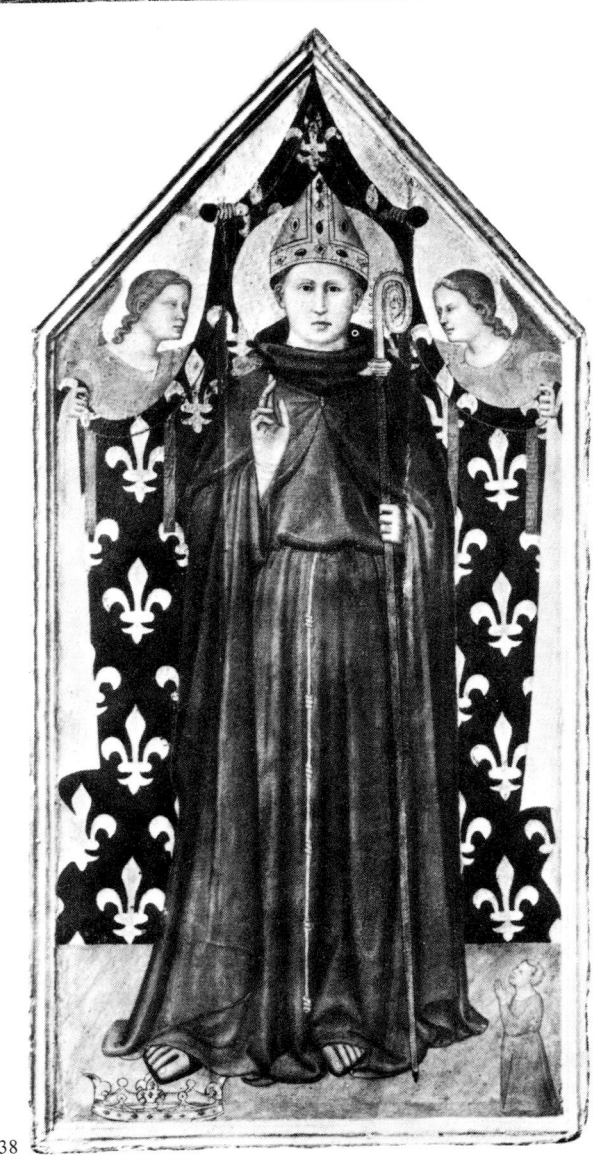

138

136. *Angel. Panel. Utrecht, Aartsbisschoppelijk Museum. no. 516. 20 × 27. Bertoni-Offner.*
137. *Angel. Panel. Utrecht, Aartsbisschoppelijk, Museum. 20 × 27. Bertoni-Offner.*
138. *St Louis of Toulouse with two Angels. Panel. Hatfield (Herts.), Walter Burns Collection. 163.3 × 73.2. Bertoni-Offner.*

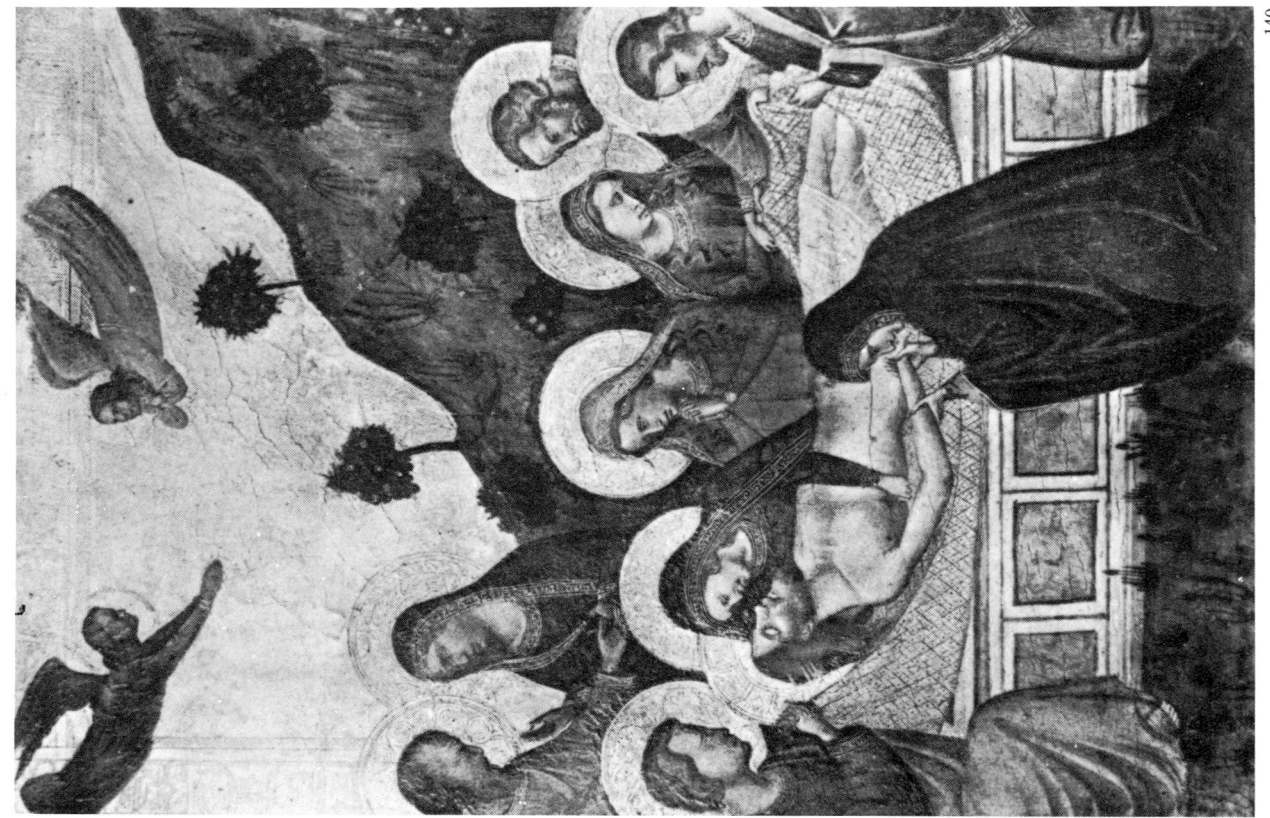

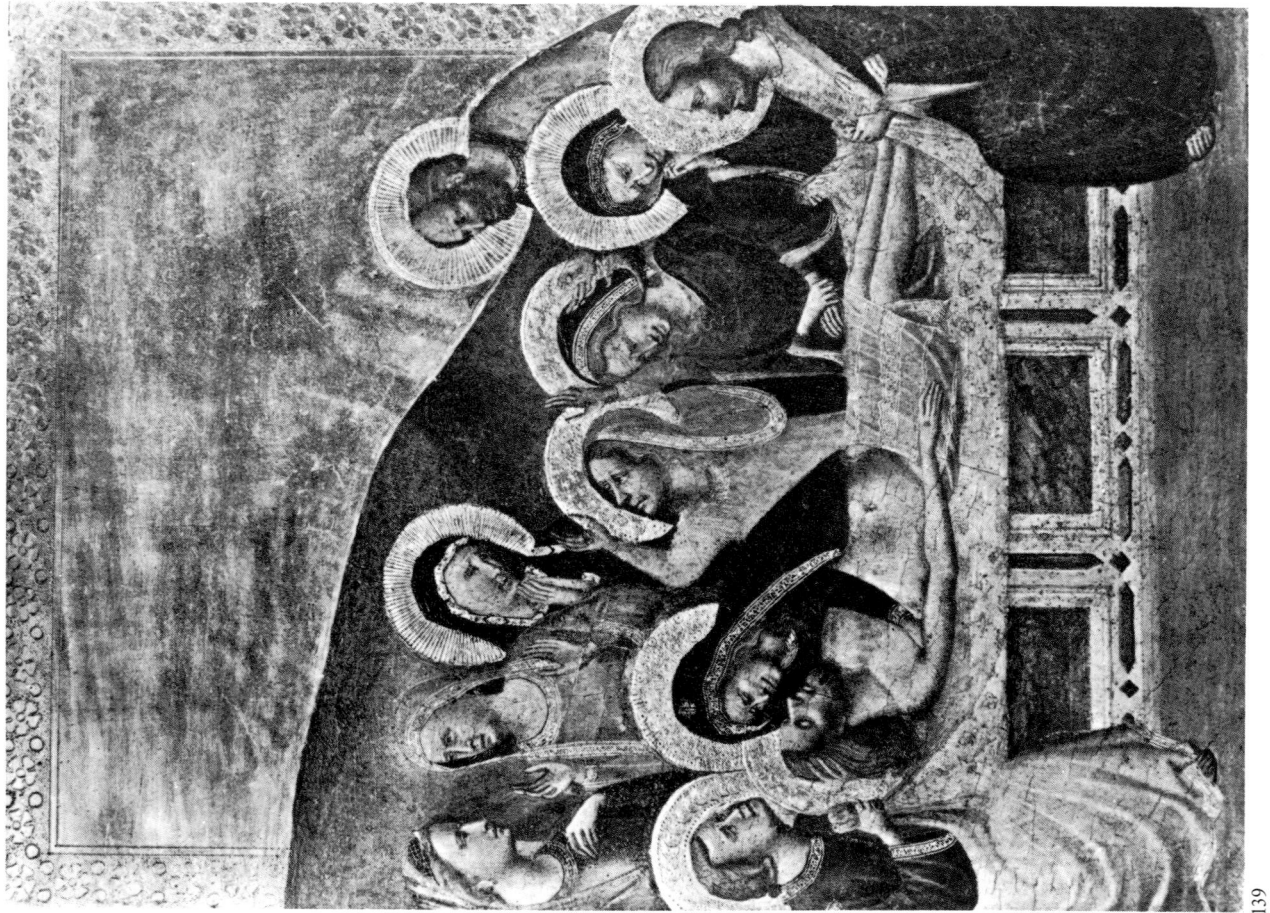

139. *Lamentation. Panel. Oxford, Ashmolean Museum, Museum Keeper's Office. no. 300. 31.1 × 22.8. Bertoni-Offner.*
140. *Lamentation. Panel. Göttingen, Kunstsammlung der Universität. no. 60. 28.5 × 20.5. Bertoni-Offner.*

TADDEO GADDI

I think that Ghiberti in the great admiration he expressed for Taddeo Gaddi was nearer to a just appreciation of this painter's merits than those who, especially of late, have severely criticised his art.

Taddeo was certainly the son of Gaddo Gaddi, the mosaicist, who may have executed the Coronation of the Virgin in the Cathedral of Florence and finished the ornamentation of the façade of Sta. Maria Maggiore, Rome.

Cennino Cennini, in his treatise on the art of painting, tells us that Giotto held Taddeo at his baptism and afterwards had him as pupil during twenty four years. He may have perhaps slightly exaggerated the length of time but the fact that Gaddi was Giotto's pupil is confirmed by a signature which Vasari saw on a painting in the old market of Florence which represented the judges pulling out the tongues of the untruthful and under which was inscribed:

> " La pura Verità, per ubbidire
> Alla Santa Giustizia che non tarda
> Cava la lingua alla falsa bugiarda
> Taddeo dipinse questo bel rigestro
> Discepol fu di Giotto il buon maestro ".

Besides this we know nothing of his life except that he died before 1366 as his wife is then mentioned as a widow; her name seems to have been Francesca di Albizzo Ormanni and in 1383 there is mention of his daughter.

Some works which have since disappeared are enumerated by Ghiberti, the Anonimo Gaddiano, Antonio Billi and their number is considerably augmented by Vasari.

They mention a fresco in Sta. Croce of the resuscitation of a child by the help of St. Francis, in which the portraits of Giotto, Dante and Taddeo himself were represented, the frescoes in the cloister of S. Spirito, a tabernacle in the via del Crocifisso, a panel in Sta. Maria dei Servi (Sta. Annunziata) and the extant works in the Baroncelli chapel of Sta. Croce, and the Lord at the age of twelve disputing with the Doctors, a painting above the door leading to the sacristy.

Vasari besides these ascribes to Taddeo the frescoes of Giovanni da Milano in the chapel of the sacristy of the same church, and those of Andrea da Firenze in the Spanish chapel which, according to this confusing biographer, Gaddi executed together with Simone Memmi (Martini) with whom he studied under Giotto; Vasari in a few moralizing words speaks of their perfect harmony in this enterprise. According to the same authority, who will forthwith be abandoned, Taddeo also adorned the chapel on the Verna mountain where St. Francis received the stigmata.....

from R. van Marle, pp. 301-302, *The Development of the Italian Schools of Painting*, Vol. III, The Hague, 1924.

In spite of his many limitations, Taddeo Gaddi is the most important painter to begin working during the last years of Giotto's life. The first notice of Taddeo, in 1332, regards the commission for the frescoes for the Baroncelli chapel in Santa Croce (in which Giotto had already placed a polyptych, signed by him, but executed in large part by his workshop, and perhaps by Taddeo Gaddi himself). These frescoes were completed in 1338. It was probably in these same years that Taddeo executed, with brilliant innovation, a very beautiful group of works: the Berlin triptych of 1334, the panels with the Stories of St. Francis for the chest of the Sacristy of Santa Croce, the frescoed lunette with the Deposition for the same church, and triptych of 1336 (Rome, Castel Sant'Angelo). His stay in Pisa in 1341-2 is documented: and in those years appeared the two great frescoes with the stories of Job, in the Camposanto there.

In 1347, he was commissioned to do the large polyptych for the Church of S. Giovanni Fuorcivitas in Pistoia. Records indicate that from 1349 to 1363 (in 1366 he was dead) he remained in Florence working for the city and for its provinces; he worked especially in the Valdelsa, executing the polyptych of Voltiggiano.... as well as the large Madonna and Child Enthroned of 1355 which was once in S. Lucchese in Poggibonsi and is now in the Uffizi Gallery in Florence. In his youth Taddeo executed the monumental Madonna and Child for Castelfiorentino. As Longhi has pointed out, Taddeo Gaddi intertwines high quality with the limits of conventional execution.....

from P. Dal Poggetto, p. 26, *Arte in Valdelsa*, Certaldo, 1963.

The most famous of Giotto's pupils and assistants. Already during his master's life time he had achieved an independent practice, his best-known early work being the decoration of the Baroncelli Chapel in Santa Croce, Florence, begun in 1332. Through him the style of Giotto was transmitted to numerous Florentine painters of the second half of the century. The somewhat vestigial nature of Giotto's influence, however, should be stressed. Taddeo Gaddi's later development tended to be towards a more decorative and Gothic approach, which was perhaps owed to Daddi, and it was this aspect of his art which is carried to greater lengths by his son Agnolo.....

from St. J. Gore, p. 7, *Art of Painting in Florence & Siena from 1250-1500*, London, 1965.

Florentine School. Active c. 1330-66. He was a pupil of Giotto and is said to have worked with him for many years. Best known are his frescoes in the Baroncelli Chapel, Santa Croce, Florence. In his panel paintings, especially, he follows the monumental conception of Giotto modified by the flowing line and gentle expression of Bernardo Daddi.

from F. R. Shapley, p. 23, *Paintings from the Samuel H. Kress Collection*, London, 1966.

" Taddeo Gaddi was a pupil of Giotto and a man of great invention who painted very many chapels and murals " (Ghiberti). He was also the most outstanding member of a family of Florentine artists active for the greater part of the fourteenth century, and unlike many of the " giotteschi ", has always enjoyed a reputation independent of his master. His hand can be traced in works from the studio of Giotto, although the first of his signed and dated works known today is a triptych of 1334 in the Kaiser Friedrich Museum, Berlin. He must have been established earlier, however; in 1327 he was admitted to the guild of Medici e Speziali, only slightly later than Giotto and his own father, Gaddo di Zanobi. In 1332 he received an important commission to paint frescoes showings scenes from the life of the Virgin in the Baroncelli Chapel of Sta. Croce, and completed these by 1338. Soon afterwards he worked in the churches of S. Miniato al Monte, Florence, and San Francesco, Pisa, and 1347-53 painted a polyptych for the church of S. Giovanni Fuorcivitas in Pistoia. A Madonna and Child from the church of S. Lucchese, Poggibonsi, signed and dated 1355, is now in the Uffizi, and a series of panels from the doors of a sacristy cupboard in Sta. Croce are distributed between Florence (Accademia), Berlin and Munich. In 1363 Gaddi painted a fresco, now lost, in the Mercanzia Vecchia, and is last mentioned in 1366.....

from P. Dal Poggetto, p. 66, *Frescoes from Florence*, London, 1969.

BIBLIOGRAPHY
BOOKS

An asterisk indicates a work listed in the General Bibliography

Pini, Milanesi*, 1876, Vol. I, no 1; *Venturi, A.**, 1907, pp. 523-52; *Khv & Salmi**, 1914, pp. 14-17; *v. Marle 1924**, pp. 301-2; *Berenson, 1932**, pp. 214-16; *Catalogo della Mostra del Tesoro di Firenze Sacra*, Florence, 1933, p. 118; *Offner, 1934**, Sec. III, Vol. IV, pp. 51, 78, 82, 96, 140, 208; Salvini, R., *L'arte di Agnolo Gaddi*, Florence, 1936, pp. 2, 9, 20-23; Sinibaldi, G., and Brunetti, G., *M. Giottesca**, 1943, pp. 429-63; *Coletti, Vol. II**, 1946, pp. 45-7, p. xlvi; *Antal**, 1948, pp. 174-6; *Vavalà, 1948**, pp. 59-63; *Galetti**, 1950, " F-O ", pp. 1013-16; *Toesca, 1951**, pp. 617-21; Oertel, R., *Die Frühzeit der Italienischen Malerei*, Stuttgart, 1953, pp. 117, 226; Baldini, U., *MAS I**, 1957, pp. 46-7; *Offner, 1958**, Sec. III, Vol. VIII, p. 116; *Camposanto**, 1960, pp. 93-102; *Borsook, 1960**, pp. 131-2; *Cracow**, 1961, pp. 45-46; *Berenson, 1963**, Vol. I, pp. 69-71; Dal Poggetto, P., *AIV**, 1963, pp. 26-7; Gore, St J., *Wildenstein**, 1965, pp. 7-8; *Marcucci**, 1965, pp. 56-68; Bianchini, M. A., *Maso di Banco* (I Maestri del Colore, 247), Milan, 1966; Boskovits, M., *La Scuola di Giotto* (I Maestri del Colore, 248), Milan, 1966; Donati, P. P., *Taddeo Gaddi* (I Diamanti dell'arte, 12), Florence, 1966; Procacci, U., *Catalogo della Mostra di Firenze ai tempi di Dante*, Florence, 1966, p. 102; Rossi, F., *Il Museo Horne a Firenze*, Milan, 1966, p. 135; *Shapley, 1966**, pp. 23-24; *Dal Poggetto**. 1967, pp. 35-8; Baldini, U., and Dal Poggetto, P., *Fresco Show*, 1968, pp. 72-7, (66-9); Gnudi, C., *L'Europe Gothique XII-XIV siècles*, Paris, 1968, pp. 194-5; *MMOA**, 1971, pp. 22-25.

JOURNALS

Sirèn, O., *AA*, VI, 1916, pp. 207-23; Sirèn, O., *BM*, 48, 1926, pp. 185-6; Hendy, P., *BM*, 52, 1928, pp. 284-95; Hendy, P., *BM*, 53, 1928, pp. 17-23; Toesca, P., *A*, XXXIII, 1930, pp. 5-15; Offner, R., *BM*, 63, 1933, p. 84; Procacci, U., *RA*, XV, 1933, pp. 224-44; Mather, R. G., *A*, XXXIX, 1936, pp. 50-64; Salmi, M., *E.*, LXXXVI, 7, 1937, pp. 349-64; Steinweg, K., *RA*, XIX, I, 1937, pp. 36-44; Marchini, G., *RA*, XX, 1938, pp. 215-41; Oertel, R., *MKIF*, V, 4/5, 1940, pp. 217-314; Procacci, U., *A*, II, XVIII, 1940, p. 45; *Edit.*, *AN*, 44, 1946, p. 36; Gronau,

H. D., *BM*, XCII, 1950, p. 322; Toesca, I., *PA*, I, 3, 1950, pp. 48-9; Baldini, L., *BA*, XXXVII, 4, 1952, pp. 173-174; Longhi, R., *PA*, III, 31, 1952, p. 23; Moriondo, M., *BA*, XXXVII, 4, 1952, pp. 51-3; de Tolnay, C., *RDA*, II, 3, 1952, pp. 151-2; Longhi, R., *PA*, VI, 65, 1955, pp. 32-6; Cohn, W., *BA*, XLI, 1956, pp. 174, 6; Gandolfo G., *NCA*, III, 13-14, 1956, pp. 32-55; S. p., *E*, CXXVI, 10, 1957, pp. 61-8; Longhi, R., *PA*, IX, 109, 1959, pp. 31-40; Longhi, R., *PA*, IX, 111, 1959, pp. 3-12; Marcucci, L., *MKIF*, IX, 3-4, 1960, pp. 141-58; Parronchi, A., *PA*, 1961, XII, 137, pp. 19-26; Borsook, E., *RA*, XXXVI, 1961-2, pp. 89-107; de Tolnay, C., *RA*, XXVI, 1961-2, pp. 3-10; Telpaz, A. M., *AB*, 46, 1964, p. 373-4; Mallory, M., *AB*, 46, 1964, p. 533; Becker, M. B., *AB*, 46, 1964, pp. 376-7; Steinweg, K., *MKIF*, XI, 2/3, 1964, pp. 194-200; Zeri, F., *BM*, CVII, 1965, p. 252; Bellosi, L., *PA*, XVII, 201/21, 1966, p. 78; Herrmann, F., *CS*, 165, 665, 1967, p. 154; Baldini, U., *La Nazione*, 1967, Dec. 6; De Benedictis, C., *AV*, 3, 1967, p. 43; Denny, D., *WCJ*, XXX, 1967, p. 146; Conti, A., *PA*, XIX, 225/45, 1968, pp. 10-20; Fahy, E., *BCMA*, LVI, 10, 1969, p. 349; Van Os, H. W., *Sim*, 4, 1970, 1, pp. 10-11; Ragghianti, C. L., *CA*, XVI, 101-102, 1969, pp. 3-80; Venturoli, P., *SDA*, 1-2, 1969, pp. 142-58; Serra, J. R., *C*, XX, 1-2, 1969, pp. 26-27; Smart, A., *AP*, XCI, 96, 1970, p. 164; Winner, M., *ZKG*, XXXIII, 4, 1970, p. 341; Gardner, J., *ZKG*, XXXIV, 2, 1971, pp. 89-114; Polzer, J., *JBM*, XIII, 1971, p. 52; Skaug, E., *MKIF*, XV, 2, 1971, pp. 141, 157-158; Boskovits, M., *MKIF*, XVII, 2-3, 1973, pp. 205, 12.

SIGNED AND DATED WORKS

1334 Berlin, Dahlem Staatliche Museen 1079-81. Portable tryptych: Madonna & Child Enthroned with Saints. s & d. (fig. 152).

1336 Rome, Castel S. Angelo, Museo. Portable triptych: Madonna & Child Enthroned with Saints. d. (fig. 151).

1355 Florence, Depositi 3. Panel: Madonna & Child Enthroned with Angels and Saints. s & d. (fig. 143).

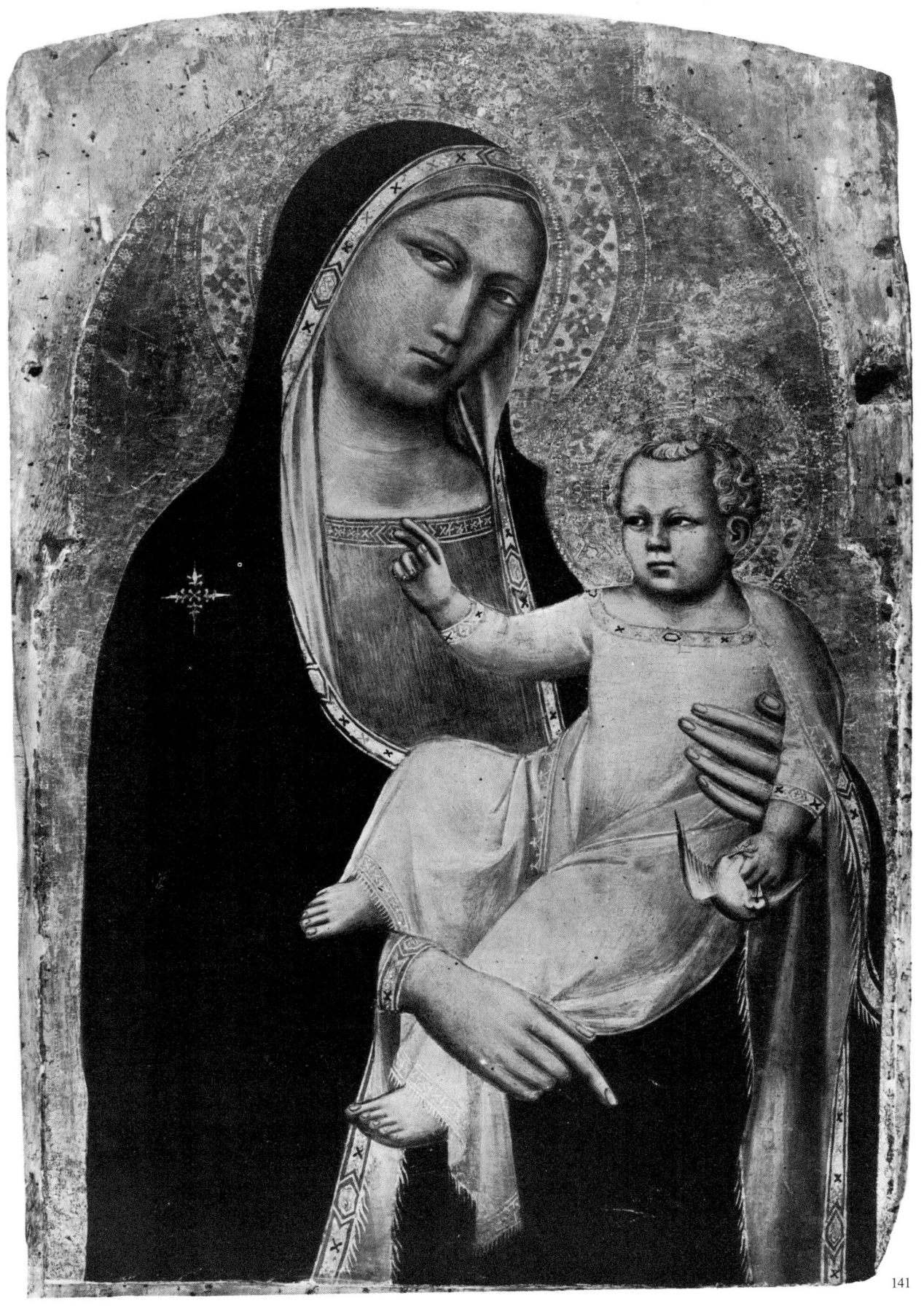

141

141. *Madonna and Child. Panel. Le Rose (Tavarnuzze, 8 kms south of Florence). S. Lorenzo. 95 × 60. SGF 26970.*

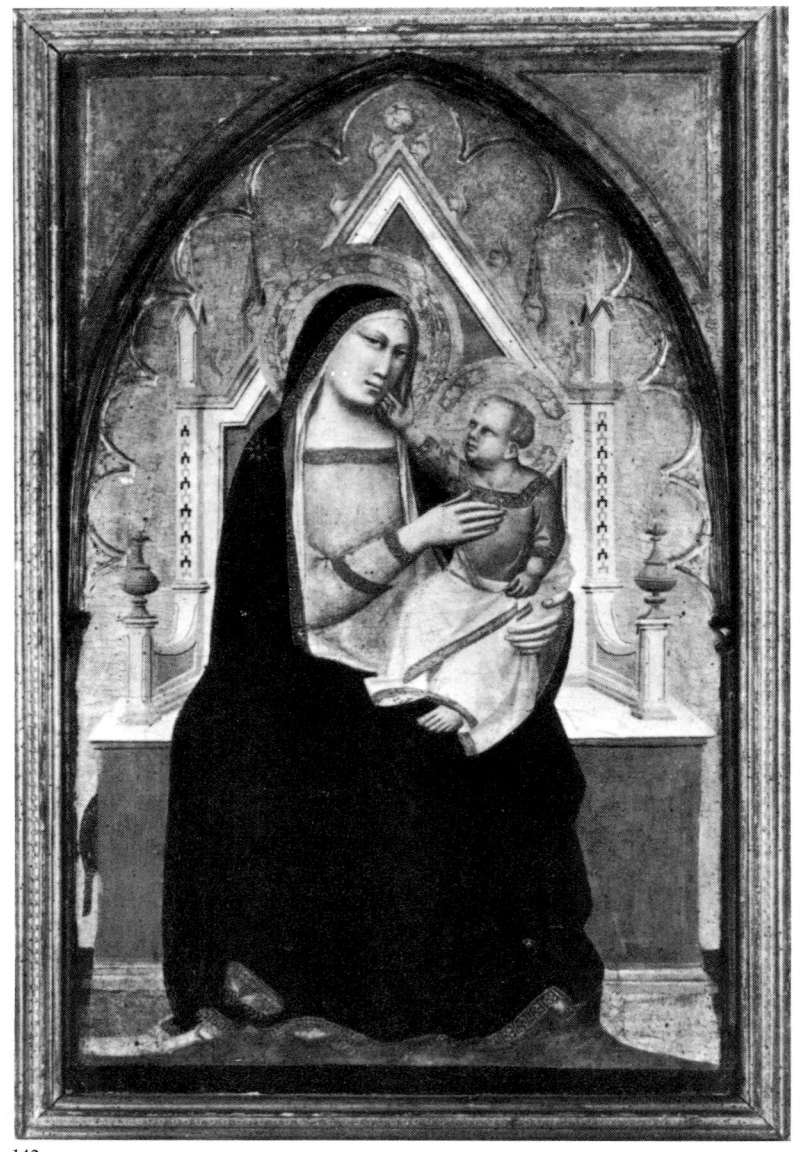

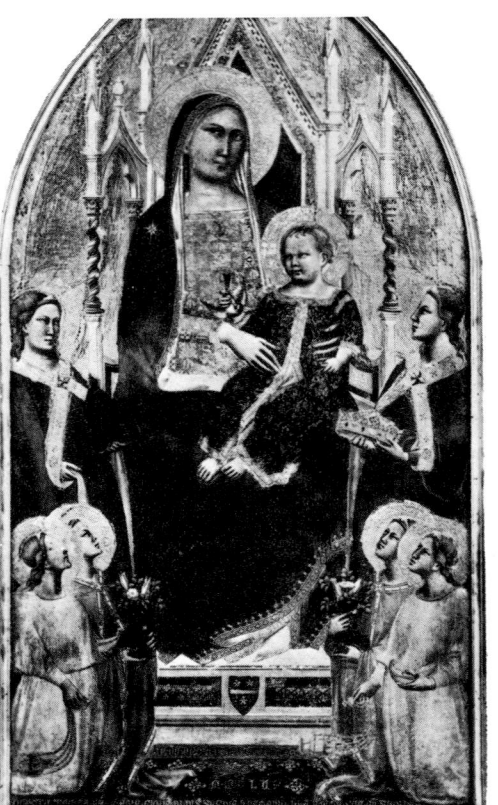

143

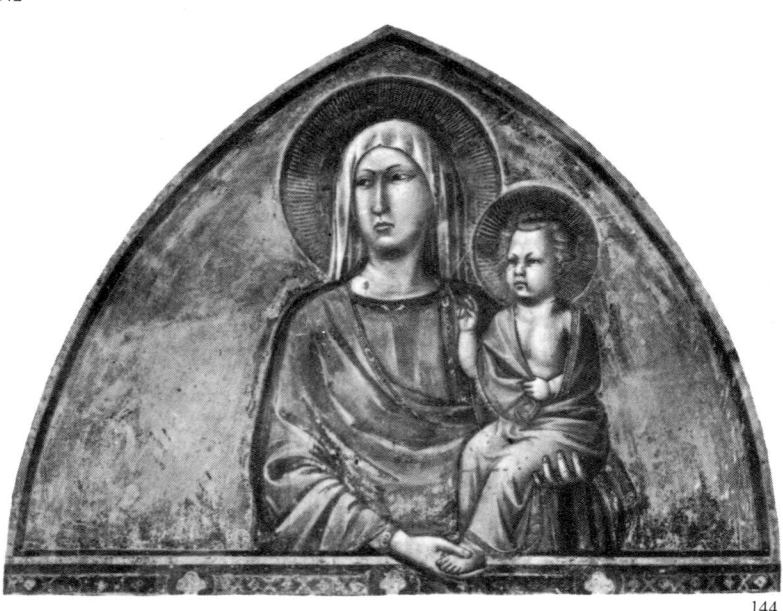

144

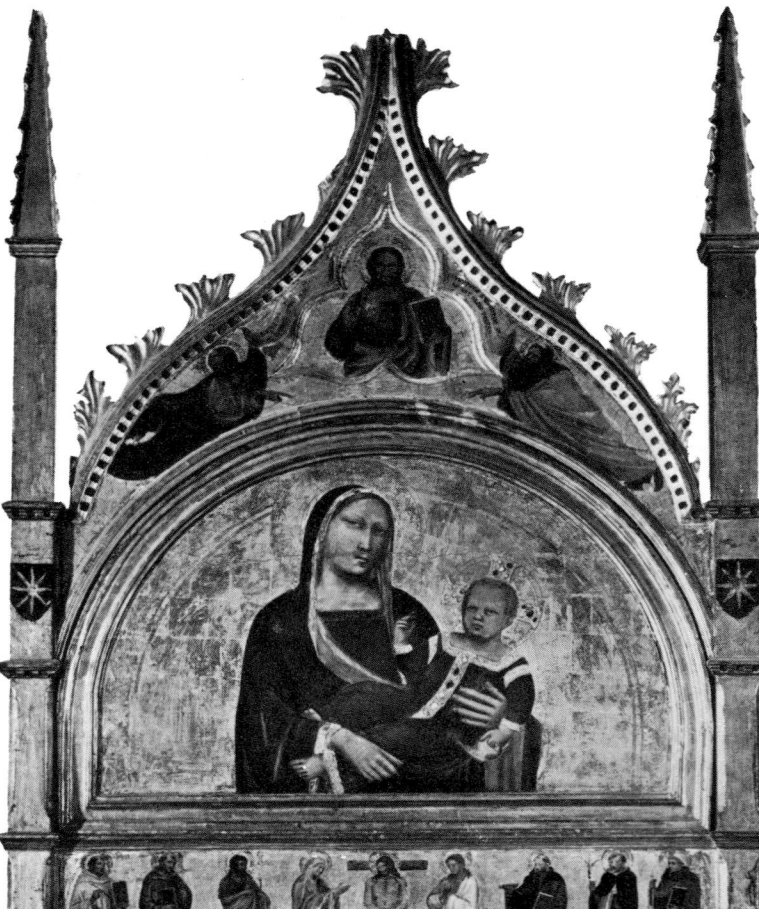

145

142. *Madonna and Child Enthroned. Panel. New Haven (Conn.), Yale University Art Gallery, Bequest of Maitland F. Griggs, 1896. no. 1943.205. 85.7 × 52.7. Museum photo.*

143. *Madonna and Child Enthroned with four Angels and two female Saints. Panel. Florence, Uffizi, Depositi. no. 3. 154 × 80. Alinari 9899. s & d. 1355.*

144. *Madonna and Child. Fresco. Florence, S. Croce, Baroncelli Tomb. SGF 117251. 1328.*

145. *Madonna and Child. (Above and predella by another hand). Panel. Florence, Accademia. no. 448. 159.5 × 127. Alinari 30510.*

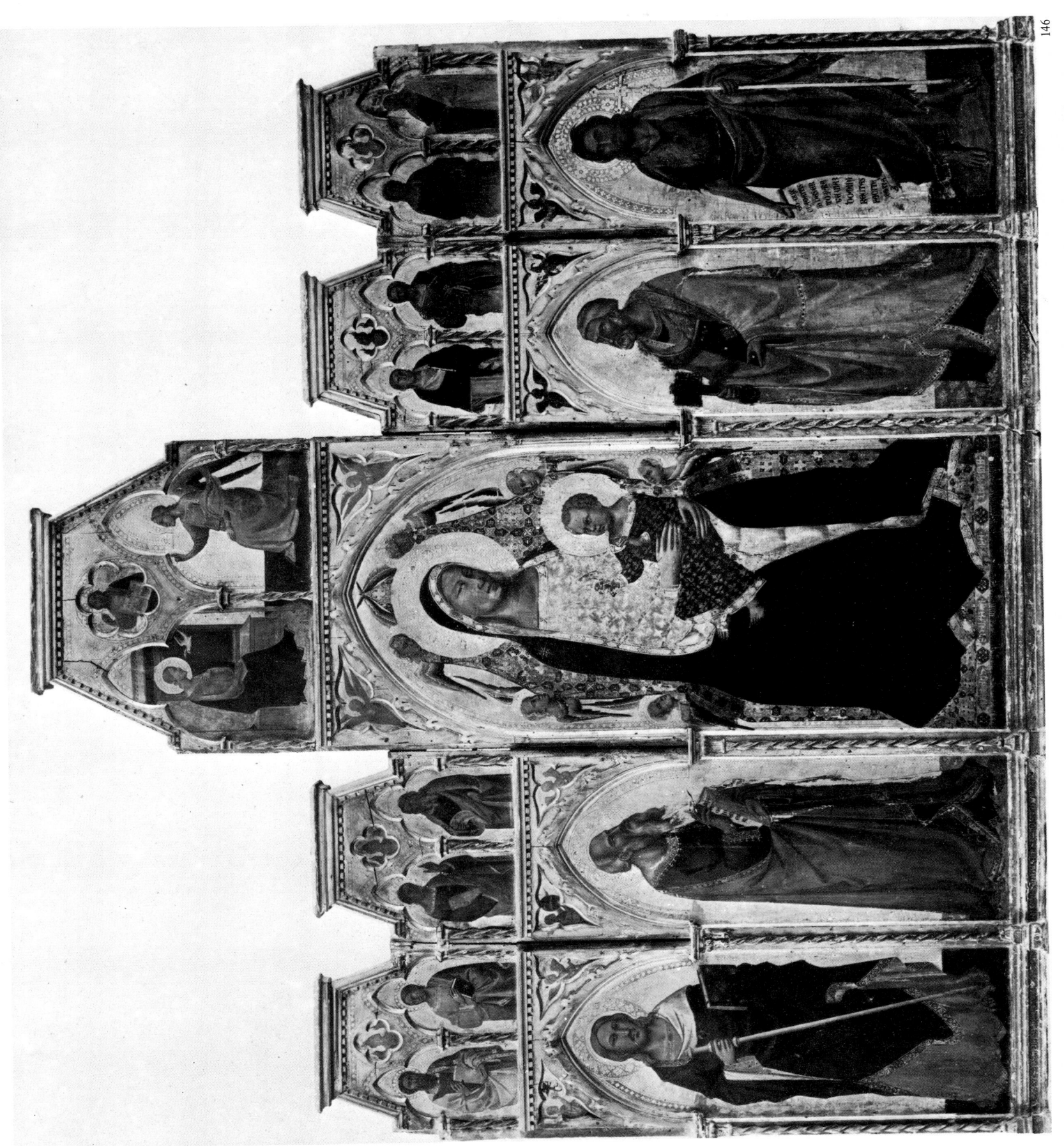

146. *Polyptych: Madonna and Child Enthroned with six Angels, Sts James, John the Evangelist, Peter and John the Baptist. Above: Christ blessing, Annunciation, eight Saints. Panel. Pistoia, S. Giovanni Fuorcivitas. 215 × 245. SGF 26963. 1353.*

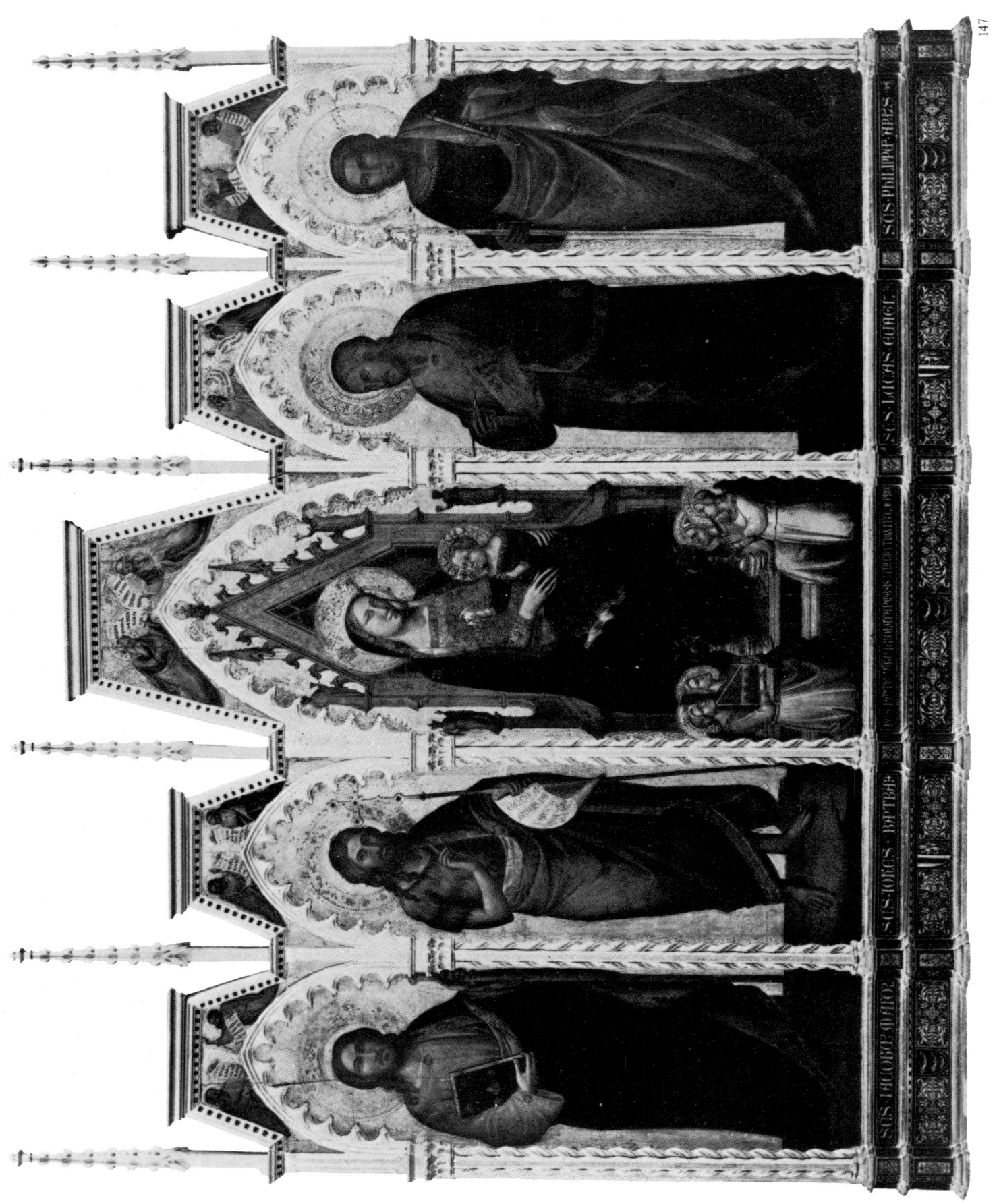

147. *Polyptych : Madonna and Child Enthroned with four Angels, Sts James, John the Baptist, Luke and Philip. Above : ten Prophets. Panel. Florence,*
S. Felicita. 212 × 270. SGF 26966.

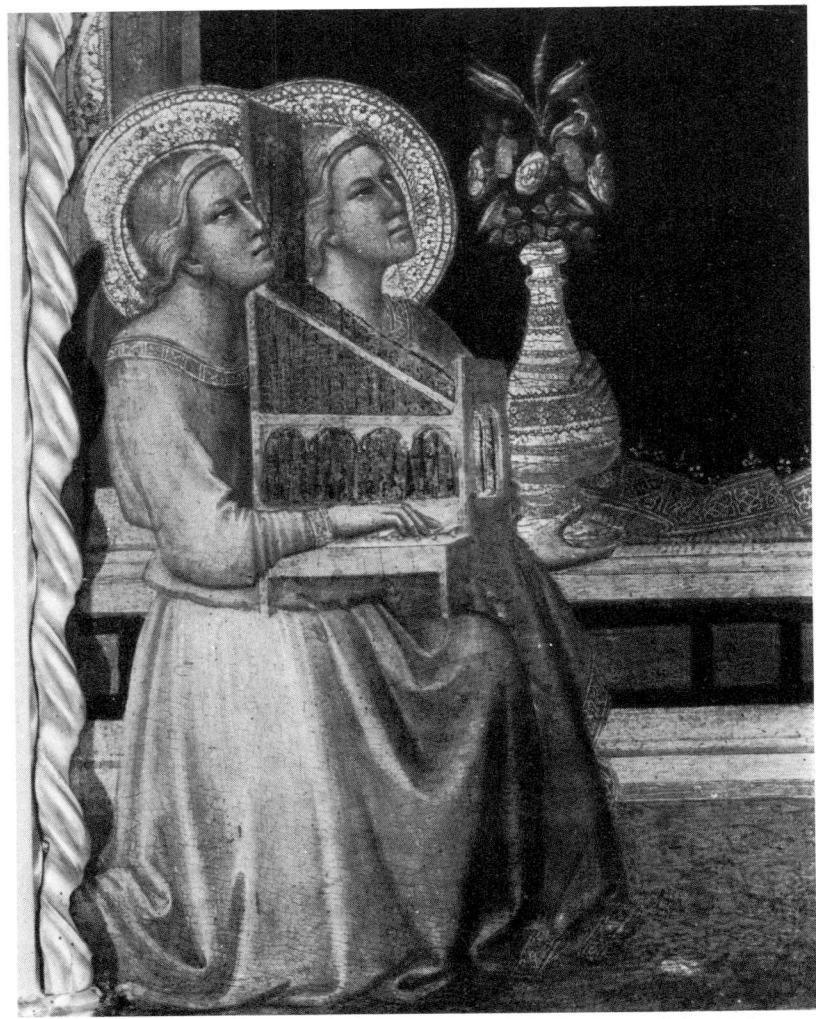

148

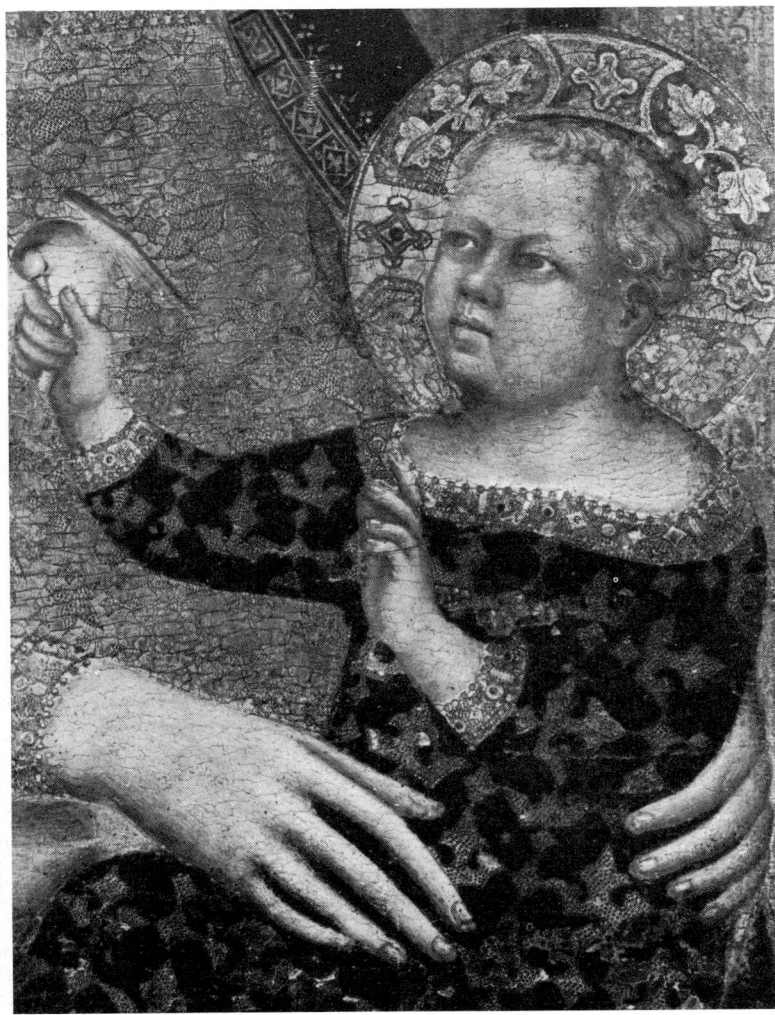

149

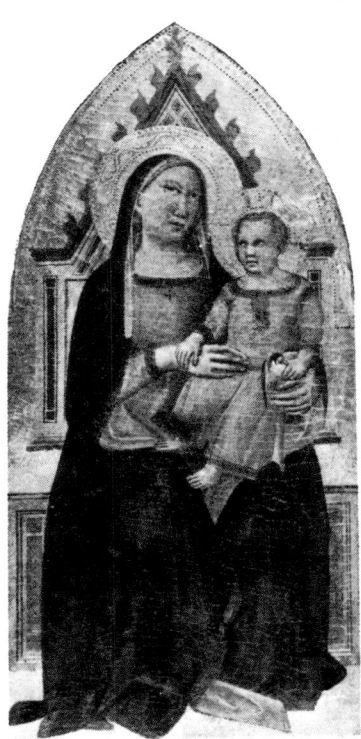

150

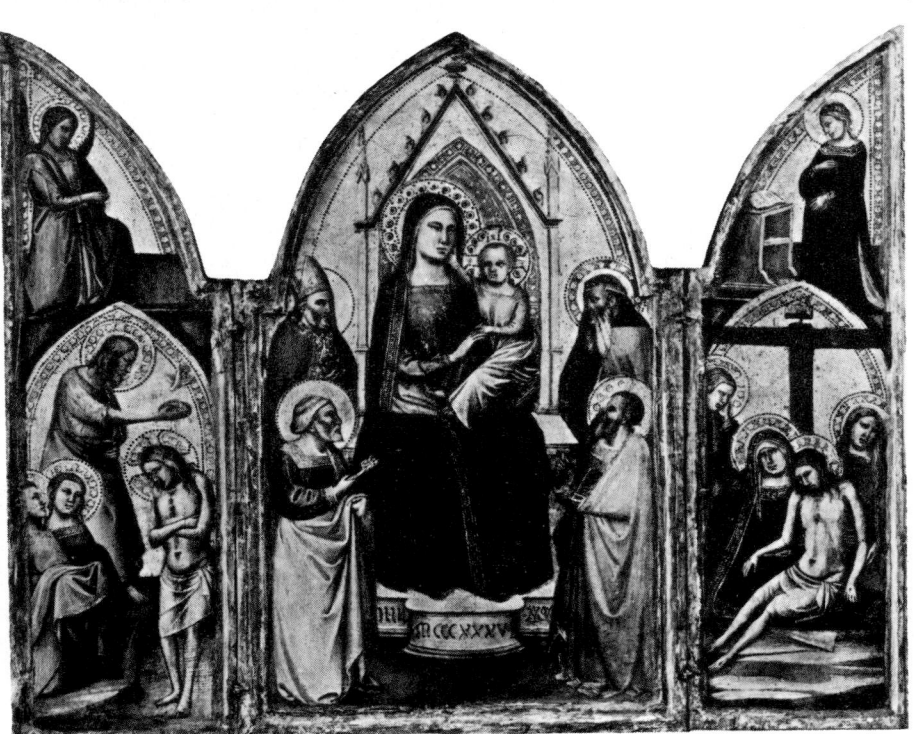

151

148. *Two Angels, detail of fig. 147. Panel. Florence, S. Felicita. SGF 49868.*
149. *Christ Child, detail of fig. 147. Panel. Florence, S. Felicita. SGF 49868.*
150. *Madonna and Child Enthroned. Panel. Paris, Musées Nationaux, Campana Collection. Campana 31. 80 × 36. Giraudon LA 23010.*
151. *Portable triptych: Madonna and Child Enthroned with Sts Peter, Paul, Anthony Abbot and a Bishop Saint, Baptism of Christ, Lamentation.*
  Above: Annunciation. Panel. Rome, Museo di Castel S. Angelo. no. III/38. 62 × 53. Anderson 26615. d. 1336.

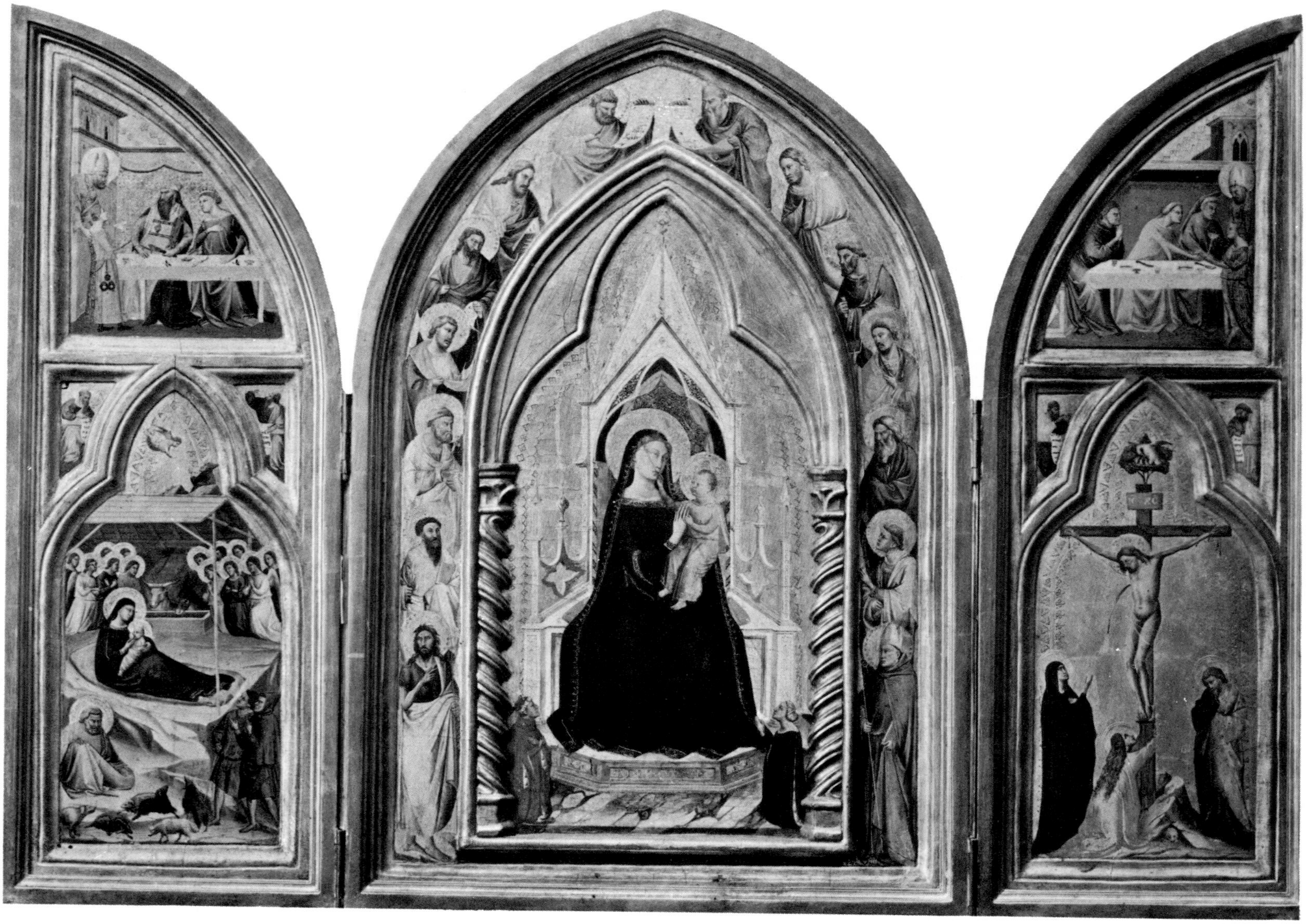

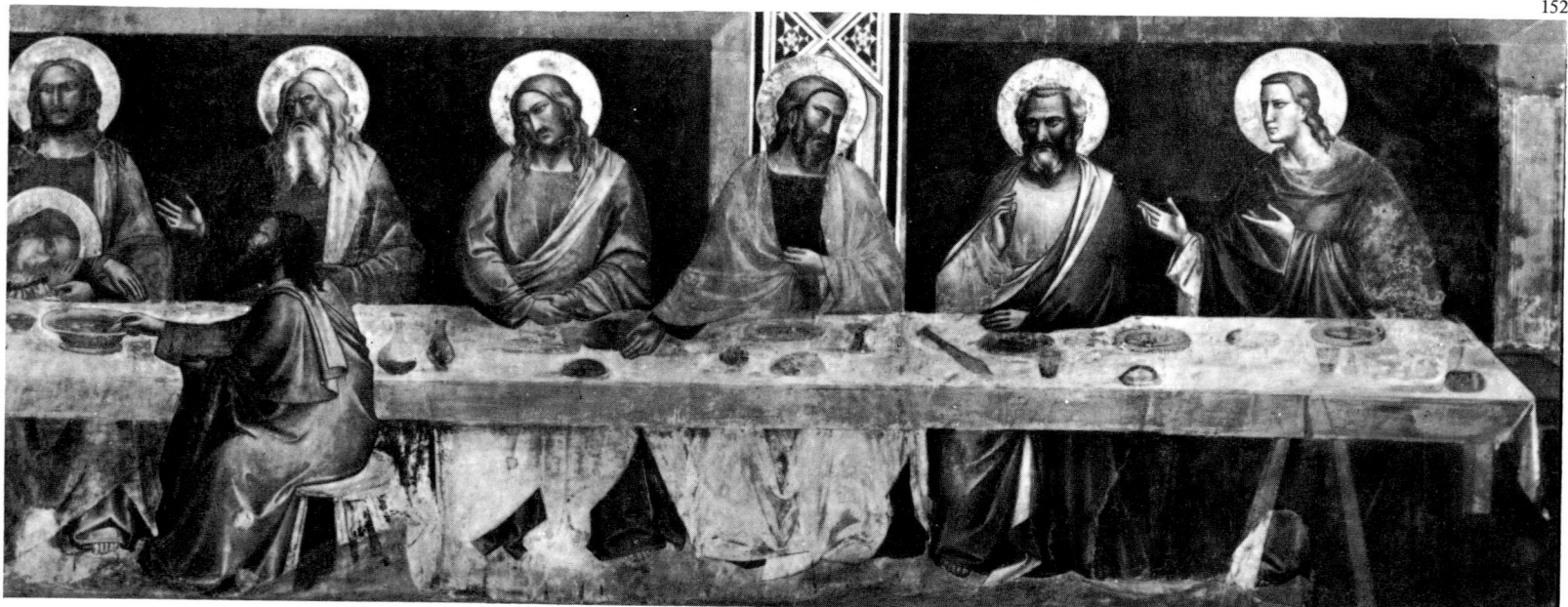

152. *Portable triptych: Madonna and Child Enthroned with fourteen Saints; St Nicholas rescuing Adeodatus from the Service of the Pagan King; Nativity. Panel. Berlin, Dahlem Staatliche Museen. no. 1079-81. cp: 61 × 38; sps: 62 × 21. Museum photo: Steinkopf. s & d. 1334.*

153. *Detail of the Last Supper. Fresco. Florence, S. Croce, Museo dell'Opera di S. Croce. Alinari 4584.*

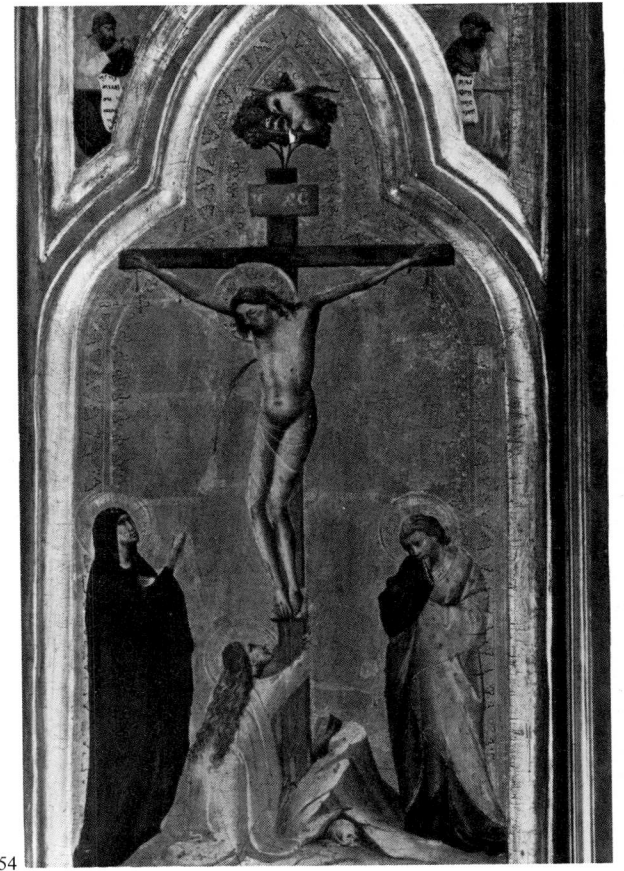

154

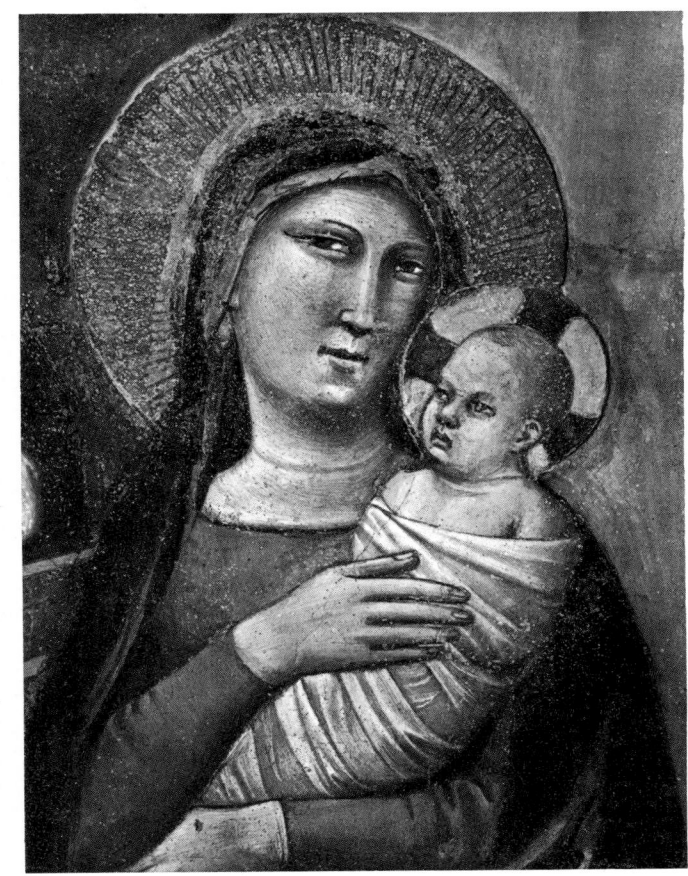

155

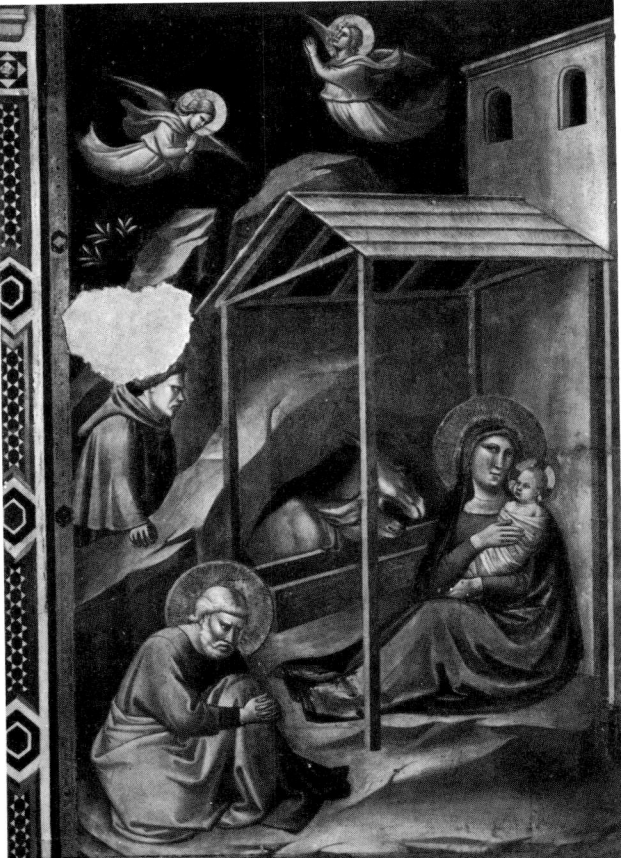

156

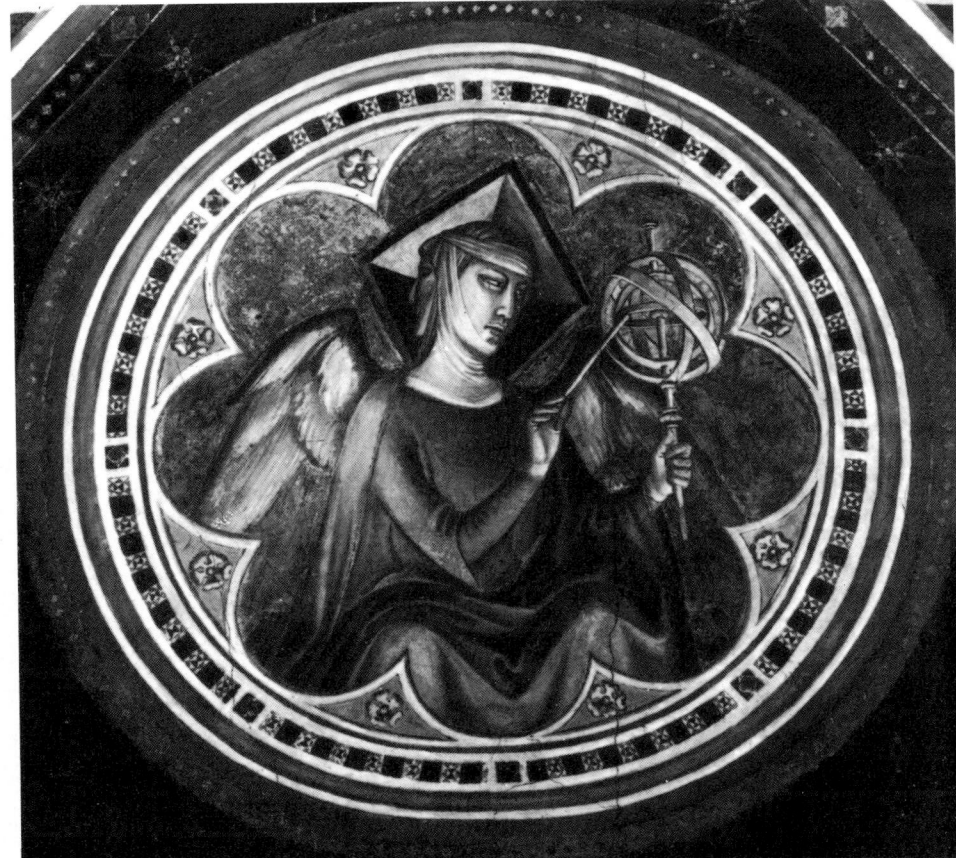

157

154. *Christ on the Cross with the Virgin, Sts John the Evangelist and Mary Magdalene, detail of fig. 152. Panel. Berlin, Dahlem, Staatliche Museen. no. 1079-81. Museum photo: Steinkopf. s & d. 1334.*
155. *Scenes from the Life of the Virgin: Virgin and Child, detail of fig. 156. Fresco. Florence, S. Croce, Baroncelli Chapel. SGF 119362. 1332-38.*
156. *Scenes from the Life of the Virgin: Nativity of Christ. Fresco. Florence, S. Croce, Baroncelli Chapel. SGF 119361. 1332-38.*
157. *Scenes from the Life of the Virgin: a Virtue. Fresco. Florence, S. Croce, Baroncelli Chapel. SGF 119325. 1332-38.*

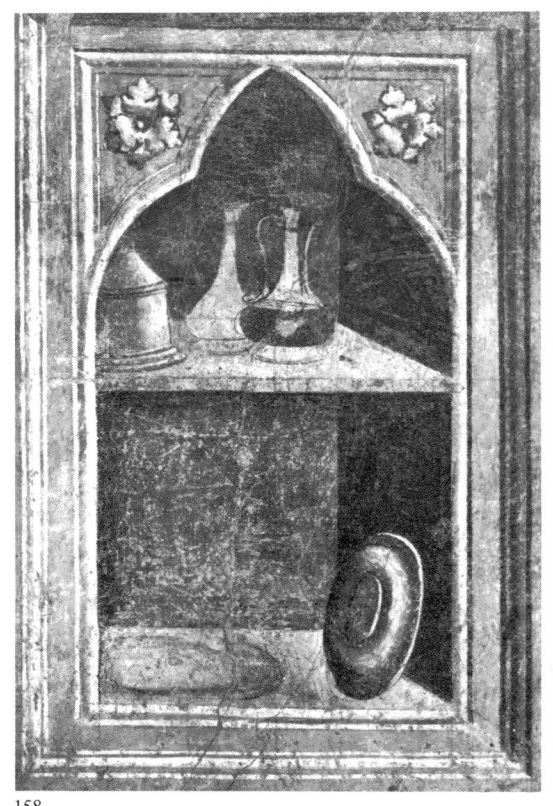

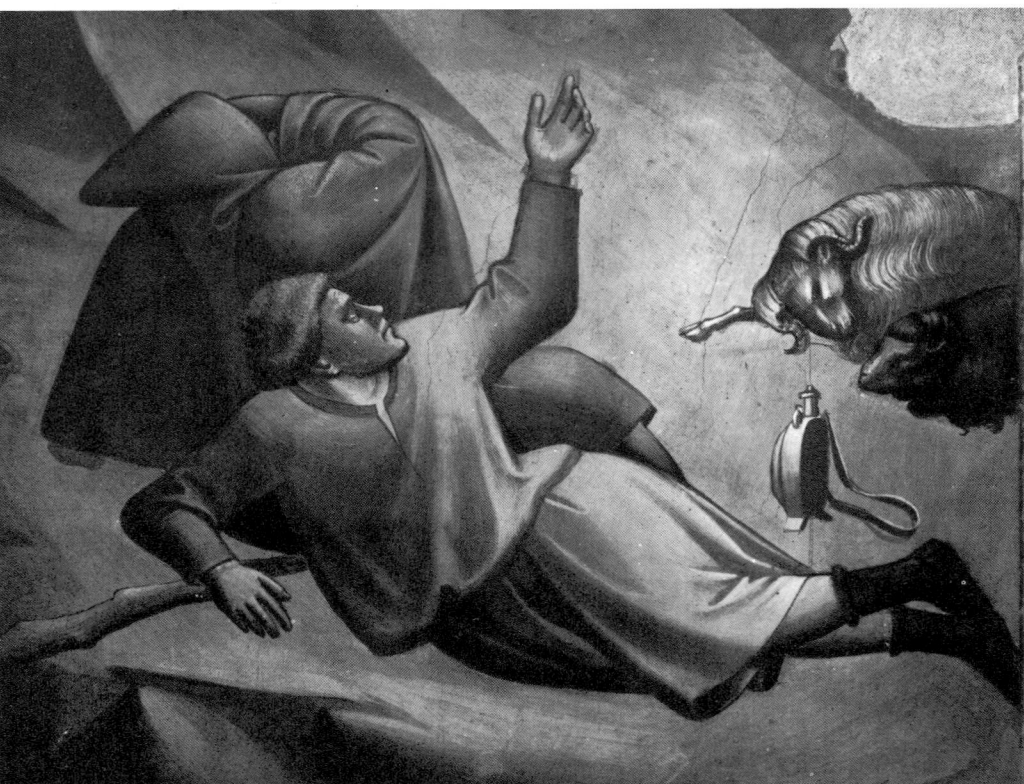

158

159

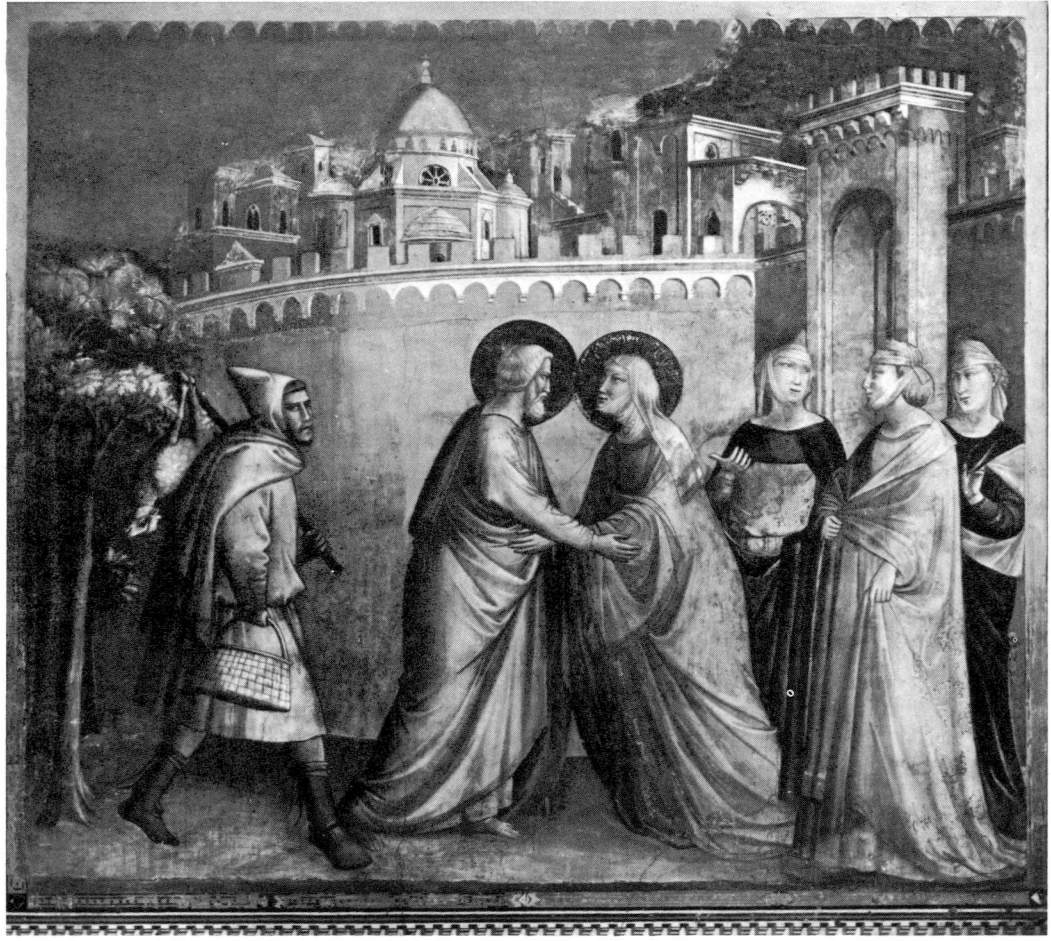

160

158.   Scenes from the Life of the Virgin: Still Life. Fresco. Florence, S. Croce, Baroncelli Chapel. SGF 119350. 1332-38.
159.   Scenes from the Life of the Virgin: Shepherd and Sheep, detail. Fresco. Florence, S. Croce, Baroncelli Chapel. SGF 119359. 1332-38.
160.   Scenes from the Life of the Virgin: Meeting at the Golden Gate.   Fresco. Florence, S. Croce, Baroncelli Chapel. Alinari 3897. 1332-38.

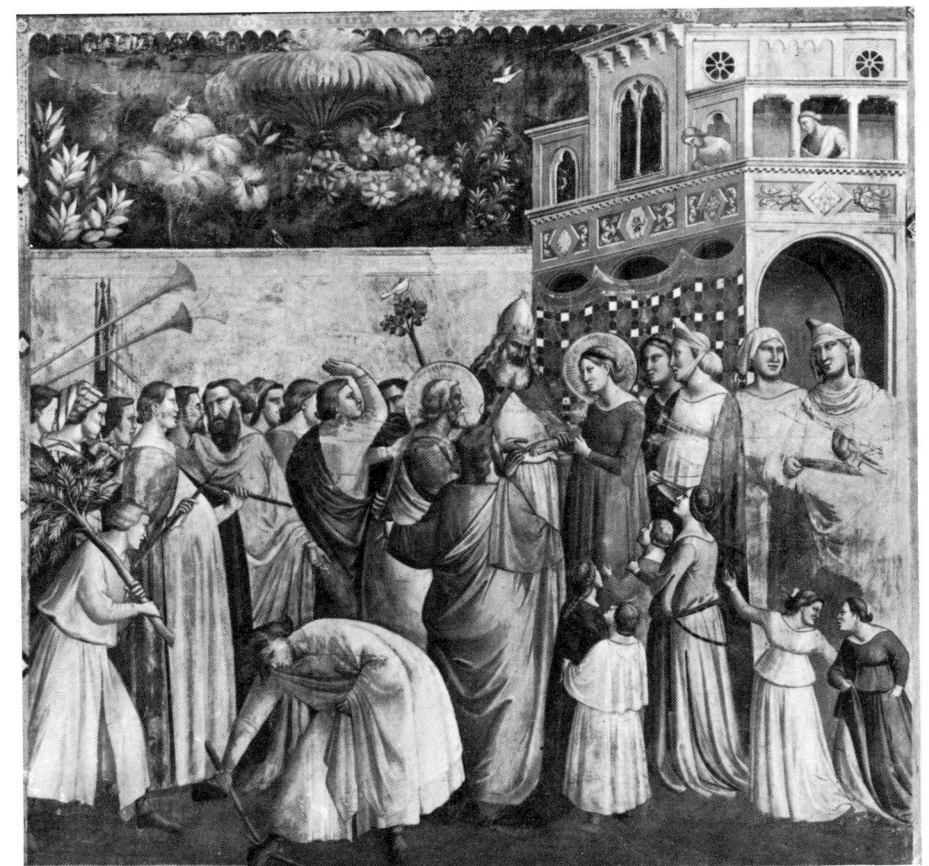

161

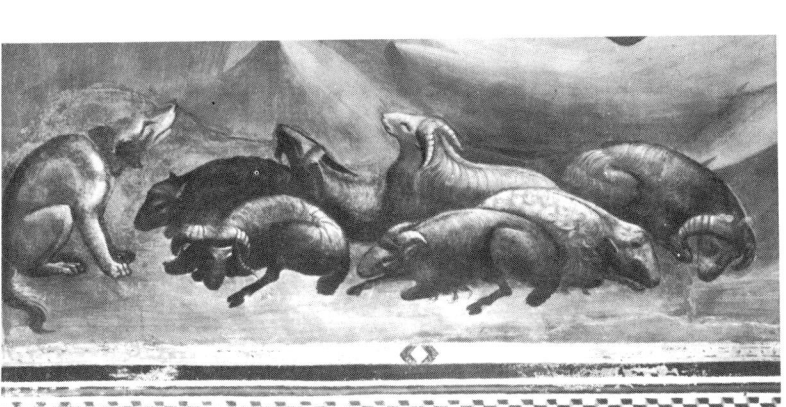

162

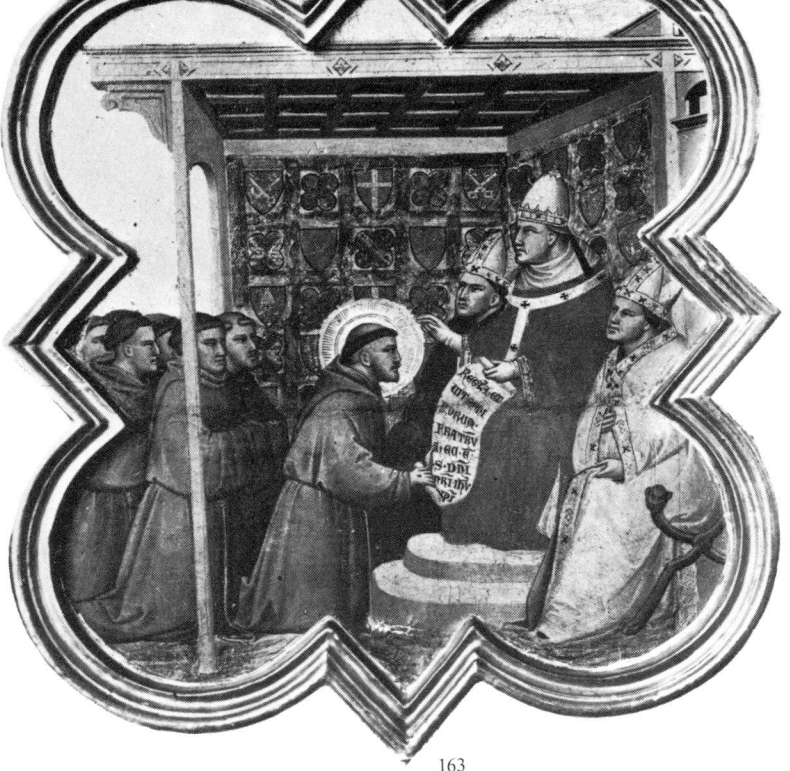

163

161. *Scenes from the Life of the Virgin: Marriage of the Virgin. Fresco. Florence, S. Croce, Baroncelli Chapel. Alinari 3900. 1332-38.*
162. *Scenes from the Life of the Virgin: Dog and Sheep, detail. Fresco. Florence. S. Croce, Baroncelli Chapel. SGF 119360. 1332-38.*
163. *Confirmation of the Rule of St Francis. Panel. Florence, Accademia. 41 × 36.5. SGF 27045.*

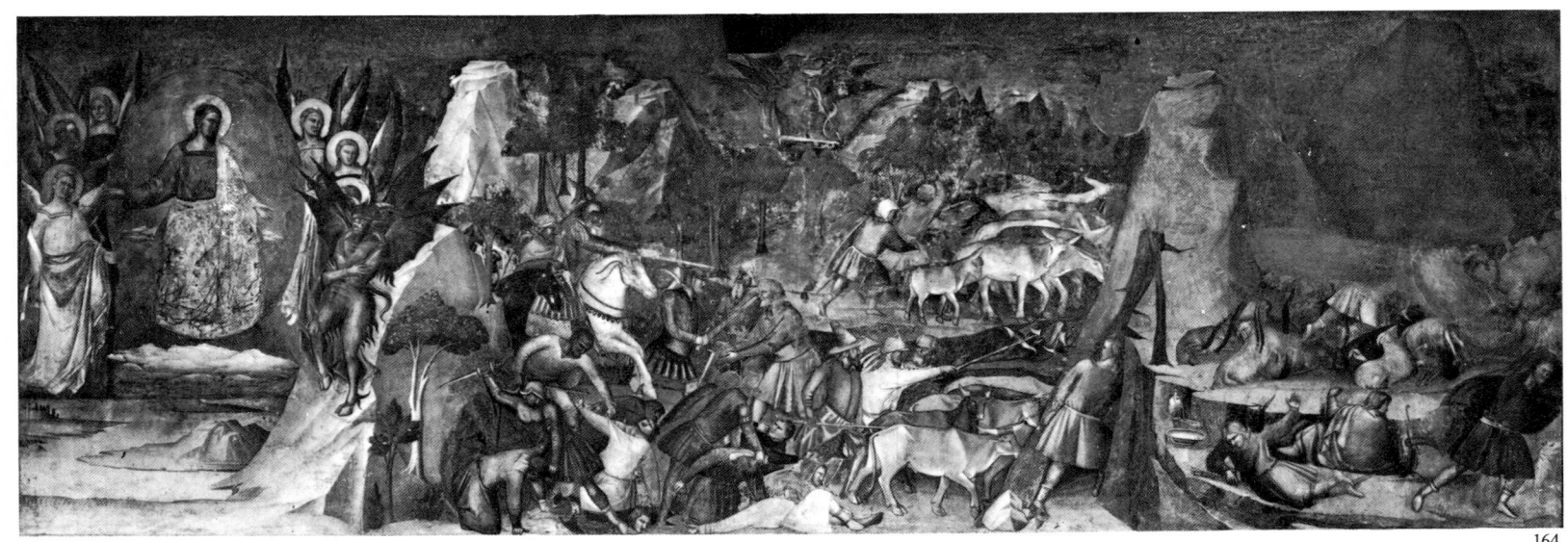

164

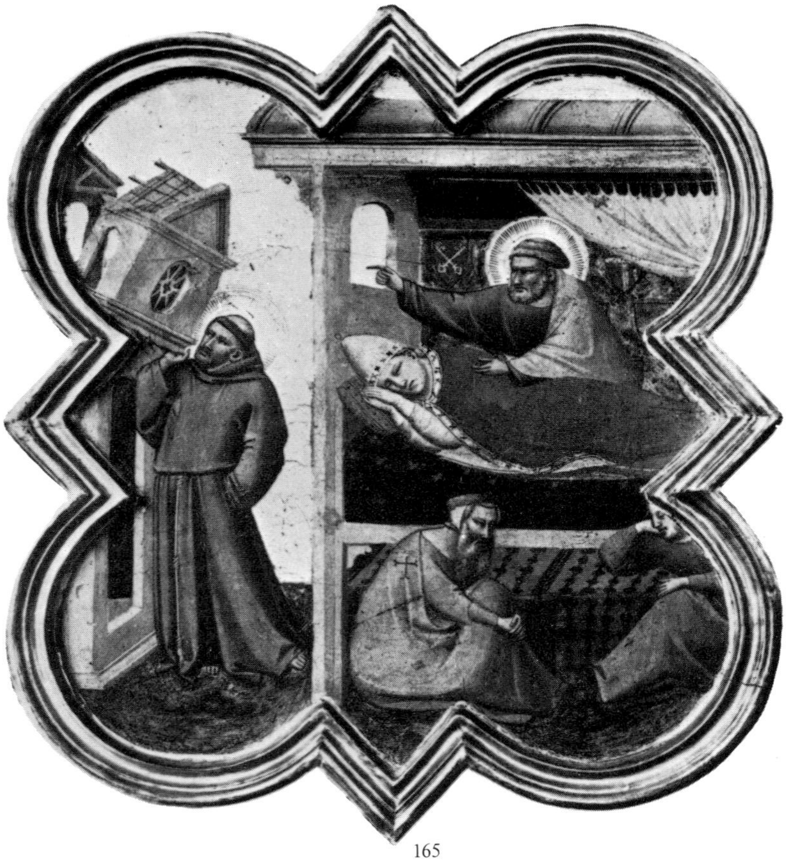

165

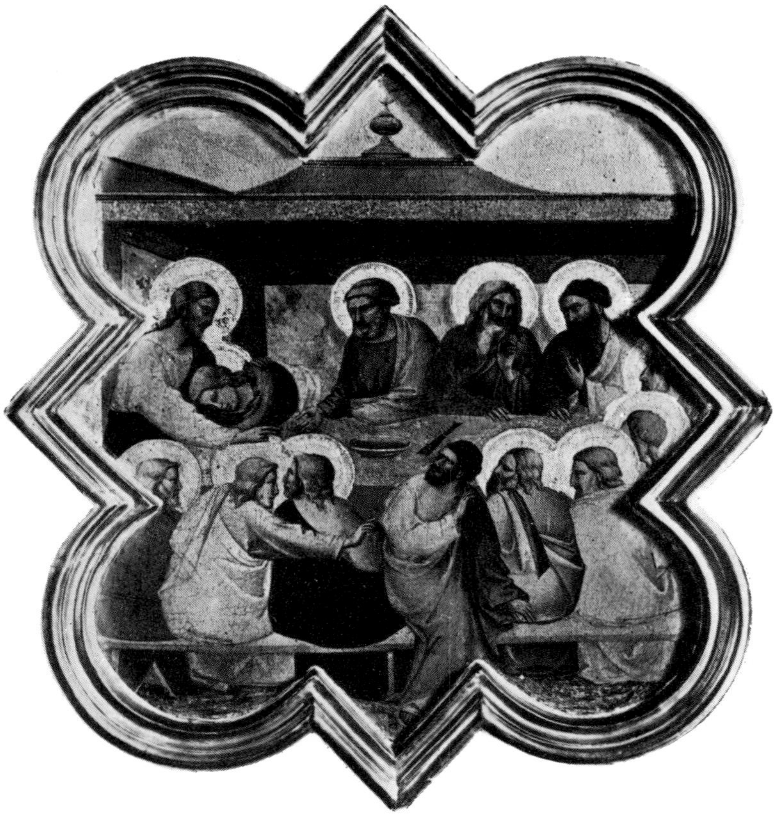

166

164. *Story of Job. Fresco. Pisa, Camposanto. Alinari 8772.*
165. *Dream of Innocent III. Panel. Florence, Accadèmia. 41 × 36.5. SGF 27041.*
166. *Scenes from the Life of Christ: Last Supper. Panel. Florence, Accademia. 40.5 × 36.5. SGF 27035.*

PUCCIO di SIMONE
(MASTER OF THE FABRIANO ALTARPIECE)

Among Daddi's numerous flock, the Master of the Fabriano Altarpiece was surely one of the youngest and gentlest of his lambs. He bleats a high note, which, while it occasionally drops, is maintained with fair consistency throughout his activity. At its best his work is shot through with a winsome, sunny lyricism rare in the period and of a particular variety that made its first Italian appearance with Daddi's early works. Our painter's color, like his humor, is pitched in an upper key and, where the subject permits it, he revels in an even blond tonality that breaks into golden lights. Although as far as we know he limited himself to sacred themes, like Daddi and the other painters of the miniaturist tendency, the Fabriano Master inclined by natural disposition to the more personal side of human behavior. But it was with a special bias that he approached it. With the large body of painting in the great religious periods, the figures have the contained and fateful air of persons who harbor some prodigious purpose. Their outward actions, accordingly, are discharged as if by temporary concession to the business in hand. Our master, on the contrary, makes the conduct of his figures explicitly relevant to the moment by showing them alive to each other's mental and physical presence. Even in his larger works, chiefly Madonna and Child subjects, they manifest a sensitive responsiveness rather than the mystical quiescence of conventional holiness.....

> from R. Offner, p. 142, *A Critical and Historical Corpus of Florentine Painting*, Sec. III, Vol. V, New York, 1957.

The personality of the Master of the Fabriano Altarpiece, as Offner named him, or of Puccio di Simone as Longhi more precisely identified him has been set out by the latter..... In the triptych of 1346, now in the National Gallery of Art in Washington, Offner recognized the presence of two distinct hands, one of the fine painter from the Marches, Allegretto Nuzi, and the other of an anonymous Florentine. To this latter, Offner transferred the principle body of works, which Berenson had attributed to the early years of Allegretto Nuzi, and added many of his own new attributions (among them the polyptych of Petrognano)..... More recently however, Longhi proposed to identify this anonymous master as Puccio di Simone. He based this identification on the strict stylistic agreement between the group and the two signed works of this artist: a Madonna with Child once in the Artaud de Montor Collection, in Paris, reproduced in an engraving in the old catalogue of the collection, as well as in Offner's catalogue of the " Maestro dell'Altare di Fabriano "; and a signed triptych in the Museum of the Accademia of Florence. These works are alike and seem to come from the same cultural environment. The painter joins elegant descriptive motifs, loose and articulate, like those of Bernardo Daddi, with the chromatically solemn treatment of forms which, as in the painting of Maso, dominate the composition and expand the space behind.
Puccio di Simone can be counted among the major artists of the second generation of the Florentine '300, the generation that began ten years after Maso, Taddeo Gaddi and Bernardo Daddi, and that saw the Orcagna family as celebrated masters.....

> from P. Dal Poggetto, p. 28, *Arte in Valdelsa*, Certaldo, 1963.

The identity of the master was established by Offner. His style bears the stamp of Daddi's *atelier* in the late 1330's and early 1340's; later he came strongly under the influence of the Cioni, Andrea and Nardo, whose own style was founded upon that of Daddi. Allegretto Nuzi, to whom paintings have been attributed which Offner considers to be by the Fabriano Master, was probably his junior. Recently Longhi has identified the master with Puccio di Simone (documented 1343/6-c. 1362), the author of a signed altarpiece in the Accademia, Florence.....

> from St. J. Gore, p. 5, *The Art of Painting in Florence and Siena from 1250-1500*, London, 1965.

Puccio di Simone was unquestionably trained in Daddi's shop, in the last years of that master's activity, probably just before 1340. He must have become one of Daddi's main collaborators, as Puccio's style can be recognized in some of Daddi's late works. The personality of Puccio was based by Longhi on the Accademia polyptych and the Artaud de Montor Madonna dated 1350 and signed by a " Puccino "; with those he grouped an impressive list of works which had led Offner to form and outline the personality of the " Master of the Fabriano Altarpiece ".

As Longhi pointed out, Puccio, starting from the teaching of Daddi, seems to develop certain stylistic elements of Maso di Banco.... at a certain moment he shows that he is aware too of the work of Giovanni da Milano, who was then working in Florence.....

from L. Marcucci, p. 71, *I Dipinti Toscani del Secolo XIV*, Rome, 1965.

Florentine School. Active probably c. 1335-c. 1365. An altarpiece of St. Antony, dated 1353, in the Pinacoteca Civica at Fabriano has suggested the now familiar designation for this painter. There has recently been an attempt to identify him as Puccio di Simone and to recognize in him a master superior to Daddi, closer to Maso. It seems more likely that his style is based on Daddi's oeuvre of the late 1330's, with modifications introduced later under the influence of Orcagna and Nardo di Cione.....

from F. R. Shapley, p. 29, *Paintings from the Samuel H. Kress Collection*, London, 1966.

BIBLIOGRAPHY
BOOKS

An asterisk indicates a work listed in the General Bibliography

Venturi, A*, Vol. V, 1907, p. 915; *Khv & Salmi**, 1914, p. 43; *v. Marle**, 1924, pp. 405-6; *Vitzhum**, 1924, p. 305; *Chiappelli**, 1925, p. 284; Romagnoli, F., *Allegretti Nuzi: littore fabrianese*, 1927; *Berenson, 1930**, pp. 63-74; *Hautecoeur**, 1931, p. 158; *Berenson, 1932**, p. 399; *Catalogo della Mostra del Tesoro di Firenze sacra*, Florence, 1933, p. 118; Gronau, H. D., *T-Becker**, 1933, XXVII, p. 442; *Venturi, L**, 1933, pls 107-111; *Offner, 1934**, Sec. III, Vol. IV, pp. 77, 207-212; Gnoli, U., *Treccani Vol. XXV**, 1935, pp. 86-7; *Berenson 1936**, pp. 343-4; *Procacci 1936**, p. 25; Quintavalle, A. O., *La Regia Galleria di Parma*, Rome, 1939, pp. 160-62; National Gallery of Art, *Preliminary Catalogue of Paintings and Sculpture*, Washington, D. C., 1941, p. 128; *Coletti, Vol. II**, 1946, p. 59; *Offner 1947**, Sec. III, Vol. V, pp. 141-229; *Galetti**, " A-E ", 1950, pp. 1779-80; *Galetti**, " P-Z ", 1950, p. 2053; *Oertel 1950**, p. 52; *Toesca 1951**, p. 624; Suida, W. E., *Catalogue of the Birmingham Museum of Art*, Birmingham, (Ala.), 1952, pp. 16-17; Suida, W. E., *Paintings of the Renaissance*, Portland Art Museum, Portland, (Oregon), 1952, pp. 20-1; *Offner 1957**, Sec. III, Vol. V, p. 142; *Offner 1958**, Sec. III, Vol. VIII, pp. 165, 192; Suida, W. E., *Catalogue of the Birmingham Museum of Art*, Birmingham, (Ala.), 1959, pp. 14-15; *Gregori**, 1960, pp. 5-6; Shapley, F. R., *Catalogue of the North Carolina Museum of Art*, Raleigh, 1960, pp. 48-51; *Berenson, 1963**, Vol. I, p. 182; Dal Poggetto, P., *AIV*, 1963, pp. 28-29; *Marcucci**, 1965, pp. 70-3; Bologna, F., *La Pittura del Medioevo* (I Maestri del Colore, 251), Milan, 1966; Gore, St. J., *Wildenstein**, 1965, pp. 5, 14, 47-8, 56, 70-7; *Shapley**, 1966, pp. 29-30, 75-76.

JOURNALS

Venturi, A., *A*, XI, 1908, p. 139; Post, C. R., *AA*, III, 1915, pp. 213-222; Chiappelli, A., *MKIF*, III, 1919-32, p. 193; Berenson, B., *BA*, II, 1922, 7, pp. 296-309; Sirèn, O., *BM*, XLV, 1924, pp. 285-91; Chiappelli, A., *DD*, X, 1929-1930, pp. 199-228; Procacci, U., *RA*, XV, 1933, pp. 224-44; Gamba, C., *BA*, XXVII, 1933, pp. 145-63; Gamba, C., *RA*, XV, 1933, pp. 70-71; Suida, W. E., *AP*, XX, 1934, p. 120; Molajoli, B., *RA*, XVI, 1934, p. 350; Meiss, M., *AB*, XVIII, 1936, p. 442; Zeri, F., *BA*, XXXIV, 4, 1949, pp. 21-22; Longhi, R., *PA*, I, 7, 1950, p. 49; Marabottini, A., *RA*, XXVII, 1951-2, pp. 23-55; Cohn, W., *BA*, XLII, 4, 1957, pp. 175-6; Longhi, R., *PA*, III, 1959, pp. 3-12; Procacci, U., *RA*, XXXIII, 1958, pp. 121-39; Rozycka-Bryzek, A., *A.*, LXI, 27/3-4, 1962, pp. 115-124; Zeri, F., *BA*, XLVIII, 4, 1963, p. 246; Longhi, R., *PA*, XVI, 183, 1965, pp. 8-16; Vertova, L., *BM*, CIX, 1967, pp. 668-72; Sacconi, G. V., *PA*, XX, 227, 1969, pp. 63-4.

SIGNED AND DATED WORKS

Florence, Accademia 8569. Polyptych: Madonna of Humility with Sts. Lawrence, Humphrey, James & Bartholomew s. (fig. 175).

1353 Fabriano, Pinacoteca. Panel: St Anthony. d. (fig. 168).

1354 Washington, D. C., National Gallery 6. Triptych: Madonna & Child with Saints. d. (fig. 181).

1360 Whereabouts unknown. Panel: Madonna nursing the Child. s & d. (fig. 167).

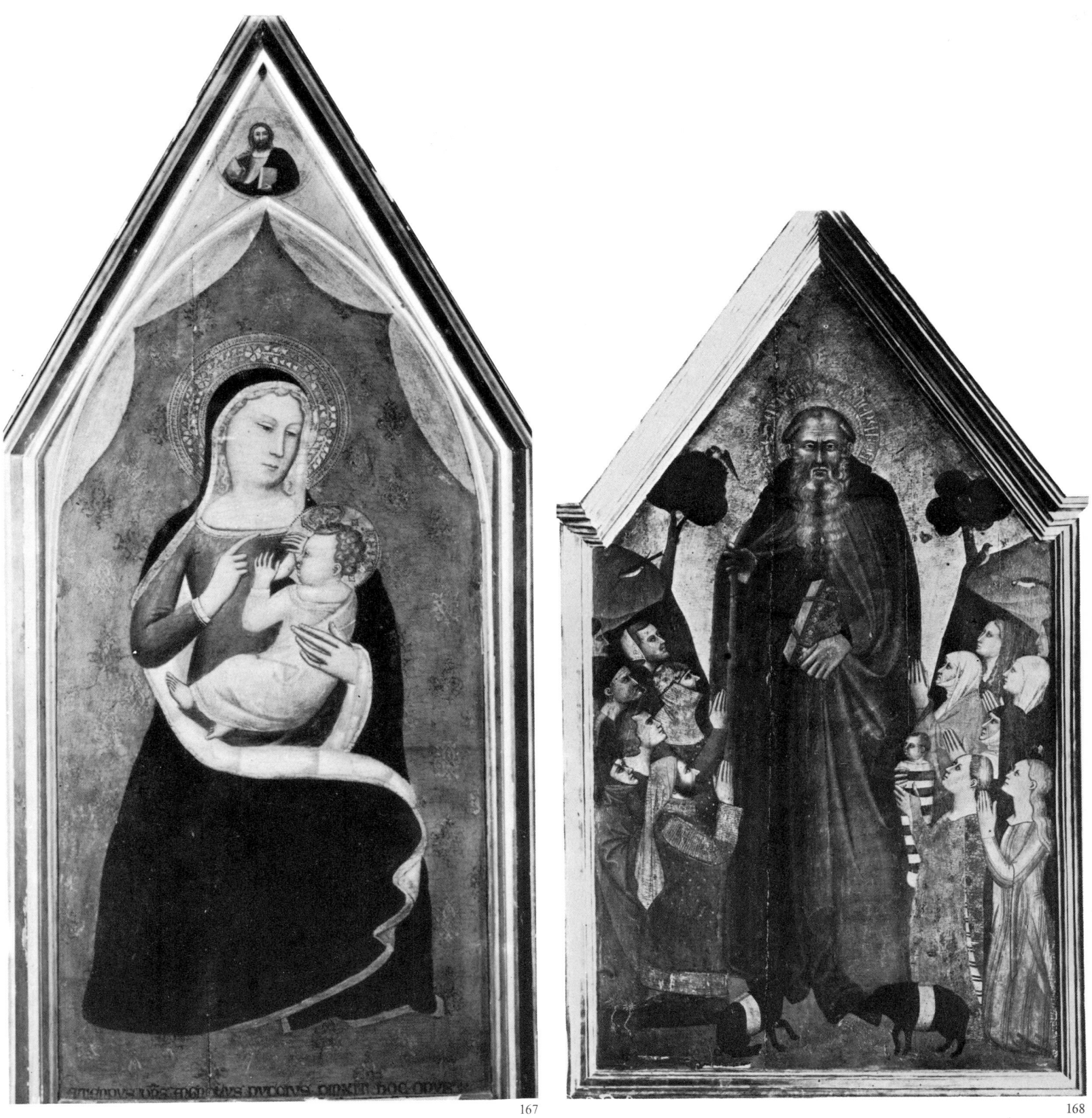

167

168

167. *Madonna nursing the Child. Panel. Whereabouts unknown. Sotheby A5839. s & d. 1360.*
168. *St Anthony. Panel. Fabriano, Pinacoteca. 202 × 113. GFN C2605. d. 1353.*

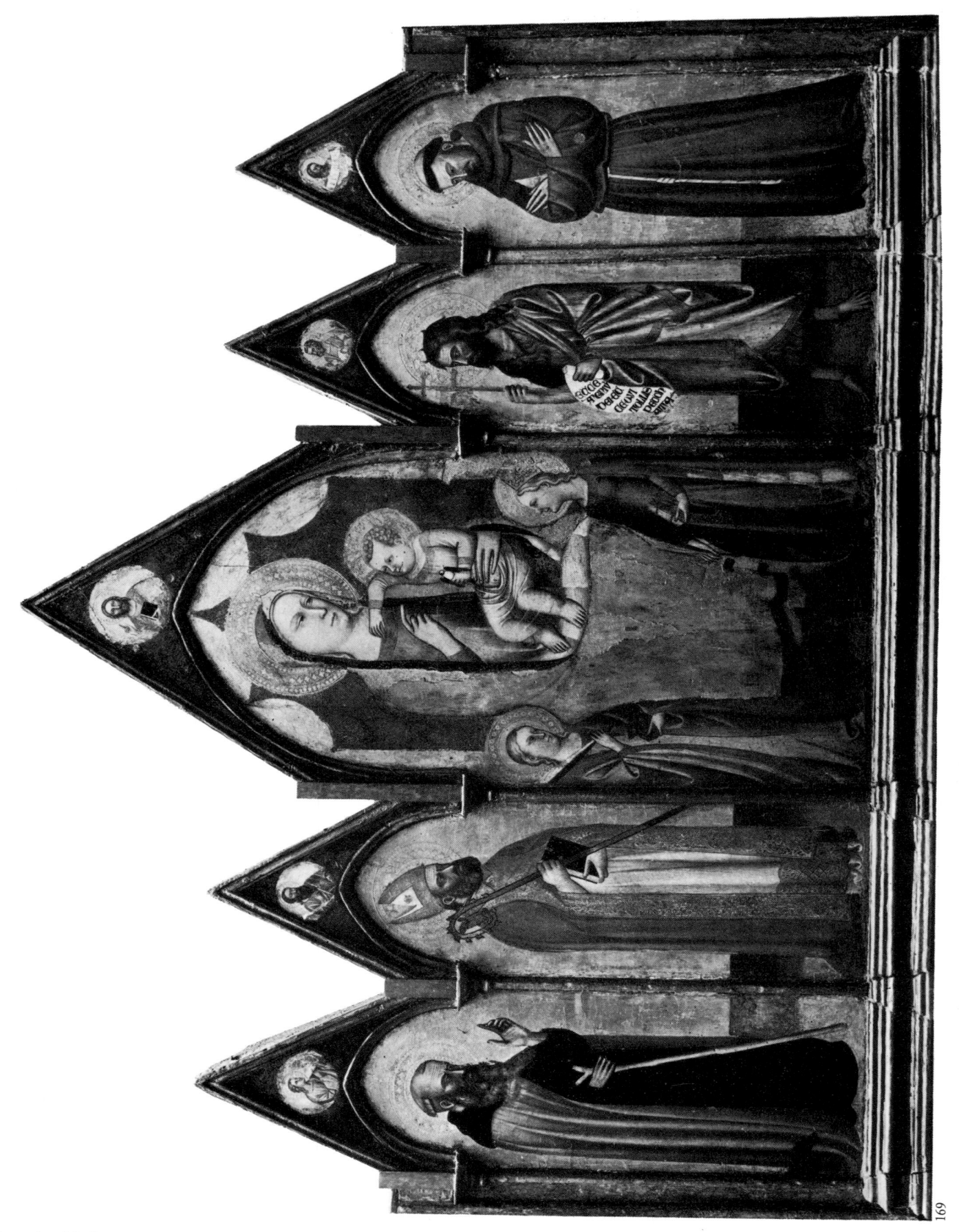

169. *Polyptych: Madonna and Child Enthroned with Sts Lucy, Catherine, Anthony Abbot, Nicholas, John the Baptist and Francis. Above: Christ blessing, the four Evangelists. Panel. San Donnino, Certaldo. cp: 144 × 57; sps: 111 × 31. SGF 69431.*

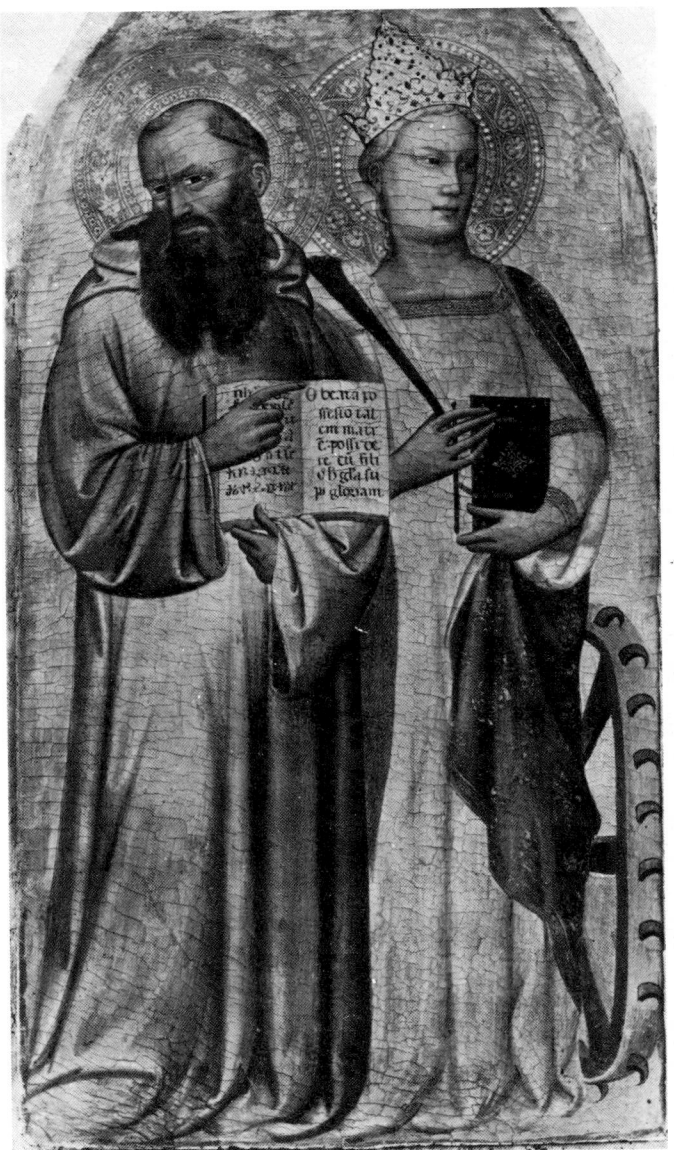

170

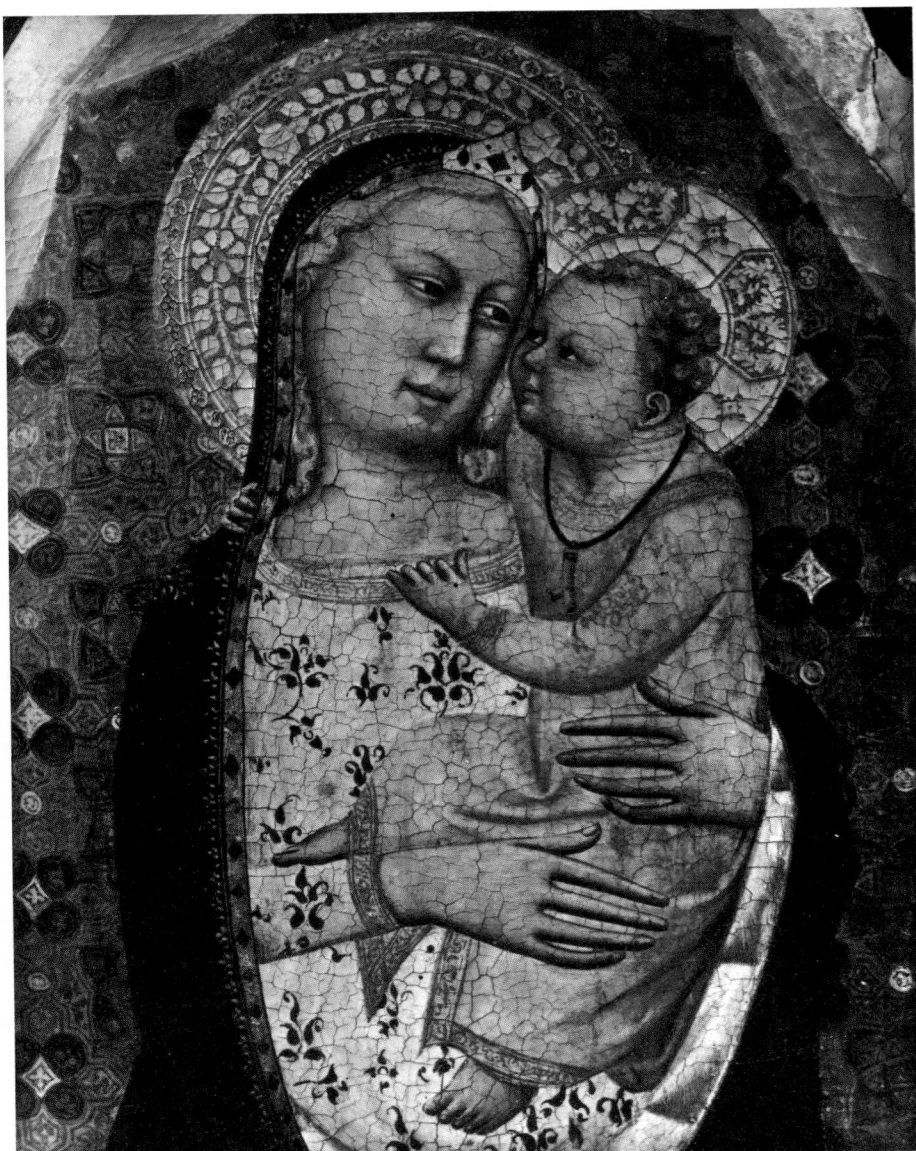

171

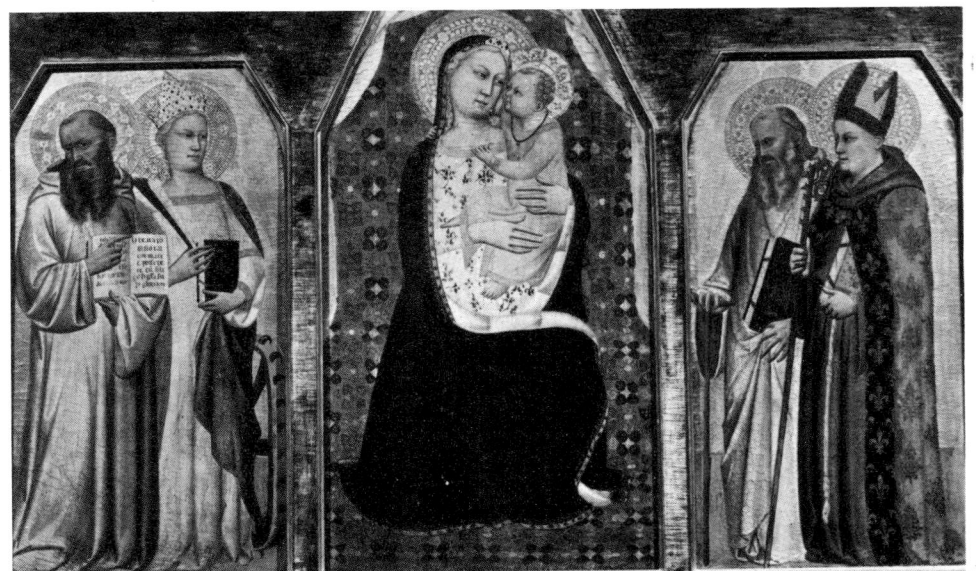

172

170. *Sts Benedict and Catherine, detail of fig. 172. Panel. Venice, Cini Collection. no. 7006. 89 × 49.3. Cini Foundation photo.*
171. *Madonna and Child, detail of fig. 172. Panel. Venice, Cini Collection. no. 7006. Cini Foundation photo.*
172. *Madonna and Child with Sts Benedict, Catherine, Romuald and Louis of Toulouse. Panel. Venice, Cini Collection. no. 7006. lp: 89 × 49.3; cp: 105 × 57.7; rp: 90.3 × 49.8. Cini Foundation photo.*

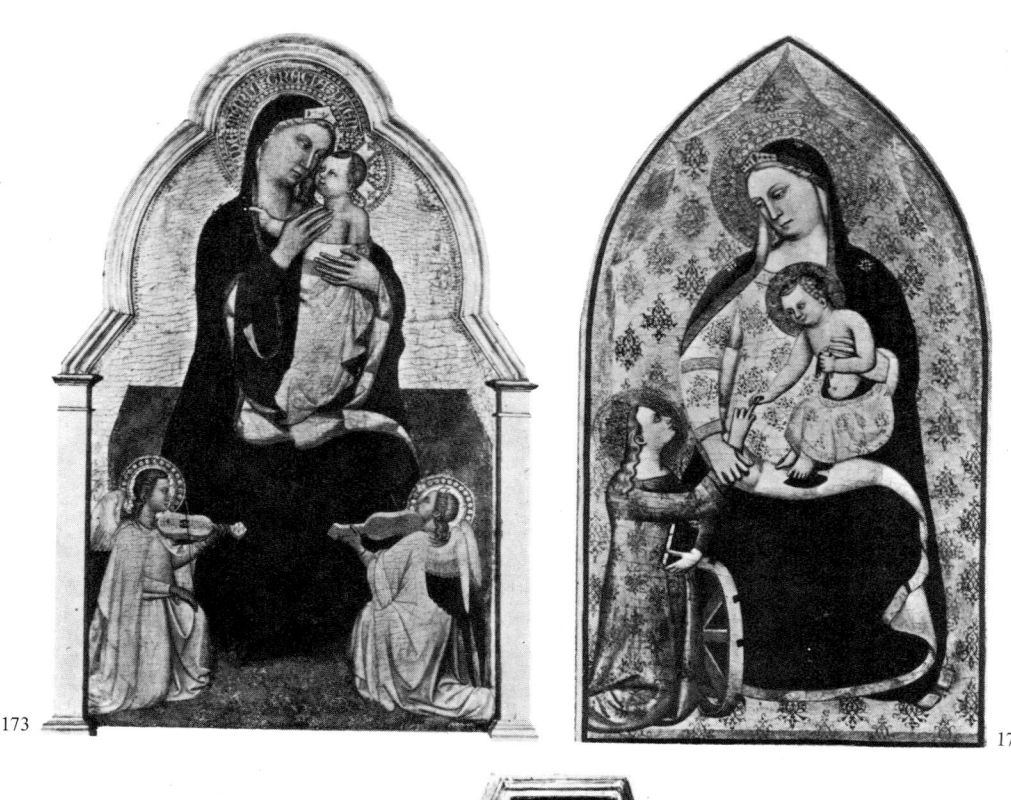

173

174

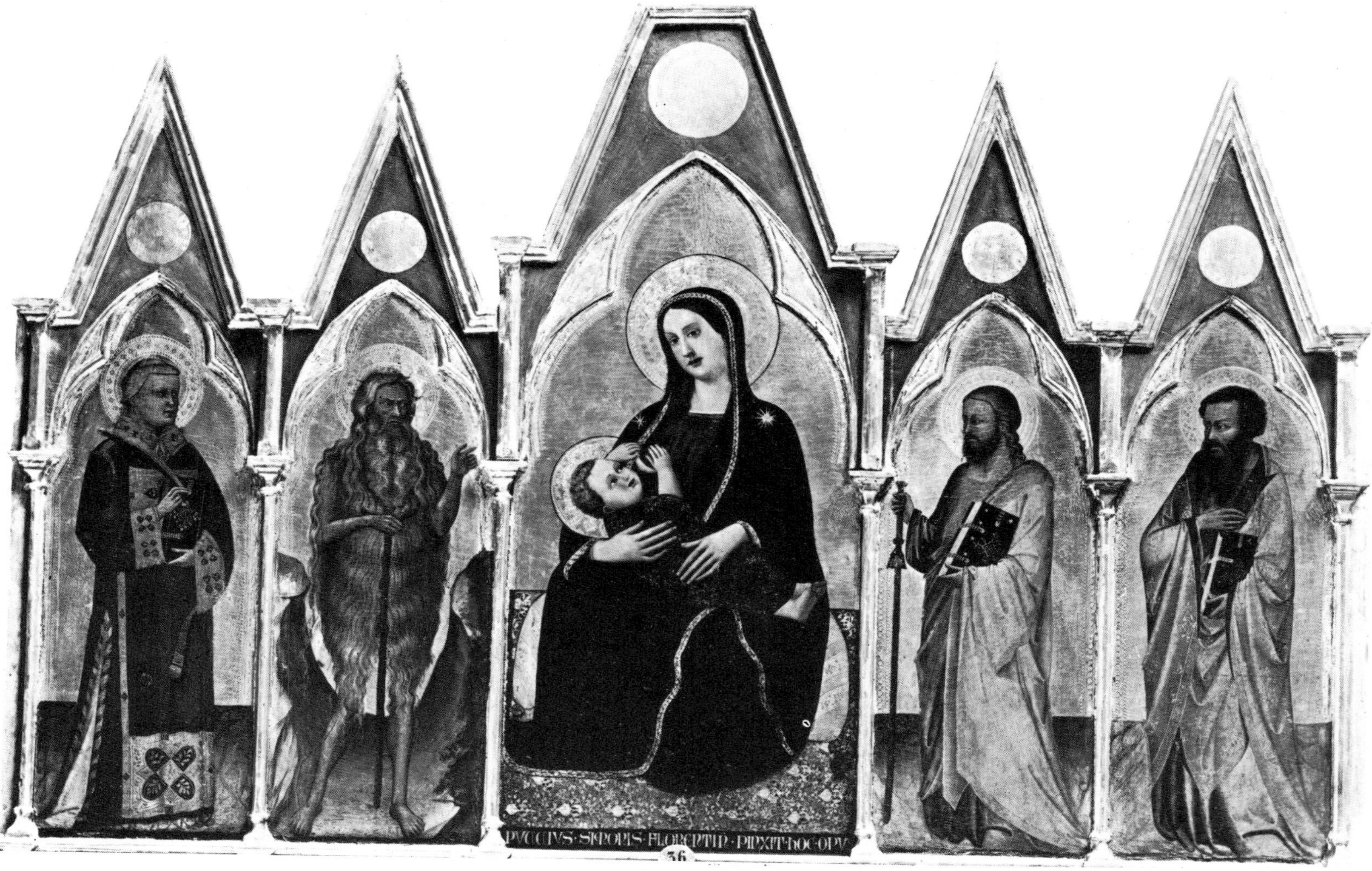

36

175

173.   *Madonna and Child with two music-making Angels. Panel. Los Angeles (Calif.), Los Angeles County Museum of Art. 91.3 × 54. Bertoni-Offner.*
174.   *Mystical Marriage of St Catherine. Panel. Berlin, Paul Bottenwieser Collection.   101.4 × 54.6.   Bertoni-Offner.*
175.   *Polyptych: Madonna of Humility with Sts Lawrence, Humphrey, James and Bartholomew.   Panel.   Florence, Accademia.   no. 8569. 132 × 191. Alinari 1605. s.*

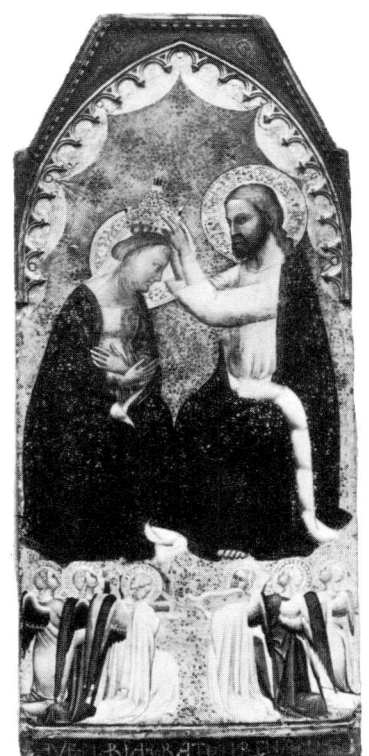
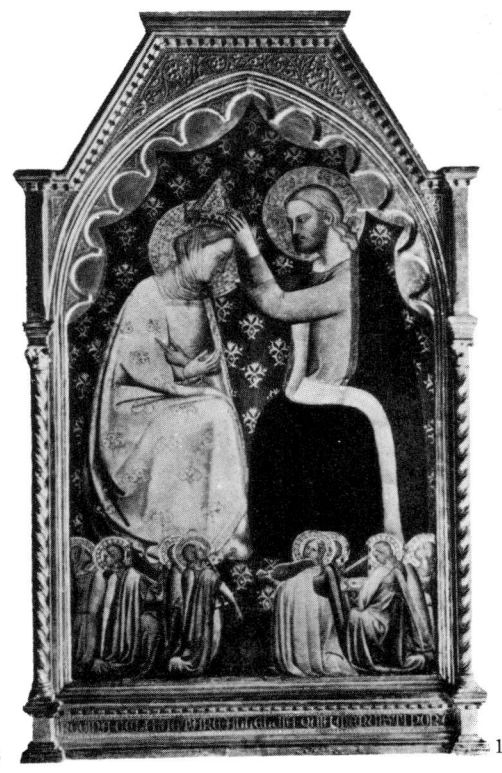

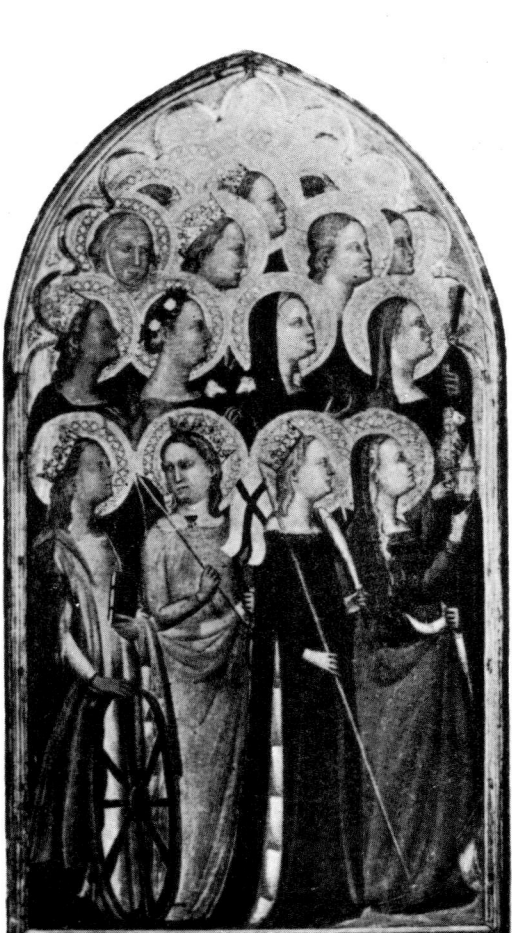
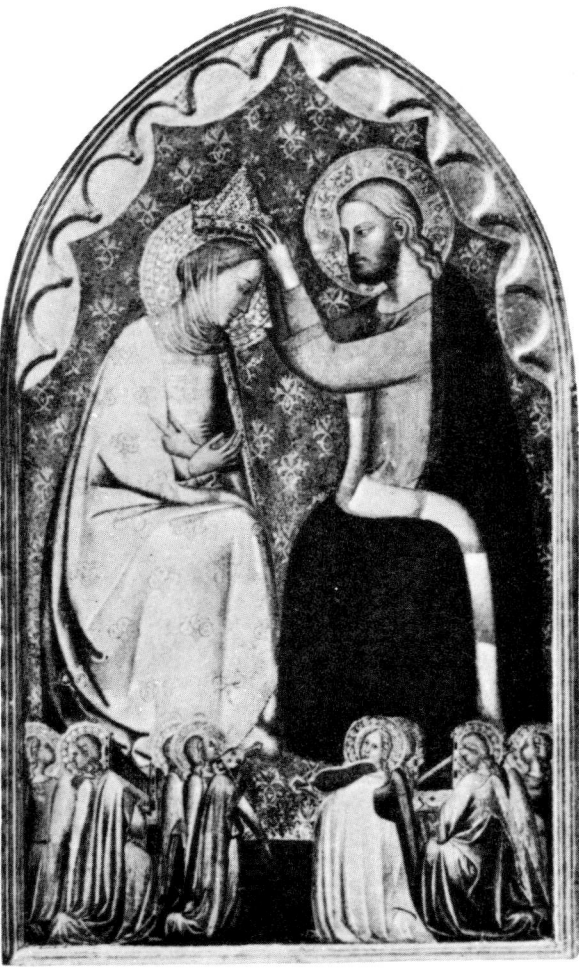
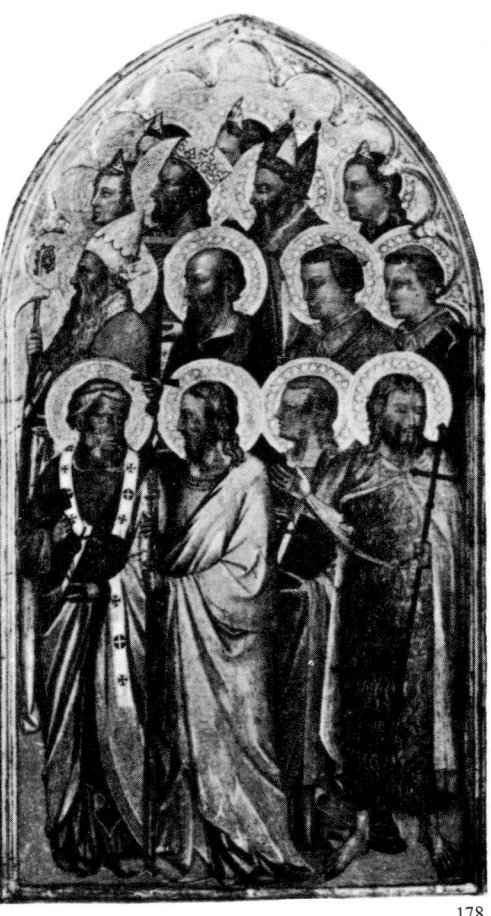

176. *Coronation of the Virgin with six music-making Angels. Panel. Ghent, Musée. no. 1903 A. 152 × 61. Museum photo.*
177. *Coronation of the Virgin and eight music-making Angels. Panel. Lucca, Conte Cenami-Spada Collection. 126 × 76. Bertoni-Offner.*
178. *Coronation of the Virgin with Angels and Saints. Three panels. cp: Lucca, Conte Cenami-Spada Collection (see fig. 177); sps: Parma, Galleria Nazionale. Bertoni-Offner.*

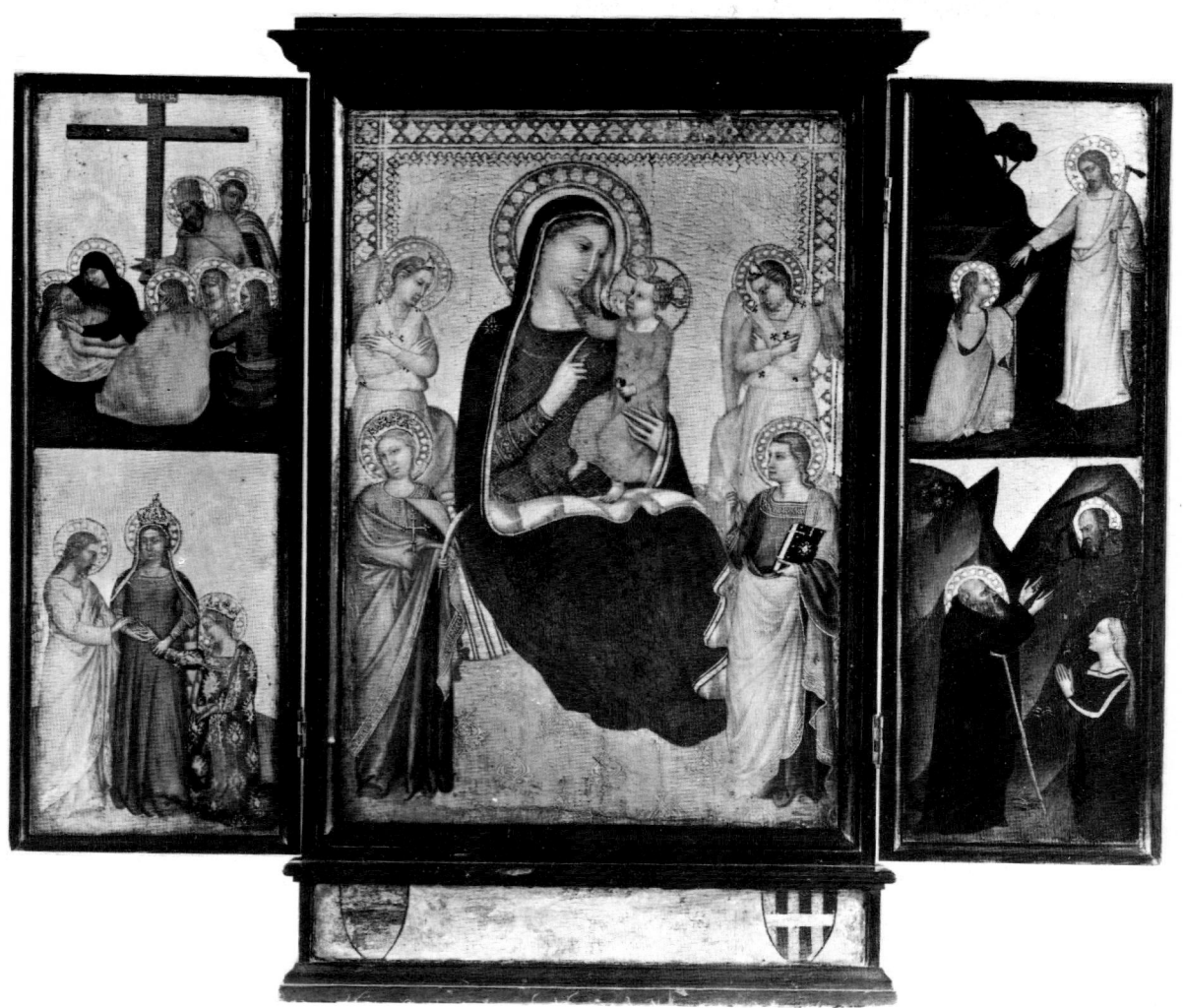

179

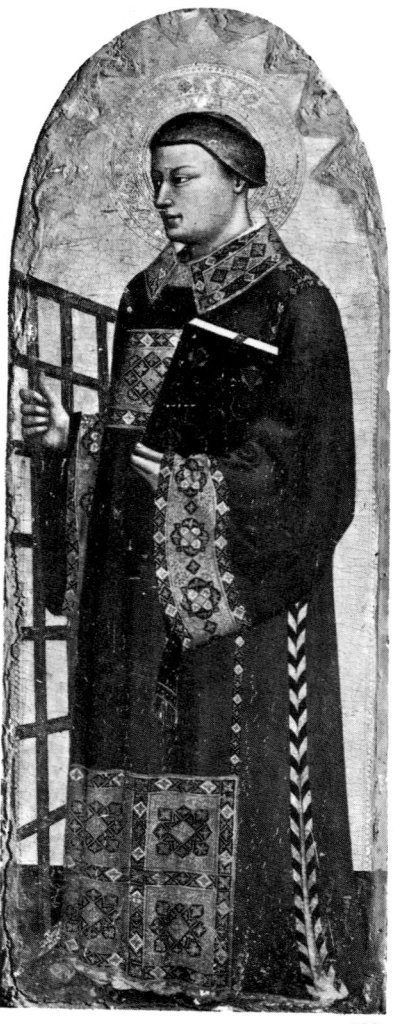

180

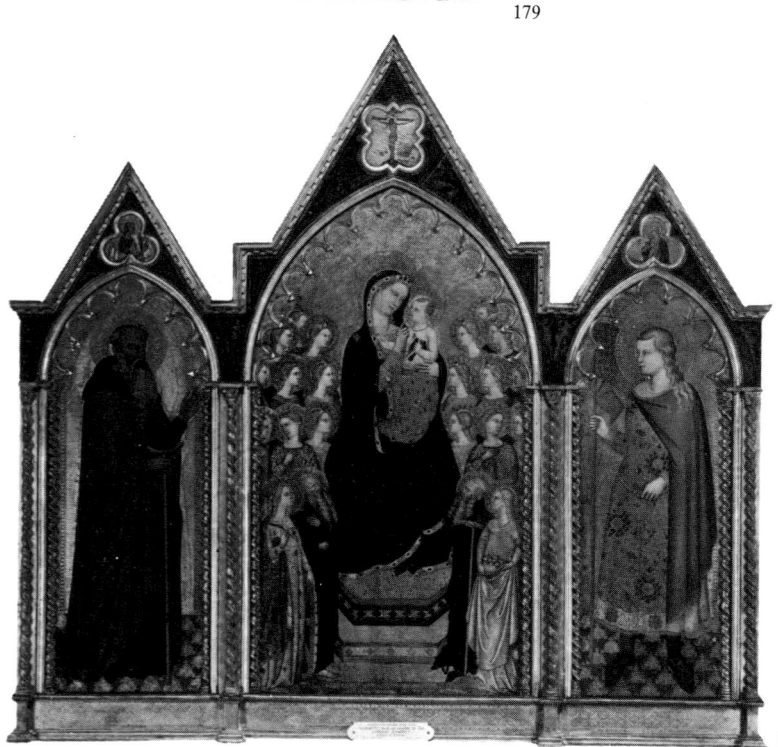

181

179. *Madonna of Humility with Sts Margaret, John the Evangelist and two Angels. Wings: Pietà; Marriage of St Catherine; Noli me tangere; Sts Anthony Abbot, and Paul the Hermit with female Donor. Panel. Corsham Court (Wilts.), Lord Methuen Collection.* cp: 39.5 × 26.2; sps: 39.5 × 12.9. *Bertoni-Offner.*

180. *St. Lawrence. Panel. Bagno a Ripoli (3 km south-east of Florence), S. Maria a Quarto. Accademia.* no. 8707. 103 × 39. SGF 76521.

181. *Triptych: Madonna and Child Enthroned with Saints, and with Sts Anthony Abbot, Stephen. Above: Christ on the Cross, Annunciation. Panel. Washington (D.C.), National Gallery, Mellon Collection.* no. 6. 108.6 × 59.4. *Museum photo. (left panel by another hand).* d. 1354.

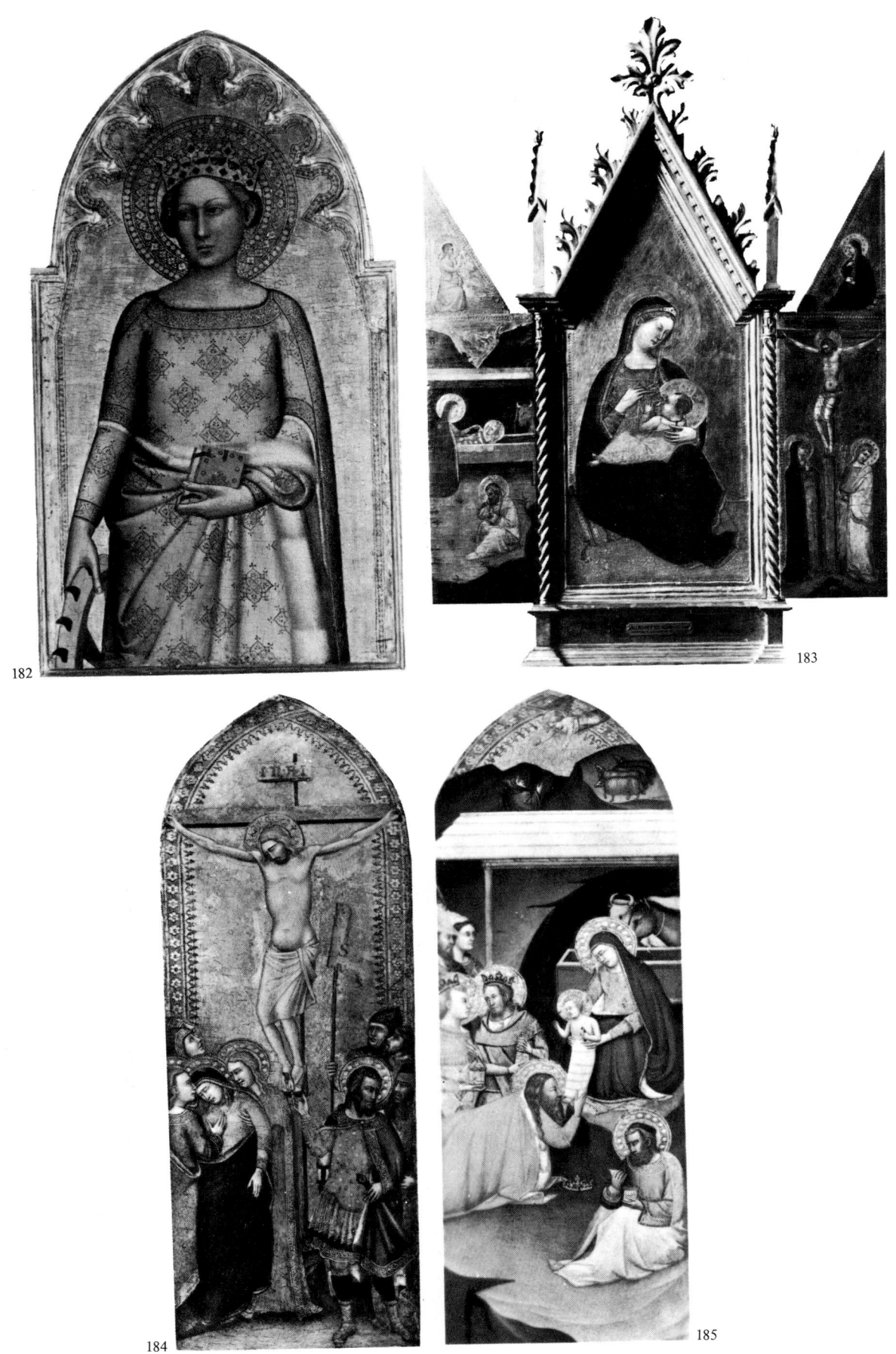

182. *St Catherine. Panel. Locko Park (Derbys.), Drury-Lowe Collection. no. 267. Sotheby 304123.*
183. *Portable triptych: Madonna of Humility: Nativity; Christ on the Cross. Above: Annunciation. Panel. Paris, Musées Nationaux. no. 28. cp: 78 × 55; sps: 58 × 13. Photo Musée de Dijon.*
184. *Christ on the Cross. Panel. Notre Dame (Ind.), University of Notre Dame, Kress Study Collection. K263. 39.3 × 14.2. Kress Foundation photo.*
185. *Adoration of the Magi. Panel. Worcester (Mass.), Worcester Art Museum, Ellis Collection. no. 1940.34. 40.6 × 15.2. Museum photo.*

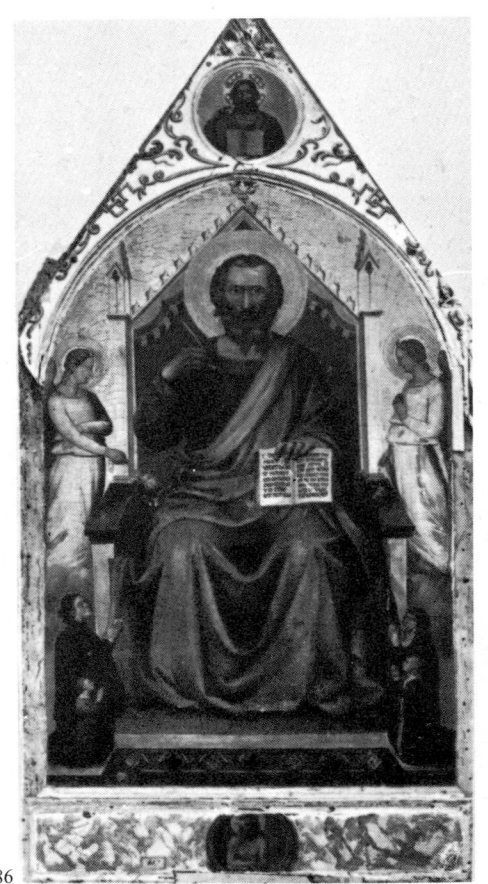

186

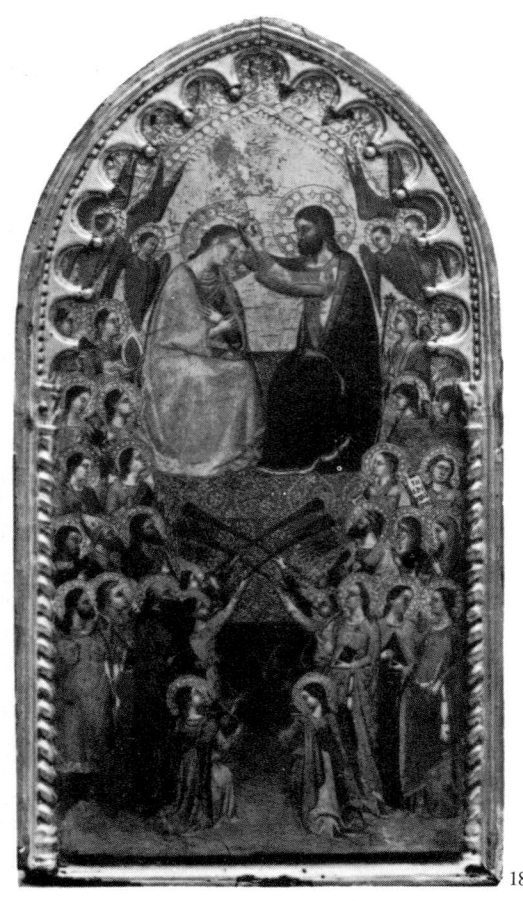

187

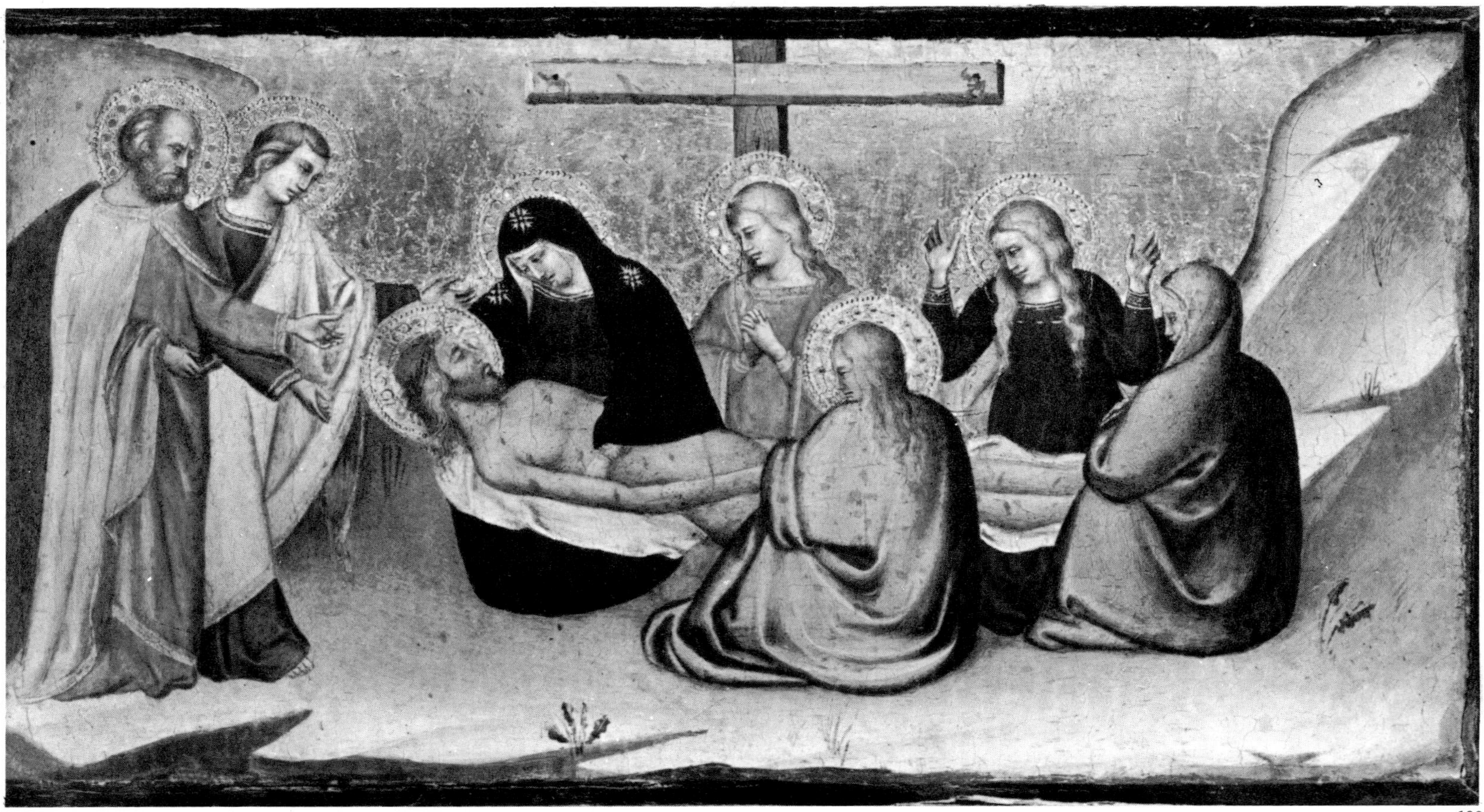

188

186. *St. Matthew, central panel of triptych. Panel. Florence, Uffizi, Depositi. no. 5063. 185 × 95. SGF 117705.*
187. *Coronation of the Virgin. Panel. Paris, Louvre. 63 × 34. Réunion des Musées Nationaux 70 EN1730.*
188. *Lamentation. Panel. Berlin, Dahlem, Staatliche Museen. no. 1059. Museum photo.*

MASTER OF TERENZANO

Anonymous provincial whose panel in S. Maria Novella furnishes the earlier of two dates we possess for him, that of 1336 as a terminus post quem for the picture. The polyptych in Viscount Lee's collection bears a mutilated date of which MCCCXL shows clearly, and which may originally have recorded any additional numeral between this and 1349. The painter tends to the miniature style and continues in the shop-conventions of the Biadaiolo Illuminator, whom he resembles so closely at times that we are tempted to regard him his associate or pupil. His works show him evolving parallel to Jacopo del Casentino, and lingering evolutionistically behind Daddi, whose influence he cannot altogether escape. Although confused repeatedly with the Cione School, and oddly enough even with Traini, this master has been recognized independently in a small number of panels by Dr. Osvald Sirèn, published in an article, until recently unknown to me.... under the name of the Master of the Lee Polyptych. He was formed under the direct influence of Pacino di Bonaguida.....

> from R. Offner, p. 49, *A Critical and Historical Corpus of Florentine Painting*, Sec. III, Vol. II, Part I, New York, 1930.

A hasty transcriber of style and motifs he found among his older and younger contemporaries among others the Biadaiolo Illuminator, the Master of the Dominican Effigies, Jacopo del Casentino and Bernardo Daddi. His schooling he received very probably in the shop of Pacino di Buonaguida, but the influence of Bernardo Daddi reorganizes his manner and is variously reflected in all of the works attributed to him here.

> from R. Offner, p. 73, *A Critical and Historical Corpus of Florentine Painting*, Sec. III, Vol. II, Part I, New York, 1930.

There is another polyptych which is undoubtedly by the same hand. It is still today *in situ*, in the parish church of Terenzano, behind Settignano. Without being so identical that they seem stamped out, these polyptychs are unquestionably by the same artist; and that he was an artist and not a simple artisan we know from exactly that diversity within their similarity. At Terenzano for example he reminds us a good deal of a contemporary of his who was perhaps a few years older; like him he is close to Daddi and approaches Jacopo del Casentino; this contemporary is the author of a polyptych in the Accademia in Florence which has a modern inscription under the central panel, copied (how accurately?) from an older one: he is Pacino di Bonaguida.
As this last-mentioned work [at Terenzano] was the first to attract my attention, wondering who was the artist, as it is the least likely to be moved, and as the name I propose is not unsuitable, I will call him the Master of Terenzano.....

> from B. Berenson, p. 980, *Dedalo*, XI, 4, 1930-31.

The denomination of the miniaturist and panel painter of the Dominican Effigies on the panel in Santa Maria Novella (which must have been painted after 1336, because among the blessed is included Maurizio d'Ungheria who was beatified in that year; probably it was in fact painted after 1340) is due to Offner who assigns to the painter a number of mediocre paintings without any great craft (including the polyptych in the collection of Viscount Lee which is dated 1340), as well as a numerous series of miniatures some of which would seem to be by the same hand as the pictures, while others are of a higher quality, which I believed to be by Jacopo di Casentino.....

> from M. Salmi, p. 39, *La Miniatura Fiorentina Gotica*, Rome, 1954.

The polyptych originates from the Church of S. Paolino in Florence, as recorded in the *Sepoltuario Strozziano*. This document also aids us in establishing an exact date for the picture — 1345 — Strozzi, in fact gives the following as the inscription on the picture:

Mater Dei Ora Pro Nobis 1345 —, which gives us a new fixed point for the chronology of the works of the Master of the Dominican Effigies.....

from W. Cohn, pp. 67-68, *Rivista d'Arte*, Vol. XXX, 1955.

The name of this artist, who painted small pictures as well as miniatures, is derived from a panel of *Christ and the Virgin adored by Dominican Saints*, executed shortly after 1336 and now in the Sacristy of Santa Maria Novella, Florence. According to Offner he developed on similar lines to Jacopo del Casentino, the chief influence on his style being that of Daddi. For hypotheses concerning the identity of this master, see Levi d'Ancona, M., *Miniatura a Firenze*.....

from St. J. Gore, p. 7, *The Art of Painting in Florence and Siena from 1250-1500*, London, 1965.

With the name of " Master of the Dominican Effigies ", from the picture in the church of S. Maria Novella, Offner outlined the personality of an artist who had already been identified by Sirèn as the " Master of the Lord Lee Polyptych ". It would, however, seem practical to add under this name " Master of the Dominican Effigies " all the works which Offner gives to the " Biadaiolo Master " and to the " Master of the Cappella Medici ": this is in fact what Berenson started to do, with his " Terenzano Master " of 1931, in which he joins the Master of the Dominican Effigies and the Master of the Cappella Medici; Procacci has continued Berenson's idea of a single master, adding to the work of a single figure also those works of the Biadaiolo Master.....

from L. Marcucci, p. 69, *I Dipinti Toscani del Secolo XIV*, Rome, 1965.

BIBLIOGRAPHY

BOOKS
An asterisk indicates a work listed in the General Bibliography

Offner, 1930*, Sec. III, Vol. II, Part I, pp. 49-68; *Venturi, 1931**, pl. 34; *Procacci, 1936**, p. 25; *M. Giottesca**, 1943, p. 551; *Antal**, 1948, p. 266; *Galetti**, " F-O ", 1950, p. 1465; *Toesca, 1951**, p. 807; Catalogue: *Mostra Storica Nazionale della Miniatura*, Rome, 1953, pp. 215-16; *Salmi, 1954**, pp. 13-4, 27, 34, 36, 39-40, 42; Salmi, M., *La Miniatura Italiana*, Milan, 1955, p. 17; *Offner, 1957**, Sec. III, Vol. VII, pp. 29-80; *Marcucci**, 1965, pp. 68-70; Gore, St. J., *Wildenstein**, 1965, p. 7; *Klesse**, 1967, pp. 329, 367; *Dutch Show**, 1974, pp. 11, 86.

JOURNALS

Sirèn, O., *JBK*, IV, 1926, pp. 13-28; Berenson, B., *DD*, XI, 4, 1930-1, pp. 957-88; Suida, W, *B*, XXI, 2, 1932, p. 128; Levi, E. L., *Bib*, XLVIII, 1946, pp. 9-20; Cohn, W., *RA*, XXXI, 6, 1951, p. 67; Salmi, M., *ABI*, XX, 1952, p. 14; Baldini, U., *BA*, XXXVIII, 1953, pp. 277-8; Cohn, W., *RA*, XXXI, 1956, pp. 41-72; Procacci, U., *RA*, XXXIII, 1958, pp. 121-39; Boskovits, M., *AV*, X, 5, 1971, pp. 3-4, 9, notes 4, 5.

DATED WORK

1340 London, Courtauld Institute of Art. Polyptych: Madonna & Child Enthroned with Saints. d. (fig. 202).

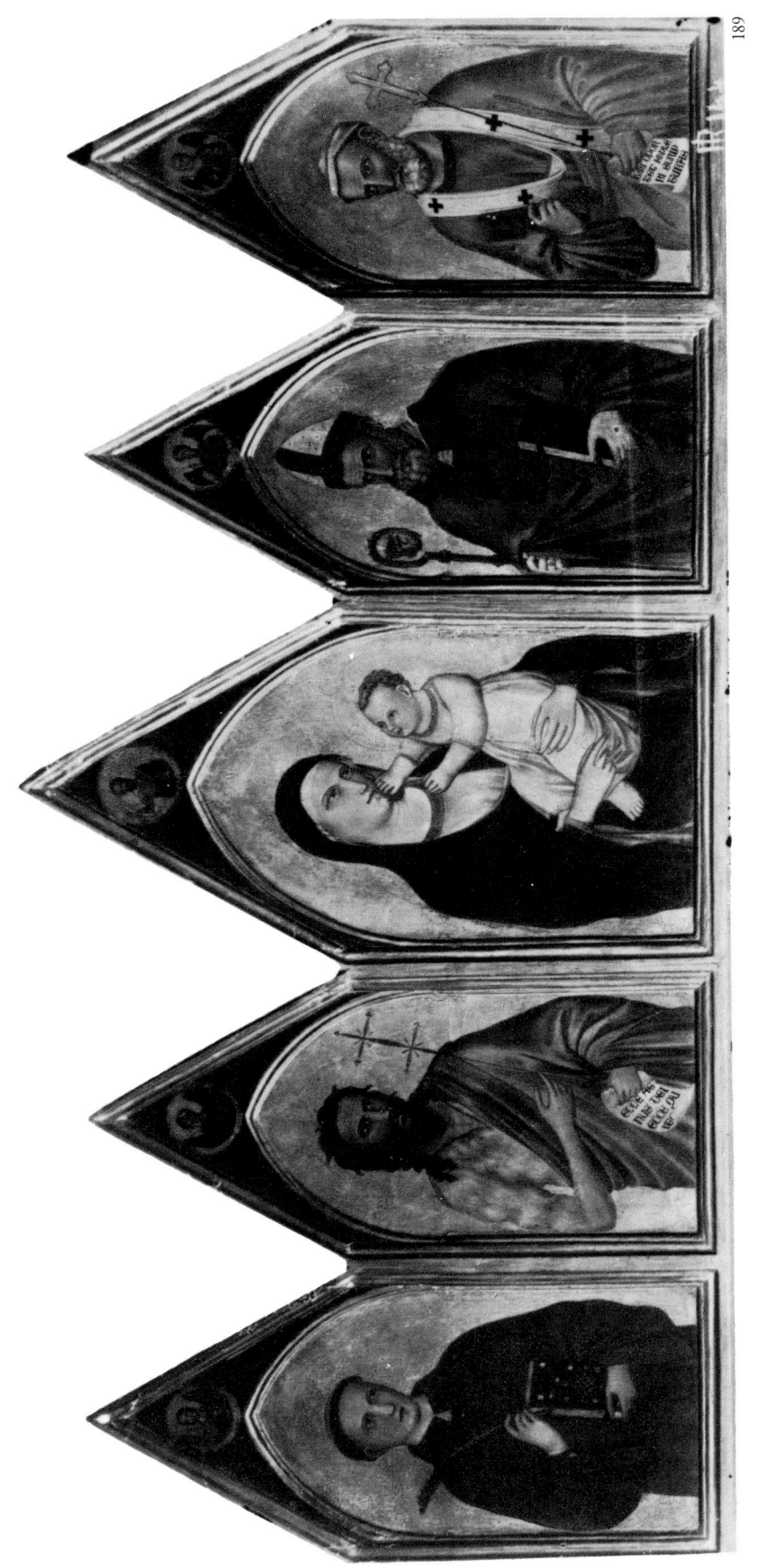

189. *Madonna and Child with Sts Lawrence, John the Baptist, Zenobius, and Peter. Above: Christ blessing, four Angels. Panel. Terenzano (1.5 km from Settignano, near Florence), S. Martino. cp: 91 × 21.6; sps: 83.5 × 21.6. SGF 21117.*

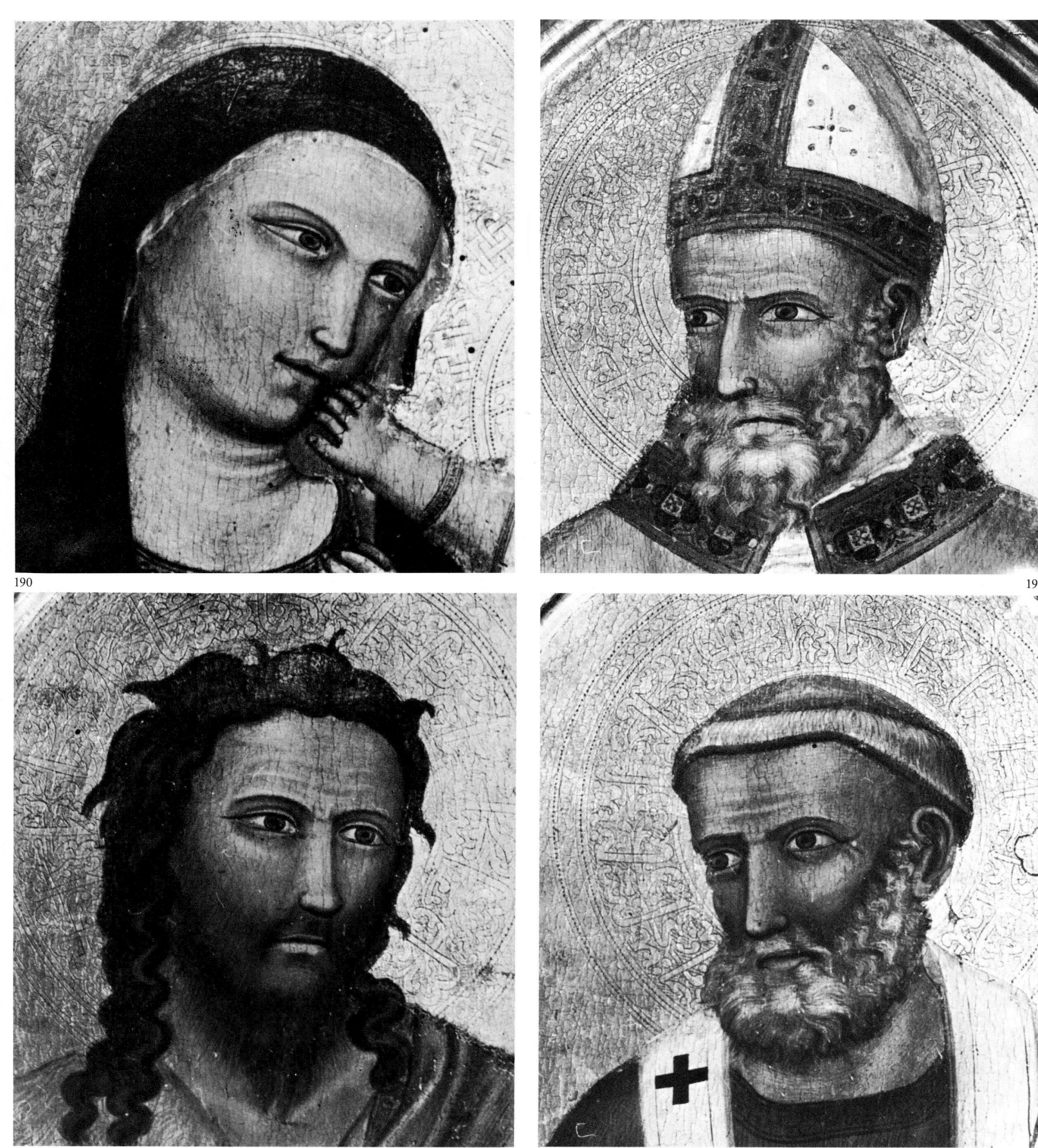

190. Head of Madonna, detail of fig. 189. Panel. Terenzano, S. Martino. Author's photo.
191. St Martin, detail of fig. 189. Panel. Terenzano, S. Martino. Author's photo.
192. St John the Baptist, detail of fig. 189. Panel. Terenzano, S. Martino. Author's photo.
193. St Peter, detail of fig. 189. Panel. Terenzano, S. Martino. Author's photo.

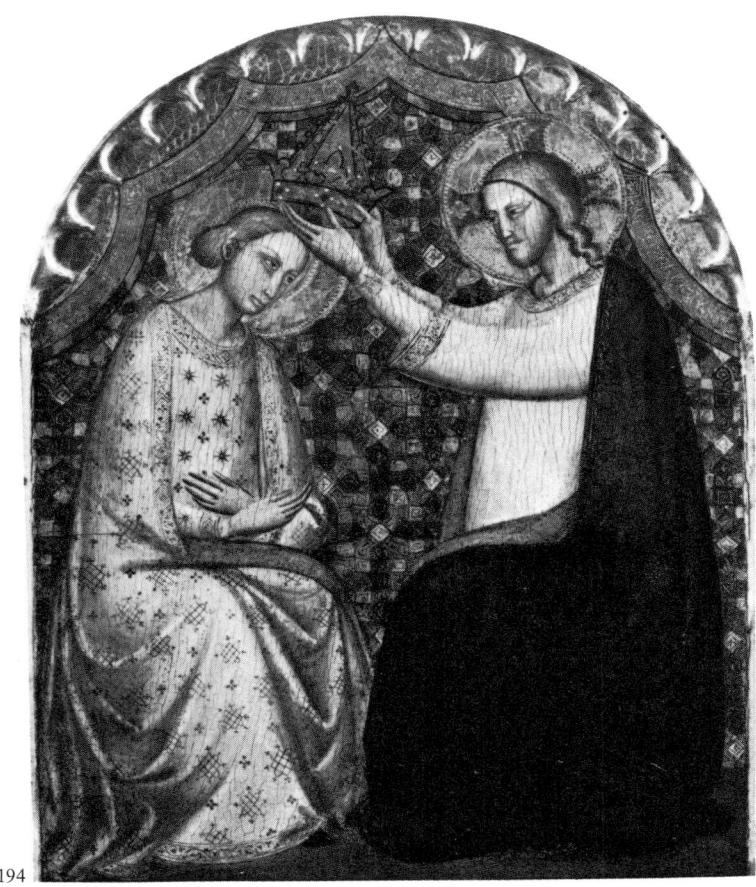

194

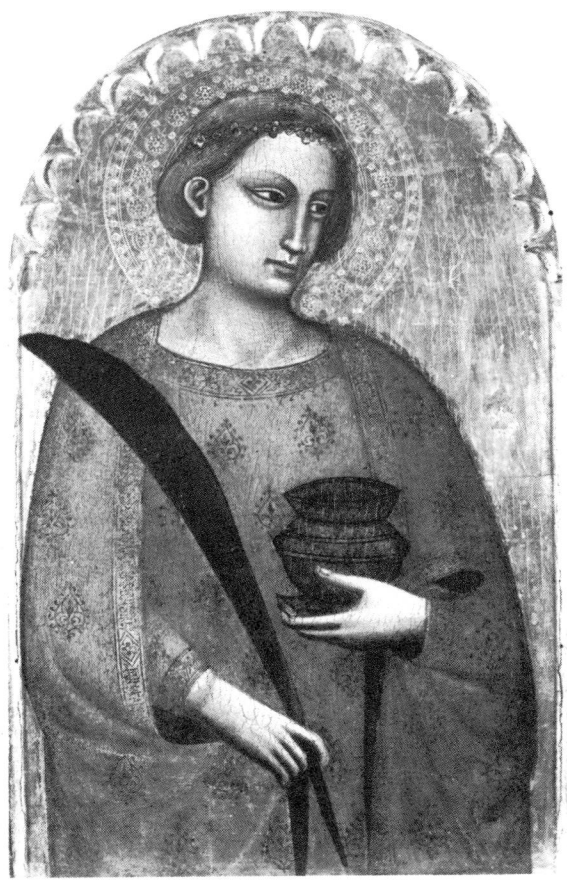

195

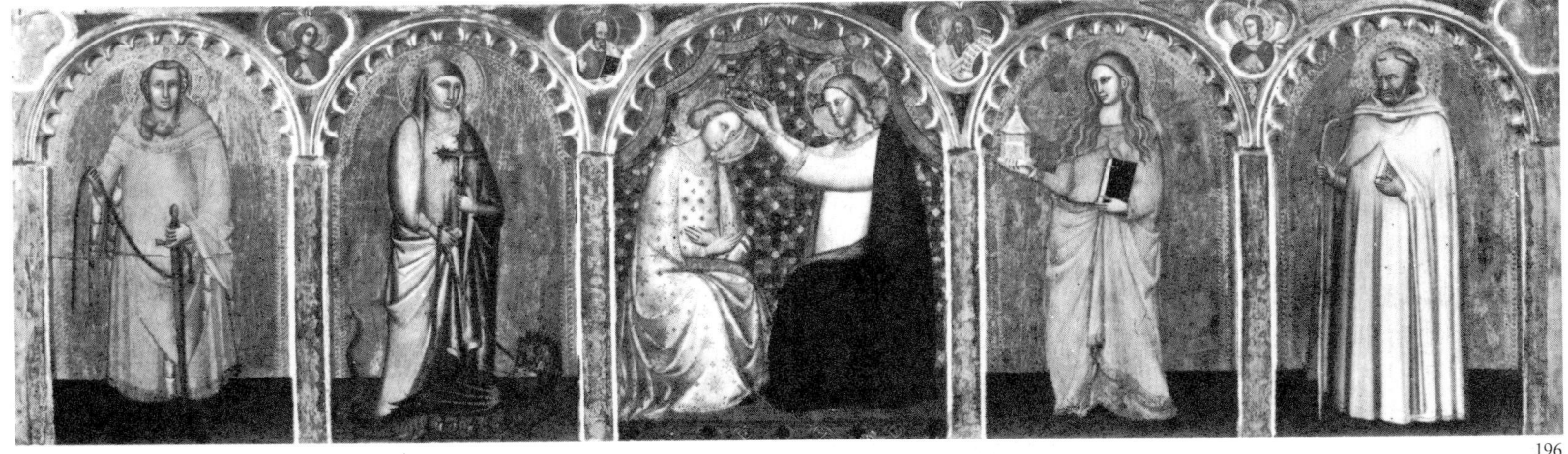

196

194. *Coronation of the Virgin, detail of fig. 196. Panel. Florence, Accademia. no. 4634. SGF 117782.*
195. *St Lucy, detail of fig. 199. Panel. Florence, Accademia. no. 4633. SGF 118617.*
196. *Coronation of the Virgin with Saints. Above: two Prophets, two Angels. Panel. Florence, Accademia. no. 4634. 64 × 193. SGF 117779 (verso of fig. 199).*

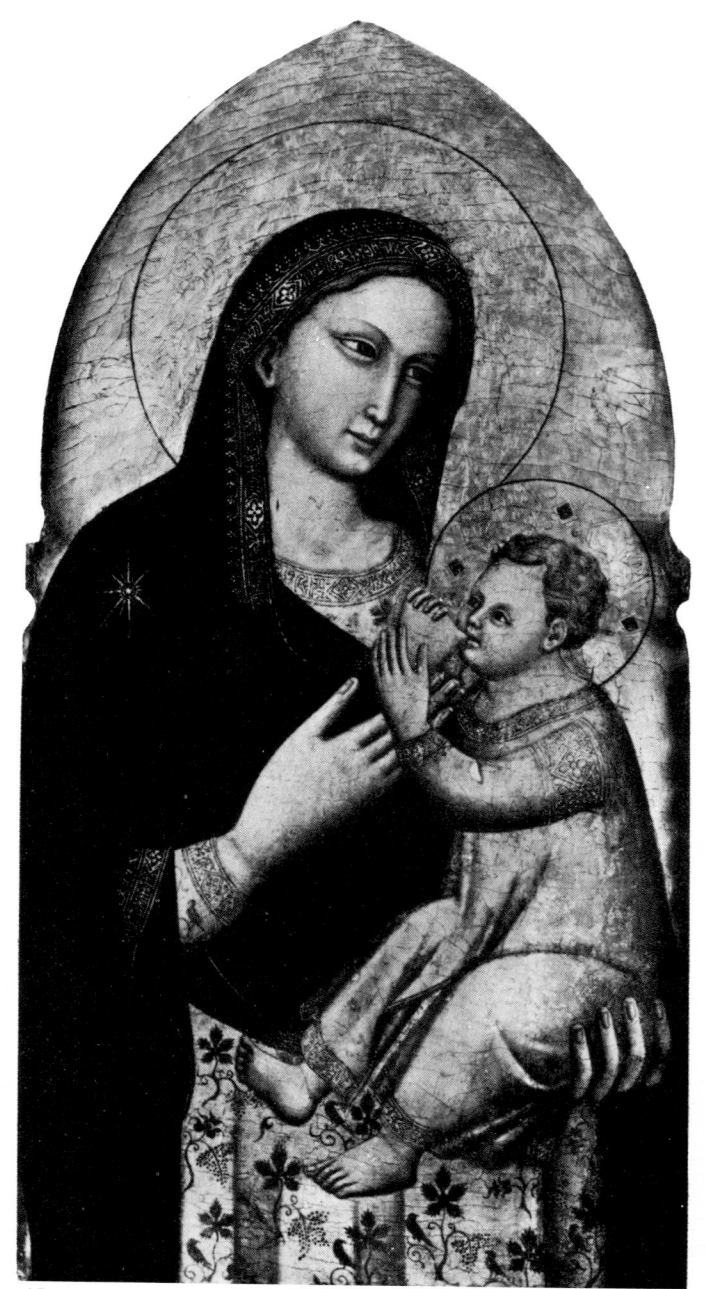

197

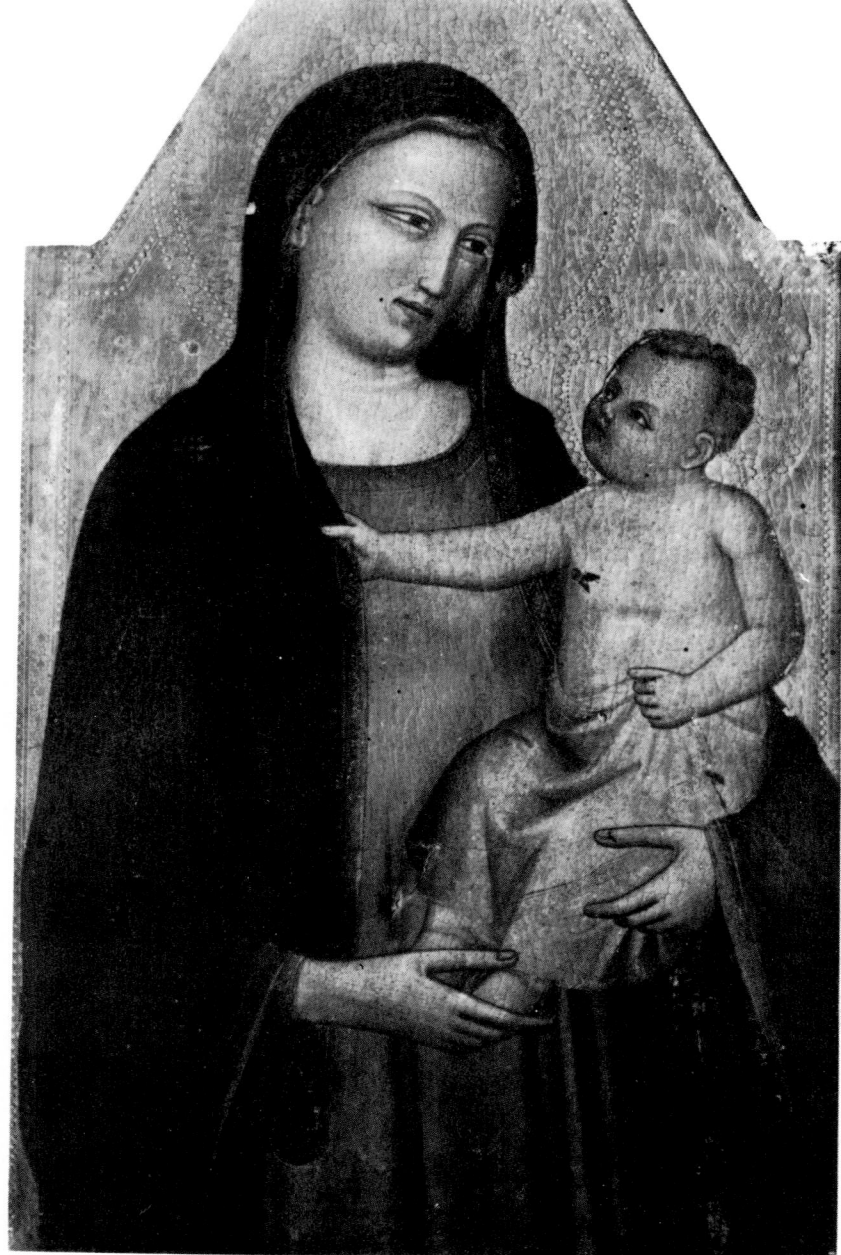

198

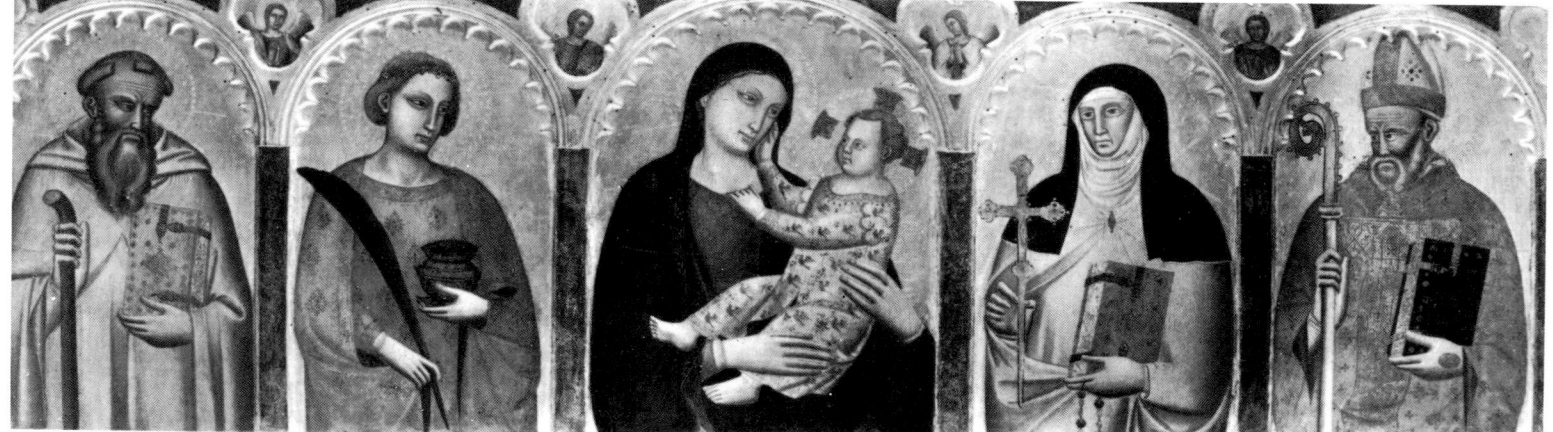

199

197. *Madonna nursing the Child. Panel. Private Collection. Reali.*
198. *Madonna and Child. Panel. Florence, S. Croce, Medici Chapel. 84 × 44. Brogi 22076.*
199. *Madonna and Child with Sts Benedict, Lucy, Margaret, Zenobius. Above: four Angels. Panel. Florence, Accademia. no. 4633. 64 × 193. SGF 118607 (recto of fig. 196).*

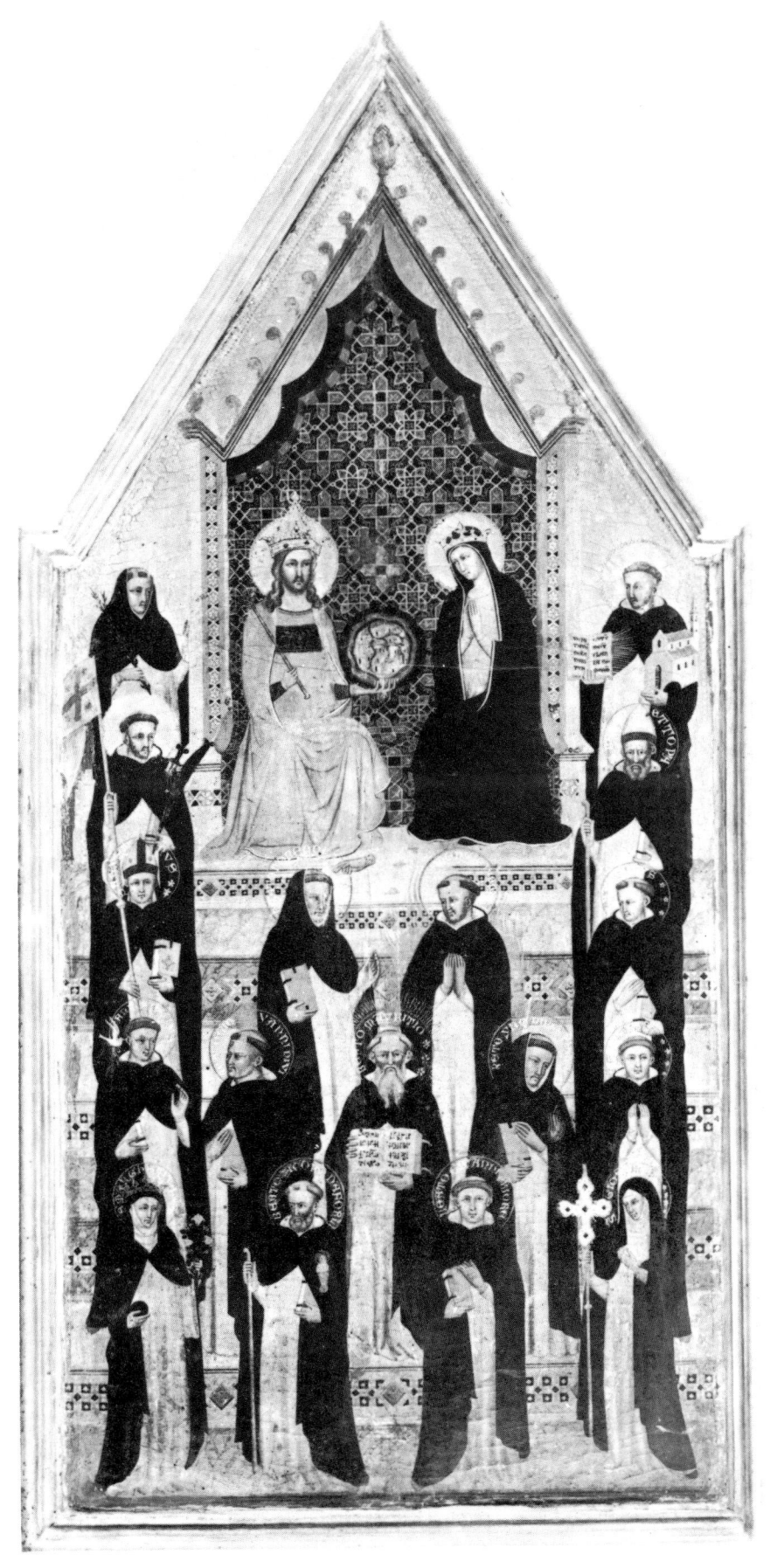

206

206.   *Christ and the Virgin Enthroned with seventeen Dominican Saints. Panel. Florence, S. Maria Novella, Sacristy. 125 × 45. SGF 27015.*

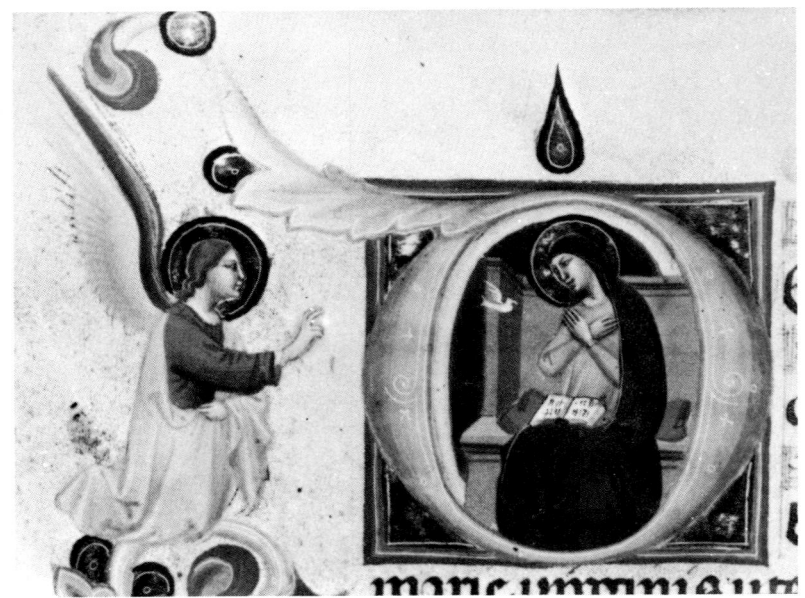

207

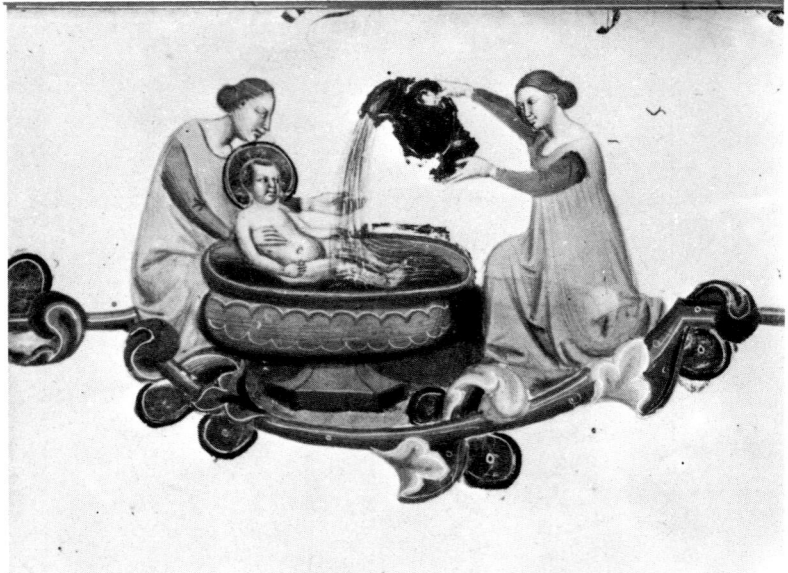

208

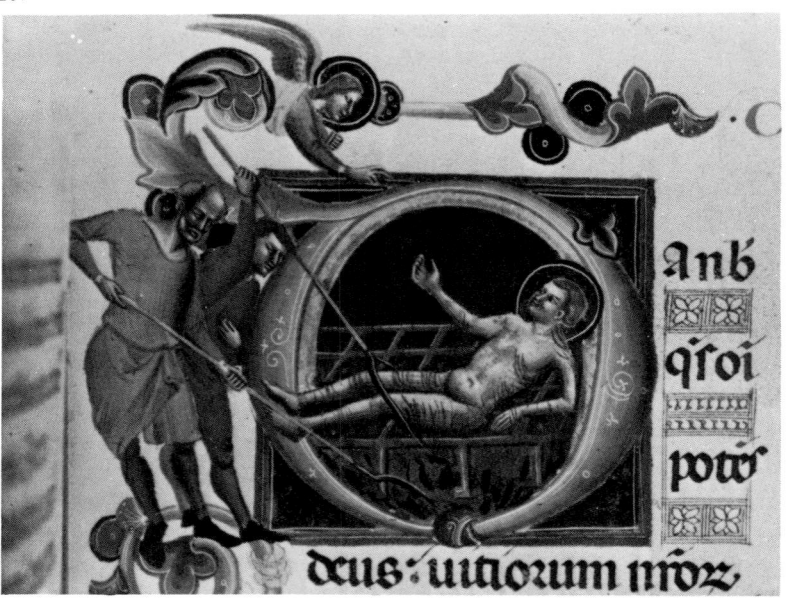

209

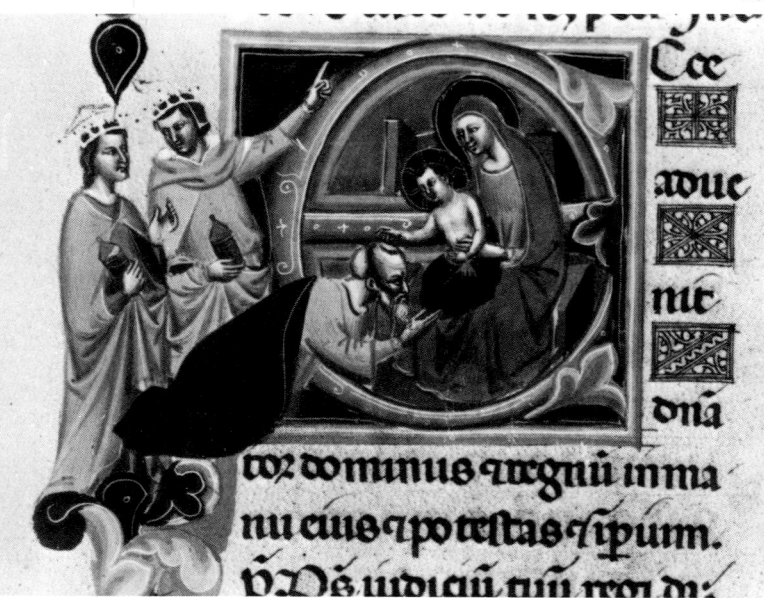

210

207. *Miniature: Annunciation. Parchment. Florence, Seminario Maggiore, Missal, p. 225. SGF 95276.*
208. *Miniature: Bathing the Infant Virgin. Parchment. Florence, Seminario Maggiore, Missal, p. 255. SGF 95296.*
209. *Miniature: Martyrdom of St Lawrence. Parchment. Florence, Seminario Maggiore, Missal, p. 248. SGF 95291.*
210. *Miniature: Adoration of the Magi. Parchment. Florence, Seminario Maggiore, Missal, p. 18. SGF 95239.*

MASTER OF FIGLINE
(MASTER OF THE FOGG PIETÀ)

In the works so far assembled the artistic personality is determined and differentiated by a certain eccentric energy in the statement and shape. The heavy mould is outlined by the cut of an emphatic contour, and a graduated light that renders the flexibility of the flesh. The same mould, the same decisive line, the same chiaroscuro, reappear in the Fogg Pietà. But if these analogies are general and do not suggest their significance at once, their radical importance will proclaim itself in a confrontation of details.....
All these panels join, by the analogies that have been pointed out, in a single artistic personality. But they also express a common tradition and a common period. The formative influence of their master, it must be admitted, cannot be as easily ascertained, possibly because of the idiosyncracies of a genius which, wanting in supreme characters, was nevertheless as original as any in Florence. It is a type of genius, that sacrifices the sublime or the exquisite qualities of the greatest expression for qualities so vigorous and so individual, that they require an appraisal by standards of their own. Accordingly, if he has undergone a deserved neglect beside his most illustrious contemporaries, his integrated oeuvre now marks a claim to high rank...

from R. Offner, pp. 53, 55, *Studies in Florentine Painting*, New York, 1927.

Finally, there is the most unusual figure of the Master of the Fogg Pietà, one of the most masterful reconstructions of Offner, particularly noteworthy for its clarifications on this para-Giottesque ground. He was a master of not uncommon vigour and character who certainly worked in Florence as is proved by the Crucifix in S. Croce and the stupendous panel at Figline (but why should he not more correctly be called the *Master of Figline*?). He is an incisive draughtsman, even becoming harsh in certain realistic details. His drawing is so subtle and alive that it is not comprehensible without admitting an influence by Simone Martini from whose style we recall certain brusque articulations such as the way that he makes cloth fall. There is also an influence of Ambrogio whom one can see clearly in the figure of the Saint with her lap full of roses..... There are traces of an inscription on the frame which we hope Procacci will be able to decipher; if so, it may solve the enigma of this master whose work in any case must pass over into the second half of the century.....

from L. Coletti, p. 65, *Bollettino d' Arte*, XXXI, 1937.

The painting [in S. Francesco at Assisi] is of a large Madonna and Child upon a large throne, at the sides of which are, above, two angels and below Sts. Francis and Clare; the attribution to the master called " of the Fogg Pietà ", by American students and by us, in a more Italianate manner, " of Figline ", from his greatest work, is immediate and sure; we know this to be especially true because of the extremely close similarity of the angels and saints with those placed in the same positions in the picture at Figline.

from A. Graziani, p. 66, *Proporzioni*, I, 1943.

A much greater density of composition and content is achieved in the small painting by the Master of the Fogg Pietà in the Fogg Museum. A few landscape features are present, but the figures are placed hieratically under the single, centrally located Cross. They are composed symmetrically, close to the foreground. Christ is stretched out on the ground, His body, not truly resting, but tilted into the picture plane in what might be called an *ostentatio mortui*. He is flanked by Sts. John and Mary Magdalene. Above him, in the center, the Virgin is supported by female saints on either side. And the composition ends at the right and the left in the standing, isolated and grieving figures of Nicodemus and Joseph. This careful and controlled arrangement finds further monumentality in the composed and balanced poses of the figures: from the horizontal Christ with the flanking crouching saints, via the half raised figures of the three Maries to the vertical of the two standing saints.....

from K. M. Birkmeyer, p. 474, *Gazette des Beaux-Arts*, LX, VI, 1962.

The author of this significant addition to the group of major wall paintings uncovered in Florence in the last years, is the most dramatic painter in that city between Cimabue and Masaccio, the Master of the Fogg Pietà. This painter, whose artistic activity has been reconstructed by Richard Offner, and who is sometimes called the Figline Master, from his greatest work, had without question a line which gave both immediate structure to a figure as well as an intense feeling of life.....

from M. Meiss, p. 149, *Bollettino d' Arte*, LI, 3/4, 1966.

In 1926, Offner singled out a group of paintings which he attributed to the " Master of the Fogg Pietà ", named after a panel in the Fogg Art Museum, Cambridge (Mass.). He included a Madonna Enthroned in the church of S. Francesco in Figline Valdarno, which provides the second name, " Maestro di Figline ", normally used by Italian critics. His other attributions consisted of a Crucifix in Sta. Croce, two panels (St. Philip and St. Francis) in Worcester (Mass.), a King David in Rennes Museum and a fragment from a Crucifix in the Mason Perkins Collection, now normally rejected. Offner regarded this artist as a Florentine follower of Giotto, active after 1320. Later critics have endorsed and amplified Offner's original suggestions. The most substantial contribution was made by Graziani, who added to the oeuvre a fresco of the Madonna with Saints Francis and Clare in the Basilica of S. Francesco at Assisi and an Assumption in Sta. Croce, Florence, dating both as early works, around 1320.....

from M. Meiss, p. 84, *Frescoes from Florence*, London, 1969.

BIBLIOGRAPHY
BOOKS

An asterisk indicates a work listed in thè General Bibliography

Offner, *Studies**, 1927, pp. 49-57; *Handbook of the Fogg Art Museum*, Harvard University, Cambridge, 1931, p. 34; *Paatz**, 1940, pp. 285-6, 310, 571, 600-8; *M. Giottesca**, 1943, pp. 553-65; *Coletti, Vol. II**, 1946, pp. 35-6; Catalogue: *Mostra di Opere d' Arte Trasportate a Firenze durante la Guerra e di Opere d' Arte restaurate*, Florence, 1947, p. 24; *Antal**, 1948, p. 221; *Galetti**, "F-O ", 1950, pp. 1460-5; *Toesca, 1951**, pp. 642-3; Oertel, R., *Die Frühzeit der Italienischen Malerei*, Stuttgart, 1953, p. 232; Marchini, G., *Le Vetrate Italiane*, Milan, 1955, p. 31; *Offner, 1956**, Sec. III, Vol. VI, pp. 65-100; Bellosi, L., *La Pittura dell'Italia Centrale nell'Età Gotica* (I Maestri del Colore, 252), Milan, 1966; *Dal Poggetto**, 1967, pp. 48-50; Meiss, M., *Fresco Show**, 1968, pp. 90-3 (84-7); Schlegel, U., *Congresso VII**, 1971, pp. 161-7, and Marchini, G., pp. 67-77.

JOURNALS

Chiappelli, A., *RADA*, IX, 5, 1909, pp. 71-3; Offner, R., *AA*, XIV, 1926, pp. 160-76; Salmi, M., *RA*, XI, 1929, p. 137; Suida, W., *P*, XX, 1937, p. 350; Salmi ,M., *E*, LXXXVI, 1937, pp. 349-64; Coletti, L., *BA*, XXXI, 3, 1937, pp. 49-72; Oertel, R., *ZKG*, VI, 1937, pp. 218-38; Graziani, A., *Prop.*, I, 1943, p. 79, n. 8; Graziani, A., *BM*, LXXXVIII, 1946, p. 172; Levi, E. L., *BIB*, XLVIII, 1946, p. 9-20; Longhi, R., *Prop*, 11, 1948, p. 53; Oertel, R., *ZKG*, XII, 1949, pp. 128-30; Baldini U., *BA*, XXXVIII, 3, 1953, pp. 277-8; Bologna, F., *BA*, XLI, 4, 1956, pp. 193-99; Procacci, U., *RA*, XXXII, 1958, pp. 126-7; Birkmeyer, K. M., *GBA*, LX, VI, 1962, p. 474; Marcucci, L., *AV*, I, 4, 1962, pp. 11-19; Marcucci, L., *JBM*, V, 1963, pp. 14-43; Volpe, C., *PA* XIV, 157, 1963, pp. 3-14; Bellosi, L., *PA*, XVII, 201/21, 1966, p. 77; Meiss, M., *BA*, LI, 5, 1966, pp. 149-50; Serra, J. R., *C*, XX, 1-2, 1969, pp. 20-36; Volpe, C., *PA*, XXIII, 267, 1972, pp. 6, 10, 11; Volpe, C., *PA*, XXIV, 277, 1973, pp. 3-23.

There are no known dated works by the Master of the Fogg Pietà.

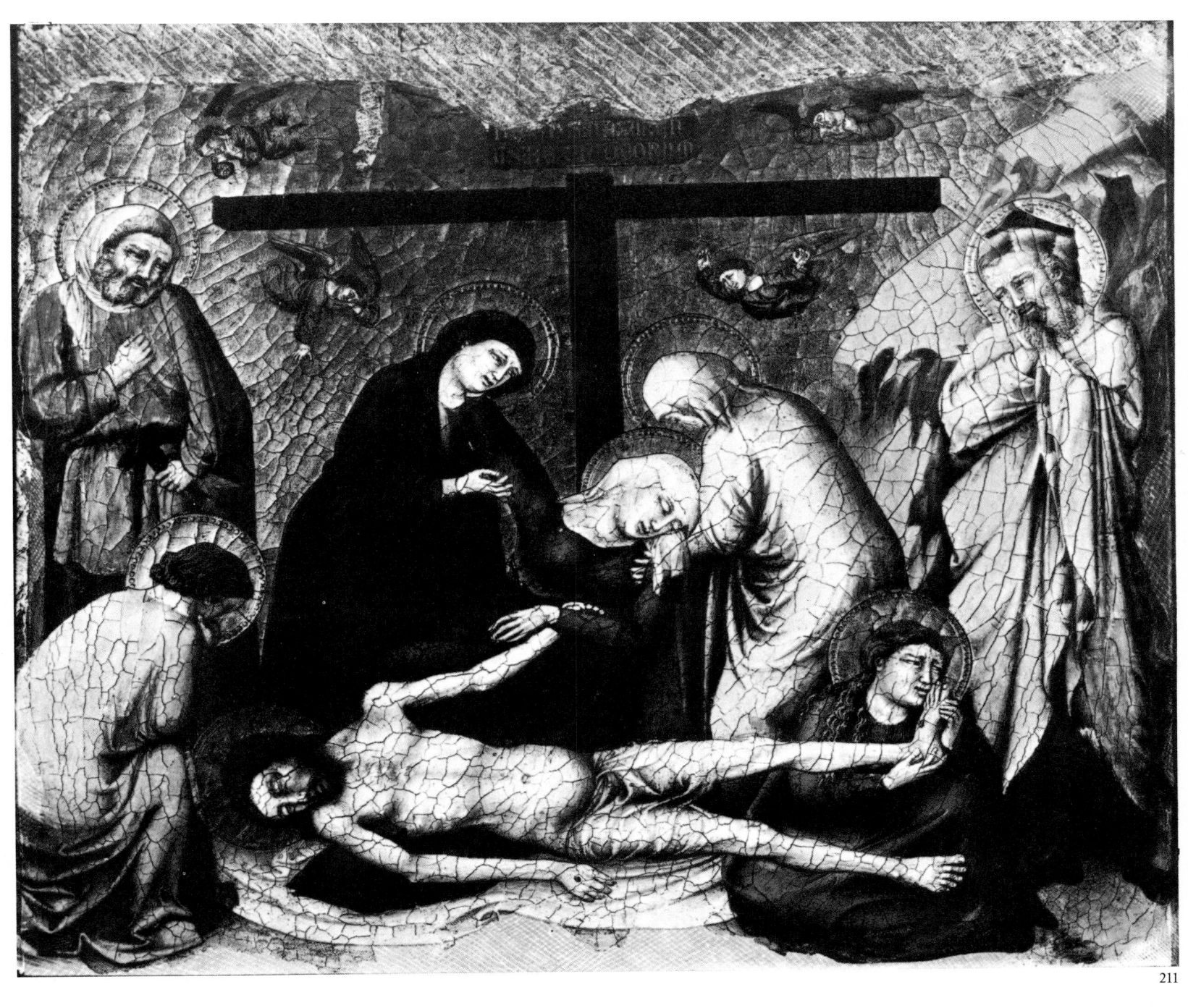

211

211. *Lamentation. Panel. Cambridge (Mass.), Fogg Art Museum, Sachs Gift. no. 1927.306. 43 × 50. Brogi 25934.*

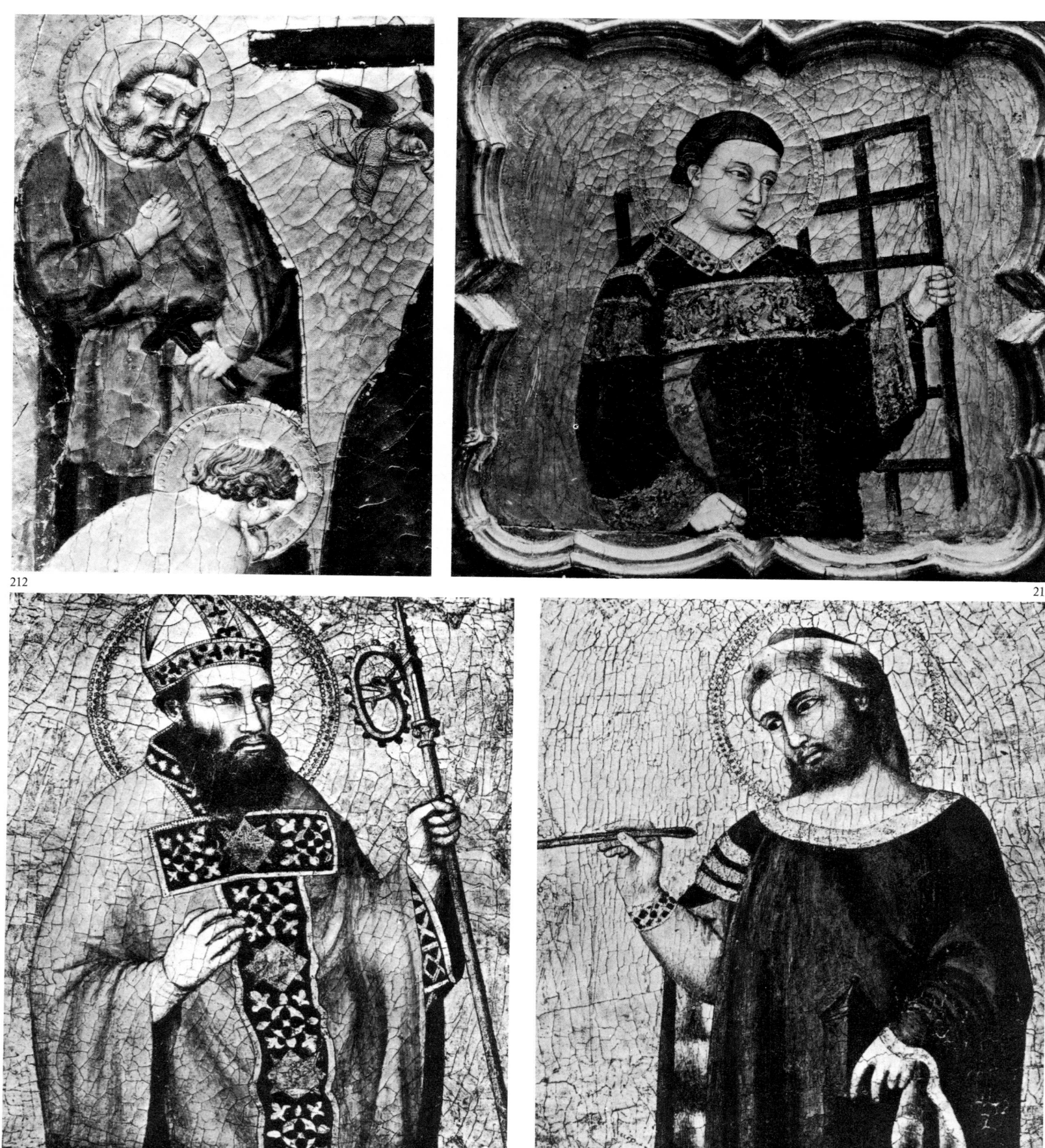

212. *Joseph of Arimethea, detail of fig. 211. Panel. Cambridge (Mass.), Fogg Art Museum. no. 1927.306. Bertoni-Offner.*
213. *St Lawrence. Panel. London, Courtauld Institute of Art, Lee of Fareham Collection. no. 4. 44.7 × 48.8 (w.f.). Fototeca Berenson.*
214. *Bishop Saint. Panel. Private Collection. 37.5 × 37.5. Bertoni-Offner.*
215. *Male Saint. Panel. Rome, Private Collection. 37.5 × 37.5. Bertoni-Offner.*

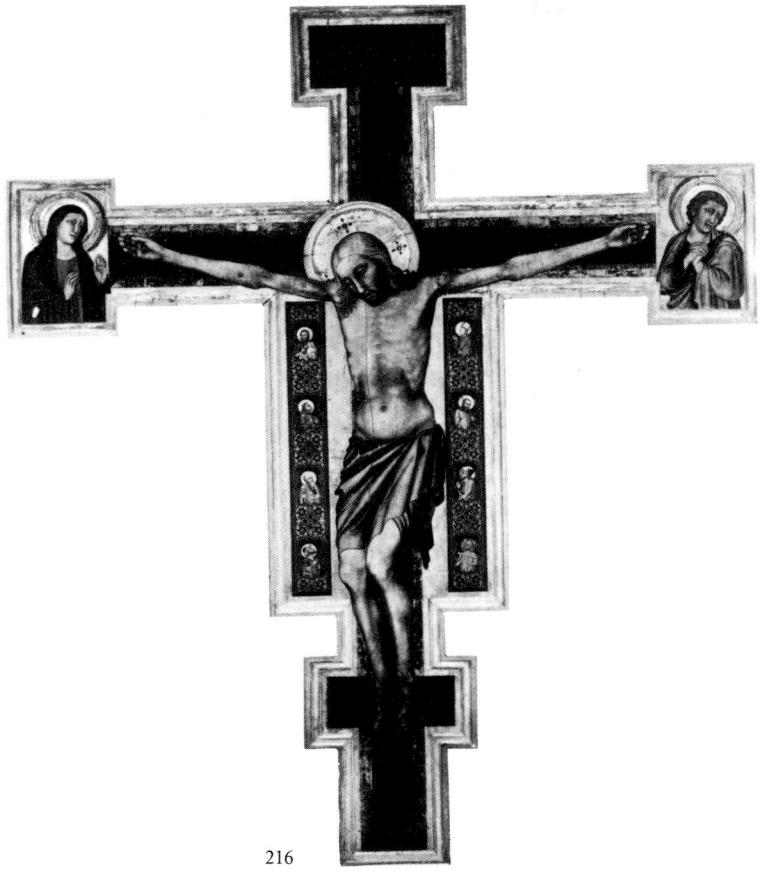

216

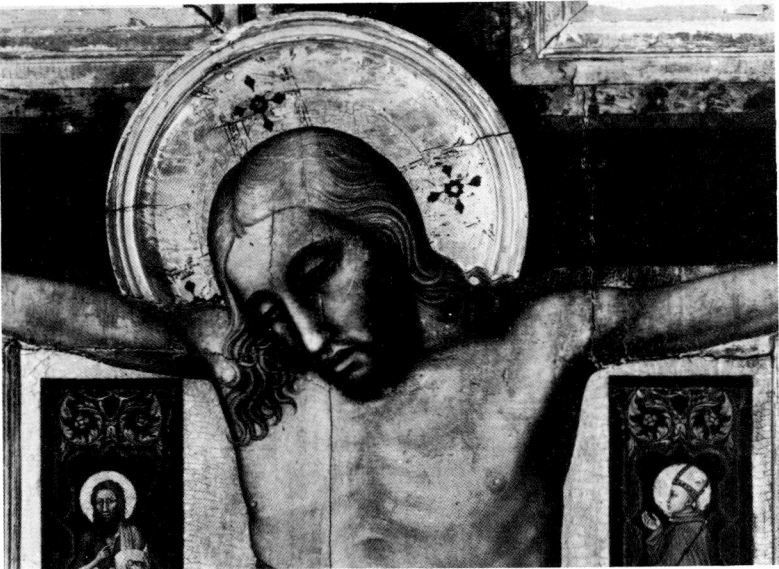

217

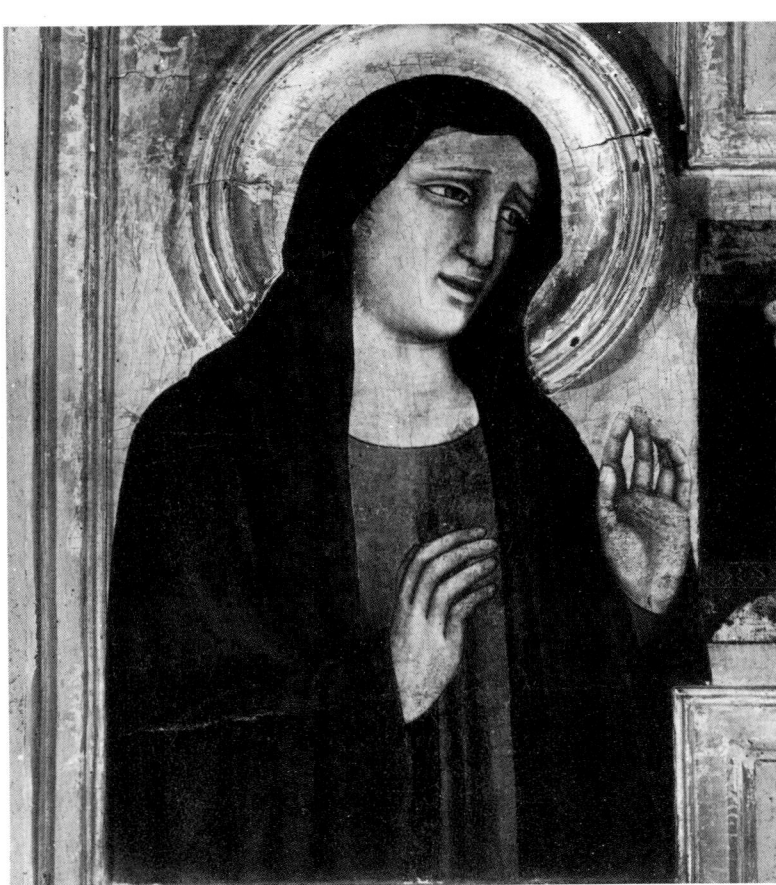

218

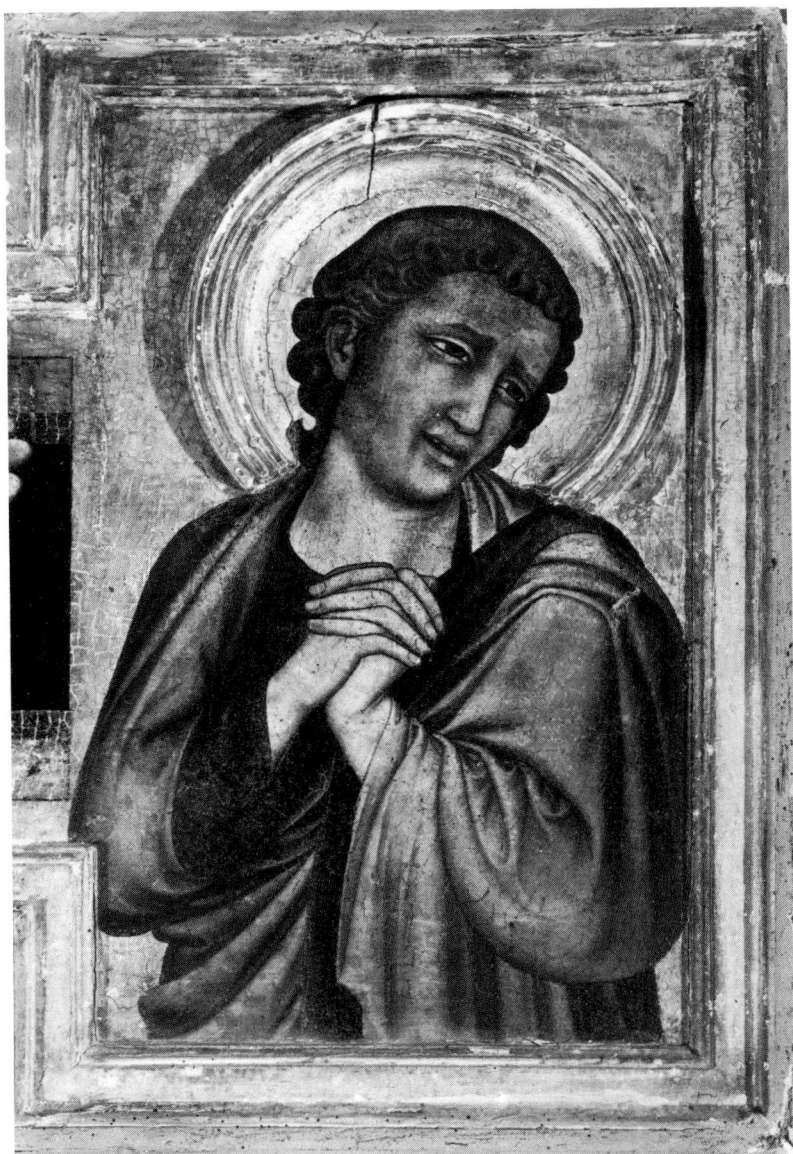

219

216. *Painted Crucifix. Panel. Florence, S. Croce, Choir. 473 × 384. SGF 26952.*
217. *Christ on the Cross, detail of fig. 216. Panel. Florence, S. Croce, Choir. SGF 26953.*
218. *The Virgin, detail of fig. 216. Panel. Florence, S. Croce, Choir. SGF 26954.*
219. *St John, detail of fig. 216. Panel. Florence, S. Croce, Choir. SGF 26955.*

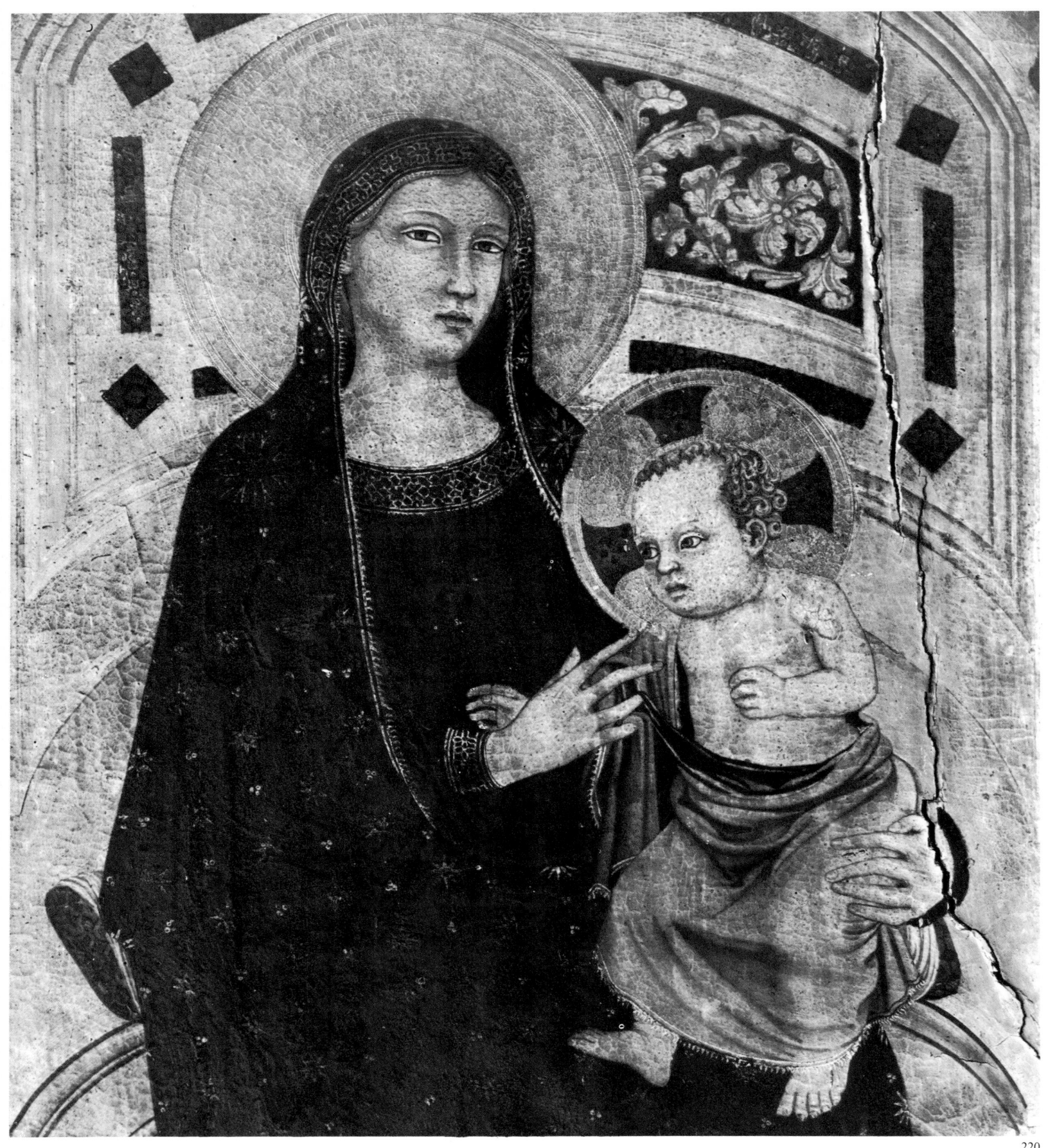

220. *Madonna and Child, detail of fig. 221. Panel. Figline, Collegiata di S. Maria. Brogi 25848.*

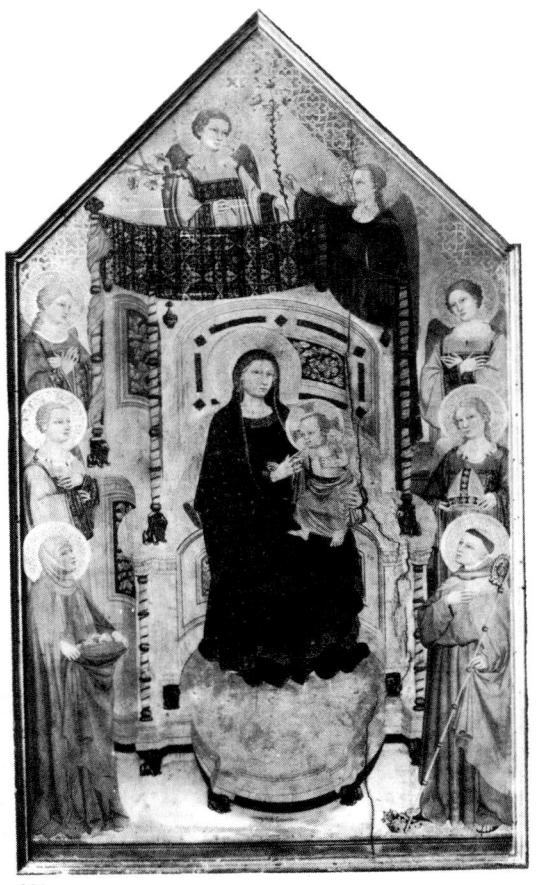

221

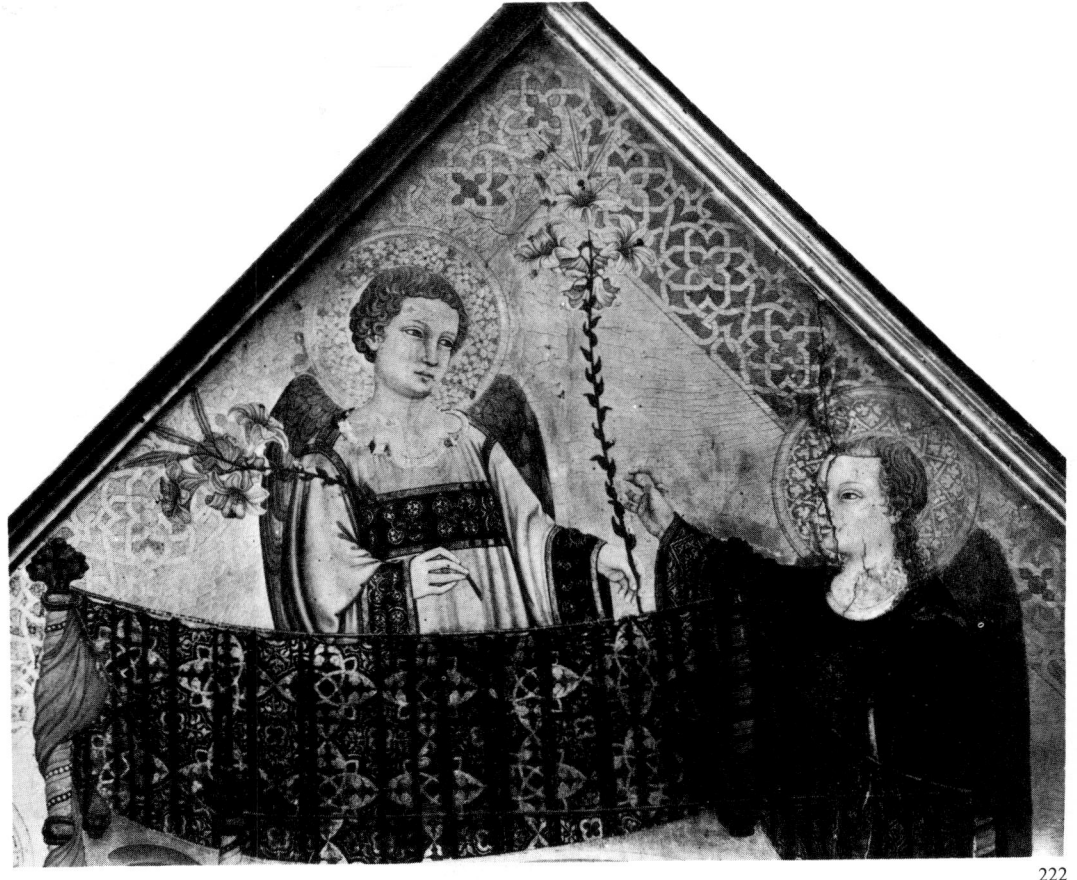

222

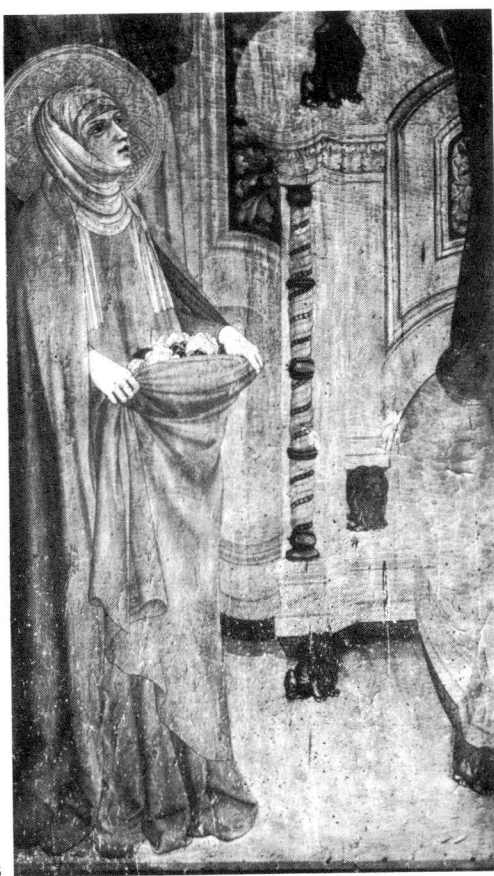

223

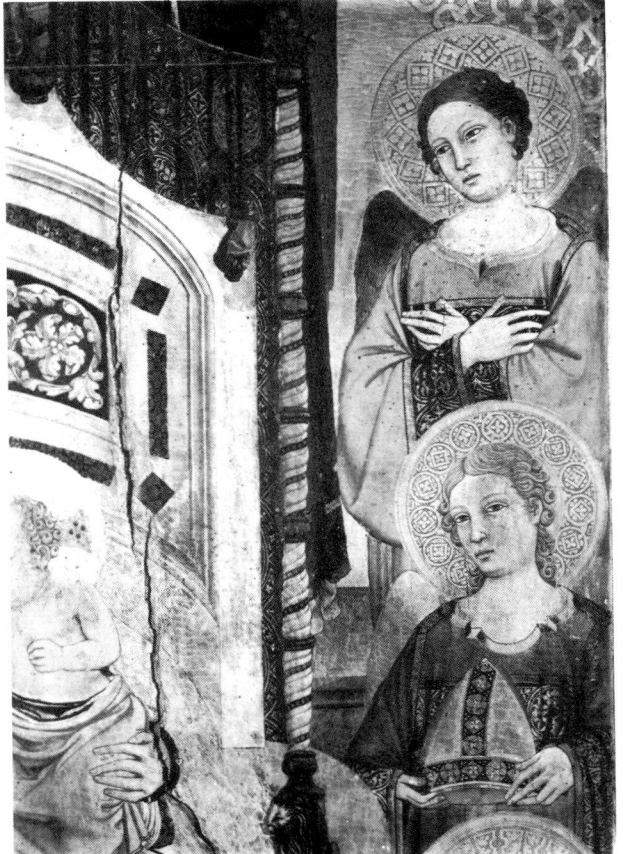

224

221. *Madonna and Child Enthroned with Saints and Angels. Above: Annunciation. Panel. Figline (Upper Valdarno), Collegiata di S. Maria. 300 × 176. SGF 26949.*

222. *Annunciation, detail of fig. 221. Panel. Figline, Collegiata di S. Maria. SGF 26950.*

223. *St Elizabeth of Hungary, detail of fig. 221. Panel. Figline, Collegiata di S. Maria. Brogi 25850.*

224. *Saint and Angel, detail of fig. 221. Panel. Figline, Collegiata di S. Maria. SGF 26951.*

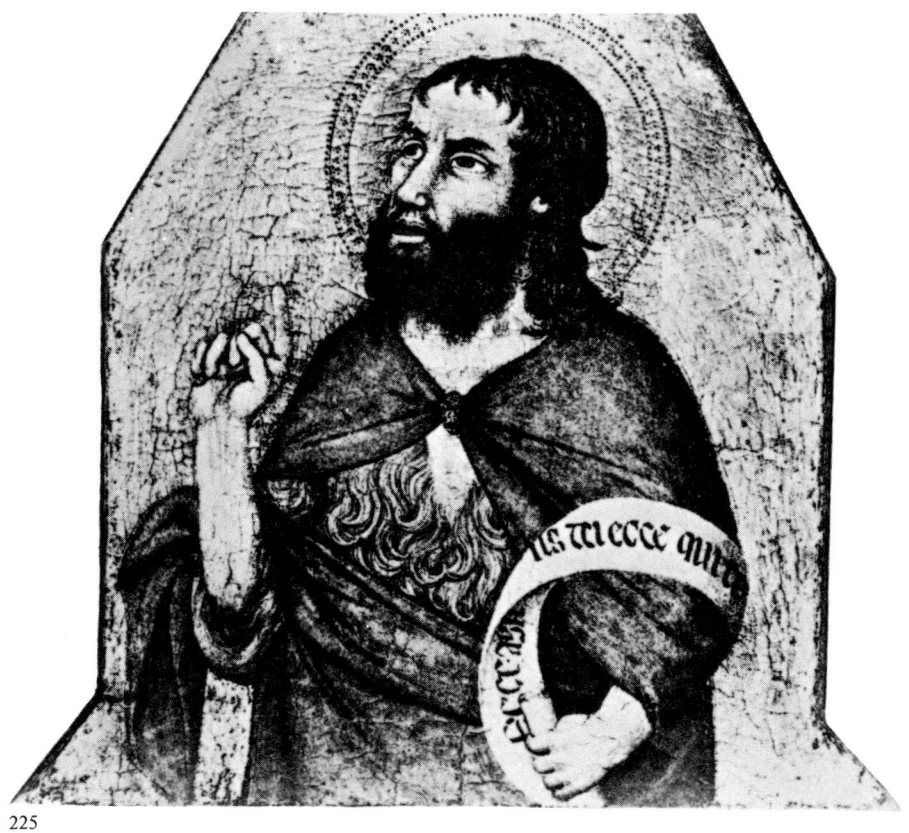

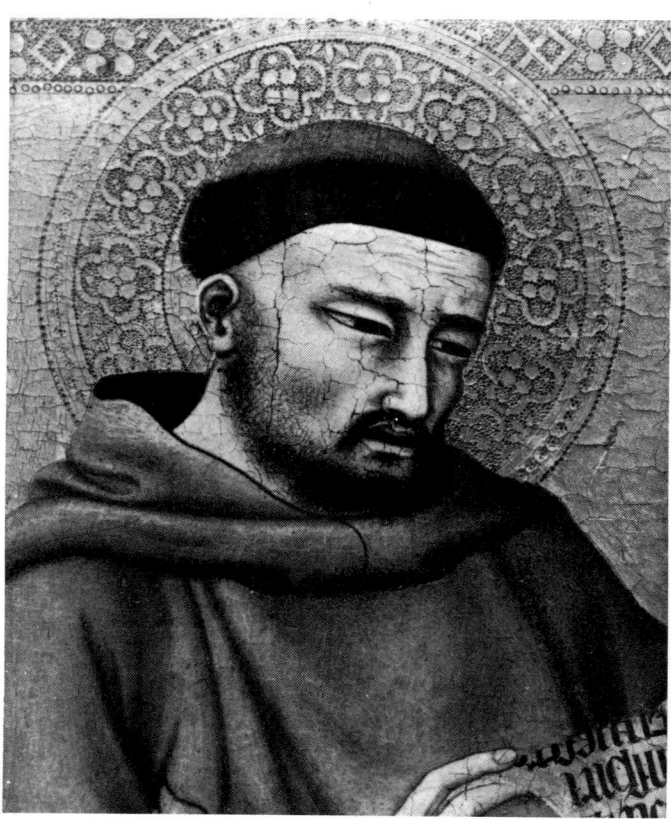

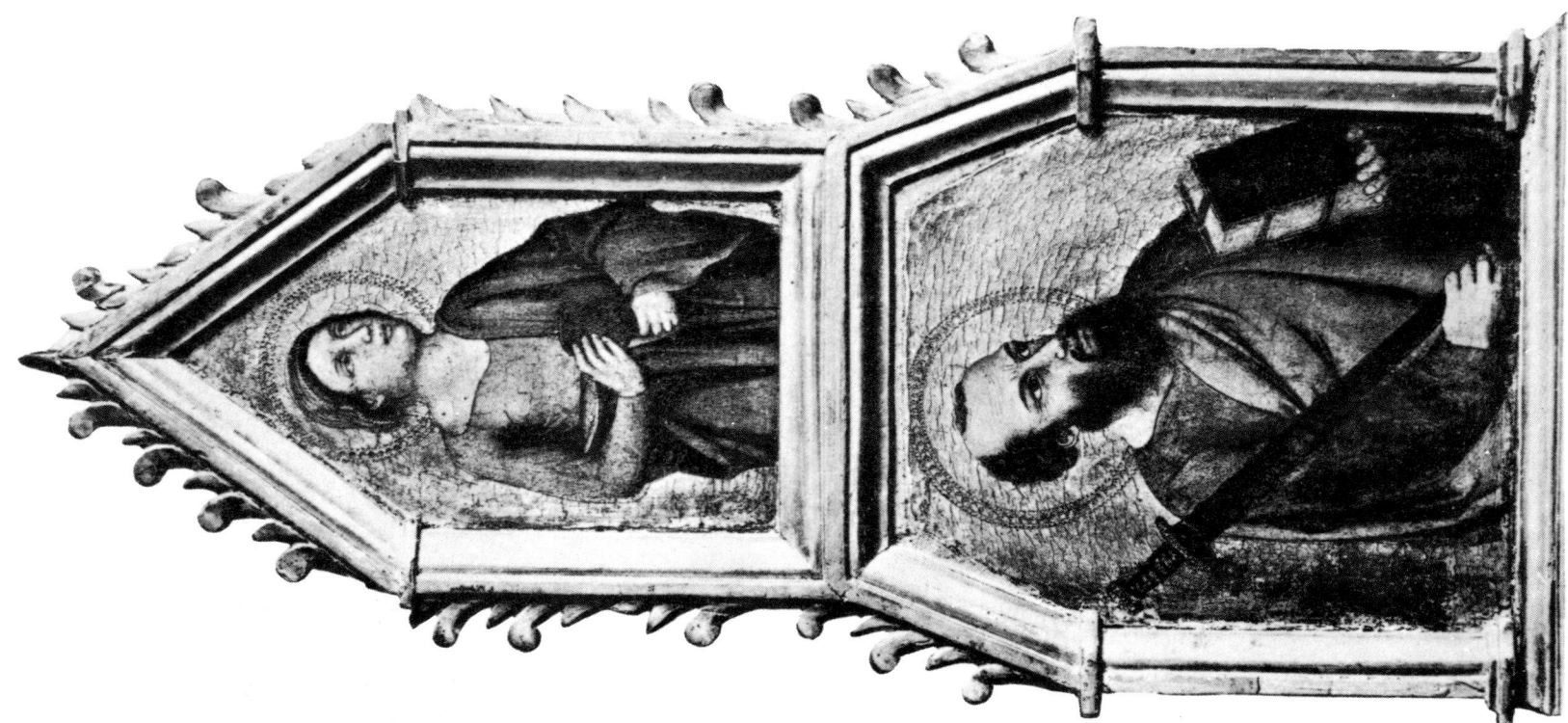

225

226

227

225. *St John the Baptist. Panel. Whereabouts unknown, (formerly Genoa, Gnecco Collection). 26 × 23.3. Bertoni-Offner.*
226. *St Francis, detail of fig. 228. Panel. Worcester (Mass.), Worcester Art Museum. no. 1923.19. Museum photo.*
227. *Sts Lucy and Paul. Panel. 's-Heerenberg, Holland, Dr J. H. van Heek Collection. Above: 27.3 × 15.4; below: 27.3 × 23.3. Bertoni-Offner.*

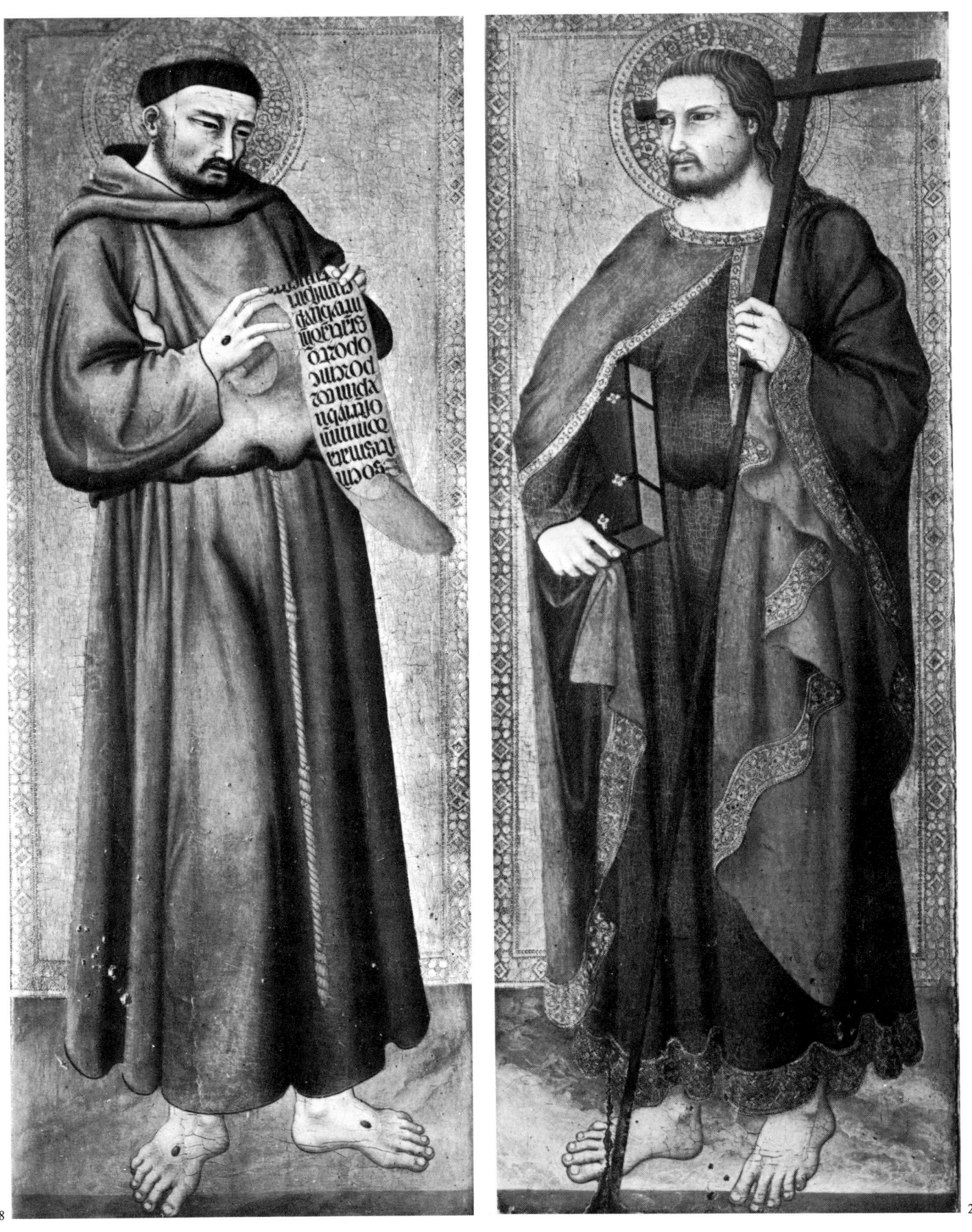

228

229

228. *St Francis. Panel. Worcester (Mass.), Worcester Art Museum. no. 1923.19. 96 × 36. Museum photo.*
229. *St Philip. Panel. Worcester (Mass.), Worcester Art Museum. no. 1923.18. 96 × 36. Museum photo.*

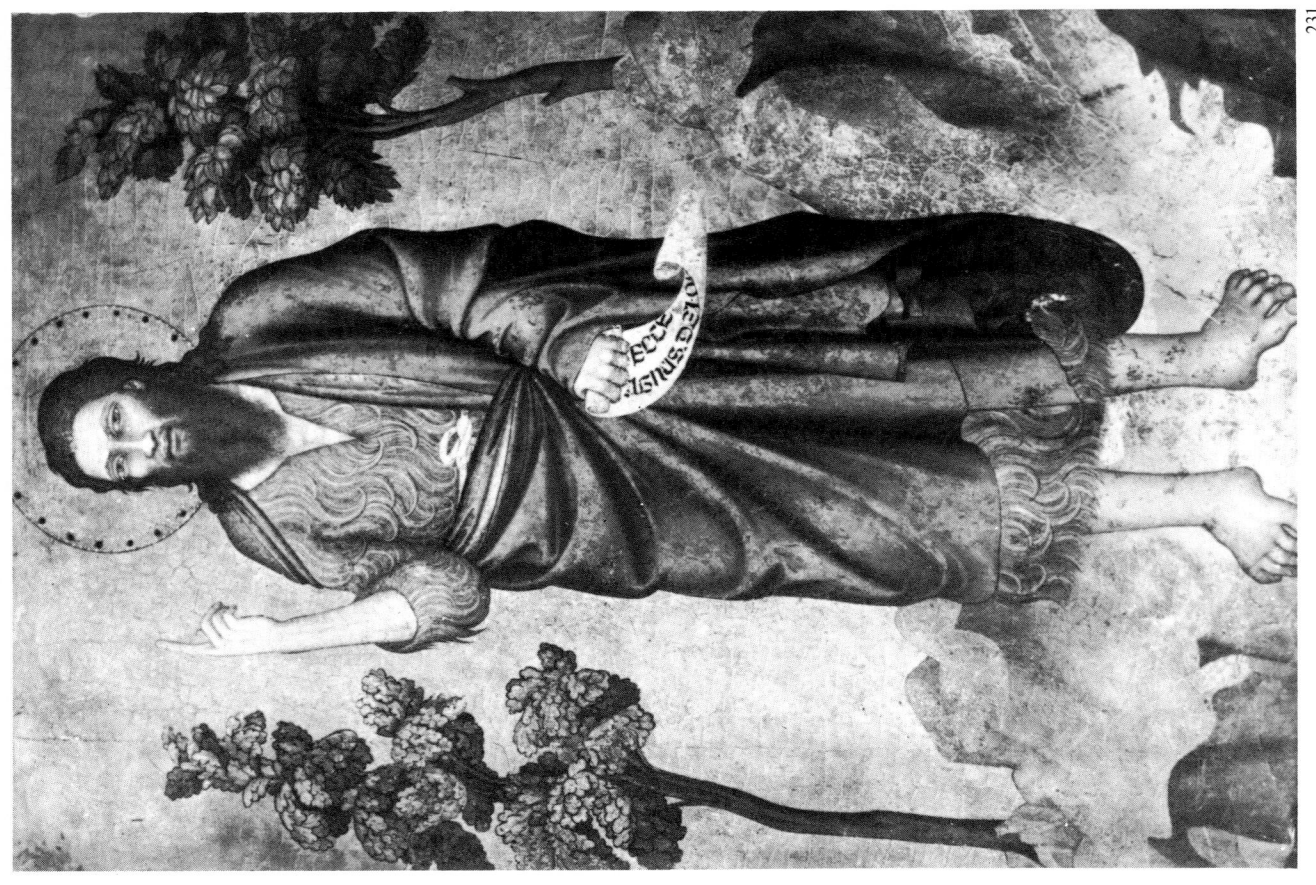

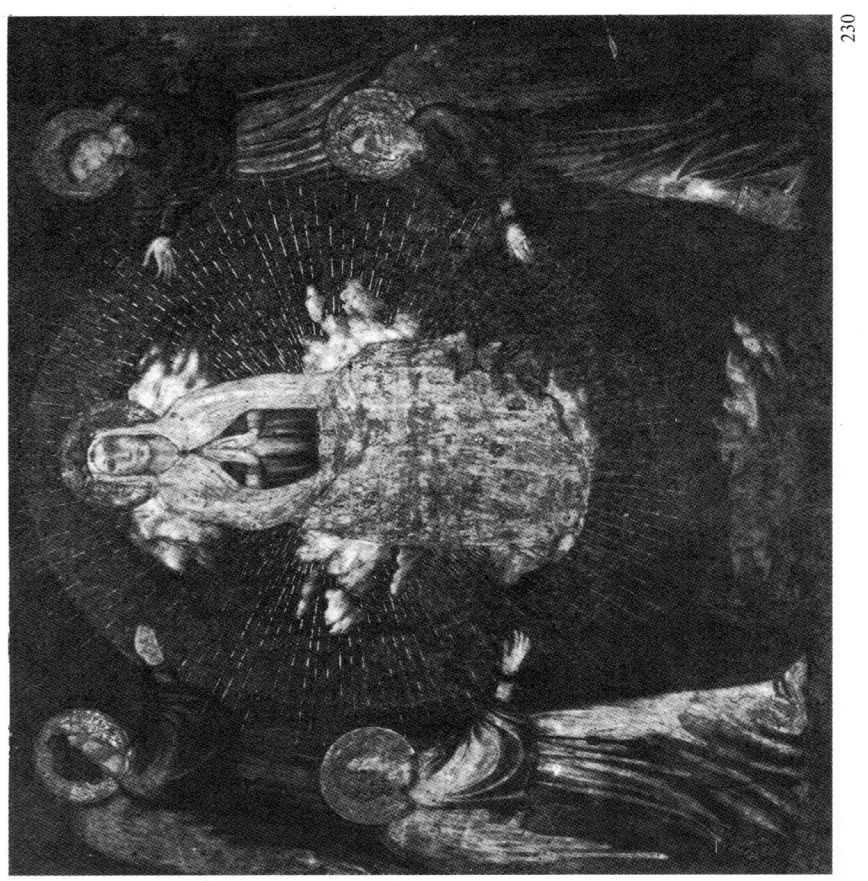

230. *Madonna in Glory with four Angels. Fresco. Florence, S. Croce, Tosinghi Chapel. SGF 48689.*
231. *St John the Baptist. Panel. Ferrara, Duke of Massari-Zavaglia Collection. Frick 23940.*

JACOPO del CASENTINO

Amongst the four counsellors, who, with four captains and two secretaries, signed the " ordinamenti " of the painters' corporation of Florence, which very probably dates from 1339, appears the name of " Jacopo di Chasentino " which proves that at that moment this painter was well-known in Florence and not very young. Vasari tells us in his first edition that he died at Pratovecchio in 1358 at the age of 65, in which case the year of his birth would be 1293; but in the second edition he makes the painter live until the age of 80. Horne has produced documents which prove that he probably died in 1349, anyhow certainly before 1354; he is still found mentioned in a report of 1347.
Vasari tells us that Jacopo was a pupil of Taddeo Gaddi's which is far from the truth because not only does the style of his painting refute this statement, but from what has been said it appears that these two artists were almost contemporary, and, if anything, Jacopo slightly earlier than Taddeo. The Anonimo Gaddiano places him amongst the immediate pupils of Giotto and in so doing assigns him his rightful place.....
Having abolished that part of Jacopo's career which was supposed to have taken place at Arezzo and those works which we are now certain were not executed by him, the artist becomes a very comprehensible member of the Giottesque group of painters.
We need not then mention all the numerous works at Arezzo which Vasari ascribes to Jacopo, but limit ourselves to those at Florence which the biographer attributes to this artist. They are: the ornamentation of the vaults of Or San Michele; the tabernacle dei Tintori representing the Madonna between angels; and the Madonna between angels and saints, with the Coronation of the Virgin above, on the angle of the Palazzo dell'Arte della Lana...

from R. van Marle, pp. 294-296, *The Development of the Italian Schools of Painting*, Vol. III. The Hague, 1924.

Whereas Horne inclines to 1349 for Jacopo's death the Annali Camaldolensi (if we may trust Beni's Guida Illustrata del Casentino, 1908) put it at 1358 and at the age of eighty, which is the age Vasari adopts in his second edition. This would tend to shift the date of Jacopo's beginnings to about 1300, long before his first mention in 1339. The stylistic evidence in Jacopo's earlier works, as well as his consistent development, would encourage the hypothesis of a long activity, and an early period — not quite as early as 1300, however — for his origins. Prolific, ambitious, assimilative, eclectic, archaistic, his provincial genius is ill-adjusted to the advancing tempo of Florentine evolution. He was naturally inclined to small scale, but was won by the pondus and monumentality of the Giotteschi. Formed probably in Arezzo under mixed Sienese and Florentine influences, he gives way completely with time to the enchantments of Daddi's painting. But most persistent in his style are the elements inherited from the welter of earlier tradition, of which the most prominent exponent is the St. Cecilia Master. Occasional though conspicuous analogies of type with the Master of the Dominican Effigies (with whom Jacopo has recently been confused) may be due to reciprocal borrowing, and a sympathy between the two masters which could neither have been profound nor enduring. Jacopo's influence, however, seems seldom to have reached very far beyond the shop-precincts.....

from R. Offner, p. 87, *A Critical and Historical Corpus of Florentine Painting*, Sec. III, Vol. II, Part II, New York, 1930.

Died 1349 (or 1358?). Possibly a pupil of Meo da Siena; influenced by Bolognese artists by the S. Cecilia Master and later by Daddi.

from B. Berenson, p. 100, *Italian Pictures of the Renaissance. Florentine School*, Vol. I, London, 1963.

Although this painter signed his paintings " Jacobus de Casentino ", he must have been active prevalently in Florence. The first record we have of him dates from 1339, when he was counsellor of the Compagnia di San Luca. But if he died in 1349 (as Horne proposed in 1909, and Offner agreed), then he must have begun to paint around 1320 or shortly thereafter, under a strictly Giottesque influence. There are only two sure works by this painter: the signed triptych in the Cagnola alla Gazzada Collection (Varese) and the Madonna and Child with Saints in the Tabernacle of Palazzo dell'Arte della Lana in Florence. Today, chiefly through the work of Offner, we recognize his artistic personality through a number of reliable attributions.

In Florence, in the first half of the '300, the figure of Jacopo del Casentino occupies a special place among his contemporaries, from Maso to Bernardo Daddi and Taddeo Gaddi. He shows a particular interest in the most French Gothic aspects of Giotto's art..... In fact, in the tabernacle of Palazzo dell'Arte della Lana, one can recognize not only many details but even entire scenes from the Assisi work..... At S. Miniato in Florence, the lateral stories are really miniatures..... On the one hand, they show certain precise references to the Stories of St. Francis by Giotto, and on the other, they emphasise this " Gallicism ".
Jacopo del Casentino must have been particularly important in determining the new direction given to Giottesque art towards the middle of the century by the Orcagna brothers.....

from P. Dal Poggetto, pp. 24-25, *Arte in Valdelsa*, Certaldo, 1963.

Florentine School. Active first half of fourteenth century. In 1339 Jacopo was one of the founders, along with Bernardo Daddi and others, of the painters' Corporation of St. Luke in Florence. Vasari says that he was a pupil and assistant of Taddeo Gaddi, whom he resembles stylistically; but he was also influenced by the Master of St. Cecilia, by Giotto, and later by Bernardo Daddi and Sienese painters. He was perhaps the most prolific panel painter in fourteenth century Florence. Undoubtedly, he made much use of studio assistants.....

from F. R. Shapley, p. 24, *Paintings from the Samuel H. Kress Collection*, London, 1966.

BIBLIOGRAPHY
BOOKS

An asterisk indicates a work listed in the General Bibliography

Coretti-Miniati, G. G., *Vita di Jacopo di Casentino*, Florence, 1913; *Khv & Salmi**, 1914, p. 25; Sirèn, O., *Giotto and Some of his Followers*, Vol. I, Cambridge, 1917, pp. 189-92; *v. Marle, 1924**, pp. 294-300; *Offner, Studies**, 1927, pp. 23-42; *Toesca, 1929**, p. 64; *Offner, 1930**, Sec. III, Vol. II, Part II; *Berenson, 1932**, pp. 271-3; Waldmann, E., *Die Bremen Kunsthalle*, Kassel, 1938, p. 36; Catalogue: *Gemälde und Bildhauerwerke in der Kunsthalle zu Bremen*, Bremen, 1939, pp. 83-4; *Preliminary Catalogue of Painting and Sculpture*, National Gallery of Art, Washington, D.C., 1941, pp. 101-2; *M. Giottesca**, 1943, pp. 465-71; *Coletti, Vol. II**, 1946, p. 35; *Antal**, 1948, pp. 186-7; Busch, C., *Handbuch der Kunsthalle, Bremen*, Bremen, 1948, pp. 18-19; *Vavalà, 1948**, pp. 59-63; *Galetti**, " F-O ", 1950, p. 1270; *Oertel, 1950**, pp. 45-6; Suida, W. E., *Paintings and Sculpture from the Kress Collection*, Washington, 1951, pp. 34-5; *Toesca, 1951**, p. 626; Suida, W. E., *Catalogue of the William Rockhill Nelson Gallery of Art*, Kansas City, 1952, p. 24; Suida, W. E., *The Samuel H. Kress Collection in the Honolulu Academy of Arts*, Honolulu, 1952, pp. 12-13; Busch, C., *Handbuch der Kunsthalle Bremen*, Bremen, 1954, pp. 18-19; Suida, W. E., *Catalogue of the University of Arizona Collection*, Tucson, 1957, no 4; *Offner, 1957**, Sec. III, Vol. VII, pp. 93-134; *Gregori**, 1960, pp. 4-5; Shapley, F. R., *Catalogue of the El Paso Museum of Art*, El Paso, 1961, no 2; Dal Poggetto, P., *AIV**, 1963, pp. 24-6; *Berenson, 1963**, Vol. I, pp. 100-3; *Marcucci**, 1965, pp. 50-6; Rossi, F., *Il Museo Horne a Firenze*, Milan, 1966, p. 136; *Shapley**, 1966, p. 24; *Dal Poggetto**, 1967, pp. 31-2; Procacci, U., *AIE, 1966**, Vol. I, p. 304; *Dutch Show**, 1974, pp. 59-60.

JOURNALS

Toesca, P., *A*, 1, 1904; Gamba, C., *RADA*, IV, 12, 1904, pp. 177-86; Suida, W., *K*, XVII, 21, 1906, p. 335; Horne, P. H., *RA*, VI, 1909, pp. 95-112; Sirèn, O., *BM*, XXVI, 1914, pp. 77-83; Dami, L., *BA*, VIII, 1915, pp. 216-44; Offner, R., *BA*, III, 1, 1923-24, pp. 248-84; Salmi, M., *B*, V, 1924, pp. 119-23; de Térey, G., *BM*, XLVII, 1925, pp. 251-2; Gronau, H. D., *BM*, LIII, 1928, pp. 78-87; Salmi, M., *Bib*, XXX, 1928, pp. 369-82; Salmi, M., *MKIF*, III, 1919-32, pp. 145-6; Suida, W., *B*, XV, 1929, pp. 329-30; Salmi, M., *RA*, IX 1929, pp. 134-5; Toesca, P., *A*, XXXIII, 5, 1930, p. 15; Berenson, B., *IS*, XCVII, 1930, pp. 33-35; Berenson, B., *DD*, XI, I, 1930-31, pp. 263-84; Comstock, H., *CS*, CVII, 1941, pp. 72-3; *Edit.*, *K*, II, 1949, p. 66; Longhi, R., *PA*, I, 7, 1950, p. 46; Gronau, H. D., *BM*, XCII, 1950, p. 322; Busch, G., *K*, V, 1952, p. 32; Berti, L., *BA*, XXXVII, 1952, pp. 55-57; Micheletti, E., *BA*, XXXIX, 4, p. 360; Eisenberg, M. J., *PR*, XIV, 1955, pp. 4-8; Cohn, W., *BA*, XLI, 4, 1956, pp. 172-4; *Edit.*, *BM*, 102, supp. 1, 1960, plate III; Donati, P. P., *AV*, V, 2, 1966, pp. 16-22; Donati, P. P., *AV*, 2, 1967, pp. 12-16; De Benedictis, C., *AV*, 3, 1967, p. 42; Donati, P. P., *C*, XVIII, 4, 1967, pp. 290-96; Skaug, E., *MKIF*, XV, 2, 1971, pp. 141-60; Van Os, H. W., *C*, XXII, 1, 1971, p. 74; De Benedictis, C., *AV*, XI, 4, 1972, pp. 6-8; Cole, B., *GBA*, LXXX, 114, 1972, pp. 91-96; Cole, B., *MKIF*, XVII, 2-3, 1973, p. 236, 245-6.

SIGNED AND DATED WORKS

Florence, Uffizi 9258. Triptych: Madonna & Child Enthroned with Saints and Angels. s. (fig. 244).
1330 Kansas City (Mo.), William Rockhill Nelson Gallery of Art. Panel: Infant Christ presented in the Temple for Circumcision. d. (fig. 235).
1345 Budapest, Musée des Beaux-Arts. Panel: Madonna & Child Enthroned, with Saints and Angels. d. (fig. 242).

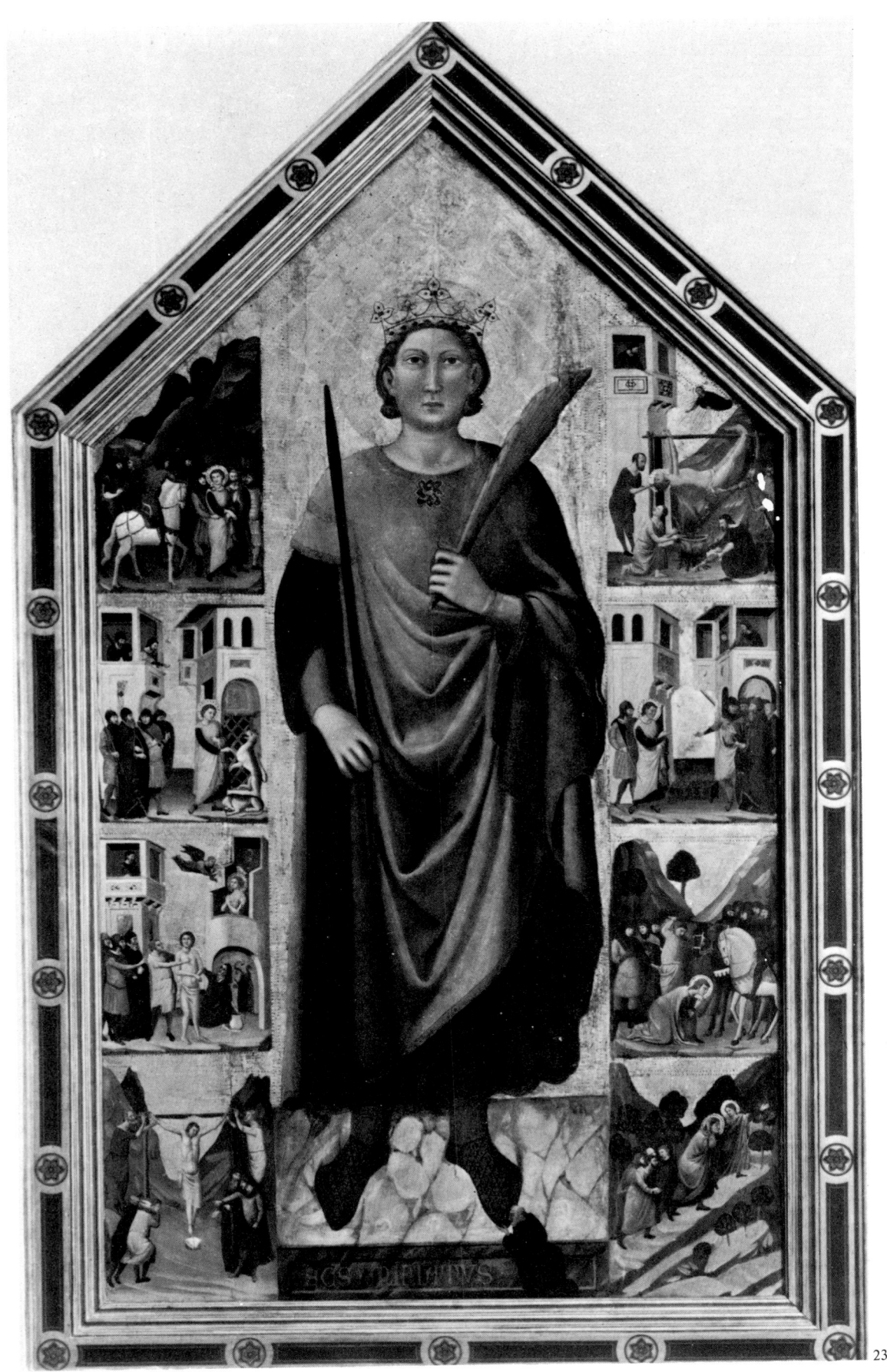

232. *St Minias and Scenes from his Life: Arrest of St Minias; Death of the Leopard; Torture of St Minias in an oven, on the gallows, and over a fire; Refusal of the Bribe; Beheading of St Minias; St Minias carrying his head to the site of his Church. Panel. Florence, S. Miniato al Monte. 185 × 106. Alinari 44368.*

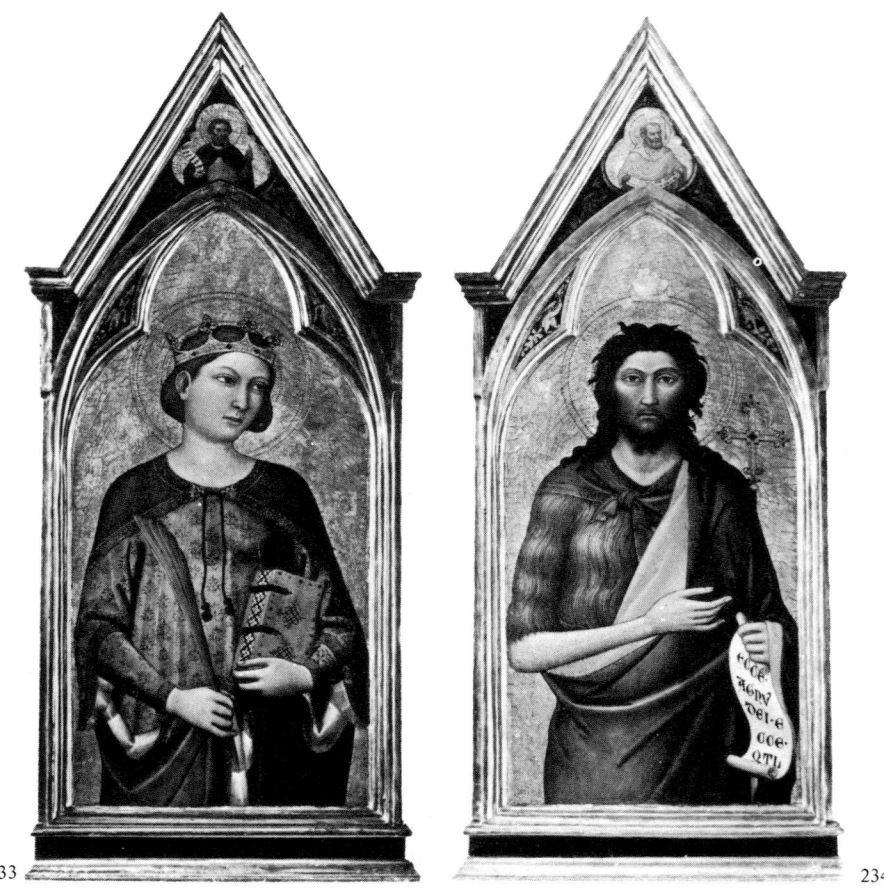

233   234

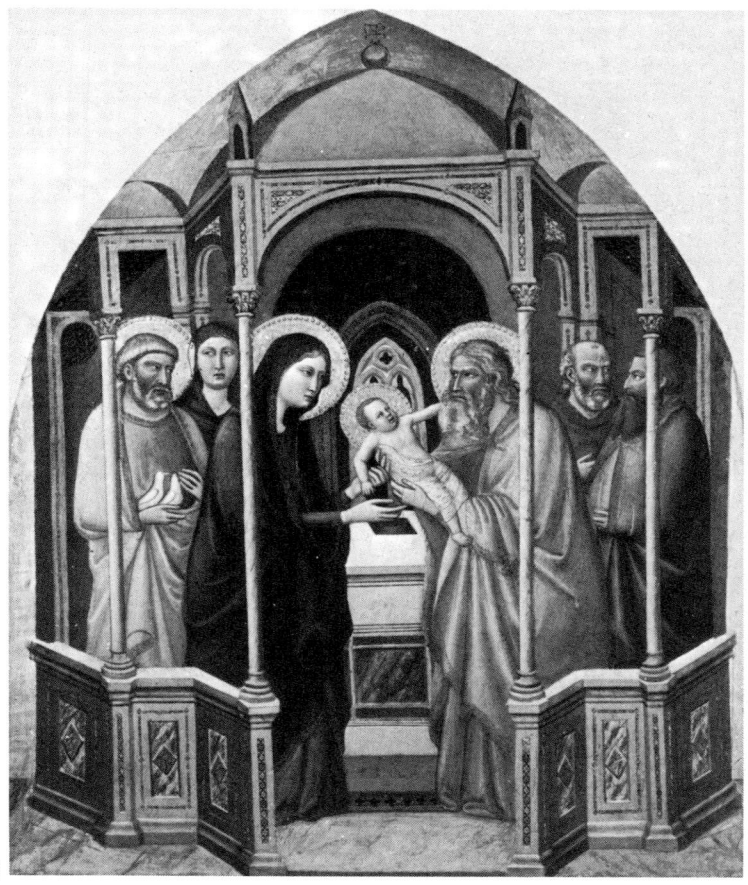

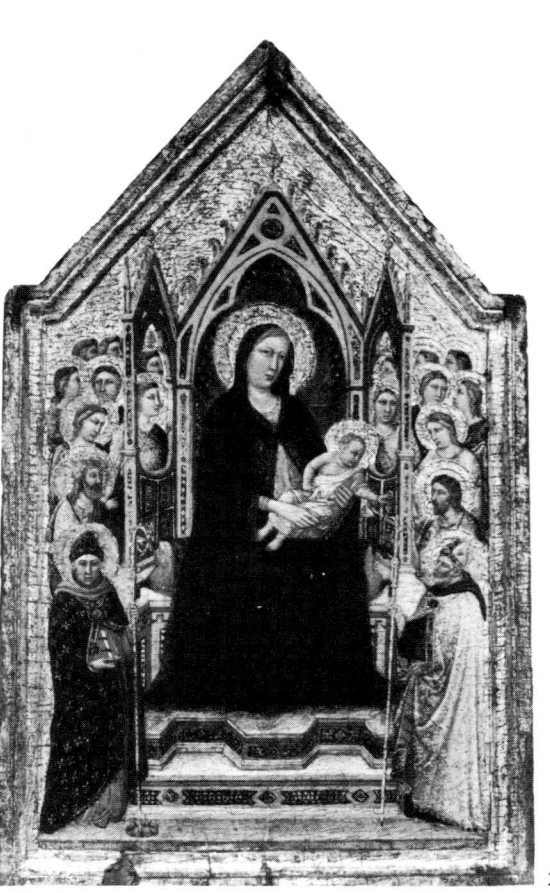

235   236

233. *St Catherine. Above: Prophet. Panel. Houston (Tex.), Rice University, Institute for the Arts, Menil Foundation Collection. 114.3 × 43.8. Museum photo 60-01(D).*

234. *St John the Baptist. Above: Prophet. Panel. Houston (Tex.), Rice University, Institute for the Arts, Menil Foundation Collection. 114.3 × 34.8. Museum photo 60-01 (A).*

235. *The Infant Christ presented in the Temple for Circumcision. Panel. Kansas City (Mo.), Wm. Rockhill Nelson Gallery of Art, Samuel H. Kress Collection. K 446. 74.6 × 59.7. Kress Foundation photo. d. 1330.*

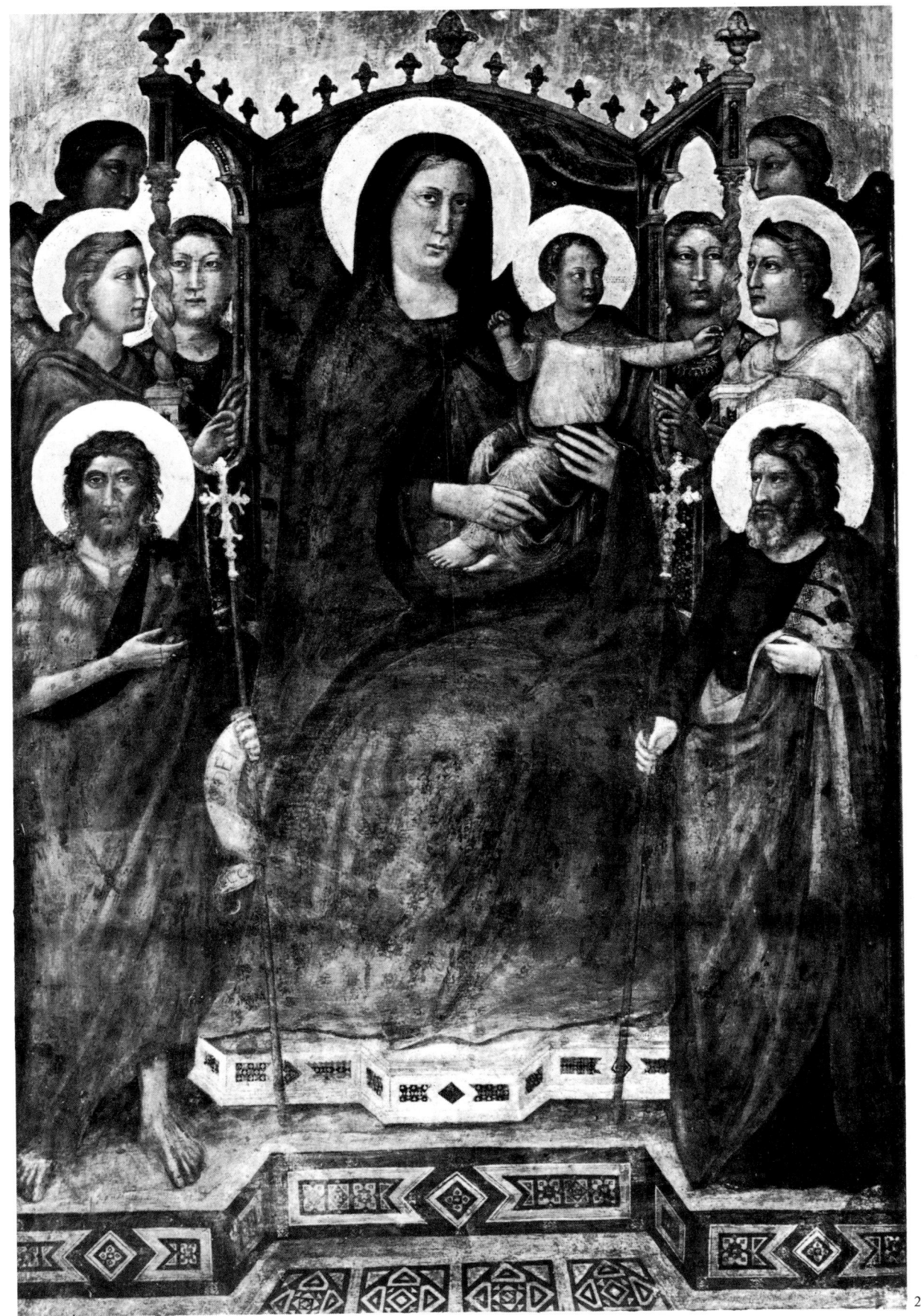

237

236. *Madonna and Child Enthroned with Saints and Angels. Panel. Ann Arbor (Mich.), University of Michigan, Museum of Art. no. 1960/2.123.*
   56.5 × 32.4. Museum photo.
237. *Madonna and Child Enthroned with Sts John the Baptist and John the Evangelist and six Angels. Panel. Florence, Palazzo dell' Arte della Lana.*
   238 × 120. SGF 26984 (see Master of the Arte della Lana, fig. 665).

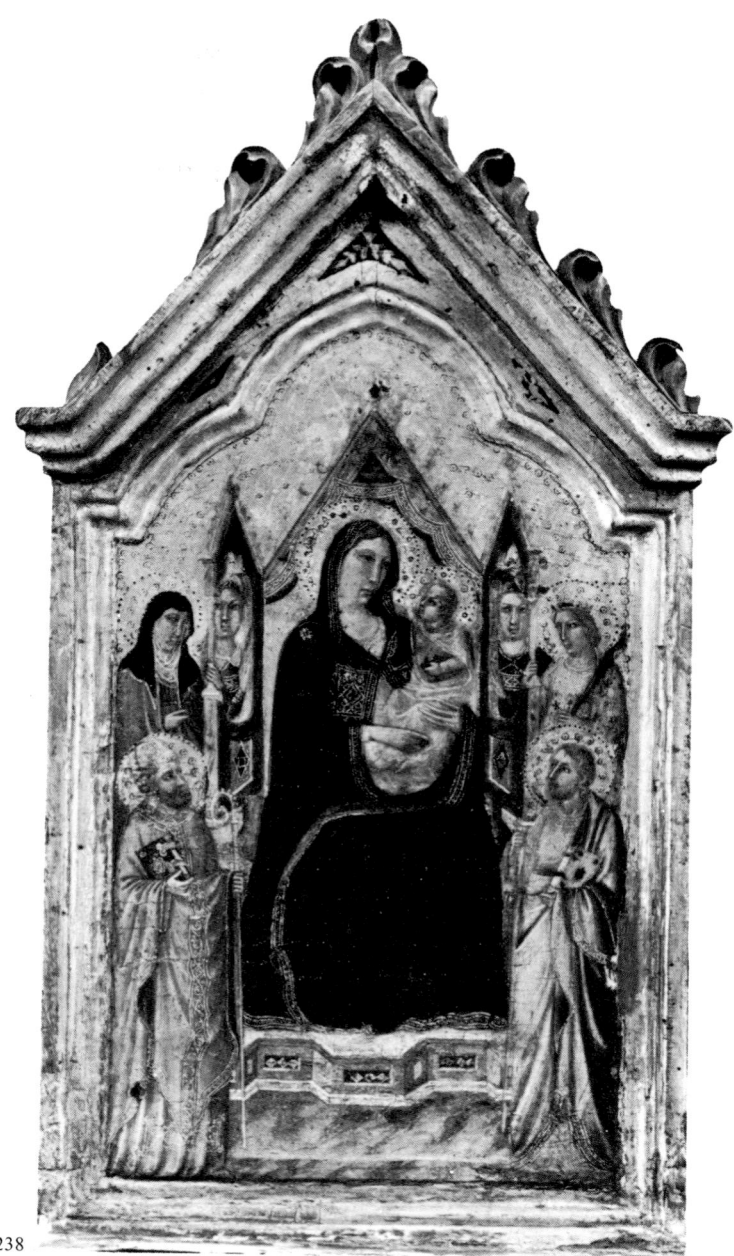

238

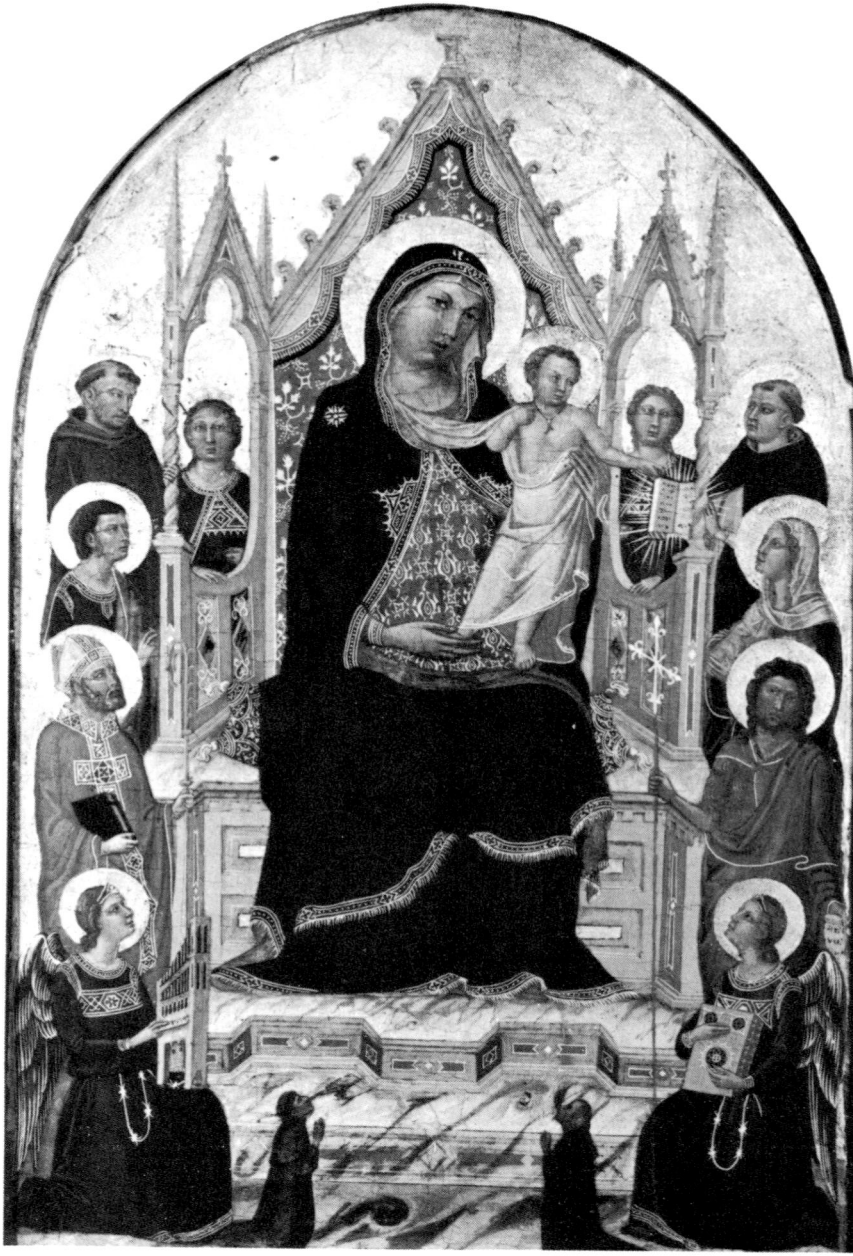

239

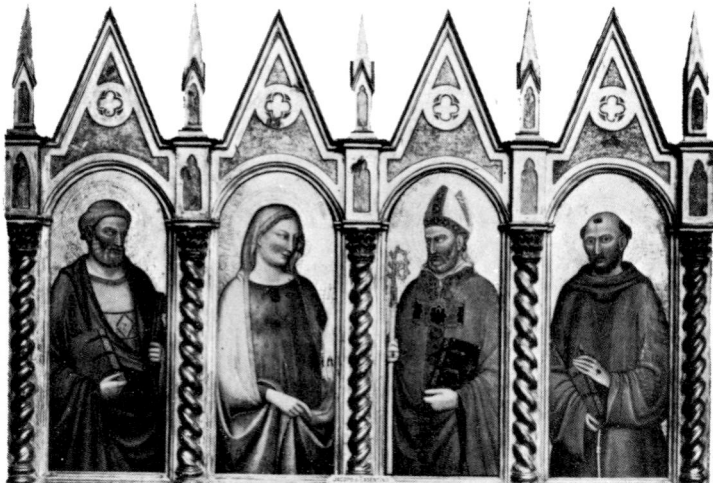

240

238. *Madonna and Child Enthroned with Sts Clare, a Bishop Saint, Catherine, James Major, and two other figures. Panel. Whereabouts unknown. Reali.*
239. *Madonna and Child Enthroned with six Saints, four Angels and two Donors. Panel. Berlin, Dahlem, Staatliche Museen. no. 1096. 50 × 32. Museum photo.*
240. *Polyptych: St Peter, female Saint, Bishop Saint and St Francis. Panel. Whereabouts unknown. 150 × 195. Fototeca Berenson.*

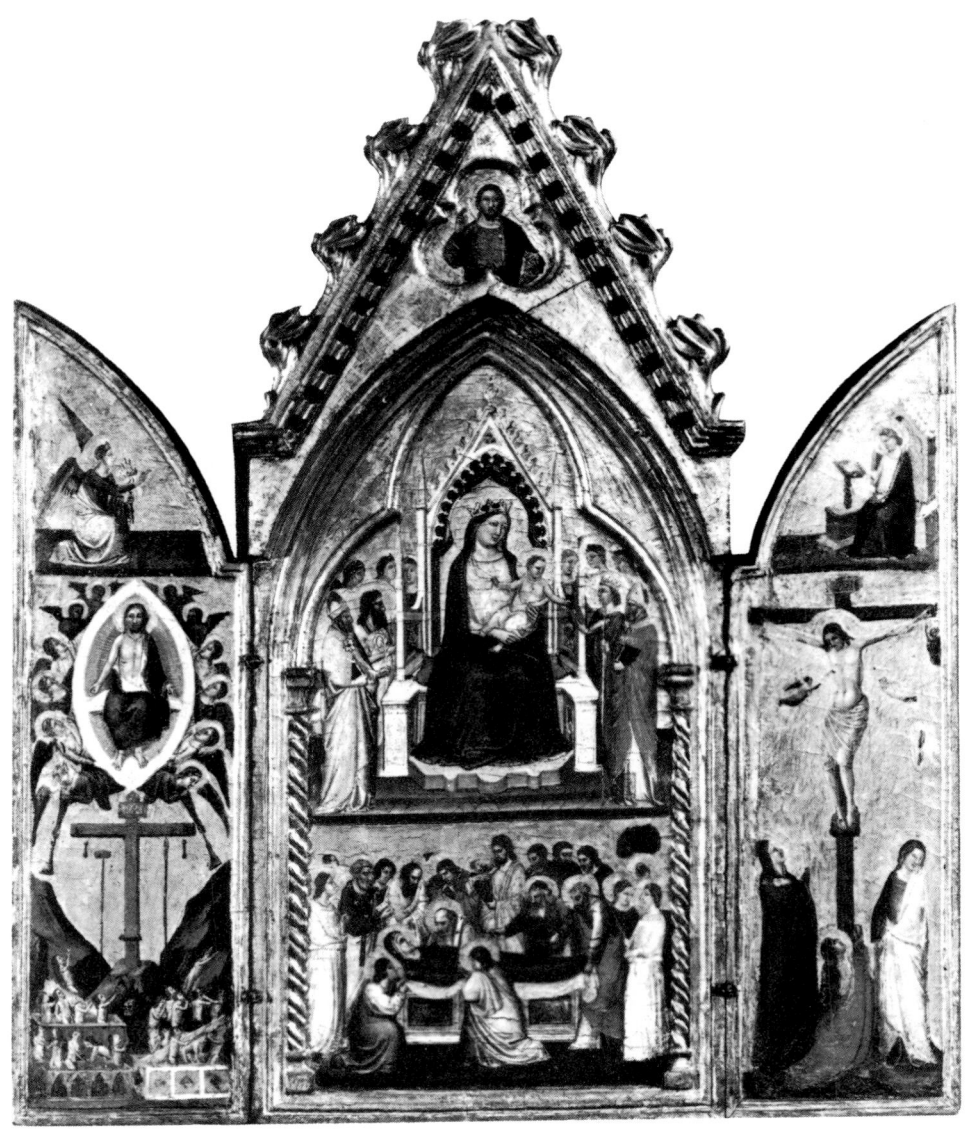

241

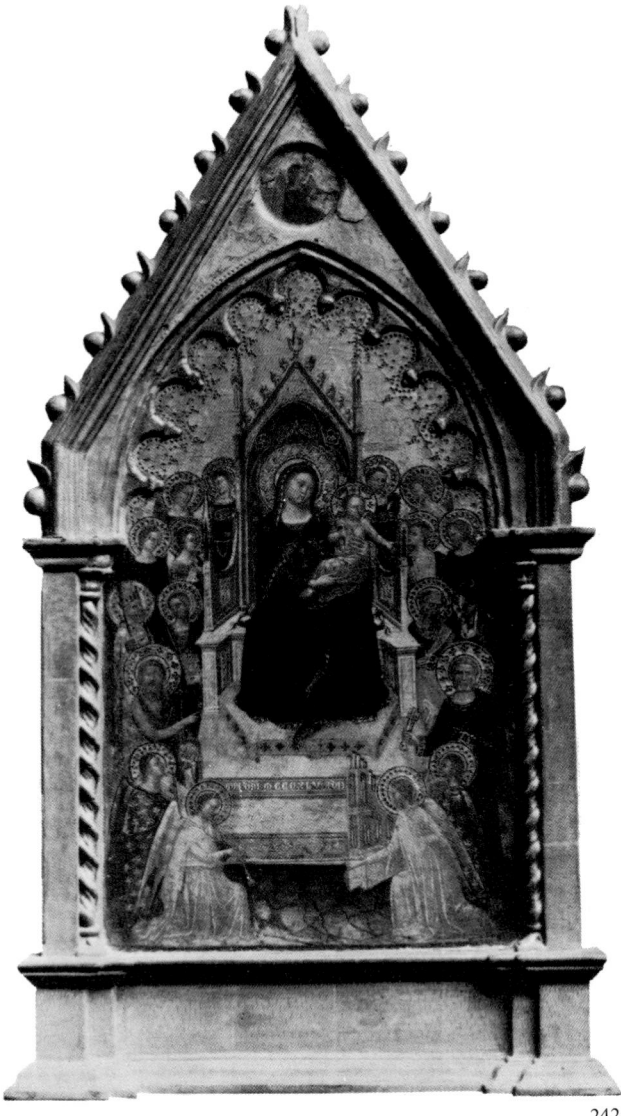

242

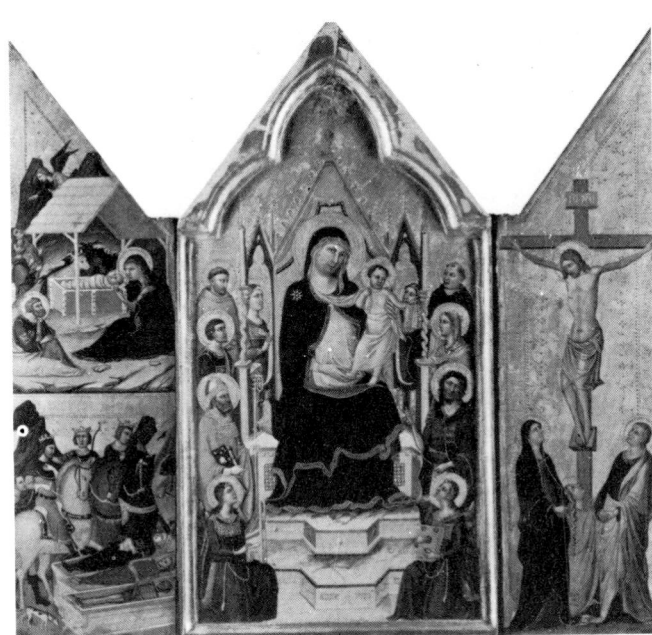

243

241. *Triptych: Madonna and Child Enthroned with four Saints and six Angels; Dormition of the Virgin. sps: Last Judgement, Christ on the Cross with the Virgin, Sts John the Evangelist and Mary Magdalene; Annunciation. Pinnacle: Christ blessing. Panel. Bremen, Kunsthalle. no. 292. 77.5 × 28.5. Museum photo: Stickelmann 197.*

242. *Madonna and Child Enthroned with ten Saints and eight Angels. Panel. Budapest, Musée des Beaux-Arts. no. 6006. 62 × 30. Museum photo. d. 1345.*

243. *Triptych: Madonna and Child with six Saints and four music-making Angels; Nativity; three dead Kings and three living Kings; Christ on the Cross with the Virgin, Sts John Evangelist and Mary Magdalene. Panel. Berlin, Dahlem, Staatliche Museen. no. 1091. 51 × 125. Museum photo.*

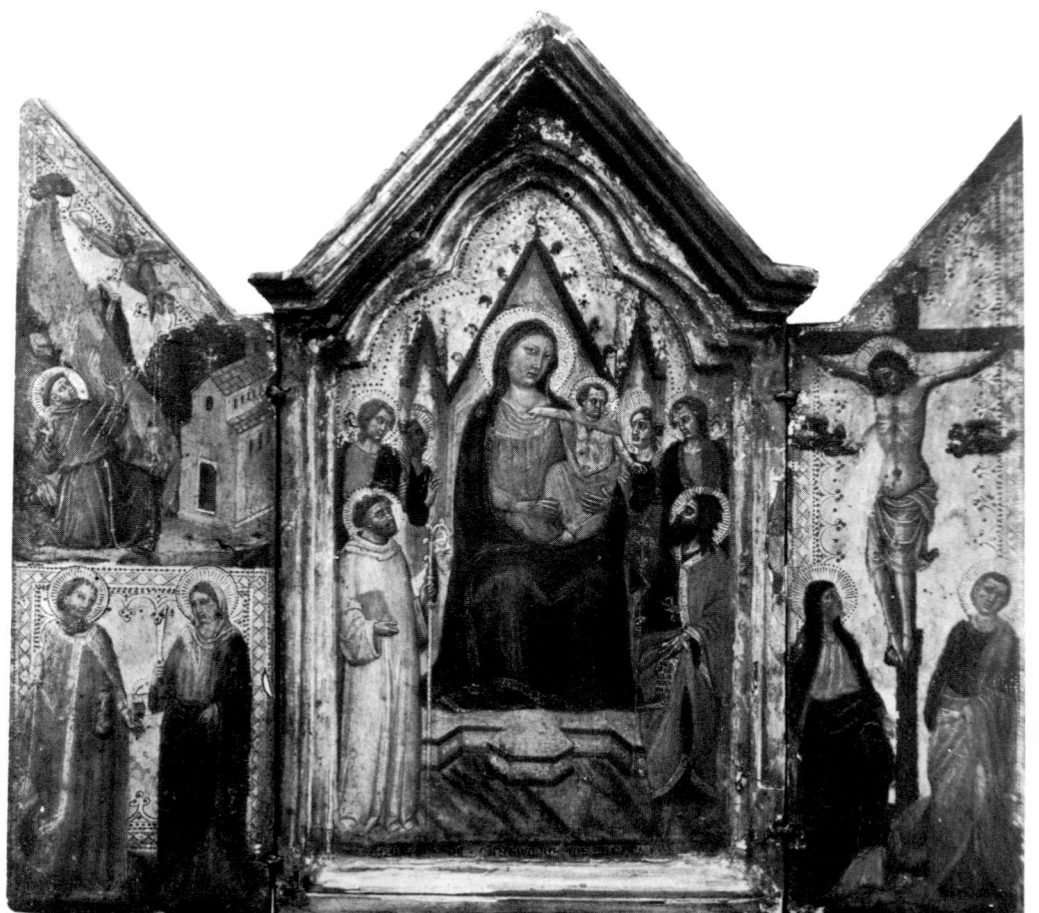

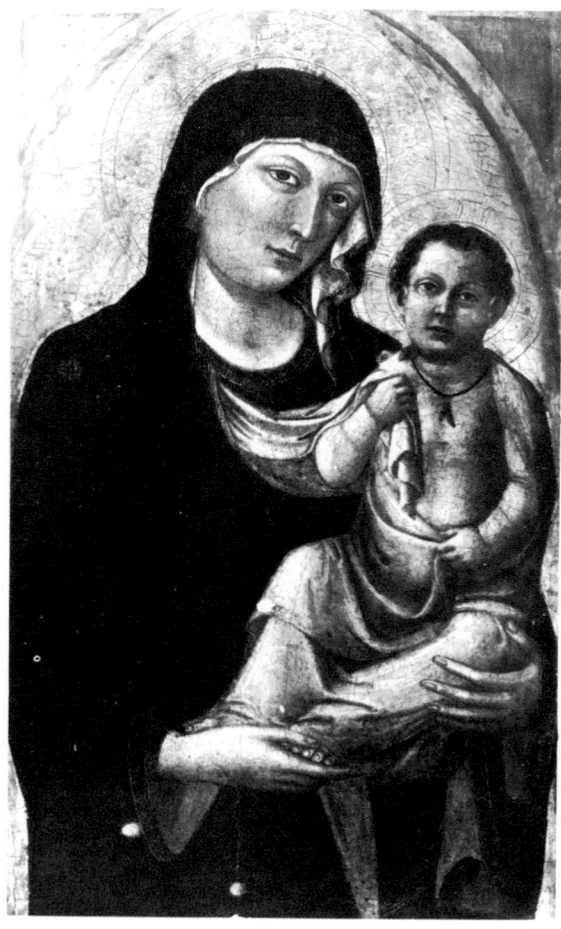

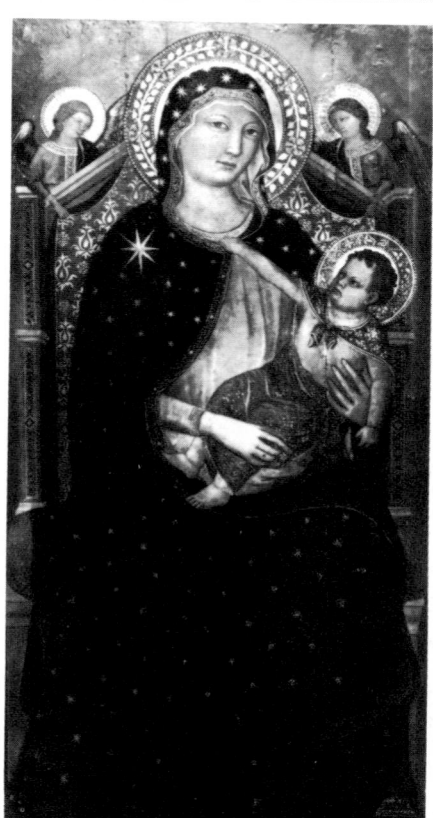

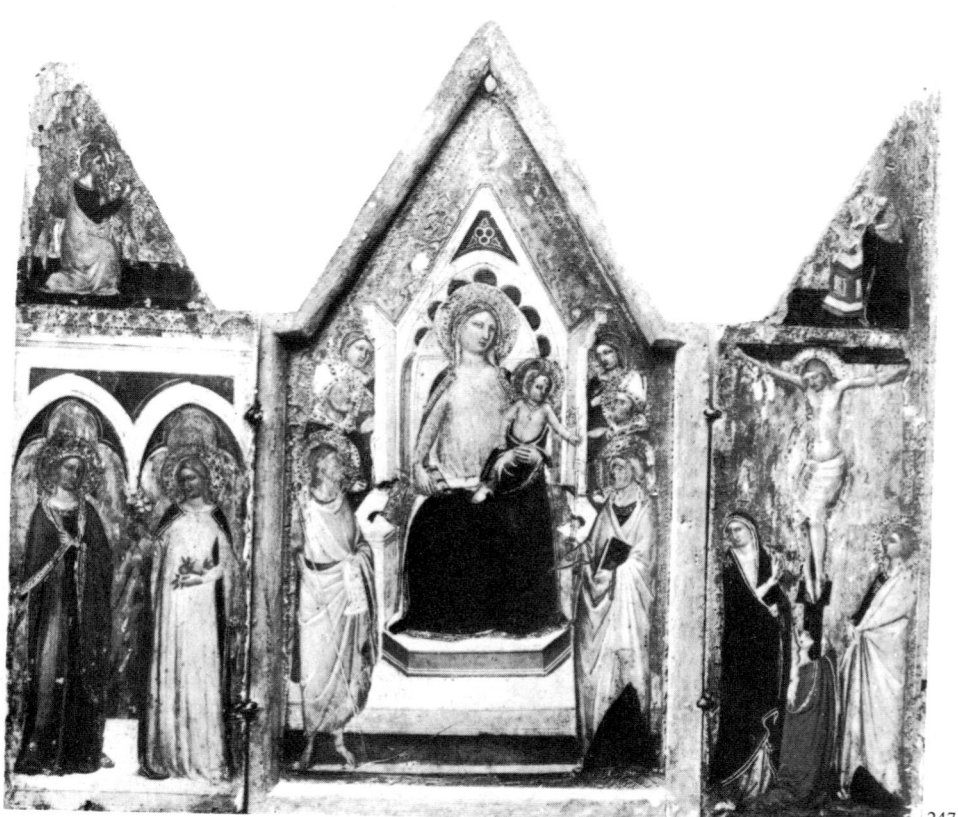

244. *Portable triptych: Madonna and Child Enthroned with Sts John Gualbert, John the Baptist and four Angels; Stigmatization of St Francis; two female Saints; Christ on the Cross with the Virgin and St John the Evangelist. Panel. Florence, Uffizi. no. 9258. 39.2 × 42.2. SGF 66630. s.*

245. *Madonna and Child. Panel. Florence, Horne Museum. no. 46. 83 × 46. SGF 6287.*

246. *Madonna and Child Enthroned with two Angels. Panel. Scarperia, Madonna dell Grazie. 145 × 85. Alinari 45544.*

247. *Portable triptych: Madonna and Child Enthroned with four Saints and two Angels; Christ on the Cross; Sts Catherine and Elizabeth of Hungary; Annunciation. Panel. Whereabouts unknown (formerly Vienna, Emil Weinberger). cp: 39.5 × 24.5; sps: 37 × 12. Fototeca Berenson.*

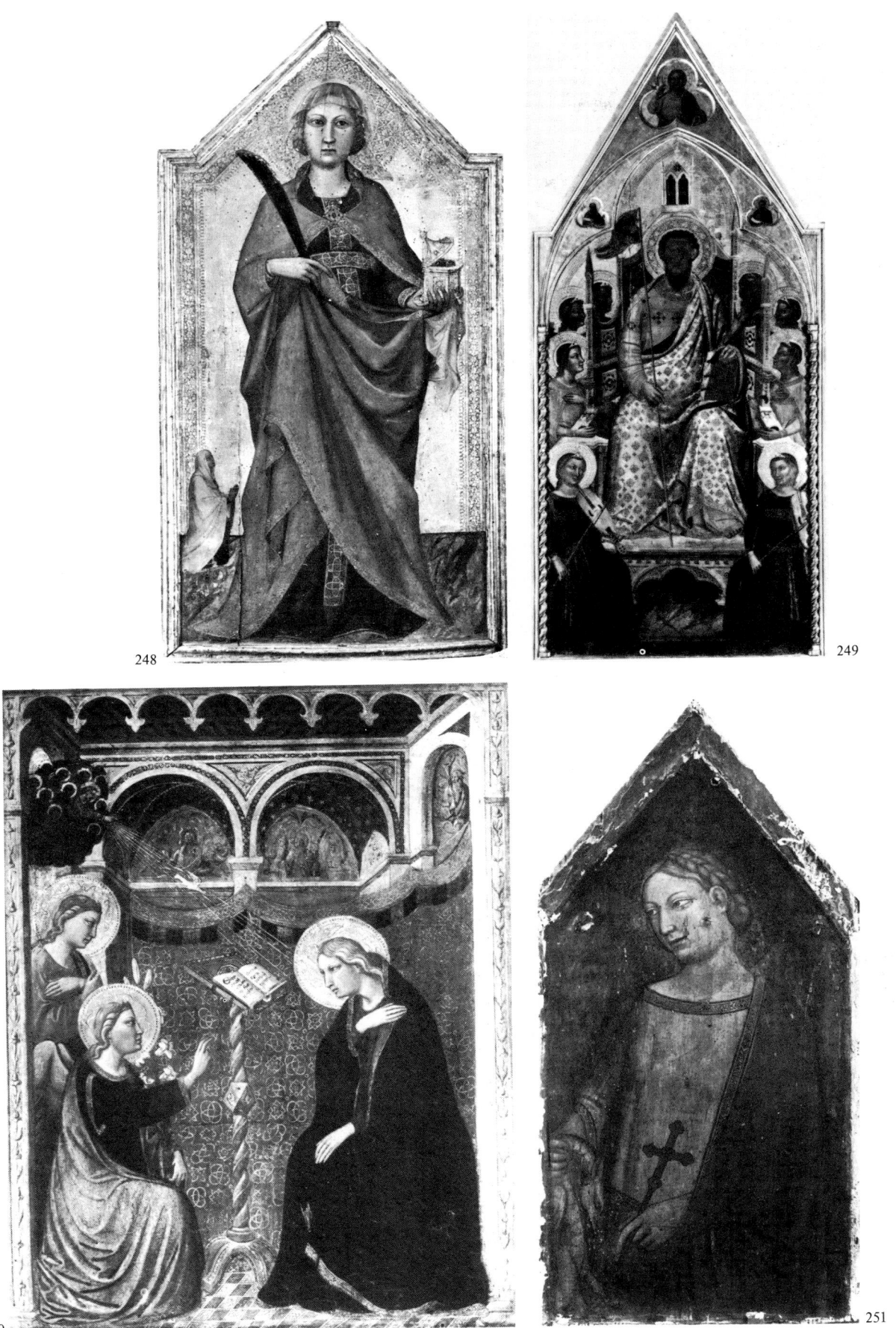

248. *St Lucy. Panel. Gravenhage, Dienst 's-Rijks Verspreide Kunstvoorwerpen. no. NK 1423. 130 × 67.8. Museum photo.*
249. *St Bartholomew Enthroned with eight Angels. Above: Christ blessing. Panel. Florence, Accademia. no. 440. 266 × 122. SGF 106601.*
250. *Annunciation. Panel. Whereabouts unknown (formerly Florence, Loeser Collection). SGF 55135.*
251. *St Margaret. Panel. Ughi (Rignano sull' Arno), S. Maria. 88 × 44. SGF 125573.*

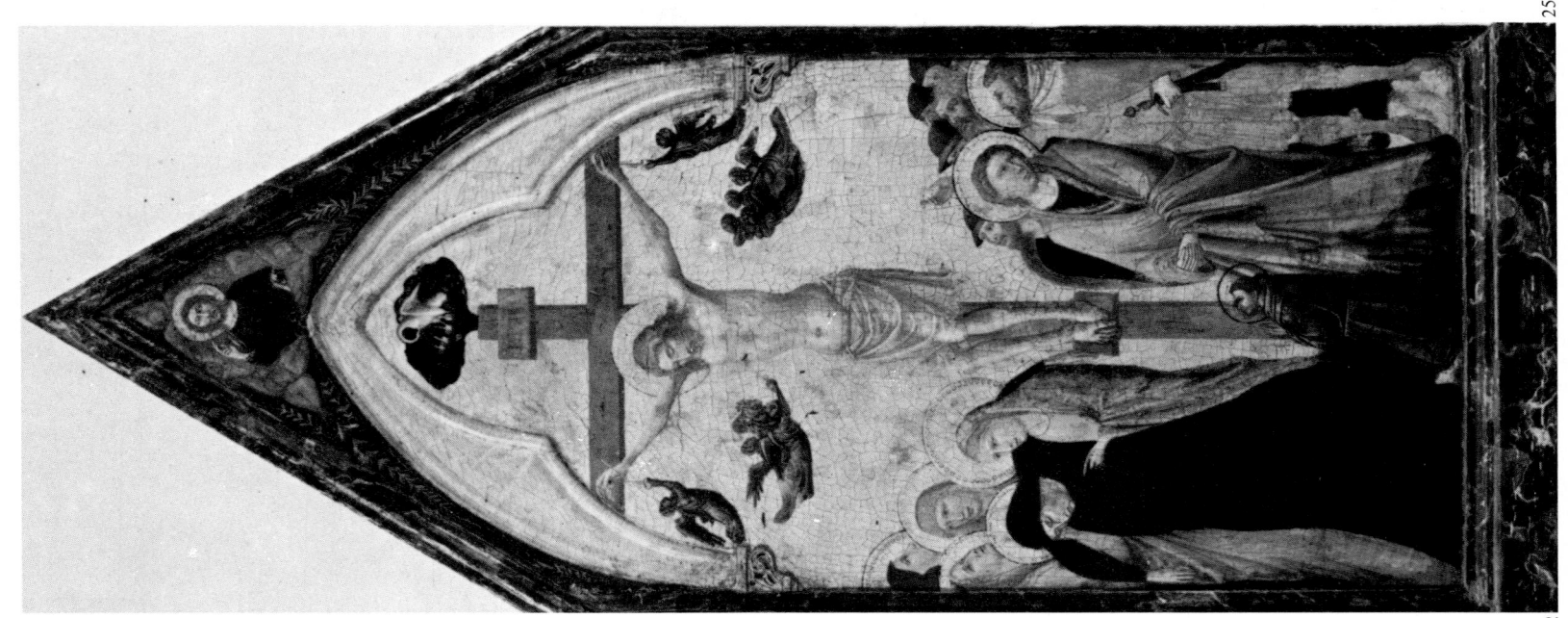

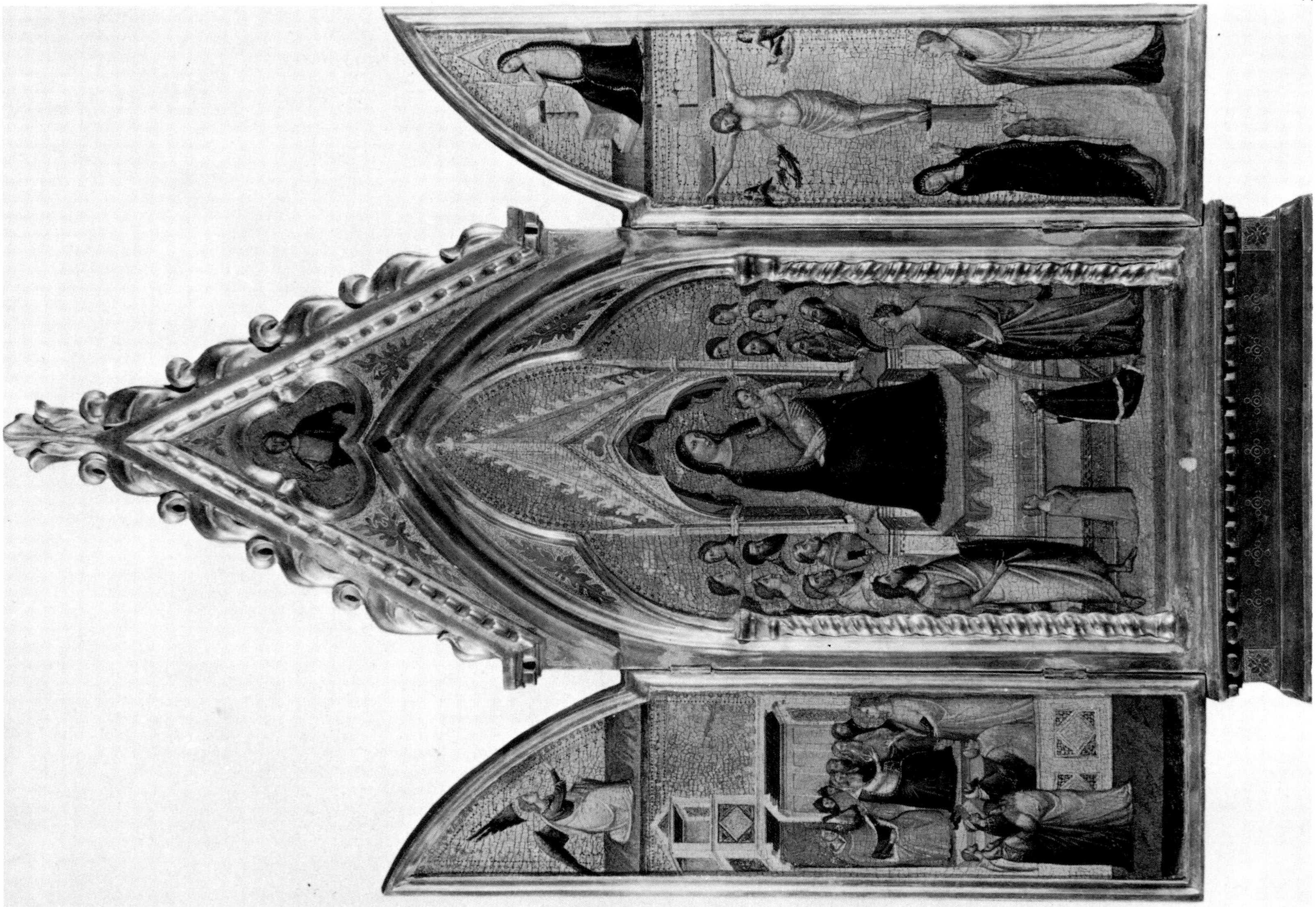

252. *Triptych: Madonna and Child Enthroned with fourteen Saints and two Donors; Disputation of St Catherine of Alexandria; Christ on the Cross with the Virgin and St John the Evangelist; Annunciation. Above: Christ blessing. Panel. Tucson (Ariz.). University of Arizona, Museum of Art, Samuel H. Kress Collection. no. K 572. cp: 47 × 21.6; sps: 41.9 × 12.1. Kress Foundation photo.*

253. *Christ on the Cross with the Virgin, Saints and a Donor. Panel. Princeton (N.J.), Mrs Douglas Delanoy Collection. 110.5 × 44.4. Photo Taylor and Dull, Inc., N.Y.*

MASO di BANCO

In the Matricola of the Florentine painters, we find two different Masos both of whose names are accompanied by the date 1350; they are Maso di Ciacco who inhabited the quarter of Porta S. Reparata, and Maso di Bancho or Banchi. The latter is also found mentioned in 1341 when his belongings in the shop of Sandro di Giovanni were sequestered on demand of Rodolfo dei Bardi. Among his goods there were two parts of an altar-piece representing the Madonna, the Baptist and St. Francis, and also painting utensils. He first matriculated in 1343 and his name appears again in 1346, but we do not know to which of these Masos the various authors attribute different works.

Both Villani and Ghiberti sing this artist's praises; the latter tells us that he was a pupil of Giotto's and that there were only few of his works which were not perfect.....

A great factor on which to build is the date. On the whole it seems probable that the Maso — be he di Ciacco or di Banco — mentioned between 1340 and 1350, was a generation previous to Giottino. Not only did the latter matriculate in 1368, that is to say twenty-five years later than Maso di Banco, but the fact that he was the son of a contemporary of Giotto and that his own son died at the beginning of the 15th century make us imagine that he was an artist who flourished in the third quarter of the 14th century, while Maso must have been active in the second quarter.

This last period is also the one in which, in all probability, the frescoes of the Bardi chapel, the only work still existing of those Ghiberti attributed to Maso, were executed.....

from R. van Marle, pp. 409-412, *The Development of the Italian Schools of Painting*, Vol. III, The Hague, 1924.

Pupil of Giotto, Maso is a painter whom Vasari... confused with Giottino. Filippo Villani,... Cristoforo Landini, ... and Ghiberti all name Maso in terms of high praise — the two first shortly, the third... at some length. Ghiberti then says that Maso painted a chapel in fresco in the church of Sto. Spirito: the "Descent of the Holy Ghost", over the principal entrance of the church, and a Madonna with many surrounding figures in a tabernacle at the entrance of the adjoining piazza. His works in Sto. Spirito were destroyed in the great fire of 1471, and the tabernacle has disappeared. In Sta. Croce, Ghiberti continues, Maso decorated a chapel with stories of S. Sylvester and the Emperor Constantine. Of this work a Deposition from the Cross and a Christ in Glory, retouched, are still visible. Ghiberti adds that Maso had many pupils, whose names, however, we are unable to indicate, and that he was a master in both the arts of painting and sculpture.....

from D. E. Colnaghi, p. 175, *Dictionary of Florentine Painters*, London, 1928.

Maso di Banco (Florence, known from 1341). Among the followers of Giotto, he was especially praised by Ghiberti, and is among the major artists of the 14th century in Florence. Art historians are still divided about the extent of his corpus and attribute some of Vasari's list to Giottino (about whom there is also confusion, but it may simply be one of names); and to Stefano, the father of Giottino, whose work has recently been reconstructed by Longhi. All of this is a very involved problem which is not yet solved.....

from U. Baldini, p. 47, *Iᵃ Mostra di Affreschi Staccati*, Florence, 1957.

Maso di Banco — painter and sculptor. Among the Florentine painters of the 14th century of the name Maso, a certain Maso di Banco can be identified as the follower of Giotto who is so often praised. The artist in 1341 (and not 1346, as Toesca wrote in 1951) lived in the district of San Lorenzo in Florence. And on September 29th of that year, two painted panels and other painter's furnishings were confiscated at the instigation of Ridolfo de' Bardi and Company..... We also know that between January and April of 1346 Maso joined the Guild of Physicians and Apothecaries. It has also been conjectured that he was already dead in 1347, as his name does not appear in a Pistoiese record of that year, which listed the major Florentine painters who would be worthy of executing a panel for the church of San Giovanni Fuorcivitas in Pistoia.....

from M. Salmi, p. 918, *Enciclopedia Universale dell' Arte*, Vol. III, Rome-Venice, 1958.

Active first half of fourteenth century. Pupil of Giotto; in a later phase strongly influenced by the Lorenzetti.

from B. Berenson, p. 135, *Italian Pictures of the Renaissance, Florentine School*, Vol. I, London, 1963.

A substantial contribution to the solution of the intricate historical and stylistic problem [of Maso and Giottino] was made finally by Longhi and by Coletti: these studies establish a clear distinction between Maso and the " Master of the San Remigio panel " — that is Giottino, ...

from L. Marcucci, p. 88, *I Dipinti Toscani del Secolo XIV*, Rome, 1965.

BIBLIOGRAPHY
BOOKS

An asterisk indicates a work listed in the General Bibliography

Sirèn, O., *Giotto*, Stockholm, 1906, pp. 129-48; *Venturi, A.**, 1907, p. 499; Sirèn, O., *Giottino*, Leipzig, 1908; *Khv & Salmi**, 1914, pp. 18-20; Sirèn, O., *Giotto and some of his Followers*, Vol. I, Cambridge, 1917, pp. 209-13; *v. Marle 1924**, pp. 409, 412; *Colnaghi**, 1928, p. 175; *Toesca, 1929**, pp. 64-5; *T-Becker**, Vol. XXIV, 1930, pp. 208-210; Brunetti, G., *M. Giottesca**, 1943, pp. 472-89; Bettini, S., *Giusto de' Menabuoi, e l'Arte del Trecento*, Padua, 1944, pp. 25-7; *Coletti, Vol. II**, 1946, pp. 43-4; Morisani, O., *Pittura del Trecento in Napoli*, Naples, 1947, pp. 63, 140; *Antal**, 1948, p. 225; *Vavalà, 1948**, pp. 67-70; *Galetti**, " F-O ", 1950, pp. 1602-7; *Toesca, 1951**, pp. 626-34; *Paatz**, Vol. V, 1953, pp. 11, 17; Baldini, U., *MAS I**, 1957, pp. 47-8; Longhi, R., in *Catalogo della Mostra di " Arte Lombarda dai Visconti agli Sforza "*, Milan, 1958, p. xxiv; Salmi, M., *EUA**, 1958, p. 918; *Borsook**, 1960, p. 131; Bucci, M., *Camposanto**, 1960, many refs; Procacci, U., p. 30, in *Scritti di Storia dell'Arte in onore di Mario Salmi*, Vol. II, Rome, 1962; *Berenson, 1963**, Vol. I, pp. 135-6; *Marcucci**, 1965, pp. 88-92; Bianchini, M. A., *Maso di Banco* (I Maestri del Colore, 247), Milan, 1966; Bianchini, M. A., *La Pittura dell'Italia Centrale nell'Età Gotica* (I Maestri del Colore 256), Milan, 1966; *MMOA**, 1971, pp. 20-22; Meiss, M., in *Congresso VII**, 1971, pp. 401-418; Gilbert, C., *History of Renaissance Art throughout Europe*, New York, 1973, p. 73; Toesca, P., *Gli affreschi della Cappella di San Silvestro in Santa Croce a Firenze*, Florence, s. d.

JOURNALS

Suida, W., *RKW*, XXVII, 1904, p. 483; Wulff, O., *RKW*, XXIX, 1906, pp. 477-8; Suida, W., *RKW*, XXXI, 1908, p. 205; Venturi, A., *A*, 1908, pp. 137-8; Sirèn, O., *MKW*, 1, 1908, pp. 501-10; *Edit.*, *RA*, IX, 5, 1909, pp. 71-3; Suida, W., *MKW*, VII, 1, 1914, pp. 1-2; Offner, R., *MKIF*, III, 1919-32, pp. 186-7; Sirèn, O., *DD*, VIII, 1827-8, pp. 395-424; Longhi, R., *Pin*, I, 1928, p. 143; Offner, R., *BM*, LIV, 1929, pp. 224-45; Berenson, B., *DD*, XI, 4, 1930-1, pp. 957-88, 1039-73; Coletti, L., *RA*, XIII, 1931, pp. 331-2; Valentiner, W. R., *A*, XXVIII, 1935, pp. 3-29; Meiss, M., *AB*, XVIII, 1936, p. 442; Coletti, L., *BA*, XXXI, 1937, 111, pp. 49-72; Salmi, M., *E*, LXXXVI, 7, 1937, pp. 349-64; Longhi, R., *CA*, V, 1940, pp. 145-91; Coletti, L., *E*, XCV, 11, 1942, pp. 460-78; Lucignani, E. L., *RA*, XXIV, 1942, pp. 107-24; Coletti, L., *E*, XCVI, 11, 1942, pp. 460-78; Salmi, M., *ACOL*, I, 1943-6, pp. 415-421; Salmi, M., *ACOL*, XII, 1947, pp. 415-32; Valentiner, W. R., *AQ*, XII, 1, 1949, pp. 48-73; Coletti, L., *CA*, VIII, 6, 1950, pp. 443-54; Beccherucci, L., *RA*, XXVI, 1950, pp. 223-6; Levi, E. L., *RA*, XXVI, 1950, pp. 193-7; Longhi, R., *PA*, II, 13, 1951, pp. 19-40; Ragghianti, C. L., *NCA*, I, 3, 1954, pp. 293-9; s.p., *E*, CXXVI, 10, 1957, pp. 61-8; Longhi, R., *PA*, IX, 109, 1959, pp. 31-40; Longhi, R., *PA*, IX, 111, pp. 3-12, 1959; Birkmeyer, K. M., *GBA*, LX, 6, 1962, p. 461; Gallotti Minola, M., *E*, CXXXVII, 822, 1963, pp. 254-60; Marcucci, L., *JBM*, V, 1963, pp. 14-43; *Edit.*, *A*, III, 1963, pp. 226-231; Arslan, E., *BA*, XLVIII, 4, 1963, pp. 221-38; Zeri, F., *BA*, XLVIII, 4, 1963, pp. 245-58; Vayer, L., *AHA*, XI, 1965, pp. 217-39; Bellosi, L., *PA*, XVI, 187/7, 1965, pp. 18-43; Gregori, M., *AV*, V, 6, 1966, pp. 25-32; Donati, P. P., *C*, XVII, 1-3, 1966, pp. 56-72; De Benedictis, C., *AV*, 3, 1967, p. 45; Bellosi, L., *PA*, XVIII, 203/23, 1967, p. 85; Conti, A., *PA*, XIX, 225/45, 1968, pp. 10-20; Conti, A., *PA*, XIX, 215/35, 1968, p. 11; Mellini, G. L., *CA*, XV, 98, 1968, pp. 49-64; Zeri, F., *GBA*, LXXI, 110, 1968, pp. 70-71; Wilkins, D., *BM*, CXI, 1969, pp. 83-6; Venturoli, P., *SDA*, 1-2, 1969, pp. 142-58; *Edit.*, *GBA*, LXXIII, 111, 1969, pp. 50-51 (supplement), nos. 219, 220; Boskovits, M., *AI*, III, 25/26, 1970, pp. 32-47; Gonzales-Palacios, A., *AP*, XCI, 95, 1970, p. 76; Meiss, M., *BM*, CXIII, 817, 1971, p. 185.

There are no known signed and/or dated works by Maso di Banco.

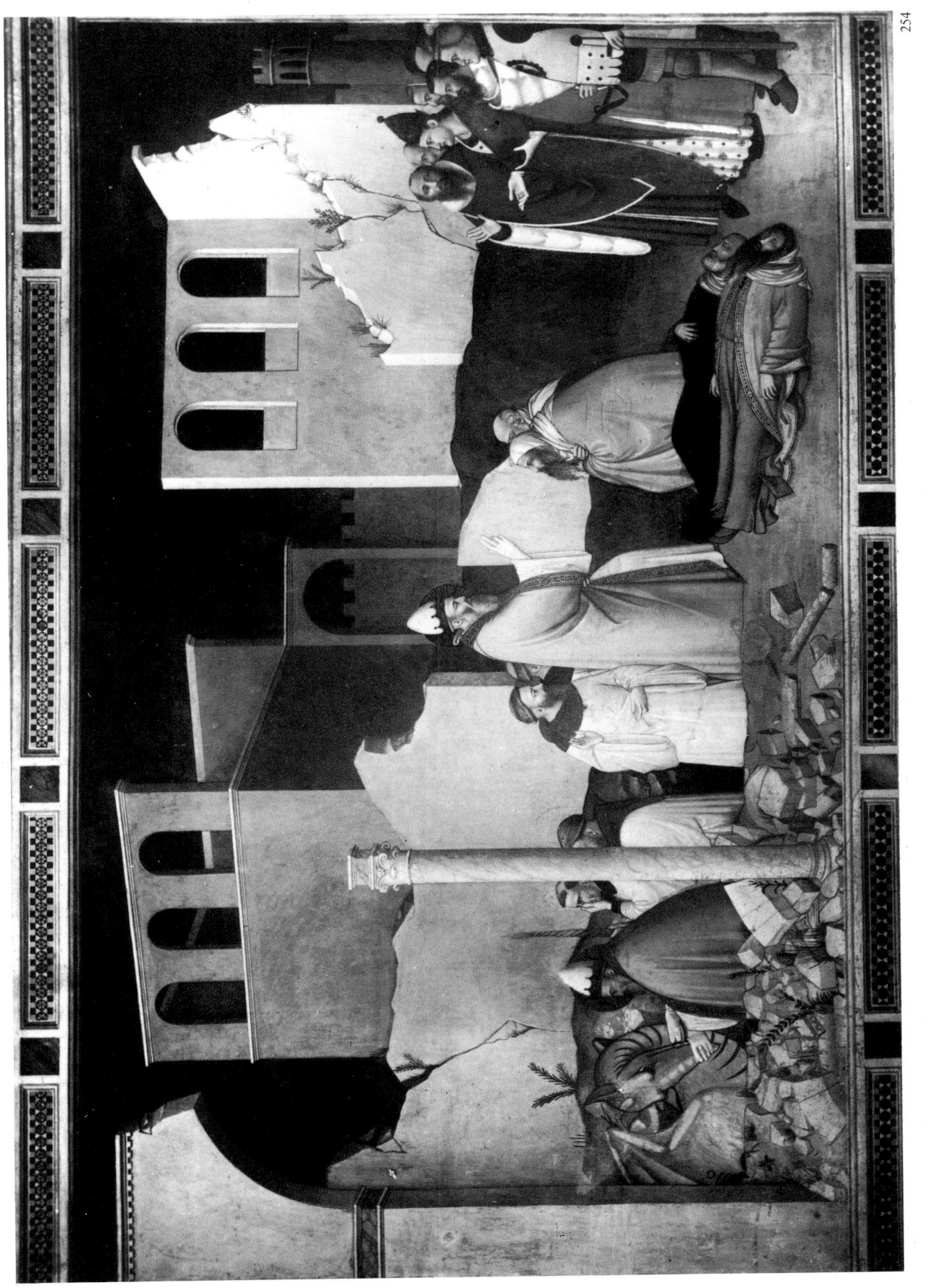

254. *St Sylvester subduing the Dragon and resuscitating two Priests. Fresco. Florence, S. Croce, Bardi di Vernio Chapel. SGF 25573. 1335-45.*

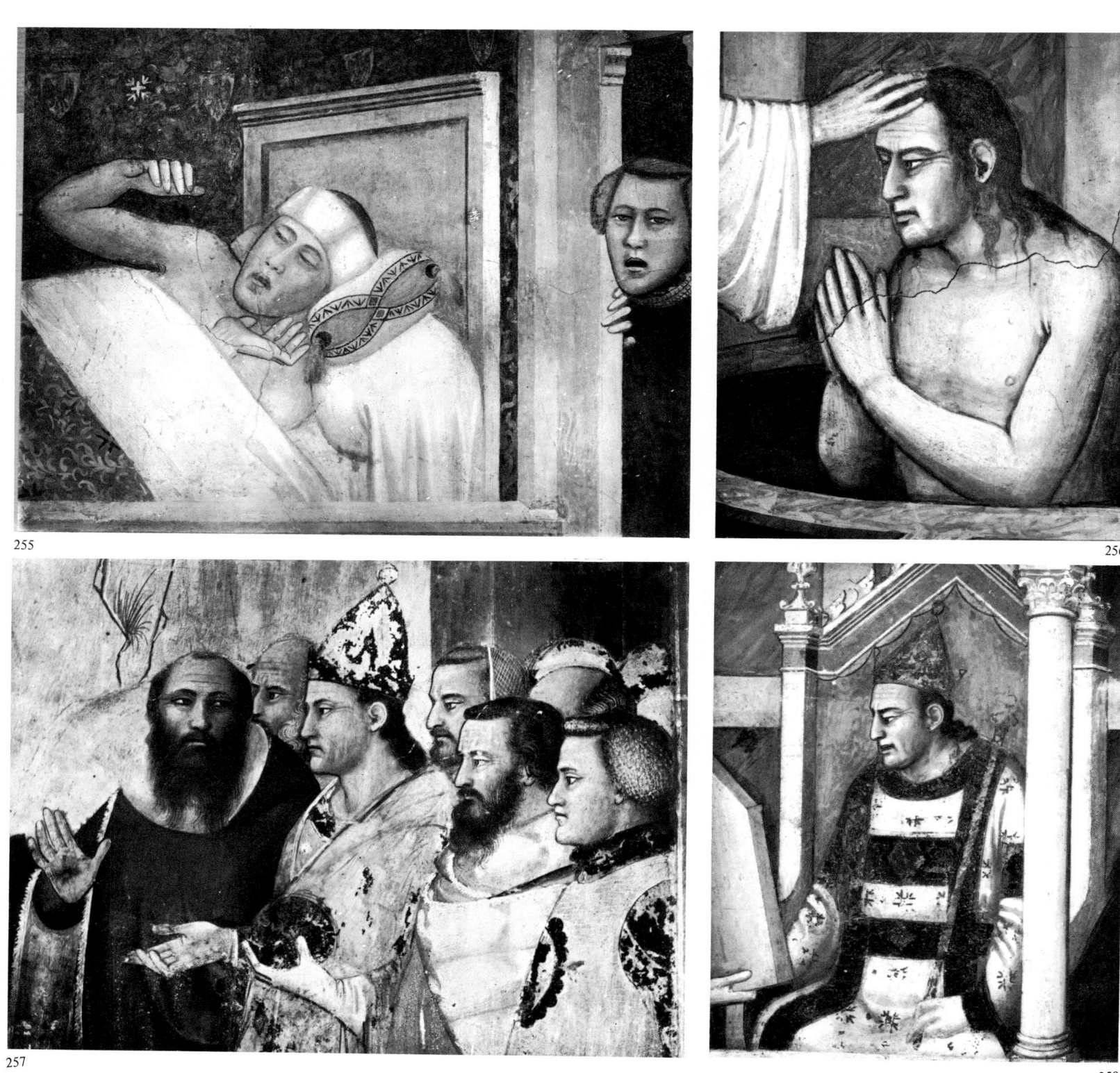

255

256

257

258

255. *Dream of Constantine, detail of fig. 259. Fresco. Florence, S. Croce, Bardi di Vernio Chapel. SGF 25486. 1335-45.*
256. *Baptism of Constantine, detail of fig. 260. Fresco. Florence, S. Croce, Bardi di Vernio Chapel. SGF 25455. 1335-45.*
257. *Onlookers, detail of fig. 254. Fresco. Florence, S. Croce, Bardi di Vernio Chapel. SGF 73517.*
258. *Recognition of the portraits of Peter and Paul, detail of fig. 260. Fresco. Florence, S. Croce, Bardi di Vernio Chapel. SGF 25450. 1335-45.*

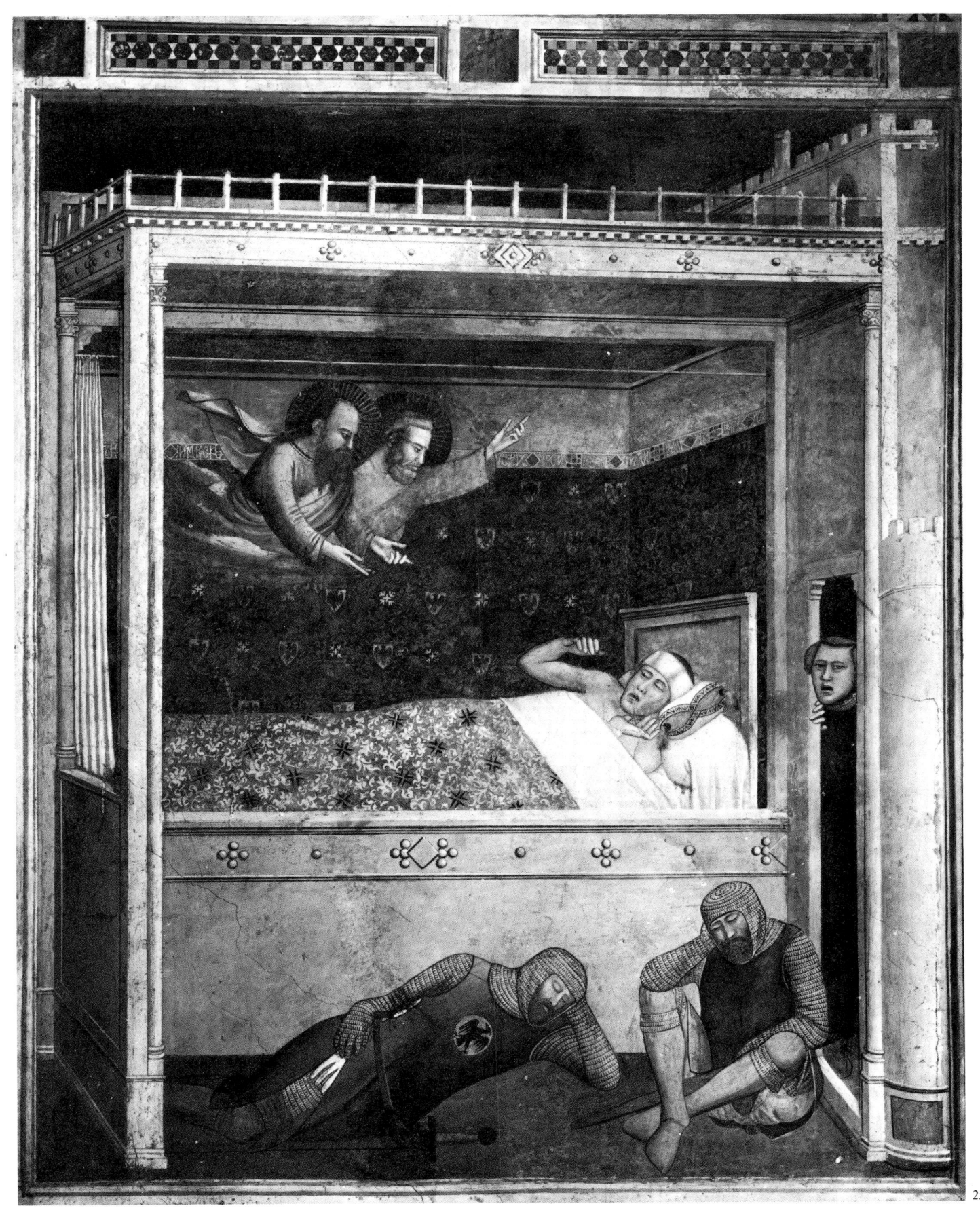

259. *Dream of Constantine. Fresco. Florence, S. Croce, Bardi di Vernio Chapel. SGF 25562. 1335-45.*

259

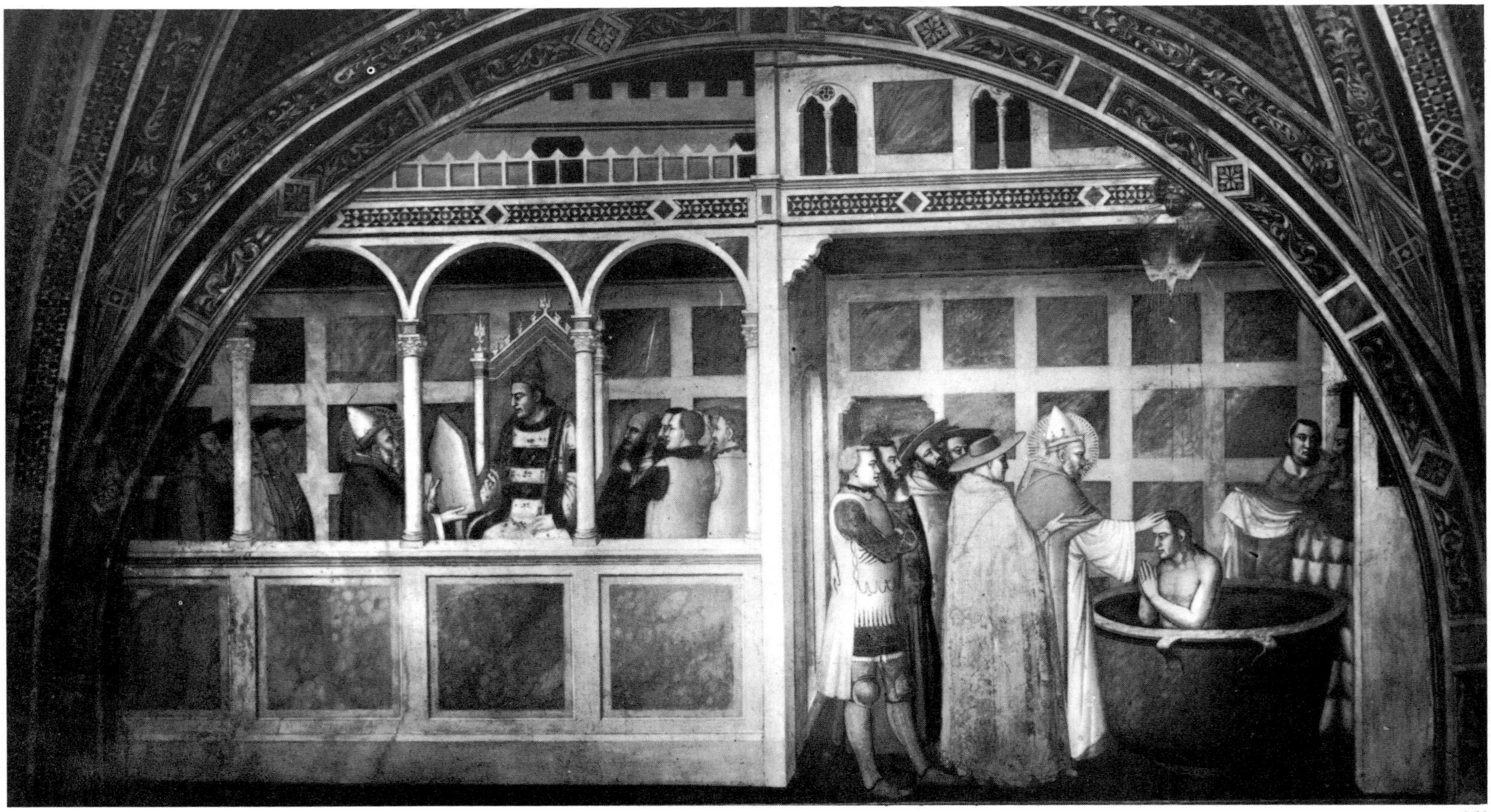

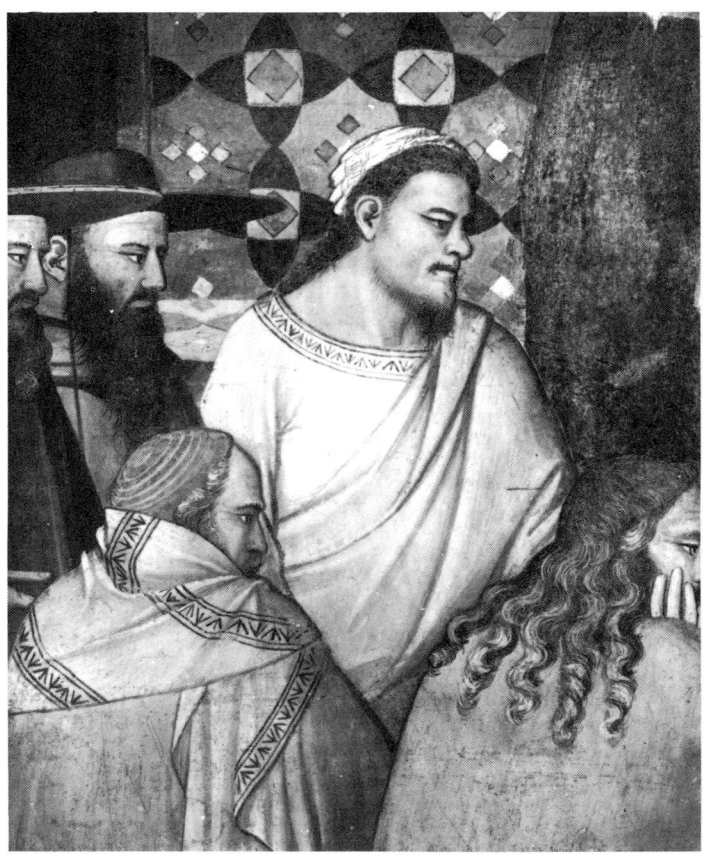

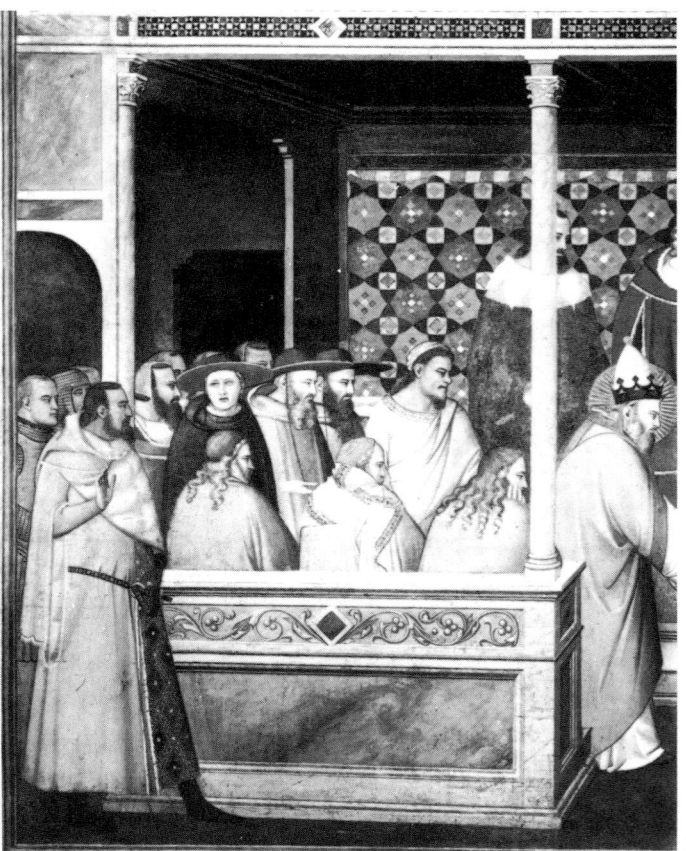

260. *Recognition of the portraits of Peter and Paul, and Baptism of Constantine. Fresco. Florence, S. Croce, Bardi di Vernio Chapel. SGF 25446. 1335-45.*
261. *Onlookers, detail of fig. 263. Fresco. Florence, S. Croce, Bardi di Vernio Chapel. SGF 25459. 1335-45.*
262. *Onlookers, detail of fig. 263. Fresco. Florence, S. Croce, Bardi di Vernio Chapel SGF 25566. 1335-45.*

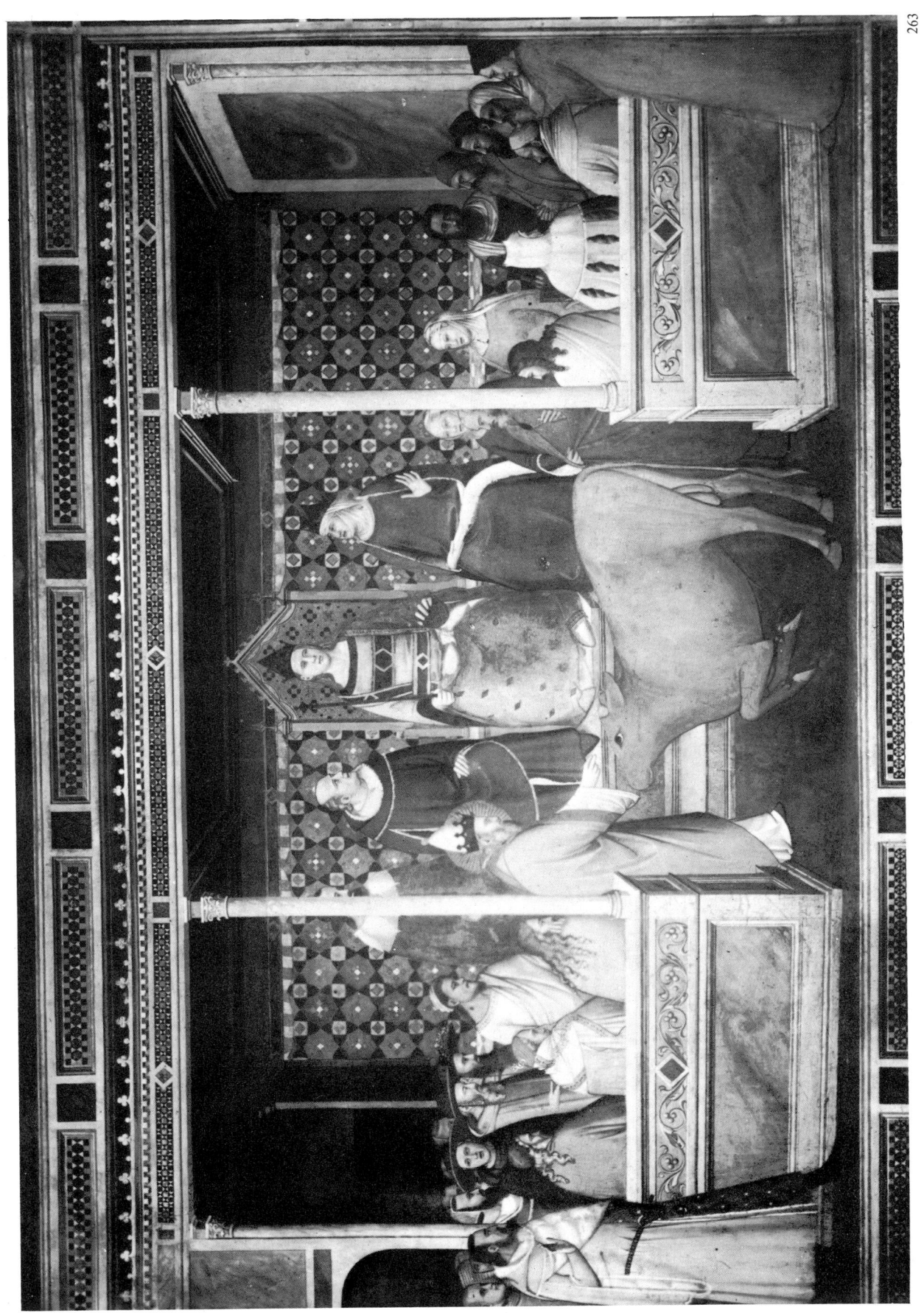

263. *Raising of the Bull. Fresco. Florence, S. Croce, Bardi di Vernio Chapel. SGF 25565. 1335-45.*

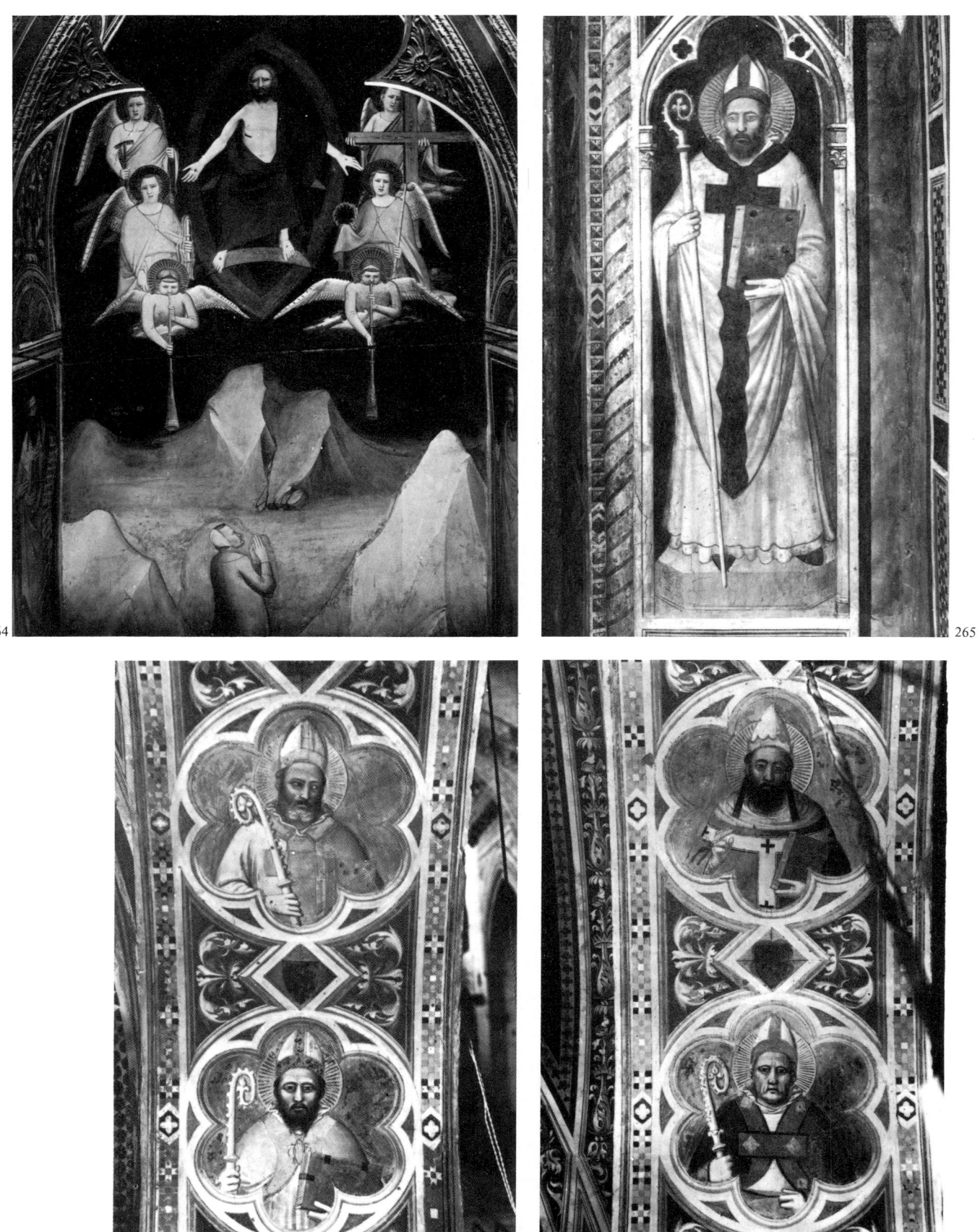

264. *Last Judgement with six Angels and Bettino Bardi kneeling below. Fresco. Florence, S. Croce, Bardi di Vernio Chapel. SGF 25563. 1335-45.*
265. *Bishop Saint. Fresco. Florence, S. Croce, Bardi di Vernio Chapel. SGF 25572. 1335-45.*
266. *Two Bishop Saints. Fresco. Florence, S. Croce, Bardi di Vernio Chapel. SGF 25442. 1335-45.*
267. *Two Bishop Saints. Fresco. Florence, S. Croce, Bardi di Vernio Chapel. SGF 25443. 1335-45.*

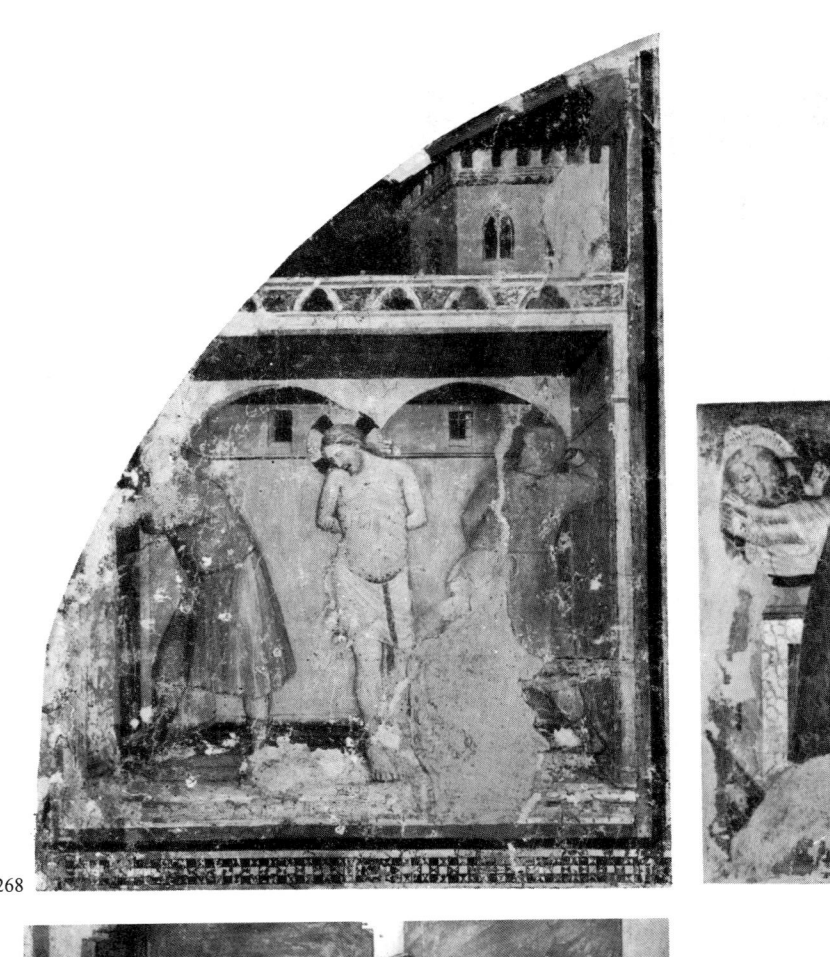

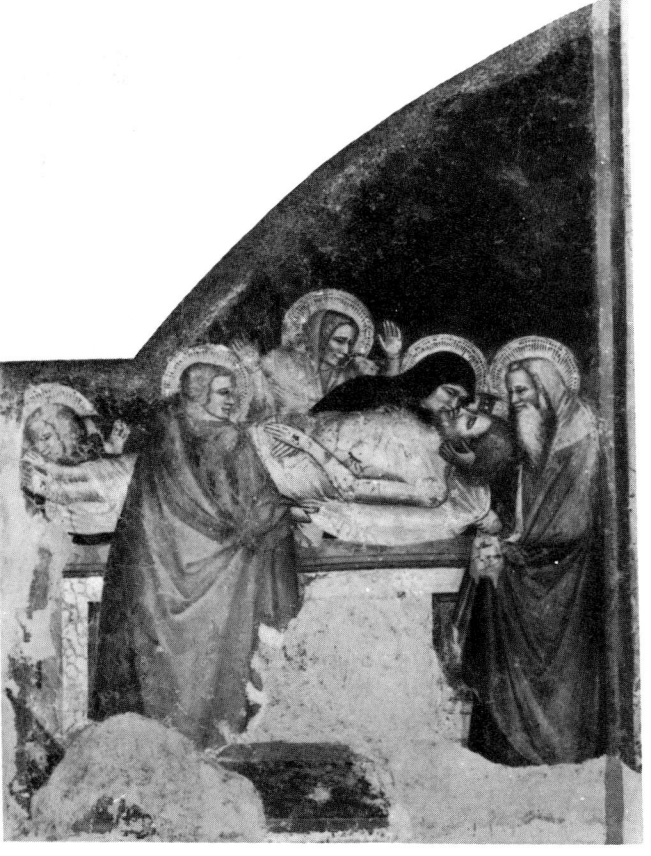

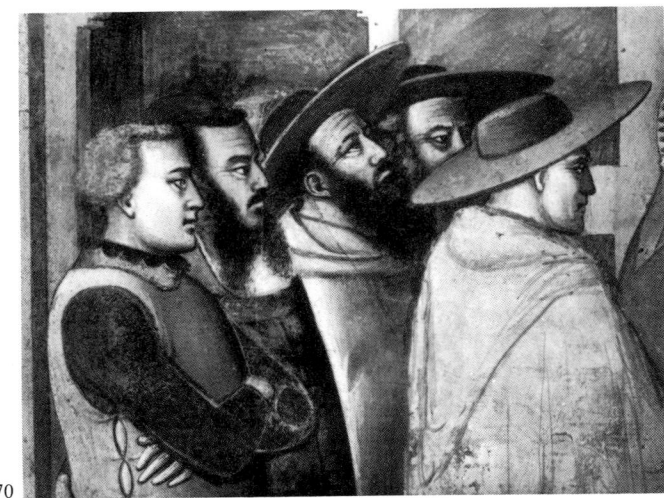

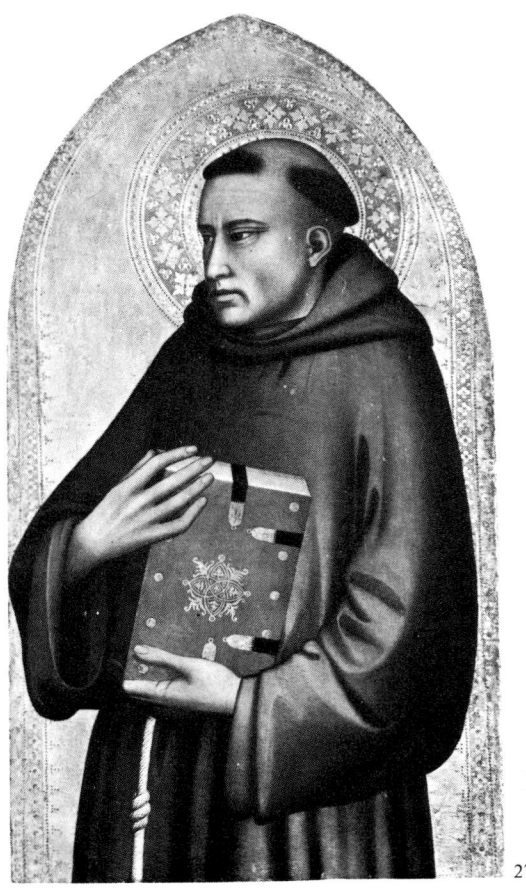

268. *Flagellation of Christ. Fresco. Assisi, S. Rufinuccio. Foto de Giovanni 51/1.*
269. *Entombment. Fresco. Assisi, S. Rufinuccio. Foto de Giovanni 51/3.*
270. *Onlookers, detail of fig. 260. Fresco. Florence, S. Croce, Bardi di Vernio Chapel. SGF 25453. 1335-45.*
271. *St Anthony. Panel. New York (N.Y.), Metropolitan Museum of Art, Griggs Collection. no. 43.98.13. 74.3 × 40.6. Museum photo 131060.*

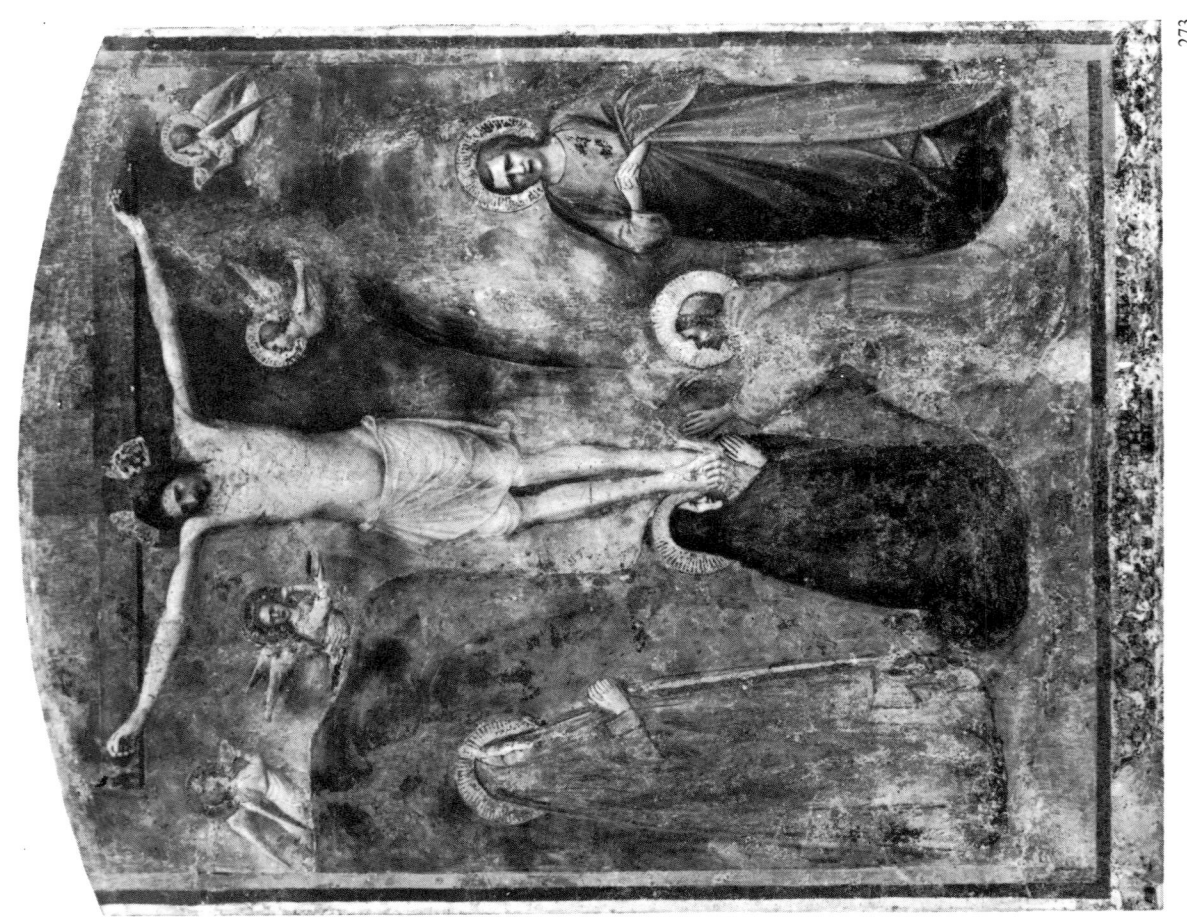

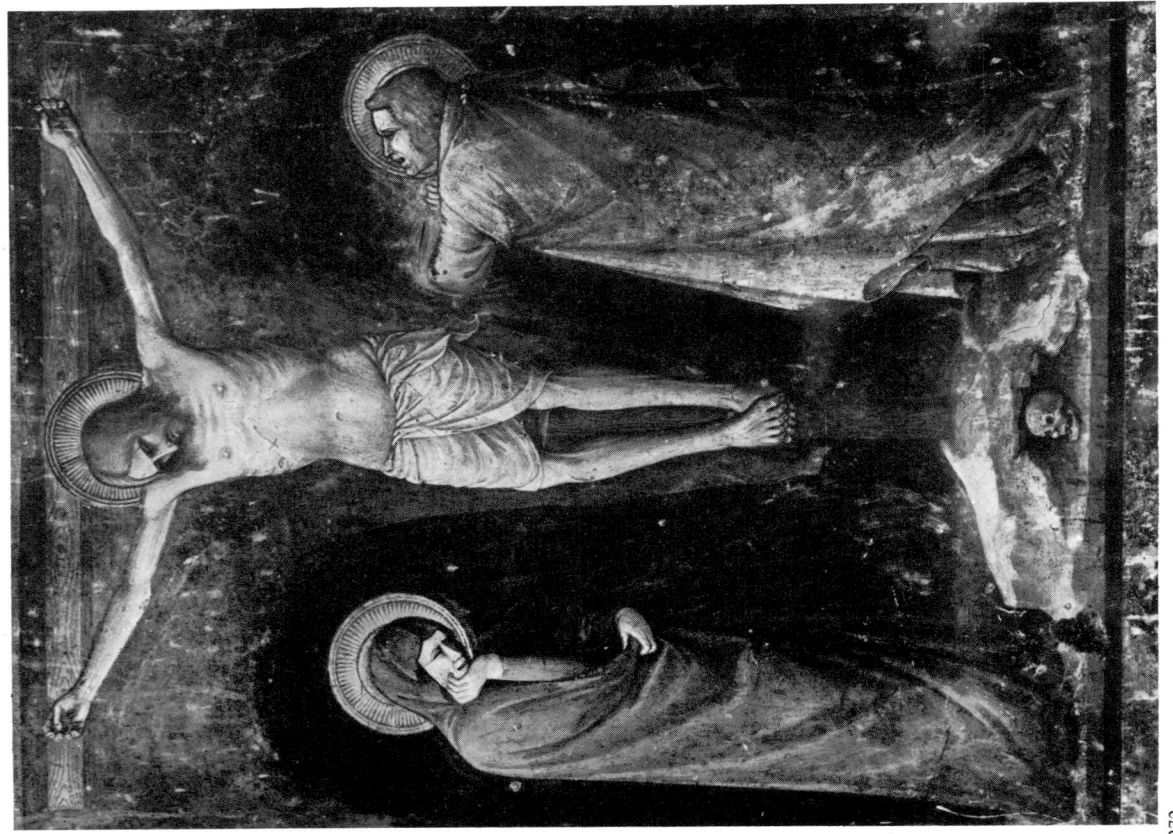

272. *Christ on the Cross, with the Virgin and St John. Fresco. Assisi, S. Francesco, Lower Church, St Stanislaus Chapel. Foto de Giovanni 56/1.*
273. *Christ on the Cross with the two Marys, St John the Baptist, Francis, and four Angels. Fresco. Assisi, S. Rufinuccio. Foto de Giovanni 51/4.*

ANDREA ORCAGNA

The tradition that Andrea Orcagna and his brothers form but one artistic individuality goes as far back as the year 1347 when amongst the five Florentine painters who were taken into consideration for the execution of the altar-piece in S. Giovanni Fuorcivitas at Pistoia, with which it will be remembered Taddeo Gaddi was charged, we find mentioned " Maestro Orchagia e Maestro Nardo in (porta di) Balla ". It is the only instance in this little list in which two painters are named together, it was evidently known that they worked in cooperation.

In Ghiberti, however, we find no confirmation of this. Andrea Orcagna is discussed at length and his brothers just mentioned at the end of the description. Vasari on the other hand leads us to suppose that the one hardly ever worked without the other and this tradition of almost six centuries has again recently been followed by Mr. Berenson, speaking, in his " Florentine Painters " of " Andrea Orcagna and his brothers" without any attempt to differentiate the productions of the three individuals whom we know to have existed. The utmost caution is required in dealing with these painters because we have only one authentic painting by Andrea, none by Nardo and probably none by Jacopo, for we are not certain which part we can attribute to him of the two pictures at which we know he worked, but which we are equally sure are only partly by him. It is particularly regrettable that we have no better information about these artists who, as will be seen, played a very important part in the progress of painting in Florence.

Happily our comprehension of Andrea is greatly aided by the fact that he has left us an important piece of plastic art signed and dated: the ciborium in Or San Michele; while for Nardo we have Ghiberti's elucidatory attribution of the frescoes in the Strozzi chapel. However, the reason of the fusion of the three artistic personalities may be explained by the complete domination of Andrea over the painters surrounding him, resulting in a connection somewhat similar to that which existed at Siena between Simone Martini and Lippo Memmi and, had we been unaware of the existence of Nardo, many of his works would have been attributed to Andrea and others to his school.....

from R. van Marle, pp. 454-455, *The Development of the Italian Schools of Painting*, Vol. III, The Hague, 1924.

The most impressive Florentine painting of the third quarter of the fourteenth century that has come down to us is the altarpiece in the Strozzi Chapel of S. M. Novella, painted by Andrea Orcagna between 1354 and 1357. A landmark in the history of style, it is also unprecedented in subject, at least among Florentine and Sienese retables of the great epoch in painting that began with Giotto and Duccio. Of the dozens of altarpieces that were painted by them and their successors during the first half of the fourteenth century, none so far as I know represents the full-length adult Christ in the central field. Nor does any of these earlier altarpieces show Christ in the act of disseminating doctrine and granting ecclesiastical authority.

from M. Meiss, p. 9, *Painting in Florence and Siena after the Black Death*, Princeton, 1951.

This painter, architect, and sculptor belongs among the great painters of the second half of the Florentine Trecento still under the force of Giottesque relief. The most important sure work of Orcagna is the panel (1354-1357) in the Strozzi Chapel in S. Maria Novella. Through a series of important critical studies which first confirmed and then invalidated the information which has been handed down to us about this artist, we are now able to construct a fairly clear "curriculum" of his activity as a painter and fresco painter. Salvini has written, Orcagna is always " charged with an intense but controlled energy, wherein one finds a tension between values of plastic intensity and values of chromatic richness; between the form, which tends to achieve perfect volumetric rotundity, and the line which cuts it drily and contains it by force. It is always psychic spiritual tension between a desire for complete spiritualization and a tenacious affection for the nature of man, seen above all as being endowed with will and capable of action ". One can recognize Orcagna's importance through the execution of whole projects by workshops and masters who for a long time worked for him; the Cappella Maggiore of S. Maria Novella (destroyed to make room for the beautiful Florentine work of Ghirlandaio) must have been an important school for many: as the few rediscovered fragments of this work seem to demonstrate.

from U. Baldini, p. 31, *Iª Mostra di Affreschi Staccati*, Florence, 1957.

Andrea di Cione, traditionally known as Orcagna, is a single case of a great master enjoying wide recognition in his day and a settled posthumous reputation as a painter whose work has come most of the way down to us founded upon one sole panel, the Strozzi altarpiece.....

Yet the voluminous documents bearing on him remove whatever doubt may remain regarding his real merits and rest his renown upon much firmer foundation. They make it clear in their concreteness, extent and continuity that his contemporary fame did not derive from the practice of a specific art, certainly not from painting alone, for besides being a painter, he was a poet, but notably an architect, and certainly pre-eminent in the Italy of his day in solid accomplishment. Witness to this is not only his direction of the building of the Cathedral of Orvieto, of Or S. Michele, but notably his share in certain phases of the construction of the Florentine Cathedral, to which he was attached also as counsellor.....

The date of his birth is unknown. Milanesi's surmise of 1308 is arrived at from Vasari's statement that Orcagna was sixty years old at his death, which occurred about 1368, but which Vasari puts at 1389, thus dislocating completely Orcagna's chronology. But if the year of his birth has eluded Vasari, the period of Orcagna's activity may be reckoned on the available evidence. For though Vasari was here misled, he must have had reason for placing Orcagna after Taddeo Gaddi in the chronological sequence of his *Vite*, since this accords with the order of their mention in the famous Pistoiese document of c. 1347 presumably according to age. The commission for the Pistoiese polyptych, moreover, went to the older painter Taddeo Gaddi, possibly because of his seniority. And indeed, that Orcagna was still a young man at this time is beyond doubt, as he appears a maximum of four years before in the registers of the guild of the Medici and Speziali, between 1343 and 1346, which is, besides, the earliest date we possess for him.

It is at this date — and this entry — that Orcagna's artistic career may be said to have begun, although it is not until 1350 that the first commission to come down to us, follows. Being a commission for a work as important as the decoration of the choir of S. Maria Novella, it must have been preceded by a number of others now lost. Whereas he is mentioned by implication — and in documents only — as sculptor and architect, it is of some significance that he appears consistently in the documents, and in the signature to his sculptured tabernacle, under the specific denomination of his preferred craft either as *pictor* or *dipintore*.

from R. Offner, pp. iii-v, *A Critical and Historical Corpus of Florentine Painting*, Sec. IV, Vol. I, New York, 1962.

Andrea di Cione, called Orcagna (presumably a corruption of Arcangelo). Florentine School. Active 1344-68. A painter, sculptor, and architect, Orcagna was the outstanding artist of his time in Florence. His brothers Nardo di Cione and Jacopo di Cione are known to have collaborated with him and only one extant panel painting, the Strozzi altarpiece in Santa Maria Novella, Florence, is documented as by him alone. The style of the work suggests the strong influence of Bernardo Daddi, under whom Orcagna may have studied.

from F. R. Shapley, p. 31, *Paintings from the Samuel H. Kress Collection*, London, 1966.

Orcagna, the son of a goldsmith, was to become the most prominent Florentine painter, sculptor and architect of the mid-fourteenth century. He matriculated in the guild in 1352. In 1354 he was commissioned to paint an altarpiece for the Strozzi chapel in Sta. Maria Novella, which is signed and dated 1357. In September 1367 he received a commission for an altarpiece taken over by his younger brother Jacopo. This is now in the Uffizi. In 1355 he was the superintending architect of Orsanmichele and with another brother, Matteo, was responsible for the sculpture of the tabernacle in the guild oratory. In 1357 he was appointed architect for the Duomo in Florence and in 1358 went to Orvieto where he supervised the mosaic decoration of the façade of the cathedral, again with his brother Matteo, between 1359 and 1360. Returning to Florence, he resumed his post at the Duomo from 1364-6. As a painter, his work is often cited as typical of Florence in the third quarter of the fourteenth century, reacting under the pressure of the Black Death against the optimism and innovation of the previous generation....

from P. Dal Poggetto, p. 70, *Frescoes from Florence*, London, 1969.

BIBLIOGRAPHY

BOOKS

An asterisk indicates a work listed in the General Bibliography

Venturi, A.*, 1907, pp. 767-77; *v. Marle, 1924**, pp. 454-535; Chiapelli, A., *Arte del Rinascimento*, Rome, 1925, pp. 90-113; *Offner Studies**, 1927, p. 97; *Colnaghi**, 1928, pp. 192-5; Steinweg, K., *Andrea Orcagna*, Strasburg, 1929; *Toesca, 1929**, p. 67; *Venturi, L.**, 1933, no 43; Gronau, H. D., *Andrea Orcagna und Nardo di Cione*, Berlin, 1937; *Berenson, 1932**, pp. 403-4; *Paatz**, Vol. I, 1940, p. 551 (with preceding bib.); *Coletti, Vol. II.* 1946, pp. 50-1; *Antal**, 1948, pp. 170, 191-3; *Vavalà, 1948**, pp. 71-5; Beccherucci, L., Catalogue: *Affreschi dell'Orcagna e sculture del Trecento*, Florence, 1949; *Galetti**, " F-O ", 1950, pp. 178-9; *Toesca, 1951**, pp. 635-7, 650-679; Suida, W. E., *Paintings & Sculpture of the Samuel H. Kress Collection, Denver Art Museum*, Denver, (Colo.), 1954, pp. 110-11; Baldini, U., *MAS I**, 1957, pp. 31-3; *Davies**, 1961, pp. 389-99; *Offner, 1962**, Sec. IV, Vol. I; Vigni, G., pp. 114-17 in *EUA**, 1963; *Berenson, 1963**, Vol. I, pp. 106, 163; Gore, St J., *Wildenstein**, 1965, p. 10; *Offner, 1965**. Sec. IV, Vol. III, pp. 107-8; *Marcucci**, 1965, pp. 77-88; Oertel, R., *Die Frühzeit der Italienischen Malerei* (2nd ed.), Stuttgart, 1966, pp. 174-6; *Shapley 1966**, pp. 31-33; *Dal Poggetto**, 1967, pp. 56-60; Gnudi, C., Catalogue: *L'Europe Gothique XII-XIV siècles*, Paris, 1968, pp. 199-200; Dal Poggetto, P., *Fresco Show**, 1968, pp. 78-83 (70-9); *Meiss, 1970**, pp. 92-5; Zeri, F., *Diari di Lavoro*, Bergamo, 1971, p. 16; Gilbert, C., *History of Renaissance Art throughout Europe*, New York, 1973, pp. 46-47; *Dutch Show**, 1974, pp. 27-28.

JOURNALS

Sirèn, O., *BM*, XIV, 1908, p. 193; Bombe, W., *MKIF*, 1912, II, 1; Berenson, B., *DD*, XI, 4, 1930-1, pp. 1039-73; Tosi, L. M., *BA*, XXVII, 1934, 3, pp. 512-26; Salvini, R., *A*, XL, 1937, pp. 16-45; Steinweg, K., *BM*, LXXII, 1938, pp. 96-7; Beccherucci, L., *BA*, XXXIII, 4, 1948, pp. 143-56; Valentiner, W. R., *AQ*, XII, 1949, 1, pp. 48-73; Valentiner, W. R., *AQ*, XII, 2, 1949, pp. 113-28; Frankfurter, A. M., *AN*, 49, 1951, pp. 23-5; Offner, R., *MKIF*, VII, 3-4, 1953-6, pp. 173-92; Ragghianti, C. L., *NCA*, I, 1, 1954, pp. 1-18; Cohn, W., *BA*, XLI, 1956, p. 175; Levi d'Ancona, M., *RA*, XXXII, 1957, pp. 3-37; Klesse, B., *MKIF*, VIII, 4, 1959, pp. 247-52; Stöckelová, G., *A*, LIX, 25/4, 1960, pp. 277-88; Pini, U., *AC*, I, 1960-1, pp. 7-37; Steinweg, K., *MKIF*, X, 2, 1961, pp. 122-7; Saalman, H., *AB*, XLVI, 1964, p. 480; White, J., *BM*, CVI, 1964, p. 516; King, E. S., *BWAG*, XVII, 4, 1965, p. 4; Bellosi, L., *PA*, XVII, 201, 1966, pp. 77-8; Donati, P. P., *C*, XVII, 1-3, 1966, pp. 56-72; De Benedictis, C., *AV*, 3, 1967, p. 43; Boskovits, M., *MKIF*, XIII, 1-4, 1967-8, p. 50; White, J., *BM*, CXI, 794, 1969, p. 380; Boskovits, M., *AI*, III, 25/26, 1970, pp. 32-47; Pieper, P., *ZKG*, XXXIII, 1, 1970, p. 84; Boskovits, M., *BM*, CXIII, 818, 1971, pp. 239-251; Gardner, J., *ZKG*, XXXIV, 2, 1971, p. 91; Skaug, E., *MKIF*, XV, 2, 1971, p. 145; Fehm, S., *MKIF*, XVII, 2-3, 1973, p. 258; Bellosi, L., *MKIF*, XVII, 2/3, p. 188; Procacci, U., *MKIF*, XVII, 2/3, p. 318.

SIGNED AND DATED WORKS

1346 Private Collection. Panel: Annunciation with Donor. s & d. (fig. 294).

1350 Utrecht, Aartsbisschoppelijk Museum. Triptych: Madonna nursing the Child with two Angels & Sts. Mary Magdalene and Ansanus. d. (fig. 289).

1357 Florence, S. Maria Novella, Strozzi Chapel. Polyptych: Christ in Glory with four music-making Angels, Cherubs, Saints and the Virgin. s & d. (fig. 274).

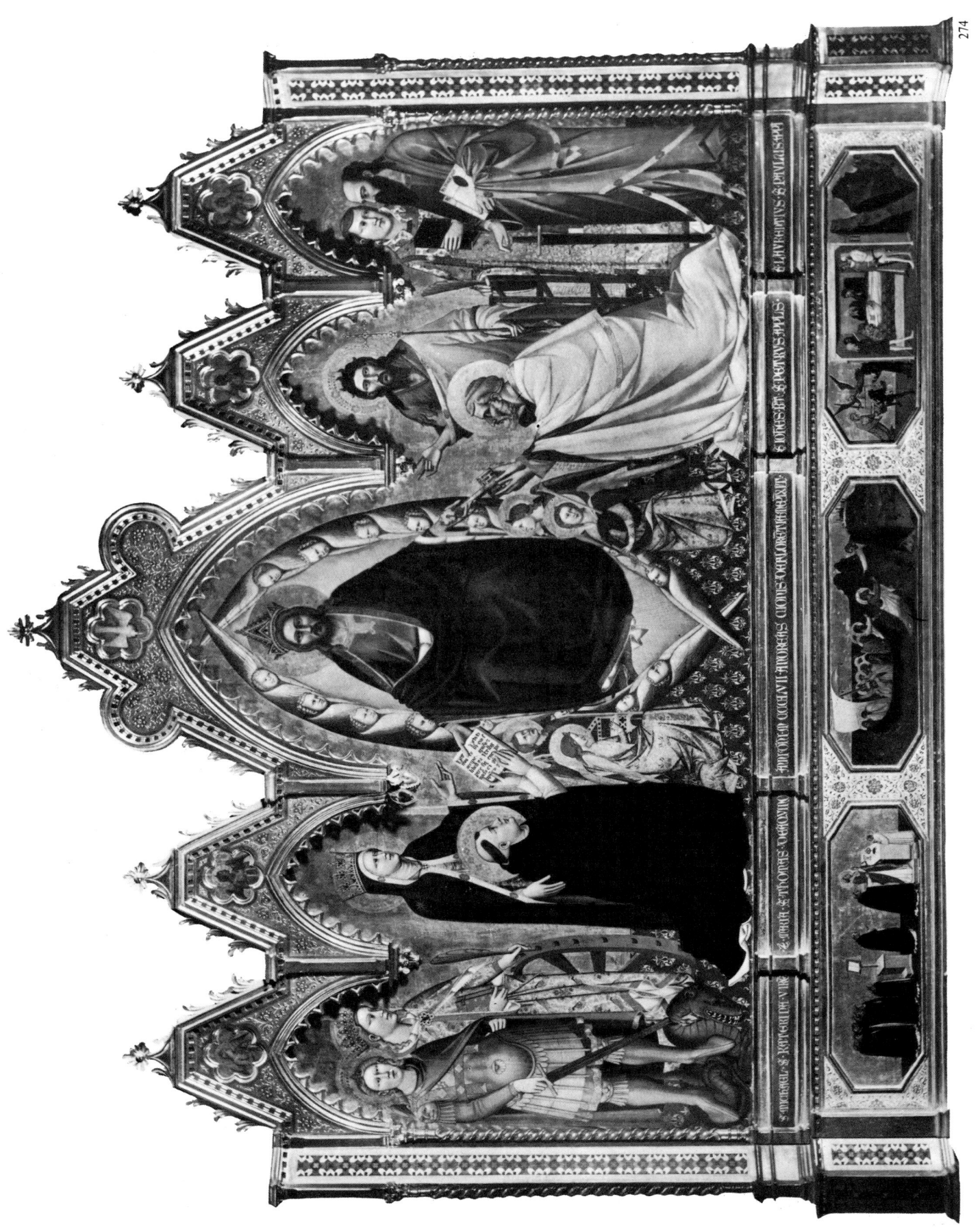

274. *Polyptych: Christ in Glory with four music-making Angels and winged heads of Cherubs forming mandorla, and Sts Michael, Catherine, the Virgin, Thomas Aquinas, Peter, John the Baptist, Lawrence and Paul. Above: Holy Spirit and four Angels. Predella: Mass of St Thomas; Calling of St Peter; Death of Emperor and Lawrence redeeming his Soul. Panel. Florence, S. Maria Novella, Strozzi Chapel. cp: 160 × 296; sps: 128 × 296. Alinari 4045. s & d 1357.*

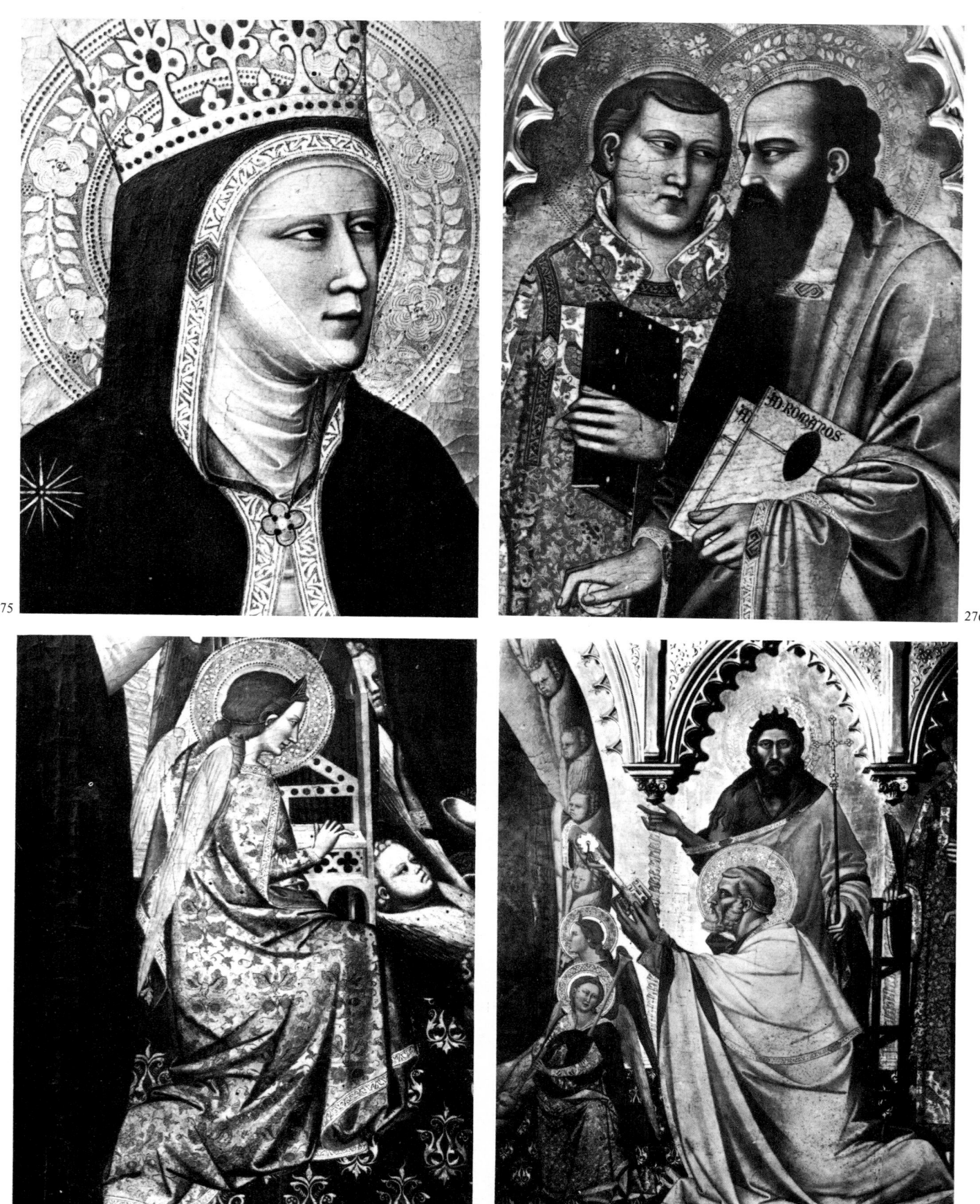

275. *Head of Virgin, detail of fig. 274. Panel. Florence, S. Maria Novella, Strozzi Chapel. Brogi 17234c. s & d. 1357.*
276. *Sts Lawrence and Paul, detail of fig. 274. Panel. Florence, S. Maria Novella, Strozzi Chapel. Brogi 17234. s & d. 1357.*
277. *Music-making Angel, detail of fig. 274. Panel. Florence, S. Maria Novella, Strozzi Chapel. Brogi 17234f. s & d. 1357.*
278. *Sts Peter and John the Baptist, detail of fig. 274. Panel. Florence, S. Maria Novella, Strozzi Chapel. Brogi 25584. s & d. 1357.*

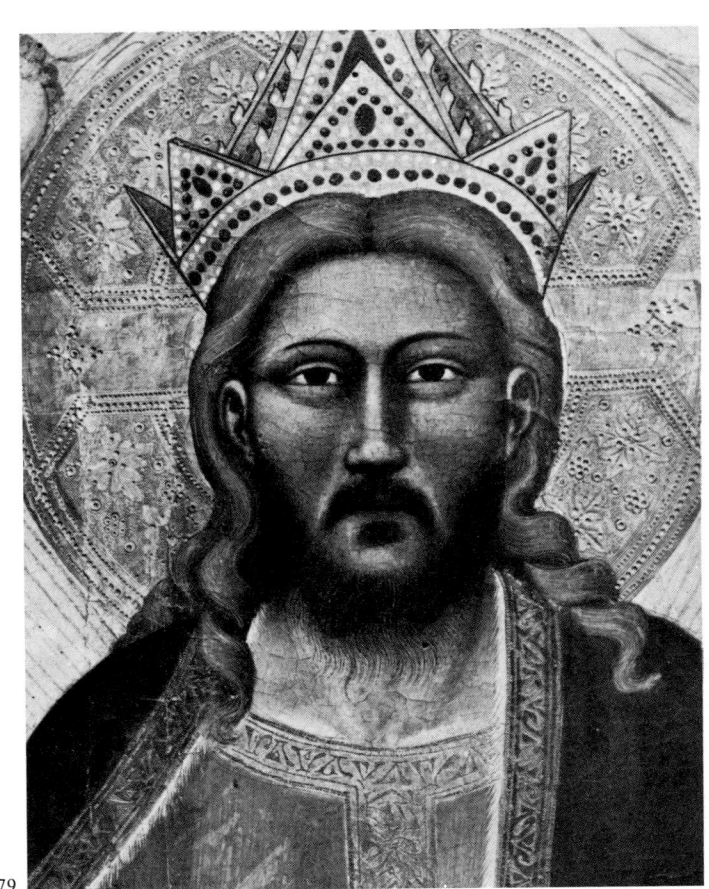

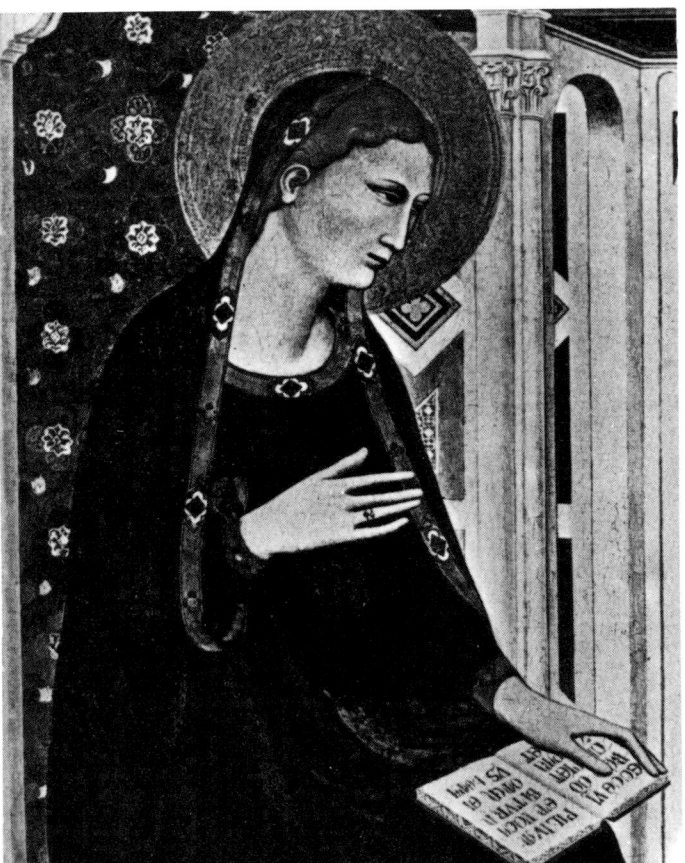

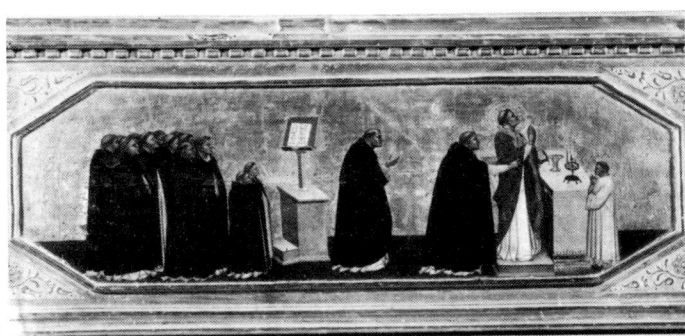

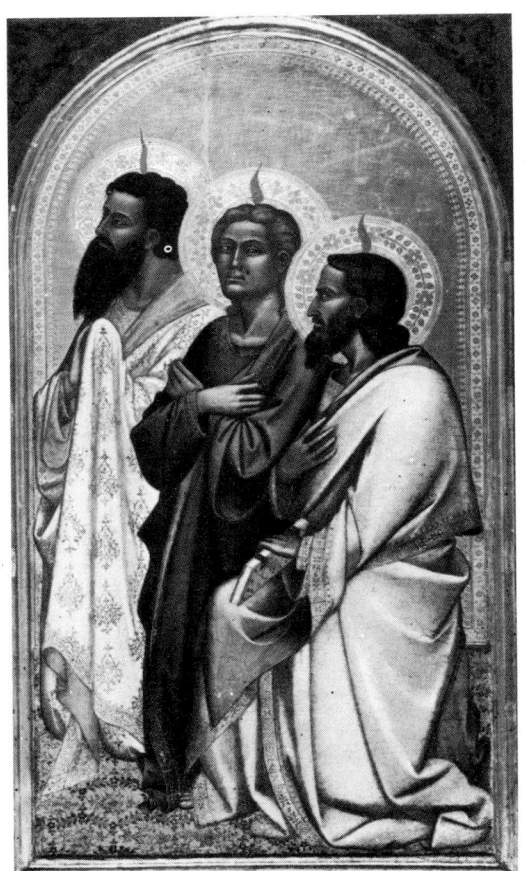

279. *Head of Christ, detail of fig. 274. Panel. Florence, S. Maria Novella, Strozzi Chapel. Brogi 17234e. s & d. 1357.*
280. *Virgin Annunciate, detail of fig. 294. Panel. Private Collection. Collection photo. s & d. 1346.*
281. *Predella scene: Mass of St Thomas, detail of fig. 274. Panel. Florence, S. Maria Novella, Strozzi Chapel. Brogi 19960. s & d. 1357.*
282. *Three Apostles, detail of fig. 292. Panel. Florence, Accademia. Depositi no. 165. S G F 95465.*

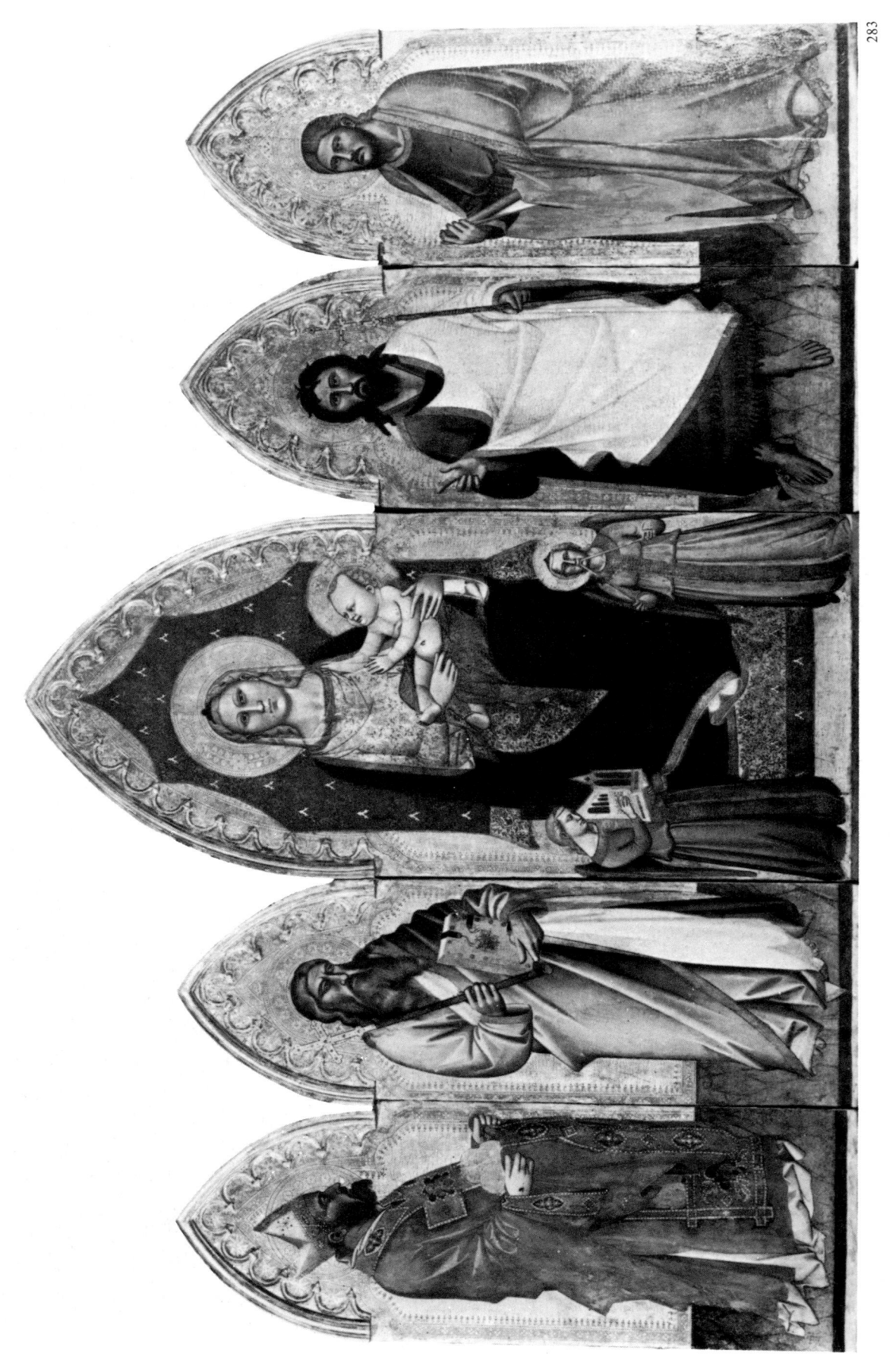

283. *Polyptych: Madonna and Child with two music-making Angels, and Sts John the Baptist, James, Nicholas and Peter. Panel. Florence, Accademia, no. 3469. cp: 127 × 56.5; sps: 104 × 37. SGF 69634.*

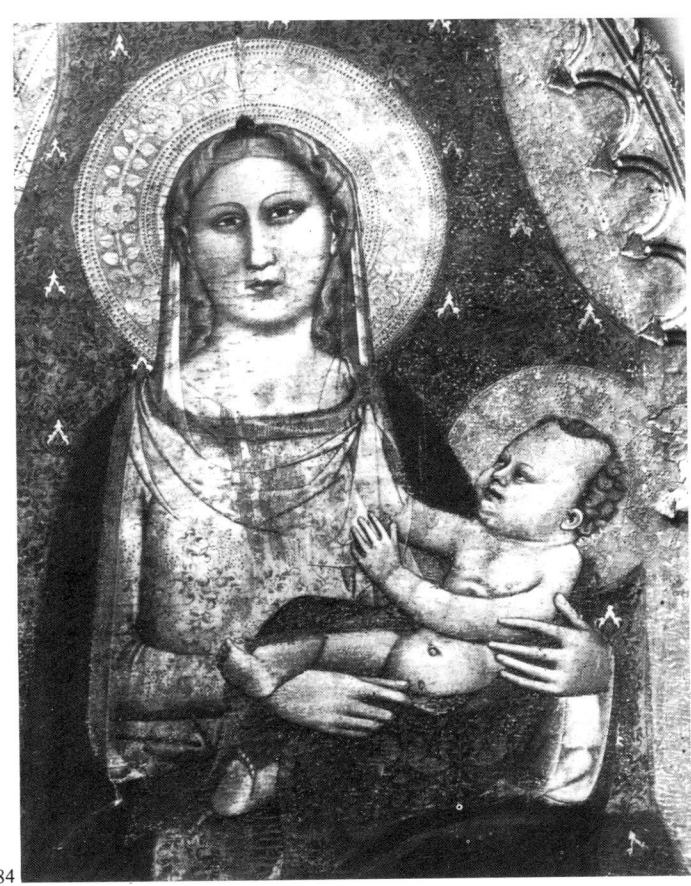

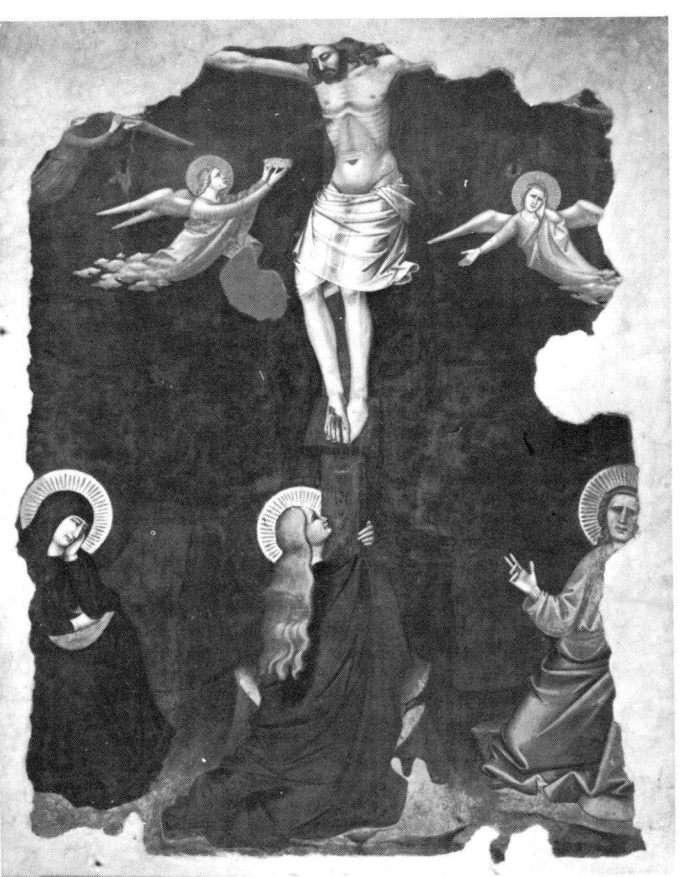

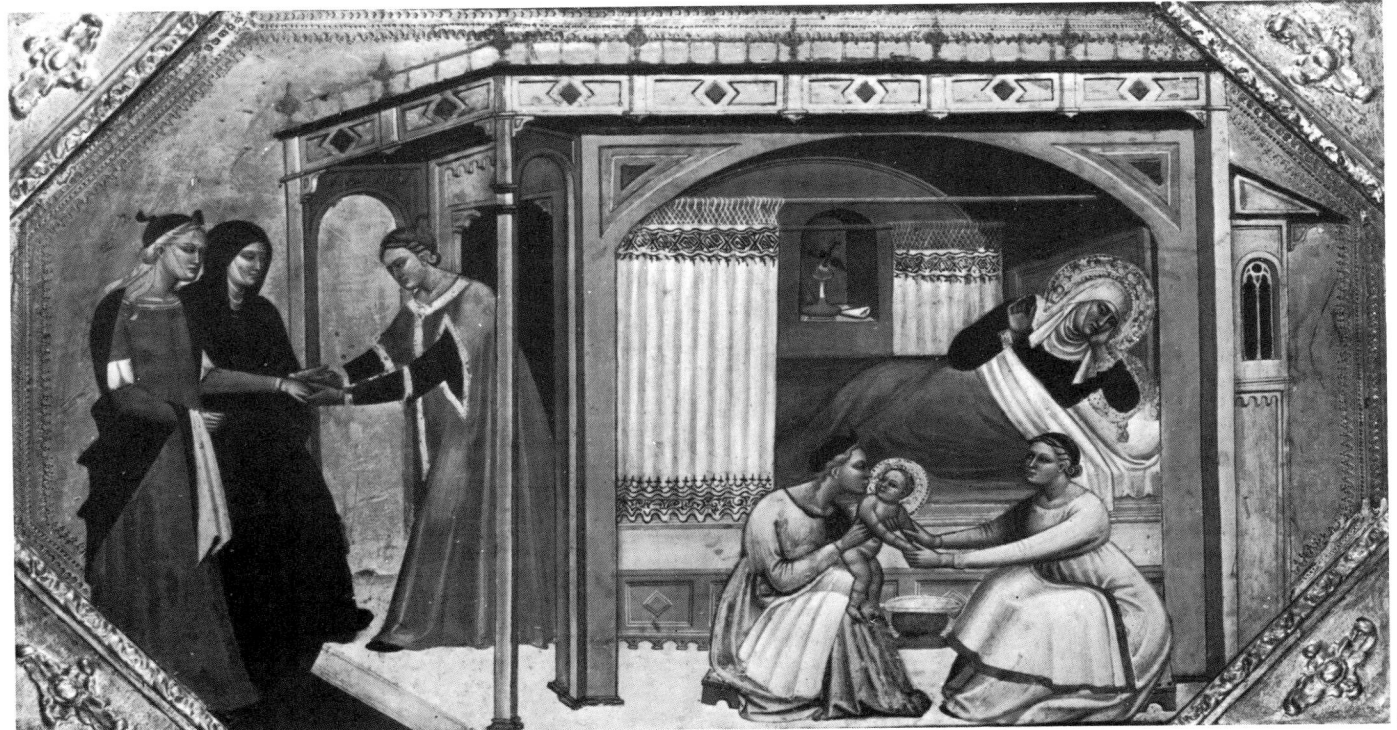

284. *Madonna and Child, detail of fig. 283. Panel. Florence, Accademia. no. 3464. SGF 20930.*
285. *Christ on the Cross with St John and the two Marys. Fresco. Florence, Conservatorio di S. Marta. SGF 130414.*
286. *Predella scene: Birth of the Virgin. Panel. Oxford, Ashmolean Museum. no. 306. 37 × 55. Museum photo.*

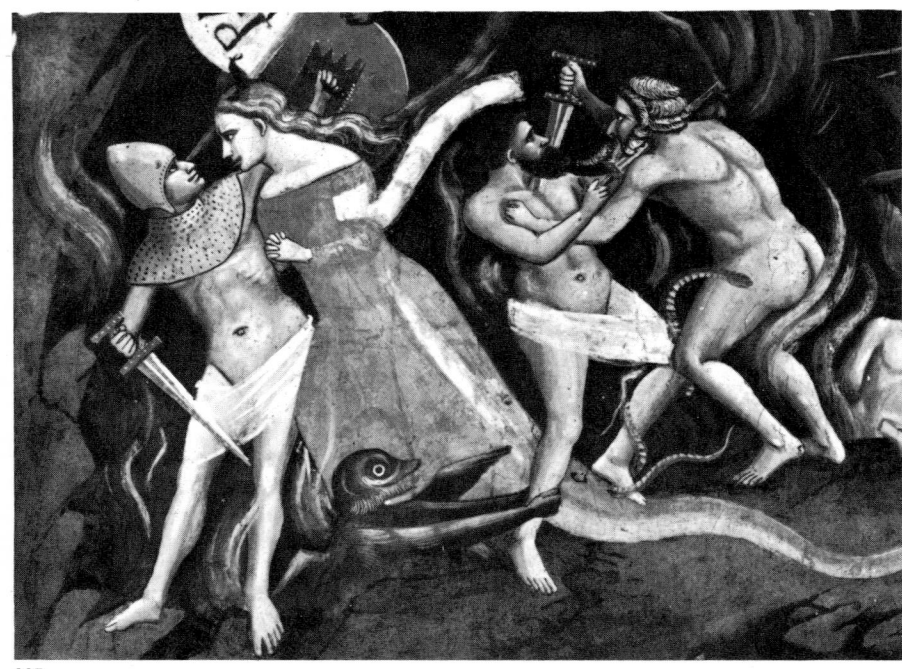

287

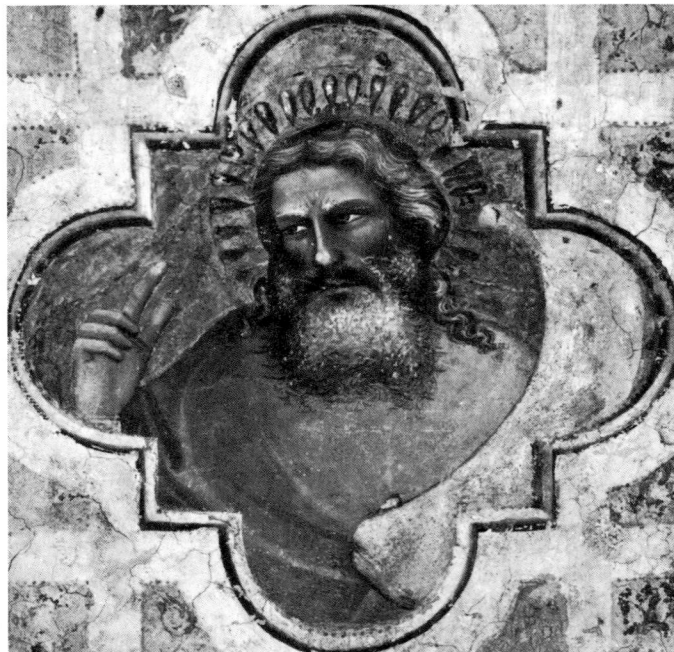

288

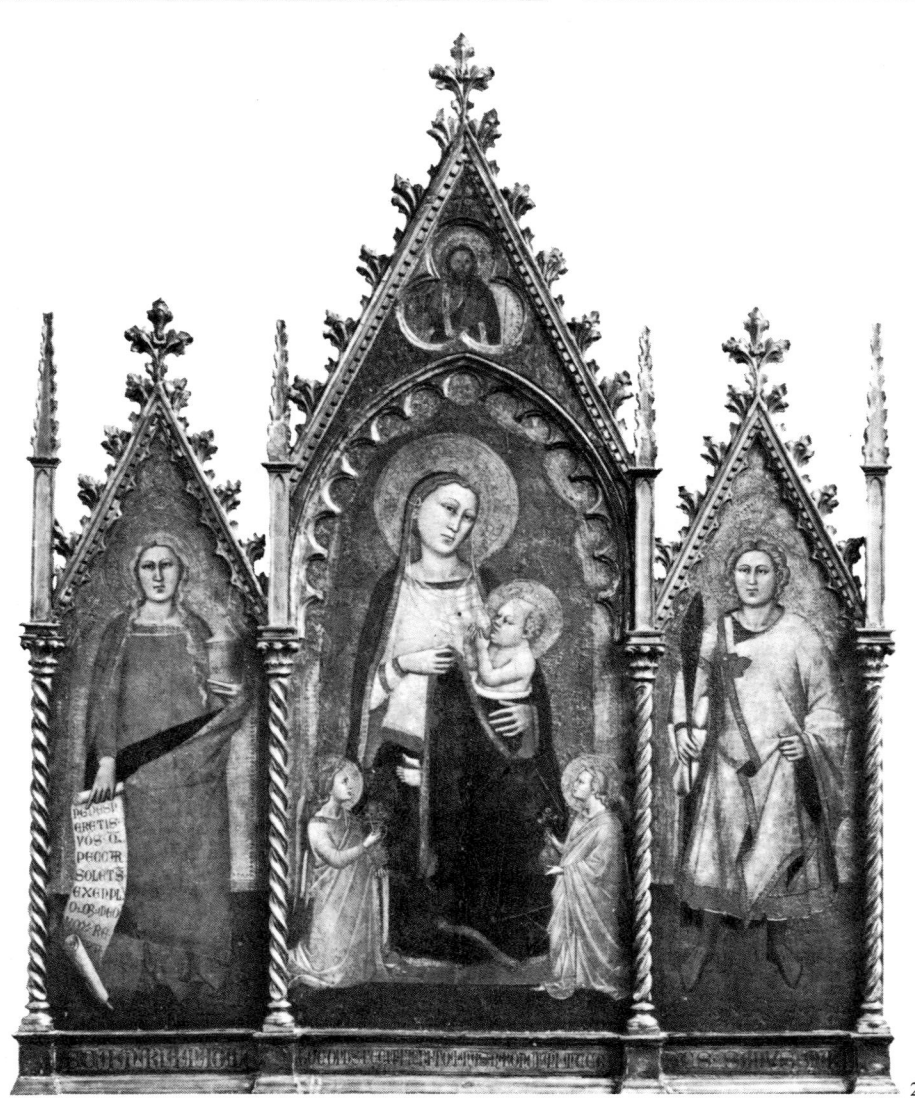

289

287. *Scene from the Inferno. Fresco. Florence, Museo dell'Opera di S. Croce. SGF 108146.*
288. *A Prophet. Fresco. Florence, S. Maria Novella, Choir. SGF 105780.*
289. *Triptych: Madonna nursing the Child, with two Angels and Sts Mary Magdalene and Ansanus. Above: Christ blessing. Panel. Utrecht, Aartsbisschoppelijk Museum. no. 296. 115 × 135. Museum photo: Hans Sibbelee. d. 1350.*

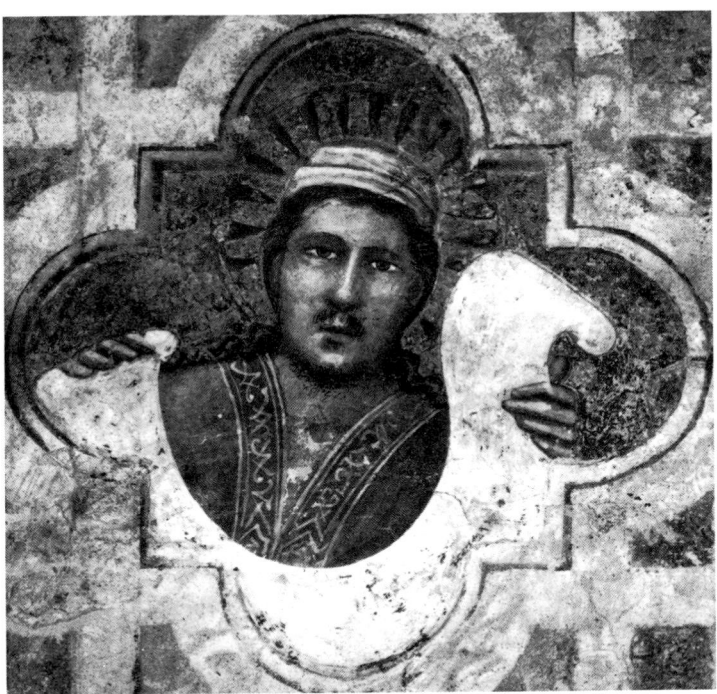

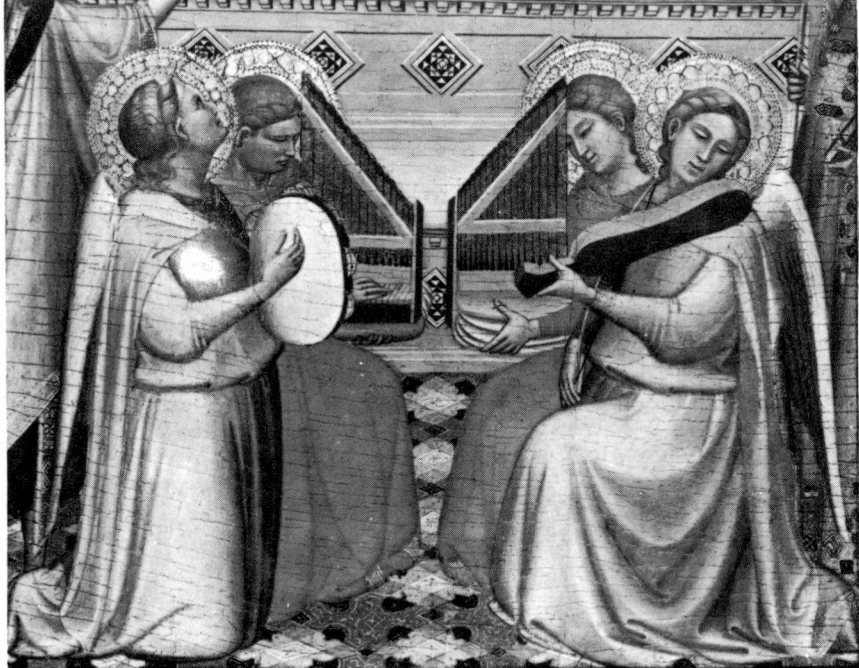

290

291

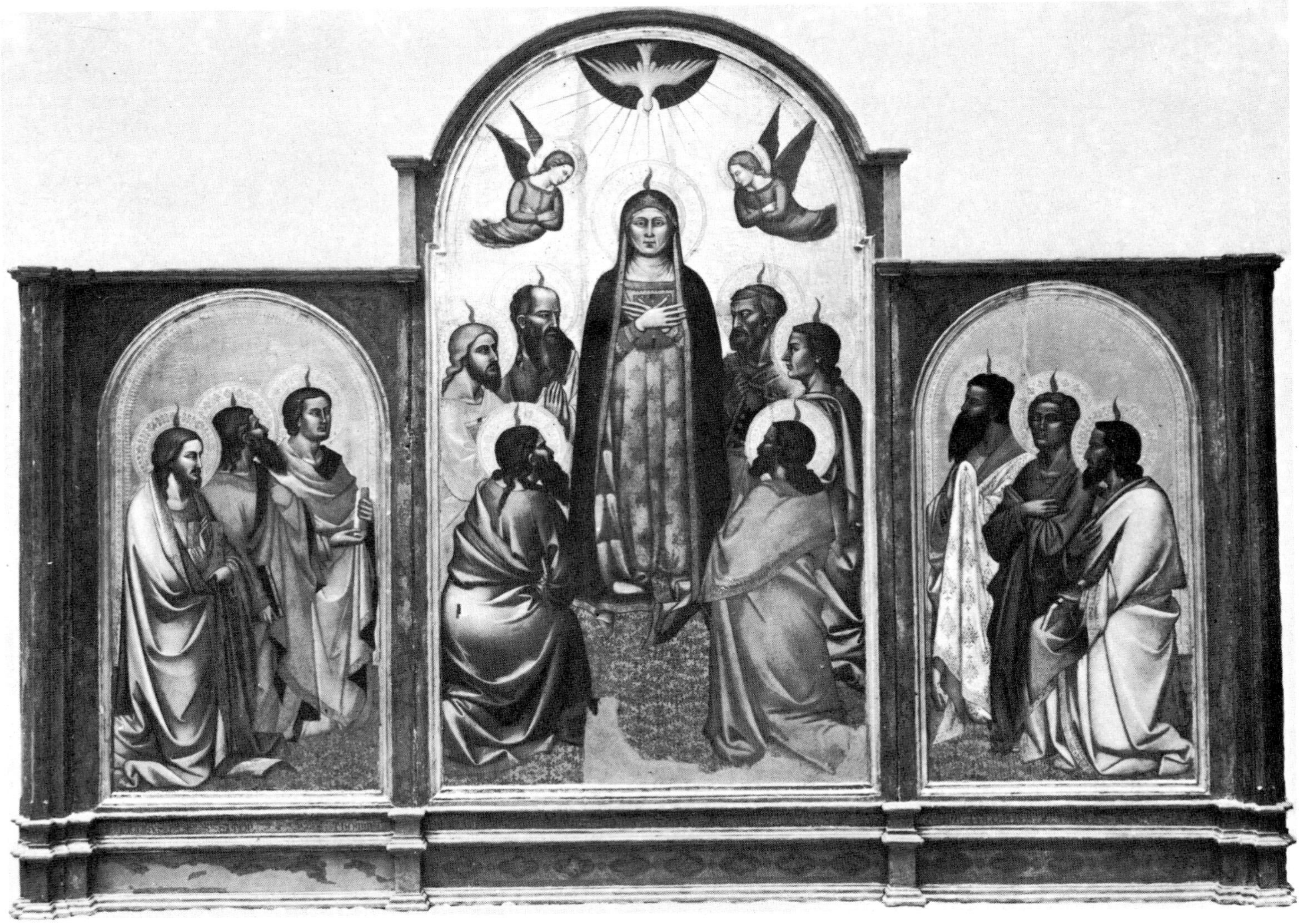

292

290. *A Prophet. Fresco. Florence, S. Maria Novella, Choir. SGF 105772.*
291. *Four music-making Angels. Panel. Oxford, Christ Church. no. 5. 44 × 54.3. Collection photo.*
292. *Triptych: Assumption with twelve Apostles and two Angels. Panel. Florence, Accademia. Depositi no. 165 . cp : 194 × 102; sps : 140 × 87. SGF 95462.*

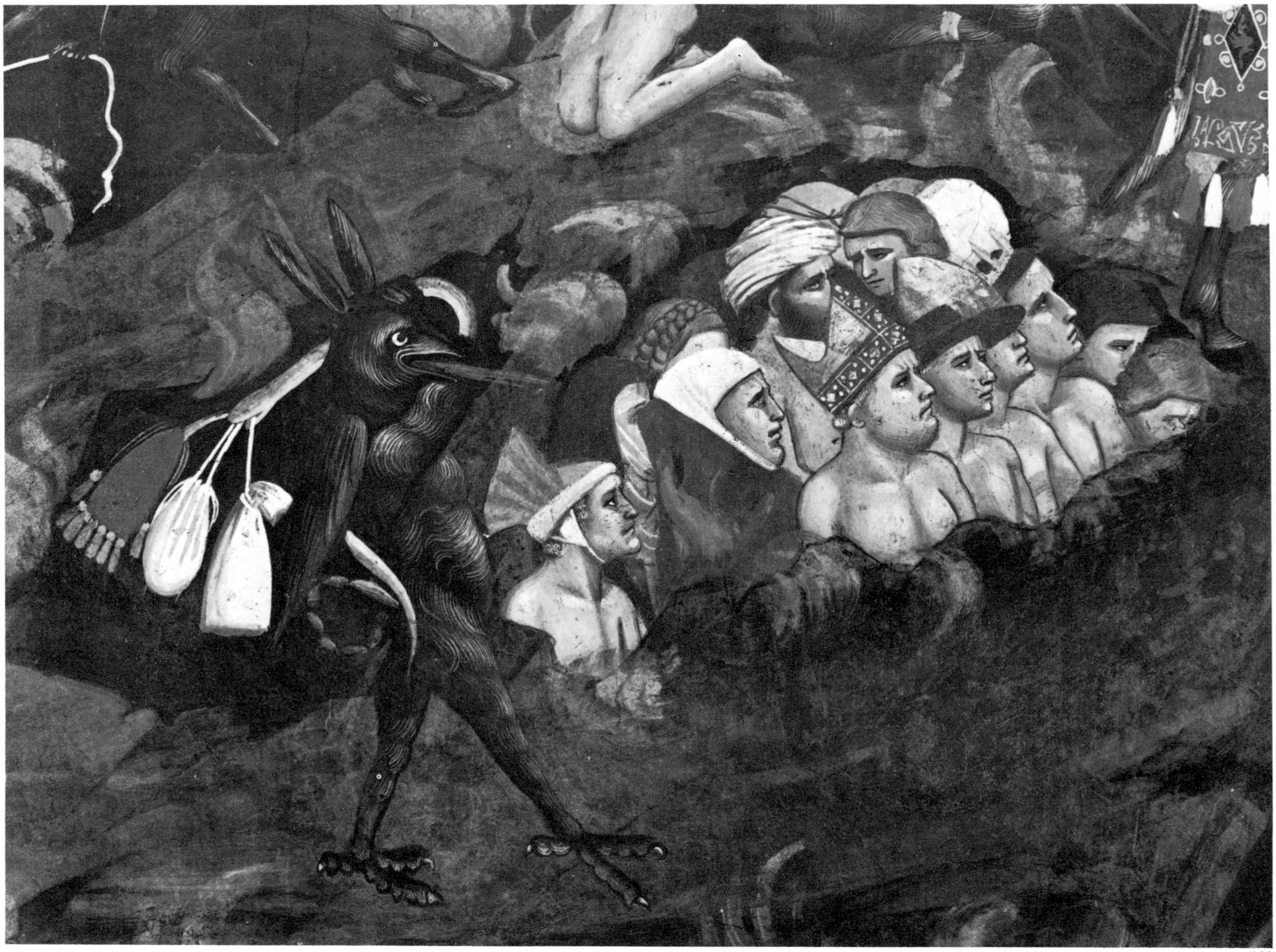

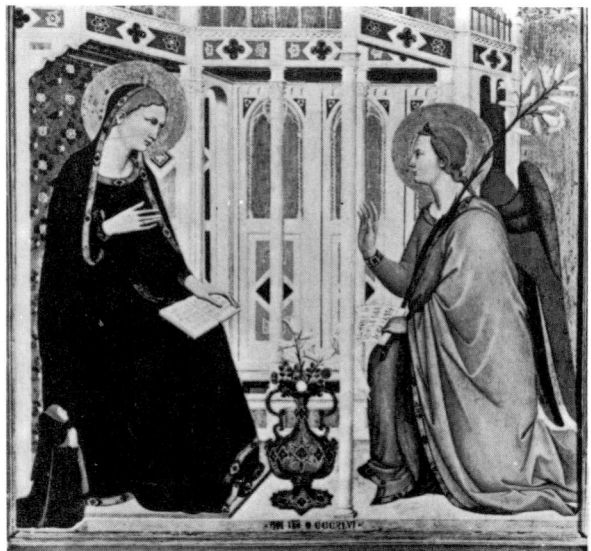

293. *Detail of Souls in Hell. Fresco. Florence, Museo dell'Opera di S. Croce. SGF 108142.*
294. *Annunciation with Donor. Panel. Private Collection. Fototeca Berenson. s & d. 1346.*

NARDO di CIONE

Nardo di Cione is one of the most delightful fresco painters of the Trecento. A follower of Maso, he deviates from him, softening the former's relief, and minimizing his sense of depth. Nardo uses a less vibrant coloration, suffused with delicate chiaroscuro. His greatest work — the Strozzi Chapel in S. Maria Novella, with the Judgment, Paradise, and the Inferno — achieves a delicate refinement and spatiality through chiaroscuro and through the use of intense colour. It proceeds towards a graceful idealization of form which one can see also in the great Crucifixion of the Cenacolo di S. Spirito, where Nardo collaborated with his brother Andrea. The Resurrection of the Chiostrino dei Morti — (the stories of the Madonna are also by him) — is tangible proof of delicate linear modulation and of his ability to synthesize spatial construction and subdued chromatic harmony. The calm which pervades his compositions can be recognized even in the most worn surface.....

from U. Procacci, p. 30, *II^a Mostra di Affreschi Staccati*, Florence, 1958.

Although Nardo di Cione kept faith with the artistic tradition of his native Florence throughout his career, he must have been something of an anomaly to his contemporaries. And he has remained so until relatively recent times except for Ghiberti (c. 1452-1455) alone. Because Ghiberti's attribution of the Strozzi frescoes, Nardo's capital work, to Nardo became submerged under the weight of Andrea's mounting fame only the twentieth century has learned to recognize him. Vasari could only have had a dim notion of Nardo's style, if we judge his views on the subject by his incongruous attributions to Orcagna and to Nardo. Vasari's confusion took refuge behind the conventional formula of Nardo as collaborator of Orcagna, which had, and today has, no basis in visual experience or in explicit documentary mention. Considering the fact that Vasari's view persisted until the late nineteenth century, it is perhaps not mere chance that Baldinucci at the end of the seventeenth in his life of Nardo is found ascribing the direction of the Strozzi frescoes to Nardo (*Bernardo.... prese in aiuto Andrea....*) although the epochs following revert to Vasari's allotment of the Strozzi frescoes to the two brothers. It may be this deviation from traditional opinion that is echoed in Fantozzi, in 1842, and in François in 1850, who put " Bernardo " before Andrea in assigning responsibility for the painting of the Paradise and the Inferno. Such priority may have had its origin in the totally unverified notion that Nardo was the elder of the two brothers. A modest contribution is made by Cavalcaselle, in 1864, who is the first to subject the Strozzi Chapel frescoes to a study of their style and condition. And although he fails to attribute them to Nardo, to decide for a single authorship throughout is a significant advance made prior to Milanesi (1878). This writer invokes Ghiberti's attribution of the Strozzi Chapel to Nardo although he considers Andrea's collaboration possible. It is, however, Wickhoff (1889) who first declares himself — without reservation and without immediate adherents — for Nardo, and who brings the problem into proper focus for the first critically discerning inquiry on him by Suida (1905 and 1908), followed by Sirén who at an early stage of research on this master (between 1907 and 1919) had the merit of adding at least five panels to the small stock of his acceptable works. A few years afterwards in 1924, and later in 1927, I was able to add five more, thus rendering Nardo's artistic personality more intelligible in terms chiefly of a continuing development. Since then, apart from the justifiable claim for Nardo of the Prague polyptych by Berenson and Gronau (1932), Nardo has hardly received his due as artist and influence.....

from R. Offner, p. III, *A Critical and Historical Corpus of Florentine Painting*, Sec. IV, Vol. II, New York, 1960.

Nardo's influence was prodigious. In a world still unrecovered from the ravages of the great plague, his domination of north Tuscan painting, shared to be sure with his brother Andrea, was almost complete. Virtually all the Florentine painters of the second half of the fourteenth century can trace their sources back to these two masters.....

from R. Offner, p. IX, *A Critical and Historical Corpus of Florentine Painting*, Sec. IV, Vol. II, New York, 1965.

Brother of Andrea di Cione (Orcagna). To some extent his style depended upon that of his brother, but he is less sculptural and austere. A canon for his work is provided by Ghiberti's evidence that he was responsible for the frescoes in the Strozzi Chapel in Santa Maria Novella, Florence. He may have been a pupil of Maso (a Giotto follower.....) whose manner of painting he sometimes recalls, but his roots were primarily in Daddi and the non-Giottesque tradition. He and his brother were the main influence in Tuscan painting during the second half of the century.....

from St. J. Gore, p. 11, *The Art of Painting in Florence and Siena from 1250-1500*, London, 1965.

The date of his birth is unknown, but according to Milanesi and Frey, Nardo di Cione was the oldest brother of Andrea di Cione, called Orcagna. In 1343 he matriculated in the guild of Medici e Speziali, and in 1347 his name appeared on the list of artists who competed for the commission to paint an altarpiece for the Church of S. Giovanni Fuorcivitas at Pistoia. In October 1363 he was employed to decorate the vault of an oratory of the Compagnia del Bigallo and in 1364 joined the guild of St. Luke. On May 21, 1365, Nardo di Cione made his will, and is referred to a year later as dead. According to Ghiberti he painted the frescoes in the Strozzi Chapel of Sta. Maria Novella, although Vasari attributes them to Orcagna " in conjunction with his brother ". Scholars have tended to agree with Ghiberti, and it is by comparison with these frescoes that attributions to Nardo are usually made. These include frescoes in the Chiostro de' Morti of Sta. Maria Novella and in the Giochi-Bastari chapel in the Badia. Although Nardo di Cione probably worked within the framework of the family workshop, his own style seems to have remained more Giottesque than that of his younger brother.....

from P. Dal Poggetto, p. 81, *Frescoes from Florence*, London, 1969.

BIBLIOGRAPHY
BOOKS

An asterisk indicates a work listed in the General Bibliography

Venturi, A.*, 1907, pp. 759-67; v. Marle 1924*, pp. 475-6; Offner Studies*, 1927, p. 97; Suida, W. E., *Die Florentinische Malerei des XIV Jahrhunderts*, Munich, 1929, pp. 59, 61; Toesca, 1929*, p. 66; Steinweg, K., *Andrea Orcagna*, Strasburg, 1929; Venturi, L.*, 1933, pls 44, 45; Berenson, 1932*, p. 363; Gronau, H. D., *Andrea Orcagna und Nardo di Cione*, Berlin, 1937; Coletti, Vol. II*, 1946, pp. 51-3; Offner, 1947*, Sec. III, Vol. V, pp. 28, 150, 296; Antal*, 1948, pp. 189-191; Vavalà, 1948, pp. 75-6; Galetti*, " F-O ", pp. 1790-2; Oertel, 1950*, p. 51; Toesca, 1951*, pp. 636-8; Paatz*, Vol. III, 1952, p. 126; Procacci, U., *MAS II**, 1958, p. 30; Offner, 1960*, Sec. IV, Vol. II; Davies*, 1961, pp. 382-4; Berenson, 1962*, p. vii; Vigni, C., p. 117, in *EUA**, Vol. V, 1963; Berenson, 1963*, Vol. I, pp. 151-2; Gore, St J., Wildenstein*, 1965, p. 11; Offner, 1965*, Sec. IV, Vol. III, p. 97; Marcucci*, 1965, pp. 73-7; Bianchini, M. A., *Maso di Banco* (I Maestri del Colore, 247), Milan, 1966; Shapley*, 1966, pp. 34-5; Dal Poggetto*, 1967, pp. 54-6; Gnudi, C., Catalogue: *L'Europe Gothique XII-XIV siècles*, Paris, 1968, pp. 195-6; Dal Poggetto, P., *Fresco Show**, 1968, pp. 84-9 (80-1); Meiss, 1970*, p. 97; Gilbert, C., *History of Renaissance Art throughout Europe*, New York, 1973, p. 46.

JOURNALS

Sirèn, O., *AA*, 1914, p. 325; Bodmer, H., *MKIF*, III, 1919-32, pp. 194-5; Offner, R., *AA*, 1924, pp. 99-112; Berenson, B., *DD*, XI, 4, 1930-1, pp. 957-88, 1039-73; Suida, W. E., *P*, XXVI, 1940, p. 274; Coletti, L., *CA*, VIII, 6, 1950, pp. 443-54; Offner, R., *MKIF*, VII, 3/4, 1953-6, pp. 173-92; Middeldorf, U., *MKIF*, VII, 1, 1953-6, pp. 169-172; Baldini, U., *BA*, XL, 4, 1955, pp. 79-81; s. p., *E*, CXXVI, 10, 1957, pp. 61-8; Coor, G., *AB*, 44, 1962, pp. 340-342; Gallotti Minola, M., *E*, CXXXVII, 822, 1963, pp. 254-60; Gregori, M., *AV*, V, 6, 1966, pp. 40-9; De Benedictis, C., *AV*, 3, 1967, p. 46; Kiel, H., *P*, XXVII, 5, 1969, p. 421; White, J., *BM*, CXI, 794, 1969, p. 380; (photograph), *GBA*, LXXIII, III, 1969, (Supplement), n. 220; van Os, H. W., *Sim*, 4, 1970, 1, pp. 10-11; Fehm, S., *MKIF*, XVII, 2-3, 1973, pp. 258; Procacci, U., *MKIF*, XVII, 2-3, 1973, pp. 307-24.

DATED WORKS

1365 Florence, Academia 8464. Triptych: Trinity with Sts. Romuald and John the Evangelist. d. (fig. 311).
1365 Florence, S. Croce (Uffizi dep. 170), Sacristy. Triptych: Madonna of Humility with St. Gregory and Job. d. (fig. 315).

There are no known signed works by Nardo di Cione.

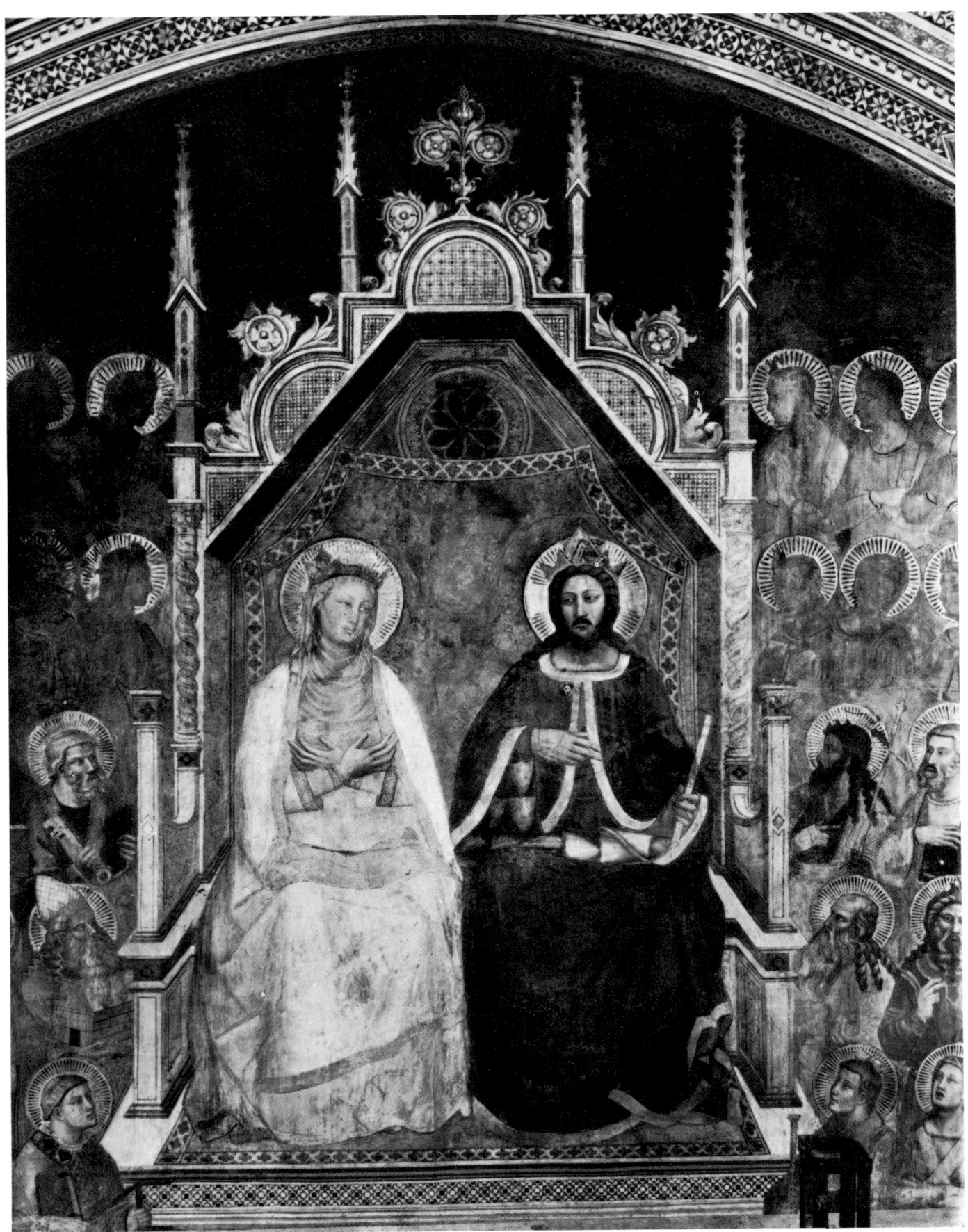

295. *Madonna and Christ Enthroned, detail. Fresco. Florence, S. Maria Novella, Strozzi Chapel. SGF 66060.*

295

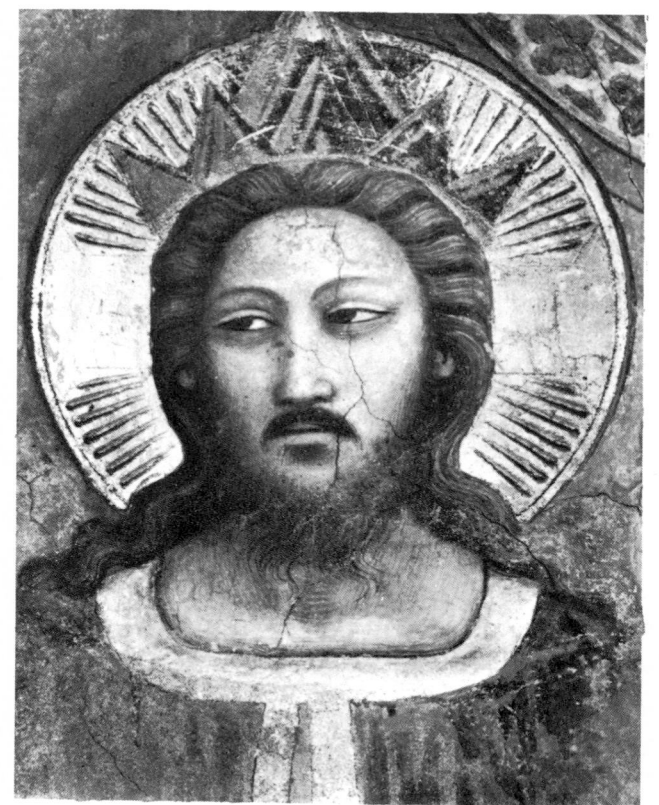

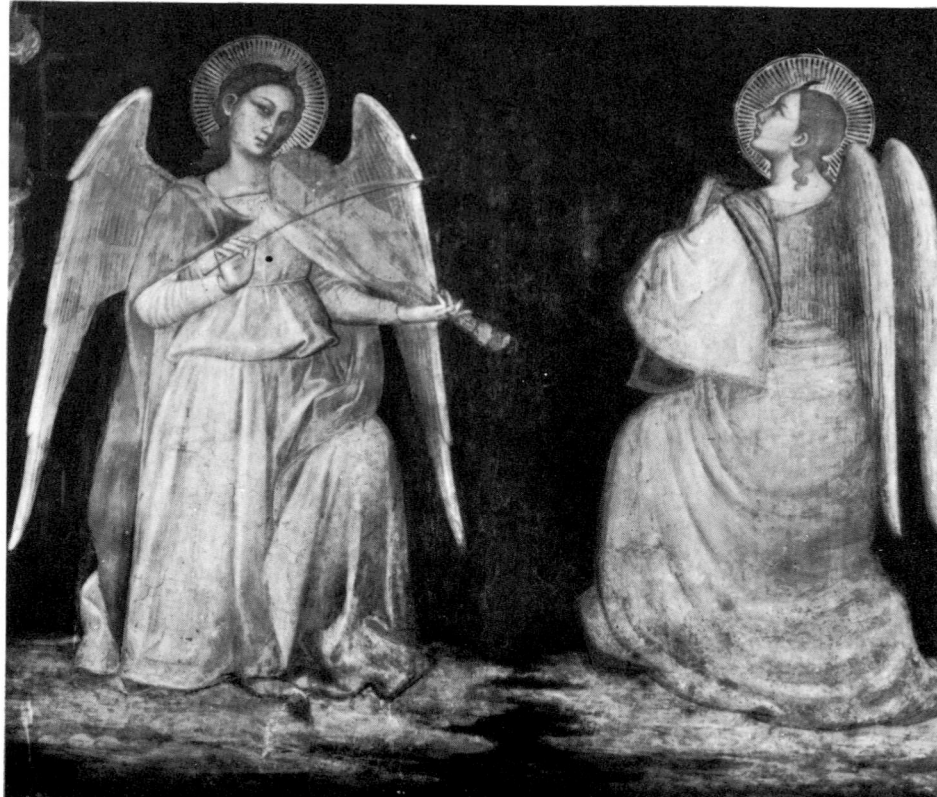

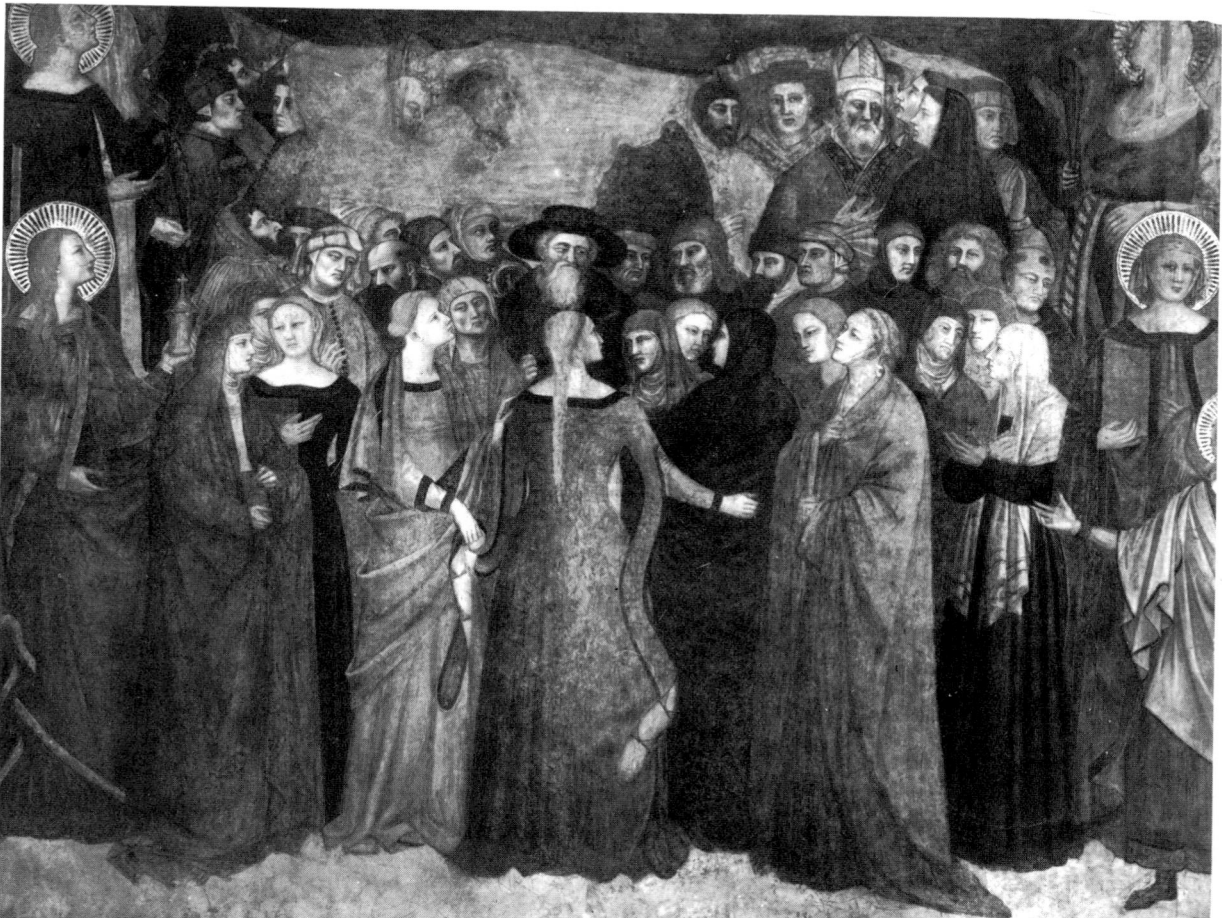

296. *Head of Christ, detail of fig. 301. Fresco. Florence, S. Maria Novella, Strozzi Chapel. SGF 66062.*
297. *Two Angels, detail. Fresco. Florence, S. Maria Novella, Strozzi Chapel. SGF 66243.*
298. *Scene from Paradise, detail. Fresco. Florence, S. Maria Novella, Strozzi Chapel. SGF 66306.*

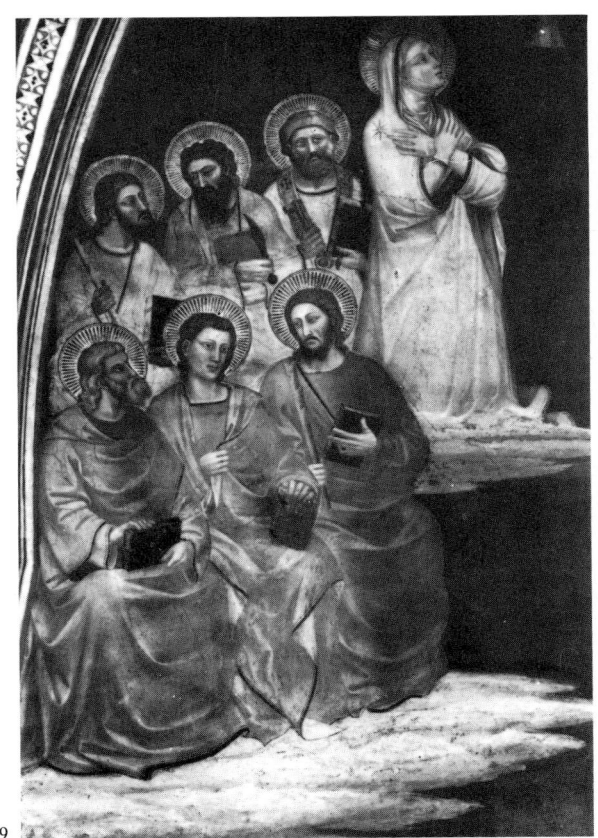

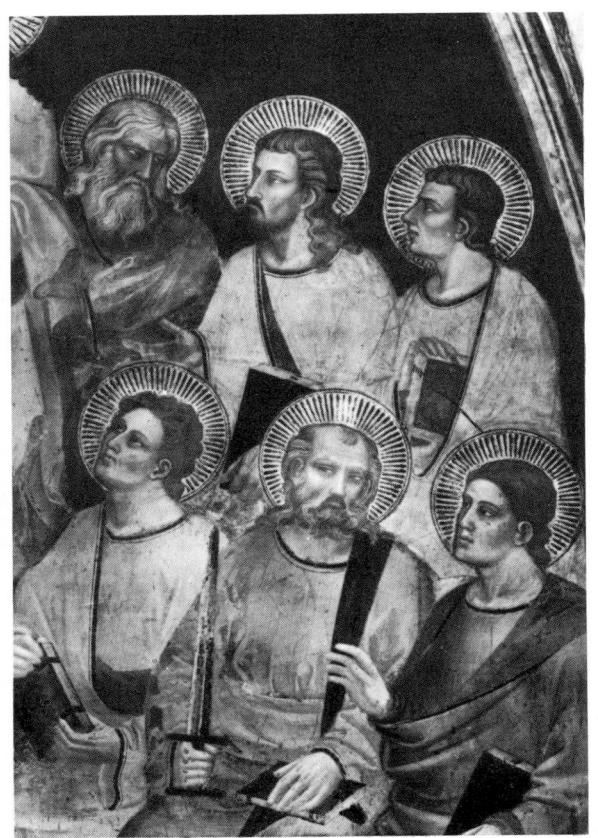

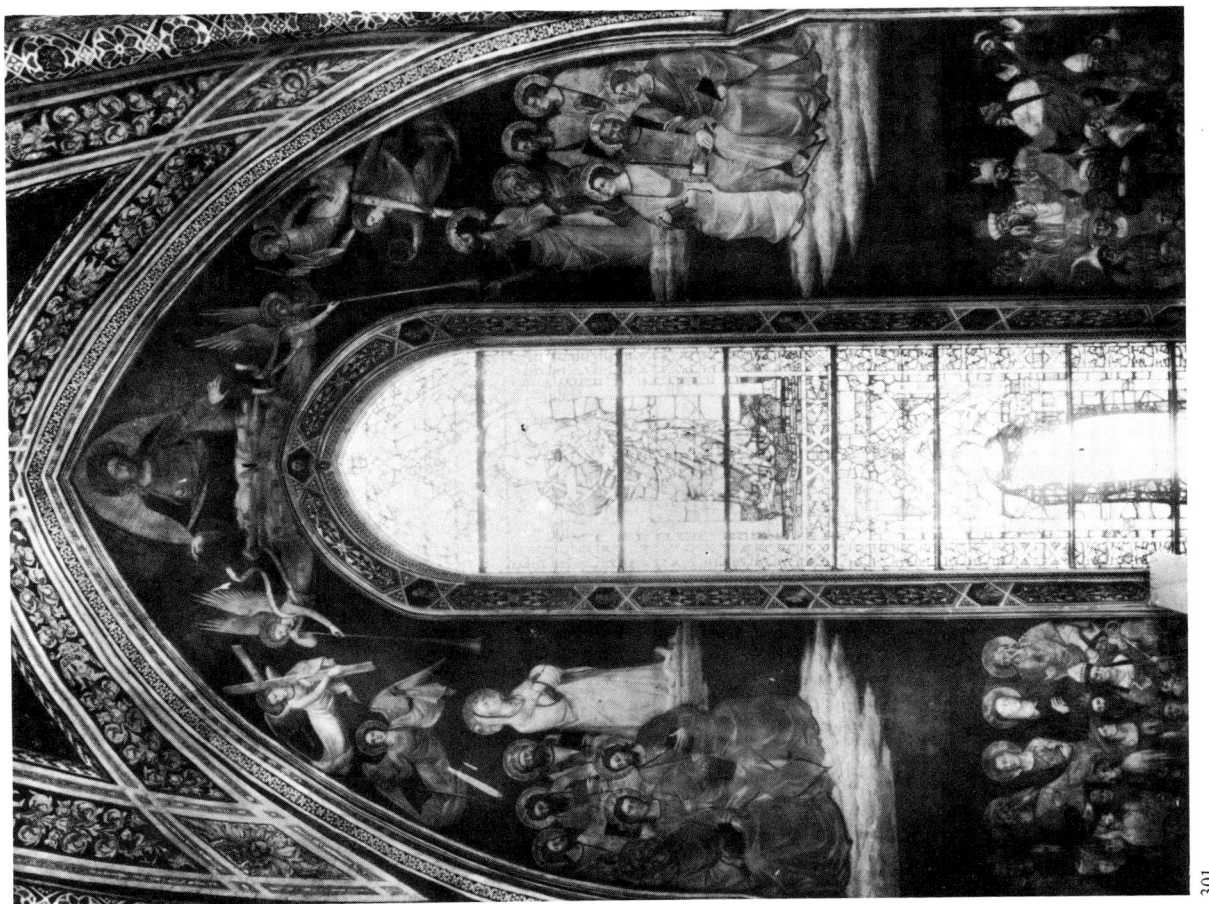

299. *Apostles and the Virgin, detail of fig. 301. Fresco. Florence, S. Maria Novella, Strozzi Chapel. SGF 66099.*
300. *Heads of Apostles, detail of fig. 301. Fresco. Florence, S. Maria Novella, Strozzi Chapel. SGF 66073.*
301. *The Last Judgement, detail. Fresco. Florence, S. Maria Novella, Strozzi Chapel. SGF 66246.*

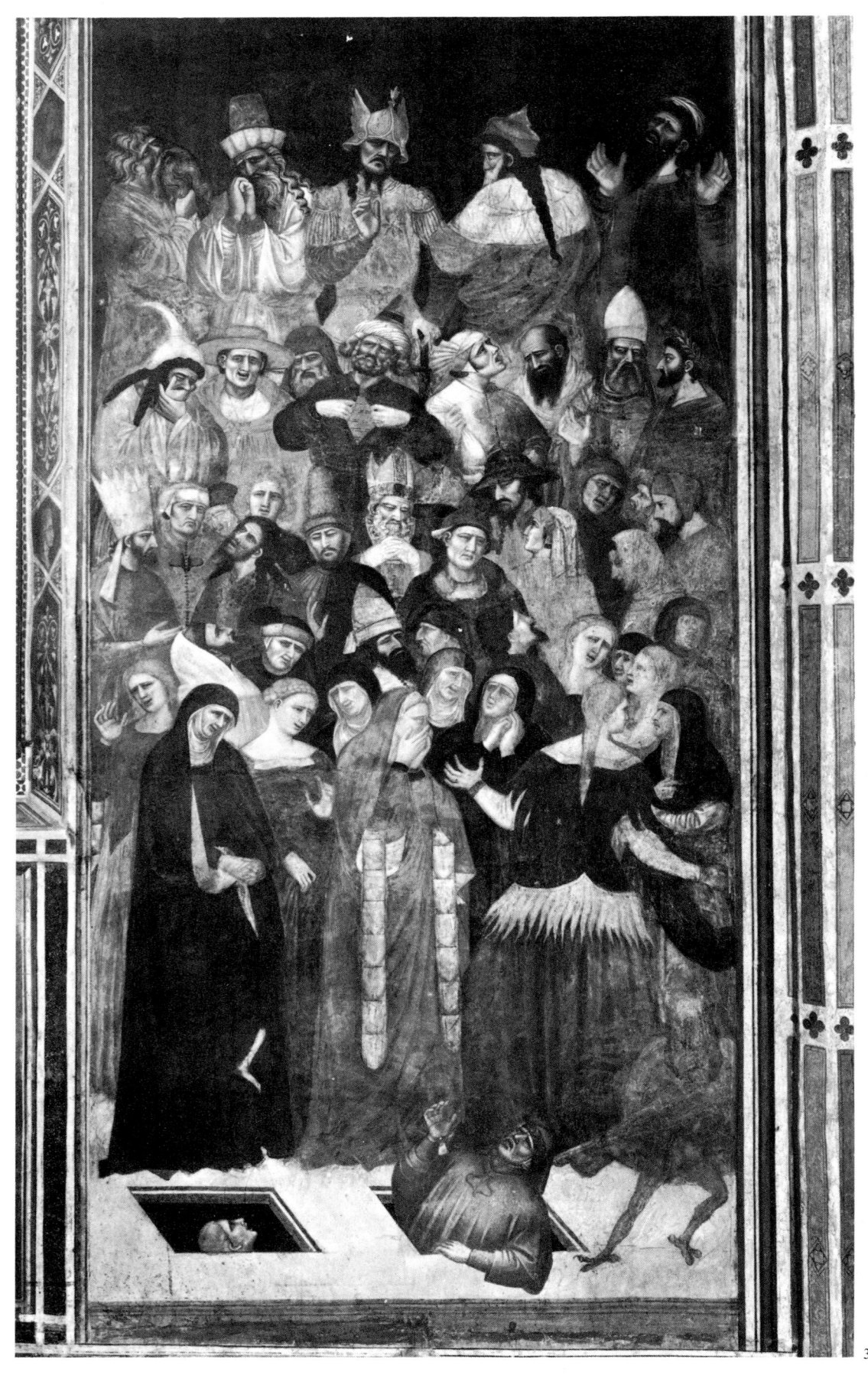

302

302. *Scene from the Last Judgement, detail. Fresco. Florence, S. Maria Novella, Strozzi Chapel. SGF 66309.*

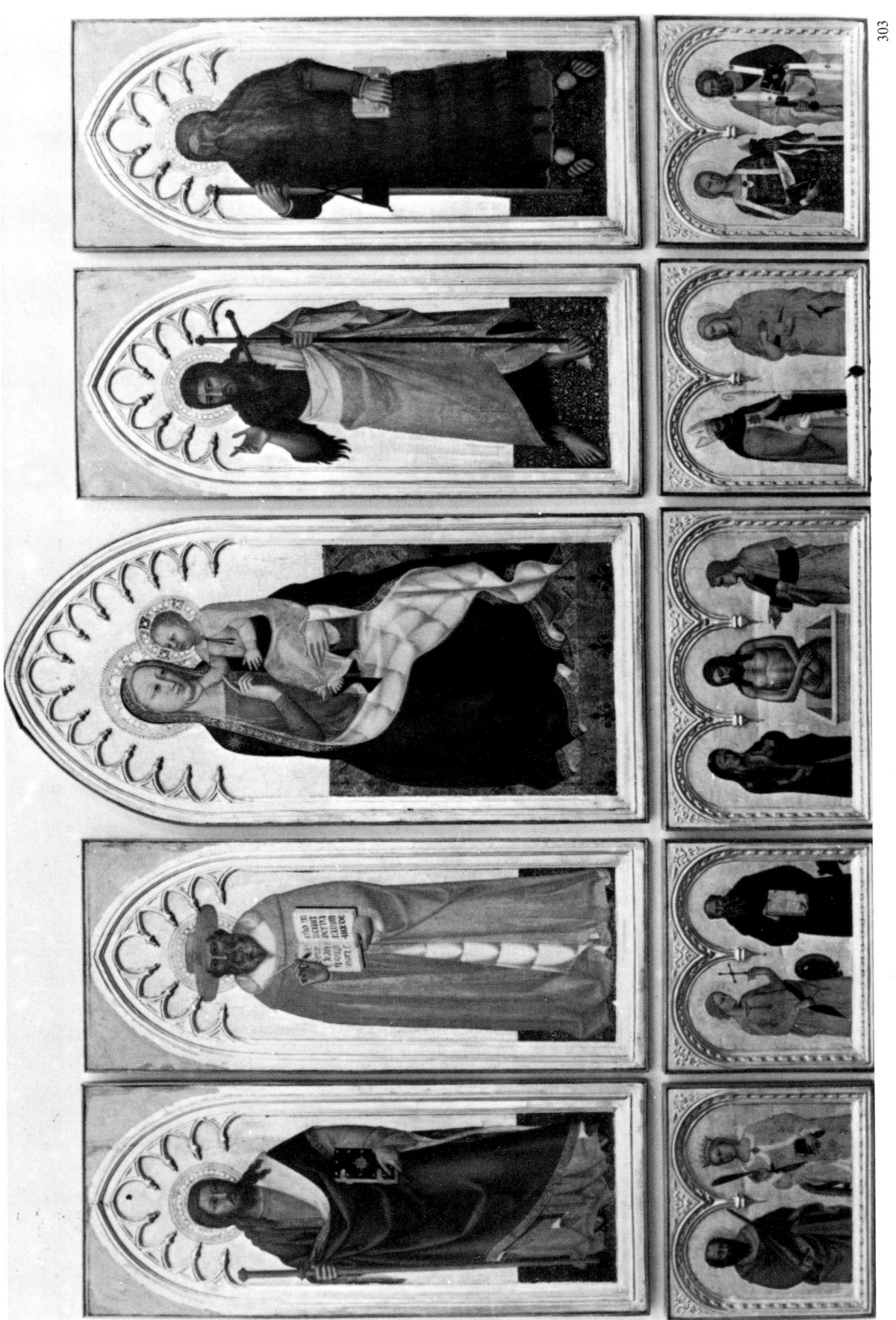

303. *Polyptych: Madonna of Humility with Sts James, Jerome, John the Baptist and Jacob the Hermit. Predella: Man of Sorrows with the Virgin and St John, and Sts Paul, Catherine, Margaret, Anthony Abbot, Nicholas, Mary Magdalene, Lucy and Peter. Panel. Prague, Narodni Galerie. no. 0-2376-85. cp: 117 × 59; sps: 103 × 44. Predella: cp: 38 × 61; sps: 38 × 44. Museum photo 49.047.*

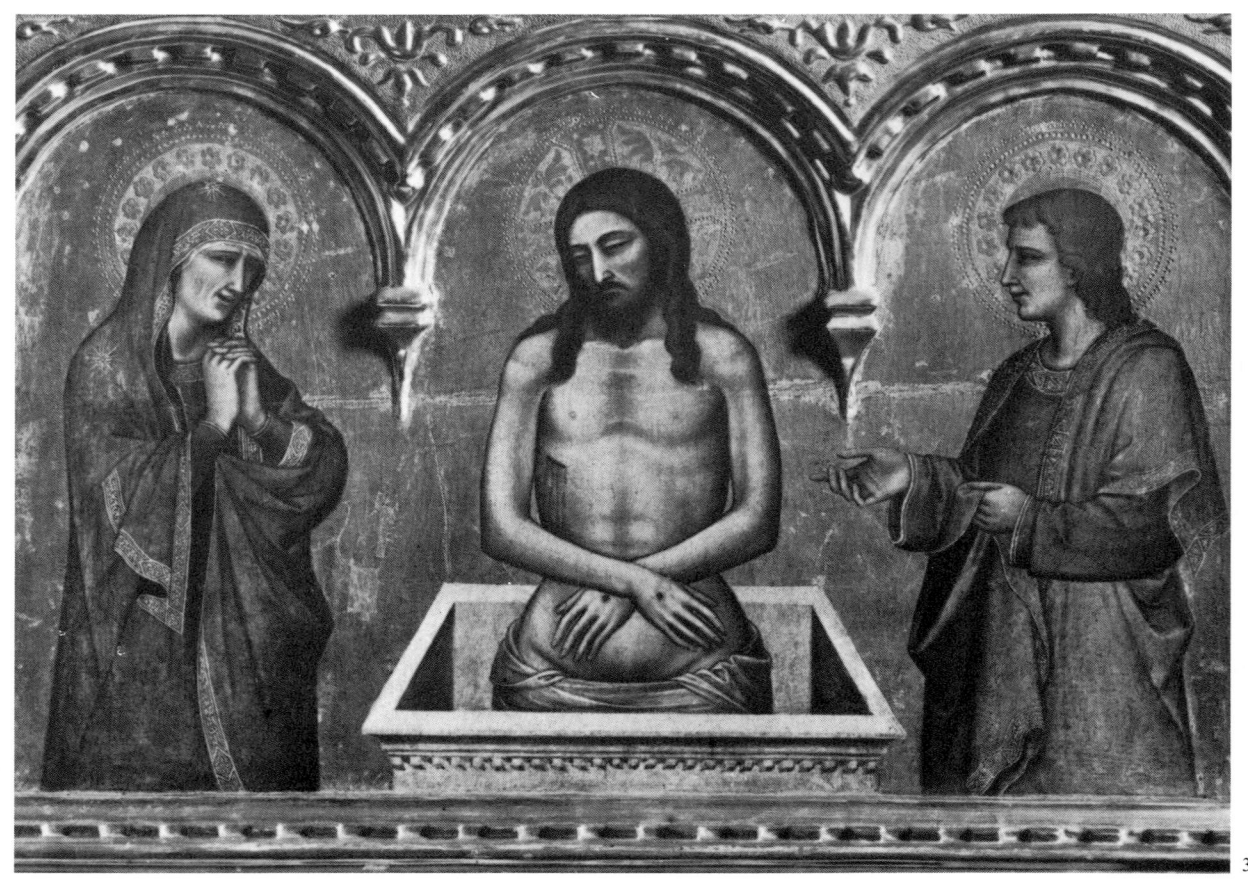

304

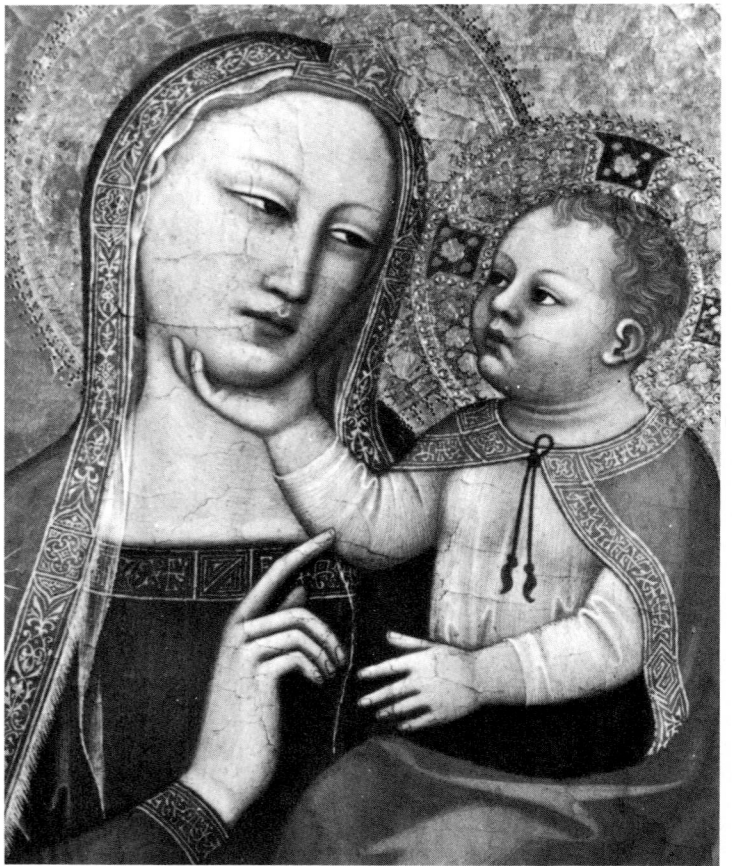

305

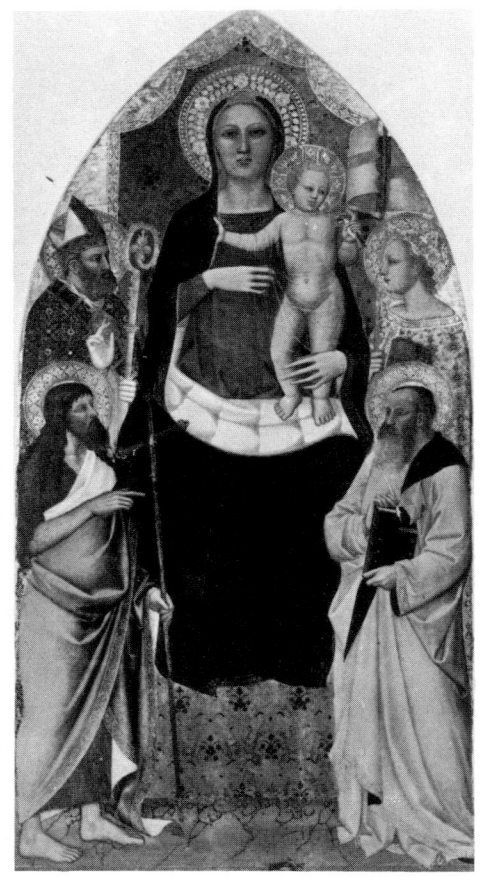

306

304. *Man of Sorrows with the Virgin and St John the Evangelist, detail of fig. 303. Panel. Prague, Narodni Galerie. no. O-2376-85. Museum photo 4.492.*
305. *Heads of the Madonna and Child, detail of fig. 303. Prague, Narodni Galerie. no. O-2376-85. Museum photo 4.866.*
306. *Madonna and Child Enthroned with Sts Zenobius, John the Baptist, Reparata and John the Evangelist. Panel. New York (N.Y.), New York Historical Society. no. 1867.3. 195 × 98. Collection photo 1420.*

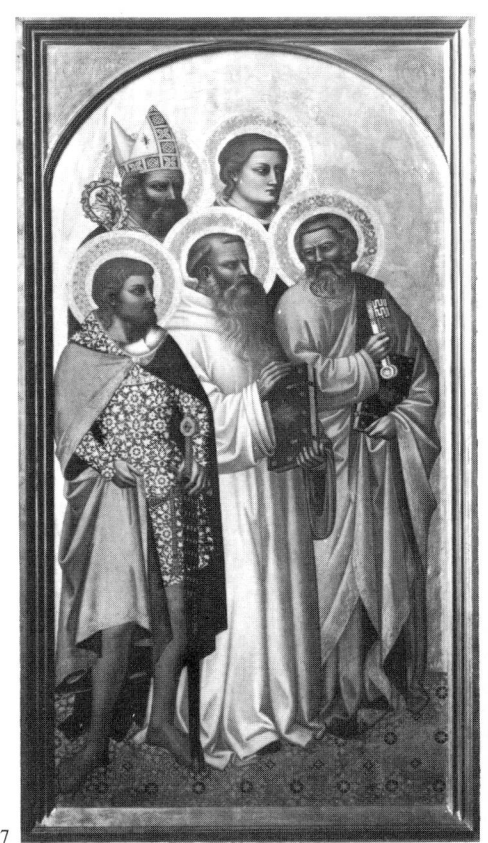

307

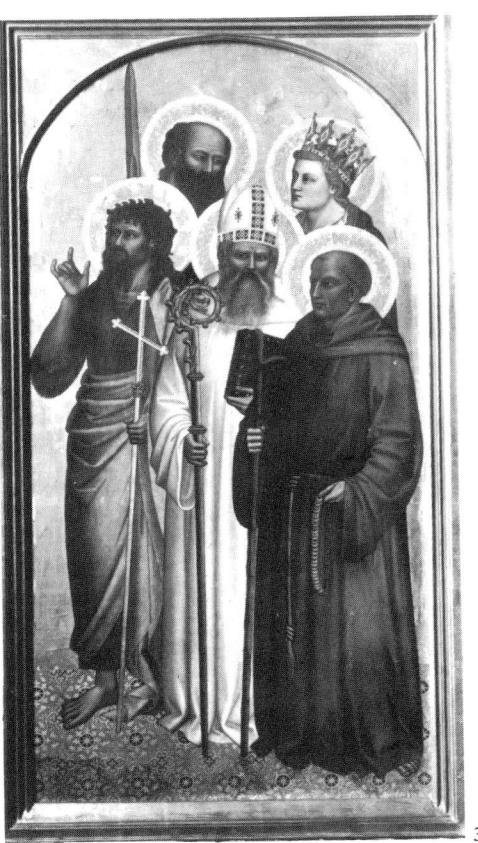

308

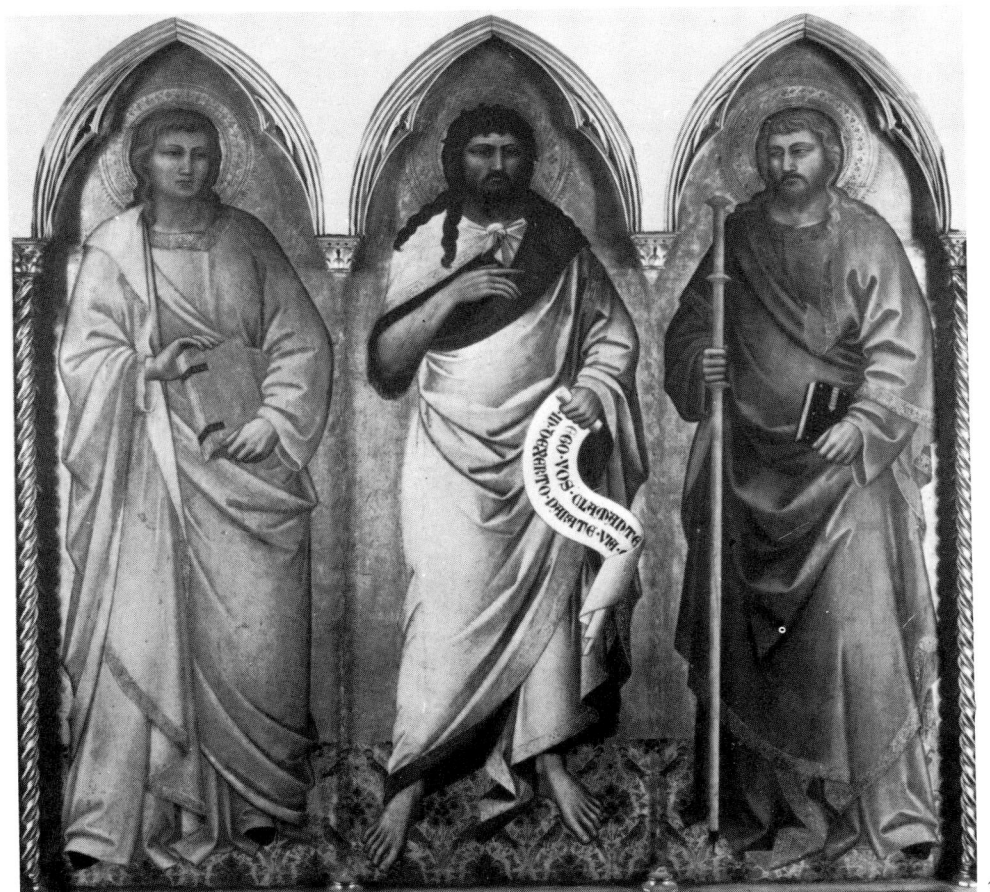

309

307. *Sts Julian, Benedict, Peter, a Bishop Saint and young Deacon Saint. Panel. Munich, Alte Pinakothek. no. WAF 1027. 142 × 70. Museum photo.*
308. *Sts John the Baptist, Paul, Ambrose, Catherine, and Gerard of Villamagna. Panel. Munich, Alte Pinakothek. no. WAF 1028. 142 × 70. Museum photo.*
309. *Sts John the Evangelist, John the Baptist and James. Panel. London, National Gallery. no. 581. 160 × 148. Museum photo.*

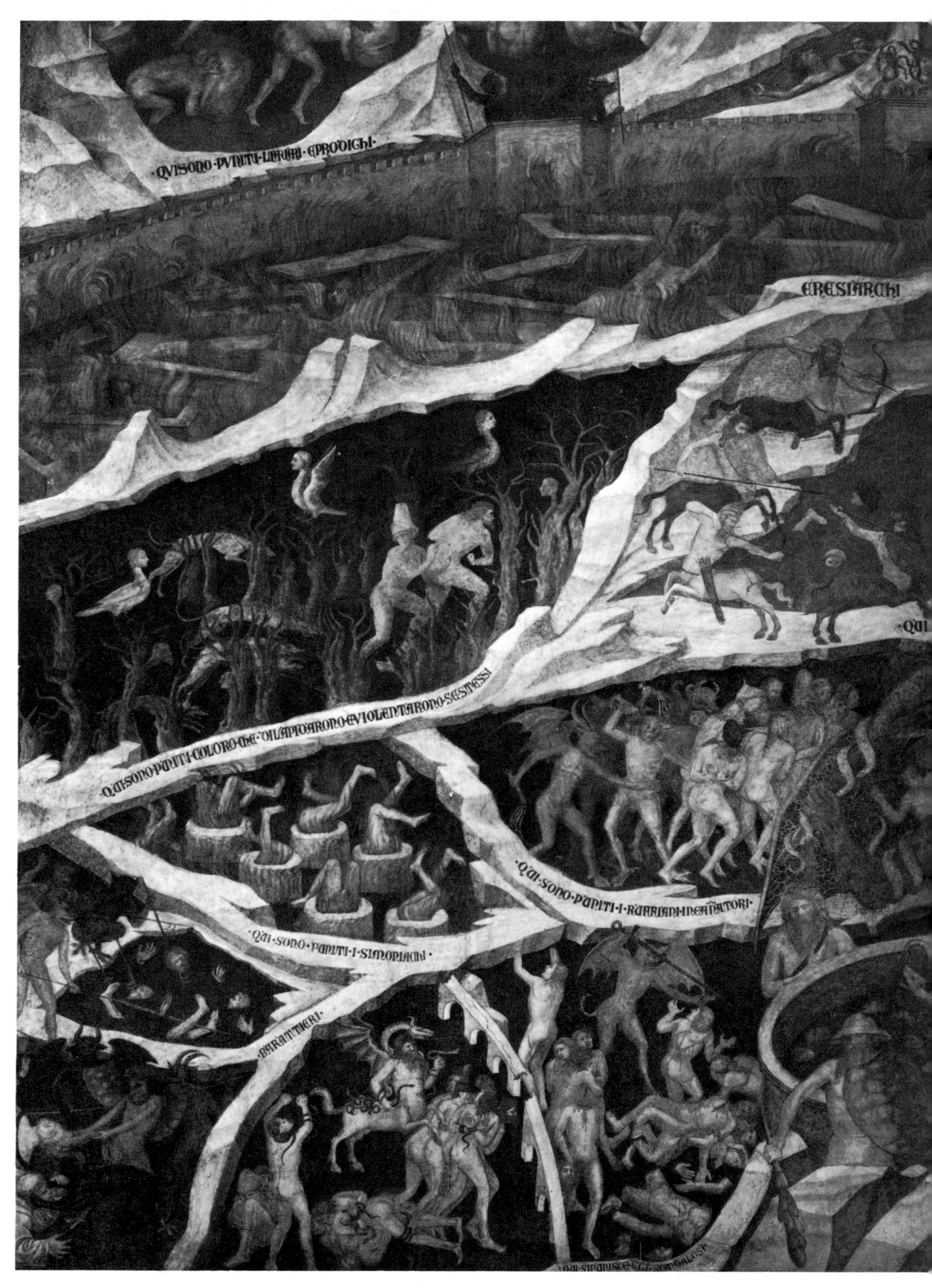

310. *Hell, detail. Fresco. Florence, S. Maria Novella, Strozzi Chapel. SGF 66311, 66313.*

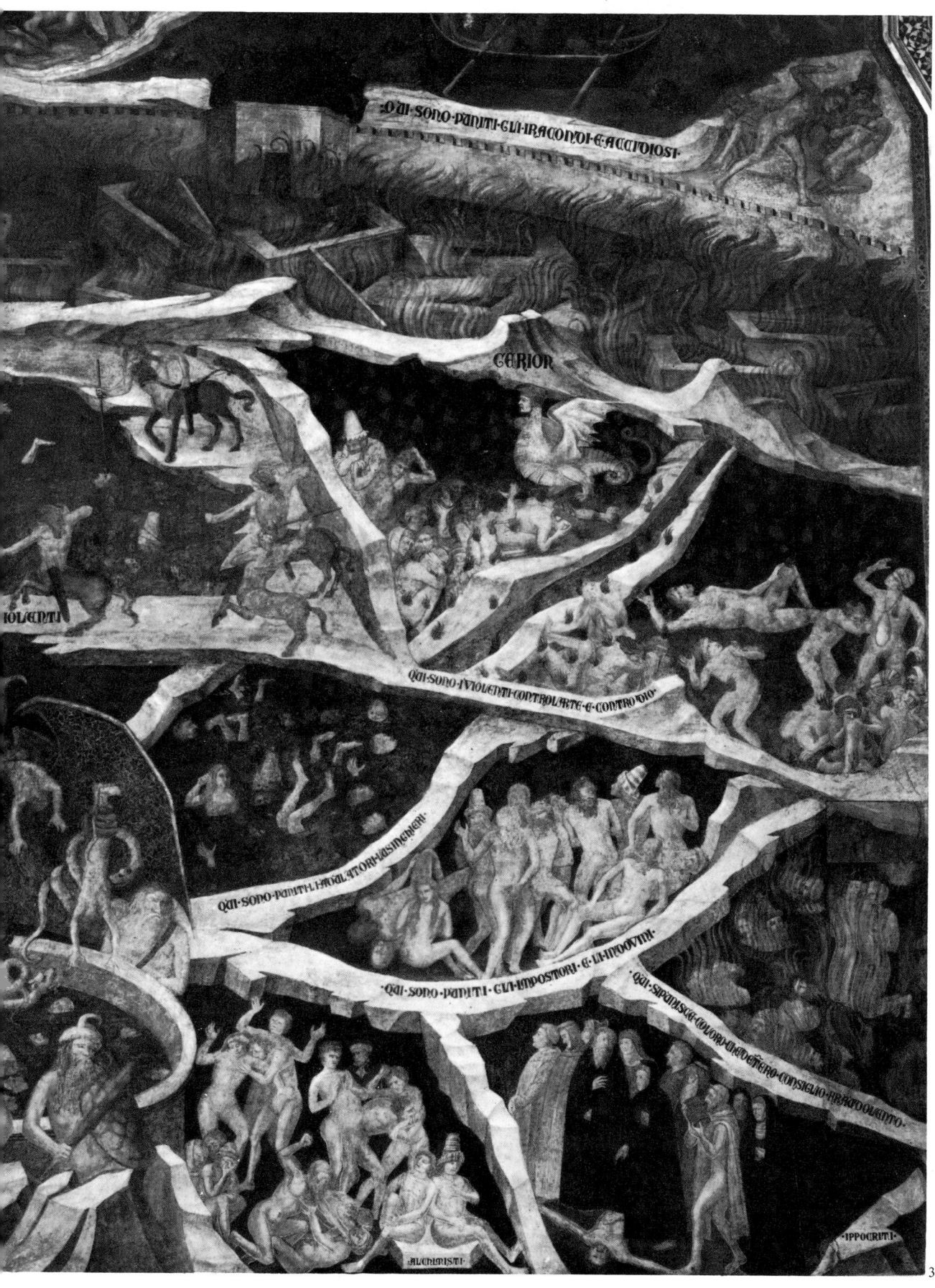

·O·QUI·SONO·PUNITI·GLI·IRACONDI·E·ACCIDIOSI·

GERION

IOLENTI

QUI·SONO·I·VIOLENTI·CONTRO·L'ARTE·E·CONTRO·DIO·

QUI·SONO·PUNITI·LI·FALSATORI·LUSINGHIERI·

·QUI·SONO·PUNITI·GLI·IMPOSTORI·E·LI·INDOVINI·

QUI·SI·PUNISCA·COLORO·CHE·DETTERO·CONSIGLIO·FRAUDOLENTO·

·IPPOCRITI·

ALCHIMISTI

310

157

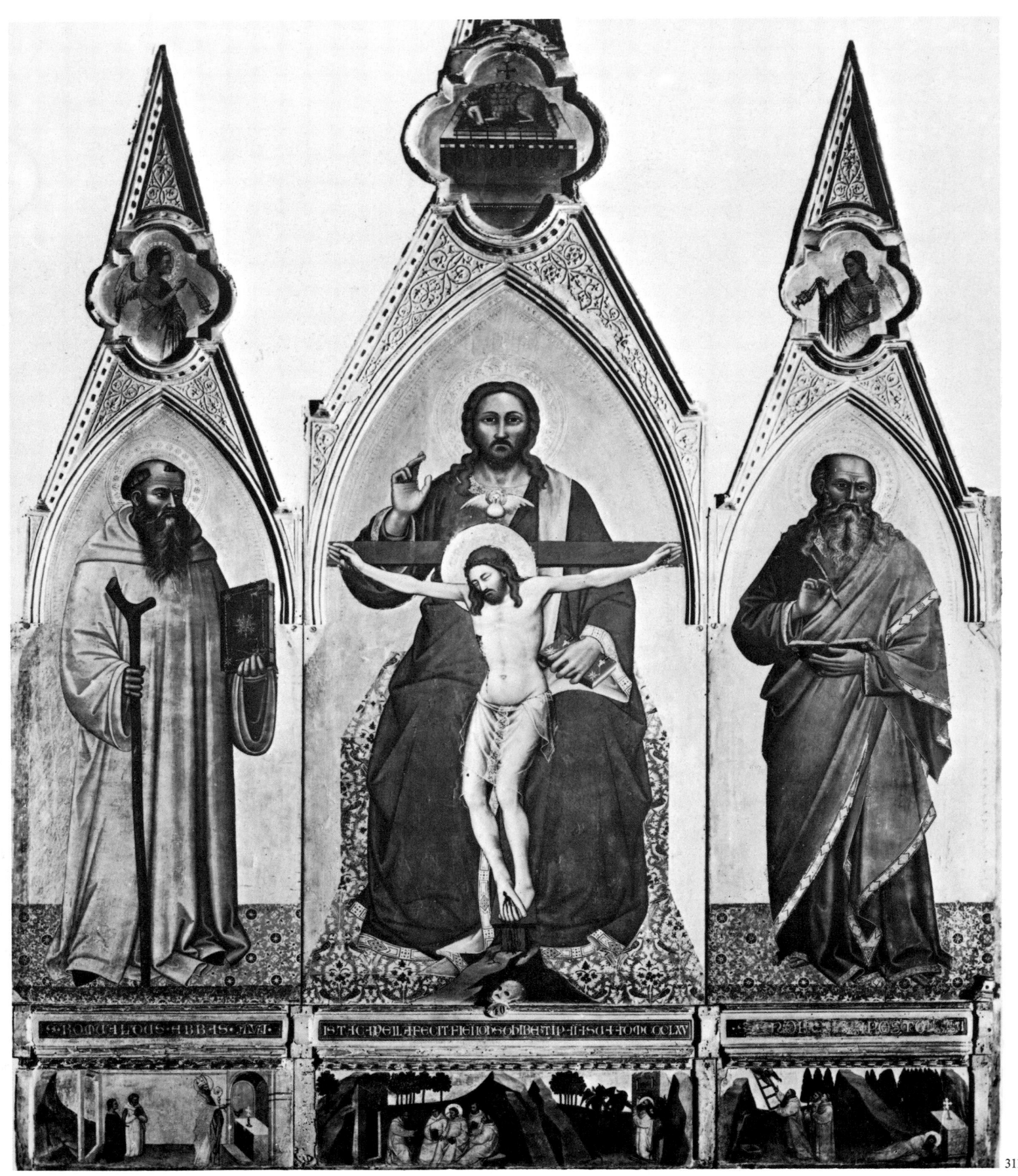

311

311. *Triptych: Trinity; Sts Romuald and John the Evangelist. Pinnacles: Agnus Dei and two censing Angels. Predella: St Romuald's vision of St Apollinaris; St Romuald chastened by a Hermit and molested by devils; Dream of St Romuald. Panel. Florence, Accademia. no. 8464. 292 × 212. Alinari 1478. d. 1365.*

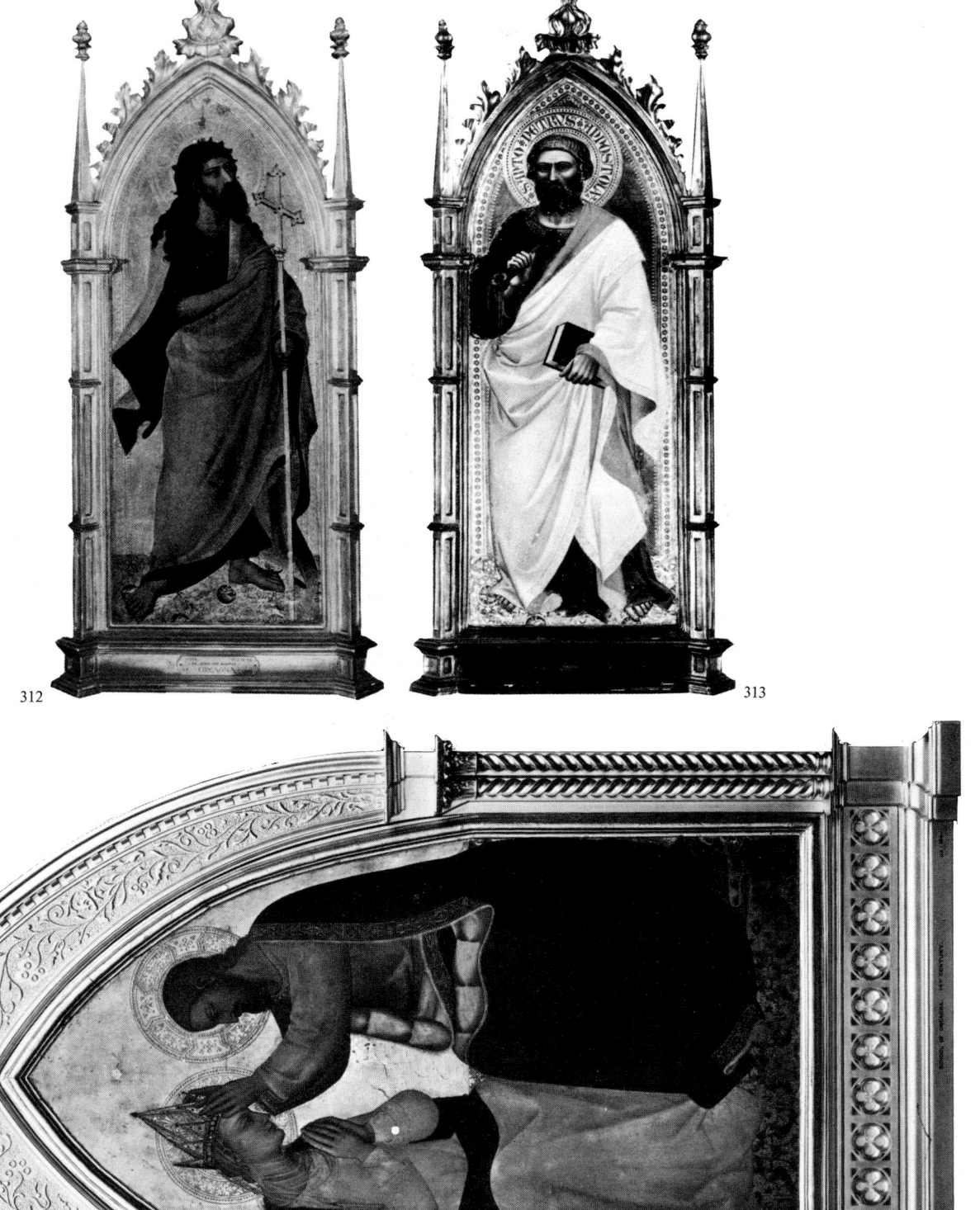

312. *St. John the Baptist. Panel. New Haven (Conn.), Yale University Art Gallery, J. J. Jarves Collection. no. 1871.14. 99.1 × 40. Museum photo.*
313. *St Peter. Panel. New Haven (Conn.), Yale University Art Gallery, J. J. Jarves Collection. no. 1871.13. 99.1 × 40. Museum photo.*
314. *Coronation of the Virgin. Panel. London, Victoria and Albert Museum. no. 104. 118.1 × 77.5. Museum photo 63505.*

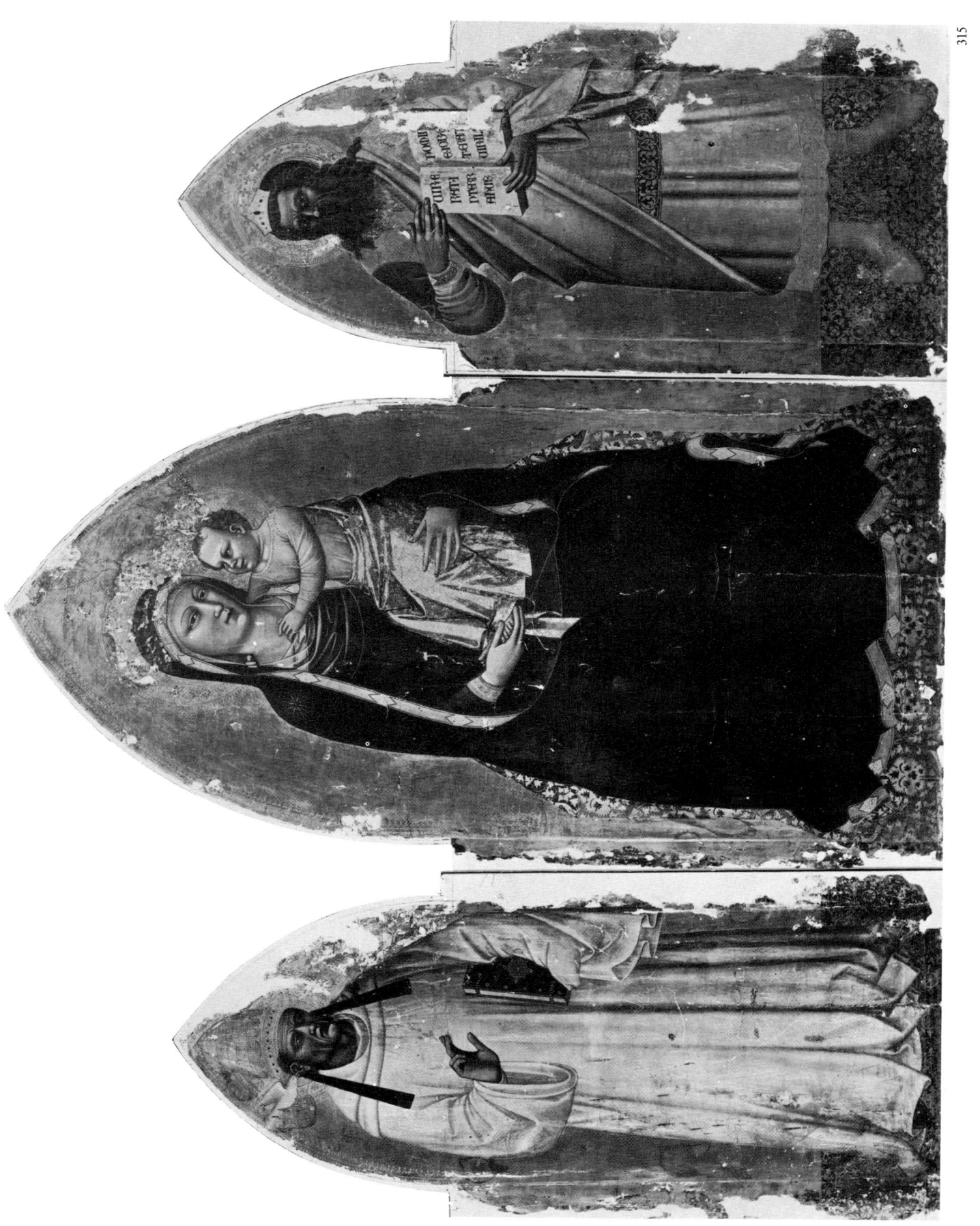

315. *Three panels from a triptych: Madonna of Humility Enthroned with St Gregory and the Prophet Job. Panel. Florence, S. Croce. 164 × 88. SGF 29913,*
29914. d. 1365.

JACOPO di CIONE

Jacopo di Cione was evidently much younger than either Andrea or Nardo because we find him first mentioned after Nardo's death and only occasionally at the end of Andrea's career. The earliest documentary evidence we have of his existence as a painter is in 1368 when he is charged to finish a panel of St Matthew begun by his brother Andrea, then too ill to continue the work. In 1368-9 he matriculates in the corporation of Medici Speciale e Merciai; in a document of 1373 he is found working with Niccolò di Pietro Gerini. For fourteen years we can discover no trace of him; the next record is in 1387 when he is mentioned amongst the six consuls of the corporation, while the following year he becomes a member of the St. Lucas guild. In 1389 he colours and ornaments four marble statues for the Cathedral and in 1390 we find him paying for marble which his brother Matteo had ordered but which only arrived after his death. Vasari pretends that Jacopo too was also a sculptor. In 1394, he is mentioned for the last time.....

from R. van Marle, p. 491, *The Development of the Italian Schools of Painting*, Vol. III, The Hague, 1924.

In the case of the S. Pier Maggiore painting [in the National Gallery, London], the artist has long since been recognized as Jacopo di Cione. In every morphological detail, the altarpiece corresponds closely with the two authenticated works by Jacopo, the St Matthew.... altarpiece from Orsanmichele, in the Uffizi, which he is known to have completed after it had been left unfinished by Orcagna, at the latter's death at the end of 1368, and the large *Coronation* panel in the Accademia in Florence (from the Mint), which Jacopo executed in 1372-3. In the execution of the S. Pier Maggiore altarpiece, Jacopo certainly had the help of assistants, who may well have been the Matteo di Pacino and Tuccio (di Vanni) named in the records. But, although certain parts of the painting, notably the main side panels, suggest the collaboration of some weaker hand, the style is uniform throughout and excludes the cooperation of an independent fellow artist.....

from H. D. Gronau, p. 140, *Burlington Magazine*, LXXXVI, 1945.

Mentioned 1365-1398, but probably active considerably before the first date. Brother and assistant of Andrea Orcagna. His independent manner was based more upon Andrea's sculpture than on his paintings. Influenced overpoweringly by Maso, then by his brother Nardo and later by Niccolò di Pietro Gerini.

from B. Berenson, p. 103, *Italian Pictures of the Renaissance, Florentine School*, Vol. I, London, 1963.

Jacopo, the youngest of the Cione brothers, was first mentioned in 1365 in the draft of his older brother Nardo's will. Therein he was cited as one of the heirs along with his brothers Andrea and Matteo. When in 1368 Jacopo was commissioned to complete a panel painting begun by Andrea di Cione, it appears that he was not yet officially recognized as a master working entirely on his own. It was only as a consequence of this commission that he was received into the *Arte dei Medici e Speziali* on January 12th, 1369. Judging by the date of his admission into the painter's guild, it is probable that Jacopo was not born until the end of the fourth decade of the fourteenth century. Jacopo is last mentioned in 1398, and since no annual payment under his name was acknowledged in the Prestanza list for the year 1400, it can be assumed that he died between May 2nd, 1398 and the end of 1400. Thus Jacopo survived his brothers, Nardo (died 1366) and Andrea (died 1368), by about thirty years.....

Among Jacopo's works five panel paintings are mentioned, the descriptions of which are so vague that they cannot be identified (March 6th, 1386). The earliest certain point of reference is the above-mentioned St Matthew triptych which Andrea di Cione began and Jacopo had to complete (August 25th, 1368). This picture was probably finished only in 1369. It has survived and is today in the Uffizi Gallery. But here Jacopo's share in the picture must first be established on the basis of stylistic criteria. In 1383 Jacopo di Cione worked together with Niccolò di Pietro Gerini on the fresco of the Annunciation in the Palazzo dei Priori in Volterra. This work is in such a miserable state that unfortunately it now reveals nothing of the character of either master.....

from R. Offner & K. Steinweg, p. 1, *A Critical and Historical Corpus of Florentine Painting*, Sec. IV, Vol. III, 1965.

Also called Robiccia. Florentine School. Active c. 1368-98. Jacopo was probably the youngest of three brothers, the other two known as Andrea Orcagna and Nardo di Cione. The brothers collaborated, and no extant painting is documented as the work of Jacopo alone. Both he and Nardo obviously followed the style of their elder brother, Andrea.

from F. R. Shapley, p. 33, *Paintings from the Samuel H. Kress Collection*, London, 1966.

BIBLIOGRAPHY
BOOKS
An asterisk indicates a work listed in the General Bibliography

Khv & Salmi*, 1912, pp. 31-2; Sirèn, O., *Descriptive Catalogue of the Pictures in the Jarves Collection*, New Haven, 1916, pp. 43-6; Sirèn, O., *Giotto, and some of his Followers*, Cambridge, Mass., 1917, pp. 256-62; *v. Marle, 1924**, pp. 491-508; *Berenson, 1932**, pp. 273-5; *Venturi, A.**, 1933, pp. 44-5; *Coletti, Vol. II**, 1946, p. 51; Offner, R., *Studies, Museum of Art of the Rhode Island School of Design in Providence*, Rhode Island (R.I.), U.S.A., 1947, pp. 43-61; *Antal**, 1948, p. 194; *Vavalà, 1948**, pp. 71-5; Marabottini, A., *Giovanni da Milano*, Florence, 1950, pp. 96-7; *Galetti**, "F-O", 1950, pp. 1788-90; *Toesca, 1951**, p. 637; Shorr, D. C., *The Christ Child in Devotional Images*, New York, 1954, p. 80; *Offner, 1962**, Sec IV, Vol. I, p. 73; *Berenson, 1962**, p. x; *Berenson, 1963**, Vol. I, pp. 103-6, 163, *Marcucci**, 1965, pp. 99-102; *Offner, 1965**, Sec. IV, Vol. III; *Shapley**, 1966, pp. 31-4; Bianchini, M. A., *Maso di Banco* (I Maestri del Colore, 247), Milan, 1966.

JOURNALS
Berenson, B., *DD*, XI, 4, 1930-31, pp. 1039-73; Offner, R., *BM*, LXIII, 1933, pp. 83-4; Gronau, H. D., *BM*, LXXXVI, 1945, pp. 139-45; Meiss, M., *AB*, XXVIII, 1946, p. 13; *Edit.*, *BM*, 96, supp. 2, 1954; Levi d'Ancona, M., *RA*, XXXII, 1957, pp. 3-37; Steinweg, K., *R*, XXX-XXXI, 1957-59, pp. 231-44; Cappellini, I., *Cronache d'altri tempi*, 1964, n. 119; Simson, O. v., *JBM*, VIII, 1966, p. 138; Fahy, E., *CB*, LVI, 1969, pp. 348-53; *Edit.*, *GBA*, LXXIII, III, 1969 (supplement), n. 22; Huter, C., *AVN*, XXIV, 1970, pp. 29-30; Bellosi, L., *MKIF*, XVII, 2-3, 1973, p. 187, note 11; Procacci, U., *MKIF*, XVII, 2-3, 1973, p. 318; Fehm, S. A., *MKIF*, XVII, 2-3, 1973, p. 271.

DATED WORKS

1362 Formerly Brussels, Stoclet Collection. Panel: Madonna nursing the Child. d. (fig. 335).
1383 Florence, SS. Apostoli (Uffizi 8607). Polyptych: Madonna & Child with Saints & Angels. d. (fig. 334).
1386 Florence, Miari-Pelli-Fabbroni Collection. Panel: Madonna of Humility with 2 Angels. d. (fig. 336).

There are no known signed works by Jacopo di Cione.

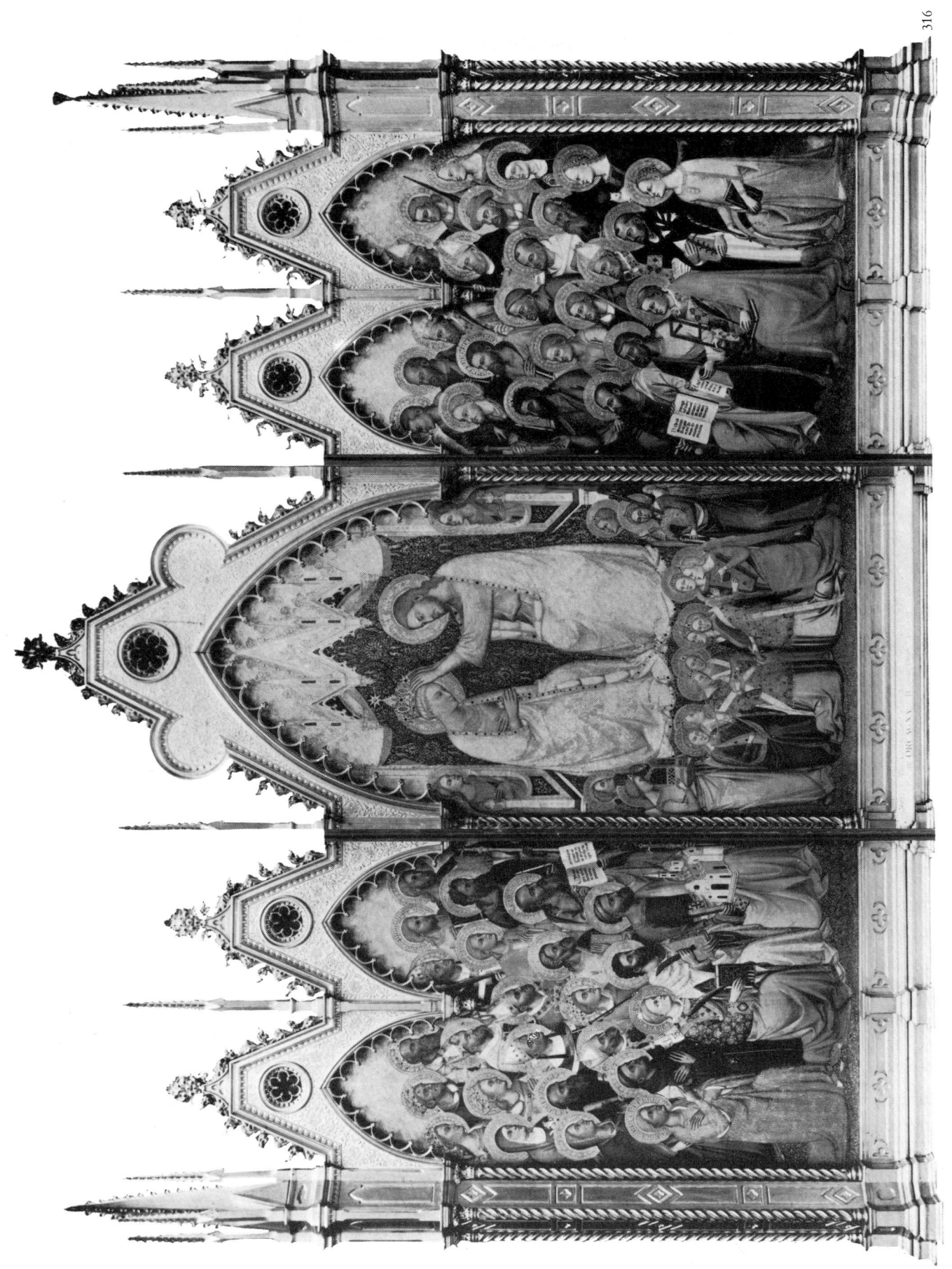

316. *Triptych: Coronation of the Virgin with music-making Angels and Saints. Panel. London, National Gallery. no. 569. cp: 207 × 113.7; sps: 168.9 × 112.4. Museum photo. 1370-71.*

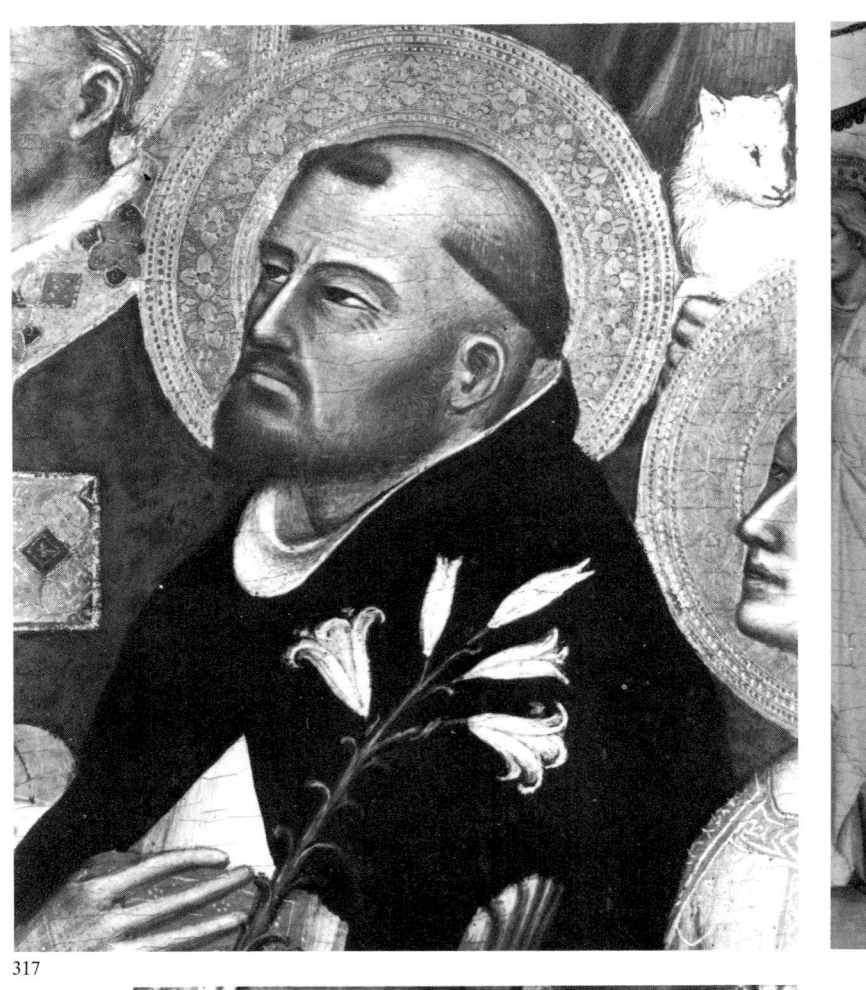

317

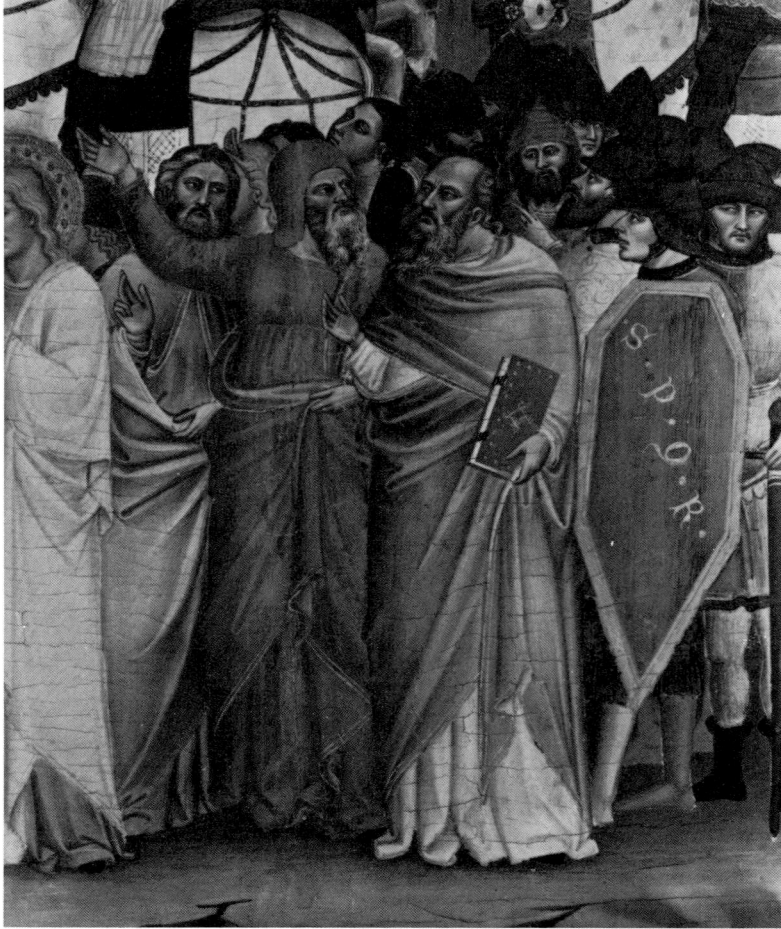

318

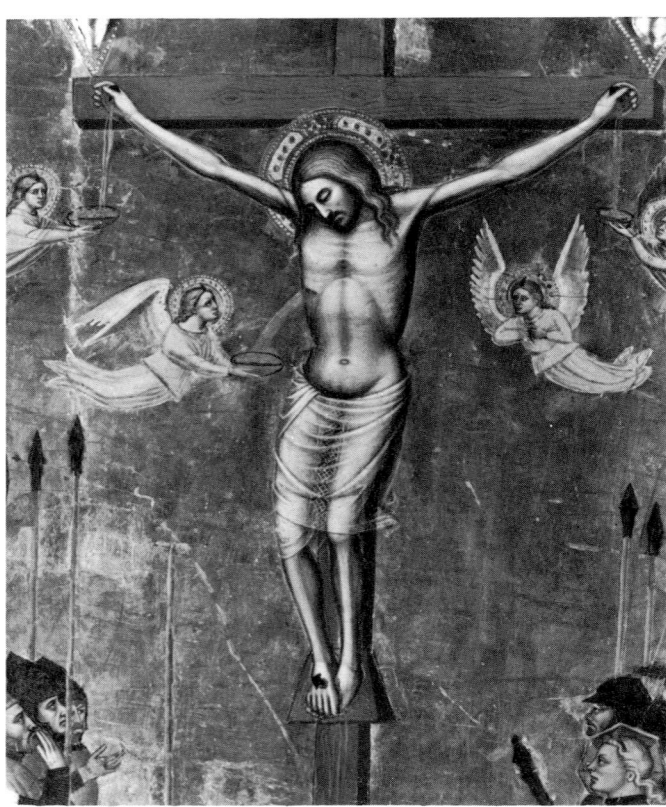

319

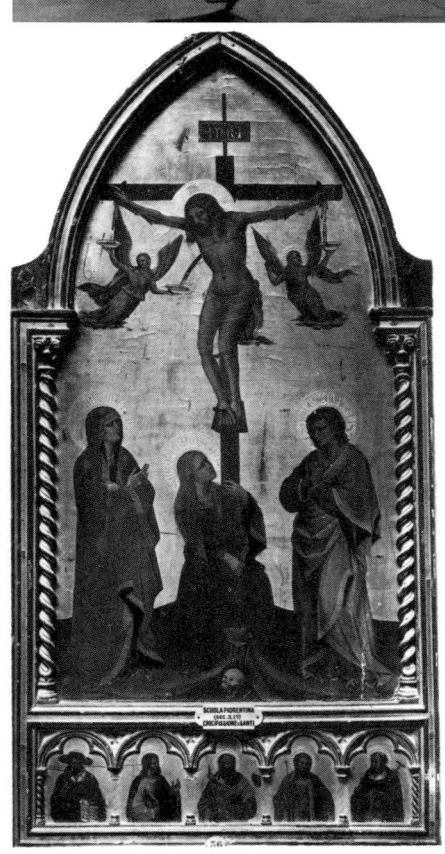

320

317. Head of a Saint, detail of fig. 316. Panel. London, National Gallery. no. 569. Museum photo. 1370-71.
318. Figures at the foot of the Cross, detail of fig. 321. Panel. London, National Gallery. no. 1468. Museum photo.
319. Christ on the Cross, detail of fig. 321. Panel. London, National Gallery. no. 1468. Museum photo.
320. Christ on the Cross with the Virgin, Sts Mary Magdalene and John the Evangelist. Predella: five Saints. Panel. Florence, Accademia. no. 3515. 123 × 64. SGF 88966.

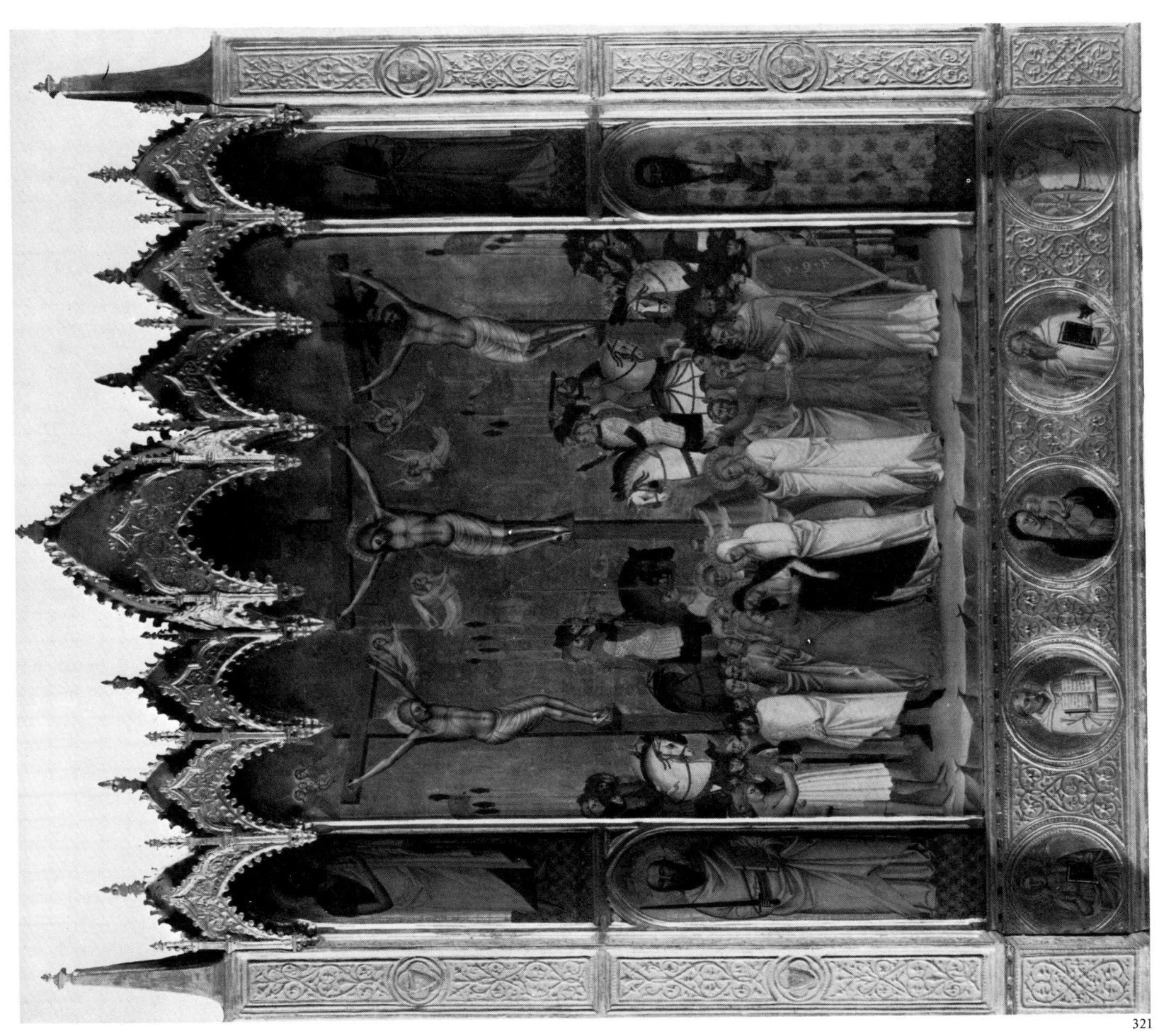

321

321. *Crucifixion. Pilasters: Sts John the Baptist, Paul, James and Bartholomew. Predella: Madonna and Child and four Saints. Panel. London, National Gallery. no. 1468. 108 × 83.8. Museum photo.*

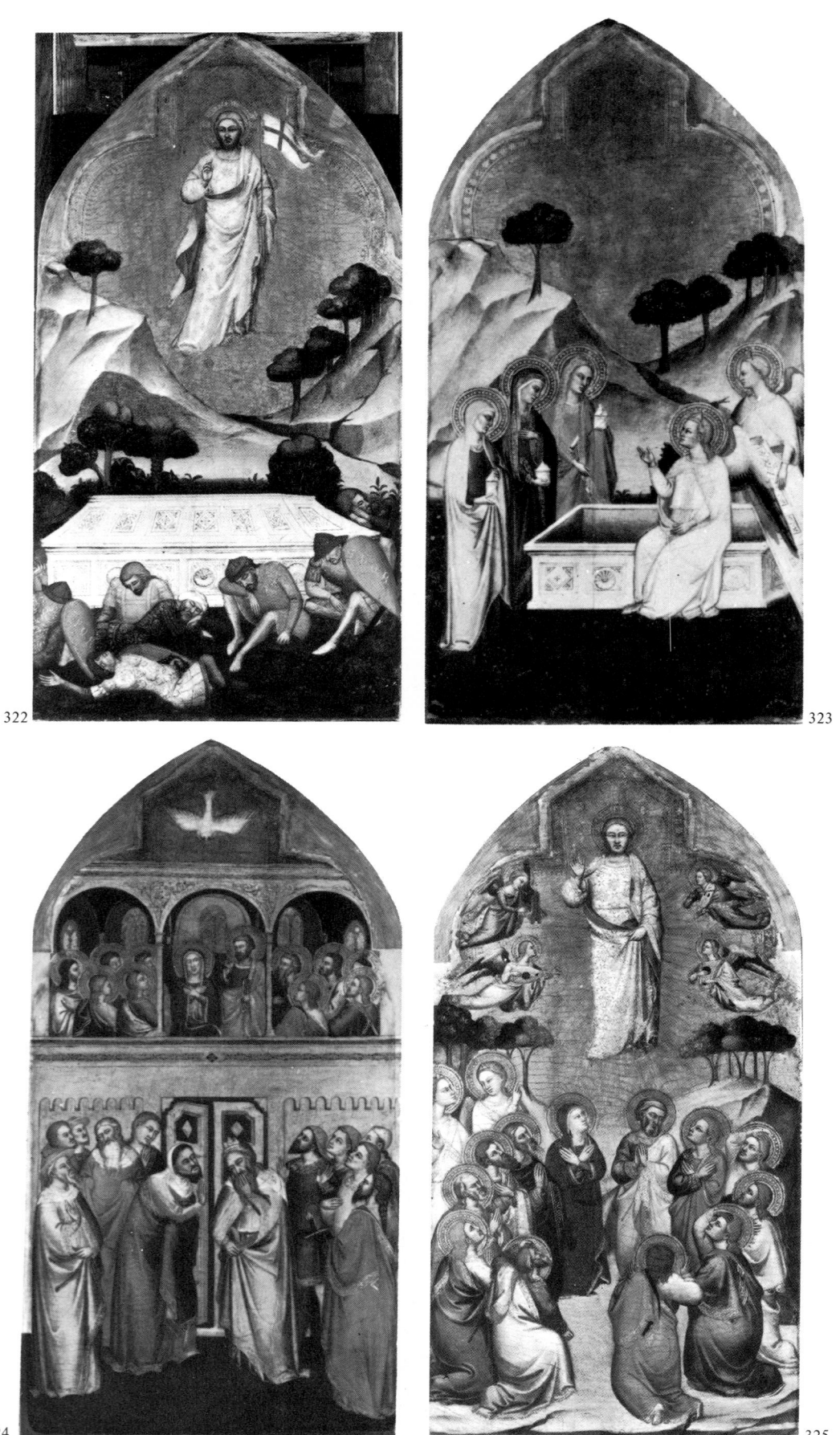

322. *Resurrection. Panel. London, National Gallery. no. 575. 95.2 × 49.5. Museum photo. 1370-71.*
323. *Three Marys at the Tomb with two Angels. Panel. London, National Gallery. no. 576. 95.2 × 48.2. Museum photo. 1370-71.*
324. *Descent of the Holy Spirit. Panel. London, National Gallery. no. 578. 95.2 × 49.5. Museum photo. 1370-71.*
325. *Ascension. Panel. London, National Gallery. no. 577. 95.2 × 49.5. Museum photo. 1370-71.*

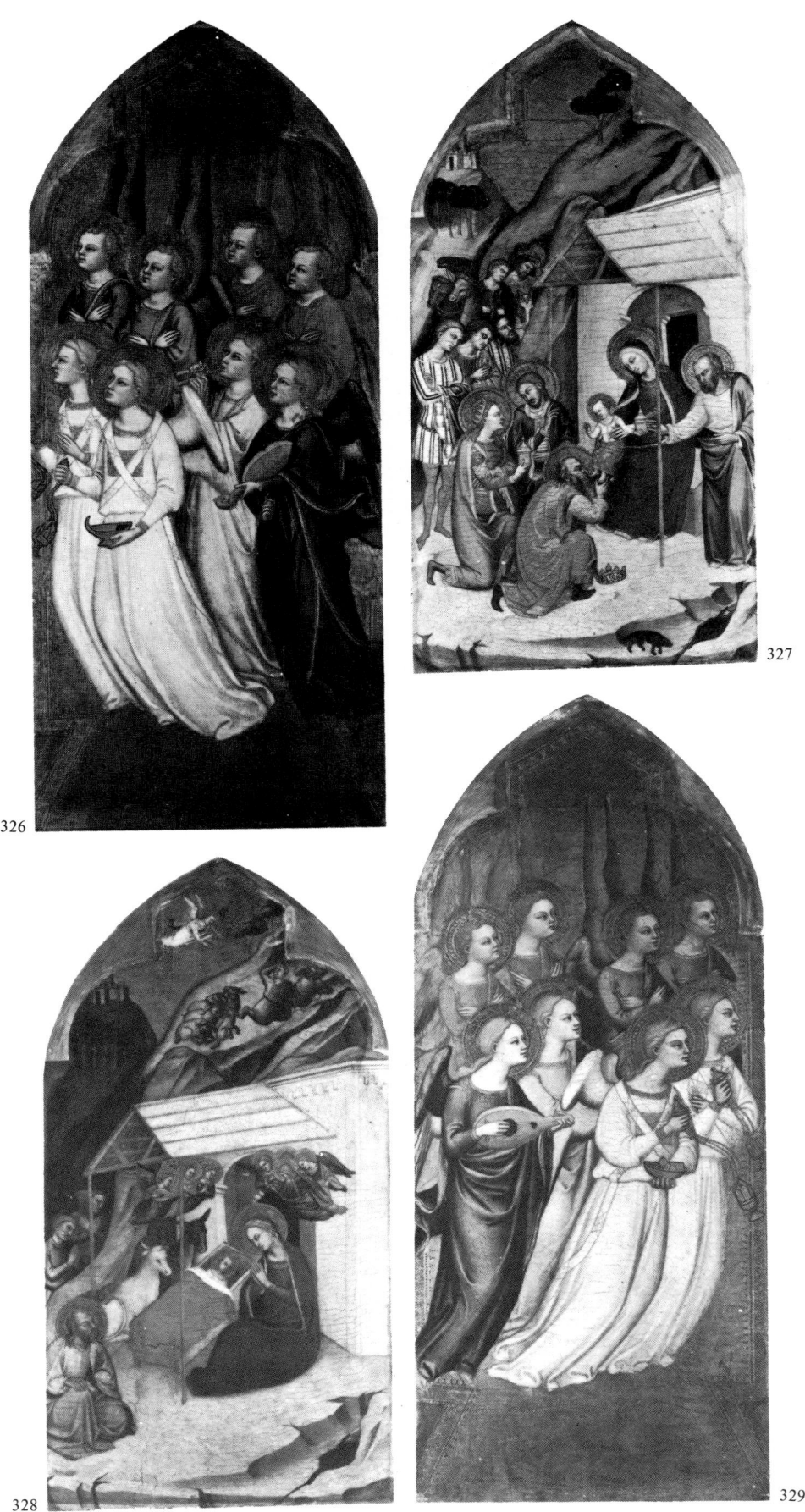

326. *Eight Angels. Panel. London, National Gallery. no. 572. 87 × 37.5. Museum photo. 1370-71.*
327. *Epiphany. Panel. London, National Gallery. no. 574. 87 × 40. Museum photo. 1370-71.*
328. *Nativity. Panel. London, National Gallery. no. 573. 95.2 × 49.5. Museum photo. 1370-71.*
329. *Eight Angels. Panel. London, National Gallery. no. 571. 87 × 37.5. Museum photo. 1370-71.*

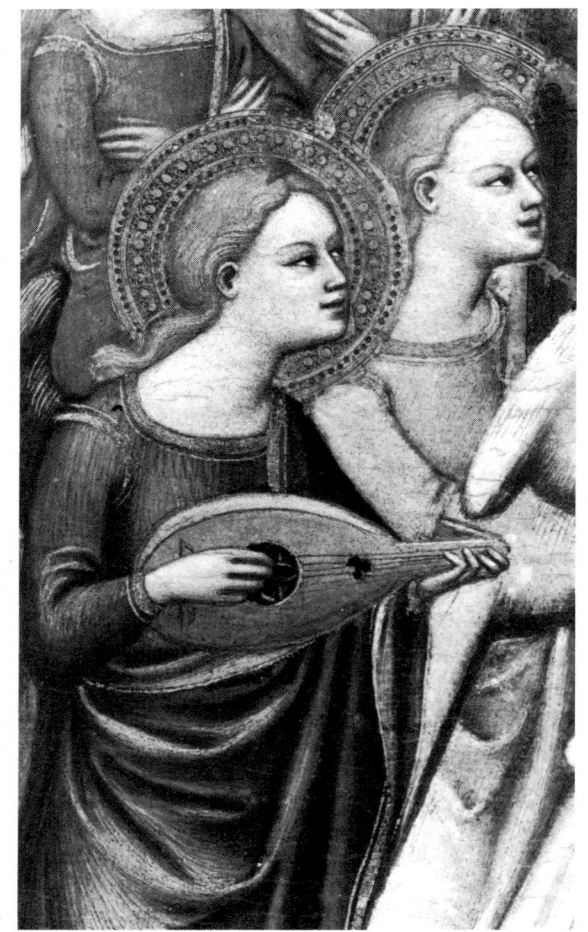

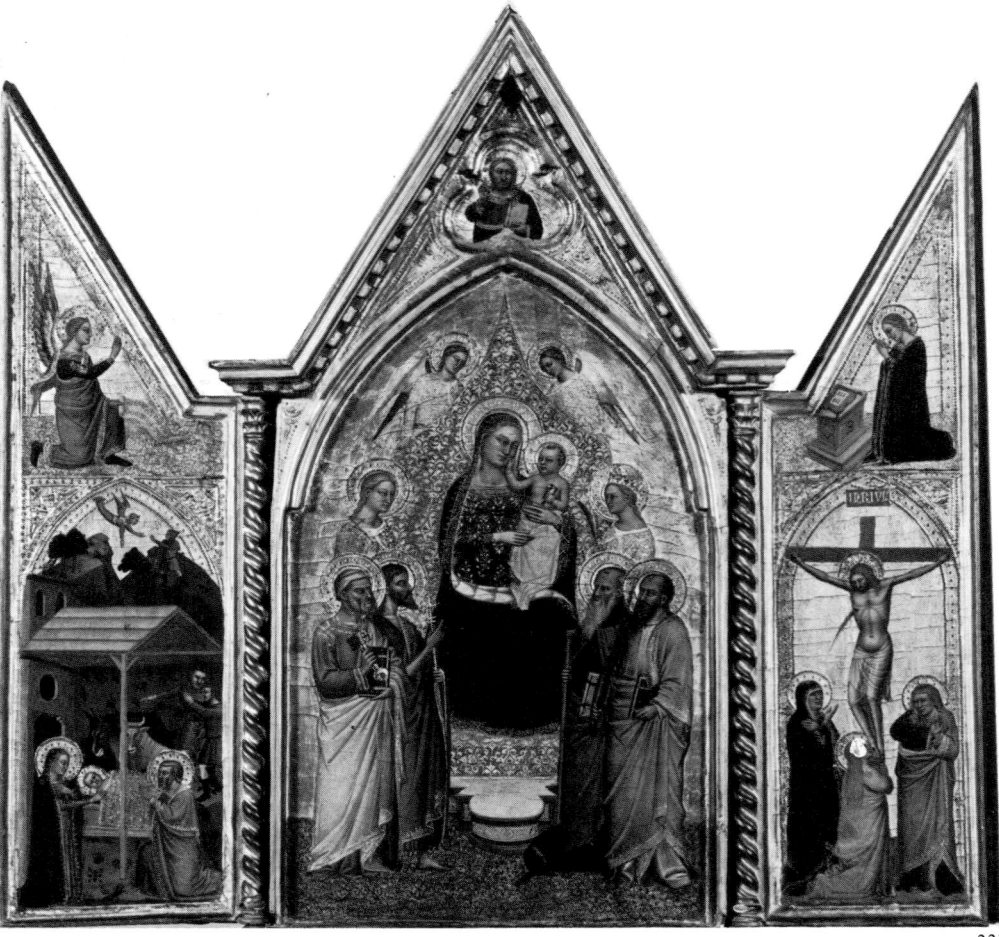

330

331

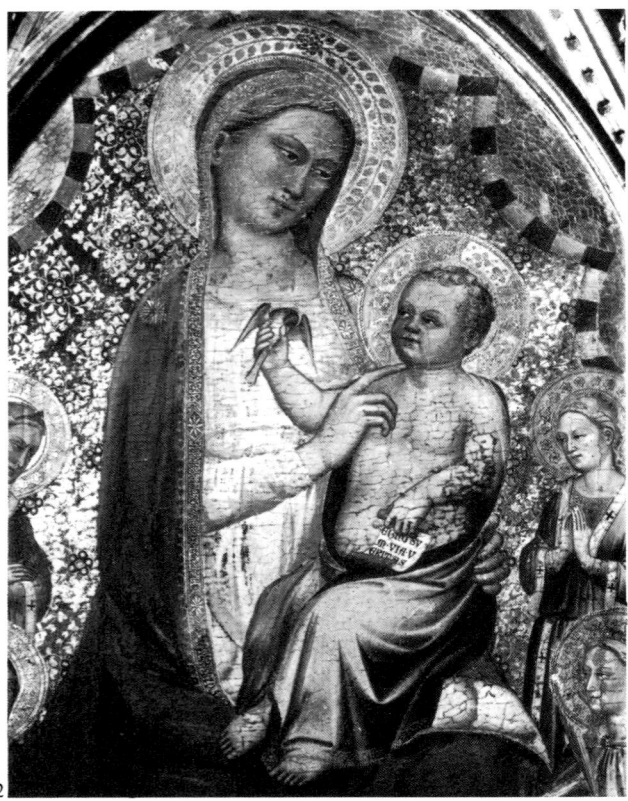

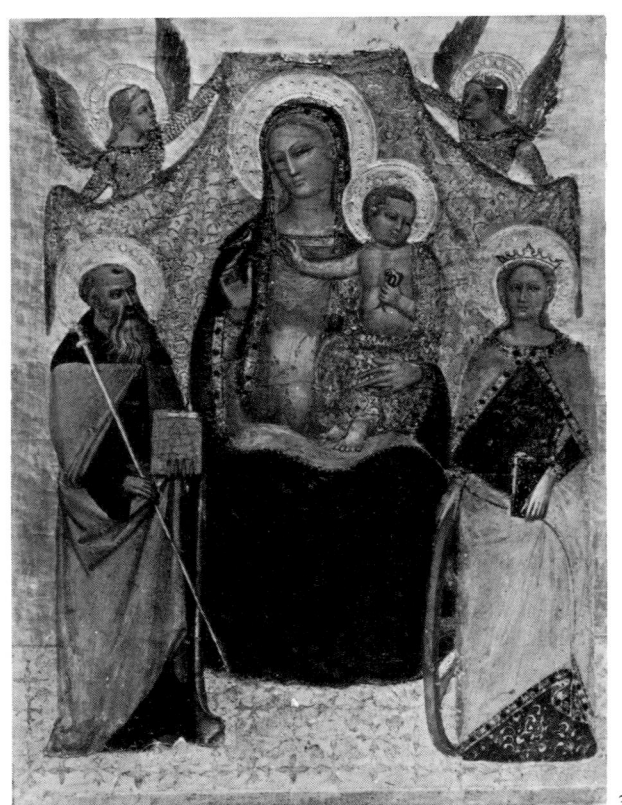

332

333

330. *Music-making Angels, detail of fig. 326. Panel. London, National Gallery. no. 571. Museum photo. 1370-71.*
331. *Portable triptych: Madonna and Child Enthroned with Sts Peter, John the Baptist, Anthony Abbot, Paul, Catherine, Margaret and two Angels; Nativity; Christ on the Cross. Above: Christ blessing and Annunciation. Panel. Ottawa, National Gallery of Canada. no. 15000. 76.5 × 69.2. Museum photo.*
332. *Madonna and Child, detail of fig. 334. Panel. Florence, SS. Apostoli. Uffizi. no. 8607. Brogi 24205. d. 1383.*
333. *Madonna and Child Enthroned with Sts Anthony Abbot and Catherine and two Angels. Panel. Florence, Acton Collection. no. 131. 175 × 23.5. Reali.*

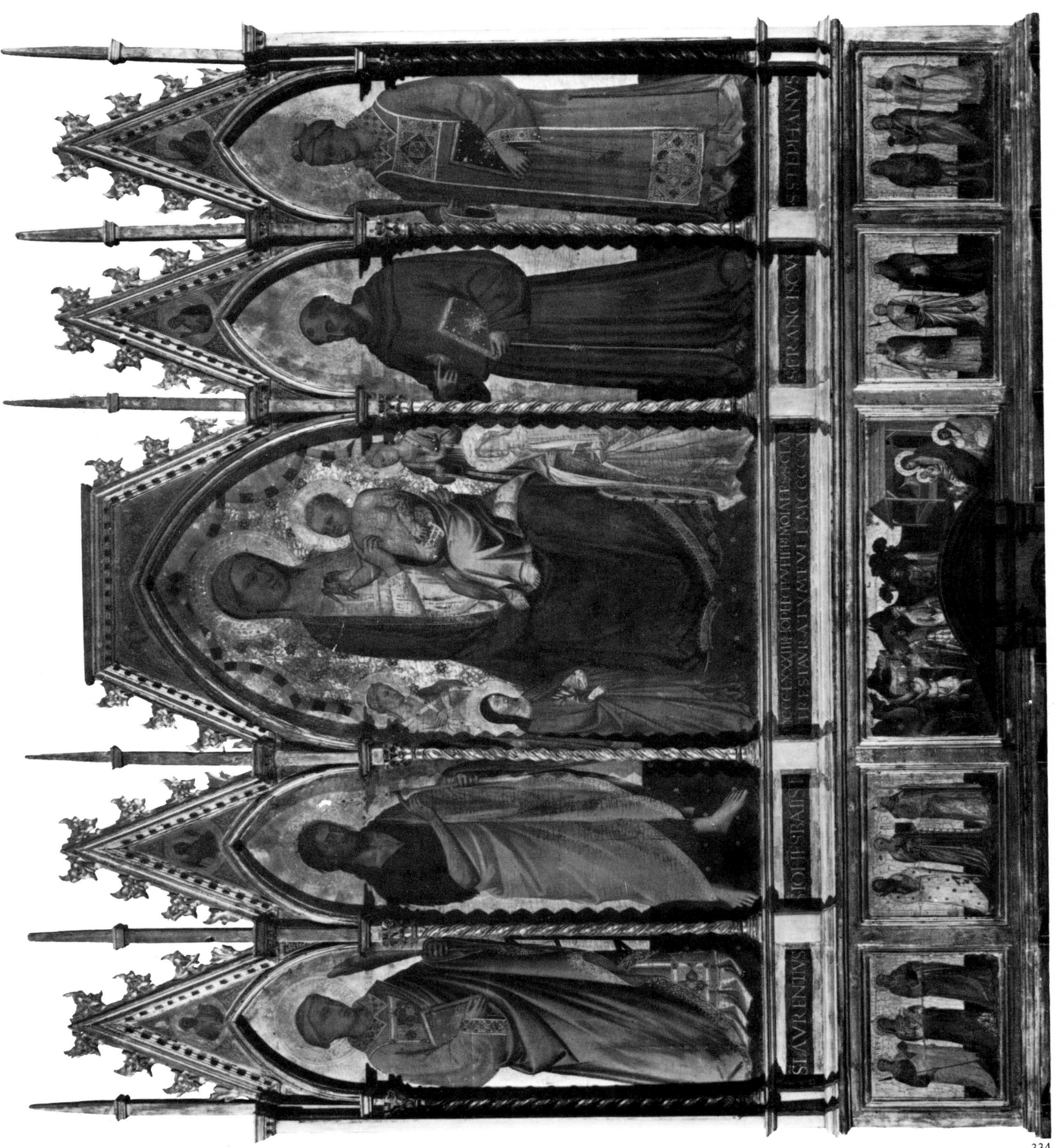

334. *Polyptych: Madonna and Child with Sts Euphrasia and Catherine, and two Angels. Wings: Sts Lawrence, John the Baptist, Francis and Stephen. Pinnacles: Annunciation; Sts Peter and Paul. Predella: twelve Saints; Adoration of the Magi. Panel. Florence, SS. Apostoli. Uffizi. no. 8607. 204 × 229. SGF 117721. d. 1383.*

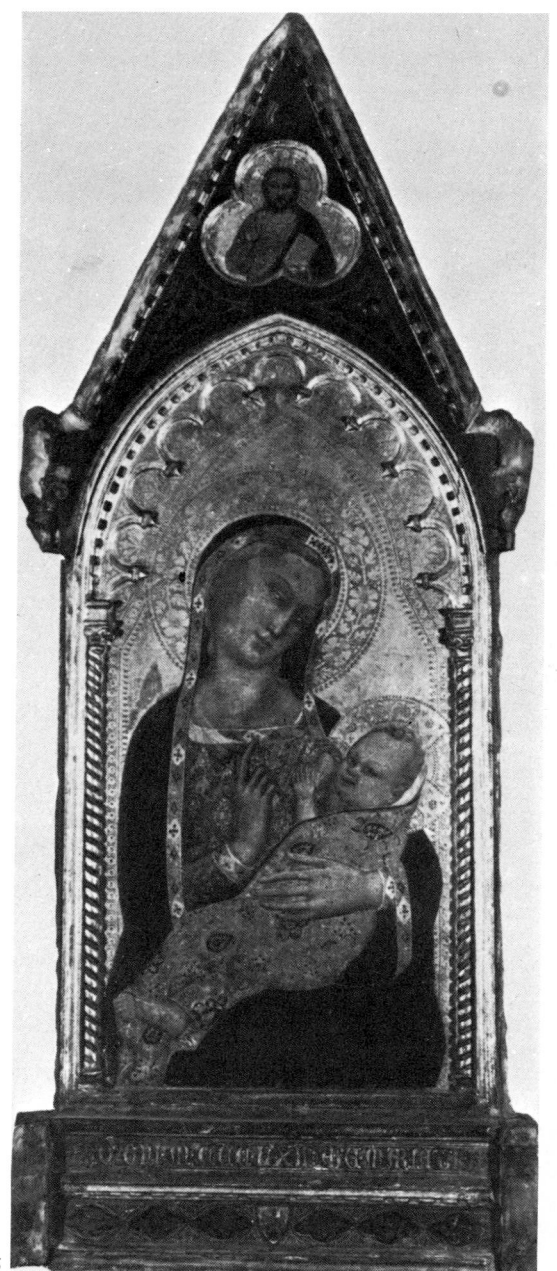

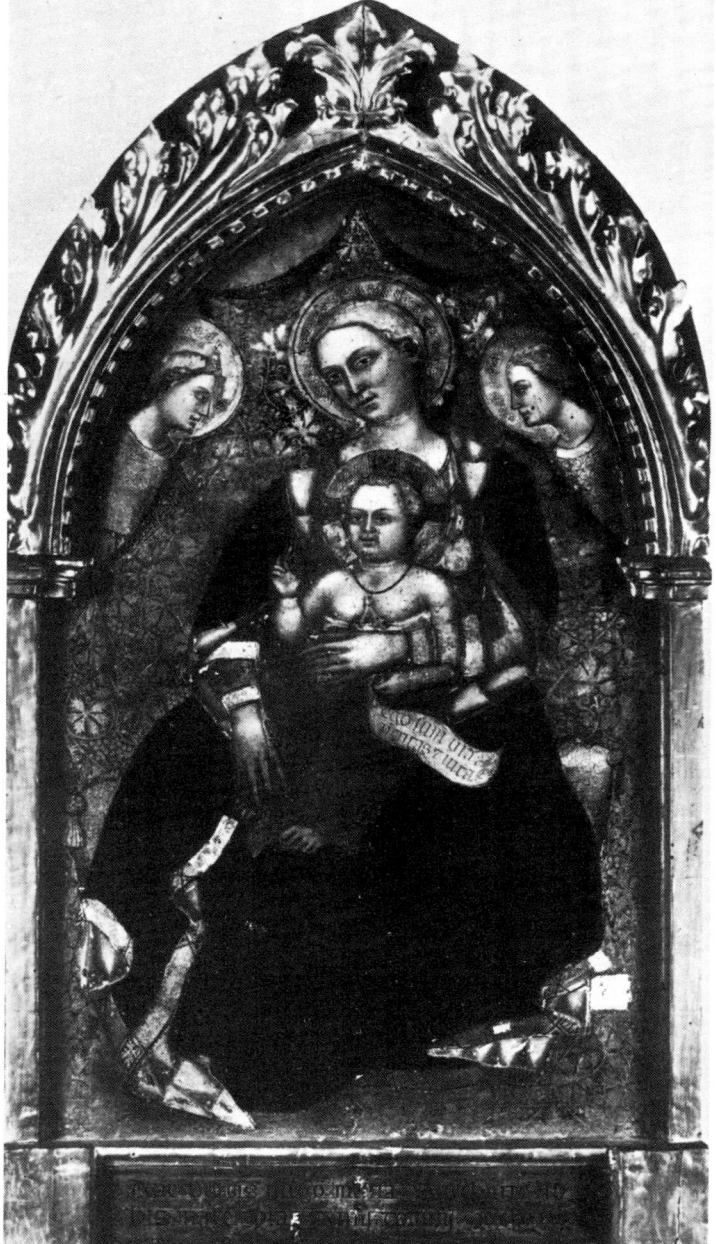

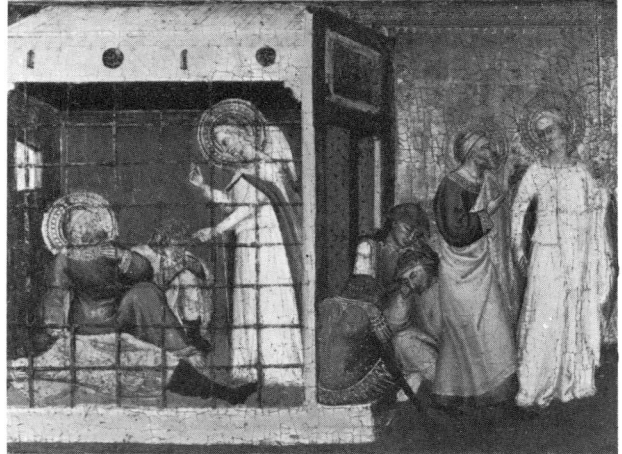

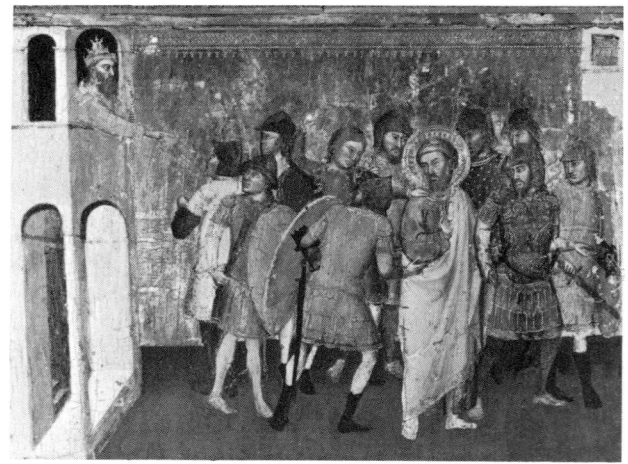

335. *Madonna nursing the Child. Panel. Whereabouts unknown (formerly Brussels, Stoclet Collection). Sotheby A7694. d. 1362.*
336. *Madonna of Humility with two Angels. Panel. Florence, Miari-Pelli-Fabbroni Collection. Fototeca Berenson. d. 1386.*
337. *Predella scene: St Peter freed from prison. Panel. Philadelphia (Pa.), Museum of Art, John G. Johnson Collection. no. 4. 38.7 × 52.1. Collection photo. 1370-71.*
338. *Predella scene: St Peter taken prisoner. Panel. Providence (R.I.), Museum of Art, Rhode Island School of Design. no. 22047. 32.2 × 52.7. Museum photo. 1370-71.*

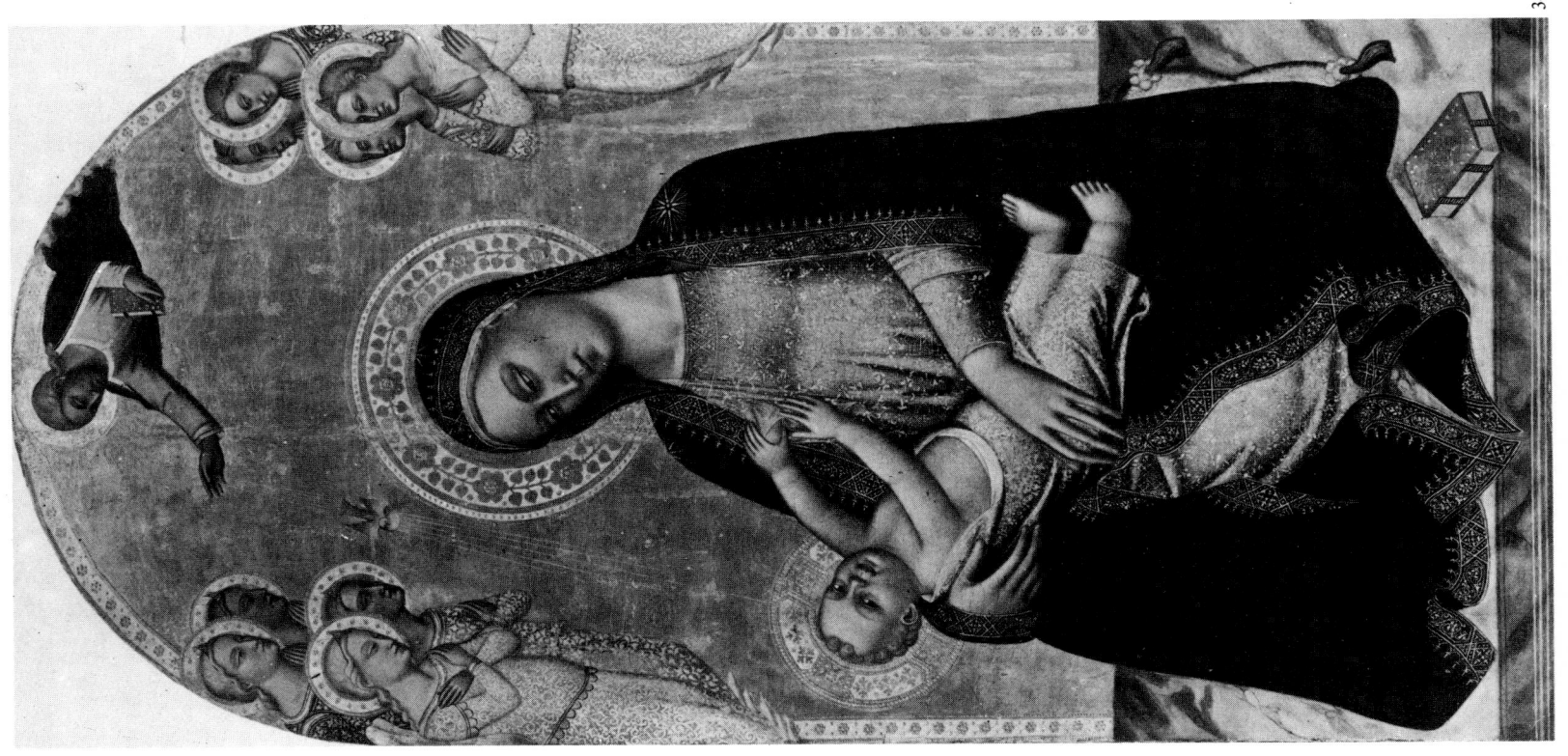

339. *Coronation of the Virgin with ten Saints. Above: two Prophets. Panel. Florence, Accademia. no. 456. 350 × 190. Brogi 6656. 1373.*
340. *Madonna of Humility nursing the Child with eight Angels. Above: God the Father and Holy Spirit. Panel. Washington, National Gallery, Samuel H. Kress Collection. no. 814. 141 × 69. Museum photo.*

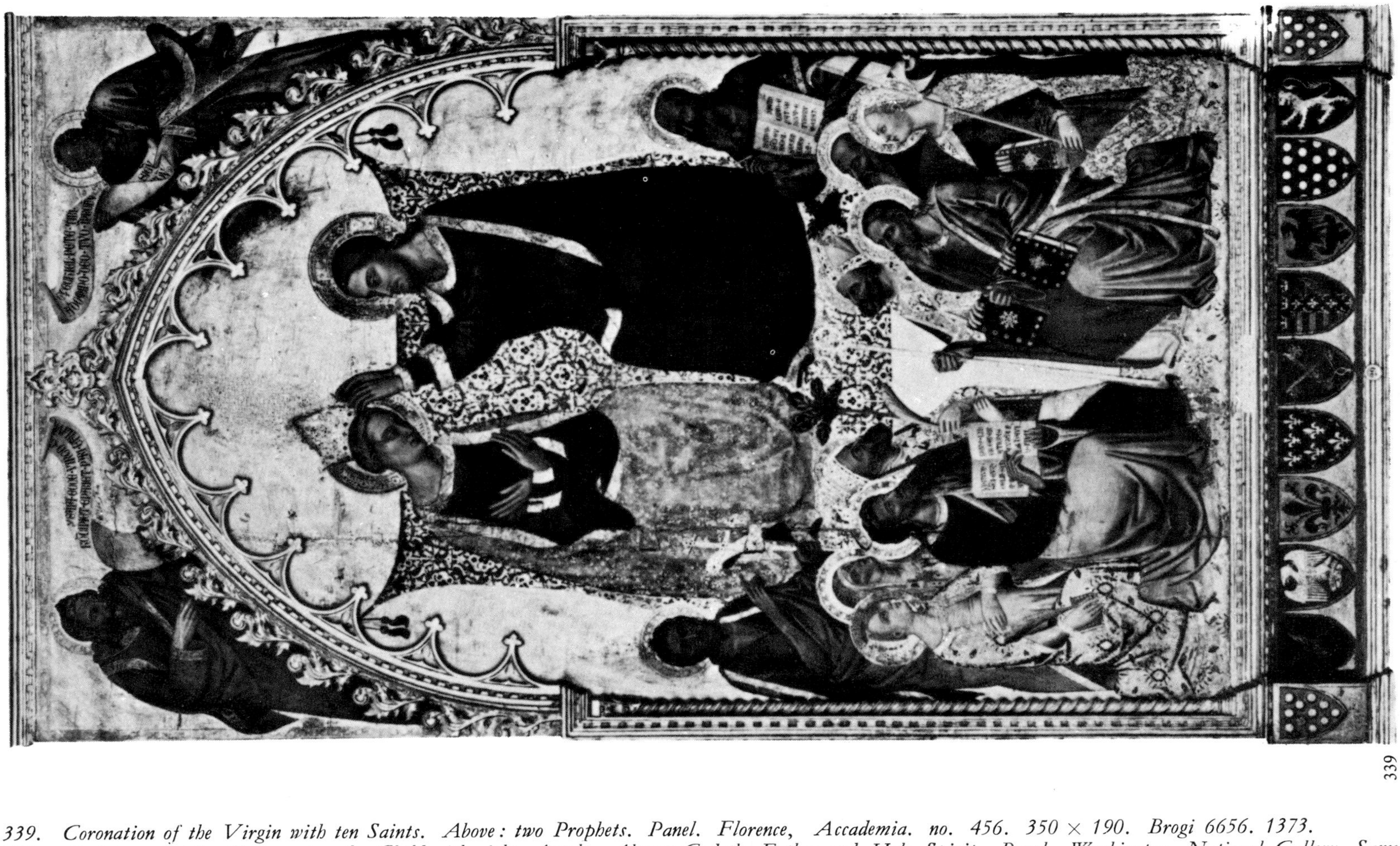

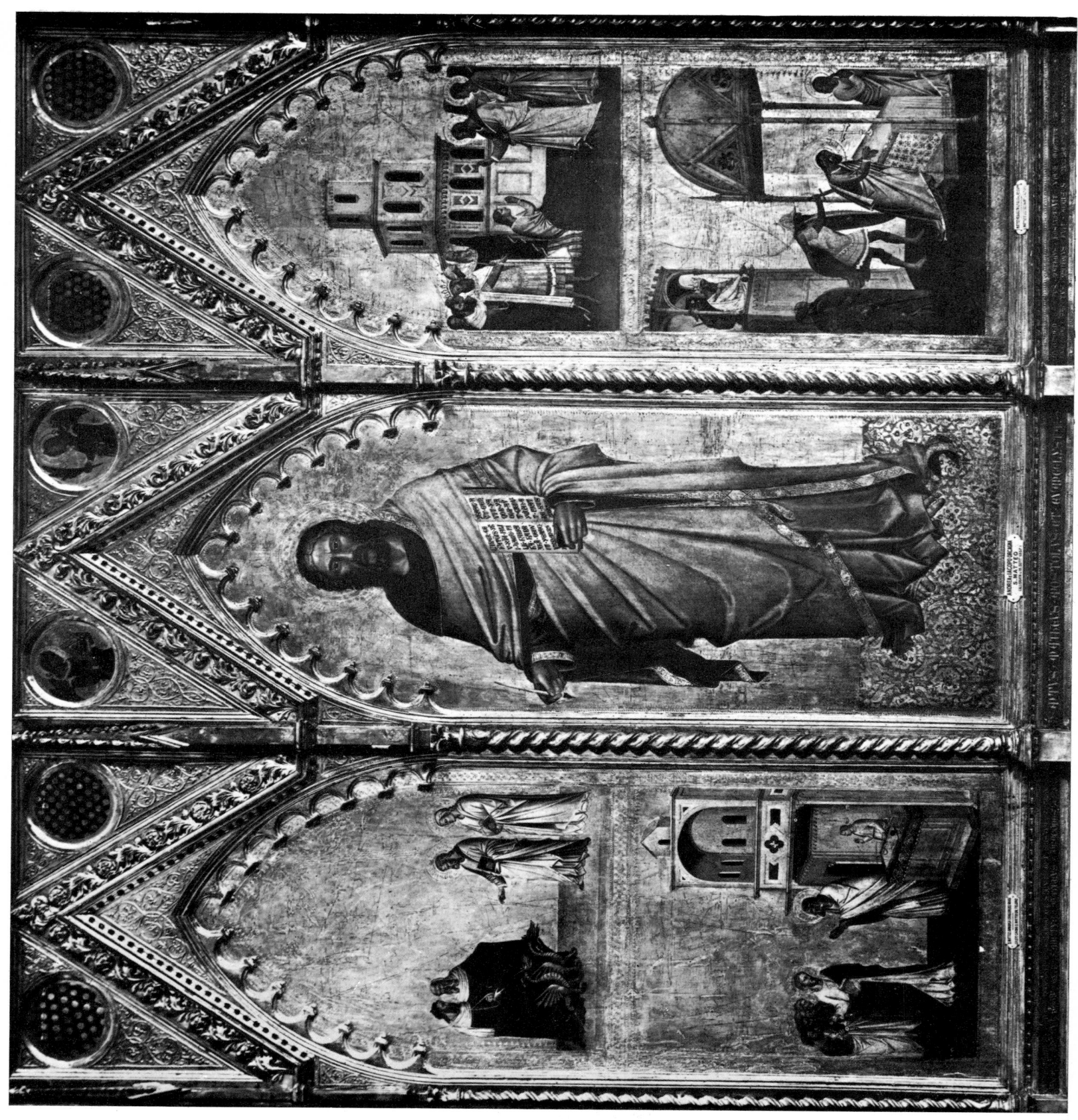

341. *Triptych: St Matthew and scenes from his Life: St Matthew overcoming two Dragons by making the Sign of the Cross, thus putting an end to the power of the Magicians; St Matthew's Vocation; he raises to life the King's Child; he is stabbed by Hirtacus before the Altar. Above: two Angels. Panel. Florence, Uffizi. no. 3163. 291 × 265. Brogi 22171. 1367-68 (started by Orcagna).*

NICCOLÒ di TOMMASO

Niccolò di Tommaso is one of the many painters whose advice was asked in 1366 for the construction of the Cathedral of Florence and in 1365 he was one of the witnesses in the drawing up of Nardo di Cione's will. His signature and the date 1371 appear on an altarpiece in the church of S. Antonio, Naples: " MCCCLXXI Nicholaus Tomasi di Flore picto ".....
The painter was obviously inspired by Nardo but this influence is not perhaps sufficiently strong here for us to admit that Niccolò was a pupil. We can, however, notice the same artistic aspiration and attempt to produce beautiful faces with religious expressions; the drapery also to a certain extent reproduces the Orcagnesque plasticity and the taste for decoration seems to have been taken from the same source; but the proportions are somewhat more elongated.

from R. van Marle, pp. 534-535, *The Development of the Italian Schools of Painting*, Vol. III, The Hague, 1924.

His activity as a painter might have begun around 1330. If it did, then none of his earlier works has yet been identified. All those I attribute to him would seem to fall into the third quarter of the Trecento. And oddly enough, the two documents bearing on him, are of the same period, that is of the years 1365 and 1366. Their contents imply middle life and a settled reputation at the time of their drawing up. In 1365 he is a witness at the proving of the will of Nardo di Cione. Under the following year, 1366, he is recorded with Orcagna — among others — in a list of artists consulted by the Operai del Duomo..... These assimilations from Nardo, and Niccolò's dependence on him, express a deeper temperamental affinity between master and pupil. Both possess a tendency to sink the action in a pervading mood, and each object, as in a piece of still-life, becomes steeped in a life beyond itself, the life of its suggestions and associations. This poetic factor in Niccolò's paintings, in a stylistic context so explicitly Nardesque, urges the conclusion that only Nardo's example could be responsible for it.
With this dependence once admitted, there still remains a quality in Niccolò's painting which, if wanting in original genius, yields a unique savor and makes him an extraordinary figure among his contemporaries. In an age when art was not a personal but a traditional expression, Niccolò, pursuing a path struck by his master, evolves an art that draws on intimate experience. His painting is neither determined to an idea, nor does it liberate a direct force; his figures release a mood, and spread an atmosphere about themselves. They have their being in an ante-motor world, in which the monotonous bliss of life has not yet felt the vehemence of the heart, nor reached the light of full consciousness. In a final reckoning, it is an ingenuous insinuating but unevolved expression, still in the stage of the protoplasmic dream, dumbly shaping its half-formed images. How inaccessible and unreal the Giottesque idealism of his day must have seemed to this provincial little Florentine, whose only reality was the drifting state of the feelings and the instincts...

from R. Offner, pp. 118-119, *Studies in Florentine Painting*, New York, 1927.

Florentine, born 13- -, died - -. Painter, member of the Physicians and Apothecaries Guild between 1320-45/6. Member of the Company of Saint Luke (? if he is the Niccolaio di Maso entered on the roll in 1405, probable date of death). Pupil? of Nardo di Cione. Niccolò was among the painters called in council by the Board of Works of Sta. Reparata in 1366-67..... Niccolò di Tommaso, popolo of S. Giorgio, was one of the witnesses to the will of Nardo di Cione, his friend and probable master on May 21, 1365, and he is possibly the Niccolaio who in Sacchetti's record took part in the discussion between several artists at S. Miniato al Monte on the decay of painting in Florence, when Maestro Alberto Arnoldi showed that the Florentine ladies were the best painters of the day in the adornment of their faces..... If the date on the Roll of S. Luke is correct, he evidently ended his life in Florence.....

from D. E. Colnaghi, pp. 190-191, *A Dictionary of Florentine Painters*, London, 1928.

Active ca 1343-1376. His identified works show him coming out of Nardo and veering toward Jacopo di Cione and Giovanni del Biondo; influenced by Giovanni da Milano.

from B. Berenson, p. 161, *Italian Pictures of the Renaissance, Florentine School*, Vol. I, London, 1963.

Florentine School. Active c. 1343-1405. He is now credited with some paintings which were formerly attributed to Giovanni da Milano; but the strongest influence upon his style came from Nardo di Cione.

from F. R. Shapley, p. 35, *Paintings from the Samuel H. Kress Collection*, London, 1966.

BIBLIOGRAPHY
BOOKS
An asterisk indicates a work listed in the General Bibliography

Khv & Salmi*, 1914, p. 36; *v. Marle, 1924**, pp. 534-5; *Offner, Studies**, 1927, pp. 109-24; *Colnaghi**, 1928, pp. 190-191; *Toesca, 1929**, p. 66; *Berenson, 1932**, p. 397; *Coletti, Vol. II**, 1946, p. 54; *Antal**, 1948, pp. 197-9; Marabottini, A., *Giovanni da Milano*, Florence, 1950, p. 99; Shorr, D. C., *The Christ Child in Devotional Images*, New York, 1954 pp. 46, 57; *Berenson, 1963**, Vol. I, p. 161; *Marcucci**, 1956, pp. 102-3; *Shapley**, 1966, p. 35; Procacci, U., in *Edit.*, *Atti del 2º Convegno Internazionale di Studi* (*Il Gotico a Pistoia nei suoi rapporti con l'arte gotica italiana*), Pistoia-Rome 1966, pp. 247-260, 375-6; Prokopp, M., in *Edit.*, *Evolution Générale et Développements Regionaux en Histoire de l'Art* (*Actes du XXIIº Congrès International d'Histoire de l'art*) Budapest, 1969, Vol. 1, pp. 583-86; *MMOA**, 1971, pp. 34-35; Procacci, U., in *Congresso VII**, 1971, pp. 349-363; Palumbo, G., *Collezione Federico Mason Perkins*, Rome, 1973, p. 45; *Dutch Show**, 1974, pp. 95-96.

JOURNALS

Salazar, L., *NN*, XIV, 4, 1905, p. 54; Offner, R., *AA*, XIII, 1924, pp. 19-35; Offner, R., *AA*, XIII, 1925, pp. 21-37; Sandberg-Vavalà, E., *AA*, XV, 1927, pp. 273-87; Lasareff, V., *AA*, XVI, 1928, pp. 25-40; Salmi, M., *RA*, XI, 1929, pp. 142-4; Arslan, W., *DD*, XII, 2, 1932, pp. 467-70; Berenson, B., *DD*, XI, 4, 1930-31, pp. 1039-73; Gronau, H. D., *B*, XVII, 2, 1930, pp. 96-7; Colasanti, A., *BA*, XXVII, 1934, pp. 337-50; Meiss, M., *AB*, XXVIII, 1946, p. 13; Offner, R., *MKIF*, VII, 3/4, 1956, pp. 173-92; Kup, K., *PMB*, LV, 263/4, 1959-60, pp. 14-16; Guerrieri, F., *BSP*, LXXII, V, 1, 1970, pp. 3-20; Gai, L., *BSP*, LXXII, V, 2, 1970, pp. 75-94; Kiel, H., *P.*, XXVIII, II, 1970, p. 161; *Edit.*, *BM*, 103, Suppl. 1, 1961; Schlegel, U., *MKIF*, XI, 2/3, 1964, pp. 63-70; Boskovits, M., *MKIF*, XIII, 1-4, 1967-68, pp. 34, 36, 55; *Edit.*, *BSP*, LXXII, V, 1, 1970, pls. 11-16; Bellosi, L., *MKIF*, XVII, 2/3, 1973, p. 182.

SIGNED AND DATED WORKS

1360 Pistoia, Palazzo Comunale. Fresco: St James & Bishop Saint with Madonna and Child and 2 Angels. d. (fig. 361).

1367 Formerly, Arezzo, Pinacoteca (destroyed). Panel: Madonna & Child with female Donor. d. (fig. 343).

1371 Naples, Museo di S. Martino. Triptych: St Anthony Abbot Enthroned with Angels & Saints. s & d. (fig. 346-8).

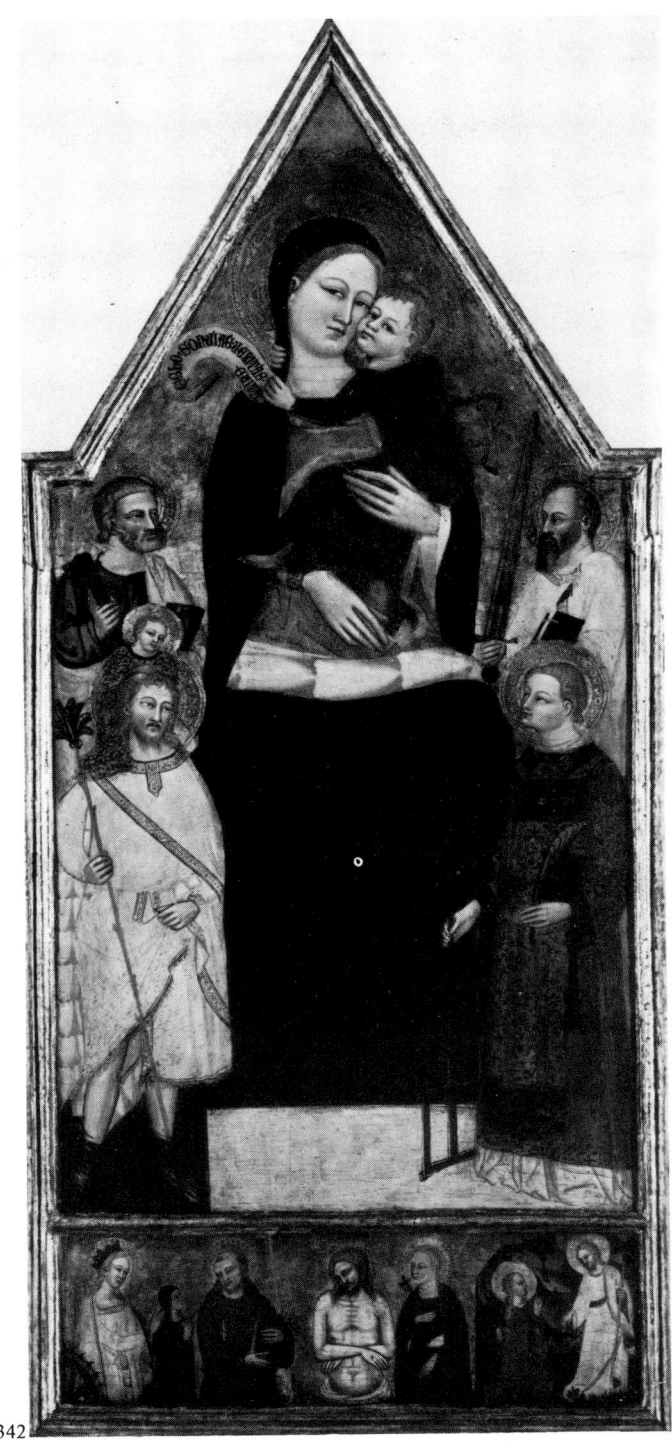

342

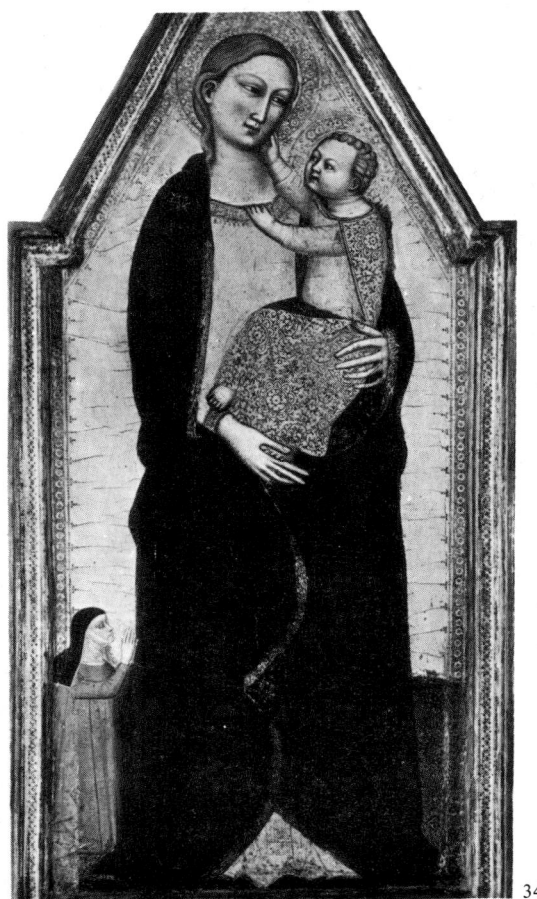

343

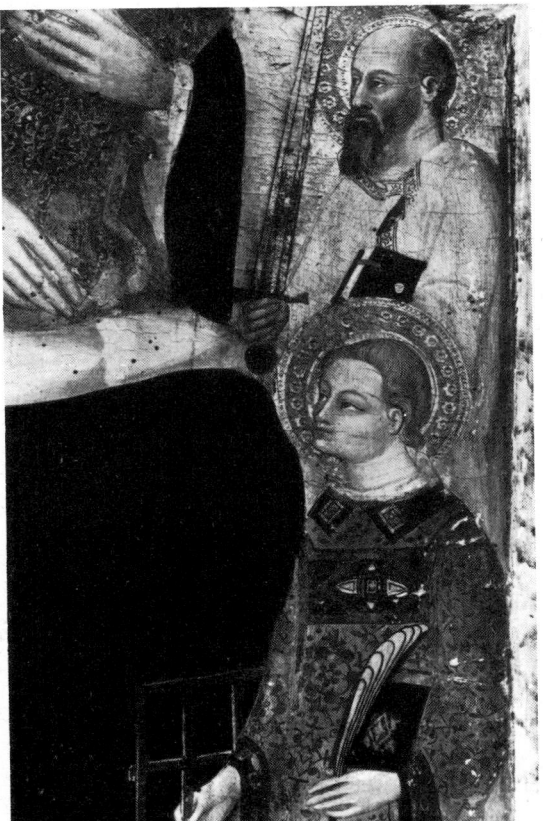

345

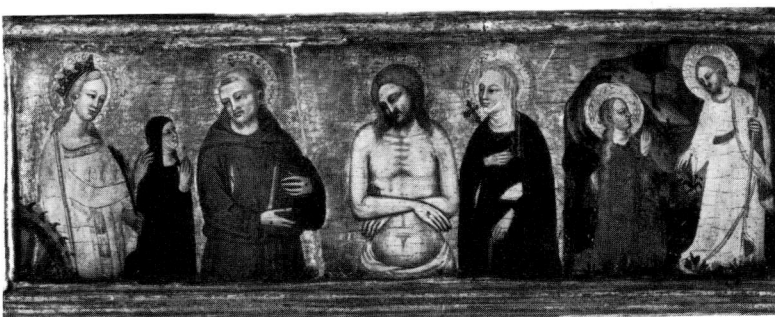

344

342. *Madonna and Child with Sts Peter, Christopher, Paul and Lawrence. Predella: Man of Sorrows with Sts Catherine, Francis, a female Donor, female Saint, and Noli me tangere. Panel. Florence, Ospedale di S. Maria Nuova, Administration Office. no. 116. 135 × 67. SGF 143334.*
343. *Madonna and Child with female Donor. Panel (destroyed). Arezzo, Pinacoteca. no. 13. Alinari 60954. d. 1367.*
344. *Predella scene: Man of Sorrows with Sts Catherine, Francis, female Donor, female Saint, and Noli me tangere, detail of fig. 342. Panel. Florence, Ospedale di S. Maria Nuova, Administration Office. SGF 143335.*
345. *Sts Paul and Lawrence, detail of fig. 342. Panel. Florence, Ospedale di S. Maria Nuova, Administration Office. Brogi 24363.*

175

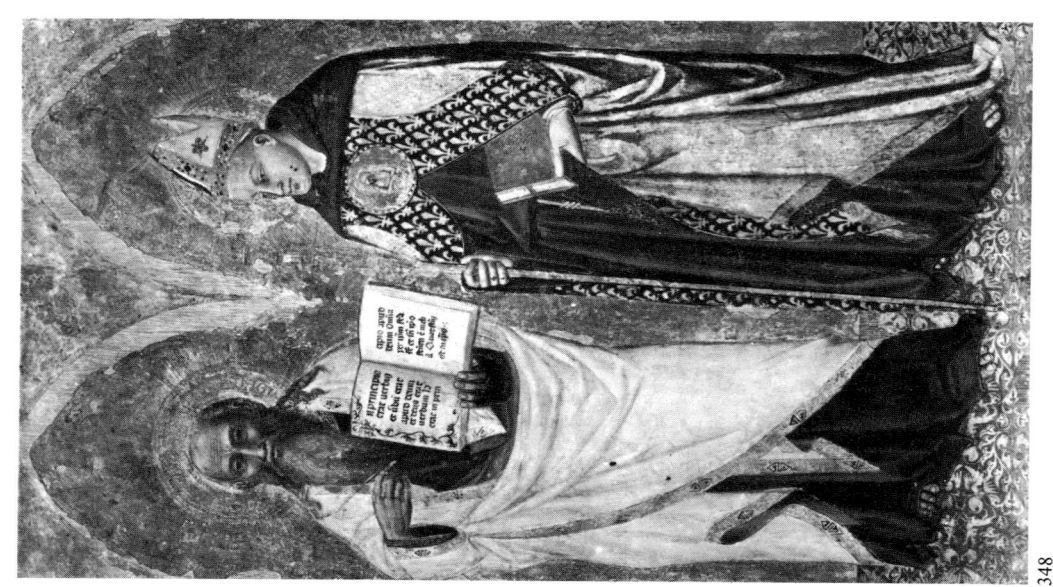

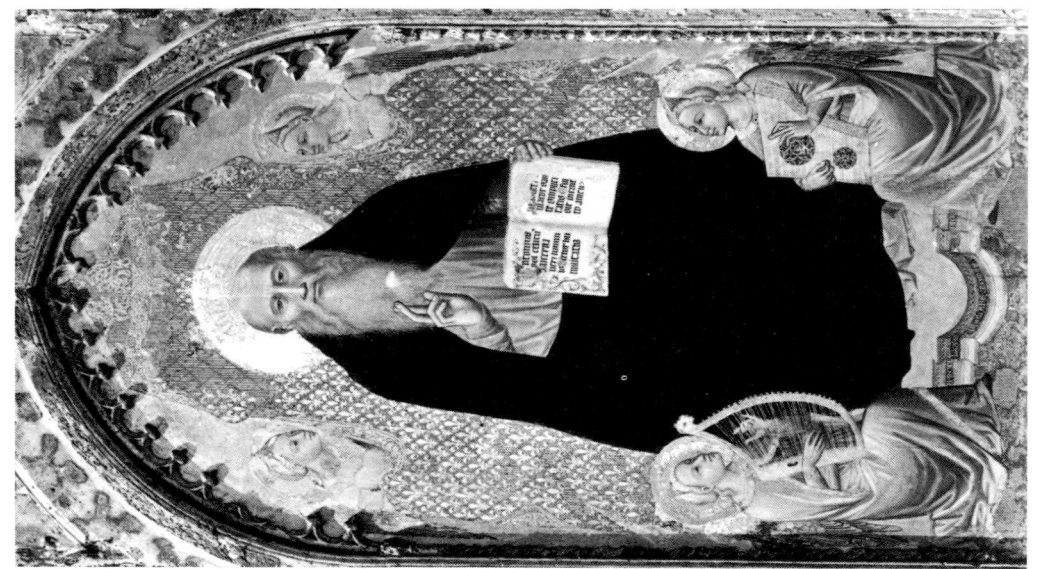

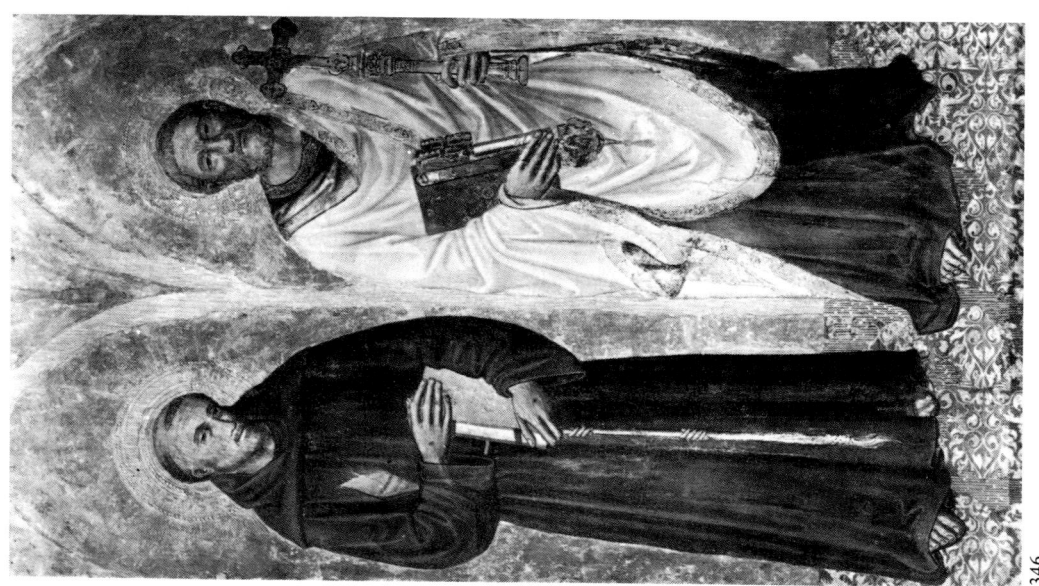

346. *Left wing of a triptych: Sts Francis and Peter. Panel. Naples, Museo di S. Martino. 118 × 68. SGN 4887. s & d. 1371.*
347. *Central panel of a triptych: St Anthony Abbot Enthroned with four Angels. Panel. Naples, Museo di S. Martino. 162 × 101. SGN 4869. s & d. 1371.*
348. *Right wing of a triptych: Sts John the Evangelist and Louis of Toulouse. Panel. Naples, Museo di S. Martino. 118 × 68. SGN 4888. s & d. 1371.*

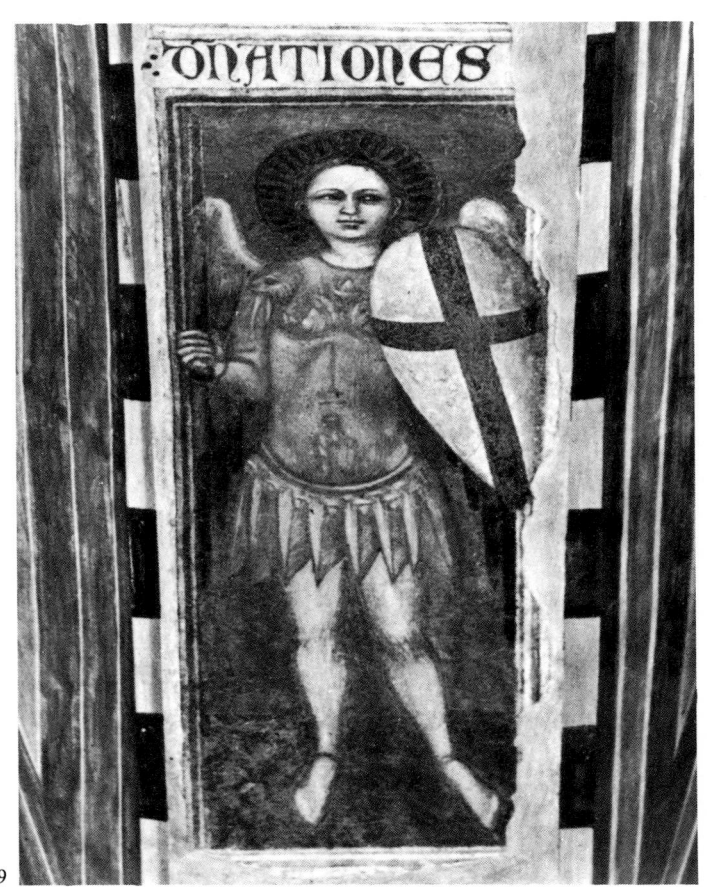

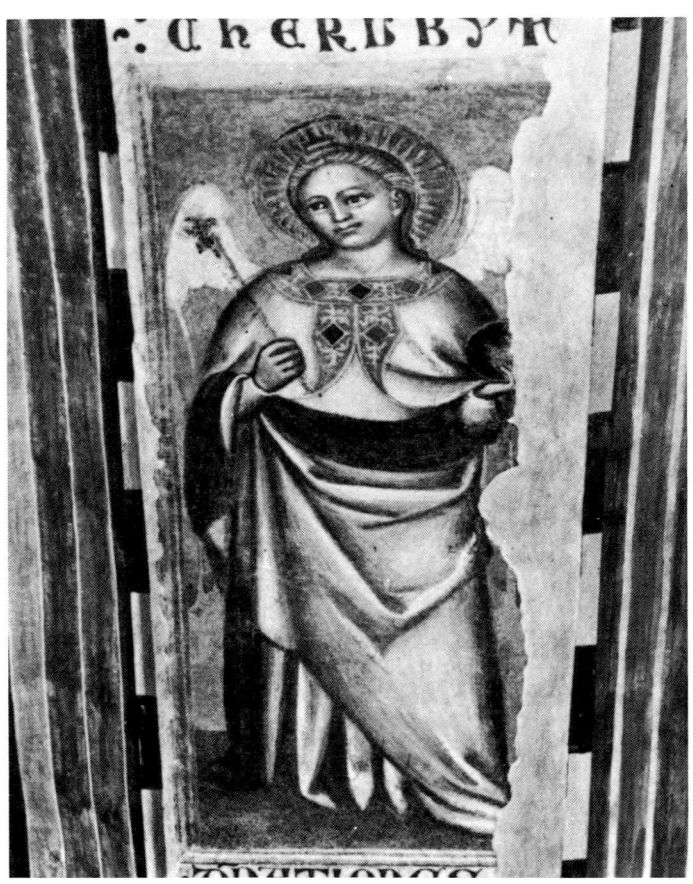

349

350

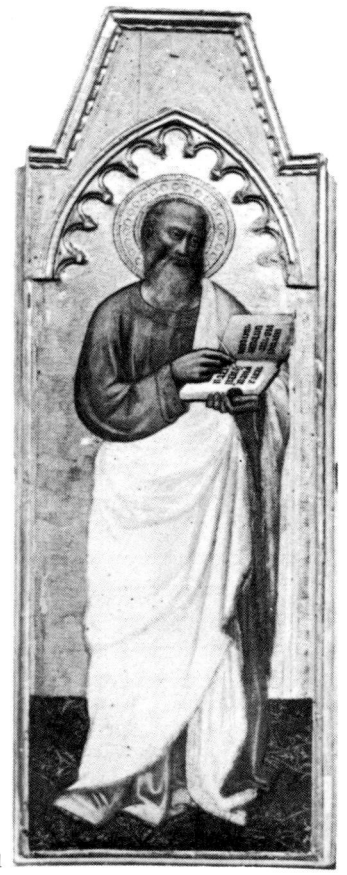

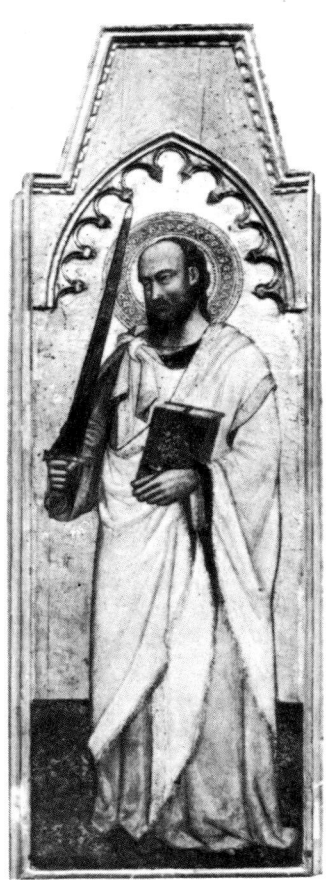

351

352

349. *St George. Fresco. Florence, S. Maria Novella. Fototeca Berenson.*
350. *Angel. Fresco. Florence, S. Maria Novella. Fototeca Berenson.*
351. *St John the Evangelist. Panel. Florence, Horne Museum. no. 75. 153 × 41.5. Fototeca Berenson.*
352. *St Paul. Panel. Florence, Horne Museum. no. 76. 153 × 41.5. Fototeca Berenson.*

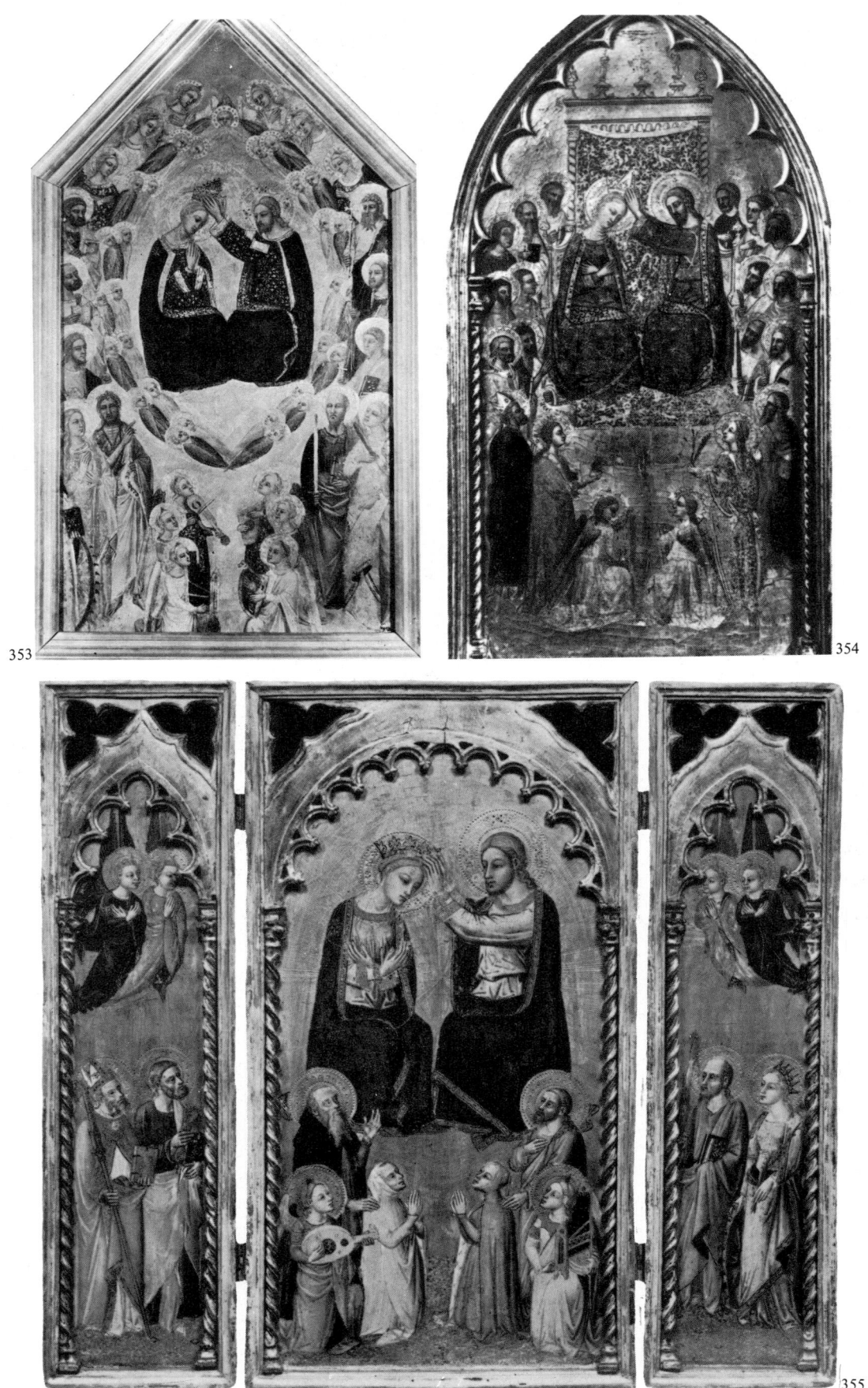

353. *Coronation of the Virgin. Panel. Prague, Narodni Galerie. no. O-11.889. 71 × 37. Museum photo.*
354. *Coronation of the Virgin with Saints and Angels. Panel. Florence, Accademia. no. 8580. 58 × 28. SGF 20946.*
355. *Portable triptych: Coronation of the Virgin with Saints and Angels. Panel. Baltimore (Md.), Walters Art Gallery. no. 37.718. 66.5 × 73.5. Museum photo H '59.*

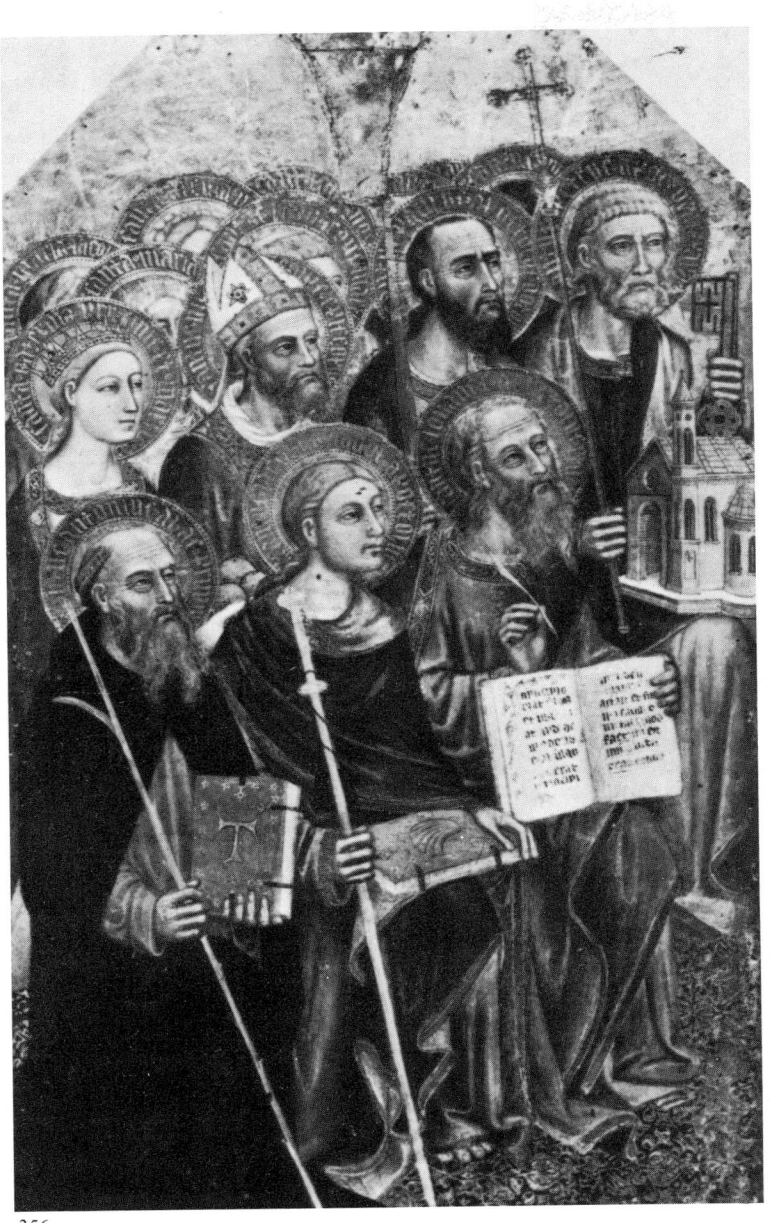

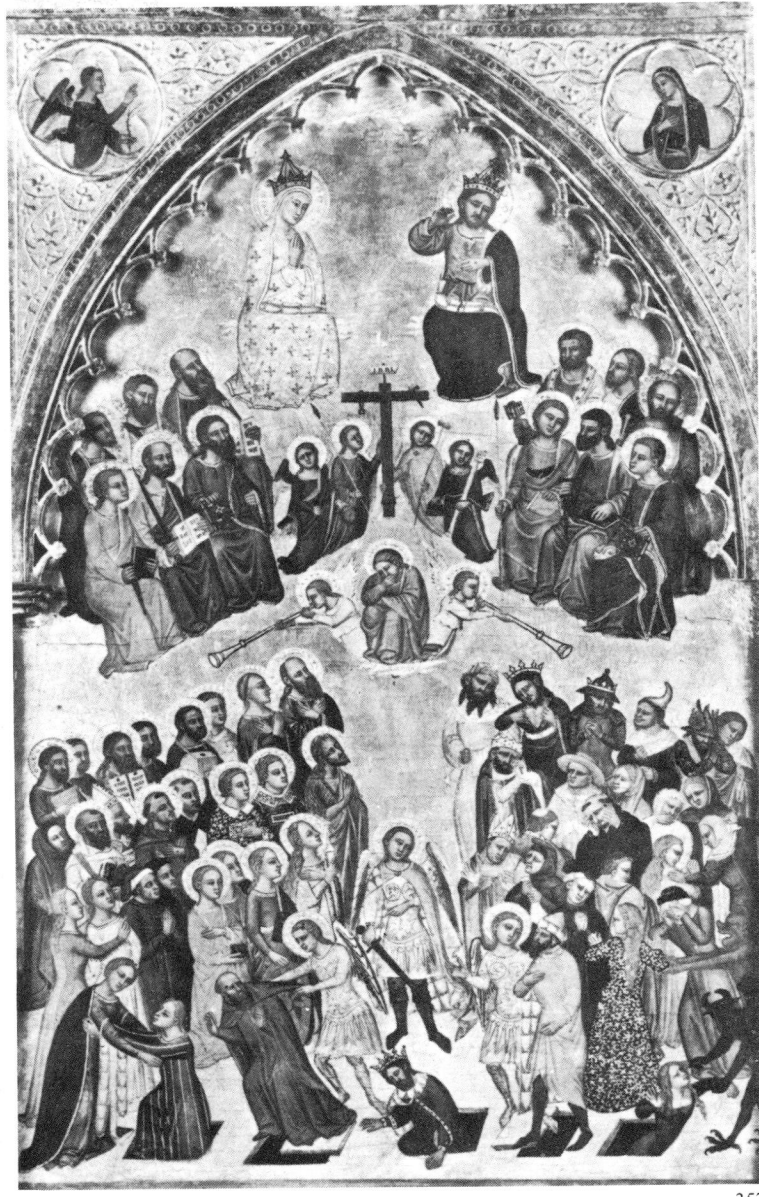

356

357

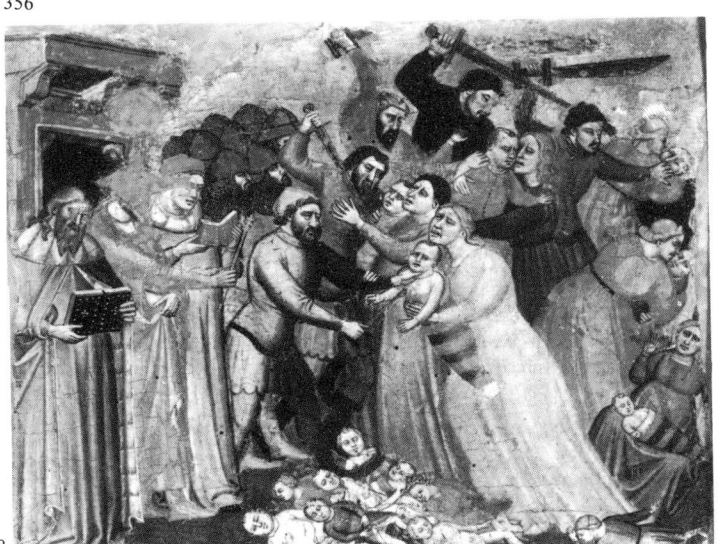

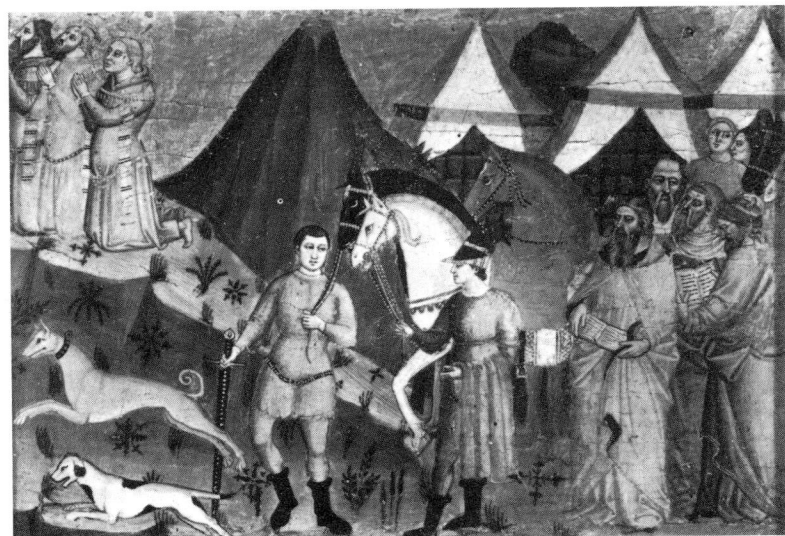

358

359

356. *Fifteen Saints. Panel. Whereabouts unknown. Fototeca Berenson.*
357. *Last Judgement. Panel. Whereabouts unknown (formerly Livorno, Larderel Collection). Fototeca Berenson.*
358. *Predella scene: Massacre of the Innocents. Panel. Fiesole, Museo Bandini. no. 23 D. 25.8 × 33.1. SGF 69403.*
359. *Predella scene: Journey of the Magi. Panel. Fiesole, Museo Bandini. no. 23 C. 25.8 × 33.1. SGF 69424.*

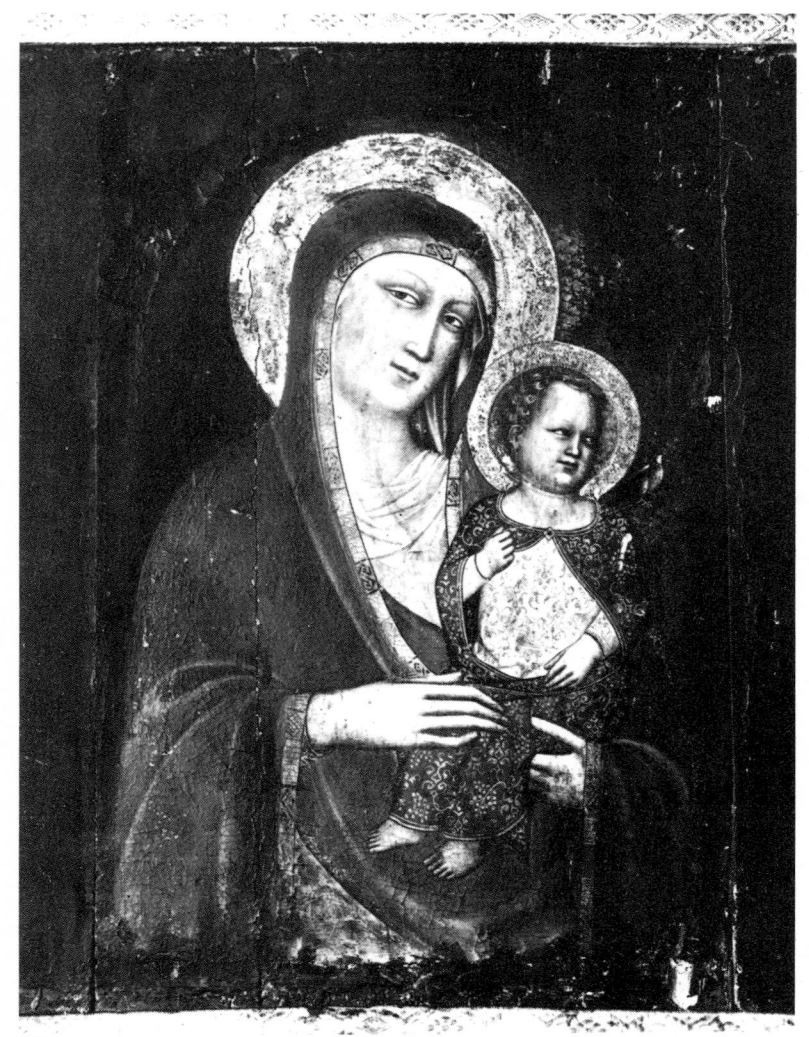

360

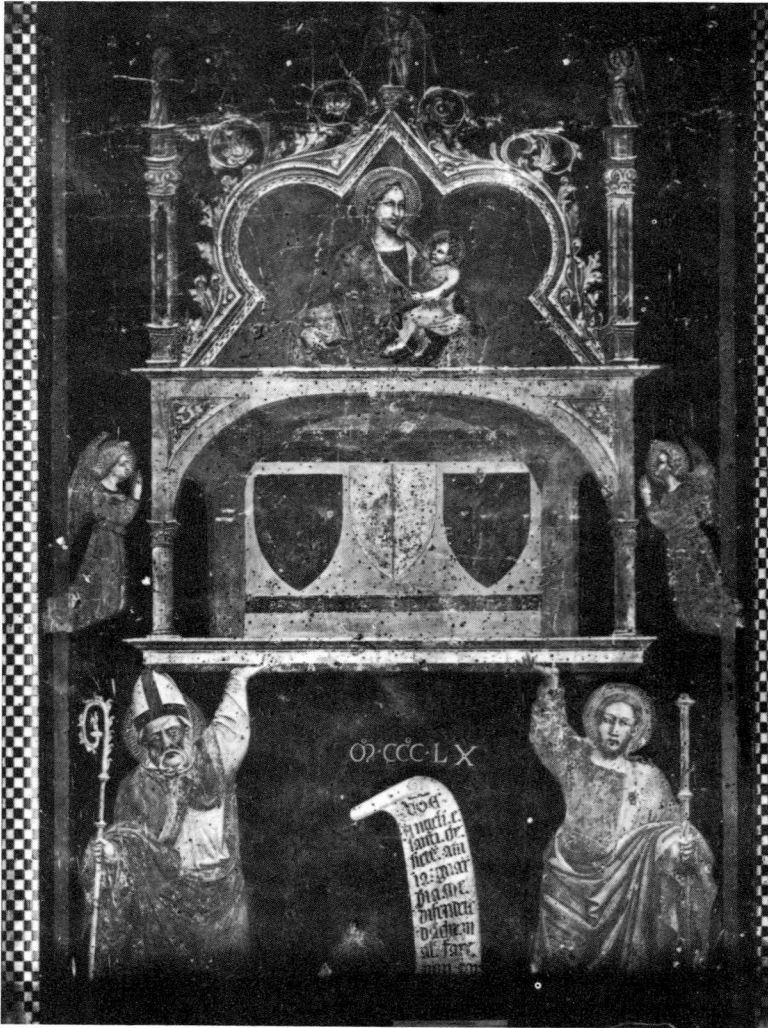

361

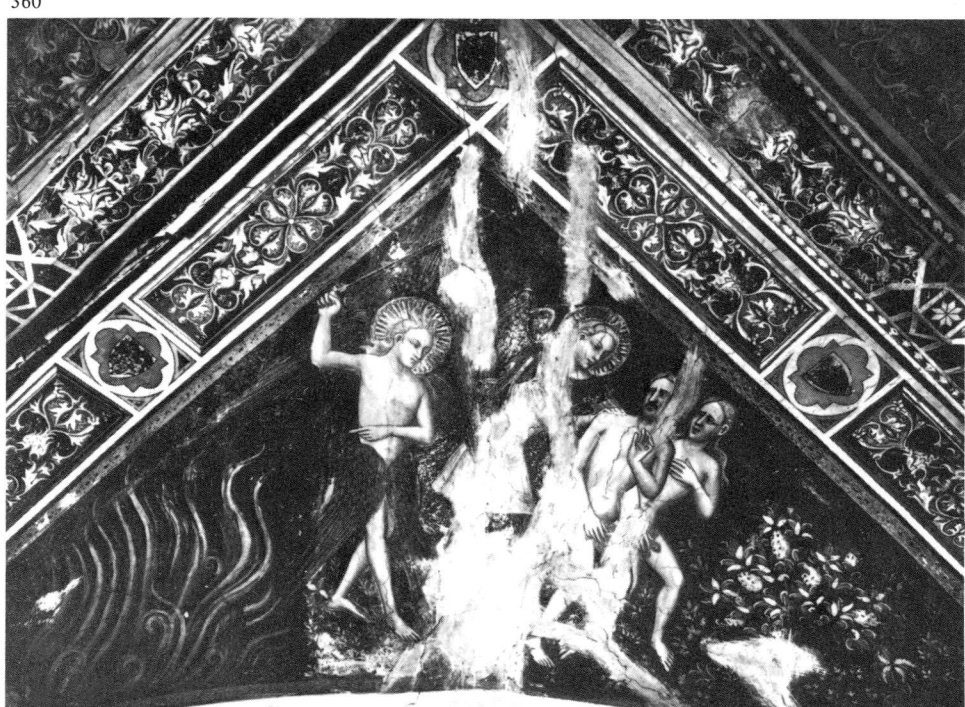

362

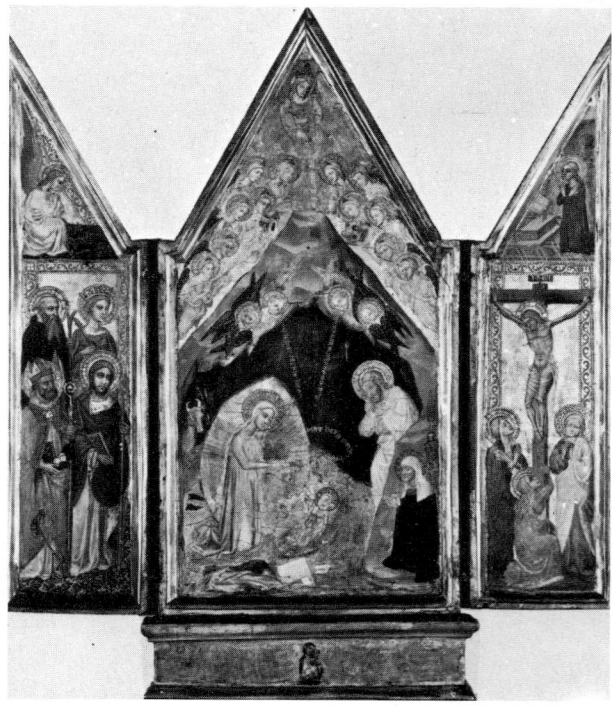

363

360. *Madonna and Child. Panel. Carteano (near Prato), S. Paolo. 76 × 90 . Alinari 60961.*
361. *Madonna and Child with two Angels, St James and Bishop Saint. Fresco. Pistoia, Palazzo Comunale. Alinari 6280. d. 1360.*
362. *Expulsion of Adam and Eve. Fresco. Pistoia, Convento del " T " (formerly). Brogi 6259.*
363. *Portable triptych: St Bridget's Vision of the Nativity; Annunciation; four Saints; Crucifixion. Panel. Philadelphia (Pa.), Museum of Art, John G. Johnson Collection. no. 120. 55.8 × 52.4. Museum photo.*

GIOVANNI da MILANO

Giovanni da Milano moulded his style to a certain extent on that of Taddeo Gaddi, with whom he lived for many years in the position of journeyman. But Giovanni had been bred in the north of Italy; he had never quite acquired the Tuscan manner, and his constant aim had evidently been to correct the conventionalism of the rigidly Giottesque school by a more careful appeal to nature, a more finished contour, and a more conscientious shaping of form. It is not too much to say that the stress which he laid upon these material parts of painting contributed to the marked expansion which characterised Florentine art under Orcagna.

> from J. A. Crowe and G. B. Cavalcaselle, p. 181, *A History of Painting in Italy*, Vol. II, New York, 1903.

Johannes Jacobi de Como is included in a list of foreign painters living in Florence in 1350. This is without question the same artist who on the 25th June 1363 appears registered in the Arte dei Medici e Speziali under the name of Giovanni di Giacomo di Guido da Como. The 25th December of the same year Giovanni makes a tax return to the Estimo. He was living in the " Gonfalone " Chiavi, " Quartiere " of San Giovanni, in the via del Canto alla Briga, "popolo" of San Pier Maggiore; he owned at Tizzano in the "piviere" of Ripoli, three parcels of land: il Castagnaccio, Il Canneto, il Querciolo. In 1365 he signed the picture of the *Pietà* which is today in the Accademia in Florence: " Io Giovanni da Melano depinsi questa tavola in MCCCLXV ". The 26th May of the same year a memorandum of the Capitani di Orsanmichele conceded to " Johannes pictor de kaversaio " a prolongation until " ad Kal. novembris proxime secuturas " to finish the frescoes which he had already begun in the sacristy of Santa Croce.....

> from A. Marabottini, p. 17, *Giovanni da Milano* Florence, 1950.

Mentioned in Florence 1346-1366, in Rome 1369. Probably trained by Lombard Giotteschi, but influenced by Orcagna and Nardo.

> from B. Berenson, p. 89, *Italian Pictures of the Renaissance, Florentine School*, Vol. I, London, 1963.

The life and artistic activity of Giovanni da Milano are illustrated by a very few documents which, unfortunately, are not even well known.
Of primary importance is the document discovered by Procacci which refers to Florentine artists living in Florence, among whom is mentioned Johannes Jacobi de Commo, born at Caversaccio, a small town in the territory of Como. At that date [1350], he was therefore already in Florence, although nothing is known of his preceding artistic formation in Lombardy..... It is more probable that Giovanni da Milano's style was formed in Lombardy in contact with painters of the Giottesque movement, active in Milan between 1335 and 1345. Those influences were grafted onto the artistic culture of Lombardy which was also being influenced by the continental trends—that is, the styles of France and Avignon.....
There is no other certain information about his life until the 23rd of June 1363, when Giovanni is taken into the Guild of Physicians and Apothecaries in Florence.....
On 26 December in the same year, 1365, Giovanni da Milano declared his assets, from which we know that he was the owner of land and farms. On the 22nd of April in the year 1366 he received citizenship for himself and for his sons. The last date which refers to him is 1369. In this document he is mentioned in Rome together with other Florentine artists, among whom are Agnolo and Giovanni Gaddi and Giottino the son of Stefano, in order to decorate two chapels in the Vatican for Urban V.
The information given by Vasari (even though it has been accepted by several scholars among whom is Toesca) that Giovanni da Milano, at the end of his career " went away to Milan, completed many works of tempera and fresco there and finally died there " is highly unlikely.

> from L. Castelfranchi-Vegas, p. 1, *Giovanni da Milano* (I Maestri del Colore 111), Milan, 1965.

Having arrived in Florence, Giovanni da Milano encountered the solemn frescoes of Giotto, as well as those of Maso and of other followers of Giotto. He was certainly also aware that the style of these artists was at that point considered conservative and no longer satisfied modern requirements. In 1347, among the best painters mentioned in a Pistoiese document, the only "traditionalist" of importance is Taddeo Gaddi, at that moment under the influence of Maso di Banco; the others that we recognize are of the second post-Giotto generation: Andrea di Cione and his brother Nardo, Puccio and a certain Francesco, a collaborator of Orcagna. Stefano, who figures in the second place after Taddeo, was a pupil of Giotto, although from what we know from documents, his style was quite different from that of the Master.....

from M. Boskovits, p. 8, *Giovanni da Milano*, Florence, 1966.

BIBLIOGRAPHY
BOOKS

An asterisk indicates a work listed in the General Bibliography

C-Cavalcaselle II*, 1903, p. 181; *Suida, 1905**, pp. 28-39; *Venturi, A.**, 1907, pp.891-916; *v. Marle, 1924**, pp. 220-244; *Toesca, 1929**, p. 65; *Hautecoeur**, 1931, p. 168; Toesca, P., *Treccani Vol. XVII*, 1933, pp. 248-49; Berenson B., *Pitture Italiane del Rinascimento*, Milan, 1936, pp. 243-44; Bettini, S., *Giusto de' Menabuoi*, Padua, 1944; *Coletti, Vol. III**, 1947, pp. 65-8; *Antal**, 1948, pp. 196-7; *Vavalà, 1948*, pp. 64-7; Marabottini, A., *Giovanni da Milano*, Florence, 1950; *Galetti**, "F-O", 1950, pp. 1154-60; *Toesca, 1951**, pp. 762-7; Salmi, M., *Storia di Milano*, Vol. V, Milan, 1955; *Laclotte**, 1956, pp. 8-9; Russoli, F., and others, *Catalogo della Mostra " Arte Lombarda dai Visconti agli Sforza "*, Milan, 1958, pp. 19-24; Mazzini, F., and Matalon, S., *Affreschi del Trecento e Quattrocento in Lombardia*, Milan, 1958, pp. 11, 19, 37, 75, 76; Castelfranchi-Vegas, L., *L'Abbazia di Viboldone*, Milan, 1959; Rasmo, N., pp. 120-124 in *Scritti di storia dell'arte in onore di Mario Salmi*, Vol. II, Rome, 1961; *Berenson, 1962**, p. ix; *Berenson, 1963**, Vol. I, pp. 89-90; Castelfranchi-Vegas, L., *Giovanni da Milano (I Maestri del Colore, 111)*, Milan, 1965; *Marcucci**, 1965, pp. 83-8; Gregori, M., *Giovanni da Milano alla Cappella Rinuccini (L'Arte Racconta, 30)*, Milan, 1965; Boskovits, M., *Giovanni da Milano (I Diamanti dell'Arte 15)*, Florence, 1966; Castelfranchi-Vegas, L., *Il Gotico Internazionale in Italia*, Rome-Dresden, 1966, pp. 164-5; Segre Montel, C., *La Pittura dell'Italia Settentrionale nell'Età Gotica (I Maestri del Colore, 253)*, Milan, 1966; *Shapley**, 1966, p. 39; *Klesse**, 1967, pp. 288, 301-2; *Prato 1969**, pp. 26-7; *Meiss, 1970**, p. 98; *MMOA**, 1971, pp. 33-34; *Dutch Show**, 1974, pp. 17, 41, 53-54.

JOURNALS

Sirèn, O., *RADA*, 1914, p. 232; Offner, R., *AA*, VII, 1919, pp. 190-1; van Marle, R., *BM*, XLVI, 1925, p. 188; Salmi, M., *RA*, XI, 1929, pp. 144-5; Berenson, B., *DD*, XI, 4, 1930-3, pp. 1039-1073; Coletti, L., *E*, XCVI, 2, 1942, pp. 460-78; Longhi, R., *CA*, V, 1940, pp. 145-91; Bartarelli, A., *ASP*, XXXI, 1955, p. 53; Baratti, A.A., *A*, LIX, 1960, pp. 7-15; Marcucci, L., *Como*, IV, Inv. 1960, p. 7-14; Procacci, U., *AAM*, 13/16, 1961, pp. 49-66; Marcucci, L., *AV*, I, 4, 1962, pp. 11-19; Smith, M. Q., *BM*, 104, 1962, p. 110; Birkmeyer, K. M., *GBA*, LX, 1962, 6, pp. 475-80; Marabottini, A., *C*, XVI, 1/2, 1965, pp. 23-34; Longhi, R., *PA*, XVI, 183, 1965, pp. 8-16; Bellosi, I., *PA*, XVI, 187/7, 1965, pp. 18-43; Boskovits, M., *ZKG*, XXXI, 4, 1968, p. 278; Boskovits, M., *AI*, III , 25/26, 1970, p. 43, note 13; Boskovits, M., *RDA*, II, 1971, pp. 55-58; Boskovits, M., *RAAM*, II, 1971, pp. 56-57; Fahy, E., *MM*, XXIX, 10, 1971, p. 433; Gonzalez-Palacios, A., *AV*, X, 3, 1971, pp. 3-9; *Edit.*, *GBA*, LXXVII, 113, Feb. 1971, p. 137, no. 633 (supplement); Fahy, E., *MM*, XXIX, 10, June 1971, p. 433; Gregori, M., *PA*, XXIII, Mar. 1972, pp. 3-35; Bellosi, L., *MKIF*, XVII, 2-3, 1973, pp. 180, 190.

SIGNED AND DATED WORKS

Prato, Galleria Comunale 5. Polyptych: Madonna & Child Enthroned with Sts. Catherine, Bernard, Bartholomew & Barnabas. s. (fig. 380).
1365 Florence, Accademia 8467. Panel: *Pietà*. s & d. (fig. 378).

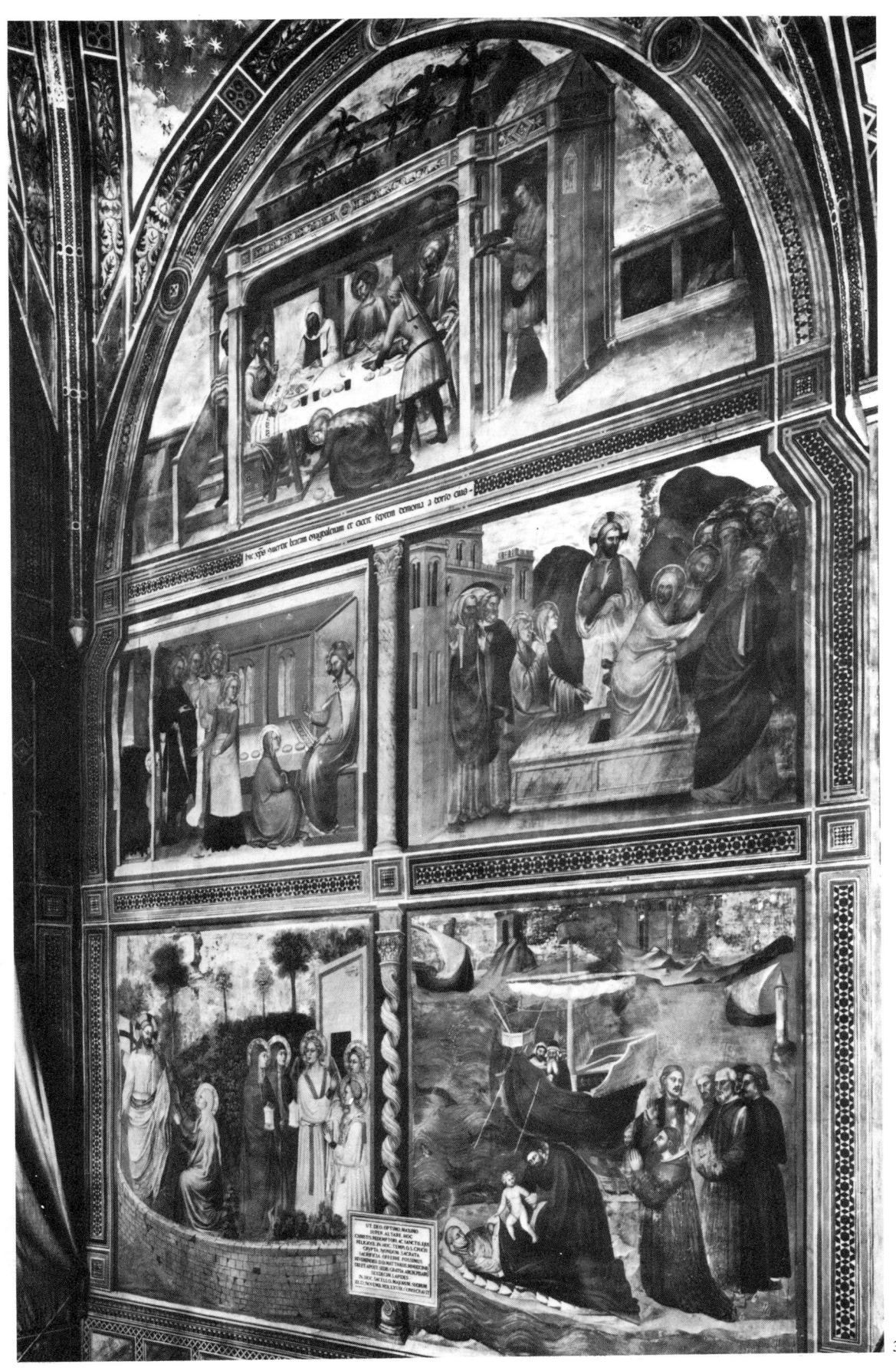

364

364.   *Scenes from the Lives of the Virgin and St Mary Magdalene: Feast in the House of Simon; Christ in the House of Mary and Martha of Bethany;*
Raising of Lazarus; Noli me tangere; Story of the Prince of Marseilles. Fresco. Florence, S. Croce, Sacristy, Rinuccini Chapel. Alinari 3961.
(Three upper scenes by Giovanni da Milano; two lower by the Master of the Rinuccini Chapel: see figs. 385-407.

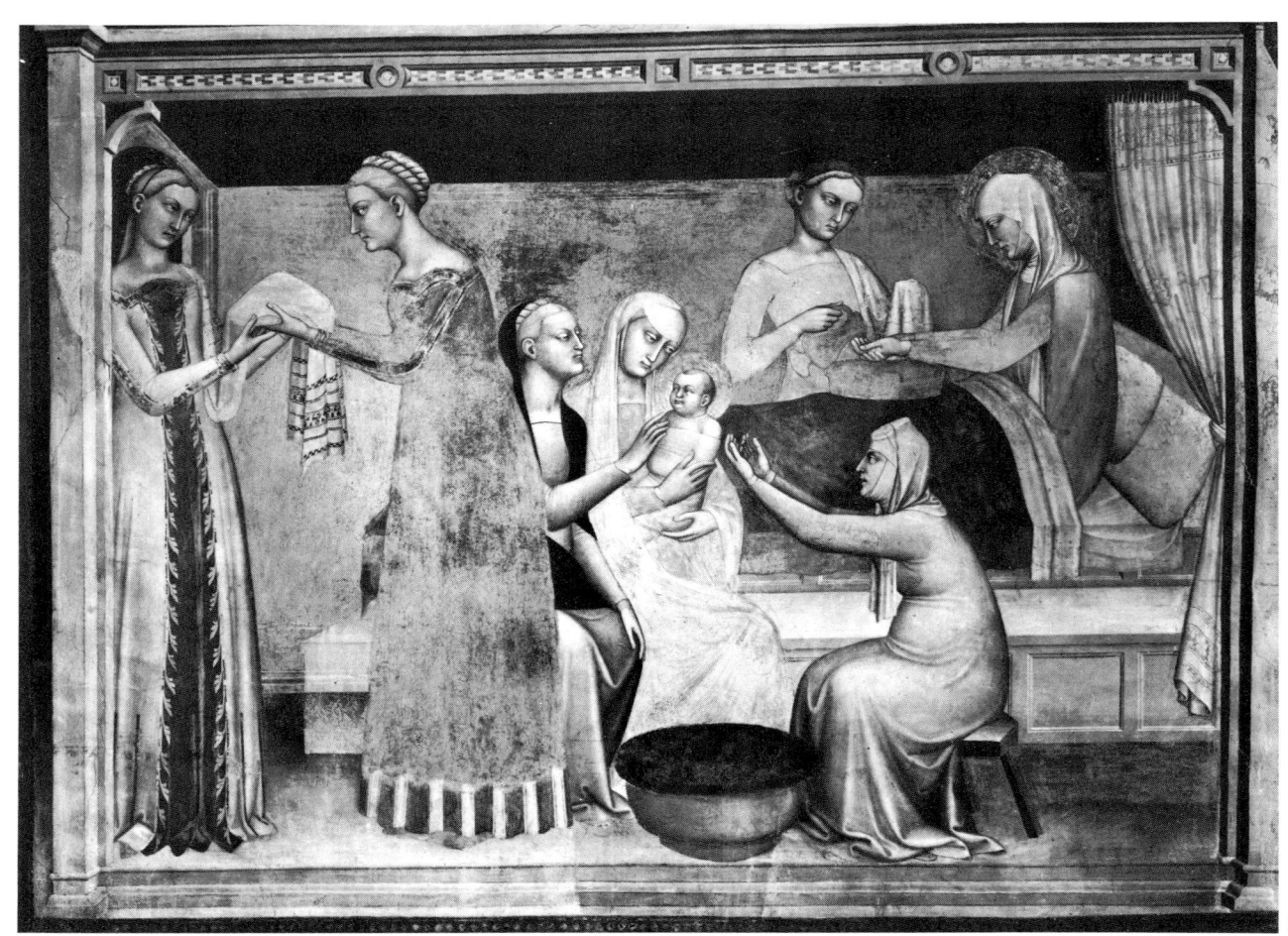

365

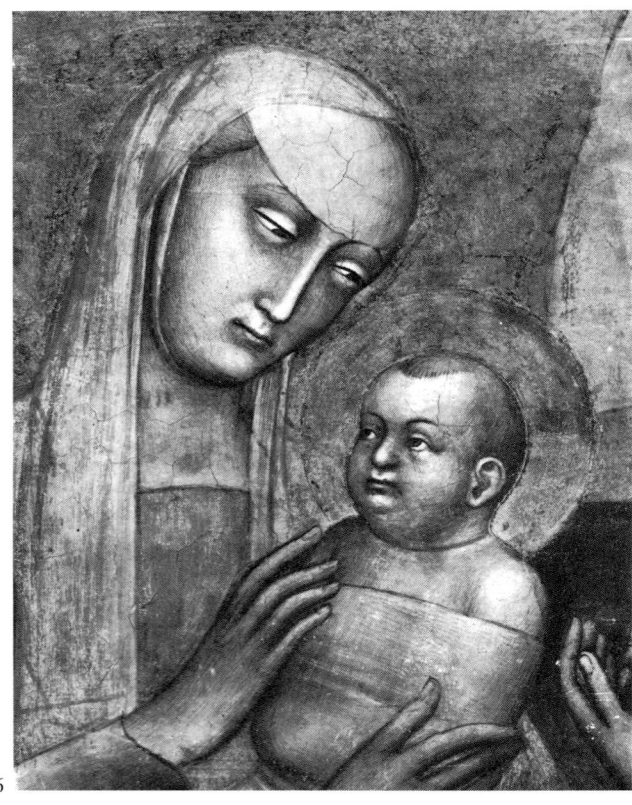

366

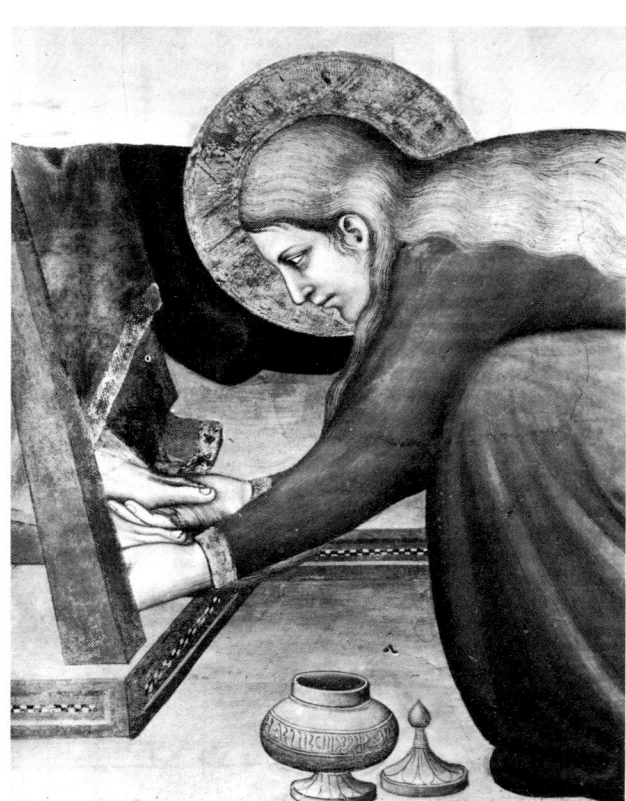

367

365. *Birth of the Virgin. Fresco. Florence, S. Croce, Sacristy, Rinuccini Chapel. SGF 116599. 1360-65.*
366. *Woman and Child, detail of fig. 365. Fresco. Florence, S. Croce, Sacristy, Rinuccini Chapel. SGF 116609. 1360-65.*
367. *St Mary Magdalene annointing Christ's Feet, detail of fig. 365. Fresco. Florence, S. Croce, Sacristy, Rinuccini Chapel. SGF 116631. 1360-65.*

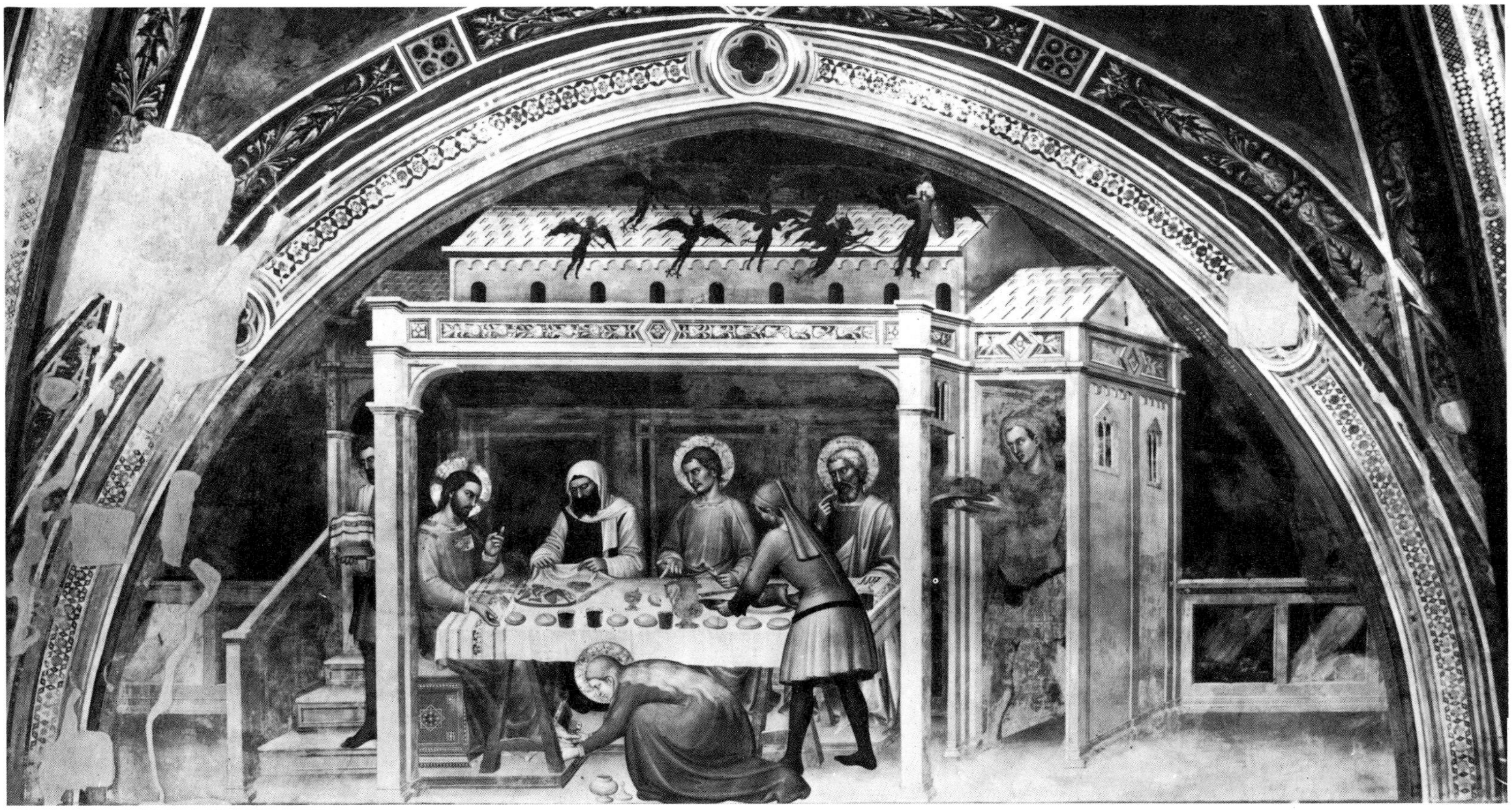

368

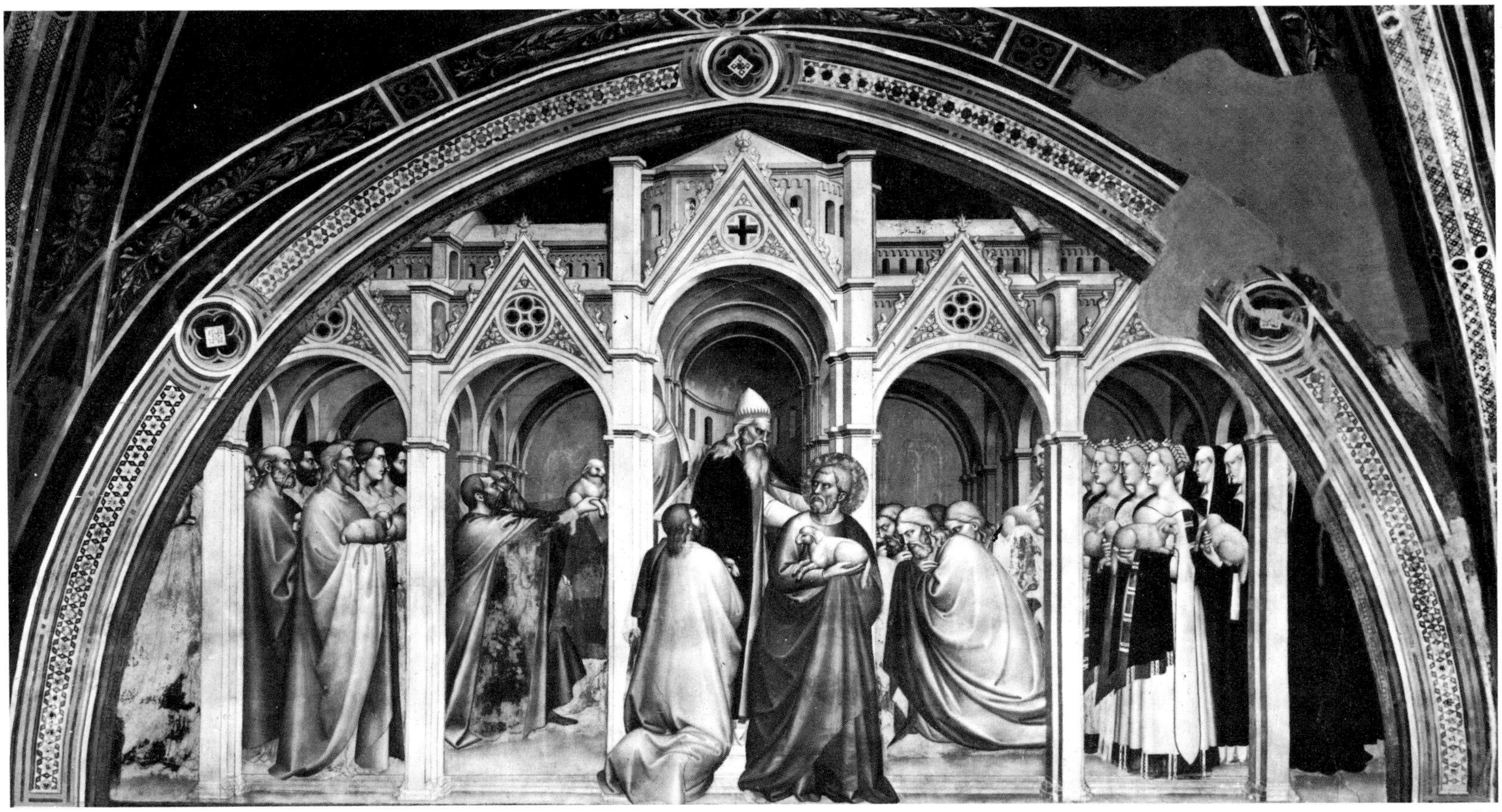

369

368.   Feast in the House of Simon. Fresco. Florence, S. Croce, Sacristy, Rinuccini Chapel. SGF 116619. 1360-65.
369.   Expulsion of Joachim from the Temple. Fresco. Florence, S. Croce, Sacristy, Rinuccini Chapel. SGF 116556. 1360-65.

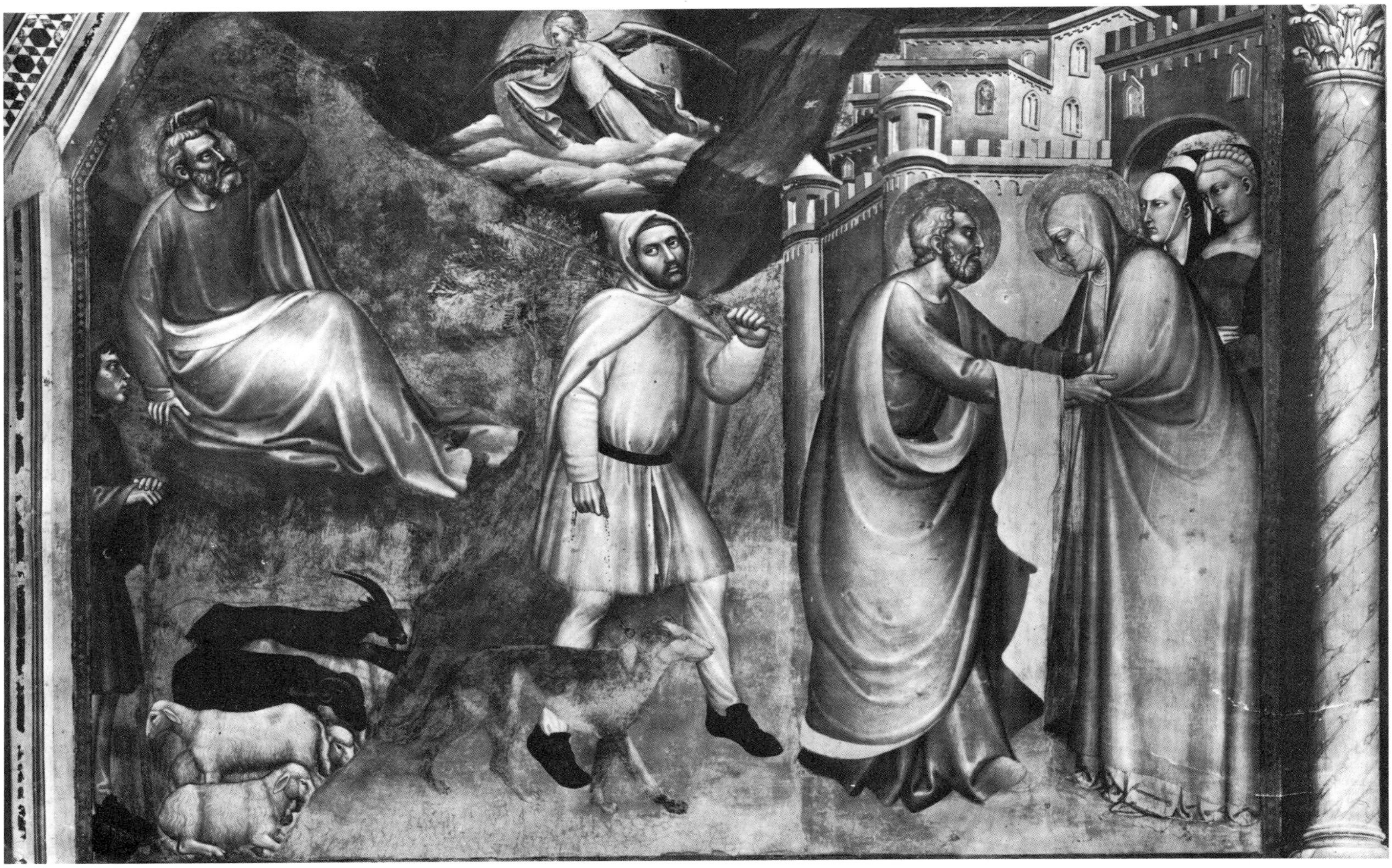

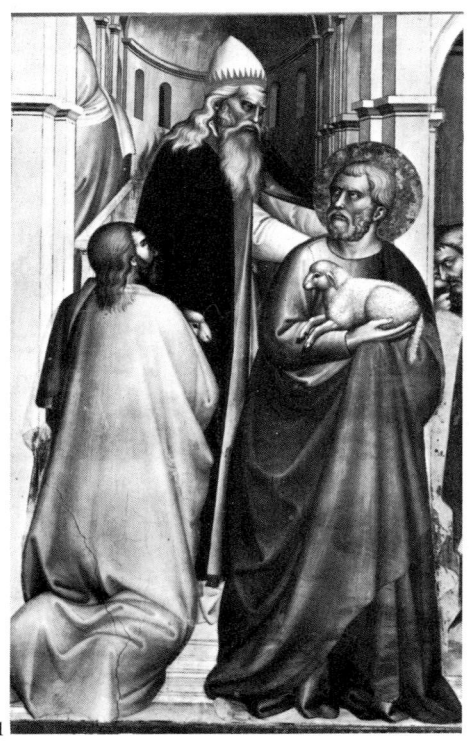

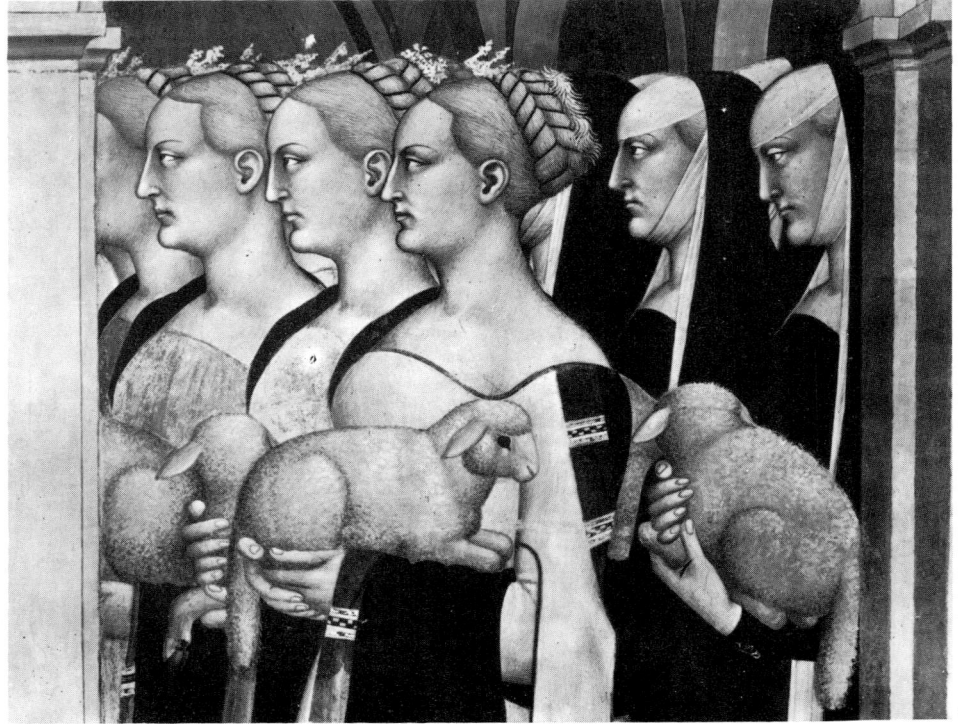

370. *Annunciation to Joachim and the Meeting at the Golden Gate. Fresco. Florence, S. Croce, Sacristy, Rinuccini Chapel. SGF 116582. 1360-65.*
371. *Expulsion of Joachim, detail of fig. 369. Fresco. Florence, S. Croce, Sacristy, Rinuccini Chapel. SGF 116567. 1360-65.*
372. *Woman carrying lambs, detail of fig. 369. Fresco. Florence, S. Croce, Sacristy, Rinuccini Chapel. SGF 116577. 1360-65.*

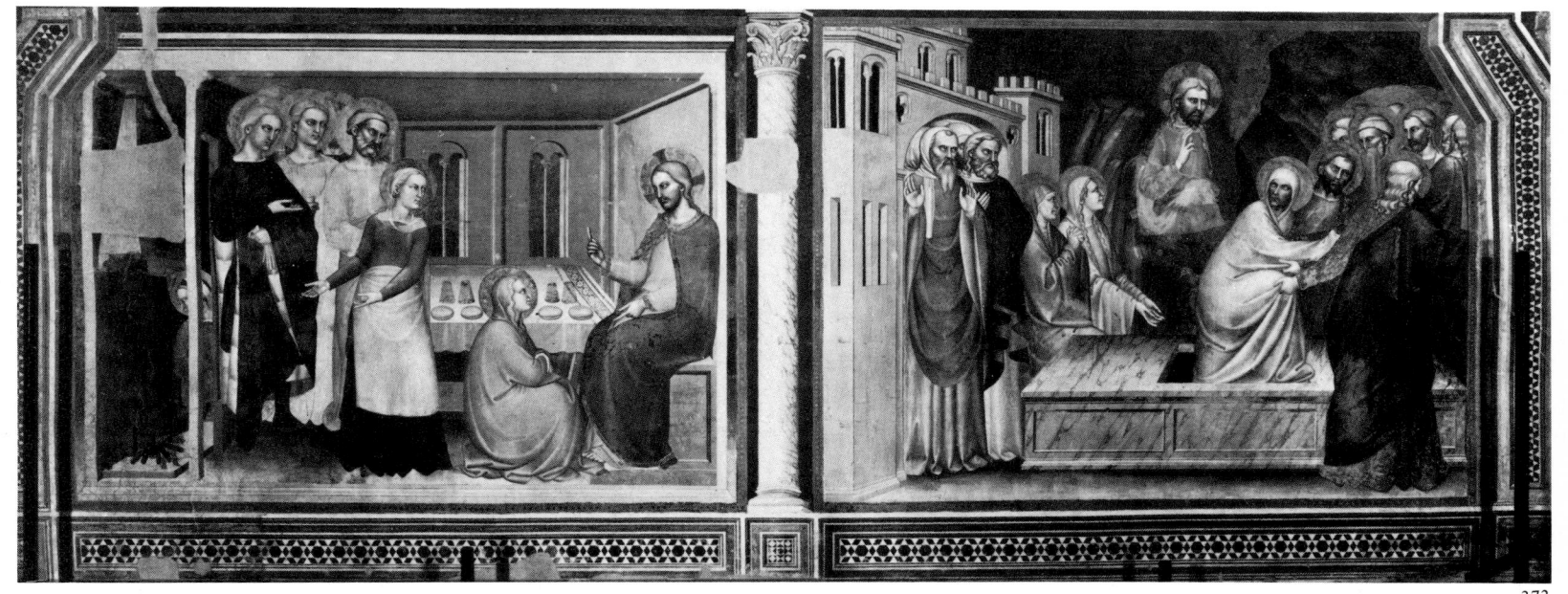

373

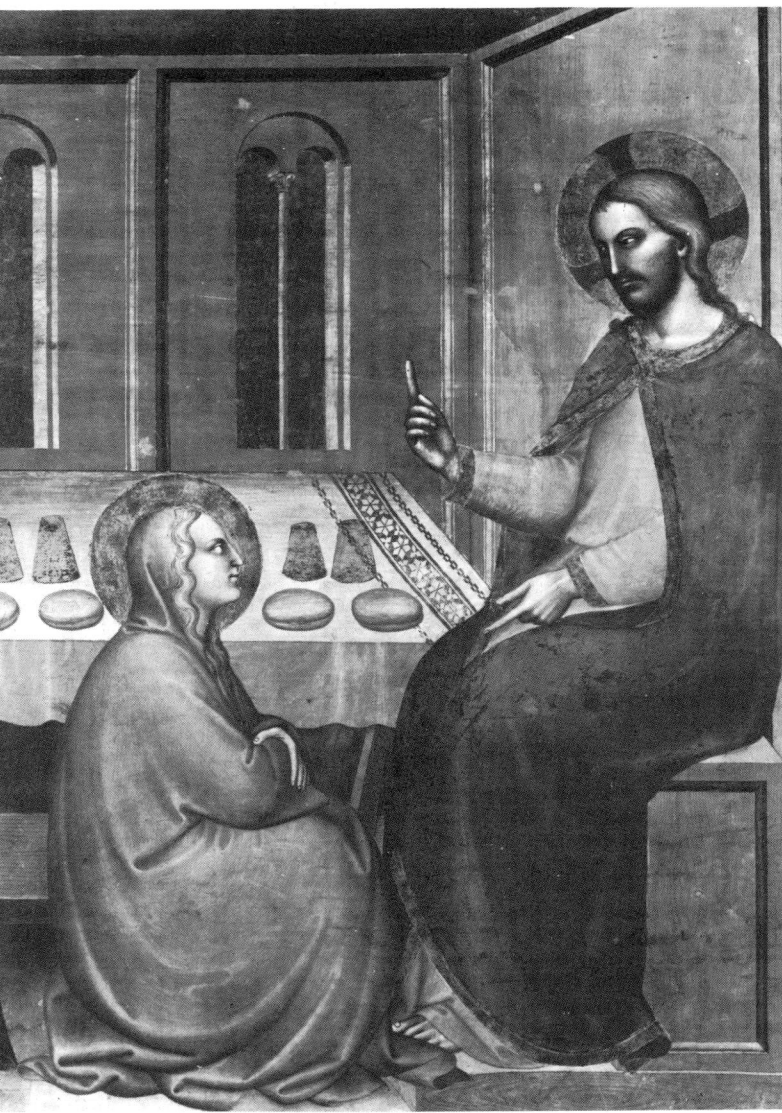

374

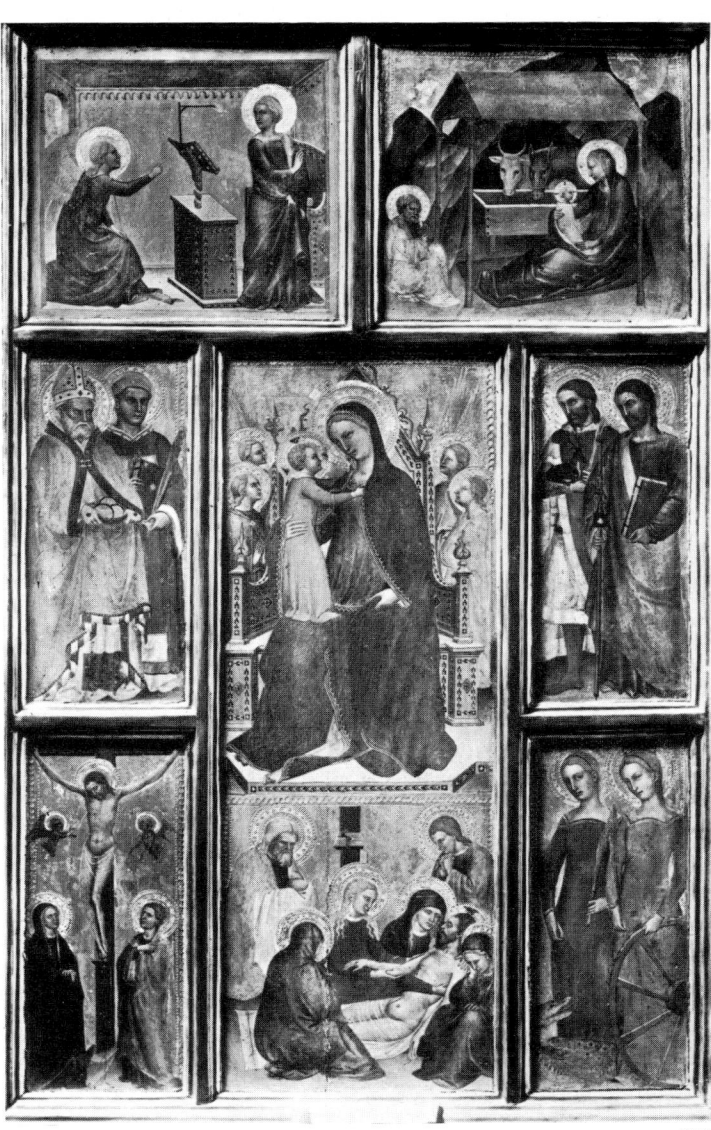

375

373.   *Christ in the House of Mary and Martha of Bethany and the Raising of Lazarus. Fresco. Florence, S. Croce, Sacristy, Rinuccini Chapel. SGF 116554. 1360-65.*

374.   *Mary listening to Christ, detail of fig. 373. Fresco. Florence, S. Croce, Sacristy, Rinuccini Chapel. SGF 116665. 1360-65.*

375.   *Madonna and Child Enthroned with four Angels, Annunciation, Nativity, Sts Nicholas and Lawrence, Sts Eustace and James, Christ on the Cross with the Virgin and St John, Lamentation, Sts Margaret and Catherine. Panel. Rome, Galleria Nazionale (Palazzo Barberini), no. FN 695. 87 × 55.   Alinari 40791.*

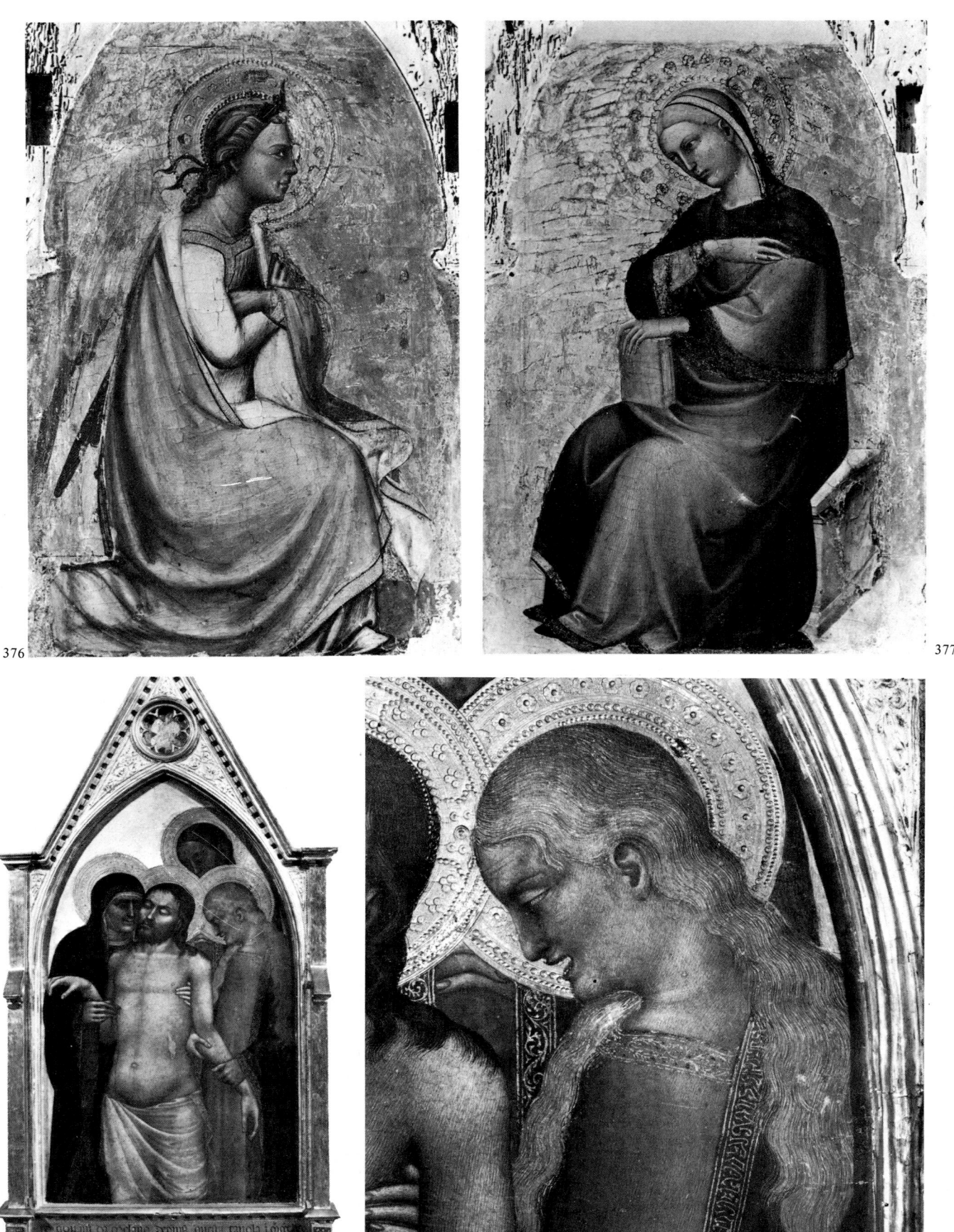

376. *Announcing Angel. Panel. Pisa, Museo Nazionale di S. Matteo. no. 1709. 50 × 32. SGPLLM 2895.*
377. *Virgin Annunciate. Panel. Pisa, Museo Nazionale di S. Matteo. no. 1709. 50 × 32. SGPLLM 2898.*
378. *Pietà. Panel. Florence, Accademia, no. 8467. 58 × 22. SGF 105238. s & d. 1365.*
379. *Head of St Mary Magdalene, detail of fig. 378. Panel. Florence, Accademia. no. 8467. SGF 145345. s & d. 1365.*

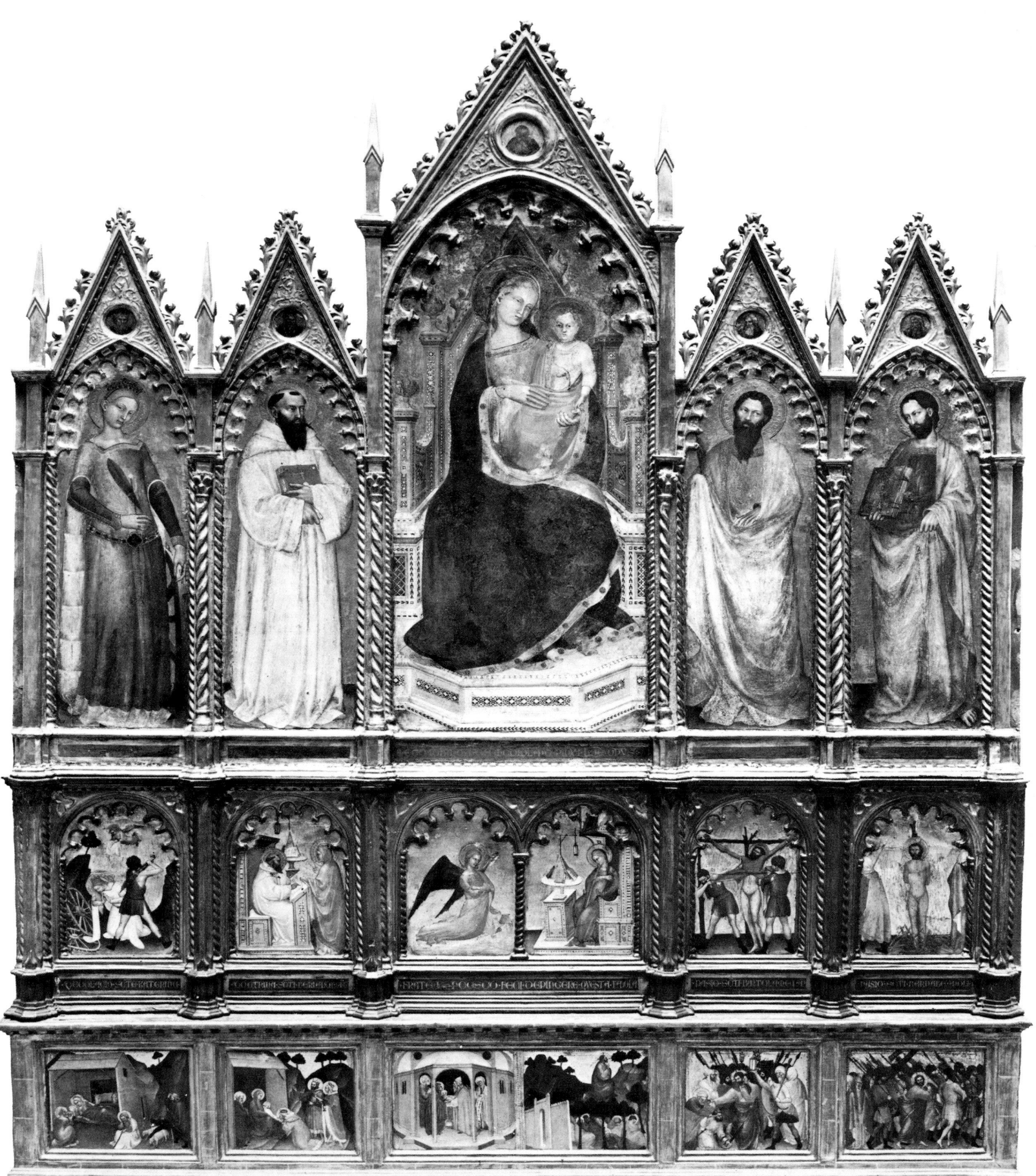

380. *Polyptych: Madonna and Child Enthroned with Sts Catherine, Bernard, Bartholomew and Barnabas. Above: five Prophets. First predella: Beheading of St Catherine, Vision of St Bernard, Annunciation, Flaying of St Bartholomew, Martyrdom of St Barnabas. Second predella: Nativity, Adoration of the Magi, Circumcision, Agony in the Garden, Betrayal of Christ, Way to Calvary. Panel. Prato, Galleria Comunale. no. 5. cp : 112 × 51 ; lp 78 × 27.5. SGF 107520. s.*

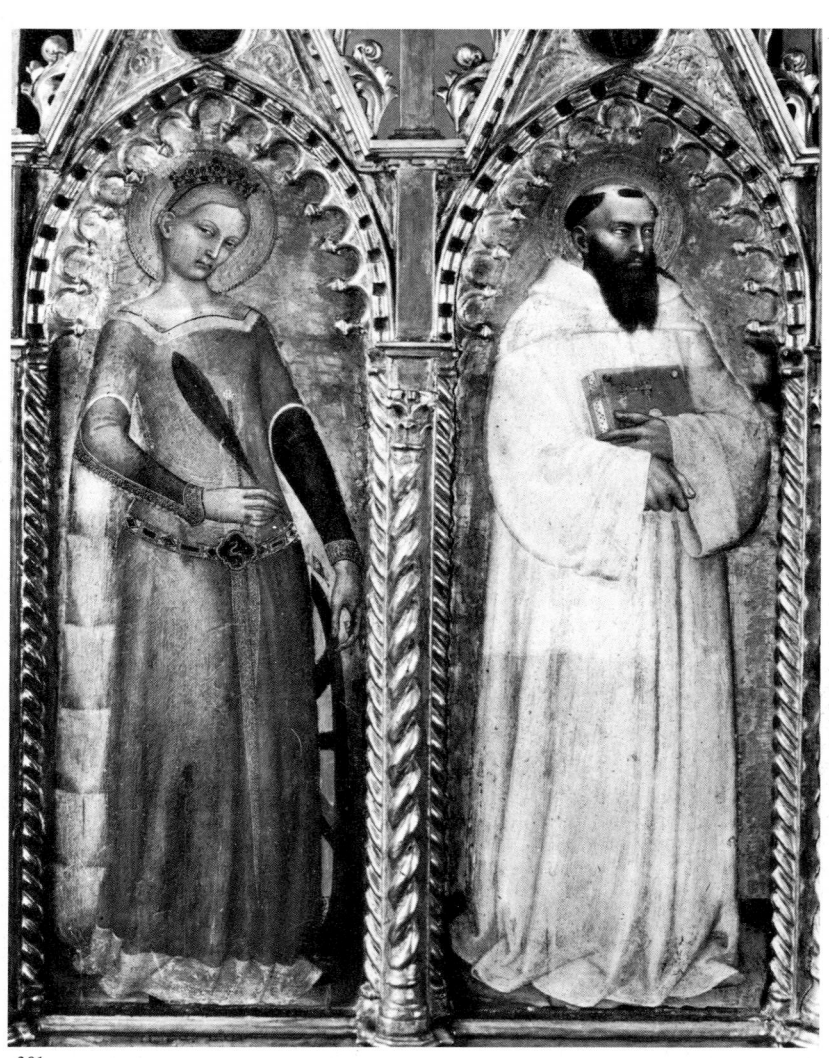

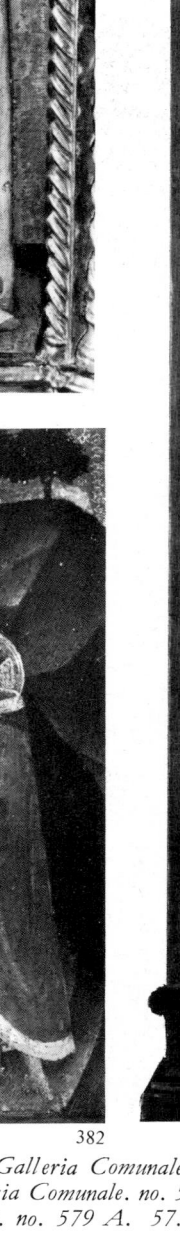

381

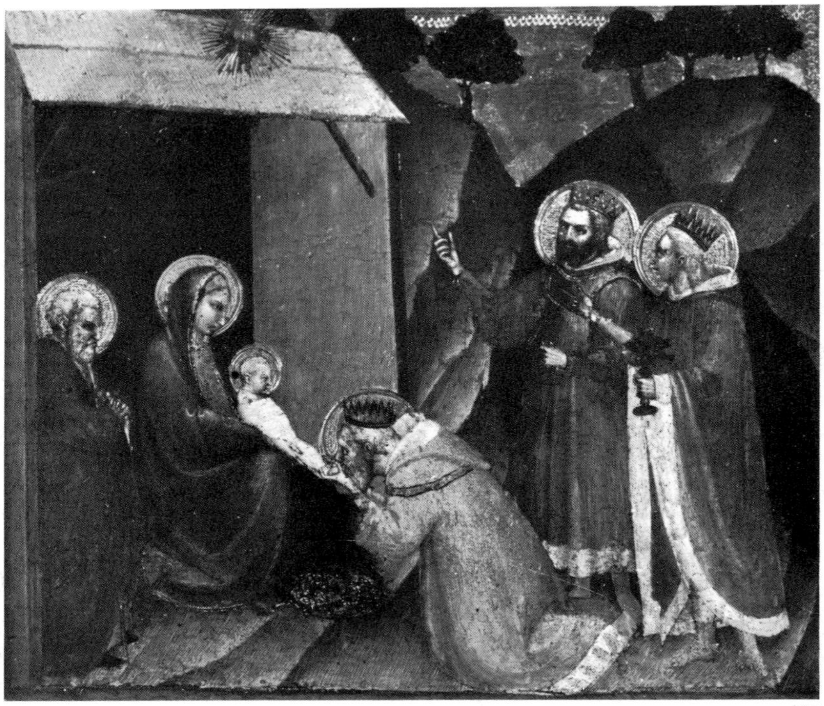

382

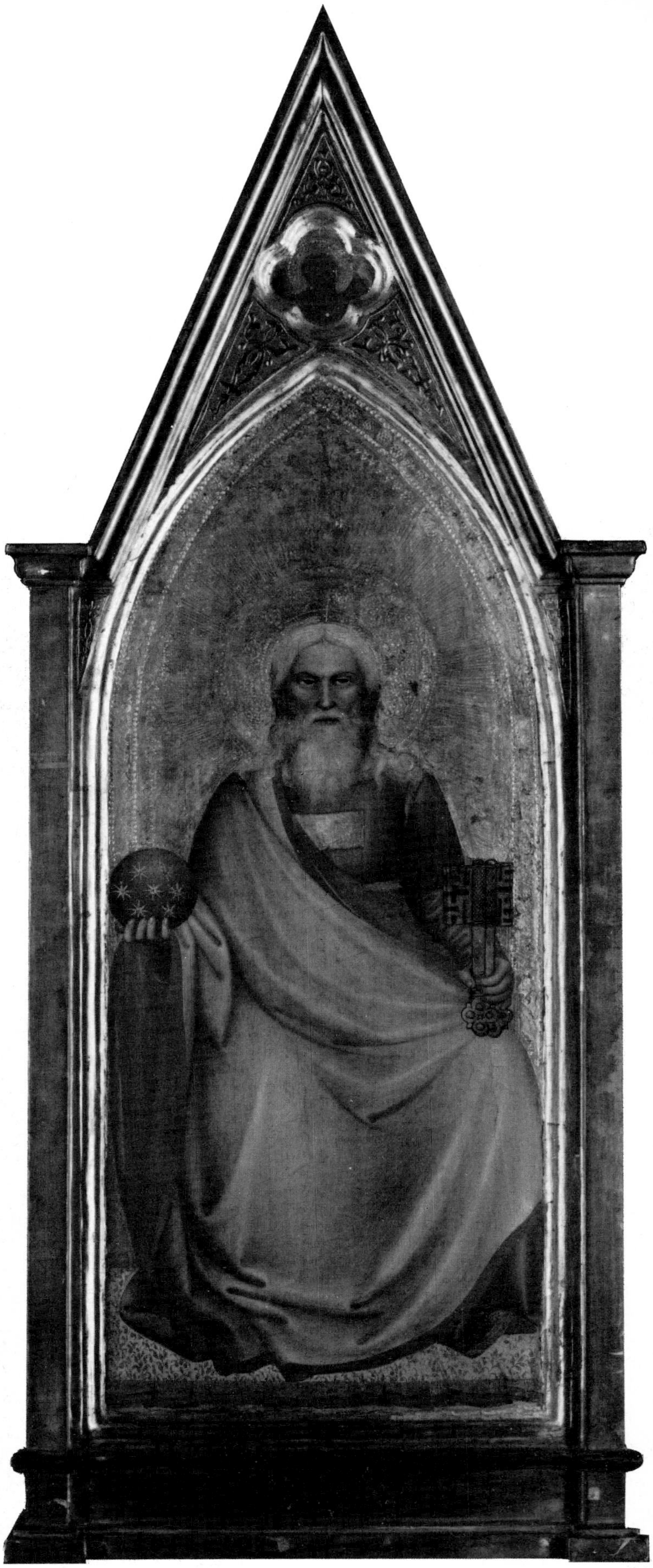

383

381. *Sts Catherine and Bernard, detail of fig. 380. Panel. Prato, Galleria Comunale. no. 5. SGF 107804. s.*
382. *Adoration of the Magi, detail of fig. 380. Panel. Prato, Galleria Comunale. no. 5. SGF 96914. s.*
383. *Pinnacle: God the Father. Panel. London, National Gallery. no. 579 A. 57.8 × 25.4. Museum photo.*

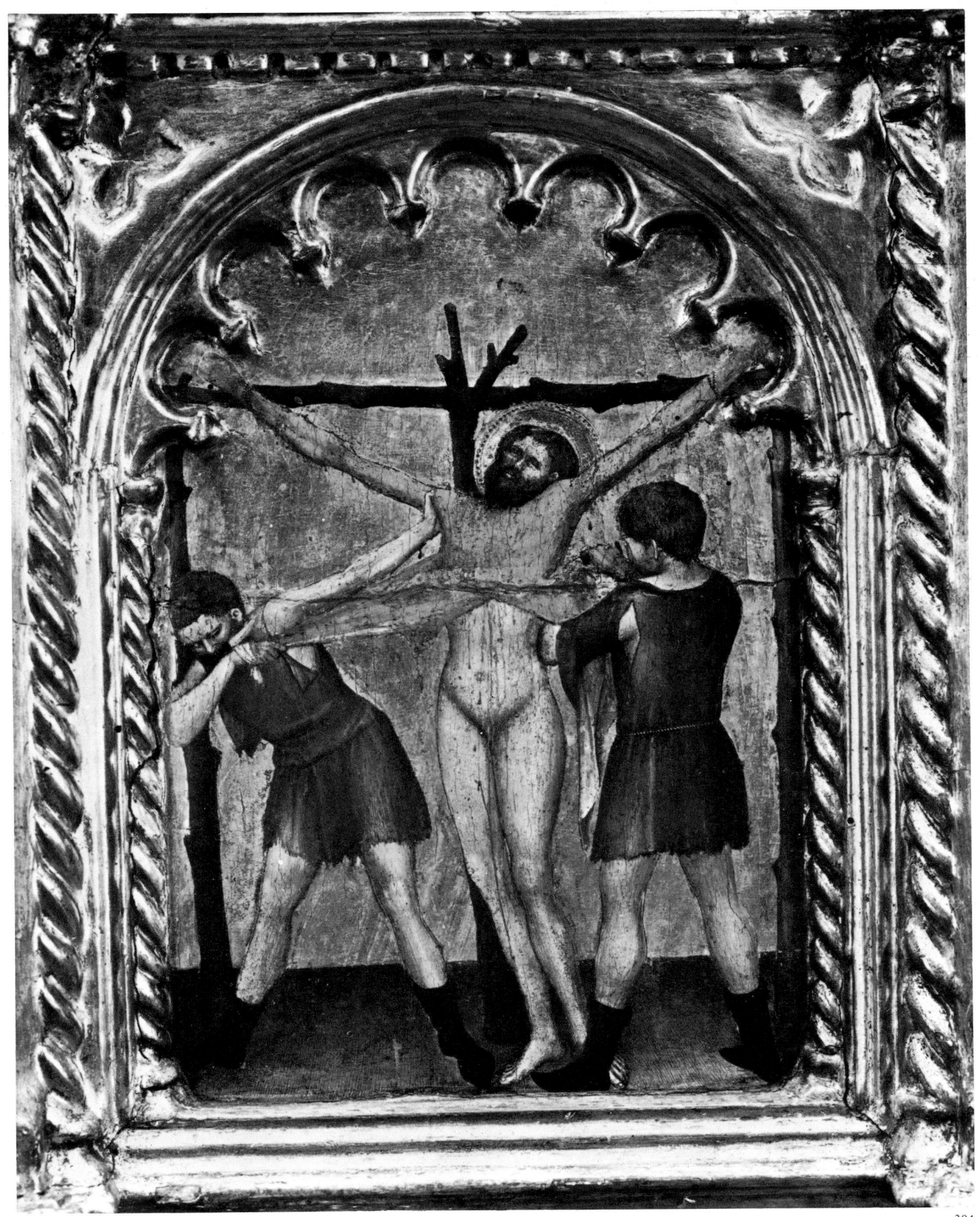

384. *Martyrdom of St Bartholomew, detail of fig. 380. Panel. Prato, Galleria Comunale. no. 5. SGF 115812.*

MASTER OF THE RINUCCINI CHAPEL

It had escaped him that the significant fact about this painter of the lowest tier in the Rinuccini Chapel, is not the fortuitous one that he helped Giovanni, but rather that he was an autonomous master, intrinsically independent of him. Giovanni, it must be remembered, was a foreigner, with a foreign manner and a foreign accent; the painter of the lowest tier was, on the contrary, formed on indigenous Florentine traditions.....
If the master who undertook to complete the series was of different affinities and character, his share of it on the other hand, reveals that he pledged himself to carry the painting forward so far as possible on Giovanni's plans, and what is clearer still, in Giovanni's palette. It is this adherence to Giovanni's color that has been deluding most eyes. But leaving the color for the present out of our reckoning, notice how wide the disparity between the two styles really is.
Giovanni's figures are organized to a rhythmic coherence on the flat from left to right by the flowing lines of their clean-edged patterns. Such organization implies a direct scale-relation of these to the area and its limits. Every object is in the compositional system and becomes a directly operative factor in it.
But the figures are at the same time organized in depth — in a way that reveals depth and surface to be correlated manifestations of the same organizing principle. Everything is further harmonized by a fluid and binding chiaroscuro, by a physical atmosphere, by a poetic and sensitive vision which is of a different racial quality than that of his Florentine successor. In this atmosphere, the individual figure — of the texture and consistency of which Giovanni had a northern sense — is modulated to a soft, swelling plasticity, which together with the line, liberates it from the mere heaviness of mass.
Such a way of seeing is radically diverse from that of the master who finished the Rinuccini cycle. In his share of the frescoes there is by contrast, a rude heaviness of bulk, a modelling that always uncovers the raw saliences of the figure, but never becomes qualitative. No linear melody unites the elements of the surface; in fact there is no such linealistic consciousness in this painter, as in the Sienizing Giovanni, and none of his optical sensibility. The action, which in Giovanni's frescoes moves with an ideal dramatic progression, becomes in the lowest tier, scattered and manifold, to produce the illusion of a fullness and variety of life. There is no gradation of accents, and no swiftly seizable relief of its determinants in an ideally unified action as in Giovanni, whose poetry is here replaced by an austere, somewhat crabbed prose. Passing from the upper to the lowest tiers, the total effect is starkly realistic.....

from R. Offner, p. 120-121, *Studies in Florentine Painting*, New York, 1927.

We now attribute to Giovanni all these paintings [in the Rinuccini Chapel in Santa Croce], except for three: the two lower ones on the left wall, and the lowest one on the right wall; these are by another painter, who is called the Master of the Rinuccini Chapel.....

from F. Rossi, p. 85, *Arte Italiana in Santa Croce*, Florence, 1962.

A painter between Orcagna and Giovanni del Biondo, active in the third quarter of the fourteenth century.

from B. Berenson, p. 143, *Italian Pictures of the Renaissance. Florentine School*, Vol. I, London, 1963.

The latest studies by Procacci (1961) have revealed that, contrary to what was believed, the commission for the frescoes in the Rinuccini Chapel in Santa Croce was not given to Giovanni by the Rinuccini family. Recent restoration work has brought to light the crest of the Guidalotti family frescoed under the tempera crest of the Rinuccini family. This unforeseen discovery has made Procacci suggest that the commission for the frescoes of the chapel was given to Giovanni through the wish expressed in a will of some member of the Guidalotti family, probably a certain Lupo di Lizio. The change of patronage from the Guidalotti to the Rinuccini family was the reason the decoration of the chapel was not finished by Giovanni da Milano, but by an unknown, mediocre painter chosen by the new patron; the artist today is known by the name " Master of the Rinuccini Chapel ".....

from L. Castelfranchi-Vegas, p. 1, *Giovanni da Milano* (I Maestri del Colore, 111), Milan, 1965.

Florentine School. Active second half of fourteenth century. This anonymous painter's style is revealed in the lowest tier of frescoes in the Rinuccini Chapel of Santa Croce, Florence. He was influenced by Orcagna and even more by Nardo di Cione.

> from F. R. Shapley, p. 35, *Paintings from the Samuel H. Kress Collection*, London, 1966.

On the 27th of October, 1367, at a crowded meeting of more than three hundred Florentines — brought together to give their opinions of two models of Santa Reparata — was present among others the painter, Matteo di Pacino. He had matriculated in the Arte dei Medici e Speziali on the 25th of June 1359; much later, in 1394 (and this is the last notice we have of him), he joined the Company of San Luca....
From what one can judge in a not very good photograph of the whole triptych [signed by Matteo Pacino, once in the Stroganoff collection in Rome] the characteristics of this lead directly to that anonymous artist who finished the frescoes of Giovanni da Milano in S. Croce, named by Offner the " Master of the Rinuccini Chapel "....

> from L. Bellosi, pp. 180-181, *Mitteilungen des Kunsthistorischen Institutes in Florenz*, XVII, 2-3, 1973.

BIBLIOGRAPHY
BOOKS
An asterisk indicates a work listed in the General Bibliography

*Offner, Studies**, 1927, pp. 109-26; *Berenson, 1932**, p. 237; *Procacci, 1936**, p. 28; *Paatz**, 1940, Vol. I, p. 292; *Coletti, Vol. II**, 1946, p. 51; *Antal**, 1948, pp. 225-6; *Galetti**, " F O ", 1950, p. 1453; Marabottini, A., *Giovanni da Milano*, Florence, 1950, pp. 103, 105-6; *Meiss, 1951**, p. 77; *Toesca, 1951**, pp. 644, 763; Shapley, F. R., *Catalogue of the North Carolina Museum of Art*, Raleigh, 1960, p. 36; Rasmo, N., pp. 120-4, in *Scritti di Storia dell' Arte in Onore di Mario Salmi*, Vol. II, Rome, 1962; Rossi, F., *Arte Italiana in Santa Croce*, Florence, 1962, *Berenson, 1963**, Vol. I, p. 143; *Marcucci**, 1965, pp. 93-7; *Shapley**, 1966, pp. 35-6; Castelfranchi-Vegas, *Giovanni da Milano* (I Maestri del Colore, 111), Milan, 1965.

JOURNALS
Salmi, M., *RA*, XI, 1929, pp. 144-5; Berenson, B., *DD*, XII, 1, 1933, p. 22; Marchini, G., *RA*, XX, 1938, pp. 215-241; Oertel, R., *MKIF*, V, 4/5, 1940, pp. 217-314; Winner, M., *ZKG*, XXXIII, 4, 1970, p. 341; Bellosi, L., *MKIF*, XVII, 2-3, 1973, pp. 179-182.

There are no known dated works by the Master of the Rinuccini Chapel.

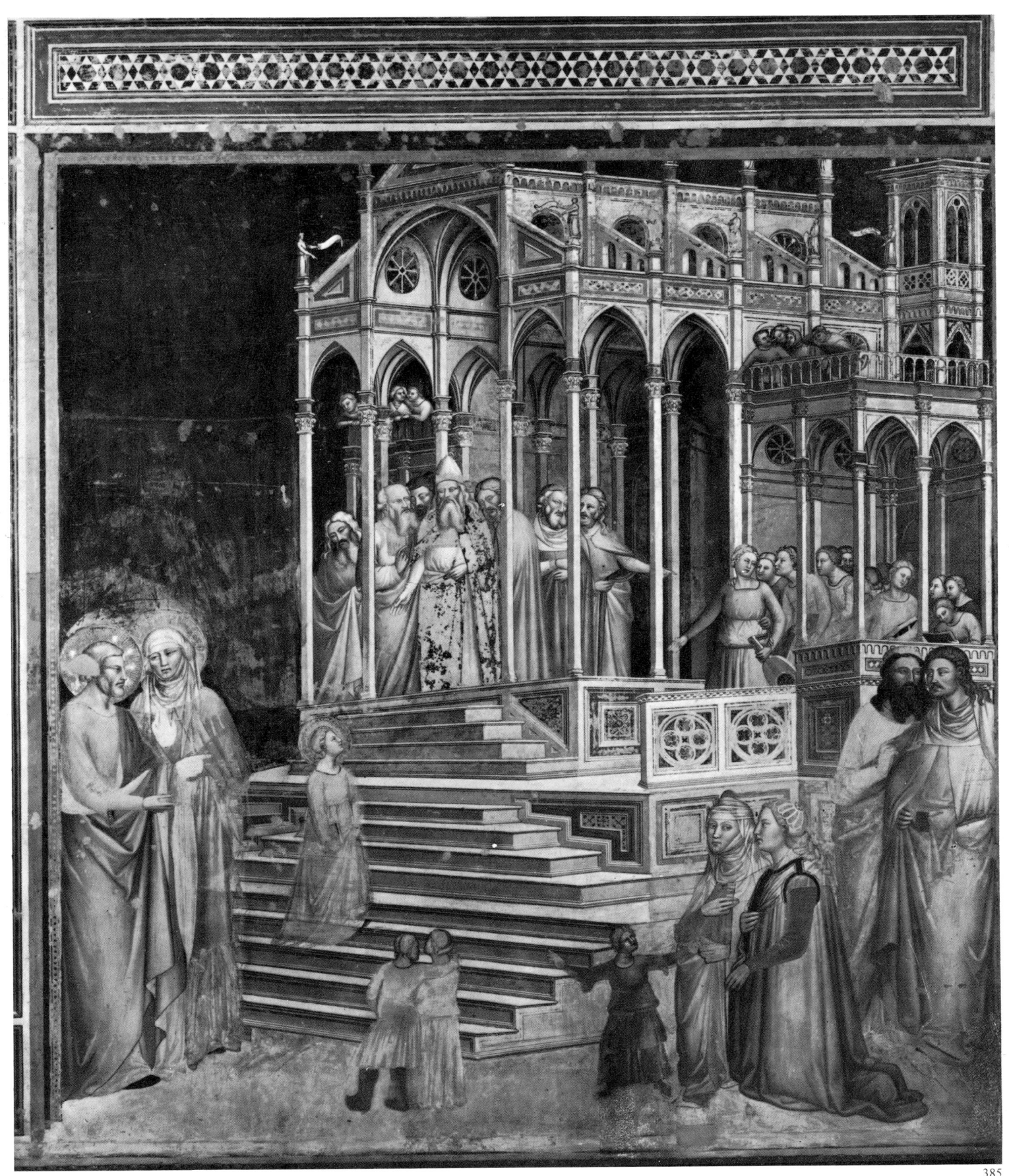

385. *Presentation of the Virgin in the Temple. Fresco. Florence, S. Croce, Sacristy, Rinuccini Chapel. Alinari 54503.*

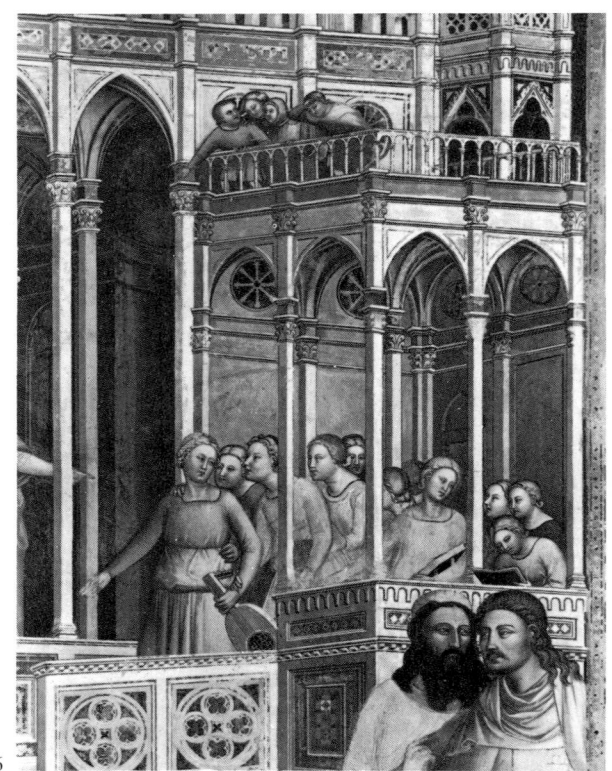

386

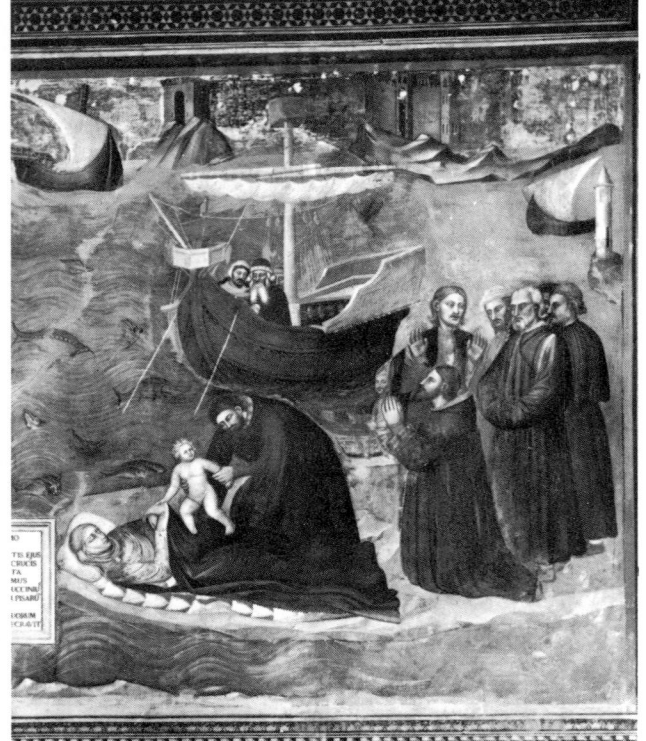

387

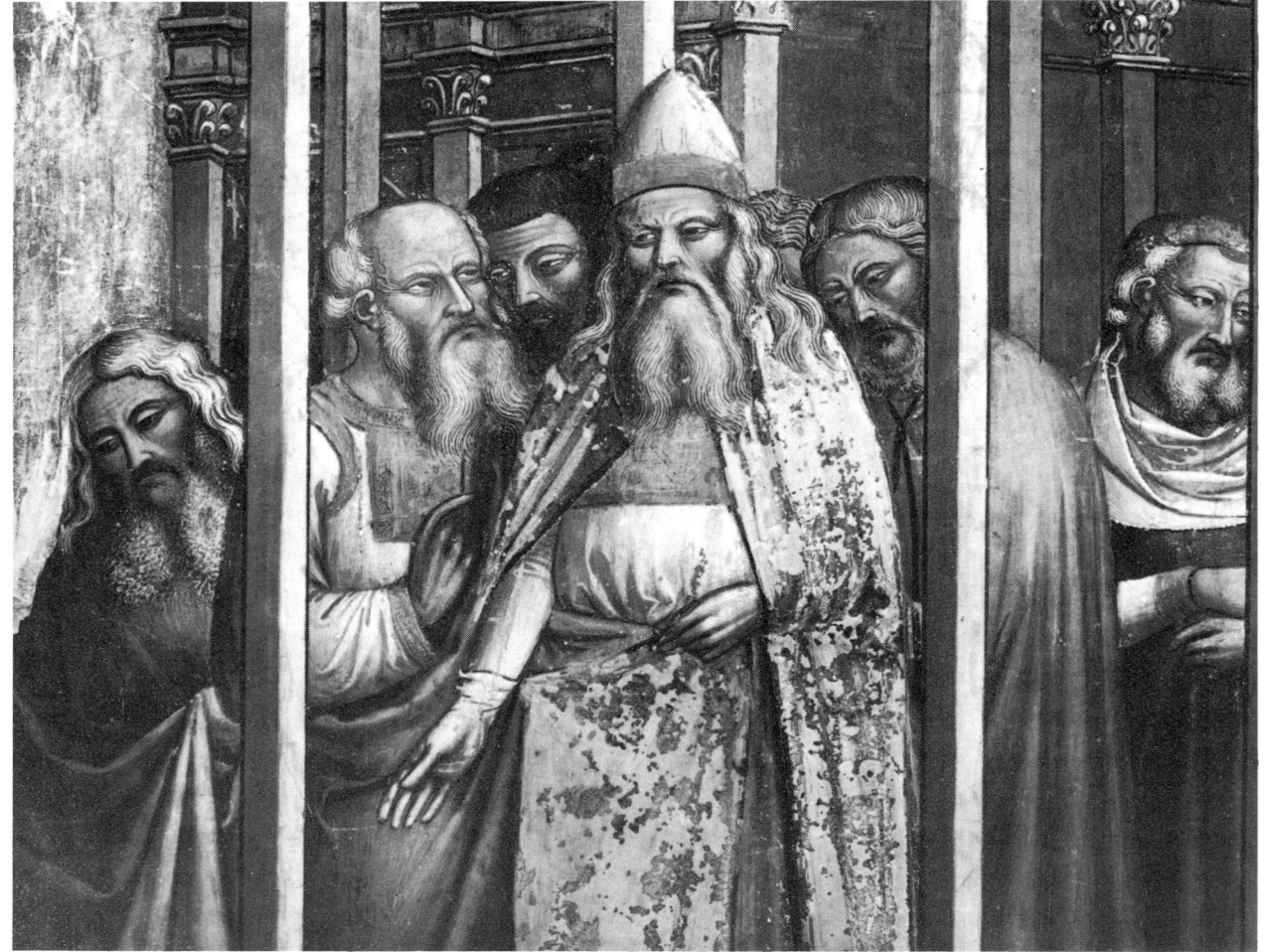

388

386. *Presentation of the Virgin in the Temple, detail of fig. 385. Fresco. Florence, S. Croce, Sacristy, Rinuccini Chapel. Alinari 54506.*
387. *Story of the Prince of Marseilles, detail of fig. 364. Fresco. Florence, S. Croce, Sacristy, Rinuccini Chapel. Alinari 3960.*
388. *Presentation of the Virgin in the Temple, detail of fig. 385. Fresco. Florence, S. Croce, Sacristy, Rinuccini Chapel. Brogi 25520.*

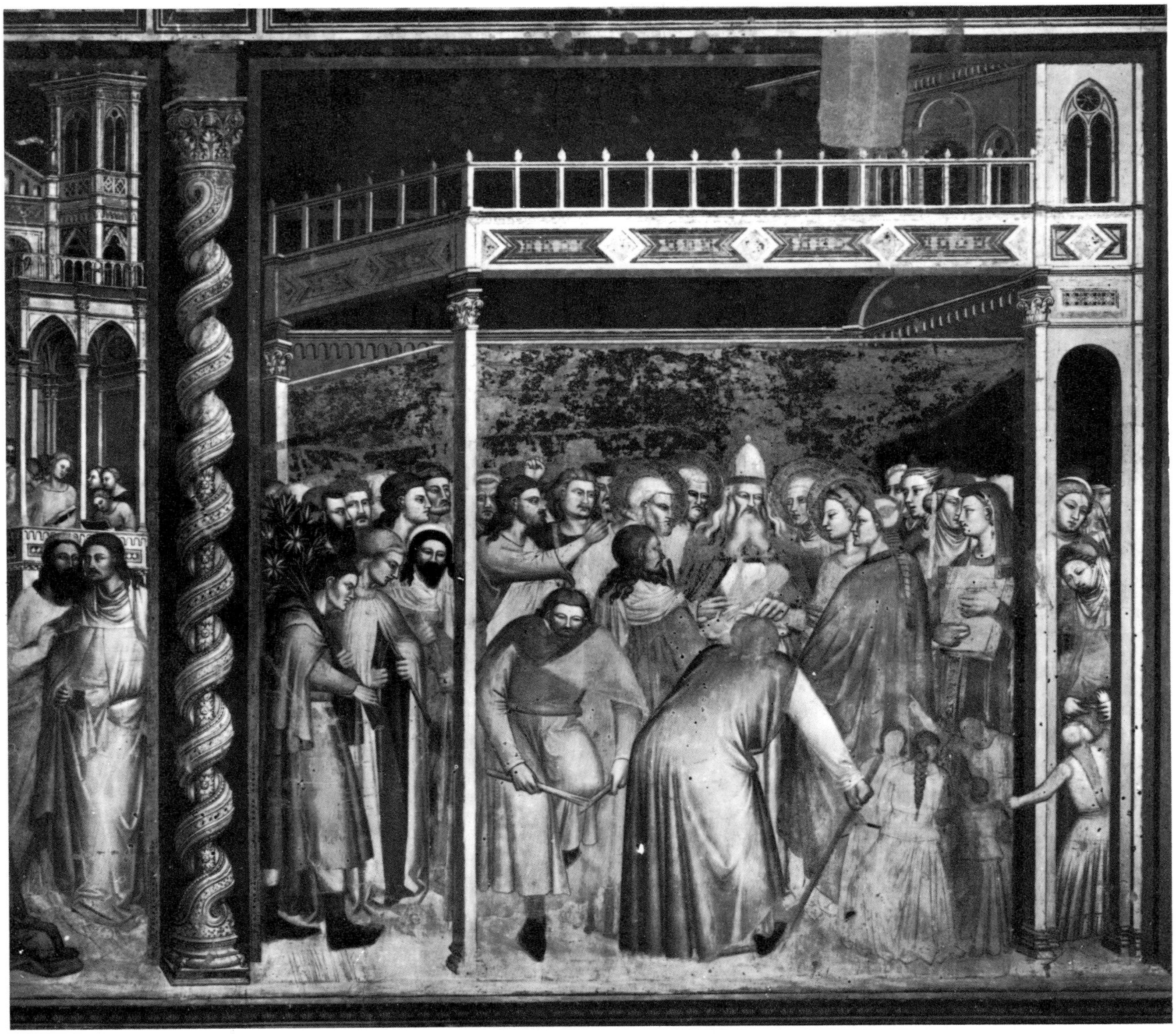

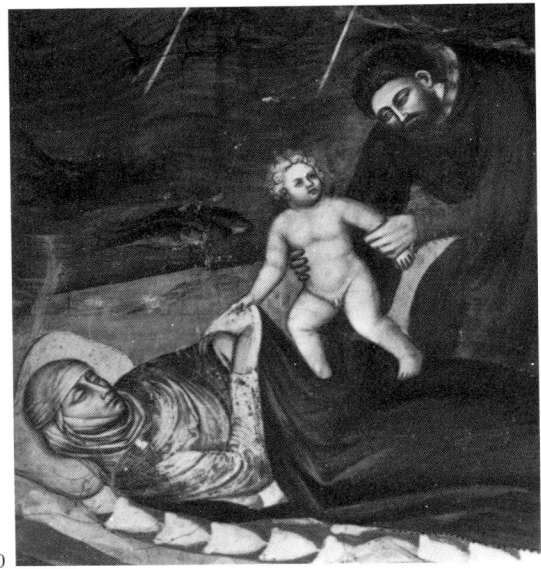

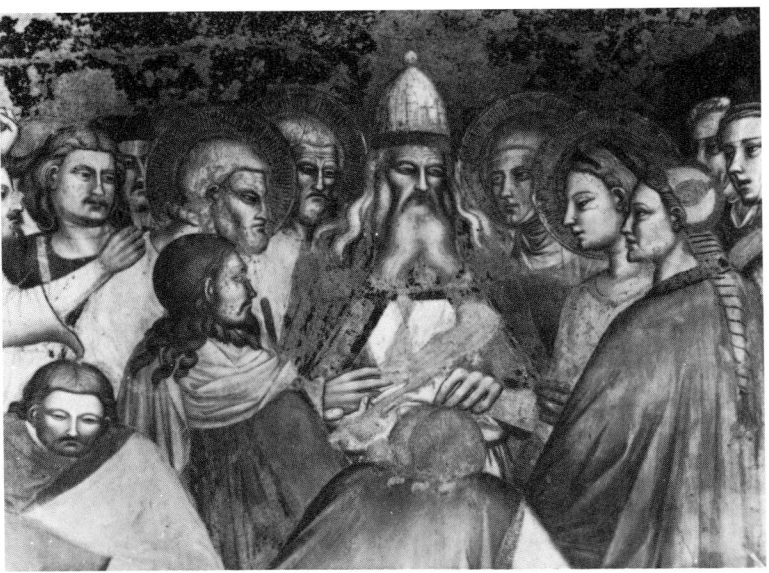

389. *Marriage of the Virgin. Fresco. Florence, S. Croce, Sacristy, Rinuccini Chapel. SGF 116685.*
390. *Story of the Prince of Marseilles, detail of fig. 364. Fresco. Florence, S. Croce, Sacristy, Rinuccini Chapel. Brogi 1936.*
391. *Marriage of the Virgin, detail of fig. 389. Fresco. Florence, S. Croce, Sacristy, Rinuccini Chapel. Alinari 54509.*

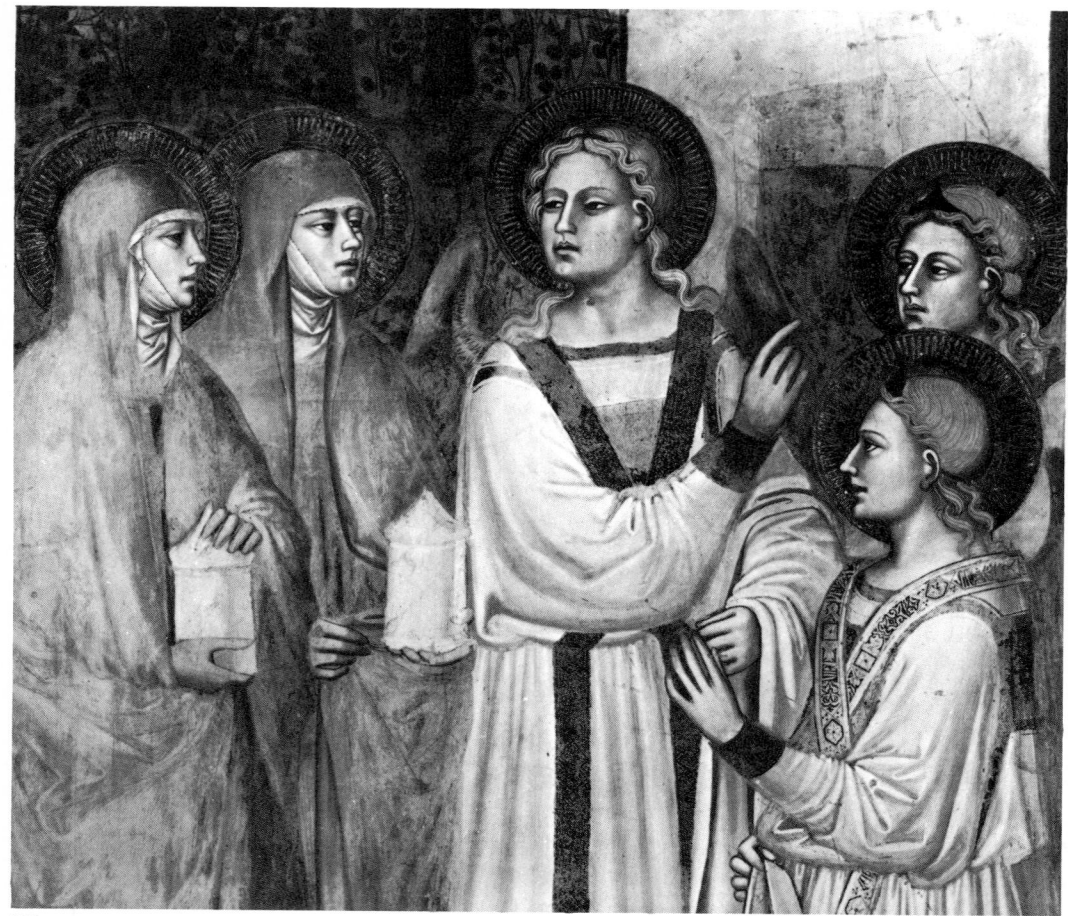

392

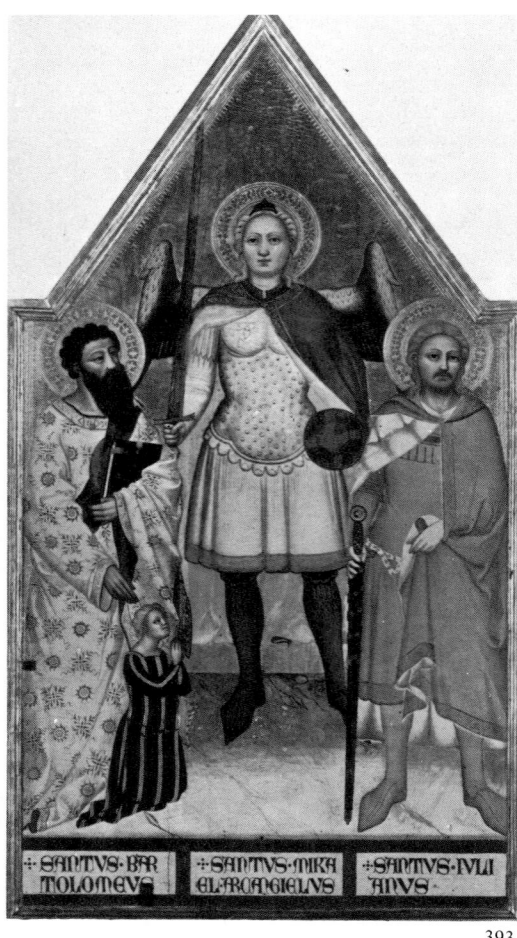

393

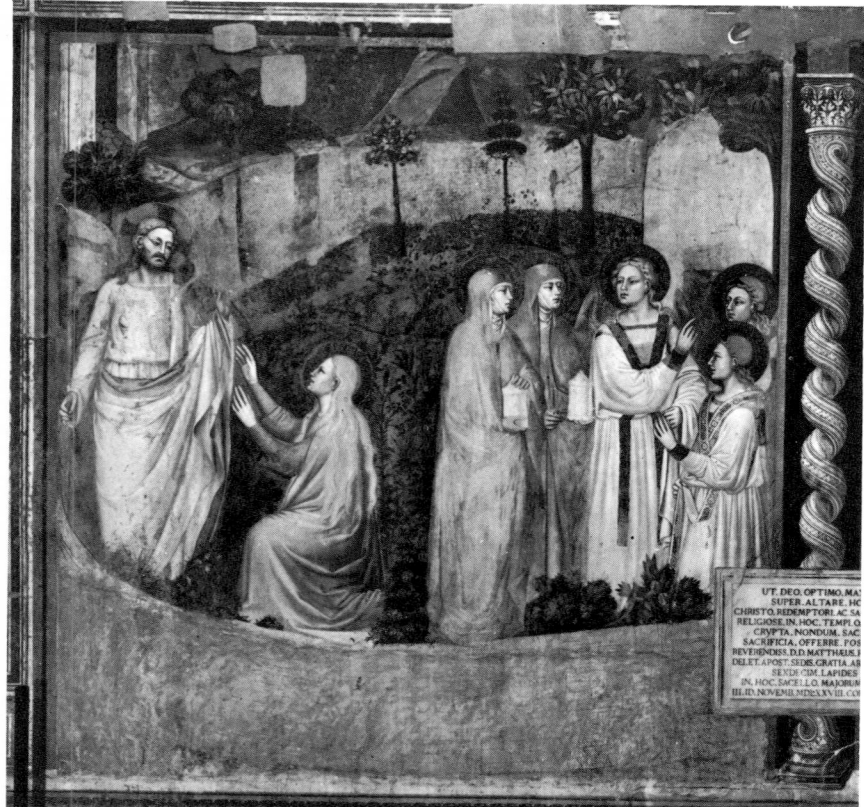

394

392. *Three Marys at the Tomb. Fresco. Florence, S. Croce, Sacristy, Rinuccini Chapel. Alinari 54511.*
393. *St Michael the Archangel with Sts Bartholomew and Julian, and Donor. Panel. Florence, Accademia. no. 6134. 156 × 87. SGF 118848.*
394. *Noli me tangere, and three Marys at the Tomb. Fresco. Florence, S. Croce, Sacristy, Rinuccini Chapel. SGF 116686.*

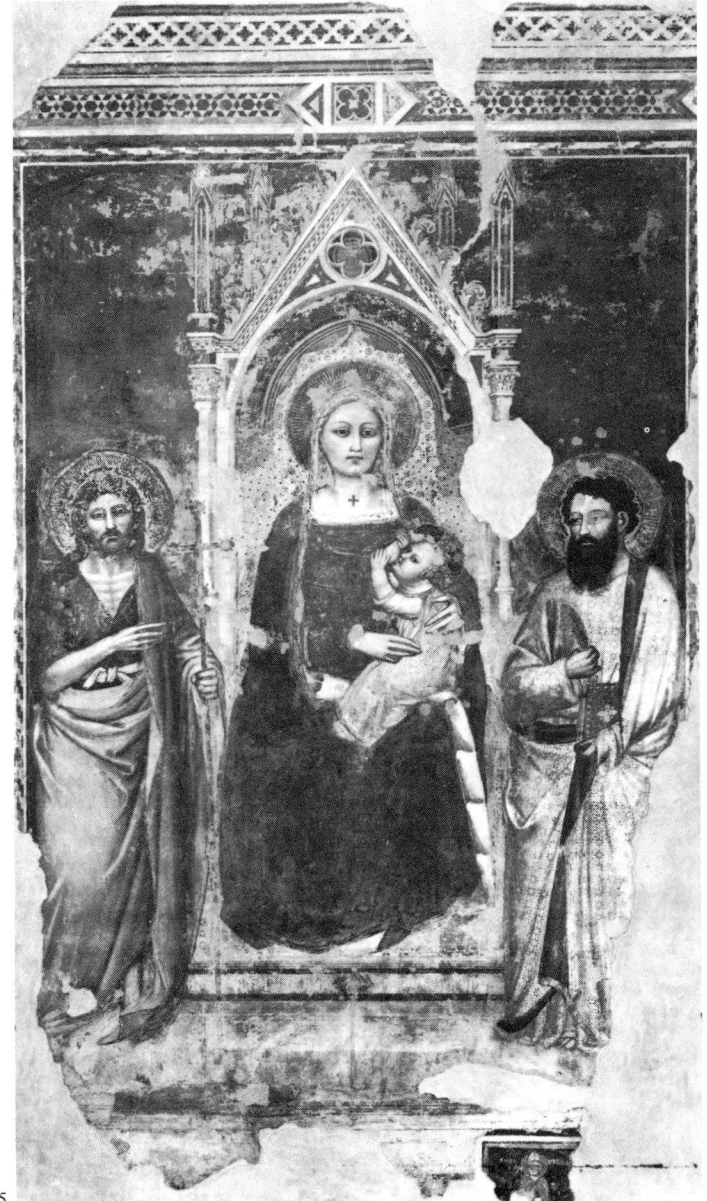

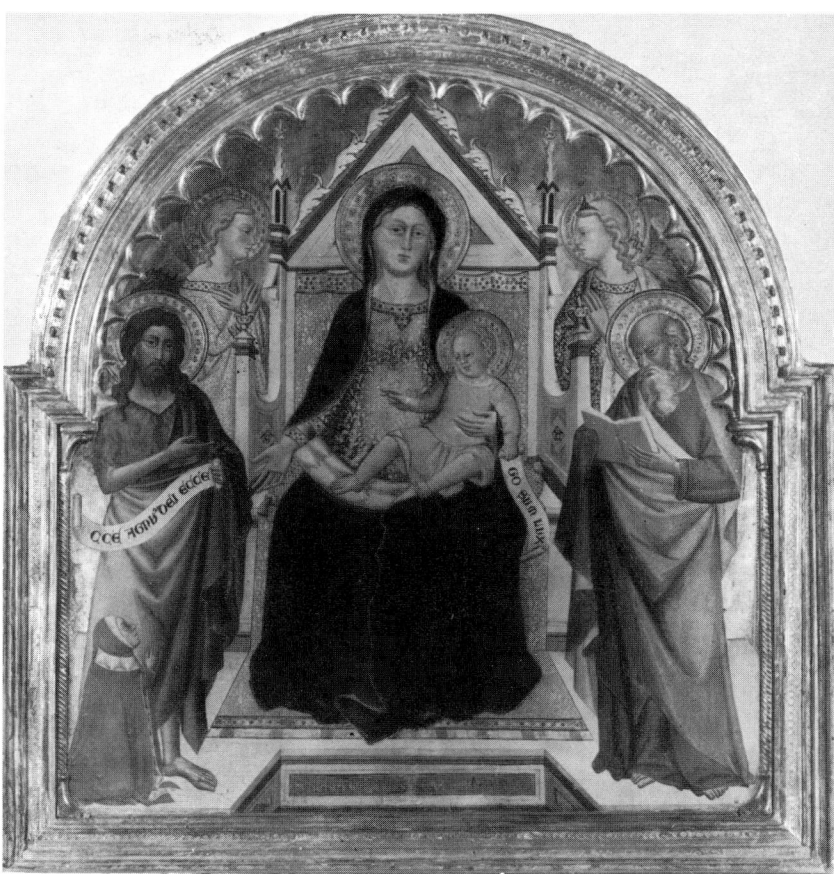

396

395

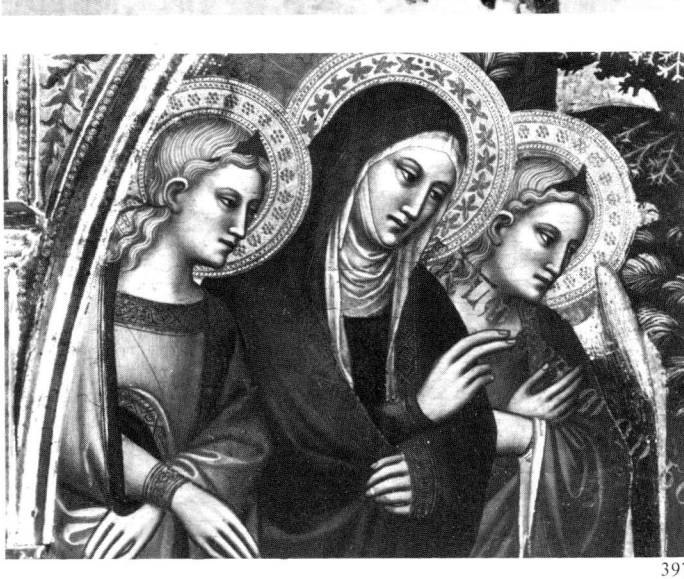

397

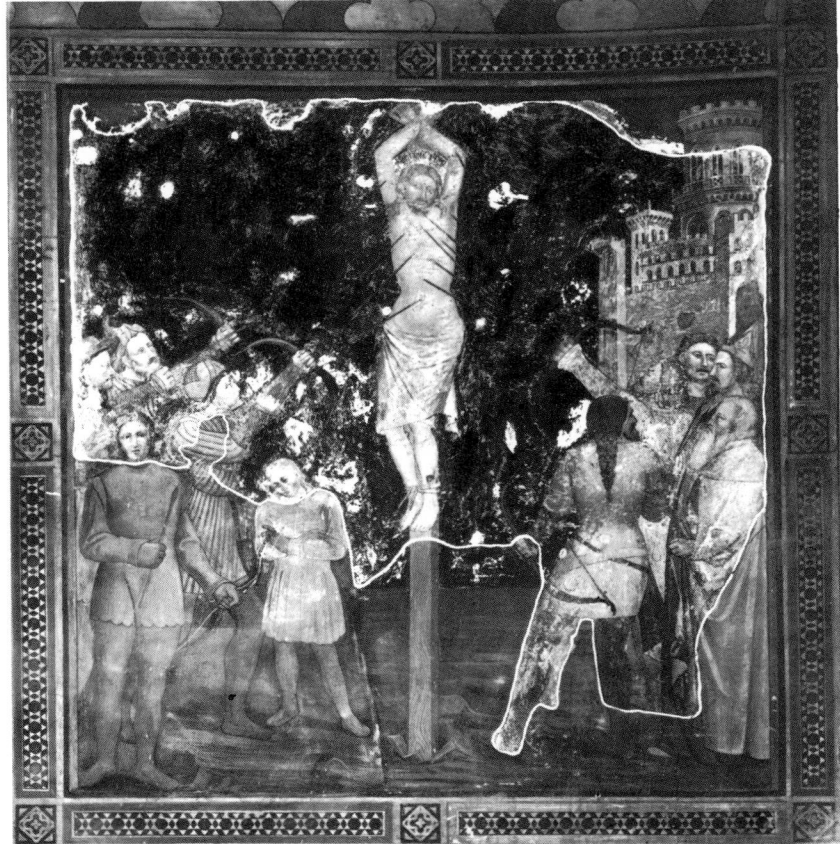

398

395. *Madonna and Child Enthroned with Sts John the Baptist and Bartholomew, Fresco. Florence, S. Ambrogio. SGF 132970.*

396. *Madonna and Child Enthroned, with Sts John the Baptist, John the Evangelist, two Angels and Donor. Panel. Los Angeles (Calif.), County Museum of Art, Samuel H. Kress Collection. no. L.2100.39-551 (K1121). 96.2 × 80. Kress Foundation photo. (Sts John the Baptist and John the Evangelist are by another painter).*

397. *Virgin and two Angels, detail of fig. 403. Panel. Florence, Accademia. no. 8463. Brogi 24201.*

398. *Martyrdom of St Sebastian. Fresco. Florence, S. Donato in Polverosa. SGF 129595.*

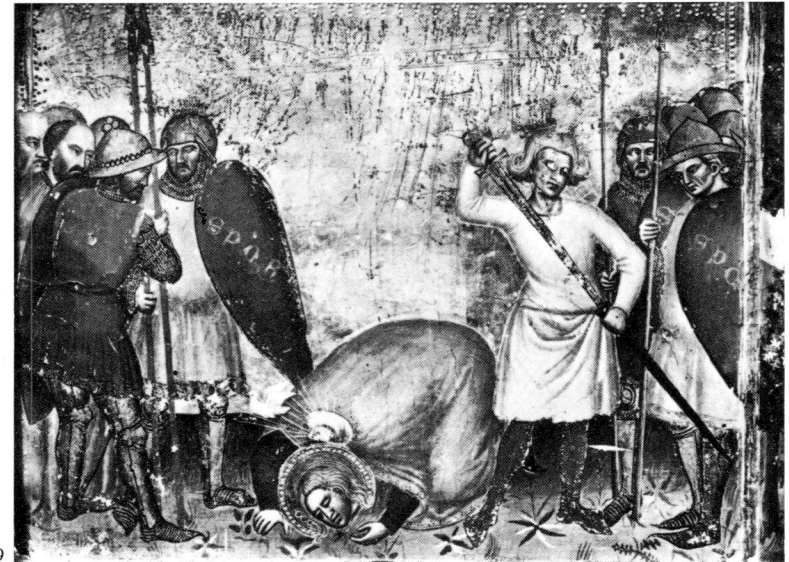

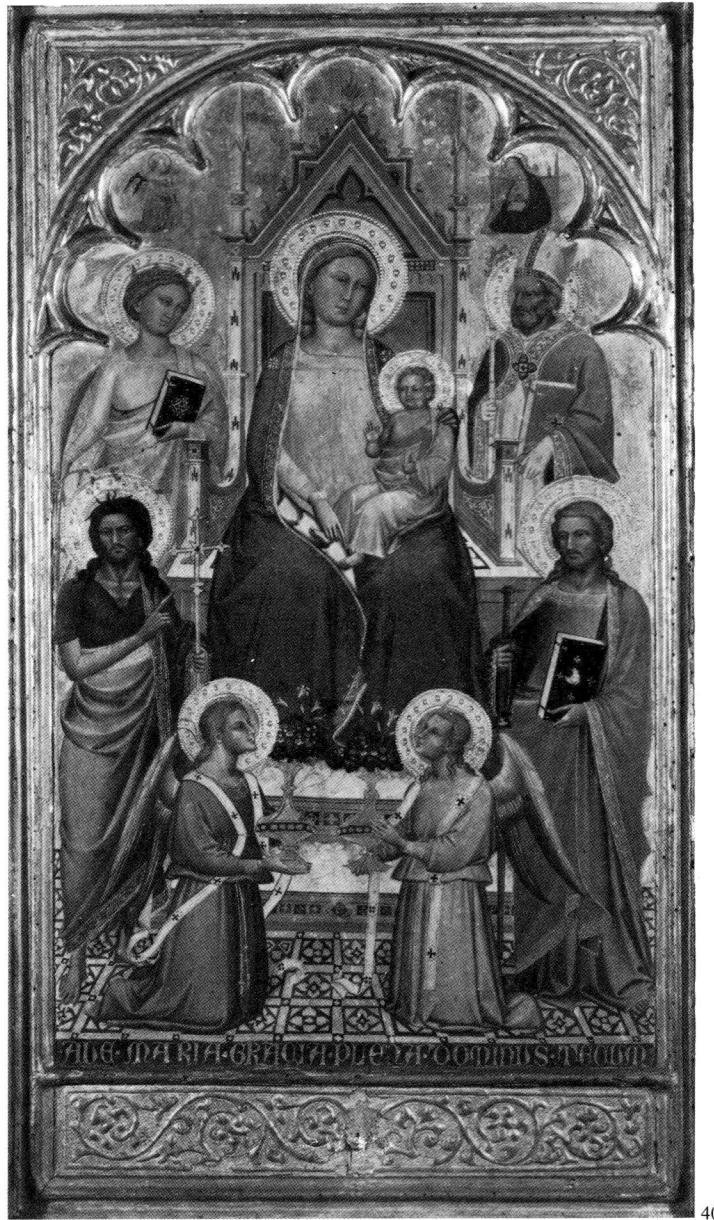

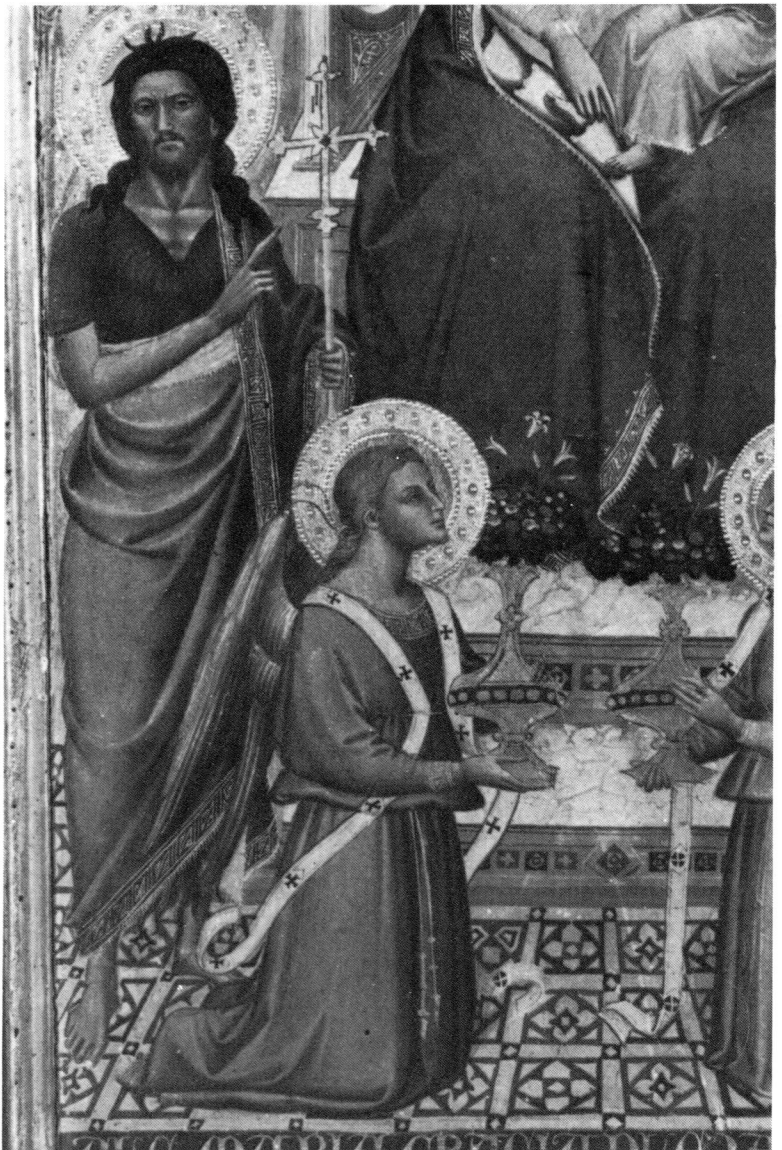

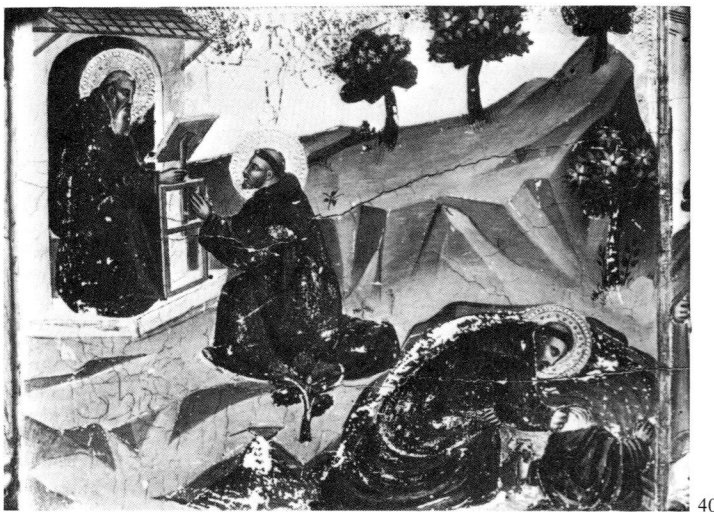

399. *Predella scene: Beheading of St Quentin, detail of fig. 403. Panel. Florence, Accademia. no. 8463. Bertoni-Berenson.*
400. *Madonna and Child Enthroned with Sts Catherine, John the Baptist, Nicholas, James and two Angels. Above: Announcing Angels and Virgin Annunciate. Panel. Private Collection. A. C. Cooper 150054.*
401. *St John the Baptist and an Angel, detail of fig. 400. Panel. Private Collection. A. C. Cooper 150054.*
402. *Predella scene: St Placidus praying, and his miraculous Rescue. Panel. Florence, Accademia. no. 8463. Bertoni-Berenson.*

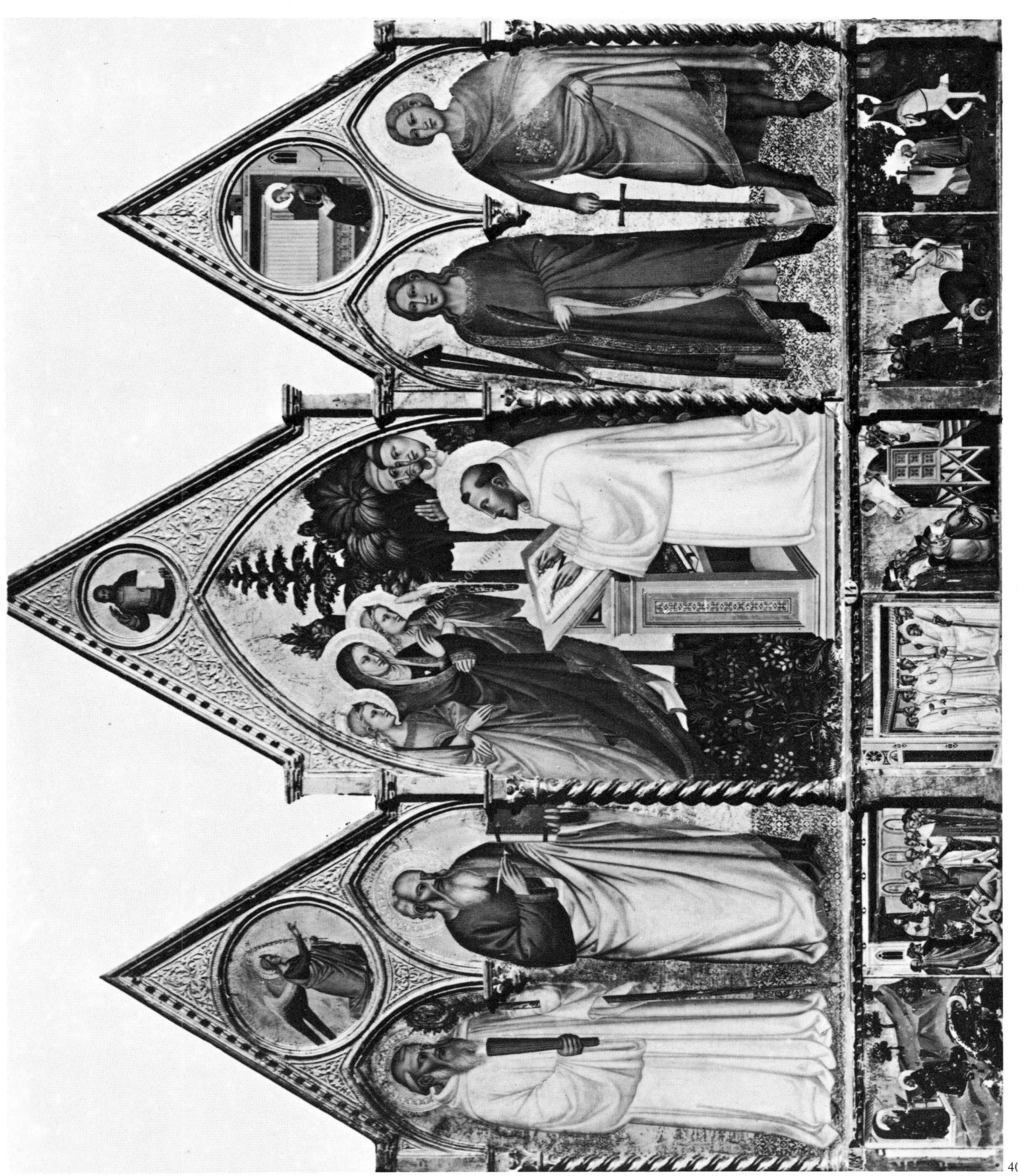

403

403. *Triptych: Vision of St Bernard with Sts Benedict, John the Evangelist, Quentin and Galganus. Above: Christ blessing; Annunciation. Predella: Miraculous Rescue of St Placidus; St John and the poisoned Wine; St Bernard and his Brothers; St Bernard preaching at Sarlat; Beheading of St Quentin; St Galganus adoring his Sword in the Rock. Panel. Florence, Accademia. no. 8463. 175 × 200. Alinari 1570.*

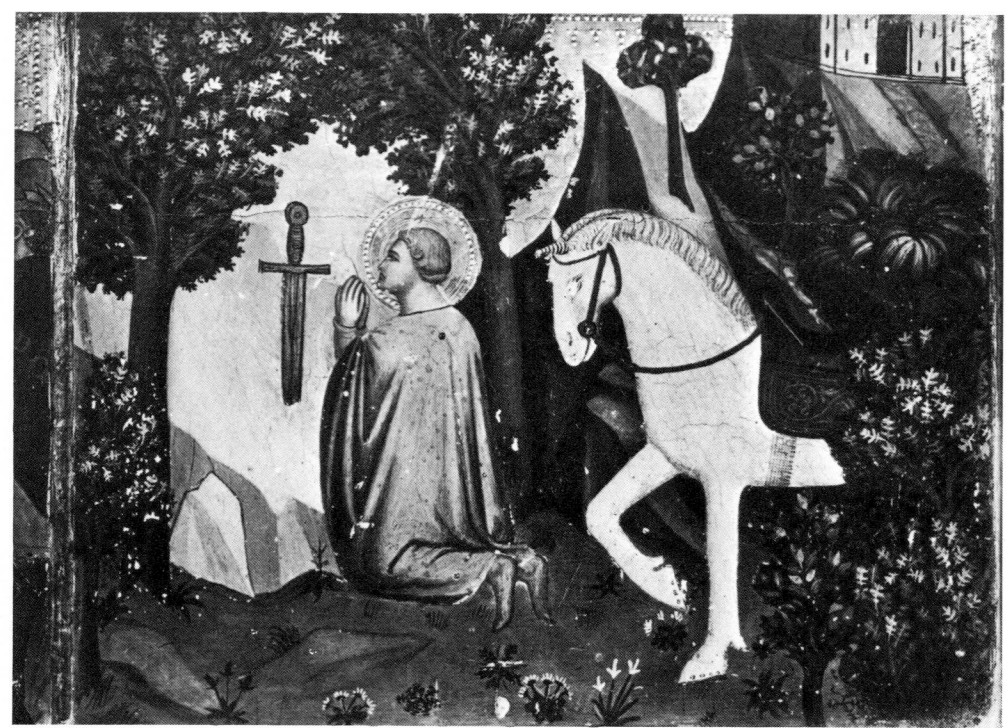

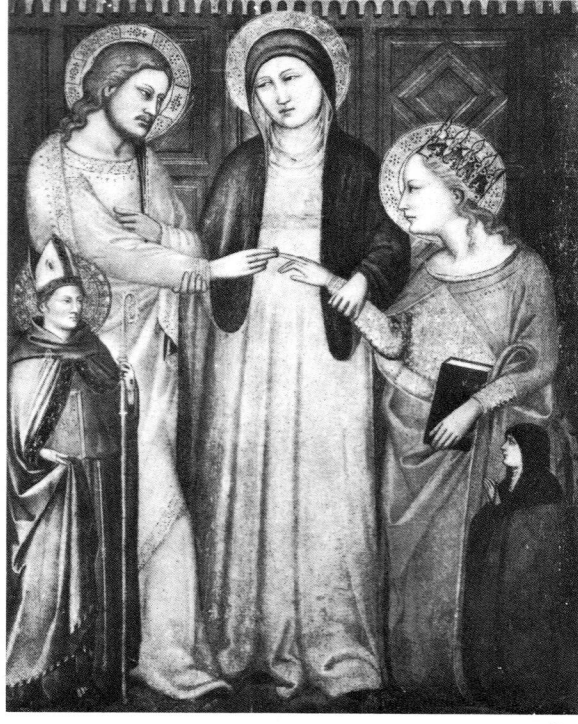

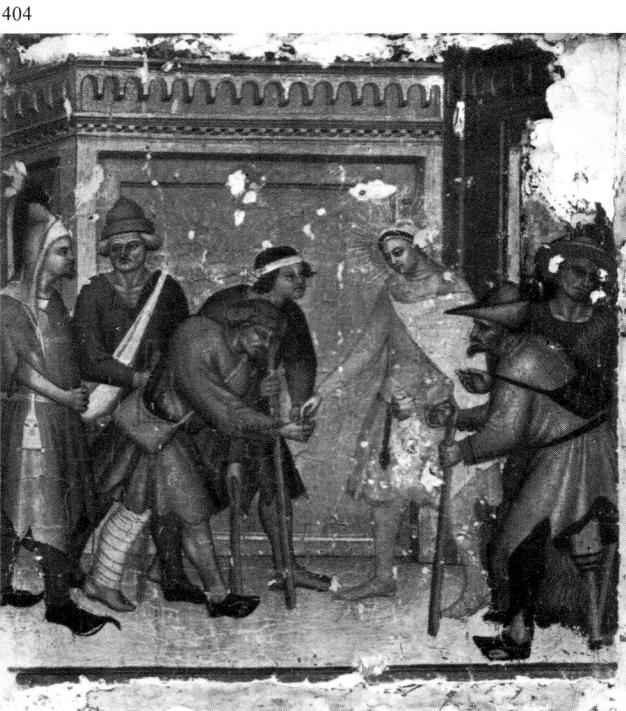

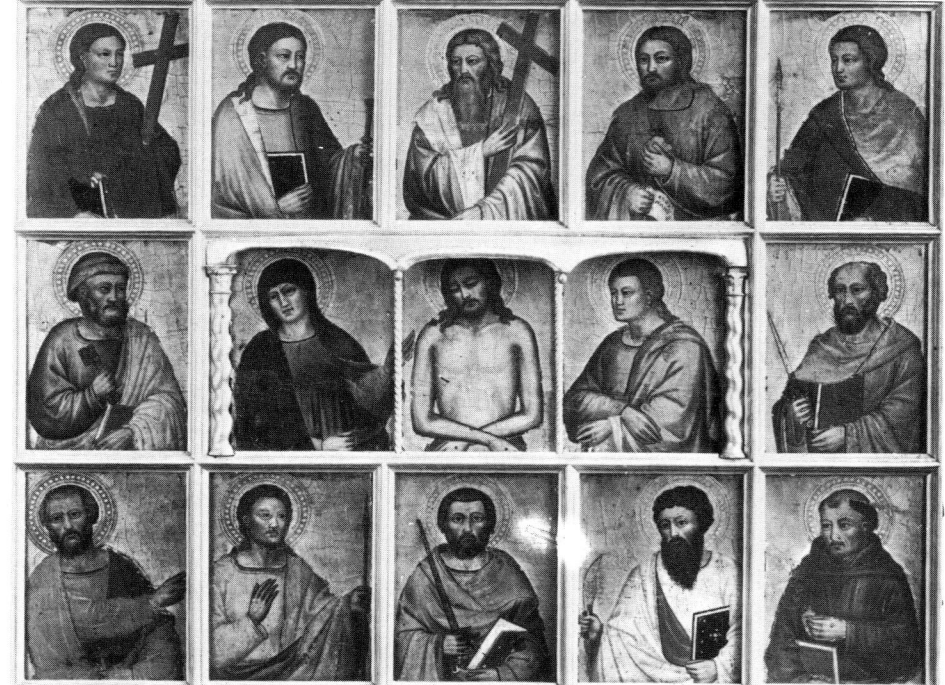

404. *Predella scene: St Galganus adoring his Sword in the Rock. Panel. Florence, Accademia. no. 8463. Bertoni-Berenson.*
405. *Mystical Marriage of St Catherine. Philadelphia (Pa.), Museum of Art, John G. Johnson Collection. 81 × 63. Collection photo.*
406. *St Anthony Abbot distributes alms to the Poor. Panel. Florence, Accademia. no. 460. 39.5 × 35.2. SGF 105050.*
407. *Man of Sorrows, with the Virgin, St Francis and the twelve Apostles. Panel. Rome, Vatican, Pinacoteca, Depositi. Alinari 38143.*

ANDREA da FIRENZE

Andrea da Firenze, who according to Bonaini was Andrea Ristori del Popolo di San Pancrazio (1333-1392) and according to Milanesi, Andrea Bonaiuti (1343-1377), is representative even more than Bernardo Daddi and Nardo di Cione of the penetration of Florentine art by the Sienese..... [He], in the Spanish Chapel in S. Maria Novella illustrates how Sienese artistic principles affected Florentine painting.....

> from A. Venturi, pp. 777-778, *Storia dell' Arte Italiana*, Vol. V, Milan, 1907.

Andrea Buonaiuti, who certainly is not the same as the Andrea Ristori, mentioned between 1333 and 1392, with whom he is sometimes identified, is known to us through several documents and two important authentic works. He matriculated in the corporation of " Medici e speciali " in the year 1343 and possibly is the Andrea who, in 1339, ornamented a Gonfalone with events from the life of the Madonna for the Company of St Peter Martyr of Sta. Maria Novella, for which he received 1 lib. 16 soldi. In 1358 his name appears on the roll of painters in the parish of Sta. Maria Maggiore and in 1365 we find him signing the contract for the frescoes in the Spagnoli chapel; in 1366 he formed part of the commission which directed the construction of the Cathedral and we thus have proof of the favour in which he was held. He might be the Andrea da Firenze who worked in Orvieto at the end of 1368. In 1370 he witnesses a testament; four years later he is mentioned with Orcagna in the St. Lucas company, while in 1377 he receives 529 lire, 10 soldi from Ludovico Orselli for the frescoes of the legend of St Ranieri which he painted in the Campo Santo of Pisa.....

> from R. van Marle, p. 425, *The Development of the Italian Schools of Painting*, Vol. III, The Hague, 1924.

Among the several painters of the name of Andrea who flourished in Florence in the latter half of the fourteenth century, data are wanting to recognize the artist who, in 1377, commenced the series of frescoes in the Campo Santo of Pisa, illustrating the life of St. Ranieri, which were subsequently completed by Antonio Veneziano. Messrs. Crowe and Cavalcaselle, from a resemblance in style between the Pisan frescoes and those of the Spanish chapel in the cloister of the Florentine church of Sta Maria Novella, conjecture that Andrea da Firenze may have been one of the artists employed in executing the frescoes in this chapel, which have been erroneously attributed to the Sienese painter, Simone Martini.....

> from D. E. Colnaghi, p. 14, *A Dictionary of Florentine Painters*, London, 1928.

The wording of the document found by Fr Innocenzo Taurisano according to which on 30th December 1365 Andrea di Buonaiuto was engaged to paint " all the chapter-room " within two years certainly does not mean that all the work had to be by Andrea. The closeness of part of the chapel to sure works by Andrea, and the difference between other parts of the chapel and the same sure work leaves no doubt whatsoever about this, even if Venturi and more recently van Marle consider the whole chapel by the same hand. This is not a question of fluctuations within an homogeneous style due to work done by assistants under the direction of a master, but of enormous differences; these were clearly pointed out by Cavalcaselle, as well as by Vasari long before, who erroneously wrote that three walls were by Simone Martini. He correctly saw however, that the style was near that of the " Stories of St Ranierius " in Pisa, which a document found by Bonaini showed were works of Andrea Buonaiuto as Cavalcaselle had guessed; the other wall — this is still Vasari's opinion — and the vaults, were supposed to be by Taddeo Gaddi.....

> from L. Coletti, p. LIV, *I Primitivi*, Vol. II, Novara, 1946.

After 1343 he appears registered in the Arte dei Medici e Speziali in Florence; in 1366, there having been created a committee of eight painters to give advice " supra facto hedificationis ecclesiae " of S. Maria dei Fiori, the name of Andrea di Buonaiuto appears on the list immediately after that of Taddeo Gaddi; he must have made an impression on the council, for on the 20th August of the same year, together with four colleagues, he received the commission to draw up plans for the cathedral; from September to December of 1372, he was consul of the painters' guild; two years later he appears registered in the Company of St Luke; in 1368 he was summoned to Orvieto; in 1377 he went to Pisa to paint the " Stories from the life of St Ranierius " in the Camposanto, for which he was paid the same year, before making his will on the 2nd November, 1377, a few days before his death.....

from U. Galetti and E. Camesasca, p. 68,
Enciclopedia della Pittura Italiana, " H-E ",
Cernusco sul Naviglio, 1950.

BIBLIOGRAPHY
BOOKS

An asterisk indicates a work listed in the General Bibliography

C-Cavalcaselle II*, 1883, pp. 349-52; *Venturi, A.**, 1907, pp. 777-816; *v. Marle, 1924**, p. 425; *Colnaghi**, 1928, p. 14; Poggi, G., *Treccani, Vol. III**, 1929, p. 200; *Toesca, 1929**, p. 66; *Berenson, 1932**, p. 11; *Venturi, L**, 1933, Vol. I, pl. 58; *Coletti, Vol. II**, 1946, pp. 54-7, 68; *Antal**, 1948, pp. 199-203; *Galetti**, 1950, " A-E ", pp. 68-73; *Toesca, 1951**, pp. 638-42; *Paatz**, 1952, Vol. IV, pp. 495-99; Bertolini, L., *Camposanto**, 1960, pp. 69-76; *Borsook, 1960**, pp. 140-2; Cecchi, E., *Piaceri della Pittura*, Venice, 1960, pp. 220-22; Carli, E., *Pittura pisana del Trecento: la seconda metà del secolo*, Milan, 1961, p. 22; *Oertel, 1961**, p. 119; *Cracow**, 1961, p. 44; *Berenson 1963**, Vol. I, p. 4; *Marcucci**, 1965, p. 97.

JOURNALS

Dami, L., *BA*, 1915, 8, pp. 216-44; Devlin, M. A., *S*, 4, 1929, pp. 270-81; Berenson, B., *DD*, XI, 4, 1930-1, pp. 1039-1073; Levi, E. L., *RA*, XXV, 1950, pp. 193-7; Matteoli, A., *BAE*, XV, 26, 1950, pp. 40-41, Cohn, W., *MKIF*, VIII, 2, 1958, pp. 65-77; Cohn, W., *Weltkunst*, 1960, p. 5; Rozycka-Bryzek, A., *Biuletin Historii Sztuki*, XXII, 1960, pp. 203-18; Bellosi, L, *PA*, XVIII, 203/23, 1967, pp. 85-6; Luttrell, A., *BM*, CXIV, 831, 1972, pp. 362-369; von Holst, N., *MKIF*, XVI, 3, 1972, pp. 261-68.

There are no known signed and/or dated works by Andrea da Firenze.

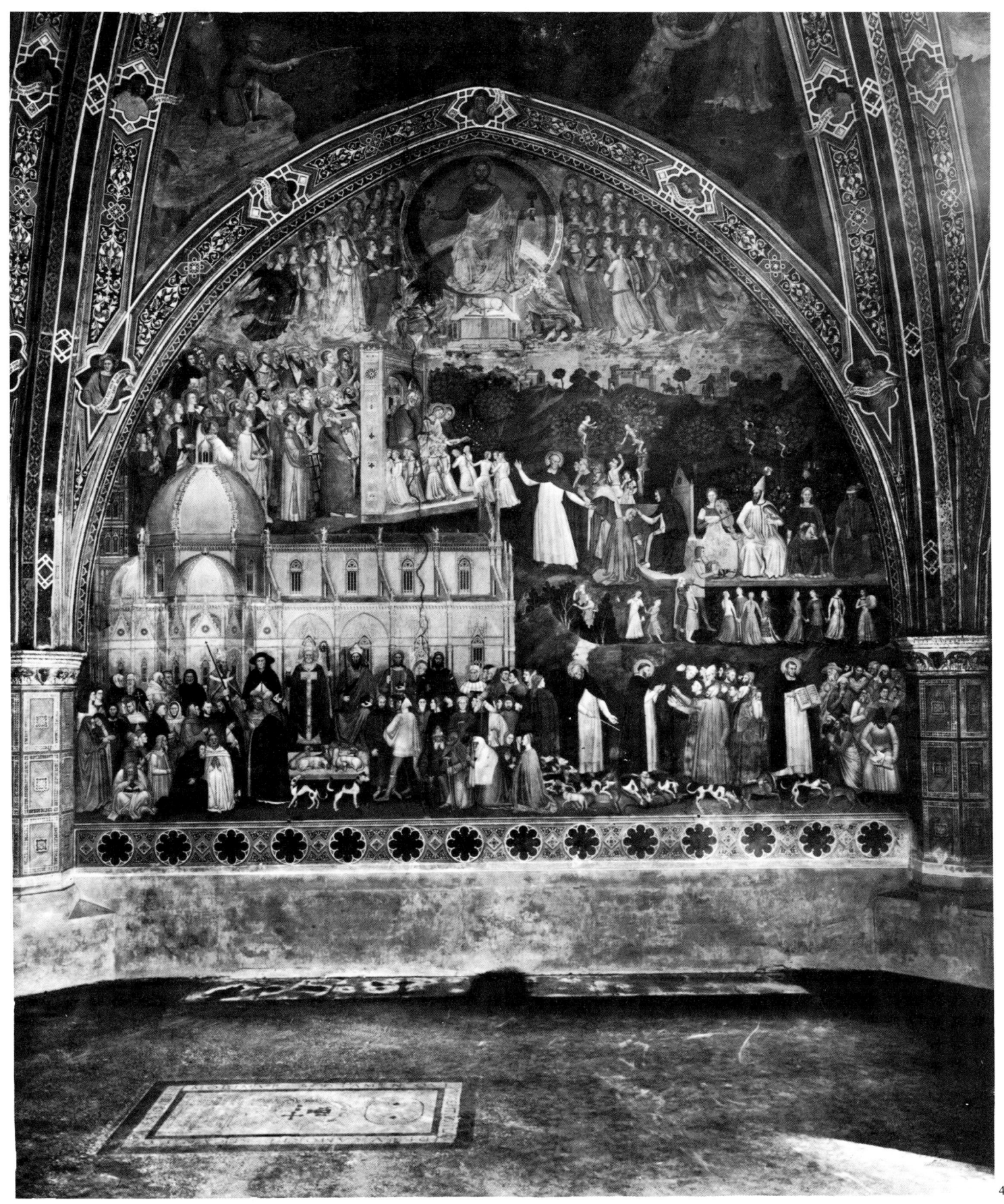

408. *Church Militant and Church Triumphant, Via Veritatis. Fresco. Florence, S. Maria Novella, Cloister, Spanish Chapel. SGF 104656. 1366-68.*

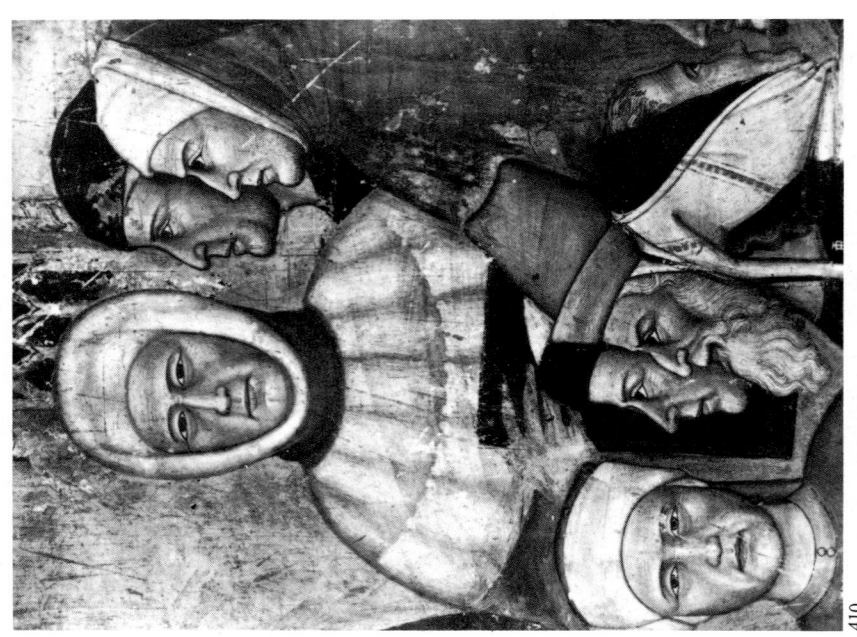

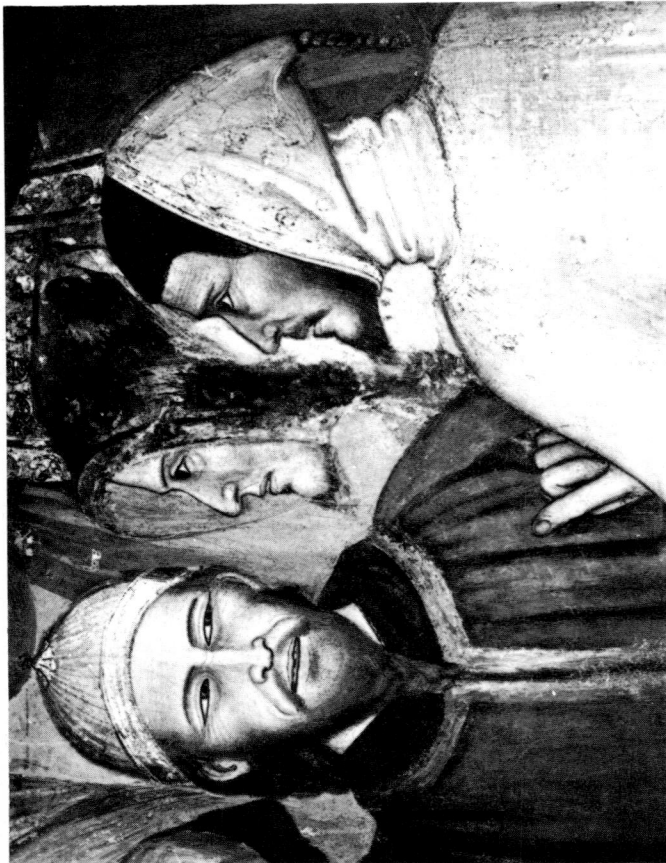

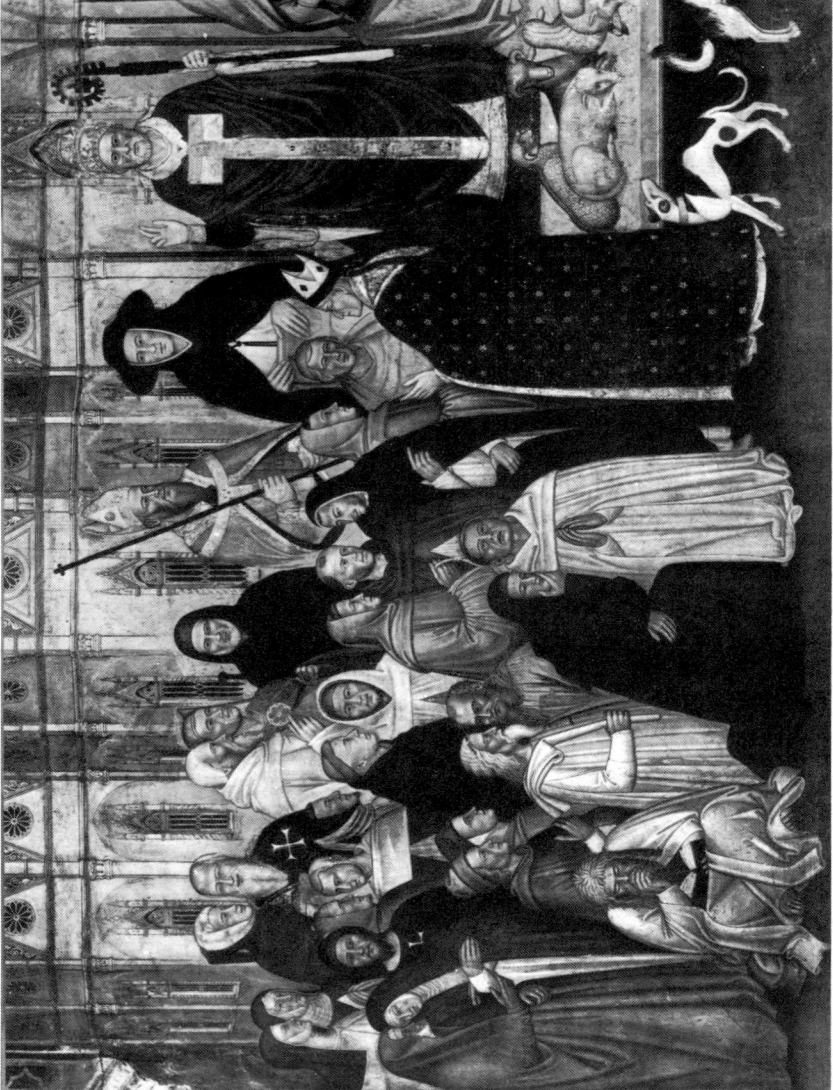

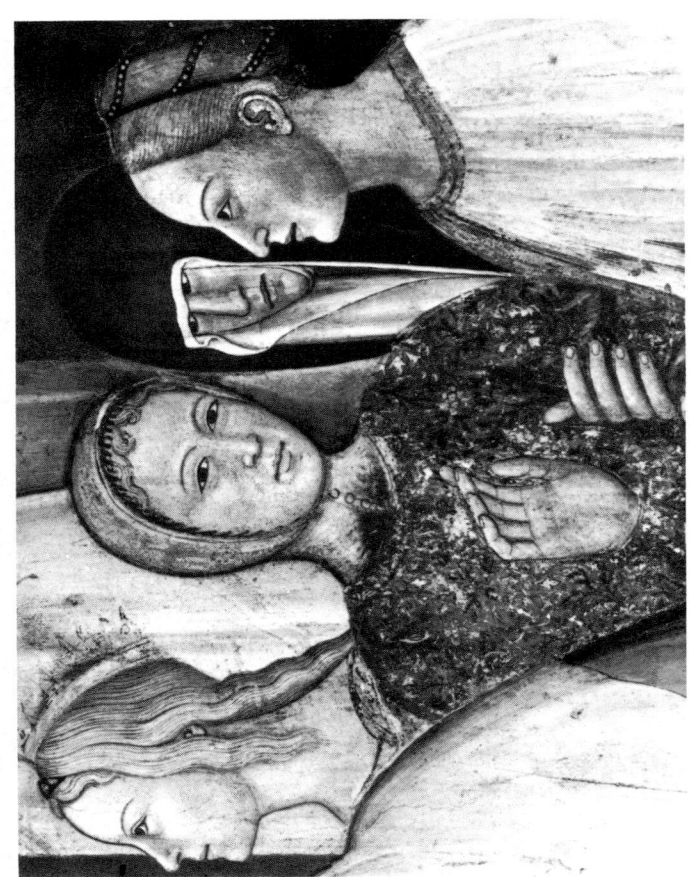

409. *Pope and Ecclesiastical Authority, detail of fig. 408. Fresco. Florence, S. Maria Novella, Cloister, Spanish Chapel. Alinari 4101. 1366-68.*

410. *Presumed portraits of Boccaccio, Petrarch, and others, detail of fig. 408. Fresco. Florence, S. Maria Novella, Cloister, Spanish Chapel. Alinari 58167. 1366-68.*

411. *Presumed portraits of Beatrice, Laura, Fiammetta and Beata Villana, detail of fig. 408. Fresco. Florence, S. Maria Novella, Cloister, Spanish Chapel. Alinari 4106. 1366-68.*

412. *Presumed portraits of Cimabue, Giotto and Taddeo Gaddi, detail of fig. 408. Fresco. Florence, S. Maria Novella, Cloister, Spanish Chapel. Alinari 4104. 1366-68.*

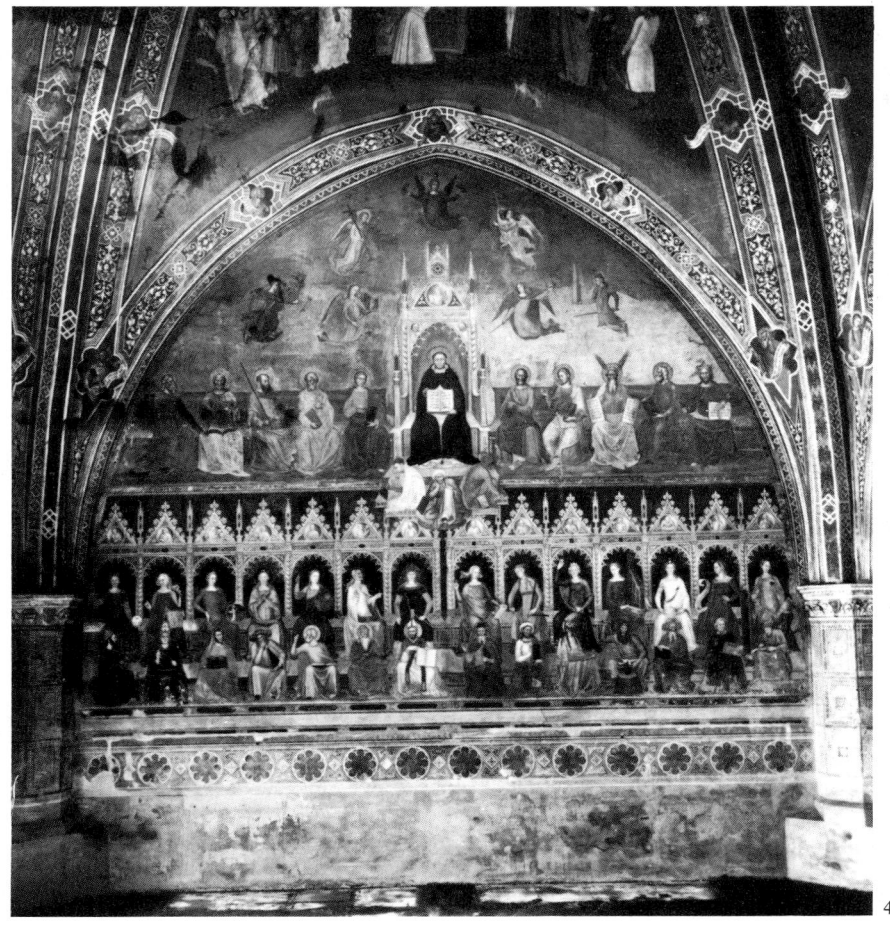

413

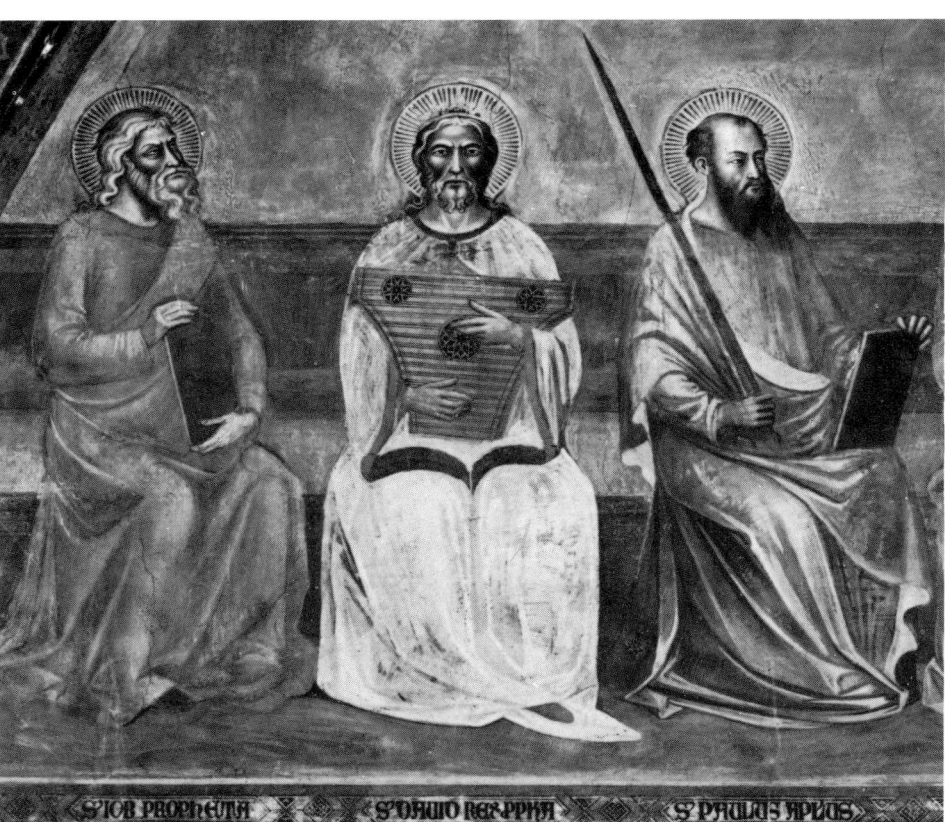

414

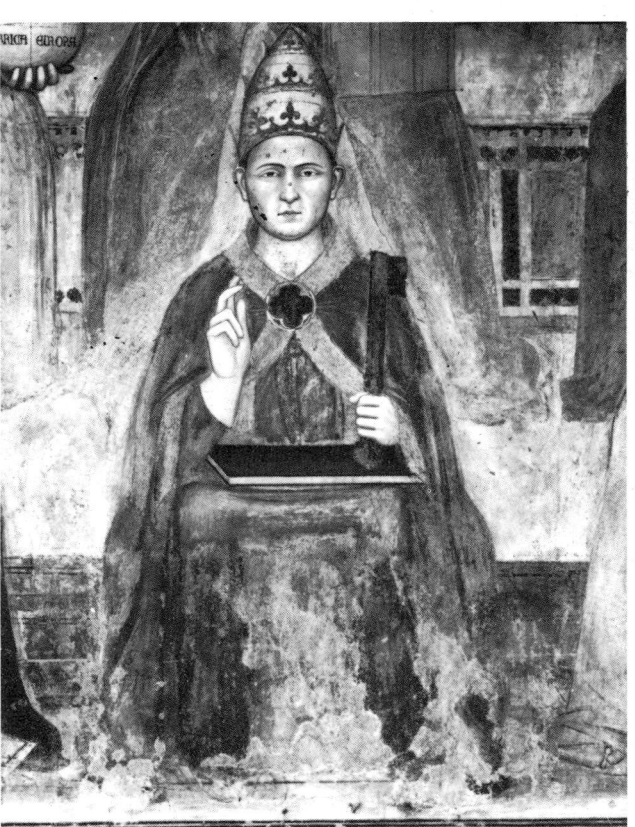

415

413. *Triumph of St Thomas Aquinas. Fresco. Florence, S. Maria Novella, Cloister, Spanish Chapel. SGF 104654. 1366-68.*
414. *Holy Men, detail of fig. 413. Fresco. Florence, S. Maria Novella, Cloister, Spanish Chapel. Alinari 4087. 1366-68.*
415. *Innocent IV representing Canon Law, detail of fig. 413. Fresco. Florence, S. Maria Novella, Cloister, Spanish Chapel. SGF 123303. 1366-68.*

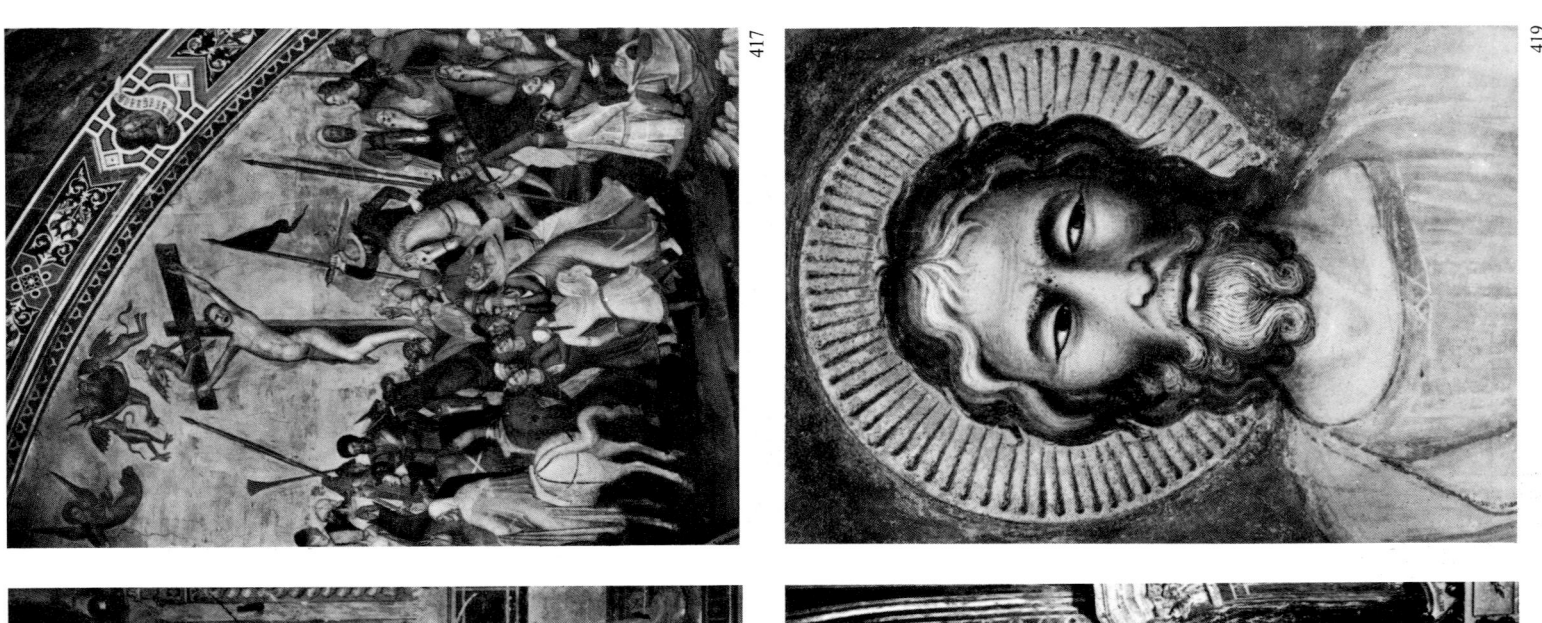

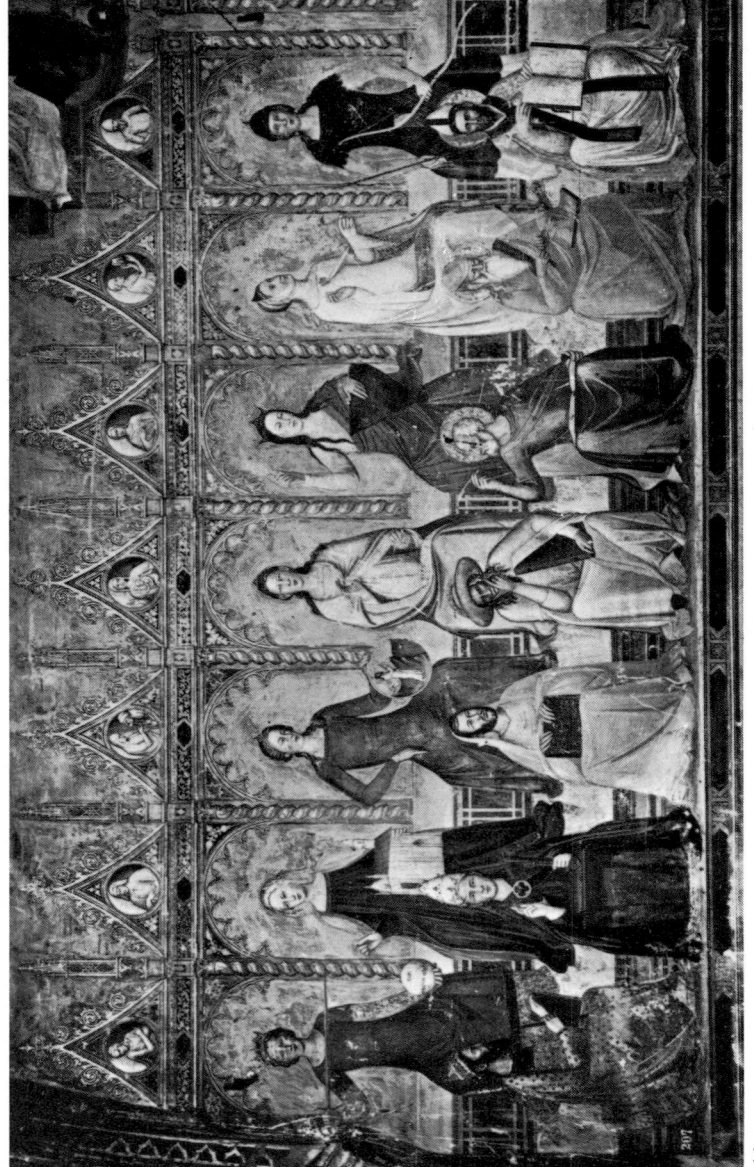

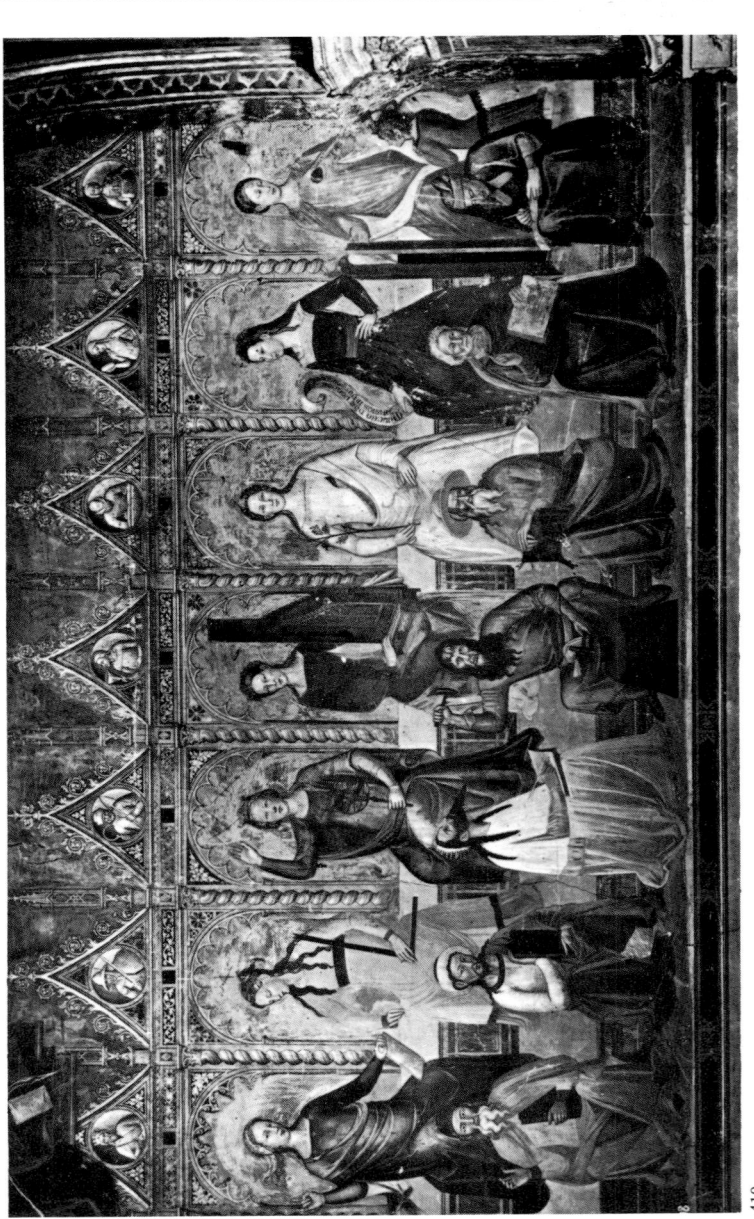

416. *Allegorical figures of the Liberal Arts: Civil Law, Justinian; Canon Law, Innocent IV; Physics, Hippocrates; History, St Jerome; Dogmatics, St Dionysius the Areopagite; Ethics, St John Chrysostom; Mystical Inspiration, St Augustine; detail of fig. 413. Fresco. Florence, S. Maria Novella, Cloister, Spanish Chapel. SGF 52736. 1366-68.*

417. *Crucifixion, detail of fig. 420. Fresco. Florence, S. Maria Novella, Cloister, Spanish Chapel. Alinari 4113.*

418. *Allegorical figures of the Liberal Arts: Arithmetic, Pythagoras; Geometry, Euclid; Astronomy, Ptolomy; Music, Tubalcain; Dialectic, Zeno; Rhetoric, Cicero; Grammar, Priscian; detail of fig. 413. Fresco. Florence, S. Maria Novella, Cloister, Spanish Chapel. SGF 52737. 1366-68.*

419. *Head of a Saint, detail of fig. 413. Fresco. Florence, S. Maria Novella, Cloister, Spanish Chapel. SGF 112846. 1366-68.*

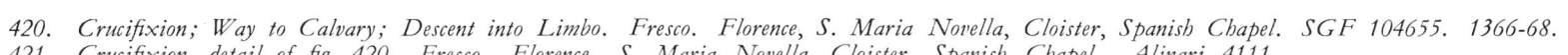

420. *Crucifixion; Way to Calvary; Descent into Limbo. Fresco. Florence, S. Maria Novella, Cloister, Spanish Chapel. SGF 104655. 1366-68.*
421. *Crucifixion, detail of fig. 420. Fresco. Florence, S. Maria Novella, Cloister, Spanish Chapel. Alinari 4111.*
422. *Holy Women and St John, detail of fig. 420. Fresco. Florence, S. Maria Novella, Cloister, Spanish Chapel. Brogi 25590. 1366-68.*

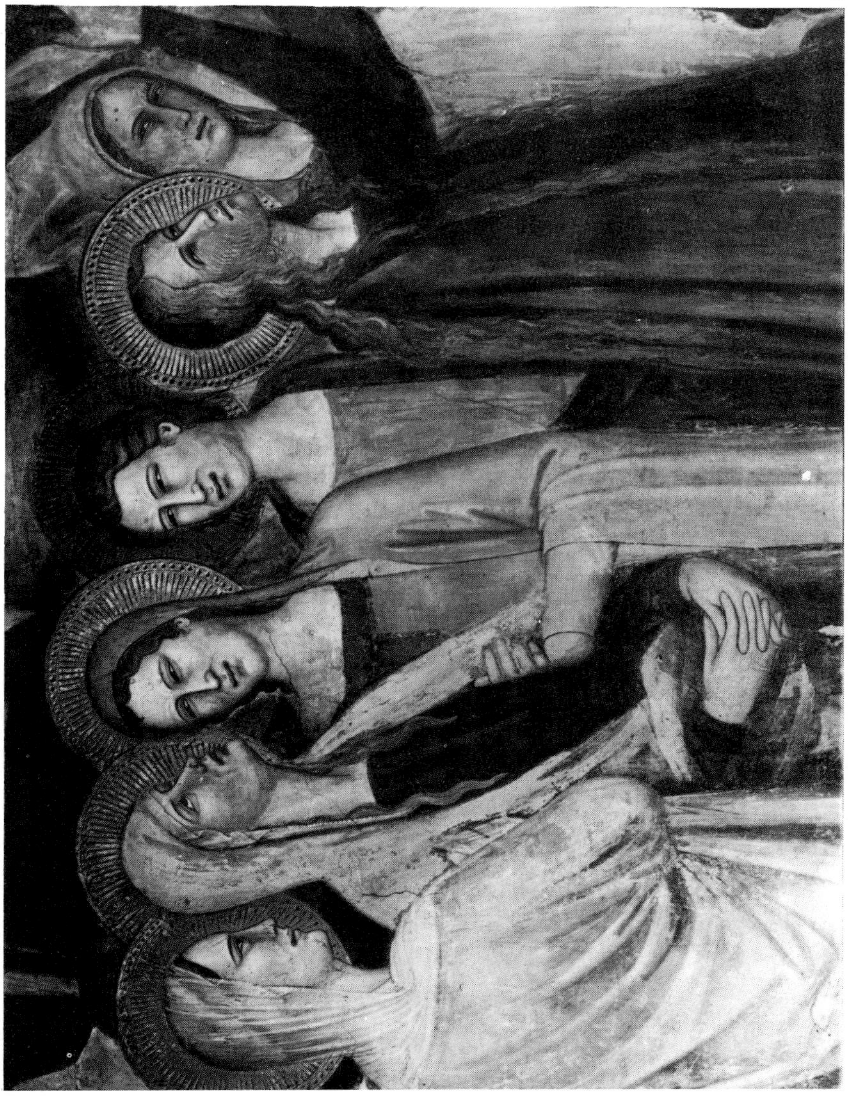

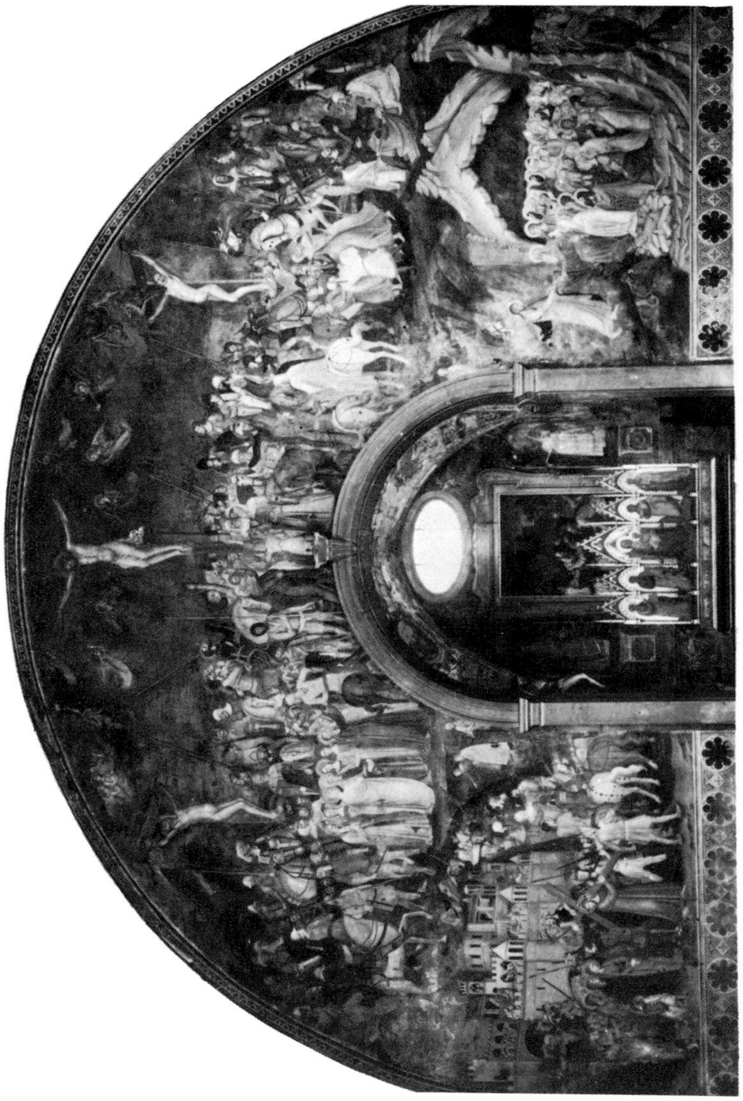

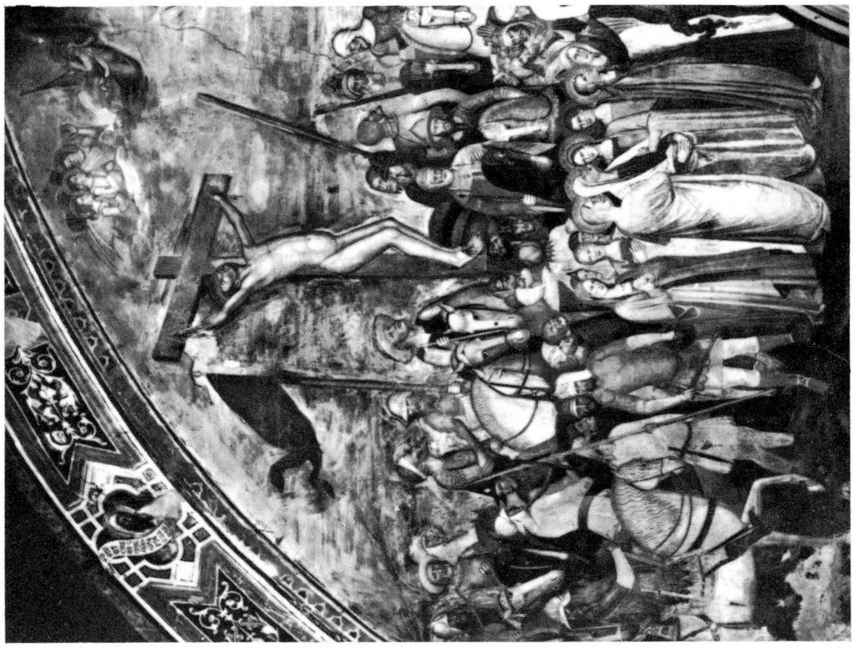

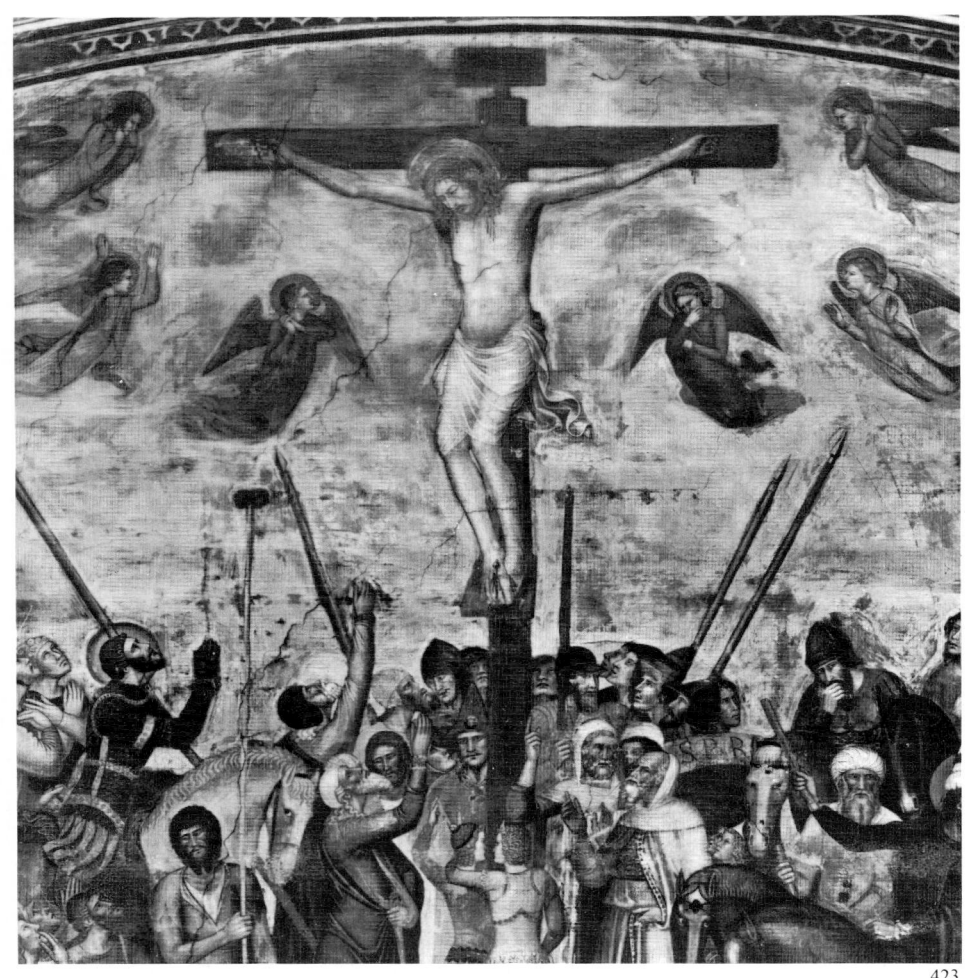

423

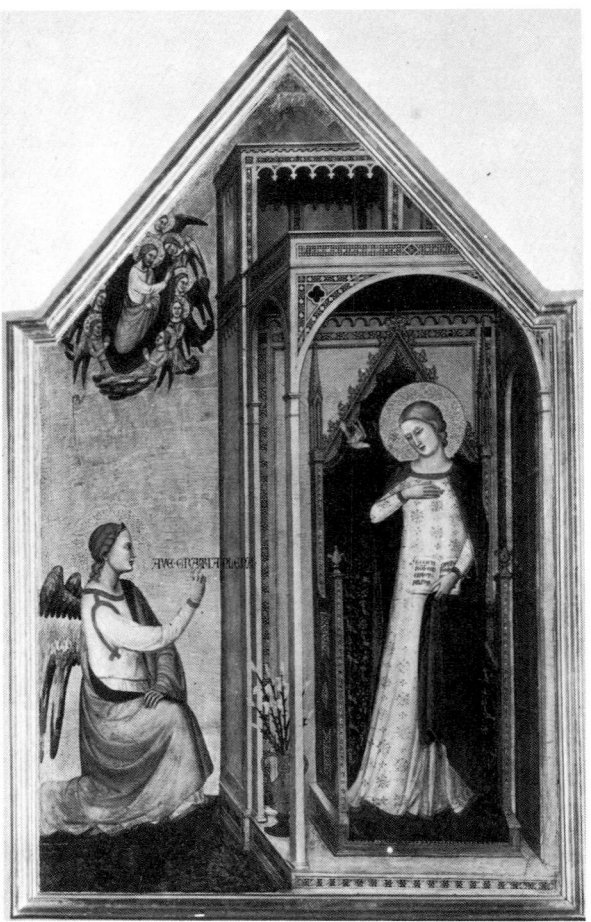

424

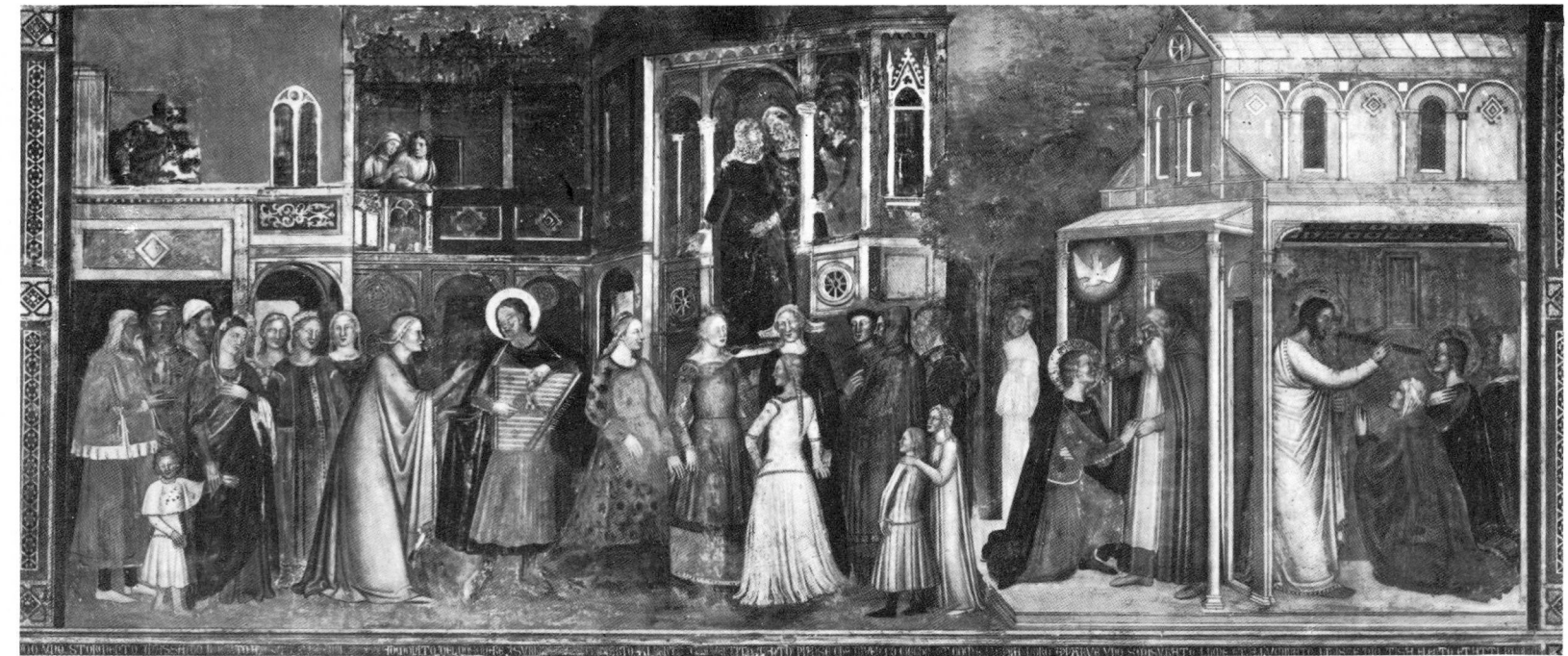

425

423. *Crucifixion, detail of fig. 420. Fresco. Florence, S. Maria Novella, Cloister, Spanish Chapel. Alinari 4112. 1366-68.*
424. *Annunciation. Panel. Florence, Accademia. no. 455. 216.5 × 114.5. SGF 5050.*
425. *Scenes from the Legend of St Raynerius: Vocation of the Saint and Restoration of his Eyesight. Fresco. Pisa. Camposanto. Alinari 8761. 1375-77.*

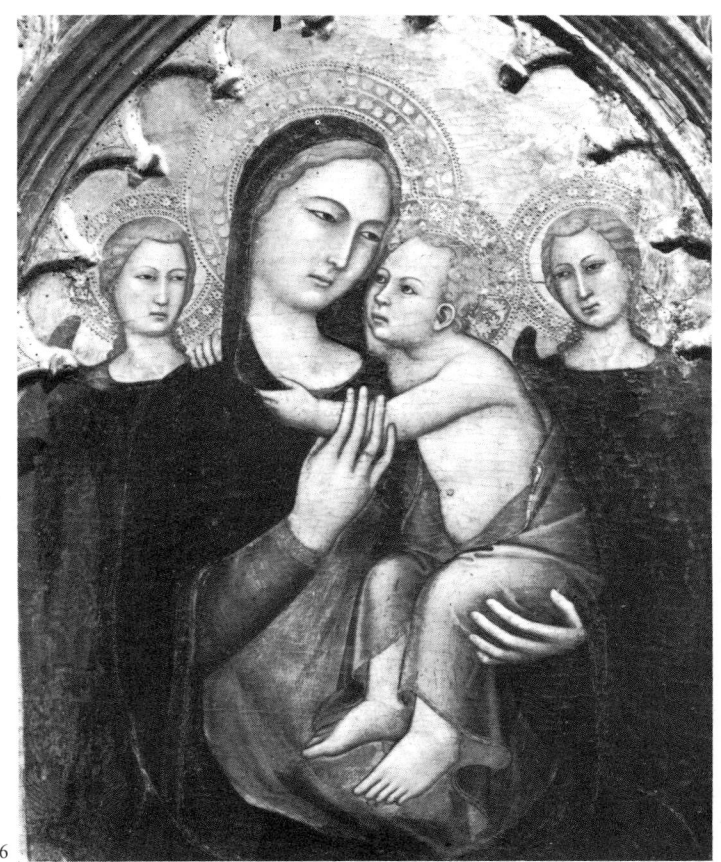

426

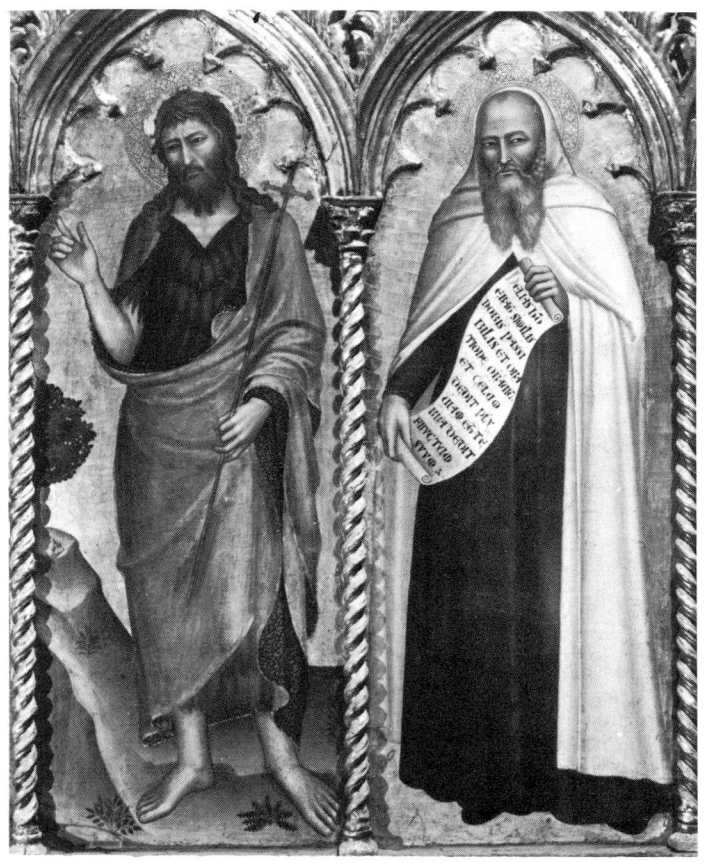

427

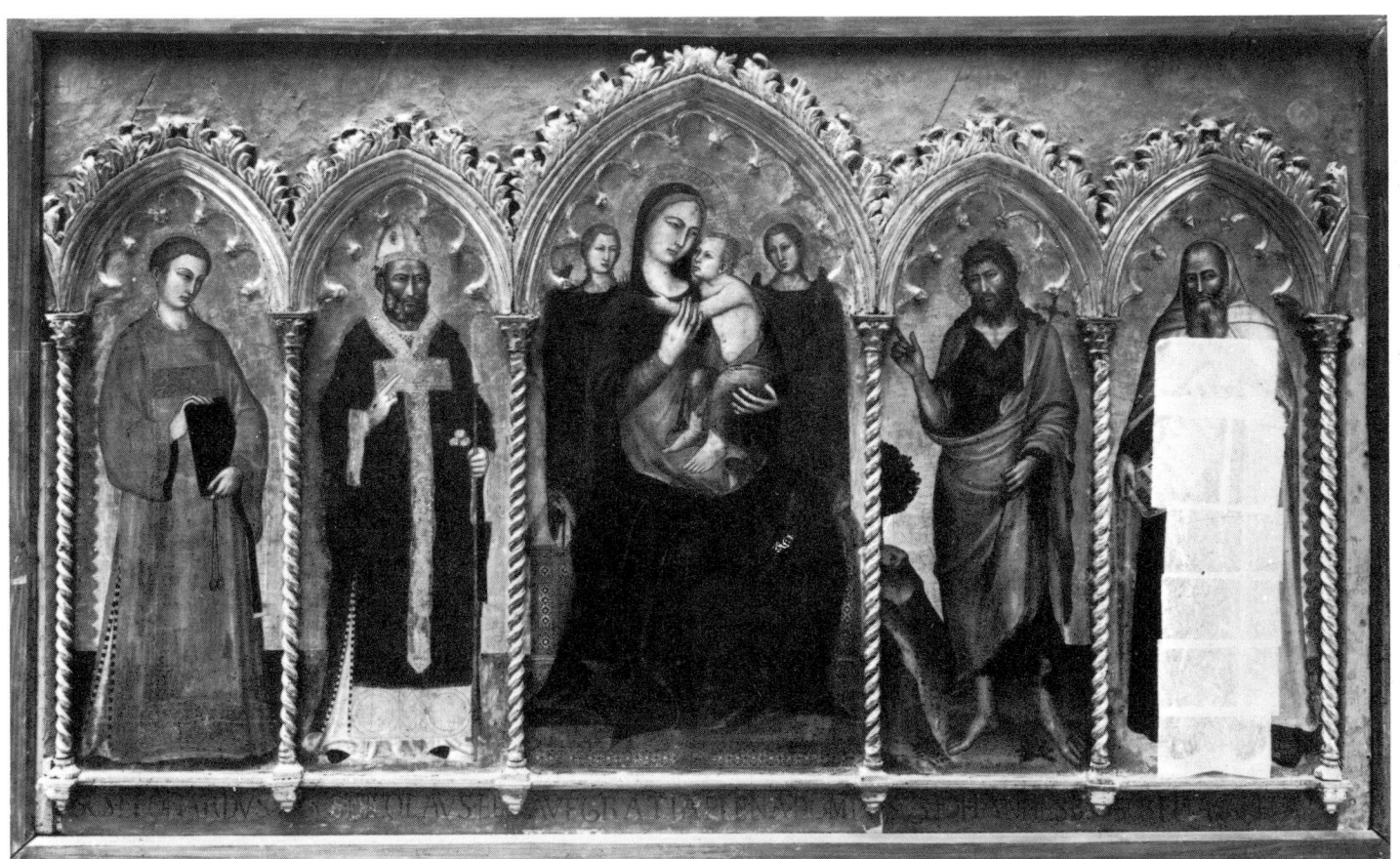

428

426. *Madonna and Child and two Angels, detail of fig. 428. Panel. Florence, S. Maria del Carmine, Sacristy. SGF 161802.*
427. *St John the Baptist and Elijah the Prophet, detail of fig. 428. Panel. Florence, S. Maria del Carmine, Sacristy. SGF 161801.*
428. *Polyptych: Madonna and Child with two Angels, Sts Leonard, Nicholas, John the Baptist, and Elijah the Prophet. Panel. Florence, S. Maria del Carmine, Sacristy. 144 × 228. SGF 95179.*

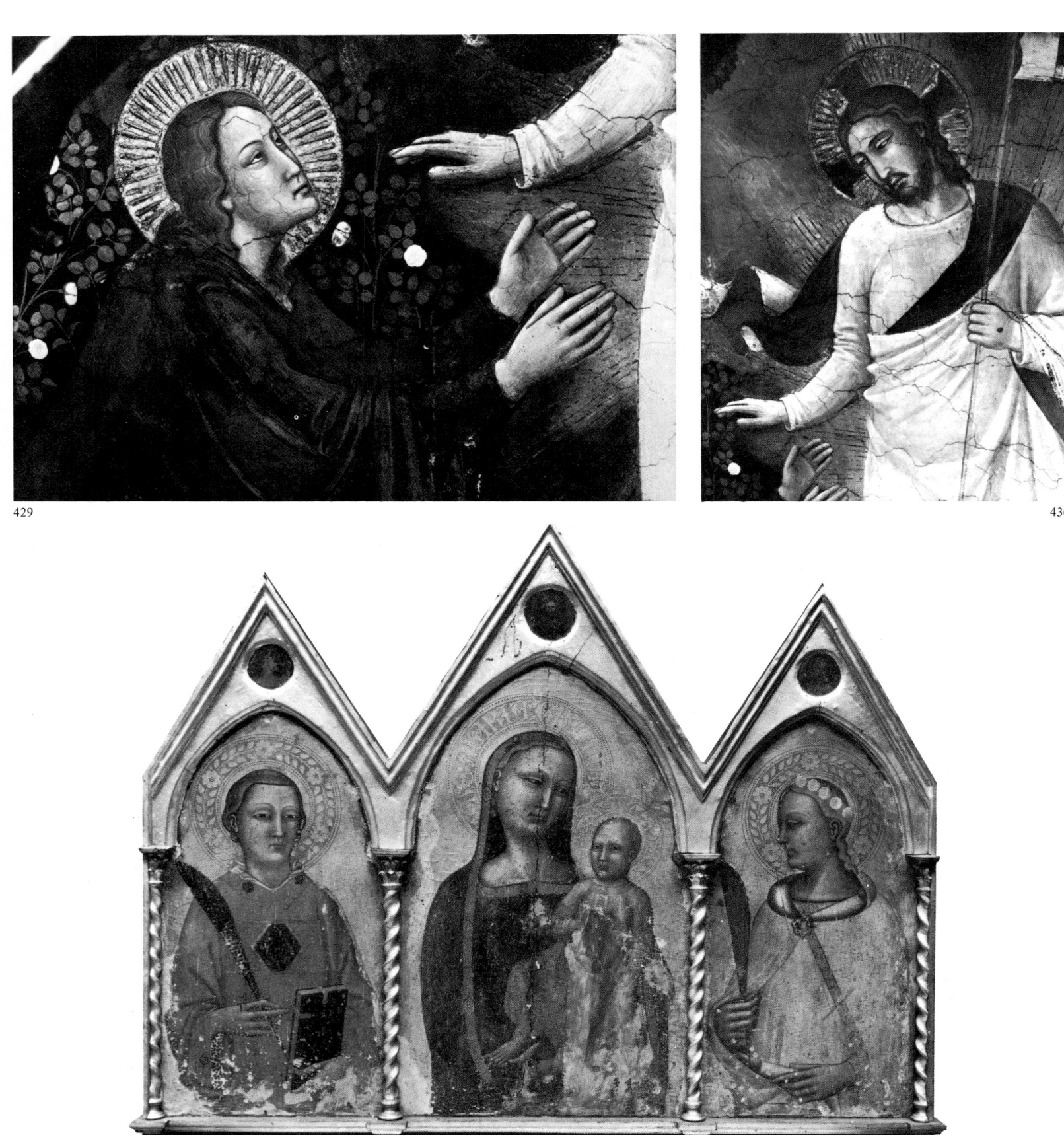

429

430

431

429. *Head of Mary Magdalene, detail of Noli me tangere. Fresco. Florence, S. Maria Novella, Cloister, Spanish Chapel. SGF 118537.*
430. *Christ, detail of Noli me tangere. Fresco. Florence, S. Maria Novella, Cloister, Spanish Chapel. SGF 118538.*
431. *Triptych: Madonna and Child, Deacon Martyr, and St Dorothy. Panel. Cracow, Muzeum Narodowe. no. XII-185 (226). 103 × 120. Museum photo.*

GIOVANNI BONSI

Considerably more refined and belonging to a more advanced stage of evolution, showing in the plasticity of the figures an Orcagnesque influence, is the painter Giovanni
Bonsi, of whom we only possess one authentic work, a polyptych in the Vatican Gallery
depicting the Virgin enthroned between SS. Onophrius, Nicholas, Bartholomew and
John the Evangelist. This is signed....

> from R. van Marle, p. 406, *The Develop-
> ment of the Italian Schools of Painting*, Vol. III,
> The Hague, 1924.

Giovanni di Bonsi (Bonsignore), Florentine, born 13- -, died - -. Painter, member of the
Physicians and Apothecaries Guild between 1353-58. Giovanni was evidently an artist
of some reputation in his day. He was one of the painters deputed by the Physicians and
Apothecaries Guild on July 13, 1366, at the request of the Board of Works, to advise on
the construction of the church of St. Reparata. On May 31, 1367, Giovanni was one of the
thirteen sworn experts — masters of stone, goldsmiths, painters and citizens — called to
advise with regard to the lights of the central nave of the church, and to give their opinion
on the respective merits of the two models of the cupolas or croce (transept) that were
on view for approval.....

> from D. E. Colnaghi, p. 129, *A Dictionary
> of Florentine Painters*, London, 1928.

The only document about this painter that we have is the Vatican picture: it tells us all
— the period, the school, the style. But not the painter himself — he must remain obscure
until other documents appear to throw light upon his personality, which has so far remained hidden.....

> from — —, p. 6, *Guida della Pinacoteca Va-
> ticana*, 1933.

Documented from 1351 to 1371. Belongs to the Gaddi school.

> from B. Berenson, p. 32, *Italian Pictures
> of the Renaissance, Florentine School*, Vol. I,
> London, 1963.

The facts upon which the historical survival of the fourteenth century painter Giovanni
Bonsi depend are few and of different sorts: a signed work and a few archive documents.....
In 1366 Bonsi is mentioned immediately after Taddeo Gaddi, Andrea di Cione (alias Orcagna), Niccolò di Tommaso, and before Andrea Bonaiuti (followed by names which
today have lost their meaning, Neri di Mone, Nuccio di Jacopo and Paolo Soldini) in
a debate of the Opera of Santa Maria del Fiore, when it asked the commission formed of
these people its opinion on how the construction of the new Cathedral should be continued; and again in 1367, Bonsi appears in the list of thirteen citizens and masters representing the *Operai* who were asked to make a choice of one of the models put forward as
ways of finishing the most important sacred building in Florence. As for the only pictorial text to have survived, it has the artist's signature and the date 1371; it is in the Vatican
Pinacoteca, where it has been since the last century; originally it came from the Cappella
Morali in the church of SS. Jacopo and Lucia, in San Miniato, between Florence and
Pisa.....

> from F. Zeri, p. 224, *Bollettino d' Arte*, XLIX,
> IV, 1964.

Also dating from 1372 is the Vatican triptych of Giovanni Bonsi, still caught up in a
dry Orcagnesque style — although a few lively passages permit one to see an opening towards the later characteristics of the Master of San Martino a Mensola (this last painter's

works include a fresco fragment in the Museum of Santa Croce, dated 1387, Madonna and Child with Angels in the Acton Collection (both in Florence) and the triptych at San Martino a Mensola, dated 1395, near Florence).....

from L. Bellosi, p. 19, *Paragone*, XVI, 187/7, 1965.

BIBLIOGRAPHY
BOOKS

An asterisk indicates a work listed in the General Bibliography

D'Achiardi, P., *Guida della Pinacoteca Vaticana*, Rome, 1913, pp. 18-19; *Khv & Salmi**, 1914, p. 42; Sirèn, O., and Brockwell, M. W., *Catalogue of a Loan Exhibition of Italian Primitives*, Kleinberge Galleries, New York, 1917, p. 38; *v. Marle, 1924**, pp. 406-8; *Colnaghi**, 1928, p. 129; *Toesca, 1929**, p. 53; *Firenze, 1933**, p. 32; *Galetti**, " A-E ", 1950, p. 384; *Gregori**, 1960, pp. 6-7; *Berenson, 1963**, Vol. I, p. 32; *Marcucci**, 1965, pp. 132-3.

JOURNALS

Rondoni, G., *MSV*, XII, 1904, p. 24; Sirèn, O., *RADA*, VI, 5, 1906, pp. 81-7; Bernardini, G., *RADA*, IX, 6, 1909, pp. 89-94; Dami, L., *BA*, IX, 1915, p. 228; Poggi, G., *RA*, XI, 1929, pp. 289-91; Procacci, U., *RA*, XV, 1933, p. 240; Matteoli, A., *BAE*, XV, 1950, pp. 39-43; Baldini, U., *BA*, XXXVII, 4, 1952, pp. 349-50; Zeri, F., *BA*, XLIX, 4, 1964, pp. 224-8; Bellosi, L., *PA*, XVI, 187/7, 1965, p. 19; Boskovits, M., *MKIF*, XIII, 1-4, 1967-8, pp. 55-56; Zeri, F., *GBA*, LXXI, 110, 1968, pp. 73-74.

SIGNED AND DATED WORKS

1371 Rome, Vatican, Pinacoteca, Polyptych: Madonna & Child Enthroned with Saints. s & d. (fig. 436).
1380 Florence, Acton Collection. Panel: St Humphrey with Donor. d. (fig. 448).

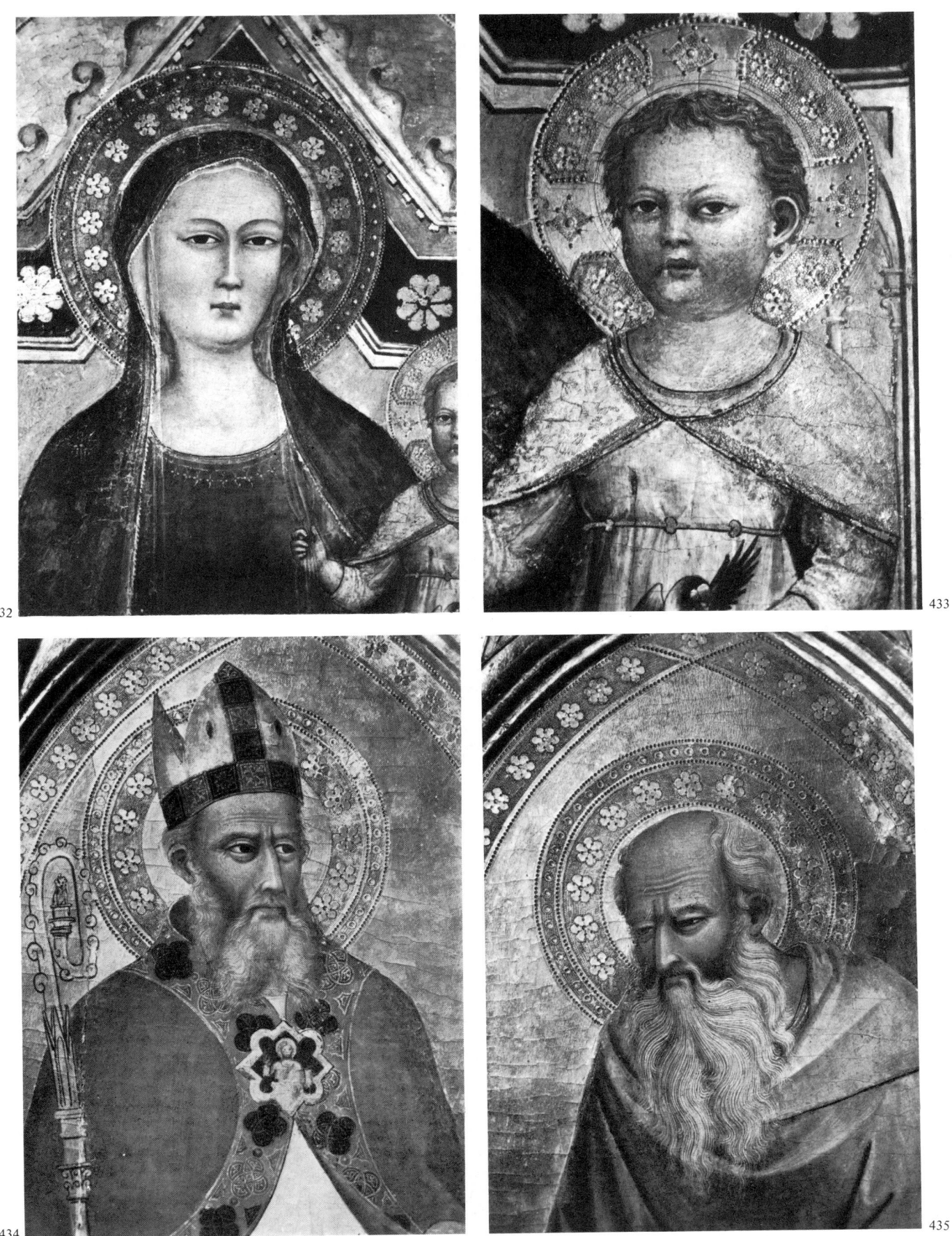

432. *Head of Madonna, detail of fig. 436. Panel. Rome, Vatican, Pinacoteca. no. 9. Museum photo, XXX. 15.45. s & d. 1371.*
433. *Infant Christ, detail of fig. 436. Panel. Rome, Vatican, Pinacoteca. no. 9. Museum photo, XXX.15.46. s. & d. 1371.*
434. *St Nicholas, detail of fig. 436. Panel. Rome, Vatican, Pinacoteca. no. 9. Museum photo, XXX.15.44. s & d. 1371.*
435. *St John the Evangelist, detail of fig. 436. Panel. Rome, Vatican, Pinacoteca. no. 9. Museum photo, XXX.15.48. s & d. 1371.*

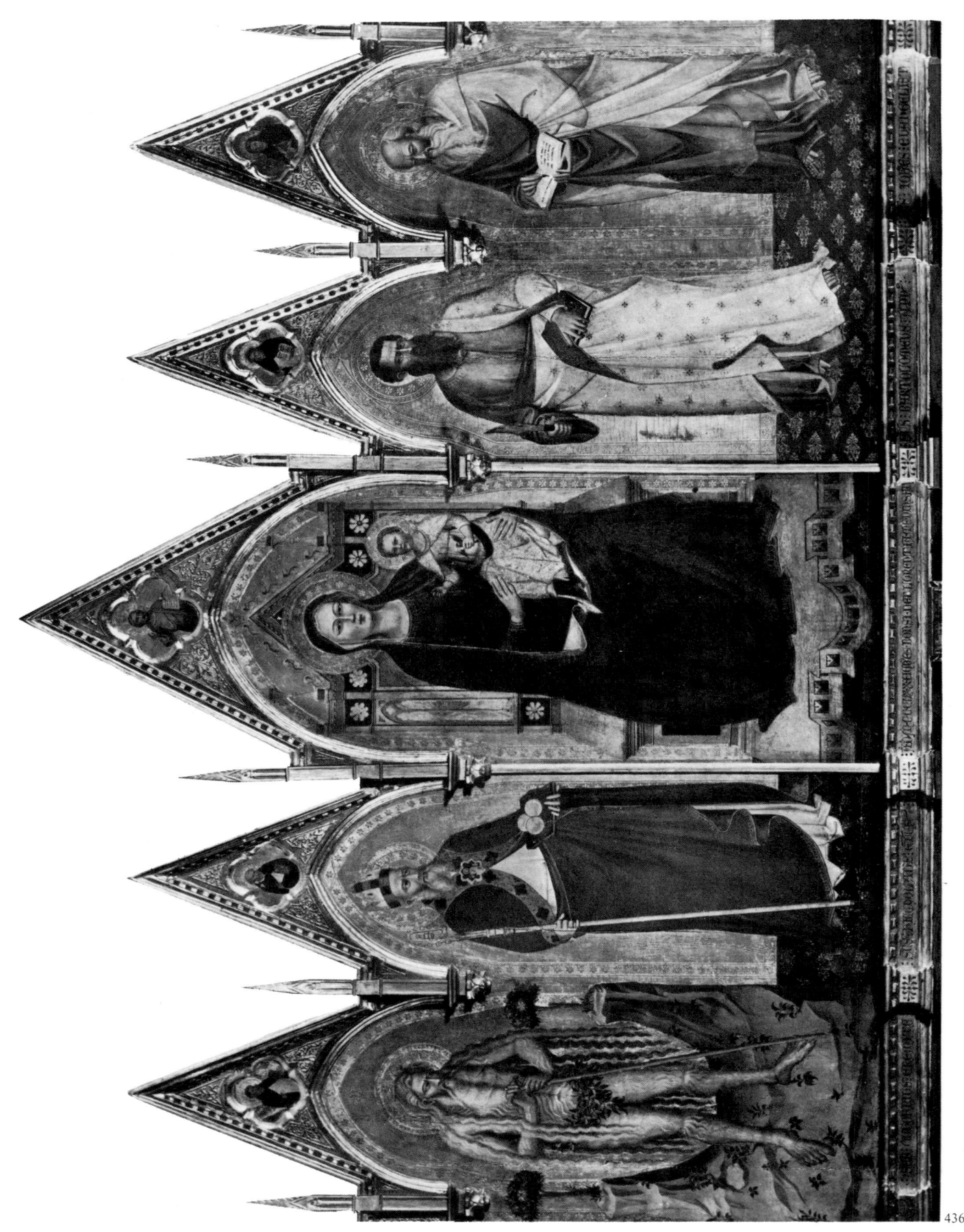

436. *Polyptych: Madonna and Child Enthroned with Sts Humphrey, Nicholas, Bartholomew and John the Evangelist. Above: Christ blessing, and four monastic Saints. Panel. Rome, Vatican, Pinacoteca. no. 9. 166 × 232. Alinari 28134. s & d. 1371.*

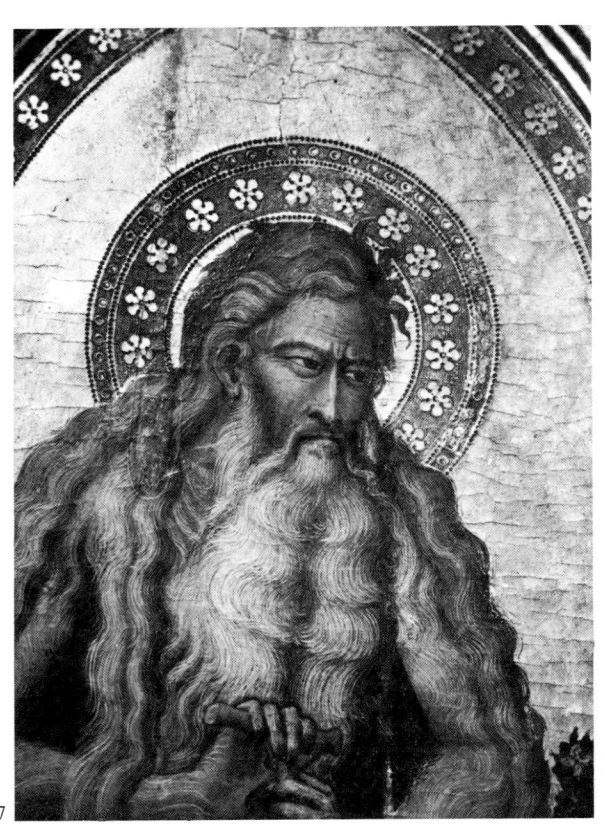

437

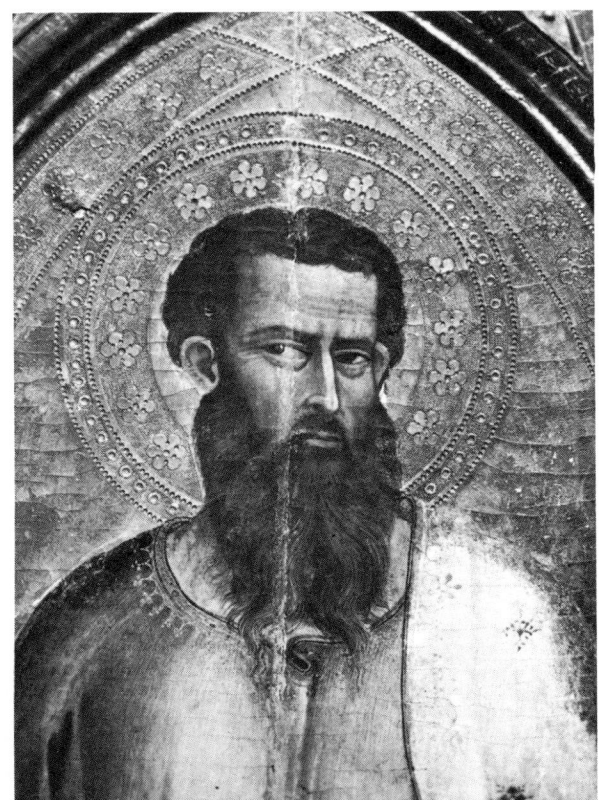

438

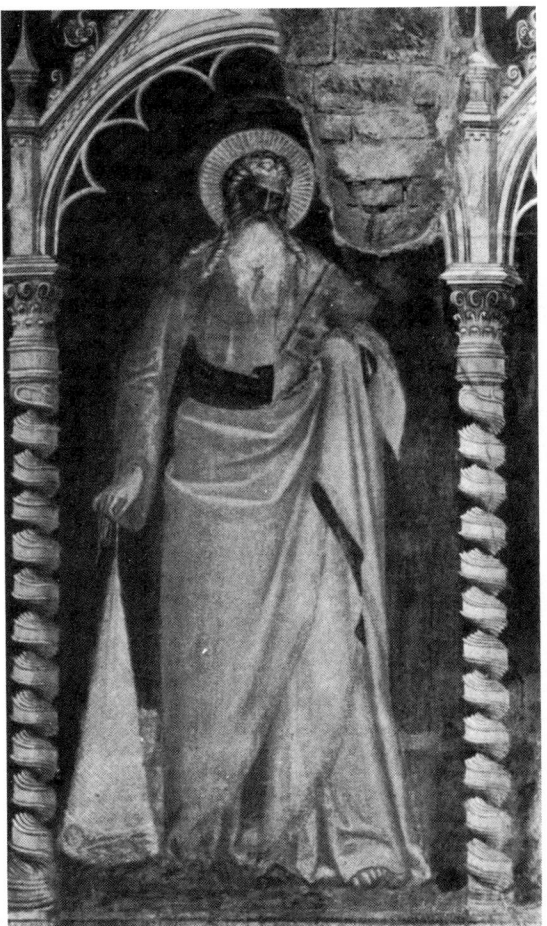

439

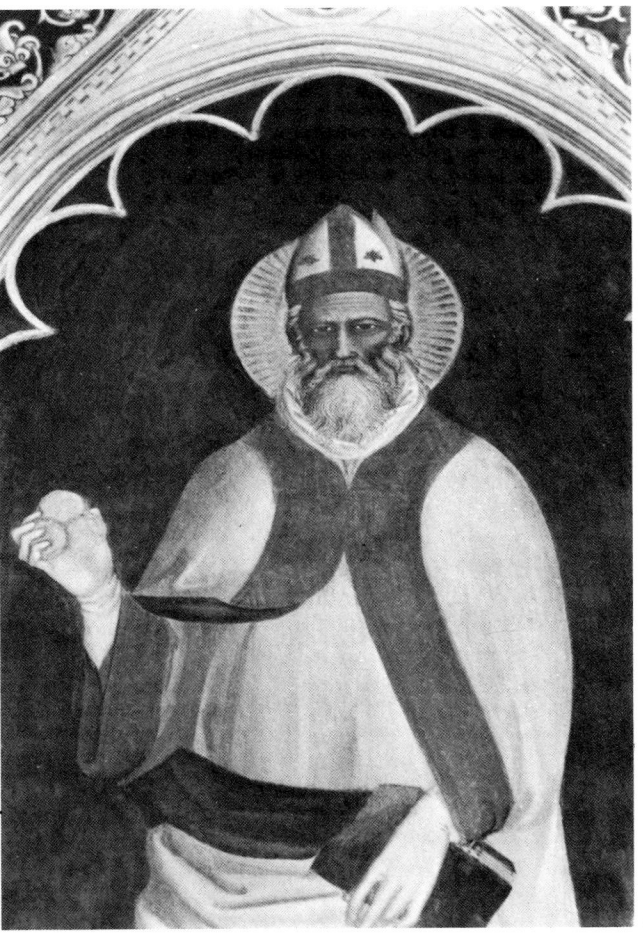

440

437. *St Humphrey, detail of fig. 436. Panel. Rome, Vatican, Pinacoteca. no. 9. Museum photo, XXX.15.43. s & d. 1371.*
438. *St. Bartholomew, detail of fig. 436. Panel. Rome, Vatican, Pinacoteca. no. 9. Museum photo, XXX.15.47. s & d. 1371.*
439. *St Pancras (?), detail of a frescoed triptych (see figs 440, 446-47). Florence, S. Miniato al Monte. Author's photo.*
440. *St. Nicholas, detail of a frescoed triptych (see figs 439, 446-47). Florence, S. Miniato al Monte. Author's photo.*

217

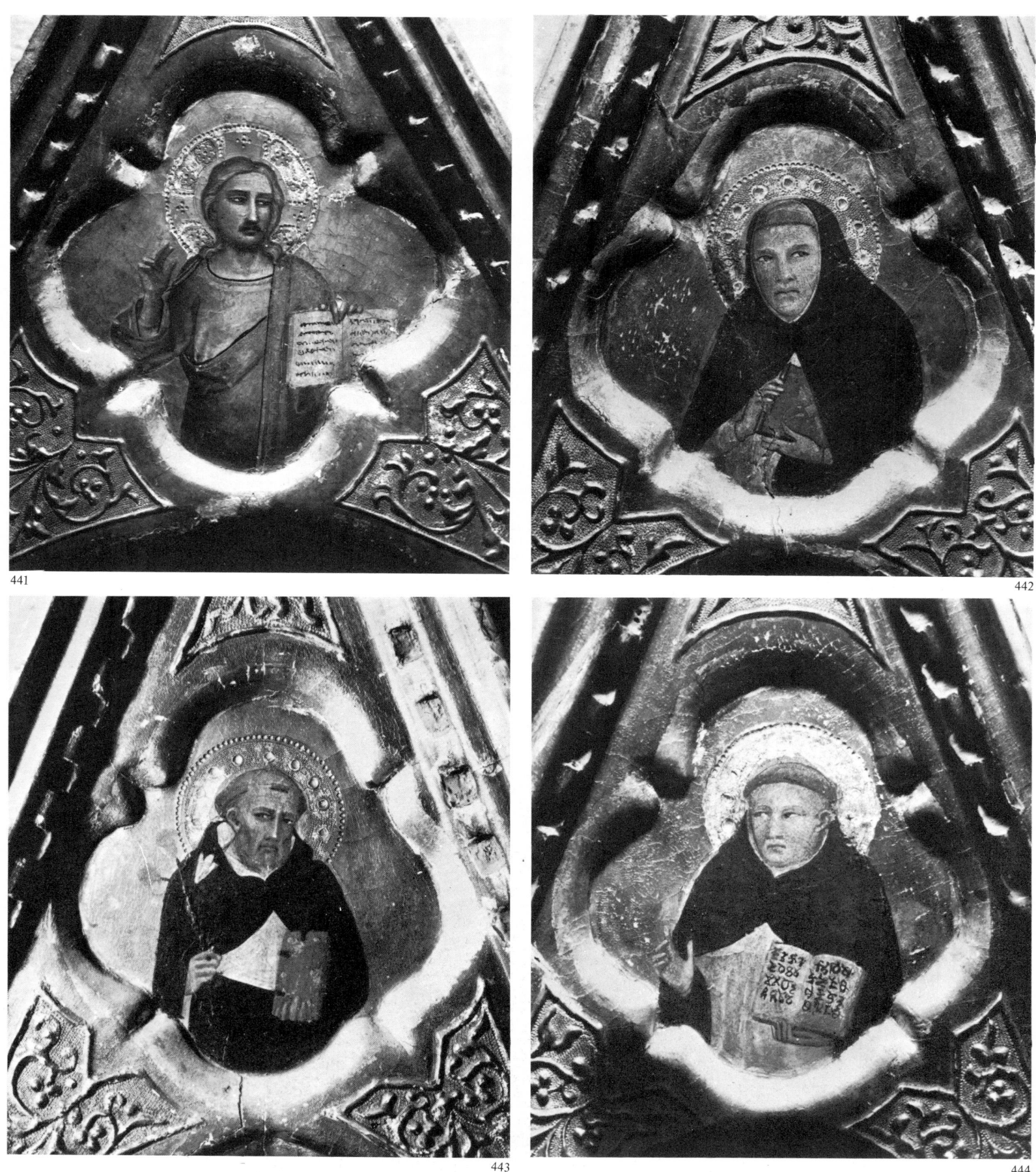

441. *Christ blessing*, *detail of fig. 436. Panel. Rome, Vatican, Pinacoteca. no. 9. Museum photo, XXX.16.99. s & d. 1371.*
442. *Monastic Saint, detail of fig. 436. Panel. Rome, Vatican, Pinacoteca. no. 9. Museum photo, XXX.16.101. s & d. 1371.*
443. *Monastic Saint, detail of fig. 436. Panel. Rome, Vatican, Pinacoteca. no. 9. Museum photo, XXX.16.98. s & d. 1371.*
444. *Monastic Saint, detail of fig. 436. Panel. Rome, Vatican, Pinacoteca. no. 9. Museum photo, XXX.16.100. s & d. 1371.*

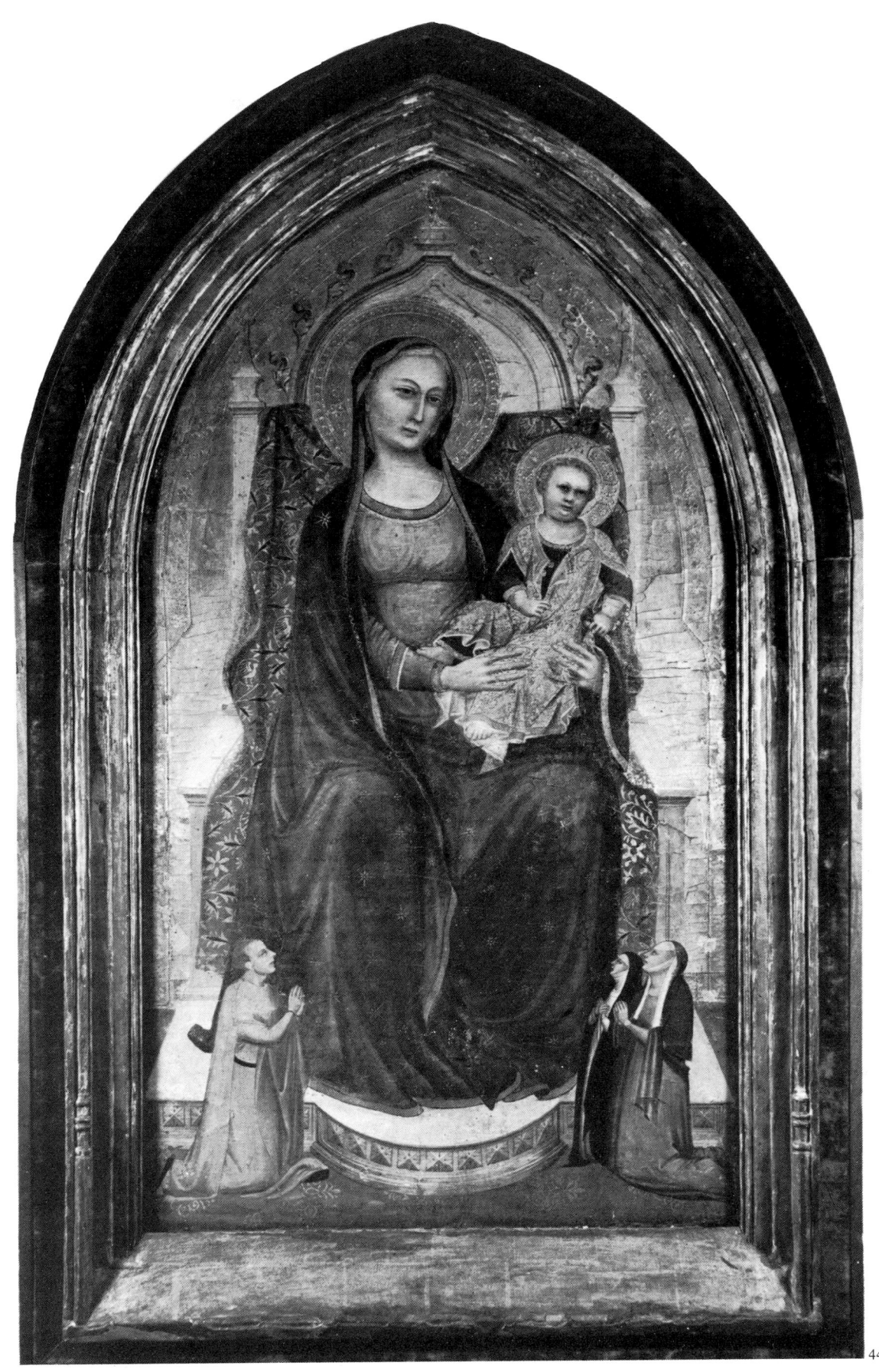

445

445. *Madonna and Child Enthroned with three Donors. Panel. Denver (Colo.), Denver Art Museum. no. E-113. 109.2 × 59.7. Museum photo.*

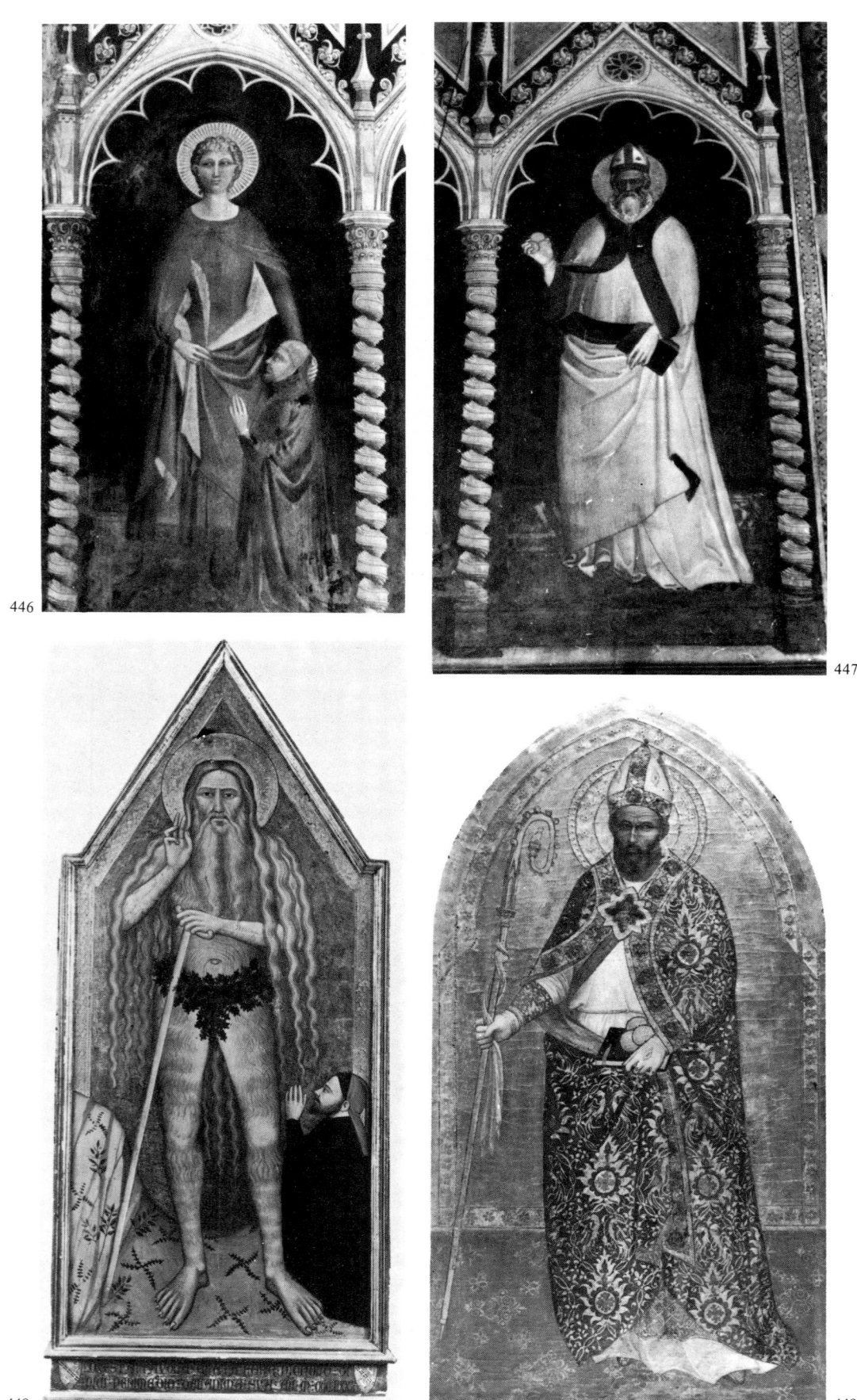

446. *St Minias with a Donor, detail of a frescoed triptych (see figs 439, 440-47). Florence, S. Miniato al Monte. Author's photo.*
447. *St Nicholas, detail of a frescoed triptych (see figs 439, 440-46). Florence, S. Miniato a Monte. Author's photo.*
448. *St Humphrey with Donor. Panel. Florence, Acton Collection. 137 × 60. Reali. d. 1380.*
449. *St Nicholas of Bari. Panel. San Diego (Calif.), Fine Arts Gallery. no. 50:89. 111.7 × 64.7. Museum photo..*

MASTER OF THE GIRALDI TABERNACLE

.... the tabernacle in via dei Giraldi, at the corner of Borgo degli Albizi, of the Madonna and Child with Saints is by an unknown fourteenth century master who was a fine painter.....

from A. J. Rusconi, p. 158, *Emporium*, XLVIII, 4, 1942.

The closeness of the style of the Giraldi tabernacle leads us to consider it to be by the same hand as the Perticaia triptych.....
The painter has the usual luggage of his age: traces of Orcagna, of the Cioni, of Gerini. But there is also a particular manner of painting which is fairly clear, a draughtsmanship quite definitely his: this gives us a precise focal point for identifying the work of the painter and shows us that he is more developed in the Giraldi tabernacle than in the triptych at Perticaia. From this comes the name we would suggest provisionally for him — Master of the Giraldi Tabernacle. He is secondary but capable and we should soon be able to attribute to him other works.....

from U. Baldini, p. 349, in *Bollettino d' Arte*, XXXVII, 4, 1952.

In 1370 Andrea Orcagna and Nardo di Cione had only recently ceased working; Andrea Bonaiuti had finished his frescoes in S. Maria Novella. The Florentine artistic world was alive with activity. Jacopo di Cione was also fully employed (his Uffizi polyptych dates from two years before and about 1370 he was working with Niccolò di Pietro Gerini on the *Coronation of the Virgin*, now in London); Giovanni del Biondo was already established, while Giovanni Bonsi was about to begin work on his Vatican polyptych.

From artists such as these spring the sources of our modest painter. Nardo, Jacopo and Niccolò Gerini are the painters who influence him decisively. Jacopo must have fascinated him with certain elements of control over movement and with his clear tight draughtsmanship, Nardo with his delicacy of colour and sometimes almost manneristic treatment of clothing, Gerini with his free narrative style. Perhaps even Giovanni Bonsi influenced him, although that artist's Vatican polyptych dates from only a year later.....

from U. Baldini, p. 350, *Bollettino d' Arte*, XXXVII, 4, 1952.

The picture is by the same hand as an altarpiece in the parish church of S. Pietro in Perticaja, near Florence. In that triptych the Virgin is seen in full length, seated in the center panel. St Catherine and St Christopher are represented in the wings. This attribution was supported by most of the scholars consulted by the Kress Foundation. The one scholar who expressed a different opinion was Bernard Berenson, who suggested Bartolommeo Cristiani as the author. The " Perticaja " master must have been a Florentine painter of the late 14th century, influenced by both Orcagna and Daddi. The Perticaja triptych, according to William Suida, is dated 1370 and the present panel is probably not much later. It represents well the languid style of Florentine art in the later 14th century, after it had absorbed some Sienese influences.

The significance of this panel is all the greater as it seems to be in an unusually fine state of preservation.

from J. S. Held, no. 3, *The Samuel H. Kress Collection of Italian and Spanish Paintings*, Ponce, Puerto Rico, 1962.

The figures [in the Madonna and Child in Ponce, Puerto Rico] are so closely paralleled in a *Madonna and Child with Angels* in the Louvre as to suggest that both panels are by the same follower of Niccolò di Pietro Gerini. Probable identity of authorship with a triptych of the *Madonna and Child with Saints*, dated 1370, in San Pietro, Perticaia, near Florence, has suggested the designation Master of the Perticaia Triptych for the anonymous painter [of the Ponce panel], with a date around 1370-80.

from F. R., Shapley, pp. 43-44, *Paintings from the ˎSamuel H. Kress Collection*, London, 1966.

BIBLIOGRAPHY
BOOKS

An asterisk indicates a work listed in the General Bibliography

Offner, R., *Studies**, 1927, pp. 83-96; Rusconi, A. J., *E*, XLVIII, 4, 1942, pp. 158-9; Baldini, U., *BA*, XXXVII, 4, 1952, pp. 349-50; Held, J. S., *Museo de Arte de Ponce*, Puerto Rico, 1962, no. 3; *Shapley**, 1966, pp. 43-44.

DATED WORK

1370 Perticaia, Rignano sull'Arno. S. Cristofano, Polyptych: Madonna & Child with Sts. Christopher and Margaret. d. (fig. 461).

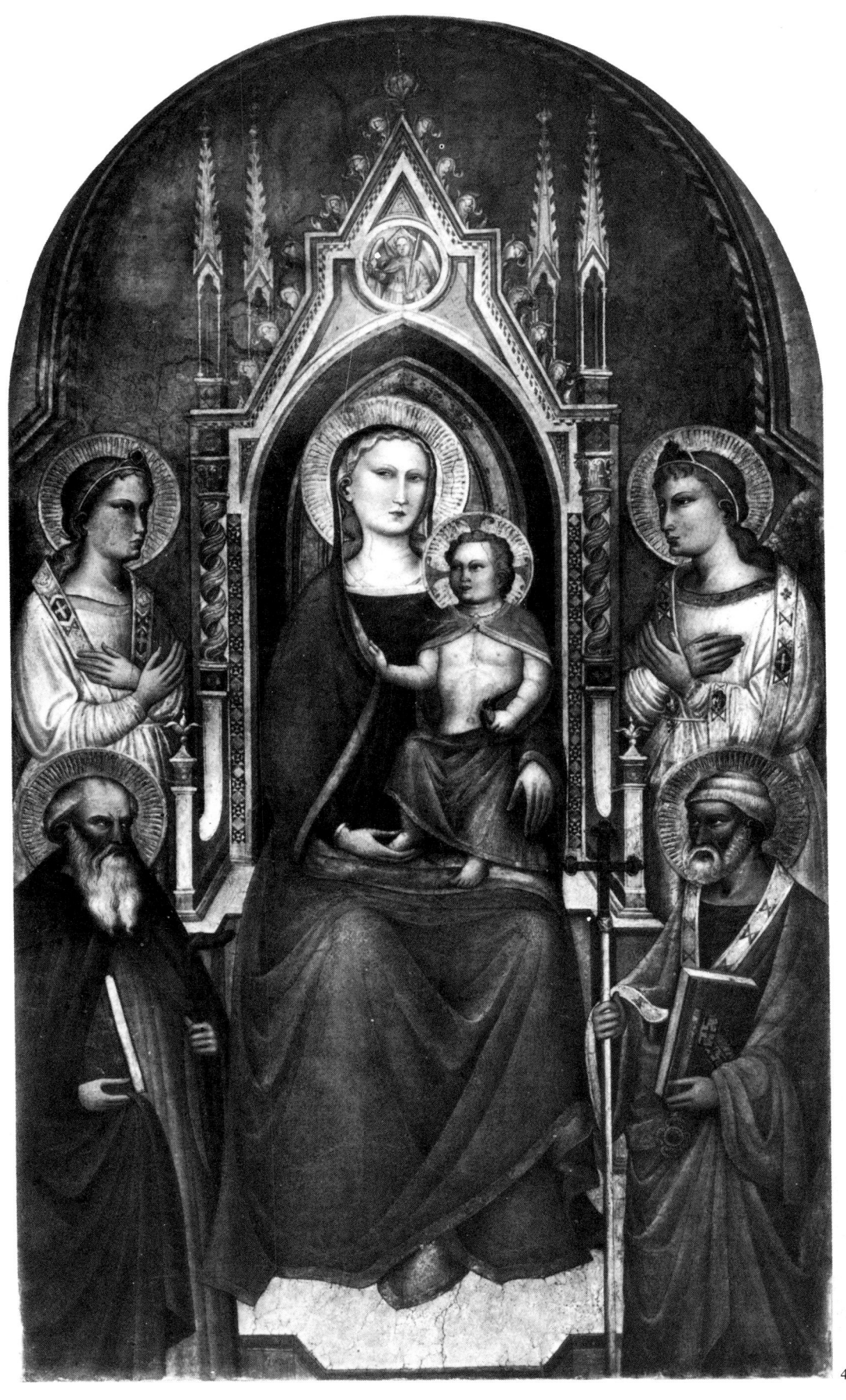

450

450. Tabernacle: Madonna and Child Enthroned with Sts Anthony Abbot and Peter and two Angels. Fresco. Florence, corner of via dei Giraldi and Borgo degli Albizi. SGF 93994.

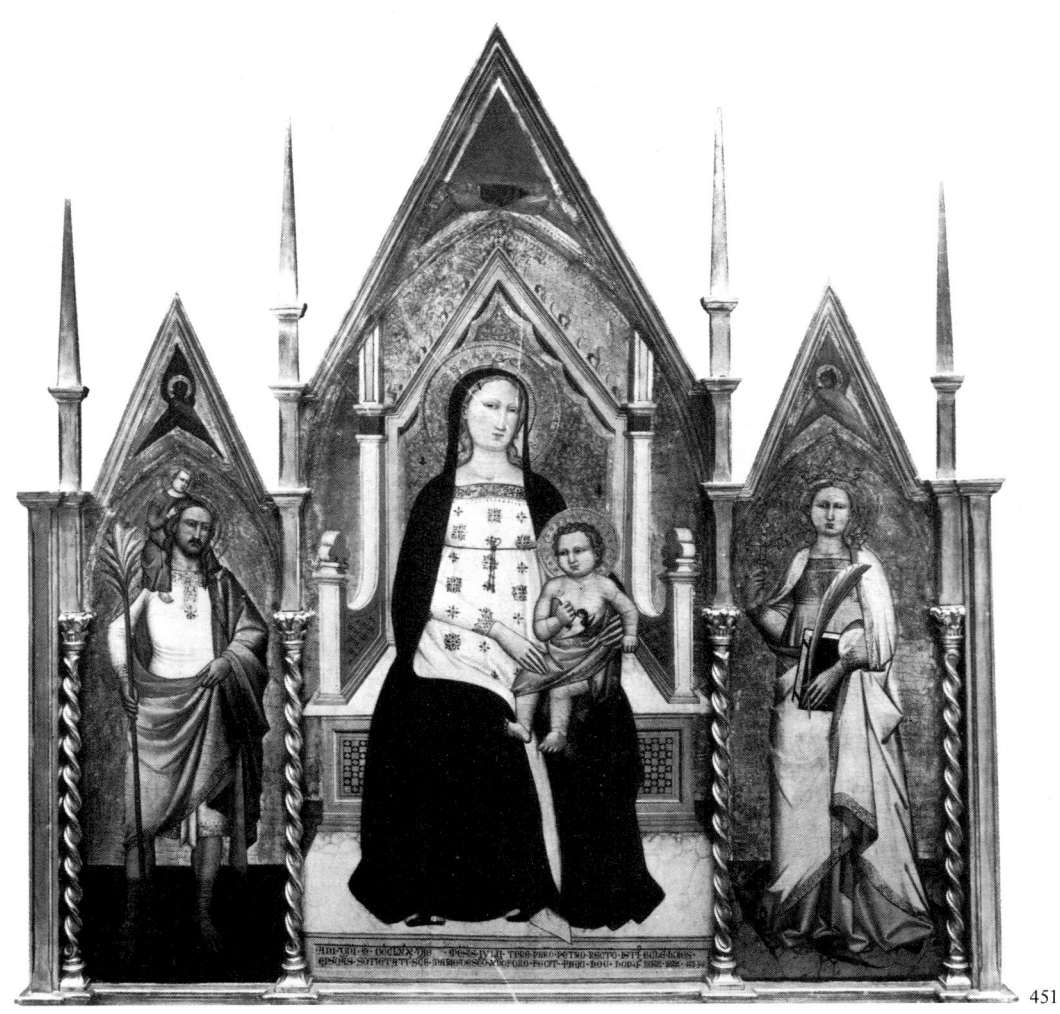

451

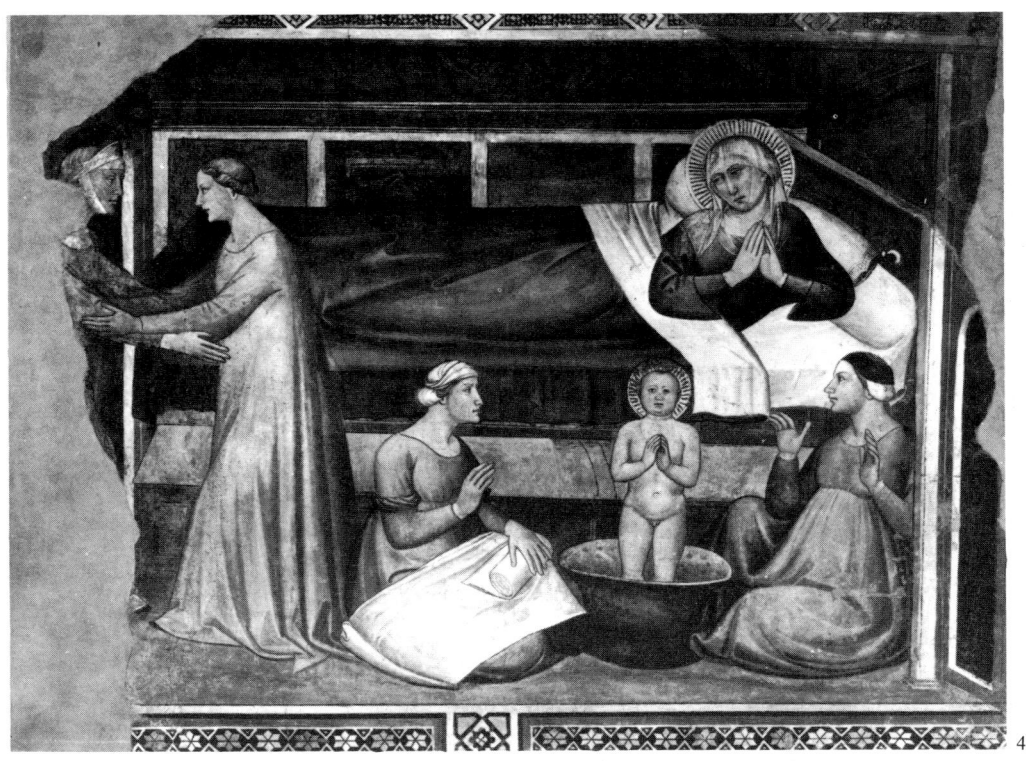

452

451. *Triptych: Madonna and Child Enthroned with Sts Christopher and Margaret. Panel. Perticaia, Rignano sull' Arno, S. Cristofano. cp: 148 × 67; sps: 108 × 37. SGF 25030. d. 1370.*
452. *Birth of St John the Baptist. Fresco. Florence, S. Simone. SGF 174093.*

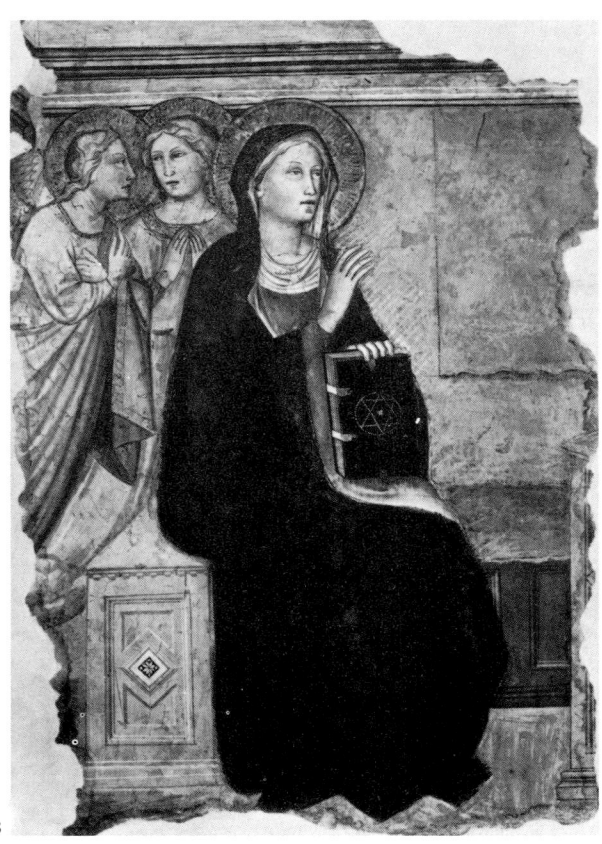

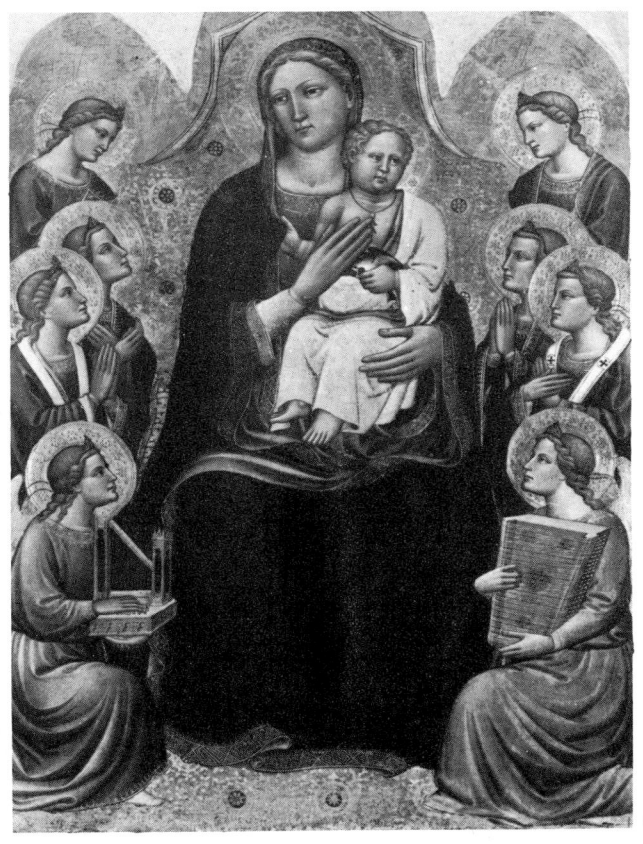

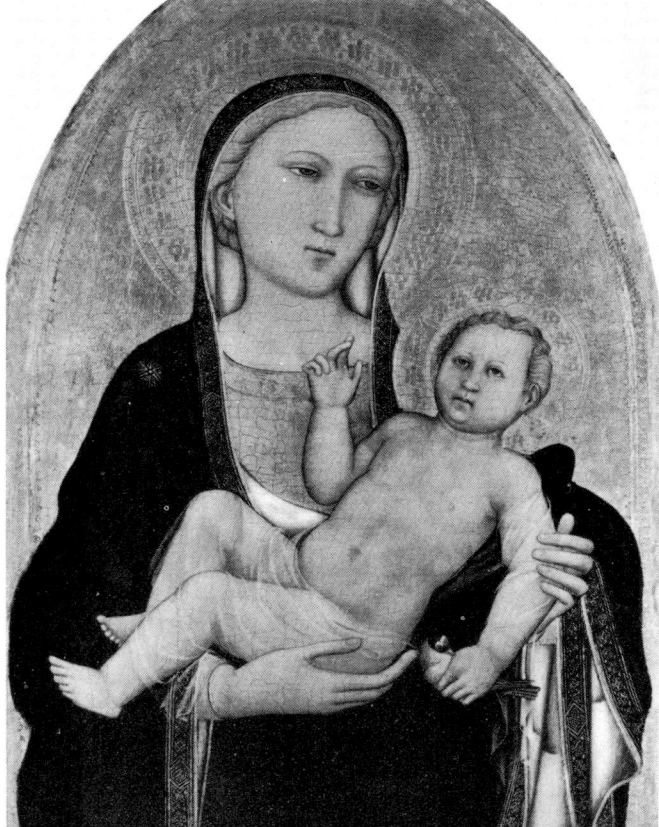

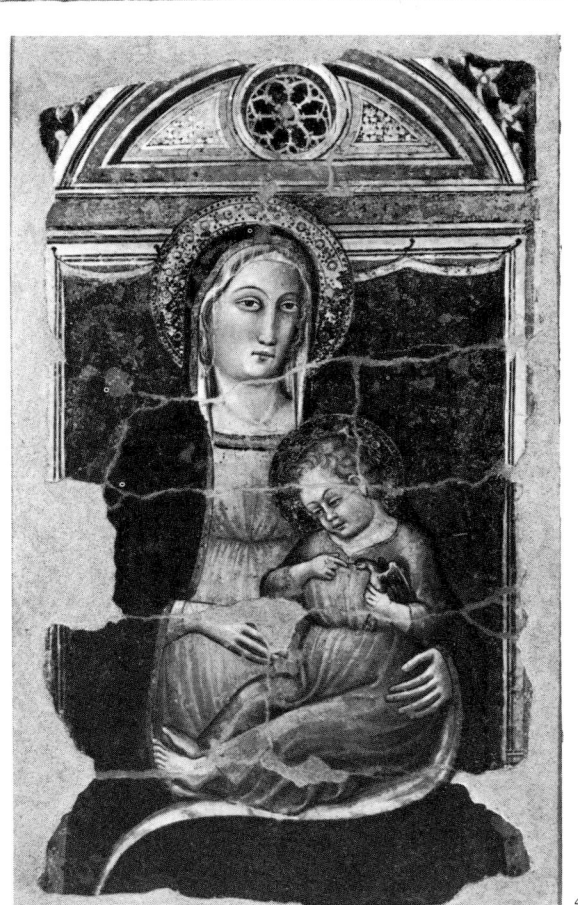

453. *Virgin Annunciate. Fresco. Montevarchi, Chiesa di Cernana. SGF 132694.*
454. *Madonna and Child Enthroned with eight Angels. Panel. Paris, Musée du Louvre. no. 1316. 85 × 61. Museum photo.*
455. *Madonna and Child. Panel. Ponce (Puerto Rico), Museo de Arte, Kress Study Collection. no. K.1119. 56.5 × 38.4. Kress Foundation photo.*
456. *Madonna and Child. Fresco. Arezzo, Duomo. SGF 132696.*

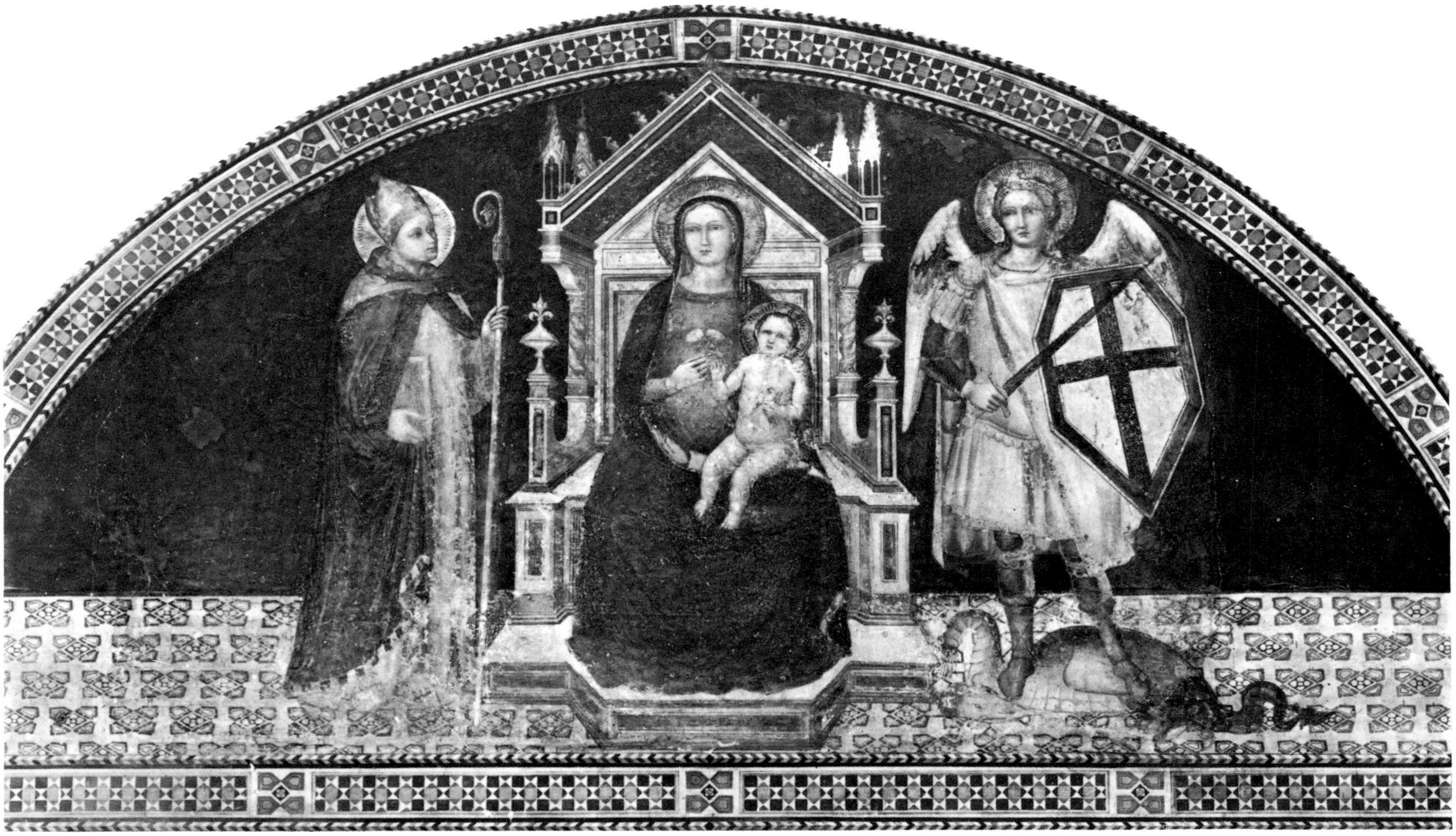

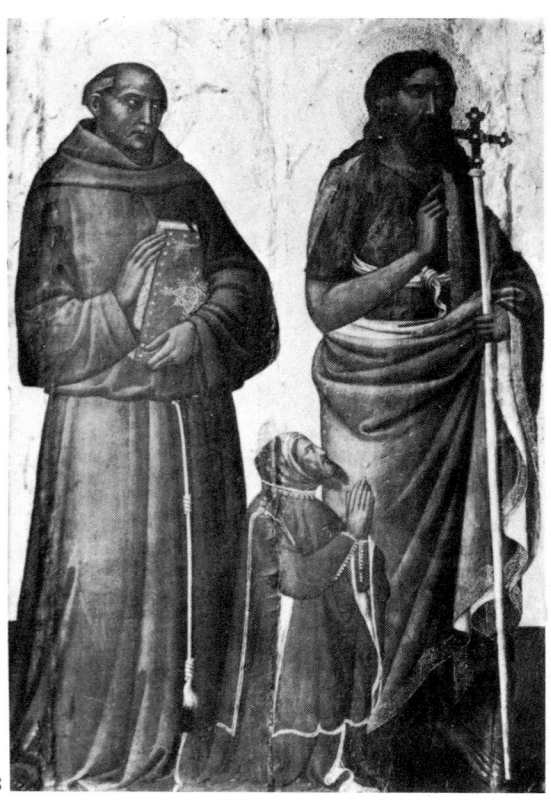
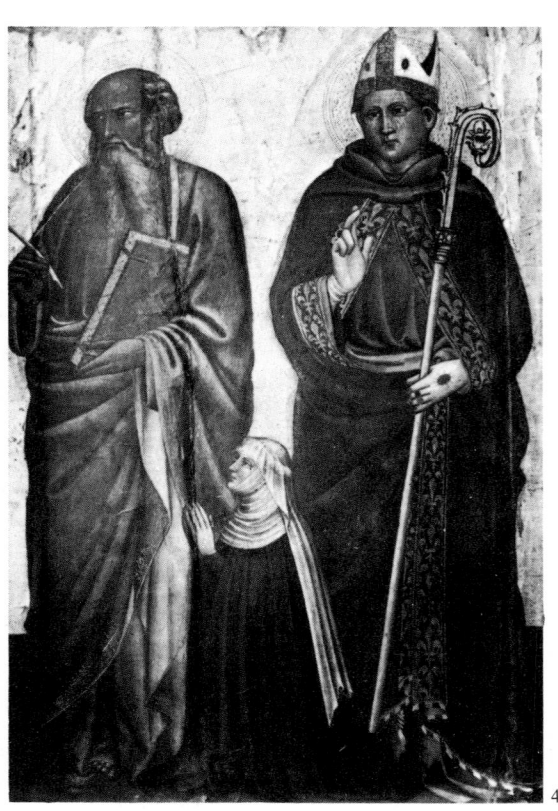

457. *Madonna and Child Enthroned with Sts Martin and George. Fresco. Florence, S. Croce, Cloister. Alinari 3971.*
458. *Sts Bernardino, John the Baptist and Donor (see fig. 459). Panel. Rouen, Musée, Campana Collection. Campana no. 103. Fototeca Berenson.*
459. *Sts Louis of Toulouse, John the Evangelist and Donor (see fig. 458). Panel. Rouen, Musée, Campana Collection. Campana no. 102. 84 × 57. Fototeca Berenson.*

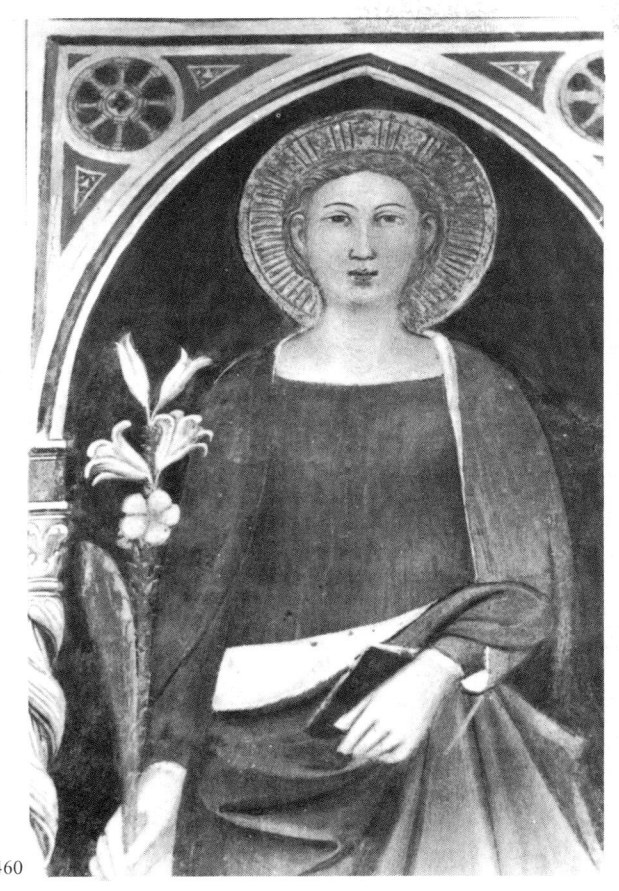

460

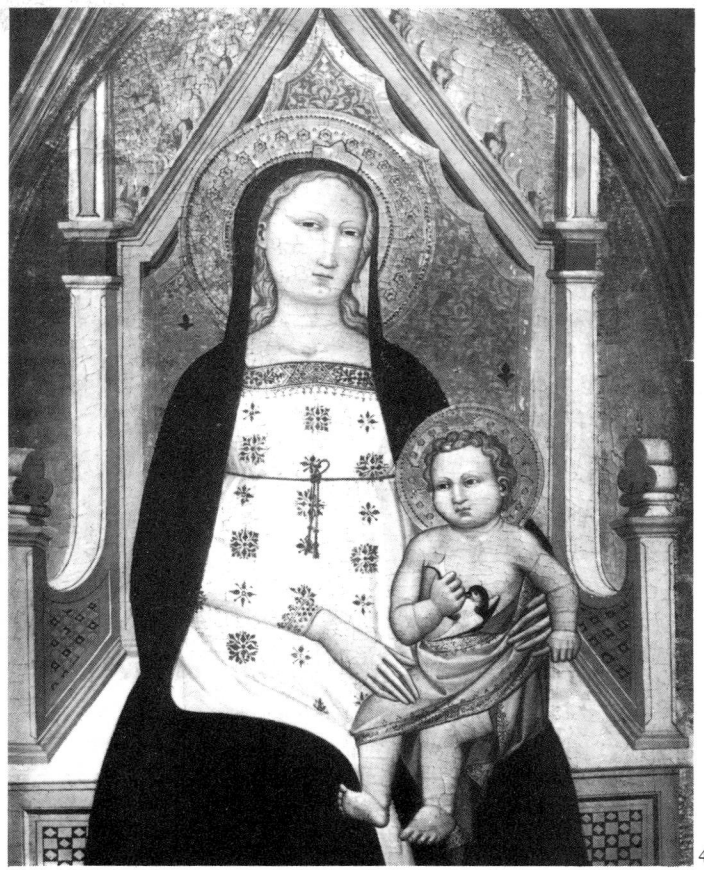

461

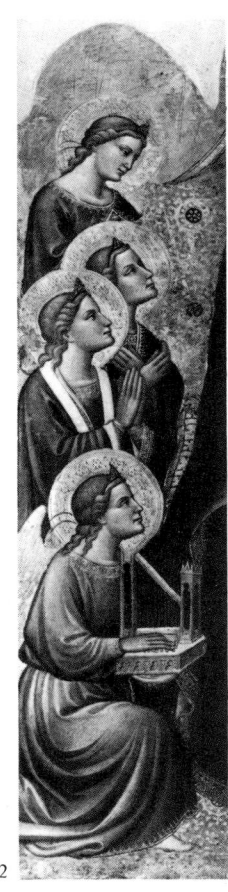

462

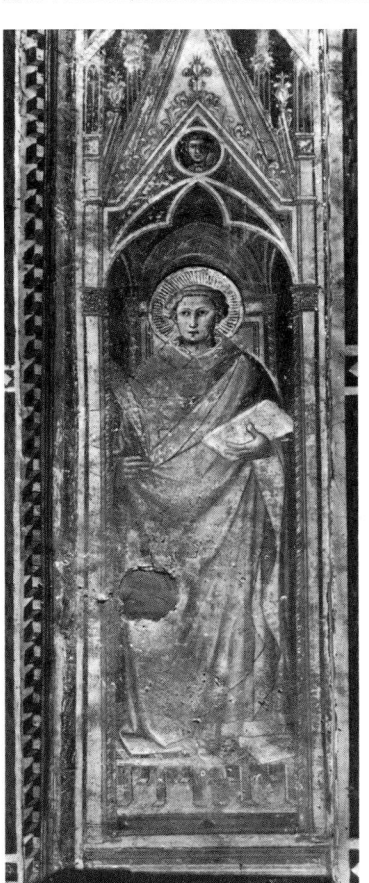

463

460. *Detail: St Catherine of Alexandria. Fresco. Florence, S. Miniato al Monte. Author's photo.*
461. *Madonna and Child, detail of fig. 451. Panel. Perticaia, Rignano sull' Arno, S. Cristofano. SGF 25031. d. 1370.*
462. *Four Angels, detail of fig. 454. Panel. Paris, Musée du Louvre. no. 1316. Museum photo.*
463. *St Lawrence. Fresco. Florence, S. Croce, Castellani Chapel. Brogi 19260.*

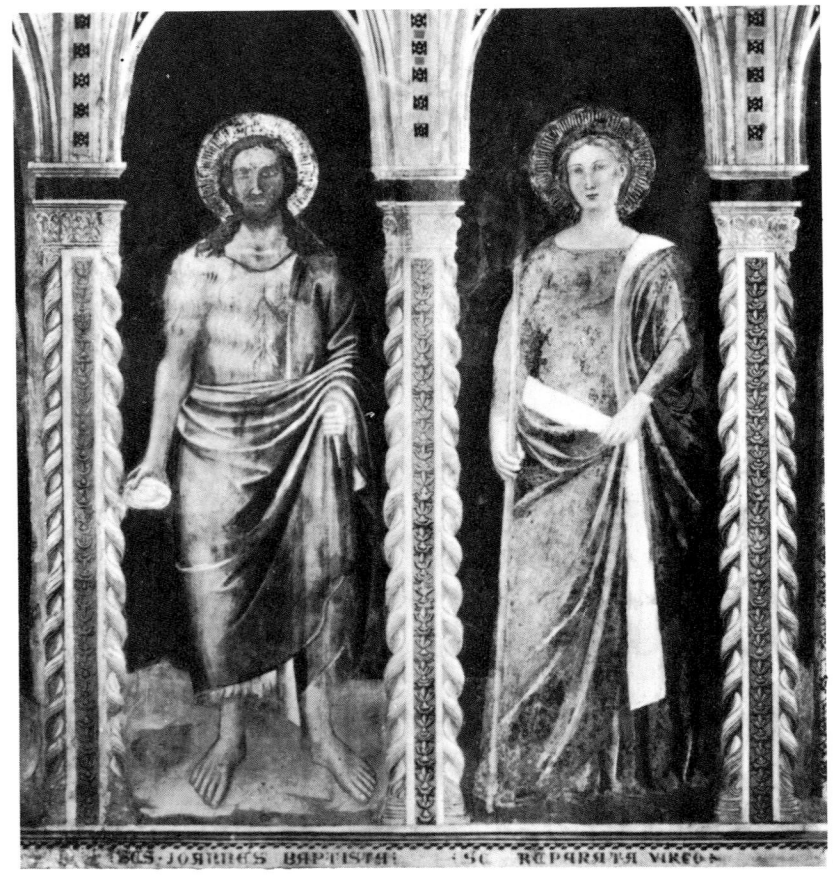

464

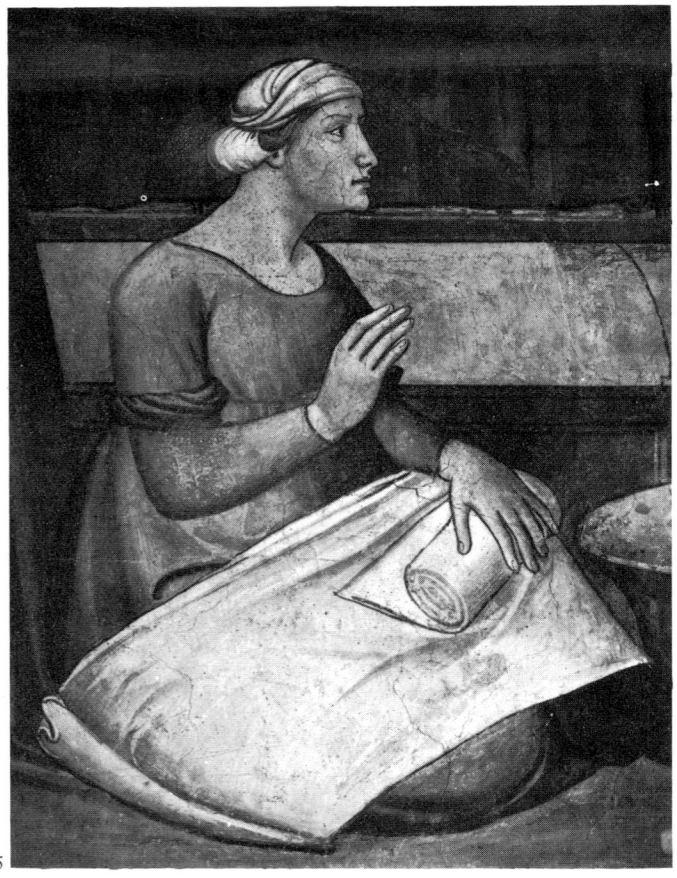

465

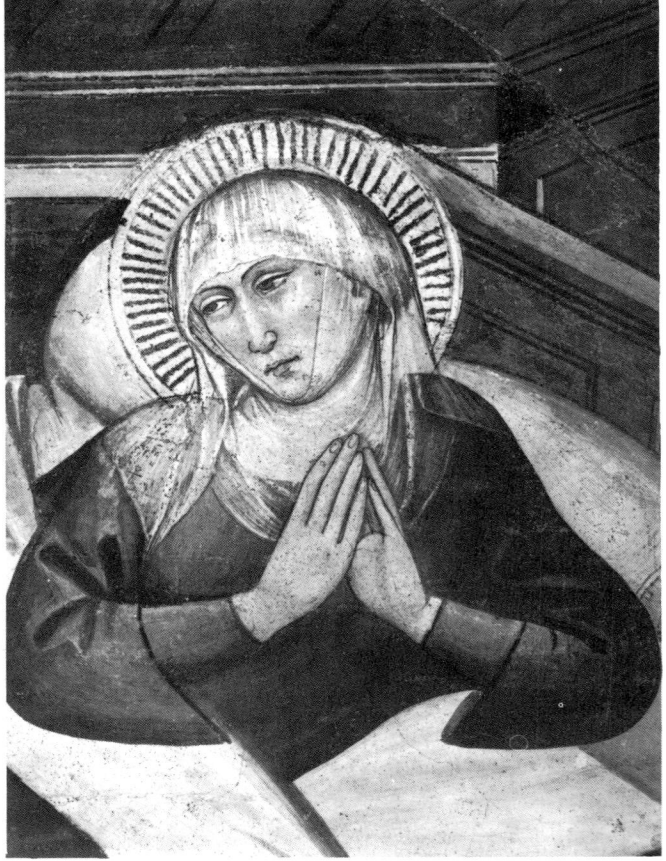

466

464. *Two Saints. Fresco. Florence, S. Miniato al Monte. Author's photo.*
465. *Seated woman, detail of fig. 452. Fresco. Florence, S. Simone. SGF 174101.*
466. *Head of St Elizabeth, detail of fig. 452. Fresco. Florence, S. Simone. SGF 174097.*

ANTONIO VENEZIANO

Of weaker fibre than Orcagna, but gifted with a very delicate taste, Antonio Veneziano went beyond his precursors in accuracy of observation and power in realising detail, distinguishing the texture as well as the folding of varieties of stuffs, colouring surfaces in tender shades of tints, and perfecting the processes of manipulation in pure fresco.....

from J. A. Crowe & G. B. Cavalcaselle, p. 17, *A History of Painting in Italy*, Vol. IV, London, 1911.

Antonio Veneziano is à painter about whom we possess a certain amount of documentary evidence but whose artistic activities are known to us through three works, the frescoes in the Campo Santo of Pisa, those in the tabernacle of the so-called Torre degli Agli in the neighbourhood of Florence, and a panel in Palermo under which part of his signature seems still to be visible.
Antonio, according to Vasari, was Venetian by birth but received his artistic instruction in Florence. He returned to his native town and was charged by the council with the execution of an important wall-painting which, on account of its excellence, caused so much jealousy that Antonio left Venice for ever.....

from R. van Marle, p. 443, *The Development of the Italian Schools of Painting*, Vol. III, The Hague, 1924.

To find a combination of Sienese and Florentine characteristics one often has to go to Pisa, and it is in Pisa, in the Camposanto, that we find our master, in three damaged scenes from the life of S. Ranieri. Admitting natural disparities between fresco and tempera, and assuming a discrepancy in the dates of the two paintings, the manner, the types and the aesthetic content of our picture betray the same artistic personality.
Antonio Veneziano has a Florentine understanding of physical density, and the modelling shadow within, or beyond the edge, in the Camposanto series, is a Florentine convention that goes back to the thirteenth century, and in its persistence in the typically Florentine low marble-relief, manifests its suitability to a peculiarly Florentine, feeling for plasticity. This mode renders the figure in flat masses, as in the Obsequies of S. Ranieri, where it best shows its desired effects of architectural solidity and breadth.....

from R. Offner, pp. 71-72, *Studies in Florentine Painting*, New York, 1927.

He was closely tied to Florentine culture, whether one takes his name to refer to his place of birth (Vasari), or simply to indicate that he spent a long time in Venice — neither hypothesis is documented by any works which have come down to us. All we know of him has to with Tuscany: he is in Siena in 1369, working in the Duomo with Andrea Vanni; in Florence in 1374; and then in Pisa from 1384 to 1386 in the Camposanto to finish the cycle of the history of St. Ranierius which had been begun by Andrea Bonaiuti.....

from U. Baldini, p. 89, *IIª Mostra di Affreschi Staccati*, Florence, 1958.

Antonio di Francesco da Venezia, worked in Siena with Andrea Vanni 1369-70, is documented in Florence in 1374 and in Pisa from 1384 to 1388. Must have come under the influence of Orcagna's following in Florence, of Traini in Pisa, and of Vanni in Siena.....

from B. Berenson, p. 16, *Italian Pictures of the Renaissance, Florentine School*, Vol. I, London, 1963.

Tuscan School although his name would indicate Venetian derivation. Mentioned 1369-1388, in Siena, Florence, and Pisa. · He worked in all three cities and felt the influence of their painters. The chief touchstone for his style had been the frescoes which he painted between 1384 and 1387 in the Campo Santo, Pisa. Destroyed during World War II, these frescoes must now be studied in reproduction.....

from F. R. Shapley, p. 46, *Paintings from the Samuel H. Kress Collection*, London, 1966.

BIBLIOGRAPHY
BOOKS

An asterisk indicates a work listed in the General Bibliography

C-Cavalcaselle II*, 1903, pp. 279-95; *Venturi, A.**, 1907, pp. 915-20; Fogolari, G., *T-Becker**, 1908, Vol. II, pp. 13-15; *v. Marle, 1924**, pp. 443-53; *Offner, Studies**, 1927, pp. 67-81; *Offner, 1927**, p. 21; *Colnaghi**, 1928, p. 274; *Berenson, 1932**, p. 238; *Venturi, L.**, 1931, pls. 48-49, 87-90; Marcazzan, M., *Treccani, Vol. XXXV**, 1937, p. 78; *Coletti, Vol. II**, 1946, pp. 57-8; *Antal**, 1948, p. 205; *Galetti**, " A-E ", 1950, pp. 129-33; *Oertel, 1950**, p. 24; *Toesca, 1951**, pp. 668-9; *MAS II**, 1958, p. 89; Bertolini, L., *Camposanto**, 1960, pp. 77-82; Carli, E., *Pittura pisana del Trecento: la seconda metà del secolo*, Milan, 1961, pp. 22-4; *Berenson 1963**, Vol. I, p. 16; *Shapley**, 1966, p. 46; Paolucci, A., *Il diffondersi della visione prospettica* (I Maestri del Colore, 257), Milan, 1966.

JOURNALS

Offner, R., *AA*, VIII, 3, 1920, pp. 98-103; Offner, R., *AA*, 1923, pp. 216-228; Salmi, M., *BA*, VIII, 7, 1929, pp. 433-52; Angulo Inigiez, D., *AE*, XIX, 1931, p. 27; Brandi, C., *MKIF*, III, 1919-32, pp. 441-4; Gamba, C., *RA*, XIV, 1932, pp. 55-74; Cohn, W., *Berliner Museen*, VII, 1957, pp. 52-3; Steinweg, K., *W*, XXXII, 24, 1962, p. 17; Steinweg, K., *Berliner Museen*, XV, 1, 1965, pp. 4-6; Boskovits, M., *ZKG*, XXXI, 4, 1968, p. 278; (*advertisement*), *AP*, XCI, June 1970, p. CXVIII; Fremantle, R., *AV*, XII, I, 1973, pp. 12-13; Fremantle, R., *BM*, CXVI, 858, 1974, pp. 526-29.

SIGNED AND DATED WORK

1388 Palermo, S. Niccolò Reale, Museo Diocesano. Panel: Flagellation of Christ; Virgin, St John, Evangelists and Prophets. s & d. (fig. 480).

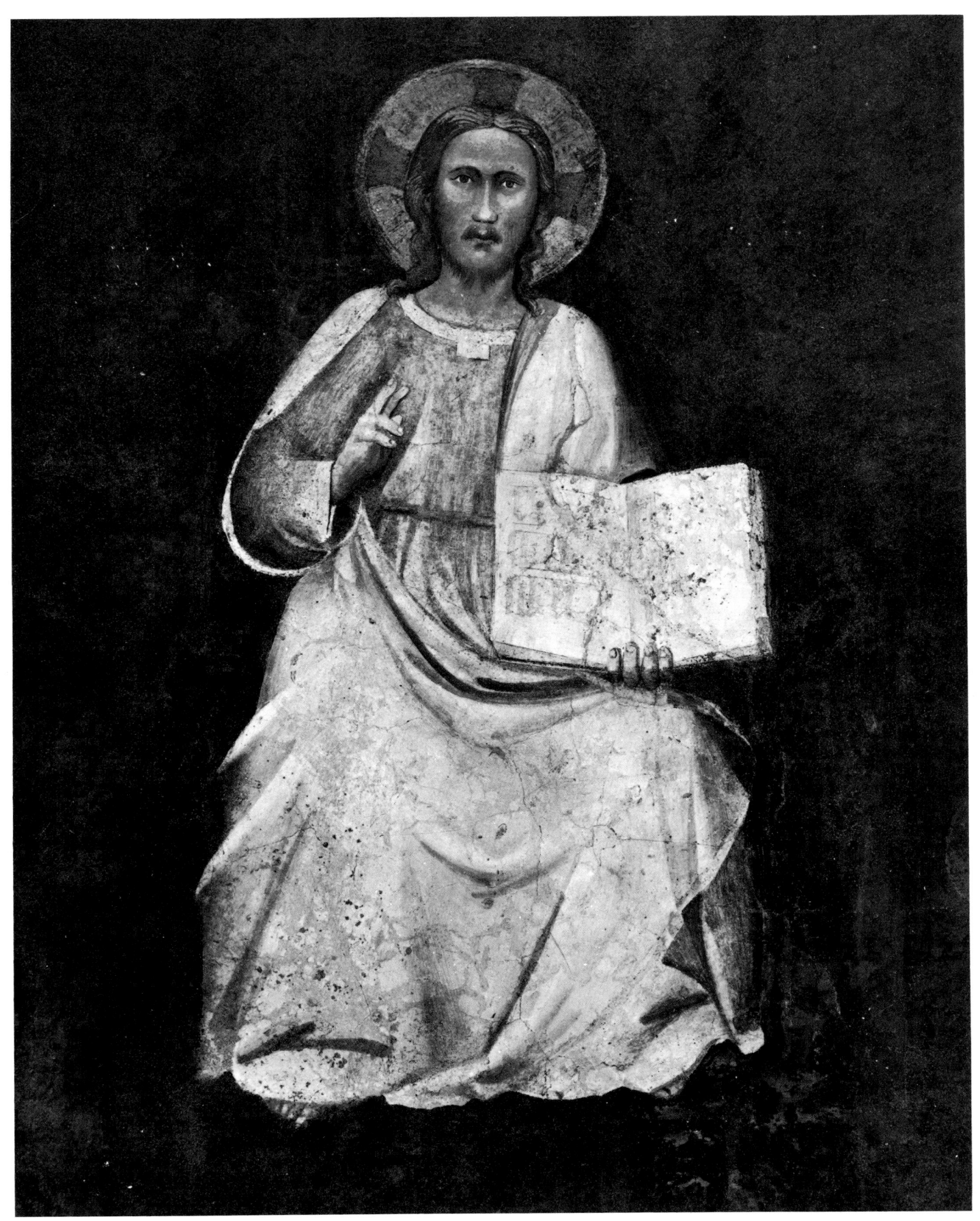

467. *Christ the Redeemer, detail of fig. 481. Fresco. Florence, Forte di Belvedere (formerly Torre degli Agli). SGF 108167.*

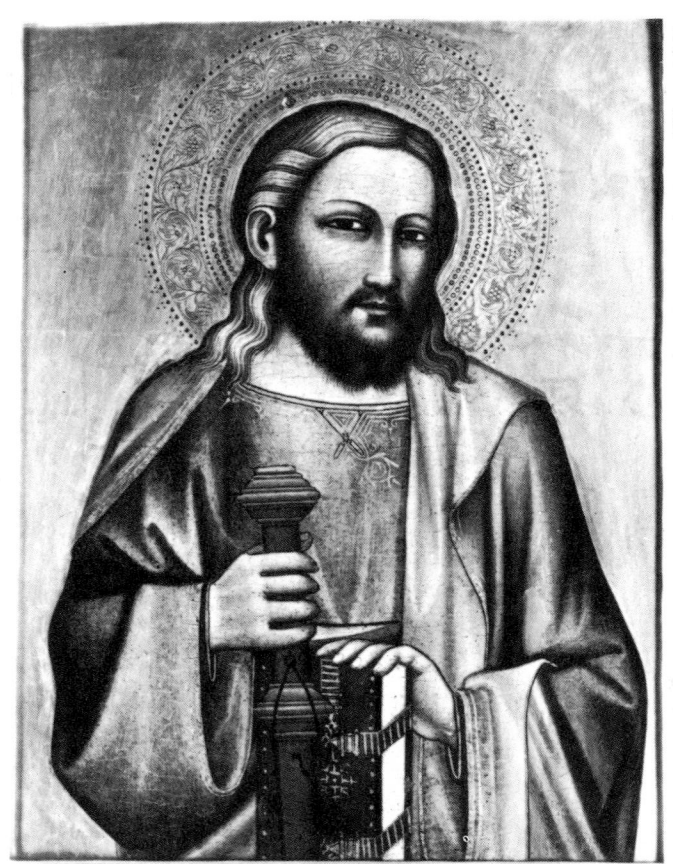

468

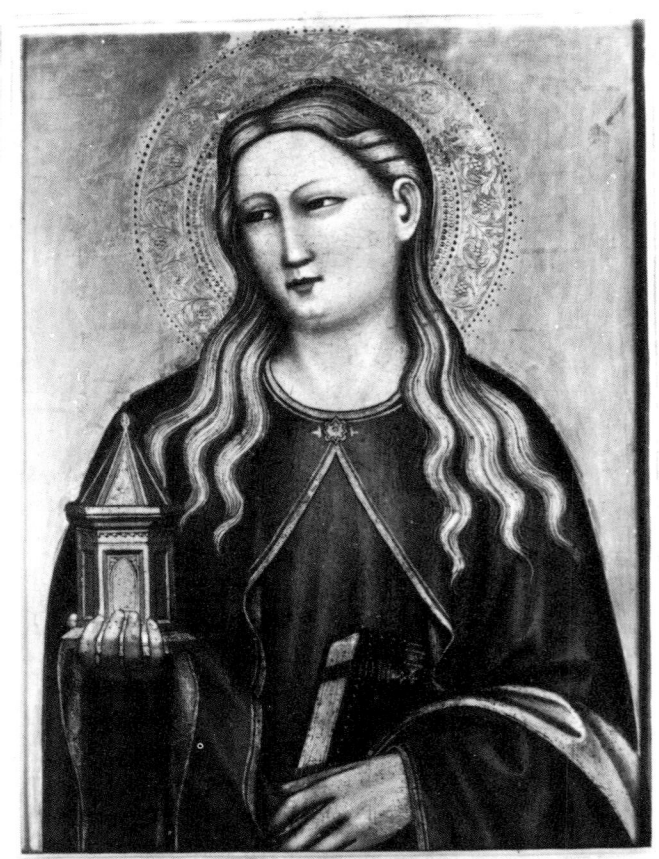

469

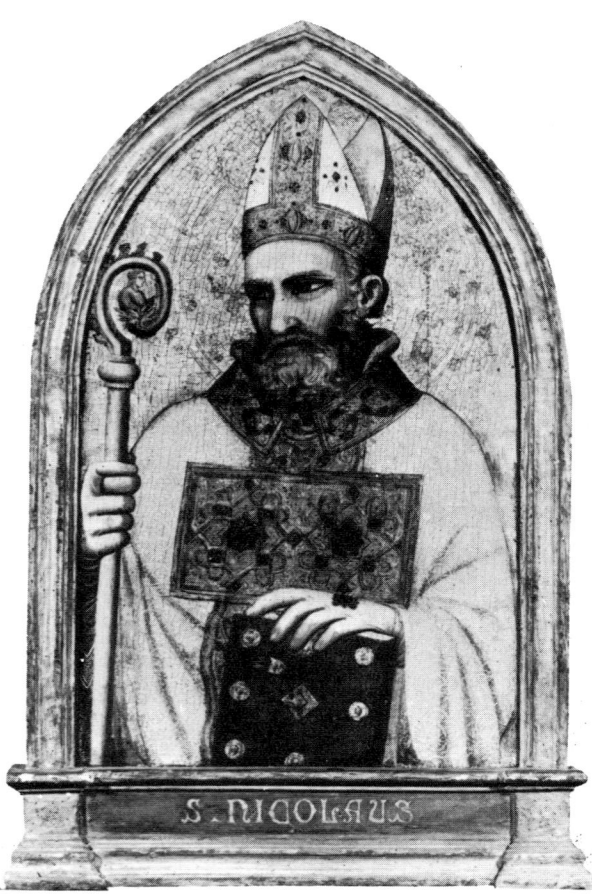

470

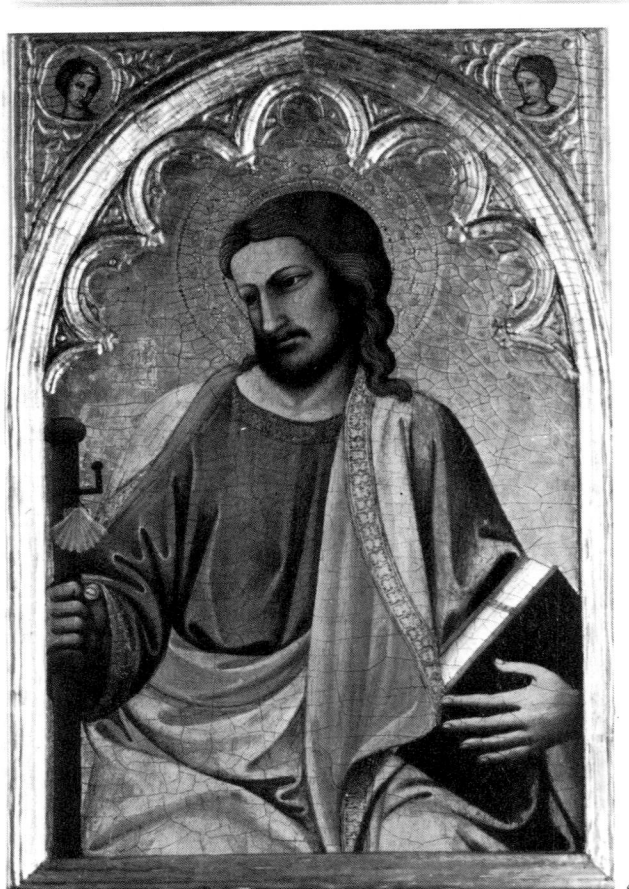

471

468. *St James Major. Panel. Rome, Vatican, Pinacoteca. no. 16 . 57 × 43. Alinari 38180.*
469. *St Mary Magdalene. Panel. Rome, Vatican, Pinacoteca. no. 19. 56.6 × 43.1. Alinari 38181.*
470. *St Nicholas. Panel. Private Collection. 61 × 36.2. Fototeca Berenson.*
471. *St James. Panel. Göttigen, Stadtmuseen, Kunstsammlung der Georg-August-Universität (on loan from Berlin, Dahlem). no. 181. 51 × 35.5. Museum photo : Steinkopf.*

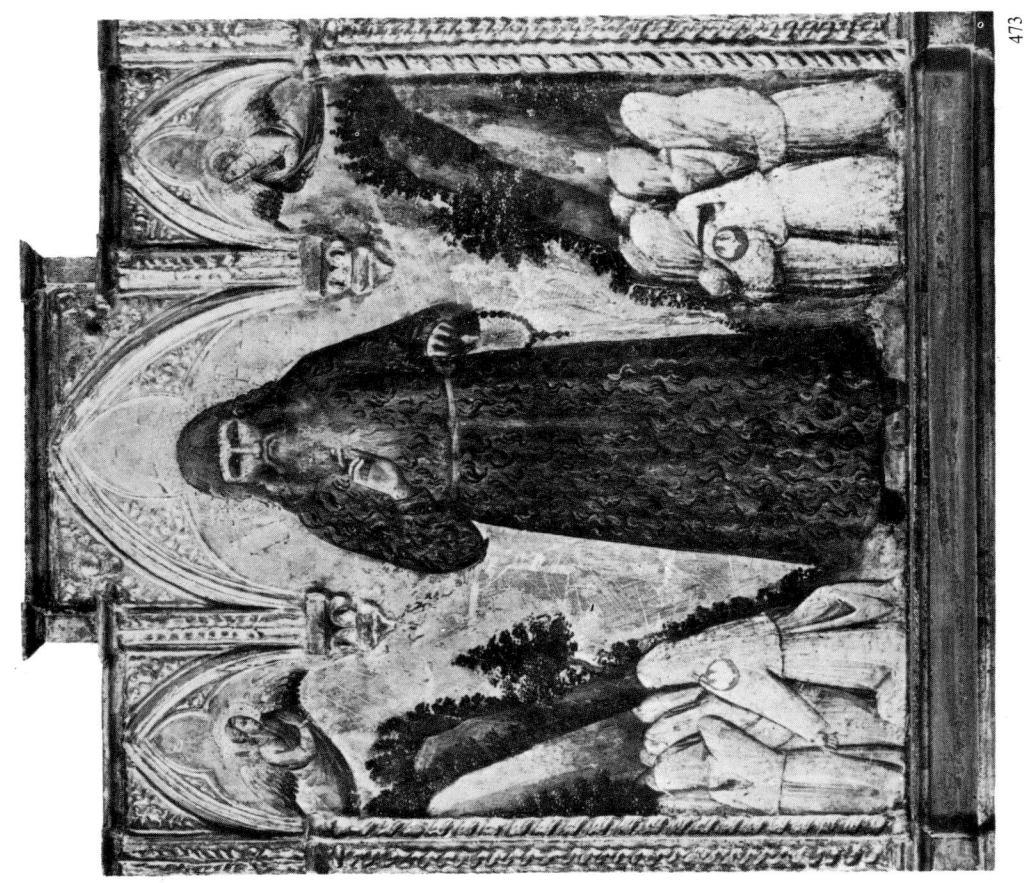

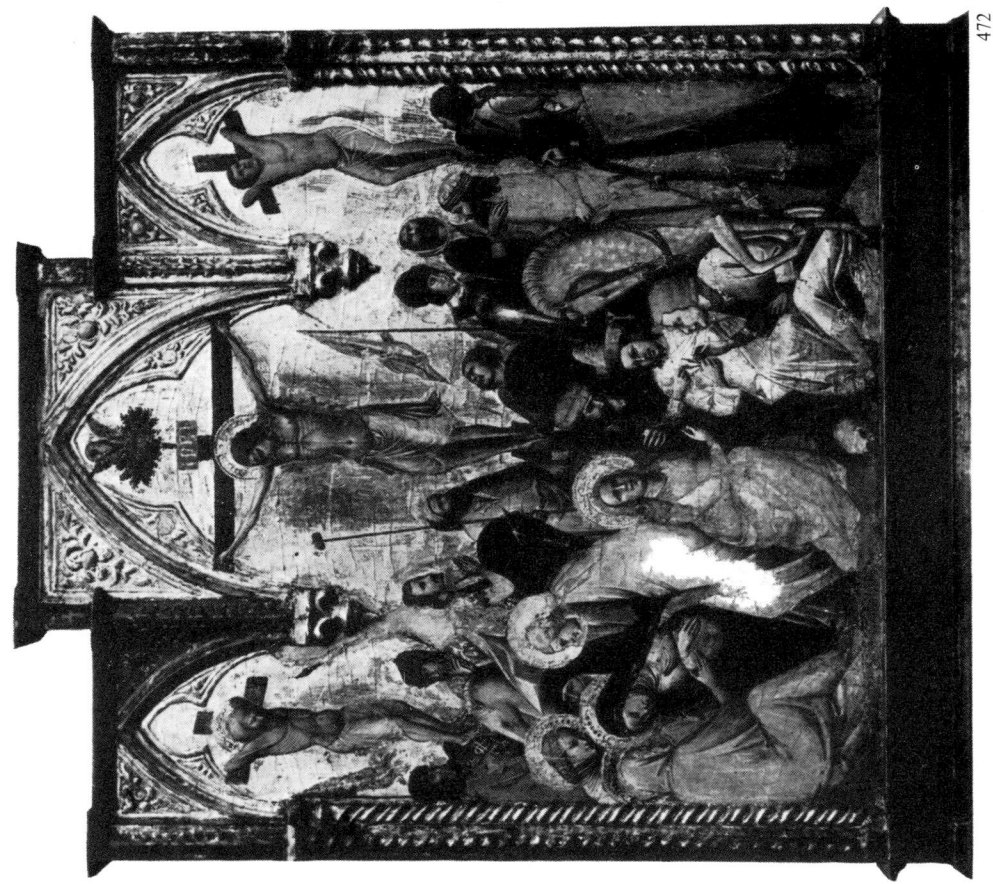

472. *Crucifixion. Panel, recto of fig. 473. Pisa, Museo Nazionale di S. Matteo. no. 1160. 68 × 64. SGPLLM 4023.*
473. *St. Remigius. Panel, verso of fig. 472. Pisa, Museo Nazionale di S. Matteo. no. 1160. 68 × 64. Brogi 19369.*

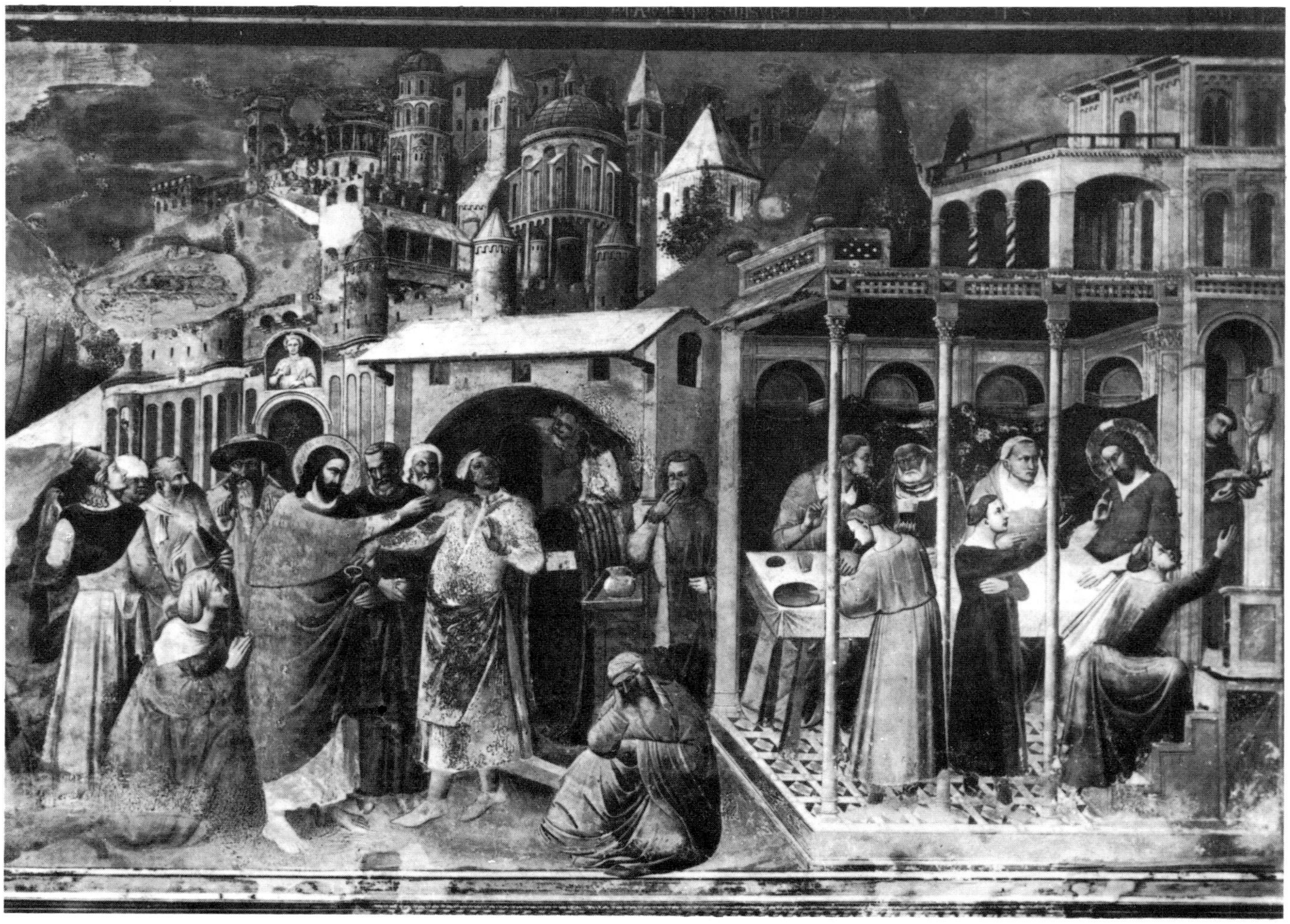

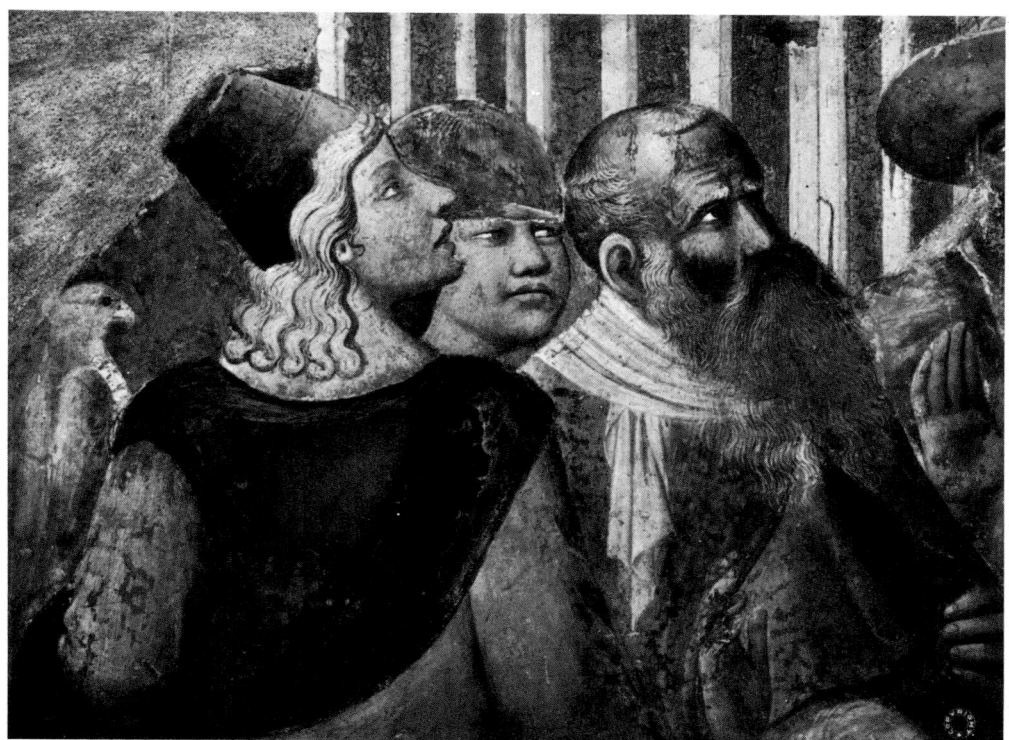

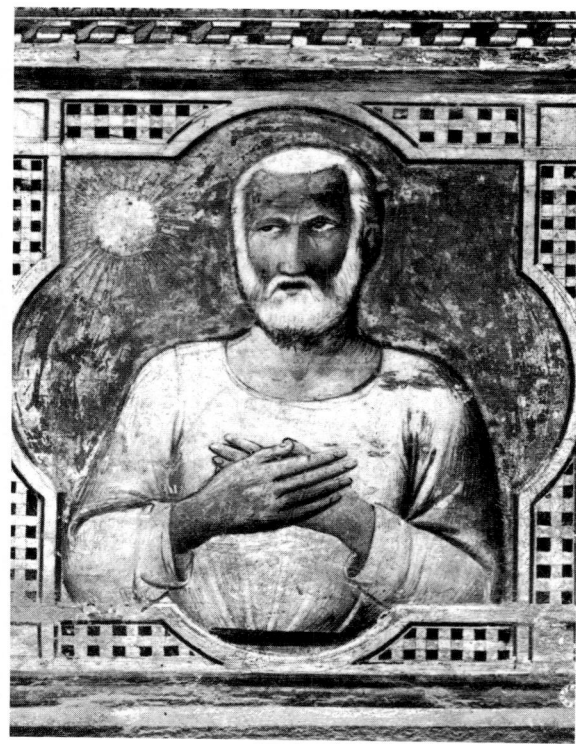

474. *St Raynerius with the dishonest Innkeeper, and dining with the Canons of the Cathedral. Fresco. Pisa, Camposanto. Alinari 8764A. 1384-86.*
475. *Heads of Onlookers, detail of fig. 474. Fresco. Pisa, Camposanto. Anderson 28155. 1384-86.*
476. *Male Saint, detail of border decoration. Detail: St Raynerius and the dishonest Innkeeper. Fresco. Pisa, Camposanto. Anderson 28156. 1384-86.*

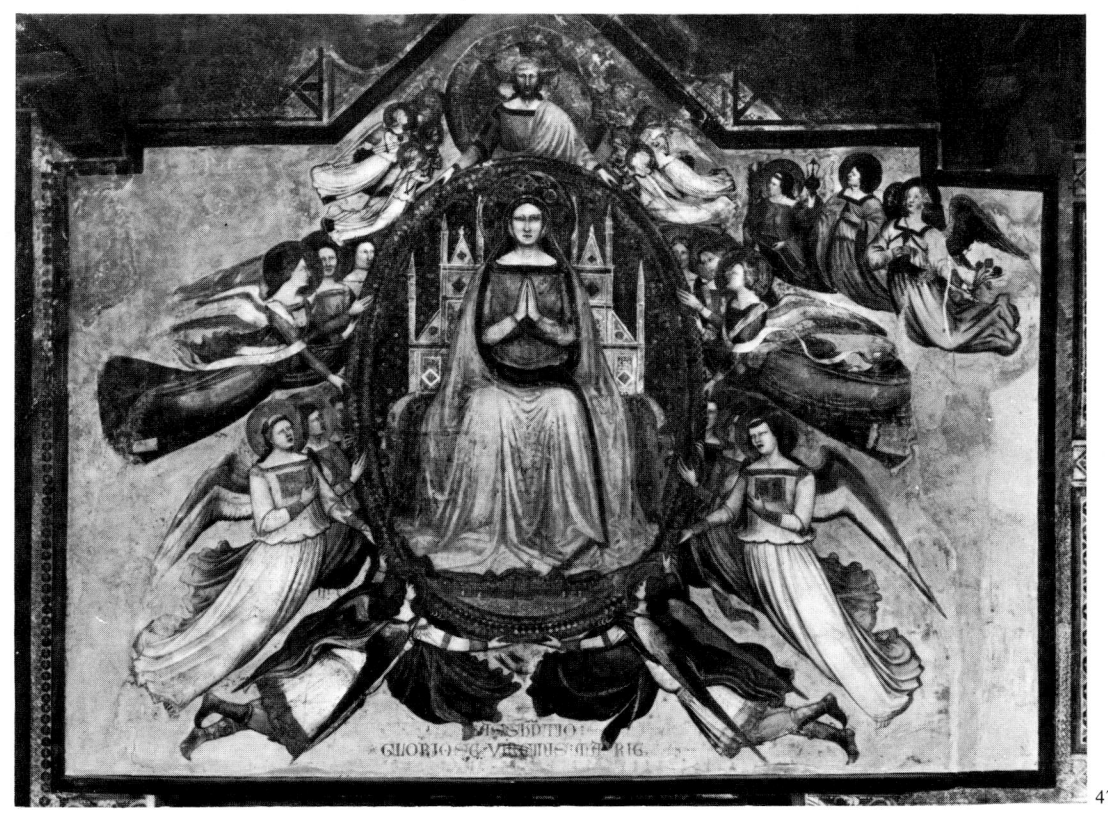

477

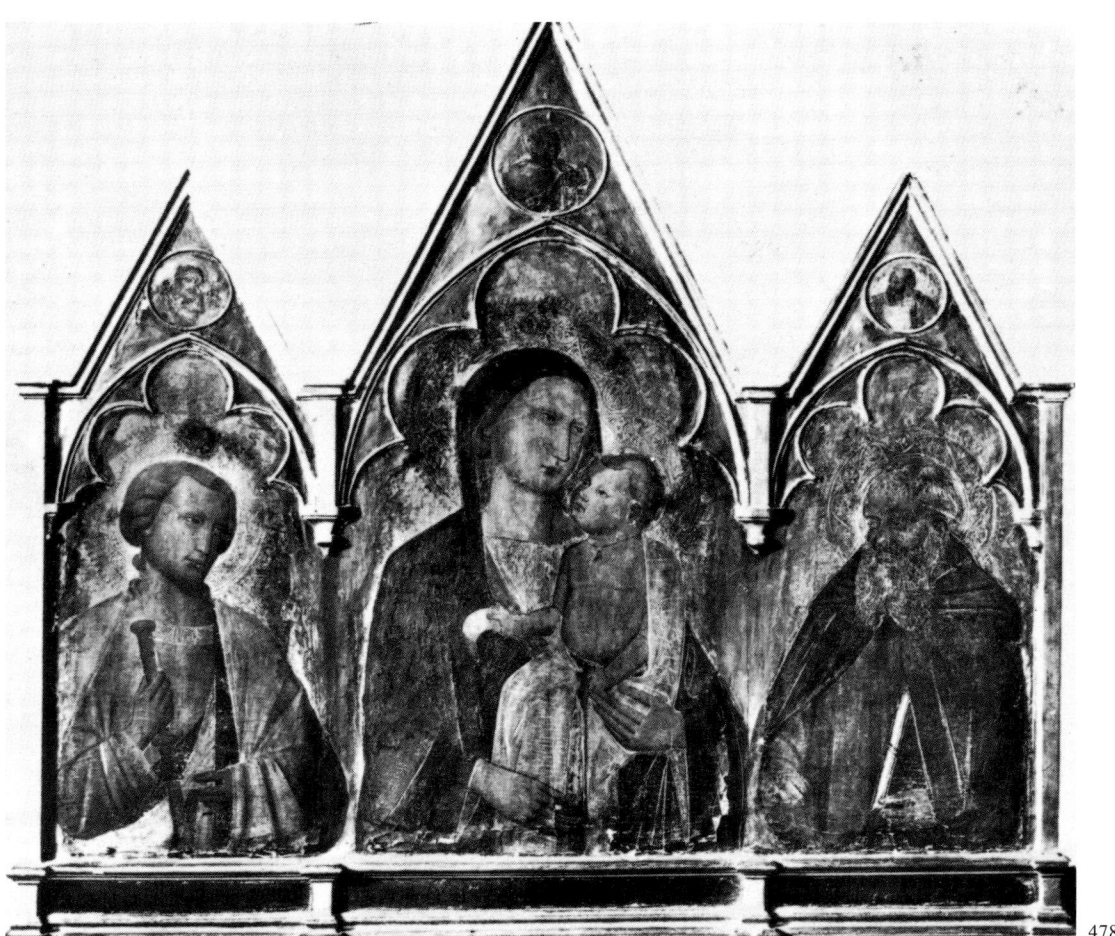

478

477. *Assumption of the Virgin with Angels and Christ above. Fresco. Pisa, Convento di S. Tommaso. Alinari 8832.*
478. *Triptych: Madonna and Child with two Saints. Above: three Saints. Panel. Private Collection. Reali.*

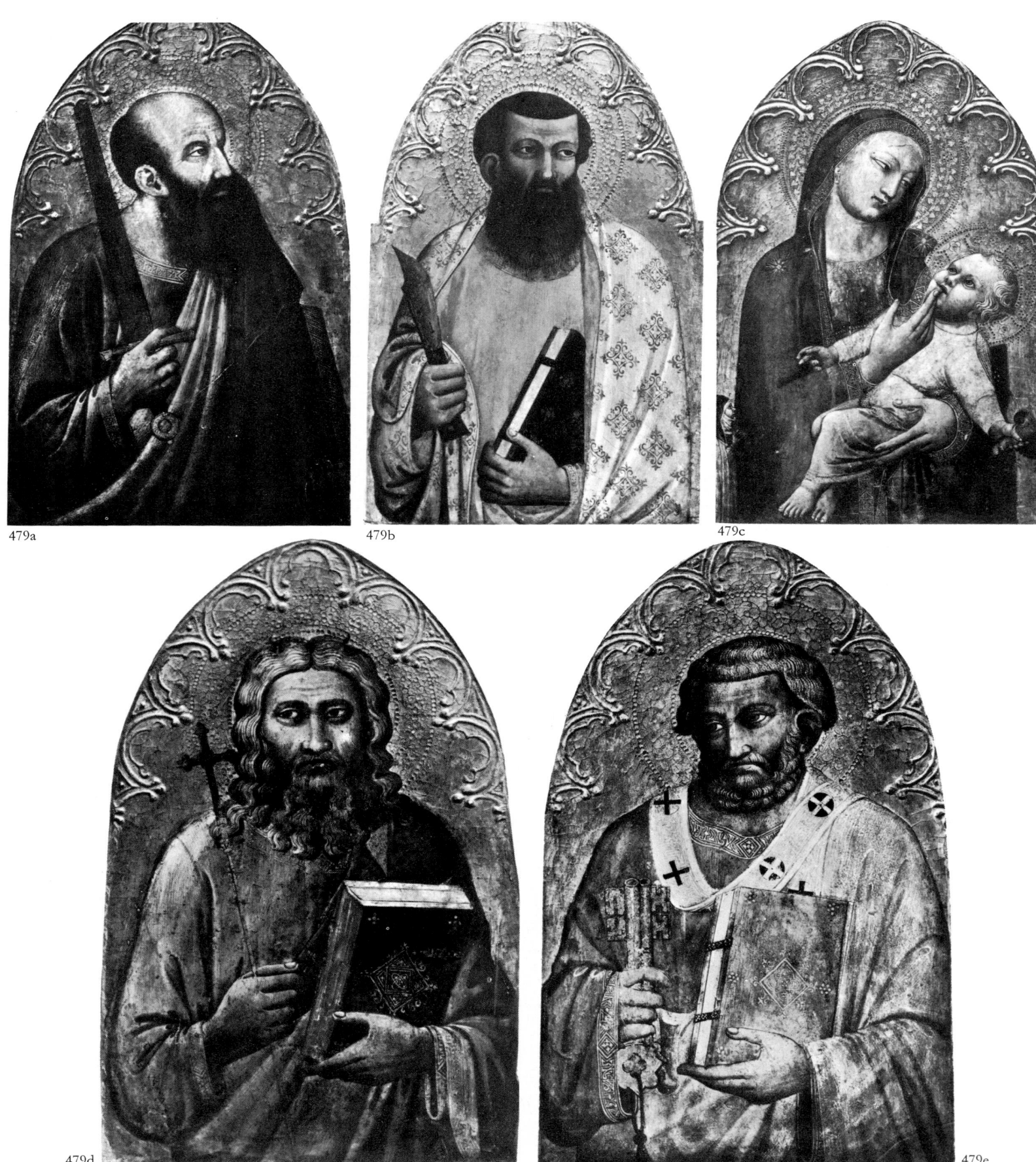

479a. *St Paul. Panel. Florence, formerly Loeser Collection. 43.5 × 29.5. SGF 55324.*
479b. *St Bartholomew. Panel. Auckland (N.Z.), Auckland Art Gallery. no. 4538. 43.5 × 29.5. Museum photo: S. Newbery 015355.*
479c. *Madonna and Child with Donor. Panel. Boston, Museum of Fine Arts. no.84.293. 58.7 × 39.4. Museum photo.*
479d. *St Andrew. Panel. Whereabouts unknown. 46 × 31.5. Fototeca Berenson.*
479e. *St Peter. Panel. Florence, formerly Loeser Collection. 43.5 × 29.5. SGF 55326.*

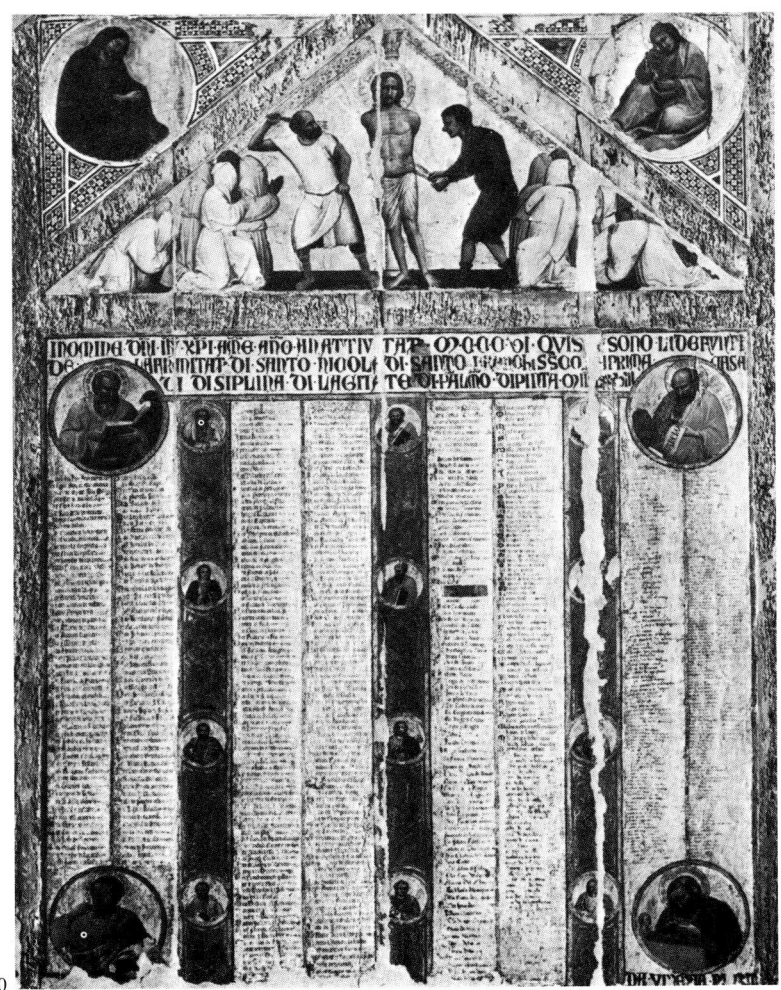

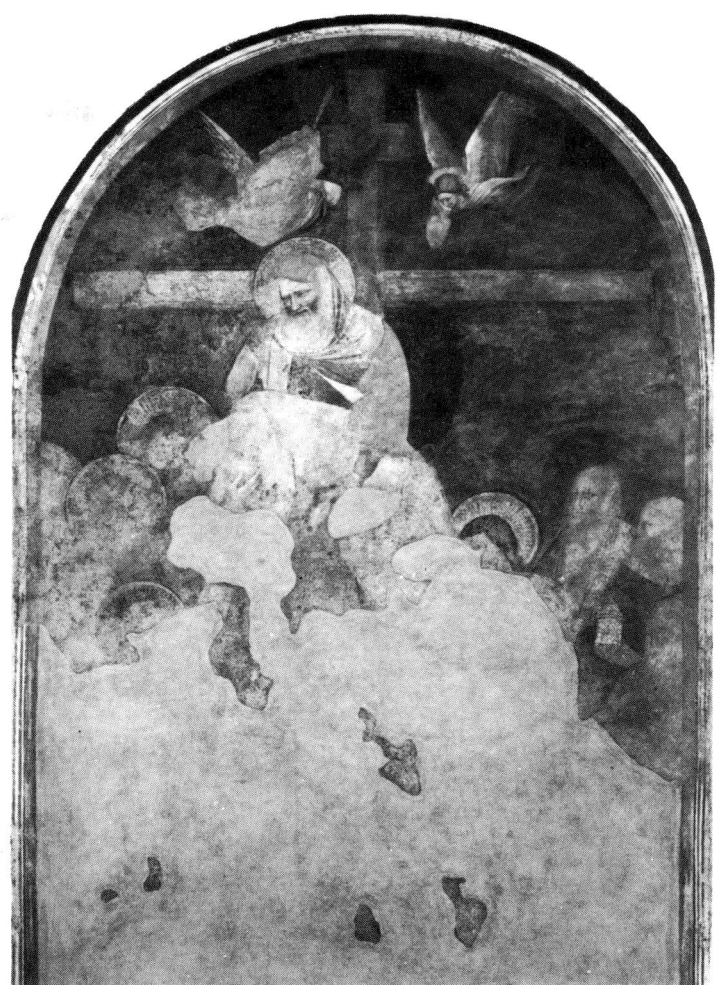

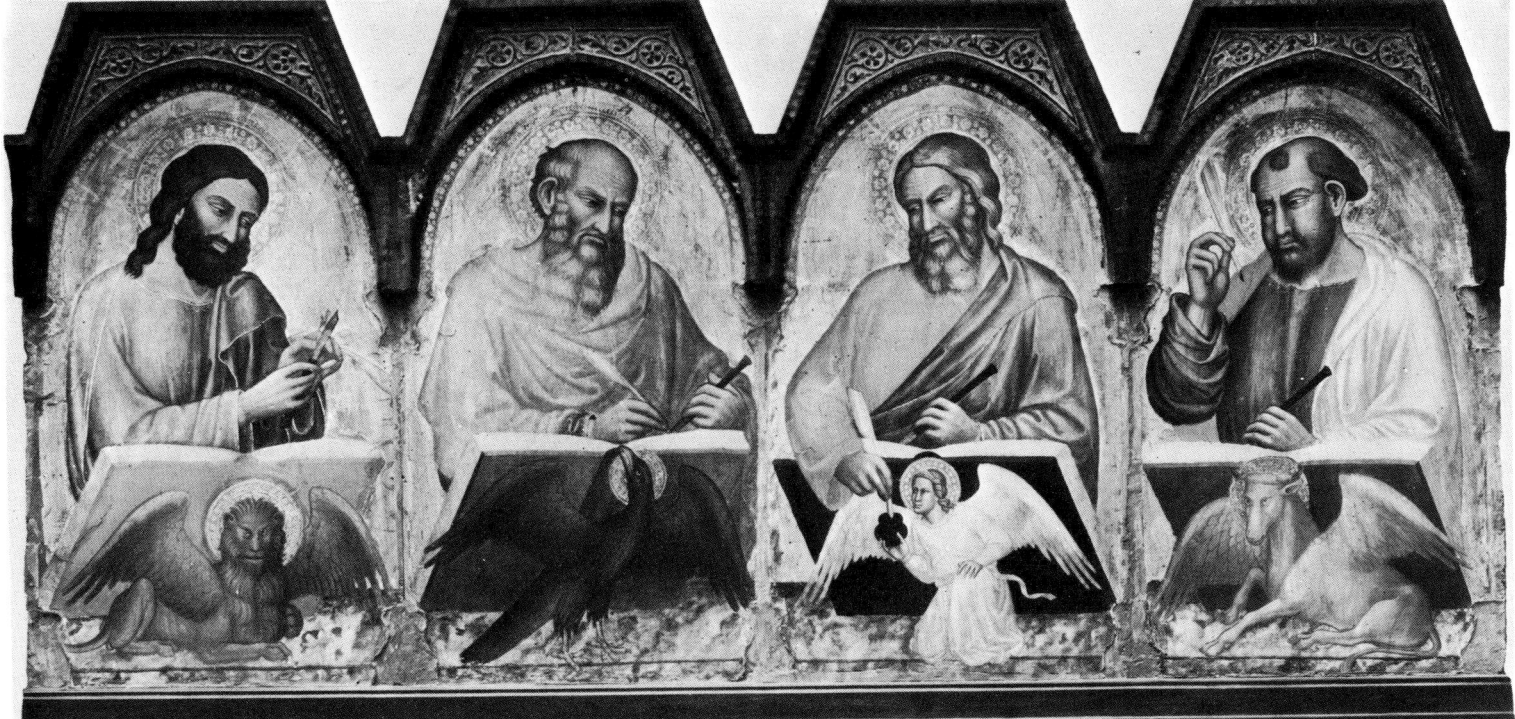

480. *Flagellation; Virgin, St John, Evangelists and Prophets. Panel. Palermo, S. Niccolò Reale, Museo Diocesano. 126 × 169. Publifoto. s & d.* **1388.**
481. *Deposition. Fresco. Florence, Forte di Belvedere (formerly Torre degli Agli). 285 × 173. SGF 113799.*
482. *Polyptych: the Four Evangelists. Panel. Siena, Pinacoteca Nazionale. no. 110. 81 × 176. Alinari 39923. 1365-70.*

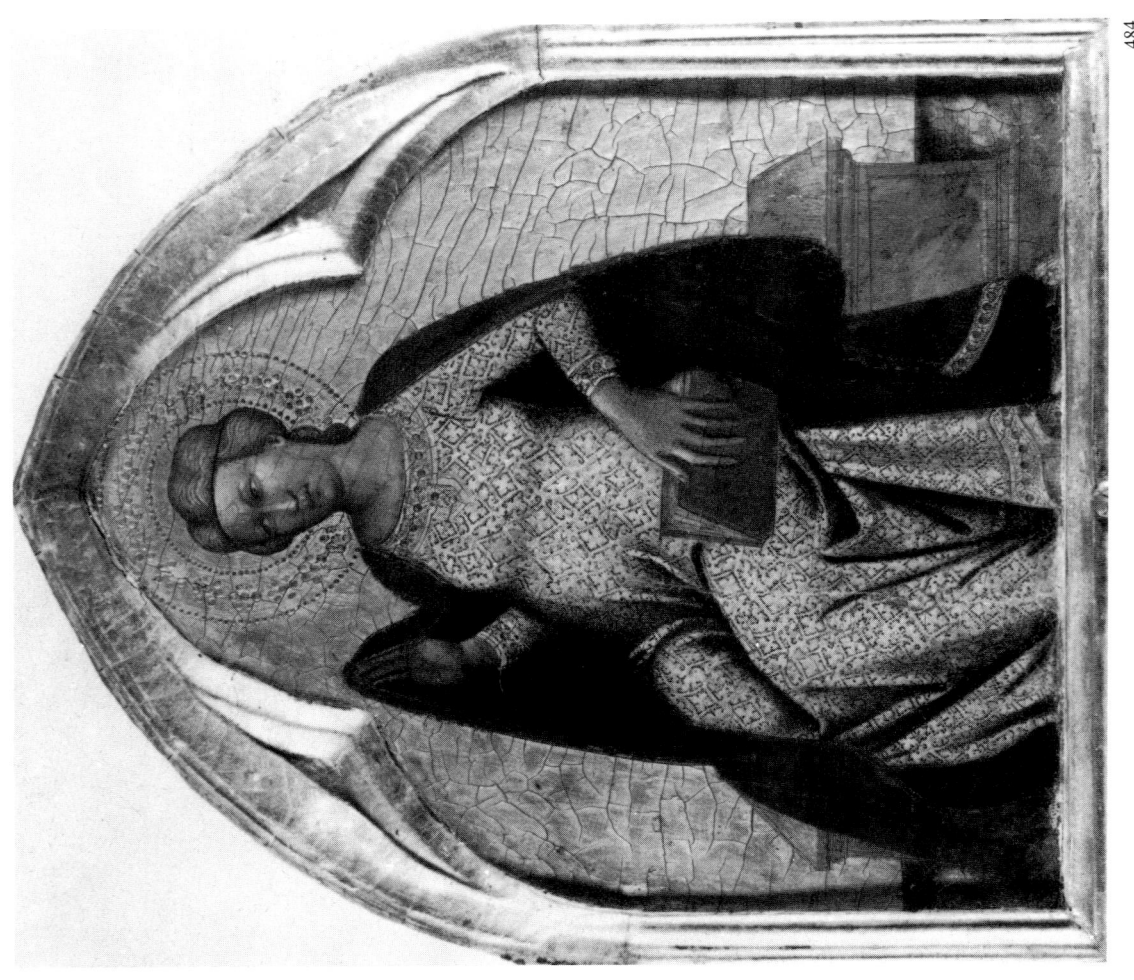

484

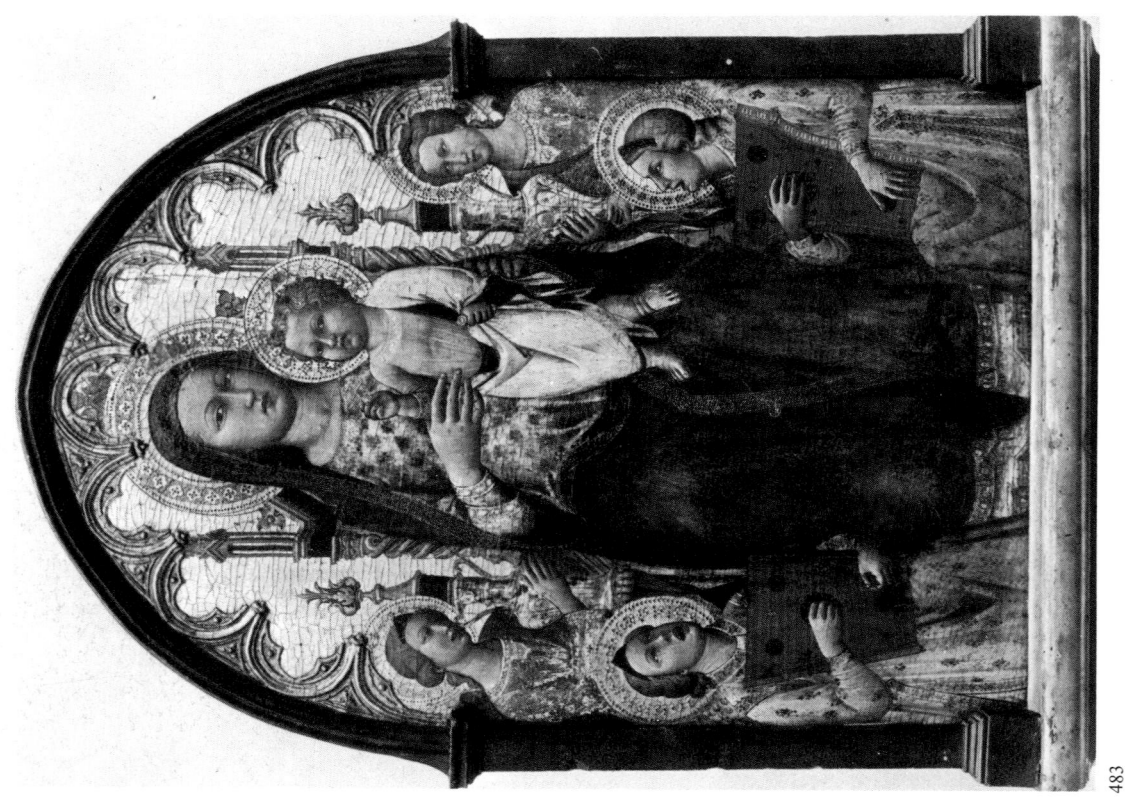

483

483. *Madonna and Child Enthroned with four Angels. Panel. Hanover, Niedersachsische Landesgalerie. no. 86. 94 × 64. Museum photo B3699.*
484. *Virgin Annunciate. Panel. Berlin, Dahlem, Staatliche Museen. no. 1336. 18 × 13. Museum photo: Steinkopf.*

238

GIOVANNI del BIONDO

Active ca. 1356-1399. Probably a pupil of the Gaddi; influenced by Daddi in his early work, and later by the Orcagna brothers.

from B. Berenson, p. 84, *Italian Pictures of the Renaissance, Florentine School*, Vol. I, London, 1963.

Giovanni del Biondo is one of numerous painters who, like Niccolò di Tommaso, Niccolò di Pietro Gerini, Mariotto di Nardo, and Angelo Gaddi, populated the artistic scene of Florence in the second half of the '300. We have records of him from 1356 to 1392. If it is true, as Offner has strongly proposed, that we must recognize Giovanni's assistance in vaults of the Strozzi chapel in S. Maria Novella, then the artistic beginnings of the painter were in the environment of the Orcagna family. His first works, dated from 1360 to '70, the frescoes of Castelfiorentino, the sides of the polyptych of the high altar of S. Croce in Florence, the little stories of S. Benedict attributed by Offner (1956) and by Zeri (1952), reveal a fresh narrative vein which, finding no satisfaction in the formal and spatial abstraction of the Orcagna family, reunites with the Giottesque " naturalism " of the Taddeo Gaddi tradition. This is the finest moment of his activity. Later he adheres fully to the art of Andrea Orcagna and of Nardo di Cione, deriving from the first rigidity of form and negation of space, from the other an elongation of faces and figures, and a characteristic chromatic scheme. He must have had reservations on the expressiveness of that art, for his interpretation assumed at first a benign tone, and then an ironic one, irrational and grotesque, (as in the Martyrdom of St. Sebastian of the Museo dell'Opera del Duomo in Florence). The characters, depicted with the humoristic inventiveness of popular stories, lose their heaviness through the use of dry, lively colours.....

from P. Dal Poggetto, p. 30, *Arte in Valdelsa*, Certaldo, 1963.

Suida was the first to establish the artistic personality of Giovanni del Biondo but his name being unknown at that time, he called this painter after the most important work of art in which he discovered his hand the " master of the Rinuccini altarpiece " and to him he rightly attributed eight paintings, suggesting even a ninth. Shortly after this, two works signed by this master came to light.....
Documentary evidence affords us the following facts about the artist: in October 1356 he becomes a citizen of Florence, in 1360 he makes an altar-polyptych for Castelfiorentino; we find the date 1372 on an altar-piece — a Madonna and four saints — in the chapel to the left of the choir in Sta. Croce; the polyptych of S. Ansano, Fiesole, now in the Bandini Museum bears the date 1373, while in 1376 Giovanni appears among the taxpayers of the St. John's quarter, Gonfalone Vajo, popolo di S. Maria Alberighi; the Madonna in the Gallery of Siena is signed and dated 1377, the Rinuccini altar-piece bears the date 1379, an Annunciation between two saints in the Innocenti Hospital of Florence that of 1385, altered into 1485 by the repainter of the frame, and a Madonna at S. Felice a Ema near Florence, 1387. In 1389, his name is said to appear in the scroll of painters of Siena as " Giovanni de Biondi da Fiorenza pittore " and in 1392 he signed the panel of the Madonna at Figline in the Val d'Arno Superiore, about which the old records have been found.....
Only one of the critics who have dealt with Giovanni del Biondo has observed that a fragment of the altar-piece, which the painter executed in 1360 for Castelfiorentino, still exists. It was a polyptych representing the Madonna, SS. Francis, John the Evangelist, Sophia and Verdiana, made for the church of Sta. Sophia of this city and was signed " *Giovanni Biondi Fiorentino* ".
In the sacristy of the church of Sta. Verdiana of Castelfiorentino we still find a panel representing this saint which no doubt formed part of this altar-piece. The much damaged picture shows us the saint standing between two snakes. Even if we did not find clear traces of it in his later works, this picture would prove that Giovanni's manner is an outcome of the art of Andrea and Nardo di Cione; this explains also its attribution to Andrea. Del Biondo's own manner is here still very much dominated by that of his two more gifted predecessors which would lead us to believe that at the time he was only a young artist; this supposition is corroborated by the fact that we find him still active more than thirty years after this date.....

from R. van Marle, pp. 518-19, *The Development of the Italian Schools of Painting*, Vol. III, The Hague, 1924.

A minor, prolific and essentially popular Florentine artist, who drew upon earlier sources, producing a synthesis of the styles of Taddeo Gaddi, Daddi, and Orcagna.

from St. J. Gore, pl. 3, *The Art of Painting in Florence & Siena from 1250-1500*, London, 1965.

Florentine. School. Active from 1356; died 1399. He was early influenced by Bernardo Daddi and later by the Cione brothers; especially Nardo, whom he seems to have assisted in the Strozzi Chapel of Santa Maria Novella, Florence. He was a prolific painter, characterized by sweet, mystic expression.....

from F. R. Shapley, p. 36, *Paintings from the Samuel H. Kress Collection*, London, 1966.

BIBLIOGRAPHY
BOOKS

An asterisk indicates a work listed in the General Bibliography

D'Achiardi, P., *Guida della Pinacoteca Vaticana*, Rome, 1913, pp. 34-5; *Khv & Salmi**, 1914, pp. 33-5; *v. Marle, 1924**, pp. 518-34; *Offner, 1927**, p. 18; *Toesca, 1929**, p. 66; *Hautecoeur**, 1931, p. 168; *Berenson, 1932**, pp. 241-2; *Catalogo della Mostra del Tesoro di Firenze Sacra*, Florence, 1933, p. 120; Procacci, U., *La Reale Galleria dell' Accademia di Firenze*, Rome, 1936, p. 27; *Coletti, Vol. II**, 1946, p. 54; *Offner, 1947**, Sec. III, Vol. V, p. 228; *Antal**, 1948, pp. 205-6; *Vavalà, 1948**, p. 76; Marabottini, A., *Giovanni da Milano*, Florence, 1950, pp. 106-7; Salmi, M., and Moriondo, M., Catalogue: *Mostra d'Arte Sacra delle Diocesi e della Provincia dal secolo XI al secolo XVIII*, Arezzo, 1950, p. 95; *Galetti**, 1950, "A-E", p. 347; *Toesca, 1951**, p. 644; Suida, W. E., *Catalogue of the Isaac Delgado Museum of Art*, New Orleans, 1953, pp. 12-13; Shorr, D. C., *The Christ Child in Devotional Images*, New York, 1954, p. 79; Wescher, P., *Catalogue of the Los Angeles County Museum of Art*, Los Angeles, 1954, p. 12; Gabelentz, H.-C., Catalogue: *Italienische Malerei der Vor-und Frührenaissance in Staatlichen Lindenau-Museum*, Altenburg, 1956, p. 55; Baldini, U., *MAS I**, 1957, pp. 51-2; Carli, E., *Guida della Pinacoteca di Siena*, Milan, 1958, p. 48; *Procacci, 1958**, p. 26; Suida, W. E., *Catalogue of the Brooks Memorial Art Gallery*, Memphis, (Tenn.), 1958, pp. 20-21; Baldini, U., *MAS II**, 1958, pp. 47-48; Berti, L., *Il Museo della Basilica a S. Giovanni Valdarno*, Florence, 1959, pp. 7, 11-12; *Vavalà, 1959**, Part I; *Procacci, 1960**, p. 39; Shapley, F. R., *Catalogue of the Allentown Art Museum*, Allentown, (Pa.), 1960, pp. 44-5; *Oertel, 1961**, pp. 119-21; Santi, F., pp. 51-60, in *Scritti di Storia dell' Arte in Onore di Mario Salmi*, Vol. II, Rome, 1962; Dal Poggetto, P., *AIV**, 1963, pp. 30-1; *Berenson, 1963**, Vol. I, pp. 84-7; Gore, St J., *Wildenstein**, 1965, p. 13; *Marcucci**, 1965, pp. 117-22; Ciardi, R. P., *La Raccolta Cagnola*, Cremona, 1965, p. 26; Held, J. S., *Museo de Arte de Ponce, Catalogue I*, Ponce, Puerto Rico, 1965, pp. 12-13; Wadsworth Atheneum, *An Exhibition of Italian Panels and Manuscripts from the 13th and 14th Centuries, in Honor of Richard Offner*, Hartford (Conn.), 1965, p. 14; *White**, 1966, p. 371; *Shapley, 1966**, pp. 36-8; Zeri, F., *Tesori d'Arte delle grandi famiglie*, Milan, 1966, pp. 28-9; *Offner, 1967**, Sec. IV, Vol. IV, Part I; *Klesse, B.**, Berne, 1967, pp. 232-3, 476; *Offner, 1969**, Sec. IV, Vol. V, Part II; *Dutch Show**, 1974, pp. 51-2.

JOURNALS

Sirèn, O., *A*, IX, 1906, p. 322; Gamba, C., *RA*, V, 1-2, 1907, pp. 22-25; Poggi, G., *RA*, V, 1-2, 1907, pp. 26-28; Bernardini, G., *RADA*, IX, 6, 1909, pp. 89-94; Salmi, M., *A*, XVI, 1913, pp. 208-27; Suida, W., *MKW*, I, 1914, pp. 1-2; Sirèn, O., *AA*, VI, 1916, pp. 207-23; Sirèn, O., *BM*, XXXVII, 1920, pp. 289-303; Salmi, M., *RA*, XI, 1929, pp. 268-9; Berenson, B., *DD*, XI, 5, 1930-31, pp. 1286, 1318; Gamba, C., *BA*, XXVII, 1933, pp. 145-63; Meiss, M., *AB*, XVIII, 1936, pp. 462-3; Marchini, G., *RA*, XX, 1938, pp. 215-41; Schorr, D. C., *AB*, XXVIII, 1946, p. 30; Salmi, M., *C*, II, 3-4, 1951, pp. 169-81; Chiarelli, R., *E*, CXIII, 1, 1951, pp. 3-16; Baldini, U., *BA*, XXXVII, 4, 1952, pp. 350-1; Offner, R., *MKIF*, VII, 1, 1953-6, pp. 173-92; Cohn, W., *BA*, XLI, 1956, p. 171; Cohn, W., *RA*, XXXI, 1956, pp. 55-7, 70; Cohn, W., *K*, XII, 1959, p. 272; Asano Fabbi, D., *RA*, XXXIV, 1959, pp. 109-122; Klesse, B., *MKIF*, VIII, 1959, p. 248; Klesse, B., *ZKG*, XXV, 1962, pp. 270-1; Zeri, F., *PA*, XIII, 149, 1962, pp. 14-20; Dal Poggetto, P., *AV*, II, 8, 1963, pp. 52-3; Steinweg, K., *MKIF*, XI, 2-3, 1964, pp. 194-200; Zeri, F., *BA*, XLIX, 1964, pp. 127, 130; Acton, H., *AP*, LXXXII, 1965, pp. 278-9; Bellosi, L., *PA*, XVI, 187/7, 1965, p. 19; Salmi, M., *BA*, LII, 5, 1967, pp. 222-24; Bellosi, L., *PA*, XVIII, 203/23, 1967, p. 86; von Erffa, H. M., *K*, XX, 1967, p. 190; Boskovits, M., *MKIF*, XIII, 1-4, 1967-68, p. 56; Boskovits, M., *ZKG*, XXXI, 4, 1968, p. 275; Friedmann, H., *Sim*, 3, 1968-69, 1, pp. 6-14; White, J., *BM*, CXI, 794, 1969, p. 308; (Photograph), *O*, 169, 1969, p. 72; Boskovits, M., *AI*, III, 25/26, 1970, p. 43, note 14; Cole, B., *AB*, LII, 2, 1970, pp. 200-202; Kiel, H., *P*, XXVIII, 2, 1970, p. 161; Corti, G., *C*, XXII, 1, 1971, p. 85. (*Edit.*), *BM*, CXIII, 821, 1971, p. 435; Luttrell, A., *BM*, CXIV, 831, 1972, pp. 366-7; White, J., *BM*, CXIV, 830, 1972, pp. 338-41; Bellosi, L., *MKIF*, XVII, 2-3, 1973, p. 188.

SIGNED AND DATED WORKS

1363 Florence, S. Croce, High Altar. Panels: Fathers of the Church: Sts. Ambrose, Gregory, Augustine and Jerome
   d. (fig. 493).

1364 Florence, Accademia 8462. Triptych: Presentation of Christ in the Temple. d. (fig. 485).

1372 Formerly, Richmond, Surrey, Cook Collection. Panels: Coronation of the Virgin. d. (figs. 499-501).

1372 Florence, S. Croce, Tosinghi Chapel. Polyptych: Madonna & Child with Sts. Augustine, Anthony Abbot, Bartholomew and Lawrence. d. (fig. 491).

1373 Fiesole, Duomo, Sacristy. Triptych: Coronation of the Virgin with Saints and Angels. d. (fig. 490).

1375 San Donato in Poggio (near Tavarnelle, Val di Pesa), Pieve, Baptistery. Panel: Coronation of the Virgin with Saints, a Donor and four Angels. d. (fig. 494).

1377 Siena, Pinacoteca Nazionale 584. Panel: Madonna & Child. s & d. (fig. 496).

1379 Florence, S. Croce, Sacristy, Rinuccini Chapel. Polyptych: Madonna & Child Enthroned with Saints. d. (fig. 488).

1387 Florence, S. Felice a Ema (near Impruneta). Panel: Madonna & Child with 16 figures in adoration. d. (fig. 497).

1392 Figline (Upper Valdarno), S. Francesco, Misericordia. Panel: Madonna & Child Enthroned. s & d. (fig. 498).

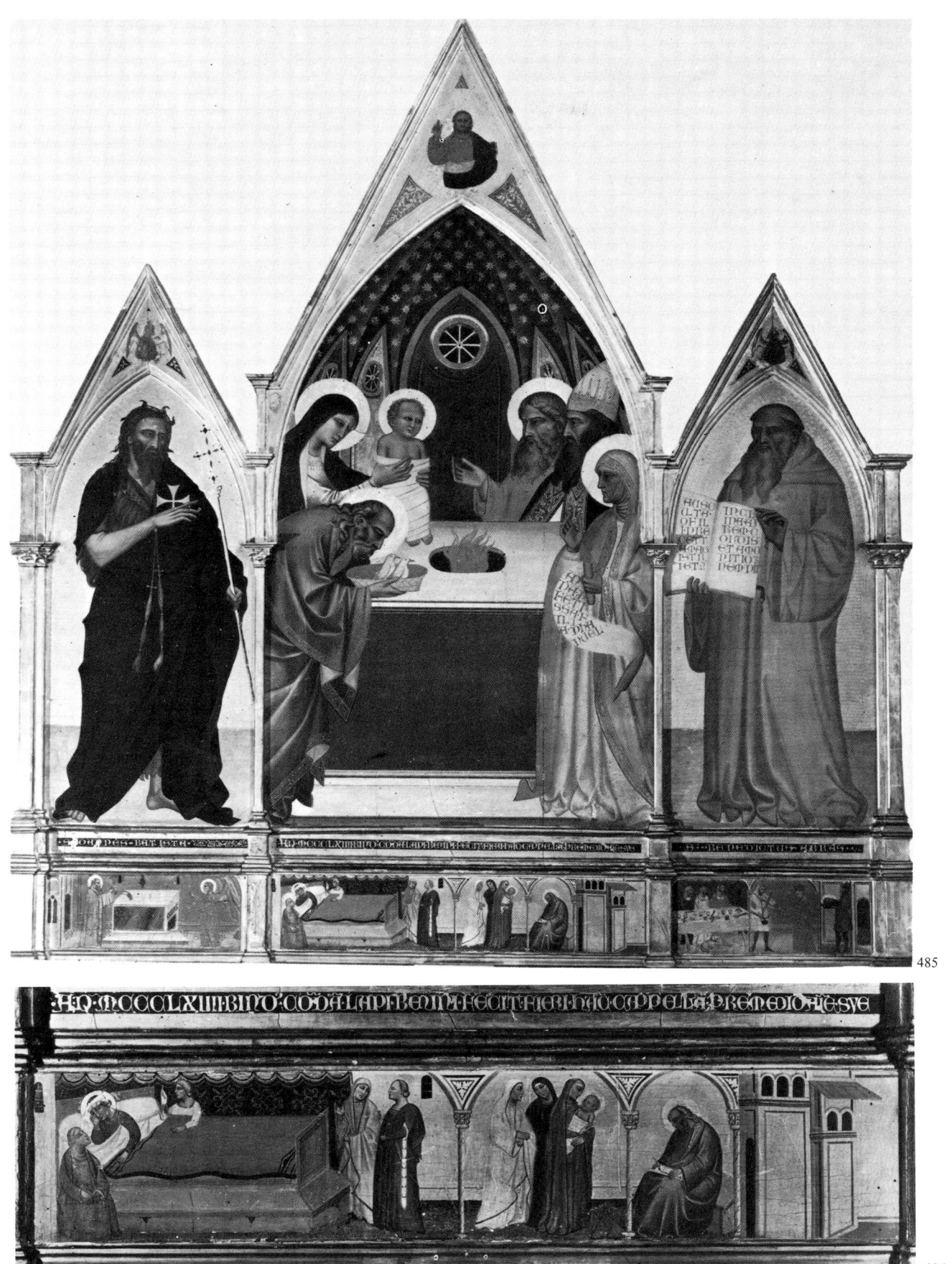

485

486

485. *Triptych: Presentation of Christ in the Temple with Sts John the Baptist and Benedict. Predella: scenes from the Life of St John the Baptist. Panel. Florence, Accademia. no. 8462. 215 × 186. Alinari 50196. d. 1364.*

486. *Predella scene: Birth and the Naming of St John the Baptist, detail of fig. 485. Panel. Florence, Accademia. no. 8462. SGF 103705. d. 1364.*

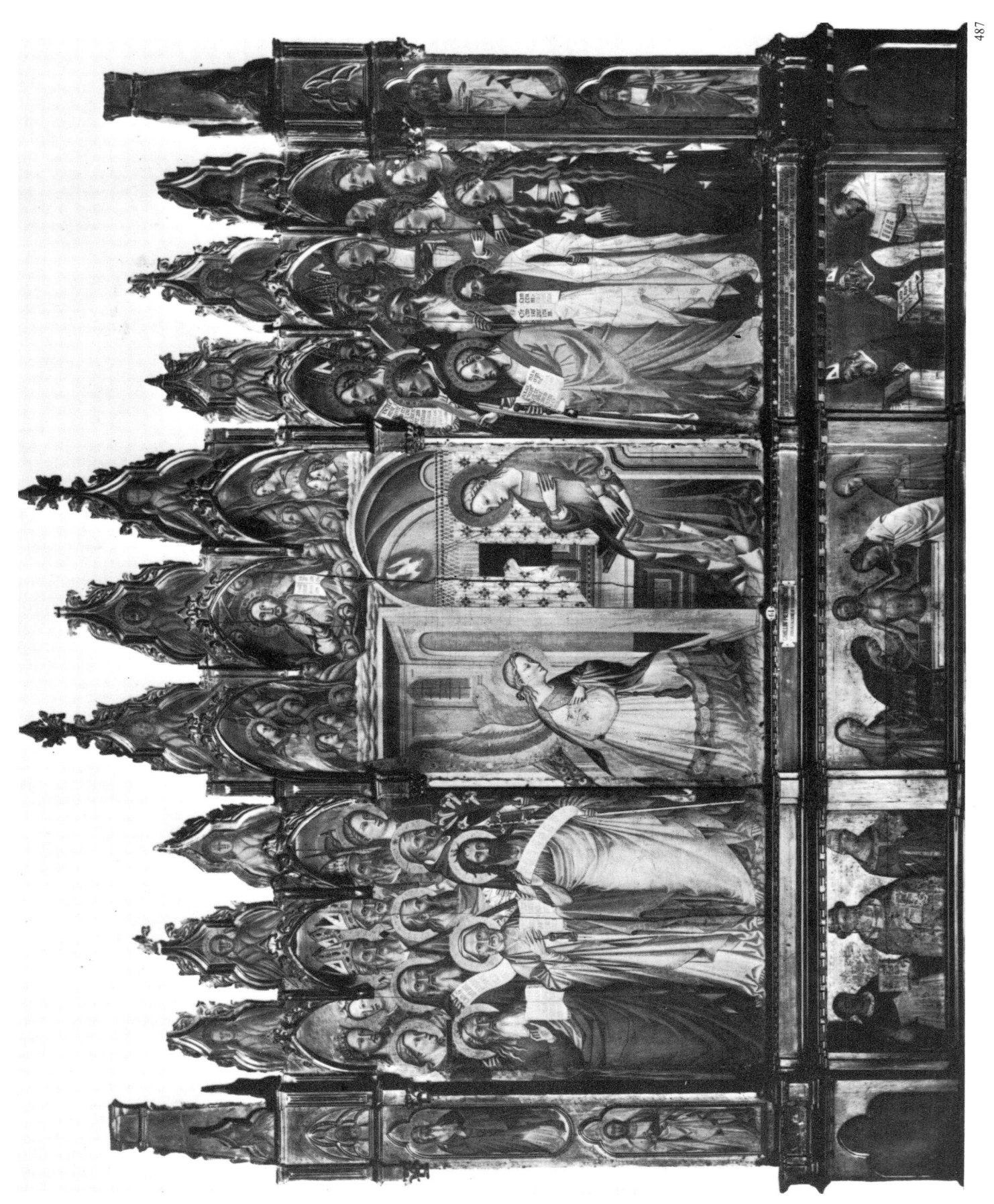

487. *Triptych: Annunciation with Sts John the Evangelist, Peter, John the Baptist, James Major, Bartholomew and other Saints. Above: God the Father,*
Angels. Pilasters: six Saints. Predella: Man of Sorrows, the three Marys and six Doctors of the Church. Panel. Florence, Accademia. no. 8606.
406 × 377. Brogi 7564. 1378.

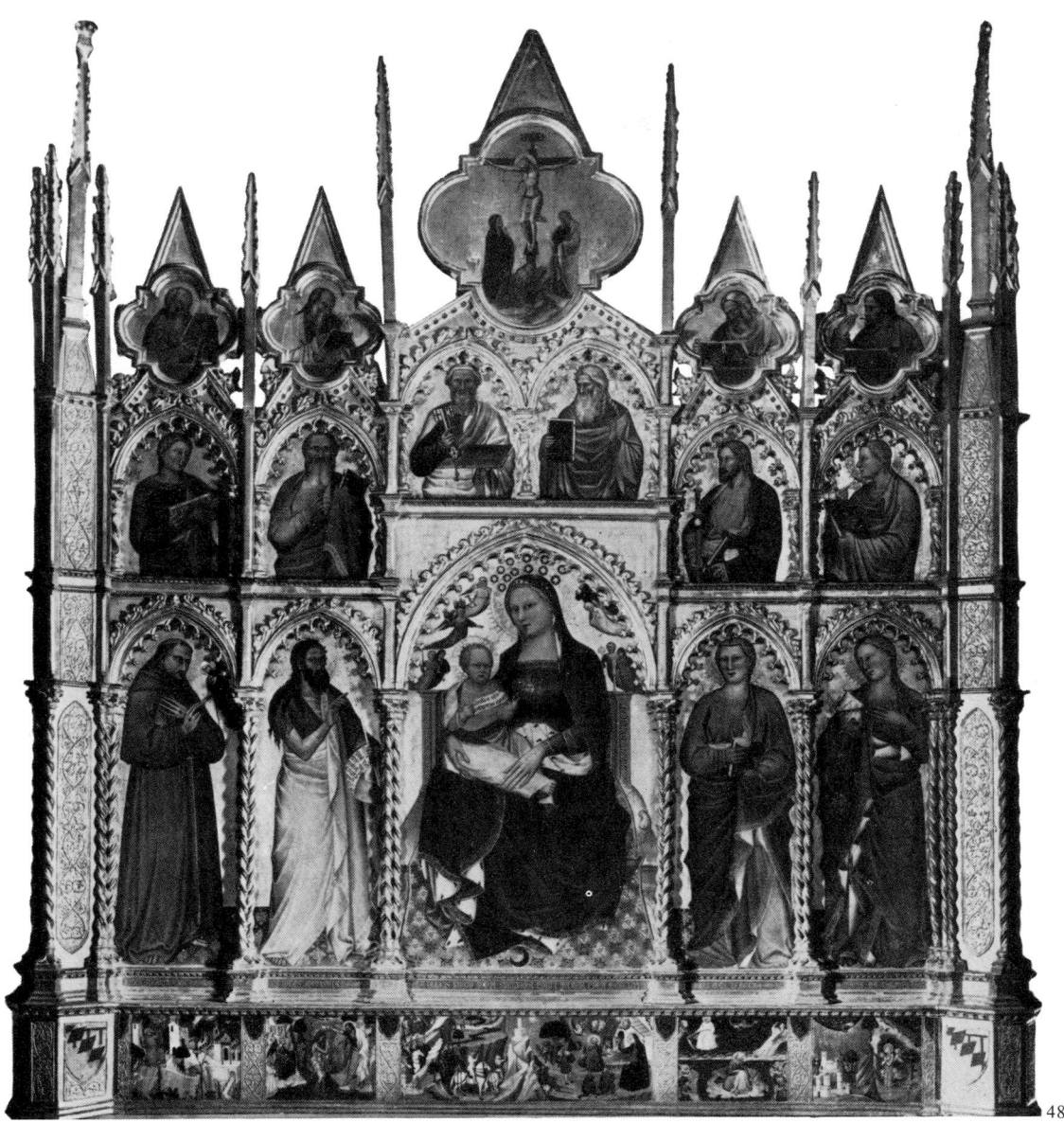

488

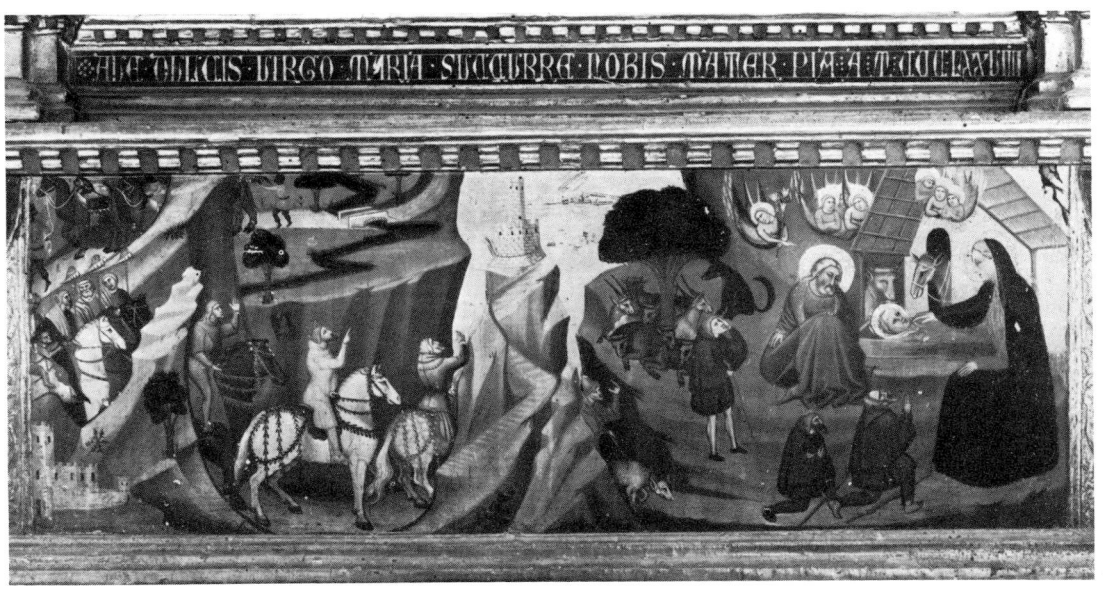

489

488. *Polyptych: Madonna and Child Enthroned with Sts Francis, John the Baptist, John the Evangelist, Mary Magdalene. Above: Christ on the Cross, six Apostles, four Prophets. Predella: Stigmatization of St Francis; Baptism of Christ; Journey of the Magi; Nativity, St John on Patmos; Ecstasy of Mary Magdalene. Panel. Florence, S. Croce, Sacristy, Rinuccini Chapel. cp: 136 × 83; sps: 111 × 42. Alinari 3962. d. 1379.*
489. *Predella scene: Journey of the Magi; the Nativity, detail of fig. 488. Panel. Florence, S. Croce, Sacristy, Rinuccini Chapel. SGF 100451. d. 1379.*

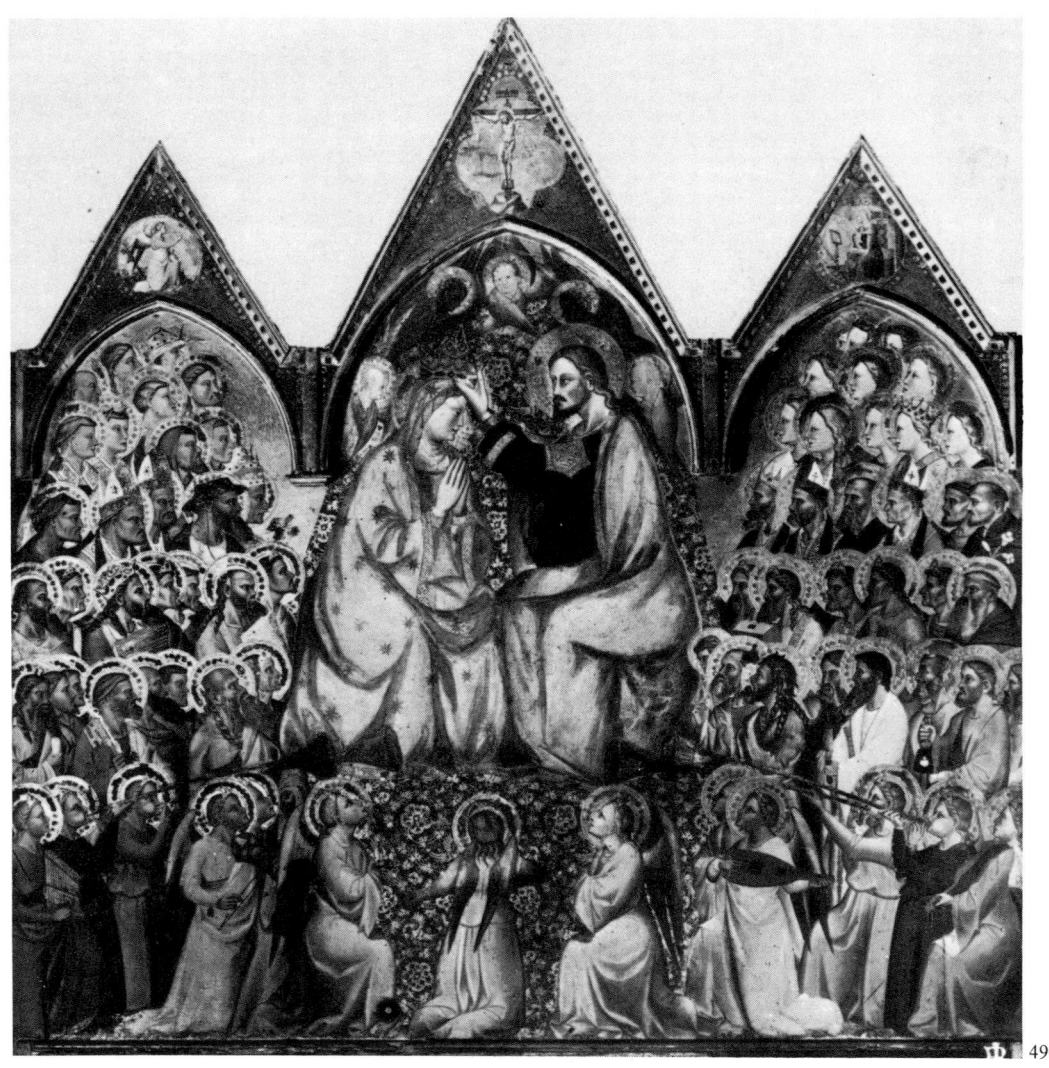

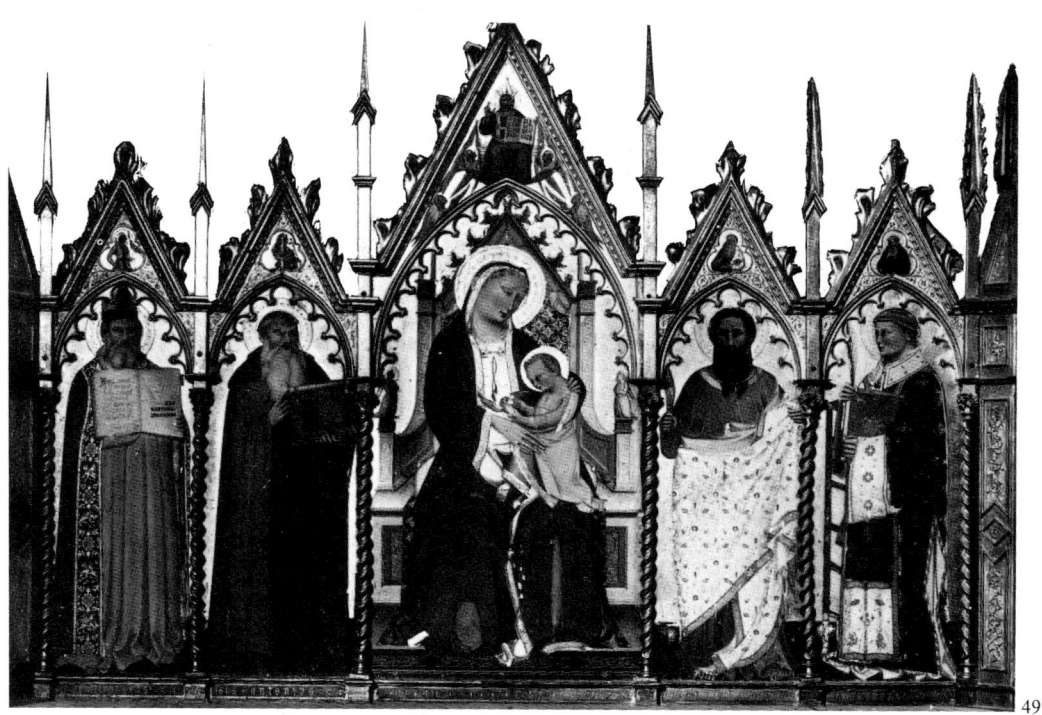

490. *Triptych: Coronation of the Virgin with Saints and Angels. Panel. Fiesole, Duomo. 210 × 201. Alinari 7741. d. 1373.*
491. *Polyptych: Madonna and Child Enthroned with Sts Augustine, Anthony, Bartholomew and Lawrence. Panel. Florence, S. Croce, Tosinghi Chapel. Alinari 61686. d. 1372.*

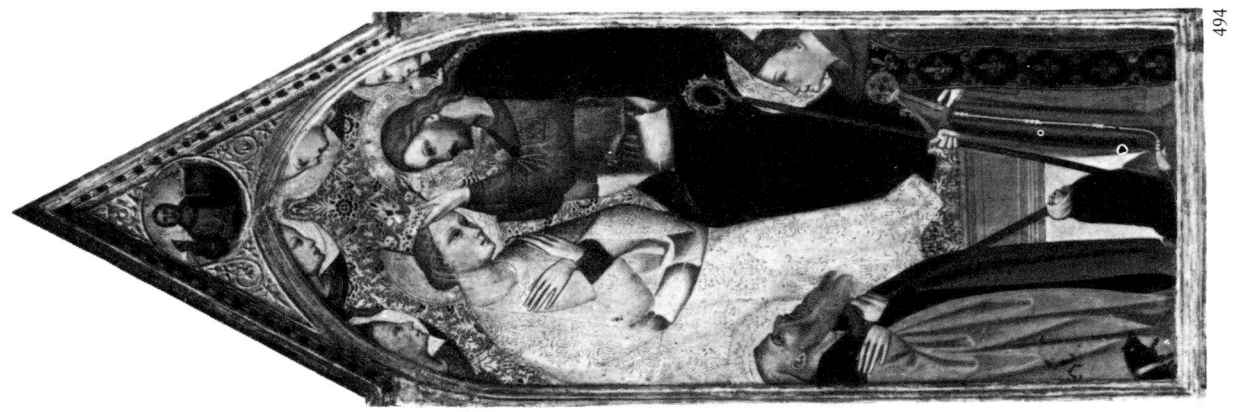

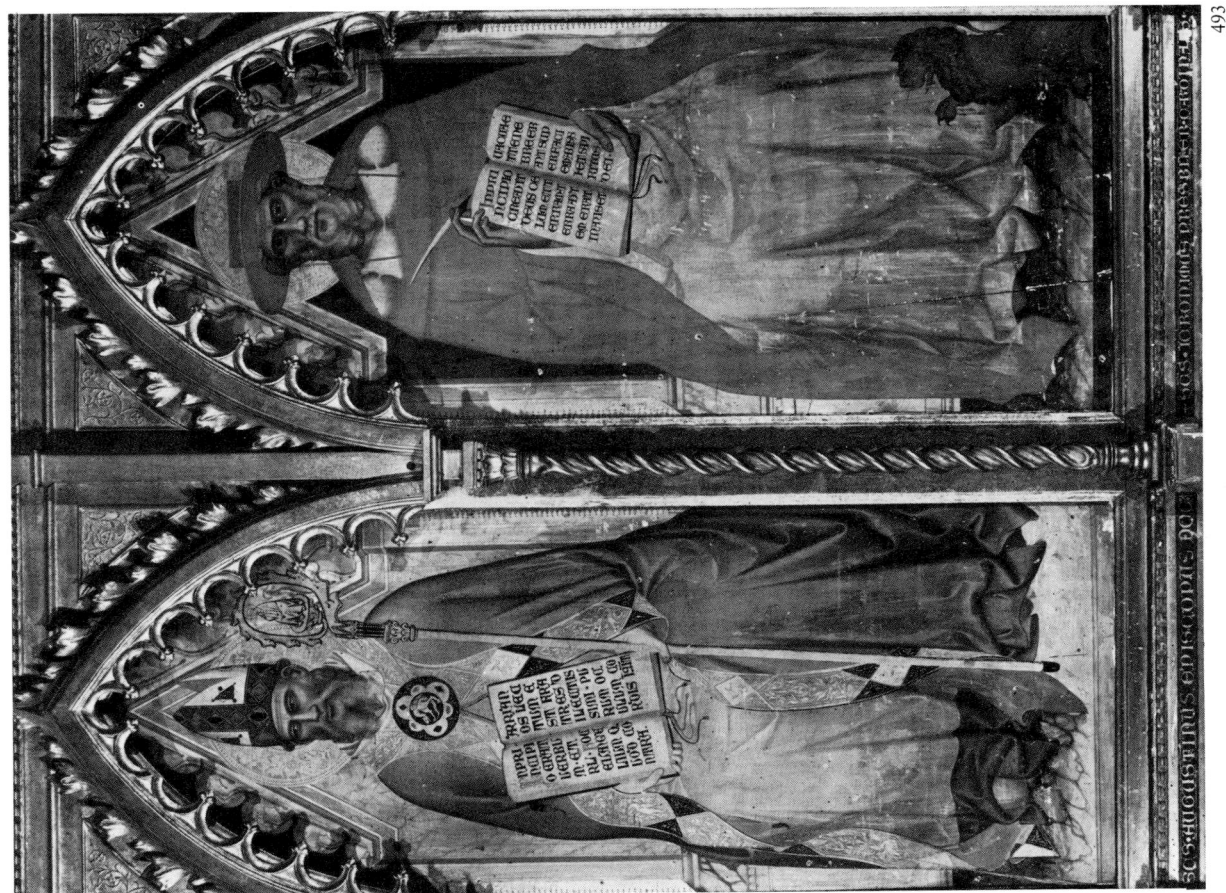

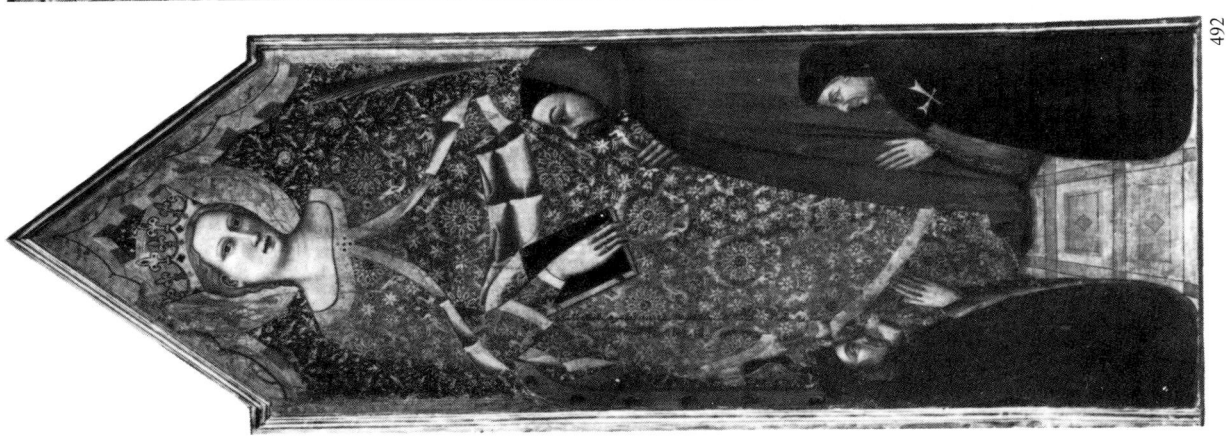

492. *St Catherine Enthroned with three members of the Bischeri Family. Panel. Florence, Museo dell'Opera del Duomo. no. 90. Original part: 163 × 66. Alinari 17265. 1370. (Scene in the frame by another hand).*

493. *Sts Augustine and Jerome, side panels of an altarpiece (see also figs 200-1, 204). Panel. Florence, S. Croce, High Altar. SGF 100448. d. 1363.*

494. *Coronation of the Virgin with Sts Anthony Abbot and Louis, a female Donor, four Angels. Above: Christ blessing. Panel. San Donato in Poggio (near Tavarnelle, Val di Pesa), Pieve, Baptistery. 159 × 51.5. SGF 12418. d. 1375.*

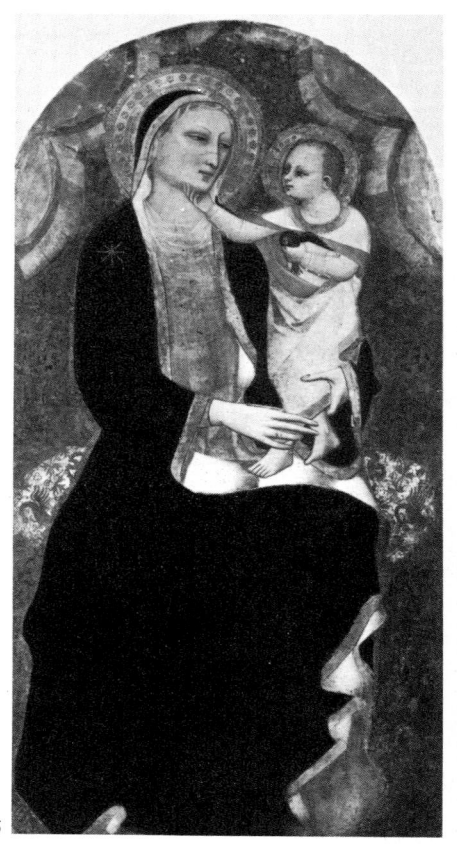

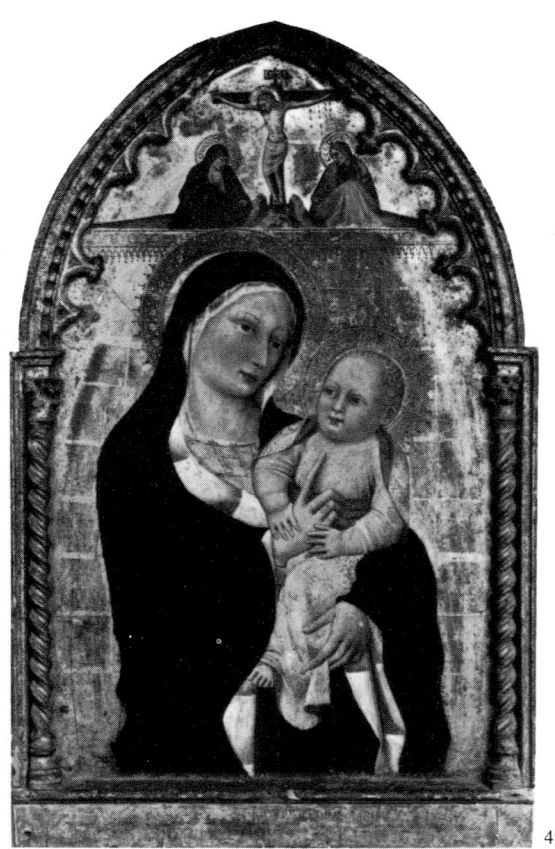

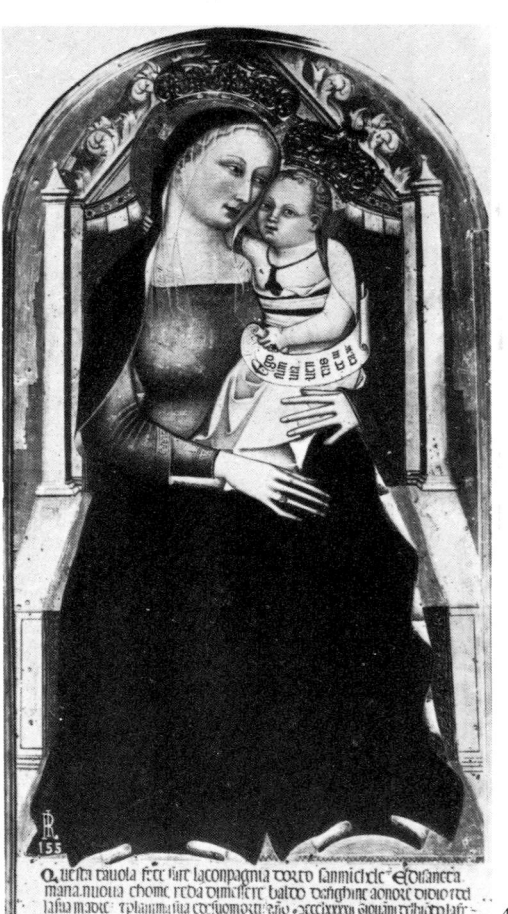

495. *Madonna of Humility. Panel. Florence, S. Felicita, Sacristy. 120 × 62. SGF 115540. 1360-65.*

496. *Madonna and Child. Above: Christ on the Cross. Panel. Siena, Pinacoteca Nazionale. no. 584. 56 × 92. Fototeca Berenson. s & d. 1377.*

497. *Madonna and Child with sixteen figures in adoration. Above: Angels holding crown. Predella: Man of Sorrows. Panel. Florence, S. Felice a Ema (near Impruneta). 125 × 64. SGF 06964. d. 1387.*

498. *Madonna and Child Enthroned. Panel. Figline (Upper Valdarno), S. Francesco, Misericordia. 126 × 65. SGF 21158. s & d. 1392.*

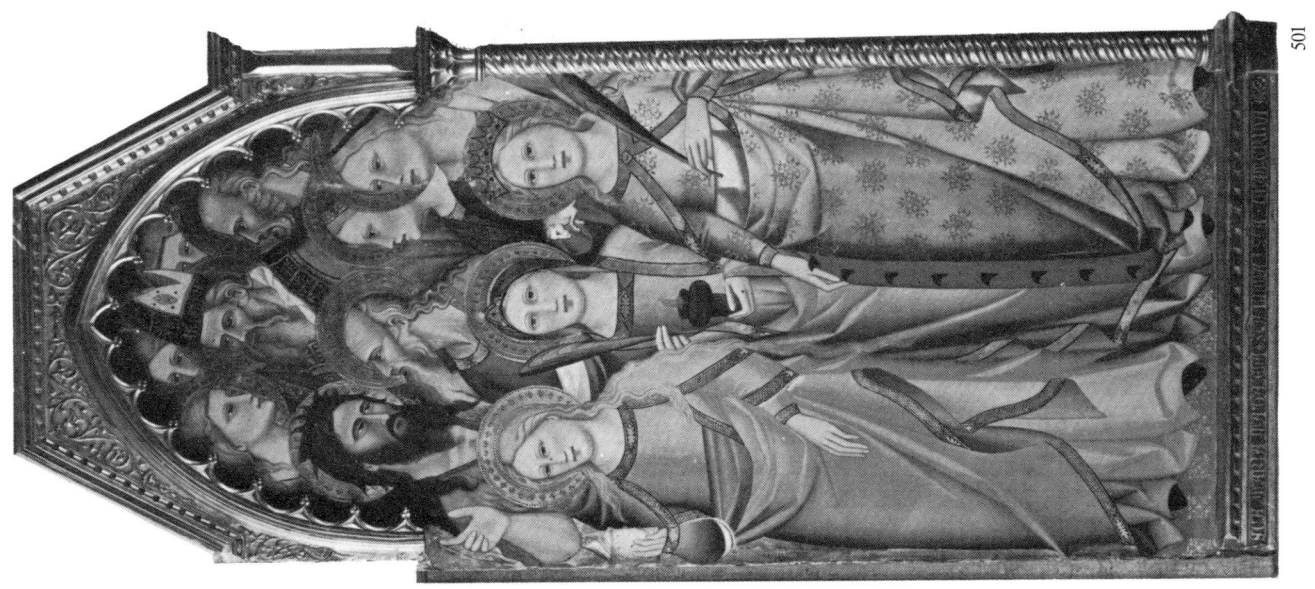

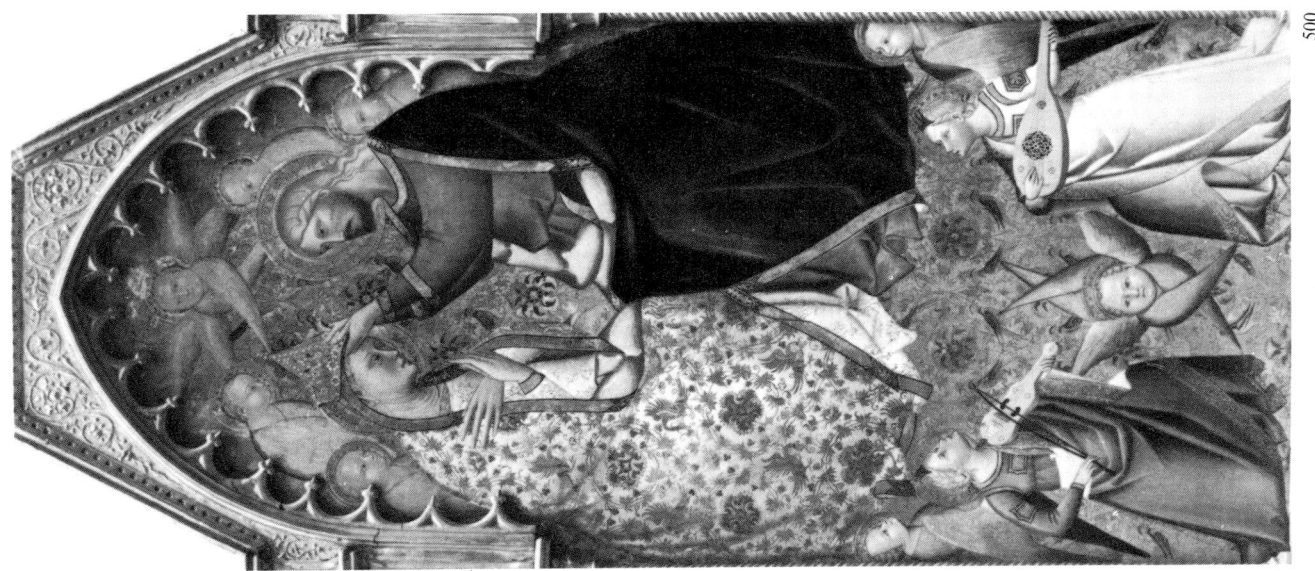

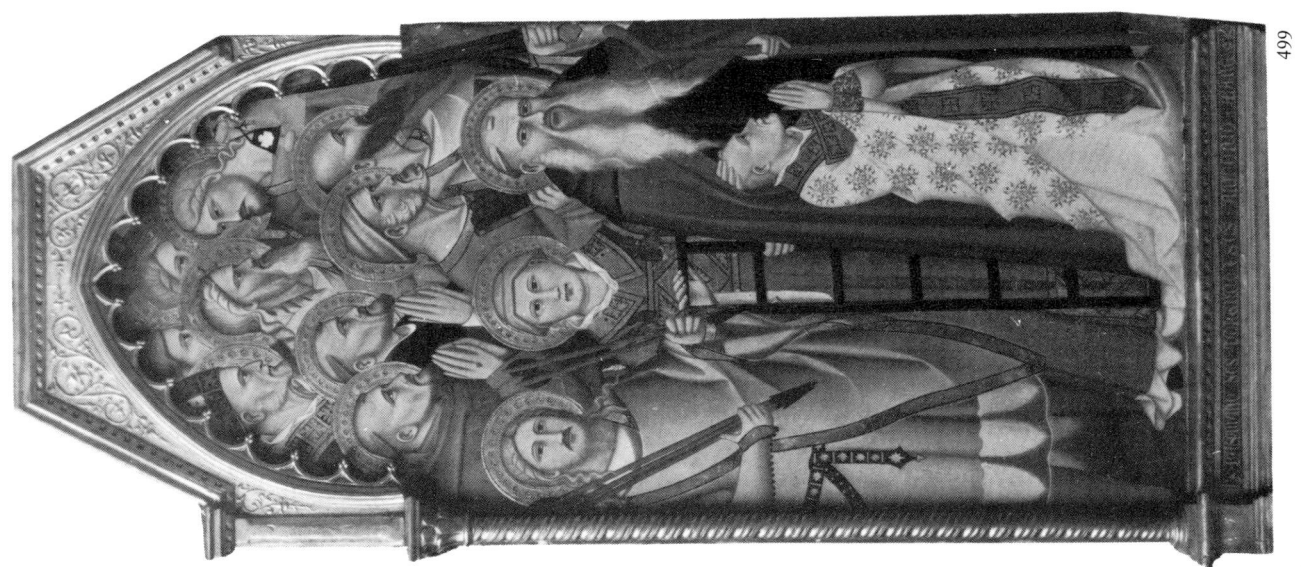

499. *Sts Sebastian, Lawrence and Anthony Abbot, with other Saints, and Guglielmo Geri de Spinis, Prior of Peretola (panel of triptych, see figs 500-1). Panel. Formerly Richmond, (Surrey), Cook Collection. no. 12. Sotheby 129620. d. 1372.*

500. *Coronation of the Virgin, two music-making Angels and other Angels (panel of triptych, see figs 499, 501). Panel. Formerly Richmond, (Surrey), Cook Collection. no. 12. Sotheby 130018. d. 1372.*

501. *Sts Mary Magdalene, Lucy and Catherine, with other Saints (panel of triptych, see figs 499-500). Panel. Formerly Richmond, (Surrey), Cook Collection. no. 12. Sotheby 129378. d. 1372.*

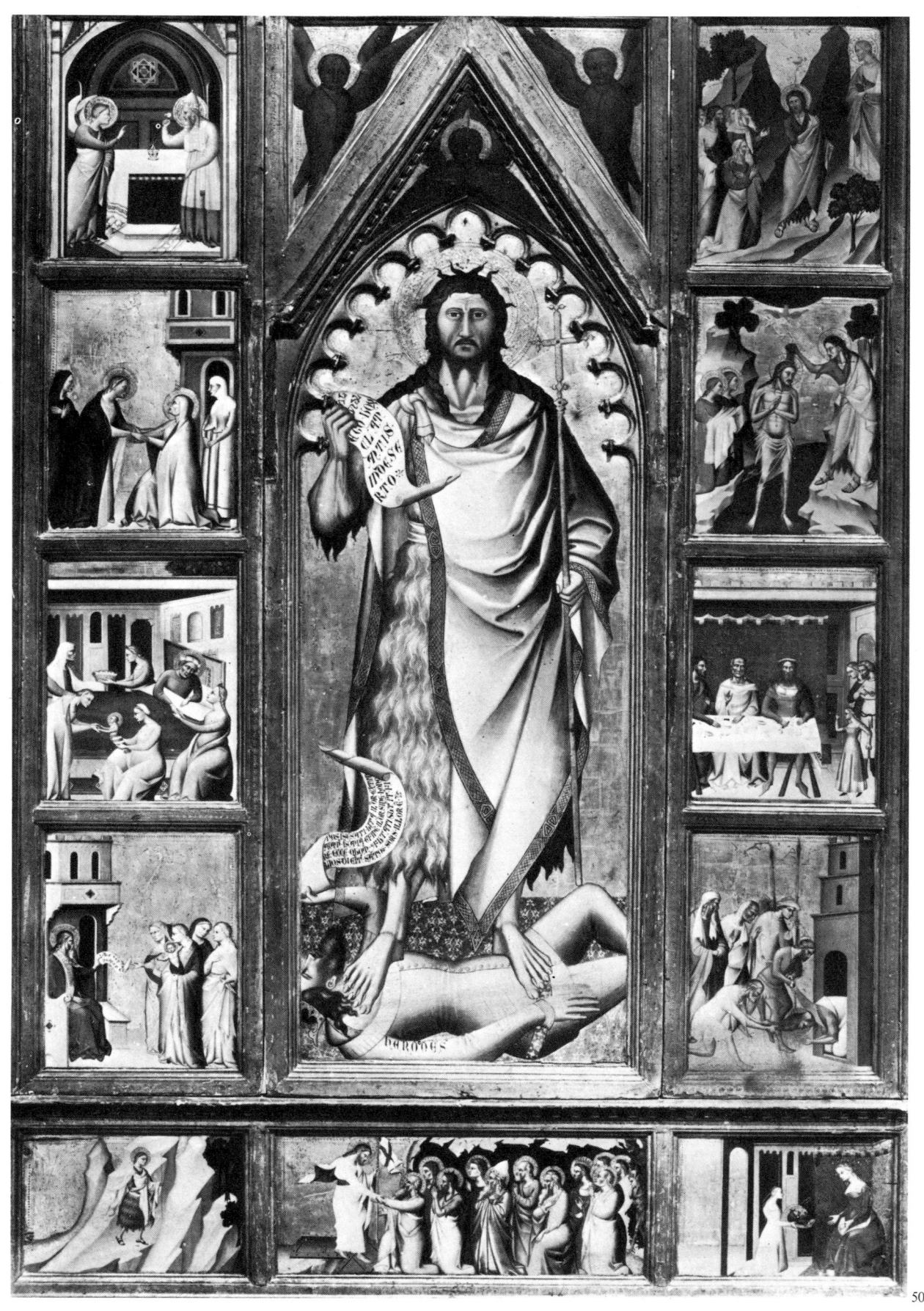

502. *St John the Baptist and scenes from his Life. Panel. Florence, Palazzo Pitti, Contini-Bonacossi Collection. 194 × 57. Reali.*

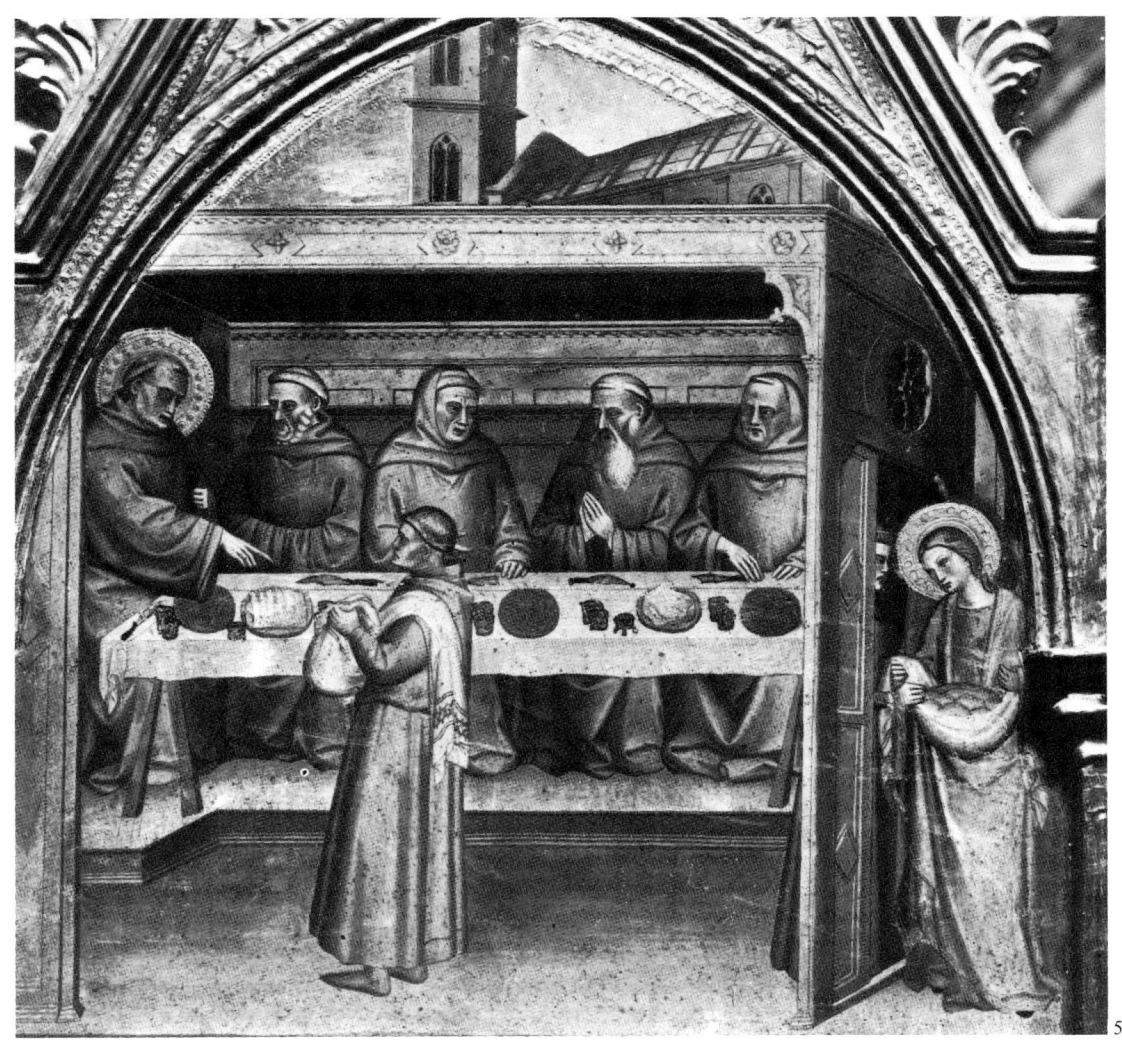

503

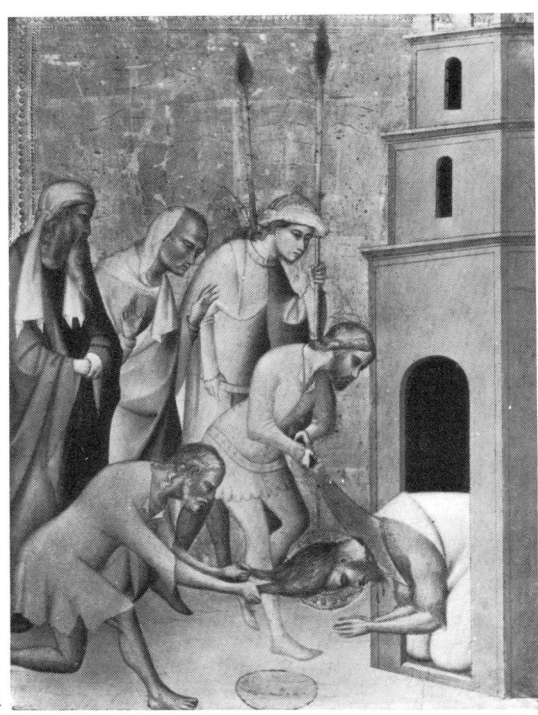

504

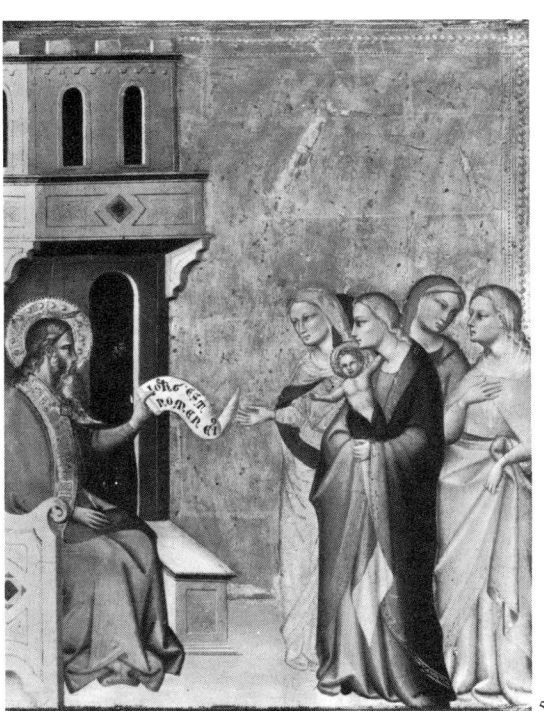

505

503. *An Angel brings bread to a monastery on a day of abstinence, detail of fig. 506. Panel Florence, S. Croce, Bardi di Vernio Chapel. Brogi 22064.*
504. *Beheading of St John, detail of fig. 502. Panel. Florence, Uffizi. Reali.*
505. *Naming of St John, detail of fig. 502. Panel. Florence, Uffizi. Reali.*

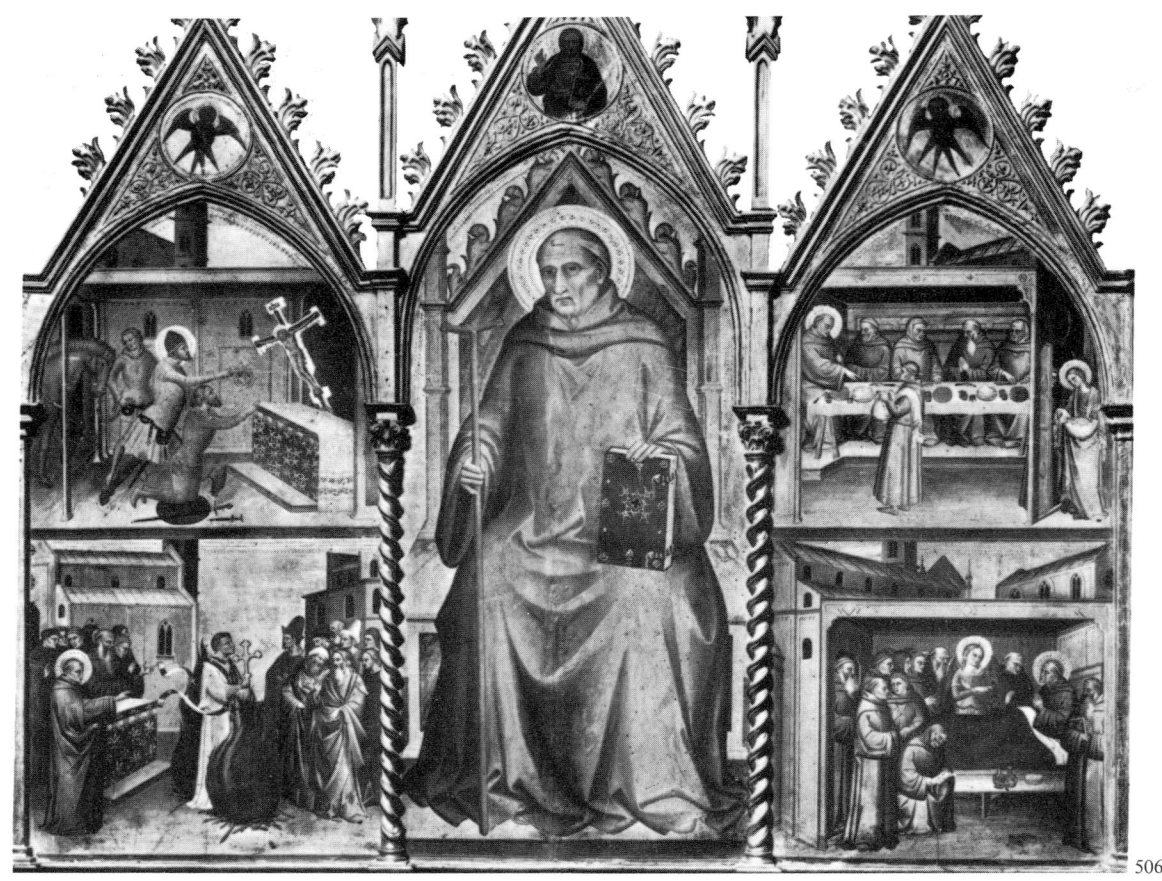

506

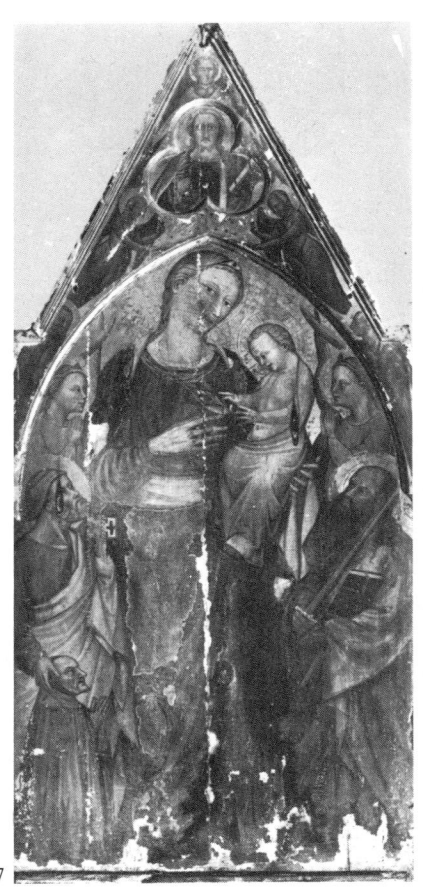

507

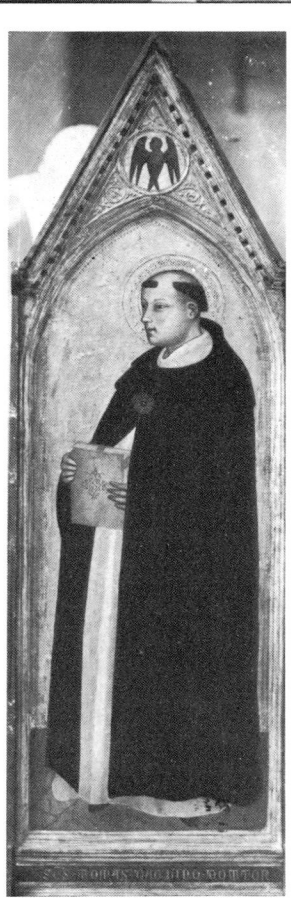

508

506. *Triptych: St John Gualbert and scenes from his Life: Christ speaks to him from the Cross; he assists in the ordeal of fire of Blessed Peter Igneus. An Angel brings bread to a monastery on a day of abstinence; his Death. Above: Christ blessing and two Angels. Panel. Florence, S. Croce, Bardi di Vernio Chapel. 199 × 180. Brogi 22061.*

507. *Centre panel of a polytych: Madonna and Child with Sts Peter and Paul, a Donor and two Angels. Above: Christ blessing and five Angels. Panel. Romena (Casentino), Pieve di S. Pietro. 173 × 77. SGF 15157. 1386.*

508. *St Thomas Aquinas. Panel. San Donato in Poggio (near Tavarnelle, Val di Pesa), Pieve, Baptistery. 137.5 × 41.5. SGF 12417. d. 1375.*

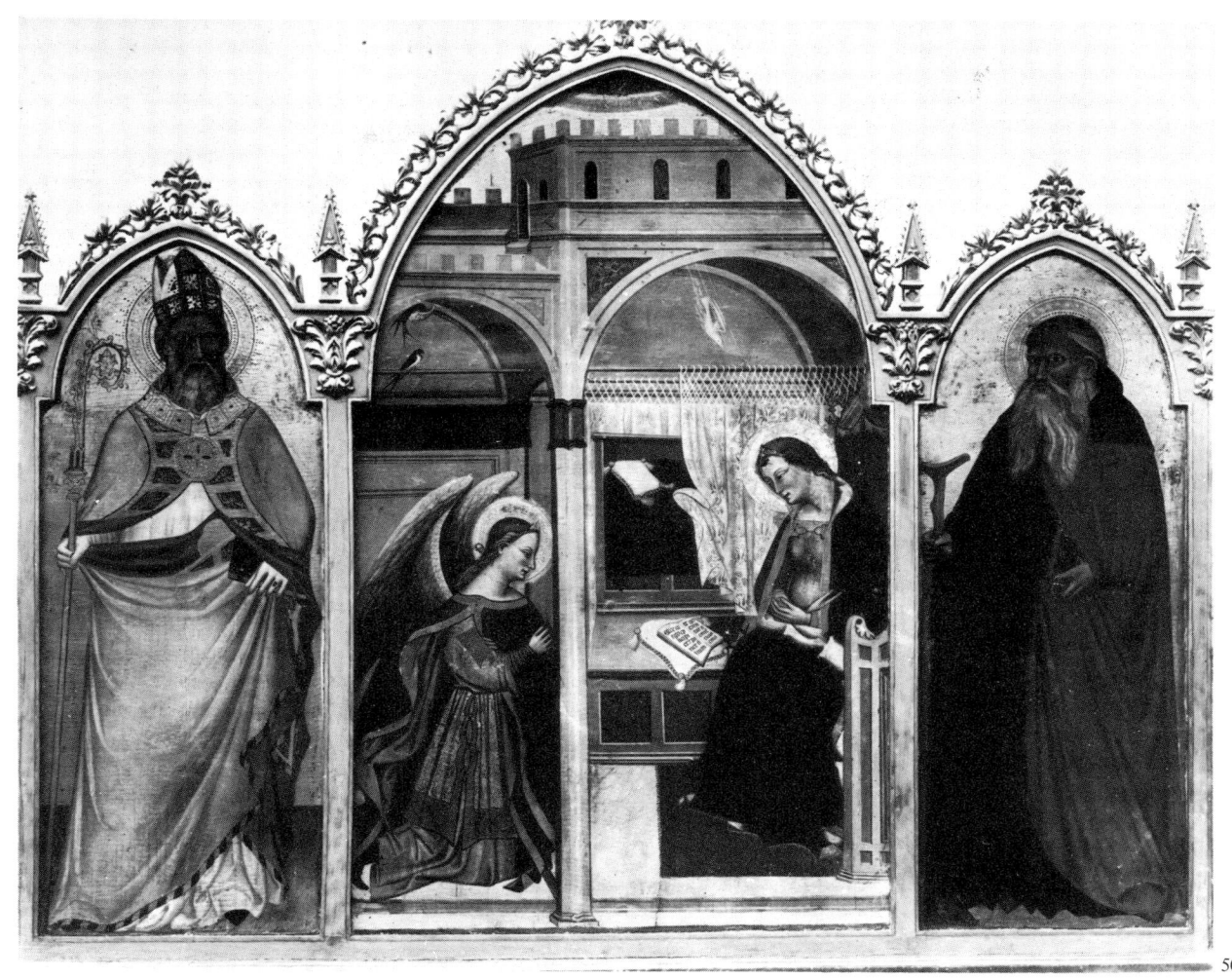

509

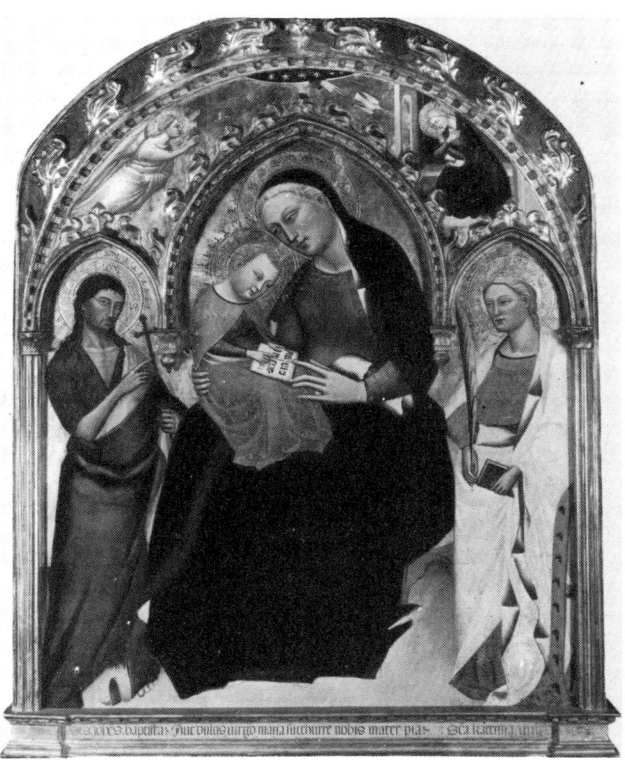

510

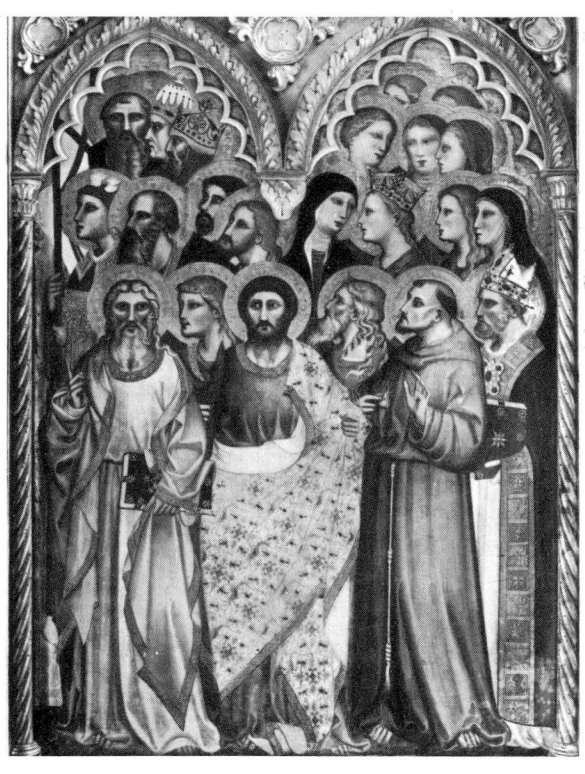

511

509. *Triptych: Annunciation with Sts Nicholas and Anthony Abbot. Panel. Florence, Ospedale degli Innocenti. no. 122. 185 × 240. SGF 21029. 1385.*
510. *Madonna and Child Enthroned with Sts John the Baptist and Catherine. Above: Annunciation. Panel. Memphis (Tenn.), Brooks Memorial Art Gallery, Samuel H. Kress Collection. no. K259. 86.1 × 76.8. Kress Foundation photo.*
511. *Sts John the Evangelist, Bartholomew and Francis (in front row) with Saints. Panel. Rome, Vatican, Pinacoteca. no. 13. 100 × 36. Anderson 23954.*

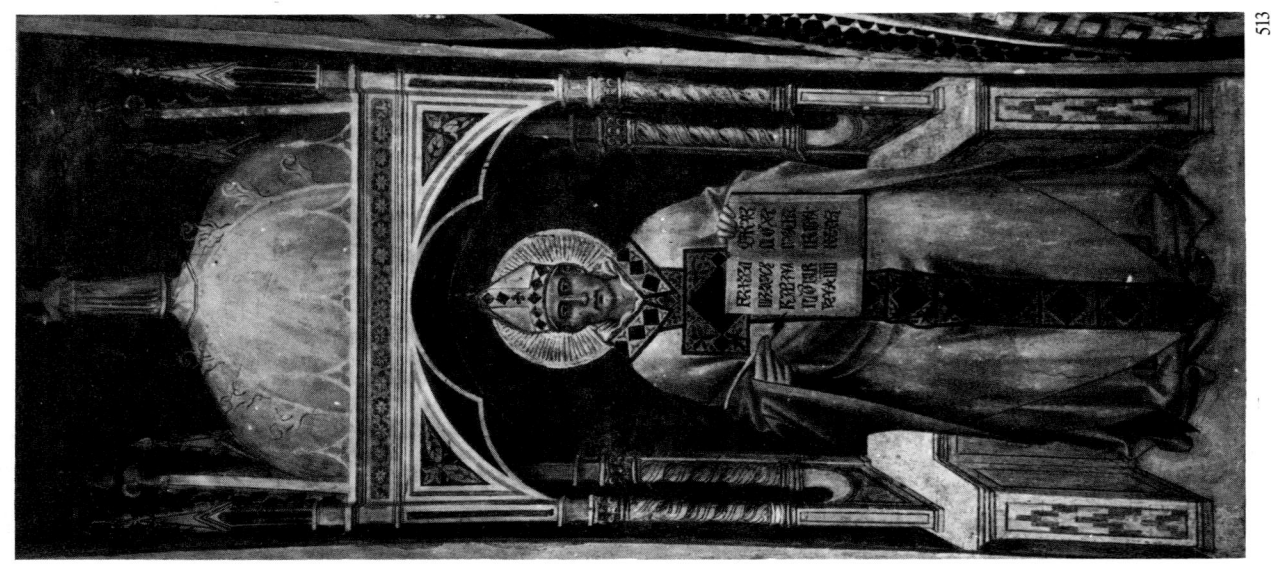

512. *Triptych: Coronation of the Virgin with Angels and Saints. Above: Christ on the Cross, Annunciation, two Prophets. Panel. San Giovanni Valdarno, S. Maria delle Grazie. no. 1. 182 × 297. Alinari 8909.*
513. *St Augustine. Fresco. Florence, S. Maria Novella, Strozzi Chapel. SGF 66079.*

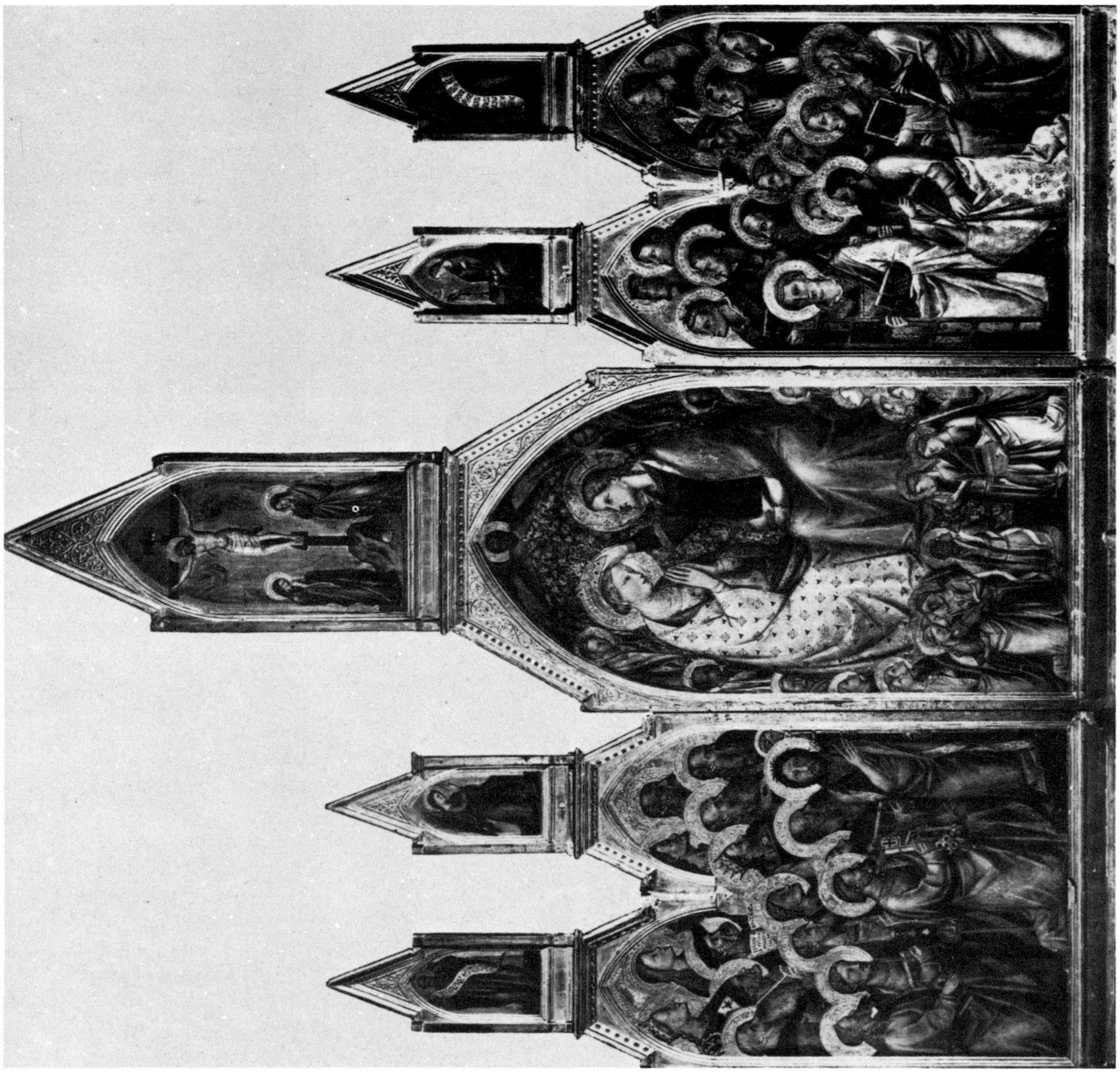

CRISTIANI

Pistoia, born 13- -, died - -. Painter, Vasari mentions a Giovanni da Pistoia, who may probably be identified with Cristiani, calling him a pupil of Pietro Cavallini. Master, probably, of his sons, Bartolommeo and Jacopo....
1389, Giovanni had painted three standards for the " Opera " of the Duomo of Pisa, for which he was paid 3 lire 10 soldi Pisan currency..... In 1394 the Board of Works of the chapel of S. Jacopo in the Duomo of Pistoia commissioned him to design the new shape and figure to be given to the silver altar, for which he appears to have made a drawing in 1395..... From 1396 to 1398 Giovanni was engaged in decorating, in fresco, the residence of the Pistojese confraternity known as " La Disciplina de' Rossi ". In a deed, referring to his son, Giovanni is styled Painter of the parish of S. Paolo of Pistoia. He was the son of a tailor; in 1366 he married his first wife, Margherita di Bonacorso di Vantino, by whom he had two sons and one daughter, born blind in 1382. Giovanni was one of the Anziani of Pistoia in 1374.....

> from D. E., Colnaghi, pp. 82-3, *A Dictionary of Florentine Painters*, London, 1928.

Giovanni di Bartolomeo Cristiani, Pistoiese, signed the *dossale* of St John the Evangelist, which was probably placed under a polyptych by the workshop of Taddeo Gaddi, in the church of San Giovanni Fuorcivitas. He was a follower of Orcagna. He painted the *dossale* in 1370. It may have been used to lift up the polyptych, as upon it were carefully painted by Giovanni scenes from the life of the saint. A panel of 1390 is also by this competent Pistoiese painter, which had been kept in the oratory of Nerli at Montemurlo and now is the property of the Gerardi Pieraccini; besides these, several paintings in the house attached to the cathedral have been attributed to him; as time passes many other works will be attributed to him, which are now generally assigned to the school of Orcagna.....

> from A. Venturi, pp. 836-7, *Storia dell' Arte Italiana*, Vol. V, Milan, 1907.

Giovanni di Bartolomeo Cristiani was an associate, rather than a pupil of Agnolo Gaddi. One can easily see in his signed picture of St John the Evangelist and eight episodes from his legend, that he was a pupil of Taddeo Gaddi, who underwent a strong influence by Nardo di Cione. However his works mentioned in early documents are all lost. Happily Professor Offner has identified his hand and style in a triptych belonging to Arthur Acton in Florence; it places Giovanni among the most distinguished painters of the last decades of the Florentine Trecento, if not even the very best painter himself.....

> from B. Berenson, pp. 1308-9, *Dedalo*, V, XI, 1930-1.

We only know of Giovanni di Bartolomeo Cristiani between 1366 and 1398, although he certainly worked over a longer period. His known works are relatively few in number. Attributions are generally based upon his best known work, the picture in the church of San Giovanni Fuorcivitas in Pistoia, which depicts scenes from the life of St John and which the painter signed and dated 1370. In this painting he follows closely the compositional scheme used by Orcagna's shop; he brings everything up close to the spectator, placing it all in the nearest plane of the picture; the figures are wrapped in folds which fall heavily with a soft effect of light and dark, making them hard, almost metallic forms. His facial types mirror, besides characteristics that have been inherited from Nardo, an influence from Giovanni del Biondo; from him, too, the manner of depicting buildings, which recalls the architectonic forms of Giovanni di Bartolomeo.....

In the 80's and 90's of the Trecento, the style of Giovanni di Bartolomeo Cristiani undoubtedly loses some of its elegance. In the Acton triptych, in the tabernacle in Via Buonarroti in Florence (now in the Church of Sant'Ambrogio), in the panels of saints at the Museo Bandini in Fiesole, as well as in the mural paintings of the " Incredulity of St Thomas " in the Duomo of Pistoia, one can see that the figures are a bit too drily modelled and elongated, with the outlines and features too simplified, but also with a further emphasizing of the characteristics of each individual type which have been described above.....

According to sources already published, Giovanni di Bartolomeo Cristiani begins to be mentioned in written documents in 1366 on the occasion of his first marriage. But since a source, which until now has never been published, informs us that Giovanni " commits himself to help Maestro Nardo every time that he has to work outside of Florence " it is clear that his ties with Nardo di Cione go back to many years before; this master is recorded dead on the 16th May, 1366.....

> from M. Boskovits, pp. 69, 70, 92, *Acta Historiae Artium*, XI, 1-2, 1965.

Florentine School. Active 1367-98, chiefly in Florence and Pistoia. His style was formed under the influence of Orcagna and of Taddeo and Agnolo Gaddi.

> from F. R. Shapley, p. 40, *Paintings from the Samuel H. Kress Collection*, London, 1966.

BIBLIOGRAPHY
BOOKS
An asterisk indicates a work listed in the General Bibliography

Venturi, A.*, 1907, pp. 836-7; *Khv & Salmi**, 1914, p. 37; *v. Marle, 1925**, pp. 302-5; *Toesca, 1929**, p. 66; *Colnaghi**, 1928, pp. 82-3; Chiti, A., *Pistoia*, Pistoia, 1931, p. 46; Giglioli, O. H., *Fiesole*, Rome, 1933, pp. 211-12; *Galetti**, " F-O ", 1950, p. 1148; *Toesca, 1951**, p. 657; *Berenson, 1963**, Vol. I, pp. 50-1; *Marcucci**, 1965, p. 131; *Shapley**, 1966, pp. 40-1; *Klesse**, 1967, pp. 340, 358, 361, 362, 462; *MMOA**, 1971, pp. 39-42.

JOURNALS

Lasareff, V., *AA*, XVI, 1928, pp. 25-40; Berenson, B., *DD*, III, XI, 5, 1930-31, pp. 1286-1318; Offner, R., *MKIF*, VII, 1953-6, 3-4, pp. 173-92; Zeri, F., *BA*, XLVI, 4, 1961, pp. 219-23; Steinweg, K., *MKIF*, XI, 2-3, 1964, pp. 194-200; Boskovits, M., *AHA*, XI, 1965, pp. 69-94; Bellosi, L., *RA*, XVII, 201, 1966, p. 75; Boskovits, M., *AI*, III, 25/26, 1970, p. 43; Bellosi, L., *MKIF*, XVII, 2-3, 1973, pp. 192.

SIGNED AND DATED WORKS

Unknown, Private Collection: Madonna & Child with Sts Nicholas & John the Baptist. s. (fig. 526).
Pistoia, Museo Civico. Panel: Madonna & Child with angels & s. (fig. 515).
1370 Pistoia, S. Giovanni Fuorcivitas. Panel: St. John the Evangelist & Scenes from his Life. s & d. (fig. 527).
1388 Pistoia, Duomo. Fresco: Incredulity of St Thomas, with Saints. d. (fig. 521).

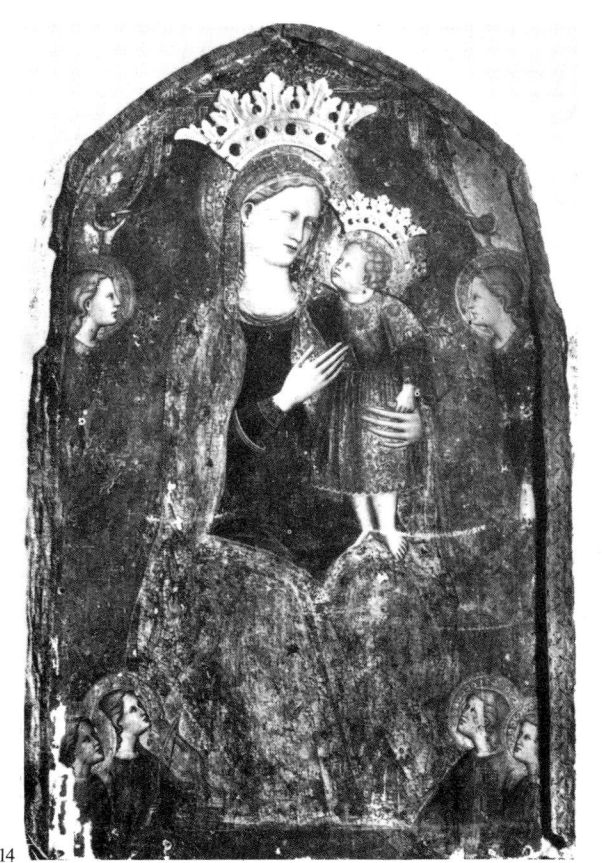

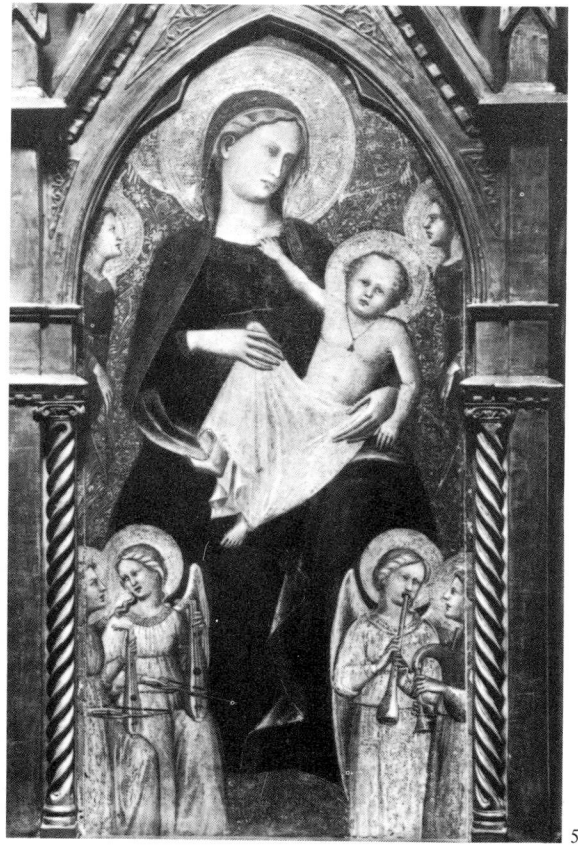

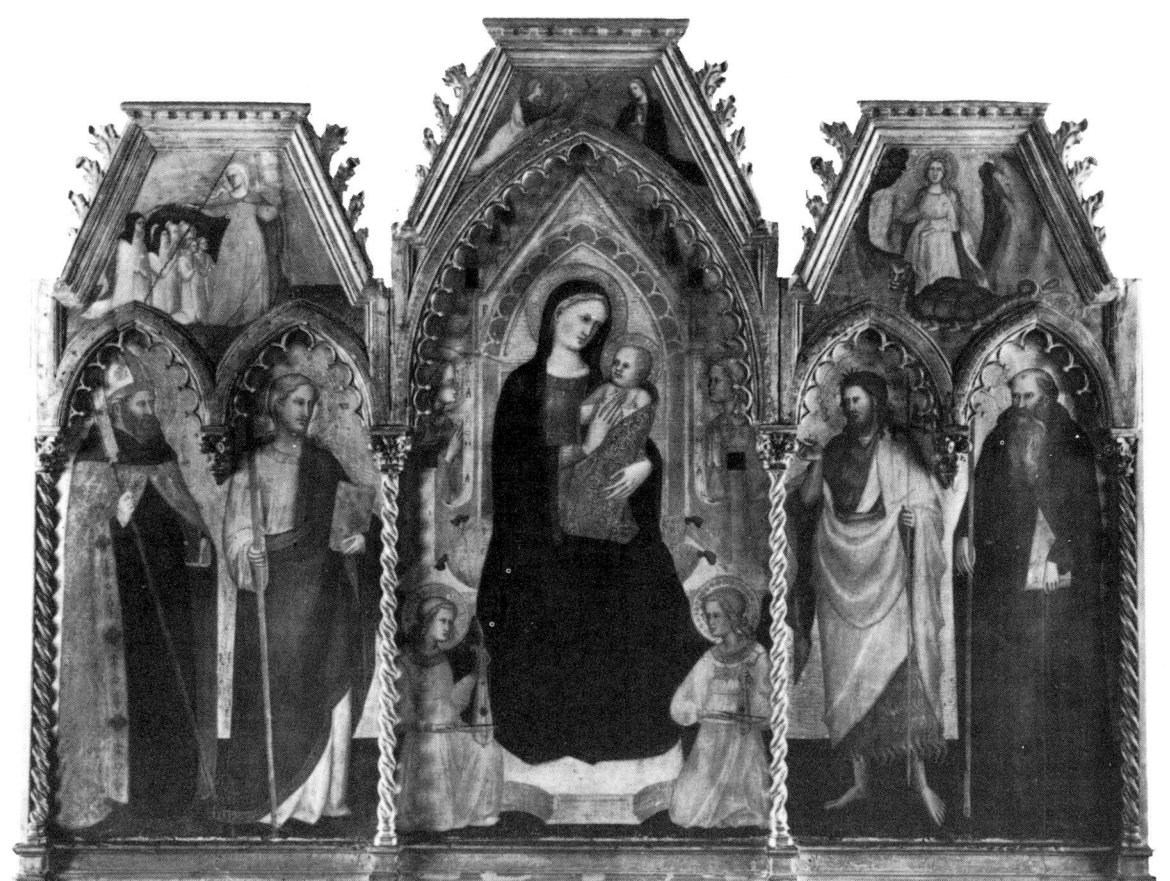

514. *Madonna and Child Enthroned with six Angels. Panel. Crespina (20 kms south-east of Pisa), S. Michele Arcangelo. 109 × 79. SGF 71779.*
515. *Madonna and Child with four music-making Angels and two other Angels. Panel. Pistoia, Museo Civico. no. 474B. 198 × 87.5. Brogi 22466. s.*
516. *Triptych: Madonna and Child Enthroned with four Angels, and Sts James, John the Baptist, Anthony Abbot and a Bishop Saint. Above: Annunciation and two female Saints. Panel. Florence, Acton Collection. cp: 171 × 214; sps: 155 × 214. Reali.*

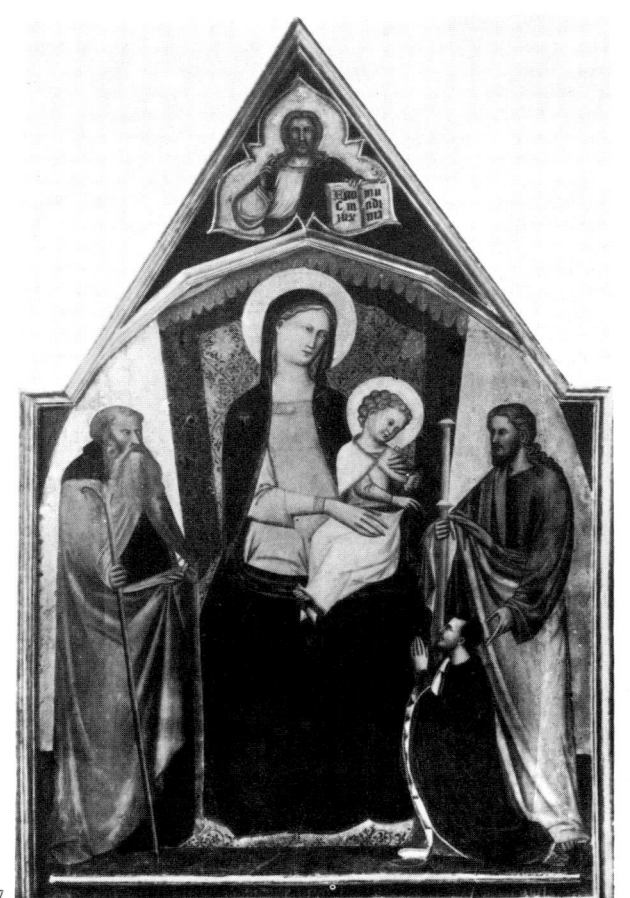

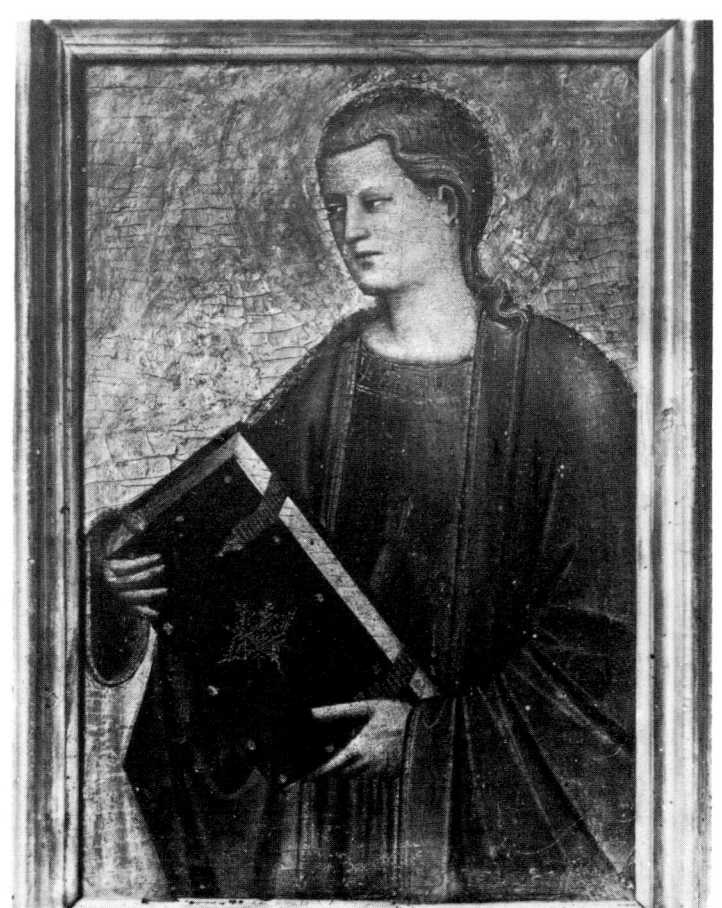

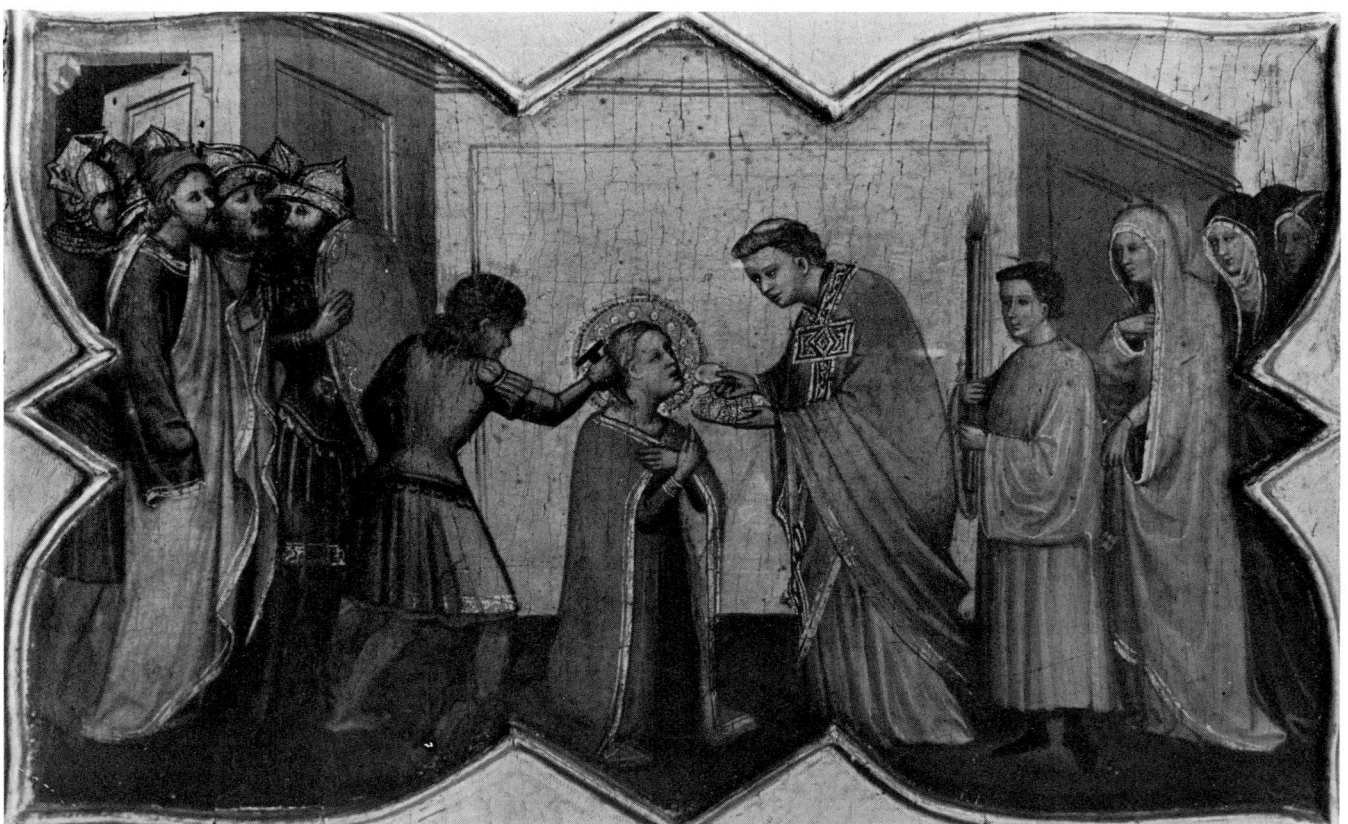

517. *Madonna and Child Enthroned with Sts Anthony Abbot, James and Donor. Above: Christ blessing. Panel. Florence, S. Ambrogio. 155 × 132.5. Alinari 31053.*

518. *St John the Evangelist. Panel. Pistoia, Museo Civico. Brogi 22445.*

519. *Predella scene: Martyrdom of St Lucy (see fig. 533). Panel. Private Collection. 24.7 × 38.1. Sotheby A 5844.*

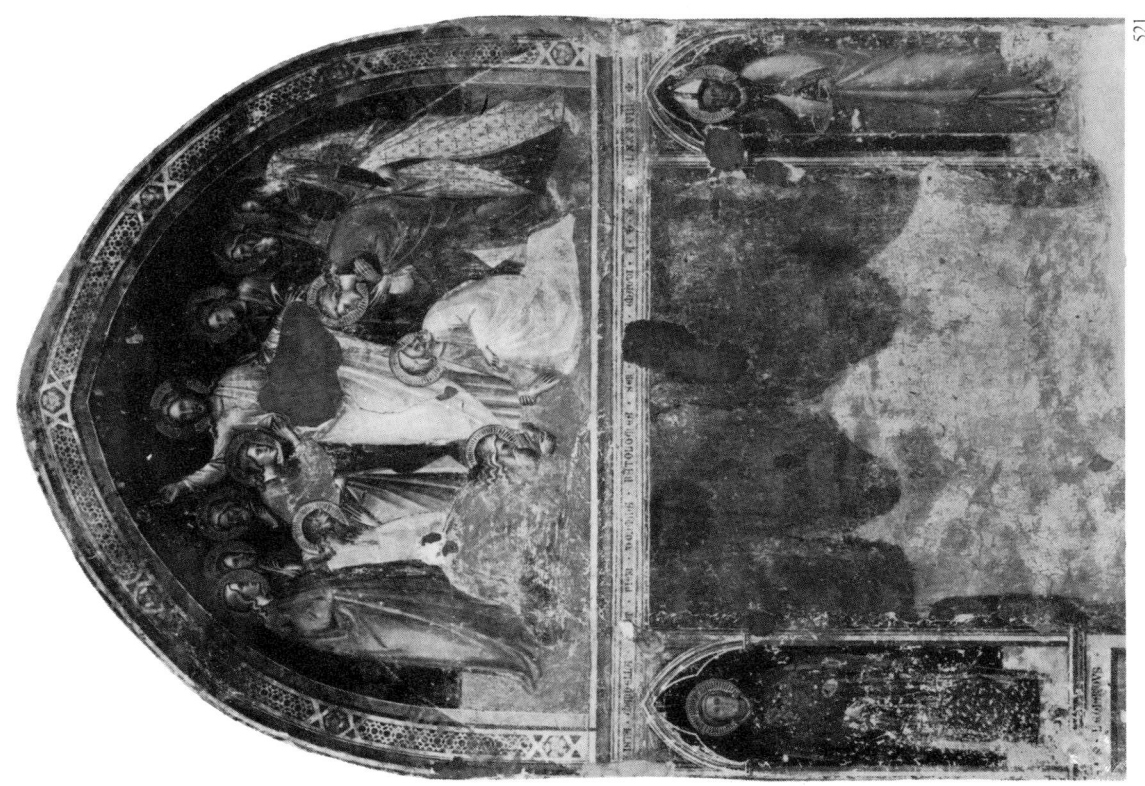

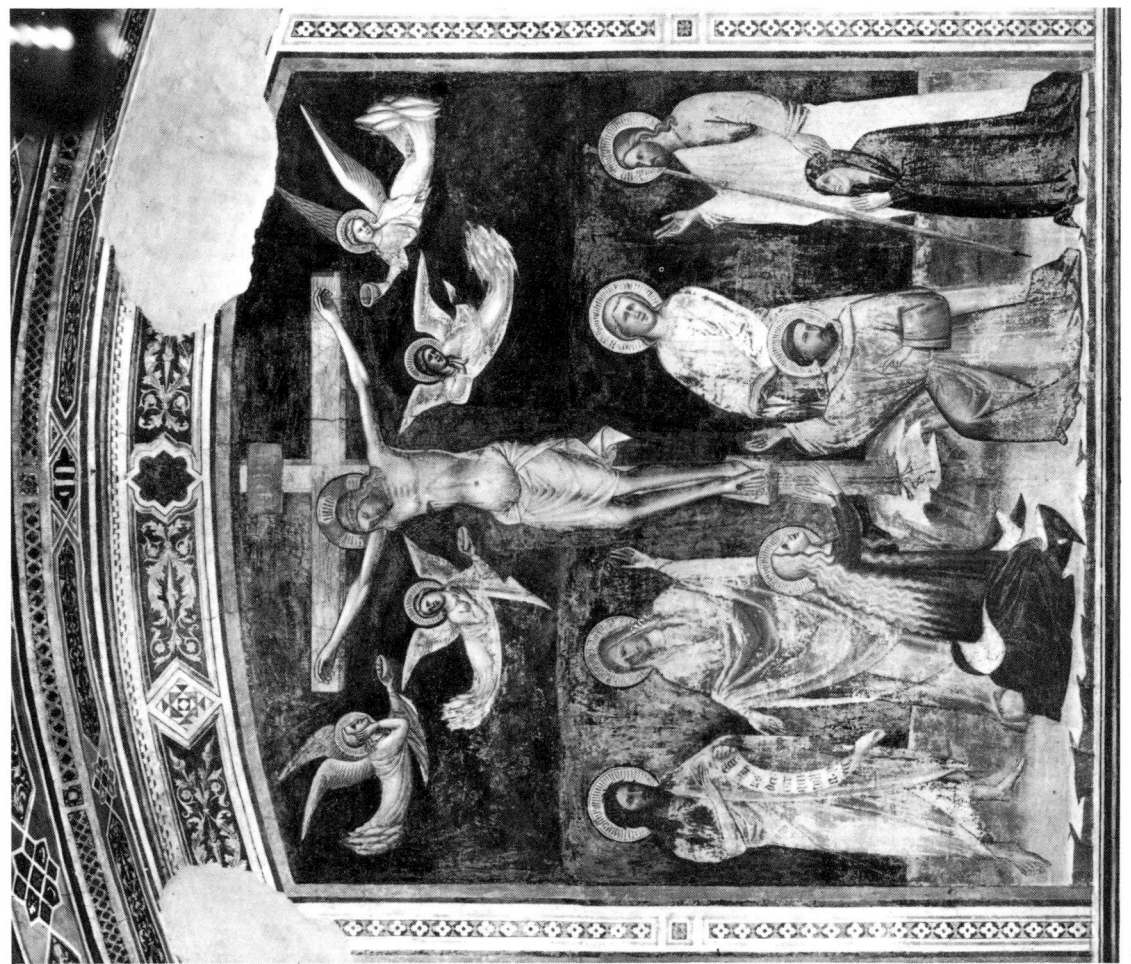

520. *Christ on the Cross with St John the Baptist, the three Marys, Sts Francis, John the Evangelist and a Nun. Fresco. Pistoia, S. Francesco, Sacristy. SGF 101533.*

521. *Incredulity of St Thomas with two Saints. Pistoia, Duomo. SGF 111002. d. 1388.*

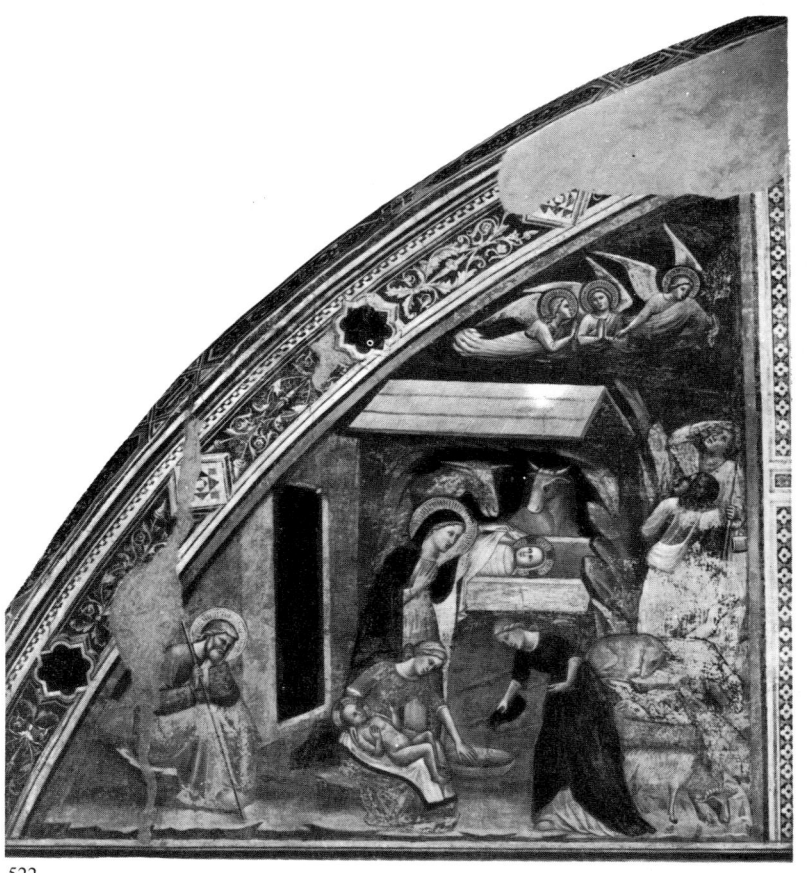

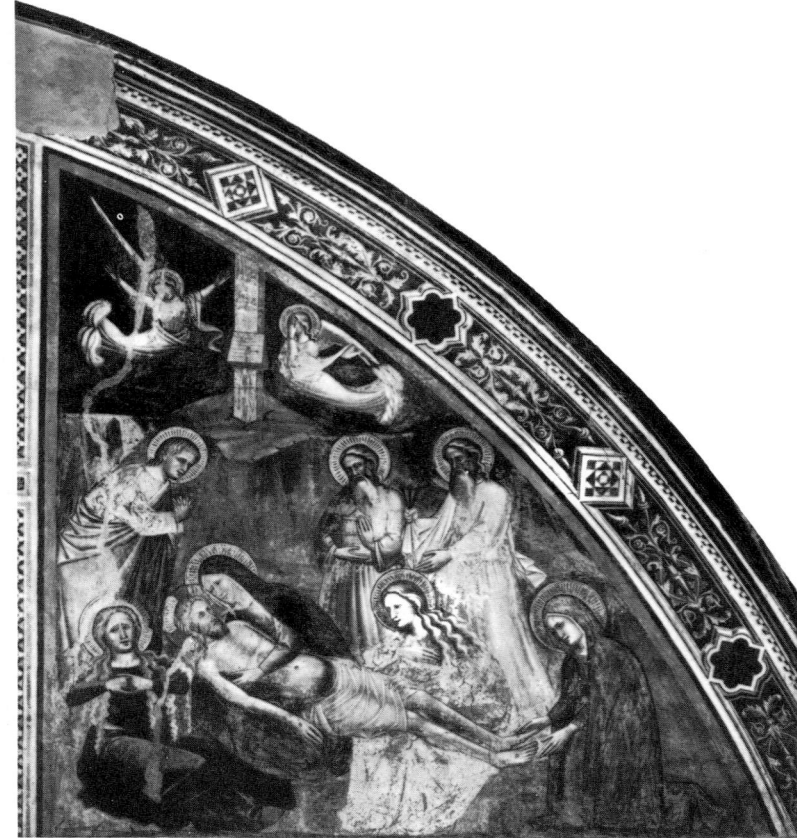

522

523

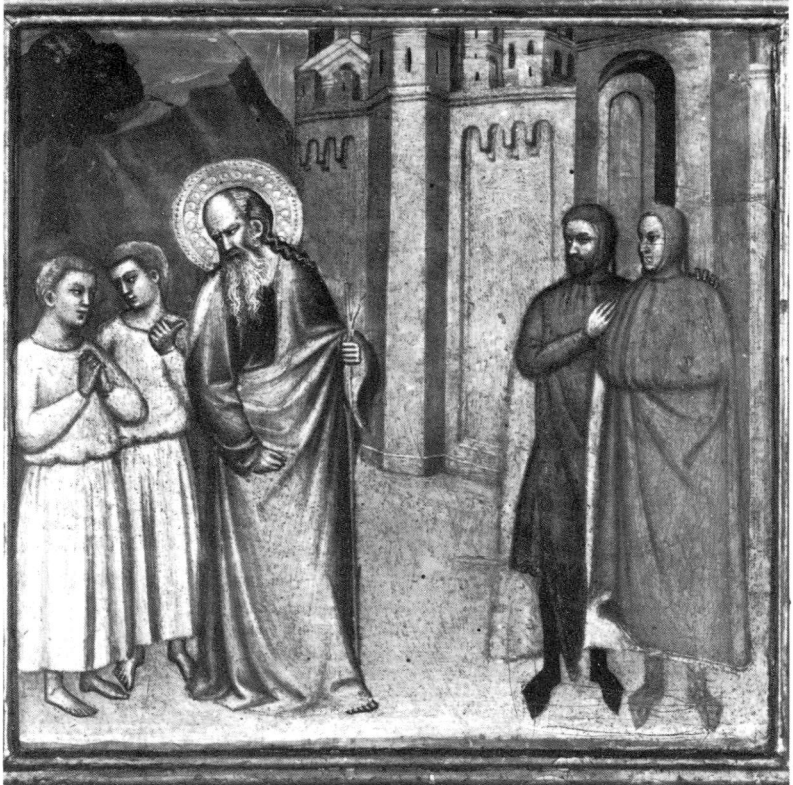

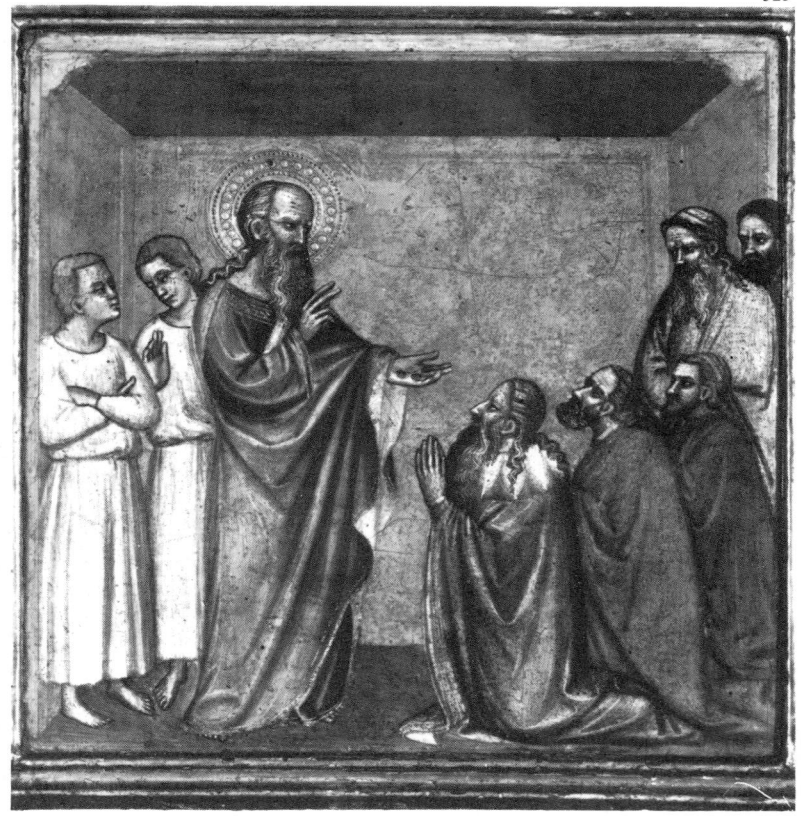

524

525

522. *Nativity. Fresco. Pistoia, S. Francesco, Sacristy. SGF 101534.*
523. *Lamentation. Fresco. Pistoia, S. Francesco, Sacristy. SGF 101535.*
524. *Acteus and Eugenius meeting their Servants, detail of fig. 527. Panel. Pistoia, S. Giovanni Fuorcivitas. SGF 149700.*
525. *Conversion of Crato and his Followers, detail of fig. 527. Panel. Pistoia, S. Giovanni Fuorcivitas. SGF 149698.*

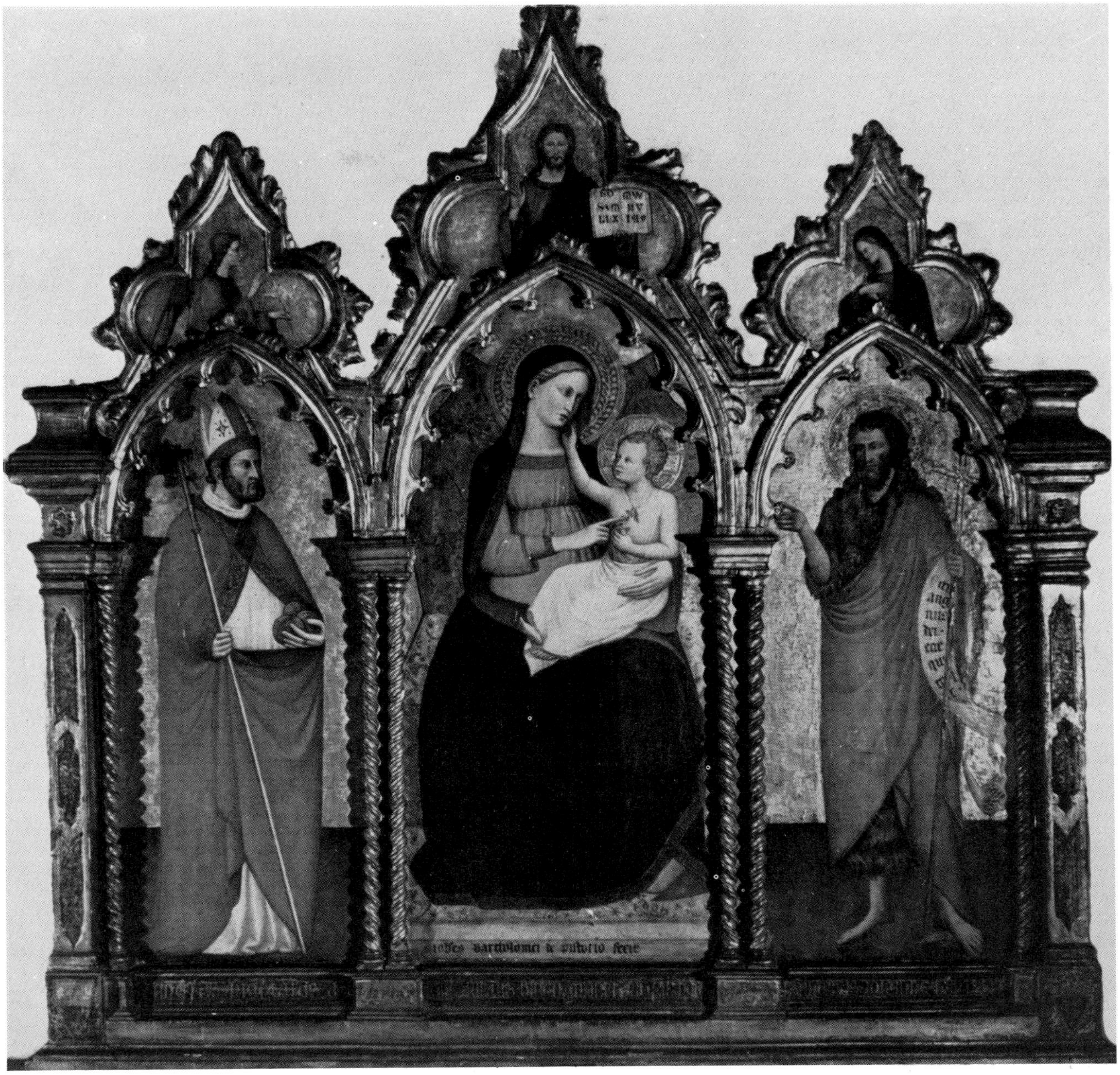

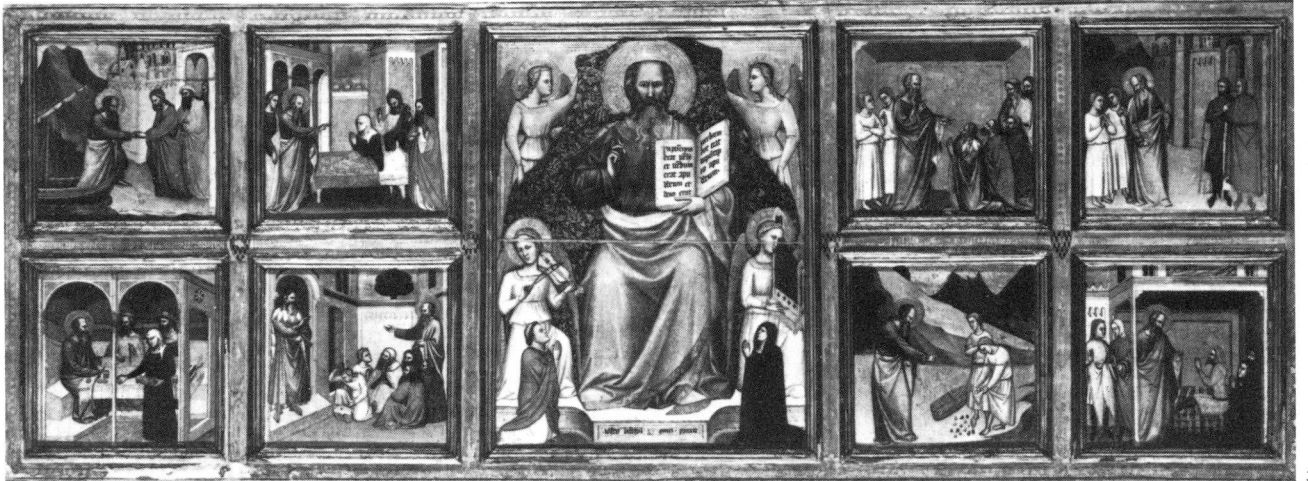

526

527

526. *Triptych: Madonna and Child Enthroned with Sts Nicholas and John the Baptist. Above: the Annunciation and the Redeemer. Panel. Private Collection. 187 × 183. Collection photo. s.*

527. *St John the Evangelist and scenes from his Life: Arrival at Ephesus; Raising of Drusiana; Drusiana serving St John; Crato's followers destroying their Patrimony; Conversion of Crato and his Followers; Acteus and Eugenius meeting their former Servants; St John restoring their Wealth; Raising of Saltheus. Panel. Pistoia, S. Giovanni Fuorcivitas. SGF 149684. s & d. 1370.*

261

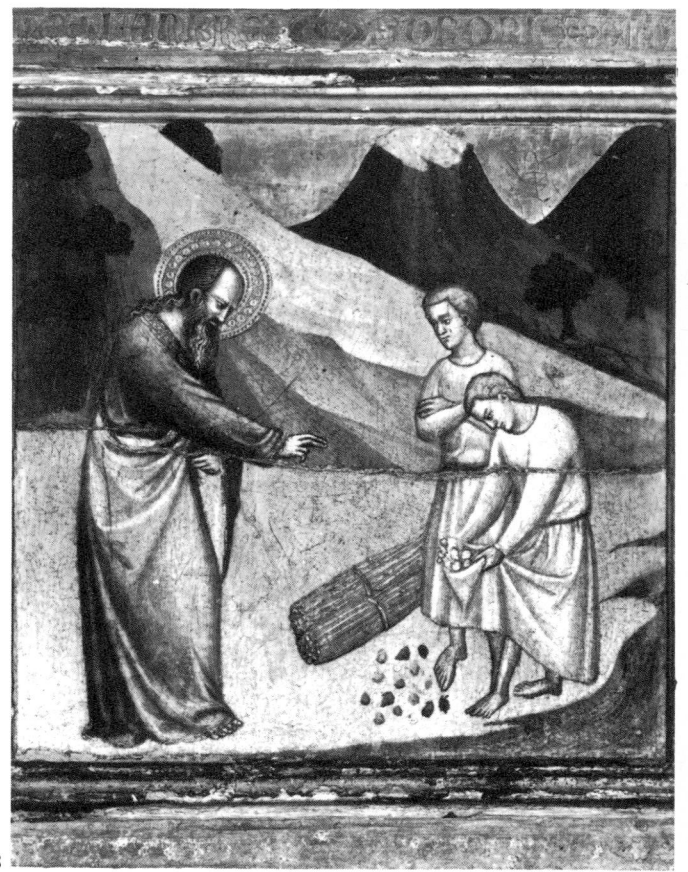

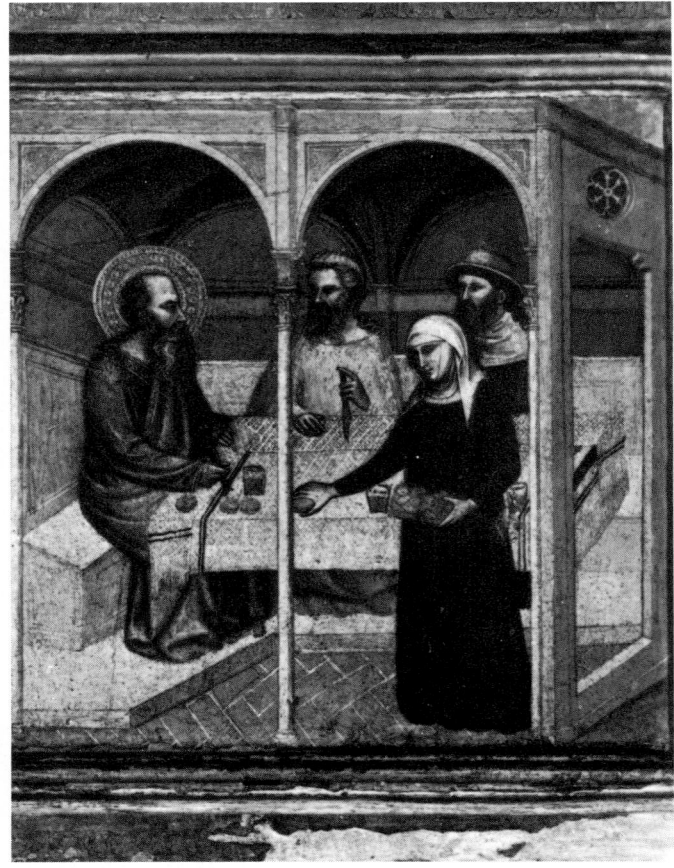

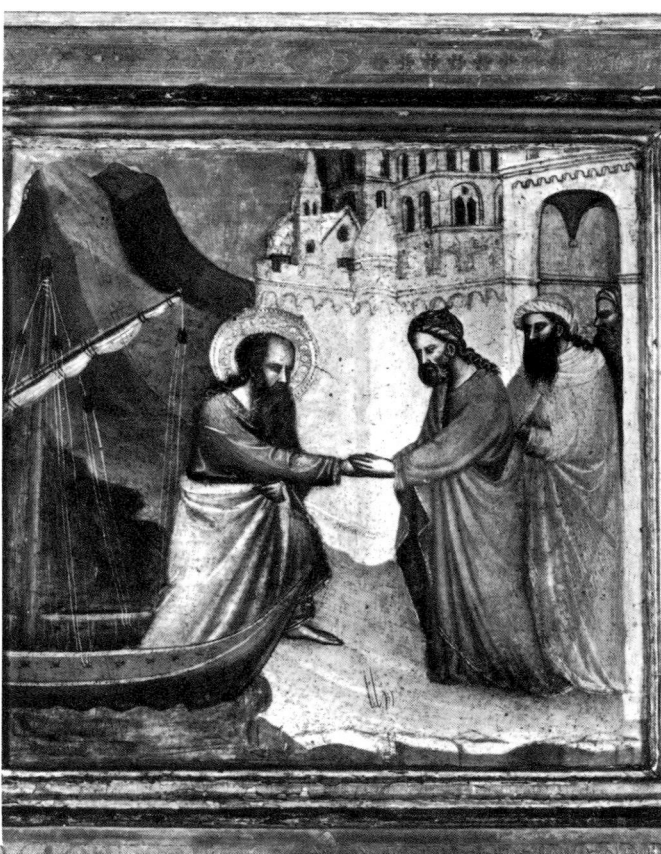

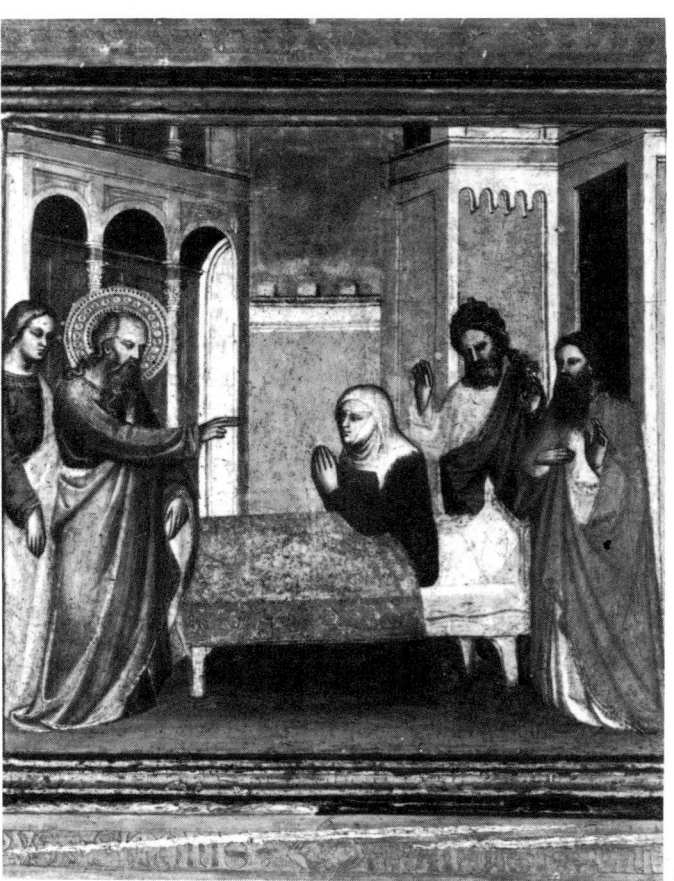

528. *St John restoring the Wealth of Acteus and Eugenius, detail of fig. 527. Panel. Pistoia, S. Giovanni Fuorcivitas. SGF 149702. s & d. 1370.*
529. *Drusiana serving St John, detail of fig. 527. Panel. Pistoia, S. Giovanni Fuorcivitas. SGF 149694. s & d. 1370.*
530. *St John arriving at Ephesus, detail of fig. 527. Panel. Pistoia, S. Giovanni Fuorcivitas. SGF 149690. s & d. 1370.*
531. *Raising of Drusiana, detail of fig. 527. Panel. Pistoia, S. Giovanni Fuorcivitas. SGF 149692. s & d. 1370.*

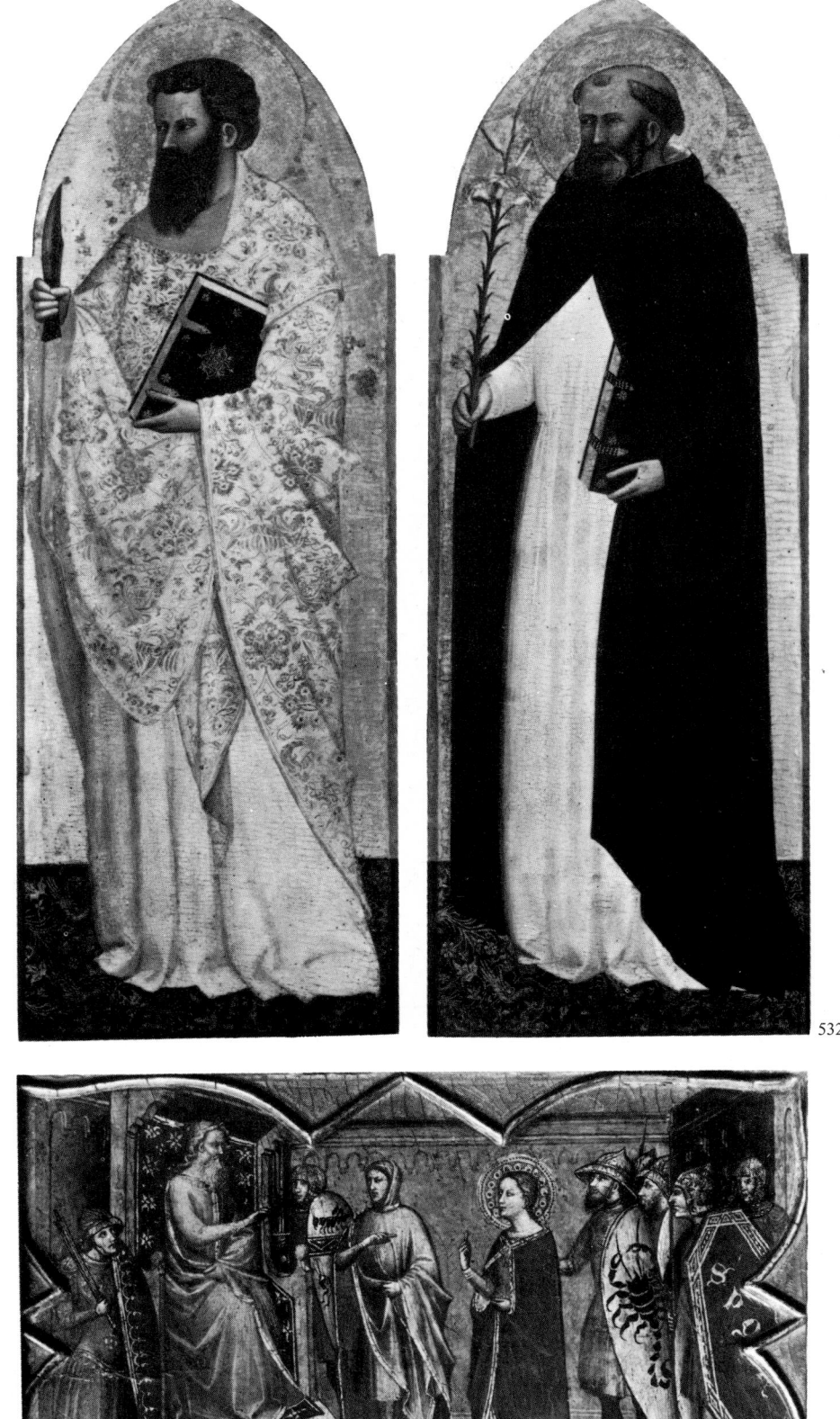

532

533

532. *Sts Bartholomew and Dominic. Panel. Fiesole, Museo Bandini. no. 15. 122 × 42.6 each. SGF 69737.*
533. *St Lucy before the Prefect (see fig. 519). Panel. New York (N.Y.), Metropolitan Museum of Art, Rogers Fund. no. 12.41.1. 24.1 × 38.7. Museum photo 12323.*

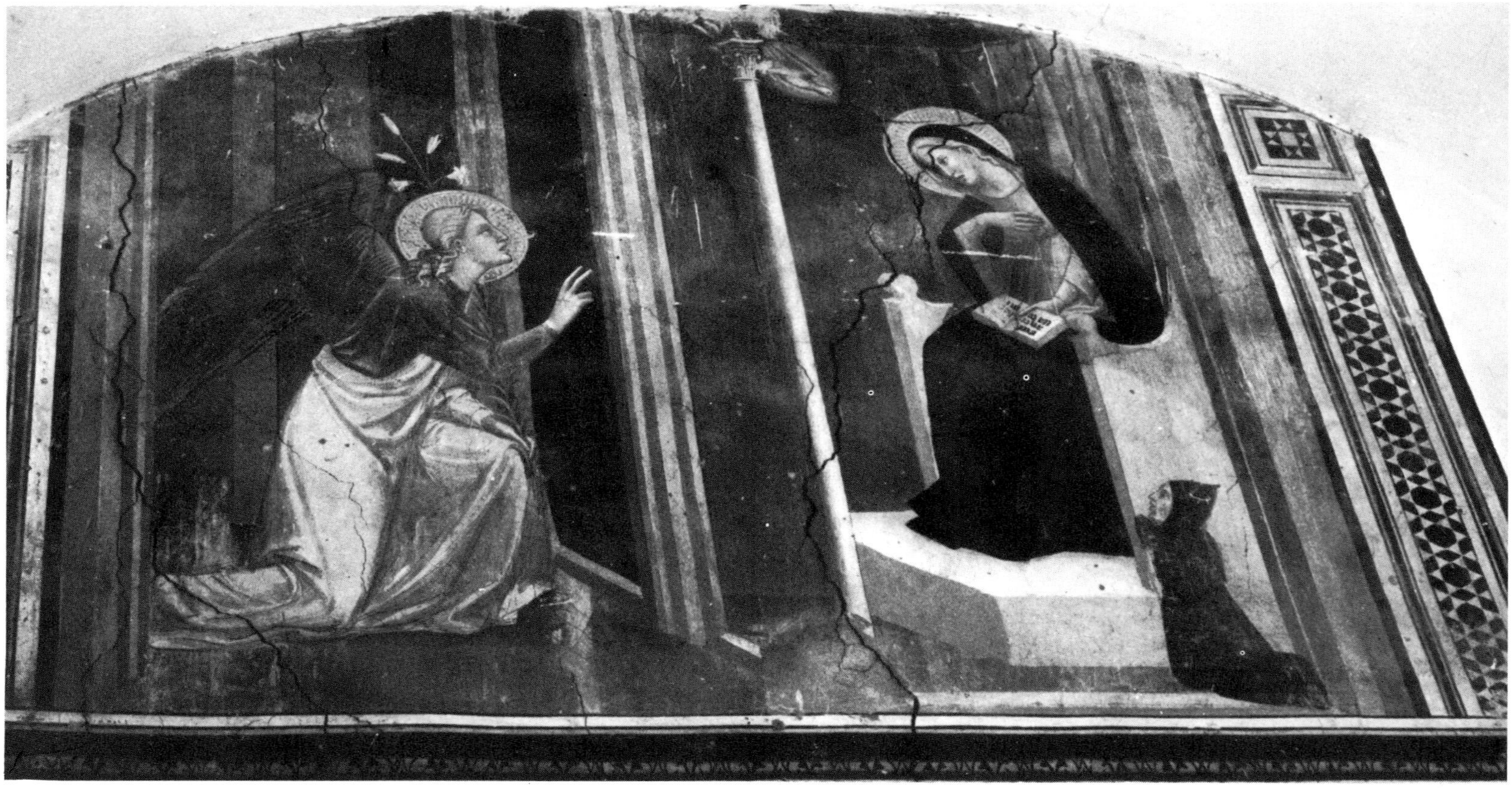

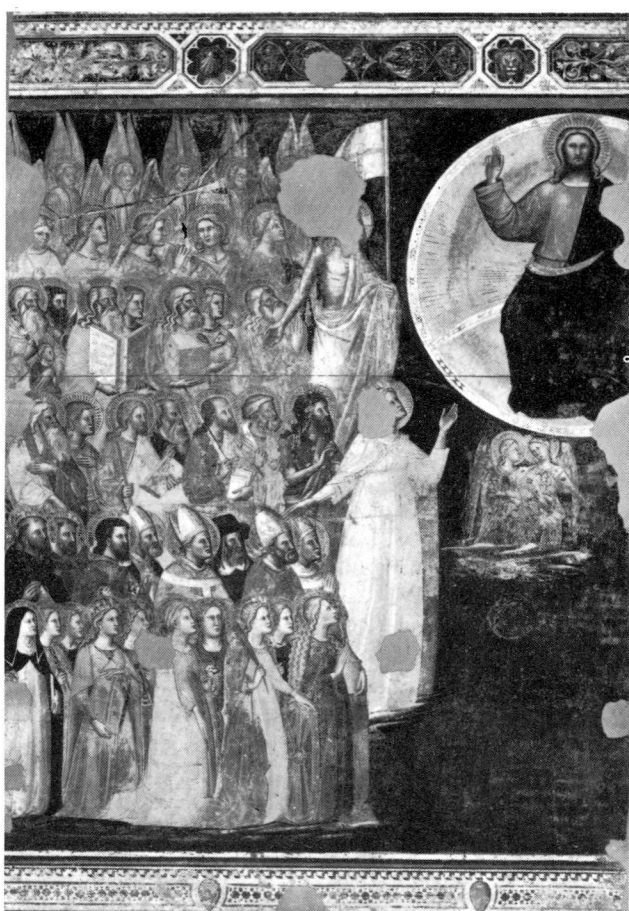

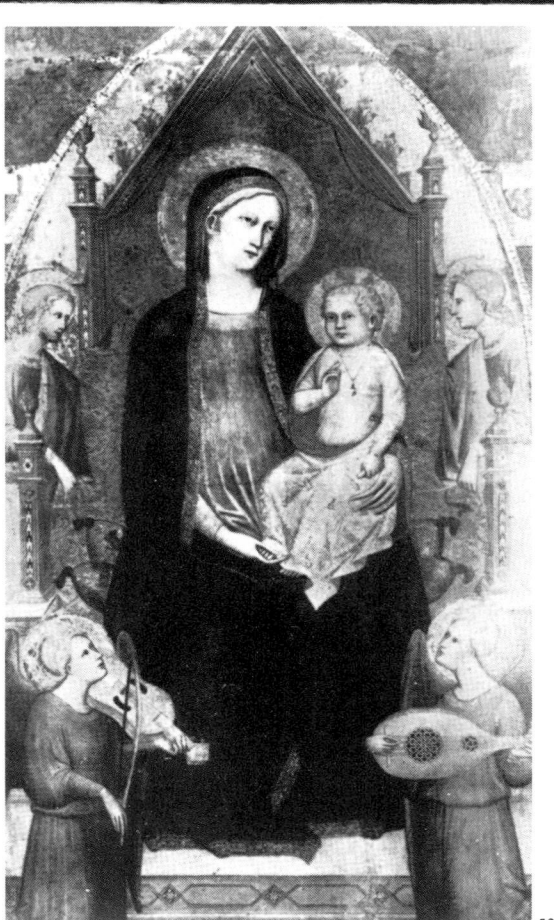

534. *Annunciation. Fresco. Pistoia, SS. Annunziata. SGF 146149. 1396.*
535. *Detail: Paradise. Fresco. Pistoia, S. Domenico. SGF 133018.*
536. *Madonna of Humility with four Angels. Panel. Moscow, Puškin Museum. no. 176. 164 × 92.˙ Museum photo.*

AGNOLO GADDI

Agnolo must have been a well-known artist in 1380 when he was charged to make designs for the plastic decoration of the Loggia dei Lanzi. From 1383 until 1386 he is busy drawing and colouring the statues of Faith, Hope, Prudence and Charity which were executed in stone by Jacopo di Piero Guidi and Piero di Giovanni. Between 1370 and 1380 his name appears several times in the tax registers and in 1387 he becomes a member of the S. Lucca corporation.

During the period that Agnolo worked in Florence we also find him active at Prato where he went for the first time about 1385 with Tommaso del Mazza in connection with some work which had to be executed for Francesco Marco Datini, a man who evidently did not part easily with his money, as pressing letters of 1391 clearly prove. On the other hand there exists a letter from Datini to a certain Stoldo di Lorenzo, full of complaints about the painters who were working for him, and ending with the melancholy phrase " .... mai non farò più dipignere ", which would lead us to believe that the artists had little consideration for their employer.....

> from R. van Marle, p. 537, *The Development of the Italian Schools of Painting*, Vol. III, The Hague, 1924.

Agnolo di Taddeo Gaddi, Florentine. Born 1333? died Oct. 15, 1396. Painter. Company of S. Luke 1387. Pupil of his father and assistant to his brother Giovanni.....

> from D. E. Colnaghi, p. 111, *A Dictionary of Florentine Painters*, London, 1928.

We are too well aware of his limits to try to claim that he was an innovator, the maker of a new spiritual position. However we are forced to recognize his place as the head of a new movement in the world of Florentine painting, the first of a new style, a precursor. A number of new and traditional elements, indigenous and foreign, are cast together in his painting: the result is a new fairytale world, that of the High Gothic....

> from R. Salvini, pp. 171-2, *L'Arte di Agnolo Gaddi*, Florence, 1936.

Son of Taddeo and probably his pupil. In 1369 he was working at the Vatican as an assistant to his brother Giovanni. According to Vasari, who expatiated upon the success and fortune of the Gaddi family of painters, he was also taught by Giovanni da Milano.... His chief works are frescoes in Santa Croce, Florence, and in the Cathedral at Prato (1392-95). Through his father he was an heir to the Giottesque tradition. Nevertheless his style became more purely decorative and deviated from Giotto's austerity and plasticity.....

> from St. J. Gore, p. 8, *The Art of Painting in Florence and Siena from 1250-1500*, London, 1965.

Florentine School. Active from 1369; died 1396. One of the artist sons of Taddeo Gaddi, Agnolo studied under his father and also under Giovanni da Milano. He worked in Rome, Florence, and Prato, frescoes in the Prato Cathedral being definitely documented. Among the assistants who helped in the execution of his work there has been an attempt to identify Gherardo Starnina. But since this identification remains theoretical, the so-called Starnina paintings are here treated as representing a phase of Agnolo Gaddi and his school.....

> from F. R. Shapley, p. 39, *Paintings from the Samuel H. Kress Collection*, London, 1966.

BIBLIOGRAPHY
BOOKS   *An asterisk indicates a work listed in the General Bibliography*

Venturi, A.*, 1907, pp. 816-28; *v. Marle 1924*, p. 537; *Colnaghi**, 1928, p. 111; Wulff, O., pp. 156-90 in *Italienische*

Studien (Schubring-Festschrift), Leipzig, 1929; *Venturi, L.**, 1931, Vol. I, pls 50-52; Salvini, R., *L'arte di Agnolo Gaddi*, Florence, 1936; *Coletti, Vol. II**, 1946, pp. 59-60; *Antal**, 1948, pp. 203-4; *Vavalà, 1948**, pp. 76-8; *Galetti**, " F-O ", 1950, pp. 1010-12; *Toesca, 1951**, pp. 646-8; Suida, W. E., *Catalogue of the University of Arizona Collection*, Tucson, (Ariz.), 1957, no. 2; *Oertel, 1961**, pp. 124-5; *Berenson, 1963**, Vol. I, pp. 66-9; Gore, St. J., *Wildenstein**, 1965, p. 8; *Marcucci**, 1965, pp. 138-44; *Shapley**, 1966, pp. 39-40; Bellosi, L., *La Pittura Tardogotica in Toscana* (I Maestri del Colore, 239), Milan, 1966; *MMOA**, 1971, pp. 46-49; Zeri, F., *Diari di Lavoro*, Bergamo, 1971, p. 16; *Dutch Show**, 1974, p. 42, 8; Zeri, F., *AP*, XCIX, 144, 1974, p. 93.

JOURNALS

Dami, L., *BA*, 1915, 8, pp. 216-44; Tosi, L. M., *BA*, IX, 7, 1930, pp. 538-44; Piattoli, R., *RA*, XI, 1929, 221-53, 396-437, 537-79; XII, 1930, pp. 97-150; Nicholson, A., *AB*, Sept, 1930, XII, 3, pp. 270-300; Berenson, B., *DD*, XI, 1930-31, 5, pp. 1286-1318; Gamba, C., *RA*, XIV, 1932, pp. 55-74; Piattoli, R., *RA*, XIV, 1932, pp. 377-82; *Edit.*, *RA*, XIV, 1932, pp. 355-76; Procacci, U., *MKIF*, March, 1919-32, III, p. 194; Procacci, U., *RA*, XV, 1933, pp. 151-90; Salvini, R., *RA*, XVI, 1934, pp. 29-44, 205-228; Salvini, R., *BA*, XXIX, 1935, pp. 279-94; Procacci, U., *RA*, XVII, 1935, pp. 333-84; Lipman, J., *AB*, XVIII, 1936, pp. 54-102; Procacci, U., *RA*, XVIII, 1936, pp. 77-94; Sandberg-Vavalà, E., *AB*, XVIII, 1936, 420-3; Ragghianti, C. L., *CA*, II, 1937, pp. 185-189; Sandberg-Vavalà, E., *AA*, XXVII, 1939, pp. 105-11; Lane, A., *BM*, Feb, 1949, XCI, pp. 43-8; Gronau, H. D., *PR*, 1950, III, pp. 41-7; Baldini, U., *BA*, Apr.-June, 1952, XXXVII, 4, pp. 173-4; Dresser, L., *BWAM*, XXV, 3, 1959; Bellosi, L., *PA*, XVI, 1965, pp. 21-23; Bellosi, L., *RA*, XVII, 201, 1966, p. 76; Boskovits, M., *MKIF*, 1-2, XIII, 1967, pp. 31-60; Cole, B., *MKIF*, XIII, 1-2, 1967, pp. 61-82; Salmi, M., *BA*, LII, 5, 1967, pp. 222-24; Boskovits, M., *ZKG*, XXXI, 4, 1968, p. 276; Boskovits, M., *AV*, VII, 3, 1968, pp. 3-13; Boskovits, M., *BM*, Apr, 1968, CX, pp. 208-15; Cole, B., *MKIF*, XIII, 3-4, 1968, pp. 289-300; Boskovits, M., *AI*, III, 25/26, 1970, pp. 32-47; Clark, K., *AP*, XCI, Apr, 1970, p. 262; Kiel, H., *P*, XXVIII, II, Apr, 1970, pp. 161-2; *Edit.*, *BM*, CXIII, 821, 1971, p. 435; Boskovits, M., *MKIF*, XVII, 2/3, 1973, pp. 201-22; *Edit.*, *AV*, XII, 2, 1973, p. 72.

There are no known signed and/or dated works by Agnolo Gaddi.

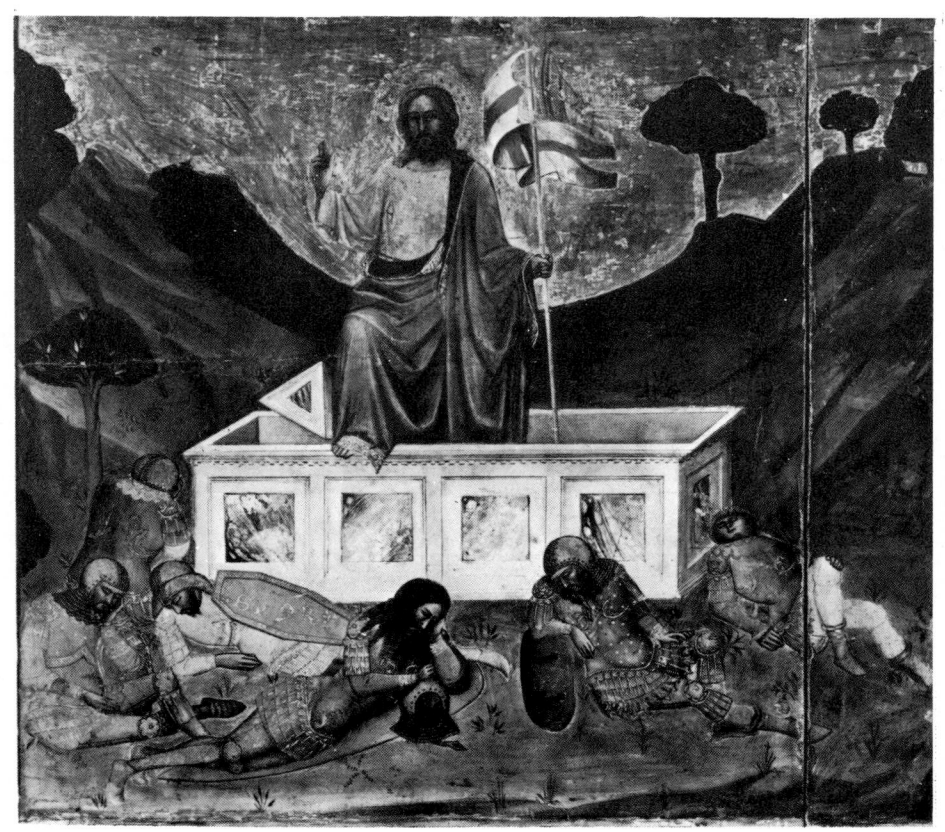

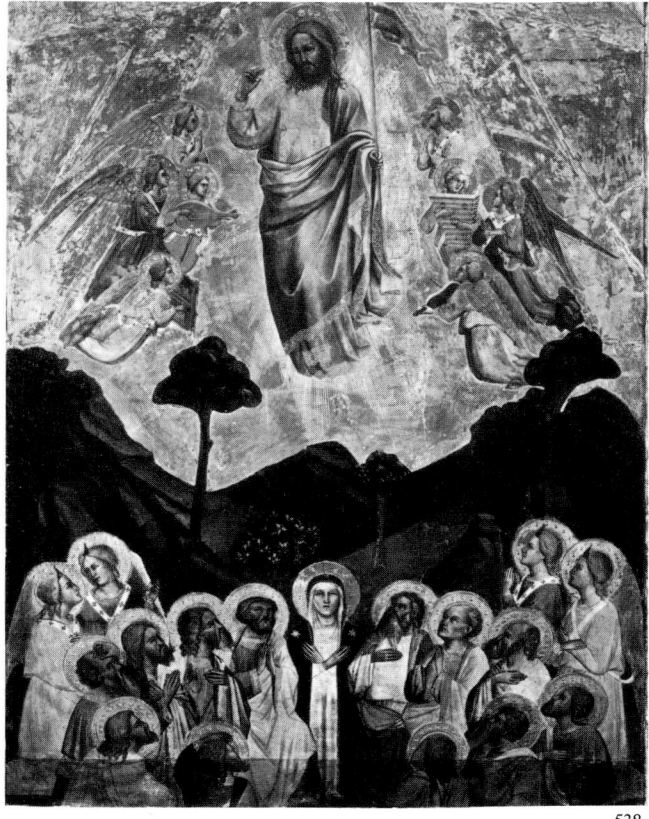

537

538

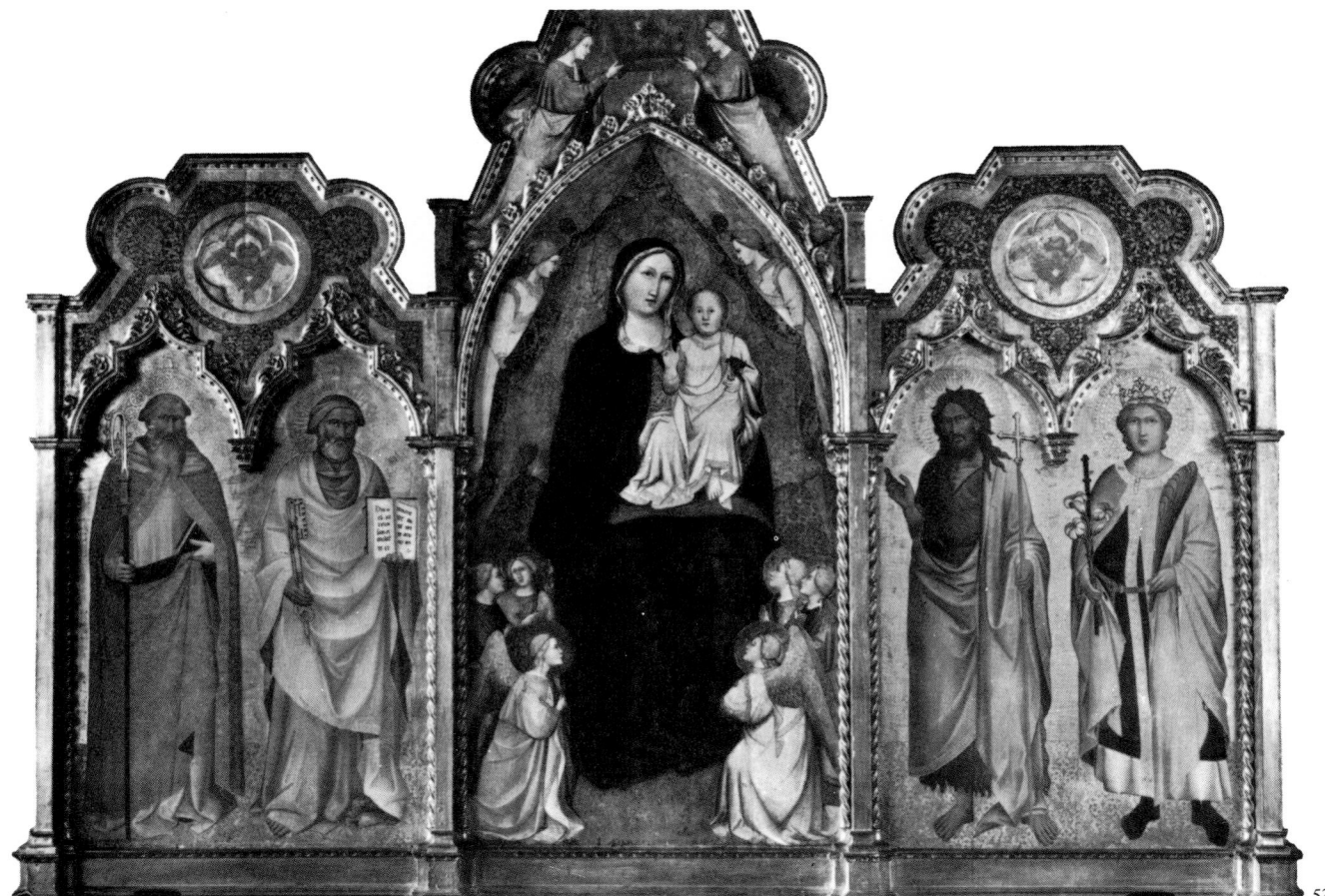

539

537. *Resurrection of Christ. Panel. Florence, S. Miniato al Monte, Cappella del Crocifisso. SGF 128812. 1396.*
538. *Ascension of Christ. Panel. Florence, S. Miniato al Monte, Cappella del Crocifisso. SGF 128806. 1396.*
539. *Triptych: Madonna and Child Enthroned with eight Angels and a Bishop Saint, Sts Peter, John the Baptist, Minias. Above, two Angels. Panel. Florence, Palazzo Pitti, Contini-Bonaccossi Collection. 222 × 290. Reali.*

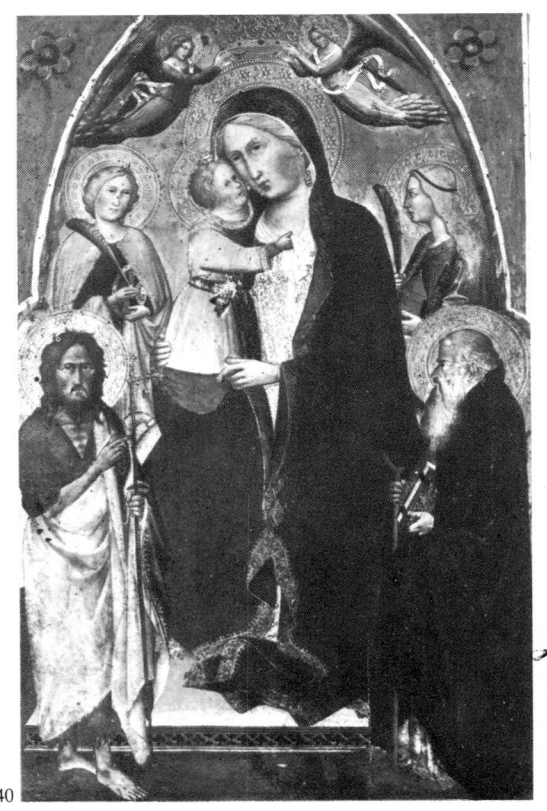
540

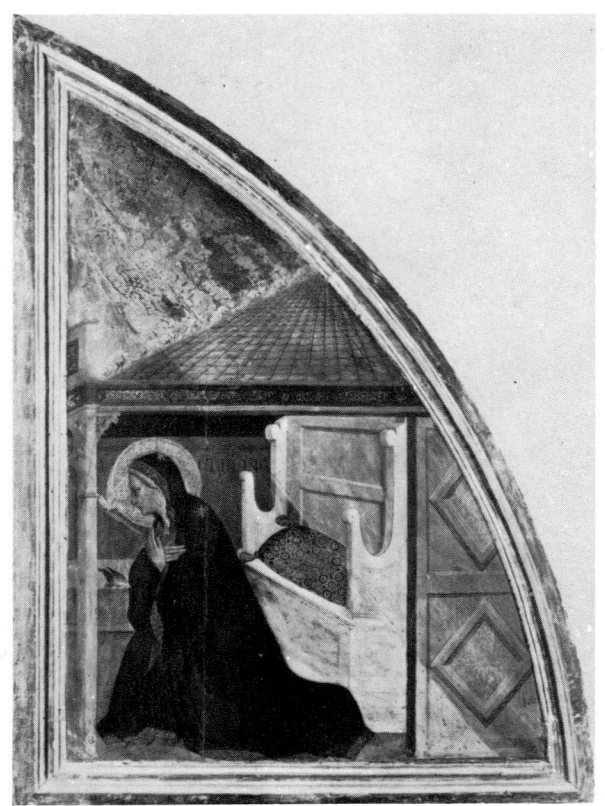
541

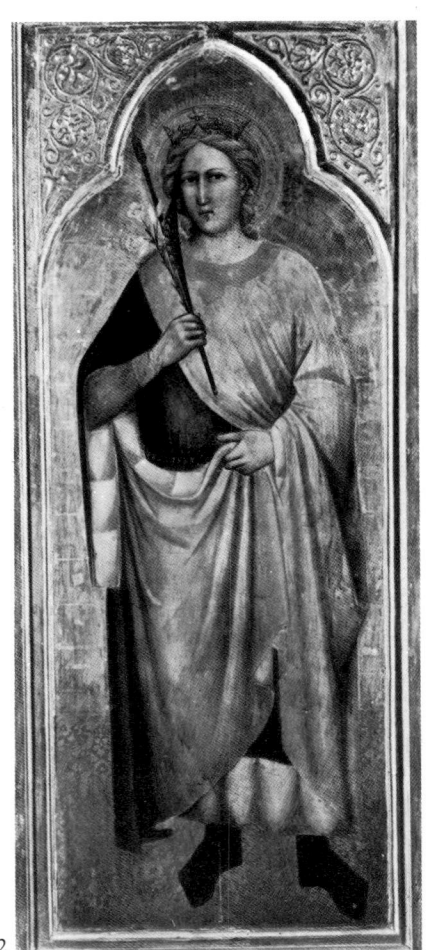
542

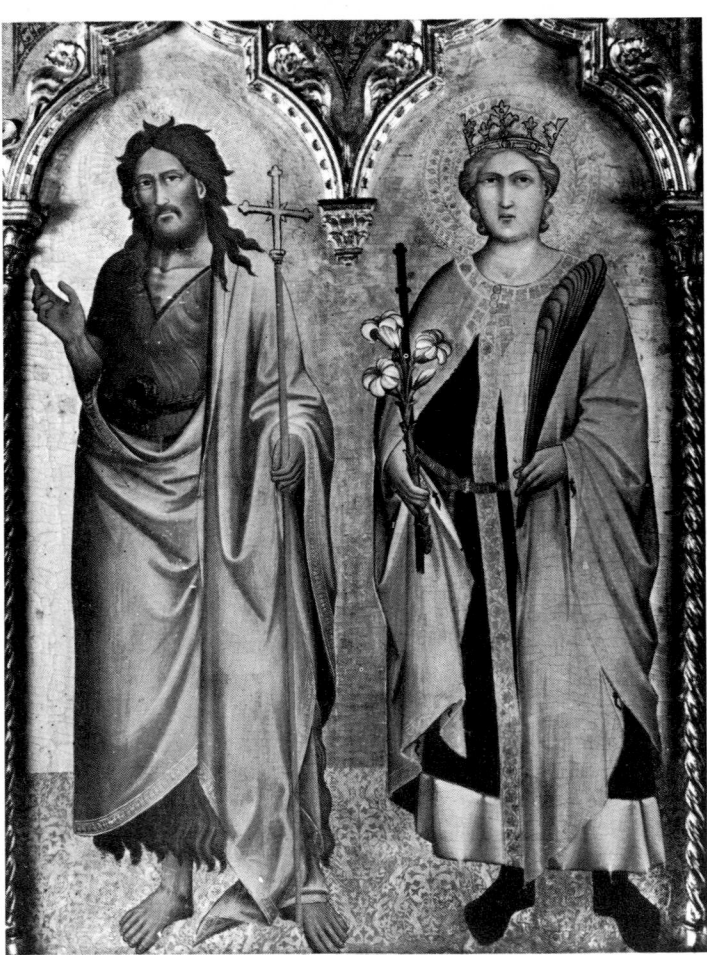
543

540. *Madonna and Child with Sts John the Baptist, Catherine, Anthony Abbot, Mary Magdalene. Above: two Angels. Panel. Fiesole, Museo Bandini. no. I,11. 83.7 × 54. SGF 21114.*

541. *Detail: Virgin Annunciate. Panel. Florence, S. Miniato al Monte, Cappella del Crocifisso. SGF 128807. 1396.*

542. *Detail: St Minias. Panel. Florence, S. Miniato al Monte, Cappella del Crocifisso. SGF 128810. 1396.*

543. *Sts John the Baptist and Minias: detail of fig. 539. Panel. Florence, Palazzo Pitti, Contini-Bonacossi Collection. Reali.*

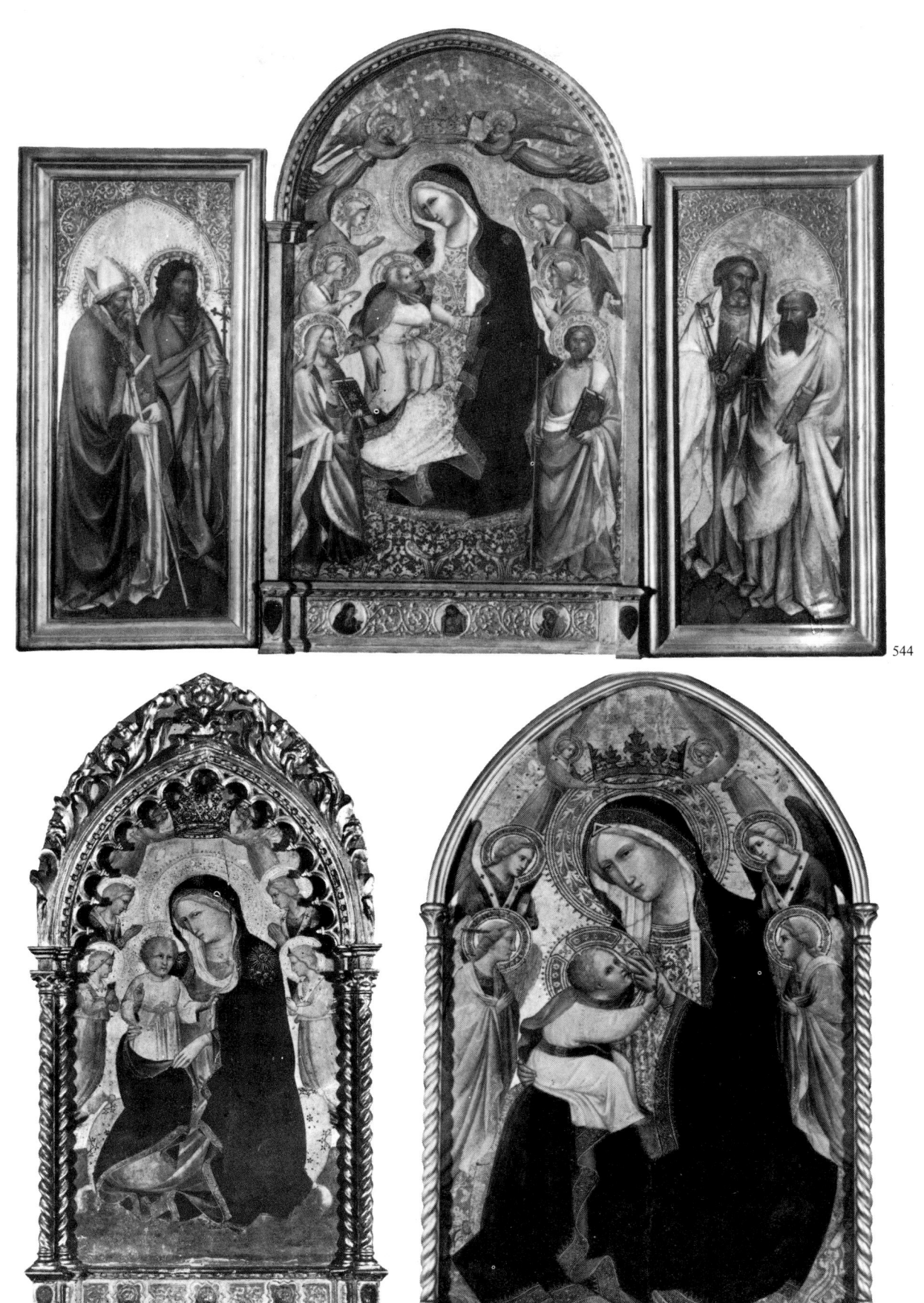

544. *Triptych: Madonna of Humility nursing the Child with Sts James, Andrew and six Angels. Panel. Perugia, Museo dell'Opera del Duomo. no. 16. cp: 120 × 70; lp: 97 × 46; rp: 97 × 45. Anderson 15704.*

545. *Madonna of Humility with six Angels. Panel. Florence, Accademia. no. 1890:461. 118 × 58. SGF 112688.*

546. *Madonna of Humility nursing the Child, with six Angels. Panel. London, Courtauld Institute of Art. no. Gambier-Parry 114. 69.5 × 43. Museum photo B66/1047.*

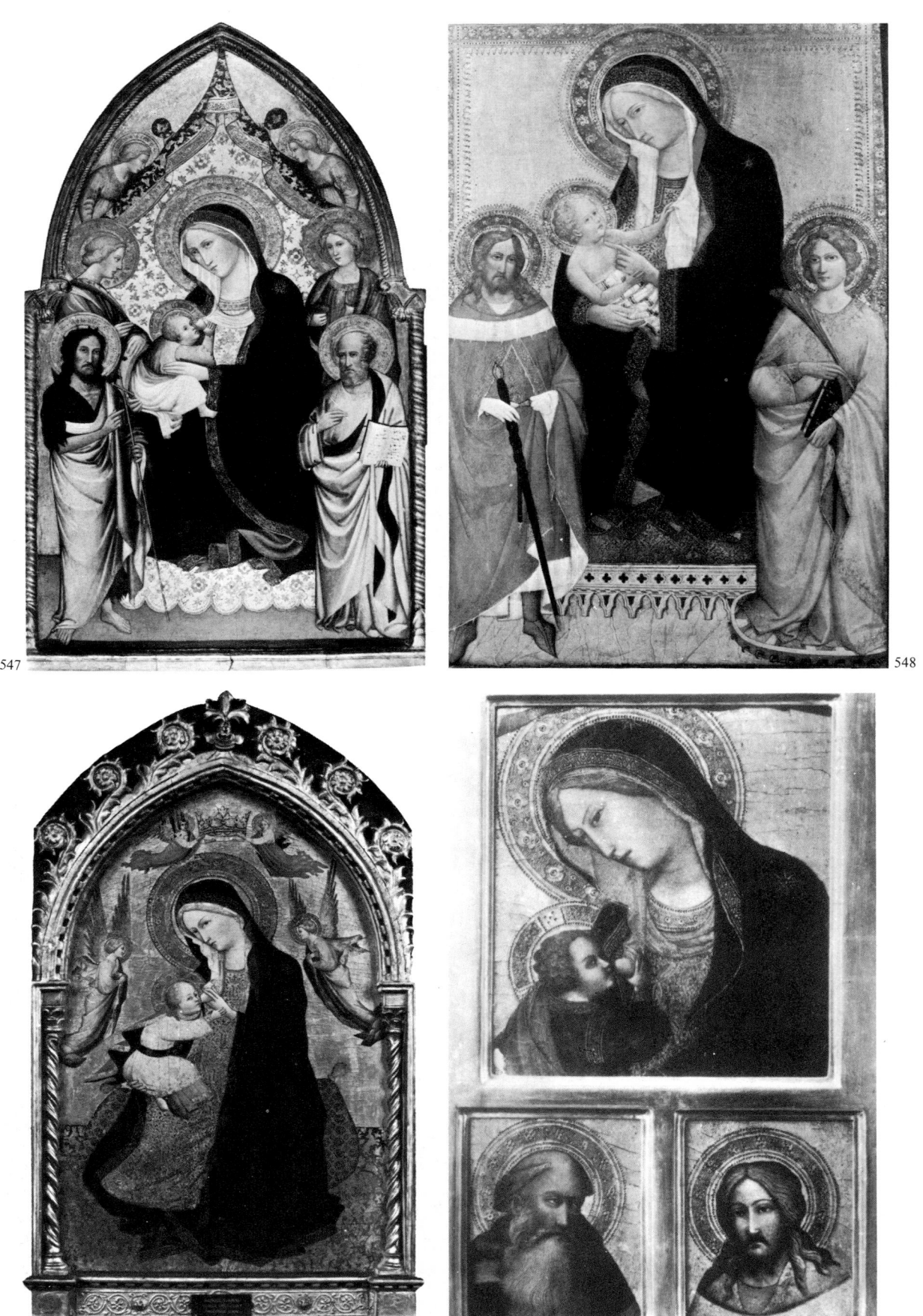

547. *Madonna of Humility nursing the Child with Sts Catherine, John the Baptist, Lucy, a male Saint and four Angels. Panel. Worcester (Mass.),*
Worcester Art Museum. no. 1959.103. 84.7 × 50.5. Museum photo.
548. *Madonna and Child with Sts Julian and Catherine. Panel. Private Collection. 76.2 × 49.8. A. C. Cooper 708442.*
549. *Madonna of Humility nursing the Child with four Angels. Panel. Amsterdam, Rijksmuseum. no. 2228-BI. 76.5 × 53.5. Museum photo 2256.*
550. *Three fragments: Madonna nursing the Child; two Saints. Panel. Florence, Museo Nazionale del Bargello, Carrand Collection. no. 2013-15. Madonna:*
20 × 24; Saints: 13 × 11. SGF 32963.

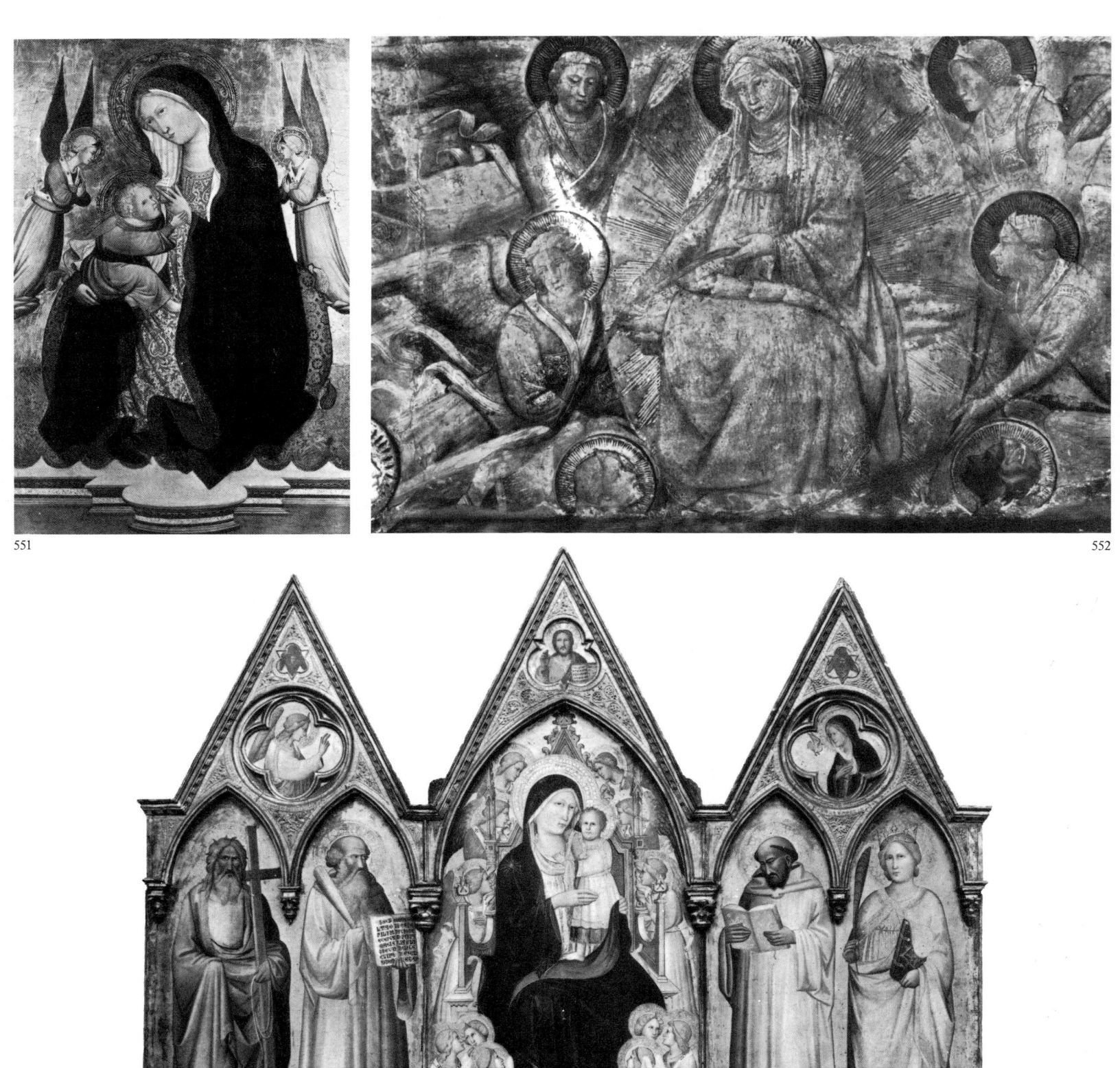

551. *Detail: Madonna of Humility nursing the Child, with two Angels. Panel. Tucson (Ariz.), University of Arizona Art Gallery, Samuel H. Kress Collection. K. 563. Whole panel: 70.8 × 47.6. Kress Foundation photo.*
552. *Assumption of the Virgin with six Angels. Fresco. Prato, Duomo, Cappella del Sacro Cingolo. Alinari 30750. 1394-96.*
553. *Triptych: Madonna and Child Enthroned with twelve Angels, and Sts Andrew, Benedict, Bernard and Catherine. Above: Annunciation and Christ blessing. Panel. Washington (D.C.), National Gallery of Art, Mellon Bequest. no. 4. 205 × 245. Museum photo.*

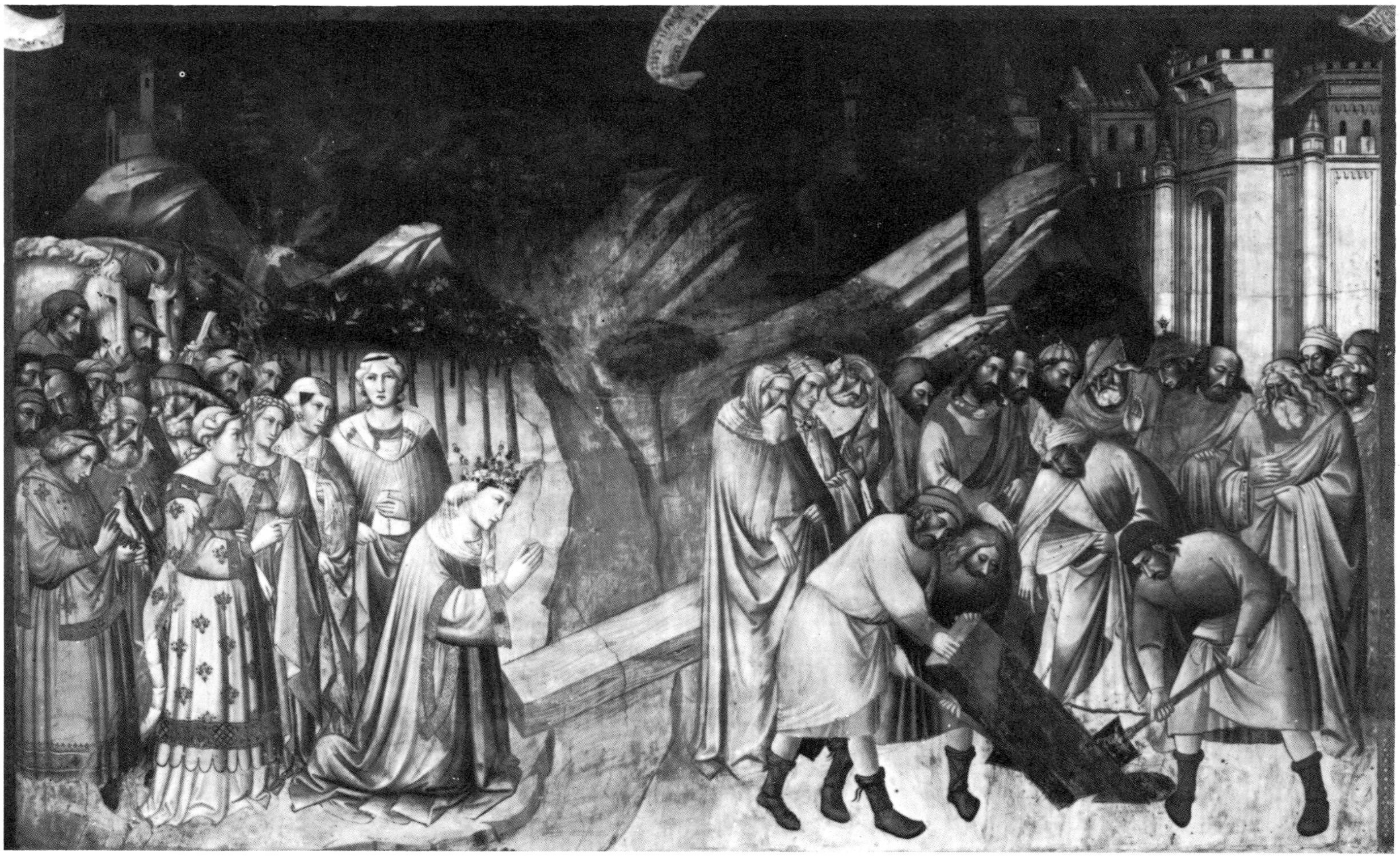

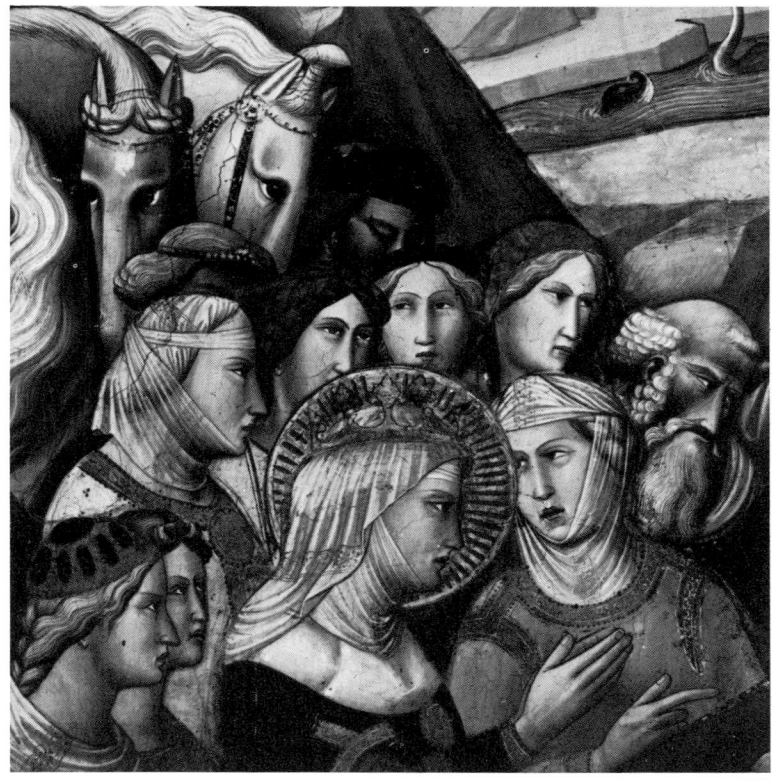

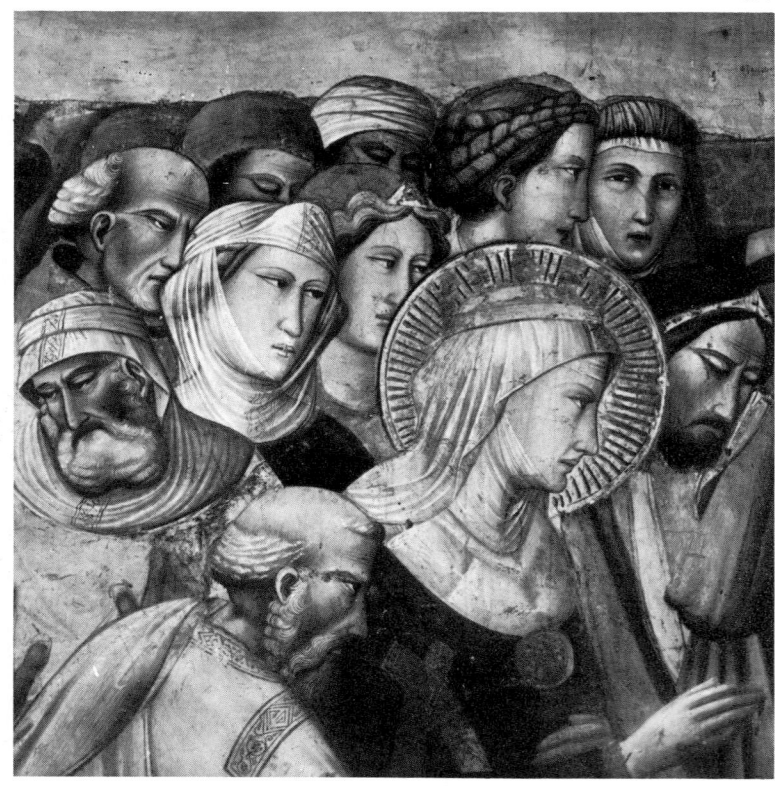

554. *Recognition and Burial of the Holy Wood. Fresco. Florence, S. Croce, Choir. Alinari 3886. 1385-95.*
555. *Detail: Invention of the True Cross. Fresco. Florence, S. Croce, Choir. Alinari 16095. 1385-95.*
556. *Detail: Invention of the True Cross. Fresco. Florence, S. Croce, Choir. Alinari 16094. 1385-95.*

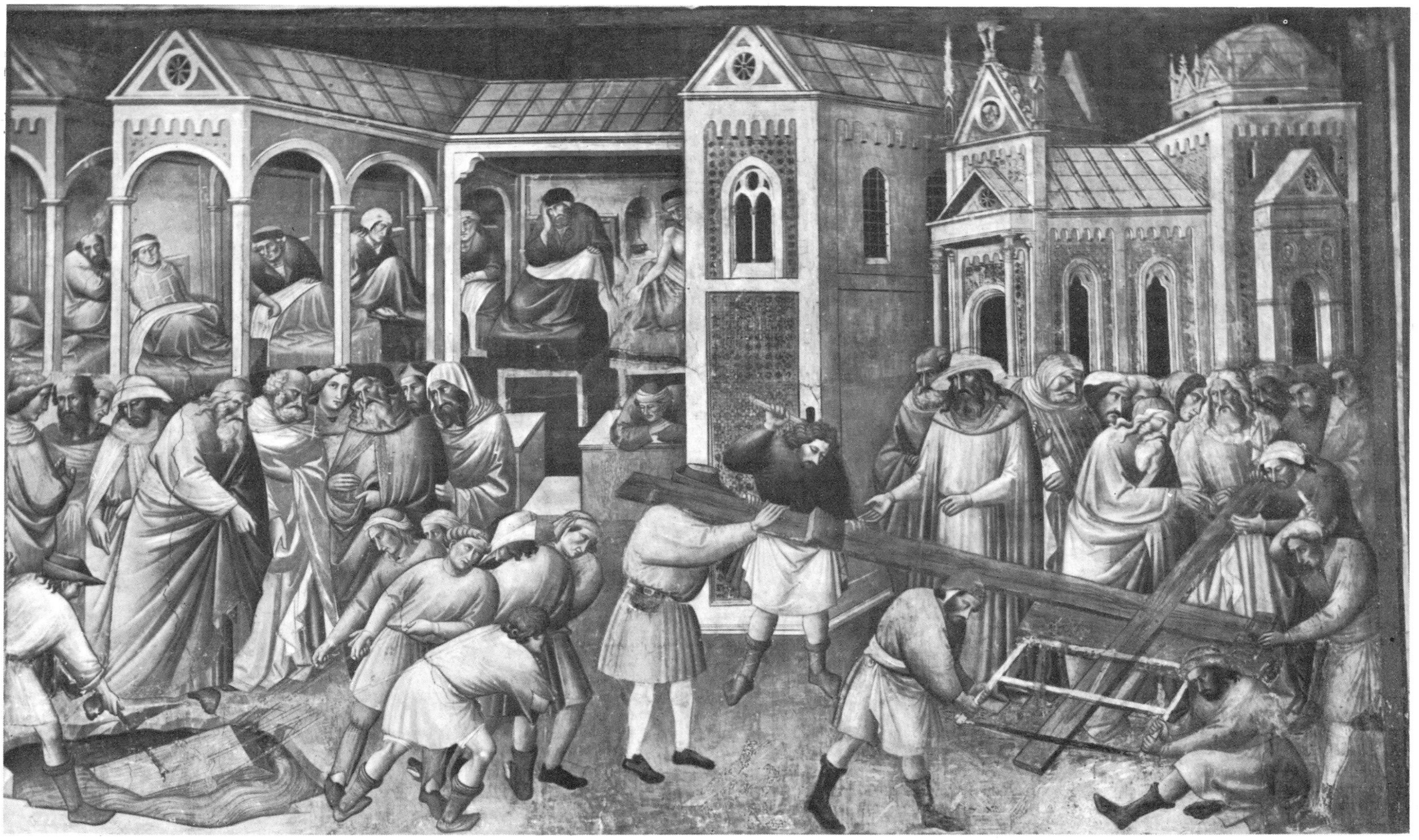

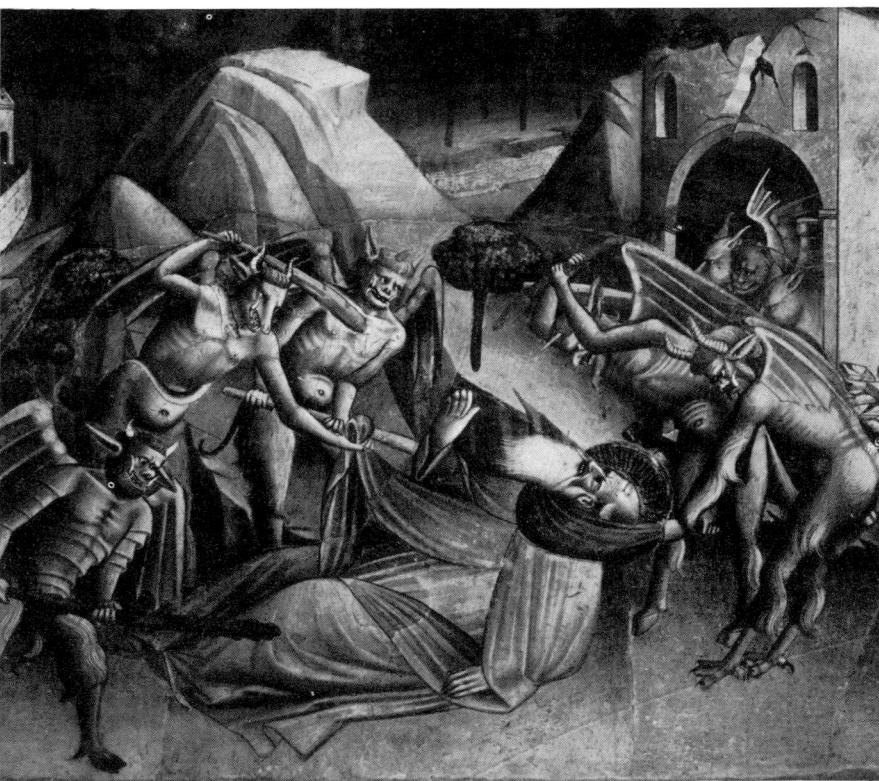

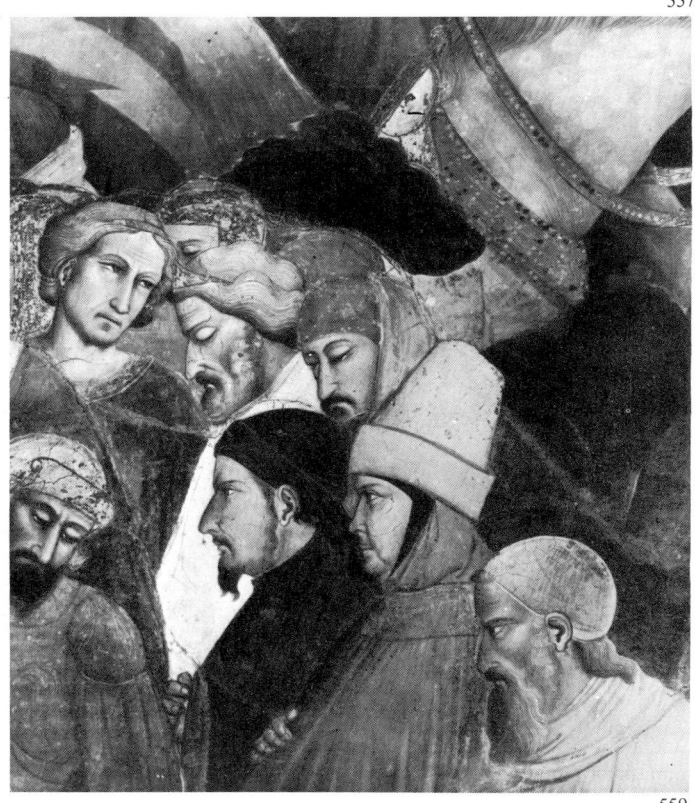

557. *Recovery of the Wood and Manufacture of the Cross. Fresco. Florence, S. Croce, Choir. Alinari 3887. 1385-95.*
558. *Temptation of St Anthony. Fresco. Florence, S. Croce, Castellani Chapel. Alinari 46092.*
559. *Male heads and half-figures, detail of the Beheading of King Cosroes, (the figure in a dark hat may be a self-portrait of the painter). Fresco. Florence, S. Croce, Choir. SGF 47478. 1385-95.*

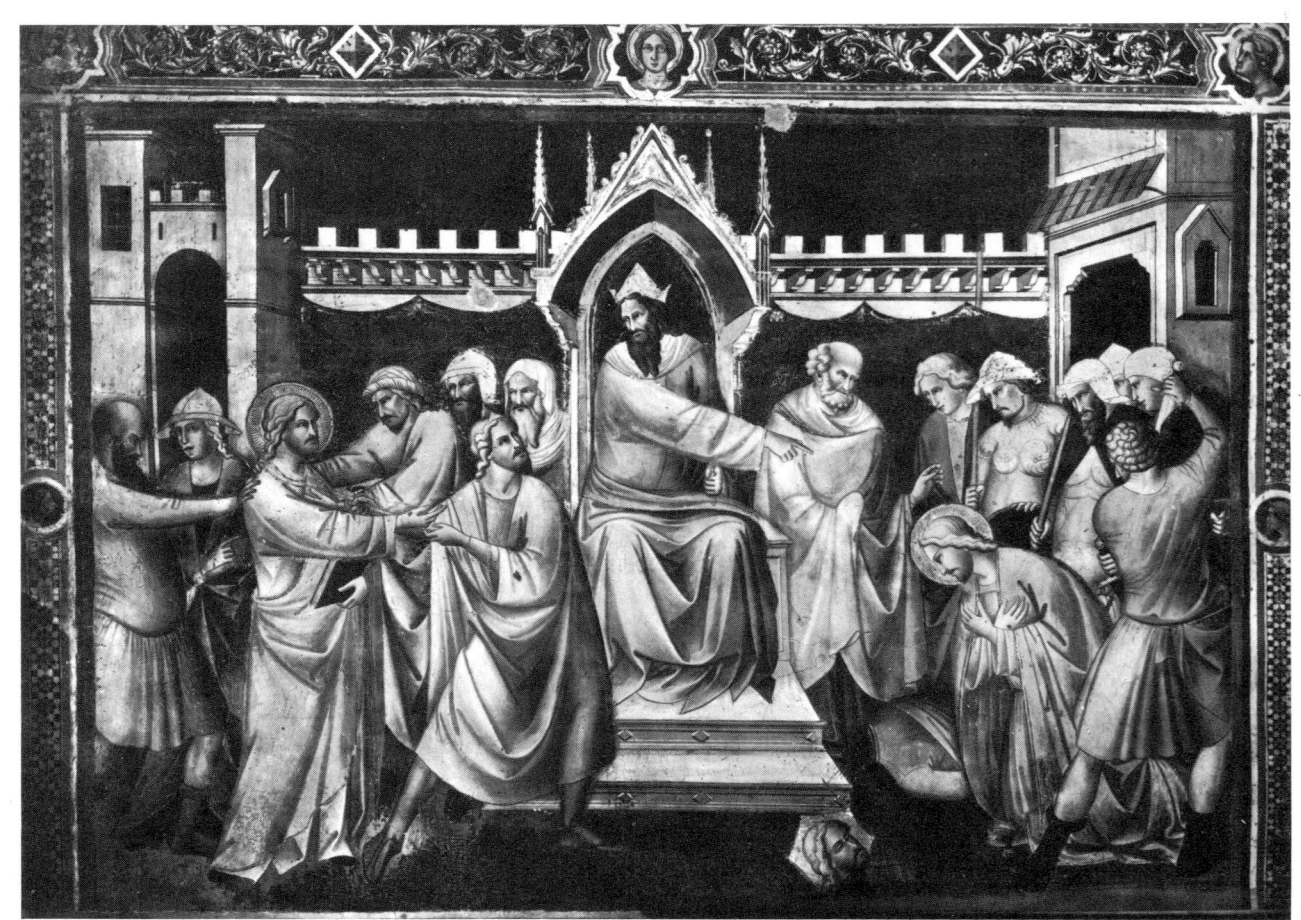

560

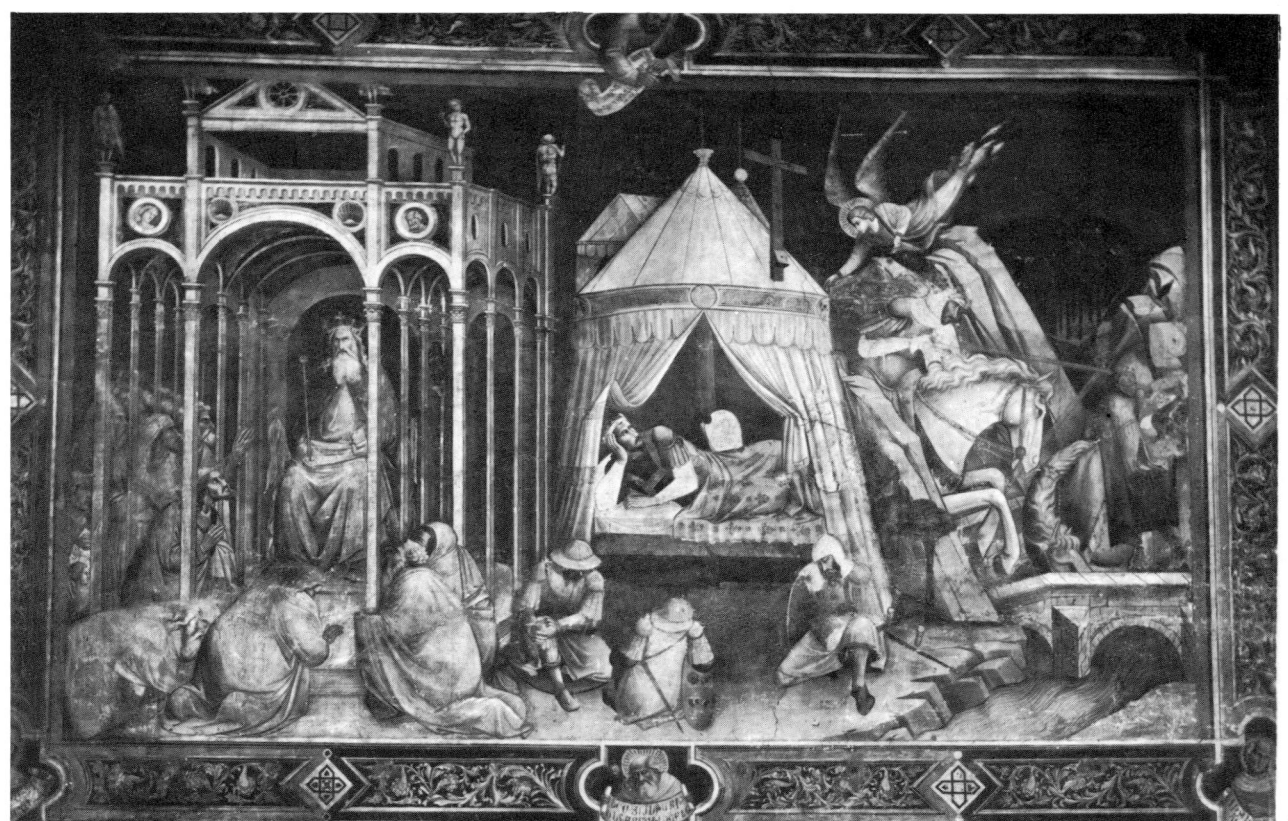

561

560. *Arrest and Beheading of St James. Fresco. Prato, Duomo, Cappella Manassei. Alinari 10408.*
561. *Throne of Cosroes, Dream of Heraclius and Defeat of Cosroes. Fresco. Florence, S. Croce, Choir. Alinari 3892. 1385-95.*

MASTER OF S. MARTINO A MENSOLA

Another important Florentine painter of the early fifteenth century, who unites fourteenth century elements from Gaddi with the late Gothic, is the master who painted the *Madonna and Child Enthroned* from the Villa Arcivescovile at Scandicci.
He makes the Infant strong and herculean, with curly hair and a round puffy face, and a roundish protruding chin and very curved eyebrows.....

> from U. Procacci, p. 240, *Rivista d'Arte*, XV, 1933.

In the shadow of the paintings of such artists as Agnolo Gaddi, Gherardo Starnina, Spinello Aretino and Niccolò di Pietro Gerini work many unknown masters, who are more or less dependent upon these unknown painters for example. But one of these anonymous figures holds himself aloof from these influences. He gives his pictures an individual appearance by looking back farther, to earlier works and uses his own talents to create personal forms which stand apart from those of his contemporaries: this unusual painter is the Master of the high-altarpiece at San Martino a Mensola.....

> from B. Klesse, p. 247, *Mitteilungen der Kunsthistorischen Institutes in Florenz*, VIII, IV, 1959.

Of the many fine works of the late Trecento, in part by unknown masters, let us take as an example the half-length *Madonna and Child* in Warsaw. It strikes us not only because the Infant Christ is completely naked (it is one of the earliest examples of this) but also for its strong characteristic style, from which we recognize without difficulty the hand of the Master of San Martino a Mensola.....

> from B. Klesse, p. 276, *Zeitschrift für Kunstgeschichte*, XXV, 1962.

Also dating from 1372 is the Vatican triptych of Giovanni Bonsi, still caught up in a dry Orcagnasque style — although a few lively passages permit one to see an opening towards the later characteristics of the Master of San Martino a Mensola (this last painter's works include a fresco fragment in the Museum of Santa Croce, dated 1387, Madonna and Child with Angels in the Acton Collection (both in Florence) and the triptych at San Martino a Mensola, dated 1395, near Florence).....

> from L. Bellosi, p. 19, *Paragone*, XVI, 187/7, 1965.

In his altarpiece dated 1391 at S. Martino a Mensola — a polyptych representing the Madonna standing with saints and donors — he gives us his most colourful and fantastic version of cloth design, upon which birds are represented with their wings spread, upon a background of waving oriental squiggles. The present writer has already attempted to put together the known works of this master, basing the study upon this sort of stencil that he uses. The master did not however use it in all his works: it can be found in a panel of the *Madonna and Child with Donors*, in the Bellini Gallery in Florence, as well as in another panel again of the *Madonna and Child with Sts George and Lawrence*, in the Pardo Gallery, in Paris.....

> from B. Klesse, pp. 146-48, *Seidenstoffe in der Italienischen Malerei des 14. Jahrhunderts*, Bern, 1967.

The Master of S. Martino a Mensola is named for the high altar-piece in the small church of S. Martino, just above Ponte a Mensola, near Settignano. The painting is clearly dated 1391, and is by a painter who seems to have been influenced by foreign forms, probably Spanish.

As noted before, the Master of S. Martino a Mensola seems to have been an almost exact contemporary of Starnina, and to have had a similar training and similar activity. The difficulties in comparing their work come from the fact that although we know quite a lot about the Mensola Master, we still know almost nothing about Starnina.

Although the idea that the Mensola Master and Starnina are the same person is tempting indeed and although the evidence of their similar dates and activity is interesting, we cannot certainly identify them as a single painter at the moment.....

from R. Fremantle, pp. 3-13, *Antichità Viva*, XII, 1, 1973.

BIBLIOGRAPHY
BOOKS

An asterisk indicates a work listed in the General Bibliography

Puccinelli, P., *Vita ed atti del B. Andrea di Scotia*, Milano, 1645; Carocci, G., *I Dintorni di Firenze*, Vol. I, Florence, 1906, p. 55; *v. Marle, 1924**, figs 276, 277, 295; *Offner, Studies**, 1927, p. 90; Steinweg, K., *Andrea Orcagna*, Strasburg, 1929, pp. 63-5; *Firenze, 1933**, p. 6; Hönigmann, S., *Die Umgebrung von Florenz*, Florence, 1938, p. 223; *Kaftal, 1952**, p. 50; *Shorr**, 1954, p. 37; *Cracow**, 1961, p. 52, pl. 31; *Marcucci**, 1965, p. 144, no. 103; *Klesse**, 1967, pp. 363-4.

JOURNALS

Gregori, M., *RA*, 1933, p. 240; Rusconi, A. J., *E*, XLVIII, I, 1942, p. 74; Klesse, B., *MKIF*, VIII, 4, 1959, pp. 247-252; Klesse, B., *ZKG*, 1962, pp. 275-6; Bellosi, L., *PA*, XVI, 187/7, 1965, p. 19; Conti, A., *PA*, XIX, 225/45, 1968, pp. 11, 16; Wilckens, L., *ZKG*, XXXI, 2, 1968, p. 168; Zeri, F., *GBA*, LXXI, 110, Janvier, 1968, pp. 71-73, 76, no. 103; van Os, H. W., *Sim*, 4, 1970, 1, p. 11; Boskovits, M., *MKIF*, XVII, 2-3, 1973, pp. 204, note 9, 219; Fremantle, R., *AV*, XII, 1, 1973, pp. 3-13.

DATED WORKS

1385 Florence, Acton Collection. Panel: Madonna & Child Enthroned with Angels. d. (fig. 581).
1387 Florence, S. Croce, second altar, right of nave. Fresco: Madonna & Child Enthroned with Saints. d. (fig. 568).
1391 Florence, S. Martino a Mensola. Triptych: Madonna & Child with Saints. d. (fig. 565).
1395 Whereabouts unknown. Panel: Madonna & Child with 2 Donors. d. (fig. 579).

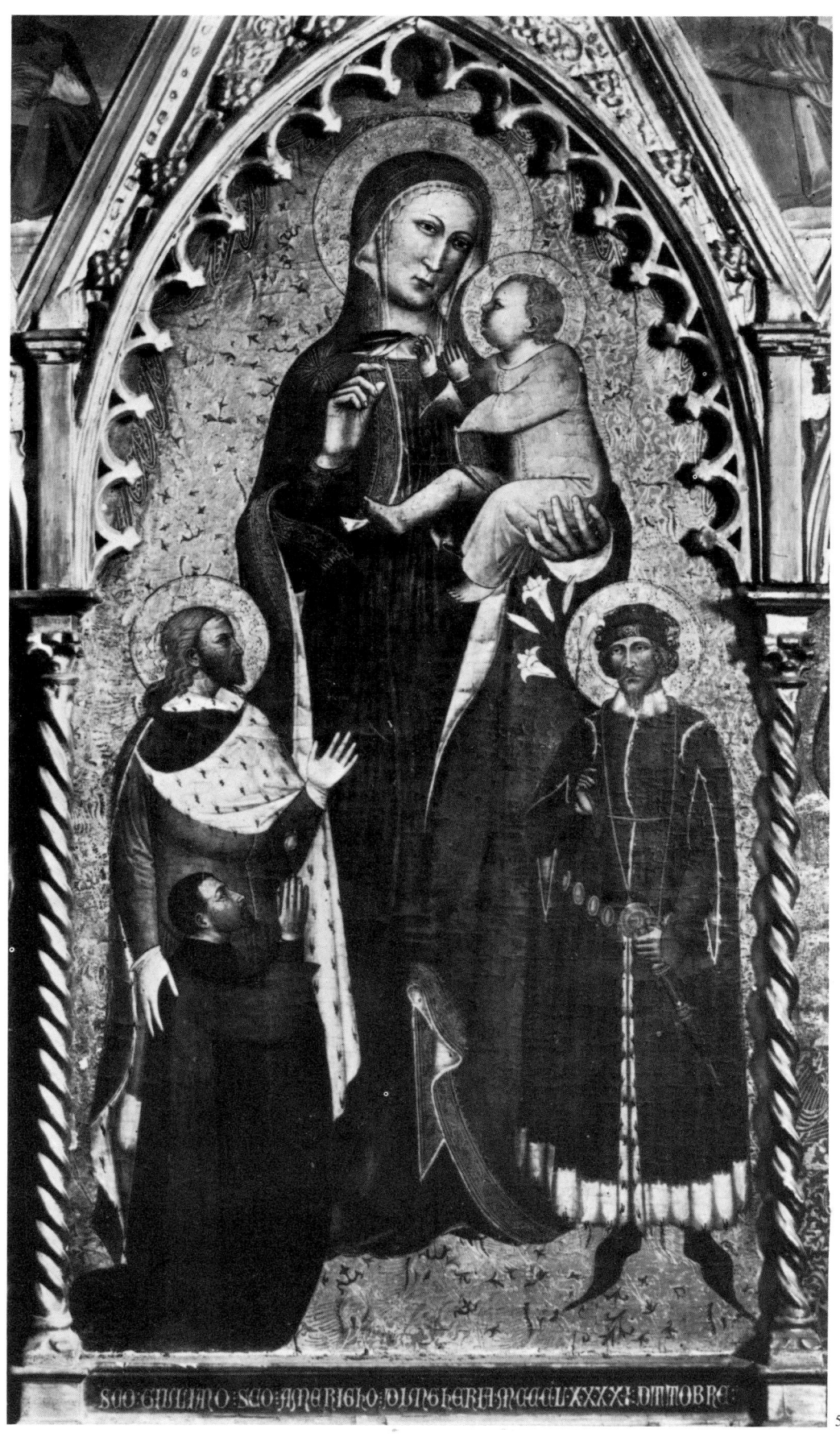

562

562. *Madonna and Child with Sts Julian, Henry of Hungary and a Donor, detail of fig. 565. Panel. Florence, S. Martino a Mensola. Brogi 23458. d. 1391.*

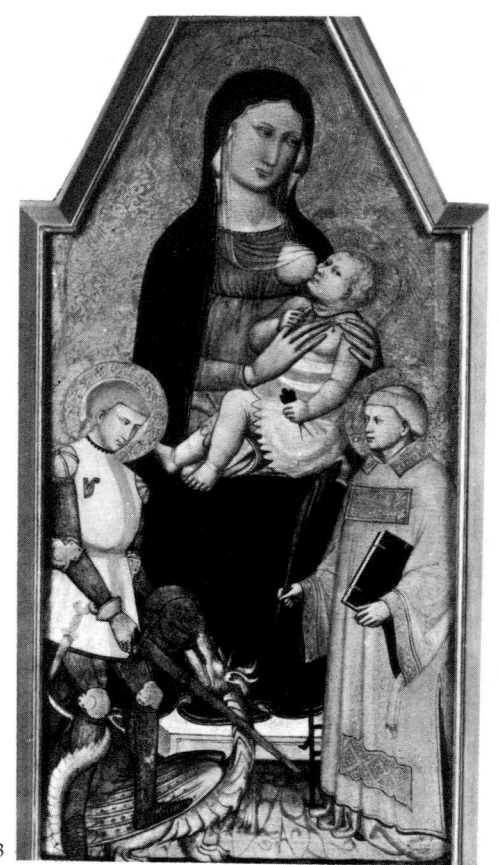

563

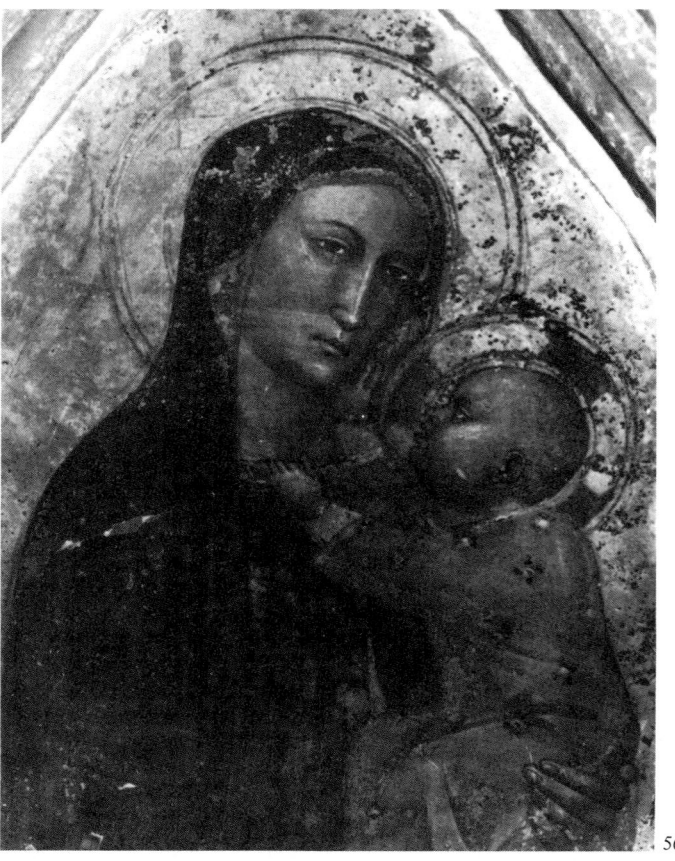

564

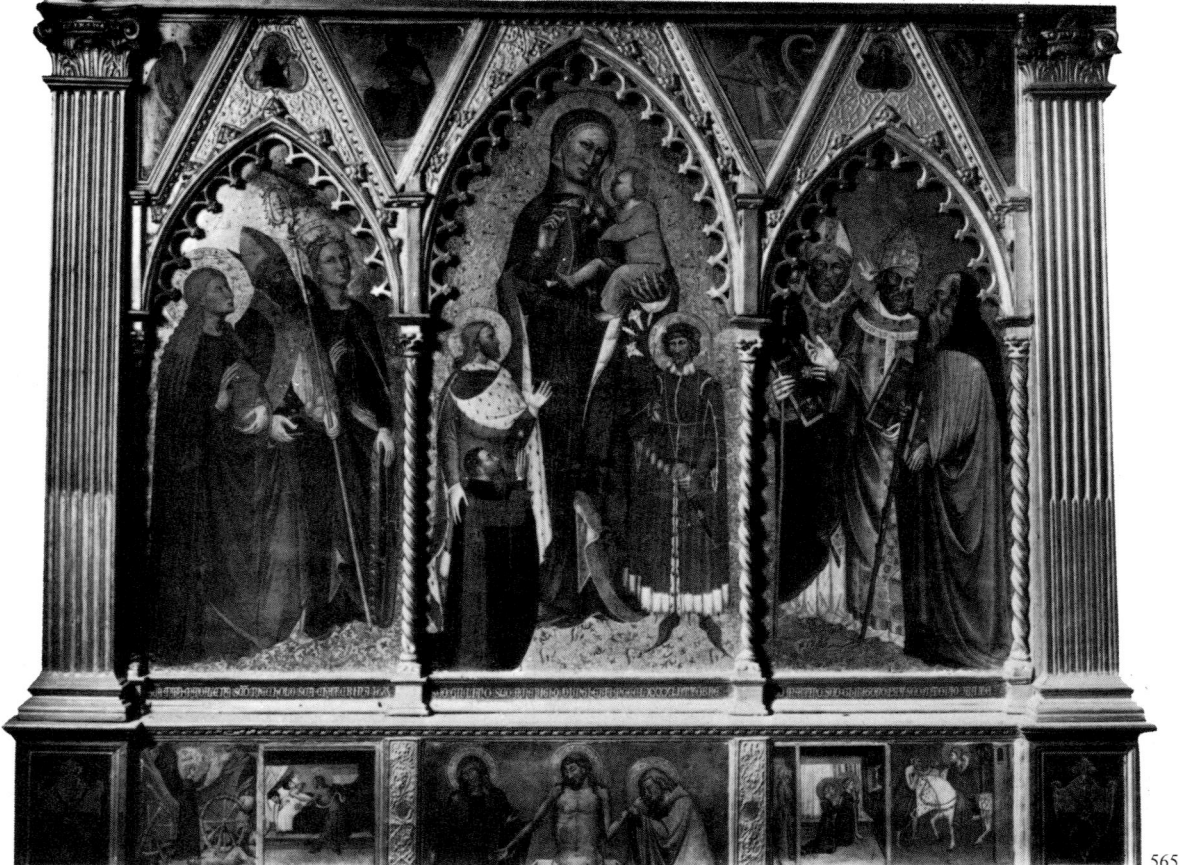

565

563. *Madonna nursing the Child with Sts George and Lawrence. Panel. Private Collection. 115 × 56. Reali.*
564. *Madonna and Child, detail of fig. 569. Fresco. Terenzano (1.5 km. from Settignano, near Florence), S. Martino. Author's photo.*
565. *Triptych: Madonna and Child, Sts Julian, Henry of Hungary and a Donor, with Sts Mary Magdalene, Nicholas, Catherine, Martin, Gregory and Anthony Abbot. Above: Annunciation. Predella: Martyrdom of St Catherine; St Julian murdering his Parents; Man of Sorrows with the Virgin and St John the Evangelist; St Henry taking the vow of Continence with his Wife; St Martin dividing his Cloak with a Beggar. Panel. Florence, S. Martino a Mensola. 104.5 × 146. SGF 2294. d. 1391.*

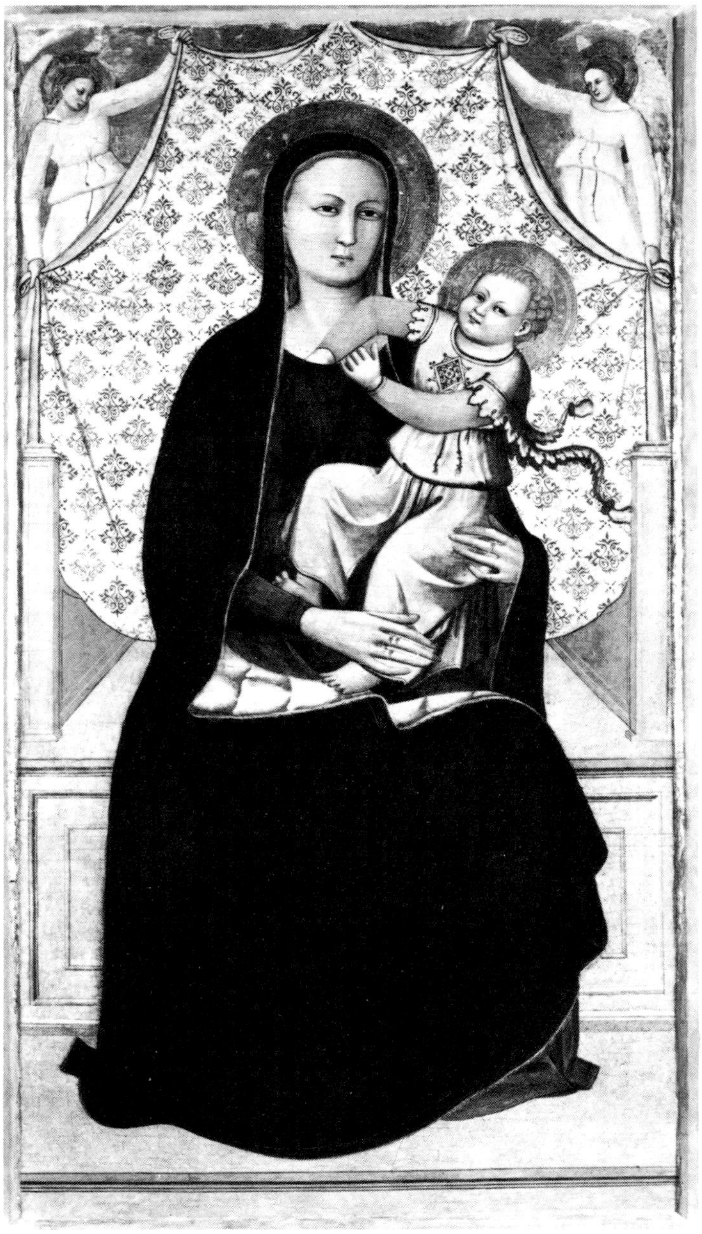

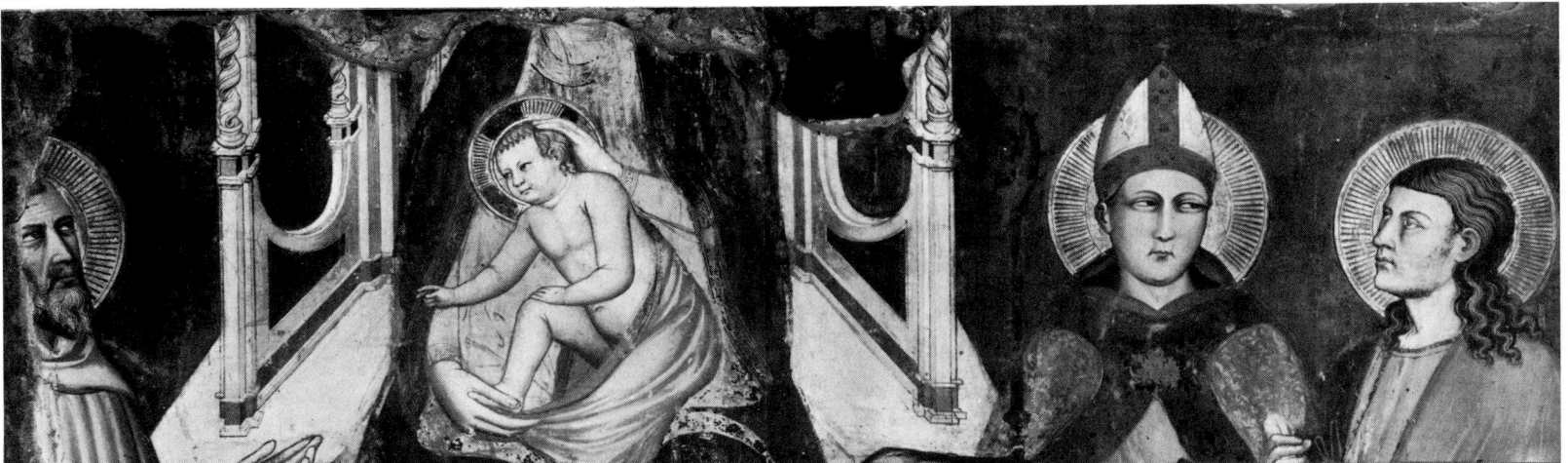

566

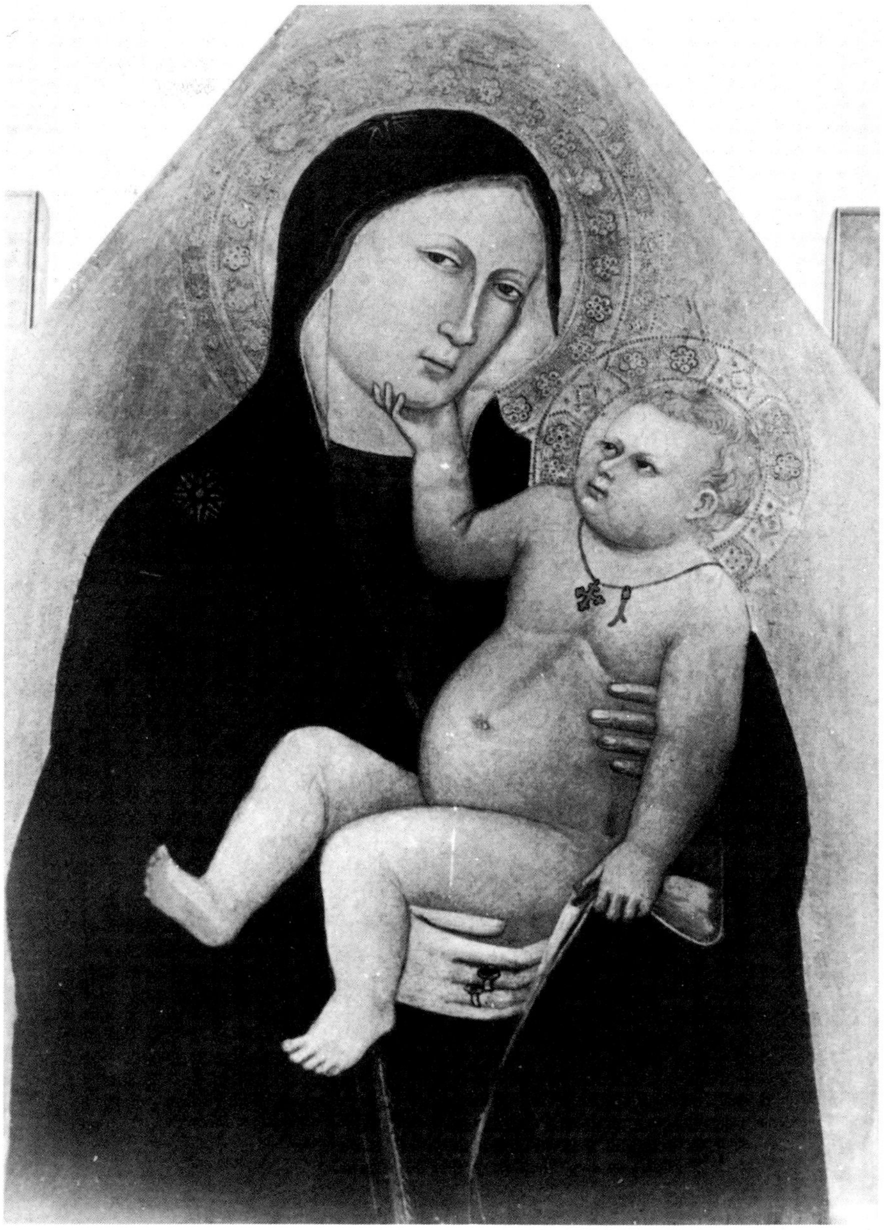

567

568

566.   *Madonna and Child Enthroned with two Angels. Panel. Florence, Sacro Cuore (via Capo di Mondo). 156 × 98. SGF 96806.*
567.   *Madonna and Child. Panel. Warsaw, Muzeum Narodowe. no. 1969/70 1618. 110 × 76. Museum photo.*
568.   *Infant Christ with three male Saints. Florence, S. Croce, second altar, right hand wall of nave. Fresco. SGF 66207. d. 1387.*

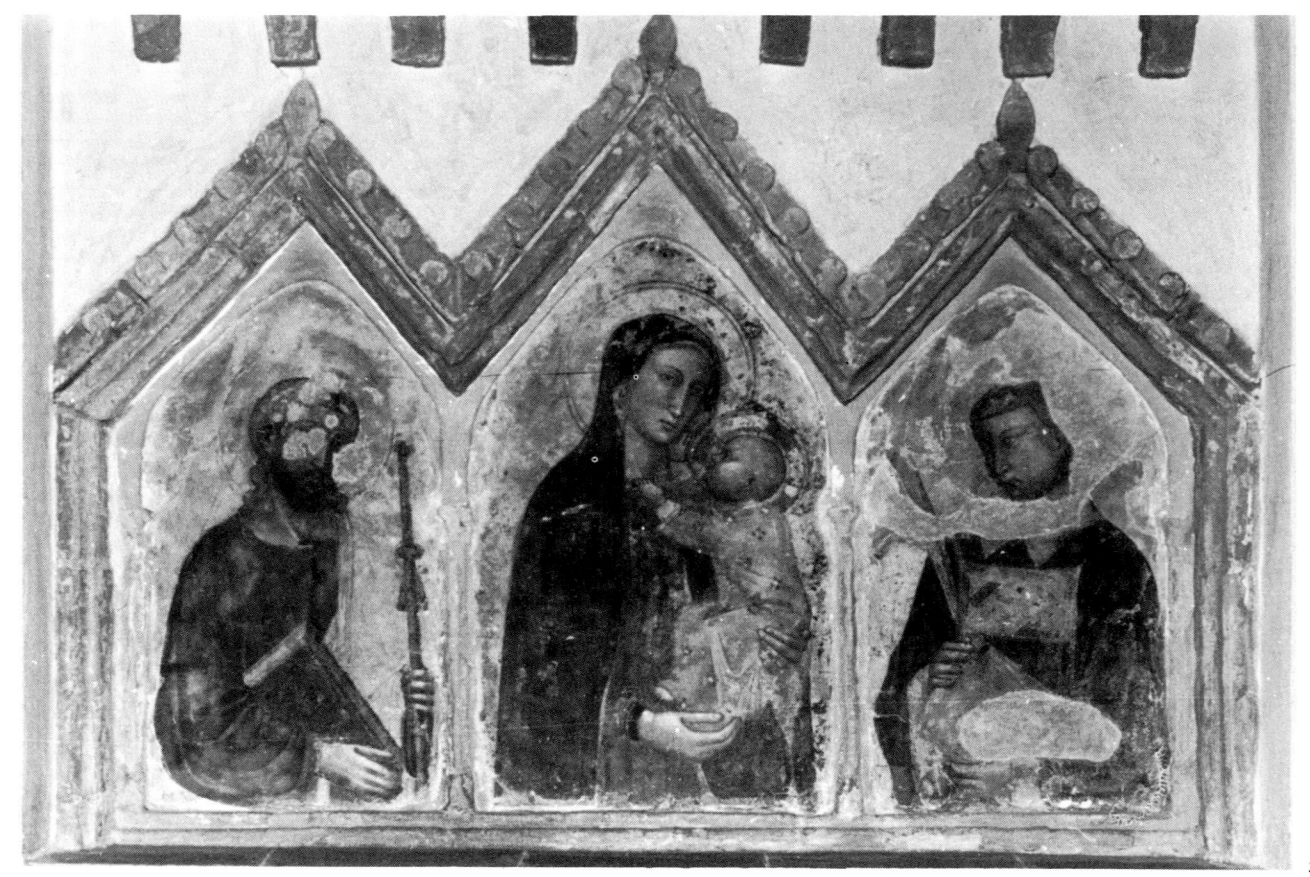

569

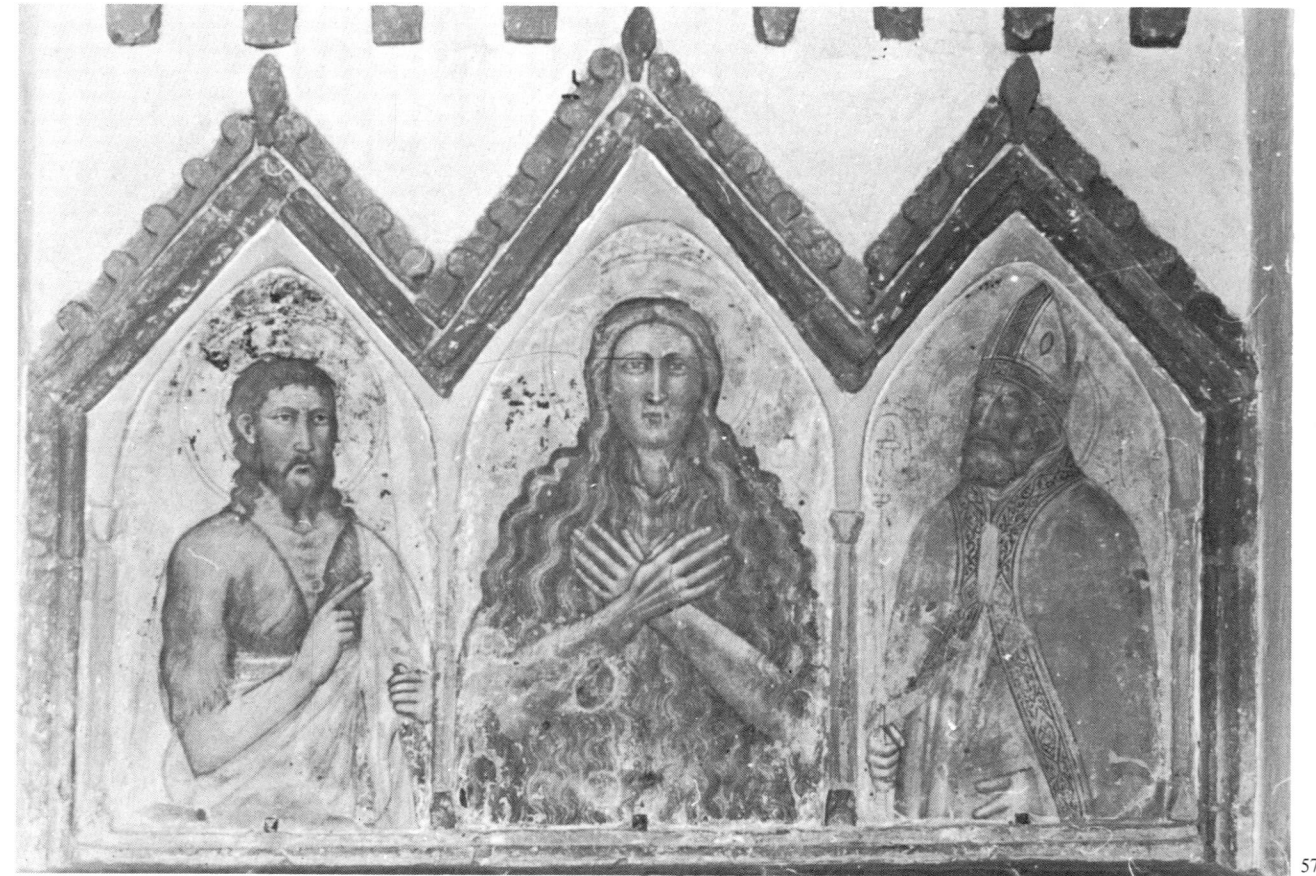

570

569. *Madonna and Child with Sts James and Lawrence. Fresco. Terenzano, S. Martino. Author's photo.*
570. *St Mary Magdalene with Sts John the Baptist and Martin. Fresco. Terenzano, S. Martino. Author's photo.*

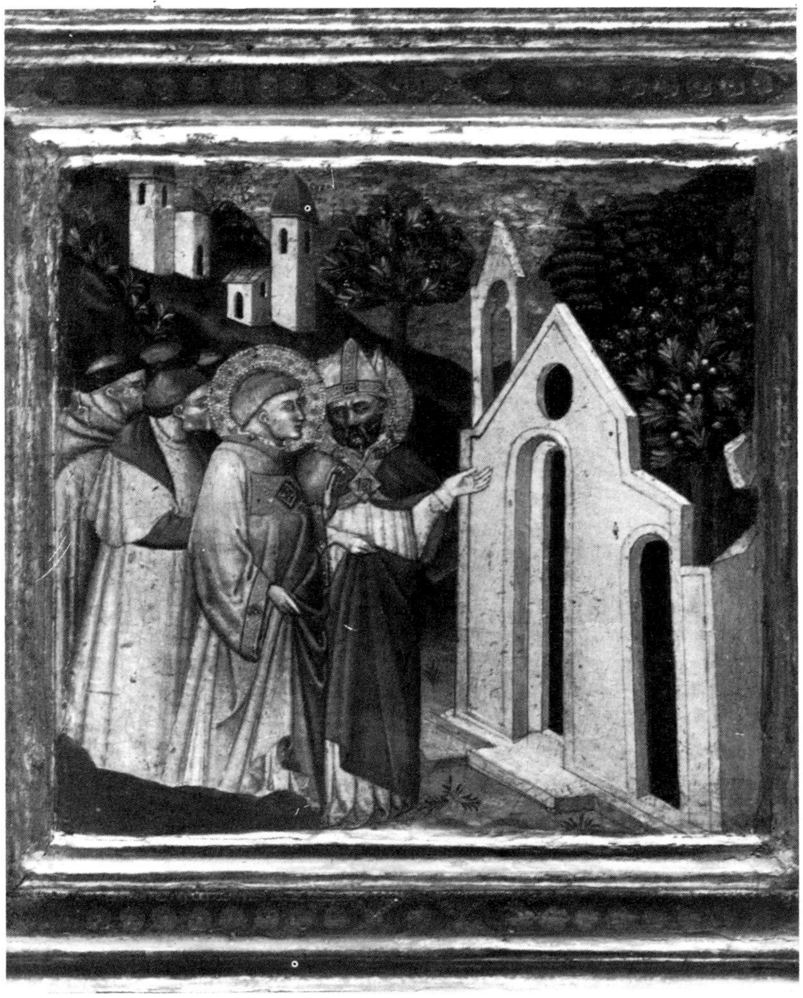

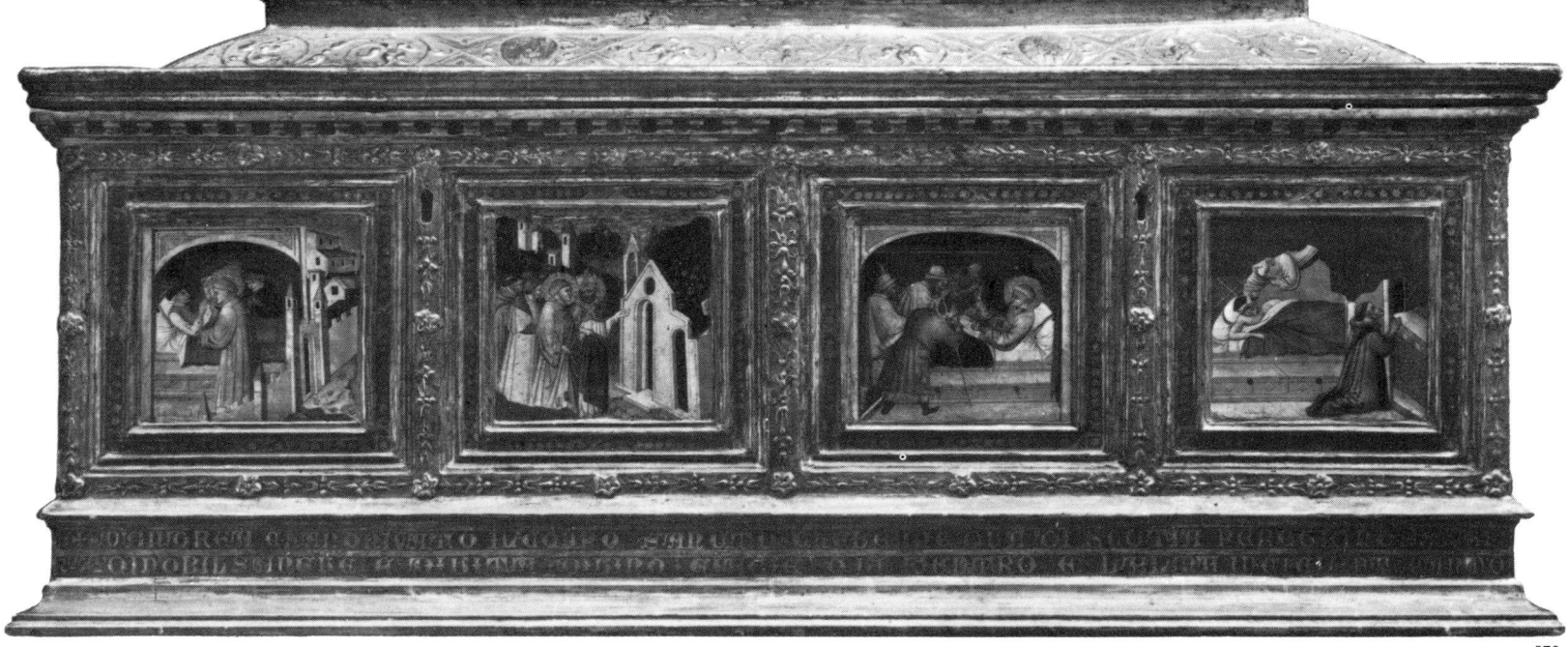

571

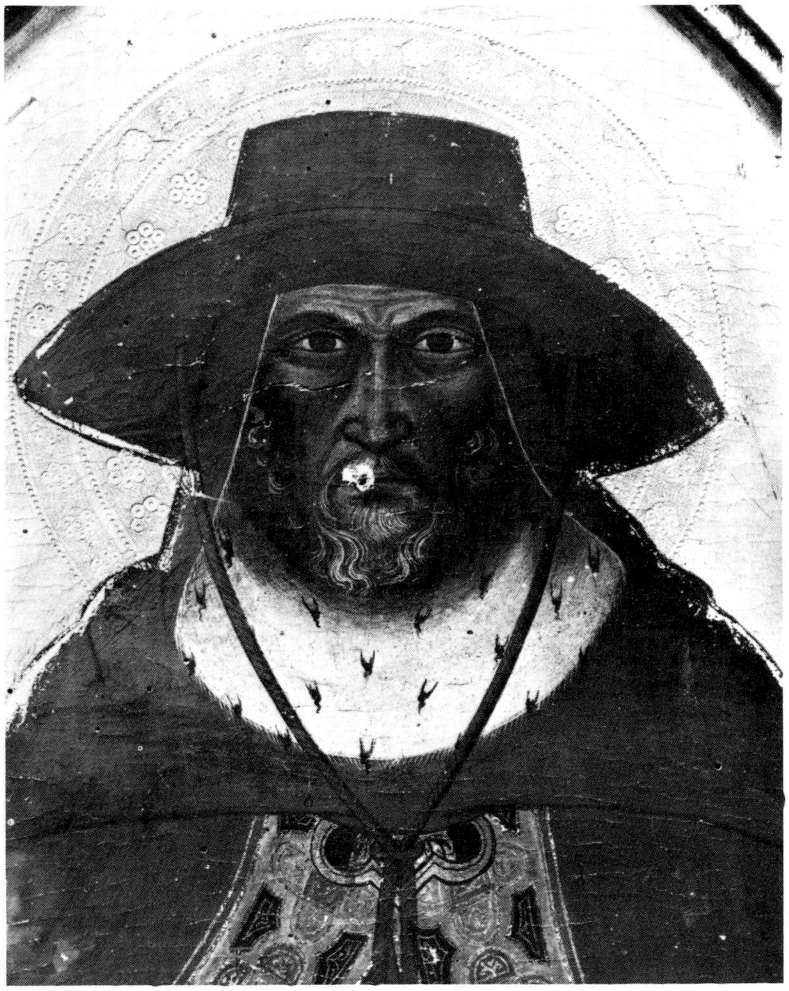

572

573

571.   *Cassone: St Donatus gives Andrew permission to restore the church of St Martino a Mensola, detail of fig. 573.   Panel.   Florence, S. Martino a Mensola.*
   SGF 28037.
572.   *Head of St Jerome, detail of fig. 582.   Panel.   Carrara, Accademia.   SGF 76493.*
573.   *Cassone: Four scenes from the life of St Andrew.   Panel.   Florence, S. Martino a Mensola.   59 × 127.   SGF 28035.*

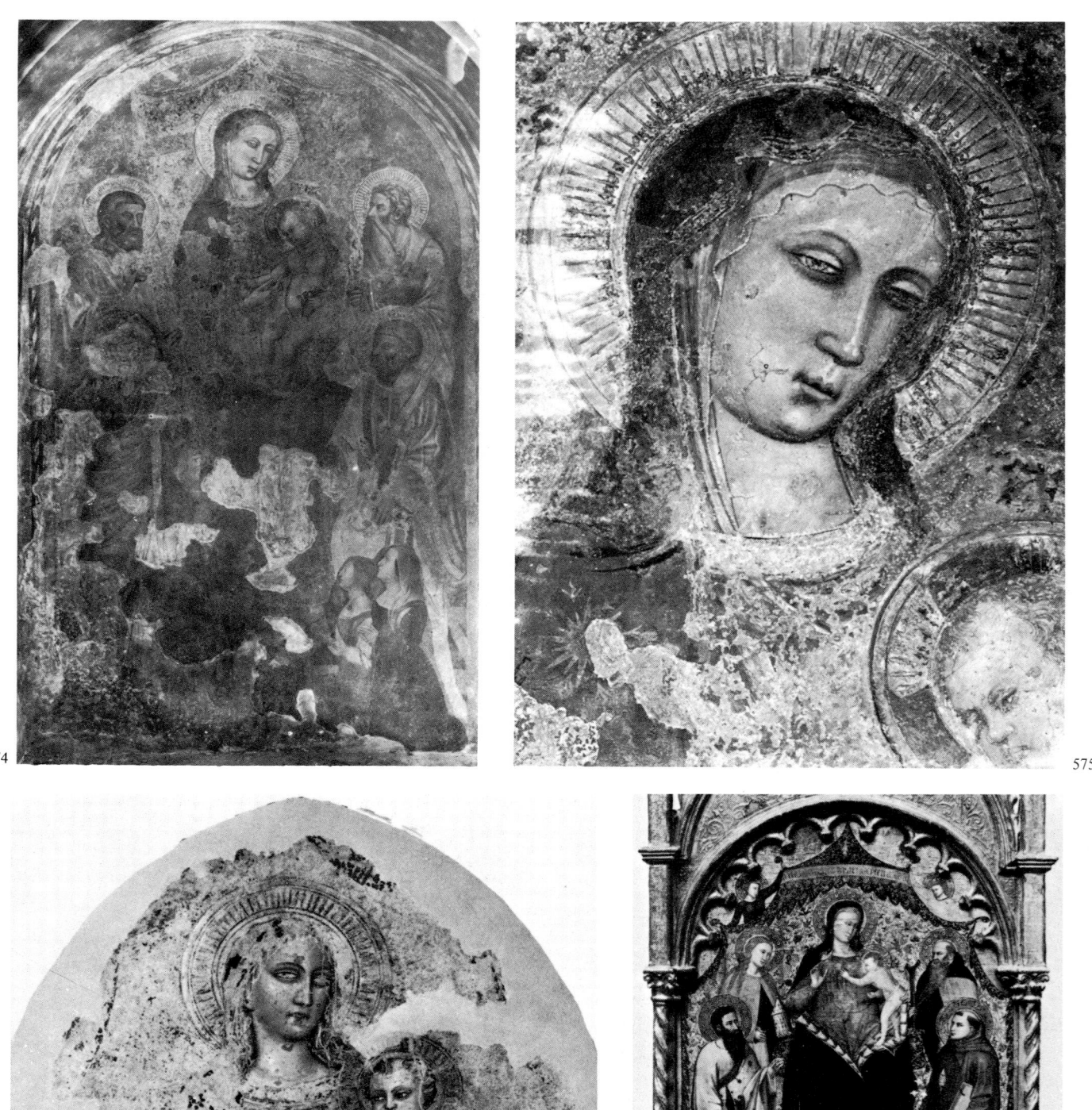

574. *Tabernacle: Madonna and Child with six Saints and Donors. Fresco. Florence, Piazza del Carmine. SGF 31273.*
575. *Head of Madonna, detail of fig. 574. Fresco. Florence, Piazza del Carmine. SGF 31275.*
576. *Madonna and Child. Fresco. Fucecchio, Museo. 118 × 88. SGF 151867.*
577. *Madonna and Child with four Saints, Angels and a Donor. Two predella scenes: Adoration of the Magi and Flight into Egypt. Panel. Main panel:*
130 × 89; predellas 45 × 95. Photo Galleria Bellini.

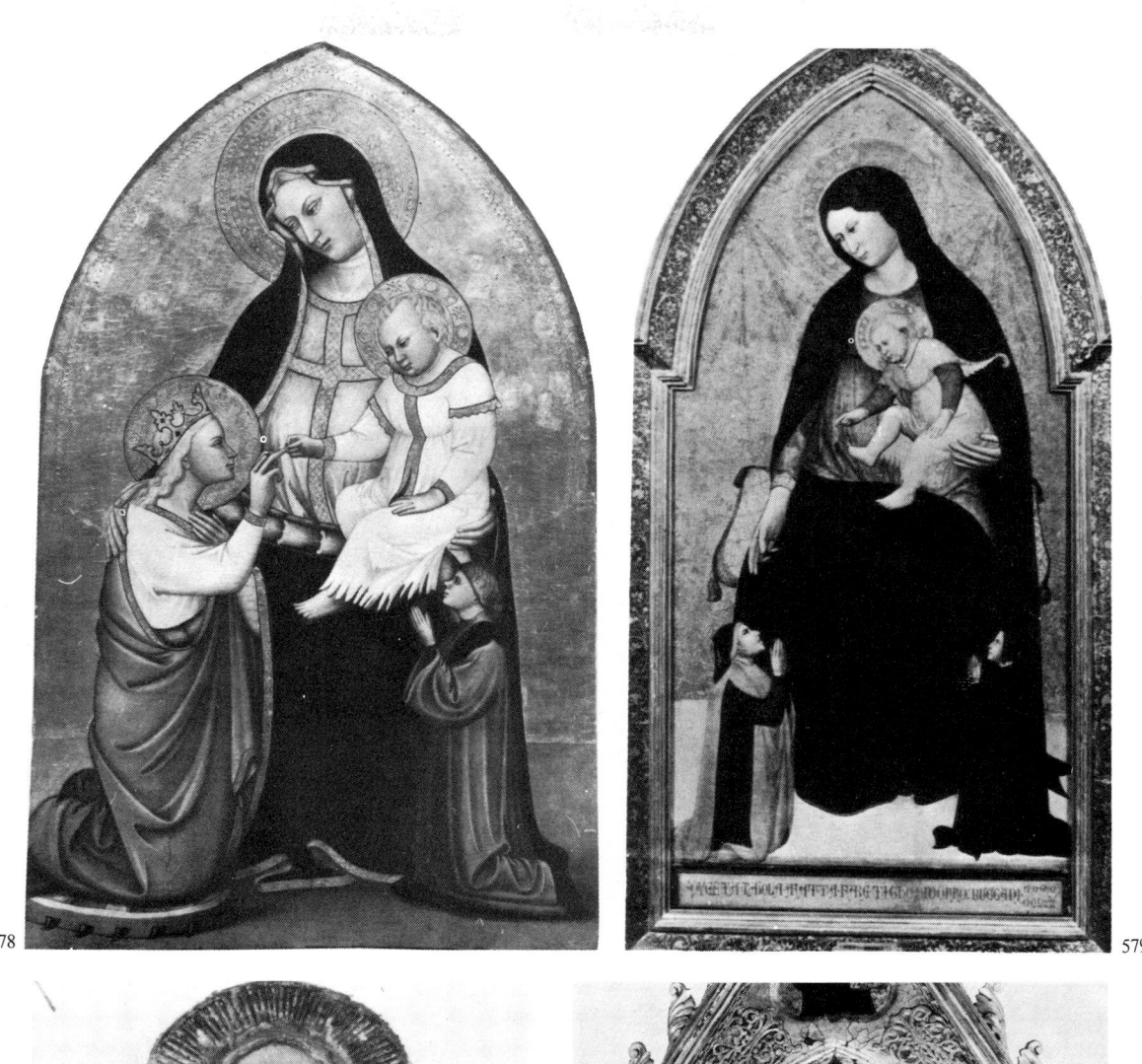

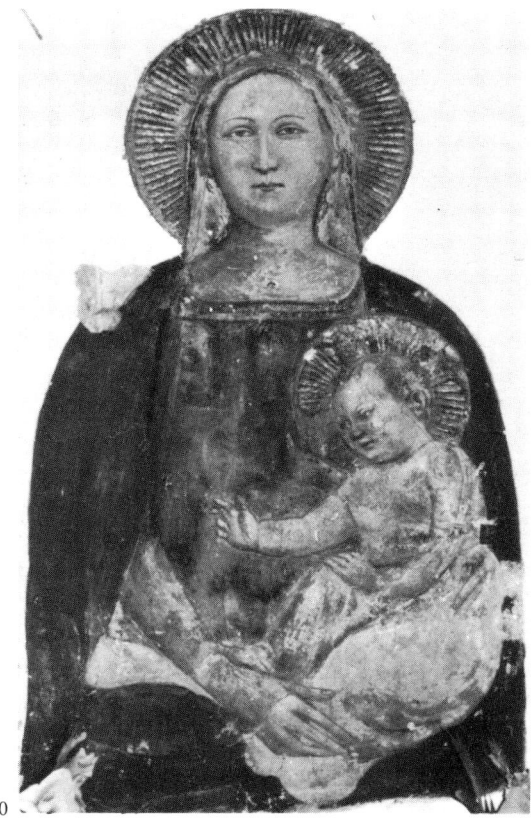

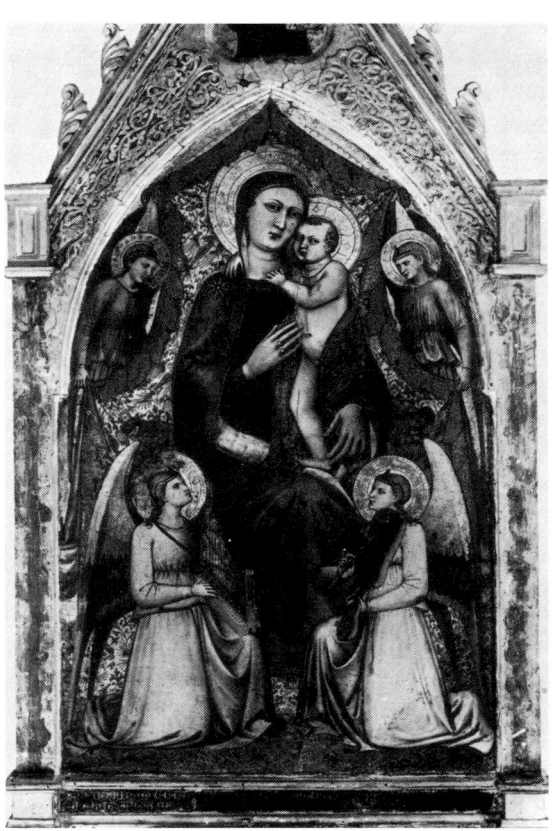

578. *Mystical Marriage of St Catherine. Panel. Whereabouts unknown. 116 × 65. Courtauld photo.*
579. *Madonna and Child with Donors. Panel. Whereabouts unknown. 116 × 64. Photo Kunsthistorisches Institut in Florenz. d. 1395.*
580. *Madonna and Child. Fresco. S. Pietro a Quintole (near Rovezzano). Author's photo.*
581. *Madonna and Child Enthroned with two music-making Angels and two Angels holding canopy. Panel. Florence, Acton Collection. 168 × 90. Brogi 594/40. d. 1385.*

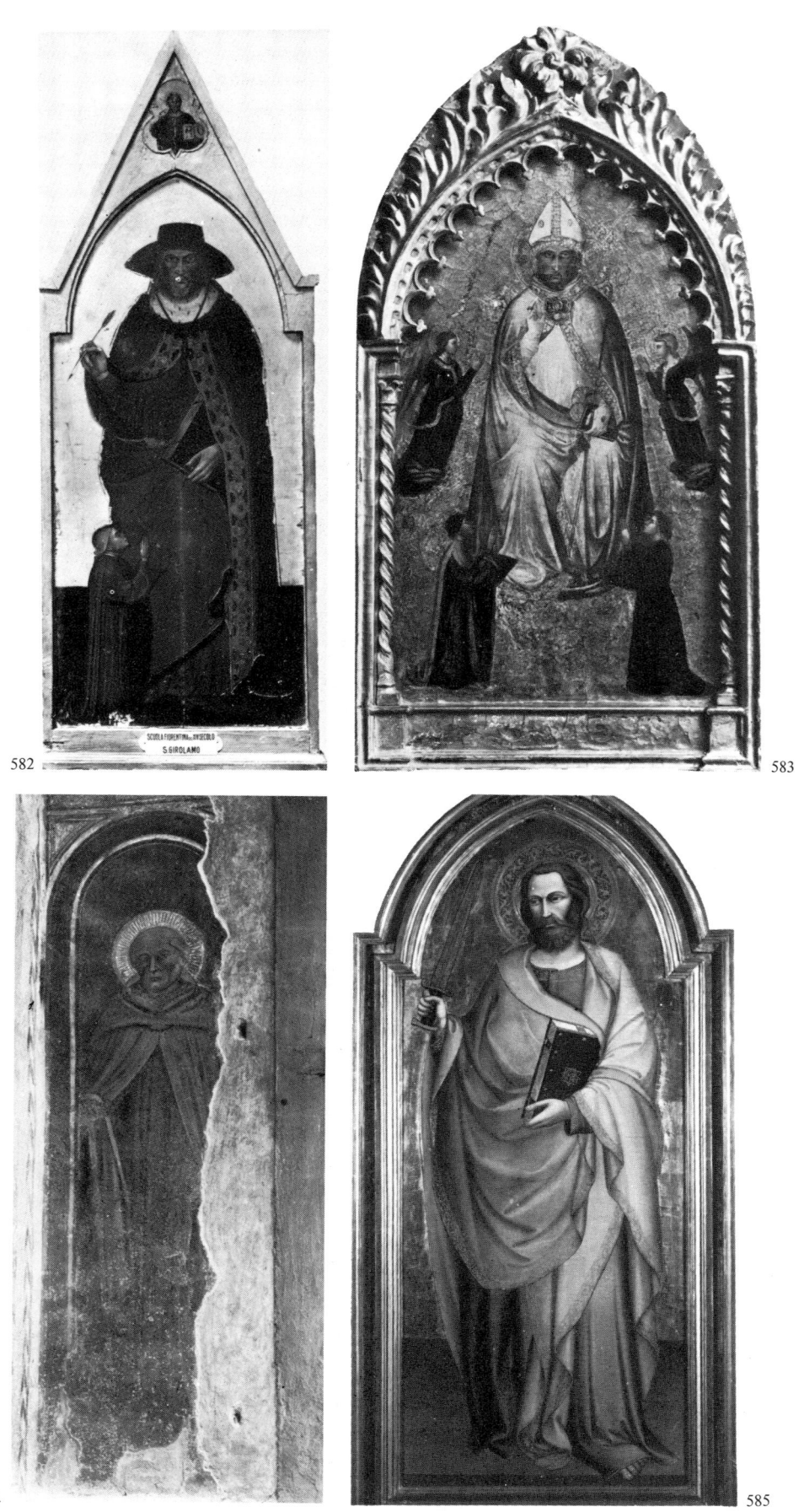

582   583

584   585

582. *St Jerome. Panel. Carrara, Accademia. 106 × 57. SGF 76492.*
583. *St Nicholas Enthroned with two Angels and two Donors. Panel. Whereabouts unknown. no. Soprintendenza Firenze 4336. 79 × 43. Photo Julius Böhler.*
584. *St Andrew of Anagni (see also fig. 574). Fresco. Florence, Piazza del Carmine. SGF 31286.*
585. *St Paul. Panel. San Francisco (Calif.), M. H. de Young Memorial Museum, Kress Gift. no. 61.44.4 K 429. 107.3 × 44.2. Kress Foundation photo.*

STARNINA

The so-called Starnina is the most important figure among the adherents of Agnolo Gaddi and no doubt the one who most closely co-operated with him.

That the otherwise anonymous painter whose principal work is the decoration of the Castellani chapel in Sta. Croce might be Gherardo Starnina, as Vasari alone affirms, is far from certain. Two documents, however, guarantee the existence of a painter of this name. He is found first in 1387 in the register of the guild of S. Luca as " Gherardo d iacopo Starna dipintore " and in February of 1408 the Compagnia della Nunziata charge him with the decoration of a chapel in the church of S. Stefano at Empoli.

Vasari tells us that he was born in 1354 and was the pupil of Antonio Veneziano; in 1378 he fled to Spain because he was implicated in the strife of the Ciompi. When asked to return to execute certain works in Pisa he sent Antonio Vita in his place. He was the master of Masolino, died in 1408 and was buried in S. Jacopo Sopra Arno. Besides the frescoes in the Castellani chapel, old authors, like Richa and Baldinucci as well as Vasari, speak of his paintings in the chapel of S. Gerolamo in the Carmine church in which he introduced Spanish costumes and which betray the versatility of his character, and of the fresco he depicted in the Palace of the Guelf party in remembrance of the sale of Pisa to the Florentines, in which St. Dionysius and two angels were to be seen above the purchased city.....

from R. van Marle, p. 565, *The Development of the Italian Schools of Painting*, Vol. III, The Hague, 1924.

To the grandeur of his forms Starnina begins to unite a sense of space in the background which, it seems to me, is the first step towards the imminent art of the Renaissance. His work in painting corresponds to what Nanni di Banco accomplished in sculpture. We can no longer accept the legend that Starnina, having returned from Spain, brought back the style of high Gothic which in a few years conquered all of Italy, and in a certain sense opposed the beginning of the Renaissance. This affirmation is based upon the few fragments of sinopia on the façade of the Palazzo di Parte Guelfa which, before being foolishly knocked down, showed St Dionysius with two angels. I have been told that this consisted in only a few remnants of cloth. These certainly gave a false idea of the art of the master. This highly developed art does, however, appear in the frescoes at the Church of S. Maria del Carmine, which are antecedent by only two years, and in the *Tebaide* which can be placed in about the same period of time; Starnina's style in these pictures is certainly far from the delicacies and flourishes of the late Gothic. Even if high Gothic was examined and studied by Starnina, it certainly didn't change the artist's solemn and grandiose style. Perhaps it only served to give a greater sense of gracefulness to the squared figures and the rough landscapes. The advocate of high Gothic in Florence was quite a different artist: Lorenzo Monaco.....

from U. Procacci, p. 80, *Gherardo Starnina*, Florence, 1936 (extract in *Rivista d'Arte*, XV, 1933; XVII, 1935; XVIII, 1936).

It is to Starnina that from time to time one tries to attribute the well-known picture in the Uffizi, the *Tebaide*. In the text I have tried to show that the picture is in fact by Angelico, datable about 1420, when Starnina had already been dead for a number of years. Any general view of the problem of Starnina, which has been so very carefully researched by Dott. Procacci, cannot avoid the fact that Vasari places his " Life of Starnina " among those of the " first age ", that is among artists who do not in any way pass beyond the spirit of the Trecento. And Vasari knew the frescoes of the chapel of St Jerome in the Carmine a great deal better than ever we shall be able, given the flimsy remains which have come to light. From them we can only suppose that Starnina, returning from his time spent in Spain, was the first to introduce into Florence in the early years of the Quattrocento, new forms of an extremely linear and exotic Gothic.....

from R. Longhi, p. 182, *Critica d'Arte*, V, 1940.

In October of 1404, the decoration of the Cappella di S. Gerolamo in the church of the Carmine, was finished; its author, Gherardo Starnina, became " famous in all of Tuscany, and in fact, in all of Italy " (Vasari). This cycle has been almost completely destroyed.

The fortuitous and precious discovery by Procacci of the remaining fragments is sufficient to make us regret the loss even more. Because of the loss, we must go back to original documents in order to learn something of him; a follower of Agnolo, pupil of Antonio Veneziano who was his master, and master himself, in his turn, of Masolino. Other records include the fact that he worked upon a fresco in the Palazzo di Parte Guelfa (destroyed), in the Cappella Castellani with Agnolo Gaddi, in S. Agostino at Empoli, and in Spain at Toledo and Valencia (1398-1408). Critics first attempted to single out his personality in the circle of Agnolo and from this a group of works was later attributed to the so-called Master delle Madonne. Following this, new contacts and attributions were suggested (among which, the most important remains the traditional one of the Tebaide in the Uffizi, about which not everyone agrees). From the few fragments which we have by him (including those recently discovered by Procacci, and now in the museum at Empoli), his personality is not yet absolutely clear; from them, however, we can see that he must have moved within the world of the high Gothic.....

from U. Baldini, p. 44, *II^a Mostra di Affreschi Staccati*, Florence, 1958.

.... that Starnina participated in the decoration of the Castellani chapel in Santa Croce can only be hypothetical; those frescoes seem to show only the characteristics of work by Agnolo Gaddi and helpers. As for the suggestion that Starnina is the author of the *Tebaide* of the Uffizi, this should be firmly rejected, if only on the question of quality; there is no sign whatsoever in that painting of the Spanish 'international Gothic'; besides because of the sky with clouds in it, and the heavy solidity of the figures, it must have been painted after 1420 (Starnina died before 1413): these things are inexplicable unless they follow Masaccio's work....

from L. Bellosi, p. 76, in *Paragone*, XVII, 201, 1966.

Vasari writes that Starnina was born in Florence and became a pupil of Antonio Veneziano, that his early work in Sta. Croce earned him the admiration of visiting Spaniards, and that as a result he was persuaded to go to Spain as a royal protegé. It has since been suggested that he was a member of the Gaddi workshop, but he appears to have been active in Toledo and Valencia in 1398-1401. In October 1404 he was back in Florence, employed in painting the St. Jerome chapel in Sta. Maria del Carmine, and in 1409 worked on another cycle of frescoes, this time in the church of S. Stefano at Empoli. A document dated October 18th, 1413 refers to him as dead, " cut off at the height of his powers " according to Vasari. The problem since has been to make reliable attributions to Starnina. His importance for the Quattrocento is clear; the absence of authenticated works has deprived him of the reputation he should perhaps enjoy.....

from P. Dal Poggetto, p. 94, *Frescoes from Florence*, London, 1969.

The identification of the Maestro del Bambino Vispo with Starnina makes it possible to define this artist's role in Florentine painting at the beginning of the Quattrocento. This will require further research, from which it may appear that Starnina's return from Spain, which took place after 1401 and before 1404, was of decisive importance for the spread of the International Style at Florence.

from J. van Waadenoijen, p. 90, in *The Burlington Magazine*, CXVI, 851, 1974.

BIBLIOGRAPHY
BOOKS   *An asterisk indicates a work listed in the General Bibliography*

Venturi, A.*, Vol. VII, 1911, p. 29; *v. Marle, 1924**, p. 565; *Colnaghi**, 1928, p. 257; *Toesca, 1929**, p. 67; Wulff, O., pp. 156-90 in *Italienischen Studien* (Festschrift for Paul Schubring), Leipzig, 1929; Procacci, U., *Gherardo Starnina*, Florence, 1936; Toesca, P., in *Treccani*, Vol. *XXXII**, 1937, p. 486; *Antal**, 1948, p. 205; *Vavalà, 1948** pp. 103-5; *Galetti**, " P-Z ", 1950, pp. 2349-50; Baldini, U., *MAS I**, 1957, pp. 53-4; Baldini, U., *MAS II**, 1958, p. 44; *Shapley**, 1966, pp. 39-40; Bellosi, L., *La Pittura Tardogotica in Toscana* (I Maestri del Colore, 239), Milan, 1966; Dal Poggetto, P., *Fresco Show**, 1968, pp. 102-5 (94-7); *Meiss, 1970**, pp. 102-3; *Dutch Show**, 1974, p. 48.

JOURNALS

Giglioli, H. O., *RA*, III, 1905, pp. 19-21; Tormo, E., *Boletino de la Società Española de Excurciones*, 1910, pp. 82-101; Schmarsow, A., *AS*, XXX, 1911, pp. 205-6; Mather, J. F., Jr., *AA*, I, 1913, pp. 179-81; Vegue y Goldoni, A., *AE*, VI, 1930, pp. 199-203; Tosi, L. M., *BA*, IX, II, 1930, pp. 538-54; Vegue y Goldoni, A., *AE*, VI, 1930, pp. 277-79; Angulo Iniguez, D., *AE*, VII, 1931, pp. 23-9; Gamba, C., *RA*, XIV, 1932, pp. 55-74; Procacci, U., *RA*, XV, 1933, pp. 151-90; Procacci, U., *BA*, XXVII, 1934, pp. 327-34; Procacci, U., *RA*, XVII, 1935, pp. 333-384; Salvini, R., *BA*, XXIX, III, 1935, pp. 279-94; Procacci, U., *RA*, XVIII, 1936, pp. 77-94; Pudelko, G., *AA*, XXVI, 1, 1938, pp. 47-63; Longhi, R., *CA*, V, 1940, pp. 145-91; Salmi, M., *C*, I, 2, 1950, pp. 75-81; Bellosi, L., *PA*, XVII, 201/21, 1966, pp. 75-76; Parronchi A., *AAM*, XXXIII, 1966, pp. 45-57; Middeldorf, U., *BM*, LXIII, 815, 1971, pp. 74-75; Volpe, C., *MKIF*, XVII, 2-3, 1973, p. 355; van Waadenoijen, J., *BM*, CXVI, 851, 1974, pp. 82-91.

There are no known signed and/or dated works by Starnina.

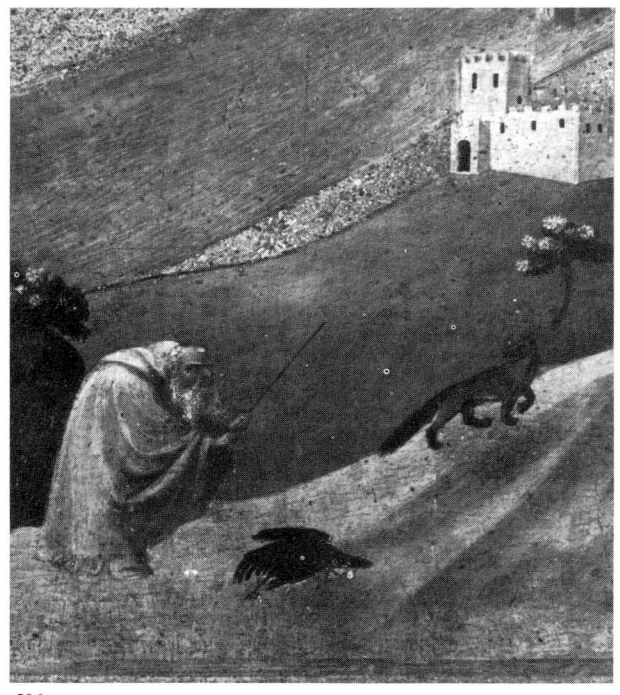

586

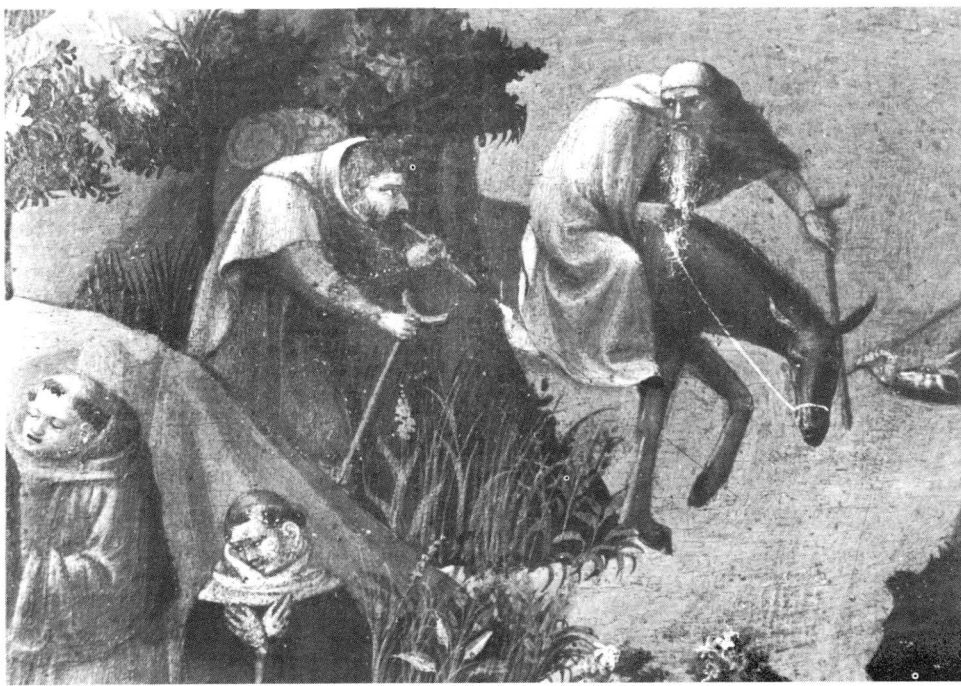

587

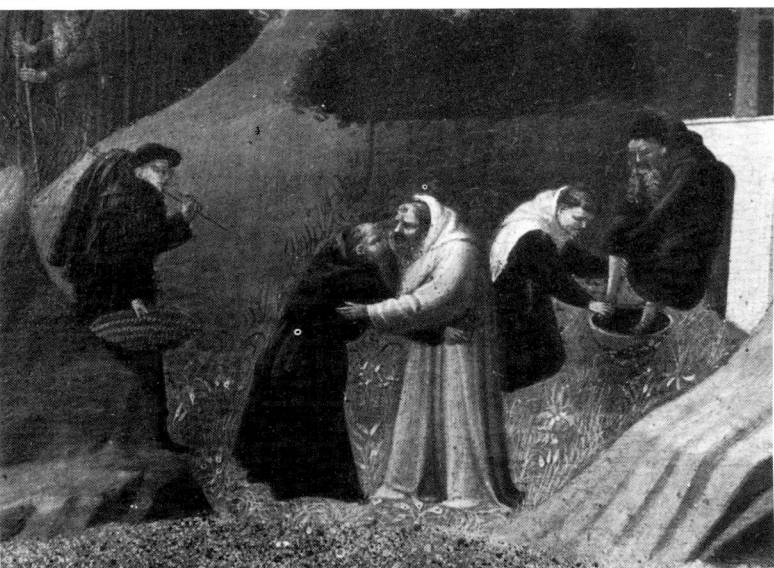

588

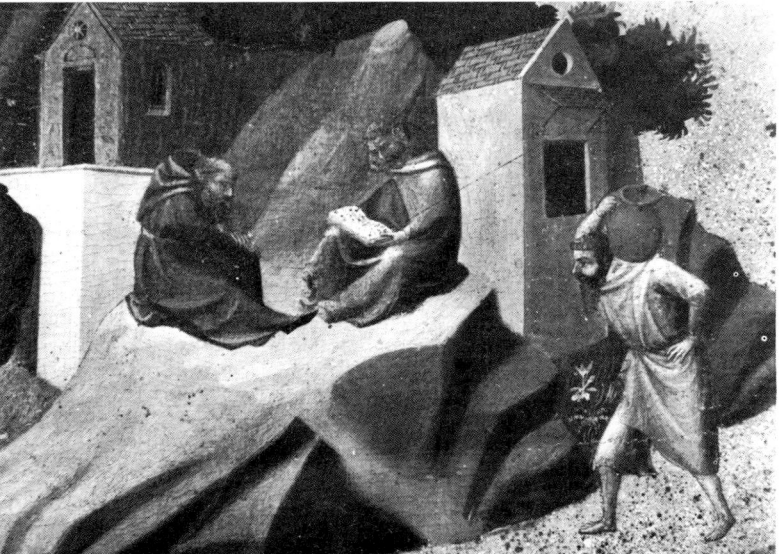

589

586. The Thebaid, detail of fig. 590. Panel. Florence, Uffizi. no. 447. SGF 140959.
587. The Thebaid, detail of fig. 590. Panel. Florence, Uffizi. no. 447. SGF 140953.
588. The Thebaid, detail of fig. 590. Panel. Florence, Uffizi. no. 447. SGF 140957.
589. The Thebaid, detail of fig. 590. Panel. Florence, Uffizi. no. 447. SGF 140958.

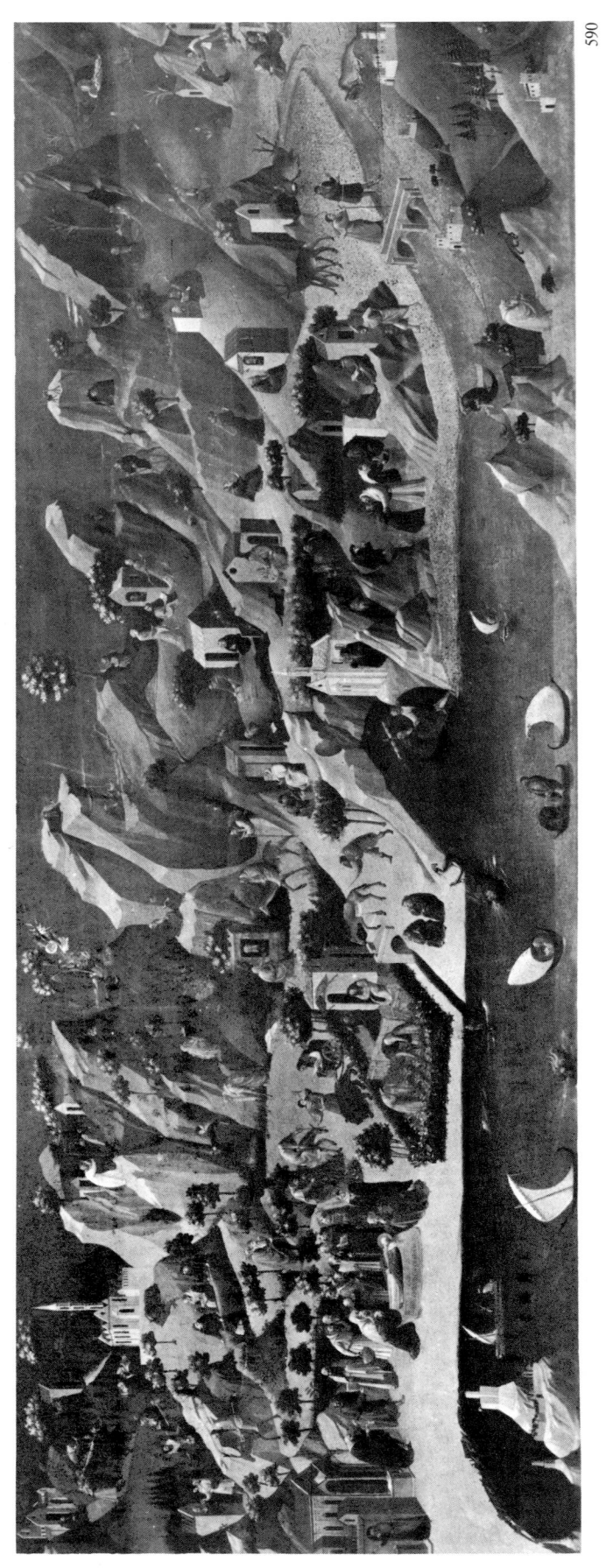

590. *The Thebaid, or the Anchorites in the Desert. Panel. Florence, Uffizi. no. 447. 75 × 208. SGF 140949.*

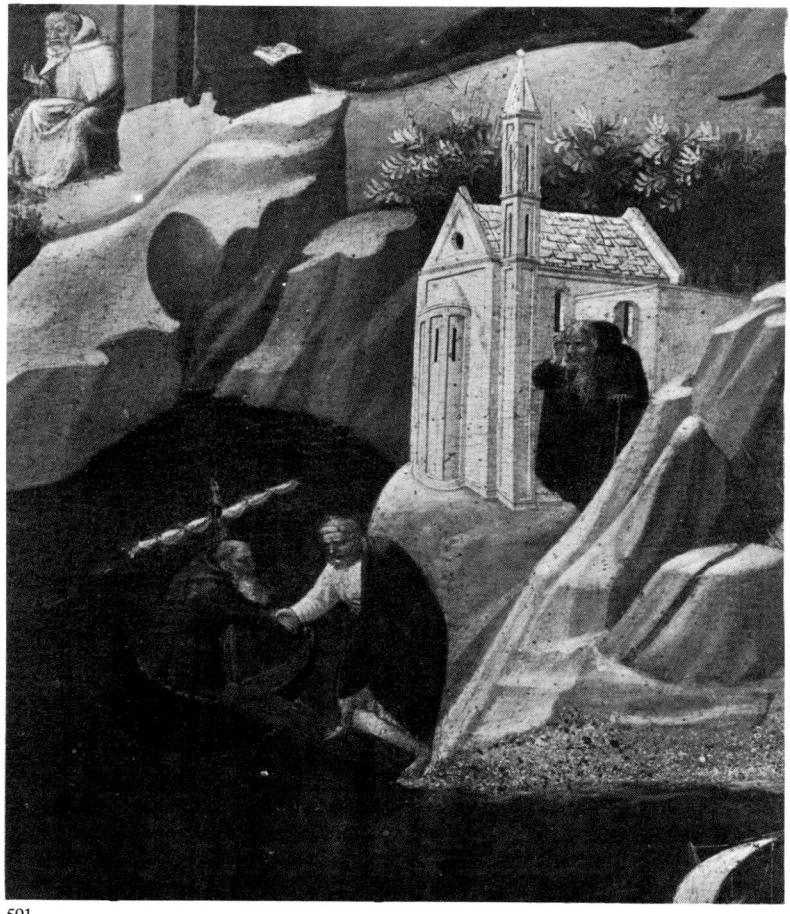

591

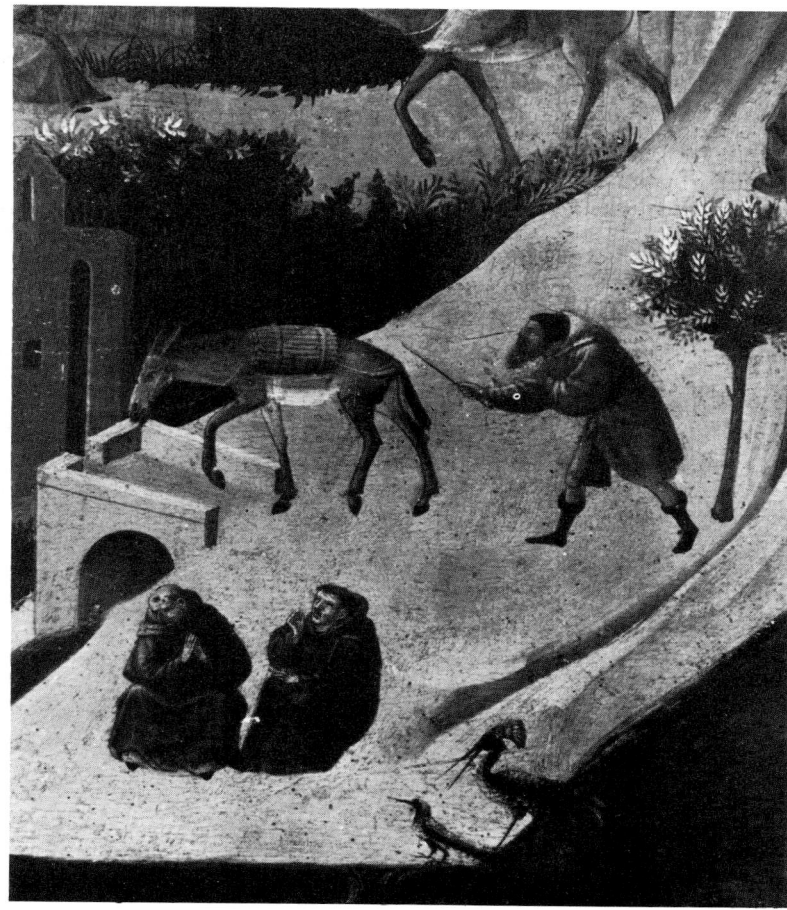

592

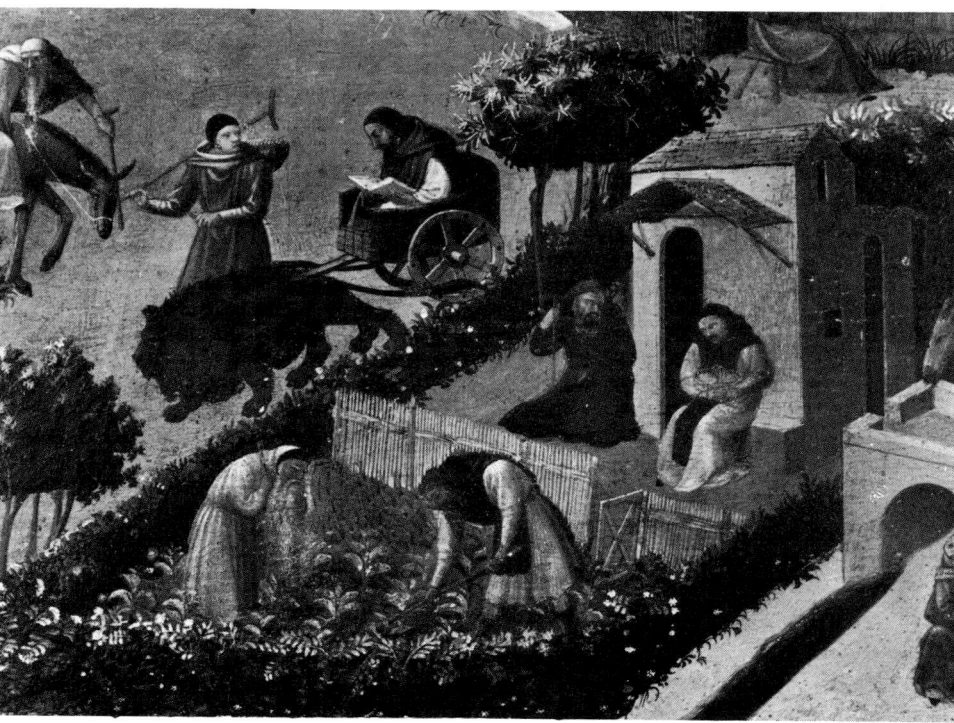

593

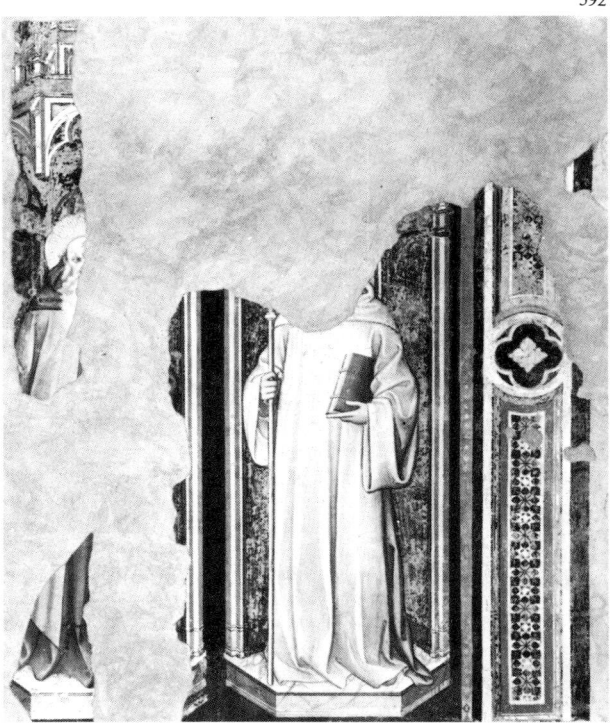

594

591. *The Thebaid, detail of fig. 590. Panel. Florence, Uffizi. no. 447. SGF 140956.*
592. *The Thebaid, detail of fig. 590. Panel. Florence, Uffizi. no. 447. SGF 140955.*
593. *The Thebaid, detail of fig. 590. Panel. Florence, Uffizi. no. 447. SGF 140954.*
594. *Fragment. Fresco. Florence, S. Maria del Carmine. SGF 132693.*

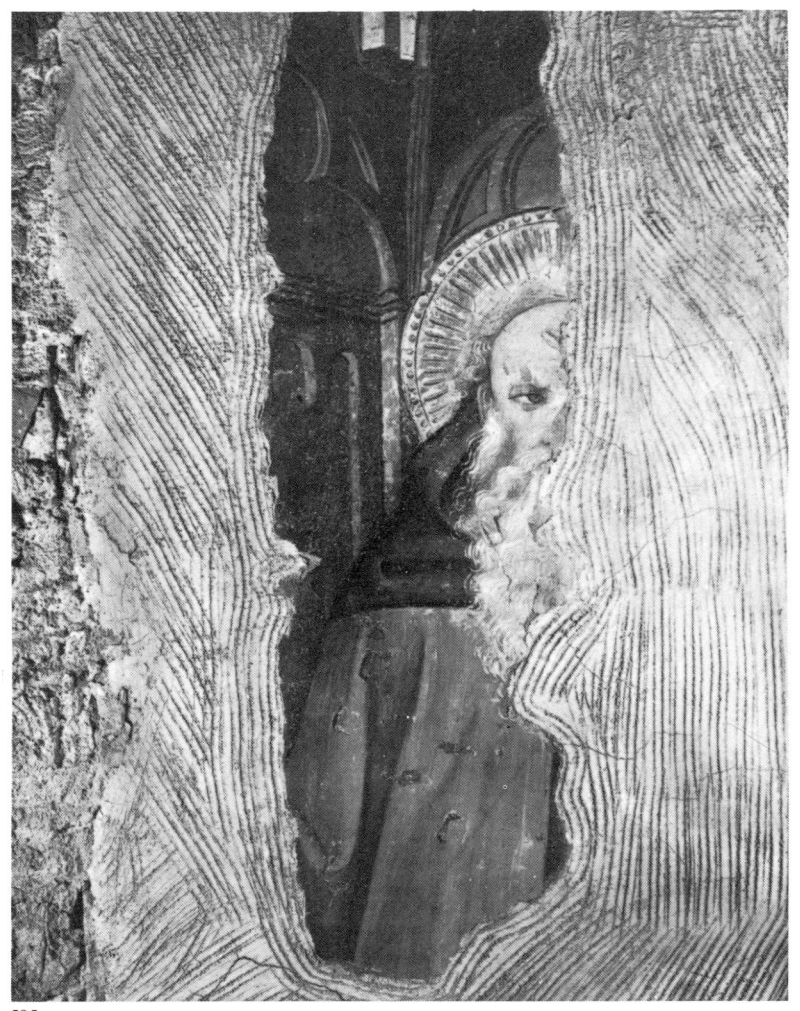

595

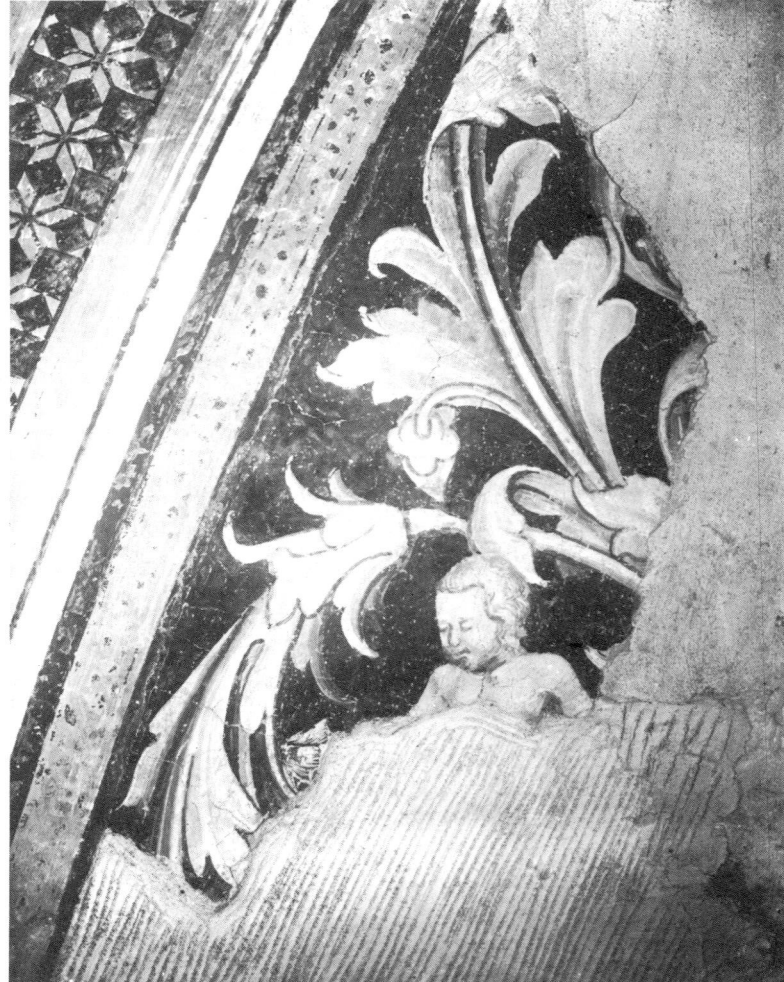

596

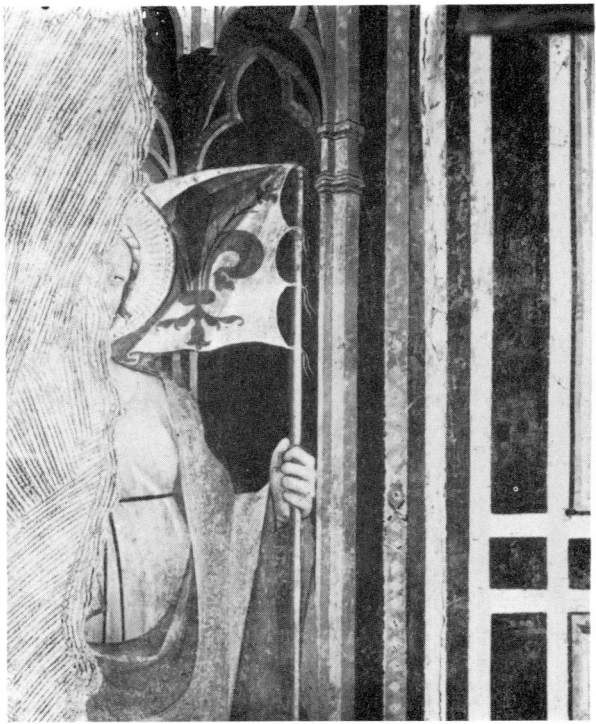

597

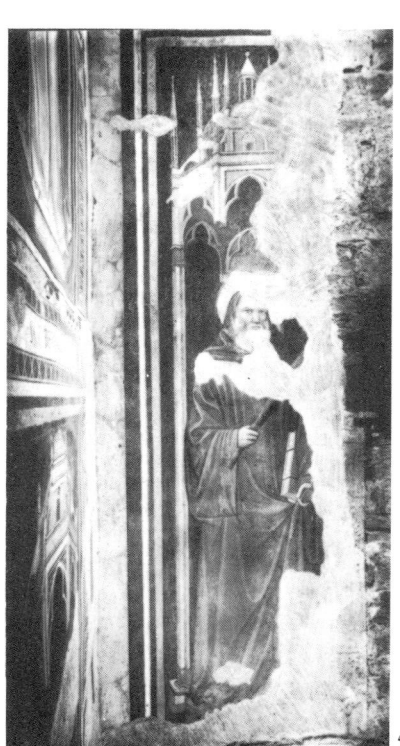

598

595. *Fragment. Fresco. Florence, S. Maria del Carmine. SGF 88143.*
596. *Fragment. Fresco. Florence, S. Maria del Carmine. SGF 85148.*
597. *Fragment. Fresco. Florence, S. Maria del Carmine. SGF 85137.*
598. *St Benedict. Fresco. Florence, S. Maria del Carmine. SGF 85139.*

MASTER OF SANTA VERDIANA PANEL

One of the important followers of the great founder of the Florentine School, Giotto, here [in Birmingham, Alabama] presents an altarpiece typical of the teachings of his master. The Madonna of Humility and the Child are solidly constructed, with features of the sort Giotto used in his new humanism, and with gorgeous robes. They are surrounded by a heavenly choir of angels playing lute and viol, and by a spacious " mandorla" as well as carefully tooled haloes, the whole outlined by the disembodied seraphim and cherubim with wings and faces of rich but soft red and blue. The throne is heaven itself, symbolically indicated by curious little cloud forms.....

There exists quite a group of paintings by this same easily recognizable artist, which, when assembled by scholars, will enrich our knowledge of the Florentine School toward 1400.....

> from W. Suida, p. 23, *The Samuel H. Kress Collection*, Birmingham Museum Of Art, Birmingham, Alabama, 1952.

This pseudonym is the provisional designation of a Tuscan painter, evidently a follower of Agnolo Gaddi, who in his latest works shows influences from Lorenzo Monaco. The name suggested by W. Suida derives from a painting in the Samuel H. Kress Collection, now in the Atlanta Art Association Galleries, representing the Madonna and Child with six Saints, among them the rarely represented St Verdiana with two serpents. Recently R. Longhi and F. Zeri have added more paintings to the group by this master, accepting the pseudonym the " Santa Verdiana Master ".....

> from W. Suida, p. 20, *The Samuel H. Kress Collection*, Birmingham Museum of Art, Birmingham, Alabama, 1959.

That the author of the two panels in Greenville began his work close to Agnolo Gaddi is proven by SS John the Evangelist and Paul: they are very Agnolesque in type and in execution, so much so that they even point to an eventual presence of the same hand in certain of the large and numerous undertakings on panels and in fresco, which Gaddi planned and directed, but which he himself only partly executed.....

> from F. Zeri, p. 35, *Studies in the History of Art Dedicated to William E. Suida on his eightieth Birthday*, London, 1959.

A whole series of Madonna pictures produced probably during the 1390's display great similarity in composition to this panel [in Esztergom]. Most of them show affinity to a greater or lesser extent with works of the workshop of Agnolo Gaddi. It is believed, however, that these pictures are not from his workshop but from that of another artist, referred to as the Master of the Santa Verdiana, whose early works show the influence of the Orcagna tradition....

> from M. Boskovits, p. 31, *Early Italian Panel Paintings*, Budapest, 1966.

In the case of the Master of Santa Verdiana we can't give the painter a name. The almost forty pictures of fairly good quality that we may attribute to him are a good enough basis to attempt an outline of his development and to indicate his place in the history of Florentine painting.

Anyone who has studied the painting of the years at the end of the 14th and beginning of the 15th centuries will be familiar with this painter.....

If one compares all the panels which have been published by the Verdiana Master — sometimes he is called the Master of the Louvre Coronation — then it becomes necessary to enlarge upon F. Zeri's opinion of the painter's position, making a few small corrections. While the influence of Agnolo does unquestionably dominate in some works by the painter, we find in others many features which point instead to an Orcagnesque origin to his style.....

from M. Boskovits, pp. 31-2, *Mitteilungen des Kunsthistorischen Institutes in Florenz*, XIII, I-II, Dec. 1967.

BIBLIOGRAPHY
BOOKS

An asterisk indicates a work listed in the General Bibliography

Suida, W. E., *Catalogue of the Birmingham Museum of Art*, Birmingham, (Ala.), 1952, pp. 22-3; *Offner, 1952**, Sec. IV, Vol. III; Suida, W. E., *Catalogue of the Atlanta Art Association*, Atlanta, (Ga.), 1958, pp. 14-15; Suida, W. E., *Catalogue of the Birmingham Museum of Art*, Birmingham, (Ala), 1959, pp. 19-21; Zeri, F., pp. 35-40, *Studies in the History of Art Dedicated to William E. Suida*, London, 1959; *Offner, 1965**, Sec. IV, Vol. III, p. 107; *Shapley**, 1966, pp. 41-2; Boskovits, M., *Early Italian Panel Paintings*, Budapest, 1966, p. 31; Fredericksen, B. B., *Catalogue of the Paintings in the J. Paul Getty Museum*, Malibu (Calif.), 1972, p. 8.

JOURNALS

Sirèn, O., *BM*, Dec. 1914, p. 113; Berenson, B., *DD*, XI, 5, 1930-1, pp. 1286-1318; Procacci, U., *RA*, XIV, 1932, pp. 341-49; Bellosi, L., *PA*, XVI, 187/7, 1965, p. 34; Boskovits, M., *MKIF*, XIII, 1-4, 1967-1968, pp. 31-60; Zeri, F., *GBA*, LXXI, 110, 1968, p. 71; Zeri, F., *AP*, XCIX, 144, Feb., 1974, pp. 93, 96.

There are no known dated works by the Master of S. Verdiana.

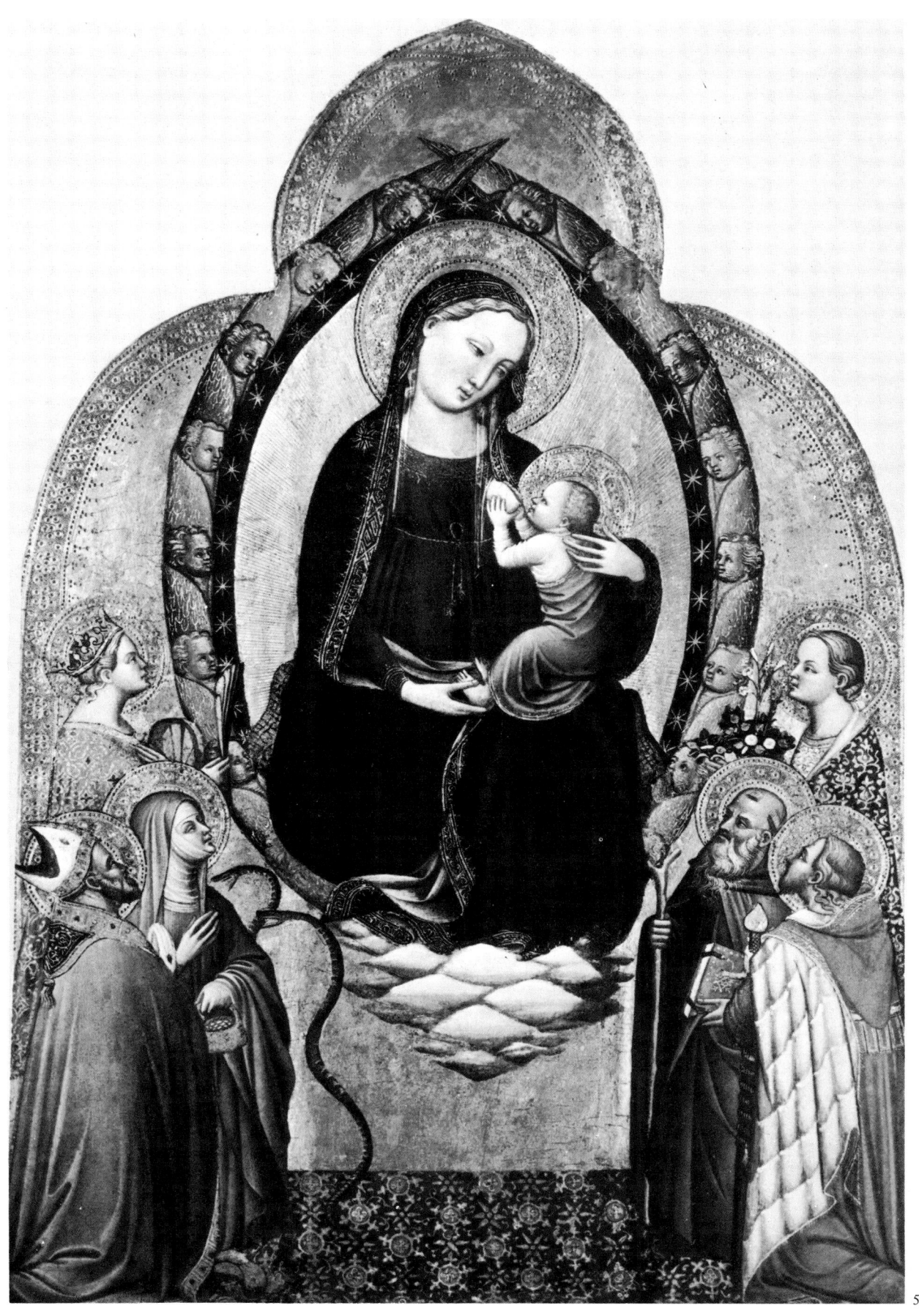

599

599. *Madonna in Glory nursing the Child, with six Saints, including S. Verdiana. Panel. Atlanta (Ga.), High Museum of Art, Samuel H. Kress Collection. no. K 1054. 80.6 × 54.3. Kress Foundation photo.*

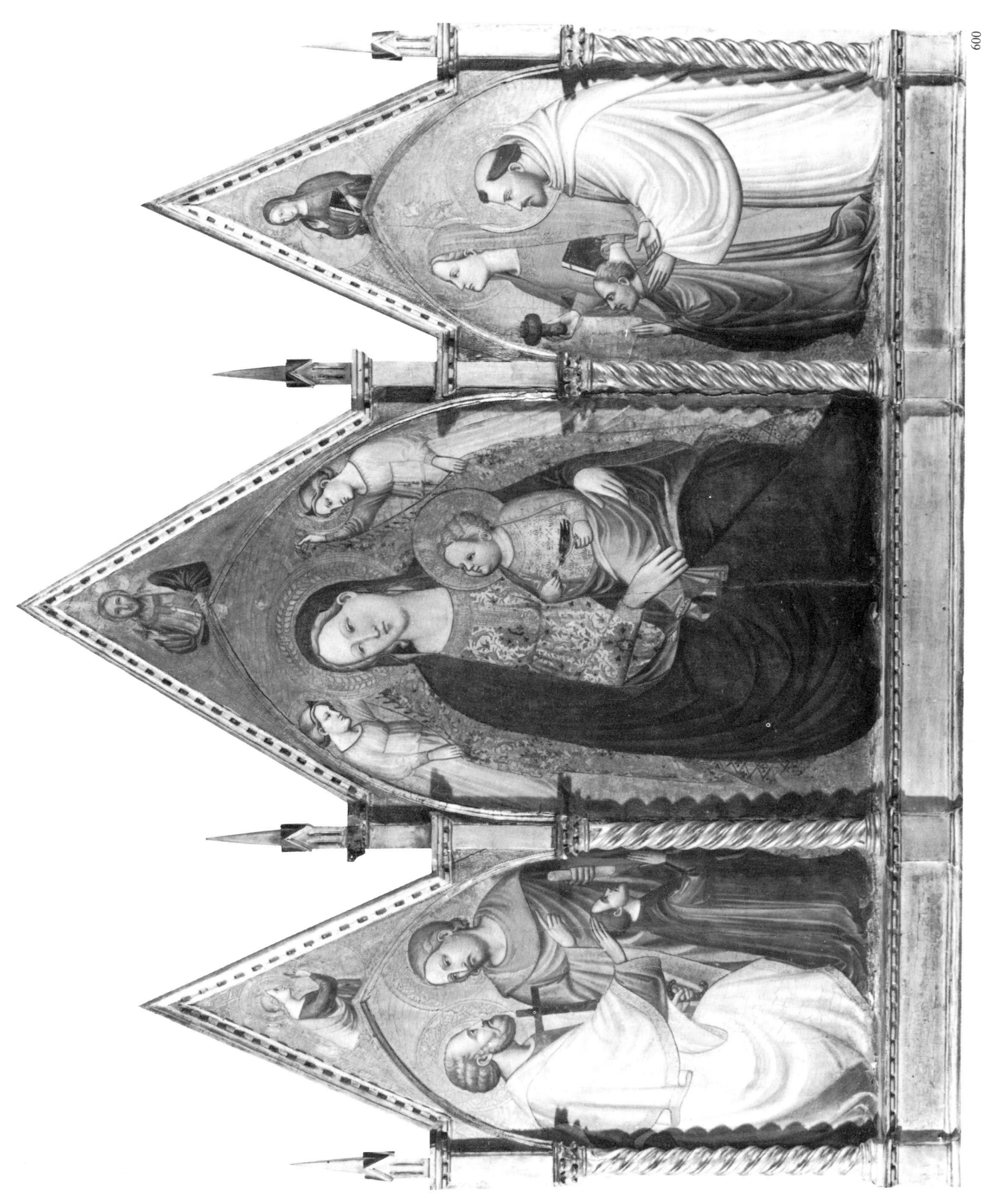

600. *Triptych: Madonna of Humility with Saints and Angels. Pinnacles: Christ blessing; Annunciation. Panel. Dublin, National Gallery of Ireland. no. 1201. 111 × 153. Museum photo.*

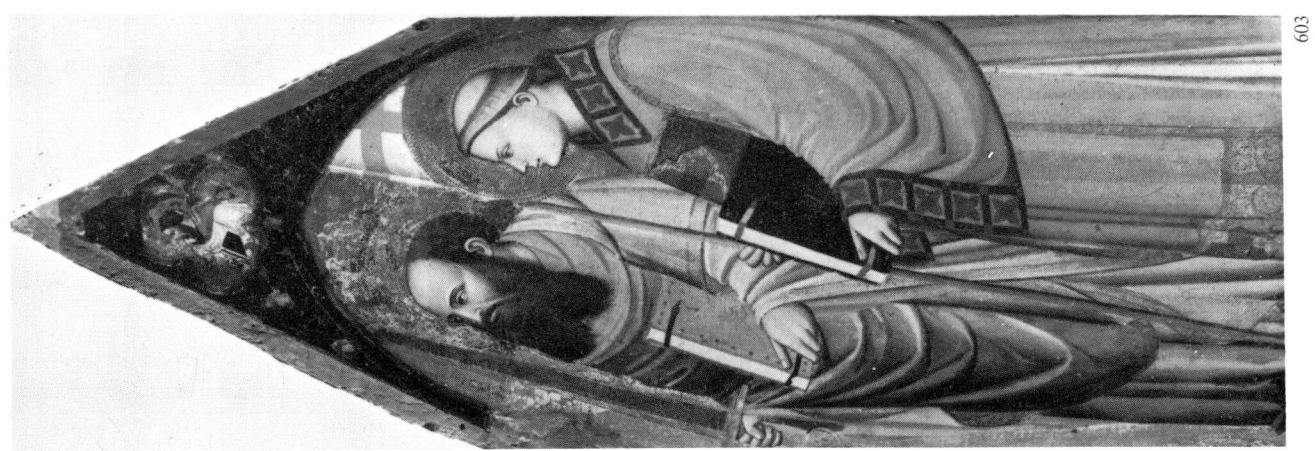

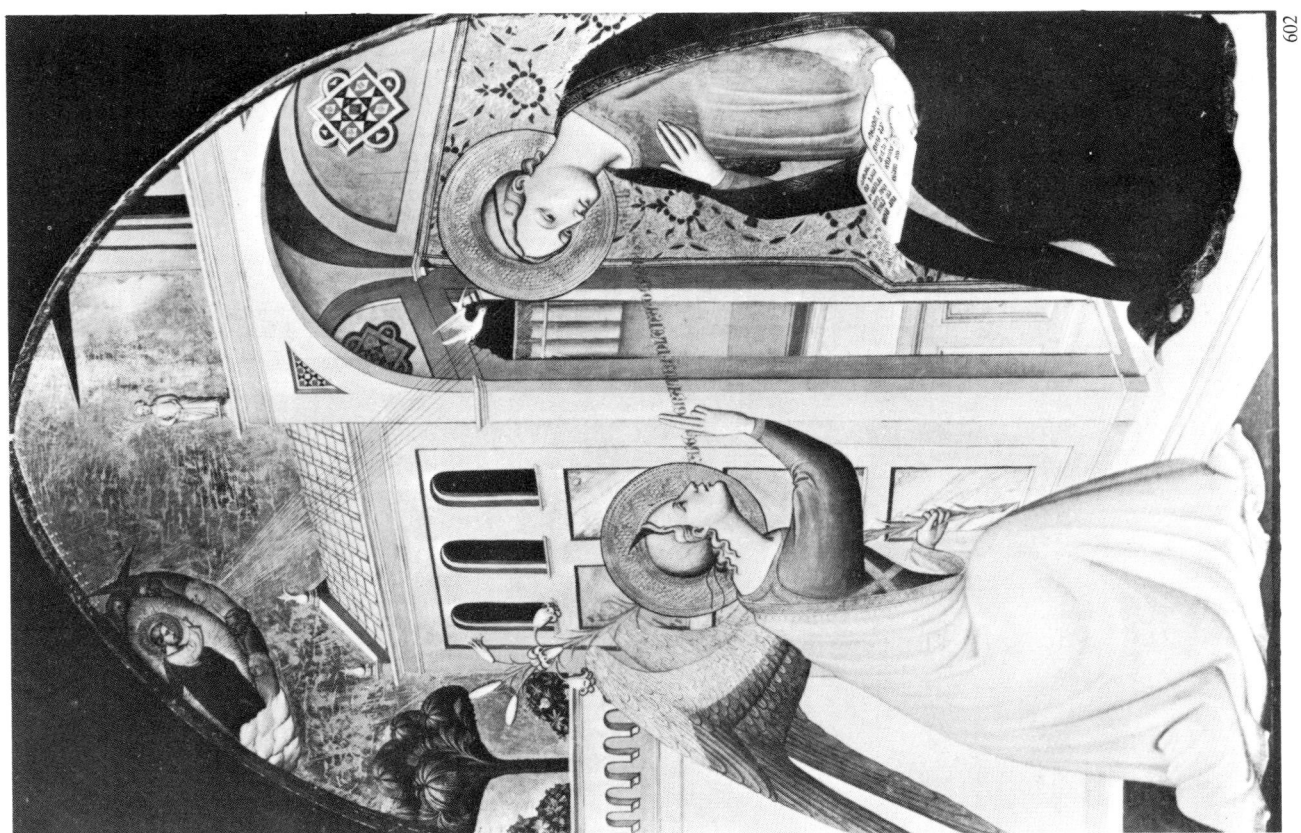

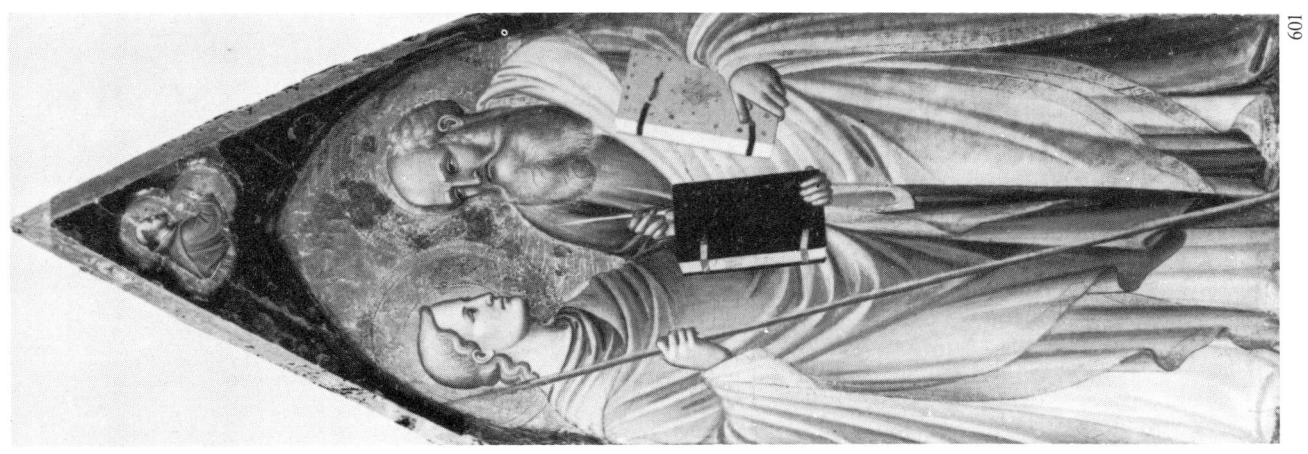

601. *Sts James the Less and John the Evangelist. Panel. Greenville (S.C.), Bob Jones University. 121.9 × 50.8. Museum photo.*
602. *Annunciation. Panel. Malibu (Calif.), J. Paul Getty Museum. no. 9. 128.2 × 92. Photo Kunsthistorisches Institut in Florenz 3266.*
603. *Sts Paul and Stephen. Panel. Greenville (S.C.), Bob Jones University. 121.9 × 50.8. Museum photo.*

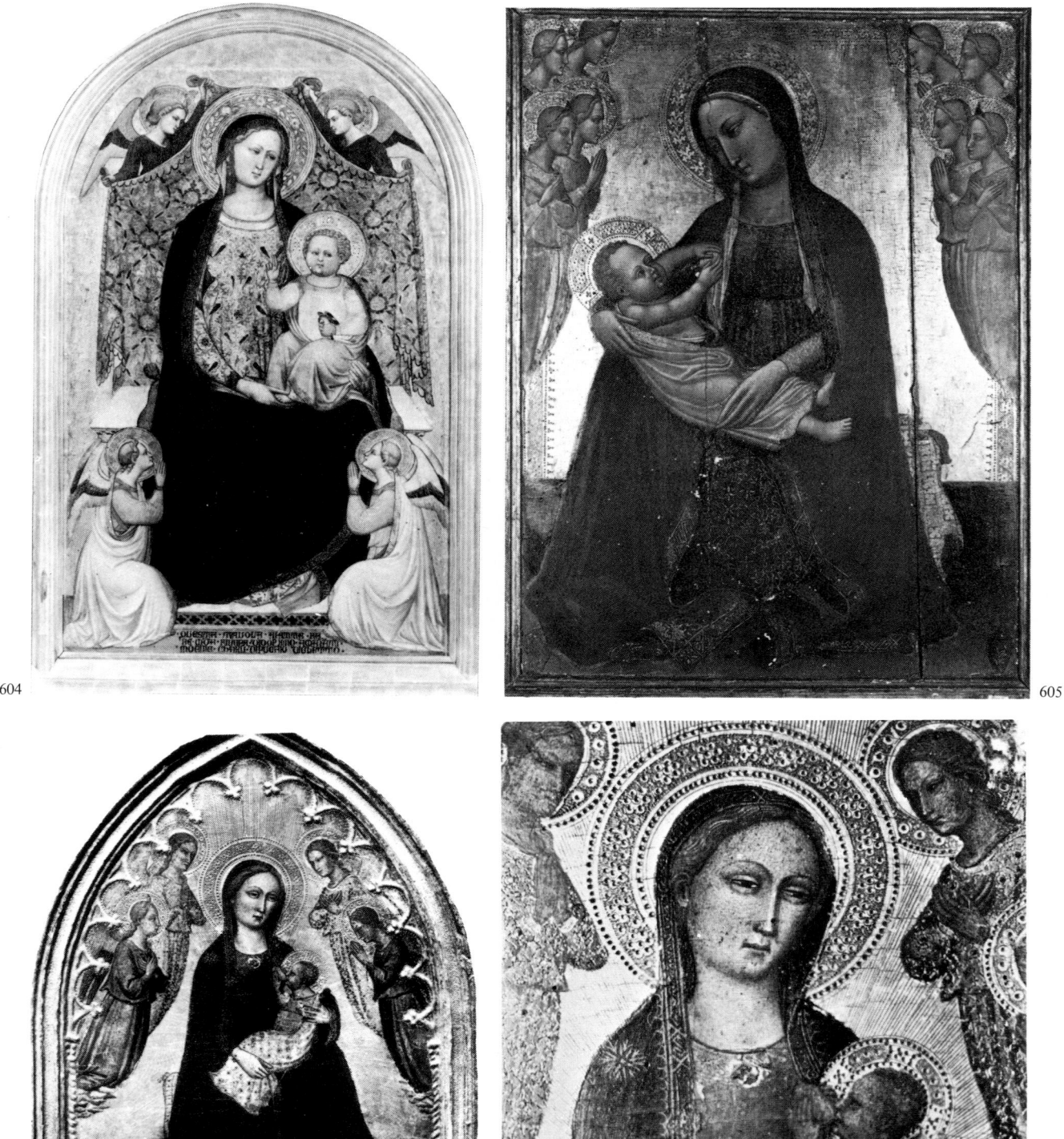

604. *Madonna and Child with four Angels. Panel. Private Collection.* 113×72.5. *Sotheby 0796.*
605. *Madonna of Humility with eight Angels. Panel. Philadelphia (Pa.), Museum of Art, Barnard Collection. no. '45-25-119.* 89.5×64.7 *(w.f.). Museum photo.*
606. *Madonna and Child in Glory with six Saints and four Angels. Panel. Florence, Accademia. no. 1890: 3156.* 87×49. *SGF 20949.*
607. *Madonna and Child, detail of fig. 606. Panel. Florence, Accademia. no. 1890 :3156. Author's photo.*

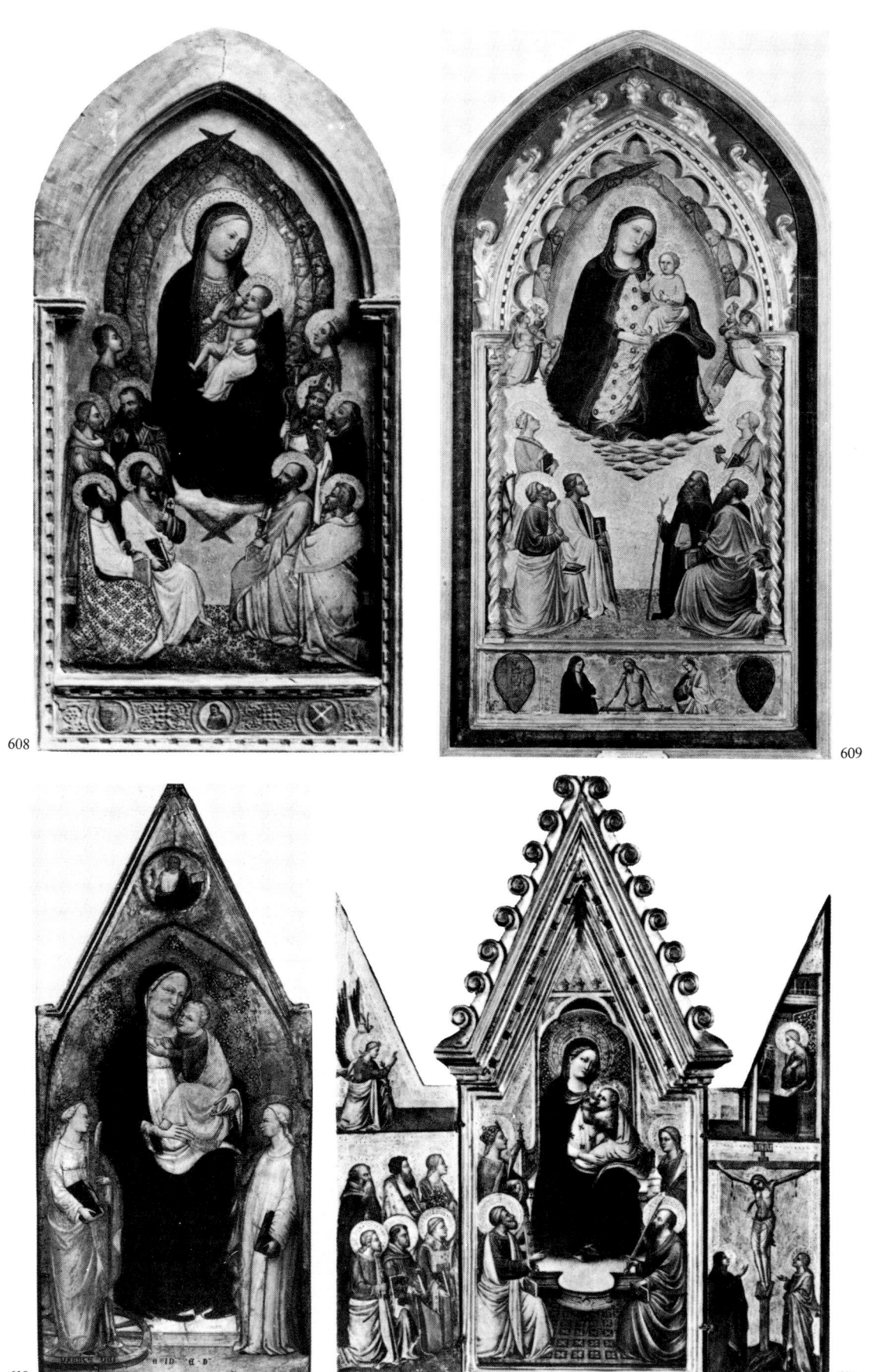

608.   *Madonna in Glory nursing the Child, with ten Saints.   Panel.   Budapest,   Musée des Beaux-Arts.   82 × 43.   Museum photo.*
609.   *Madonna and Child in Glory with six Saints and four music-making Angels.   Below: Man of Sorrows.   Panel.   Birmingham (Ala.), Birmingham Museum of Art, Samuel H. Kress Collection.   no. K 261.   96.5 × 53.3.   Kress Collection photo.*
610.   *Madonna and Child with Sts Catherine and Lucy.   Above: Christ blessing.   Panel.   Private Collection.   Perotti 21124.*
611.   *Portable triptych: Madonna and Child with four Saints, Annunciation, six Saints, and Christ on the Cross.   Panel.   Rome, Galleria Nazionale.   cp: 56.5 × 14; lp: 50.5 × 13; rp: 55 × 13.   Alinari 27444.*

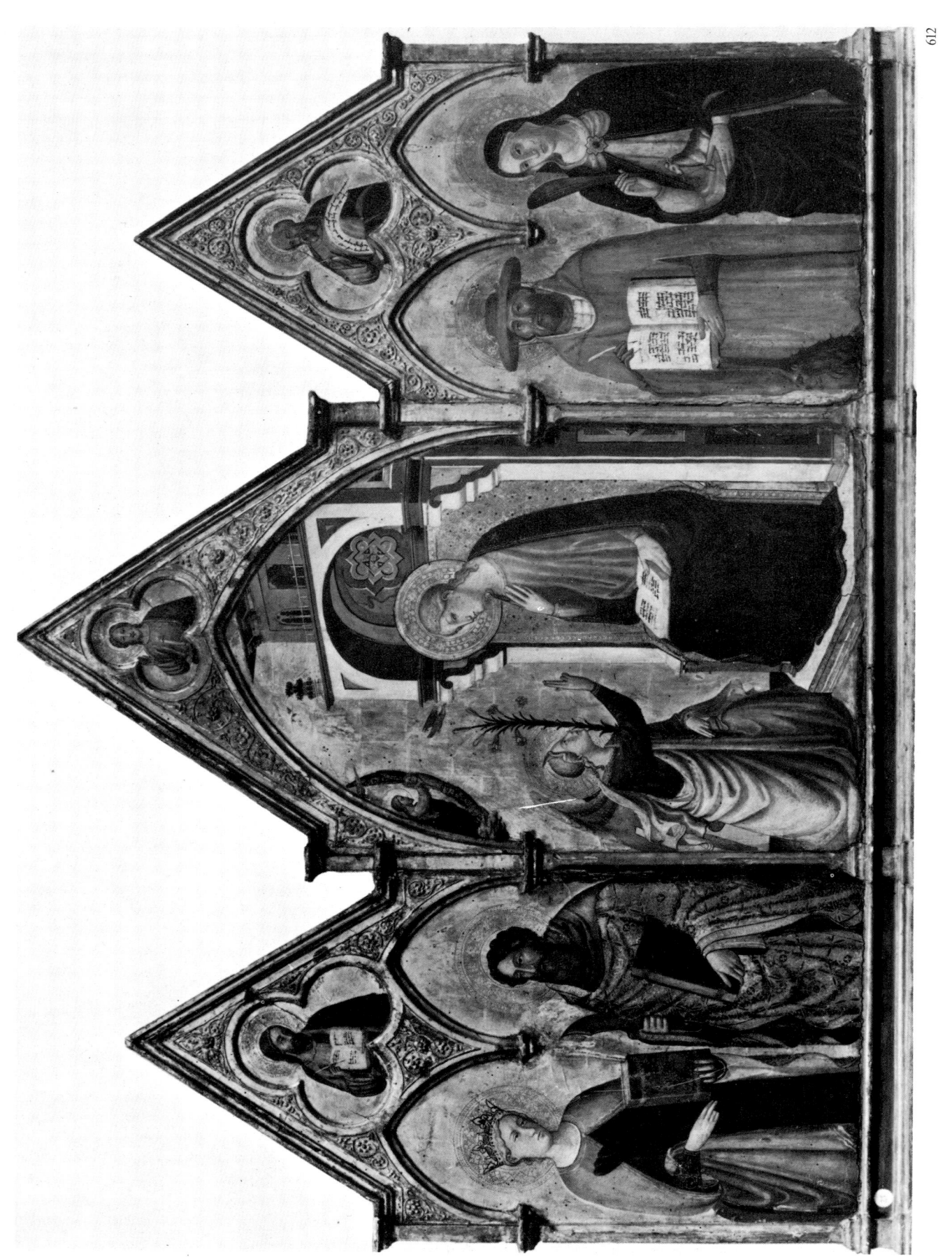

612. *Triptych: Annunciation with Sts Catherine, Bartholomew, Jerome and a male Saint. Above: God the Father, two Prophets. Panel. Private Collection. Perotti 21117.*

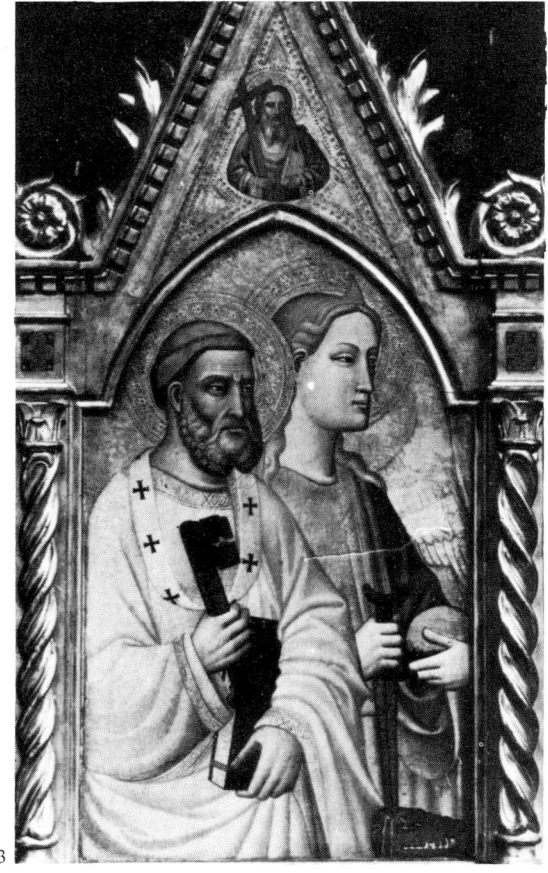

613

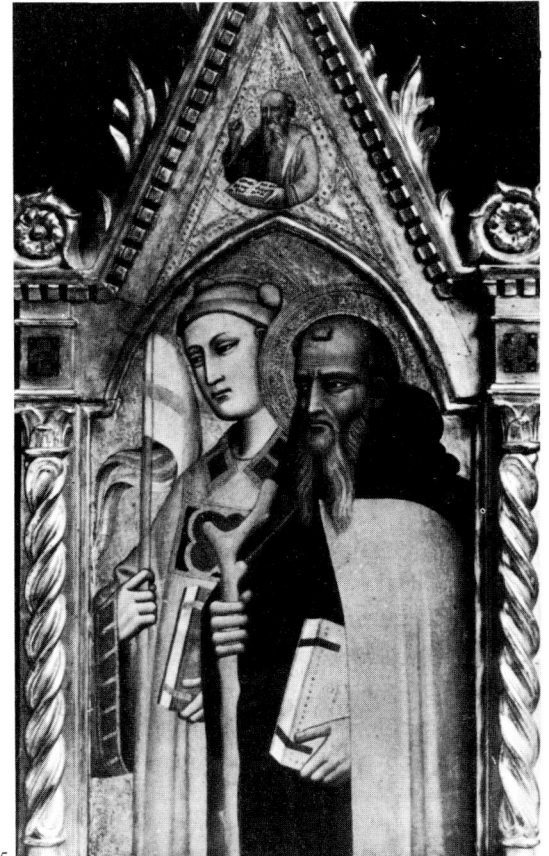

615

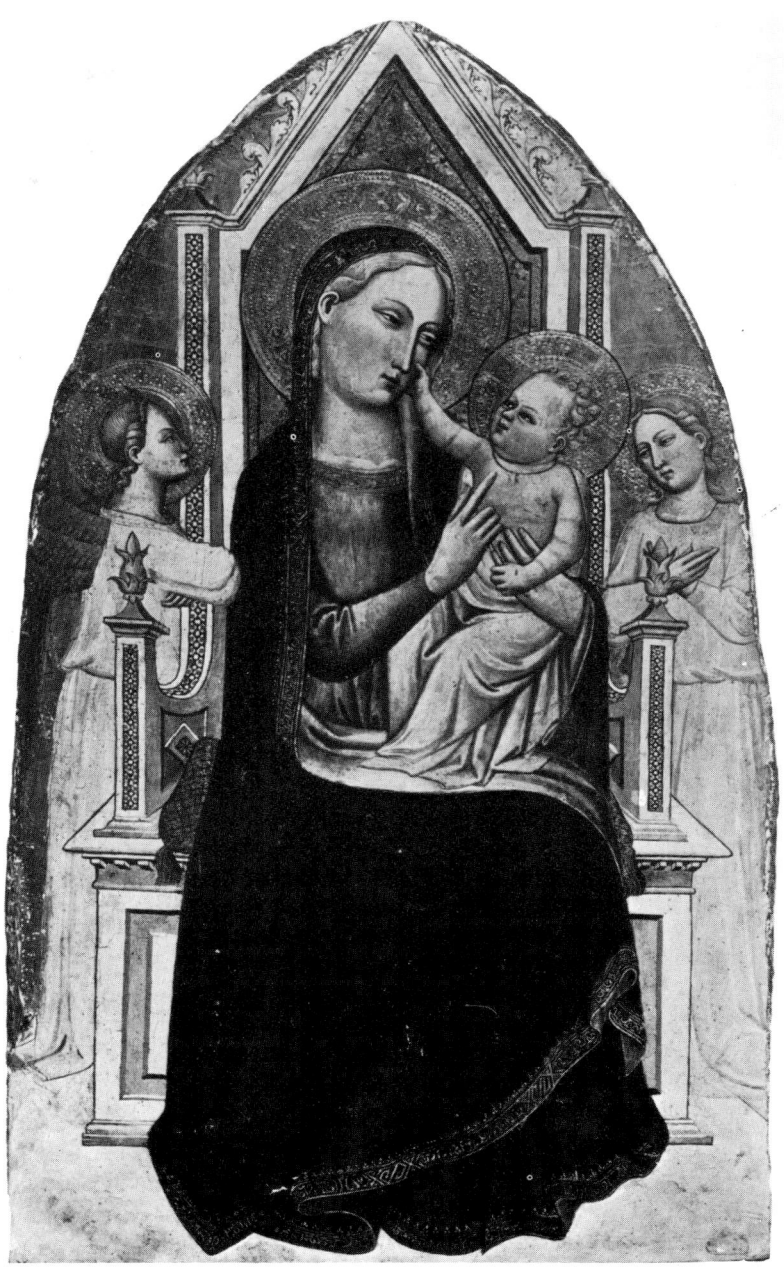

614

613. *Sts Peter and Michael Archangel. Panel. Private Collection. 124.5 × 57.2. Courtauld. photo.*
614. *Madonna and Child Enthroned with two Angels. Panel. Private Collection. Courtauld photo.*
615. *Sts Anthony Abbot and Stephen. Panel. Private Collection. 124 × 57.2. Courtauld photo.*

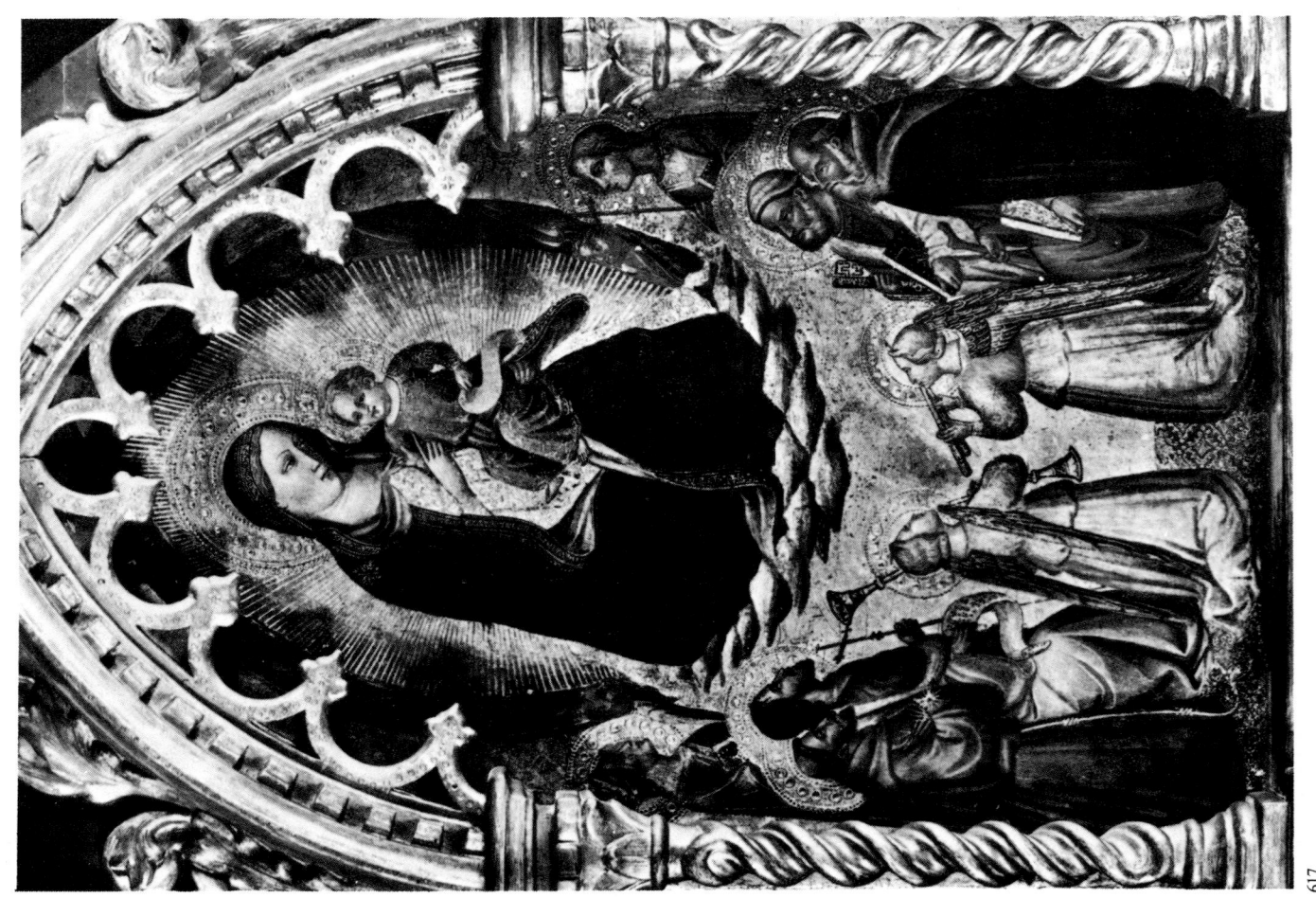

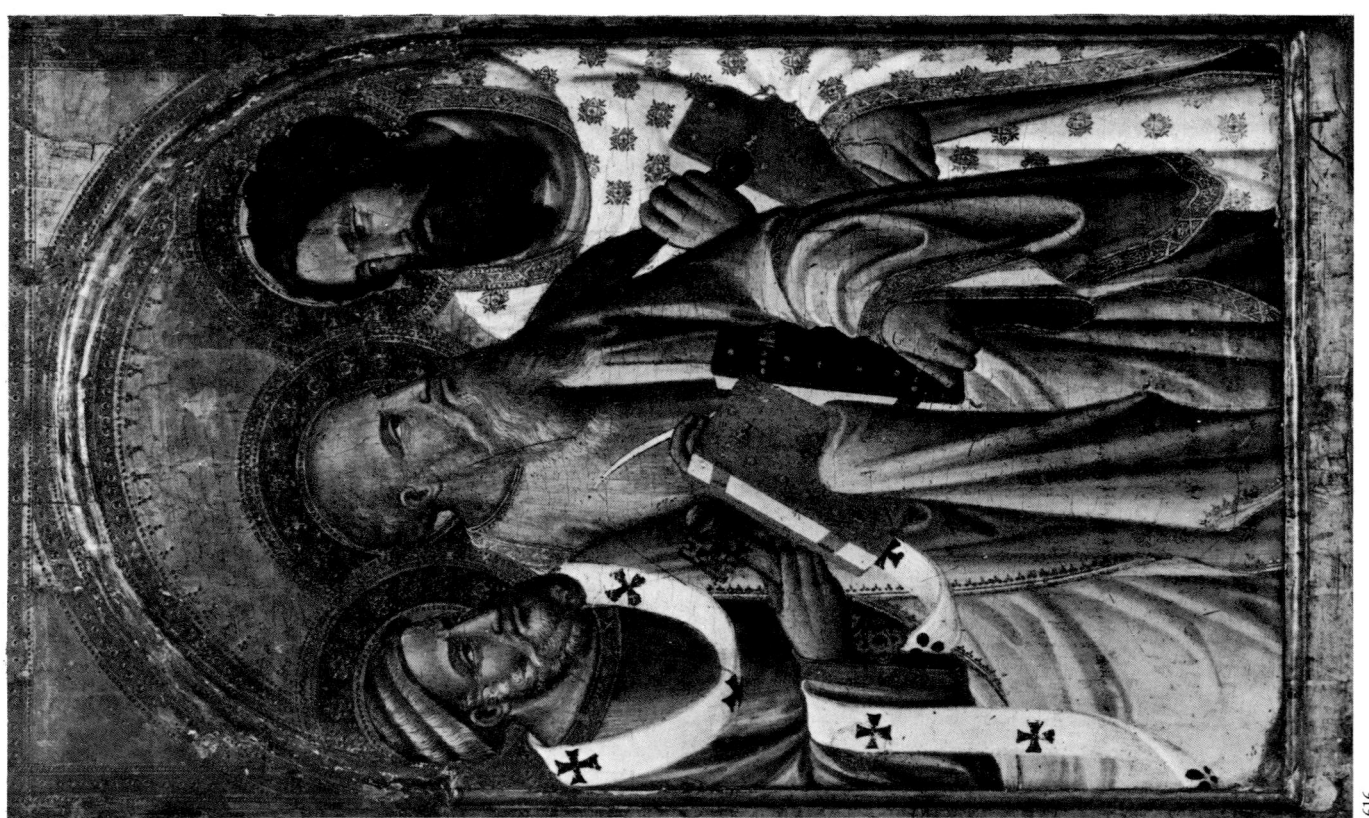

616. *Three Saints. Panel. Ottawa, National Gallery of Canada. no. 2024. 66 × 43. Museum photo.*
617. *Madonna and Child in Glory with six Saints and two music-making Angels. Below: Man of Sorrows. Panel. Florence, Museo Stibbert. no. 10294.*
    80 × 46. Brogi 22134.

MASTER OF THE STRAUS MADONNA

Although this painter (to be known here as the Master of the Straus *Madonna*) is all milk and roses, he lavishes these profanities on representations of a purely devotional character — almost without exception the *Madonna and Child* — for we have thus far found no episodic representation by him. His soft world of pouting women professes a remote Sienese ancestry, only that their Sienese forbears still remember the light of Paradise, while our master's figures have kept only the flavour of its forbidden fruit. But his wares have often grown over-ripe, and though often exquisitely insinuating, in general he is not sustained and occasionally lapses into a heavy bathos.....

The twenty-three works I attribute to him show him one of the prolific painters of his day, working chiefly under the influence of Agnolo Gaddi and of his cult of feminine refinement. But he has refashioned Agnolo's type, giving it a longish oval face, unprojecting thin nose, a narrow mouth and a dainty chin, which communicate to the face the appearance of budding maturity. The children are helpless little muslin dolls with tight woollen curls. The hair of the adults, of a stiffish fibre, rolls back from the temples diagonally down along the cheek in a heavy mass. The haloes and borders reveal a taste for rich patterning upon a ground punched with a tiny disk peculiar to him; but most commonly the halo has a twig circling within it with small sharp leaves springing symmetrically from it. He is fond of a rich all-over design of unmodelled affronted or averted birds and animals, as in the S. Giuseppe, Vatican, Berlin, and the Florentine Private Collection panels. The scalloped edging in the haloes and borders is especially characteristic.....

> from R. Offner, pp. 169-70, *The Burlington Magazine*, LXIII, 1933.

In his painting from Galiga [recently on temporary show in the Uffizi], the painter adds some personal elements to a style which is essentially Orcagnesque in its line and plasticity; he adds especially his own sense of colour.....

Out of this comes a composition which is essentially on the surface, the delicate modulation being one of colour values and of delicate comparisons, and one of drawn out flowing forms, prompted by quiet plastic sounds, which in the painting at Valcava, will become more intense, approaching once again Florentine forms. It is for this reason that we think the painting at Citille just previous to that at Valcava: the punches in the haloes of the two works are identical.....

> from U. Baldini, p. 60, *Bollettino d'Arte*, XXXVII, 4, 1962.

The master was first identified by Offner who accumulated twenty-three related paintings which he named after a Madonna then in the Straus collection, New York. This fragrant artist, whose masterpiece is an Annunciation in the Academy, Florence, worked chiefly under the influence of Agnolo Gaddi, emphasizing his cult of feminine refinement. All his pictures are of the Madonna and to quote Offner: " His soft world of pouting women professes a remote Sienese ancestry ".....

> from St. J. Gore, p. 9, *The Art of Painting in Florence & Siena from 1250-1500*, London, 1965.

Florentine School. Active late fourteenth and early fifteenth century. So called from a half-length " Madonna " formerly in the Percy S. Straus Collection (now in the Museum of Fine Arts, Houston), this master is identical with the one sometimes called the Master of the Innocenti (from his " Coronation " in the Gallery of the Innocenti, Florence) and Master of the Accademia Annunciation (from a painting in the Accademia, Florence). He was a follower of Agnolo Gaddi, with whose style he sought to combine the calligraphic elegance of Lorenzo Monaco, arriving at an effect comparable to that of the Master of the Bambino Vispo.....

> from F. R. Shapley, p. 41, *Paintings from the Samuel H. Kress Collection*, London, 1966.

The painter known as the Master of the Straus Madonna was an interesting figure of "late Gothic eclecticism". He may well be regarded as eclectic in style, for he drew on a most varied series of artistic sources. His direct master was probably Agnolo Gaddi, whose influence can be strongly felt in his work; but he was inspired none the less by the formal solutions of earlier masters, and his pictures display marks of the influence which the Florentine Daddi and also Simone Martini's circle exercised on his painting. His figures, elongated in proportions, are graceful of movement and often seem almost to float in his pictures; their relief effect is produced by fine tones which, at the same time, tend to stylize into smooth, mild surfaces the forms of human figures, and develops uniform, regular ripples in the folds of the draperies. His compositions are conservative and avoid, as far as possible, the emphatic suggestion of spatial depth.....

from M. Boskovits, no. 32, *Early Italian Panel Paintings*, Budapest, 1966.

BIBLIOGRAPHY
BOOKS

An asterisk indicates a work listed in the General Bibliography

Antal*, 1948, p. 334; *Galetti**, "F-O", 1950, p. 1468; Suida, W. E., *Catalogue of the Seattle Art Museum*, Seattle, 1952, p. 13; Suida, W. E., *Catalogue of the Seattle Art Museum*, Seattle, 1954, p. 24; Gore, St. J., *Wildenstein**, 1965, p. 9; Bellosi, L., *La Pittura Tardogotica in Toscana* (I Maestri del Colore, 239), Milan, 1966; *Shapley**, 1966, p. 41; Boskovits, M., *Early Italian Panel Paintings*, Budapest, 1966, no. 32; *Dutch Show**, 1974, pp. 22, 89-90; *Maetzke**, 1974, pp. 72-74.

JOURNALS

Longhi, R., *Pin*, I, 1928-29, p. 34; Berenson, B., *DD*, XI, 5, 1930-31, pp. 1286-1318; Berenson, B., *DD*, XII, 1, 1932, pp. 5-34; Offner, R., *BM*, LXIII, 1933, pp. 169-70; Procacci, U., *RA*, XV, 1933, pp. 224-44; Salvini, R., *RA*, XVI, 1934, pp. 205-28; Baldini, U., *BA*, XXXVII, 4, 1952, p. 60; Asano Fabbi, D., *RA*, XXXIV, 1959, pp. 109-122; Smith, M.Q., *BM*, CIV, 1962, pp. 62-6; Zeri, F., *BA*, XLVIII, 4, 1963, p. 247; Zeri, F., *BM*, CVII, 1965, p. 255; Bellosi, L., *PA*, XVI, 187/7, 1965, p. 38; Boskovits, M., *ZKG*, XXIX, 1, 1966, pp. 51-66; Conti, A., *PA*, XIX, 223/43, 1968, p. 17; (photograph), *BM*, CXI, 799, 1969, p. lviii; Huter, C., *AVN*, XXIV, 1970, p. 30; Boskovits, M., *AI*, III, 25/6, 1970, pp. 32-47; *Edit.*, *GBA*, LXXVII, 113, 1917, p. 60 (supplement), n. 280; Volpe, C., *MKIF*, XVII, 2-3, 1973, p. 358.

There are no known dated works by the Master of the Straus Madonna.

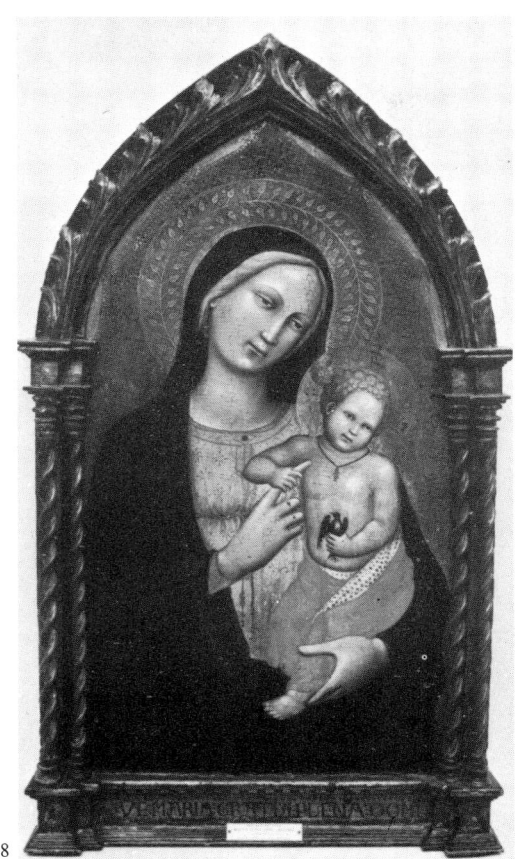

618

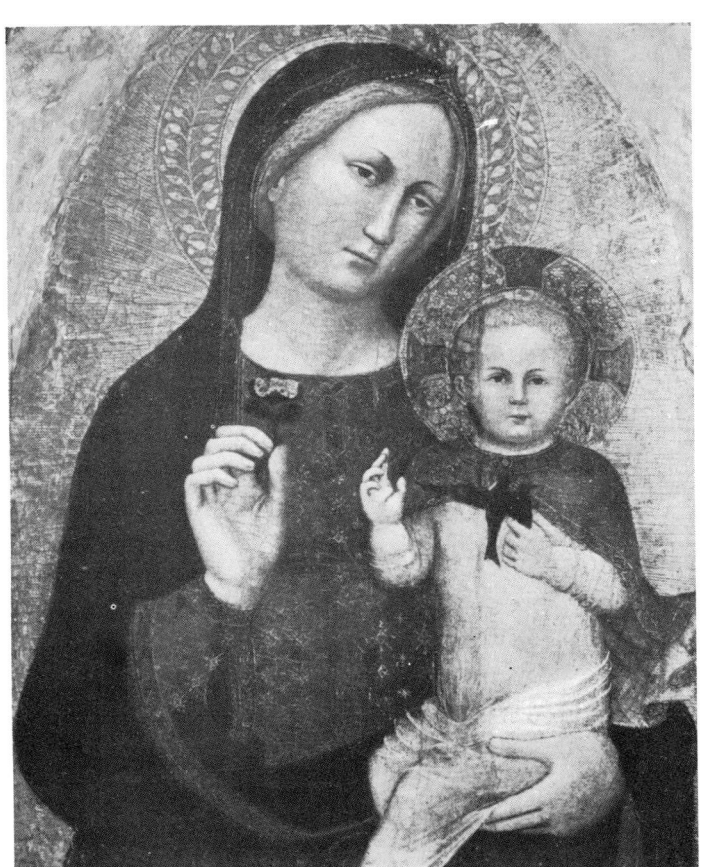

619

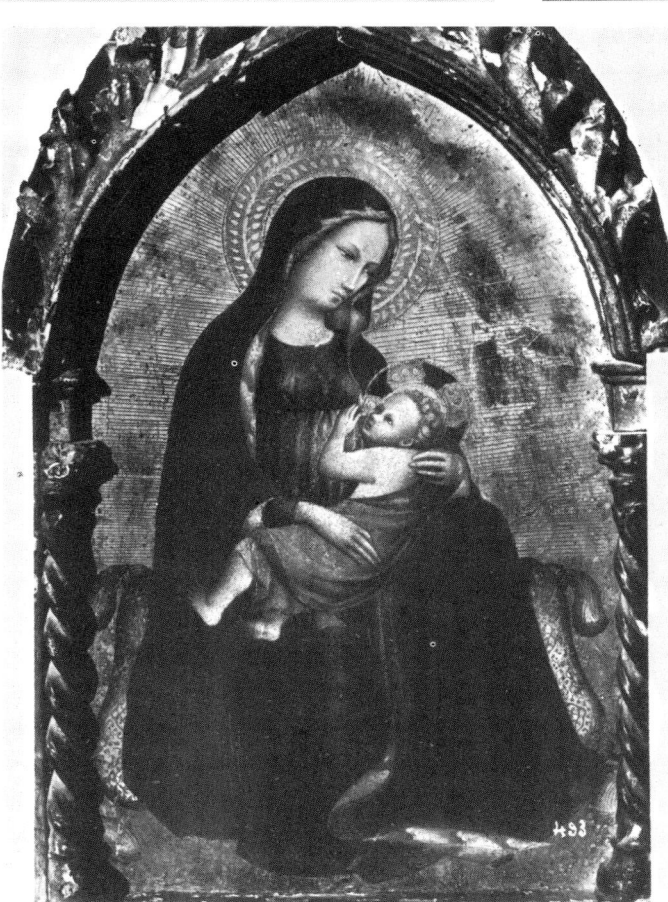

620

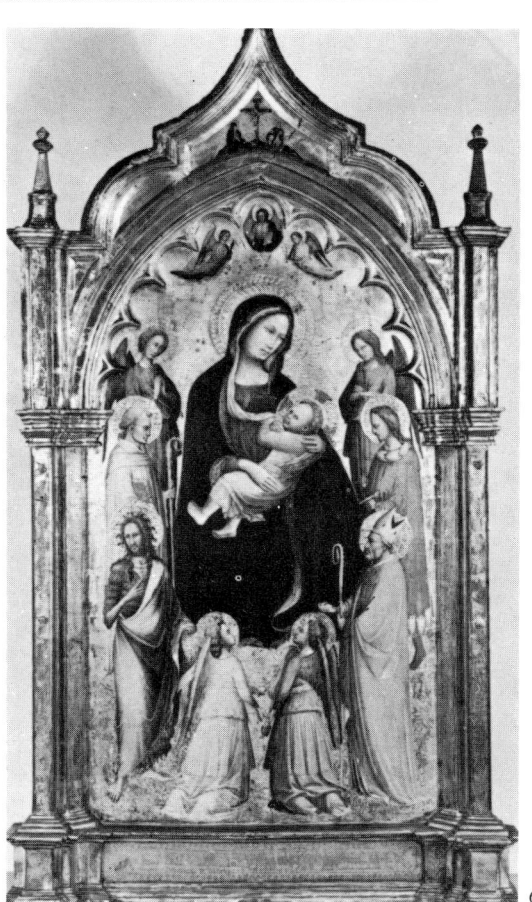

621

618. *Madonna and Child. Panel. Houston (Tex.), Museum of Fine Arts, Straus Collection. no. 44-565. 90.2 × 48.2. Museum photo: A. Mewbourn.*
619. *Madonna and Child. Panel. Whereabouts unknown. Fototeca Berenson.*
620. *Madonna of Humility. Panel. Florence, Museo Nazionale del Bargello, Carrand Collection. no. 2016C. 71 × 40. SGF 21043.*
621. *Madonna and Child with Sts Bernard, Julian, John the Baptist, Nicholas and four Angels. Above: Christ on the Cross with the Virgin and St John, Christ blessing, two Angels. Panel. Baltimore (Md.), Walters Art Gallery. no. 729. 130.3 × 73.3. Museum photo.*

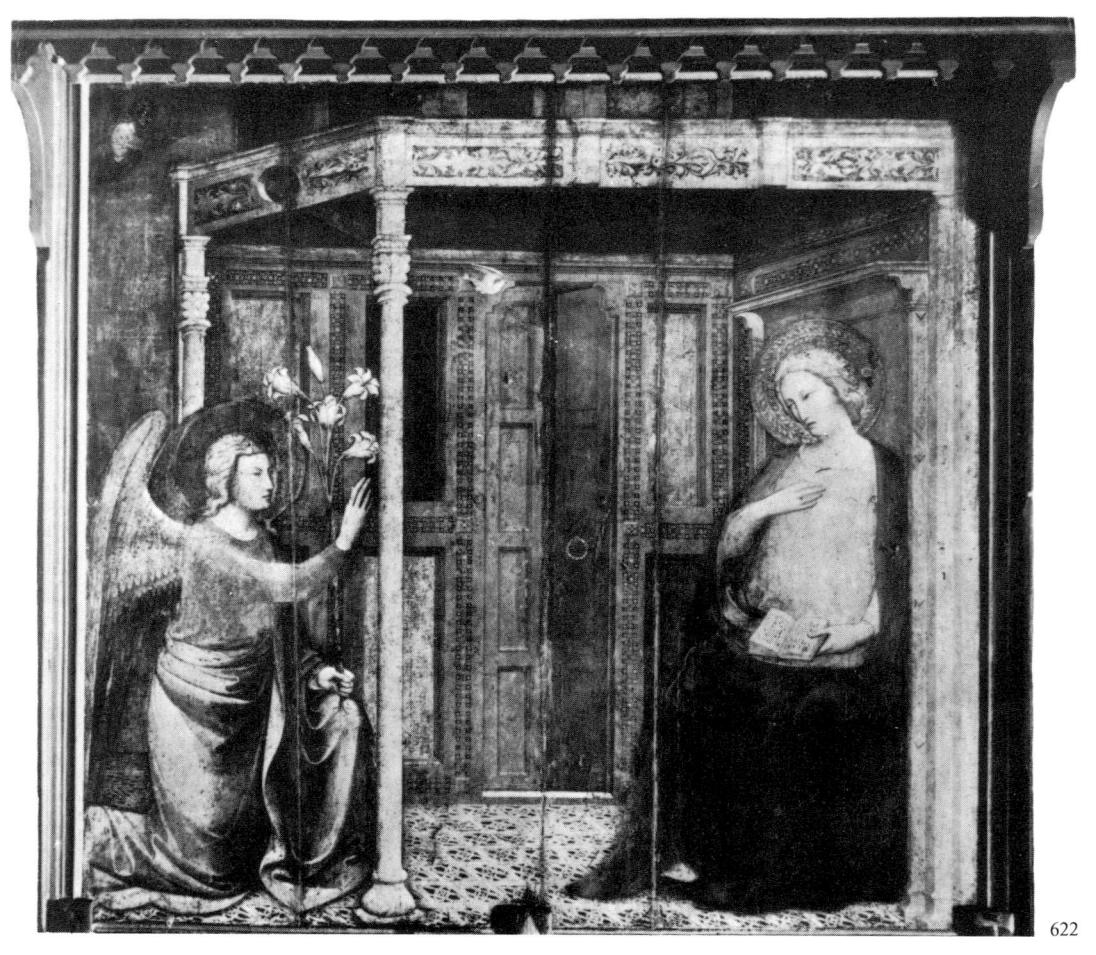

622

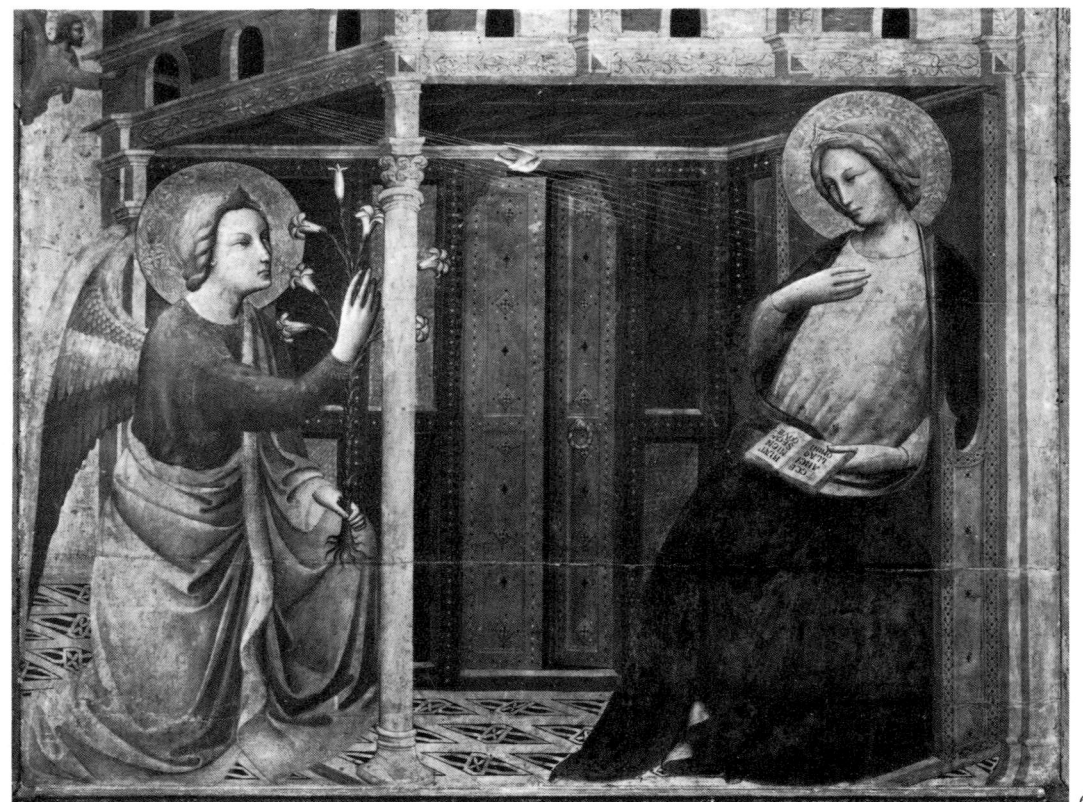

623

622. *Annunciation. Panel. Florence, Accademia. no. 3146. 210 × 220. Fototeca Berenson.*
623. *Annunciation. Panel. Sesto Fiorentino, S. Maria. 139 × 167. SGF 118723.*

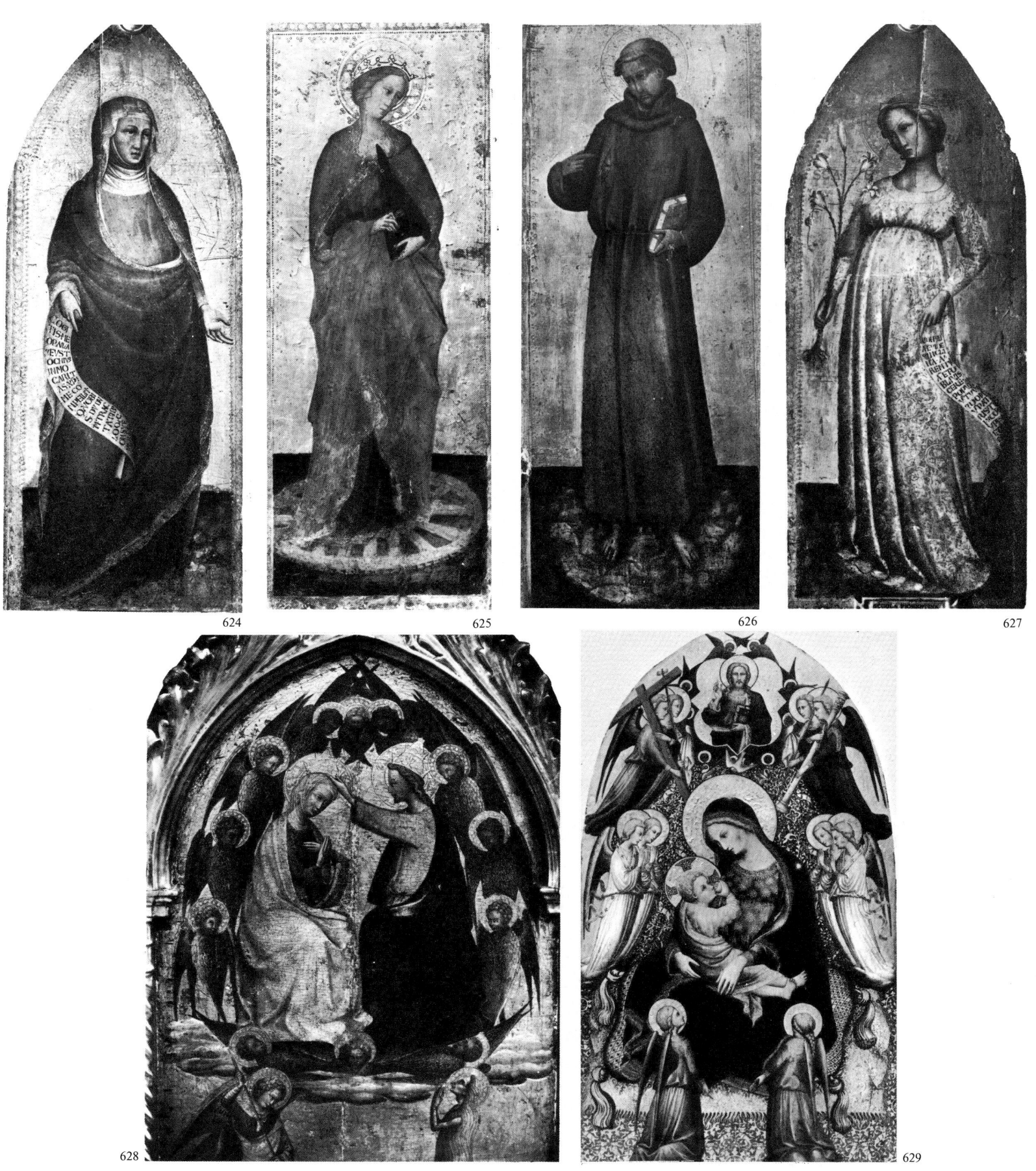

624. *St Paula. Panel. Rome, Vatican, Pinacoteca. 95 × 36. Alinari 38051.*
625. *St Catherine. Panel. Florence, Accademia. Alinari 49229.*
626. *St Francis. Panel. Florence, Accademia. Alinari 49229.*
627. *St Eustacia. Panel. Rome, Vatican, Pinacoteca. 95 × 36. Alinari 38052.*
628. *Detail: Coronation of the Virgin with Saints and Angels. Panel. Florence, Ospedale degli Innocenti. 128 × 68. SGF 21033.*
629. *Madonna of Humility nursing the Child, with six Angels. Above: Christ blessing and four Angels with symbols of the Passion. Panel. (destroyed 1945). Berlin, Bodestrasse, Staatliche Museen. no. 1118. 90 × 52. Museum photo.*

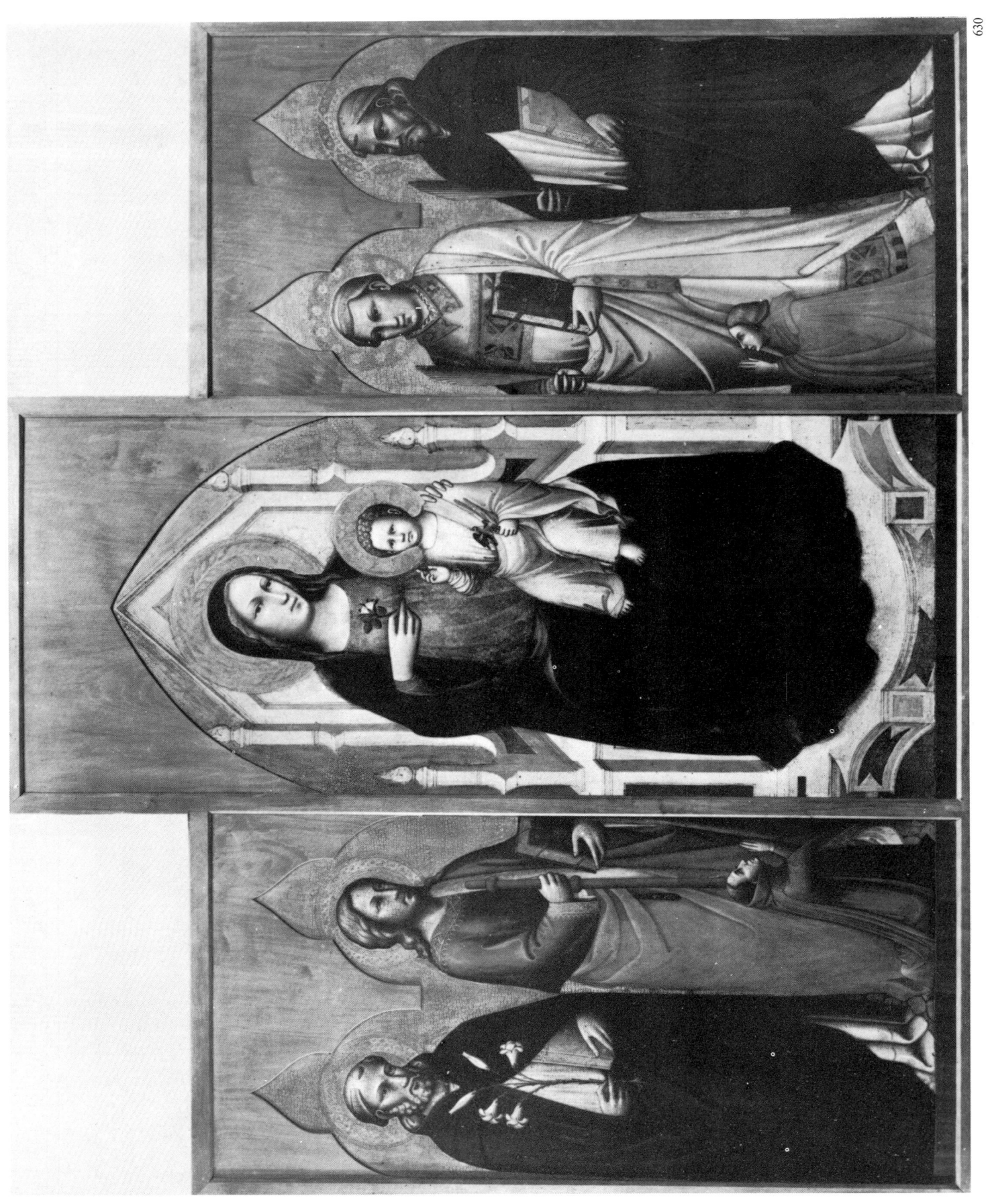

630. *Triptych: Madonna and Child Enthroned with four Saints and two Donors. Panel. Florence, Uffizi. 160 × 228. SGF 69696.*

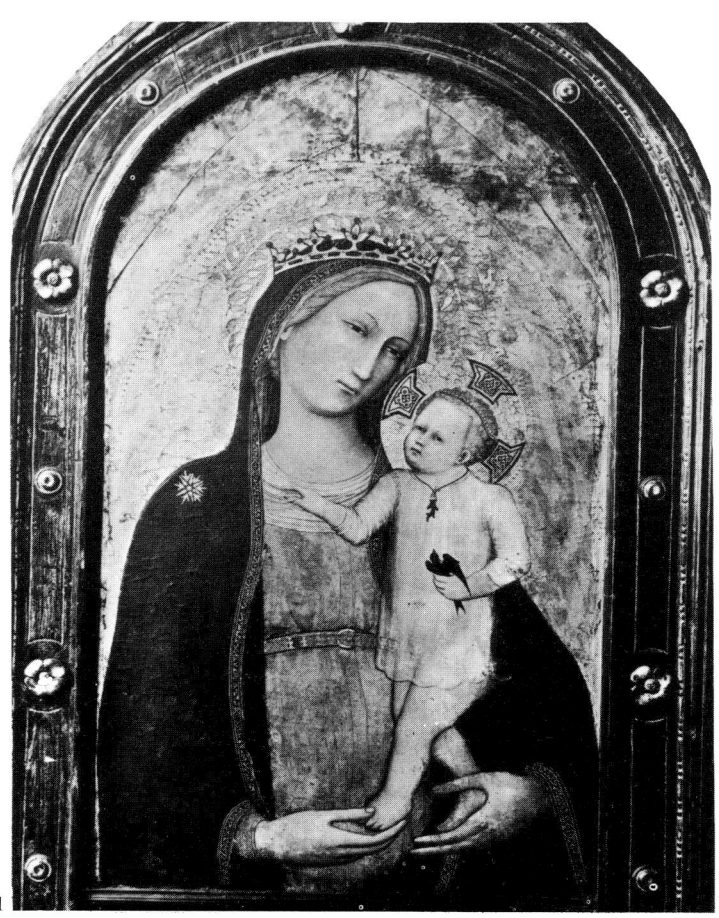

631

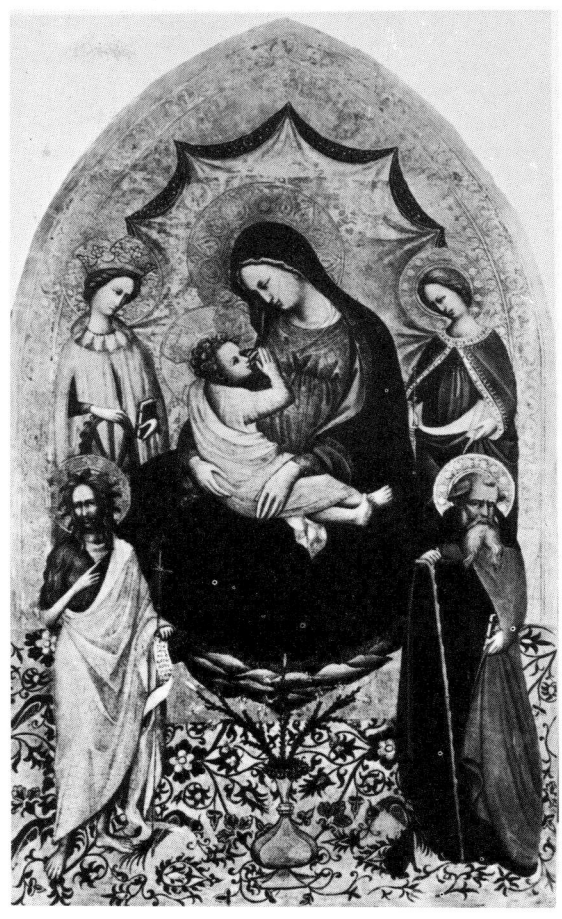

632

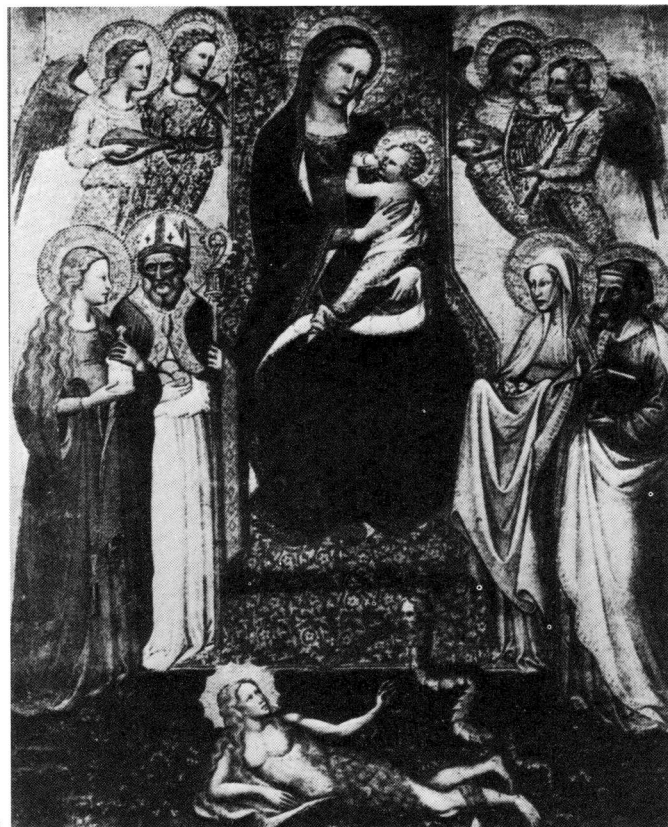

633

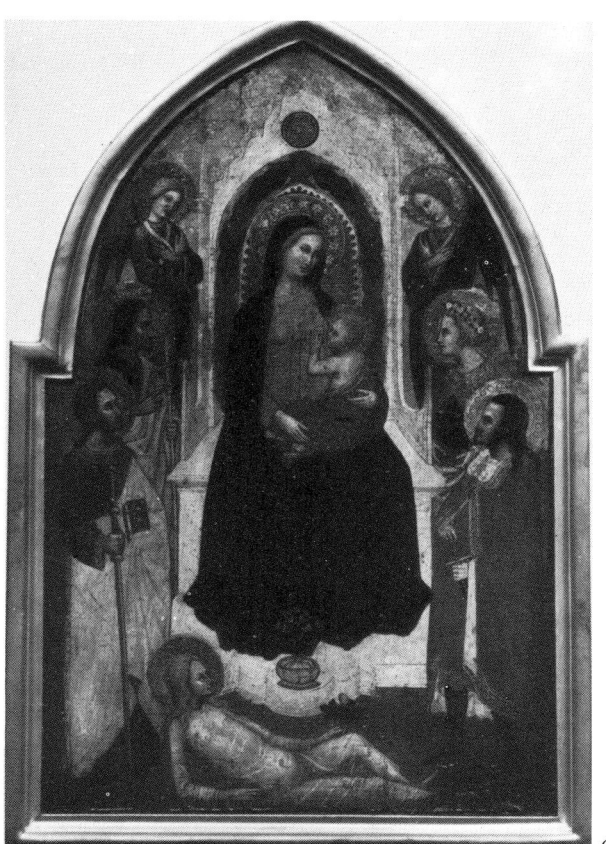

634

631. *Madonna and Child. Panel. Private Collection. 97 × 56. Courtauld photo.*
632. *Madonna nursing the Child with Sts John the Baptist, Catherine, Margaret, Anthony Abbot. Panel. Private Collection. Fototeca Berenson.*
633. *Madonna and Child Enthroned with four Saints and four Angels, and Eve. Panel. Paris, Musée du Louvre. Courtauld photo.*
634. *Madonna and Child Enthroned with two Angels, Sts James, John the Baptist, Dorothy and Eve. Panel. Stalybridge, Cheshire, Astley Cheetham Art Gallery.*
   no. 22. 67.5 × 43. Museum photo.

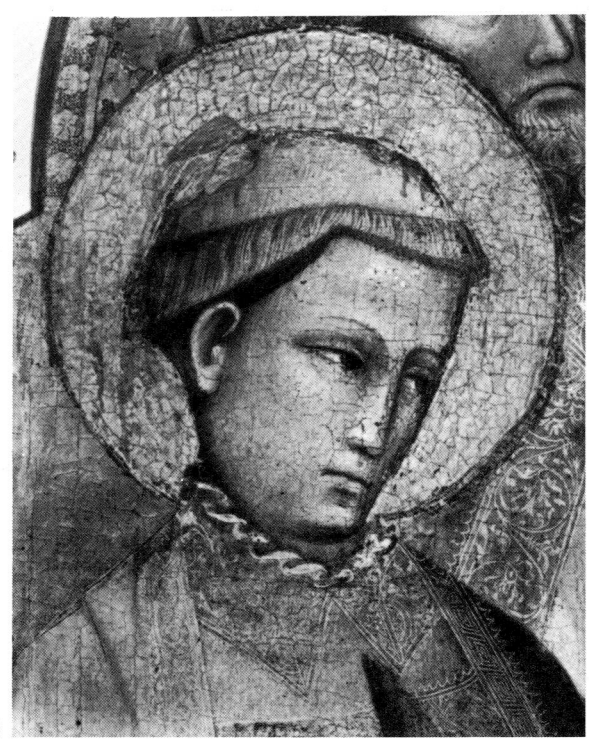

635

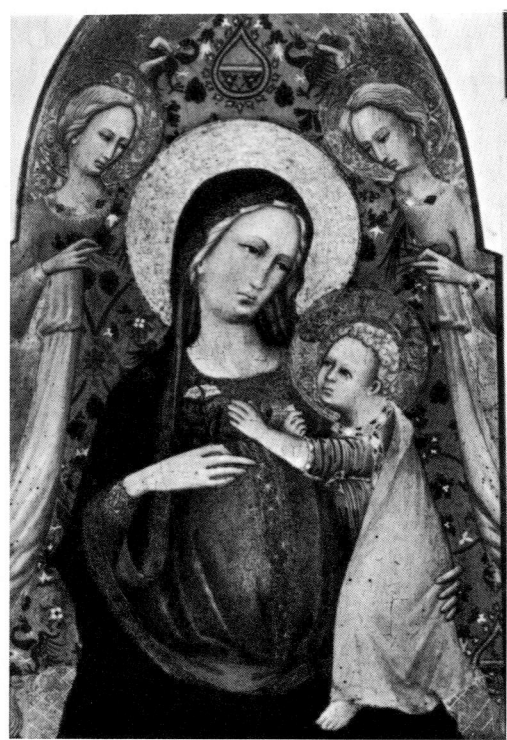

636

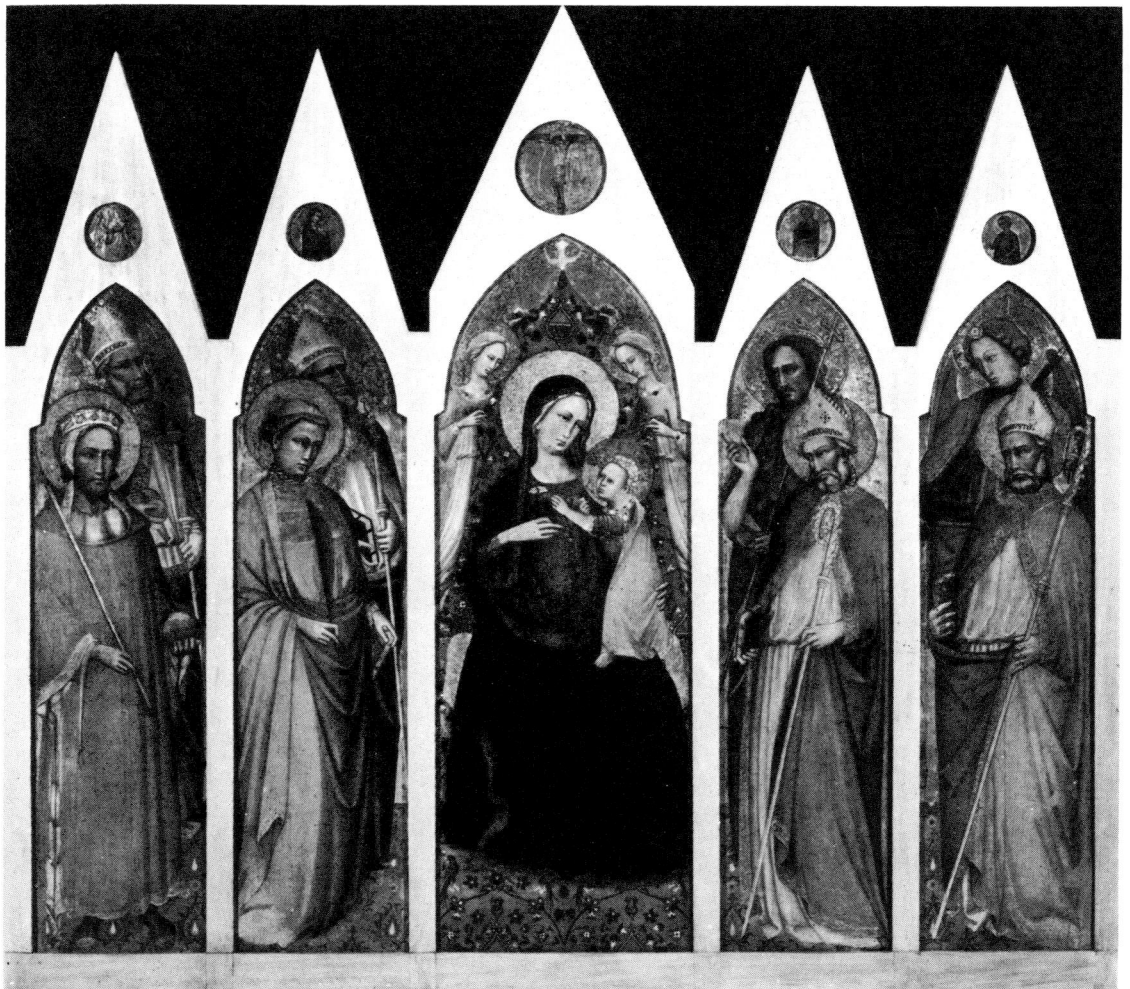

637

635, *Head of St Stephen, detail of fig. 637. Panel. Citille, S. Donato. SGF 68859.*
636. *Madonna and Child with two Angels, detail of fig. 637. Panel. Citille, S. Donato. SGF 68858.*
637. *Polyptych: Madonna and Child Enthroned with eight Saints and two Angels. Panel. Citille (Greve), S. Donato. 190 × 228. SGF 68574.*

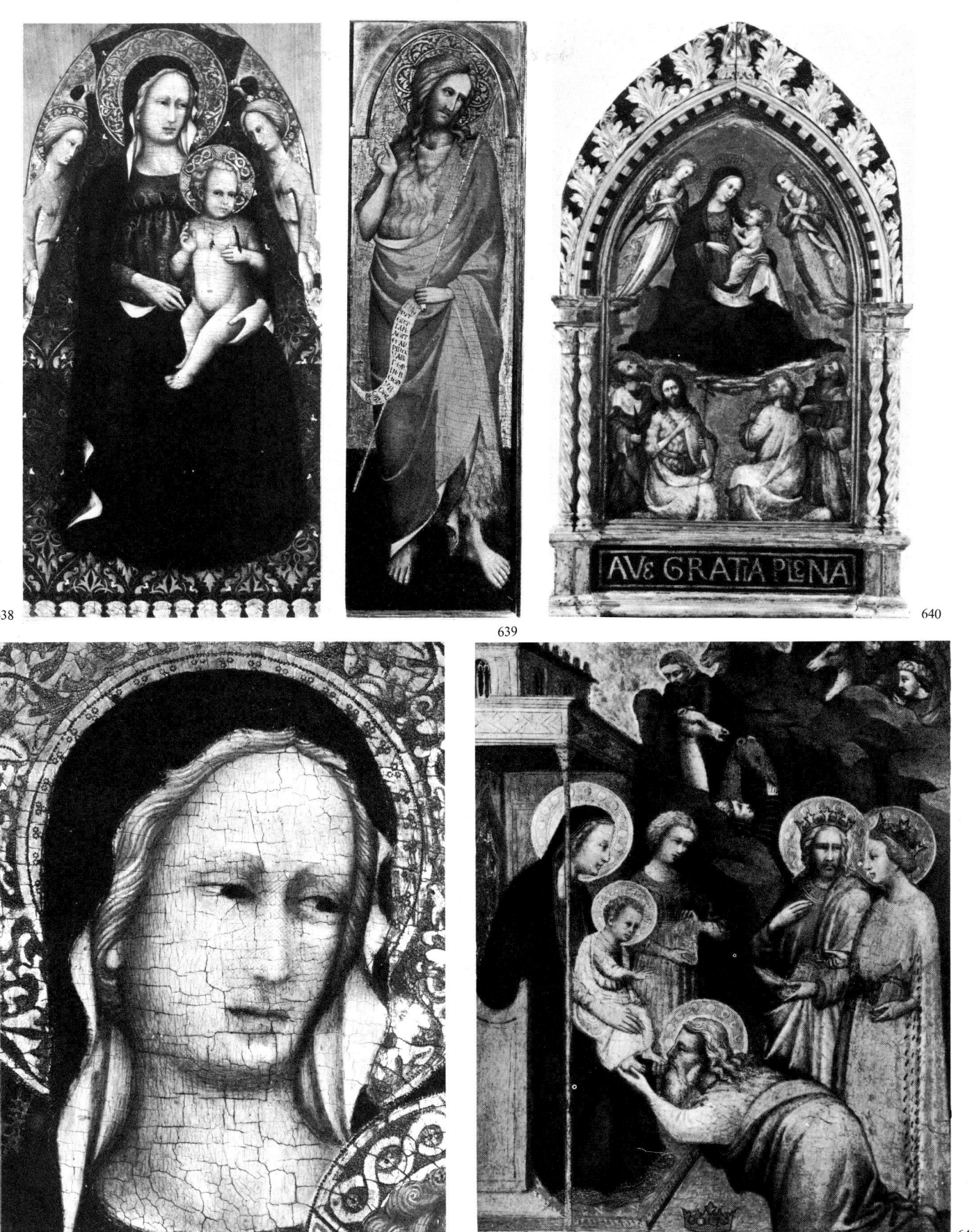

638. *Madonna of Humility with two Angels. Panel. San Cresci in Valcava, Pieve (4 kms south of Borgo San Lorenzo). 120 × 60. SGF 162820.*
639. *St John the Baptist. Panel. Christ Church, Oxford. no. 14. 99.2 × 26.8. Museum photo.*
640. *Madonna of Humility in Glory with Sts Bartholomew, John the Baptist, a male Saint and St Francis. Panel. Ontario, Art Gallery, Larkin Bequest 1961. 96.5 × 53.4. Photo Ron Vickers. no. 16778-9.*
641. *Head of the Virgin, detail of fig. 638. Panel. San Cresci in Valcava, Pieve. SGF 162822.*
642. *Adoration of the Magi. Panel. Seattle (Wash.), Art Museum, Samuel H. Kress Collection. no. K. 1546. 34.3 × 27. Kress Foundation photo.*

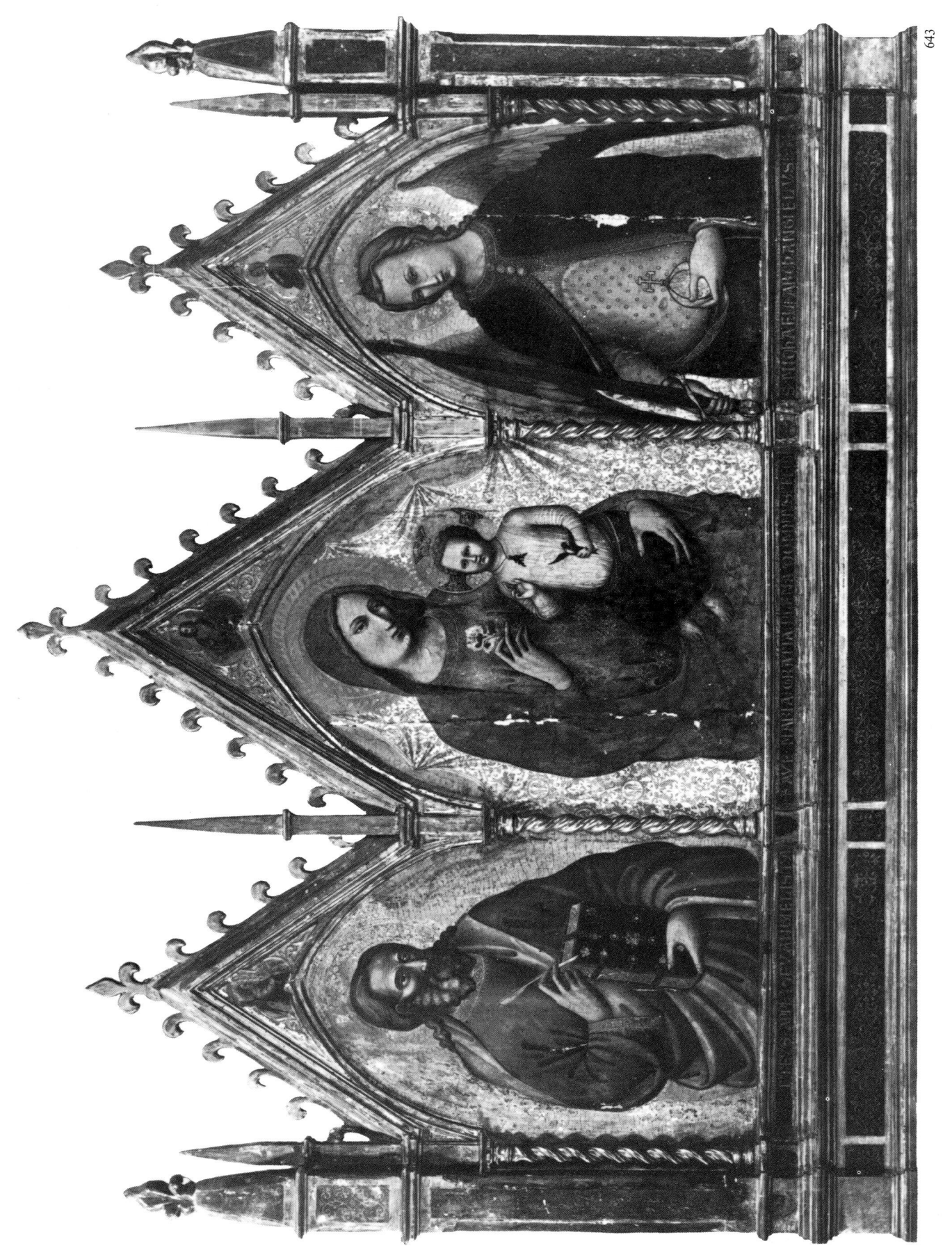

643. *Triptych: Madonna and Child, Sts Matthew and Michael the Archangel. Above: Christ blessing and Annunciation. Panel. Florence, S. Giuseppe.* 50.5 × 78. Brogi 22108.

NICCOLÒ di PIETRO GERINI

Niccolò di Pietro Gerini is probably the artist who contributed most to the persistence in the 15th century of the early Florentine manner of painting, because at the same time as he worked, for his period, in a very archaic manner, he was also exceedingly active and did not only produce a great quantity of works but also directed the training of many assistants and pupils. He thus helped to form a generation of artists who were to prolong the life of the Giottesque tradition contemporaneous with the activities of Masaccio.

A great number of dates connected with the life and works of Niccolò di Pietro are known to us. The earliest is 1368 when his name appears in the ledgers of the Corporation of Medici e Speziali...

In 1411 we find him again in Prato, this time decorating the façade of the Palazzo del Ceppo; in 1414, his name appears in the records of the Florentine painters' guild; in the same year " Niccolò di Piero dipintore " receives payment for the decoration of a chapel in Sta. Maria Nuova, while he must have died before February 1416, because at that time the balance of what was due for the execution of the altar-piece of Sta. Verdiana, Florence, is handed over to his heirs.

Niccolò di Pietro Gerini must have attained a great age. We have proof of this not only in the fact that forty-seven years separate the date when he is first mentioned (1368) from the year of his death (1415) but that in his earliest works we find obvious traces of his having studied under Taddeo Gaddi who died in 1366, and he followed a modified Giottesque tradition in the Madonna of 1372 in Sta. Croce.....

> from R. van Marle, pp. 611-13, *The Development of the Italian Schools of Painting*, Vol. III, The Hague, 1924.

Florentine School. Active from 1368; died 1415. Niccolò early collaborated with Jacopo di Cione but was influenced especially by Taddeo Gaddi, Orcagna, and Nardo di Cione. He later collaborated with his son, Lorenzo di Niccolò, and with Spinello Aretino. Through his many pupils, Niccolò helped prolong the Giottesque tradition to the time of Masaccio.

> from F. R. Shapley, p. 42, *Paintings from the Samuel H. Kress Collection*, London, 1966.

Active ca. 1368-1415. Follower of the Gaddi and Orcagna traditions.

> from B. Berenson, p. 158, *Italian Pictures of the Renaissance, Florentine School*, Vol. I, London, 1963.

This minor and conservative Florentine artist was a prolific painter with a large workshop. He is generally said to have been a pupil of Taddeo Gaddi, but the Orcagna tradition is more relevant to his style, and he has been associated with the " Niccolaio " who collaborated in the early 1370's with Jacopo di Cione (brother of Andrea and Nardo, who had probably inherited their practices). He worked in Pisa and Prato...

> from St. J. Gore, p. 16, *The Art of Painting in Florence & Siena from 1250-1500*, London, 1965.

As did all painters in Florence, Niccolò joined the Guild of Physicians and Apothecaries; he did so in 1368, and in 1370 he executed his first important work with the help of Jacopo di Cione: the polyptych of the Church of S. Pierino in Florence, now in the National Gallery of London. We also know that he collaborated (in 1386) with Ambrogio di Baldese in the external decoration of the Confraternity of the Bigallo, between 1390 and 95 he worked off and on in Prato with Agnolo Gaddi for Francesco Datini while the former was painting the story of the sacred girdle in the Duomo at Prato.....

Niccolò Gerini was a highly valued and very active artist in the last quarter of the 14th century and played the important role of being the last to support the Giottesque tradition. He did so until the beginning of the Renaissance, through his characters of monumental dignity. Although Niccolò's role was played in a rather academic manner, this impression is due more to the external form than to the spiritual content of his painting. His attitude is revealed in a letter which he wrote to Datini praising a Crucifix which he himself had painted for the latter, in which he says that it is " painted so well that even if Giotto had painted it, it couldn't have been done better ". He also revealed himself as a worthy disciple of Taddeo Gaddi. He continued this painter's tradition, even if he was also under the rigidly academic Orcagnesque influence of his collaborator, Jacopo di Cione, as may be seen in the London polyptych.....

from G. Marchini, p. 31, *Due Secoli di Pittura Murale*, Prato, 1969.

BIBLIOGRAPHY

BOOKS

An asterisk indicates a work listed in the General Bibliography

Pini, Milanesi*, 1876, no 8; D'Achiardi, P., *Guida della Pinacoteca Vaticana*, Rome, 1913, pp. 12-3, 27; *Khv & Salmi*, 1914, pp. 55-7; Sirén, O., *T-Becker**, 1920, XIII, pp. 465-7; *v. Marle, 1924**, pp. 611-27; *Offner, Studies**, 1927, pp. 83-95; *Offner, 1927**, pp. 3, 18, 20, 83-106; *v. Marle, 1927**, pp. 611-13; *Toesca, 1929**, p. 66; Ciaranfi, A. M., *Treccani, Vol. XVI**, 1932, pp. 665-6; *Berenson, 1932**, pp. 394-96; Longstreet, G. W., *General Catalogue: The Isabella Stewart Gardner Museum, Fenway Court*, Boston, 1935, p. 95; *Paatz**, 1940, I, p. 28; *Coletti Vol. II**, 1946, p. 54; *Antal**, 1948, pp. 210-2, 328-9; *Oertel, 1950**, p. 43; *Galetti**, 1950, " F-O ", p. 1066; *Toesca 1951**, p. 46; Suida, W. E., *Catalogue of the Birmingham Museum of Art*, Birmingham, (Ala.), 1952, pp. 24-5; Suida, W. E., *Catalogue of the Denver Art Museum*, Denver, (Colo.), 1954, pp. 14-5; Suida, W. E., *Catalogue of the Birmingham Museum of Art*, Birmingham, (Ala.), 1959, pp. 22-4; *Gregori**, 1960, pp. 7-8; *Cracow**, 1961, pp. 46-47; *Oertel, 1961**, pp. 128-9; *Berenson, 1963**, Vol. I, pp. 158-61; *Marcucci**, 1965, pp. 64-5, 106-15; Gore, St J., *Wildenstein**, 1965, p. 16; *Shapley, 1966**, pp. 42-4; Procacci, U., *AIE, 1966**, p. 304; Steinweg, K., pp. 52-9, in Kosegarten, A., *Festschrift Ulrich Middeldorf*, Berlin, 1968; Prato, 1969, p. 31; *Dutch Show**, 1974, p. 94.

JOURNALS

Sirén, O., *A*, VII, 1904, pp. 338-9; Poggi, G., *RA*, III, 1905, pp. 126-8; Sirén, O., *RADA*, VI, 5, 1906, pp. 81-7; Supino, I. B., *RA*, V, 1907, pp. 134-8; Bernardini, G., *RA*, IX, 6, 1909, pp. 89-94; Sirén, O., *AA*, IV, 1916, pp. 221-2; Offner, R., *AA*, IX, 1921, pp. 148-55, 233-40; Borenius, T., *BM*, XLI, 1922, pp. 156-8; Lavagnino, E., *BA*, IX, 1, 1929, pp. 39-44; Piattoli, R., *RA*, XI, 1929, pp. 221-53, 396-437, 537-8; Piattoli, R., *RA*, XII, 1930, pp. 97-150; Berenson, B., *DD*, XII, 1, 1932, pp. 5-34; Offner, R., *BM*, LXIII, 1933, pp. 166-9; Procacci, U., *RA*, XV, 1933, pp. 224-44; Marchini, G., *RA*, XX, 1938, pp. 215-41; Salmi, M., *C*, II, 3-4, 1951, pp. 169-81; Cohn, W., *BA*, XLI, 1956, pp. 174, 176; Cohn, W., *RA*, XXXI, 1956, pp. 66-67; *Edit.*, *BM*, CI, supp. 1, 1959; Boskovits, N., *BHA*, 21, 1962, pp. 21-30; Kiel, H., *P*, XXII, 5, 1964, p. 351; Muraro, M., *RA*, XXX, 1965, pp. 167-82; Cole, B., *MKIF*, XIII, 1-2, 1967, pp. 61-82; Bellosi, L., *RA*, XVII, 201, 1966, p. 78; Boskovits, M., *MKIF*, 1-4, 1967-1968, pp. 42-3; Boskovits, M., *ZKG*, XXXI, 4, 1968, p. 276; Zeri, F., *GBA*, LXXI, 6, 1968, p. 71; Boskovits, M., *AI*, III, 25/6, 1970, p. 44, note 25; Corti, G., *C*, XXII, 1, 1971, pp.84, 91; Bellosi, L., *MKIF*, XVII, 2-3, 1973, pp. 183-94; Bisogni, F., *MKIF*, XVII, 2-3, 1973, pp. 195-200; Boskovits, M., *MKIF*, XVII, 2-3, 1973, p. 219, note 46; Fehm, S., *MKIF*, XVII, 2-3, 1973, p. 258.

DATED WORK

1409 (Florentine Style: January 1408) Rovezzano, Sant'Andrea. Fresco: Madonna & Child with Saints. d. (fig. 647).

There are no known signed works by Niccolò di Pietro Gerini.

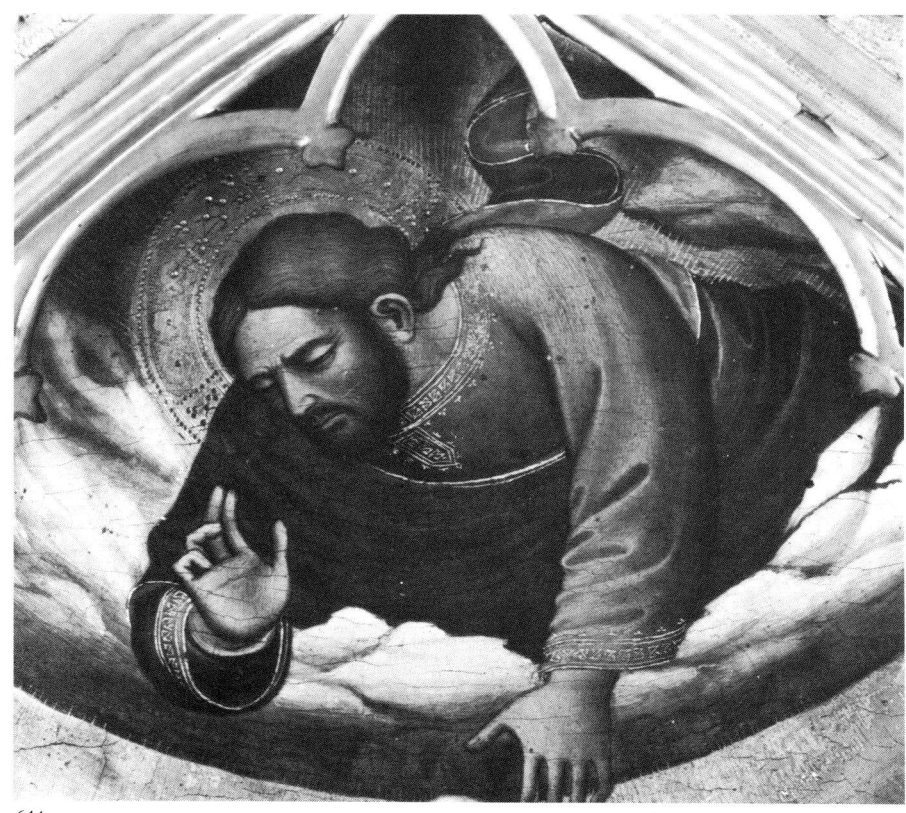

644

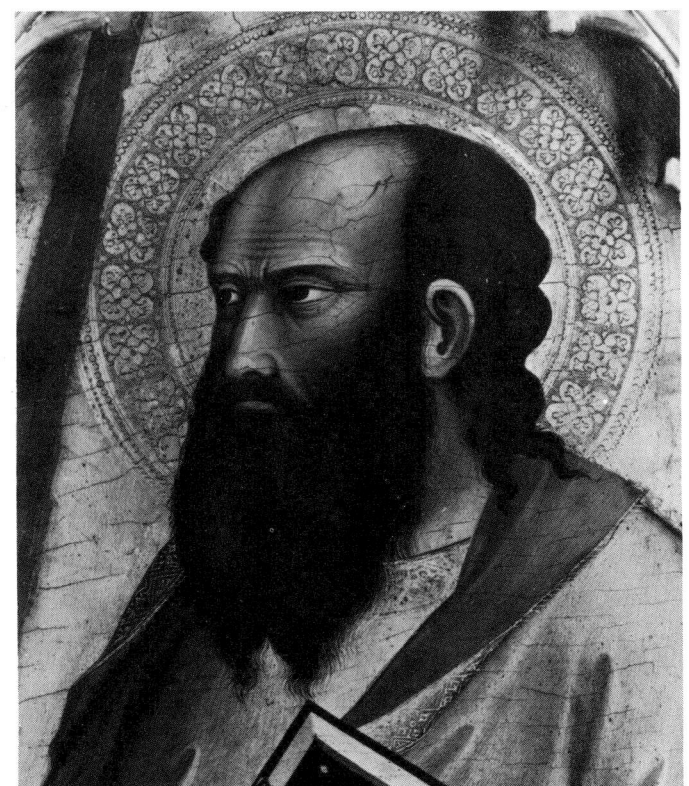

645

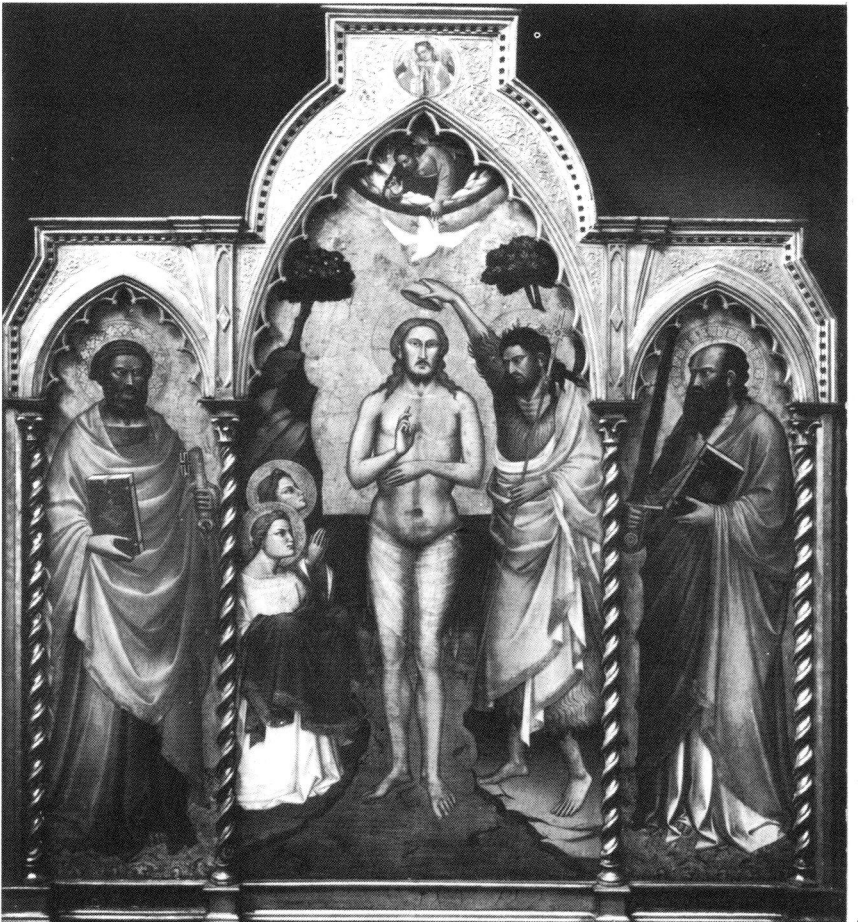

646

644. *God the Father, detail of fig. 646. Panel. London. National Gallery. no. 579. Museum photo.*
645. *St Paul, detail of fig. 646. Panel. London, National Gallery. no. 579. Museum photo.*
646. *Triptych: Baptism of Christ, with Sts Peter and Paul. Above: God the Father and the Holy Spirit. Panel. London, National Gallery. no. 579.*
  cp: 190.5 × 171.4. Museum photo.

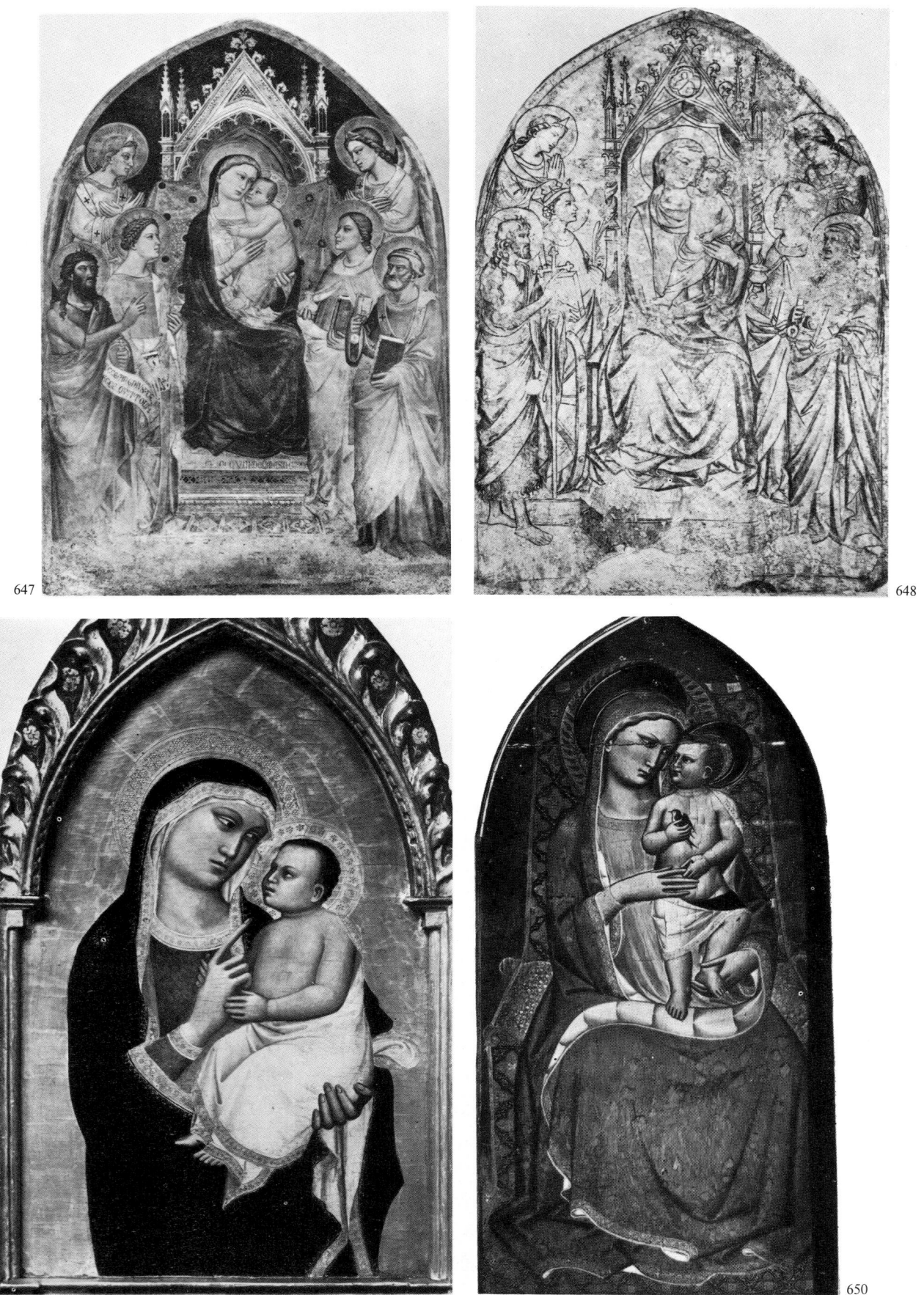

647. *Tabernacle: Madonna and Child Enthroned with Sts John the Baptist, Catherine, Lucy and Peter, and two Angels. Fresco. Rovezzäno (6 kms east of Florence), S. Andrea. SGF 110713. d. 1408.*

648. *Madonna and Child Enthroned with Sts John the Baptist, Catherine, Lucy, Peter, and two Angels. Sinopia. Rovezzano, S. Andrea. SGF 110714 (see fig. 647).*

649. *Madonna and Child. Panel. Careggi (3 kms north of Florence), Nuovo Convento delle Oblate. no. 128. 106 × 59. Alinari.*

650. *Madonna and Child Enthroned. Panel. Vincigliata (near Settignano, 6 kms east of Florence), S. Lorenzo. 116 × 55. Brogi 22221.*

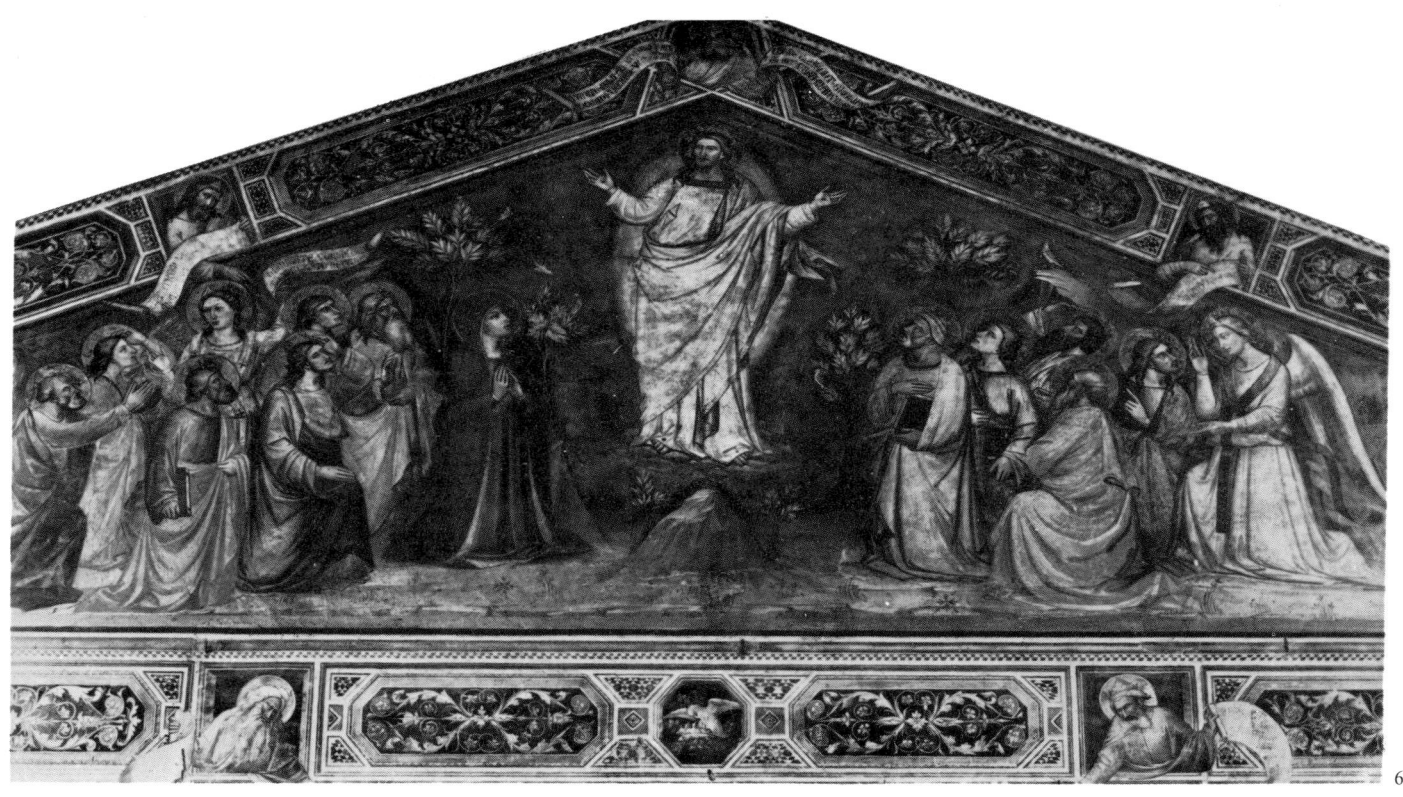

651

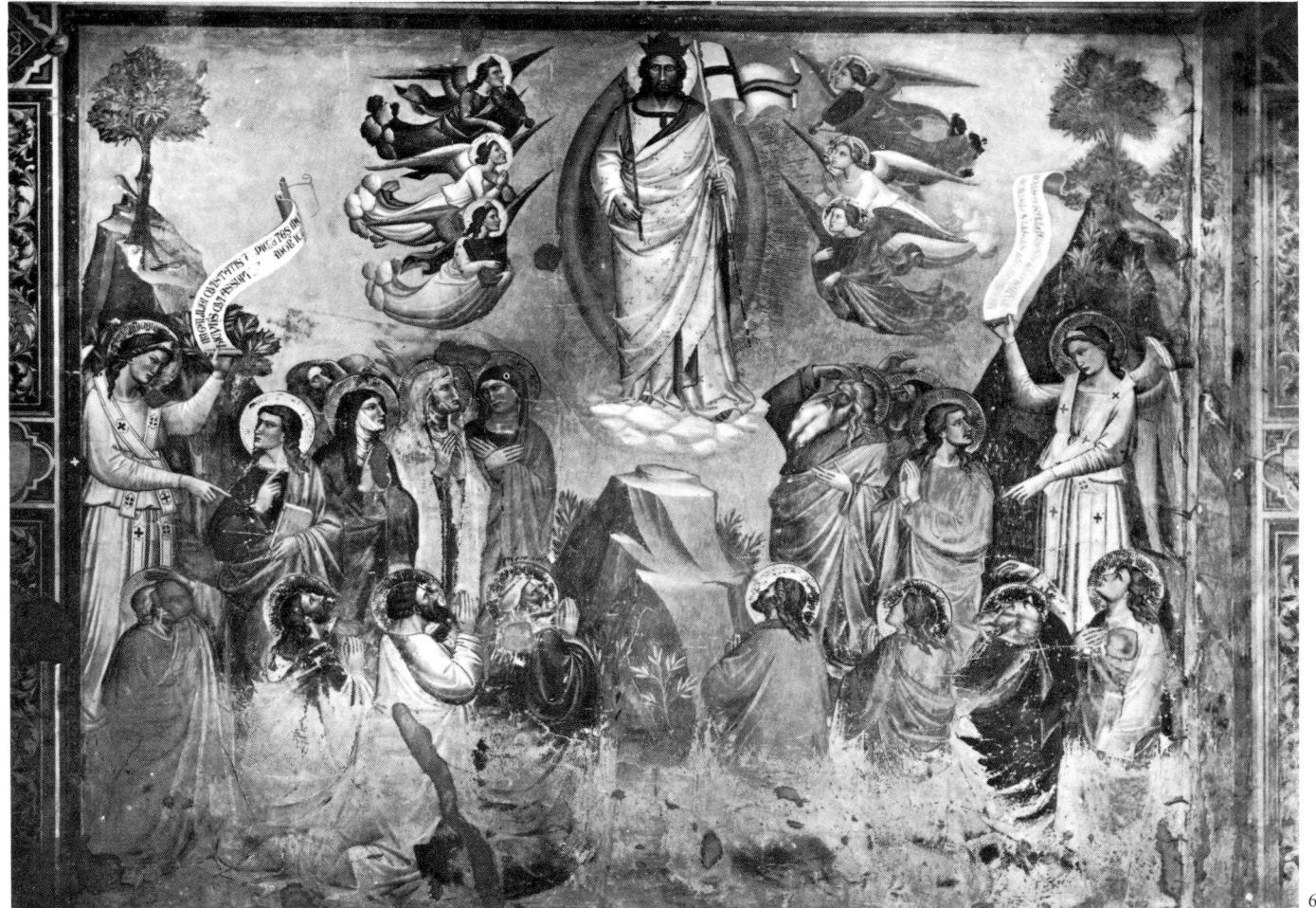

652

651. *Ascension. Fresco. Florence, S. Croce, Sacristy. Alinari 3915.*
652. *Ascension. Fresco. Pisa, S. Francesco, Chapter Room. Alinari 8865.*

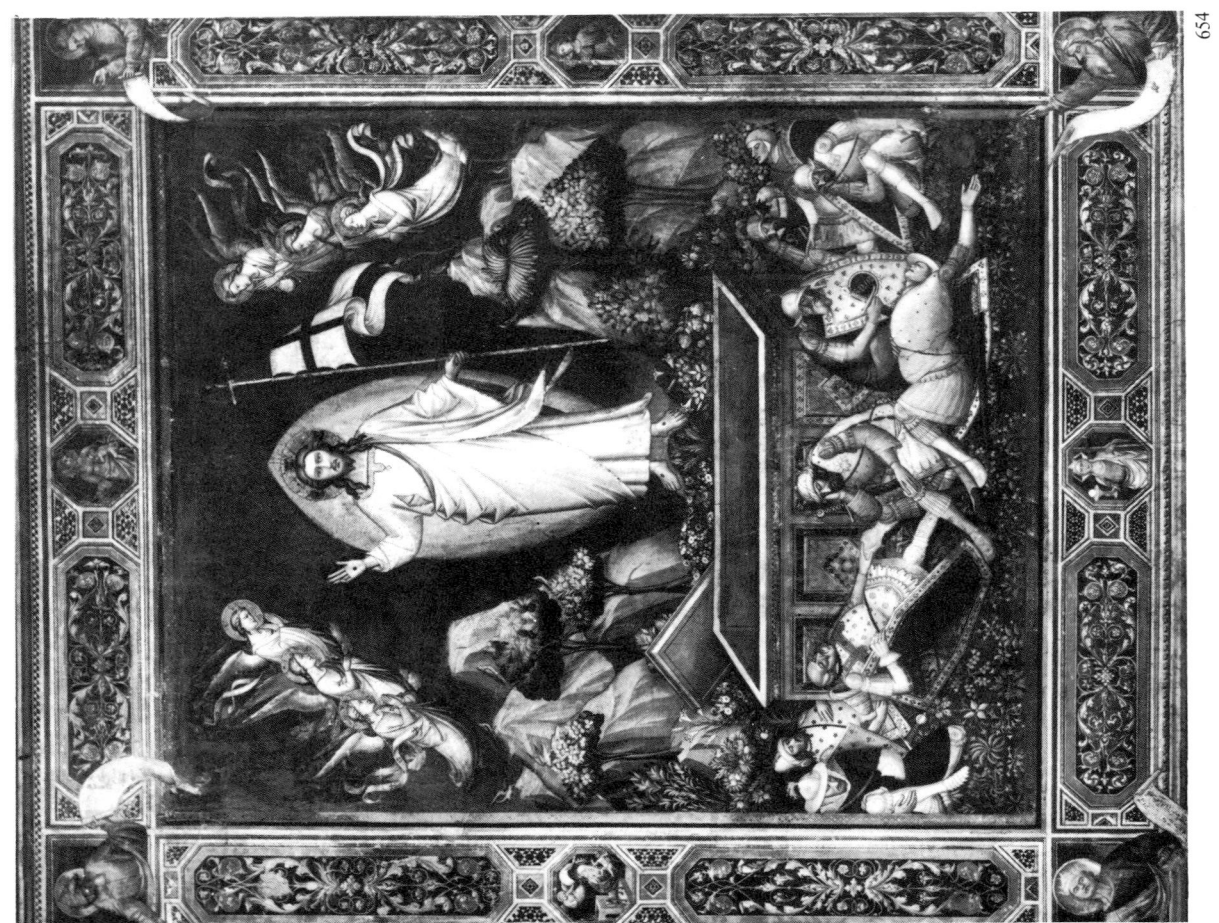

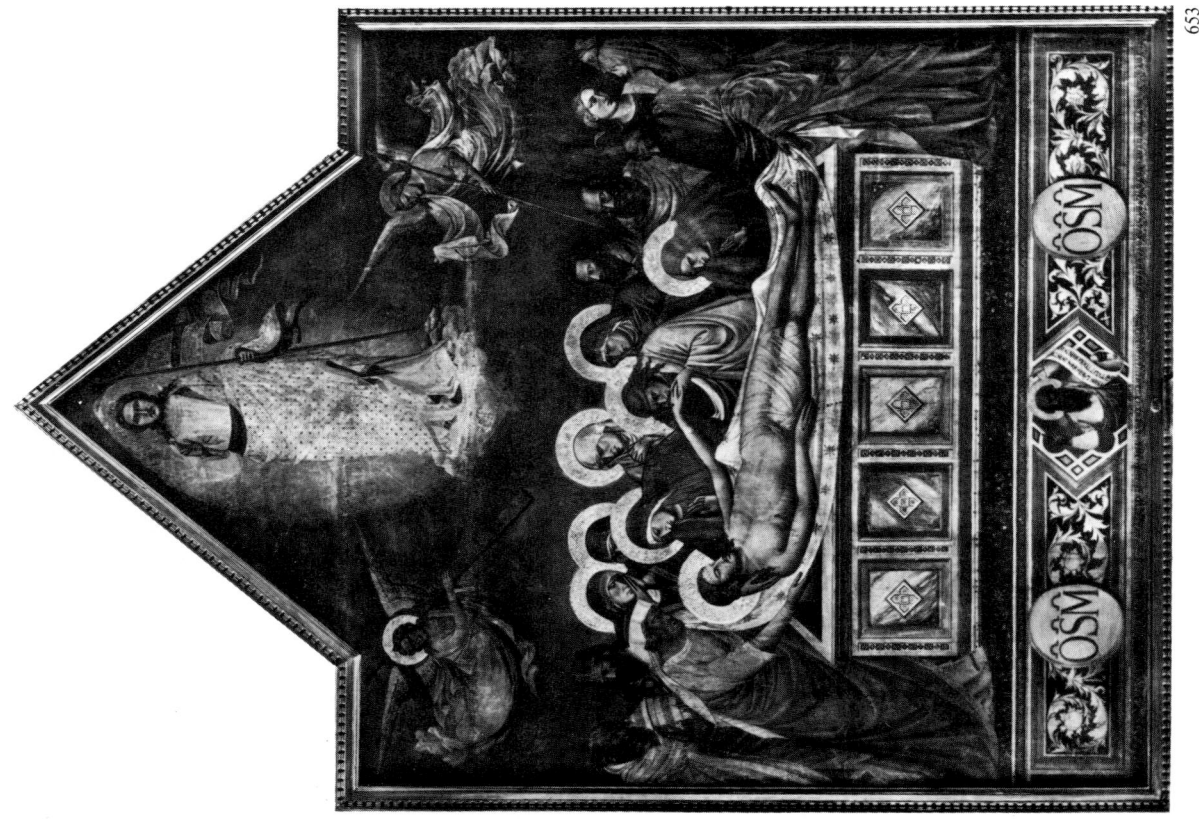

653. *Entombment and Ascension. Panel. Florence, Accademia (presently in S. Carlo dei Lombardi). no. 8469. 395 × 286. Brogi 2400.*
654. *Resurrection. Fresco. Florence, S. Croce, Sacristy. Alinari 3914.*

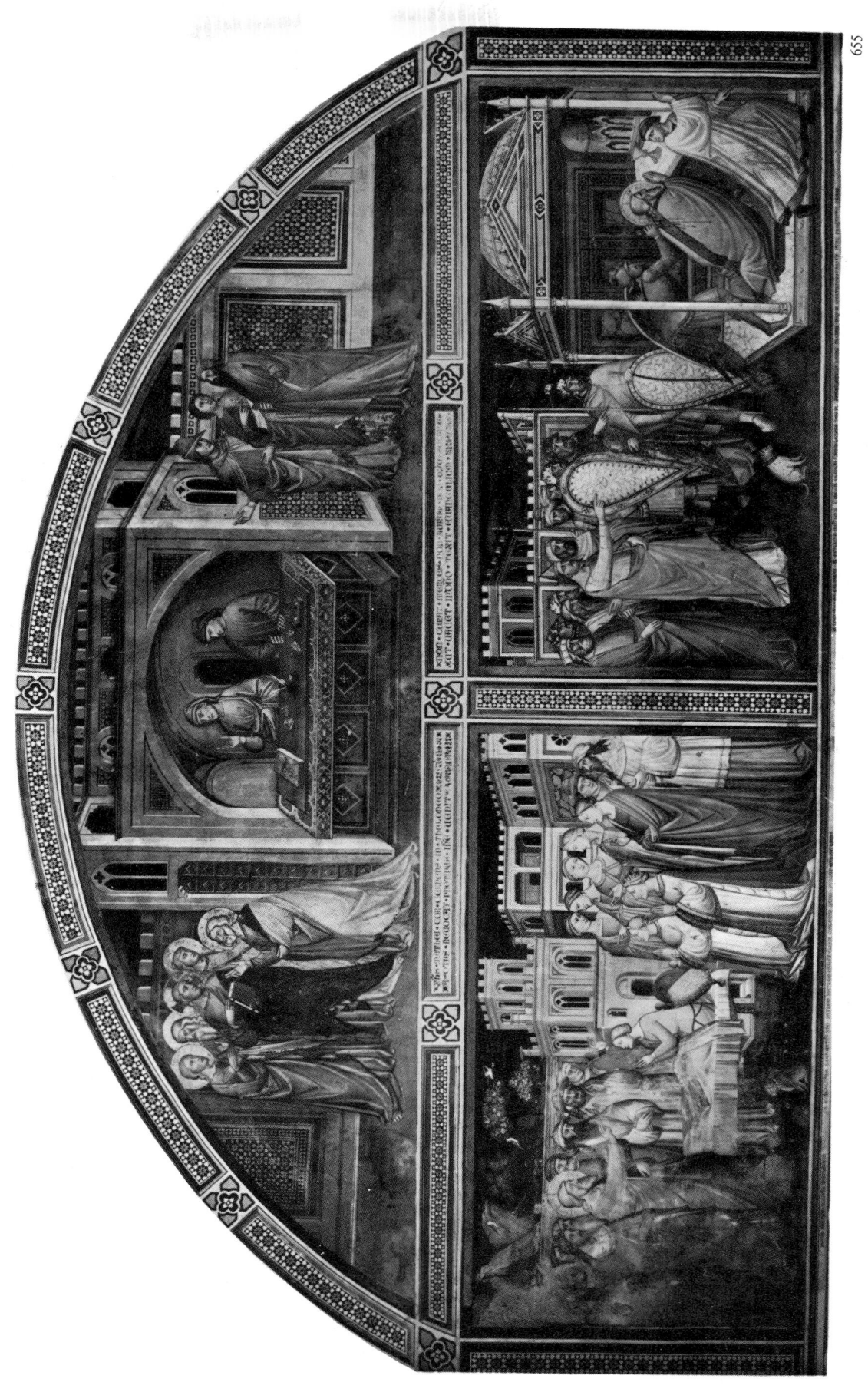

655. *Calling of St Matthew; St Matthew raises the King's son from the dead; Martyrdom of St Matthew. Fresco. Prato, S. Francesco, Chapter Room. SGF 109019.*

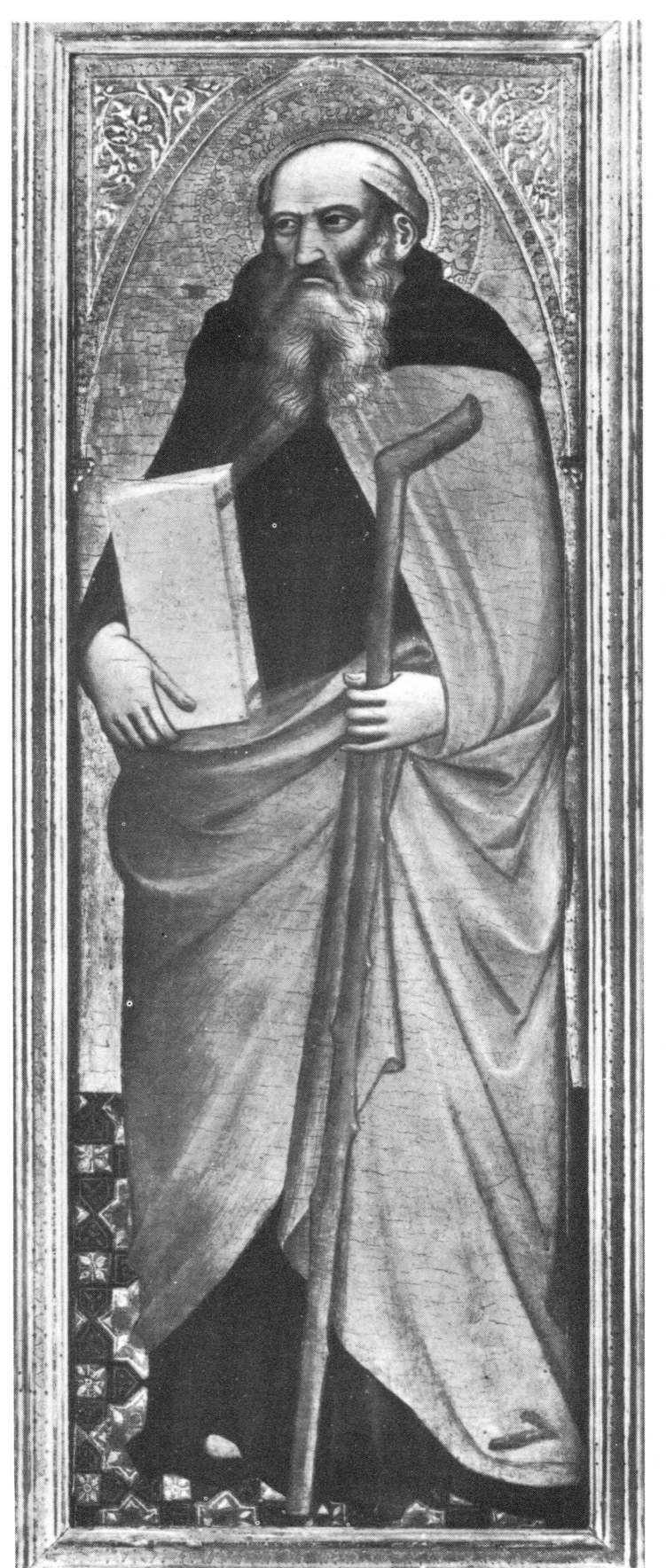

656

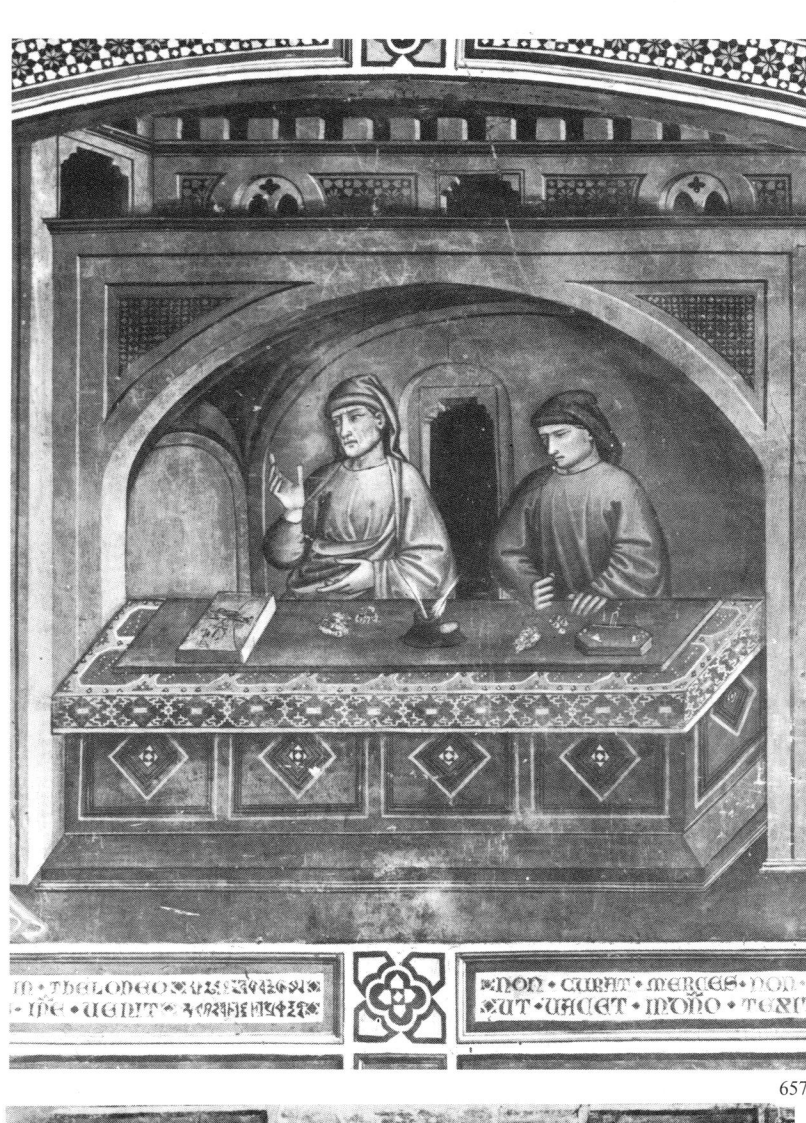

657

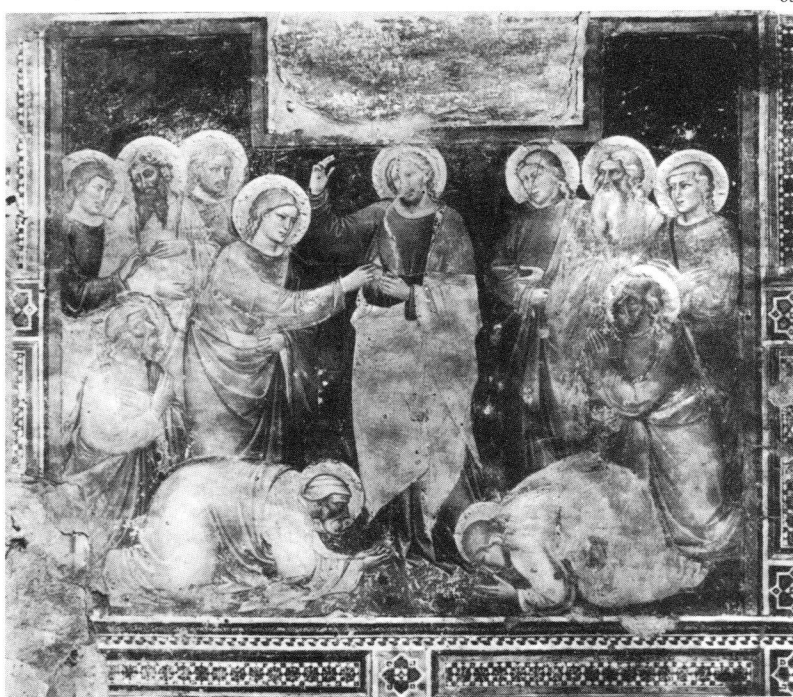

658

656. *St Anthony Abbot. Panel. Florence, Acton Collection. 97 × 33. Reali.*
657. *St Matthew's counting house, detail of fig. 655. Fresco. Prato, S. Francesco, Chapter Room. SGF 109021.*
658. *Incredulity of St Thomas. Fresco. Florence (near Bagno a Ripoli), Paradiso degli Alberti. Fototeca Berenson.*

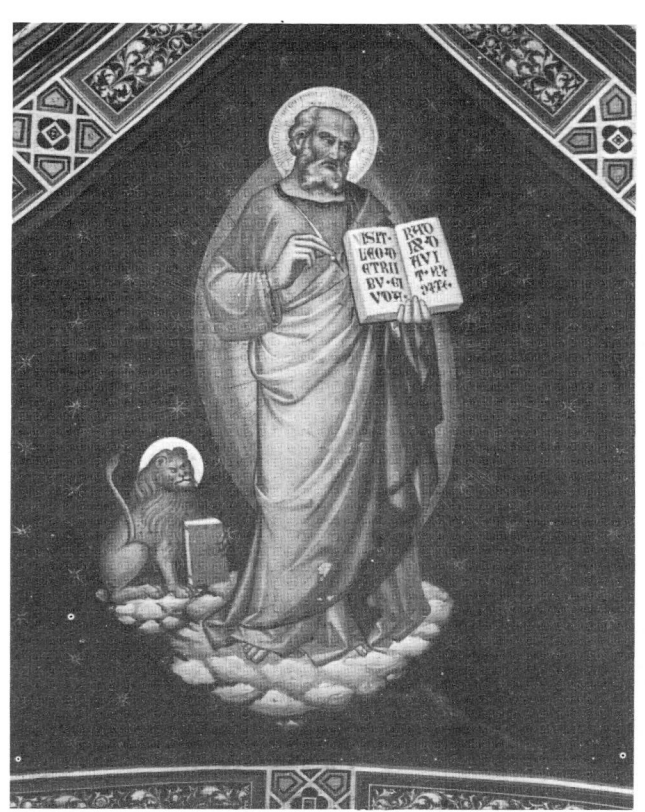

659

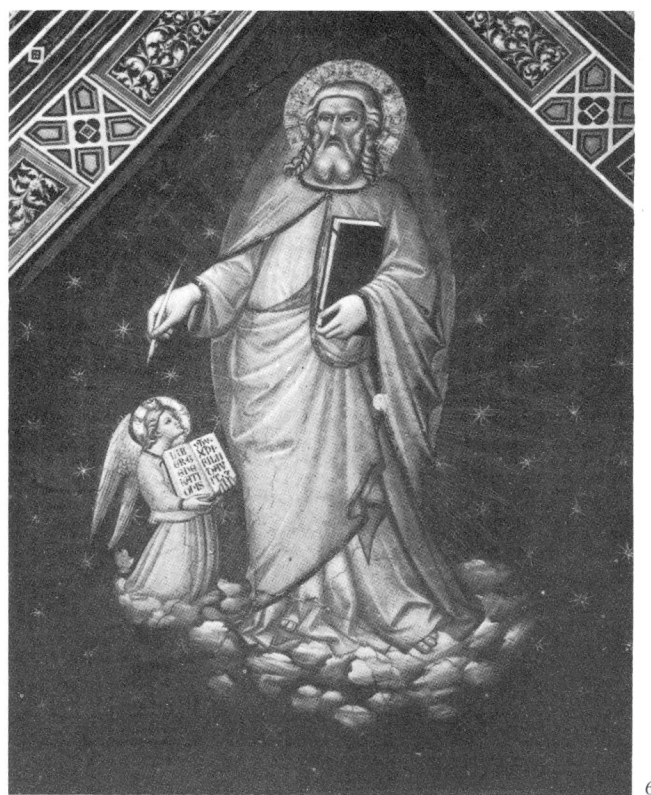

660

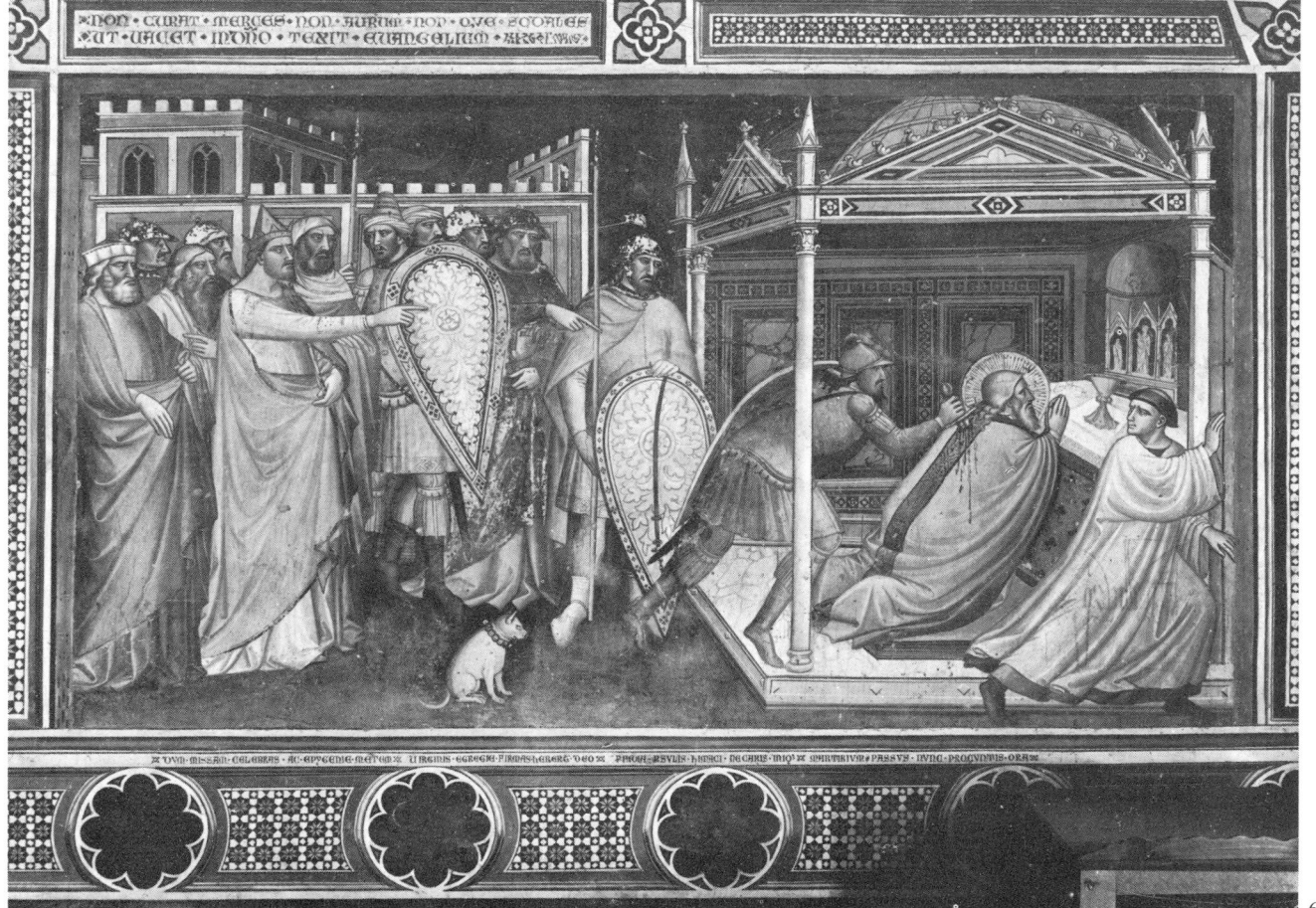

661

659. Vault: St Mark. Fresco. Prato, S. Francesco, Chapter Room. SGF 108994.
660. Vault: St Matthew. Fresco. Prato, S. Francesco, Chapter Room. SGF 108997.
661. Martyrdom of St Matthew, detail of fig. 655. Fresco. Prato, S. Francesco, Chapter Room. SGF 109027.

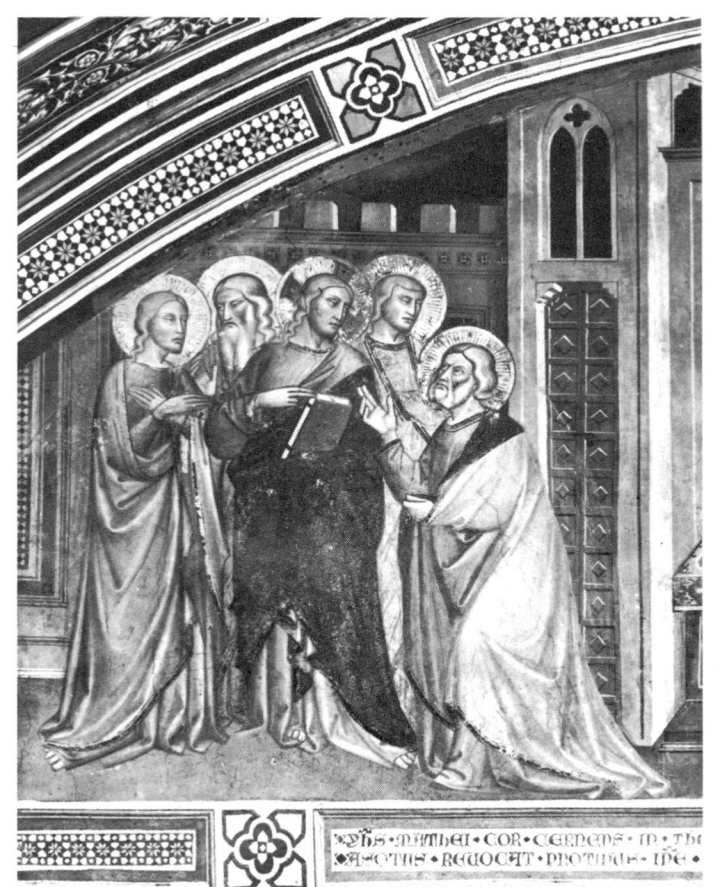

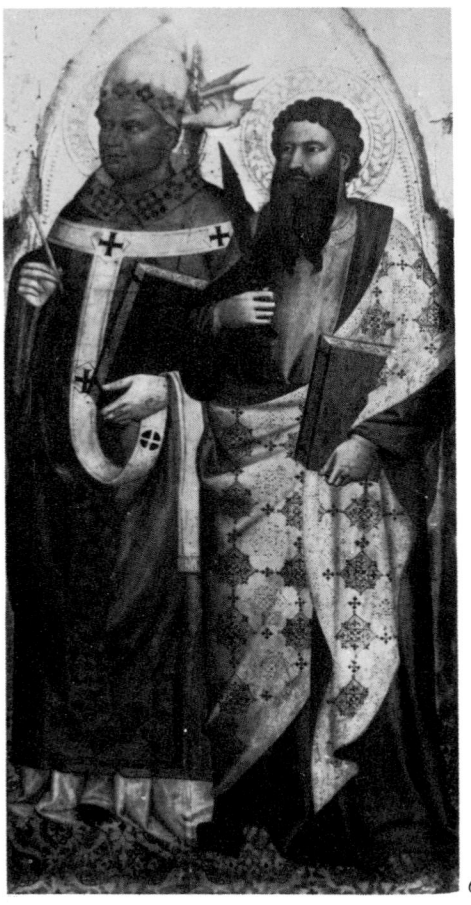

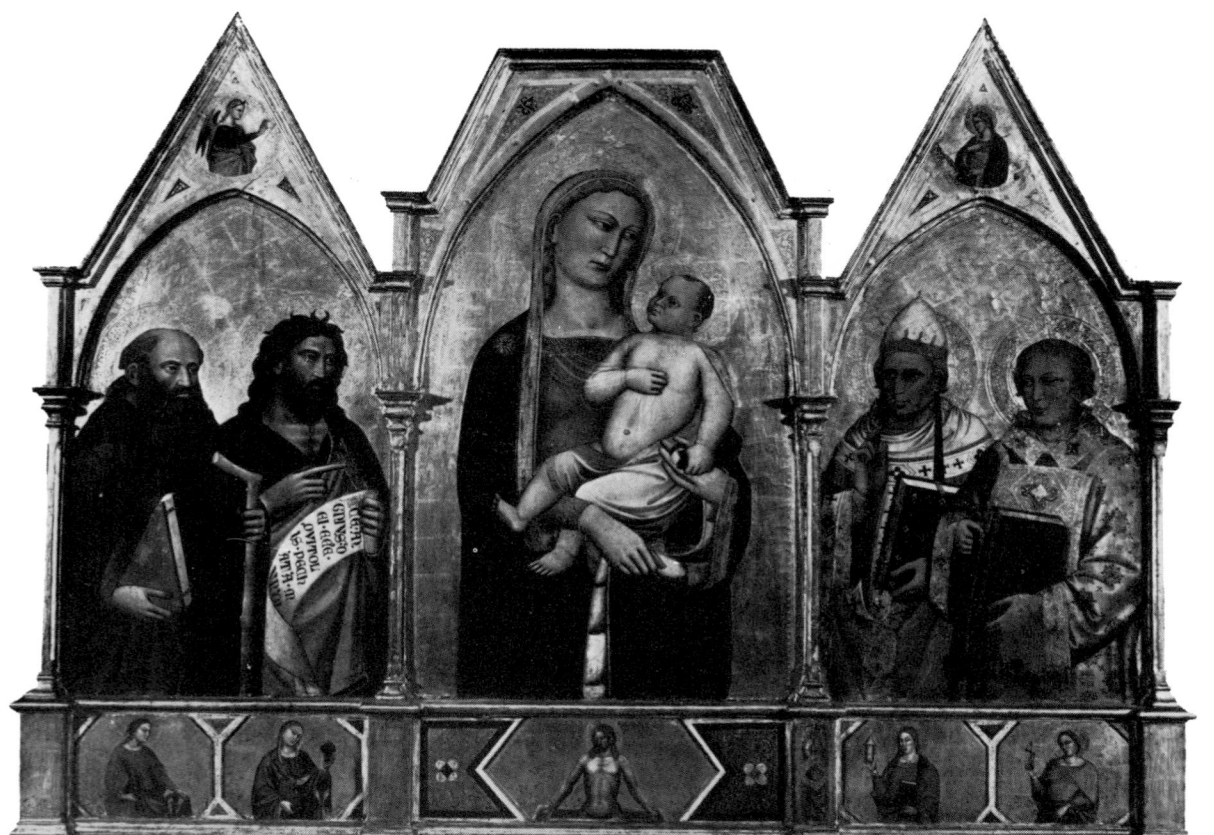

662. *Calling of St Matthew, detail of fig. 655. Fresco. Prato, S. Francesco, Chapter Room. SGF 109020.*

663. *Sts Gregory and Bartholomew. Panel. Verona, Museo di Castelvecchio. no. 788. 55 × 17.5. Museum photo.*

664. *Triptych: Madonna and Child with Sts Anthony Abbot, John the Baptist, Gregory and Leonard. Above: Annunciation. Predella: Man of Sorrows with four Saints. Panel. Empoli, Museo della Collegiata. no. 14. 137 × 182. SGF 69439.*

MASTER OF THE ARTE DELLA LANA

Florence, Palazzo dell'Arte della Lana: Altarpiece in a street tabernacle: Madonna and Child with SS. John the Baptist, John the Evangelist and six Angels.
The lunette representing the Coronation and Angels is by a close follower of Niccolò di Pietro Gerini....
This altarpiece is to be identified with the one in the Oratory or Tabernacle of S. Maria della Tromba since before 1361....
The altarpiece continues to be noticed in this church (although some writers have overlooked it) until it is moved to the Uffizi not long before 1891. In 1903 it is in the Museo dell'antica Firenze in S. Marco. It is finally (in 1905) placed in the tabernacle of the Palazzo dell'Arte della Lana, its present site.....

> from R. Offner, p. 104, *Corpus of Florentine Painting*, Sec. III, Vol. II, New York, 1930.

Follower of Niccolò di Pietro Gerini. Possibly an early phase of Lorenzo di Niccolò.

> from B. Berenson, p. 138, *Italian Pictures of the Renaissance, Florentine School*, Vol. I, London, 1963.

Both artists seem to have begun their careers in the shop of Niccolò di Pietro Gerini and this may account for some of the outward similarity between their paintings. But the quality of the fine panel at the Convento delle Suore Oblate clearly demonstrates that the Master of the Arte della Lana Coronation cannot be identified with the less talented Lorenzo di Niccolò.....

> from B. Cole, pp. 215-16, *The Burlington Magazine*, CX, 781, 1968.

The same stylistic features which link the panels are seen in most of the works grouped under the name of the Master of the Arte della Lana Coronation by Berenson. He has stated that the paintings of this artist may be early works by Lorenzo di Niccolò.....
A good example of Lorenzo's style is the signed and dated (1402) triptych of the *Madonna and Child with Saints Zanobi and Lawrence* in the church of San Martino at Terenzano.
At first glance this painting seems quite close to the two just discussed, but detailed examination reveals a number of fundamental differences. Perhaps the most striking discrepancy is the stiff, almost wooden quality of the Virgin and Child, noted at once in the rigid right arm of the Madonna or in the clumsy arch formed by the arms of the baby.

> from B. Cole, p. 215, *The Burlington Magazine*, CX, 781, 1968.

BIBLIOGRAPHY
BOOKS   *An asterisk indicates a work listed in the General Bibliograpy*

de Ricci, S., *Peintures du Louvre*, I, Paris, 1913, p. 68; Nicolle, M., *Le Musée de Rouen*, Paris, 1920, p. 19; *Edit.*, *Catalogue of Paintings, Museum of Fine Arts*, Boston, 1921, p. 30; D'Achiardi, P., *I Quadri Primitivi della Pinacoteca Vaticana*, Rome, 1929, p. 4; *Offner 1930**, Sec. III, Vol. II, p. 104; *Oertel 1961**, pp. 122-24, 128; *Berenson, 1963**, Vol. I, p. 138.

JOURNALS

Berenson, B., *DD*, XII, 1932, p. 13; Procacci, U., *RA*, XV, 1933, p. 229; Cole, B., *BM*, CX, 781, 1968, pp. 215-16.

DATED WORK

1404 Boston, (Mass.), Museum of Fine Arts 16.64. Panel: Madonna & Child Enthroned. d. (fig. 683).

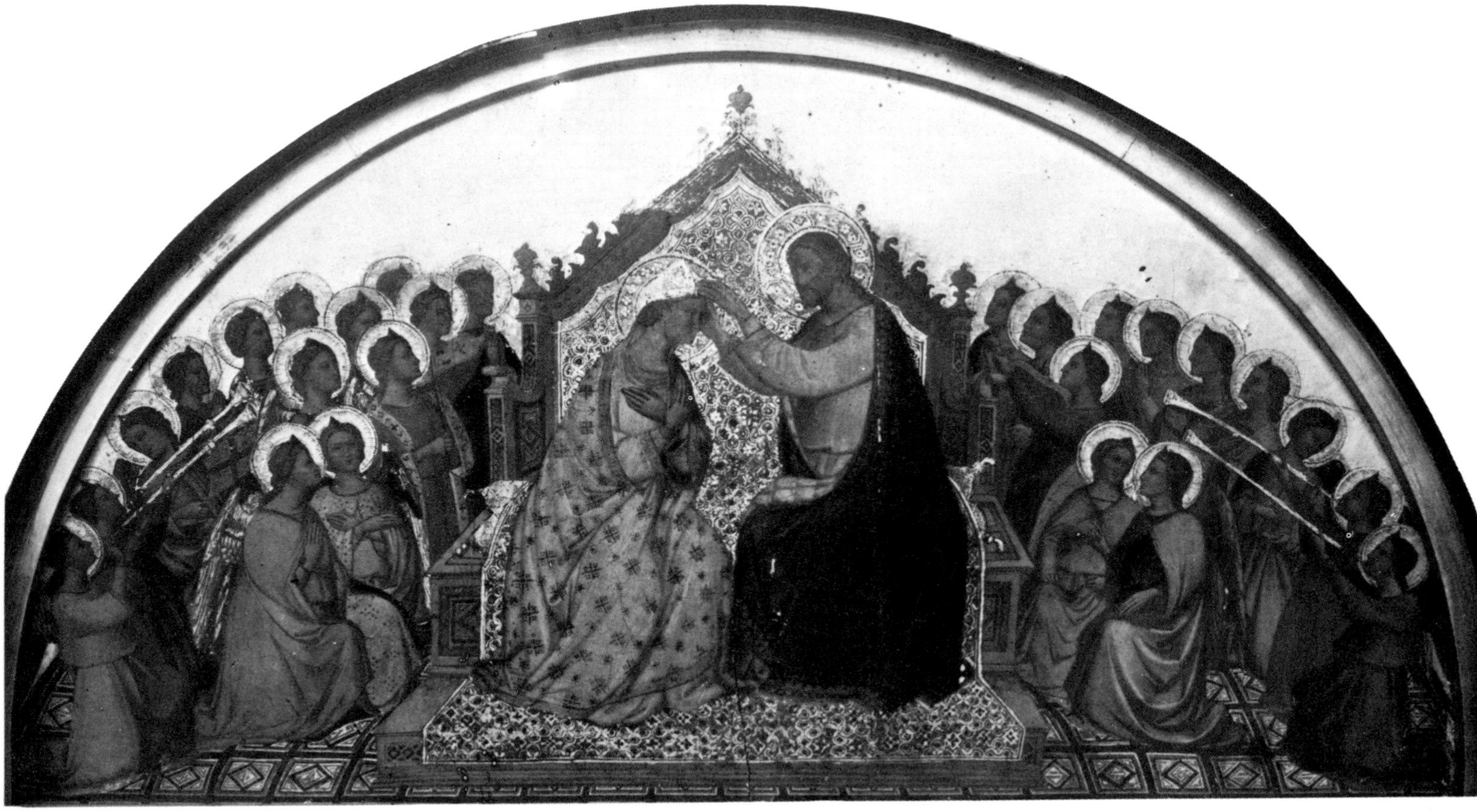

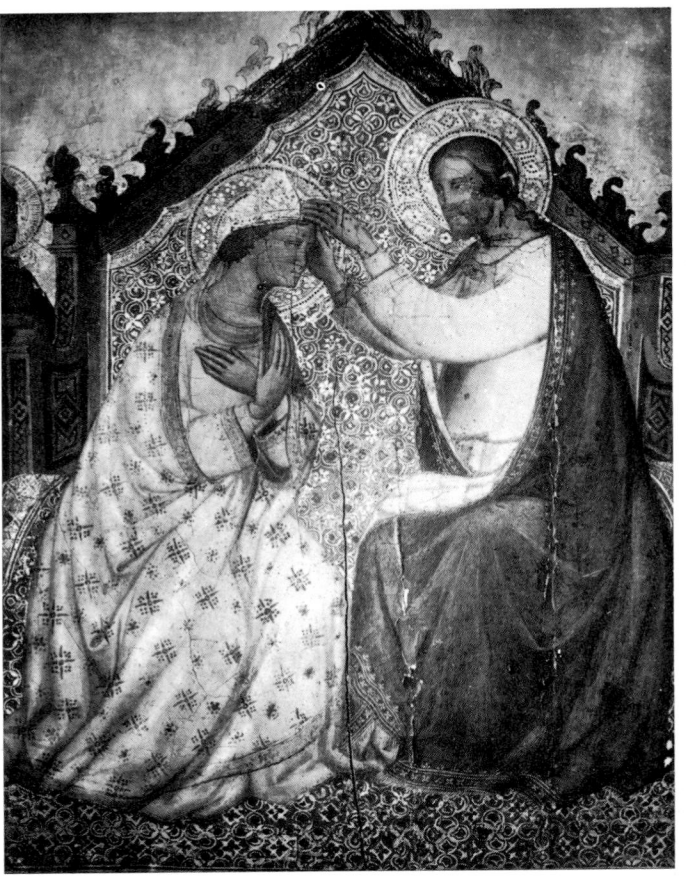

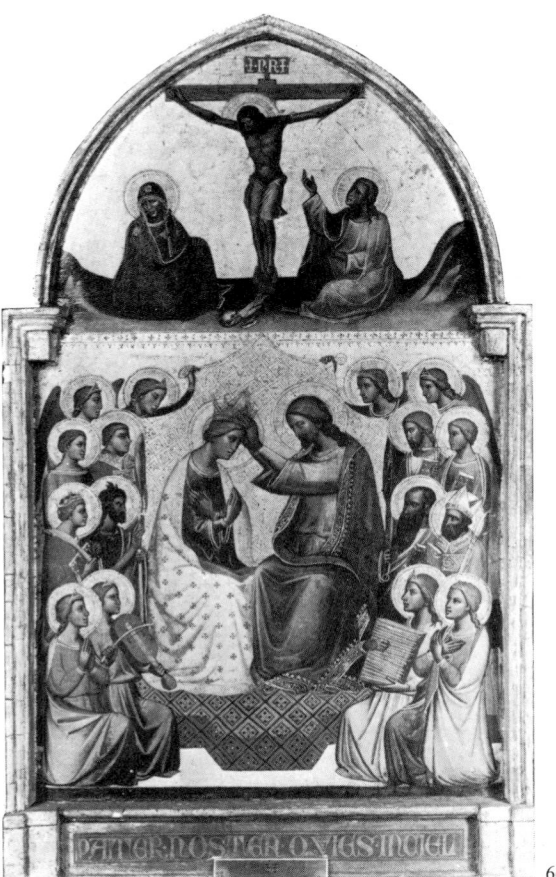

665. *Coronation of the Virgin. Panel. Florence, Palazzo dell' Arte della Lana. 153 × 274. SGF 6880 (see also fig. 237).*
666. *Coronation of the Virgin, detail of fig. 665. Panel. Florence, Palazzo dell' Arte della Lana. Brogi 22135.*
667. *Coronation of the Virgin. Panel. Altenburg, Staatliches Lindenau Museum 36. 108 × 55.5. Museum photo, Deutsche Fotothek Dresden.*

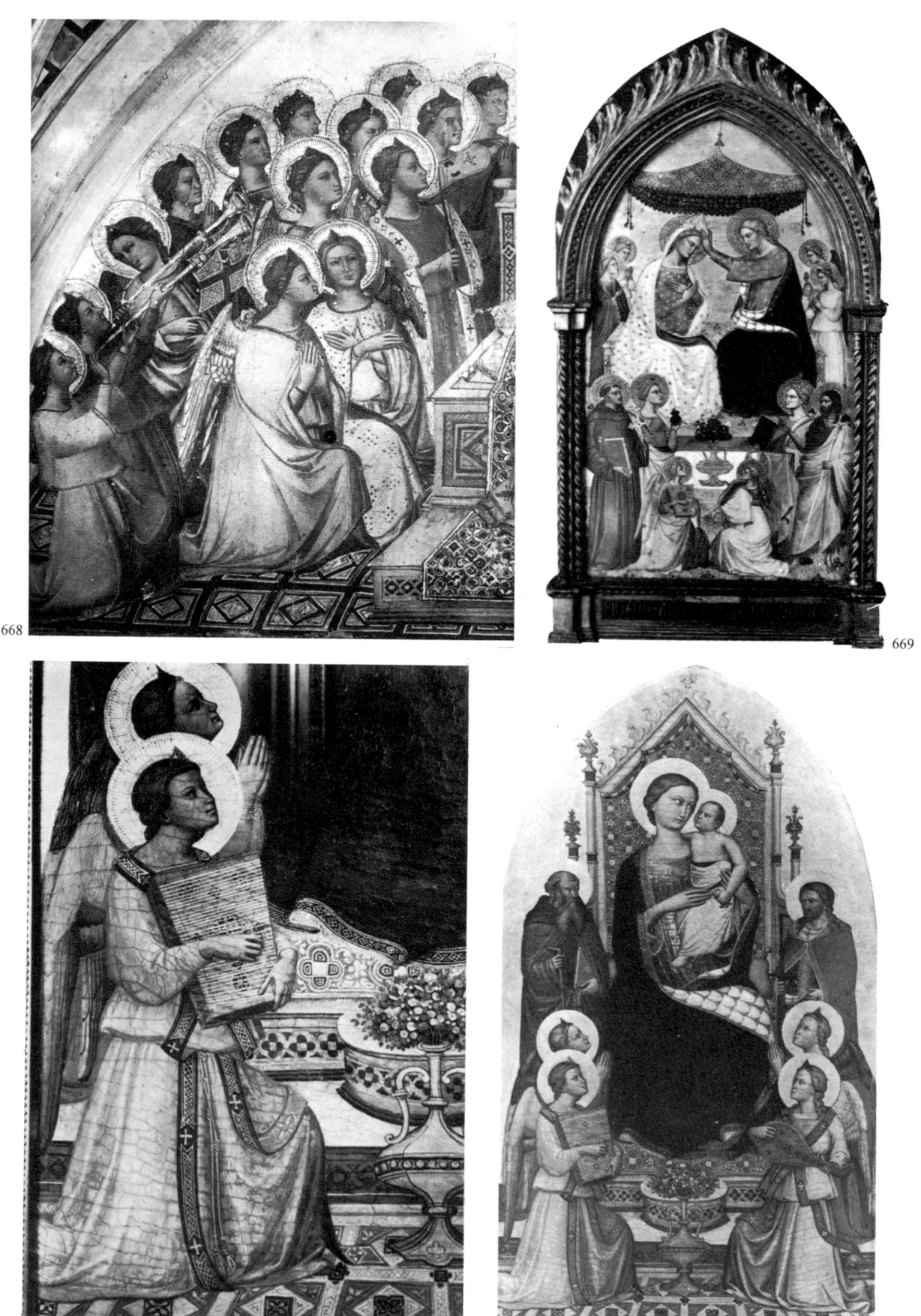

668. *Adoring Angels, detail of fig. 665. Panel. Florence, Palazzo dell' Arte della Lana. Brogi 22136.*

669. *Coronation of the Virgin with Sts Francis, Lucy, Catherine and John the Baptist and six Angels. Panel. Montreal (Quebec), Museum of Fine Arts, no. 1059. 90.1 × 50.8. Museum photo.*

670. *Two Angels, detail of fig. 671. Panel. Altenburg, Staatliches Lindenau Museum. no. 68. Museum photo, Deutsche Fotothek Dresden.*

671. *Madonna and Child Enthroned with Sts Anthony Abbot, Julian and four Angels. Panel. Altenburg, Staatliches Lindenau Museum. no. 68. 94 × 52. Museum photo, Deutsche Fotothek Dresden.*

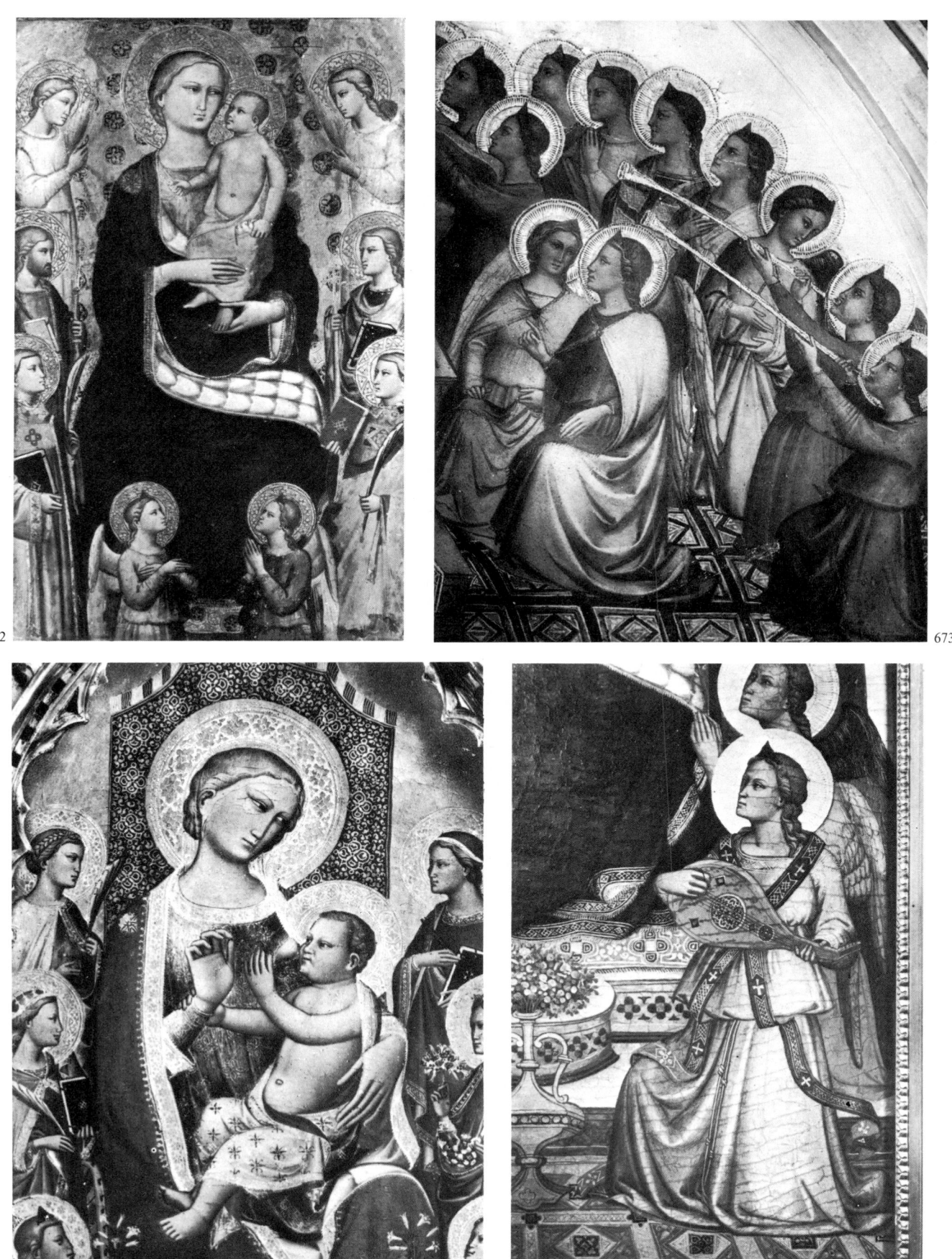

672. *Madonna and Child Enthroned with four Saints and four Angels. Panel. Leningrad, Hermitage. no. 269. 62.5 × 37. Museum photo.*
673. *Adoring Angels, detail of fig. 665. Panel. Florence, Palazzo dell' Arte della Lana. Brogi 22137.*
674. *Madonna nursing the Child, detail of fig. 676. Panel. Rome, Vatican, Pinacoteca. no. 10. Anderson 24027.*
675. *Two Angels, detail of fig. 671. Panel. Altenburg, Staatliches Lindenau Museum. no. 68. Museum photo, Deutsche Fotothek Dresden.*

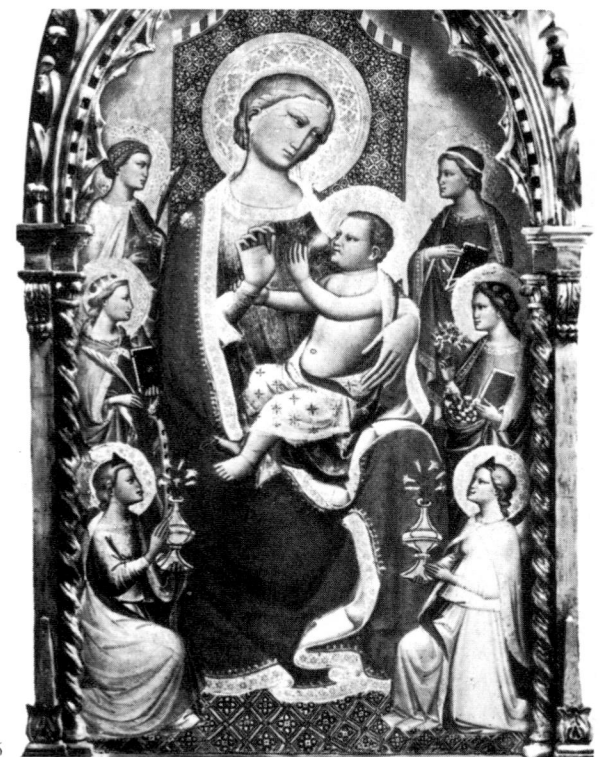

676

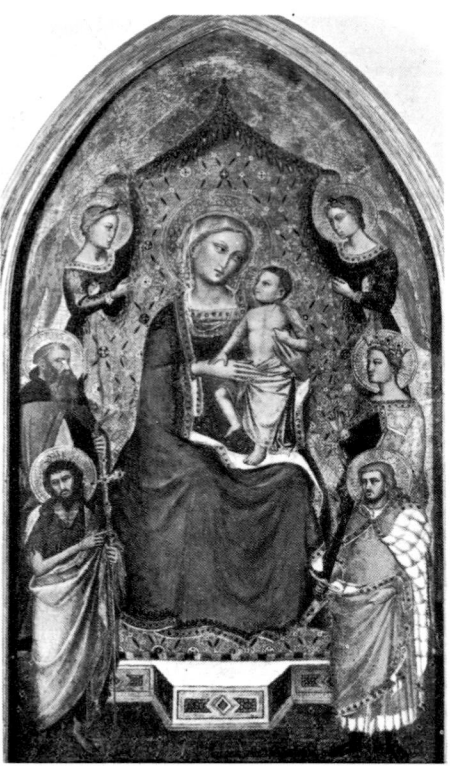

677

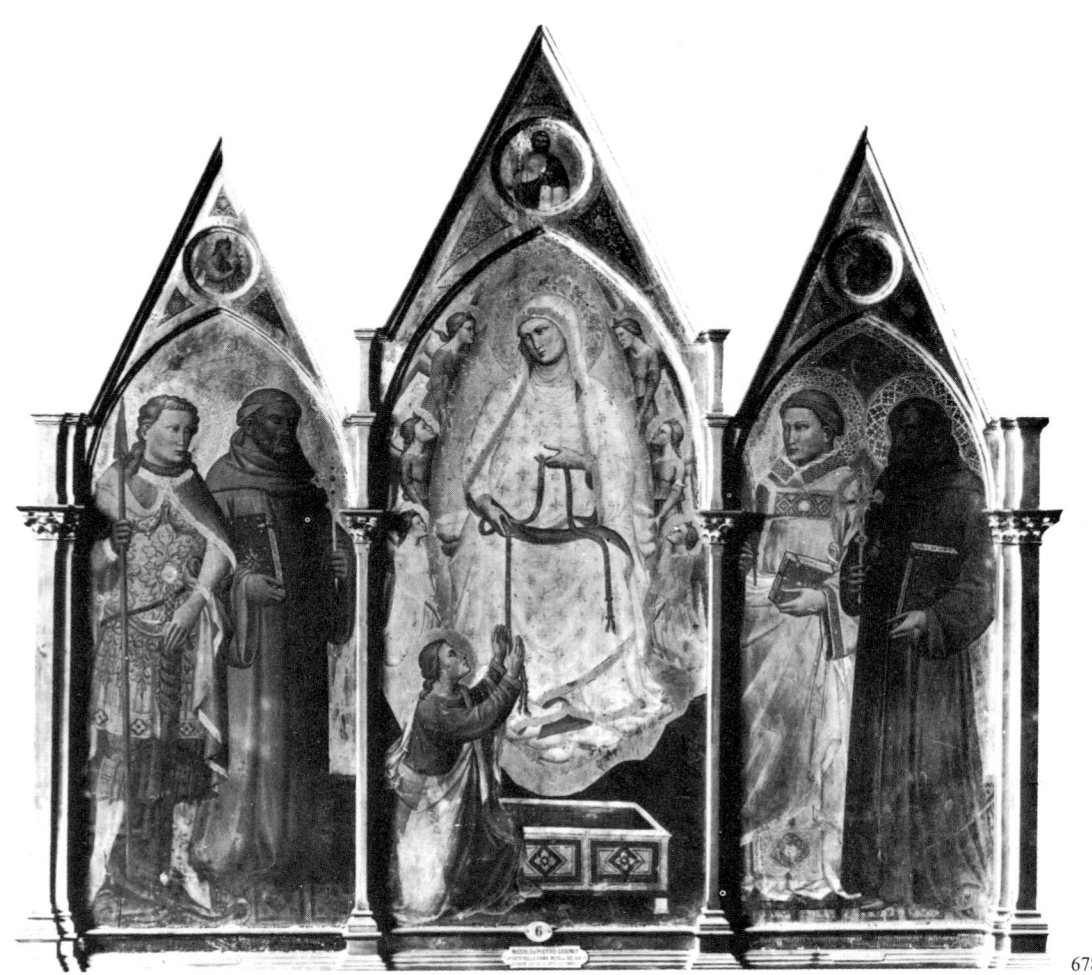

678

676. *Madonna Enthroned nursing the Child with four Saints and two Angels. Panel. Rome, Vatican, Pinacoteca. no. 10. 115 × 58. Anderson 24027.*
677. *Madonna and Child Enthroned with two Angels and four Saints. Panel. Oxford, Christ Church. no. 10. 102.5 × 60.7. Museum photo.*
678. *Triptych: Madonna giving the Holy Girdle to St Thomas with Sts Michael, John Gualbert, Lawrence, Francis and six Angels. Panel. Florence, Accademia. no. 8578. cp: 185.9 × 67; sps: 167.5 × 55. SGF 72132.*

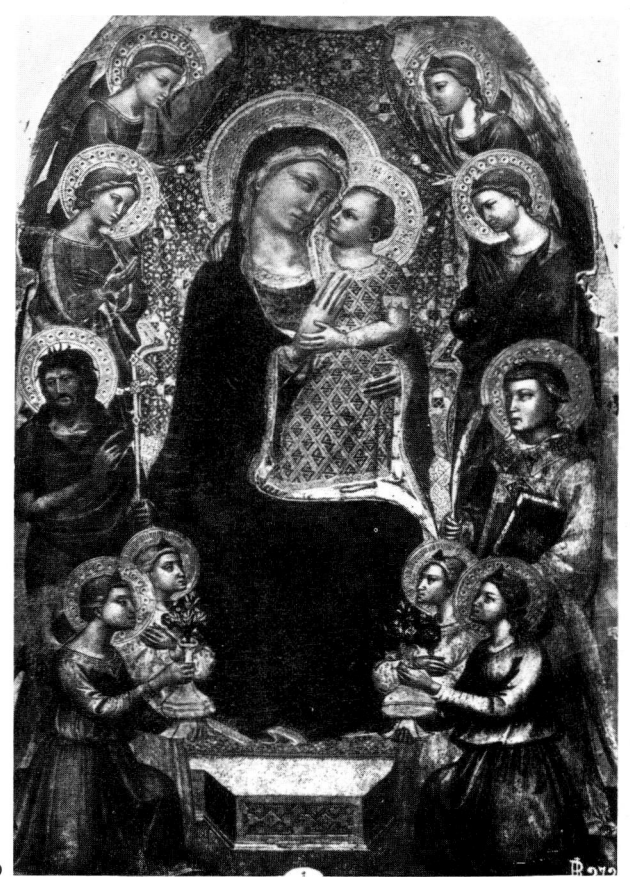

679

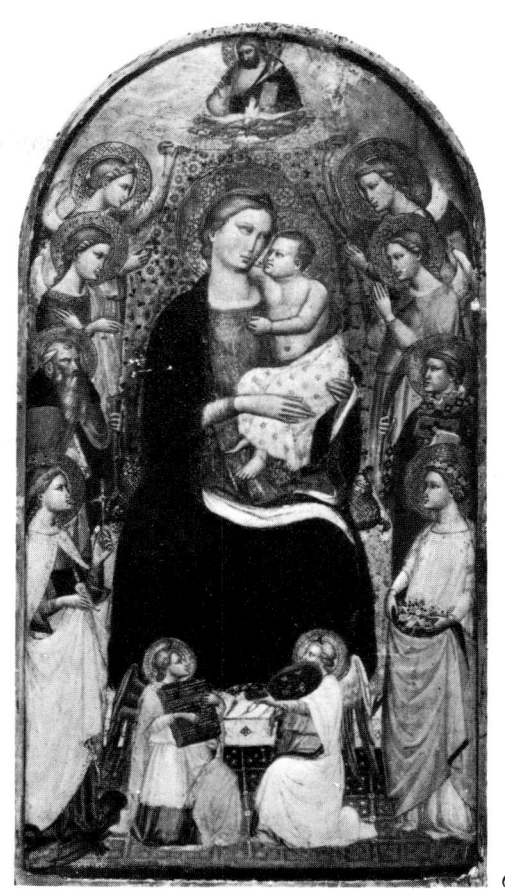

680

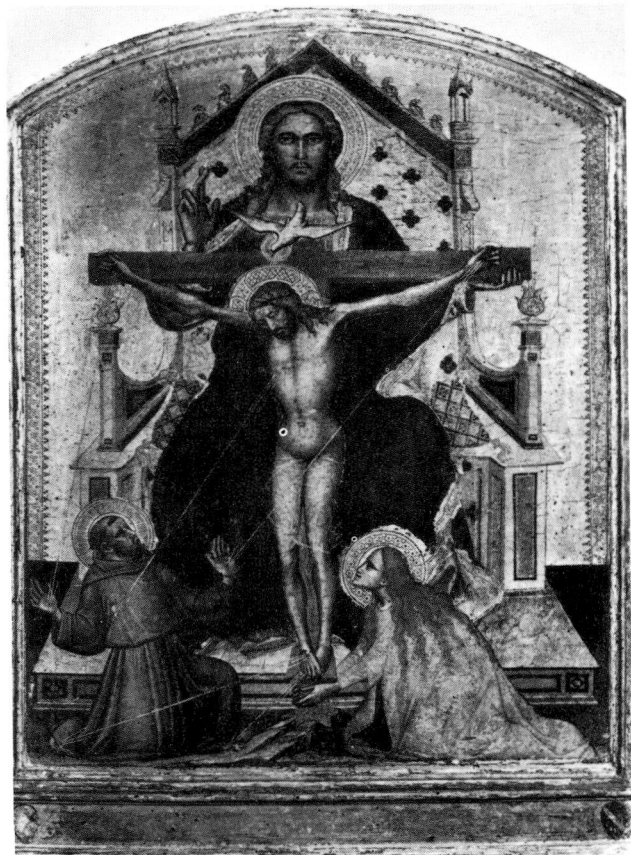

681

679. *Madonna and Child Enthroned with Sts John the Baptist and Stephen and eight Angels. Panel. Florence, Museo Nazionale del Bargello. Carrand Collection 2010. SGF 21042.*

680. *Madonna and Child Enthroned with four Saints and six Angels. Above: Christ blessing and the Holy Spirit. Panel. Private Collection. A. C. Cooper 736688.*

681. *The Trinity with Sts Francis and Mary Magdalene. Panel. Fiesole, Museo Bandini. no. I.22. 76 × 60. SGF 69864.*

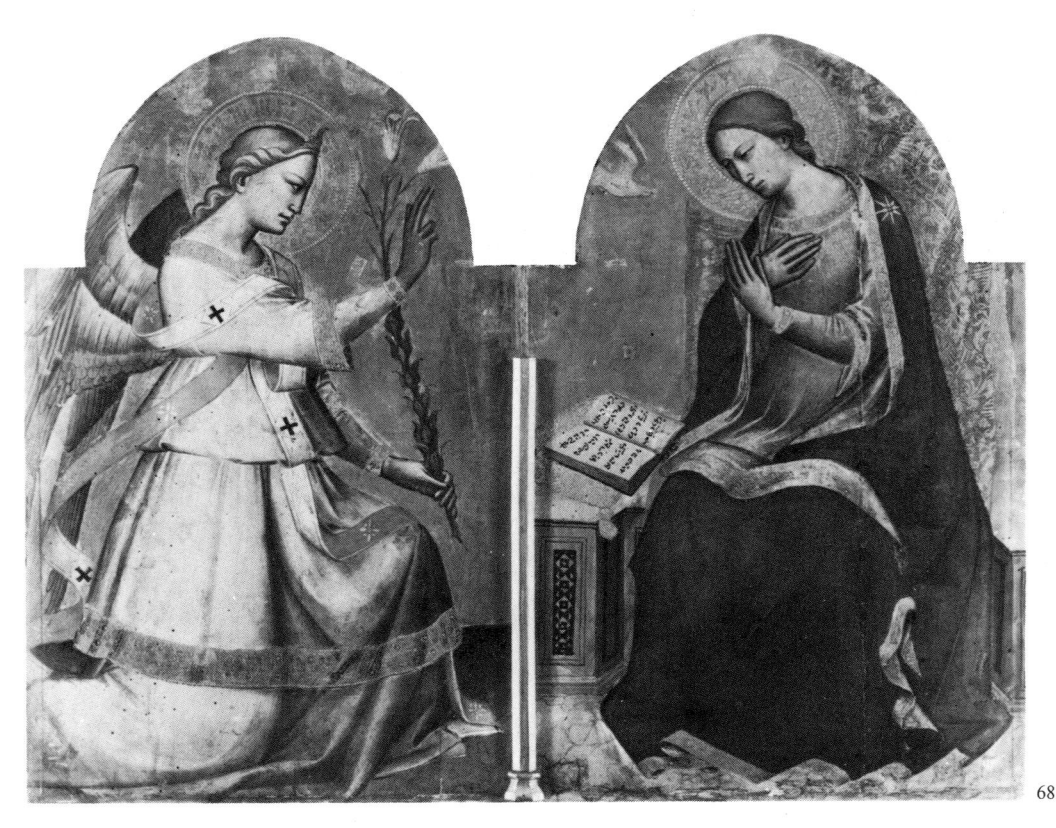

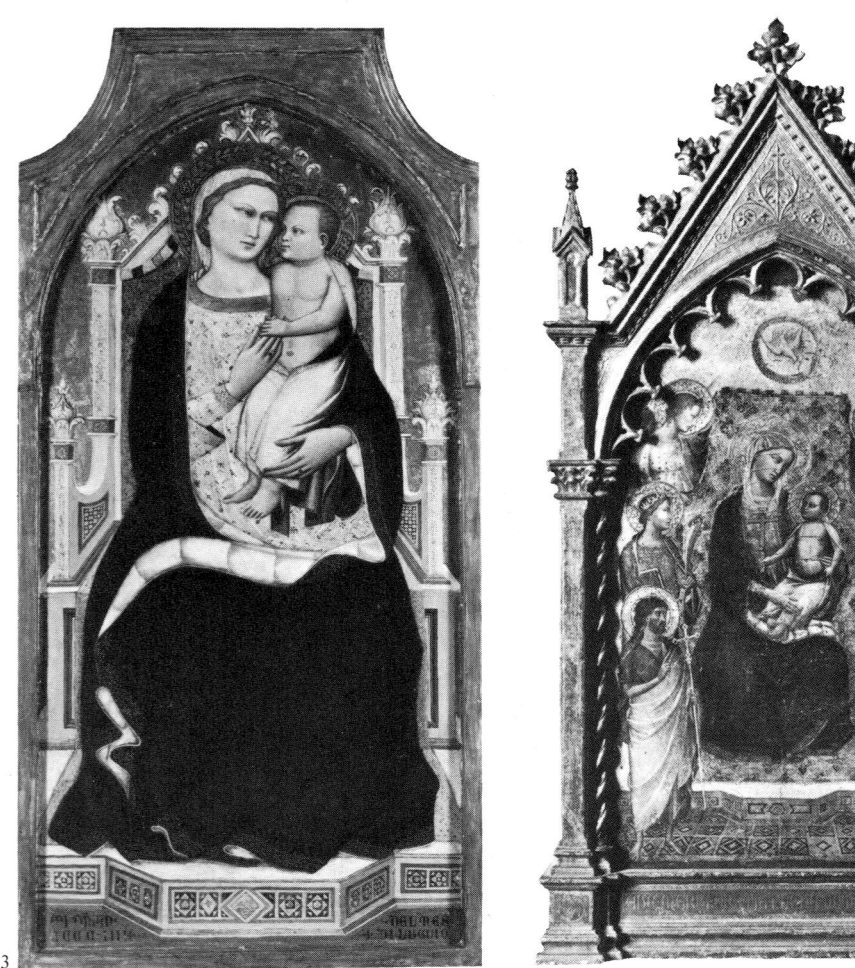

682. *Annunciation. Panel. Cambridge, Fitzwilliam Museum. no. 550. 80 × 50.8. Museum photo, Stearn & Sons FMS 5599.*
683. *Madonna and Child Enthroned. Panel. Boston (Mass.), Museum of Fine Arts. no. 16.64. 146 × 70.5. Museum photo, C 14750. d. 1404.*
684. *Madonna and Child Enthroned with six Saints. Panel. Whereabouts unknown. SGF 04509.*

PIETRO NELLI (and Tommaso del Mazza)

Until 1382 this painter had a shop together with Tommaso del Mazza, author of a panel for Sant'Antonio at Pisa; in 1382 he was matriculated in the Guild of *Medici e Speziali*; two years later he received payment for his altarpiece at Impruneta; in 1397 he was awarded the contract for the frescoes in the main chapel of the same church; in 1411 he was registered in the Company of Painters, and in 1416 he did a fresco in the refectory of the Hospital of Bonifazio. He must have been trained in the school of Taddeo Gaddi and influenced by the painting of Niccolò Gerini.....

from B. Khvoshinsky and M. Salmi, p. 63,
I Pittori Toscani, Rome, 1912.

Piero Nelli and Tommaso del Mazza are only known to us through one enormous polyptych in the Pieve of Impruneta. Documents, published by Milanesi however, offer us further information concerning these two artists.

Beside the date of 1375 on the altar-piece, we know that until 1382 they kept a shop together. That same year Pietro matriculated in the corporation of " medici e speciali ", in 1384 he received payment for the Impruneta picture and in 1397 was charged with the decoration of the choir of the same Pieve. In 1411 he was inscribed in the company of S. Lucca and in 1416 painted a fresco for the refectory of the hospital of S. Bonifazio. He died in 1419.

Milanesi identifies Tommaso del Mazza with Tommaso di Marco; he matriculated in 1377 and for the same hospital in which Nelli painted the fresco, he executed a panel in 1391. Milanesi affirms that he ornamented with six frescoes the chapel to the left of the choir in the Cathedral of Prato.

Vasari tells us that Tommaso was a pupil of Andrea Orcagna and in 1392 made a panel which in his time was to be found in the church of S. Antonio, Pisa.

We can only judge the merits of these two painters from the polyptych mentioned above, in the centre of which the Virgin is represented enthroned and surrounded by angels, while of the three panels to either side each contains two figures of Apostles. Below, the predella is divided into seven compartments, the central one showing us the Lord standing dead in His tomb. Above, an equal number of panels illustrate events from the youth of the Virgin and of the Saviour while in the middle we find the Death of the Madonna depicted. Only two of the pinnacles now remain.

Instead of connecting our artists with Taddeo Gaddi and Niccolò Gerini as has been done, I see in them late imitators of Bernardo Daddi. Not only is the polyptych in its ensemble modelled on Bernard's altar-piece now in the Uffizi, but the proportions, types, expressions and general feeling all reflect Daddi's art.

It is not devoid of interest to observe that at the close of the 14th century we find at the same time that Lorenzo di Niccolò Gerini revived, as it were, Taddeo Gaddi's manner, two other painters were drawing their inspiration from Taddeo's greatest contemporary, who however, was representative of quite another tendency.

That there were artists at that time who selected their masters from painters of a bygone generation may have resulted from their consciousness of the downfall of the Florentine school.

Artists like Lorenzo di Niccolò, Pietro Nelli and Tommaso del Mazza form the link between the great Florentine Trecento tradition and those painters who, like Bicci di Lorenzo, who died in 1452, produced during a great part of the 15th century, works in which the Giottesque elements are really of more importance than those borrowed from their contemporaries or immediate predecessors.

from R. van Marle, pp. 646-49, *The Development of the Italian Schools of Painting*, Vol. III, The Hague, 1924.

Piero (or Pietro) di Nello da Rubatta in Mugello. B. c. 1345, d. 1419. For some years Piero was in partnership with Tommaso del Mazza their connection terminating in 1382. In 1375 Piero painted for the high altar of the parish church of Sta. Maria dell'Impruneta, near Florence, a large composite panel in compartments, representing the Virgin enthroned with Infant and Angels, the Coronation of the Virgin, Apostles, Saints and various subjects from the life of the Virgin, etc. In this work Piero was assisted by his partner, Tommaso. The panel was painted at the expense of the Pievano Stefano and the men of the Company of Sta. Maria dell'Impruneta. In 1384 Piero was paid 8 lire, balance of 5 flor.

due to him for having painted the upper compartment of the above panel..... The only work by Pietro known to be extant is the panel at Impruneta, now preserved in the sacristy of the church.

In 1381, Piero married Francesca di Giovanni Matini, stovigliaio (potter), of Rubatta and had a daughter Tita, married in 1409 to Ser Bartolo Giannini, notary, her father giving her a dowry of 500 flor. Not having any sons, Piero " si commise " to the Company of Sta. Maria del Bigallo on June 5, 1412, making over to the Company his house and " podere " at Rubatta. After Piero's death the Company sold the property to Jacopo Malagonelle, and with the proceeds, erected an oratory at Rubatta.....

from D. E. Colnaghi, p. 214, *A Dictionary of Florentine Painters*, London, 1928.

I have been speaking of Pietro Nelli as if in the altarpiece at Impruneta one could distinguish his work from that of Tommaso del Mazza. In fact it seems to me that the two painters in this work are quite separate: one is so near to Niccolò di Pietro that we can hardly tell that he is, in fact, another hand, while the other is an orcagnesque painter. Vasari, in fact, tells us that Tommaso was a pupil of Orcagna, and it could be that this current of painting continued right up to the middle of the Cinquecento. Since I can easily see two separate hands in the painting at Impruneta and since I care little for the names that artists may have had in the world of beings, if I am able to distinguish their individuality in the world of the spirit — names are after all but useful and reasonable conventions — I do not hesitate to designate Pietro Nelli as the author of those parts of the picture which are by a close follower of Niccolò.....

from B. Berenson, pp. 11-12, *Dedalo*, XII, 1, 1932.

Tommaso del Mazza, the more Orcagnesque of the painters, did six of the panels in the Impruneta polyptych: the *Birth of the Virgin*, the *Presentation in the Temple*, the *Marriage of the Virgin*, the *Annunciation*, the *Nativity*, the *Adoration of the Magi*. The central panel of the Assumption is by Pietro Nelli, as are the angels above the Marriage of the Virgin. He also did the rest of the polyptych, with the exception of the *Coronation of the Virgin*, above the Annunciation, and he was aided in the predella.....

from B. Berenson, p. 34, note 2, *Dedalo*, XII, 1, 1932.

The painting, which is inscribed as having been painted in 1375 and paid for by Pievano Stefano and by the members of the company of Santa Maria dell'Impruneta, stood on the main altar of the Basilica until 1534, was then removed to the sacristy, only to return to its original location towards the end of the 19th century.....

from U. Baldini, p. 13, *X^a Mostra di Opere d'arte Restaurate*, Florence, 1959.

The painting of the Impruneta polyptych was done by two quite different painters who divided the commission, each one working quite autonomously. One of the two, who uses forms difficult to distinguish from those of Niccolò di Pietro Gerini, is the author of the Madonna and Child with angels, in the centre of the polyptych, of the Dormition of the Virgin above this, and of the whole predella. The second who is almost a rustic, much-later-Bernardo Daddi, is responsible for the six side panels with two saints each and for the six stories from the life of the Virgin, above these....

In either case, Pietro Nelli's part in the Impruneta polyptych remains the six lateral panels and the six cusps above them....

About ten years before the Impruneta polyptych, the painter had executed in the Church of S. Lorenzo at Signa a sequence of votive frescoes, each one ordered by a different patron. Under the figures of a male saint and St. Catherine is inscribed the name of the patron, Benozzo di N... (Niccolò?) linaiuolo, and the date: ANNI M. CCCLXVI....

from L. Bellosi, pp. 183, 187, *Mitteilungen des Kunsthistorischen Institutes in Florenz*, XVII, 2-3, 1973.

BIBLIOGRAPHY

BOOKS

An asterisk indicates a work listed in the General Bibliography

Milanesi, G., *Memorie intorno a Pietro Nelli*, Florence, 1872; *Pini, Milanesi**, 1876, no 11 (Tommaso del Mazza, no 9); *Khv & Salmi**, 1914, p. 63; *Toesca, 1951**, p. 644; *v. Marle 1924**, pp. 459, 537, 646-49; *Colnaghi**, 1928, p. 214 (Tommaso del Mazza, p. 261); Shorr, D. C., *The Christ Child in Devotional Images*, New York, 1954, p. 114; Baldini, U., *Xª Mostra di Opere d'arte Restaurate*, Florence, 1959, p. 13; Zeri, F., *Diari di Lavoro*, Bergamo, 1971, p. 16.

JOURNALS

Sirén, O., *A*, 1904, p. 342; Sirén, O., *RADA*, VI, 5, 1906, pp. 81-7; Berenson, B., *DD*, XII, 1, 1932, pp. 5-34; Marchini, G., *RA*, XX, 1938, pp. 215-41; Bellosi, L., *PA*, 187/7, 1965, p. 19; Bellosi, L., *MKIF*, XVII, 2-3, 1973, p. 183-194.

DATED WORKS

1366 Signa, S. Lorenzo. Fresco. St Julian and St Catherine. d. (fig. 705).
1375 Impruneta, Chiesa Collegiata. Polyptych: Madonna & Child with Saints. d. (fig. 686).

There are no known signed works by these painters.

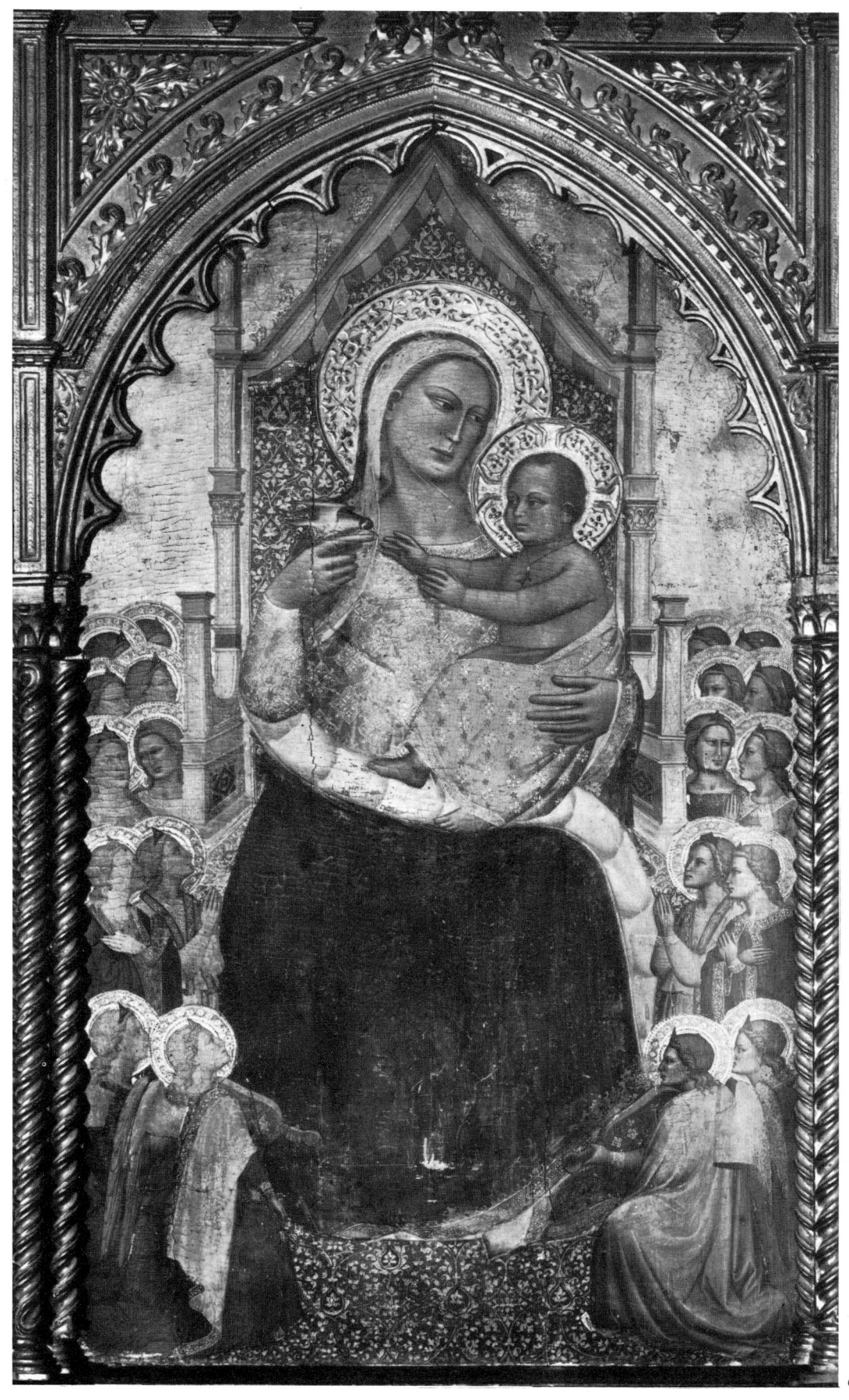

685

685.   *Madonna and Child Enthroned with Angels, detail of fig. 686. Panel. Impruneta, Collegiata di S. Maria.   Alinari 43948.   d. 1375.*

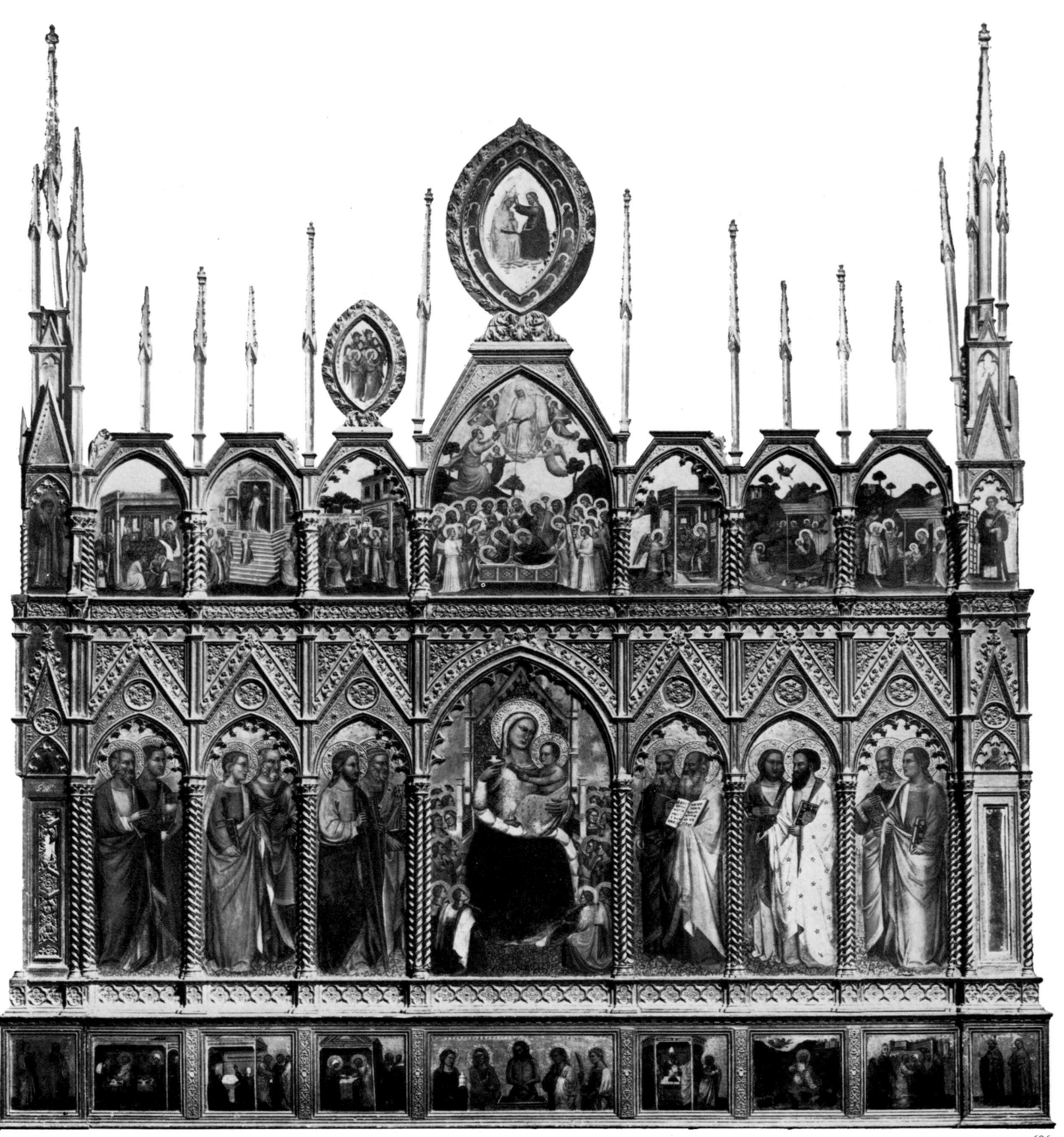

686

686. *Polyptych: Madonna and Child Enthroned with Saints and Angels and scenes from the Lives of the Virgin and Joseph. Panel. Impruneta (14 kms south of Florence), Collegiata di S. Maria. Alinari 4658. d. 1375.*

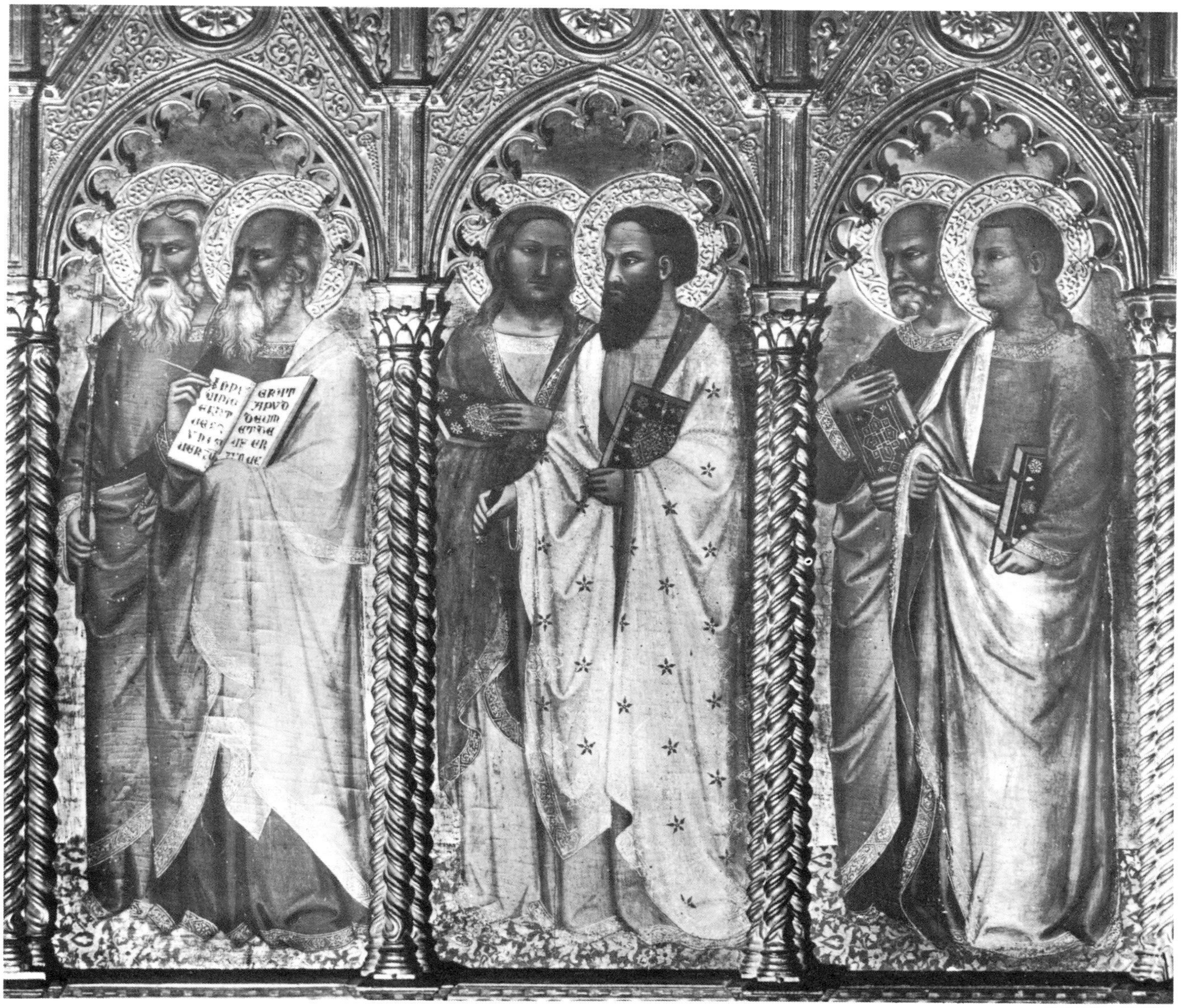

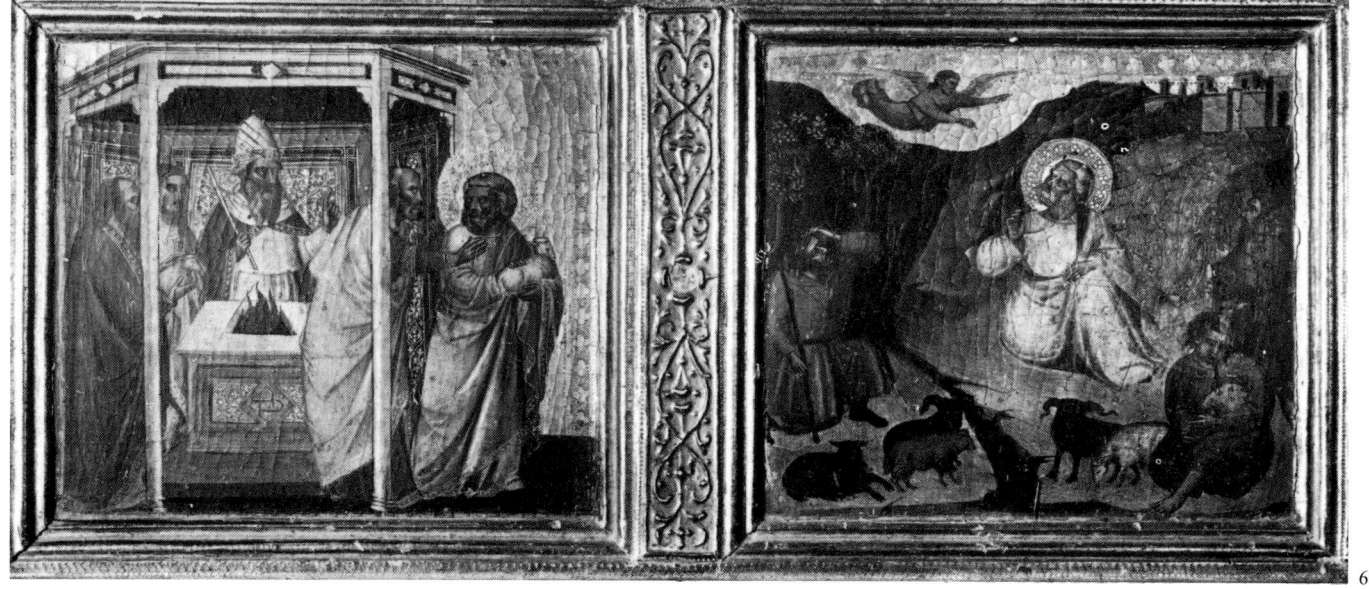

687

688

687. *Six Saints, detail of fig. 686. Panel. Impruneta, Collegiata di S. Maria. Alinari 43950. d. 1375.*
688. *Scenes from the Life of Joseph, detail of fig. 686. Panel. Impruneta, Collegiata di S. Maria. Alinari 43954. d. 1375.*

337

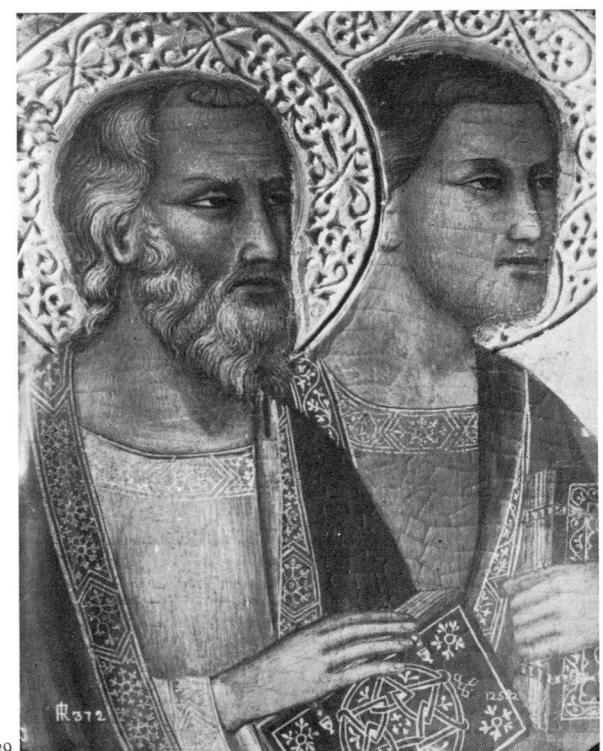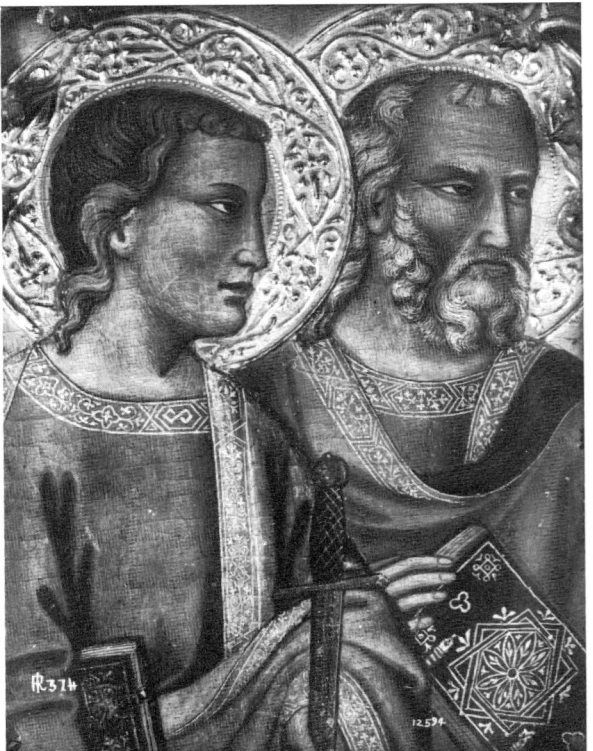

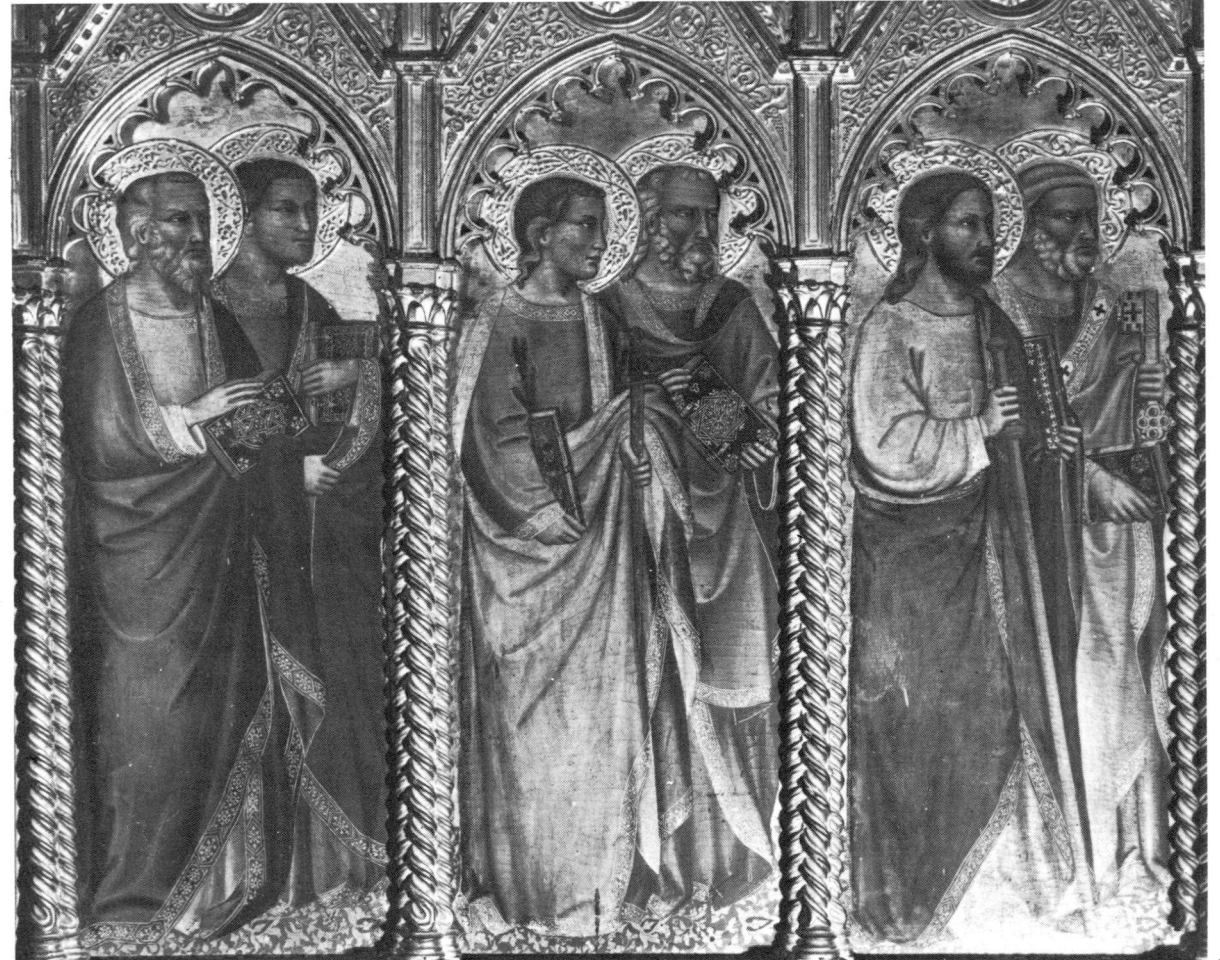

689. *Heads of two male Saints, detail of fig. 686. Panel. Impruneta, Collegiata di S. Maria. Frick 12592. d. 1375.*
690. *Heads of two male Saints, detail of fig. 686. Panel. Impruneta, Collegiata di S. Maria. Frick 12594. d. 1375.*
691. *Six Saints, detail of fig. 686. Panel. Impruneta, Collegiata di S. Maria. Alinari 43949.*

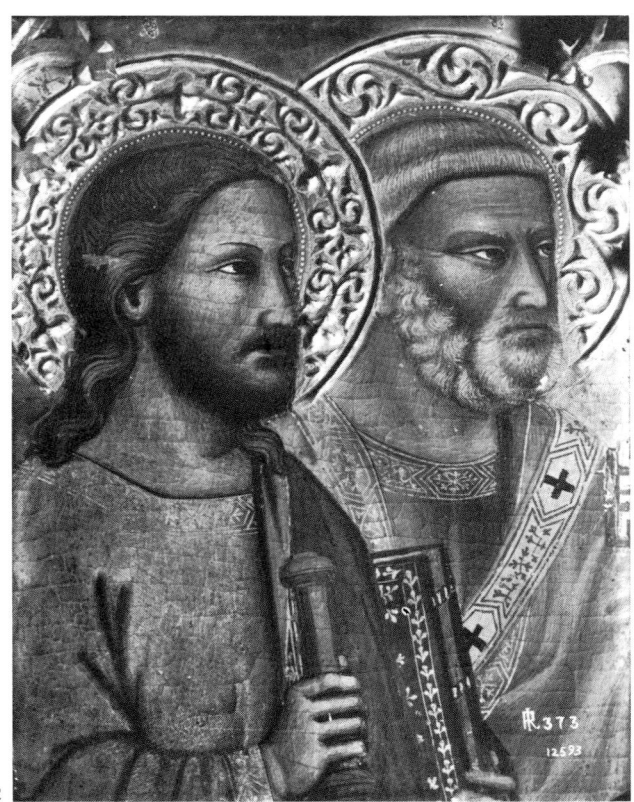

692

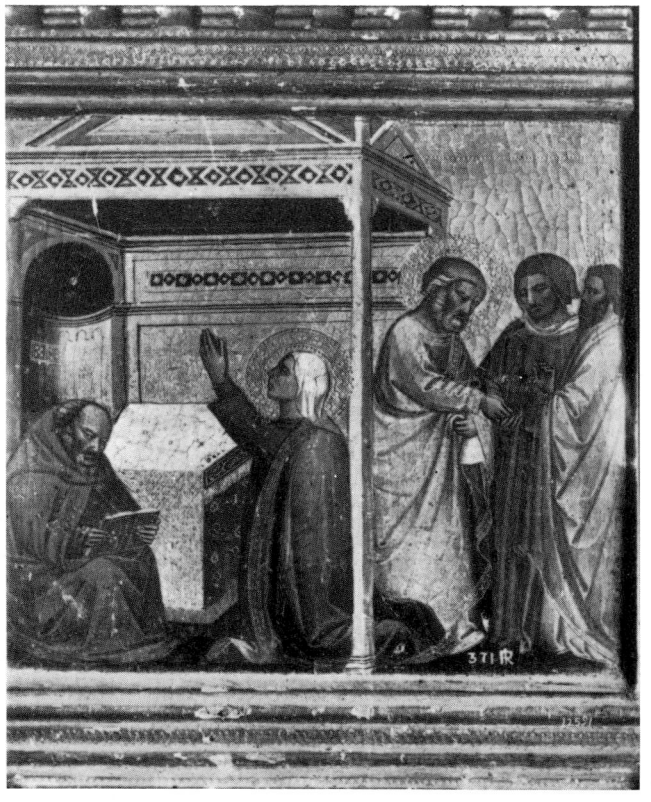

693

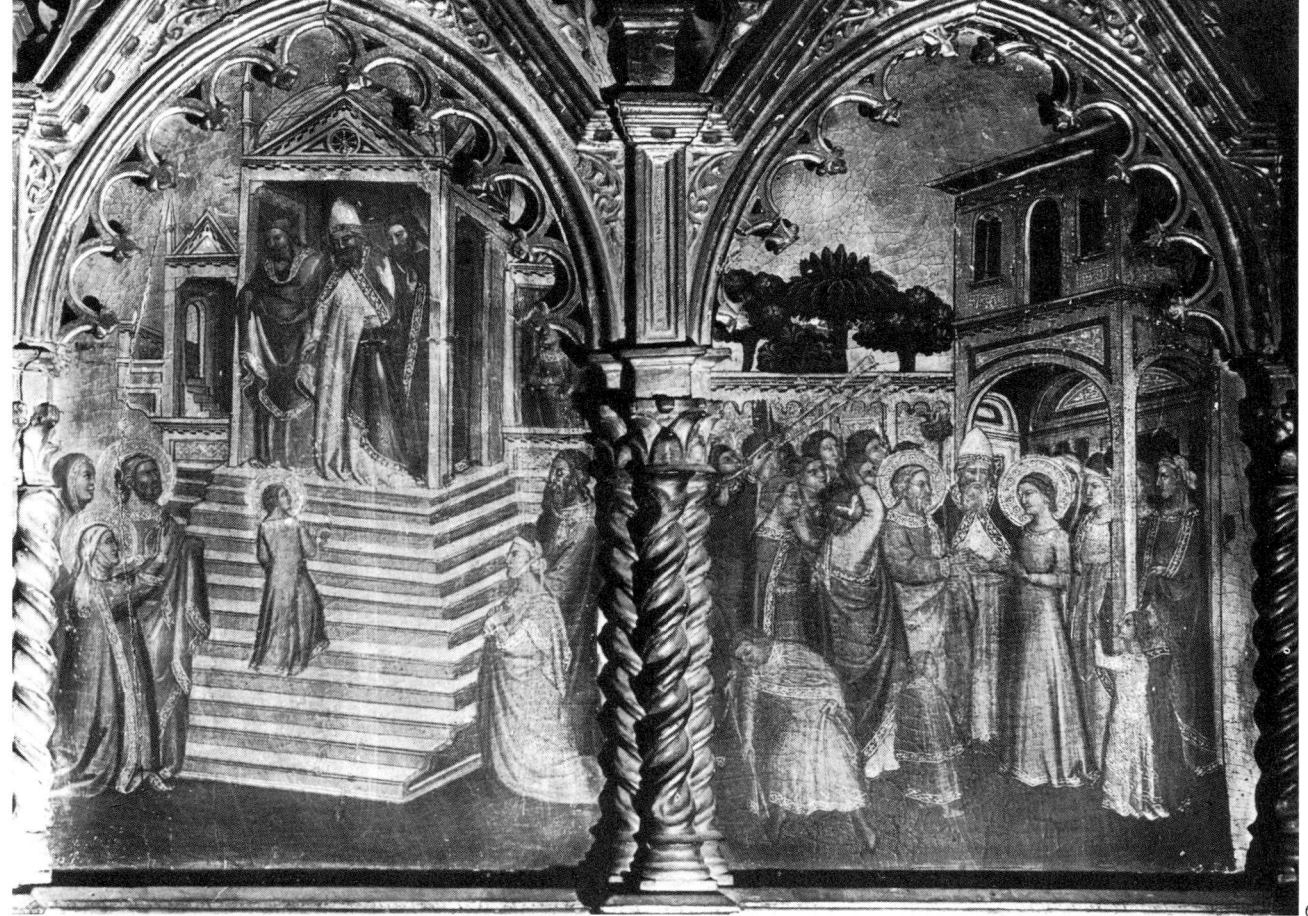

694

692. *Heads of two male Saints, detail of fig. 686. Panel. Impruneta, Collegiata di S. Maria. Frick 12593. d. 1375.*
693. *Prayer of St Anne, detail of fig. 686. Panel. Impruneta, Collegiata di S. Maria. Frick 12591. d. 1375.*
694. *Presentation of the Virgin in the Temple and Marriage of the Virgin, detail of fig. 686. Panel. Impruneta, Collegiata di S. Maria. Alinari 43958. d. 1375.*

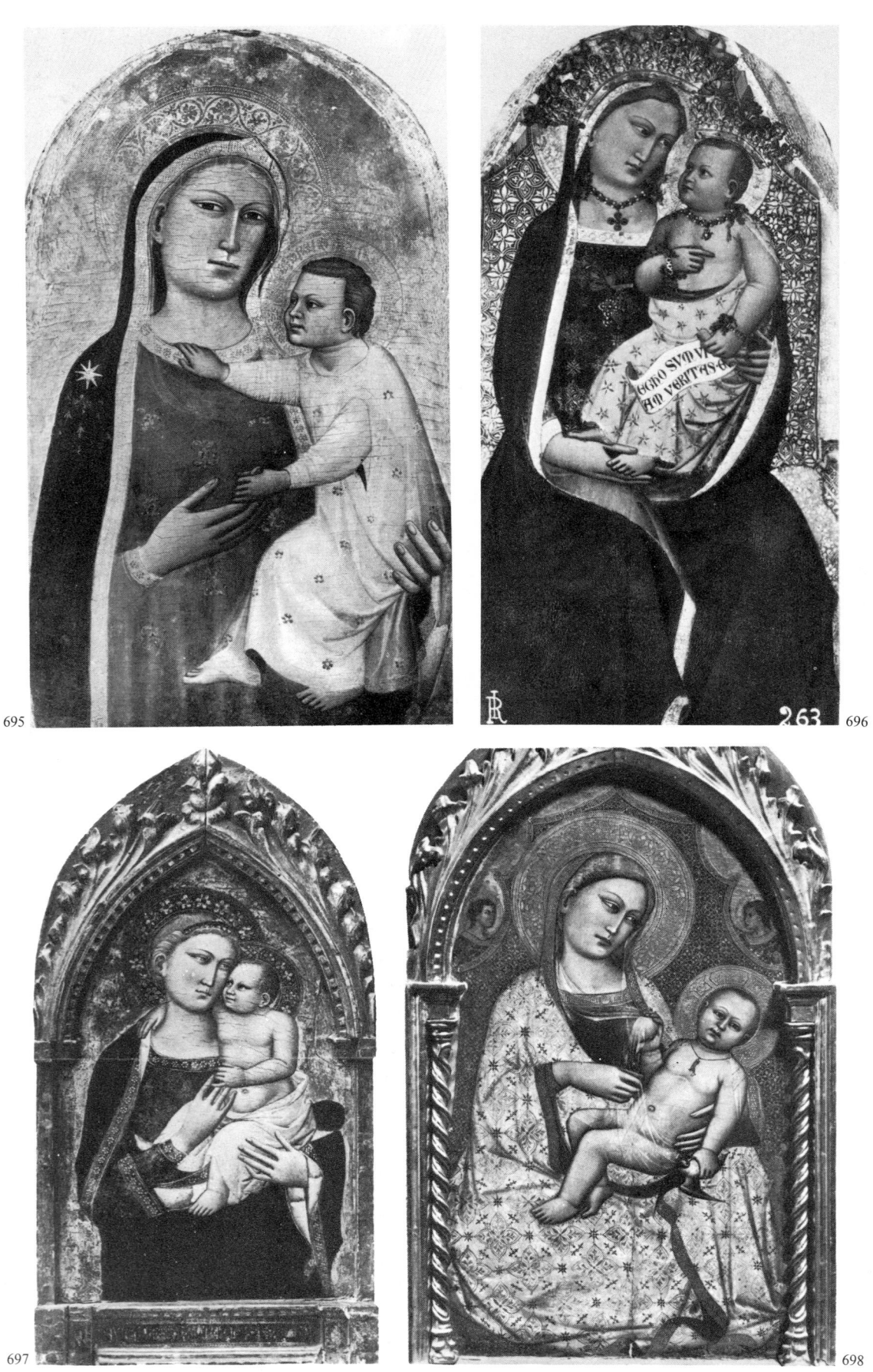

695 263 696

697 698

695. *Madonna and Child. Panel. Borgo San Lorenzo (Mugello), S. Lorenzo. SGF 24555.*
696. *Madonna and Child Enthroned. Panel. Pelago (5 kms west of Pontassieve), Chiesa di Magnale. Reali.*
697. *Madonna and Child. Panel. Whereabouts unknown. Fototeca Berenson.*
698. *Madonna nursing the Child. Panel. Montalve, Istituto della Quiete, Grande Salone. 80 × 50. Brogi 24782.*

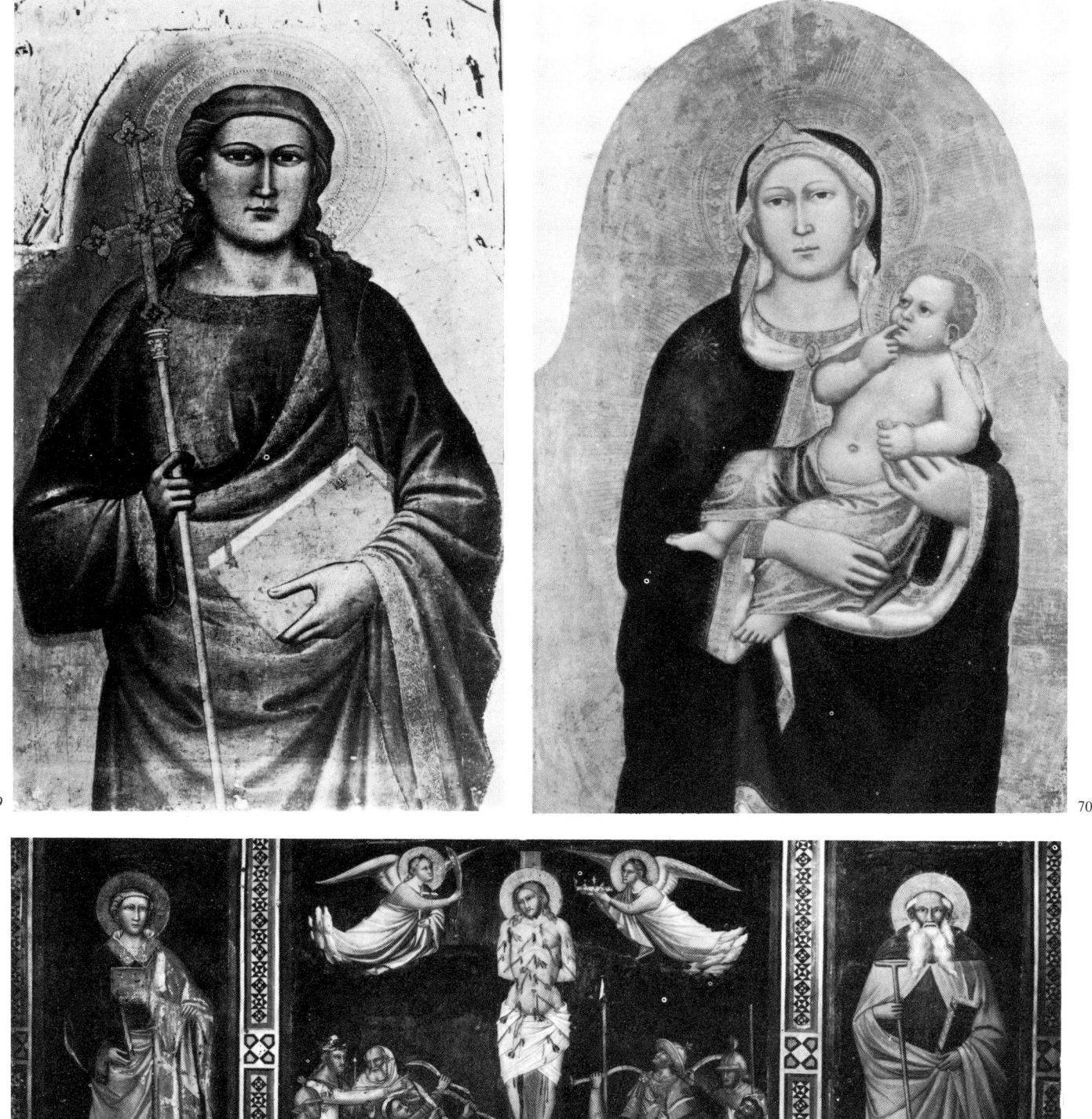

699

700

701

699. *St Philip. Panel. Oxford, Christ Church. no. 12. 64.7 × 39.3. Fototeca Berenson.*
700. *Madonna and Child. Panel. Colorado Springs (Colo.), Fine Arts Center, Samuel H. Kress Collection. no. K1004. 79.3 × 45.7. Kress Foundation photo.*
701. *Martyrdom of St Sebastian, with Sts Lawrence and Anthony Abbot. Fresco. Signa, S. Lorenzo. Alinari 31179.*

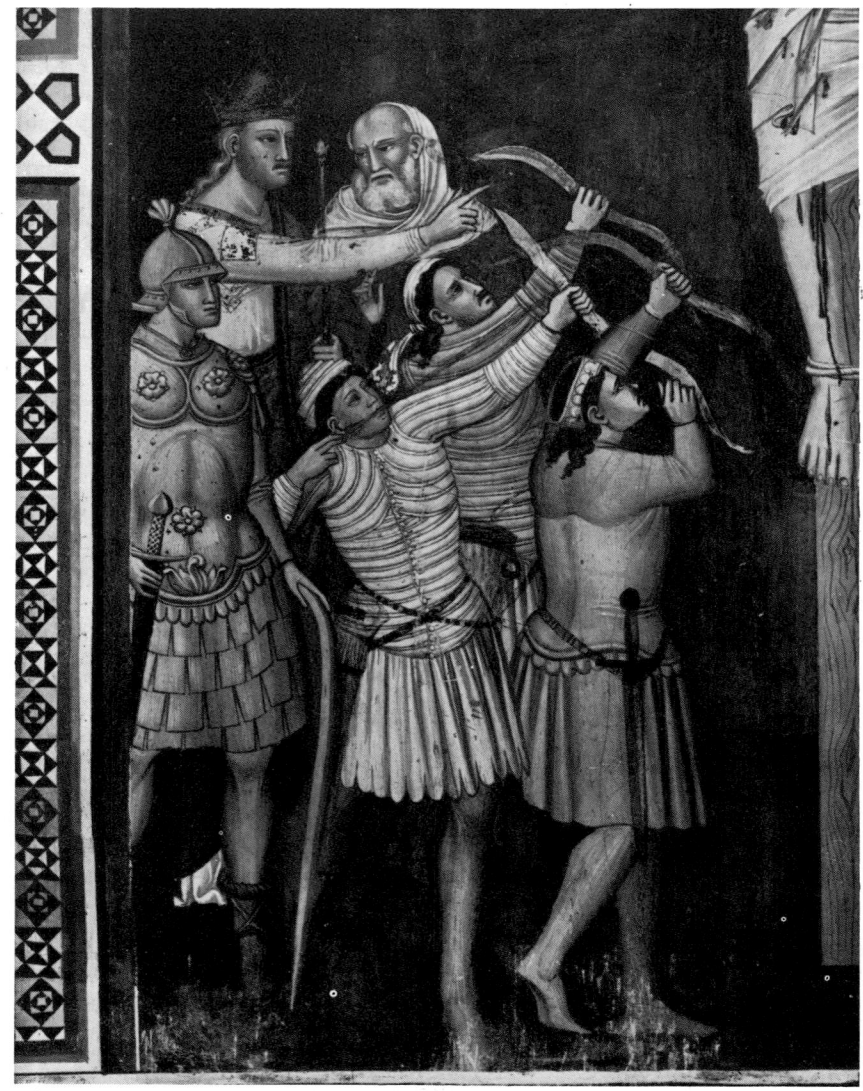

702

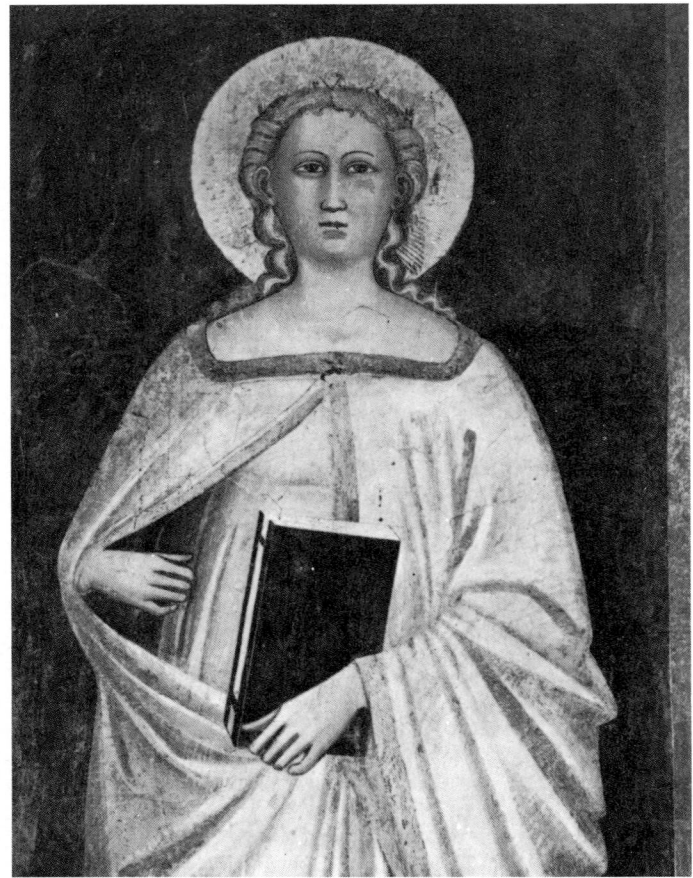

703

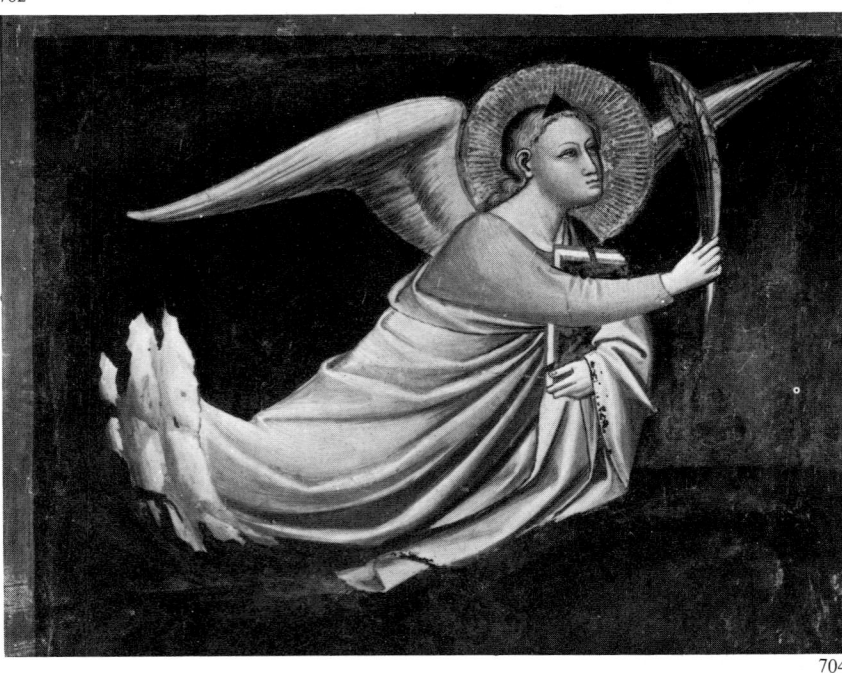

704

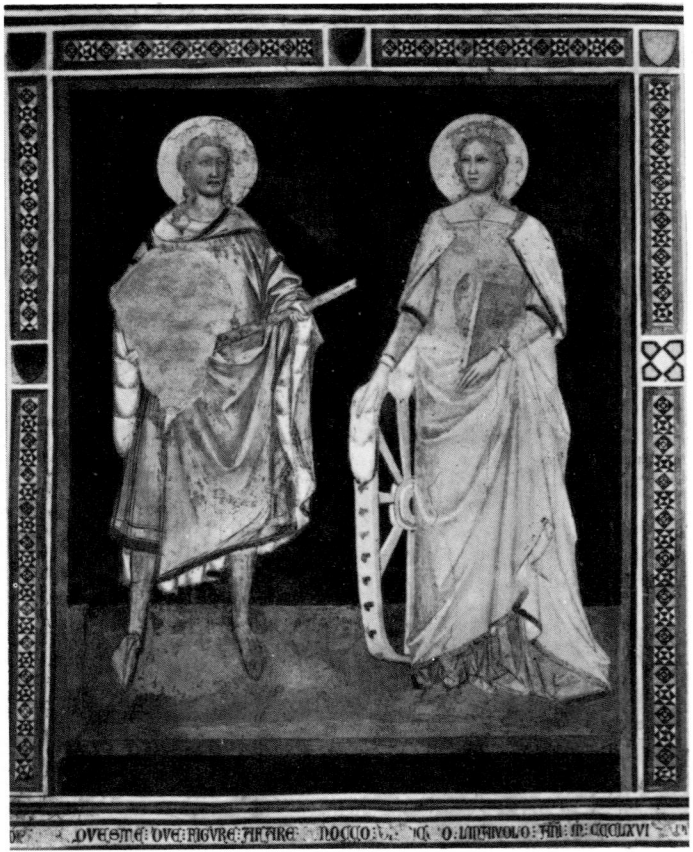

705

702. *Martyrdom of St Sebastian, detail of fig. 701. Fresco. Signa, S. Lorenzo. SGF 131308.*
703. *St Margaret, detail. Fresco. Signa, S. Lorenzo. SGF 131323.*
704. *An Angel, detail of fig. 702. Fresco. S. Lorenzo. SGF 131305.*
705. *Sts Julian and Catherine. Fresco. Signa, S. Lorenzo. SGF 131296. d. 1366.*

SPINELLO ARETINO

One of the must gifted Florentine painters of the later part of the 14th century was Spinello Aretino, born, as the name indicates, at Arezzo; we know also that his father's name was Lucca and that he belonged to a family of goldsmiths. Not only his father and grandfather but an uncle and a brother as well, followed this trade.

Notwithstanding the fact that Vasari and Spinello were natives of the same town, the biographer does not seem to have been better informed about this artist than about any other painter of the Trecento. He calls him a pupil of Jacopo del Casentino....

Spinello's father married in 1344 or '45, so the painter cannot very well have been born much before 1346 and the date of 1361 is therefore hardly admissible for the altar-piece that he made for the monastery of Camaldoli, which in 1639 was replaced by one of Vasari's own productions. In 1373 he is found buying landed property and in 1375 he is charged by the confraternity of Sta. Maria with the execution of frescoes in the chapel of Francesco degli Accettanti in the Pieve, Arezzo, for which he was to receive the sum of fifty-six golden guilders.

The first dated work we have of this artist is the altar-piece he executed in 1385 for Monte Oliveto. It is probable that he married in the following year and that sons were born to him in 1387, 1398 and 1406; Spinello remarried after the death of his first wife. In 1386 Spinello appears also as witness in an act of Arezzo.

The frescoes in the sacristy of S. Miniato al Monte and those in Sta. Caterina of Antella were ordered from Spinello by Benedetto degli Alberti who was exiled, but in his will of July 1387 makes arrangements for the finishing of the latter, from which it may be assumed that the former were then already executed.

In 1391 Parasone Grassi, one of the surveyors of the Cathedral, called Spinello to Pisa to make the still existing frescoes in the Campo Santo, for which he received forty or fifty guilders a piece; this money was paid to him in 1391 and 1392.

The signed polyptych, now in the Accademia, Florence, but originally at Lucca, is dated 1391 and might very well have been made during his sojourn in Pisa; at the end of 1395 and beginning of 1396 we find him again in Arezzo where he executed a now much damaged but still visible fresco of the Pietà above the door of the palace of the Fraternity and two figures in the " Udienza " for which he was paid three gold florins.

In 1399 he undertook to make a triptych of the Coronation of the Virgin between saints for the monastery of Sta. Felicità, Florence, which he executed with the assistance of Niccolò di Pietro Gerini and his son Lorenzo di Niccolò. This picture, now in the Accademia of Florence, bears the date 1401.

The same year, 1401, he was charged with the ornamentation of two chapels in the Pieve of Arezzo, for which work he was to be paid thirty Aretine guilders; of this he received part in that same year and part in 1404.

In November 1404, on the occasion of the reception of the new bishop, Piero dei Ricci, at Arezzo, great festivities were organised and the decoration, among which were painted flags, was entrusted to Spinello, for which he was paid, in February, 1405, six golden guilders. At the beginning of 1405 he went with Parri to Siena and worked seven and a half months at eleven and a half guilders a month in the Cathedral, but of these paintings nothing remains.

In 1407 Spinello with his son Parri contracted for the extant frescoes in the Sala di Balia of the Palazzo Pubblico at Siena for which they were to receive forty-four florins a month; they were started about March 1408, a certain Bettus Benedicti, indicating the subjects which should be represented, and these were probably accomplished before Spinello's death which took place in March two years later, because at that moment we find him back again in Arezzo. Vasari's fertile fantasy tells us the cause of death was a dream Spinello had in which he saw a figure of Lucifer just as he had depicted him. He was buried in the church of Morello.....

from R. van Marle, pp. 577-80, *The Development of the Italian Schools of Painting*, Vol. III, The Hague, 1924.

After a primary formation in the city of his birth, through which influences from both Siena and Florence crossed, he must have passed through a Florentine Orcagnesque period; but he also must have had some Sienese contacts, as they are evident in his polyptych of Monteoliveto, today dismantled. The episodes of St Benedict's life of 1387, frescoes in the sacristy of St. Miniato al Monte, mark the happiest point in Spinello's work. They are of a lovely narrative technique which recalls the prose of Sacchetti, and are of a high quality which somehow anticipates the subtleties of Lorenzo Monaco.....

The principal stages of Spinello after 1387 and the sacristy of San Miniato are the frescoes in the oratory of S. Caterina at Antella, near Florence: these seem not too distant in date, later, rather than earlier; the triptych dated 1491 which is in the Accademia of Florence; the frescoes of the Camposanto in Pisa with the lives of Saints Efisius and Potitus, which are roughly of the same date; the large triptych of 1401, also at the Accademia in Florence, which marks a collaboration with Niccolò Gerini; and finally, the life of Pope Alexander III frescoed in the Palazzo Pubblico of Siena (1407-8).....

> from L. Berti, p. 21, *II^a Mostra di Affreschi Staccati*, Florence, 1958.

Ca. 1350-1410. Probably a pupil of Agnolo Gaddi; principally influenced by the Orcagna school, and to a lesser degree by Luca di Tommé. Assisted in his late years by his son, Parri.

> from B. Berenson, p. 202, *Italian Pictures of the Renaissance, Florentine School*, Vol. I, London, 1963.

A native of Arezzo, as his name implies. He was employed at Pisa and Siena, as well as working in Florence, where he may have been a pupil of Agnolo Gaddi. The Florentine tradition, notably that of Orcagna, was the predominant influence on his style.....

> from St. J. Gore, p. 15, *The Art of Painting in Florence & Siena from 1250-1500*, London, 1965.

Spinello di Luca Spinelli, called Spinello Aretino. Florentine School. Born ca. 1346; died 1410/11. Although he came from Arezzo, his style was developed under Orcagnesque influence in Florence. He was active there and also in Pisa and Siena.

> from F. R. Shapley, p. 45, *Paintings from the Samuel H. Kress Collection*, London, 1966.

Spinello Aretino was born in Arezzo around 1346, where he may have received a local workshop training, although at an early stage in his work the Florentine influences of Orcagna and Nardo di Cione can be detected. During the years 1384-5 he painted a polyptych for the church of Monteoliveto Maggiore, parts of which are preserved in the Pinacoteca in Siena, the Fogg Art Museum and Budapest. Two fresco cycles, one in a small church at Antella near Florence and the other, illustrating the life of St. Benedict, in S. Miniato al Monte, Florence, both date from around 1387. In 1391 Spinello painted a triptych for the church of S. Andrea, Lucca, in co-operation with Lorenzo di Niccolò, and towards the end of his life worked in Pisa (the Camposanto), Arezzo, and Siena where he frescoed scenes from the life of Pope Alexander III in the Sala di Balia of the Palazzo Pubblico. An accurate assessment of Spinello Aretino has often been hampered by the readiness of scholars to attach his name to anonymous fragments of late Gothic fresco. His authentic work, while representative of the late Trecento, is in fact more vigorous than many of the rather insipid attributions from which he suffers. Particularly in his later frescoes, the Giottesque element is one of advance towards a style which has more in common with Masaccio than with Agnolo Gaddi.....

> from P. Dal Poggetto, p. 90, *Frescoes from Florence*, London, 1969.

BIBLIOGRAPHY
BOOKS

An asterisk indicates a work listed in the General Bibliography

Pini, Milanesi*, 1876, no 6; *v. Marle 1924**, pp. 577-80; Gombosi, G., *Spinello Aretino*, Budapest, 1926; *Toesca, 1929**, p. 67; *Berenson, 1932**, pp. 574-9; *Venturi, L.**, 1931, pl. 50; Berenson, B., in *T-Becker**, 1937, XXXI, pp. 385-7; Gombosi, G., in *Treccani, Vol. XXXII**, 1937, p. 337; *Coletti, Vol. II**, 1946, pp. 58-9; *Antal**, 1948, pp. 207-10, 357-8; *Galetti**, " P-Z ", 1950, pp. 2342-3; *Oertel, 1950**, p. 57; *Toesca, 1951**, pp. 650-2; Berti, L., *MAS II**, 1958, p. 21; Bucci, M., *Camposanto**, 1960, pp. 83-92; *Gregori**, 1960, p. 7; *Davies**, 1961, pp. 498-501; *Berenson, 1963**, Vol. I, pp. 202-6; Gore, St J., *Wildenstein**, 1965, pp. 15-16; *Marcucci**, 1965, pp. 125-6; Bellosi, L., *La Pittura Tardogotica in Toscana* (I Maestri del Colore, 239), Milan, 1966; Chiarini, M., *Masaccio e la pittura del '400 in Toscana* (I Maestri del Colore, 256), Milan, 1966; *Shapley**, 1966, pp. 45-6; Dal Poggetto, P., *Fresco Show**, 1968, pp. 98-101 (90-3); *MMOA**, 1971, pp. 42-46; Zeri, F., *Diari di Lavoro*, Bergamo, 1971, pp. 28-32; Calderoni Masetti, A. R., *Spinello Aretino Giovane*, Florence-Pisa, 1973; *Dutch Show**, 1974, pp. 103-4; *Maetzke**, 1974, pp. 61-67.

JOURNALS

Del Vita, A., *RAAM*, II, XV, 1915, pp. 75-88, 110-20; Pasqui, U., *RA*, X, 1917-18, pp. 53-68; Lasareff, V., *AA*, XVI, 1928, pp. 25-40; Burroughs, A., *MM*, XXIII, 1928, pp. 274-8; Del Vita, A., *BA*, VIII, VII, 1929, pp. 385-95; Procacci, U., *IV*, II, 1, 1928-9, pp. 35-48; Procacci, U., *RA*, XI, 1929, pp. 273-87; degli Azzi, G., *IV*, 1930, III, pp. 216-21; Berenson, B., *DD*, XI, 5, 1930-1, pp. 1286-1318; Procacci, U., *RA*, XIV, 1932, pp. 141-232; Colasanti, A., *BA*, XXVII, 1934, pp. 337-50; Oertel, R., *MKIF*, V, 4/5, 1940, pp. 217-314; Pouncey, P., *BM*, 88, 1946, pp. 168-72; Gettens, R. J., *BFM*, X, 6, 1947, pp. 188-93; Coor, G., *WRJ*, XVIII, 1956, pp. 111-131; Zeri, F., *PA*, IX, 105, 1958, pp. 63-7; Vaughan, M., *CS*, CXLIV, 1959, pp. 206-7; Longhi, R., *PA*, XI, 131, 1960, pp. 33-5; Coor, G., *PMB*, LVI, 1961, pp. 56-60; Eisenberg, M., *AQ*, XXVI, 3, 1963, pp. 299-305; Donati, P. P., *AV*, III, 1964, pp. 11-24; Previtali, G., *O*, 121, 1965, p. 3; Bellosi, L., *PA*, XVI, 187/7, 1965, pp. 18-43; Gonzalez-Palacios, A., *PA*, XVI, 187/7, 1965, pp. 44-51; Longhi, R., *PA*, XVI, 187/7, 1965, pp. 52-55; Bellosi, L., *PA*, XVII, 201, 1966, pp. 76-9; Donati, P. P., *C*, XVII, 1966, pp. 56-72; Zeri, F., *BM*, 107, 1965, p. 255; Boskovits, M., *AV*, V, 2, 1966, pp. 23-28; Donati, P. P., *AV*, V, 2, 1966, pp. 16-22; Boskovits, M., *MKIF*, XIII, 1-4, 1967-68, p. 53; Donati, P. P., *AV*, VI, 2, 1967, pp. 21-16; *Edit.*, *BM*, 109, 1967, Dec, Ad. Section, plate 17; Boskovits, M., *AV*, VII, 3, 1968, pp. 3-13; Donati, P. P., *PA*, XIX, 221/41, 1968, pp. 10-21; van Os, H.W., *BM*, CXI, 1969, pp. 513-4; Avery, C., *AI*, II, 19/20/21, 1969, pp. 4-5; Henderson, N. R., *AQ*, XXXII, 1969, pp. 393-410; Kiel, H., *P.*, XXVII, 5, 1969, p. 421; Donati, P. P., *PA*, XXI, 247, 1970, pp. 3-11; Bellosi, L., *MKIF*, XVII, 2-3, 1973, p. 186, note 10; Bisogni, F., *MKIF*, XVII, 2-3, 1973, pp. 198, 9; Boskovits, M., *MKIF*, XVII, 2-3, 1973, p. 201; Carli, E., *MKIF*, XVII, 2-3, 1973, p. 226; Fehm, S., *MKIF*, XVII, 2-3, 1973, p. 257-72; Zeri, F., *MKIF*, XVII, 2-3, 1973, p. 369.

SIGNED AND DATED WORKS

Cambridge (Mass.), Fogg Art Museum 1917.3. Panel: Madonna & Child with Angels. s. (fig. 708).

1377 Arezzo, Museo Diocesano, formerly, S. Agostino. Fresco: Madonna & Child with Sts James, Antony Abbot and Kneeling Warrior. d. (fig. 715).

1385 Budapest, Musée des Beaux-Arts, 36. Panel: Sts Nemesius and John the Baptist. d. (fig. 709).

1385 Cambridge (Mass.), Fogg Art Museum 1915.12a, b, c. Panel: Sts Benedict and Lucilla. d. (fig. 712).

1391 Florence, Accademia 8461. Triptych: Madonna & Child Enthroned with Saints and Angels. s & d. (fig. 723).

1393 Quinto (near Sesto Fiorentino), S. Maria, L. Wall. Triptych: Madonna & Child Enthroned with Sts Peter, Philip, James and Lawrence. d. (fig. 716).

1407 Arezzo, S. Domenico. Fresco: Virgin Annunciate. d. (fig. 724).

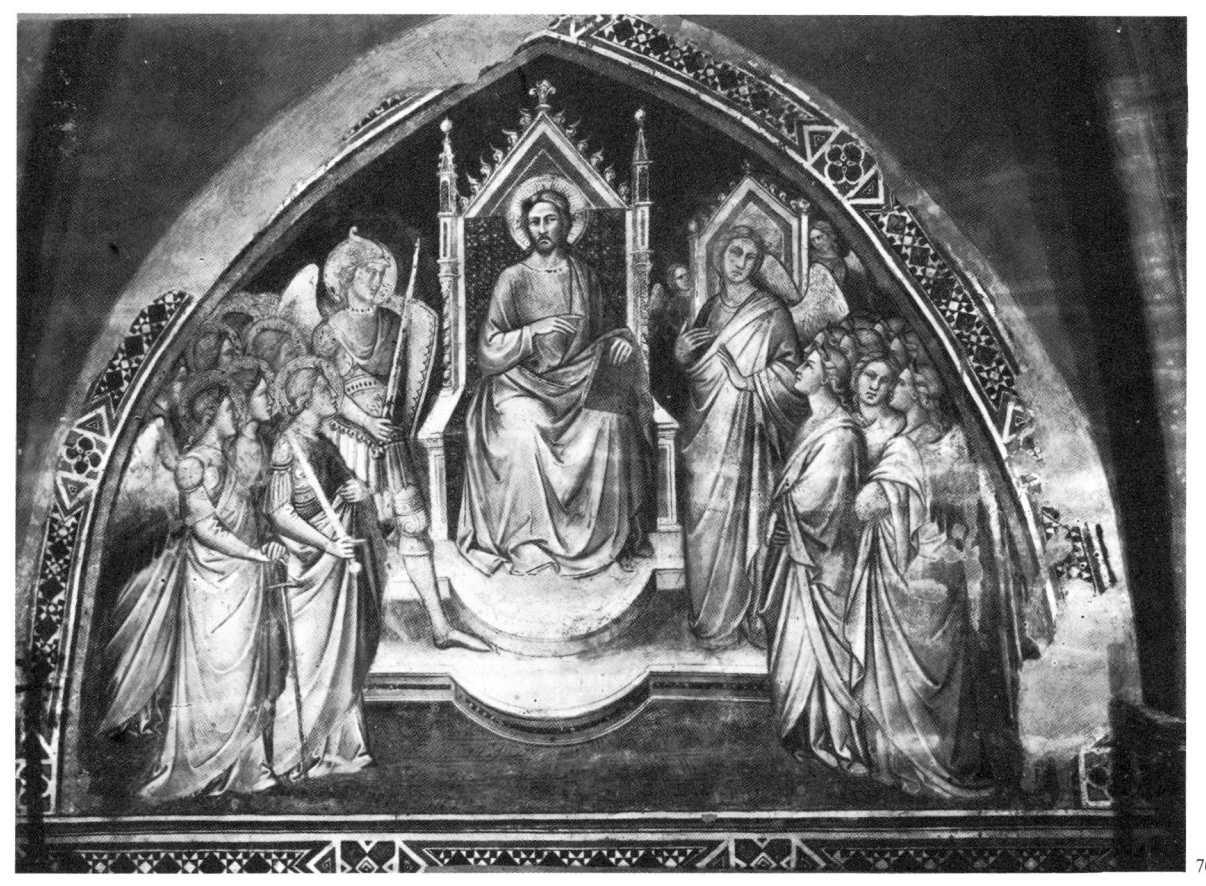

706

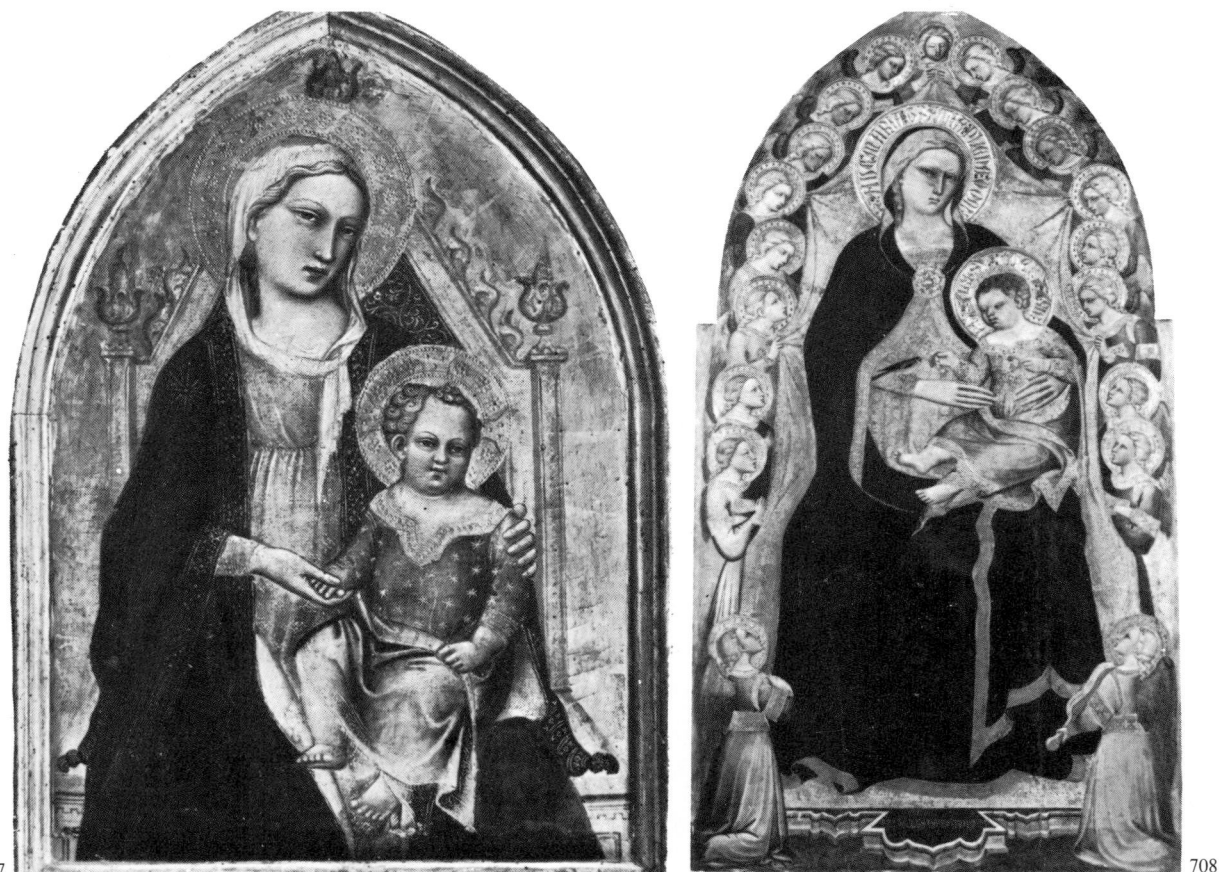

707   708

706. *Christ Enthroned with Angels and Saints. Fresco. Arezzo, S. Francesco. SGF 133155.*
707. *Madonna and Child Enthroned. Panel. Pisa, Museo Nazionale di S. Matteo. no. 133. 71 × 50. Brogi 19409.*
708. *Madonna and Child Enthroned with Angels. Panel. Cambridge (Mass.), Fogg Art Museum. no. 1917.3. 215.5 × 92.3. Museum photo. s.*

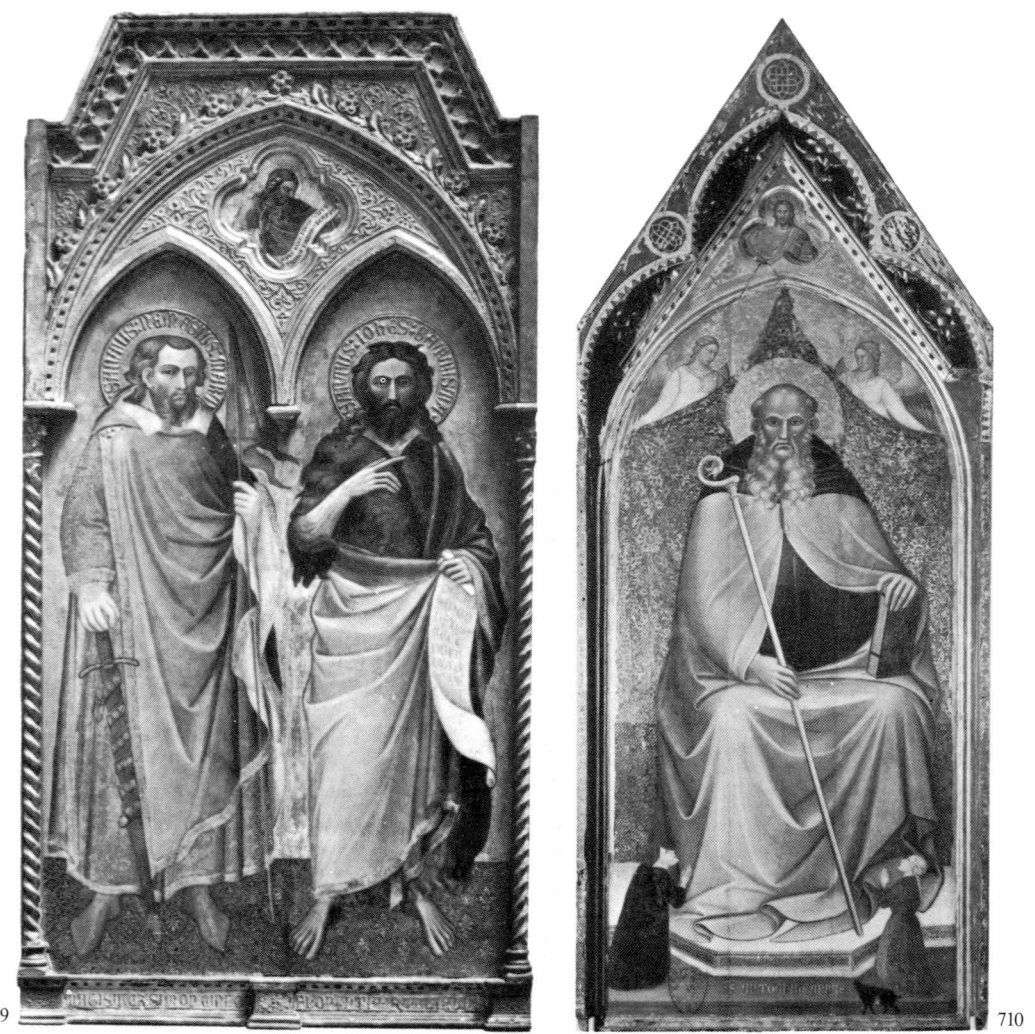

709   710

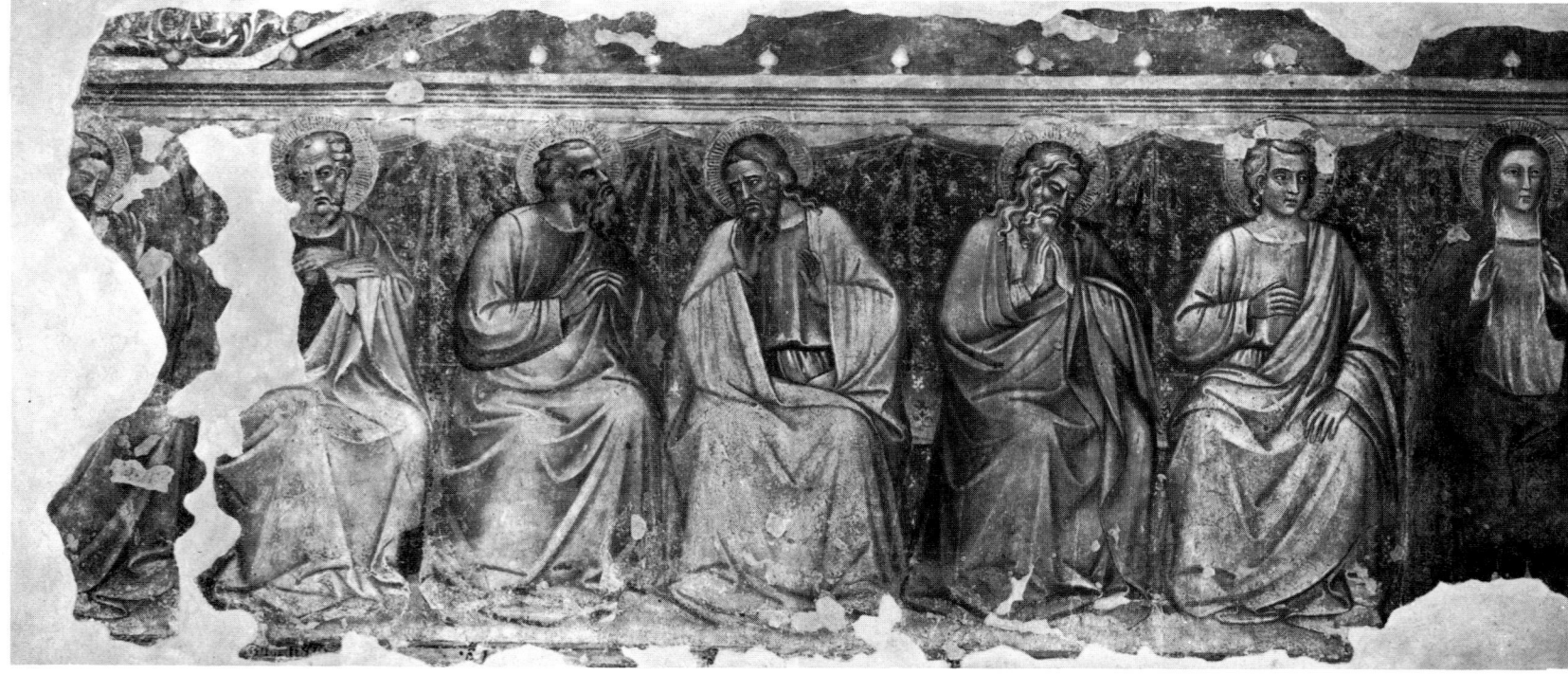

709. *Sts Nemesius and John the Baptist. Above: a Prophet. Panel. Budapest, Musée des Beaux-Arts. no. 36. 194 × 94.5. Museum photo. d. 1385.*
710. *St Anthony Abbot Enthroned with two Angels and two Donors. Above: Christ blessing. Panel. Providence (R.I.), Museum of Art, Rhode Island School of Design. no. 16.243. 229.8 × 91.1. Museum photo.*
711. *Pentecost. Fresco. Arezzo, S. Francesco. SGF 125015-6.*

348

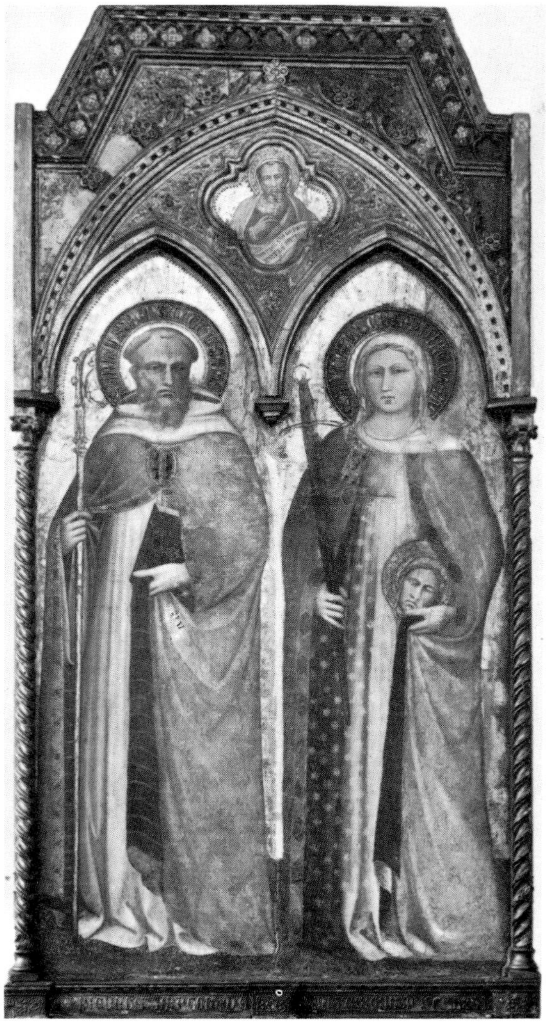

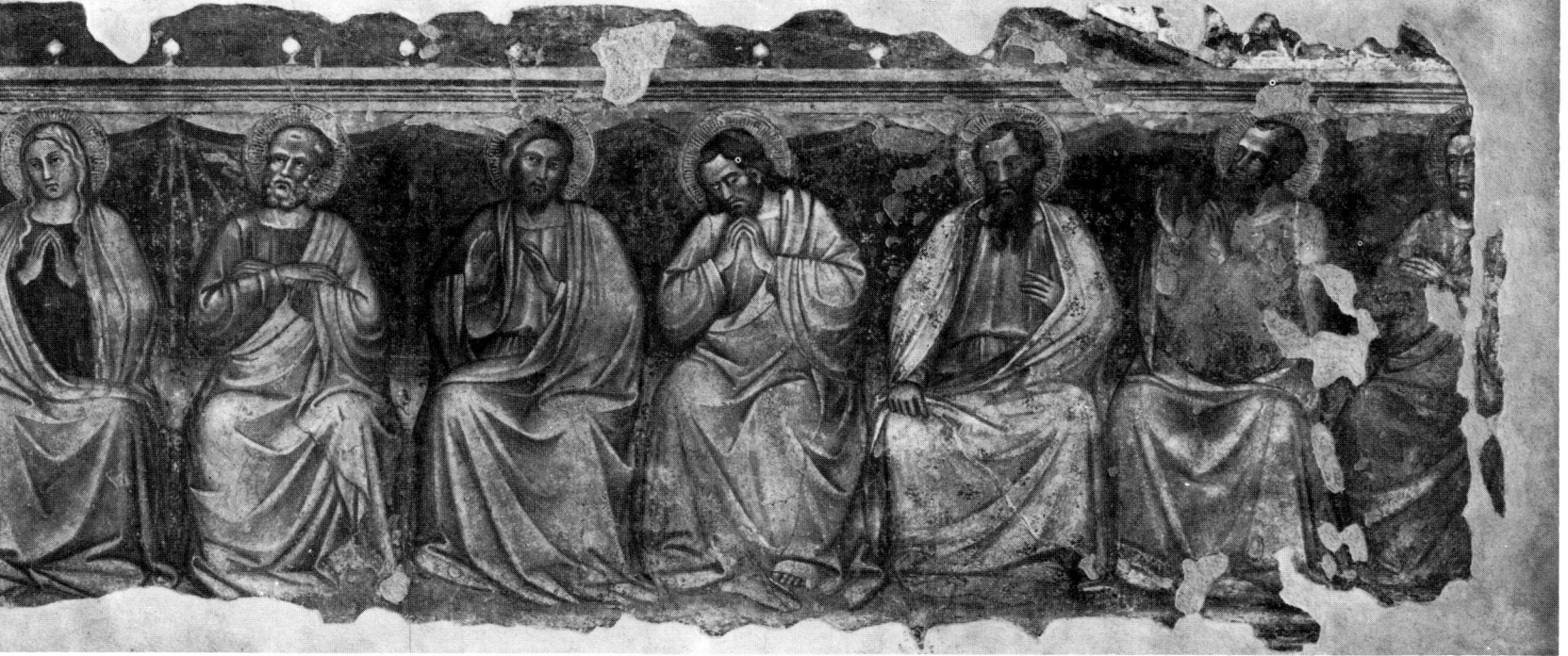

712.   Sts Benedict and Lucilla. Panel. Cambridge (Mass.), Fogg Art Museum. no. 1915.12A and B. 189.5 × 92. Museum photo. d. 1385.
713.   Predella scenes: Beheading of St Nemesius; a Saint; Feast of Herod, predella from fig. 709. Panel. Budapest, Musée Beaux-Arts. no. 36.
lp: 35 × 32.7;   cp: 32 × 8;   rp: 35 × 34.3.   Museum photo. d. 1385.
714.   Predella scene: Death of St Benedict; St Augustine; Martyrdom of St Lucilla, predella from of fig. 712. Panel. Cambridge (Mass.), Fogg Art
Museum.   no. 1915.12B: ca. 96 × 76.   Museum photo. d. 1385.

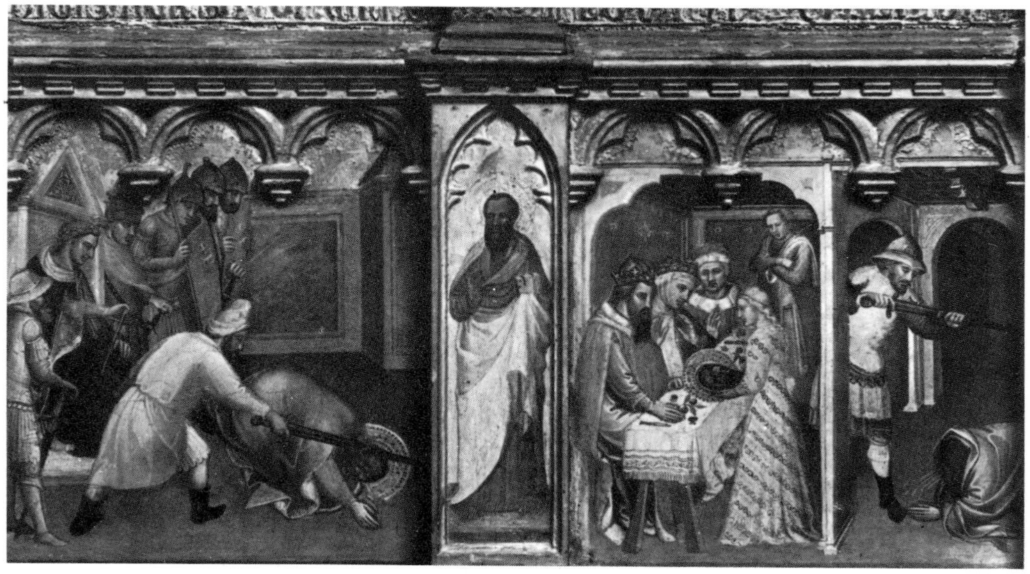

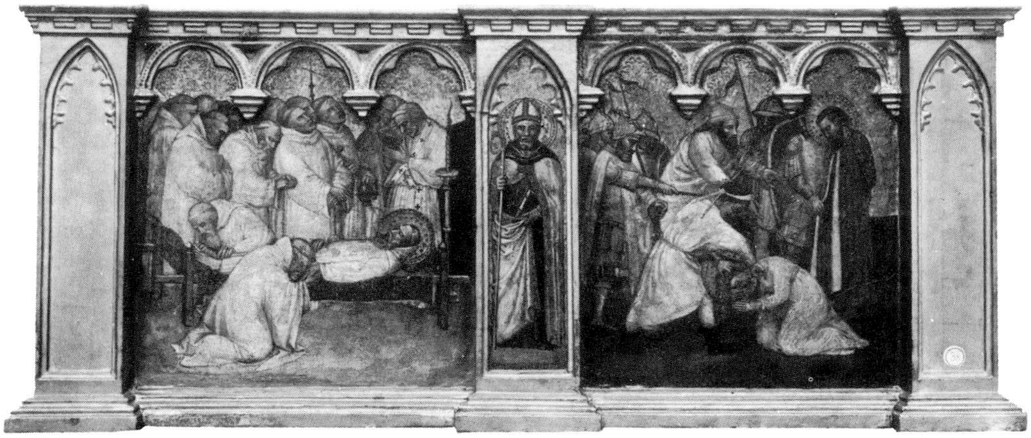

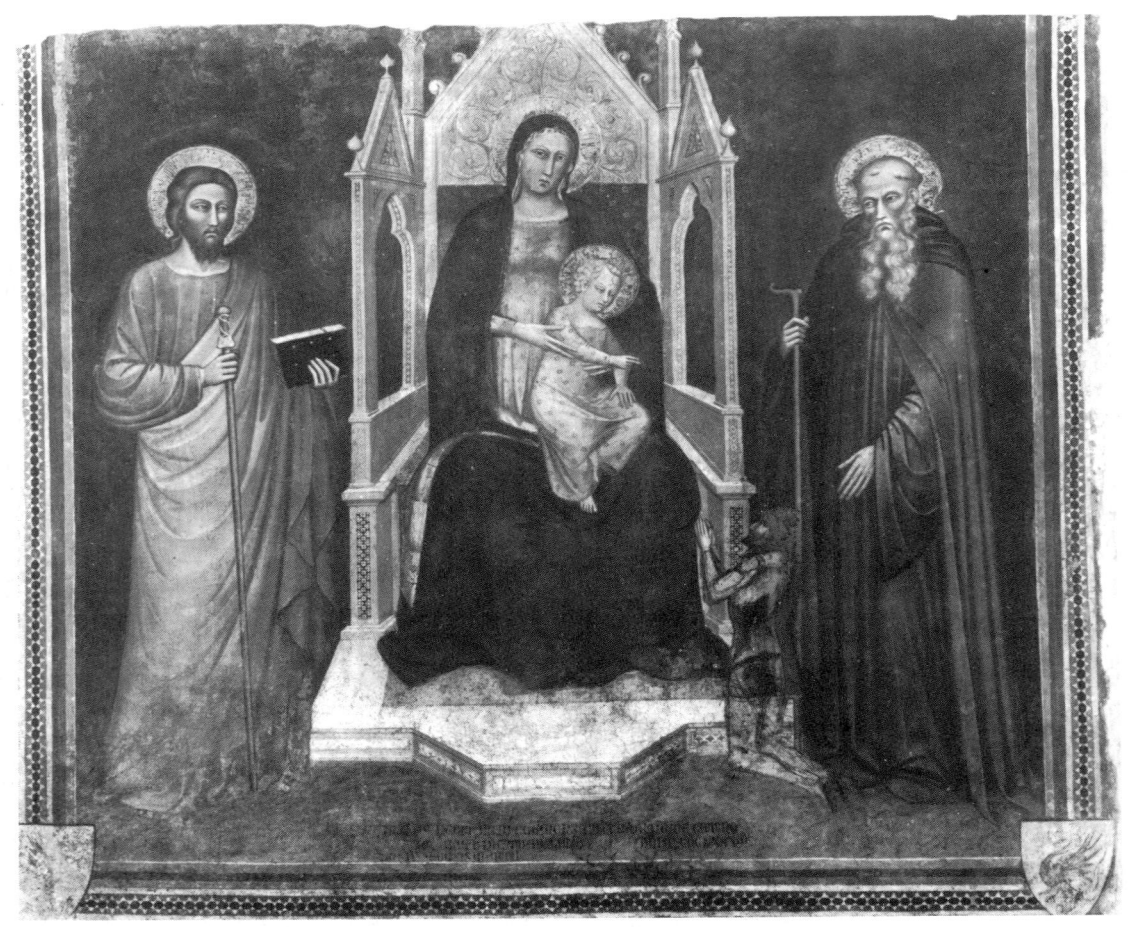

715

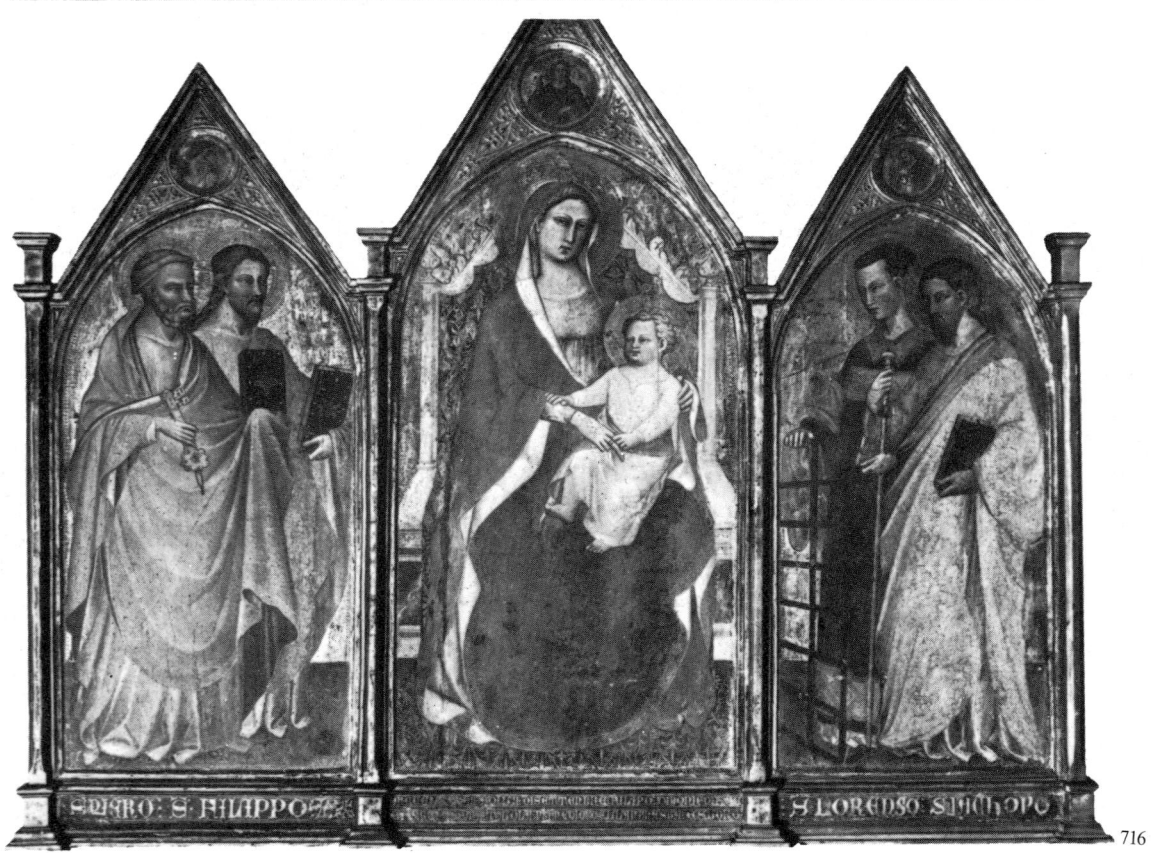

716

715. *Madonna and Child Enthroned with two Saints and a kneeling Warrior. Fresco. Arezzo, Museo Diocesano (formerly S. Agostino). SGF 124814. d. 1377.*
716. *Triptych: Madonna and Child Enthroned with Sts Peter, Philip, Lawrence and James. Panel. Quinto, (near Sesto Fiorentino), S. Maria. 170 × 152. Brogi 24793. d. 1393.*

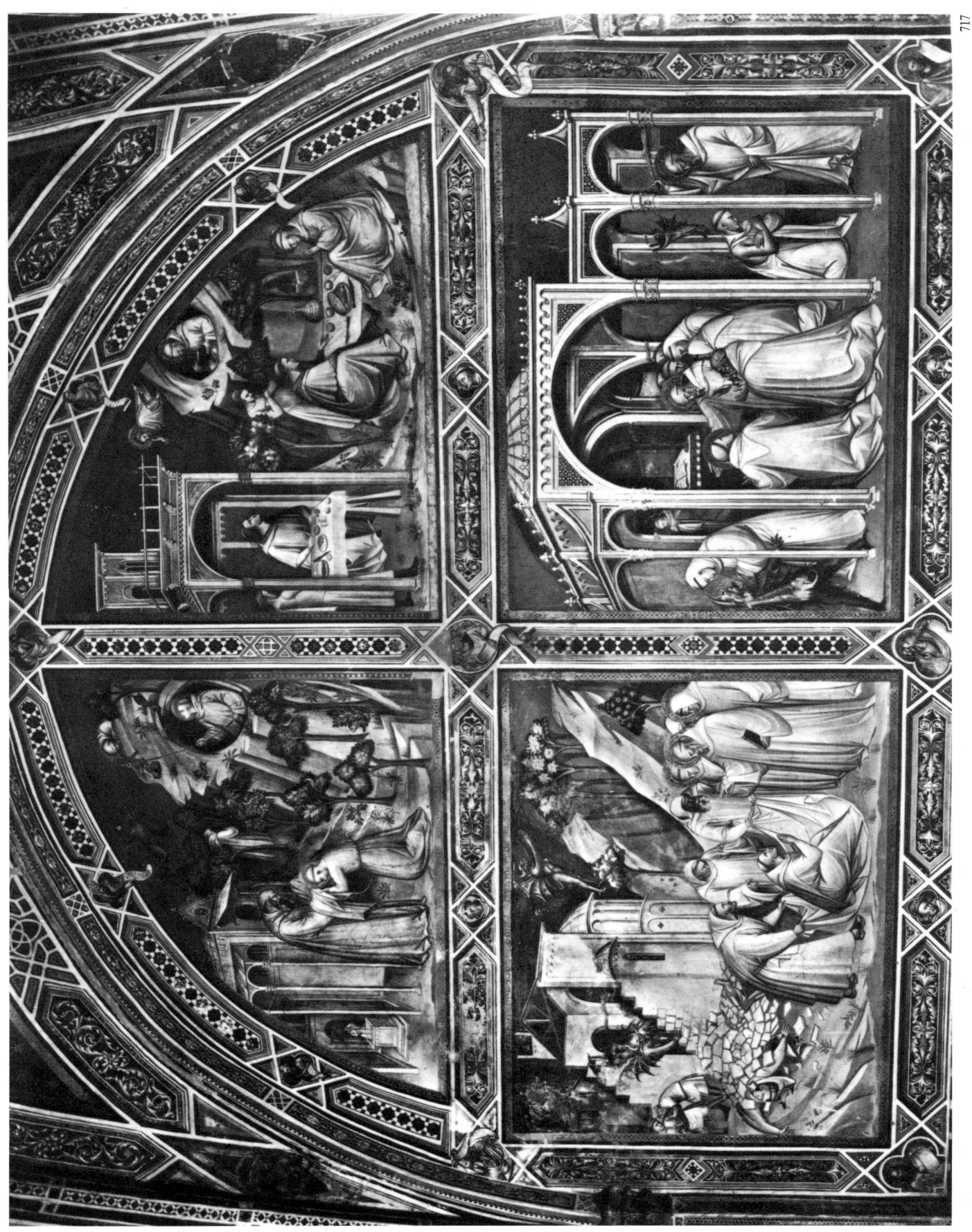

717. *Four scenes from the Life of St Benedict : St Benedict retires to Subiaco and is given the Habit by the monk Romano; on Easter Day St Benedict is visited by a monk sent by God; St Benedict founds Monte Cassino and brings back to life a monk crushed by a falling wall; St Benedict exorcises a possessed monk. Fresco. Florence, S. Miniato al Monte. Alinari 4508. 1386-87.*

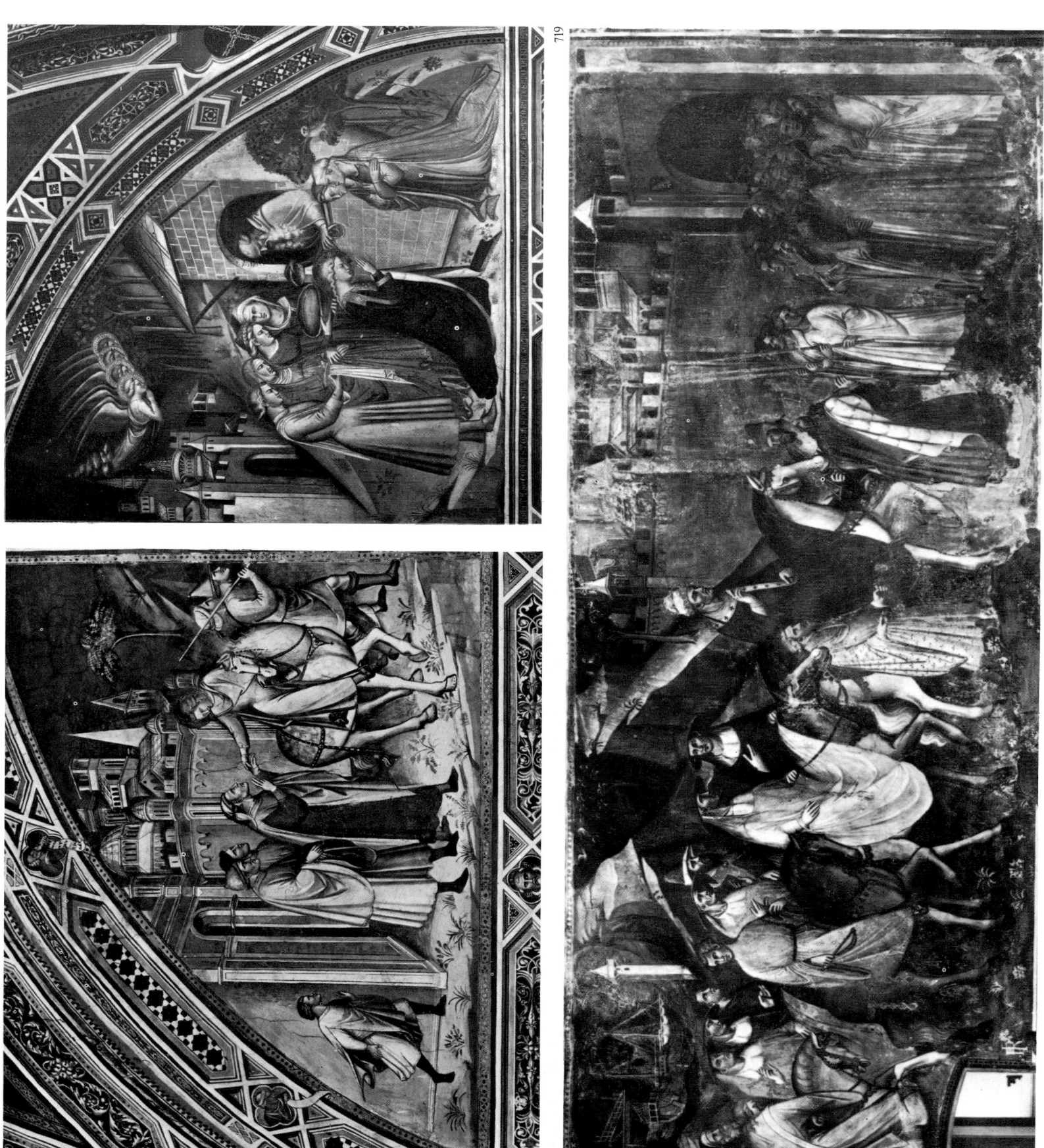

718. *Scene from the Life of St Benedict: he leaves his home. Fresco. Florence, S. Miniato al Monte. Alinari 4504. 1386-87.*
719. *Scene from the Life of St Catherine: St Catherine baptised by the Hermit. Fresco. Antella, Oratorio di S. Caterina. SGF 100728. 1387.*
720. *Scene from the Life of Alexander III: Alexander entering Rome. Fresco. Siena, Palazzo Pubblico, Sala di Balia. Brogi 15071. 1408-10.*

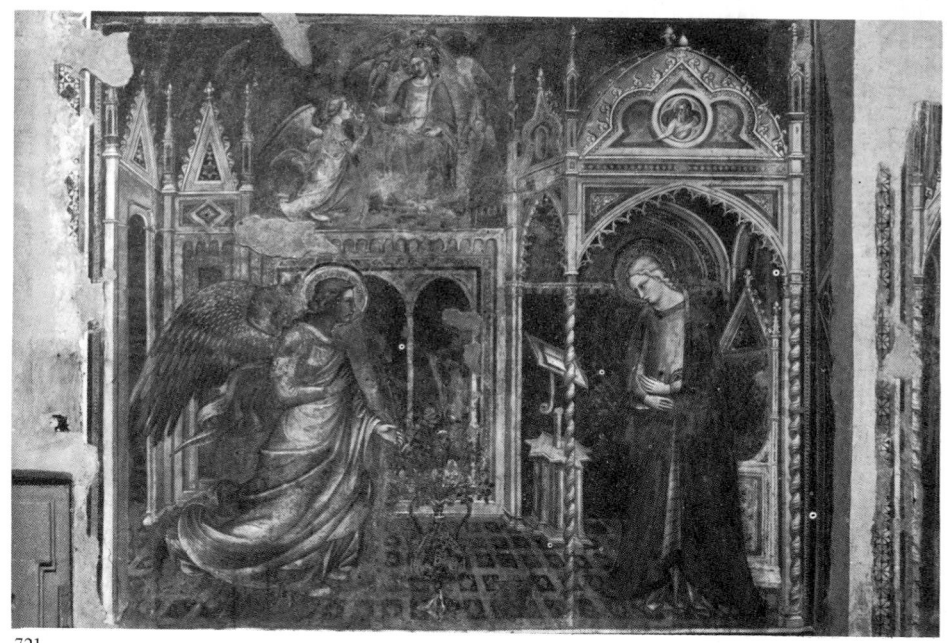

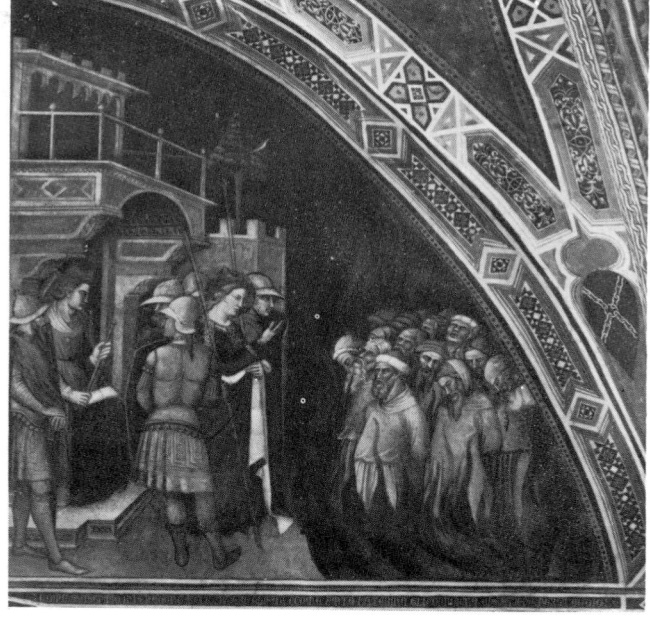

721

722

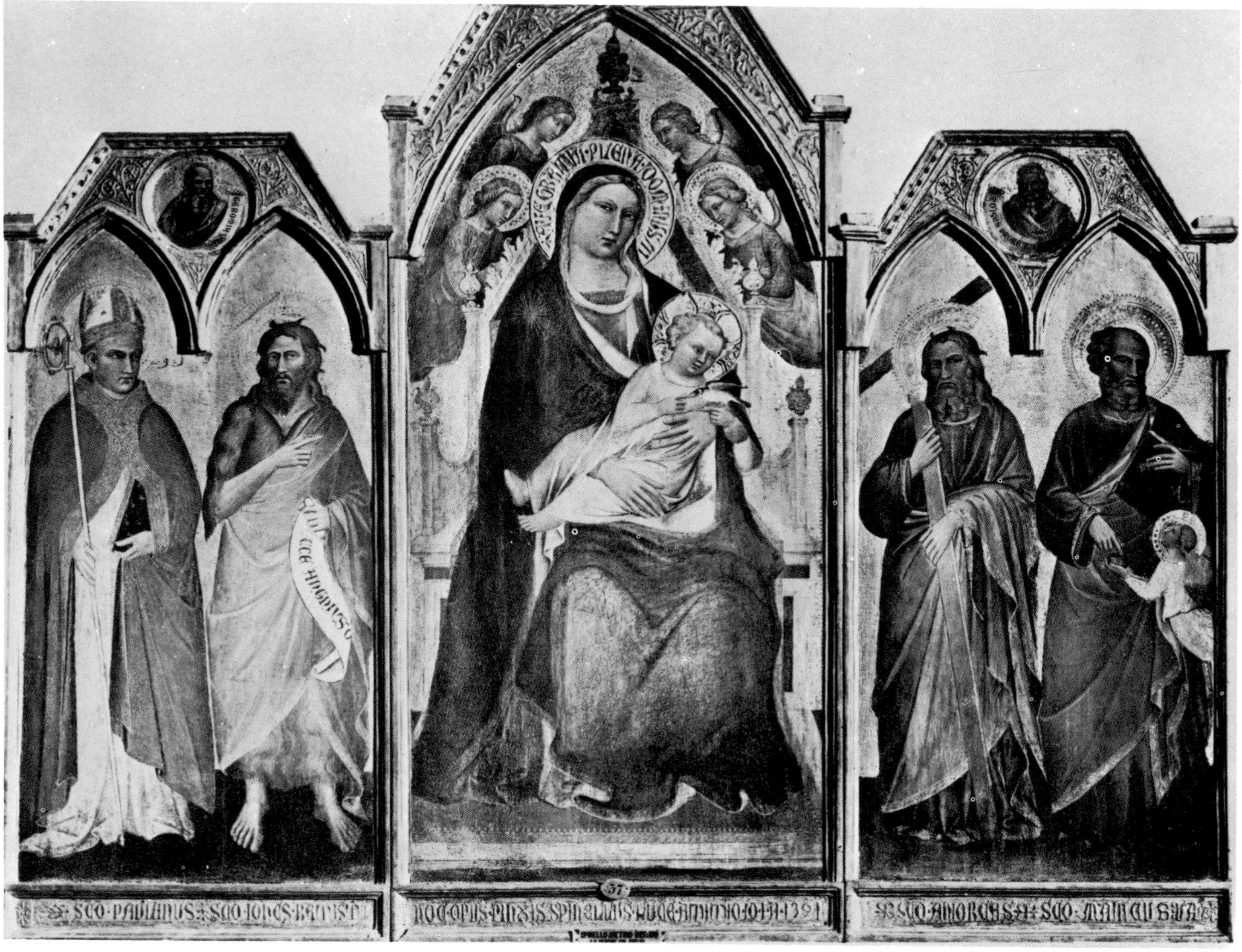

723

721. *Annunciation. Fresco. Arezzo, S. Francesco. SGF 129575.*
722. *Scene from the Life of St Catherine: Martyrdom of the converted Philosophers. Fresco. Antella (8 kms south-east of Florence), Oratorio di S. Caterina.
SGF 100709. 1387.*
723. *Triptych: Madonna and Child Enthroned with four Angels and Sts Paulinus, John the Baptist, Andrew and Matthew. Above: two Prophets. Panel.
Florence, Accademia no. 8461. 109 × 209. Alinari 1620. s & d. 1391.*

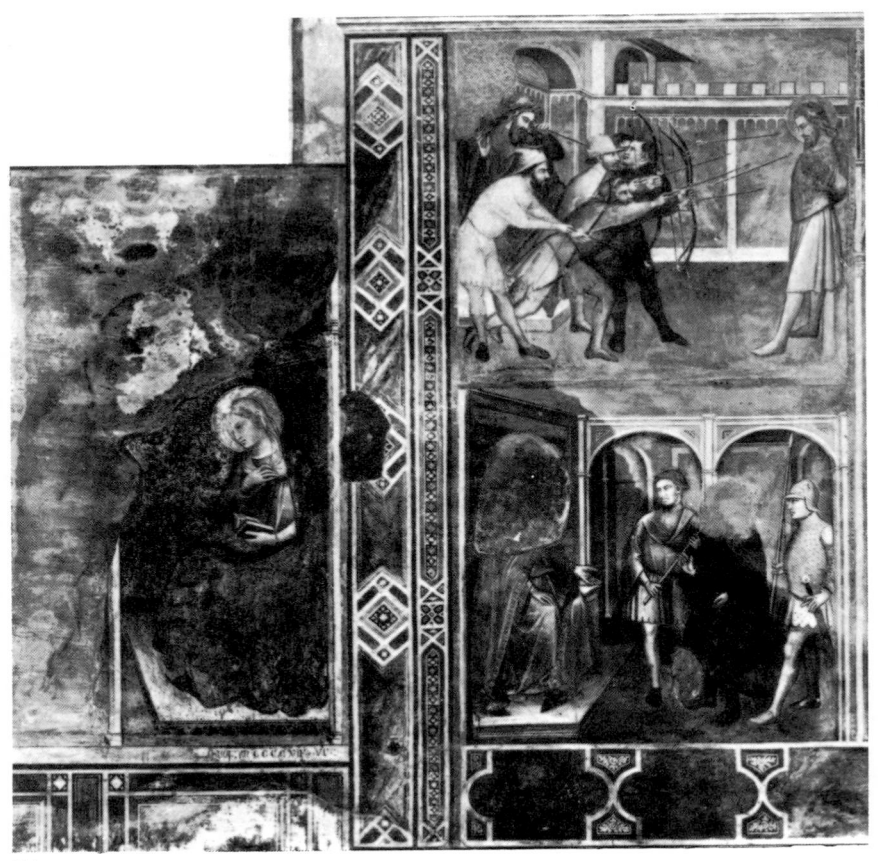

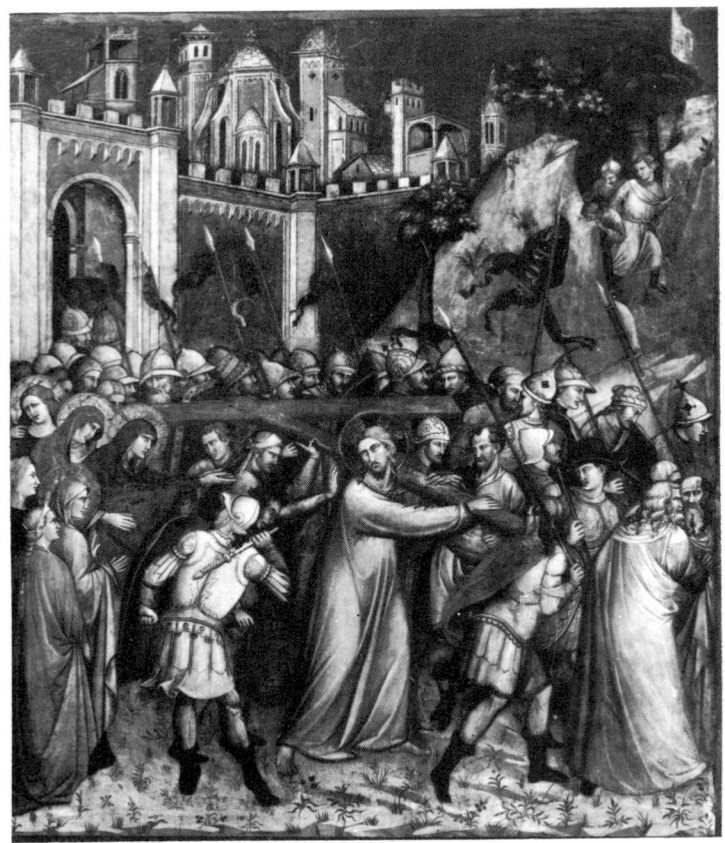

724

725

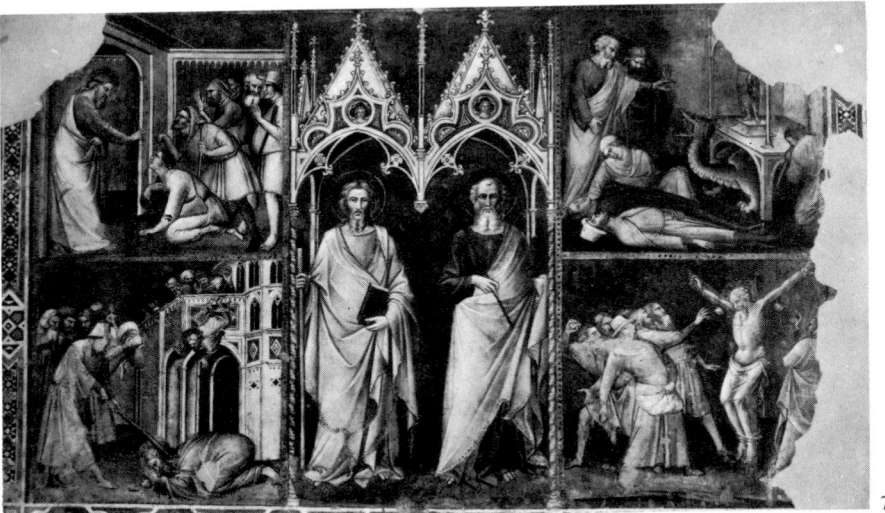

726

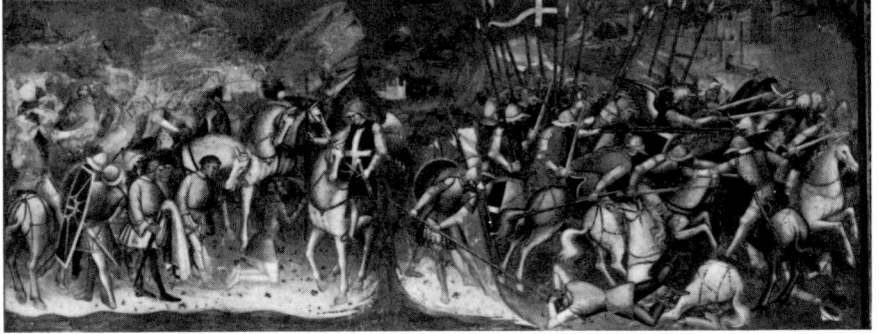

727

724. *Various damaged scenes, including a dated Virgin Annunciate. Fresco. Arezzo, S. Domenico. SGF 12247. d. 1407.*
725. *Way to Calvary. Fresco. Florence, S. Croce, Sacristy. Alinari 3912.*
726. *Sts James and Philip; St James heals Cripples; his Beheading; St Philip exorcises the Temple of Hierapolis; his Crucifixion. Fresco. Arezzo, S. Domenico. SGF 159349.*
727. *Conversion of St Ephysius in Battle and Rout of the Pagans in Sardinia. Fresco. Pisa, Camposanto. Alinari 8852. 1391-92.*

GIOVANNI dal PONTE

Already Vasari attributed to his Giovanni dal Ponte some frescoes in the Scali chapel of Sta. Trinita, now it is known that this decoration was executed in 1434 by Giovanni di Marco and his companion Smeraldo di Giovanni and since the frescoes, parts of which are in a good state of preservation, have been discovered in this chapel, the personality of this artist is no longer wrapped in mystery, Vasari calls his painter Giovanni di Stefano a Ponte; his real name was Giovanni di Marco and he had his studio near S. Stefano a Ponte. We possess several documents concerning him, from which we learn that he was born in 1385, that in 1408 he was member of the compagnia di S. Lucca... Between 1427 and 1433 we find him paying taxes and running a studio together with Smeraldo di Giovanni who died in 1444 at the age of seventy-nine. Giovanni di Marco died seven years before his companion who continued to pay taxes until 1442.....

> from R. van Marle, p. 68, *The Development of the Italian Schools of Painting*, Vol. IX, The Hague, 1927.

The triptych by Giovanni da Ponte from Rosano shows the same current of evolution a little farther along in time, in a moment of revived Gothicism to which Lorenzo Monaco, a painter with a purer and simpler note that Gentile's — who may have had some influence on Bicci — led the way. Here, in the *Annunciation*, the angel alights imponderably, bringing the breath of the morning with him; but while he has caught something of Lorenzo's exquisite grace, the Virgin, unable to rise to the poetic exigencies of the situation, betrays only too clearly the typical limitations of Giovanni.....

> from R. Offner, p. 170, *The Burlington Magazine*, Vol. LXIII, July-Dec., 1933.

1358-after 1437. Probably a pupil of Spinello Aretino; strongly influenced by Lorenzo Monaco, and subsequently by Fra Angelico and Masaccio. Close to the Master of the Bambino Vispo.

> from B. Berenson, p. 90, *Italian Pictures of the Renaissance, Florentine School*, Vol. I, London, 1963.

His name arose from his occupying a studio near Santo Stefano al Ponte Vecchio, Florence. According to Berenson he may have been a pupil of Spinello Aretino; he was influenced by Lorenzo Monaco and later by Angelico and Masaccio. Paintings of a rather mannered and sophisticated Gothicism seem to have been collected under his name. His only documented work is a series of frescoes of the early 1430's in Santa Trinita, Florence.....

> from St. J. Gore, p. 21, *The Art of Painting in Florence & Siena from 1250-1500*, London, 1965.

Giovanni di Marco, called Giovanni dal Ponte, from the location of his studio, near Santo Stefano a Ponte, Florence. Florentine School. Born ca. 1385; died 1437?. His consistent, somewhat *retardataire* style has been recognized in a large number of paintings, although only a few are documented or signed and these date in his last years, after 1430. He may have been a pupil of Spinello Aretino but was influenced chiefly by Lorenzo Monaco and Fra Angelico. His nearest of kin among the minor Gothic painters of his class is the Master of the Bambino Vispo.....

> from F. R. Shapley, p. 91, *Paintings from the Samuel H. Kress Collection*, London, 1966.

.... only a half-decade after the death of Masaccio, artists like Giovanni dal Ponte attempted to reconcile the revolutionary new vision of Masaccio with features of the past art, features which had never entirely ceased to be valid but which in the 1430's were again very deliberately asserted and applied. Giovanni dal Ponte, along with other contemporaries, thus invented a style which, in retrospect can be considered the foundation upon which a Fra Filippo Lippi or a Domenico Veneziano, greater as artists but faced with artistic problems not so dissimilar to Giovanni's, created what amounts to the Early Renaissance style of the second quarter of the fifteenth century in Florence.

from C. Shell, p. 42, *The Art Bulletin*, LIV, I, 1972.

BIBLIOGRAPHY

BOOKS

An asterisk indicates a work listed in the General Bibliography

Venturi, A.*, 1911, p. 26; Sirén, O., *Descriptive Catalogue of the Pictures in the Jarves Collection*, New Haven, 1916, pp. 77-78; *v. Marle, 1927**, pp. 85-6; *Antal**, 1948, p. 331; *Vavalà, 1948**, pp. 101-3; *Galetti**, 1950, " F-O ", p. 1152; *Oertel, 1950**, p. 45; Suida, W. E., *Art of the Italian Renaissance* (Catalogue of the Columbia Museum of Art, Columbia, (S. Carolina), 1954, pp. 14-15; Suida, W. E., *Catalogue of the M. H. De Young Memorial Museum*, San Francisco, 1955, p. 36; *Gregori**, 1960, p. 11; Contini-Bonacossi, A., *Art of the Renaissance* (Catalogue of the Columbia Museum of Art Columbia, (S. Carolina), 1962, pp. 31-33; *Berenson, 1963**, Vol. I, pp. 90-2; Gore, St J., *Wildenstein**, 1965, p. 21; Bellosi, L., *La pittura Tardogotica in Toscana* (I Maestri del Colore, 239), Milan, 1966; *Shapley**, 1966, pp. 91-2; *MMOA**, 1971, pp. 56-57; *Dutch Show**, 1974, p. 55.

JOURNALS

Toesca, P., *A*, 1904, pp. 49-58; Gamba, C., *RADA*, IV, 12, 1904, pp. 177-86; Horne, H. P., *BM*, IX, 1906, pp. 332-7; Sirén, O., *RADA*, VI, 5, 1906, pp. 81-7; Gamba, C., *RA*, IV, 10-12, 1906, pp. 164-8; Sirén, O., *BM*, XIV, 1909, pp. 325-6, Bernardini, G., *RADA*, IX, 6, 1909, pp. 89-94; Sirén, O., *RADA*, 1914, p. 234; Berenson, B., *DD*, XII, 1, 1932, pp. 173-93; Offner, R., *BM*, LXIII, July-Dec., 1933, p. 170; Boschetto, A., *Musées Royaux des Beaux-Arts, Bulletin*, III, 1954, p. 21; Berti, L., *C*, XII, 2, 1961, pp. 84-107; Blunt, A., *AP*, 81, 1965, p. 292; Guidi, F., *PA*, XIX, 223/43, 1968, pp. 27-46; Guidi, F., *PA*, XXI, 239, 1970, pp. 11-23; Shell, C., *AB*, LIV, 1, 1972, pp. 41-6.

DATED WORKS

1410 Chantilly, Musée Condé. Triptych: Coronation of the Virgin with God the Father, Angels and Saints. d. (fig. 739).

1430 Rosano (Pontassieve), S. Annunziata. Triptych: Annunciation with Sts. Eugenius, Benedict, John the Baptist and Nicholas. d. (fig. 741).

1435 Rome, Vatican, Pinacoteca. Triptych: Annunciation with Sts. Louis of Toulouse and Anthony of Padua. d. (fig. 750).

There are no known signed works by Giovanni dal Ponte.

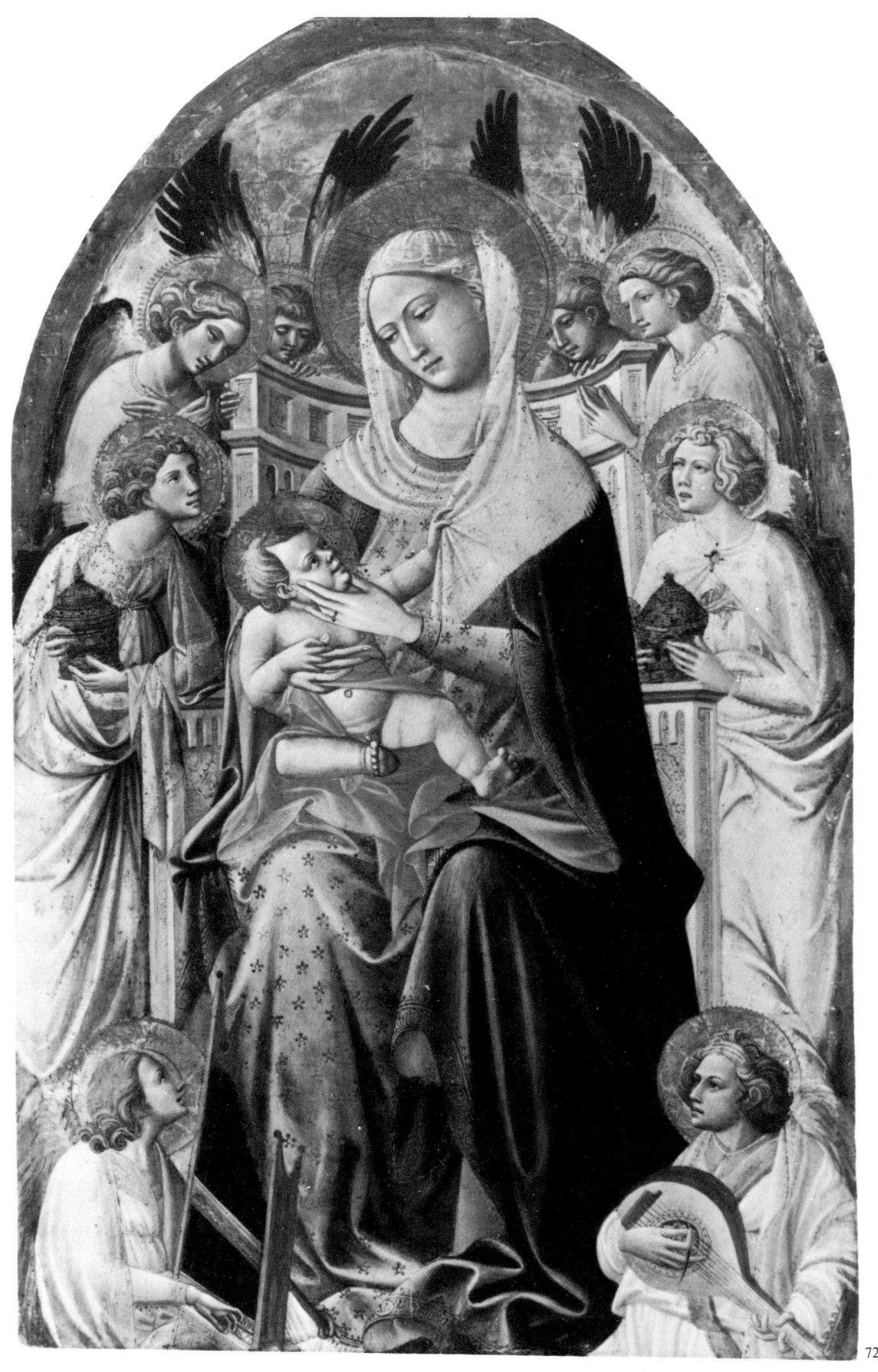

728

728. *Madonna and Child Enthroned with eight Angels. Panel. Cambridge, Fitzwilliam Museum. no. 551. 139.1 × 85.7. Museum photo: Stearn & Sons FMS 4895.*

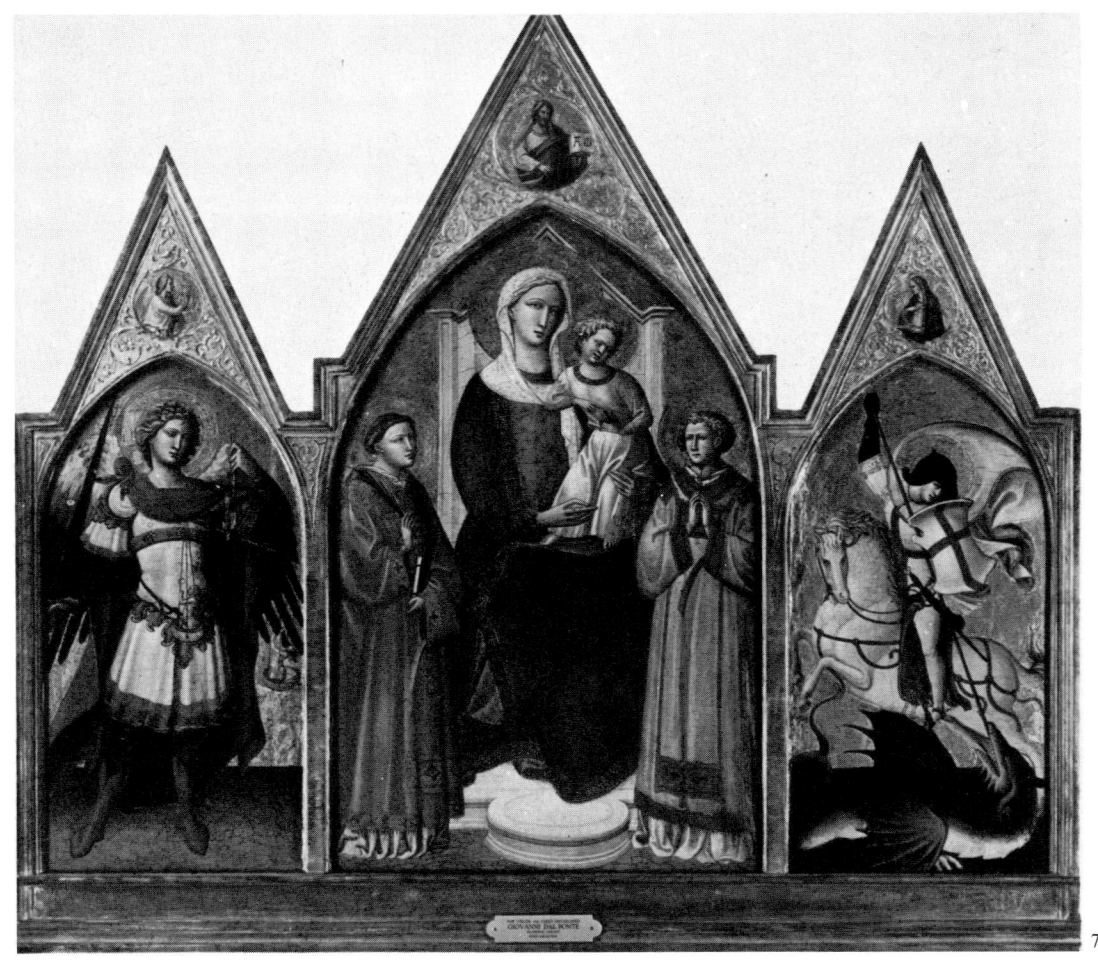

729

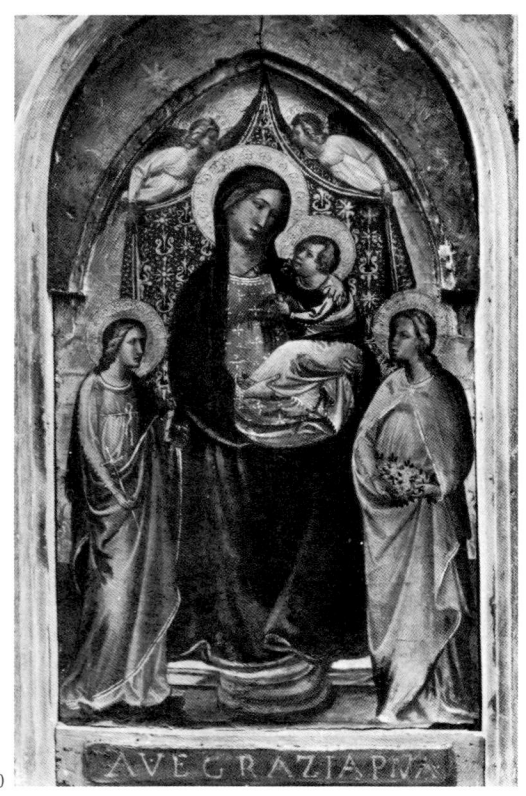

730

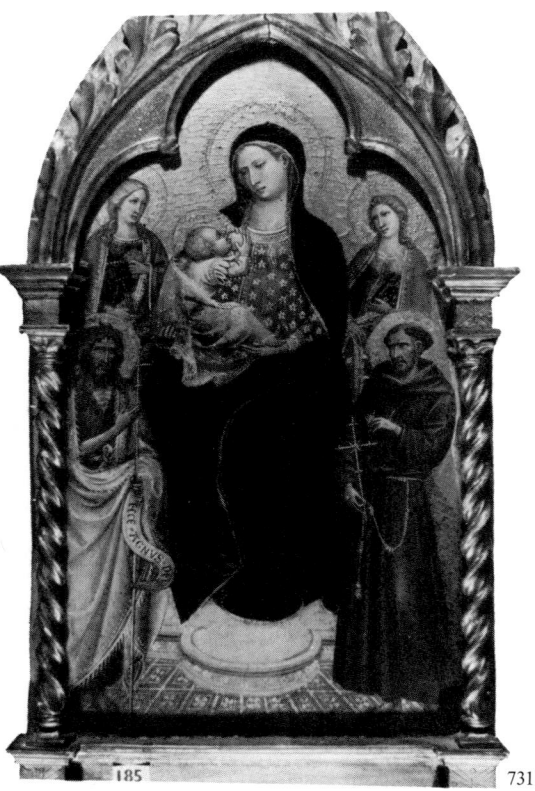

185 731

729. *Triptych: Madonna and Child Enthroned with Sts Stephen and Lawrence, Michael the Archangel and George. Above: Christ blessing and Annunciation. Panel. Columbia (S.C.), Museum of Art, Samuel H. Kress Collection. no. K300. cp: 92.7 × 58.4; sps: 70.1 × 35.2. Kress Foundation photo.*
730. *Tabernacle: Madonna and Child with two Angels and two female Saints. Panel. Florence, via de' Tavolini. Alinari 29196.*
731. *Madonna nursing the Child with Sts Lucy, John the Baptist, Catherine and Francis. Panel. Oakly Park (Shrops.), Earl of Plymouth Collection. 63.5 × 35.5. Courtauld B65/584.*

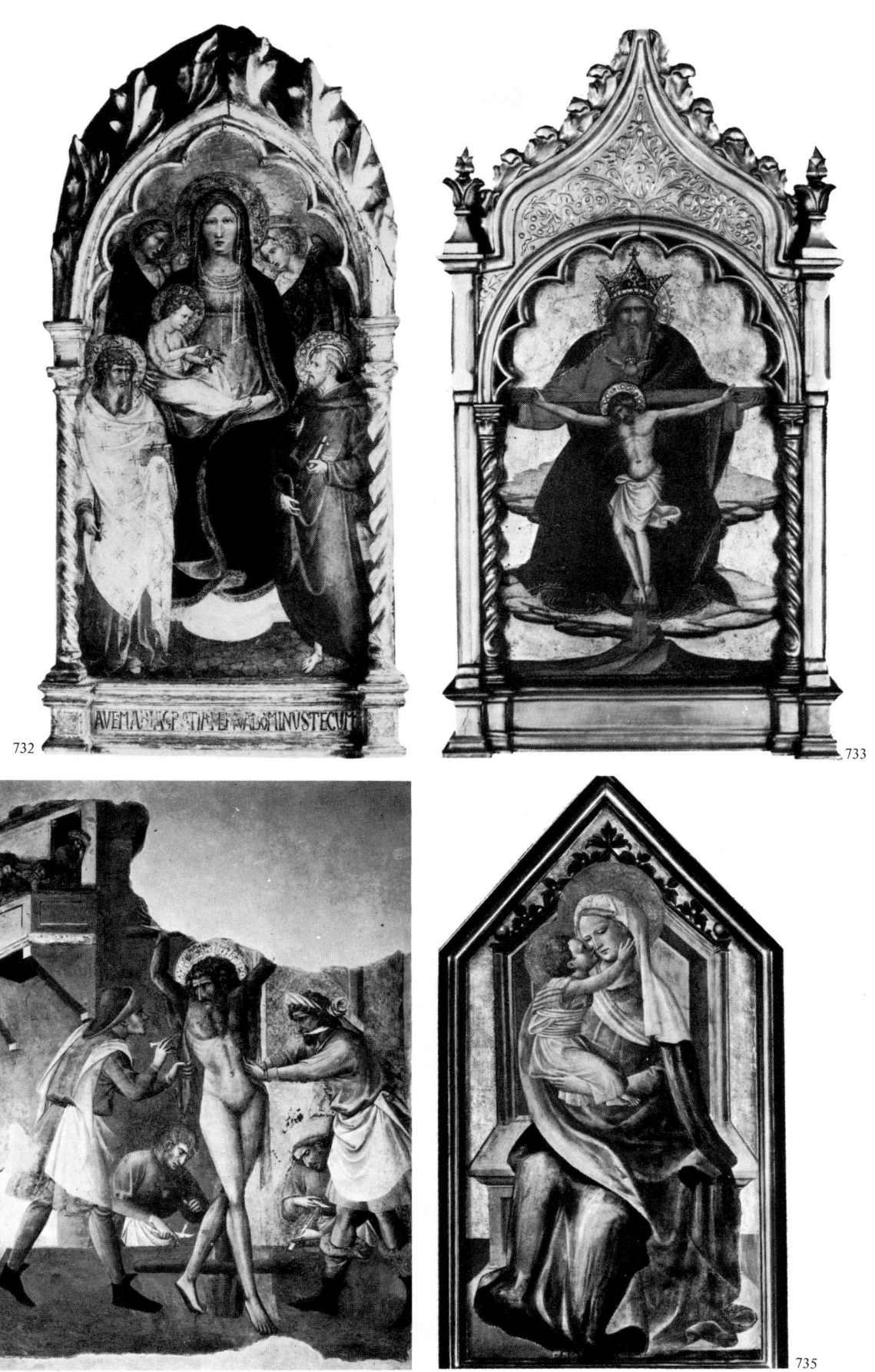

732. *Madonna and Child Enthroned with Sts Bartholomew and Francis and two Angels. Panel. Whereabouts unknown (formerly Perugia, van Marle Collection). Brogi 25663.*

733. *Pinnacle: Trinity, detail of fig. 738. Panel. London, National Gallery. no. 580 A. 43.1 × 27.3. Museum photo.*

734. *Skinning of St Bartholomew. Fresco. Florence, S. Trinita, Chapel of Our Lady of Lourdes. SGF 193409.*

735. *Madonna and Child Enthroned. Panel. Galluzzo (4 kms south of Florence), Certosa, Museo del Convento. 126 × 61. Brogi 6237.*

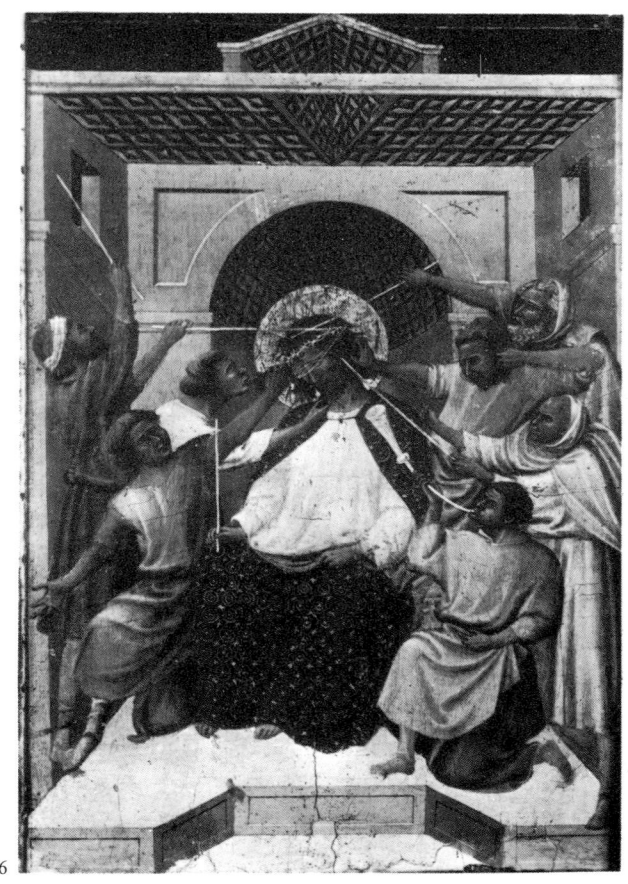

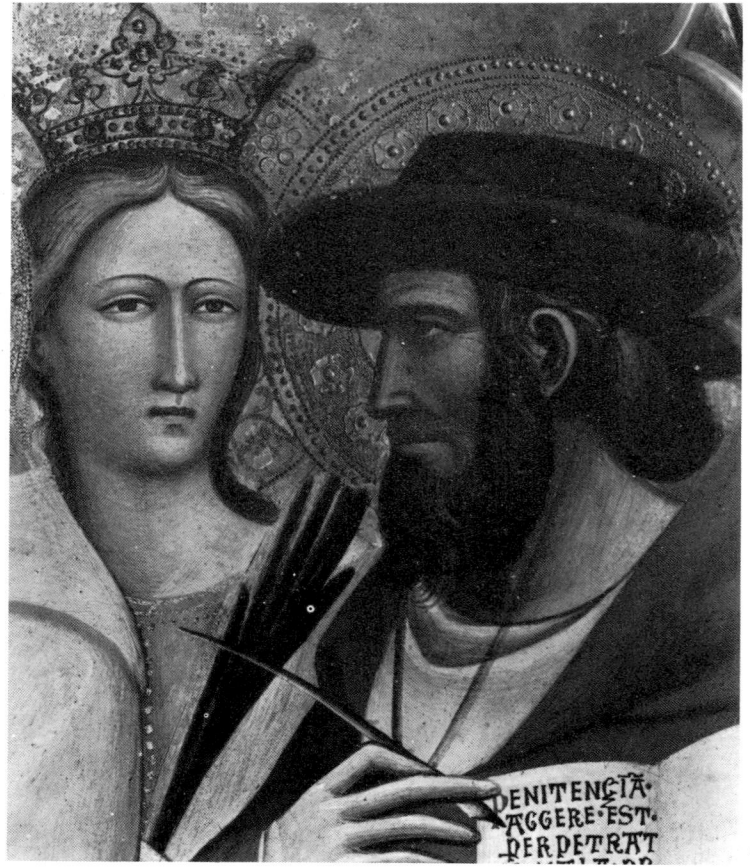

736

737

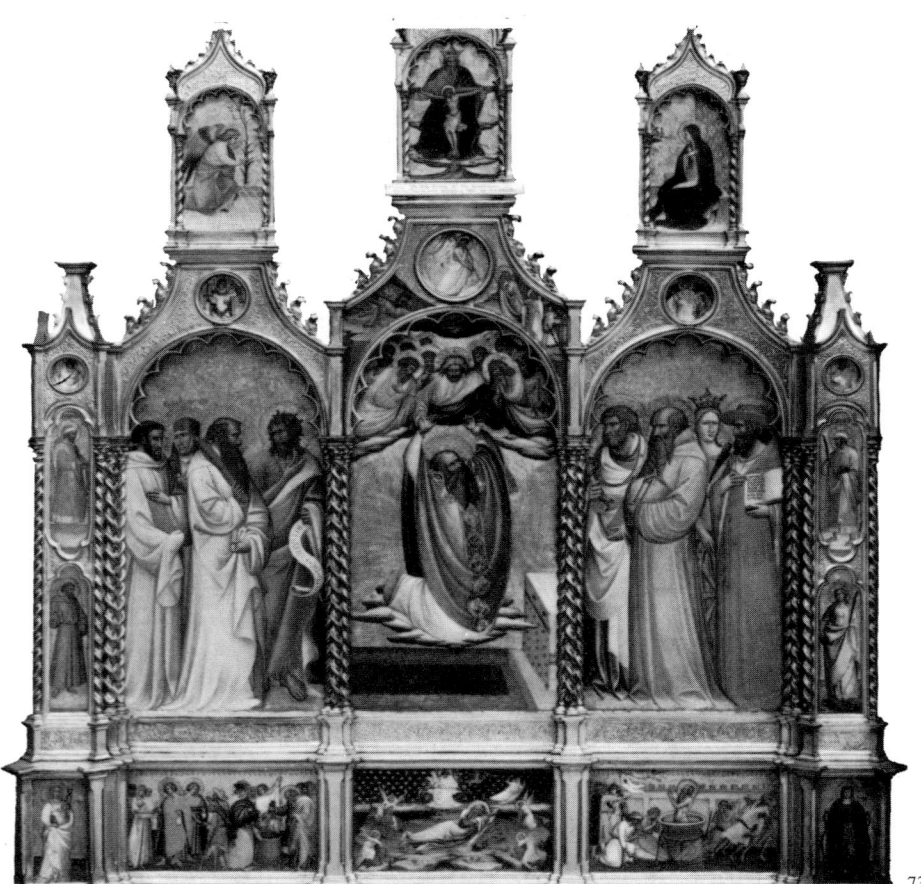

738

736. *Mocking of Christ. Panel. Strasbourg, Musée de Ville. no. 207. 38 × 26. Museum photo.*
737. *Heads of Sts Catherine and Jerome, detail of fig. 738. Panel. London, National Gallery. no. 580. Museum photo.*
738. *Triptych: Assumption of St John the Evangelist with Sts Bernard, Scholastica, Benedict, John the Baptist, Peter, Romuald, Catherine, and Jerome.*
 Pilasters: six Saints. Above: Trinity, Annunciation, Descent into Limbo, and two Saints. Predella: St Apollonia; Mission of the Apostles; St John
 on Patmos; St John in the pot of boiling oil; S. Verdiana. Panel. London, National Gallery. no. 580, 580 A. 166.3 × 249.5. Museum photo.

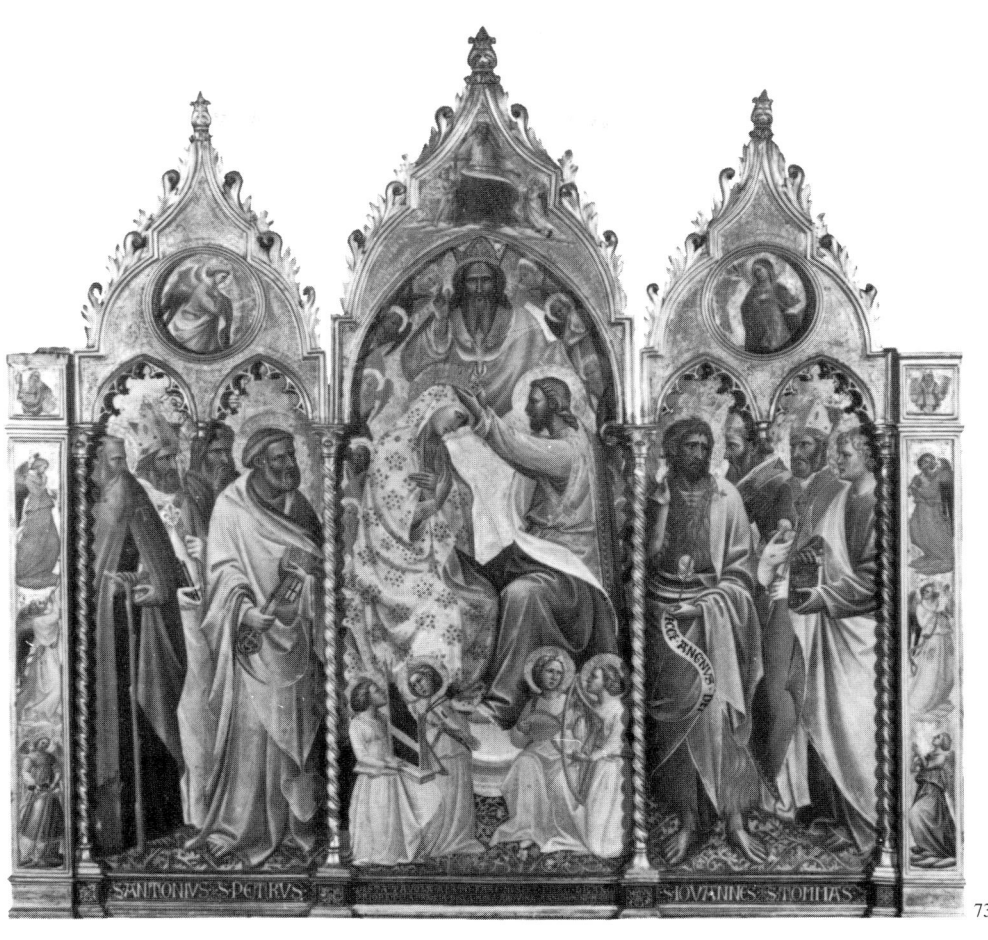

739

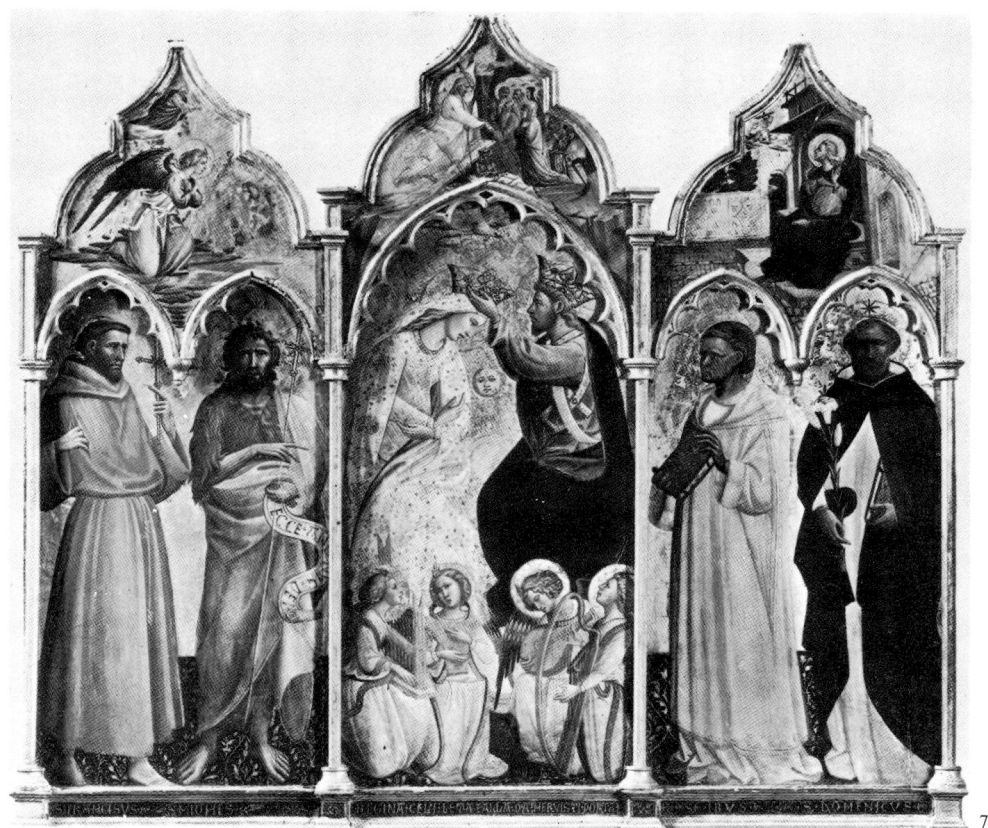

740

739. *Triptych: Coronation of the Virgin with God the Father, four music-making Angels and four Saints. Pinnacles: Annunciation and God the Father. Panel. Chantilly, Musée Condé. no. 3. 178 × 215. Giraudon 22490 LA. d. 1410.*

740. *Triptych: Coronation of the Virgin with four music-making Angels and Sts Francis, John the Baptist, Ives and Dominic. Above: Descent into Limbo, Annunciation. Panel. Florence, Accademia. no. 458. 182 × 207.5. Alinari 988.*

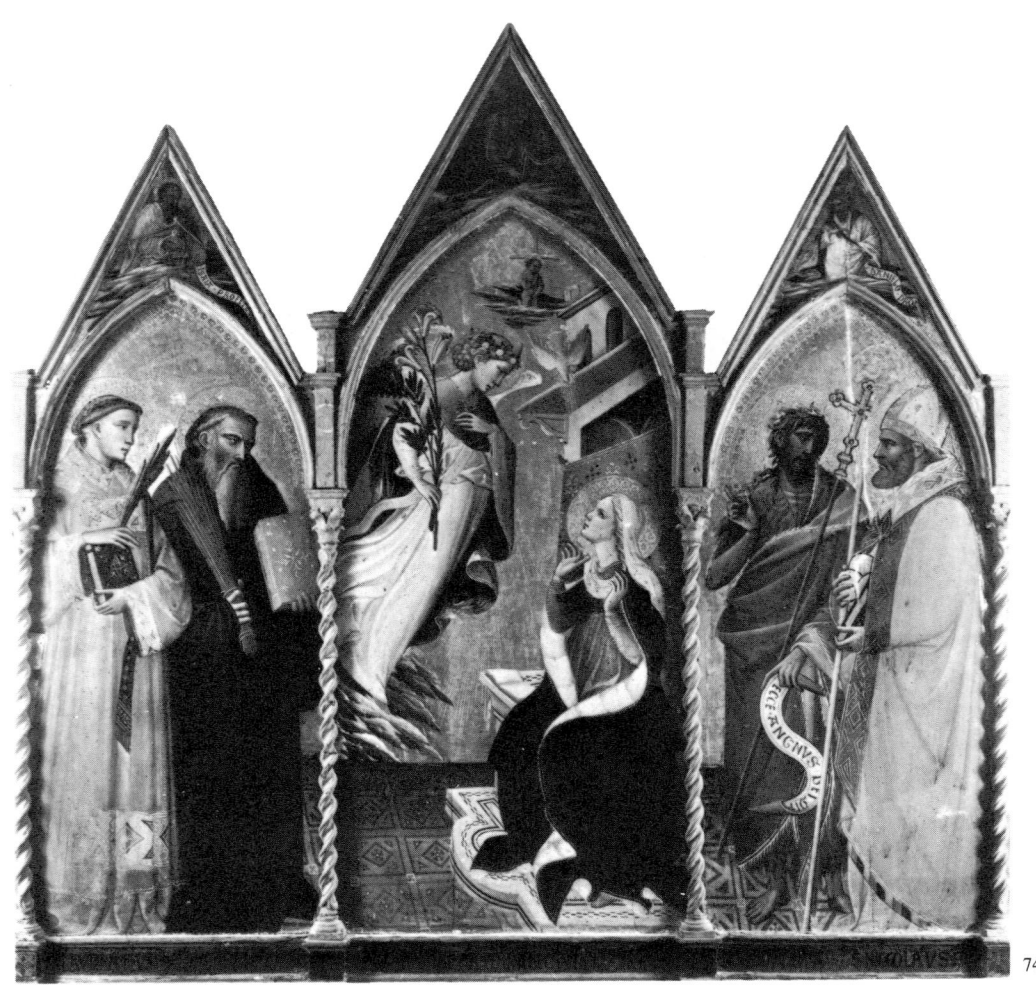

741

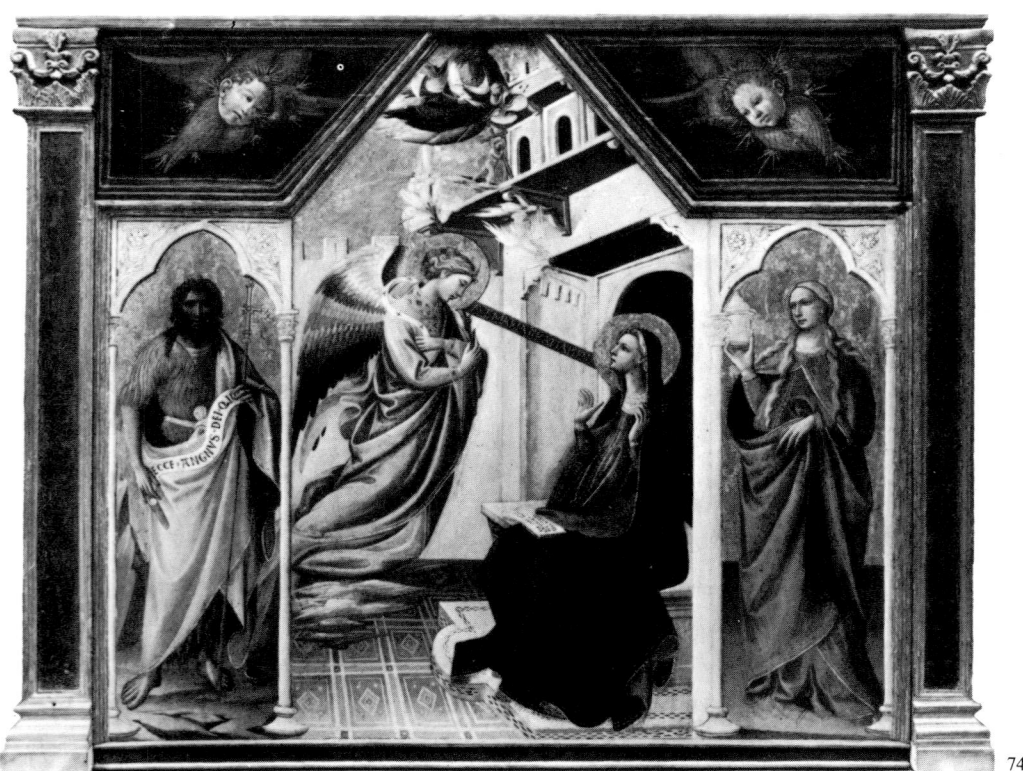

742

741. *Triptych: Annunciation with Sts Eugenius, Benedict, John the Baptist and Nicholas. Above: Christ blessing and two Prophets. Rosano (Pontassieve),*
SS. Annunziata. SGF 23641. d. 1430.
742. *Annunciation with Sts John the Baptist and Mary Magdalene. Panel. Poppiena (Casentino), Badia. 150 × 184. SGF 28175.*

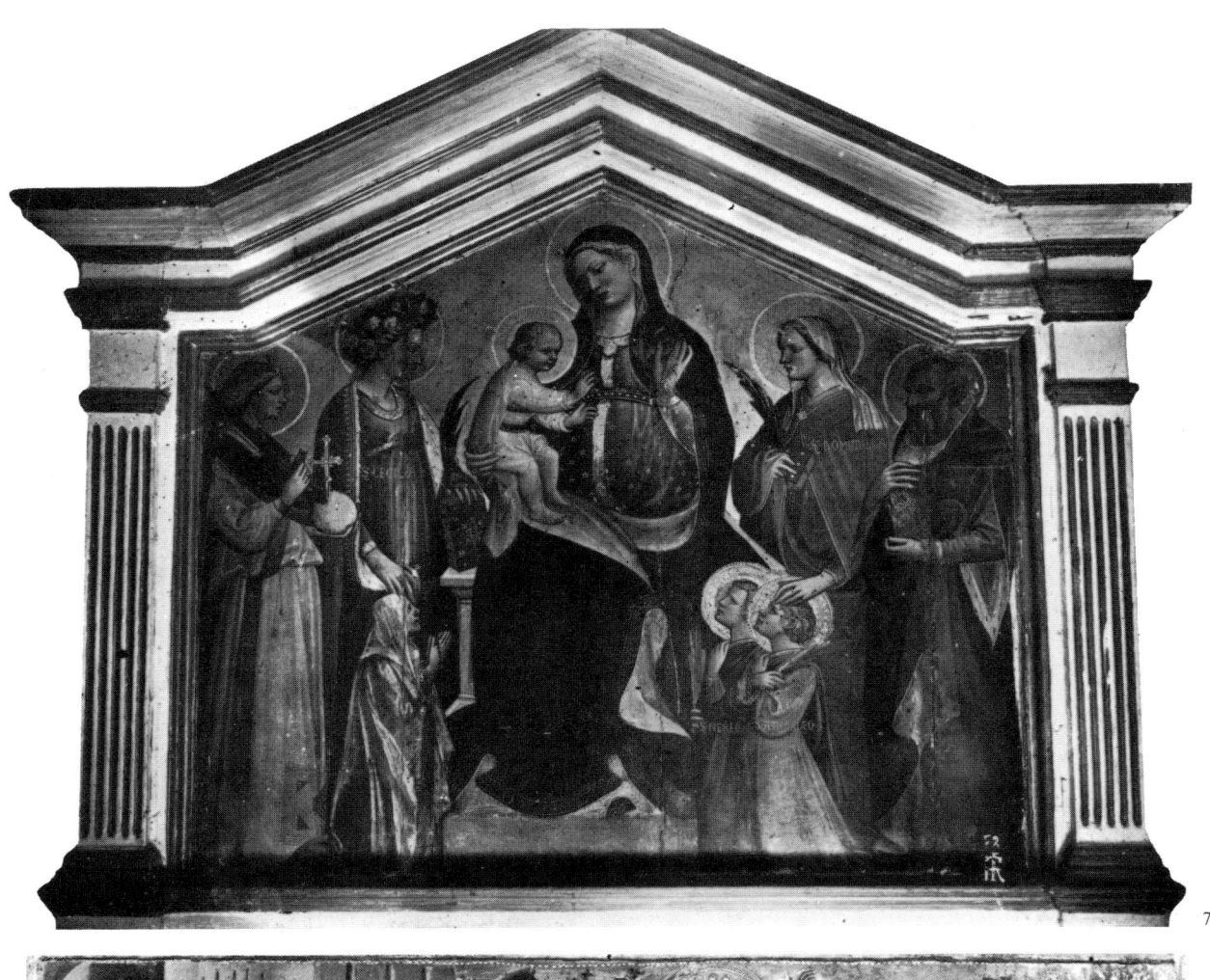

743

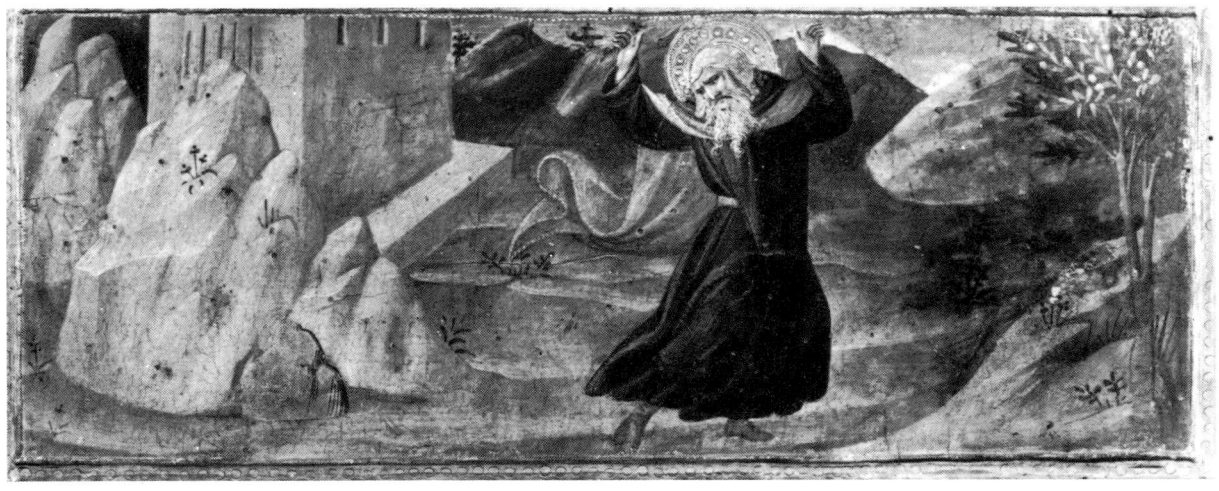

744

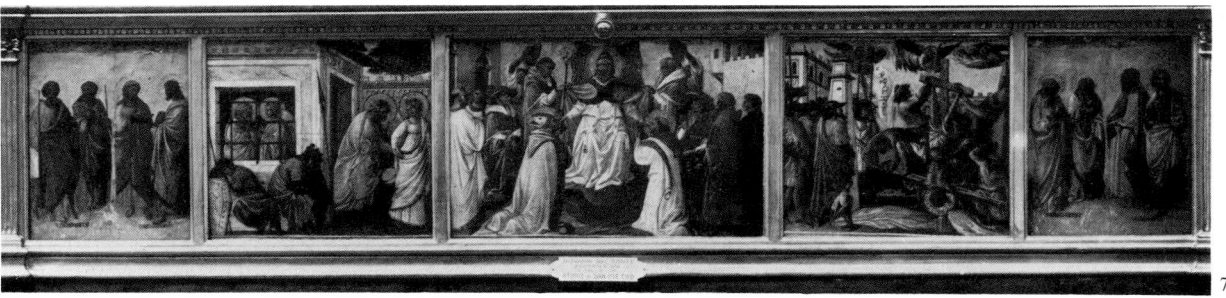

745

743. *Madonna and Child Enthroned with Sts Michael, Cecilia, a female Donor, St Domitilla, a male Saint and Sts Achilleus and Nereus. Panel. Florence, S. Salvatore al Monte. 158 × 181. SGF 20996.*

744. *Predella scene: Temptation of St Anthony. Panel. Brussels, Musée des Beaux-Arts. no. 631. 20 × 50. Museum photo: ACL 203338.*

745. *Predella: Sts Thomas, James the Less, Luke and James Major; Liberation of St Peter; Cattedra Petri; Martyrdom of St Peter: Sts Andrew, Joseph, Matthew and Philip. Panel. Florence, Uffizi. no. 1620. 44 × 249. SGF 10412.*

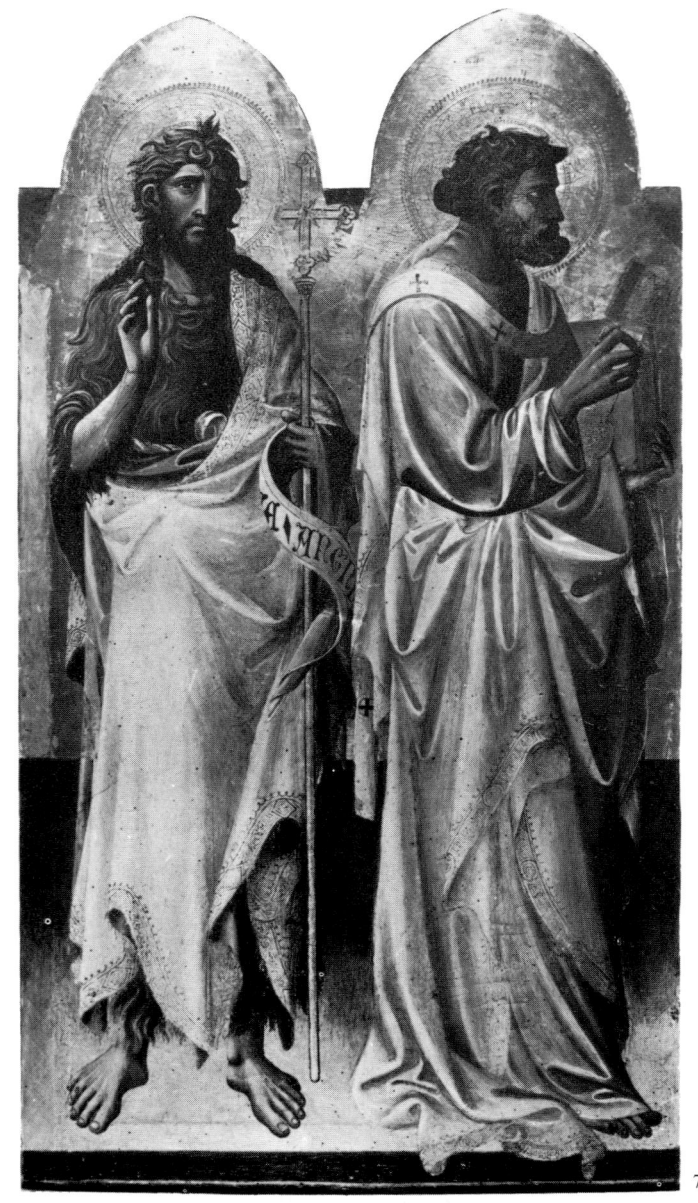

746

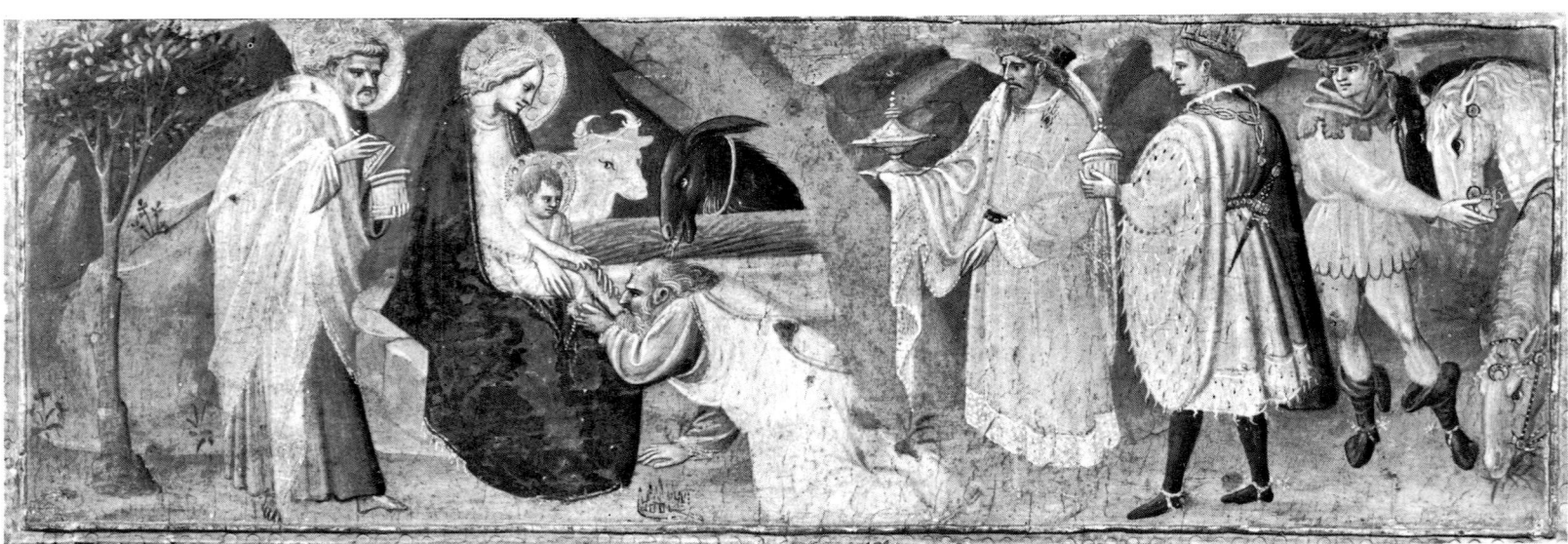

747

746. *Detail: Sts John the Baptist and Peter. Panel. Fiesole, Museo Bandini. no. II, 13. 139.9 × 73. SGF 69729.*
747. *Predella scene: Adoration of the Magi. Panel. Brussels, Musée des Beaux-Arts. no. 631. 20 × 57.5. Museum photo: ACL 2033371.*

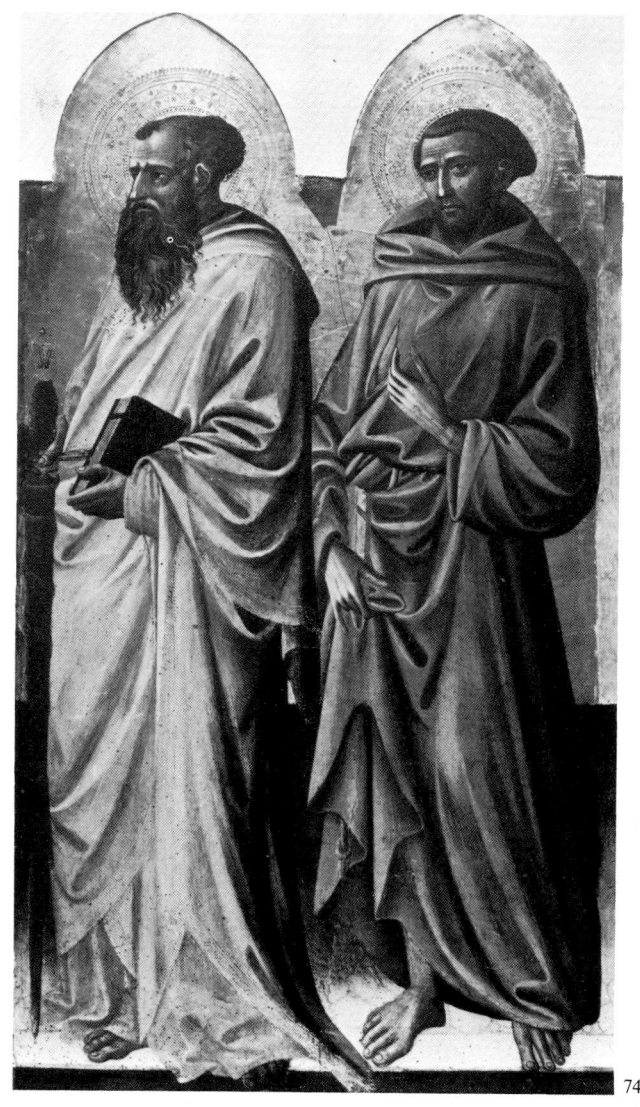

748

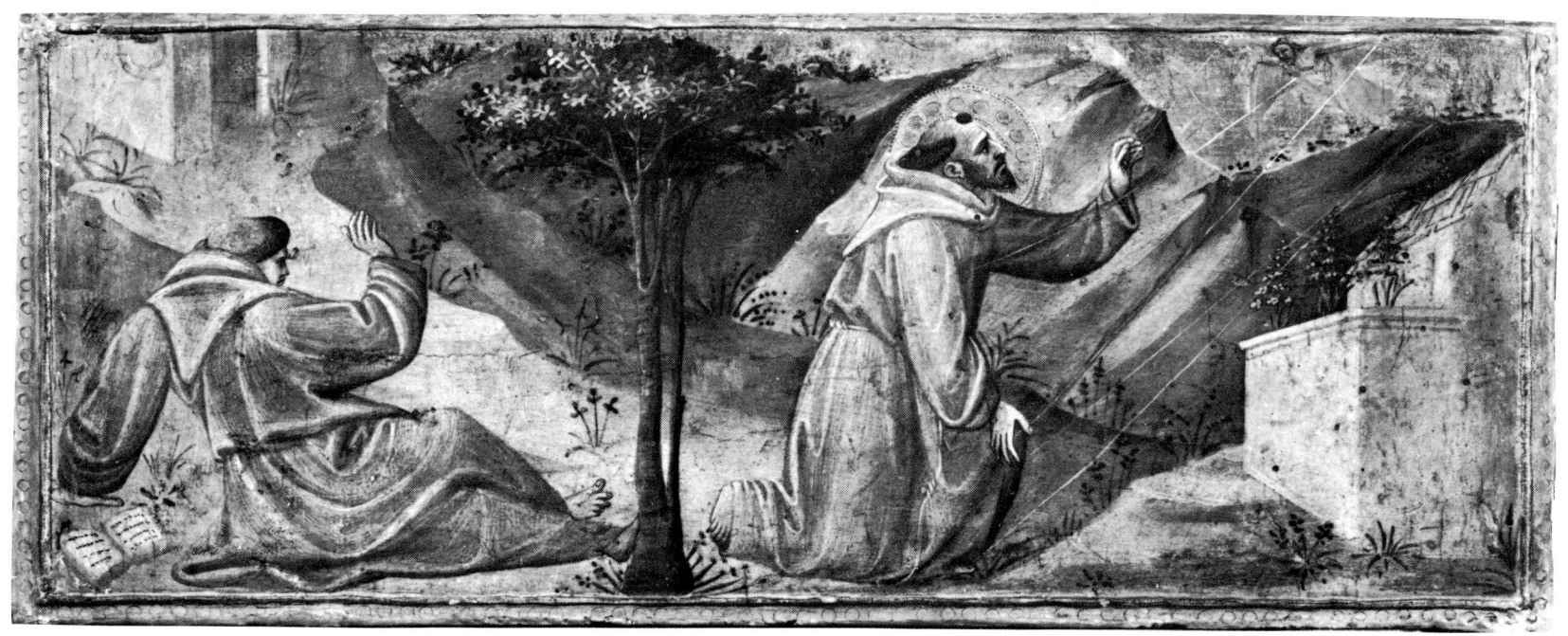

749

748.   *Detail: Sts Paul and Francis. Panel. Fiesole, Museo Bandini. no. II, 14. 139.9 × 73. SGF 69730.*
749.   *Predella scene: Stigmatization of St Francis. Panel. Brussels, Musée des Beaux-Arts. no. 631. 20.5 × 49.5. Museum photo: ACL 20336V.*

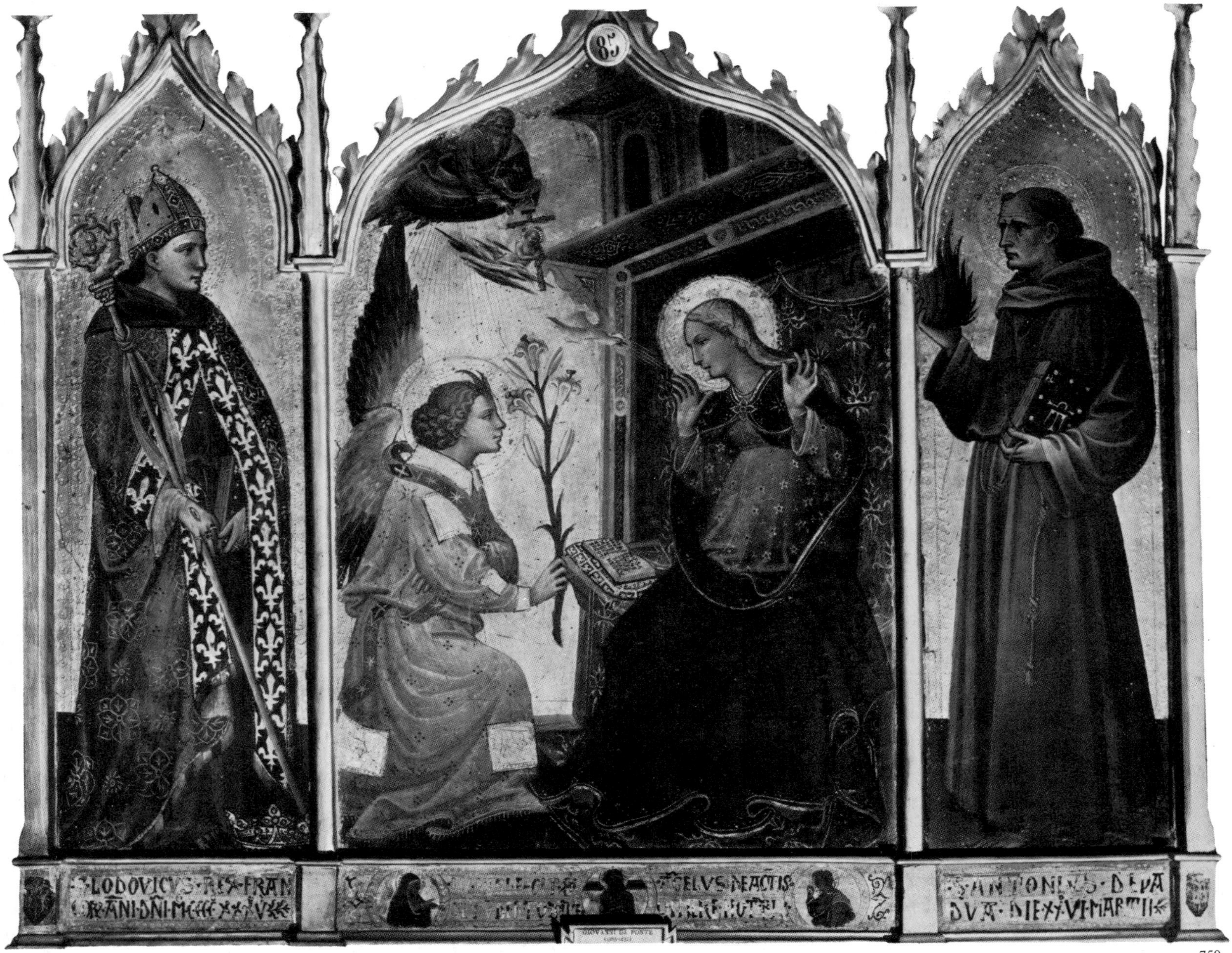

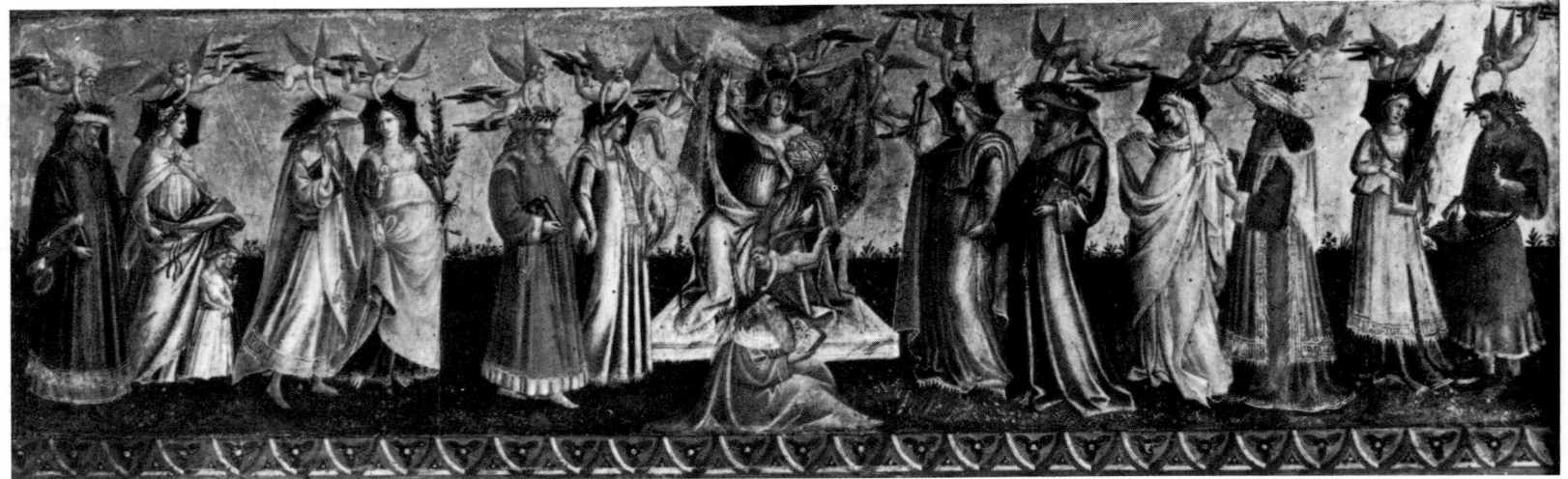

750. *Triptych: Annunciation with Sts Louis of Toulouse and Anthony of Padua. Predella: Man of Sorrows, the Virgin and St John. Panel. Rome, Vatican, Pinacoteca. no. 11. 127.3 × 150.3. Alinari 38097. d. 1435.*

751. *Cassone: Seven Liberal Arts. Panel. Madrid, Prado. no. 2844. 30 × 144. Museum photo.*

LORENZO MONACO

Lorenzo (Don) Monaco (in the world Piero di Giovanni). Siena, born c. 1370, died 1425? Painter, miniaturist. The Sienese origin of Don Lorenzo is determined by Milanesi's discovery of an entry in the book of records which belonged to the monastery degli Angioli, and which is now preserved in the Archivio di Stato Fiorentino, that " on Jan. 29, 1414/15, is sold for life to Don Lorenzo, painter of Siena of our order, a house with a *sporto* (projecting first floor) situate opposite to us "....

Don Lorenzo professed in the Monastery degli Angeli (Order of Camaldoli) on Dec. 10, 1391, after a year's novitiate. Before 1399, probably, he left the monastery, never to return alive, to commence the more extended artistic career from which his reputation is derived..... 1425 is the presumed year of Don Lorenzo's death. If he was twenty-one years of age at the date of his profession in 1391, which is probable, but not certain, he would have been born about 1370, and so have been fifty-five years old at the date of his death, as stated by Vasari.....

from D. E. Colnaghi, pp. 161-62, *A Dictionary of Florentine Painters*, London, 1928.

Lorenzo Monaco is the most important Quattrocento painter in Florence before Masolino and Masaccio. It is therefore surprising to find that so little is known about his life and works. Few facts are known about him. He was born in Siena, and came to Florence at an unknown date. In Florence he lived in the parish of San Michele Visdomini until he entered the Monastery of Santa Maria degli Angeli in 1390. His secular name was Piero di Giovanni, and he changed it to Lorenzo when he became a monk at Santa Maria degli Angeli in 1390 after a year there as a novice. In 1392 he was ordained subdeacon and in 1396, deacon. In 1406 he is said to have been living in the parish of San Bartolo al Corso The date of his departure from the monastery is not specified, nor are the reasons for his leaving. Vasari tells us that he left on account of his poor health. In 1414 he bought a house from the Monastery, opposite Santa Maria Nova, and he lived there until his death. The exact date of his death is unknown. He was still alive in 1422, and he must have died between 1422 and 1424.....

from M. Levi D'Ancona, p. 175, *The Art Bulletin*, XL, 3, 1958.

In 1391 he entered the Camaldolese Monastery of Santa Maria degli Angeli in Florence, where he was engaged on the illumination of manuscripts. This early training and his fervid religious feeling distinguish all his work. He was a painter of great refinement, and while not unaware of the Florentine advances in art — Ghiberti has been cited as an influence on him — he owed more to the French Gothic style. Spiritually he remained a Trecento artist; and it is the Sienese grace of Simone Martini, allied with the more angular type of Gothicism current in Florence, that is the hall-mark of his style.....

from St. J. Gore, p. 17, *The Art of Painting in Florence & Siena from 1250-1500*, London, 1965.

Don Lorenzo di Giovanni, who before entering the Convent of Santa Maria degli Angeli as a novice in 1390 lived at Florence in the parish of San Michele Visdomini, made his profession in the Florentine monastery of the Camaldolese order on the 19th December 1391. In the same month he received the four minor orders; the 21st of September, the year after, he received the sub-deaconry and only on the 26th of February 1396, the deaconry. This is the first documentary evidence we have on the Camaldolese painter who in secular life had the name Piero and who, we really should call Don Lorenzo, as did his contemporaries, rather than calling him Lorenzo Monaco according to the convention begun in the second half of the 19th century.

He was probably born around 1370 (however not later than 1371 because in order to have became sub-deacon in 1392 he would have had to have been at least 21); he was born at Siena, it would appear, according to a document that calls him a " Sienese painter ". In 1402, the same year in which he became a member of the guild of painters under the secular name of Piero di Giovanni, he was living in San Bartolo al Corso and therefore in the meantime he must have abandoned the convent. This was probably done without " shedding the robes " as is said today, but instead, having probably obtained a dispensation from the life of the cloister while maintaining his title of brother of the order of Angeli and keeping his authority.....

The last information on the Camaldolese monk is from the 3rd of March 1433 when the heirs of the Cardinal Pietro Corsini commissioned a panel for the Chapel of San Lorenzo in the church of Santa Maria del Fiore to be painted in 18 months by the " monk of the Angeli " or by another painter who was " sufficient or better ". This panel was then executed by the Master of the Bambino Vispo, perhaps because Lorenzo Monaco had died in the meantime. As for his last works, it is possible that May 24, considered as the date of his death according to information derived from the Archives of Santa Maria degli Angeli, without indication of the year could be the same 1423 or at the latest 1424....

> from L. Bellosi, p. 1, *Lorenzo Monaco* (I Maestri del Colore, 73), Milan, 1965.

Piero di Giovanni, called Lorenzo Monaco (he took his vows and the name of Lorenzo at the Camaldolese Monastery of Santa Maria degli Angeli, Florence, in 1391). Florentine School. Born c. 1370; died 1422/24. He came from Siena to Florence, where he was influenced by Agnolo Gaddi, became the most important painter at the beginning of the fifteenth century, and influenced the stylistic formation of Masolino and Fra Angelico. Panel paintings, frescoes, and illuminations, characterized by the flowing line of the International Style, make up his very considerable oeuvre.....

> from F. R. Shapley, p. 89, *Paintings from the Samuel H. Kress Collection*, London, 1966.

BIBLIOGRAPHY
BOOKS
An asterisk indicates a work listed in the General Bibliography

Sirén, O., *Dom Lorenzo Monaco*, Strasburg, 1905; *Venturi, A.**, Vol. VII, 1911, pp. 3-21; Golzio, Vincenzo, *Lorenzo Monaco*, Rome, 1931; *Venturi, L.**, 1931, nos 142, 143; Ciaranfi, A. M., *Treccani, Vol. XXI**, 1934, p. 502; *Antal** 1948, pp. 315-24; *Vavalà, 1948**, pp. 95-101; *Galetti**, 1950, " F-O ", pp. 1409-10; *Toesca, 1951**, pp. 654-6; Suida, W. E., *Catalogue of the Seattle Art Museum*, Seattle, (Washington), 1952, p. 14; Suida, W. E., *Paintings and Sculpture of the Samuel H Kress Collection*, Tulsa, (Okla), 1953, p. 18; Suida, W. E., *Catalogue of the Seattle Art Museum*, Seattle, (Washington), 1954, p. 28; Amerio, R., in *EUA**, 1958, pp. 700-702; *Cracow**, 1961, pp. 53-54; *Oertel 1961**, pp. 130-132; *Berenson 1962**, p. xxxii; Santi, F., pp. 58-9, in *Scritti di Storia dell'Arte in Onore di Mario Salmi*, Vol. II, Rome, 1962; *Berenson, 1963**, Vol. I, pp. 117-21; Bellosi, L., *Lorenzo Monaco*, (I Maestri del Colore, 73), Milan, 1965; Gore, St. J., *Wildenstein**, 1965, pp. 17-8; Bellosi, L., *La Pittura Tardogotica in Toscana* (I Maestri del Colore, 239), Milan, 1966; *Castelfranchi-Vegas**, 1966, p. 169; *Shapley**, 1966, pp. 89-90; *Meiss, 1970**, p. 104; *MMOA**, 1971, pp. 62-68; Gilbert, C., *History of Renaissance Art throughout Europe*, New York, 1973, pp. 57-8; Palumbo, G., *Collezione Federico Mason Perkins*, Rome, 1973, p. 50; *Dutch Show**, 1974, pp. 12, 68-74.

JOURNALS

Borenius, T., *BM*, 40, 1922, p. 134; Borenius, T., *AP*, XI, 1930, pp. 91-6; Milliken, W. M., *BCMA*, XVII, 1930, pp. 131-33; Ciaranfi, A. M., *A*, III, 1932, pp. 285-317, 379-99; Berenson, B., *DD*, XII, 1, 1932, pp. 5-34; Pudelko, G., *AA*, XXVI, 1, 1938, pp. 47-63; Pudelko, G., *BM*, LXXIII, 1938, pp. 237-48; Pudelko, G., *BM*, LXXIV, 1939, pp. 76-81; Sandberg-Vavalà, E., *AA*, XXVII, 1939, pp. 106-111; Longhi, R., *CA*, V, 1940, pp. 145-91; Oertel, R., *MKIF*, V, 4-5, 1940, pp. 217-314; Glazer, C., *GBA*, XXII, 6, 1942, pp. 149-64; *Edit.*, *AN*, XLVI, 1947, p. 33; Davies, M., *CA*, VIII, 3, 1949, pp. 202-10; Milliken, W. M., *BCMA*, XXXVII, 1950, pp. 43-6; Gronau, H. D., *BM*, XCII, 1950, pp. 183-88, 216-224; Chiarelli, R., *E*, CXIII, 1, 1951, pp. 3-16; Cohn, W., *RA*, XXX, I, 6, 1951, p. 68; Berti, L., *BA*, XXXVII, 4, 1952, p. 175; Eisenberg, M. J., *AQ*, XVIII, 1955, pp. 45-9; Baldini, U., *BA*, XL, 4, 1955, pp. 81-2; Eisenberg, M. J., *BA*, XLI, 4, 1956, pp. 333-5; Cohn, W., *RA*, XXXI, 1956, pp. 41-72; Rosenthal, E., *C*, VII, 2, 1956, pp. 71-7; Eisenberg, M. J., *AB*, XXXIX, 1957, pp. 49-52, and correction p. 168; Levi d'Ancona, M., *AB*, XL, 1958, pp. 175-191; Meiss, M., *BM*, C, 1958, pp. 190-8, 359; Jurlaro, R., *A*, LVII, 1958, pp. 243-6; V. C., *E*, CXXVIII, 765, 1958, pp. 115-20; Eisenberg, M. J., *AB*, XLI, 1959, pp. 127-9; Vaughn, M., *CS*, CXLIV, 1959, pp. 206-7; Rozycka-Bryzek, A., *Biuletin Historii Sztucki*, 22, 1960, pp. 203-18; Stöckelová, G., *A*, LIX, 25/4, 1960, p. 277-88; Zeri, F., *BM*, CVI, 1964, pp. 554-8; Zeri, F., *BM*, CVII, 1965, pp. 3-11; Neumeyer, A., *AQ*, XXVIII, 1965, pp. 5-16; Bellosi, L., *PA*, XVI, 187, 1965, pp. 18-43; Murray, P., *AP*, 81, 1965, pp. 284-5; Blunt, A., *AP*, 81, 1965, p. 292; *Edit.*, *MM*, XXIV, 2, 1965, pp. 40-1; Bellosi, L., *RA*, XVII, 201, 1966, pp. 76, 77, 78; Donati, P. P., *C*, XVII, 1-3, 1966, pp. 56-72; de Montebello, G.-P., *MM*, XXV, 4, 1966, pp. 155-69; Zeri, F., *BA*, LI, 5, 1966, pp. 150-1; Bellosi, L., *PA*, XVIII, 203/23, 1967, p. 87; Baxandall, D., *SAR*, XI, 1, 1967, pp. 6-7; Guidi, F., *PA*, XIX, 223/43, 1968, pp. 27-46; Fremantle, R., *AV*, IX, 6, 1970, pp. 39-49; Boskovits, M., *AI*, III, 25/26, 1970, pp. 32-47; Gonzalez-Palacios, A., *PA*, XXI, 241, 1970, pp. 27-36; Gonzalez-Palacios, A., *AV*, X, 3, 1971, pp. 3-9; Bellosi, L., *MKIF*, XVII, 2-3, 1973, p. 194; Bisogni, F., *MKIF*, XVII, 2-3, 1973, p. 199; Boskovits, M., *MKIF*, XVII, 2-3, 1973, p. 204, note 8; Volpe, C., *MKIF*, XVII, 2-3, 1973, pp. 347, 51, 57-8; Zeri, F., *MKIF*, XVII, 2-3, 1973, pp. 364, 6, 70.

SIGNED AND DATED WORKS

MCCC- - [incomplete]. Berlin, Staatliche Museen. Panel: Madonna & Child with Angels & Sts John the Baptist and Nicholas. d. (destroyed 1945). (fig. 753).

1400 Moscow, Puskin Museum 144. Panel: Madonna of Humility with 2 Angels. d. (fig. 752).

1404 Empoli, Museo della Collegiata. Triptych: Madonna of Humility with Saints. d. (fig. 754).

1404 Florence, Academia 467. Panel: Man of Sorrows with the Virgin, St John the Baptist and Symbols of the Passion. d. (fig. 755).

1405 Florence, Ponte a Mensola, Berenson Collection. Panel: Madonna of Humility. d. (fig. 760).

1408 Florence, Accademia 470. Panel: Madonna & Child Enthroned with Saints and Angels. d. (fig. 758).

1408 Paris, Louvre 1384a. Side panels of portable triptych: Agony in the Garden, and the Marys at the Tomb. d. (fig. 762).

1408 Seattle, Museum of Art, Kress Collection K 1654. Panel: Crucifixion. d. (fig. 763).

1408 Turin, Museo Civico 152 (3023). Painting on glass: Madonna & Child with St John the Baptist and another Saint d. (fig. 757).

1410 Florence, Palazzo Davanzati. Triptych: Madonna & Child with two Angels & Sts Bartholomew, John the Baptist, Thaddeus and Benedict. d. (fig. 766).

1412 Pisa, Museo Nazionale di S. Matteo. Panel: Madonna of Humility with six Angels. d. (fig. 764).

1413 Washington, D.C., National Gallery K 1293, Samuel H. Kress Collection. Panel: Madonna of Humility. d. (fig. 765).

1414 Florence, Uffizi 885. Altarpiece: Coronation of the Virgin with Saints and Angels. s & d. February 1413 (Florentine Style). (fig. 767).

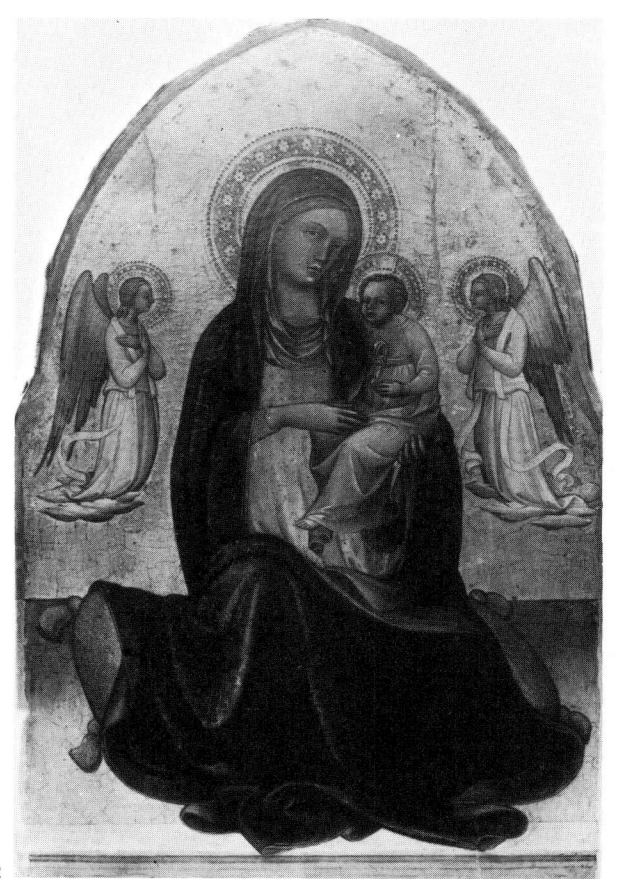

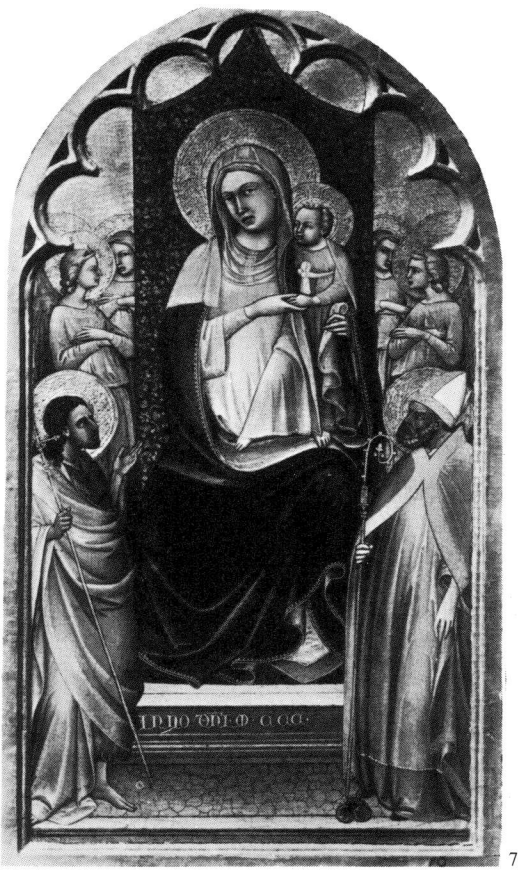

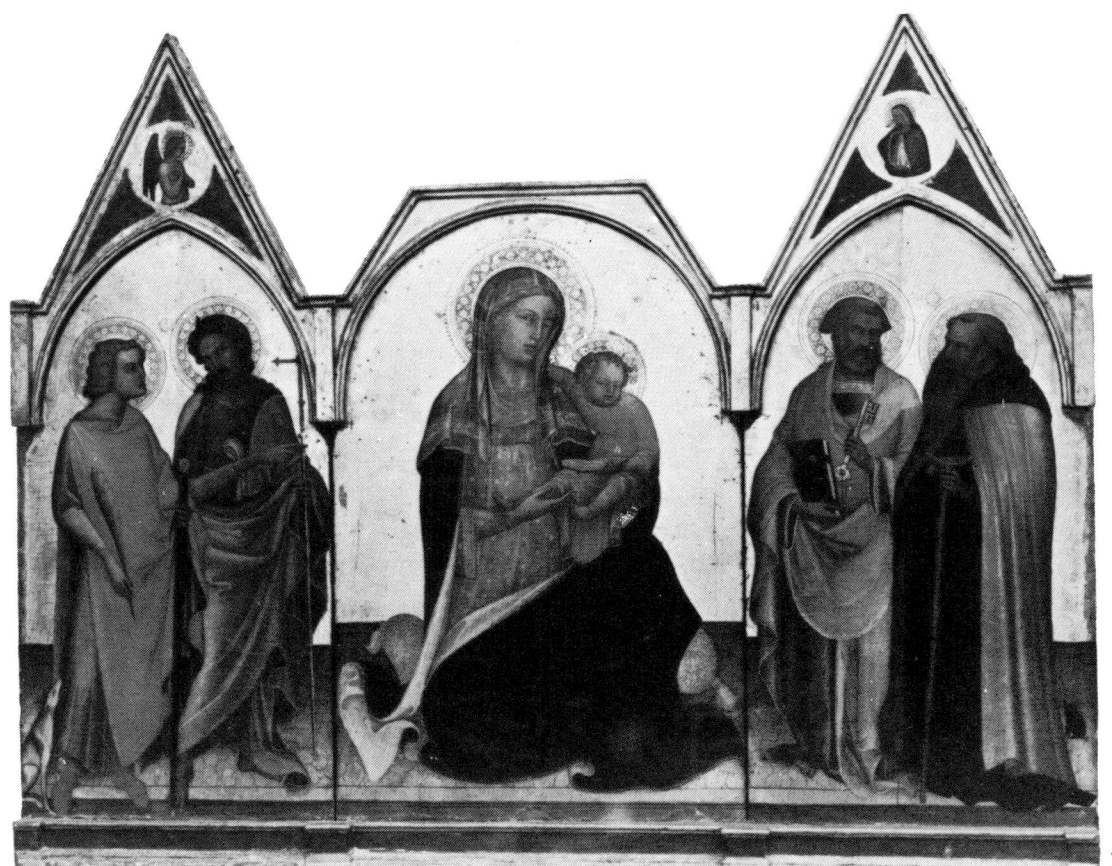

752. *Madonna and Child with two Angels. Panel. Moscow, Puskin Museum. no. 144. 73 × 46. Museum photo. d. 1400.*

753. *Madonna and Child with Angels and Sts John the Baptist and Nicholas of Bari. Panel (destroyed 1945). Berlin, Staatliche Museen no. 1119. SGF 67697. d. MCCC?*

754. *Triptych: Madonna of Humility with Sts Donnino, John the Baptist, Peter and Anthony Abbot. Above: Annunciation. Panel. Empoli, Museo della Collegiata. no. 2. 157 × 197. Museum photo. d. 1404.*

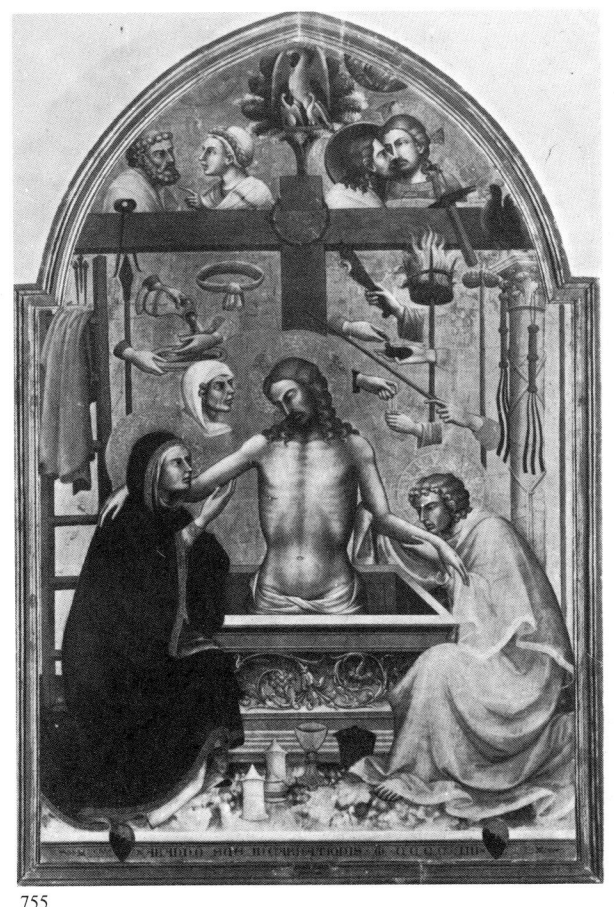

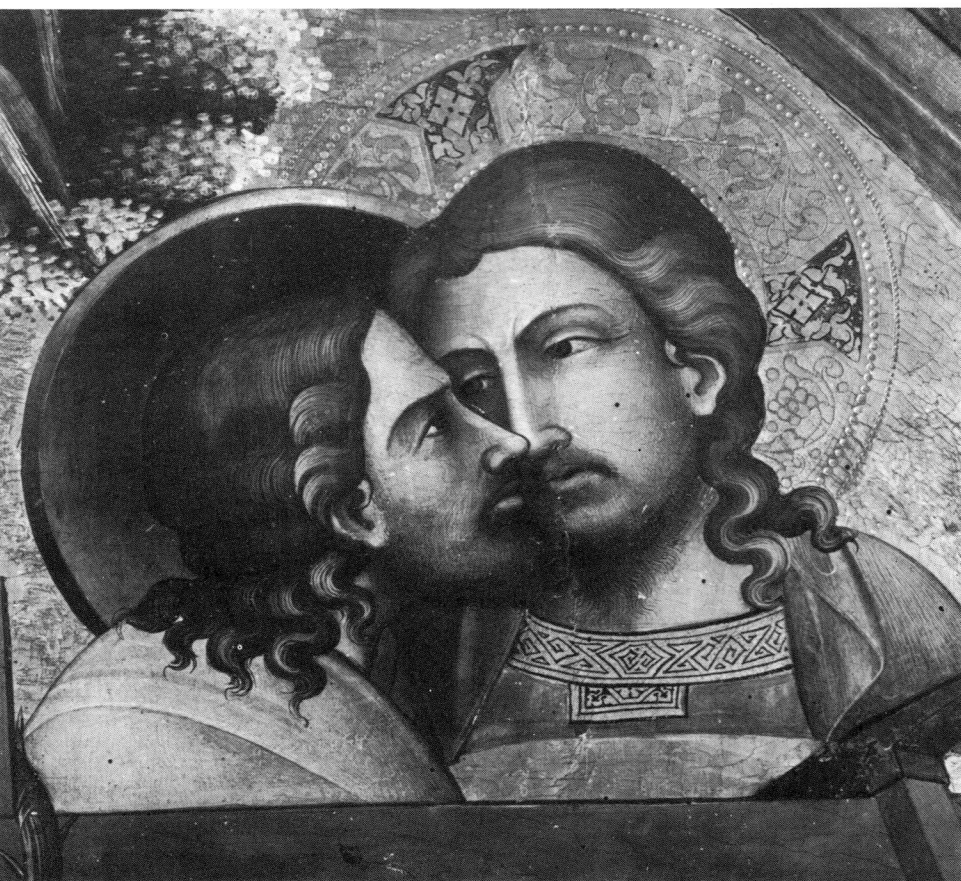

755

756

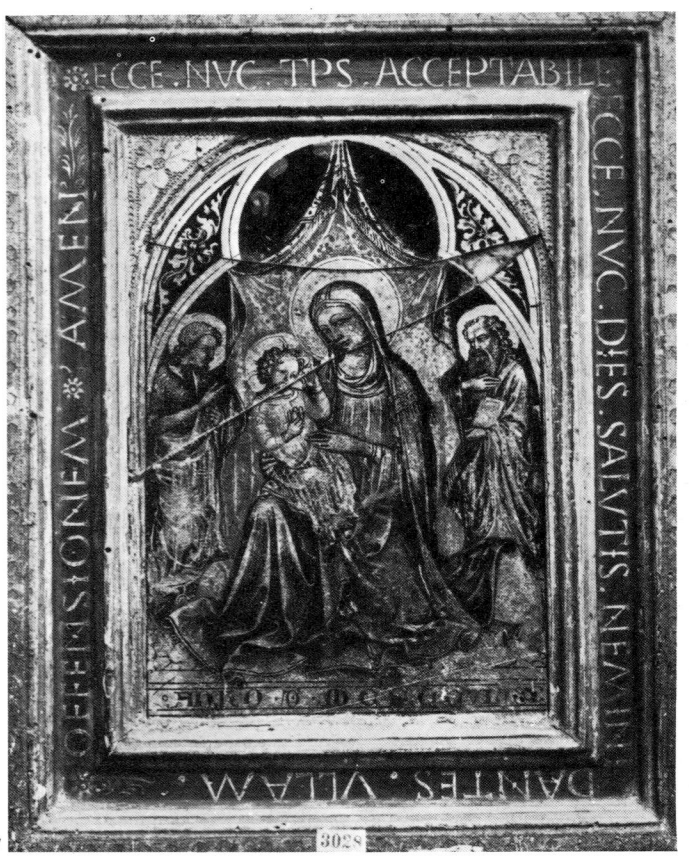

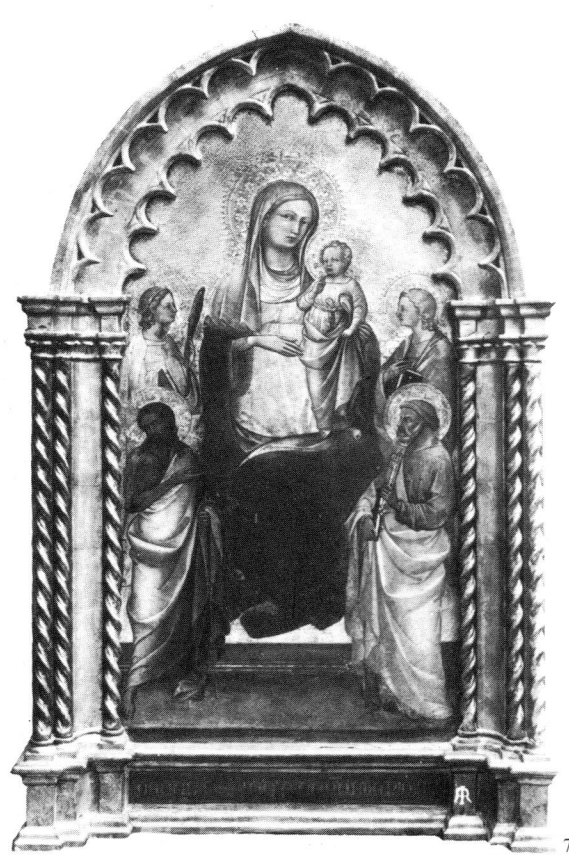

757

758

755. *Man of Sorrows with the Virgin, St John the Evangelist and Symbols of the Passion. Panel. Florence, Accademia. no. 467. 267 × 171. SGF 111652. d. 1404.*

756. *Kiss of Judas, detail of fig. 755. Panel. Florence, Accademia. no. 467. SGF 111657. d. 1404.*

757. *Madonna and Child Enthroned with two Saints. Glass. Turin, Museo Civico. no. 152 (3023). 13.5 × 20. Museum photo. d. 1408.*

758. *Madonna and Child Enthroned with Sts John the Baptist and Peter and two Angels. Panel. Florence, Accademia. no. 470. 90 × 47. Alinari 7408. d. 1408.*

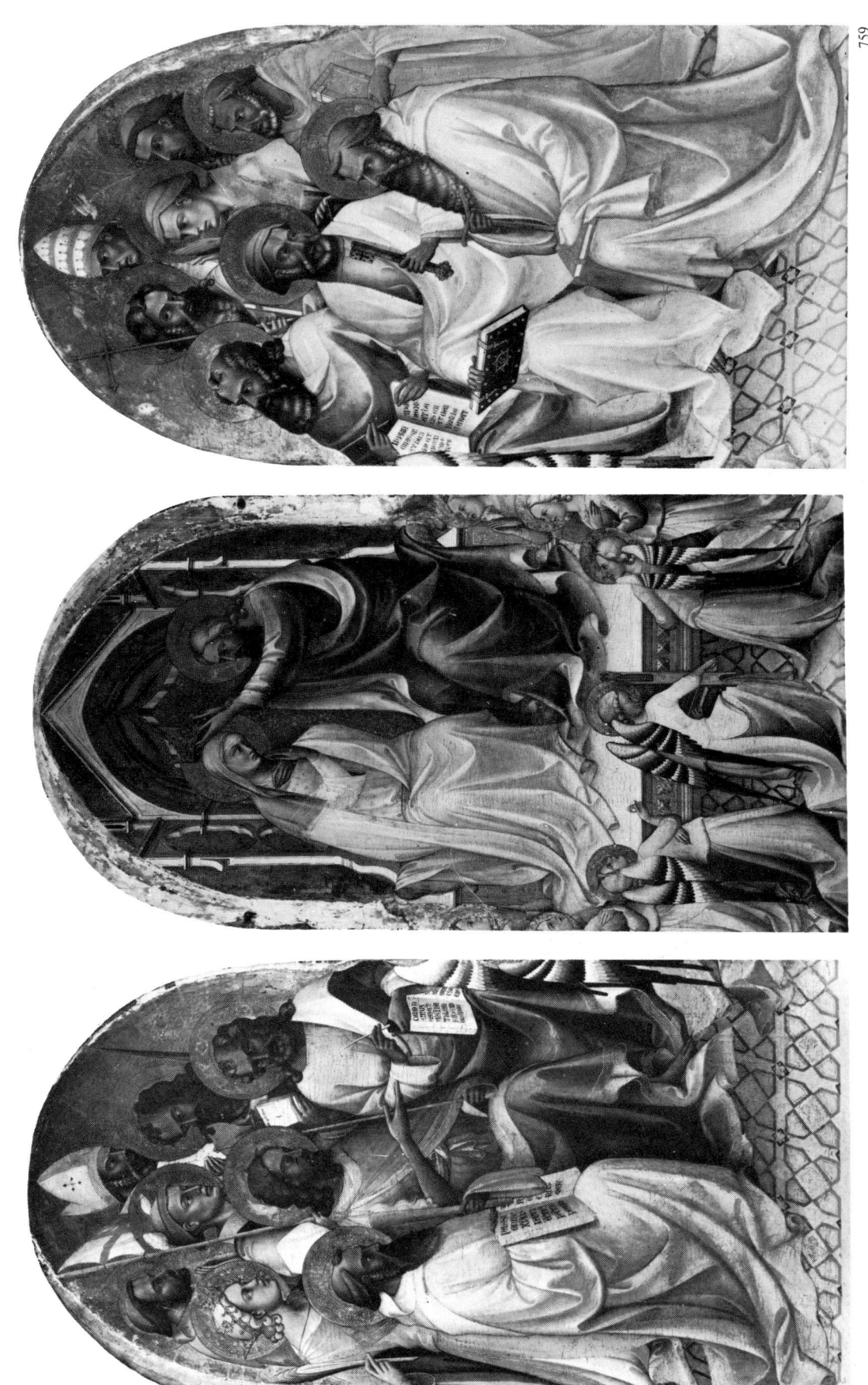

759. *Three panels from a triptych: Eight Saints; Coronation of the Virgin with Angels; Eight Saints. London, National Gallery. nos. 215, 1897 and 216.*
lp: 180 × 102; cp: 215 × 102; rp: 177 × 102. Museum photos.

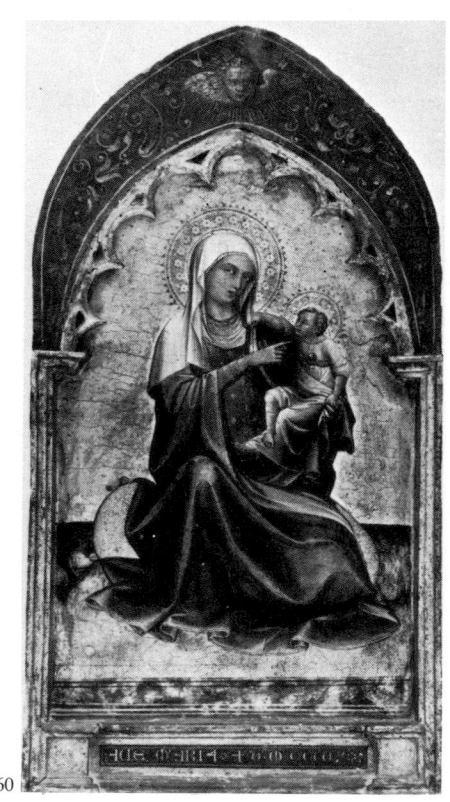

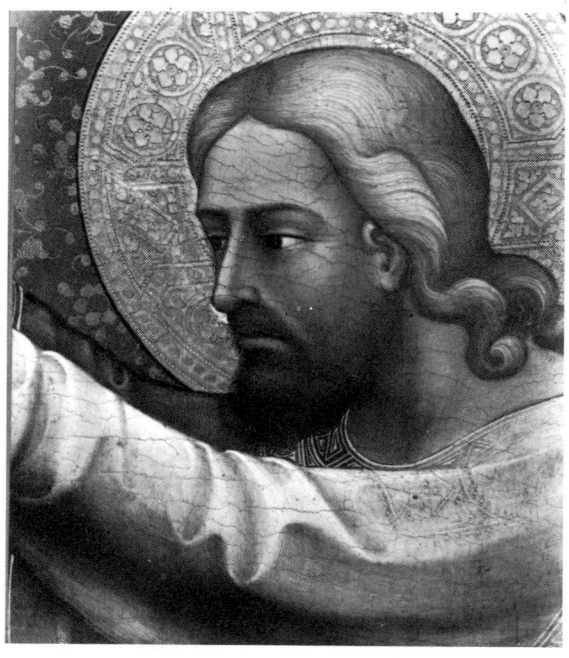

761

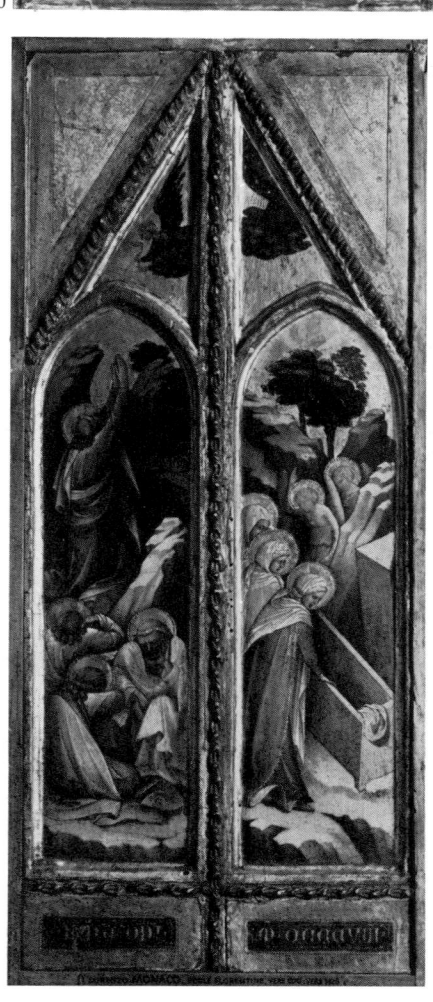

762

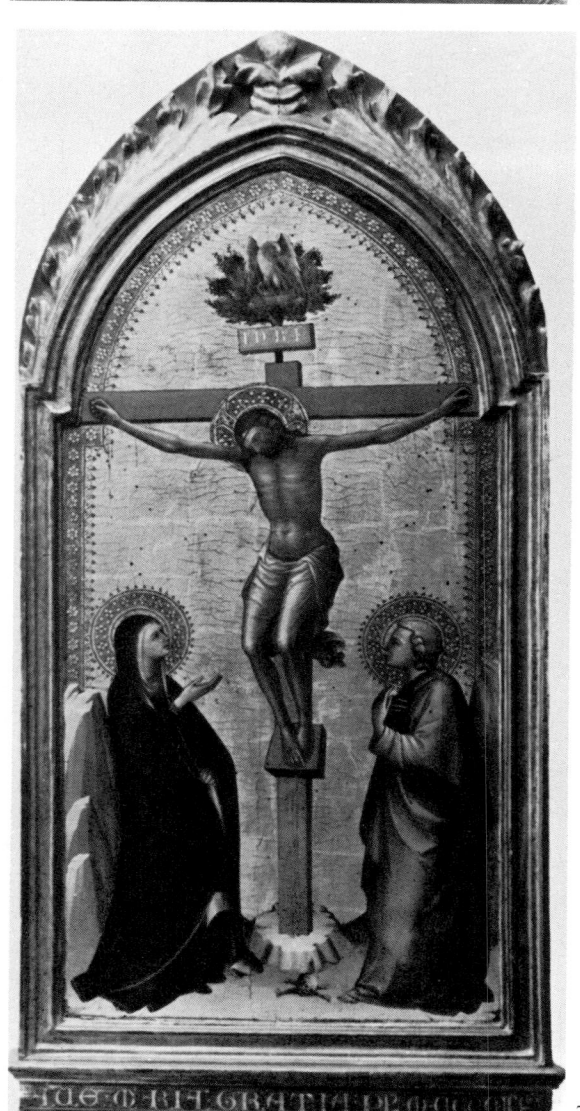

763

760. *Madonna of Humility. Panel. Florence, Ponte a Mensola (near Settignano), Berenson Collection. 78.5 × 41. SGF 54871. d. 1405.*
761. *Head of Christ, detail of fig. 759. Panel. London, National Gallery. no. 1879. Museum photo.*
762. *Wings from a portable triptych: Agony in the Garden; the three Marys at the Sepulchre. Panel. Paris, Musée du Louvre. no. 1348 A. 60 × 20. Museum photo. d. 1408.*
763. *Crucifixion. Panel. Seattle (Washington), Seattle Art Museum, Samuel H. Kress Collection 1949: no. K. 1645. 125.7 × 59.6. Kress Foundation photo. d. 1408.*

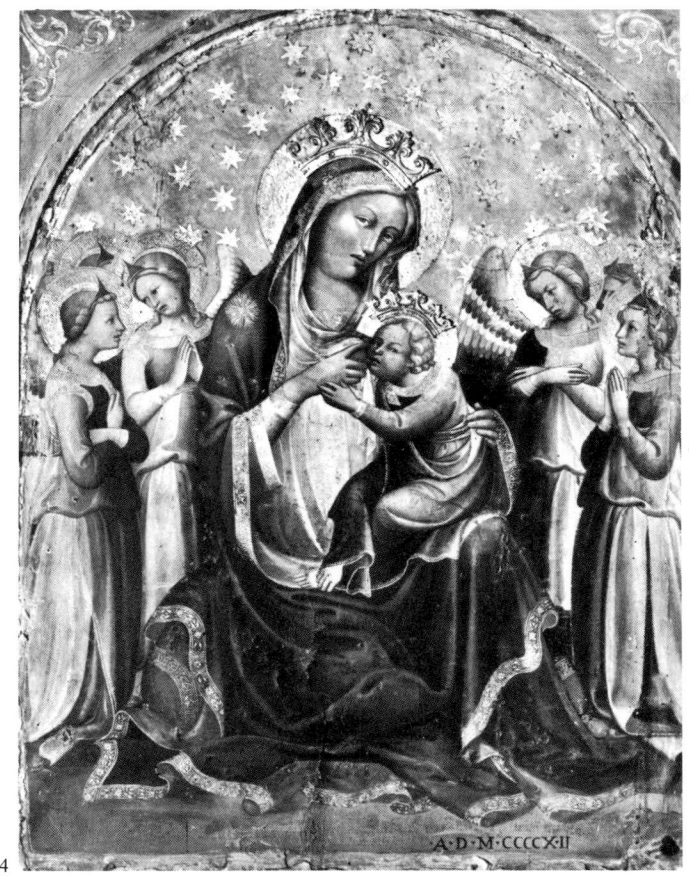

764

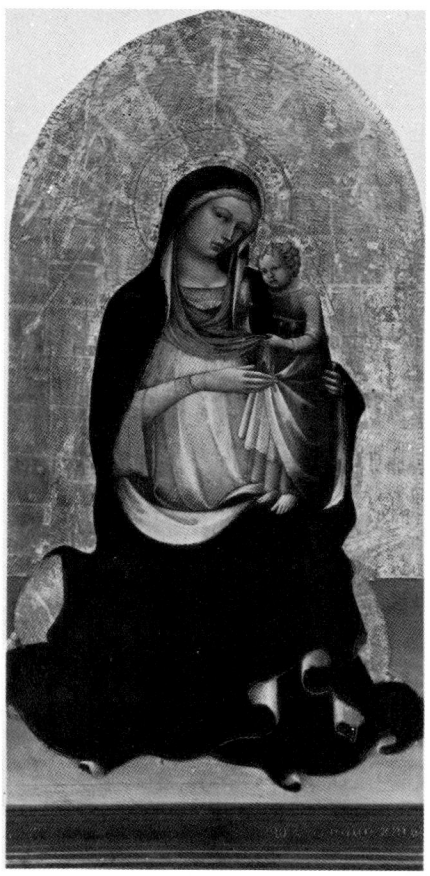

765

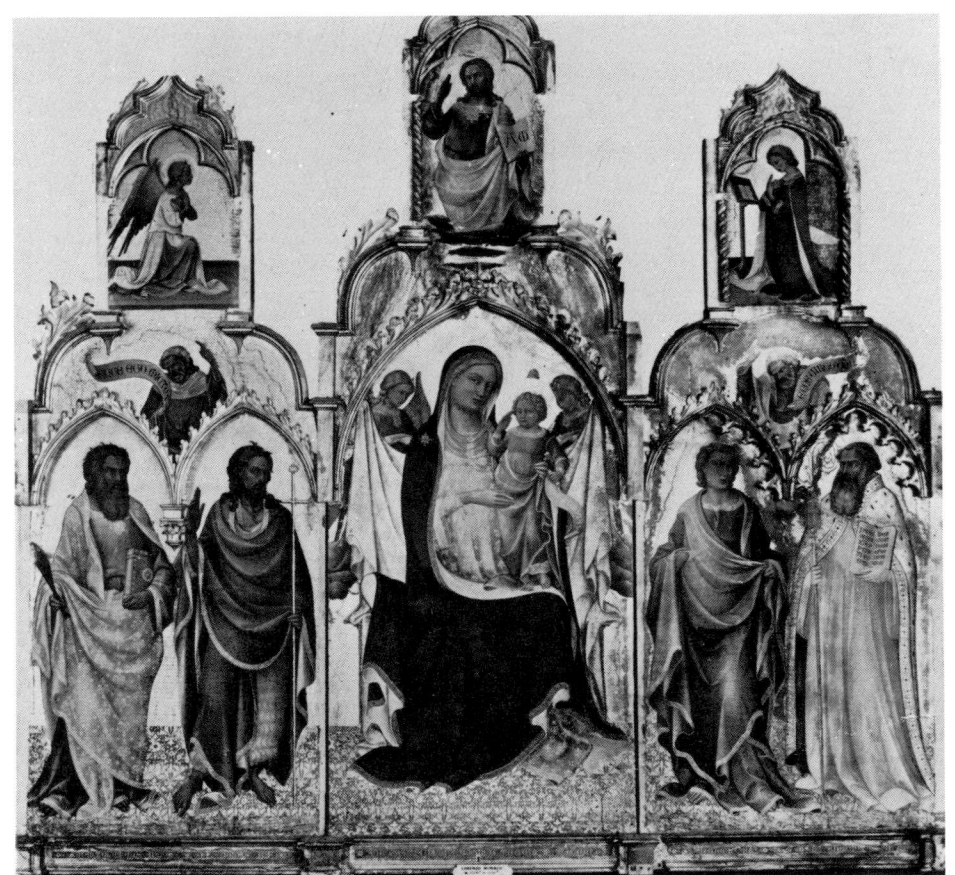

766

764. *Madonna nursing the Child with six Angels. Panel. Pisa, Museo Nazionale di S. Matteo. 140 × 107. Brogi 19345. d. 1412.*
765. *Madonna of Humility. Panel. Washington (D.C.), National Gallery of Art, Samuel H. Kress Collection. no. 1939. 116.8 × 55.2. Museum photo. d. 1413.*
766. *Triptych: Madonna and Child with two Angels, Sts Bartholomew, John the Baptist, Thaddeus and Benedict. Above: Christ blessing; Angel and Virgin of Annunciation; two Prophets. Panel. Florence, Palazzo Davanzati. no. 168. 277 × 235. Alinari 797. d. 1410.*

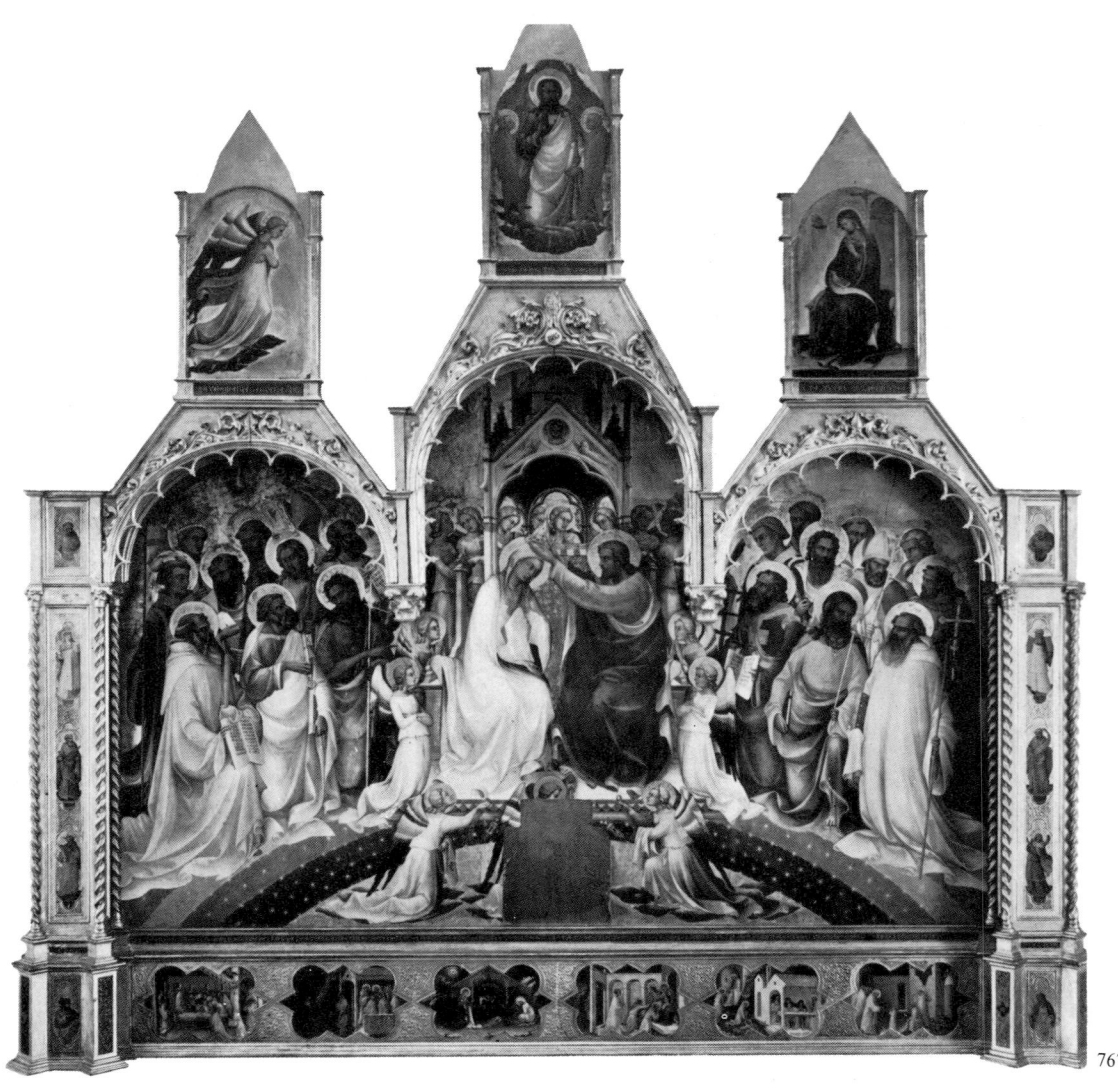

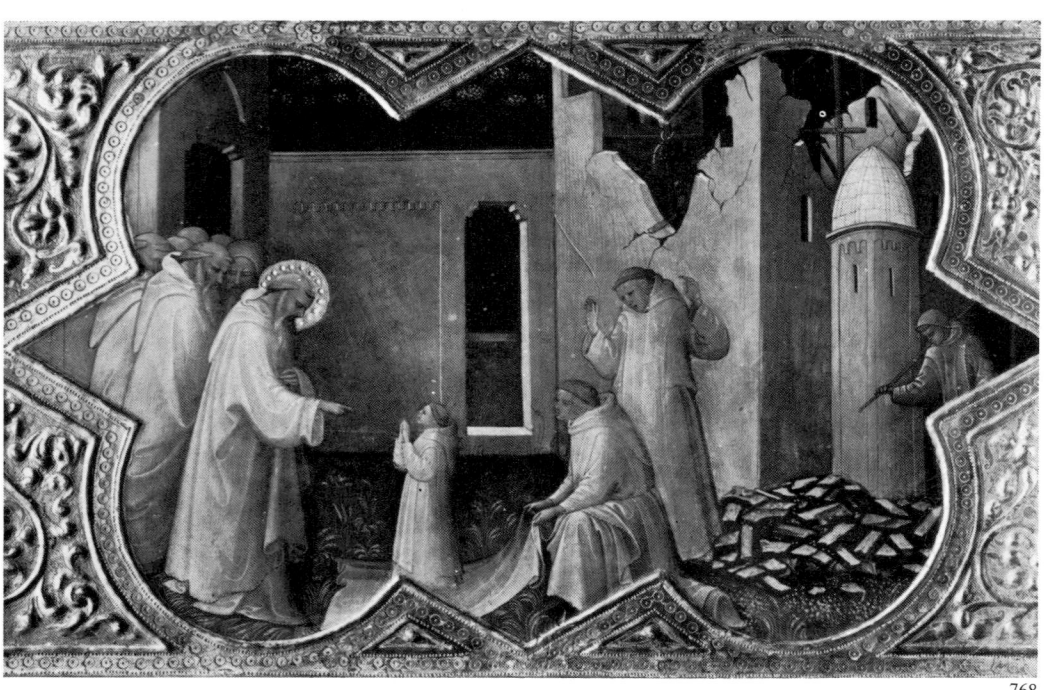

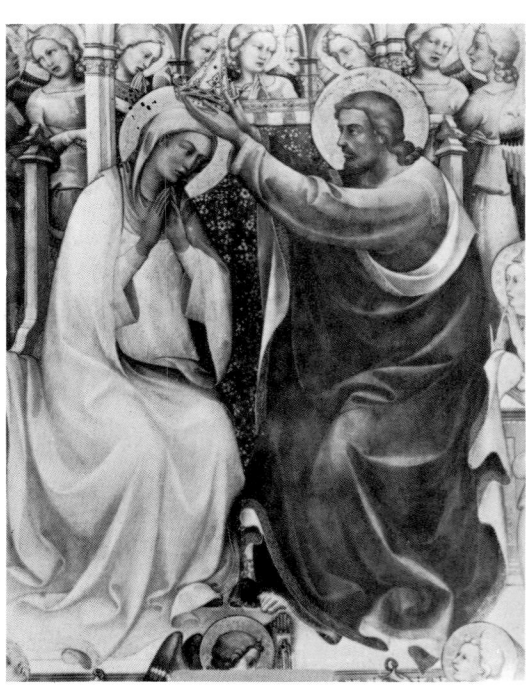

767. *Coronation of the Virgin. Panel. Florence, Uffizi. no. 885. 247 × 373. SGF 112697. s & d. February 1413 (Florentine style; new style 1414).*
768. *Predella scene: Raising of a Monk from the Ruins of Montecassino, detail of fig. 767. Panel. Florence, Uffizi. no. 885. SGF 112706. s & d. February 1413.*
769. *Coronation of the Virgin, detail of fig. 767. Panel. Florence, Uffizi. no. 885. Alinari 793. s & d. February 1413.*

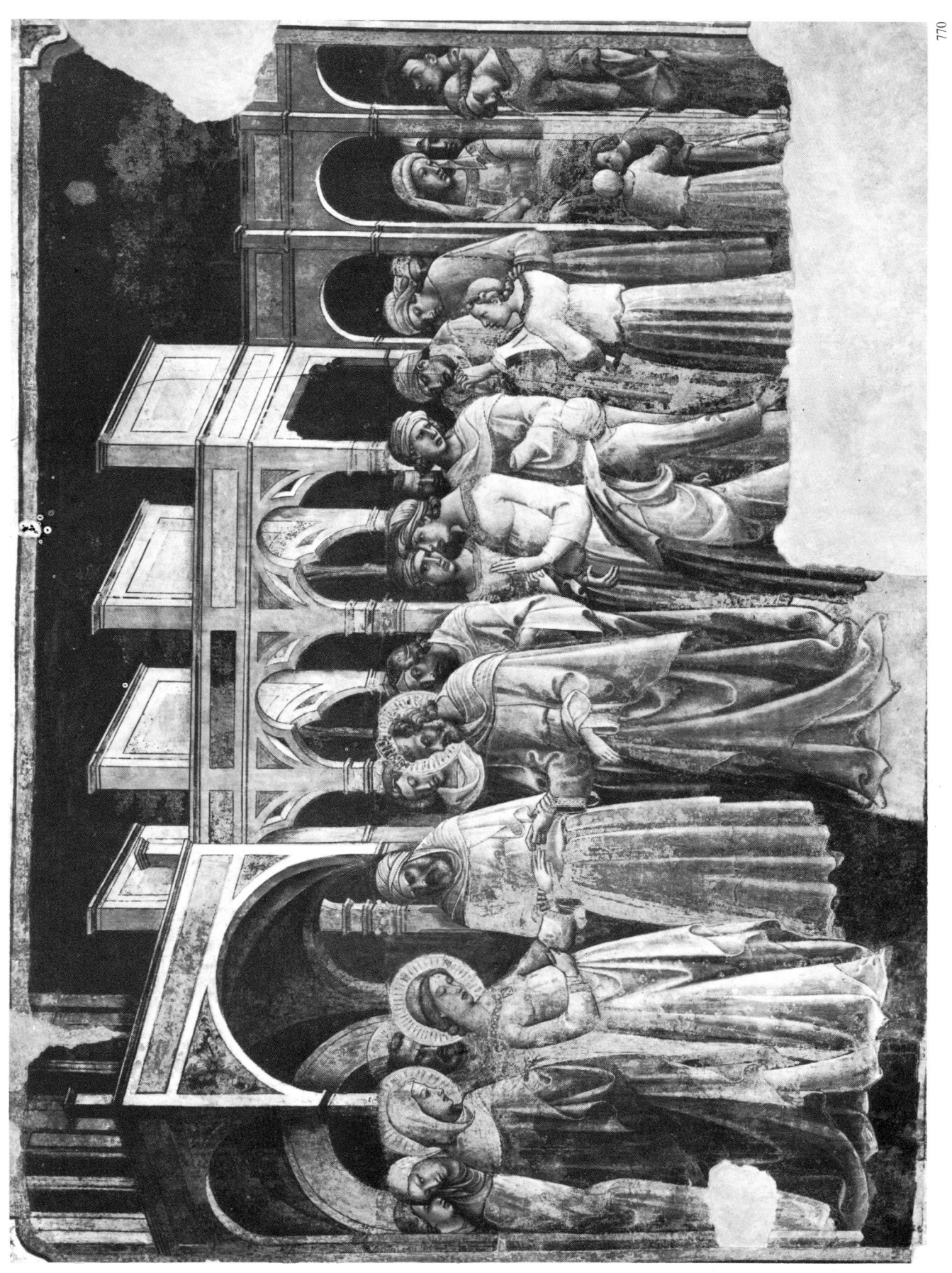

770. *Marriage of the Virgin. Fresco. Florence, S. Trinita, Bartolini Chapel. SGF 119702. 1422-25.*

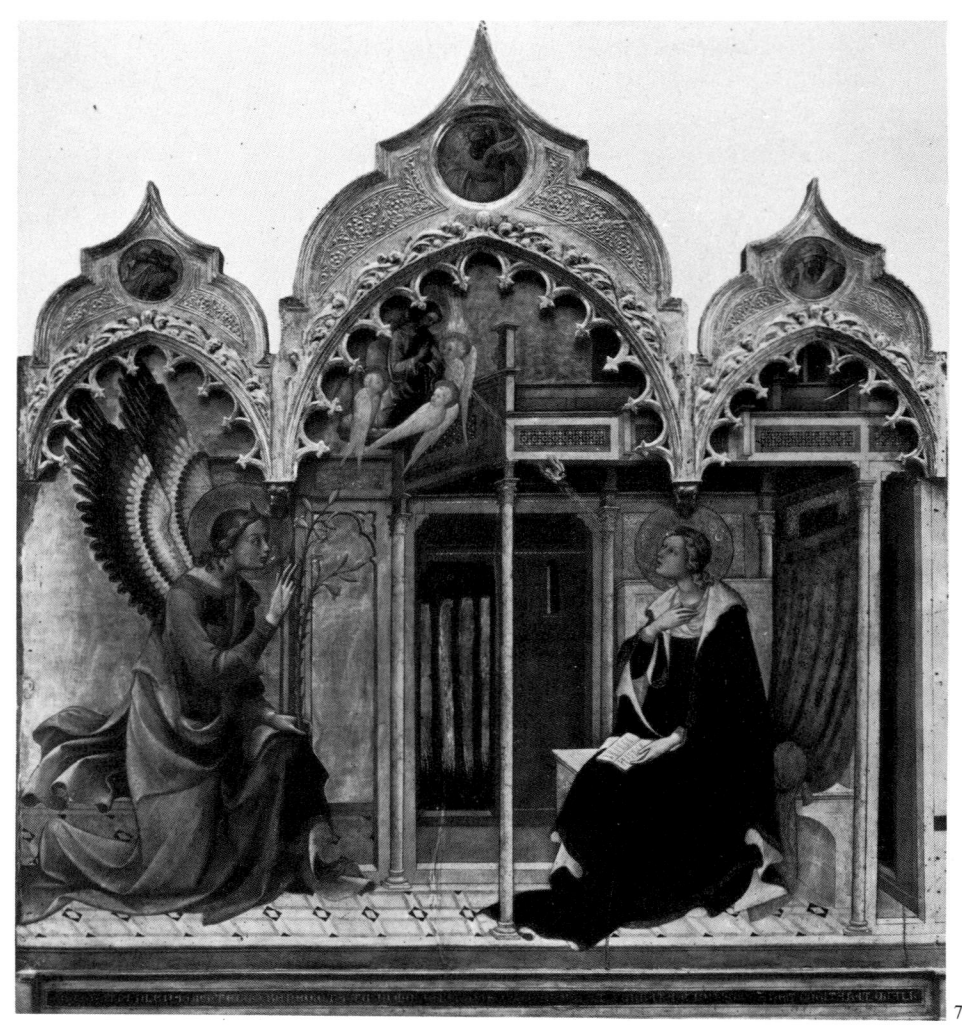

771

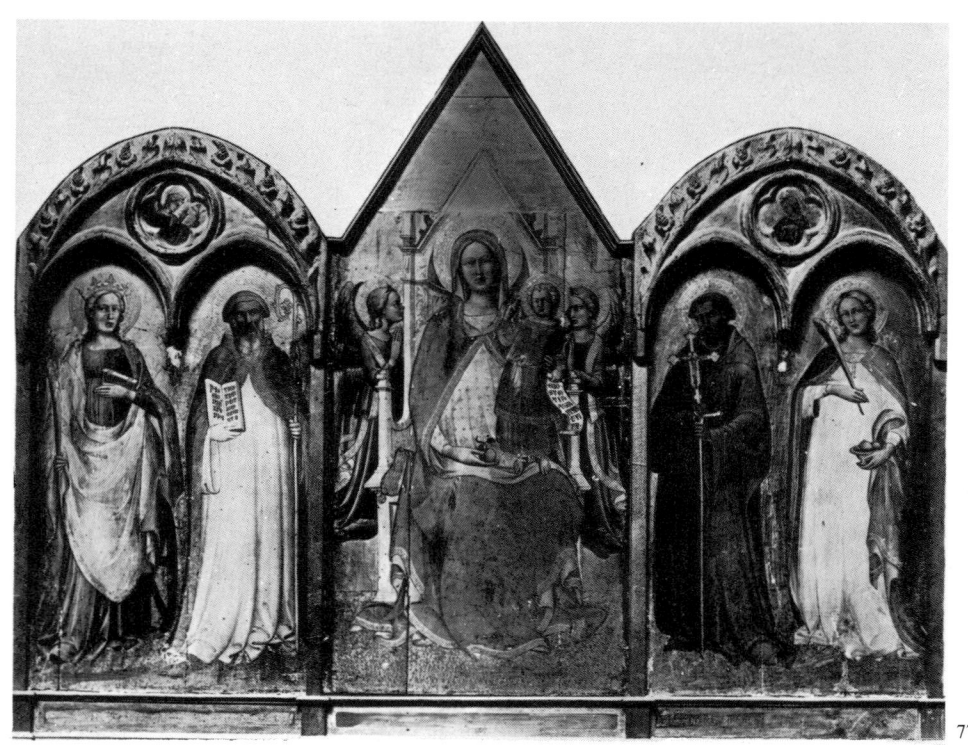

772

771. *Annunciation. Above: three Prophets. Panel. Florence, S. Trinita, Bartolini Chapel. 300 × 264. SGF 120388. 1422-25.*
772. *Triptych: Madonna and Child Enthroned with two Angels. Sts Catherine, Benedict, John Gualbert and Agatha. Above: Annunciation. Panel. Prato, Galleria Comunale. no. 7. cp: 110 × 69; sps: 139.5 × 63. GFN C 1723.*

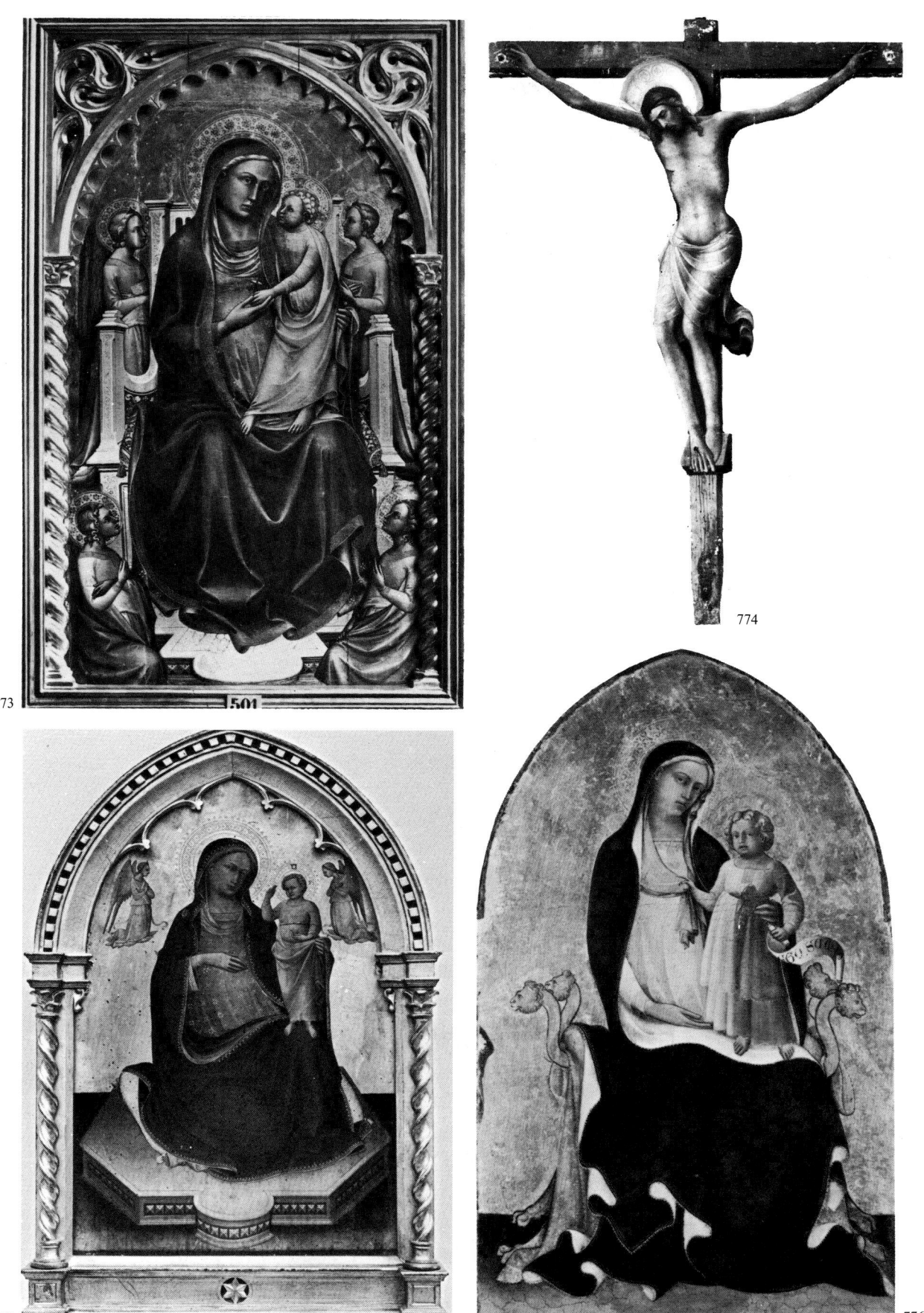

773. *Madonna and Child Enthroned with four Angels. Panel. Bologna, Pinacoteca Nazionale. no. 501. 133 × 78. Alinari 37999.*
774. *Painted crucifix. Panel. Monte San Savino (east of Siena, near Asciano), S. Maria delle Vertiche. 110 × 85. SGF 29035.*
775. *Madonna of Humility with two Angels. Panel. Assisi, F.M. Perkins Collection. 103 × 70. Foto de Giovanni.*
776. *Madonna and Child. Panel. Edinburgh, National Gallery of Scotland. 101.6 × 61. Museum photo: Annan.*

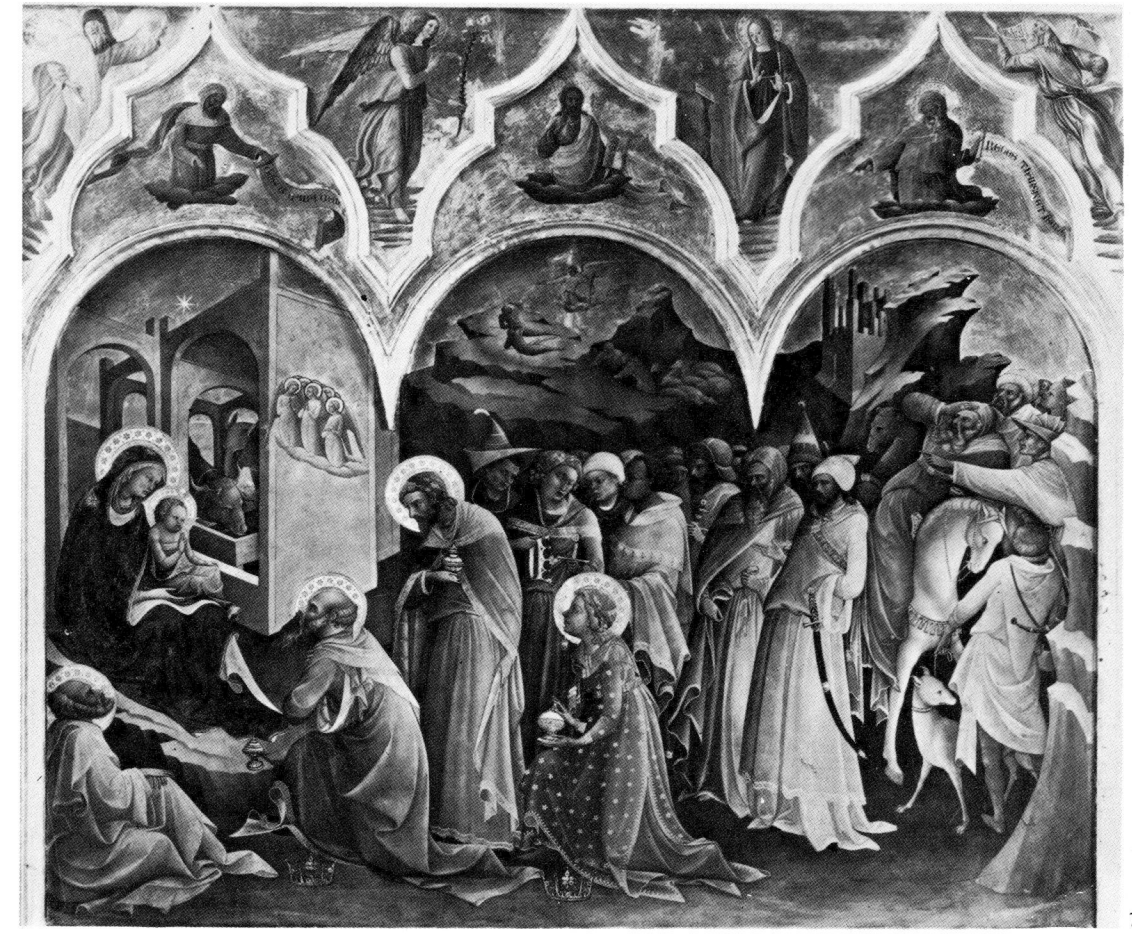

777

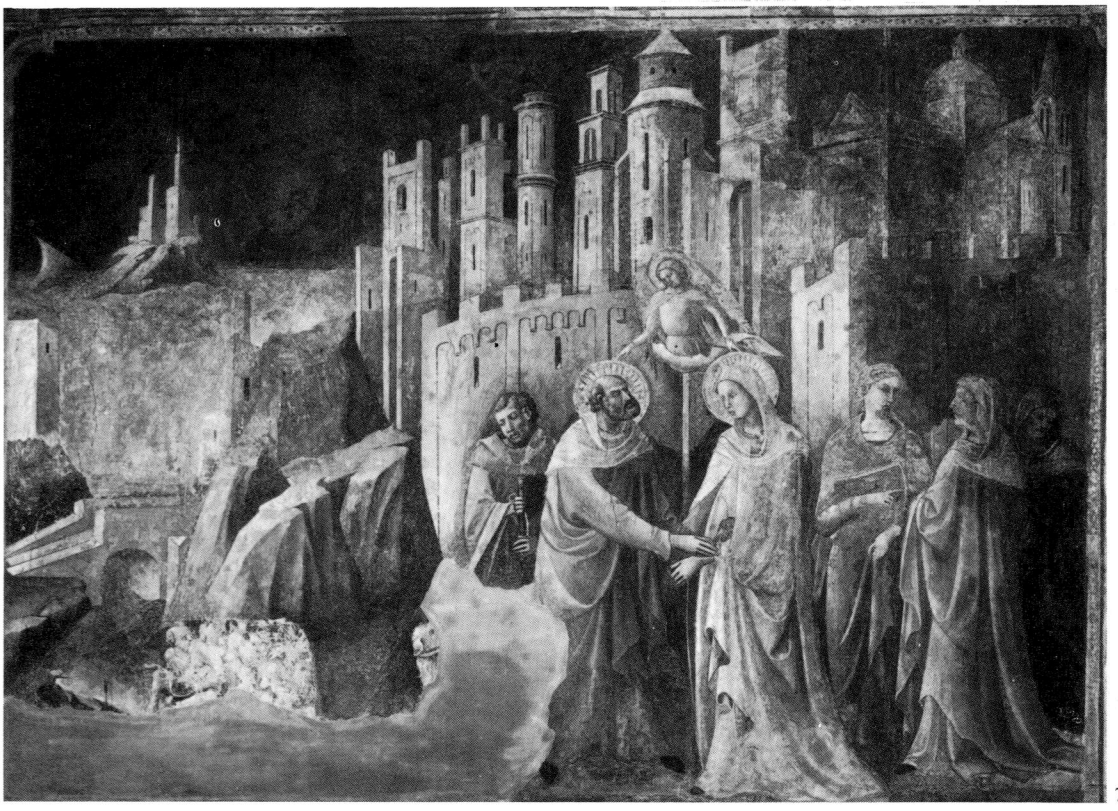

778

777. *Adoration of the Magi. Above: Christ blessing and two Prophets. Panel. Florence, Uffizi. no. 466. 144 × 177. Alinari 796.*
778. *Meeting at the Golden Gate. Fresco. Florence, S. Trinita, Bartolini Chapel. SGF 24496. 1422-25.*

CENNI di FRANCESCO di SER CENNI

Cenni di Francesco di Ser Cenni, inscribed in 1415 among the painters of Florence, is of more importance to us because we have at least one large work from his hand which shows him to have been a faithful follower, almost an imitator of Agnolo Gaddi, but not a great artist.

In the chapel of the Compagnia della Croce di Giorno in the church of S. Francesco at Volterra, this artist decorated the walls with scenes from the life of the Madonna, the youth of the Saviour and with some frescoes freely copied from Agnolo's legend of the Cross. The work is signed and dated 1410; the inscription also mentions the part that Jacopo di Firenze took in the decoration.

Of Agnolo's art this painter has preserved some of the types, the hardness of design and the decorative tendencies which he exaggerates into still more confused and obscure compositions. His designs and colours are coarse, his figures flat and his details and expressions vulgar.....

> from R. van Marle, p. 561, *The Development of the Italian Schools of Painting*, Vol. III, The Hague, 1924.

Once confused with Cennino Cennini, this Agnolesque master was registered among the Florentine painters in 1415, and is noted for the frescoes of the Stories of the Cross in S. Francesco di Volterra, where his signature affirms his authorship of the entire cycle together with a painter named Jacopo da Firenze. He was singled out by Cavalcaselle, and most recent criticism has assigned to him a noteworthy number of works which show us his pleasingly gaudy colouristic, discorsive qualities. They also show him aware of both Gothic innovations from north of the Alps and Sienese taste.....

> from U. Baldini, p. 34, *Iϊ Mostra di Affreschi Staccati*, Florence, 1957.

The only sure information we have about this Florentine painter, who in 1410 signed and dated a delightful fresco cycle in S. Francesco in Volterra, is that in 1415 he was registered among the Florentine painters. Today, due in great part to the numerous unpublished findings of Baldini (1958) we know of other works (some dated). These are all found in Valdelsa (in Castelfiorentino, in Montalbino, in Lucardo, in S. Martino a Maiano) and in the vicinity of Empoli: they testify to Cenno's long artistic career and a real ' iter ' in that area. In particular, the triptych of S. Giusto at Montalbino, which is dated 1400, indicates that the artistic activity of Cenno must have begun at least in the last decade of the '300. His personality, once vague enough to be confused with that of Cennino Cennini, is now clearly defined. He is one of the more lyrical, lively and sensitive interpreters of a Florentine culture at the end of the century, influenced by the Nardesque tradition and by Agnolo Gaddi. His Stories of the Cross and of Jesus at Volterra vie with the famous cycle of Agnolo Gaddi in Santa Croce in Florence. They have the same precise unrestrained and animated composition, the same spirit of refined invention (see the Flight of Cosroes, in the Annunciation to the Shepherds) and the same lovely impasto of colours.....

> from P. Dal Poggetto, pp. 36-37, *Arte in Valdelsa*, Certaldo, 1963.

Follower of Agnolo Gaddi, documented 1415.

> from B. Berenson, p. 47, *Italian Pictures of the Renaissance, Florentine School*, Vol. I, London, 1963.

Cenni di Francesco di Ser Cenni. Florentine School. Active first quarter of fifteenth century in Volterra. He was a follower and imitator of Agnolo Gaddi and shows parallels also with Giovanni del Biondo and Niccolò di Pietro Gerini.....

> from F. R. Shapley, p. 42, *Paintings from the Samuel H. Kress Collection*, London, 1966.

BIBLIOGRAPHY

BOOKS

An asterisk indicates a work listed in the General Bibliography

Venturi, A.*, 1907, pp. 827-8; *Khv & Salmi**, 1914, p. 49; *v. Marle, 1924**, pp. 561-3; *Colnaghi**, 1928, p. 69; National Gallery of Art, *Preliminary Catalogue of Paintings and Sculpture*, Washington D. C., 1941, p. 38; *Antal**, 1947, pp. 330-1; *Galetti**, " A-E ", 1950, p. 630; *Toesca, 1951**, p. 648; Baldini, U., and Berti, L., *MAS I**, 1957, p. 34; Baldini, U., *MAS II**, 1958, p. 71; Dal Poggetto, P., *AIV**, 1963, pp. 36-8; *Berenson, 1963**, Vol. I, pp. 47-8; *Marcucci**, 1965, p. 145; *Shapley**, 1966, p. 42; *Klesse**, 1967, p. 334; Fredericksen, B. B., *Catalogue of the Paintings in the J. Paul Getty Museum*, Malibu (Calif.), 1972, pp. 8-9.

JOURNALS

G. D., *VA*, III, 1910, p. 149; Matteoli, A., *BAE*, XV, 1961-62, pp. 101-4; Zeri, F., *BA*, XLVIII, 4, 1963, pp. 246-255; Bellosi, L. *PA*, XVII, 201/21, 1966, p. 79; Boskovitz, M., *AV*, V, 2, 1966, pp. 23-8; Boskovits, M., *MKIF*, XIII, 1-2, 1967, pp. 31-60; Boskovits, M., *ZKG*, XXXI, 4, 1968, pp. 273-92; Cole, B., *BM*, CXI, 1969, p. 83; Wilkins, D., *BM*, CXI, pp. 83-5, 1969; Boskovits, M., *AI*, III, 25/26, 1970, pp. 42, note 6, 44-45, note 25; Boskovits, M., *MKIF*, XVII, 2-3, 1973, p. 204.

SIGNED AND DATED WORKS

1383 Florence, San Donato in Polverosa. Fresco: Adoration of the Magi. d. (fig. 798).
1393 San Miniato al Tedesco (val d'Elsa), Palazzo Comunale. Fresco: Madonna nursing the Child. d. (fig. 779).
1400 Montalbino, S. Giusto. Triptych: Madonna nursing the Child with Saints. d. (fig. 784).
1408 Volterra, Pinacoteca. Triptych: Madonna of Humility with Saints. d. (fig. 781).
1410 Volterra, S. Francesco, Oratorio della Compagnia della Croce di Giorno. Fresco: Legend of the True Cross and Life of the Virgin. s & d. (figs. 785, 788-96).

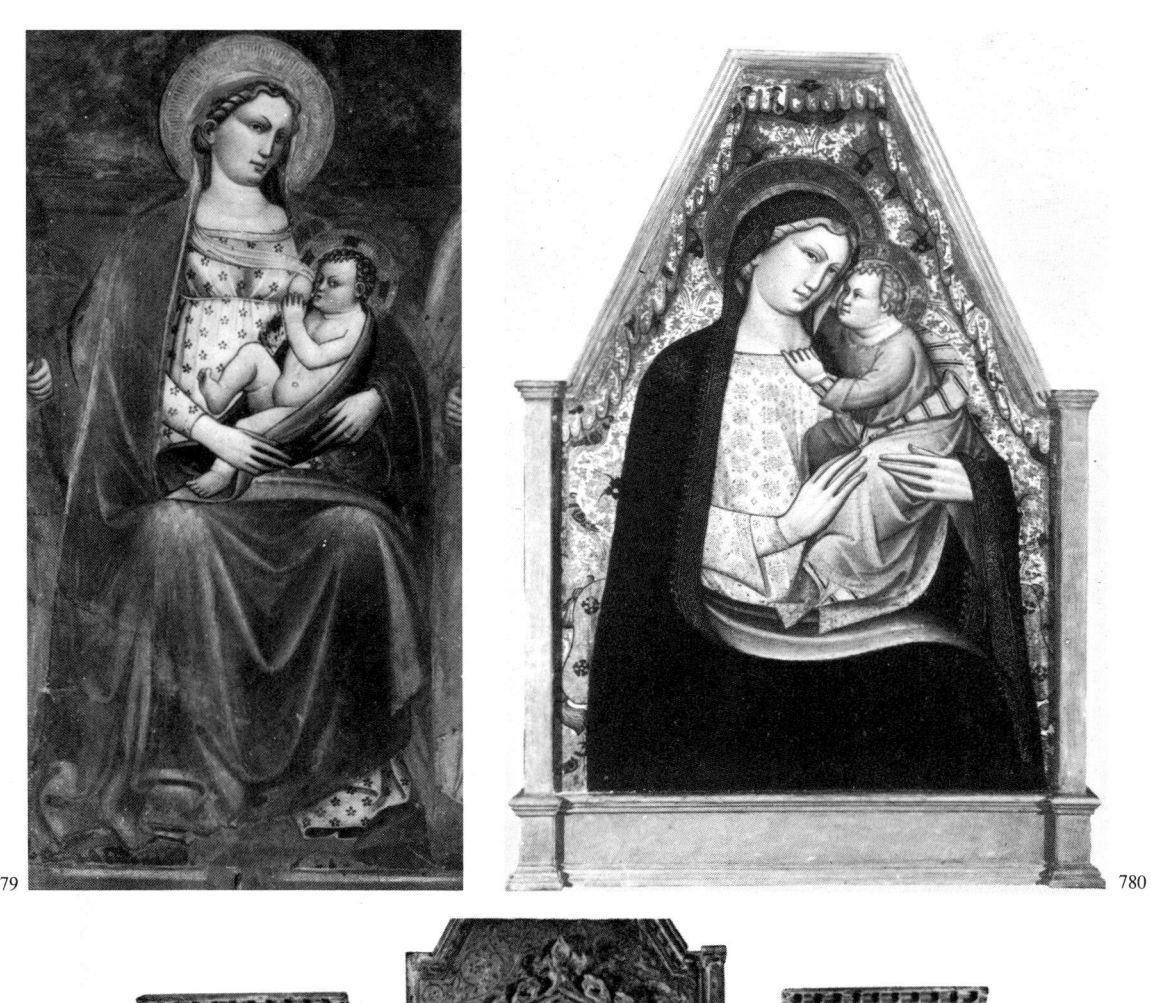

779

780

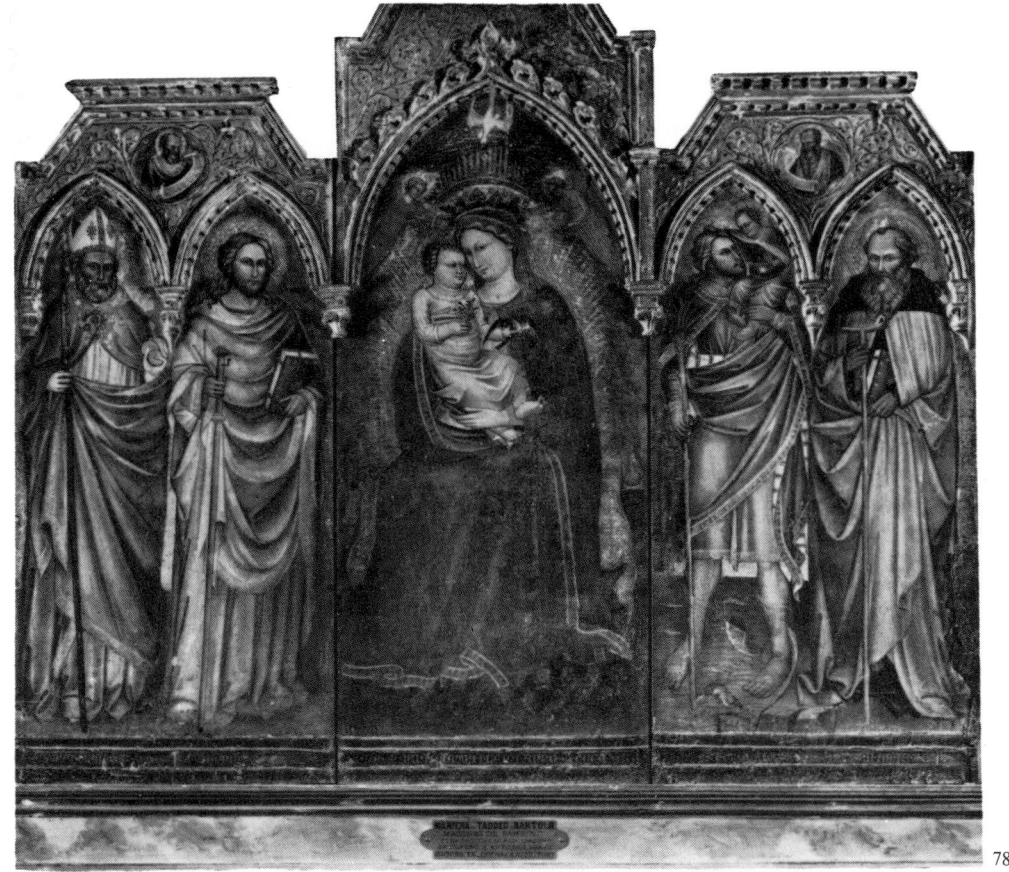

781

779. *Detail: Madonna nursing the Child. Fresco. San Miniato al Tedesco (Val d'Elsa), Palazzo Comunale. Alinari (detail) 19274. d. 1393.*
780. *Madonna and Child. Panel. Argiano (Val di Pesa), S. Martino. SGF 94691.*
781. *Triptych: Madonna of Humility with Sts Nicholas, James, Christopher and Anthony Abbot. Above: two Angels holding the Virgin's crown, and two Prophets. Panel. Volterra, Pinacoteca. no. 19. 192 (w. predella) × 192. Alinari 34628. d. 1408.*

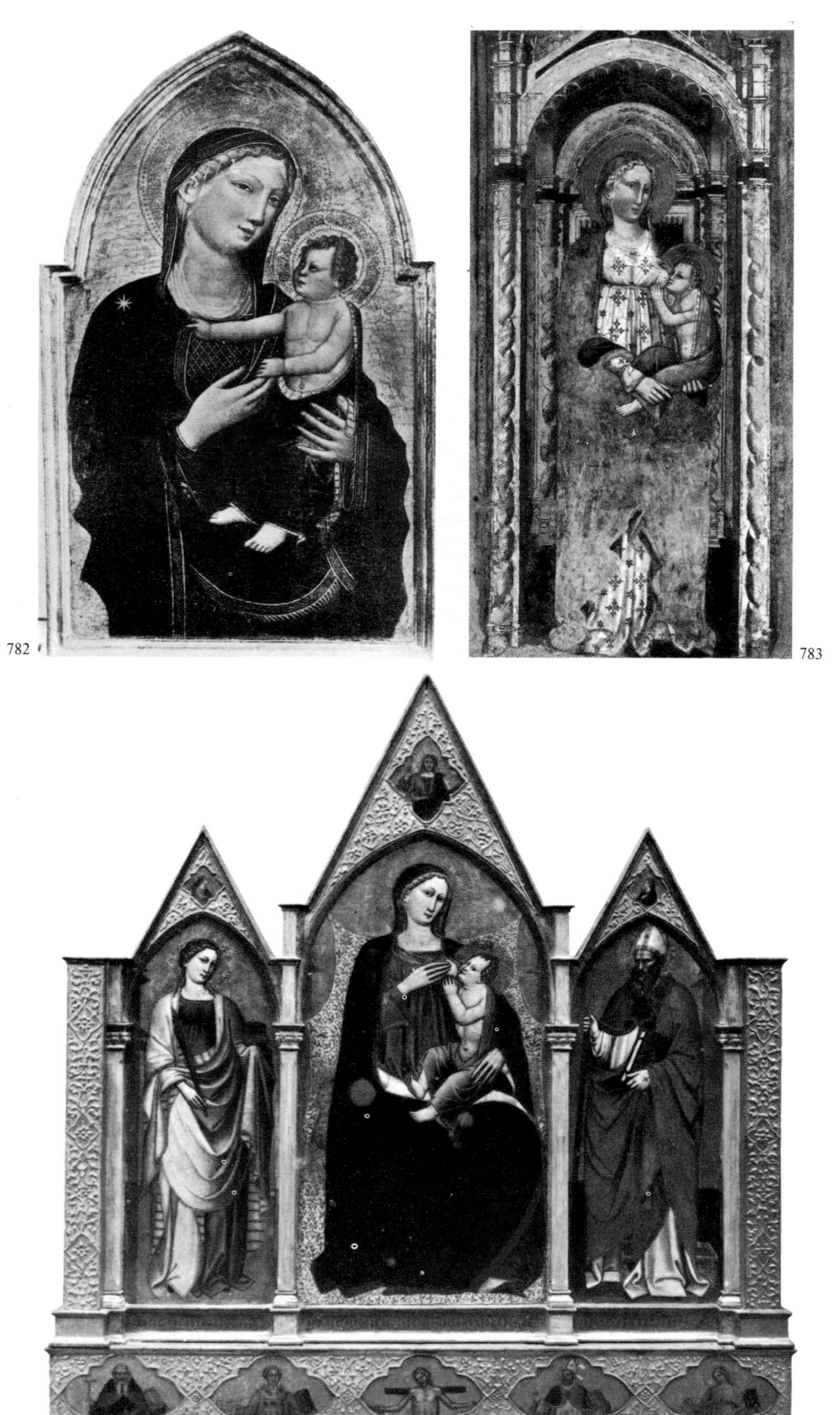

782. *Madonna and Child. Panel. Whereabouts unknown (formerly Rome, S. Basilio). Fototeca Berenson.*
783. *Madonna nursing the Child. Fresco. San Martino a Maiano (between Certaldo and Castelfiorentino, Val d'Elsa), Pieve. SGF 122560.*
784. *Triptych: Madonna nursing the Child with Sts Lucy and Justus. Predella: Man of Sorrows, Sts Anthony Abbot, Lawrence, a Bishop, Catherine. Above: Christ blessing and Annunciation. Panel. Montalbino (near Montespertoli), S. Giusto. 155 × 142. SGF 109560. d. 1400.*

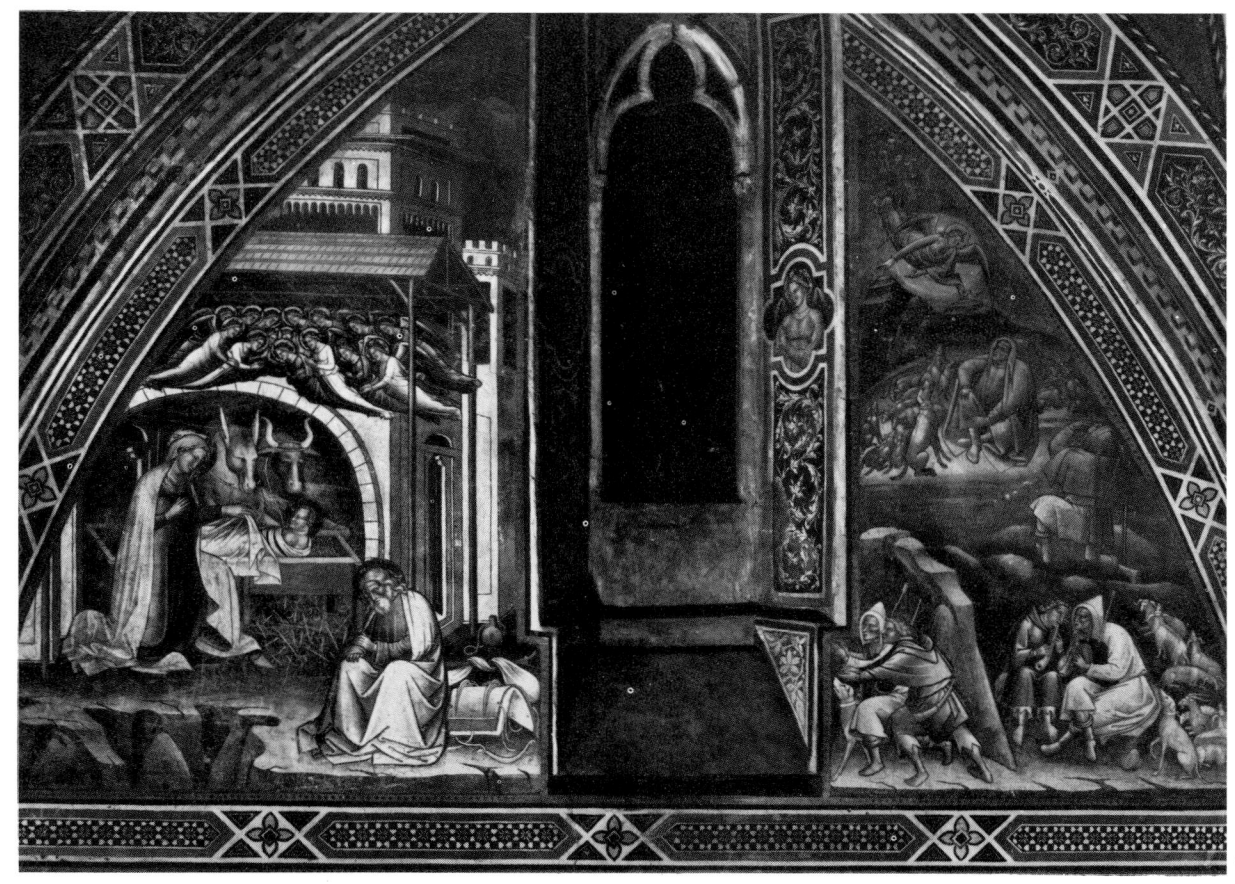

785

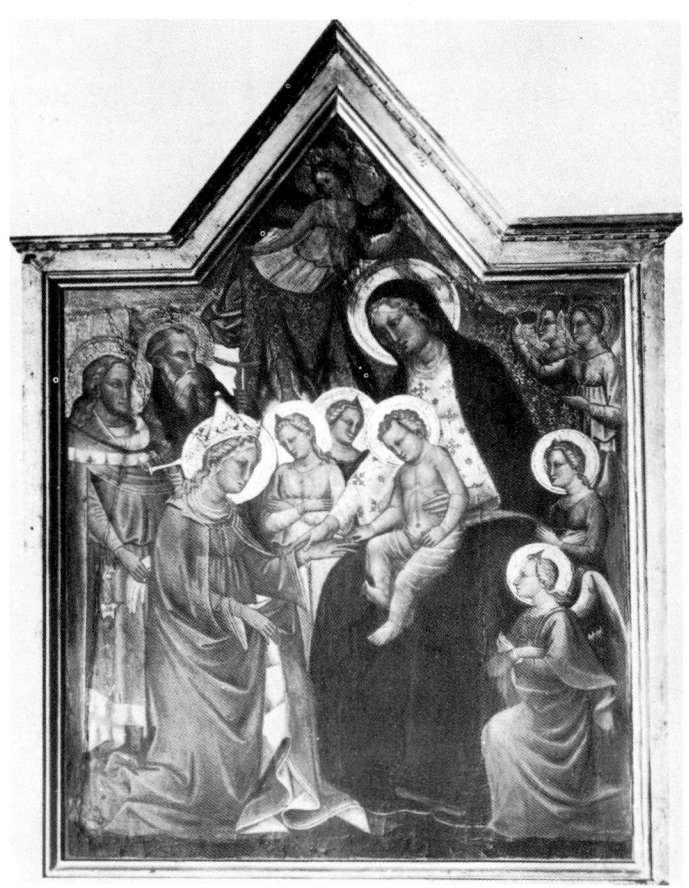

786

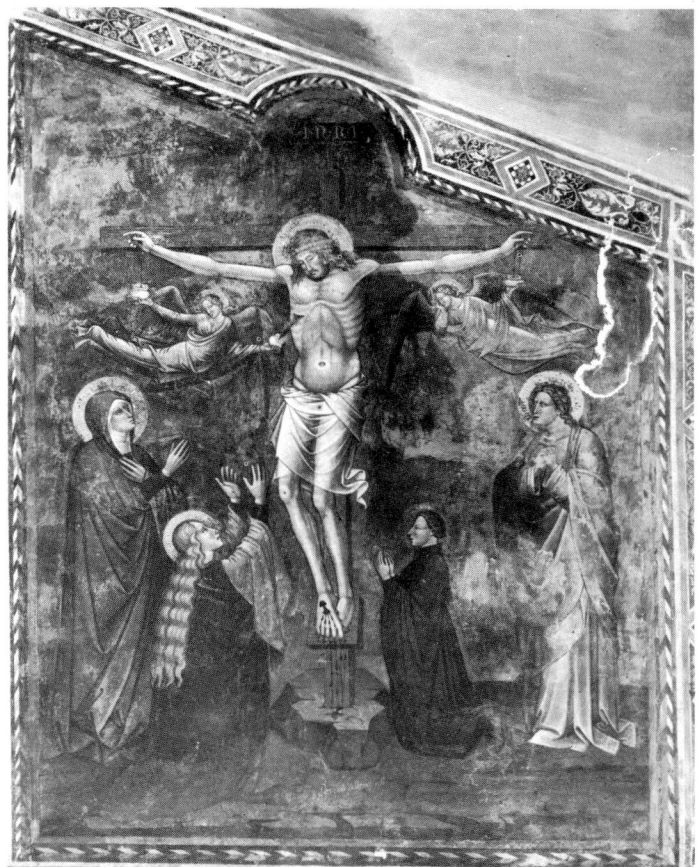

787

785. *Nativity. Fresco. Volterra, S. Francesco, Oratorio della Compagnia della Croce di Giorno. Brogi 15354. s & d. 1410.*
786. *Mystical Marriage of St Catherine. Panel. Fiesole, S. Francesco. 147 × 109. Alinari 1934.*
787. *Christ on the Cross with the Virgin, Sts John the Evangelist, Mary Magdalene, and a Donor. Fresco. San Gimignano, S. Lorenzo in Ponte. Frick 6652.*

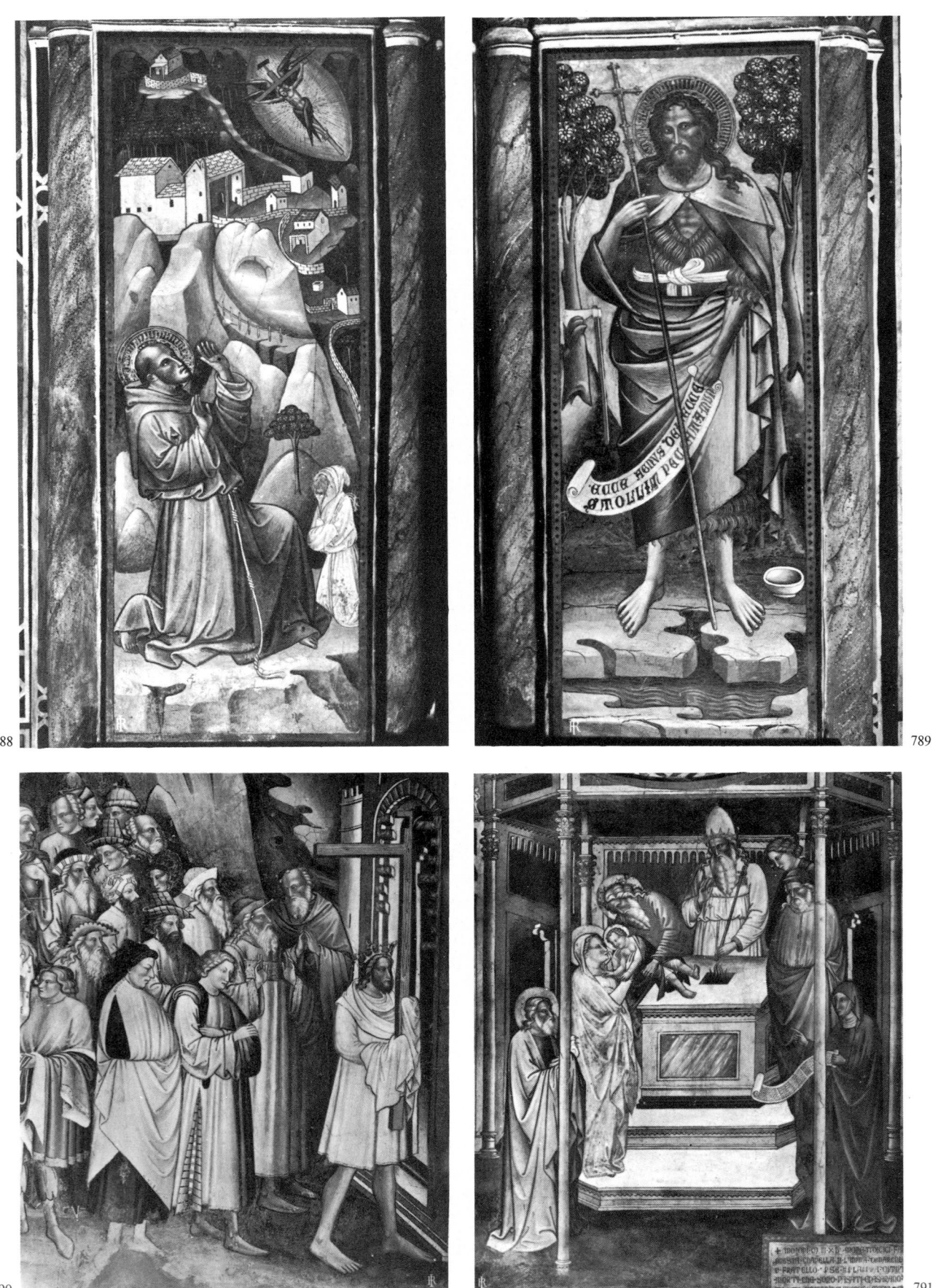

788   *St. Francis receiving the Stigmata. Fresco. Volterra, S. Francesco, Oratorio della Compagnia della Croce di Giorno. Brogi 15359. s & d. 1410.*
789   *St John the Baptist. Fresco. Volterra, S. Francesco, Oratorio della Compagnia della Croce di Giorno. Brogi 15360. s & d. 1410.*
790   *Detail: Heraclius carries the True Cross back to Jerusalem. Fresco. Volterra, S. Francesco, Oratorio della Compagnia della Croce di Giorno. Brogi 15346. s & d. 1410.*
791   *Circumcision. Fresco. Volterra, S. Francesco, Oratorio della Compagnia della Croce di Giorno. Brogi 15355. s & d. 1410.*

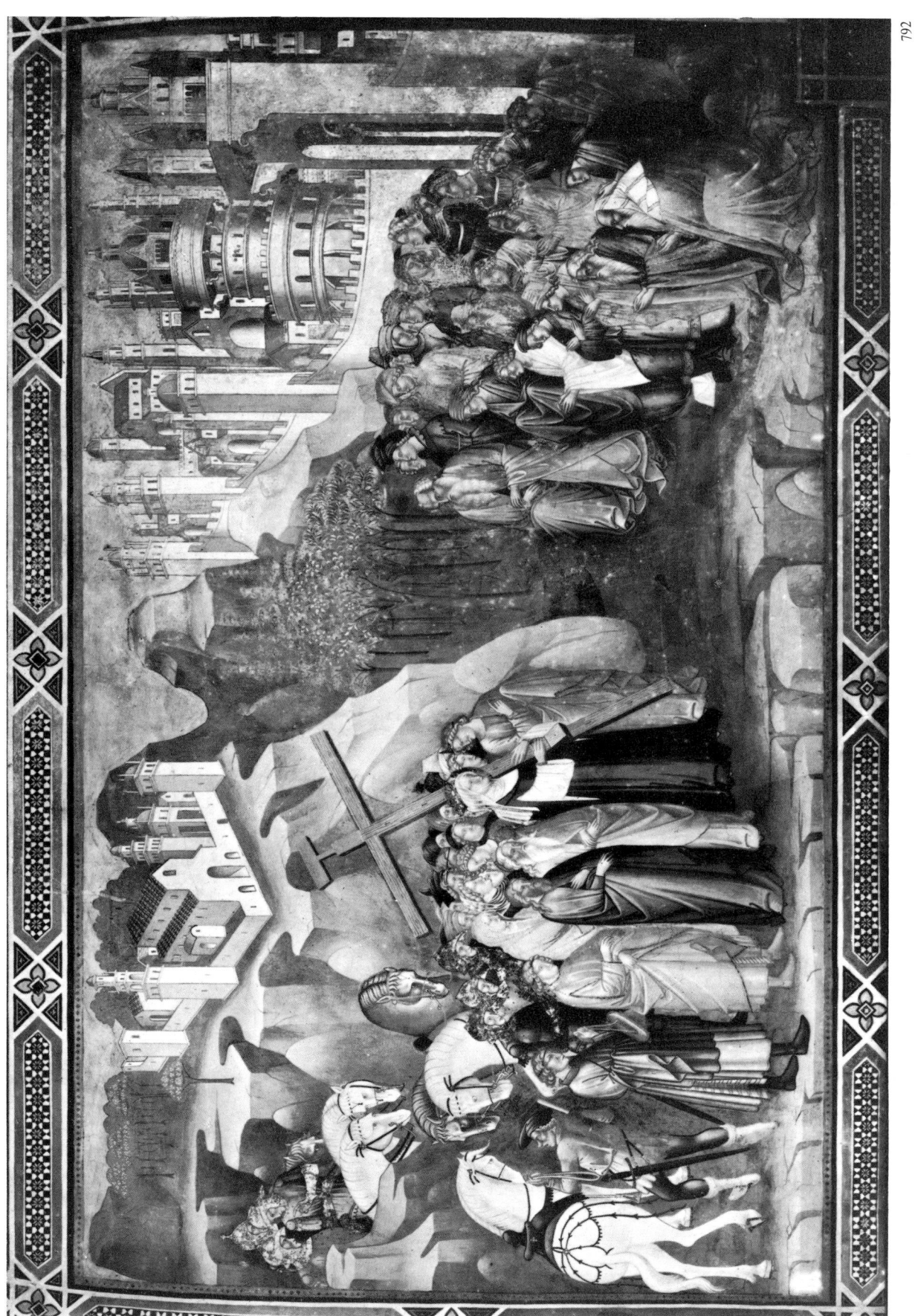

792. *St Helen carries the True Cross to Jerusalem. Fresco. Volterra, S. Francesco, Oratorio della Compagnia della Croce di Giorno. Brogi 15348. s & d. 1410.*

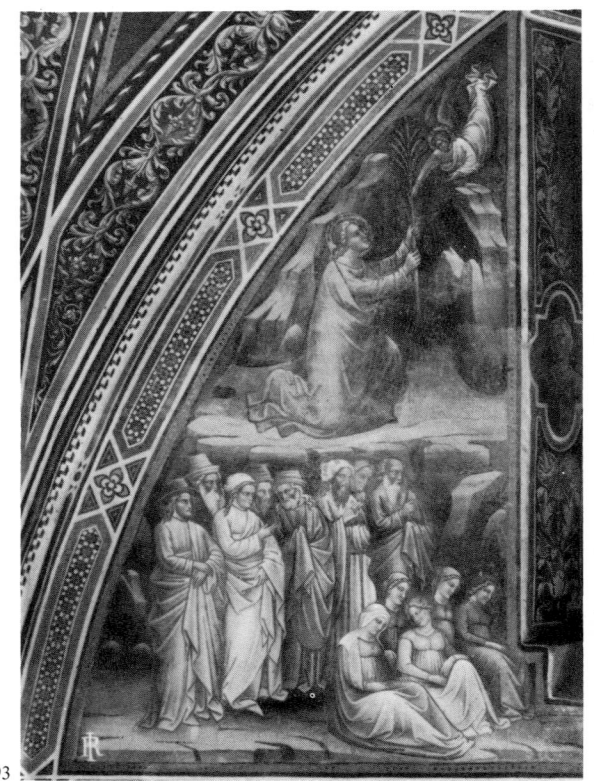
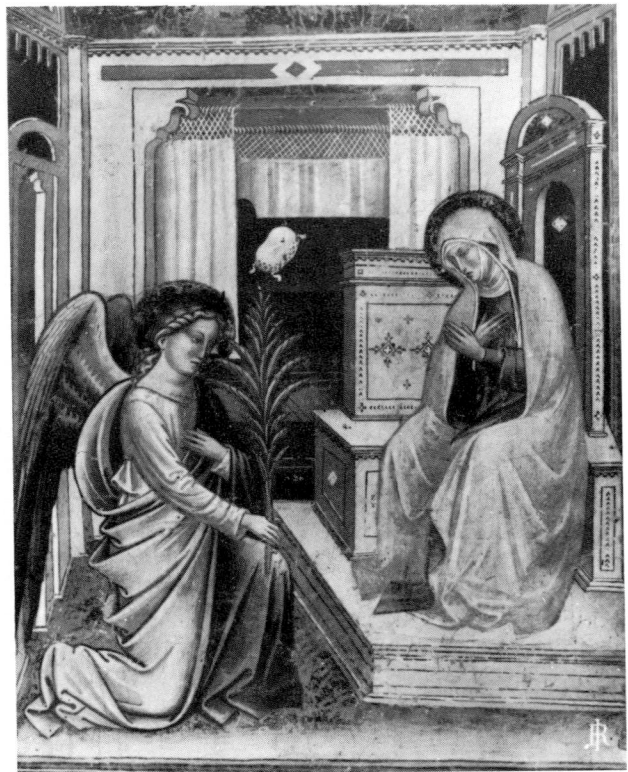

793. *Seth receives a branch of the Tree of Knowledge. Fresco. Volterra, S. Francesco, Oratorio della Compagnia della Croce di Giorno. Brogi 15347. s & d. 1410.*

794. *Annunciation. Fresco. Volterra, S. Francesco, Oratorio della Compagnia della Croce di Giorno. Brogi 15353. s & d. 1410.*

795. *Detail: Massacre of the Innocents. Fresco. Volterra, S. Francesco, Oratorio della Compagnia della Croce di Giorno. Brogi 15357. s & d. 1410.*

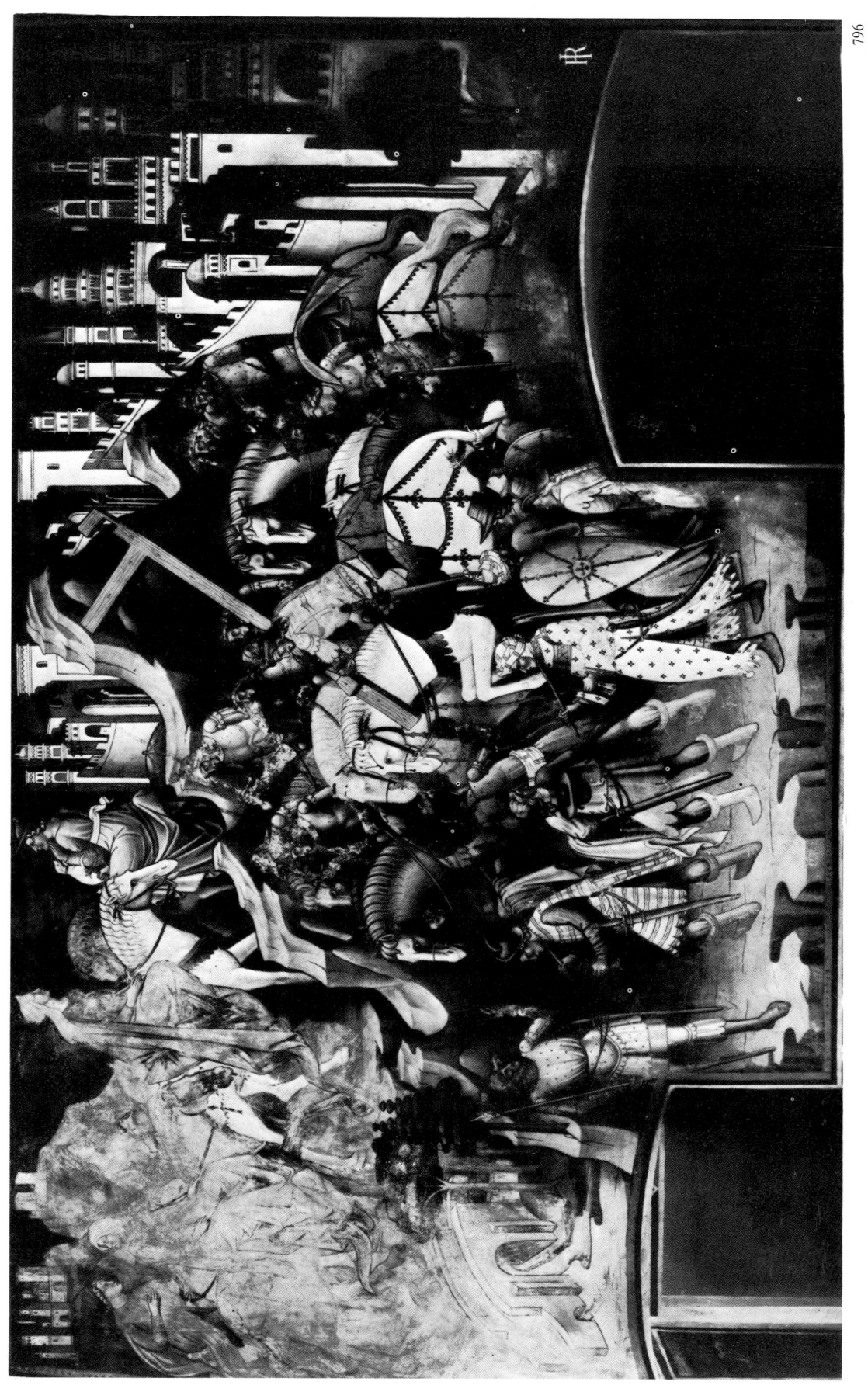

796. *Two scenes from the Legend of the True Cross: Queen of Sheba preaches the future of the True Cross; Cosroes steals the True Cross. Fresco. Volterra, S. Francesco, Oratorio della Compagnia della Croce di Giorno. Brogi 15351. s & d. 1410.*

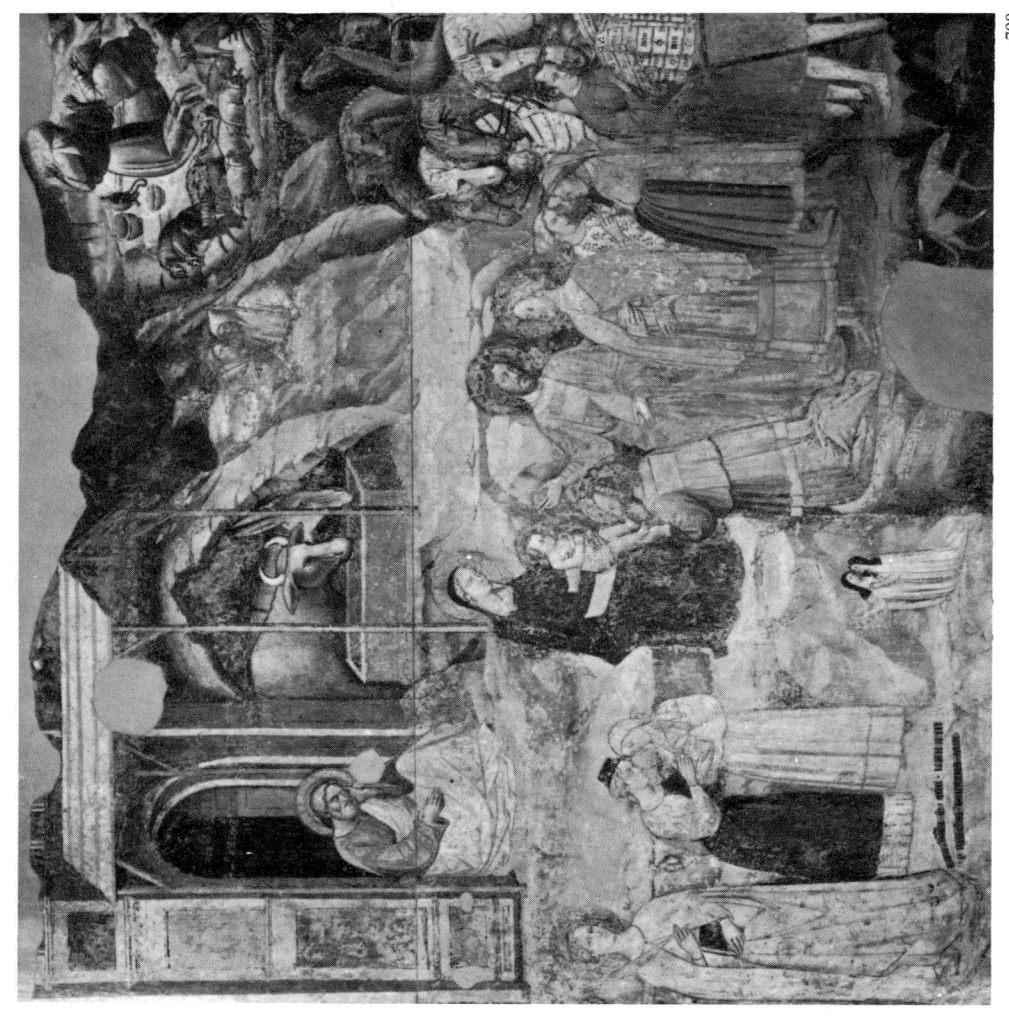

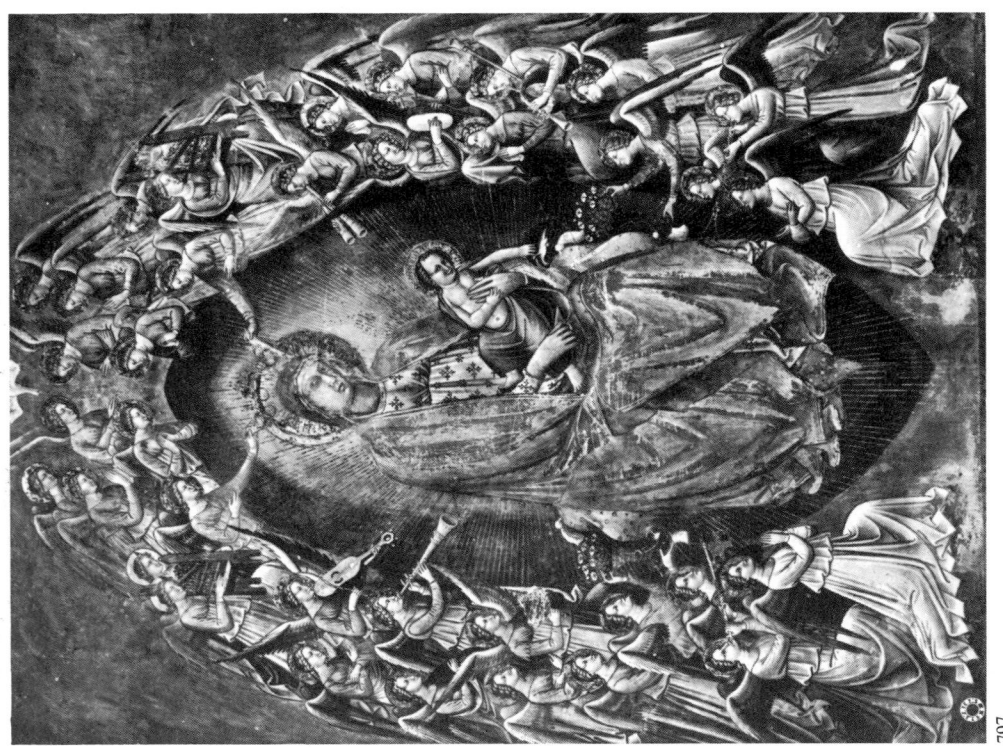

797. *Madonna and Child in Glory surrounded with Angels. Above: Holy Spirit. Fresco. San Gimignano, S. Lorenzo in Ponte. Anderson 31458.*
798. *Adoration of the Magi. Fresco. Florence, San Donato in Polverosa. SGF 129592. d. 1383.*

LORENZO di NICCOLÒ

Lorenzo di Niccolò was the son, but only a somewhat distant follower, of Niccolò di Pietro Gerini.

We find him first mentioned in 1392 as Niccolò's helper in his activities for Datini at Prato and between 1399 and 1401 he executed with his father and Spinello the altar-piece of the Coronation of the Virgin, now in the Accademia.

The signed picture representing St. Bartholomew and scenes from his legend in the Gallery of San Gimignano is dated 1401, while in 1402 he painted the altar-piece for the church of S. Marco, Florence, now in S. Domenico, Cortona and the same year signed the Madonna between four half-length figures in the church of Terenzano near Settignano. In 1408 Lorenzo matriculated in the guild of "medici e speciali" and two years later in that of S. Lucca. He is mentioned for the last time in 1411 when he receives six lire for the repainting of certain frescoes in S. Pietro Maggiore,.....

With Lorenzo di Niccolò's early manner, Trecento painting revives for one moment only to disappear again very suddenly. The artist, as we have observed, had many qualities which he must have acquired by studying and appreciating painters of an earlier period than the one to which his father belonged, and than whom Lorenzo was really a better and less vulgar artist. He was a more skilled draughtsman and a better colorist, and he attempted, with a fair amount of success to follow his illustrious predecessors, even in the more delicate particularities of their technique. He grasped the value of sober concentrated compositions for dramatic effects, and as a narrator he may be called the last adherent of that tradition which goes straight back to Giotto himself.....

> from R. van Marle, pp. 632-33, 646, *The Development of the Italian Schools of Painting*, Vol. III, The Hague, 1924.

Florentine, born 13- -, died 14- -. Painter. Physicians Apothecaries between 1386-1408..... Influenced by Spinello Aretino, partner in art of Niccolò di Piero Gerini. This partnership had already commenced in 1391-92, between which date and 1395 Niccolò and Lorenzo were engaged on various works at Prato for Francesco di Marco Datini..... On Jan. 25, 1401-2, Lorenzo was commissioned to paint a panel for the high altar of the church of S. Marco, which, removed to make way for the panel of the Virgin, Infant and Saints by Fra Angelico, was presented by Cosimo and Lorenzo de' Medici in 1440 to the convent of S. Domenico of Cortona, where it still remains. It is a rich Gothic altar-piece, divided into several compartments, with the Coronation of the Virgin in the centre, bearing the inscription "LAVRENTIVS. NICHOLA. ME. PINSIT".....

> from D. E. Colnaghi, p. 163, *A Dictionary of Florentine Painters*, London, 1928.

Recorded 1391-1411. Pupil of his father Niccolò di Pietro Gerini; influenced by Spinello Aretino and Lorenzo Monaco. (See also Master of Arte della Lana Coronation).

> from B. Berenson, p. 121, *Italian Pictures of the Renaissance, Florentine School*, Vol. I, London, 1963.

The pupil of his father, Niccolò di Pietro Gerini. He collaborated with Spinello Aretino and their styles are somewhat close. Later, Gothic elements, as in the exhibited painting, feature more prominently in his work, perhaps as a result of his having seen pictures by Lorenzo Monaco or Barna. According to Berenson he may be the same as the artist described as the Master of the Arte della Lana Coronation.....

> from St. J. Gore, p. 46, *The Art of Painting in Florence & Siena from 1250-1500*, London, 1965.

A good example of Lorenzo's style is the signed and dated (1402) triptych of the *Madonna and Child with Saints Zanobi and Lawrence* in the church of San Martino at Terenzano. At first glance this painting seems quite close to the two just discussed, but detailed examination reveals a number of fundamental differences. Perhaps the most striking discrepancy is the stiff, almost wooden quality of the Virgin and Child, noted at once in the rigid right arm of the Madonna or in the clumsy arch formed by the arms of the baby..... Contrary to popular belief Lorenzo di Niccolò was not the son of Niccolò di Pietro Gerini. His full name was Lorenzo di Niccolò di Martino.

from B. Cole, p. 215, *The Burlington Magazine*, CX, 1968.

He is named for the first time in a document of 1392 which records him as a helper of Niccolò di Pietro Gerini (whose son, according to some critics, he was); between 1399 and 1401 he worked on an altar panel for the Florentine church of S. Felicità (which is now in the Accademia Gallery in Florence), the principal painters of which were Gerini and Spinello Aretino. In his works of these years (at San Gimignano, at Cortona and at Terenzano, near Florence) there is, besides the influence of Niccolò, another influence of Spinello (especially in the frescoes at " Paradiso degli Alberti " at Bandino near Florence) and still the suggestion, in a Quattrocento already well on its way, of the painting and narrative characteristics of Taddeo Gaddi; a little bit later, the loose elegance of the painting of Lorenzo Monaco mingles with the former influences emphasizing certain of the rigid qualities of the painter's earlier production, creating a decorative sense characteristic of the new full Gothic tastes. Typical of this period is the Coronation of the Virgin of 1408, in Santa Croce in Florence.....

from M. L. Moriondo, pp. 17-18, *Arte in Valdichiana dal XIII al XVIII secolo*, Cortona, 1970.

BIBLIOGRAPHY
BOOKS

An asterisk indicates a work listed in the General Bibliography

Pini, Milanesi*, 1876, no 10; *Khv & Salmi**, 1914, pp. 58-9; *v. Marle 1924**, pp. 632-3; *Colnaghi**, 1928, p. 163; *Galetti**, " F-O ", 1950, p. 1065; *Oertel, 1950**, pp. 42-3; Suida, W. E., *Catalogue of the Birmingham Museum of Art*, Birmingham, (Ala.), 1959, pp. 25-6; Shapley, F. R., *Catalogue of the North Carolina Museum of Art*, Raleigh, 1960, p. 38; *Oertel, 1961**, pp. 128-9; *Berenson, 1963**, Vol. I, pp. 121-4; Dal Poggetto, P., *AIV*, 1963, p. 34; Gore, St J., *Wildenstein**, 1965, p. 16; *Marcucci**, 1965, pp. 109-14; *Shapley**, 1966, pp. 44-5; Moriondo, M. L., *Arte in Valdichiana dal XIII al XVIII secolo*, Cortona, 1970, pp. 17-8; *MMOA**, 1971, pp. 52-56; Palumbo, G., *Collezione Federico Mason Perkins*, Rome, 1973, p. 66; *Dutch Show**, 1974, pp. 75-76.

JOURNALS

Sirén, O., *A*, VII, 1904, pp. 338-42; Sirén, O., *RA*, VI, 5, 1906, pp. 81-7; Sirén, O., *BM*, XIV, 1908, p. 193; Sirén, O., *A*, XI, 1908, p. 179; Bernardini, G., *RA*, IX, 6, 1909, pp. 89-94; Salmi, M., *A*, XVI, 1913, pp. 208-27; Sirén, O., *AA*, VI, 1916, pp. 207-23; Sirén, O., *BM*, XXXVI, 1920, pp. 72-8; Lasareff, V., *AA*, XVI, 1928, pp. 25-40; Salmi, M., *RA*, XI, 1929, pp. 138-40; Piattoli, R., *RA*, XI, 1929, pp. 221-53, 396-437, 537-58; Biagetti, B., *L'Illustrazione Vaticana*, I, 1930, pp. 39-43; Piattoli, R., *RA*, XII, 1930, pp. 97-150; Berenson, B., *DD*, XII, 1, 1932, pp. 5-34; Offner, R., *BM*, LXIII, 1933, p. 169; Procacci, U., *RA*, XV, 1933, pp. 224-44; Salmi, M., *RA*, XVI, 1934, pp. 168-186; Rogers, M. R., *SLB*, XXIII, 1938, pp. 2-5; Cohn, W., *RA*, XXXI, 6, 1951, p. 41; Salmi, M., *C*, II, 3-4, 1951, pp. 169-81; Baldini, U., *BA*, XXXVII, 4, 1952, pp. 349-50; Cohn, W., *RA*, XXXI, 1956, pp. 41-72; Cohn, W., *BA*, XLI, 1956, p. 1; Boschetto, A., *Musées Royaux des Beaux-Arts, Bulletin*, III, 1954, pp. 20-1; Gherardini, P., *MSV*, 1957, p. 77; *Edit.*, *MM*, XVIII, 1959, p. 37; Boskovits, N., *BHA*, 21, 1962, pp. 21-30; Zeri, F., *BA*, XLVIII, 4, 1963, p. 247; Baldini, U., *AV*, V, 6, 1966, pp. 25-32; Bellosi, L., *PA*, XVII, 201, 1966, p. 74; Eisenberg, M. J., *MIAB*, 55, 1966, p. 16; Bellosi, L., *PA*, XVIII, 203/23, 1967, pp. 86-7; Boskovits, M., *AV*, VII, 3, 1968, pp. 21-31; Cole, B., *BM*, CX, 1968, pp. 215-16; Zeri, F., *GBA*, LXXI, 110, 1968, pp. 66-67; Wilkins, D., *BM*, CXI, 791, 1969, pp. 83-85; Cole, B., *AQ*, XXXIII, 2, 1970, pp. 114-19; Polzer, J., *JBM*, XIII, 1971, p. 49; Zeri, F., *MKIF*, XVII, 2-3, 1973, p. 369.

SIGNED AND DATED WORKS

1401 San Gimignano, Museo Civico. Triptych: St Bartholomew Enthroned and scenes from his life. d. (fig 819).
1402 Terenzano, S. Martino. Triptych: Madonna & Child with Sts. Martin and Lawrence. s & d. (fig. 815).
1404 Venice, Cini Collection 336. Polyptych: Madonna & Child with four Saints d. (fig. 806).
1409 Florence, S. Croce, Medici Chapel. Panel: Madonna & Child Enthroned, with the Infant Christ holding the Cross. d. (fig. 804).
1412 Mezzomonte (near Pozzolatico), S. Lorenzo in Collina. Polyptych: Madonna & Child Enthroned with Saints. d. (fig. 820).

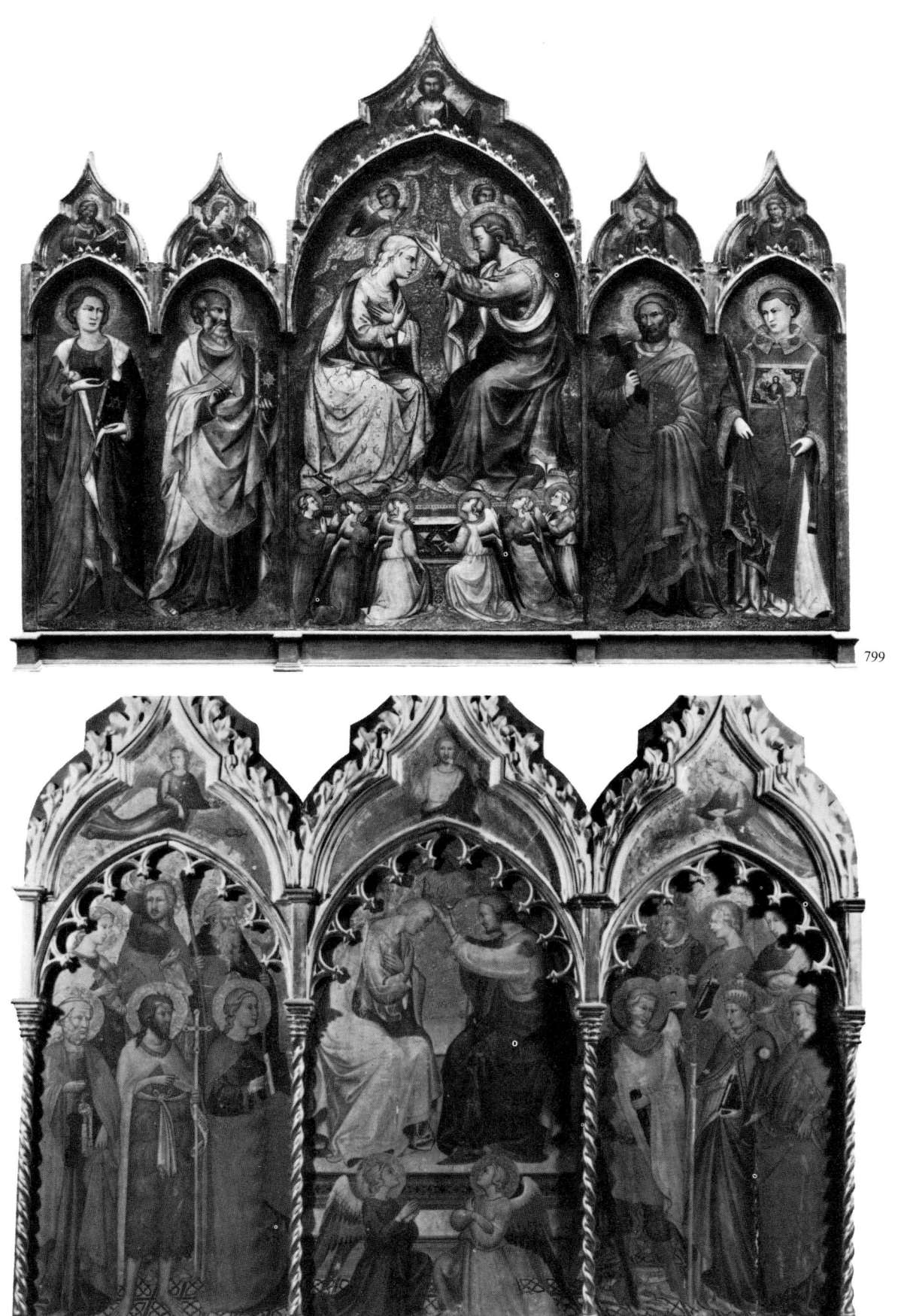

799

800

799. *Polyptych: Coronation of the Virgin with Sts Peter, John the Evangelist, Lucy, and Lawrence. Above: Christ blessing. Pinnacles: Annunciation and two Prophets. Panel. Florence, Museo di S. Croce. SGF 108889.*

800. *Triptych: Coronation of the Virgin with two Angels and Sts Catherine, Christopher, Anthony Abbot, Peter, John the Baptist, Lucy, Michael the Archangel, Agatha and four other Saints. Above: Christ blessing and two Angels. Panel. Private Collection. 174 × 179. Sotheby 211410.*

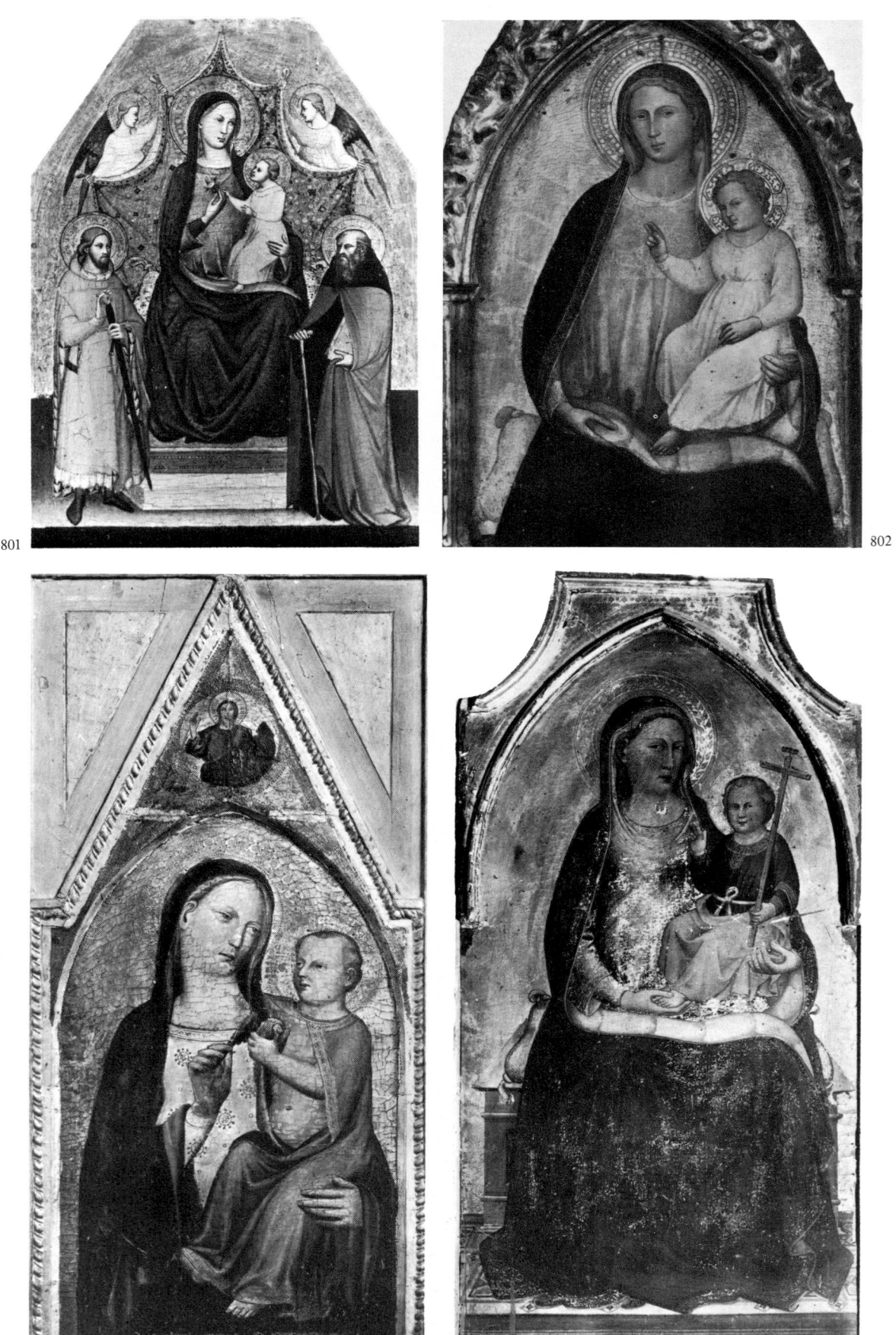

801. *Madonna and Child Enthroned with Sts Julian and Anthony Abbot, and two Angels. Panel. Berea (Ky.), Berea College, Samuel H. Kress Collection. no. K 108. 68 × 47.5. Kress Foundation photo.*
802. *Madonna of Humility. Panel. Florence, Acton Collection. no. 33. 56 × 78. Reali.*
803. *Madonna and Child. Above: Christ blessing. Panel. Parma, Galleria Nazionale. no. 445. 75 × 33.7. Alinari 44507.*
804. *Madonna and Child Enthroned with the Infant Christ holding the Cross. Panel. Florence, S. Croce, Medici Chapel. Brogi 19954. d. 1409.*

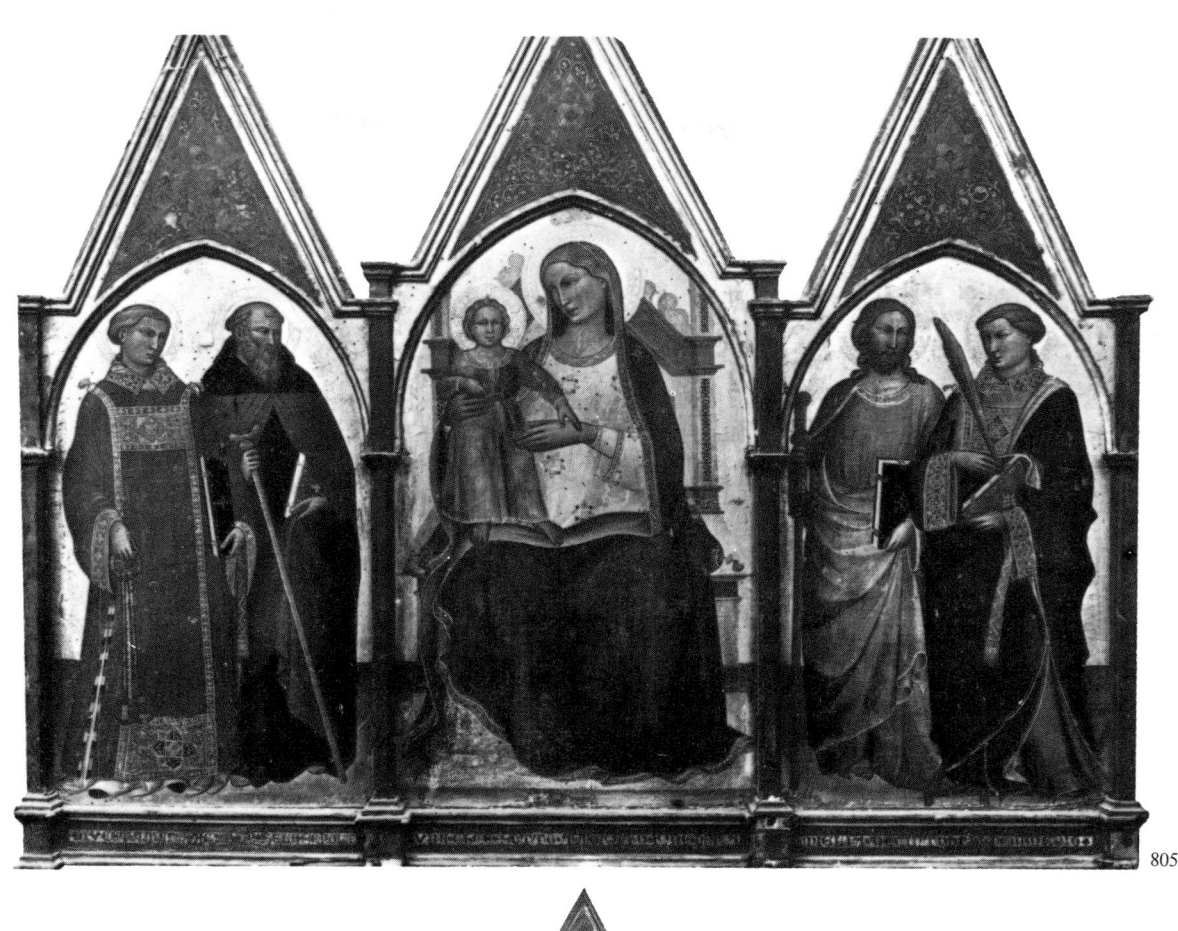

805

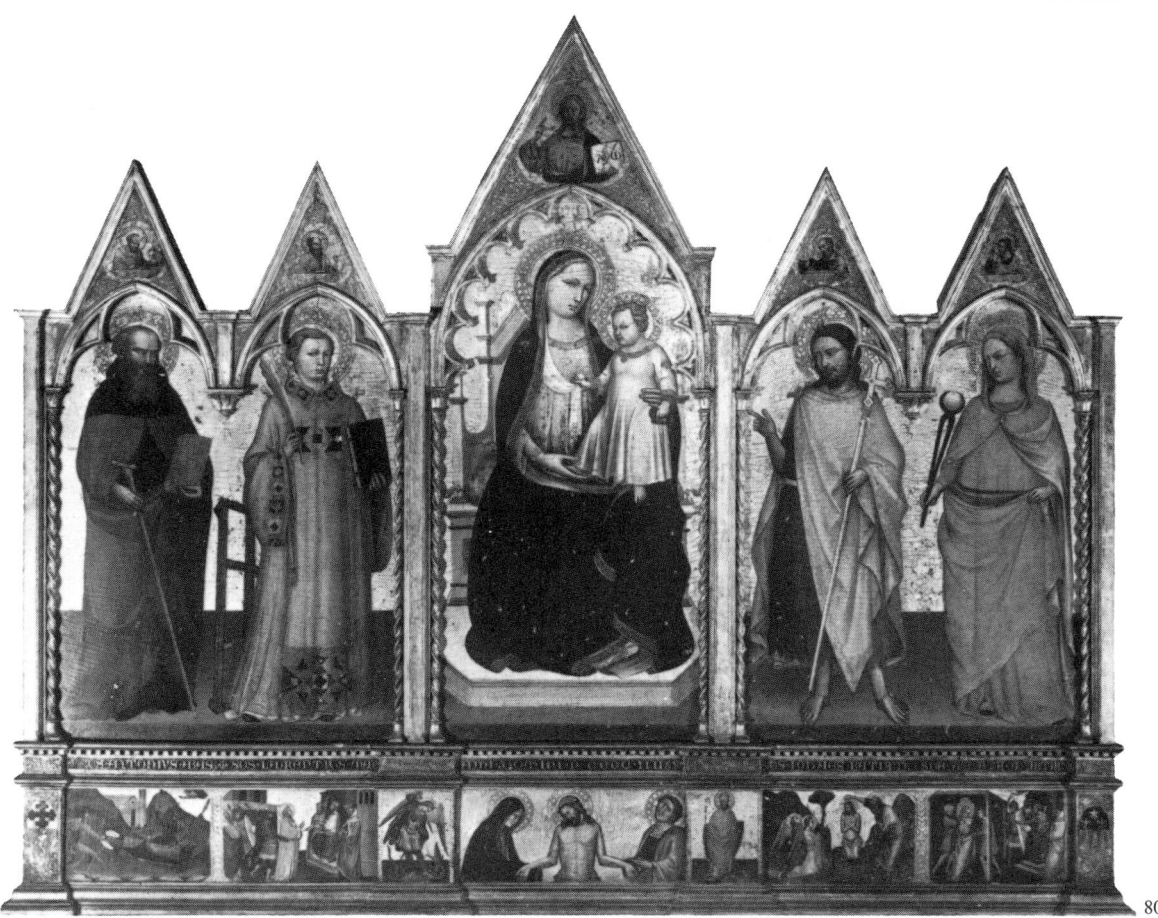

806

805. *Triptych: Madonna and Child Enthroned with Sts Leonard, Anthony Abbot, James and Lawrence. Panel. Florence, Arcetri, S. Leonardo. SGF 2125.*
806. *Polyptych: Madonna and Child Enthroned with Sts Anthony Abbot, Lawrence, John the Baptist, Agatha. Predella: Scenes from the Lives of the Saints above, and Man of Sorrows. Panel. Venice, Cini Collection. no. 336. 208 × 170. Collection photo. d. 1404.*

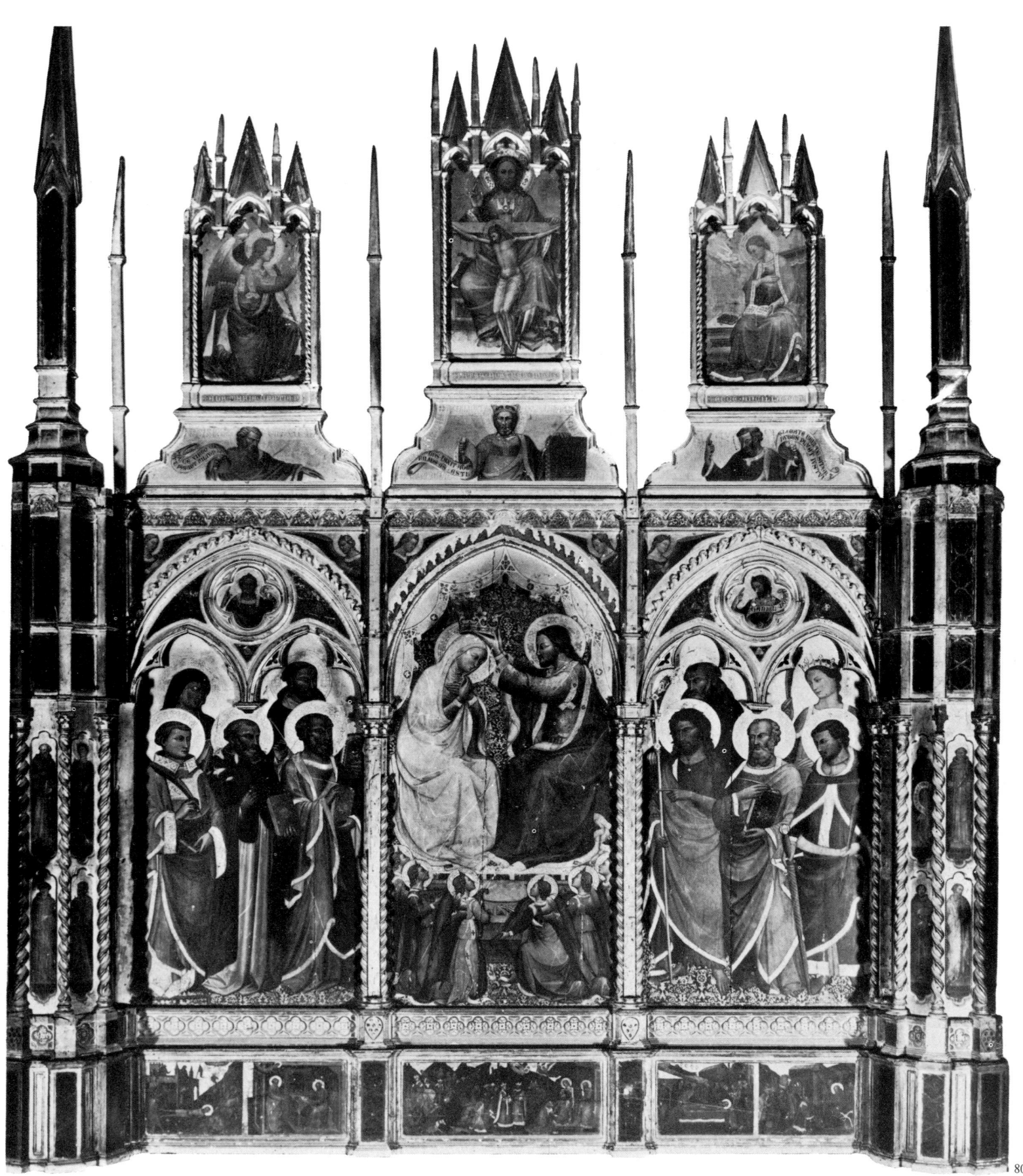

807

807. *Polyptych: Coronation of the Virgin with four music-making Angels, and Sts Lawrence, Catherine of Siena, Dominic, Thomas Aquinas, Mark, John the Baptist, Benedict, John the Evangelist, Catherine of Alexandria, and Julian. Above: two Prophets and heads of six Angels. Predella: Martyrdom of St Lawrence; St Peter dictating to St Mark; Adoration of the Magi; Death of St John the Evangelist; Totila before St Benedict. Pinnacles: the Trinity, the Annunciation, two Prophets and Christ the King. Pilasters: twelve Saints. Panel. Cortona, S. Domenico. Alinari 42421. 1402.*

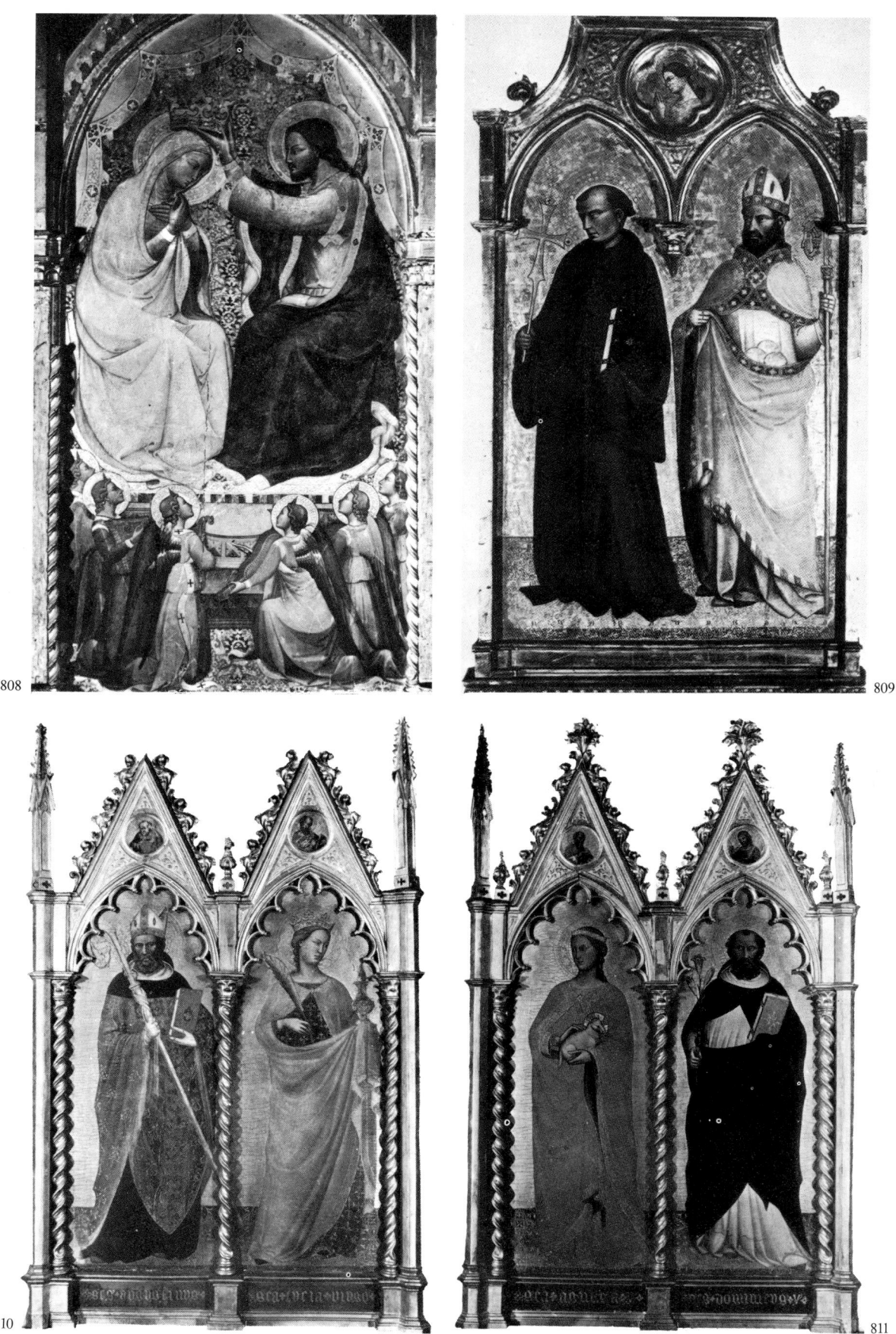

808. *Coronation of the Virgin with four music-making Angels, detail of fig. 807. Panel. Cortona, S. Domenico. Alinari 42422. 1402.*
809. *Sts John Gualbert and Nicholas of Bari. Panel. Assisi, F. M. Perkins Collection. no. 56. 122 × 85. Foto de Giovanni.*
810. *Sts Lucy and Augustine. Panel. New Haven (Conn.), Yale University Art Gallery, J. J. Jarves Collection. no. 1871.27. 109.2 × 63.2. Museum photo.*
811. *Sts Agnes and Dominic. Panel. New Haven (Conn.), Yale University Art Gallery, J. J. Jarves Collection. no. 1871.28. 111.4 × 63.8. Museum photo.*

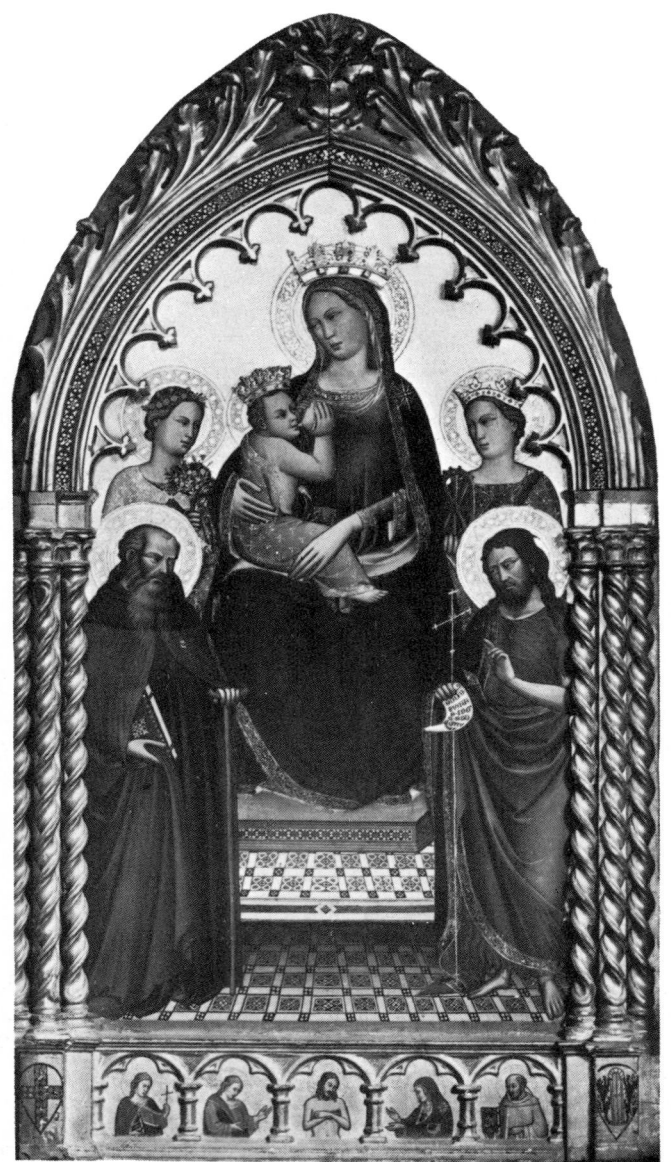

812

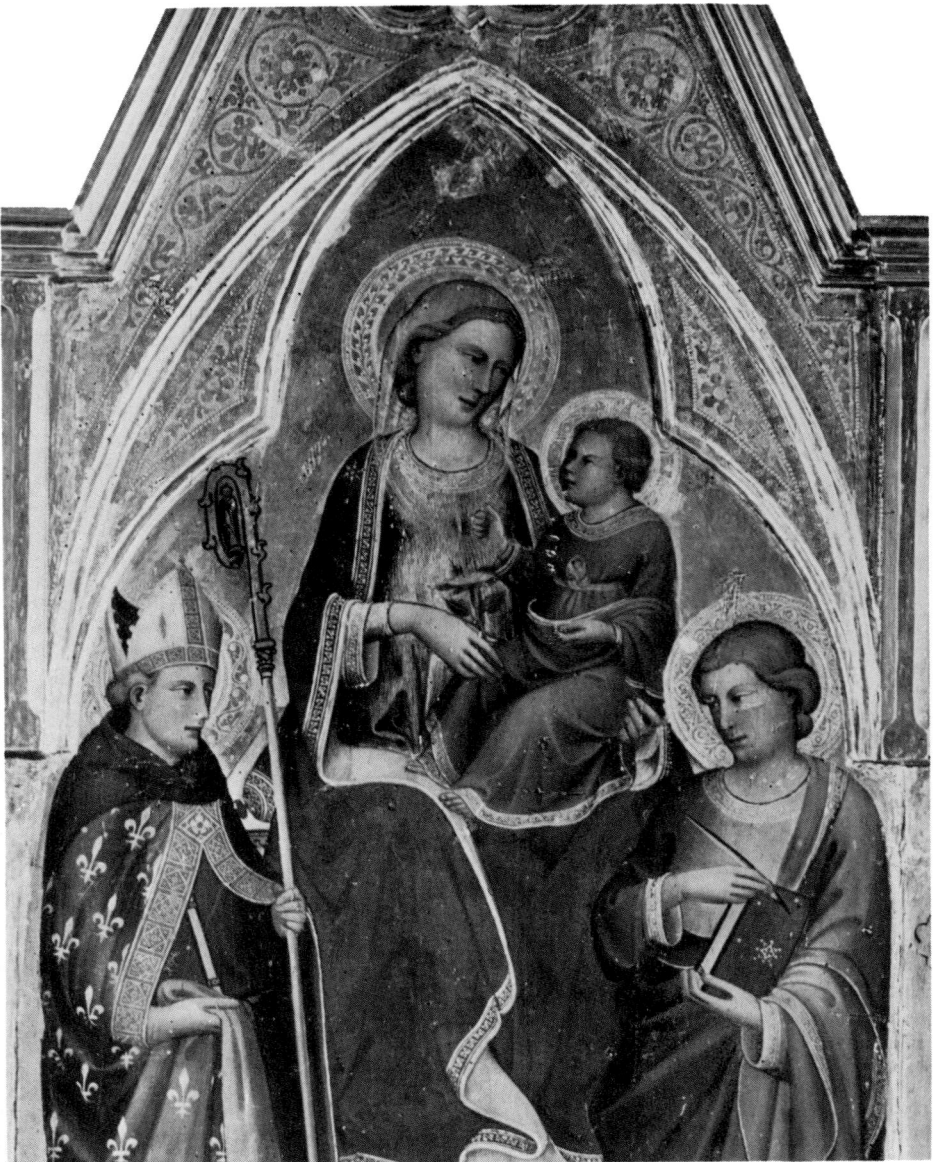

813

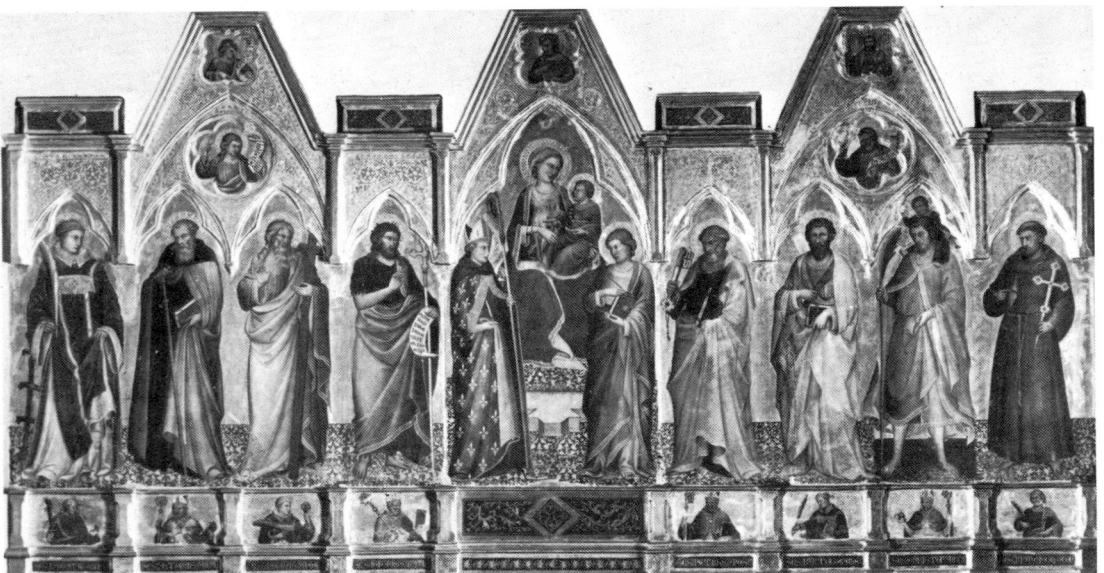

814

812. *Madonna Enthroned nursing the Child with Sts Catherine, John the Baptist, Dorothy and Anthony Abbot. Predella: Man of Sorrows and four Saints.*
Panel. Stia (Casentino), S. Maria delle Grazie. 110 × 58. Alinari 8529.
813. *Madonna and Child Enthroned with Sts Louis of Toulouse and John the Evangelist, detail of fig. 814. Panel. Florence, S. Croce, Sacristy. Alinari (detail) 3964.*
814. *Polyptych: Madonna and Child Enthroned with Sts Louis of Toulouse and John the Evangelist, Christopher, Francis, Lawrence, Anthony Abbot, Andrew,*
John the Baptist, Peter, Bartholomew. Above: five Prophets. Predella: eight Saints. Panel. Florence, S. Croce, Sacristy. Alinari 3964.

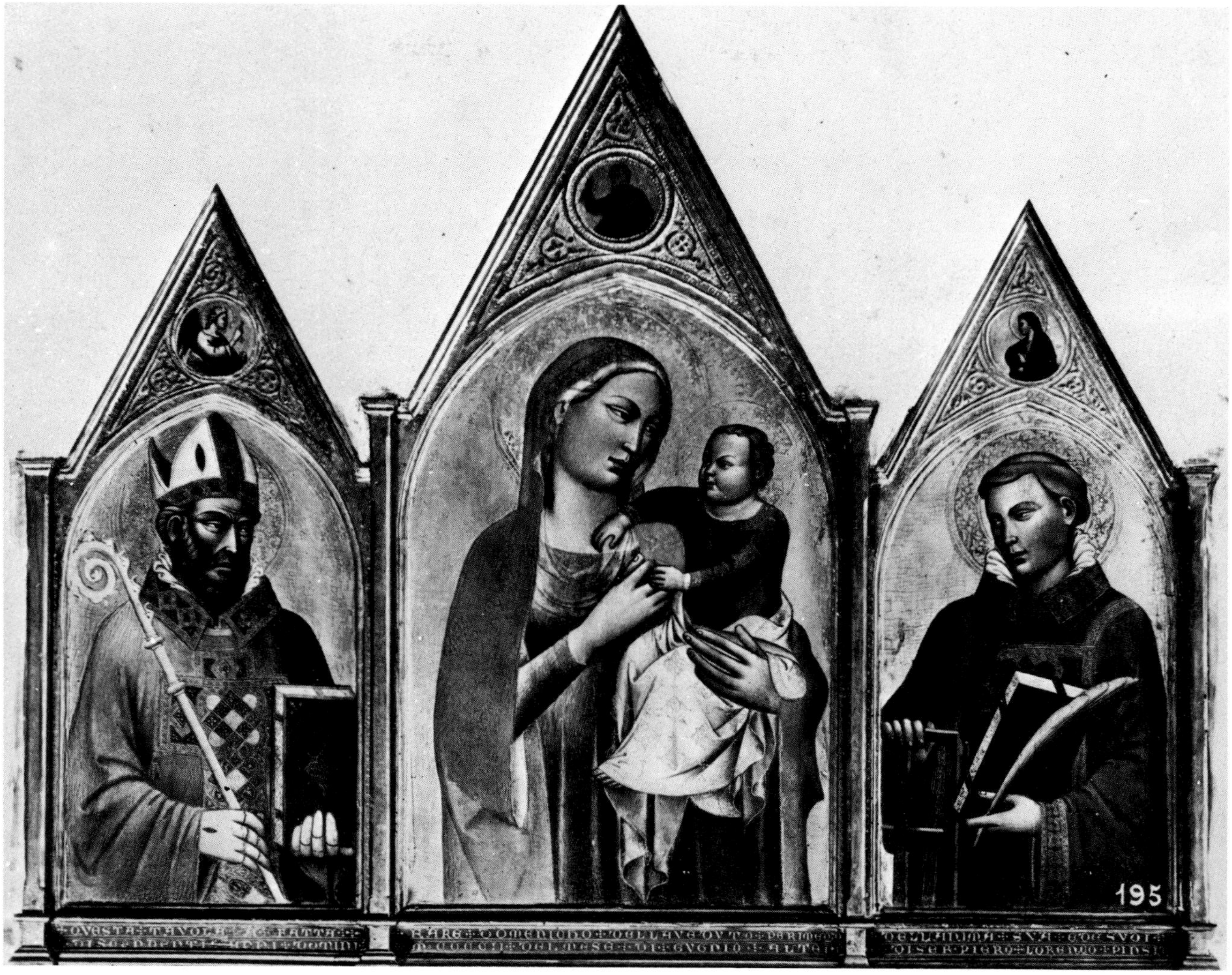

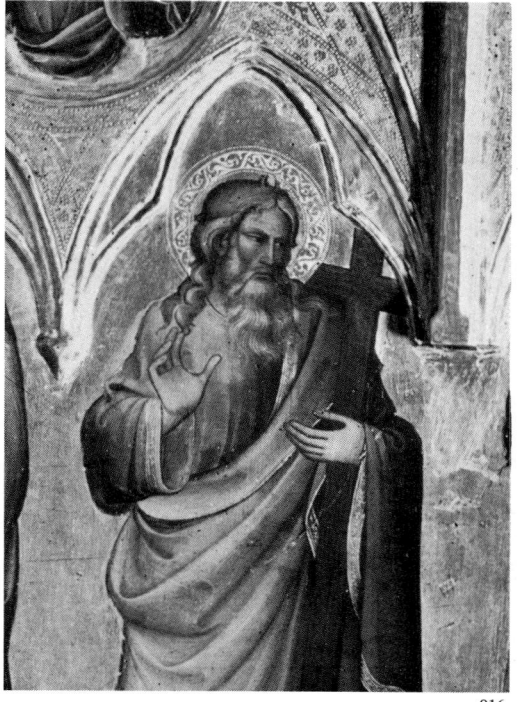

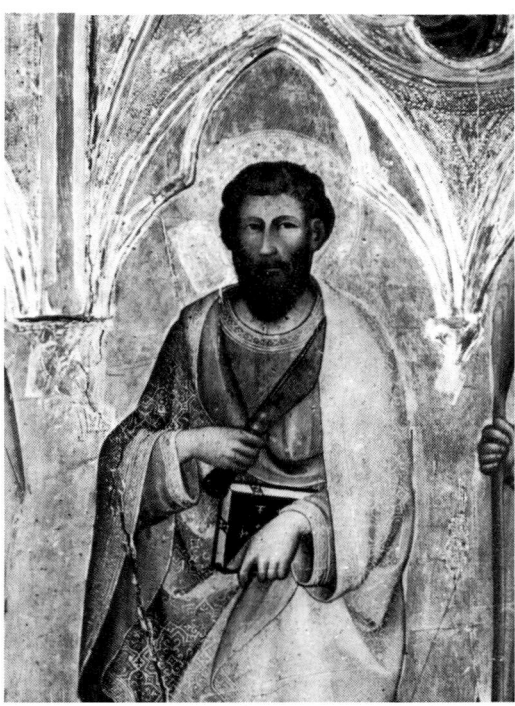

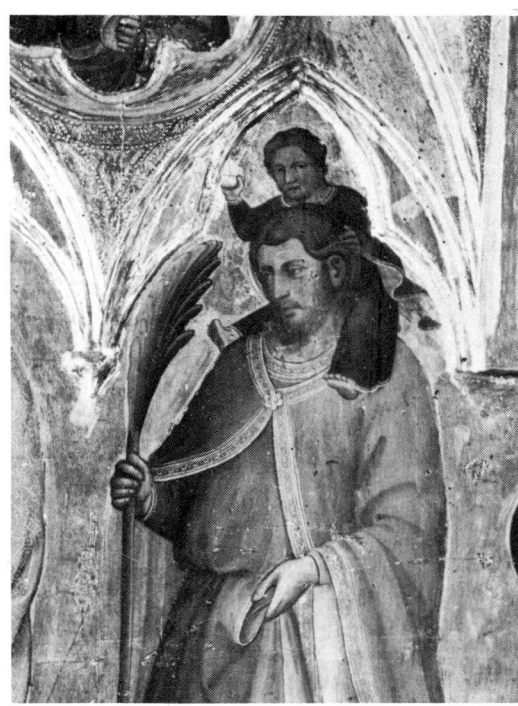

815. *Triptych: Madonna and Child with Sts Martin and Lawrence.   Above: Christ blessing; Annunciation. Panel. Terenzano (1.5 km from Settignano, near Florence), S. Martino. 117 × 141. SGF 21118. s & d. 1402.*

816. *St Andrew, detail of fig. 814. Panel. Florence, S. Croce, Sacristy. Alinari (detail) 3964.*

817. *St Bartholomew, detail of fig. 814. Panel. Florence, S. Croce, Sacristy. Alinari (detail) 3964.*

818. *St Christopher, detail of fig. 814. Panel. Florence, S. Croce, Sacristy. Alinari (detail) 3964.*

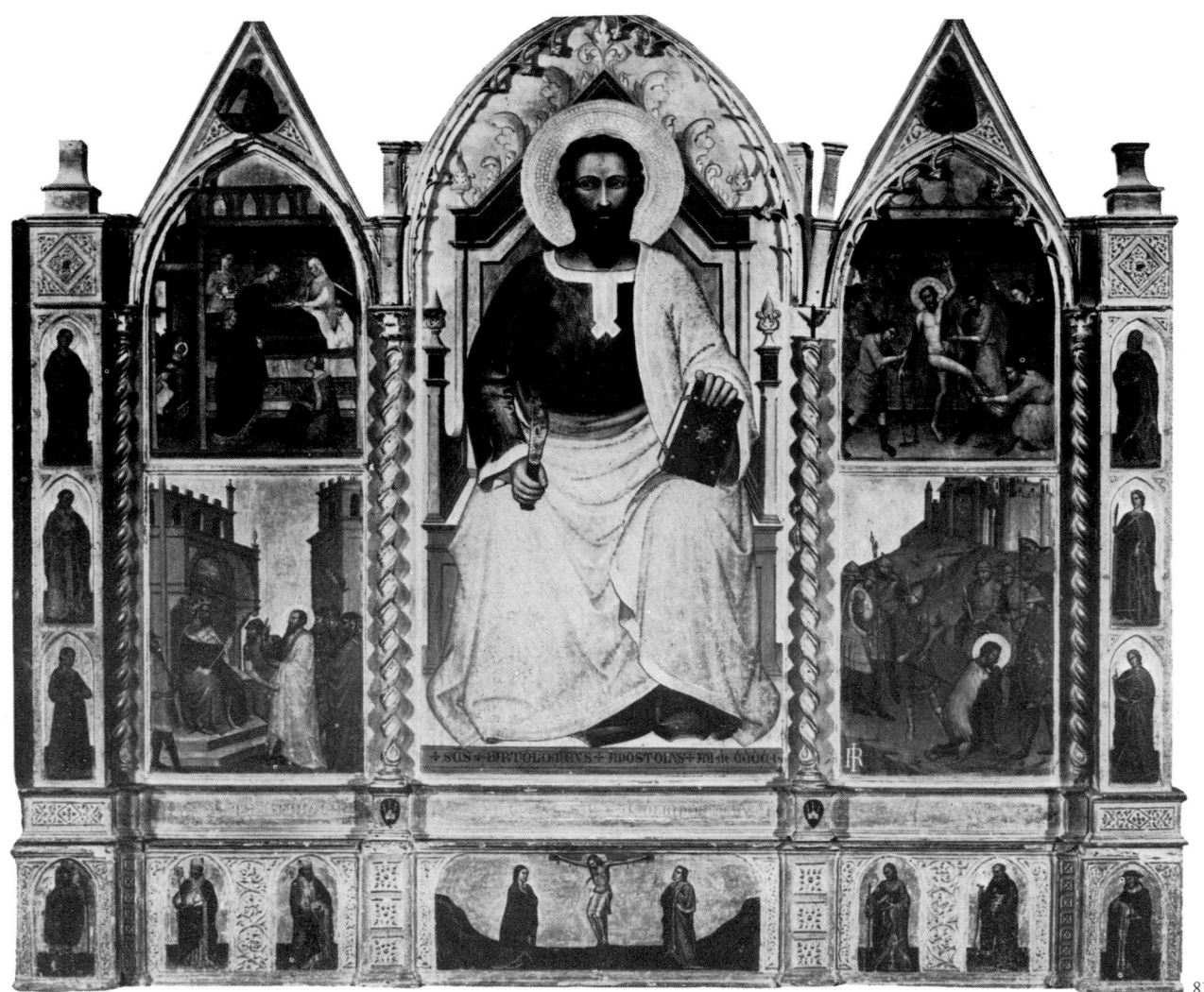

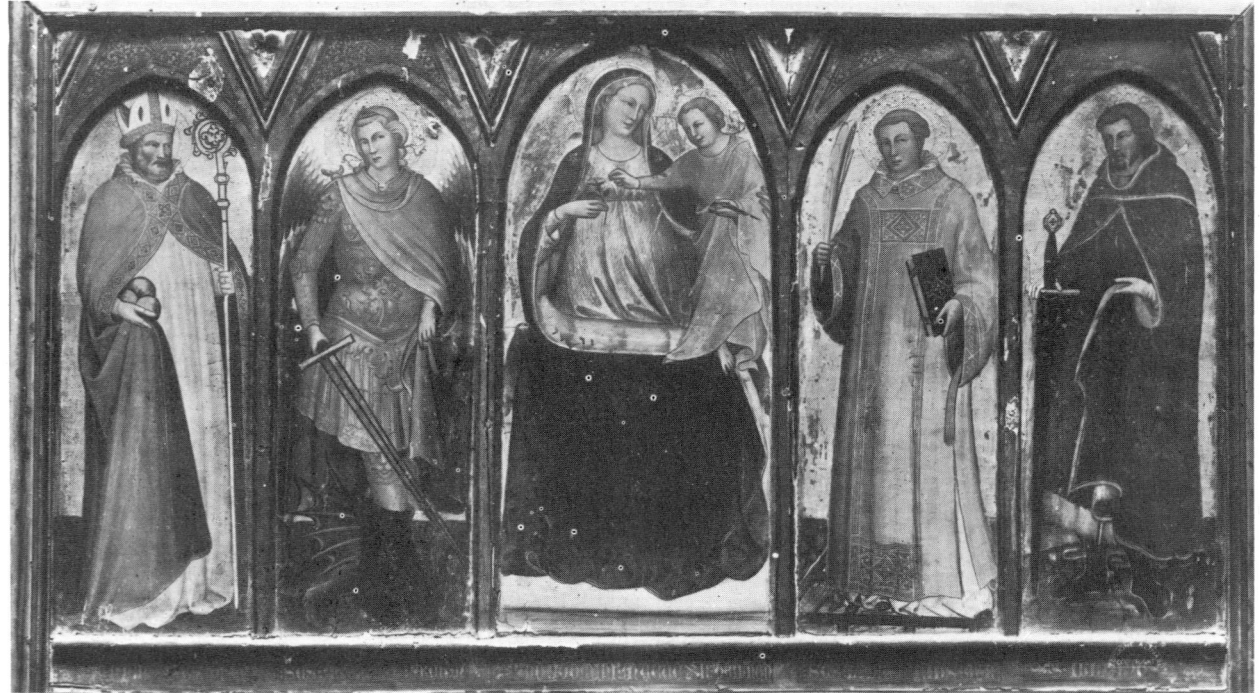

819. *Triptych: St Bartholomew Enthroned and scenes from his Life. Above: Annunciation. Pilaster: six Saints. Predella: Christ on the Cross, six Saints. Panel. San Gimignano, Museo Civico. no. 14. 215 × 190. Brogi 15287. d. 1401.*

820. *Polyptych: Madonna and Child Enthroned with Sts Nicholas, George, Lawrence and Julian. Panel. Mezzomonte (Pozzolatico), S. Lorenzo a Collina. 91 × 152. Alinari 44087. d. 1412.*

PIETRO di MINIATO

The painter is mentioned in documents from Prato, and it would seem that he never left his native land. In 1409 he painted frescoes in San Domenico; in the following year he did work for Francesco di Marco Datini.....
From 1411 to 1420 he lived in via del Ceppo; in 1427 he was living in the country near Prato where he left some of his rather ordinary work, which derives more from Agnolo Gaddi than from Niccolò Gerini.....

from B. Khvoshinsky and M. Salmi, p. 64, *I Pittori Toscani*, Rome, 1912.

Pietro di Miniato is known to us through a large altar-piece which he painted in 1413; he was born in 1366 and is mentioned in documents of 1409, 1411, 1418 and 1427. We find him always active in the vicinity of Prato and as far as we know he never left this town. The tabernacle which he made for the monastery of S. Matteo is now in the Pinacoteca of Prato; it shows in the centre a not ungraceful Coronation of the Virgin with two cherubs above the throne and two angelic musicians kneeling at the foot; on the side panels are represented the somewhat heavy figures of SS. Matthew and Matthias; the two others, SS. Peter and Paul, have disappeared. The twelve handsome little panels of the predella show, still more than the larger figures, the artist's dependence on Agnolo Gaddi especially in their diffuse action and decorative graceful figures. Apart from the Adoration of the Magi all the other panels illustrate incidents from the lives of the saints who figure on the picture above. Pietro di Miniato died between 1430 and 1446.....

from R. van Marle, pp. 559-60, *The Development of the Italian Schools of Painting*, Vol. III, The Hague, 1924.

Piero di Miniato di Piero di Meglio, known as Piero Miniati. Prato, born c. 1366, died June, 1430. Painter. Member of the Physicians and Apothecaries Guild between 1386-1408 (as Piero di Donato [for Miniato?] di Meglio da Prato). Member of the Company of Saint Luke 1392. Pupil of Agnolo Gaddi or of Niccolò di Piero Gerini, who were both working at Prato towards the close of the fourteenth century. It is not known that Piero ever abandoned his native city. Piero worked at Prato for Francesco di Marco Datini, and for the Rectors of the Spedale del Ceppo, which Datini had bequeathed to his native city..... Piero in the same year [1413] also received 34 florins for painting a panel of the Coronation of the Virgin, with two predelle, a curtain and all the ornaments of the same for the monastery of S. Matteo..... He probably died after 1430 and before 1446.....

from D. E. Colnaghi, pp. 183-84, *A Dictionary of Florentine Painters*, London, 1928.

1366-ca 1450. Documented 1409-27, mainly active in Prato. Follower of Agnolo Gaddi.

from B. Berenson, p. 177, *Italian Pictures of the Renaissance, Florentine School*, Vol. I, London, 1963.

We know that the painter Piero di Miniato was commissioned to paint the arms of Louis [of Anjou, King of Sicily]. These were hung over the main entrance to the palace and must have contained the crown and lilies of the house of Anjou.....

from B. Cole, p. 80, *Mitteilungen des Kunsthistorischen Institutes in Florenz*, XIII, 1/2, 1967.

BIBLIOGRAPHY
BOOKS

An asterisk indicates a work listed in the General Bibliography

Khv & Salmi*, Vol. I, 1912, p. 64; *v. Marle ,1924**, pp. 559-60; *Colnaghi**, 1928, pp. 183-4; *Berenson, 1963** Vol. I, p. 177.

JOURNALS

Salvini, R., *RA*, XVI, 1934, pp. 205-28; Cole, B., *MKIF*, XIII, 1/2, 1967, p. 80; Boskovits, M., *AI*, 25/6, 1970, pp. 40-1.

There are no known signed and/or dated works by Pietro di Miniato.

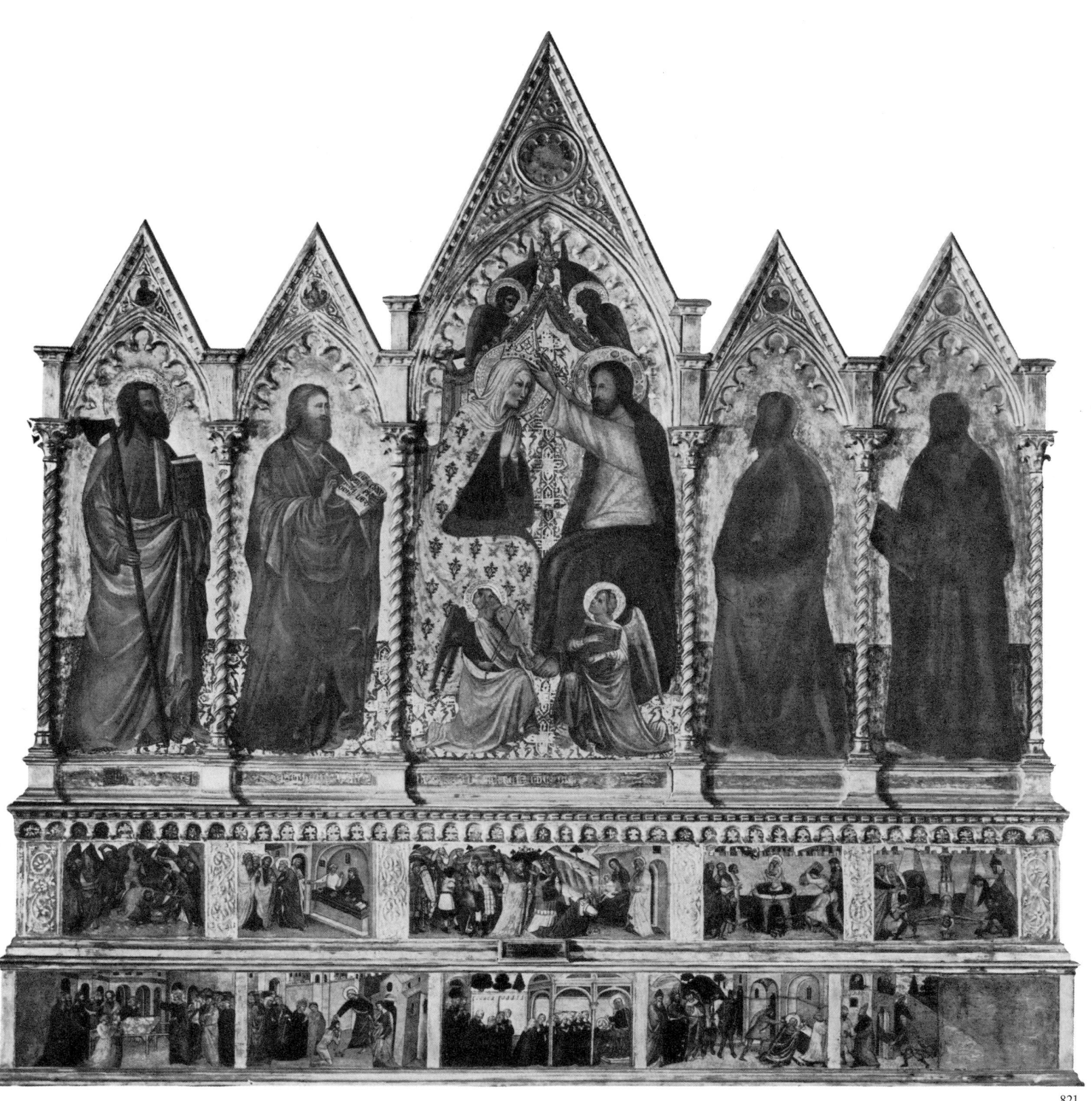

821

821. *Polyptych: Coronation of the Virgin with two Angels and Sts Matthias, Matthew, John the Evangelist and Peter. Below ten predella scenes. Panel. Prato, Galleria Comunale. no. 6. cp. 139 × 66.5; sps: 139 × 75. Alinari 31208. 1412.*

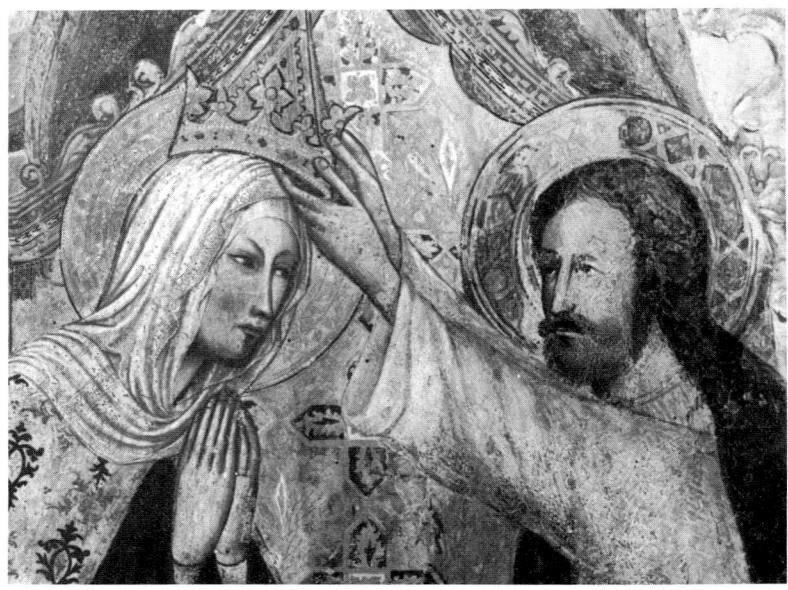

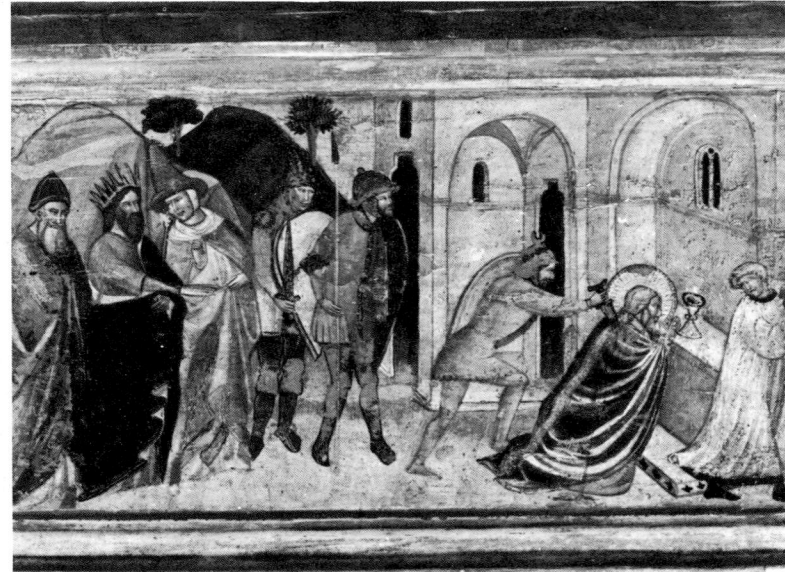

822

823

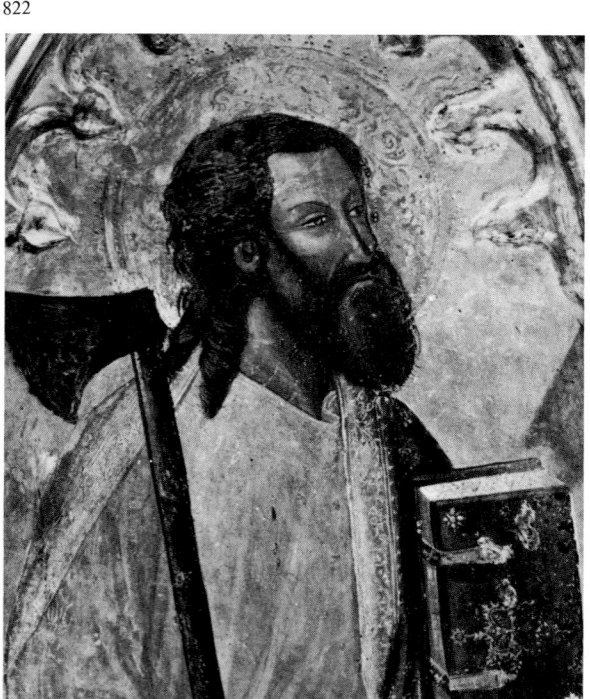

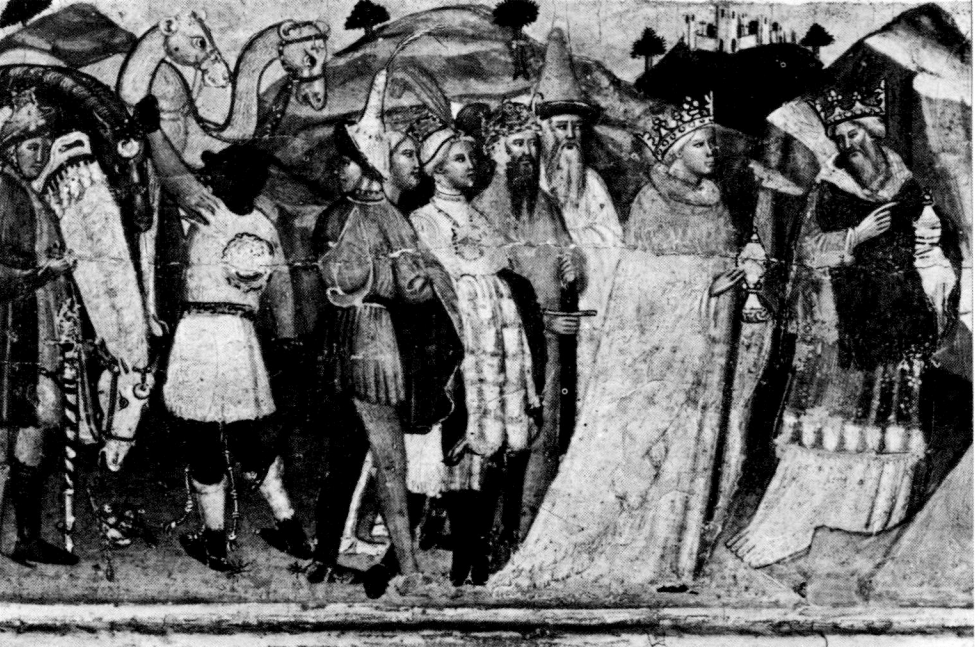

825

824

822. *Coronation of the Virgin, detail of fig. 821. Panel. Prato, Galleria Comunale. no. 6. Bertoni. 1412.*
823. *Predella scene: St Matthew is stabbed by Hirtacus before the Altar, detail of fig. 821. Panel. Prato, Galleria Comunale. no. 6. Bertoni. 1412.*
824. *St Matthias, detail of fig. 821. Panel. Prato, Galleria Comunale. no. 6. Bertoni. 1412.*
825. *Predella scene: Adoration of the Magi, detail of fig. 821. Panel. Prato, Galleria Comunale. no. 6. Bertoni. 1412.*

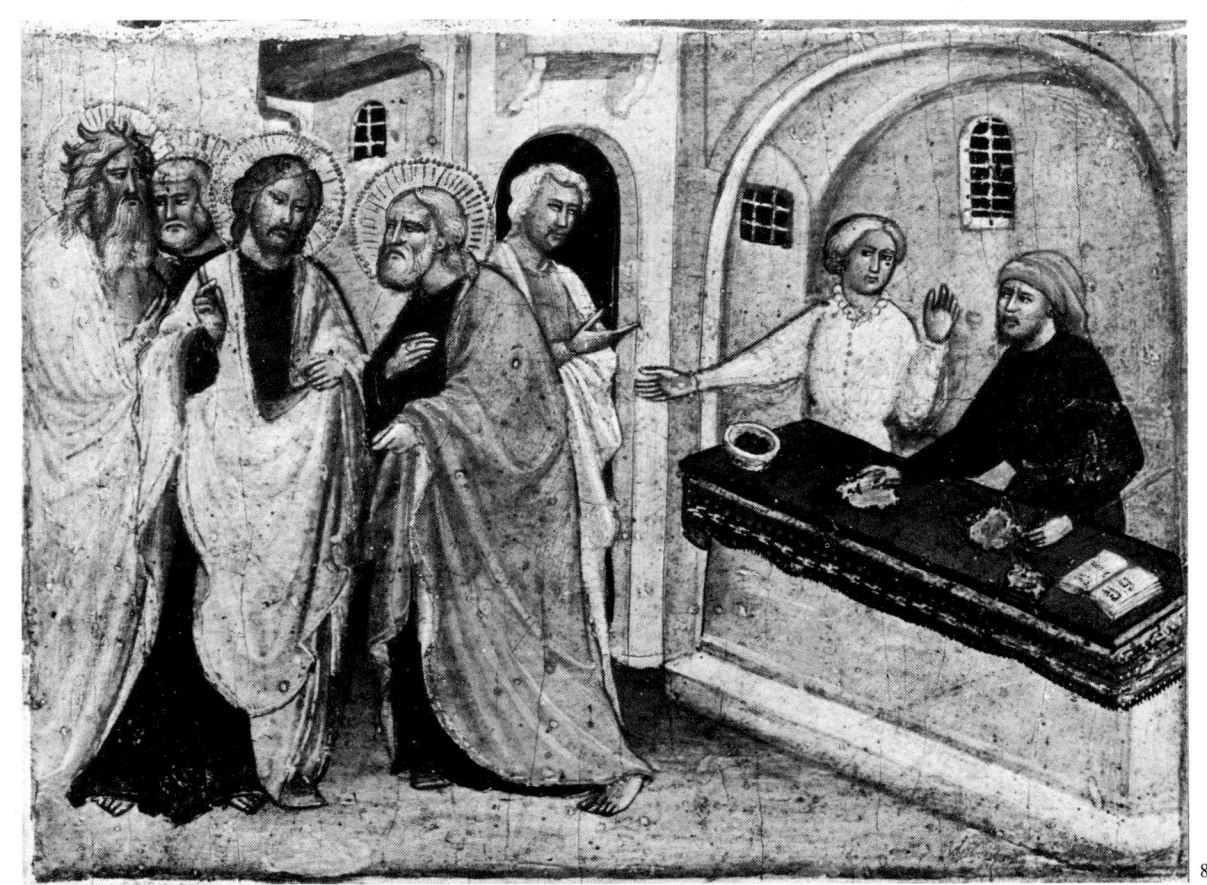

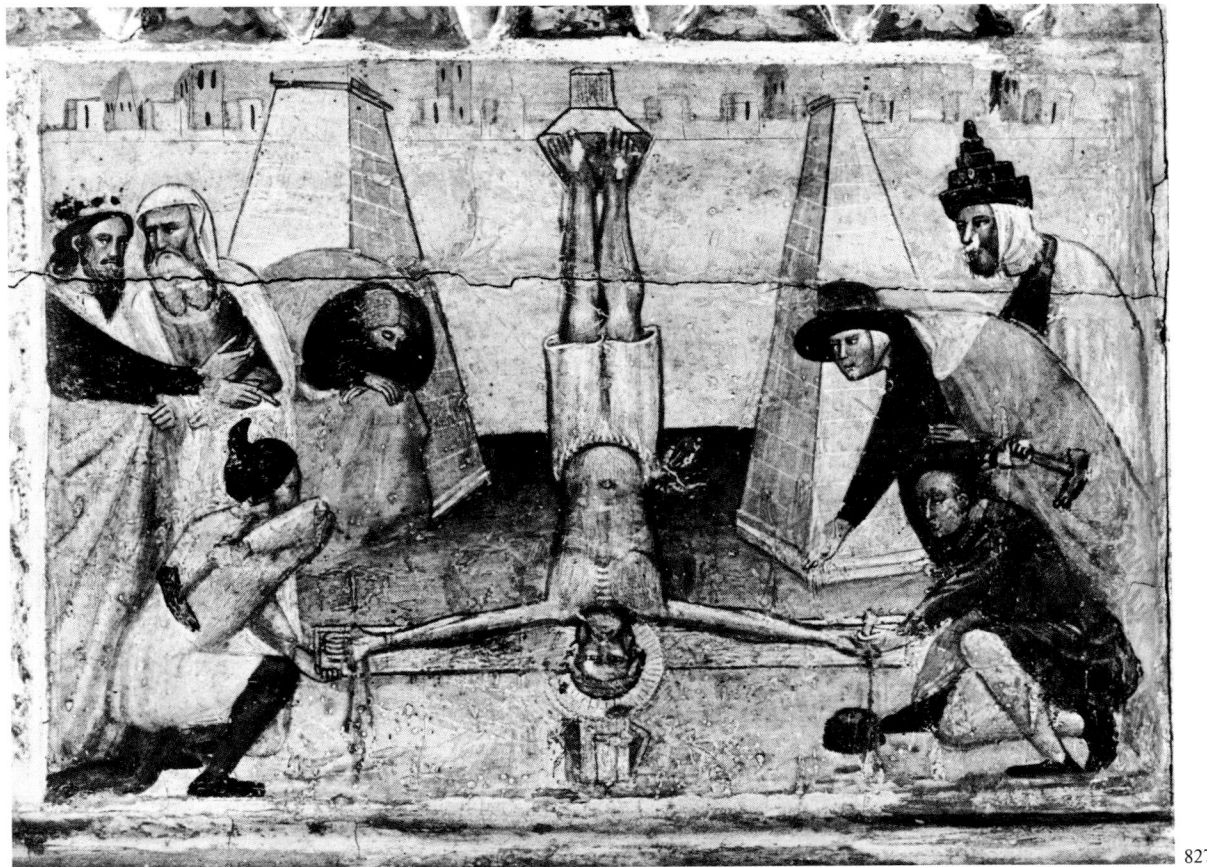

826. Predella scene: *Calling of St Matthew, detail of fig. 821. Panel. Prato, Galleria. Comunale. no. 6. Bertoni. 1412.*
827. Predella scene: *Martyrdom of St Peter, detail of fig. 821. Panel. Prato, Galleria Comunale. no. 6. Bertoni. 1412.*

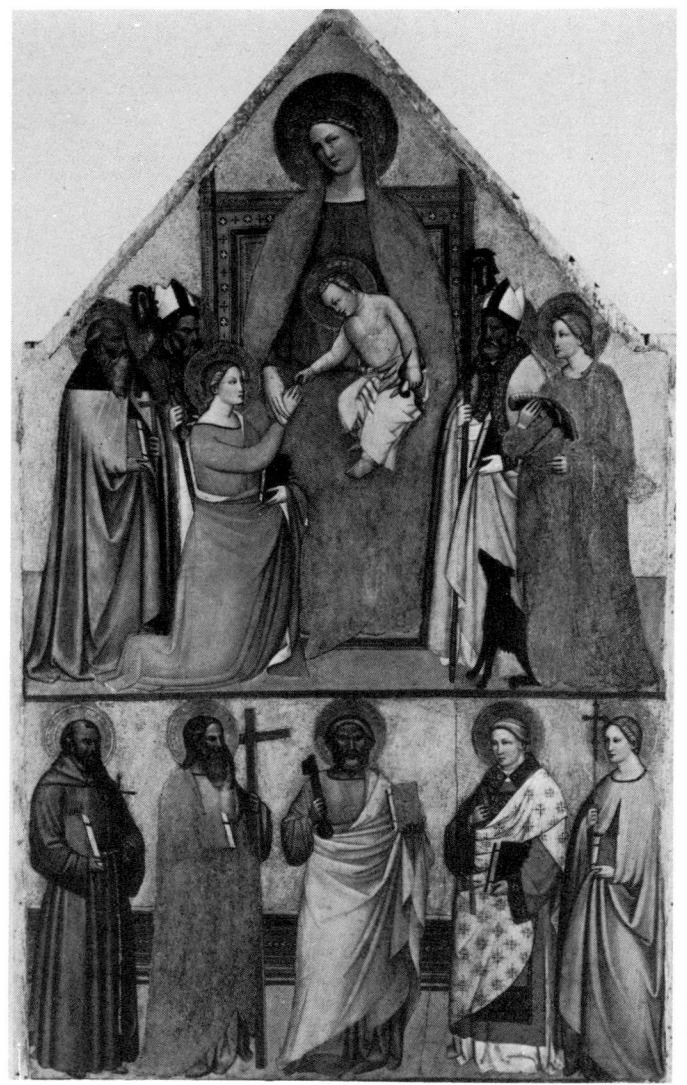

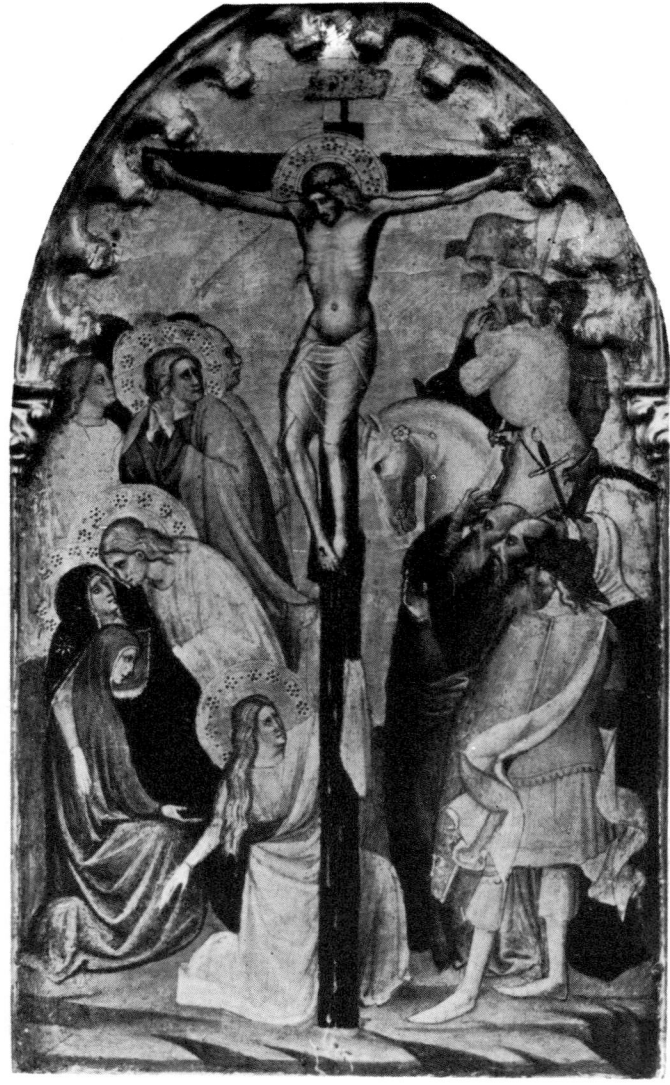

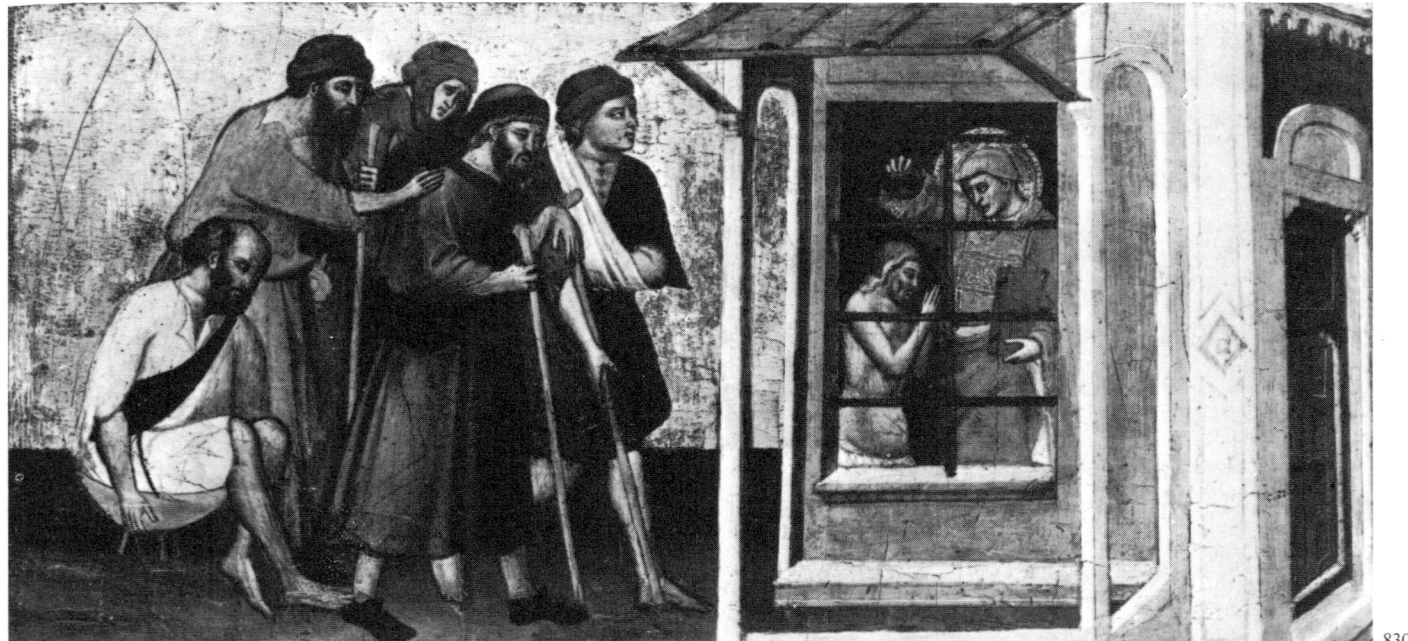

828. *Mystical Marriage of St Catherine with Sts Anthony Abbot, Nicholas, Donatus of Fiesole, Margaret. Below: Sts Francis, Andrew, Peter, Lawrence and Margaret. Panel. Vicchio di Rimaggio (near Greve), S. Lorenzo. 225 × 159. SGF 131623.*
829. *Crucifixion. Panel. Whereabouts unknown. Reali.*
830. *Cassone scene: St Lawrence in Prison, baptises his Jailer Hippolytus, Lucillus and others. Panel. Paris, Musée du Louvre. no. MI 389. Réunion des Musées Nationaux 70 EN 1634.*

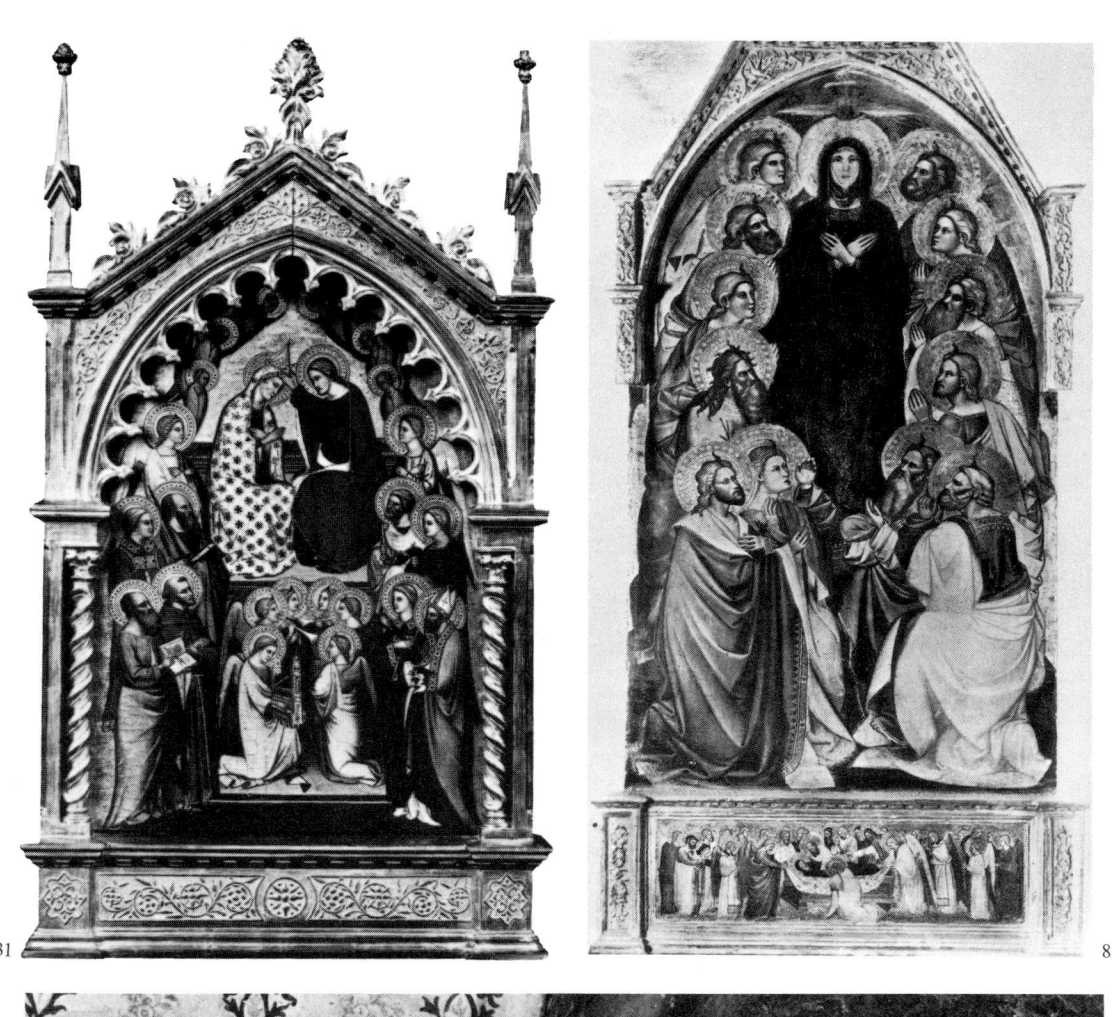

831

832

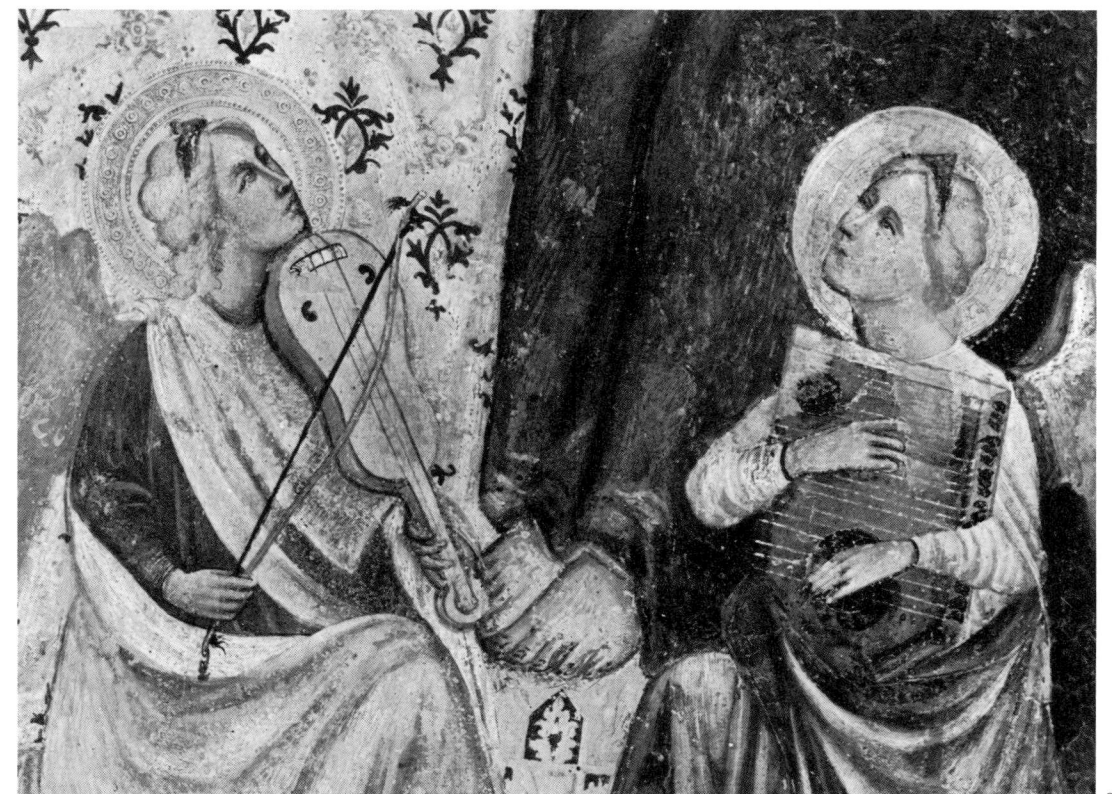

833

831.   Coronation of the Virgin with Angels and Saints. Panel. Florence, Uffizi, Depositi SGF 08178.
832.   Assumption. Below: Dormition of the Virgin. Panel. Sesto Fiorentino, S. Martino. Alinari 45949. SGF 1934.
833.   Predella scene: Two Angels playing musical instruments, detail of fig. 821. Panel. Prato, Galleria Comunale. no. 6. Bertoni. 1412.

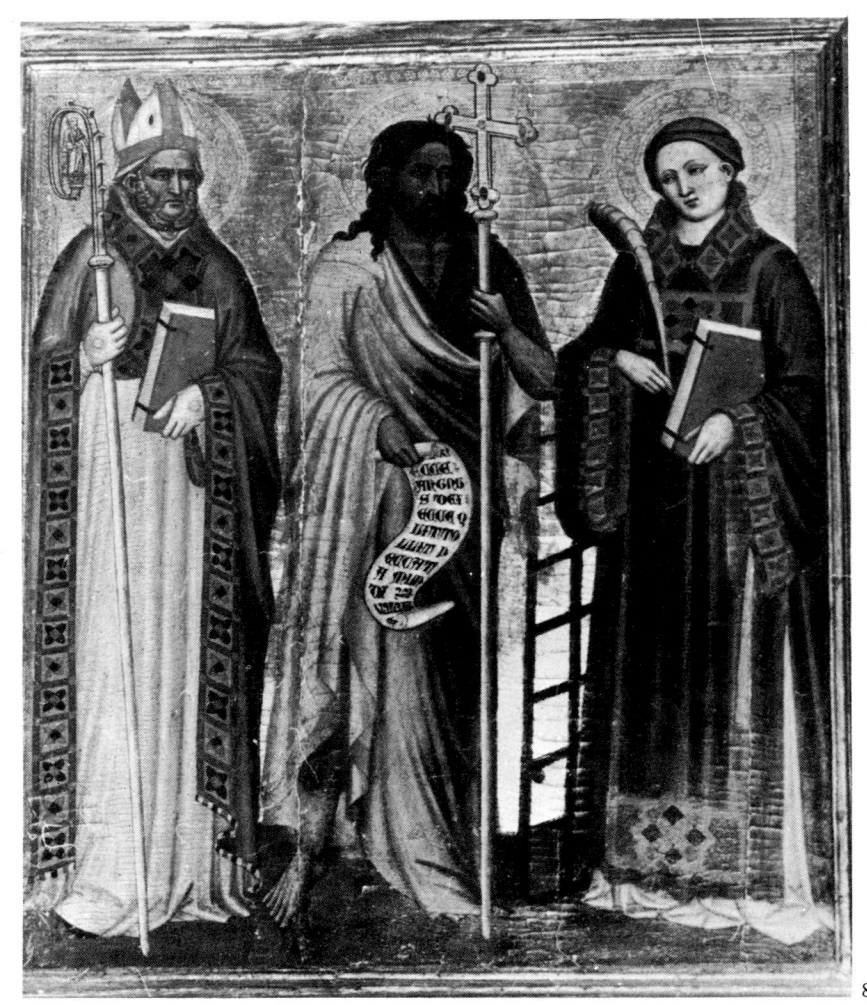

834

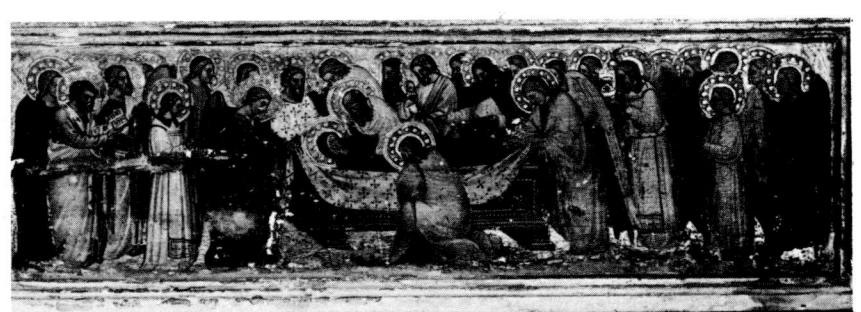

835

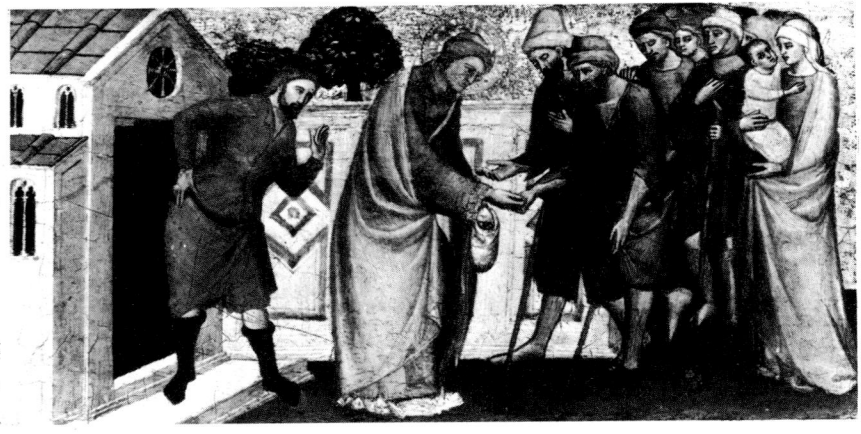

836

834. *Sts Martin, John the Baptist and Lawrence. Panel. Terenzano (1.5 km from Settignano, near Florence), S. Martino. 109 × 90. Author's photo.*
835. *Predella scene : Dormition of the Virgin, detail of fig. 832. Panel. Sesto Fiorentino, S. Martino. 160 × 81. SGF 1935.*
836. *Cassone scene : St Lawrence distributes the Treasure of the Church to the Poor. Panel. Paris, Musée du Louvre. no. MI 388. Réunion des Musées Nationaux 70 EN 1633.*

LORENZO di BICCI

So little has come down to us of the artistic activity of Lorenzo di Bicci that we need not dwell at length on this painter whom Vasari had confused with his son Bicci di Lorenzo. Lorenzo di Bicci is mentioned in documents of 1370, 1375, 1386, 1409, when he was inscribed in the corporation of S. Lucca, and again in 1427, the year of his death. He is also found in 1387, together with Agnolo Gaddi and Spinello, making designs of statues for the Cathedral, while between 1388 and 1391 he painted statues for the Loggia dei Lanzi, designed by Agnolo and executed by Piero di Giovanni. In 1399 he executed a Crucifixion for the Compagnia della Croce at Empoli.

In 1398 we find him receiving ninety golden guilders in payment of works executed for the Cathedral of Florence, parts of which are the only authentic productions we now possess by Lorenzo di Bicci. These are three half-length figures of Evangelists in medallions, and are rather commonplace, although they show some effort to express dignity which does not altogether fail. Crowe and Cavalcaselle believed that Lorenzo began the paintings in the vault and entrance arch of the choir of S. Francesco at Arezzo, and that his son Bicci di Lorenzo only continued and finished them.....

from R. van Marle, pp. 573-74, *The Development of the Italian Schools of Painting*, Vol. III, The Hague, 1924.

The figure of Lorenzo di Bicci, a Florentine painter who belongs to the generation of Lorenzo di Niccolò Gerini, and of Mariotto di Nardo, has long been confused, because of Vasari's error, with that of his son Bicci di Lorenzo; today we recognize him, by merit of Poggi, who in 1905 and in 1909, discovered the documents for two paintings and identified them (Crucifixion, St. Stefano at Empoli; and the half-figures of the Evangelists in medallions, in the Duomo of Florence). This permitted the attribution of numerous other works by Salmi, Salvini (1932) and Gronau (1933). The art of Lorenzo di Bicci appears to be linked with that group of artists who, like Niccolò di Pietro Gerini, his son Lorenzo, and Mariotto di Nardo, had all studied under Nardo but refused to follow the extreme spatial and linear abstraction which Agnolo Gaddi had, coming from the same sources, employed. They preferred rather to return to the great Florentine tradition of strict observation, personified by Giottesques like Taddeo Gaddi and Bernardo Daddi. Still, Lorenzo's frequent contact with Agnolo Gaddi brought about his acceptance from this artist of a certain fluid rhythm and a slightly dismal rosy tonality.....

from P. Dal Poggetto, p. 35, *Arte in Valdelsa*, Certaldo, 1963.

Vasari says that Lorenzo was a pupil of Spinello Aretino: but it is much more likely that his early training was in the shop of Andrea Orcagna.....

Although limited as a painter, Lorenzo is nonetheless of very serious professionalism, who knows the techniques of his art to perfection and who works in a genuine orcagnesque tradition; he uses this knowledge to give to all his forms effects of weight and volume — from cloth to metals, even to beards and hair, building up or limiting the colour, obtaining an attractive result of good artisanship. This is particularly notable in works from his best period which would run from about 1380 to 1400.

from L. Marcucci, p. 127, *I Dipinti Toscani del Secolo XIV*, Rome, 1965.

Florentine School, mentioned from 1370; died 1427. He collaborated with Agnolo Gaddi and Spinello Aretino and was strongly influenced by Niccolò di Pietro Gerini.

from F. R. Shapley, p. 46, *Paintings from the Samuel H. Kress Collection*, London, 1966.

Documents show that Lorenzo di Bicci was active as a painter in Florence by 1370, and references to him continue into the fifteenth century. In 1385 he was working with other artists on the Loggia dei Lanzi in Florence, and was paid 90 gold florins in 1386 for paintings in S. Maria del Fiore. In 1389 he appears to have painted a Crucifixion for the Compagnia della Croce, in the church of S. Stefano at Empoli, and in 1412 a S. Nicholas for the hospital of S. Matteo in Florence. Between 1386 and 1408 Lorenzo di Bicci joined the guild of Medici e Speziali and in 1409 his name appears on the register of the guild of S. Luke. Not many of his works can now be identified, and it is generally accepted that the frescoes in S. Maria del Carmine in Florence and S. Francesco in Arezzo which Vasari attributed to him were in fact the work of his son Bicci di Lorenzo (1373-1452).....

from U. Procacci, p. 98, *Frescoes from Florence*, London, 1969.

BIBLIOGRAPHY
BOOKS
An asterisk indicates a work listed in the General Bibliography

v. Marle 1924*, pp. 573-74; *Berenson, 1932**, p. 82; *Antal**, 1948, pp. 152, 217, 229; *Vavalà, 1948**, p. 78; *Galetti**, " F-O ", 1950, pp. 1403-4; *Meiss, 1951**, p. 138; *Toesca, 1951**, p. 646; *Paatz**, 1952, Vol. IV, p. 126; Procacci, U., *Sinopie e Affreschi*, Florence, 1960, pp. 65, 235; Dal Poggetto, P., *AIV**, 1963, p. 35; *Marcucci**, 1965, pp. 126-30; *Shapley**, 1966, pp. 46-7; *Klesse**, 1967, p. 363; Borsook, E., p. 61, in Kosegarten, R., *Festschrift Ulrich Middeldorf*, Berlin, 1968; Procacci, U., *Fresco Show**, 1968, pp. 106-11, (98-101).

JOURNALS
Perkins, F. M., *RA*, VI, 1910, p. 40; Berenson, B., *RA*, V, 1917, p. 97; Berenson, B., *AA*, VI, 1918, p. 52; de Nicola, G., *RA*, VI, 1919, p. 99; Berenson, B., *GBA*, I, 1924, p. 257; Heil, W., *BDIA*, XI, 1929, p. xxv-xxviii; Salmi, M., *RA*, XII, 1930, pp. 81-6; Salvini, R., *RA*, XIV, 1932, pp. 475-83; Deusch, W. R., *RA*, XIV, 1932, pp. 111-13; Gronau, H. D., *MKIF*, IV, 2/3, 1932, pp. 103-18; Salmi, M., *RA*, XVI, 1934, pp. 65-76; Meiss, M., *AB*, VIII, 1936, p. 447; Sinibaldi, G., *RA*, XXVI, 1950, pp. 199-205; Sinibaldi, G., *BA*, XXXVII, 4, 1952, pp. 57-59; Baldini, U., *BA*, XXXVIII, 4, 1953, p. 278; Cohn, W., *BA*, XLI, 4, 1956, pp. 171-7; Zeri, F., *PA*, IX, 105, 1958, pp. 67-71; Cohn, W., *K*, 1959, pp. 272-3; Zeri, F., *BA*, XLVIII, 4, 1963, p. 247; Zeri, F., *GBA*, LXXI, 110, 1968, p. 73.

There are no signed and/or dated works by Lorenzo di Bicci.

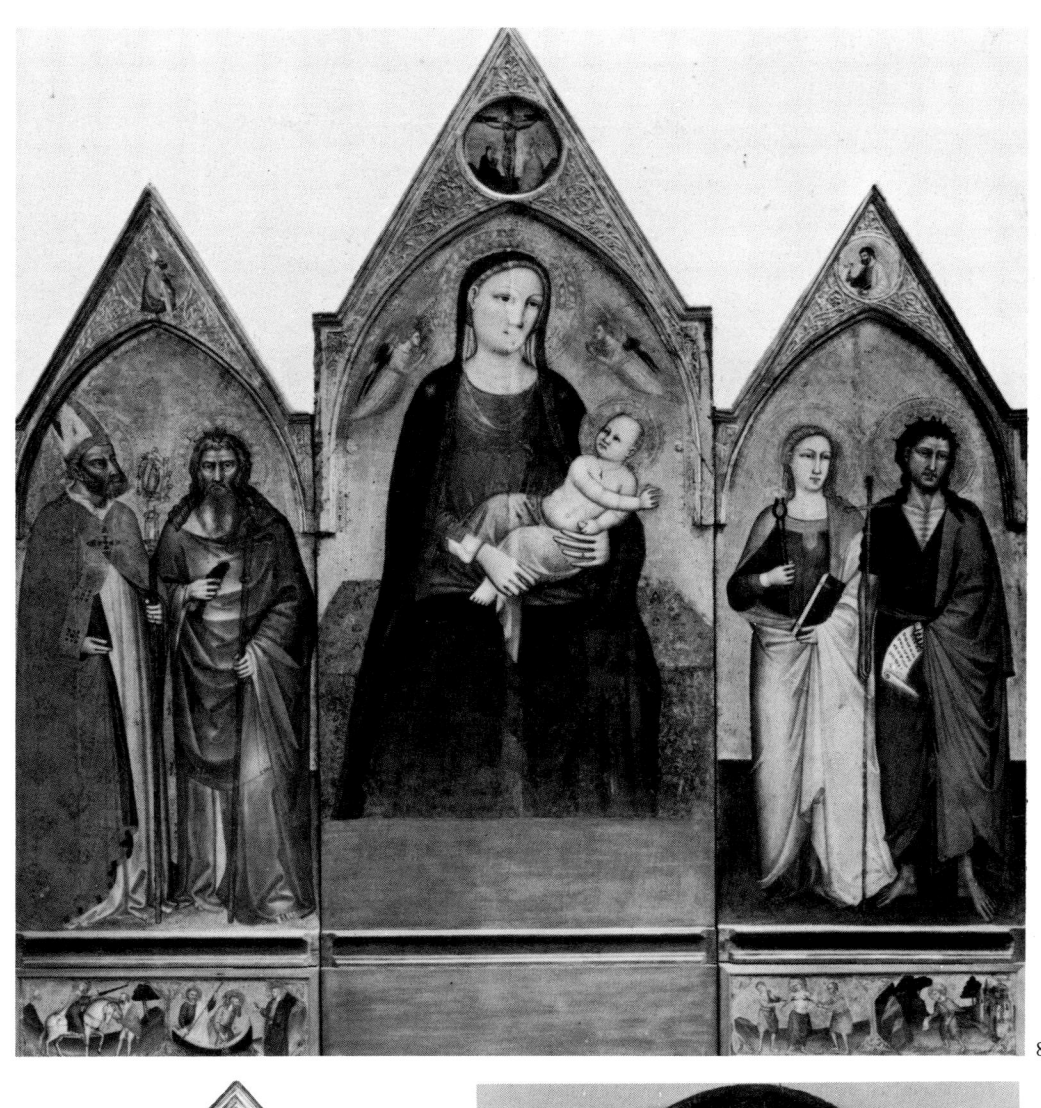

837

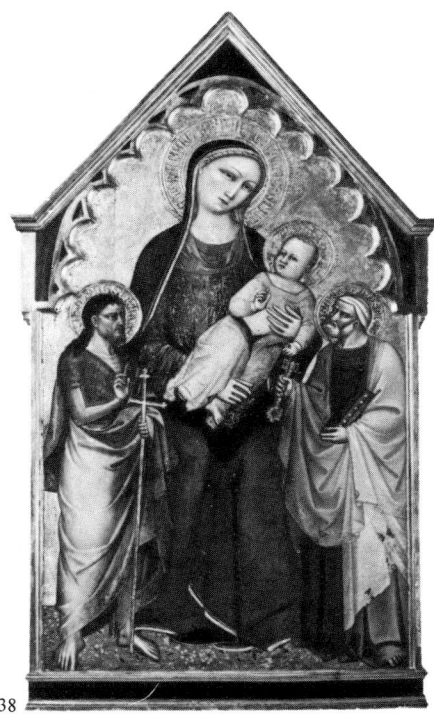

838

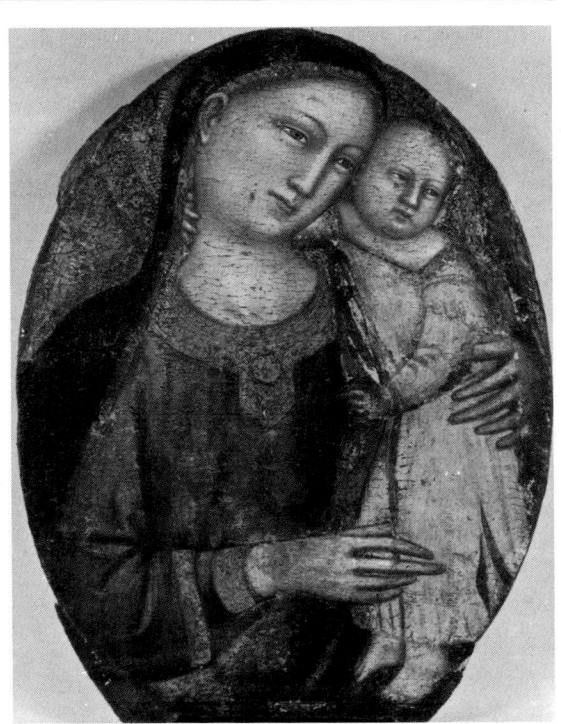

839

837. *Triptych: Madonna and Child with Sts Martin, Andrew, Agatha and John the Baptist. Panel. Empoli, Museo della Collegiata. no. 10,12. 200 × 205. SGF 29937.*

838. *Madonna and Child with Sts John the Evangelist and Peter. Panel. Whereabouts unknown (formerly, Hereford, Eastnor Castle, Lord Somers Collection). 57.1 × 35.5. Foteteca Berenson.*

839. *Madonna and Child. Panel. Baltimore (Md.), Walters Art Gallery. no. 37.478. 56.8 × 41.9. Museum photo.*

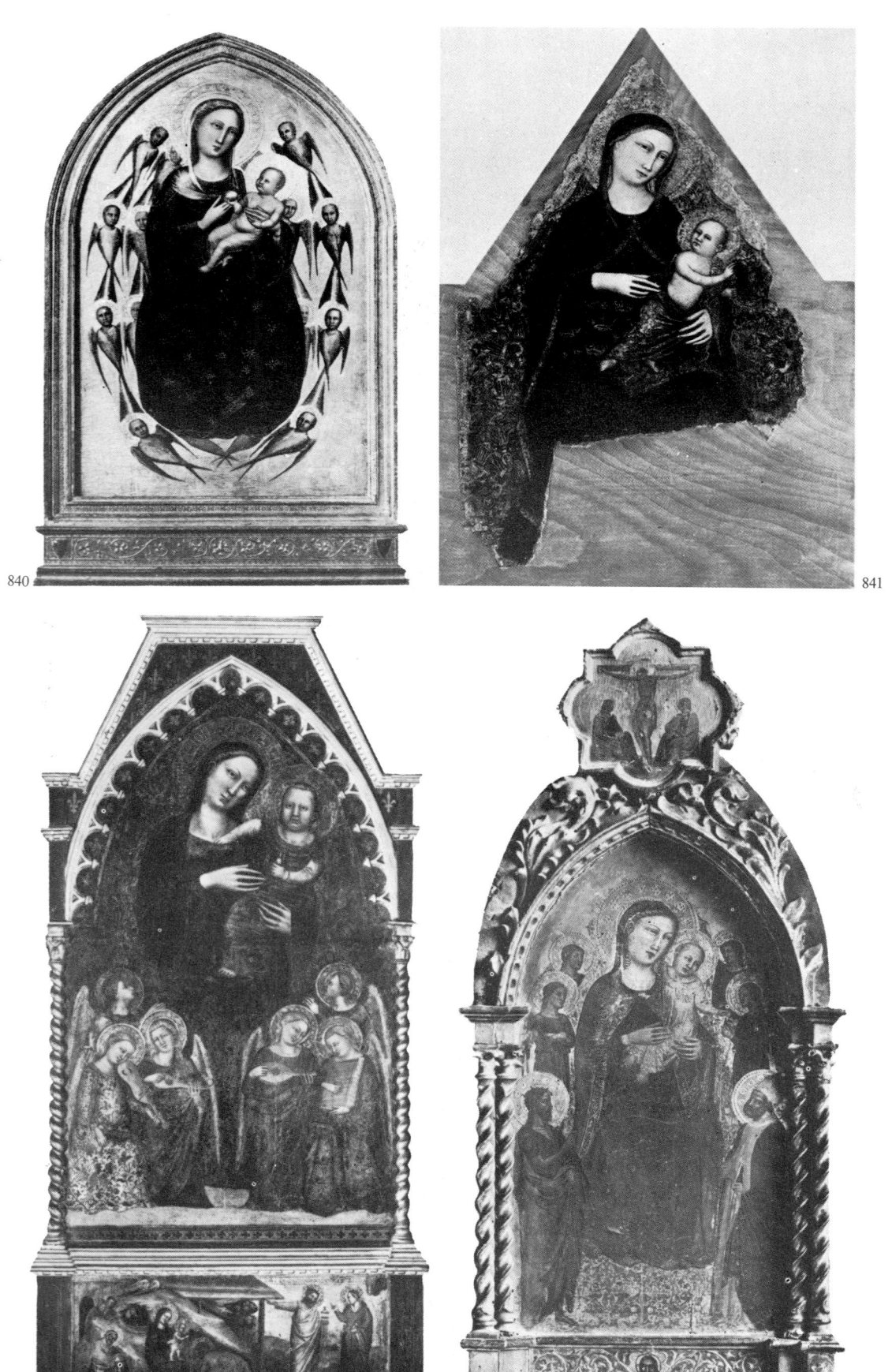

840. *Madonna in Glory, nursing the Child. Panel. Whereabouts unknown (formerly, Rome, Conte Giuseppe Primoli Collection). 57.1 × 35.5. Fototeca Berenson.*
841. *Madonna and Child. Panel. Volognano, S. Michele. 88.8 × 58.4. SGF 169784.*
842. *Madonna and Child with six music-making Angels. Predella: Adoration of the Magi. Panel. Pescia, S. Stefano. 200 × 90. SGF 19763.*
843. *Madonna and Child with two Saints and four Angels. Above: Christ on the Cross. Below: Head of Christ. Panel. Whereabouts unknown. Brogi 35/40.*

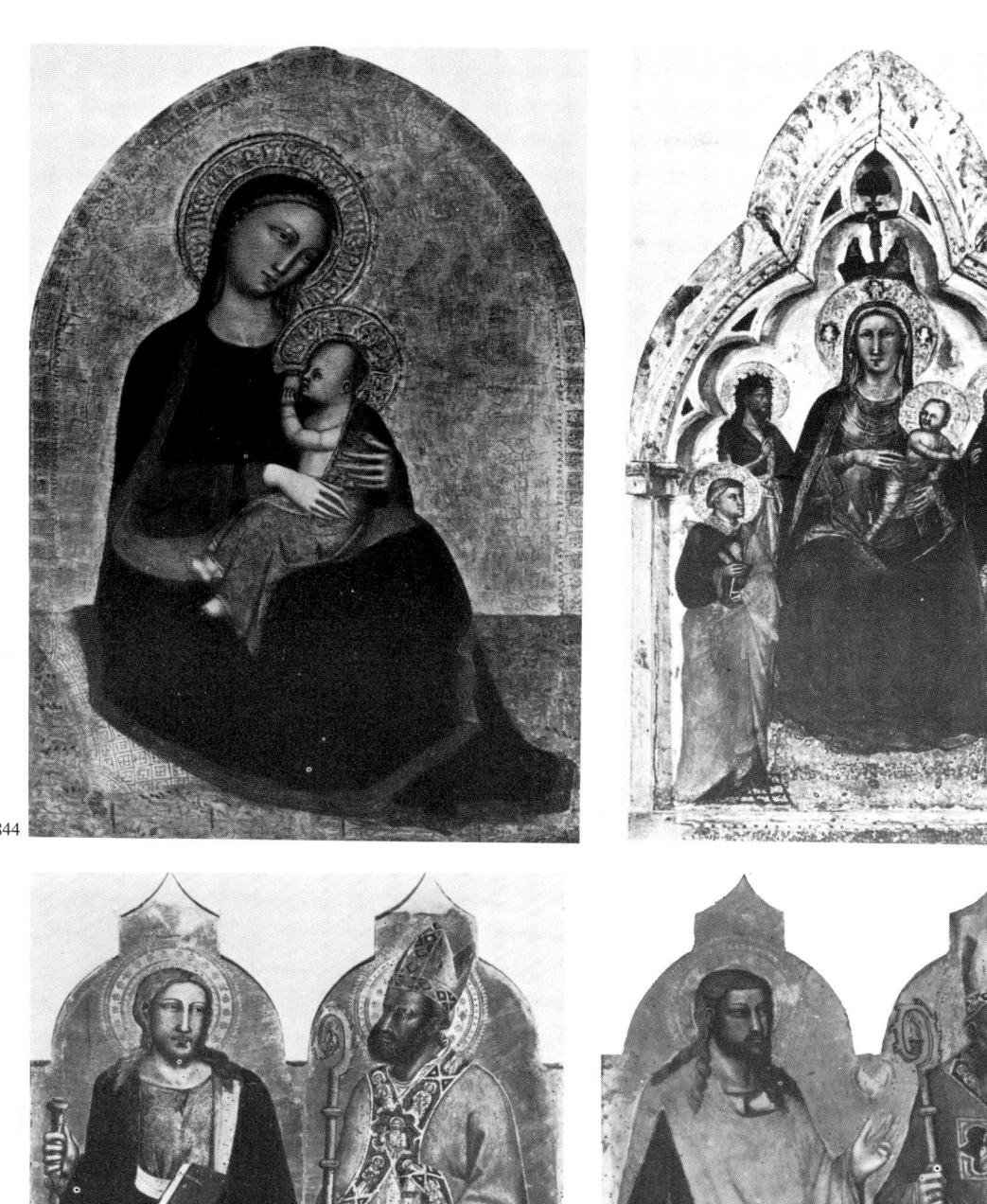

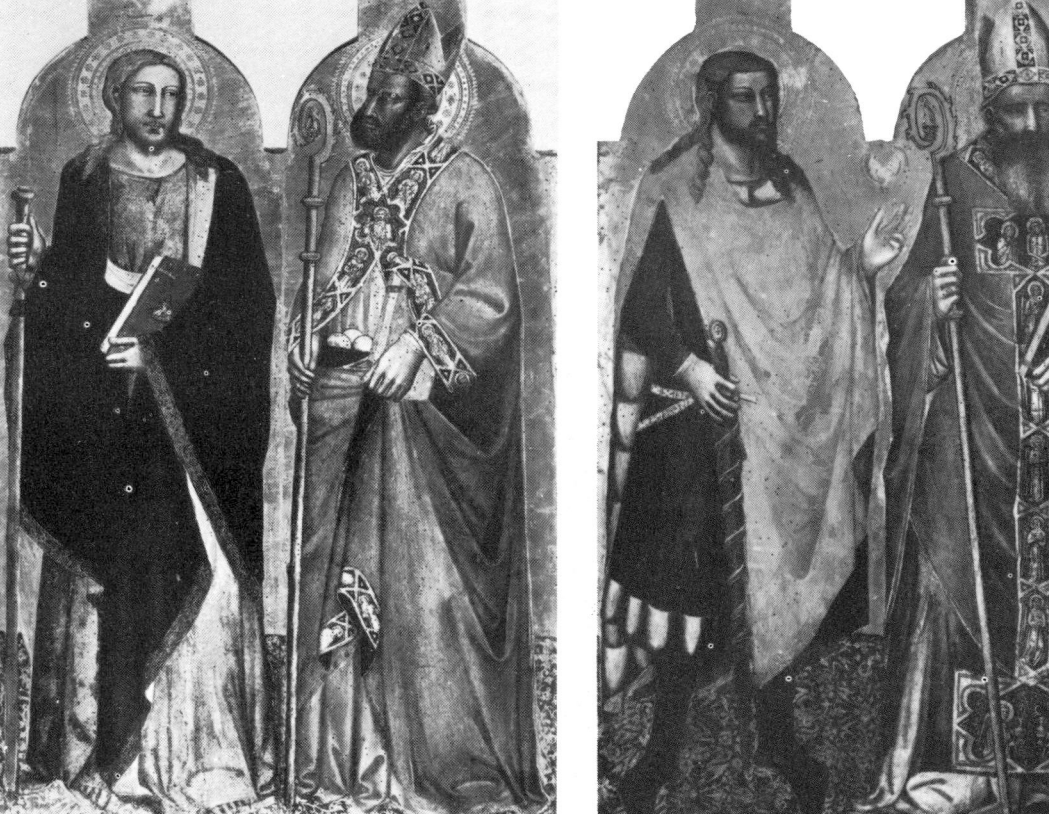

844. *Madonna of Humility. Panel. Private Collection. Perotti 20132.*
845. *Madonna and Child Enthroned, with Sts Lawrence, John the Baptist, Anthony Abbot and Nicholas. Panel. Villore, near Poggibonsi, Cappella di S. Giusto. 115 × 65. Fototeca Berenson.*
846. *St James and St Nicholas. Panel. Fiesole, Museo Bandini. Uffizi no. 5410. 114.7 × 40.2. SGF 69738.*
847. *Two male Saints. Panel. Fiesole, Museo Bandini. Uffizi no. 5410. 114.7 × 40.2. SGF 98570.*

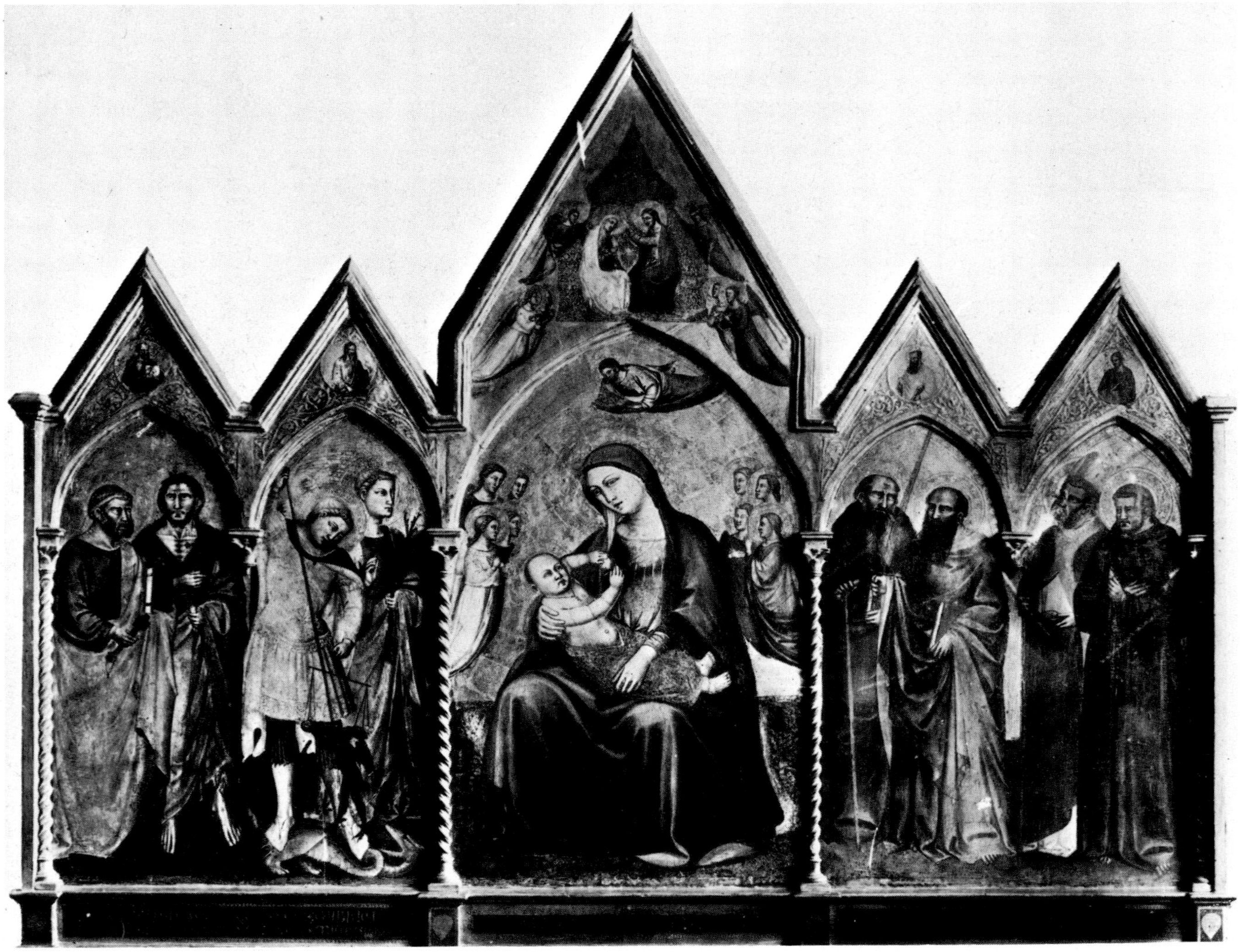

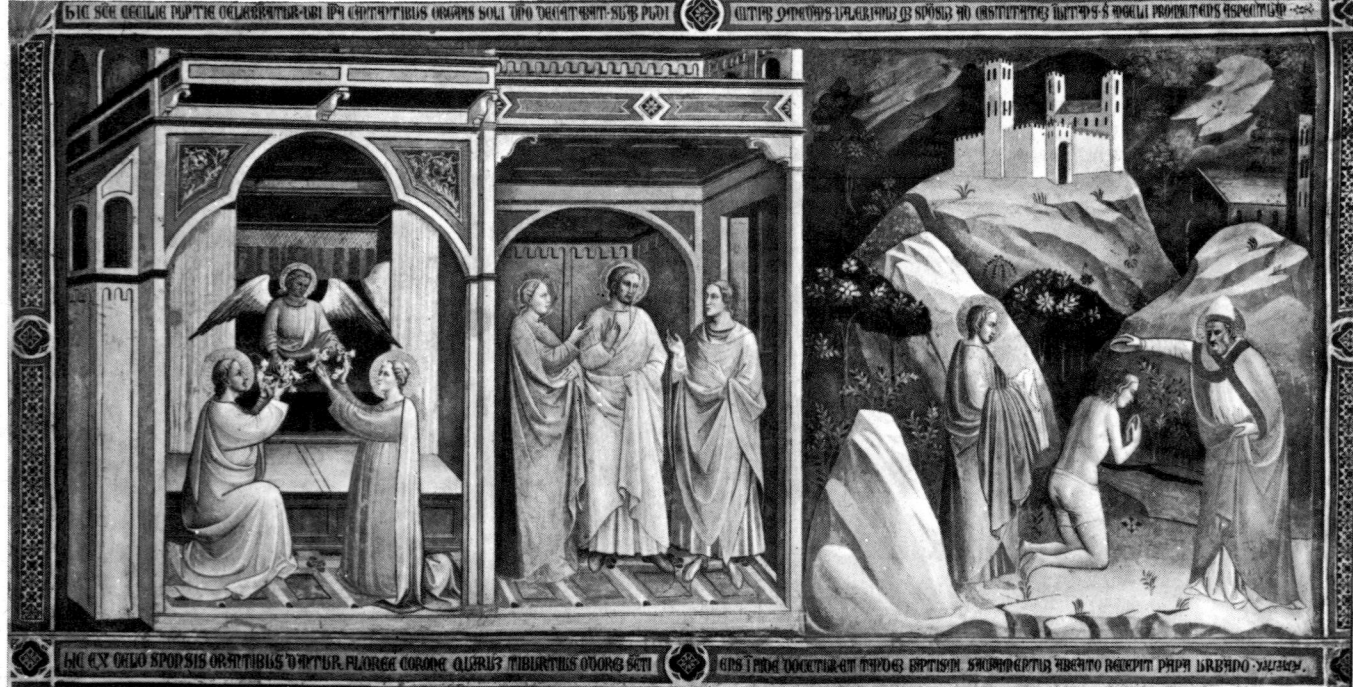

848. *Polyptych: Madonna of Humility and Child, with eight Angels, and Sts John the Baptist, Peter, Gabriel, Michael, Anthony, Paul, Nicholas and Francis. Pinnacles: the Four Evangelists and the Coronation of the Virgin with six Angels. Panel. Loro Ciuffenna (Pratomagno, north of Montevarchi), S. Maria Assunta. 180 × 210. SGF 18764.*

849. *Marriage of St Cecilia and Valerian; Baptism of Tiburtius. Fresco. Florence, S. Maria del Carmine, Sacristy. Brogi 19806.*

414

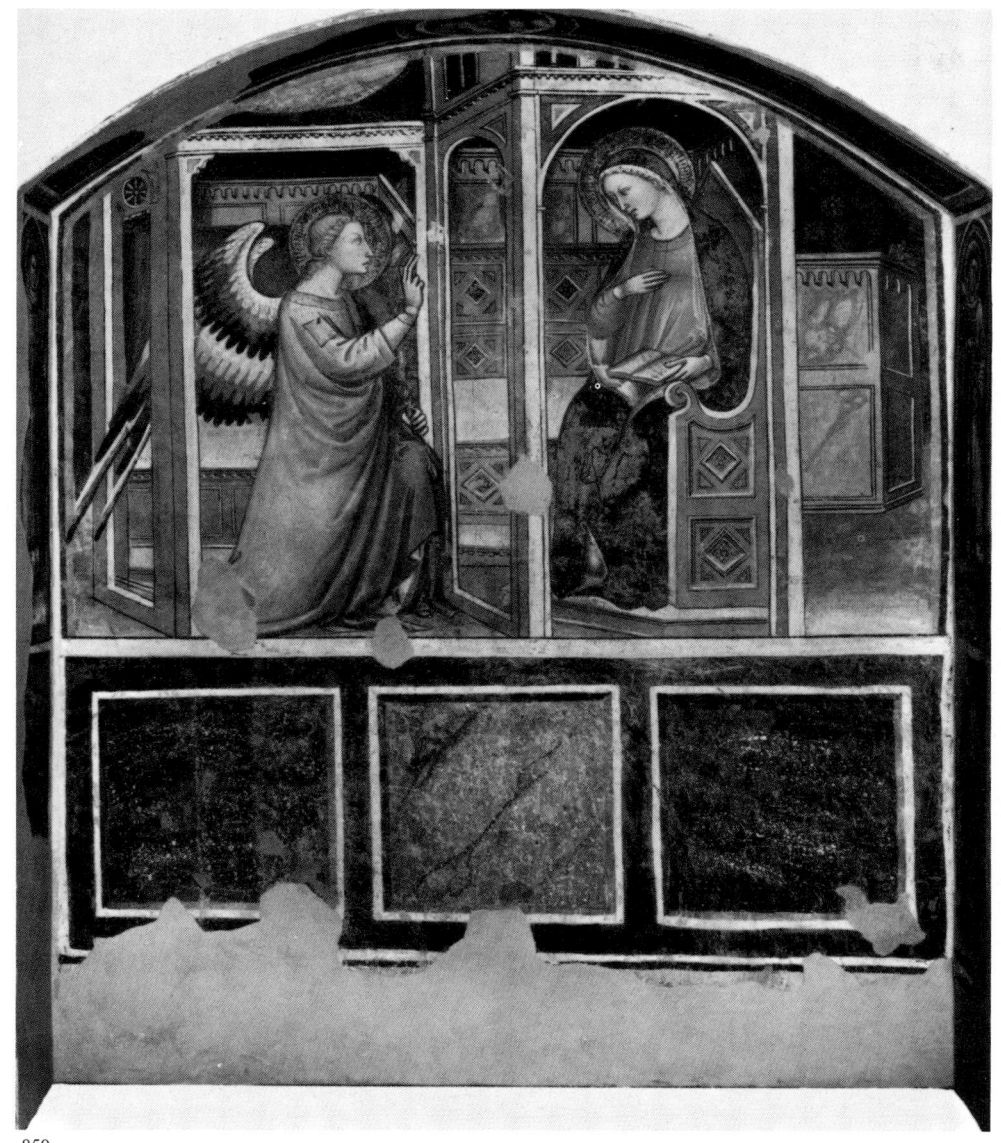

850

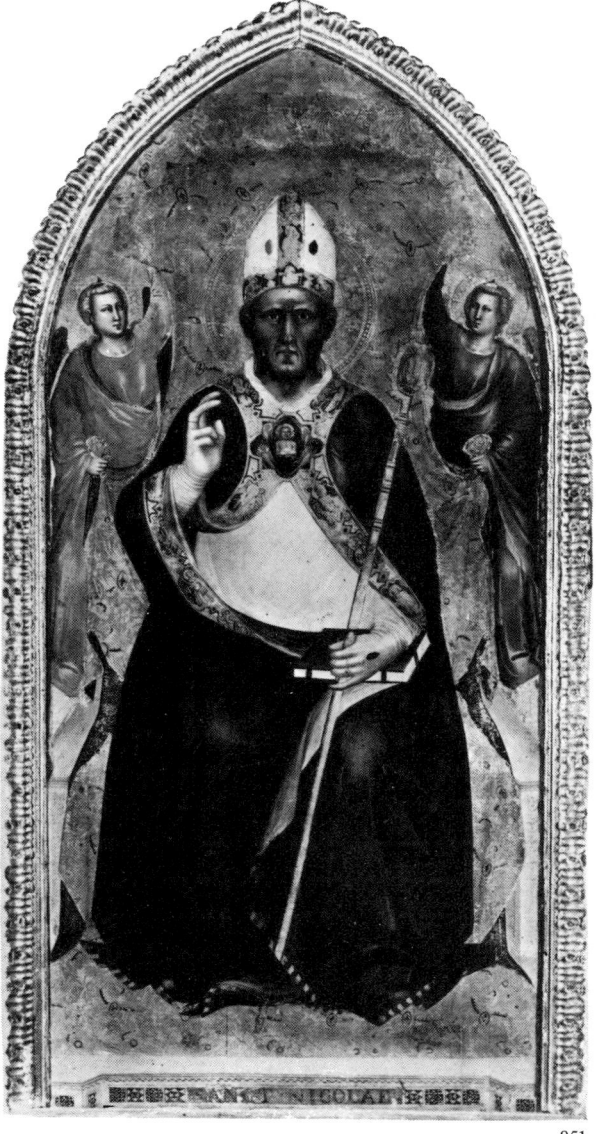

851

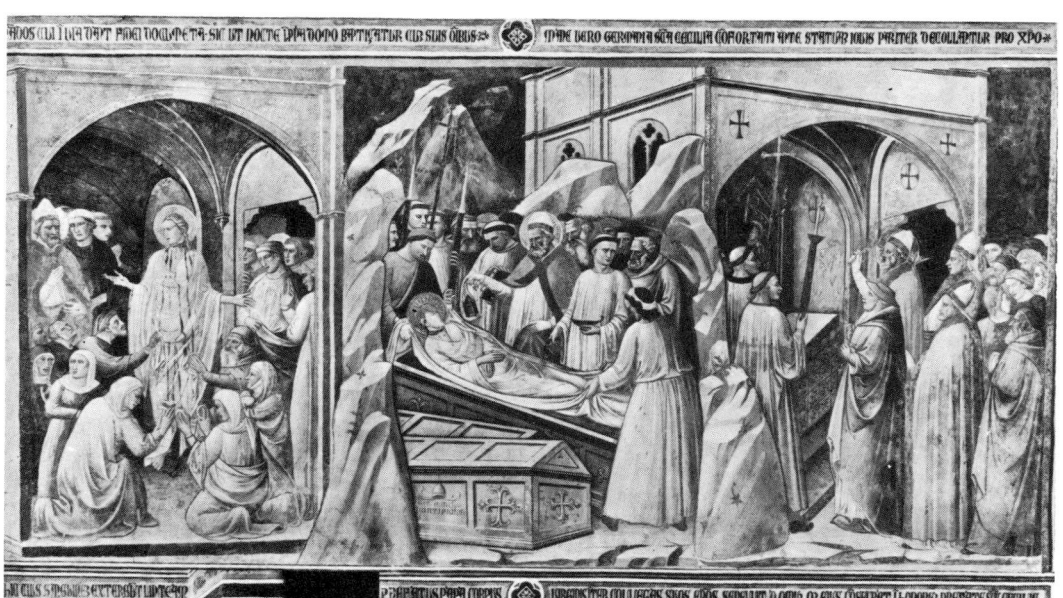

852

850. *Annunciation. Fresco. Florence, S. Simone. SGF 174059.*
851. *St Nicholas, with two Angels. Panel. Ferraglia (Vaglia), Parrocchiale. SGF 99375.*
852. *Death and Apotheosis of St Cecilia. Fresco. Florence, S. Maria del Carmine, Sacristy. Brogi 19805.*

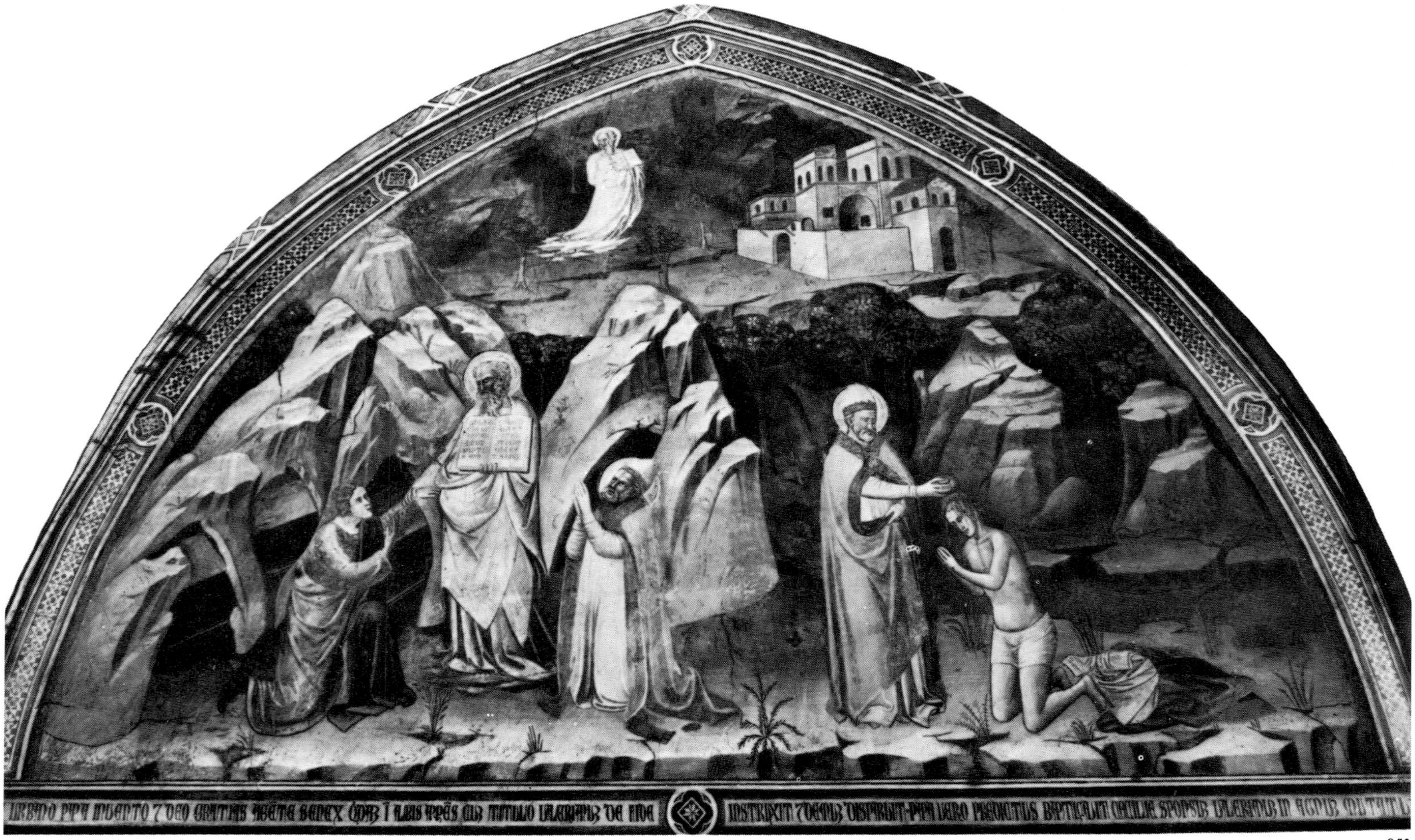

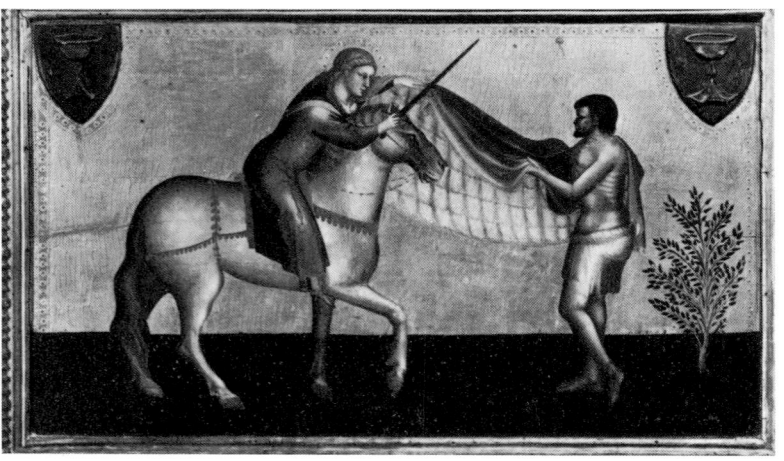

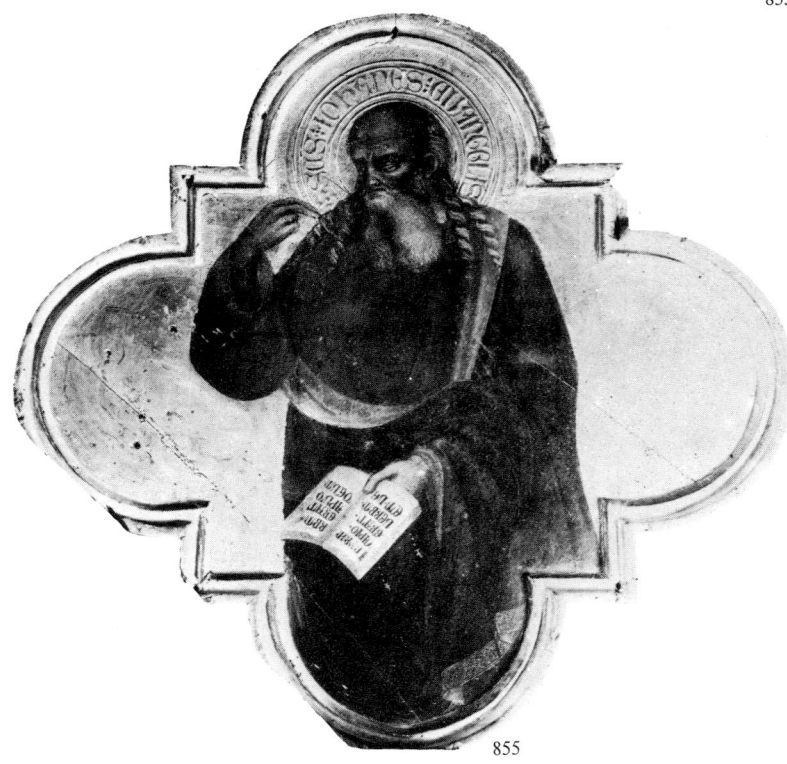

853. *Conversion and Baptism of Valerian. Fresco. Florence, S. Maria del Carmine.* Brogi 19804.
854. *St Martin and the Beggar. Panel. Florence, Accademia. Uffizi 462. 10 × 25.6.* SGF 102744.
855. *St John the Evangelist. Panel. Florence, Duomo, Sacristy. 100 × 100.* Alinari 58064.

PSEUDO AMBROGIO di BALDESE

This master's manner of painting the figure is, in fact, a very significant mixed product of trecento and quattrocento methods. Although an older colleague of Lorenzo Monaco, he tried to adopt something of the realism of the awakening Renaissance in his figure modelling. His personal predeliction, however, seems chiefly directed to the elegant and ornamental..... Ambrogio Baldese is, without doubt, one of the most skilful and sensitive painters who were active in Florence during the transition from the fourteenth to the fifteenth century.....

> from O. Sirén, p. 326, *The Burlington Magazine*, XIV, 71, 1909.

He was probably active already in the seventies of the XIV century, though we have no definite records of his works before the middle of the eighties. Of the frescoes he executed at that time, in company with Niccolò di Pietro Gerini, on the façade of the Bigallo in Florence, an important fragment remains, which was transferred in 1777 from its original place to the interior of the building, in order to be better protected.....

> from O. Sirén, p. 59, *A Descriptive Catalogue of the Pictures in the Jarves Collection*, New Haven, 1916.

Mr Sirén identified the personality of Ambrogio di Baldese who also worked in the Or San Michele with the anonymous author of a great number of Madonnas and saints executed, I should say, between 1420 and 1440. On account of their late date I do not think his hypothesis can be correct....

> from R. van Marle, p. 612, *The Development of the Italian Schools of Painting*, Vol. III, The Hague, 1924.

A painter of this group, perhaps a little earlier, or in any case a little less forward looking than the others, was the so-called Pseudo-Baldese. Dr van Marle in the IX Volume of his *Italian Schools* spoke of him and anticipated my own attribution to him of a *Madonna* in the Worcester museum (U.S.A.). This picture is so advanced and so similar to those of Rossello di Jacopo Franchi, that it must belong to the end of the career of this little artist, and be perhaps his finest work.
I have seen several " homeless " *Madonnas* of his, which show him to be nearer to Lorenzo Monaco's early career, to Alvaro Portoghese and to Martino di Bartolomeo.....

> from B. Berenson, p. 176, *Dedalo*, XII, 1, 1932.

I have already alluded to (the) proposed identification of Ambrogio di Baldese and the author of a certain number of paintings of the second quarter of the 15th century, inspired chiefly by Bicci di Lorenzo, for which reason I think he belonged to the generation following that of Ambrogio who was born in 1352 and died in 1429 and of whose activity we are unable to find any evidence after 1417. Consequently he was a contemporary of Spinello Aretino and Niccolò di Pietro Gerini and he collaborated with the latter in the execution of a fresco in the Bigallo, an important fragment of which has come down to us. This work reveals him as a faithful adherent of the 14th century tradition, as indeed the dates of his activity alone would have led us to conclude.
As for the other painter whom Mr. Sirén wished to identify with Ambrogio di Baldese, he is an artistic individuality generally fairly easily recognised. Mr. Sirén emitted his theory in connexion with a large polyptych in the Jarves collection, Yale University, New Haven, which shows in the centre the Virgin enthroned with two angelic musicians kneeling below and in the lateral panels SS. Anthony of Padua, Peter, John the Baptist and Anthony Abbot; in the three medallions above we see God the Father bestowing a blessing and the two figures of the Annunciation. Below, an inscription gives the date 1370 but as Mrs. Logan

Berenson, who includes this painting in the list of Bicci di Lorenzo's works and Mr. Sirén himself have already remarked, this cannot possibly be the correct date because the picture can hardly be prior to the beginning of the 15th century.....

from R. van Marle, p. 87, *The Development of the Italian Schools of Painting*, Vol. IX, The Hague, 1927.

An unknown Florentine painter, active about 1410-1420, influenced by Bicci di Lorenzo; for a time erroneously identified with Ambrogio di Baldese....

from R. Oertel, p. 134, *Frühe Italienische Malerei in Altenburg*, Berlin, 1961.

BIBLIOGRAPHY
BOOKS
An asterisk indicates a work listed in the General Bibliography

Venturi, A., *Storia dell' Arte Italiana*, VII, Milan, 1911, p. 28; Sirén, O., *Descriptive Catalogue of the Pictures in the Jarves Collection*, New Haven, 1916, pp. 58-61; *v. Marle, 1924**, p. 612; *v. Marle, 1927**, pp. 86-92; *Offner, 1927**, pp. 19-20; *Toesca, 1929**, p. 68; *Galetti**, 1950, " A-E ", p. 48; *MASA**, 1961, p. 7; *Oertel, 1961**, pp. 134-5; Dal Poggetto, P., *AIV**, 1963, pp. 42-3.

JOURNALS
Poggi, G., *RA*, II, 10-11, 1904, pp. 189-244; Sirén, O., *BM*, XIV, 1909, p. 326; R. W., *BWAM*, XII, 1922, p. 62; Henniker-Heaton, R., *AA*, XII, 1924, pp. 211-15; E. S. S., *BWMM*, XVII, 1927, pp. 86-88; Longhi, R., *Pin*, I, 1928-9, p. 34; Piattoli, R., *RA*, XI, 1929, pp. 221-53, 396-437, 537-79; Piattoli, R., *RA*, XII, 1930, pp. 97-150; Berenson, B., *DD*, XII, 1, 1932, pp. 5-34, 173-93, Procacci, U., *RA*, XV, 1933, pp. 224-44; Pudelko, G., *AB*, XVIII, 1935, pp. 83-9; Zeri, F., *BA*, XLVIII, IV, 3, 1963, pp. 256-57; Zeri, F., *BA*, XLVIII, 4, 1963, p. 247.

There are no known signed and/or dated works by Pseudo Ambrogio di Baldese.

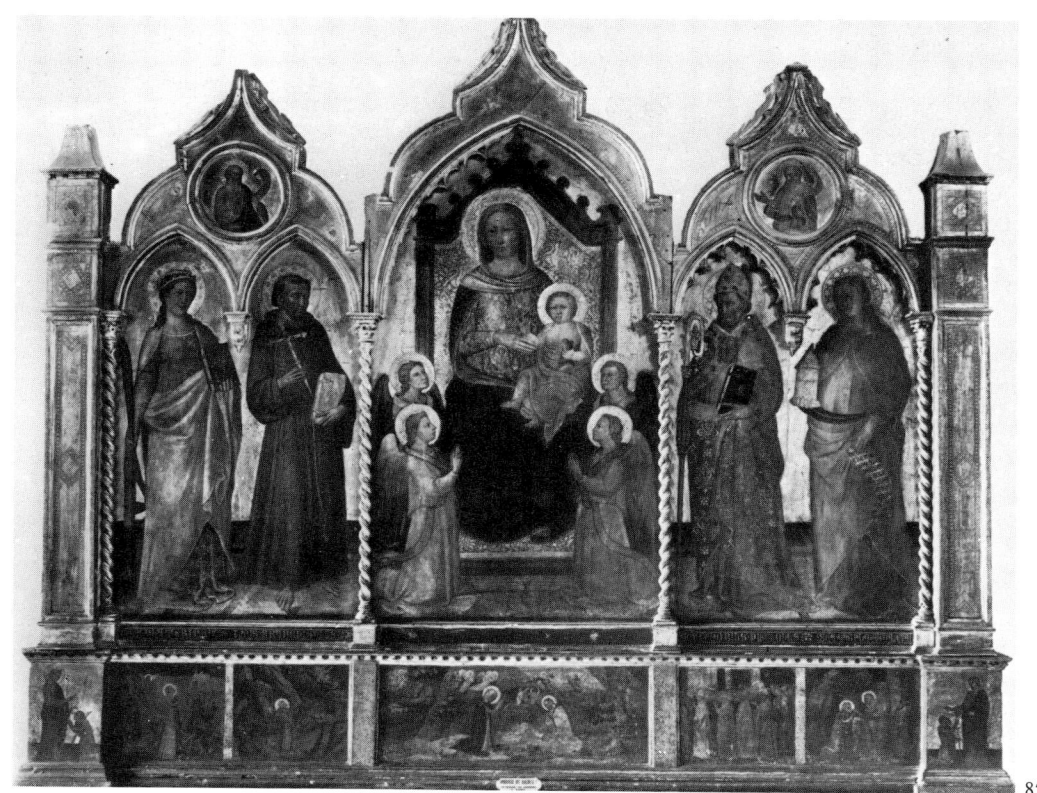

856

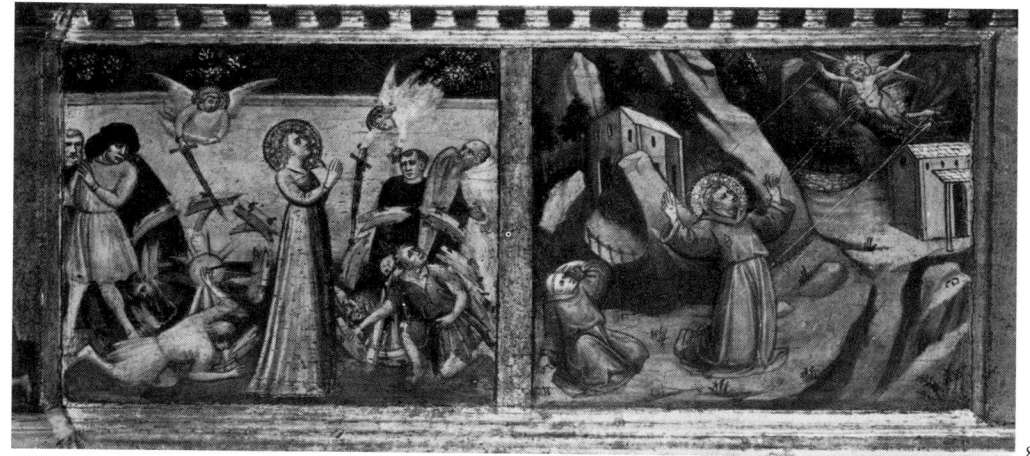

857

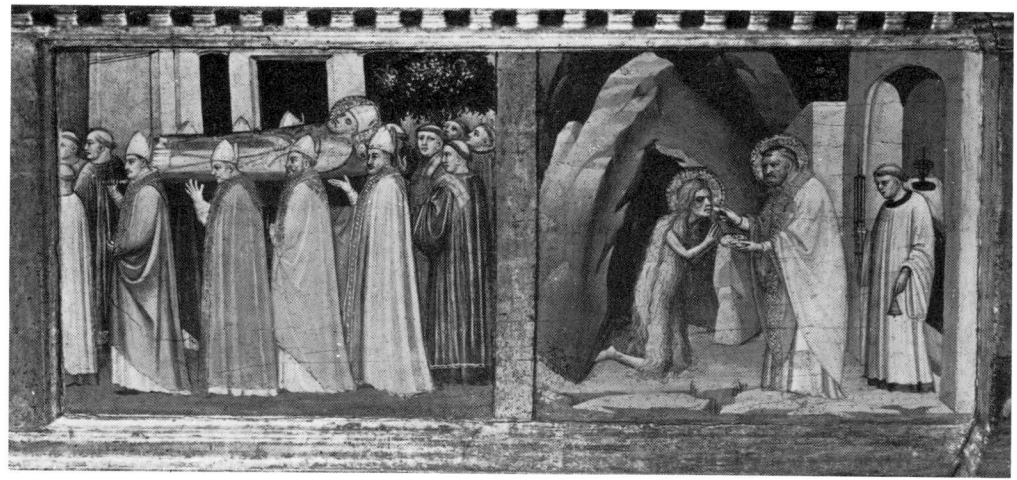

858

856. *Triptych: Madonna and Child Enthroned with Sts Catherine, Francis, Zenobius, Mary Magdalene and four Angels. Above: two Prophets. Predella: five scenes referring to figures above, two scenes of Christ blessing. Panel. Florence, Accademia. no. 8655. 191 × 273. SGF 102864.*
857. *Predella scene: Attempted Martyrdom of St Catherine, Stigmatization of St Anthony, detail of fig. 856. Panel. Florence, Accademia. no. 8655. SGF 106638.*
858. *Predella scene: Funeral of a Bishop Saint; Last Communion of Mary Magdalene, detail of fig. 856. Panel. Florence, Accademia. no. 8655. SGF 106639.*

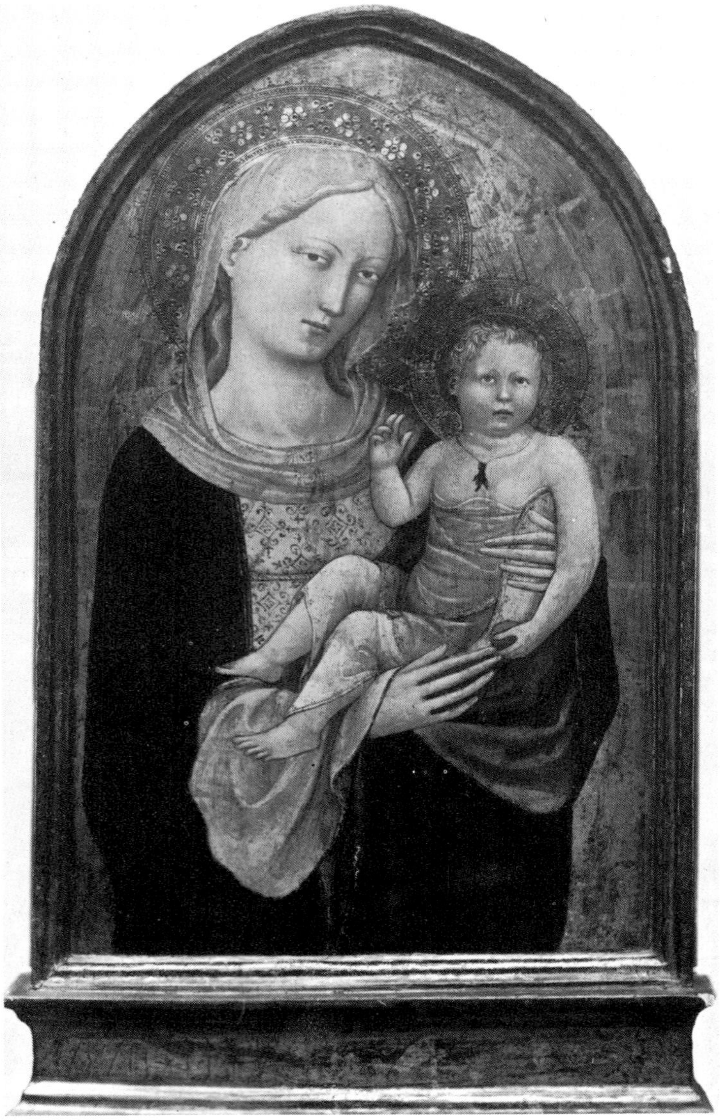

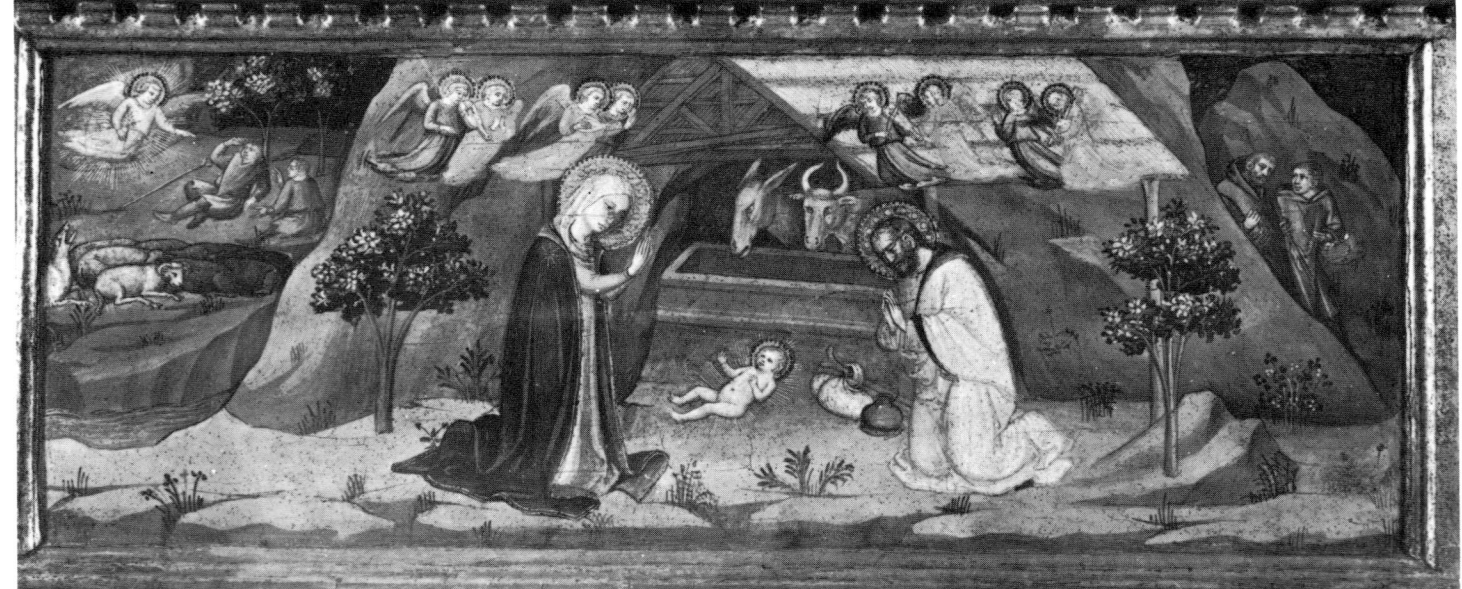

859

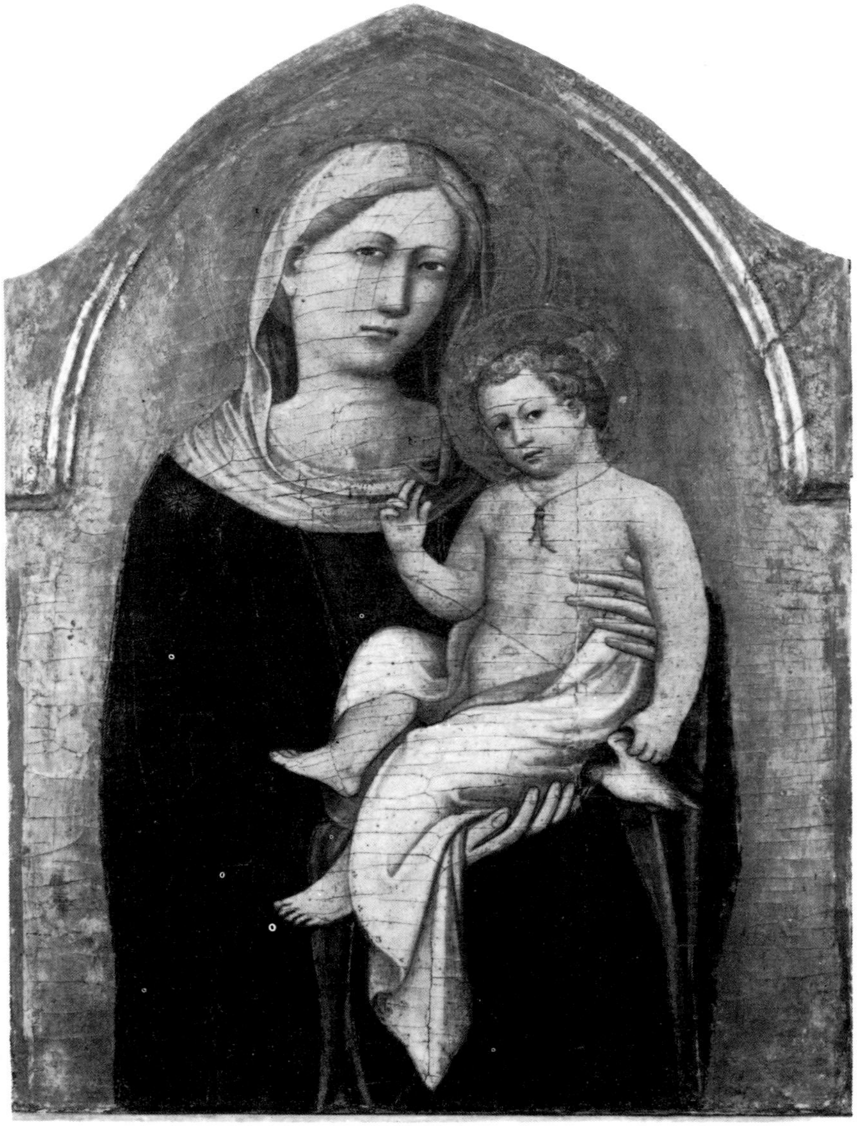

860

861

859. *Madonna and Child. Panel. Worcester (Mass.), Worcester Art Museum. no. 1921.58. 72.8 × 44.4. Museum photo.*
860. *Madonna and Child. Panel. Pastine (between Barberino Valdelsa and Poggibonsi), S. Martino. 74 × 48. SGF 110328.*
861. *Predella scene: Nativity, detail of fig. 856. Panel. Florence, Accademia. no. 8655. SGF 106637.*

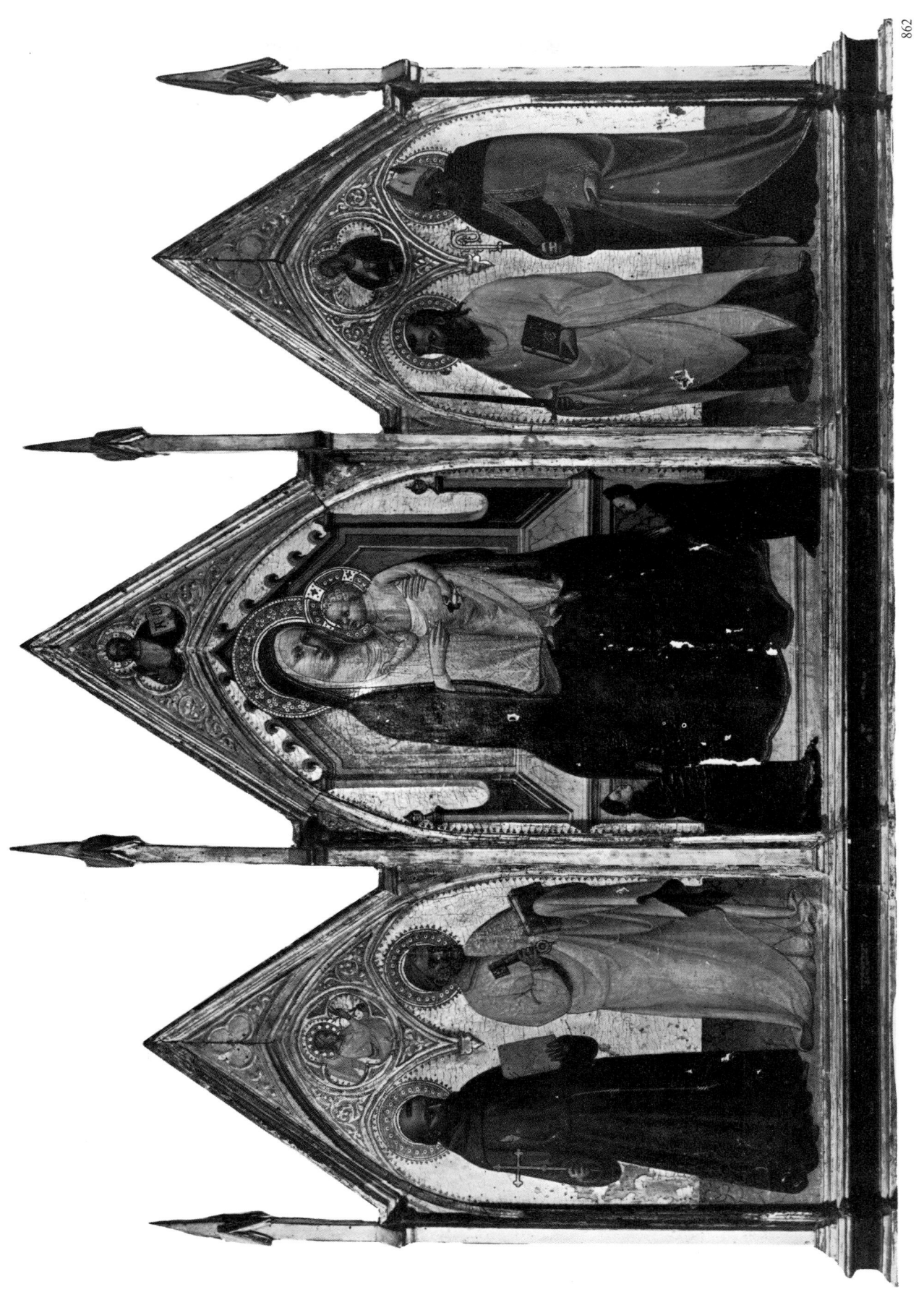

862. *Triptych: Madonna and Child Enthroned with two Donors, and Sts Francis, Peter, Paul and a Bishop Saint. Above: Christ blessing, Annunciation. Panel. Cedda (near Poggibonsi), S. Pietro. cp: 107 × 52; sps: 93 × 46.5. SGF 122523.*

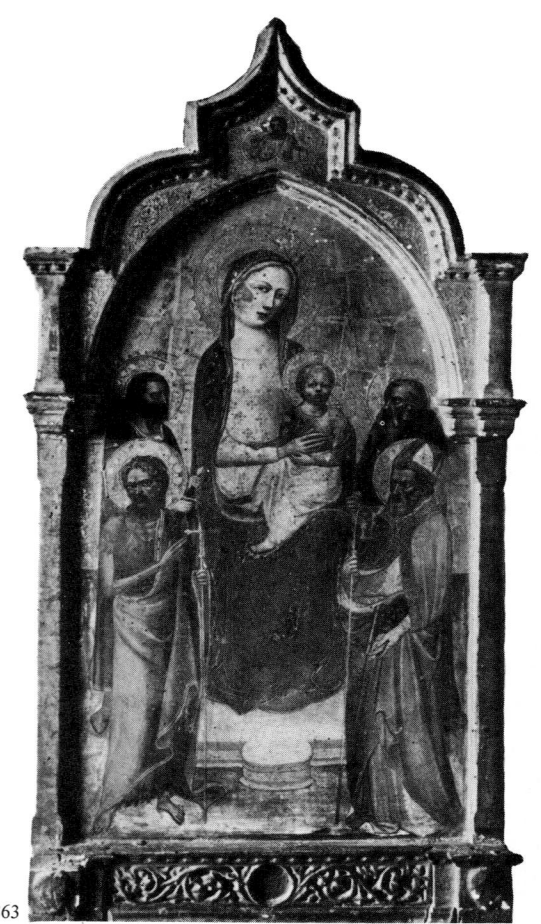

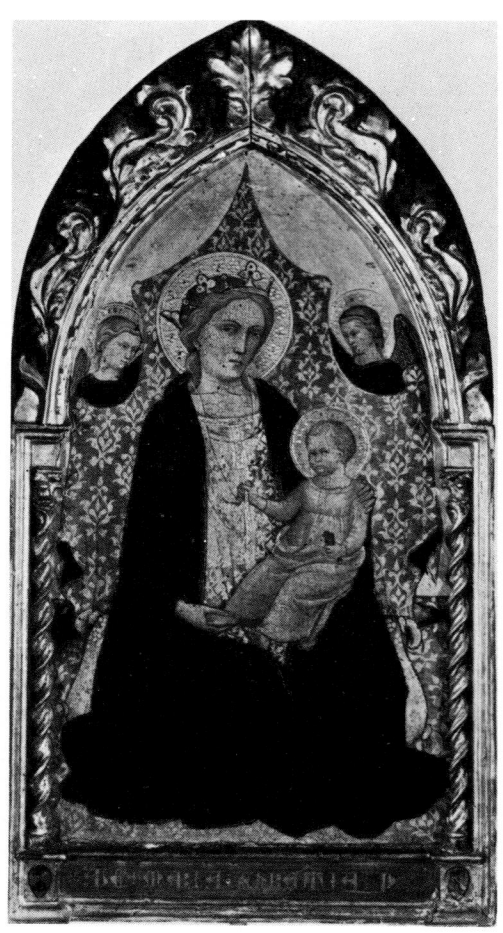

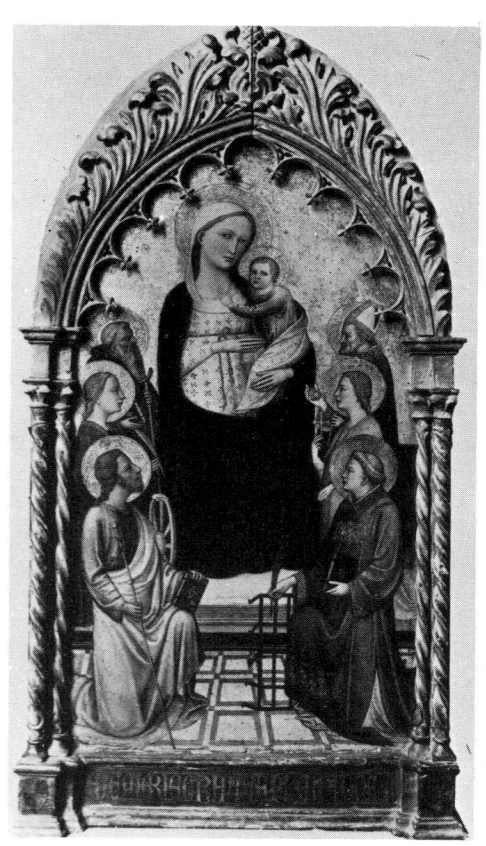

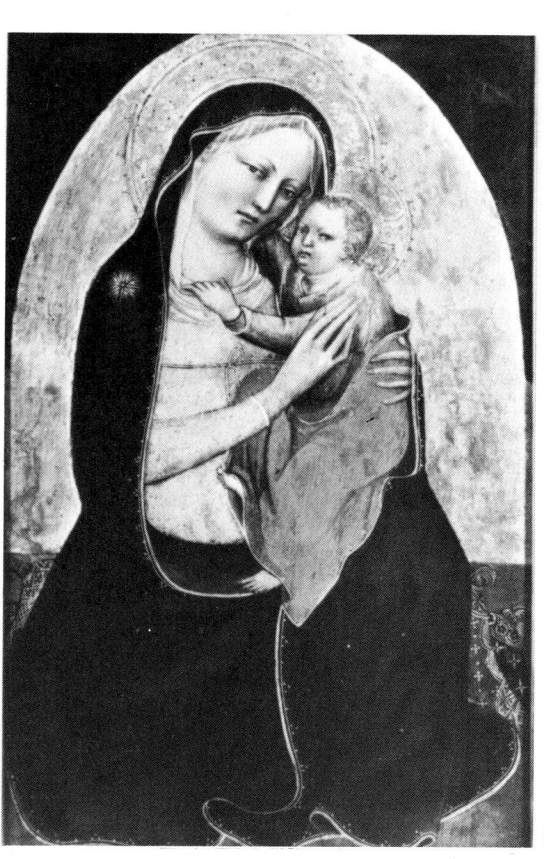

863. *Madonna and Child Enthroned with Sts John the Baptist, Julian, Anthony Abbot and Nicholas. Panel. Whereabouts unknown. Fototeca Berenson.*
864. *Madonna of Humility with two Angels. Panel. Pistoia, Museo Civico. no. 497. 100 × 54. SGF 154574.*
865. *Madonna and Child with six Saints. Panel. Private Collection. Reali.*
866. *Madonna of Humility. Panel. Whereabouts unknown. 78.7 × 49.5. Courtauld photo.*

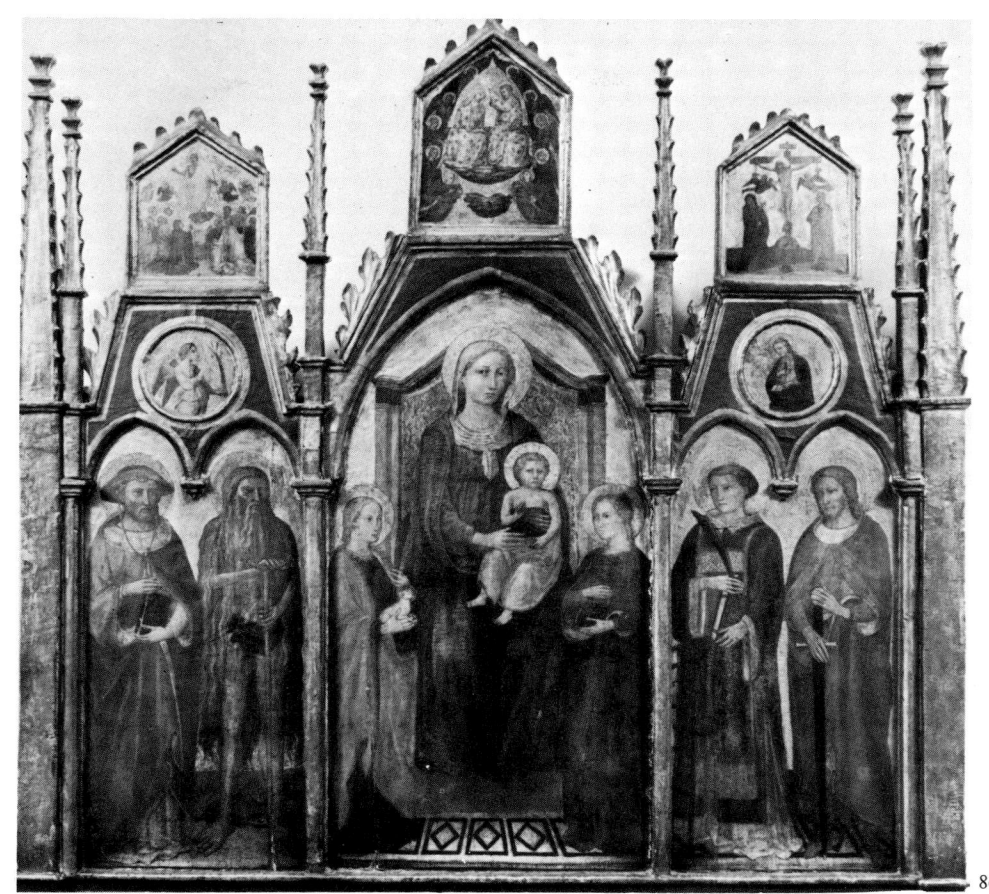

867

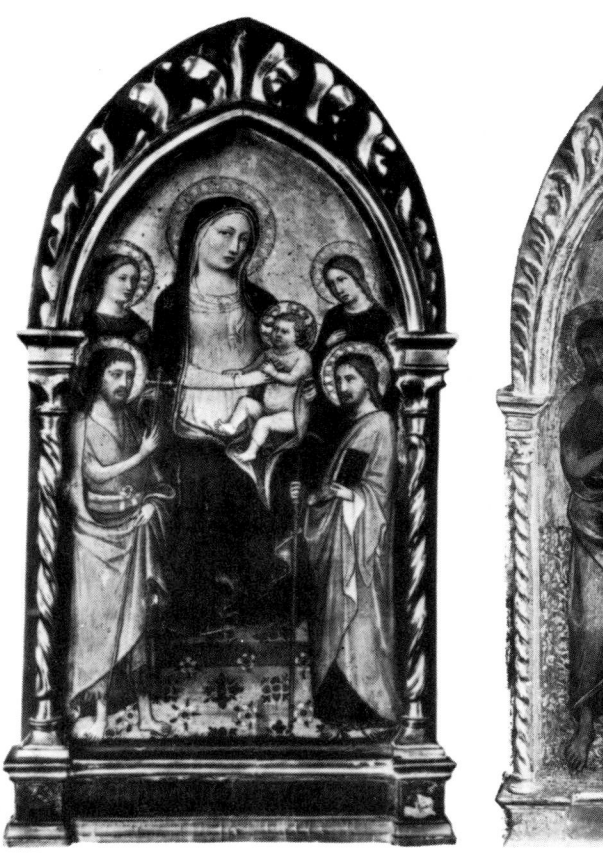

868

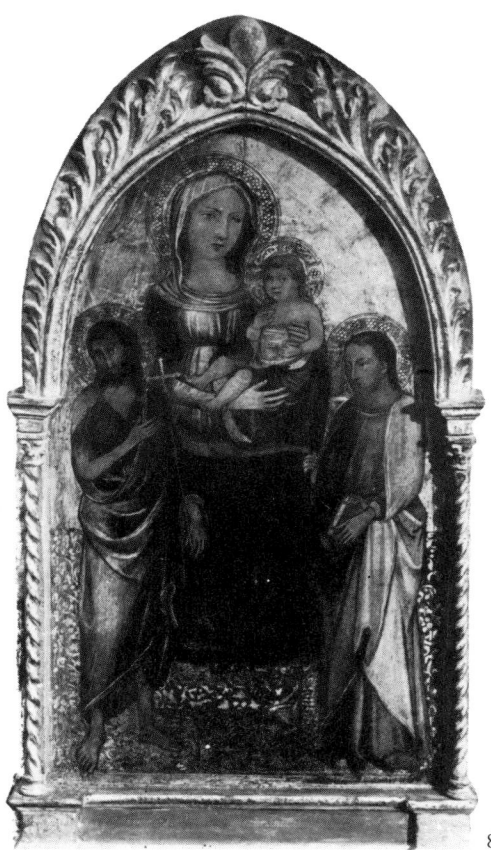

869

867. *Triptych: Madonna and Child with six Saints. Above: Ascension; Coronation of the Virgin; Christ on the Cross; Annunciation. Panel. Private Collection. cp: 103.5 × 56.5; sps: 78.7 × 38.7. Sotheby A7300.*

868. *Madonna and Child Enthroned with two Saints and two Angels. Panel. Florence, Marchese Bagneri Collection. SGF 113313.*

869. *Madonna and Child with St John the Baptist and another Saint. Panel. Vincigliata (near Settignano, east of Florence), Castello. 54 × 109. SGF 21155.*

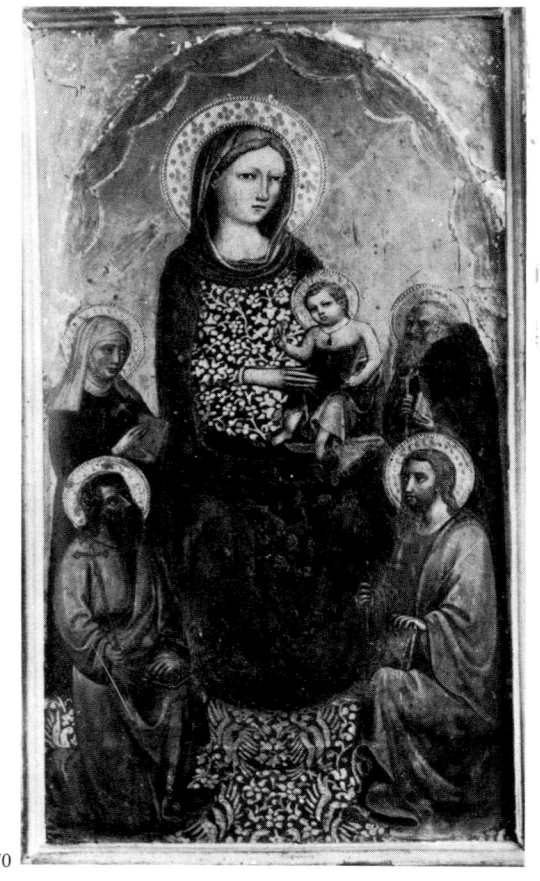

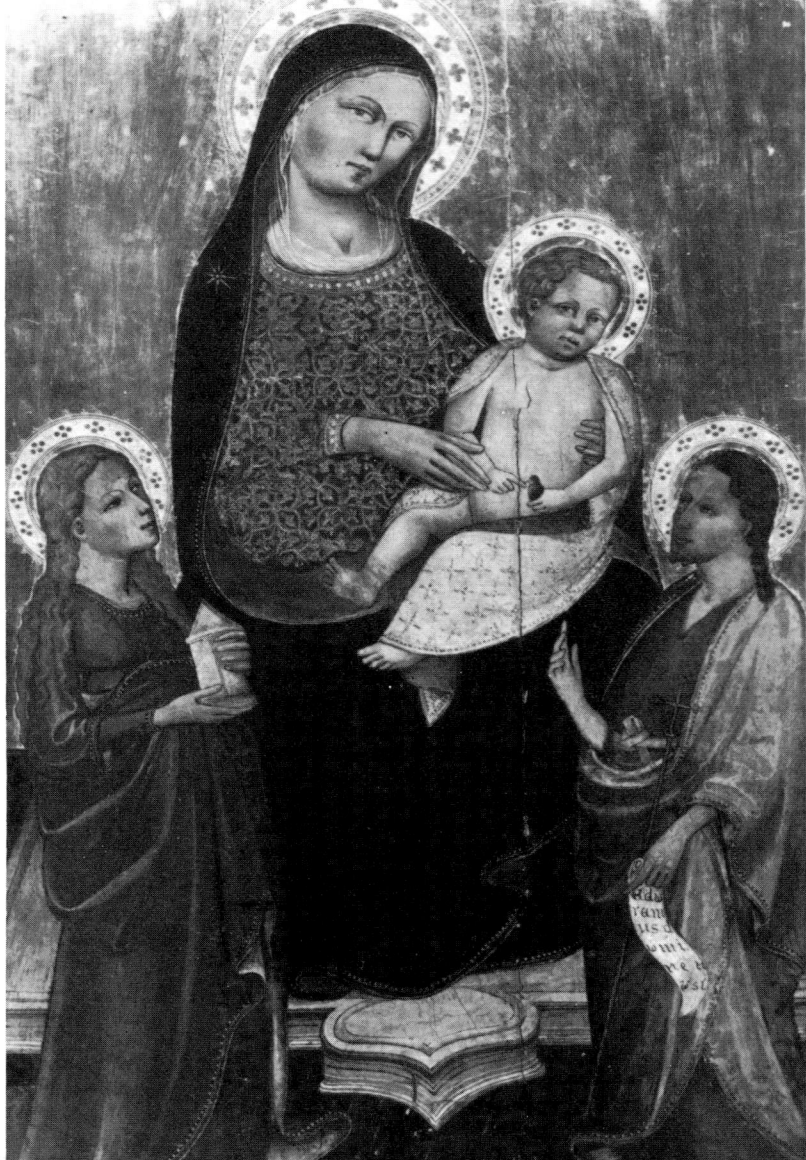

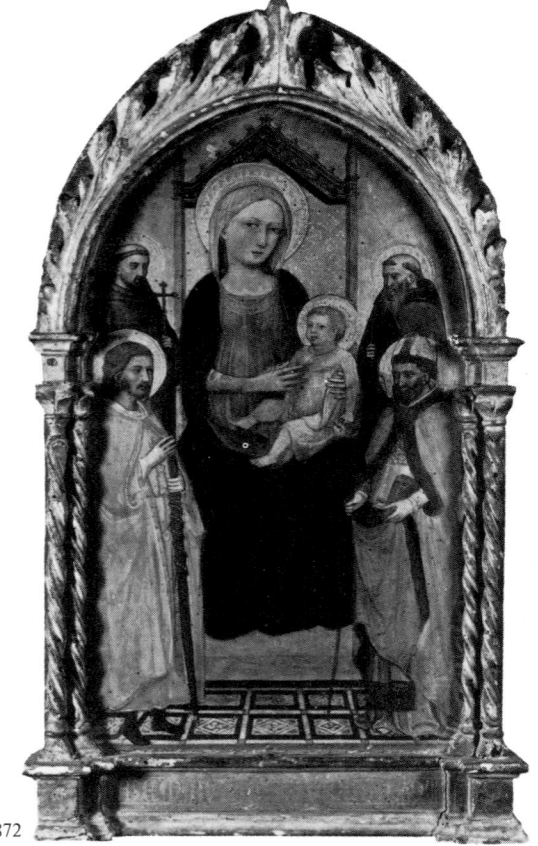

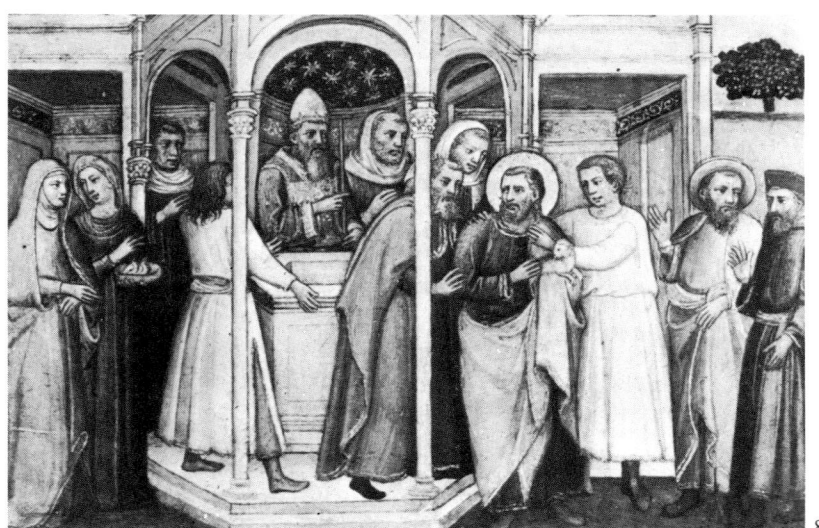

870. *Madonna and Child with four Saints. Panel. Whereabouts unknown. Fototeca Berenson.*
871. *Madonna and Child Enthroned with Sts Mary Magdalene and John the Baptist. Panel. Boston (Mass.), Museum of Fine Arts. no. 03.564.*
80 × 50.1. Museum photo C 4732.
872. *Madonna and Child Enthroned with four Saints. Panel. Private Collection. 91 × 48.5. Finarte, Milan 12694.*
873. *Expulsion of Joachim from the Temple. Panel. Knonopist (Czech.), Museum. no. 22468. 28.5 × 41.4. Fototeca Berenson.*

424

FRANCESCO di ANTONIO

Florentine, born 13- -, died 14- -. Painter, member of the Guild of Physicians and Apothecaries Nov. 21, 1429. In 1412 Francesco painted a panel of the Virgin, Infant and Saints for Don Gabriele, signed Franciscus. Antonii. De. Fl. Pinsit. On June 17, 1429, Francesco received 18 florins of gold for painting the shutters of Or San Michele; these shutters and the altar-piece mentioned above were formerly in the Toscanelli collection at Pisa, which was dispersed in Florence in 1883. Francesco is probably the Francesco Fiorentino mentioned by Vasari as a pupil of Don Lorenzo Monaco, and to whom he attributes the tabernacle at the corner of the Piazza of Sta. Maria Novella and the Via della Scala, which is still extant, although repainted.

from D. E. Colnaghi, p. 34, *A Dictionary of Florentine Painters*, London, 1928.

A painter called Francesco d'Antonio di Bartolomeo seems to have been registered in the Arte dei Medici e Speziali, in 1409; and if he were, as I think possible, the painter in question, his work of the second decade of the quattrocento would be his youthful activity. His was a personality too weak to develop coherently or consistently. From a trecentesque base, he is made more sensitive by contact with Lorenzo Monaco; then — although remaining essentially Gothic in colour and form — he comes into contact with Masolino, and even with Masaccio, although he has no understanding of him whatsoever. His " angels " for Orsanmichele, which are his best formal work, show us that his art is carried on by Paolo Schiavo, especially with this latter's " Annunciation " in the Berlin Museum. The relationship is so close that we may suppose that Paolo learned his art with Francesco d'Antonio.....

from M. Salmi, pp. 23-4, *Rivista d'Arte*, II, I, 1929.

Francesco d'Antonio Banchi must have begun his career with Lorenzo Monaco, or under his guidance, but he was moulded by Masolino and Masaccio, and sealed, to use an expression, by Paolo Uccello and Domenico Veneziano.....
If I had written three years ago, I would still have been forced to establish who Francesco di Antonio Banchi was, how many signed works by him are known, etc. By good luck, this duty has been done by Professor Mario Salmi of the University of Florence, and it has been done excellently.....
Out of the fear that I will be accused of having wasted my time on such an unimportant artist, I point out that more than thirty years ago I already began to suspect that he in fact painted certain pictures which were noted either for their own merits or for the lofty attributions by which they were known. For example, during the first years in which I was in Florence, there was on exhibition at the Uffizi, as a thing of some importance, an elliptical cassone, attributed to Matteo de' Pasti; and the *Marriage of an Adimari* (in the Accademia) was one of the most popular paintings in Florence, at least for the Anglo-Saxons. There is, too, a *desco da parto*, with a *Triumph of Fame* painted on it, the finest of all for quality, painted in 1449 for the birth of Lorenzo il Magnifico, now in the Historical Society of New York. Today I am of the opinion that these and various similar paintings are by Francesco d'Antonio Banchi, even if, in the case of the *desco*, he almost certainly worked on a design of Domenico Veneziano.....

from B. Berenson, pp. 529, 532, *Dedalo*, XII, 2, 1932.

Florentine School. Known from documents 1393-1433. Secondary painter, but one who has the merit after having followed Lorenzo Monaco and then Masolino, of understanding, or at least imitating, certain of the discoveries of Masaccio; although he certainly did this in a minor key, he did it at a time when such comprehension was still exceptional.....

from M. Laclotte, p. 49, *De Giotto à Bellini*, Paris, 1956.

Francesco d'Antonio, but a few years older than Masaccio, shows in his earliest surviving works remarkable affinity to Lorenzo Monaco and a close adherence to the Florentine species (more abstract, crystalline, joyless and more trecentesque) of the " International Style ". This phase is best exemplified in his frescoes at San Francesco in Figline Valdarno which date around 1418. The style yielded to by Francesco was not one indigenous to Florence, where it was accepted by only a few artists, who themselves received it primarily as a reflection from the work of Ghiberti and Lorenzo Monaco. In Francesco's work it was quickly superceded by another phase in which the energetic line of the International Style is slowed, its calligraphy simplified, but in which line becomes more nearly congruous with its descriptive function. This more quiet mode results in a greater lyric calm and in a kind of stateliness and decorum.....

> from C. Shell, pp. 467-68, *The Art Bulletin*, 1965, Vol. XLVII.

A minor Florentine painter of the early Quattrocento, Francesco d'Antonio's style reacted to a series of contemporary influences. He began, perhaps as a follower of Lorenzo Monaco, but was then influenced by Gentile da Fabriano who worked in Florence between 1422 and 1425. A polyptych in the church of S. Niccolò in Florence for which Gentile painted his Quaratesi altarpiece (1424-5) has been attributed to Francesco d'Antonio, because of its obvious debt to Gentile. Like the fresco exhibited here it was probably painted soon after 1425, because by 1429, when Francesco d'Antonio was paid for decorating the organ of Orsanmichele, his style had once more shifted, under the influence of Masolino and Masaccio. His Madonna della Cintola in S. Vito a Loppiano in Valdarno can probably be placed slightly earlier. The head of a Virgin which he painted in a shrine in the Piazza Santa Maria Novella recalls Masolino's Madonna at Todi of 1432, and frescoes at Montemarciano first attributed to Francesco d'Antonio by Lindberg are dependent upon Masaccio.....

> from P. Dal Poggetto, p. 111, *Frescoes from Florence*, London, 1969.

BIBLIOGRAPHY
BOOKS
An asterisk indicates a work listed in the General Bibliography

Sirén, O., *Don Lorenzo Monaco*, Strasburg, 1905, pp. 162-3; Constable, W. G., *Catalogue of Pictures in the Marlay Bequest, Fitzwilliam Museum, Cambridge*, Cambridge, 1927, p. 31; *Colnaghi**, 1928, p. 34; *v. Marle, 1937**, pp. 190-2; Salmi, M., *Masaccio*, Milan, 1948, pp. 218-19 with bibliography; *Galetti**, " F-O ", 1950, p. 980; Suida, W. E., *Catalogue of the the Denver Art Museum*, Denver, (Colo.), 1954, pp. 16-7; *Laclotte**, 1956, p. 49; Berti, L., *MAS II**. 1958, p. 5; *Gregori**, 1960, p. 12; *Berenson, 1963**, Vol. I, pp. 62-4; Bellosi, L., *La Pittura Tardogotica in Toscana* (I Maestri del Colore, 239), Milan, 1966; Chiarini, M., *Masaccio e la pittura del '400 in Toscana* (I Maestri del Colore, 256), Milan, 1966; *Shapley**, 1966, pp. 92-3, 106; Dal Poggetto, P., *Fresco Show**, 1968, pp. 122-5 (111-13); Klesse, B., *Katalog der Italienischen, Französischen und Spanischen Gemälde bis 1800 im Wallraf-Richartz Museum*, Cologne, 1973, p. 47.

JOURNALS

Constable, W. G., *BM*, XLVII, 1925, p. 281; Sirén, O., *BM*, XLIX, 1926, p. 121; Salmi, M., *RA*, XI, 1929, pp. 1-24, 291; Poggi, G., *RA*, XI, 11, 1929, p. 291; Berenson, B., *DD*, XII, 1932, pp. 512-41; Gronau, G., *RA*, XIV, 1932, pp. 382-5; Longhi, R., *CA*, V, 1940, pp. 145-91, 186-7, n. 4; Carità, R., *BA*, XXXVI, 1949, pp. 272-3; Zeri, F., *BA*, XXXIV, 1949, pp. 22-6; Berti, L., *BA*, XXXVII, 1952, pp. 175-8; Gombrich, E. H., *WCJ*, XVIII, 1955, pp. 16-34; Berti, L., *C*, XII, 2, 1961, pp. 84-107; Shell, C., *AB*, XLVII, 1965, pp. 465-9; Boskovits, M., *AI*, 13/14, 1969, pp. 4-13; Friedmann, H., *Sim*, 3, 1968-69, 1, p. 7; Kiel, H., *P*, XXVII, 5, 1969, p. 421; Gonzalez-Palacios, A., *AP*, XCI, 95, 1970, p. 76.

SIGNED AND DATED WORKS

Figline, S. Francesco, Misericordia. Fresco: Coronation of the Virgin with five Angels and a Donor, Annunciation with Donor. s. (fig. 885).

1415 Cambridge, Fitzwilliam Museum. Triptych: Madonna & Child Enthroned with Sts Lawrence and John Gualbert. s & d. (fig. 876).

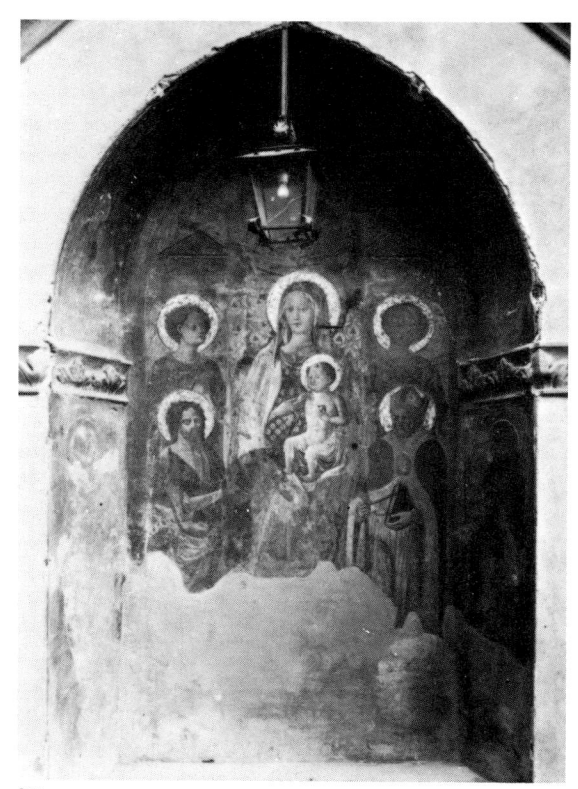

874

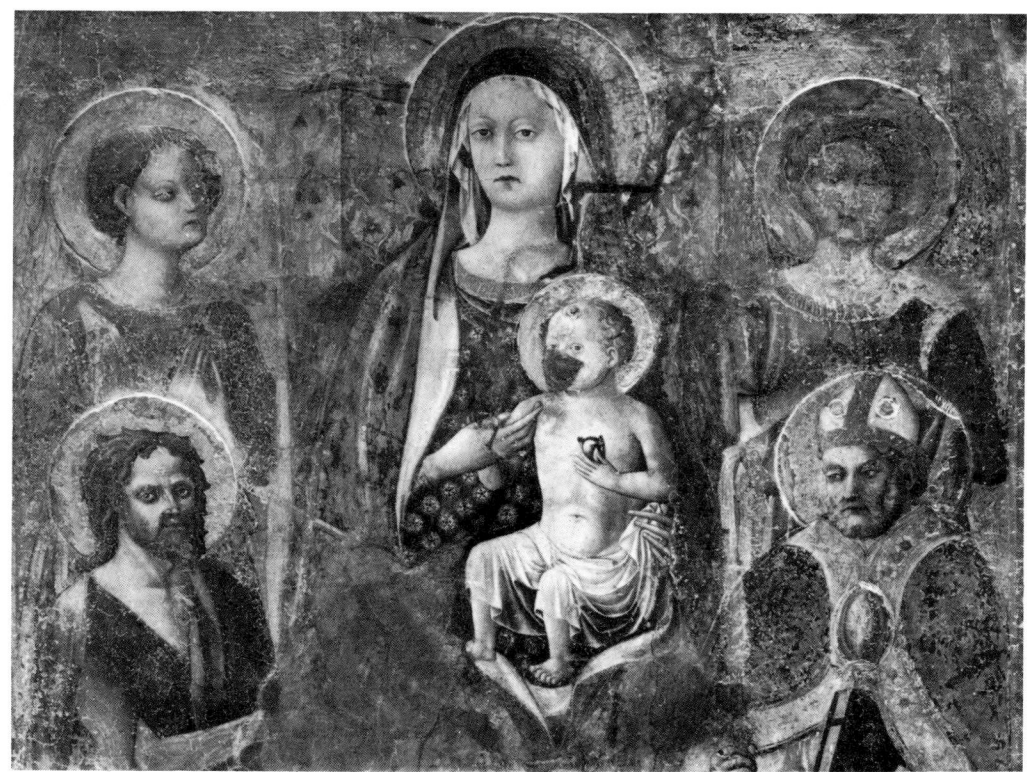

875

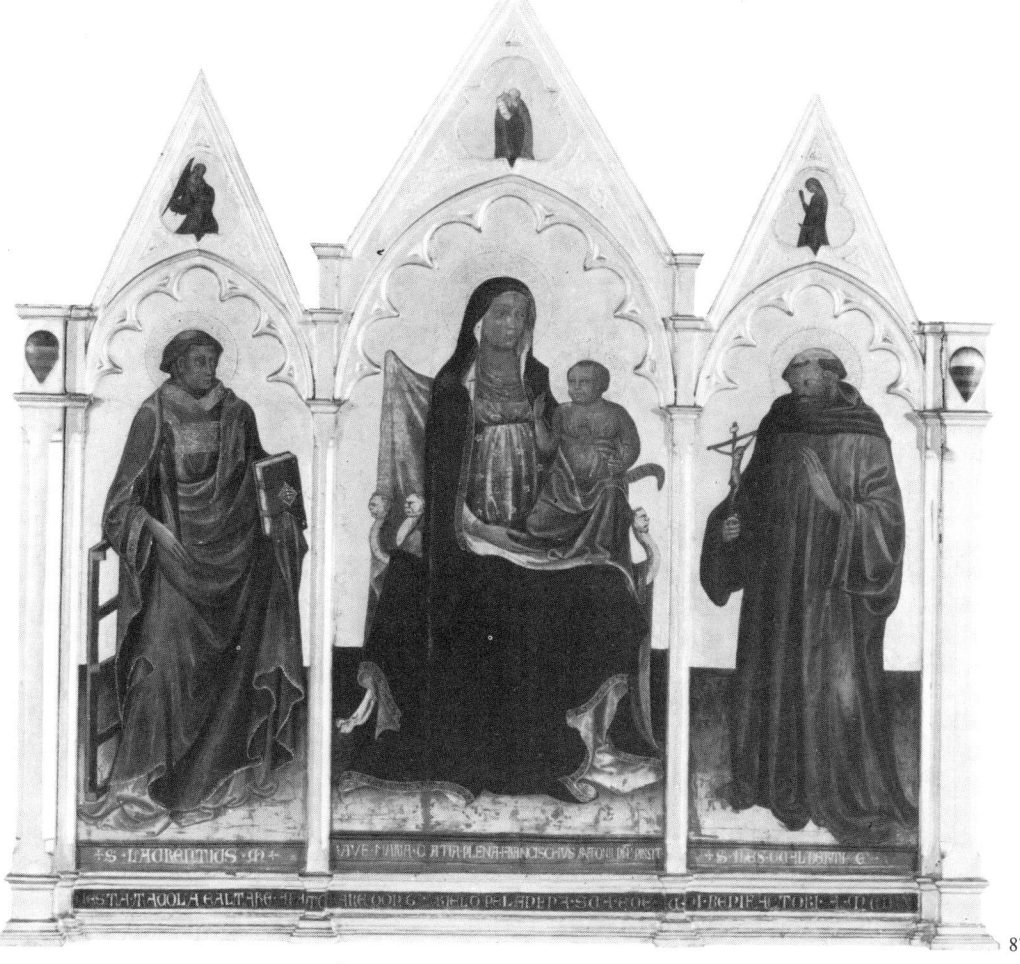

876

874. *Tabernacle: Madonna and Child Enthroned with two Angels, St John the Baptist and Bishop Saint. Fresco. Florence, corner of Piazza S. Maria Novella and via della Scala. 333 × 188. SGF 108065.*

875. *Madonna and Child, two Angels and St John the Baptist and Bishop Saint, detail of fig. 874. Fresco. Florence, corner of Piazza S. Maria Novella and via della Scala. Alinari 29182.*

876. *Triptych: Madonna and Child Enthroned with Sts Lawrence and John Gualbert. Panel. Cambridge, Fitzwilliam Museum. no. M33. cp: 163.2 × 50.2; lp: 91.7 × 34.3; rp: 89.8 × 34.6. Museum photo: Stearn & Sons: FMS 4992. s & d. 1415.*

427

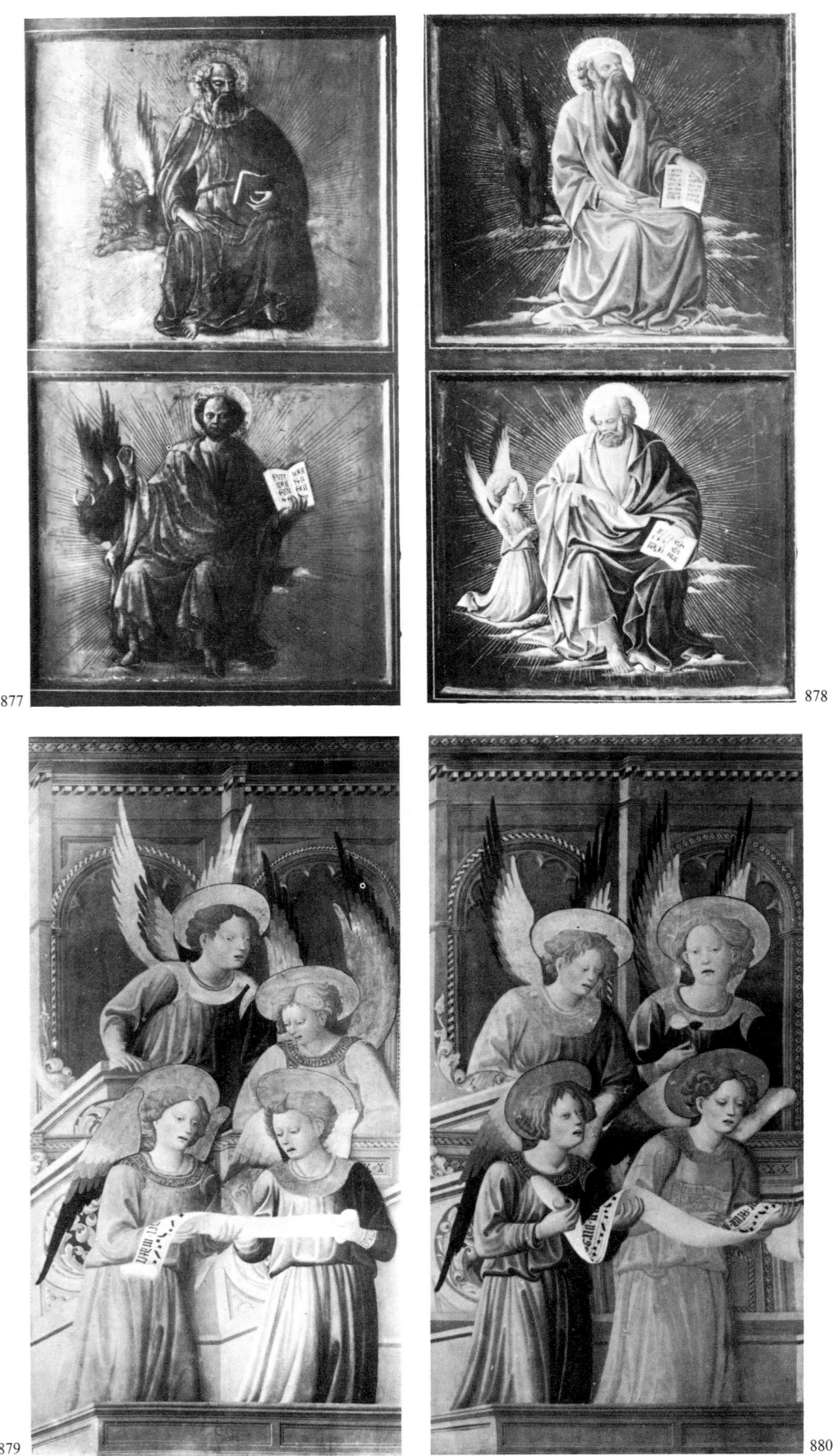

877

878

879

880

877. *Organ shutter, exterior: Sts Mark and Luke. Panel (lost). Florence, Accademia. no. 9272. 192 × 105. SGF 17625. 1429.*
878. *Organ shutter, exterior: Sts John the Evangelist and Matthew. Panel. Florence, Accademia. no. 9271. 192 × 105. SGF 26276. 1429.*
879. *Organ shutter, inside face: four singing Angels. Panel. Florence, Accademia. no. 9271. 192 × 105. SGF 26273. 1429.*
880. *Organ shutter, inside face: four singing Angels. Panel (lost). Florence, Accademia. no. 9272. 192 × 105. SGF 26270. 1429.*

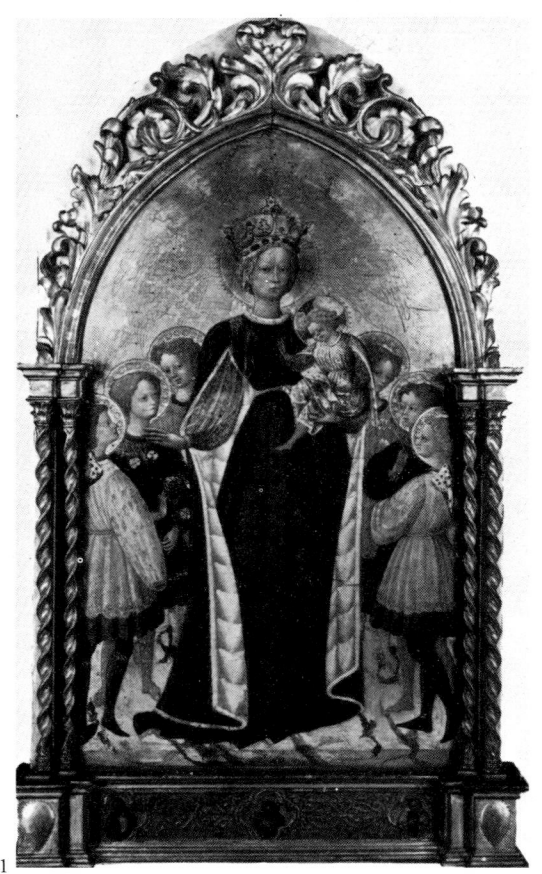

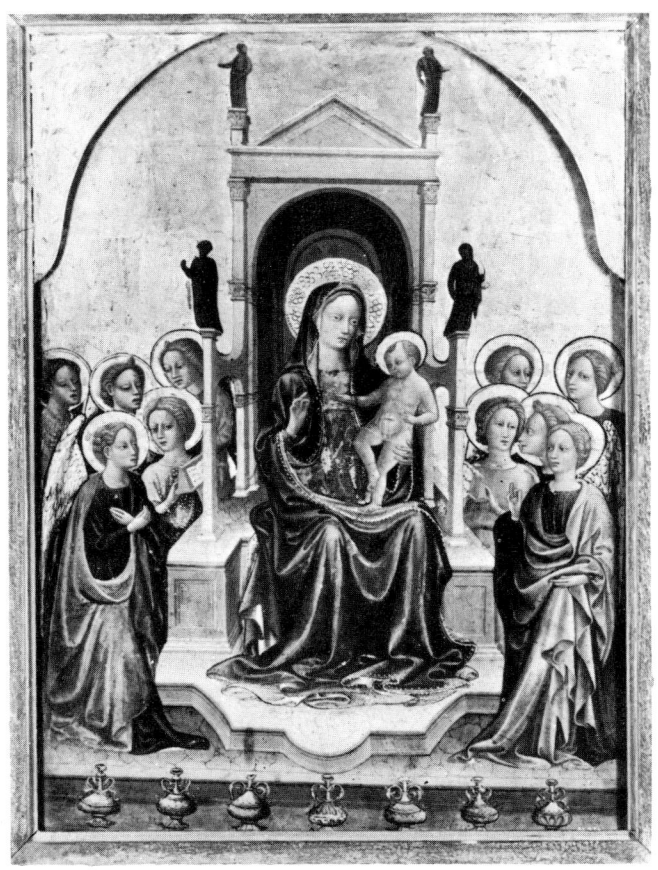

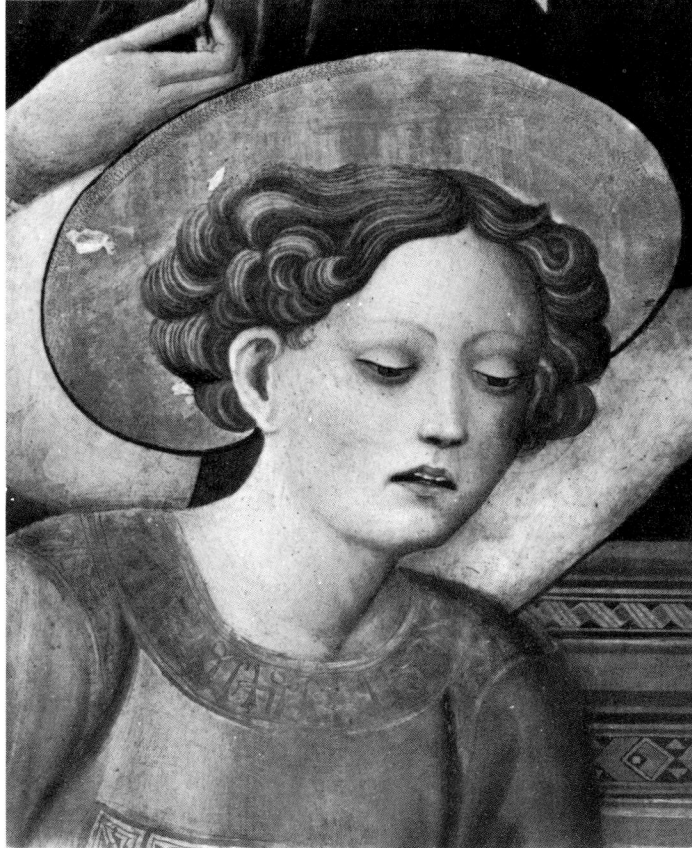

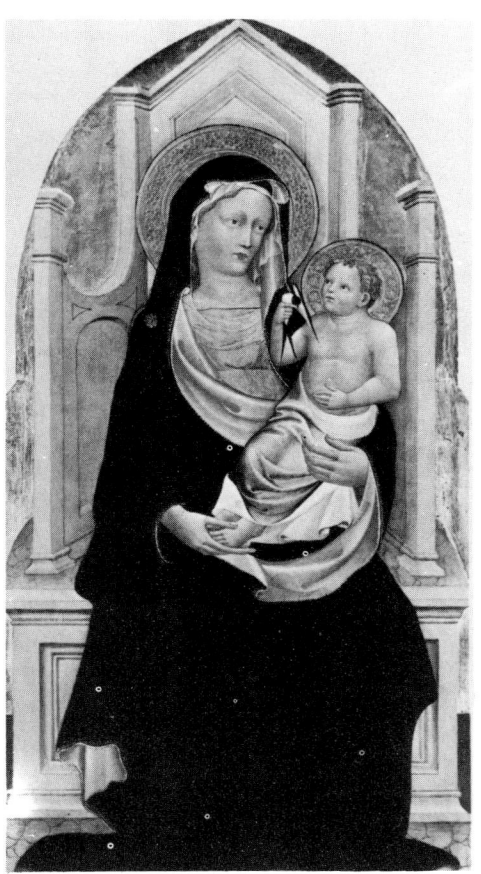

881. *Madonna and Child with six Angels. Panel. London, National Gallery. no. 1456. 85.1 × 54. Museum photo.*
882. *Madonna and Child Enthroned with ten Angels. Panel. Cologne, Wallraf-Richartz-Museum. no. 731. 58 × 41. Museum photo: 93697.*
883. *Head of Angel, detail of fig. 880. Panel (lost). Florence, Accademia. no. 9272. SGF 26272. 1429.*
884. *Madonna and Child Enthroned. Panel. Denver (Colo.), Denver Art Museum, Samuel H. Kress Collection. no. 543. 112.7 × 54. Kress Foundation. photo.*

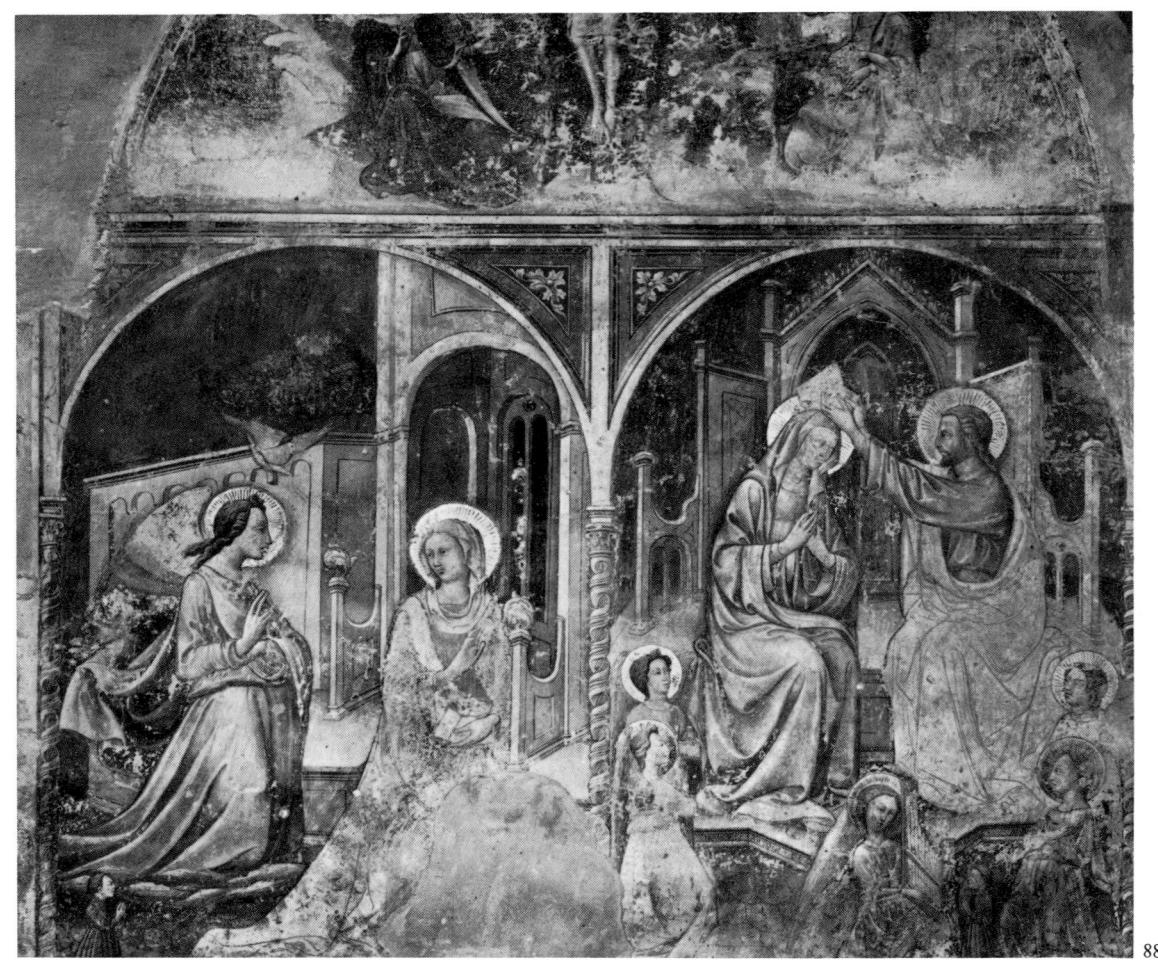

885

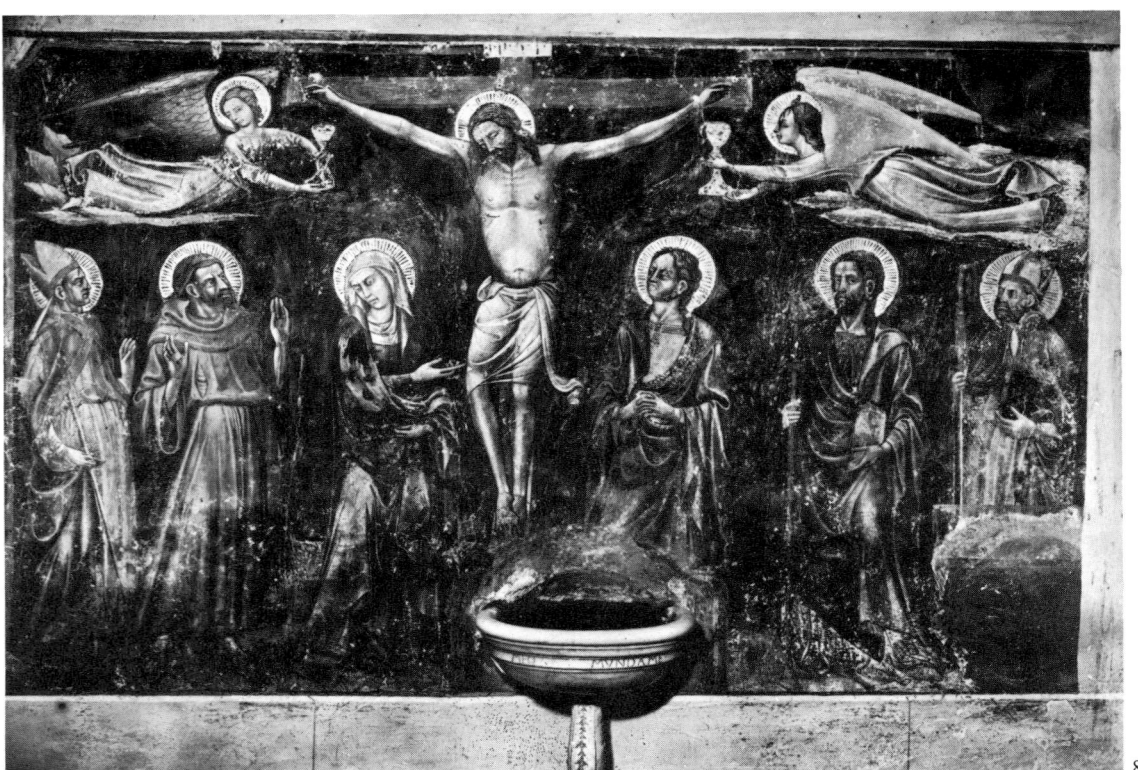

886

885. *Two scenes: Annunciation with Donor: Coronation of the Virgin with five Angels and Donor. Fresco. Figline (Upper Valdarno), S. Francesco. SGF 96104. s.*

886. *Christ on the Cross with a Bishop Saint, St Francis, the Virgin, Sts John the Evangelist, James, a Bishop Saint and two Angels. Fresco. Figline, S. Francesco. Alinari 41432.*

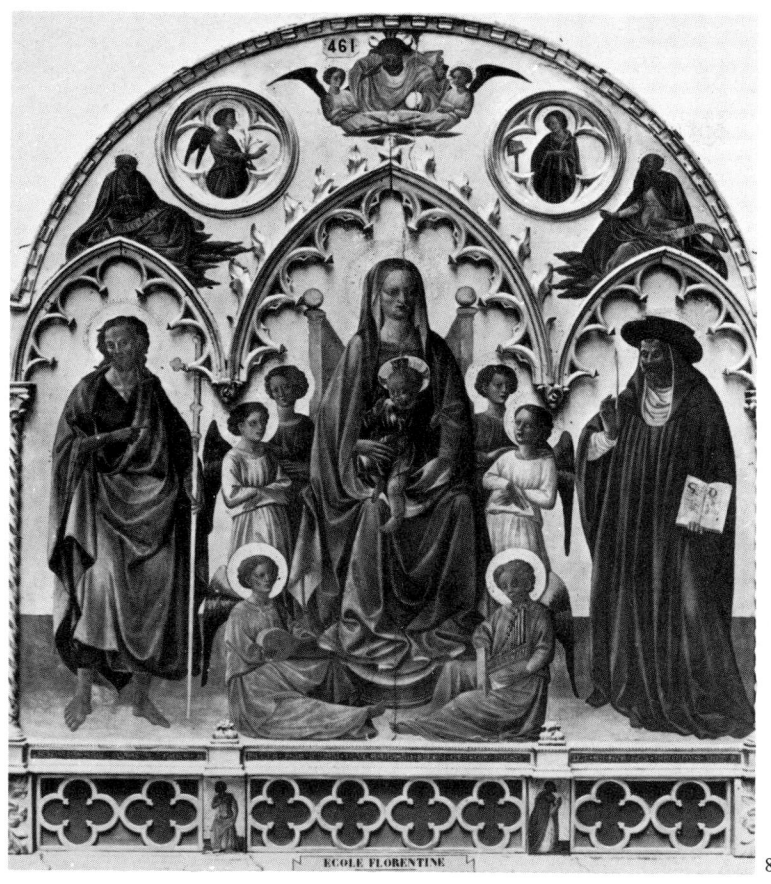

887

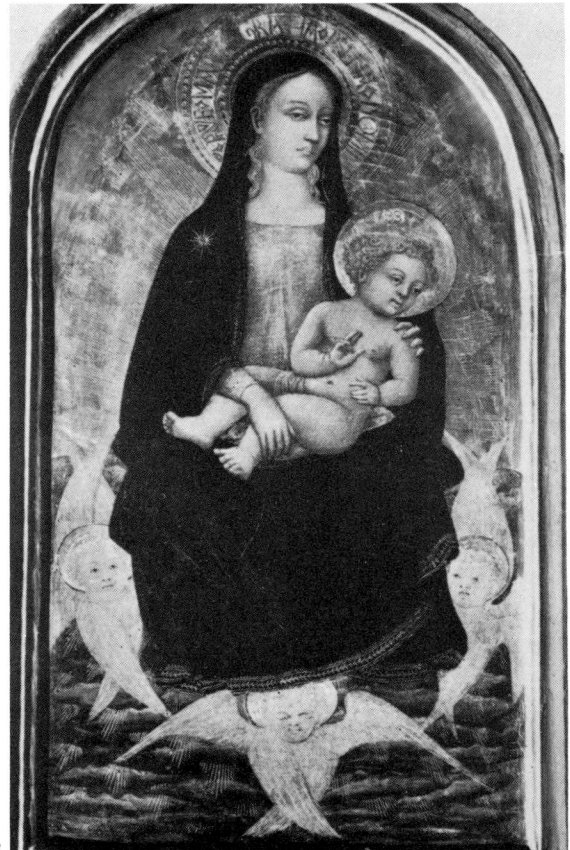

888

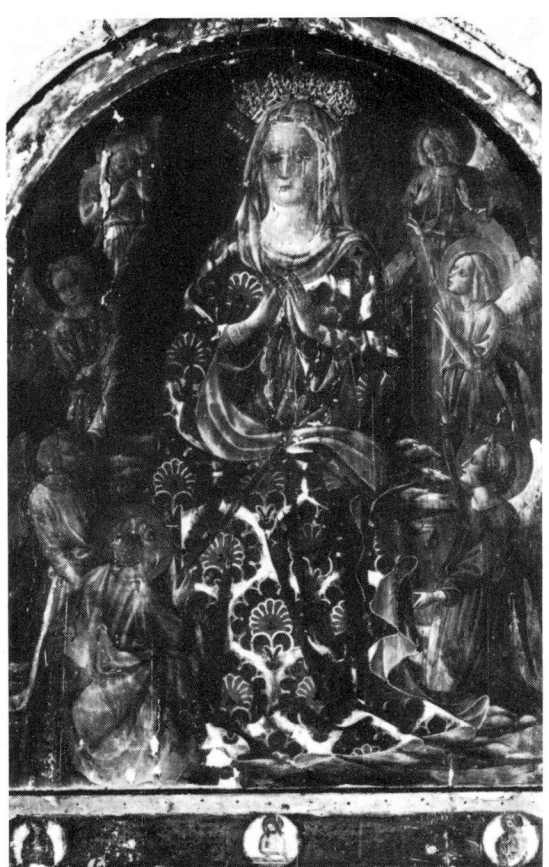

889

887. *Madonna and Child Enthroned with six Angels and Sts John the Baptist and Jerome. Above: God the Father; Annunciation; two Prophets. Panel. Grenoble, Musée de Peinture et de Sculpture. Campana no. 106. 182 × 168. Museum photo.*
888. *Madonna and Child in Glory with Cherubs. Panel. Florence, Mrs. C. H. Coster Collection. Fototeca Berenson.*
889. *Madonna of the Girdle with six Angels and a Saint. Panel. Loppiano (Incisa Valdarno), S. Vito. SGF 1422.*

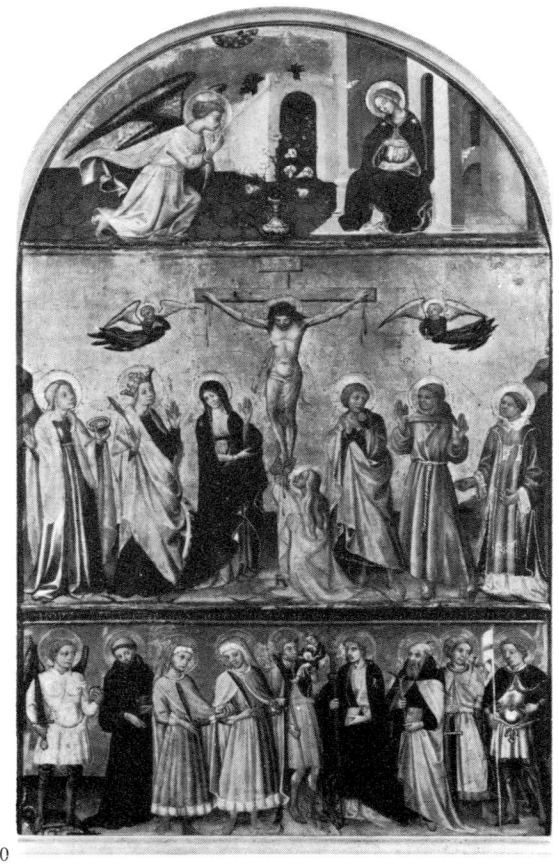

890

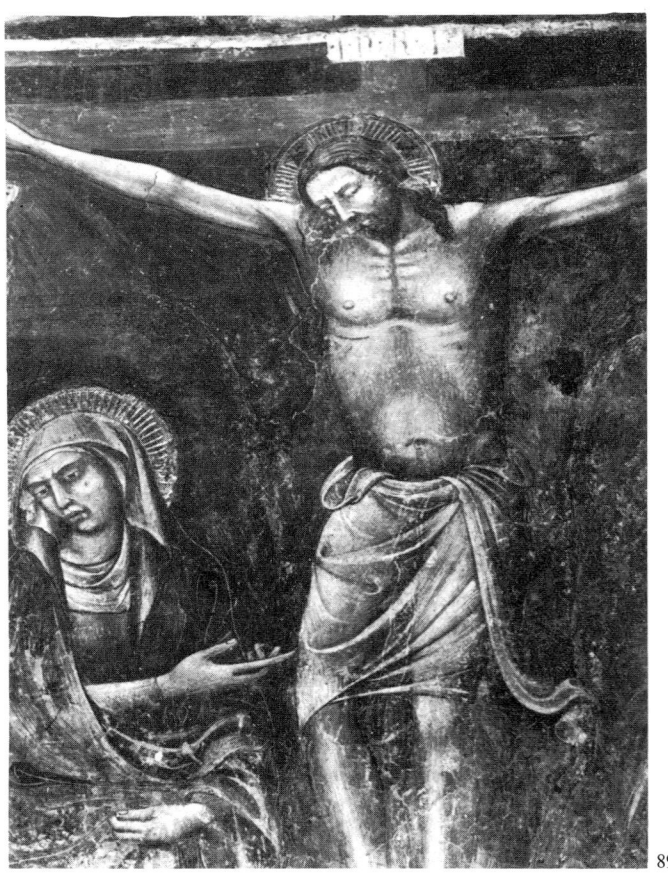

891

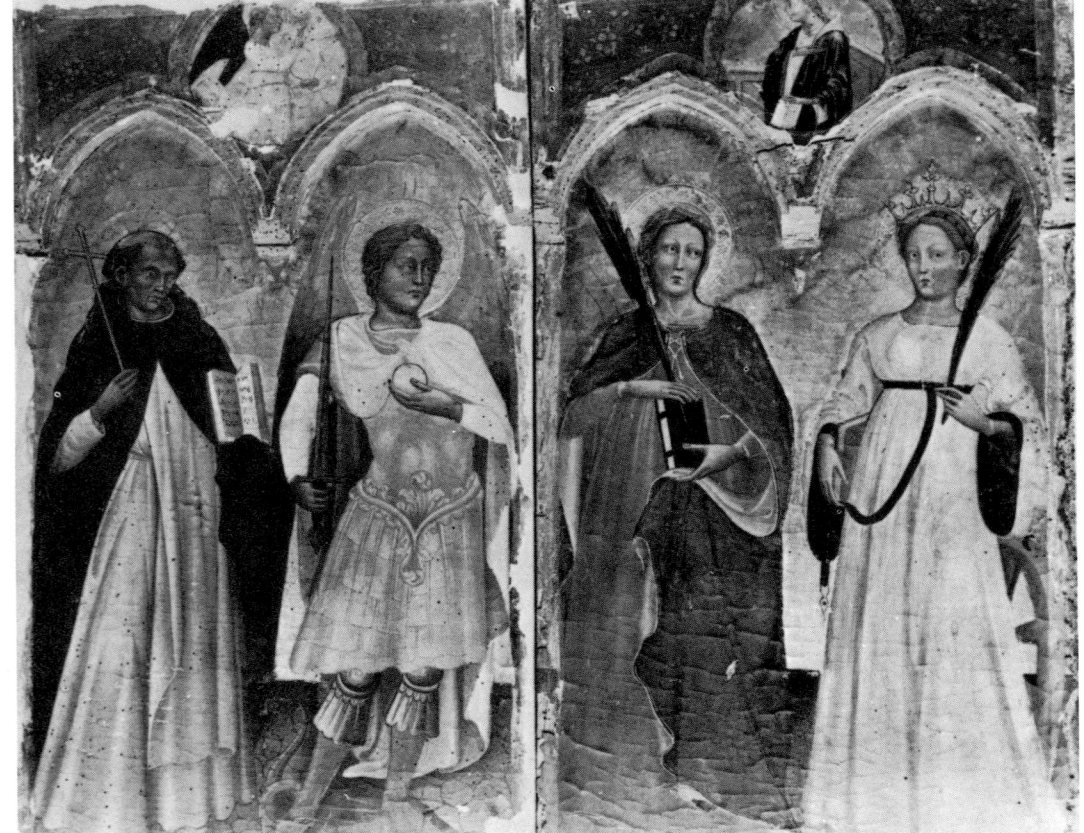

892

890. *Annunciation, Christ on the Cross, Saints. Panel. Montgomery (Ala.), Montgomery Museum of Fine Arts, Samuel H. Kress Collection. K. 1046. 70.8 × 44.4. Kress Foundation photo.*

891. *Christ on the Cross, with the Virgin, detail of fig. 886. Fresco. Figline, S. Francesco. Author's photo.*

892. *Sts Dominic, Michael, a female Saint and Catherine. Panel. Pisa, Museo Nazionale di S. Matteo. nos. 114, 115. 96 × 54 each. Museum photo 2639.*

432

ALVARO PORTOGHESE

Alvaro Pirez d'Evora di Portogallo, commonly known as Alvaro di Pietro, born 13- -, died 14- -. Painter, named by Vasari as a pupil of Taddeo Bartoli and as having painted several pictures at Volterra, one in S. Antonio of Pisa and others elsewhere, which did not demand any special mention. In 1411 Alvaro worked with Niccolò di Pietro Gerini and other Florentine painters on the façade of the Palazzo del Ceppo at Prato. He cannot have been, as has been stated, painter to the King, Dom Emanuel, who began to reign in 1495, but he may possibly have been in the service of an earlier Portuguese monarch.....

> from D. E. Colnaghi, p. 12, *A Dictionary of Florentine Painters*, London, 1928.

We know of several painters who.... visited Italy, where they left some of their works, sometimes even apparently settling in that country. The most important of these artists was Alvaro Pires de Evora, who is mentioned by Vasari and whose works are still to be seen in Pisa, Nicosia and Volterra.... Alvaro Pires actually belongs more to Italian than to Portuguese painting.....

> from C. de Azevedo, p. 930, *Journal of the Royal Society of Arts*, 5015, CV, 25 October, 1957.

Alvaro embodies the end of a stylistic epoch which is still full of mediaeval tradition. It's not surprising that his works reflect the various influences of Tuscan art; at Pisa, one of the principal centres of activity for the artist, the various currents which determined the style of Florence and Siena, came together. Alvaro was also conscious of contemporary style; and from this comes his gothic tendency; but by anything which indicated the future, he was untouched.....

> from K. Steinweg, pp. 39-55, *Rivista d'Arte*, XXXII, 1957.

Alvaro di Piero di Evora da Portogallo, also known as Alvaro Pirez, probably Portuguese in origin, is known to have been in 1411 in Prato, in 1423 in Volterra. His last dated work is the little triptych from 1434 in the Brunswick Museum.....

> from R. Oertel, p. 138, *Frühe Italienische Malerei in Altenburg*, Berlin, 1961.

Alvaro di Pietro, Alvaro Pirez d'Evora, active in the earliest decades of the fifteenth century, is documented in Prato with other Florentine artists in 1411. Formed his style under the influence of Lorenzo Monaco and the Sienese School.....

> from B. Berenson, p. 4, *Italian Pictures of the Renaissance, Florentine School*, Vol. I, London, 1963.

BIBLIOGRAPHY
BOOKS

An asterisk indicates a work listed in the General Bibliography

Venturi, A.*, 1911, pp. 29-30; Dos Santos, R., *Alvaro Pires d'Evora, pintor quatrocentista em Italia*, Lisbon, 1922; v. Marle, *1927**, p. 581-86; *Colnaghi**, 1928, p. 12; *Galetti**, "A-E", 1950, p. 46; *Oertel, 1950**, p. 25; Dos Santos, R., *L'Art Portugais*, Paris, 1953, p. 54; Shorr, D. C., *The Christ Child in Devotional Images in Italy during the XIV Century*, New York, 1954, pp. 26-7; Carli, E., *Pittura pisana del Trecento: la seconda metà del secolo*, Milan, 1961, p. 33; *Oertel, 1961**, pp. 138-40; *Cracow**, 1961, pp. 58-59; Bellosi, L., *La Pittura Tardogotica in Toscana* (I Maestri del Colore, 239), Milan, 1966; Castelfranchi-Vegas, L., *Il Gotico Internazionale in Italia*, Dresden-Rome, 1966, p. 169; *Bosquet**, 1968, p. 84.

JOURNALS

Battistini, M., *LA*, XXIV, 1921, pp. 124-5; " V. M. ", *A*, XXVIII, 1925, p. 79; Schiff, R., *Lusitania*, Oct., 1925; Salmi, M., *LC*, II, 1929, pp. 267-81; Piattoli, R., *RA*, XII, 1930, pp. 97-150; de Saralegin, L., *Archivio de Arte Valenciana*, 1935, pp. 3-68; de Saralegin, L., *Archivio de Arte Valenciana*, 1936, pp. 3-39; Procacci, U., *BA*, XXIX, 1936, III, p. 373; Brandi, C., *RAI*, 1940, p. 166; de Saralegin, L., *AEA*, 1944, pp. 104-23; Longhi, R., *PA*, I, 7, 1950, p. 47; Steinweg, K., *K*, VI, 1953, p. 328; Zeri, F., *PA*, 5, 59, 1954, pp. 44-7; de Azevedo, C., *Journal of the Royal Society of Arts*, CV, 5015, 1957, p. 930; Steinweg, K., *RA*, XXXII, 1957, pp. 39-55; Rozycka-Bryzek, A., *A*, LXI, 27/3-4, 1962, pp. 115-24; Zeri, F., *MKIF*, XVII, 2-3, 1973, pp. 361-370.

SIGNED AND DATED WORKS

Pisa, S. Croce a Fossabanda. Panel: Madonna & Child Enthroned with six Angels. s. (fig. 894).

Nicosia, Chiesa dei Francescani. Panel: Madonna & Child Enthroned with two Angels. s. (fig. 893).

1423 Volterra, Pinacoteca. Triptych: Madonna & Child Enthroned with Sts. Nicholas, John the Baptist, Christopher and Michael. s & d. (fig. 895).

1434 Brunswick, Herzog Anton Ulrich Museum. Portable triptych: Madonna Enthroned nursing the Child with Sts. John the Baptist and Anthony Abbot. s & d. (fig. 894).

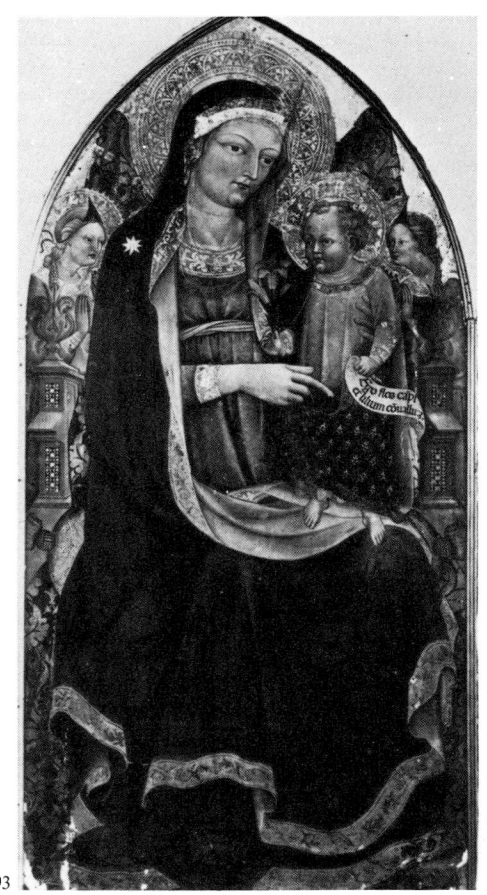

893

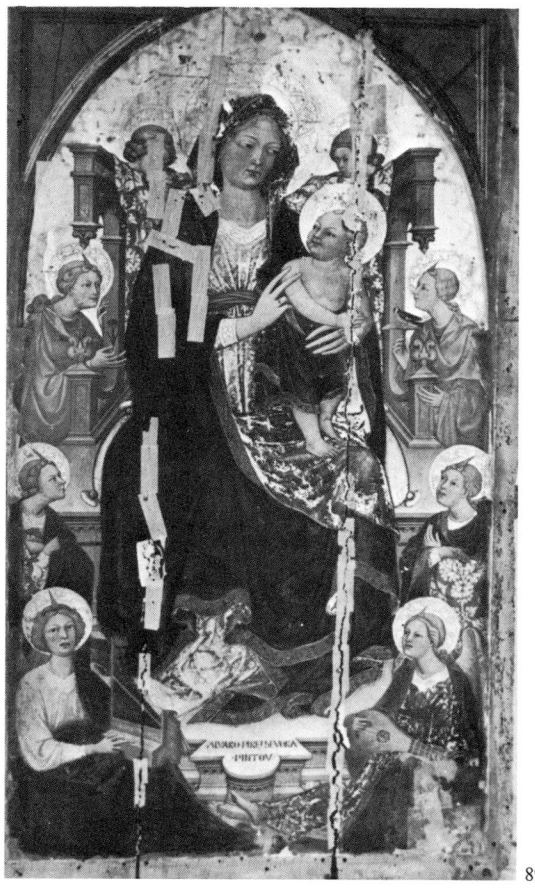

894

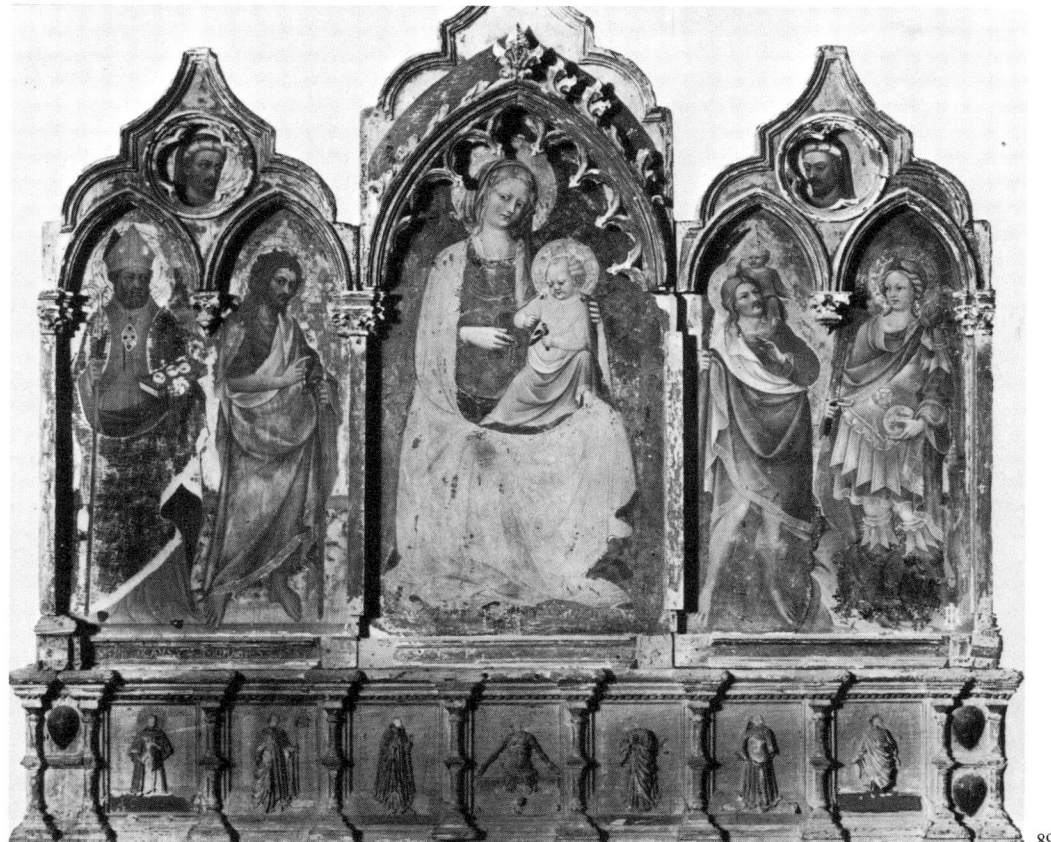

895

893. *Madonna and Child Enthroned with two Angels. Panel. Nicosia (12 kms south-east of Pisa), Chiesa dei Francescani. 150 × 73. SGPLLM 2641. s.*
894. *Madonna and Child Enthroned with six Angels. Panel. Pisa, S. Croce a Fossabanda. 220 × 140. SGPLLM 4716. s.*
895. *Triptych: Madonna and Child Enthroned with Sts Nicholas, John the Baptist, Christopher, and Michael. Above: heads of Sts Cosmas and Damian. Panel. Volterra, Pinacoteca. no 13. 235 × 245. Brogi 15325. s & d. 1423.*

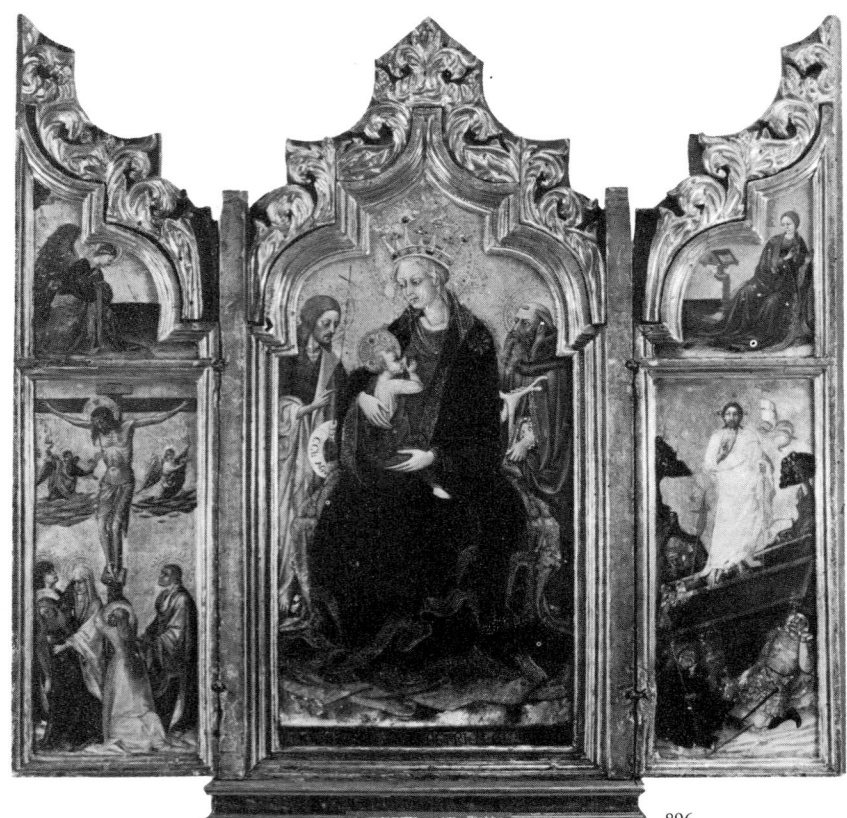

896

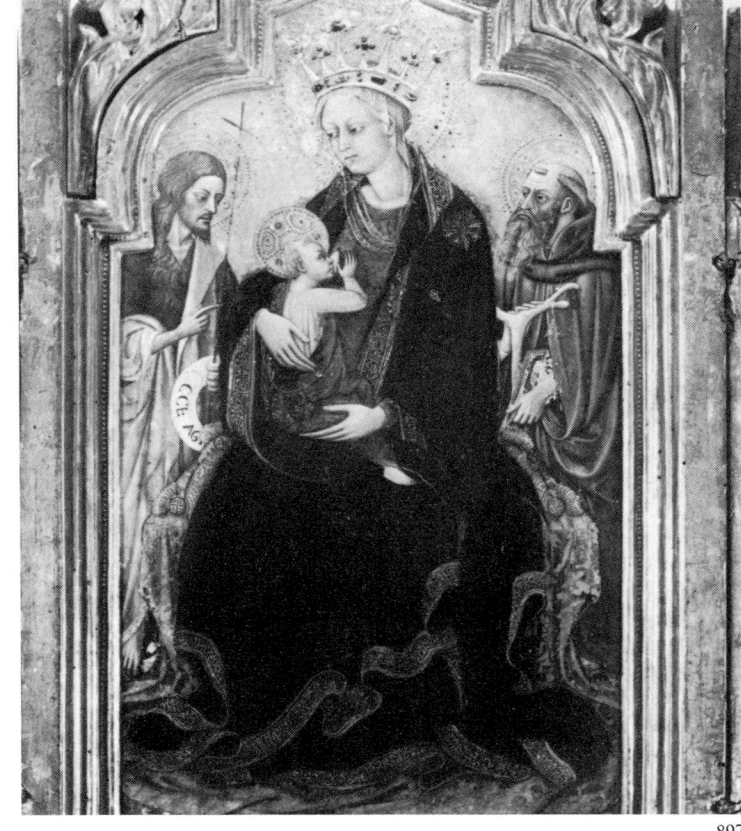

897

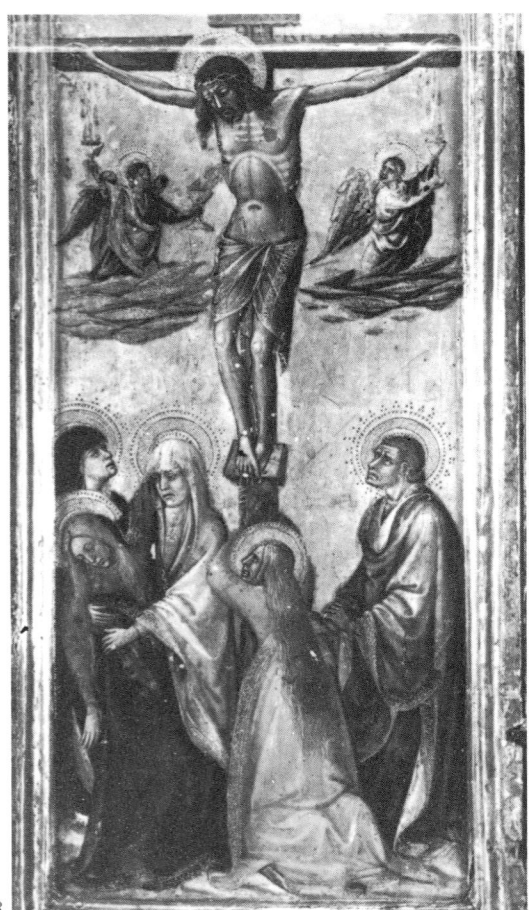

898

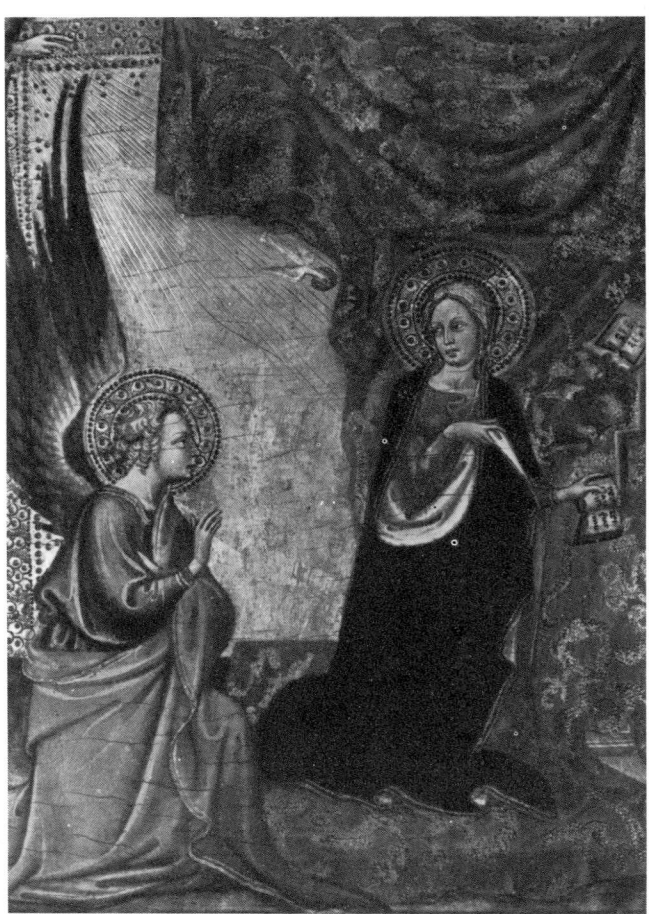

899

896. *Portable triptych: Madonna Enthroned nursing the Child with Sts John the Baptist and Anthony Abbot; Wings: Christ on the Cross with the Virgin, St John and the three Marys; Resurrection and Annunciation. Panel. Brunswick, Herzog Anton Ulrich Museum. cp: 74 × 44; sps: 73 × 22. Museum photo. s & d. 1434.*

897. *Madonna Enthroned nursing the Child with Sts John the Baptist and Anthony Abbot, detail of fig. 896. Panel. Brunswick, Herzog Anton Ulrich Museum. no. 6. Museum photo. s & d. 1434.*

898. *Christ on the Cross with the Virgin, St John, the three Marys and two Angels, detail of fig. 896. Panel. Brunswick, Herzog Anton Ulrich Museum. no. 6. Museum photo. s & d. 1434.*

436

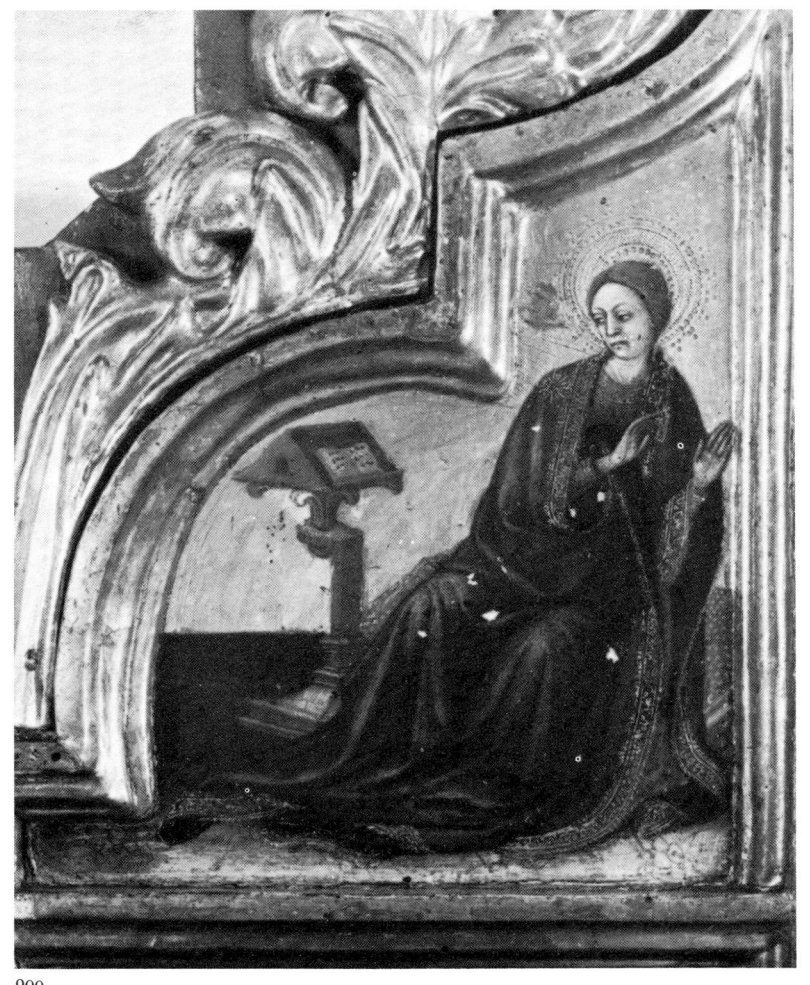

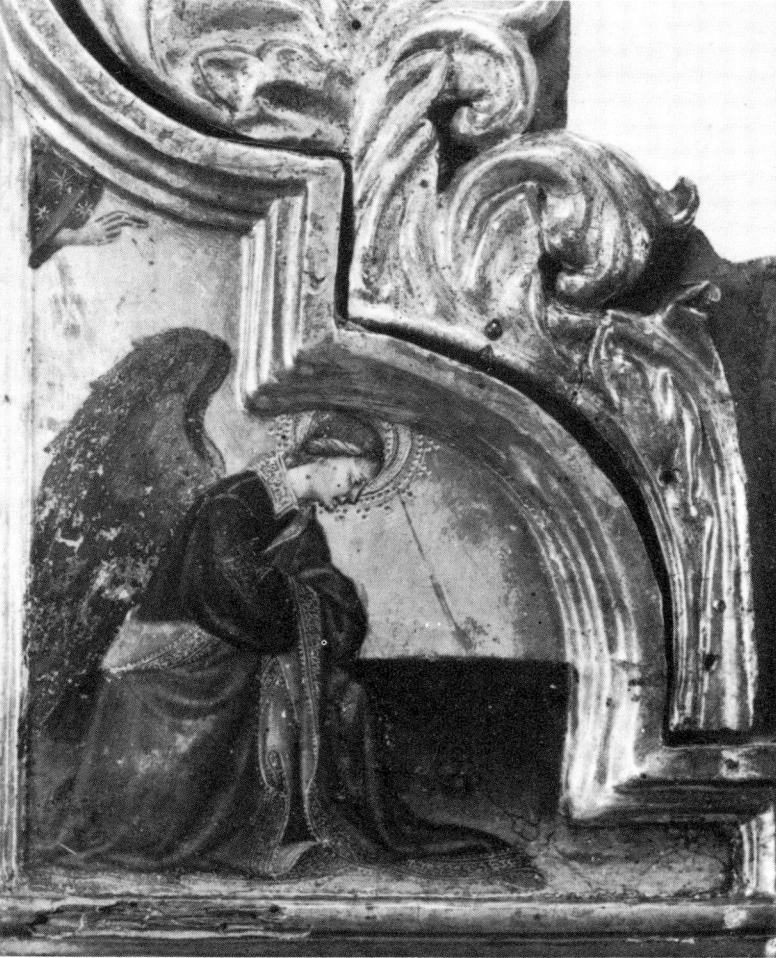

900

901

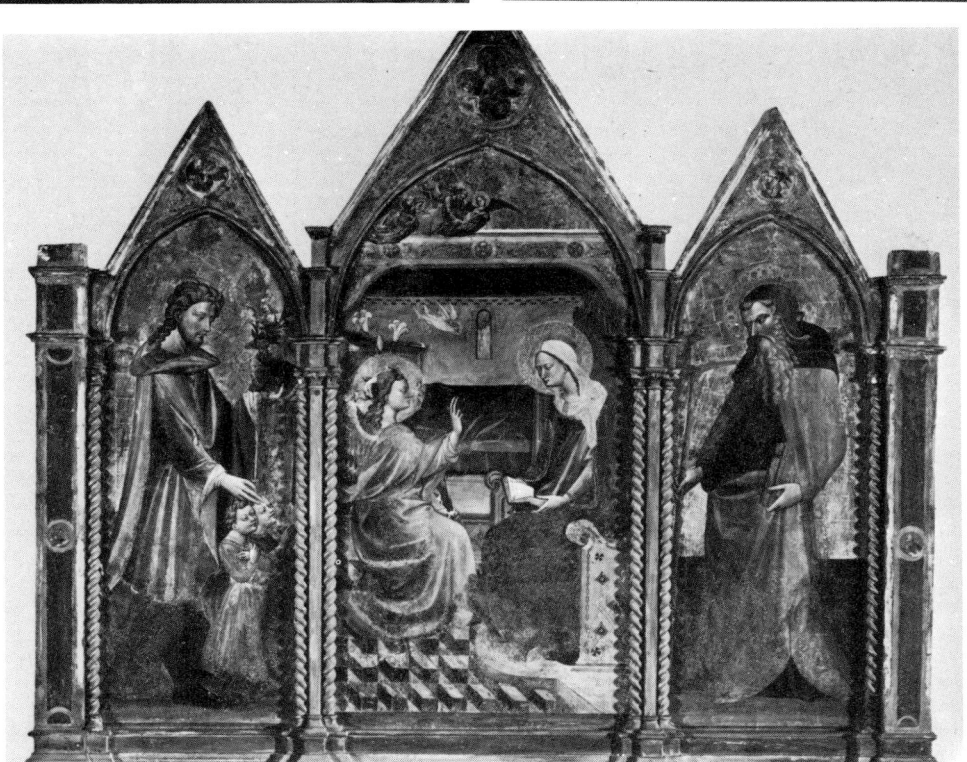

902

899. *Annunciation. Panel. Whereabouts unknown. A. C. Cooper 724427.*
900. *Announcing Angel, detail of fig. 896. Panel. Brunswick, Herzog Anton Ulrich Museum. no. 6. Museum photo. s & d. 1434.*
901. *Virgin Annunciate, detail of fig. 896. Panel. Brunswick, Herzog Anton Ulrich Museum. no. 6. Museum photo. s & d. 1434.*
902. *Triptych: Annunciation with Sts Eustace and Anthony Abbot. Above: Christ blessing and two Angels. Panel. Brozzi (5 kms west of Florence),*
    S. Andrea. cp: 158 × 85; sps: 145 × 58. Alinari 20322.

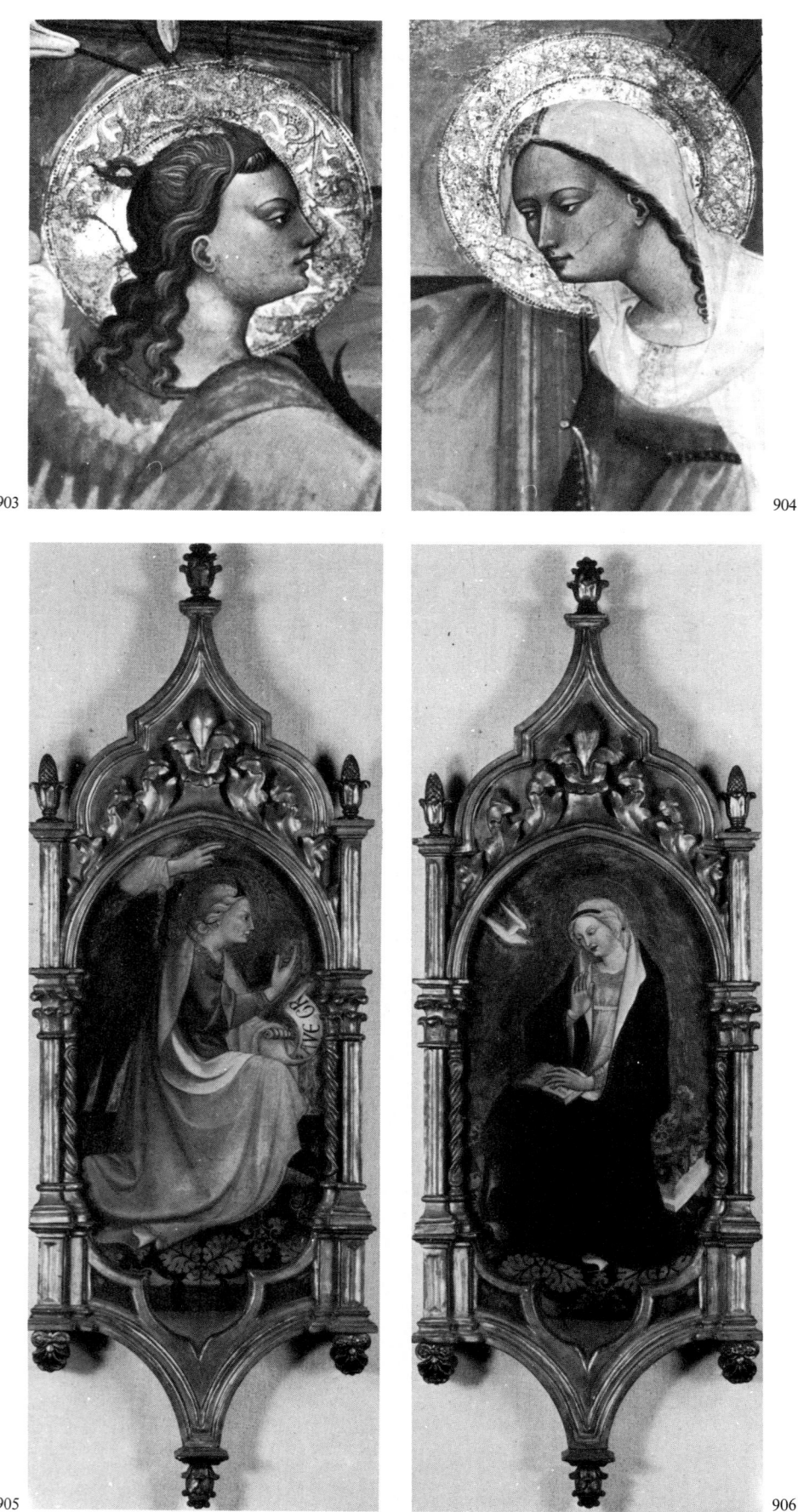

903. *Head of the Angel Gabriel, detail of fig. 902. Panel. Brozzi, S. Andrea. Author's photo.*
904. *The Virgin, detail of fig. 902. Panel. Brozzi, S. Andrea. Author's photo.*
905. *Announcing Angel. Panel. Sarasota (Fla.), Ringling Museum of Art. State no. 11. 127.6 × 47.6. Museum photo.*
906. *Virgin Annunciate. Panel. Sarasota (Fla.), Ringling Museum of Art. State no. 10. 127 × 47.2. Museum photo.*

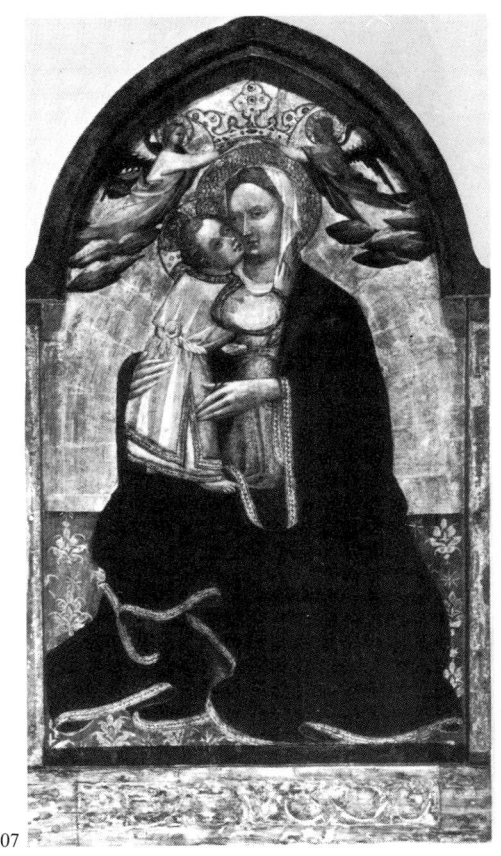

907

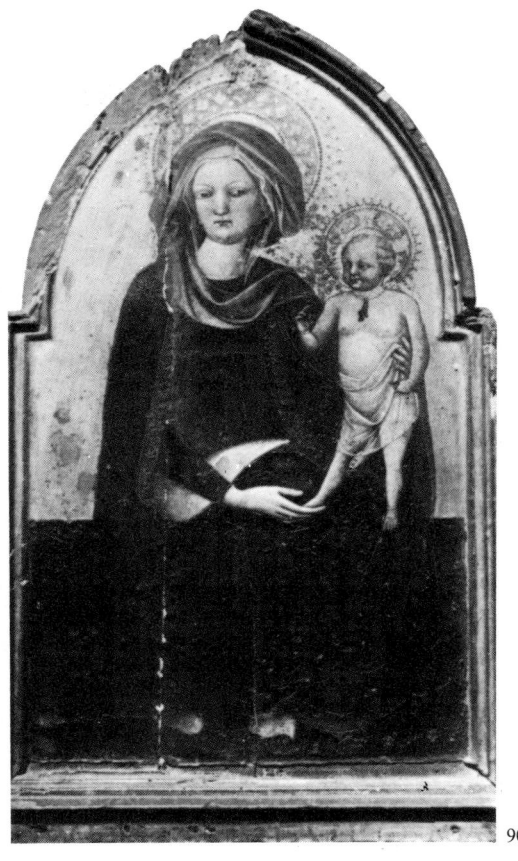

908

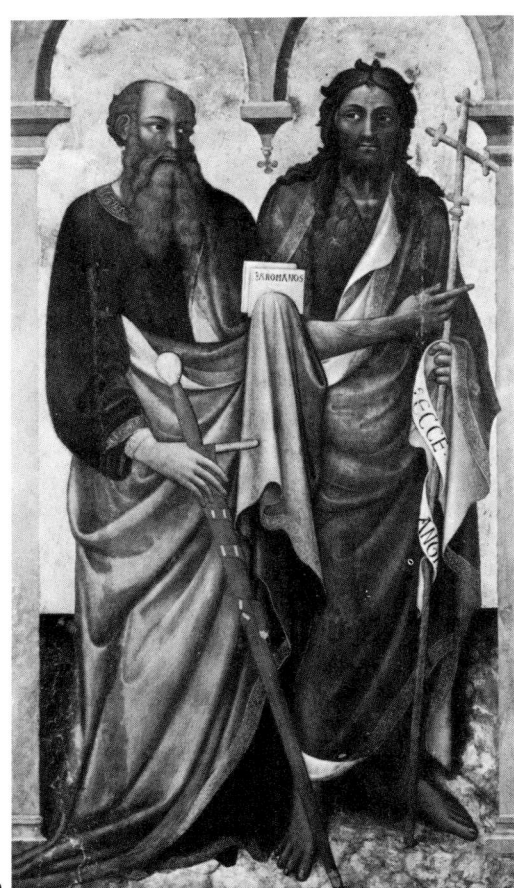

909

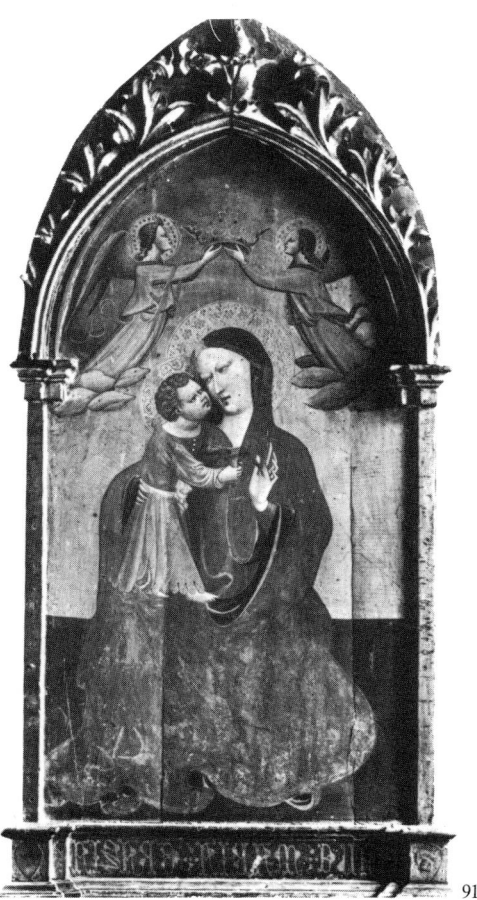

910

907. *Madonna of Humility with two Angels. Panel. Florence, S. Niccolò Oltrarno. SGF 155461.*
908. *Madonna and Child. Panel. Rome, Fabrizio Massimo Collection. Fototeca Berenson.*
909. *Sts Paul and John the Evangelist. Panel. Altenburg, Staatliches Lindenau Museum. no. 37. 145 × 82. Museum photo.*
910. *Madonna and Child crowned by two Angels. Panel. Whereabouts unknown. Brogi 17001/25.*

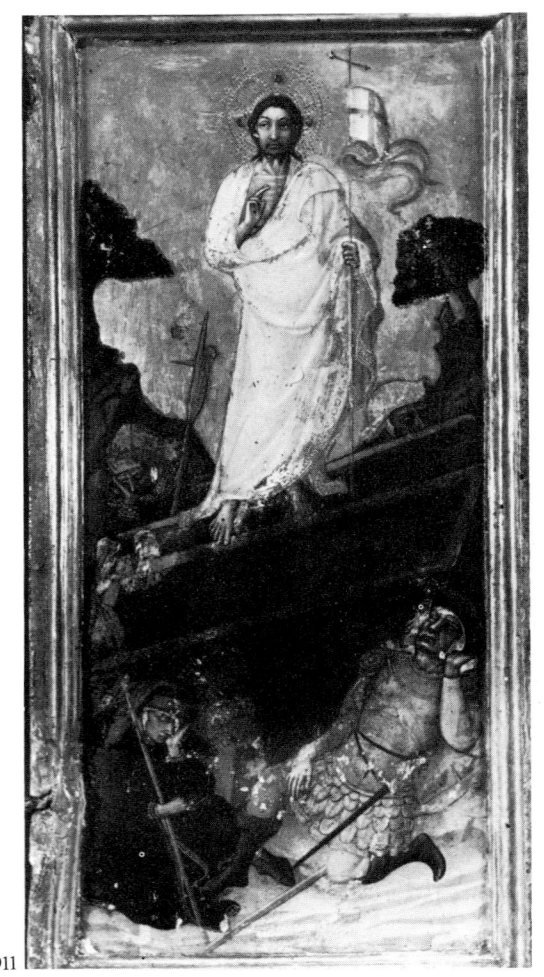

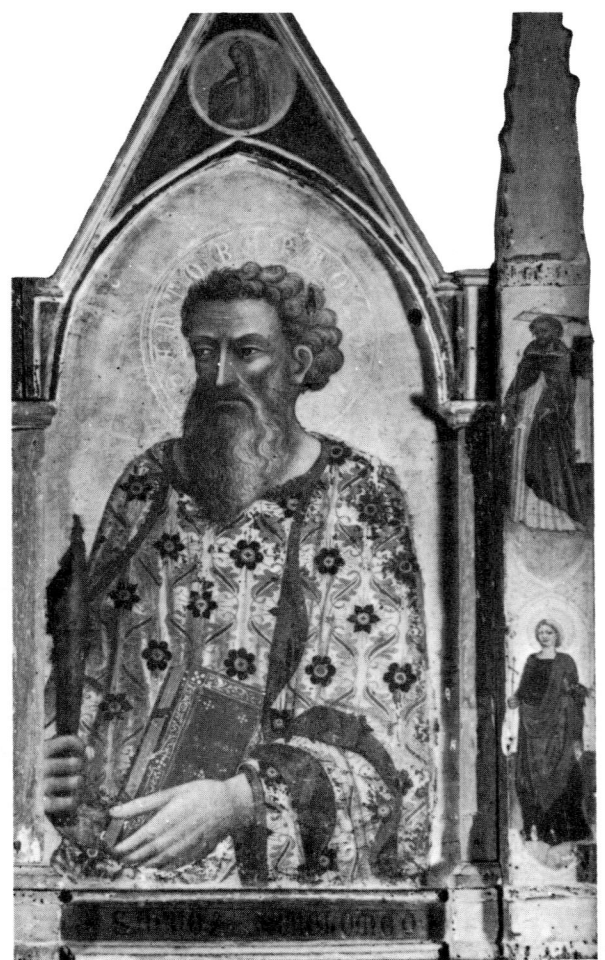

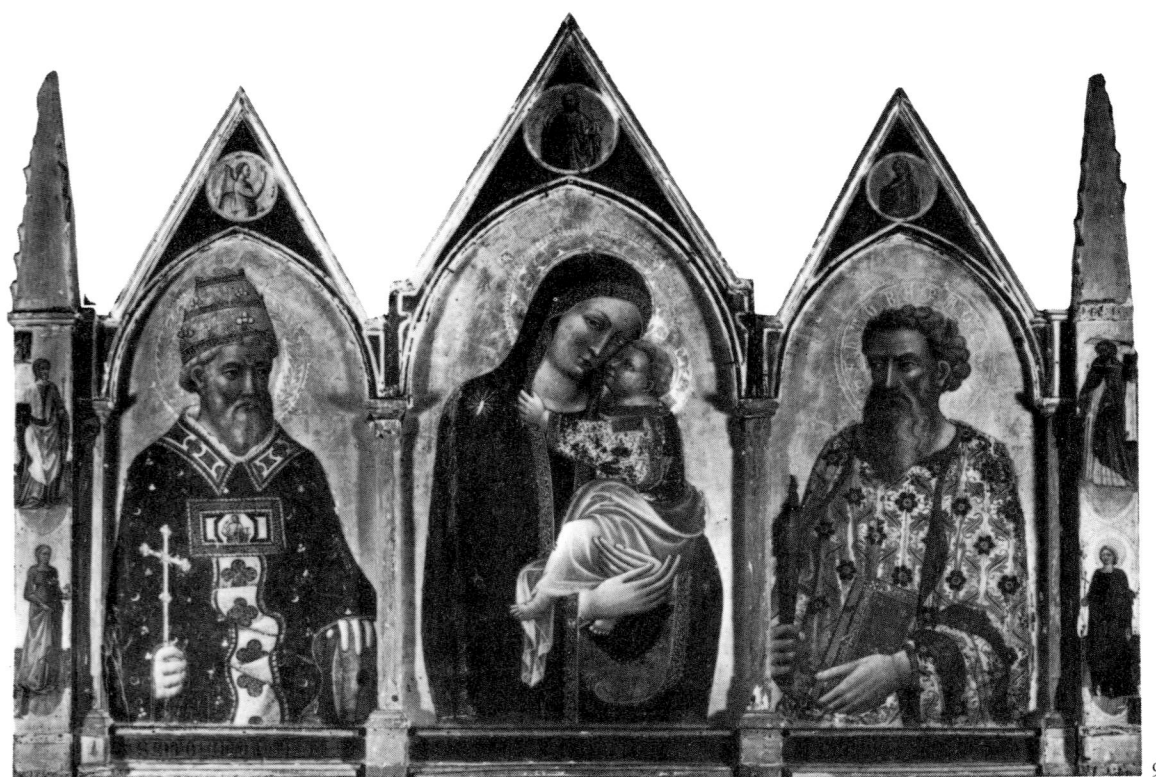

911. *Resurrection, detail of fig. 896. Panel. Brunswick, Herzog Anton Ulrich Museum. no. 6. Museum photo. s & d. 1434.*
912. *St Bartholomew, detail of fig. 913. Panel. Colle, Val d'Elsa, Museo Diocesano. Alinari (detail) 37341.*
913. *Triptych: Madonna and Child with Sts Clement and Bartholomew. Above: Christ blessing, Annunciation. Pilasters: four Saints. Panel. Colle, Val d'Elsa, Museo Diocesano. 126 × 180. Alinari 37341.*

440

MASTER OF THE BAMBINO VISPO

The Maestro del Bambino Vispo as an artistic personality is not difficult to realize. He was a painter who, at the beginning of his career was inspired by Florentine art of the 14th century, in particular by the manner of Agnolo Gaddi, but who at a later stage came under the influence of Lorenzo Monaco whose contemporary he must have been for a considerable number of years, but in all probability the " Maestro del Bambino Vispo " lived longer than Lorenzo; in any case certain elements in some of his pictures lead us to place them in the second quarter of the 15th century sooner than in the first..... Personally I am of the opinion that this master's manner is devoid of any features typical of Sienese Art.....

> from R. van Marle, pp. 200-3, *The Development of the Italian Schools of Painting*, Vol. IX, The Hague, 1927.

The " Master of the Bambino Vispo " was christened so by Dr Sirén. More than once this latter has given in to the temptations to identify the painter with one name or another, known by a signature or in documents; but since the author of this group of pictures could not have also executed those pictures which.can be attributed to Pietro di Domenico da Montepulciano, and even less those of Parri Spinelli, let us just leave him with the name " Master of the Bambino Vispo ".
He is so different, so gracious, so romantic, and sometimes he surprises us so unexpectedly that we are justified not only in our deep admiration, but also in trying to find his origins outside of Italy, in Bourgogne, in Westphalia, and perhaps less capriciously, in Valencia. I would not guarantee that he was a Tuscan, even though his activity in Tuscany is proven by the continued presence of polyptychs designed if not executed by him, in the churches for which they were painted, or near them, and by a fresco representing the *Resurrection of Lazarus* now in the Museum of Santa Croce, which was certainly done by him for that convent. He may have been a Spaniard, but certainly not identical to that other and closer follower of Lorenzo Monaco, whose best things are in the Museum at Valencia.

> from B. Berenson, pp. 177-80, *Dedalo*, XII, 1, 1932.

G. Pudelko has given us an elegant appreciation of this painter; it is a pity to see the writer somewhat unappreciated because of his abstract historical diversions such as the one where, by simple chronological precedence, he arrives at the point of assuming that the " cosmopolitan " style — to which this delicate and whimsical master belongs — was one of the preliminary conditions which enabled Masaccio to complete his revolution; or that the " cosmopolitan " style lived right through the whole Quattrocento, as he would have the works of Botticelli prove.....

> from R. Longhi, p. 183, *Critica d'Arte*, V, 1940.

An unknown painter who worked about 1422 in Florence, before which he was probably an active painter in Spain; he is named for the " lively " infant in his pictures of the Madonna; leader of the " gentle manner " among Tuscan painters.

> from R. Oertel, p. 136, *Frühe Italienische Malerei in Altenburg*, Berlin, 1961.

From that point to identifying Miguel Alcañiz with the Master of the Bambino Vispo was but a short distance; Gudiol refers to it indirectly in '55 in his ninth volume of *Ars Hispaniae* and in '65 Laclotte comes back to it again, in the catalogue of Spanish painting in France, shown at the Pavillon de Marson.....

> from R. Longhi, p. 39, *Paragone*, 181/1, 1965.

Florentine School. Active early fifteenth century. The name, meaning " Master of the Lively Child ", was coined to express this anonymous artist's treatment of the Christ Child in a number of paintings assigned to him. His style is closely related to that of Lorenzo Monaco. There is evidence that he worked not only in Florence but also in Spain: one of his paintings, which dates 1415, comes from Majorca, and there is a Spanish flavor in his style.....

from F. R. Shapley, p. 90, *Paintings from the Samuel H. Kress Collection*, London, 1966.

The discussion, summarized above, on the artist's identity and origin clearly demonstrates how difficult it is to situate his work in Florentine painting of the early fifteenth century. Yet, it cannot be denied that his art is strongly rooted in the Florentine Trecento tradition as far as iconography, composition and colour-scheme are concerned. This fact is only partly disguised by the long elegant folds of the International Style. Who, then was this artist, who took an active part in the development of Florentine painting and whose influence on his contemporaries has been established? Where did he come from and how are the non-Florentine features in his work to be explained?

I should like to venture the hypothesis that the author of the important and influential *oeuvre* attributed till now to the anonymous Maestro del Bambino Vispo was none other than Gherardo Starnina.....

from J. van Waadenoijen, p. 85, in *The Burlington Magazine*, CXVI, 851, 1974.

BIBLIOGRAPHY
BOOKS
An asterisk indicates a work listed in the General Bibliography

v. Marle, *1927**, pp. 200-3; *Toesca, 1929**, p. 68; *Antal**, 1948, pp. 333-4; *Galetti**, " F-O ", 1950, pp. 1450-2; *Oertel, 1950**, p. 49; Suida, W. E., *Catalogue of the William Rockhill Nelson Collection*, Kansas City, (Mo.), 1952, p. 26; *Paatz**, Vol. III, 1953, pp. 406-7; *Davies**, 1961, pp. 361-3; *Oertel, 1961**, pp. 136-7; *Berenson, 1963**, Vol. I, pp. 138-41; Oertel, R., pp. 205-20, in *Studien zur Toskanischen Kunst*, Munich, 1964; Bellosi, L., *La Pittura Tardogotica in Toscana* (I Maestri del Colore, 239), Milan, 1966; Castelfranchi-Vegas, L., *Il Gotico Internazionale in Italia* (I Maestri del Colore, 255), Milan, 1966; Castelfranchi-Vegas, *Il Gotico Internazionale in Italia*, Rome-Dresden, 1966, p. 169; *Shapley**, 1966, pp. 90-1; *Dutch Show**, 1974, pp. 42, 83-84.

JOURNALS

Sirèn, O., *A*, VII, 1904, pp. 349-52; Sirèn, O., *A*, VIII, 1905, p. 48; Sirèn, O., *BM*, 24, 1914, pp. 323-30; Sirèn, O., *BM*, 25, 1914, pp. 15-24; Henniker-Heaton, R., *AA*, XII, 1924, pp. 211-15; Sirèn, O., *BM*, XLIX, 1926, pp. 117-24; Berenson, B., *DD*, XII, 1, 1932, pp. 173-93; Colasanti, A., *BA*, XXVII, 1934, pp. 337-50; Pudelko, G., *AA*, XXVI, 2, 1938, pp. 47-63; Longhi, R., *CA*, V, 1940, pp. 145-91; Refice, C., *C*, II, 3-4, 1951, pp. 196-200; de Saralegni, L., *AE*, XXVI, 1953, pp. 237-42; Puppi, L., *E*, CXXXVII, 1963, pp. 243-253; Longhi, R., *PA*, XVI, 185/5, 1965, pp. 38-40; Bellosi, L., *PA*, 193/13, 1966, pp. 44-58; Bellosi, L., *PA*, XVII, 201, 1966, pp. 75-76; Guidi, F., *PA*, XIX, 223/43, 1968, pp. 27-46; Zeri, F., *GBA*, LXXI, 110, 1968, p. 89; Fahy, E., *BCMA*, 1969, pp. 205-20; Boskovits, M., *Ai*, III, 25/26, 1970, pp. 32-47; Gonzalez-Palacios, A., *AV*, X, 3, 1971, pp. 3-9; Volpe, C., *MKIF*, XVII, 2-3, 1973, pp. 347-360; Zeri, F., *MKIF*, XVII, 2-3, 1973, pp. 370; van Waadenoijen, J., *BM*, CXVI, 1974, pp. 82-91.

DATED WORK

1423 Borgo alla Collina (Casentino), S. Donato. Triptych: Mystical Marriage of St. Catherine, with Sts Francis, Tobias and Angel, Michael and Louis of Toulouse. d. (figs. 922-3). (*If the supposition that the Master of the Bambino Vispo is, in fact Starnina, is correct, then this work must be by a follower*).

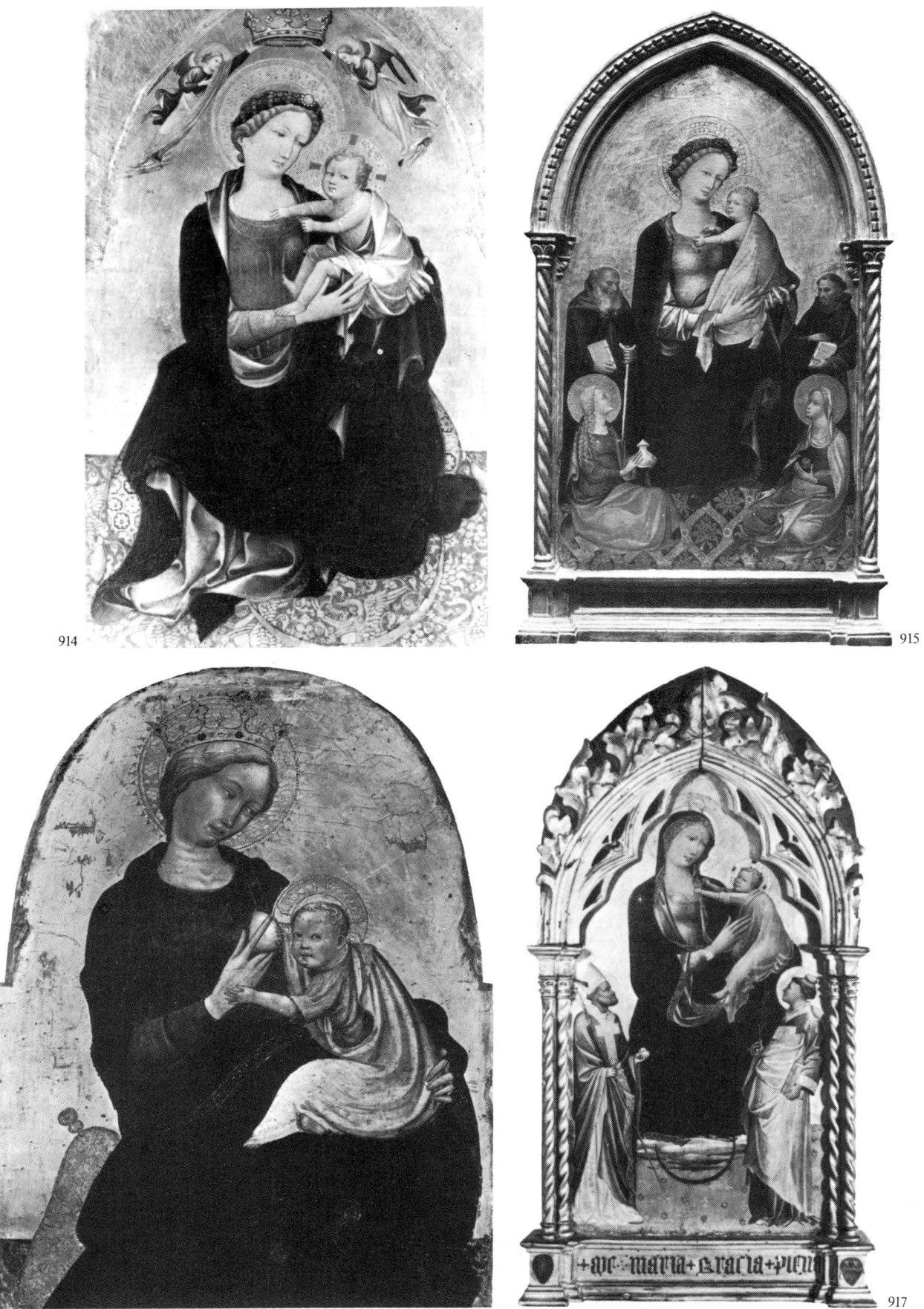

914. *Madonna of Humility crowned by two Angels. Panel. Oxford, Christ Church Library. no. 20. 82.2 × 50.4. Collection photo.*

915. *Madonna and Child with Sts Anthony Abbot, Francis, Mary Magdalene, and Lucy. Panel. Lugano-Castagnola, Galerie Thyssen. no. 251. 109 × 55. Gallery photo: Brunel.*

916. *Madonna of Humility. Panel. Private Collection. Perotti 20194.*

917. *Madonna and Child in Glory with Sts Nicholas of Bari and Stephen. Panel. Lucerne, Kofler-Truniger Collection. 96 × 50.5. Collection photo.*

443

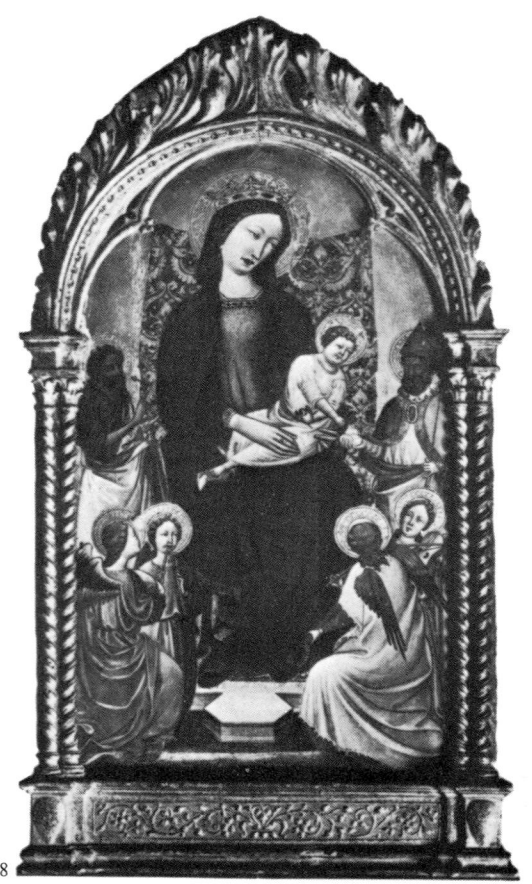
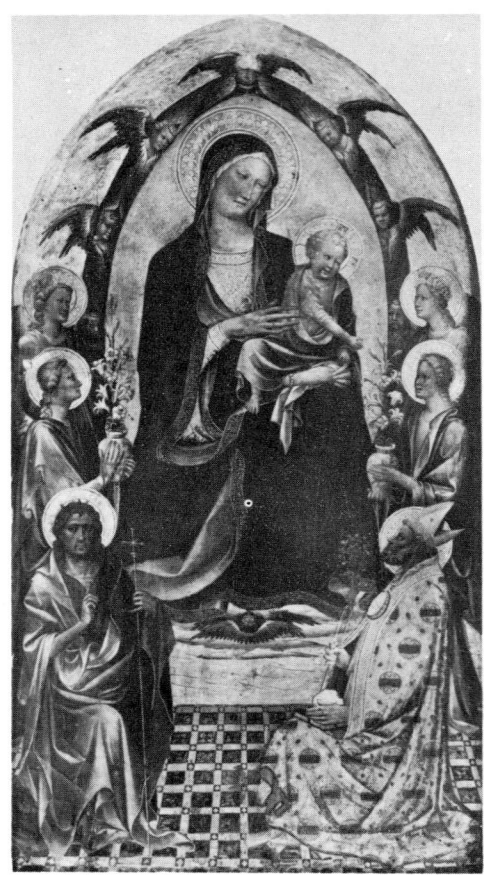
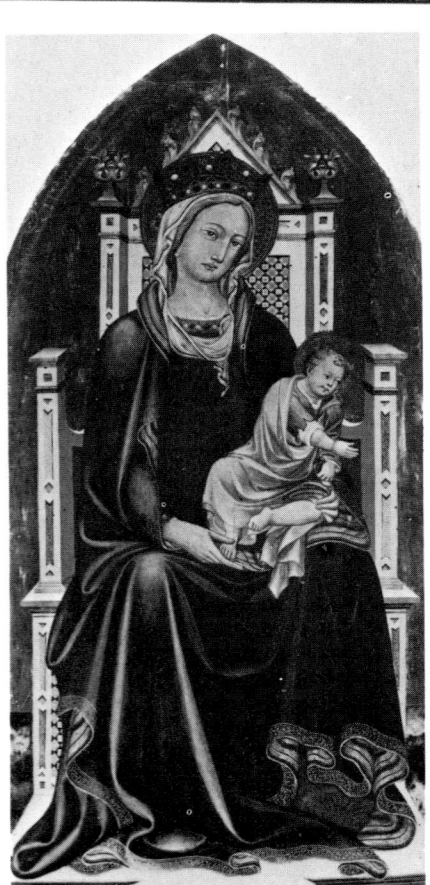
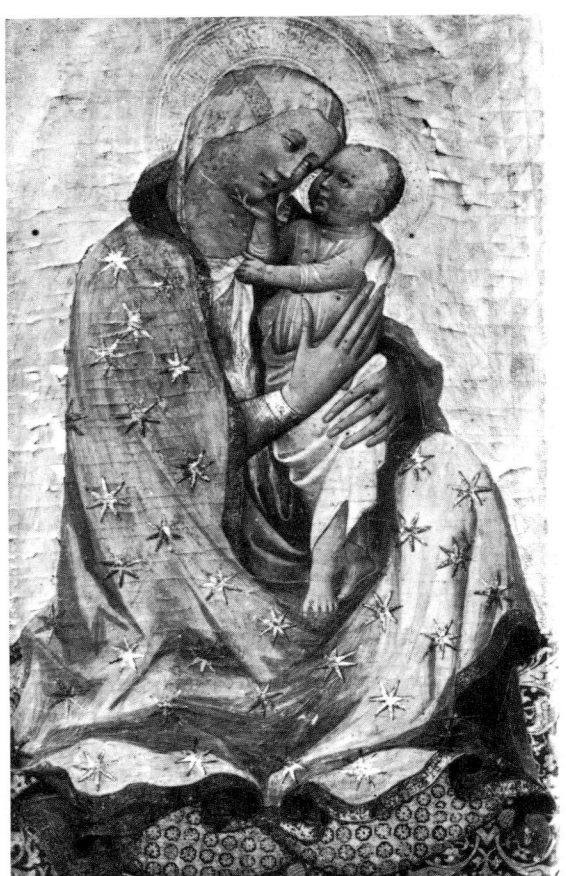

918

919

920

921

918. *Madonna and Child Enthroned with Sts John the Baptist and Nicholas, and four music-making Angels. Panel. Whereabouts unknown. Bertoni-Berenson.*
919. *Madonna and Child in Glory with four Angels and Sts John the Baptist and Nicholas. Panel. Florence, Accademia, no. 441. 98 × 52. Alinari 989.*
920. *Madonna and Child Enthroned. Panel. Greenville (S.C.), Bob Jones University. no. 8. 118.1 × 54.6. Collection photo: Unusual Films.*
921. *Madonna of Humility. Panel. Florence, Depositi Gallerie Fiorentine. Accademia 6270. SGF 72197.*

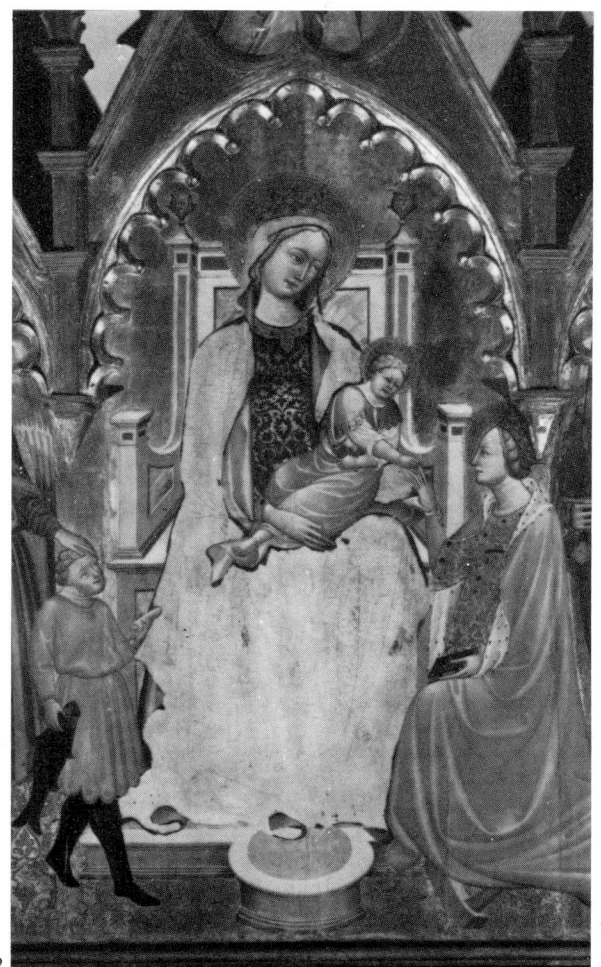

922

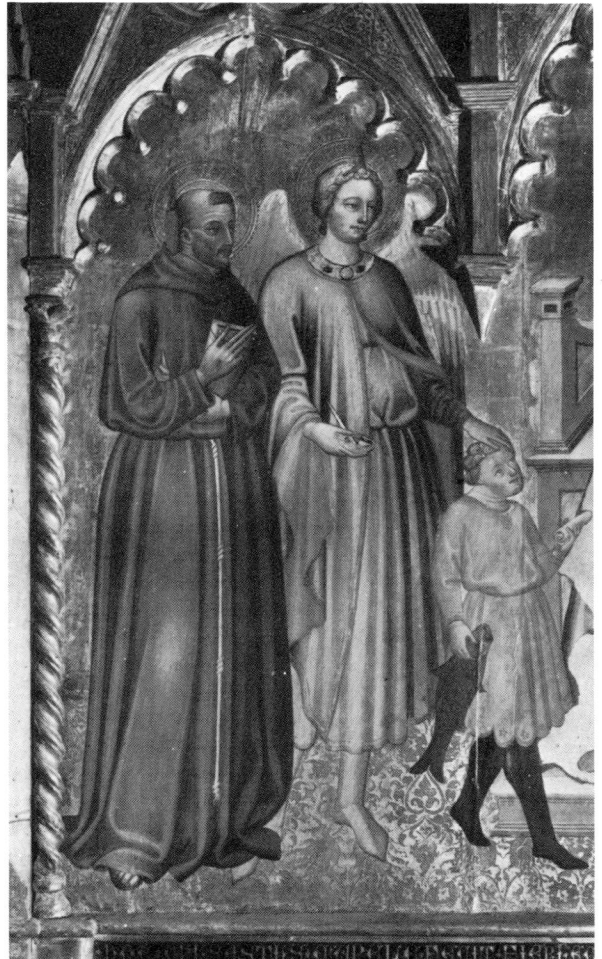

923

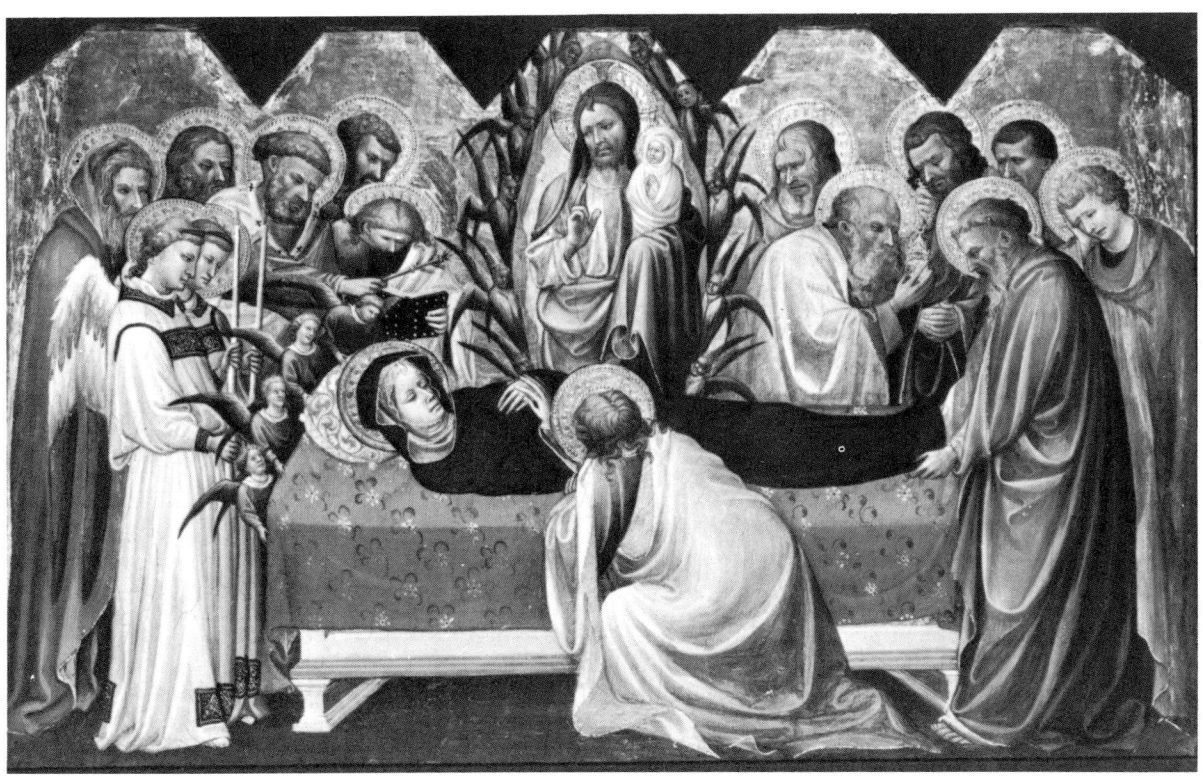

924

922. Detail: *Mystical Marriage of St Catherine with Sts Francis, Tobias and the Angel, and Sts Michael and Louis of Toulouse. Panel. Borgo alla Collina (Casentino), S. Donato. 190 × 173. SGF 172698. d. 1423.*
923. Detail: *Sts Francis and Tobias and the Angel. Panel. Borgo alla Collina, S. Donato. SGF 172697. d. 1423.*
924. Predella *scene: Dormition of the Virgin. Panel. Chicago (Ill.), Art Institute, Ryerson Collection. no. 33.1017. 41.6 × 65.1. Museum photo, negative C28215.*

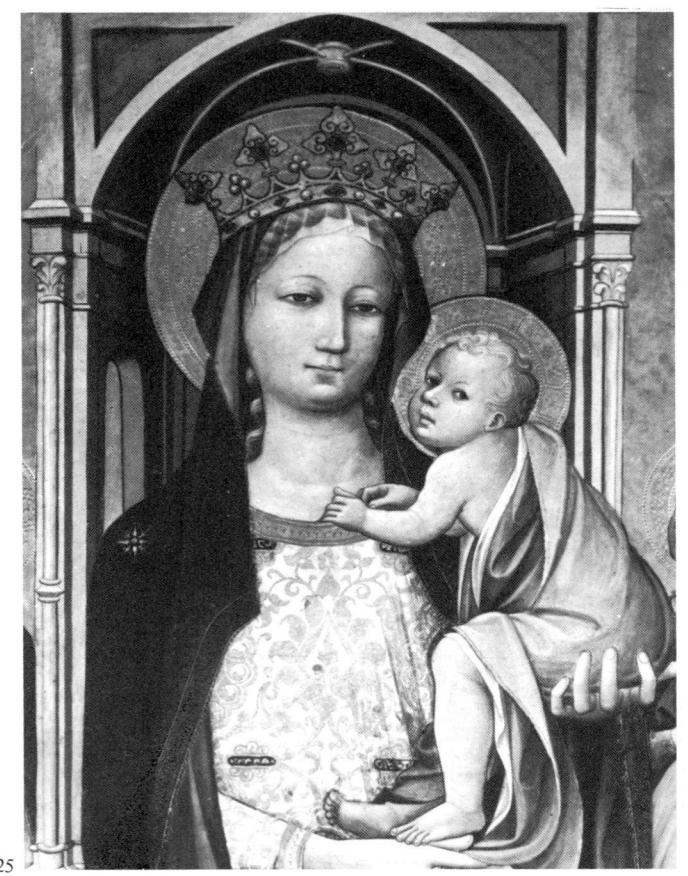

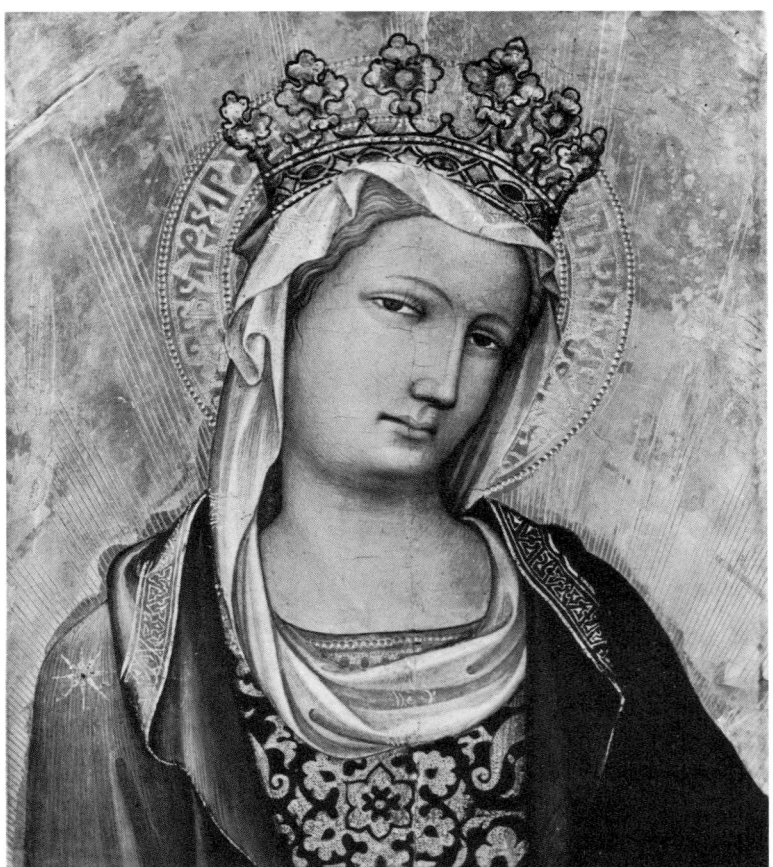

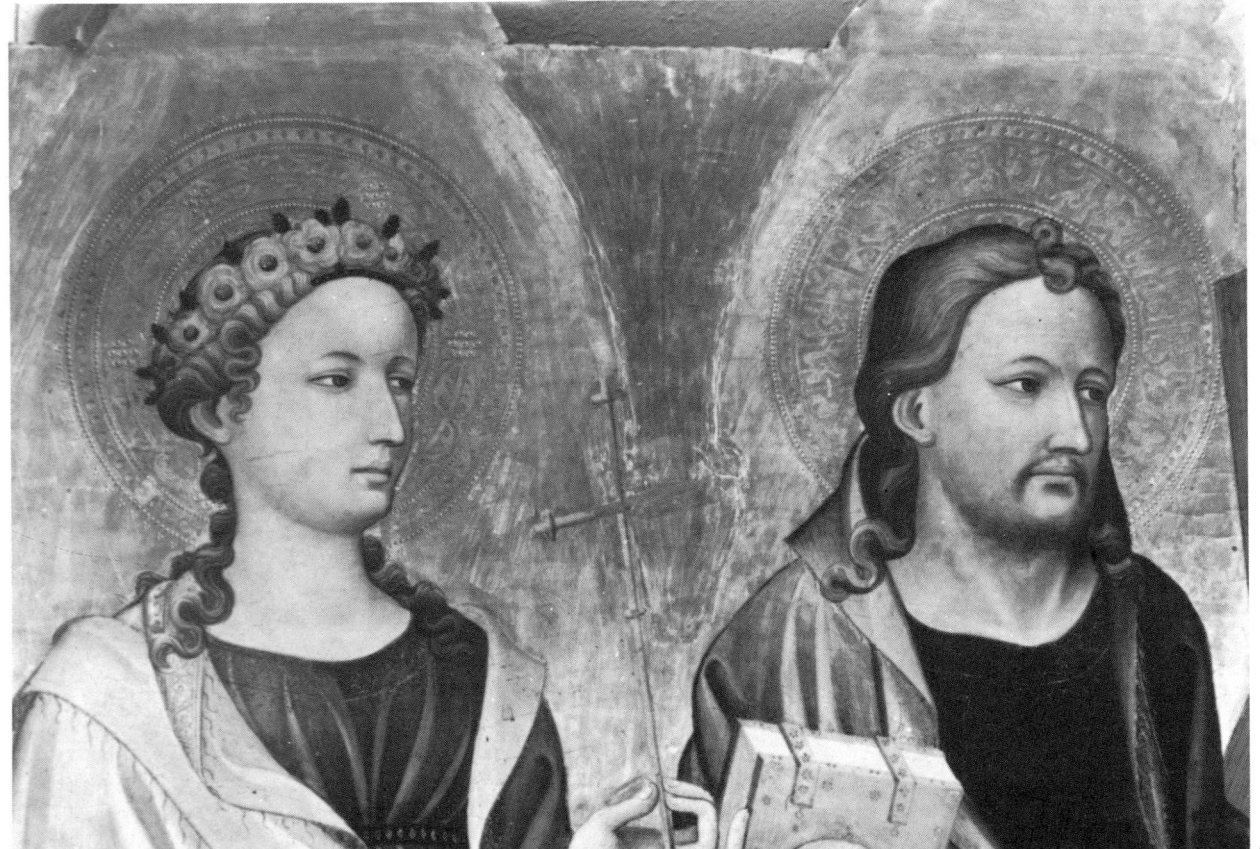

925. *Madonna and Child, detail of a triptych. Panel. Würzburg, Martin von Wagner Museum. no. 89. Museum photo: Gundermann 14705.*
926. *Head of the Virgin. Panel. Dresden, Staatliche Kunstsammlungen. no. 30. 35 × 29. Museum photo, negative C780.*
927. *Heads of Sts Margaret and Andrew, detail of a triptych. Panel. Würzburg, Martin von Wagner Museum. no. 89. Museum photo: Gundermann 14707.*

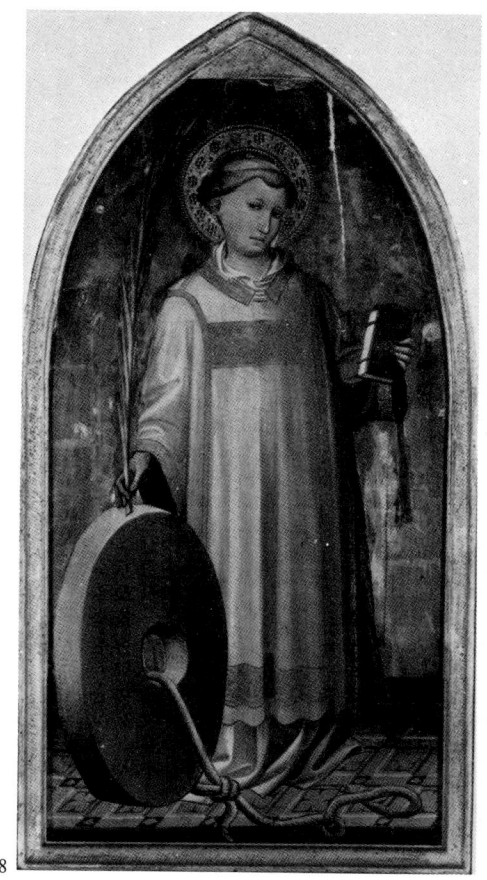

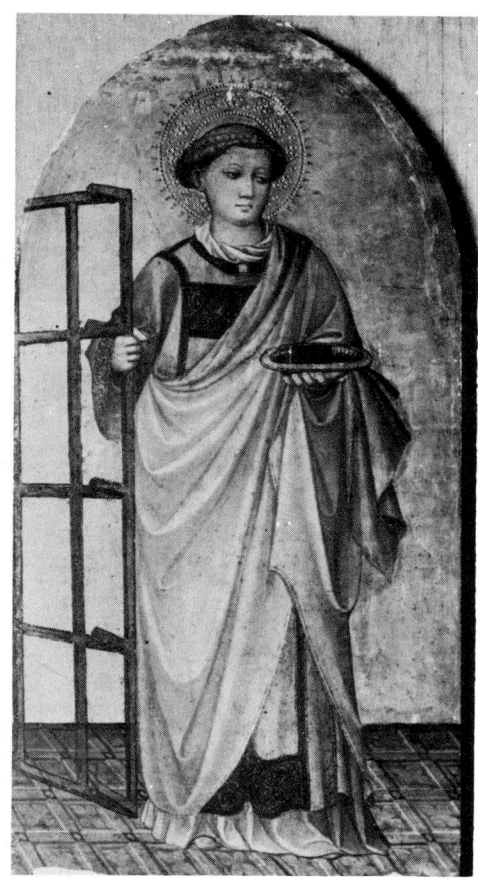

928

929

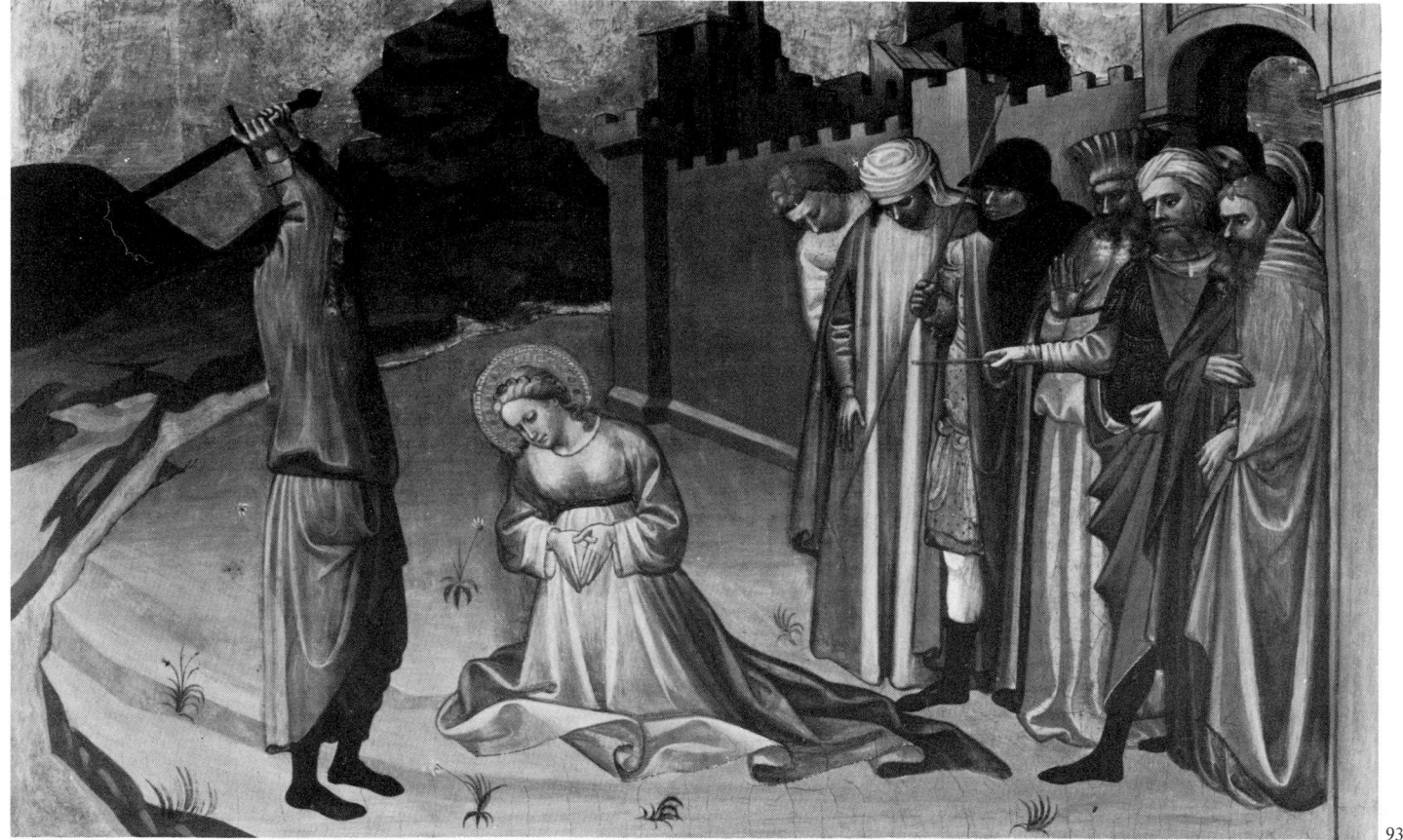

930

928. *St Vincent. Panel. Boston (Mass.), Museum of Fine Arts. no. 20.1855a. 68 × 34. Museum photo, negative C6057.*
929. *St Lawrence. Panel. Assisi, Convento di S. Francesco. no. 8. 65.5 × 33.5. Collection photo.*
930. *Predella scene: Martyrdom of St Catherine. Panel. London, National Gallery. no. 3926. 40.6 × 62.8. Museum photo.*

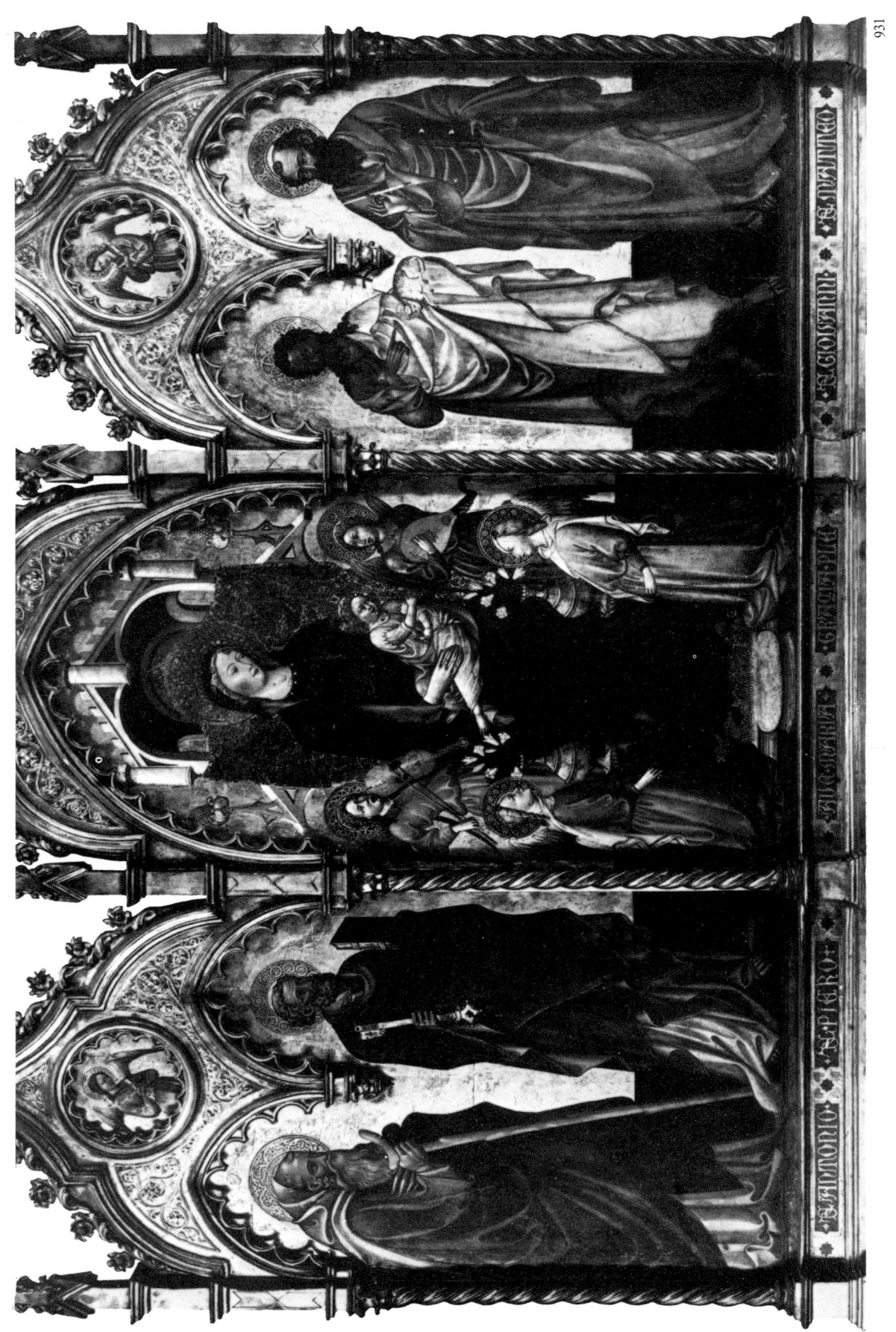

931. *Triptych: Madonna and Child Enthroned with four Angels and Sts Anthony Abbot, Peter, John the Baptist, Matthew. Above: Annunciation. Panel. Rome, Galleria Doria Pamphilj. cp: 143 × 78; sps: 112 × 77. GFN 8858.*

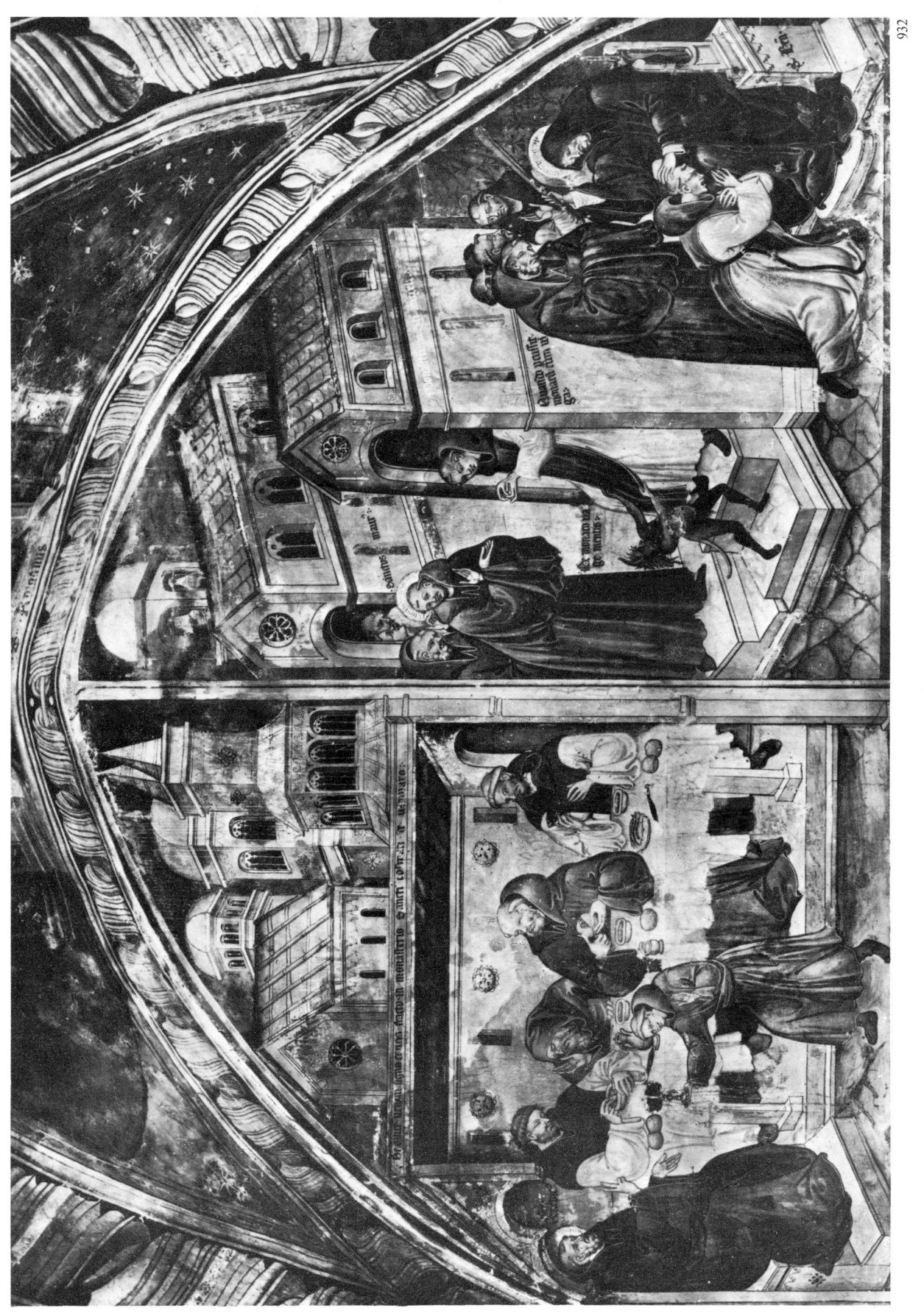

932

932. *Scenes from the Life of St Benedict: the Poisoned Cup breaks; St Benedict exorcises a Devil which had tempted a young Monk from prayer. Fresco.*
Subiaco, Lazio, Sacro Speco. Alinari 26234.

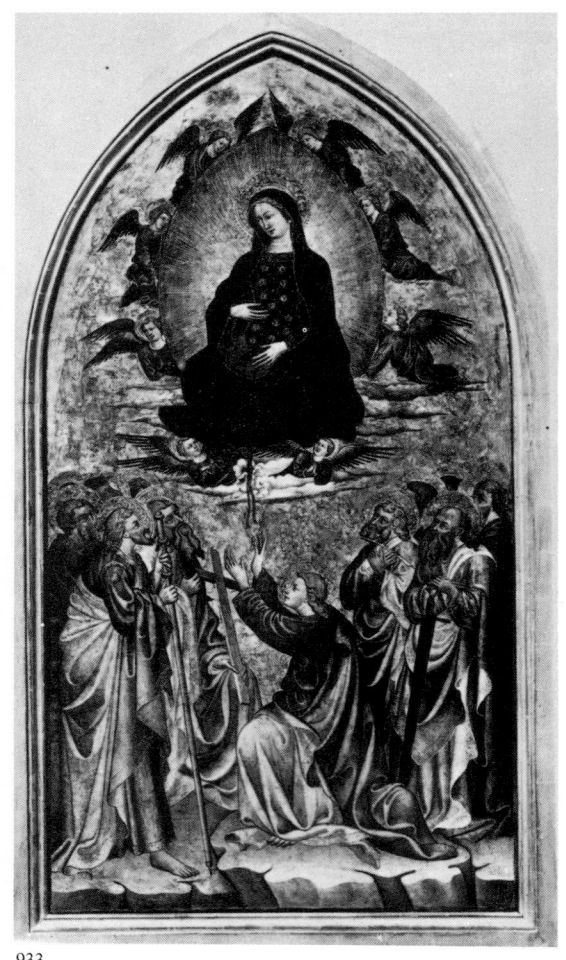

933

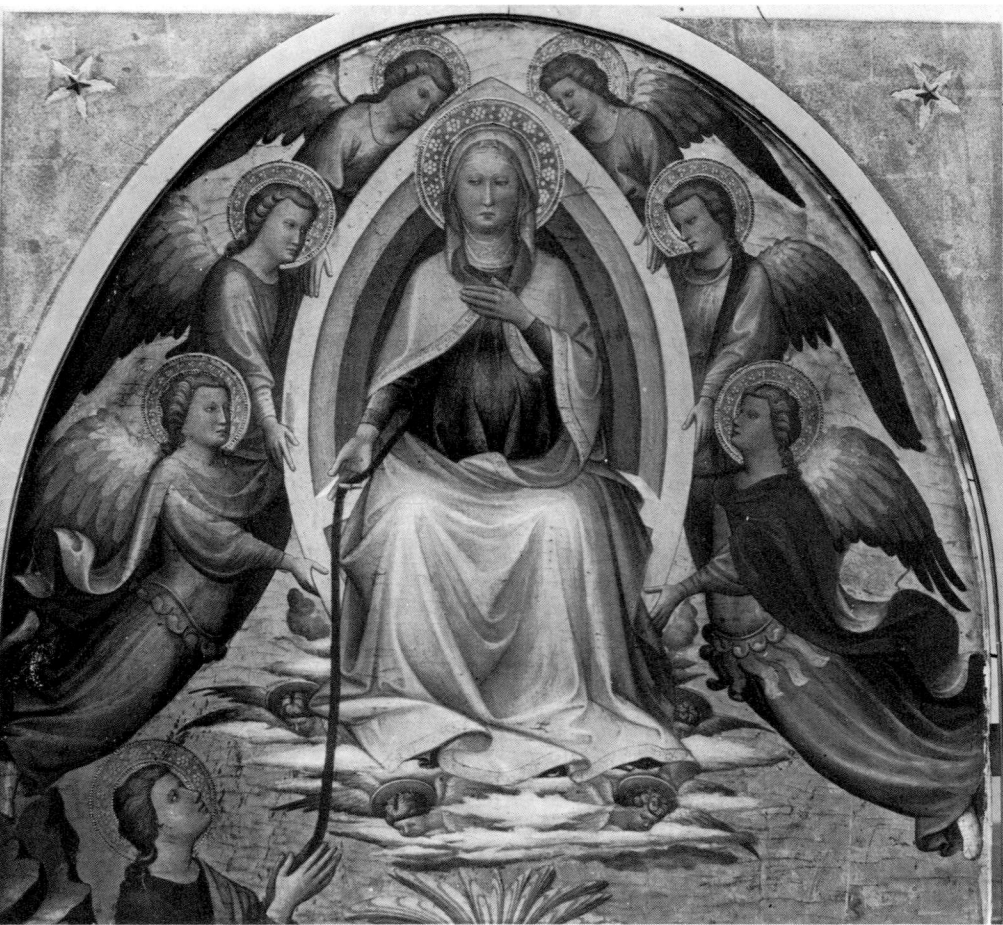

934

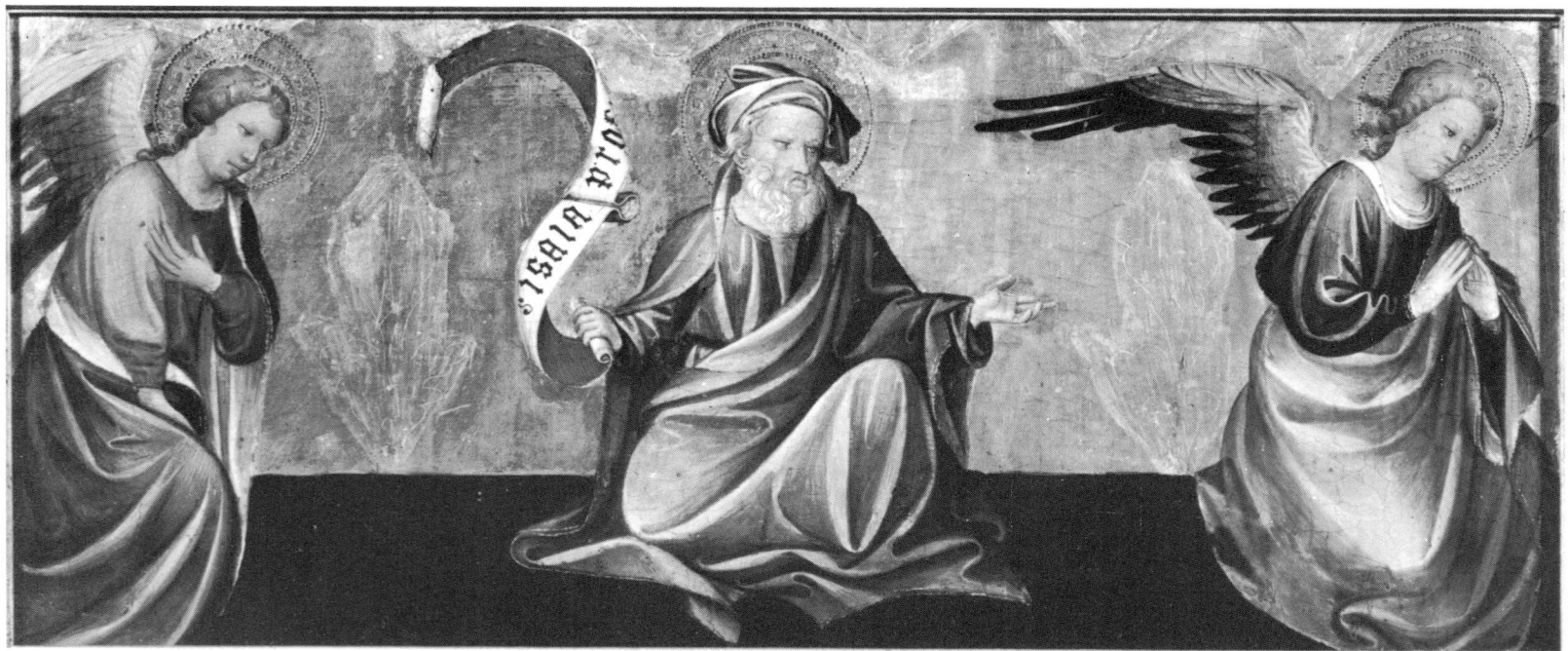

935

933. *Madonna of the Holy Girdle with St Thomas, Apostles and Angels. Panel. Stia (Casentino), Propositura di S. Maria Assunta. 155 × 80. SGF 22273.*
934. *Lunette: Madonna of the Holy Girdle with St Thomas and six Angels. Cambridge (Mass.), Fogg Art Museum. 1920.1. 77.5 × 82.5. Museum photo.*
935. *Predella scene: Isaiah with two Angels. Panel. Boston (Mass.), Museum of Fine Arts. no. 20.1856. 32 × 74. Museum photo, negative C6055.*

MARIOTTO di NARDO

With regard to Mariotto di Nardo we possess a large number of documents. He was the son of a stone-cutter called Nardo, who worked in Siena in 1380 and in Volterra in 1381, and in all likelihood had nothing to do with the di Cione family, although for very long it was thought that he was the son of Nardo di Cione. Vasari informs us that he was the grand-son of Andrea Orcagna. The earliest records of his activities are in documents of 1394 and 1395 when he executed the extant altar-piece for the church of S. Donnino in Villamagna... We find that during this year, 1404, he signed one of the figures of the stained-glass window in S. Domenico, Perugia, as follows: " hoc opus Marioctus Nardi de Florentia pinsit MCCCCIV....etc. etc. ". This signature is inscribed on the hem of the robe of St. Catherine but in all probability he designed a large part of the window; however, the signature of Fra Bartolommeo di Pietro, accompanied by the date 1411, which fills up the lower part of the window, is much more important. It would be useless to attempt to make any hypotheses on the question of this collaboration, because the entire window is so much restored that we can learn nothing from it regarding the art of these two masters.... In 1424, the master being seriously ill, makes his will, after which there is no further documentary evidence concerning him.....

> from R. van Marle, pp. 206-209, *The Development of the Italian Schools of Painting*, Vol. IX, The Hague, 1927.

Mariotto di Nardo (or Lionardo) di Cione. Florentine, born 13- -, died 1424. Painter, member of the Physicians and Apothecaries Guild between 1386-1408. Member of the Company of Saint Luke 1408. In 1398 Mariotto painted an altar-piece for the chapel of the Madonna della Neve in the Duomo of Florence, by commission of the Board of Works. The picture was commenced in 1397, in which year he received 15 florins in part payment of a panel he is executing for the " opera " of Sta. Reparata for the altar of the new chapel of the Virgin Mary.... The last work entrusted to Mariotto of which there is any record was a panel which, on March 2, 1415/16, the Captains of the Company of Sta. Maria del Bigallo commissioned him to paint for the altar of their Oratory.....

> from D. E. Colnaghi, p. 172, *A Dictionary of Florentine Painters*, London, 1928.

In the artistic circle of Spinello Aretino, one of the most able Tuscan painters of the second half of the '300; he participated actively in a precise artistic direction which originated in Florence. Its aim was essentially an archaistic " romantic " recovery of the great Giottesque culture, in reaction to the sterile graphic amusements of Agnolo Gaddi. From his early works, such as the large polyptych in the church of S. Donnino at Villamagna (1394-1395), which is his first known undertaking, to the large polyptych in the Serristori house in Florence, dated 1424 (the year of his death), Mariotto preferred to arrange his short, broad and powerful figures, who move their heavy burdens with the finest possible grace in a large spatial scheme. In the first decade of the century, however, he lightens the weight of his figures through more supple and elegant use of the line and through very fine chromatic delineations. In these new elements one finds a reflexion of the parallel (but much more important) artistic development of Lorenzo Monaco.....

> from P. Dal Poggetto, p. 36, *Arte in Valdelsa*, Certaldo, 1963.

Recorded 1394-1431. Close follower of Jacopo di Cione; influenced by Niccolò di Pietro Gerini, and later by Lorenzo Monaco.

> from B. Berenson, p. 129, *Italian Pictures of the Renaissance, Florentine School*, Vol. I, London, 1963.

Florentine School. Active from 1394; died probably 1424. Much of his work adheres to the fourteenth-century tradition, especially in the manner of Niccolò di Pietro Gerini, with close relationship also to Spinello Aretino. His later style was somewhat influenced by Lorenzo Monaco.....

from F. R. Shapley, p. 46, *Paintings from the Samuel H. Kress Collection*, London, 1966.

BIBLIOGRAPHY
BOOKS

An asterisk indicates a work listed in the General Bibliography

v. Marle, 1927*, pp. 206-9; Colnaghi*, 1928, p. 172; *Catalogo della Mostra del tesoro di Firenze sacra*, Florence, 1933, p. 116; Antal*, 1948, pp. 329-30; Galetti*, " F-O ", 1950, pp. 1570-1; Gregori*, 1960, p. 8; Cracow*, 1961, pp. 47-48; MASA*, 1961, p. 14; Oertel, 1961*, pp. 132-4; Dal Poggetto, P., AIV*, 1963, p. 36; Berenson, 1963*, Vol. I, pp. 129-133; Shapley*, 1966, p. 46; Algranti, G., *Antologia di dipinti di cinque secoli*, Milan, 1971; Fredericksen, B. B., *Catalogue of the J. Paul Getty Museum*, Malibu (Calif.), 1972, pp. 7-8; Palumbo, G., *Collezione Federico Mason Perkins*, Rome, 1973, pp. 33, 67; Dutch Show*, 1974, pp. 42, 79-81; Maetzke*, 1974, pp. 74-75.

JOURNALS

Sirèn, O., A, XI, 1908, pp. 179-96; Salmi, M., A, XVI, 1913, pp. 208-27; Piattoli, R., RA, XI, 1929, pp. 221-253, 396-437, 537-79; Piattoli, R., RA, XII,1930, pp. 97-150; Berenson, B., DD, XI, 5, 1930-1, pp. 1286-1318; Offner, R., BM, LXIII, 1933, p. 169; Procacci, U., RA, XV, 1933, pp. 224-44; Pouncey, P., BM, LXXXVIII, 1946, pp. 71-3; Eisenberg, M. J., PR, VIII, 1949, pp. 6-14; Cohn, W., RA, XXXI, 6, 1951, p. 68; Eisenberg, M. J., *Oberlin College Bulletin*, IX, 1, 1951, pp. 9-16; Moriondo, M., BA, XXXVII, 4, 1952, p. 351; Salmi, M., RA, XXX, 1955, pp. 147-52; Cohn, W., RA, XXXI, 1956, p. 68; Eisenberg, M. J., PR, XVIII, 2, 1959, pp. 61-4; Rozycka-Bryzek, A., A, LXI, 27/3-4, 1962, pp. 115-24; Zeri, F., JWG, XXVII-XXVIII, 1964-65, pp. 74-9; Spychalfka-Boczkowska, A., BMNV, IX, 2, 1968, pp. 29-36; Bury, A., CS, CLX, 1965, p. 255; Bellosi, I., PA, XVII, 201, 1966, p. 74; Simson, O. V., JBM, VIII, 1966, pp. 119-59; Eisenberg, M. J., MIAB, 55, 1966, pp. 9-24; Edit., BM, CIX, supp. I, 1967; Boskovits, M., AV, VII, 5, 1968, pp. 3-13; Boskovits, M., AV, VII, 6, 1968, pp. 21-31; Boskovits, M., MKIF, XIII, 1-4, 1967-68; p. 56; Zeri, F., GBA, LXXI, 110, 1968, p. 69; Fehm, S., MKIF, XVII, 2-3, 1973, p. 258; Procacci, U., MKIF, XVII, 2-3, 1973, p. 320.

DATED WORKS

1398 Fiesole, Oratorio di Fontelucente. Triptych: Madonna of the Holy Girdle with Saints and Angels. d. (fig. 955).
1400 Pesaro, Museo Civico. Triptych: Madonna & Child Enthroned with Angels and Saints. d. (fig. 942).
1404 Assisi, Convento di S. Francesco. Panel: Madonna and Child Enthroned with two Donors. d. (fig. 945).
1406 Florence, S. Trinita, High Altar. Triptych: Trinity, Sts Anthony Abbot, Michael, Francis & Julian. d. (fig. 952).
1408 Minneapolis (Minn.). Institute of Art. Panels: Coronation of the Virgin; Sts Bartholomew and Anthony (from ex-Hatton Garden Altarpiece, London). d. (fig. 957) (see also Grand Rapids [Mich.] 51.1.4).
1418 Florence, Accademia 473. Panel: Madonna & Child Enthroned with Sts. Philip and John the Baptist. d. (fig. 947).
1418 Florence, Academia 3460. Panel: Madonna in Glory with Sts. Stephen and Reparata. d. (fig. 944).
1418 Impruneta, Collegiata. Panel: Trinity with two Donors. d. (fig. 950).
1421 Panzano, Pieve di S. Leolino. Triptych: Madonna & Child Enthroned with Angels and Saints. d. (fig. 941).
1422 Florence, Acton Collection. Panel: Madonna of Humility. d. (fig. 946).
1424 Florence, Serristori Collection. Triptych: Madonna and Child with Angels and Saints. d. (fig. 938).
1431 Florence, Acton Collection. Panel: Coronation of the Virgin. d. (fig. 956).

There are no known signed works by Mariotto di Nardo.

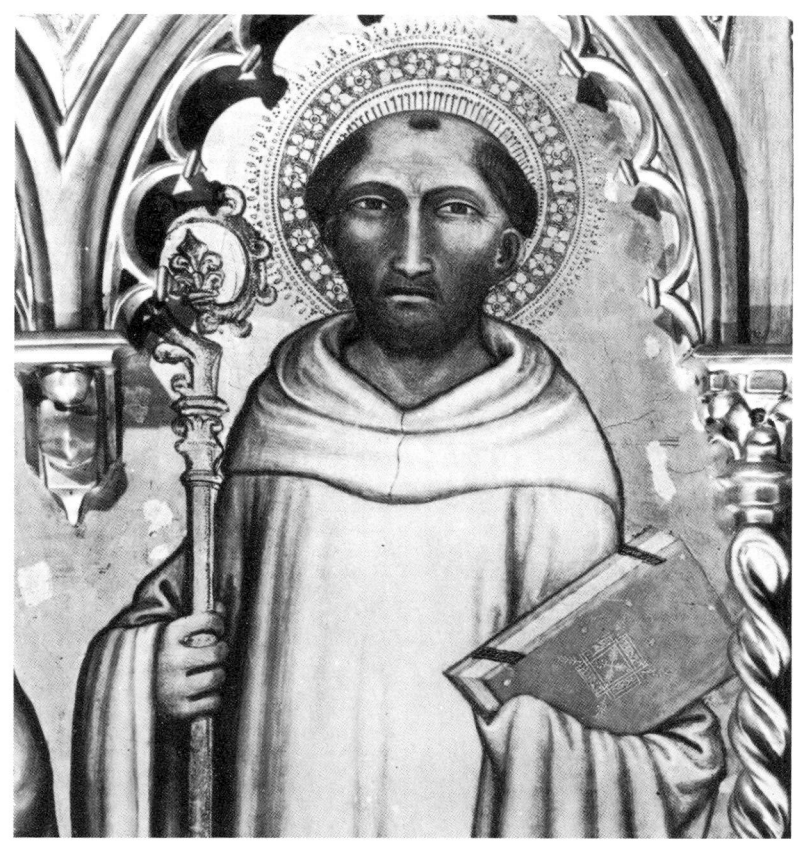

936

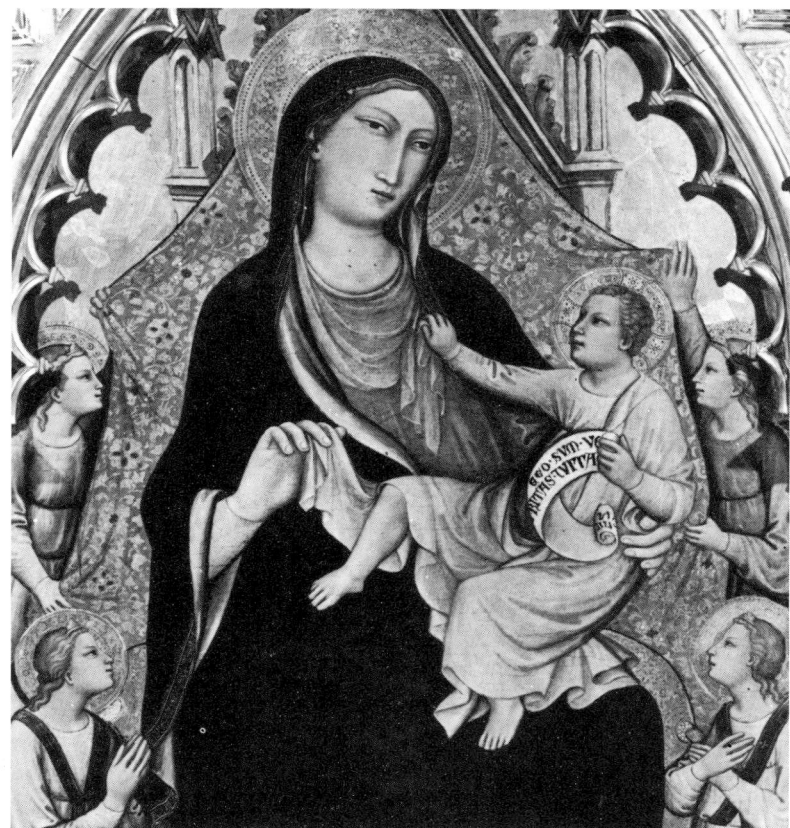

937

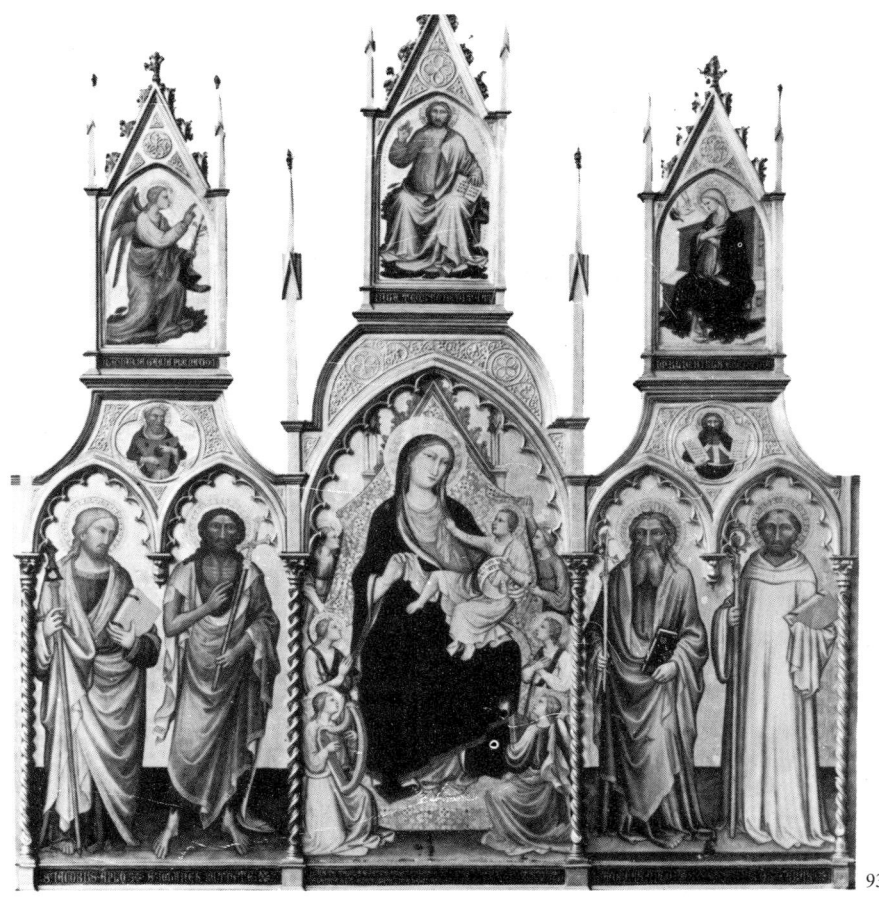

938

936. *St Bernard, detail of fig. 938. Panel. Florence, Serristori Collection. Bertoni. d. 1424.*
937. *Madonna and Child with Angels., detail of fig. 938. Panel. Florence, Serristori Collection. Bertoni. d. 1424.*
938. *Triptych: Madonna and Child with six Angels and Sts James, John the Baptist, Andrew and Bernard. Above: Christ blessing, Annunciation, two Prophets. Panel. Florence, Serristori Collection. Whole: 278 × 254. cp: 145 × 79; sps (each): 116 × 74. Bertoni. d. 1424.*

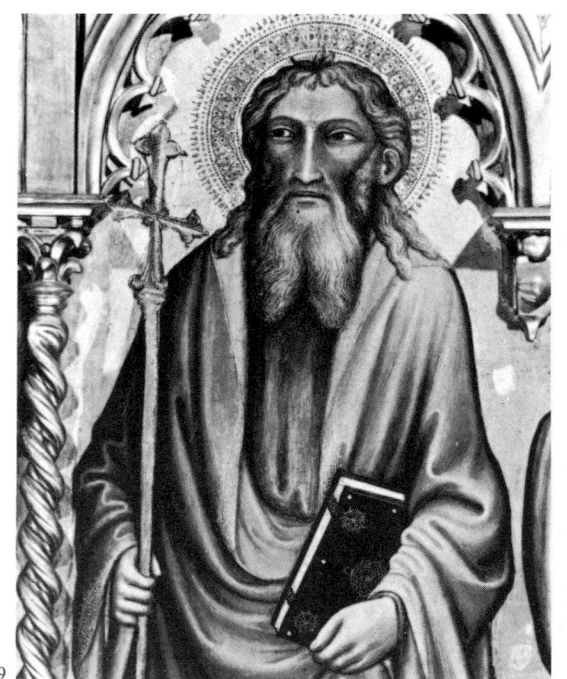

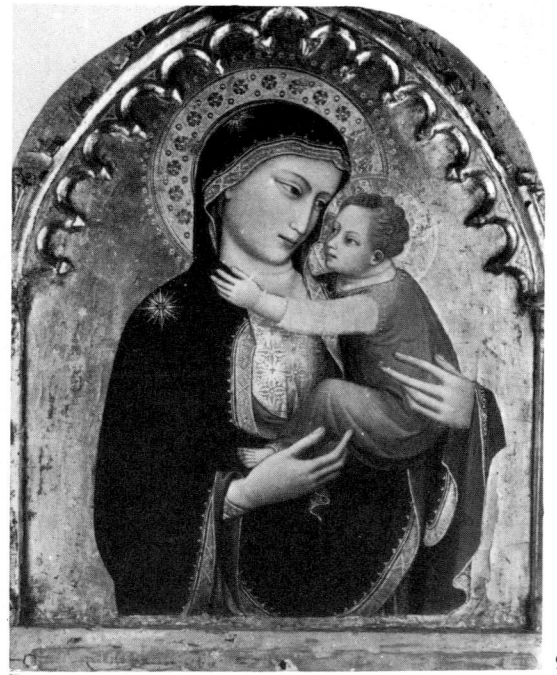

939 940

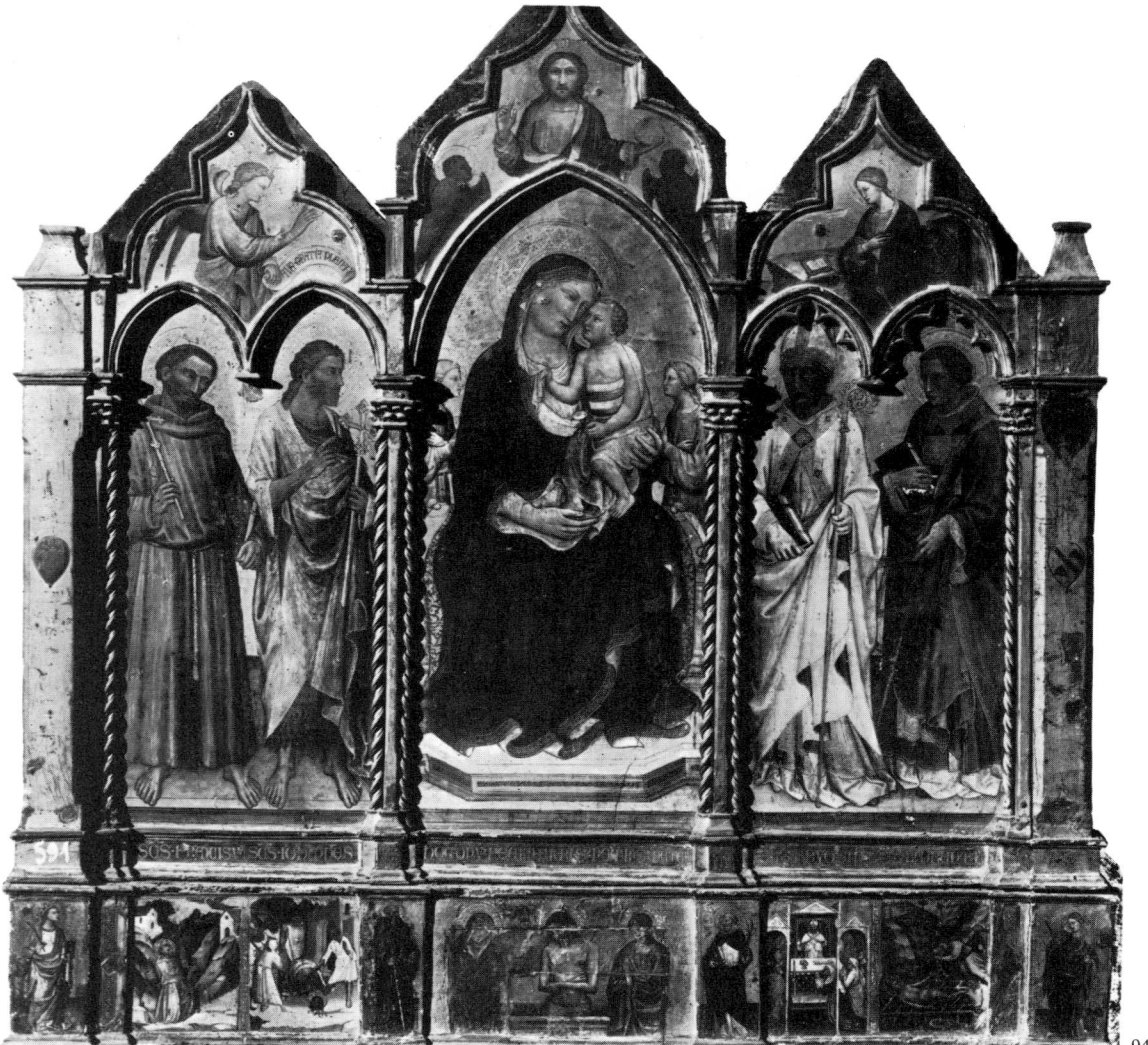

941

939. *St Andrew, detail of fig. 938. Panel. Florence, Serristori Collection. Bertoni. d. 1424.*
940. *Madonna and Child. Panel. Pagnana (near Empoli), S. Cristina. 61 × 46. SGF 23636.*
941. *Triptych: Madonna and Child Enthroned with two Angels and Sts Francis, John the Baptist, Euphrosynus and Lawrence. Above: Christ blessing;*
    Annunciation. Predella: St Catherine; Stigmatization of St Francis; Beheading of St John; St Anthony Abbot; Man of Sorrows; St Dominic;
    scene from the Life of St Euphrosynus; Martyrdom of St Lawrence; St Lucy. Panel. Panzano (near Greve), Pieve di S. Leolino. 160 × 200.
    SGF 21084. d. 1421.

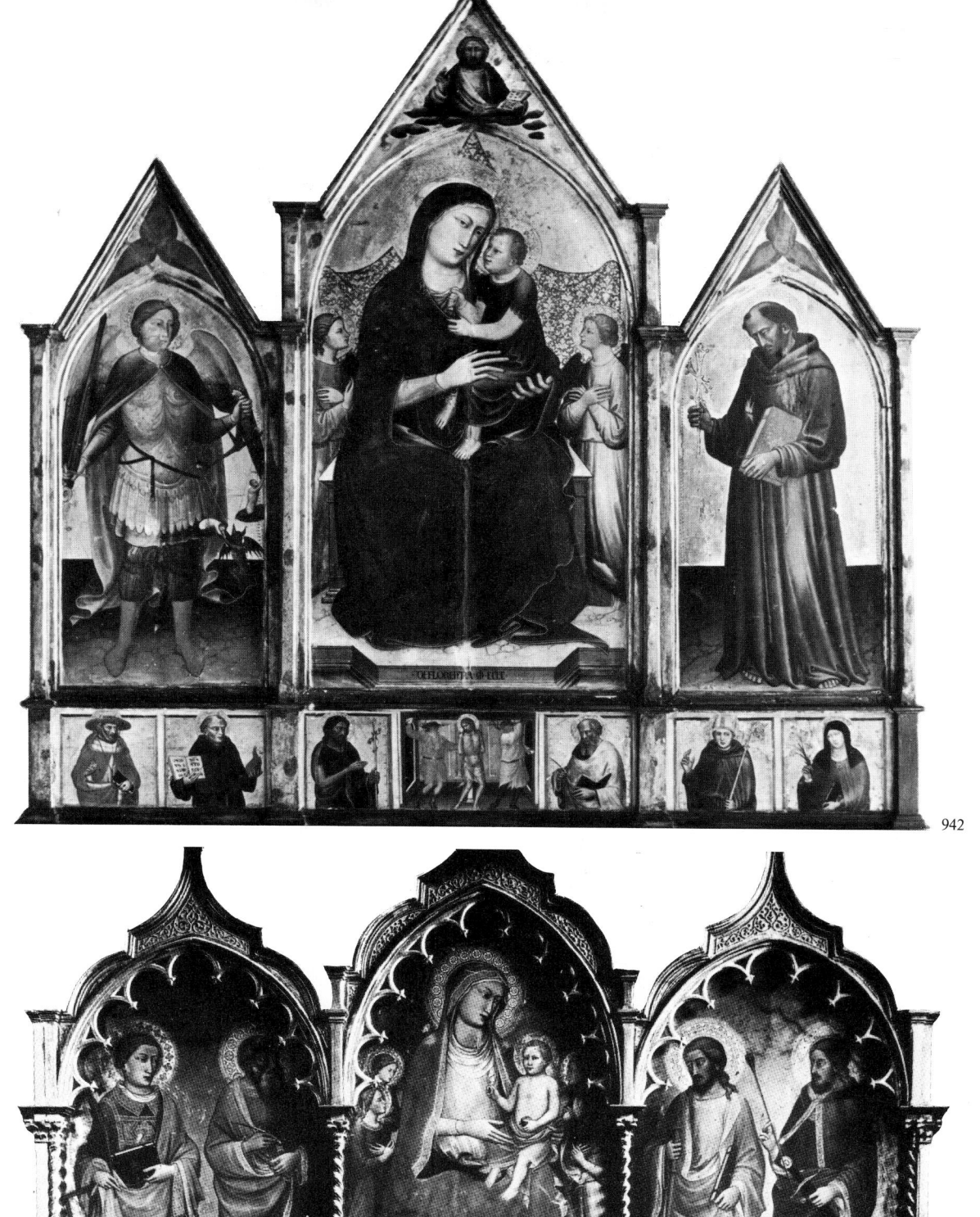

942

943

942. *Triptych: Madonna and Child Enthroned with two Angels, Sts Francis and Michael. Predella: Sts Jerome, Anthony of Padua, John the Baptist, John the Evangelist, Louis of Toulouse, Clare; Flagellation. Panel. Pesaro, Museo Civico. no. 23. cp: 183 × 74; sps: 145 × 50. Museum photo. d. 1400.*

943. *Triptych: Madonna and Child Enthroned with four Angels and four Saints. Predella: Annunciation to Joachim; Birth of the Virgin; Dormition of the Virgin; Presentation in the Temple; Marriage of the Virgin. Panel. Florence, Accademia. Triptych, no. 139, predella, no. 138. 177 × 254. SGF 3280.*

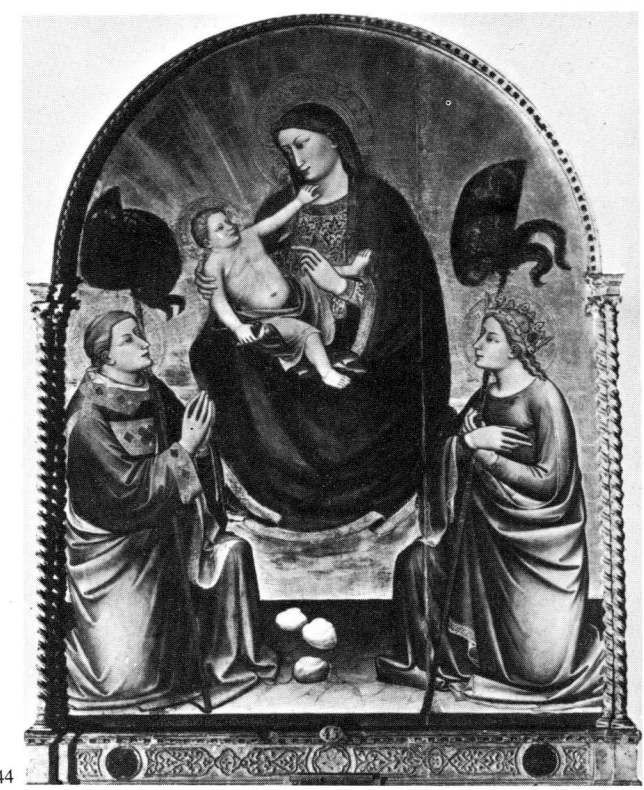

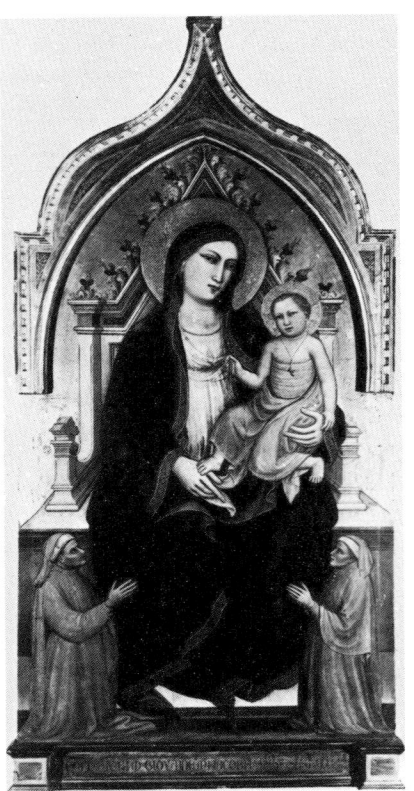

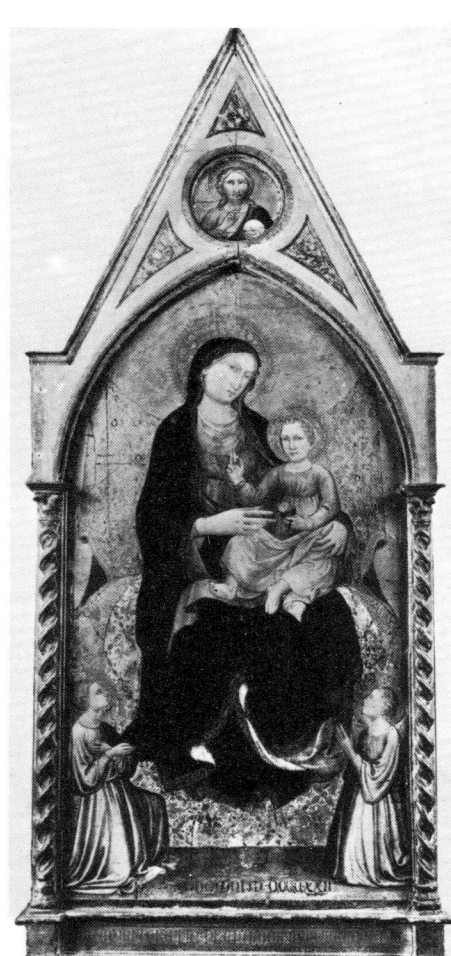

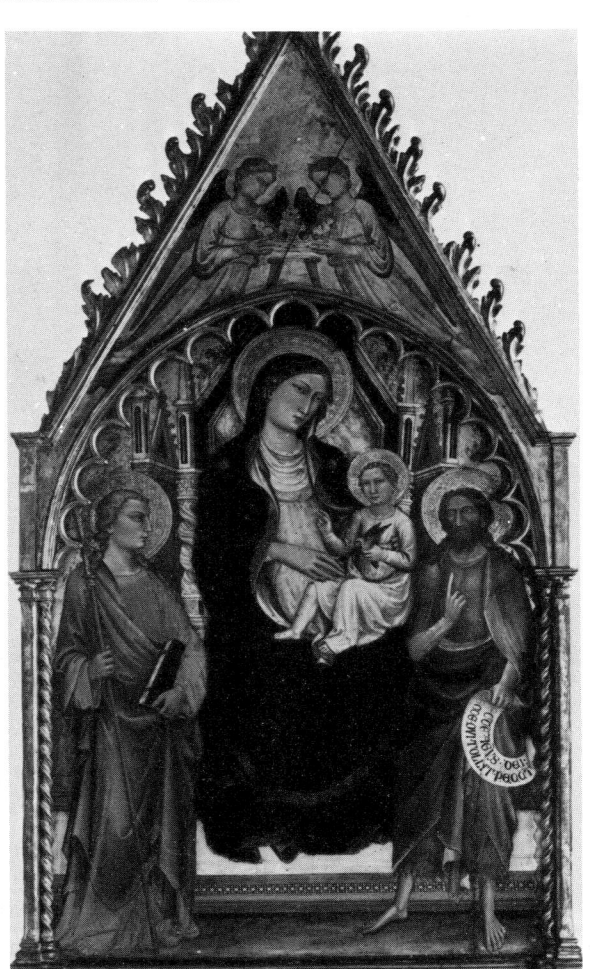

944. *Madonna in Glory, with Sts Stephen and Reparata. Panel. Florence, Accademia. no. 3460. 161 × 118. Alinari 1479. d. 1418.*
945. *Madonna and Child Enthroned with two Donors. Panel. Assisi, Convento di S. Francesco, F. M. Perkins Collection. no. 57. 180 × 95. Collection photo. d. 1404.*
946. *Madonna of Humility with two Angels. Above: Christ blessing. Panel. Florence, Acton Collection. 198.5 × 86. Reali. d. 1422.*
947. *Madonna and Child Enthroned with Sts Philip and John the Baptist. Above: two crowning Angels. Panel. Florence, Accademia. no. 473. 177 × 245. Alinari 50197. d. 1418.*

456

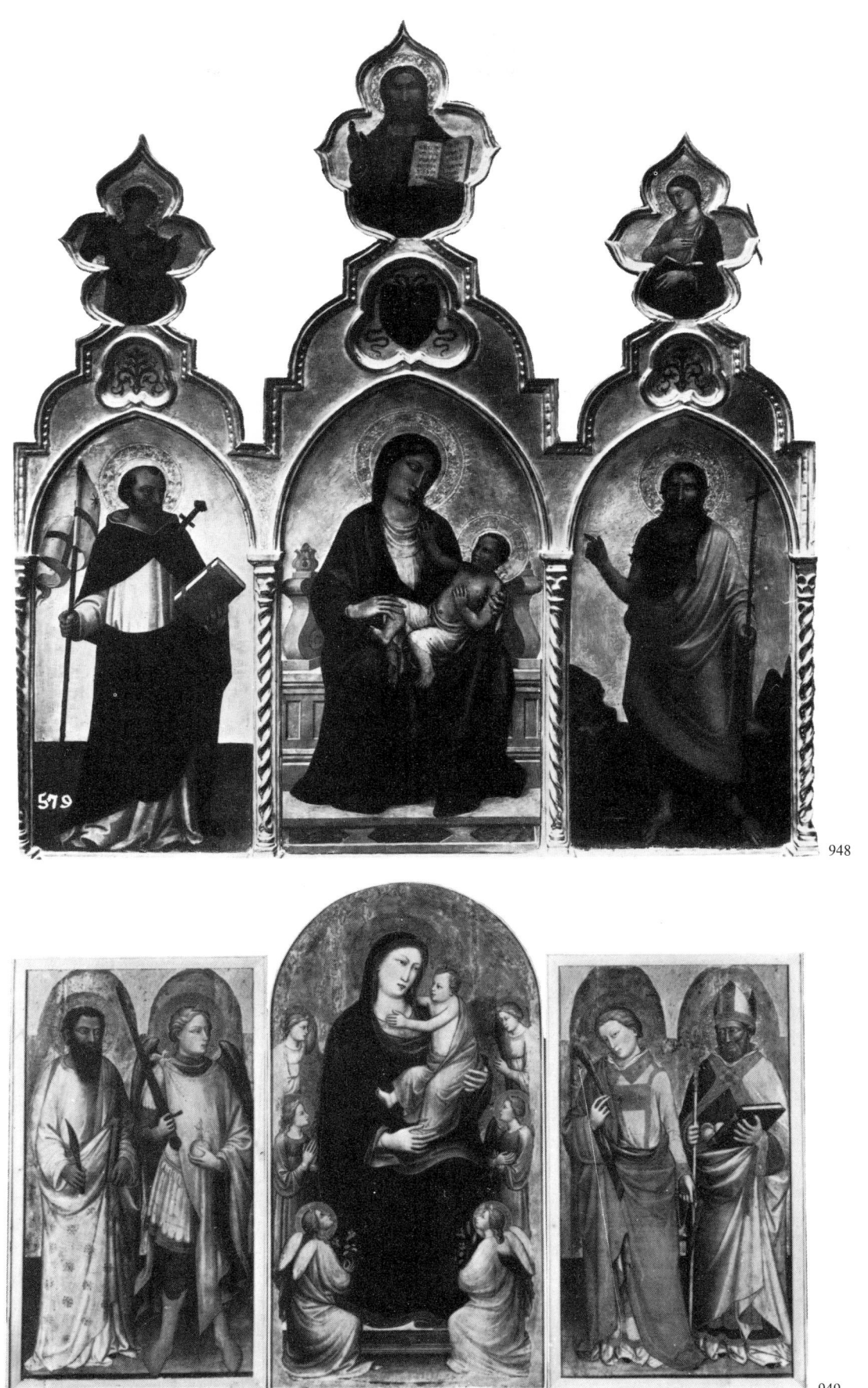

948. *Triptych: Madonna and Child Enthroned with Sts John the Baptist and Peter Martyr. Above: Christ blessing, Annunciation. Panel. Whereabouts unknown. SGF 0922.*

949. *Triptych: Madonna and Child Enthroned with six Angels; Sts Bartholomew, Michael, Lawrence and Nicholas. Panel. Legnaia (between Florence and Scandicci), S. Arcangelo. 152 × 82. SGF 69348.*

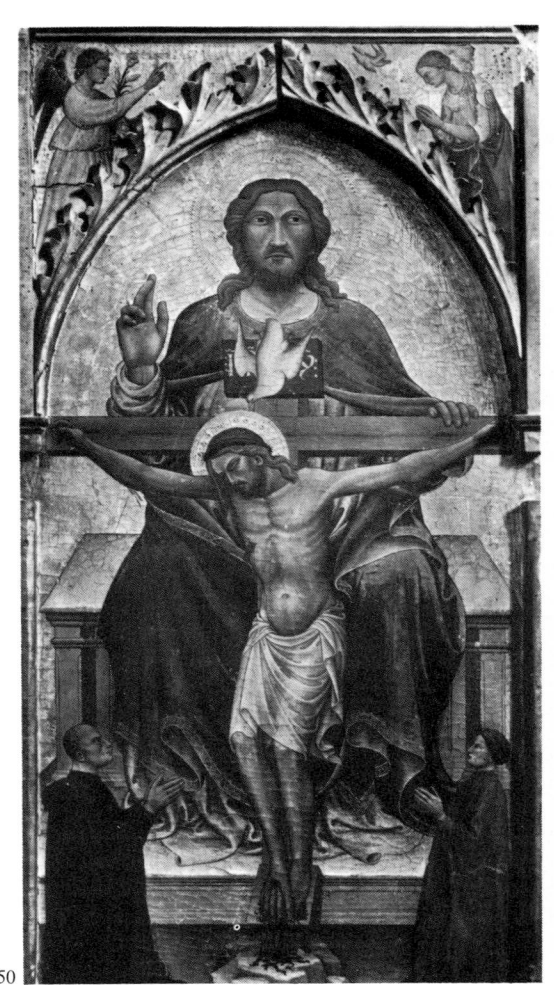
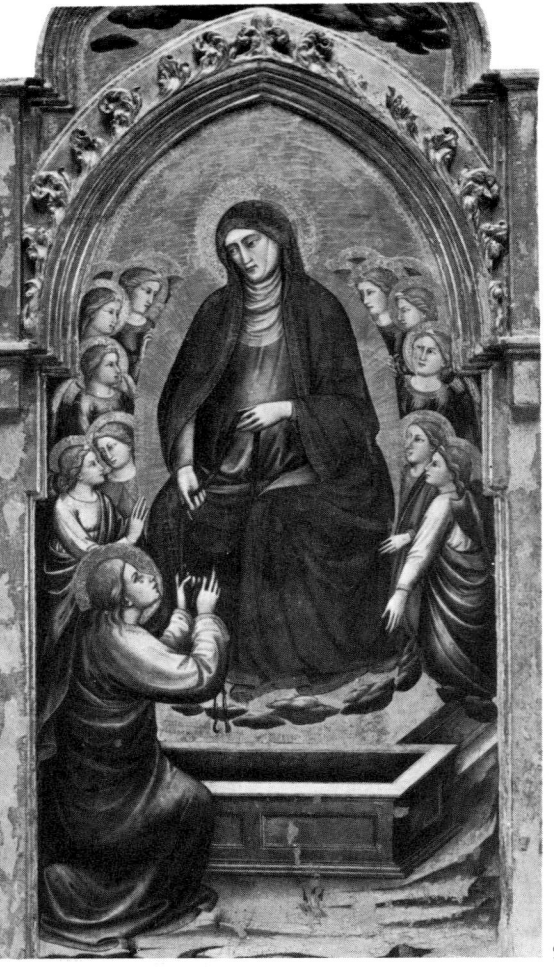

950 951

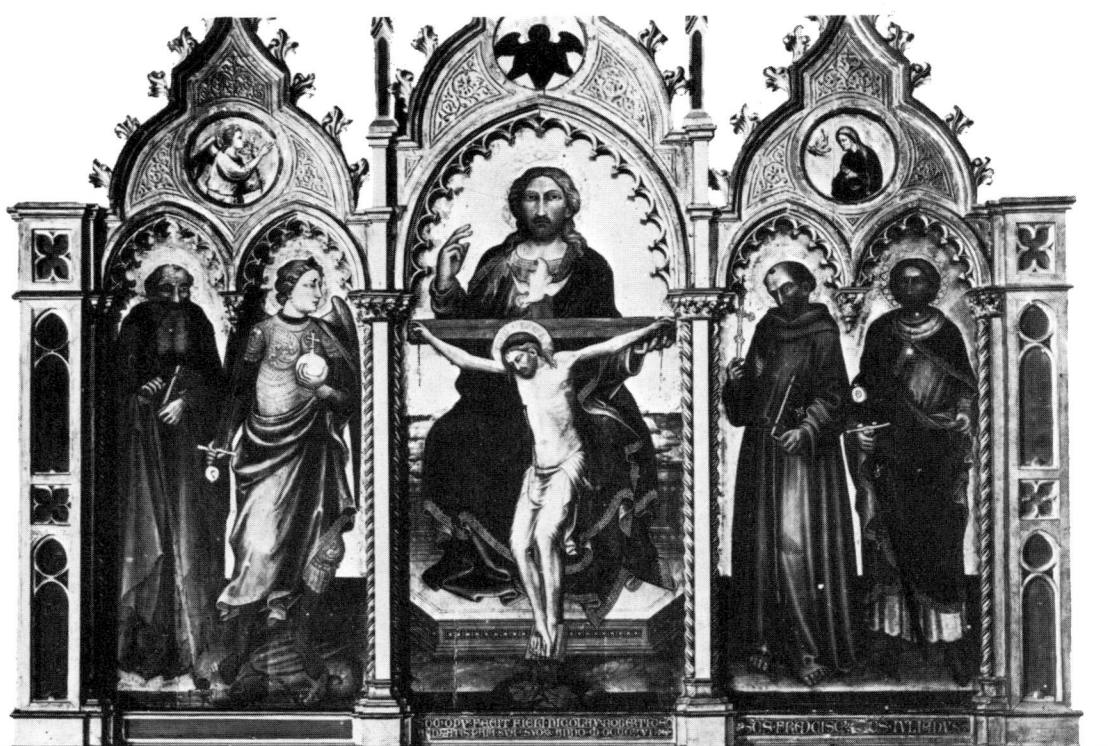

952

950. *Trinity with two Donors. Panel. Impruneta (8 kms south of Florence), Collegiata. Alinari 8962. d. 1418.*
951. *Madonna of the Holy Girdle, detail of fig. 955. Panel. Fiesole, Oratorio di Fontelucente. SGF 125815. d. 1398.*
952. *Triptych: Trinity; Sts Anthony Abbot, Michael, Francis and Julian. Above: Annunciation. Panel. Florence, S. Trinita, High Altar. Whole: 243 × 266; cp: 155 × 76; sps: 127 × 70. SGF 3547. d. 1406.*

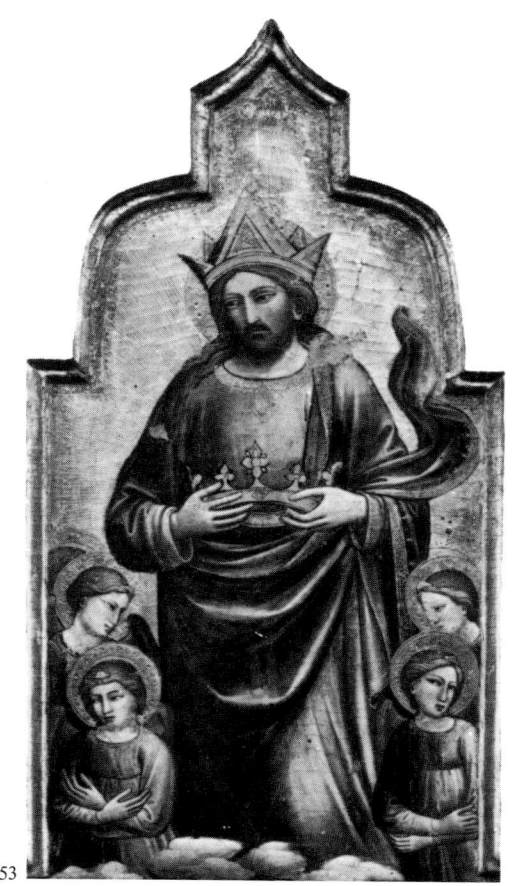

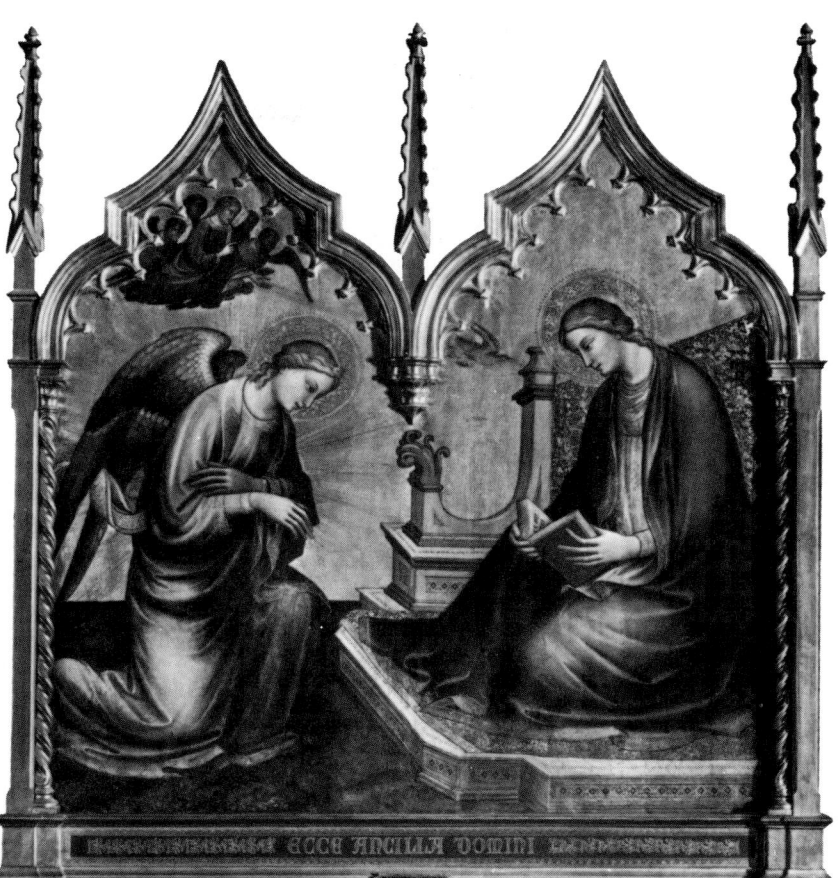

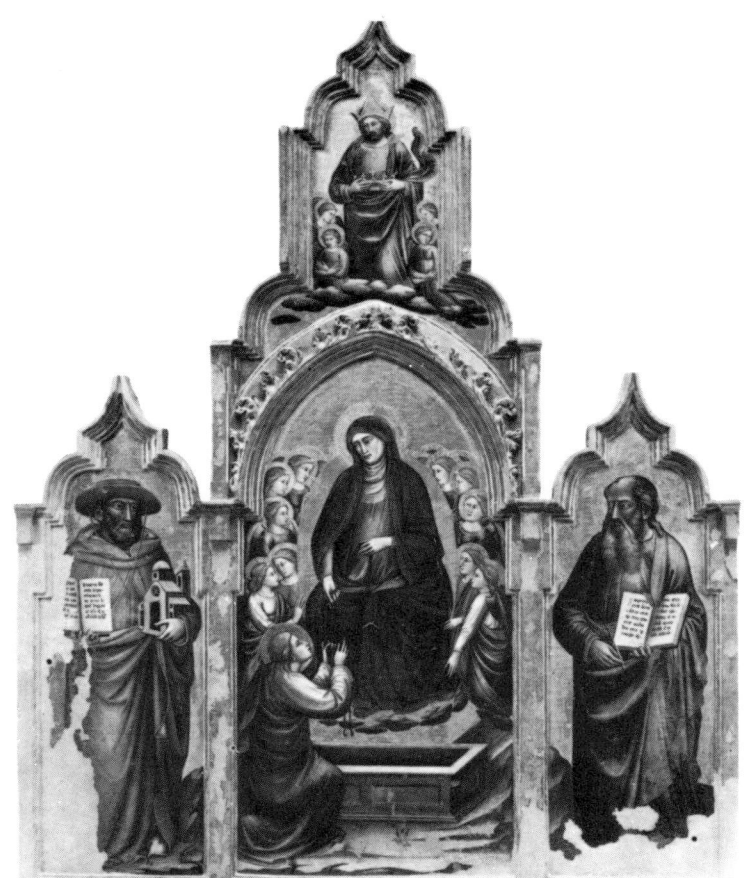

953. *Christ with Angels, detail of fig. 955. Panel. Fiesole, Oratorio di Fontelucente. SGF 125813. d. 1398.*

954. *Annunciation. Panel. Florence, Accademia. 136 × 134.5. Alinari 30512.*

955. *Triptych: Madonna of the Holy Girdle with St Thomas and Angels, and Sts Jerome and John the Evangelist. Above: Christ with Angels. Panel. Fiesole, Oratorio di Fontelucente. Whole panel: 240 × 180; cp: 240 × 80; sps: 143 × 50. SGF 125812. d. 1398.*

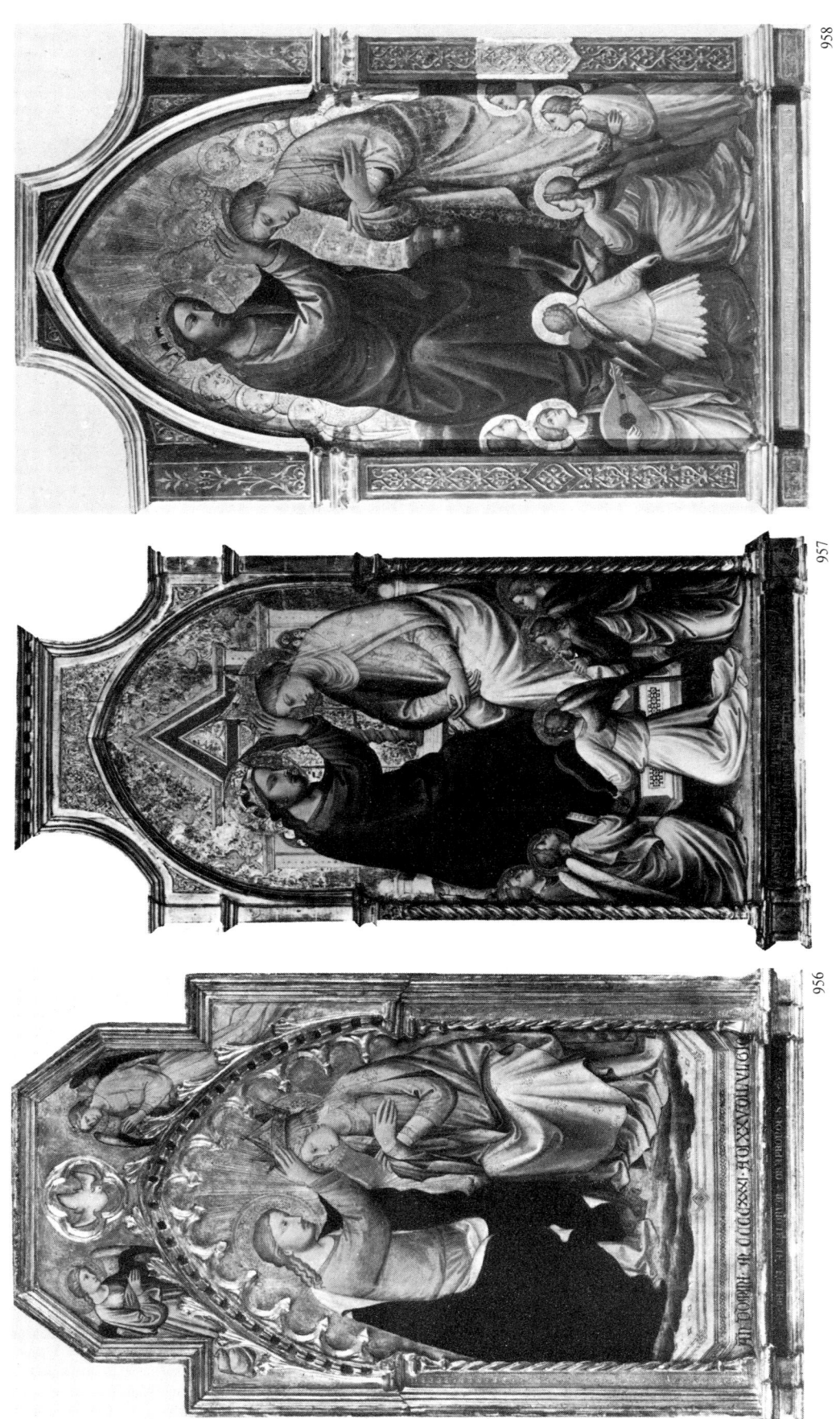

956. *Coronation of the Virgin. Above: Holy Spirit, two Angels. Panel. Florence, Acton Collection. 136.5 × 82. Reali. d. 1431.*
957. *Coronation of the Virgin. Panel. Minneapolis (Minn.), Minneapolis Institute of Art. no. 65.37. 131.7 × 68.6. Museum photo 12-971. d. 1408.*
958. *Coronation of the Virgin with six music-making Angels. Panel. Galluzzo, Certosa, Museo del Convento. 120 × 93. SGF 118517.*

ROSSELLO di JACOPO FRANCHI

Some painters are considered to be followers of Don Lorenzo Monaco by the analogies between their own late forms and his; others imitated him directly, copied him, reduced him to forms which were freer and more acceptable. Among them are the many that gave a more motherly expression to the Madonna, or more elegance to the figures taken from Lorenzo's triptychs, or developed further his Gothic forms. An example of such a follower of Don Lorenzo is Rossello di Jacopo Franchi, a master who is all curls, with the hair of his figures in rounded tufts, the faces squared, the foreheads high and convex, the little mouths drawn up in anger. His cylindrical figures, not sharp like those of Don Lorenzo, wear burdensome clothes which hang heavily as if drawn down by their weight and which don't stay loose from the narrow bodies or flutter freely. In his *Madonna & Child* at the Uffizi, there are comparisons between the adoring angels at the foot of the throne, with those in Lorenzo's *Adoration* also in the Uffizi, although the former lack the latter's ease and rapidity of his fleeing forms.....

from A. Venturi, p. 19, *Storia dell' Arte Italiana*, Vol. III, Milan, 1911.

Rossello di Jacopo Franchi, a painter very superior to Dello Delli and Paolo di Stefano, was obviously also inspired by Bicci di Lorenzo.
Rossello was born in all probability about 1376, because on his tombstone in the church of S. Lorenzo, an inscription informs us that he died in 1457 at the age of eighty. His name is recorded in several documents; from them we learn that he was active for the Bigallo in 1426 together with his brother Giunta di Jacopo Franchi who was born in 1379 and who is found enrolled in the corporation of Florentine painters in 1424. Rossello married in 1427 and in 1429 together with Matteo Torelli he executed miniatures for the Bigallo and for the cathedral of Prato; in 1435 he collaborated with Bicci di Lorenzo and Lippo di Corso in the execution of the figures of the Twelve Apostles in the cathedral of Prato; and in 1445 and 1446 he is again working for the Bigallo, first with his brother Giunta and then with Ventura di Moro; he painted the frescoes from the life of St. Peter the Martyr, some of which are still visible.....
There are still a few other productions by this master who was a serene painter of little talent but not without charm; he created a morphological type of his own, full of originality and expression but the result is that all his figures resemble one another. Rossello was even less of an innovator than Bicci di Lorenzo. He felt little of the influence of the more modern movement which flourished in Florence, particularly towards the end of his career; nor was he very much dominated by the cosmopolitan Gothic manner, not even by Lorenzo Monaco. His art derives from Agnolo Gaddi and the knowledge of Bicci's painting is clearly manifest in his work.....

from R. van Marle, pp. 52, 64, *The Development of the Italian Schools of Painting*, Vol. IX, The Hague, 1927.

.... the most dull innocent could not help but recognize the standard type among his works, best illustrated by the signed painting which I had the good luck to discover at Staggia. Now that the signature OPUS ROSSELLI FRANCHISC has given a name to some paintings which were grouped together by Professor Sirén and other critics, the painting in question has quite an interest for us. Unfortunately shortly after its publication, the painting was stolen. We reproduce it in the hope that the person who presently owns it will give it back to Italy, and especially to Florence, as it is so important a document of Florentine art. The artistic merit of the picture, as pleasant and even delightful as it is, certainly falls below its historical interest.....

from B. Berenson, p. 189, *Dedalo*, XII,1, 1932.

Rossello, who was born around 1377 and died in 1458, evolves as an artist within the circle of Bicci di Lorenzo, from whom he then breaks away to pursue his own delightful poetic inclinations, though he is not insensitive to the finer elegance of the international gothic. His colours, light and delicate even when he intends the boldest contrasts, are always consistent with his fine and elegantly linear drawing, producing painting of great sensitivity and grace. He is among the best and most personal of the minor Florentine painters of the early Quattrocento. Little is known about him as a fresco painter and his activity in this field probably was not great, since his art adapts itself better to the richness of gold backgrounds and to fine coloristic harmony on smooth surfaces.....

> from U. Baldini, p. 29, *I ͣ Mostra di Affreschi Staccati*, Florence, 1957.

Until a few decades ago, Rossello di Jacopo Franchi was known through a wealth of documents which testified to his prolonged artistic activity for the Compagnia del Bigallo and for the Duomo of Florence, but which in no way served to identify any of his works. Finally Gamba and Berenson (1905) published respectively the Coronation of the Virgin of the Pinacoteca of Siena, signed and dated 1439, and the Tabernacle of Staggia Senese (Madonna & Child with two angels), also signed. On the basis of these, the corpus of the painter has enlarged considerably.
The style and the artistic development of Rossello are extremely linear; and consequently he never changed his flowery style closely related to Lorenzo Monaco; on the contrary, he brings himself up to date with the late activity of Lorenzo. The fascination of his art is his absolute faith in the beauty of the late Gothic linear rhythm, with an almost plastic effect of pushing the figures forward on the surface, as one can see even in the Madonna of Ortimino, where the halo seems to want to leave the surface of the painting, placing the group in a superimposed plane.....

> from P. Dal Poggetto, p. 39, *Arte in Valdelsa*, Certaldo, 1963.

BIBLIOGRAPHY
BOOKS
An asterisk indicates a work listed in the General Bibliography

Venturi, A.*, Vol. VIII, 1911, p. 19; v. Marle, *1927**, p. 64; Firenze, *1933**, p. 124; Antal*, 1948, p. 331; Galetti*, " P-Z ", 1950, pp. 2164-5; Oertel, *1950**, p. 54; Baldini, U., *MAS I*, 1957, pp. 29-30; Santi, F., pp. 51-60 in *Scritti di Storia dell'arte in onore di Mario Salmi*, Vol. II, Rome, 1962; Berenson, *1963**, Vol. I, p. 192; Dal Poggetto, P., *AIV**, 1963, pp. 39-40; Bellosi, L., *La Pittura Tardogotica in Toscana* (I Maestri del Colore, 39), Milan, 1966.

JOURNALS

Poggi, G., *RA*, II, 10-11, 1904, pp. 196, 203, 239, 241; Berenson, B., *RADA*, V, 1, 1905, pp. 9-11; Salmi, M., *A*, XVI, 1913, pp. 208-27; Lasareff, V., *AA*, XVI, 1928, pp. 25-40; Berenson, B., *DD*, XII, 1, 1932, pp. 173-93; Gamba, C., *BA*, XXVII, 1933, III, pp. 145-63; Castelfranco, G., *RA*, XV, 1933, pp. 78-82; Offner, R., *BM*, LXIII, 1933, p. 173; Salmi, M., *RA*, XVI, 1934, pp. 168-86; Cohn, W., *RA*, XXXI, 1956, pp. 41-72; Berti, L., *C*, XII, 2, 1961, pp. 84-107; Bellosi, L., *PA*, 193/13, 1966, pp. 44-58; Friedmann, H., *SIM*, 3, 1968-1969, 1, p. 7; Volpe, C., *MKIF*, XVII, 2-3, 1973, p. 357.

SIGNED AND DATED WORKS

Formerly Staggia, S. Maria Assunta (stolen 1920). Panel: Madonna & Child Enthroned with two Angels. s. (fig. 970).
1420 Florence, Accademia 8460. Triptych: Coronation of the Virgin with Archangels, Angels and Saints. d. (fig. 973).
1439 Siena, Pinacoteca Nazionale 608. Panel: Coronation of the Virgin with Angels. s & d. (fig. 977).

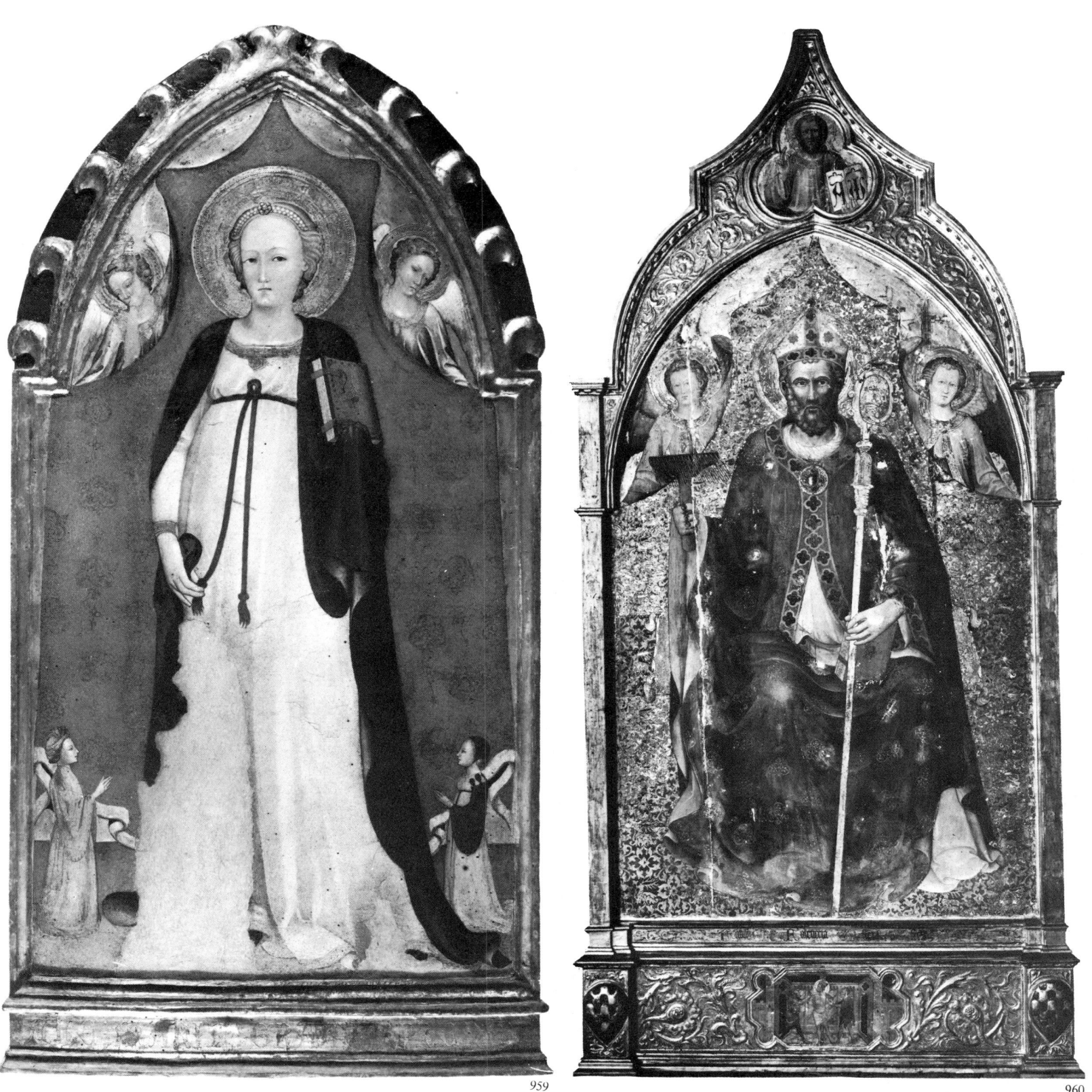

959

960

959.   *Madonna del Parto with two Angels and two Donors. Panel. Florence, Palazzo Davanzati. no. 1021. 121 × 61. SGF 94621.*
960.   *St Blaise Enthroned with two Angels. Above : Christ blessing. Predella : Martyrdom of St. Blaise. Panel. Florence, Duomo. SGF 71967. 1408.*

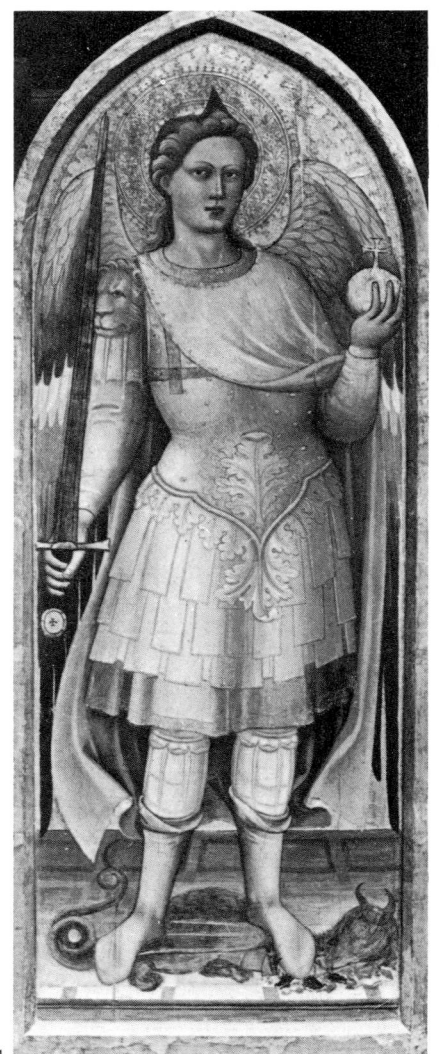
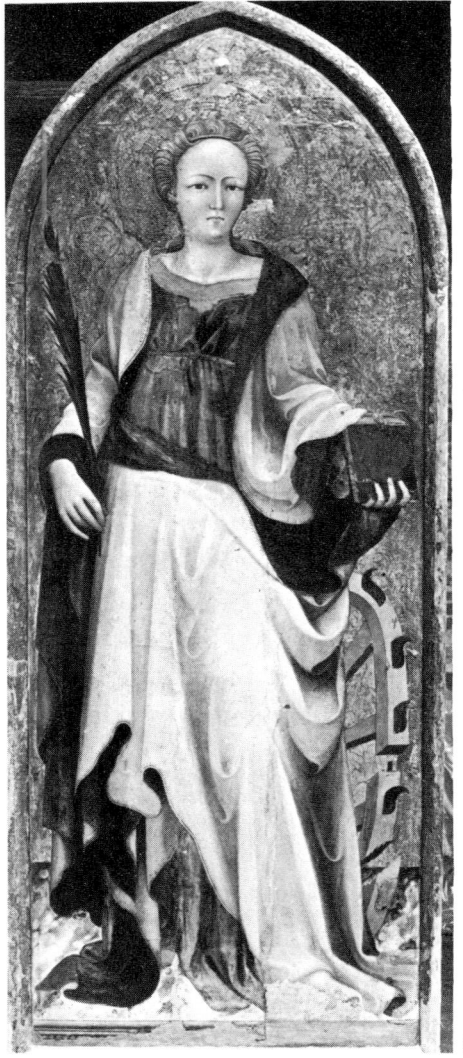
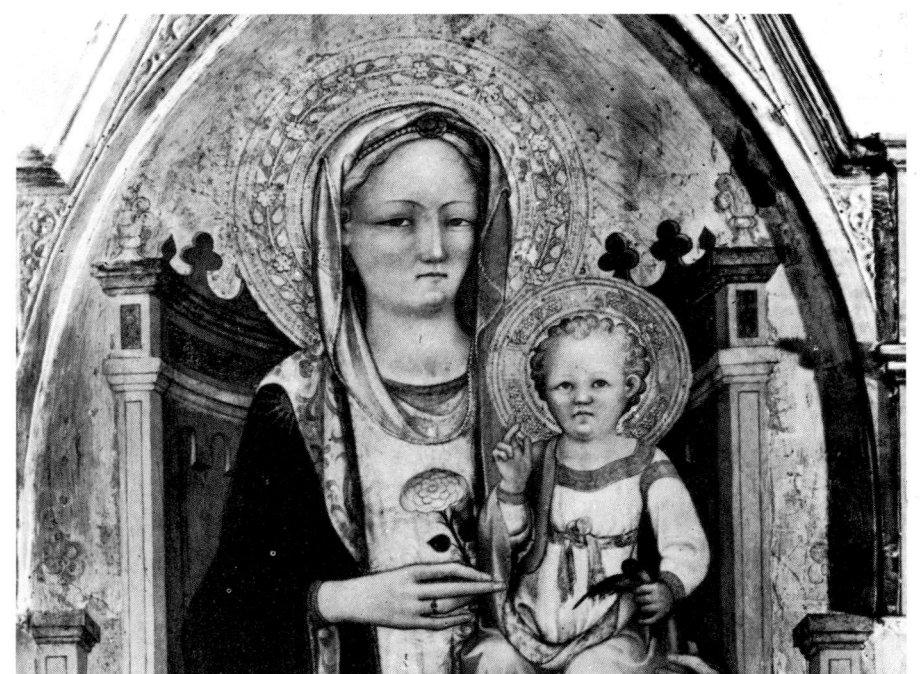

961. *St Michael the Archangel. Panel. San Miniato al Tedesco (Pisa), S. Domenico. SGPL 13049.*
962. *St Catherine. Panel. San Miniato al Tedesco (Pisa), S. Domenico. SGPL 13044.*
963. *Half-figures of Madonna and Child, detail of fig. 972. Panel. Florence, Accademia. no. 475. Alinari (detail) 994.*

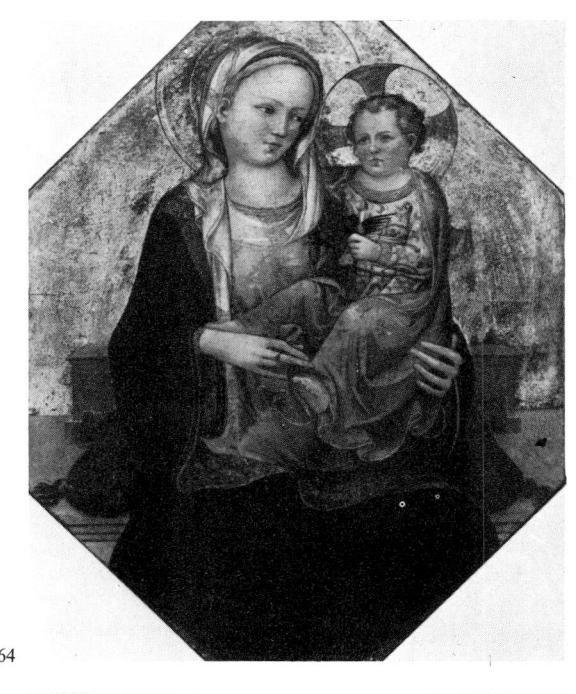

964

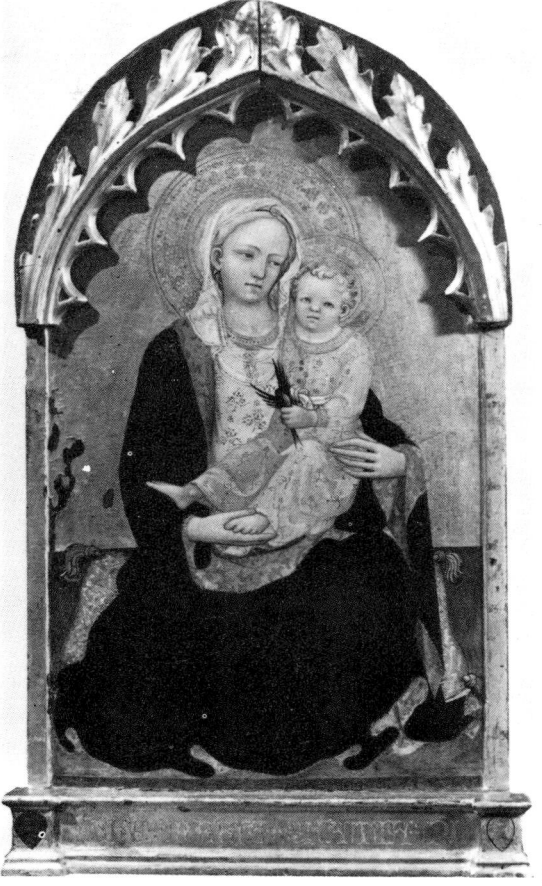

965

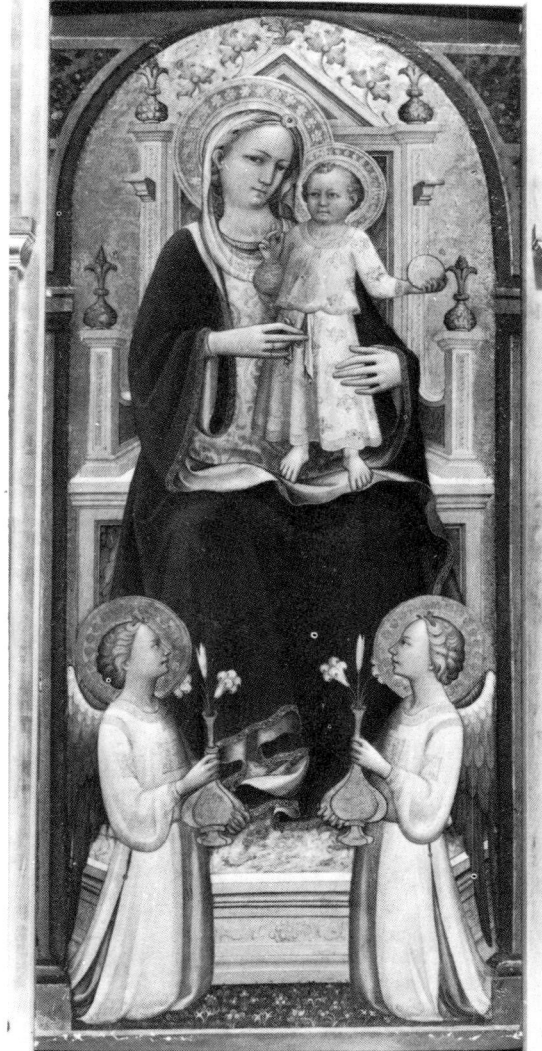

966

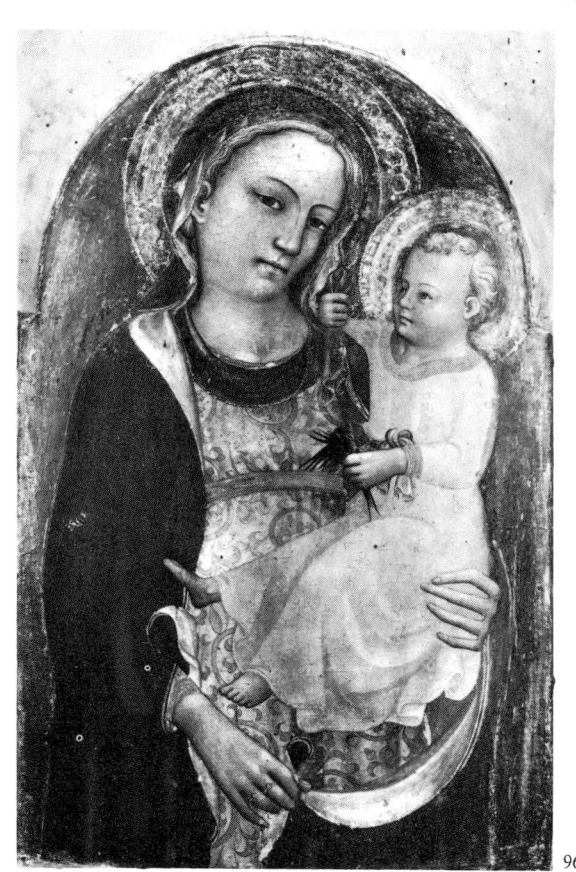

967

964. *Madonna of Humility. Panel. Cleveland (Ohio), Museum of Art, Holden Collection. no. 16.814. 69.5 × 55.5. Museum photo 2392.*
965. *Madonna of Humility. Panel. Florence, De Carlo Collection. 95 × 54. Collection photo.*
966. *Madonna and Child Enthroned with two Angels. Panel. London, Courtauld Institute of Art, Gambier-Parry Collection. no. 52. 128 × 55.5. Museum photo B66/1270.*
967. *Madonna and Child. Panel. Ortimino (near Montespertoli, Val d'Elsa), S. Vito. 77 × 47. SGF 123449.*

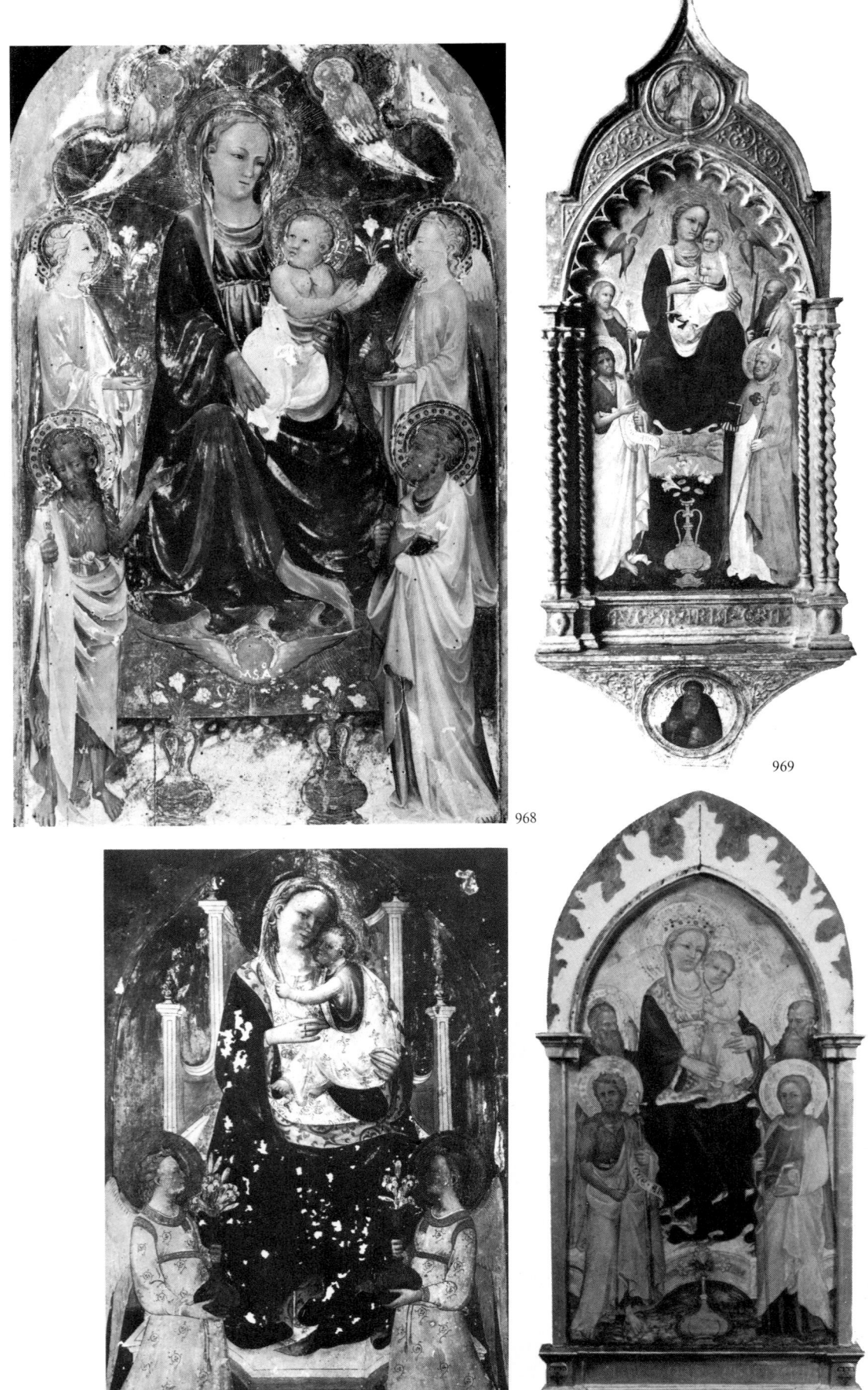

968

969

970

971

968.   Madonna and Child in Glory with two Angels and Sts John the Baptist and Peter.   Panel.   New Haven, Yale University Art Gallery.   no. 1943.219.
        89 × 50.9.   Museum photo.
969.   Madonna and Child Enthroned with Sts James, John the Baptist, Paul and a Bishop Saint.   Above: God the Father.   Predella: St Anthony Abbot.
        Panel.   Barcelona, Museu d'Arte de Cataluña.   no. MAB 15932.   167 × 63.   Museum photo: 15273.
970.   Madonna and Child Enthroned with two Angels.   Panel.   Formerly Staggia (Poggibonsi), S. Maria Assunta; stolen 1920.   SGF 10088.   s.
971.   Madonna and Child Enthroned with Sts Andrew, John the Baptist, a hermit Saint, and James.   Cambridge, Fitzwilliam Museum.   no. 1129.   85.7 × 48.5.
        Museum photo: Stearn & Sons FMS 4773.

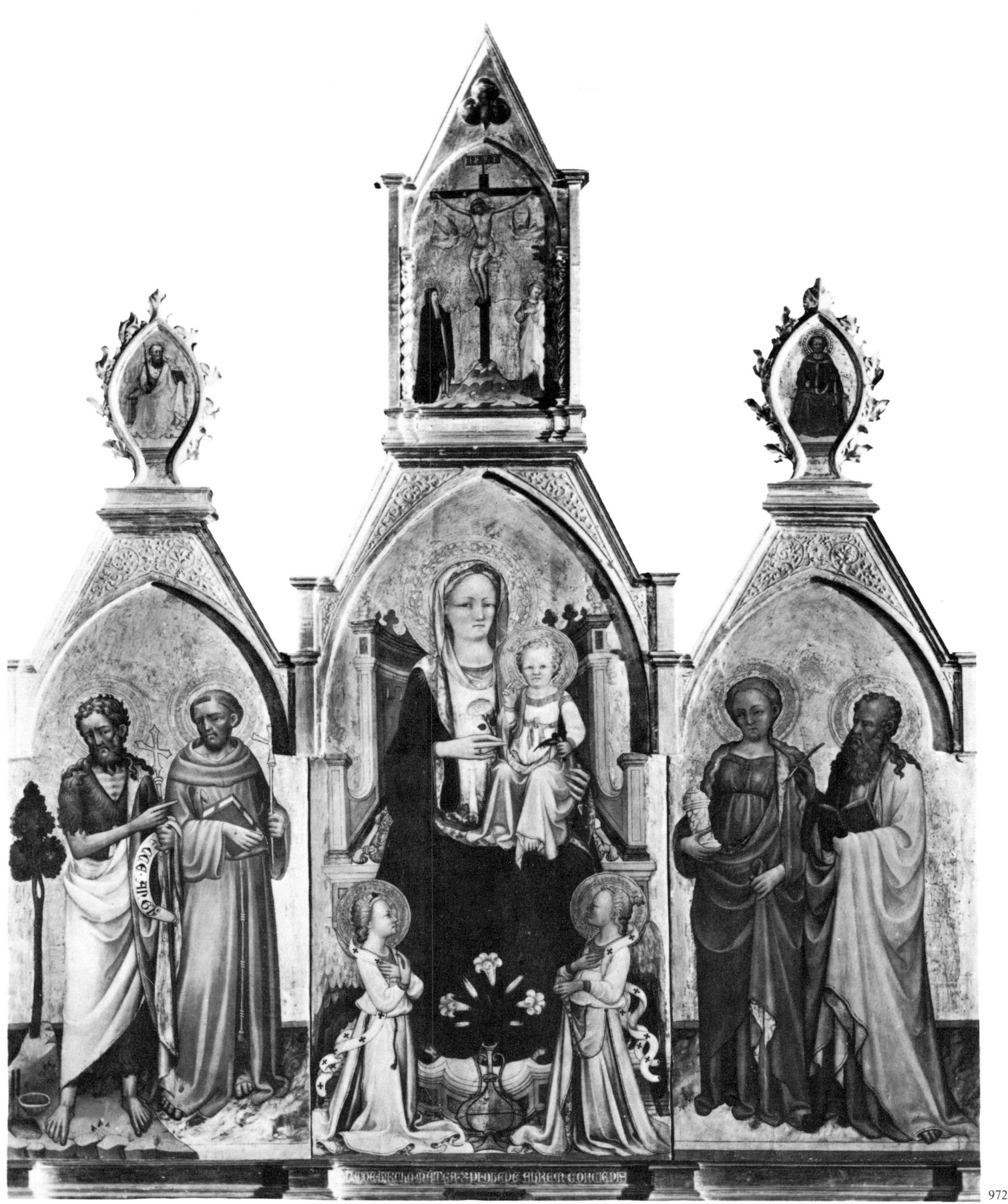

972. *Triptych: Madonna and Child Enthroned with two Angels, Sts John the Baptist, Francis, Mary Magdalene and Matthew. Above: Christ on the Cross and Sts Paul and Peter. Panel. Florence, Accademia, no. 475. 239 × 196. Alinari 994.*

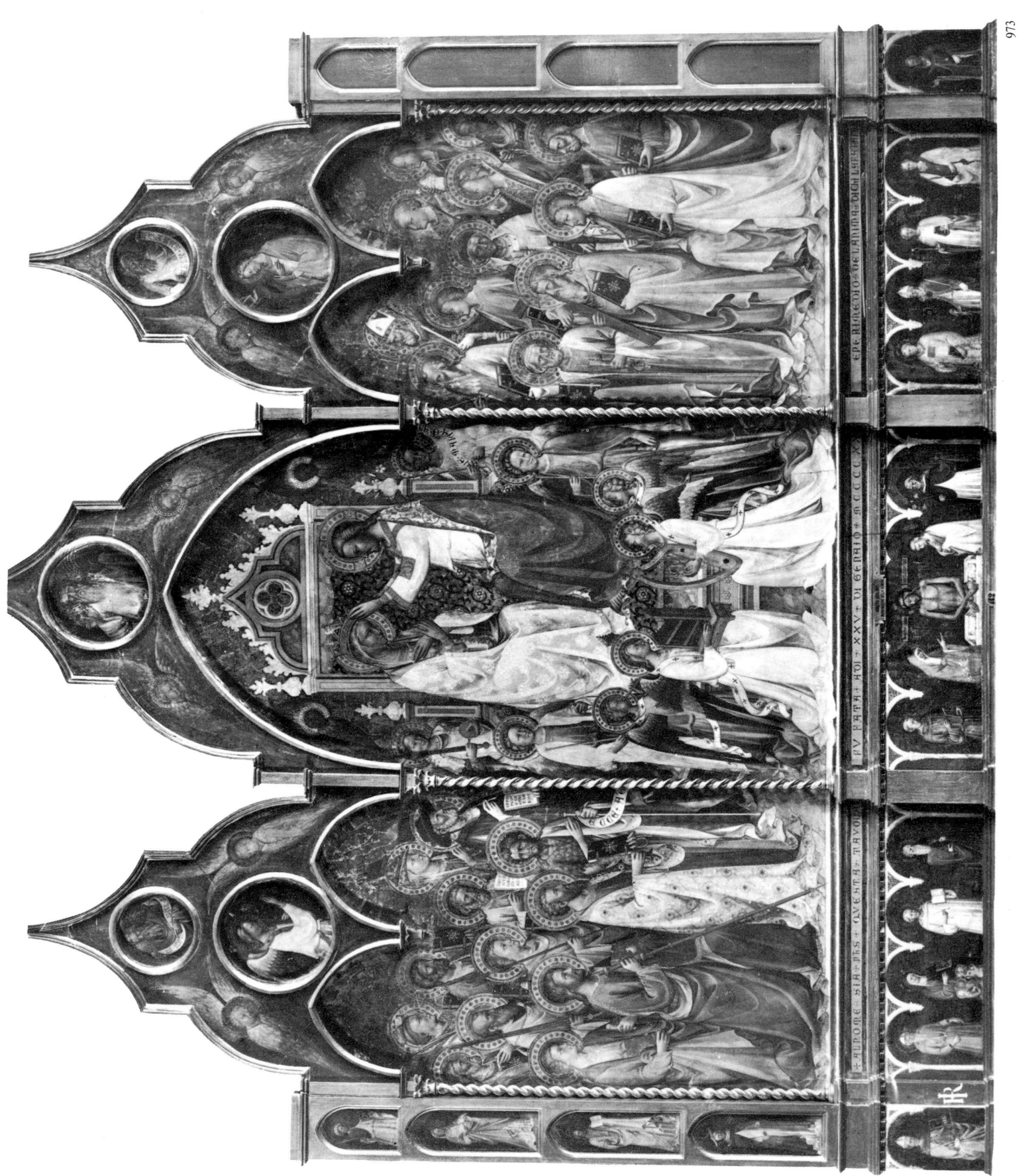

973. *Triptych: Coronation of the Virgin with Archangels Michael and Gabriel, six Angels and twenty-four Saints. Above: God the Father, two Prophets, Annunciation. Left pilaster: four Saints. Predella: Man of Sorrows with Virgin, St John and twelve Saints. Panel. Florence, Accademia, no. 8460. 334 × 390. Brogi 7565. d. 1420.*

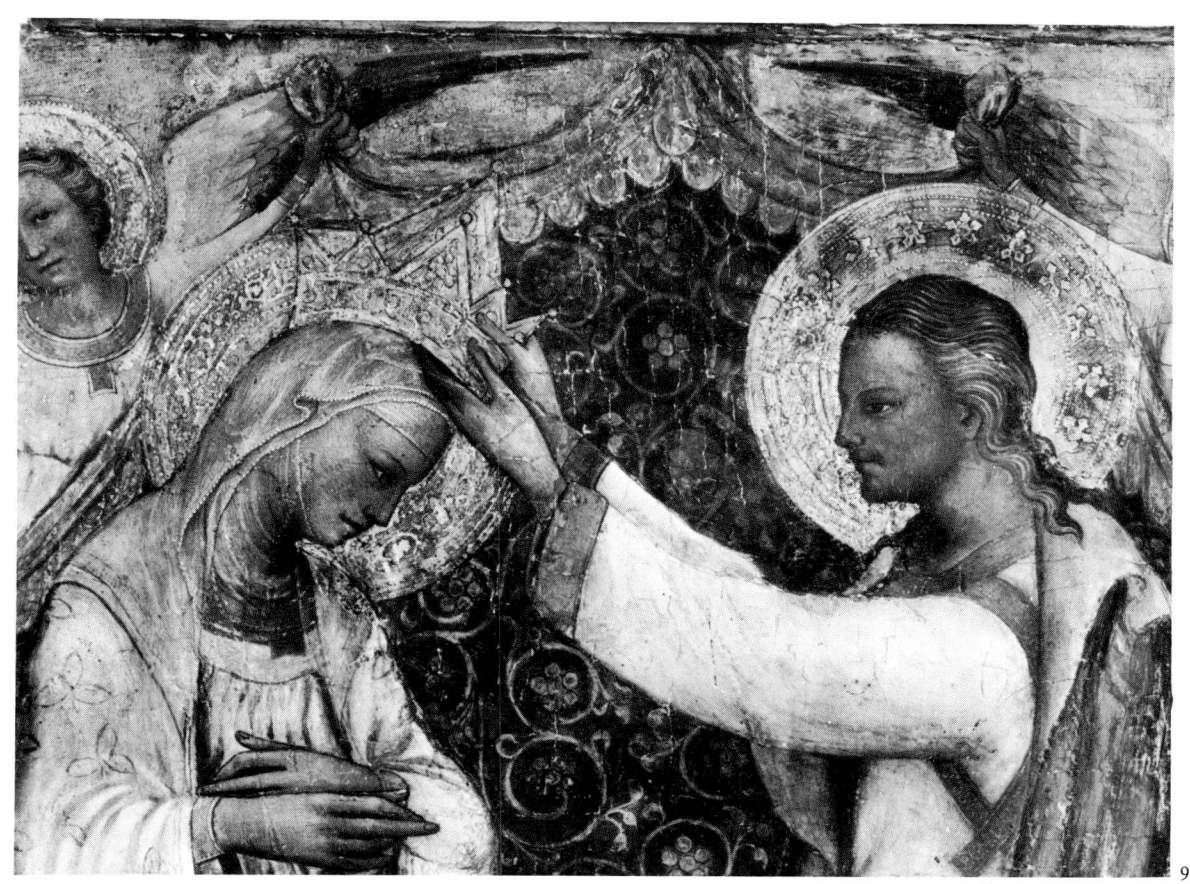

974

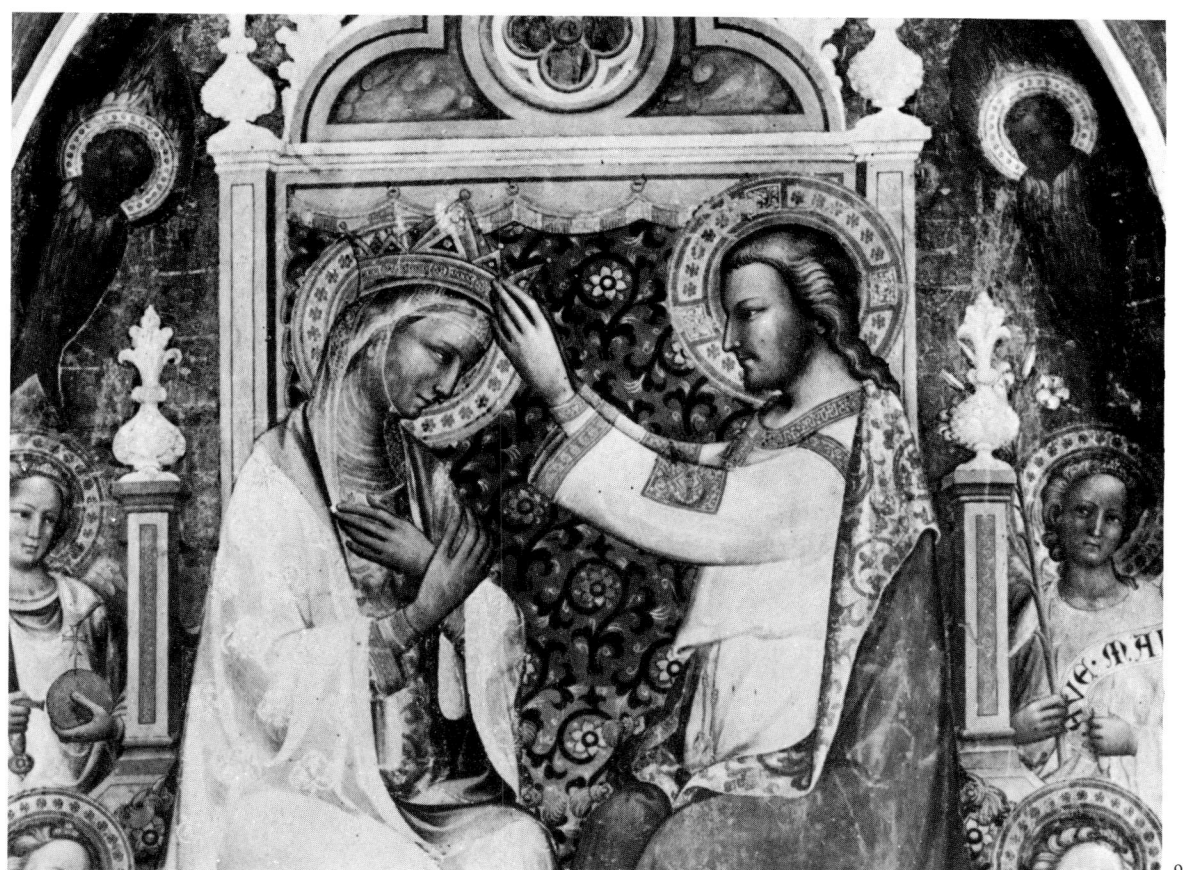

975

974. *Christ crowning the Virgin, detail of fig. 977. Panel. Siena, Pinacoteca Nazionale no. 608. Alinari (detail) 39987. s & d. 1439.*
975. *Christ crowning the Virgin, detail of fig. 973. Panel. Florence, Accademia. no. 8460. Brogi (detail) 7565. d. 1420.*

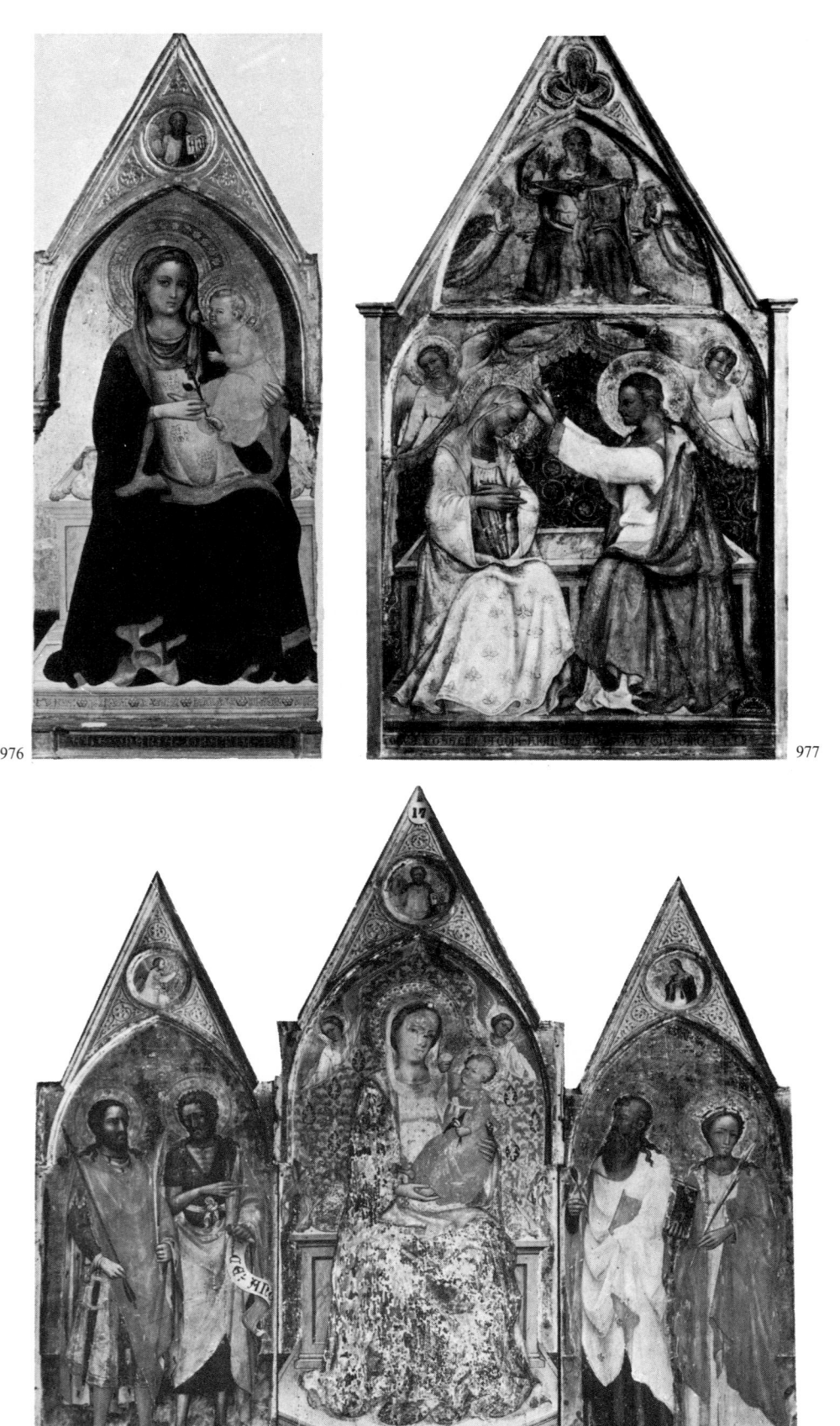

976. *Madonna and Child. Above: God the Father. Panel. Whereabouts unknown. A. C. Cooper 706806.*

977. *Coronation of the Virgin with two Angels. Above: a Prophet, the Trinity adored by two Angels. Panel. Siena, Pinacoteca Nazionale. no. 608. 140 × 75. Alinari 39987. s & d. 1439.*

978. *Madonna and Child with two Angels and Sts Sebastian, John the Baptist, John the Evangelist and Domitilla. Panel. Empoli, Museo della Collegiata. no. 17. Alinari 42370.*

BICCI di LORENZO

As several writers have remarked, Milanesi in the first place, Vasari confused Bicci di Lorenzo with his father, Lorenzo di Bicci and almost all the data he gives regarding Lorenzo,
concern the son; he even adds to the confusion by including some facts from the life of
Neri di Bicci, the son of Bicci di Lorenzo and not his brother as Vasari imagined.
The knowledge we have of the career of Bicci di Lorenzo is very considerable, thanks to
the researches of Milanesi.....
The more important facts are that he was born in 1373, that his son Neri was born in 1418,
that his wife was called Benedetta di Amato Amati and that he died in May 1452 and was
buried in the church of Sta. Maria del Carmine. All the other documents refer to his paintings and his constant activity. Between 1420 and 1446, there are but very few years for
which Milanesi does not provide us with documentary evidence of Bicci's diligence and
often there is more than one record for each year.....

> from R. van Marle, pp. 1-2, *The Develop-*
> *ment of the Italian Schools of Painting*, Vol. IX,
> The Hague, 1927.

Florentine, born 1373, died May 6, 1452. Painter, member of the Physicians' and Apothecaries' Guild between 1386-1408. Member of the Guild of St Luke, 1424. Pupil of his father
Lorenzo; influenced(?) by Spinello Aretino. Master of his son Neri, Antonio di Tommaso.
Andrea di Giusto [Manzini] was his garzone in 1423-24. Bonaiuto di Giovanni and Stefano
d'Antonio were his assistants and worked in his bottega.....

> from D. E. Colnaghi, p. 42, *A Dictionary of*
> *Florentine Painters*, London, 1928.

The voluble Bicci di Lorenzo has his rapturous moments of limpid and luscious colour as,
e.g., in his triptych in the Perugia Gallery, which has general affinities with the not altogether happy *Annunciation* from S. Angelo a Legnaia.....

> from R. Offner, p. 170, *The Burlington Magazine*,
> Vol. LXIII, July-Dec. 1933.

To list, even briefly, the pictorial activity of this apt and amiable painter, active in the first
half of the XV century, would be impossible in a few lines. His vast production, spread
through every region of Tuscany, was entrusted in part also to the collaboration of a most
organized workshop; further, the stylistic variations that he displayed in his active career
were so slight, that they roused but limited interest. The most evident characteristic of his
painting arises from the calm slackness in his use of the formulas of the late gothic art,
which he adapts, however in the most simple way. In his beginnings he appears in fact
very closely linked with the example of his father, Lorenzo di Bicci (see the first dated
work, *The Annunciation* in S. Lorenzo a Porciano of 1414). But he is a more modern version
of his father with fluid linear rhythm and tenuous drafting of colours, elements which he
derived from the environment of Lorenzo Monaco. Later, from the end of the third decade
to the beginning of the fourth, he experienced a fascination for Gentile da Fabriano (and
like Andrea di Giusto, he even executed copies of Gentile's work); he was also influenced
by Masolino. He was indifferent to innovations of the Renaissance, although he had close
contact with them when he collaborated with Domenico Veneziano in the S. Egidio cycle
(1438).....

> from P. Dal Poggetto, p. 45, *Arte in Val-*
> *delsa*, Certaldo, 1963.

A conservative Florentine artist, the pupil of his father Lorenzo di Bicci, and father of the
painter Neri di Bicci. To some extent he must have been influenced by Lorenzo Monaco.
He carried the Gothic style methodically into the middle of the fifteenth century and its
continuing popularity, at a time when Alberti was publishing the first treatise of painting
on the new humanist style, is attested by numerous commissions throughout Tuscany.

Had he not died when he did the frescoes of Piero della Francesca in San Francesco, Arezzo, would never have been executed. His manner of painting is generally of a hard and angular type, characteristic of Florentine Gothic. The International Gothic style, with its sinuous and flowing lines, made known to Florence by the visit of Gentile da Fabriano in 1423, was apparently admired but littled heeded by conventional artists such as Bicci di Lorenzo.....

> from St. J. Gore, p. 20, *The Art of Painting in Florence & Siena from 1250-1500*, London, 1965.

Florentine School. Born 1373; died 1452. The son of Lorenzo di Bicci and the father of Neri di Bicci, he appears in his early work as a follower of Agnolo Gaddi. Later he was influenced by Gentile da Fabriano's Florentine sojourn of the 1420's and soon after 1440 he collaborated with Domenico Veneziano.....

> from F. R. Shapley, p. 47, *Paintings from the Samuel H. Kress Collection*, London, 1966.

BIBLIOGRAPHY
BOOKS

An asterisk indicates a work listed in the General Bibliography

*Pini, Milanesi**, 1876, no 22; Venturi, A., *Storia dell' Arte Italiana*, VII, Milan, 1911, pp. 24-5; *v. Marle, 1927**, IX, pp. 1-106; *Colnaghi**, 1928, p. 42; Salmi, M., *Treccani, Vol. VI**, 1930, p. 973; *Berenson, 1932**, pp. 82-6; Longstreet, G. W., *General Catalogue: The Isabella Stewart Gardner Museum, Fenway Court*, Boston, 1935, p. 97; *Antal**, 1947, pp. 331-2; *Galetti** 1950, " A-E ", p. 343; Berti, L., *MAS I**, 1957, pp. 62-3; *Cracow**, 1961, pp. 48-49; *Berenson 1963**, Vol. I, p. 27; Dal Poggetto, P., *AIV**, 1963, pp. 45-6; Gore, St J., *Wildenstein**, 1965, pp. 20-1; *Shapley**, 1966, p. 47; Procacci, U., *Fresco Show**, 1968, pp. 106-11 (98-101); Klesse, B., *Katalog der Italienischen, Französischen und Spanischen Gemälde bis 1800 im Wallraf-Richartz Museum*, Cologne, 1973, p. 24; Palumbo, G., *Collezione Federico Mason Perkins*, Rome, 1973, pp. 62-63; *Maetzke**, 1974, pp. 75-77.

JOURNALS

Fiocco, G., *RA*, XI, 1929, pp. 25-42; Procacci, U., *RA*, XI, 1929, pp. 119-27; Berenson, B., *DD*, XII, 1, 1932, pp. 173-193; Offner, R., *BM*, LXIII, 1933, p. 170; Colasanti, A., *BA*, XXVII, 1934, pp. 337-50; Salmi, M., *RA*, XVI, 1934, pp. 168-86; Suida, W. E., *AP*, XX, 1934, p. 120; Constable, W. G., *BMB*, XLIII, 1945, pp. 71-5; Mather, R. G., *AB*, 30, 1948, pp. 20-65; Ragghianti, C. L., *NCA*, I, 1954, pp. 293-99; Cohn, W., *RA*, XXXI, 1956, pp. 41-72; Cohn, W., *BA*, XLIV, 1959, pp. 61-8; Rozycka-Bryzek, A., *Biuletin Historii Sztuki*, XXII, 1960, pp. 203-18; Berti, L., *C*, XII, 1961, pp. 84-107; Rozycka-Bryzek, A., *A*, LXI, 27/3-4, 1962, pp. 115-124; Laclotte, M., *RDL*, 14, 1964, p. 185; Acton, H., *AP*, LXXXII, 1965, pp. 278-9; Martelli, G., *BA*, L, 5, 1965, p. 137; Bellosi, L., *PA*, XVIII, 1967, 203/23, pp. 86-7; Brigstocke, H., *York Review*, XXI, 82, 1968, p. 759; Beck, J. H., *AB*, LIII, 2, 1971, pp. 181, 184-89; *MMOA**, 1971, pp. 68-72; Procacci, U., *MKIF*, XVII, 2-3, 1973, p. 319.

DATED WORKS

1414 Stia, Propositura di S. Maria Assunta. Triptych: Annunciation with Sts Michael, James the Less, Margaret and John the Evangelist. d. (fig. 979).
1423 Berlin. Panels: St Salvi healing plague-stricken, Nativity, S. Bernardo degli Uberti (destroyed 1945). d. (fig. 980).
1430 Florence, Porta S. Giorgio. Fresco. Lunette: Madonna & Child Enthroned with Sts. George and Leonard. d. (fig. 988).
1430 Vertine, S. Bartolomeo. Triptych: Madonna and Child with two Angels and Sts Bartholomew, John the Evangelist, Mary Magdalene and Anthony Abbot. d. (fig. 989).
1433 Parma, Pinacoteca 456. Three panels from triptych: Madonna & Child Enthroned with four Angels and Saints. c.p. d. (fig. 990).
1434 Velletri, Museo del Duomo. Panel: Visitation. d. (fig. 993).
1435 Bibbiena (Casentino), Propositura. Triptych: Madonna Enthroned nursing the Child with Saints. d. (fig. 996).
1435 Florence, S. Giovannino dei Cavalieri. Panel: Nativity. d. (fig. 1003).
1440 Legnaia, Florence, S. Arcangelo. Panel: Annunciation. d. (fig. 1000).

There are no known signed works by Bicci di Lorenzo.

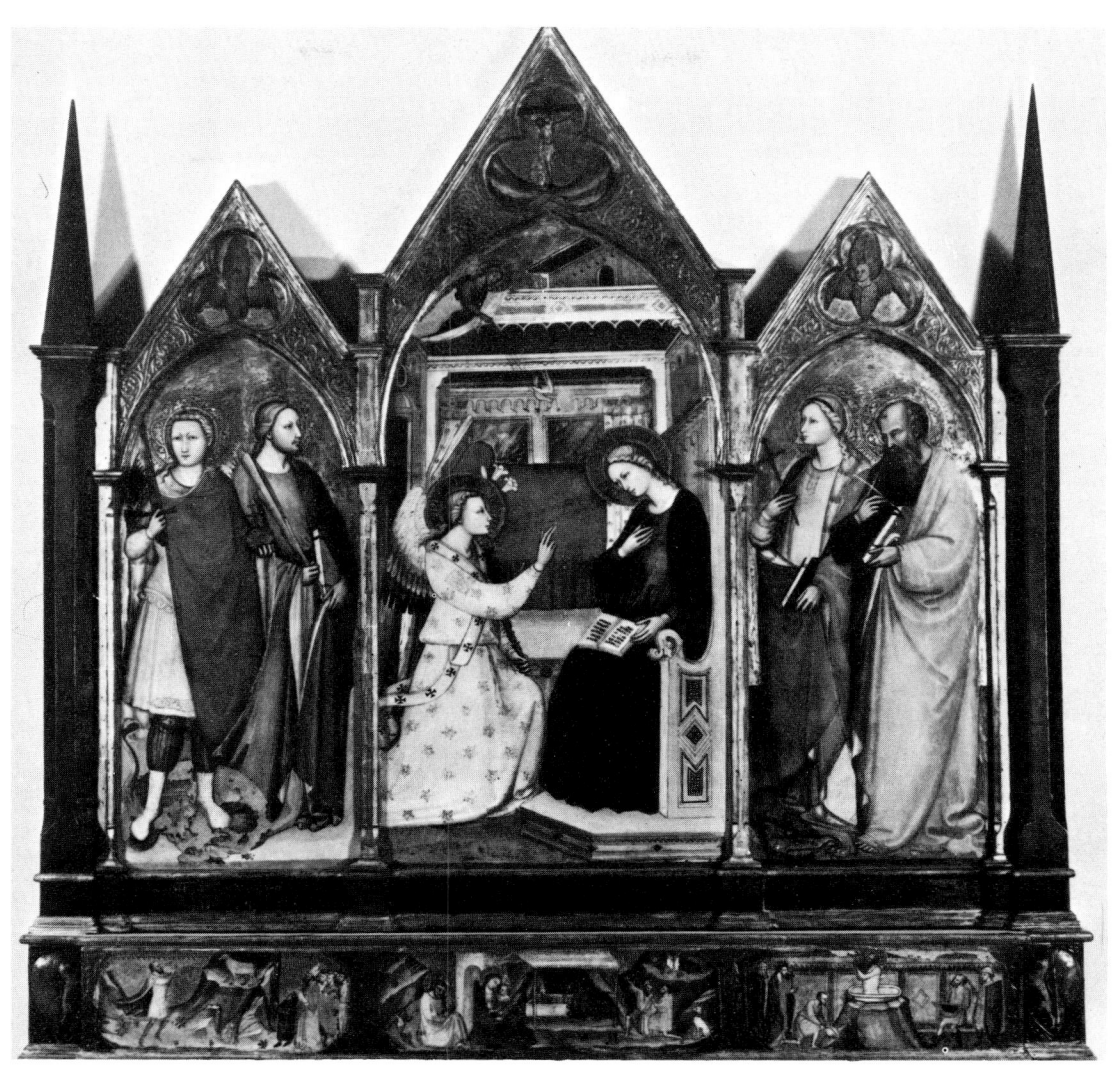

979

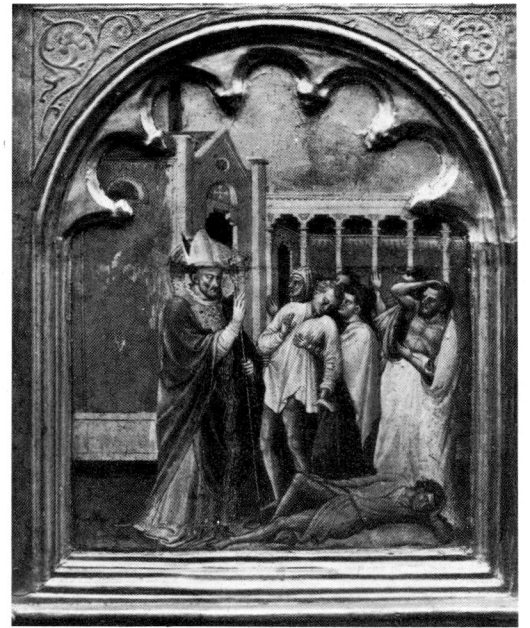
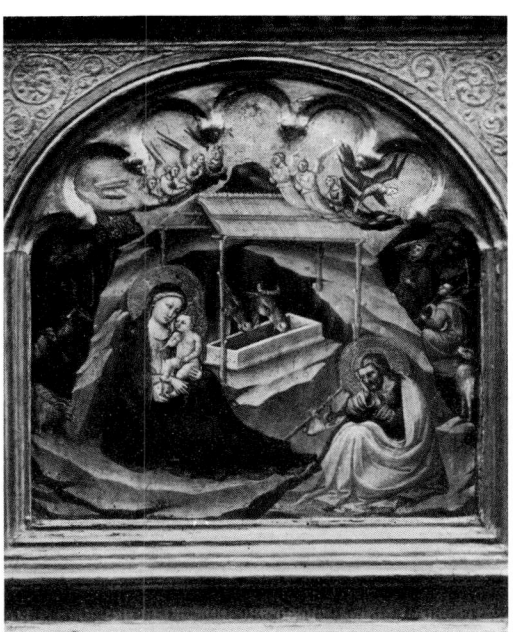
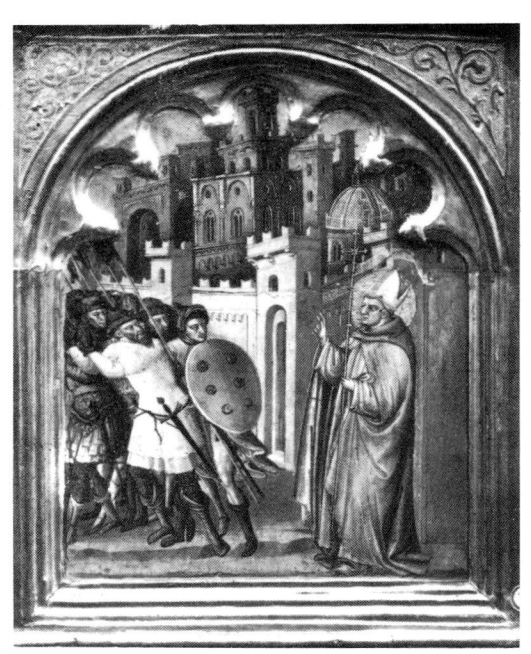

980

979. *Triptych: Annunciation with Sts Michael, James the Less, Margaret and John the Evangelist. Above: Christ on the Cross; Cherubim and Seraphim. Predella: Miracle of the Bull of Gargano; Nativity; St John in the Cauldron of Boiling Oil. Panel. Stia, near Pratovecchio (Casentino), Propositura di S. Maria Assunta. 190 × 180. SGA 11660. d. 1414.*

980. *Three predella scenes: St Salvi healing the Plague-stricken (41 × 32); Nativity (41 × 40); S. Bernardo degli Uberti defending Rome (41 × 32). Panels. Berlin, Bodestrasse, Staatliche Museen, no. 1046A. Museum photo. d. 1423 (destroyed 1945).*

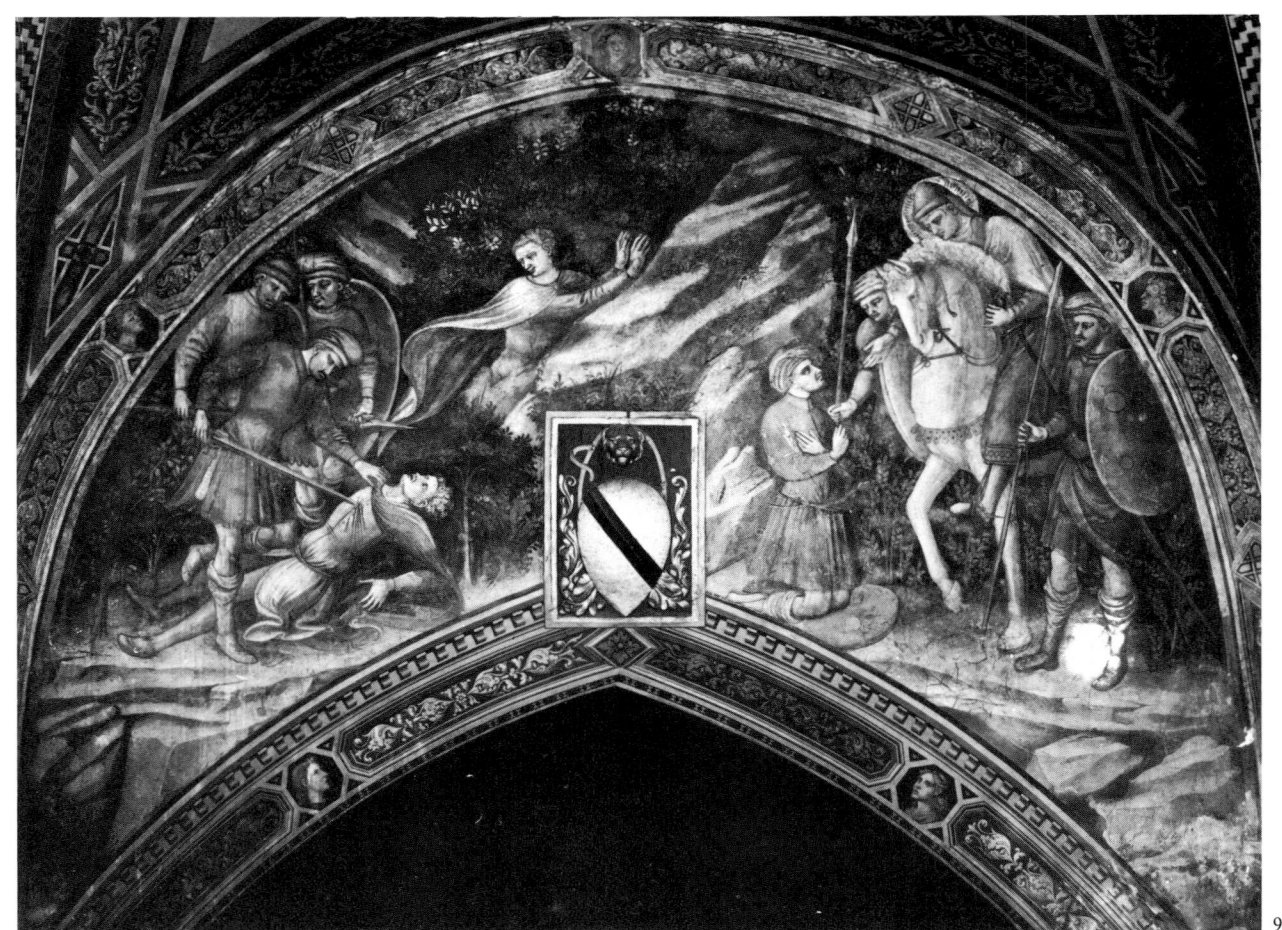

981

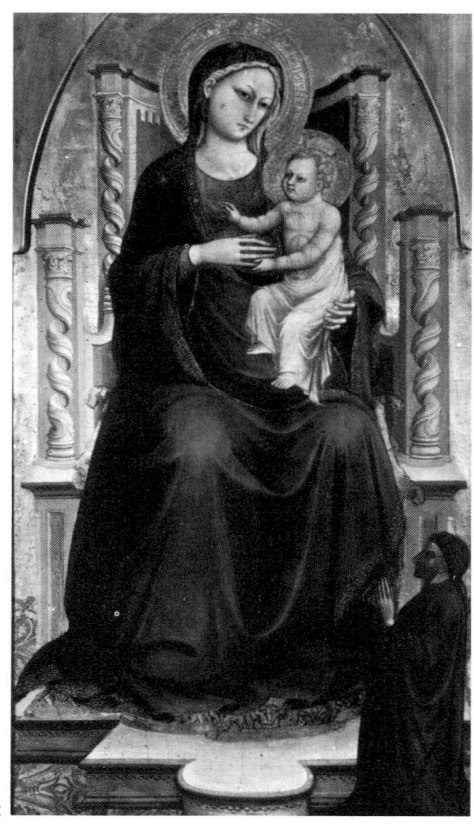

982

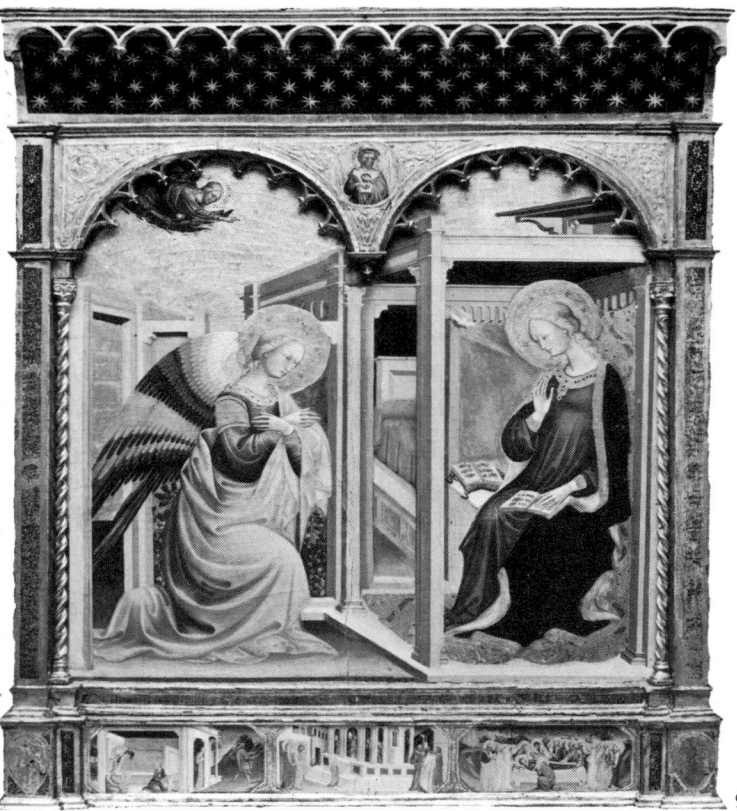

983

981. *Killing of the brother of St John Gualbert; St John Gualbert forgives his brother's assassin. Fresco. Florence, S. Trinita. SGF 111602.*
982. *Madonna and Child Enthroned with Simone Guiducci di Specchio as Donor. Panel. Empoli, Museo della Collegiata. no. 18. 130 × 78. SGF 69535. 1423.*
983. *Annunciation. Predella: scenes from the Life of the Virgin: Birth, Presentation in the Temple; Dormition. Panel. Baltimore (Md.), Walters Art Gallery. no. 37.448. 164.5 × 144.7. Museum photo H 47.*

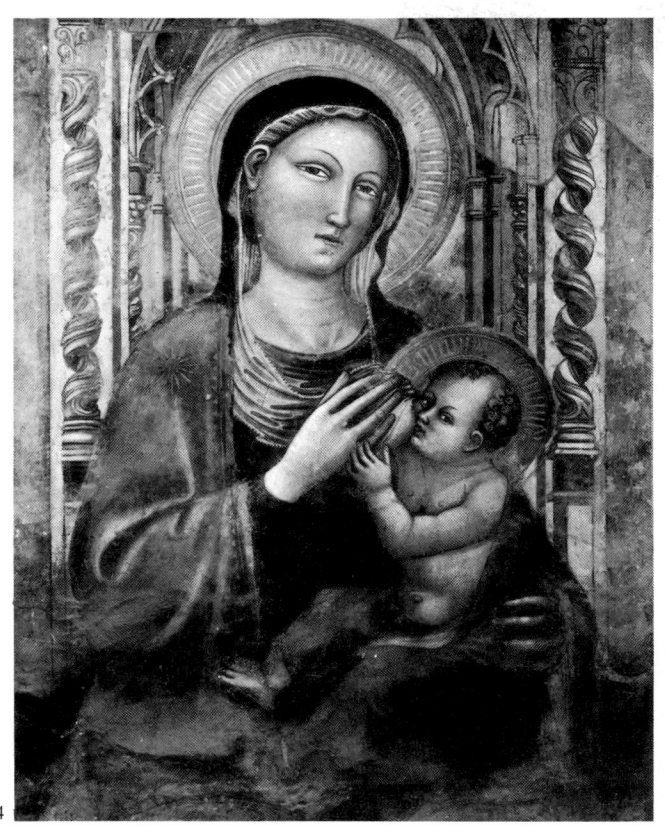

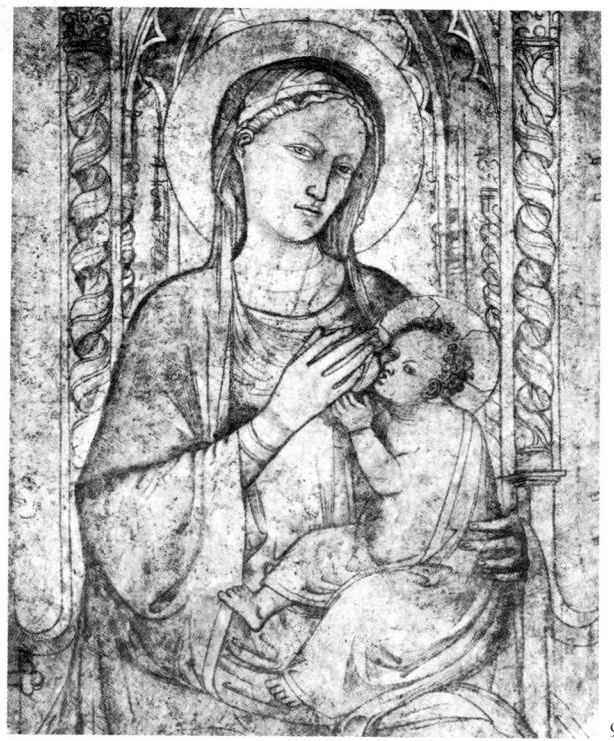

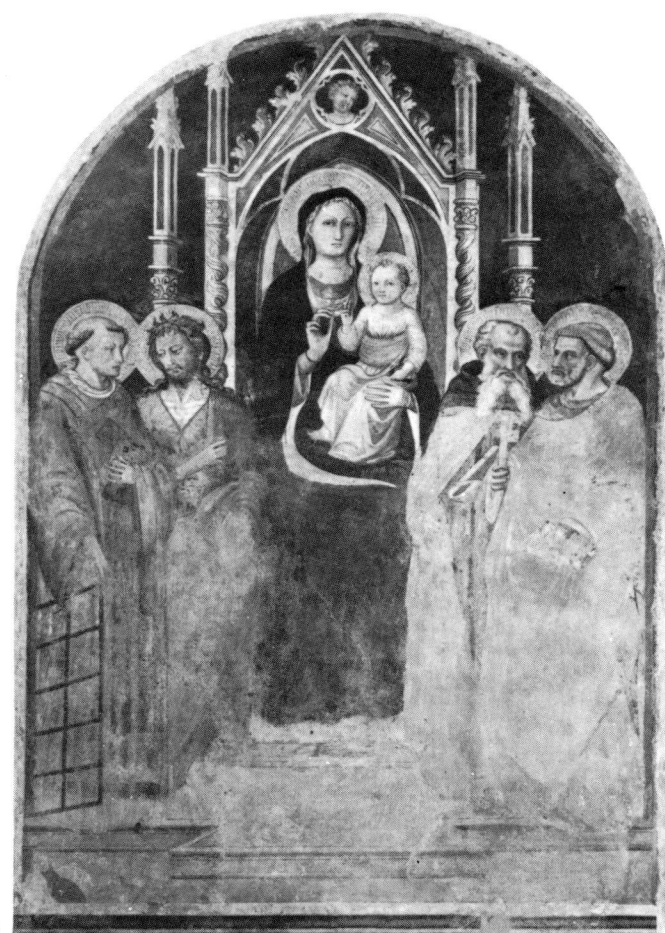

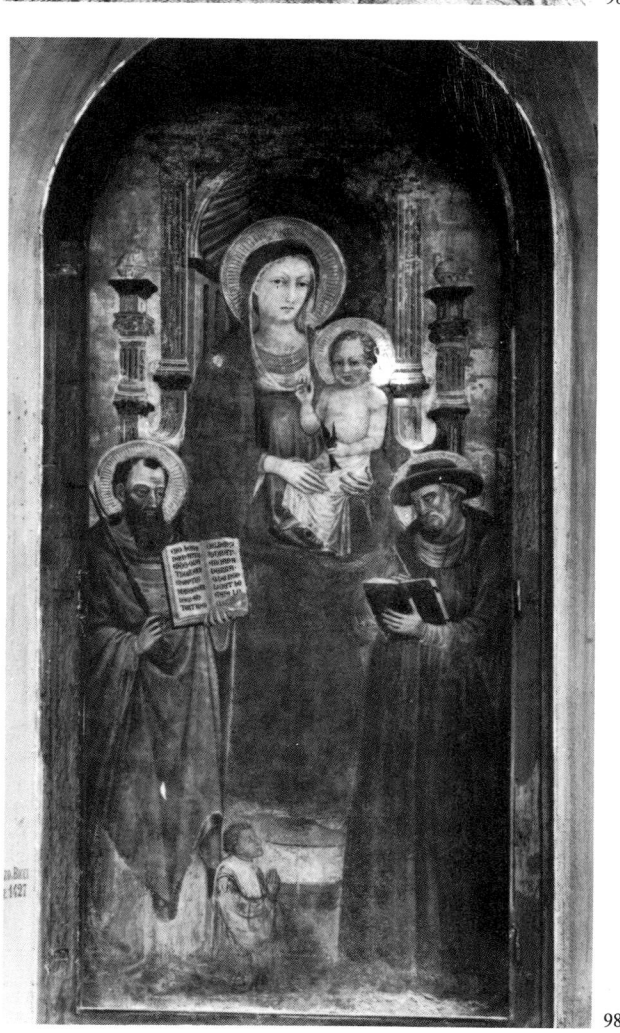

984. Tabernacle: Madonna nursing the Child. Fresco. Florence, corner via Aretina and via S. Salvi. Alinari 29174. 1427.
985. Tabernacle: Sinopia of fig. 984. Madonna and Child. Fresco. Florence, corner via Aretina and via S. Salvi. SGF 113199.
986. Tabernacle: Madonna and Child Enthroned with Sts Lawrence, John the Baptist, Anthony Abbot and Peter. Fresco. Ponte a Greve (near Florence), via Pisana. SGF 108410.
987. Tabernacle: Madonna and Child Enthroned with Sts Paul and Jerome and Donor. Fresco. Florence, corner of via de' Serragli and via S. Monaca. Alinari 29168. 1427.

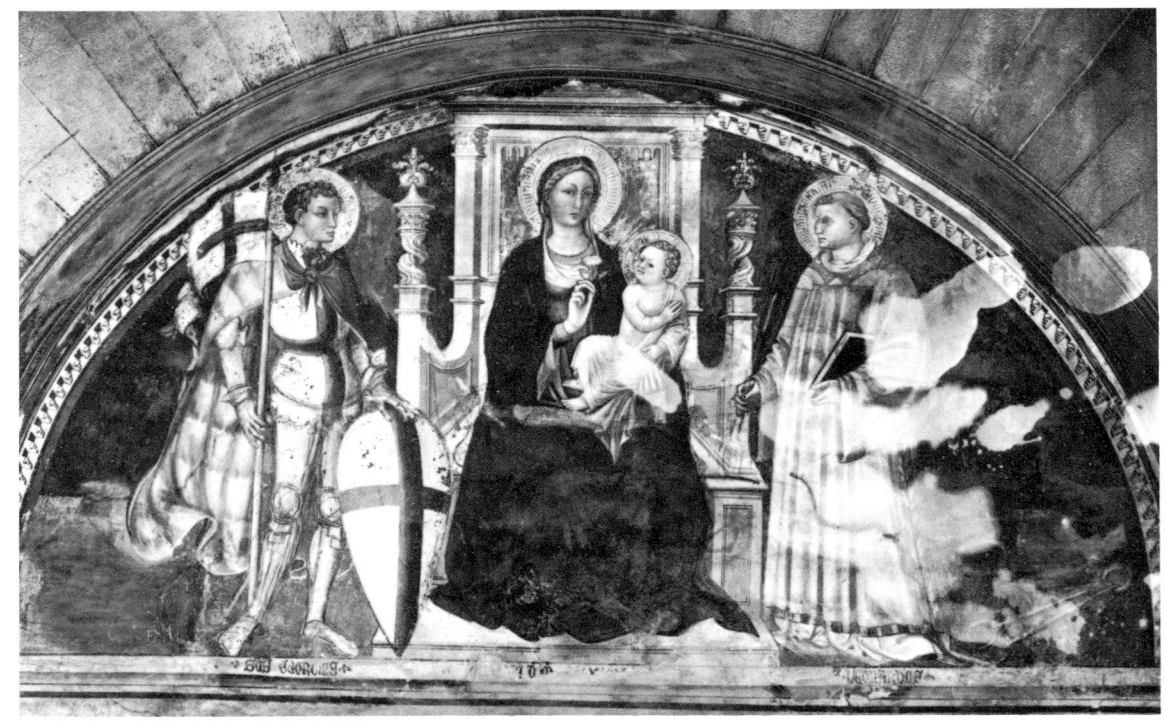

988

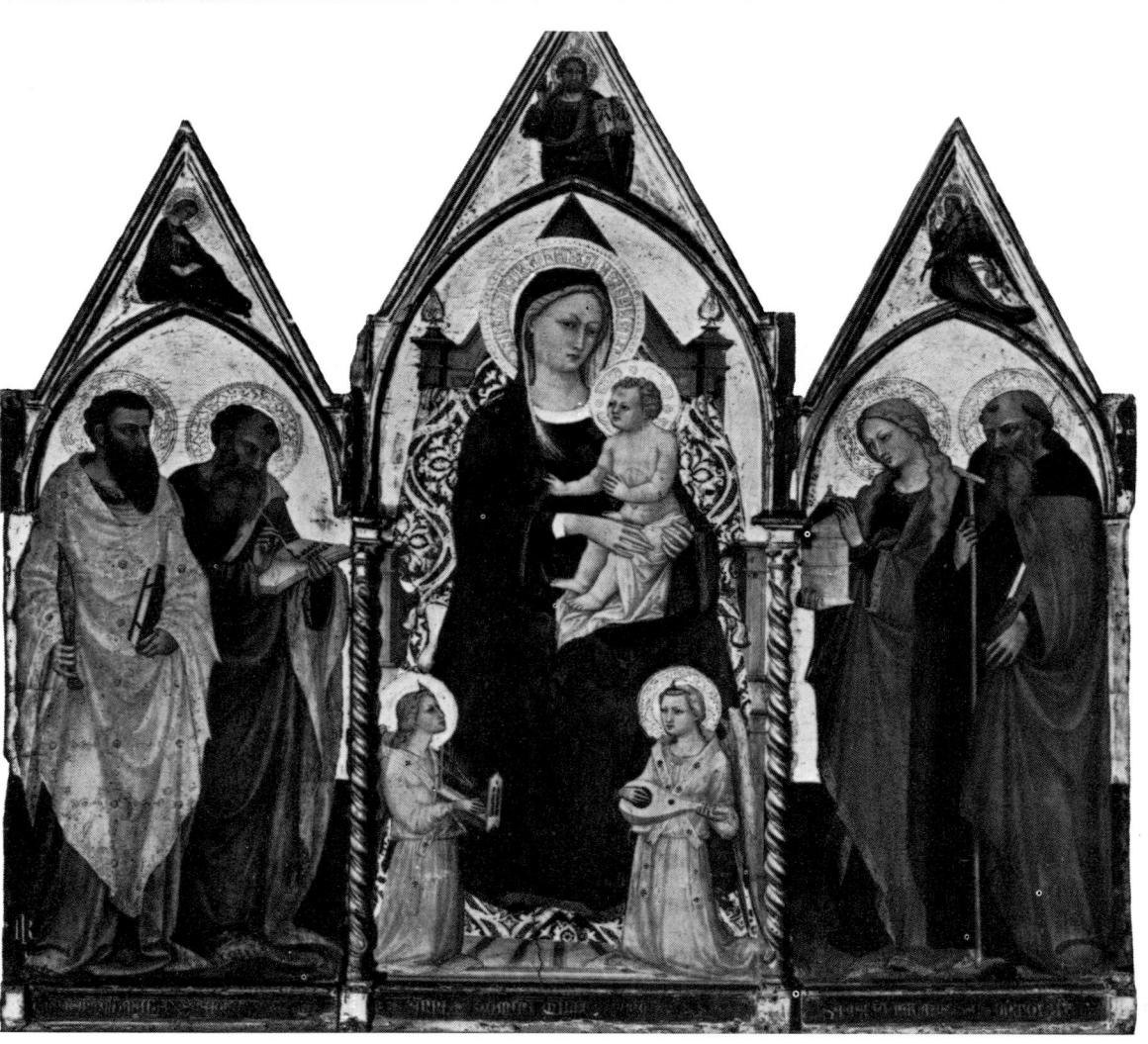

989

988. *Lunette: Madonna and Child Enthroned with Sts George and Leonard. Fresco. Florence, Porta S. Giorgio. 243 × 451. Alinari 4698. d. 1430.*
989. *Triptych: Madonna and Child Enthroned with two music-making Angels and Sts Bartholomew, John the Evangelist, Mary Magdalene and Anthony. Panel. Siena, Pinacoteca Nazionale. 183 × 74. Brogi 14934. d. 1430 (on loan from Vertine, Chianti).*

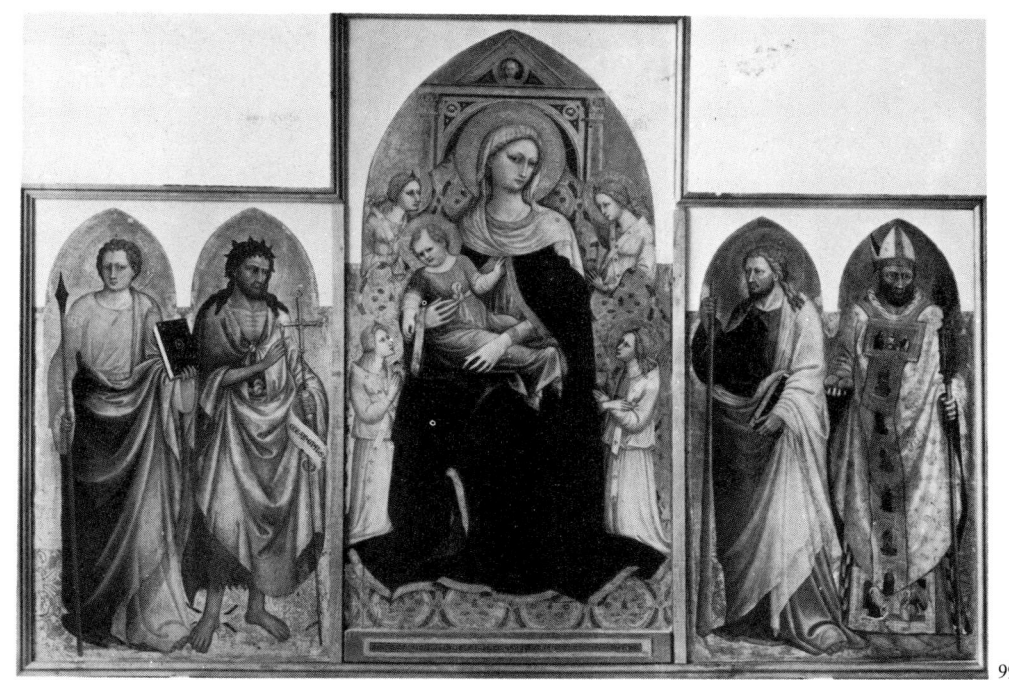

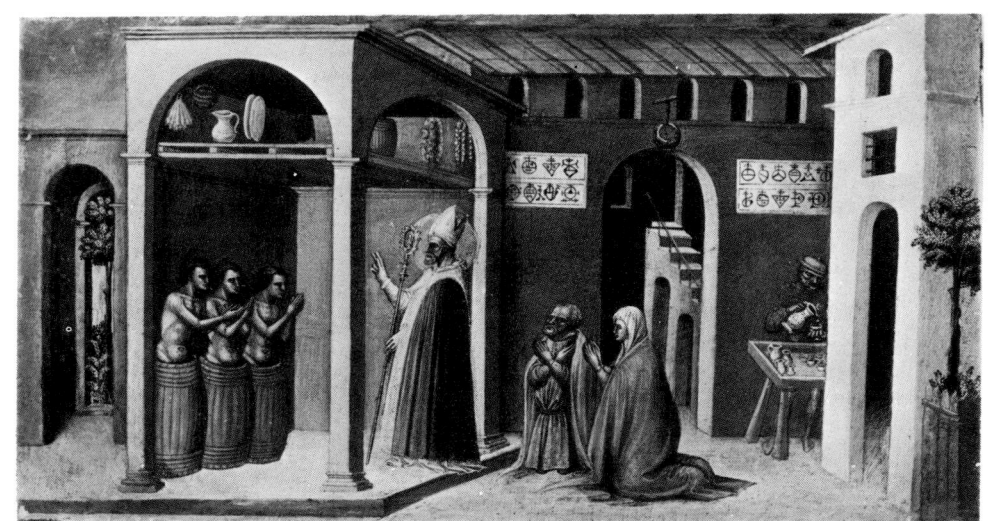

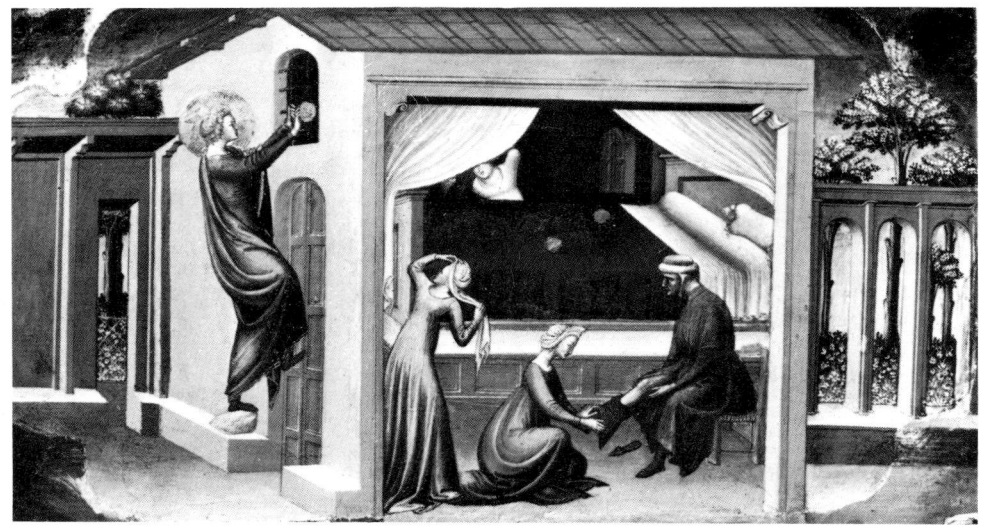

990. *Three panels from a triptych: Madonna and Child Enthroned with four Angels, Sts Thomas, John the Baptist, James the Less and Nicholas of Bari.*
cp: Parma, Galleria Nazionale. no. 456. 171 × 81.7. sps: Parma, Congregazione di S. Filippo Neri, Pinacoteca Stuard. nos. 5 and 6. Museum
photo: AI 11/3. cp. d. 1433.

991. *St Nicholas reviving three Youths. Panel. New York (N.Y.), Metropolitan Museum of Art, Francis Kleinberger Gift. no. 16.121. 30.5 × 57.1:*
Museum photo 34341. 1433.

992. *St Nicholas providing Dowries. Panel. New York (N.Y.), Metropolitan Museum of Art. no. 88.3.89, Coudert Brothers Gift. 30.4 × 57.1. Museum*
photo 8511. 1433.

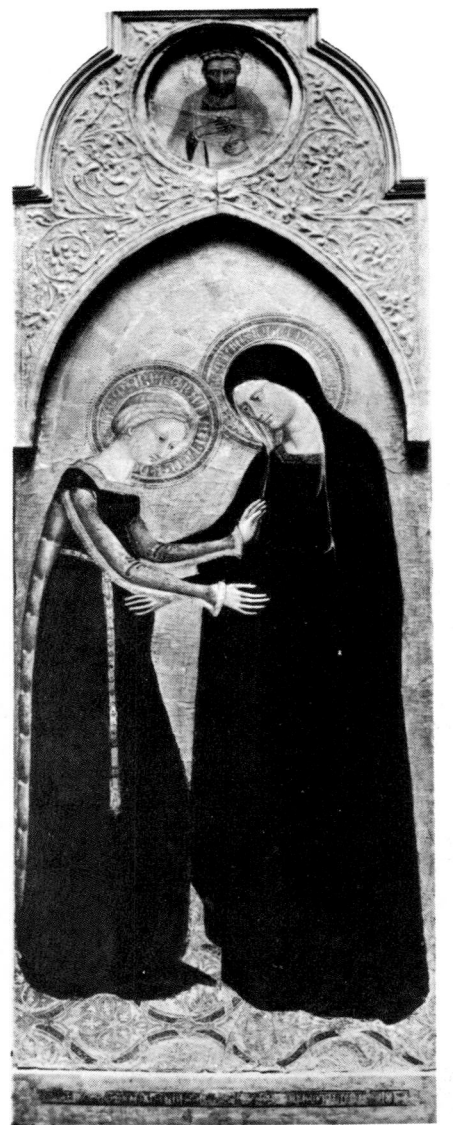

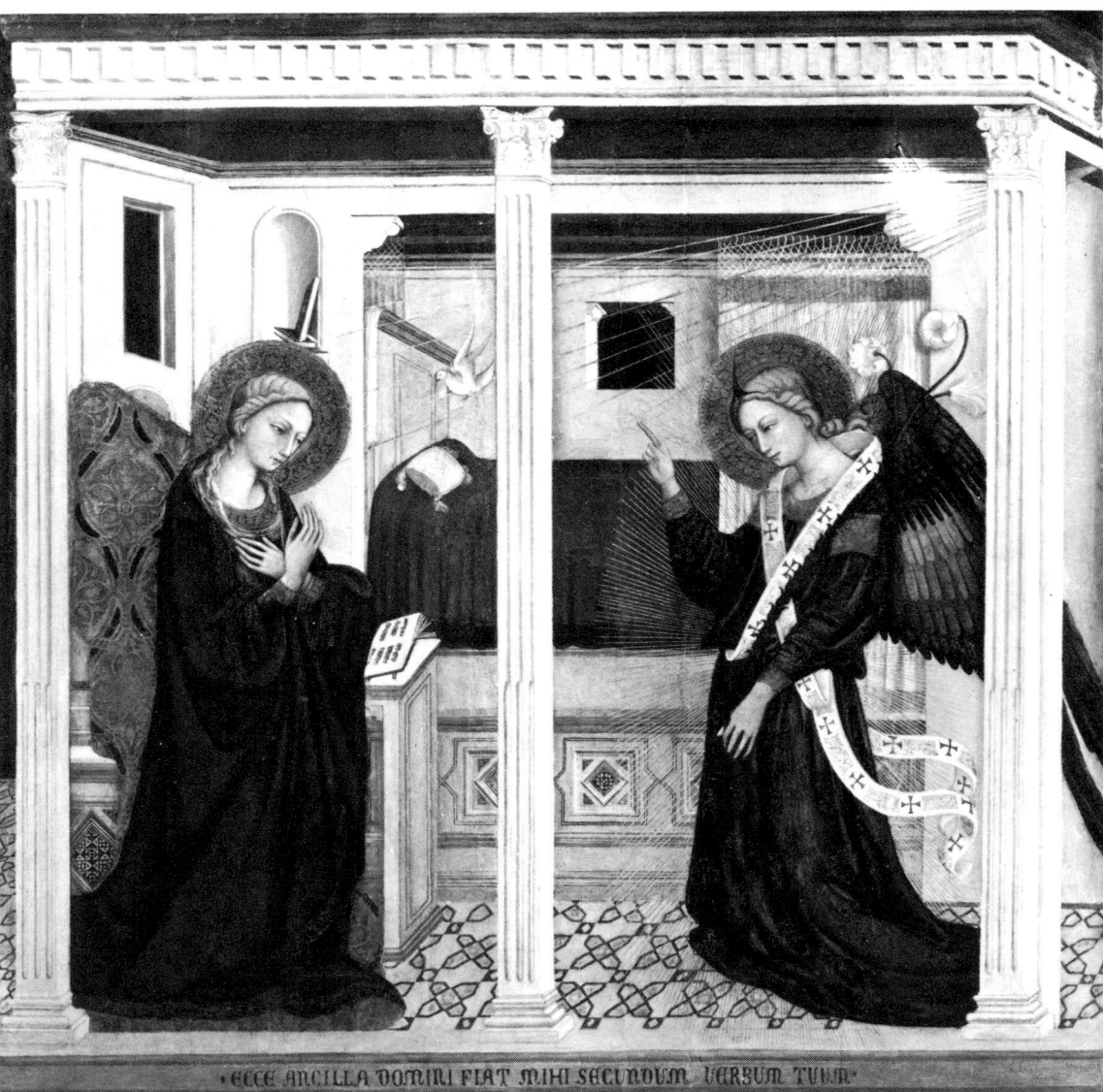

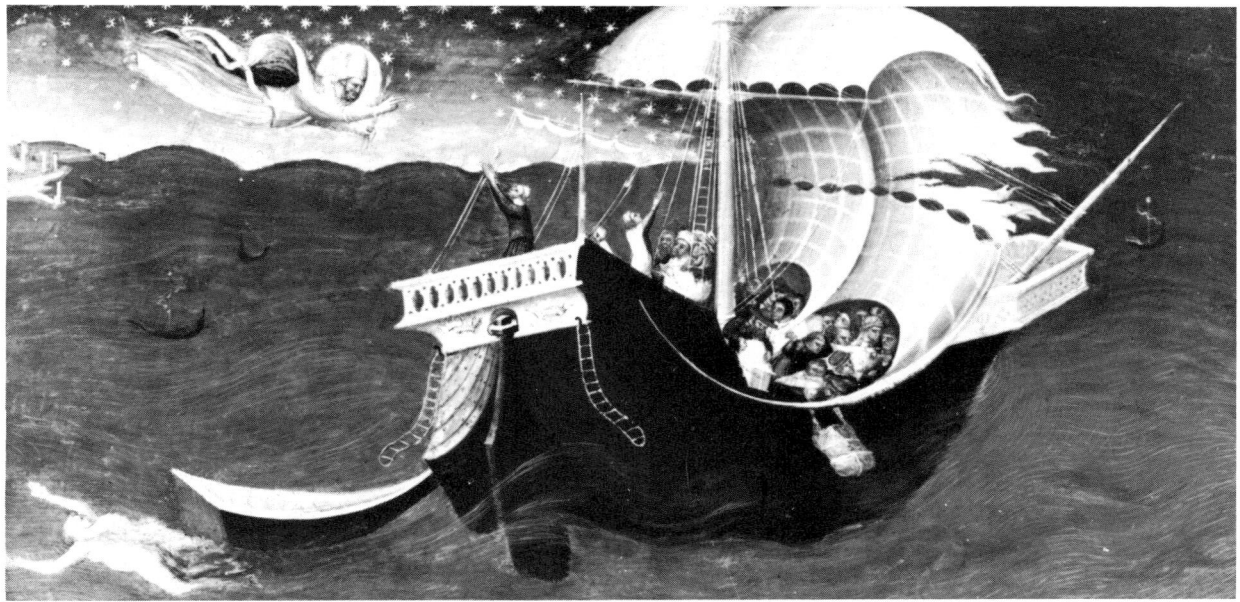

993. *Visitation. Above: David. Panel. Velletri, Museo del Duomo. Fototeca Berenson. d. 1434.*
994. *Annunciation. Panel. Boston (Mass.), Museum of Fine Arts. no. 43.218. 146 × 144.1. Museum photo C11723.*
995. *Miracle of St Nicholas of Bari, saving the Ship. Panel. Oxford, Ashmolean Museum. no. 60. 71.1 × 49.8. Museum photo. 1433.*

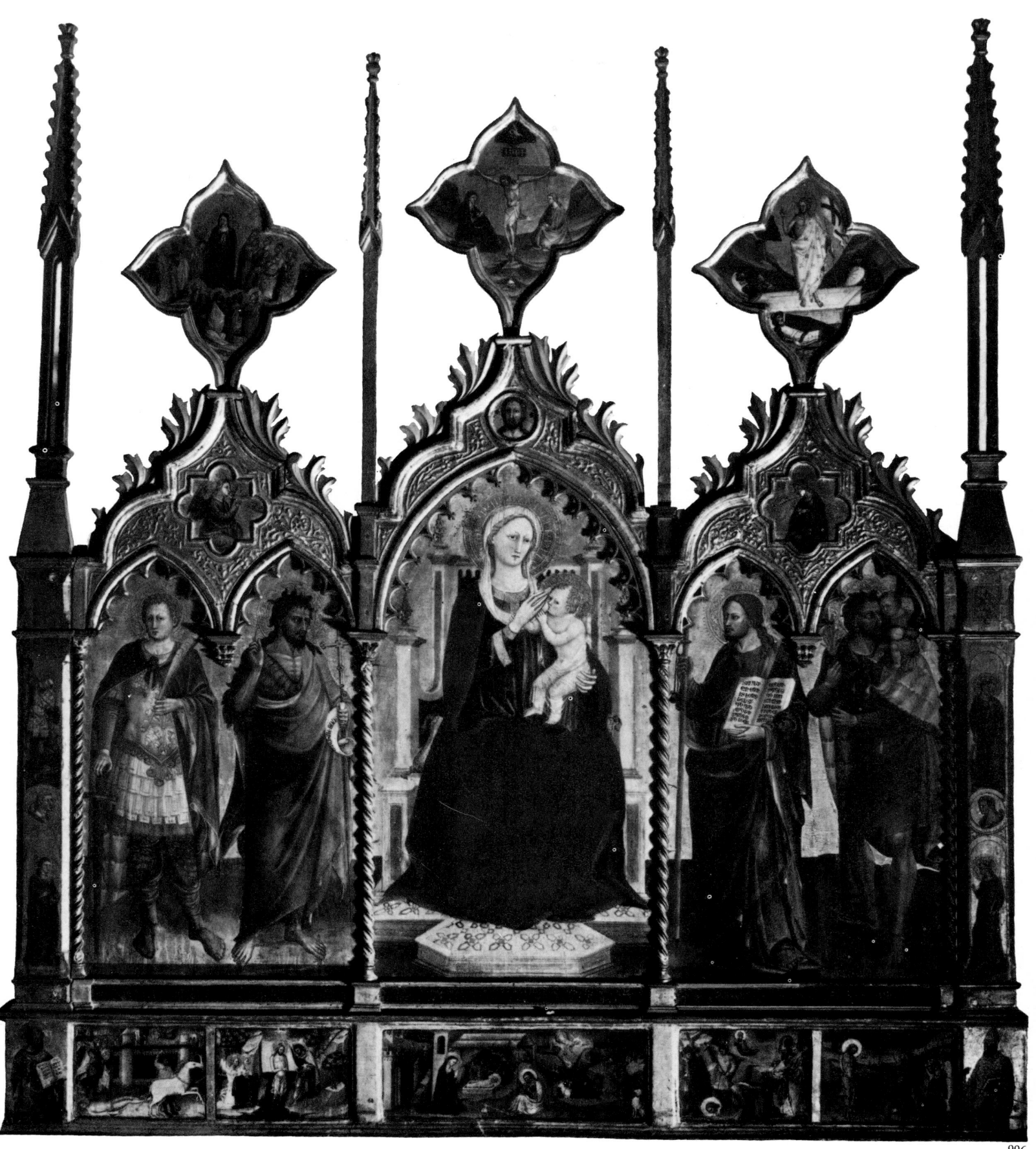

996. *Triptych: Madonna Enthroned nursing the Child, with Sts Hippolytus, John the Baptist, James and Christopher. Above: Assumption; Christ on the Cross with the Virgin and St John; Resurrection. Pilasters: four Saints, two Angels' heads. Predella: an Evangelist, Martyrdom of St Hippolytus, Baptism of Christ, Nativity, Beheading of St James, Attempted Martyrdom of St Christopher. Panel. Bibbiena (Casentino), Propositura, Pieve di S. Ippolito. 280 × 250 (incl. spires). SGF 80662. d. 1435.*

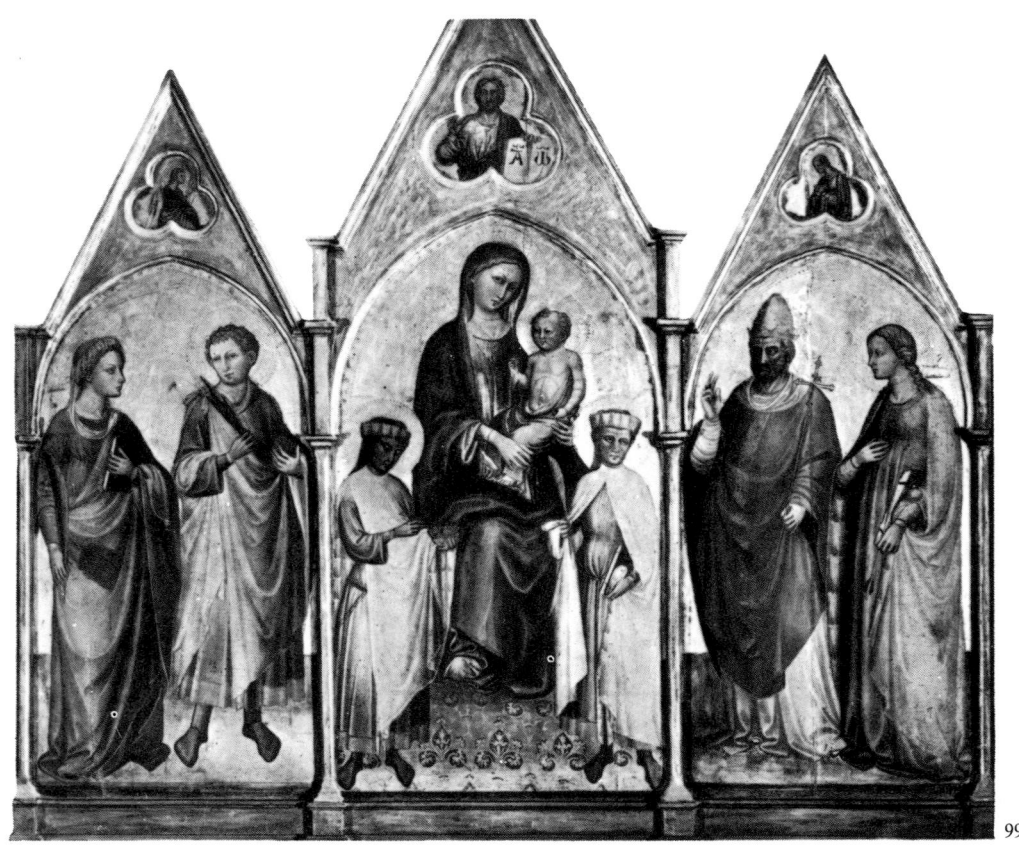

997

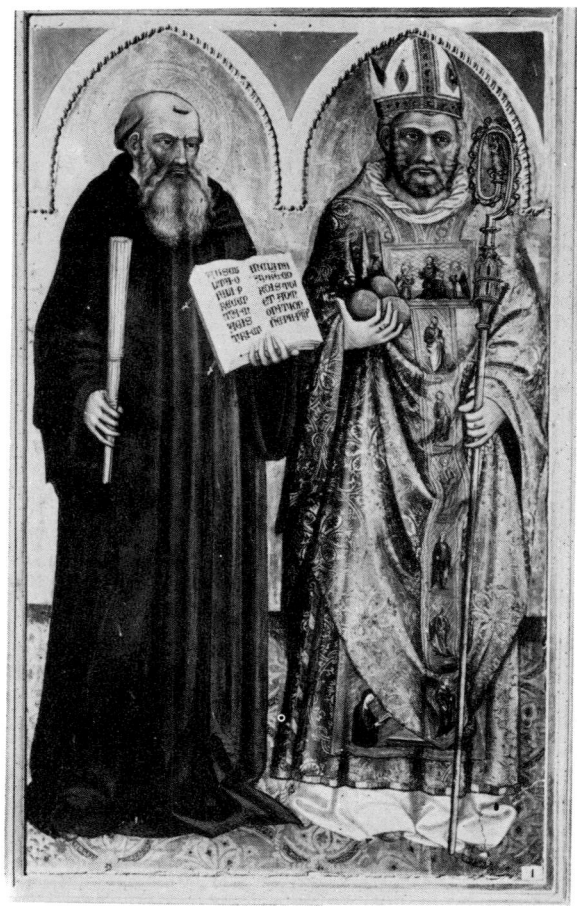

998

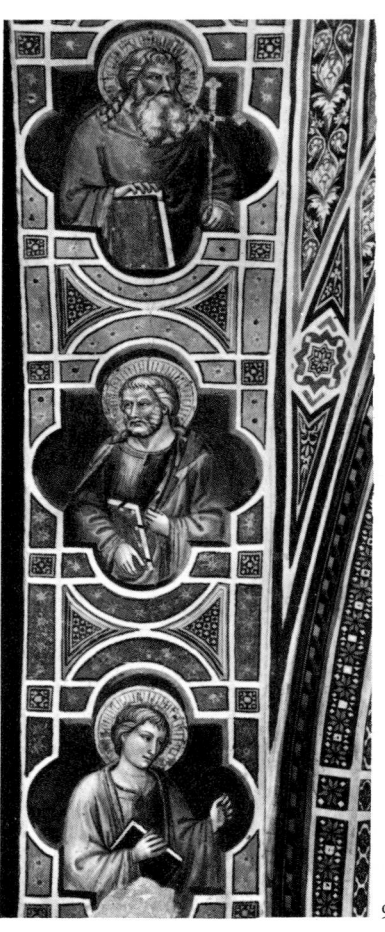

999

997. *Triptych: Madonna and Child with Sts Cosmas and Damian, a female Saint, Sts Ansanus, Clement and Ursula. Above: Christ blessing; Annunciation.*
Panel. Florence, S. Ambrogio. 175 × 184. Alinari 36341.
998. *Sts Benedict and Nicholas of Bari. Panel. Grottaferrata (near Frascati), Badia. 125 × 75. GFN E1267. d. 1433.*
999. *Three half-figures of saints. Fresco. Pescia (Lower Valdarno), S. Antonio Abbate. SGF 129618.*

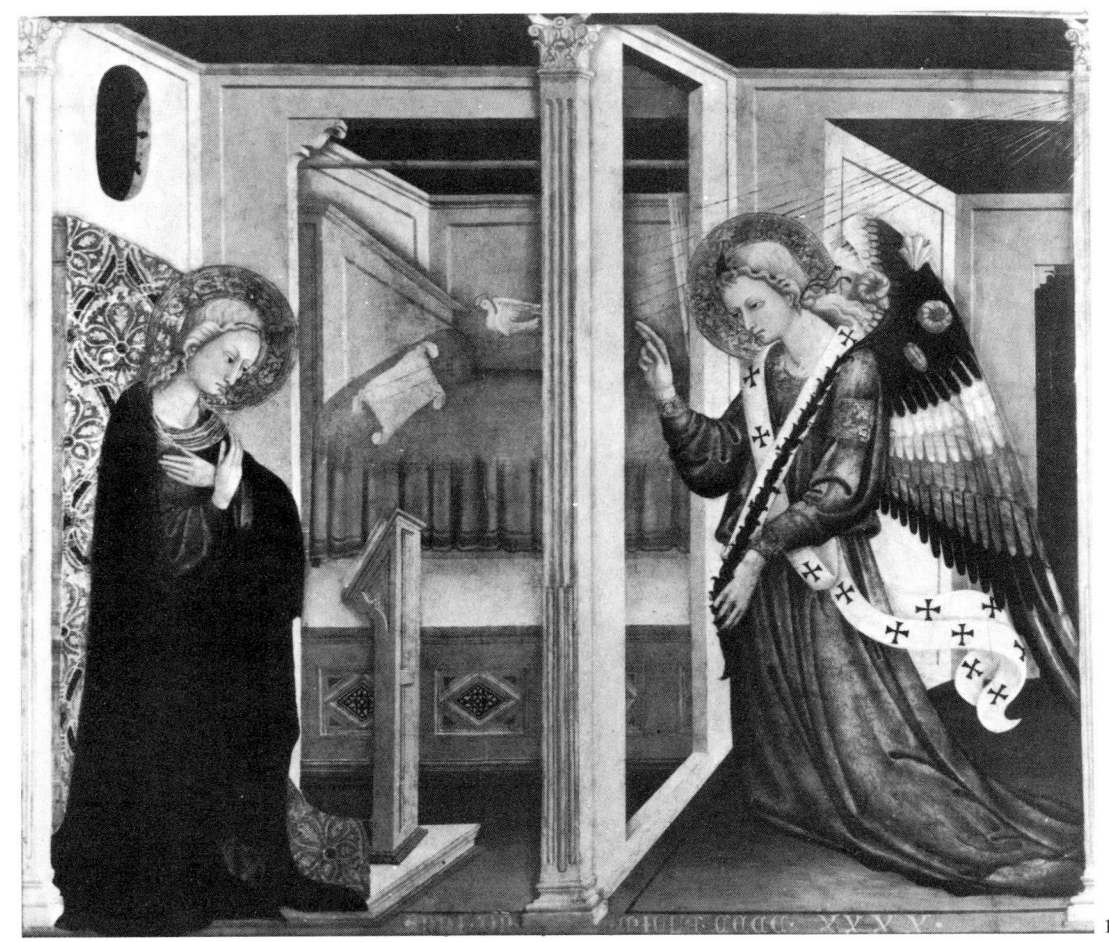

1000

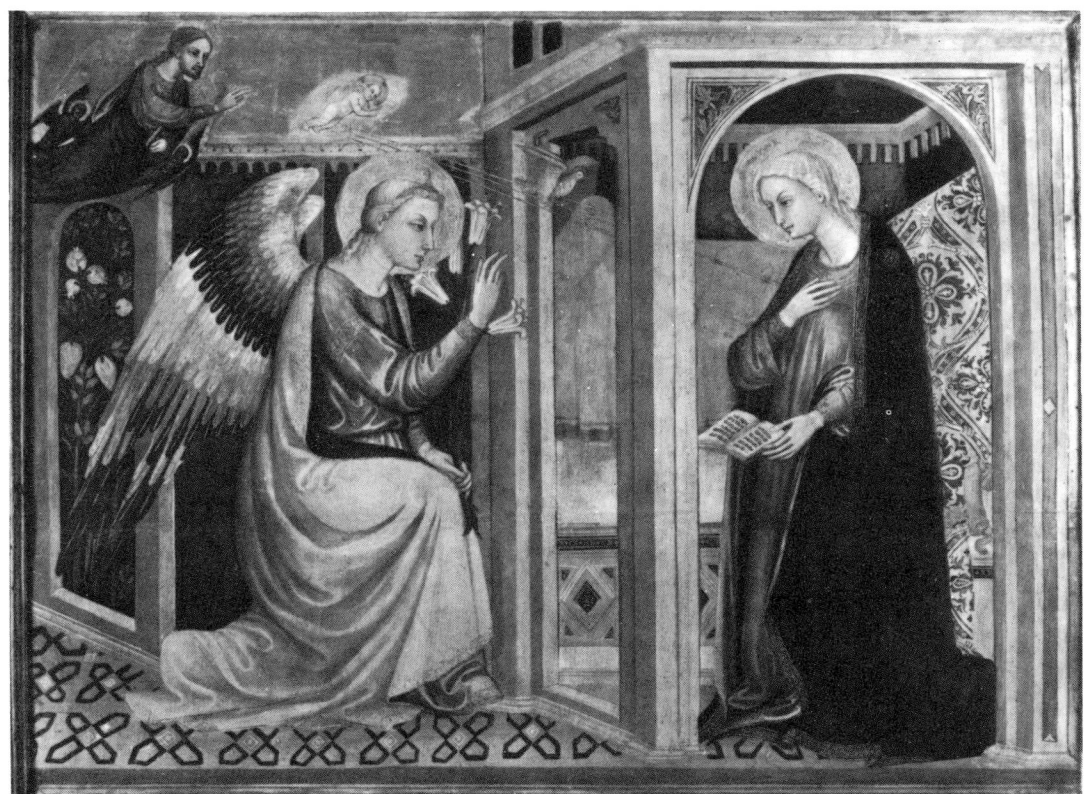

1001

1000. *Annunciation. Panel. Legnaia (Florence), S. Arcangelo. 130 × 150. SGF 68767. d. 1440.*
1001. *Annunciation. Panel. Private Collection. Reali.*

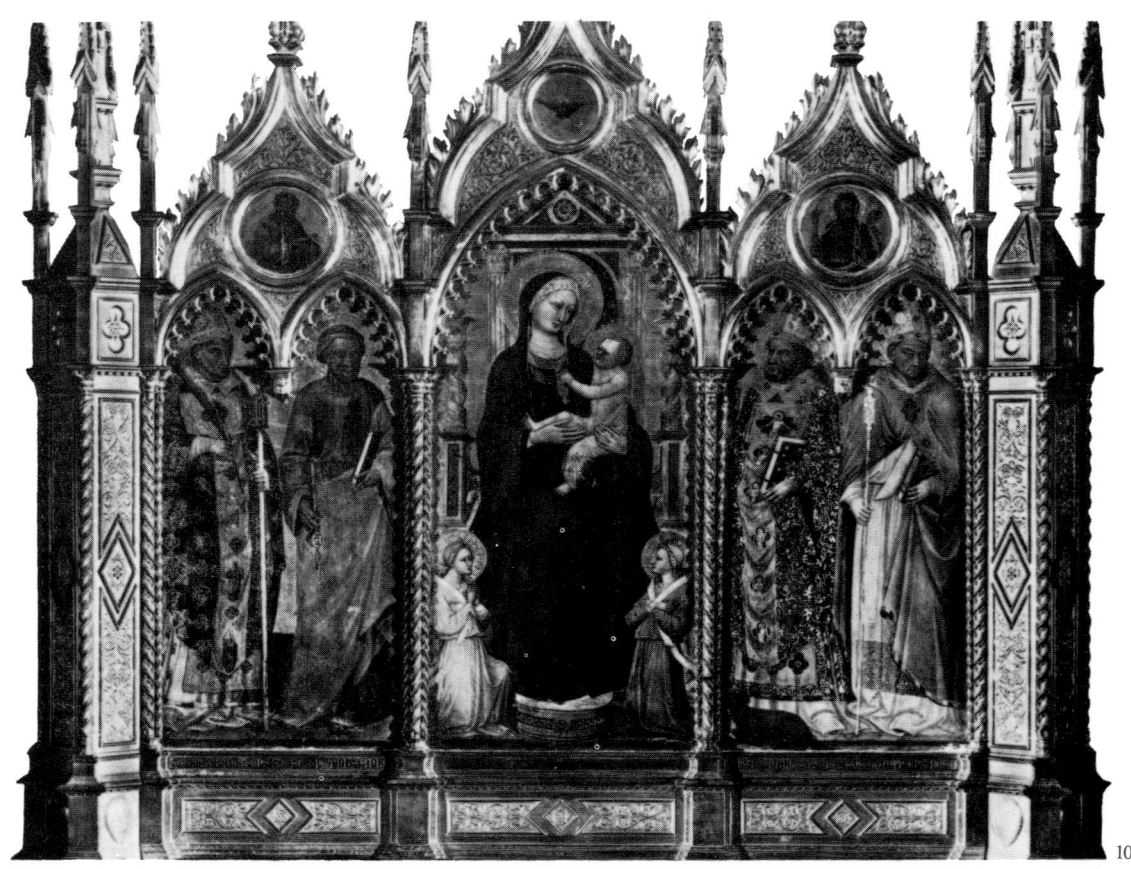

1002

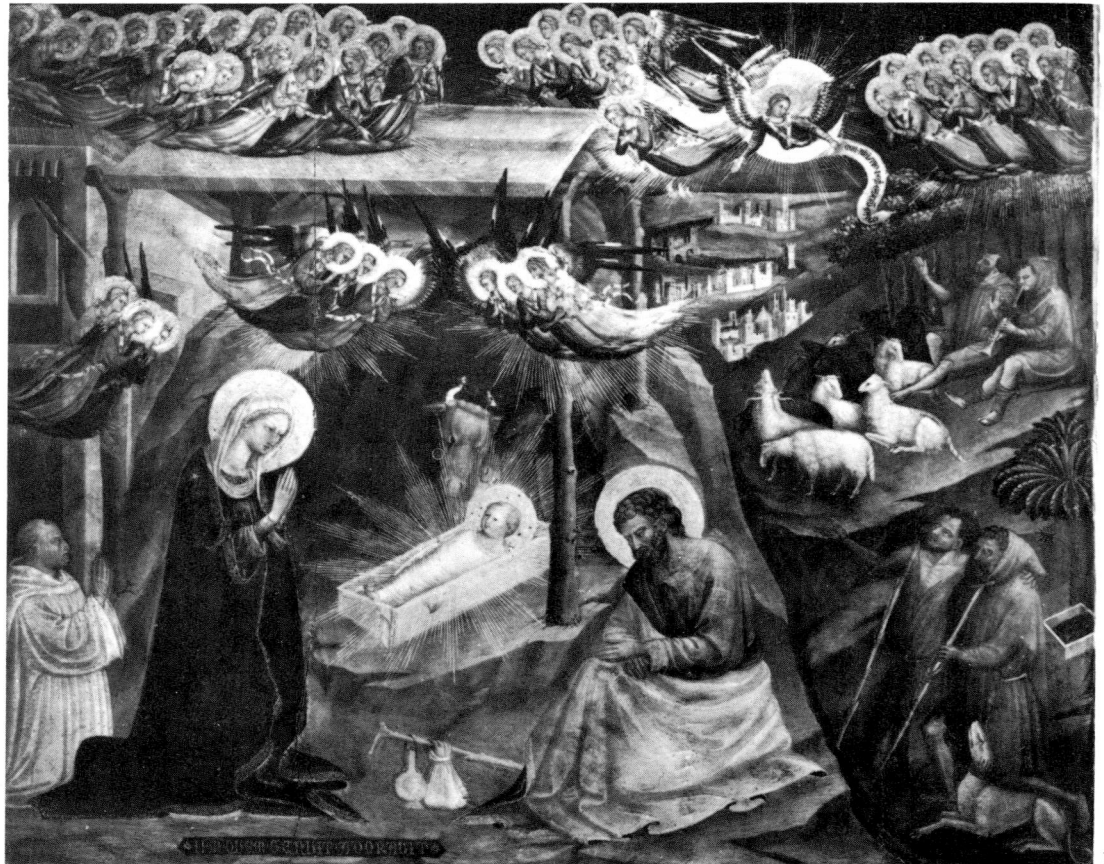

1003

1002. Triptych: Madonna and Child Enthroned with two Angels and Sts Alexander, Peter, Donatus and Romulus. Above: Holy Spirit, an Evangelist and John the Baptist. Panel. Fiesole, Duomo. cp: 172.5 × 81.5; sps: 138.5 × 74. Alinari 20349. d. 1450.
1003. Nativity. Panel. Florence, S. Giovannino dei Cavalieri. 190 × 190 (predella included). Alinari 20306. d. 1435.

MASOLINO

We have a few basic facts about Tommaso di Cristoforo Fini, called [Panicale] after the place he came from either in Valdelsa or in Valdarno. He was born in 1383; in 1424 he was registered in the Arte degli Speziali and was working in Empoli for the Company of the Holy Cross; in 1427 he was still in Hungary where he'd gone to work for Pippo Spano, the viceroy of Temesvar, an adventurous Florentine merchant who had been a *condottiero* for the Emperor Sigismond; he probably died in 1447. Luckily, we have a sure work of his, and thus an exact point of departure for anyone wishing to know his style — a cycle of frescoes..... at Castiglione d'Olona, a tiny village between Tradate and Varese, which Cardinal Branda Castiglione, at the beginning of the Quattrocento, made blessed by Art.....

> from P. Toesca, p. 11, *Masolino da Panicale*, Bergamo, 1908.

Masolino, Tommaso di Cristofano di Fino — called Masolino. Painter. Born at Panicale (Valdarno) in 1383, died in 1440 or 47 as is illustrated in the book of the dead in Santa Maria del Fiore. Certainly Ghiberti and contemporary sculpture influenced his formation, which is not sufficiently clear. There is, therefore, no particular reason not to believe the sources which say that Masolino helped Ghiberti on the second door of the Baptistery. However, Milanesi and Colnaghi have hypothesized that the Maso di Cristofano who was cited in the agreements of 1403 and 1407 between Ghiberti and the Merchant's Guild, referred to the goldsmith Tommaso di Cristofano di Braccio who died January 13, 1430. An indirect, although not decisive proof of collaboration with Ghiberti would be, according to Salmi, Masolino's late entry into the Guild of Physicians and Apothecaries. Neither can one completely deny the possibility of his having been apprenticed to the almost mythical Starnina.....

> from U. Baldini, p. 919, *Enciclopedia Universale dell' Arte*, Vol III, Venice-Rome, 1958.

The name of Tommaso di Cristofano di Fino, called Masolino is so well known that one needs add but essential biographical data. After the Madonna of Bremen in 1423, Masolino's artistic development is evidenced first by a fresco fragment [in Empoli " Group of young girls "] followed by the Pietà della Collegiata at Empoli, in which however the use of chiaroscuro to render the forms more plastic reveals perhaps Masolino's first contact with Masaccio. As has been noted he collaborated with Masaccio in the years 1424-25 on the S. Anna Metterza at the Uffizi and the upper part of the frescoes of the Brancacci chapel. But it is now universally accepted that the finest, most highly poetic moment in Masolino's artistic career occurs not, as Vasari had thought and as was believed for a long time, when he worked beside the talent of Masaccio, but rather when he was free to imagine his own bright visions, pleasantly abstract and at the same time delightfully intimate. These moments are represented by the early frescoes at Empoli, unfortunately almost entirely lost, by the frescoes of the Basilica di San Clemente at Rome and the Baptistery and Collegiata of Castiglione Olona in Lombardy, executed shortly before the end of his active existence in about 1440.....

> from P. Dal Poggetto, p. 40, *Arte in Valdelsa*, Certaldo, 1963.

Tommaso di Cristofano di Fino, called Masolino. Florentine School. Born 1383/84; active to 1432. He was influenced by Lorenzo Monaco and also by Ghiberti, of whom he was possibly an assistant. He worked in Florence, Castiglione d'Olona, Empoli, Todi, Rome, and in Hungary.

> from F. R. Shapley, p. 93, *Paintings from the Samuel H. Kress Collection*, London, 1966.

Masolino was born in Panicale near S. Giovanni Valdarno, the same district as Masaccio, with whom his name is often linked. One of the major Florentine painters of the early Quattrocento, his art began with, and later reverted to, a style which was more Gothic than that of his associate. Masolino probably trained in Florence, perhaps in the workshop of Gherardo Starnina. He had certainly joined the Ghiberti shop before 1407, and in 1423 he enrolled in the guild of Medici e Speziali. In 1424 he received a payment for frescoes in the church of S. Stefano at Empoli and his association with Masaccio appears to have begun soon afterwards. The Virgin and Child executed with St. Anne now in the Uffizi is their first joint work. Together they executed the fresco cycle in the Brancacci chapel of Sta. Maria del Carmine. Both artists went to Rome in 1428; Masaccio died there and Masolino carried out a cycle of frescoes in the Branda chapel of S. Clemente. After the death of Masaccio, Masolino returned to a more Gothic style which presents affinities to that of the sculptor Ghiberti. His last recorded works are the frescoes in the Baptistery and Collegiata at Castiglione d'Olona, completed by 1435.....

from P. Dal Poggetto, p. 102, *Frescoes from Florence*, London, 1969.

BIBLIOGRAPHY
BOOKS

An asterisk indicates a work listed in the General Bibliography

Toesca, P., *Masolino da Panicale*, Bergamo, 1908; Lindberg, H., *To the Problem of Masolino and Masaccio*, 2 vols., Stockholm, 1931; *Venturi, L.**, 1933, pls 185-90; Pittaluga, M., *Masaccio*, Florence, 1935 (with preceding bibliography); Wassermann, G., *Masaccio und Masolino*, Strasburg, 1935; Toesca, P., *Masolino a Castiglione Olona*, Milan, 1946; Salmi, M., *Masaccio*, Milan, 1930, 1948; *Galetti**, " F-O ", 1950, pp. 111-17; *Vavalà, 1948**, pp. 1607-12; Salmi, M., *Masaccio, Masolino, Filippino Lippi. La Cappella Brancacci a Firenze*, Milan, s. d. (ca. 1951), Vol. I; *Marangoni**, 1957, pp. 167-175; Baldini, U., *EUA**, 1958, p. 919; Baldini, U., *MAS II**, 1958, pp. 34-8; Micheletti, E., *Masolino da Panicale*, Milan, 1959 (with bibliography); *Borsook, 1960**, pp. 146-7; *Procacci, 1960**, figs. 62-70, p. 227; *Davies**, 1961, pp. 355-61; Lajor, V., *Masolino és Róma*, Budapest, 1962; *Berenson, 1963**, Vol. I, pp. 136-7; Dal Poggetto, P., *AIV**, 1963, pp. 40-1; Meiss, M., pp. 169-90, in *Studien zur Toskanischen Kunst. Festschrift für Ludwig Heydenreich*, Munich, 1964; Oertel, R., pp. 205-20, in *Studien zur Toskanischen Kunst. Festschrift für Ludwig Heydenreich*, Munich, 1964; Salvini, R., *Quattrocento Toscano e Quattrocento Fiammingo*, Florence (Dispense: Istituto di Storia dell'Arte), 1964; Martini, A., *Masolino*, (L'Arte Racconta, 3), Milan, 1965; Bianchini, M. A., *Masolino* (I Maestri del Colore, 80), Milan, 1965; Procacci, U., *Masolino* (Forma e Colore, 6), Florence, 1965; Castelfranchi-Vegas, L., *Il Gotico Internazionale in Italia*, Rome-Dresden, 1966, p. 169; Castelfranchi-Vegas, L., in *Il Gotico Internazionale in Italia* (I Maestri del Colore, 255), Milan, 1966; Bologna, F., *Masaccio* (I Maestri del Colore, 166), Milan, 1966; *Shapley**, 1966, pp. 93-4; Dal Poggetto, P., and Baldini, U., *Fresco Show**, 1968, pp. 112-20 (102-9); Meiss, M., in Kosegarten, A., *Festschrift Ulrich Middeldorf*, Berlin, 1968, pp. 116-17; *Meiss, 1970**, p. 107; *Dutch Show**, 1974, p. 44.

JOURNALS

Borenius, T., *BM*, 29, 1916, p. 45; Brockhaus, H., *MKIF*, III, 1919-32, pp. 160-82; R. W., *BWAM*, XII, 1922, pp. 62-5; Toesca, P., *BA*, 1923-24, pp. 3-6; Schmarsow, A., *B*, VII, 1925, pp. 145-57; Salmi, M., *DD*, VIII, 1927-1928, pp. 227-44; Salmi, M., *DD*, IX, 1928-9, pp. 3-30; Beenken, H., *ZBK*, 1929-30, pp. 112-19, 156-65; Steckow, W., *ZBKKK*, Feb., 1930, II, pp. 125-7; Berenson, B., *DD*, XII, 2, 1932, pp. 512-41; Beenken, H., *ZBK*, 1931-2, pp. 219-220; Morassi, A., *P*, XIX, 1937, pp. 72-80; Longhi, R., *CA*, V, 1940, pp. 145-91; Pope-Hennessy, J., *BM*, LXXXII, 1943, pp. 28, 30, 31; Lavagnino, E., *E*, XCVII, 3, 1943, pp. 96-112; Mather, F. J., Jr., *AB*, XXVI, 4, 1944, pp. 275-277; Mather, F. J., Jr., *AB*, XXVI, 3, 1944, pp. 175-87; Meiss, M., *AB*, XXVI, 4, 1944, pp. 274-5; Pope-Hennessy, J., *BM*, LXXXVIII, 1946, p. 173; Clark, K., *BM*, XCIII, 1951, pp. 339-47; Paccagnini, G., *BA*, XXXVII, 4, 1952, pp. 115-26; Meiss, M., *AN*, 51, 1952, pp. 24-5; Salmi, M., *C*, III, 1, 1952, pp. 14-21; Pope-Hennessy, J., *BM*, XCIV, 1952, pp. 31-2; Longhi, R., *PA*, III, 25, 1952, pp. 8-16; Silvestri, O., *A*, XVIII, 1952-3, pp. 16-7; Procacci, U., *RA*, XXVIII, 1953, pp. 3-55; Baldini, U., *BA*, XXXIX, 4, 1954, pp. 221-40; Spencer, J. R., *AB*, XXXVII, 1955, pp. 279-80; Bologna, F., *PA*, LXV, 1955, pp. 36-40; Urbani, G., *CS*, CXXXVI, 1955, pp. 155-60; Wolters, C., *K*, IX, 1956, pp. 33-5; *Edit.*, *AN*, 55, 1956, p. 74; *Edit.*, *BIR*, VI, 23-4, 1955, pp. 187-91; Carità, R., *BIR*, IX, 36, 1958, pp. 164-7; Berti, L., *C*, XII, 2, 1961, pp. 84-107; Parronchi, A., *PA*, XII, 133, 1961, pp. 18-48; Parronchi, A., *PA*, XII, 137, 1961, pp. 19-26; de Tolnay, C., *RA*, XXXVI, 1961-2, pp. 3-10; Scholler, R. W., *RJB*, X, 2-3, 1962 pp. 56-67; Vayer, L., *AHA*, VIII, 1962, pp. 45-53; Gioseffi, D., *E*, CXXXV, 806, 1962, pp. 50-72; Salmi, M., *AL*, VIII, 2, 1963, pp. 93-103; Mazzini, F., *BA*, XLIX, 4, 1964, pp. 266-7; *Edit.*, *PR*, XXIII, 1964, p. 44; Shell, C., *AB*, XLVII, 4, 1965, pp. 465-9; Vayer, L., *AHA*, XI, 1965, pp. 217-39; Genthon, I., *AHA*, XI, 1965, pp. 209-15; de Tolnay, C., *AL*, X, 1965, pp. 69-74; Bernier, R., *O*, 123, 1965, p. 33; Vayer, L., *Nachrichten der Gesellschaft für Vergleichende Kunstforschung in Wien*, VII, 1965; Berti, L., *AV*, V, 3, 1966, pp. 3-12; Bogyay, T. v., *ZKG*, 1966, XXIX, 1, pp. 71-6; von Einem, H., *AHA*, XIII, 1967, pp. 187-90; Gengaro, M. L., *AL*, XII, 2, 1967, pp. 25-32; Boskovits, M., *MKIF*, XIII, 1-1967-68, p. 56; Gendel, M., *AN*, 67, 1968, p. 28; Cole, B., *MKIF*, XIII, 3-4, 1968, pp. 289-300; Zeri, F., *AV*, VIII, 6, 1969, pp. 5-15; Fremantle, R., *AV*, IX, 6, 1970, pp. 39-49; Winner, M., *ZKG*, XXXIII, 4, 1970, p. 344; Eiko Wakayama, M. L., *AL*, XVI, 1971, pp. 1-16; Eiko Wakayama, M. L., *AL*, XVII, 1972, pp. 56-61, 83-87; Mode, R. L., *BM*, CXIV, 831, 1972, pp. 368-78; Pogány-Balás, E., *AHA*, XVIII, 1-2, 1972, pp. 107-24; Watkins, L., *MKIF*, XVII, 1, 1973, pp. 65-74; Zanoli, A., *PA*, XXIV, 277, 1973, pp. 40-41; Volpe, C., *MKIF*, XVII, 2-3, 1973, pp. 357, 9.

SIGNED AND DATED WORKS

Castiglione d'Olona (near Varese, Lombardy), Collegiata. Fresco: Marriage of the Virgin, Nativity & Annunciation. s. (fig. 1024-6).

1423 Bremen, Kunsthalle 164. Panel: Madonna of Humility. d. (fig. 1014).

1435 Castiglione d'Olona (near Varese, Lombardy), Baptistery. Fresco: Scenes from the Life of St John the Baptist. d. (figs. 1010, 11, 18, 23).

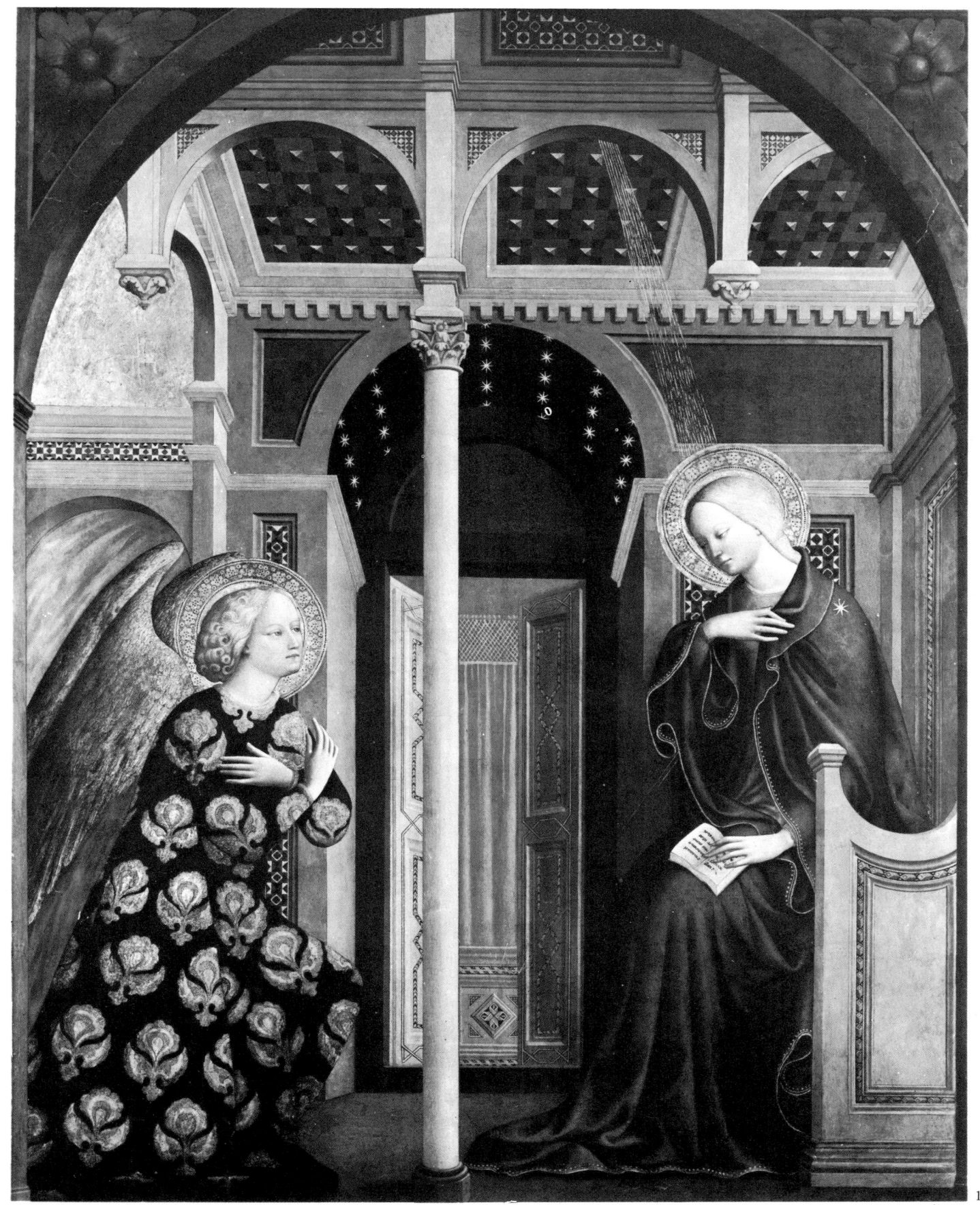

1004. *Annunciation. Panel. Washington (D.C.), National Gallery, Mellon Collection. no. 16. 148 × 115. Museum photo.*

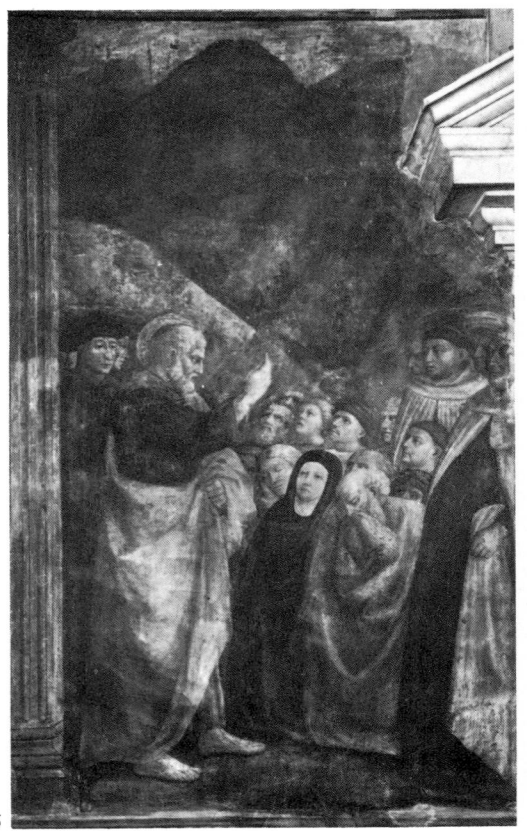

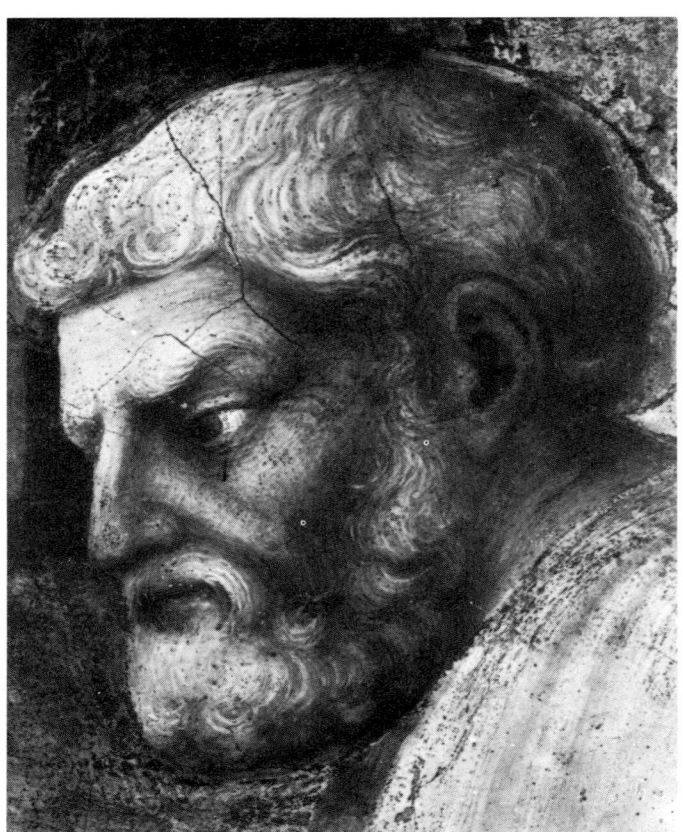

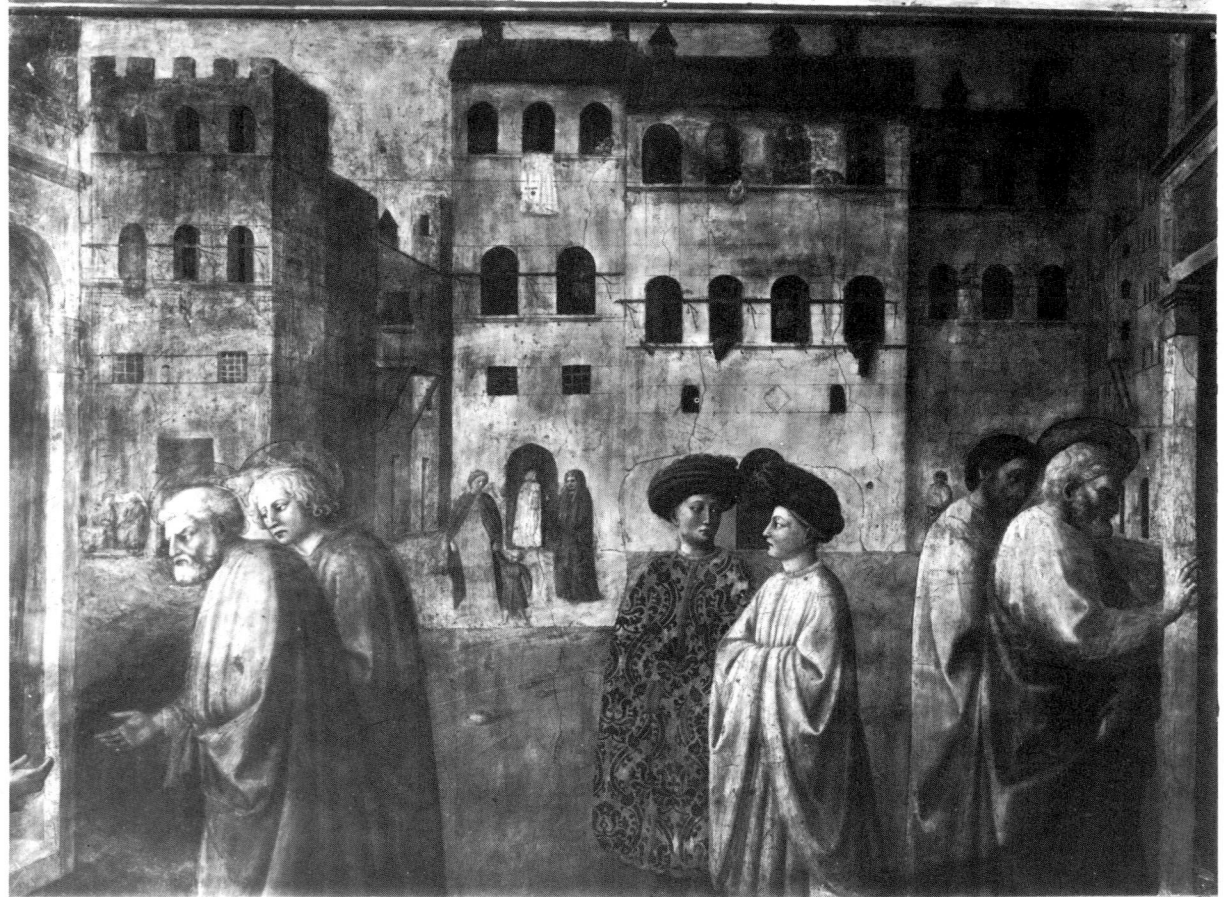

1005. *St Peter preaching. Fresco. Florence, S. Maria del Carmine, Brancacci Chapel. SGF 43465.*
1006. *Head of St Peter, detail of fig. 1007. Fresco. Florence, S. Maria del Carmine, Brancacci Chapel. SGF 78011.*
1007. *Detail: Resurrection of Tabitha and Healing of a Cripple. Fresco. Florence, S. Maria del Carmine, Brancacci Chapel. SGF 41492.*

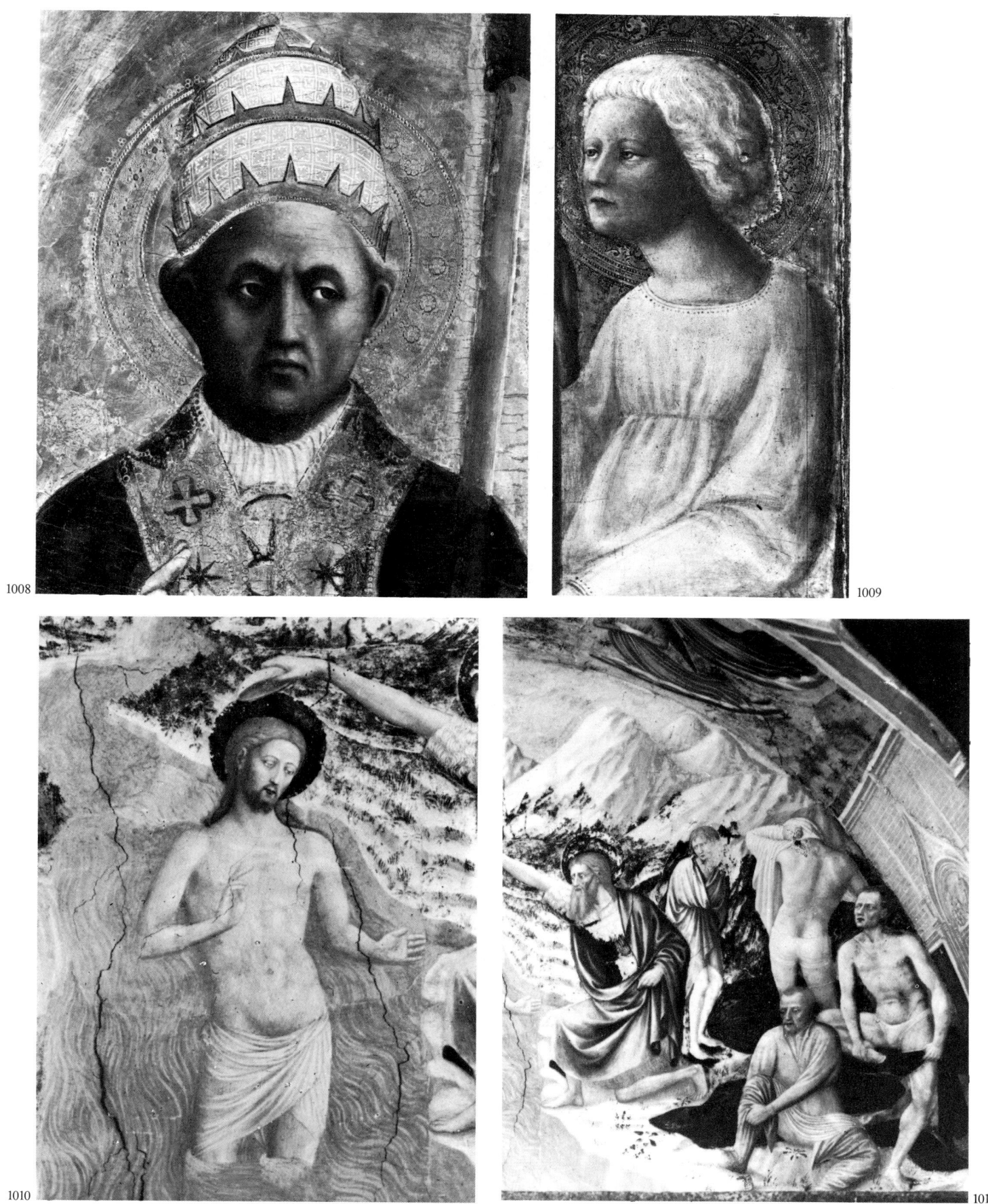

1008. *Detail: Head of Pope Martin V. Panel. London, National Gallery. no. 5963. Museum photo.*
1009. *An Angel, detail of fig. 1057. Panel. Florence, Uffizi. no. 8386. SGF 97724.*
1010. *Detail: Baptism of Christ. Fresco. Castiglione d'Olona, Baptistery. Alinari (detail) 18412. d. 1435.*
1011. *Detail: Baptism scene. Fresco. Castiglione d'Olona (near Varese, in Lombardy), Baptistery. Alinari (detail) 18412. d. 1435.*

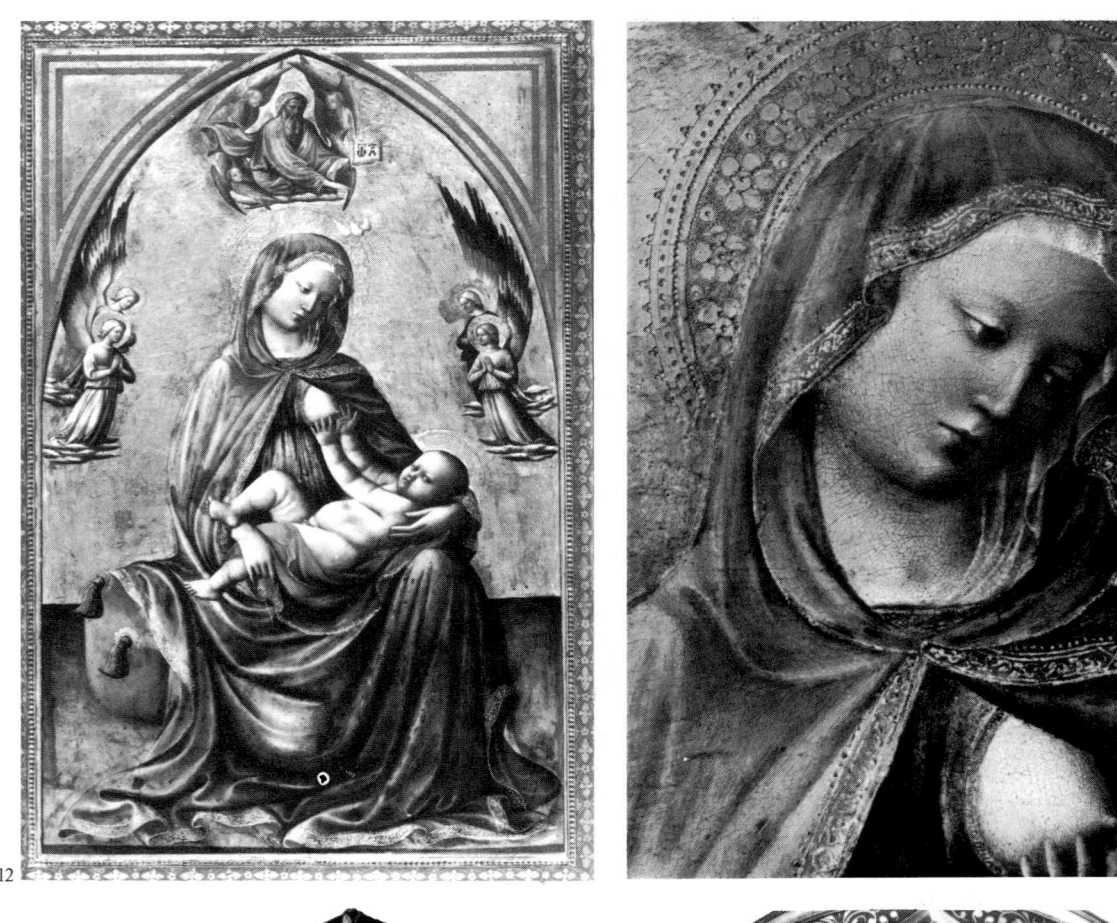

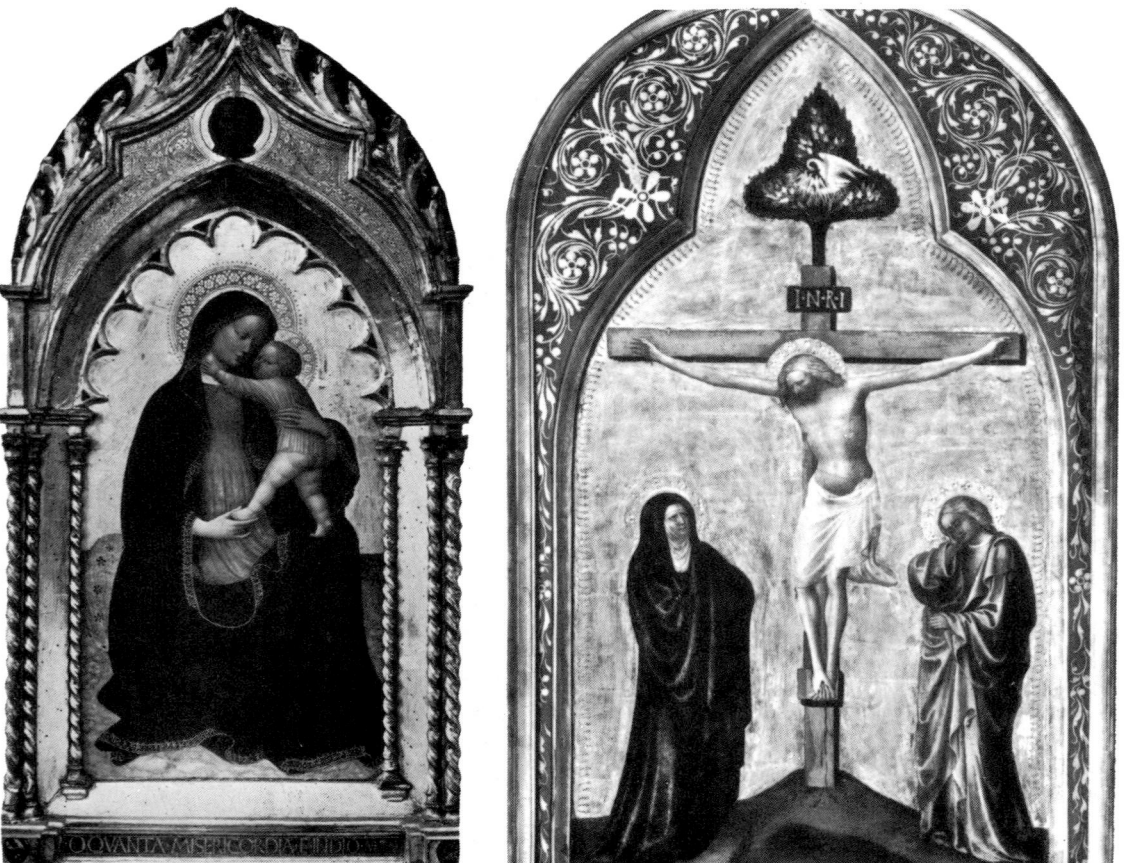

1012. *Madonna of Humility nursing the Child with adoring Angels and God the Father. Panel. Munich, Alte Pinakothek. no. WAF 264. 95 × 57. Museum photo: Bayer.*

1013. *Head of Madonna, detail of fig. 1012. Panel. Munich, Alte Pinakothek. no. WAF 264. Museum photo: Bayer.*

1014. *Madonna of Humility. Panel. Bremen, Kunsthalle. no. 164. 96 × 52. Museum photo: Stickelmann no. 92. d. 1423.*

1015. *Christ on the Cross with the Virgin and St John the Evangelist. Panel. Rome, Vatican, Pinacoteca. no. 260. Anderson 23976.*

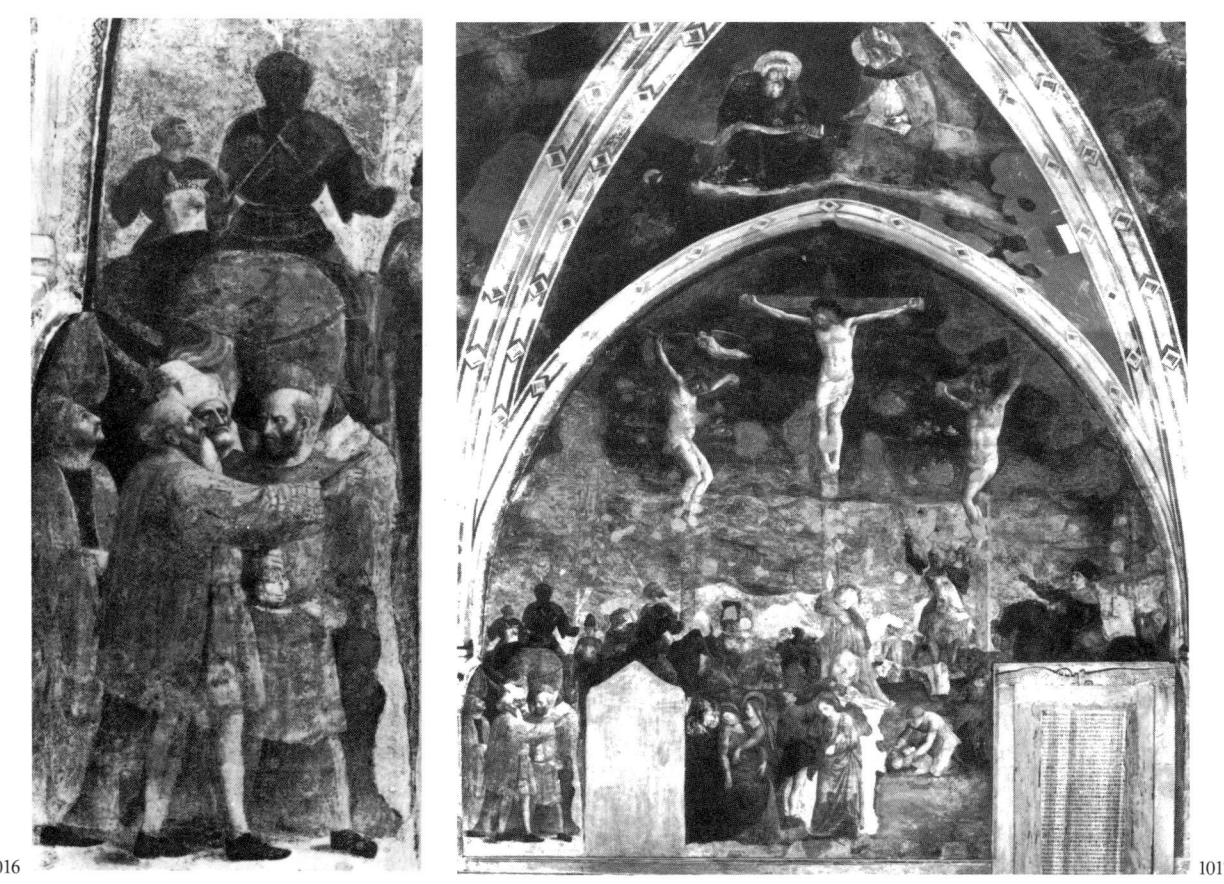

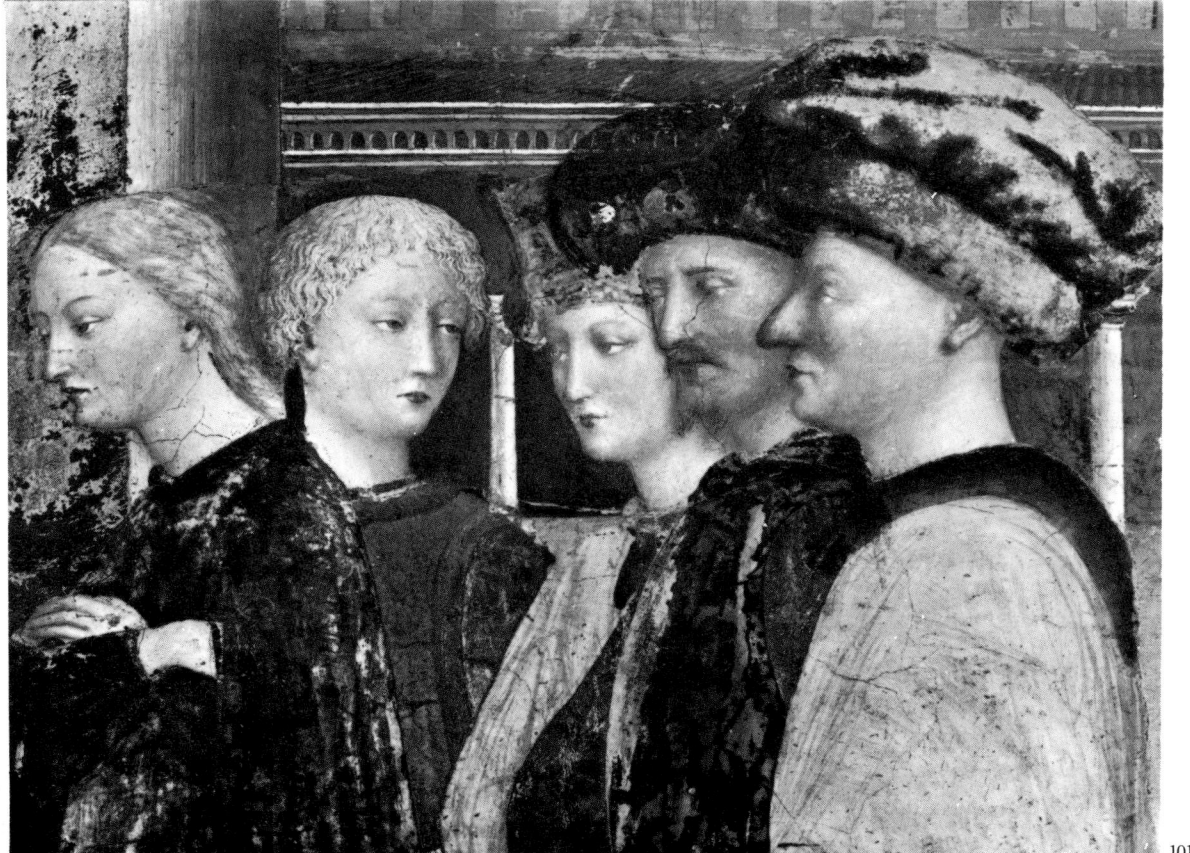

1016. *Mounted and standing figures, detail of fig. 1017. Fresco. Rome, S. Clemente. GFN E44510.*
1017. *Crucifixion. Fresco. Rome, S. Clemente. GFN E44509.*
1018. *Detail: Bystanders at Feast of Herod. Fresco. Castiglione d'Olona, Baptistery. Alinari 18410. d. 1435.*

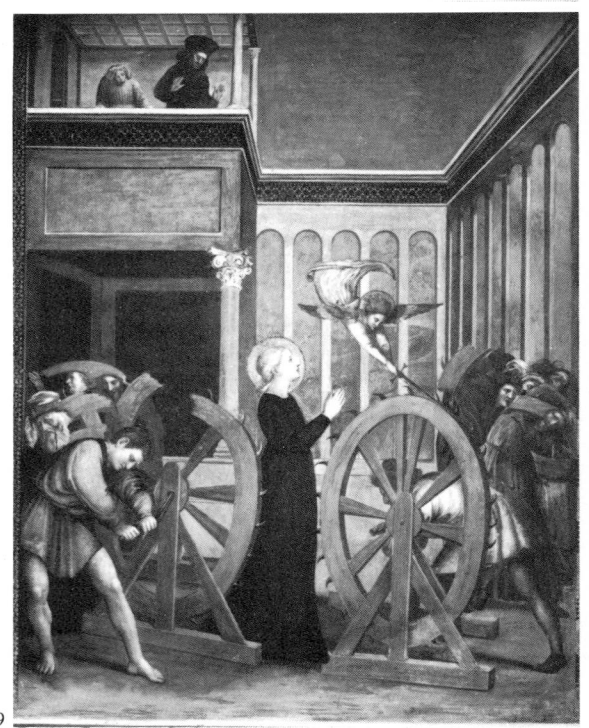

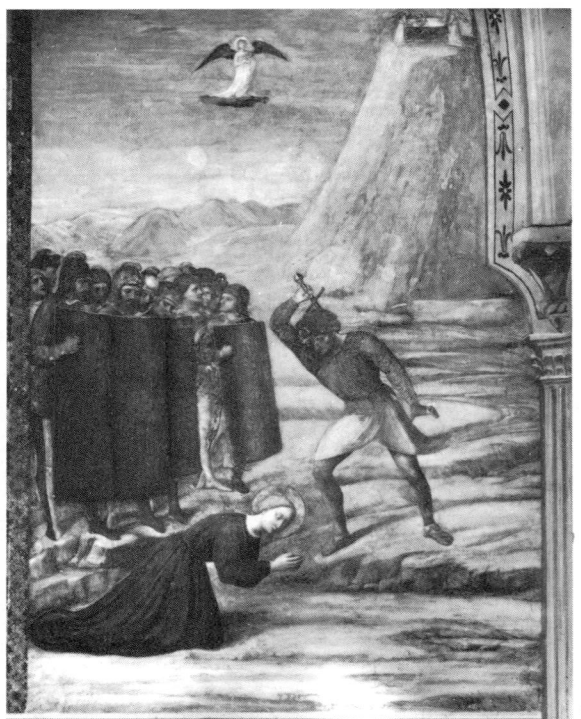

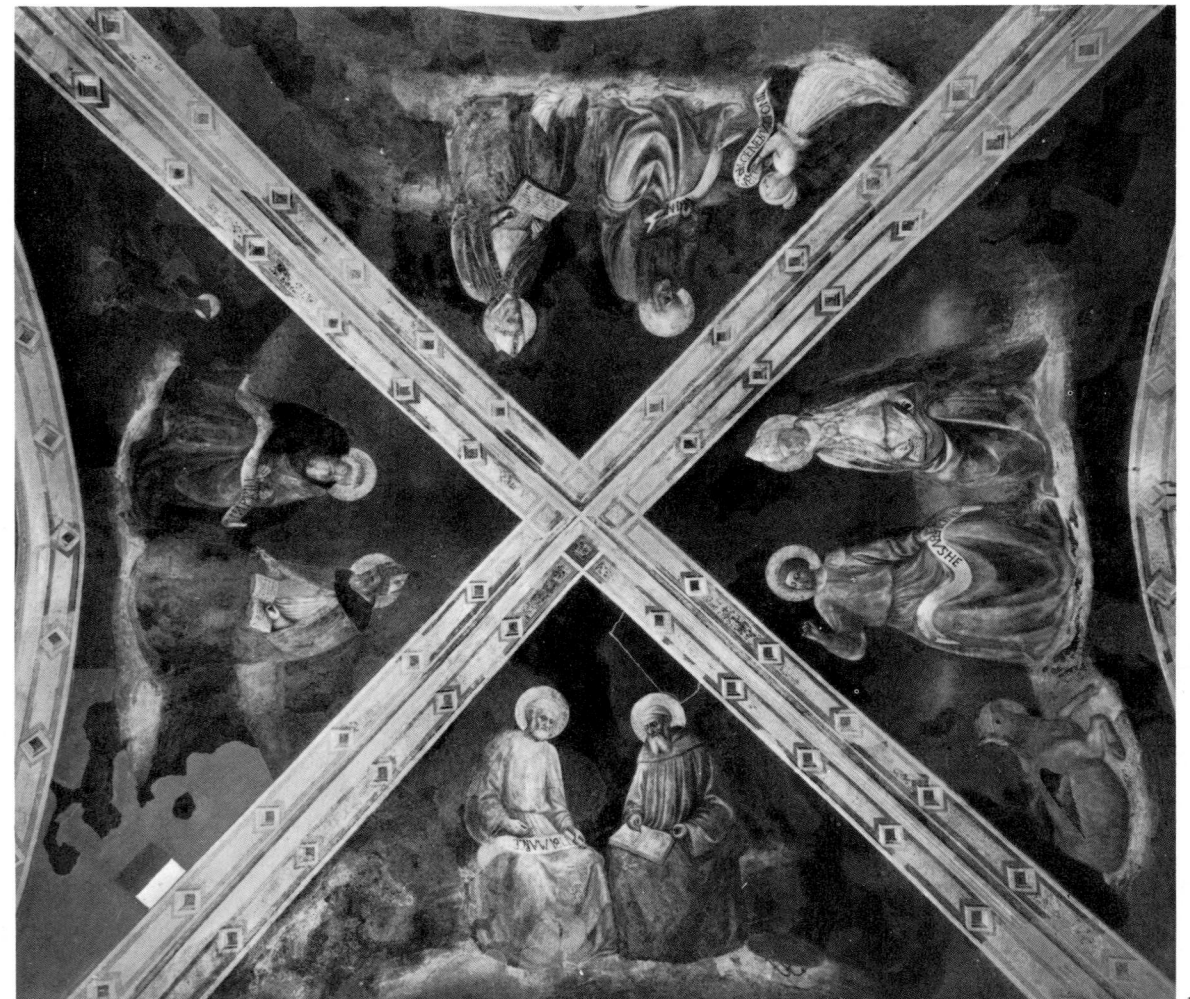

1019. *Attempted Martyrdom of St Catherine. Fresco. Rome, S. Clemente. Alinari 8088.*
1020. *Beheading of St Catherine. Fresco. Rome, S. Clemente. Alinari 8089.*
1021. *Vault: Evangelists and Doctors of the Church. Fresco. Rome, S. Clemente. GFN E26660.*

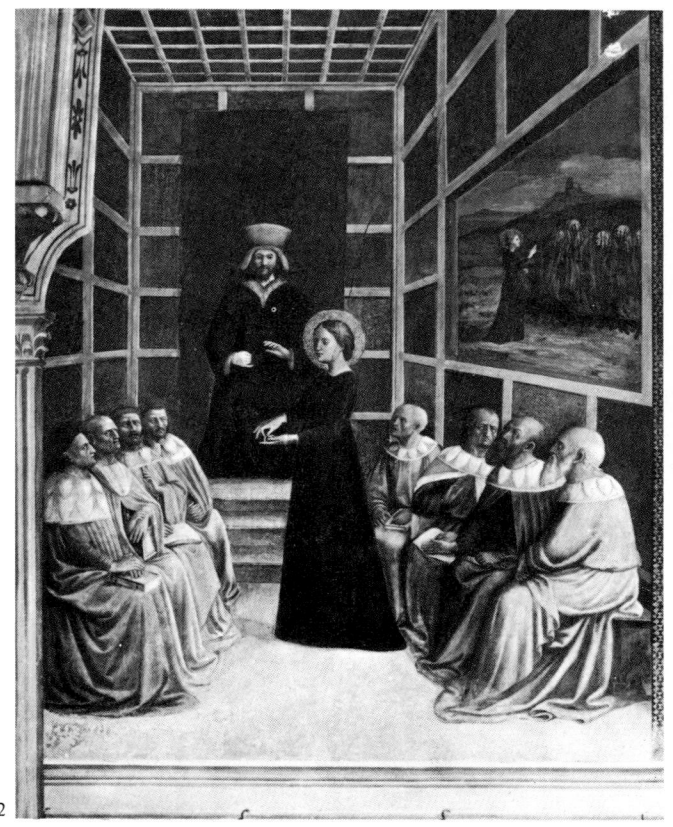

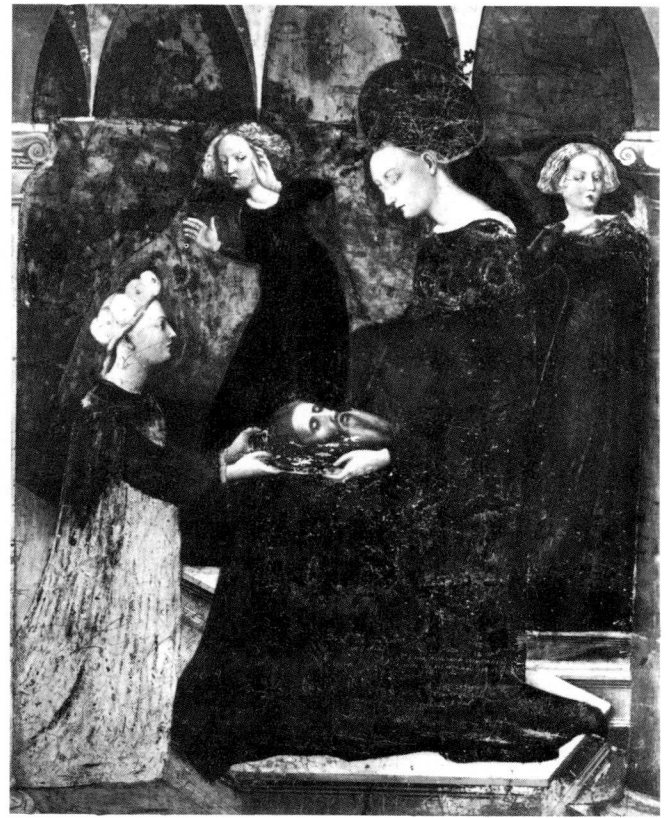

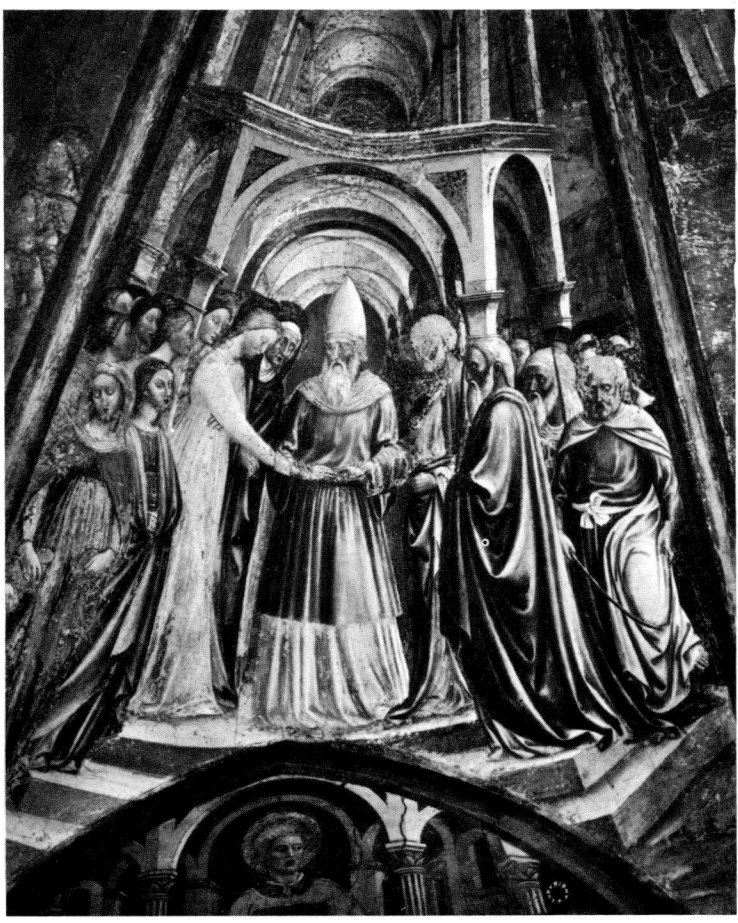

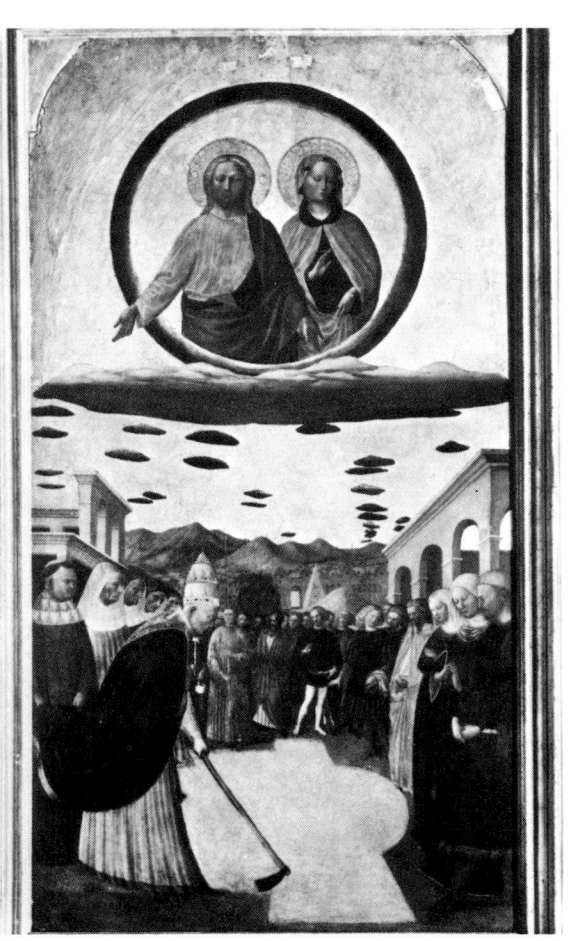

1022. *St Catherine disputes with the Doctors. On wall: their Martyrdom. Fresco. Rome, S. Clemente. Alinari 8084.*
1023. *Detail: Salome presents the Baptist's Head to her Mother. Fresco. Castiglione d'Olona, Baptistery. Alinari 18411. d. 1435.*
1024. *Vault: Marriage of the Virgin. Fresco. Castiglione d'Olona, Collegiata. Anderson 32269. s.*
1025. *Foundation of S. Maria Maggiore. Panel. Naples, Museo Nazionale di Capodimonte. no. 35. 144 × 107.6 Alinari 12077.*

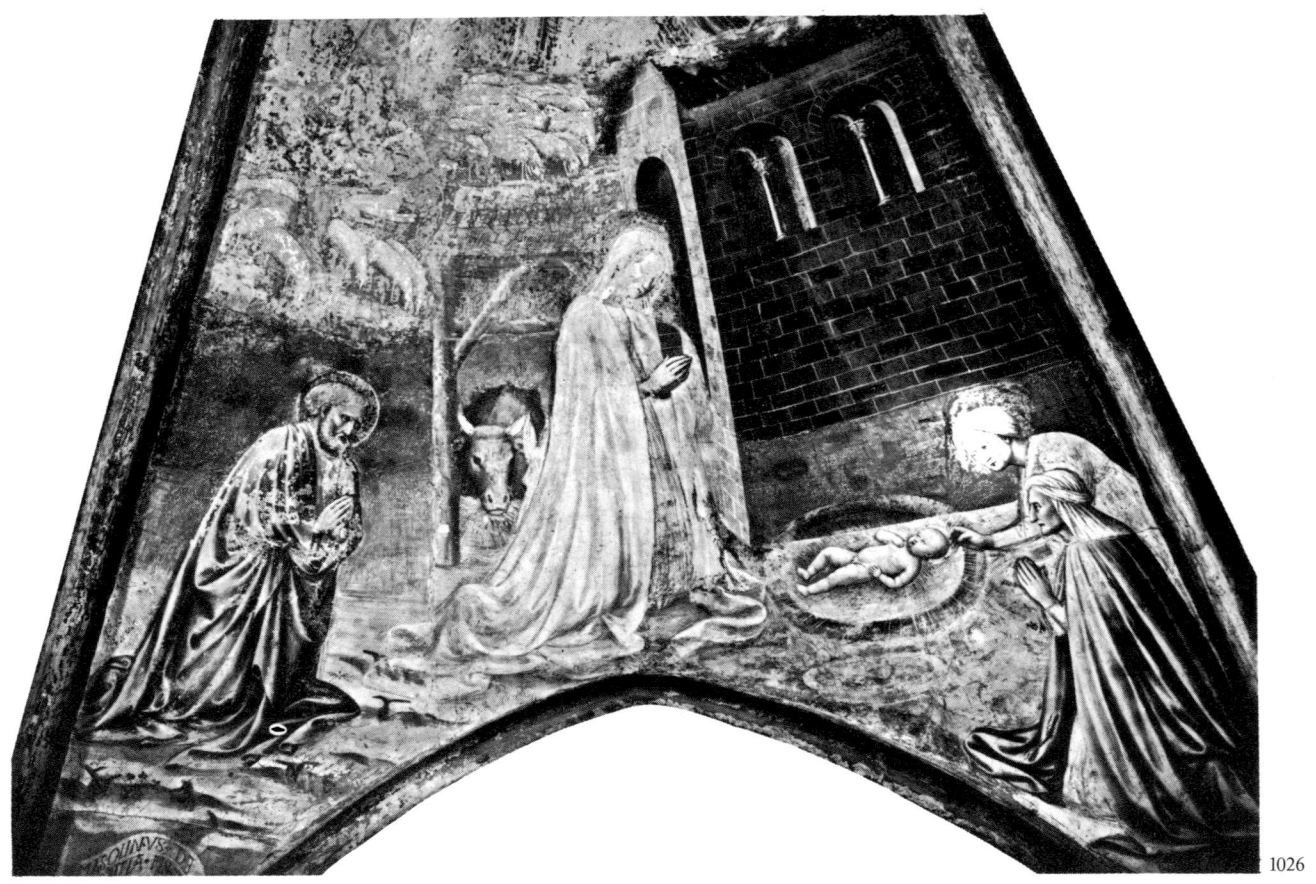

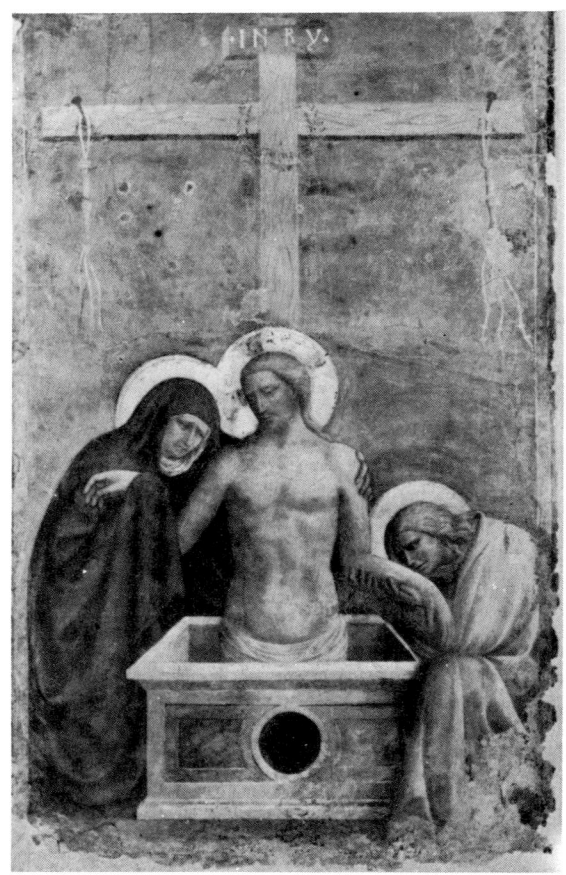

1026. *Nativity. Fresco. Castiglione d'Olona, Collegiata. Anderson 32271. s.*
1027. *Man of Sorrows with the Virgin and St John. Fresco. Empoli, Museo della Collegiata. no. 95. Photo: Città di Empoli.*

GIOVANNI TOSCANI

Giovanni — and after his death, Madonna Niccolosa, his wife — both note in their declarations to the Catasto of 1427 and 1430 that he completed the paintings in the Ardinghelli chapel in S. Trinita, which had been begun by a " frate Domenico ", that he began a painting of the Annunciation for Simone Buondelmonti which was finished after his death by Giuliano, called Pesello, and finally that he executed another painting for the Lord of Urbino. Giovanni died being nearly sixty years old, May 2nd 1430, and was buried in the church of S. Maria del Fiore.

from *Giornale Storico degli Archivi Toscani*, IV, 1860, p. 91.

Giovanni di Francesco Toscani, Florentine, born 1372, died May 2, 1430. Painter, member of the Physicians' and Apothecaries' Guild Company of Saint Luke 1424 (?). Pupil of Giottino. According to Vasari, Giovanni was an Aretine and painted in the manner of his master throughout Tuscany, but especially in Arezzo. He also painted some panels for the Duomo of Pisa. Though Giovanni may have been of Aretine origin, his returns to the Catasto seem to point to himself being a Florentine..... Vasari ascribes to Don Lorenzo Monaco some frescoes in the Ardinghelli chapel in the church of Sta. Trinita (Florence), which were executed by Giovanni (?) c. 1413, by commission of Neri and Piero di Neri degli Ardinghelli. The vault had previously been painted by a Frate Domenico.

from D. E. Colnaghi, p. 262, *A Dictionary of Florentine Painters*, London, 1928.

The works of this painter, whom I will call the Master of the Griggs Crucifixion, reveal a raw, vigorous personality among the younger painters born in the fourteenth and active within the second, third and fourth decades of the fifteenth century. He builds upon the remnants of the Orcagnesque tradition and upon Gothic sculpture, and allows the mood and colour of Lorenzo Monaco, Masolino and Angelico to win him. Finally the works of Arcangelo di Cola betray their influence in the Christ of the Griggs and Uffizi storeroom *Crucifixions* and in the halos of the former. He is lively, and borrows what he finds to his taste. He has a freshness and a profane humour as conspicuous as his lack of real artistic qualities. And his looseness is in part due to creative lassitude, in part certainly to an effort to escape the conventions of his time. And in this respect fate may be said to have favoured him, especially when he painted the Griggs Crucifixion, which, by its formal and original handling, evokes an unexpected moment of this sacred event, wherein a human tragedy is seen rending the hearts of a few people within the hollow made round them by the stony pagan horsemen.....

from R. Offner, p. 173, *The Burlington Magazine*, Vol. LXIII, July-Dec., 1933.

Prof. Offner has given us a competent list of this painter's work while pointing out his relationship to Arcangelo di Cola. The painting where the junction of the styles of the two artists appears to me most certain is the " Adoration of the Magi " in the Dodge Collection in London, not mentioned by Offner but recognized by Pudelko and published by Berenson as a dubious work of Rossello di Jacopo.....

from R. Longhi, p. 185, *Critica d'Arte*, V, 1940.

With this conventional name we indicate an unknown Florentine master whose major work is in the collection of Maitland Griggs in New York. The work of this painter was first noted by Salmi; Offner dedicated time to it also, making a list of his works, and defining his style. He is noted among the painters born in the '300 but active until the fourth decade of the '400, for his vigour. His origins are orcagnesque, but he adopts the colours of Lorenzo Monaco, Masolino and Angelico and the shading of Arcangelo di Cola.

from U. Procacci, p. 6, *Iᵃ Mostra di opere d'arte Restaurate*, Florence, 1946.

In the first three decades of the '400, we find a large group of minor artists in Tuscany who are content to cultivate in their work very elegant variations of the extreme gothic style. One of the most enchanting painters of this group is the Master of the Griggs Crucifixion. He is the anonymous author of a number of stylistically homogenous works, grouped by Offner around a Crucifixion in the Griggs Collection in New York. Most of these works were already known under various conflicting attributions. The Master of the Griggs Crucifixion has a precise physiognomy inherited from the preceding century and from Lorenzo Monaco. From this latter he derives most of his exuberant linear abstractions, transforming them into simpler, more elongated and more exquisitely profane rhythms. In his search for a fresh but refined elegance, his trained eye led him to the works of those artists who, like Masolino, Gentile da Fabriano and Arcangelo di Cola, in those years, were depicting Nature in a new light.....

> from P. Dal Poggetto, p. 41, *Arte in Valdelsa*, Certaldo, 1963.

Among the artists of the first decades of the Quattrocento who skirted and almost touched the first Renaissance ideas, is one particularly fascinating: the sweet eccentric painter who goes under the name of the " Master of the Griggs Crucifixion ", or elliptically, of " the Griggs Master ".....
The innate ambiguity [in his work] is demonstrated by the fact that a critic as knowledgeable as Berenson distributed the works of this group between Rossello di Jacopo and Arcangelo di Cola da Camerino; and that whereas both the " Master of the Bambino Vispo " and " Master of the Straus Madonna " have been well known for some time (although even today it is not sure which, for this latter, is the correct nomenclature) for the " Griggs Master " it was only at a relatively late date that we have had an unobjectionable and rational list of his works, thanks to Offner.....
No one has ever thought of attributing to this painter the two badly damaged frescoes which are in the Cappella Ardinghelli in Santa Trinita in Florence..... Today we know that these are by Giovanni di Francesco Toscani and date precisely from the years 1423-1424.....

> from L. Bellosi, pp. 44, 50, *Paragone*, XVII, 193/13, 1966.

BIBLIOGRAPHY
BOOKS

An asterisk indicates a work listed in the General Bibliography

Colnaghi*, 1928, p. 262; Salmi, M., *Masaccio*, Rome, 1930, p. 134; *Berenson, 1932**, pp. 493-4; *Catalogo della Mostra del Tesoro di Firenze sacra*, Florence, 1933, p. 117; Procacci, U., *MAS I**, 1946, p. 6; *Galetti**, " F-O ", 1950, p. 1457; *Berenson, 1963**, Vol. I, p. 192; Dal Poggetto, P., *AIV**, 1963, pp. 41-2; *Shapley**, 1966, pp. 99-100; Bellosi, L., *La Pittura Tardogotica in Toscana* (I Maestri del Colore, 239), Milan, 1966.

JOURNALS

Milanesi, G., *GSAT*, IV, 1860, pp. 191-94, 210; Berenson, B., *DD*, X, 1929-30, pp. 133-42; Berenson, B., *DD*, XI, 4, 1930-1, p. 974; Berenson, B., *DD*, XII, 1932, pp. 173-93; Castelfranco, G., *RA*, XV, 1933, pp. 80-81; Offner, R., *BM*, LXIII, 1933, pp. 172-3; Salmi, M., *RA*, XVI, 1934, pp. 168-86; Pudelko, G., *AA*, 1938, p. 63; Longhi, R., *CA*, V, 1940, pp. 145-91; Marchini, G., *ASP*, XX, III-IV, 1942, pp. 98-100; Friedmann, H., *Buffalo Gallery Notes*, XII, 1, 1947, pp. 19-26; Berti, L., *C*, XII, 2, 1961, pp. 84-107; Zeri, F., *BA*, XLVIII, 4, 1963, pp. 248-257; Bellosi, L., *PA*, XVII, 193/13, 1966, pp. 44-58; Boskovits, M., *ZKG*, XXIX, 1, 1966, pp. 51-66; Boskovits, M., *MKIF*, XIII, 1-4, 1967-68, p. 56; Zeri, F., *GBA*, LXXI, 110, 1968, p. 68; Fahy, E., *MM*, XXIX, 10, 1971, p. 433; *MMOA**, 1971, pp. 73-7; Watson, P. F., *WCJ*, XXXIV, 1971, pp. 331-3; Bellosi, L., *MKIF*, XVII, 2-3, 1973, p. 189; Volpe, C., *MKIF*, XVII, 2-3, 1973, pp. 354, 7, 8.

There are no known signed and/or dated works by Giovanni Toscani.

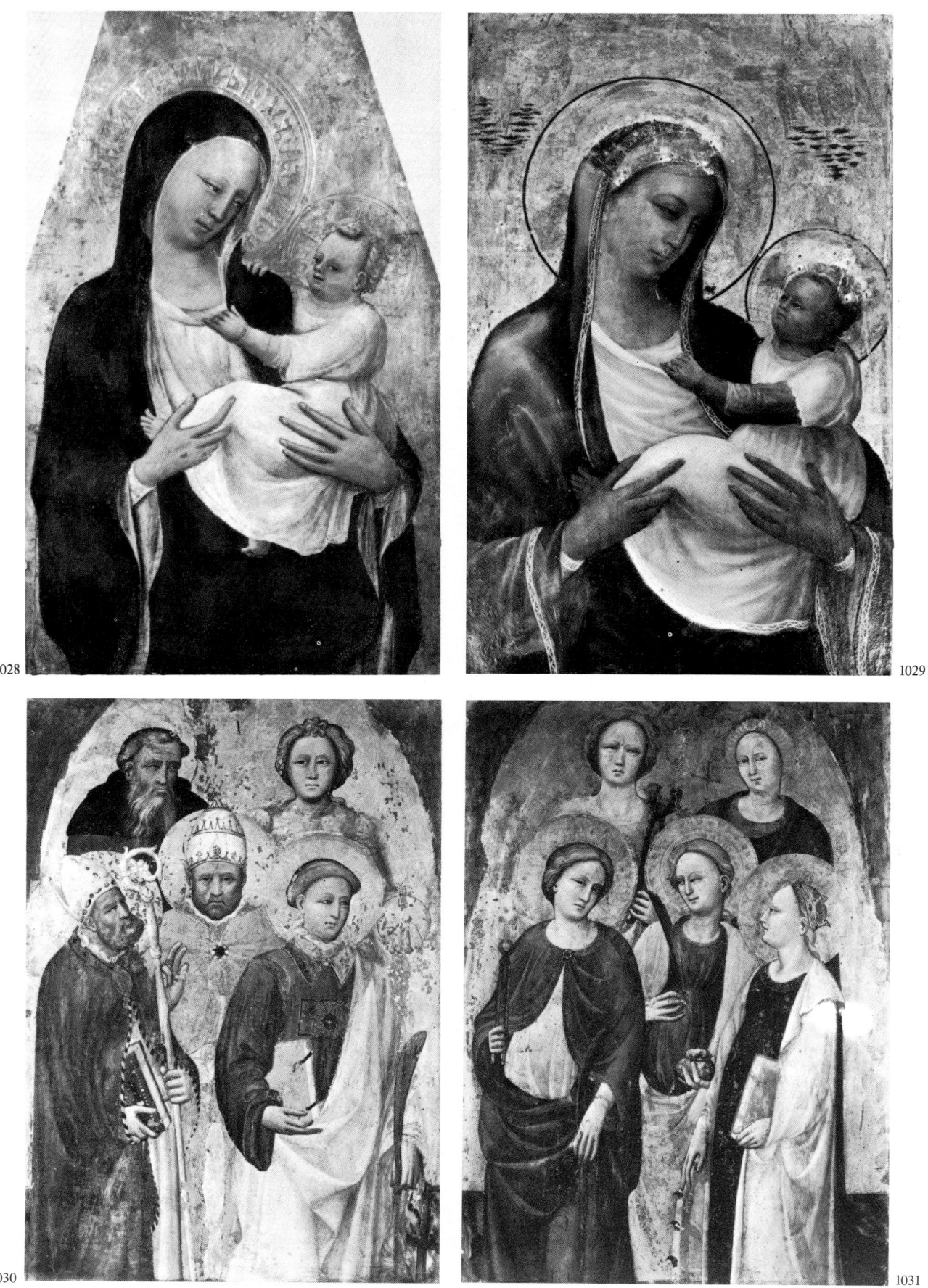

1028. *Madonna and Child. Panel. Montemignaio (6 kms south of Consuma), Pieve di S. Maria. 82 × 51. SGF 120262.*
1029. *Madonna and Child. Panel. Calenzano (near Prato), S. Donato. 95 × 60. SGF 127309.*
1030. *Five male Saints. Panel. Pontorme (Empoli), S. Martino. 60 × 40. SGF 123451.*
1031. *Five male Saints. Panel. Pontorme (Empoli), S. Martino. 60 × 40. SGF 123450.*

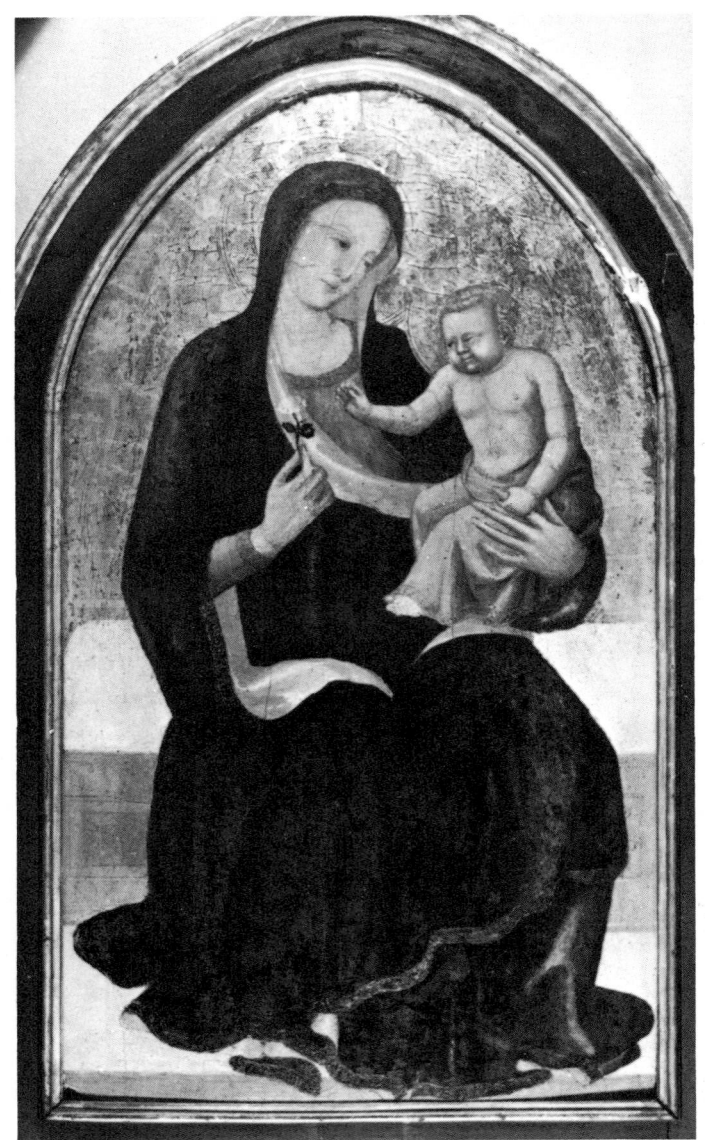

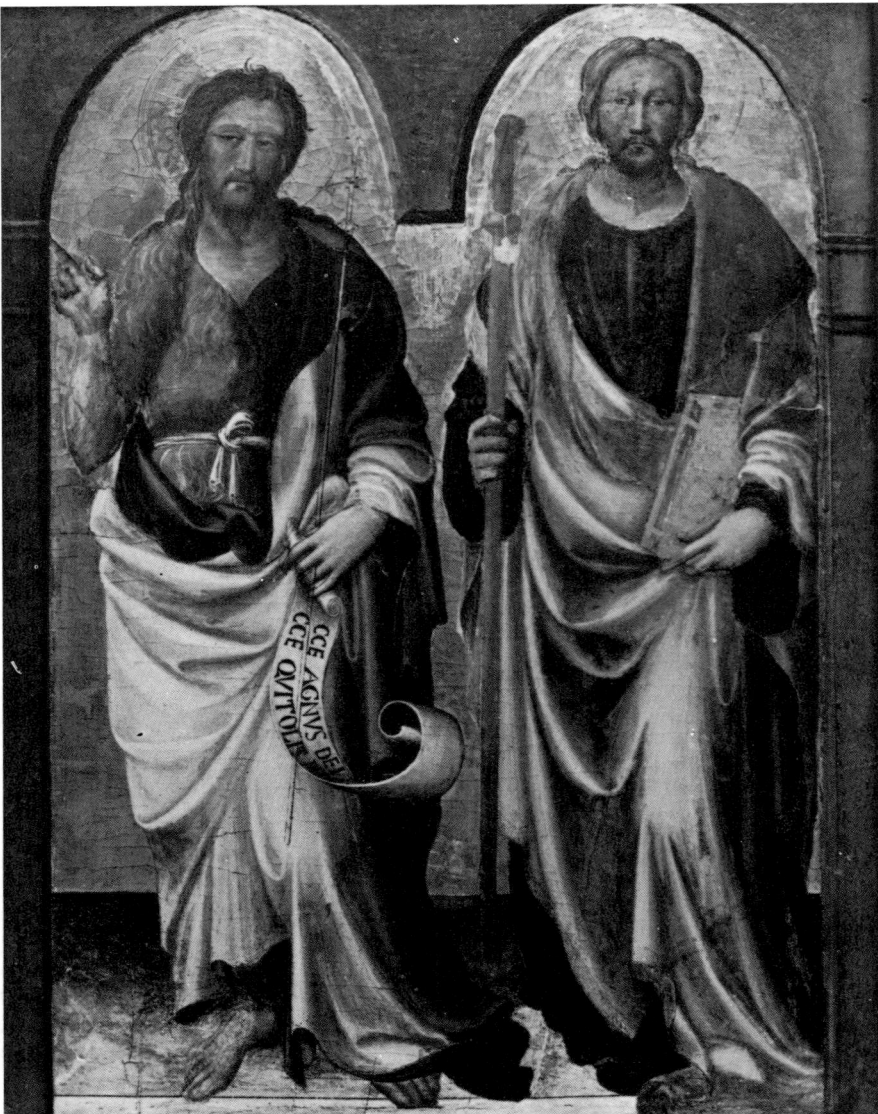

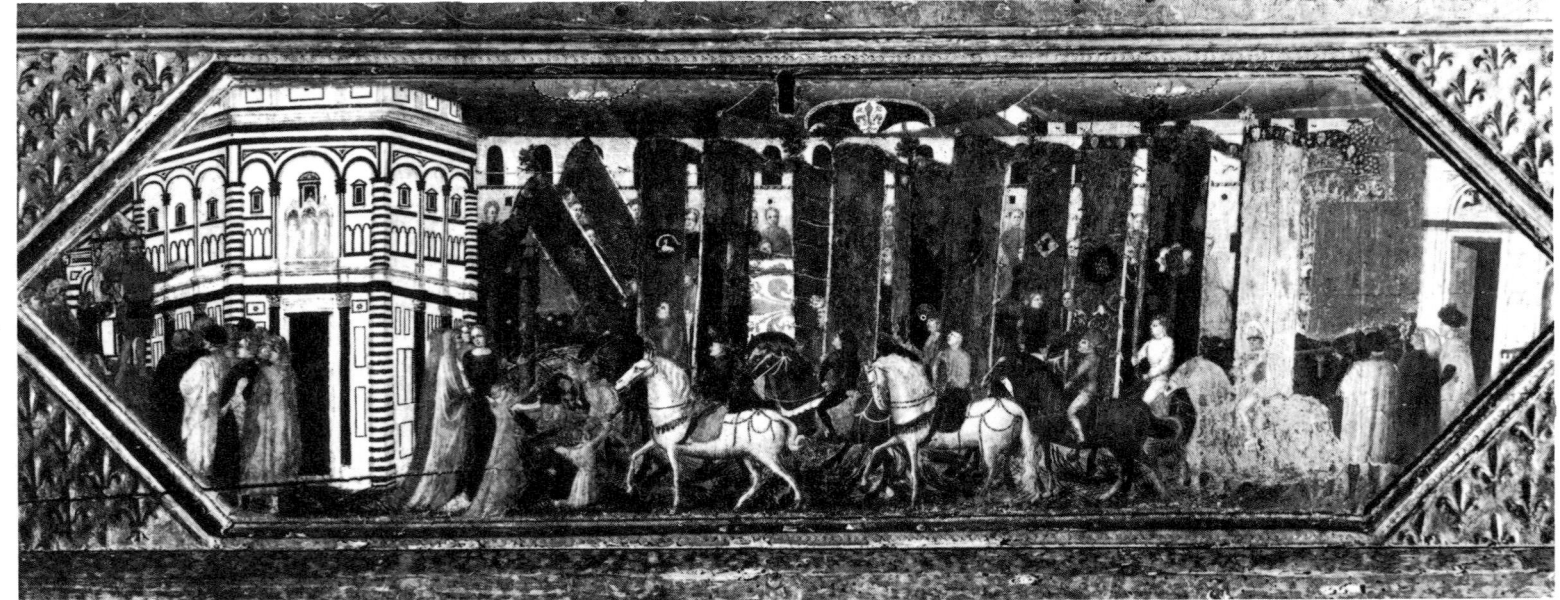

1032.   *Madonna and Child Enthroned. Panel. Melbourne, National Gallery of Victoria. no. 557/4. 121.9 × 68.2. Museum photo.*
1033.   *St John the Baptist and St James Major. Panel. Baltimore (Md.), Walters Art Gallery. no. 37.632. 101.9 × 76.1. Museum photo.*
1034.   *Cassone : Procession of banners (Pali) in the Piazza del Duomo, in Florence. Panel. Florence, Museo Nazionale del Bargello. 185 × 60.   Alinari 20394a.*

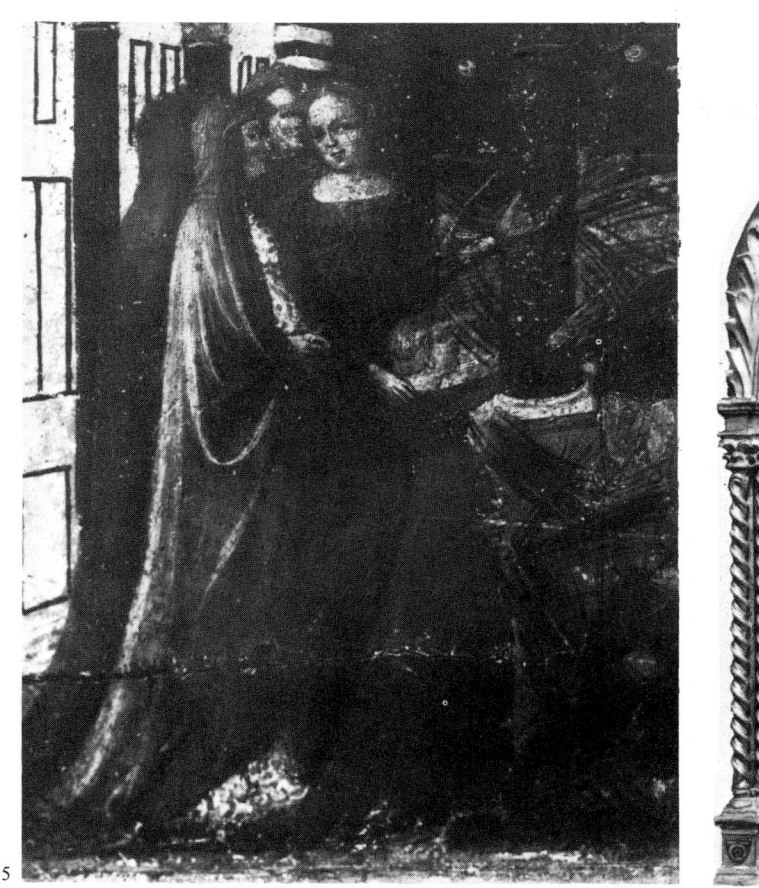

1035

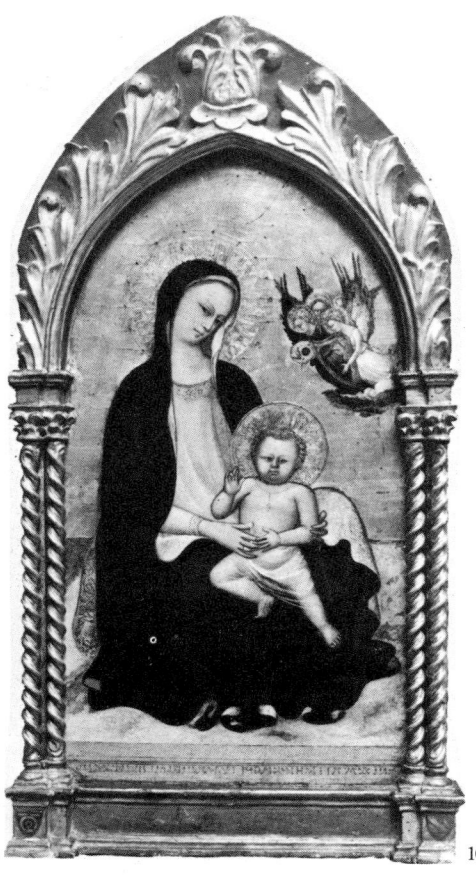

1036

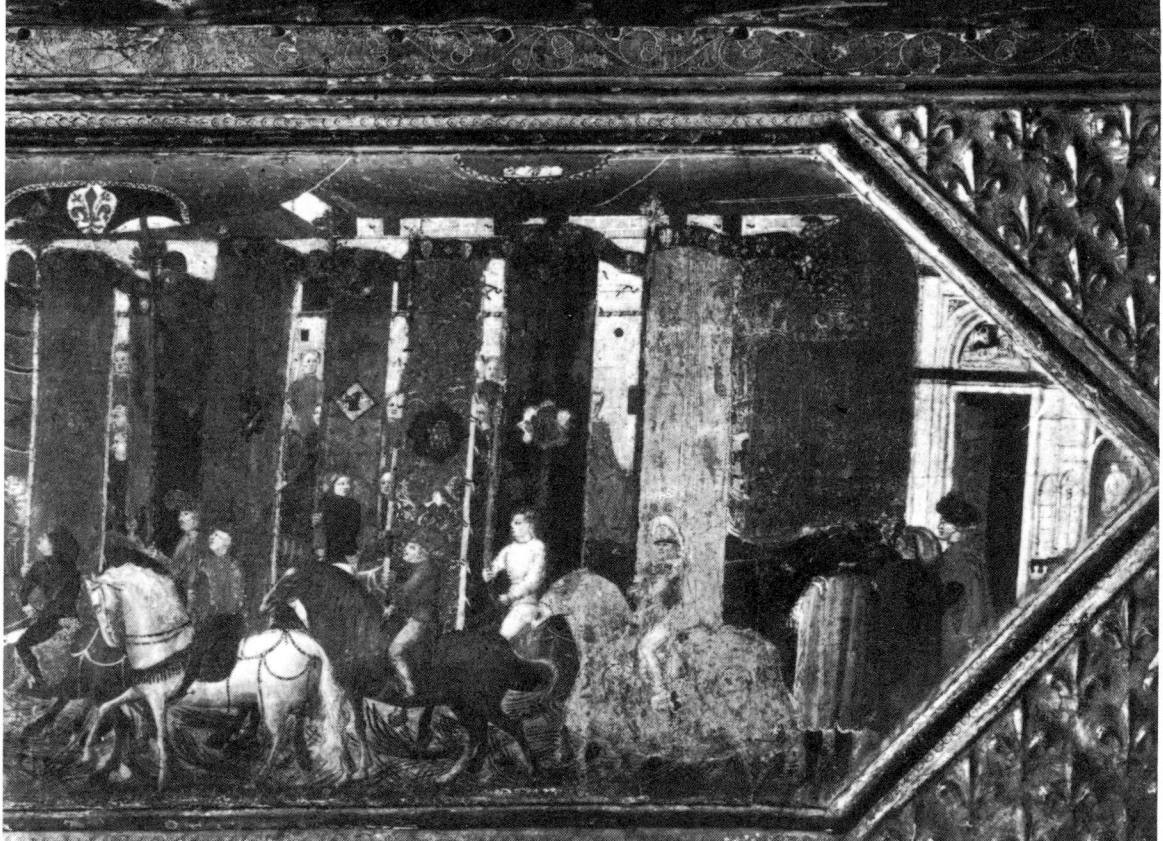

1037

1035. *Female figures, detail of fig. 1034. Panel. Florence, Museo Nazionale del Bargello. SGF 73672.*
1036. *Madonna of Humility with Angels. Panel. Buffalo (N.Y.), Albright-Knox Art Gallery. no. 27.34. 114.2 × 55.8 (w.f.) Gallery photo.*
1037. *Cassone: Offering of Banners (Pali) in the Piazza del Duomo, detail of fig. 1034. Panel. Florence, Museo Nazionale del Bargello. no. 161. SGF 13902.*

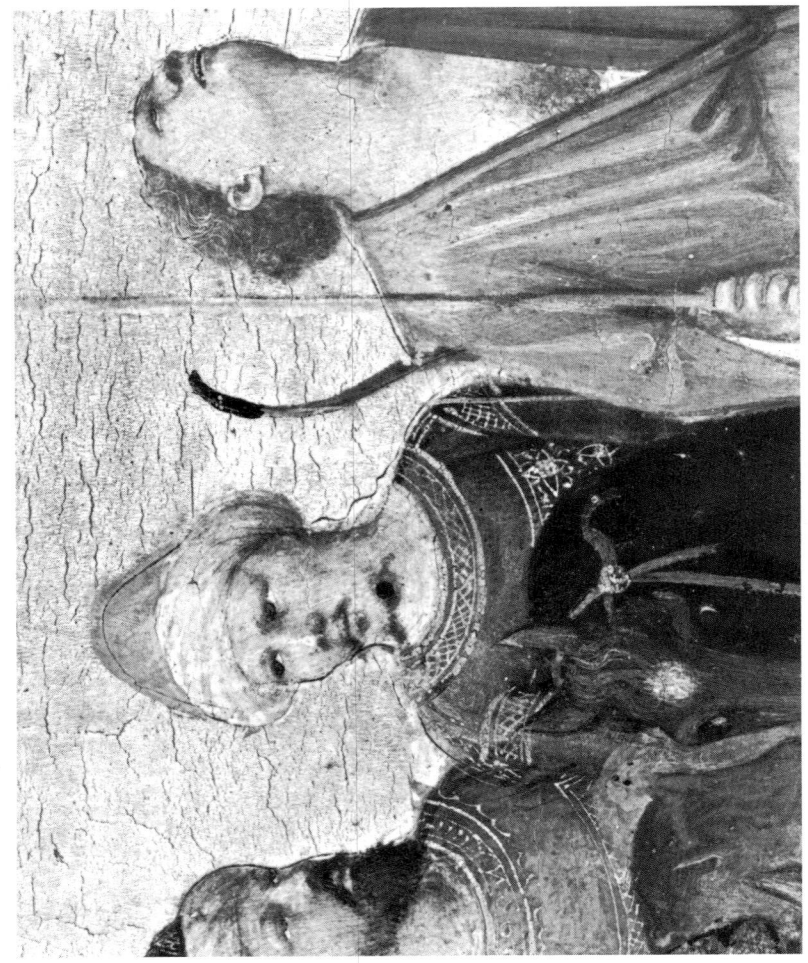

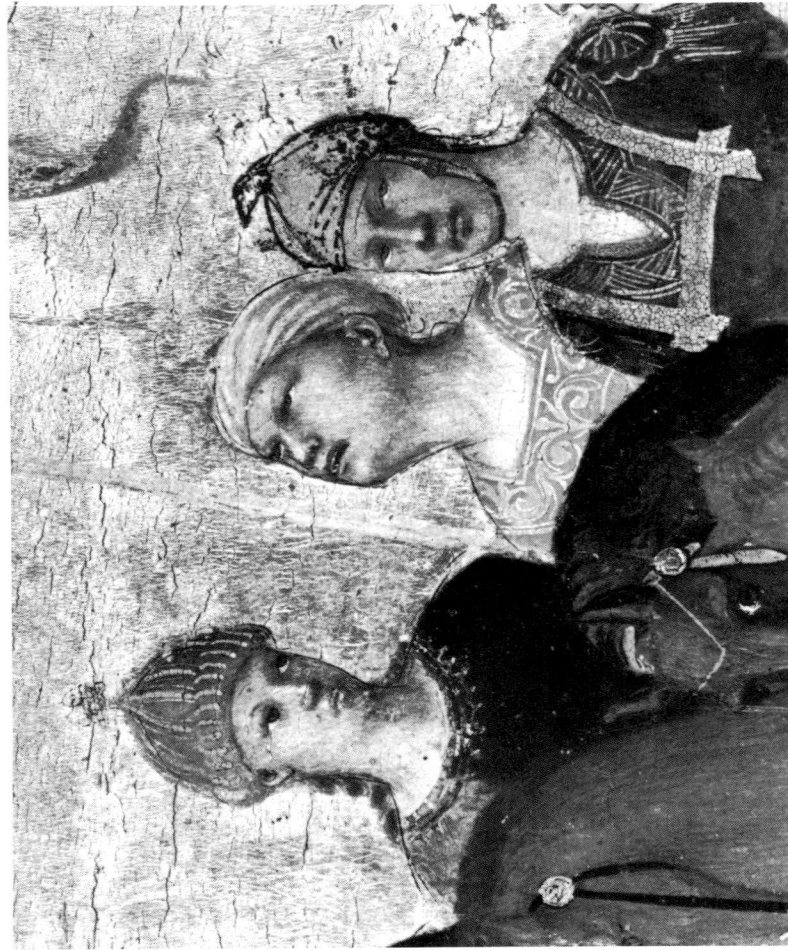

1039

1040

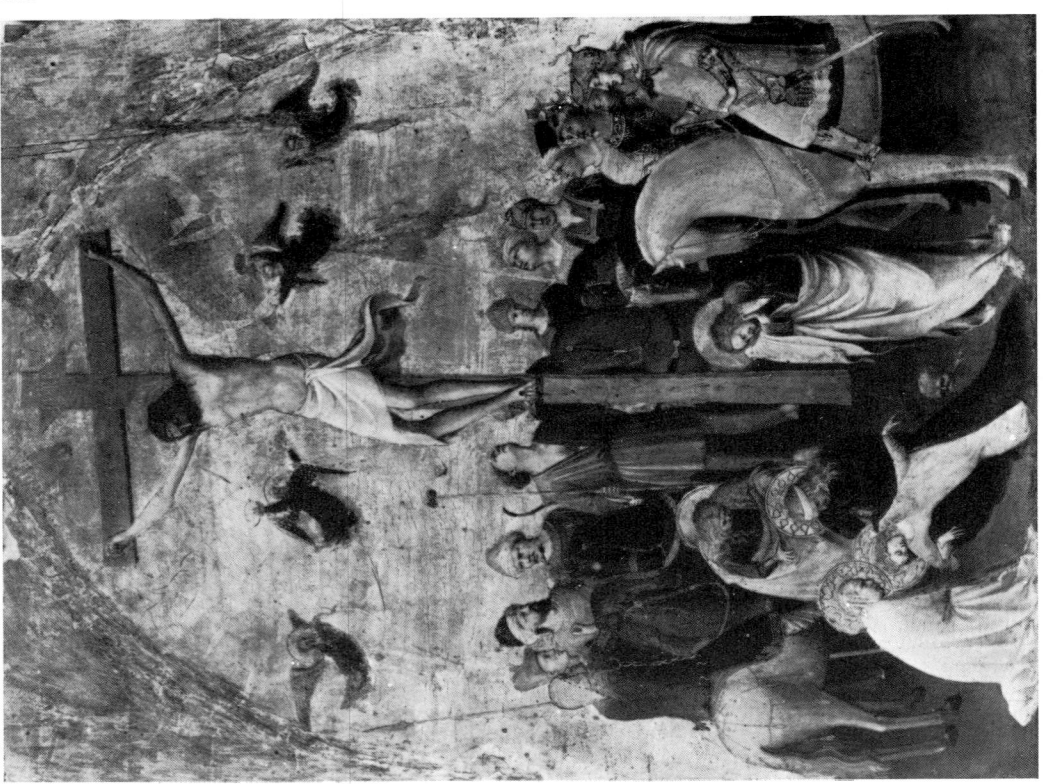

1038

1038. *Crucifixion. Panel. New York (N.Y.), Metropolitan Museum of Art, Griggs Gift. no. 43.98.5. 63.4 × 48.2. Museum photo 131378.*
1039. *Soldiers at the foot of the Cross, detail of fig. 1038. Panel. New York (N.Y.), Metropolitan Museum of Art. no. 43.98.5. Museum photo 134164.*
1040. *Soldiers at the foot of the Cross, detail of fig. 1038. Panel. New York (N.Y.), Metropolitan Museum of Art. no. 43.98.5. Museum photo 134163.*

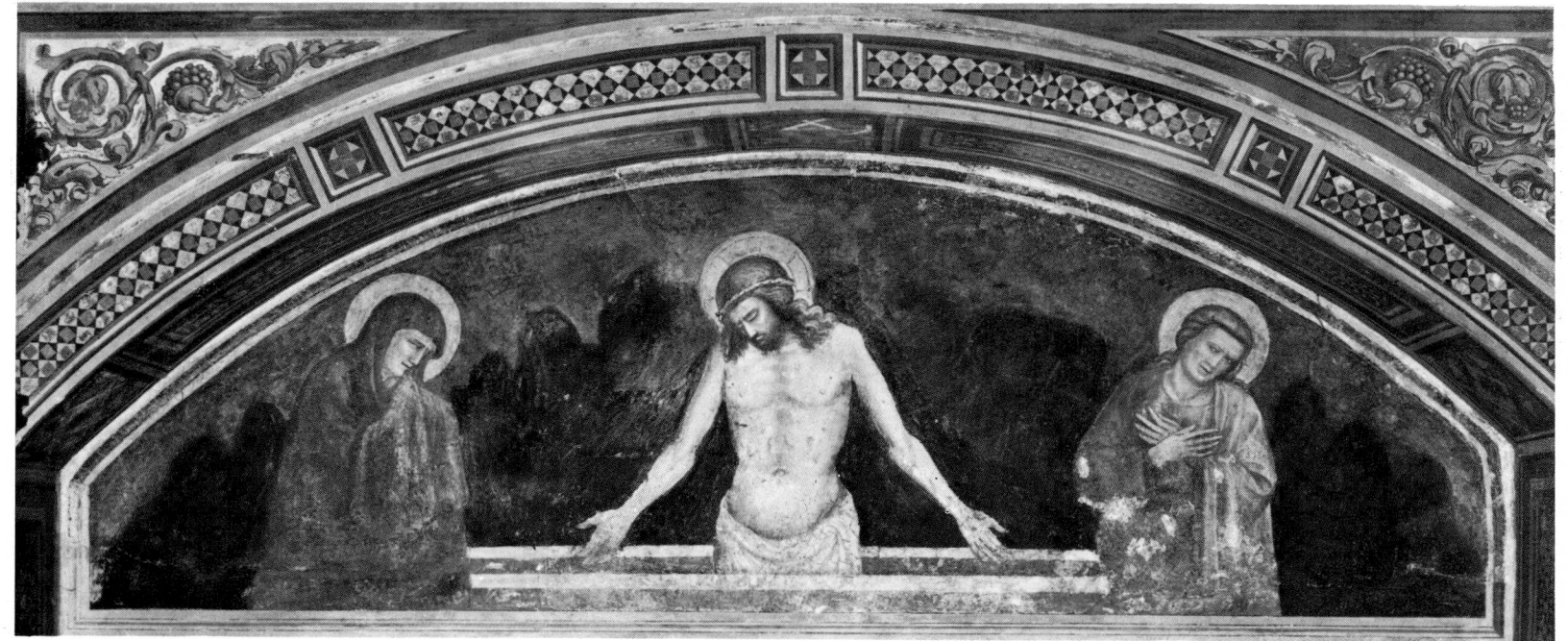

1041

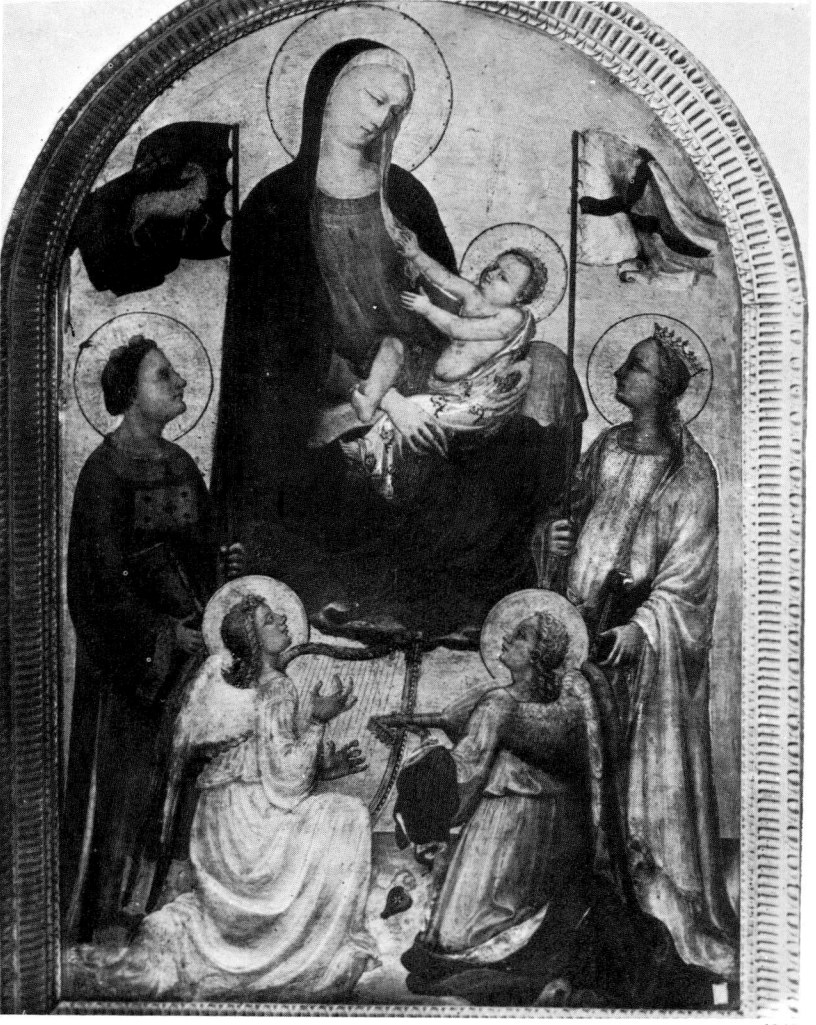

1042

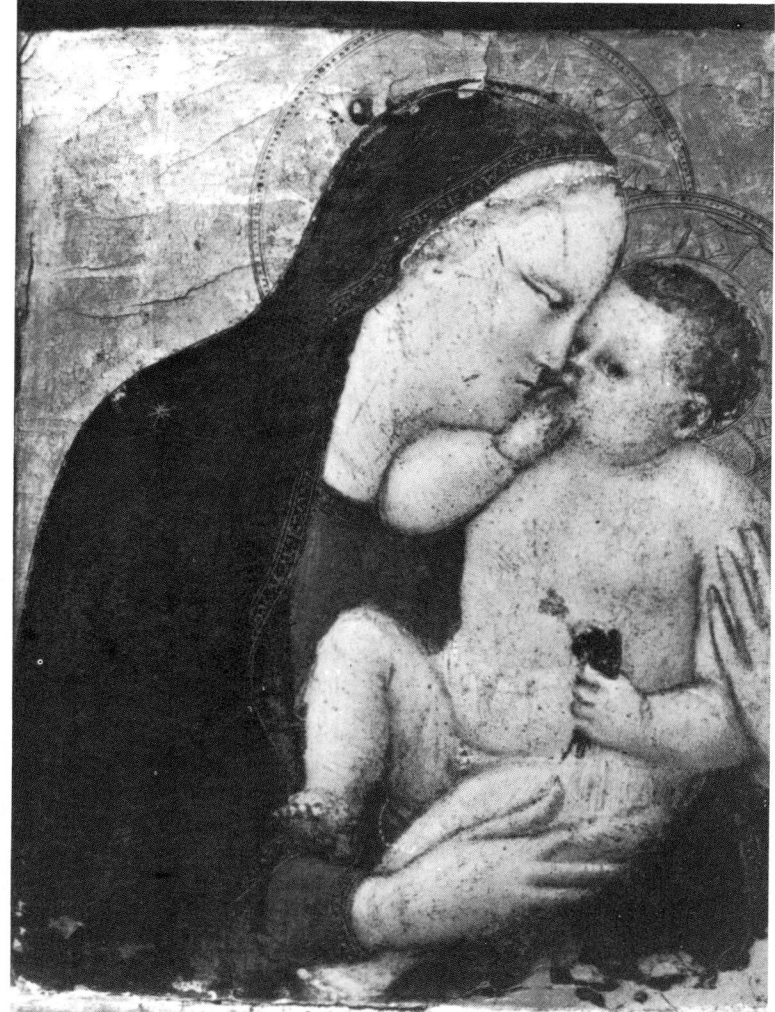

1043

1041. *Man of Sorrows. Fresco. Florence, S. Trinita. 105 × 302. SGF 106619.*
1042. *Madonna and Child with two Saints and two Angels. Panel. Pescia, Museo Civico. no. Soprintendenza Firenze 5917. 185 × 97. Alinari 60984.*
1043. *Madonna and Child. Panel. Whereabouts unknown. Photo: Galleria Bellini 1562.*

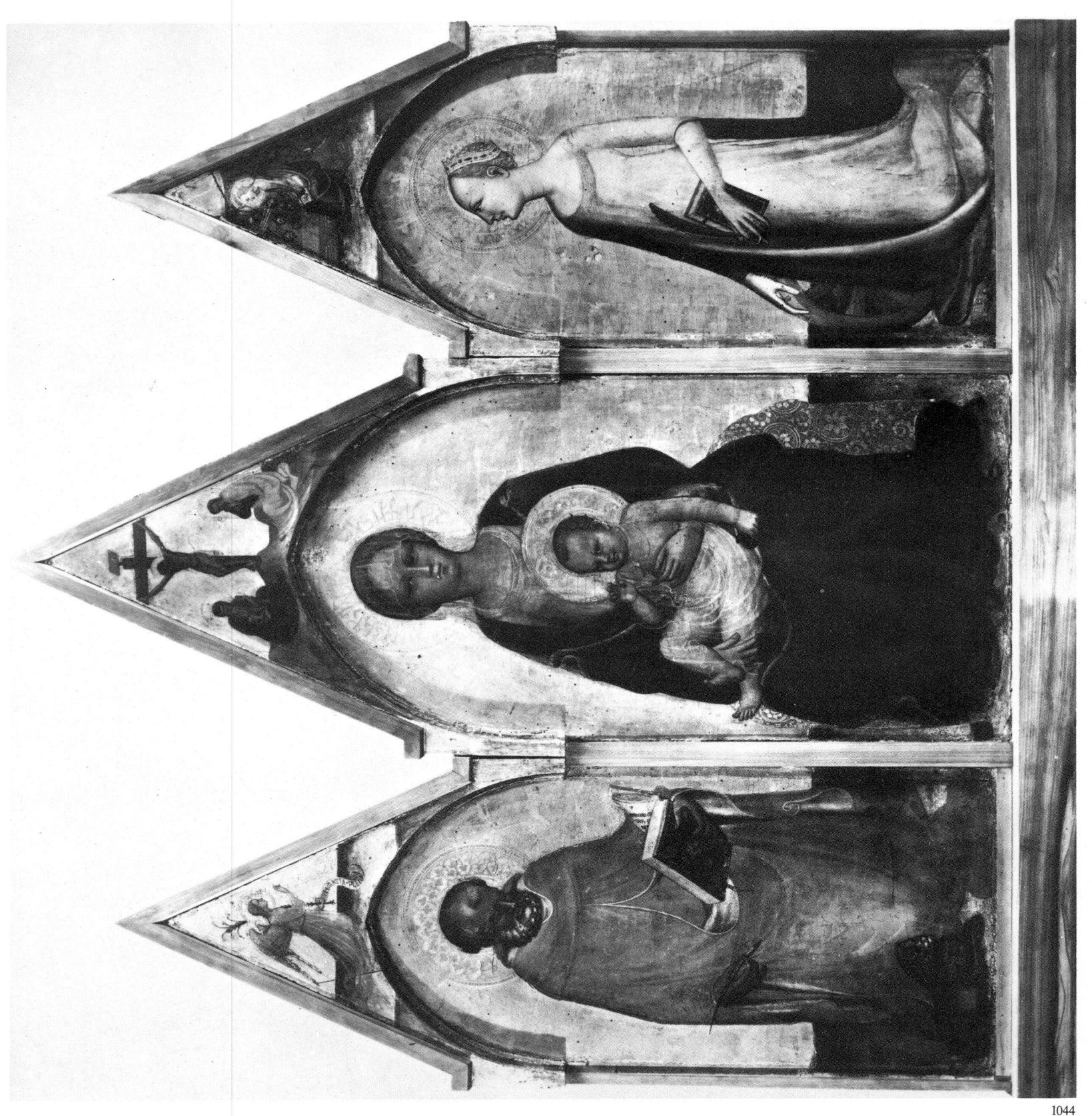

1044

1044. *Triptych: Madonna of Humility with Sts Jerome and Catherine. Above: Christ on the Cross, Annunciation. Panel. Florence, Ospedale degli Innocenti, Pinacoteca. 142 × 163. SGF 69632.*

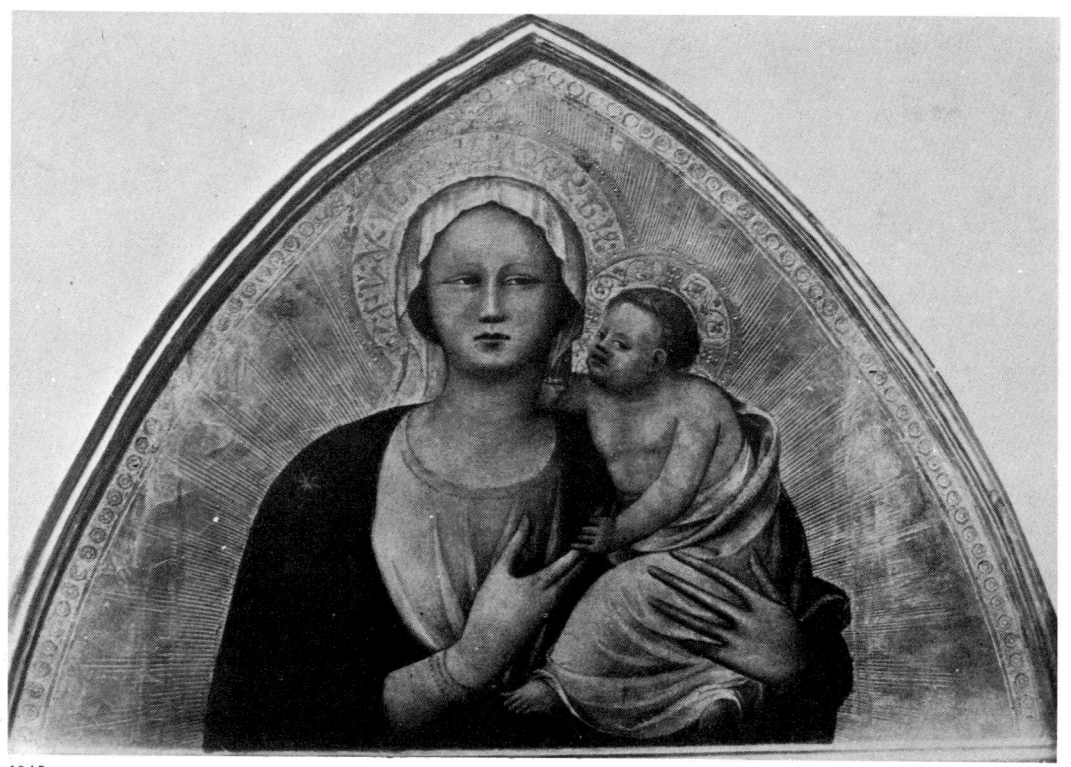

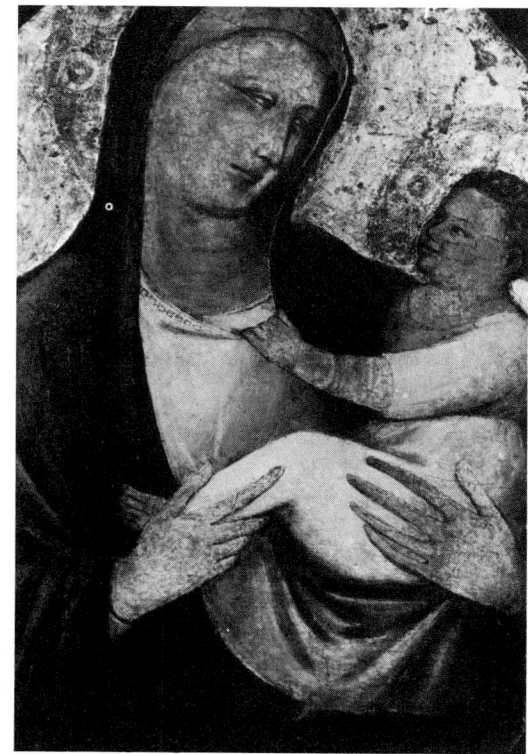

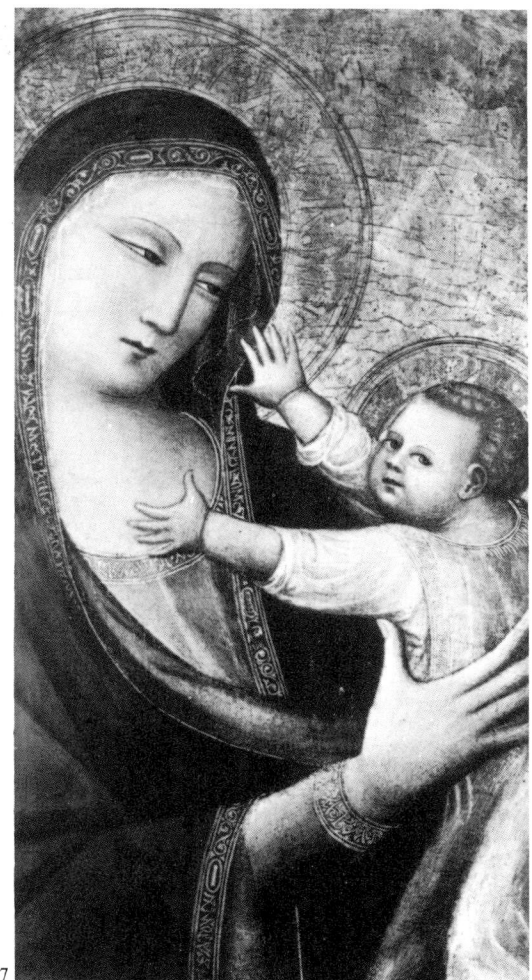

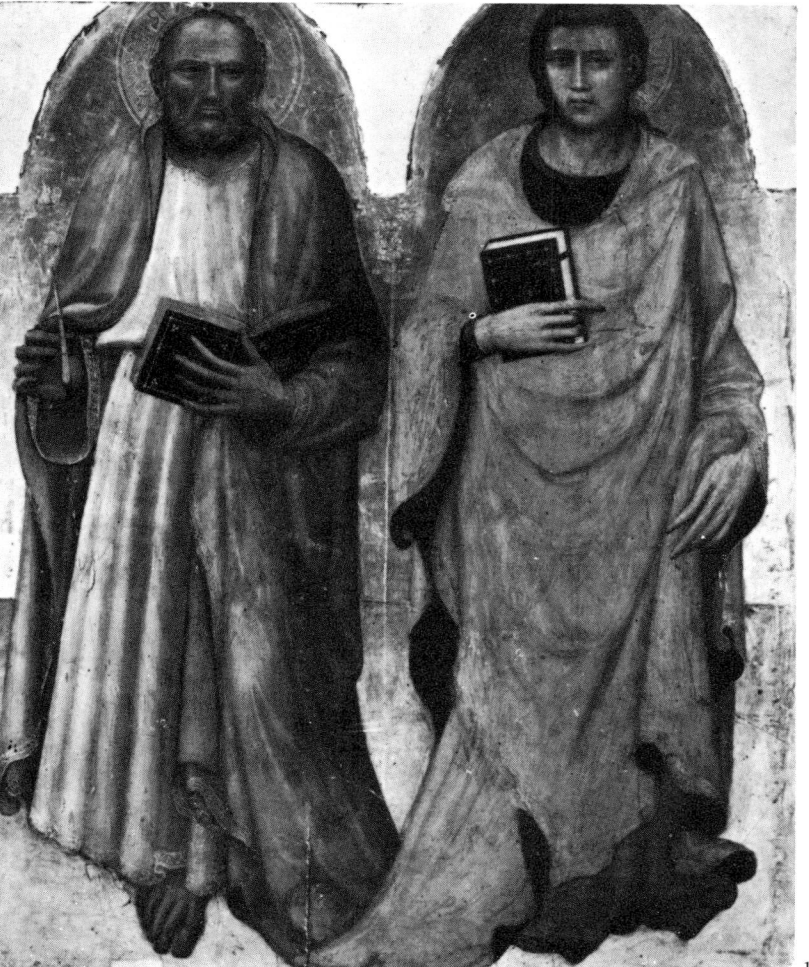

1045. *Lunette: Madonna and Child. Panel. Florence, Palazzo Vecchio. 63.5 × 89. Fototeca Berenson.*
1046. *Madonna and Child. Panel. Esztergom, Kereszteny Muzeum. no. 55.163. 55 × 37.5. Museum photo.*
1047. *Madonna and Child. Panel. Philadelphia (Pa.), Museum of Art. no. 43.40.45. 52.1 × 26.6. Museum photo.*
1048. *Two male Saints. Panel. Prato, Museo dell'Opera del Duomo. 103 × 75.5. Foto Barone 10447.*

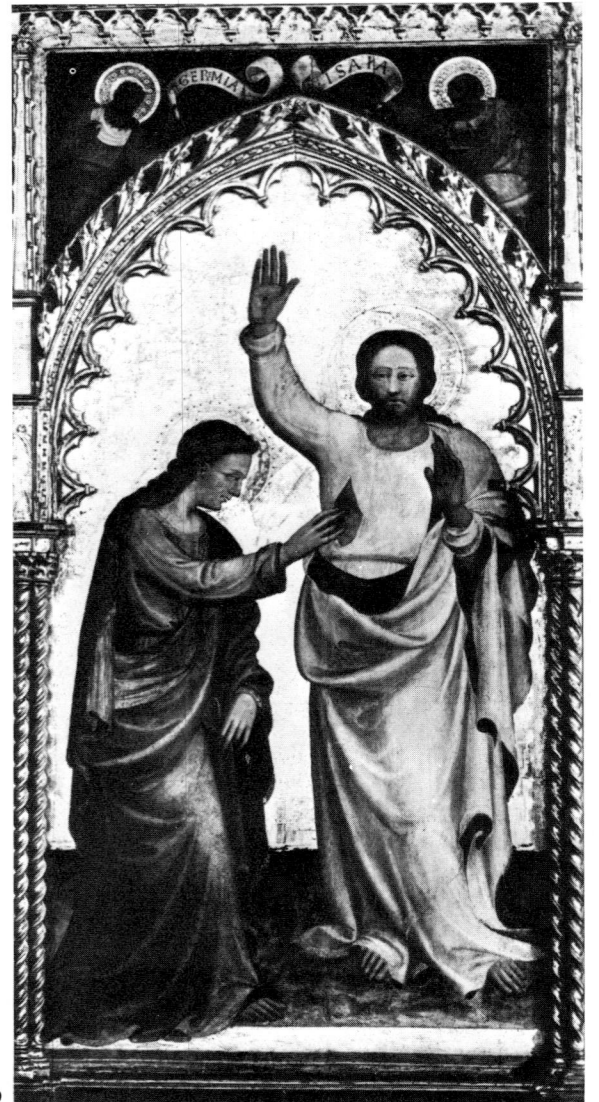

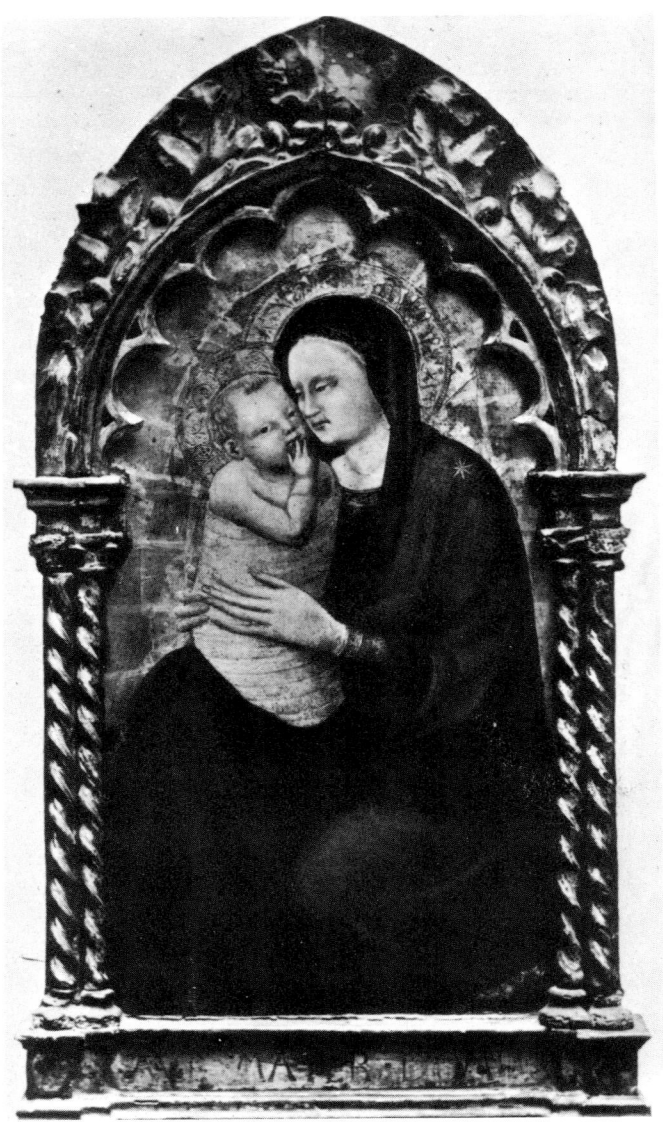

1049   1050

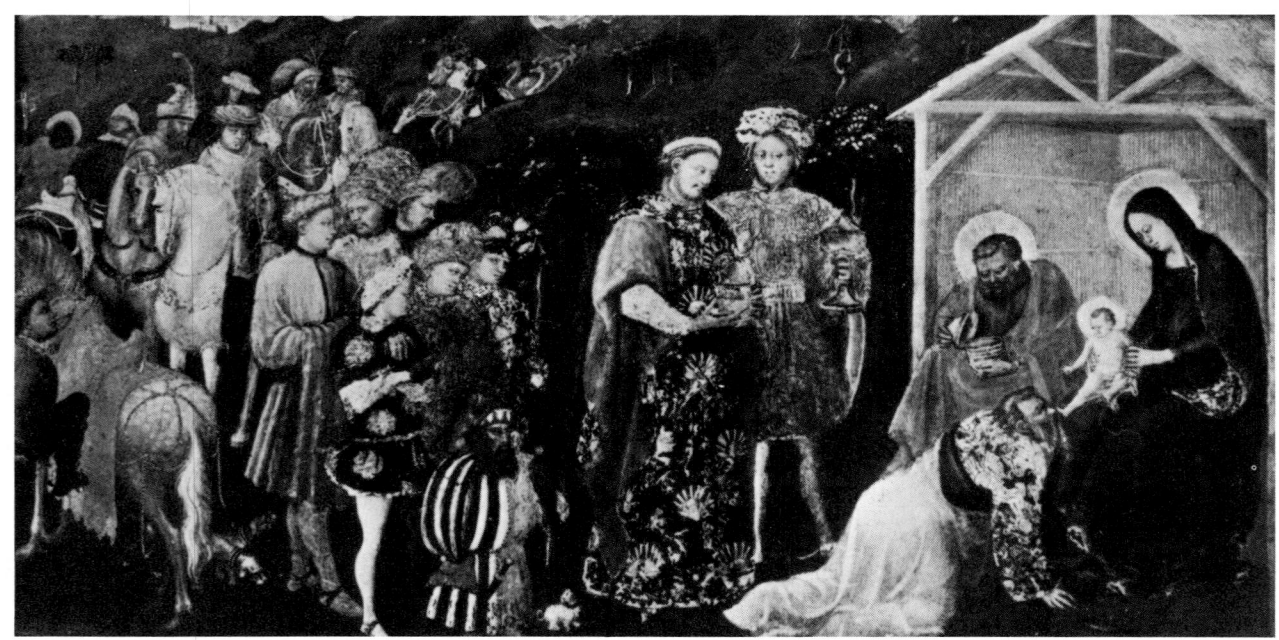

1051

1049. *Incredulity of St Thomas. Above: two Prophets. Panel. Florence, Accademia. no. 457. 242 × 121. Alinari 629.*
1050. *Madonna and Child (probably by Giovanni Toscani together with Masaccio). Panel. Whereabouts unknown (formerly Rome, Marinucci Collection).*
        SGF69851.
1051. *Adoration of the Magi. Panel. Whereabouts unknown (formerly London, Dodge Collection). Fototeca Berenson.*

MASACCIO

Masaccio is one of the great names in the history of Italian art. He exercised an immeasurable influence on the development of Florentine painting during the whole of the 15th century, and following that on the later development of European art. He was considered a master and an innovator by successive generations of painters, respected as a spiritual ancestor by the highest geniuses of the Renaissance and he was celebrated as the first painter of the "new manner" by the earliest historians of the age. In spite of all that, he died young, at an age when the painters of our own day only just begin to know themselves, and are stumbling, uncertain, just out of school, torn by different influences. His works are meagre in number. One of them, saved for us by a miracle, is enough to show the measure of his genius and to have been a model for all his successors....

from J. Mesnil, p. 1, *Masaccio et les débuts de la Renaissance*, The Hague, 1927.

Certain works of art are elevated to such a height that they overcome every limit of time and every accident of style. The transitory and ephemeral elements which are necessarily united to their origin appear to us as eternal conquests of the human genius and always maintain their true value. Among these works are the frescoes of Masaccio in the Brancacci Chapel. But if we consider the artist in the society in which he lived and worked, we see him dominate, as a genius who synthesized past experiences and who proceeded alone along a way which is opposed to that of the refined tastes of the late Gothic period, in order to create a new world: the world of the Renaissance. Masaccio appears even more prodigious to us if we think that he lived little more than twenty-six years. His art is so novel and so personal that he has forever a prominent place in art criticism. But in so much of this praise, usually generic and limited in the most commonplace manner, we can only remark that what belongs to him has always been separated from what belongs to others. A just selection of attributions has made the starting point with which one can measure, through the examination of single paintings, the greatness of the master and with which one can perceive the true range of his accomplishments.....

from M. Salmi, p. 7, *Masaccio*, Milan, 1947.

Masaccio was born on December 21, 1401, on the Feast Day of St. Thomas, in Castel San Giovanni " on the hill " (the modern San Giovanni Valdarno), which was a large and prosperous village in the region of Florence. His father, Ser Giovanni was, at his birth, a very young notary aged twenty. His mother, Monna Iacopa, was even younger. She was the daughter of Martinozzo, an innkeeper of Barberino di Mugello.....
The family's name was not Guidi, as is still widely believed. This name was chosen by Masaccio's brother, Giovanni (called *lo Scheggia*), in his old age, during a period when most families of the lower and middle classes of Florence were choosing their own surnames. Guidi was a very common one, and may have been the surname of one of Giovanni's two wives.
At the end of the fourteenth century the Mone family was still lacking a full surname. Only at the beginning of the Quattrocento did its various members, including Masaccio and his brother Giovanni, begin to be described in official documents as *Cassai* (chest-makers) from the profession of their elders. But the surname *Cassai* was soon to vanish, as Giovanni relinquished it later in favor of Guidi, and the other members of the family died childless.....
Nothing is known about his early youth. The only information available proves that in 1422, when he was over twenty years old, Masaccio became a member of the Florentine Guild of Doctors and Apothecaries, which also included painters. But we can only speculate about his artistic beginnings (whether, for instance, he began to paint in Castello or went at an early age to Florence), for on this subject there is no information.....

from U. Procacci, pp. 7-9, *All the Paintings of Masaccio*, London, 1962.

When a great revolutionary event appears in art, it is always difficult, where there is a lack of evidence, to explain how it came about. It is a question of distinguishing the elements which form it from those upon which it reacts. But Masaccio's revolution contains elements which are destructive only in their power, in the act. It is a revolution which appears as a rapid maturing of preceding elements. In contrast with the style of the time — that which today is known as International Gothic — and in accordance with the few artists that counted, it selected and isolated elements in the painting of the preceding century: that of Giotto and the first artists of the Trecento. It is enough to reflect that Masaccio's art never needed academic instruction. It was forced to follow its own evolution even if rapid, graded.....

from A. Parronchi, p. 7, *Masaccio* (I Diamanti dell'Arte, 24), Florence, 1966.

It was Masaccio the painter who single-handedly translated the principles and discoveries of his older contemporaries to a two-dimensional surface and thereby established the guidelines for Renaissance painting. Within a space of ten years at most, Masaccio created a revolution in painting that still, after more than five hundred years retains much of its original validity.....

from J. Beck, p. 179, *The Art Bulletin*, LVII, 2, 1971.

The nude preoccupies Florentine painting from Giotto in the fourteenth century to Michelangiolo in the sixteenth. Giotto opens up a spatial world; Masaccio puts man into it. Michelangiolo makes man into a colossus which dominates and eliminates it. This image [the Expulsion from Paradise] of Masaccio's is the essence of the Florentine search: the stark reality of man's anguish before a nature which he most combat to live, but which, in death, will destroy him.....

from R. Fremantle, p. 111, *Florentine Painting in the Uffizi*, Florence, 1971.

BIBLIOGRAPHY
BOOKS

An asterisk indicates a work listed in the General Bibliography

Schmarsow, A. H., *Masaccio*, Kassel, 1909; Mesnil, J., *Masaccio et les débuts de la renaissance*, The Hague, 1927; v. Marle, 1928*, pp. 251-3; Salmi, M., *Masaccio*, Rome, 1930; Lindberg, H., *To the Problem of Masolino and Masaccio*, 2 vols, Stockholm, 1931; Oertel, R., *Masaccio's Frühwerke*, Marburg, 1933; Wassermann, G., *Masaccio und Masolino*, Strasburg, 1935; Pittaluga, M., *Masaccio*, Florence, 1935 (with preceding bibliography); Cecchi, E., *Giotto*, Milan, 1937; *Procacci, 1946**, pp. 45-50; Salmi, M., *Masaccio*, Milan, 1947; Steinbart, K., *Masaccio*, Vienna, 1948; *Vavalà, 1948**, pp. 111-7; Pope-Hennessy, J., *Donatello's Relief of the Ascension*, London, 1949, pp. 10-12; *Galetti**, " F-O ", 1950, pp. 1588-1607; Salmi, M., *Masaccio, Masolino, Filippino Lippi: La Cappella Brancacci a Firenze*, Vol. I, Milan, s. d. (ca. 1951); Procacci, U., *Tutta la Pittura di Masaccio*, Milan, 1951; *Paatz**, 1952, Vol. III, pp. 201-9; *Salvini**, 1952, p. 16; Baldini, U., pp. 3-7, in *Catalogo della Mostra di Quattro Maestri del primo Rinascimento*, Florence, 1954; Orlandi, S., *Necrologia di Santa Maria Novella*, Vol. II, Florence, 1955, pp. 193-195, 613; Procacci, U., pp. 211-22, in *Scritti di Storia dell'Arte in Onore di Lionello Venturi*, Vol. I, Rome, 1956; Hendy, P., *Masaccio: frescoes in Florence*, Greenwich, (Conn.), 1956; Salmi, M., *Italia. Gli affreschi a Firenze*, Paris, (UNESCO) 1956; De Libero, L., *Masaccio*, Ivrea, 1956; Offner, R., pp. 66-72, in *Studies in the History of Art Dedicated to William E. Suida*, London, 1959; Shell, C., pp. 150-7, in Kosegarten, A., *Festschrift Ulrich Middeldorf*, Berlin, 1968; *Borsook, 1960**, pp. 143-6; Carli, E., *Capolavori del Museo di Pisa*, Torino, 1961, p. 127, tav. XXXVI; *Davies**, 1961, pp. 347-351; *Oertel, 1961**, pp. 140-2; Middeldorf, U., pp. 286-9, in *Scritti di Storia dell'Arte in Onore di Mario Salmi*, Vol. II, Rome, 1962; Procacci, U., *All the Paintings of Masaccio*, London, 1962; Baldini, U., pp. 866-77, in *EUA**, Vol. VIII, 1962; Meiss, M., pp. 123-45, in *Studies in Western Art*, Vol. II, Princeton, 1963; Oertel, R., pp. 146-59, in *Studies in Western Art*, Vol. II, Princeton, 1963; Berti, L., *Masaccio*, Milan, 1964 (Eng. trans. Penn State University, U.S.A., 1966); Hartt, F., pp. 117 ff., in *Essays in Memory of Karl Lehman* (Marsyas Supplement No 1, ed. Sandler, L. F.), New York (Institute of Fine Arts, New York University), 1964; Meiss, M., pp. 169-90, in *Studien zur Toskanischen Kunst, Festschrift für Ludwig Heydenreich*, Munich, 1964; Salvini, R., *Quattrocento Toscano e Quattrocento Fiammingo*, Florence (Dispense Istituto di Storia dell'Arte), 1964; Procacci, U., *Masaccio: La Cappella Brancacci* (Forma e Colore, 6), Florence, 1965; Bianchini, M. A., *Masaccio* (I Maestri del Colore, 80), Milan, 1965; Procacci, U., *Masaccio*, 2 vols, New York, 1966; Bologna, F., *Masaccio e la Pittura del '400 in Toscana*, (I Maestri del Colore, 256), Milan, 1966; Chiarini, M,. *Masaccio e la Pittura del '400 in Toscana* (I Maestri del Colore, 256), Milan, 1966; Gilbert, C., pp. 333-40, in *Arte in Europa: Scritti di Storia dell'Arte in Onore di Edoardo Arslan*, Milan, 1966; Parronchi, A., *Masaccio* (I Diamanti dell'Arte, 24), Florence, 1966; Procacci, U., pp. 15-20 in *Atti del VIII Convegno Internazionale di Studi sul Rinascimento*, (Donatello e il suo tempo), Florence-Padua, 1966-68; Gombrich, E. H., pp. 71-82, in *Essays in the History of Art Presented to Rudolph Wittkower*, London, 1967; Janson, H. W., pp. 83-88, in *Essays in the History of Art Presented to Rudolph Wittkower*, London, 1967; von Einem, H., *Masaccio's " Zinsgroschen "*, Cologne, 1967; Berti, L., *L'Opera Completa di Masaccio* (Classici dell'Arte, 24), Milan, 1968; Meiss, M., pp. 112-8; in Kosegarten, A., *Festschrift Ulrich Middeldorf*, Berlin, 1968; Meiss, 1970* , pp. 113-5; Fremantle, R., *Florentine Painting in the Uffizi*, Florence, 1971, pp. 3, 48-50, 106-16; Martindale, A., *Rise of the Artist in the Middle Ages and Early Renaissance*, London, 1972, p. 122; Gilbert, C., *History of Renaissance Art throughout Europe*, New York, 1973, pp. 74-5.

JOURNALS

Hadeln, D. V., *MKW*, 2, 1908, pp. 785-9; Fontana, P., *MKIF*, III, 1919-32, pp. 357, 365-72; Brockhaus, H., *MKIF*, III, 1919-32, pp. 160-82; Schmarsow, A., *B*, VII, 1925, pp. 145-57; Beenken, H., *B*, X, 1926, pp. 167-78; Mesnil, J., *BM*, 48, 1926, pp. 91-8; Schmarsow, A., *B*, XII, 1928, pp. 103-16; Beenken, H., *ZBK*, 1929-30, pp. 112-9, 156-65; Berenson, B., *DD*, X, 1929-30, pp. 331-6; Berenson, B., *DD*, X, 1929-30, pp. 133-42; Stechow, W., *ZBKKK*, Feb. 1930, II, pp. 125-7; Venturi, L., *BM*, 57, 1930, pp. 21-7; Beenken, H., *ZBK*, 1931-32, pp. 219-20; Carrà, C., *IV*, IV, 1931, pp. 12-19; Procacci, U., *RA*, XIV, 1932, pp. 141-232; Procacci, U., *RA*, XIV, 1932, pp. 489-503 and XVII, 1935, pp. 91-111; Serra, L., *BA*, XXIX, 1935, p. 32; Longhi, R., *CA*, V, 1940, pp. 145-91; Oertel, R., *MKIF*, V, 4/5, 1940, pp. 217-314; Lavagnino, E., *E*, XCVII, 3, 1943, pp. 96-112; Mather, F. J., Jr., *AB*, XXVI, 3, 1944, pp. 175-87; Meiss, M., *AB*, XXVI, 4, 1944, pp. 274-5; Lanyi, J., *BM*, LXXXIV-V, 1944, pp. 87-93; Toesca, E. B., *AF*, I, Oct. 1945, pp. 148-50; Pope-Hennessy, J., *BM*, LXXXVIII, 1946, p. 173; Procacci, U., *BM*, LXXXIX, 1947, pp. 309-10; Gilbert, C., *GBA*, XXXIV, 6, 1948, pp. 389-404 (trs. pp. 449-55); Longhi, R., *PA*, I, 5, 1950, pp. 3-5; Longhi, R., *PA*, I, 9, 1950, pp. 3-7; Pittaluga, M., *RA*, XXVI, 1950, pp. 229-231; Oertel, R. *ZKG*, LIV, 1951, pp. 167-73; Meiss, M., *AN*, 51, 1952, pp. 24-5; Clark, K., *BM*, XCIII, 1951, pp. 339-47; Salmi, M., *C*, II, 3-4, 1951, pp.182-3; Grassi, L., *PA*, II, 15, 1951, pp. 23-30; Longhi, R., *PA*, III, 35, 1952, pp. 10-37; Salmi, M., *C*, III, 1, 1952, pp. 14-21; Pope-Hennessy, J., *BM*, XCIV, 1952, pp. 31-2; Longhi, R., *PA*, III, 25, 1952, pp. 8-16; Procacci, U., *RA*, XXVIII, 1953, pp. 3-55; Baldini, U., *BA*, XXXIX, 4, 1954, pp. 221-40; Salmi, M., *C*, V, 1, 1954, pp. 65-78; Spencer, J. R., *AB*, XXXVII, 1955, pp. 273-80; *Edit.*, *AN*, 55, 1956, p. 74; Nyberg, D., *MA*, VII, 1957, pp. 1-7; Schlegel, U., *RA*, XXXII, 1957, pp. 77-106; Parronchi, A., *PA*, LXXXIX, 1957, pp. 4-7; Cohn, W., *BA*, XLIII, 4, 1958, pp. 64-8; Weisstein, V., *CAJ*, 17, 3, 1958, pp. 331-2; Parronchi, A., *PA*, CVII, 1958, pp. 3-32; Previtali, G., *PA*, IX, 113, 1959, pp. 3-32; Parronchi, A., *PA*, CIX, 1959, pp. 3-32; Virch, C., *MM*, XIX, 7, 1961, pp. 185-93; Shell, C., *AB*, 43, 1961, pp. 197-209; Meller, P., *AC*, III, 1961, pp. 186-227; Meller, P., *AC*, IV, 1961, pp. 273-312; Borsook, E., *BM*, CIII, 1961 pp. 212-15; Parronchi, A., *PA*, XII, 137, 1961, pp. 19-26; Parronchi, A., *PA*, XII, 133, 1961, pp. 18-48; de R., N., *AC*, II, 1961-2, pp. 70-1; Berti, L., *AC*, II, 1962, pp. 149-65; Bottari, S., and Berti, L., *AAM*, 18, 1962, pp. ii-iv; Shearman, J., *ZKG*, XXV, 1, 1962, pp. 13-47; Chiarini, M., *PA*, XIII, 149, 1962, pp. 53-6; Gioseffi, D., *E*, CXXXV, 806, 1962, pp. 50-72; Boskovits, M., *AHA*, VIII, 1963, pp. 241-60; Boskovits, M., *AHA*, IX, 1963, pp. 139-62; Schlegel, U., *AB*, XLV, 1963, pp. 19-33; Martinelli, V., *C*, XIV, 1, 1963, pp. 211-26; Shell, C., *AB*, XLVII, 4, 1965, pp. 465-9; Vayer, L., *AHA*, XI, 1965, pp. 217-39; de Tolnay, C., *AL*, X, 2, 1965, pp. 69-74; Hatfield, R., *AB*, XLVII, 1965, pp. 315-24; Murray, P., *AP*, LXXXI, 1965, pp. 299-300; Longhi, R., *PA*, XVI, 185/5, 1965, pp. 38-40; Romanini, A. M., *C*, XVII, 4, 1966, pp. 290-323; Boskovits, M., *ZKG*, XXIX, 1966, 1, pp. 51-66; Shearman, J., *BM*, CVIII, 1966, pp. 449-55; Bellosi, L., *PA*, 193/13, 1966, pp. 49-50; Bellosi, L., *PA*, 201, 1966, p. 76; Coolidge, J., *AB*, XLVIII, 1966, pp. 382-4; Parronchi, A., *RIA*, I, 2, 1966, pp. 29-42; Simson, O. v., *JBM*, VIII, 1966, pp. 119-59; Berti, L., *AV*, V, 3, 1966, pp. 3-12; Smart, A., *AP* LXXXIII, 1966, p. 263; von Einem, H., *AHA*, XIII, 1967, pp. 187-90; Kardos, T., *AHA*, XIII, 1967, pp. 137-48; Shearman, J., *PA*, XVIII, 203/23, 1967, p. 28; Linnenkamp, R., *P*, XXV, 1967, pp. 126-7; Conti, A., *PA*, XIX, 223/43, 1968, p. 5; Cole, B., *MKIF*, XIII, 3-4, 1968, pp. 289-300; Weiss, G., *A*, II, 1968, pp. 5-25; Conti, A., *PA*, XIX, 215/35, 1968, p. 14; Kosegarten, A., *JBM*, X, 1968, pp. 14-100; (photograph), *K*, XXI, 1968, p. 215; Friedmann, H., *Sim*, 3, 1968-9, 1, pp. 11, 13; Boskovits, M., *AI*, II, 13/14, 1969, pp. 4-13; Schneider, L., *AQ*, XXXII, 1, 1969, p. 27; Gilbert, C., *SDA*, 3, 1969, pp. 260-78; Calvesi, M., *SDA*, 1-2, 1969, pp. 158-61; Fremantle, R., *CA*, XVI, 103, 1969, pp. 39-56; Fremantle, R., *AV*, VIII, 6, 1969, pp. 22-5; Boskovits, M., *AI*, II, 13/14, 1969, pp. 4-13; Fremantle, R., *AV*, IX, 6, 1970, pp. 39-49; Paoletti, J., *C*, XXI, 1-2, 1970, pp. 55-58; Beck, J., *AB*, LVII, 2, 1971, pp. 177-95; Cole, B., & Middeldorf, U., *BM*, CXIII, 822, 1971, pp. 500-7; Middeldorf, U., *BM*, CXIII, 1971, 815, p. 72; Polzer, J., *AB*, LIII, 1971, pp. 36-40; Polzer, J., *JBM*, XIII, 1971, pp. 18-59; Dempsey, C., *AB*, LIV, 3, 1972, pp. 279-81; Shell, C., *AB*, LIV, 1, 1972, pp. 41-46; Cole, B., *MKIF*, XVII, 2-3, 1973, p. 229; Volpe, C., *MKIF*, XVII, 2-3, 1973, pp. 357-8; Fremantle, R., *BM*, CXV, 845, 1973, pp. 516-8; Zeri, F., *MKIF*, XVII, 2-3, 1973, p. 362; Welliver, W., *AQ*, XXXVI, 1/2, 1973, pp. 1-30; Watkins, L., *MKIF*, XVII, 1, 1973, pp. 65-74.

DATED WORK

1422 San Giovenale (Reggello). Triptych: Madonna & Child with Sts. Giovenale, Anthony, Bartholomew and Blaise. d. (fig. 1054).

There are no known signed works by Masaccio.

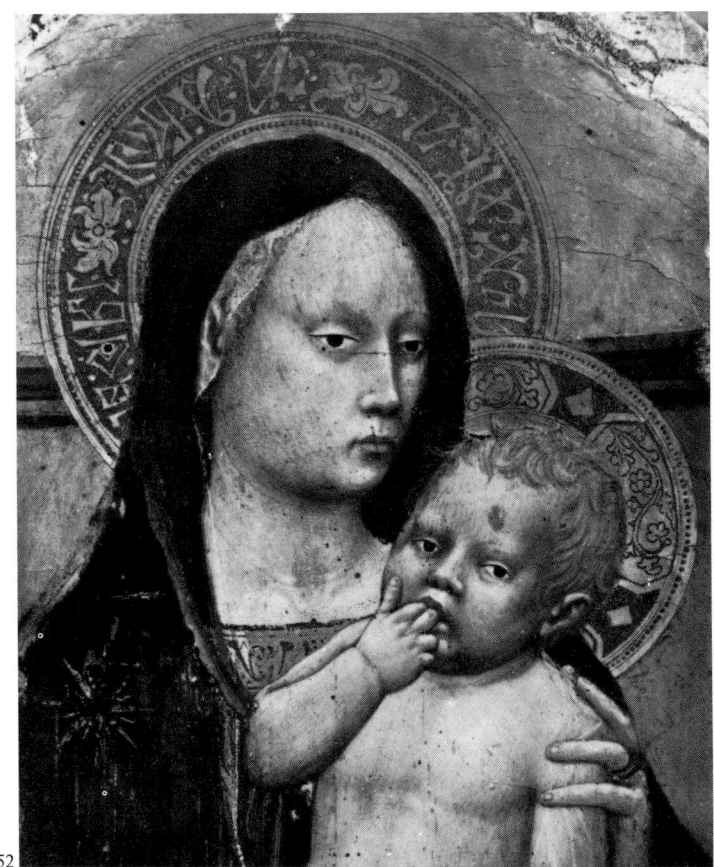

1052

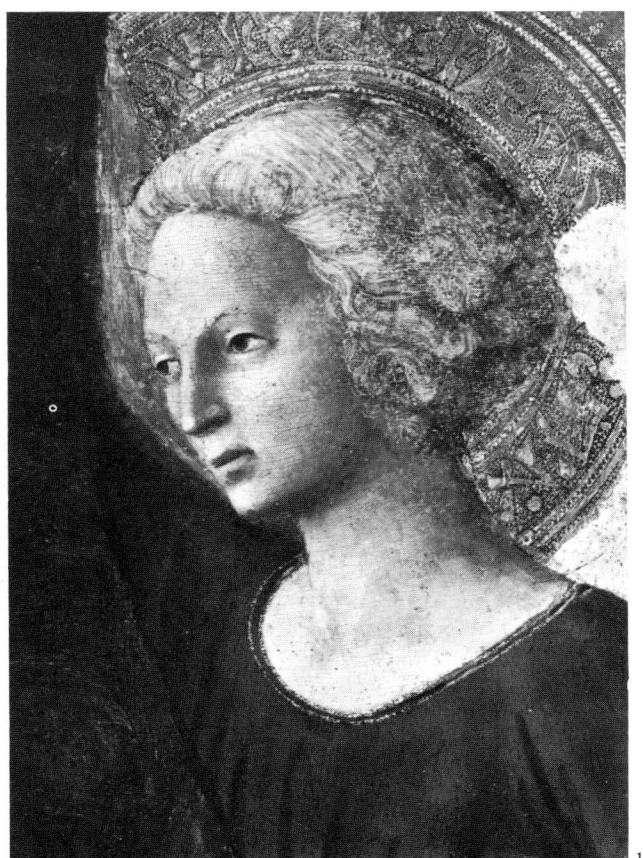

1053

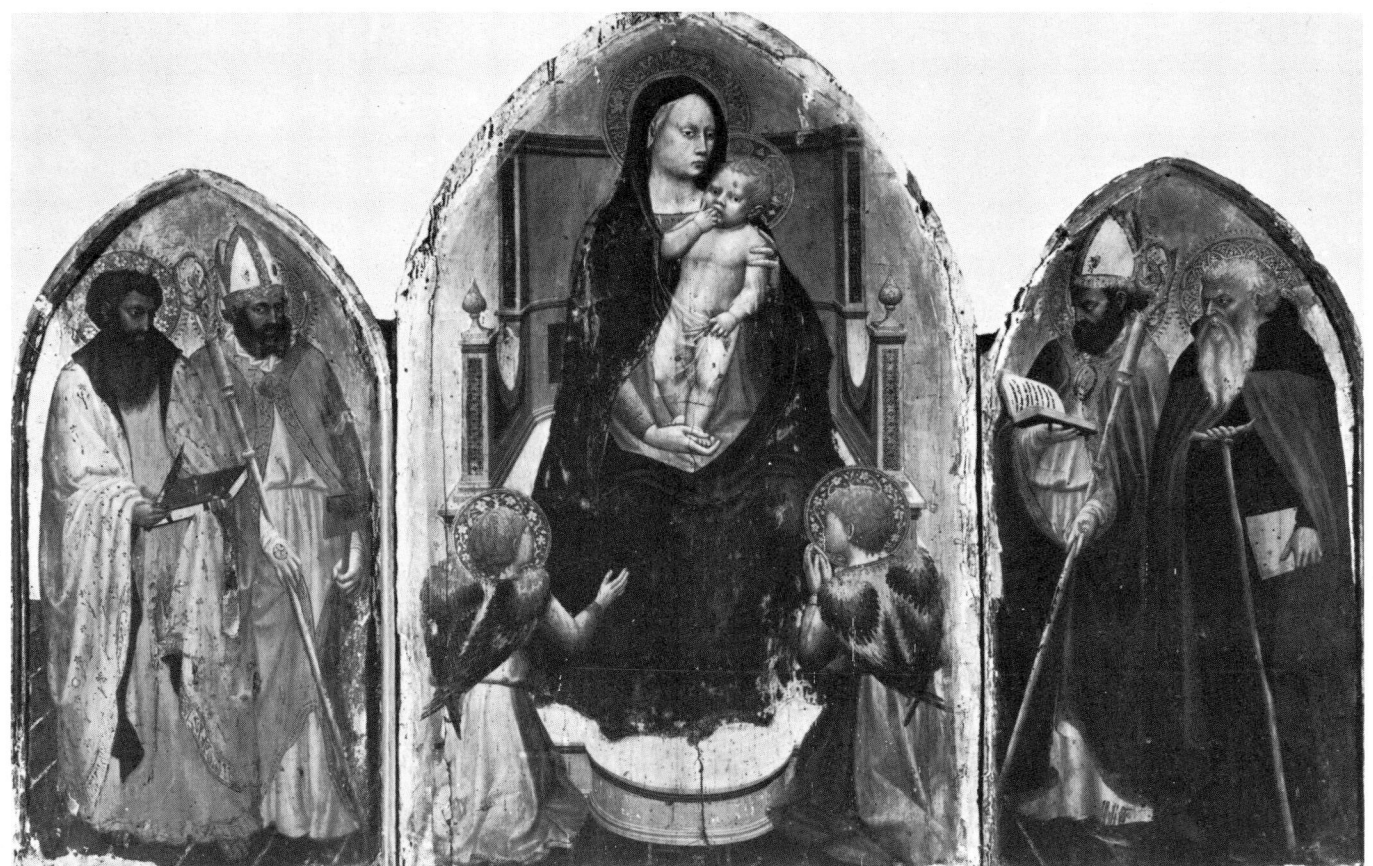

1054

1052. *Madonna and Child, detail of fig. 1054. Panel. San Giovenale, Chiesa. SGF 11763. d. 1422.*
1053. *Head of an Angel, detail of fig. 1057. Panel. Florence, Uffizi. no. 8386. SGF 97722.*
1054. *Triptych: Madonna and Child with Sts Bartholomew, Blaise, Giovenale and Anthony Abbot. Panel. San Giovenale (near Reggello in Pratomagno),*
       Chiesa. SGF 117156. d. 1422.

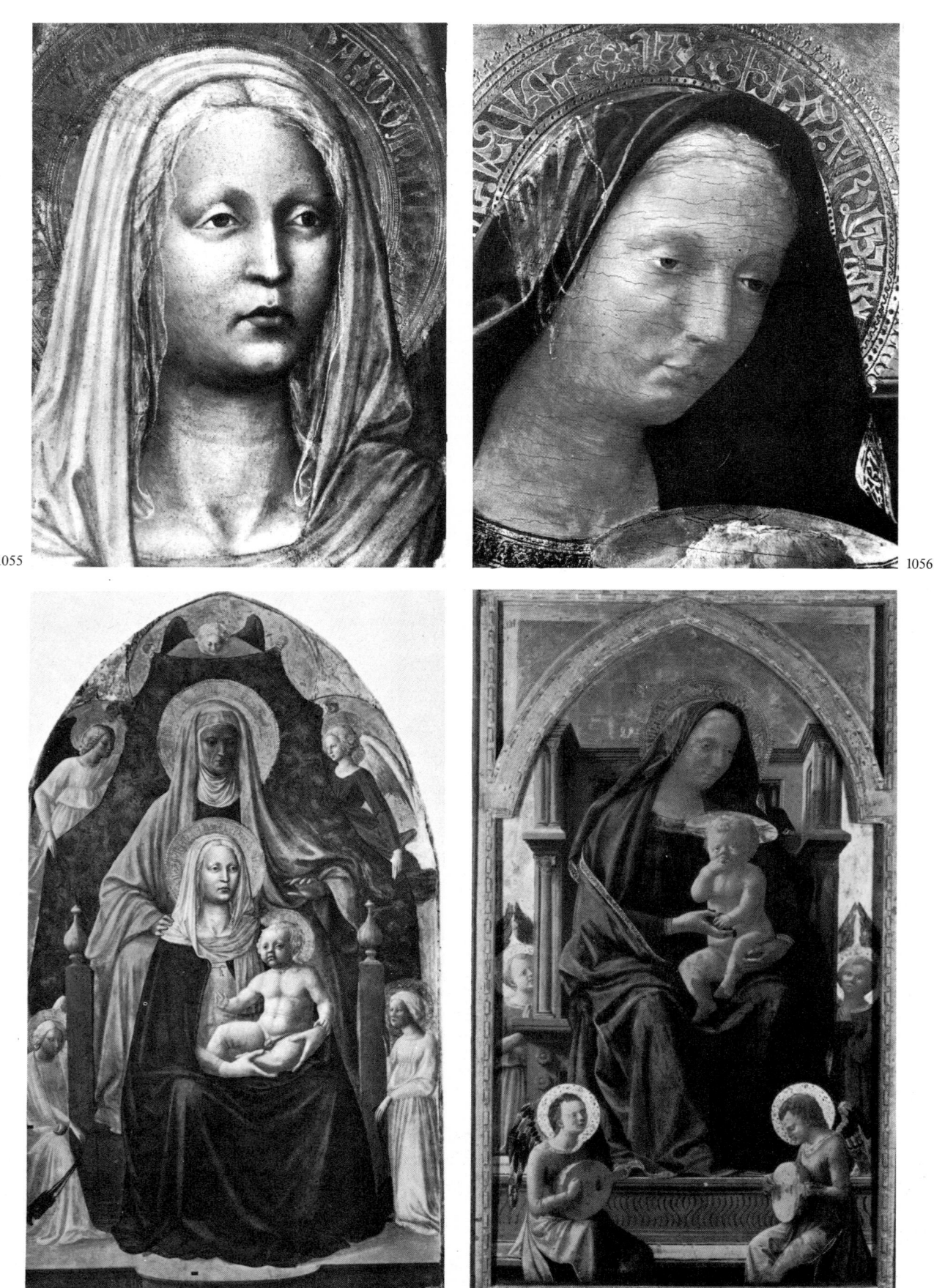

1055.   *Head of Madonna, detail of fig. 1057. Panel. Florence, Uffizi. no. 8386. SGF 97714.*
1056.   *Head of Madonna, detail of fig. 1058. Panel. London, National Gallery. no. 3046. Museum photo. 1426.*
1057.   *Madonna and Child Enthroned with St Anne and five Angels. Panel. Florence, Uffizi. no. 8386. 175 × 103. SGF 97490.*
1058.   *Madonna and Child Enthroned with four Angels. Panel. London. National Gallery. no. 3046. 135.2 × 60.3. Museum photo. 1426.*

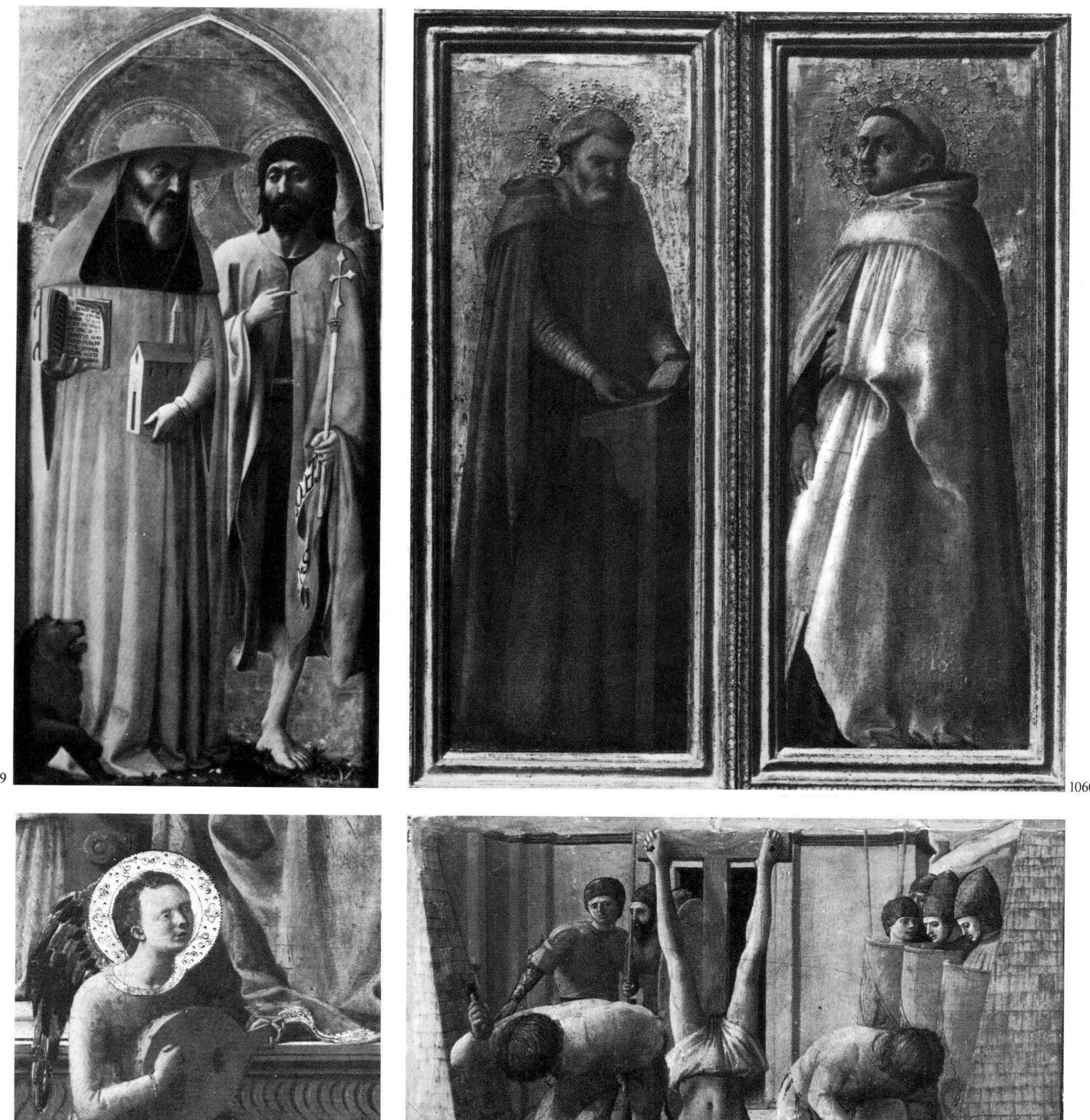

1059. *Sts Jerome and John the Baptist. Panel. London, National Gallery. no. 5962. 114.3 × 54.6. Museum photo.*
1060. *Two Carmelite Saints. Panel. Berlin, Dahlem, Staatliche Museen. no. 58 D. 38 × 12.5. Museum photo: Steinkopf. 1426.*
1061. *Music-making Angel, detail of fig. 1058. Panel. London, National Gallery. no. 3046. Museum photo. 1426.*
1062. *Martyrdom of St Peter. Panel. Berlin, Dahlem, Staatliche Museen. no. 58 A. 21 × 61. Museum photo: Steinkopf. 1426.*

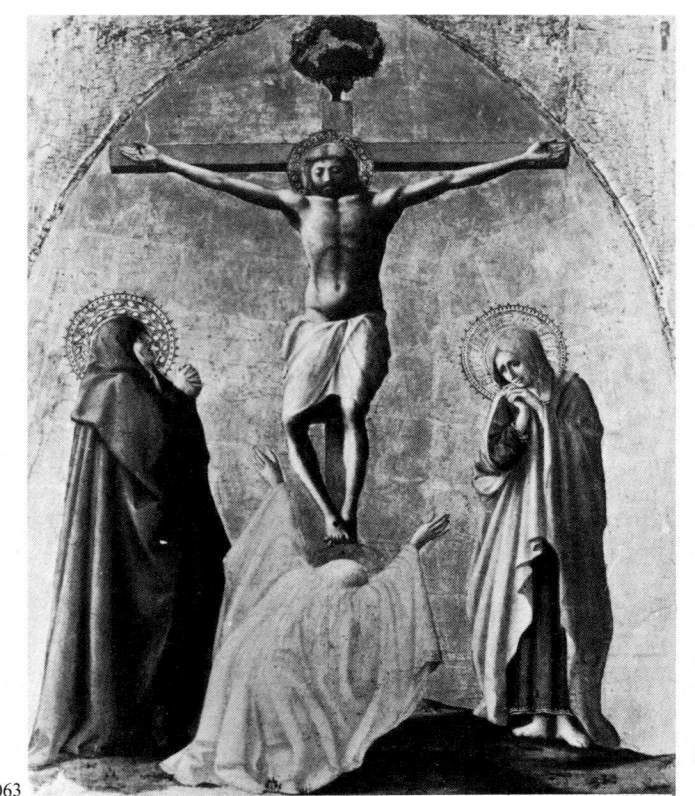

1063

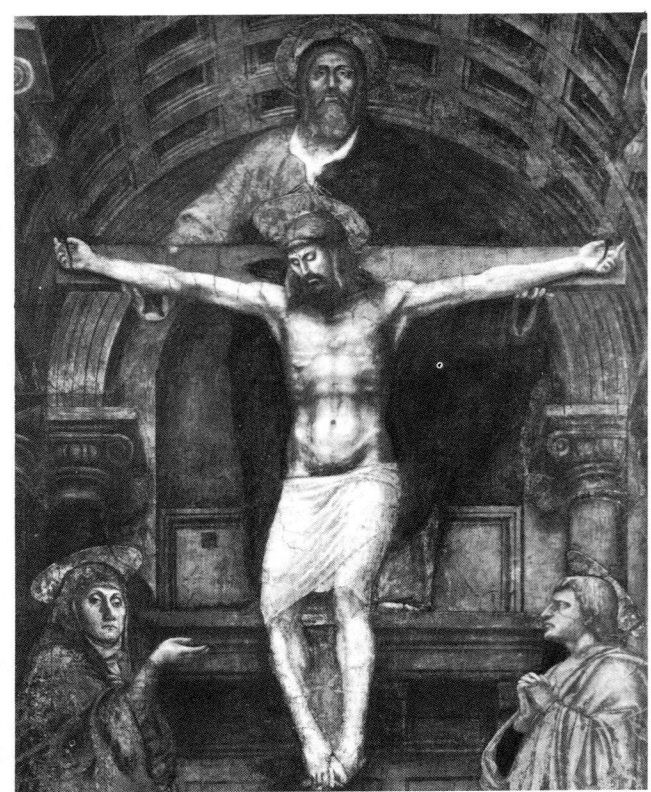

1064

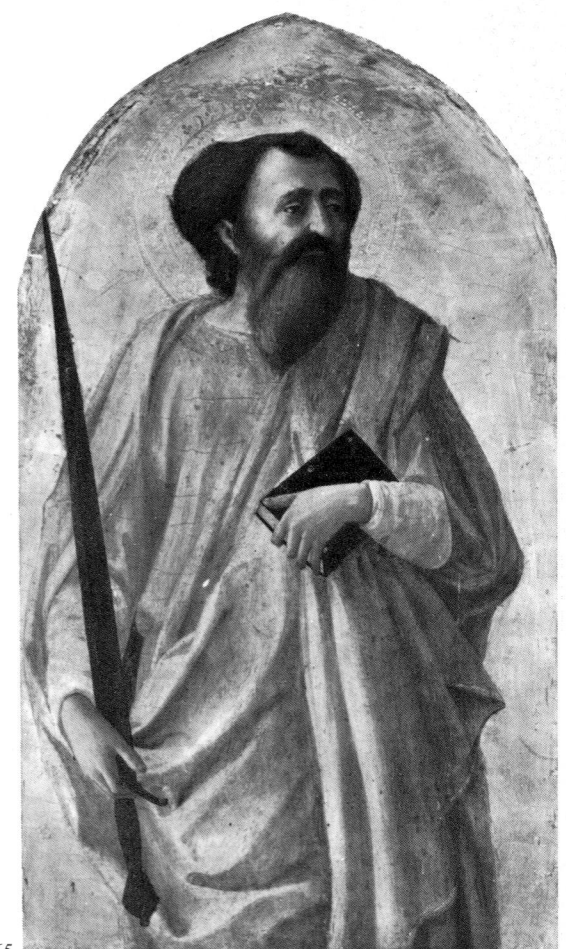

1065

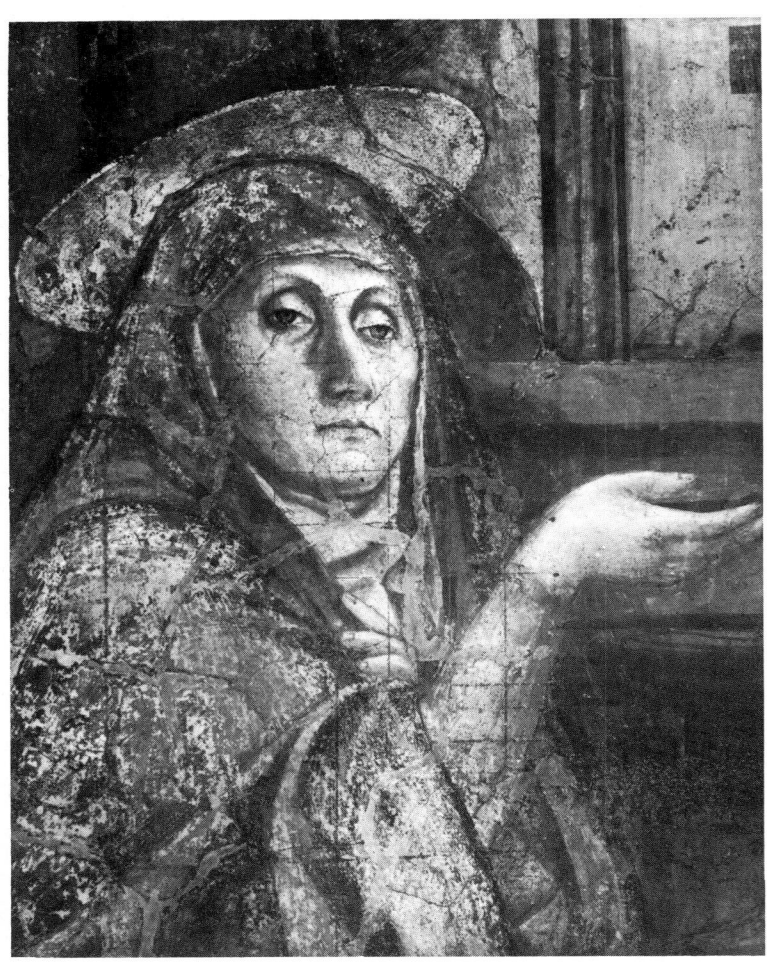

1066

1063. *Lamentation at the Crucifixion. Panel. Naples, Museo Nazionale di Capodimonte. Courtauld photo.*
1064. *Trinity, the Virgin and St John the Evangelist, detail of fig. 1069. Fresco. Florence, S. Maria Novella. SGF 67553.*
1065. *St Paul. Panel. Pisa, Museo Nazionale di S. Matteo. no. 1720. 59 × 34. SGF 104371. 1426.*
1066. *The Virgin, detail of fig. 1069. Fresco. Florence, S. Maria Novella. SGF 67562.*

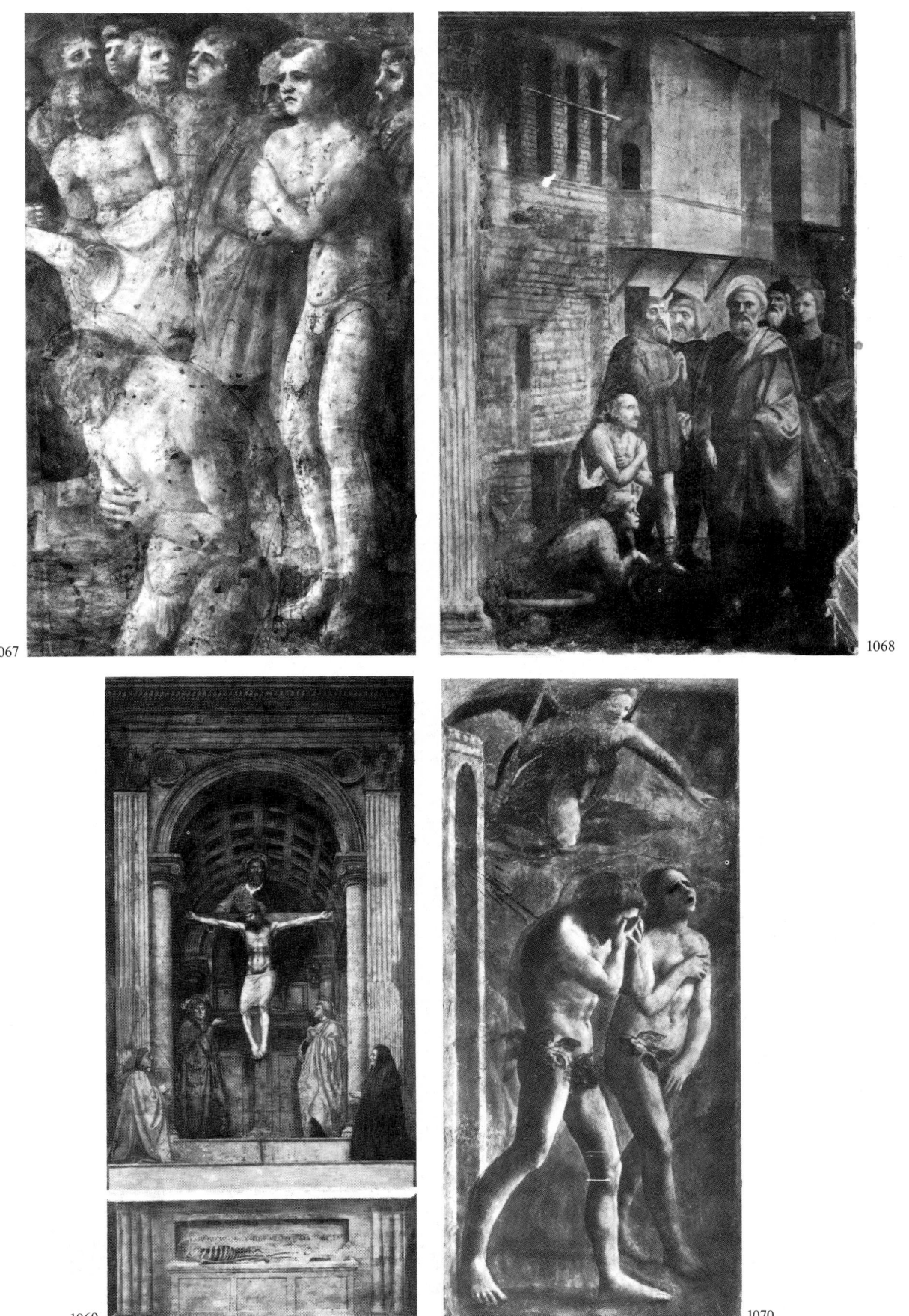

1067. *St Peter baptizing. Fresco. Florence, S. Maria del Carmine, Brancacci Chapel. SGF 43480.*
1068. *St Peter healing with his Shadow. Fresco. Florence, S. Maria del Carmine, Brancacci Chapel. SGF 43474.*
1069. *Trinity with the Virgin, St John the Baptist, two Donors. Predella: Momento mori. Fresco. Florence, S. Maria Novella. SGF 104648.*
1070. *Expulsion from Paradise. Fresco. Florence, S. Maria del Carmine, Brancacci Chapel. SGF 54492.*

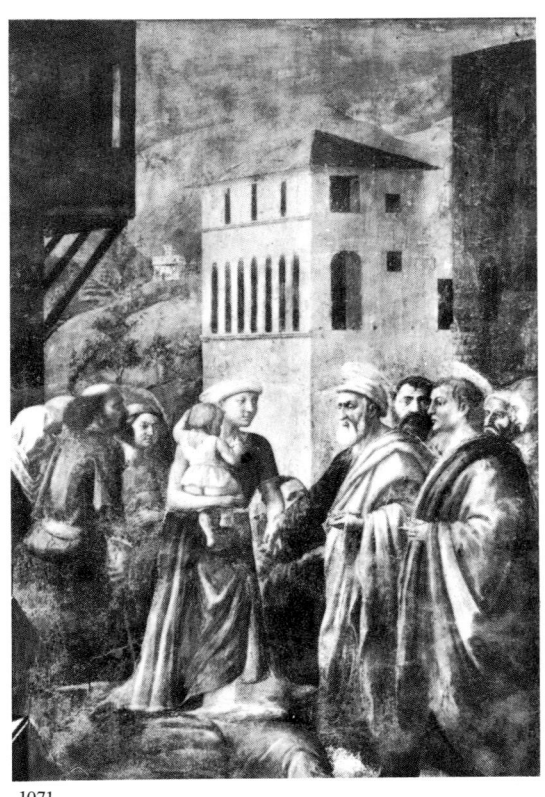

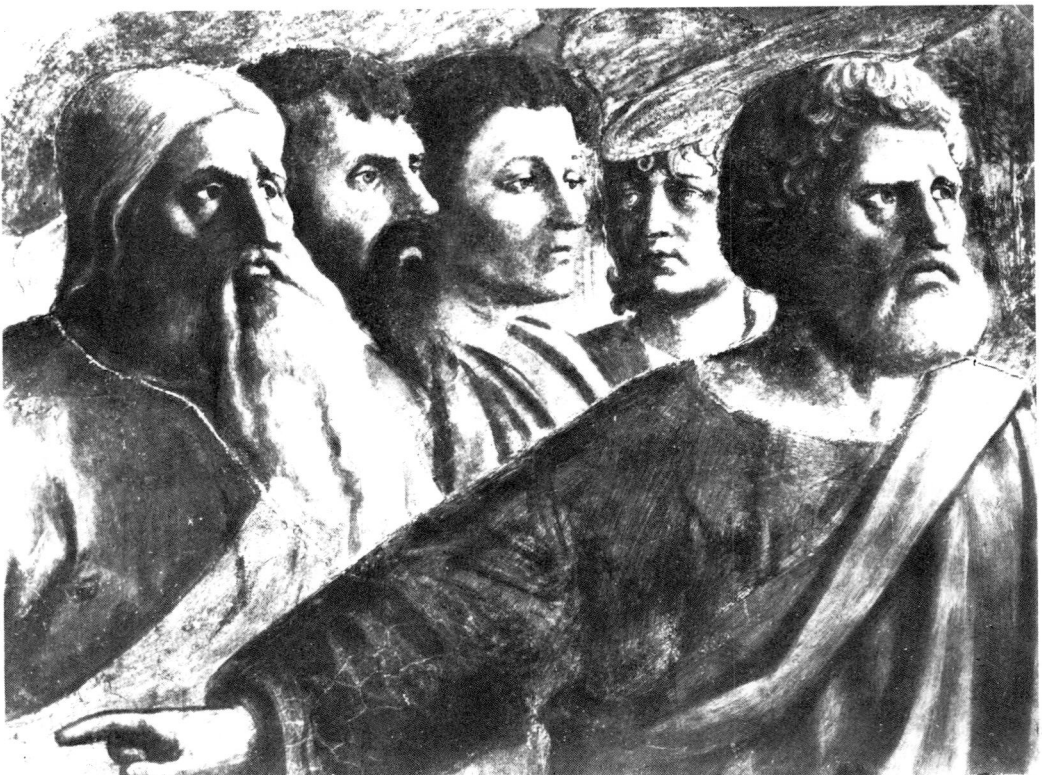

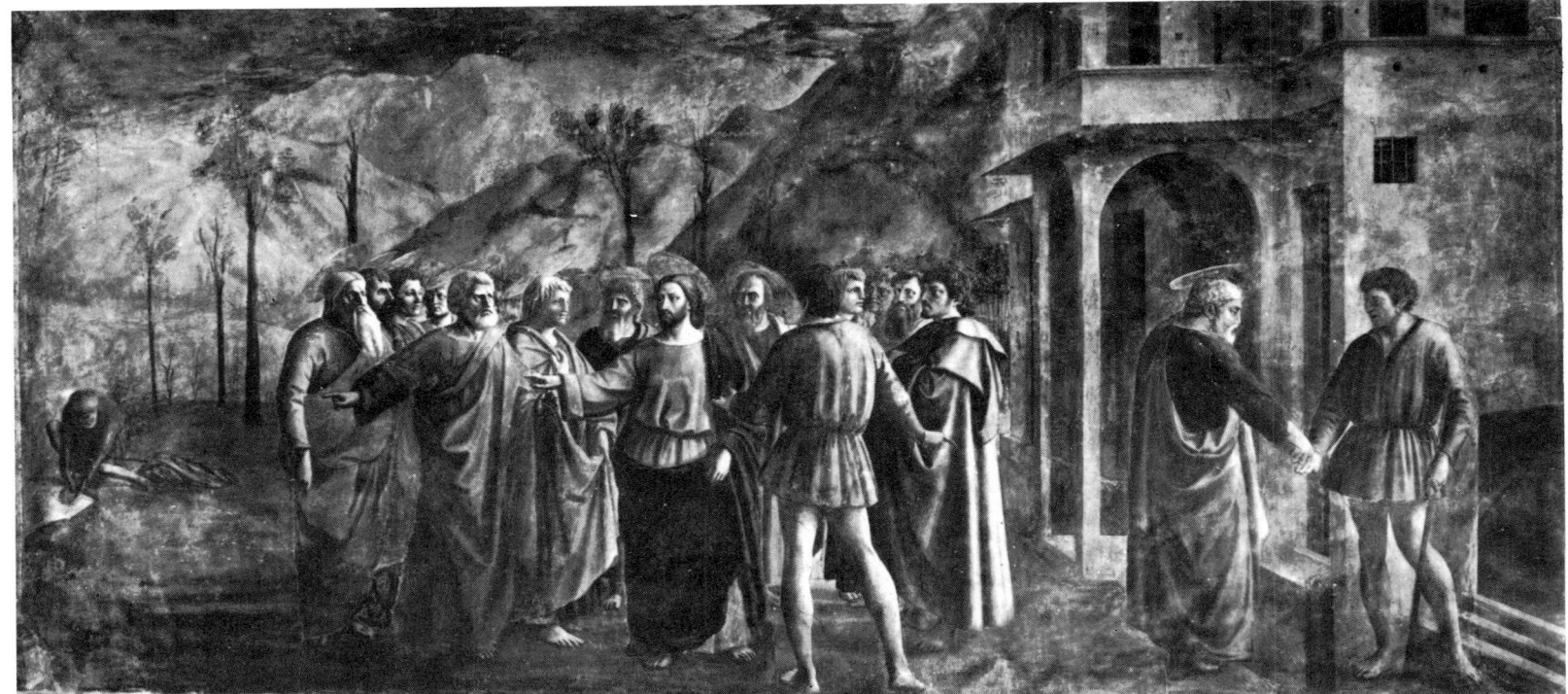

1071. *St Peter distributing Alms. Fresco. Florence, S. Maria del Carmine, Brancacci Chapel. SGF 54512.*
1072. *Heads of St Peter and four Apostles, detail of fig. 1073. Fresco. Florence, S. Maria del Carmine, Brancacci Chapel. SGF 54503.*
1073. *Tribute Money. Fresco. Florence, S. Maria del Carmine, Brancacci Chapel. SGF 54501.*

ANDREA di GIUSTO

Andrea di Giusto Manzini was an eclectic artist who began his career as a follower of Lorenzo Monaco. He is recorded for the first time in 1424 when he collaborated with Bicci di Lorenzo and again in 1426 working with Masaccio at Pisa. Between 1427 and 1447 his name appears regularly in the roll of taxes and in 1436 he is mentioned as a member of the " Arte di Calimala ". The same year he makes a contract to execute an altarpiece for the church of Sta. Maria dei Magnoli, Florence; we possess works dating from 1426, 1435, and 1437; the artist died in 1455.....

> from R. van Marle, pp. 238-40, *The Development of the Italian Schools of Painting*, Vol. IX, The Hague, 1927.

Manzini, Andrea di Giusto, Florentine, born 13- -, died Sept. 2, 1450. Painter, Arte of Physicians and Apothecaries, March 8, 1428/9. Popolo of San Simone (as Andrea di Giusto Bugli). Saint Luke (date uncertain, ? c. 1424). Pupil possibly of Bicci di Lorenzo, assistant of Masaccio, and perhaps also of Fra Angelico and Don Lorenzo Monaco. He is probably the Andrea da Firenze, living in the fifteenth century, to whom the works of this date, thus signed, may be attributed.....

> from D. E. Colnaghi, p. 169, *A Dictionary of Florentine Painters*, London, 1928.

There is a small typical Madonna by Andrea di Giusto from S. Giusto a Montalbino that shows him as inept and threadbare as in his other works.

> from R. Offner, p. 174, *The Burlington Magazine*, LXIII, July-Dec, 1933.

In the Berenson Catalogue are many pictures attributed to this little painter which are certainly not his, and some of which we have already placed elsewhere.....
When the above works have been severed from the small but real body of Andrea di Giusto's work, he, after a brief contingency with Masaccio, appears between '30 and '40 as a rustic interpreter of Angelican ideas. While under the influence of Masaccio, he painted the well known parts of the Pisan predella and the " Miracle of the Possessed " in the Johnson Collection. As time passed, it would seem that he approached the loose gigantic " quaternary " forms of Paolo Uccello; with this last painter he in fact collaborates, about 1445, on the frescoes of the Cappella dell'Assunta in the Duomo of Prato.....

> from R. Longhi, p. 183, *Critica d'Arte*, V, 1940.

The artistic career of Andrea di Giusto, which can be traced at least to the time of the Prato Polyptych of 1435, reveals the incredible ease with which he mastered every old and new element, in order to compensate for his lack of imagination. Indeed, in his vascillating artistic achievement, he is credited with having observed, with a certain curiosity, the great events of the Renaissance, though misunderstanding their significance and degrading their quality. In the Prato Polyptych of 1435, for example, he places in the predella a literal replica of that " Masaccesque " masterpiece of Angelico, " The Naming of the Baptist "; and next to it, a Nativity which differs little from that of Gentile da Fabriano in the Strozzi altarpiece. The " Assunta " of '37, in the Accademia in Florence, already reveals a reflection of Paolo Uccello, and in the predella, Andrea recopies Masolino's " Dormitio Virginis " for the polyptych of the Nevi. In fact, although he definitely collaborated in 1426 with Masaccio, and at the end of his life with Paolo Uccello, in the frescoes of the Chapel of the " Assunta " in the Duomo of Prato, it was Angelico and Masolino, filled with Masaccio's inspiration, who left an indelible mark on his artistic physiognomy.....

> from P. Dal Poggetto, p. 44, *Arte in Valdelsa*, Certaldo, 1963.

Andrea di Giusto Manzini. Florentine School. Active from 1422; died 1455. He was an eclectic, chiefly influenced by Lorenzo Monaco, also by Fra Angelico. He worked with Bicci di Lorenzo, and, in 1426, with Masaccio on the predella of the altarpiece which Masaccio painted for the Church of the Carmine, Pisa.....

from F. R. Shapley, p. 98, *Paintings from the Samuel H. Kress Collection*, London, 1966.

BIBLIOGRAPHY
BOOKS

An asterisk indicates a work listed in the General Bibliography

Supino, J. B., *T-Becker**, I, 1907, pp. 453-4; Venturi, A., *Storia dell' Arte Italiana*, VII, Milan, 1911, pp. 28-9; *v. Marle, 1927**, pp. 238-56; *Colnaghi**, 1928, p. 169; Tosi, M., *Treccani Vol. III**, 1929, p. 203; *Catalogo della Mostra del Tesoro di Firenze Sacra*, Florence, 1933, p. 123; *Galetti**, " A-E ", 1950, p. 74; Suida, W. E., *Catalogue of the Philbrook Art Center*, Tulsa, (Okla.), 1953, p. 28; *Cracow**, 1961, pp. 59-60; *Berenson, 1962**, p. xxxiii; *Berenson, 1963**, Vol. I, pp. 5-7; Dal Poggetto, P., *AIV**, 1963, pp. 44-5; Procacci, U., *AIE, 1966**, p. 304; *Shapley**, 1966, pp. 98-99; Chiarini, M., *Masaccio e la pittura del '400 in Toscana* (I Maestri del Colore, 256), Milan, 1966; *Prato 1969**, pp. 51-133.

JOURNALS

Sirén, O., *A*, VII, 1904, pp. 342-5; Hadeln, D. v., *MKW*, 1908, 2, pp. 785-9; Sirén, O., *BM*, XIV, 1909, p. 326; Diaz, E., *RADA*, IX, 1909, p. 200; De Nicola, *GRAAN*, V, 1918, pp. 69-73; Borenius, T., *BM*, LXI, 1922, pp. 104-9; T. B., *AP*, I, 1925, p. 312; Longhi, R., *Pin*, I, 1928-9; p. 38; Berenson, B., *DD*, XII, 2, 1932, pp. 512-541; Gamba, C., *BA*, XXVII, 1933, pp. 145-63; Offner, R., *BM*, LXIII, 1933, p. 174; Castelfranco, G., *RA*, XV, 1933, pp. 82-8; Longhi, R., *CA*, V, 1940, pp. 145-91; Salmi, M., *C*, I, 3, 1950, pp. 146-56; Ragghianti Collobi, L., *NCA*, II, 7, 1955, pp. 22-47; Cohn, W., *RA*, XXXI, 1956, pp. 53-54; Rozycka-Bryzek, A., *Biuletin Historii Sztuki*, XXII, 1960, pp. 203-18; Berti, L., *C*, XII, 2, 1961, pp. 84-107; *BM*, CIV, suppl. 1, Dec., 1962; *AC*, 1963, I, pp. 61-79; Boskovits, M., *AI*, III, 25/26, 1970, p. 42, note 8, p. 45, notes 29-30.

SIGNED AND DATED WORKS

1435 Prato, Galleria Comunale. Triptych: Madonna & Child Enthroned with two Angels & Saints. d. (fig. 1074).

1436 Figline, S. Andrea a Ripalta. Triptych: Madonna & Child with the Magi & Sts. Andrew, John the Baptist, James & Anthony Abbot. d. (fig. 1082).

1437 Florence, Accademia 3236. Panel: Madonna of the Holy Girdle with St. Thomas and eleven Angels, Sts. Catherine and Francis. s & d. (fig. 1085).

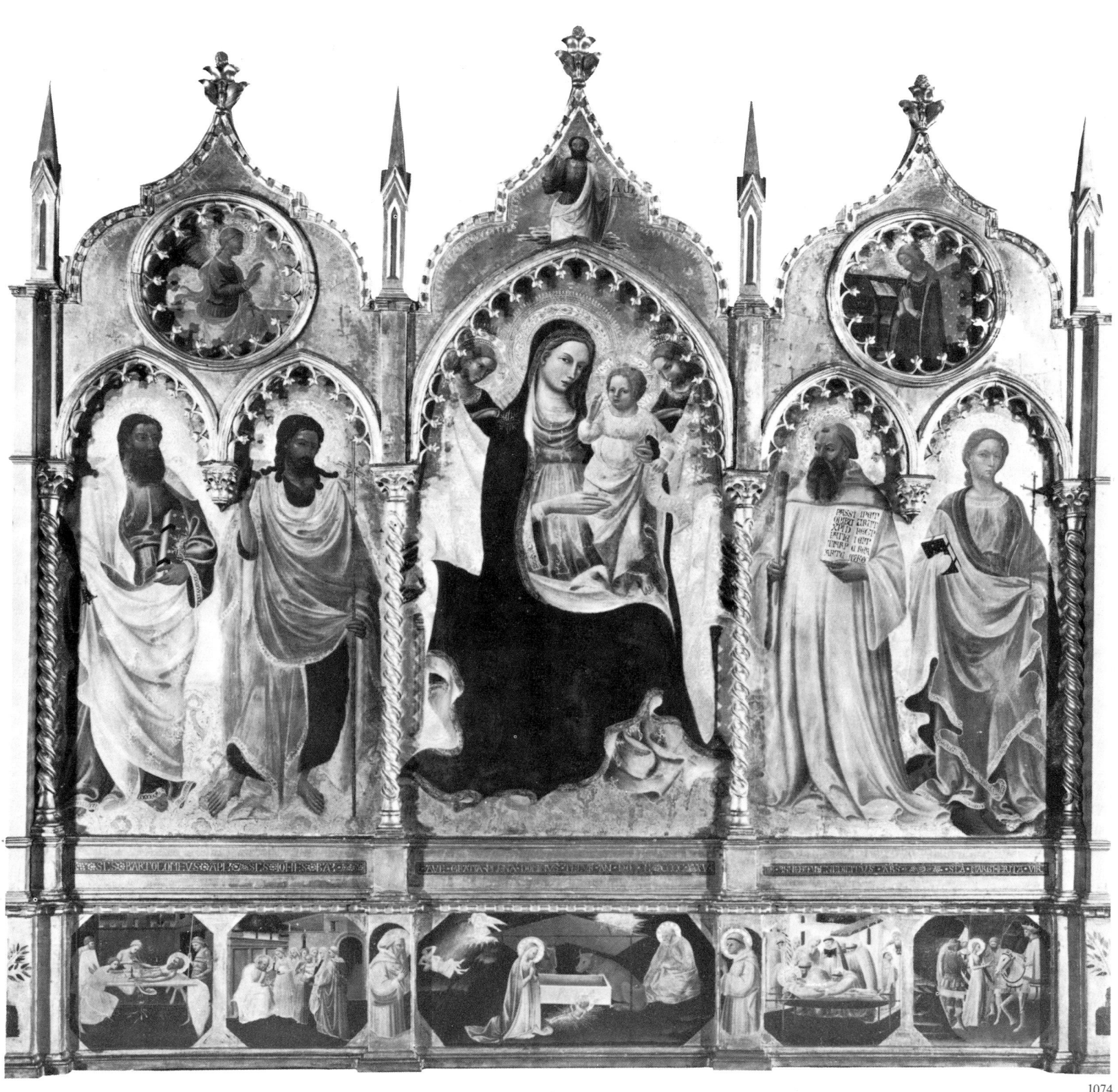

1074. *Triptych: Madonna and Child Enthroned with two Angels, and Sts Bartholomew, John the Baptist, Benedict and Margaret. Above: Christ blessing, Annunciation. Predella: Martyrdom of St Bartholomew; Naming of the Baptist; St Maurus; Nativity; St Placidus; Death of St Benedict; Abduction of St Margaret. Panel. Prato, Galleria Comunale. no. 8. c p: 196.5 × 76; sps: 187.5 × 78. SGF 107518. d. 1435.*

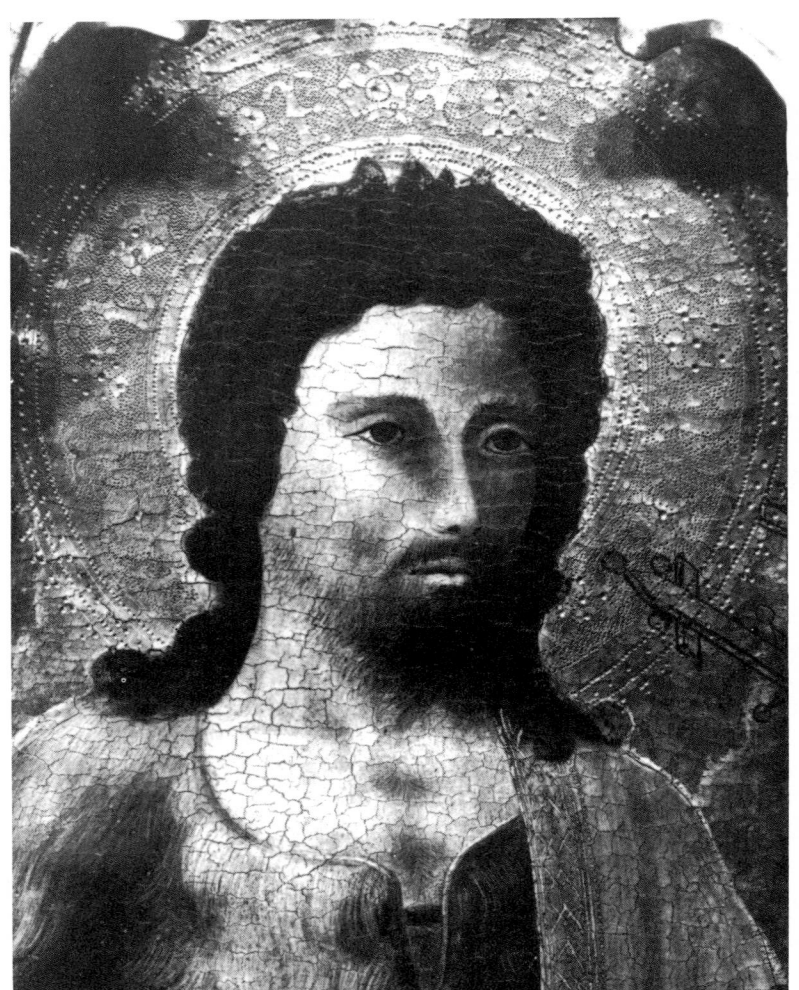

1075

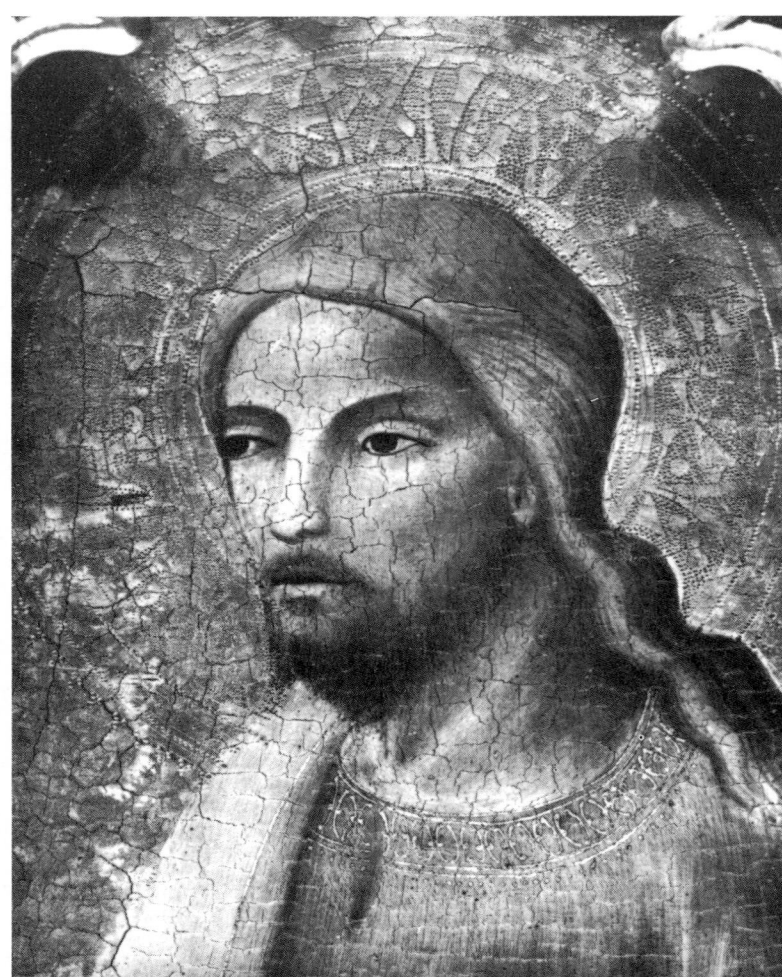

1076

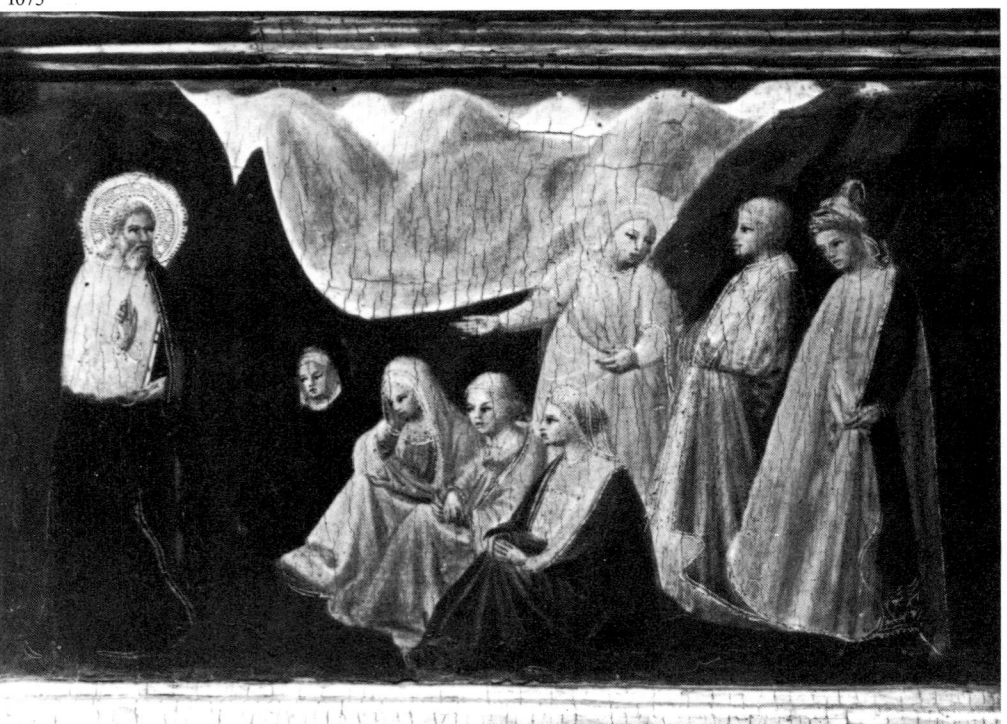

1077

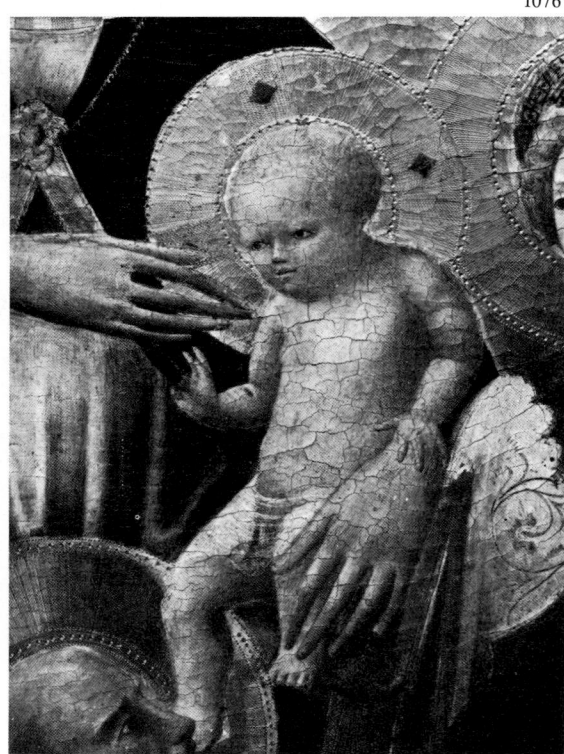

1078

1075. *Head of St John the Baptist, detail of fig. 1082. Panel. Figline, S. Andrea a Ripalta. SGF 124567. d. 1436.*
1076. *Head of St James, detail of fig. 1082. Panel. Figline, S. Andrea a Ripalta. SGF 124574. d. 1436.*
1077. *St Andrew preaching, detail of fig. 1082. Panel. Figline, S. Andrea a Ripalta. SGF 124585. d. 1436.*
1078. *Infant Christ, detail of fig. 1082. Panel. Figline, S. Andrea a Ripalta. SGF 124569. d. 1436.*

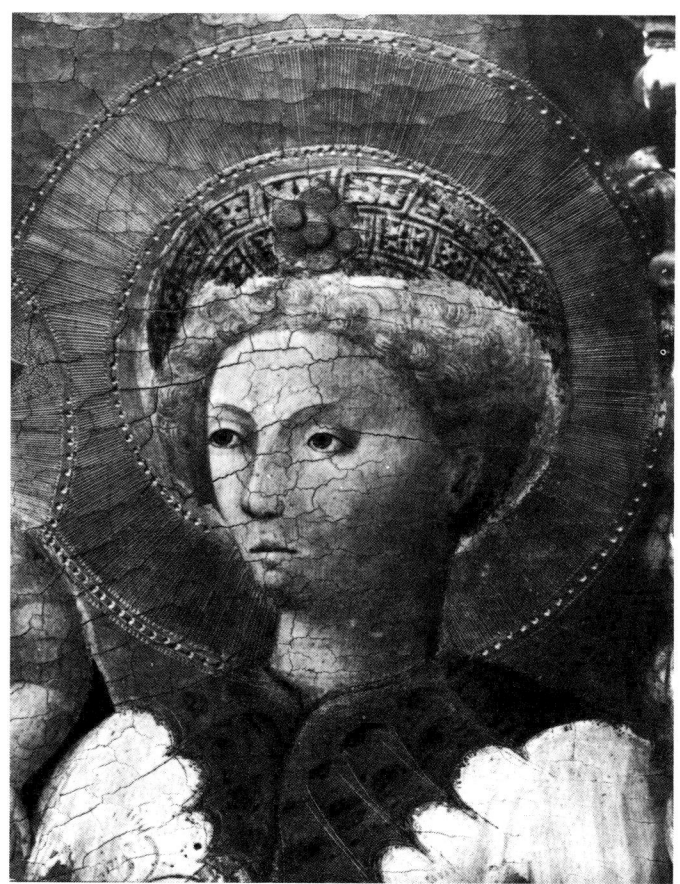

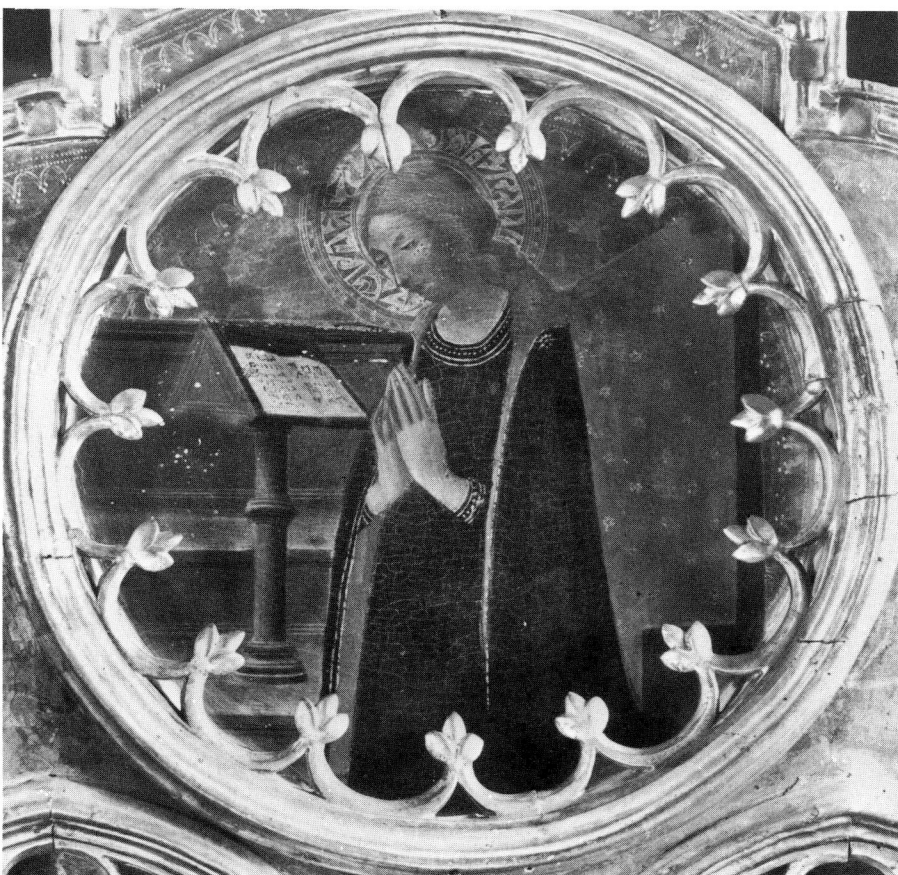

1079

1080

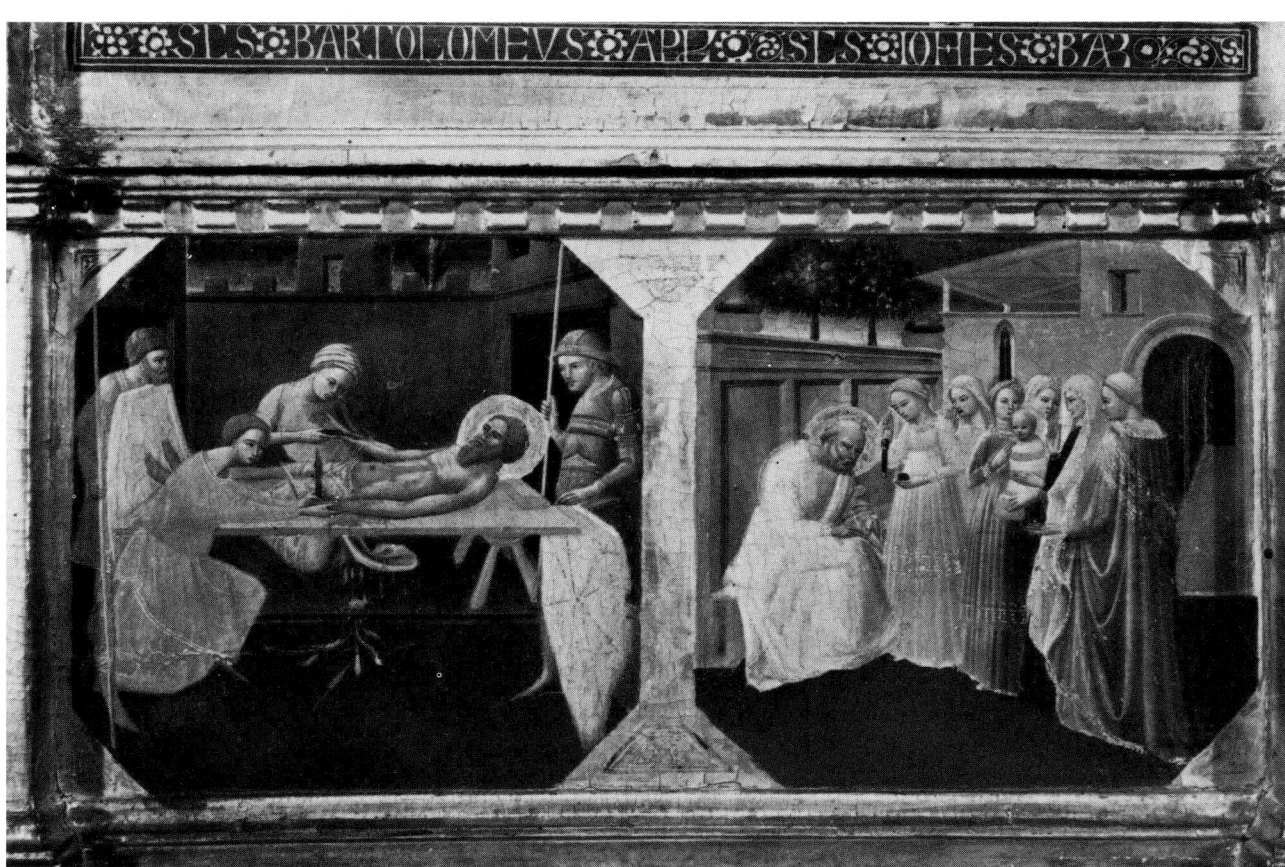

1081

1079. *Head of a King, detail of fig. 1082. Panel. Figline, S. Andrea a Ripalta. SGF 124571. d. 1436.*
1080. *Virgin Annunciate, detail of fig. 1074. Panel. Prato, Galleria Comunale. no. 8. SGF 96929. d. 1435.*
1081. *Martyrdom of St Bartholomew, Naming of the Baptist, detail of fig. 1074. Panel. Prato, Galleria Comunale. no. 8. SGF 96930. d. 1435.*

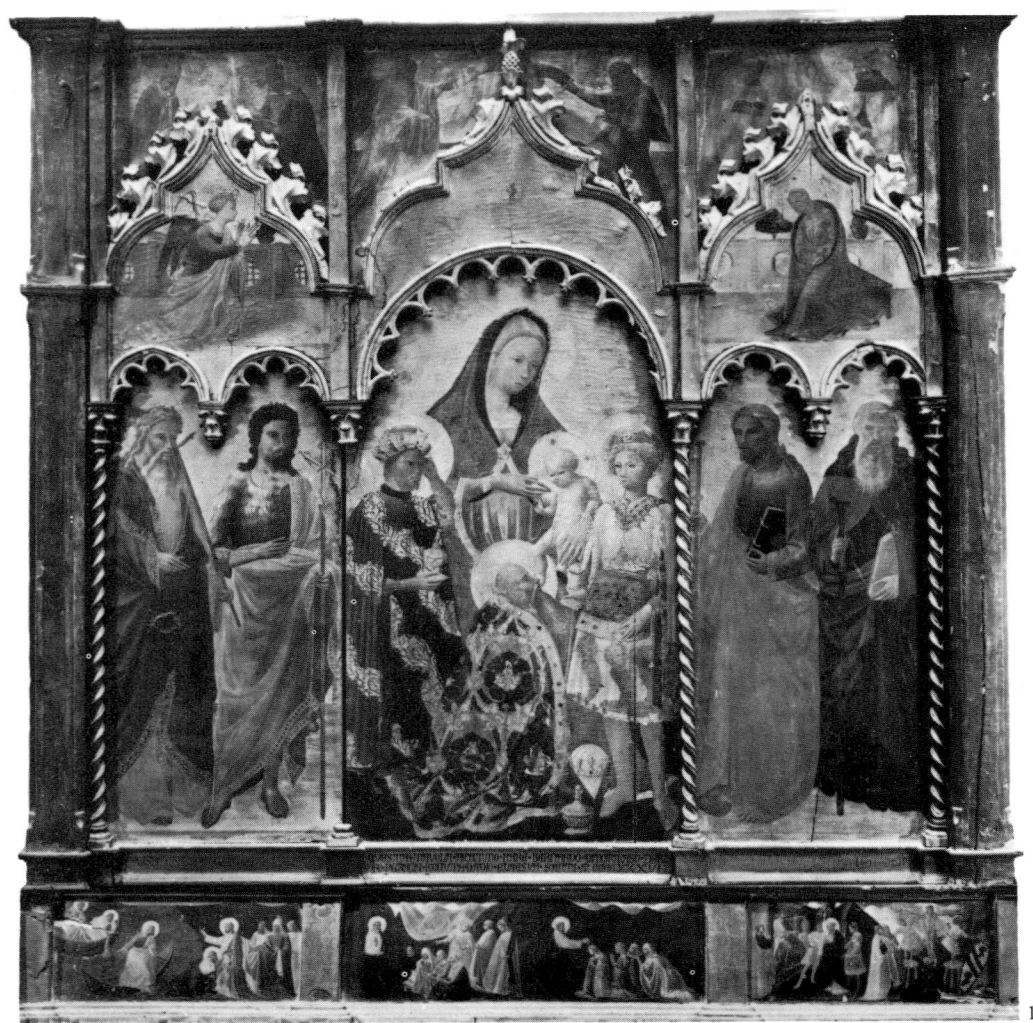

1082

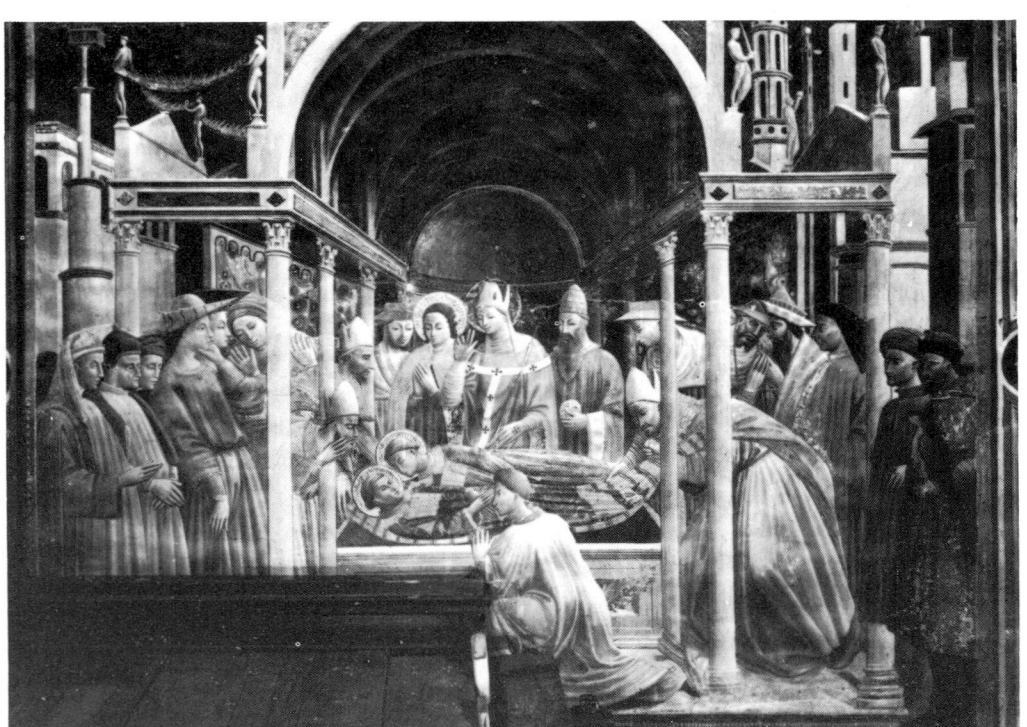

1083

1082. *Triptych: Madonna and Child with the Magi, Sts Andrew, John the Baptist, James and Anthony Abbot. Above: Annunciation, six Prophets and Saints; Predella: Donors; Calling of Sts Peter and Andrew; St Andrew preaching and baptising; and the Judgement and Crucifixion of St Andrew. Panel. Figline, (Upper Valdarno), S. Andrea a Ripalta. SGF 121351 and 121362. d. 1436.*
1083. *Burial of St Stephen. Fresco. Prato, Duomo, Cappella dell'Assunta. SGF 124765.*

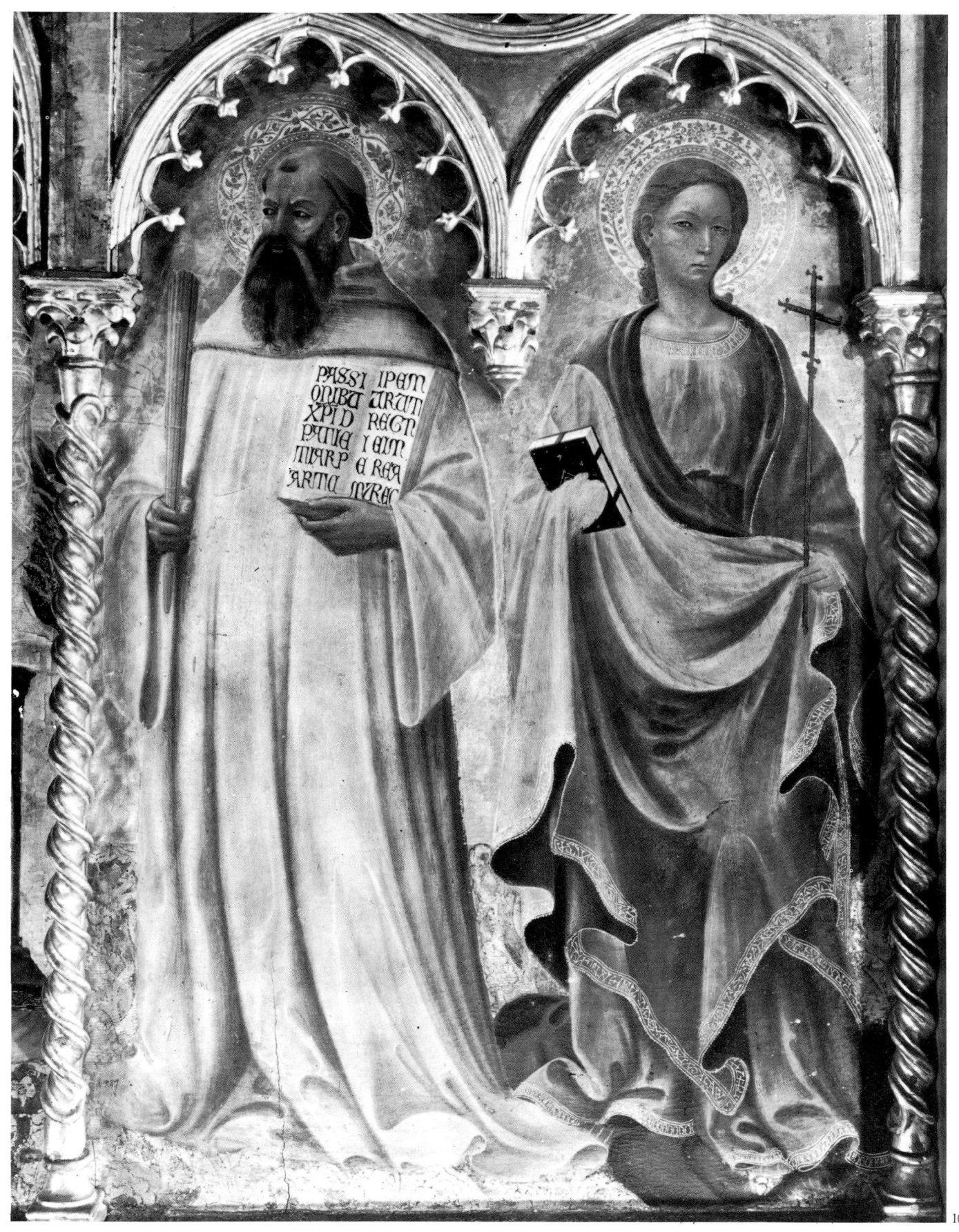

PASSI IPQM
ONIBT ARVTI
XPID REGT
PNIQ IQIM
MARP Q RGQ
ARITQ MRQC

1084

1084. *Sts Benedict and Margaret, detail of fig. 1074. Panel. Prato, Galleria Comunale. no. 8. SGF 96926. d. 1435.*

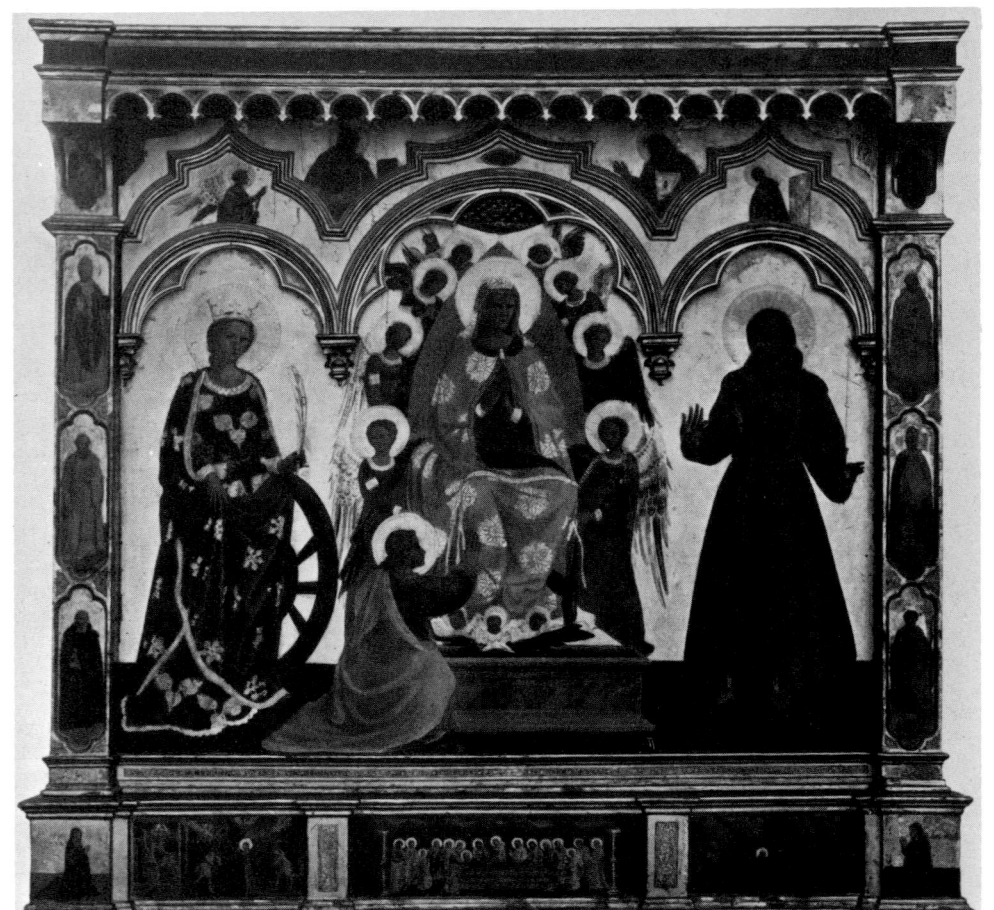

1085

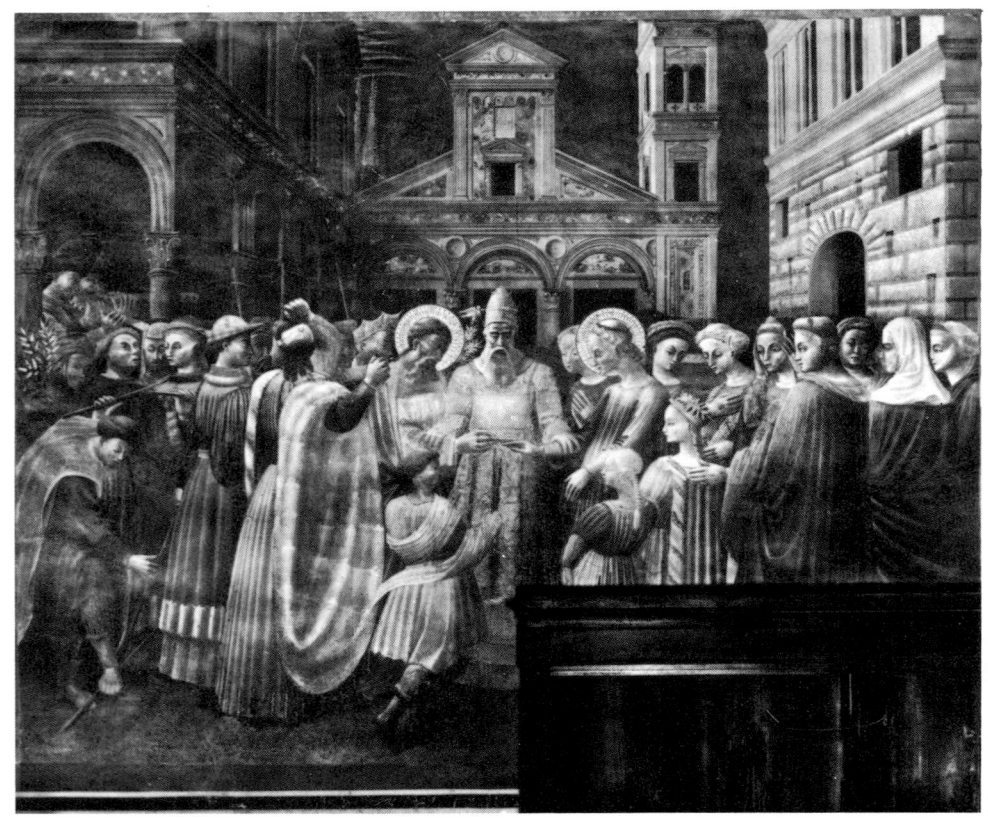

1086

1085. *Madonna of the Holy Girdle with St Thomas and eleven Angels, Sts Catherine and Francis. Above: Annunciation and Holy Spirit. Pilasters: Saints. Predella: Donors; Martyrdom of St Catherine; Dormition of the Virgin; Stigmatization of St Francis. Panel. Florence, Accademia. no. 3236. 183 × 213. SGF 145936. s & d. 1437.*
1086. *Marriage of the Virgin. Fresco. Prato, Duomo, Cappella dell'Assunta. Alinari 30742.*

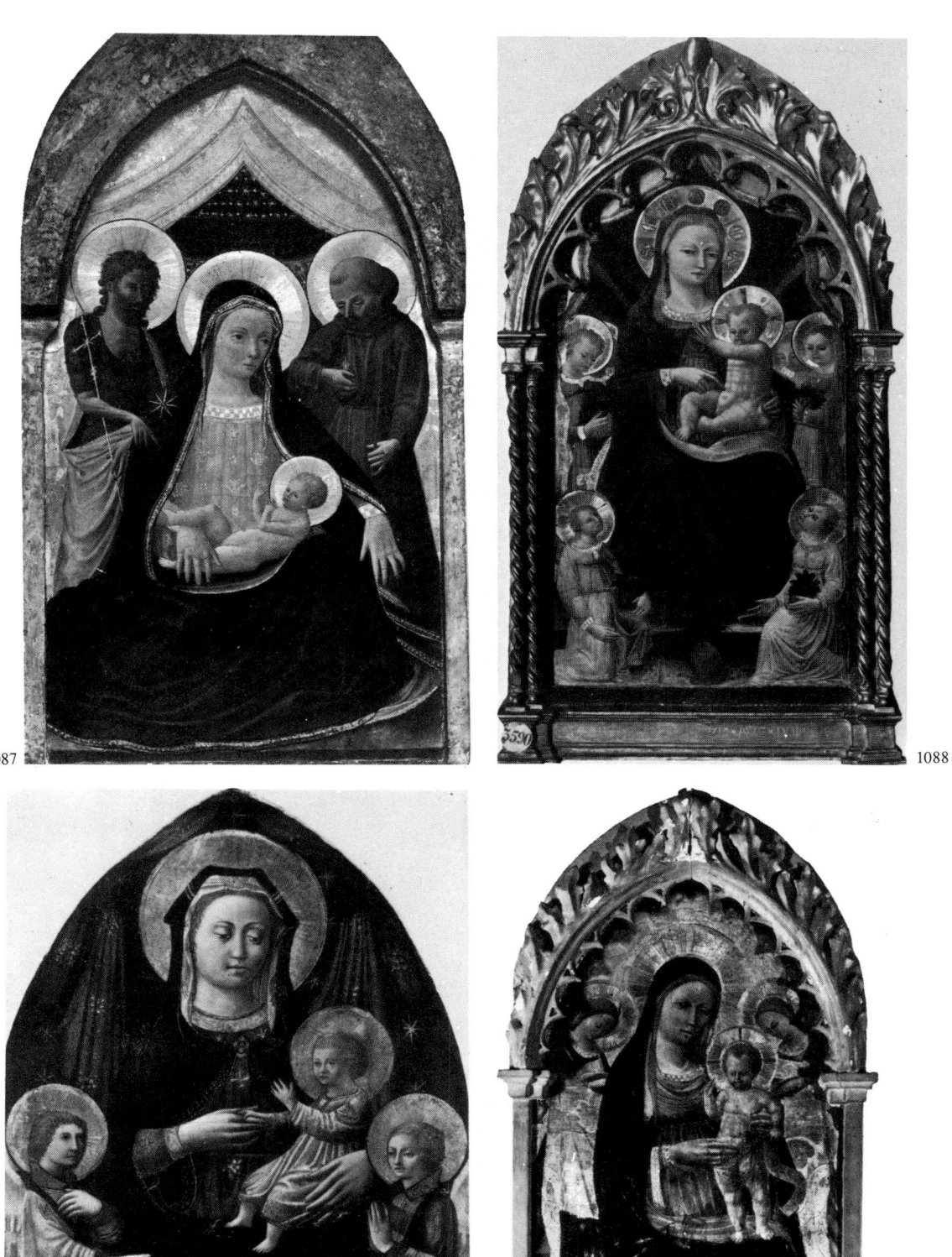

1087. *Madonna of Humility with Sts John the Baptist and Francis. Panel. Copenhagen, Statens Museum for Kunst. no. 1750. 77.5 × 43.5. Museum photo 17.*
1088. *Madonna and Child Enthroned with six Angels. Panel. Florence, Museo Stibbert. no. 3590. 120 × 65. Museum photo.*
1089. *Madonna and Child with two Angels. Panel. Private Collection. Reali.*
1090. *Madonna and Child with two Angels. Panel. Florence, Accademia. no. 3169. 115 × 61. SGF 97627.*

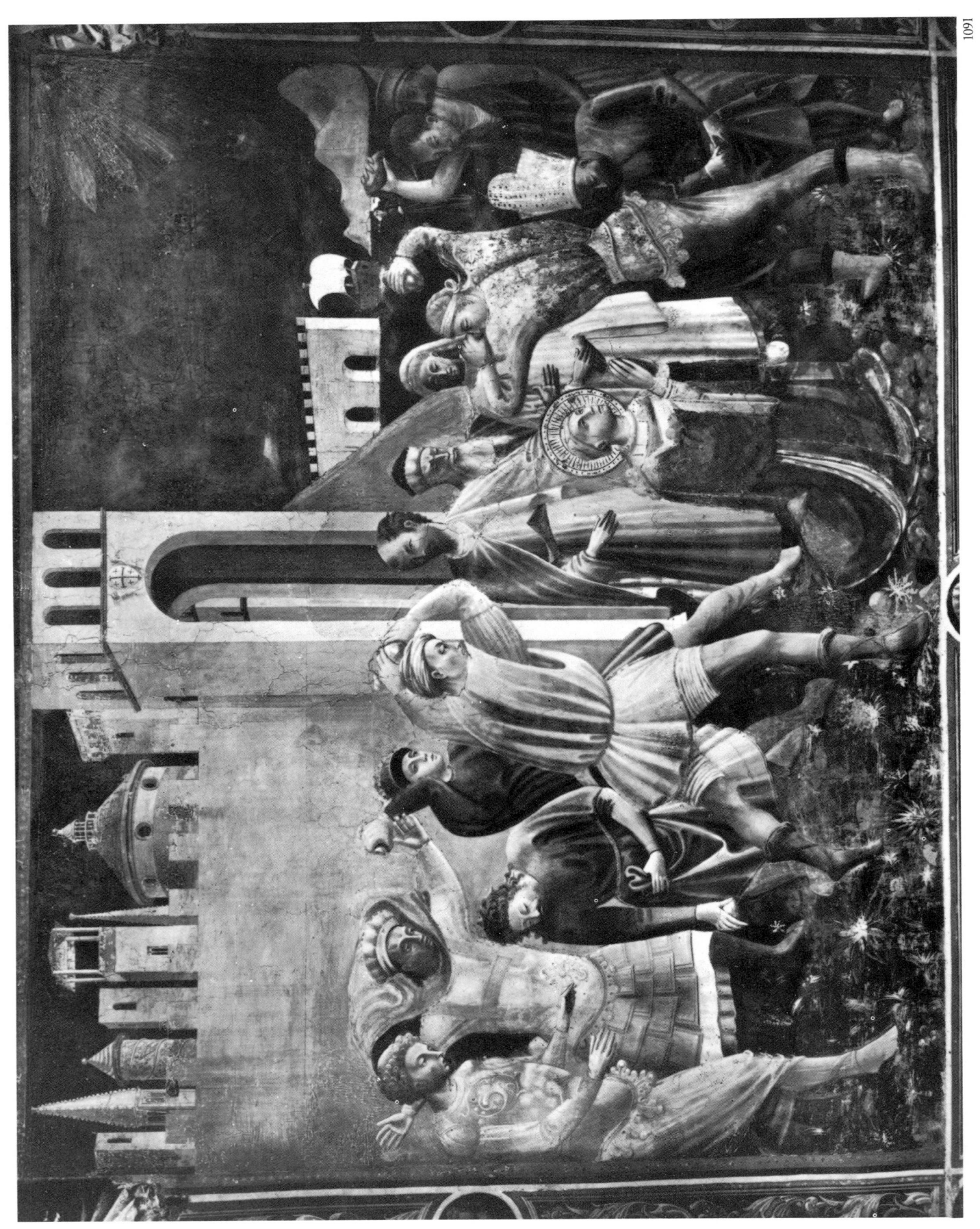

1091. *Martyrdom of St Stephen. Fresco. Prato, Duomo, Cappella dell' Assunta. Alinari 30743.*

PAOLO SCHIAVO

Was Paolo di Stefano Badaloni. Florentine, born 1397, died 1478. Member of the Physicians and Apothecaries Guild Dec. 8, 1429. Company of Saint Luke. A Follower of Masolino da Panicale. Paolo painted a fresco in a tabernacle on the Canto de' Gori at the entrance of the Via dell'Ariento. The spot is now termed " Le Cantonelle ", a corruption of the neighbouring Canto de' Nelli. This fresco, which represents the Virgin, Infant and Saints, is still extant, but has been repainted.... Paolo died in Pisa. He may have received the surname of Schiavo from his family having been of Sclavonian origin.....

> from D. E. Colnaghi, p. 200, *A Dictionary of Florentine Painters*, London, 1928.

Born in 1397, that is a few years before Masaccio, Paolo Schiavo was registered as a painter only in 1429, after he was 30 years old; it is probable then that he had an earlier period, which has yet to be discovered. In 1436 he is mentioned in Florentine sources, and he signs his fresco in San Miniato al Monte; thus his work in the Collegiata at Castiglione would seem to have to be placed in the period 1437-38, certainly not before 1436.....
The early period of Schiavo's life should be studied for his relationship to Alvaro Pirez, whose polyptych in Volterra would suggest that Schiavo was still within the orbit of Lorenzo Monaco. This calculation could be correct because Alvaro's work in Volterra is documented in 1422 when Schiavo was already 25 years old.....
It was Offner who discovered that Schiavo was also a miniaturist (and thus there is another parallel with Francesco d'Antonio and another confirmation of a common origin); it can be added that he also supplied drawings for embroiderers: one of his loveliest compositions, of the decade '30 to '40, is that which can be seen in the embroidery of " The Coronation of the Virgin " in the Lederer Collection in Vienna.....

> from R. Longhi, p. 188, *Critica d'Arte*, V, 1940.

Paolo di Stefano Badaloni, known as Paolo Schiavo, born 1397 in Florence, probably a pupil of Masolino, greatly influenced by Masaccio; active in Florence, Pistoia and Pisa, where he died in 1478.....

> from R. Oertel, p. 142, *Frühe Italienische Malerei in Altenburg*, Berlin, 1961.

Paolo di Stefano was born in Florence in 1397. Vasari suggests that he was a pupil of Masolino. He enrolled in 1429 in the guild of Medici e Speziali, and probably painted his best-known work, the frescoes in the Collegiata at Castiglione d'Olona, between 1429 and 1436. A fresco of the Madonna with four Saints in the church of S. Miniato al Monte in Florence, appears to be later, and carries an incomplete date which is normally read as 1436. A small tabernacle of the Madonna and Child is in the Fitzwilliam Museum, Cambridge. In 1448 Schiavo worked in Pistoia on frescoes in the Cappella dell'Assunta and documents prove his activity in Pisa around 1462. He died there in 1478.

> from U. Baldini, p. 132, *Frescoes from Florence*, London, 1969.

Paolo di Stefano Badaloni, called Paolo Schiavo, born in Florence in 1397, matriculated in the Arte dei Medici e Speziali in 1429; the last notice of him is in 1462, at Pisa. His early training must have been in the shop of Lorenzo Monaco, but he was soon attracted towards a circle of more modern painting, that of Masolino da Panicale, and he even shows an interest in Masaccio; many of his paintings from the 30's such as the small panels in the Kress collection in New York, the Madonna and Child with saints in Santa Croce in Florence, or some of the frescoes in the Collegiata of Castiglione Olona, are the enchanting result of this education. The fresco of the Madonna and Child with saints in the church of San Miniato al Monte in Florence, the date of which should probably be read 1436, attained such a sense of monumentality that it even interested the youthful Andrea del Castagno.....

> from L., Bellosi, p. 20, *Arte in Valdichiana dal XIII al XVIII secolo*, Cortona, 1970.

BIBLIOGRAPHY

BOOKS

An asterisk indicates a work listed in the General Bibliography

Colnaghi, 1928*, p. 200; Pudelko, G., *T-Becker**, 1936, Vol. XXX, pp. 46-7; *Galetti**, " P-Z ", 1950, p. 2244; *Oertel, 1961**, pp. 142-3; *Berenson, 1963**, Vol. I, pp. 165-6; Bianchini, M. A., *Masolino* (I Maestri del Colore, 80), Milan, 1965; Chiarini, M., *Masaccio e la Pittura del '400* (I Maestri del Colore, 256), Milan, 1966; *Shapley**, 1966, p. 105; Baldini, U., *Fresco Show**, 1968, pp. 131-5; Bellosi, L., *Arte in Valdichiana dal XIII al XVIII secolo*, Cortona, 1970, p. 20.

JOURNALS

Dami, L., *BA*, 8, 1915, pp. 216-44; Salmi, M., *DD*, IX, 1928-29, pp. 3-30; Salmi, M., *RA*, XI, 1929, pp. 267-273; Berenson, B., *DD*, XII, 2, 1932, pp. 512-41; Procacci, U., *RA*, XIV, 1932, pp. 348-52; Longhi, R., *CA*, V, 1940; pp. 145-91; Pouncey, P., *BM*, LXXXVIII, 1946, p. 228; Berti, L., *BA*, XXXVII, 4, 1952, pp. 178-81; Berti, L., *BA*, XXXVIII, 4, 1953, pp. 278-9; Bologna, F., *PA*, VI, 65, 1955, pp. 36-40; Linnenkamp, R., *RA*, XXXIII, 1958, pp. 27-33; Berti, L., *C*, XII, 2, 1961, pp. 84-107; Gregori, M., *AV*, V, 6, 1966, pp. 40-9; Shearman, J., *PA*, XVIII, 203/23, 1967, p. 27; Zeri, F., *MKIF*, XVII, 2-3, 1973, pp. 364, 70.

SIGNED AND DATED WORKS

1436 Florence, S. Miniato al Monte. Fresco: Madonna & Child Enthroned with Saints. s & d. (fig. 1101).
1448 Florence, Museo di Andrea del Castagno. Fresco: Christ on the Cross with two Angels & Nuns. s & d. (fig. 1102).
1460 Florence, Monticelli, Oratory of S. Maria della Querce. Panel: Assumption of the Virgin. s & d. (fig. 1095).

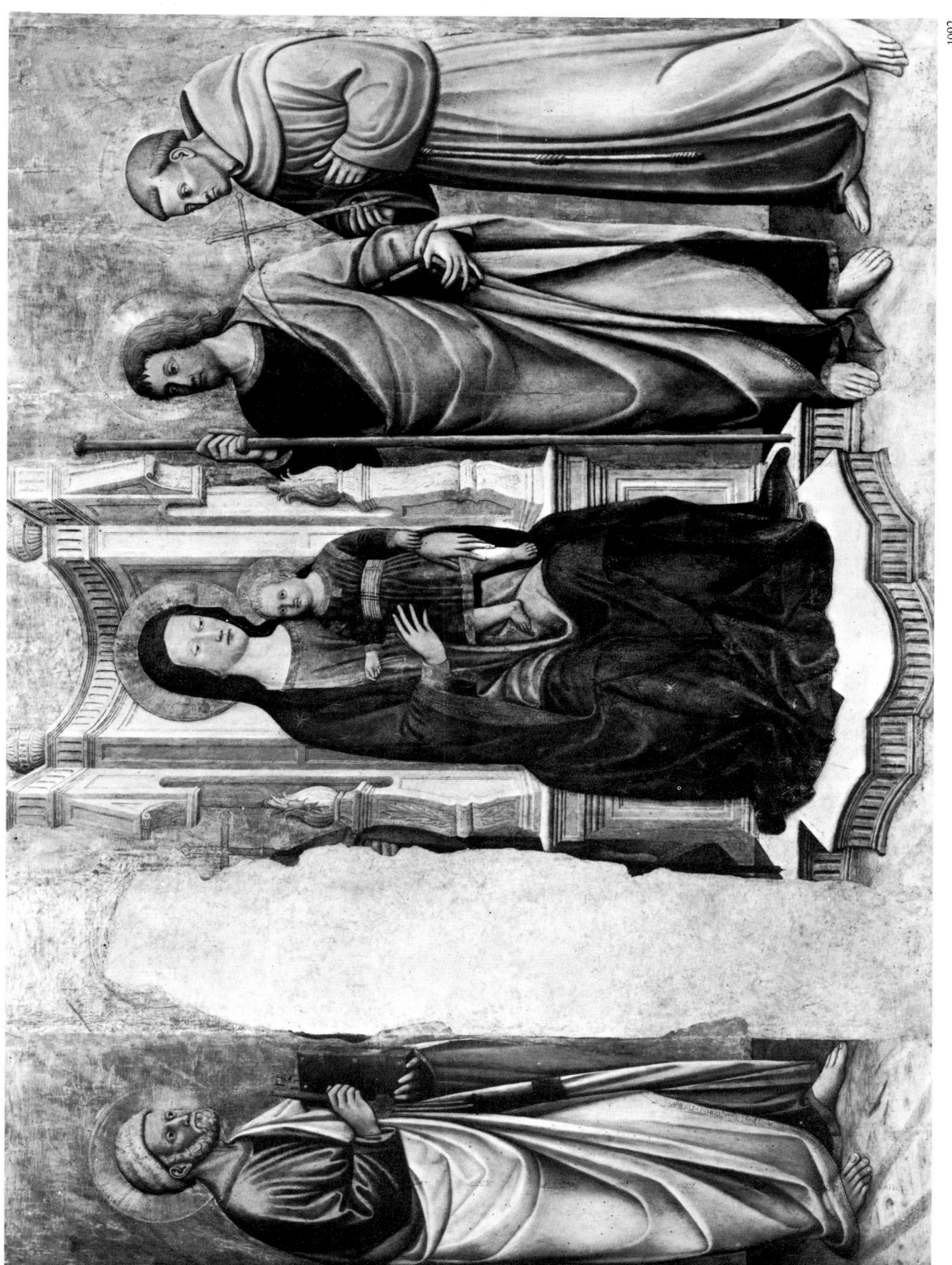

1092. *Madonna and Child Enthroned with four Saints. Panel. Florence, Museo di S. Croce. 195 × 262. SGF 104912.*

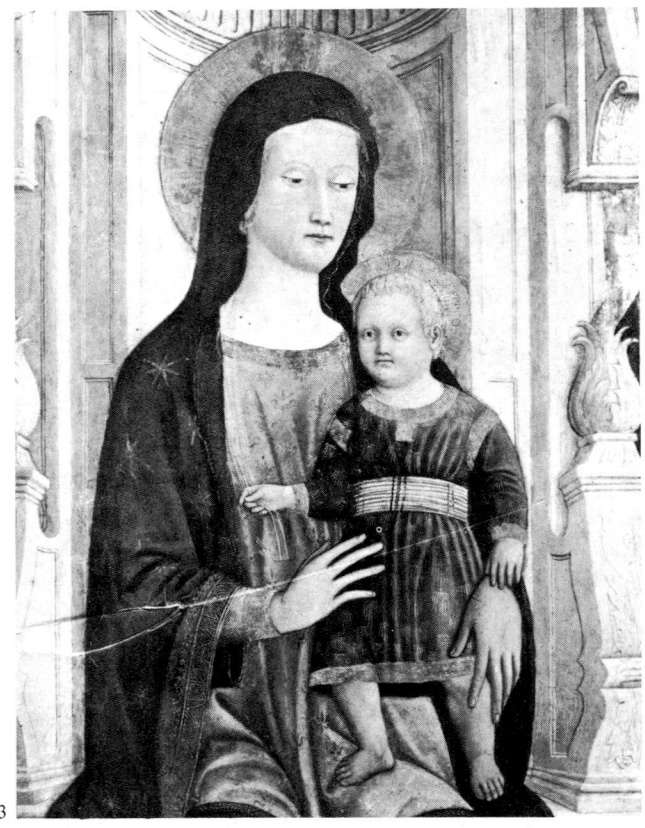

1093

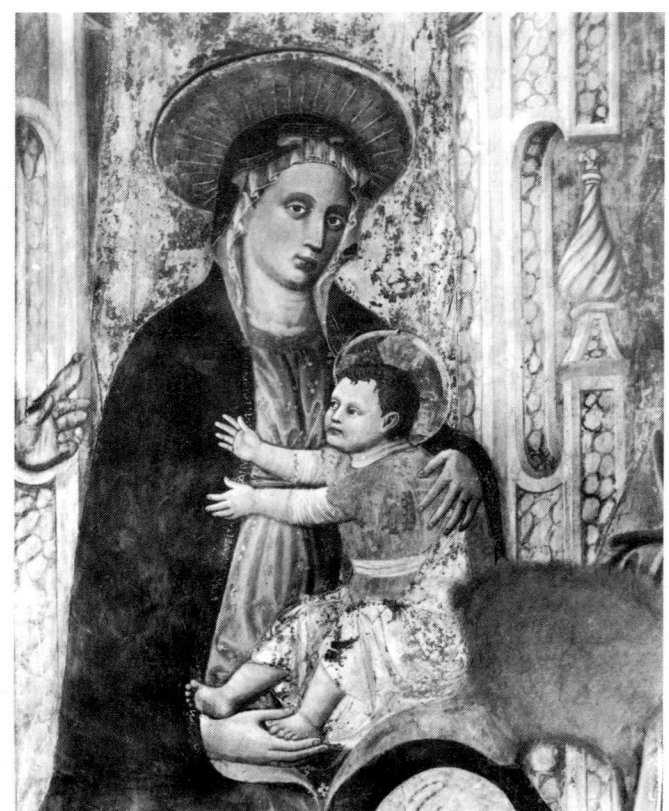

1094

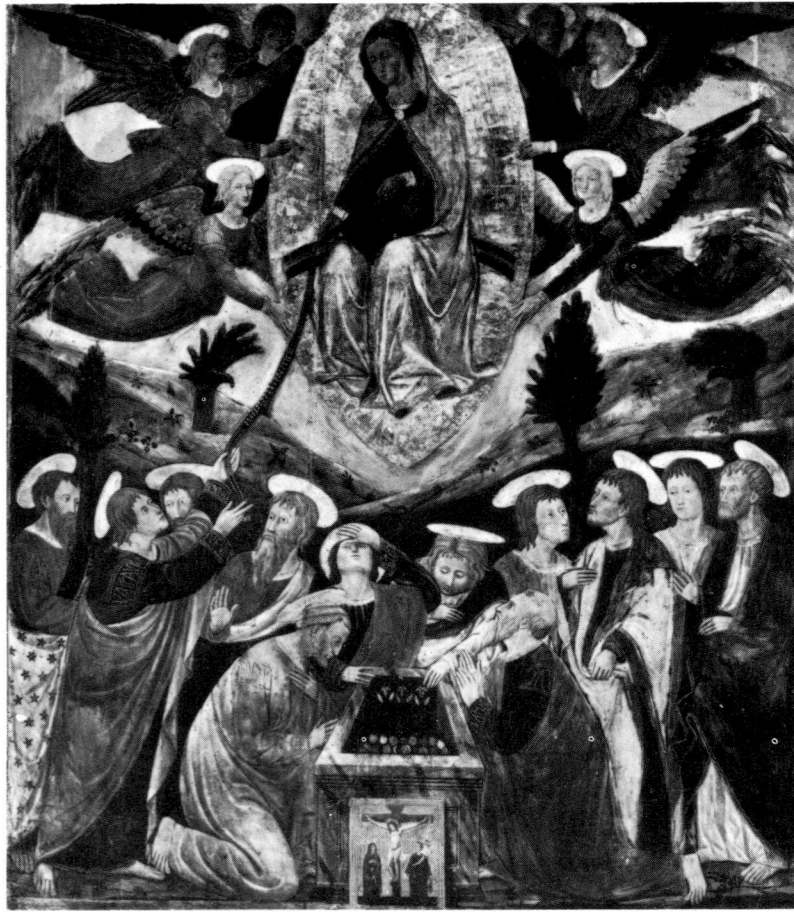

1095

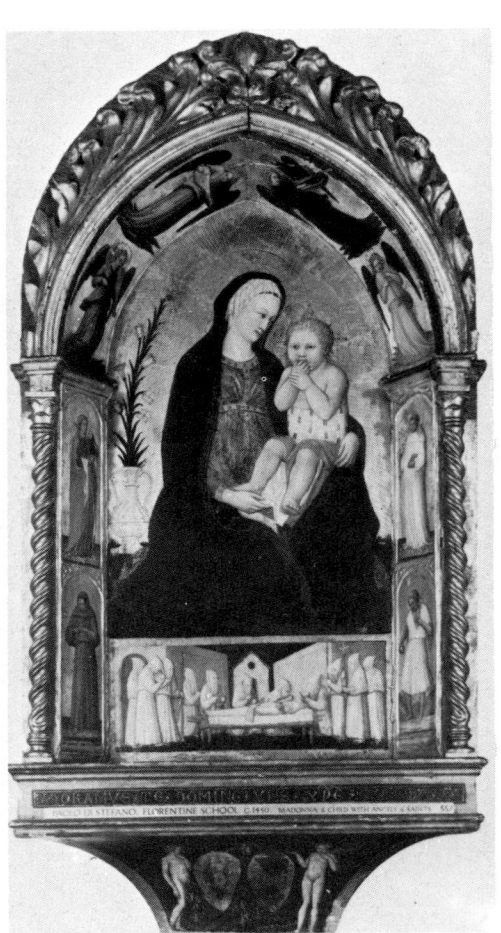

1096

1093. *Madonna and Child, detail of fig. 1092. Fresco. Florence, Museo di S. Croce. SGF 104913.*
1094. *Madonna and Child, detail of fig. 1101. Fresco. Florence, S. Miniato al Monte. Brogi 26467.*
1095. *Assumption of the Virgin, giving the Holy Girdle to St Thomas. In foreground, small Christ on the Cross, mourned by the Virgin and St John. Panel. Monticelli (outskirts of Florence, on the via Pisana), Oratorio di S. Maria della Querce. SGF 29003. s & d. 1460.*
1096. *Madonna of Humility. Above: four Angels. Pilaster: Sts Francis, Mary Magdalene, Jerome, Bernard. Predella: Funeral scene with members of a Confraternity of Flagellants. Console: Fall of Man. Panel. Cambridge, Fitzwilliam Museum. no. 557. 143.5 × 71. Museum photo: Stearn & Sons FMS 3133.*

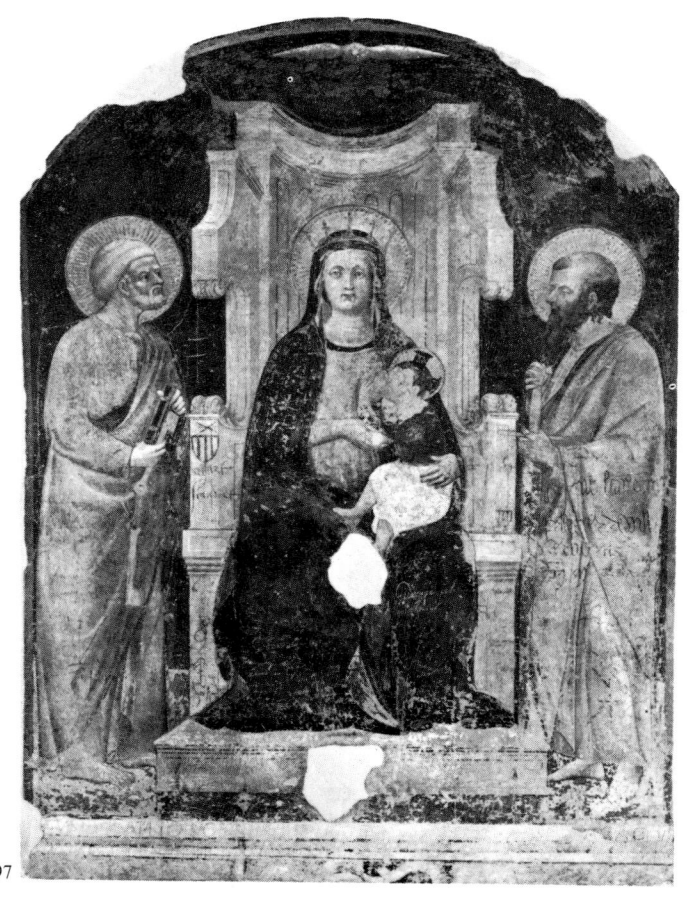

1097

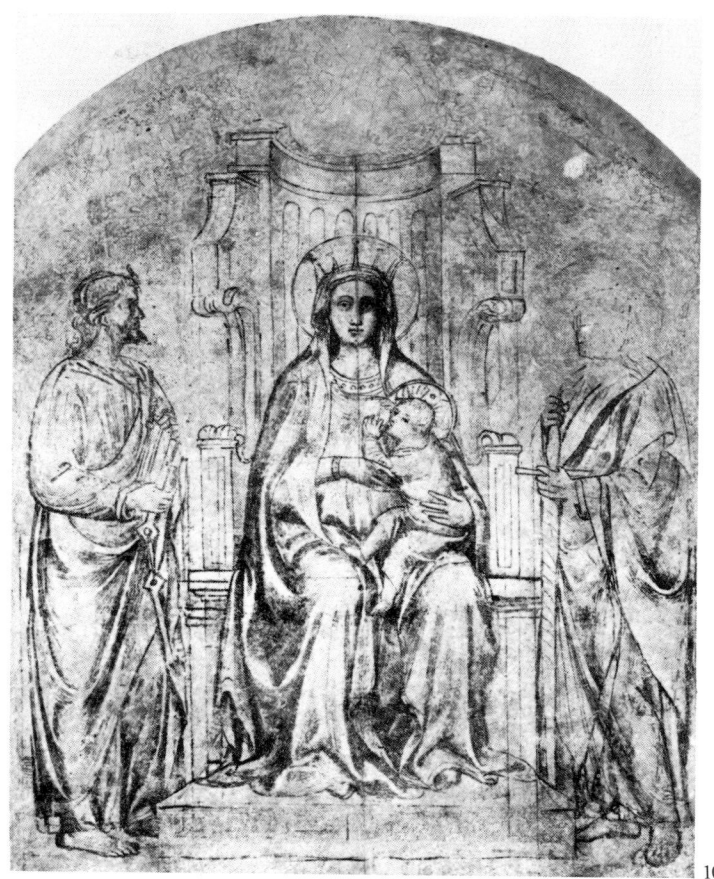

1098

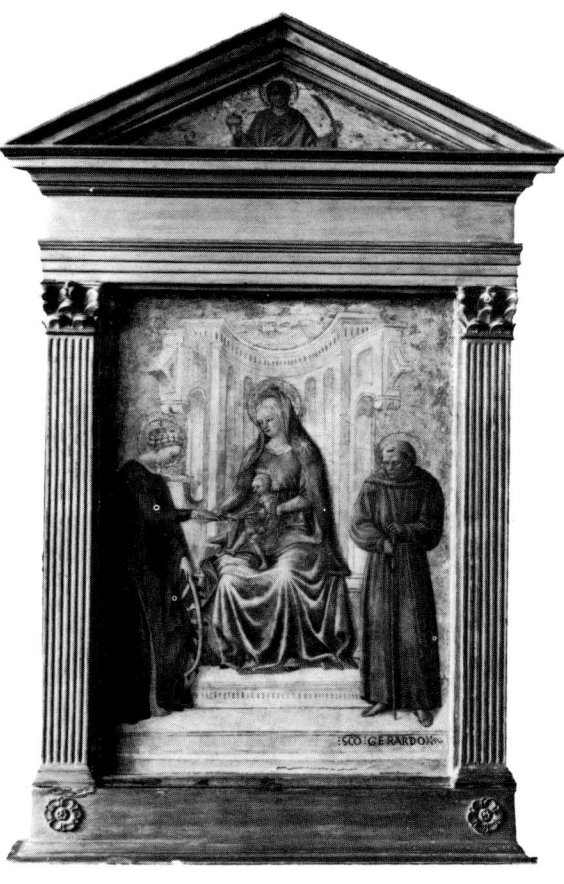

1099

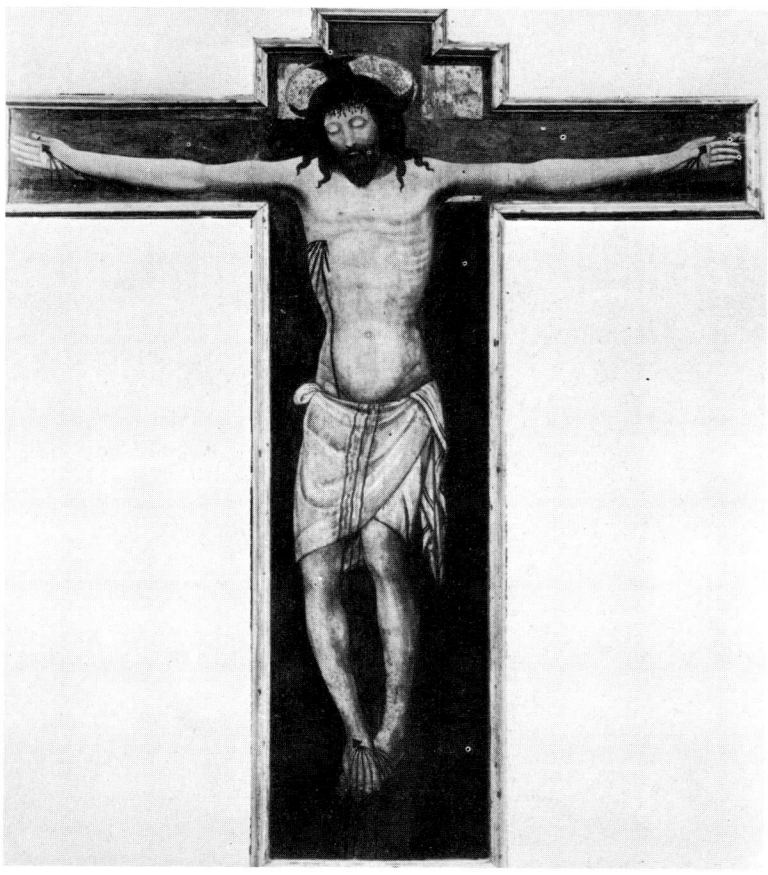

1100

1097. *Madonna Enthroned nursing the Child with Sts Peter and Paul. Fresco. Whereabouts unknown, formerly San Piero a Sieve, Mugello, Tabernacolo delle Mozzette. SGF 133004.*

1098. *Madonna Enthroned nursing the Child with Sts Peter and Paul. Sinopia. Whereabouts unknown, formerly San Piero a Sieve, Mugello, Tabernacolo delle Mozzette (see fig. 1097). SGF 113822.*

1099. *Mystical Marriage of St Catherine with St Gerard of Villamagna. Panel. Altenburg, Staatliches Lindenau Museum. no. 80. 86 × 43 (w.f.). Museum photo.*

1100. *Painted Crucifix. Panel. Pisa, Museo Nazionale di S. Matteo. 177 × 142. Museum photo 2163.*

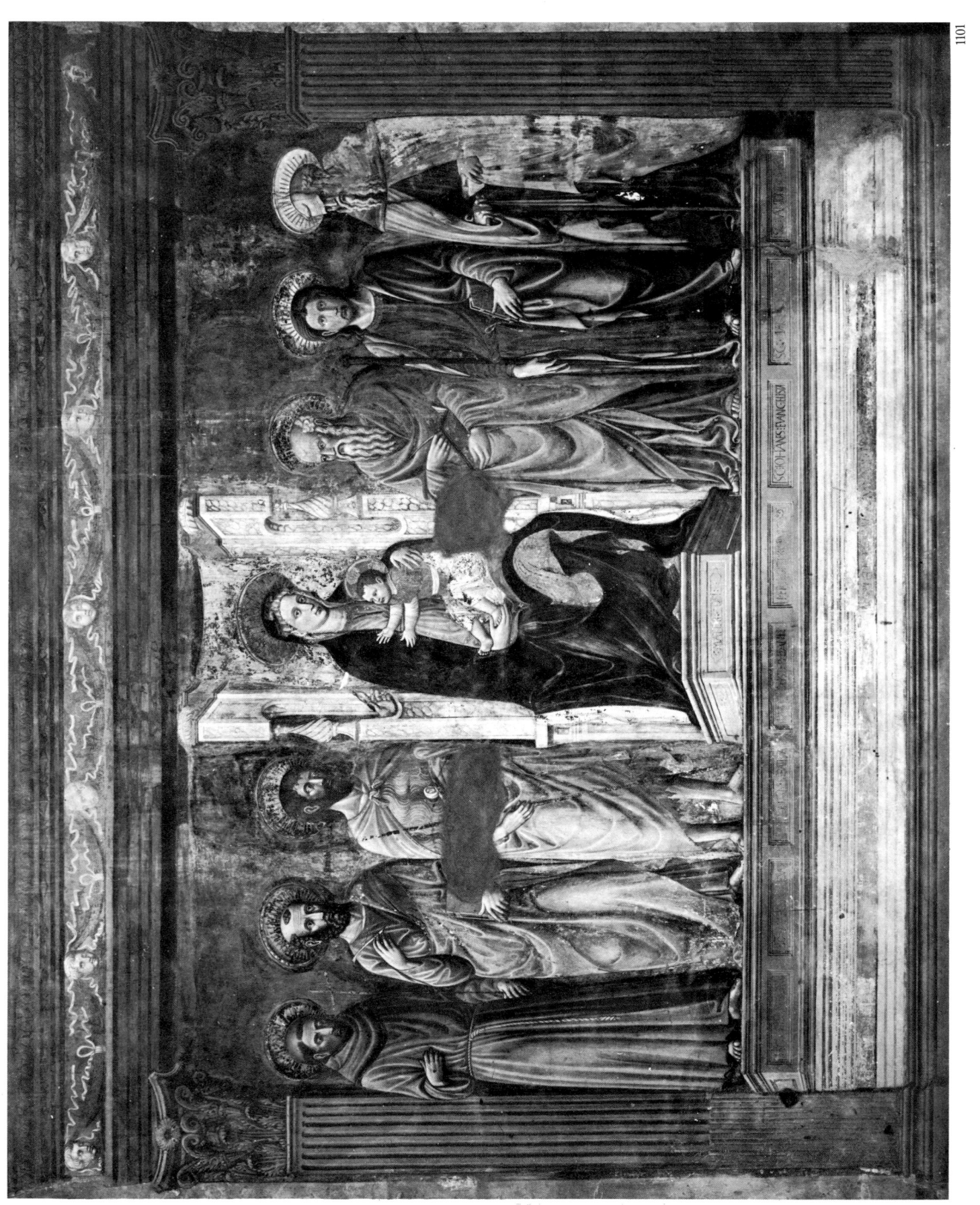

1101. *Madonna and Child Enthroned with Sts Francis, Mark, John the Baptist, John the Evangelist, James and Anthony Abbot. Fresco. Florence, S. Miniato al Monte. SGF 2321. s & d. 1436.*

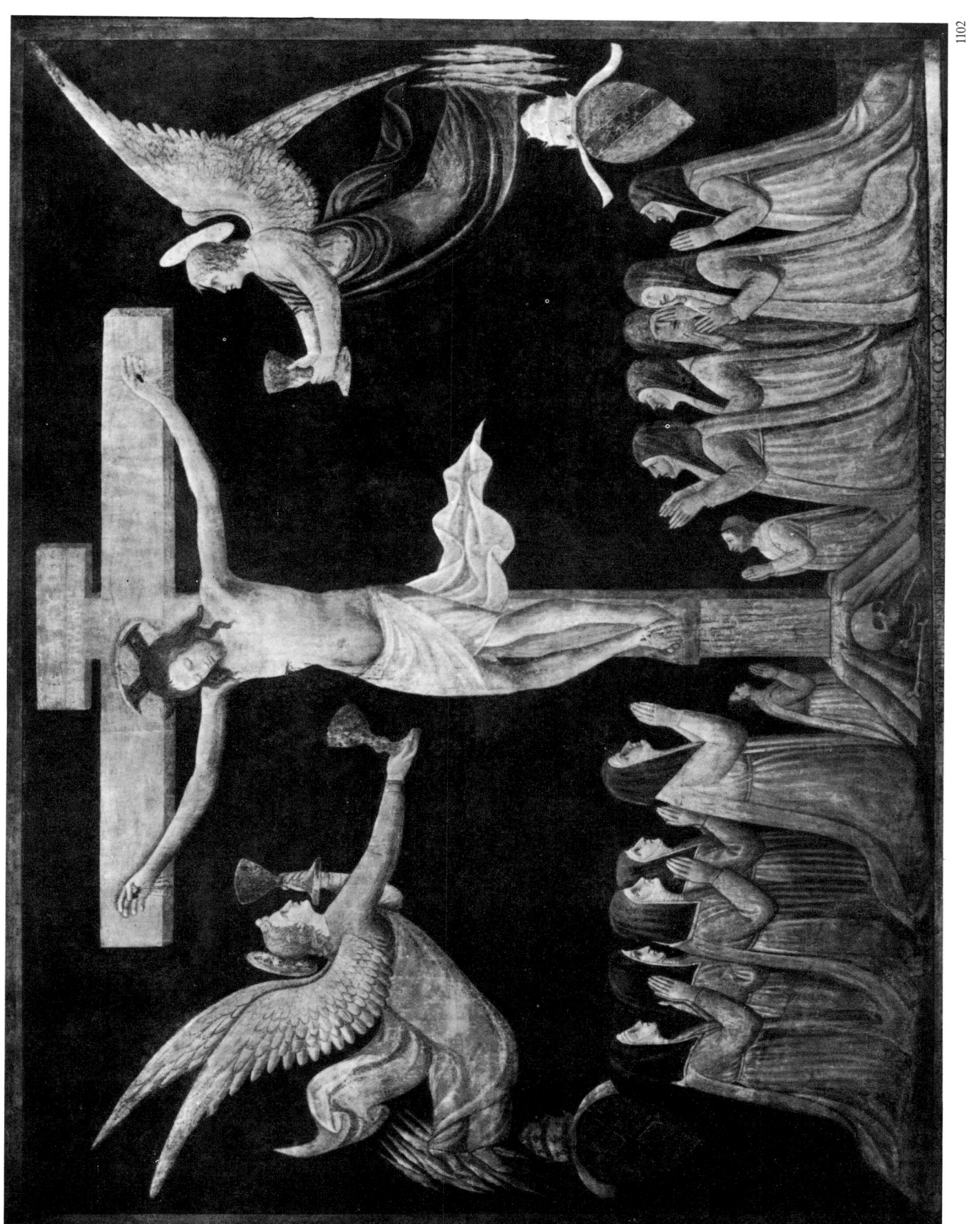

1102. *Christ on the Cross, with two Angels and adoring Nuns. Fresco. Florence, Museo di Andrea del Castagno, Cenacolo di Sant' Apollonia. Alinari 30682. s & d. 1448.*

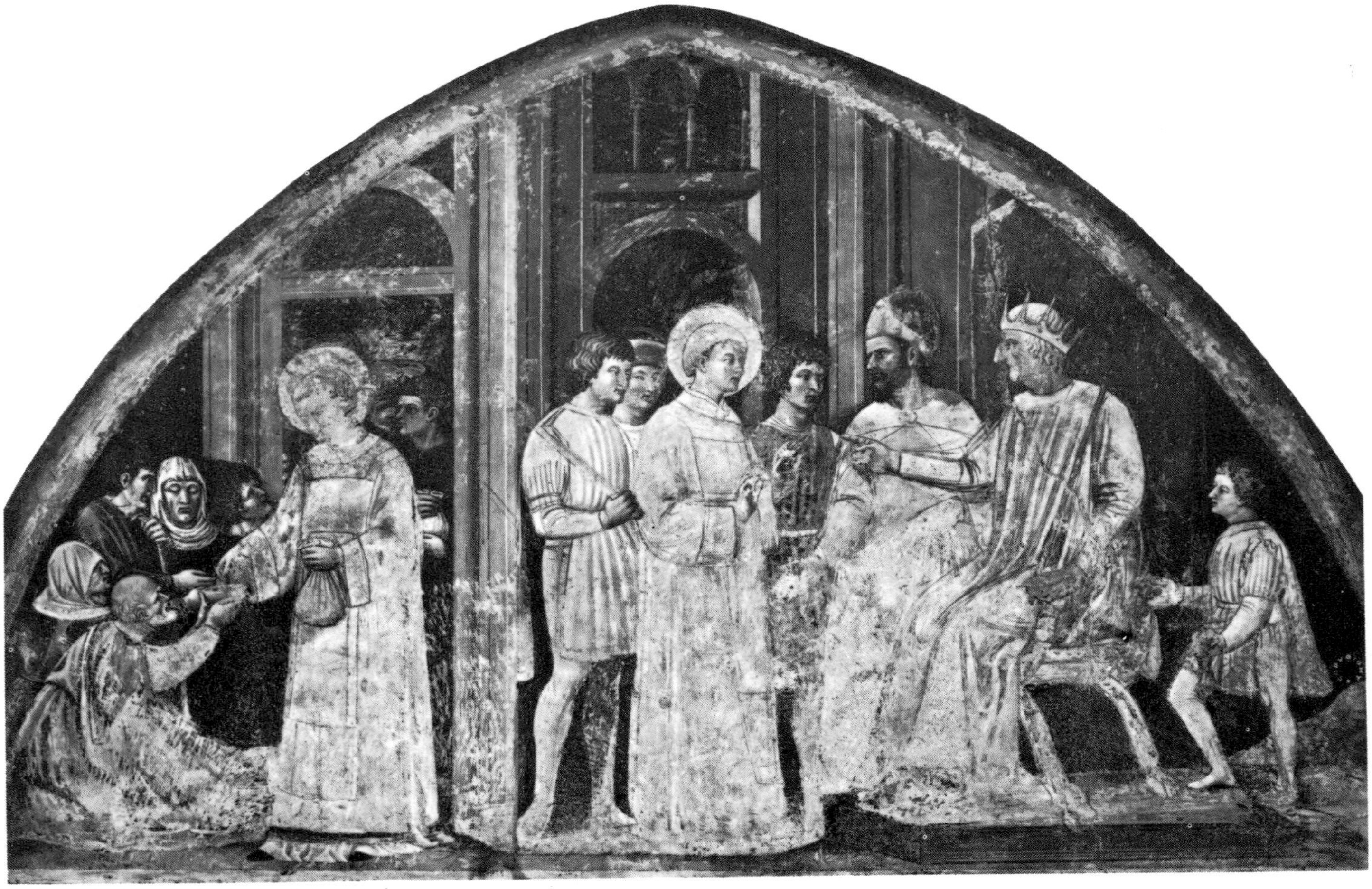

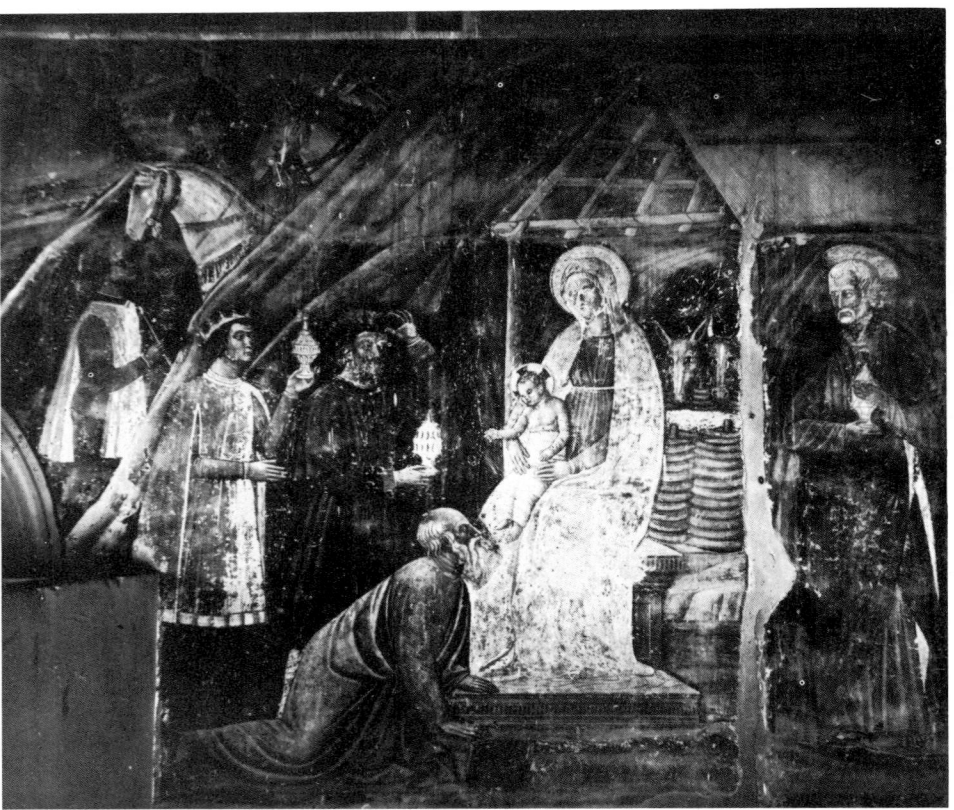

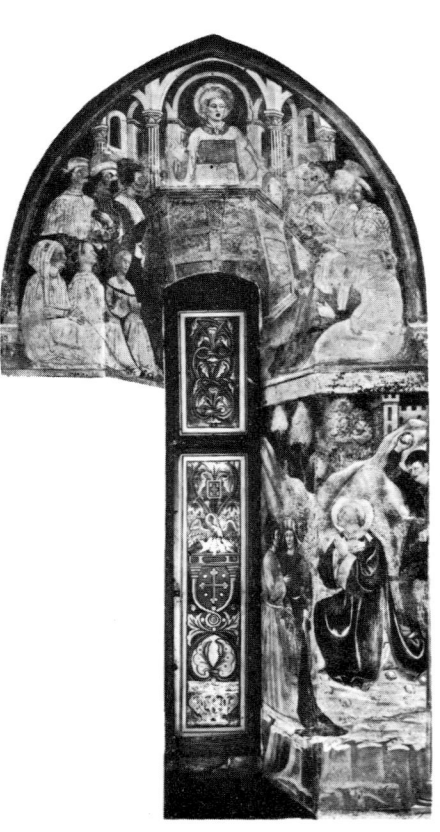

1103. *Lunette: scenes from the Life of St Lawrence: St Lawrence giving alms, St Lawrence before Decius. Fresco. Castiglione d'Olona (near Varese, Lombardy), Collegiata, Apse. Anderson 32280.*
1104. *Adoration of the Magi. Fresco. Monticelli, Oratorio di S. Maria della Querce. SGF 2145.*
1105. *Two Stories in the Life of St Stephen: St Stephen preaching; Martyrdom of Stephen. Fresco. Castiglione d'Olona, Collegiata. Anderson 32277.*

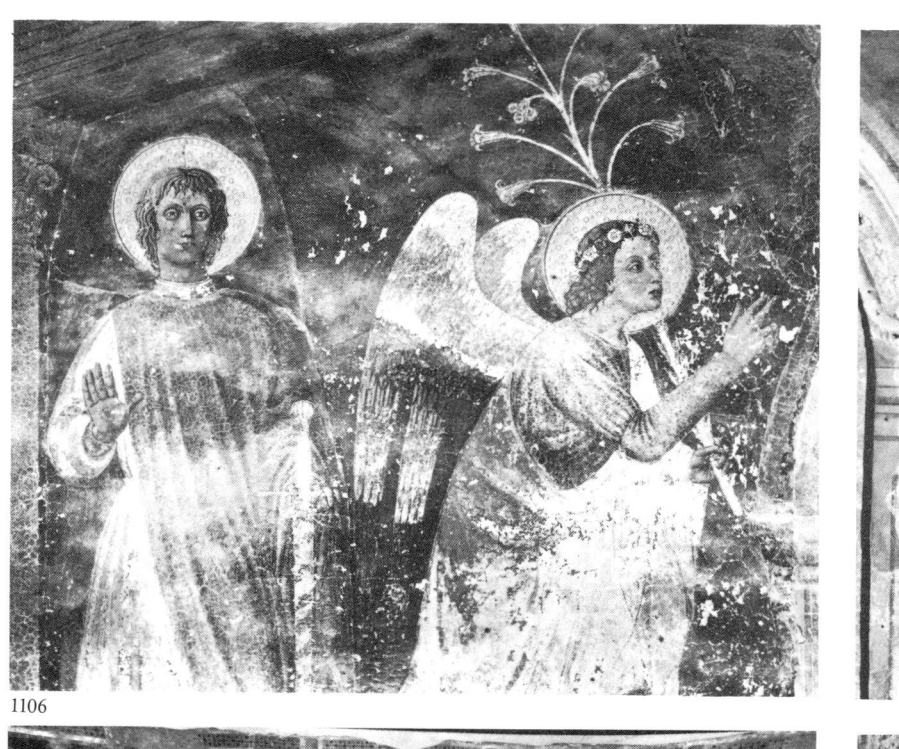

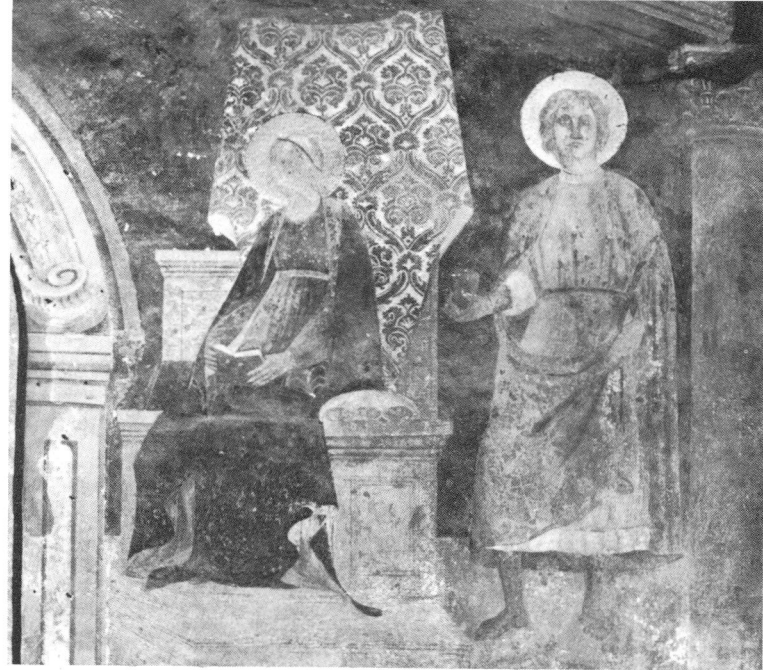

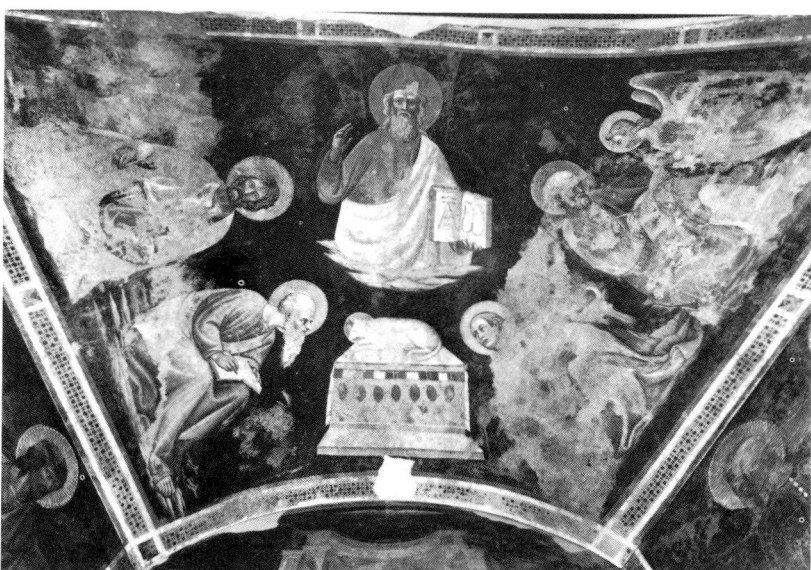

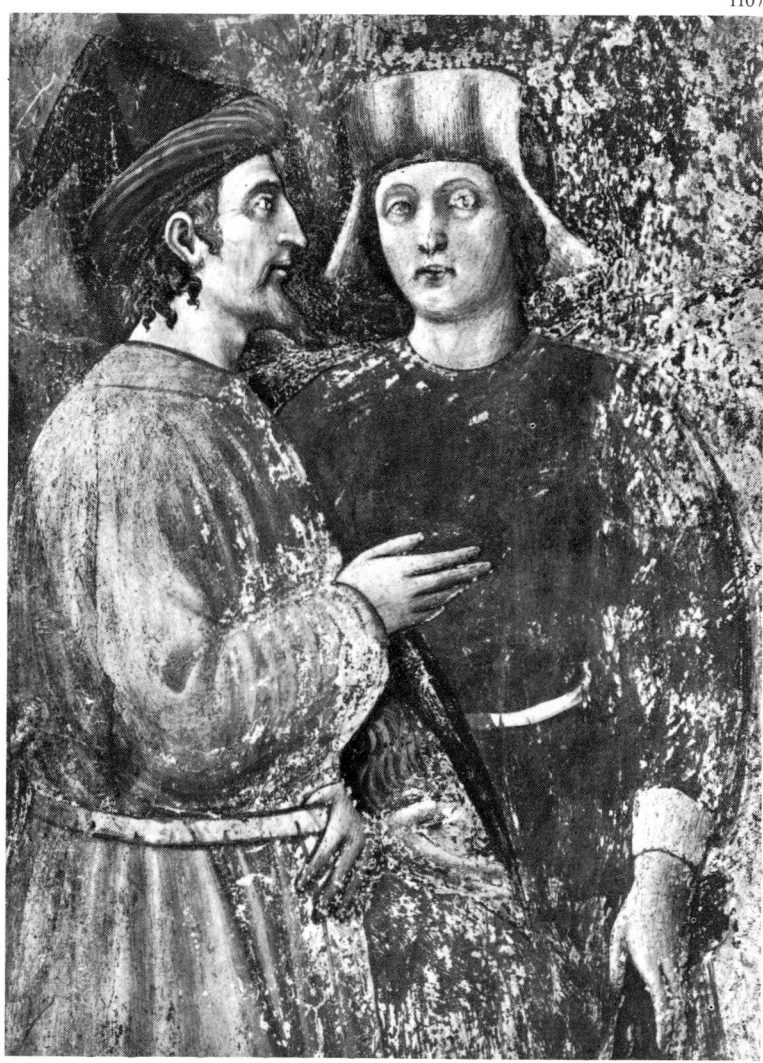

1106. *St Julian and Announcing Angel (see fig. 1107). Fresco. Castello (near Florence), Tabernacolo dell'Olmo. SGF 71759.*
1107. *Virgin Annunciate and St Ansanus (see fig. 1106). Fresco. Castello, Tabernacolo dell'Olmo. SGF 152782.*
1108. *Detail: God the Father, Paschal Lamb, and the four Evangelists. Fresco. Formerly San Piero a Sieva, Tabernacolo delle Mozzette. SGF 133007.*
1109. *Spectators of the Stoning of St Stephen, detail of fig. 1105. Fresco. Castiglione d'Olona, Collegiata. Anderson 32279.*

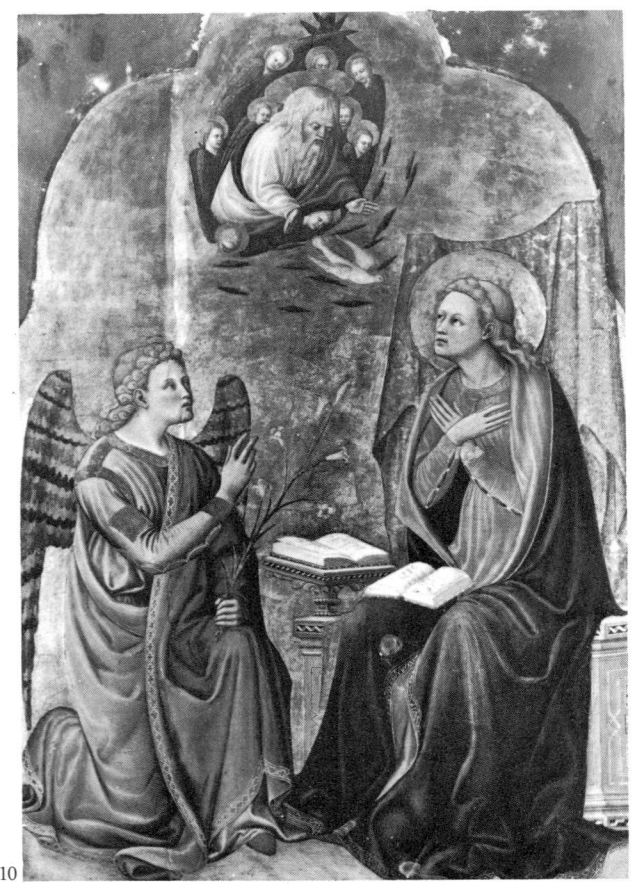

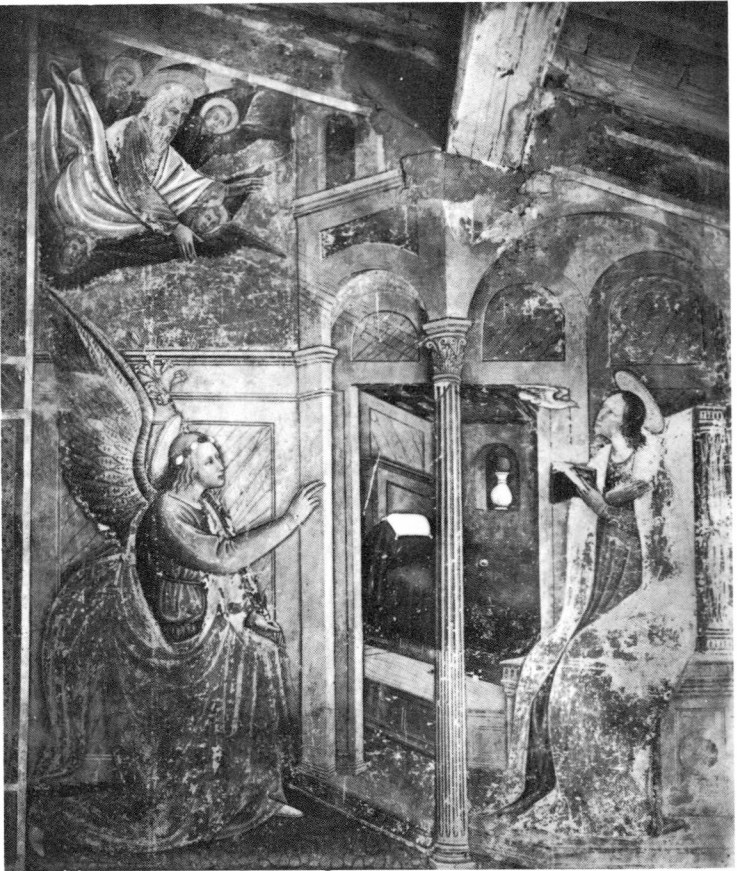

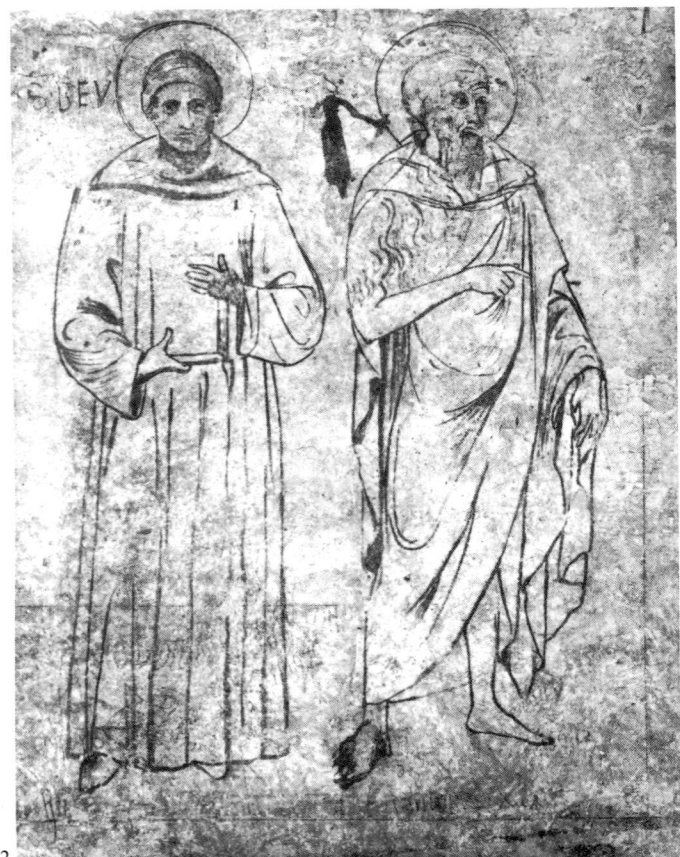

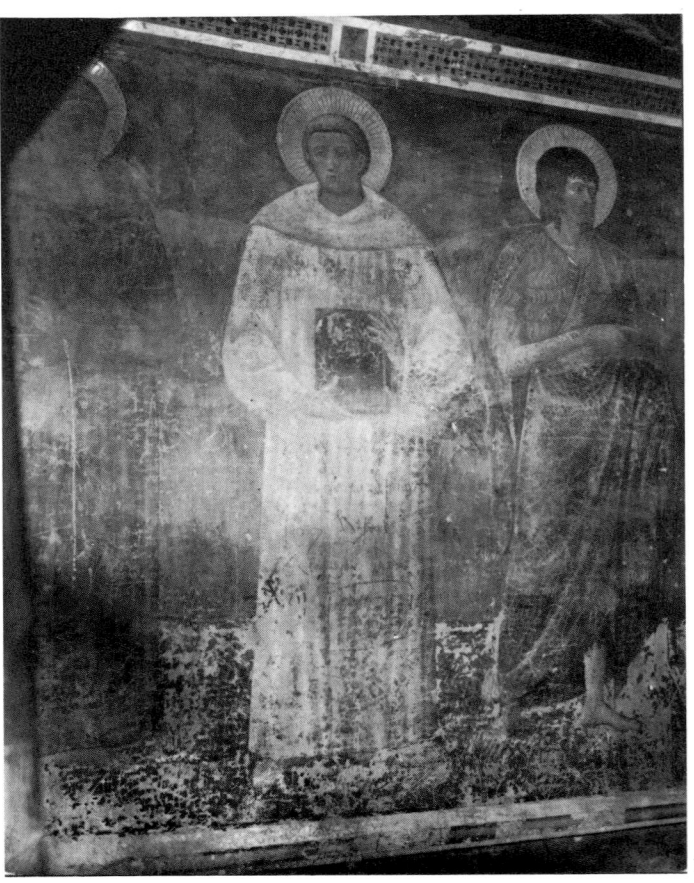

1110. *Annunciation. Panel. Berlin, Dahlem, Staatliche Museen 1136. 103 × 69. Museum photo: Steinkopf.*
1111. *Annunciation. Fresco. Monticelli, Oratorio di S. Maria della Querce. SGF 2140.*
1112. *Monastic Saint and St John the Baptist. Sinopia (see fig. 1113). Formerly San Piero a Sieve, Tabernacolo delle Mozzette. SGF 113824.*
1113. *St Francis, another Saint, and John the Baptist. Fresco. Formerly San Piero a Sieve, Tabernacolo delle Mozzette. SGF 28163.*

PARRI SPINELLI

Whether it was due to neurasthemia which afflicted him for a long time and prevented him from working, or to disagreements with his relatives—even to the point of their assaulting him physically—Parri watched as the wealth left to him by his father disappeared. In the *estimo* of 1433 he is no longer registered among the landowners of the town; Baldassare, who from 1427 onwards we find as a salaried worker, in 1435 is separated from his brother and living with his mother and his other uterine brother, Vanni di Andrea di Chese.

Parri died at 66 years of age (and not the 56 noted by Vasari) in 1453, and was buried on 9th January in S. Marco di Murello. This is noted thus in the necrology of the Fraternity of S. Maria:

" 1452 die VIII mensis ianuarii Parrus Spinelli pictor sepultus in ecclesia Morelli ".

from U. Pasqui, p. 77, *Rivista d' Arte*, X, 1917-1918.

Parri, whose real name was Gasparri, was born in 1387; this we know from a cadastral document of 1427 and from a record of his age at death and the year he died.....
According to Vasari, Parri was of a melancholy, lonesome nature, too much engrossed in his art and his work; the same authority informs us that Mario da Montepulciano, Bicci di Lorenzo's assistant, painted Parri's portrait. He is far from right when he tells us that the painter died at the age of fifty-six and was buried in the church of S. Agostino, in his father's tomb, because we have documents which prove that he died on the 9th June 1453 and was buried in the church of Murello. Milanesi affirms that Parri suffered from a nervous disease but he does not give us the source of this information.....

from R. van Marle, pp. 221-223, *The Development of the Italian Schools of Painting*, Vol. IX, The Hague, 1927.

Guasparre (Parri) di Spinello. Arezzo (possibly born in Florence), born 1387, died 1452. Painter, pupil of his father Spinello, to whom he was greatly inferior; a friend of Masolino da Panicale. His figures were particularly long and slender. In 1407 and 1408 Parri was his father's assistant at Siena..... Parri died at Arezzo and was buried in the same tomb as his father at Murello. He does not appear to have been married.....

from D. E. Colnaghi, p. 225, *A Dictionary of Florentine Painters*, London, 1928.

We owe to Salmi the most important contributions about the activity of this painter from Arezzo who was born in 1387 and died in 1453. He was the son of Spinello Aretino and notable as a fresco painter. As a young man he worked with his father on the frescoes of the Palazzo Pubblico in Siena. But his most important works in fresco are in his native town of Arezzo.....

from U. Baldini, pp. 37-38, *I^a Mostra di Affreschi Staccati*, Florence, 1957.

Returning to his native Arezzo after a long absence during the period of his artistic training, Parri developed a tendency to the artificial and neurotic. He became insensitive to the progression of time and to the arrival in Arezzo of renaissance innovations..... Among his works are the Madonna of Mercy in S. Maria delle Grazie, done perhaps in 1428; the panel of the same subject today in the Museum of Arezzo of 1435-7; what is left of the *Maestà* of the Guild of the Nunziata, in the same Museum; the Crucifixion in the convent school of S. Caterina of 1444; the Madonna of Mercy in the Fraternity, perhaps of 1448. Moreover, there are the splendid drawings in the Uffizi which some critics once wished to attribute to a Veronese painter, but which, as is shown by a sinopia, can be securely attributed to him. In these last works there is the macabre sensibility and exasperation, and the paradoxical stylistics of a Cinquecento mannerist. Parri was morbidly paranoid due to a practical joke of some of his relatives. He was considered " of a melancholy nature, lonely and too dedicated to the study of art and his work ". He died shortly after Piero della Francesca had begun to paint the S. Francesco cycle. But had he lived longer, it would, in my opinion, have been better for him to have remained shut up with his dreams of yesterday, than become modern of the low level of a painter like Lorentino.....

> from L. Berti, p. 62, *II^a Mostra di Affreschi Staccati*, Florence, 1958.

Born in Arezzo in 1387, Parri Spinelli was the son and pupil of Spinello Aretino. In 1407 he helped his father to paint the frescoes in the Sala di Balia in the Palazzo Pubblico of Siena. He returned to Arezzo, where he continued to paint in the tradition which he derived from Spinello Aretino and from his contact with the Florentine followers of Lorenzo Monaco. His workshop must have been a prominent one in Arezzo. He worked for a number of local churches, among them S. Francesco and S. Domenico. He painted a Madonna della Misericordia in fresco for the Confraternità dei Laici around 1448 and the fresco of the Crucifixion in the Palazzo Comunale. The museum in Arezzo has a number of panels attributed to him, and a group of drawings in the Uffizi appear to be his. He died in Arezzo on June 9, 1453.....

> from P. Dal Poggetto, p. 123, *Frescoes from Florence*, London, 1969.

BIBLIOGRAPHY
BOOKS

An asterisk indicates a work listed in the General Bibliography

*Pini, Milanesi**, 1876, no. 19; *v. Marle, 1927**, pp. 221-3; *Colnaghi**, 1928, p. 255; *Galetti**, " P-Z ", 1950, pp. 2341-2342; Baldini, U., *MAS I**, 1957, pp. 37-8; Berti, L., *MAS II**, 1958, p. 61; *Procacci, 1960**, pp. 60-1; *Borsook**, 1960, p. 27; *Berenson, 1963**, Vol. I, p. 166; Castelfranchi-Vegas, L., *Il Gotico Internazionale in Italia*, Rome-Dresden, 1966, p. 169; *Shapley**, 1966, p. 91; Bellosi, L., *La Pittura Tardogotica in Toscana* (I Maestri del Colore, 239), Milan, 1966; Dal Poggetto, P., and Berti, L., *Fresco Show**, 1968, pp. 136-43 (123-31); *Meiss 1970**, p. 106.

JOURNALS

Salmi, M., *A*, XVI, 1913, pp. 61-4; Del Vita, A., *RADA*, XIII, 5, 1913, pp. 84-6; Sirén, O, *BM*, XXIV, 1913, pp. 323-30; Sirén, O., *BM*, XXV, 1914, pp. 15-24; Del Vita, A., *RADA*, II, XV, 1915, pp. 84-7; Pasqui, U., *RA*, X, 1917-18, pp. 53-68, 76-78; Del Vita, A., *BA*, VIII, VII, 1929, pp. 385-95; Refice, C., *C*, II, 3-4, 1951, pp. 196-200; Virch, C., *MM*, 19, 1961, pp. 185-93; Richards, L. S., *BCMA*, 49, 1962, pp. 167-9; Donati, P. P., *AV*, 4, 1964, pp. 15-23; Bellosi, L., *PA*, XVI, 187/7, 1965, p. 23; Bellosi, L., *PA*, XVII, 201, 1966, pp. 75-78; Donati, P. P., *C*, XVII, 1-3, 1966, pp. 56-72; Donati, P. P., *PA*, XIX, 221/41, 1968, pp. 10-21; Kiel, H., *P*, XXVIII, IV, 1970, pp. 337-8.

DATED WORK

1444 Arezzo, Conservatorio di S. Caterina. Fresco: Crucifixion. d. (fig. 1124).
There are no known signed works by Parri Spinelli.

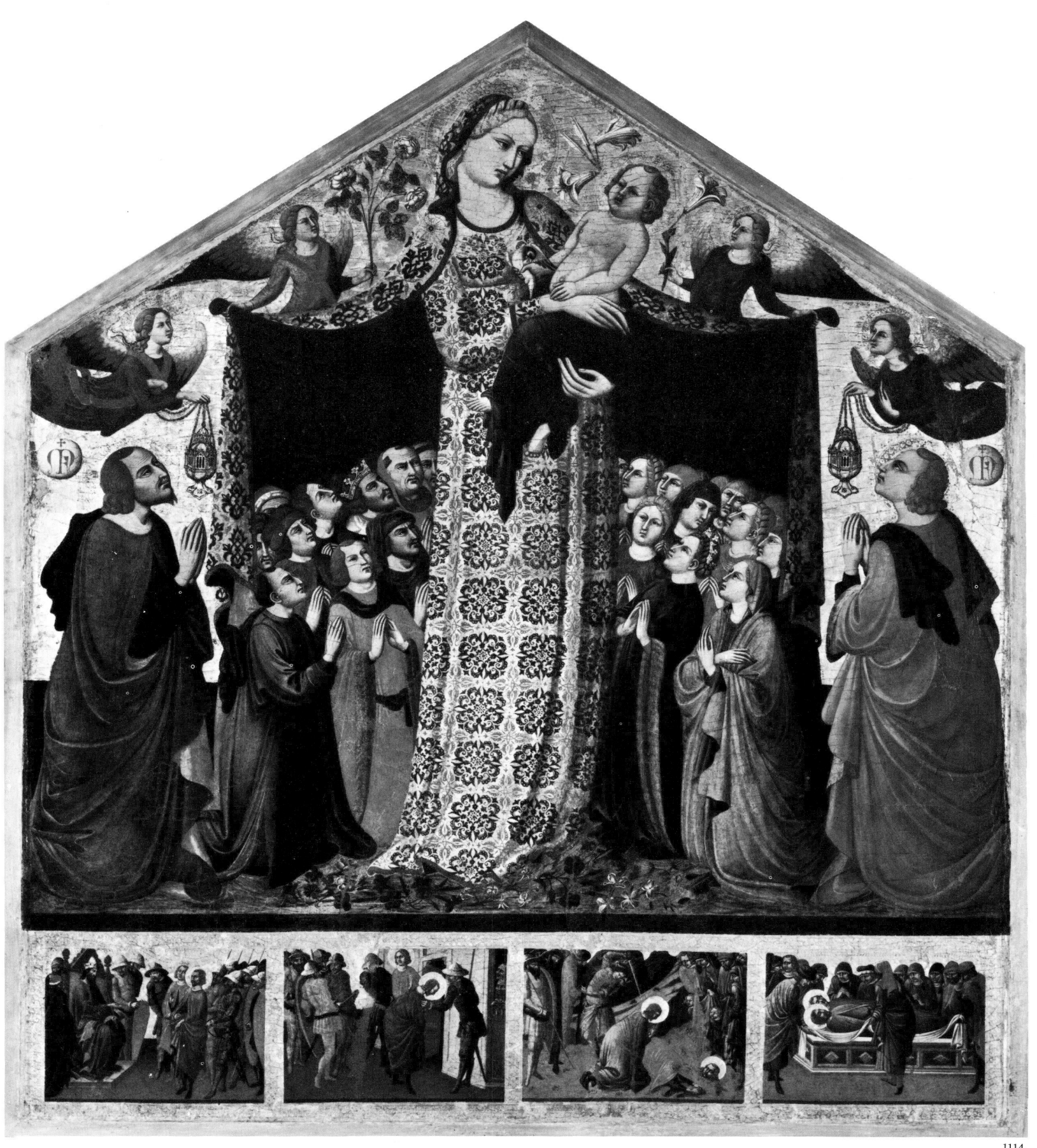

1114

1114. *Madonna of Mercy with the Infant Christ, four Angels and Sts. Pergentius and Laurentianus. Predella: Condemnation, Imprisonment, Beheading and Burial of Sts Pergentius and Laurentianus. Panel. Arezzo, Pinacoteca, no. 21. 199.5 × 174. SGA. 1435-37.*

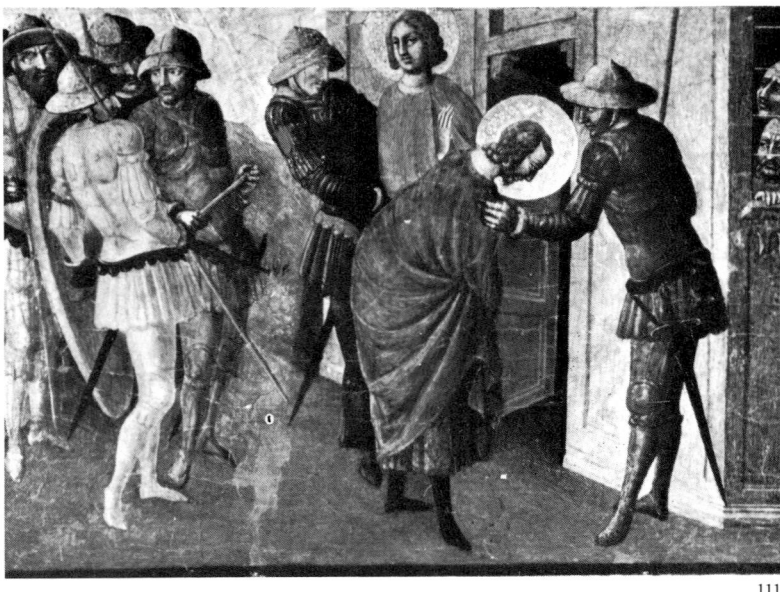

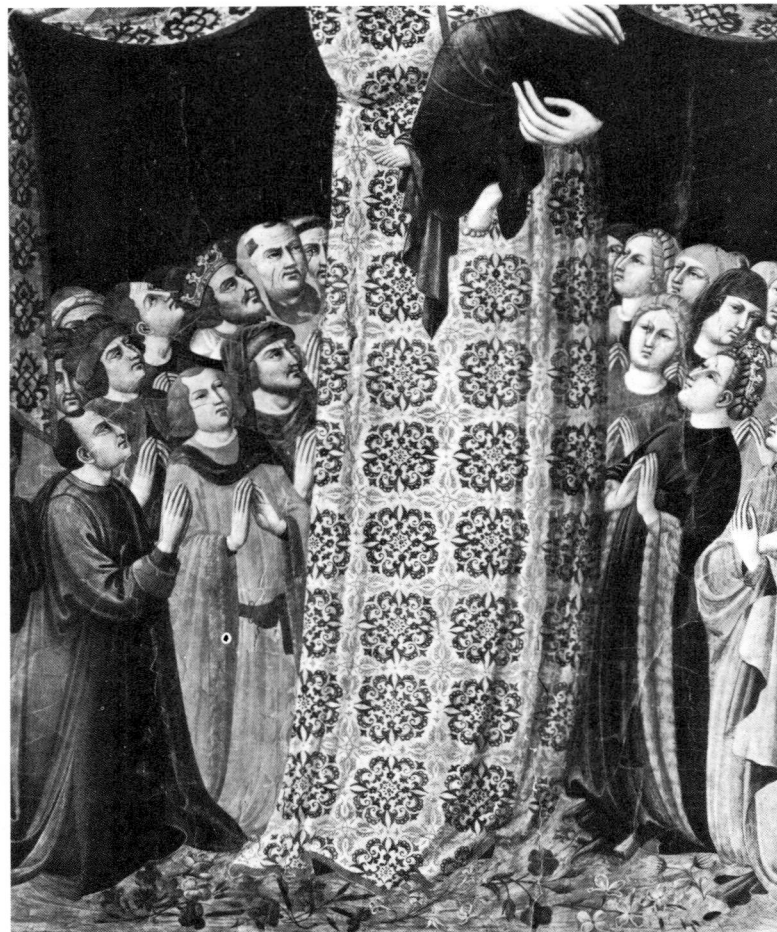

1115

1116

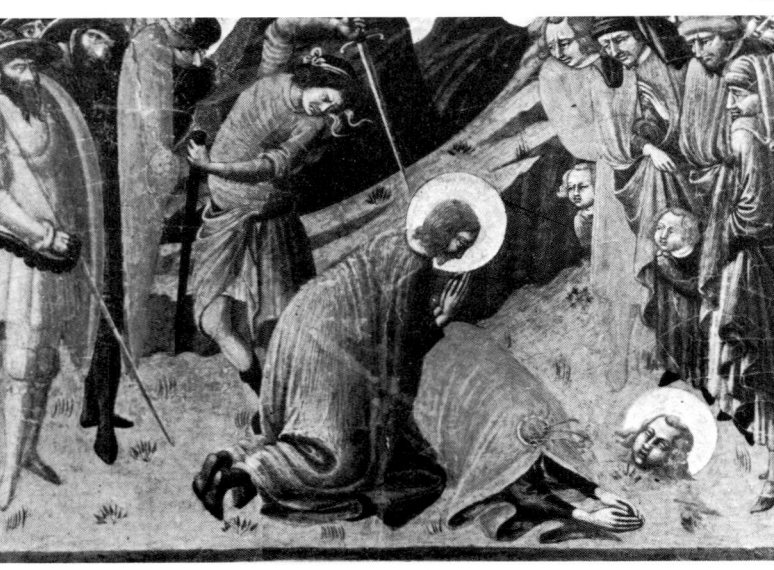

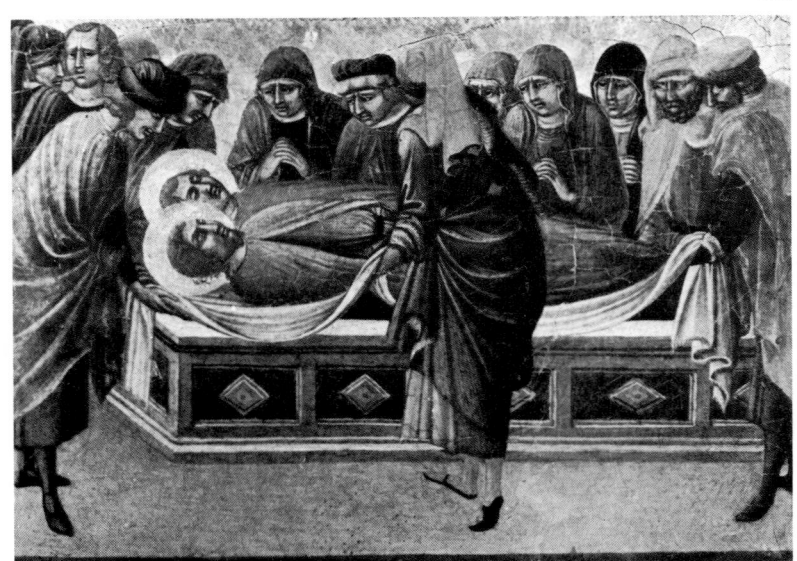

1117

1118

1115. *Imprisonment of Sts Pergentius and Laurentianus, detail of fig. 1114. Panel. Arezzo, Pinacoteca. no. 21. SGA 1810. 1435-37.*
1116. *Faithful and the Virgin, detail of fig. 1114. Panel. Arezzo, Pinacoteca. no. 21. Museum photo. 1435-37.*
1117. *Beheading of Sts. Pergentius and Laurentianus, detail of fig. 1114. Panel. Arezzo, Pinacoteca. no. 21. SGA 1811. · 1435-37.*
1118. *Burial of Sts. Pergentius and Laurentianus, detail of fig. 1114. Panel. Arezzo, Pinacoteca. no. 21. SGA 1812. 1435-37.*

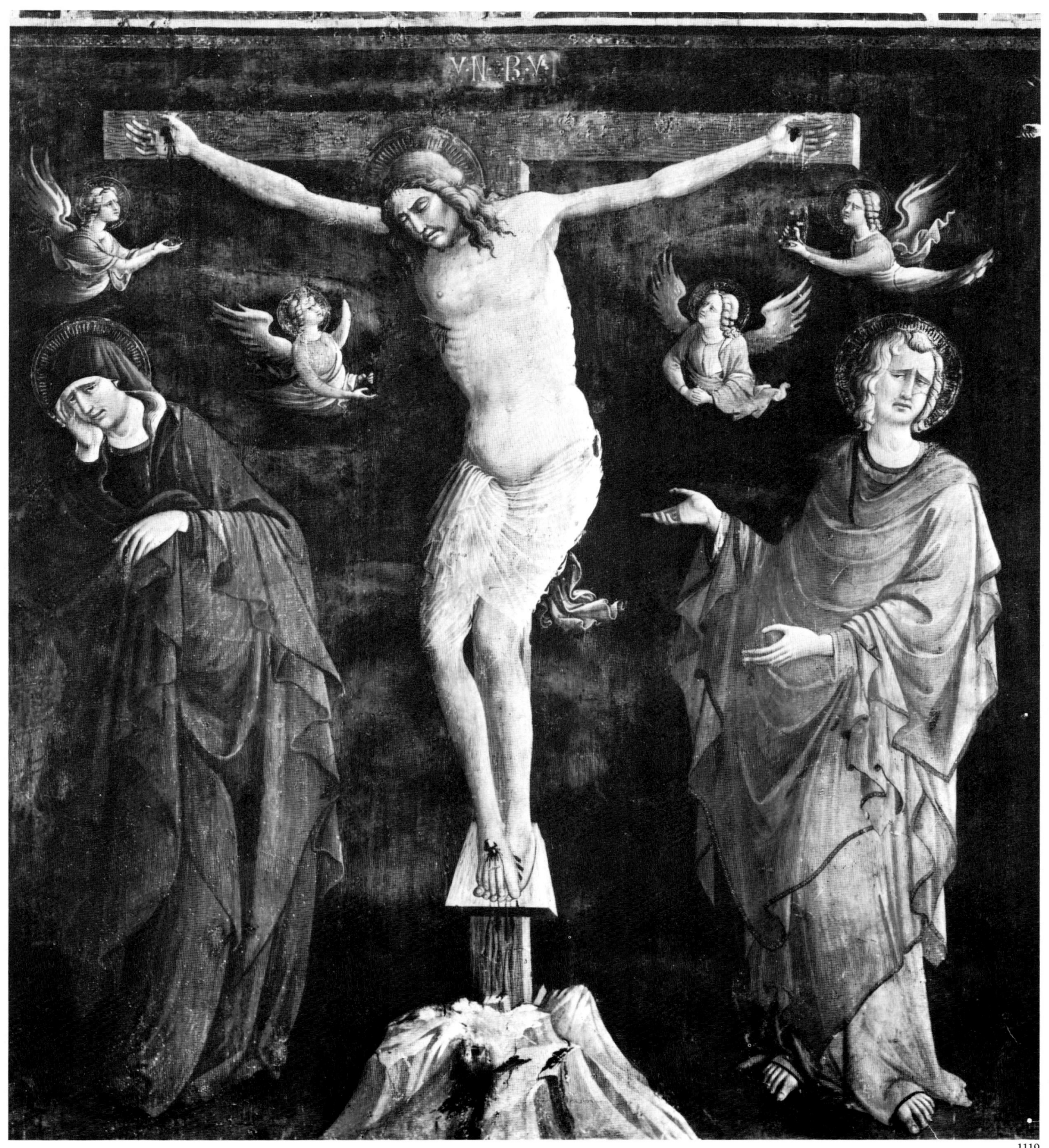

1119. *Detail: Christ on the Cross with the Virgin and St John. Fresco. Arezzo, S. Domenico. Anderson 17269.*

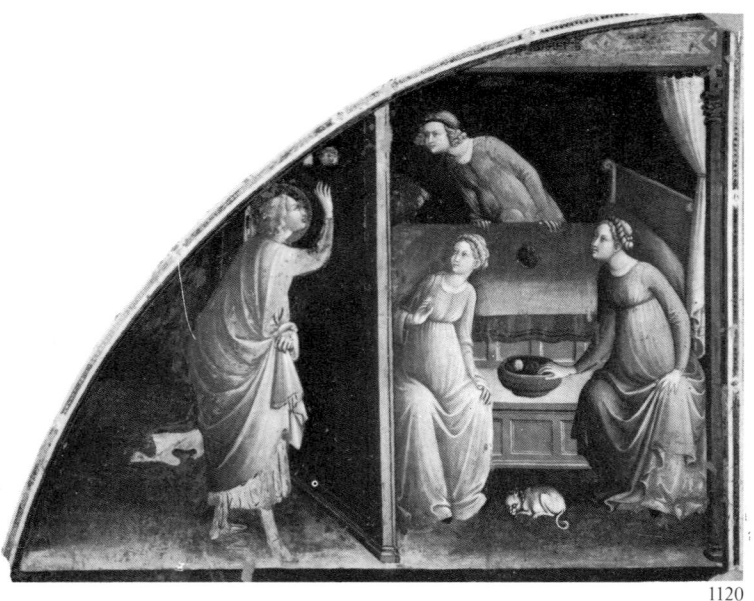

1120

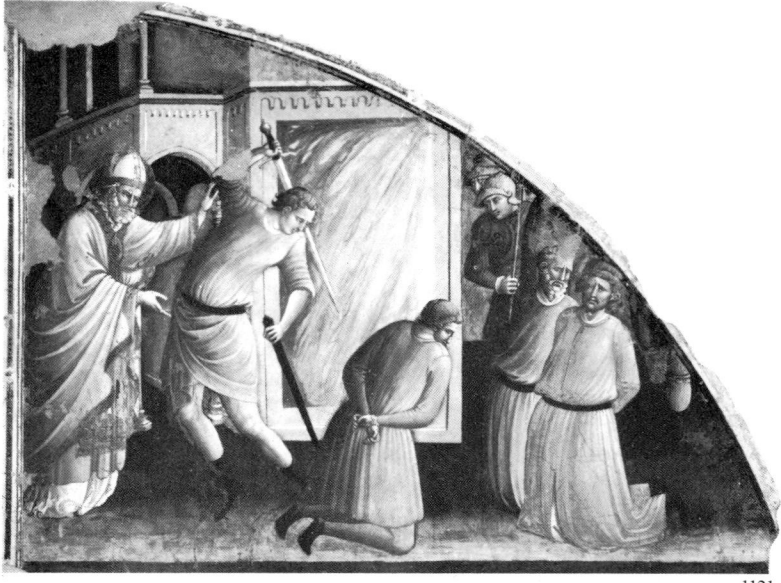

1121

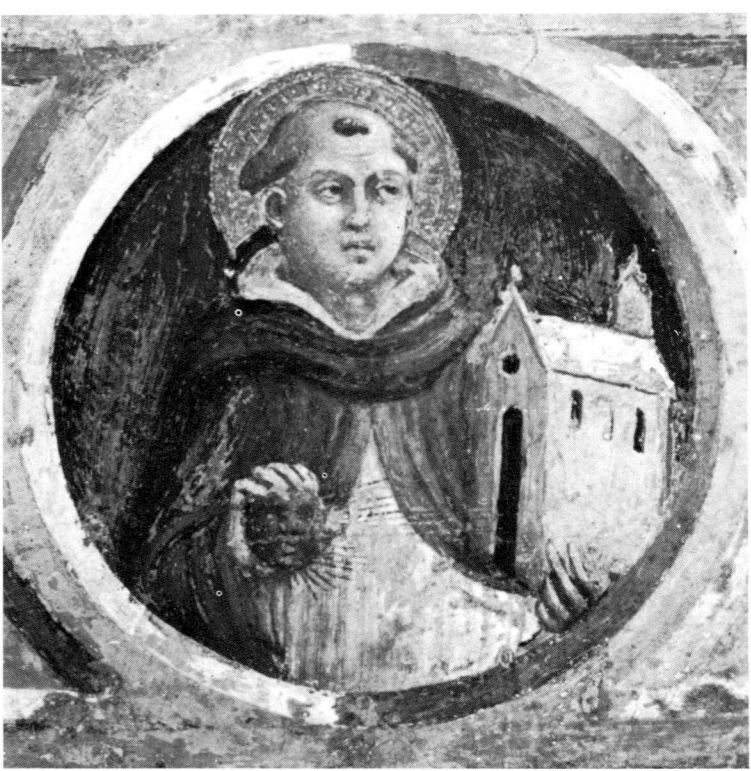

1122

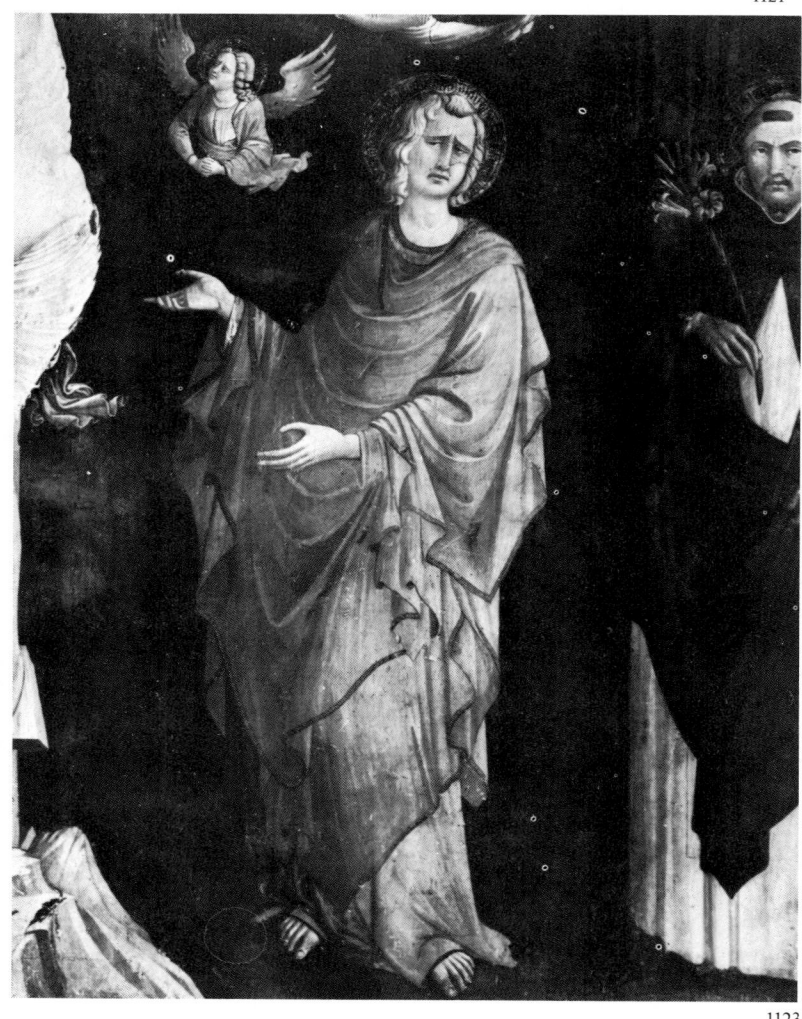

1123

1120. *St Nicholas throwing Gold to the Maidens, detail of a fresco. Fresco. Arezzo, S. Domenico. SGF 143274.*
1121. *Scene from the Life of St Nicholas of Bari, detail of a fresco. Fresco. Arezzo, S. Domenico. SGF 143275.*
1122. *St Dominic, detail of border decoration, fig. 1119. Fresco. Arezzo, S. Domenico. Author's photo.*
1123. *St. John, detail of fig. 1119. Fresco. Arezzo, S. Domenico. Anderson 17269.*

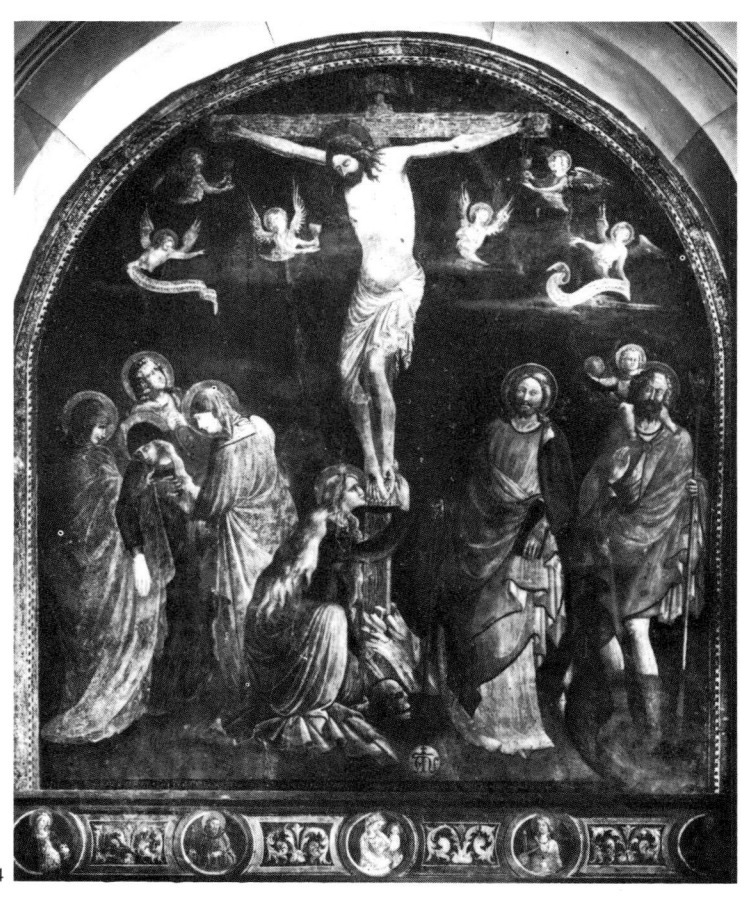

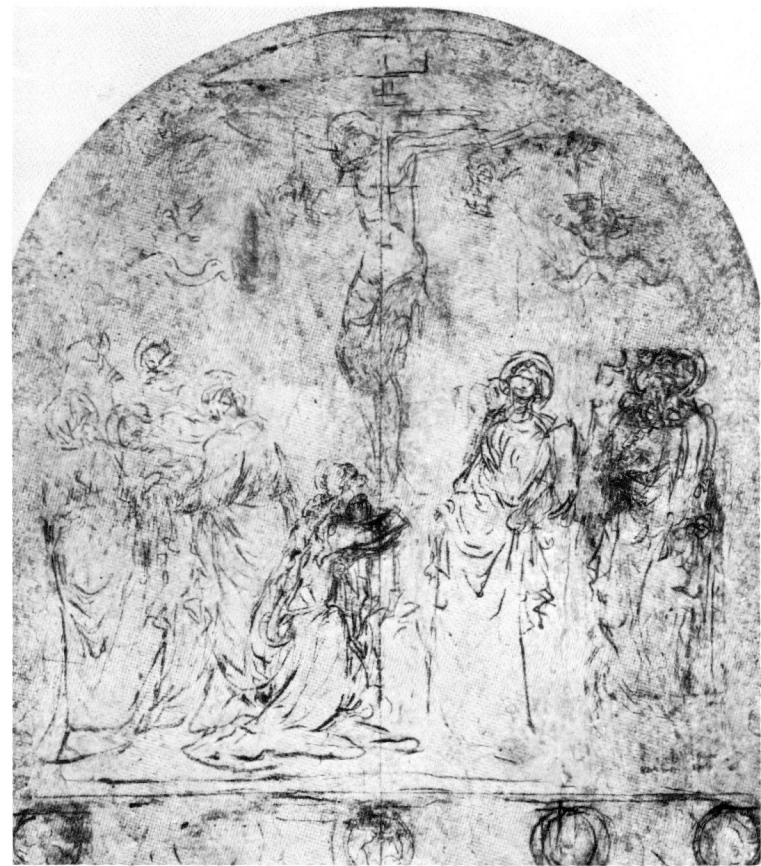

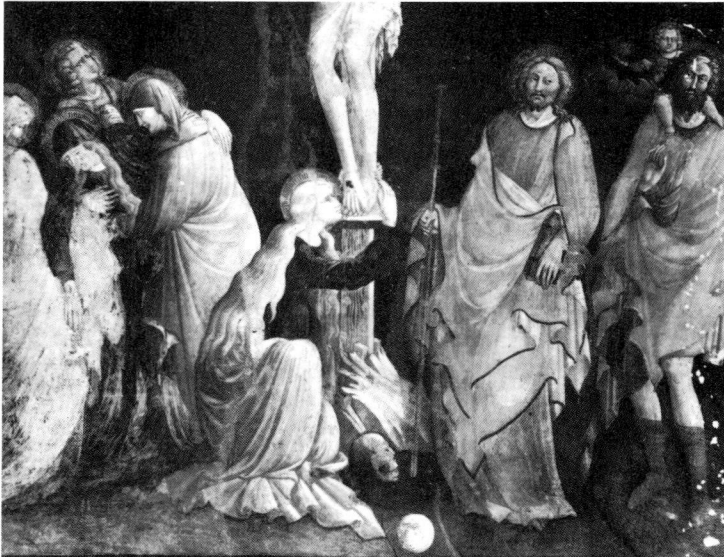

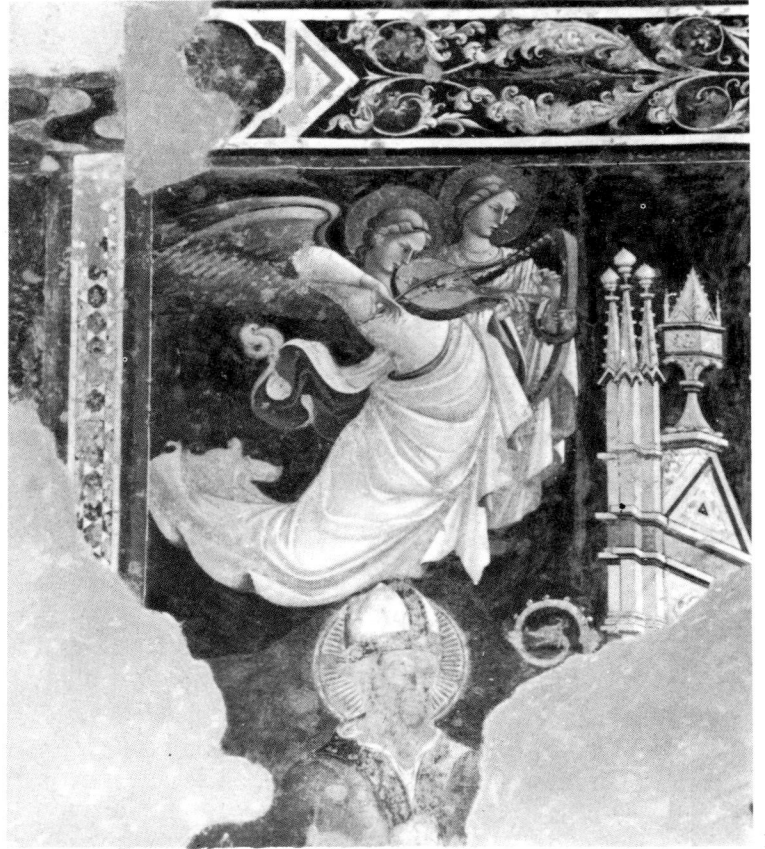

1124. *Crucixion. Fresco. Arezzo, Conservatorio di S. Caterina. SGF 35. d. 1444.*
1125. *Crucifixion. Sinopia. Arezzo, Conservatorio di S. Caterina. SGF 113830. d. 1444.*
1126. *Crucifixion, detail of fig. 1124. Fresco. Arezzo, Conservatorio di S. Caterina. SGF 113960. d. 1444.*
1127. *Detail: music-making Angels. Fresco. Arezzo, S. Domenico. Author's photo.*

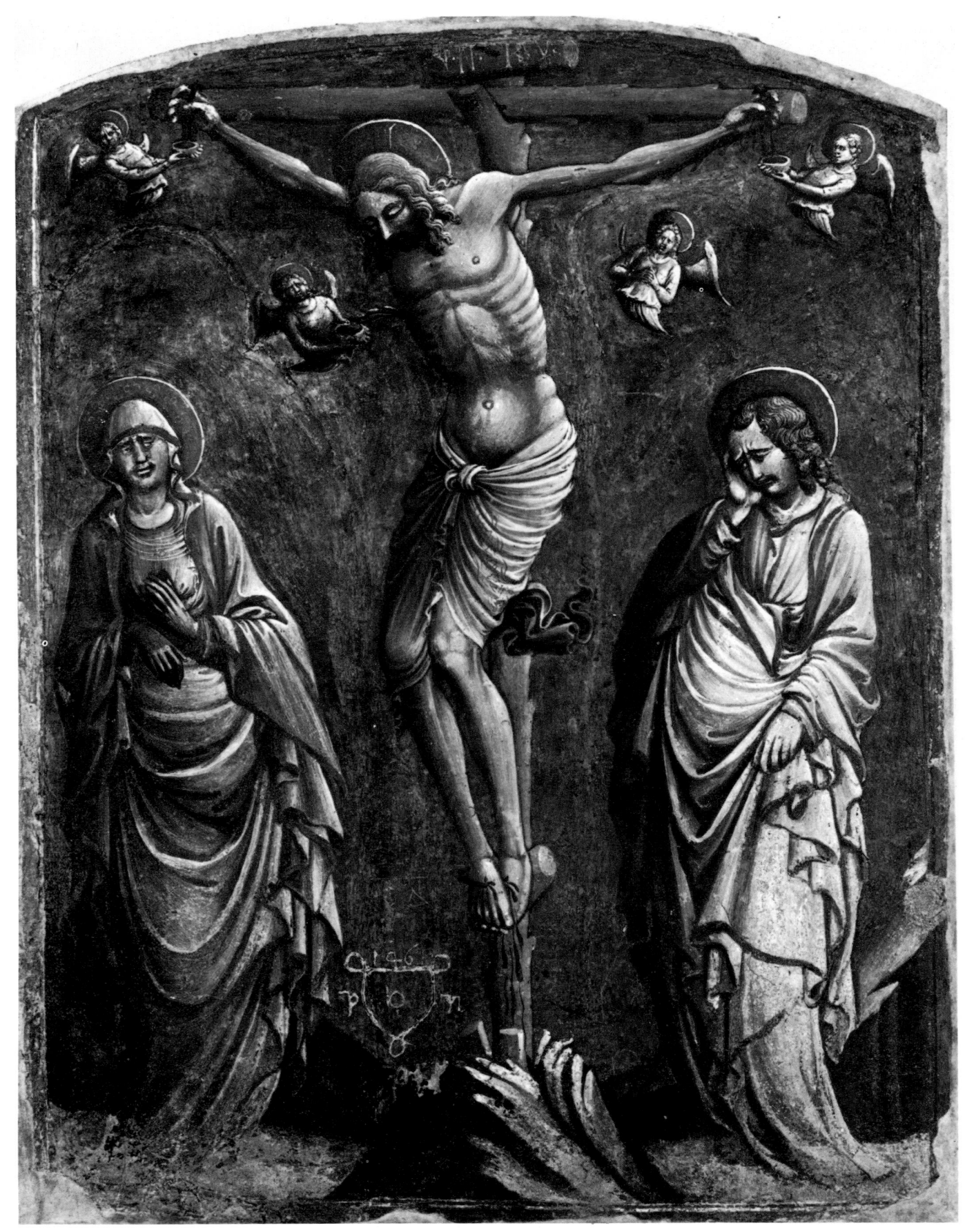

1128. *Christ on the Cross between the Virgin and St John the Evangelist. Fresco. Arezzo, Palazzo dei Priori. SGF 108190.*

1128

540

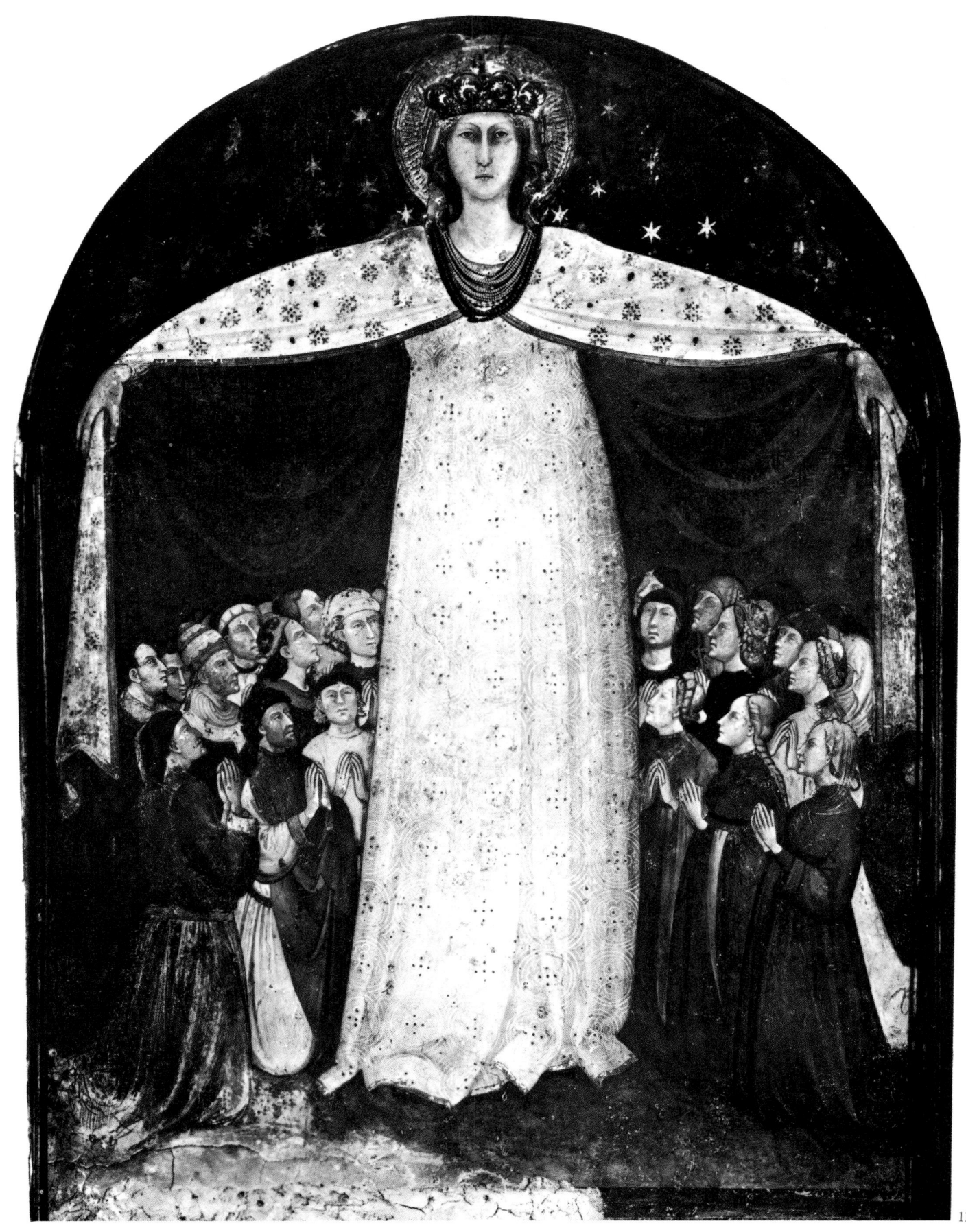

1129. Madonna of Mercy. Fresco. Arezzo, S. Maria delle Grazie. Alinari 9976. 1428.

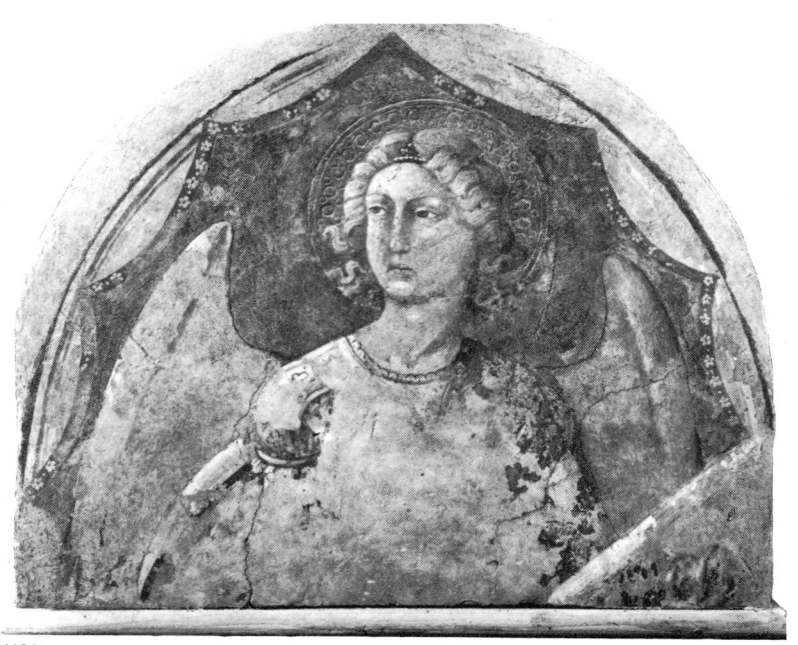

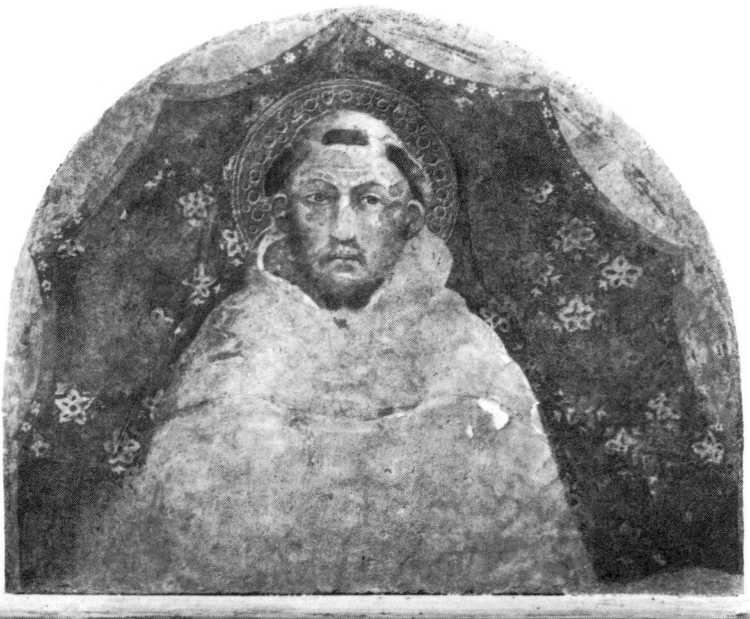

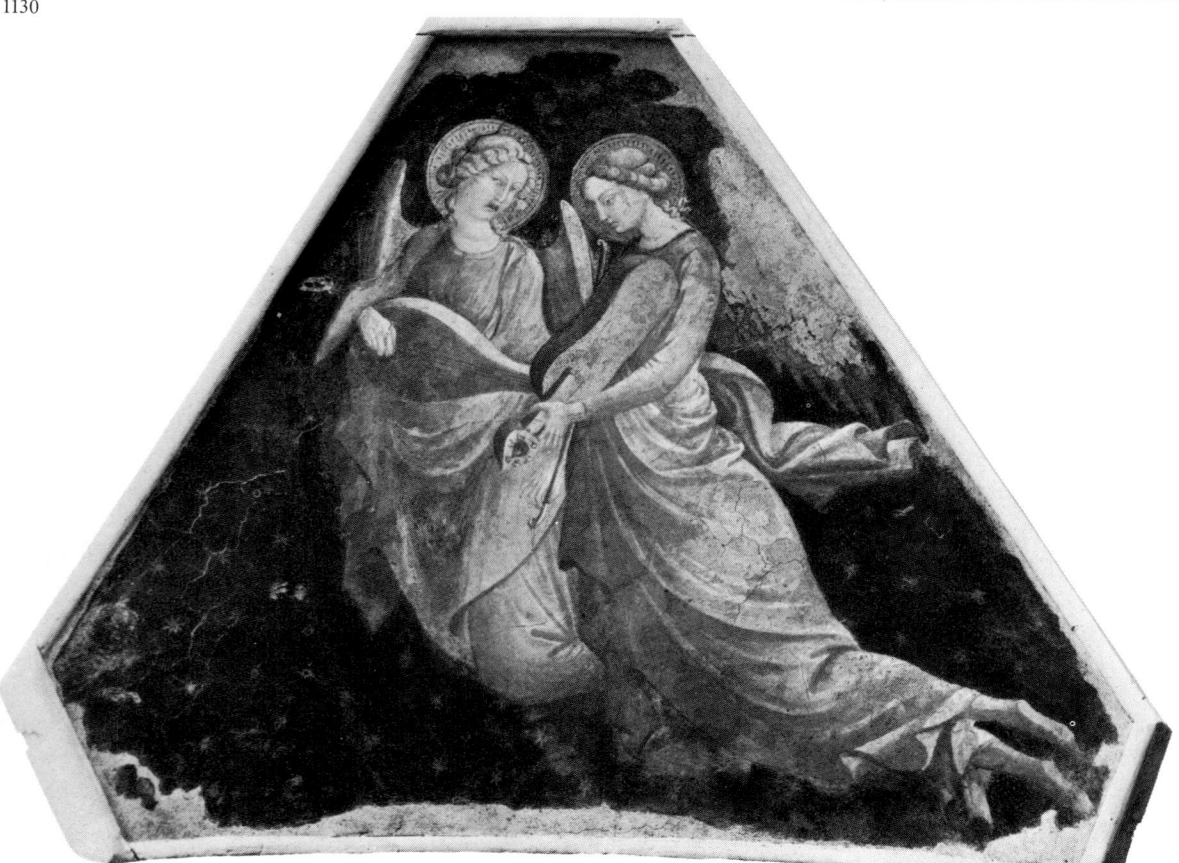

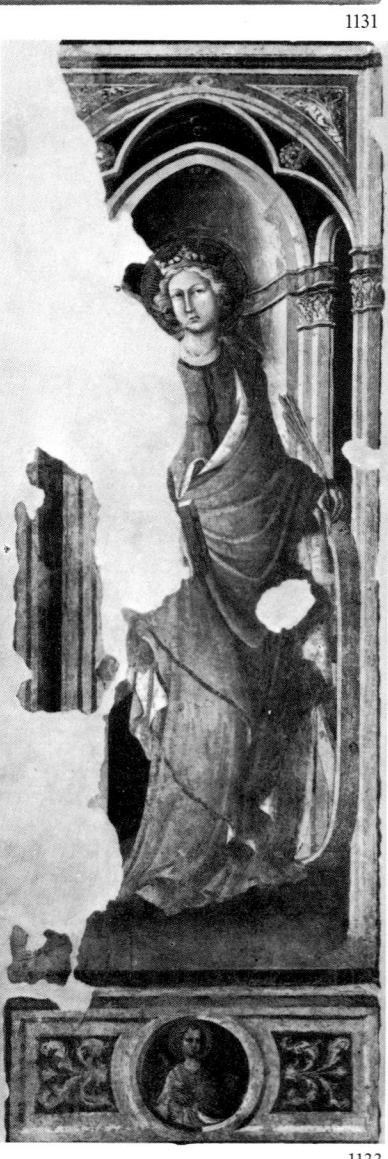

1130. *Head of St Michael. Fresco. Arezzo, Pinacoteca. SGF 49849.*
1131. *Head of St Leonard. Fresco. Arezzo, Pinacoteca. SGF 49848.*
1132. *Two music-making Angels. Fresco. Arezzo, Pinacoteca. SGF 49846.*
1133. *St Catherine. Fresco. Arezzo, S. Domenico. SGF 100810.*

542

MASTER OF FUCECCHIO

The formal spirit which was so close to Sienese art of 1450, I have already pointed out, in that immensely attractive painter of Florentine and Aretine " cassoni ", who also did the following works which even if they are not of the first order, are unforgettable: the " Triumph of Fame " in the collection of the New York Historical Society; the Cassone known as that of the " Adimari-Ricasoli wedding ", in the Uffizi; the round chest with various triumphal scenes on it, formerly in the Uffizi, now in the small Horne Museum, the Madonna and Child in Fucecchio; and also the tabernacle with musical angels in the Oratory of the Virgin at San Giovanni Valdarno.....

from R. Longhi, p. 38, *Pinacoteca*, 1929.

The Master of Fucecchio has been named after an altar-piece in the sacristy of the cathedral of this town. Mr Berenson, who has dedicated a few pages to this little master, believes that he is the same as Francesco di Antonio Fiorentino (to whom the family name Banchi has erroneously been given), a mediocre follower of Lorenzo Monaco, by whom a signed triptych exists in the Fitzwilliam Museum, Cambridge. He is mentioned by Vasari and several other paintings can, with good reason, be attributed to him.
Mr Berenson explains the much more evolved appearance of the picture at Fucecchio by endowing Francesco with a career of forty or fifty years. However, I find altogether too much difference between the authentic works of Francesco, who is a typical adherent of the school of Lorenzo Monaco, and the picture at Fucecchio which shows no connexion with that particular manner.....

from R. van Marle, pp. 191-2, *The Development of the Italian Schools of Painting*. Vol. XVI, The Hague, 1937.

Francesco d'Antonio e il Maestro del Cassone degli Adimari. Prof. Salmi, in his essay on the artist in *Rivista d'Arte*, 1929, clearly defines Francesco d'Antonio; he also corrects an earlier confusion of mine to do with the triptych in Grenoble and with Andrea di Giusto. There is no doubt whatsoever that Francesco di Antonio di Bartolomeo (and not Banchi as in Berenson's lists....) who was born in 1393 and of whom we have mention until 1433, was trained under Lorenzo Monaco.....
It is not necessary to repeat that one must remove from Berenson's lists the many pictures [which he attributes to Francesco di Antonio] which are really by the Master of the *Adimari Cassone*. They are by a vivacious artist, of a younger generation (confirmed by the sure date of 1449 for the *tondo* " The Triumph of Fame " in the New York Historical Society) who, in my opinion, was trained about 1435-40 in the circle of Vecchietta and Paolo Schiavo.....

from R. Longhi, pp. 186-7, *Critica d'Arte*, V, 1940.

B. Berenson, *Dedalo*, 1932, believes that the " Master of Fucecchio " is the same person as Francesco di Antonio (erroneously called Banchi), by whom there exists a signed Madonna dated 1415.
R. van Marle distinguishes between this older painter, a pupil of Lorenzo Monaco, and the " Master of Fucecchio " who was young enough to be influenced by Masaccio, Uccello, Domenico Veneziano and others. R. Longhi and W. Suida agree with van Marle.....

from W. Suida, p. 31, *The Samuel H. Kress Collection*, Birmingham, Alabama, 1952.

But who is the Master of the Adimari Cassone? He is named for this celebrated cassone in the Accademia in Florence. At one point he was mistakenly identified with Francesco di Antonio; successively he had another name — the Master of Fucecchio — but this too seemed wrong, as in that town there is only one of his paintings, not among his best. Recently it has again been suggested that he might be Lazzaro Vasari, great-grandfather of Giorgio, who was a saddler and painter among the followers of Piero della Francesca.

But a surviving fresco by Lazzaro in S. Domenico at Arezzo would eclude this identification. It is noteworthy that the painter has a number of works here in San Giovanni, and in the neighbourhood: besides the two paintings in this museum, there are two frescoed saints and a panel of the Madonna & Child of his in the church of S. Lorenzo, and a frescoed Annunciation in the church which was formerly the Badia of Soffena, near Castelfranco. So many nearby commissions would perhaps suggest someone from the Valdarno: if so, the Master should be searched for amongst that band of painters which went down from San Giovanni to Florence after Masolino and Masaccio.....

from L. Berti, p. 13, *Il Museo della Basilica a San Giovanni Valdarno*, Florence, 1959.

The personality of the " Master of Fucecchio " was invented by van Marle in 1937, who gathered together a fairly homogeneous group of paintings from the " corpus " of Francesco d'Antonio, brought together by Berenson in his " lists " in 1932.....

The training and background of the " Master of Fucecchio " (as I prefer to call him — while waiting for a more correct nomenclature to appear, in deference to both his most distinctive picture and to the most satisfactory grouping of his works under this name — by van Marle) was, according to van Marle, influenced by Francesco di Antonio and by the early work of Masaccio. Longhi, on the other hand, first saw a close relationship to Sienese painting of about 1450; then he invented his " Master of the Cassone degli Adimari " (including in this group, the picture in Fucecchio), and placed him in the same *ambiente* as Paolo Schiavo and Vecchietta.....

The " Master of Fucecchio " certainly worked with Paolo Schiavo, as can be seen by the two organ shutters from San Giovanni Valdarno: one is by Paolo Schiavo and the other by the author of the panel in Fucecchio.....

from P. Dal Poggetto, p. 10, *Museo di Fucecchio*, Città di Fucecchio, 1969.

BIBLIOGRAPHY
BOOKS

An asterisk indicates a work listed in the General Bibliography

Schubring, P., *Cassoni*, Leipzig, 1923; Longhi, R., *Piero della Francesca*, Rome, 1927, pp. 109, 120, 145; *v. Marle, 1927**, pp. 102-3; Pudelko, G., *Catalogue: Exposition de l'art italien de Cimabue à Tiepolo*, Paris, 1935, p. 165; *v. Marle, 1937**, Vol. XVI, pp. 192, 196; Ragghianti, L. C., *Catalogue: Lorenzo il Magnifico e le Arti*, Florence, 1949, p. 28; *Galetti**, "F-O", 1950, p. 980; *T-Becker**, Vol. XXXVII, 1950, p. 109; *Procacci, 1951**, pp. 40-1; Suida, W. E., *Catalogue of the Birmingham Museum of Art*, Birmingham, (Ala.), 1952, pp. 30-3; Suida, W. E., *Catalogue of the Seattle Art Museum*, Seattle, 1954, p. 32; Berti, L., *MAS II**, 1958, p. 5; Suida, W. E., *Catalogue of the Birmingham Museum of Art*, Birmingham, (Ala.), 1959, p. 40; Berti, L., *Il Museo della Basilica a San Giovanni Valdarno*, Florence, 1959, p. 13; *TCI, 1959**, p. 104; *Berenson, 1963**, Vol. I, p. 62-64; Castelfranchi-Vegas, L., *Il Gotico Internazionale in Italia* (I Maestri del Colore, 255), Milan, 1966; *Shapley**, 1966, pp. 105-6; Marcucci, L., *Cassone Adimari*, Milan (s. d.); *Fresco Show**, 1968, pp. 122-5 (111-3); Dal Poggetto, P., *Catalogue: Museo di Fucecchio*, Città di Fucecchio, 1969, pp. 10-2.

JOURNALS

Schubring, P., *ZBK*, LIX, 1925-6, pp. 162-9; Longhi, R., *CA*, 1940, p. 187; Kiel, H., *P*, XXVII, 5, 1969, p. 421. Gonzales-Palacios, A., *AP*, XCI, 1970, pp. 69-70.

There are no known dated works by the Master of Fucecchio.

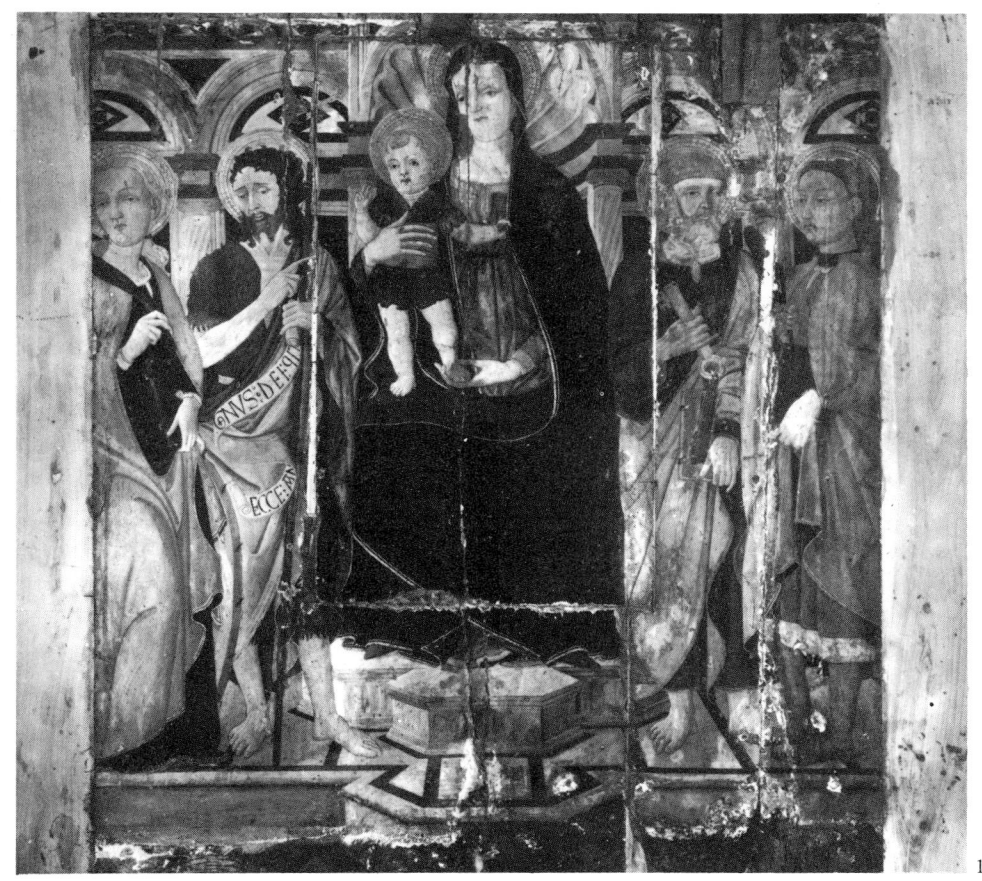

1134

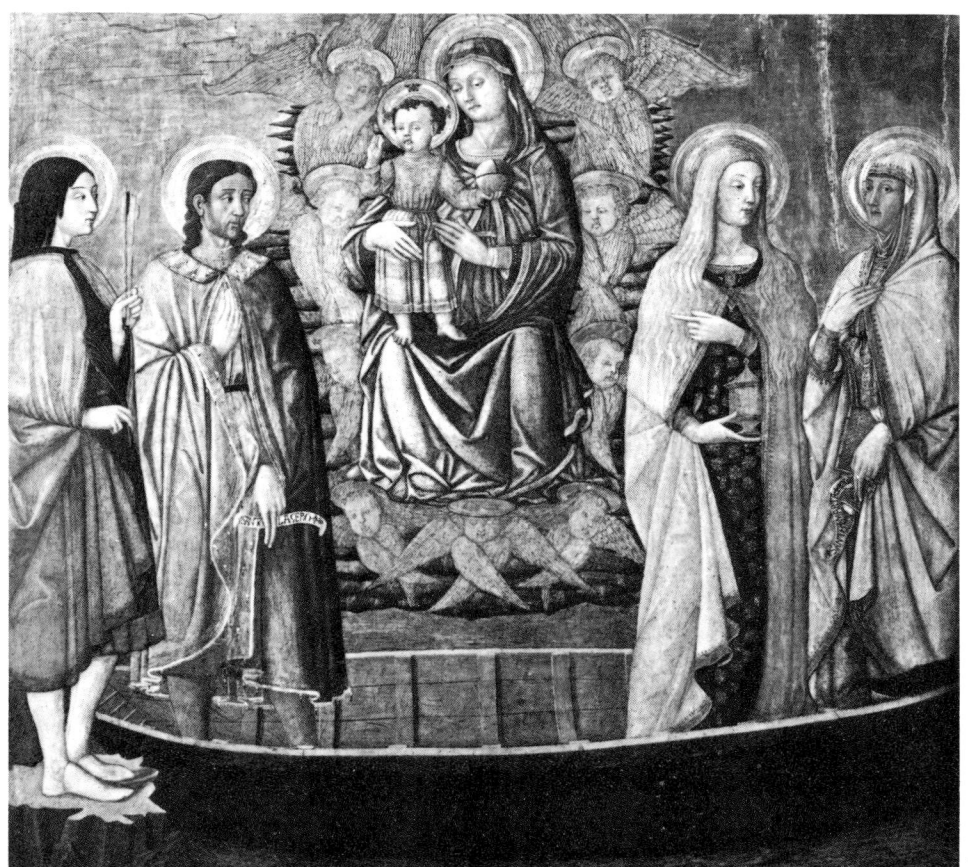

1135

1134. *Madonna and Child Enthroned with Sts Catherine, John the Baptist, Peter and Ansanus. Panel. San Giovanni Valdarno, S. Maria delle Grazie. 243 × 106. SGF 68085.*

1135. *Madonna and Child appearing to Sts Lazarus, Mary Magdalene, and Martha on their way to Marseilles, and St Sebastian. Panel. Fucecchio (10 kms west of Empoli, on the Arno), Collegiata. no. 3. 200 × 195. SGF 113902.*

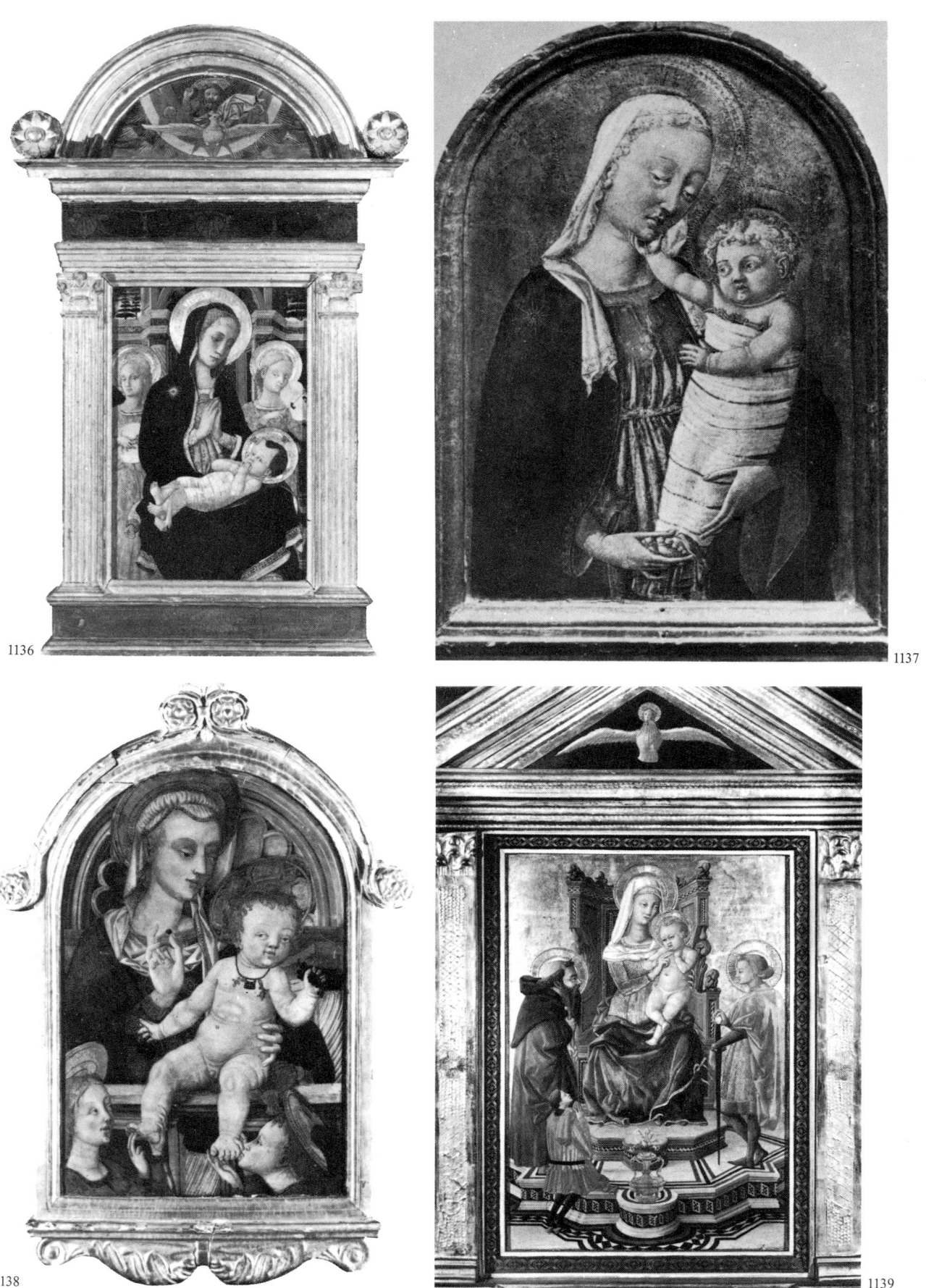

1136. *Madonna and Child with two Angels. Panel. Arezzo, Museo Comunale.* 44 × 67. *SGF 68930.*
1137. *Madonna and Child. Panel. Whereabouts unknown. Fototeca Berenson.*
1138. *Madonna and Child with two Angels. Panel. Whereabouts unknown. Sotheby photo.*
1139. *Madonna and Child Enthroned with two Saints and a Donor. Panel. London, Courtauld Institute of Art.* 44.2 × 30. *Museum photo B66/1018.*

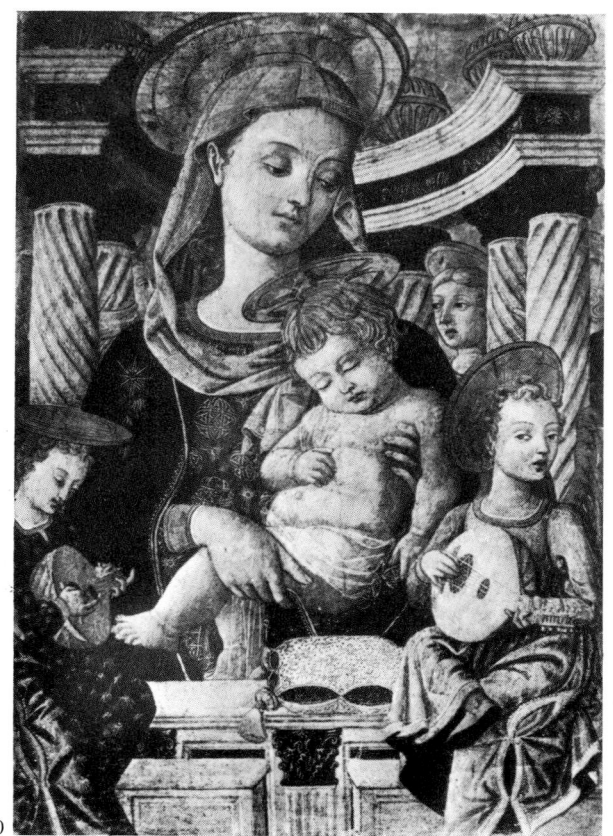

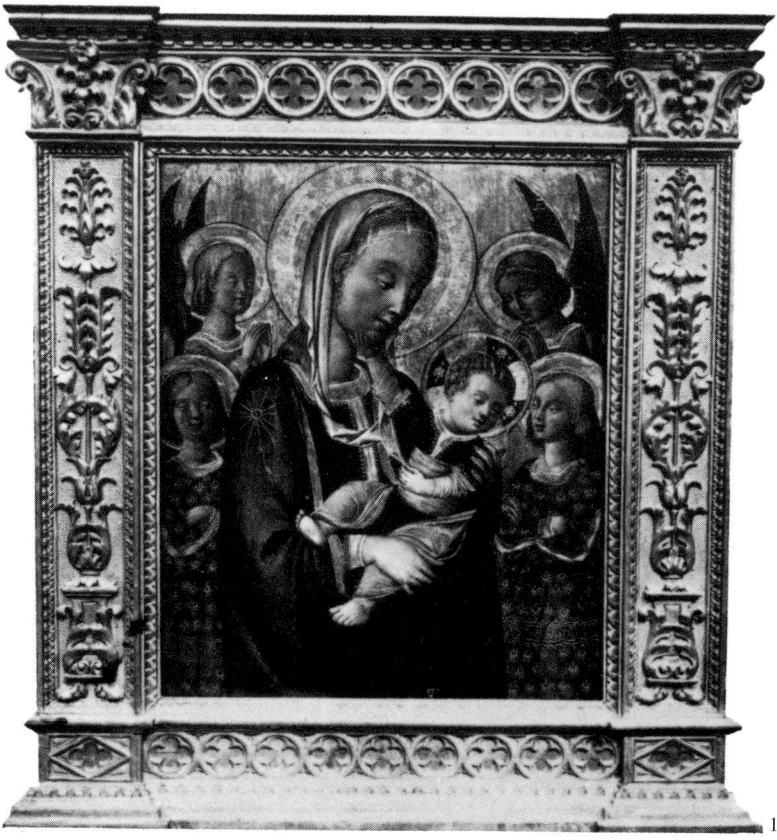

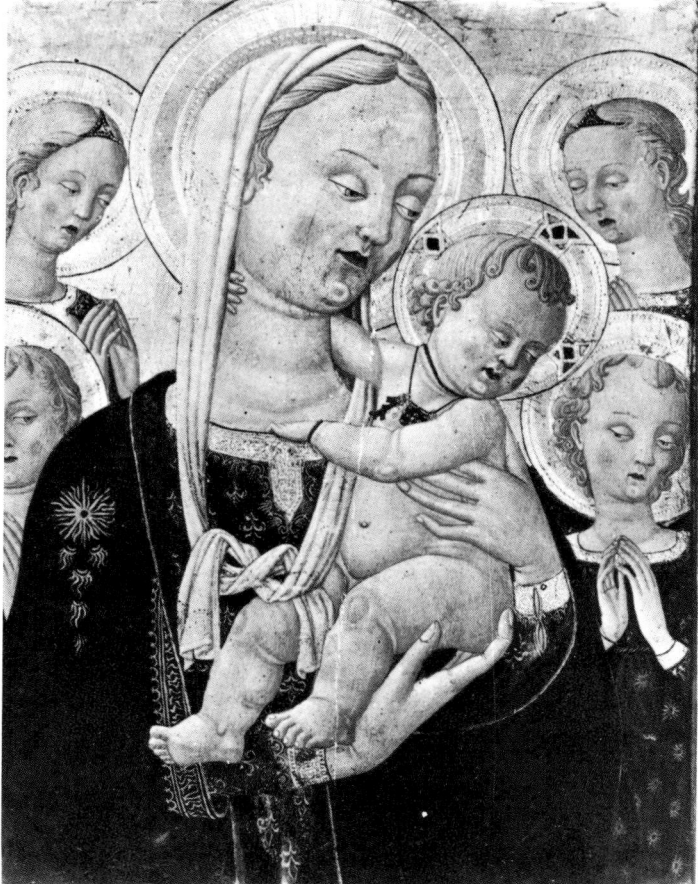

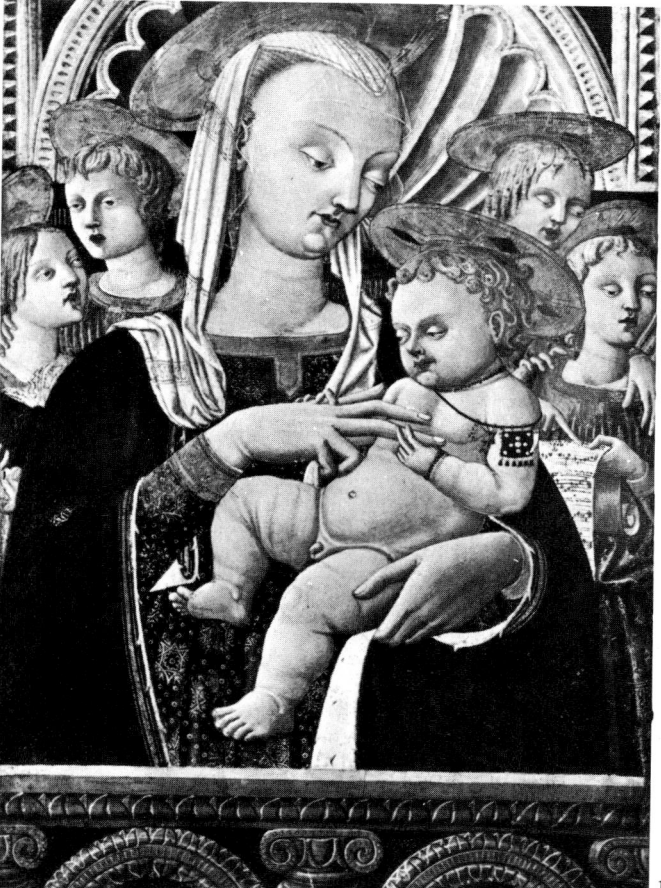

1140. *Madonna and Child Enthroned with music-making Angels. Panel. Lisbon, J. P. Leacock Collection. Fototeca Berenson.*
1141. *Madonna and Child with four Angels. Panel. Florence, S. Trinita, Sacristy. Fototeca Berenson.*
1142. *Madonna and Child with Angels. Panel. Whereabouts unknown. Fototeca Berenson.*
1143. *Madonna and Child with Angels. Panel. Whereabouts unknown. Fototeca Berenson.*

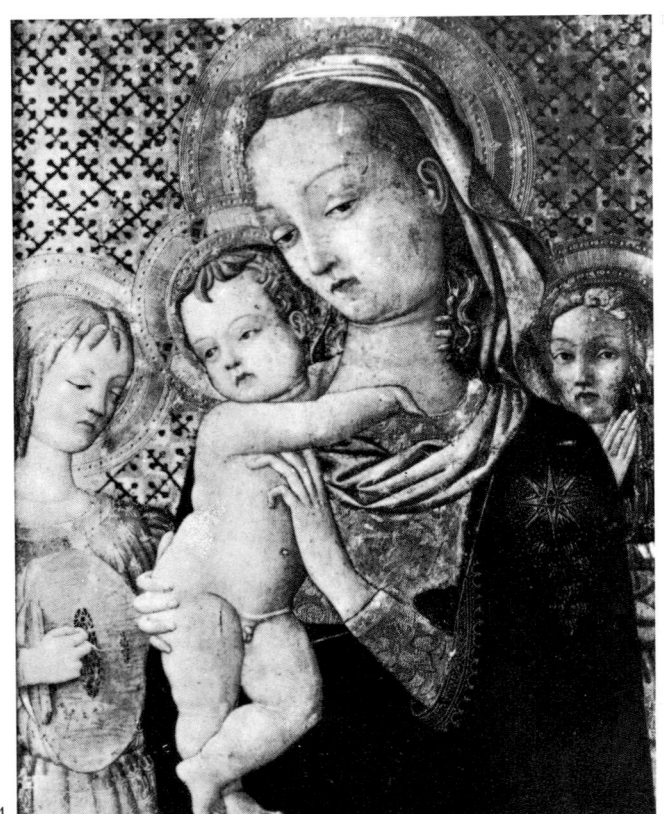

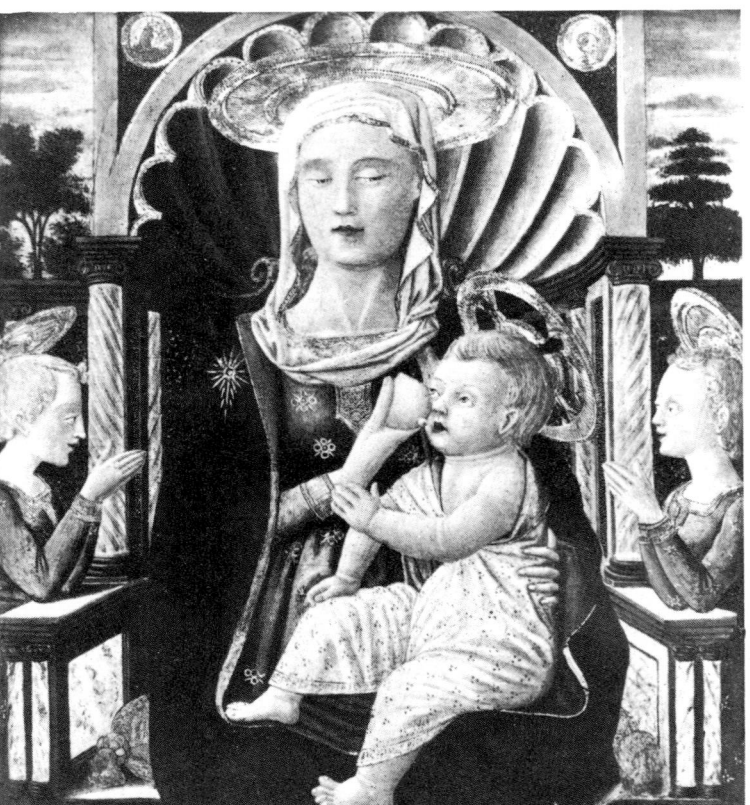

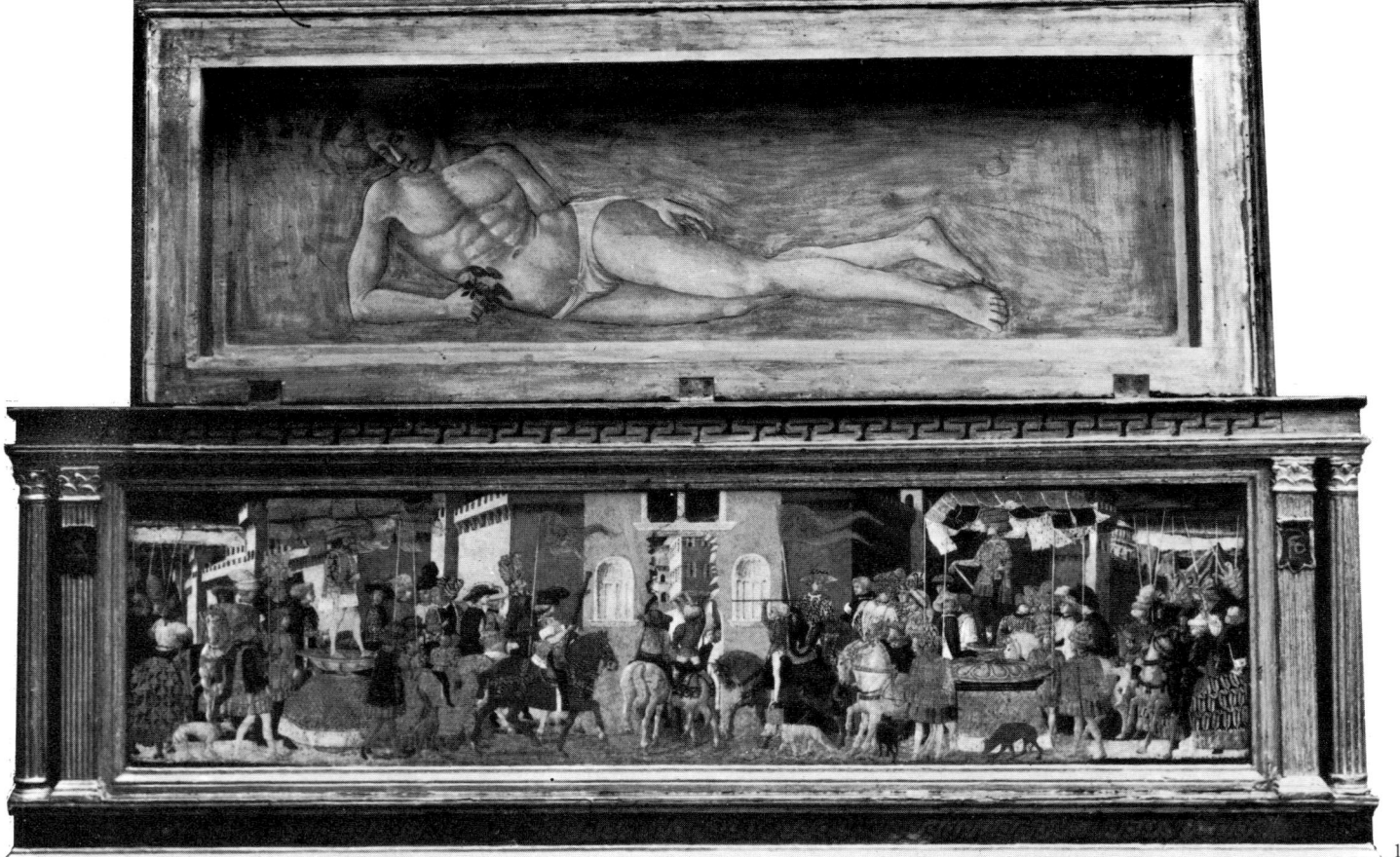

1144. *Madonna and Child with Angels. Panel. Cherbourg, Musée Thomas Henry, Campana Collection. Campana. no. 75. 63 × 70. Museum photo.*
1145. *Madonna nursing the Child with two Angels. Panel. Whereabouts unknown. Fototeca Berenson.*
1146. *Cassone scene: The Reconciliation of two Families. Lid: Reclining Nude. Panel. Copenhagen, Statens Museum for Kunst. no. 4786. 77.5 wide, 207.6 long, 87.6 deep. Museum photo.*

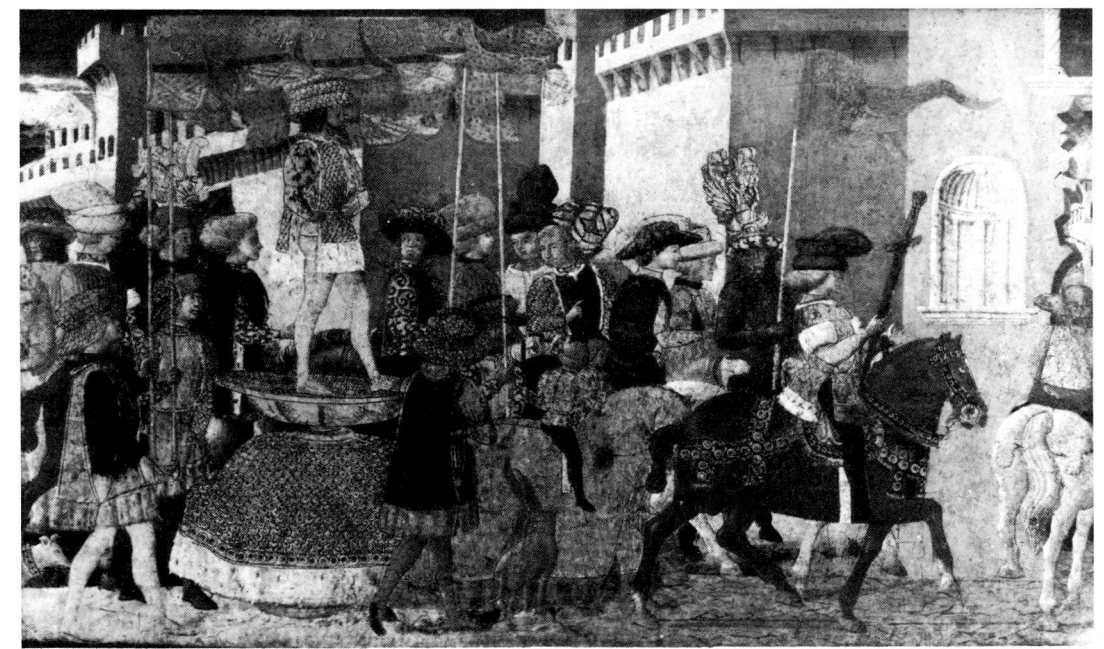

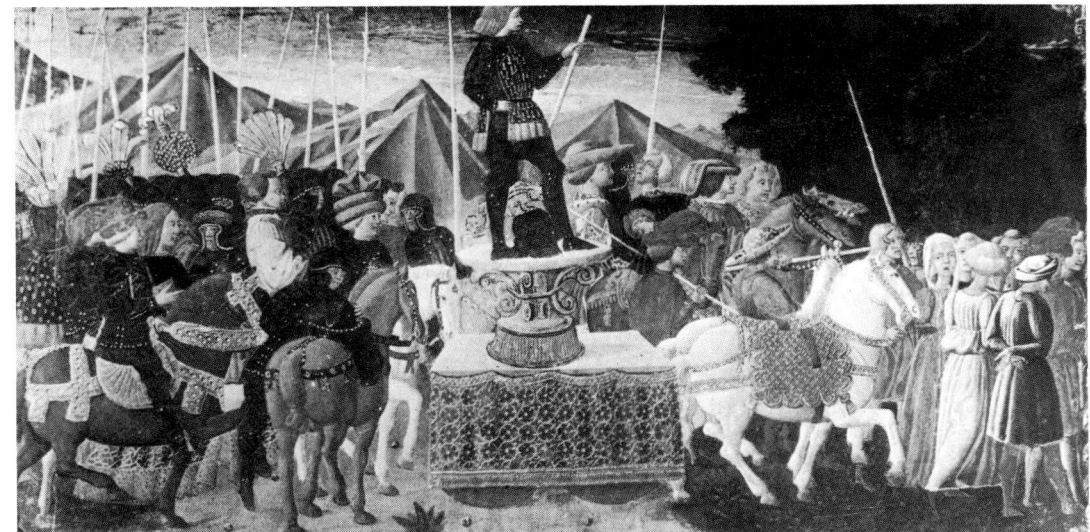

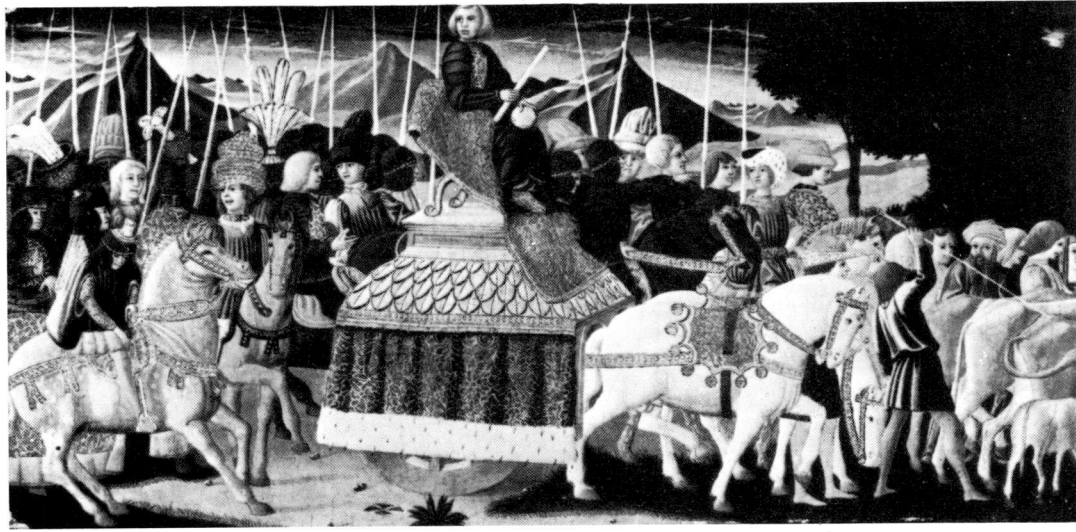

1147. *Cassone scene: Family Procession, detail of fig. 1146. Panel. Copenhagen, Statens Museum for Kunst. no. 4786. Museum photo.*
1148. *Cassone scene: Triumph of young Heroes. Panel. Whereabouts unknown (formerly Milan, Chiesa Collection). 43.5 × 83. Fototeca Berenson.*
1149. *Cassone scene: Roman Triumph. Panel. Los Angeles (Calif.), Los Angeles County Museum of Art, Hearst Collection. no. 46.4.1. 43.8 × 85.1. Museum photo.*

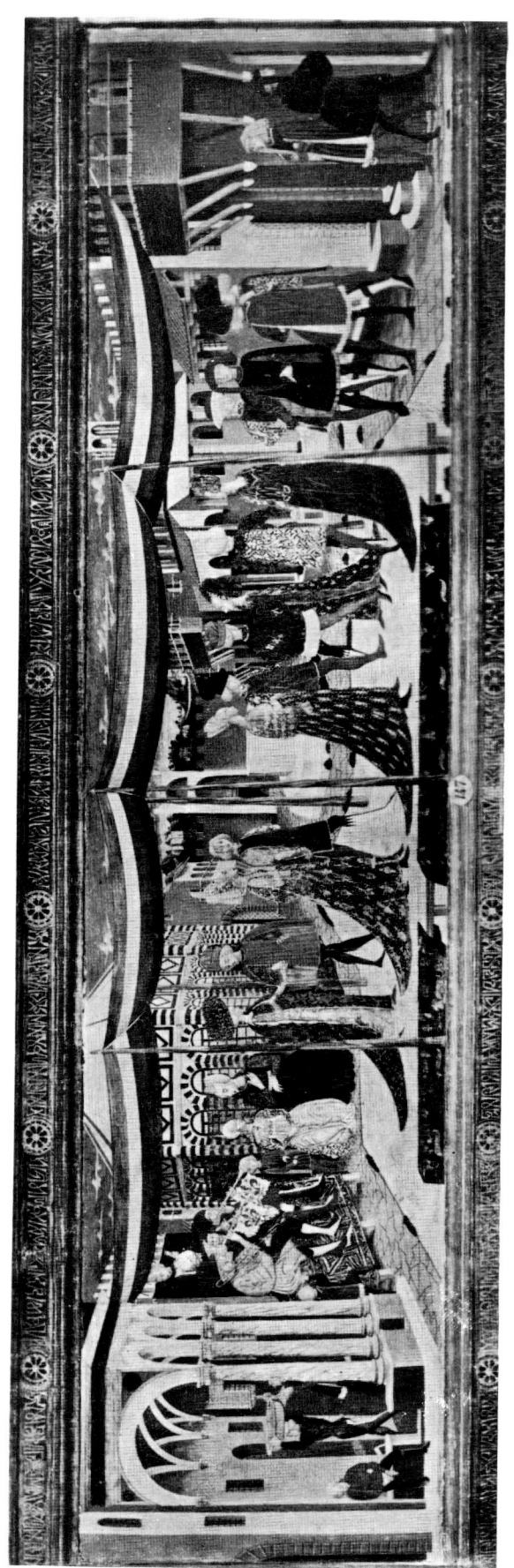

1150. "*Adimari*" *cassone. Panel. Florence, Accademia. no. 8457. 89.5 × 305. SGF 72130.*

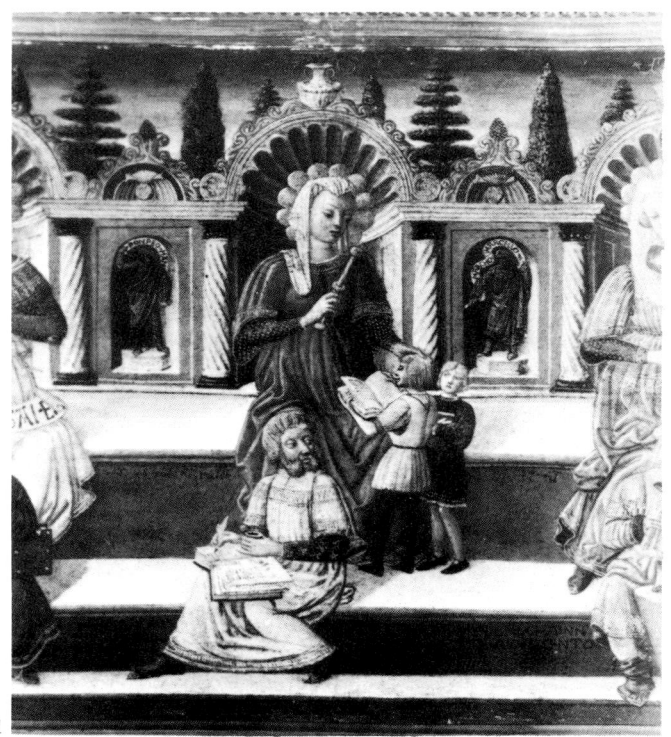

1151

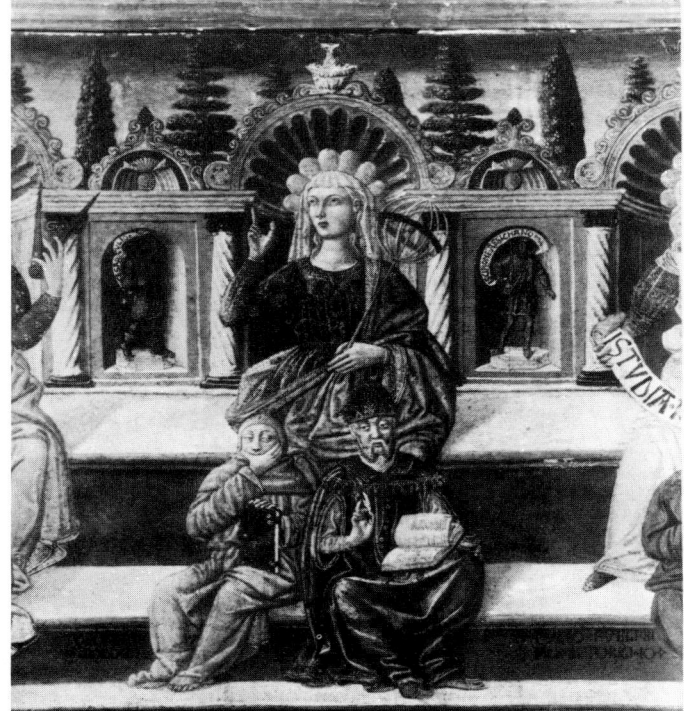

1152

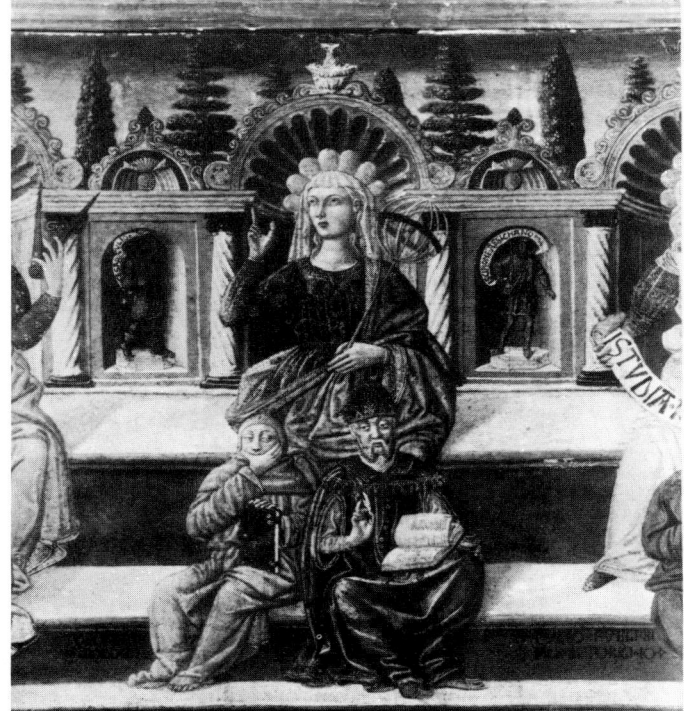

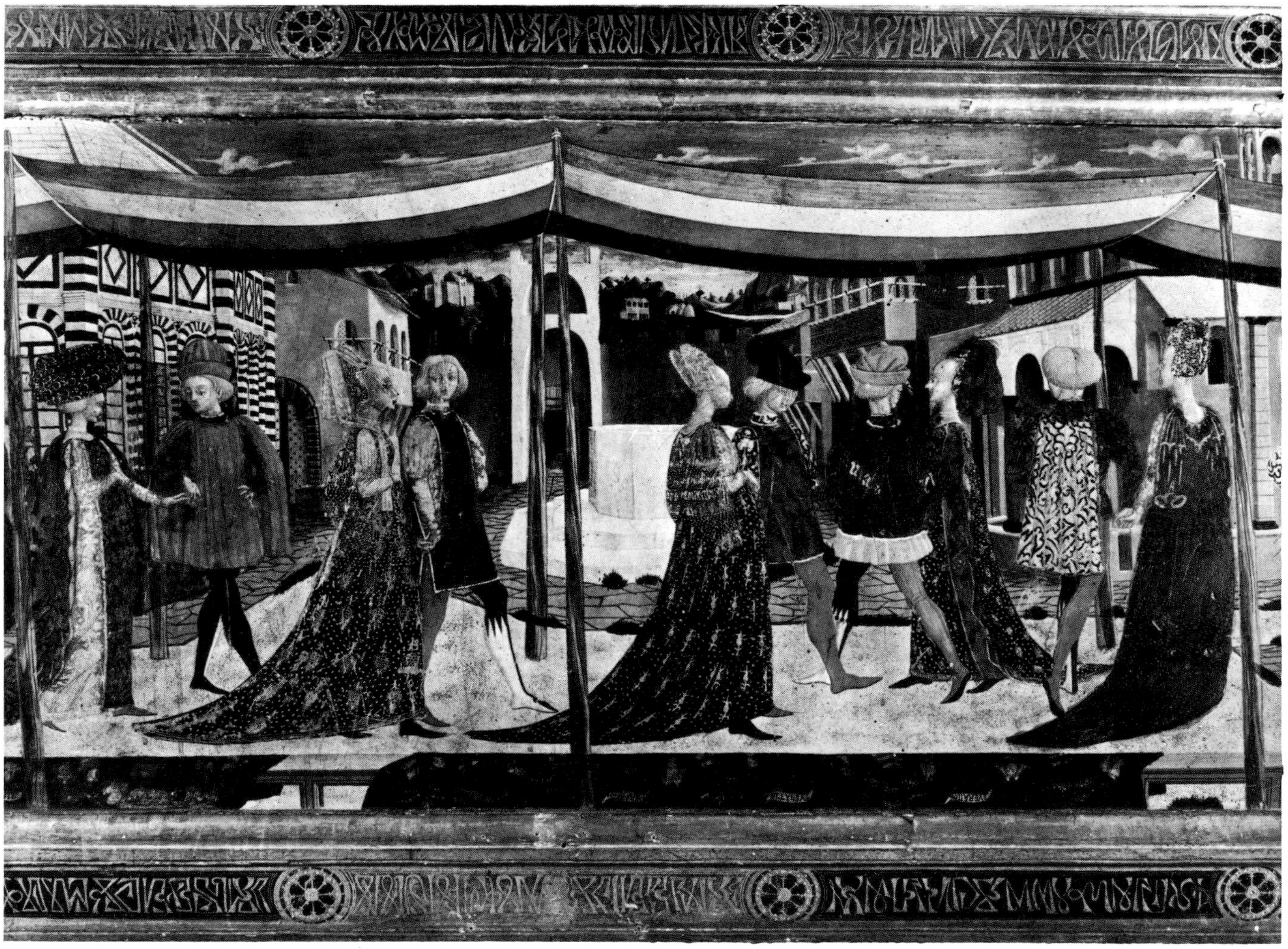

1153

1151.   Detail: Seven Liberal Arts. Panel. Barcelona, Museo d'Arte Cataluña, Cambò Bequest. Whole panel: 156 × 47. Fototeca Berenson.
1152.   Detail: Seven Liberal Arts. Panel. Barcelona, Museo d'Arte Cataluña, Cambò Bequest. Fototeca Berenson.
1153.   Dancing figures, detail of fig. 1150. Panel. Florence, Accademia. no. 8457. SGF 123306.

551

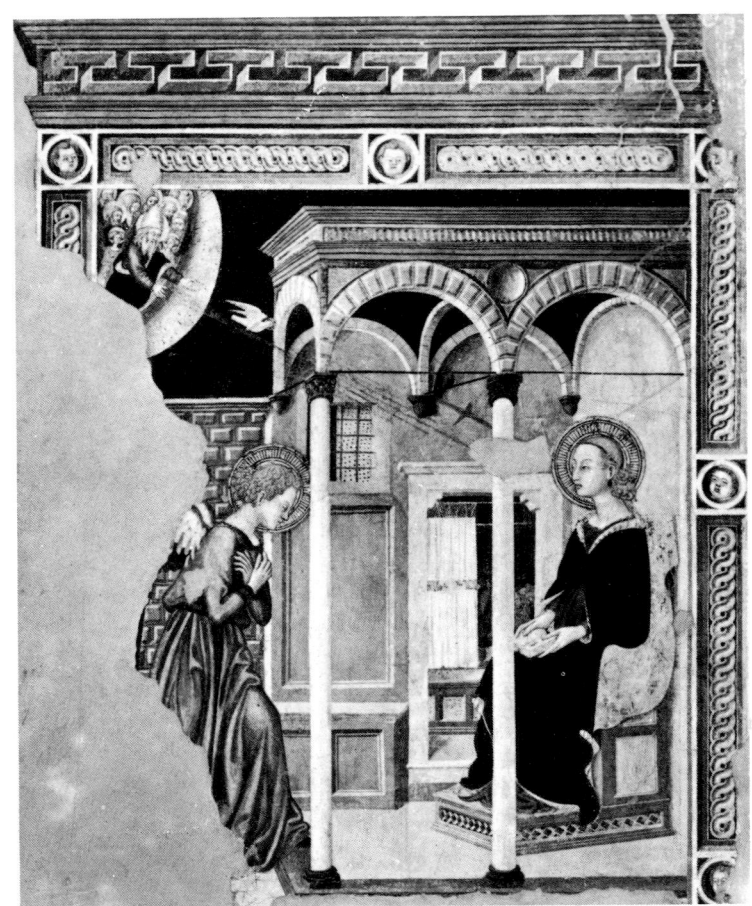

1154

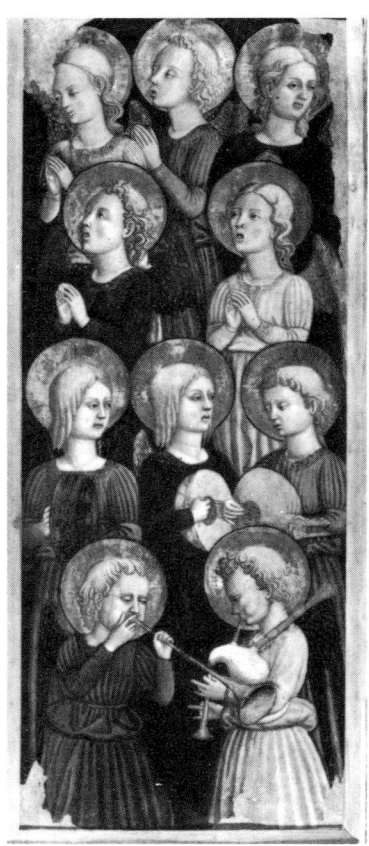

1155

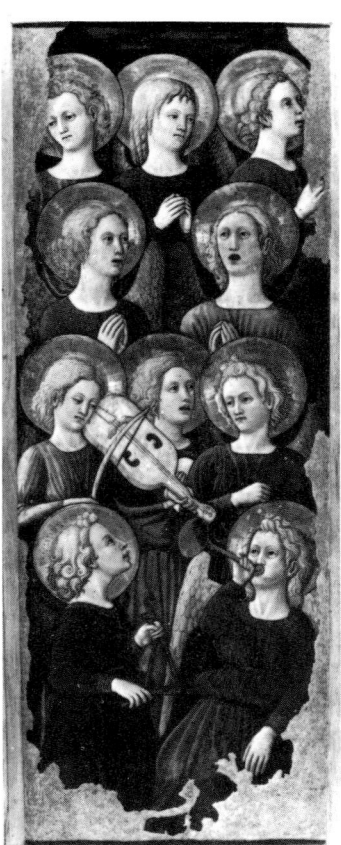

1156

1154. *Annunciation. Fresco. Castelfranco di Sopra, Badia a Soffena. SGF 133021.*
1155. *Choir of Angels. Panel. San Giovanni Valdarno, S. Maria delle Grazie. 154 × 57. SGF 95171.*
1156. *Choir of Angels. Panel. San Giovanni Valdarno, S. Maria delle Grazie. 154 × 57. SGF 95170.*

MARIOTTO di CRISTOFANO

Mariotto di Cristofano is mentioned as " Mariotus Cristofori pictor " in the [Aretine] *liber custodie* of 1413, together with his father. He is not to be found in any other [Aretine] document of the time.

from U. Pasqui in *Rivista d' Arte*, X, 1917-18, p. 70.

Mariotto di Cristofano, da Castel San Giovanni in Val d'Arno, born 1393, died 1457. Member of the Company of Saint Luke 1418. On April 26, 1454, Mariotto was commissioned to paint a banner " da Disciplinanti " for the church of St. Maria degli Angeli at San Gimignano, to contain a figure of Our Lady, for which he was to be paid 3 florins larghi.....

from D. E. Colnaghi, p. 172, *A Dictionary of Florentine Painters*, London, 1928.

The artistic stature which is behind these works is certainly not very high. Mariotto appears a painter of receptive rather than creative character; in his art are mirrored very different currents, making the outlines of his personality unclear. The influence of Beato Angelico was certainly decisive, and especially predominant in the scenes from the " Life of the Madonna ". There are also Masolinesque traces in his painting (the " Redentore " of San Miniato comes particularly to mind), and his style sometimes borders with the manner of the pictures by the so-called " Pseudo Ambrogio di Baldese ": all these contacts should be more carefully investigated. In the type of soldier who watches over the tomb, of the Resurrection, one can even seen northern influences perhaps stemming from the activity of Gentile da Fabriano in Florence. That there are various influences which come together in his painting is also clear from the number of names which have been put forward for the authorship of these pictures.....

from W. Cohn, pp. 64-8, *Bollettino d' Arte*, XLIII, IV, 1958.

S. Giovanni Valdarno 1393-Florence 1457. Brother-in-law of Masaccio, active in Florence from 1419. Influenced by Angelico and Paolo Schiavo.

from B. Berenson, p. 129, *Italian Pictures of the Renaissance, Florentine School*, Vol. I, London, 1963.

Later on Monna Jacopa [Masaccio's mother] took another husband, Tedesco del Maestro Feo, a druggist already sixty years old, who also came from Castel San Giovanni; he had been a widower twice and had two daughters; one of these, Caterina, was to marry another artist, Mariotto di Cristofano — he, too, from Castel San Giovanni (born in 1393) who in 1419 was already a known painter in Florence. The work and style of this almost-brother-in-law of Masaccio, who lived until 1457, has been identified (by W. Cohn), but he would not seem to have had any contact with Masaccio nor any influence upon Masaccio's work.

from L. Berti, p. 83, *L'Opera Completa di Masaccio*, Milan, 1968.

When Werner Cohn found in the Archivio di Stato of Florence a document making it possible for him to identify a few works by Mariotto di Cristofano — a painter until then quite unknown — he saw quite clearly that he had unearthed a very modest personality. " Mariotto appears a painter of receptive rather than creative character ", he wrote quite justifiably in his introductory article, while adding, " in his art are mirrored very different currents making the outline of his character unclear ". There is, however, an unusual neglected interest in the life of this modest artist: that concerning his contacts with Masaccio. We already knew — from Procacci's investigations — that one of the daughters of Masaccio's stepfather married a fellow-townsman, the very same Mariotto di Cristofano. Eight years older than Masaccio, his step-brother-in-law, Mariotto was already an established painter in Florence in 1419; there would have been nothing more natural, therefore, than that Masaccio, having about 1420, chosen to go to Florence, in order to begin his career as a painter, put himself in contact as soon as possible with his already established city connection.....

In order to understand more clearly the work of Mariotto di Cristofano during a period of exceptional importance to Florentine painting, it seems to me that there is an even better example than that at San Giovanni Valdarno which is so tied to an abstract idea; it is one that has never been published before, now in Rome in Palazzo Venezia. It is a Madonna & Child, adored by eight saints, which in spite of its obviously excellent quality, its lively figures and its dazzling colour, has until now, remained anonymous. It seems to me quite clear that this is one of the best pictures of the painter; although it is clearly not to be confronted with the work of Masaccio, it can easily be compared with that of Francesco d'Antonio, who after an initial Gothic period adapts his forms to the stylistic requirements of Florence in the third decade of the 15th century.....

from M. Boskovits, pp. 4, 6, *Arte Illustrata*, II, 13/14, 1969.

BIBLIOGRAPHY
BOOKS   *An asterisk indicates a work listed in the General Bibliography*

Ridolfi, E., *Le Gallerie Nazionali Italiane*, IV, 1899, pp. 172-3; *v. Marle 1927**, pp. 34, 66; *v. Marle 1928**, pp. 155-8; Procacci, U., *La Reale Galleria dell' Accademia di Firenze*, Florence, 1936, p. 34; Santi, F., p. 58, in *Scritti di Storia dell'Arte in Onore di Mario Salmi*, Vol. II, Rome, 1962; Middeldorf, U., p. 282, in *Scritti di Storia dell'Arte in Onore di Mario Salmi*, Vol. II, Rome, 1962; *Maetzke**, 1974, pp. 85-88.

JOURNALS

Salmi, M., *A*, XVI, 1913, p. 221; Pasqui, U., *RA*, X, 1917-18, p. 70; Procacci, U., *RA*, XVII, 1935, pp. 91-111; Collobi-Ragghianti, L., *CA*, VIII, 1950, p. 467; Procacci, U., *RA*, XXVIII, 1954, p. 32; Salmi, M., *C*, V, 1, 1954, p. 68; Cohn, W., *BA*, XLIII, 1, 1958, pp. 64-68; Berti, L., *C*, XII, 2, 1961, pp. 84-107; Bellosi, L., *PA*, XVIII, 203/23, 1967, p. 87; Boskovits, M., *AI*, II, 13/14, 1969, pp. 4-13.

There are no known signed and/or dated works by Mariotto di Cristofano.

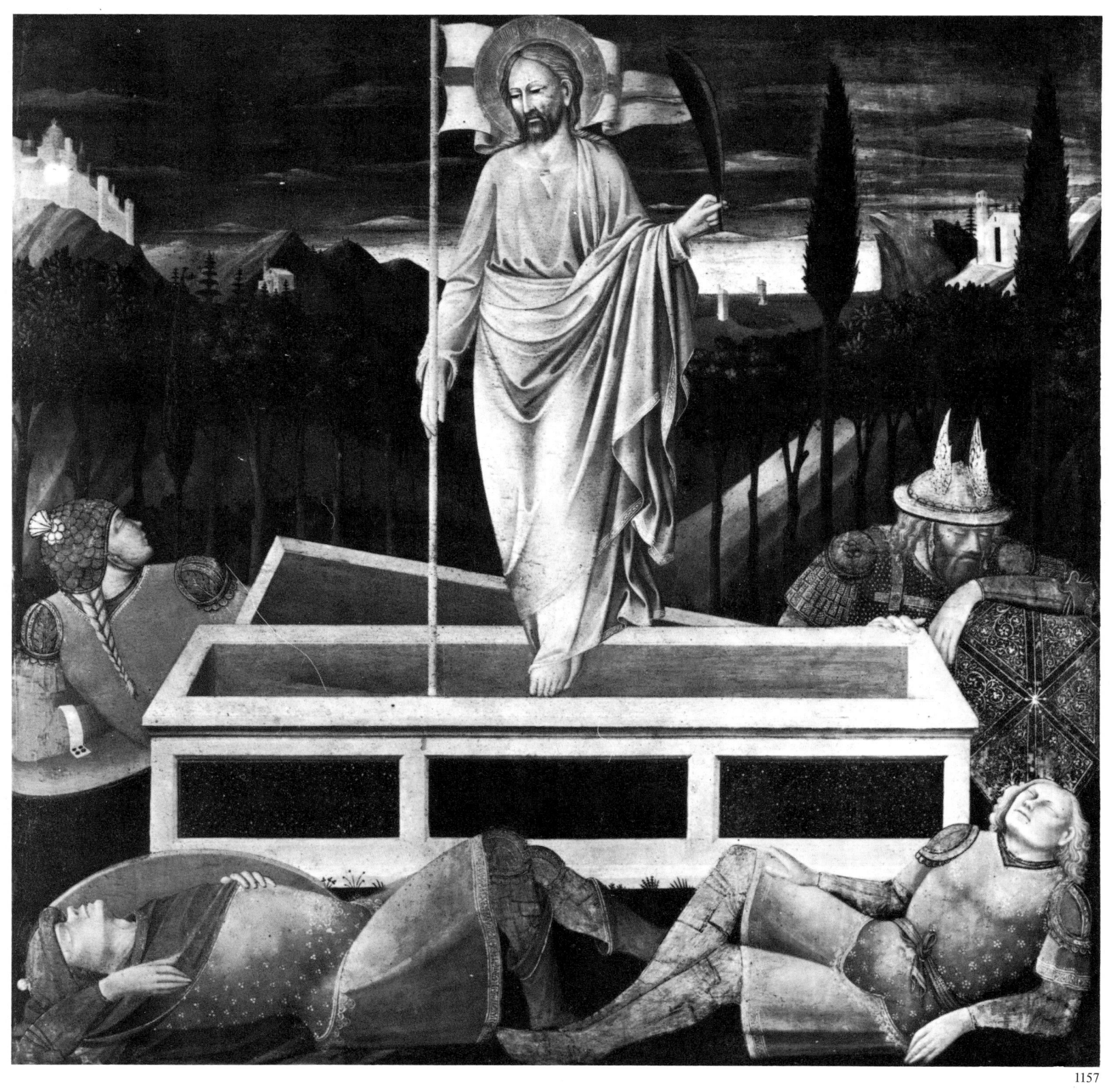

1157

1157. *Resurrection of Christ (verso of fig. 1158). Panel. Florence, Accademia. no. 3164. 160 × 159. SGF 117560. 1445-47.*

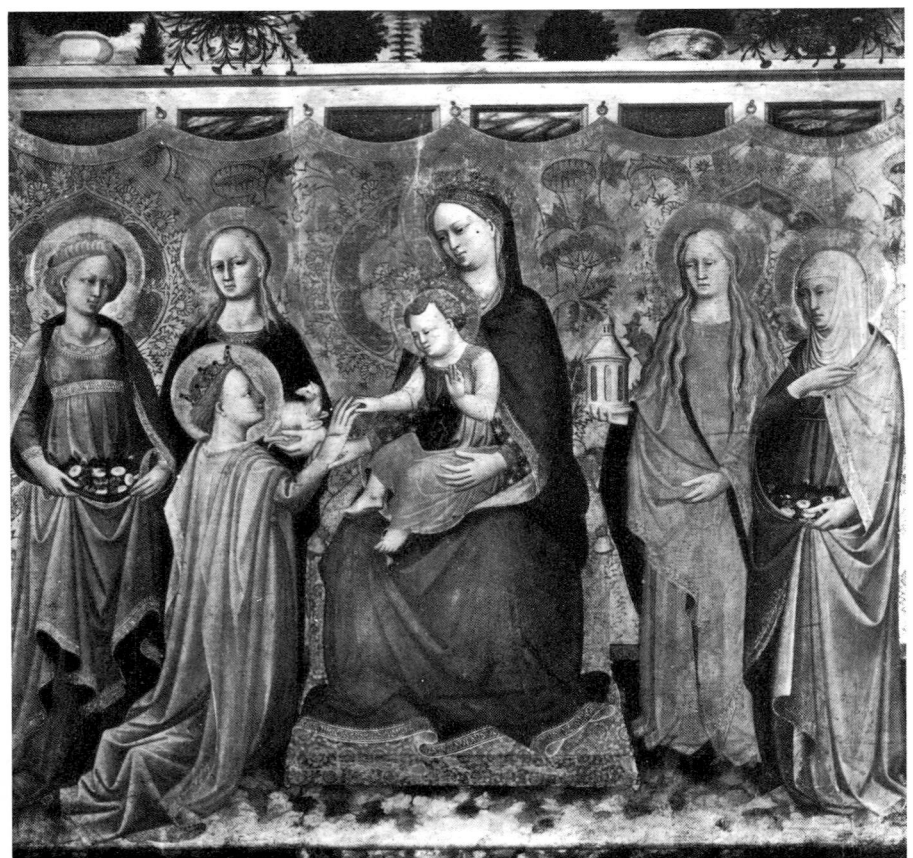

1158

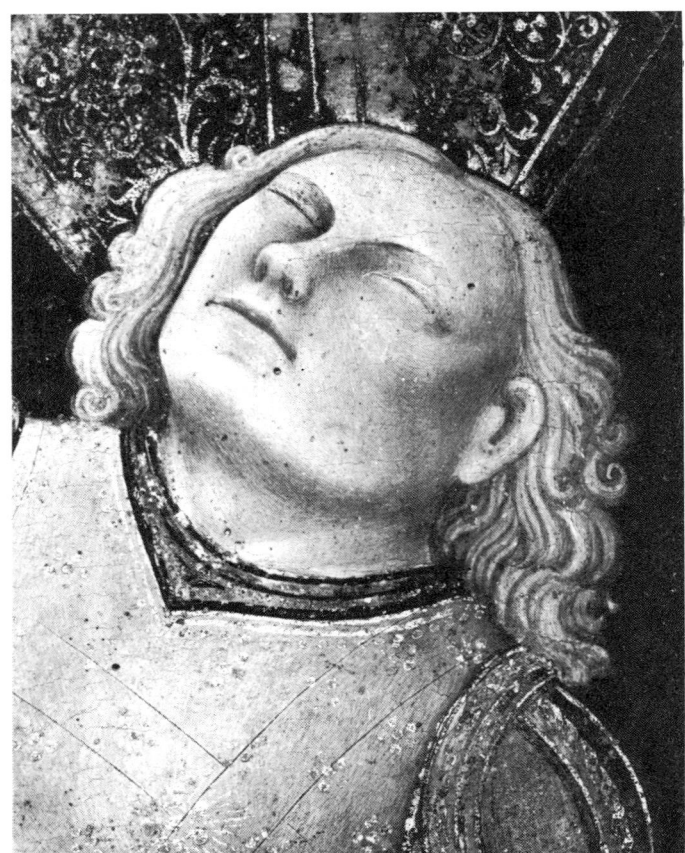

1159

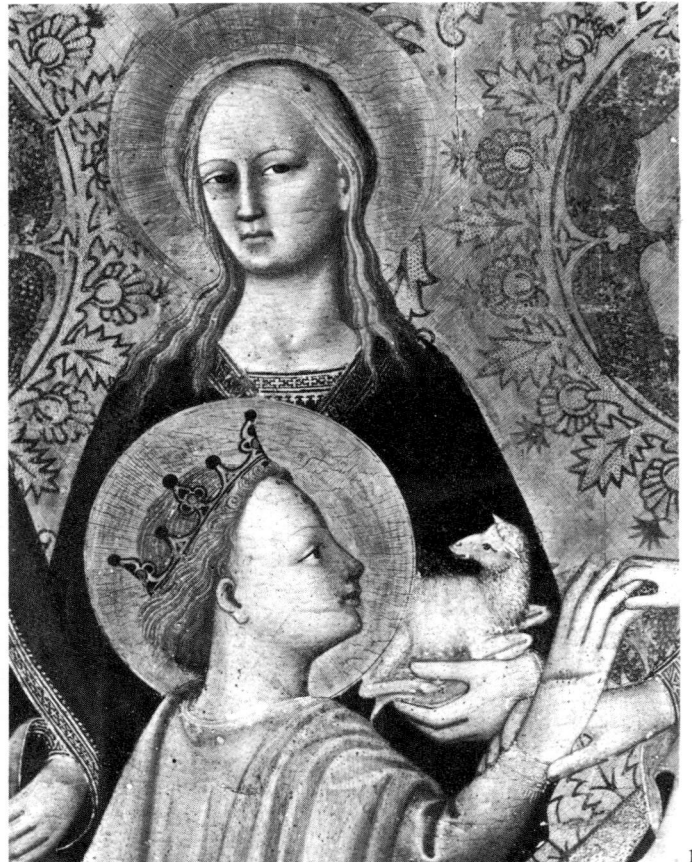

1160

1161

1158.   *Mystical Marriage of St Catherine with four female Saints (recto of fig. 1157). Panel. Florence, Accademia. no. 3162. 160 × 152. SGF 117561. 1445-47.*
1159.   *Head of sleeping Soldier, detail of fig. 1157., Panel. Florence, Accademia. no. 3164. Bertoni. 1445-47.*
1160.   *Sts Mary Magdalene and Elizabeth of Hungary, detail of fig. 1158. Panel. Florence, Accademia. no. 3162. Fototeca Berenson. 1445-47.*
1161.   *Heads of Sts Agnes and Catherine, detail of fig. 1158. Panel. Florence, Accademia. no. 3162. Bertoni. 1445-47.*

556

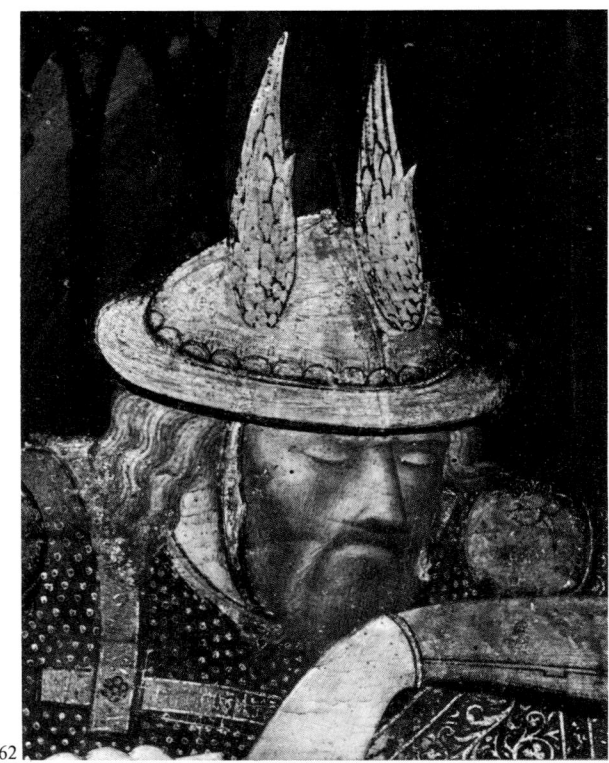

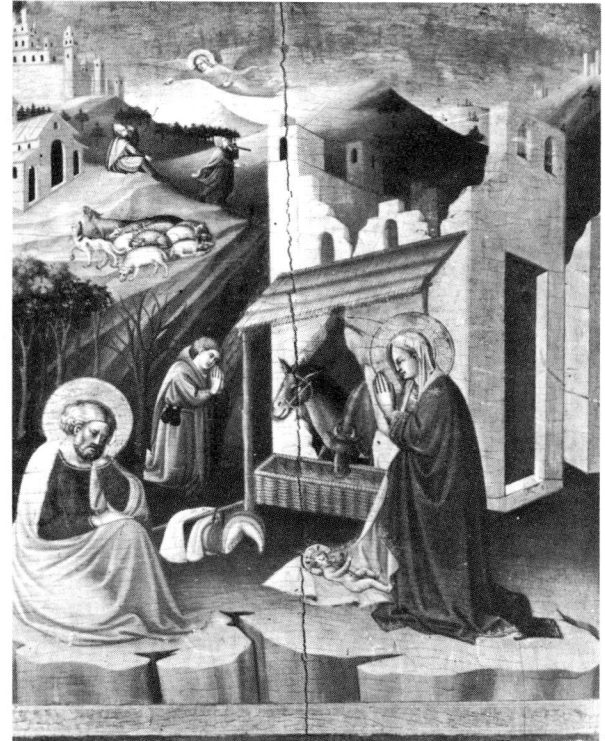

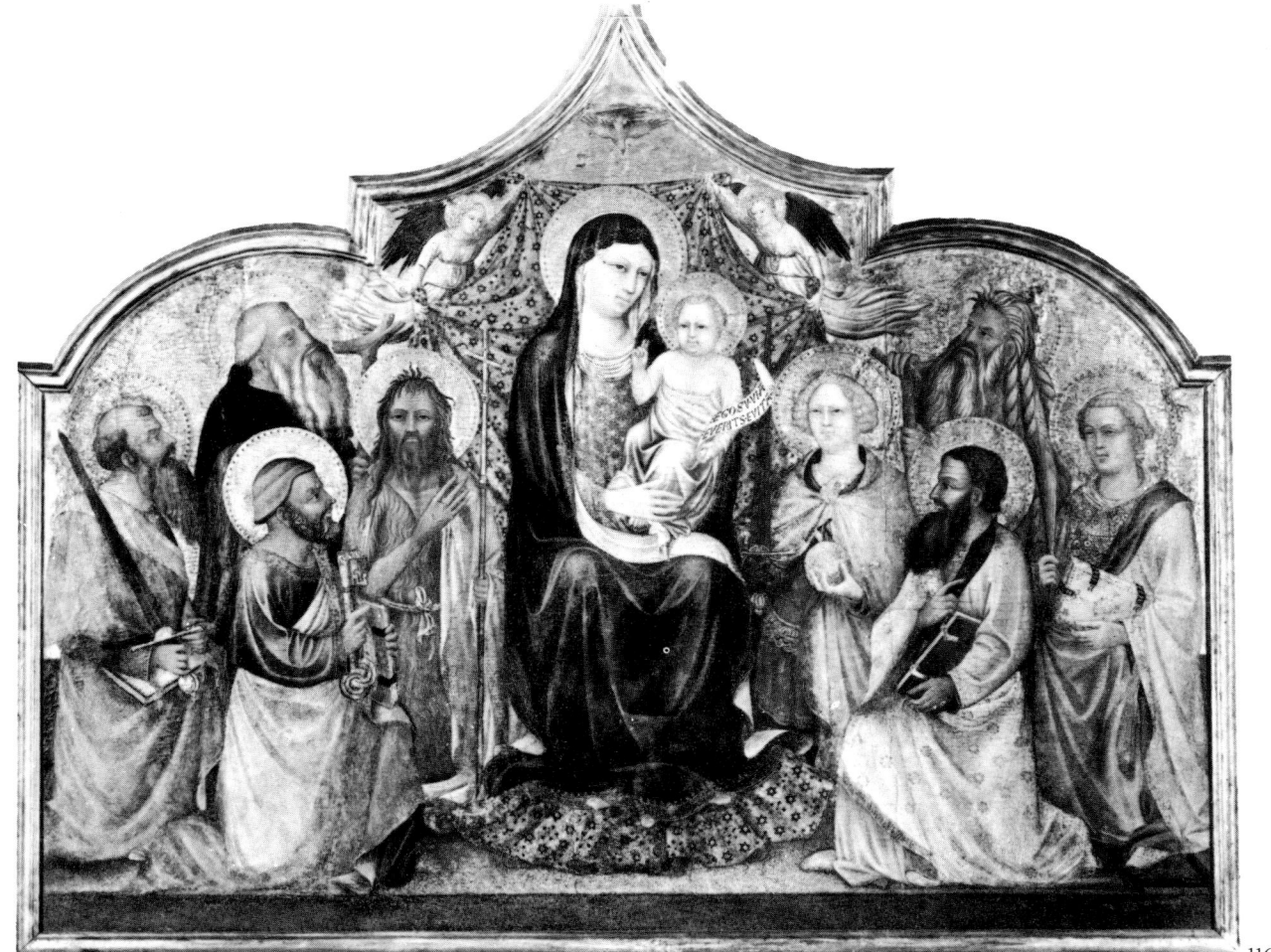

1162. *Head of sleeping Soldier, detail of fig. 1157. Panel. Florence, Accademia. no. 3164. Bertoni. 1445-47.*
1163. *Nativity, detail of fig. 1165. Panel. Florence, Accademia. no. 8508. Bertoni.*
1164. *Madonna and Child Enthroned with eight male Saints and two Angels. Panel. Rome, Museo di Palazzo Venezia. no. P.V. 10227. 132 × 169.*
GFN E26511.

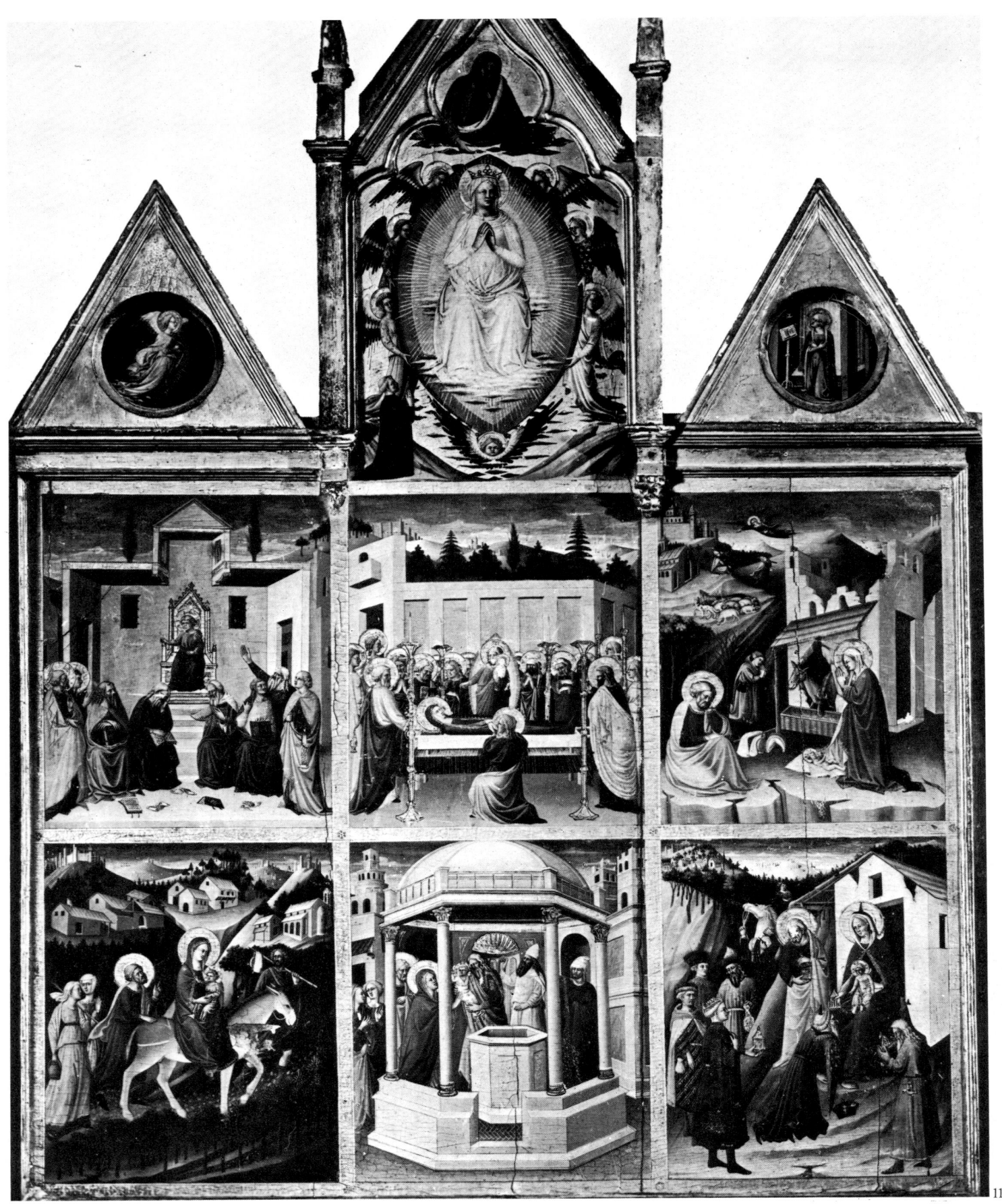

1165. *Polyptych: The Seven Joys of Mary: Christ among the Doctors; Dormition of the Virgin; Nativity; Flight into Egypt; Presentation in the Temple; Adoration of the Magi. Above: Assumption with Donor; Annunciation. Panel. Florence, Accademia. no. 8508. 253 × 192. Alinari 1572.*

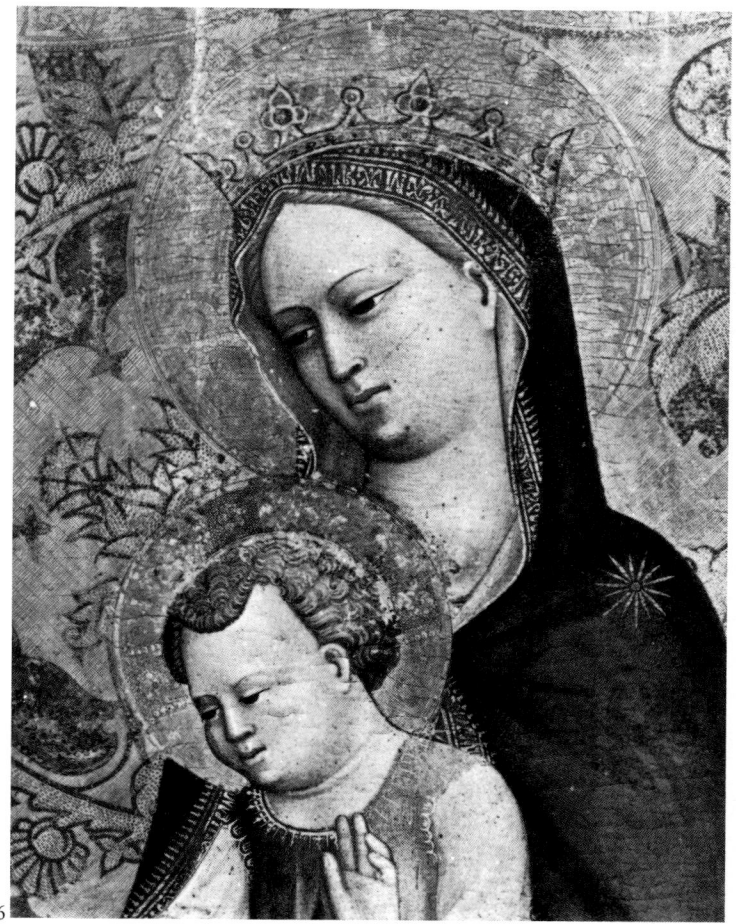

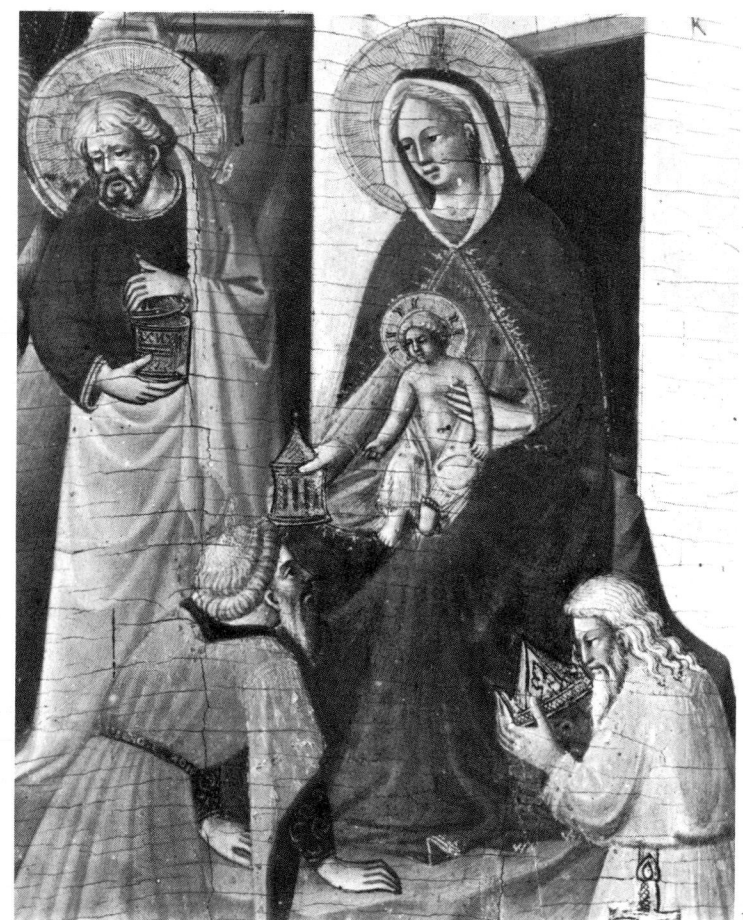

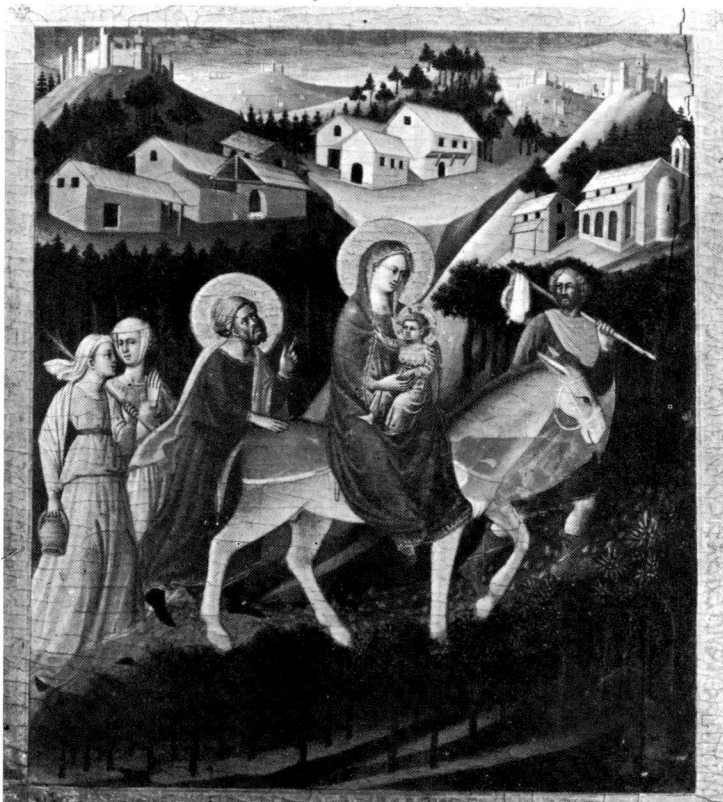

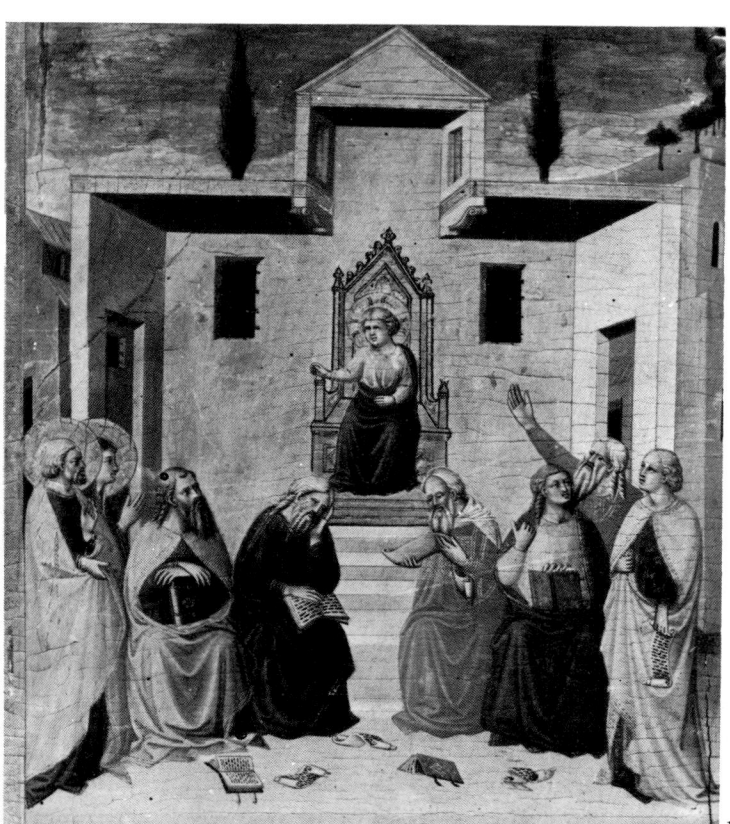

1166. *Madonna and Child, detail of fig. 1158. Panel. Florence, Accademia. no. 3162. Bertoni. 1445-47.*
1167. *Adoration of the Magi, detail of fig. 1165. Panel. Florence, Accademia. no. 8508. Bertoni.*
1168. *Flight into Egypt, detail of fig. 1165. Panel. Florence, Accademia. no. 8508. Bertoni.*
1169. *Christ among the Doctors, detail of fig. 1165. Panel. Florence, Accademia. no. 8508. Bertoni.*

559

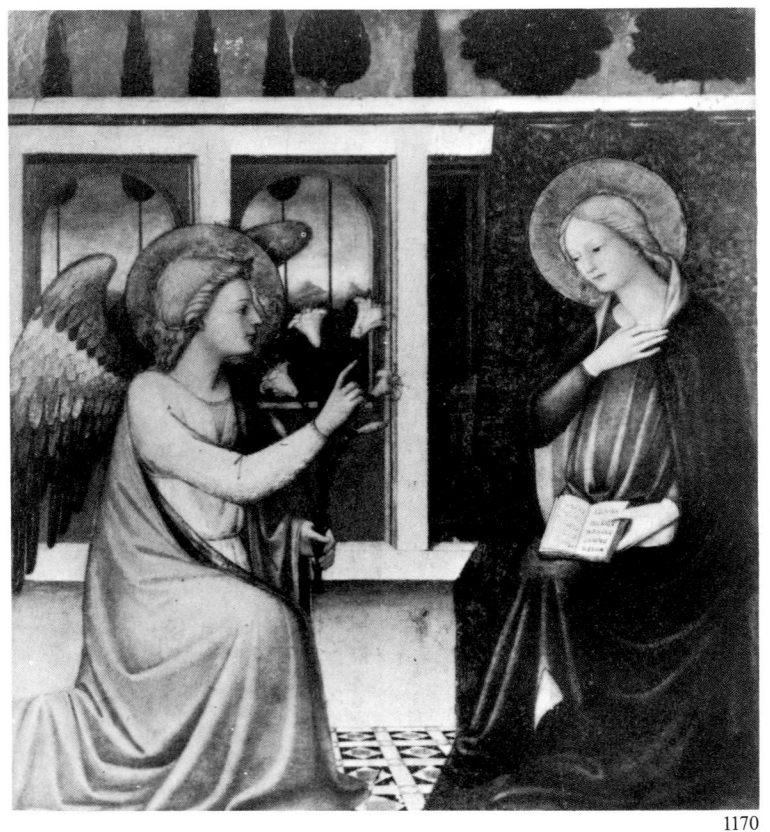

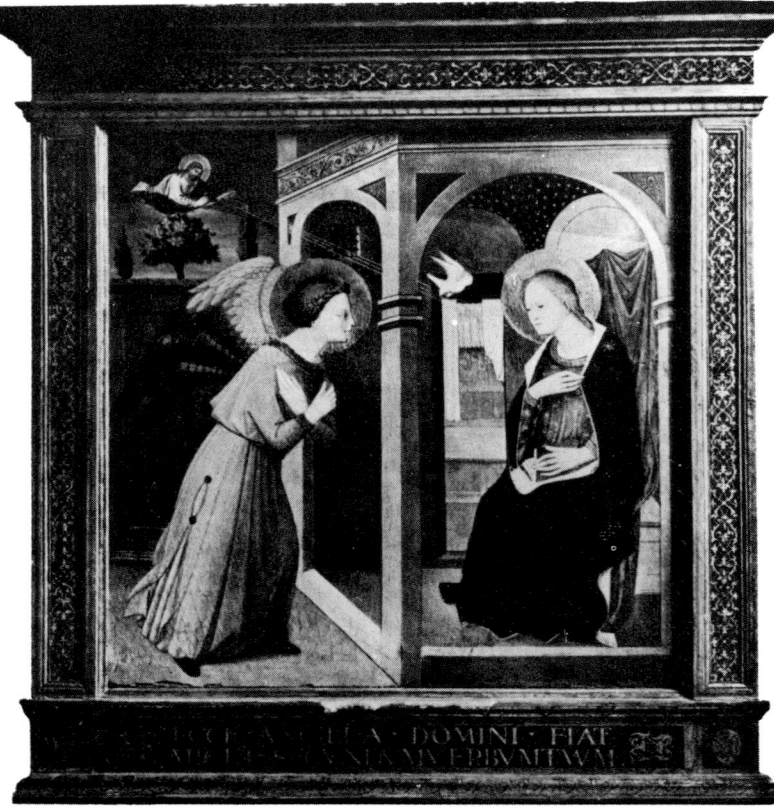

1170

1171

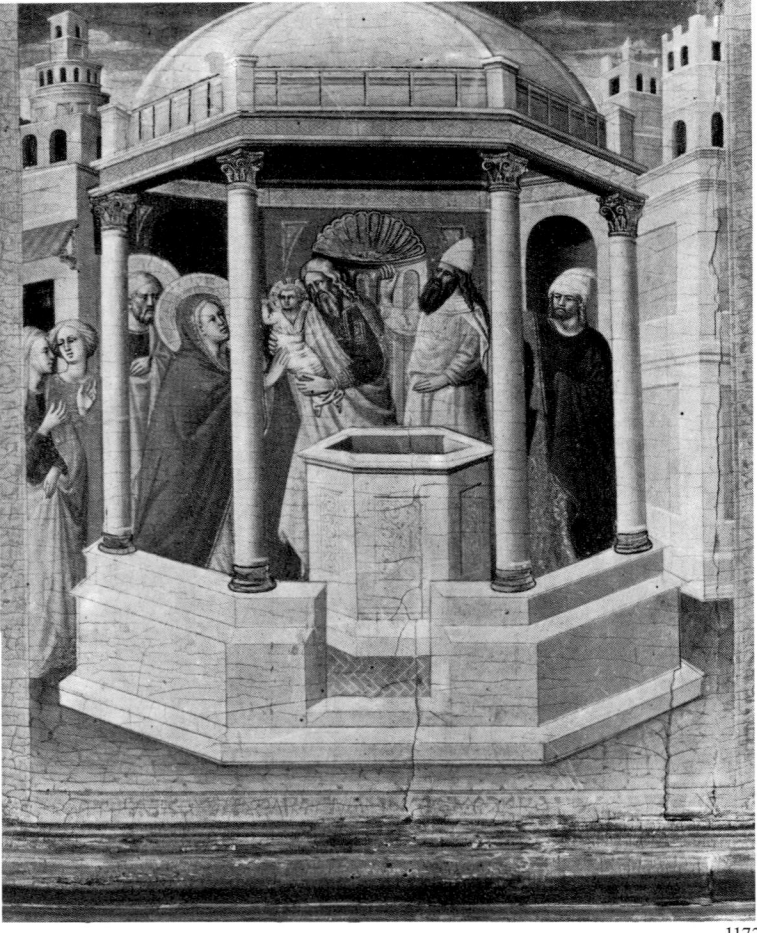

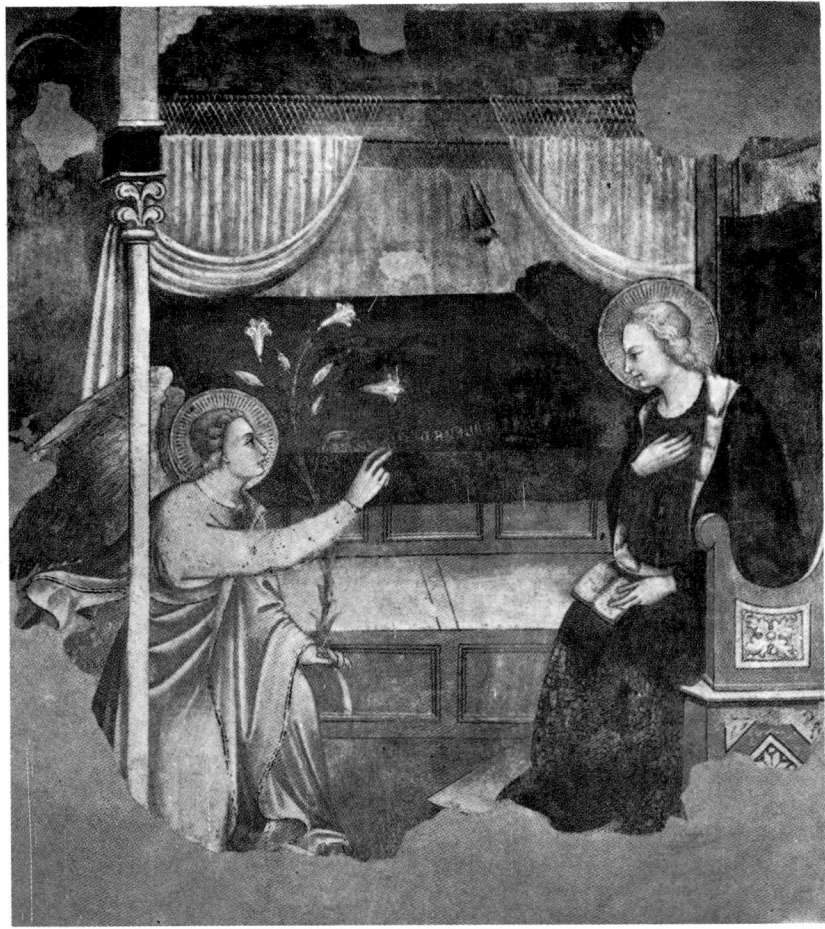

1172

1173

1170. *Annunciation. Panel. Whereabouts unknown. Fototeca Berenson.*
1171. *Annunciation. Panel. Whereabouts unknown, formerly, Amsterdam, Lanz Collection. Fototeca Berenson.*
1172. *Presentation in the Temple, detail of fig. 1165. Panel. Florence, Accademia. no. 8508. Bertoni.*
1173. *Annunciation. Fresco. Cascia (near Reggello, upper Valdarno), Parrochiale. Author's photo.*

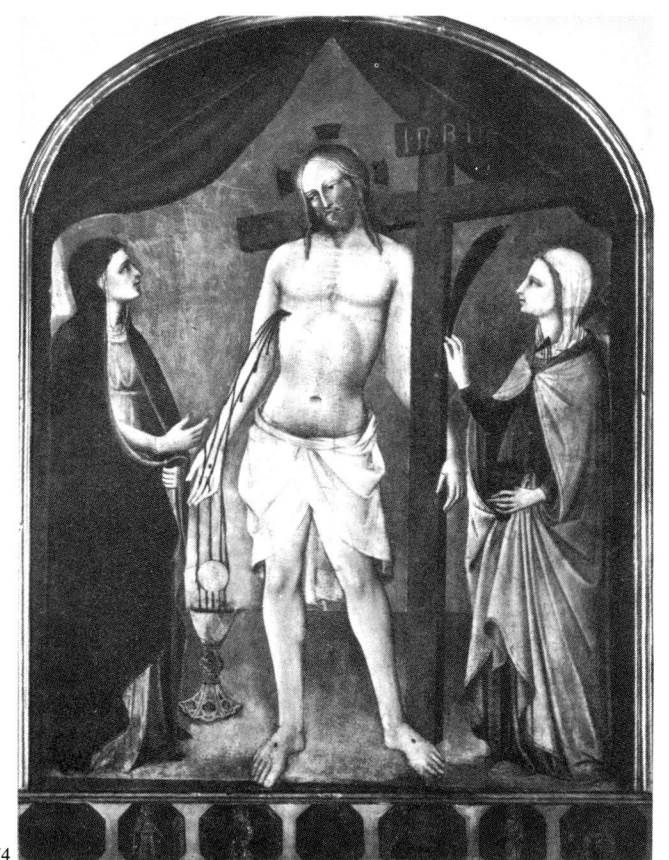

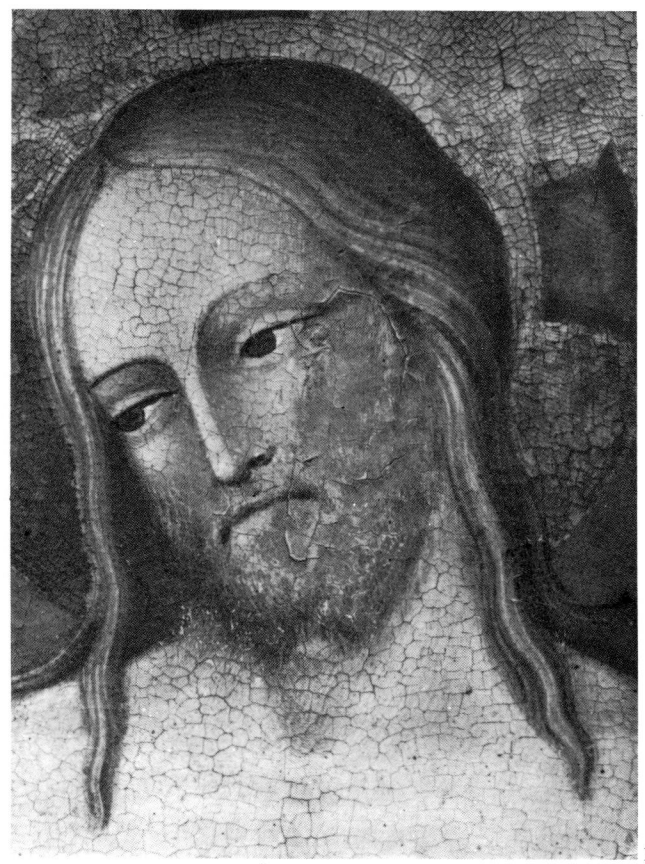

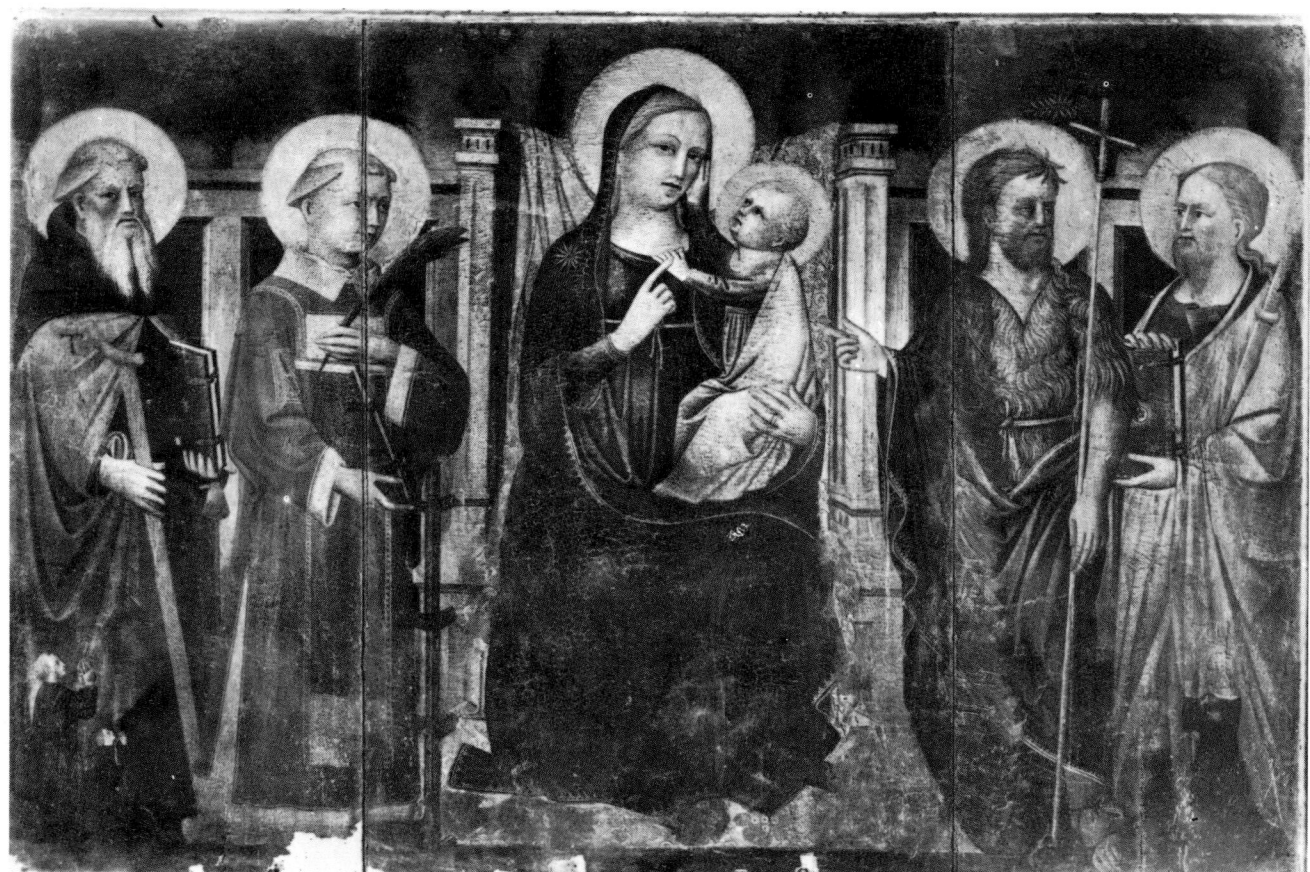

1174. *Christ with the Cross and two Saints. Panel. San Giovanni Valdarno, S. Maria delle Grazie. 194 × 143. Alinari 8917.*
1175. *Head of Christ, detail of fig. 1174. Panel. San Giovanni Valdarno, S. Maria delle Grazie. SGF 66370.*
1176. *Polyptych: Madonna and Child with Sts Anthony Abbot, Lawrence, John the Baptist and John the Evangelist, and four Donors. Panel. San Giovanni Valdarno, S. Maria delle Grazie. 117 × 167. Alinari 8915.*

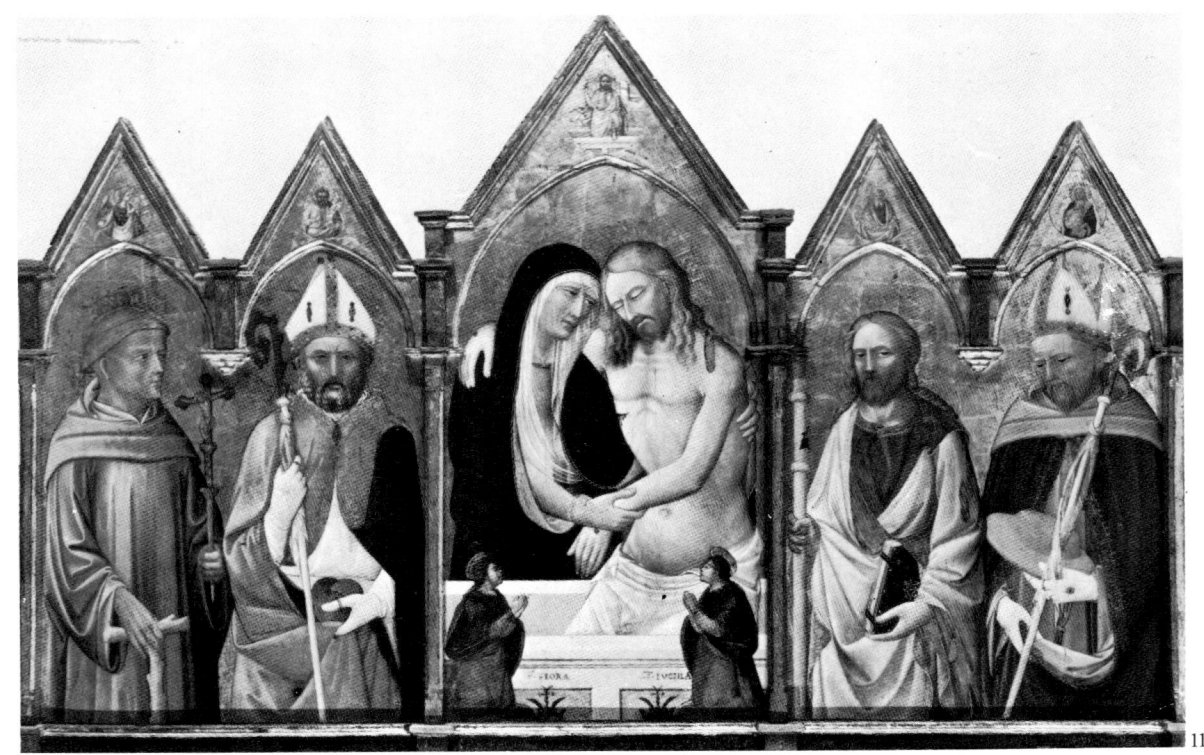

1177

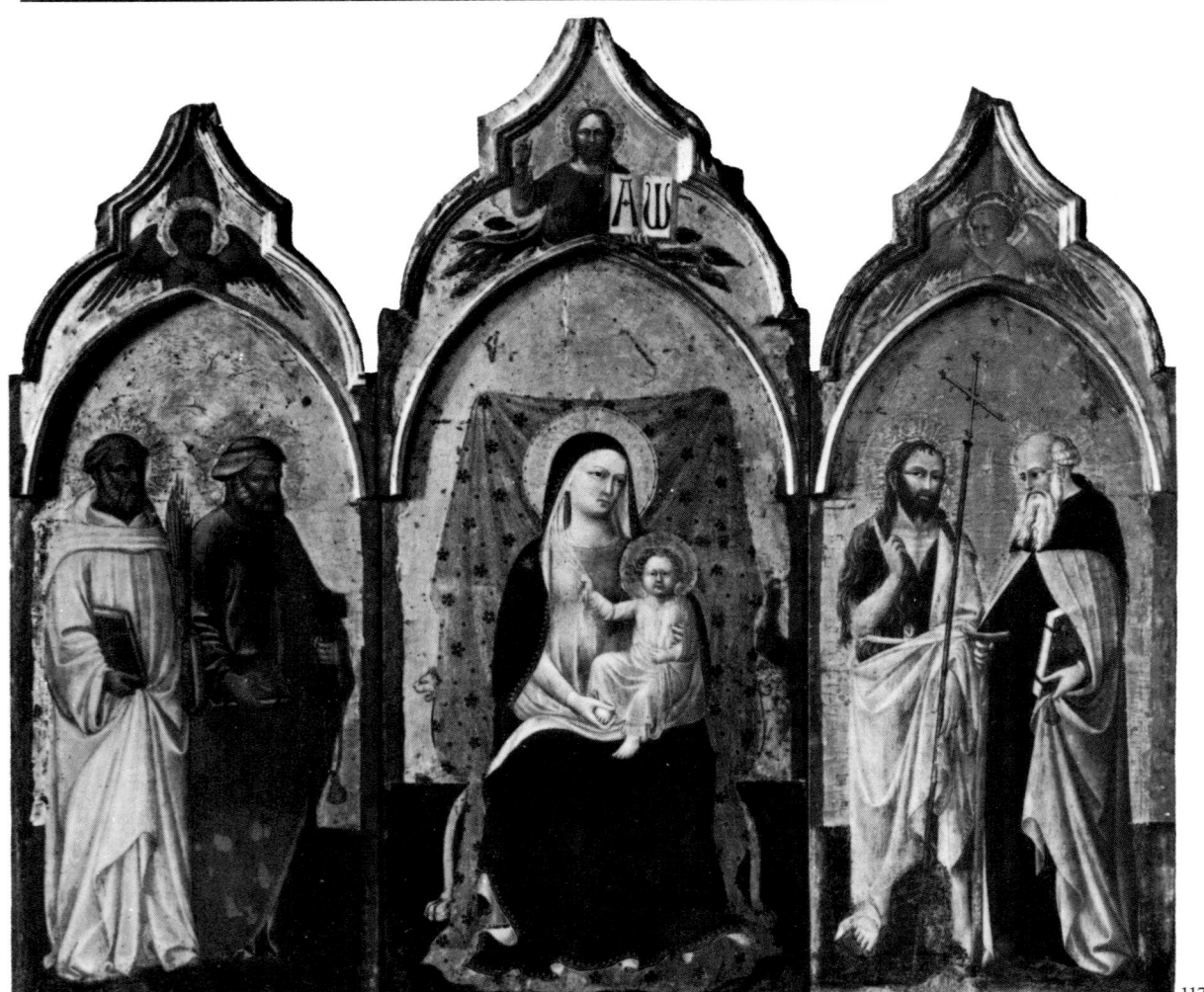

1178

1177. Triptych: Pietà with Sts Florahand Lucilla, Anthony Abbot, Nicholas of Bari, John the Evangelist and Jerome. Panel. Carda (south of Bibbiena, Pratomagno), Parrocchiale. 128 × 194. SGA.

1178. Triptych: Madonna and Child Enthroned with four male Saints. Panel. Whereabouts unknown, formerly Preci (near Norcia, Umbria), S. Maria. Foto Fiorucci.

APPENDICES

APPENDIX A

An asterisk indicates a work listed in the General Bibliography

Some painters who worked in or near Florence immediately before and after the period of this compendium. Also, many painters who are either almost completely unknown, or too well-known to have been included in the main section of the book, who worked in and near Florence *during* the period of this compendium.

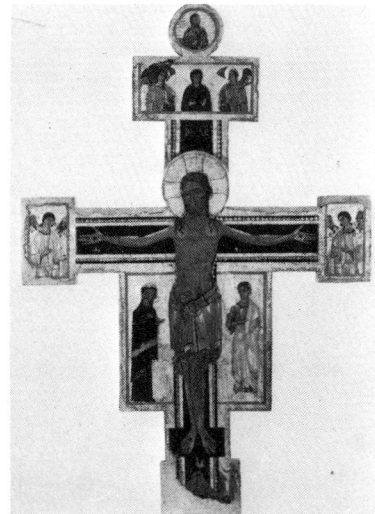

Master of the Bigallo
Florentine of the first half of the 13th century, whose name is based on a crucifix in the Museo del Bigallo, Florence.
See *M. Giottesca**, 1943, pp. 166-173.

1179 Master of the Bigallo. Painted Crucifix. Panel. Florence, Museo del Bigallo. 179 × 121. SGF 94622.

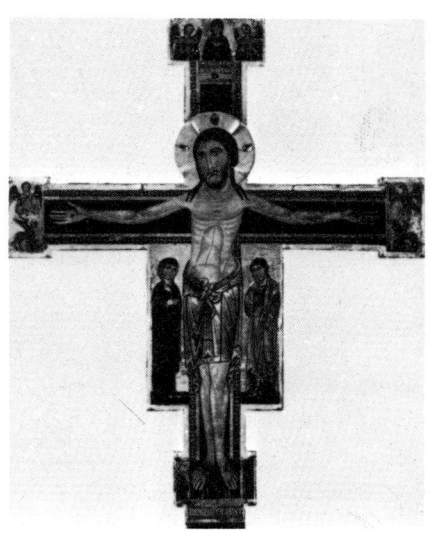

Berlinghiero
Lucchese of the first half of the 13th century.
See Zeri, F. and Gardner, E. E., in *MMOA**, 1971, pp. 1-2.

1180 Berlinghiero. Painted Crucifix. Panel. Lucca, Museo Nazionale di Villa Guinigi. SGF 26702. s.

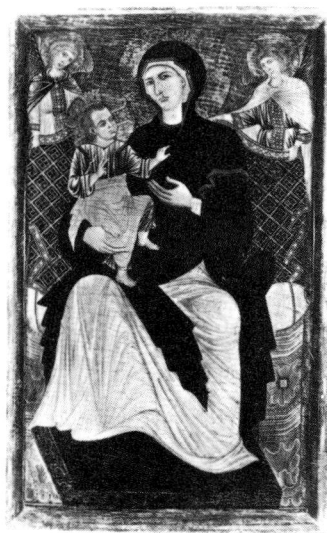

Master of S. Martino
Thirteenth century Pisan named for a panel now in the Museo Nazionale di S. Matteo, Pisa.
See Longhi, R., *Prop*, II, 1948, p. 15, pls. 11-18.

1181 Master of S. Martino. Madonna and Child with two Angels. Panel. Florence, Acton Collection. no. 10.
65 × 105. Reali.

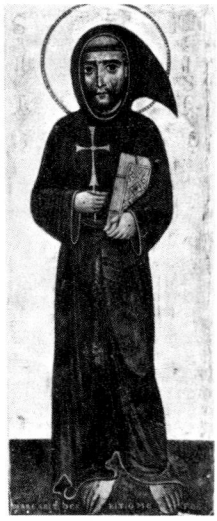

Margarito d' Arezzo
Aretine, working in the mid-thirteenth century.
See *Maetzke**, 1974, pp. 15-31.

1182   Margarito d'Arezzo. St Francis. Panel. Montepulciano, Museo Civico. Alinari 55144. s.

Lapo da Firenze
Perhaps actually Pistoiese, of the mid-thirteenth century.
See *Fresco Show**, 1969 (Eng. ed.), p. 50.

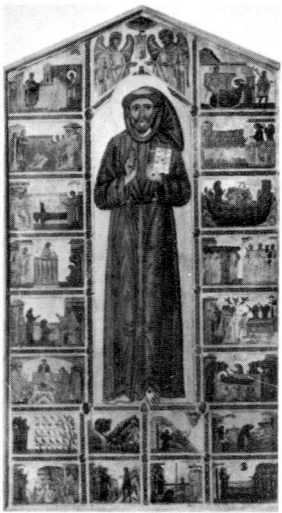

Master of Vico l' Abate
Mid-thirteenth century painter named for an altar-frontal in the church of S. Angelo, Vico l'Abate.
See Offner, R., *BM*, LXIII, 2, 1933, p. 79 and pl. IIB.

1183   Master of Vico l'Abate. St Francis and Scenes from his Life. Panel. Florence, S. Croce, Cappella Bardi.
         SGF 26784.

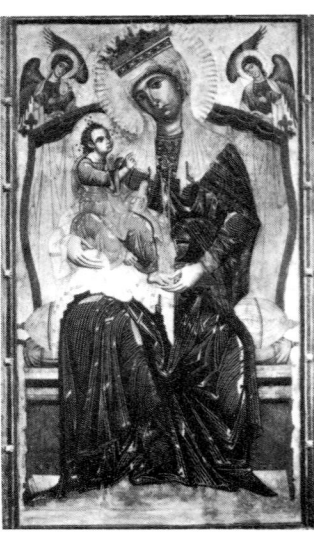

Coppo di Marcovaldo
Florentine, also working in Siena, active 1250-1276.
See *M. Giottesca**, 1943, pp. 184-197.

1184   Coppo di Marcovaldo. Madonna and Child with two Angels. Panel. Orvieto, Chiesa dei Servi. SGF 26790.

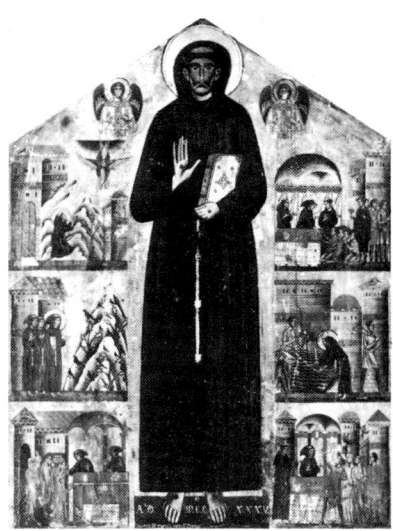

Bonaventura Berlinghieri
Son of Berlinghiero, active in the second and third quarters of the thirteenth century.
See *M. Giottesca**, 1943, pp. 14-27.

1185   Bonaventura Berlinghieri. St Francis and Scenes from his Life. Panel. Pescia, S. Francesco. 160 × 126. SGF 14855. s & d. 1235.

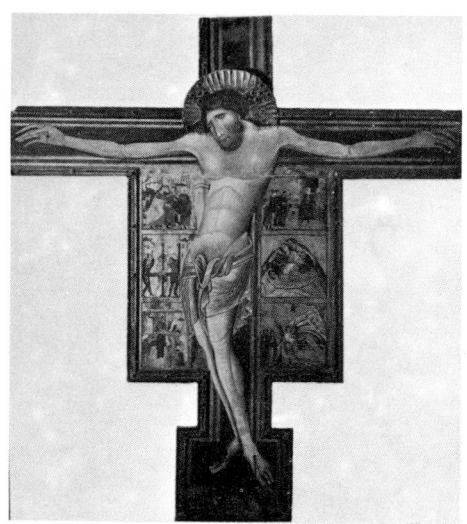

Salerno di Coppo
Son of Coppo di Marcovaldo, active during the second half of the thirteenth century.
See *M. Giottesca**, 1943, pp. 198-201.

1186   Salerno di Coppo (and Coppo di Marcovaldo). Painted Crucifix. Panel. Pistoia, Duomo. Alinari 43437.

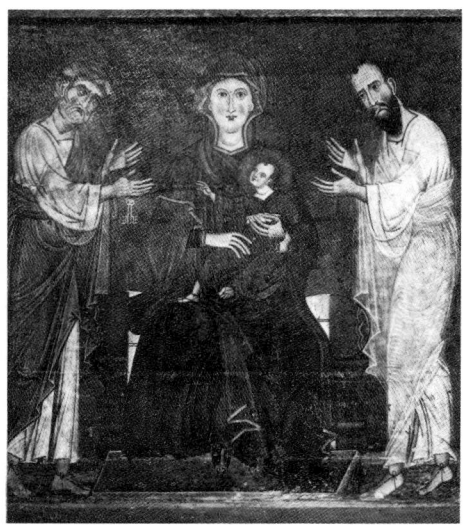

Master of Panzano
Painter of a davanzale in S. Leolino, Panzano, active in the second half of the thirteenth century. It has been suggested that he may be Meliore Toscano. He should not be confused with the Sienese painter of the mid-fourteenth century, with the same designation.
See *M. Giottesca**, 1943, pp. 212-5.

1187   Master of Panzano. Detail of a dossale: Madonna and Child Enthroned with Sts Peter and Paul. Panel. Panzano (35 kms south of Florence), S. Leolino.   Alinari 44383.

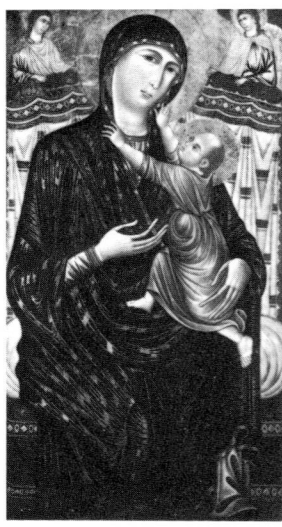

Master of S. Remigio
Near to the Master of Mosciano and named for a painting from this church in Florence. Active in the second half of the thirteenth century. Not to be confused with the painter of the fourteenth century *Pietà* now in the Uffizi.
See Toesca, P., *Storia dell' Arte Italiana*, I, III, 1927, Turin, p. 1041, no. 48.

1188   Master of S. Remigio. Madonna and Child. Panel. Florence, S. Remigio. SGF 24660.

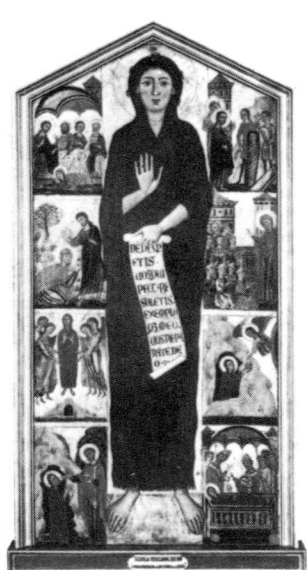

Master of the Maddalena
Florentine, active in the second half of the thirteenth century.
See *Maetzke**, 1974, pp. 31-34.

1189   Master of the Maddalena. St Mary Magdalene and Scenes from her Life. Panel. Florence, Accademia.
       no. 8466. SGF 26816.

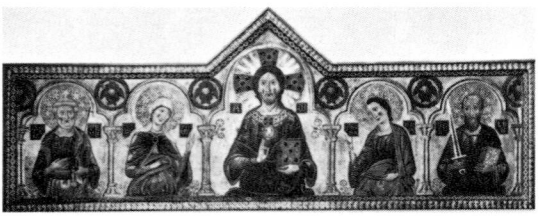

Meliore Toscano
Active during the second half of the thirteenth century; it has been suggested that his name was Megliore di Jacopo.
See *M. Giottesca**, 1943, pp. 216-218.

1190   Meliore Toscano. Dossale: Christ the Redeemer and four Saints. Panel. Florence, Accademia. Alinari
       44395.

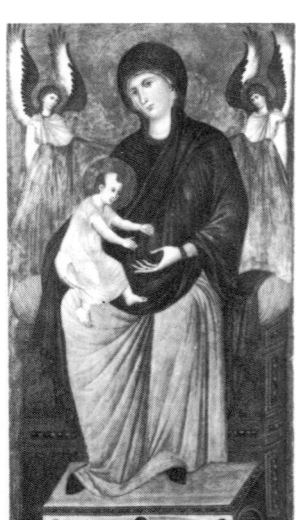

Master of Mosciano
Named for a Madonna & Child Enthroned in S. Andrea di Mosciano, near Scandicci, outside Florence; active in the late thirteenth century.
See Perkins, F. M., *RA*, XVI, 1961, p. 121.

1191   Master of Mosciano. Madonna and Child Enthroned with two Angels. Panel. Mosciano, S. Andrea. SGF
       193106.

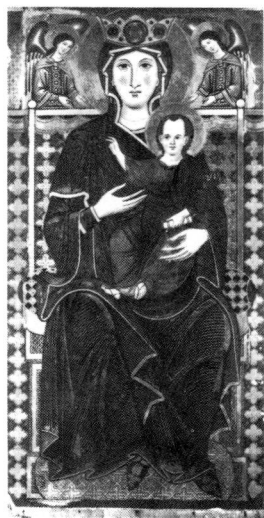

Master of Bagnano
Florentine, active in the last quarter of the thirteenth century, and named for a picture in S. Maria a Bagnano.
See Baldini, U., in *VII Mostra di Opere d'Arte Restaurate*, Florence, 1953, p. 14.

1192   Master of Bagnano. Madonna and Child Enthroned with two Angels. Panel. Certaldo, S. Maria a Bagnano.
SGF 24618.

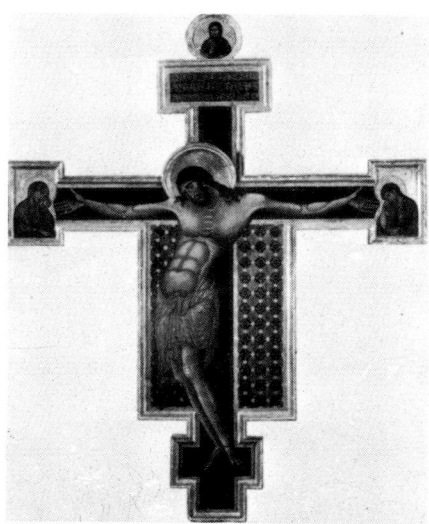

Cimabue
Named Cenni di Pepi, he worked in Rome at the end of the thirteenth century and in Pisa in the early part of the next century.
See Battisti, E., *Cimabue*, Milan, 1963.

1193   Cimabue. Painted Crucifix. Panel. Arezzo, S. Domenico. SGF 26832.

Andrea Tafi
He was a mosaicist, friend to Cimabue, who worked on the ceiling of the Florentine Baptistery.
See Mather, F. J., Jr., *The Isaac Master*, Princeton, 1932, pp. 78-81.

Jacopo Torriti
May have worked in Assisi with Cimabue.
See Hueck, I., *MKIF*, XIII, 1-4, 1967-8, pp. 1-30.

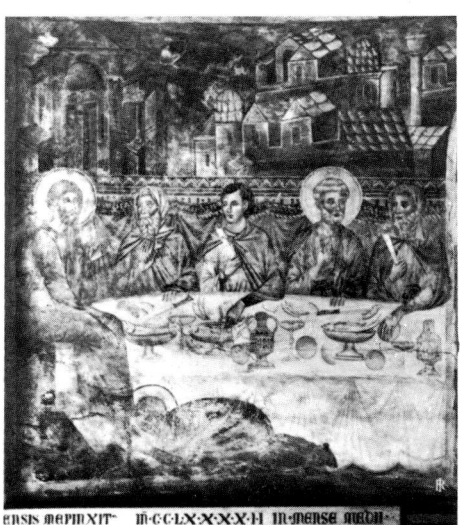

Manfredino da Pistoia
Pupil and close follower of Cimabue, active at the end of the thirteenth century.
See Longhi, R., *Prop*, II, 1948, p. 19, pl. 38b.

1194   Manfredino da Pistoia. Last Supper. Panel. Genoa, Accademia delle Belle Arti. 229 × 202. SGF 86596.
d. 1292.

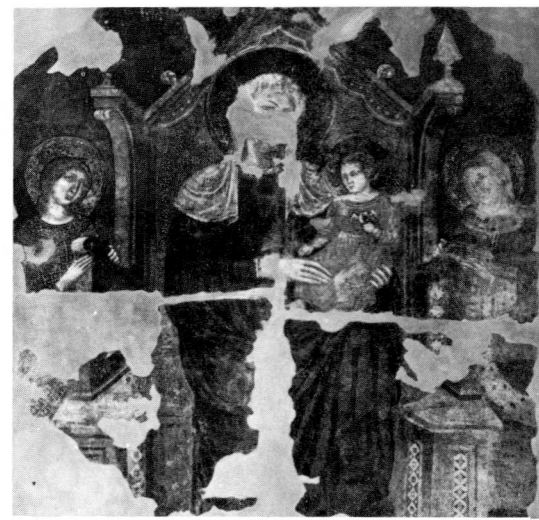

Maestro della Cappella dei Velluti
Florentine, at the end of the thirteenth century, named for a chapel in S. Croce.
See Volpe, C., *PA*, XIV, 157, 1963, pp. 3-14.

1195   Maestro della Cappella dei Velluti. Madonna & Child Enthroned with two Angels. Fresco. Florence, Museo di S. Croce.   SGF 105656.

Corso di Buono
Pupil of Cimabue.
See Longhi, R., *Prop*, II, 1948, p. 19.

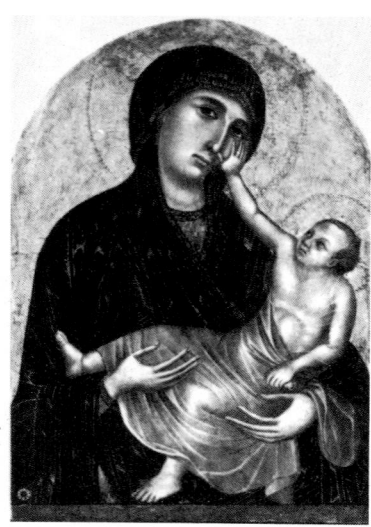

Master of Castelfiorentino
Florentine of the late thirteenth century, near to Cimabue.
See Procacci, U., *RA*, XIV, 1932, p. 463.

1196   Master of Castelfiorentino. Madonna and Child. Panel. Castelfiorentino (Val d'Elsa, south of Empoli), S. Verdiana, Pinacoteca. Anderson 40715.

Cavallini
Active in Rome and Naples from about 1270 to 1320.
See Sindona, E., *Pietro Cavallini*, Milan, 1958.

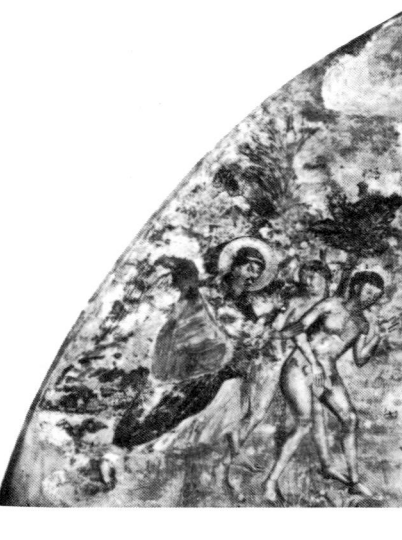

1197   Cavallini (?). Expulsion from Paradise. Fresco. Assisi, Convento di S. Francesco, Upper Church. SGF 86580.

Deodato Orlandi
Lucchese, active in the late thirteenth and early fourteenth centuries, influenced by Cimabue.
See Longhi, R., *Prop*, II, 1948, pp. 31-32.

Master of S. Chiara
A painter working in the last quarter of the 13th century.
See Gregori, M., Longhi, R., *PA*, XXIV, 281/3, 1973, p. 12.

Gaddo Gaddi
A contemporary and associate of Giotto, the father of Taddeo Gaddi; it has been suggested that he is the "Isaac Master".
See Mather, F. J., Jr., *The Isaac Master*, Princeton, 1932; Mather, R. G., *A.*, XXXIX, 7, 1936, pp. 50-64.

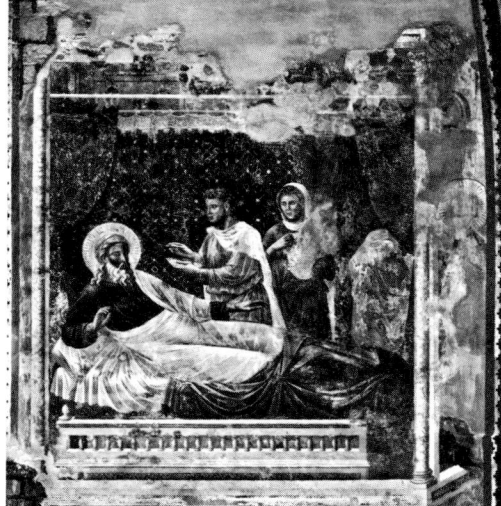

Isaac Master
Active during the last decade of the thirteenth century, he worked in the Upper Church at Assisi and has been tentatively identified as the young Giotto.
See Salmi, M., *RA*, XIX, 200, 1937, pp. 193-200. See also Gaddo Gaddi.

1198   Isaac Master. Esau carries the bowl of lentils to his father. Fresco. Assisi, Convento di S. Francesco, Upper Church. Alinari 5246.

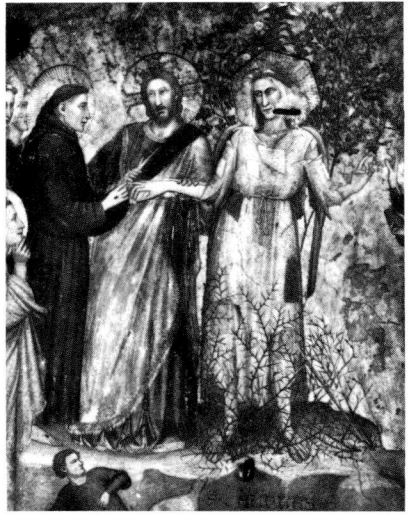

Maestro delle Vele
Named for vault scenes in the Lower Church at Assisi of Poverty, Chastity, Obedience and Triumph of St Francis.
See *Khv* & *Salmi**, 1914, pp. 11-12.

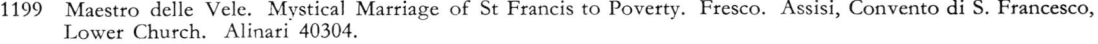

1199   Maestro delle Vele. Mystical Marriage of St Francis to Poverty. Fresco. Assisi, Convento di S. Francesco, Lower Church. Alinari 40304.

Master of Varlungo
Florentine, active at the turn of the thirteenth century.
See Zeri, F. and Gardner, E. E., *MMOA**, 1971, pp. 10-11.

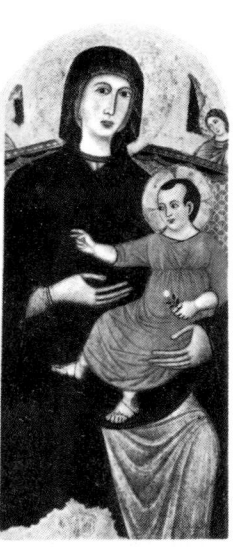

1200   Master of Varlungo. Madonna and Child. Panel. Varlungo (outskirts of Florence, on the via Aretina), S. Pietro. SGF 101758.

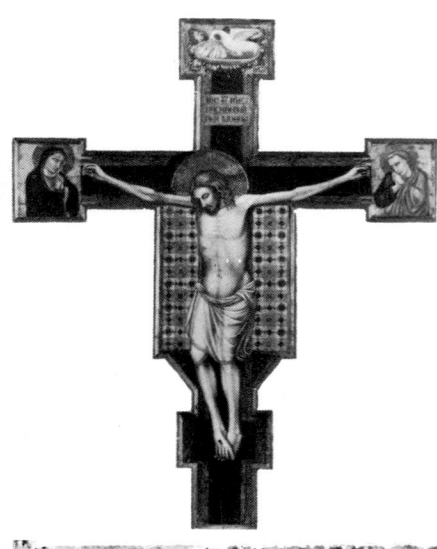

Master of the Corsi Crucifix
Florentine, active during the early years of the fourteenth century.
See Boskovits, M., *AV*, X, 5, 1971, pp. 3, 9, no. 4.

1201   Master of the Corsi Crucifix. Painted Crucifix. Panel. Stuttgart, Staatsgalerie. Courtauld photo.

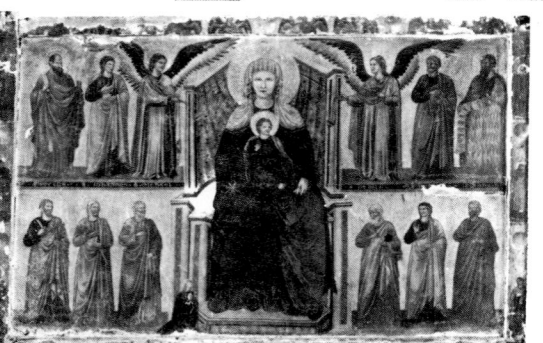

Master of Cesi
Named for a retable in S. Maria, Cesi (Terni), dated 1308, and active in the first decade of the fourteenth century.
See Meiss, M., in *Scritti di Storia dell' Arte in onore di Mario Salmi*, Rome, 1962, Vol. II, pp. 75-111.

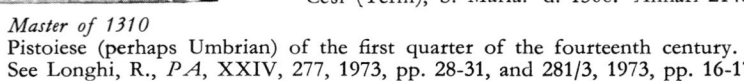

1202   Master of Cesi. Madonna and Child Enthroned with ten Saints, two Angels, and Donor. Panel.
Cesi (Terni), S. Maria. d. 1308. Alinari 21482.

Master of 1310
Pistoiese (perhaps Umbrian) of the first quarter of the fourteenth century.
See Longhi, R., *PA*, XXIV, 277, 1973, pp. 28-31, and 281/3, 1973, pp. 16-17.

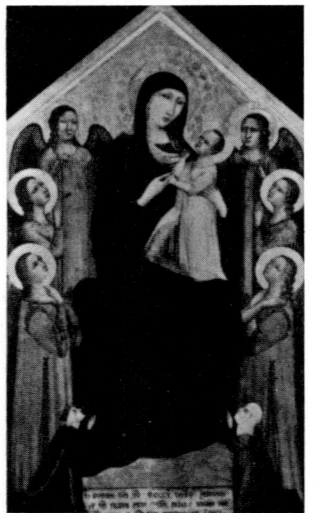

1203   Master of 1310. Madonna and Child Enthroned with six Angels and and two Donors. Panel. (Formerly)
Angers, Musée. Author's photo. d. 1310.

Buffalmacco
Florentine, believed to have painted the much-ruined frescoes at Settimo, dated 1315. He has recently been identified
with the Maestro del Trionfo della Morte, at Pisa.
See Bellosi, L., *Buffalmacco e il Trionfo della Morte*, Turin, 1974.

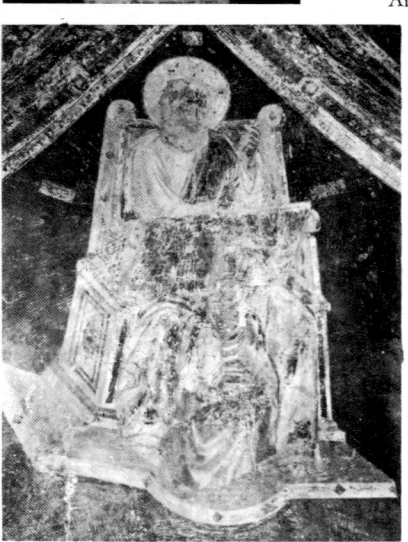

1204   Buffalmacco (?). Vault: An Evangelist Enthroned. Fresco. Florence, Badia a Settimo, Cappella di S. Jacopo.
SGF 122900. d. 1315.

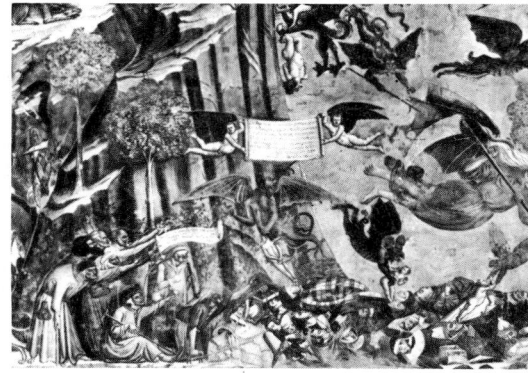

Maestro del Trionfo della Morte.
The painter of a large fresco in the Camposanto at Pisa; recently identified with Buffalmacco.
See Bellosi, L., *Buffalmacco e il Trionfo della Morte*, Turin, 1974.

1205 Maestro del Trionfo della Morte. Detail of the Triumph of Death. Fresco. Pisa, Camposanto. Brogi 2244.

Buonamico
Active during the first half of the fourteenth century and should perhaps be identified with Buffalmacco.
See Donati, P. P., *C*, XVIII, 4, 1967, pp. 290-296.

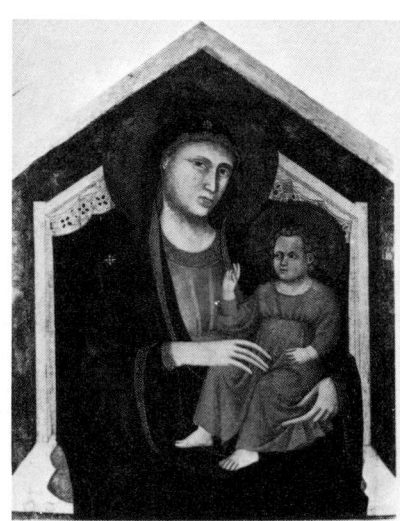

Master of the Horne Triptych
Named for a triptych in the Horne Museum, Florence; is sometimes identified with the Master of S. Cecilia.
See Offner, R., *Corpus**, Sec. III, Vol. I, 1931, pp. 67-84; Sec. III, Vol. VI, pp. 103-114. (See also fig. 85, herein).

1206 Master of the Horne Triptych. Madonna and Child Enthroned with female Saints. Panel. Bibbione (San Casciano), Chiesa di S. Colombano. SGF 123801.

Master of S. Giorgio alla Costa
Near to Giotto and may be the Master of S. Cecilia.
See *M. Giottesca**, 1943, pp. 356-358.

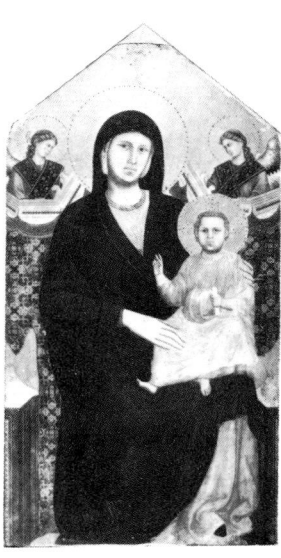

1207 Master of S. Giorgio alla Costa. Madonna and Child Enthroned with two Angels. Panel. Florence, S. Giorgio. 180 × 90. SGF 26928.

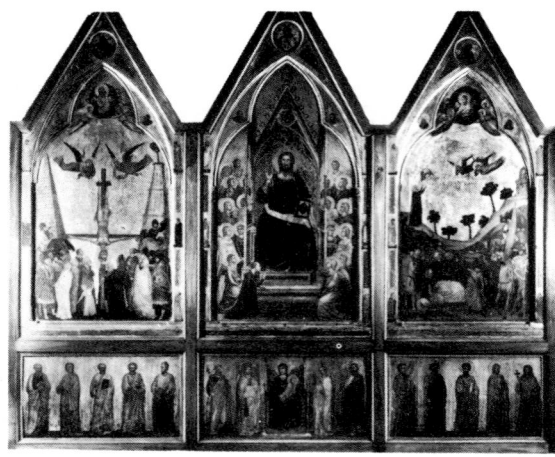

Master of Stefaneschi Altarpiece
In Giotto's workshop, named for a polyptych in the Vatican Pinacoteca.
See Gioseffi, D., *Congresso VII**, Rome, 1971, pp. 221-231.

1208 Master of the Stefaneschi Altarpiece. Triptych: Christ blessing with Angels, Saints and Donor; Martyrdom and Burial of St Peter. Below: ten male Saints, and Madonna and Child Enthroned with two Angels and Sts Peter and John the Evangelist. Panel. Rome, Vatican, Pinacoteca. Museum photo, XIII.20.15.

Stefano Fiorentino
According to Vasari, the father of Giottino.
See Gabrielli, M., *RA*, XXXI, 6, 1956, pp. 3-23.

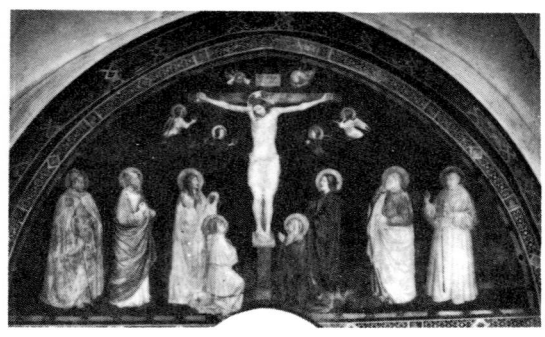

Maestro Colorista di Assisi
Perhaps a follower of Giotto.
See Coletti, L., *CA*, VIII, 1949-50, pp. 443-454.

1209 Maestro Colorista di Assisi. Christ on the Cross with the two Marys, six Saints and six Angels. Fresco. Assisi, Collegio Principe di Napoli. Alinari 20041.

Giottino
Follower of Giotto, whose *oeuvre* is disputed.
See *Dal Poggetto**, 1967, pp. 51-53.

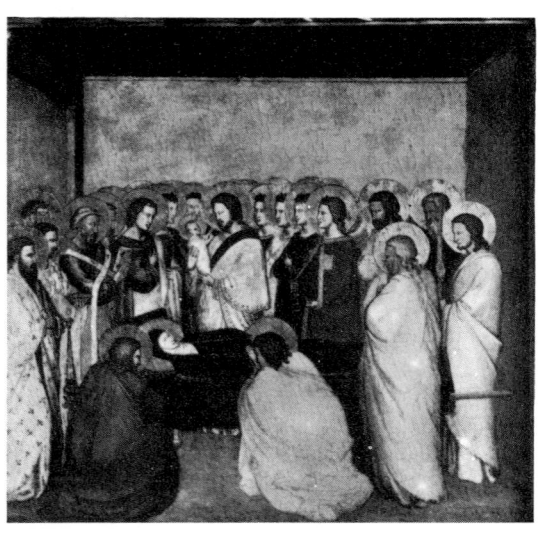

Master of Chantilly
Follower of Giotto, named for a painting in Chantilly.
See *M. Giottesca**, 1943, pp. 370-371.

1210 Master of Chantilly. Dormition of the Virgin. Panel. Chantilly, Musée Condé. 44 × 48. Alinari 42203.

Maestro dell' Altare di S. Spirito
A painter near to Maso, probably the same artist as the Master of Chantilly.
See Suida, W., *RA*, V, 1907, pp. 45-46.

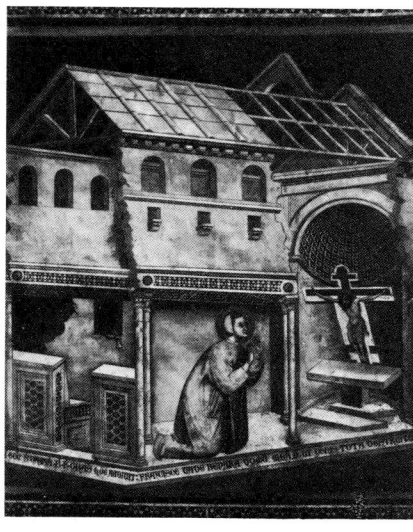

Puccio Capanna
Active early fourteenth century. Supposedly a disciple of Giotto who may have executed the frescoes in the church of S. Francesco, Pistoia, recently attributed to the Bolognese, Dalmasio, c. 1343.
See Chiappelli, A., *DD*, X, 1929-30, pp. 199-228.

1211   Puccio Capanna (?). St Damian and his Adoration of the Cross. Fresco. Pistoia, S. Francesco. Brogi 30261.

Master of Montefalco
A painter near to Puccio Capanna who worked in the second quarter of the 14th century.
See Scarpellini, P., *PA*, XXIV, 279, 1973, pp. 9-21.

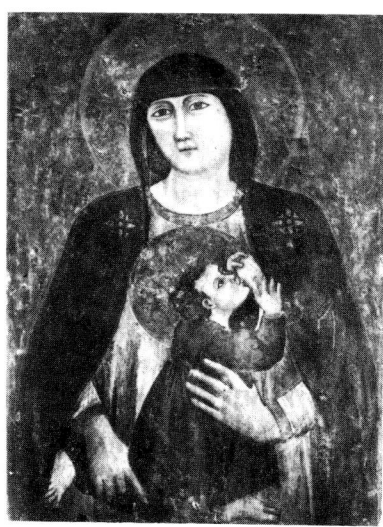

Master of the S. Lorenzo Madonna
Follower of the Master of S. Cecilia.
See Offner, R., *Corpus**, Sec. III, Vol. I, 1931, pp. 92-94.

1212   Master of the S. Lorenzo Madonna. Madonna nursing the Child. Panel. Florence, S. Lorenzo, Cappella della Madonna di S. Zanobi. 86 × 56. Bertoni-Offner.

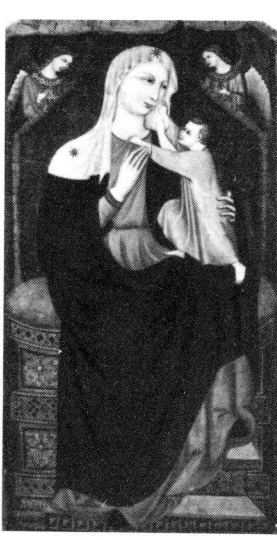

Vicchio-Paris Master
Follower of the Master of S. Cecilia.
See Offner, R., *Corpus**, Sec. III, Vol. VI, 1956, pp. 118-120.

1213   Vicchio-Paris Master. Madonna and Child with two Angels. Panel. Vicchio a Rimaggio, S. Lorenzo. 165 × 86. SGF 120056.

Master of Vicchio a Rimaggio
See *Vicchio-Paris Master.*
See Volpe, C., *PA*, XIV, 157, 1963, pp. 3-14.

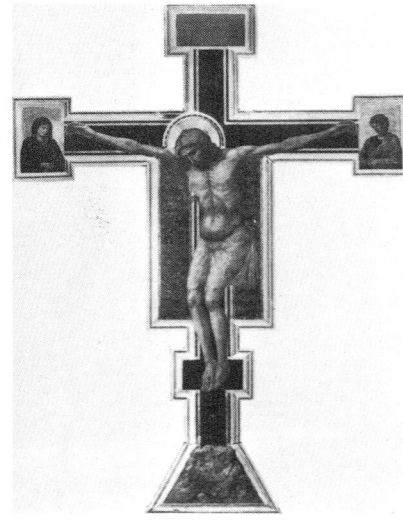

Master of the S. Maria Novella Cross
Follower of the Master of S. Cecilia. May also be the painter of the Madonna & Child in the church of S. Giorgio alla Costa: see this Master.
See Offner, R., *Corpus**, Sec. III, Vol. VI, 1956, pp. 3-18.

1214   Master of the S. Maria Novella Cross. Painted Crucifix. Panel. Florence, S. Maria Novella, Sacristy. 578 × 406. SGF 26884.

Master of S. Pietro in Monticelli
Follower of the Master of the S. Maria Novella Cross.
See Cole, B., *MKIF*, XV, 3, 1971, pp. 259-264.

Master of the Oberlin Cross
Follower of the Master of the S. Maria Novella Cross.
See Cole, B., *MKIF*, XV, 3, 1971, pp. 259-264.

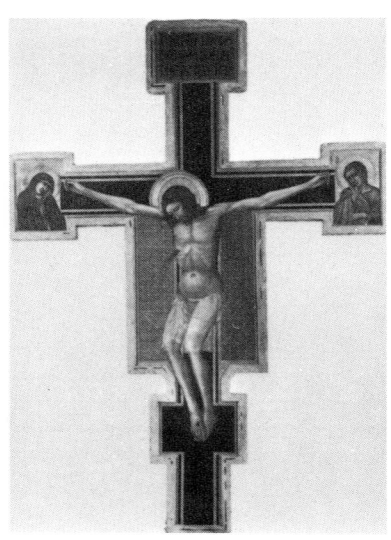

Master of the Da Filicaia Cross
Follower of the Master of S. Cecilia.
See Offner, R., *Corpus**, Sec. III, Vol. VI, 1956, pp. vii, 49-56.

1215   Master of the Da Filicaia Cross. Painted Crucifix. Panel. Florence, Museo di S. Croce. no. 15. 428 × 313. SGF 112782.

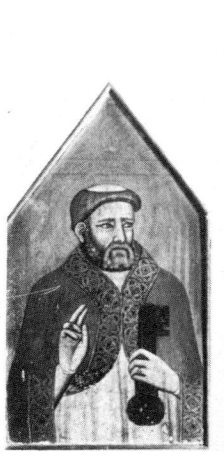
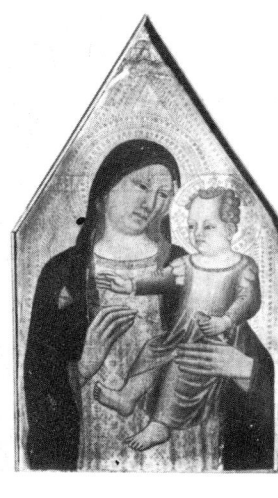

Master of Mezzana
Follower of the Master of S. Cecilia.
See Offner, R., *Corpus**, Sec. III, Vol. VI, 1956, pp. IX, 57-63.

1216 Master of Mezzana. Two panels: Madonna and Child, and St Peter. Panel. Mezzana, near Prato, Chiesa Parrocchiale. SGF 22465.

Giovanni di Bonino
Active in the first half of the fourteenth century; identified with the *Master of the Fogg Pietà* (or *Master of Figline*).
See Marchini, G., *Congresso VII**, 1971, pp. 67-77.

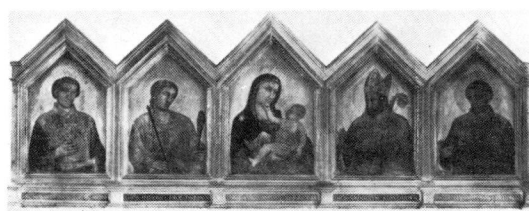

Master of the S. Reparata Polyptych
Florentine, near to the *Fogg Master*, named for painting now in the Duomo, Florence.
See *M. Giottesca**, 1943, pp. 363-365.

1217 Master of the S. Reparata Polyptych. Polyptych: Madonna and Child with Sts Eugenius, Minias, Zenobius and Crescentius. Panel. Florence, Duomo. 94 × 242. SGF 26946.

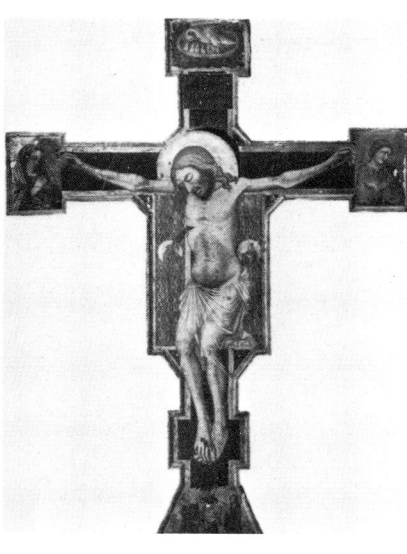

Master of S. Quirico
Active in the first half of the fourteenth century and named for a crucifix in S. Quirico, Ruballa.
See Offner, R., *Corpus**, Sec. III, Vol. I, 1931, pp. 95-98.

1218 Master of S. Quirico. Painted Crucifix. Panel. Ruballa (Bagno a Ripoli), S. Quirico. Brogi 24848.

Master of Ruballa
See *Master of S. Quirico*.

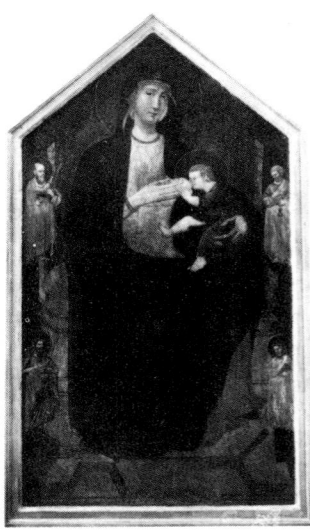

Master of S. Gaggio
Active in the first half of the fourteenth century.
See Longhi, R., *Prop*, II, 1948, p. 19, pl. 36.

1219 Master of S. Gaggio. Madonna nursing the Child, with Sts Peter, Paul, John the Baptist and John the Evangelist. Panel. Florence, Accademia. no. 6115. SGF 75693.

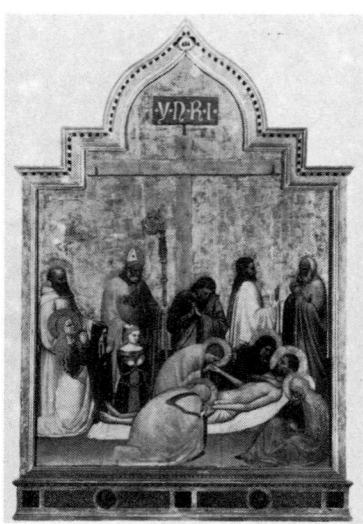

Master of S. Remigio
Active second quarter of the fourteenth century; named after the *Pietà* formerly in S. Remigio, now in the Uffizi. Not to be confused with a painter of this name active mid-thirteenth century.
See Coletti, L., *RA*, XIII, 1931, pp. 331-339.

1220 Master of S. Remigio. Lamentation. Panel. Florence, Uffizi. no. 454. SGF 145037.

Biadaiolo Illuminator
Influenced by Bernardo Daddi, active about 1340.
See Offner, R., *Corpus**, Sec. III, Vol. II, Part I, pp. 43-48.

Master of the Corsini Triptych
Considered to be a follower of Daddi.
See Sirén, O., *BM*, XXVI, 1914-15, p. 107.

Master of the Dominican Effigies
See *Master of Terenzano*.

Amico di Daddi
See *Master of S. Martino alla Palma*.

Master of the Lord Lee Polyptych
See *Master of Terenzano*.

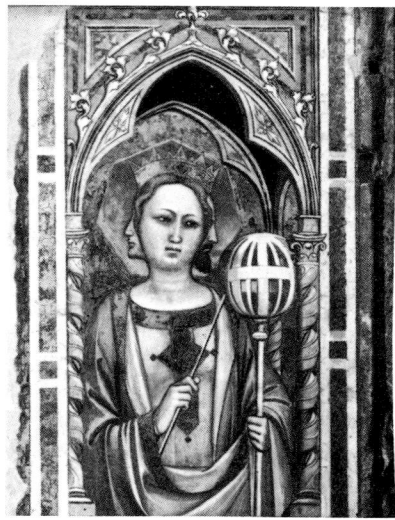

Alessio d'Andrea
Pratese, active c. 1340-60.
See Procacci, U., in *Studien zur Toskanischen Kunst* (Festschrift Ludwig Heydenreich), Munich, 1964, pp. 244-254.
and *Prato* 1969*, pp. 21-24; also *Maestro del Tau*, and *Bonaccorso di Cino*.

1221   Alesso d'Andrea (?). Detail of an allegorical figure. Fresco. Pistoia, Duomo. SGF 122257.

Maestro del Giudizio dell'Ospedale
See *Alessio d'Andrea*.

Bonaccorso di Cino
Florentine, registered in the company of St Luke in 1341; active in Pistoia in 1347. Worked on frescoes in the chapel of S. Jacopo in the Duomo, Pistoia and may also be the *Maestro del Tau*
See Meiss, M., pp. 401-418; and Procacci, U., in *Congresso VII*, 1971, pp. 349-363, and his appendix to, *Edit.*, *Atti del 2º Convegno Internazionale di Studi* (*Il Gotico a Pistoia nei Suoi Rapporti con l'arte gotica italiana*), Pistoia-Rome, 1966, (pp. 247-260), pp. 375-6.

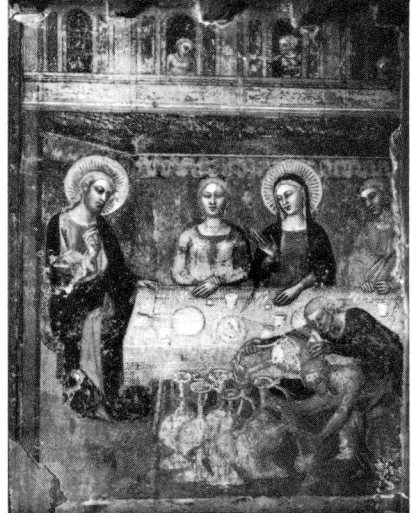

Maestro del Tau
This painter has been identified with Niccolò di Tommaso. He is the painter of the frescoes in the " Cappella del Tau " in Pistoia. He may also have been Antonio di Vita Ricci.
See Tuci, M., in *Pistoia*, I, May 1964, pp. 4-6.
See also *Bonaccorso di Cino*, and Gai, L., *BSP*, LXXII, V, 2, 1970, pp. 75-94.

1222   Maestro del Tau (Maestro del Convento del T). Detail: The Miracle of the Wine. Fresco. Pistoia, Chiesa del Tau. SGF 131996. (See also fig. 362).

Maestro del Convento del T
See *Bonaccorso di Cino*, and *Maestro del Tau*.

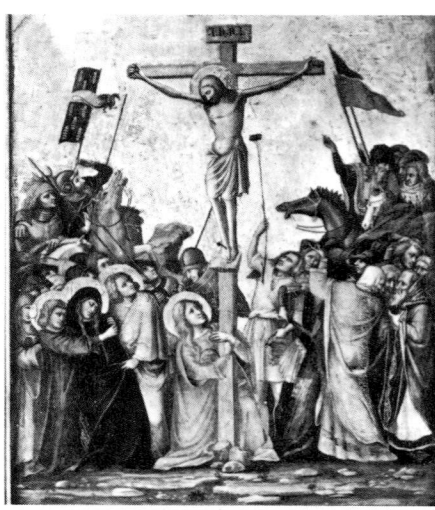

Dalmasio
Bolognese, c. 1340-1375, known to have worked in Pistoia; may have executed frescoes (ca. 1343) in the main chapel of S. Francesco, Pistoia. See also *Puccio Capanna*.
See Mellini, G. L., *AI*, III, 27/28/29, 1970, pp. 40-55.

1223   Dalmasio (?). Crucifixion. Panel. Florence, Acton Collection. Reali.

Master of the S. Spirito Refectory
Active mid-fourteenth century; Offner distinguished him as a separate painter working with the Master of the Pentecost in S. Spirito, Florence.
See Offner, R., *Corpus**, Sec. IV, Vol. I, 1962, pp. 65-67, pls V^1-V^{15}.

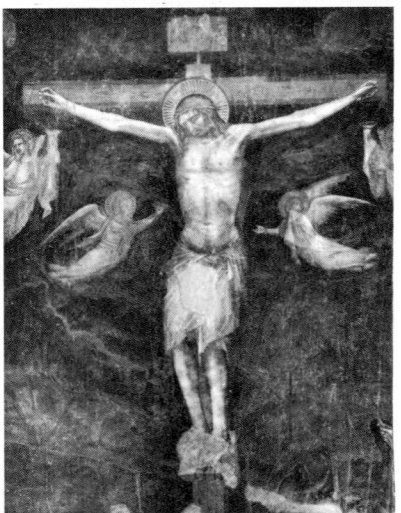

1224   Master of the S. Spirito Refectory. Detail: Christ on the Cross. Fresco. Florence, S. Spirito, Refectory. SGF 32489.

Master of the Pentecost
Follower of Andrea Orcagna and painter of the triptych of this name, now in the Accademia. Also worked in the refectory of S. Spirito.
See Offner, R., *Corpus**, Sec. IV, Vol. I, 1962, pp. 61-80, pls V^{16}-V^{28} and VI^1-VI^{12}.

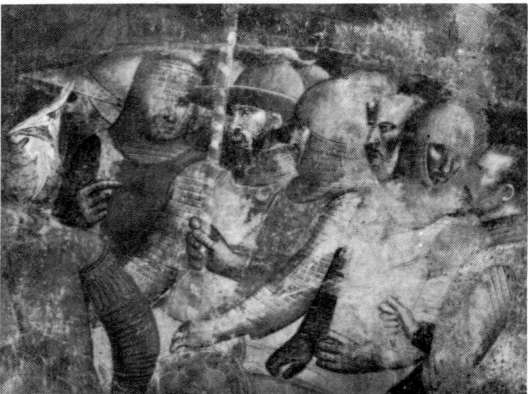

1225   Master of the Pentecost. Detail: Heads of Soldiers. Fresco. Florence, S. Spirito, Refectory. SGF 32555.

Master of the Cini S. Paolo
Follower of Orcagna named for a polyptych in the Cini collection in Venice.
See Carli, E., *Pittura Pisana del Trecento*, Milan, 1961, pp. 18-19, and pls 19-23.

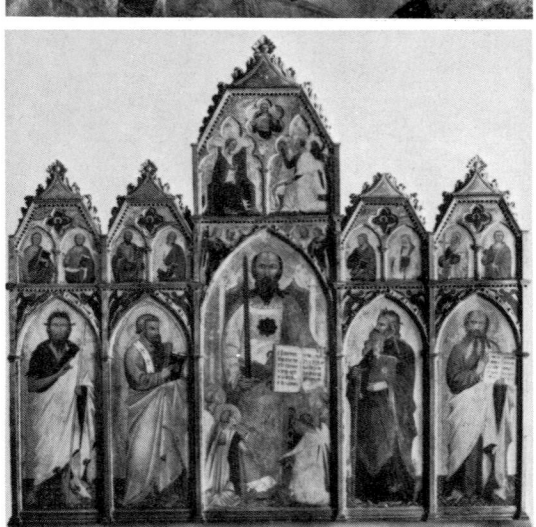

1226   Master of the Cini S. Paolo. Polyptych: St Paul Enthroned with four Angels and twelve Saints. Above: Annunciation. Panel. Venice, Cini Collection. no. 2880 (86). 260 × 274. Collection photo.

Master of Campodonico
Marchigian, active mid-fourteenth century.
See Donnini, G., *C*, XXII, 1971, pp. 326-34.

Master of S. Biagio in Caprile
See *Master of Campodonico.*

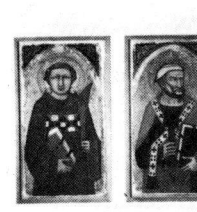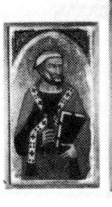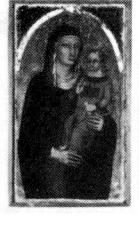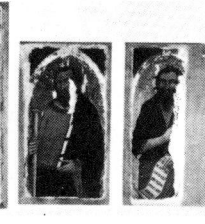

Master of Popiglio
Pistoiese; named for a painting in S. Maria Assunta di Popiglio, near Bagni di Lucca.
See Baldini, U., *Guida alla visita del Museo della Collegiata di Empoli*, Empoli, 1964, p. 26.

1227   Master of Popiglio. Madonna & Child & four male Saints. Panel. Pistoia, Museo Civico. SGF 177002.

Master of the Fabriano Altarpiece
See *Puccio di Simone*, (p. 85).

Maestro Universitas Aurificum.
A Pisan who worked in the second half of the fourteenth century.
See *Marcucci**, 1965, pp. 175-6.

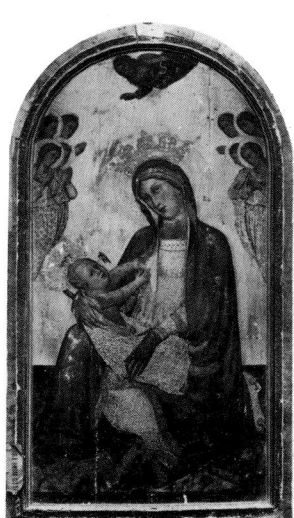

Don Silvestro dei Gherarducci (1339-1396)
Florentine of the second half of the fourteenth century; also miniaturist in S. Maria degli Angeli.
See Boskovits, M., *PA*, XXIII, 265, 1972, pp. 35-61.

1228   Don Silvestro dei Gherarducci. Madonna of Humility nursing the Child, with eight Angels. Above: Christ blessing. Panel. Carrara, Accademia. SGF 76483.

Master of the Cionesque — or Orcagnesque — Humility; or Master of the Accademia Humility
See *Don Silvestro dei Gherarducci.*

Master of the Virgin of Mercy
See Berenson, B., *DD*, XI, 1931, p. 1058.

Don Simone
Florentine miniaturist of the last quarter of the fourteenth and early fifteenth centuries.
See Boskovits, M., *PA*, XXIII, 265, 1972, pp. 35-61.

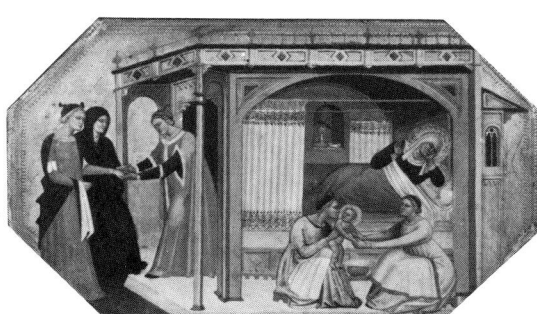

Master of the Ashmolean Predella
Named after the painting which the museum attributes to Orcagna.
See *Catalogue of Paintings in the Ashmolean Museum*, Oxford, 1961, p. 161.

1229   Master of the Ashmolean Predella. Nativity of the Virgin. Panel. Oxford, Ashmolean Museum. Museum photo. (See also fig. 286).

Francesco Ghissi
Marchigian, active 1359-1395, influenced by Allegretto Nuzi.
See Gore, St J., *Wildenstein**, 1965, pp. 14-15.

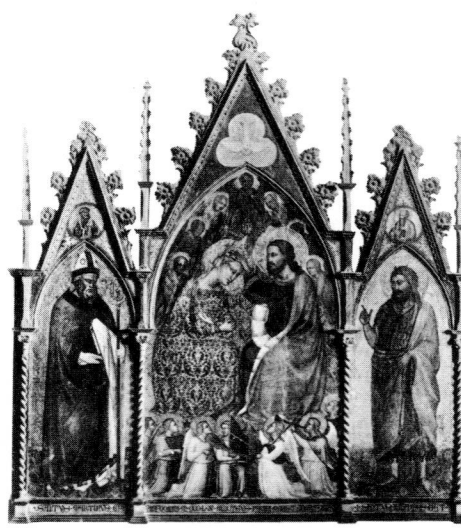

Matteo Pacini
Follower of Daddi and collaborator of the Cioni. It has recently been suggested that he is the Master of the Rinuccini Chapel (pp. 193-204).
See Bellosi, L., *MKIF*, XVII, 2-3, 1973, pp. 179-182.

1230   Matteo Pacini. Triptych: Coronation of the Virgin with Angels and Sts Martin and John the Baptist. Above: Sts Peter and Paul and the Holy Spirit. Panel. Formerly, Rome. Stroganoff Collection. 160 × 180. Fototeca Berenson. s & d. 1360.

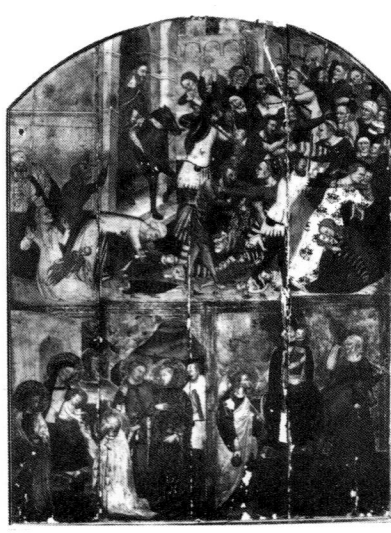

Master of the Infancy of Christ
Florentine, sometimes identified with Niccolò di Tommaso, active c. 1360-1390.
See *Marcucci**, 1965, no. 62, pp. 103-105.

1231   Master of the Infancy of Christ. Massacre of the Innocents, Epiphany, Flight into Egypt. Panel. Florence, Uffizi, Depositi. no. 5887. 141 × 101. SGF 79927.

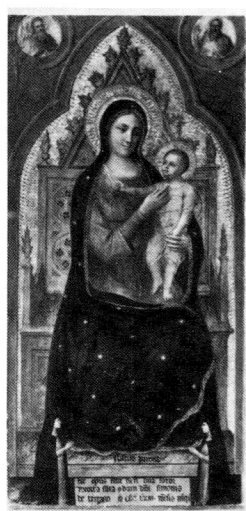

Giusto de' Menabuoi
Florentine, active in northern Italy, 1363-1391.
See Bettini, S., *Le pitture di Giusto de' Menabuoi nel Battistero del Duomo di Padova*, Venice, 1960.

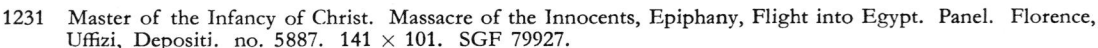

1232   Giusto di Menabuoi. Madonna and Child Enthroned. Panel. Private Collection. Reali. d. 1363.

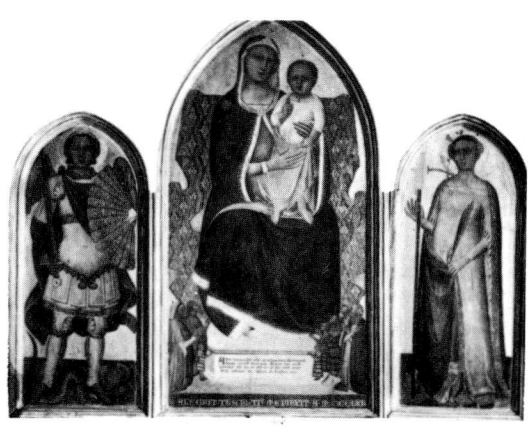

Allegretto Nuzi
Marchigian; may have worked in Florence. His work has been confused with that of Puccio di Simone.
See Rossi, A., in *Pittura nel Maceratese dal Duecento al Tardo Gotico* (catalogue), Macerata, 1971, pp. 53-64.

1233 Allegretto Nuzi. Triptych: Madonna and Child with eight Donors and St George and a female Saint. Panel. Rome, Vatican, Pinacoteca. Alinari 38206. s & d. 1365.

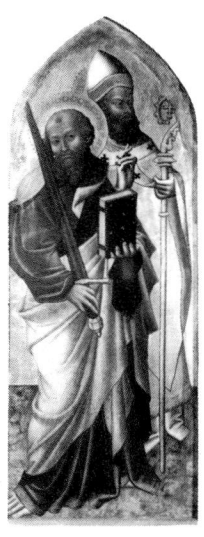

Angelo Puccinelli
Lucchese, active in the second half of the Trecento.
See Gonzalez-Palacios, A., *AV*, X, 3, 1971, pp. 3-9.

1234 Angelo Puccinelli. Two male Saints. Panel. Antwerp, Musée Mayer van der Bergh. Museum photo 98990.

Ser Monte
Probably a miniaturist of the second half of the fourteenth century.
See Boskovits, M., *PA*, XXIII, 265, 1972, p. 43.

Tommaso del Mazza
Worked with Pietro Nelli.
See that painter.

Corsino di Bonaiuto
Father of Bonaiuto di Corsino; active in the third quarter of the fourteenth century.
See Procacci, U., *RA*, XXXV, 10, 1960, pp. 18-19.

Master of the Louvre Nativity
Aretine, active in the third quarter of the fourteenth century. Another painter of this name is also active in the second half of the fifteenth century.
See Boskovits, M., *AV*, X, 5, 1971, p. 6, 12.

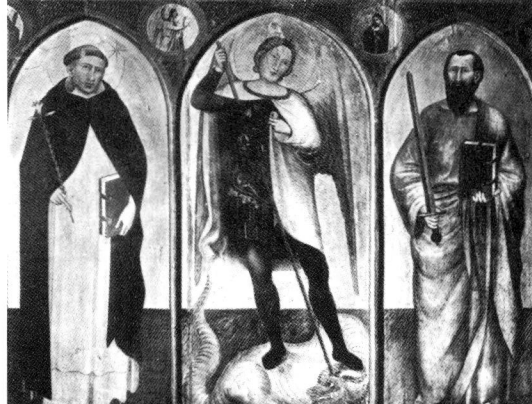

Master of Vescovado
Aretine, close to the Master of the Louvre Nativity, active in the third quarter of the fourteenth century.
See *Maetzke**, 1974, pp. 53-61.

1235 Maestro del Vescovado. Sts Michael, Dominic & Paul. Panel. Arezzo, S. Domenico. SGF 12264.

Master of the Vincigliata Madonna
The painter of a Madonna in the parish church at Vincigliata near Settignano, since identified as Niccolò di Pietro Gerini.
See Gamba, C., *RA*, V, 1907, p. 24.

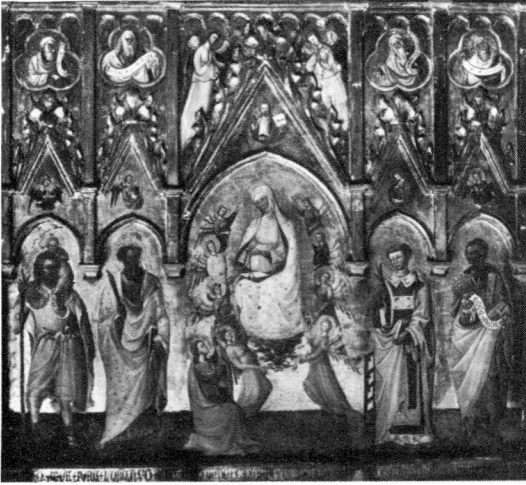

Master of Montefloscoli
Named for a polyptych in S. Maria a Montefloscoli, near S. Piero a Sieve. Active in the last quarter of the fourteenth century.
See Offner, R., *BM*, LXIII, 367, 1933, p. 174, note 23.

1236   Master of Montefloscoli. Madonna of the Holy Girdle with Sts Christopher, Bartholomew, Lawrence and John the Baptist. Panel. Montefloscoli (near San Piero a Sieve), S. Maria. Alinari 45546.

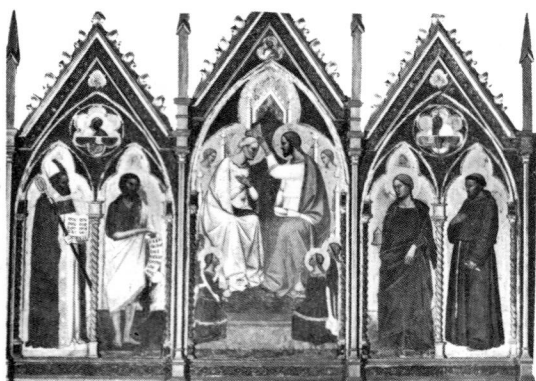

Master of S. Lucchese
Offner distinguishes this painter from Orcagna.
See Offner, R., *Corpus**, Sec. III, Vol. IV, p. 20, note 1, and Brandi, C., *La Regia Pinacoteca di Siena*, Rome, 1933, p. 172 and no. 317.

1237   Master of S. Lucchese. Triptych: Coronation of the Virgin with Sts Zenobius, John the Baptist, Mary Magdalene and Francis. Panel (destroyed 1944). Formerly Poggibonsi (outskirts), S. Lucchese. Alinari 37340.

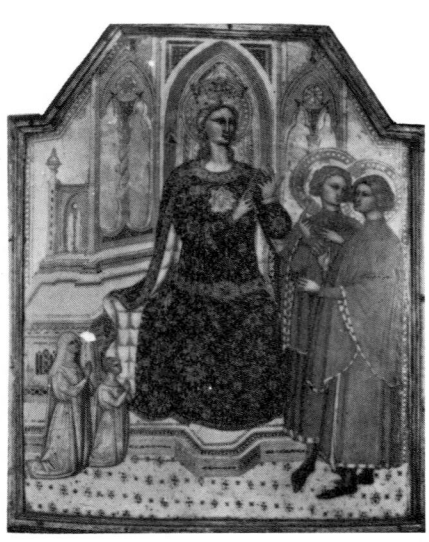

Master of the Kahn St Catherine
Florentine, active last quarter of the fourteenth century.
See Venturi, L., *Pitture Italiane in America*, Milan, 1931, Vol. I, pl. LIII.

1238   Master of the Kahn St Catherine. Madonna Enthroned with two Saints and two Donors. Panel. 53.3 × 43.2. Cleveland (Ohio), Museum of Art. Fototeca Berenson.

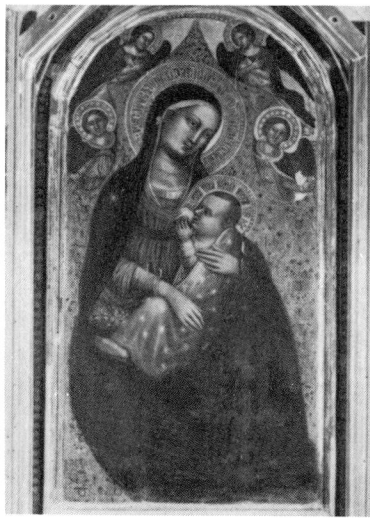

Master of the St Nicholas Altarpiece
Follower of Orcagna, active last quarter of the fourteenth century. See also, Maestro Francesco.
See *Marcucci**, 1965, p. 106, and p. 130, scheda 91.

1239 Master of the St Nicholas Altarpiece. Madonna nursing the Child with four Angels. Panel. Latera (Barberino di Mugello), S. Niccolò. 107 × 62. SGF 119131.

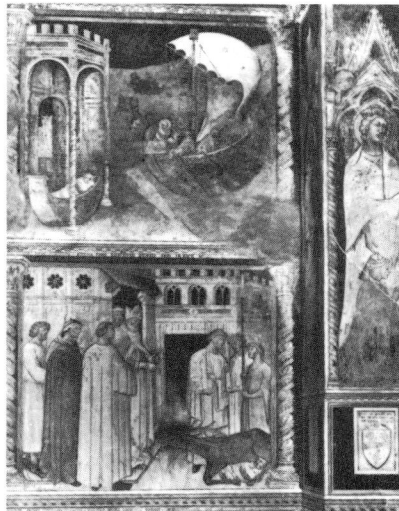

Cennino Cennini
No generally accepted attributions have been made to this painter. Known chiefly for his *Libro dell'Arte*. Active c. 1372-1400.
See Boskovits, M., *MKIF*, XVII, 2-3, 1973, pp. 201-222.

1240 Cennino Cennini (?). Three Scenes. Fresco. Poggibonsi (outskirts), S. Lucchese. Alinari 37339.

Master of S. Giacomo
Active late fourteenth century in Padua; it has been suggested that he may be Cennino Cennini.
See Coletti, L., *RA*, XIII, 1931, pp. 306-331.

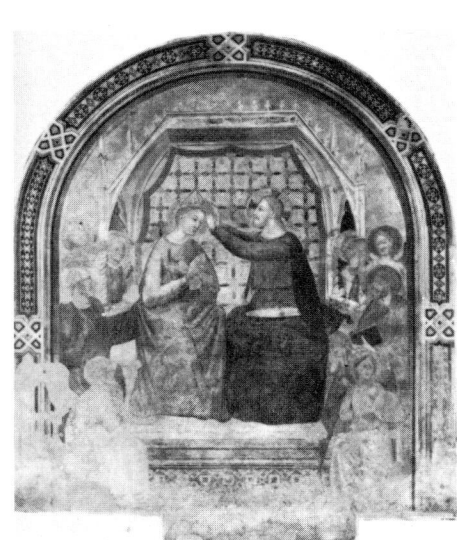

Francesco di Michele Colonnata
Painter of a tabernacle of 1385 at Colonnata, near Florence. May be the painter of the 1394 triptych by the so-called Brunelleschi Master.
See Salmi, M., *RA*, XVI, 1934, pp. 70-71, 73-76.

1241 Francesco di Michele Colonnata. Coronation of the Virgin with Saints and Angels. Fresco. Colonnata, Sesto Fiorentino, Tabernacolo dei Logi. SGF 107438.

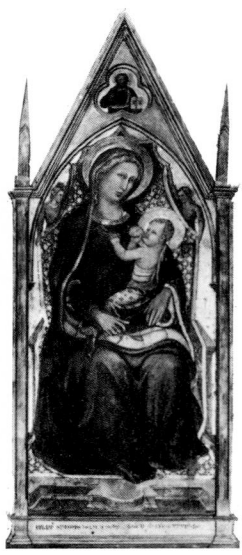

Giuliano di Simone
Lucchese, active at the turn of the fourteenth century.
See Gonzalez-Palacios, A., *AI*, IV, 45/46, 1971, pp. 49-59; Meloni Trkulja, S., *PA*, XXII, 255, 1971, pp. 61-4.

1242   Giuliano di Simone. Madonna and Child Enthroned with two Saints. Above: Christ blessing. Castiglione Garfagnana (Lucca), S. Michele. SGF 20301. s & d. 1389.

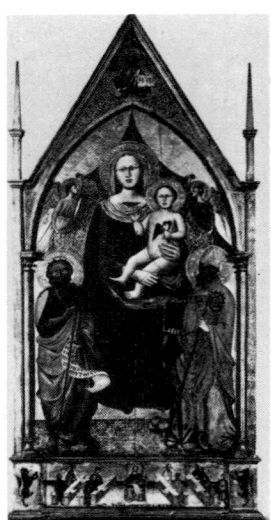

Maestro Francesco
Active at the end of the fourteenth century; he painted the s & d. 1391 panel of the Madonna and Child Enthroned with Saints in S. Maria a Quarto, Bagno a Ripoli; see also, *Maestro del Cristo Docente*, and the *Master of the St Nicholas Altarpiece*.
See Borsook, E., in *Festschrift Ulrich Middeldorf*, Berlin, 1968, Vol. I, pp. 60-63.

1243   Maestro Francesco. Madonna and Child enthroned with Sts John the Baptist and Nicholas of Bari. Panel. Florence, Accademia, on loan to Bagno a Ripoli, S. Maria a Quarto. 215 × 96. SGF 110977. s & d. 1391.

Maestro del Cristo Docente
A painter of the end of the fourteenth century related to Agnolo Gaddi; he has been identified as Maestro Francesco.
See Zeri, F., *GBA*, LXXI, 110, 1968, pp. 71-73.

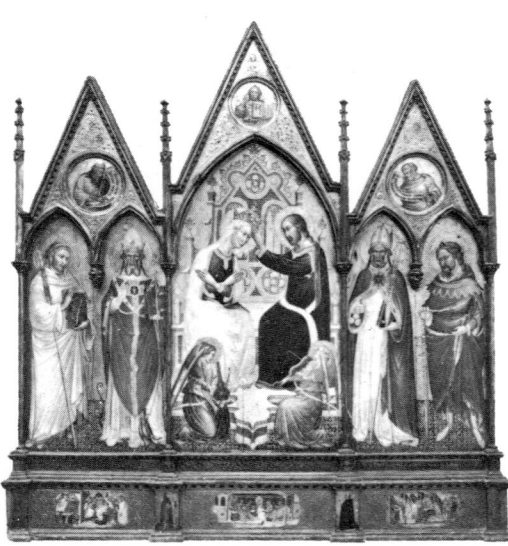

Brunelleschi Master
Named after the altarpiece dated 1394, commissioned by Alderotto Brunelleschi.
See Zeri, F and Gardner, E. E., *MMOA**, 1971, pp. 49-52.

1244   Brunelleschi Master. Triptych: Coronation of the Virgin with Sts Bernard, Sylvester, Nicholas, Julian and two music-making Angels. Above: Annunciation and Christ blessing. Predella: Apparition of Sts Peter and Paul to Constantine; Raising of the Bull; Binding of the Dragon; Raising of the two Pagan Priests; two Donors, members of the Brunelleschi family. Panel. New York (N.Y.), Metropolitan Museum of Art, Lehman Gift. no. 50.229.2. 191 × 193. Museum photo: 149124. d. 1394.

Jacopo d' Agnolo
Worked in the Palazzo Datini in Prato with Dino di Puccio, in 1389.
See Cole, B., *MKIF*, XIII, 1-4, Dec. 1967-Oct. 1968, pp. 76 ff.

Dino di Puccio
Worked in the Palazzo Datini in Prato with Jacopo d'Agnolo in 1389.
See Cole, B., *MKIF*, XIII, 1-4, Dec. 1967-Oct. 1968, pp. 76 ff.

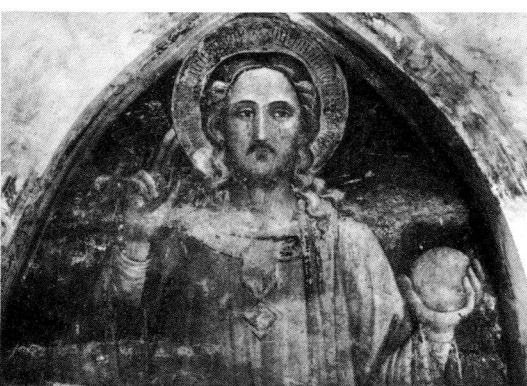

Bartolomeo Bertozzo
Worked with Agnolo Gaddi in the Palazzo Datini in Prato, in 1391.
See Cole, B., *MKIF*, 1-4, Dec. 1967-Oct. 1968, pp. 64-82.

1245   Bartolomeo Bertozzi (?). Christ the Redeemer. Fresco. Prato, Palazzo Datini. SGF 106681.

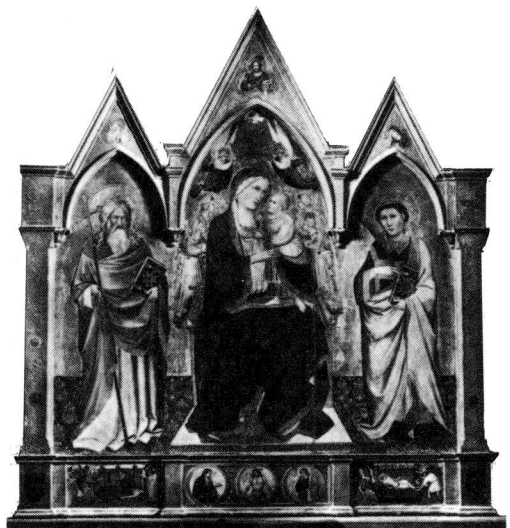

Master of the Madonnas
Close to Agnolo Gaddi, active late fourteenth century.
See Baldini, U., *Xª Mostra di Opere d'arte Restaurate*, Florence, 1959, pp. 14-15; and *Prato* 1969*, pp. 42-3.

1246   Master of the Madonnas. Triptych: Madonna and Child Enthroned with Sts Philip and Lawrence, six Angels and the Holy Spirit. Above: Christ blessing, Annunciation. Predella: Miracle of St Philip; Man of Sorrows. Panel. Florence, Uffizi, Depositi. 184 × 170. Alinari 4499.

Compagno d' Agnolo
See *Master of the Madonnas*; Sirén, O., *BM*, XXVI, 1914-1915, p. 113.

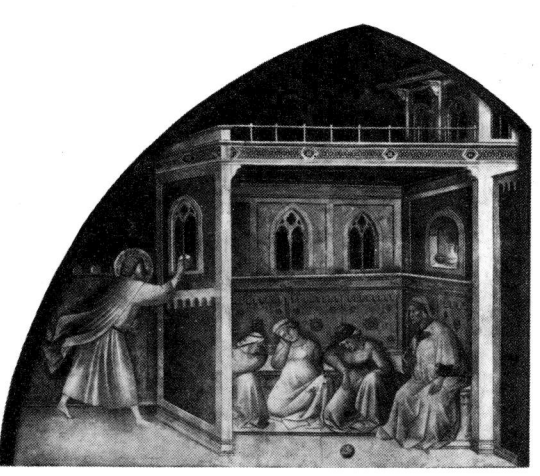

Meo di Frusino
Worked with Agnolo Gaddi in the Cappella del Sacro Cingolo. Also a miniaturist. May be the Maestro delle Storie di S. Niccolò.
See Salvini, R., *RA*, XVI, 1934, pp. 210-216.

1247   Meo di Frusino. St Nicholas and the three Maidens. Fresco. Florence, S. Croce, Castellani Chapel. Alinari 16256.

Maestro delle Storie di S. Niccolò
Worked in the Castellani Chapel in S. Croce, Florence.
See Tosi, L. M., *BA*, IX, 1929-30, pp. 538-554.

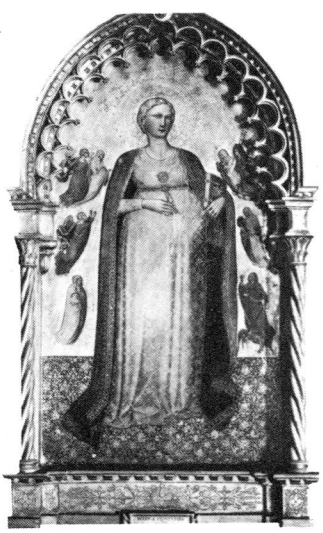

Maestro Vaticano
Named for a panel of the *Madonna del Parto* (or *Madonna delle Virtù*) in the Vatican. Active late fourteenth century.
See Salvini, R., *RA*, XVI, 1934, pp. 216-228.

1248   Maestro Vaticano.   Madonna del Parto.   Panel.   Rome, Vatican, Pinacoteca.   Alinari 38069.

Master of the Rovezzano Tabernacle
Perhaps an assistant of Niccolò di Pietro Gerini.
See *Marcucci**, 1965, p. 112, and fig. 647 herein.

Maestro di S. Girolamo
A reference to the painter of a panel of St Jerome in the Accademia in Florence, since attributed to the Master of
San Martino a Mensola.
See *Marcucci**, 1965, p. 128, fig 582 herein.

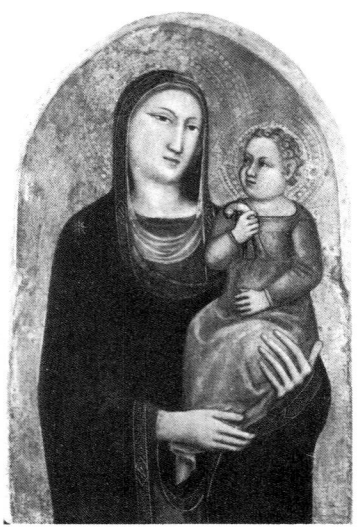

Master of the Barberino Madonna
A painter of the end of the fourteenth century.
See Zeri, F., *BA*, XLVIII, 1963, pp. 245-247.

1249   Master of the Barberino Madonna.   Madonna and Child.   Panel.   Barberino Val d'Elsa (35 kms. S-W of
Florence), S. Bartolomeo.   SGF 122489.

Lippo Fiorentino
Active at the end of the fourteenth century.   Work not universally agreed upon.
See Procacci, U., *BA*, XXVIII, 1933-34, pp. 327-334.

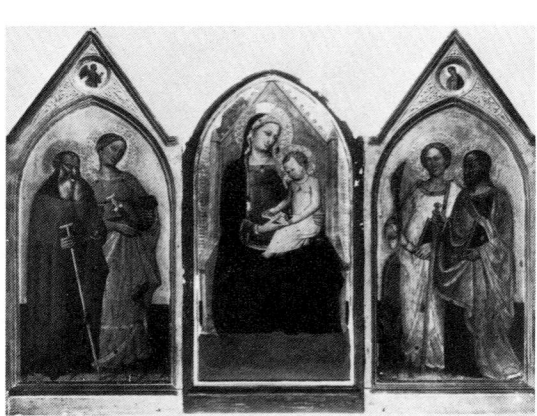

Master of S. Jacopo a Mucciana
Influenced by Agnolo Gaddi; active at the end of the fourteenth century.
See Zeri, F., *BA*, XLVIII, IV, 3, 1963, pp. 247, 256, note 6.

1250   Master of S. Jacopo a Mucciana.   Triptych: Madonna and Child with four Saints.   Panel.   Mucciana
(San Casciano), S. Jacopo.   SGF 23631.

Master of the Accademia Annunciation
See the *Master of the Straus Madonna* and *Shapley**, 1966, p. 41.

Master of the Innocenti Madonna
See the *Master of the Straus Madonna* and *Shapley**, 1966, p. 41.

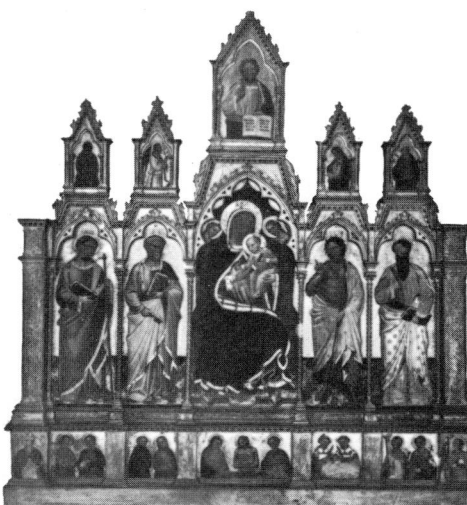

Francesco di Andrea Anguilla
Lucchese, active at the end of the fourteenth century.
See Gonzalez-Palacios, A., *AI*, IV, 45/46, 1971, p. 49.

1251   Francesco di Andrea Anguilla. Polyptych: Madonna and Child with Sts Peter, John the Baptist, Bartholomew and James. Panel. Camaiore (Lucca), Badia di S. Pietro. SGF 8089.

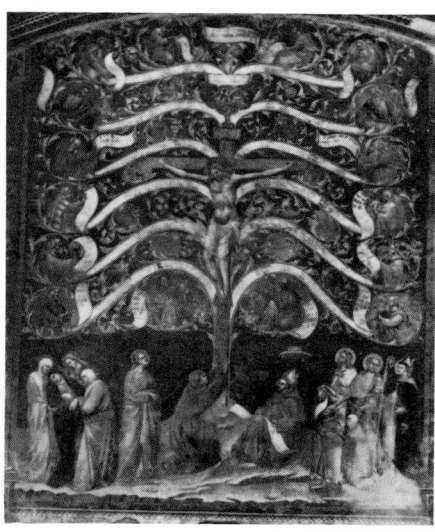

Antonio di Vita Ricci or *Antonio Vite*
See *Maestro del Tau*, and *Bonaccorso di Cino*; Gai, L., *BSP*, III, 6, 1971, pp. 125-30.

1252   Antonio Vite (?). The Crucifixion and Tree of Life. Fresco. Pistoia, S. Francesco, Chapter Room. Alinari 10473.

Master of Figline di Prato
A painter at the end of the fourteenth century, perhaps the Master of the St Nicholas Altarpiece.
See Gurrieri, F., and Maetzke, G., *La Pieve di Figline di Prato*, figs 33-35.

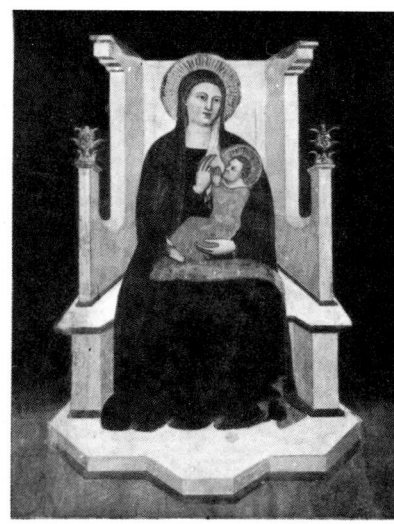

Master of the Figline di Prato Madonna
A painter of about 1400.
See Gurrieri, F., and Maetzke, G., *La Pieve di Figline di Prato*, fig. 44.

1253   Master of the Figline di Prato Madonna. Madonna and Child. Fresco. San Miniato al Tedesco, Misericordia. SGF 21191.

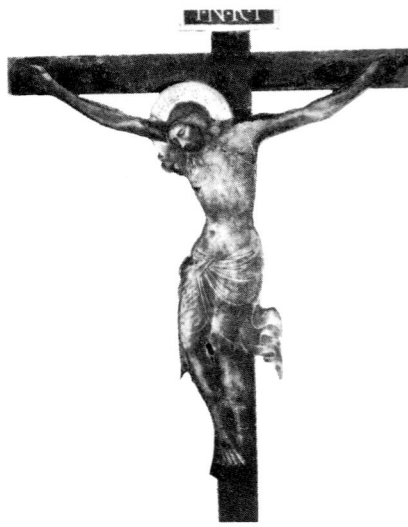

Bartolommeo di Frosino
Florentine panel painter and miniaturist, active late fourteenth, early fifteenth century.
See Watson, P. F., *AB*, LVI, 1, 1974, pp. 4-9.

1254   Bartolomeo di Frosino (?). Painted Crucifix. Panel. Florence, Accademia. Brogi 24227. d. 1411.

Torelli
Family name of a number of Florentine painters and miniaturists at the end of the fourteenth and first half of the
fifteenth century.
See *Colnaghi**, 1928, pp. 261-262, and Boskovits, M., *PA*, XXIII, 265, 1972, pp. 44-46.

Bonaiuto di Corsino
Florentine, son of Corsino di Bonaiuto. Active at the turn of the fourteenth century.
See Ugo, P., *RA*, XXXV, 10, 1960. pp. 18-19.

Master of S. Eligio
Named for a panel in the Cambò Collection in Barcelona; perhaps à follower of Lorenzo di Niccolò. May be the same
painter as the Master of the Orcagnesque Misericordia.
See *Marcucci**, 1965, no. 95, pp. 133-136.

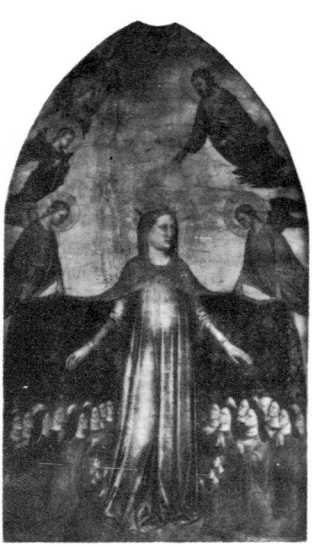

Master of the Orcagnesque Misericordia
Named for a panel in the Accademia; active late fourteenth century.
See *Master of S. Eligio.*
See Zeri, F., and Gardner, E. E., *MMOA**, 1971, p. 38.

1255   Master of the Orcagnesque Misericordia.   Madonna of the Misericordia.   Panel.   Florence, Accademia.
         no. 8562. 63 × 34. SGF 5067.

Master of the Accademia Misericordia
See the *Masters of the Orcagnesque Misericordia* and *S. Eligio.*

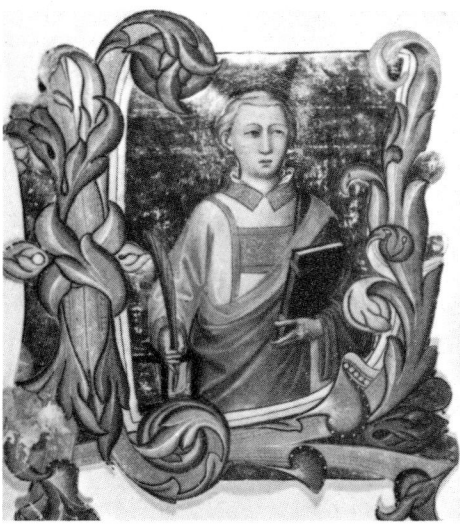

Maestro delle Canzoni
Florentine miniaturist, active end of the fourteenth and beginning of the fifteenth century.
See Levi D'Ancona, M., *RA*, XXXII, 1957, pp. 28-37.

1256   Maestro delle Canzoni. Miniature: St. Lawrence. Parchment. Cambridge, Fitzwilliam Museum. Museum photo no. S 3759.

Battista da Pisa
Named Battista di Gerio; style similar to those of Bicci di Lorenzo and Rossello di Jacopo Franchi.
See Carli, E., *Pittura Pisana del Trecento*, Milan, 1961, p. 97, pl. 81.

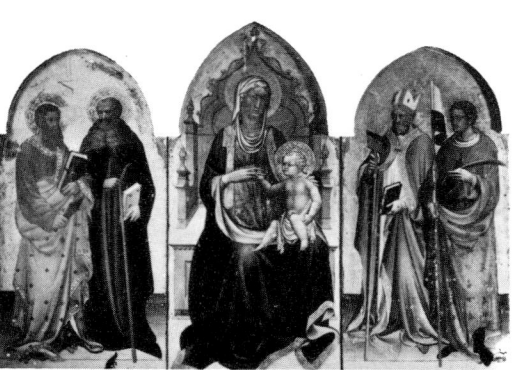

1257   Battista da Pisa. Madonna and Child Enthroned with Sts Bartholomew, Anthony Abbot, Blaise and a fourth saint. Panel. Camaiore (Lucca), Pieve. SGF 29797. s & d. 1409.

Ambrogio di Baldese (1352-1429)
Contemporary and collaborator of Niccolò di Pietro Gerini.
See *Colnaghi**, 1928, pp. 13-14.

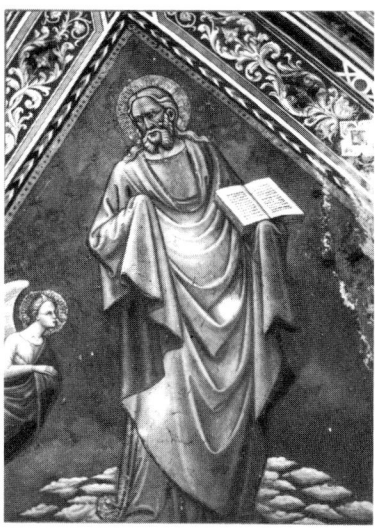

Jacopo da Firenze
Apparently a collaborator of Cenni in Volterra, who did the signed vaults in the Oratorio della Compagnia della Croce di Giorno in S. Francesco; dated 1410.
See *Khv & Salmi**, 1914, p. 50.

1258   Jacopo da Firenze. Evangelists. Fresco. Volterra, S. Francesco, Oratorio della Compagnia della Croce di Giorno. Author's photo. s & d. 1410.

Arrigo di Niccolò
Pratese, working in the Palazzo Datini in about 1409.
See Cole, B., *MKIF*, XIII, 1-4, Dec. 1967-Oct. 1968, pp. 78-82.

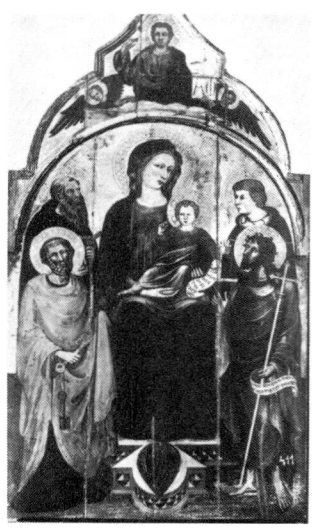

Master of 1416
Named for a dated panel of the *Madonna and Child with four Saints* in the Accademia in Florence.
See Zeri, F., *GBA*, LXXI, 110, 1968, pp. 66-70.

1259   Master of 1416. Madonna and Child Enthroned with Sts Peter, John the Baptist and two other male Saints.
Above: Christ blessing. Panel. Florence, Accademia. no. 4635. 132 × 68. SGF 20955. d. 1416.

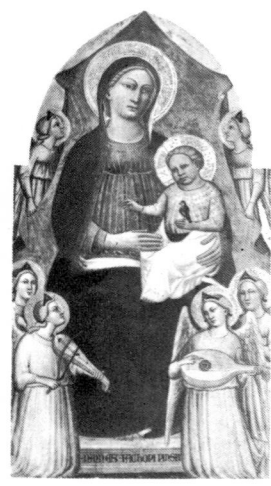

Nanni di Jacopo
Painter of the early fifteenth century, who executed a signed painting in the Museo di Palazzo Venezia.

1260   Nanni di Jacopo. Madonna and Child with six Angels. Panel. Rome, Museo di Palazzo Venezia. 132 × 68.
GFN E26509. s.

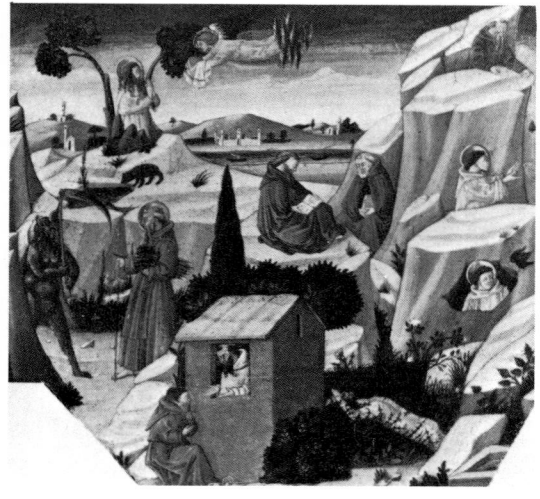

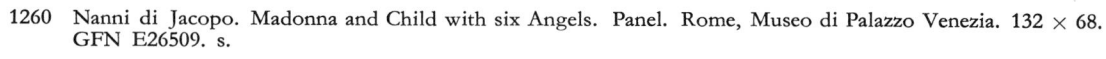

Crawford-Thebaid Master
Named for panels of the Thebaid in the collection of the Earl of Crawford and Balcarres.
See *Byam Shaw**, 1967, pp. 40-46.

1261   Crawford-Thebaid Master. Scenes from the Life of St Benedict, Abbâ Macarius and others. Panel.
Oxford, Christ Church. no. 21. 34 × 44 (approx.). Museum photo.

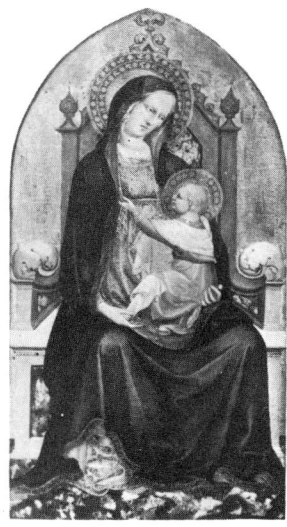

Master of 1419
Florentine, named for the dated central panel of an altarpiece now in Cleveland.
See Cohn, W., *RA*, XXXI, 1956, pp. 41-72.

1262 Master of 1419. Madonna and Child Enthroned. Panel. Cleveland (Ohio), Museum of Art. 195.6 × 68.6.
Museum photo. d. 1419.

Pesello (1367-1446)
Florentine.
See *Colnaghi**, 1928, pp. 206-207.

Calvano di Cristofano
Close contemporary of Pesello.
See Procacci, U., *RA*, XXXV, 10, 1960, pp. 18 ff.

Stefano di Lorenzo
Close contemporary of Pesello.
See Procacci, U., *RA*, XXXV, 10, 1960, pp. 18 ff.

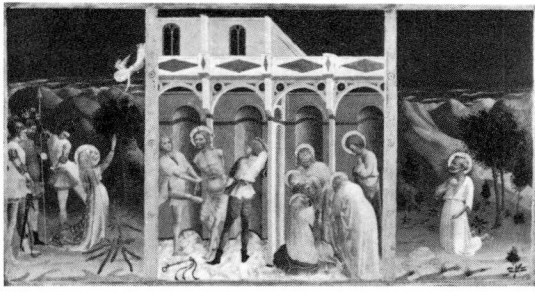

Master of the Sherman Predella
Florentine; appears to have worked in the second decade of the fifteenth century.
See Longhi, R., *PA*, XVIII, 211/31, Sept. 1967, pp. 38-40.

1263 Master of the Sherman Predella. Beheading of a female Saint; Flagellation, and Swooning of the
Virgin; St Jerome in the Wilderness. Panel. Boston (Mass.), Museum of Fine Arts, Gift of Zoe
Oliver Sherman. n. 22.635. Museum photo C 14390.

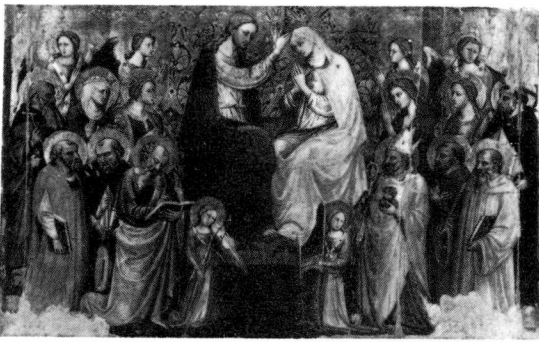

Pietro Chellini (1387-1459)
Florentine, close to Bicci di Lorenzo.
See Cohn, W., *BA*, XLV, 4, 1960, pp. 180-185.

1264 Pietro Chellini. Coronation of the Virgin with twelve Saints and six Angels. Panel. Montelupo,
Pieve. Depositi Gallerie Fiorentine no. 1890, n. 611. SGF 122094.

Giunta di Jacopo Franchi
Brother of Rossello di Jacopo Franchi.
See *v. Marle**, 1927, Vol. IX, pp. 52-64.

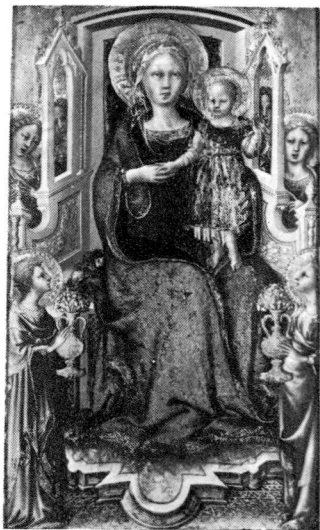

Arcangelo di Cola da Camerino
Marchigian, also working in Florence in the second and third decades of the fifteenth century.
See Zampetti, P., *La Pittura Marchigiana*, Venice, s. d. (c. 1971), pp. 75-80, and *Maetzke**, 1974, pp. 81-85.

1265   Arcangelo di Cola da Camerino. Madonna and Child Enthroned with four Angels. Panel. New York, Miss Helen C. Frick Collection. Frick Art Reference Library photo. s.

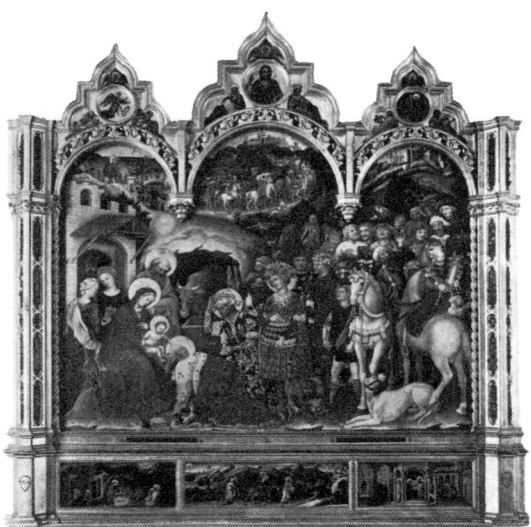

Gentile da Fabriano
Marchigian, active in Florence in the 1420's.
See Grassi, L., *Tutta la pittura di Gentile da Fabriano*, Milan, 1953.

1266   Gentile da Fabriano. Adoration of the Magi. Panel. Florence, Uffizi. 300 × 282. SGF 160314. s & d. 1423.

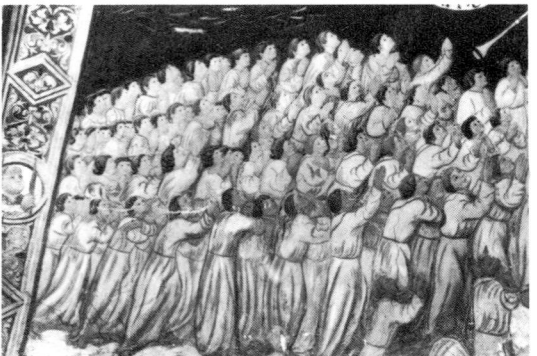

Dello Delli (and brother *Delli Samsone*)
Florentines of the second and third quarters of the fifteenth century, who also worked in Spain.
See de Bosque, A., *Artisti Italiani in Spagna*, Milan, 1968, pp. 111-132.

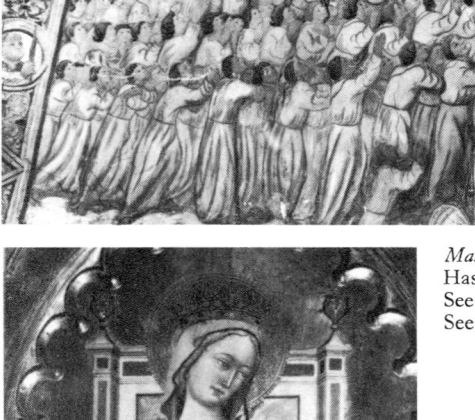

1267   Dello Delli. Detail: Last Judgement. Fresco. Salamanca, Catedral Vieja. Foto Mas 49994.

Master of Borgo alla Collina
Has been identified with the Master of the Bambino Vispo.
See Master of the Bambino Vispo, triptych, d. 1423, at Borgo alla Collina (fig. 922).
See Pudelko, G., *AA*, XXVI, 26, 1, 1938, pp. 47-63, and *Maetze**, 1974, pp. 77-80.

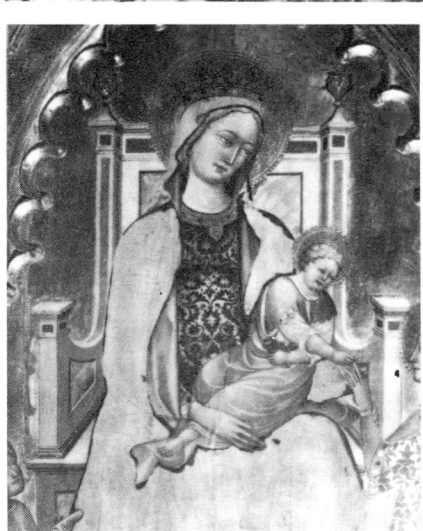

1268   Master of Borgo alla Collina. Detail: Madonna and Child. Panel. Borgo alla Collina, Casentino, S. Donato. SGF 172700. d. 1423. (See fig. 922).

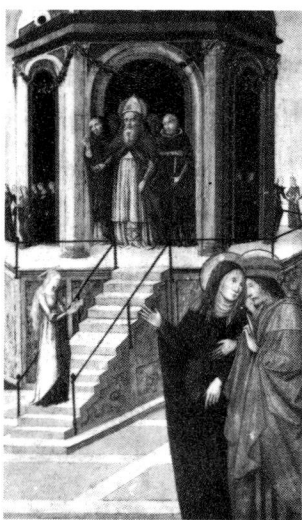

Maestro di Marradi
Minor Florentine of the second quarter of the fifteenth century.
See Zeri, F., *Diari di Lavoro*, Bergamo, 1971, pp. 66-69.

1269   Maestro di Marradi. Presentation of the Virgin at the Temple. Panel. Geneva, Musée d'Art et d'Histoire.
        no. 5.222. 81.5 × 47.5. Museum photo.

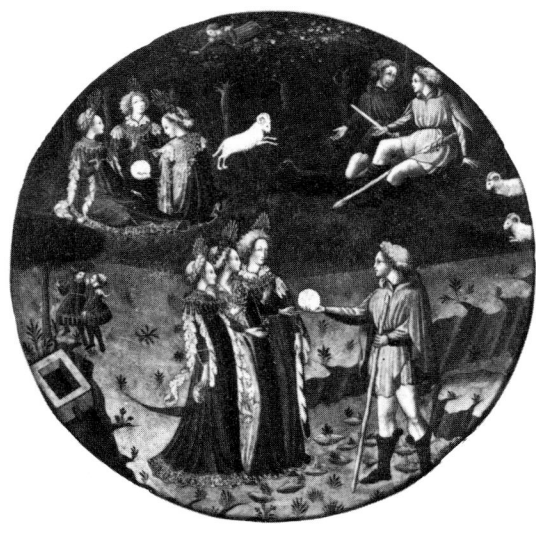

Maestro del Giudizio di Paride
Painter of a *tondo* in the Bargello, Florence; active in the second quarter of the fifteenth century.
See Bellosi, L., *La Pittura tardogotica in Toscana* (Maestro del Colore, 239), Milan, 1966, p. 5.

1270   Maestro del Giudizio di Paride. Tondo: Judgement of Paris. Panel. Florence, Museo Nazionale del
        Bargello, Carrand Collection. Alinari 4638.

Master of the Bargello Tondo
See *Maestro del Giudizio di Paride*.

Jacopo di Cristofano, Giuliano di Jacopo, Ventura di Moro, Marco di Filippo.
Florentines working in the second quarter of the fifteenth century.
See Procacci, U., *RA*, XXXV, 10, 1960, pp. 21 ff.

Master of the Life of the Virgin
Author of a painting in the Accademia in Florence, now attributed to Mariotto di Cristofano, Masaccio's stepsister's
husband (see fig. 1165).

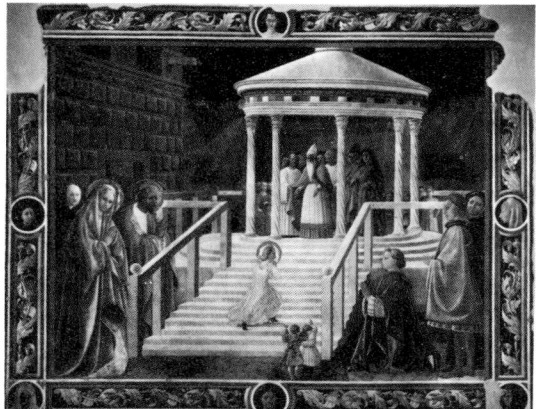

Prato Master
Worked in the Cappella dell'Assunta, in the Cathedral of Prato between 1443 and 1455. Has been identified
as a painter close to Uccello, or perhaps the young Uccello himself.
See *Marchini**, 1969, catalogue, pp. 51-132.

1271   Prato Master. Presentation of the Virgin in the Temple. Fresco. Prato, Duomo. SGF 150152.

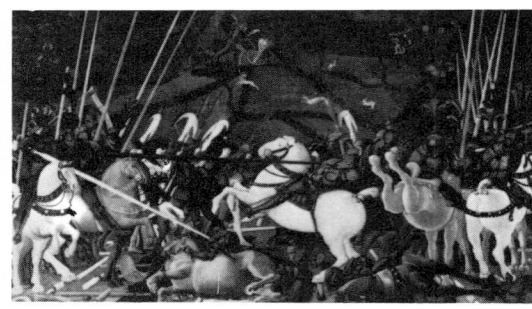

Paolo Uccello
Paolo di Dono, called Uccello, born at the end of the fourteenth century and died in 1475.
See Sindona, E., and Procacci, U., *A*, XVII, 1972, pp. 4-100.

1272   Uccello. Battle of S. Romano. Panel. Florence, Uffizi. no. 479. 182 × 323. SGF 97499.

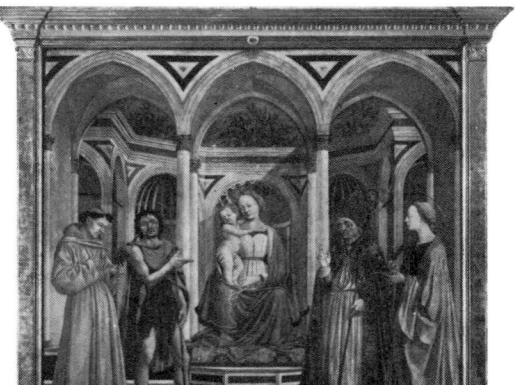

Domenico Veneziano
Active in the second and third quarters of the fifteenth century.
See Salmi, M., *Paolo Uccello, Andrea del Castagno, Domenico Veneziano*, Milan, 2nd ed., 1938.

1273   Domenico Veneziano. Madonna and Child Enthroned with Sts Francis, John the Baptist, Zenobius and
       Lucy. Panel. Florence, Uffizi. no. 884. 209 × 213. SGF 97824.

Master of Pratovecchio
Active c. 1440-1460, influenced by Domenico Veneziano.
See Longhi, R., *PA*, III, 35, 1952, pp. 10-37.

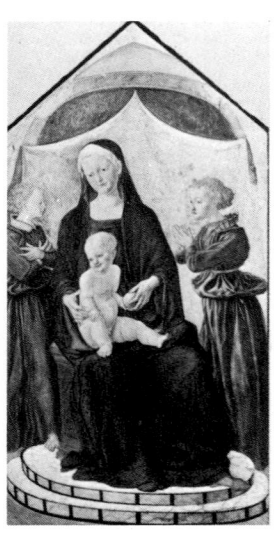

1274   Master of Pratovecchio. Madonna and Child with two Angels. Panel. Sutton Place, J. Paul Getty Collection.
       Sotheby photo A2078.

Maestro degli Arcangeli
See *Master of Pratovecchio*

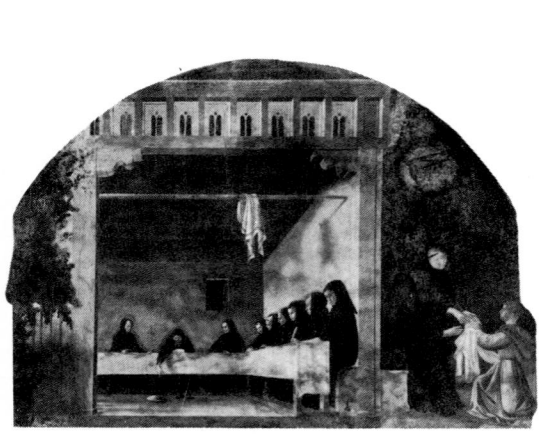

Master of the Chiostro degli Aranci
Painter of frescoes in the cloister of the Badia Fiorentina, Florence, for which he is named, possibly of Spanish
or Portuguese origin.
See Henderson, N. R., *AQ*, XXXII, 1969, pp. 393-410.

1275   Master of the Chiostro degli Aranci. Scene from the Life of St Benedict: the Raven saves his Life.
       Fresco. Florence, Badia, Chiostro degli Aranci. SGF 104227.

Giovanni di Consalvo
Portuguese painter who may be the Master of the Chiostro degli Aranci.
See Chiarini, M., *Prop*, 4, 1963, pp. 1-24.

Master of Karlsruhe
Follower of Paolo Uccello.
See Pope-Hennessy, J., *Paolo Uccello*, London, 1950, pp. 162-167.

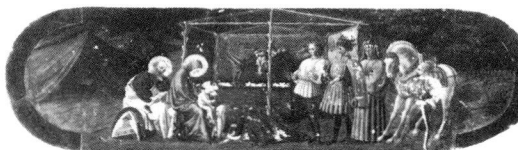

Master of the Quarata Predella
Follower of either Uccello or Domenico Veneziano.
See Pope-Hennessy, J., *Paolo Uccello*, London, 1950, pp. 162-163.

1276   Master of the Quarata Predella. Adoration of the Magi. Panel. Bagno a Ripoli, S. Bartolomeo a Quarata. 20.5 × 17.8. SGF 19827.

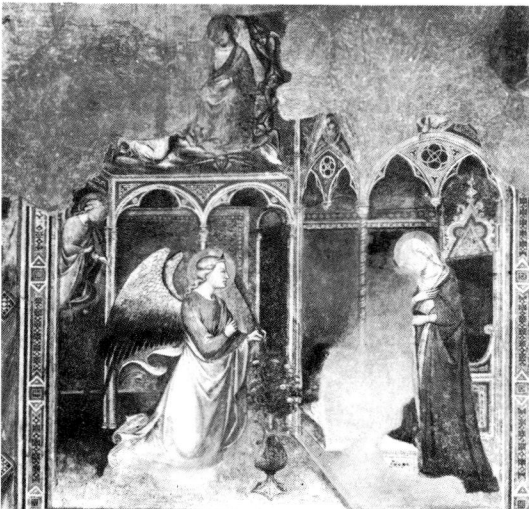

Giovanni d' Agnolo di Balduccio
Aretine of the first half of the fifteenth century.
See Donati, P. P., *AV*, III, 9-10, 1964, pp. 32-46.

1277   Giovanni di Agnolo di Balduccio (?). Annunciation. Fresco. Arezzo, S. Domenico. SGF 12250.

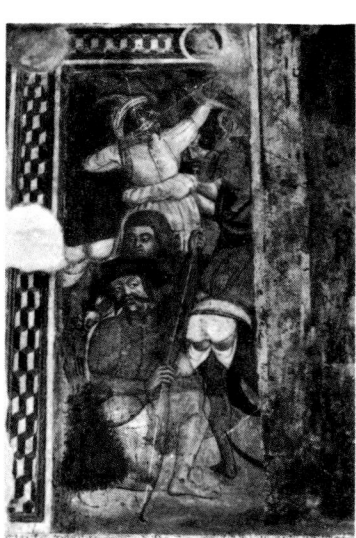

Giovanni di Ser Giovanni
Born 1406, he was called " lo Scheggia ". Brother of Masaccio and perhaps the author of some frescoes in
S. Lorenzo at San Giovanni Valdarno.
See Bellosi, L., *Mostra d' Arte Sacra della Diocese di S. Miniato* (*BAE*, XXXII, 41, 1969), pp. 56-57, and *Maetzke**,
1974, pp. 88-91.

1278   Giovanni di Ser Giovanni. Detail: Battle scene with Archers. Fresco. San Giovanni Valdarno, S. Lorenzo.
Author's photo. s.

Lo Scheggia
See *Giovanni di Ser Giovanni*.

Master of the Adimari Cassone
See *Master of Fucecchio* and *Giovanni di Ser Giovanni*.

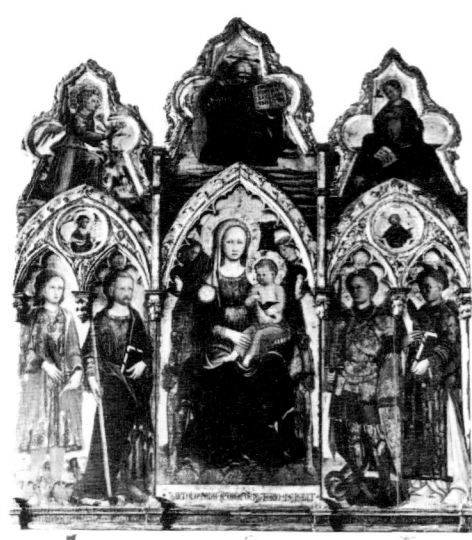

Bartolommeo d'Andrea Bocchi
Pistoiese, born in 1406, and active in the second and third quarters of the fifteenth century.
See Procacci, U., *RA*, XIV, 1932, pp. 395-399.

1279   Bartolomeo di Andrea Bocchi. Triptych: Madonna and Child Enthroned with two Angels, Sts Hippolytus, James, Michael the Archangel, Stephen.   Above: Christ blessing, Annunciation, two Saints.   Panel.   Serravalle (Pistoia), S. Michele.   cp: 228 × 70; sps: 211 × 62. Collection photo. s & d. 1439.

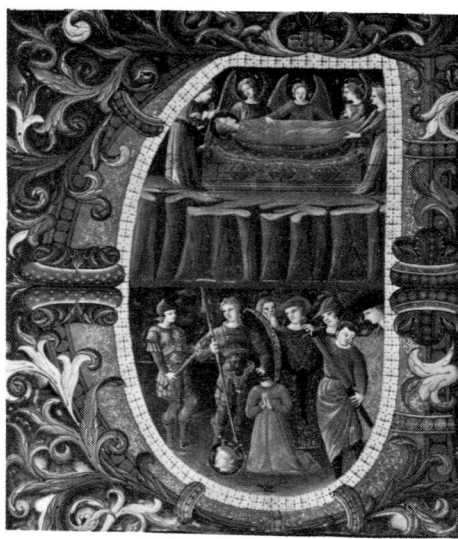

Jacopo di Antonio
Florentine, born 1427, died 1454.
See Procacci, U., *RA*, XXXV, 10, 1960, pp. 3-70.

1280   Jacopo di Antonio (?).   Miniature: Beheading and Death of St Catherine.   Parchment.   Florence, Biblioteca Corsini. f. 32v.   SGF 101628.

Jacopo del Corso
See *Jacopo di Antonio*

Cipriani di Simone
Collaborator of Jacopo di Antonio.
See Procacci, U., *RA*, XXXV, 10, 1960, pp. 20-21.

Giuliano d'Arrigo
Collaborator of Jacopo di Antonio.
See Procacci, U., *RA*, XXXV, 10, 1960, pp. 20-21.

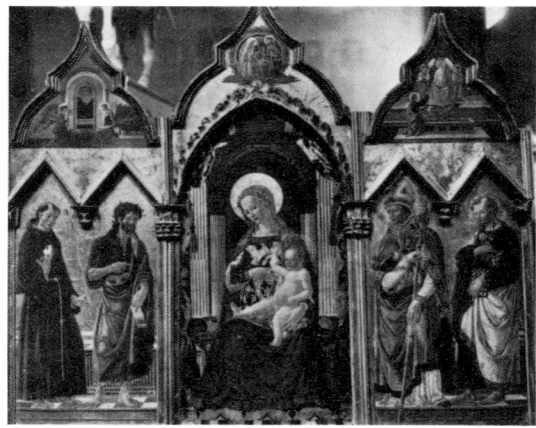

Giovanni di Francesco
Mid-fifteenth century painter influenced by Domenico Veneziano and others.
See Giovannozzi, V., *RA*, XVI, 1934, pp. 337-365.

1281   Giovanni di Francesco. Triptych: Madonna and Child Enthroned with Sts Francis, John the Baptist, Zenobius and Paul.   Panel.   Florence, Museo Nazionale del Bargello.   no. 2025.   SGF 52277.

Master of the Carrand Triptych
See *Giovanni di Francesco.*

Master of the Contini Madonna
See *Giovanni di Francesco.*

Stefano d' Antonio di Vanni
c. 1407-1483, pupil and assistant of Bicci di Lorenzo.
See Cohn, W., *BA*, XLIV, 4, 1959, pp. 61-68.

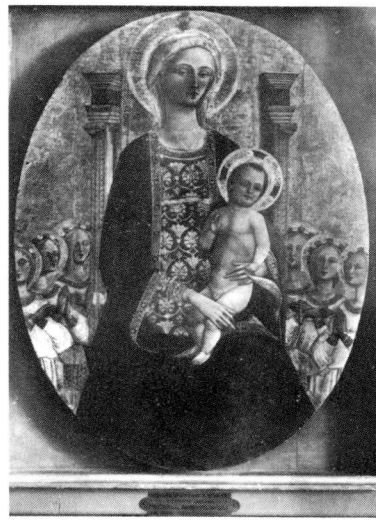

1282   Stefano di Antonio di Vanni. Madonna and Child Enthroned with six Angels. Panel. Volterra, Pinacoteca.
        Museum photo.

Angelico
Active second and third quarters of the fifteenth century.
See Baldini, U., *L'opera completa dell'Angelico*, Milan, 1970.

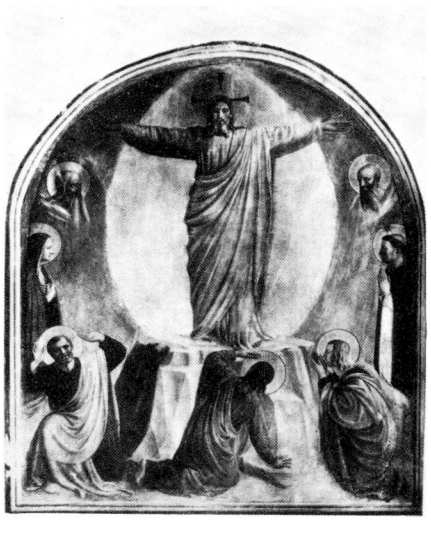

1283   Angelico. Transfiguration. Fresco. Florence, S. Marco, Sixth Cell. SGF 07799.

Battisti di Biagio Sanguigni
Miniaturist and friend of Angelico. Born 1392.
See Cohn, W., *RA*, XXX, 1955, pp. 211-215.

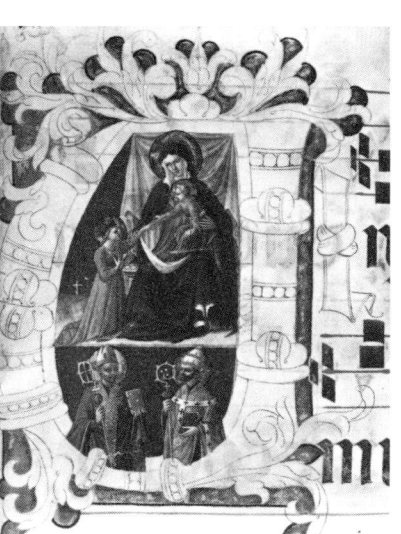

1284   Battista di Biagio Sanguigni (?). Miniature: Marriage of St Catherine. Parchment. Florence, Biblioteca
        Corsini. f. 38v. SGF 101631.

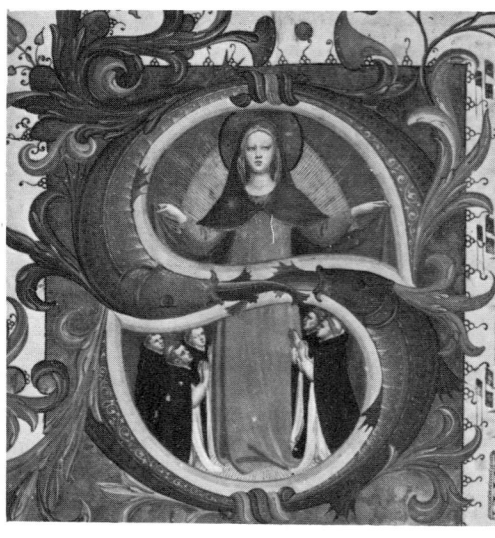

Zanobi Strozzi (1412-1468)
Collaborator of Battista di Biagio Sanguigni.
See Ciardi Dupré Dal Poggetto, M. G., *AV*, XII, 4, 1973, pp. 3-10.

1285 Zanobi Strozzi. Miniature: Virgin protects the Dominicans. Parchment. Florence, Museo di S. Marco. no. 558. c. 156v. SGF 118662.

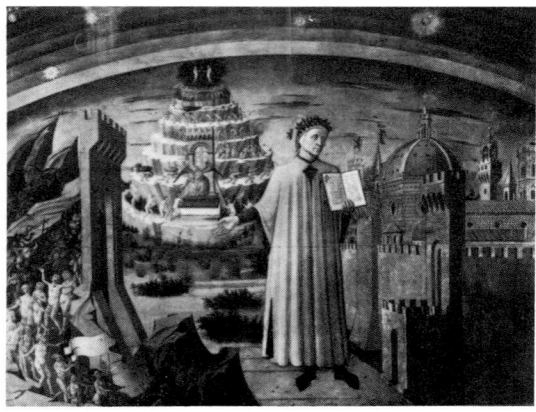

Domenico di Michelino (1417-1491)
Strongly influenced by Angelico.
See Zeri, F., and Gardner, E. E., *MMOA**, 1971, pp. 105-106.

1286 Domenico di Michelino. Dante holding open The Divine Comedy which casts a light over the city of Florence. Panel. Florence, Duomo. no. 131. SGF 131853.

Pseudo Domenico di Michelino
See Zeri, F., *AP*, XCIX, 144, Feb., 1974, pp. 92, 4.

Master of the Buckingham Palace Madonna
This painter is the same as Pseudo-Domenico di Michelino - a close follower of Angelico.
See also *Domenico di Michelino*.

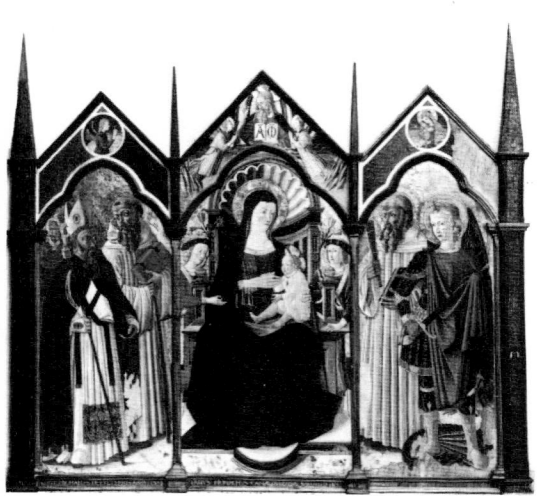

Giuliano Amadei
The painter of a signed triptych at Pieve a Tifi, Caprese, Mugello. Apparently a miniaturist influenced by Angelico and a colleague of Piero della Francesca.
See *Maetzke**, 1974, pp. 94-6.

1287 Giuliano Amadei. Triptych: Madonna and Child Enthroned with two Angels and four Saints. Panel. Caprese (Casentino), Pieve a Tifi. SGA 17183.

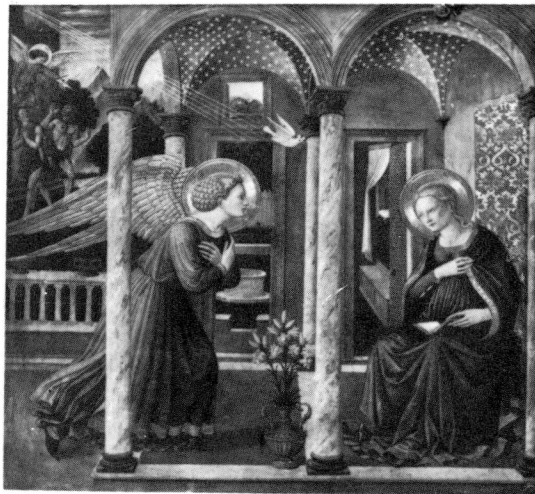

Zanobi Macchiavelli
Active mid-fifteenth century, influenced by Angelico and Filippo Lippi.
See Matteoli, A., *BAE*, XXXIII, 42, 1972, pp. 137-145.

1288 Zanobi Machiavelli. Annunciation. Panel. Ponte a Mensola (near Settignano), S. Martino. Brogi 19217.

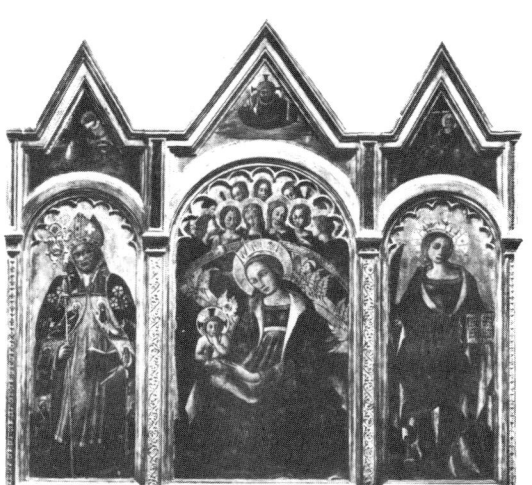

Antonio da Firenze
Active after c. 1440, tracing his origins in Angelico's work.
See Zeri, F., *PA*, XI, 123, 1960, pp. 50-57.

1289 Antonio da Firenze. Triptych: Madonna & Child with two Saints. Ponte a Mensola (near Settignano), Berenson Collection. SGF 54676.

Master of S. Miniato
Follower of Angelico, also influenced by Botticelli.
See Castelfranchi, G., *RA*, 1933, II, V, pp. 88-92.

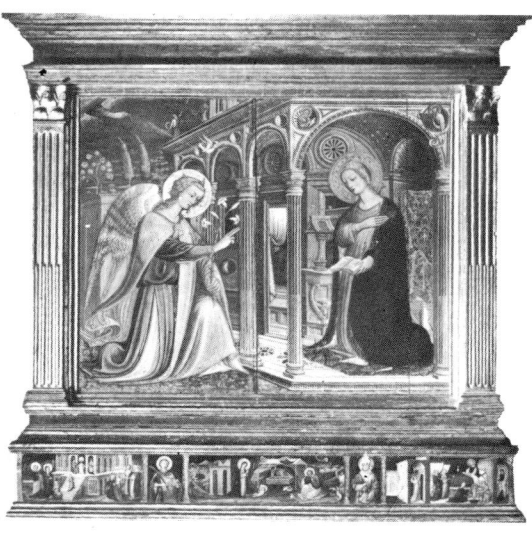

Master of Signa
Florentine, a follower of Bicci di Lorenzo.
See Zeri, F., *BA*, XLVIII, IV, 1963, pp. 248-249, 257-258, n. 13.

1290 Master of Signa. Annunciation. Panel. Ponte a Mensola (near Settignano), Berenson Collection.
SGF 56803.

Apollonio di Giovanni
Kept a shop with Marco del Buono in the mid-fifteenth century, making painted marriage chests.
See Zeri, F., and Gardner, E. E., *MMOA**, 1971, pp. 100-105.

603

Marco del Buono
See *Apollonio di Giovanni.*

Master of the Cassoni
See *Apollonio di Giovanni*

Master of the Jarves Cassone
See *Apollonio di Giovanni*

Virgil Master
See *Apollonio di Giovanni.*

Dido Master
See *Apollonio di Giovanni.*

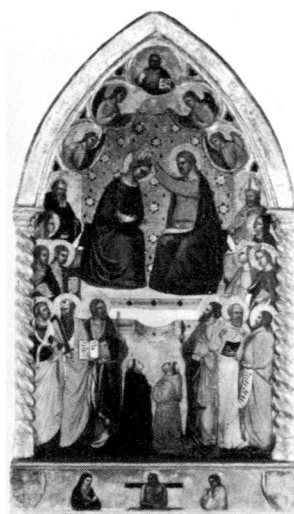

Master of the Christ Church Coronation
Active mid-fifteenth century.
See *Byam Shaw**, 1967, pp. 33-34, pl. 9.

1291 Master of the Christ Church Coronation. Coronation of the Virgin with Saints. Panel. Oxford, Christ Church. no. 7. 91.1 × 48. Museum photo.

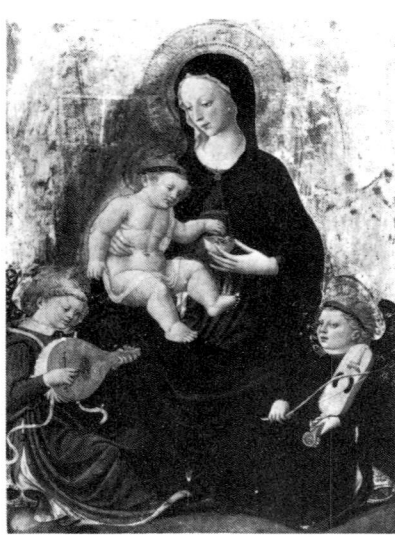

Pesellino (1422-1457)
(*Francesco di Stefano*). Follower of Angelico; he worked with Filippo Lippi in 1455.
See Zeri, F., and Gardner, E. E., *MMOA**, 1971, pp. 95-98.

1292 Pesellino. Madonna and Child with two music-making Angels. Panel. Ponte a Mensola (near Settignano), Berenson Collection. SGF 54940.

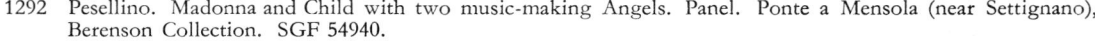
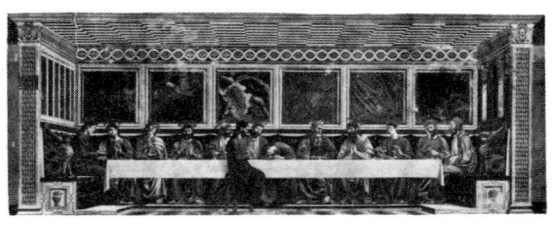

Andrea del Castagno
Born near Florence, and painted in the 1440's and 1450's. Influenced by the early renaissance painters. Died in 1457.
See *Fresco Show**, 1969 (Eng. ed.), pp. 146-153.

1293 Andrea del Castagno. Last Supper. Fresco. Florence, Cenacolo di S. Apollonia, Museo di Andrea del Castagno. SGF 123794.

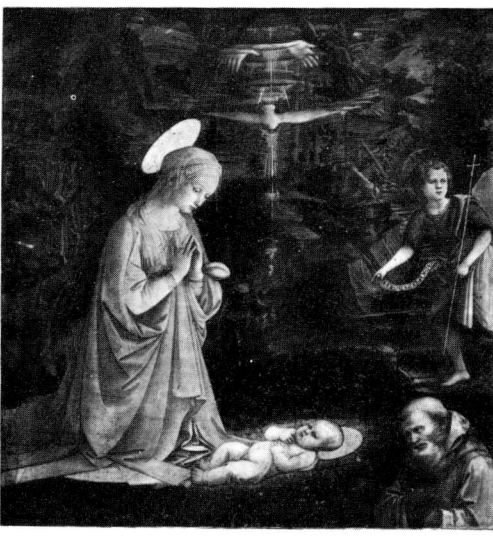

Filippo Lippi (*c. 1406-1469*)
Young contemporary of Masaccio.
See Zeri, F., and Gardner, E. E., *MMOA**, 1971, pp. 82-94.

1294   Filippo Lippi. Adoration of the Infant Christ with Infant St John and St Bernard. Panel. Florence, Uffizi. no. 8353. 140 × 131. SGF 105953.

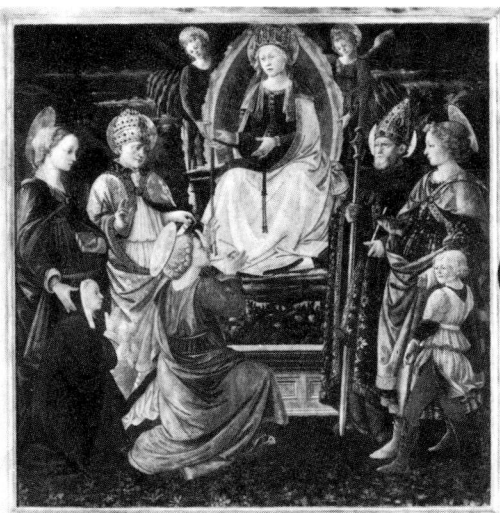

Fra Diamante
Associate of Filippo Lippi.
See Pittaluga, M., *Fra Diamante collaboratore di Filippo Lippi* (pamphlet: Bibliopolis), Florence, 1941.

1295   Fra Diamante. Madonna of the Holy Girdle with St Thomas, four other Saints, two Angels and Donor. Panel. Prato, Galleria Comunale. Alinari 10443.

Master of the Louvre Nativity
Named after a painting in the Louvre, by a close associate of Filippo Lippi. Not to be confused with a painter of the same name, active in the third quarter of the fourteenth century.
See Busignani, A., *E*, LXIV, 127, 1958, pp. 146-156.

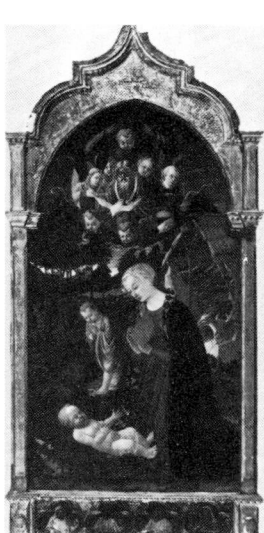

Master of the Castello Nativity
Active in Florence from c. 1445 to 1475. Influenced by Masaccio, Lippi and Domenico Veneziano.
See Zeri, F., and Gardner, E. E., *MMOA**, 1971, pp. 114-116; Meiss, M., *GBA*, LXX, 109, 1967, pp. 213-218.

1296   Master of the Castello Nativity. Adoration of the Infant Christ with Infant St John. Above: God the Father and Holy Ghost. Predella: four Prophets. Florence, Accademia, Depositi. no. 171. SGF 94693.

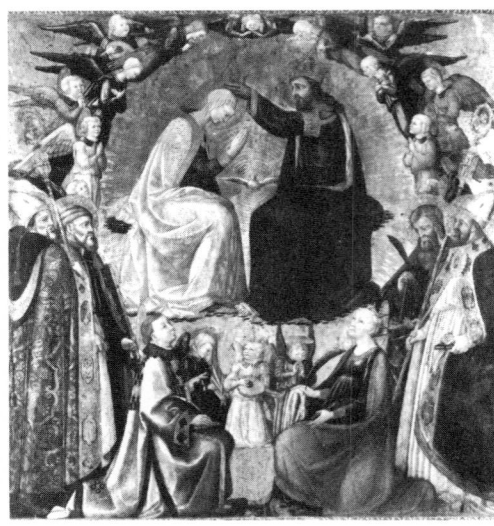

Neri di Bicci (1419-1491)
Son of Bicci di Lorenzo.
See *Galetti**, 1950, Vol. II, pp. 1764-1765.

1297　Neri di Bicci. Coronation of the Virgin with Sts Lucy, Catherine, Bartholomew, and Andrew. Panel. Florence, Museo dell'Ospedale degli Innocenti. SGF 136621.

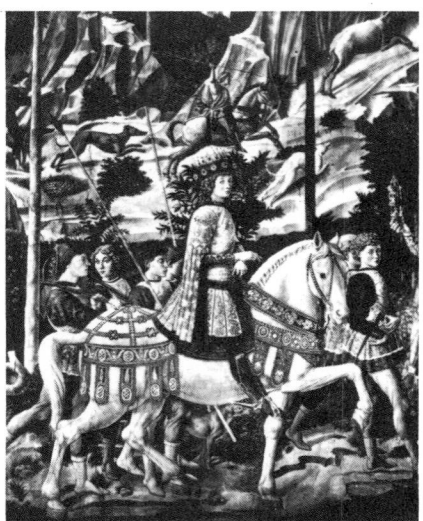

Benozzo Gozzoli (1420-1497)
Called *Benozzo di Lese*, he was a collaborator of Ghiberti and Angelico.
See Rizzo, A. D., *Benozzo Gozzoli Pittore Fiorentino*, Florence, 1972.

1298　Benozzo Gozzoli. Detail: Lorenzo the Magnificent. Fresco. Florence, Palazzo Medici Riccardi, Cappella. SGF 53870.

Additions

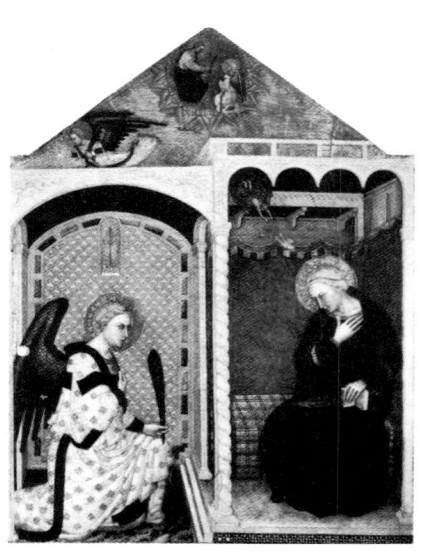

Andrea di Nerio
An Aretine of the mid-14th century, recently identified.
See *Maetzke**, 1974, pp. 53-61.

Andrea di Nerio. Annunciation. Panel. Arezzo. Museo Diocesano. s. SGA. 7892.

DATED WORKS BY UNKNOWN PAINTERS

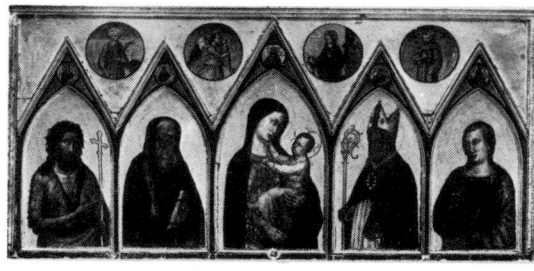

1299 Unknown painter near to Daddi. Polyptych: Madonna & Child with four Saints. Panel. San Godenzo (Mugello), Basilica. SGF 10794. d. 1333.

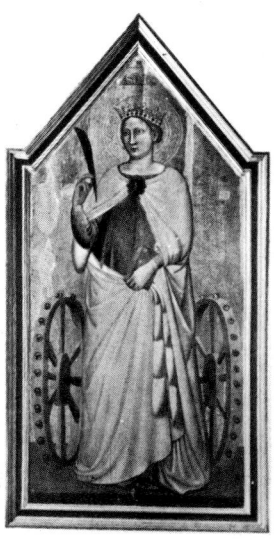

1300 Unknown painter near to Daddi. St Catherine. Panel. Formerly Hatfield (Herts.), N. Mymms, Burns Collection. d. 1333.

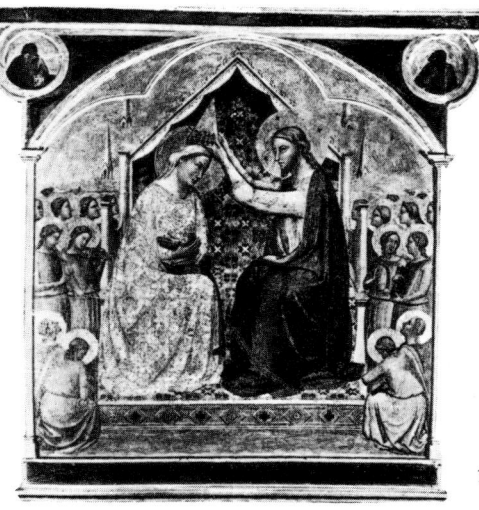

1301 Unknown painter near to Daddi. Coronation of the Virgin with twenty-four Angels. Panel. Milan, Private Collection. Collection photo. d. 1338.

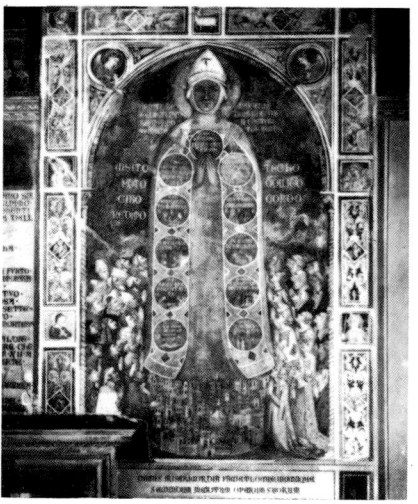

1302 Unknown painter. Madonna della Misericordia. Fresco. Florence, Opera del Bigallo. SGF 142912. d. 1342. (or 1352).

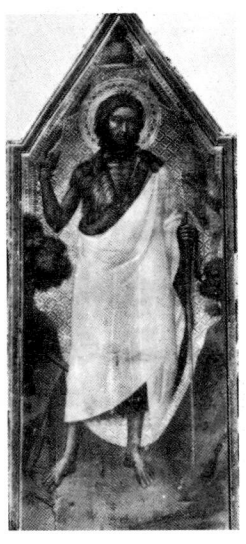

1303   Unknown painter near to Daddi. St John the Baptist. Panel. Gangalandi (near Lastra a Signa), S. Martino. Frick Art Reference Library photo no. 12780. d. 1346.

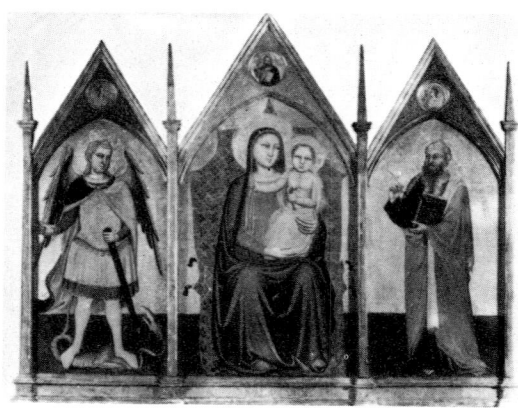

1304   Unknown painter near to Giovanni del Biondo. Triptych: Madonna & Child with two Saints. Panel. Vertelli, S. Michele. SGF 24523. d. 1357.

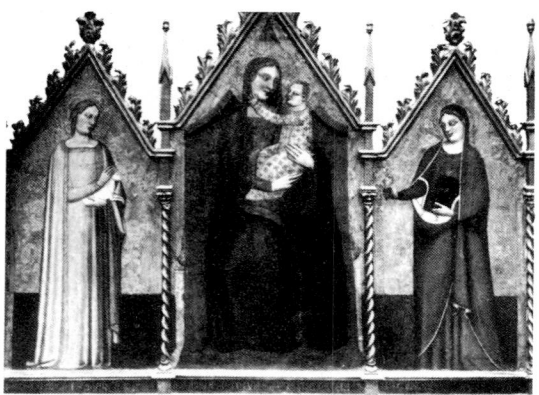

1305   Unknown painter near to Andrea da Firenze. Triptych: Madonna & Child Enthroned with Sts Agnes and Catherine. Panel. Florence, Museo Bardini, Corsi Collection. Reali. d. 1358.

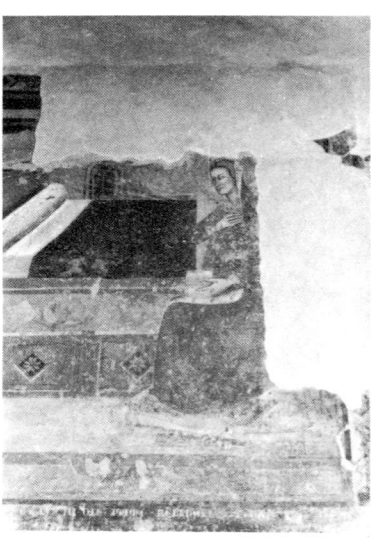

1306   Unknown painter. Fresco: Virgin Annunciate, Figline di Prato, Pieve. Author's photo. d. 1363.

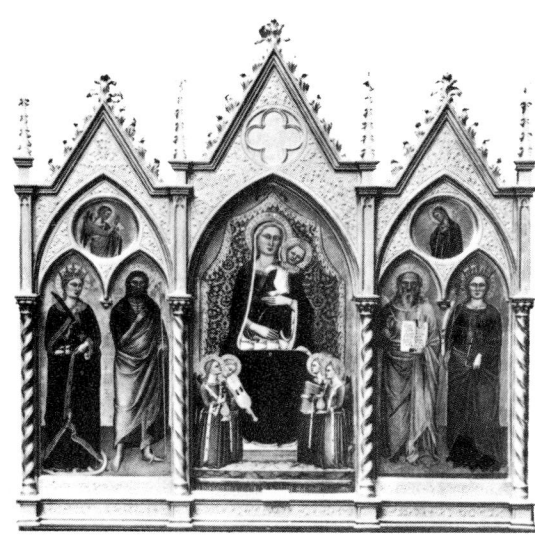

1307 Unknown painter near to Jacopo di Cione. Triptych: Madonna & Child with four Saints. Panel. Whereabouts unknown. Fototeca Berenson. d. 1379.

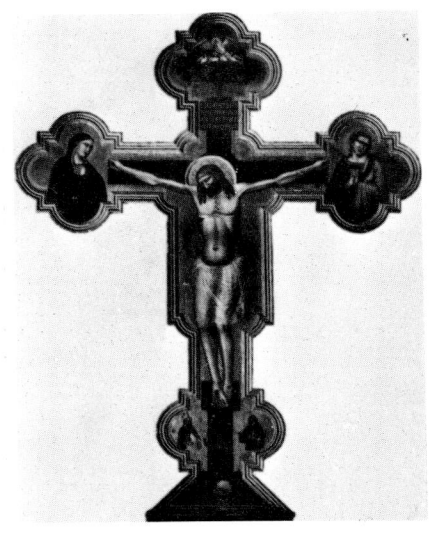

1308 Unknown painter near to Niccolò di Pietro Gerini. Painted Crucifix. Panel. Florence, S. Croce, Castellani Chapel. Alinari 3916. d. 1380.

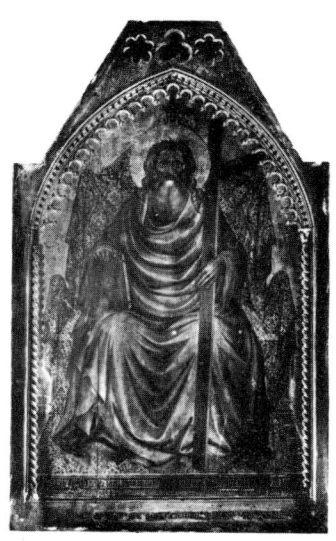

1309 Unknown painter. St Andrew. Panel. Faltignano (Val di Pesa), S. Bartolomeo. SGF 1806. d. 1380.

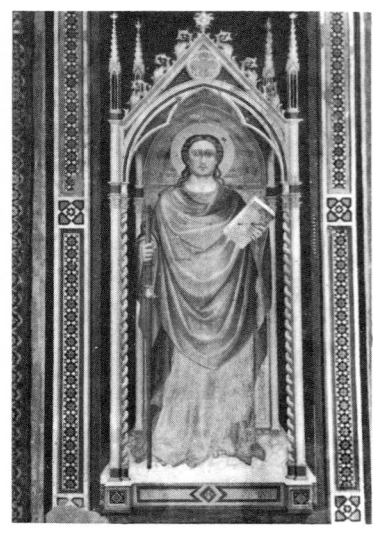

1310   Unknown painter. St James. Fresco. Florence, S. Miniato al Monte. Author's photo. d. 1387.

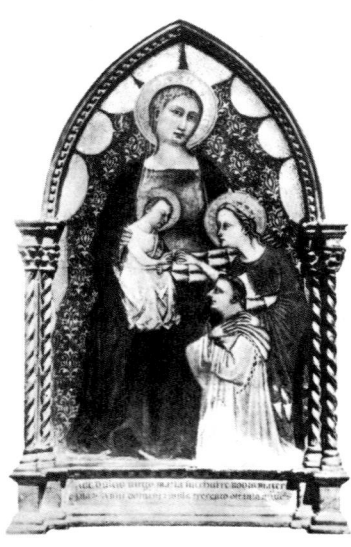

1311   Unknown painter near Giovanni del Biondo. Marriage of St Catherine. Panel. Formerly San Domenico di Fiesole, Lucas Collection. d. 1389.

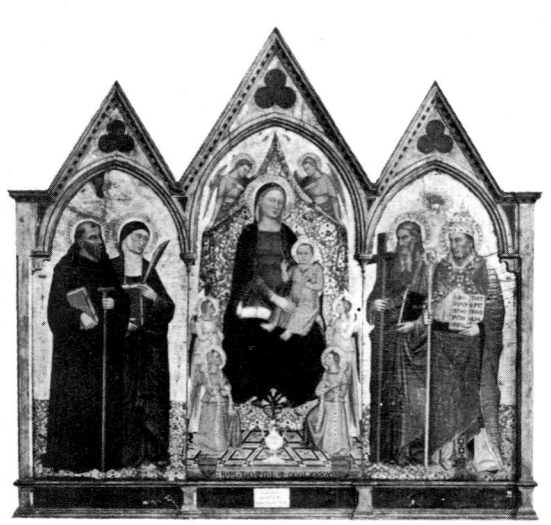

1312   Unknown painter near to Nardo di Cione. Triptych: Madonna & Child with four Saints and six Angels. Panel. Honolulu, Academy of Arts 2834. Museum photo. d. 1391.

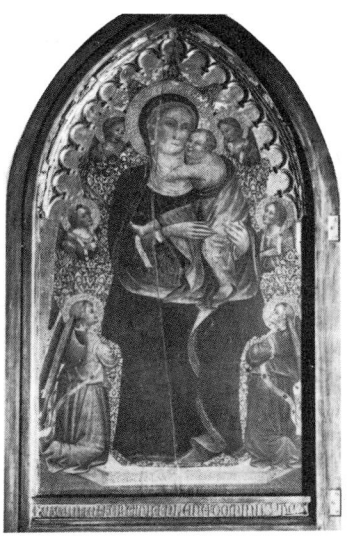

1313 Unknown painter. Madonna & Child with six Angels. Panel. Figline (Upper Valdarno), Ospedale Serristori. Alinari 41424. d. 1399.

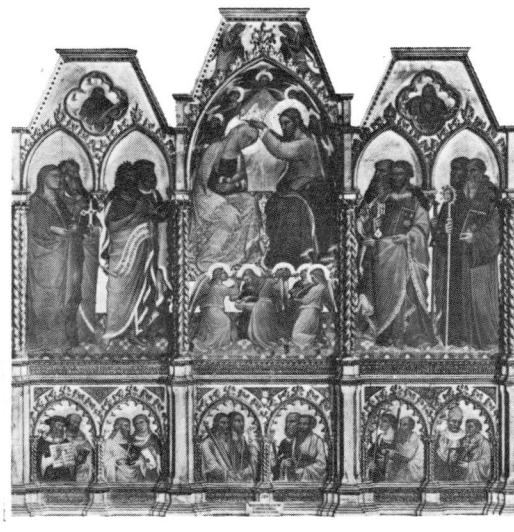

1314 Lorenzo di Niccolò, Niccolò di Pietro Gerini and Spinello Aretino. Polyptych: Coronation of the Virgin with twenty Saints and four Angels. Florence, Accademia 8468. Brogi 2391. d. 1401.

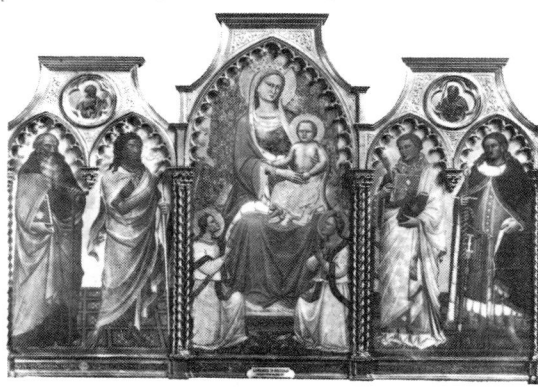

1315 Unknown painter near to Niccolò di Pietro Gerini. Triptych: Madonna & Child with two Angels and Saints. Florence, Accademia 8610. Brogi 22281. d. 1404.

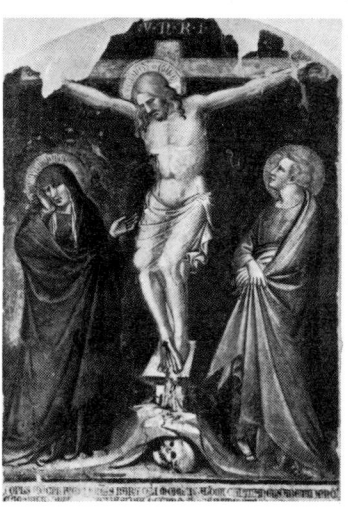

1316 Unknown painter near to Spinello Aretino. Christ on the Cross with the Virgin & St John the Evangelist. Fresco. Arezzo, S. Domenico. SGF 144949. d. 1408.

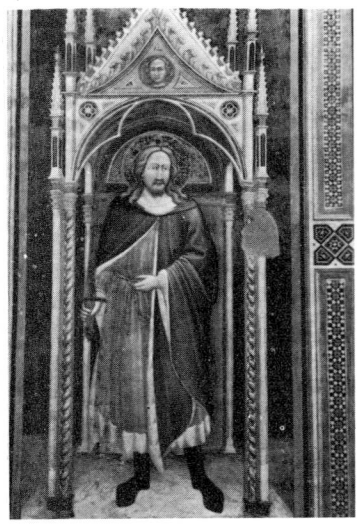

1317 Unknown painter. St Julian. Fresco. Florence, S. Miniato al Monte. Author's photo. d. 1409.

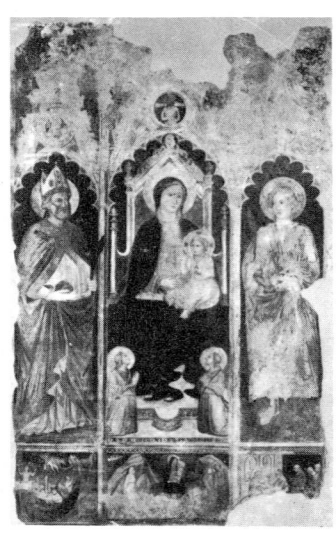

1318 Unknown painter near Cristiani. Frescoed triptych: Madonna & Child with two Saints and Angels; three scenes below. Prato, Palazzo dell'Arte della Lana. SGF 118701. d. 1411.

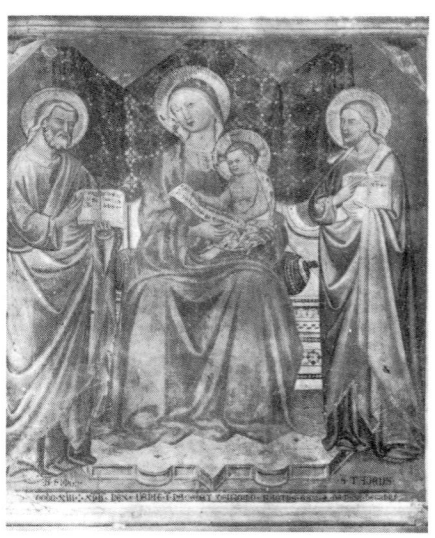

1319 Unknown painter. Madonna & Child Enthroned with Sts Simon & Thaddeus. Fresco. San Donato in Poggio (near Passignano), Val di Pesa. SGF 18412. d. 1413.

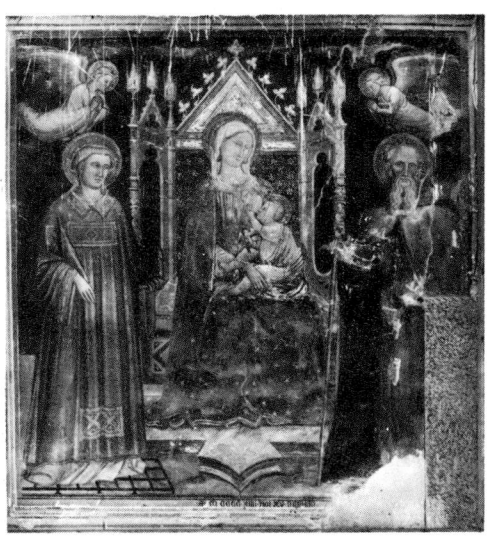

1320 Unknown painter. Madonna & Child Enthroned with Sts Lawrence & Anthony Abbot. Fresco. Arezzo, Museo. SGF 14071. d. 1414.

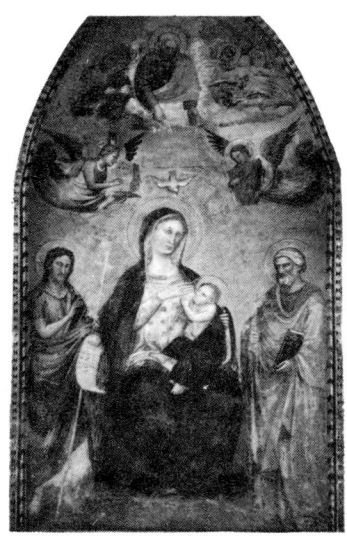

1321 Unknown painter. Tabernacle: Madonna nursing the Child with Sts John the Baptist and Peter, God the Father and two Angels. Fresco. Florence, via Lippi, near Caciolle. Alinari 29207. d. 1416.

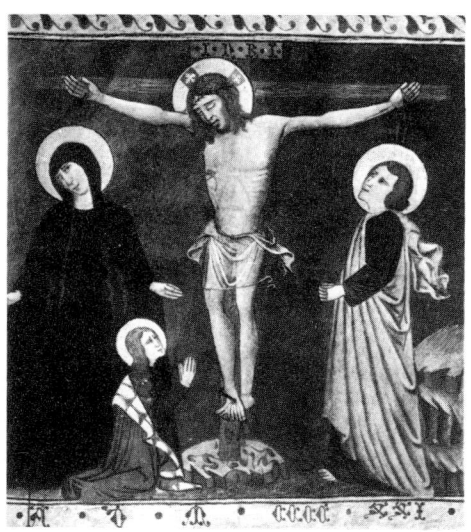

1322 Unknown painter. Christ on the Cross with the Virgin, Sts John the Evangelist and Mary Magdalene. Fresco. Sestino (Stia), S. Pancrazio. SGF 20809. d. 1421 (?).

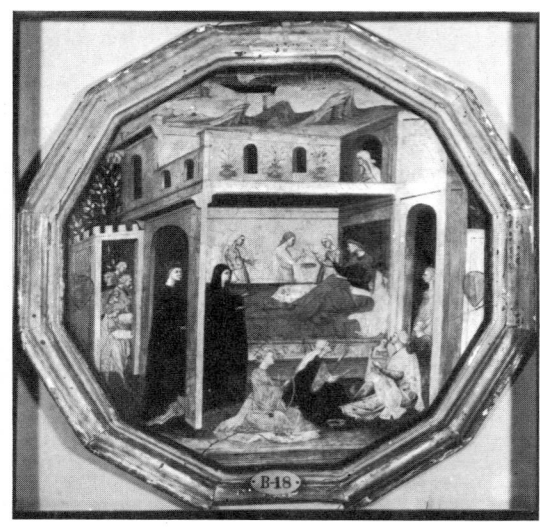

1323 Unknown painter. Desco da parto: Birth of St John the Baptist. Panel. New York, Historical Society 1867.18. Museum photo 259. d. 1428.

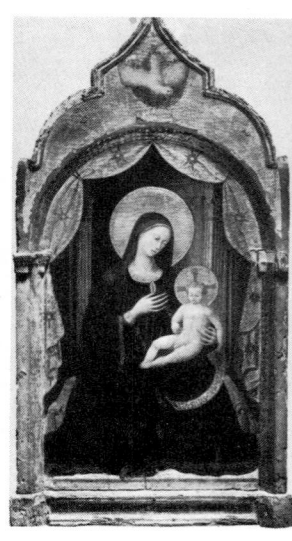

1324 Unknown painter near to Andrea di Giusto. Madonna & Child. Panel. Florence, Berenson Collection, Fototeca Berenson. d. 1435 (?).

Additions

APPENDIX B

GLOSSARY

Abba (Aramaic). In the New Testament, a patriarchal figure; sometimes applied to God; from it we have such words as *abbot*, and *abbé*.

Ab incarnatione. The manner of dating the year from 25th March, the Feast of the Annunciation; in many cities in Tuscany in the late Middle Ages and Renaissance, the calendar year began with this feast. It is sometimes also called " old style " or " Florentine style ". Florence, Siena and Prato used this dating system as did Pisa; however, this last city also anticipated the date by one year. See *a nativitate.*

A fresco, affresco, al fresco. A method of wall painting, for which earth colours are used, mixed with water. A rough layer of plaster called *arriccio* is first applied to the wall, on which, when the wall is thoroughly dry, the *sinopia* is drawn. A final layer, of plaster, called *intonaco*, is then applied wet, on which the outline is redrawn; paint is put on while the plaster is still damp so that the colours sink into the wall drying as part of the wall itself.

Al secco. Painting with tempera onto a plaster wall which is already dry.

A nativitate. The manner of dating the year from 25th December. This method was used in Pistoia, Arezzo and Lucca. See *ab incarnatione.*

Ancona. This is a panel painting with the mouldings integrally part of it; it may be of any size, and of one or more panels. As were *panels*, anconas were usually made of poplar, linden or willow.

Antiphonary. A book, usually a codex containing antiphons, that is verses of psalms to be sung.

Arcosol tomb. A grave or tomb which has been placed in a vaulted niche in a wall: often the wall above the grave is decorated.

Arriccio. The rough first layer of plaster put on a wall which is being prepared for fresco painting. It is on the *arriccio* that the *sinopia* is drawn when dry. The final layer of plaster (see *intonaco*), is placed wet on top, ready for the painter to use.

Arte dei Medici e Speziali (lit. *Guild of Doctors and Apothecaries*). This is the guild to which painters in Florence belonged, as painters depended upon apothecaries for their pigments. The first corporation of painters dates from the early fourteenth century. In 1339 *L'Arte de' Pittori* is incorporated, dependent upon the *Arte dei Medici e Speziali*. In 1349 it becomes the *Compagnia e Fraternità di S. Luca* under the special protection of the Virgin Mary, St John the Baptist, St Zenobius and St Reparata. This company met in S. Matteo and sometimes called themselves *La Confraternità de' Pittori.*

Arzica. Yellow.

Azurite. Blue carbonate of copper, an ore similar to malachite.

Bargello. A chief of police; the word also refers to the building in Florence which is now the National Museum of Sculpture. Built about 1255, it was the town hall until the Palazzo della Signoria was constructed. It served as the prison for many years.

Biacca. A white lead.

Biffo. A colour made by mixing *lac* and blue.

Binder. (lit. something which holds together). In painting, glue; the substance mixed with *pigment* and *medium* to help them adhere to a surface.

Bole. An earth or clay; there are various kinds, coloured red, yellow or brown; Cennini's *bole* may simply be an astringent earth.

Bottega. Studio or workshop of a painter; it refers also to works done by assistants and pupils.

Bozzetto. A sketch.

Braccia. A measurement, about two feet.

Brazil, brazilin. Originally a red wood from the East Indies; the country was named for a similar wood: a red dye from the tree.

Bon fresco. True fresco as opposed to *mezzo fresco* or painting *al secco*: see *al fresco.*

Burnish. To shine, to make bright either by rubbing or with a tool; to furbish.

Calimala. The guild of cloth merchants in Florence. This guild worked cloth, both local and imported.

Camposanto (Ital. *holy field*). A cemetery.

Canna. A measurement, about forty-five inches.

Cartone (lit. a large sheet of paper, or cardboard, or a cartoon). See also *sinopia.* A preliminary drawing for a painting ready to be transferred onto a panel or wall; usually on a large sheet of paper.

Cartouche. A scroll ornament with rolled-up ends, inscribed.

Cassone. A renaissance marriage chest for the storage of linen. It is generally oblong in shape, 4' to 6' by 1½' to 2', about 2' high.

Cast. A mould; also the action of pouring a liquified solid into a mould.

Cattedra. A bishop's throne.

Cenacolo. Scene of the Last Supper.

Cenotaph (Greek, empty *tomb*). A tomb-like monument for someone buried elsewhere.

Chapter-room. The room in a religious community where " chapters " of holy books were read; it was a room also used for administrative meetings of the brethren.

Chiaroscuro (Ital. *light-dark*). Gradation from light to shadow or vice versa, used to depict volume or contour.

Cinabrese. An Italian term for a red earth colour commonly used in fresco work, and for colouring wood, or earth tiles.

Cinnaber. Red mercuric sulphide; vermilion.

Cinquecento (five hundred). Fifteen hundreds, or sixteenth century: from *millecinquecento.*

Company of St Luke. The company to which painters in Florence belonged; see *Arte dei Medici e Speziali.*

Company of St Nicholas of Bari. A company which seems to have been founded in 1334. Its members met in a small chapel dedicated to St Nicholas under the main altar of the church of Santa Maria del Carmine.

Console. A support or bracket sometimes found below panel paintings. Its function is support when the picture is hung on a wall. Often decorated.

Continuous representation. The depiction of successive incidents of a story within one painting.

Craquelure (French). Fine cracks on paintings due to shrinkage of the surface.

Crook. A tool used in gilding.

Cufic or *pseudo-cufic.* Primitive or inaccurate form of arabic alphabet used in inscriptions, and as decoration for hems of garments, haloes, edges of gold-panelled pictures, etc.

Davanzale. A window sill or ledge.

Desco da parto (Ital. *birth plate*). A circular tray, for carrying gifts, presented to a woman who had just given birth.

Diadem. A crown; also sometimes a band round the head used to support a crown, or symbol of a crown.

Dies natalis (Lat. *anniversary*). Day on which a saint's feast (anniversary of his death or burial), is celebrated.

Distemper. Paint made by mixing powdered colour with size; also the technique of using this type of paint.

Diptych. A devotional object made up of two pictures hinged together.

Doratura. For Cennino Cennini, this was a kind of gold shellac. It may also have been made from gold and mercury. It is probably a synonym for *vermeil.*

Dossal. An altar frontal, often carved or painted.

Dugento (Variation of Ital. *duecento*, two hundred). Twelve hundreds, or thirteenth century; from *milleduecento.*

Duomo. The principal church in a town, often a cathedral; from *domus*, house.

Faulting. When gilding a panel, the repairing of imperfections after having laid on the gold leaf.

Florentine style. See *ab incarnatione.*

Florin (Ital. *fiorino*). The gold *florin* was the basis of Florentine finances (see also *lira*). It was worth about $3\frac{1}{2}$-4 *lire* in 1400; about $5\frac{1}{5}$-6 in 1500. Also called a *ducat.*

Fondo d'oro. Gold background which appears in many early paintings, also used as a name for these early pictures.

Forzerinaio. One who painted small boxes, called *forzerini.*

Forzerino. A small painted box.

Friars (Lat. *frater, brother*). Members of religious orders combining ministry " in the work " with contemplative life.

Friars minor. Franciscans.

Friars preachers. Dominicans.

Gamboge. A gum or resin used for yellow.

Garzone (Ital. *apprentice*). A young boy learning the trade in a shop.

Gesso (Ital. *chalk*). A chalk, or plaster substance often used in sculpture.

Gesso bolognese and *volteriano* seem both to have been the same as *gesso grosso*, a coarse plaster.

Gesso sottile. Fine plaster.

Giallorino. A yellow.

Gilding. The process of colouring a panel (or anything else) with real gold.

Giornata (Ital. *period of a whole day*). Amount of fresco painting achieved in one day. On the average, perhaps a yard square. The *giornate* can be easily counted, and their sequence known by the technical necessity of making the edges of a day's plastering overlap the plaster applied the previous day.

Glue. Various glues were used in the 14th and 15th centuries: Cennino Cennini describes how to make glues from flour, from mastic and wax, from varnish, from white lead and verdigris, from fish, from goat or sheep, or from lime and cheese.

Gold leaf. Thin sheets of gold applied to the surface of panel paintings.

Gonfaloniere. (Ital. *standard bearer*). The head of a Florentine guild; the term was also used to name the chief magistrate in the Palazzo Vecchio.

Graffito or *sgraffito.* An outline for a wall painting which has been scratched into wet plaster (Ital. *graffiare, to scratch*). A graffito can be a finished scratched drawing in itself, and often refers to all kinds of wall marks and writings.

Grisaille. Method of painting in monotone in order to depict on the two dimensional plane the three dimensional quality of objects; the colour is often grey.

Grospoint. A method of embroidery on open-grained coarse canvas.

Grotesque. Ornament for the decoration of borders; usually a vine of foliage in which appear human heads, fantastic animals, flowers, fruit, etc. The word cames from the discovery in Rome, during the Renaissance, in " grottos " — that is in excavated Roman buildings — of many such decorations.

Guild. These were divided into two classes — merchant guilds and craft guilds. The members of the merchant guilds were *maestri* (masters) and *discipuli* (apprentices), and of the craft guilds, *maestri, lavoranti* (workmen) and *garzoni* (apprentices).

Hagiography (Greek). Literature, i.e. lives and legends, of saints.

Halo. A disc of light about the head of holy figures, a *nimbus.*

Hatching. Usually a series of fine parallel lines used in drawing, for shading.

Hieronymianum. Catalogue of martyrs and saints in date order, i.e. the date of each saint's feast day. Compiled before 600 A.D.

Iconoclasm (Greek). The breaking or destruction of images.

Imago Pietatis (Lat. *image of sorrow*). The Dead Christ standing in the Tomb showing His Wounds. He is sometimes with the Virgin, and with Saints and Symbols of the Passion.

Impalcatura. See *pontata.*

In situ (Lat. *in place*). Used adjectively to describe a painting which is in the place for which it was executed.

Intonaco (Ital. *plaster*). Final layer of wet plaster to which paint is applied, when painting al fresco. It is damp, so that the paint may be absorbed into the plaster and become part of the wall.

Intrados. The underside of an arch. In early Tuscan churches it was often decorated.

Kermes. A crimson.

Lac, or *Lake,* a red colour.

Laccio. This usually refers to a pattern, but may also indicate a net or mesh-like arrangement. It can also refer to making an opening in a painted surface to see what is beneath.

Libro delle Matricole. A list of matriculated members of a guild; often used in the history of Florentine painting to refer to the list of members of the *Compagnia di San Luca.*

Life mask. An imprint taken of a person's face, usually in plaster or wax, while they are alive. A *death mask* is one taken from a dead person.

Lire. Florentine money was calculated in *lire, soldi* and *dinari,* abbreviated *l. s. d;* the system persisted until recently in England: 12 *dinari* made one *soldo;* twenty *soldi* made one *lira.* For the value of the *lira* see *Florin.*

Lunette. A space, usually semi-circular, above a door or window, often decorated.

Madonna in Glory. A representation of the Virgin in heaven; often there are symbolic clouds under Her.

Madonna of the Holy Girdle. A representation of the Virgin in Glory, handing Her girdle to St Thomas.

Madonna of Humility. A representation of the Virgin seated on a cushion; the cushion is usually on the ground.

Madonna del Latte. A representation of the Virgin giving suck to the Infant Jesus.

Maestà (Ital. *majesty*). Portrayal of the Virgin and Child enthroned in majesty with saints and angels.

Malachite. Hydrous carbonate of copper, of a green colour. The ore is similar to azurite.

Mandorla (Ital. *almond*). An almond-shaped form encircling the figure of Christ Resurrected or the Virgin of the Assumption.

Man of Sorrows. See *Imago Pietatis.*

Martelli natura or *punzecchiatura.* Method of roughening, either by hammer (*martello*) or denting (*punzecchiatura*), a plaster surface already laid so that the intonaco will better adhere to it.

Massicot. A colour, yellow oxide of lead.

Mastic. A gum or resin; or cement; sometimes a pale yellow.

Matrix (lit. *an enclosing mass*). For artisans a mould used in moulding or casting.

Medium. The liquid in which pigments are mixed, e.g. oil, water; also techniques of painting, such as water colour, oil, painting, etc. In Italian, *media.*

Memento mori (Lat. " remember that you must die "). In paintings, images that remind one of death, such as skulls, skeletons, etc.

Minium. Vermilion, red lead.

Miniver. Very fine fur from the animal of this name, used for making brushes.

Monk (Greek *monos,* alone). Member of male religious community bound under vows of chastity, obedience and poverty.

Monte. A pawnbroker or lending house. The *Monte* in Florence was the communal public debt, founded in 1345 and paying 5% annually.

Mordant. A substance used for fixing colours and goldleaf.

Navicella (Ital. *little boat*). The boat-shaped urn in which incense is kept; it can refer to other boat-shaped objects; the term also refers specifically to a lost mosaic, once at Old St. Peter's in Rome, by Giotto, of Christ walking on the sea, saving St Peter.

Net. See *squaring.*

New style. See *ab incarnatione.*

Nimbus or *nimbo.* A cloud of glory, or a halo.

Noli me tangere (Bib. lat. " Touch me not "). The scene of Christ's appearance to Mary Magdalene after the Resurrection. He says that she should not touch Him.

Nun. Member of female religious community, see *Monk.*

Observants. Members of the stricter form of the Rule of St Francis as opposed to the moderate Conventuals.

Opera (Ital. *work*; Fr. *oeuvre*). Collective work of an artist; also refers to a single work. May also refer to the committee which ran the affairs of an Italian church, e.g. *Opera del Duomo,* the office of the Governors of the Cathedral.

Orpiment. A yellow.

P., Pinx., Pinxit (Lat., *he painted*). Written by a painter after his name on a picture, and signifying that he painted the work. Also sometimes, *pinsit.*

Pala (Ital.). A large panel or altarpiece.

Paletta. Probably the origin of the modern " palette ": it was a small card with rounded corners, with which gold leaf was applied to panels.

Pall. A cloth hung over something and decorated; a coffin or tomb cover, a canopy, an altar-cloth.

Palm. A measurement, about five inches.

Panel, or panel painting. This term refers to pictures which are apparently painted on wooden panels: in fact the wood serves as a base to a layer of glue, canvas and plaster, upon which the picture is painted and the gold leaf laid. See *tavola, ancona, triptych,* etc. Panels were usually made of poplar, linden or willow.

Pannello (Ital.) A panel painting. See above.

Parchment. The skin of a goat or sheep dried and prepared for writing or decoration; the term also refers to a piece of this material which has been written upon or decorated. In Italian *pergamena.*

Parrocchia. A parish.

Pentiptych. A five-panelled devotional painting (Ital. *pentittico*).

Pergamena (Ital.). *parchment.* See above.

Pernambuco, and *fernambuco* (or fernambuck). Brazil, verzino.

Perspective. This usually refers to a system of representation upon a plane surface, so arranged as to produce on that surface an illusion of three-dimensional space. During the fourteenth and fifteenth centuries, painters became progressively fascinated with its various elements and possibilities. Some examples of perspective are *serial, linear, isometric, angular* and *oblique.* The word in its general sense, however, means a manner of seeing, or a science of optics.

Petit-point. A method of embroidery using fine canvas.

Piazza. A town square, or open area in a town.

Pietà (Ital. *pity*). Dead Christ portrayed lying across His Mother's lap.

Pieve (Ital. *parish*). It is usually a country church not far outside a town; from *plebs,* a people.

Pigments. Coloured substances used in making paints.

Piscopio. See *vescovado.*

Plastic (lit. *capable of being moulded*). This term is used in painting to describe two-dimensional forms which appear three-dimensional or seem to have the quality of three-dimensional objects.

Podestà. Administrative head of an Italian city, roughly equivalent to a mayor but with more absolute power.

Polyptych. Devotional painting made up of several panels hinged together.

Pontata. In order to best use the scaffolding (*ponte, ponteggio, impalcatura*) which he has set up, the fresco painter begins at the top of the wall, and works horizontally until he has reached the end of the wall. He then lowers his platform (ponte) a convenient distance, and once again paints horizontally to the end of the wall. Because of the need to employ only fresh, wet plaster, his work is on a series of patches of plaster, placed horizontally each one attached to the previous one, and usually of roughly the same size. These are called " pontate ".

Ponte, ponteggio. See *pontata.*

Porporino. Usually the colour purple; it can also mean resplendent, and thus refer to glowing colours, particularly gold.

Predella. A wooden stand for an altarpiece upon which has been painted a number of small scenes. The scenes are usually representations of some event from the life or legend of the figure directly above. These scenes are generally wider than high, and the *predella* frames them.

Presepio. The manger or crib. The Nativity scene is often given this name.

Punching. The tooling of the gold leaf on panel paintings, particularly of the haloes and borders.

Punzecchiatura. See *martelli natura.*

Quattrocento (Ital. *four hundred*). Fourteen hundreds or fifteenth century; from *mille quattrocento.*

Raffietti or *raschiaii.* Tools for working plaster.

Raschiaii. See *raffietti.*

Realgar. A yellow.

Refectory. An eating-room.

Reliquary. An object in which relics are kept.

Reredos. An altar frontal.

Retable. This is usually an elaborate, carved wooden frame or screen with painted panels, to stand, or to be hung behind an altar.

Rete. See *squaring.*

Saffron. A yellow.

Sgraffito. See *graffito.*

Simony. Derived from the New Testament *Simon Magus.* It is the buying and selling of Church favours.

Sinopia. A sketch executed in red ochre as a preliminary to the final fresco painting. It is drawn upon the *arriccio* or first, dry layer of plaster. The name comes from the town of Sinopie in Asia Minor which originally supplied the reddish pigment of this colour, called *sinoper.*

Size. In painting, a glaze. Size is a gelatinous matter which is also used as a *binder* when mixing *pigments* and water. See also *distemper.*

Spandrel. The space between the (usually) rectangular frame of an arch, and the arch itself; in Gothic altarpieces this space is often decorated with angels, looking down upon the figures within the arches; in Italian Gothic architecture such spaces are often decorated.

Speziale (Ital. *apothecary*). It was to the Guild of *Medici e Speziali* that the painters belonged.

Spolvero (Ital. *dusting*). After a cartoon has been drawn, holes are pricked into the outline, the cartoon is held up to the wall to be painted, and chalk dust is snapped through the holes. This procedure, called *spolvero,* enables the painter to transfer the outline of a large drawing to the wall he wishes painted.

Squaring. The use of *squaring* or a *grid* or a *net* (*rete* in Italian) replaced the use of *sinopia.* It enabled the painter to transfer accurately, a small drawing to a large wall. The drawing was covered with enough parallel horizontal and vertical lines to cover it with squares. A large sheet of paper (or the wall itself) was covered with an identical number of squares which were consequently larger in scale. The painter then transferred the small drawing, square by square, to the larger surface. There was also a similar system, using a smallish veil made of fine cloth with lines painted onto it (or sewn into it) which was transparent. The artist hung it between himself and whatever he wished to copy, thus seeing the object criss-crossed by squares. As before he had merely to copy what he saw onto the larger surface, square by square.

Stacco. This is a term used to designate a method of removing frescoes from walls, named from the Italian *staccare,* to detach. A fine cloth is attached with water-soluble glue to the fresco to be detached. Other cloths, each one more coarse than the one before, are attached with the same water-soluble glue, to the first, and to each other until a sufficiently strong support has been built up. The glue is allowed to dry very hard and the many-layered cloth is then pulled away from the wall. Because the painted plaster is in fact a separate layer, which had been placed upon the *arriccio* as the painter orked, this layer of painted wall comes away from the rest usually with the aid of a knife to help separate from behind the two layers of plaster. Since it is firmly glued to the multiple cloth it can be preserved upon this until it is to be replaced, or mounted on a new support. The glued cloths are simply soaked with water and removed.

Stigmata. Marks corresponding to Christ's wounds which appeared on the body of St Francis of Assisi, and others.

Strappo (Ital. *to tear away*). A method of detaching only the pigment of a fresco painting. A cloth is glued to the fresco and then stripped off: it pulls, glued to it, the whole top layer of colour which has sunk into the plaster. See also *stacco*.

Stucco. Plaster.

Style. A pointed instrument for drawing, or for engraving, often made of bone.

Synod (Greek, *sunodos*, meeting). A church council or convention of clergy.

Tabernacle. In tre- and quattrocento painting, a covered niche or recess in a structure made to contain an image.

Tavola. A *tavola* is a panel painting without mouldings; see *ancona*.

Tela. (Ital. *canvas*). Sometimes used to refer to a picture.

Tempera. Paint which is made from pigments, water and egg; the technique using this kind of paint.

Terracotta (Ital. *cooked earth*). Baked clay.

Terra verde (Ital. *green earth*). A green pigment sometimes used for monotone fresco painting, or for under-painting.

Tertiary. Third Order. Lay men and women bound together for religious purposes and associated with first order friars. Nuns constituted the " second orders ".

Tirocinio (Ital. *apprenticeship*). This term applies to apprenticeship within the guilds, see *garzone, guilds*.

Tondo (Ital. *rotondo*, round). A circular painting.

Tracery. The decorative metal braces in stained glass windows, the carved shapes, the upper parts of wooden paintings, and sometimes the painted decoration in vaults.

Trecento (Ital. *three hundred*). Thirteen hundreds or fourteenth century; from *mille-trecento*.

Triptych (Ital. *trittico*). Devotional painting consisting of three panels linked together, or a single panel clearly broken into three parts.

Tympanum. A space above a door or window, often decorated, usually semicircular.

Tufa, or *tufo*. A volcanic rock of cellular or rough texture, very porous. It is light and easy to cut, and can be seen used in many different kinds of construction in Italy, for example in Volterra and Orvieto.

Veil. See *squaring*.

Vele (Ital. *sails*). Refers to the sail-shaped sections of vaults; in Italian churches these were often painted.

Verdaccio. A green pigment used as a base in fresco painting. See *terra verde*.

Verdigris. A green obtained from the action of acetic acid on copper.

Vermeil. See *doratura*.

Verzino. See *brazil*.

Vescovado, piscopio. A bishopric or sometimes cathedral church; in any case this refers to the residence of a bishop.

Additions

SAINTS AND THEIR SYMBOLS

If a saint is not associated within the picture itself by an object known to symbolize him, it is often difficult or even impossible today to identify him precisely. Originally his name might have been written somewhere in the painting or under it. One might still perhaps identify him from the predella scenes below, or from the church or chapel for which the picture was made. So many pictures have been damaged or removed, or broken into separate panels that in the absence of an accompanying symbol it may be that some figures are no longer identifiable. Below is a list of some common saints including all those who appear in the handbook with their usual symbols when known.

For further reference, the following books are recommended:

de Bles, A., *How to Distinguish the Saints in Art*, New York, 1925.
Coulson, J., and Noël, B., *Dictionnaire Historique des Saints*, Paris, 1964.
Daniel, H., *Encyclopaedia of Themes and Subjects in Painting*, London, 1971.
Englebert, O., *The Lives of the Saints* (trans. by C. and A. Fremantle), London, 1951.
Ferguson, G., *Signs and Symbols in Christian Art*, Oxford, 1961.
Istituto Giovanni XXIII, *Biblioteca Sanctorum* (13 vols.), Rome, 1961.
Jameson, Mrs., *History of Our Lord* (2 vols.), London, 1864.
    Legends of the Madonna, London (2nd ed.), 1857.
    Legends of the Monastic Orders, London, 1900.
    Sacred and Legendary Art, London, 1848.
Kaftal, G., *The Iconography of Saints in Tuscan Art*, Florence, 1952.
Kerler, D. H., *Die Patronate der Heiligen*, Hildesheim, 1968.
Künstle, K., *Ikonographie der Christlichen Kunst* (2 vols.), Freiburg, 1928.
van Marle, R., *The Development of the Italian Schools of Painting*, Vol. VI, The Hague, 1925.
Menzies, L., *The Saints in Italy*, London, 1924.
Molsdorf, W., *Christliche Symbolik der Mittelalterlichen Kunst*, Leipzig, 1926.
Murray, P. and L., *A Dictionary of Art and Artists*, Harmondsworth, 1958.
Reau, L., *Iconographie de l' Art Chrétien* (3 vols.), Paris, 1955-59.
Sales Doyé, F. von, *Heiligen und Seilige* (2 vols.), Leipzig, 1928-30.

Some symbols are common to many saints; the most usual of these are:

the palm (or sword)	to martyrs
the pen and/or book	to learned saints
the pastoral staff (and/or mitre)	to bishops
the Church	to founders of churches or orders
the lily	to virgins
the habit	to religious

Orders

Augustinian	black
Benedictine	black (original order) white (reformed)
Camaldoli	white
Cistercian	white
Clare	grey robe with black veil, & waist cord
Dominican	black and white
Franciscan	brown
Vallombrosan	grey

Angels

First hierarchy (represent the love of God)

Seraphim	usually red, holding burning candles
Cherubim	yellow or blue
Thrones	carry a staff

619

Second hierarchy (guardians of heaven and earth)

Dominations	crowns, and carry symbols of authority
Virtues	carry lilies
Powers	dressed in armour

Third hierarchy (guardians of man and executors of God's will)

All these angels carry symbols of messengers. The most frequently represented are the four Archangels:

Gabriel	carries a lily or sceptre; the words *Ave Maria Gratia Plena* also often appear
Michael	a winged knight with sword or lance, a vanquished dragon, scales, sometimes a crown
Raphael	a pilgrim or traveller, wearing sandals, carrying a staff, sword, or sometimes a casket or wallet
Uriel	usually carries a book

All the Virtues are portrayed as women

Faith	with a chalice; with St Peter
Hope	with wings; with St James Major
Charity	with children and a heart; with St John the Evangelist
Temperance	with a sword; with Scipio Africanus
Prudence	with two heads, a mirror, a serpent; with Solon
Fortitude	carries a symbol of force, usually a sword or club and sometimes Hercules' lion skin; with Samson
Justice	carries a balance and sword; with Trajan

The manner of portrayal of the Vices varies, as do the vices themselves. In Englishspeaking countries the seven vices are usually: Pride, Wrath, Envy, Lust, Gluttony, Avarice, Sloth; in the Scrovegni Chapel, Giotto portrays the following: Inconstancy, Infidelity, Envy, Despair, Injustice, Foolishness, Wrath.

SAINTS	SYMBOLS

A

Achilleus	He is always depicted with St Nereus; they are both very young martyrs.
Agatha	A young virgin martyr with a long veil. She carries a palm branch as a symbol of victory; a dish containing two breasts, shears or pincers.
Alexander	An elderly bishop; the patron saint of Fiesole.
Ambrose	A middle-aged bishop with a crosier and mitre, carrying a book. He is sometimes depicted holding a sphere with a Church in it, a whip, or a bee-hive.
Agnes	She is usually young, with long hair and a lamb and sword are often depicted by her.
Andrew	He is an old apostle with long white hair and a divided beard. Sometimes he is portrayed enthroned; he holds a cross saltire, a crucifix, a fish or fisherman's net. In earlier paintings, he holds either a crucifix or a cross in the shape of a Y; later representations show him with a cross saltire.

Andrew of Anagni	An elderly Franciscan friar; somewhere near him a cardinal's hat.
Andrew of Ireland	He is a young deacon (also called Bl. Andrew of Scotland).
Anne	The mother of the Virgin. She is elderly, in a green cloak and red dress, and sometimes holds a book.
Ansanus	A beardless martyr. He holds a banner with a cross and fountain, or baptismal cup. He sometimes carries a cluster of grapes.
Anthony Abbot	An elderly or old monk with a blue Tau-shaped crutch and bell. Sometimes depicted with a small hog or pig (the symbol of greed and lust), or with penitents. Flames are often shown under his feet.
Anthony of Padua	He wears the robes of the Franciscan Order. He carries a lily, a flowered crucifix, a fish, a book with the Tau-cross, or a heart. He sometimes carries the Christ Child holding a flame. A kneeling ass is also sometimes shown.
Appollinaris	A young bishop martyr.
Apollonia	A virgin martyr carrying the palm of martyrdom and pincers holding a tooth.
Augustine	One of the four great Doctors of the Church. An old bearded bishop, wearing a pallium. He is shown holding a book and blessing. He wears a monk's habit under bishop's robes, and has a short dark beard. He carries a book and pen and sometimes a flaming heart with an arrow through it.

B

Barnabas	An elderly bearded apostle, holding an olive branch.
Bartholomew	An apostle, dark haired and bearded, sometimes holding a large butcher's knife, a banner and carrying a human skin over his arm. He is also depicted enthroned.
Barbara	She sometimes carries the chalice and wafer or a peacock feather. A tower is often depicted.
Benedict	An elderly Benedictine abbot with a long beard. (The original Benedictine habit is black; the reformed order, white). He holds an aspergillum, book and a cup. He is often enthroned, and a raven appears with him.
Bernard	An elderly Cistercian monk, holding a book or pen. He is sometimes seen with a demon in chains, three mitres, a bee-hive, the Cross and instruments of the Passion of Our Lord.
Bernardo degli Uberti	A middle-aged beardless cardinal.
Bernardino da Siena	An elderly ascetic Franciscan bearing a tablet, sun or book, with the letters inscribed IHS: " Jesu Salvator Homines ".
Blaise	An elderly white bearded bishop, often enthroned. He holds an iron comb and lighted candle (or two crossed candles) and a panisellus tied to his staff.
Bonaventure	A Franciscan friar or bishop with a cardinal's hat by him. He holds a crucifix and chalice. An angel carrying the Host is sometimes depicted.

C

Caius	An middle-aged bearded Pope.
Catherine of Alexandria	A virgin princess martyr, usually crowned (by angels), carrying the palm of victory and a sword. A spiked wheel is generally by her side.
Catherine of Siena	She wears Dominican robes and holds a crucifix, rosary and letters with a lily or heart. She is often depicted with the stigmata and sometimes with a crown of thorns. Her mystical marriage is often related. She is also seen with her foot on a dragon. In pictures with the Madonna & Child, she is often seen kneeling, receiving a ring from the Christ Child.
Cecilia	A young martyr, often wearing a crown of roses and with wounds in her neck. She appears with Sts Valerian and Tiburtius. She is also depicted enthroned holding a book.
Christina of Bolsena	A virgin martyr holding a book.
Christopher	A giant warrior martyr, holding a flowered staff. He is generally shown wading through water, carrying the Christ Child.
Clare	She wears a grey robe with a black veil and waist-cord of St Francis. She carries the lily of purity, pyx, palm of victory, a monstrance and a crucifix.
Clement	He is an elderly pope, holding a crucifix and keys and with an anchor or millstone round his neck or by him. He is often shown with a lamb or fountain.
Constantine the Great	He appears as either an Emperor or as a mounted knight in armour.
Constantius	An elderly bearded bishop.
Cosmas	A young martyr of oriental appearance, always shown with his brother Damian. He wears the red gown and cap of physicianship and sometimes carries a mortar and

Crescentius	pestle or surgical instruments. A young deacon seen with Sts Zenobius and Eugenius, holding a chalice or censer.
Cyril	He appears as a white-robed elderly bearded monk with a book in his hand.

D

Damian	See Cosmas.
Dominic	He is generally young, wearing the black and white habit of his Order. He has a star on his forehead or in his halo, has a short beard or is cleanshaven. He is also sometimes shown as elderly with a long beard. He carries a rosary, lily and a loaf of bread. A dog with a lighted torch in its mouth is sometimes by him.
Domitilla	A young virgin martyr, shown holding a plaque with Christ's initials on it.
Donatus of Arezzo	A middle-aged bishop, holding a broken chalice. He is often depicted kneeling in front of an altar.
Donatus of Fiesole	An elderly bishop with a dragon at his feet.
Donnino	A young martyr holding a small cross. He usually has a dog by his side. He is also depicted holding a chalice.
Dorothy	She carries roses, or is seen with an angel holding a basket of roses and apples. She is sometimes seen tied to a stake.

E

Elizabeth	An elderly woman present in scenes of the Visitation and the Birth of St John the Baptist.
Elizabeth of Hungary	A middle-aged Franciscan nun with a basket of roses or apron-full. She is sometimes seen with the three crowns which symbolise royalty.
Ephysius	A young warrior martyr.
Eugenius	A young deacon with Sts Zenobius and Crescentius.
Eulalia	A young virgin martyr with a book and the lily of purity in her hand.
Euphemia	A lion, a bear, and a sword are depicted with her.
Euphrasia	A young nun in black with a white collar-piece, holding a book and lily.
Euphrosynus	A middle-aged bishop.
Eustace (Placidus)	He is depicted either as a knight on horseback or a soldier. He is often with hounds, and a stag with a crucifix between its horns. He is sometimes shown with a brazen bull.
Eustochium	She is dressed in white, either as a laywoman or as a young nun holding a lily.

F

Fabian	An elderly pope, sometimes with St Sebastian.
Felicitas (Felicity)	She wears nun's robes, is shown with her children and holds a book.
Felix of Nola	A young priest in robes used for the Mass.
Fina	A young virgin holding flowers and a model of the town of San Gimignano or a book. Her symbol is a rat.
Flora	A young nun dressed in black, holding a flower and a lamp.
Florentius	An elderly bishop with a short beard.
Florian	His symbol is a millstone.
Fortunatus of Todi	An elderly bishop.
Francis	He is sometimes depicted as a deacon but is generally bearded, wearing the brown robes of his Order. He shows the signs of the stigmata and is seen carrying a lily, crucifix, wolf, lamb or skull.
Frediano	He diverted the Serchio river with a rake from flooding Lucca. A middle-aged bishop with rake, or bishop's staff and a panisellus.

G

Galganus	He is depicted as a young knight; his symbol is a sword thrust into a rock.
Gaudentius	He is a middle-aged bishop with his deacon, Culmatus. He is sometimes shown wearing a papal crown.
Geminianus (Gimi-gnano)	An elderly bishop, holding a model of the town of San Gimignano.
George	He is usually shown as a knight in armour with a banner showing a red cross on a white field. He is depicted slaying the dragon with a sword or lance or holding a shield and lance.
Gerard of Villamagna	An old Franciscan friar, barefoot, and carrying beads, a crutch, cherry blossom or a stick.

Giles	An old abbot or Benedictine monk in white. He carries a lily, with a deer by his side.
Giovenale	A middle-aged bearded bishop, carrying a staff and reading the book in his hand.
Gregory	He wears papal robes and holds a crosier with a double cross. He sometimes carries a church and a pen. A dove is also depicted. He is a Father of the Church.

H

Helen	She wears a crown and carries a cross with hammer and nails. She is also seen with the True Cross and a model of the Holy Sepulchre.
Henry	A young prince with a short beard and holding a lily.
Herculanus	A middle-aged bishop.
Hilarion	An old bearded monk carrying beads
Hippolytus	A young warrior martyr.
Humilitas	She wears the robes of a Vallombrosan nun, black veil and a white collar.
Humphrey	See Onuphrius.

I

Ignatius of Antioch	An elderly bishop holding a heart with the inscription IHS: " Jesu Salvator Homines ".
Ives	A middle-aged or young cleanshaven lawyer. He wears a white cloak over a red tunic and a red cap. He holds a book.

J

James Major	He carries a pilgrim's staff, a gourd and a scallop shell. He often holds a scroll.
James the Less	An apostle, often similar to the Christ figure, but sometimes elderly and bearded. He holds a club.
Jerome	An old monk. He is often depicted as a hermit in the desert with a crucifix and skull. A lion is always shown with him. He is a Father of the Church and is seen praying or writing. An owl is often shown nearby.
Joachim	He is the father of the Virgin, husband of St Anne. His symbols are doves, lambs and lilies.
John the Baptist	He is usually shown covered in animal skins, carrying a crucifix. He sometimes carries a lamb and scroll with " Ecce Agnus Dei ". A plate bearing his head is often shown.
John Chrysostom	One of the four great Doctors of the Church. He is middle-aged with a short beard, wearing a mitre and cope.
John the Evangelist	An elderly Evangelist enthroned. His symbol is an eagle and he is often shown with a cup.
John Gualbert	A young bearded monk of the Vallombrosan Order, in grey. He is sometimes enthroned and carries a crucifix or sword.
Joseph	He is elderly or old, carrying a staff, carpenter's tools and a lily. He often carries doves in a basket.
Jude	His attribute is a heavy sword or lance.
Julian	He is a young bearded warrior, wearing a cloak, or is a huntsman with a stag. A boat and a river are often shown.
Justus	Elderly bishop with grey hair and beard, sometimes holding loaves of bread.

L

Ladislas	A young King (of Hungary), holding a banner.
Laurentianus	A young warrior martyr, always seen with St Pergentius.
Lawrence	A middle-aged deacon, sometimes enthroned. He usually carries a palm and gridiron, or a plate of coins, crucifix or censer. He is often shown with St Stephen.
Leo the Great	An elderly bishop wearing triple tiara, carrying a crosier with a double cross.
Leolino	He was a bishop and martyr who preached in the valley of the Sieve, and whose symbols are those of a bishop carrying a palm.
Leonard	A young deacon carrying broken fetters and often depicted with penitents.
Louis of Toulouse	A bishop with a fleur-de-lys in his hand or by him. A crown and sceptre lie at his feet.
Louis IX	He wears a crown of thorns or the crown of France. He holds a crucifix, sword, fleur-de-lys and a knotted cord.
Lucilla	She is either a nun in black robes, very similar to Flora, and holding a burning lamp; or she is a young virgin martyr holding a sword.

Lucy	She is often depicted carrying her eyes on a dish. She has a wound in her neck and holds a burning lamp or dagger.
Luke	An Evangelist, he is either middle-aged and bearded or elderly, bald and bearded. He carries his gospels and is often shown painting the Virgin. His symbol is a winged ox which is almost always shown.

M

Margaret	A young virgin martyr usually crowned and holding a crucifix and palm. She is often shown with a dragon.
Marinus	A middle-aged, bearded mason, holding a hammer.
Mark	A middle-aged, bearded Evangelist, holding a pen and book of his gospel. His symbol is a winged lion, usually shown by him.
Martha	(Sister of Lazarus). She is portrayed either as a nun, white gown with a black cloak, or as a mediaeval lady in a cloak. She carries keys and a ladle and is sometimes shown with a dragon and a cup.
Martin	He is depicted as either a bishop with a goose by his side or as a soldier on horseback, dividing his cloak to give to a beggar. He often wears a cloak with his initial on the border.
Mary Magdalene	She is portrayed with loose unbound hair and often with a box of ointment in her hand or by her side. She may also hold a crucifix.
Mary	The three Marys depicted at the Tomb are: Mary Magdalene Mary, mother of James Mary, wife of Cleophas.
Mary of Egypt	An elderly lined woman with long tresses carrying three loaves, sometimes with a lion at her side.
Matthew	He is elderly and bearded, and often shown with a book, pen, or bag of money. He is enthroned. When the four Evangelists are depicted, his symbol is a book.
Maurice	A young warrior.
Maurus	An elderly Benedictine monk in white robes.
Michael	A winged knight, holding a sword or lance. He is shown standing with a vanquished dragon. He also holds scales. He sometimes wears a crown.
Minias	A young knight, crowned, holding a sceptre, feather quill or lily. He also carries his own head.
Monica	She appears as a a nun in scenes with St Augustine, her son.

N

Nemesius	An elderly warrior martyr carrying a banner.
Nereus	See Achilleus.
Nicholas of Bari	A bishop carrying three golden balls or purses. A boat or anchor are often shown.
Nicholas of Tolentino	An Augustinian monk in black robes with a star on his chest. He carries a crucifix. A model of the town of Empoli is sometimes shown in his hands, or at his feet.

O

Onuphrius (Humphrey)	An old hermit figure, holding a crutch. Two lions are often depicted.
Pancras	A young warrior martyr.
Paphnutius	An elderly monk with a long beard. He wears a grey cassock, holding a book, and blessing.

P

Paul the Hermit	An old hermit with long white hair and beard, similar to Onuphrius (Humphrey). A raven and loaf of bread are often depicted.
Paul	A middle-aged bearded apostle, carrying a sword and book of his letters.
Paula	An elderly woman.
Paulinus	A middle-aged beardless bishop.
Peregrinus	An elderly pilgrim with beads.
Pergentius	A young warrior martyr, always depicted with St Laurentianus.
Peter	An elderly bearded apostle, wearing a yellow cloak. He holds the Keys to Heaven and is sometimes enthroned.
Peter Martyr	A young beardless Dominican monk, often with his finger to his lips. He carries a palm and often a knife or sword.
Philip	A young apostle, sometimes bearded. He carries a cruci-

	fix or sometimes a Tau-cross. A dragon is occasionally shown with him.
Placidus	A young Benedictine (see Eustace).
Pontianus	A young bearded warrior martyr.
Procolus	He is either a middle-aged bishop or monk; or else a young warrior martyr.

Q

Quentin	A young early martyr, depicted with two spits by his side.
Quiricus	An early martyr.
Quirinus	A young warrior with shield and banner with nine balls depicted on each.

R

Raymond de Peñaforte	Middle-aged Dominican friar, holding a book and bâton as symbol of teaching authority.
Raynerius	A young pilgrim with a hairshirt and staff holding beads; or an old bearded pilgrim.
Regulus	A middle-aged bearded bishop.
Remigio (Rémy)	An elderly bearded bishop.
Reparata	A virgin martyr holding a lily and a banner. She is sometimes crowned. A dove, representing her spirit, is often shown flying from her mouth.
Roch	A pilgrim with a hound. A staff and plague sores are often depicted; also a cockleshell or wallet.
Romuald	An old bearded monk or abbot of the Camaldoli Order (white). He holds a crutch, book, reliquary and a model of the monastery. A ladder to Heaven is shown sometimes, as well as a devil under his feet.
Rufinus	Elderly bishop with short grey beard, holding a book and blessing.

S

Salvius	An elderly bishop.
Satan	He is often also represented as a serpent.
Scholastica	She wears the white or black robes of the Benedictine Order (being the twin sister of St Benedict), and holds a lily or cross, with a dove beside her.
Sebastian	A young warrior martyr, shown with many arrows piercing his body, often tied to a stake.
Simon Zelote	An apostle, sometimes with a staff, otherwise a cross or large saw.
Stephen	A deacon holding the palm of martyrdom and often with a stone in his head. He is frequently shown with St Lawrence.
Sylvester	A middle-aged or elderly pope carrying a crosier and book, with a bull or dragon at his feet.

T

Thaddeus	A young apostle holding a book.
Thomas	A young cleanshaven apostle holding a spear. He is often shown with the Virgin giving him Her girdle or with his hand in Christ's side. His attributes can also be the builder's rule or square.
Thomas Aquinas	A Dominican monk (white and/or black robes), often enthroned, carrying a book or scales and a crown or chalice. He sometimes holds a model of the Church. His clothing may be emblazoned with an ox.
Thomas Becket	An elderly bishop.
Tibertius	An early martyr; shown in scenes from the life of St Cecilia.

U

Urban I	An elderly bearded pope; shown in scenes from the life of St Cecilia.
Ursula	A crowned young woman, carrying a pilgrim's staff with a white banner and red cross. She is often depicted protecting followers with a cloak.

V

Valerian	An early martyr, husband of St Cecilia; shown in scenes of her life.
Venantius	A young martyr sometimes with a book or quill, or holding a banner.

Verdiana	A middle-aged nun carrying a basket. Two snakes are generally shown with her.
Veronica	She appears in the Crucifixion scenes holding a cloth with the portrait of Christ on it.
Victor	An elderly pope holding a double cross and olive branch.
Vincent	A deacon with the palm of martyrdom in his hand. Two crows are often depicted, as are a whip, chain, grill or millstone.

Z

Zeno	A bishop with fish hanging from his staff.
Zenobius	A middle-aged bishop with lilies in his halo. He is often enthroned. He can be depicted carrying a dead child. A flowering tree is sometimes shown.
Zita	A servant, carrying keys, or a pail or jug.

APPENDIX C

INDICES TO BERENSON AND OFFNER

Section III of A CORPUS OF FLORENTINE PAINTING is confined in period to the fourteenth century. The material contained in it embodies a distinct current within the school from its beginnings through the Renaissance, which runs in a clear course alongside the deeper and fuller central Florentine stream represented by Giotto and his school. This category, which might be called the Miniaturist Tendency, evolves out of the narrative conventions of the middle ages and out of the storied crosses and altarfrontals of the thirteenth century. Determined in its mode of presentation largerly by book-illumination, this tendency constitutes a phase that is separated by the continuity of its proper tradition, as well as by a direct opposition of taste and of aesthetic, from the intellectualized materialism of monumental (or of fresco) painting in Florence. By temper and disposition more conservative than their contemporaries, the monasters of the Miniaturist Tendency reach their completest expression in the small scenes, which stand in columns over one another on either side of a central sainted figure in earlier, or run in a course under it, in later periods.

Offner, R., *A Critical and Historical Corpus of Florentine Painting*, New York, 1931. Introduction to Section III. Section III, Vol. I, p. xv.

As opposed to Section II, Section IV is devoted exclusively to that phase of non-monumental style in Florence, which is of Cionesque origin, and of its ramifications.

Since the workshop of Orcagna was the chief source for the painting in Florence following him till the end of the century, he fittingly provides the historical transition from the first to second half of the Trecento. He and his brother Nardo divided the field between them and determined essentially the course of Florentine evolution for some time to come. Although the principal works of the later part of this period are monumental in scale, the figure tends to fall short of the plastic integrity characteristic of the Florentine tradition and inherited from its Greco-Roman past.

The Florentine monumental fresco of the earlier Trecento — in the Giotto tradition — breaches the wall, and extends the living space into the wall and beyond it. The painting appropriates the scale and the substance of life. Its plasticity concentrates volume and weight in the solid forms, which are reduced to a readily commanded composition. While it maintains an alliance to life by using its materials, it raises them to a higher power and locks them within a determinate structure. The whole imposes itself upon us because of its implications of a universal stability and permanence. But these major qualities tend to disappear from the moral painting of the second half of the Trecento. In their stead we have painting, in both fresco and panel, that is primarily either narrative or explanatory.

Offner, R., *A Critical and Historical Corpus of Florentine Painting*, New York, 1962. Introduction to Section IV. Section IV, Vol. I, p. 1.

The Lists in previous editions, although revised from time to time were all based on the conviction that the hand of the artist never faltered, even if his head did occasionally nod. The execution, on this theory, tended to weigh more than the creative mental effort. The question of questions was whether a painting was autograph. If it was not, it did not count, unless indeed it betrayed the hand of another painter, in which case it was included in that painter's work. An artistic personality thus shrank to a composite of those pictures only where hand and mind were one....

But now, fortified with this experience of the artist at his highest, one may well afford to relax from the earlier severity, and include every work that shows the distinct trace of his creative purpose, whether largely or only in small part by his own hand, whether done in his studio on his indications, or whether mere copies of lost works.

Berenson, B., *Italian Pictures of the Renaissance*, Oxford, 1932. Preface to the Edition of 1932.

Painters listed by Berenson (1963) page and plate numbers; and by Offner, section, volume and sometimes page number:

Painter	Berenson	Offner
Alvaro Portoghese	p 4; pls 466-8	
Andrea (Bonaiuto) da Firenze	pp 4-5; pls 235-49	
Andrea di Giusto	p 57; pls 640-7	
Angelico	pp 10-16; pls 591-625	
Antonio Veneziano	pp 16-17; pls 250-64	
Bicci di Lorenzo	pp 27-32; pls 497-514	
Bartolomeo di Andrea Bocchi	p 32; pls 648-9	
Bonsi (Giovanni da Firenze)	p 32; pl 306	
Buffalmacco		Sec. III, Vol. I, pp 39-46
Cenni di Francesco di Ser Cenni	pp 47-8; pls 359-62	Sec. III, Vol. IV, pp 39-46

Painter	Berenson	Offner
Cristiani, Giovanni di Bartolomeo	pp 50-1; pls 325-35	
Daddi, Bernardo	pp 51-8; pls 162-84	Sec. III, Vol. III-IV; Sec. III, Vol. V, pp. 55-140 Sec. III, Vol. VIII, pp 1-34
Domenico Veneziano	pp 61-2; pls 701-10	
Francesco di Antonio (di Bartolomeo, erroneous-ly read Banchi).	pp 62-4, pls 711-33B	
Gaddi, Agnolo	pp 66-9; pls 336-54	

Gaddi, Taddeo	pp 69-71; pls 112-17; 119-32	
Giotto	pp 79-81; pls 24-45; 48-62	
Giotto's Assistants	pp. 81-3; pls 63-71	
Giotto's Anonymous Contemporaries & Immediate Followers	pp 83-4; pls 72-80; 111	Sec. IV, Vol. IV and V
Giovanni del Biondo	pp 84-7; pls 286-98	
Giovanni da Milano	pp 89-90; pls 265-79	
Giovanni (di Marco, called) dal Ponte	pp 90-92; pls 483-96	
Jacopo del Casentino	pp 100-3; pls 98-110	Sec. III, Vol. II, Part II, pp 87-152 / Sec. III, Vol. VII, pp 93-127 / Sec. IV, Vol. III
Jacopo di Cione	pp 103-6; pls 216-34	Sec. III, Vol. VI, pp 27-45
Lippo di Benivieni	p 114; pls 95-7	
Lorenzo Monaco	pp 117-21; pls 429-65	
Lorenzo di Niccolò	pp 121-4; pls 386-96	
Mariotto di Cristofano	p 129; pls 650-1	
Mariotto di Nardo	pp 129-33; pls 515-32	
Masaccio	pp 134-35; pls 579-90	
Maso di Banco	pp 135-6; pls 133-58	
Masolino	pp 136-7; pls 553-78	
Master of the Arte della Lana Coronation	p 138; pls 382-5	
Master of the Bambino Vispo	pp 138-41; pls 469-82	
Master of the Cappella Medici Polyptych (Berenson: Master of Terenzano)		Sec. III, Vol. II, Part II, pp 73-84 / Sec. III, Vol. VI, pp 103-14 / Sec. III, Vol. VII, pp 83-92
Master of the Corsi Crucifix		Sec III, Vol. I, pp 59-62; Sec. III, Vol. VI. p 26
Master of the Dominican Effigies (Berenson: Master of Terenzano)		Sec. III, Vol. II, Part II, pp 49-68; / Sec. III, Vol. III, Part II, pp 239-61; / Sec. III, Vol. VII, pp 27-82
Master of the Da Filicaia Cross		Sec. III, Vol. VI pp 47-54
Master of the Fabriano Altarpiece (Puccio di Simone)		Sec. III, Vol. V, pp 141-237; / Sec. III, Vol. VIII, pp 165-92
Master of the Fogg Pietà (Figline)		Sec. III, Vol. VI, pp 65-100
Master of the Horne Triptych		Sec. III, Vol. I, pp 67-76
Mezzana Master		Sec. III, Vol. VI pp 103-14
Master of the Pentacost		Sec. III, Vol. VI, pp 57-63
Master of the Rinuccini Chapel	pp 143-4; pls 280-5	Sec. IV, Vol. I, pp 61-80
Master of S. Cecilia	pp 144-5; pls 81-93	Sec. III, Vol. I, pp 15-37; 47-109; Sec. III, Vol. VI, pp 20-4
Master of the S. Lorenzo Madonna		Sec. III, Vol. VI, pp 1-26
Master of the S. Maria Novella Cross		Sec. III, Vol. I pp 91-94
Master of San Martino alla Palma		Sec. III, Vol. VI, pp 3-18
Master of the San Quirico Crucifix		Sec. III. Vol. V, pp 1-53 / Sec. III, Vol. I pp 95-8; Sec. III, Vol. VIII pp 123-34

Master of the Straus Madonna	pls 355; 357-8	
Vicchio-Paris Master		Sec. III, Vol. VI, pp 115-20
The Biadaiolo Illuminator		Sec. III, Vol. VII, pp 1-20; Sec. III, Vol. II, Part I, pp 43-8; Sec. III, Vol. VII, pp 1-19
Nardo di Cione	pp 151-2; pls 191-208	Sec. IV, Vol. II
Niccolò di Pietro Gerini	pp 158-61; pls 363-80; 386	
Niccolò di Tommaso (Master of the Convento del T)	pp 161-3; pls 308-26	
Orcagna (Andrea di Cione, called)	p 163; pls 209-15	Sec. IV, Vol. I
Pacino di Bonaguida	p 164; pl 94	Sec. III, Vol. II, Part I, pp 1-20; Sec. III, Vol. VI, pp 121-264
Paolo Schiavo	pp 165-6; pls 652-56	
Parri Spinelli (or di Spinello)	p 166; pls 47; 426-8	
Pietro di Miniato	p 177; pls 397-9	
Puccio di Simone	p 182; pls 188-90	Sec. III, Vol. V, pp 141-240; Sec. III, Vol. VIII, pp 165-92
Rossello di Jacopo ('Franchi')	pp 192-4; pls 533-45; 547-9	
Spinello Aretino	pp 202-6; pls 400-25	
Unidentified Florentines ca. 1350-1420	pp 213-16	
Unidentified Florentines ca. 1420-1465	pp 217-20	

Titles of the fourteen volumes so far published of:

A Critical and Historical Corpus of Florentine Painting by Richard Offner

The Fourteenth Century, Section III, Vols I-VIII:

Vol. I	(1931):	The Master of Santa Cecilia and School, Buffalmacco, Master Corsi, Horne, S. Lorenzo, S. Quirico
Vol. II, Part 1	(1930):	Pacino di Bonaguida, School, and Elder Contemporaries of Daddi, Master Cappella Medici, Domenican Effigies, Jacopo del Casentino
Vol. II, Part 2	(1930):	Jacopo di Casentino and School, Pacino di Bonaguida
Vol. III	(1930):	Bernardo Daddi
Vol. IV	(1934):	School of Daddi
Vol. V	(1947):	Master of San Martino alla Palma / Assistant of Daddi and School / Master of the Fabriano Altarpiece and School
Vol. VI	(1956):	Master of Santa Cecilia, and School / Lippus Benivieni, Master of the Fogg Pietà / Pacino di Bonaguida and School, Master S. Maria Novella Cross, Corsi Crucifix, Da Filicaia Cross, Mezzana, Fogg, Horne, Vicchio-Paris.
Vol. VII	(1957):	Master of the Dominican Effigies, Cappella Medici Jacopo del Casentino, Biadaiolo Illuminator
Vol. VIII	(1958):	Daddi and School, Master of San Martino alla Palma, Master of the Fabriano Altarpiece, Puccio di Simone.

The Fourteenth Century, Section IV, Vols I-V:

Vol. I	(1962):	Andrea di Cione and Following
Vol. II	(1960):	Nardo di Cione and Following
Vol. III	(1965):	Jacopo di Cione and Following
Vol. IV	(1967):	Giovanni del Biondo and Following: Dated and Earlier Works
Vol. V	(1969):	Giovanni del Biondo and Following: Later Works.

APPENDIX D

LIST OF SIGNED AND DATED WORKS

I. A chronological list of extant dated works 1300-1450 by the Florentines in the main body of this compendium, as well as dated works of the same period by Florentines in Appendix A; the works listed at the end of Appendix A, by unknown hands, are also included herein. (See also various dated and/or signed works by other artists in Appendix A).

DATED WORKS

1307 Master of S. Cecilia: Florence, S. Simone. Panel: St Peter Enthroned (fig. 83).

1315 Buffalmacco (?): Florence, Badia a Settimo, Vault Fresco: Evangelist (fig. 1204).

1328 Bernardo Daddi: Florence, Uffizi 3073. Panel: Madonna & Child s. (fig. 90).

1330 Jacopo del Casentino: Kansas City (Mo.), Wm. Rockhill Nelson Gallery of Art 47.1952. Panel: Infant Christ Presented for Circumcision (fig. 235).

1333 Bernardo Daddi: Florence, Museo del Bigallo. Triptych: Madonna & Child with Saints (fig. 94).
Bernardo Daddi: Florence, Uffizi (Depositi 6170). Panel: Madonna & Child with Sts John the Baptist, John the Evangelist & 2 Angels (fig. 93).
Bernardo Daddi: Washington, D.C., Mellon Collection 3. Panel: St Paul & Donors. 133(3)? (fig. 92).
Unknown Painter close to Daddi: ex Hatfield, (Herts.), Burns Collection. Panel: St Catherine (fig. 1300).
Unknown Painter close to Daddi: San Godenzo (Mugello), Basilica. Polyptych: Madonna & Child with Saints (Uffizi Inv. 8745) (fig. 1299).

1334 Bernardo Daddi: Cambridge (Mass.), Fogg Art Museum 1918.33. Portable triptych: Christ on the Cross; Agony in the Garden. (fig. 97).
Bernardo Daddi: Florence, Museo dell'Opera del Duomo. Panel: Madonna of the Magnificat (fig. 98).
Bernardo Daddi: Florence, Uffizi 8564. Panel: Madonna & Child with Sts Peter & Paul and 8 Angels s. (fig. 99).
Bernardo Daddi: Philadelphia, John G. Johnson Collection. Triptych: Madonna & Child with Saints (fig. 96 b).
Taddeo Gaddi: Berlin, Dahlem Staatliche Museen 1079-81. Triptych: Madonna & Child with Saints s. (fig. 152).

1336 Bernardo Daddi: Osteria Nuova (Bagno a Ripoli), S. Giorgio a Ruballa. Panel: Madonna & Child with four Angels, Sts Mattias, George and Donor (fig. 100).
Bernardo Daddi: Siena, Pinacoteca 60. Portable triptych: Madonna & Child with Saints (fig. 106).
Taddeo Gaddi: Rome, Museo di Castel S. Angelo. Portable triptych: Madonna & Child with Saints (fig. 151).

1337 Bernardo Daddi: Washington, Dumbarton Oaks. Panel: Madonna & Child with Saints (fig. 105).

1338 Bernardo Daddi: Edinburgh, National Gallery of Scotland 1904. Portable triptych: Nativity; Madonna & Child (fig. 113).
Bernardo Daddi: London, Count Seilern Collection. Portable triptych: Madonna & Child with Saints (fig. 114-5).
Bernardo Daddi: Minneapolis (Minn.), Art Institute. Portable triptych: Madonna & Child with Saints (fig. 117).
Unknown painter near to Bernardo Daddi: Milan. Private Collection. Panel: Coronation of the Virgin (fig. 1301).

1340 Master of Terenzano: London, Courtauld Institute Galleries. Polyptych: Madonna & Child Enthroned with Saints (fig. 202).

1342 (or 1352?) Unknown Painter: Florence, Opera del Bigallo. Fresco: Madonna della Misericordia (fig. 1302).

1343 Bernardo Daddi: Florence, Accademia 8570. Panel: Christ on the Cross with the Virgin & Saints (fig. 111).

1344 Bernardo Daddi: Florence, S. Maria Novella, Cloister, Spanish Chapel. Polyptych: Madonna & Child with Saints. s. (fig. 119).

1345 Jacopo del Casentino: Budapest, Musée des Beaux-Arts 6006. Panel: Madonna & Child with Saints and Angels (fig. 242).

1346 Orcagna: Private Collection. Panel: Annunciation with Donors. s. (fig. 294).
Unknown Painter close to Daddi: Gangalandi (near Lastra a Signa), S. Martino. Panel: St John the Baptist (fig. 1303).

1348 Bernardo Daddi: London, Courtauld Institute Galleries. Polyptych: Crucifixion. s. (fig. 120).

1350 Orcagna: Utrecht, Aartsbisschoppelijk Museum. Triptych: Madonna nursing the Child with Saints (fig. 289).

1353 Puccio di Simone: Fabriano, Pinacoteca. Panel: St Anthony (fig. 168).

1354 Puccio di Simone: Washington (D.C.), no. 6. Triptych: Madonna & Child Enthroned with two Saints (fig. 181).

1355 Taddeo Gaddi: Florence, Uffizi (Depositi 3). Panel: Madonna & Child with four Angels & two female Saints. s. (fig. 143).

1357 Orcagna: Florence, S. Maria Novella, Strozzi Chapel. Polyptych: Christ in Glory with Saints & the Virgin. s. (fig. 274).
Unknown Painter near to Giovanni del Biondo. Triptych: Madonna and Child with two Saints. Panel. Vertelli, S. Michele (fig. 1304).

1358 Unknown Painter near to Andrea da Firenze: Florence, Museo Bardini, Corsi Collection. Triptych: Madonna & Child with two Saints. (fig. 1305).

1360 Matteo Pacini: formerly Rome, Stroganoff Collection. Panel: Coronation of the Virgin with Saints. s. (fig. 1230).
Niccolò di Tommaso: Pistoia, Palazzo Comunale. Fresco: St James & a Bishop Saint with Madonna & Child & Angels. (fig. 361).
Puccio di Simone: Unknown. Panel: Madonna nursing the Child. s. (fig. 167).

1362 Jacopo di Cione: Formerly Brussels, Stoclet Collection. Panel: Madonna nursing the Child. (1362?) (fig. 335).

1363 Giovanni del Biondo: Florence, S. Croce. Panels: Four Church Fathers (part of High Altarpiece) (fig. 493).
Giusto de Menabuoi: Private Collection. Panel: Madonna & Child with two Nuns (fig. 1232).
Unknown Painter. Figline di Prato, Pieve. Fresco: Virgin Annunciate. (fig. 1306).

1364 Giovanni del Biondo: Florence, Accademia 8462. Triptych: Presentation of Christ (fig. 485).

1365 Giovanni da Milano: Florence, Accademia 8467. Panel: Pietà. s. (fig. 378).
Nardo di Cione: Florence, Accademia 8464. Triptych: Trinity with two Saints (fig. 311).
Nardo di Cione: Florence, Museo dell'Opera di S. Croce (Uffizi Inv. 170 dep.). Triptych: Madonna of Humility with Sts Gregory & Job (fig. 315).

1366 Pietro Nelli: Signa, Pieve Vecchia di S. Lorenzo. Frescoes: Sts Julian & Catherine, Martyrdom of St Sebastian (figs. 701, 5).

1367 Niccolò di Tommaso: formerly Arezzo, Pinacoteca (destroyed). Panel: Madonna & Child with female Donor. (fig. 343).

1370 Cristiani: Pistoia, S. Giovanni Fuorcivitas. Panel: St John & Scenes from his Life. s. (fig. 527).
Master of the Giraldi Tabernacle: Perticaia, Rignano sull'Arno, S. Cristofano. Triptych: Madonna & Child with Saints (fig. 451).

1371 Giovanni Bonsi: Rome, Vatican, Pinacoteca. Polyptych: Madonna & Child with Saints. s. (fig. 436).
Niccolò di Tommaso: Naples, Museo di S. Martino. Triptych: St Anthony Abbot with Saints. s. (figs. 346-8).

1372 Giovanni del Biondo: Florence, S. Croce, Tosinghi Chapel. Polyptych: Madonna & Child with Saints (fig. 491).
Giovanni del Biondo: formerly Richmond (Surrey), Cook Collection. Panel: Coronation of the Virgin (fig. 499).

1373 Giovanni del Biondo: Fiesole, Duomo. Triptych: Coronation of the Virgin with Saints (fig. 490).

1375 Giovanni del Biondo: San Donato in Poggio (near Tavarnelle, Val di Pesa), Pieve, Baptistery. Panel: Coronation of the Virgin with Saints (figs. 494, 508).
Pietro Nelli (and Tommaso del Mazza): Impruneta, Chiesa Collegiata. Polyptych: Madonna & Child with Saints (figs. 685-6).

1377 Giovanni del Biondo: Siena, Pinacoteca 584. Panel: Madonna & Child. s. (fig. 496).
Spinello Aretino: Arezzo, Museo Diocesano (formerly S. Agostino). Fresco: Madonna & Child with two Saints & a kneeling Warrior (fig. 715).

1379 Giovanni del Biondo: Florence, S. Croce, Sacristy, Rinuccini Chapel. Polyptych: Madonna & Child with Saints (fig. 488).
Unknown Painter near Jacopo di Cione: Whereabouts unknown. Triptych: Madonna & Child with four Saints and four Angels (fig. 1307).

1380 Giovanni Bonsi: Florence, Acton Collection. Panel: St Humphrey with Donor (fig. 448).
Unknown Painter near to Niccolò di Pietro Gerini: Florence, S. Croce, Castellani Chapel. Painted Crucifix (fig. 1308).
Unknown Painter: St Andrew. Panel. Faltignano (Val di Pesa), S. Bartolomeo (fig. 1309).

1383 Cenni di Francesco di Ser Cenni: Florence, San Donato in Polverosa. Fresco: Adoration of the Magi (fig. 798).
Jacopo di Cione: Florence, SS. Apostoli (Uffizi 8607). Polyptych: Madonna & Child with Saints & Angels (fig. 334).

1385 Master of S. Martino a Mensola: Florence, Acton Collection. Panel: Madonna & Child (fig. 581).

Spinello Aretino: Budapest, Musée des Beaux-Arts. Panel: Sts Nemesius & John the Baptist (fig. 709).

Spinello Aretino: Cambridge (Mass.), Fogg Art Museum 1915.12 a b c. Panel: Sts Benedict & Lucilla (fig. 712).

1386 Jacopo di Cione: Florence, Miari-Pelli-Fabbroni Collection. Panel: Madonna of Humility with two Angels (fig. 336).

1387 Giovanni del Biondo: Florence, S. Felice a Ema (near Impruneta). Panel: Madonna & Child with 16 figures (fig. 497).

Master of San Martino a Mensola: Florence, S. Croce, second altar, right of nave. Fresco: Madonna & Child with Saints (fig. 568).

Unknown Painter: St James. Fresco. Florence, S. Miniato al Monte (fig. 1310).

1388 Antonio Veneziano: Palermo, S. Niccolò Reale, Museo Diocesano Panel: Flagellation; Virgin, St John, Evangelists & Prophets. s. (fig. 480).

Cristiani: Pistoia, Duomo. Fresco: Incredulity of St Thomas with Saints (fig. 521).

1389 Unknown Painter close to Giovanni del Biondo: ex San Domenico di Fiesole, Lucas Collection. Panel: Marriage of St Catherine (fig. 1311).

1391 Master of S. Martino a Mensola: Florence, S. Martino a Mensola. Triptych: Madonna & Child with Saints (fig. 565).

Spinello Aretino: Florence, Accademia 8461. Triptych: Madonna & Child with Saints (fig. 723).

Unknown Painter near to Nardo di Cione: Honolulu, Academy of Arts 2834. Triptych: Madonna & Child with Saints (fig. 1312).

Maestro Francesco: Florence, Accademia 6154. Panel: Madonna & Child with Sts John Baptist and Nicholas (presently at Bagno a Ripoli, S. Maria a Quarto). s. (fig. 1243).

1392 Giovanni del Biondo: Figline (Upper Valdarno), S. Francesco, Misericordia. Panel: Madonna & Child. s. (fig. 498).

1393 Cenni di Francesco di Ser Cenni: San Miniato al Tedesco (Val d'Elsa), Palazzo Comunale. Panel: Madonna nursing the Child (fig. 779).

Spinello Aretino: Florence, Quinto (Sesto Fiorentino), S. Maria. Triptych: Madonna & Child with Saints (fig. 716).

1394 Brunelleschi Master: New York, Metropolitan Museum of Art 52.229.2. Triptych: Coronation of the Virgin with Saints (fig. 1244).

1395 Master of San Martino a Mensola: Whereabouts unknown. Panel: Madonna & Child with two Donors (fig. 579).

1398 Mariotto di Nardo: Fiesole, Oratorio di Fontelucente. Triptych: Madonna of the Holy Girdle (fig. 955).

1399 Unknown Painter: Figline (Upper Valdarno), Ospedale Serristori. Panel: Madonna & Child with six Angels (fig. 1313).

MCCC- [incomplete], Lorenzo Monaco: Berlin, Staatliche Museen. Panel: Madonna & Child with Angels & Saints (destroyed 1945) (fig. 753).

1400 Cenni di Francesco di Ser Cenni: Montalbino, S. Giusto. Triptych: Madonna nursing the Child with Saints (fig. 784).

Lorenzo Monaco: Moscow, Puskin Museum 144. Panel: Madonna of Humility (fig. 752).

Mariotto di Nardo: Pesaro, Museo Civico. Triptych: Madonna & Child with Saints (fig. 942).

1401 Lorenzo di Niccolò, Niccolò di Pietro Gerini & Spinello Aretino: Florence, Accademia 8468. Triptych: Coronation of the Virgin with Saints (fig. 1314).

Lorenzo di Niccolò: San Gimignano, Museo Civico. Triptych: St Bartholomew & Scenes from his Life (fig. 819).

1402 Lorenzo di Niccolò: Terenzano (near Settignano), S. Martino. Triptych: Madonna & Child with Saints. s. (fig. 815).

1404 Lorenzo Monaco: Empoli, Pinacoteca Collegiata 2. Triptych: Madonna of Humility with Saints (fig. 754).

Lorenzo Monaco: Florence, Accademia 467. Panel: Man of Sorrows with the Virgin & St John the Baptist (fig. 755).

Lorenzo di Niccolò: Venice, Cini Collection 336. Polyptych: Madonna & Child with Saints (fig. 806).

Mariotto di Nardo: Assisi, Convento di S. Francesco. Panel: Madonna & Child with two Donors (fig. 945).

Master of the Arte della Lana: Boston (Mass.), Museum of Fine Arts 16.64. Panel: Madonna & Child Enthroned (fig. 683).

Unknown Painter near Niccolò di Pietro Gerini & the Master of the Arte della Lana: Florence, Accademia 8610. Triptych: Madonna & Child with Saints (fig. 1315).

1405 Lorenzo Monaco: Florence, Ponte a Mensola, Berenson Collection. Panel: Madonna of Humility (fig. 760).

1406 Mariotto di Nardo: Florence, S. Trinita, High Altar. Triptych: Trinity with Saints (fig. 952).

1407 Spinello Aretino: Arezzo, S. Domenico. Fresco: Virgin Annunciate (fig. 724).

1408 Cenni di Francesco di Ser Cenni: Volterra, Pinacoteca. Triptych: Madonna of Humility with Saints. (1408?) (fig. 781).

Lorenzo Monaco: Florence, Accademia 470. Panel: Madonna & Child with Saints (fig. 758).

Lorenzo Monaco: Paris, Musée du Louvre 1348A. Two panels: Agony in the Garden; Marys at the Tomb (fig. 762).

Lorenzo Monaco: Seattle (Wash.), Museum of Art K 1654, Samuel H. Kress Collection. Panel: Crucifixion (fig. 763).

Lorenzo Monaco: Turin, Museo Civico 3023. Painting on glass: Madonna & Child (fig. 757).

Mariotto di Nardo: Minneapolis (Minn.), Institute of Art. Panel:

Coronation of the Virgin (from altarpiece formerly in Hatton Garden Church, London) (fig. 957).

Unknown Painter near to Spinello Aretino: Arezzo, San Domenico. Fresco: Christ on the Cross with the Virgin and St John Evangelist (fig. 1316).

1409 Lorenzo di Niccolò: Florence, S. Croce, Medici Chapel. Panel: Madonna & Child (fig. 804).

Niccolò di Pietro Gerini: Rovezzano, S. Andrea. Fresco: Madonna & Child Enthroned with four Saints & two Angels (fig. 647).

Unknown Painter: Florence, S. Miniato al Monte. Fresco: St Julian. (fig. 1317).

1410 Cenno di Francesco di Ser Cenni: Volterra, S. Francesco, Oratorio della Compagnia della Croce di Giorno. Frescoes: Legend of the True Cross, Life of the Virgin. s. (figs. 785, 788-96).

Jacopo da Firenze: Volterra, S. Francesco, Oratorio della Compagnia della Croce di Giorno. Vault frescoes. Evangelists. s. (fig. 1258).

Giovanni dal Ponte: Chantilly, Musée Condé. Triptych: Coronation of the Virgin with Saints (fig. 739).

Lorenzo Monaco: Florence, Palazzo Davanzati (Uffizi 468). Triptych: Madonna & Child with Saints (fig. 766).

Bartolomeo di Frusino (?): Florence, Accademia. Painted Crucifix (fig. 1254).

Unknown Painter near to Cristiani: Prato, Palazzo dell'Arte della Lana. Frescoed triptych: Madonna & Child with two Saints & Angels (fig. 1318).

1412 Lorenzo Monaco: Pisa, Museo Nazionale di S. Matteo. Panel: Madonna of Humility (fig. 764).

Lorenzo di Niccolò: Florence, Mezzomonte (near Pozzolatico), S. Lorenzo in Collina. Polyptych: Madonna & Child with Saints. (fig. 820).

1413 Lorenzo Monaco: Washington, National Gallery K 1293, Samuel H. Kress Collection. Panel: Madonna of Humility (fig. 765).

Unknown Painter: San Donato in Poggio. Fresco: Madonna & Child with Sts Simon & Thaddeus (fig. 1319).

1414 Bicci di Lorenzo: Stia, Propositura di S. Maria Assunta. Triptych: Annunciation with four Saints (fig. 979).

Lorenzo Monaco: Florence, Uffizi 885. Triptych: Coronation of the Virgin with Saints. (Florentine Style: Feb. 1413). s. (fig. 767).

Unknown Painter: Arezzo, Museo. Fresco: Madonna & Child Enthroned, with Sts Lawrence & Anthony Abbot. (fig. 1320).

1415 Francesco di Antonio: Cambridge, Fitzwilliam Museum. Triptych: Madonna & Child with Saints. s. (fig. 876).

1416 Master of 1416: Florence, Accademia 4635. Panel: Madonna & Child with Sts Anthony Abbot, Peter, John the Baptist & Julian (fig. 1259).

Unknown Painter: Florence, via Lippi near Caciolle. Fresco: Tabernacle: Madonna nursing the Child, with Sts John Baptist & Peter, God the Father & two Angels. (fig. 1321).

1418 Mariotto di Nardo: Florence, Accademia 473. Panel: Madonna & Child with Saints (fig. 947).

Mariotto di Nardo: Florence, Accademia 3460. Panel: Madonna in Glory with Saints (fig. 944).

Mariotto di Nardo: Impruneta, Collegiata. Panel: Trinity with two Donors (fig. 950).

1419 Master of 1419: Cleveland Museum of Art 54.834. Panel: Madonna & Child Enthroned (fig. 1262).

1420 Rossello di Jacopo Franchi: Florence, Accademia 8460. Triptych: Coronation of the Virgin with Saints (fig. 973).

1421 Mariotto di Nardo: Panzano, Pieve di S. Leolino. Triptych: Madonna & Child with four Saints (fig. 941).

1421 (?) Unknown Painter: Sestino (Stia), S. Pancrazio. Fresco: Christ on the Cross with the Virgin, Sts John Evangelist & Mary Magdalene. (fig. 1322).

1422 Mariotto di Nardo: Florence, Acton Collection. Panel: Madonna of Humility (fig. 946).

Masaccio: San Giovenale (Reggello), S. Giovenale. Triptych: Madonna & Child with Saints (fig. 1054).

1423 Alvaro Portoghese: Volterra, Pinacoteca. Triptych: Madonna & Child with Saints. s. (fig. 895).

Bicci di Lorenzo: Berlin, Bodestrasse, Staatliche Museen. Three panels: S. Salvi healing; Nativity; S. Bernardo degli Uberti. (Destroyed 1945). (fig. 980).

Masolino: Bremen, Kunsthalle 164. Panel: Madonna of Humility. (fig. 1014).

Master of the Bambino Vispo or Master of Borgo alla Collina: Borgo alla Collina (Casentino), S. Donato. Triptych: Marriage of St Catherine with Saints (fig. 922, 1268).

1424 Mariotto di Nardo: Florence, Serristori Collection. Triptych: Madonna & Child with Saints (fig. 938).

1428 Unknown Painter: New York, Historical Society B-18 (1867.18). Panel: Desco da Parto. Birth of St John the Baptist (fig. 1323).

1430 Bicci di Lorenzo: Florence, Porta S. Giorgio. Fresco: Madonna & Child with Saints (fig. 988).

Bicci di Lorenzo: Vertine, S. Bartolomeo. Triptych: Madonna & Child with Saints (temporarily in the Pinacoteca Nazionale, Siena). (fig. 989).

Giovanni dal Ponte: Rosano, Pontassieve, SS. Annunziata. Triptych: Annunciation with Saints (fig. 741).

1431   Mariotto di Nardo: Florence, Acton Collection. Panel: Coronation of the Virgin (fig. 956).

1433   Bicci di Lorenzo: Parma, Pinacoteca 456. Panel: Madonna & Child Enthroned (fig. 990).

1434   Alvaro Portoghese: Brunswick, Herzog Anton Ulrich Museum S. 26. Panel: Madonna Enthroned nursing the Child. s. (fig. 896).

Bicci di Lorenzo: Velletri, Museo del Duomo. Panel: Visitation. (fig. 993).

1435   Andrea di Giusto: Prato, Galleria Comunale 8. Triptych: Madonna & Child with Saints (fig. 1074).

Bicci di Lorenzo: Bibbiena, Propositura. Panel: Madonna & Child Enthroned (fig. 996).

Bicci di Lorenzo: Florence, S. Giovannino dei Cavalieri. Panel: Nativity (fig. 1003).

Unknown Painter near to Andrea di Giusto: Florence, Ponte a Mensola, Berenson Collection. Panel: Madonna of Humility (fig. 1323).

Giovanni dal Ponte: Rome, Vatican, Pinacoteca. Triptych: Annunciation with Saints (fig. 750).

Masolino: Castiglione d'Olona (near Varese, Lombardy), Baptistery. Frescoes: Scenes from the Life of St John the Baptist (figs. 1010-1, 18, 23).

1436   Andrea di Giusto: Figline, S. Andrea a Ripalta. Triptych: Madonna & Child with Saints (fig. 1082).

Paolo Schiavo: Florence, S. Miniato al Monte. Fresco: Madonna & Child with Saints. s. (fig. 1101).

1437   Andrea di Giusto: Florence, Accademia 3236. Triptych: Madonna of the Holy Girdle. s. (fig. 1085).

1439   Rossello di Jacopo Franchi: Siena, Pinacoteca 608. Panel: Coronation of the Virgin. s. (fig. 977).

1440   Bicci di Lorenzo: Florence, Legnaia, S. Arcangelo. Panel: Annunciation (fig. 1000).

1444   Parri Spinelli: Arezzo, Conservatorio di S. Caterina. Fresco: Crucifixion (fig. 1124).

1448   Paolo Schiavo: Florence, Museo di Andrea del Castagno. Fresco: Christ on the Cross with two Angels and Nuns. s. (fig. 1102).

NOTES AND ADDITIONS

II. Three lists, arranged by artist, of works by the Florentines in the main body of this compendium, and those who appear in Appendix A, 1300-1450, which are:

1) signed
2) dated
3) signed and dated.

SIGNED WORKS

Alvaro Portoghese
    Pisa, S. Croce a Fossabanda. Panel: Madonna & Child (fig. 894).
    Pisa, Nicosia, Chiesa dei Francescani. Panel: Madonna & Child (fig. 893).
    Brunswick, Herzog Anton Ulrich Museum S 26. Panel: Madonna Enthroned nursing the Child. d. 1434 (fig. 896).
    Volterra, Pinacoteca. Triptych: Madonna & Child with Saints. d. 1423 (fig. 895).

Andrea di Giusto
    Florence, Accademia 3236. Panel: Madonna of the Holy Girdle. d. 1437 (fig. 1085).

Antonio Veneziano
    Palermo, S. Niccolò Reale, Museo Diocesano. Panel: Flagellation; Virgin, St John Evangelist & Prophets. d. 1388 (fig. 480).

Bernardo Daddi
    Florence, Uffizi 3073. Panel: Madonna & Child. d. 1328 (fig. 90).
    Florence, Uffizi 8564. Panel: Madonna & Child. d. 1334 (fig. 99).
    Florence, S. Maria Novella, Cloister, Spanish Chapel. Panel: Madonna & Child. d. 1344 (fig. 119).
    London, Courtauld Institute of Art. Polyptych: Crucifixion. d. 1348 (fig. 120).

Cenno di Francesco di Ser Cenni
    Volterra, S. Francesco, Oratorio della Compagnia della Croce di Giorno. Fresco: Legend of the True Cross; Life of the Virgin. d. 1410 (figs. 785, 788-96).

Cristiani
    — Private Collection. Triptych: Madonna & Child with Saints (fig. 526).
    Pistoia, Museo Civico. Panel: Madonna & Child (fig. 515).
    Pistoia, S. Giovanni Fuorcivitas. Panel: St John and Scenes from his Life. d. 1370 (fig. 527).

Francesco di Antonio
    Cambridge, Fitzwilliam Museum. Triptych: Madonna & Child with Saints. d. 1415 (fig. 876).
    Figline, S. Francesco, Misericordia. Fresco: Annunciation with Donor; Coronation of the Virgin with Angels and Donor (fig. 885).

Giotto (Shop)
    Bologna, Pinacoteca Nazionale 102. Polyptych: Madonna & Child with Saints (fig. 25).
    Florence, S. Croce, Baroncelli Chapel. Polyptych: Coronation of the Virgin with Saints & Angels (fig. 24).
    Paris, Louvre 1312. Panel: Stigmatization of St Francis (fig. 23).

Giovanni del Biondo
    Siena, Pinacoteca Nazionale 584. Panel: Madonna & Child. d. 1377 (fig. 496).
    Figline, S. Francesco, Misericordia. Panel: Madonna & Child. d. 1392 (fig. 498).

Giovanni Bonsi
    Rome, Vatican, Pinacoteca. Polyptych: Madonna & Child with Saints. d. 1371 (fig. 436).

Giovanni da Milano
    Florence, Accademia 8467. Panel: Pietà. d. 1365 (fig. 378).
    Prato, Galleria Comunale 5. Polyptych: Madonna & Child Enthroned (fig. 380).

Giovanni di Ser Giovanni
    San Giovanni Valdarno S. Lorenzo. Fresco: Battle Scene with Archers (fig. 1278).

Jacopo del Casentino
    Florence, Uffizi 9258. Portable triptych: Madonna & Child Enthroned with Saints; Nativity & Crucifixion (fig. 244).

Jacopo da Firenze
  Volterra, S. Francesco, Oratorio della Compagnia della Croce di Giorno. Vault frescoes: Evangelists. d. 1410 (fig. 1258).

Lippo di Benivieni
  Florence, Acton Collection. Panel: Madonna & Child with Saints (fig. 59).
  Florence, Conte Carlo degli Alessandri Collection. Panel: Madonna & Child (fig. 49).
  Florence, Conte Cosimo degli Alessandri Collection. Two panels: Sts Peter & Paul (fig. 57-8).

Lorenzo Monaco
  Florence, Uffizi 885. Triptych: Coronation of the Virgin with Saints. d. 1414 (Florentine style Feb. 1413) (fig. 767).

Lorenzo di Niccolò
  Terenzano, (near Florence), S. Martino. Triptych: Madonna & Child with Saints. d. 1402 (fig. 815).

Maestro Francesco
  Florence, Accademia 6154 (actually at Bagno a Ripoli, S. Maria a Quarto). Panel: Madonna and Child with Saints and Angels. d. 1391 (fig. 1243).

Masolino
  Castiglione d'Olona (near Varese, Lombardy), Collegiata. Frescoes: Marriage of the Virgin, Nativity & Annunciation (fig. 1024, 6).

Nanni di Jacopo
  Rome, Museo di Palazzo Venezia. Panel: Madonna and Child with six Angels. (fig. 1259).

Niccolò di Tommaso
  Naples, Museo di S. Martino. Triptych: St Anthony Abbot with Saints. d. 1371 (fig. 346-8).

Orcagna
  Private Collection. Panel: Annunciation with Donor. d. 1346. (fig. 294).
  Florence, S. Maria Novella, Strozzi Chapel. Polyptych: Christ in Glory with Saints and Virgin. d. 1357 (fig. 274).

Pacino di Buonaguida
  Florence, Accademia 8568. Polyptych: Christ on the Cross with the Virgin and St John, & Saints. d. 13?? (fig. 26).

Paolo Schiavo
  Florence, S. Miniato al Monte. Fresco: Madonna & Child with Saints. d. 1436 (fig. 1101).
  Florence, Museo di Andrea del Castagno. Fresco: Christ on the Cross with two Angels & Nuns. d. 1448 (fig. 1102).

Puccio di Simone
  Florence, Accademia 8569. Polyptych: Madonna of Humility with Saints (fig. 175).
  Whereabouts unknown. Panel: Madonna nursing the Child. d. 1360 (fig. 167).

Rossello di Jacopo Franchi
  Siena, Pinacoteca Nazionale 608. Panel: Coronation of the Virgin. d. 1439 (fig. 977).
  Formerly *Staggia*, S. Maria Assunta (stolen 1920). Panel: Madonna & Child (fig. 970).

Spinello Aretino
  Cambridge (Mass.), Fogg Art Museum 1917.3. Panel: Madonna & Child (fig. 708).
  Florence, Accademia 8461. Triptych: Madonna & Child with Saints. d. 1391 (fig. 723).

Taddeo Gaddi
  Berlin, Dahlem, Staatliche Museen 1079-81. Portable triptych: Madonna & Child with Saints. d. 1334 (fig. 152).
  Florence, Depositi no. 3. Panel: Madonna & Child with Saints. d. 1355. (fig. 143).

NOTES AND ADDITIONS

DATED WORKS LISTED ALPHABETICALLY

by known Florentine Masters; see also the list of various " Master ofs " in Appendix A, as well as the list of dated works by unknown hands at the end of that Appendix.

Alvaro Portoghese
  1423   Volterra, Pinacoteca. Triptych: Madonna & Child with Saints. s. (fig. 895).
  1434   Brunswick, Herzog Anton Ulrich Museum S. 26. Panel: Madonna Enthroned nursing the Child. s. (fig. 896).

Andrea di Giusto
  1435   Prato, Galleria Comunale 8. Triptych: Madonna & Child with Saints (fig. 1074).
  1436   Figline, S. Andrea a Ripalta. Triptych: Madonna & Child with Saints (fig. 1082).
  1437   Florence, Accademia 3236. Triptych: Madonna of the Holy Girdle with Saints (fig. 1085).

Antonio Veneziano
  1388   Palermo, S. Niccolò Reale, Museo Diocesano. Panel: Flagellation; Virgin, St John, Evangelists & Prophets. s. (fig. 480).

Bartolomeo di Frusino (?)
  1411   Florence, Accademia. Painted Crucifix (fig. 1254).

Bernardo Daddi
  1328   Florence, Uffizi 3073. Panel: Madonna & Child. s. (fig. 90).
  1333   Florence, Museo del Bigallo. Triptych: Madonna & Child with Saints (fig. 94).
  1333   Florence, Uffizi (Depositi 6170). Panel: Madonna & Child with Sts John the Baptist, John the Evangelist and Angels (fig. 93)
  1333 (?) Washington, National Gallery, Mellon Collection. Panel: St Paul & Donors (fig. 92).
  1334   Cambridge (Mass.), Fogg Art Museum 1918.3. Portable triptych: Christ on the Cross; Agony in the Garden (fig. 97).
  1334   Florence, Museo dell'Opera del Duomo. Panel: Madonna of the Magnificat (fig. 98).
  1334   Florence, Uffizi 8564. Panel: Madonna & Child. s. (fig. 99).
  1334   Philadelphia, John G. Johnson Collection. Triptych: Madonna & Child with Saints (fig. 96b).
  1336   Osteria Nuova (Bagno a Ripoli), S. Giorgio a Ruballa. Panel: Madonna & Child with Saints (fig. 100).

1336   Siena, Pinacoteca 60. Portable Triptych: Madonna & Child with Saints (fig. 106).

1337   Washington, Dumbarton Oaks. Panel: Madonna & Child with Saints (fig. 105).

1338   Edinburgh, National Gallery 1904. Portable Triptych: Nativity, Madonna & Child (fig. 113).

1338   London, Count Seilern. Portable triptych: Madonna & Child with Saints (fig. 114, 5).

1338   Minneapolis (Minn.), Art Institute. Portable triptych: Madonna & Child with Saints (fig. 117).

1343   Florence, Accademia 8570. Panel: Christ on the Cross with Virgin & Saints (fig. 111)

1344   Florence, S. Maria Novella, Cloister, Spanish Chapel. Polyptych: Madonna & Child with Saints. s. (fig. 119).

1348   London, Courtauld Institute. Polyptych: Crucifixion. s. (fig. 120).

Bicci di Lorenzo
1414   Stia, Propositura di S. Maria Assunta. Triptych: Annunciation with four Saints (fig. 979).

1423   Berlin (destroyed 1945), St Salvi healing, Nativity, St Bernardo degli Uberti (fig. 980).

1430   Florence, Porta S. Giorgio. Fresco: Madonna & Child (fig. 988).

1430   Vertine, S. Bartolomeo. Triptych: Madonna & Child with Saints (fig. 989).

1433   Parma, Pinacoteca. Panel: Madonna & Child Enthroned (fig. 990).

1434   Velletri, Museo del Duomo. Panel: Visitation (fig. 993).

1435   Bibbiena, Propositura. Panel: Madonna & Child Enthroned with Saints (fig. 996).

1435   Florence, S. Giovannino dei Cavalieri. Panel: Nativity (fig. 1003).

1440   Legnaia (Florence), S. Arcangelo. Panel: Annunciation (fig. 1000).

Buffalmacco (?)
1315   Florence, Badia a Settimo. Vault fresco: Evangelist (fig. 1204).

Cenni di Francesco di Ser Cenni
1383   Florence, San Donato in Polverosa. Fresco: Adoration of the Magi (fig. 798).

1393   San Miniato al Tedesco (Val d'Elsa), Palazzo Comunale. Panel: Madonna nursing the Child (fig. 779).

1400   Montalbino, S. Giusto. Triptych: Madonna nursing the Child with Saints (fig. 784).

1408 (?) Volterra, Pinacoteca. Triptych: Madonna of Humility with Saints (fig. 781).

1410   Volterra, S. Francesco, Oratorio della Compagnia della Croce di Giorno. Frescoes: Legend of the True Cross, Life of the Virgin. s. (figs. 785, 88-96).

Cristiani
1370   Pistoia, S. Giovanni Fuorcivitas. Panel: St John and Scenes from his Life. s. (fig. 527).

1388   Pistoia, Duomo. Fresco: Incredulity of St Thomas with two Saints. (fig. 521).

Francesco di Antonio
1415   Cambridge, Fitzwilliam Museum. Triptych: Madonna & Child with Saints. s. (fig. 876).

Giovanni del Biondo
1363   Florence, S. Croce. Panels: Four Church Fathers: Sts Ambrose, Gregory, Augustine, Jerome (fig. 493).

1364   Florence, Accademia 8462. Triptych: Presentation of Christ with Saints (fig. 485).

1372   Florence, S. Croce, Tosinghi Chapel. Polyptych: Madonna & Child with Saints (fig. 491).

1372   Formerly Richmond (Surrey), Cook Collection. Panel: Coronation of the Virgin (fig. 499).

1373   Fiesole, Duomo. Triptych: Coronation of the Virgin with Saints (fig. 490).

1375   San Donato in Poggio (near Tavarnelle, Val di Pesa), Pieve, Baptistery. Panel: Coronation of the Virgin with Saints (figs. 494, 508).

1377   Siena, Pinacoteca Nazionale 584. Panel: Madonna & Child. s. (fig. 496).

1379   Florence, S. Croce, Sacristy, Rinuccini Chapel. Polyptych: Madonna & Child with Saints (fig. 488).

1387   Florence, S. Felice a Ema (near Impruneta). Panel: Madonna & Child with 16 figures (fig. 497).

1392   Figline (Upper Valdarno), S. Francesco, Misericordia. Panel: Madonna & Child. s. (fig. 498).

Giovanni Bonsi
1371   Rome, Vatican, Pinacoteca. Polyptych: Madonna & Child with Saints. s. (fig. 436).

1380   Florence, Acton Collection. Panel: St Humphrey with Donor (fig. 448).

Giovanni dal Ponte
1410   Chantilly, Musée Condé, 3. Triptych: Coronation of the Virgin with Saints (fig. 739).

1430   Rosano (Pontassieve), SS. Annunziata. Triptych: Annunciation with Saints (fig. 741).

1435   Rome, Vatican, Pinacoteca. Triptych: Annunciation with Saints (fig. 750).

Giovanni da Milano
1365   Florence, Accademia 8467. Panel: Pietà, s. (fig. 378).

Jacopo del Casentino
1330   Kansas City (Mo.), Wm. Rockhill Nelson Gallery of Art. Panel: Infant Christ presented in the Temple for Circumcision (fig. 235).

1345   Budapest, Musée des Beaux-Arts. Panel: Madonna & Child Enthroned with Saints & Angels. (fig. 242).

Jacopo di Cione
1362   Whereabouts unknown (formerly Brussels, Stoclet Collection). Panel: Madonna nursing the Child (fig. 335).

1383   Florence, SS. Apostoli (Uffizi 8607). Polyptych: Madonna & Child with Saints and Angels (fig. 334).

1386   Florence, Miari-Pelli-Frabbroni Collection. Panel: Madonna of Humility with two Angels (fig. 336).

Jacopo da Firenze
1410   Volterra, S. Francesco, Oratorio della Croce di Giorno, Vault frescoes: Evangelist (fig. 1258).

Lorenzo Monaco
MCCC- (incomplete), Berlin ex-Staatliche Museen, destroyed 1945. Panel: Madonna & Child with Saints (fig. 753).

1400   Moscow, Puskin Museum. Panel: Madonna of Humility (fig. 752).

1404   Empoli, Museo della Collegiata 2. Triptych: Madonna of Humility with Saints (fig. 754).

1404   Florence, Accademia 467. Panel: Man of Sorrows with the Virgin & the Baptist (fig. 755).

1405   Ponte a Mensola (Florence), Berenson Collection. Panel: Madonna of Humility (fig. 760).

1408   Florence, Accademia 470. Panel: Madonna & Child with Saints (fig. 758).

1408   Paris, Louvre 1348 A. Side panels to a triptych: Agony in the Garden; Marys at the Tomb (fig. 762).

1408   Seattle (Wash.), Museum of Art K 1654, Samuel H. Kress Collection. Panel: Crucifixion (fig. 763).

1408   Turin, Museo Civico 3023. Painting on glass: Madonna & Child (fig. 757).

1410   Florence, Palazzo Davanzati. Triptych: Madonna & Child with Saints (fig. 766).

1412   Pisa, Museo Nazionale di S. Matteo. Panel: Madonna of Humility (fig. 764).

1413   Washington, National Gallery K 1293, Samuel H. Kress Collection. Panel: Madonna of Humility (fig. 765).

1414   (Florentine Style, Feb. 1413), Florence, Uffizi 885. Triptych: Coronation of the Virgin with many Saints. s. (fig. 767).

Lorenzo di Niccolò
1401   San Gimignano, Museo Civico. Triptych: St Bartholomew & Scenes from his Life (fig. 819).

1402   Terenzano (near Florence), S. Martino. Triptych: Madonna & Child with Saints. s. (fig. 815).

1404   Venice, Cini Collection 336. Polyptych: Madonna & Child with Saints (fig. 806).

1409   Florence, S. Croce, Medici Chapel. Panel: Madonna & Child (fig. 804).

1412   Mezzomonte (Pozzolatico), S. Lorenzo a Collina. Polyptych: Madonna & Child with Saints (fig. 820).

Maestro Francesco
1391   Florence, Accademia 6154. Madonna & Child with Saints & Angels. s. (fig. 1243).

Mariotto di Nardo
1398   Fiesole, Oratorio di Fontelucente. Triptych: Madonna of the Holy Girdle (fig. 955).

1400   Pesaro, Museo Civico. Triptych: Madonna & Child with Saints (fig. 942).

1404   Assisi, Convento di S. Francesco. Panel: Madonna & Child with two Donors (fig. 945).

1406   Florence, S. Trinita, High Altar. Triptych: Trinity with Saints (fig. 952).

1408   Minneapolis (Minn.), Institute of Art. Panel: Coronation of the Virgin (part of ex-Hatton Garden Church triptych, d. 1408) (fig. 957).

1418   Florence, Accademia 473. Panel: Madonna & Child with Saints (fig. 947).

1418   Florence, Accademia 3460. Panel: Madonna in Glory with Saints (fig. 944).

1418   Impruneta, Collegiata. Panel: Trinity with two Donors (fig. 950).

1421   Panzano, Pieve di S. Leolino. Triptych: Madonna & Child with Saints (fig. 941).

1422   Florence, Acton Collection. Panel: Madonna of Humility (fig. 946).

1424   Florence, Serristori Collection. Triptych: Madonna & Child with Saints (fig. 938).

1431   Florence, Acton Collection. Panel: Coronation of the Virgin (fig. 956).

Masaccio
1422   San Giovenale (Reggello), Pieve. Triptych: Madonna & Child with Saints (fig. 1054).

Masolino
1423   Bremen, Kunsthalle 164. Panel: Madonna of Humility (fig. 1014).
1435   Castiglione d'Olona (near Varese, Lombardy), Baptistery. Frescoes: Scenes from the Life of St John the Baptist (figs. 1010-1, 1018, 1023).

Master of the Arte della Lana
1404   Boston (Mass.), Museum of Fine Arts. Panel: Madonna & Child Enthroned (fig. 683).

Master of the Bambino Vispo (or Master of Borgo alla Collina)
1423   Borgo alla Collina, Casentino, S. Donato. Triptych: Marriage of St Catherine with Saints (fig. 922).

Master of the Giraldi Tabernacle
1370   Rignano sull'Arno, Perticaia, S. Cristofano. Polyptych: Madonna & Child with Sts Christopher & Margaret (fig. 451).

Master of S. Cecilia
1307   Florence, S. Simone. Panel: St Peter Enthroned (fig. 83).

Master of S. Martino a Mensola
1385   Florence, Acton Collection. Panel: Madonna & Child (fig. 581).
1387   Florence, S. Croce, second altar, right of nave. Fresco: Madonna & Child Enthroned with Saints (fig. 568).
1391   Florence, S. Martino a Mensola. Triptych: Madonna & Child with Saints (fig. 565).
1395   Whereabouts unknown. Panel: Madonna & Child with two Donors (fig. 579).

Master of Terenzano
1340   London, Courtauld Institute of Art. Polyptych: Madonna & Child Enthroned with Saints (fig. 202).

Nardo di Cione
1365   Florence, Accademia 8464. Triptych: Trinity with two Saints (fig. 311).
1365   Florence, S. Croce (Uffizi 170 dep.), Sacristy. Triptych: Madonna of Humility with two Saints (fig. 315).

Niccolò di Pietro Gerini
1409   Rovezzano, Sant'Andrea. Fresco: Madonna & Child with Saints (fig. 647).

Niccolò di Tommaso
1360   Pistoia, Palazzo Comunale. Fresco: St James & Bishop Saint with Madonna & Child & Angels (fig. 361).
1367   Formerly Arezzo (destroyed), Pinacoteca. Panel: Madonna & Child with female Donor (fig. 343).
1371   Naples, Museo di S. Martino. Triptych: St Anthony Abbot with Saints. s. (figs. 346-8).

Orcagna
1346   Private Collection. Panel: Annunciation with Donor. s. (fig. 294).
1350   Utrecht, Aartsbisschoppelijk Museum. Triptych: Madonna nursing the Child with Saints (fig. 289).
1357   Florence, S. Maria Novella, Strozzi Chapel. Polyptych: Christ in Glory with Saints and the Virgin. s. (fig. 274).

Pacino di Bonaguida
13 ? ?   Florence, Accademia 8568. Polyptych: Christ on the Cross with the Virgin & St John, & Saints. s. (fig. 26).

Paolo Schiavo
1436   Florence, S. Miniato al Monte. Fresco: Madonna & Child with Saints. s. (fig. 1101).
1448   Florence, Museo di Andrea del Castagno. Fresco: Christ on the Cross with two Angels and Nuns. s. (fig. 1102).
1460   Florence, Monticelli, Oratory of S. Maria della Querce. Panel: Assumption. s. (fig. 1095).

Parri Spinelli
1444   Arezzo, Conservatorio di S. Caterina. Fresco: Crucifixion (fig. 1124).

Pietro Nelli
1366   Signa, Pieve Vecchia di S. Lorenzo. Frescoes: Sts Julian & Catherine, Martyrdom of St Sebastian (figs. 701, 5).
1375   Impruneta, Chiesa Collegiata. Polyptych: Madonna & Child with Saints (fig. 686), (and Tommaso del Mazza).

Puccio di Simone
1353   Fabriano, Pinacoteca. Panel: St Anthony (fig. 168).
1354   Washington (D.C.), no. 6. Triptych: Madonna & Child Enthroned with two Saints (fig. 181).
1360   Whereabouts unknown. Panel: Madonna nursing the Child s. (fig. 167).

Rossello di Jacopo Franchi
1420   Florence, Accademia 8460. Triptych: Coronation of the Virgin with Saints (fig. 973).
1439   Siena, Pinacoteca Nazionale 608. Panel: Coronation of the Virgin. s. (fig. 977).

Spinello Aretino
1377   Arezzo, Museo Diocesano (formerly S. Agostino). Fresco: Madonna & Child with two Saints and a kneeling Warrior (fig. 715).
1385   Budapest, Musée des Beaux-Arts. Panel: Sts Nemesius & John the Baptist (fig. 709).
1385   Cambridge (Mass.), Fogg Art Museum 1915.12 a b c. Panel: Sts Benedict & Lucilla (fig. 712).
1391   Florence, Accademia 8461. Triptych: Madonna & Child with Saints (fig. 723).
1393   Quinto (Sesto Fiorentino), S. Maria. Triptych: Madonna & Child with Saints (fig. 716).
1407   Arezzo, S. Domenico. Fresco: Virgin Annunciate (fig. 724).

Taddeo Gaddi
1334   Berlin, Dahlem Staatliche Museen 1079-81. Triptych: Madonna & Child with Saints. s. (fig. 152).
1336   Rome, Museo di Castel S. Angelo. Portable triptych: Madonna & Child with Saints (fig. 151).
1355   Florence, Depositi 3. Panel: Madonna & Child with four Angels & two female Saints. s. (fig. 143).

NOTES AND ADDITIONS

SIGNED AND DATED WORKS

Alvaro Portoghese
1423 Volterra, Pinacoteca. Triptych: Madonna & Child with Saints (fig. 895).
1434 Brunswick, Herzog Anton Ulrich Museum, S 26. Panel: Madonna Enthroned nursing the Child (fig. 896).

Andrea di Giusto
1437 Florence, Accademia 3236. Panel: Madonna of the Holy Girdle (fig. 1085).

Antonio Veneziano
1388 Palermo, S. Niccolò Reale, Museo Diocesano. Panel: Flagellation; Virgin, St John, Evangelists & Prophets (fig. 480).

Bernardo Daddi
1328 Florence, Uffizi 3073. Panel: Madonna & Child (fig. 90).
1334 Florence, Uffizi 8564. Panel: Madonna & Child Enthroned with Saints (fig. 99).
1344 Florence, S. Maria Novella, Cloister, Spanish Chapel. Polyptych: Madonna & Child with Saints (fig. 119).
1348 London, Courtauld Institute. Polyptych: Crucifixion with Saints (fig. 120).

Cenni di Francesco di Ser Cenni
1410 Volterra, S. Francesco, Cappella della Croce di Giorno. Frescoes (figs. 785, 88-96).

Cristiani
1370 Pistoia, S. Giovanni Fuorcivitas. Panel: St John & Scenes from his Life (fig. 527).

Francesco di Antonio
1415 Cambridge, Fitzwilliam Museum. Triptych: Madonna & Child with Saints (fig. 876).

Giovanni del Biondo
1377 Siena, Pinacoteca Nazionale 584. Panel: Madonna & Child (fig. 496).
1392 Figline, S. Francesco (Upper Valdarno), Misericordia. Panel: Madonna & Child (fig. 498).

Giovanni Bonsi
1371 Rome, Vatican, Pinacoteca. Polyptych: Madonna & Child with Saints (fig. 436).

Giovanni da Milano
1365 Florence, Accademia 8467. Panel: Pietà (fig. 378).

Jacopo da Firenze
1410 Volterra, S. Francesco, Oratorio della Croce di Giorno. Vault frescoes: Evangelists (fig. 1258).

Lorenzo Monaco
1414 (Florentine Style, Feb. 1413), Florence, Uffizi 885. Triptych: Coronation of the Virgin with Saints (fig. 767).

Lorenzo di Niccolò
1402 Terenzano (near Florence), S. Martino. Triptych: Madonna & Child with Saints (fig. 815).

Maestro Francesco
1391 Florence, Accademia 6154. Panel: Madonna & Child with Saints & Angels (fig. 1243).

Niccolò di Tommaso
1371 Naples, Museo di S. Martino. Triptych: St Anthony Abbot with Saints (fig. 346-8).

Orcagna
1346 Private Collection. Panel: Annunciation with Donor (fig. 294).
1357 Florence, S. Maria Novella, Strozzi Chapel. Polyptych: Christ in Glory with Saints and the Virgin (fig. 274).

Pacino di Bonaguida
13?? Florence, Accademia 8568. Polyptych: Christ on the Cross with the Virgin and St John, and Saints (fig. 26).

Paolo Schiavo
1436 Florence, S. Miniato al Monte. Fresco: Madonna & Child (fig. 1101).
1448 Florence, Museo di Andrea del Castagno. Fresco: Christ on the Cross with two Angels & Nuns (fig. 1102).

Puccio di Simone
1360 Whereabouts unknown. Panel: Madonna nursing the Child (fig. 167).

Rossello di Jacopo Franchi
1439 Siena, Pinacoteca Nazionale 608. Panel: Coronation of the Virgin (fig. 977).

Spinello Aretino
1391 Florence, Accademia 8461. Triptych: Madonna & Child with Saints (fig. 723).

Taddeo Gaddi
1334 Berlin, Dahlem, Staatliche Museen 1079-81. Portable triptych: Madonna & Child with Saints (fig. 152).
1355 Florence, Uffizi (Depositi no. 3). Panel: Madonna & Child with Saints (fig. 143).

NOTES AND ADDITIONS

III. A chronological list, by year 1300-1450, which includes, by Florentines:
— all dated works reproduced in this compendium
— most documented works
— works with tentative dates, suggested by Berenson, Marcucci, Offner.

Pictures in this list include most works which are either dated, or documented, or for which dates have been suggested by Berenson, Marcucci or Offner; BBD denotes a suggested date by Berenson, MD by Marcucci, and OD by Offner. The letter 'D' denotes that the work is dated, and 'S', signed.

Painting which are known but permanently lost are not included with the exception of the 1433 Bicci di Lorenzo panels formerly in Berlin, photographs of which exist.

1300-1320	Master of S. Cecilia: Florence, Uffizi 449. Panel: St Cecilia Enthroned with Scenes from her Life. ca 1300-10 MD; pre-1304 OD. Giotto: Padua, Scrovegni Chapel. Frescoes: Scenes from the Lives of Christ & the Virgin. ca 1305-6. BBD. Pacino di Bonaguida: Florence, Accademia 8459. Panel: Tree of Life. ca 1305-10. MD.
1307	Master of S. Cecilia: Florence, S. Simone. Panel: St Peter Enthroned. D.
1315	Buffalmacco (?): Florence, Badia a Settimo. Vault Fresco. Evangelist.
1315	Pacino di Bonaguida: Florence, Accademia 8568. Polyptych: Christ on the Cross with Saints. 1315 MD; 13?? BBD.
Post 1317	Giotto: Florence, S. Croce, Bardi Chapel. Frescoes: Scenes from the Life of St Francis. BBD.
About 1320	Pacino di Bonaguida: Florence. Accademia 6146. Panel: Madonna & Child. About 1320. MD.
1328	Bernardo Daddi: Florence, Uffizi 3073. Panel: Madonna & Child. S & D. Taddeo Gaddi: Florence, S. Croce, Baroncelli Tomb. Fresco. ca 1328. BBD.
1329	Maso di Banco: Naples, Castelnuovo, Cappella Palatina. Fragments of frescoes. 1329-32. BBD.
1330	Jacopo del Casentino: Kansas City (Mo.), Wm. Rockhill Nelson Gallery of Art 47.1952. Panel: Infant Christ Presented for Circumcision. D. Jacopo del Casentino: Arezzo, Pinacoteca 8571,2,3. Three panels: Sts John the Baptist, Nicholas, John the Evangelist. About 1330. MD.
Post 1330	Jacopo del Casentino: Florence, Accademia 440. Panel: St Bartholomew. 1330-40. MD.

NOTES AND ADDITIONS

1331	
Before 1332	Pacino di Bonaguida: Florence, Accademia 8698, 8700. Panels: Sts Nicholas, John the Evangelist & Proculus. Before 1332. MD.
1332	Taddeo Gaddi: Florence, S. Croce, Baroncelli Chapel. Frescoes. 1332-38. BBD.
1333	Bernardo Daddi: Florence, Museo del Bigallo. Triptych: Madonna & Child with Saints. D. Bernardo Daddi: Florence, Uffizi (Depositi 6170). Panel: Madonna

& Child with Sts John the Baptist, John the Evangelist & 2 Angels. D.
Bernardo Daddi: Washington, D.C., Mellon Collection 3. Panel: St Paul & Donors. 133(3)?. D.
Unknown Paniter close to Daddi: Formerly Hatfield (Herts.), Burns Collection. Panel: St Catherine. D.
Taddeo Gaddi: Florence, Accademia 8581-8593. Panels: Lunette & twelve quatrefoils with Scenes from the Life of Christ; 8594-8603, panels: ten scenes from the Life of St Francis. 1333-34. MD.
Unknown Painter close to Daddi: San Godenzo (Mugello), Basilica. Polyptych: Madonna & Child with Saints (Uffizi Inv. 8745). D.
Unknown Painter close to Bernardo Daddi: formerly Lecore (near Florence), S. Pietro. Panel: Madonna & Child Enthroned. 1333-34. OD.
Unknown Painter close to Bernardo Daddi: formerly Marburg, Schloss Plansdorf, von Goldammer Collection. Panel: Madonna & Child with four Saints. 1333-36. OD.

1334 Bernardo Daddi: Cambridge (Mass.), Fogg Art Museum 1918.33. Portable triptych: Christ on the Cross; Agony in the Garden. D.
Bernardo Daddi: Florence, Museo dell'Opera del Duomo. Panel: Madonna of the Magnificat. D.
Bernardo Daddi: Florence, Uffizi 8564. Panel: Madonna & Child with Sts Peter & Paul & eight Angels. S & D.
Bernardo Daddi: Philadelphia, John G. Johnson Collection. Triptych: Madonna & Child with Saints. D.
Taddeo Gaddi: Berlin, Dahlem, Staatliche Museen 1079-81. Triptych: Madonna & Child with Saints. S & D.
Bernardo Daddi: Cambridge (Mass.), Fogg Art Museum 1936.56. Panel: St Gregory. BBD.
Bernardo Daddi: Sherborn (Mass.), Mrs Carl Pickhardt. Panel: St Francis. BBD.

1335 Bernardo Daddi: Florence, Accademia 3466. Panel: Madonna & Child. 1335-40. MD.
Maso di Banco: Florence, S. Croce, Bardi di Vernio Chapel. Frescoes: Scenes from the Life of St Sylvester. ca 1335-45. BBD.
Taddeo Gaddi: Cortona, Accademia Etrusca (Uffizi Inv. 3144). Two panels: Annunciation, Madonna & Child, two Saints. About 1335. MD.
Taddeo Gaddi: Florence, Accademia 164 dep. Panel: Madonna & Child with Saints. 1335. MD.

1336 Bernardo Daddi: Osteria Nuova (Bagno a Ripoli), S. Giorgio a Ruballa. Panel: Madonna & Child with four Angels, Sts Matthias, George & Donor. D.
Bernardo Daddi: Siena, Pinacoteca 60. Portable triptych: Madonna & Child with Saints. D.
Taddeo Gaddi: Rome, Museo di Castel S. Angelo. Portable triptych: Madonna & Child with Saints. D.
Bernardo Daddi: Rome, Visconti Venosta Collection. Portable triptych: Madonna & Child with Saints. BBD.
Giotto's assistant: Assisi, S. Francesco, Lower Church, Crossing Vault. Fresco: Allegory of Chastity. 1335-40. BBD.
Master of the Dominican Effigies: Florence, S. Maria Novella, Sacristy. Panel: Dominican Saints. After 1336. OD.

1337 Bernardo Daddi: Washington (Dumbarton Oaks). Panel: Madonna & Child with Saints. D.
Andrea da Firenze: Pisa, Camposanto. Frescoes. ca 1337. OD.

1338 Bernardo Daddi: Edinburgh, National Gallery of Scotland 1904. Portable triptych: Nativity; Madonna & Child. D.
Bernardo Daddi: London, Count Seilern Collection. Portable triptych: Madonna & Child with Saints. D.
Bernardo Daddi: Minneapolis (Minn.), Art Institute. Portable triptych: Madonna & Child with Saints. D.
Unknown painter near to Daddi: Milan, Private Collection. Panel: Coronation of the Virgin. D.
Bernardo Daddi: Berlin, Dahlem, Staatliche Museen 1094. Predella: St Thomas resisting Temptation. 1338? BBD.
Bernardo Daddi: New Haven (Conn.), Yale University Art Gallery 1871.6. Predella: St Dominic's Vision. 1338? BBD.
Bernardo Daddi: Paris, Musée des Arts Decoratifs. Predella: Preaching of St Peter Martyr. 1338? BBD.
Bernardo Daddi: Poznan, Museum, Mo. 11. Predella: St Dominic Saving a Ship. 1338? BBD.
Bernardo Daddi: Florence, Accademia 8563. Panel: Crucifixion; St Christopher. 1338-40. MD.
Bernardo Daddi: Florence, Uffizi 8458, 6127-8. San Pancrazio polyptych. Probably before 1338-40. MD.

1339

NOTES AND ADDITIONS

1340   Master of Terenzano: London, Courtauld Institute Galleries. Polyptych: Madonna & Child Enthroned with Saints. D.

Master of the Dominican Effigies: Florence, Accademia 4633, 4634. Dossale (painted on both sides): Madonna & Child with Saints; Coronation of the Virgin with Saints. ca 1340. MD.

Master of S. Martino alla Palma: Florence, Uffizi 6165. Panel: Madonna del Parto " La Ninna '. ca 1340. MD.

Taddeo Gaddi: Florence, Uffizi 448. Panel: Madonna & Child. 1340-1345. MD.

Bernardo Daddi: Florence, Accademia 3449. Panel: Coronation of the Virgin. 1340-48. MD.

1341
1342   Unknown Painter: Florence, Opera del Bigallo. Fresco: Madonna della Misericordia. D. (or 1352).

Taddeo Gaddi: Pisa, S. Francesco, Choir. Frescoes: St Francis & six Saints. BBD.

Taddeo Gaddi: Florence, S. Miniato al Monte, Crypt. Frescoes in vault. 1341-42. BBD.

1343   Bernardo Daddi: Florence, Accademia 8570. Panel: Christ on the Cross with the Virgin & Saints. D.

Bernardo Daddi: Florence, Accademia 442. Painted Crucifix. About 1343. MD.

1344   Bernardo Daddi: Florence, S. Maria Novella, Cloister, Spanish Chapel. Polyptych: Madonna & Child with Saints. S & D.

About 1344 Assistant of Bernardo Daddi: Florence, Duomo. Panel: St Catherine with Donor. OD.

1345   Jacopo del Casentino: Budapest, Musée des Beaux-Arts 6006. Panel. Madonna & Child with Saints & Angels. D.

1346   Orcagna: Private Collection. Panel: Annunciation with Donors. S & D.

Unknown Painter close to Bernardo Daddi: Gangalandi (near Lastra a Signa), S. Martino. Panel: St John the Baptist. D.

1347   Bernardo Daddi: Florence, Orsanmichele. Panel: Madonna & Child with eight Angels. BBD; OD.

1348   Bernardo Daddi: London, Courtauld Institute Galleries. Polyptych: Crucifixion. S & D.

Puccio di Simone: Florence, Accademia 8569. Polyptych: Madonna & Child with Saints. 1348-50. MD.

Bernardo Daddi (& shop): Barga, Conservatorio di S. Elisabetta (Uffizi Inv. 6140). Four panels: Sts Mary Magdalene, Michael, Julian & Martha. Post 1348. MD.

1349

NOTES AND ADDITIONS

1350   Orcagna: Utrecht, Aartsbisshoppelijk Museum. Triptych: Madonna nursing the Child with Saints. D.

1351
1352
1353   Puccio di Simone: Fabriano, Pinacoteca Civica. Panel: St Anthony. D.

Taddeo Gaddi: Pistoia, S. Giovanni Fuorcivitas. Polyptych: Madonna & Child with Saints. BBD.

Orcagna: Florence, Accademia 3469. Triptych: Madonna & Child with Saints. 1353-55. MD.

1354   Puccio di Simone: Washington (D.C.), no. 6. Triptych: Madonna & Child Enthroned with 2 Saints. D.

1355   Taddeo Gaddi: Florence, Uffizi (Depositi 3). Panel: Madonna & Child with four Angels & two female Saints. S & D.

1356
1357   Orcagna: Florence, S. Maria Novella, Strozzi Chapel. Polyptych: Christ in Glory with Saints & the Virgin. S & D.

Unknown painter near to Giovanni del Biondo: Vertelli, S. Michele. Triptych: Madonna & Child with two Saints. D.

1358   Unknown Painter: Florence, Museo Bardini, Corsi Collection. Triptych: Madonna & Child with two Saints. D.

1359   Orcagna: Florence, Orsanmichele. Marble tabernacle. S & D.

NOTES AND ADDITIONS

1360   Matteo Pacini: formerly Rome, Stroganoff Collection. Panel: Coronation of the Virgin with Saints. S & D.

Niccolò di Tommaso: Pistoia, Palazzo Comunale. Fresco: St James & Bishop Saint with Madonna & Child & Angels. D.

Puccio di Simone: Whereabouts unknown. Panel: Madonna nursing the Child. S & D.

Giottino (?), Florence, Museo del Bargello (Carrand 2009). Panel: Coronation with six Angels. ca 1360. MD.

Master of the Rinuccini Chapel: Florence, Accademia 6134. Panel: St Michael Archangel with two Saints & a Donor. ca 1360 MD.

Puccio di Simone (?): Florence, Depositi 3229. Panel: St Bartholomew. ca 1360. MD.

Giottino (?): Florence, Uffizi 454. Panel. Lamentation. ca 1360-1365. MD.

Nardo di Cione: Florence, S. Maria Novella, Strozzi Chapel. Frescoes. ca 1360. OD.

1361
1362   Jacopo di Cione: formerly Brussels, Stoclet Collection. Panel: Madonna nursing the Child. 1362 (?). D.

1363   Giovanni del Biondo: Florence, S. Croce. Panels: Four Church Fathers (part of High Altarpiece). D.

Giusto de Menabuoi: formerly Pisa, Schiff Collection. Panel: Madonna & Child with two Nuns. D.

Giovanni da Milano: Florence, S. Croce, Rinuccini Chapel. Frescoes: Scenes from the Life of the Virgin & St Mary Magdalene. 1363-65. BBD.

Unknown Painter: Figline di Prato, Pieve. Fresco: Virgin Annunciate. D.

1364   Giovanni del Biondo: Florence, Accademia 8462. Triptych: Presentation of Christ. D.

Jacopo di Cione: Florence, S. Trinita, Cappella Davanzati. Fresco: St Catherine. 1364 (?). BBD.

1365   Giovanni da Milano: Florence, Accademia 8467. Panel: Pietà. S & D.

Nardo di Cione: Florence, Accademia 8464. Triptych: Trinity with two Saints. D.

Nardo di Cione: Florence, Museo dell'Opera di S. Croce (Uffizi Inv. 170 dep.). Triptych: Madonna of Humility with St Gregory & Job. D.

Antonio Veneziano: Siena, Pinacoteca Nazionale 110. Panel: Four Evangelists. 1365. BBD.

Matteo Pacini: Florence, Accademia 437. Panel: Madonna & Child Sts Peter & Paul; predella scenes. ca 1365. MD.

Giovanni da Milano: Florence, S. Croce, Rinuccini Chapel. Frescoes. Unfinished in 1365. BBD.

Master of the Rinuccini Chapel: Florence, Accademia 8463. Triptych: Vision of St Bernard. ca 1365-70. MD.

Niccolò di Tommaso: Pistoia, Cappella del Tau. Frescoes. 1365-70. OD.

Allegretto Nuzi: Rome, Vatican, Pinacoteca. Triptychi. Madonna and Child with eight Donors, St George and a female Saint. S & D.

1366 Pietro Nelli: Signa, Pieve Vecchia di S. Lorenzo. Frescoes: Sts Julian & Catherine, Martyrdom of St Sebastian. D.

Andrea da Firenze: Florence, S. Maria Novella, Spanish Chapel. Frescoes. ca 1366-68. BBD.

Andrea da Firenze: Florence, S. Maria Novella, Spanish Chapel. Frescoes. Before 1366-67. OD.

1367 Niccolò di Tommaso: formerly Arezzo, Pinacoteca (destroyed). Panel: Madonna & Child with female Donor. D.

Orcagna & Jacopo di Cione: Florence, Uffizi 3163. Triptych: St Matthew & Scenes from his Life. ca 1367-69. MD.

1368
1369

NOTES AND ADDITIONS

1370 Cristiani: Pistoia, S. Giovanni Fuorcivitas. Panel: St John & Scenes from his Life. S & D.

Master of the Giraldi Tabernacle: Perticaia, Rignano sull'Arno, S. Cristofano. Triptych: Madonna & Child with Saints. D.

Giovanni del Biondo: Florence, Museo dell'Opera del Duomo 90. Panel: St Catherine. ca 1370. BBD.

Jacopo di Cione: London, National Gallery 569-578. Triptych: Coronation of the Virgin. 1370-71. BBD.

Jacopo di Cione: Philadelphia, Johnson Collection 4. Predella: Freeing of St Peter. 1370-71. BBD.

Jacopo di Cione: Providence (R.I.), Rhode Island School of Design. Predella: Arrest of St. Peter. 1370-71. BBD.

Jacopo di Cione: formerly Radensleben, von Quast Collection. Predella: Final Meeting of Sts Peter & Paul. 1370-71. BBD.

Jacopo di Cione: Rome, Vatican, Pinacoteca 107 & 113. Predellas: St Peter in Cattedra; Rising of the son of Theophilus. 1370-71. BBD.

1371 Giovanni Bonsi: Vatican, Pinacoteca. Polyptuch: Madonna & Child with Saints. S & D.

Niccolò di Tommaso: Naples, Museo di S. Martino. Triptych: St Anthony Abbot with Saints. S & D.

1372 Giovanni del Biondo: Florence, S. Croce, Tosinghi Chapel. Polyptych: Madonna & Child with Saints. D.

Giovanni del Biondo: formerly Richmond (Surrey), Cook Collection. Panel: Coronation of the Virgin. D.

1373 Giovanni del Biondo: Fiesole, Duomo. Triptych: Coronation of the Virgin with Saints. D.

Jacopo di Cione: Florence, Accademia 456. Panel: Coronation of the Virgin with Saints & Prophets. 1373 BBD; 1373-4 MD; 1383 OD.

1374
1375 Giovanni del Biondo: San Donato in Poggio (near Tavarnelle, Val di Pesa), Pieve, Baptistery. Panel: Coronation of the Virgin with Saints. D.

Pietro Nelli (and Tommaso del Mazza): Impruneta, Chiesa Collegiata. Polyptych: Madonna & Child with Saints. D.

1376
1377 Giovanni del Biondo: Siena, Pinacoteca 584. Panel: Madonna & Child. S & D.

Spinello Aretino: Arezzo, Museo Diocesano (formerly S. Agostino). Fresco: Madonna & Child with two Saints & a kneeling Warrior. D.

Andrea da Firenze: Pisa, Camposanto. Frescoes: Scenes from the

Life of St Raynerius. 1377. BBD.

1378 Giovanni del Biondo: Florence, Accademia 8606. Triptych: Annunciation with Saints. ca 1378. BBD.

1379 Giovanni del Biondo: Florence, S. Croce, Sacristy, Rinuccini Chapel. Polyptych: Madonna & Child with Saints. D.

Unknown Painter near Jacopo di Cione: Unknown. Triptych: Madonna & Child with four Saints & four Angels. D.

NOTES AND ADDITIONS

1380 Giovanni Bonsi: Florence, Acton Collection. Panel: St Humphrey with Donor. D.

Jacopo di Cione: Florence, Accademia 132 Dep. Panel: Madonna & Child. ca 1380 (?). MD.

Master of the Infancy of Christ: Florence, Accademia 8465. Tabernacle: Madonna & Child with Saints. ca 1380. MD.

Niccolò di Pietro Gerini: Florence, Accademia 4670. Panel: Christ on the Cross. ca 1380 MD.

Niccolò di Pietro Gerini: Florence, S. Carlo dei Lombardi. Panel: Deposition. ca 1380-88. MD.

Unknown Painter near to Niccolò di Pietro Gerini: Florence, S. Croce, Castellani Chapel. Painted Crucifix. D.

Unknown Painter: Faltignano (Val di Pesa), S. Bartolomeo. Panel: St. Andrew.

1381
1382
1383 Cenni di Francesco di Ser Cenni: Florence, San Donato in Polverosa. Fresco: Adoration of the Magi. D.

Jacopo di Cione: Florence, SS. Apostoli (Uffizi 8607). Polyptych: Madonna & Child with Saints & Angels. D.

Jacopo di Cione (with Niccolò di Pietro Gerini): Volterra, Palazzo dei Priori. Fresco: Annunciation. OD.

1384 Antonio Veneziano: Pisa, Camposanto. Frescoes: Three Scenes from the Life of St Raynerius. 1384-86. BBD.

1385 Master of S. Martino a Mensola: Florence, Acton Collection. Panel: Madonna & Child. D.

Spinello Aretino: Budapest, Musée des Beaux-Arts. Panel: Sts Nemesius & John the Baptist. D.

Spinello Aretino: Cambridge (Mass.), Fogg Art Museum 1915.12 a b c. Panel: Sts Benedict & Lucilla. D.

Spinello Aretino: Siena, Pinacoteca 119. Panel: Coronation of the Virgin. BBD.

Spinello Aretino: Siena, Pinacoteca 125. Panel: Dormition of the Virgin. BBD.

Giovanni del Biondo: Florence, Ospedale degli Innocenti. Triptych: Annunciation. BBD.

Agnolo Gaddi: Florence, S. Croce, Choir. Frescoes. ca 1385-95. BBD.

Lorenzo di Bicci: Ferraglia, S. Niccolò (Uffizi Inv. 174, dep 462). Panels: St Martin; St Martin divides his cloak. 1385-86. MD.

Niccolò di Pietro Gerini: Cortona, Accademia Etrusca (Uffizi Inv. 6112). Panel: Bishop Saint. 1385-90. MD.

1386 Jacopo di Cione: Florence, Miari-Pelli-Fabbroni Collection. Panel: Madonna of Humility with two Angels. D.

Giovanni del Biondo: Romena, S. Pietro. Panel: Madonna & Child with Saints. BBD & OD.

Niccolò di Pietro Gerini: Florence, Museo del Bigallo. Fresco: The Brethren with their charges. BBD.

Spinello Aretino: Florence, S. Miniato al Monte, Sacristy. Frescoes: Scenes from the Life of St Benedict. 1386-87. BBD.

1387 Giovanni del Biondo: Florence, S. Felice a Ema (near Impruneta). Panel: Madonna & Child with 16 figures. D.

Unknown Painter: Florence, S. Miniato al Monte. Fresco: St James. D.

Niccolò di Pietro Gerini: London, National Gallery 579. Triptych: Baptism of Christ. BBD.

Spinello Aretino: Antella (near Florence), S. Caterina. Frescoes: Scenes from the Life of St Catherine. BBD.

Antonio Veneziano: Pisa, Convento di S. Tommaso. Panel: Assumption. ca 1387. BBD.

Master of San Martino a Mensola: Florence, S. Croce, second altar, right of nave. Fresco: Madonna & Child with Saints. D.

1388 Antonio Veneziano: Palermo, S. Niccolò Reale, Museo Diocesano. Panel: Flagellation; Virgin, Sts John, Evangelist & Prophets. S & D.

Cristiani: Pistoia, Duomo. Fresco: Incredulity of St Thomas with Saints. D.

1389 Unknown Painter close to Giovanni del Biondo: ex San Domenico di Fiesole, Lucas Collection. Panel: Marriage of St Catherine. D.

Giuliano di Simone: Castiglione Garfagnana (Lucca), S. Michele. Panel. Madonna and Child Enthroned whith two Saints. S. & D.

NOTES AND ADDITIONS

1390 Agnolo Gaddi: Florence, S. Croce. Frescoes. OD.

1391 Maestro Francesco: Florence, Accademia 6154; on loan to Bagno a Ripoli, S. Maria a Quarto. Panel: Madonna & Child with Saints & Angels. S & D.

Lorenzo di Niccolò: Florence, Uffizi 8461. Triptych: Madonna & Child with Saints. BBD.

Master of S. Martino a Mensola: Florence, S. Martino a Mensola. Triptych: Madonna & Child with Saints. D.

Spinello Aretino: Florence, Accademia 8461. Triptych: Madonna & Child with Saints. D.

Spinello Aretino: Pisa, Camposanto. Frescoes: Scenes from the Life of St Ephysius. 1391-92. BBD.

Unknown Painter near to Nardo di Cione: Honolulu, Academy of Arts 2834. Triptych: Madonna & Child with Saints. D.

1392 Giovanni del Biondo: Figline (Upper Valdarno), S. Francesco, Misericordia. Panel: Madonna & Child. S & D.

Niccolò di Pietro Gerini: Pisa, S. Francesco. Frescoes: Scenes from the Life of Christ. BBD & OD.

1393 Cenni di Francesco di Ser Cenni: San Miniato al Tedesco (Val d'Elsa), Palazzo Comunale. Panel: Madonna nursing the Child. D.

Spinello Aretino: Florence, Quinto (Sesto Fiorentino), S. Maria. Triptych: Madonna & Child with Saints. D.

1394 Unknown Painter near to Jacopo di Cione: New York, Metropolitan Museum of Art 52.229.2. Triptych: Coronation of the Virgin with Saints. D.

Lorenzo Monaco: Florence, Biblioteca Laurenziana, Codice Cor. Laurenziana 5. Illuminated initial: St Jerome. ca 1394. BBD.

Mariotto di Nardo: S. Donnino di Villamagna (near Florence). Triptych: Madonna & Child with Saints & Angels. 1394-95. BBD.

Agnolo Gaddi: Prato, Duomo, Cappella del Sacro Cingolo. Frescoes. 1394-96. BBD.

1395 Master of San Martino a Mensola: Whereabouts unknown. Panel: Madonna & Child with two Donors. D.

Niccolò di Pietro Gerini: Prato, S. Francesco, Chapter Room. Frescoes: Scenes from Lives of Sts Anthony Abbot, Benedict & Matthew. BBD.

Lorenzo Monaco: Florence, Biblioteca Laurenziana, Codice Cor. Lauziana 8. Three illuminated initials: Sts Romuald, Paul and David. ca 1395. BBD.

1396 Agnolo Gaddi: Florence, S. Miniato al Monte, Cappella del Crocifisso: Sts John Gualbert & Minias, & Scenes from the Life of Christ. Unfinished in 1396. BBD.

Niccolò di Pietro Gerini: Prato, S. Francesco. Frescoes. After 1396. OD.

1397
1398 Mariotto di Nardo: Fiesole, Oratorio di Fontelucente. Triptych: Madonna of the Holy Girdle. D.

Niccolò di Pietro Gerini: Florence, Paradiso degli Alberti (formerly Convento di SS. Salvatore e Brigida al Bandino). Frescoes: Scenes from the Life of Christ. 1398-9. BBD.

1399 Unknown Painter: Figline (Upper Valdarno), Ospedale Serristori. Panel: Madonna & Child with Six Angels. D.

1400 Cenni di Francesco di Ser Cenni: Montalbino, S. Giusto. Triptych: Madonna nursing the Child with Saints. D.

Lorenzo Monaco: Moscow, Puskin Museum, 144. Panel: Madonna of Humility. D.

Lorenzo Monaco: Berlin, Staatliche Museen. Panel: Madonna & Child with Angels & Saints. MCCC- [incomplete]. (Destroyed 1945). D.

Mariotto di Nardo: Pesaro, Museo Civico. Triptych: Madonna & Child with Saints. D.

Niccolò di Pietro Gerini: Arezzo, S. Francesco (Uffizi Inv. 8720). Triptych: Madonna & Child with four Saints. ca 1400. MD.

Niccolò di Pietro Gerini: Florence, Accademia 3152. Triptych: Crucifixion with six Saints. After 1400. MD.

1401 Lorenzo di Niccolò, Niccolò di Pietro Gerini & Spinello Aretino: Florence, Accademia 8468. Triptych: Coronation of the Virgin with Saints. D.

Lorenzo di Niccolò: San Gimignano, Museo Civico. Triptych: St Bartholomew & Scenes from his Life. D.

1402 Lorenzo di Niccolò: Terenzano (near Settignano), S. Martino. Triptych: Madonna & Child with Saints. S & D.

Lorenzo di Niccolò: Cortona, S. Domenico. Triptych: Coronation of the Virgin. BBD.

1403
1404 Lorenzo Monaco: Empoli, Pinacoteca Collegiata 2. Triptych: Madonna of Humility with Saints. D.

Lorenzo Monaco: Florence, Accademia 467. Panel: Man of Sorrows with the Virgin & St John the Baptist. D.

Lorenzo di Niccolò: Venice, Cini Collection 336. Polyptych: Madonna & Child with Saints. D.

Mariotto di Nardo: Assisi, Convento di S. Francesco. Panel: Madonna & Child with two Donors. D.

Master of the Arte della Lana: Boston (Mass.), Museum of Fine Arts 16.64. Panel: Madonna & Child Enthroned. D.

Mariotto di Nardo: Perugia, S. Domenico, Choir. Windows: Various scenes. BBD.

Niccolò di Pietro Gerini: Arezzo, Museo (Uffizi Inv. 6148). Panel: Man of Sorrows with the Symbols of the Passion. 1404-10. MD.

Unknown Painter near to Niccolò di Pietro Gerini. Triptych: Madonna and Child with Angels and Saints. Florence, Accademia 8610. D.

1405 Lorenzo Monaco: Florence, Ponte a Mensola, Berenson Collection. Panel: Madonna of Humility. D.

Lorenzo Monaco: New York, Metropolitan Museum of Art. Four panels: King David, Abraham, Noah, Moses. 1405-10. BBD.

1406 Mariotto di Nardo: Florence, S. Trinita, High Altar. Triptych: Trinity with Saints. D.

1407 Spinello Aretino: Arezzo, S. Domenico. Fresco: Virgin Annunciate. D.

Lorenzo Monaco: Paris, Musée du Louvre 1348. Triptych: St Lawrence Enthroned with Saints. BBD.

Lorenzo Monaco: Vatican, Pinacoteca 215-7. Predellas: Three scenes. BBD.

1408 Cenni di Francesco di Ser Cenni: Volterra, Pinacoteca. Triptych: Madonna of Humility with Saints. (1408?) D.

Lorenzo Monaco: Florence, Accademia 470. Panel: Madonna & Child with Saints. D.

Lorenzo Monaco: Paris, Musée du Louvre 1348A. Two panels: Agony in the Garden; Marys at the Tomb. D.

Lorenzo Monaco: Seattle (Wash.), Museum of Art K 1654, Samuel H. Kress Collection. Panel: Crucifixion. D.

Lorenzo Monaco: Turin, Museo Civico 3023. Painting on glass: Madonna & Child. D.

Mariotto di Nardo: Grand Rapids (Mich.), Art Gallery 51.1.4. Panel: St Sylvester & Bishop Saint; Sts Francis & Dominic (panel from altarpiece formerly in Hatton Garden Church, London). D.

Mariotto di Nardo: Minneapolis (Minn.), Institute of Art. Panels: Coronation of the Virgin; Sts Bartholomew & Anthony (panels from altarpiece formerly in Hatton Garden Church, London). D.

Rossello di Jacopo Franchi: Florence, Duomo. Panel: St Blaise Enthroned. BBD.

Niccolò di Pietro Gerini: Florence, Orsanmichele. Fresco: Trinity; Pentecost. 1408-9. BBD.

Spinello Aretino: Siena, Palazzo Pubblico, Sala di Balìa. Frescoes: Scenes from the Life of Pope Alexander III. 1408-10 BBD.

Unknown Painter near to Spinello Aretino: Arezzo, San Domenico. Fresco: Christ on the Cross with the Virgin & St John Evangelist. D.

1409 Lorenzo di Niccolò: Florence, S. Croce, Medici Chapel. Panel: Madonna & Child. D.

Niccolò di Pietro Gerini: Rovezzano, Sant'Andrea. Fresco: Madonna & Child with Saints. D.

Battista da Pisa: Camaiore (Lucca), Pieve. Triptych: Madonna & Child with four Saints. S & D.

Lorenzo Monaco: Florence, Biblioteca Laurenziana. Codice Cor. Laurenziana 3. Eight initials: Prophets. ca 1409. BBD.

Unknown Painter: Florence, S. Miniato al Monte. Fresco: St Julian. D.

NOTES AND ADDITIONS

1410 Cenni di Francesco di Ser Cenni: Volterra, S. Francesco, Oratorio della Compagnia della Croce di Giorno. Frescoes: Legend of the True Cross, Life of the Virgin. S & D.

Jacopo da Firenze: Volterra, S. Francesco, Oratorio della Croce di Giorno. Vault frescoes: Evangelists. D.

Giovanni dal Ponte: Chantilly, Musée Condé. Triptych: Coronation of the Virgin with Saints. D.

Lorenzo Monaco: Florence, Palazzo Davanzati (Uffizi 468). Triptych: Madonna & Child with Saints. D.

1411 Bartolomeo di Frusino (?): Florence, Accademia. Painted crucifix. D.

Unknown Painter near to Cristiani. Prato, Palazzo dell'Arte della Lana. Frescoed Triptych: Madonna & Child with two Saints and Angels. D.

1412 Lorenzo Monaco: Pisa, Museo Nazionale di S. Matteo, Panel: Madonna of Humility. D.

Lorenzo di Niccolò: Mezzomonte (Pozzolatico), S. Lorenzo a Collina. Polyptych: Madonna & Child with Saints. D.

Pietro di Miniato: Prato, Pinacoteca. Polyptych: Coronation of the Virgin with Saints. Doc.

Lorenzo Monaco: Florence, Museo del Bargello. Manuscript: S. Maria Nuova Codice E 70. Illuminated initials. BBD.

Rossello di Jacopo Franchi: Florence, Museo del Bargello. Manuscript: Codice H 74. Resurrection. 1412-13 (?) BBD.

1413 Lorenzo Monaco: Washington, National Gallery K 1293, Samuel H. Kress Collection. Panel: Madonna of Humility. D.

Unknown Painter: San Donato in Poggio. Fresco: Madonna & Child with Sts Simon & Thaddeus. D.

1414 Bicci di Lorenzo: Stia, Propositura di S. Maria Assunta. Triptych: Annunciation with four Saints. D.

Lorenzo Monaco: Florence, Uffizi 885. Triptych: Coronation of the Virgin with Saints. (Florentine Style: Feb. 1413). S & D.

Unknown Painter: Arezzo, Museo. Fresco: Madonna & Child with Sts Lawrence & Anthony Abbot. D.

1415 Francesco di Antonio: Cambridge, Fitzwilliam Museum. Triptych: Madonna & Child with Saints. S & D.

Mariotto di Nardo: Florence, Compagnia del Bigallo. Triptych (stolen): Madonna & Child with Saints. 1415-16. BBD.

Master of the Bambino Vispo: Munich, Alte Pinakothek 10201. Panel: Last Judgement. 1415(?) BBD.

1416 Master of 1416: Florence, Accademia 4635. Panel: Madonna & Child

with Sts Anthony Abbot, Peter, John the Baptist and Julian. D.

Unknown Painter. Florence, via Lippi near Caciolle. Tabernacle: Madonna nursing the Child, with Sts. John Baptist and Peter, God the Father & two Angels. Fresco. D.

1417
1418 Mariotto di Nardo: Florence, Accademia 473. Panel: Madonna & Child with Saints. D.

Mariotto di Nardo: Florence, Accademia 3460. Panel: Madonna in Glory with Saints. D.

Mariotto di Nardo: Impruneta, Collegiata. Panel: Trinity with two Donors. D.

1419 Master of 1419: Cleveland Museum of Art 54.834. Panel: Madonna & Child Enthroned. D.

NOTES AND ADDITIONS

1420 Rossello di Jacopo Franchi: Florence, Accademia 8460. Triptych: Coronation of the Virgin with Saints. D.

Lorenzo Monaco: Florence, Uffizi 466. Altarpiece: Adoration of the Magi. 1420-22 (?) BBD.

1421 Mariotto di Nardo: Panzano, Pieve di S. Leolino. Triptych: Madonna & Child with four Saints. D.

Unknown Painter. Sestino (Stia), S. Pancrazio. Fresco: Christ on the Cross with the Virgin, Sts John Evangelist & Mary Magdalene. D.

1422 Mariotto di Nardo: Florence, Acton Collection. Panel: Madonna of Humility. D.

Masaccio: San Giovenale (Reggello), S. Giovenale. Triptych: Madonna & Child with Saints. D.

Lorenzo Monaco: Florence, S. Trinita, Bartolini Chapel. Altarpiece: Annunciation. 1422-25. BBD.

Lorenzo Monaco: Florence, S. Trinita, Bartolini Chapel. Frescoes: Scenes from the Life of the Virgin. 1422-25. BBD.

1423 Alvaro Portoghese: Volterra, Pinacoteca. Triptych: Madonna & Child with Saints. S & D.

Bicci di Lorenzo: Berlin, Bodestrasse, Staatliche Museen. Three panels: S. Salvi healing; Nativity; S. Bernardo degli Uberti. (Destroyed 1945). D.

Gentile da Fabriano: Florence, Uffizi 8364. Panel: Adoration of the Magi. S. & D.

Masolino: Bremen, Kunsthalle 164. Panel: Madonna of Humility. D.

Master of the Bambino Vispo (or Master of Borgo alla Collina): Borgo alla Collina, Casentino, S. Donato. Triptych: Marriage of St Catherine with Saints. D.

Bicci di Lorenzo: Empoli, Museo Collegiata 18. Triptych: Madonna & Child with Saints. BBD.

Master of the Bambino Vispo: Berlin, Dep 1123. Panel: Sts Mary Magdalene & Lawrence. 1423(?) BBD.

Master of the Bambino Vispo: Douai, Musée 35. Predella: Adoration of the Magi. 1423(?) BBD.

Master of the Bambino Vispo: London, National Gallery 3926. Panel: Head of the Virgin. 1423(?) BBD.

Master of the Bambino Vispo: Rome, Visconti Venosta Collection. Panel: Miracle of St Zenobius. 1423(?) BBD.

Master of the Bambino Vispo: Rome, Colonna Collection. Predella: Death of St Lawrence. 1423(?) BBD.

Master of the Bambino Vispo: Rotterdam, Museum Boymans van Beuningen 2557. Panel: Two Angels. 1423(?) BBD.

Master of the Bambino Vispo: Stockholm, National Museum 2678. Panel: Sts Zenobius & Benedict. 1423(?) BBD.

Master of the Bambino Vispo: Dresden, Gemäldegalerie 30. Panel: Head of the Virgin. 1423(?) BBD.

Masolino: Washington (D.C.), National Gallery, Mellon Collection 16. Panel: Annunciation. 1423. BBD.

1424 Mariotto di Nardo: Florence, Serristori Collection. Triptych: Madonna & Child with Saints.   D.

Masolino: Empoli, S. Stefano, 1st Chapel right. Fresco fragments. 1424.   BBD.

Masolino: Empoli, Museo Collegiata 95. Fresco: Man of Sorrows. ca 1424.   BBD.

Masolino: Empoli, S. Stefano, entrance to Sacristy. Fresco: Madonna & Child with two Angels. ca 1424.   BBD.

Masolino: Washington D.C., National Gallery of Art, Mellon Collection. Panel: Annunciation. ca 1423-5.   BBD.

Masolino: Whereabouts unknown, formerly Florence, Novoli, S. Maria. Panels: Madonna & Child; Florence, Seminario Maggiore: St Julian: Montaubon, Musée Municipal 116: St Julian murdering his Parents. 1424-25.   BBD.

After 1424 Bicci di Lorenzo: Florence, Ospedale di S. Maria Nuova. Fresco: Pope Martin V consecrating Sant'Egidio. After 1424.   BBD.

1425 Masolino: Florence, S. Maria del Carmine, Cappella Brancacci. Frescoes. ca 1425.   BBD.

Masolino: Munich, Alte Pinakothek WAF 264. Panel: Madonna of Humility. ca 1425 BBD.

1426 Andrea di Giusto: Berlin, Dahlem Staatliche Museen 58 E. Panel: St Nicholas & the three Maidens.   Doc.

Andrea di Giusto: Berlin, Dahlem. Staatliche Museen 58 E. Panel: St. Julian murdering his Parents.   Doc.

Masaccio: Berlin, Dahlem Staatliche Museen 58 A,B. Predella panels: Adoration of the Magi; Crucifixion of St Peter & Beheading of St John the Baptist. Doc. 1426.

Masaccio: Berlin, Dahlem Staatliche Museen 58 D. Panels: Sts Augustine, Jerome & two Carmelite Saints. 58 E, predella scenes: St Julian murdering his Parents: St. Nicholas & the three Maidens (with the hand of Andrea di Giusto).   Doc.

Masaccio: London, National Gallery 3046. Panel: Madonna & Child Enthroned with Angels.   Doc.

Masaccio: Naples, Museo Nazionale di Capodimonte 36. Panel: Crucifixion.   Doc.

Masaccio: Pisa, Museo Nazionale di S. Matteo. Panel: St Paul.   Doc.

1427 Bicci di Lorenzo: Florence, via Serragli & via S. Monaca. Tabernacle fresco: Madonna & Child with Saints.   BBD.

Masolino: Stockholm, National Museum 5173. Panel: Madonna & Child.   1427(?)   BBD.

1428 Unknown Painter: New York, Historical Society B-18 (1867.18). Desco da Parto: Birth of St John the Baptist.   D.

Parri Spinelli: Arezzo, S. Maria della Grazie. Fresco: Madonna of Mercy.   1428(?)   BBD.

Masolino: Rome, S. Clemente. Fresco: Annunciation; Scenes from the Lives of St Catherine & Ambrose; Crucifixion. 1428-31.   BBD.

1429 Francesco di Antonio: Florence, Accademia 9271. Panel: Four Singing Angels.   BBD.

Francesco di Antonio: Florence, Accademia 9272. Panel: Four Singing Angels (lost).   BBD.

Giovanni dal Ponte: Florence, S. Trinita, Cappella dell'Abbaco. Fresco: Christ Enthroned with Saints & Angels. 1429-30.   BBD.

Giovanni dal Ponte: Florence, S. Trinita, Cappella Ficozzi. Fresco: Ascension. 1429-30.   BBD.

NOTES AND ADDITIONS

1430 Bicci di Lorenzo: Florence, Porta S. Giorgio. Fresco: Madonna & Child with Saints.   D.

Bicci di Lorenzo: Vertine, S. Bartolomeo. Triptych: Madonna & Child with Saints.   D.

Giovanni dal Ponte: Rosano, Pontassieve, SS. Annunziata. Triptych: Annunciation with Saints.   D.

Bicci di Lorenzo: Florence, Duomo. Panel: Sts Cosmas & Damian. BBD.

Masolino: London, National Gallery 5963. Panel: A Pope & St Matthias. ca 1430.   BBD.

Masolino: Naples, Museo Nazionale di Capodimonte 33,35. Panels: Assumption; Foundation of S. Maria Maggiore. ca 1430.   BBD.

Masolino: Philadelphia, Museum of Art, Johnson Collection 408, 409. Panels: Sts Peter & Paul; St Martin & Evangelist. ca 1430. BBD.

After 1430 Bicci di Lorenzo: Florence, S. Martino a Gangalandi. Frescoes. After 1430.   BBD.

1431 Mariotto di Nardo: Florence, Acton Collection. Panel: Coronation of the Virgin.   D.

1432 Masolino: Todi, S. Fortunato. Fresco: Madonna & Child.   BBD.

1433 Bicci di Lorenzo: Parma, Pinacoteca 456. Panel: Madonna & Child Enthroned.   D.

Bicci di Lorenzo: Grottaferrata, Badia. Panel: Sts Benedict & Nicholas.   BBD.

Bicci di Lorenzo: New York, Lehman Collection. Panel: Sts John the Baptist & John the Evangelist.   BBD.

Bicci di Lorenzo: Oxford, Ashmolean Museum 60. Predella panel: St Nicholas saving a ship at sea.   BBD.

Angelico: Florence, Museo di S. Marco. Tabernacle: Madonna & Child (Linaiuoli Tabernacle).   BBD.

1434 Bicci di Lorenzo: Velletri, Museo del Duomo. Panel: Visitation.   D.

Alvaro Portoghese: Brunswick, Herzog Anton Ulrich Museum S 26. Panel: Madonna Enthroned nursing the Child.   S & D.

Giovanni dal Ponte: Florence, S. Trinita, Cappella Scali. Frescoes: Martyrdom of St Bartholomew, Beheading of a Saint. 1434-35. BBD.

1435 Andrea di Giusto: Prato, Galleria Comunale 8. Triptych: Madonna & Child with Saints.   D.

Bicci di Lorenzo: Bibbiena, Propositura. Panel: Madonna & Child Enthroned.   D.

Bicci di Lorenzo: Florence, S. Giovannino dei Cavalieri. Panel: Nativity.   D.

Giovanni dal Ponte: Rome, Vatican, Pinacoteca. Triptych: Annunciation with Saints.   D.

Masolino: Castiglione d'Olona (near Varese, Lombardy), Baptistery. Frescoes: Scenes from the Life of St John the Baptist.   D.

Parri Spinelli: Arezzo, Pinacoteca 21. Panel: Madonna of Mercy. Doc. 1435-37.

Unknown Painter near to Andrea di Giusto: Florence, Ponte a Mensola, Berenson Collection. Panel: Madonna of Humility.   D.

1436 Andrea di Giusto: Figline, S. Andrea a Ripalta. Triptych: Madonna & Child with Saints.   D.

Paolo Schiavo: Florence, S. Miniato al Monte. Fresco: Madonna & Child with Saints.   S & D.

Parri Spinelli: Arezzo, Pinacoteca 21. Panel: Madonna of Mercy with Saints. Doc. 1435-37.

1437 Andrea di Giusto: Florence, Accademia 3236. Triptych: Madonna of the Holy Girdle.   S & D.

Angelico: Vatican, Pinacoteca 251-252, Panel: St Nicholas of Bari. BBD.

Angelico: Perugia, Pinacoteca Nazionale 91. Triptych: Madonna & Child with four Angels & Saints.   BBD.

1438 Angelico: Dublin, National Gallery of Ireland 242. Panel: Attempted Martyrdom of Sts Cosmas & Damian by fire. 1438-40.   BBD.

Angelico: Florence, Museo di S. Marco. S. Marco Altarpiece. 1438-40.   BBD.

Angelico: Munich, Alte Pinakothek WAF 36-38 A. Four predella panels. 1430-40.   BBD.

Angelico: Paris, Musée du Louvre 1290. Panel: Coronation of the Virgin.   BBD.

Angelico: Paris, Musée du Louvre 1293. Predella: Beheading of Sts Cosmas & Damian. 1438-40.   BBD.

Angelico: Washington (D.C.), National Gallery of Art K 1387, Samuel H. Kress Collection. Predella: Healing of Palladia by Sts Cosmas & Damian. 1438-40.   BBD.

NOTES AND ADDITIONS

1439	Bartolomeo di Andrea Bocchi: Serravalle Pistoiese, S. Michele. Triptych: Madonna & Child with Saints & Angels. S & D.
	Rossello di Jacopo Franchi: Siena, Pinacoteca 608. Panel: Coronation of the Virgin. S & D.
	Angelico: Florence, Museo di S. Marco. Cell Frescoes. ca 1439-45. BBD.
1440	Bicci di Lorenzo: Florence, Legnaia, S. Arcangelo. Panel: Annunciation. D.
1441	Bicci di Lorenzo: Poppi (Casentino), Castello. Fresco: Madonna & Child with Saints. BBD.
1442	
1443	
1444	Parri Spinelli: Arezzo, Conservatorio di S. Caterina. Fresco: Crucifixion. D.
1445	Bicci di Lorenzo: Empoli, Museo Collegiata 91. Panel: St Nicholas of Tolentino defends Empoli. BBD.
	Mariotto di Cristofano: Florence, Accademia 3162, 3164. Altarpiece painted on both sides: Marriage of St Catherine; Resurrection. Doc. 1445-47.
1446	
1447	Angelico: Rome, Vatican, Chapel of Nicholas V. Frescoes: Scenes from the Lives of St Stephen & Lawrence. BBD.
	Angelico: Orvieto, Duomo, Cappella di S. Brizio. Frescoes: Christ in Judgement & 16 Prophets. BBD.
1448	Paolo Schiavo: Florence, Museo di Andrea del Castagno. Fresco: Christ on the Cross with two Angels and Nuns. S & D.
	Parri Spinelli: Arezzo, Palazzo dei Priori. Fresco: Christ on the Cross. 1448(?) BBD.
	Parri Spinelli: Arezzo, Fraternità dei Laici. Fresco: Madonna of Mercy. BBD.
1449	Master of Fucecchio: New York, Historical Society B-5. Desco da Parto: Triumph of Fame. BBD.
1450	Bicci di Lorenzo: Fiesole, Duomo. Triptych: Madonna & Child with Saints. ca 1450. BBD.

NOTES AND ADDITIONS

APPENDIX E

DETAILED MAPS OF THE ARNO VALLEY ADJACENT AREAS

*These maps are reproduced
through the kindness of the Istituto Geografico Militare
(autorizzazione n. 754), and of the
Touring Club Italiano, authorized reproduction.*

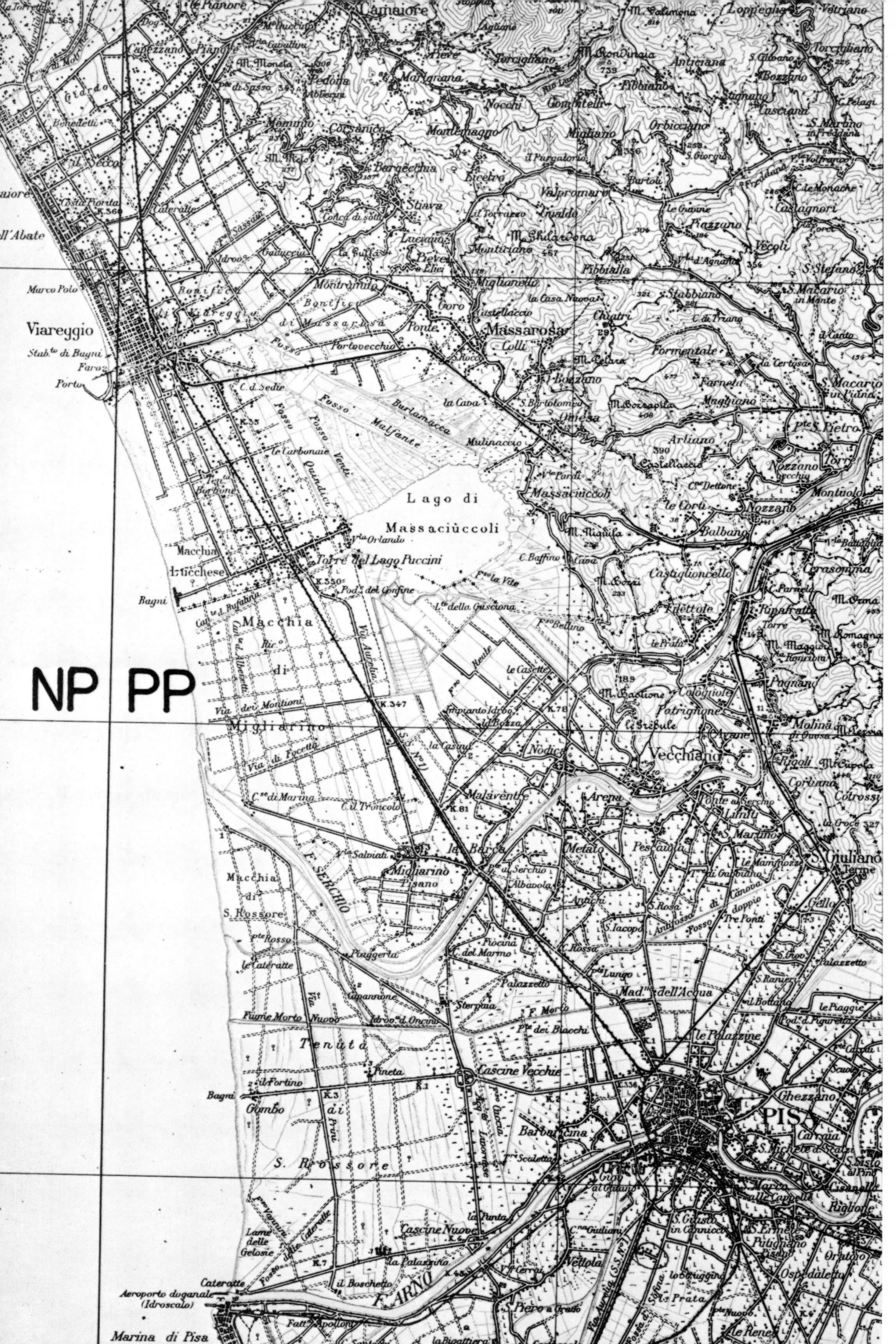

NP PP

647

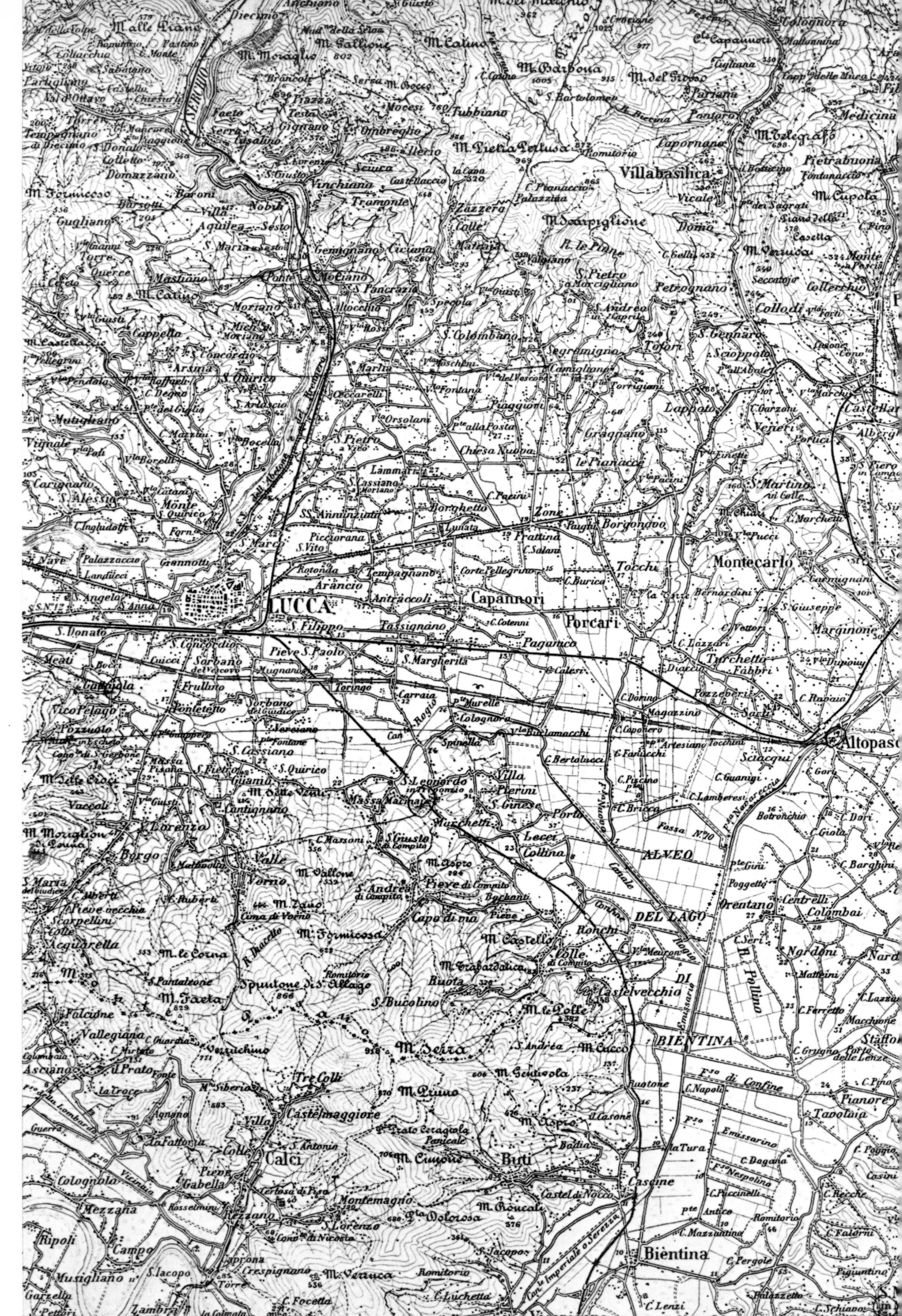

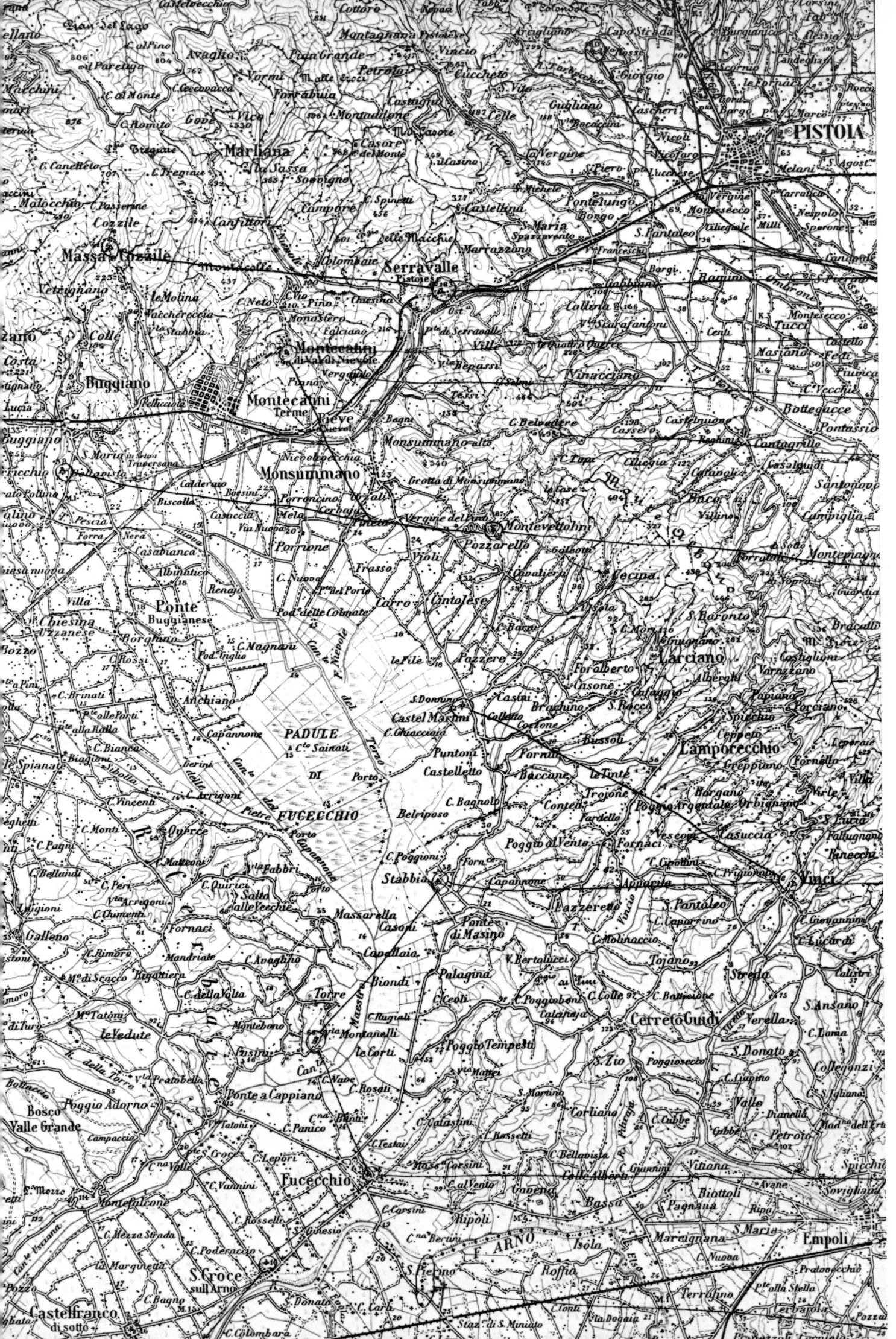

649

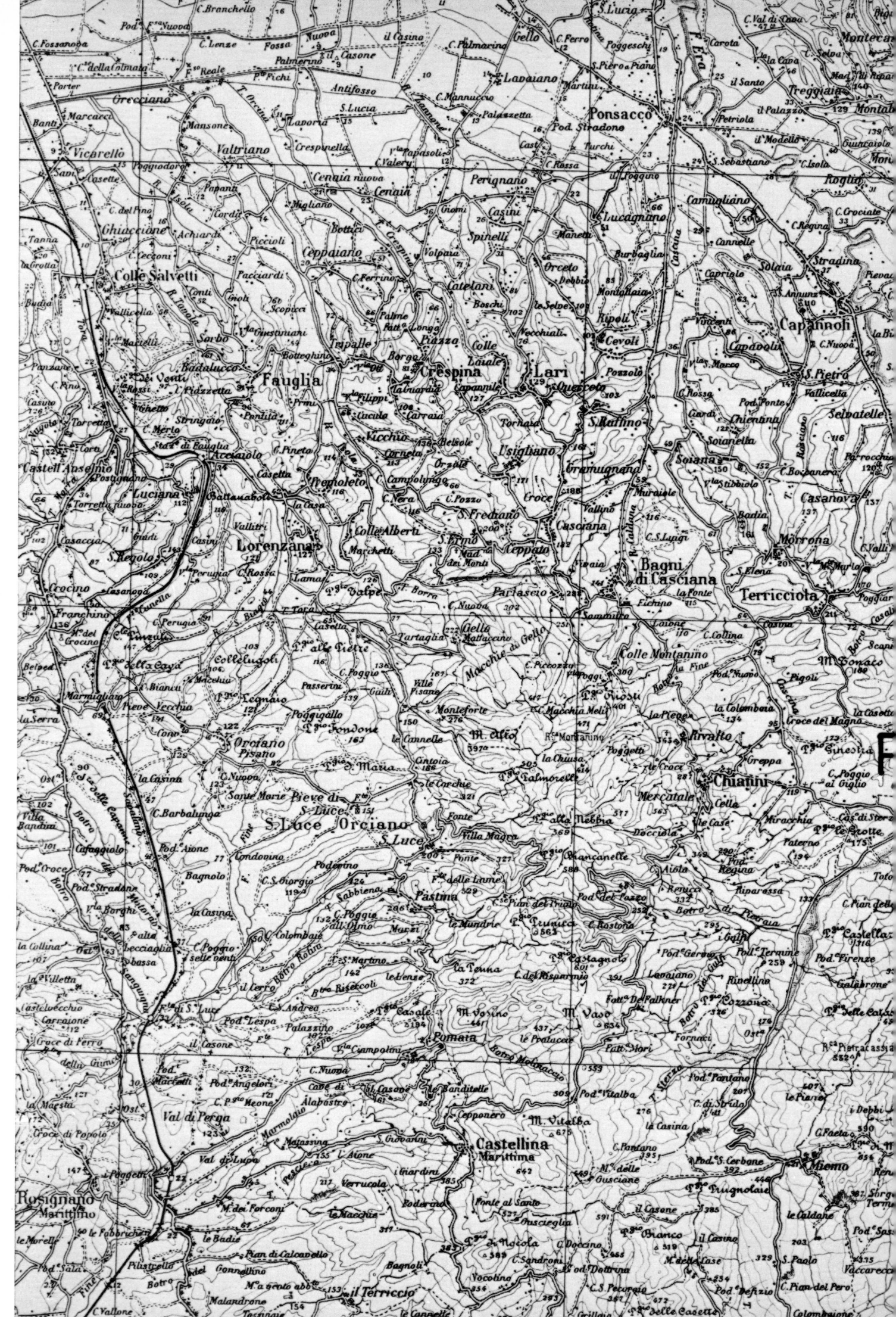

650

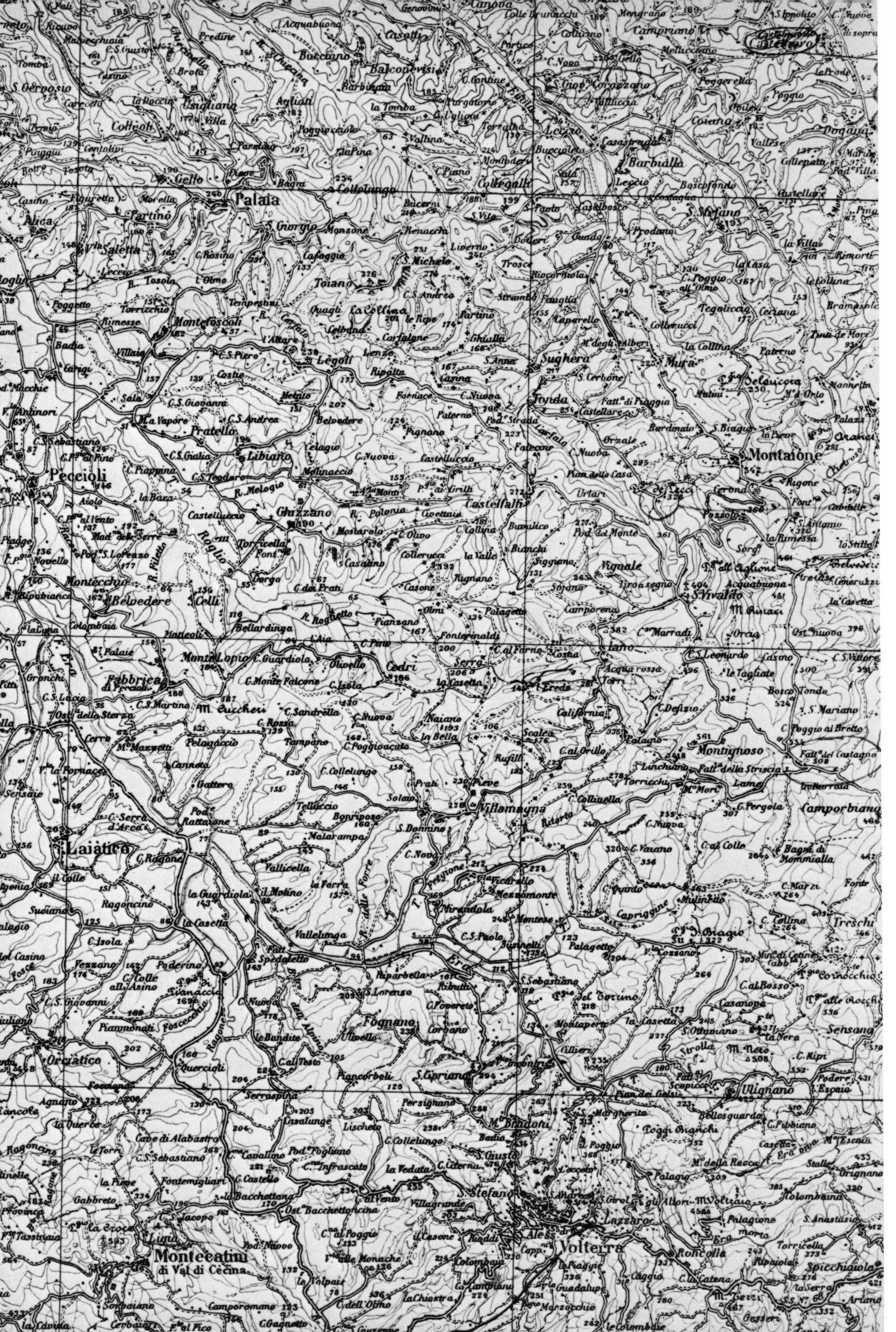

651

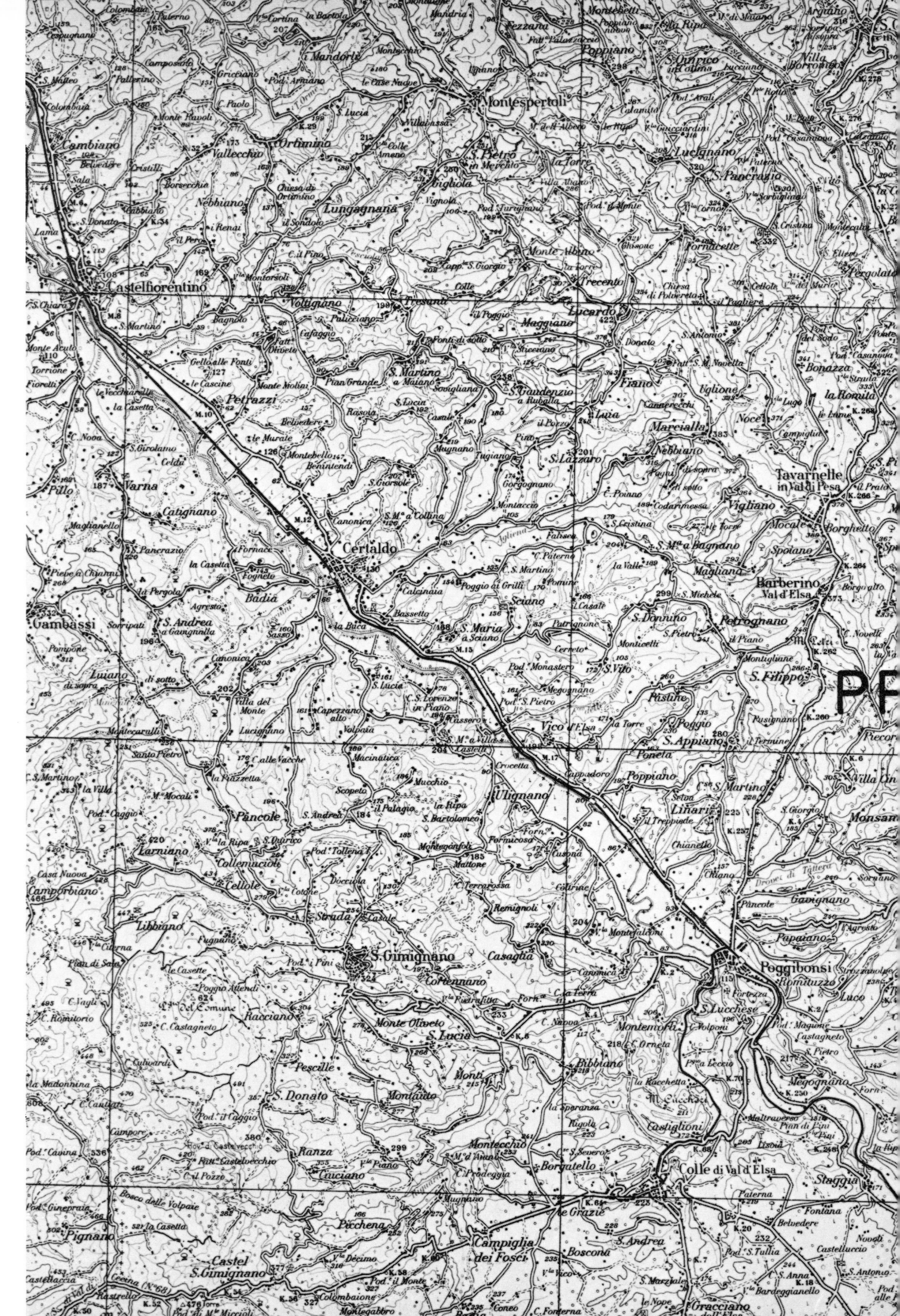

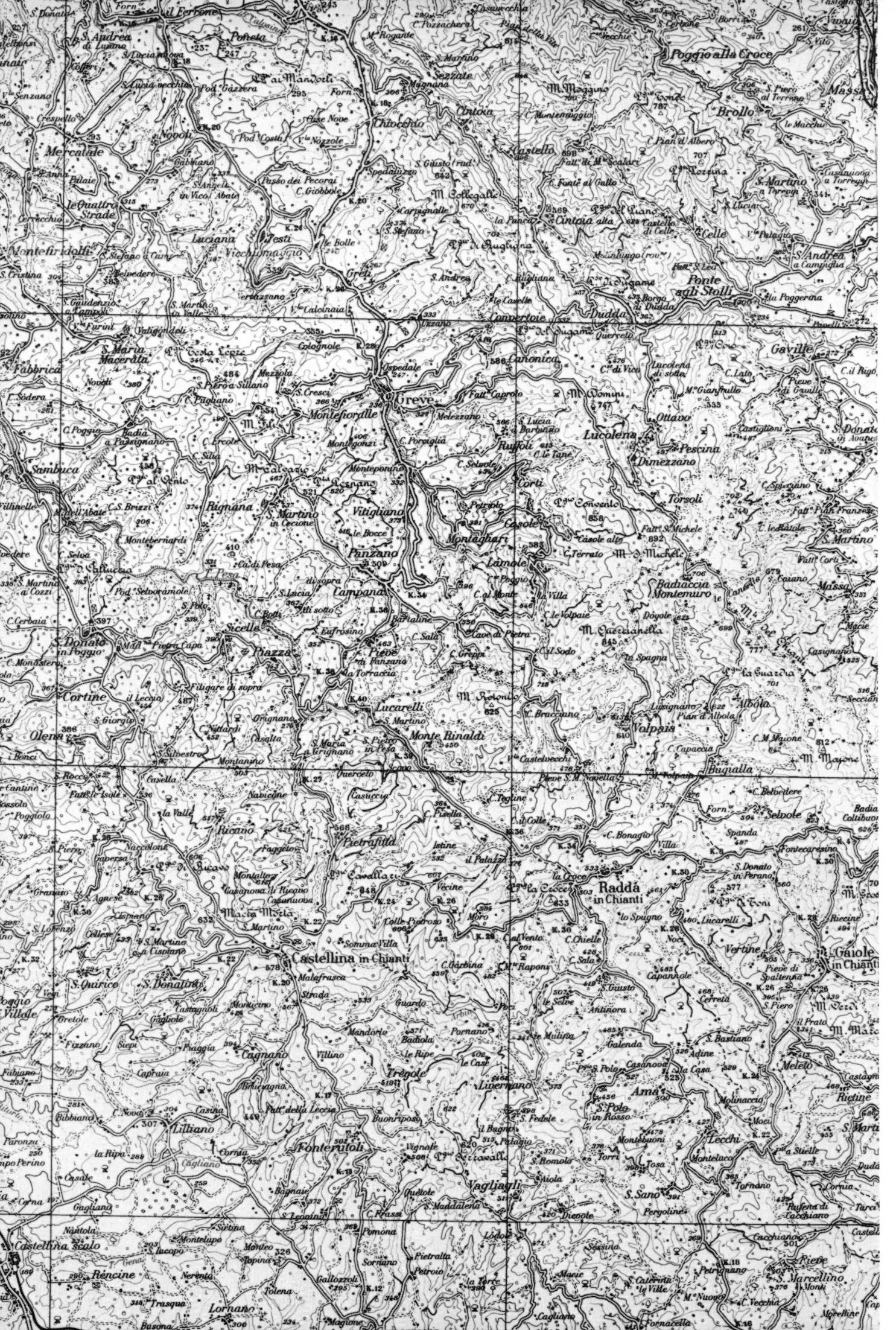

653

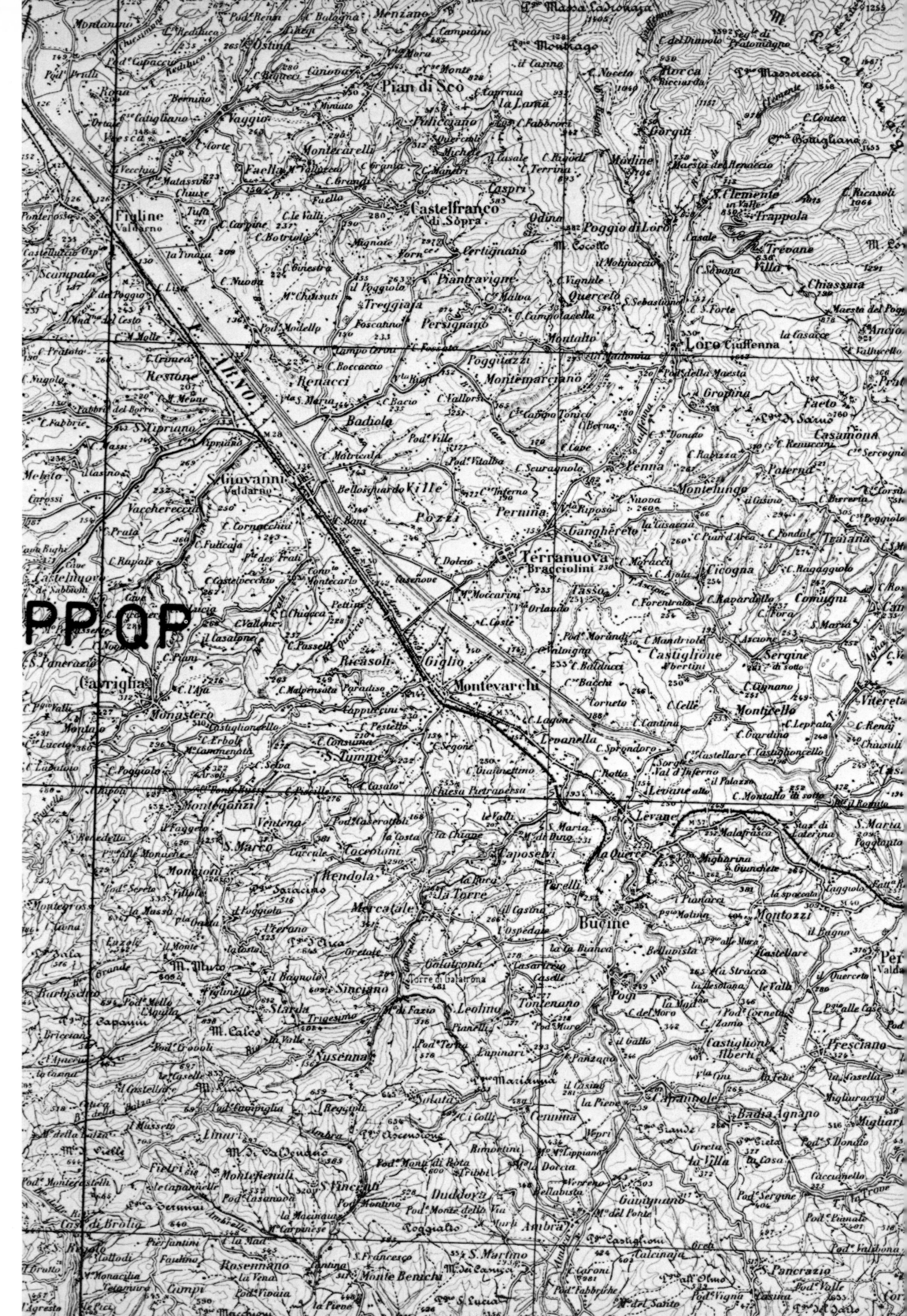

654

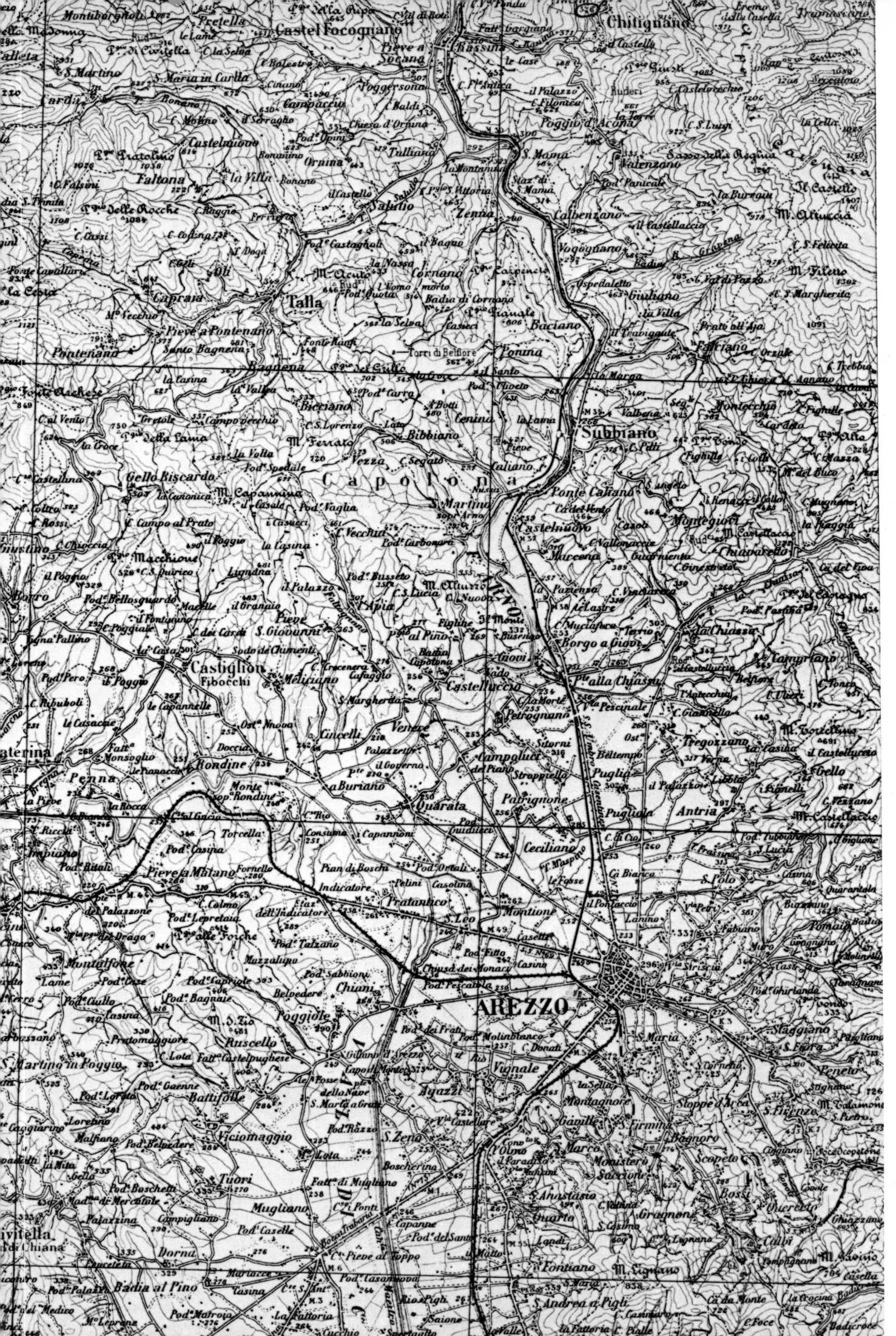

655

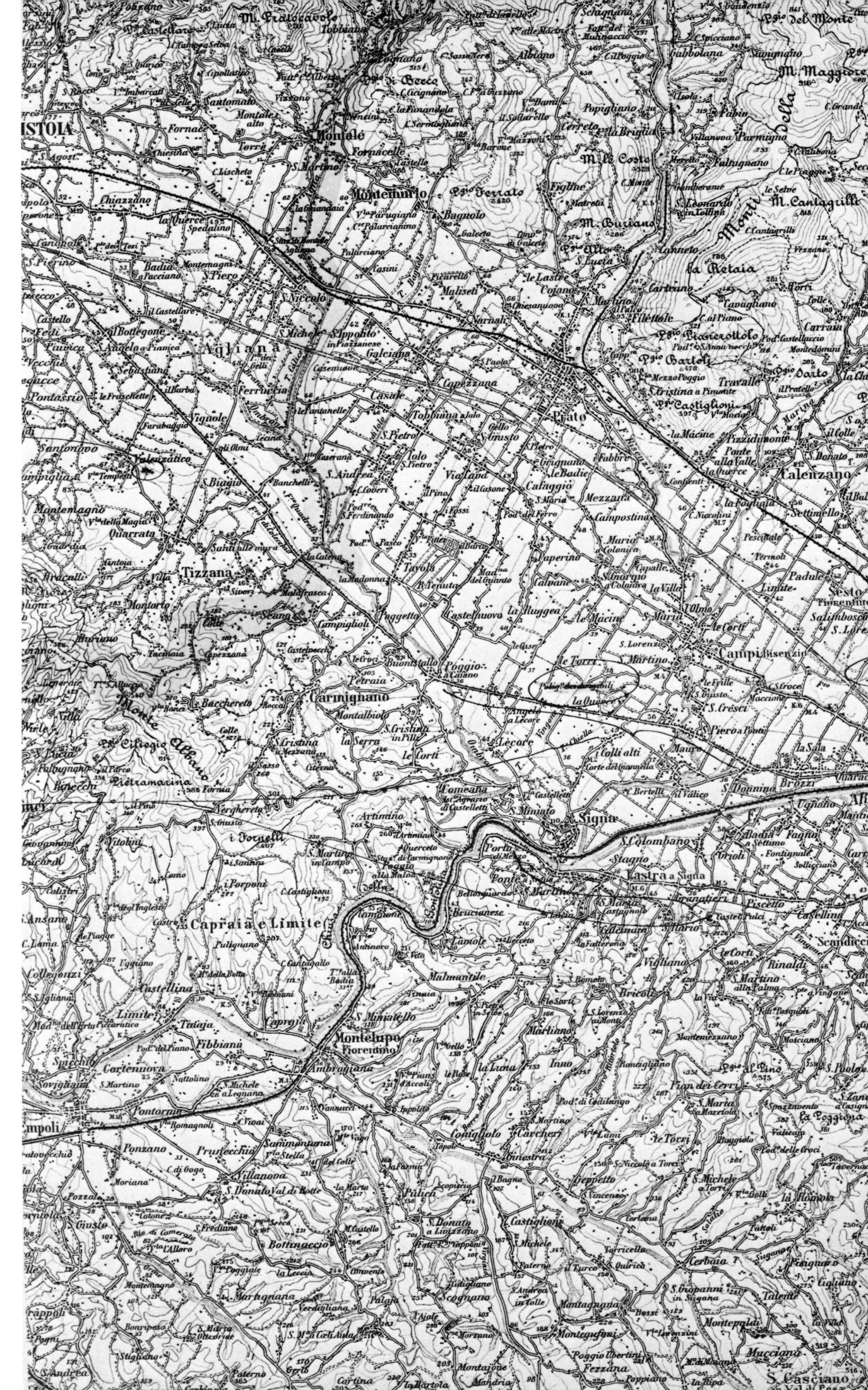

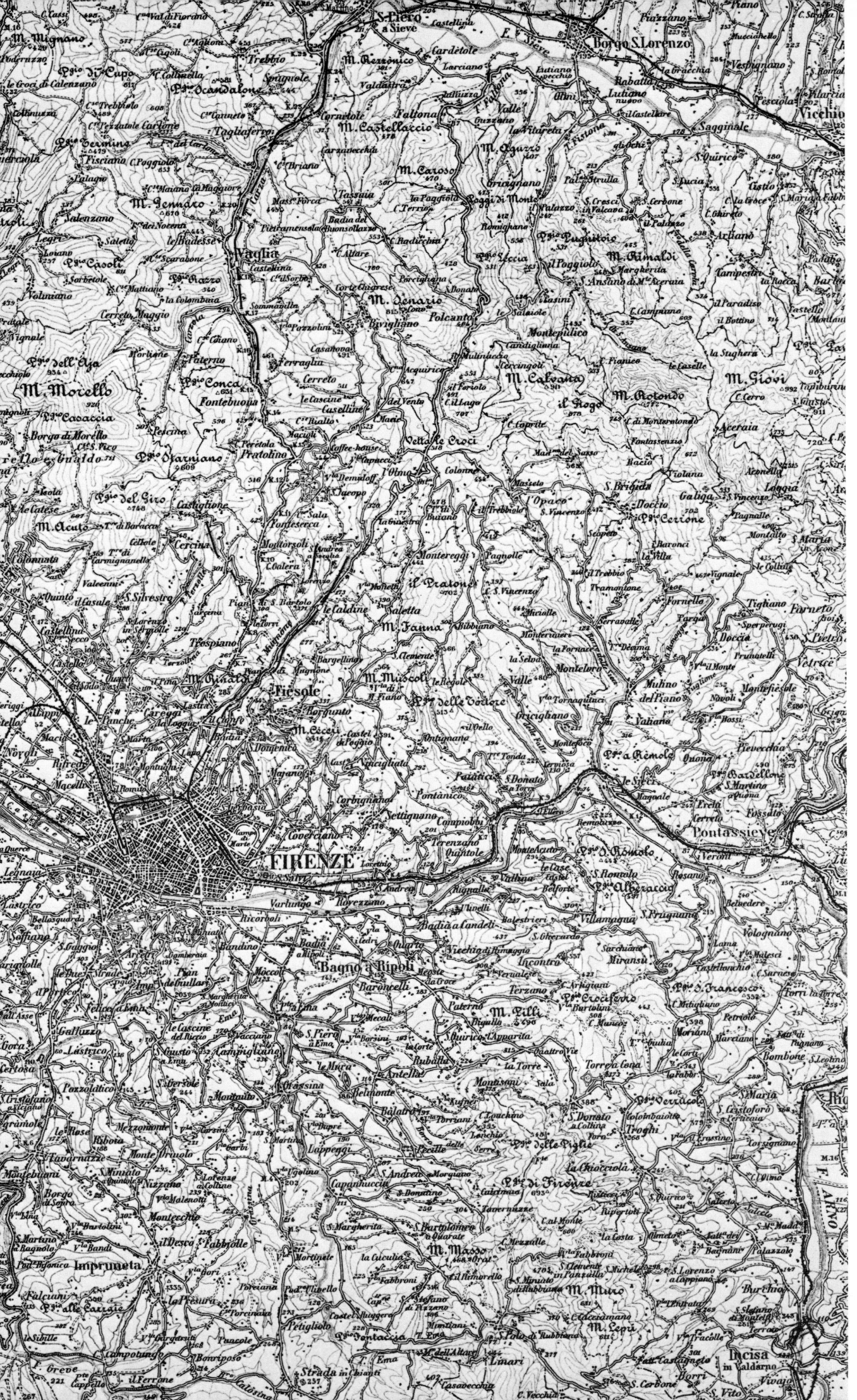

657

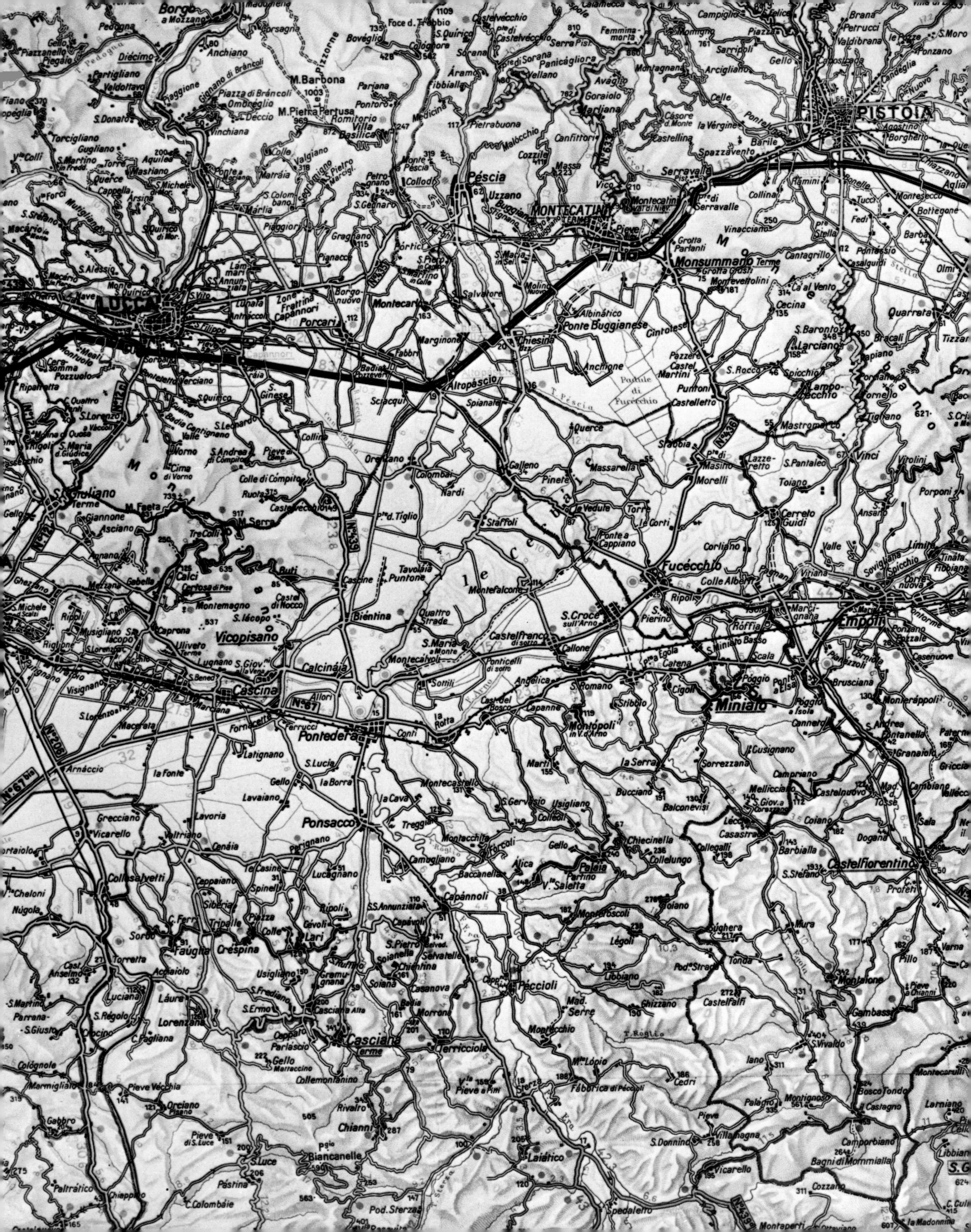

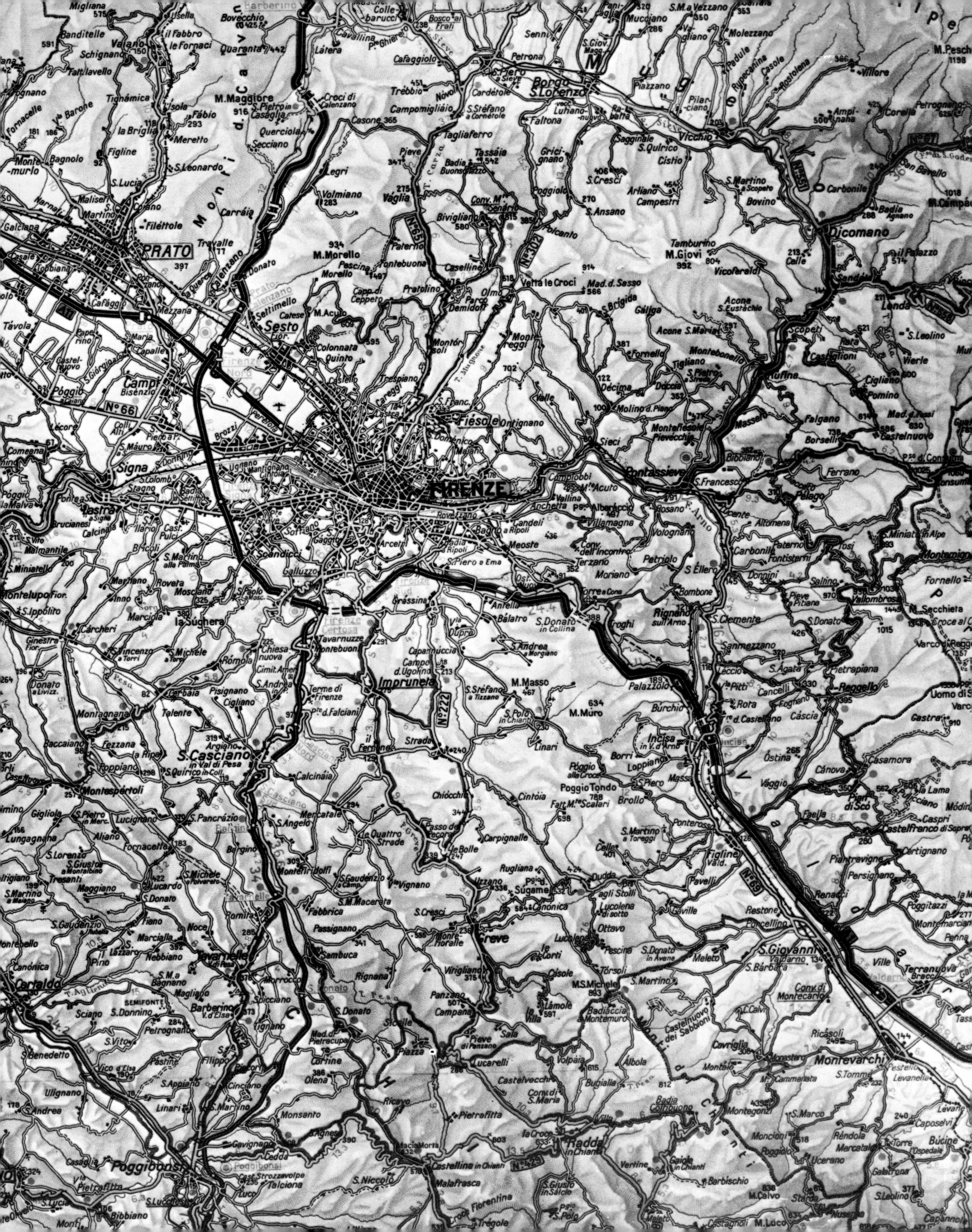

LIST OF PHOTOGRAPHERS

Abbreviation

Arezzo	SGA	Archivio Fotografico — Sez. Gallerie Soprintendenza ai Monumenti e Gallerie, Arezzo.
Assisi		Foto de Giovanni, via S. Francesco 26, 06081 Assisi.
Barcelona	MAS	MAS, Piso 3, Freneria 5, Barcelona 2.
Bremen		Photo Stickelmann, Meyerstr. 141, Bremen.
Cambridge (*Eng.*)		Stearn & Sons, Photographess. c/o Eaden Lilley & Co. Market St., Cambridge. tel: 50677.
Edinburgh-Glasgow		T. & R. Annan 130 W. Campbell, St.. Glasgow.
Florence	Alinari, Brogi Anderson	Alinari I.D.E.A., (including Brogi & Anderson), via Nazionale 6, Florence 50100.
	Foto Barone	Gaetano Barone, via Veracini 30/G, Florence 50144.
	Foto Bertoni	Marcello Bertoni, Fotografo, viale E. Duse 9, Florence 50137.
	Fototeca Berenson	Photograph Librarian, Fototeca Berenson, Villa I Tatti, via di Vincigliata, 26, Ponte a Mensola, Settignano, Florence.
	KHIF	Kunsthistorisches Institut in Florenz, via Giusti 44, Florence.
	Rodolfo Reali	This firm is no longer in business.
	Scala	V. Chiantigiana, Ponte a Niccheri, Antella, (Florence).
	SGF	Gabinetto Fotografico della Soprintendenza alle Galleria, Piazzale degli Uffizi, Florence.
London	A. C. Cooper	A. C. Cooper Ltd., 10 Pollen Street, London W.l.
	Courtauld	Courtauld Institute of Art, 20 Portman Square, London W.1.
	Sotheby	Sotheby and Co., 34 & 35 New Bond St., London, W.1.
Lugano	Foto Brunel	c/o Thyssen Collection Villa Favorita, 6976 Castagnola.

Milan	Perotti	Mario Perotti, Galleria Vittorio Emanuele, (Angolo Piazza Scala) Milan.
Naples	SGN	Laboratorio Fotografico della Soprintendenza alle Gallerie, Naples.
New York	Frick	Frick Art Reference Library, 10 East 71st Street, New York, N.Y. 10021.
	Kress	Samuel H. Kress Foundation, 221 West 57th Street, N.Y. 10019. Taylor & Dull, Inc., 980 Madison Avenue, N.Y. 10021.
Palermo	Publifoto	via Mariano Stabile, 273, Palermo.
Paris		Giraudon, 9 rue des Beaux-Arts, Paris 6^e.
Perugia	Foto Fiorucci	Foto Carlo Fiorucci, via Pinturicchio 76, 06100 Perugia.
Pescia	Foto Tredici	Milo Tredici, via D. Anzilotti 5, Pescia.
Pisa	SGPLLM	Gabinetto Fotografico della Soprintendenza di Pisa, Livorno, Lucca e Massa Carrara, Lungarno Pacinotti 46, Pisa.
Rome	GFN	Gabinetto Fotografico Nazionale, via in Miranda 5, Rome.
Toronto		Ron Vickers Ltd., 168 Davenport Road, Toronto 5, Ontario.
Utrecht		Hans Sibbelee Pr. Marijkelaan 11, Maartensdijk.
Venice		Fotografo Osvaldo Böhm, Salizzada, San Moise 1349-50, Venice.
	AFI	Agenzia Fotografica Industriale, San Marco 628, Venice.
Würzburg		Foto-Verlag, Gundermann, Bahnhofstrasse 3, Würzburg, FDR.

TOPOGRAPHICAL LIST

Photographs have been reproduced through the courtesy of keepers of paintings
in the following locations:

Agnano (Pisa), S. Jacopo
Altenburg, Staatliches Lindenau Museum
Amsterdam, Rijksmuseum
      (formerly) Lanz Collection
Ann Arbor (Mich.), University of Michigan, Museum of Art
Antwerp, Musée Mayer van den Bergh
Arezzo, Museo Comunale
      Pinacoteca
      Palazzo dei Priori, S. Maria delle Grazie
      Museo Diocesano
      S. Domenico
      Conservatorio di S. Caterina
Argiano (Val di Pesa), S. Martino
Assisi, Collegio Principe di Napoli
      Convento di S. Francesco
      S. Stanislaus Chapel
      S. Rufinuccio
      F. M. Perkins Collection
Atlanta (Ga.), High Museum of Art
Auckland (N.Z.), Art Gallery
Baltimore (Md.), Walters Art Gallery
Barberino (Valdelsa), S. Bartolomeo
Barcelona, Museo d'Arte Cateluña
Berea (Ky.), Berea College
Berlin, DDR, Staatliche Museen zu Berlin (Bodestrasse)
      FDR, Berliner Staatlichen Museum (Dahlem)
      Paul Bottenweiser Collection
Bibbiena (Casentino), Propositura, Pieve di S. Ippolito
Bibbione (San Casciano), S. Colombano
Birminghau (Ala.), Museum of Art
Bologna, Pinacoteca Nazionale
Borgo alla Collina (Casentino), S. Donato
Borgo S. Lorenzo (Mugello), S. Lorenzo
Boston (Mass.), Museum of Fine Arts
Bremen, Kunsthalle
Brunswick, Herzog Anton Ulrich Museum
Brussels, Musée des Beaux-Arts
      (formerly) Stoclet Collection
Budapest, Musée des Beaux-Arts
Buffalo (N.Y.), Albright-Knox Art Gallery
Caldine, S. Maria Maddalena
Calenzano (Prato), S. Donato
Camaiore (Lucca), Badia di S. Pietro; Pieve
Cambridge, Fitzwilliam Museum
Cambridge (Mass.), Fogg Art Museum
Caprese (Casentino), Pieve a Tifi
Carda (Pratomagno), Parrocchiale
Carrara, Accademia
Carteano (Prato), S. Paolo
Cascia (Reggello), S. Pietro
Castelfiorentino (Val d'Elsa), Chiesa di S. Verdiana (Pinacoteca)
Castelfranco di Sopra, Badia a Soffena
Castiglione d'Olona (Lombardy), Collegiata, Baptistery
Castiglione Garfagnana (Lucca), S. Michele
Cedda (Poggibonsi), S. Pietro
Certaldo, S. Maria a Bagnano
Cesi (Terni), S. Maria
Chantilly, Musée Condé
Cherbourg, Musée Thomas Henry
Chicago (Ill.), Art Institute
Citille (Greve), S. Donato
Cleveland (Ohio), Museum of Art
Colle Val d'Elsa, Museo Diocesano
Colorado Springs (Colo.), Fine Arts Center
Columbia (S.C.), Museum of Art
Copenhagen, Statens Museum for Kunst
Corsham Court (Wilts.), Lord Methuen Collection
Cortona, S. Domenico
Cracow, Muzeum Narodowe
Crespina (Pisa), S. Michele Arcangelo
Denver (Colo.), Art Museum
Detroit, Institute of Arts
Dijon, Musée
Dresden, Staatliche Kunstsammlungen
Dublin, National Gallery of Ireland

Eastnor Castle (Hereford), formerly Lord Somers Collection
Edinburgh, National Gallery of Scotland
Empoli, Museo della Collegiata
Esztergom, Kereszteny Muzeum
Fabriano, Pinacoteca
Faltignano (Val di Pesa), S. Bartolomeo
Ferraglia (Vaglia), Parrocchiale
Ferrara, Duke of Massari-Zavaglia Collection
Fiesole, Museo Bandini
      Duomo
      (formerly) Lucas Collection
      Oratorio di Fontelucente
      S. Francesco
Figline (Upper Valdarno), S. Andrea a Ripalta
      S. Francesco (Misericordia)
      Collegiata di S. Maria
      Ospedale Serristori
Florence
  Galleries, Museum & Palaces
      Galleria dell'Accademia
      Galleria degli Uffizi
      Galleria Palatina di Palazzo Pitti
      Museo Bardini
      Museo Nazionale del Bargello
      Museo del Bigallo
      Museo di Andrea del Castagno
      Museo Horne
      Museo dell'Ospedale degli Innocenti
      Museo di S. Croce
      Museo di S. Marco
      Museo Stibbert
      Palazzo dell'Arte della Lana
      Palazzo Davanzati
      Palazzo Medici-Riccardi
      Palazzo Vecchio

  Tabernacles
      Forte di Belvedere, Torre degli Agli
      Piazza del Carmine
      Porta S. Giorgio
      via Aretina & S. Salvi
      via dei Giraldi & Borgo degli Albizi
      via Lippi, near Caciolle
      via de' Serragli & S. Monaca
      via dei Tavolini

  Private Collections
      Acton Collection
      Marchese Bagneri Collection
      Berenson Collection (now in the keeping of the Fellows and Trustees of Harvard University)
      Conte Alessandro Contini-Bonacossi
      Corsini Library
      Mrs C. H. Coster
      De Carlo Collection
      Conte Cosimo degli Alessandri
      Finaly Collection
      ex-Charles Loeser Collection
      Miari-Pelli-Fabbroni Collection
      Serristori Collection

  Churches
      Duomo
      S. Ambrogio
      SS. Apostoli
      S. Arcangelo (Legnaia)
      Badia, Chiostro degli Aranci
      S. Croce, Sacristy
          Bardi Chapel
          Baroncelli Chapel
          Castellani Chapel
          Choir
          High Altar
          Medici Chapel
          Peruzzi Chapel

Pulci & Beraldi Chapels
Rinuccini Chapel
Tosinghi Chapel
(Museo di Santa Croce)
S. Cuore
S. Donato in Polverosa
S. Felice a Ema
S. Felicita, Sacristy
S. Giorgio
S. Giovannino dei Cavalieri
S. Giuseppe
S. Lorenzo, Cappella della Madonna di S. Zanobi
S. Margherita a Montici (Arcetri)
S. Marco, Museo
Monastery
S. Maria del Carmine, Sacristy
Brancacci Chapel
S. Maria Novella, Sacristy
Cloister, Spanish Chapel
Strozzi Chapel
S. Miniato al Monte
S. Niccolò Oltrarno
S. Remigio
S. Salvatore al Monte
S. Simone
S. Spirito, Refectory
S. Trinita, Sacristy
Bartolini Chapel
Accademia della Toscana di Scienze Letterarie " La Colombaria "
Conservatorio di S. Marta
Orsanmichele
Ospedale degli Innocenti
Ospedale di S. Maria Nuova
Nuovo Convento delle Oblate (Careggi)
Seminario Maggiore

Outskirts
Antella, Oratorio di S. Caterina
Badia a Settimo, Cappella di S. Jacopo
Bagno a Ripoli, S. Bartolomeo a Quarata
S. Maria a Quarto
Villa del Paradiso (degli Alberti)
Brozzi, S. Andrea
Castello (Sesto Fiorentino), S. Michele a Castello
Tabernacolo dell'Olmo
Colonnata (Sesto Fiorentino), Tabernacolo dei Logi
Galluzzo, Certosa, Museo del Convento
Le Rose (Tavarnuzze), S. Lorenzo
Mezzomonte (Pozzolatico), S. Lorenzo a Colline
Montalve, Istituto della Quiete
Mosciano, S. Andrea
Osteria Nuova (Bagno a Ripoli), S. Giorgio a Ruballa
Quinto (Sesto Fiorentino), S. Maria
Rosano (Pontassieve), SS. Annunziata
Ruballa (Bagno a Ripoli), S. Quirico
San Martino alla Palma, Pieve
S. Pietro a Quintole (Rovezzano)
Sesto Fiorentino, S. Martino
Signa, Oratorio di S. Lorenzo
Terenzano, S. Martino
Vincigliata, Castello
S. Lorenzo
Fucecchio (Valdarno), Collegiata Museo
Gangalandi (Lastra a Signa), S. Martino
Geneva, Musée d'Art et d'Histoire
Genoa, Accademia delle Belle Arti
formerly Gnecco Collection
Ghent, Musée.
Göttingen, Stadtmuseen, Kunstsammlungen der Georg-August-Universität
Gravenhage, Dienst 'S-Rijks Verspreide Kunstvoorwerpen
Greenville (S.C.), Bob Jones University Gallery
Grenoble, Musée de Peinture et de Sculpture
Grottaferrata (Roma), Badia
Hanover, Niedersachsische Landesgalerie
Hatfield (Herts.), Walter Burns Collection (formerly)
Honolulu, Academy of Arts
Houston (Texas), Museum of Fine Arts
Rice University, Institute for the Arts
Impruneta, Collegiata di S. Maria
Kansas City (Mo.), William Rockhill Nelson Gallery of Art
Knonopist (Czechoslovakia), Museum
Latera (Barberino di Mugello), S. Niccolò
Leningrad, Hermitage
Lisbon, J. P. Leacock Collection
Livorno, formerly Larderel Collection
Locko Park (Derbys.), Drury-Lowe Collection
London, National Gallery
Courtauld Institute Galleries

Victoria & Albert Museum
(formerly) Dodge Collection
Count Antoine Seilern Collection
Loppiano (Incisa Valdarno), S. Vito
Loro Ciuffenna (Pratomagno), S. Maria Assunta
Los Angeles (Calif.), County Museum of Art
Lucca, Museo Nazionale di Villa Guinigi
Conte Cenami-Spada Collection
Lucarelli (Chianti), S. Martino
Lucerne, Kofler-Truniger Collection
Lugano-Castagnola, Galerie Thyssen
Madrid, Prado
Malibu (Calif.), J. Paul Getty Museum
Melbourne, National Gallery of Victoria
Memphis (Tenn.), Brooks Memorial Art Gallery
Mezzana (Prato), Chiesa Parrocchiale
Milan, (formerly) Chiesa Collection
Galleria Finarte
Minneapolis (Minn.), Institute of Art
Montalbino (Montespertoli), S. Giusto
Montefloscoli (San Piero a Sieve), S. Maria
Montelupo, Pieve
Montemignaio (Consuma), Pieve di S. Maria
Montepulciano, Museo Civico
Monte San Savino (Siena), S. Maria delle Vertiche
Montevarchi, Chiesa di Cernana
Montgomery (Ala.), Museum of Fine Arts
Monticelli, Oratorio di S. Maria della Querce
Montreal (Quebec), Museum of Fine Arts
Moscow, Puskin Museum
Mucciana (San Casciano), S. Jacopo
Munich, Alte Pinakothek
Naples, Museo Nazionale di Capodimonte
Museo di S. Martino
Castelnuovo, Cappella Palatina
New Haven (Conn.), Yale University Art Gallery
New York (N.Y.), Metropolitan Museum of Art
Historical Society
Miss Helen C. Frick Collection
Maurice Salomon Collection
Nicosia (Pisa), Chiesa dei Francescani
Notre Dame (Ind.), University
Oakly Park (Shrops.), Earl of Plymouth Collection
Ontario, Art Gallery
Ortimino, S. Vito
Orvieto, Chiesa dei Servi
Ottawa, National Gallery of Canada
Oxford, Ashmolean Museum
Christ Church
Padua, Arena Chapel
Pagnana (Empoli), S. Cristina
Palermo, S. Niccolò Reale, Museo Diocesano
Panzano (Greve), Pieve di S. Leolino
Paris, Musées Nationaux
Musée du Louvre
Parma, Galleria Nazionale
Congregazione di S. Filippo Neri (Pinacoteca Stuard)
Pastine, S. Martino
Pelago (Pontassieve), Chiesa di Magnale
Perticaia (Rignano sull'Arno), S. Cristoforo
Perugia Museo dell'Opera del Duomo
(formerly) van Marle Collection
Pesaro, Museo Civico
Pescia, Museo Civico
Museo della Biblioteca Comunale
S. Antonio Abate
S. Francesco
S. Stefano
Philadelphia (Pa.), Museum of Art
John G. Johnson Collection
Pisa, Museo Nazionale di S. Matteo
Camposanto
S. Croce a Fossabanda
Convento di S. Tommaso
S. Francesco (Chapter Room)
Pistoia, Museo Civico
Duomo
Palazzo Comunale
SS. Annunziata
S. Domenico
S. Francesco
S. Giovanni Fuorcivitas
Convento (or Chiesa) del T
Poggibonsi, S. Lucchese
Ponce (Puerto Rico), Museo de Arte
Pontorme (Empoli), S. Martino
Poppiena (Casentino), Badia

Prague, Narodni Galerie
Prato, Galleria Comunale
    Duomo, Cappella del Sacro Cingolo
        Cappella Manassei
        Museo dell'Opera
    S. Francesco (Chapter Room)
    Palazzo Datini
    Palazzo dell'Arte della Lana
Pratovecchio (Casentino), Propositura di S. Maria Assunta
Preci, S. Maria
Princeton (N.J.), Mrs Douglas Delanoy
Providence (R.I.), Rhode Island School of Design, Museum of Art
Reggello, S. Pietro in Cascia
Rennes, Musée des Beaux-Arts
Richmond (Surrey), formerly Cook Collection
Rome, Galleria Nazionale (Palazzo Barberini)
    Galleria Doria Pamphilj
    Museo del Castel S. Angelo
    Museo di Palazzo Venezia
    Pinacoteca Capitolina
    Vatican, Pinacoteca
    (formerly) S. Basilio
    S. Clemente
    S. Giorgio
    Fabrizio-Massimo Collection
    (formerly) Count Giuseppe Primoli Collection
    (formerly) Marinucci Collection
    (formerly) Stroganoff Collection
Romena (Casentino), Pieve di S. Pietro
Rosano (Pontassieve), SS. Annunziata
Rouen, Musée
Salamanca, Catedral Vieja
Santa Brigida all'Opaco, Pieve
San Cresci in Valcava, Pieve
San Diego (Calif.), Fine Arts Gallery
San Donato in Poggio (Val di Pesa), Pieve
San Donnino (Certaldo), Parrochiale
San Francisco (Calif.), M. H. de Young Memorial Museum
San Gimignano, Museo Civico
    S. Lorenzo in Ponte
San Giovanni Valdarno, S. Lorenzo, S. Maria delle Grazie
San Giovenale (Reggello), Chiesa
San Godenzo (Mugello), Basilica
San Martino a Maiano (Val d'Elsa), Pieve

San Miniato al Tedesco (Pisa), Misericordia
        Palazzo Comunale
        S. Domenico
San Piero a Sieve (Mugello), Tabernacolo delle Mozzette
São Paolo, Museu
Sarasota (Fla.), Ringling Museum of Art
Scarperia (Mugello), Madonna delle Grazie
Seattle (Wash.), Art Museum
Serravalle (Pistoia), S. Michele
Sestino (Stia), S. Pancrazio
'S-Heerenberg (Holland), Dr J. H. van Heek Collection
Sherborn (Mass.), Mrs R. F. Pickhardt Collection
Siena, Pinacoteca Nazionale
    Palazzo Pubblico
Signano (Scandicci), S. Giusto
Staggia (Poggibonsi), S. Maria Assunta
Stalybridge (Ches.), Astley Cheetham Art Gallery
Stia (Casentino), S. Maria delle Grazie
        Propositura di S. Maria Assunta
Strasbourg, Musée de Ville
Stuttgart, Staatsgalerie
Subiaco (Lazio), Sacro Speco
Sutton Place (Surrey), J. Paul Getty Collection
Tucson (Ariz.), University of Arizona Art Gallery
Turin, Museo Civico
Ughi (Rignano sull'Arno), S. Maria
Utrecht, Aartsbisschoppelijk Museum
Varlungo, S. Pietro
Velletri, Museo del Duomo
Venice, Conte Vittorio Cini Collection
Verona, Museo di Castelvecchio
Vertelli, San Michele
Vicchio di Rimaggio (Greve), S. Lorenzo
Vienna, (formerly) Emil Weinberger Collection
Villore (Poggibonsi), Cappella di S. Giusto
Vincigliata, Castello
    S. Lorenzo
Volognano (Pontassieve), S. Michele
Volterra, Pinacoteca
    S. Francesco, Oratorio della Croce di Giorno
Warsaw, Muzeum Narodowe
Washington (D.C.), National Gallery of Art
        Dumbarton Oaks
Worcester (Mass.), Art Museum
Würzburg, Martin von Wagner Museum

Printed in Italy - July, 1975
by Industria Grafica L'Impronta, S.p.A.
Scandicci - Firenze